Random House
SPANISH-ENGLISH
ENGLISH-SPANISH
Dictionary
Second Edition

Edited by
Margaret H. Raventós, M.A.
*Special Lecturer in Spanish
at the University of
Manchester*

Revised and Updated by
David L. Gold
*Doctor in Romance
Philology
University of Barcelona*

BALLANTINE BOOKS • NEW YORK

A Ballantine Book
Published by The Ballantine Publishing Group
Copyright © 1999, 1996 by Random House, Inc.

www.randomhouse.com/BB/

Library of Congress Catalog Card Number: 96-96206

ISBN 0-345-40547-1

Manufactured in the United States of America

Second Ballantine Books Edition: March 1999

15 14 13 12 11 10

Contents

Jackson
Hoose

Preface

This is a revised Second Edition of *Random House Spanish-English English-Spanish Dictionary*, first published in 1995. New to this edition are pronunciations for all Spanish and English main entries, using IPA (International Phonetic Alphabet) symbols. The IPA symbols are explained in the pronunciation key for English on page viii and for Spanish on page xiv. Also included in this dictionary are detailed guides to the pronunciation of both languages.

Spanish Spelling and Alphabetization

On January 1, 1959, the Spanish language academies changed certain spelling rules and on April 27, 1994, they eliminated **ch** and **ll** as separate letters of the alphabet. Thus, whereas words like **chico** and **chocolate** were formerly alphabetized under their own letter (**ch**, which came between **c** and **d**) and words like **llamar** and **llegar** were formerly alphabetized under their own letter (**ll**, which came between **l** and **m**), words containing **ch** or **ll**, in whatever part of the word they may appear, are now alphabetized as they would be in English (**chico** therefore now appears under **c** and **llegar** under **l**).

Field Labels

Only essential field labels are given in this dictionary. For example, the label *medicine* or *pathology* is unnecessary at **flebitis** "phlebitis" (in the Spanish-English section) because both the Spanish and English words refer only to the medical condition so called in those languages.

In contrast to that entry, we do need a label at **foca** "seal" (in the Spanish-English section) because English **seal** has several meanings and only the zoological one is intended here. English speakers looking up **foca** thus need the label *zoology* (Spanish speakers need no label because they know that **foca** is the name of an animal, and so they will correctly assume that **seal** is intended only in its zoological sense).

Regional Labels for Spanish

Regional labels are given in this dictionary when a less than universal usage is found in a certain region or country. A regional label should be interpreted as meaning that the usage so labeled is found in that particular place, but it may also be found elsewhere. For instance, the regional label *Mexican* means that the usage so labeled is found in Mexico, but further research would be necessary to determine whether the usage is present or absent in other countries. The label *West. Hem.* is used for Spanish terms that are in general use throughout the Western Hemisphere.

Subentries

If a main entry head is repeated in a subentry in exactly the same form, it is abbreviated to its first letter (for instance, at **fin** in the Spanish-English section we find **a f. de,** which stands for **a fin de**). If the main entry head appears in any other form, the full form is given in the subentry (thus, at **fin,** the subentry head **a fines de** is spelled without abbreviation).

Irregular Spanish Verbs and the Direction "See . . ."

If a Spanish verb is irregular, it has been treated in one of two ways: either its principal parts are shown (see for example the end of the entry for **caber**) or you are referred to an analogous irregular verb for guidance (see for example the end of the entry for **comparecer,** where you are directed to **conocer**). Thus, since the irregular form **conozco** is shown at **conocer** (it being irregular in the sense that it has a **z**), you may infer that **comparecer** has the irregular form **comparezco.**

One of the consequences of the changes in Spanish spelling is that a new kind of orthographically irregular verb has come into existence (for example, **ahijar, ahincar, ahitar, ahuchar, ahumar, ahusar, cohibir, desahuciar, prohibir, prohijar, rehilar, rehusar, sahumar, sobrehilar,** and **trashumar**).

If "See . . ." is all you find at an entry, you are being directed to a synonym. Thus, "**descompasarse** See **descomedirse**" means that the translations of **descomedirse** are those of **descompasarse** too.

Spanish Equivalents of "you"

Today's Spanish, when taken as a whole, has at least six equivalents of "you": **tú, vos, usted** (abbreviated to **Vd.**), **su merced** (all of which are used in addressing one person), **ustedes** (abbreviated to **Vds.**), **vosotros, vosotras,** and **sus mercedes** (all used in addressing more than one person).

When **you** occurs in this dictionary, usually only one of those words has been chosen to translate it, though three are never used here: **su merced, sus mercedes,** because they are now limited to only a small area of the Spanish-speaking world (the Cundinamarca Savanna, in Colombia) and even there they are now obsolescent, and **vos,** because the verb forms corresponding to this pronoun often vary from country to country.

Usually, the selection of one pronoun or another in this dictionary has been arbitrary, in which case any of the others could just as easily have been chosen. For example, for **How are you?** the translation "¿Cómo está Vd.?" is offered, yet any of the other pronouns could appear instead (with, in certain cases, a different verb form, for instance "¿Cómo están Vds.?").

In certain cases, however, not all pronouns (whether actually used or just implicit) would be appropriate. For example, among the translations of **please** . . . are imperative forms of **servirse**. . . . Because **servirse** in this sense is a formal usage (found mostly in impersonal writing like application blanks), it is not found in any familiar form of the imperative. The dictionary therefore gives **¡sírvase . . . !** (where the understood subject is **usted,** a formal pronoun). It could also have given **¡sírvanse . . . !** (where the understood subject is **ustedes,** likewise a formal pronoun), but not any form in which the subject were an informal pronoun.

Masculine and Feminine, Male and Female

A growing number of Spanish nouns formerly used only in the masculine gender are being used in the feminine too. This dictionary thus labels **nauta, paracaidista, púgil, pugilista, recluta, reservista,** and **seminarista,** for example, as both masculine and feminine (the gender to be chosen depending on the gender of the person in question). The gender of Spanish nouns is indicated not only in the Spanish-English section but also in the English-Spanish one.

The editors are always grateful to receive suggestions for new words to add to subsequent editions. Any suggestions or queries should be sent to:

Random House Reference & Information Publishing
201 East 50th Street
New York, NY 10022

Símbolos de Pronunciacíon por los Sonidos del inglés

Pronunciation Symbols for the Sounds of English

Símbolos del AFI IPA Symbols	Ejemplos Key Words
/æ/	*Eng.* hat
/ei/	*Eng.* stay; *Fr.* cité; *Ger.* bequem; *It.* fréccia; *Sp.* reina
/ɛə/ [followed by /r/]	*Eng.* hair; *Fr.* frère; *Ger.* mehr; *It.* mercante; *Sp.* ver
/ɑ/	*Eng.* father; *Fr.* tasse; *Ger.* Vater; *It.* pasta; *Sp.* casa
/ɛ/	*Eng.* bet; *Fr.* gazelle; *Ger.* Bett; *It.* freschezza; *Sp.* entre
/i/	*Eng.* bee; *Fr.* difficile; *Ger.* Wiegen; *It.* limone; *Sp.* vida
/ɪə/ [followed by /r/]	*Eng.* hear; *Fr.* rire; *Ger.* hier
/ɪ/	*Eng.* sit; *Ger.* ist
/ai/	*Eng.* try; *Ger.* zeigen; *It.* operaio; *Sp.* ay
/ɒ/	*Eng.* hot
/o/	*Eng.* boat; *Fr.* chapeau; *Ger.* Mond
/ɔ/	*Eng.* saw; *Fr.* donner; *Ger.* doch; *It.* oglio; *Sp.* nota
/ɔi/	*Eng.* toy; *Ger.* Deutsch; *Sp.* hoy
/ʊ/	*Eng.* book
/u/	*Eng.* too; *Fr.* tout; *Ger.* tun; *It.* inutile; *Sp.* luna
/au/	*Eng.* cow; *Ger.* aus; *Sp.* pausa
/ʌ/	*Eng.* up
/ɜ/ [followed by /r/]	*Eng.* burn; *Fr.* fleur; *Ger.* böse
/ə/	*Eng.* alone; *Fr.* demain; *Ger.* stehen
/ᵊ/	*Eng.* fire (fiᵊr); *Fr.* bastille
/æ̃/, /ɔ̃/, /ɛ̃/, /ɑ̃/ [A tilde over a vowel shows that it is nasalized]	As in *Fr.* un bon vin blanc
/b/	*Eng.* boy; *Fr.* bête; *Ger.* backen; *It.* buio; *Sp.* boca
/tʃ/	*Eng.* child; *It.* cibo; *Sp.* mucho
/d/	*Eng.* dad; *Fr.* danse; *Ger.* dieser; *It.* destra; *Sp.* doy
/f/	*Eng.* for; *Fr.* fête; *Ger.* fahren; *It.* fretta; *Sp.* fecha
/g/	*Eng.* give; *Fr.* garde; *Ger.* gut; *It.* seguito; *Sp.* gato

Símbolos del AFI / IPA Symbols	Ejemplos / Key Words
/h/	*Eng.* happy; *Ger.* heben; *It.* hascisc
/dʒ/	*Eng.* just; *It.* giugno
/k/	*Eng.* kick; *Fr.* capable; *Ger.* Kirche; *It.* amichevole; *Sp.* kilogramo
/l/	*Eng.* love; *Fr.* lait; *Ger.* lieben; *It.* lira; *Sp.* libro
/m/	*Eng.* mother; *Fr.* manger; *Ger.* Mann; *It.* meandro; *Sp.* limbo
/n/	*Eng.* now; *Fr.* noble; *Ger.* nach; *It.* nulla; *Sp.* noche
/ŋ/	*Eng.* sing; *Ger.* singen; *It.* vengo
/p/	*Eng.* pot; *Fr.* parfum; *Ger.* Post; *It.* pacc; *Sp.* papa
/r/	*Eng.* read; *Fr.* rouge; *Ger.* Rat; *It.* ricco; *Sp.* para
/s/	*Eng.* see; *Fr.* santé; *Ger.* essen; *It.* sérpo; *Sp.* hasta
/ʃ/	*Eng.* shop; *Fr.* chercher; *Ger.* Schlaf; *It.* scelto
/t/	*Eng.* ten; *Fr.* tête; *Ger.* Teil; *It.* topo; *Sp.* tomar
/θ/	*Eng.* thing; *Sp.* (in Spain) cerdo
/ð/	*Eng.* father; *Sp.* codo
/v/	*Eng.* victory; *Fr.* vie; *Ger.* was; *It.* voi; *Sp.* verdad
/w/	*Eng.* witch; *Fr.* oui; *It.* guardare
/y/	*Eng.* yes; *Fr.* yeux; *Ger.* jung; *Sp.* yacer
/z/	*Eng.* zipper; *Fr.* zéro; *Ger.* Sieg
/ʒ/	*Eng.* pleasure; *Fr.* jeune

Los sonidos del inglés americano

Vocales y diptongos

a　Cuando representa el sonido /æ/, se pronuncia más cerrada que la *a* de *paro* (por ejemplo: **act, at, bat, hat, marry**); también se encuentra este sonido en palabras deletreadas con: -ah- (d*ah*lia), -ai- (pl*ai*d), -al- (h*al*f), -au- (l*au*gh), -ua- (g*ua*rantee).

a　Cuando representa el sonido /ei/, se pronuncia más cerrada que la *e* de *hablé* y como si fuera seguido de *i* (por ejemplo: **age, gate, rate**); también se encuentra este sonido en palabras deletreadas con: -ai- (r*ai*n, *ai*r), -aigh- (str*aigh*t), -au- (g*au*ge), -ay- (s*ay*), -ea- (st*ea*k), -ei- (v*ei*l, w*ei*gh), -ey- (ob*ey*).

a /ɑ/　Equivale aproximadamente a la *a* de *sentado* y *bajo* (por ejemplo: **ah, father, part**); también se encuentra este sonido en palabras deletreadas con: -al- (c*al*m), -e(r)- (s*er*geant), -ea(r)- (h*ear*t), -ua- (g*ua*rd).

a /ə/　Equivale aproximadamente a la *e* de las palabras francesas *de* y *le* (por ejemplo: **alone, about**); también se encuentra este sonido en palabras deletreadas con: -e- (syst*e*m), -i- (eas*i*ly), -o- (gall*o*p), -u- (circ*u*s), -y- (mart*y*r).

e /ɛ/　Equivale aproximadamente a la *e* de *templo* y *perro* (por ejemplo: **edge, set, merry**); también se encuentra este sonido en palabras deletreadas con: a-, -a- (*a*ny, m*a*ny), -ai- (s*ai*d), -ay- (s*ay*s), -ea- (l*ea*ther), -ei- (h*ei*fer), -eo- (j*eo*pardy), -ie- (fr*ie*nd).

e /i/　Equivale aproximadamente a la *i* de *Chile* (por ejemplo: **be, equal, secret**); también se encuentra este sonido en palabras deletreadas con: ea- *(ea*ch, t*ea*), -ee- (f*ee*, k*ee*p), -ei- (rec*ei*ve), -eo- (p*eo*ple), -ey- (k*ey*), -ie- (f*ie*ld), -y (cit*y*).

i /ɪ/　Se pronuncia menos cerrada que la *i* de *Chile* (por ejemplo: **if, big, fit, mirror**); también se encuentra este sonido en palabras deletreadas con: e- (*E*ngland), -ee- (b*ee*n), -ei- (counterf*ei*t), -ia- (carr*ia*ge), -ie- (s*ie*ve), -o- (w*o*man), (b)u(s)- (b*u*siness), -y- (s*y*mpathetic).

i /ai/　Equivale aproximadamente a la *ai* de *aire, baile* (por ejemplo: **bite, ice, pirate**); también se encuentra este sonido en palabras deletreadas con: ais- (*ai*sle), -ei- (h*ei*ght, st*ei*n), -eye- *(eye)*, -ie (p*ie*), -igh- (h*igh*), is- (*i*sland), -uy (b*uy*), -y (cycle, sky), -ye (l*ye*).

o /ou/　Se pronuncia más cerrada que la *o* de *supo* (por ejemplo: **hope, go, oh, over**); también se encuentra este sonido en palabras deletreadas con: -au- (m*au*ve), -aux (f*aux* pas), -eau- (b*eau*), -ew (s*ew*), -oa- (r*oa*d), -oe (t*oe*), -oo- (br*oo*ch), -ot (dep*ot*), -ou- (s*ou*l), -ow (fl*ow*), -owe- *(owe)*.

o /ɔ/　Se pronuncia más cerrada que la *o* de *corre* (por ejemplo: **alcohol, order, raw**); también se encuentra este sonido en palabras deletreadas con: -a- (t*a*ll), -al- (w*al*k), au- (*au*thor, v*au*lt), -augh- (c*augh*t), -oa- (br*oa*d), -oo- (fl*oo*r), -ough- (s*ough*t).

oi /oi/　Equivqale aproximadamente a la *oy* de *doy* (por ejemplo: **oil, joint, voice**); también se encuentra este sonido en palabras deletreadas con: -awy- (l*awy*er), -oy- (b*oy*).

oo /ʊ/　Se pronuncia menos cerrada que la *u* de *insulto* (por ejemplo: **book, foot**); también se encuentra este sonido en palabras deletreadas con: -o- (w*o*lf), -ou- (t*ou*r), -u- (p*u*ll).

oo /u/	Se pronuncia más larga que la *u* de *susto* (por ejemplo: **too, ooze, fool**); también se encuentra este sonido en palabras deletreadas con: -eu- (mane*u*ver), -ew (gr*ew*), -o (wh*o*), -o. . .e (m*o*ve), -oe (can*oe*), -ou- (tr*ou*pe), -u. . .e (r*u*le), -ue (fl*ue*), -ui- (s*ui*t).
ou /au/	Equivale aproximadamente a la *au* de *aurora* (por ejemplo: **loud, out**); también se encuentra este sonido en palabras deletreadas con -ow (br*ow*, c*ow*, pl*ow*).
u /iu/	Equivale aproximadamente a la *iu* de *ciudad* (por ejemplo: **cue, use, utility**); también se encuentra este sonido en palabras deletreadas con: -eau- (b*eau*ty), -eu- (f*eu*d), -ew (f*ew*), (h)u- (h*u*man), (h)u. . .e (h*u*ge), -iew (v*iew*), you *(you)*, yu. . .e *(yule)*.
u /ʌ/	Es sonido intermedio entre la *o* de *borro* y la *a* de *barro*, algo parecido a la pronunciación de la *eu* francesa de *peur;* (por ejemplo: **up, sun, mud**); también se encuentra este sonido en palabras deletreadas con: o- (*o*ther), -o- (s*o*n), -oe- (d*oe*s), o. . .e (l*o*ve), -oo- (bl*oo*d), -ou (tr*ou*ble).

Consonantes

b	Se pronuncia igual que la *p* española salvo que en la pronunciación de la *b* suenan las cuerdas vocales. La *b* inglesa es más fuerte (más aspirada) que la española. Se encuentra en palabras escritas con *b* (**bed, amber, rub**) y también en palabras deletreadas con -bb- (ho*bb*y).
c	Como la *c* española, lleva dos sonidos, /s/ y /k/. La /s/ se pronuncia igual que la *s* española y se encuentra en palabras deletreadas con ce- (**center**) y ci- (**city**). La /k/ es semejante a la *c* española cuando aparece delante de -a, -o, y -u *(católica, cómo, cuándo)* pero se pronuncia más fuerte (más aspirada). La /k/ se encuentra en palabras deletreadas con ca-, co-, y cu- (**cat, account, cut**).
ch	Equivale aproximadamente a la *ch* española (por ejemplo: **chief, beach**); también se encuentra en palabras deletreadas con: -tch- (ca*tch*, bu*tch*er), -te- (righ*teo*us), -ti- (ques*ti*on), -tu- (na*tu*ral). A veces equivale a la /š/ de la palabra francesa *chèrie* (**chef**), o a la /k/ de *cómo* (**character**).
d	Equivale aproximadamente a la *d* de *onda* (por ejemplo: **do, odor, red**); también se encuentra en palabras deletreadas con -dd- (la*dd*er) y -de- (fa*de*). La *d* inglesa es siempre más fuerte (más aspirada) que la española y no se pronuncia nunca /ʤ/ como la *d* de *padre* o las *d*'s de *Madrid*.
f	Equivale aproximadamente a la *f* española (por ejemplo: **feed, safe**); también se encuentra en palabras deletreadas con -ff- (mu*ff*in) y -fe (li*fe*).
g	Equivale aproximadamente a la *g* de *globo* (por ejemplo: **give, fog**); también se encuentra en palabras deletreadas con -gg (e*gg*), gh- (*gh*ost), y -gue (pla*gue*). La *g* cuando cae delante de -i y -e se pronuncia /ʤ/ (**George, gem, legitimate**). El sonido /ʤ/ es semejante a, pero más fuerte que, la *y* y la *ll* españolas de *yo* y *llevar*. Véase *j*.
h	Se pronuncia más aspirada pero menos áspera que la *j* española en *jabón* (por ejemplo: **hit, hope**); también se encuentra en palabras deletreadas con wh- (*wh*o).

j   Equivale aproximadamente a la *y* de *yo* en su pronunciación enfática (p.ej. . . . *yo, y yo sólo soy el dueño aquí!*) o como la *y* de *cónyuge* en ciertas modalidades del español (por ejemplo: **just, joke**); también se encuentra en palabras deletreadas con -dg- (ju*dg*e), -di- (sol*di*er), -ge (sa*g*e), -gg- (exa*gg*erate), gi- (*gi*n). La pronunciación de la *j* y de la *g* delante de -i y -e /dʒ/ es igual que la de la *ch* española, salvo que suenan las cuerdas vocales en la pronunciación del sonido /dʒ/.

k   (Por ejemplo: **keep, make, token**) equivale a la *qui-* y *que* españolas pero se pronuncia más fuerte (más aspirada). La *k* inglesa no se pronuncia cuando cae delante de una *n* (**knife, knight, knee**).

l   Se pronuncia aproximadamente como la *l* de *lago* (por ejemplo: **leap, sail**); también se encuentra en palabras deletreadas con -le (mi*le*) y -ll (ca*ll*).

m   Equivale aproximadamente a la *m* española (por ejemplo: **more, drum, him, summer**). Tengan cuidado de pronunciar la *m* al final de una palabra igual que se pronuncia en medio de la palabra y de no convertir el sonido en *n*.

n   Equivale aproximadamente a la *n* de *bueno* (por ejemplo: **now, sunny**); también se encuentra en palabras deletreadas con gn- (*gn*at) y kn- (*kn*ife).

ng   (Por ejemplo: **sing, Washington**) equivale aproximadamente a la *n* de *blanco*.

p   (Por ejemplo: **pool, spool, supper, stop**) tras consonante equivale aproximadamente a la *p* española, pero lleva más aspiración. La *p* delante de una *s* (**psychologist, psyche**) no se pronuncia.

r   Se pronuncia con la punta de la lengua elevada hacia el paladar (sin tocarlo) y doblada para atrás (por ejemplo: **red, hurry, near**); también se encuentra en palabras deletreadas con: -re (pu*re*), rh- (*rh*ythm), y wr- (*wr*ong).

s   Equivale aproximadamente a la *s* de *salir*, pero algo más tensa y larga (por ejemplo: **see, kiss**).

sh   Equivale aproximadamente a la *ch* de las palabras francesas *changer* and *chapeau* (por ejemplo: **ship, wash**); también se encuentra en palabras deletreadas con: -ce (o*ce*an), -ch- (ma*ch*ine), -ci- (spe*ci*al), s(u)- (*s*ugar), -sci- (con*sci*ence), -si- (man*si*on), -ss- (ti*ss*ue, mi*ss*ion), -ti- (ca*ti*on).

t   (Por ejemplo: **team, ten, steam, bit**) tras consonante equivale aproximadamente a la *t* española salvo con más aspiración; también se encuentra en palabras deletreadas con: -bt (dou*bt*), -cht (ya*cht*), -ed (tal*k*ed), -ght (bou*ght*), -te (bi*te*), th- (*th*yme), -tt- (bo*tt*om), tw- (*tw*o).

th   (Por ejemplo: **thin, ether, path**) equivale aproximadamente a la *z* española en el norte de España.

th   (Por ejemplo: **that, the, either, smooth**) equivale aproximadamente a la *d* de *adoptar*.

v   (Por ejemplo: **voice, river, live**) equivale aproximadamente a la *b* de *haba* pero es labiodental en vez de bilabial. La pronunciación de la *v* inglesa es igual que la de la *f*, salvo que suenan las cuerdas vocales en la pronunción de la *v*.

w   (Por ejemplo: **west, witch, away**) equivale aproximadamente a la *u* de *puesto*.

y   (Por ejemplo: **yes, beyond**) equivale aproximadamente a la *i* de *bien;* también se encuentra en palabras deletreadas con -i- (on*i*on, un*i*on), -j- (hallelujah), y -ll- (torti*lla*).

z   Tiene dos sonidos: /z/ y /zh/. La /z/, la más común (por ejemplo: **zoo, lazy, zone**), equivale aproximadamente a la *s* de *isla* y *mismo* en ciertas modalidades del español, pero con más sonoridad. Este sonido se pronuncia igual que la *s* española, salvo que en la pronunciación de la /z/ suenan las cuerdas vocales. Se encuentra el sonido /z/ en algunas palabras deletreadas con: -s- (ha*s*), -se (ri*se*), x- (*x*ylophone), y -zz- (buzzard, fuzz). El sonido /zh/ que se encuentra en **azure** y **brazier** equivale aproximadamente a la *ll* del español de la gente mayor de la cuidad de Buenos Aires (o sea, como la *j* de la palabra francesa *bonjour*). El sonido /zh/ también se encuentra en ciertas palabras deletreadas con -ge (gara*ge*, mira*ge*), -si- (vi*si*on), y su- (plea*su*re).

Pronunciation Symbols for the Sounds of Spanish

Símbolos de Pronunciacíon por los Sonidos del español

IPA Symbols Símbolos del AFI	Key Words Ejemplos	Key Words Ejemplos
a	albo, banco, cera	father, depart
e	esto, del, parte	rain, eight
i	ir, fino, adiós, muy	beet, conceive
o	oler, flor, grano	telephone, goal
u	un, luna, cuento	fool, group
b	bajo, vaca	by, abet
β	hablar, escribir, lavar	
d	dar, desde, dos, dueña	deal, adept
ð	pedir, Pedro, verdad	that, gather
f	fecha, afectar, golf	fan, after
g	gato, grave, gusto, largo	garden, ugly
h	gemir, giro, junta, bajo, relojes	horse, loch
k	cacao, claro, cura, cuenta, que, quinto	kind, actor
l	lado, lente, habla, papel	lot, altar
ʎ	llamar, calle, olla	million, civilian
m	mal, amor	more, commit
n	nada, nuevo, mano, bien	not, enter
ɲ	ñaques, año	canyon, companion
ŋ	angosto, aunque	ring, anchor
p	peso, guapo	pill, applaud
r	real, faro, deber	rice, carpet
s	sala, espejo, mas	say, clasp
θ	cena, hacer, cierto, cine, zarzuela, lazo, vez	thin, myth
t	tocar, estado, cenit	table, attract
y	ya, ayer	you, voyage
tʃ	chica, mucho	chill, batch

Diphthongs

ai, ay	baile, hay	high, rye
au	auditor, laudar	out, round
ei	veinte, seis	aim, ray
eu	euscaro, deuda	
oi, oy	roido, hoy	coin, loyal
ue	buena, suerte	sway, quaint
ie	miel, tambien	fiesta, pieta

The Basics of Standard Spanish Pronunciation

Whereas the fit between English spelling and pronunciation has for centuries been less than ideal (think, for example, of the various pronunciations of -ough, as in although, bough, cough, and slough), the fit between today's Spanish spelling and pronunciation is quite good, thanks to the regulatory efforts of the Spanish academies.

The following instructions thus take spelling as their starting point. Pronunciation is described in two ways: with phonetic symbols (enclosed in slashes) and by way of approximate comparisons with English. A wavy line separates variants (like esnob ~ snob). A stress mark (') means that the syllable following it is stressed (as in /re'lo/). An asterisk indicates a nonexistent form (like English *llion). A right-facing "arrow" (>), or "greater than" sign, means "became in Spanish" (as in English rum and French rhum > ron ~ romo).

As may be expected of a language that has been used for many centuries, over a vast area, and by many diverse people, Spanish is now pronounced in various ways. Of the many current pronunciations, two are offered as most suitable for speakers of Spanish as a second language. The two standards are identical to a large extent, differing chiefly with respect to the pronunciation of c before e; c before i; z in any position; and, optionally, ll, g, and j.

To the extent that the two standards differ, features belonging to just one of them are labeled either *Standard 1* or *Standard 2* below.

Features labeled *Standard 1* are accepted as standard in Spain but not in the Western Hemisphere. Features labeled *Standard 2* are accepted as standard in the Western Hemisphere but not in Spain. If you speak Spanish mostly with Spaniards or mostly with people from the Western Hemisphere, your choice of standard will thus be straightforward. If you speak with people from both areas, you can either try to master both standards or, if you want to follow just one of them no matter to whom you speak, pick Standard 2.

a is pronounced /a/, which is similar to the second vowel of the English interjection aha! and the vowel of the English interjection ah, although much shorter in duration. See also "Diphthongs and Triphthongs" below.

b has three pronunciations. At the beginning of an utterance, after /m/ (whether represented by m or by n), or after /n/ (whether represented by n or by m), the letter b is pronounced /b/, which is similar to the pronunciation of the first consonant of English beach, broth, pebble, etc. For example, in the sentence Bulgaria envió a ambos embajadores en un barco japonés, each of the four instances of b (and the one instance of v) is pronounced in this way.

At the end of a word, more than one pronunciation of b may be heard. For example, club may be /klub/, /kluβ/, or /klu/. Its plural, clubs, may be /klups/, /klus/, and possibly /kluβs/, unless the plural clubes is used, whose universal pronunciation is /kluβɛs/ (see the next paragraph for interpreting /β/, and e for interpreting /ɛ/). All of the foregoing holds for compounds of club, like aeroclub. In esnob ~ snob, the final b is pronounced /b/.

In all other positions (for example, hablas, hablar, and habré), b is pronounced /β/, a sound absent in English, which is made by bringing the lips close together without letting them touch each other (as if you were blowing dust away or blowing out a match or candle), expelling air through the mouth, and vibrating the vocal cords. This sound is thus similar to /v/ (as in English very and vowel), except that the latter is made by making the lower lip touch the upper teeth. English-speakers should not mistake Spanish /β/ for English /v/.

It follows from the foregoing that if the position of **b** in the utterance changes, its pronunciation may change. For example, when the word **baba** is pronounced in isolation, the first **b** is rendered /b/ and the second one /β/, but in the phrase **la baba**, the first **b** is no longer at the beginning of an utterance (nor is it preceded by the sounds /m/ or /n/), hence the phrase is pronounced /laβaβa/.

These rules of pronunciation also hold true for the letter **v**, which is pronounced /b/ at the beginning of words, and /β/ in the middle. See also **v**.

c has several pronunciations. If it is followed by **e** or **i**, the letter **c** is pronounced /θ/ in Standard 1 and /s/ in Standard 2. The pronunciation of /θ/ in Spanish is similar to that of **th** in English **thatch**, **think**, etc., but made with somewhat more protrusion of the tongue. The sound /s/ is similar to the pronunciation of **s** in English **say**, **simple**, etc.

Although Standard 1 has /θ/ for **c** before **e** or **i**, people who use that pronunciation will not be put off if they hear you pronounce the **c** as /s/, because the latter is widespread (though not standard) in Spain. In the Western Hemisphere, **c** before **e** or **i** is always pronounced /s/ and never /θ/. Speakers of Western Hemispheric Spanish will react to /θ/ either as "the correct pronunciation" ("though we don't use it") or as a pretentious pronunciation (unless it comes from people to the manner born, i.e., many Spaniards). Thus, whereas it is desirable though not obligatory that you use Standard 1 in Spain, you would be well advised to use only Standard 2 in the Western Hemisphere, where /θ/ is bound to elicit a sharp reaction of one kind or another (as sharp as British **drawing pin**, **lorry**, or **trunk call** instead of **thumbtack**, **truck**, and **long-distance call** would probably elicit in the United States).

ch, wherever it is found, is always pronounced as /tʃ/, which is similar to the pronunciation of **ch** in English **church**, **child**, etc.

If **c** ends a syllable (for instance, **accionista**, **facsimíl**, and **técnico**), **c** is pronounced as /k/. Spanish /k/ is similar to the pronunciation of **c** in English **escape**, **scandal**, etc. To achieve a good rendition of Spanish /k/, hold your open palm in front of your mouth and pronounce first **cape** and **coop**, then **escape** and **scandal**. When pronouncing the first two words, you felt a noticeable puff of air on your palm, but in the last two words you felt almost no puff at all. A noticeable puff of air accompanying a speech sound is called *aspiration*; sounds pronounced with aspiration are *aspirated*, and those pronounced without it are *unaspirated*. Spanish /k/ (like Spanish /p/ and /t/) is always unaspirated, wherever it occurs. Thus, you should have no trouble with Spanish **escapar** and **escandalo** because here /k/ occurs after /s/, and as an English speaker you will automatically pronounce it as unaspirated, just as you would the **c** of the English cognates of those words: **escape** and **scandal**. It is in other positions that you have to be careful not to aspirate: **claro**, **crear**, etc. (contrast them with their English cognates, both of which have an aspirated /k/: **clear**, **create**).

See also **k**, **ll** (under **l**), **q**, **s**, and **z**.

d has several pronunciations. At the beginning of an utterance, after /n/, or after /l/, this letter is pronounced /d/, which is similar to the pronunciation of **d** in English **dear**, **dust**, etc., with this difference: in the production of Spanish /d/, the tongue touches the lower edge of the upper front incisors.

When between two vowels, when preceded by a vowel and followed by **r**, or when at the end of a word and not preceded by **r** (as in **pedir, Pedro,** and **libertad**), the letter **d** is pronounced /ð/, which is similar to the pronunciation of **th** in English **that, there,** etc., but less interdental than English /ð/ (in the production of the Spanish sound, the tip of the tongue gently touches the lower edge of the upper incisors).

It follows from the foregoing that if the position of **d** in the utterance changes, its pronunciation may change. Contrast, for example, these three utterances: (1) **Dinamarca mandó embajadores a doce países,** (2) **En Dinamarca viven unos cuantos americanos,** and (3) **Iremos a Dinamarca.** In (1), the **d** of **Dinamarca** is pronounced /d/ because it comes at the beginning of an utterance; in (2) the same **d** is also pronounced /d/ because it comes after /n/; but in (3) the same **d** is pronounced /ð/ because none of the conditions for pronouncing it /d/ is met. Similarly, when the word **dedo** is pronounced in isolation, the first **d** is rendered /d/ (and the second one /ð/), but in the phrase **mi dedo,** the first **d** is no longer at the beginning of an utterance (nor is it preceded by /n/ or /l/); hence the phrase is pronounced /miðeðo/.

e has two pronunciations. The instruction given in some books that **e** is pronounced /e/ when stressed and /ɛ/ when unstressed does not hold true for today's Spanish and may never have been an accurate description of its pronunciation in any variety of the language.

Here are better guidelines for **e** (except when it is part of a diphthong or triphthong):

If **e** is found in a syllable ending in a consonant (see "Syllabification" below), it is pronounced /ɛ/, which is similar to the pronunciation of **è** in French or to the vowel of **bet, let, met,** etc., as pronounced in Standard English, that is, with considerable lowering of the jaw, for example, **embaldosar, fresco, hablen,** and **mestizo.**

If **e** ends a syllable and the next one begins with **r, rr,** or **t,** it is pronounced /ɛ/, for instance, **pero, caballete** (the first **e**), **cerrar,** and **jinete.**

Otherwise, **e** is pronounced /e/, which is similar to the pronunciation of **é** in French, that is, the jaw is lowered only minimally (the closest English comes to having a sound like /e/ is the vowel of **ache, rake, stake,** etc.), for example, **caballete** (the second **e**), **hablé,** and **mesa.** In this dictionary, the sounds /e/ and /ɛ/ are both represented by /e/.

See also "Diphthongs and Triphthongs" below.

f is pronounced /f/, which is similar to the pronunciation of **f** in English **fate, feet,** etc., for example, **afectar, fecha, golf, golfo, ¡uf!.**

g has several pronunciations. At the beginning of an utterance and when followed by **a, o, u,** or a consonant letter except **n** (as in **gato, goma, gusto,** or **glaciar**), **g** is pronounced /g/, which is similar to the pronunciation of **g** in English **get, go, gumption,** etc.

At the beginning of a word and when followed by **n,** the letter **g** is silent (as in **gnomo**). That pronunciation is in fact so widespread and reputable that a **g**-less spelling is now acceptable and is in fact preferred in this dictionary (see "Miscellaneous" below).

When **g** occurs at the end of a syllable and is preceded by **n,** it is silent, as in **búmerang.** In older borrowings from other languages, that **g** was systematically or sometimes omitted, as in **sterling > esterlina, pudding > pudín.**

Before **e** or **i** (as in **gemir** and **gigante**), except if it comes at the end of a word, the letter **g** is pronounced /x/, which is absent in most varieties of current English. This sound is similar to the pronunciation of **ch** in German **Bach,** that of **ch** in Israeli Hebrew **zecher**, and that of **ch** in Scots English **loch**, **Lochaber**, etc. Press the back of the tongue against the soft palate, expel air (as if coughing), and do not vibrate the vocal chords. **g** before **e** or **i** can also be pronounced /h/, as in English **"house,"** which is common in Latin America and in southern Spain. In this dictionary, both /x/ and /h/ are represented by /h/.

If **g** ends a syllable that is not the last syllable of the word (as in **dogma** and the first syllable of **zigzag**), this letter is pronounced /g/. In such cases, the next syllable always begins with a consonant.

Otherwise, **g** is pronounced /ɣ/, a sound absent in English, which is made by bringing the back of the tongue close to the soft palate (without letting them touch), expelling air through the mouth, and vibrating the vocal chords. Examples are **hago** and **hígado**. In this dictionary, both sounds, /g/ and /ɣ/, are represented by /g/.

h is silent.

i is pronounced /i/, which is similar to the vowel of English **beet**, **feet**, **sheen**, etc., but shorter (for instance, **dicho**, **isla**, and **cursi**).
See also **y**.

j is almost always pronounced /x/, although a pronunciation as /h/ is also acceptable in parts of Latin America and southern Spain (see **g** for interpreting these symbols). A notable exception is **reloj**, which many speakers pronounce /re'lo/. That pronunciation of **reloj** is so widespread that **reló** is an alternate spelling of the singular form, but only in informal writing. In the plural, everyone pronounces /x/ or /h/ and therefore writes the **j**: **relojes**.
See **x**.

k, which is now found only in recent borrowings from other languages, is pronounced /k/ (see **c** for interpreting that symbol). The letter combination **ck** (as in **crack, flashback, shock, snack, stock**) is pronounced /k/.

l when not doubled is pronounced /l/, which is formed by putting the tip of the tongue against the sockets of the upper incisors, the remainder of the tongue lying flat. Spanish /l/ thus does not have the hollow sound of English /l/, in whose formation the back of the tongue rises toward the palate.

ll has two pronunciations, /ʎ/ and /y/, which vary by region and class rather than by placement within a word. /ʎ/, a sound similar to the Italian **gli**, has no real equivalent in English, although the **lli** of **million** comes close. While /λ/ is held to be the "correct" pronunciation by Spanish radio and television guidelines, it is almost never used in Latin America, except among some academics and the very wealthy. In Spain it is only heard in the northern regions of Castile. Much more common, and almost universally accepted today, is the pronunciation /y/, which is similar to our **y** in **yes** or **yam**.

In the Southern Cone of Latin America, a third pronunciation, /ʒ/ (like the French **Geneviève**), is also used.

m is pronounced /m/, which is similar to the pronunciation of **m** in English **make, might,** etc.

Traditionally, Spanish does not have /m/ at the end of a word when it is pronounced in isolation. However, a few words (all learned borrowings from other languages) end in **m** (for example, **álbum, factótum, ídem, médium, memorándum, ultimátum,** and **vademécum**), and that letter always appears in the Spanish names of many places outside Spanish-speaking areas, like **Bírmingham, Búckingham, Siam,** and **Vietnam**. Both /m/ and /n/ are heard in such words, depending on people's ability to pronounce /m/ at the end of a word (as more and more Spanish-speakers study other languages, they find it easier to produce that sound in that position) and their interest in maintaining the supposedly "correct" (i.e., non-Spanish) pronunciation of that letter.

n has several pronunciations. If immediately followed by a labial consonant (represented by **b, f, m, p,** or **v**) whether in the same word or in the next one, it is pronounced /m/ (as in the words **anfitrión, inmediato, anverso,** or the sentences **insiste en bucear, insiste en pelear,** and **en muchos casos hay más**). Since /m/ + /m/ is reduced to a single /m/, **en muchos casos** actually has just one /m/.

However, /m/ + /n/ (as in **insomne**) is not reduced.

Before /k/ or /g/ (as in **aunque** and **angosto**), **n** is pronounced /ŋ/, which is similar to the final consonant of **sing, long,** and **song** as pronounced in English.

In all other positions (as in **Anatolia, andan,** and **nombrar**), **n** is pronounced /n/, which is similar to the pronunciation of **n** in English **hand, near,** etc.

See also **m,** "Stress," and, "Miscellaneous" below.

ñ is pronounced /ɲ/, which is similar to the pronunciation of **ny** in English **canyon** or **ni** in English **onion.**

o is pronounced similarly to the **o** in the English words **tote** and **gloat.** English speakers, however, must be careful not to end the pronunciation of this vowel with an "off-glide" (an "off-glide," in this case, would close the **o** into a **u** sound at the end of the vowel). Thus, the Spanish **no** and the English **no** are not exactly alike, as the Spanish ends in a pure /o/ sound, while the English "off-glides" into a /u/, producing /nou/.

p, where it is pronounced, stands for /p/, which is similar to the pronunciation of **p** in English **space, spare, spook,** etc., but different from that of **p** in English **pike, peak, poke,** etc., in that it is not aspirated (see **c** for definitions of aspirated and unaspirated sounds).

Spanish **ps** at the beginning of a word is pronounced /s/.

q is always followed by **ue** or **ui.** The sequence **que** is pronounced /ke/ and **qui** is pronounced /ki/ (for example, **quince**).

To represent the sound sequences /kue/ and /kui/, Spanish has **cue** and **cui** respectively (as in **cueva** and **cuidar**).

Because **q** is always followed by **u,** if Spanish-speakers borrow words containing just **q** from other languages, that letter is changed to **k.** Thus, the Spanish names of Iraq and Qatar, for example, are **Irak** and **Katar.**

r has two pronunciations. At the beginning of a word or when it comes after **l, n,** or **s** (for example, **reir, alrededor, enrojecer,** and **Israel**), this letter has the same pronunciation as **rr** (see below).

In all other positions, **r** is pronounced with one flip of the upper part of the tongue against the sockets of the upper incisors (for instance, **leer, para, pera, pero, tercero,** and **treinta**).

rr is pronounced with a trill (several flips) of the upper front part of the tongue against the sockets of the upper incisors (for instance, **parra, perra, perro,** and **sierra**). Thus, **para** and **parra** are different words, with different meanings. The same applies to **caro** and **carro, pera** and **perra, pero** and **perro, torero** and **torrero,** and other pairs of words.

s has several pronunciations. When it represents the plural ending of nouns recently borrowed from other languages, it is silent in certain words, like **cabarets, carnets, complots, conforts, superávits, tíckets, trusts, vermuts.**

Before the letters **b, v, d, g** (but only when the letter is not followed by **e** or i), **l**, **m**, **n**, or **r** (whether any of those eight letters appear in the same word as **s** or they appear in the next word), you have an alternative in both standards if **s** is not the last letter of the word: it may be pronounced /z/ (a sound similar to the pronunciation of **z** in English **zebra**, **zoo**, etc.) or /s/ (see **c** for interpreting that symbol): **esbelto**, **esdrújulo**, **esgrimir**, **isla**, **esmalte**, **Israel**, **los baúles**, **los varones**, **los dedos**, **los guantes**, **los lagos**, **los maestros**, **los nervios**, **los ratones**, etc. If **s** is the last letter, only /s/ is found (for instance, in the family name **Pons**).

If **s** is followed by **r** (whether in the same word or in the next one), besides the two pronunciations suggested above, /s/ or /z/, a third possibility is not to pronounce the **s** at all and, as compensation, trill the **r** more. The word **Israel** (and its derivatives) thus has three pronunciations: /isrrael/, /izrrael/, and /irrrael/.

Otherwise, **s** is pronounced /s/ (as in **ese**, **especial**, **hablas**, **hasta**, **insistir**, **seco**).

If **s** is followed by **h**, the foregoing paragraph applies, except in the case of Spanish words recently borrowed from other languages or words modeled on such recently borrowed words, in which **sh** constitutes a unit, to be pronounced /ʃ/ (a sound similar to the pronunciation of **sh** in English **shall**, **sheet**, **should**, etc.). Thus, in **deshacer**, an old Spanish word not recently borrowed from another language, the instructions about **s** apply and the **h** is silent (hence the first two syllables of that word are /desa/), whereas in **riksha**, **sh** is pronounced /ʃ/.

See also **b**, **c**, **t**, **z**, and "Syllabification" below.

t is pronounced /t/, which is similar to the pronunciation of **t** in English **stoop**, **stake**, **steer**, etc., but different from that of **t** in English **take**, **teak**, **took**, etc., in that it is less aspirated (see **c**).

The Spanish /t/ is made by touching the tip of the tongue against the upper incisors (in contrast to English /t/, in whose production the tongue touches the gums). In two positions, **t** may not be pronounced as described above. First, before **l** or **m** in the same word (as in **atleta**, **aritmético**, and **ritmo**) you have an alternative: **t** may be pronounced as described or it may be pronounced /ð/ (see **d** for interpreting that symbol).

Second, the **t** at the end of a word may be silent. Probably many, most, or all Spanish-speakers pronounce it in **cenit**, **déficit**, **fagot**, **mamut**, **superavít**, and **el Tíbet ~ el Tibet**, whereas in other words the **t** is silent, for instance **cabaret**, **carnet**, **complot**, **tícket**, **trust**, and **vermut**, which are pronounced as if written *cabaré, *carné, *compló, *tique, *trus, and *vermú (the plurals are pronounced identically to their singulars). In still other words you have an alternative: **confort** is pronounced either /kom'for/ or /kom'fort/ (the plural **conforts** has both variants too).

u has two pronunciations. In the combinations **gue**, **gui**, **que**, and **qui**, the letter **u** is silent, for example, **guedeja** /geðeha/, **quedar** /keðar/, and **quien** /kien/ (see **q** and **e** on the pronunciation of those letters).

In all other cases, it is pronounced /u/, which is similar to the vowel sound of English **who** and **cool**. Thus, **puesto** and **seudónimo**, for example, are pronounced /puesto/ and /seuðonónimo/.

v has two pronunciations. At the beginning of an utterance or after **n** (which in this position is pronounced /m/), the letter **v** is pronounced /b/, which is similar to the first consonant of English **beach**, **broth**, etc. In all other positions, this letter is pronounced /β/ (see **b** for interpreting that symbol). For example, in the sentence ¿Es verdad que en el anverso de la medalla se ve un pavo real?, the second and sixth words have /b/ and the eleventh and thirteenth have /β/.

The instructions for pronouncing **b** and those for pronouncing **v** are identical (depending on the position of those letters in the utterance), as a consequence of which pairs of words like **baca** and **vaca** or **hube** and **uve** are homophones in today's Spanish and, as a further consequence of which, if you hear /b/ or /β/, you cannot tell whether it is to be represented by **b** or by **v** unless you know how to spell the word.

See also **b**.

w, which is found only in borrowings from Germanic languages and French, has several pronunciations. In several words, it is pronounced as if it were **b** or **v** and in such cases alternate spellings with **v** are found too: **wagneriano ~ vagneriano, Westfalia ~ Vestfalia**. The forms with **v** are preferable.

In at least a few words, **w** is pronounced /w/ (a sound similar to the first sound of English **win** and **won**), and for one of them an alternate spelling with **u** exists: **Malawi, Taiwán, Zimbabwe**.

In **whisky**, the letter combination **wh** is pronounced /w/ by those who want to show off their knowledge of English or, alternatively, /gw/.

x has several pronunciations. If **x** occurs before a consonant (as in **experiencia, extremidad,** and **mixto**), pronounce it /ks/. That pronunciation is probably the most frequent in words beginning with the prefix **ex-** followed by a consonant, for example **excelente**, widely pronounced /eksselente/ in Latin America, or /eksθelente/ in Castile.

If **x** occurs between vowels, you have an alternative in certain words (**examen** and **exiguo**, for example, may be pronounced with /ks/ or /gz/, but not in others (for instance, all Spanish-speakers, it seems, now pronounce **sexo** with /ks/).

At the end of a word, the pronunciation of **x** is in flux. In **ántrax, Benelux, dux, fénix, látex,** and **tórax**, /ks/ seems to be the most frequent if not universal pronunciation today, although /s/ is also heard.

At least some exceptions to those pronunciations are heard in words of Native American origin: for example, in **México** and **mexicano,** the **x** is now always pronounced /x/ (those are the spellings official and universal in Mexico; elsewhere, **Méjico** and **mejicano** are used); in **Xochimilco** (a Mexican place name), the **x** is always pronounced /s/.

Further exceptions are certain given and family names, which are found in two variants: one preserving a now archaic spelling with **x** (like **Xavier** and **Ximénez**) and the other spelled in modern fashion with **j** (**Javier** and **Jiménez**). Here, **x** is pronounced /h/, that is, just like **j**.

y has several pronunciations. In the word **y**, it is pronounced /i/ (see **i** for interpreting that symbol).

When it represents the first or last segment of a diphthong or triphthong (see "Diphthongs and Triphthongs" below), as in **ya, yegua, yunque, ley, rey, soy,** and **Paraguay,** the letter **y** is pronounced /y/ (see **ll** for interpreting that symbol).

In certain varieties of Spanish, **y** is pronounced with more occlusion, so that it has come to be close to /ʒ/ if not actually that sound (see **ll** for interpreting the latter symbol); and in still other varieties it is pronounced with so much occlusion that is has come to be close to /dʒ/ if not actually that (/dʒ/ is similar to the first consonant of English **Jacob, Jerusalem, Jew,** etc.)

Certain family names have two spelling variants, an archaic one with **y** and one spelled in modern fashion with **i** (like **Yglesias ~ Iglesias**). Here, **y** is pronounced /i/, that is, just like **i**.

z has several pronunciations. In Standard 1, you have an alternative: (1) In all positions, pronounce it /θ/ (see **c** for interpreting that symbol). Or, (2) Before the letters **b, v, d, g, l, m, n,** or **r** (whether in the same word or in the next one), pronounce it /ð/ (see **d** for interpreting that symbol), and in all other positions pronounce it /θ/.

In Standard 2, you have an alternative: (3) In all positions, pronounce it /s/ (see **c** for interpreting that symbol). Or, (4) Before the letters **b, v, d, g, l, m, n,** or **r** (whether in the same word or in the next one), pronounce it /z/, and in all other positions pronounce it /s/.

Diphthongs and Triphthongs

Spanish has fifteen diphthongs and eight triphthongs.

Eight of the diphthongs begin with a semivowel:

ia /ia/ is spelled **ya** at the beginning of a word, e.g., **desahuciar, yámbico.**

ua /ua/, e.g., **guardar.**

ie /ie/ is spelled **ye** at the beginning of a word, e.g., **agüero, bien, higiene, siete, yema.**

ue /ue/ is spelled **üe** after **g** that is not pronounced /h/, e.g., **huelga, hueste, huevo, vergüenza.**

io /io/ e.g., **biombo, piojo.** The spelling **io** at the beginning of a word is an imitation of Greek.

uo /uo/, e.g., **arduo.**

iu /iu/ is spelled **yu** at the beginning of a word, e.g., **yuca, yugo, triunfo.**

ui /ui/ (spelled **uy** in **muy**), e.g., **cuidar, muy.** For **uy** representing /uy/, see **uy** in the next section.

Take care to pronounce diphthongs beginning with a semivowel as diphthongs and not as two syllables. Thus, whereas English **barrio** has three syllables, Spanish **barrio** has two (**ba-rrio**), pronounced /barrio/.

Seven of the diphthongs end in a semivowel:

ai /ai/ is spelled **ay** at the end of most words; rarely, **ay** is found in the middle of a word, e.g., **aimará ~ aymará, hay, Raimundo, Seychelles.** If **ay** occurs before a vowel in the same word, it represents not a diphthong but /a/ + /y/, and each of those sounds belongs to a different syllable (thus, **aya** and **haya** for example are syllabified **a-ya** and **ha-ya**).

au /au/, e.g., **caudillo.**

ei is almost always pronounced /ey/ and is almost always spelled **ey** at the end of a word, e.g., **reina, rey.** A pronunciation exception is **reir,** which is pronounced as if it is spelled *reír.** If **ey** occurs before a vowel in the same word, it represents not a diphthong but /e/ + /y/, and each of those sounds belongs to a different syllable (thus, **reyes** and **leyenda** for instance are syllabified **re-yes** and **le-yen-da**).

eu /eu/, e.g., **seudonónimo.**

oi is almost always pronounced /oi/ and is spelled **oy** at the end of a word, e.g., **hoy,** and in certain family names in other positions too (like **Goytisolo**). A pronunciation exception is **oir,** which is pronounced as if spelled *oír.** If **oy** occurs before a vowel in the same word, it represents not a diphthong but /o/ + /y/ and each of those sounds belongs to a different syllable (thus, **Goya** is syllabified **Go-ya**).

uy, which always occurs at the end of a word, is almost always pronounced /ui/ (as in ¡huy!, Jujuy). The exception is **muy,** whose pronunciation is given in the previous section. If **uy** occurs before a vowel in the same word, it represents not a diphthong but /u/ + /y/ and each of those sounds belongs to a different syllable (thus, **cuyo** and **tuyas** are syllabified **cu-yo** and **tu-yas**).

The triphthongs are:

iai /iai/ e.g., **despreciáis.**

iau /iau/ e.g., **miau.**

iei /iei/ e.g., **despreciéis.**

uai /uai/ (spelled **uay** at the end of a word), e.g., **evaluáis, Uruguay.**

uau /uau/ e.g., **guau.**

uei /uei/ (spelled **uey** at the end of a word), e.g., **evaluéis, buey.**

Syllabification

Spanish is a consonant-vowel language, that is, syllables preferably end in a vowel (though many exceptions are found). Therefore, a single consonant and the vowel following it usually form a syllable or, expressed otherwise, a single consonant between two vowels usually goes with the following vowel (thus, **ba-jo, ad-he-sión**). Since **ch, ll, ñ,** and **rr** represent a single consonant, the syllabification is, for example, **mu-cha-cho, ha-llar, ni-ño, ba-rrio,** and **haz-me-rreír.**

The consonant clusters **bl, cl, dl, fl, gl, pl, tl, br, cr, dr, fr, gr, pr,** and **tr** form a syllable with the following vowel, for instance, **ha-blar, a-cla-rar, a-flo-jar, a-glo-me-rar, a-pla-zar, a-tle-ta, a-bra-zar, a-cre-di-tar, a-dre-de, a-fran-ce-sar, a-gre-gar,** and **a-pren-der.**

When representing /ʃ/, **sh** is not divided, whereas if a consonant letter + **h** is found in the middle of a word and the **h** is silent, the **h** begins a new syllable: **al-ha-ra-ca, clor-hi-dra-to, des-hi-dra-tar, in-hu-ma-ción.**

All other clusters of two consonants between vowels (including diphthongs and triphthongs) are usually divided, so that the first consonant belongs to the preceding syllable and the second consonant to the following syllable, for example, **a-cos-tar-se, ac-tuar, cuer-do, en-car-gar, es-la-vo, fras-co, Is-ra-el, llan-ta, per-di-ción, sol-da-du-ra,** and **der-vi-che.** Subject to that rule are also instances of double **c** or **n,** as in **per-fec-ción** and **en-ne-gre-cer.**

If a cluster of three or more consonants stands between vowels, the last two consonants are usually **bl, cl, fl, gl, pl, tl, br, cr, dr, fr, gr, pr,** or **tr** and they go with the following syllable, for instance, **tem-blar, ten-dré, ex-plo-tar, tem-pra-no.**

If a cluster of three or more consonants stands between vowels and if the second consonant is **s,** the **s** goes with the preceding syllable, for example **ins-tan-te** and **pers-pec-ti-va.**

If one vowel follows another and they do not constitute a diphthong (see above), they belong to separate syllables, for instance, **ma-es-tro, cre-o, le-er, to-a-lla.** Accordingly, if **i** or **u** (which represent respectively /i/ or /u/ in diphthongs and triphthongs) represents a vowel, it belongs in a separate syllable and that fact is indicated by a stress mark. Thus, **ahínco** (three syllables: **a-hín-co**), **búho** (two syllables: **bú-ho**), **desahúcio** (four syllables: **de-sa-hú-cio**), **traído** (three syllables: **tra-í-do**), **prohíbo** (three syllables: **pro-hí-bo**), **Raúl** (two syllables: **Ra-úl**), **haría** (three syllables: **ha-rí-a**), **haríais** (three syllables: **ha-rí-ais**), etc.

If **y** is preceded and followed by a vowel, it forms a diphthong with the following one and therefore belongs in the following syllable, for instance **ca-yó,** tu-yo, cre-yó. In fact, all diphthongs and triphthongs (see the list above) form syllables of their own. In contrast, identical contiguous vowels (as in **creer**) and vowels that do not form diphthongs or triphthongs (as in **leal**), as well as diphthongs or triphthongs dissolved by the stress mark (see the examples from **ahinco** to **haríais** in the previous paragraph), form separate syllables (thus, **cre-er, le-al,** etc.).

It is permissible but not obligatory to set aside the foregoing rules in the case of prefixes, which one may consider as forming syllables of their own (whether or not such would be the case if the rules were followed) or which one may subject to the rules. For example, **ab-ro-ga-ción** or **a-bro . . ., des-a-bro-char** or **de-sa . . ., ex-a-cer-ba-ción** or **e-xa . . ., sub-li-mar** or **su-bli . . .** (in each pair, the first variant reflects treatment of the prefix as a syllable in its own right, no matter what the rules should require, and the second variant shows syllabification when the rules are applied). The same applies to solid compounds: **no-so-tros, vos-o-tras** or **vo-so-tras,** etc.

The foregoing paragraph notwithstanding, the rules must be followed with respect to a succession of three consonant letters, the second of which is **s,** in which case **s** belongs with the preceding, not the following letter (thus, as already noted, **ins-tan-te, pers-pect-ti-va,** not **in-st . . ., per-sp . . .**) and with respect to prefixes if the first letter immediately following them is **h** (thus, **des-ha-cer** and **des-hi-dra-tar,** not **de-sha . . .** or **des-shi . . .**).

Stress

Most Spanish words have only one primary stress, which can be determined from the spelling according to these rules:

(1) If a word is spelled with a stress mark, stress the syllable in which it is found (like **águila, bíceps, fórceps, hablarán, Martínez**).

(2) If a word contains no stress mark:

[2.A] Stress the last syllable if the word ends in:

[2.A.i] a vowel letter + **y** (like **convoy, Uruguay, virrey**),

[2.A.ii] a consonant letter other than **n** or **s** (like **consentir, David, lateral**),

[2.A.iii] **n** not preceded by a vowel letter (like **Isern**),

[2.A.iv] **s** not preceded by a vowel letter (like **Fontanals, Casals**).

[2.B] Stress the next-to-last syllable if the word ends in:

[2.B.i] a vowel letter other than **y** (like **casi, habla, hable, hablo, fatuo, patria, sitio**),

[2.B.ii] a vowel letter + **n** (like **consienten, hablan**),

[2.B.iii] a vowel letter + **s** (like **consientes, hablas**).

The triplets **árbitro, arbitro, arbitró; público, publico, publicó; término, termino, terminó; tráfago, trafago, trafagó;** and **válido, valido, validó** illustrate several possibilities.

Miscellaneous

It is noted above that /m/ + /m/, /n/ + /n/, /p/ + /p/, and /s/ + /s/ are respectively reduced to one /m/, /p/, and /s/. Since the number of instances of /s/ + /s/ is not the same in all varieties of Spanish, the number of reductions to /s/ varies accordingly. For example, **absceso** is pronounced /apseso/ only where **c** before **e** (or **i**) is pronounced /s/ (otherwise it is rendered /apθeso/); see also **excelente** in the remarks on **x**.

Reduction of identical contiguous sounds (whether vowels or consonants) is widespread in Spanish, whether within a word or between two words.

Thus, /a/ + /a/ is reduced to /a/ both in the word **portaaviones** and in a phrase like **a ambos;** or, /e/ + /e/ is reduced to /e/ in the word **sobreexcitar.** The spellings **guardagujas, guardalmacén, remplazar, sobrentender,** etc., are in fact used too and they are preferable. In many cases, only spellings reflecting a reduction are now found, for example, **aprensión, prensil,** and **represible** (contrast those forms with their English cognates: **apprehension, prehensile,** and **reprehensible**).

English, especially British English, is a stress-timed language (it has a rhythm in which stressed syllables tend to occur at regular intervals of time, regardless of the number of intervening unstressed syllables) whereas Spanish is a syllable-timed language (with rhythm in which syllables are approximately equal in duration and thus tend to follow one another at regular intervals). Consequently, speakers of English, especially British English, tend to reduce unstressed syllables (as in the British pronunciation of **momentary, pattern, secretary**), whereas Spanish-speakers tend to pronounce each syllable distinctly and do not often slur over any of them. Spanish-speakers thus often react to English-accented Spanish as one in which **se comen las vocales** 'the vowels are swallowed up' and speakers of English (especially British English) tend to react to Spanish-accented English as "overly precise." To get an idea of the difference between stress- and syllable-timed languages, contrast American and British pronunciations of **momentary** and **secretary:** Americans pronounce each syllable of those words with more or less the same degree of distinctiveness, whereas the British pronounce only the first syllable distinctly and slur over the others; thus, American English is more syllable-timed and British English more stress-timed. To pronounce Spanish correctly, English-speakers should therefore give each vowel its full value.

Formerly, in the Spanish-speaking world, the pronunciation and spelling of words borrowed from other languages were routinely changed so that they conformed to Spanish norms. Thus for example, **bowline > bolina, coolie > culi, goal > gol,** and **kerosene > kerosen.**

Now, however, the trend is to retain non-Spanish spellings, though not necessarily non-Spanish pronunciations, with the result that the good fit between the Spanish spelling and pronunciation is in certain words absent.

List of Abbreviations Used in This Dictionary

a adjective
Abbr. abbreviation
acc accusative
adv adverb
Aer. aeronautics
Agr. agriculture
Anat. anatomy
Archit. architecture
Archeol. archeology
art. article
art art
Astron. astronomy
Astrol. astrology
Auto. automobiles
aux auxiliary
Biol. biology
Bot. botany
Cards. card games
Chem. chemistry
Com. commerce
Compar. comparative
condit conditional
conjunc conjunction
Culin. culinary
Dance. dancing
dat dative
dim diminutive
Eccl. ecclesiastical
Educ. education
Elec. electricity
Engin. engineering
Ent. entomology
Euph. euphemism
f feminine
Fig. figurative
Fig. Inf. used figuratively in informal speech or writing
fut future
gen generally; genitive

Geog. geography
Geol. geology
Geom. geometry
Gram. grammar
Gym. gymnastics
Herald. heraldry
Hist. history
Ichth. ichthyology
imperf imperfect
impers impersonal
indic indicative
indef art indefinite article
Inf. informal
infin infinitive
insep inseparable
interj interjection, exclamation
interr interrogative
Ironic. ironical
irr irregular
Law. law
Ling. linguistics
Lit. literature
m masculine
Mas. masonry
Math. mathematics
Mech. mechanics
Med. medical
Metall. metallurgy
mf masculine or feminine
Mil. military
Mineral. mineralogy
Mus. music
Myth. mythology
n noun
Naut. nautical
Nav. naval
neut neuter
Obs obsolete

Opt. optics
Ornith. ornithology
part participle
Pers. personal; person
Pharm. pharmacy
Philos. philosophy
Phonet. phonetics
Photo. photography
Phys. physics
Physiol. physiology
pl plural
Poet. poetic
Polit. political
Polit. Econ. political economy
poss possessive
prep preposition
pres present
Print. printing
pron pronoun
Psychol. psychology
Radio. radio
Rail. railway
Sew. sewing
sing singular
Spirit. spiritualism
Sports. sports
subjunc subjunctive
Superl superlative
Surg. surgery
Surv. surveying
Tan. tanning
Theat. theater
Theol. theology
v aux auxiliary verb
vi intransitive verb
vr reflexive verb
vt transitive verb
West. Hem. Western Hemispheric Spanish
Zool. zoology

Spanish-English
Dictionary

a /a/ *f*, name of the letter A

a /a/ *prep* to; at; on; by; in, into; up to; according to; if, etc. 1. Denotes the direct complement of verb before objects representing specified persons or animals, personified nouns, pronouns referring to specific persons (**alguien, entrambos, cualquiera,** etc.), demonstrative or relative pronouns, collective nouns representing persons (**el público, la muchedumbre,** etc.), names of countries, cities, rivers, etc., except where these invariably take the def. art., e.g. *Dejé a Varsovia,* I left Warsaw, *but Dejé el Perú,* I left Peru. 2. Introduces indirect obj. when this is a noun governed by a verb implying motion, or an emphatic pers. pron., e.g. *Nos conviene a ti y a mí,* It suits both you and me. It is also used before indirect obj. to avoid ambiguity when there is both an indirect and direct obj. 3. Denotes the complement of verb when this is an infin., e.g. *Enseñó a pintar a María,* He taught Mary to paint. 4. Indicates direction or destination, e.g. *Vamos a Edimburgo,* We are going to Edinburgh. 5. Signifies location, or point of time when action takes place, e.g. *Vinieron a las doce.* They came at twelve o'clock. 6. Describes position of persons or things, e.g. *Se sentaron a la puerta,* They sat down at the door. *La casa queda a lu derecha,* The house is on the right. 7. Denotes interval of time or place between one thing and another, e.g. *de tres a cinco de la tarde,* from three to five in the afternoon, *de calle a calle,* from street to street. 8. Expresses manner of action, e.g. *a la francesa,* in the French way, *bordado a mano,* embroidered by hand. 9. Indicates rate or price, e.g. *a cuatro pesetas la libra,* at four pesetas the lb. 10. Indicates difference or comparison, e.g. *Va mucho de querer a hacer,* There's a difference between wishing and doing. 11. Sometimes is synonymous with *hasta, según, hacia* and governs almost all parts of speech. Has many idiomatic uses. 12. Before infin. sometimes has conditional sense, e.g. *A haber sabido las noticias no lo hubiéramos hecho,* If we had heard the news we would not have done it. 13. With nouns and adjectives forms adverbial phrases, e.g. *poco a poco,* little by little, *a veces,* sometimes, *a ciegas,* blindly, etc. *A* + *el* becomes *al,* e.g. *al rey,* to the king. *Al* + infin. means when or on, e.g. *al marcharme yo,* when I left (on my leaving)

abacería /aβaθe'ria; aβase'ria/ *f,* grocery shop

abacero /aβa'θero; aβa'sero/ **(-ra)** *n* grocer

ábaco /'aβako/ *m, Archit.* abacus; counting frame

abajamiento /a,βaha'miento/ *m,* lowering; letting down

abajar /aβa'har/ *vt* to lower

abajo /a'βaho/ *adv* under; underneath;

A

below; down. Used immediately after noun in adverbial phrases, e.g. *cuesta a., escalera a.,* downhill, downstairs —*interj* Down with! e.g. *¡A. el rey!* Down with the king! *venirse a.,* to fall down; *Fig.* collapse

abalanzar /aβalan'θar; aβalan'sar/ *vt* to balance; impel violently; —*vr* throw oneself upon; attack, rush upon; (*with prep a*) rush into, risk. *Se abalanzó hacia ellos,* He rushed toward them

abalorio /aβa'lorio/ *m,* glass bead; bead work

abanderado /aβande'raðo/ *m,* standard-bearer; (Argentina) valedictorian

abanderizar /aβanderi'θar; aβanderi'sar/ *vt* to organize in groups; —*vr* band together

abandonado /aβando'naðo/ *a* deserted; forlorn; helpless; indolent, careless; slovenly

abandonamiento /a,βandona'miento/ *m,* desertion; forlornness; helplessness; carelessness; slovenliness

abandonar /aβando'nar/ *vt* to forsake, desert; neglect; leave; give up; renounce; —*vr* neglect oneself; grow discouraged; (*with prep a*) give oneself over to

abandono /aβan'dono/ *m,* abandonment; defenselessness; forlornness; dilapidation; renunciation; neglect; slovenliness; debauchery

abanicar /aβani'kar/ *vt* to fan

abanico /aβa'niko/ *m,* fan; anything fan-shaped; *Inf.* sword; railway signal; *Naut.* derrick, **en a.,** fan-shaped

abaniqueo /aβani'keo/ *m,* fanning; swinging, oscillation; gesticulation

abarcador /aβarka'ðor/ **(-ra)** *n* one who clasps or embraces; monopolist

abarcadura /aβarka'ðura/ *f,* **abarcamiento** /aβarka'miento/ *m,* inclusion; scope

abarcar /aβar'kar/ *vt* to clasp, encircle; include, comprise; undertake, attempt; monopolize

abarrancadero /aβarranka'ðero/ *m,* rough road; ravine, precipice; *Fig.* difficult situation

abarrancar /aβarran'kar/ *vt* to ditch; make a ravine; —*vr* fall into a pit; stick (in the mud, etc.); get into difficulties; *Naut.* run aground

abastar /aβas'tar/ *see* **abastecer**

abastecedor /aβasteθe'ðor; aβastese'ðor/ **(-ra)** *a* provisioning, supplying —*n* provider; purveyor, supplier; caterer

abastecer /aβaste'θer; aβaste'ser/ *vt irr* to supply, provide; purvey. See **conocer**

abastecimiento /aβasteθi'miento; aβastesi'miento/ *m,* providing; supply, provision; catering; supplies

abasto /a'βasto/ *m,* provisions, food; *Com.* supply —*adv* plentifully, abundantly

abatido /aβa'tiðo/ a dejected, depressed; spiritless; discouraged; crushed, humbled; *Com*. depreciated

abatimiento /aβati'miento/ m, dejection, depression; humiliation; discouragement; falling; lowering; (*Aer. Naut.*) drift

abatir /aβa'tir/ vt to knock down; overthrow; demolish; lower, take down; droop; humiliate; discourage; *Naut*. dismantle; —vi (*Naut. Aer.*) drift; —vr be despondent, despair; humble oneself; swoop down (of birds). **a. el vuelo**, to fly down

ABC /aβe'θe; aβe'se/ m, ABCs (e.g. *el ABC de la física*, the ABCs of physics)

abdicación /aβðika'θion; aβðika'sion/ f, abdication

abdicar /aβði'kar/ vt to abdicate; revoke, cancel; give up (rights, opinions)

abdomen /aβ'ðomen/ m, abdomen

abdominal /aβðomi'nal/ a abdominal

abecé /aβe'θe; aβe'se/ m, ABCs

abecedario /aβeθe'ðario; aβese'ðario/ m, ABC, alphabet; reading book, primer

abeja /a'βeha/ f, bee. **a. maestra**, queen bee. **a. obrera**, worker

abejar /aβe'har/ m, beehive

abejero /aβe'hero/ (-ra) n beekeeper

aberración /aβerra'θion; aβerra'sion/ f, deviation; error, lapse; (*Astron. Phys. Biol.*) aberration

abertura /aβer'tura/ f, opening; aperture, gap, hole; fissure, cleft; mountain pass; naturalness, frankness

abierto /a'βierto/ a free, unobstructed; open, not enclosed; open, full-blown (flowers); frank, sincere —adv openly

abigarrado /aβiga'rraðo/ a variegated; varied; speckled

abigarrar /aβiga'rrar/ vt to variegate; vary; speckle; fleck; spot; dapple

abintestato /aβintes'tato/ a *Law*. intestate

abismal /aβis'mal/ a abysmal

abismar /aβis'mar/ vt to plunge into an abyss; depress, sadden; —vr despair; be plunged in thought, be abstracted; be amazed

abismo /a'βismo/ m, chasm, abyss, gulf; hell

abjurar /aβhu'rar/ vt to forswear, retract

ablactar /aβlak'tar/ vt to wean

ablandamiento /aβlanda'miento/ m, softening; placating

ablandante /aβlan'dante/ a softening; placatory

ablandar /aβlan'dar/ vt to soften; appease, placate; loosen; relax; —vi and vr be softened; be appeased; grow less stormy; (elements) decrease in force

ablandecer /aβlande'θer; aβlande'ser/ vt irr to soften. See **conocer**

abnegación /aβnega'θion; aβnega'sion/ f, abnegation, self-sacrifice

abnegado /aβne'gaðo/ a self-sacrificing

abnegarse /aβne'garse/ vr irr to deprive oneself, sacrifice oneself. See **cegar**

abobado /aβo'βaðo/ a bewildered; foolish-looking, silly

abobar /aβo'βar/ vt to daze, bewilder; make stupid

abocado /aβo'kaðo/ a full-flavored, pleasant (of wine)

abocar /aβo'kar/ vt to seize with the mouth; bring nearer; transfer (contents of one jug to another); —vr meet, assemble; —vi *Naut*. enter (a channel, port, etc.).

abocarse (con...), to contact (...), get in touch (with...)

abochornado /aβotʃor'naðo/ a flushed (of the face); ashamed; embarrassed

abochornar /aβotʃor'nar/ vt to overheat, make flushed; shame; embarrass; —vr (plants) dry up

abofetear /aβofete'ar/ vt to slap, hit; buffet

abogacía /aβoga'θia; aβoga'sia/ f, legal profession; practice of law; advocacy

abogado /aβo'gaðo/ (-da) n lawyer

abogar /aβo'gar/ vi to defend at law; intercede for; advocate, champion

abolengo /aβo'lengo/ m, lineage, descent, family; inheritance

abolición /aβoli'θion; aβoli'sion/ f, abolition

abolir /aβo'lir/ vt to abolish; cancel; annul

abollar /aβo'ʎar; aβo'yar/ vt to bruise; dent

abollonar /aβoʎo'nar; aβoyo'nar/ vt to emboss, do raised work on; —vr (vines) sprout

abombar /aβom'bar/ vt to make convex; *Inf*. deafen, bewilder; —vr begin to putrefy; get intoxicated

abominable /aβomi'naβle/ a abominable

abominación /aβomina'θion; aβomina'sion/ f, abomination; loathing, detestation

abominar /aβomi'nar/ vt to abominate, loathe, detest

abonado /aβo'naðo/ (-da) a trustworthy, reliable; ready, prepared, inclined —n subscriber; season ticket holder (for concerts, etc.)

abonanzar /aβonan'θar; aβonan'sar/ vi impers to clear up, be fine (weather)

abonar /aβo'nar/ vt to guarantee; go surety for; improve, better; manure; ratify, confirm; pay; *Com*. place to the credit of; —vr subscribe, become a subscriber; take out (season tickets, etc.)

abonaré /aβona're/ m, *Com*. due bill; promissory note, I.O.U.

abono /a'βono/ m, subscription; voucher; guarantee; manure. **a. verde**, leaf mold. **en a. de**, in payment of; in support of

aboquillado /aβoki'kaðo; aβoki'yaðo/ a tipped (of cigarettes)

abordar /aβor'ðar/ vt *Naut*. to board a ship; *Naut*. collide, run into; accost, tackle; undertake; —vi *Naut*. put into port

aborigen /aβor'ihen/ a aboriginal

aborígenes /aβo'rihenes/ *m pl*, aborigines

aborrachado /aβorra't∫aðo/ *a* bright red; highly colored; flushed

aborrecedor /aβorreθe'ðor; aβorrese'ðor/ **(-ra)** *a* hateful —*n* hater, loather

aborrecer /aβorre'θer; aβorre'ser/ *vt irr* to hate, loathe; desert offspring (animals, birds). See **conocer**

aborrecible /aβorre'θiβle; aβorre'siβle/ *a* hateful, detestable

aborrecimiento /aβorreθi'miento; aβorresi'miento/ *m*, hate, detestation; dislike

abortar /aβor'tar/ *vt* to abort; foil (a plot); —*vi Med.* miscarry; fail, go awry

abortivo /aβor'tiβo/ *a* abortive

aborto /a'βorto/ *m*, abortion; miscarriage; monster; failure

abotonar /aβoto'nar/ *vt* to button; —*vi* bud, sprout

abra /'aβra/ *f*, cove, small bay; narrow gorge; fissure, cleft

abrasador /aβrasa'ðor/ *a* burning, flaming

abrasamiento /aβrasa'miento/ *m*, burning; ardor, heat

abrasar /aβra'sar/ *vt* to burn; dry up, parch (plants); squander, waste; shame; —*vi* burn; —*vr* be very hot, glow; burn with passion

abrasivo /aβra'siβo/ *a* and *m*, abrasive

abrazadera /aβraθa'ðera; aβrasa'ðera/ *f*, clasp; clamp

abrazamiento /aβraθa'miento; aβrasa'miento/ *m*, embracing

abrazar /aβra'θar; aβra'sar/ *vt* to embrace, clasp in one's arms; follow, adopt; engage in; seize, take advantage of; comprise, include; surround; take in hand; clamp; clasp. **abrazarse a,** to clutch, hang on to

abrazo /a'βraθo; a'βraso/ *m*, embrace

abrelatas /aβre'latas/ *m*, can opener

abrevadero /aβreβa'ðero/ *m*, watering place (for cattle)

abreviación /aβreβia'θion; aβreβia'sion/ *f*, abbreviation, shortening; summary; hastening

abreviar /aβre'βiar/ *vt* to abbreviate, shorten; hasten, accelerate; condense, abridge. **a. tiempo,** to save time. **Y para a....,** And, to cut a long story short,..

abridor /aβri'ðor/ *m*, opener; ear-ring (for keeping holes in ears open). **a. de guantes,** glove-stretcher. **a. de láminas,** engraving needle. **a. de latas,** can opener

abridura /aβri'ðura/ *f*, (act of) opening (e.g. of a trunk)

abrigada /aβri'gaða/ *f*, **abrigadero** *m*, sheltered place

abrigar /aβri'gar/ *vt* to shelter, protect (against the cold, etc.); defend, help; hold (opinions); nurse (a hope, etc.); cover; —*vr* take shelter; wrap oneself up

abrigo /a'βrigo/ *m*, shelter; defense; protection; help; sheltered place; wrap, coat; *Naut.* haven

abril /a'βril/ *m*, April; youth; *pl Poet.* years

abrillantar /aβri⋏an'tar; aβriyan'tar/ *vt* to cut in facets like a diamond; polish, burnish; cause to shine; *Fig.* improve, add luster to

abrir /a'βrir/ *vt* to open; reveal; unlock; slide the bolt of; extend, spread out; cleave; engrave; clear (the way, etc.); begin; head, lead; separate; dig; inaugurate —*vi* unfold (flowers); expand; form —**abrir y cerrar de ojos,** in the twinkling of an eye, in the wink of an eye; —*vr* open; expand; *(with con)* confide in. **a. el camino (a...),** to pave the way (for...). **abrirse camino,** to make one's way; **abrirse paso a codazos,** to elbow one's way out, (or through)

abrochamiento /aβrot∫a'miento/ *m*, buttoning; fastening

abrochar /aβro't∫ar/ *vt* to button; fasten, clasp; hook up (a dress, etc.); buckle

abrogación /aβroga'θion; aβroga'sion/ *f*, repeal, annulment

abrogar /aβro'gar/ *vt* to repeal, annul

abroncar /aβron'kar/ *vt Inf.* to bore, annoy

abrumador /aβruma'ðor/ *a* burdensome, crushing, oppressive; troublesome, tiresome; exhausting

abrumar /aβru'mar/ *vt* to weigh down; overwhelm, oppress; weary, exhaust; —*vr* grow misty

abrupto /a'βrupto/ *a* steep; rough, broken (ground); rugged

absceso /aβ'sθeso; aβ'sseso/ *m*, abscess

absentismo /aβsen'tismo/ *m*, absenteeism

absolución /aβsolu'θion; aβsolu'sion/ *f*, (*Eccl.* and *Law.*) absolution; remission, pardon

absoluta /aβso'luta/ *f*, *Mil.* discharge

absoluto /aβso'luto/ *a* absolute; categorical; *Inf.* despotic. **en a.,** absolutely

absolver /aβsol'βer/ *vt irr* to absolve; acquit (of a charge). *Law.* **a. de la instancia,** to dismiss the case. See **mover**

absorbente /aβsor'βente/ *a* and *m*, absorbent

absorber /aβsor'βer/ *vt* to absorb; consume, use up; attract, hold (the attention, etc.); imbibe

absorción /aβsor'θion; aβsor'sion/ *f*, absorption

absortar /aβsor'tar/ *vt* to amaze, dumbfound

absorto /aβ'sorto/ *a* amazed, astounded; abstracted, lost in thought

abstemio /aβs'temio/ *a* abstemious

abstención /aβsten'θion; aβsten'sion/ *f*, abstention

abstenerse /aβste'nerse/ *vr irr* to refrain; abstain. See **tener**

abstinencia /aβsti'nenθia; aβsti'nensia/ *f*, abstinence; fasting

abstinente /aβsti'nente/ a abstemious; temperate

abstracción /aβstrak'θion; aβstrak'sion/ f, abstraction; preoccupation; absent-mindedness

abstracto /aβ'strakto/ a abstract. **en a.,** in the abstract

abstraer /aβstra'er/ vt irr to abstract; consider separately; —vi (with de) do without, exclude; —vr be preoccupied; let one's thoughts wander. See **traer**

abstraído /aβstra'iðo/ a retired, recluse; preoccupied; absent-minded

abstruso /aβ'struso/ a abstruse

absurdidad /aβsurði'ðað/ f, absurdity; folly, nonsense

absurdo /aβ'surðo/ a ridiculous, absurd. m, piece of folly, nonsense

abuchear /aβutʃe'ar/ vt vi to boo, hoot, jeer

abuela /a'βuela/ f, grandmother; old woman, dame

abuelo /a'βuelo/ m, grandfather; ancestor (gen. pl); old man; pl grandparents

abulia /a'βulia/ f, lack of will-power, abulia

abultado /aβul'taðo/ a bulky, large; voluminous; exaggerated

abultamiento /aβulta'miento/ m, bulkiness; enlargement, increase; mound; exaggeration

abultar /aβul'tar/ vt to enlarge, increase; exaggerate; model in rough (sculpture); —vi be bulky; be large

abundancia /aβun'danθia; aβun'dansia/ f, abundance, plenty

abundante /aβun'dante/ a abundant, plentiful; abounding (in)

abundar /aβun'dar/ vi to be plentiful, abound

abundoso /aβun'doso/ a See **abundante**

aburrido /aβu'rriðo/ a boring, tedious, dull; tired, weary

aburrimiento /aβurri'miento/ m, boredom, dullness; wearisomeness, tediousness

aburrir /aβu'rrir/ vt to bore; Inf. spend (time, money); (birds) desert the nest; —vr grow bored; be weary

abusar /aβu'sar/ vi to abuse; exceed one's rights, go too far; (with de) take advantage of

abusivo /aβu'siβo/ a abusive

abuso /a'βuso/ m, abuse. **a. de confianza,** abuse of trust

abyección /aβyek'θion; aβyek'sion/ f, degradation, misery; abjectness, servility

abyecto /aβ'yekto/ a abject, wretched; servile

acá /a'ka/ adv hither, here; at this time, now. **a. y acullá,** hither and thither. **desde ayer a.,** from yesterday until now

acabable /aka'βaβle/ a terminable, finishable; achievable

acabado /aka'βaðo/ a complete; perfect; expert, consummate; old, worn out; ill, infirm. m, finish

acabamiento /akaβa'miento/ m, finishing, completion; end; death, decease

acabar /aka'βar/ vt to end, terminate; finish; complete, perfect; kill; (with con) destroy, finish off; suppress; squander; —vi end; die; be destroyed; (with de + infin) to have just (e.g. Acaba de salir, He has just gone out); —vr end, be exhausted; run out of; fade, grow weak; be destroyed. **Se les acabaron las dudas,** Their doubts were cleared up. **a. de desconcertar,** to nonplus completely; **a. de decidirse,** to come to a decision; **a. de saber,** to finally learn

academia /aka'ðemia/ f, academy

académico /aka'ðemiko/ (-ca) a academic —n academician. **a. de la lengua,** member of the Royal Spanish Academy

acaecer /akae'θer; akae'ser/ vi irr to happen, occur. See **conocer**

acaecimiento /akaeθi'miento; akaesi'miento/ m, happening, occurrence, event

acalambrarse /akalam'brarse/ (muscle) to contract with cramps. **Estar acalambrado,** to have cramps

acallar /aka'ʎar; aka'yar/ vt to quieten, hush; soothe, appease

acalorado /akalo'raðo/ a hot; fervent; Fig. heated

acaloramiento /akalora'miento/ m, excitement, agitation, vehemence; ardor

acalorar /akalo'rar/ vt to warm; aid, encourage; excite, stimulate; stir, move (to enthusiasm); inflame, rouse; tire (by exercise); —vr grow hot; become agitated or excited; become heated (arguments)

acamar /aka'mar/ vt to lay flat (plants by the wind); —vr be flattened (plants); lie down (animals); go rotten (fruit)

acampar /akam'par/ vi and vt to encamp

acantilado /akanti'laðo/ a steep, precipitous; shelving (ocean-bed). m, cliff

acantonar /akanto'nar/ vt to billet or quarter troops

acaparador /akapara'ðor/ (-ra) n monopolist

acaparar /akapa'rar/ vt Com. to monopolize, corner; seize, take possession of

acápite /a'kapite/ m, West. Hem. new paragraph

acarear /akare'ar/ vt to face; face up to, meet with courage

acariciador /akariθia'ðor; akarisia'ðor/ (-ra) a caressing, loving —n fondler

acariciar /akari'θiar; akari'siar/ vt to caress; brush, touch lightly; cherish, treat affectionately; toy with (a suggestion)

acarreamiento, acarreo /akarrea'miento, aka'rreo/ m, cartage, carting; transport, carriage; occasioning

acarrear /akarre'ar/ vt to cart, transport; occasion, bring (gen. evil). **La guerra acarreó la carestía,** The war brought scarcity

acaso /a'kaso/ m, chance —adv by chance; perhaps, perchance. **por si a.,** in case (e.g. *Por si a. venga*, In case he comes)

acatable /aka'taβle/ *a* venerable, worthy

acatamiento /akata'miento/ *m*, respect; reverence; observance

acatar /aka'tar/ *vt* to treat with respect, honor, revere; observe

acatarrarse /akata'rrarse/ *vr* to catch a cold

acaudalado /akauða'laðo/ *a* wealthy, well-to-do

acaudalar /akauða'lar/ *vt* to make money; hoard up wealth; acquire (learning, etc.)

acceder /akθe'ðer; akse'ðer/ *vi* (*with prep* a) to concede, grant; accede to, agree to

accesibilidad /ak,θesiβili'ðað; ak,sesiβili'ðað/ *f*, accessibility; approachableness

accesible /akθe'siβle; akse'siβle/ *a* accessible; approachable

accesión /akθe'sion; akse'sion/ *f*, agreement, acquiescence; accession; accessory; feverish attack

acceso /ak'θeso; ak'seso/ *m*, access; paroxysm, outburst; *Med.* attack

accesorio /akθe'sorio; akse'sorio/ *a* accessory

accesorios /akθe'sorios; akse'sorios/ *m pl*, accessories; *Theat.* properties

accidentado /akθiðen'taðo; aksiðen'taðo/ *a* rough, uneven; stormy, troubled (life, etc.)

accidentar /akθiðen'tar; aksiðen'tar/ *vt* to cause (someone) an accident; —*vr* be the victim of an accident; be seized by a fit

accidente /akθi'ðente; aksi'ðente/ *m*, chance; accident, mishap; illness, indisposition; *Med.* fit; *Gram.* accidence; *Mus.* accidental. **a. del trabajo**, accident at work. **por a.**, by chance, accidentally

acción /ak'θion; ak'sion/ *f*, action; battle; skirmish; *Mech.* drive; *Com.* share; gesture; lawsuit; *Lit.* action (of play, etc.); *Art.* posture, pose. **a. de gracias**, thanksgiving; *Com.* **a. liberada**, paid-up share. **a. privilegiada**, preference share

accionar /akθio'nar; aksio'nar/ *vi* to gesture, gesticulate

accionista /akθio'nista; aksio'nista/ *mf* *Com.* shareholder

acechar /aθe'tʃar; ase'tʃar/ *vt* to spy upon, watch; lie in ambush for

acecho /a'θetʃo; a'setʃo/ *m*, spying upon, watch; waylaying, ambush. **al a.**, in ambush; on the watch

acecinar /aθeθi'nar; asesi'nar/ *vt* to salt and dry (meat); —*vr* (persons) wither, dry up

acedar /aθe'ðar; ase'ðar/ *vt* to make bitter, sour; embitter, displease; —*vr* turn sour; wither (plants)

aceitar /aθei'tar; asei'tar/ *vt* to oil, lubricate; rub with oil

aceite /a'θeite; a'seite/ *m*, olive oil; oil. **a. de hígado de bacalao**, cod-liver oil. **a. de linaza**, linseed oil. **a. de ricino**,

castor-oil. **a. de trementina**, oil of turpentine

aceitera /aθei'tera; asei'tera/ *f*, woman who sells oil; oil can; oil bottle; *pl* cruet

aceitoso /aθei'toso; asei'toso/ *a* oily

aceituna /aθei'tuna; asei'tuna/ *f*, *Bot.* olive

aceitunero /aθeitu'nero; aseitu'nero/ **(-ra)** *n* olive picker; olive seller. *m*, warehouse for storing olives

aceituno /aθei'tuno; asei'tuno/ *m*, olive tree

aceleración /aθelera'θion; aselera'sion/ *f*, speed, haste; acceleration

acelerador /aθelera'ðor; aselera'ðor/ *a* accelerating. *m*, hastener; *Auto.* accelerator

acelerar /aθele'rar; asele'rar/ *vt* to hasten, speed up; accelerate

acendrado /aθen'draðo; asen'draðo/ *a* pure, unblemished, spotless

acendrar /aθen'drar; asen'drar/ *vt* to refine (metals); purify, make spotless

acento /a'θento; a'sento/ *m*, accent; tone, inflection; *Poet.* voice, words. **a. agudo**, acute accent. **a. circunflejo**, circumflex accent. **a. grave**, grave accent. **a. ortográfico**, graphic accent, written accent. **a. tónico**, tonic accent

acentuación /aθentua'θion; asentua'sion/ *f*, accentuation, stress; emphasis

acentuar /aθen'tuar; asen'tuar/ *vt* to accent; stress, emphasize; —*vr* become evident, become marked, be noticeable

acepción /aθep'θion; asep'sion/ *f*, meaning, significance, acceptation. **a. de personas**, partiality, preference

acepilladura /aθe,piλa'ðura; ase,piya'ðura/-'*f*, sweeping, brushing; planing; wood-shaving

acepillar /aθepi'λar; asepi'yar/ *vt* to sweep, brush; plane; *Inf.* brush up, polish up

aceptabilidad /a,θeptaβili'ðað; a,septaβili'ðað/ *f*, acceptability

aceptable /aθep'taβle; asep'taβle/ *a* acceptable

aceptación /aθepta'θion; asepta'sion/ *f*, acceptance; popularity; approval

aceptador /aθepta'ðor; asepta'ðor/ **(-ra)** *a* accepting. —*n* acceptor

aceptar /aθep'tar; asep'tar/ *vt* to accept; approve; accept a challenge; *Com.* honor

acequia /a'θe'kia; ase'kia/ *f*, ditch, trench; irrigation channel

acera /a'θera; a'sera/ *f*, sidewalk, pavement. **a. del sol**, sunny side of the street

acerado /aθe'raðo; ase'raðo/ *a* steel; steel-like; strong, tough; mordant, incisive

acerar /aθe'rar; ase'rar/ *vt* to steel; treat (liquids) with steel; harden, make obdurate

acerbidad /aθerβi'ðað; aserβi'ðað/ *f*, bitterness, acerbity, sourness; harshness, cruelty

acerbo /a'θerβo; a'serβo/ *a* sour, tart, bitter; cruel, harsh

acerca de /a'θerka de; a'serka de/ *adv* about, concerning

acercamiento /aθerka'miento; aserka-'miento/ *m*, approach

acercar /aθer'kar; aser'kar/ *vt* to bring nearer; —*vr* be near at hand, draw near; (*with prep a*) approach

acero /a'θero; a'sero/ *m*, steel; blade, sword; *pl* bravery, spirit; *Inf.* good appetite. **a. inoxidable,** stainless steel

acérrimo /a'θerrimo; a'serrimo/ *a superl* extremely strong, mighty; most harsh; most resolute, unflinching; very strong (taste, smell)

acerrojar /aθerro'har; aserro'har/ *vt* to lock, padlock; bolt

acertado /aθer'taðo; aser'taðo/ *a* well-aimed; fitting, suitable; wise; successful

acertar /aθer'tar; aser'tar/ *vt irr* to hit the mark; find, come across; succeed (in), achieve; guess, find out; **No acertaba a explicármelo,** I couldn't quite understand it. **a. por chambra,** to make a lucky guess —*vi* be successful; thrive (of plants); (*with prep a + infin*) happen, occur, come to pass —*Pres. Indic.* **acierto, aciertas, acierta, aciertan.** *Pres. Subjunc.* **acierte, aciertes, acierte, acierten**

acertijo /aθer'tiho; aser'tiho/ *m*, riddle

acervo /a'θerβo; a'serβo/ *m*, pile, heap; *Fig.* storehouse, wealth (e.g. of words)

acetato /aθe'tato; ase'tato/ *m*, acetate

achacar /atʃa'kar/ *vt* to attribute, impute, assign. **achacable a,** imputable to

achacoso /atʃa'koso/ *a* ailing, ill, sickly

achantarse /atʃan'tarse/ *vr Inf.* to hide from danger; put up with, bear

achaparrado /atʃapa'rraðo/ *a* stocky

achaque /a'tʃake/ *m*, ailment, illness (permanent); *Inf.* period, menstruation; pregnancy; matter, affair; pretext; failing, bad habit. **En a. de...,** Re..., concerning...

achatar /atʃa'tar/ *vt* to flatten, make flat

achicar /atʃi'kar/ *vt* to make smaller, diminish; drain, bail out; depreciate, belittle

achicarse /atʃi'karse/ *Inf.* to sing small

achicharrar /atʃitʃa'rrar/ *vt Cul.* to overcook; overheat; annoy, importune

achicoria /atʃi'koria/ *f*, chicory

achispado /atʃis'paðo/ *a Inf.* tipsy

achuchar /atʃu'tʃar/ *vt Inf.* to squeeze, hug; jostle, push against

achuchón /atʃu'tʃon/ *m*, *Inf.* shove, push; hug, squeeze

achulado /atʃu'laðo/ *a Inf.* brazen, tough

aciago /a'θiago; a'siago/ *a* unhappy, ill-omened; fateful

acibarar /aθiβa'rar; asiβa'rar/ *vt* to add bitter aloes to; embitter, sadden

acicalado /aθika'laðo; asika'laðo/ *a* polished; neat; well-groomed. *m*, polishing, burnishing (of weapons)

acicalador /aθikala'ðor; asikala'ðor/ (**-ra**) *a* polishing —*n* polisher. *m*, burnisher (machine)

acicalar /aθika'lar; asika'lar/ *vt* to burnish

(weapons); adorn, deck; —*vr* dress oneself with care

acicate /aθi'kate; asi'kate/ *m*, Moorish spur; incitement, stimulus

acicatear /aθikate'ar; asikate'ar/ *vt* to induce, spur on. **a. la curiosidad,** arouse curiosity

acidez /aθi'ðeθ; asi'ðes/ *f*, acidity, bitterness

acidia /a'θiðia; a'siðia/ *f*, indolence; sluggishness

ácido /'aθiðo; 'asiðo/ *a* acid; sour; harsh. *m*, acid. **a. fénico,** carbolic acid. **a. graso,** fatty acid

acierto /a'θierto; a'sierto/ *m*, good hit, bull's-eye; success; achievement; cleverness; dexterity, skill; wisdom, sense; tact

aclamación /aklama'θion; aklama'sion/ *f*, acclamation; shout of acclamation. **por a.,** unanimously

aclamador /aklama'ðor/ (**-ra**) *a* acclaiming —*n* applauder, acclaimer

aclamar /akla'mar/ *vt* to acclaim; applaud

aclaración /aklara'θion; aklara'sion/ *f*, explanation; elucidation

aclarado /akla'raðo/ *m*, rinse; rinsing

aclarador, aclaratorio /aklara'ðor, aklara'torio/ *a* explanatory

aclarar /akla'rar/ *vt* to clarify, purify; clear; rinse (clothes); explain; thin; —*vi* clear; (sky) clear up; dawn

aclimatación /aklimata'θion; aklimata'sion/ *f*, acclimatization

aclimatar /aklima'tar/ *vt* to acclimatize

acné /ak'ne/ *m*, acne

acobardar /akoβar'ðar/ *vt* to intimidate, frighten

acodiciar /akoði'θiar; akoði'siar/ *vt* to yearn for, covet, desire

acogedizo /akohe'ðiθo; akohe'ðiso/ *a* gathered haphazardly

acogedor /akohe'ðor/ (**-ra**) *a* welcoming, friendly; inviting (e.g. a chair or room); —*n* protector

acoger /ako'her/ *vt* to receive, welcome, admit; protect, harbor; —*vr* take refuge; (*with prep a*) make use of, resort to; **acogerse a sagrado,** seek sanctuary

acogida /ako'hiða/ *f*, reception, welcome; protection, shelter; meeting place; confluence (of waters). **tener buena a.,** to be well received

acogollar /akogo'ʎar; akogo'yar/ *vt* to protect, cover (plants); —*vi* sprout, shoot

acogotar /akogo'tar/ *vt* to fell by a blow on the neck; *Inf.* knock out

acolada /ako'laða/ *f*, accolade

acólito /a'kolito/ *m*, acolyte

acometedor /akomete'ðor/ (**-ra**) *a* capable, enterprising; aggressive —*n* aggressor, attacker

acometer /akome'ter/ *vt* to attack furiously; undertake; take in hand; overcome (of sleep, etc.)

acometida /akome'tiða/ *f*, **acometimiento** *m*, assault, onrush; undertaking

acomodable /akomo'ðaβle/ *a* easily arranged

acomodación /akomoða'θion; akomoða'sion/ *f*, adjustment; adaptation; accommodation

acomodadizo /akomoða'ðiθo; akomoða'ðiso/ *a* accommodating, easy-going

acomodado /akomo'ðaðo/ *a* suitable; convenient; wealthy, well-off; comfort-loving; moderate, low (of price)

acomodador /akomoða'ðor/ **(-ra)** *n* theater attendant, usher

acomodamiento /akomoða'miento/ *m*, agreement, transaction; accommodation

acomodar /akomo'ðar/ *vt* to arrange, adjust, accommodate; adapt; appoint; place; reconcile; employ, take on; equip, provide; lodge; —*vi* suit, be convenient; —*vr* compromise, agree

acomodaticio /akomoða'tiθio; akomoða'tisio/ *a* accommodating

acomodo /ako'moðo/ *m*, post, employment; arrangement; settlement

acompañamiento /akompaɲa'miento/ *m*, accompaniment; following, retinue; *Mus.* accompaniment; *Theat.* crowd, chorus

acompañanta /akompa'ɲanta/ *f*, chaperon; maid, servant

acompañante /akompa'ɲante/ *m*, *Mus.* accompanist

acompañar /akompa'ɲar/ *vt* to accompany; follow, escort; enclose (a letter, etc.); *Mus.* accompany

acompasado /akompa'saðo/ *a* rhythmic; deliberate, slow

acondicionado /akondiθio'naðo; akondisio'naðo/ *a* conditioned; (*with bien or mal*) in good or bad condition; of good or bad quality; good- or ill-natured. **reflejo acondicionado** *Med.* conditioned reflex

acondicionar /akondiθio'nar; akondisio'nar/ *vt* to prepare; mend, repair; —*vr* condition oneself

acongojar /akongo'har/ *vt* to sadden, grieve; oppress

aconsejable /akonse'haβle/ *a* advisable

aconsejar /akonse'har/ *vt* to advise; —*vr* (*with con*) consult, ask advice of

acontecer /akonte'θer; akonte'ser/ *vi irr impers* to happen. See **conocer**

acontecimiento /akonteθi'miento; akontesi'miento/ *m*, event, occurrence

acopio /a'kopio/ *m*, collection, store; accumulation, gathering

acopladura /akopla'ðura/ *f*, **acoplamiento** *m*, (*Mech.*) joint; coupling; yoking; mating (of animals)

acoplar /ako'plar/ *vt* to join, couple; yoke; mate (animals); reconcile (opinions); —*vr Inf.* fall in love

acoquinar /akoki'nar/ *vt Inf.* to intimidate, terrify

acorcharse /akor'tʃarse/ *vr* to dry up, shrivel; go numb (limbs)

acordadamente /akor,ðaða'mente/ *adv* by common consent, unanimously; deliberately, after due thought

acordar /akor'ðar/ *vt irr* to decide unanimously; resolve; remind; tune; harmonize (colors); —*vi* agree; —*vr* remember; come to an agreement. **Si mal no me acuerdo**, If memory serves me right —*Pres. Indic.* acuerdo, acuerdas, acuerda, acuerdan. *Pres. Subjunc.* acuerde, acuerdes, acuerde, acuerden

acorde /a'korðe/ *a* agreed; in harmony; in agreement. *m*, *Mus.* chord; harmony

acordeón /akorðe'on/ *m*, accordion; (slang) crib sheet

acordonar /akorðo'nar/ *vt* to lace; cordon off, surround; mill (coins)

acorralamiento /akorrala'miento/ *m*, corralling, penning

acorralar /akorra'lar/ *vt* to corral, pen; confine; corner, silence (in argument); frighten; harass

acorrer /ako'rrer/ *vt* to aid, assist, —*vi* run, hasten; —*vr* take refuge

acortamiento /akorta'miento/ *m*, shortening

acortar /akor'tar/ *vt* to shorten; —*vr* be speechless, be shy. **a. las velas**, to take in sail

acosador /akosa'ðor/ **(-ra)** *a* persecuting —*n* persecutor

acosamiento /akosa'miento/ *m*, persecution

acosar /ako'sar/ *vt* to persecute relentlessly; annoy, harass

acostado /ako'staðo/ *a* in bed; stretched out; *Herald.* couchant

acostar /ako'star/ *vt irr* to lay down, stretch out; put to bed; —*vi* lean, tilt; —*vr* lie down; go to bed; *Naut.* come alongside. See **contar**

acostumbrado /akostum'braðo/ *a* accustomed, usual

acostumbrar /akostum'brar/ *vt* to habituate, accustom; —*vi* be in the habit of; —*vr* (*with prep a*) become used to

acotación /akota'θion; akota'sion/ *f*, noting; marginal note; stage direction; ordnance survey number

acotar /ako'tar/ *vt* to annotate; mark out boundaries; fix, establish; accept; *Inf.* choose; testify; fill in elevation figures (on a map); —*vr* seek refuge

acre /'akre/ *a* bitter, sour; harsh; biting, mordant. *m*, acre (land measure)

acrecencia /akre'θenθia; akre'sensia/ *f*, **acrecentamiento** *m*, increase; addition

acrecentar /akreθen'tar; akresen'tar/ *vt irr* to increase; augment; promote, prefer. See **acertar**

acrecer /akre'θer; akre'ser/ *vt irr* to increase; augment. See **conocer**

acreditado /akreði'taðo/ *a* accredited, well-reputed; respected

acreditar /akreði'tar/ *vt* to prove; verify; accredit; recommend; sanction, authorize; vouch for, guarantee; *Com.* credit

acreedor /akree'ðor/ **(-ra)** *n* creditor;

claimant —*a* deserving. **a. hipotecario,** mortgagee

acreencia /akre'enθia; akre'ensia/ *f,* .debt; *Com.* claim

acribillar /akriβi'ʎar; akriβi'yar/ *vt* to riddle with holes; wound repeatedly; pelt; torment; *Inf.* pester, harass

acriminar /akrimi'nar/ *vt* to accuse, charge

acrimonia /akri'monia/ *f,* acrimony

acrisolar /akriso'lar/ *vt* to refine, purify (metals); perfect; clarify, elucidate

acrobacia /akro'βaθia; akro'βasia/ *f,* acrobatics

acróbata /a'kroβata/ *mf* acrobat

acrobático /akro'βatiko/ *a* acrobatic

acta /'akta/ *f,* minutes, record; certificate of election (as deputy to Cortes, etc.); *pl* deeds (of a martyr). **a. matrimonial,** marriage register

actitud /akti'tuð/ *f,* attitude

activar /akti'βar/ *vt* to stimulate, make active; accelerate, hasten

actividad /aktiβi'ðað/ *f,* activity; movement, bustle. **en a.,** in action; at work.

activo /ak'tiβo/ *a* active. *m, Com.* assets

acto /'akto/ *m,* act, deed, action; act, law; act (of a play); public ceremony; *pl* minutes (of a meeting), proceedings (of a conference). **a. continuo** *or* **a. seguido,** immediately afterwards. **a. vandálico,** act of vandalism. **los Actos de los Apóstoles,** Acts of the Apostles. **en a.,** in the act (of doing). **en el a.,** in the act; immediately

actor /ak'tor/ *m,* actor; *Law.* plaintiff

actriz /ak'triθ; ak'tris/ *f,* actress

actuación /aktua'θion; aktua'sion/ *f,* operation, functioning; action; *pl* legal functions, judicial acts

actual /ak'tual/ *a* present; contemporary

actualidad /aktuali'ðað/ *f,* present, present time; topic of interest. **actualidades,** current events. **en la a.,** at the present time

actuar /ak'tuar/ *vt* to operate, set in motion; —*vi* act; exercise legal functions

actuario /ak'tuario/ **(de seguros)** *m,* actuary

acuarela /akua'rela/ *f,* water-color painting

acuarelista /akuare'lista/ *mf* watercolorist

acuario /a'kuario/ *m,* aquarium; Aquarius

acuartelamiento /a,kuartela'miento/ *m,* billeting (of troops); billet, quarters

acuartelar /akuarte'lar/ *vt* to billet

acuático, acuátil /a'kuatiko, a'kuatil/ *a* aquatic

acuchillar /akutʃi'ʎar; akutʃi'yar/ *vt* to hack, cut about; stab, put to the sword; slash (sleeves, etc.); —*vr* fight with swords, daggers

acucia /a'kuθia; a'kusia/ *f,* fervor, zeal; yearning, longing

acuciar /aku'θiar; aku'siar/ *vt* to incite; goad; stimulate; encourage

acuciosidad /akuθiosi'ðað; akusiosi'ðað/ *f,* eagerness, fervor, zeal

acucioso /aku'θioso; aku'sioso/ *a* eager, fervent, keen, zealous

acuclillarse /akukli'ʎarse; akukli'yarse/ *vr* to squat, crouch

acudir /aku'ðir/ *vi* to go, repair (to); come; go or come to the aid of; attend, be present; **No me acude ningún ejemplo a la memoria,** No example comes to mind; resort (to), seek protection; reply, respond

acueducto /akue'ðukto/ *m,* aqueduct

acuerdo /a'kuerðo/ *m,* motion, resolution; decision; harmony, agreement; opinion, belief; remembrance; report; meeting (of members of a tribunal); *Art.* harmony (of colors). **de a.,** in agreement, in conformity; unanimously. **estar de a. (con),** to agree (with). **estar de acuerdo en (+ inf.),** to agree to (+ inf.) **ponerse de a.,** to come to an understanding

acumulación /akumula'θion; akumula'sion/ *f,* accumulation, collection

acumulador /akumula'ðor/ **(-ra)** *a* accumulative. *m,* accumulator, storage battery —*n* collector, accumulator

acumular /akumu'lar/ *vt* to accumulate, amass, collect; accuse, charge with

acuñación /akuɲa'θion; akuɲa'sion/ *f,* minting, coining; wedging

acuñador /akuɲa'ðor/ **(-ra)** *n* coiner, stamper; wedge. *m,* coining machine

acuñar /aku'ɲar/ *vt* to mint, stamp, coin; wedge

acuoso /a'kuoso/ *a* aqueous, watery

acurrucarse /akurru'karse/ *vr* to huddle; curl up; crouch

acusación /akusa'θion; akusa'sion/ *f,* accusation; *Law.* charge; *Law.* prosecution

acusado /aku'saðo/ **(-da)** *a* accused; prominent; well-defined; —*n* accused; *Law.* defendant

acusador /akusa'ðor/ **(-ra)** *a* accusing —*n* accuser; *Law.* prosecutor

acusar /aku'sar/ *vt* to accuse; blame; denounce; *Com.* acknowledge receipt; *Law.* prosecute; *Law.* charge. **acusarle a uno las cuarenta,** *Inf.* to give someone a piece of one's mind

acusatorio /akusa'torio/ *a* accusatory

acusón /aku'son/ **(-ona)** *n Inf.* telltale, sneak, informer

acústica /a'kustika/ *f,* acoustics

acústico /a'kustiko/ *a* acoustic

adagio /a'ðahio; *also for 2* a'ðadʒio/ *m,* adage; *Mus.* adagio

adaptar /aðap'tar/ *vt* to adapt, make suitable; —*vr* adapt oneself

adarme /a'ðarme/ *m,* tittle, jot. **por adarmes,** in bits and pieces, in drabs and driblets

adecentar /aðeθen'tar; aðesen'tar/ *vt* to make decent; tidy up; —*vr* tidy oneself

adecuación /aðekua'θion; aðekua'sion/ *f*, adequacy; suitability

adecuado /aðe'kuaðo/ *a* adequate; suitable

adecuar /aðe'kuar/ *vt* to proportion, fit; *Fig.* tailor

adefesio /aðe'fesio/ *m, Inf.* folly, absurdity (gen. *pl*); extravagant attire; guy, sight

adelantado /aðelan'taðo/ *a* precocious; forward, pert; fast (clocks); early (of fruit); excellent; capable, proficient. *m, Obs.* provincial governor *or* chief justice *or* captain-general (Spanish history). **por a.,** in advance

adelantamiento /aðelanta'miento/ *m*, promotion; furtherance; progress, advancement; betterment, improvement; *Obs.* office of **adelantado;** anticipation

adelantar /aðelan'tar/ *vt* to advance, move on; hasten; forestall; overtake; put on (the hands of clocks); improve, better; beat, excel; place in front; —*vi* progress, advance; be fast (clocks); grow, develop; —*vr* come forward

adelante /aðe'lante/ *adv* on, forward; further on; straight ahead. **¡A.!** Onward!; Come in! **de hoy en a.,** henceforth, from today

adelanto /aðe'lanto/ *m*, anticipation; progress; *Com.* payment in advance. **el a. de la hora,** moving the clock forward

adelgazamiento /aðcl,gaθa'miento; aðel,gasa'miento/ *m*, loss of weight; slenderness; thinness

adelgazar /aðelga'θar; aðelga'sar/ *vt* to make slender or thin; *Fig.* split hairs; whittle, taper; —*vi* grow slender or thin

ademán /aðe'man/ *m*, posture, attitude; gesture; *pl* behavior, manners

además /aðe'mas/ *adv* besides, in addition; moreover. **a. de,** as well as

adentro /a'ðentro/ *adv* inside, within

adentros /a'ðentros/ *m pl*, private thoughts (e.g. *Pensé para mis adentros,* I thought to myself) —*interj* **¡Adentro!** Come in!; Go in!

adepto /a'ðepto/ *a* affiliated; adept, proficient

aderezamiento /aðe,reθa'miento; aðe,resa'miento/ *m*, dressing; seasoning; embellishment

aderezar /aðere'θar; aðere'sar/ *vt* to deck; embellish; cook; *Cul.* season; *Cul.* dress; prepare; repair, mend; guide, direct; dress (cloth)

aderezo /aðe'reθo; aðe'reso/ *m*, dressing, adornment; beautifying; finery, ornament; preparation; seasoning; set of jewels; horse's trappings; gum starch (for dressing cloth); equipment

adeudar /aðeu'ðar/ *vt* to owe; be dutiable (goods); *Com.* debit; —*vi* become related (by marriage); —*vr* run into debt

adeudo /a'ðeuðo/ *m*, debt; customs duty; *Com.* debit

adherente /aðe'rente/ *a* adhesive; connected, attached. *mf* adherent, follower; *m pl.* **adherentes,** accessories, requisites

adherirse /aðe'rirse/ *vr irr* to adhere, stick; follow; believe (in). See **herir**

adhesivo /aðe'siβo/ *a* adhesive

adición /aði'θion; aði'sion/ *f*, addition

adicional /aðiθio'nal; aðisio'nal/ *a* additional, extra

adicionar /aðiθio'nar; aðisio'nar/ *vt* to add up; add to

adicto /a'ðikto/ **(-ta)** *a* addicted, fond; joint —*n* addict; follower, disciple

adiestrador /aðiestra'ðor/ **(-ra)** *n* trainer, coach; guide, teacher

adiestrar /aðies'trar/ *vt* to train, coach; guide, teach; lead; —*vr* practice, perfect oneself

adinerado /aðine'raðo/ *a* wealthy, well-off, rich

adiós /a'ðios/ *interj* Good-bye!; Hello, God be with you! (used as greeting). *m*, farewell

adiposo /aði'poso/ *a* adipose

aditamento /aðita'mento/ *m*, addition

adivinador /aðiβina'ðor/ **(-ra)** *a* prophesying, divining —*n* soothsayer

adivinanza /aðiβi'nanθa; aðiβi'nansa/ *f*, divination; riddle; puzzle. **adivinanzas,** guessing games. **no estar para jugar a las a.,** to be in no mood for guessing games

adivinar /aðiβi'nar/ *vt* to prophesy, foretell; divine, guess; solve, guess (riddles, etc.)

adjetivo /aðhe'tiβo/ *a* adjectival. *m*, adjective

adjudicación /aðhuðika'θion; aðhuðika'sion/ *f*, adjudication, award

adjudicar /aðhuði'kar/ *vt* to adjudge; award; —*vr* appropriate

adjuntar /aðhun'tar/ *vt* to enclose (with a letter, etc.)

adjunto /að'hunto/ *a* attached; enclosed, accompanying; assistant, deputy; adjectival. *m*, addition, supplement

administración /aðministra'θion; aðministra'sion/ *f*, administration; direction, control; administratorship

administrador /aðministra'ðor/ **(-ra)** *a* administrative —*n* administrator. **a. de correos,** postmaster

administrar /aðminis'trar/ *vt* to control, manage; provide, supply; administer. **administrarse el tiempo,** to budget one's time

administrativo /aðministra'tiβo/ *a* administrative, executive

admiración /aðmira'θion; aðmira'sion/ *f*, amazement; admiration; wonder; exclamation mark

admirador /aðmira'ðor/ **(-ra)** *a* admiring —*n* admirer

admirar /aðmi'rar/ *vt* to admire; surprise, amaze; to see; —*vr* (*with de*) be surprised at or by

admirativo /aðmira'tiβo/ *a* admiring; admirable, excellent

admisibilidad /aðmisiβili'ðað/ *f*, allowability, permissibility

admisible /aðmiˈsiβle/ a admissible; permissible

admisión /aðmiˈsion/ f, admission; acceptance; allowance

admitir /aðmiˈtir/ vt to admit; receive, accept; tolerate, brook; allow, permit

admonición /aðmoniˈθion; aðmoniˈsion/ f, admonition, warning; reprimand

adobar /aðoˈβar/ vt to prepare; Cul. garnish; pickle (meat); cook; dress (hides)

adobo /aˈðoβo/ m, repairing; dressing (for cloth, leather); Cul. savory sauce; pickling sauce; make-up, cosmetic

adoctrinar /aðoktriˈnar/ vt to instruct

adolecer /aðoleˈθer; aðoleˈser/ vi irr to fall ill; (with de) suffer from (diseases, defects); —vr be sorry for, regret. See **conocer**

adolescencia /aðolesˈθenθia; aðoles-ˈsensia/ f, adolescence

adolescente /aðolesˈθente; aðolesˈsente/ a and mf adolescent

adonde /aˈðonde/ adv (interr a dónde) where to, whither (e.g. ¿A dónde fuiste? Where did you go to?)

adondequiera /a,ðondeˈkiera/ adv wherever

adopción /aðopˈθion; aðopˈsion/ f, adoption

adoptador /aðoptaˈðor/ (-ra) a adopting —n adopter

adoptar /aðopˈtar/ vt to adopt (children); make one's own, embrace (opinions); take (decisions)

adoptivo /aðopˈtiβo/ a adoptive

adoquín /aðoˈkin/ m, cobble-stone; Fig. blockhead

adoquinado /aðokiˈnaðo/ m, cobbling, paving. m, cobbled pavement

adoración /aðoraˈθion; aðoraˈsion/ f, worship, adoration. **A. de los Reyes**, Adoration of the Magi; Epiphany

adorador /aðoraˈðor/ (-ra) a adoring —n adorer

adorar /aðoˈrar/ vt to adore; worship; (with en) dote on; —vi pray

adormecedor /aðormeθeˈðor; aðormeseˈðor/ a soporific, drowsy

adormecer /aðormeˈθer; aðormeˈser/ vt irr to make drowsy; soothe, lull; hush to sleep; —vr go to sleep; (limbs); fall asleep; (with en) persist in. See **conocer**

adormecimiento /aðormeθiˈmiento; aðormesiˈmiento/ m, sleepiness; lulling asleep; numbness

adormitarse /aðormiˈtarse/ vr to doze, take a nap, snooze

adornamiento /aðornaˈmiento/ m, adornment, decoration

adornar /aðorˈnar/ vt to deck, beautify; decorate; trim, embellish; adorn (of virtues, etc.)

adorno /aˈðorno/ m, decoration, adornment; ornament; trimming. **de a.**, ornamental; flowering (shrubs)

adquiridor /aðkiriˈðor/ (-ra) a acquiring —n acquirer

adquirir /aðkiˈrir/ vt irr to acquire, get; achieve, obtain —Pres. Indic. **adquiero, adquieres, adquiere, adquieren**. Pres. Subjunc. **adquiera, adquieras, adquiera, adquieran**

adquisición /aðkisiˈθion; aðkisiˈsion/ f, acquirement; acquisition. **poder de a.**, purchasing power

adquisidor /aðkisiˈðor/ (-ra) a acquiring —n acquirer, obtainer

adquisitivo /aðkisiˈtiβo/ a acquisitive

adrede /aˈðreðe/ adv on purpose, intentionally

adrenalina /aðrenaˈlina/ f, adrenaline

adscribir /aðskriˈβir/ vt to ascribe, attribute; appoint (to a post, etc.)

adscripción /aðskripˈθion; aðskripˈsion/ f, ascription, attribution; appointment

aduana /aˈðuana/ f, customs house, customs. **pasar por la a.**, to go through customs

aduanero /aðuaˈnero/ a customs. m, customs officer

aducir /aðuˈθir; aðuˈsir/ vt irr to adduce, allege, cite; add. See **conducir**

adueñarse /aðueˈɲarse/ (-de) vr to appropriate, take possession (of)

adulación /aðulaˈθion; aðulaˈsion/ f, adulation, flattery

adulador /aðulaˈðor/ (-ra) a fawning —n flatterer

adular /aðuˈlar/ vt to flatter, fawn upon, adulate

adulteración /aðulteraˈθion; aðultera-ˈsion/ f, adulteration; falsification

adulterador /aðulteraˈðor/ (-ra) a adulterant —n adulterator; falsifier; coiner

adulterar /aðulteˈrar/ vi to commit adultery; —vt adulterate; falsify

adulterio /aðulˈterio/ m, adultery

adúltero /aˈðultero/ (-ra) a adulterous; corrupt —n adulterer

adulto /aˈðulto/ (-ta) a and n adult

adusto /aˈðusto/ a extremely hot (of climate); grave, austere; standoffish, reserved

advenedizo /aðβeneˈðiθo; aðβeneˈðiso/ a foreign, alien; strange, unknown; upstart; newly rich

advenimiento /aðβeniˈmiento/ m, advent, arrival; ascension (to the throne)

advenir /aðβeˈnir/ vi irr to come, arrive; happen, befall. See **venir**

adventicio /aðβenˈtiθio; aðβenˈtisio/ a casual, accidental; Bot. adventitious

adversario /aðβerˈsario/ (-ia) n adversary, rival; opponent

adversidad /aðβersiˈðað/ f, adversity, misfortune, sorrow

adverso /aðˈβerso/ a unfavorable, contrary, adverse; opposite

advertencia /aðβerˈtenθia; aðβerˈtensia/ f, warning; introduction, preface; remark

advertido /aðβerˈtiðo/ a capable, clever; experienced; expert

advertir /aðβerˈtir/ vt irr to observe, notice; warn; advise; feel, be conscious of;

point out, indicate; inform; discover. See **sentir**

adyacente /aðya'θente; aðya'sente/ a adjacent, near-by, neighboring

aéreo /'aereo/ a aerial; airborne; airy; air; aeronautic; unsubstantial, fantastic. **correo a.**, airmail. **línea aérea** airline

aerobismo /aero'βismo/ m, aerobics

aerodinámica /aeroði'namika/ f, aerodynamics

aeronauta /aero'nauta/ mf aeronaut, balloonist

aeronáutica /aero'nautika/ f, aeronautics

aeronáutico /aero'nautiko/ a aeronautic

aeropuerto /aero'puerto/ m, airport

afabilidad /afaβili'ðað/ f, affability, geniality, friendliness

afable /a'faβle/ a affable, genial, pleasant

afamado /afa'maðo/ a famous, well known

afán /a'fan/ m, effort; manual labor; desire, anxiety **a. de mando**, thirst for power

afanar /afa'nar/ vt to press, urge on; filch; —vr toil, labor; (with por) work hard to, try to

afanoso /afa'noso/ a hard, laborious; hard-working, painstaking; eager, anxious

afear /afe'ar/ vt to make ugly; distort, deform; blame; criticize

afección /afek'θion; afek'sion/ f, fondness, affection; complaint, ailment, trouble

afectación /afekta'θion; afekta'sion/ f, affectation

afectado /afek'taðo/ a affected

afectar /afek'tar/ vt to feign, assume; affect; move, touch; Law. encumber

afectivo /afek'tiβo/ a affective

afecto /a'fekto/ a fond, affectionate; Law. encumbered; (with prep a) addicted to. m, emotion, sentiment; affection

afectuoso /afek'tuoso/ a affectionate, fond

afeitada /afei'taða/ f, shave, shaving

afeitar /afei'tar/ vt to shave; make up (one's face); adorn, beautify

afeite /a'feite/ m, cosmetic; make-up (for the complexion)

afelpado /afel'paðo/ a velvet-like, plushy

afeminado /afemi'naðo/ a effeminate

afeminar /afemi'nar/ vt to make effeminate; weaken; —vr grow effeminate

aferradamente /aferraða'mente/ adv tenaciously, persistently, obstinately

aferramiento /aferra'miento/ m, seizing, clutching; Naut. furling; Naut. grappling; mooring, anchoring; obstinacy

aferrar /afe'rrar/ vt to seize, clutch; Naut. take in, furl; Naut. grapple; —vi Naut. anchor; —vr (with con, en, a) persist in, insist on

afianzamiento /afianθa'miento; afiansa-'miento/ m, fastening, fixing; propping; grasping; guarantee, security

afianzar /afian'θar; afian'sar/ vt to fasten,

fix; prop; consolidate (e.g. one's power); guarantee, be security for; grasp

afición /afi'θion; afi'sion/ f, propensity, inclination; fondness. **tomar a. (a)**, to take a liking to

aficionado /afiθio'naðo; afisio'naðo/ (**-da**) a amateur —n amateur, fan, enthusiast. **ser a a.**, to be fond of, have a liking for

aficionar /afiθio'nar; afisio'nar/ vt to inspire liking or affection; —vr (with prep a) take a liking to, grow fond of; become an enthusiast of

afiladera /afila'ðera/ f, whetstone, grindstone

afilado /afi'laðo/ a sharp, keen (of edges)

afilador /afila'ðor/ m, grinder (of scissors, etc.); razor strop

afilalápices /afila'lapiθes; afila'lapises/ m, pencil sharpener

afilar /afi'lar/ vt to sharpen; grind, whet; taper; —vr grow thin, taper

afiliación /afilia'θion; afilia'sion/ f, affiliation

afiliar /afi'liar/ vt (with prep a) to affiliate with; —vr (with prep a) become affiliated with; join, become a member of

afiligranado /afiligra'naðo/ a filigree; delicate, fine; slender

afilón /afi'lon/ m, steel, knife sharpener; razor-strop

afín /a'fin/ a nearby, contiguous; similar, related. mf relative by marriage

afinador /afina'ðor/ m, tuning key; tuner (of pianos, etc.)

afinar /afi'nar/ vt to finish, perfect; Fig. polish, refine; tune (musical instruments); refine (metals); —vi sing in tune; —vr grow refined

afinidad /afini'ðað/ f, affinity, analogy; relationship (by marriage); Chem. affinity

afirmación /afirma'θion; afirma'sion/ f, affirmation, statement

afirmar /afir'mar/ vt to make firm; fix, fasten; affirm; —vr steady oneself; hold on to

afirmativa /afirma'tiβa/ f, affirmative

afirmativo /afirma'tiβo/ a affirmative

aflicción /aflik'θion; aflik'sion/ f, affliction, grief

aflictivo /aflik'tiβo/ a sorrowful, grievous

afligir /afli'hir/ vt to sadden; afflict, trouble; —vr lament, mourn

aflojamiento /afloha'miento/ m, slackening; loosening; diminution

aflojar /aflo'har/ vt to slacken; loosen; —vi relax, weaken; abate, diminish. **a. el paso**, to slow down

afluencia /a'fluenθia; a'fluensia/ f, crowd, concourse; eloquence, fluency

afluente /a'fluente/ a fluent, eloquent. m, tributary (river)

afluir /aflu'ir/ vi irr to crowd, swarm; flow (into). See **huir**

afonía /afo'nia/ f, Med. aphonia, loss of voice; hoarseness

afónico /a'foniko/ a hoarse

aforrador /aforra'ðor/ **(-ra)** *n* one who lines jackets, etc.

aforrar /afo'rrar/ *vt* to line (clothes, etc.); —*vr* wrap oneself up; *Inf.* gormandize

afortunado /afortu'naðo/ *a* lucky, fortunate; happy; stormy

afortunar /afortu'nar/ *vt* to bring luck to, make happy

afrancesamiento /afranθesa'miento; afransesa'miento/ *m,* adoption of the French way of life; servile imitation of everything French

afrancesar /afranθe'sar; afranse'sar/ *vt* to make French, gallicize; Frenchify; —*vr* become a Francophile

afrenta /a'frenta/ *f,* insult, affront; disgrace

afrentar /afren'tar/ *vt* to insult; —*vr* be ashamed

afrentoso /afren'toso/ *a* insulting, outrageous; disgraceful

África /'afrika/ Africa

africano /afri'kano/ **-na** *a* and *n* African

afrodisíaco /afroði'siako/ *a* and *m,* aphrodisiac

afrontar /afron'tar/ *vt* to place opposite; confront; face (danger, etc.)

afuera /a'fuera/ *adv* outside, out.

afueras /a'fueras/ *f pl,* suburbs, outskirts

agachada /aga'tʃaða/ *f,* crouch, duck; jerk

agachar /aga'tʃar/ *vt Inf.* bend, bow; —*vr Inf.* crouch down; lie low, hide

agalla /a'gaʎa; a'gaya/ *f,* oak-apple; tonsil (gen. *pl*); *Zool.* gill; *Inf.* gall, cheek

ágape /'agape/ *m,* agape; banquet, feast

agarrada /aga'rraða/ *f, Inf.* brawl, scuffle

agarradero /agarra'ðero/ *m,* handle; heft; *Inf.* influence, pull

agarrado /aga'rraðo/ *a Inf.* tight-fisted, mean

agarrar /aga'rrar/ *vt* to grip, grasp; seize, take; *Inf.* nab (jobs); —*vr* grip, hold on

agarro /a'garro/ *m,* hold; grip, grasp

agarrotar /agarro'tar/ *vt* to garrotte; tighten (ropes, etc.); press, squeeze; —*vr* (limbs) go numb

agasajar /agasa'har/ *vt* to indulge, spoil, pet; receive kindly; entertain; caress

agasajo /aga'saho/ *m,* indulgence, kindness; affability, geniality; entertainment; gift, offering

agazapar /agaθa'par; agasa'par/ *vt Inf.* to nab, catch; —*vr Inf.* squat, crouch

agencia /a'henθia; a'hensia/ *f,* influence, agency

agenciar /ahen'θiar; ahen'siar/ *vt* to negotiate, arrange; procure, manage

agenda /a'henda/ *f,* notebook; agenda

agente /a'hente/ *m,* agent. **a. de bolsa** *or* **a. de cambio,** bill broker. **a. de negocios,** business agent. **a. de policía,** police officer. **a. fiscal,** revenue officer

agestado /ahes'taðo/ *a* used generally with *advs.* **bien** *or* **mal,** well *or* ill-featured

agigantado /ahigan'taðo/ *a* enormous, gigantic; outstanding, extraordinary

ágil /'ahil/ *a* agile, nimble; easy to use (e.g. *un libro ágil,* a book easy to use)

agilidad /ahili'ðað/ *f,* agility, nimbleness

agilizar /ahili'θar; ahili'sar/ *vt* to make agile, limber; refresh one's knowledge of; to enable; —*vr* limber up

agitación /ahita'θion; ahita'sion/ *f,* shaking; agitation, excitement

agitador /ahita'ðor/ **(-ra)** *a* stirring; agitating —*n* agitator. *m,* stirrer, stirring rod

agitar /ahi'tar/ *vt* to stir; shake; agitate, excite **a. una cuestión,** raise a question; discuss a question

aglomeración /aglomera'θion; aglomera'sion/ *f,* agglomeration

aglomerado /aglome'raðo/ *m,* briquette

aglomerar /aglome'rar/ *vt* to agglomerate, amass

agnosticismo /agnosti'θismo; agnosti'sismo/ *m,* agnosticism

agnóstico /ag'nostiko/ **(-ca)** *a* and *n* agnostic

agobiar /ago'βiar/ *vt* to bow, bend down; *Fig.* weigh down, oppress; —*vr* bend (beneath a weight)

agobio /a'goβio/ *m,* bowing, bending down; oppression, burden, weight

agolparse /agol'parse/ *vr* to rush, crowd, swarm

agonía /ago'nia/ *f,* agony, anguish

agónico /a'goniko/ *a* dying; agonizing

agonizante /agoni'θante; agoni'sante/ *a* dying

agonizar /agoni'θar; agoni'sar/ *vt* to attend a dying person; *Inf.* pester, annoy; —*vi* be dying (gen. **estar agonizando**)

agorar /ago'rar/ *vt* to prophesy, foretell

agorero /ago'rero/ **(-ra)** *a* prophetic; ill-boding —*n* seer, augur

agosto /a'gosto/ *m,* August; harvest. *Inf.* **hacer su a.,** to make hay while the sun shines

agotado /ago'taðo/ *a* exhausted; out of print (of books)

agotador /agota'ðor/ *a* exhausting; exhaustive

agotar /ago'tar/ *vt* to drain off (water); empty (a glass); exhaust; run through (money); study thoroughly, examine closely (a subject)

agraciado /agra'θiaðo; agra'siaðo/ *a* graceful; pretty

agraciar /agra'θiar; agra'siar/ *vt* to lend grace to; make pretty; favor

agradable /agra'ðaβle/ *a* agreeable, pleasant

agradar /agra'ðar/ *vi* to be pleasing, like, please (e.g. *Me agrada su sinceridad,* I like his sincerity)

agradecer /agraðe'θer; agraðe'ser/ *vt irr* to be grateful for; thank for; *Fig.* repay, requite. See **conocer**

agradecido /agraðe'θiðo; agraðe'siðo/ *a* grateful; thankful

agradecimiento /agraðeθi'miento;

agradesi'miento/ *m*, gratitude; thankfulness

agrado /a'graðo/ *m*, pleasure; desire, liking; amiability, affability

agrario /a'grario/ *a* agrarian

agravación /agraβa'θion; agraβa'sion/ *f*, **agravamiento** *m*, aggravation, worsening

agravador /agraβa'ðor/ *a* aggravating; worsening; increasing

agravar /agra'βar/ *vt* to aggravate, increase; oppress (taxes, responsibilities); make worse; exaggerate; —*vr* grow worse

agraviador /agraβia'ðor/ **-ra** *a* offensive —*n* offender

agraviar /agra'βiar/ *vt* to offend; wrong; .—*vr* take offense, be insulted

agravio /a'graβio/ *m*, offense, insult; wrong, injury

agraz /a'graθ; a'gras/ *m*, unripened grape; verjuice; *Fig*. bitterness

agredir /agre'ðir/ *vt* to attack

agregación /agrega'θion; agrega'sion/ *f*, association, aggregation; total, collection, aggregate

agregado /agre'gaðo/ *m*, aggregate; assistant; attaché

agregar /agre'gar/ *vt* to add; collect, amass; appoint (to a post). **agregarse a...**, to join... (e.g. an association)

agresión /agre'sion/ *f*, aggression

agresivo /agre'siβo/ *a* aggressive

agresor /agre'sor/ **(-ra)** *a* and *n* aggressor

agreste /a'greste/ *a* rural, rustic; wild; uncouth, rude

agriar /a'griar/ *vt* to make bitter or sour; exasperate, provoke

agrícola /a'grikola/ *a* agricultural; *mf* agriculturalist, farmer

agricultura /agrikul'tura/ *f*, agriculture

agridulce /agri'ðulθe; agri'ðulse/ *a* bittersweet

agrietarse /agrie'tarse/ *vr* to crack, split

agrimensor /agrimen'sor/ *m*, surveyor

agrio /'agrio/ *a* bitter, sour; rough, uneven (ground); brittle; sharp (of color contrast); unsociable; disagreeable

agronomía /agrono'mia/ *f*, agronomy

agrónomo /a'gronomo/ *a* agronomic. *m*, agronomist

agrupación /agrupa'θion; agrupa'sion/ *f*, congregation, assembly; group; crowd; crowding, grouping

agrupar /agru'par/ *vt* to assemble, group; —*vr* crowd, cluster

agrura /a'grura/ *f*, bitterness; sourness; asperity

agua /'agua/ *f*, water; rain; slope of a roof; *pl* shot or watered effect on silks, etc.; medicinal waters; waves; water (of precious stones). **a. abajo**, down-stream. **a. arriba**, upstream. **a. bendita**, holy water. **a. cruda**, hard water. **a. de colonia**, eau de Cologne. **a. dulce**, fresh water. **a. fresca**, cold water. **a. nieve**, sleet. **a. oxigenada**, hydrogen peroxide. *Fig. Inf*. es-

tar con el a. al cuello, to be in low water. *Fig. Inf*. **estar entre dos aguas**, to be between two fires. *Naut*. **hacer a.**, to leak. **Todo eso es ya a. pasada**, That's all water under the bridge

aguacero /agua'θero; agua'sero/ *m*, heavy rainfall, shower

aguada /a'guaða/ *f*, water supply on board ship; flood (in mines); watering station; *Art*. water color

aguado /a'guaðo/ *a* watery; abstemious; watered

aguador /agua'ðor/ **(-ra)** *n* water carrier, water seller; drawer (of water)

aguafiestas /,agua'fiestas/ *mf Fig. Inf*. wet blanket

aguafuerte /,agua'fuerte/ *f*, etching

aguaje /a'guahe/ *m*, tide, waves; sea current; water supply (on board ship); wake (of a ship)

aguamanil /aguama'nil/ *m*, washstand; pitcher, ewer

aguamarina /aguama'rina/ *f*, aquamarine

aguantable /aguan'taβle/ *a* tolerable, bearable

aguantar /aguan'tar/ *vt* to bear, tolerate, endure; restrain, resist, oppose; —*vr* bear in silence, keep quiet

aguante /a'guante/ *m*, patience, endurance; resistance

aguar /a'guar/ *vt* to water down (wine, etc.); spoil (fun, etc.); —*vr* be filled with water; be flooded; become watery or thin

aguardar /aguar'ðar/ *vt* to await; expect; allow time to (debtors)

aguardentoso /aguarðen'toso/ *a* spirituous, containing, **aguardiente** hoarse, husky (of the voice)

aguardiente /aguar'ðiente/ *m*, liquor. **a. de caña**, rum

aguarrás /agua'rras/ *m*, oil of turpentine

aguatinta /agua'tinta/ *f*, aquatint

aguatocha /agua'totʃa/ *f*, pump (for water, etc.)

agudeza /agu'ðeθa; agu'ðesa/ *f*, sharpness; keenness; distinctness; alertness, cleverness; witty sally, repartee; wit; swiftness

agudo /a'guðo/ *a* sharp; alert, clever; (*Geom. Med*.) acute; fine, keen; rapid; high-pitched; strong (of scents, etc.)

agüero /a'guero/ *m*, omen, sign; prophecy, prediction

aguerrir /age'rrir/ *vt* defective to harden to war; toughen

aguijada /agi'haða/ *f*, goad, spur

aguijar /agi'har/ *vt* to prick (with a goad); urge on, encourage (animals); incite, instigate; spur on; —*vi* walk swiftly

aguijón /agi'hon/ *m*, goad; sting; thorn, prickle; spur; incitement, stimulus. **tener aguijones**, to be on pins and needles

aguijonazo /agiho'naθo; agiho'naso/ *m*, prick (with a goad)

águila /'agila/ *f*, eagle; master mind. **a. caudal** *or* **a. real**, royal eagle. **á. o sol**, heads or tails (Mexico)

aguileño /agi'leɲo/ a aquiline

aguinaldo /agi'naldo/ m, Christmas present; New Year's gift

aguja /a'guha/ f, needle; hand, pointer; hatpin; engraver's burin; switch; *Rail.* point; *Rail.* rail; obelisk; spire; bodkin; knitting needle; crochet hook; (compass) needle *pl Bot.* plumelet. **a. capotera, a. de zurcir,** darning needle. **a. de marear** *Naut.*, binnacle; mariner's compass. **a. de media,** knitting needle. **a. espartera,** packing needle

agujerear /aguhere'ar/ vt to perforate, make holes in

agujero /agu'hero/ m, hole, aperture; needle maker or seller; needle case

agujeta /agu'heta/ f, lace (for shoes, etc.); pl muscular pains, aches; tip, gratuity

aguzar /agu'θar; agu'sar/ vt to sharpen; grind, whet; stimulate, encourage; urge on, incite

aherrojar /aerro'har/ vt to put (a prisoner) in irons; oppress

aherrumbrar /aerrum'brar/ vt to give the color or taste of iron to; —vr taste or look like iron; go rusty

ahí /a'i/ adv there; over there. **de a.,** thus, so. **por a.,** somewhere about, near at hand.

ahijado /ai'haðo/ (**-da**) n godchild; protégé

ahijar /ai'har/ vt to adopt (children); mother (animals); attribute, impute; —vi bring forth offspring; *Bot.* sprout. See **prohibir**

ahincado /ain'kaðo/ a earnest, eager

ahincar /ain'kar/ vt to urge, press; —vr hurry, hasten. See **prohibir**

ahínco /a'inko/ m, earnestness, eagerness

ahitar /ai'tar/ vt to stuff with food; bore, disgust. See **prohibir**

ahíto /a'ito/ a full of food; *Fig.* fed up. m, indigestion

ahogado /ao'gaðo/ (**-da**) a drowned; suffocated; stuffy, unventilated; stifling —n drowned person; victim of suffocation

ahogamiento /aoga'miento/ m, drowning; suffocation

ahogar /ao'gar/ vt to drown; suffocate; put out (the fire); stifle (yawns, etc.); suppress, extinguish; tire; overwater (plants); —vr *Naut.* sink, founder; drown; suffocate

ahogo /a'ogo/ m, anxiety, grief; difficulty in breathing, oppression; asthma; embarrassment; suffocation; straitened circumstances

ahondamiento /aonda'miento/ m, in-depth treatment

ahondar /aon'dar/ vt to deepen; excavate, dig; go into thoroughly; go deep into, penetrate; —vi (earth) subside

ahora /a'ora/ adv now; very soon; just now, a short time ago —conjunc whether; now. **a. bien,** well now, given that. **a. mismo,** immediately, at once. **por a.,** for the present

ahorcar /aor'kar/ vt to execute by hanging, hang. *Inf.* **a. los hábitos,** to leave the priesthood, cease to be an ecclesiastic

ahormar /aor'mar/ vt to adjust, shape; break in (new shoes); make (a person) see reason

ahorquillar /aorki'ʎar; aorki'yar/ vt to prop up (trees) with forks; —vr grow forked

ahorrar /ao'rrar/ vt to free (slaves); save, economize; avoid, eschew; —vr avoid; remove clothing

ahorro /a'orro/ m, economy, thrift; pl savings

ahuciar /au'θiar; au'siar/ vt take possession of (a house)

ahuecar /aue'kar/ vt to hollow out; loosen; shake out; puff out, inflate; put on a solemn voice; hoe, dig; *Inf.* vr puff oneself out; put on airs

ahumado /au'maðo/ a smoked; smoky

ahumar /au'mar/ vt to smoke (herrings, etc.); fill with smoke; —vi smoke, burn; —vr be full of smoke; taste smoked; *Inf.* get drunk. See **desahuciar**

ahuyentar /auyen'tar/ vt to frighten off; drive away; dismiss, banish (anxiety, etc.); —vr flee

airado /ai'raðo/ a angry

airar /ai'rar/ vt to annoy, anger; —vr grow annoyed

aire /'aire/ m, air; atmosphere (sometimes pl); breeze; wind; bearing, appearance; vanity; (horse's) gait; futility, frivolity; grace, charm; gracefulness; *Mus.* air; *Mus.* tempo. **a. popular,** popular tune. **al a. libre,** in the open air, outdoors. *Inf.* **beber los aires (por),** to yearn (for)

airear /aire'ar/ vt to ventilate; aerate; —vr take the air; catch a chill

airosidad /airosi'ðað/ f, gracefulness; jauntiness

airoso /ai'roso/ a airy, open; windy, breezy, fresh; graceful; handsome; jaunty; victorious, successful

aislacionamismo /aislaθiona'mismo; aislasiona'mismo/ m, *Polit.* isolationism

aislacionista /aislaθio'nista; aislasio-'nista/ mf *Polit.* isolationist

aislado /ais'laðo/ a isolated; remote; individual; single; *Elec.* insulated

aislador /aisla'ðor/ m, *Phys.* insulator

aislamiento /aisla'miento/ m, isolation; *Phys.* insulation

aislante /ais'lante/ a isolating; insulating

aislar /ais'lar/ vt to isolate; *Elec.* insulate; —vr become a recluse; become isolated

¡ajá! /a'ha/ interj *Inf.* Aha! Good!

ajar /a'har/ vt to crease, crumple, spoil; humiliate; —vr fade, wither (flowers)

ajear /ahe'ar/ vi (partridge) to squawk (when cornered)

ajedrecista /aheðre'θista; aheðre'sista/ mf chess player

ajedrez /ahe'ðreθ; ahe'ðres/ m, chess

ajeno /a'heno/ a alien; belonging to an-

other; various, diverse; free, exempt; unsuitable; irrelevant

ajetrear /ahetre'ar/ vt to tire out, exhaust; —vr be overtired

ajetreo /ahe'treo/ m, exhaustion, fatigue

ajo /'aho/ m, garlic; Inf. make up, paint; disreputable affair, shady business; curse, oath. Inf. **revolver el a.,** to stir up trouble

ajornalar /ahorna'lar/ vt to hire by the day

ajuar /ahu'ar/ m, trousseau; household equipment

ajustado /ahus'taðo/ a exact; tight-fitting; trim

ajustador /ahusta'ðor/ **(-ra)** a adjusting —n adjuster. m, tight-fitting jacket

ajustamiento /ahusta'miento/ m, adjustment; agreement

ajustar /ahus'tar/ vt to adjust; fit; arrange; make an agreement about; reconcile, settle (accounts); engage, employ; retain (a barrister); regulate; tune up (a motor); —vr fit; —vr adapt oneself. Inf. **a. cuentas viejas,** to settle old accounts

ajuste /a'huste/ m, fitting; adjustment; agreement; arrangement; Print. make-up. reconciliation; settlement; regulation; engagement, appointment

ajusticiar /ahusti'θiar; ahusti'siar/ vt to put to death

al /al/ (contraction of a + el). 1 —prep a + m. def. art., to the, e.g. Han ido al mar, They have gone to the sea. 2 —prep a + el used as dem. pron to that, to the one, e.g. Mi sombrero se parece mucho al que tiene Vd., My hat is very similar to the one you have. al + infin. means when, as, at the same time as, e.g. Al llamar a la puerta la vi en el jardín, As I was knocking at the door, I saw her in the garden

ala /'ala/ f, Zool. wing; row, line; brim (of a hat); eaves; (Archit. Aer. Mil. Bot.) wing; blade (of propeller); fin (of fish); pl courage. **a. del corazón,** Anat. auricle. **arrastrar el a.,** to woo, flirt with. Fig. **cortar** (or **quebrar) las alas (a),** to clip a person's wings

Alá /a'la/ m, Allah

alabanza /ala'βanθa; ala'βansa/ f, praise; eulogy

alabar /ala'βar/ vt to praise; —vr brag, boast

alabastro /ala'βastro/ m, alabaster

alacena /ala'θena; ala'sena/ f, cupboard; recess; closet; safe (for food)

alacrán /ala'kran/ m, scorpion

alacridad /alakri'ðað/ f, alacrity, eagerness

alado /a'laðo/ a winged; feathered; Fig. soaring

alambicado /alambi'kaðo/ a sparing, frugal; subtle; euphuistic

alambicar /alambi'kar/ vt to distil; examine carefully, scrutinize; make over-subtle or euphuistic (of style)

alambique /alam'bike/ m, still

alambre /a'lambre/ m, wire; sheep bells. **a. espinoso,** barbed wire

alambrera /alam'brera/ f, wire fence; wire-netting; wire cover

alambrista /alam'brista/ mf tight-rope walker; (Mexico) wetback

alameda /ala'meða/ f, poplar wood or grove; avenue of poplars

álamo /'alamo/ m, poplar. **a. temblón,** aspen tree

alarde /a'larðe/ m, Mil. parade; display, ostentation. **hacer a. de,** to brag about

alargamiento /alarga'miento/ m, lengthening; stretching

alargar /alar'gar/ vt to lengthen; prolong; pass, hand (things); pay out (ropes, etc.); increase; —vr go away, depart; be wordy, spread oneself; lengthen

alarido /ala'riðo/ m, yell, shout; shriek, scream; howl; yelp; cry (of a seagull)

alarma /a'larma/ f, alarm. **a. aérea,** air-raid warning

alarmante /alar'mante/ a alarming

alarmar /alar'mar/ vt to give the alarm; frighten; —vr be alarmed

alarmista /alar'mista/ mf alarmist

alazán /ala'θan; ala'san/ a sorrel-colored. m, sorrel horse

alazo /a'laθo; a'laso/ m, flap or stroke of the wings

alba /'alβa/ f, dawn; Eccl. alb, vestment. **al a.,** at dawn

albacea /alβa'θea; alβa'sea/ mf executor, executrix; testator

albañil /alβa'ɲil/ m, mason, bricklayer

albañilería /alβaɲile'ria/ f, masonry; bricklaying

albaricoque /alβari'koke/ m, apricot

albaricoquero /alβariko'kero/ m, apricot tree

albarrada /alβa'rraða/ f, stone wall; mud fence

albear /alβe'ar/ vi to become white, whiten

albedrío /alβe'ðrio/ m, free will; fancy, caprice

alberca /al'βerka/ f, reservoir, tank; vat; artificial lake

albergar /alβer'gar/ vt to shelter; nourish, harbor; —vi and vr take refuge or shelter; lodge

albergue /al'βerge/ m, shelter, refuge; den, lair; hospitality; lodging; asylum

albóndiga /al'βondiga/ f, forced meat ball, rissole

albor /al'βor/ m, whiteness; dawnlight, dawn. **a. de la vida,** life's dawning, childhood

alborada /alβo'raða/ f, dawn; reveille; Mil. dawn attack; Mus. aubade

alborear /alβore'ar/ vi to grow light, dawn

albornoz /alβor'noθ; alβor'nos/ m, burnouse

alborotado /alβoro'taðo/ a impulsive; turbulent; noisy; excitable

alborotar /alβoro'tar/ vt to disturb; —vi

make a noise; be gay; —*vr* riot; grow rough (sea)

alboroto /alβo'roto/ *m,* noise; confusion; tumult; riot; rejoicing, gaiety; *pl* popcorn

alborozar /alβoro'θar; alβoro'sar/ *vt* to overjoy, gladden; —*vr* rejoice, be glad

alborozo /alβo'roθo; alβo'roso/ *m,* gladness, rejoicing, joy

albricias /al'βriθias; al'βrisias/ *f pl,* reward for bringer of good tidings —*interj* ¡A.! Joy! Congratulations!

álbum /'alβum/ *m,* album

albúmina /al'βumina/ *f,* albumin

albur /al'βur/ *m, Ichth.* dace; chance, risk. **al a. de,** at the risk of

alcachofa /alka'tʃofa/ *f,* artichoke

alcahueta /alka'ueta/ *f,* procuress, go-between

alcahuete /alka'uete/ *m,* procurer, go-between, pimp, pander; *Fig. Inf.* protector, screen; *Inf.* scandalmonger

alcahuetear /alkauete'ar/ *vt* to procure, act as a go-between for; —*vi* be a pimp or a procuress

alcalde /al'kalde/ *m,* mayor; magistrate. *Inf.* **tener el padre a.,** to have a friend at court

alcaldesa /alkal'desa/ *f,* mayoress

alcaldía /alkal'dia/ *f,* office or authority of an alcalde

alcance /al'kanθe; al'kanse/ *m,* reaching, attainment; range (of firearms, etc.); scope; arm's length or reach; pursuit; stop press *or* extra edition (newspapers); *Com.* deficit; importance; *pl* talent; capacity. **al a. de la voz,** within call. **hombre de cortos alcances,** a limited, dull man. **poner al a. de,** to make available to; make intelligible to

alcancía /alkan'θia; alkan'sia/ *f,* money-box; coin bank, piggy bank

alcanfor /alkan'for/ *m,* camphor

alcantarilla /alkanta'riʎa; alkanta'riya/ *f,* little bridge; sewer; culvert; bed for electric cable

alcantarillado /alkantari'ʎaðo; alkantari'yaðo/ *m,* sewage system; main sewer

alcanzable /alkan'θaβle; alkan'saβle/ *a* obtainable; attainable

alcanzadizo /alkanθa'ðiθo; alkansa'ðiso/ *a* attainable, easily reached

alcanzar /alkan'θar; alkan'sar/ *vt* to overtake; reach; range (of guns, etc.); attain, achieve; understand; *Fig.* equal (in attainments); live at the same time as, be contemporaneous with; be capable of, be able; —*vi* reach; share, participate in; be enough

alcaucil /alkau'θil; alkau'sil/ *m,* (in most places) wild artichoke; (in some places) cultivated artichoke

alcazaba /alka'θaβa; alka'saβa/ *f,* fortress (within a walled town or city), casbah

alcázar /al'kaθar; al'kasar/ *m,* fortress; royal residence, castle; *Naut.* quarterdeck

alcista /al'θista; al'sista/ *mf* speculator (on Stock Exchange)

alcoba /al'koβa/ *f,* bedroom; alcove, recess; Moorish flute

alcohol /al'kool/ *m,* alcohol; galena; eye black (cosmetic); spirits of wine. **a. desnaturalizado,** industrial alcohol, methylated spirit. **a. metílico,** wood alcohol

alcohólico /alko'oliko/ *a* alcoholic

alcoholismo /alkool'ismo/ *m,* alcoholism

Alcorán /alko'ran/ *m,* Koran

alcornoque /alkor'noke/ *m,* cork tree; dunderhead, dolt

alcorza /al'korθa; al'korsa/ *f, Cul.* icing, sugar-paste

alcorzar /alkor'θar; alkor'sar/ *vt Cul.* to ice, cover with sugar; decorate, adorn

alcurnia /al'kurnia/ *f,* lineage, family, descent

aldaba /al'daβa/ *f,* door knocker; bolt, latch; *pl* protectors, influential helpers. *Inf.* **tener buenas aldabas,** to have plenty of pull

aldabada /alda'βaða/ *f,* rap with the knocker; sudden shock

aldea /al'dea/ *f,* village

aldeano /alde'ano/ **(-na)** *a* village; country, ignorant —*n* villager; countryman, peasant

aleación /alea'θion; alea'sion/ *f,* alloy

alear /ale'ar/ *vi* to flutter, beat the wings; flap one's arms; recuperate, grow well; —*vt* alloy

aleatorio /alea'torio/ *a* accidental, fortuitous

aleccionamiento /alekθiona'miento; aleksiona'miento/ *m,* teaching, training, coaching

aleccionar /alekθio'nar; aleksio'nar/ *vt* to teach, train, coach

aledaño /ale'ðaɲo/ *a* adjoining; border. *m,* boundary, border

alegación /alega'θion; alega'sion/ *f,* allegation, statement

alegar /ale'gar/ *vt* to allege, state; cite; —*vi Law.* bring forward, adduce

alegato /ale'gato/ *m, Law.* speech (for the prosecution or defense)

alegoría /alego'ria/ *f,* allegory

alegórico /ale'goriko/ *a* allegorical

alegorizar /alegori'θar; alegori'sar/ *vt* to interpret allegorically, treat as an allegory

alegrar /ale'grar/ *vt* to make happy, gladden, rejoice; adorn, beautify; stir (fires); —*vr* be glad, rejoice; *Inf.* be merry (tipsy)

alegre /a'legre/ *a* joyful, glad; cheerful, gay; bright (colors, etc.); pretty, attractive; *Inf.* risqué; *Inf.* flirtatious, light

alegría /ale'gria/ *f,* joy, gladness; cheerfulness, gaiety; *pl* public rejoicings

alegrón /ale'gron/ *m,* sudden unexpected joy; *Inf.* flash of light —*a Inf.* flirtatious

alejamiento /aleha'miento/ *m,* placing at a distance, removal; withdrawal

Alejandría /alehan'dria/ Alexandria

alejar /ale'har/ *vt* to place at a distance, remove; withdraw; ward off (dangers, etc.); —*vr* depart, go away; withdraw.

alejarse de, to abandon (a belief, custom, superstition, etc.)

alelar /ale'lar/ *vt* to make silly or stupid

aleluya /ale'luya/ *mf*, alleluia. *m*, Eastertide. *f*, small Easter cake; *Inf.* daub, poor painting; *Inf.* doggerel; joy, rejoicing

alemán /ale'man/ **(-ana)** *a* and *n* German. *m*, German language.

Alemania /ale'mania/ Germany

alentada /alen'taða/ *f*, deep breath

alentado /alen'taðo/ *a* valiant, spirited; proud

alentador /alenta'ðor/ *a* encouraging, inspiring, stimulating

alentar /alen'tar/ *vi irr* to breathe; —*vt* encourage, inspire; —*vr* be encouraged. See **sentar**

alergia /aler'hia/ *f*, allergy

alergólogo /aler'gologo/ *m*, allergist

alero /a'lero/ *m*, projecting roof; splashboard (of carriages); eaves; gable end

alerta /a'lerta/ *adv* watchfully —*interj* Take care! Look out! **estar ojo a.**, to be on the watch

alerto /a'lerto/ *a* watchful, alert

aletargado /aletar'gaðo/ *a* lethargic; comatose

aletargamiento /aletarga'miento/ *m*, lethargy

aletargar /aletar'gar/ *vt* to cause lethargy; —*vr* become lethargic

aletazo /ale'taθo; ale'taso/ *m*, flapping, beating (of wings); *Inf.* theft

aletear /alete'ar/ *vi* to flap the wings, flutter; move the arms up and down; become convalescent

aleteo /ale'teo/ *m*, fluttering, flapping of wings; beating, palpitation (of heart)

aleve /a'leβe/ *a* See **alevoso**

alevosía /aleβo'sia/ *f*, *Law.* malice; treachery

alevoso /ale'βoso/ *a* *Law.* malicious; treacherous

alfabético /alfa'βetiko/ *a* alphabetical

alfabetización /alfaβetiθa'θion; alfaβetisa'sion/ *f*, literacy work

alfabetizador /alfaβetiθa'ðor; alfaβetisa'ðor/ *m*, literacy worker

alfabeto /alfa'βeto/ *m*, alphabet. **a. manual**, sign language

alfar /al'far/ *m*, potter's workshop; pottery, earthenware

alfarería /alfare'ria/ *f*, pottery shop; potter's workshop; potter's craft

alfarero /alfa'rero/ *m*, potter

alfeñique /alfe'nike/ *m*, *Cul.* icing, sugarpaste; *Inf.* affectation

alfil /al'fil/ *m*, bishop (in chess)

alfiler /alfi'ler/ *m*, pin; brooch with a pin; tiepin; *pl* pin-money, dress-allowance; *Fig. Inf.* **no estar uno con sus alfileres**, to have a slate loose. *Inf.* **vestido de veinticinco alfileres**, dressed to the nines

alfombra /al'fombra/ *f*, carpet; rug

alfombrado /alfom'braðo/ *m*, carpeting

alfombrar /alfom'brar/ *vt* to carpet

alfombrilla eléctrica /alfom'briʎa e'lektrika; alfom'briya e'lektrika/ *f*, electric pad or blanket

alfombrista /alfom'brista/ *m*, carpet merchant; layer of carpets

alforja /al'forha/ *f*, saddle-bag; *Mil.* knapsack

alforza /al'forθa; al'forsa/ *f*, *Sew.* tuck; *Inf.* scar

alforzar /alfor'θar; alfor'sar/ *vt* *Sew.* to tuck

alga /'alga/ *f*, alga, seaweed

algarabía /algara'βia/ *f*, Arabic; *Inf.* gibberish; din of voices, uproar

algarada /alga'raða/ *f*, troop of horse; uproar, hubbub; outcry

algarroba /alga'rroβa/ *f*, *Bot.* carob bean

algazara /alga'θara; alga'sara/ *f*, Moorish war cry; rejoicing, merriment; noise, clamor

álgebra /'alheβra/ *f*, algebra, art of bone setting

algebraico /alhe'βraiko/ *a* algebraic

algo /'algo/ *indef pron* some, something (e.g. *Se ve que hay a. que le molesta*, You can see that something is irritating him) —*adv* somewhat, a bit. **en a.**, in some way

algodón /algo'ðon/ *m*, cotton plant; cotton flower; cotton fabric; candy floss (UK), cotton candy (USA). **a. en rama**, cotton-wool. **a. hidró-filo**, absorbent cotton wool. **a. pólvora**, nitrocellulose

algodonero /algoðo'nero/ **(-ra)** *a* cotton —*n* cotton merchant

alguacil /algua'θil; algua'sil/ *m*, policeman, constable; *Obs.* city governor; short-legged spider

alguien /'algien/ *indef pron* someone, somebody, e.g. *Dime si viene a.*, Tell me if anyone comes

algún /al'gun/ *Abbr.* of **alguno** bef. *m sing* noun, e.g. *a. libro*

alguno /al'guno/ *a* (*Abbr.* **algún** bef. *m*, *sing*) some, any —*indef pron* someone, somebody; *pl* some, some people. **alguno que otro**, a few

alhaja /al'aha/ *f*, jewel; ornament; treasure, precious object; *Inf.* gem, excellent person (also ironic, e.g. *Es una a.*, He's a fine fellow)

alhajar /ala'har/ *vt* to adorn with jewels, bejewel; furnish, equip

alharaca /alar'aka/ *f*, vehemence, demonstration, fuss (gen. *pl*)

aliado /a'liaðo/ **(-da)** *a* allied —*n* ally

alianza /a'lianθa; a'liansa/ *f*, alliance; pact, agreement; relationship (by marriage); sum total, whole (of factors, etc.); wedding-ring

aliarse /a'liarse/ *vr* to join together, become allies; be associated

alicaído /alika'iðo/ *a* drooping; *Inf.* weak, exhausted; discouraged, downhearted; come down in the world

alicates /ali'kates/ *m pl*, pincers, pliers

aliciente /ali'θiente; ali'siente/ *m*, attraction, inducement

alienación /aliena'θion; aliena'sion/ *f*, alienation

alienado /alie'naðo/ *a* insane, mad

alienar /alie'nar/ *vt* See **enajenar**

aliento /a'liento/ *m*, breathing; breath; courage, spirit; encouragement. **el posterior a.**, one's last breath. **cobrar a.**, to regain one's breath; take heart. **de un a.**, in one breath; without stopping

aligación /aliga'θion; aliga'sion/ *f*, binding together, alligation

aligeramiento /a,lihera'miento/ *m*, lightening, reduction in weight

aligerar /alihe'rar/ *vt* to lighten, make less heavy; quicken, hasten; ease, alleviate; moderate; shorten, abbreviate

alígero /a'lihero/ *a Poet.* winged; fleet, swift

alimaña /ali'maɲa/ *f*, destructive animal

alimentación /alimenta'θion; alimenta-'sion/ *f*, nourishment; feeding

alimentar /alimen'tar/ *vt* to feed; nourish; encourage, foment; assist, aid; keep, support

alimenticio /alimen'tiθio; alimen'tisio/ *a* nourishing; feeding

alimento /ali'mento/ *m*, food, nourishment; stimulus, encouragement; *pl* alimony; allowance

alindar /alin'dar/ *vt* to mark the boundary of; beautify, adorn; —*vi* border, be contiguous

alineación /alinea'θion; alinea'sion/ *f*, alignment

alinear /aline'ar/ *vt* to align, range in line; dress (troops); —*vr* fall into line

aliñar /ali'ɲar/ *vt* to decorate, adorn; *Cul.* season; prepare; set (bones)

aliño /a'liɲo/ *m*, decoration, ornament; preparation; condiment, seasoning; setting (bones)

aliquebrado /alike'βraðo/ *a* brokenwinged; *Inf.* down in the mouth

alisador /alisa'ðor/ **(-ra)** *a* smoothing; polishing —*n* polisher

alisar /ali'sar/ *vt* to smooth; polish; sleek; plane; comb lightly

alisios /a'lisios/ *m pl*, trade winds

aliso /a'liso/ *m*, alder tree and wood

alistador /alista'ðor/ *m*, enroller

alistamiento /alista'miento/ *m*, enlistment; conscription; enrolment

alistar /alis'tar/ *vt* to enroll, list; enlist; conscript; prepare, get ready; —*vr* enroll; *Mil.* enlist; get ready

aliviar /ali'βiar/ *vt* to lighten; alleviate, mitigate; relieve; ease; quicken (one's step); hasten, speed up; steal

alivio /a'liβio/ *m*, lightening; relief; alleviation; ease

aljófar /al'hofar/ *m*, small irregular shaped pearl; dew-drop, raindrop, tear drop

allá /a'ʎa; a'ya/ *adv* there; to that place. **más a.**, farther on, beyond. Used in conjunction with phrases of time, indicates remoteness

allanamiento /aʎana'miento; ayana-'miento/ *m*, leveling, flattening; condescension, affability; (police) raid, (police) search acceptance of a judicial finding

allanar /aʎa'nar; aya'nar/ *vt* to level, flatten; overcome (difficulties); soothe; break into (a house, etc.); give entrance to the police; —*vr* collapse (buildings, etc.); abide by, adapt oneself (to); condescend, be affable. **a. el camino (a...)**, to pave the way (for...)

allegado /aʎe'gaðo; aye'gaðo/ **(-da)** *a* near, allied; related —*n* follower, ally

allegar /aʎe'gar; aye'gar/ *vt* to gather, collect; draw nearer; *Agr.* reap; add; —*vi* arrive

allende /a'ʎende; a'yende/ *adv* beyond; besides. **de a. el mar**, from beyond the sea

allí /a'ʎi; a'yi/ *adv* there; to that place, thereto; thereupon, then. **por a.**, through there; that way

alma /'alma/ *f*, soul; living person; essence, core; vivacity, animation; energy, vitality; spirit, ghost; core (of a rope). **a. de cántaro**, fool, ninny. **a. de Dios**, simple soul, kind person. **a. en pena**, soul in purgatory. **¡A. mía!** My darling! **con todo el a.**, with all my heart. **Lo siento en el a.**, I feel it deeply

almacén /alma'θen; alma'sen/ *m*, warehouse; store, shop

almacenaje /almaθe'nahe; almase'nahe/ *m*, cost of storage

almacenar /almaθe'nar; almase'nar/ *vt* to store; put in store; hoard

almacenero /almaθe'nero; almase'nero/ *m*, warehouseman, storekeeper

almacenista /almaθe'nista; almase'nista/ *mf* owner of a store; assistant, salesman (saleswoman)

almanaque /alma'nake/ *m*, calendar, almanac

almeja /al'meha/ *f*, *Ichth.* clam

almendra /al'mendra/ *f*, almond; kernel; crystal drop (of chandeliers, etc.); cocoon; bean (of cocoa tree, etc.). **a. garapiñada**, sugar almond

almendro /al'mendro/ *m*, almond tree

almíbar /al'miβar/ *m*, sugar syrup; nectar

almibarar /almiβa'rar/ *vt* to coat with sugar; preserve (fruit) in syrup; flatter with sweet words

almidón /almi'ðon/ *m*, starch

almidonado /almiðo'naðo/ *a* starched; *Fig. Inf.* stiff, unbending; prim, starchy

almidonar /almiðo'nar/ *vt* to starch

alminar /almi'nar/ *m*, minaret (of mosque)

almiranta /almi'ranta/ *f*, admiral's wife; flagship

almirantazgo /almiran'taθgo; almiran-'tasgo/ *m*, Admiralty; admiralship; Admiralty Court

almirante /almi'rante/ *m*, admiral

almohada /almo'aða/ f, pillow; pillow-case; cushion. *Inf.* **aconsejarse or consultar con la a.,** to think over (a matter) carefully, sleep on it

almohadilla /almoa'ðiʎa; almoa'ðiya/ f, *dim* small cushion; lace or sewing cushion; pin cushion

almohadillado /almoaði'ʎaðo; almoaði-'yaðo/ a cushioned; padded

almoneda /almo'neða/ f, auction; furniture sale

almonedear /almoneðe'ar/ vt to auction; sell off (furniture)

almorranas /almo'rranas/ f pl, hemorrhoids

almorzar /almor'θar; almor'sar/ vi irr to lunch; breakfast. See **forzar**

almuecín, almuédano /almue'θin, al'mueðano; almue'sin, al'mueðano/ m, muezzin

almuerzo /al'muerθo; al'muerso/ m, luncheon; breakfast (not so usual)

alocado /alo'kaðo/ a feather-brained, reckless; crazy, wild

alocución /aloku'θion; aloku'sion/ f, allocution, address, harangue

áloe /'aloe/ m, *Bot.* aloe

alojado /alo'haðo/ **(-da)** m, billeted soldier —n lodger

alojamiento /aloha'miento/ m, lodging; dwelling; *Mil.* billeting; *Naut.* steerage; camp, encampment

alojar /alo'har/ vt to lodge; billet, quarter (troops); insert, introduce; —vi and vr lodge; live, dwell

alpaca /al'paka/ f, alpaca (animal and fabric); nickel silver

alpargata /alpar'gata/ f, sandal with hemp sole

alpargatero /alparga'tero/ **(-ra)** n manufacturer or seller of alpargatas

Alpes, los /'alpes, los/ the Alps

alpestre /al'pestre/ a Alpine; rock (of plants); mountainous, lofty

alpinismo /alpi'nismo/ m, mountaineering

alpinista /alpi'nista/ mf mountaineer, climber

alpino /al'pino/ a Alpine

alpro /'alpro/ f, (Alianza para el Progreso)

alquería /alke'ria/ f, farmstead

alquiladizo /alkila'ðiθo; alkila'ðiso/ a rentable, hirable

alquilador /alkila'ðor/ **(-ra)** n hirer

alquilamiento /alkila'miento/ m, See **alquiler**

alquilar /alki'lar/ vt to rent; hire out; hire; —vr hire oneself out, serve on a wage basis

alquiler /alki'ler/ m, hiring out; renting; rental; hire; wages. **de a.,** for hire, on hire

alquitrán /alki'tran/ m, tar, pitch. **a. mineral,** coal tar

alquitranado /alkitra'naðo/ a tarred. m, *Naut.* tarpaulin

alrededor /alreðe'ðor/ adv around,
round about. **a. de,** around; approximately, about (e.g. *a. de cinco dólares,* about $5)

alrededores /alreðe'ðeres/ m pl, environs, surrounding country

alta /'alta/ f, certificate of discharge from hospital

altanería /altane'ria/ f, hawking; haughtiness, disdain; superciliousness

altanero /alta'nero/ a soaring, high-flying (of birds); supercilious; haughty, disdainful

altar /al'tar/ m, altar. **a. mayor,** high altar

altavoz /ˌalta'βoθ; ˌalta'βos/ m, loudspeaker; megaphone

altearse /alte'arse/ vr to rise, grow steep (of land)

alterabilidad /alteraβili'ðað/ f, alterability, changeability

alteración /altera'θion; altera'sion/ f, alteration, change; debasement (of coinage); agitation

alterar /alte'rar/ vt to change, alter; debase (coinage); disturb, agitate; —vr grow angry; become excited

altercación, /alterka'θion; alterka'sion/ f, **altercado** m, altercation, quarrel

altercar /alter'kar/ **(se)** vi and vr to quarrel, dispute, altercate

alternación /alterna'θion; alterna'sion/ f, alternation

alternado /alter'naðo/ a alternate

alternador /alterna'ðor/ a alternating. m, *Elec.* alternator

alternante /alter'nante/ a alternating

alternar /alter'nar/ vt to alternate; make one's debut as a **matador;** —vi alternate; (*with con*) have dealings with, know

alternativa /alterna'tiβa/ f, alternative, option; service performed by turns; alternation

alternativo /alterna'tiβo/ a alternative

alterno /al'terno/ a alternative; *Bot.* alternate

alteza /al'teθa; al'tesa/ f, altitude, height; sublimity, perfection; **(A.)** Highness (title)

altibajo /alti'βaho/ m, embossed velvet; pl *Inf.* rough ground; *Inf.* vicissitudes of fortune

altillo /al'tiʎo; al'tiyo/ m, hillock, eminence; garret, attic

altímetro /al'timetro/ m, *Aer.* altimeter

altiplanicie /altipla'niθie; altipla'nisie/ f, plateau; highland

altisonante /altiso'nante/ a sonorous; sublime; high-flown, pompous

altitud /alti'tuð/ f, altitude, height

altivez /alti'βeθ; alti'βes/ f, arrogance, haughtiness

altivo /al'tiβo/ a arrogant, haughty

alto /'alto/ a high; tall; difficult, arduous; sublime; deep; most serious (of crimes, etc.); dear (of price); small, early (hours). m, height; eminence, hill; story, floor; *Mil.* halt; red light (traffic light) —adv up, above, on high; loudly —interj ¡A.! *Mil.*

Halt! *Mil.* **A. Mando**, High Command. **las altas horas de la noche**, the small (or early) hours. **en alta voz**, in a loud voice. **en alto**, on high; up above. **hacer alto**, to halt, stop

altozano /alto'θano; alto'sano/ *m*, mound, hillock; viewpoint, open space

altruismo /altru'ismo/ *m*, altruism

altruista /altru'ista/ *a* altruistic. *mf* altruist

altura /al'tura/ *f*, height; altitude; *Geom.* altitude or height; top, peak; sublimity; tallness

alucinación /aluθina'θion; alusina'sion/ *f*, alucinamiento, *m*, hallucination

alucinado /aluθi'nado; alusi'nado/ *m*, person suffering from hallucinations

alucinador /aluθina'δor; alusina'δor/ *a* hallucinatory, deceptive

alucinar /aluθi'nar; alusi'nar/ *vt* to dazzle, fascinate; deceive

alud /a'luδ/ *m*, avalanche

aludir /alu'δir/ *vi* to allude (to); refer (to), cite

alumbrado /alum'braδo/ *m*, lighting; *pl* illuminati

alumbramiento /alumbra'miento/ *m*, lighting, supply of light; childbirth

alumbrar /alum'brar/ *vt* to light, illuminate; give sight to the blind; instruct, teach; inflict (blows); hoe vine roots; —*vi* give birth to a child; —*vr Inf.* grow tipsy

aluminio /alu'minio/ *m*, aluminum

alumno /a'lumno/ **(-na)** *n* ward, adopted child; pupil. **a. externo**, day pupil. **a. interno**, boarder

alunizaje /aluni'θahe; aluni'sahe/ *m*, landing on the moon, moon-landing

alunizar /aluni'θar; aluni'sar/ *vi* to land on the moon

alusión /alu'sion/ *f*, allusion

alusivo /alu'siβo/ *a* allusive, suggestive; hinting

aluvión /alu'βion/ *m*, alluvium. **de a.**, alluvial

alza /'alθa; 'alsa/ *f*, rise (of temperature, etc.); increase (in price); front sight (of guns)

alzada /al'θaδa; al'saδa/ *f*, horse's stature; mountain pasture; *Law.* appeal

alzado /al'θaδo; al'saδo/ *a* fraudulent (of bankruptcy); fixed (of price). *m*, theft; *Archit.* front elevation

alzamiento /alθa'miento; alsa'miento/ *m*, raising, lifting; higher bid (at auction); rising, rebellion; fraudulent bankruptcy

alzaprima /alθa'prima; alsa'prima/ *f*, lever; wedge; bridge (of string instruments)

alzar /al'θar; al'sar/ *vt* to raise; lift up; elevate (the Host); steal, remove; hide; gather in the harvest; build, construct; *Naut.* heave; —*vr* rise (of temperature, mercury, price, etc.); make a fraudulent bankruptcy; *Law.* appeal; (*with con*) run off with, steal. *Naut.* **a. la vela**, to set sail

ama /'ama/ *f*, mistress of the house;

owner; housekeeper; wet nurse. **a. de casa**, homemaker, housewife. **a. de leche**, foster-mother. **a. de llaves** *or* **a. de gobierno**, housekeeper. **a. seca**, children's nurse

amabilidad /amaβili'δaδ/ *f*, lovableness; kindness; niceness, goodness, helpfulness

amable /a'maβle/ *a* lovable; kind; nice, good, helpful

amador /ama'δor/ **(-ra)** *a* loving —*n* lover, admirer

amadrigar /amaδri'gar/ *vt* to welcome, receive well; —*vr* go into a burrow or lair; go into seclusion

amaestrar /amaes'trar/ *vt* to train, instruct; tame; break in (horses)

amagar /ama'gar/ *vt* and *vi* to threaten; —*vt* show signs of (diseases, etc.); —*vr Inf.* hide

amago /a'mago/ **(contra...)** threat (to...), menace (to...)

amainar /amai'nar/ *vt Naut.* to take in the sails; —*vi* drop (of the wind); —*vi* and *vt* relax (efforts, etc.)

amalgama /amal'gama/ *f*, *Chem.* amalgam

amalgamación /amalgama'θion; amalgama'sion/ *f*, amalgamation

amalgamar /amalga'mar/ *vt* to amalgamate; —*vr* be amalgamated

amamantamiento /amamanta'miento/ *m*, suckling, nursling

amamantar /amaman'tar/ *vt* to suckle

amancebado /amanθe'βaδo; amanse-'βaδo/ *m*, concubine

amancillar /amanθi'ʎar; amansi'yar/ *vt* to discredit, dishonor; tarnish; stain

amanecer /amane'θer; amane'ser/ *vi irr* to dawn; arrive *or* be somewhere *or* be doing, at dawn; appear at daybreak; begin to appear. *m*, dawn, daybreak. See **conocer**

amanerado /amane'raδo/ *a* mannered; affected

amaneramiento /amanera'miento/ *m*, manneredness; mannerism

amanerarse /amane'rarse/ *vr* to acquire mannerisms or tricks of style; become affected

amansador /amansa'δor/ **(-ra)** *a* soothing, calming —*n* appeaser

amansamiento /amansa'miento/ *m*, taming; appeasement; soothing; breaking in (horses)

amansar /aman'sar/ *vt* to tame; appease, moderate; soothe, pacify; break in (horses)

amante /a'mante/ *a* loving. *mf* lover

amanuense /ama'nuense/ *mf* amanuensis, secretary, clerk

amañar /ama'ɲar/ *vt* to execute with skill; —*vr* grow skillful

amaño /a'maɲo/ *m*, skill, dexterity; *pl* schemes, intrigues; tools, equipment

amapola /ama'pola/ *f*, poppy

amar /a'mar/ *vt* to love

amarar /ama'rar/ *vi* to alight on the water (of hydroplanes)

amargar /amar'gar/ *vi* to taste or be bitter; —*vt* make bitter; embitter

amargo /a'margo/ *a* bitter; embittered; grievous, sad. *m*, bitterness; *pl* bitters

amargor /amar'gor/ *m*, amargura, /amar'gura/ *f*, bitter taste, bitterness; trouble, affliction, pain

amarillear /amariʎe'ar/ amariye'ar/ *vi* to look yellow; turn yellow; tend to yellow

amarillento /amari'ʎento; amari'yento/ *a* yellowish, turning yellow

amarillo /ama'riʎo; ama'riyo/ *a* and *m*, yellow

amarradero /amarra'ðero/ *m*, *Naut.* mooring berth; mooring-post; hitching-post or ring

amarrar /ama'rrar/ *vt* to tie up, hitch; moor

amarre /a'marre/ *m*, mooring; hitching

amartelar /amarte'lar/ *vt* to make jealous; court, woo, make love to; —*vr* be jealous; fall madly in love

amartillar /amarti'ʎar; amarti'yar/ *vt* to hammer, knock; cock (firearms)

amasador /amasa'ðor/ **(-ra)** *a* kneading —*n* kneader

amasar /ama'sar/ *vt* to knead; massage; scheme, plot

amasijo /ama'siho/ *m*, *Cul.* dough, kneading; portion of plaster or mortar; *Inf.* hotchpotch, mixture; scheme, plot

amatista /ama'tista/ *f*, amethyst

amatorio /ama'torio/ *a* amatory

amazacotado /a,maθako'taðo; a,masako-'taðo/ *a* heavy, dense; *Fig.* stodgy (of writings, etc.)

amazona /ama'θona; ama'sona/ *f*, Amazon; independent woman; woman rider; .woman's riding habit

ambages /am'bahes/ *m pl*, maze, intricate paths; circumlocutions

ámbar /'ambar/ *m*, amber. **a. gris**, ambergris

ambición /ambi'θion; ambi'sion/ *f*, ambition

ambicionar /ambiθio'nar; ambisio'nar/ *vt* to long for; desire eagerly; be ambitious to

ambicioso /ambi'θioso; ambi'sioso/ *a* ambitious; eager, desirous

ambidextro /ambi'ðekstro/ *a* ambidextrous

ambiente /am'biente/ *a* ambient, surrounding. *m*, air, atmosphere; environment

ambigú /ambi'gu/ *m*, cold buffet; buffet (in theaters, etc.)

ambigüedad /ambigue'ðað/ *f*, ambiguity

ambiguo /am'biguo/ *a* ambiguous

ámbito /'ambito/ *m*, precincts; boundary, limit; compass, scope

ambos /'ambos,/ *a m pl*, **ambas** *a f pl*, both, e.g. *ambas casas*, both houses

ambulancia /ambu'lanθia; ambu'lansia/ *f*, ambulance. **a. de correos**, railway post office. **a. fija**, field-hospital

ambulante /ambu'lante/ *a* walking; traveling, wandering

amedrentar /ameðren'tar/ *vt* to frighten, scare; intimidate

ameliorar /amelio'rar/ *vt* to better, improve

amén /a'men/ *m*, amen, so be it. **a. de**, besides, in addition to. *Inf.* **en un decir a.**, in a trice

amenaza /ame'naθa; ame'nasa/ *f*, threat

amenazador, amenazante /amenaθa'ðor, amena'θante; amenasa'ðor, amena'sante/ *a* menacing, threatening

amenazar /amena'θar; amena'sar/ *vt* to threaten; —*vt* and *vi* presage, be pending

amenguamiento /amengua'miento/ *m*, lessening, diminution; discredit; loss of prestige

amenguar /amen'guar/ *vt* to lessen, decrease; dishonor, discredit

amenidad /ameni'ðað/ *f*, amenity; agreeableness

amenizar /ameni'θar; ameni'sar/ *vt* to make pleasant or attractive

ameno /a'meno/ *a* pleasant; entertaining; agreeable, delightful

América /a'merika/ America

América del Norte /a'merika del 'norte/ North America

América del Sur /a'merika del sur/ South America

americana /ameri'kana/ *f*, (man's) jacket

americanismo /amerika'nismo/ *m*, usage typical of Western-Hemisphere Spanish

americano /ameri'kano/ *a* American

ameritar /ameri'tar/ *vt* *West. Hem.* to deserve, merit

ametrallador /ametraʎa'ðor; ametraya-'ðor/ *m*, machine-gunner

ametralladora /ametraʎa'ðora; ametraya'ðora/ *f*, machine-gun

amianto /a'mianto/ *m*, *Mineral.* amianthus, asbestos

amiba /a'miβa/ *f*, *Zool.* ameba

amiga /a'miga/ *f*, woman friend; mistress, lover; dame, schoolmistress; dame school

amigabilidad /amigaβili'ðað/ *f*, friendliness, amicability

amigable /ami'gaβle/ *a* friendly, amicable; harmonious; suitable

amígdala /a'migðala/ *f*, tonsil

amigdalitis /amigða'litis/ *f*, tonsillitis

amigo /a'migo/ **(-ga)** *a* friendly; fond, addicted —*n* friend. *m*, lover. *Inf.* **ser muy a. de**, to be very friendly with; be very keen on or fond of

amilanar /amila'nar/ *vt* to terrify, intimidate; —*vr* grow discouraged

aminorar /amino'rar/ *vt* to diminish, lessen

amistad /amis'tað/ *f*, friendship; liaison; favor; *pl* acquaintances, friends

amistar /amis'tar/ *vt* to introduce, make

known to each other; bring about a reconciliation between or with

amistoso /amis'toso/ *a* friendly

amnesia /am'nesia/ *f*, amnesia

amnistía /amnis'tia/ *f*, amnesty

amnistiar /amnisti'ar/ *vt* to concede an amnesty, pardon

amo /'amo/ *m*, head of the house; master; owner; overlord; overseer. **a. de huéspedes,** keeper of a boarding house. **Nuestro A.** Our Lord. *Inf.* **ser el a. del cotarro,** to rule the roost

amodorramiento /amoðorra'miento/ *m*, stupor, deep sleep

amodorrarse /amoðo'rrarse/ *vr* to fall into a stupor; fall into a heavy sleep

amoladera /amola'ðera/ *f*, whetstone

amolador /amola'ðor/ *m*, scissors grinder; knife grinder; sharpener

amoladura /amola'ðura/ *f*, grinding, whetting, sharpening

amolar /amo'lar/ *vt irr* to grind, sharpen; *Inf.* pester, annoy. See **colar**

amoldar /amol'dar/ *vt* to mold; adjust; —*vr* adapt oneself

amonestación /amonesta'θion; amonesta'sion/ *f*, warning; advice. **correr las amonestaciones,** to publish bans of marriage

amonestador /amonesta'ðor/ **(-ra)** *a* warning, admonitory —*n* admonisher

amonestar /amones'tar/ *vt* to warn; advise; rebuke; *Eccl.* publish bans of marriage

amoníaco /amo'niako/ *m*, ammonia

amontillado /amonti'ʎaðo; amonti'yaðo/ *m*, kind of pale, dry sherry

amontonamiento /amontona'miento/ *m*, accumulation; gathering, collection; piling up, heaping

amontonar /amonto'nar/ *vt* to pile up, heap; gather; collect; accumulate; —*vr* *Inf.* fly into a rage

amor /a'mor/ *m*, love; beloved; willingness, pleasure; *pl* love affairs; caresses. **a. propio,** self-esteem; vanity. *Inf.* **con mil amores,** with great pleasure. **por a. de,** for love of; for the sake of

amoral /amo'ral/ *a* amoral

amoratado /amora'taðo/ *a* livid, bluish

amorcillo /amor'θiʎo; amor'siyo/ *m*, *dim* little love; unimportant love affair; Cupid

amordazamiento /amorðaθa'miento; amorðasa'miento/ *m*, muzzling; gagging

amordazar /amorða'θar; amorða'sar/ *vt* to muzzle; gag; prevent speaking

amorfo /a'morfo/ *a* amorphous

amorío /amo'rio/ *m*, *Inf.* wooing, love making; *pl* love affairs

amoroso /amo'roso/ *a* loving; gentle; mild, balmy

amorrar /amo'rrar/ *vi Inf.* to hang one's head; sulk, be sullen

amortajar /amorta'har/ *vt* to wrap in a shroud; enshroud

amortiguador /amortigua'ðor/ *m*, *Mech.* shock absorber. *Auto.* **a. de los muelles,** shock-absorber

amortiguamiento /amortigua'miento/ *m*, softening, deadening; mitigation, lessening

amortiguar /amorti'guar/ *vt* to soften, deaden; absorb (shocks); moderate, mitigate; soften (colors)

amortización /amortiθa'θion; amortisa'sion/ *f*, amortization

amortizar /amorti'θar; amorti'sar/ *vt* to amortize; recover, redeem; suppress, abolish (posts)

amoscarse /amos'karse/ *vr Inf.* to be piqued or annoyed; become agitated

amostazar /amosta'θar; amosta'sar/ *vt Inf.* to annoy; —*vi* become peeved

amotinador /amotina'ðor/ **(-ra)** *a* mutinous, rebellious —*n* rebel, mutineer; rioter

amotinar /amoti'nar/ *vt* to incite to rebellion; unbalance, unhinge (mind); —*vr* rebel; riot; *Fig.* be unhinged

amovible /amo'βiβle/ *a* movable, removable; removable (of officials, etc.)

amparador /ampara'ðor/ **(-ra)** *a* protective; sheltering —*n* protector, defender, helper; shelterer

amparar /ampa'rar/ *vt* to protect, favor, help; shelter; —*vr* take refuge, take shelter; defend oneself

amparo /am'paro/ *m*, shelter, refuge; protection, favor, help; defense

amper /am'per/ *m*, *Elec.* ampere

amperímetro /ampe'rimetro/ *m*, *Elec.* ammeter

amperio /am'perio/ *m*, *Elec.* ampere

ampliable /am'pliaβle/ *a* amplifiable

ampliación /amplia'θion; amplia'sion/ *f*, enlargement, increase, extension; *Photo.* enlargement

ampliador /amplia'ðor/ **(-ra)** *a* enlarging —*n* enlarger

ampliadora /amplia'ðora/ *f*, *Photo.* enlarger

ampliar /amp'liar/ *vt* to extend, enlarge, increase; *Photo.* enlarge

amplificación /amplifika'θion; amplifika'sion/ *f*, extension, amplification; *Photo.* enlargement

amplificar /amplifi'kar/ *vt* to enlarge; extend; increase; amplify, expatiate upon

amplio /'amplio/ *a* wide; extensive; roomy, ample; prolix

amplitud /ampli'tuð/ *f*, extension; width; spaciousness, amplitude

ampolla /am'poʎa; am'poya/ *f*, blister; ampoule; bubble; *Elec.* bulb

amputación /amputa'θion; amputa'sion/ *f*, amputation

amputar /ampu'tar/ *vt* to amputate

amuchachado /amutʃa'tʃaðo/ *a* boyish

amueblar /amue'βlar/ *vt* to furnish; provide with furniture

amuleto /amu'leto/ *m*, amulet, charm

amurallar /amura'ʎar; amura'yar/ *vt* to surround with a wall, wall

amusgar /amus'gar/ *vt* and *vi* to flatten the ears (animals); —*vt* screw up the eyes (to see better)

anacardo /ana'karðo/ *m*, cashew (nut)

anacrónico /ana'kroniko/ *a* anachronous

anacronismo /anakro'nismo/ *m*, anachronism

ánade /'anaðe/ *mf* duck

anafrodisíaco /anafroði'siako/ *a* anaphrodisiac

anagrama /ana'grama/ *m*, anagram

anales /a'nales/ *m*, *pl* annals

analfabetismo /analfaβe'tismo/ *m*, illiteracy

analfabeto /analfa'βeto/ **(-ta)** *a* and *n* illiterate

analgesia /anal'hesia/ *f*, analgesia

analgésico /anal'hesiko/ *a* and *m*, *Med.* analgesic

análisis /a'nalisis/ *m*, analysis; *Gram.* parsing

analista /ana'lista/ *mf* analyst

analizar /anali'θar; anali'sar/ *vt* to analyse

analogía /analo'hia/ *f*, analogy

analógico, análogo /ana'lohiko, a'nalogo/ *a* analogous

ananás /ana'nas/ *m*, pineapple

anaquel /ana'kel/ *m*, shelf, ledge

anaranjado /anaran'haðo/ *a* and *m*, orange (color)

anarquía /anar'kia/ *f*, anarchy

anárquico /a'narkiko/ *a* anarchical

anatema /ana'tema/ *mf*. anathema

anatomía /anato'mia/ *f*, anatomy

anatómico /ana'tomiko/ *a* anatomical

ancho /'antʃo/ *a* wide, broad. *m*, width, breadth. *Inf.* **a mis (tus, sus,** etc.) **anchas** *or* **anchos,** at my (your, his, etc.) ease, with complete freedom

anchoa /an'tʃoa/ *f*, anchovy

anchura /an'tʃura/ *f*, width, breadth; ease, freedom; extent

anchuroso /antʃu'roso/ *a* very wide; extensive; spacious

ancianidad /anθiani'ðað; ansiani'ðað/ *f*, old age; seniority; oldness

anciano /an'θiano; an'siano/ **(-na)** *a* old; ancient —*n* old person

ancla /'ankla/ *f*, anchor. **a. de la esperanza,** sheet anchor. **echar anclas,** to anchor

anclar /an'klar/ *vi* to anchor

áncora /'ankora/ *f*, anchor; refuge, haven

andada /an'daða/ *f*, wandering, roving; hard bread roll; pasture; *pl* trail, tracks. *Fig. Inf.* **volver a las andadas,** to return to one's old tricks

andaderas /anda'ðeras/ *f pl*, go-cart (for learning to walk)

andador /anda'ðor/ *a* walking; swift walking; wandering. *m*, walker; garden path; *pl* leading-strings, reins

andadura /anda'ðura/ *f*, walk, gait; pace, step

Andalucía /andalu'θia; andalu'sia/ Andalusia

andaluz /anda'luθ; anda'lus/ **(-za)** *a* and *n* Andalusian

andaluzada /andalu'θaða; andalu'saða/ *f*, *Inf.* exaggeration, tall story

andamio /an'damio/ *m*, scaffolding; stand, platform

andanada /anda'naða/ *f*, *Naut.* broadside; cheapest priced seat in a bullring; *Inf.* dressing-down, scolding

andante /an'dante/ *a* walking, strolling; errant (of knights) —*a* and *m*, *Mus.* andante

andanza /an'danθa; an'dansa/ *f*, happening, occurrence; *pl* doings, deeds. **buena a.,** good fortune

andar /an'dar/ *vi irr* to walk; move; work, operate, run (machines, etc.); progress, get along (negotiations, etc.); be, feel; elapse (of time); be occupied; behave; (*with prep a*) administer (blows, etc.); (*with en*) upset, turn over (papers, etc.); ride in or on (cars, bicycles, etc.); be engaged in; (*with con*) use, handle; —*vt* traverse. *m*, gait, walk. **a. por los cuarenta,** to be in one's forties. **a. con paños tibios,** not to be firm. **a. con pies de plomo,** to be extremely cautious. **a. tras,** to follow, go after; persecute; desire ardently (things). **andarse a la flor del berro,** to sow one's wild oats. *Fig. Inf.* **andarse por las ramas,** to beat about the bush. **¡Anda!** Get along with you!; Hurry up!; You don't say so! **¡Andando!** Let's get going!, Let's get a move on it! *Preterite* **anduve,** etc —*imperf subjunc* **anduviese,** etc.

andariego /anda'riego/ *a* swift walking; wandering, vagrant

andarín (-ina) /anda'rin/ *n* good walker; professional walker

andas /'andas/ *f pl*, kind of stretcher; bier

andén /an'den/ *m*, railway platform

andino /an'dino/ *a* Andean

andrajo /an'draho/ *m*, rag, wisp of cloth, tatter

andrajoso /andra'hoso/ *a* ragged, tattered

andurriales /andu'rriales/ *m pl*, byways, unfrequented paths; remote places

anécdota /a'nekðota/ *f*, anecdote

anegación /anega'θion; anega'sion/ *f*, drowning; flooding, inundation

anegar /ane'gar/ *vt* to drown; inundate; shipwreck; —*vr* drown; be flooded

anejo /a'neho/ *a* attached, annexed. *m*, annexed borough

anemia /a'nemia/ *f*, anemia

anémico /a'nemiko/ *a* anemic

anémona, anémone /a'nemona, a'nemone/ *f*, anemone. **anémona de mar,** sea-anemone

anestesia /anes'tesia/ *f*, anesthesia

anestesiador (-ra) /anestesia'ðor/ *n* anesthetist

anestesiar /aneste'siar/ *vt* to anesthetize

anestésico /anes'tesiko/ *a* and *m*, anesthetic

aneurisma /aneu'risma/ *mf Med.* aneurism

anexar /anek'sar/ *vt* to annex

anexión /anek'sion/ *f*, annexation

anexo /a'nekso/ *a* attached, joined. *m*, annex

anfibio /an'fiβio/ *a* amphibious. *m*, amphibian

anfiteatro /anfite'atro/ *m*, amphitheater; operating theater; dissecting room; morgue; *Theat.* dress-circle

anfitrión /anfitri'on/ *m*, *Inf.* host, one who entertains guests

angarillas /aŋga'riʎas; aŋga'riyas/ *f pl*, hand barrow; table cruet; yoke and panniers

ángel /'anhel/ *m*, angel. **á. de la guarda**, guardian angel. **estar con los ángeles**, to be in Heaven (euphem. for "to be dead")

angelical, angélico /anheli'kal, an'heliko/ *a* angelic; divine, excellent

angina /an'hina/ *f*, *Med.* angina, tonsillitis. **a. de pecho**, angina pectoris

anglicismo /aŋgli'θismo; aŋgli'sismo/ *m*, anglicism

angostar /aŋgos'tar/ *vi and vt* to narrow; tighten

angosto /aŋ'gosto/ *a* narrow; tight

angostura /aŋgos'tura/ *f*, narrowness; tightness; narrow pass; strait; *Fig.* tight corner, fix

anguila /aŋ'gila/ *f*, *Ichth.* eel; *pl Naut.* slipway, slips

ángulo /'aŋgulo/ *m*, angle. **á. inferior izquierdo**, lower lefthand corner. **á. inferior derecho**, lower righthand corner. **á. superior izquierdo**, upper lefthand corner. **á. superior derecho**, upper righthand corner. **á. recto**, right angle

anguloso /aŋgu'loso/ *a* angulate; angular, gaunt; cornered

angustia /aŋ'gustia/ *f*, anguish, grief

angustiante /aŋgus'tiante/ *a* distressing

angustiar /aŋgus'tiar/ *vt* to grieve; afflict; —*vr* be full of anguish

anhelación /anela'θion; anela'sion/ *f*, panting, hard breathing; yearning, longing

anhelar /ane'lar/ *vi* to pant, breathe with difficulty; —*vi and vt* long for, yearn for, desire

anhélito /a'nelito/ *m*, pant, hard breathing

anhelo (de) /a'nelo/ *m*, longing (for), desire (for), yearning (for)

anheloso /ane'loso/ *a* difficult, labored (of breathing); anxious, longing

anidar /ani'ðar/ *vi* to nest (birds); swell; —*vt* shelter, protect; —*vr* nest; dwell; nestle

anilla /a'niʎa; a'niya/ *f*, curtain ring; *pl* gymnastic rings

anillo /a'niʎo; a'niyo/ *m*, finger ring; small ring; coil (of serpents and ropes). *Inf.* **venir como a. al dedo**, to fit like a glove; come just at the right moment

ánima /'anima/ *f*, soul, spirit; soul in purgatory; bore (of firearms); *pl* prayer bell for the souls of the departed

animación /anima'θion; anima'sion/ *f*, liveliness, gaiety; animation, vivacity; bustle, movement

animal /ani'mal/ *m*, animal; *Inf.* dolt, brute —*a* animal; *Inf.* brutish, doltish

animalada /anima'laða/ *f*, *Inf.* stupidity, foolishness

animalidad /animali'ðað/ *f*, animalism

animar /ani'mar/ *vt* to animate; encourage, incite; invigorate, enliven; make gay, cheer up; make attractive, adorn; —*vr* take heart; make up one's mind; cheer up; grow gay

animismo /ani'mismo/ *m*, animism

ánimo /'animo/ *m*, soul, spirit; courage; endurance, fortitude; will, intention; mind. **con ánimo de + inf.**, with the intention of + *ger*. **¡Á.!** Courage!

animosidad /animosi'ðað/ *f*, hatred, animosity, dislike

animoso /ani'moso/ *a* spirited, lively; valiant

aniñado /ani'ɲaðo/ *a* childlike, childish

aniquilación /anikila'θion; anikila'sion/ *f*, destruction, annihilation; suppression; decay

aniquilador (-ra) /anikila'ðor/ *a* destructive, annihilating —*n* destroyer

aniquilamiento /anikila'miento/ *m*, See **aniquilación**

aniquilar /aniki'lar/ *vt* to annihilate, destroy completely; —*vr* waste away, decay

anís /a'nis/ *m*, aniseed, anise; anisette (liqueur)

aniversario /aniβer'sario/ *a* annual. *m*, anniversary

ano /'ano/ *m*, anus

anoche /a'notʃe/ *adv* last night; the previous night

anochecer /anotʃe'θer; anotʃe'ser/ *vi irr* to grow night; become dark; be in a place *or* be doing something at nightfall (e.g. *Anochecimos en Lérida*, We were in Lerida at nightfall) —*vr Poet.* be obscured or darkened. *m*, nightfall, dusk. See **conocer**

anochecida /anotʃe'θiða; anotʃe'siða/ *f*, dusk, late twilight

anodino /ano'ðino/ *a Med.* anodyne; ineffective, useless; inoffensive. *m*, anodyne

anomalía /anoma'lia/ *f*, anomaly, inconstancy, irregularity; *Astron.* anomaly

anómalo /a'nomalo/ *a* anomalous, abnormal, unusual

anonadar /anona'ðar/ *vt* to destroy, annihilate; suppress; *Fig.* overwhelm, depress; humble

anónimo /a'nonimo/ *a* anonymous. *m*, anonymity; anonymous letter; unsigned literary work

anormal /anor'mal/ *a* abnormal; irregular, unusual. *mf* abnormal person

anormalidad /anormali'ðað/ *f*, abnormality; irregularity, inconsistency

anotación /anota'θion; anota'sion/ f. annotation

anotador /anota'ðor/ **(-ra)** n annotator

anotar /ano'tar/ vt to annotate; note down

anquilostoma /aŋkilos'toma/ m, Med. hookworm

ansia (de) /'ansia/ f, anxiety, trouble; grief; longing (for), yearning (for); greed

ansiar /an'siar/ vt to long for, yearn for; covet, desira

ansiedad /ansie'ðað/ f, anxiety, anguish, worry

ansión /an'sion/ f, intense desire

ansioso /an'sioso/ a anxious; grievous, painful; eager, desirous; greedy

antagónico /anta'goniko/ a antagonistic

antagonismo /antago'nismo/ m, antagonism

antagonista /antago'nista/ mf antagonist, adversary

antaño /an'taɲo/ adv last year, yesteryear; long ago

ante /'ante/ m, Zool. elk; suede; buffalo

ante /'ante/ prep in the presence of, before; regarding, in the face of (e.g. a. deber tan alto, in the face of so noble a duty)

anteanoche /antea'notʃe/ adv the night before last

anteayer /antea'yer/ adv the day before yesterday

antebrazo /ante'βraθo; ante'βraso/ m, forearm

antecedente /anteθe'ðente; antese'ðente/ m, antecedent. **antecedentes** m pl background (of a case, situation, etc.)

anteceder /anteθe'ðer; antese'ðer/ vt to precede

antecesor /anteθe'sor; antese'sor/ **(-ra)** a previous —n predecessor. m, forebear, ancestor

antecoger /anteko'her/ vt to carry in front, lead before; pick too soon

antecomedor /antekome'ðor/ m, breakfast nook, breakfast room

antedatar /anteða'tar/ vt to antedate

antedicho /ante'ðitʃo/ a aforementioned, aforesaid

antelación /antela'θion; antela'sion/ f, advance, anticipation

antemano, de /ante'mano, de/ adv in advance, beforehand

antemeridiano /antemeri'ðiano/ a antemeridian, forenoon

antena /an'tena/ f, antenna; Radio. aerial

antenacido /antena'θiðo; antena'siðo/ a born prematurely

antenombre /ante'nombre/ m, title (placed before name)

anteojo /ante'oho/ m, spy-glass, small telescope; pl horse's blinkers; eyeglasses, glasses; spectacles; goggles

antepagar /antepa'gar/ vt to pay in advance

antepasado /antepa'saðo/ a previous, past. m, ancestor (gen. pl)

antepecho /ante'petʃo/ m, parapet; windowsill; railing, balustrade; front (of a theater box, etc.); Naut. bulwark

antepenúltimo /antepe'nultimo/ a antepenultimate, second from the last

anteponer /antepo'ner/ vt irr to place before; prefer, favor. See **poner**

anteproyecto /antepro'yekto/ m, first sketch, preliminary work or plan

anterior /ante'rior/ a previous, former; anterior; aforementioned, preceding

anteriormente /anterior'mente/ adv beforehand, previously

antes /'antes/ adv before; rather, on the contrary; previously. **a. bien**, rather, sooner. **a. con a.** or **cuanto a.**, as soon as possible

antesala /ante'sala/ f, antechamber

antevíspera /ante'βispera/ f, two days previously

antiaéreo /anti'aereo/ a antiaircraft. m pl **(cañones) antiaéreos**, A.A. guns

anticipación /antiθipa'θion; antisipa'sion/ f, anticipation; advance

anticipada /antiθi'paða; antisi'paða/ f, foul thrust (in fencing, etc.)

anticipadamente /antiθi,paða'mente; antisi,paða'mente/ adv in advance; prematurely

anticipado /antiθi'paðo; antisi'paðo/ a in advance; premature

anticipador /antiθipa'ðor; antisipa'ðor/ a anticipatory

anticipar /antiθi'par; antisi'par/ vt to anticipate; foresee; forestall; advance (money); lend; —vr happen before time; (with prep a) act in advance of, anticipate; get ahead of oneself

anticipo /anti'θipo; anti'sipo/ m, anticipation, advance; advance payment; sum of money lent

anticlímax /anti'klimaks/ m, anticlimax

anticonstitucional /antikonstituθio'nal; antikonstitusio'nal/ a unconstitutional

anticuado /anti'kuaðo/ a antiquated, ancient

anticuario /anti'kuario/ m, antiquarian, antique dealer

antídoto /an'tiðoto/ m, antidote

antiespasmódico /antiespas'moðiko/ a and m, Med. antispasmodic

antiestético /anties'tetiko/ a unesthetic

antietimológico /antietimo'lohiko/ a non-etymological, unetymological

antifaz /anti'faθ; anti'fas/ m, mask; face-covering

antiflogístico /antiflo'histiko/ a and m, Med. antiphlogistic

antigramatical /antigramati'kal/ a ungrammatical

antigualla /anti'guaʎa; anti'guaya/ f, antique; ancient custom; anything out-of-date

antiguamente /antigua'mente/ adv in time past, formerly

antiguamiento /antigua'miento/ *m*, seniority

antigüedad /antigue'ðað/ *f*, antiquity; ancients; length of service (in an employment); *pl* antiquities

antiguo /an'tiguo/ *a* ancient, very old; antique; senior (in an employment); former. *m*, senior member (of a community, etc.). *m pl*, ancients. **A. Testamento**, Old Testament. **de a.**, from ancient times. **en lo antiguo**, in ancient times; in former times, in days of yore

antillano /anti'ʎano; anti'yano/ **(-na)** *a* and *n* of or from the Antilles

Antillas, las /an'tiʎas, las; an'tiyas, las/ the Antilles

antílope /an'tilope/ *m*, antelope

antipalúdico /antipa'luðiko/ *a* antimalarial

antipara /anti'para/ *f*, screen, shield

antiparras /anti'parras/ *f pl*, *Inf.* spectacles, eyeglasses, glasses

antipatía /antipa'tia/ *f*, antipathy

antipático /anti'patiko/ *a* disagreeable; unattractive

antipatriótico /antipa'triotiko/ *a* unpatriotic

antípoda /an'tipoða/ *a* and *m*, or *f*, antipode

antiquísimo /anti'kisimo/ *a superl*, **antiguo,** most ancient

antisemita /antise'mita/ *a* anti-Semitic. *mf* anti-Semite

antisemitismo /antisemi'tismo/ *m*, anti-Semitism

antiséptico /anti'septiko/ *a* and *m*, antiseptic

antisifilítico /antisifi'litiko/ *a* *Med.* antisyphilitic

antisocial /antiso'ðial; antiso'sial/ *a* antisocial

antítesis /an'titesis/ *f*, antithesis

antitético /anti'tetiko/ *a* antithetic, contrasted

antojadizo /antoha'ðiθo; antoha'ðiso/ *a* capricious, fanciful, whimsical

antojarse /anto'harse/ *vr* to have a fancy for, want (e.g. *Se me antoja marcharme al campo*, I have a yen to go to the country); suspect, imagine

antojo /an'toho/ *m*, caprice, fancy, whim; desire, will; *pl* birthmark

antología /antolo'hia/ *f*, anthology

antólogo /an'tologo/ *m*, anthologist

antonomasia /antono'masia/ *f*, antonomasia. **por a.**, by analogy, by transference

antorcha /an'tortʃa/ *f*, torch, flambeau

antracita /antra'θita; antra'sita/ *f*, anthracite

ántrax /'antraks/ *m*, *Med.* anthrax

antro /'antro/ *m*, cave, cavern; *Anat.* antrum

antropología /antropolo'hia/ *f*, anthropology

antropológico /antropo'lohiko/ *a* anthropological

antropólogo /antro'pologo/ *m*, anthropologist

antruejo /antru'eho/ *m*, three days of carnival before Lent

anual /a'nual/ *a* yearly, annual

anualidad /anuali'ðað/ *f*, annuity

anuario /a'nuario/ *m*, directory, yearbook, handbook

anubarrado /anuβa'rraðo/ *a* covered with clouds, cloudy

anublado /anu'βlaðo/ *a* lowering, overcast; clouded

anublar /anu'βlar/ *vt* to cloud; darken, obscure; blight (plants); —*vr* cloud over; become blighted or mildewed

anudar /anu'ðar/ *vt* to knot; tie, fasten; join; continue; **a. amistad de,** to strike up a friendship with. **a. la corbata,** to put on one's tie, tie one's tie; —*vr* grow stunted

anulable /anu'laβle/ *a* annulable, voidable

anulación /anula'θion; anula'sion/ *f*, annulment, abrogation

anular /anu'lar/ *a* annular, ring-shaped —*vt* to annul; *Math.* cancel out

anuloso /anu'loso/ *a* annulate, formed of rings

anunciación /anunθia'θion; anunsia'sion/ *f*, *Eccl.* Annunciation; announcement

anunciador /anunθia'ðor; anunsia'ðor/ **(-ra)** *n* **anunciante** /anun'θiante; anun'siante/ *mf* announcer; advertiser

anunciar /anun'θiar; anun'siar/ *vt* to announce; publish, proclaim; advertise; foretell, presage. **Anuncian lluvia,** The forecast calls for rain

anuncio /a'nunθio; a'nunsio/ *m*, announcement; publication, proclamation; advertisement; presage, omen. **a. luminoso,** sky-sign

anzuelo /an'θuelo; an'suelo/ *m*, fishhook; *Cul.* fritter; *Inf.* attraction, inducement

añadido /aɲa'ðiðo/ *m*, hair-switch; make-weight

añadidura /aɲaði'ðura/ *f*, addition; make-weight, extra

añadir /aɲa'ðir/ *vt* to add; increase

añejo /a'ɲeho/ *a* very old

añicos /a'ɲikos/ *m pl*, fragments, small pieces. **hacer a.,** to break into fragments

añil /a'ɲil/ *m*, indigo; indigo blue

año /'aɲo/ *m*, year; *pl* birthday. **a. bisiesto,** leap-year. **a. económico,** fiscal year. **A. Nuevo,** New Year. **tener (siete) años,** to be (seven) years old. **los Años Bobos,** the period from 1874 to 1898 in Spain

añoranza /aɲo'ranθa; aɲo'ransa/ *f*, homesickness, loneliness; nostalgia

añorar /aɲo'rar/ *vi* to be homesick or lonely

añoso /a'ɲoso/ *a* very old, full of years

añublo /a'ɲuβlo/ *m*, mildew

aojar /ao'har/ *vt* to bewitch, place under a spell; spoil, frustrate

aojo /a'oho/ *m*, evil eye; magic spell

aorta /a'orta/ *f*, *Anat.* aorta

apabullante /apaβu'ʎante; apaβu'yante/ *a* crushing, flattening

apacentadero /apaθenta'ðero; apasenta'ðero/ *m*, grazing land, pasture

apacentamiento /apaθenta'miento; apasenta'miento/ *m*, pasturage; grazing

apacentar /apaθen'tar; apasen'tar/ *vt irr* to put out to grass; teach, instruct; satisfy (one's desires); —*vr* graze (cattle). See **acertar**

apacibilidad /apaθiβili'ðað; apasiβili'ðað/ *f*, agreeableness; mildness; peaceableness

apacible /apa'θiβle; apa'siβle/ *a* agreeable; mild; peaceable, calm, peaceful

apaciguamiento /a,paθigua'miento; a,pasigua'miento/ *m*, appeasement, soothing, pacification

apaciguar /apaθi'guar; apasi'guar/ *vt* to appease, pacify; calm

apadrinar /apaðri'nar/ *vt* to act as godfather to; be best man to (at a wedding); act as a second for (in a duel); sponsor; favor

apagable /apa'gaβle/ *a* extinguishable

apagado /apa'gaðo/ *a* timid, nervous; pale (of colors); dull, lusterless

apagador /apaga'ðor/ **(-ra)** *a* quenching —*n* extinguisher. *m*, candle snuffer; damper (of a piano)

apagaincendios /a,pagain'θendios; a,pagain'sendios/ *m*, ship's fire-extinguisher

apagamiento /apaga'miento/ *m*, quenching, extinguishment

apagar /apa'gar/ *vt* to extinguish, put out; *Fig.* quench, moderate; slake (lime); *Art.* tone down (colors); shut off (engines)

apagarrisas /apaga'rrisas/ *mf* crapehanger, killjoy, wet blanket

apalabrar /apala'βrar/ *vt* to make an appointment with; discuss, consider

apaleamiento /apalea'miento/ *m*, beating, thrashing

apalear /apale'ar/ *vt* to beat, thrash; knock down with a stick

apañar /apa'ɲar/ *vt* to take away, remove; seize; steal; dress, get ready; *Inf.* wrap up; patch, repair; —*vr Inf.* grow skillful

apaño /a'paɲo/ *m*, dexterity, skill; craft, guile

aparador /apara'ðor/ *m*, shop window; sideboard; workshop; *Eccl.* credence (table)

aparato /apa'rato/ *m*, apparatus; equipment, utensils; pomp, ostentation; symptoms; sign, circumstance, token. **a. digestivo**, digestive system; digestive tract. **a. fonador**, speech apparatus

aparatoso /apara'toso/ *a* showy, ostentatious. **incendio. a.**, conflagration, large

aparcería /aparθe'ria; aparse'ria/ *f*, partnership (in a farm)

aparear /apare'ar/ *vt* to match, make equal; pair; mate (animals); —*vr* form up in pairs

aparecer /apare'θer; apare'ser/ **(se)** *vi* and *vr irr* to appear; seem; be. See **conocer**

aparecido /apare'θiðo; apare'siðo/ *m*, apparition, specter

aparejador /apareha'ðor/ *m*, overseer, foreman; *Naut.* rigger

aparejar /apare'har/ *vt* to prepare, make ready; saddle (horses); prime, size; rig (a ship)

aparejo /apa'reho/ *m*, preparation, arrangement; harness, trappings; *Naut.* rigging; *Naut.* gear; priming, sizing; *Mech.* tackle; *pl* equipment

aparentar /aparen'tar/ *vt* to pretend, simulate

aparente /apa'rente/ *a* seeming, apparent; obvious, visible; suitable, proper

aparición /apari'θion; apari'sion/ *f*, appearance, arrival; apparition, phantom

apariencia /apa'ricnθia; apa'riensia/ *f*, appearance, looks, probability, likelihood; outward semblance; *pl Theat.* scenery

apartadero /aparta'ðero/ *m*, passing place for cars; railway siding; grass verge. **a. ferroviario**, railway marshaling yard

apartado /apar'taðo/ *a* distant, far off; secluded; different. *m*, post-office box; secluded room; smelting house; sorting of cattle; selection of bulls for a bullfight

apartamiento /aparta'miento/ *m*, separation; withdrawal, retiral; seclusion; apartment, flat; *Law.* withdrawal of an action

apartar /apar'tar/ *vt* to separate; remove (e.g. an obstacle), take away; *Rail.* shunt; dissuade; sort; —*vr* obtain a divorce; *Law.* withdraw an action. **apartarse de la tradición**, to depart from tradition

aparte /a'parte/ *adv* aside, on one side; separately; *Theat.* aside; besides; beyond. *m*, *Theat.* aside; paragraph; space between words. **¡Aparte!** Move to one side!

apartidario /aparti'ðario/ *a* non-partisan

apasionado /apasio'naðo/ **(-da)** *a* impassioned; fervent, devoted; passionate; enthusiastic —*n* admirer, lover; enthusiast

apasionamiento /apasiona'miento/ *m*, passion

apasionar /apasio'nar/ *vt* to arouse to passion; pain; —*vr (with por)* grow passionately fond of; become enthusiastic for

apatía /apa'tia/ *f*, apathy

apático /a'patiko/ *a* apathetic

apear /ape'ar/ *vt* to dismount; hobble (horse); survey, map out; fell a tree; *Fig.* overcome (difficulties); *Inf.* dissuade; prop; remove, bring down; scotch (a wheel); —*vr* dismount; alight, step off

apechugar /apetʃu'gar/ *vi* to push with the breast; *Inf.* put up with reluctantly

apedazar /apeða'θar; apeða'sar/ *vt* to tear; break; mend, repair

apedrear /apeðre'ar/ *vt* to stone; stone to

death; —*vi impers* hail; —*vr* be damaged by hail (crops)

apegarse /ape'garse/ *vr* to grow fond (of), become attached (to)

apego /a'pego/ *m*, fondness, inclination; affection, attachment

apelación /apela'θion; apela'sion/ *f, Law.* appeal; *Inf.* doctor's consultation

apelante /ape'lante/ *a* and *mf Law.* appellant

apelar /ape'lar/ *vi Law.* to appeal; (*with prep a*) have recourse to; —*vi* be of the same color (horses)

apellidar /apeʎi'ðar; apeyi'ðar/ *vt* to name, call; acclaim; call to arms; —*vr* be named

apellido /ape'ʎiðo; ape'yiðo/ *m*, surname; nickname; call to arms; clamor; name

apenar /ape'nar/ *vt* to grieve, afflict; cause sorrow

apenas /a'penas/ *adv* scarcely; immediately, as soon as; with trouble or difficulty

apéndice /a'pendiθe; a'pendise/ *m*, appendix, supplement; *Anat.* appendix

apendicitis /apendi'θitis; apendi'sitis/ *f*, appendicitis

apeo /a'peo/ *m*, survey; scaffolding; prop, support

apercibimiento /aperθiβi'miento; apersiβi'miento/ *m*, preparation; provision; warning; *Law.* summons

apercibir /aperθi'βir; apersi'βir/ *vt* to prepare, furnish; warn; *Law.* summon

apergaminado /apergami'naðo/ *a* parchment; parchment-like

apergaminarse /apergami'narse/ *vr Inf.* to shrivel, dry up (with old age, etc.)

aperitivo /aperi'tiβo/ *a* aperitive. *m*, aperient; aperitive, appetizer

apertura /aper'tura/ *f*, opening; inauguration; reading (of a will)

apesadumbrar /apesaðum'brar/ *vt* to sadden, afflict, grieve

apestar /apes'tar/ *vt* to infect with the plague; catch the plague; *Fig.* corrupt; *Inf.* pester, annoy; —*vi* stink

apestoso /apes'toso/ *a* stinking, putrid

apetecer /apete'θer; apete'ser/ *vt irr* to want, desire; attract. See **conocer**

apetecible /apete'θiβle; apete'siβle/ *a* attractive, desirable

apetencia /ape'tenθia; ape'tensia/ *f*, appetite; desire

apetito /ape'tito/ *m*, appetite

apetitoso /apeti'toso/ *a* appetising; tasty, savory; attractive

apiadarse /apia'ðarse/ *vr* (*with de*) to have compassion on, be sorry for

ápice /'apiθe; 'apise/ *m*, apex; peak, summit, top; orthographic accent; iota, tittle; crux (of a problem)

apicultor /apikul'tor/ **(-ra)** *n* apiarist, beekeeper

apicultura /apikul'tura/ *f*, apiculture, beekeeping

apilar /api'lar/ *vt* to pile, heap

apiñado /api'naðo/ *a* crowded, serried

apiñar /api'nar/ *vt* to group together, crowd; —*vr* crowd

apio /'apio/ *m*, celery

apisonar /apiso'nar/ *vt* to roll, stamp, flatten, ram down; tamp, pack down (e.g. tobacco in a pipe)

aplacable /apla'kaβle/ *a* appeasable, placable

aplacamiento /aplaka'miento/ *m*, appeasement

aplacar /apla'kar/ *vt* to appease, calm; moderate, mitigate

aplacible /apla'θiβle; apla'siβle/ *a* agreeable, pleasant

aplanar /apla'nar/ *vt* to flatten, level; roll (pastry); *Inf.* dumbfound, overwhelm; —*vr* collapse (buildings); lose heart

aplastar /aplas'tar/ *vt* to flatten, squash, crush; *Inf.* squash flat, floor

aplaudir /aplau'ðir/ *vt* to applaud, clap; praise, commend, approve

aplauso /a'plauso/ *m*, applause; clapping, plaudit; approbation, commendation

aplazamiento /aplaθa'miento; aplasa'miento/ *m*, postponement; appointment, summons

aplazar /apla'θar; apla'sar/ *vt* to summon, arrange a meeting; postpone; adjourn

aplicación /aplika'θion; aplika'sion/ *f*, application; diligence, assiduity; appliqué, ornamentation

aplicado /apli'kaðo/ *a* diligent, hardworking; appliqué

aplicar /apli'kar/ *vt* to apply; impute; intend, destine (for processions); *Law.* adjudge; —*vr* engage in; apply oneself. **a. el oído,** to listen intently. **a. sanciones,** *Polit.* to impose sanctions

aplomado /aplo'maðo/ *a* self-possessed, dignified; leaden, lead-colored

aplomo /a'plomo/ *m*, self-possession, dignity; sang-froid

apocado /apo'kaðo/ *a* spiritless, timid; base, mean

apocamiento /apoka'miento/ *m*, timidity, pusillanimity; depression, discouragement; shyness; baseness, meanness

apocar /apo'kar/ *vt* to diminish, reduce; humiliate, scorn

apoderado /apoðe'raðo/ *a* authorized. *m*, attorney; deputy; proxy

apoderar /apoðe'rar/ *vt* to authorize; grant powers of attorney to; —*vr* (*with de*) seize, take possession of

apodo /a'poðo/ *m*, nickname

apogeo /apo'heo/ *m*, *Astron.* apogee; *Fig.* zenith, peak (of fame, etc.)

apolillar /apoli'ʎar; apoli'yar/ *vt* to eat clothes (moths); —*vr* be moth-eaten

apologético /apolo'hetiko/ *a* apologetic

apologista /apolo'hista/ *mf* apologist

apólogo /a'pologo/ *m*, apologue, moral fable

apoplejía /apople'hia/ *f*, apoplexy

apoplético /apo'pletiko/ **(-ca)** *a* and *n* apoplectic

aporrear /aporre'ar/ *vt* to beat, cudgel; —*vr* work hard, slog away

aportación /aporta'θion; aporta'sion/ *f*, contribution; occasionalism

aportar /apor'tar/ *vt* to cause, occasion; contribute; —*vi Naut.* reach port; **El buque aportó a Nueva York,** The ship reached New York, The ship sailed into New York harbor; arrive at an unexpected place

aposentar /aposen'tar/ *vt* to lodge, give hospitality to; —*vr* lodge, settle down

aposento /apo'sento/ *m,* room; suite, apartments; lodging, accommodation; *Theat.* box

apósito /a'posito/ *m,* poultice, external application; (medical) dressing

apostar /apos'tar/ *vt irr* to bet; station (soldiers); —*vi* compete, rival. See **contar**

apostilla /apos'tiʎa; apos'tiya/ *f*, marginal note, gloss

apóstol /a'postol/ *m,* apostle

apóstrofe /a'postrofe/ *m,* or *f,* apostrophe, hortatory exclamation

apóstrofo /a'postrofo/ *m, Gram.* apostrophe

apostura /apos'tura/ *f*, neatness, spruceness

apoteosis /apote'osis/ *f*, apotheosis

apoyar /apo'yar/ *vt* (*with en*) to lean against; rest upon; —*vt* uphold, favor; confirm, bear out; droop the head (horses); second (a motion); —*vi* (*with en*) rest on; lean against; —*vr* (*with en*) rest on; lean against; **apoyarse de codos,** to lean on one's elbows; be upheld by; *Fig.* be founded on; *Fig.* depend on, lean on

apoyo /a'poyo/ *m,* support, prop; windowsill, sill; assistance; backing, support

apreciable /apre'θiaβle; apresia'βle/ *a* appreciable; estimable; important

apreciación /apreθia'θion; apresia'sion/ *f*, appreciation; valuation, estimate

apreciador /apreθia'ðor; apresia'ðor/ **(-ra)** *a* appreciatory —*n* appreciator

apreciar /apre'θiar; apre'siar/ *vt* to estimate (values); appreciate; like, esteem, have a regard for

apreciativo /apreθia'tiβo; apresia'tiβo/ *a* appreciative

aprecio /a'preθio; a'presio/ *m,* valuation, appreciation; regard

aprehender /apreen'der/ *vt* to apprehend, catch; seize (contraband); understand, grasp

aprehensión /apreen'sion/ *f*, seizure, apprehension

apremiador, apremiante /apremia'ðor, apre'miante/ *a* urgent, pressing

apremiar /apre'miar/ *vt* to hurry; urge, press; force, oblige; burden, oppress (with taxes)

apremio /a'premio/ *m,* insistence, pressure; compulsion; demand note

aprender /apren'der/ *vt* to learn. **a. de memoria,** to learn by heart

aprendiz /apren'diθ; apren'dis/ **(-za)** *n* apprentice

aprendizaje /aprendi'θahe; aprendi'sahe/ *m,* apprenticeship. **hacer el a.,** to serve an apprenticeship

aprensión /apren'sion/ *f*, capture; fear, apprehension; suspicion; fancy; prejudice, scruple

aprensivo /apren'siβo/ *a* apprehensive, nervous, fearful

apresar /apre'sar/ *vt* to nab, catch; capture (a ship); imprison; fetter

apresurar /apresu'rar/ *vt* to quicken; —*vr* hasten, be quick

apretado /apre'taðo/ *a* difficult, dangerous; tight; crabbed (of handwriting); clustered (e.g. *casas apretadas alrededor de la sinagoga,* houses clustered around the synagogue). *Inf.* mean, close-fisted. *m,* small close handwriting

apretar /apre'tar/ *vt irr* to tighten; compress; urge on, press; harass, vex, trouble; worry; speed up; squeeze; press (bells, gun triggers, etc.); —*vi* increase, grow worse (storms, heat, etc.); pinch, hurt (shoes). **a. los pasos,** to quicken one's pace. *Inf.* **a. a correr,** to take to one's heels. **¡Aprieta!** *Inf.* Nonsense! It can't be! See **acertar**

apretón /apre'ton/ *m,* squeeze, grip, pressure; *Inf.* sprint, spurt; *Inf.* fix, pickle. **a. de manos,** handshake

apretujar /apretu'har/ *vt Inf.* to squeeze, hug

aprieto /a'prieto/ *m,* crowd, crush; urgency; *Inf.* jam, trouble, fix

aprisa /a'prisa/ *adv* quickly, in a hurry

aprisionar /aprisio'nar/ *vt* to imprison; bind, fetter; tie

aprobación /aproβa'θion; aproβa'sion/ *f*, approbation, approval, commendation; ratification (of a bill); pass (in an examination)

aprobado /apro'βaðo/ *m,* pass certificate (in examinations)

aprobar /apro'βar/ *vt irr* to approve; pass (in an examination). See **contar**

apropiación /apropia'θion; apropia'sion/ *f*, appropriation; application; adaptation

apropiado /apro'piaðo/ *a* appropriate, suitable, proper

apropiar /apro'piar/ *vt* to appropriate; adapt, fit; —*vr* appropriate, take possession

aprovechable /aproβe'tʃaβle/ *a* usable, available

aprovechado /aproβe'tʃaðo/ *a* advantageous; assiduous, conscientious; capable; thrifty

aprovechador /aproβetʃa'ðor/ *a* self-seeking

aprovechamiento /aproβetʃa'miento/ *m,* utilization, employment; exploitation; profitable use

aprovechar /aproβe'tʃar/ *vi* to be advantageous or useful; be beneficial; make

progress (in studies, etc.); —*vt* use; profit
by; —*vr* take advantage of, make use of.
¡Que aproveche! May it do you good!
(said to anyone eating)

aprovisionar /aproβi'sionar/ *vt* to provision, supply

aproximación /aproksima'θion; aproksi-
ma'sion/ *f*, approximation; consolation
prize (in a lottery)

aproximar /aproksi'mar/ *vt* to bring or
draw nearer; —*vr* approach; be almost,
be approximately; draw closer

aptitud /apti'tuð/ *f*, aptitude, ability; fitness; propensity

apto /'apto/ *a* suitable, fitting; competent.
no apta para menores, not suitable for
children (of films, etc.)

apuesta /a'puesta/ *f*, bet, wager; competition

apuestas benéficas de fútbol
/a'puestas be'nefikas de 'futβol/ football
pools

apuesto /a'puesto/ *a* elegant; handsome,
well set-up

apuntador /apunta'ðor/ **(-ra)** *n* note-
taker; observer. *m, Theat.* prompter;
Theat. stage-manager

apuntalar /apunta'lar/ *vt* to prop, prop
up, underpin, bolster

apuntar /apun'tar/ *vt* to aim (a gun,
etc.); point to, indicate; note down;
mark; sketch; sharpen; bet (at cards);
fasten temporarily; *Inf.* mend; *Theat.*
prompt; suggest, hint (e.g. *La fecha está
apuntada en vanos manuscritos,* The date
is hinted at in various manuscripts); —*vi*
begin to appear. *Inf.* **a. y no dar,** to
promise and do nothing

apunte /a'punte/ *m,* abstract; note; annotation; sketch; *Theat.* prompt *or*
prompter *or* prompt book *or* cue; stake in
a card game

apuñalar /apuɲa'lar/ *vt* to stab, attack
with a dagger

apurado /apu'raðo/ *a* poor, needy; dangerous; difficult; accurate, exact; hurried

apurar /apu'rar/ *vt* to purify; drain; exhaust; finish, conclude; examine closely,
scrutinize (e.g. *apurar una materia,* to exhaust a subject, examine a subject thoroughly); irritate, make impatient; urge
on, hasten; —*vr* be anxious, fret

apuro /a'puro/ *m,* difficulty, fix; poverty,
want; anxiety, worry. **pasar apuros,** to
have a hard time

aquejar /ake'har/ *vt* to afflict; weary, beset, harass; —*vr* complain; hurry

aquel, aquella,/ *a m* **aquella,** *a f* **aquellos,** *a m pl* **aquellas** *a f pl,* that, those;
that or those over there (farther off than
ese)

aquel /a'kel/ *m,* charm, attraction, it

aquél, aquélla, aquéllos, aquéllas
/a'kel, a'keʎa, a'keʎos, a'keʎas/ *dem pron m, f,*
sing. and pl., that, the one, those, those
ones; the former. e.g. *La casa que ve
usted a lo lejos aquélla es la vivienda de*

mi tío, The house that you see in the distance, that is my uncle's dwelling. *Éste no
me gusta pero aquél sí,* I do not like the
latter, but I like the former

aquello /a'keʎo/ *dem pron neut*
that; the fact; the matter, the affair, the
former (remark, idea, etc.). e.g. *Todo a.
por fin acabó,* All that came to an end at
last. *a. de,* the fact that

aquí /a'ki/ *adv* here. **de a.,** hence the fact
that. **¡He a.!** Behold!

aquiescencia /akies'θenθia; akies'sensia/
f, consent, acquiescence

aquietar /akie'tar/ *vt* to calm, soothe

aquilatar /akila'tar/ *vt* to assay; scrutinize; examine, weigh up (persons)

aquistar /akis'tar/ *vt* to attain, acquire

ara /'ara/ *f,* altar; **en aras de,** in honor
of; for the sake of

árabe /'araβe/ *a* Arab, Arabic. *mf* Arab.
m, Arabic (language)

arabesco /ara'βesko/ *a* Arabic. *m, Art.*
arabesque

Arabia Saudita /a'raβia sau'ðita/ Saudi
Arabia

arado /a'raðo/ *m,* plow

arador /ara'ðor/ *a* plowing. *m,* plowman.
a. de la sarna, *Ent.* scabies mite

aragonés /arago'nes/ **(-esa)** *a* and *n* Ar-
agonese

arahuaco /ara'uako/ *a* and *n* Arawak, Ar-
awakian

arancel /aran'θel; aran'sel/ *m,* tariff, duty,
tax

arancelar /aranθe'lar; aranse'lar/ *vt* to
charge tuition for (e.g. *a. la universidad,*
charge tuition for college studies)

arancelario /aranθe'lario; aranse'lario/ *a*
tariff, tax; customs

arándano /a'randano/ *m, Bot.* bilberry

arandela /aran'dela/ *f,* candle-dripper;
Mech. washer; wall candelabrum

araña /a'raɲa/ *f,* spider; chandelier

arañacielos /a,raɲa'θielos; a,raɲa'sielos/
m, skyscraper

arañar /ara'ɲar/ *vt* to scratch; *Inf.* scrape
together, hoard

arañazo /ara'ɲaθo; ara'ɲaso/ *m,* scratch

arar /a'rar/ *vt* to plough. **a. en el mar,** to
labor in vain

arbitrador /arβitra'ðor/ **(-ra)** *n* arbitrator

arbitraje /arβi'trahe/ *m,* arbitration; ar-
bitrament, decision

arbitrar /arβi'trar/ *vt* to judge freely;
Law. arbitrate, mediate; devise; invent;
marshal (money, resources, etc.); draft (a
law) *vr* make shift, contrive

arbitrariedad /arβitrarie'ðað/ *f,* arbitrariness

arbitrario /arβi'trario/ *a* arbitral, mediatory; arbitrary, capricious

arbitrio /ar'βitrio/ *m,* free will; arbitration; means, way; discretion; arbitra-
ment, judgment; *pl* rates, municipal taxes

árbitro /'arβitro/ **(-ra)** *a* arbitrary —*n*
arbiter. *m, Sports.* umpire; referee

árbol /'arβol/ *m,* tree; *Mech.* shaft; *Naut.*

mast; axis of a winding stair. **a. de amor** or **a. de Judas**, Judas tree. **a. de la ciencia** (**del bien y del mal**), Tree of Knowledge (of good and evil). **a. de levas**, Mech. camshaft. **a. del pan**, breadfruit tree. Naut. **a. mayor**, mainmast. **a. motor** Mech., drivingshaft

arbolado /arβo'laðo/ a tree-covered, wooded. m, copse, woodland

arboladura /arβola'ðura/ f, Naut. masts and spars

arbolar /arβo'lar/ vt to hoist (flags); Naut. fit with masts; place upright; —vr rear, prance (horses)

arboleda /arβo'leða/ f, copse, grove, spinney

arbusto /ar'βusto/ m, shrub, woody plant

arca /'arka/ f, chest; money-box, coffer; ark; pl (treasury) vaults. **a. caudal**, strong box. **a. de agua**, water-tower. **a. de la alianza** or **a. del testamento**, Ark of the Covenant (Bible). **a. de Noé**, Noah's Ark; lumber box

arcada /ar'kaða/ f, arcade; series of arches; pl sickness, nausea

arcaico /ar'kaiko/ a archaic

arcaísmo /arka'ismo/ m, archaism

arcano /ar'kano/ a secret. m, mystery, arcanum

arce /'arθe; 'arse/ m, Bot. maple tree

archifeliz /artʃife'liθ; artʃife'lis/ a extremely happy, in bliss

archimillonario /artʃimiʎo'nario; artʃimiyo'nario/ (**-ia**) a and n multimillionaire

archipiélago /artʃi'pielaɣo/ m, archipelago

Archipiélago de Colón /artʃi'pielaɣo de ko'lon/ m, Galapagos Islands

archivar /artʃi'βar/ vt to place in an archive; file (papers)

archivero /artʃi'βero/ m, archivist, keeper of the archives; librarian; registrar; (Mexico) file cabinet, filing cabinet

archivista /artʃi'βista/ mf archivist; file clerk, filing clerk

archivo /ar'tʃiβo/ m, archives

arcilla /ar'θiʎa; ar'siya/ f, clay

arcilloso /arθi'ʎoso; arsi'yoso/ a clayey, like or full of clay

arco /'arko/ m, Geom. arc; Mil. bow; bow (of a stringed instrument); hoop (of casks, etc.); Archit. arch. **a. del cielo** or **a. de San Martín** or **a. iris**, rainbow. **a. voltaico**, electric arc. Mus. **para a.**, for strings

arder /ar'ðer/ vi to burn; shine, gleam; Fig. burn (with passion, etc.); —vt to set alight, burn

ardid /ar'ðið/ a crafty. m, trick, stratagem

ardiente /ar'ðiente/ a burning; ardent, passionate; vehement; enthusiastic; flame-colored; fiery-red

ardilla /ar'ðiʎa; ar'ðiya/ f, squirrel

ardite /ar'ðite/ m, ancient Spanish coin of little value; Fig. farthing, fig, straw. **no valer un a.**, to be not worth a straw

ardor /ar'ðor/ m, great heat; zeal, earnestness; passion, ardor; courage

ardoroso /arðo'roso/ a ardorous

arduo /'arðuo/ a arduous

área /'area/ f, area; small plot of ground; common threshing floor; arc (surface measure)

arena /a'rena/ f, sand; arena; grit, gravel. **a. movediza**, quicksand

arenal /are'nal/ m, quicksand; sand pit; sandy place

arenga /a'reŋga/ f, harangue, discourse

arenisca /are'niska/ f, sandstone

arenisco /are'nisko/ a sandy

arenque /a'renke/ m, herring

arete /a'rete/ m, earring

argamasa /arga'masa/ f, mortar

argayo /ar'gayo/ m, landslide; (Asturias) **a. de nieve**, avalanche

Árgel /'arhel/ Algiers

Argelia /ar'helia/ Algeria

argelino /arhe'lino/ (**-na**) a and n Algerian

argentado /arhen'taðo/ a silvered; silvery

argentífero /arhen'tifero/ a silver-yielding

argentino /arhen'tino/ (**-na**) a silvery —a and n Argentinian. m, Argentinian gold coin

argento /ar'hento/ m, silver. **a. vivo**, mercury

argolla /ar'goʎa; ar'goya/ f, thick metal ring (for hitching, etc.); croquet (game); stocks, pillory; hoop, iron arch

argucia /ar'guθia; ar'gusia/ f, sophism, quibble; subtlety

argüir /ar'guir/ vt irr to deduce, imply; prove; reveal, manifest; accuse; —vi argue, debate; dispute, oppose. See **huir**

argumentador /argumenta'ðor/ (**-ra**) a argumentative —n arguer

argumentar /argumen'tar/ vi to argue; dispute; oppose

argumento /argu'mento/ m, contention, case; theme (of a book, etc.); argument, discussion

aridez /ari'ðeθ; ari'ðes/ f, aridity, dryness; drought; sterility, barrenness; dullness, lack of interest

árido /'ariðo/ a dry, arid; sterile, barren; uninteresting, dull

arisco /a'risko/ a unsociable, surly; wild, shy (animals)

aristocracia /aristo'kraθia; aristo'krasia/ f, aristocracy

aristócrata /aris'tokrata/ mf aristocrat

aristocrático /aristo'kratiko/ a aristocratic

aritmética /arit'metika/ f, arithmetic

aritmético /arit'metiko/ (**-ca**) a arithmetical —n arithmetician

arlequín /arle'kin/ m, harlequin; Inf. fool, buffoon; Neapolitan ice-cream

arlequinada /arleki'naða/ f, harlequinade; buffoonery

arma /'arma/ f, weapon; Mil. arm,

branch; bull's horn; *pl* troops, army; means, way; arms, coat of arms. **a. arrojadiza,** missile. **a. blanca,** steel weapon. **a. de fuego,** fire-arm. **¡Armas al hombro!** Shoulder Arms! **armas portátiles,** small arms. *Inf.* **de armas tomar,** belligerent; resolute. **pasar por las armas,** *Mil.* to shoot. **presentar las armas,** *Mil.* to present arms. **ser a. de dos filos,** *Fig.* to cut both ways

armada /ar'maða/ *f,* navy, armada; fleet, squadron

armadía /arma'ðia/ *f,* raft, pontoon

armador /arma'ðor/ **(-ra)** *n* supplier, outfitter. *m,* shipowner; pirate, privateer; jacket; assembler, fitter

armadura /arma'ðura/ *f,* armature, armor; frame, framework; skeleton (of a building); skeleton (of vertebrates); *Phys.* armature; plate armor (of persons)

armamento /arma'mento/ *m, Mil.* armament; arms, military equipment

armar /ar'mar/ *vt* to arm; *Mech.* mount; man (guns); put together, assemble; roll (a cigarette); reinforce (concrete); *Inf.* arrange, prepare; *Inf.* occasion (quarrels); *Inf.* outfit; *Naut.* equip; commission (a ship); —*vr* prepare oneself, arm oneself. **a. caballero,** to knight. **a. los remos,** to ship the oars. *Inf.* **armarla,** to cause a row or quarrel

armario /ar'mario/ *m,* cupboard; wardrobe. **a. de luna,** wardrobe with a mirror

armatoste /arma'toste/ *m,* unwieldy piece of furniture; *Fig. Inf.* dead weight, clumsy person; snare

armazón /arma'θon; arma'son/ *f,* frame, framework; ship's hulk. *m, Anat.* skeleton

armenio /ar'menio/ **(-ia)** *a* and *n* Armenian. *m,* Armenian language

armería /arme'ria/ *f,* armory; heraldry; gunsmith's craft or shop

armisticio /armis'tiθio; armis'tisio/ *m,* armistice

armonía /armo'nia/ *f,* harmony; friendship, concord; *Mus.* harmony

armónica /ar'monika/ **(de boca)** *f,* mouth-organ

armónico /ar'moniko/ *a* harmonious —*a* and *m, Mus.* harmonic

armonio /ar'monio/ *m,* harmonium

armonioso /armo'nioso/ *a* harmonious

armonización /armoniθa'θion; armonisa-'sion/ *f, Mus.* harmonization

armonizar /armoni'θar; armoni'sar/ *vt* to bring into harmony; *Mus.* harmonize

arnés /ar'nes/ *m,* armor; harness; *pl* horse trappings; *Inf.* equipment, tools

aro /'aro/ *m,* hoop, rim (of wheel, etc.); napkin-ring; croquet hoop; *Bot.* wild arum; child's hoop. **a. de empaquetadura,** *Mech.* gasket

aroma /a'roma/ *m,* aroma, fragrance; balsam; sweet-smelling herb

aromático /aro'matiko/ *a* aromatic

arpa /'arpa/ *f,* harp. **a. eolia,** Eolian harp

arpar /ar'par/ *vt* to scratch, claw; tear, rend

arpía /ar'pia/ *f,* harpy

arpicordio /arpi'korðio/ *m,* harpsichord

arpista /ar'pista/ *mf* harpist, harp player

arquear /arke'ar/ *vt* to arch; bend; beat (wool); gauge (ship's capacity); —*vi* retch

arqueo /ar'keo/ *m,* arching; bending, curving; *Naut.* tonnage; gauging (of ship's capacity); *Com.* examination of deposits and contents of safe

arqueología /arkeolo'hia/ *f,* archeology

arqueológico /arkeo'lohiko/ *a* archeological

arqueólogo /arke'ologo/ *m,* archeologist

arquero /ar'kero/ *m, Com.* cashier, treasurer; *Mil.* archer

arquitecto /arki'tekto/ *m,* architect. **a. de jardines,** landscape gardener

arquitectónico /arkitek'toniko/ *a* architectural

arquitectura /arkitek'tura/ *f,* architecture

arrabal /arra'βal/ *m,* suburb, district; *pl* outskirts

arracimarse /arraθi'marse; arrasi'marse/ *vr* to cluster; group

arraigadamente /arrai,gaða'mente/ *adv* deeply, firmly

arraigado /arrai'gaðo/ *a* deep-rooted; firm; convinced

arraigar /arrai'gar/ *vi* to take root; —*vi* and *vr Fig.* become established, take hold; —*vr* settle; take up residence

arraigo /a'rraigo/ *m,* rooting; settlement, establishment; landed property

arrancadero /a,rranka'ðero/ *m, Sports.* starting-point

arrancar /arran'kar/ *vt* to uproot; pull out; wrench; tear off; extirpate; obtain by threats; clear one's throat; —*vt* and *vi Naut.* put on speed; —*vi* start (a race); *Inf.* leave, quit; derive, originate **¡Arrancan!** And they're off! (races)

arranque /a'rranke/ *m,* uprooting; extirpation; wrenching, pulling, seizing; stimulus (of passion); sudden impulse; *Mech.* start; *Mech.* starter. **a. automático,** self-starter

arras /'arras/ *f pl,* dowry; coins given by bridegroom to his bride; earnest money, token

arrasamiento /arrasa'miento/ *m,* demolition, destruction; leveling

arrasar /arra'sar/ *vt* to demolish, destroy; level; fill to the brim; —*vi* and *vr* clear up (sky). **ojos arrasados de lágrimas,** eyes brimming with tears

arrastrado /arras'traðo/ *a Inf.* poverty-stricken, wretched; *Inf.* knavish; unhappy, unfortunate

arrastrar /arras'trar/ *vt* to drag; trail; convince; haul; —*vi* trail along or touch the ground; trump (at cards); —*vr* crawl, creep; shuffle along; humble oneself

¡arre! /'arre/ *interj* Gee up! Get along!

arrebañar /arreβa'ɲar/ vt to pick clean, clear; eat or drink up

arrebatado /arreβa'taðo/ a precipitate, headlong; rash; flushed, red

arrebatador /arreβata'ðor/ a overwhelming; violent; bewitching, captivating; delightful

arrebatamiento /arreβata'miento/ m, abduction; seizure; fury; ecstasy

arrebatar /arreβa'tar/ vt to abduct, carry off; seize, grab; attract, charm; grip (the attention); —vr be overcome with rage

arrebato /arre'βato/ m, fit (gen. of anger); ecstasy, rapture

arrebozar /arreβo'θar; arreβo'sar/ vt to muffle; envelop

arrebujarse /arreβu'harse/ vr to huddle; wrap oneself up

arreciar /arre'θiar; arre'siar/ vi to increase in intensity; —vr grow strong

arrecife /arre'θife; arre'sife/ m, reef (in the sea); stone-paved road

arregazar /arrega'θar; arrega'sar/ (se) vt and vr to tuck up one's skirts

arreglado /arre'glaðo/ a regular; regulated; ordered; methodical

arreglar /arre'glar/ vt to regulate; arrange; adjust, put right; tidy; make up (the face); —vr (with prep a) conform to; (with con) reach an agreement with. **Me voy a a.**, I am going to make myself presentable. Inf. **arreglárselas**, to shift for oneself

arreglo /a'rreglo/ m, arrangement; rule; regulation; method, order; agreement; adjustment; compromise

arrellanarse /arreʎa'narse; arreya'narse/ vr to settle comfortably in one's chair; be happy in one's work

arremangar /arreman'gar/ vt to roll up (sleeves, trousers, etc.); —vr Inf. make a decision

arremetedor /arreme'teðor/ (-ra) n attacker, assailant

arremeter /arreme'ter/ vt to attack, assail; —vi launch oneself (at); Fig. spoil the view, shock the eye

arremetida /arreme'tiða/ f, attack, assault

arremolinarse /arremoli'narse/ vr to crowd, cluster, group

arrendador /arrenda'ðor/ (-ra) n landlord; renter; hirer; tenant

arrendamiento /arrenda'miento/ m, letting, renting; hiring; rental; agreement, lease

arrendar /arren'dar/ vt irr to let, lease; hire; rent (as a tenant); train (horses); tie up (horses); restrain; mimic, imitate. See **recomendar**

arrendatario /arrenda'tario/ (-ia) a rent, lease —n tenant; lessee; hirer. **a. de contribuciones**, tax farmer

arreo /a'rreo/ m, ornament; apparel; pl horse trappings; appurtenances, equipment

¡Arrepa! /a'rrepa/ But look!, Hold on!, Hold your horses!, Not so fast!

arrepentimiento /arrepenti'miento/ m, repentance

arrepentirse /arrepen'tirse/ vr irr to repent. See **sentir**

arrestado /arres'taðo/ a courageous, audacious, bold

arrestar /arres'tar/ vt to arrest, detain; —vr be bold, dare

arresto /a'rresto/ m, arrest; detention; imprisonment; audacity, boldness

arriada /a'rriaða/ f, lowering (of a boat); taking in (of sail)

arriar /a'rriar/ vt Naut. to strike (colors); take in (sail); pay out (ropes, etc.); lower (boats); flood, inundate

arriate /a'rriate/ m, garden border; avenue, walk; trellis (for plants)

arriba /a'rriβa/ adv up, above; overhead; upstairs; earlier, before; upwards (with prices) —interj ¡A.! Up with!; Long live! **de a. abajo**, from head to foot, from one end to the other; completely, wholly

arribada /arri'βaða/ f, Naut. arrival. **de a.**, emergency (port)

arribar /arri'βar/ vi Naut. to arrive; put into an emergency port; reach, arrive at; Inf. convalesce; attain; Naut. drift

arribista /arri'βista/ mf social climber

arribo /a'rriβo/ m, arrival

arriesgado /arries'gaðo/ a dangerous, risky; rash, daring

arriesgar /arries'gar/ vt to risk; —vr run into danger; dare, risk

arrimar /arri'mar/ vt to bring or draw near; abandon (professions, etc.); lay aside, discard; Inf. administer (blows); Naut. stow (cargo); —vr (with prep n) lean against, rest on; join, go with; seek the protection of. **Cada cual se arrima a su cada cual**, Birds of a feather flock together

arrimo /a'rrimo/ m, bringing or placing near; leaning or resting against; abandonment, giving up; protection; staff, support

arrinconado /arrinko'naðo/ a remote, secluded; forgotten; neglected

arrinconar /arrinko'nar/ vt to discard, lay aside; corner, besiege; set aside, dismiss; forsake; —vr go into retirement, withdraw

arriscado /arris'kaðo/ a craggy, rugged; bold, resolute; sprightly, handsome

arrobamiento /arroβa'miento/ m, ecstasy, rapture; trance

arrobar /arro'βar/ vt to charm, entrance; —vr be enraptured; be in ecstasy

arrodillar /arroði'ʎar; arroði'yar/ vt to cause to kneel down; —vi and vr kneel down

arrogancia /arro'ganθia; arro'gansia/ f, arrogance; courage; majesty, pride

arrogante /arro'gante/ a arrogant, haughty; courageous; proud, majestic

arrogar /arro'gar/ vt to adopt (as a son); —vr usurp, appropriate

arrojadizo /arroha'ðiθo; arroha'ðiso/ *a* easily cast or hurled; projectile

arrojado /arro'haðo/ *a* bold, determined; rash

arrojar /arro'har/ *vt* to throw, hurl, cast; shed (light, etc.; e.g. *La cuenta arroja un total de cien dólares,* The bill shows a total of a hundred dollars); *Com.* show (a balance, etc.); put out (sprouts); dismiss, send away; —*vr* cast oneself; (*with prep a*) hurl oneself against or upon; undertake, venture upon. **a. de sí (a),** to get rid of, dismiss

arrojo /a'rroho/ *m,* daring, intrepidity; boldness

arrollar /arro'ʎar; arro'yar/ *vt* to roll; make into a roll, roll up; defeat (the enemy); silence, confound; rock to sleep; bear along, carry off

arrostrar /arros'trar/ *vt* to confront, defy, face up to; —*vr* fight hand to hand. **a. las consecuencias,** *Fig.* to face the music

arroyo /a'rroyo/ *m,* stream, brook; street gutter; road, street; *Fig.* flood, plenty

arroz /a'rroθ; a'rros/ *m,* rice

arruga /a'rruga/ *f,* wrinkle; fold, pleat; crease

arrugamiento /arruga'miento/ *m,* wrinkling; fold, pleating; crumpling, creasing; corrugation

arrugar /arru'gar/ *vt* to wrinkle; pleat; corrugate; crumple, crease. **a. el ceño,** to knit one's brow, scowl

arruinamiento /arruina'miento/ *m,* ruin, decay, decline

arruinar /arrui'nar/ *vt* to ruin; destroy, damage severely

arrullar /arru'ʎar; arru'yar/ *vt* to bill and coo (doves); lull to sleep; *Inf.* whisper sweet words to, make love to

arrumaco /arru'mako/ *m,* *Inf.* embrace, caress (gen. *pl*); ornament in bad taste

arrumaje /arru'mahe/ *m,* *Naut.* stowage; clouds on the horizon

arsenal /arse'nal/ *m,* dockyard; arsenal; *Fig.* store (of information, etc.)

arsénico /ar'seniko/ *m,* arsenic

arte /'arte/ *mf,* art; skill; ability, talent; guile, craftiness. **las bellas artes,** fine arts. *Inf.* **no tener a. ni parte en,** to have nothing to do with, have no part in

artefacto /arte'fakto/ *m,* machine, mechanism, apparatus; device, appliance. **a. atómico,** atomic bomb

arteria /ar'teria/ *f,* *Med.* artery; main line (of communication)

artería /arte'ria/ *f,* craftiness, guile

arterial /arte'rial/ *a* arterial

artesano /arte'sano/ **(-na)** *n* artisan; mechanic

ártico /'artiko/ *a* Arctic

articulación /artikula'θion; artikula'sion/ *f,* joint, articulation; jointing; enunciation, pronunciation

articular /artiku'lar/ *vt* to joint, articulate; enunciate, pronounce clearly

artículo /ar'tikulo/ *m,* finger knuckle; heading; article; *Anat.* joint; *Gram.* article; *pl* goods, things. **a. de fondo,** leading article (in a newspaper). **a. de primera necesidad,** prime necessity, essential

artífice /ar'tifiθe; ar'tifise/ *mf* craftsman, artificer; author, creator; forger

artificial /artifi'θial; artifi'sial/ *a* artificial

artificio /arti'fiθio; arti'fiçsio/ *m,* skill, art; appliance, contraption, mechanism; trick, cunning device; guile, craftiness

artificioso /artifi'θioso; artifi'sioso/ *a* skilful; artificial; crafty, cunning

artillería /artiʎe'ria; artiye'ria/ *f,* artillery. **a. de costa,** coastal guns. **a. ligera, a. montada, a. rodada** *or* **a. volante,** field artillery

artillero /arti'ʎero; arti'yero/ *m,* gunner

artimaña /arti'maɲa/ *f,* trick, ruse, stratagem

artista /ar'tista/ *mf* artist; performer

artístico /ar'tistiko/ *a* artistic

artrítico /ar'tritiko/ *a* *Med.* arthritic

artritis /ar'tritis/ *f,* *Med.* arthritis

arzobispo /arθo'βispo; arso'βispo/ *m,* archbishop

as /as/ *m,* Roman copper coin; ace (*Aer.* cards, etc.)

asa /'asa/ *f,* handle; pretext, excuse

asado /a'saðo/ *m,* *Cul.* roast

asador /asa'ðor/ *m,* *Cul.* roasting-spit; roaster

asadura /asa'ðura/ *f,* *Cul.* chitterlings; offal

asaltador /asalta'ðor/ **(-ra)** *a* attacking —*n* assailant, attacker

asaltar /asal'tar/ *vt* to storm, besiege; assault, attack; occur to (ideas); come on suddenly (illness)

asalto /a'salto/ *m,* storming, besieging; assault, attack; bout (in fencing, boxing, wrestling); round (in a fight)

asamblea /asam'βlea/ *f,* congregation, assembly; meeting; legislative assembly; *Mil.* assembly (bugle call)

asambleísta /asamble'ista/ *mf* member of an assembly

asar /a'sar/ *vt* *Cul.* to roast; grill; —*vr* burning-hot; *Fig.* burn (with enthusiasm)

asaz /a'saθ; a'sas/ *adv* sufficiently, enough; very; in abundance —*a* sufficient; many

asbesto /as'βesto/ *m,* asbestos

ascalonia /aska'lonia/ *f,* *Bot.* shallot

ascendencia /asθen'denθia; assen'densia/ *f,* lineage, ancestry, origin

ascender /asθen'der; assen'der/ *vi irr* to ascend, climb; be promoted; (*with prep a*) amount to (bills, etc.); —*vt* promote. See **entender**

ascendiente /asθen'diente; assen'diente/ *mf* ancestor, forbear. *m,* influence, ascendancy

ascensión /asθen'sion; assen'sion/ *f,* ascension; promotion; *Astron.* exaltation

ascenso /as'θenso; as'senso/ *m,* ascent; promotion, preferment

ascensor /asθen'sor; assen'sor/ *m*, lift, elevator

ascensorista /asθenso'rista; assenso'rista/ *mf* elevator operator

asceta /as'θeta; as'seta/ *mf* ascetic

ascético /as'θetiko; as'setiko/ *a* ascetic

asco /'asko/ *m*, nausea; repugnance, loathing; revolting thing. *Inf.* **Me da a.,** It sickens me

ascua /'askua/ *f*, live coal, ember. **estar como una a. de oro,** to be as bright as a new pin. **estar en ascuas,** *Fig.* to be on pins

aseado /ase'aðo/ *a* clean, tidy

asear /ase'ar/ *vt* to tidy, make neat; clean up; decorate, adorn

asechanza /ase'tʃanθa; ase'tʃansa/ *f*, ambush; trick, snare, stratagem

asechar /ase'tʃar/ *vt* to ambush, waylay; *Fig.* lay snares for

asediar /ase'ðiar/ *vt* to besiege; pester, importune

asedio /a'seðio/ *m*, siege; importunity

asegurado /asegu'raðo/ **(-da)** *a* insured —*n* insured person

asegurador /asegura'ðor/ **(-ra)** *a* insuring —*n* insurer

asegurar /asegu'rar/ *vt* to fasten, make secure; pinion, grip; reassure, soothe; assert, state; *Com.* insure; guarantee; ensure, secure; —*vr Com.* insure oneself; (*with de*) make sure of

asemejar /aseme'har/ *vt* to imitate, copy; make similar to; —*vr* (*with prep a*) be like, be similar to

asenso /a'senso/ *m*, assent. **dar a.,** to believe, give credence (to)

asentaderas /asenta'ðeras/ *f pl, Inf.* buttocks, seat

asentado /asen'taðo/ *a* prudent, circumspect; permanent, stable

asentamiento /asenta'miento/ *m*, seating; settlement, residence; prudence, judgment

asentar /asen'tar/ *vt irr* to seat; place; fasten, fix; found; plant (flags); pitch (a tent); establish, make firm; smooth; hone (razors); estimate, budget, arrange, set forth; note down; affirm, believe; *Com.* enter (in an account); —*vi* fit (clothes); —*vr* seat oneself; alight (birds); settle (liquids); *Archit.* settle, subside; to be located (e.g. *El edificio se asienta en una esquina,* The building is located on a corner). **a. la mano en,** to strike hard. See **acertar**

asentimiento /asenti'miento/ *m*, assent; consent, approval

asentir /asen'tir/ *vi irr* to assent, agree; (*with en*) consent to. See **sentir**

aseñorado /aseɲo'raðo/ *a* refined, gentlemanly; ladylike; presumptuous

aseo /a'seo/ *m*, cleanliness, neatness

asequible /ase'kiβle/ *a* attainable; obtainable

aserción /aser'θion; aser'sion/ *f*, assertion

aserrar /ase'rrar/ *vt irr* to saw. See **acertar**

aserrín /ase'rrin/ *m*, sawdust

aserto /a'serto/ *m*, assertion

asesinar /asesi'nar/ *vt* to assassinate, murder

asesinato /asesi'nato/ *m*, assassination, murder

asesino /ase'sino/ *mf* assassin, murderer; murderess

asesor /ase'sor/ **(-ra)** *n* assessor

asesorar /aseso'rar/ *vt* to give advice; —*vr* take legal advice; seek advice

asestar /ases'tar/ *vt* to aim (firearms); fire; deal (a blow)

aseveración /aseβera'θion; aseβera'sion/ *f*, assertion, statement

aseveradamente /aseβeraða'mente/ *adv* affirmatively

aseverar /aseβe'rar/ *vt* to affirm, assert

asfaltado /asfal'taðo/ *m*, asphalting; asphalt pavement

asfaltar /asfal'tar/ *vt* to asphalt

asfalto /as'falto/ *m*, asphalt

asfixia /as'fiksia/ *f, Med.* asphyxia

asfixiante /asfik'siante/ *a* asphyxiating

asfixiar /asfik'siar/ *vt* to asphyxiate

así /a'si/ *adv* thus, so, in this way; like this (e.g. *en días a.,* on days like this); even if; so that, therefore. **a. a.,** middling, so-so. **a. como a.,** as well as; as soon as. **a. las cosas,** that being the case, **a. que,** as soon as, immediately; consequently, thus

asiático /a'siatiko/ **(-ca)** *a* and *n* Asiatic

asidero /asi'ðero/ *m*, hold, grasp; handle, haft; pretext, excuse

asiduidad /asiðui'ðað/ *f*, assiduity

asiduo /a'siðuo/ *a* assiduous

asiento /a'siento/ *m*, seat; place, position; site; base (of a vase, etc.); lees, sediment; indigestion; *Archit.* subsidence; settling; treaty; pact; contract; note, reminder; *Com.* entry; permanence, stability; prudence; bit (of a bridle); *pl* buttocks, seat. **estar de a.,** to be established (in a place)

asignación /asigna'θion; asigna'sion/ *f*, assignation; appropriation (of money); salary; portion, share

asignar /asig'nar/ *vt* to assign; apportion; destine, intend; appoint

asignatura /asigna'tura/ *f*, subject (of study in schools, etc.)

asilar /asi'lar/ *vt* to give shelter to, receive; put into an institution

asilo /a'silo/ *m*, shelter, refuge; sanctuary, asylum; *Fig.* protection, defense; home, institution

asimetría /asime'tria/ *f*, asymmetry

asimétrico /asi'metriko/ *a* asymmetrical

asimiento /asi'miento/ *m*, hold, grasp; attachment, affection

asimilar /asimi'lar/ *vt* to compare, liken; (*Bot. Zool. Gram.*) assimilate; —*vi* resemble, be like; *Fig.* assimilate, digest (ideas)

asimismo /asi'mismo/ *adv* similarly, like-wise

asir /a'sir/ *vt irr* to grasp, take hold of; seize; —*vi* take root (plants); —*vr* (*with de*) lay hold of; take advantage of; make an excuse to —*Pres. Indic.* **asgo, ases,** etc —*Pres. Subjunc.* **asga,** etc.

asistencia /asis'tenθia; asistensia/ *f*, presence, attendance; minimal attendance required (e.g. *Los alumnos tienen que completar una a.*, Pupils must attend a certain number of classes) assistance, help; service, attendance; medical treatment; remuneration; *pl* allowance. **a. pública,** Public Assistance. **a. social,** social work

asistenta /asis'tenta/ *f*, daily maid; waiting-maid

asistente /asis'tente/ *m*, assistant; *Mil.* orderly

asistir /asis'tir/ *vt* to accompany; assist, help; attend, treat; (*with de*) act as; —*vi* (*with prep a*) be present at, attend; follow suit (in cards)

asma /'asma/ *f*, asthma

asmático /as'matiko/ **(-ca)** *a* asthmatic —*n* asthma sufferer

asno /'asno/ *m*, ass

asociación /asoθia'θion; asosia'sion/ *f*, association; company, partnership; society, fellowship

asociado /aso'θiaðo; aso'siaðo/ **(-da)** *n* associate; member; partner

asociar /aso'θiar; aso'siar/ *vt* to associate; —*vr* associate oneself; join together; form a partnership

asolar /aso'lar/ *vt irr* to destroy, devastate, lay flat; —*vr* wither; settle (liquids). See **contar**

asolear /asole'ar/ *vt* to expose to the sun; —*vr* sun oneself; become sunburnt

asomada /aso'maða/ *f*, brief appearance; vantage point

asomar /aso'mar/ *vt* to show, allow to appear, put forth; —*vi* begin to show; —*vr* show oneself, appear; *Inf.* be flushed (with wine); (*with prep a, por*) look out of. **asomarse a la ventana,** to show oneself at, or look out of, the window

asombrar /asom'ɓrar/ *vt* to shade, shadow; darken (a color); terrify; amaze

asombro /a'sombro/ *m*, fright, terror; amazement; wonder, marvel

asombroso /asom'ɓroso/ *a* amazing; marvelous, wonderful

aspa /'aspa/ *f*, cross; sail of a windmill

aspaviento /aspa'ɓiento/ *m*, exaggerated display of emotion; gesture (of horror, etc.); **hacer aspavientos,** to make a fuss

aspecto /as'pekto/ *m*, look, appearance; aspect, outlook

aspereza /aspe'reθa; aspe'resa/ *f*, roughness, harshness; ruggedness, rockiness; severity, asperity

áspero /'aspero/ *a* rough, harsh; uneven, rocky; jarring, grating; hard, severe

aspersión /asper'sion/ *f*, *Eccl.* aspersion; sprinkling

aspiración /aspira'θion; aspira'sion/ *f*, breath; breathing; aspiration, desire; *Mus.* pause

aspirador /aspira'ðor/ **(de polvo)** *m*, vacuum cleaner

aspirante /aspi'rante/ *m*, aspirant, novice; office-seeker; applicant

aspirar /aspi'rar/ *vt* to breathe in, inhale; *Gram.* aspirate; (*with prep a*) aspire to, desire

aspirina /aspi'rina/ *f*, aspirin

asquear /aske'ar/ *vi* and *vt* to hate, loathe

asquerosidad /askerosi'ðað/ *f*, filthiness, loathsomeness; vileness, hatefulness

asqueroso /aske'roso/ *a* nauseating; loathsome, revolting; vile, hateful

asta /'asta/ *f*, lance, spear, pike; horn (of bull); antler; flagstaff; shaft. **a media a.,** at half-mast

asterisco /aste'risko/ *m*, asterisk

astigmático /astig'matiko/ *a* astigmatic

astil /as'til/ *m*, handle, pole, shaft; bar of a balance; beam feather

astilla /as'tiʎa; as'tiya/ *f*, splinter

astillero /asti'ʎero; asti'yero/ *m*, shipyard; rack for lances and pikes

astilloso /asti'ʎoso; asti'yoso/ *a* splintery, fragile

astringente /astrin'hente/ *a* astringent

astringir /astrin'hir/ *vt* to tighten up; compress; constrain

astro /'astro/ *m*, heavenly body

astrología /astrolo'hia/ *f*, astrology

astrólogo /as'trologo/ **(-ga)** *n* astrologist

astronauta /astro'nauta/ *m*, astronaut

astronomía /astrono'mia/ *f*, astronomy

astronómico /astro'nomiko/ *a* astronomical

astrónomo /as'tronomo/ *m*, astronomer

astucia /as'tuθia; as'tusia/ *f*, astuteness, guile, craftiness

astuto /as'tuto/ *a* guileful, crafty, astute

asueto /a'sueto/ *m*, day's holiday

asumir /asu'mir/ *vt* to assume; adopt, appropriate

asunción /asun'θion; asun'sion/ *f*, assumption

asunto /a'sunto/ *m*, matter, theme, subject; business, affair

astustadizo /asusta'ðiθo; asusta'ðiso/ *a* timid, nervous, easily frightened

asustar /asus'tar/ *vt* to frighten; **que asusta,** terribly (e.g. *Es de una ñoñería que asusta*, It's a terribly timid thing to do) *vr* be frightened

atacador /ataka'ðor/ **(-ra)** *a* attacking —*n* aggressor, attacker

atacar /ata'kar/ *vt* to attack; fasten, button; fit (clothes); ram (guns); *Fig.* press hard, corner (persons). **a. a los nervios,** to jar on the nerves

atadero /ata'ðero/ *m*, rope, tie, cord; hook, ring, etc. (for hitching); hindrance, impediment; hitching or fastening point

atadura /ata'ðura/ *f*, tying, stringing, fastening, tie; knot; connection

atajar /ata'har/ *vi* to take a short cut; —*vt* intercept, cut off; screen off, divide; impede, stop; interrupt (people) **atajarle la palabra a uno,** to cut somebody off, interrupt *vr* be overcome (by fear, shame, etc.)

atajo /a'taho/ *m,* short cut, quick way; cutting, abbreviation; division. *Inf.* **echar por el a.,** to go to the root of (a matter)

atalaya /ata'laya/ *f,* look out, watch tower; observation point. *m,* lookout

atalón /ata'lon/ *m,* atoll, coral island

atañer /ata'ɲer/ *vi impers* to concern, affect; belong, pertain

ataque /a'take/ *m,* (*Mil. Med.*) attack; quarrel, fight

atar /a'tar/ *vt* to tie; fasten; lace; stop, paralyse; —*vr* get in a fix; confine oneself. **a. cabos,** to put two and two together

atardecer /atarðe'θer; atarðe'ser/ *vi irr impers* to grow dusk. See **conocer**

atardecer /atarðe'θer; atarðe'ser/ *m,* dusk, evening

atarear /atare'ar/ *vt* to set to work, assign work to; —*vr* work hard

atarugar /ataru'gar/ *vt* to wedge; stop up; plug; block; *Inf.* silence, shut up; stuff, cram; —*vr Fig. Inf.* lose one's head

atasajar /atasa'har/ *vt* to cut up, jerk (beef, etc.)

atascadero /ataska'ðero/ *m,* deep rut, boggy place; impediment, obstacle

atascar /atas'kar/ *vt* to plug; block up; stop (a leak); hinder, obstruct; —*vr* stick in the mud; be held up or delayed; *Inf.* get stuck in a speech

atasco /a'tasko/ *m,* obstruction, block

ataúd /ata'uð/ *m,* coffin

ataviar /ata'βiar/ *vt* to deck, apparel, adorn

atavío /ata'βio/ *m,* get-up, dress, apparel; *pl* ornaments

ate /'ate/ *m,* (Mexico) kind of Turkish delight

ateísmo /ate'ismo/ *m,* atheism

atelaje /ate'lahe/ *m,* team, yoke (of horses); trappings, harness; *Inf.* trousseau

atemperar /atempe'rar/ *vt* to moderate, mitigate; adapt, adjust; temper, cool. **atemperarse a la realidad,** to adjust to reality

Atenas /a'tenas/ Athens

atenazar /atena'θar; atena'sar/ *vt* to grip, grasp; torture

atención /aten'θion; aten'sion/ *f,* attention; solicitude, kindness; courtesy, civility; *pl* business affairs —*interj* ¡A.! Take care! Look out!; *Mil.* Attention! **en a.** (a), taking into consideration. **estar en a.,** (patient) to be under treatment

atender /aten'der/ *vt irr* to await, expect; take care of, look after; —*vi* (*with prep a*) attend to, listen to; —*vi* remember. See **entender**

atenerse /ate'nerse/ *vr irr* (*with prep a*) to abide by; resort to, rely on. See **tener**

atentado /aten'taðo/ *a* prudent, sensible; secret, silent. *m,* infringement, violation; attempt (on a person's life); crime

atentar /aten'tar/ *vt irr* to do illegally; attempt a crime; —*vr* proceed cautiously; restrain oneself. See **acertar**

atento /a'tento/ *a* attentive; courteous, civil —*adv* taking into consideration. **su atenta** (**atta,** *Com.* your favor

atenuación /atenua'θion; atenua'sion/ *f,* attenuation, diminution

atenuante /ate'nuante/ *a* attenuating; extenuating (of circumstances)

atenuar /ate'nuar/ *vt* to attenuate, diminish; extenuate

ateo /a'teo/ **(-ea)** *a* atheistic —*n* atheist

aterirse /ate'rirse/ *vr defective* to grow stiff with cold

aterramiento /aterra'miento/ *m,* horror, terror; terrorization; *Naut.* landing; ruin, demolition

aterrar /ate'rrar/ *vt irr* to demolish; discourage; cover with earth; —*vi* land; —*vr Naut.* draw near to land. See **acertar**

aterrizaje /aterri'θahe; aterri'sahe/ *m, Aer.* landing. **a. forzoso,** forced landing. **campo de a.,** landing field

aterrizar /aterri'θar; aterri'sar/ *vi Aer.* to land, touch down

aterrorizar /aterrori'θar; aterrori'sar/ *vt* to terrify; terrorize

atesorar /ateso'rar/ *vt* to hoard, treasure up

atestación /atesta'θion; atesta'sion/ *f,* attestation, affidavit

atestar /ates'tar/ *vt irr* to stuff, cram; insert; *Inf.* stuff with food; crowd, fill with people. See **acertar**

atestar /ates'tar/ *vt* to attest, testify

atestiguación /atestigua'θion; atestigua'sion/ *f,* deposition, testimony

atestiguar /atesti'guar/ *vt* to testify, attest

atetar /ate'tar/ *vt* to suckle; —*vi* suck

atezado /ate'θaðo; ate'saðo/ *a* bronzed, sunburnt; black

atiesar /atie'sar/ *vt* to stiffen

atildar /atil'dar/ *vt* to place a tilde over; blame, criticize; decorate, ornament

atinado /ati'naðo/ *a* pertinent, relevant

atinar /ati'nar/ *vi* to find by touch; discover by chance; guess; hit the mark

atinente a... /ati'nente.a / concerning...

atisbar /atis'βar/ *vt* to spy upon; watch

atisbo /a'tisβo/ *m,* prying, watching; suspicion, hint

atisbón /atis'βon/ *a* penetrating (mind, vision)

atizador /atiθa'ðor; atisa'ðor/ *m,* poker (for the fire)

atizar /ati'θar; ati'sar/ *vt* to poke (the fire); dowse, snuff; trim (lamps); excite, rouse; *Inf.* slap, wallop

atlántico /at'lantiko/ *a* Atlantic. *m,* Atlantic Ocean

atleta /at'leta/ *m,* athlete

atlético /at'letiko/ *a* athletic

atletismo /atle'tismo/ *m*, athletics

atmósfera /at'mosfera/ *f*, atmosphere

atmosférico /atmos'feriko/ *a* atmospheric

atolladero /atoʎa'ðero; atoya'ðero/ *m*, rut; mud; bog

atolón /ato'lon/ *m*, atoll, coral island

atolondrado /atolon'draðo/ *a* scatter-brained, flighty

atolondramiento /atolondra'miento/ *m*, rashness, recklessness; bewilderment

atolondrar /atolon'drar/ *vt* to bewilder, confuse

atómico /a'tomiko/ *a* atomic

átomo /'atomo/ *m*, atom; speck, particle

atónito /a'tonito/ *a* amazed, astounded

atontar /aton'tar/ *vt* to confuse, daze; make stupid; stun

atormentador /atormenta'ðor/ **(-ra)** *a* torturing; —*n* tormentor; torturer

atormentar /atormen'tar/ *vt* to torment; torture; grieve, harass

atorrante /ato'rrante/ *a* and *mf* (Argentina) good-for-nothing

atracadero /atraka'ðero/ *m*, jetty, landingstage

atracar /atra'kar/ *vt* Inf. to stuff with food; *Naut*. tie up, moor; hold up, rob; —*vi* Naut. moor, stop; —*vr* Inf. guzzle, gorge

atracción /atrak'θion; atrak'sion/ *f*, attraction

atraco /a'trako/ **(a)** *m*, hold up (of), ambush (of)

atractivo /atrak'tiβo/ *a* attractive. *m*, attraction, charm

atraer /atra'er/ *vt irr* to attract; charm, enchant. See **traer**

atragantarse /atragan'tarse/ *vr* to choke; *Inf.* be at a loss, dry up (in conversation)

atrancar /atran'kar/ *vt* to bar the door; obstruct, block; hinder; —*vi* Inf. stride; skip (in reading)

atrapar /atra'par/ *vt* Inf. grab, seize, catch; net, obtain; deceive

atrás /a'tras/ *adv* behind, back; past; previously. **¡A.!** Back! **años a.,** years ago

atrasado /atra'saðo/ *a* slow (of clocks); backward; old-fashioned; hard-up, poor. **a. mental**, retarded person

atrasar /atra'sar/ *vt* to delay, retard; fix a later date than the true one; put back (clocks) —*vi* be slow (clocks); —*vr* be late; be left behind

atraso /a'traso/ *m*, delay; backwardness, dullness; slowness (clocks); lateness; *pl* arrears. **El reloj lleva cinco minutos de a.,** The watch is five minutes slow

atravesado /atraβe'saðo/ *a* slightly squint-eyed; mongrel, crossbreed; half-caste; ill-intentioned

atravesar /atraβe'sar/ *vt irr* to lay across, put athwart; cross, traverse; pierce; obstruct; *Naut*. lie to; —*vr* be among, mingle (with); interrupt; interfere, take part; quarrel; occur, arise. See **confesar**

atrayente /atra'yente/ *a* attractive

atreverse /atre'βerse/ *vr* to dare, risk, venture; be overbold or insolent

atrevido /atre'βiðo/ *a* bold, audacious; hazardous, dangerous; brazen, impudent

atribución /atriβu'θion; atriβu'sion/ *f*, attribution; perquisite, attribute

atribuible /atri'βuiβle/ *a* attributable

atribuir /atri'βuir/ *vt irr* to impute, attribute; assign, turn over to; —*vr* take upon oneself, assume. See **huir**

atributo /atri'βuto/ *m*, attribute, quality

atril /a'tril/ *m*, lectern, reading desk; music stand

atrincherar /atrintʃe'rar/ *vt* to protect with entrenchments; —*vr* entrench oneself

atrio /'atrio/ *m*, atrium; hall, vestibule; *Archit*. parvis

atrocidad /atroθi'ðað; atrosi'ðað/ *f*, atrocity, cruelty; *Inf*. terrific amount; enormity, crime

atrofia /a'trofia/ *f*, atrophy

atronar /atro'nar/ *vt irr* to deafen, stun with noise; confuse, daze. See **tronar**

atropellado /atrope'ʎaðo; atrope'yaðo/ *a* rash, foolhardy

atropellar /atrope'ʎar; atrope'yar/ *vt* to trample upon; thrust out of the way; knock down; disregard, violate (feelings); insult, abuse; transgress; do hastily; —*vr* act rashly

atropello /atro'peʎo; atro'peyo/ *m*, trampling; road accident; knocking over; upsetting; violation; outrage

atroz /a'troθ; a'ntros/ *a* atrocious, savage; monstrous, outrageous; *Inf*. terrific, enormous

atún /a'tun/ *m*, tuna

aturdido /atur'ðiðo/ *a* reckless, scatter-brained, silly; thoughtless; stunned

aturdimiento /aturði'miento/ *m*, daze; confusion, bewilderment

aturdir /atur'ðir/ *vt* to daze; confuse, bewilder; amaze; stun

atusar /atu'sar/ *vt* to trim (hair, beard); *Agr*. prune; smooth down (hair); —*vr* dress over-carefully

audacia /au'ðaθia; au'ðasia/ *f*, audacity

audaz /au'ðaθ; au'ðas/ *a* audacious, daring

audibilidad /auðiβili'ðað/ *f*, audibility

audición /auði'θion; auði'sion/ *f*, audition

audiencia /au'ðienθia; au'ðiensia/ *f*, audience, hearing; *Law*. audience; audience chamber

audífono /au'ðifono/ *m*, hearing aid

audioteca /auðio'teka/ *f*, audio library

auditivo /auði'tiβo/ *a* auditory

auditorio /auði'torio/ *a* auditory. *m*, audience

auge /'auhe/ *m*, *Fig*. zenith, height; *Astron*. apogee

aula /'aula/ *f*, lecture or class room; *Poet*. palace

aullar /au'ʎar; au'yar/ *vi* to howl; bay

aullido /au'ʎiðo; au'yiðo/ *m*, howl; baying

aumentar /aumen'tar/ **(se)** *vt vi vr* to increase, augment

aumentativo /aumenta'tiβo/ *a Gram.* augmentative

aumento /au'mento/ *m,* increase; progress; enlargement. **ir en a.,** to increase; advance, progress; prosper

aun /a'un/ *adv* even. **A. los que viven lejos han de oíros,** Even those who live far must hear you. **a. así** *or* **a. siendo así,** even so. **a. ayer,** only yesterday. **a. cuando,** even if. **más a.,** even more. **ni a. si,** not even if.

aún /a'un/ *adv* still, yet. **A. no te creen** *or* **No te creen a.,** They still don't believe you ¿A. se lo darás? *or* ¿Se lo darás a.? Will you still give it to her?

aunque /'aunke/ *conjunc* although, even if, even though. It takes the Indicative referring to statement of fact and Subjunctive referring to a hypothesis, e.g. *A. vino, no lo hizo,* Although he came, he did not do it. *A. él cantase yo no iría allí,* Even though he sang (were to sing), I should not go there

auricular /auriku'lar/ *a* auricular. *m,* little finger; receiver, ear-piece (of a telephone); earphone (radio)

aurora /au'rora/ *f,* dawn; genesis, beginnings. **a. boreal,** aurora borealis, Northern Lights

auscultar /auskul'tar/ *vt Med.* to auscultate

ausencia /au'senθia; au'sensia/ *f,* absence. **en ausencia de,** in the absence of

ausentar /ausen'tar/ *vt* to send away; —*vr* absent oneself

ausente /au'sente/ *a* absent. *mf* absent person

auspicio /aus'piθio; aus'pisio/ *m,* augury, prediction; favor, patronage; *pl* auspices

austeridad /austeri'ðað/ *f,* austerity; mortification of the flesh

austero /aus'tero/ *a* austere, ascetic; severe, harsh; honest, upright

australiano /austra'liano/ **(-na)** *a* and *n* Australian

austríaco /aus'triako/ **(-ca)** *a* and *n* Austrian

autenticación /autentika'θion; autentika'sion/ *f,* authentication

autenticar /autenti'kar/ *vt* to authenticate, attest; prove genuine

autenticidad /autentiθi'ðað; autentisi'ðað/ *f,* authenticity

auténtico /au'tentiko/ *a* authentic

auto /'auto/ *m, Law.* sentence, decision; *Theat.* one-act allegory (gen. religious); *pl* proceedings. **a. de fe,** auto-da-fé. **a. de reconocimiento,** search-warrant. **a. sacramental,** one-act religious drama on theme of mystery of the Eucharist. **hacer a. de fe de,** to burn

autobiografía /autoβiogra'fia/ *f,* autobiography

autobús /auto'βus/ *m,* motor bus, bus

autocitarse /autoθi'tarse; autosi'tarse/ *vr* to quote from one's own works

autoclave /auto'klaβe/ *m,* pressure cooker

autocracia /auto'kraθia; auto'krasia/ *f,* autocracy

autócrata /au'tokrata/ *mf* autocrat

autocrático /auto'kratiko/ *a* autocratic

autodescubrimiento /autoðeskuβri'miento/ *m,* self-discovery

autodidacto /autoði'ðakto/ *a* autodidactic; self-educated, self-taught

autógeno /au'toheno/ *a* autogenous, self-generating

autografía /autogra'fia/ *f,* autography

autográfico /auto'grafiko/ *a* autographic, in lithographic reproduction

autógrafo /au'tografo/ *a* autographical. *m,* autograph

autoinducción /autoinduk'θion; autoinduk'sion/ *f,* self-induction

autómata /au'tomata/ *m,* automaton

automático /auto'matiko/ *a* automatic. *m, Sew.* press stud

automatismo /automa'tismo/ *m,* automatism

automejoramiento /autome,hora'miento/ *m,* self-improvement

automóvil /auto'moβil/ *m,* automobile, motor car —*a* automatic

automovilismo /automoβi'lismo/ *m,* motoring

automovilista /automoβi'lista/ *mf* motorist

autonombrarse /autonom'βrarse/ *vr* to call oneself, go by the name of

autonomía /autono'mia/ *f,* autonomy

autónomo /au'tonomo/ *a* autonomous

autopista /auto'pista/ *f,* motor road

autopsia /au'topsia/ *f, Med.* autopsy, post-mortem

autor /au'tor/ **(-ra)** *n* agent, originator; author; inventor; *Law.* perpetrator

autoridad /autori'ðað/ *f,* authority; pomp, show

autoritario /autori'tario/ *a* authoritarian; authoritative

autorización /autoriθa'θion; autorisa'sion/ *f,* authorization

autorizado /autori'θaðo; autori'saðo/ *a* approved, authorized, responsible

autorizar /autori'θar; autori'sar/ *vt* to authorize; *Law.* attest, testify; cite, prove by reference; approve; exalt

autorretrato /autorre'trato/ *m,* self-portrait

autostopista /autosto'pista/ *mf* hitch-hiker (Spain)

autosugestión /autosuhes'tion/ *f,* auto-suggestion

auxiliador /auksilia'ðor/ **(-ra)** *a* assistant; helpful —*n* helper, assistant

auxiliar /auksi'liar/ *vt* to help, aid; attend (the dying). *m, Educ.* lecturer —*a* assisting

auxilio /auk'silio/ *m,* help, aid, assistance

aval /a'βal/ *m, Com.* endorsement; voucher

avalar /aβa'lar/ *vt* to enhance. **avalado por la tradición,** hallowed by tradition

avalentado /aβalen'taðo/ *a* boastful, bragging

avalorar /aβalo'rar/ *vt* to value, estimate; put spirit into, encourage

avance /a'βanθe; a'βanse/ *m,* advance; advance payment; balance sheet; attack

avanzada /aβan'θaða; aβan'saða/ *f, Mil.* advance guard

avanzado /aβan'θaðo; aβan'saðo/ *a* advanced, progressive

avanzar /aβan'θar; aβan'sar/ *vt* to advance; promote; —*vi* advance; attack; grow late (time)

avanzo /a'βanθo; a'βanso/ *m,* balance sheet; price estimate

avaricia /aβa'riθia; aβa'risia/ *f,* greed, avarice

avaricioso, avariento /aβari'θioso, aβa'riento; aβari'sioso, aβa'riento/ *a* avaricious, greedy

avaro /a'βaro/ **(-ra)** *a* miserly; greedy —*n* miser

avasallador /aβasaʎa'ðor; aβasaya'ðor/ *a* dominating; *Fig.* overwhelming; enslaving

avasallar /aβasa'ʎar; aβasa'yar/ *vt* to subdue, dominate; —*vr* become a vassal; surrender, yield

ave /'aβe/ *f,* bird. **a. de paso,** migratory bird; *Fig.* bird of passage. **a. de rapiña,** bird of prey. **a. fría,** *Ornith.* plover. **ave cantora,** songbird

avecinarse /aβeθi'narse; aβesi'narse/ *vr* to be approaching (e.g. *el año que avecina,* the coming year)

avellana /aβe'ʎana; aβe'yana/ *f,* hazel nut

avellanarse /aβeʎa'narse; aβeya'narse/ *vr* to shrivel

avellano /aβe'ʎano; aβe'yano/ *m, Bot.* hazel

avemaría /aβema'ria/ *f,* Hail Mary (prayer); Angelus; rosary bead. *Inf.* **en un a.,** in a trice

avena /a'βena/ *f,* oats; *Poet.* oaten pipe. **a. loca,** wild oats

avenar /aβe'nar/ *vt* to drain (land); drain off (liquids)

avenencia /aβe'nenθia; aβe'nensia/ *f,* agreement, arrangement; transaction; conformity, harmony

avenida /aβe'niða/ *f,* flood, spate; avenue; abundance; way, approach (to a place)

avenido /aβe'niðo/ *a* (*with* bien *or* mal) well *or* ill-suited

avenidor /aβeni'ðor/ **(-ra)** *n* arbitrator, mediator

avenir /aβe'nir/ *vt irr* to reconcile; —*vi* happen (used in infinitive and third singular and plural); —*vr* be reconciled; agree; compromise, give way; harmonize (things); (*with* con) get on with, agree with. See **venir**

aventador /aβenta'ðor/ *m, Agr.* winnower; pitchfork

aventajado /aβenta'haðo/ *a* outstanding, talented; advantageous. *m, Mil.* private who enjoys extra pay

aventajar /aβenta'har/ *vt* to improve, better; promote, prefer; excel; —*vr* (*with prep a*) surpass, excel. **Te aventajo en diez años,** I'm ten years older than you

aventura /aβen'tura/ *f,* adventure; chance, luck; risk, danger

aventurar /aβentu'rar/ *vt* to risk, hazard

aventurero /aβentu'rero/ **(-ra)** *a* adventurous; unscrupulous, intriguing; undisciplined (of troops) —*n* adventurer

avergonzar /aβergon'θar; aβergon'sar/ *vt irr* to shame; make shy, abash; —*vr* be ashamed; be shy or sheepish —*Pres. Indic.* avergüenzo, avergüenzas, avergüenza, avergüenzan. *Pres. Subjunc.* avergüence, avergüences, avergüence, avergüencen

avería /aβe'ria/ *f,* aviary; damage (to merchandise); loss, harm; *Elec.* fault; breakdown. **a. gruesa,** general average (marine insurance)

averiarse /aβe'riarse/ *vr* to be damaged; deteriorate; break down

averiguable /aβeri'guaβle/ *a* examinable, investigable; discoverable

averiguación /aβerigua'θion; aβerigua'sion/ *f,* inquiry, investigation; discovery

averiguar /aβeri'guar/ *vt* to investigate, inquire into; discover, ascertain. **¡averigüelo Vargas!** Beats me!, Search me!

averío /aβe'rio/ *m,* flock of birds

aversión /aβer'sion/ *f,* aversion, repugnance

avestruz /aβes'truθ; aβes'trus/ *m,* ostrich

avezar /aβe'θar; aβe'sar/ *vt* to accustom; —*vr* grow accustomed (to)

aviación /aβia'θion; aβia'sion/ *f,* aviation

aviador /aβia'ðor/ *m,* aviator

aviar /a'βiar/ *vt* to outfit, equip; prepare, make ready; *Inf.* speed up; caulk (ship). *Fig. Inf.* **estar aviado,** to be in a mess

avidez /aβi'ðeθ; aβi'ðes/ *f,* avidity, greed; longing, desire

ávido /'aβiðo/ *a* avid, greedy

avieso /a'βieso/ *a* twisted, crooked; illnatured; sinister

avillanado /aβiʎa'naðo; aβiya'naðo/ *a* countrified; gross, vulgar; boorish

avío /a'βio/ *m,* preparation, provision; picnic lunch; money advanced (to miners or laborers); *pl Inf.* equipment, tools. **avíos de pesca,** fishing tackle

avión /a'βion/ *m,* airplane; *Ornith.* martin or swift. **a. de bombardeo,** bomber. **a. de caza,** fighter plane. **a. de combate nocturno,** night fighter. **a. de hostigamiento,** interceptor. **a. de reacción,** jet airplane. **a. de transporte,** *Aer.* transport. **a. en picado,** dive-bomber. **a. taxi,** air taxi. **por a.,** by airmail **«Avión»** "Airmail"

avioneta /aβio'neta/ *f,* light airplane, small airplane

avisado /aβi'saðo/ *a* shrewd, sensible. **mal a.**, ill-advised, imprudent

avisar /aβi'sar/ *vt* to inform, acquaint; warn; advise

aviso /a'βiso/ *m,* notice, announcement; warning; advice; care, caution; attention; shrewdness, prudence. **estar sobre a.**, to be on call; be on the alert

avispa /a'βispa/ *f,* wasp

avispado /aβis'paðo/ *a* Inf. smart, clever, quick; wide-awake

avispar /aβis'par/ *vt* to goad, prick; Inf. rouse, incite; —*vr* be uneasy, fret

avispero /aβis'pero/ *m,* wasp's nest; swarm of wasps; Fig. Inf. hornet's nest

avistar /aβis'tar/ *vt* to descry, sight, spot; —*vr* avistarse con, to interview

avituallar /aβitua'ʎar/ aβitua'yar/ *vt* to victual, supply with food

avivar /aβi'βar/ *vt* to enliven; stimulate, encourage; stir (fire), trim (wicks); brighten (colors); inflame; vivify, invigorate; —*vi* revive, recover

avizor /aβi'θor; aβi'sor/ *m,* watcher, spy —*a* watchful, vigilant

avizorar /aβiθo'rar; aβiso'rar/ *vt* to watch, spy upon

axila /ak'sila/ *f,* Bot. axil; Anat. axilla, armpit

axioma /ak'sioma/ *m,* axiom

axiomático /aksio'matiko/ *a* axiomatic

¡ay! /ai/ *interj* Alas! Woe is me! *m,* complaint, sigh

aya /'aya/ *f,* governess

ayer /a'yer/ *adv* yesterday; a short while ago; in the past. *m,* past

ayo /'ayo/ *m,* tutor

ayuda /a'yuða/ *f,* help, assistance; enema; clyster; watch dog. *m,* **a. de cámara,** valet

ayudador /ayuða'ðor/ **(-ra)** *a* helping, assisting —*n* helper

ayudante /ayu'ðante/ *m,* assistant; teaching assistant; Mil. adjutant. **a. a cátedra,** Educ. assistant lecturer. **a. de plaza,** post adjutant

ayudar /ayu'ðar/ *vt* to assist; help, aid; —*vr* make an effort; avail oneself of another's help

ayunador /ayuna'ðor/ **(-ra)** *a* fasting —*n* faster; abstainer

ayunar /ayu'nar/ *vi* to fast

ayuno /a'yuno/ *m,* fast —*a* fasting; ignorant, unaware. **en a.** *or* **en ayunas,** before breakfast, fasting; Inf. ignorant, unaware

ayuntamiento /ayunta'miento/ *m,* meeting, assembly; municipal government; town hall; sexual union

azabache /aθa'βatʃe; asaβatʃe/ *m,* Mineral. jet

azada /a'θaða; a'saða/ *f,* Agr. spade; hoe

azafata /aθa'fata; asa'fata/ *f,* queen's waiting-maid Obs.; flight attendant

azafate /aθa'fate; asa'fate/ *m,* flat basket; small tray

azafrán /aθa'fran; asa'fran/ *m,* Bot. saffron; crocus

azahar /a'θaar; a'saar/ *m,* flower of orange, lemon or sweet lime tree

azar /a'θar; a'sar/ *m,* chance, hazard; unexpected misfortune; losing card or throw of dice

azararse /aθa'rarse; asa'rarse/ *vr* to go wrong, fail (negotiations, etc.); grow nervous; become confused; blush

azaroso /aθa'roso; asa'roso/ *a* unlucky, ill-omened; hazardous

ázimo /'aθimo; 'asimo/ *a* unleavened (bread)

ázoe /'aθoe; 'asoe/ *m,* nitrogen

azogar /aθo'gar; aso'gar/ *vt* to silver (mirrors, etc.); slake lime; —*vr* suffer from mercury poisoning; Inf. grow uneasy, be agitated

azogue /a'θoge; a'soge/ *m,* Mineral. mercury, quick-silver; market-place

azolve /a'θolβe; a'solβe/ *m,* silt

azoramiento /aθora'miento; asora'miento/ *m,* alarm, terror; confusion, stupefaction; incitement

azorar /aθo'rar; aso'rar/ *vt* to alarm, terrify; confuse, stun, dumbfound; excite, stimulate; encourage

azotacalles /aθota'kaʎes; asota'kayes/ *mf* Inf. idler, street loafer

azotar /aθo'tar; aso'tar/ *vt* to whip, beat, flog; scourge, ravage; knock against or strike repeatedly

azote /a'θote; a'sote/ *m,* whip; scourge; lash, blow with a whip; spank, slap, misfortune, disaster. Inf. **azotes y galeras,** monotonous diet

azotea /aθo'tea; aso'tea/ *f,* flat terrace roof

azozador /aθoθa'ðor; asosa'ðor/ party whip, whip

azteca /aθ'teka; as'teka/ *a* and *mf* Aztec

azúcar /a'θukar; a'sukar/ *m,* sugar. **a. blanco** *or* **a. de flor,** white sugar. **a. de pilón,** loaf sugar. **a. moreno,** brown sugar. **a. quebrado,** brown sugar. **a. y canela,** sorrel gray (of horses)

azucarado /aθuka'raðo; asuka'raðo/ *a* sugary; sugared, sugar-coated; Inf. honeyed, flattering

azucarar /aθuka'rar; asuka'rar/ *vt* to coat with sugar; sweeten; Inf. soften, mitigate; —*vr* crystallize; go sugary (jam)

azucarero /aθuka'rero; asuka'rero/ *a* sugar-producing (e.g. province)

azucarillo /aθuka'riʎo; asuka'riyo/ *m,* Cul. bar made of white of egg and sugar for sweetening water

azufre /a'θufre; a'sufre/ *m,* sulphur

azul /a'θul; a'sul/ *a* and *m,* blue. **a. celeste,** sky blue, azure. **a. de mar** *or* **a. marino,** navy blue. **a. de ultramar,** ultramarine. **a. turquí,** indigo

azulejo /aθu'leho; asu'leho/ *m,* ornamental glazed tile

azuzar /aθu'θar; asu'sar/ *vt* to set on (dogs); irritate, provoke; incite, urge

B

babador, babero /baβa'ðor, ba'βero/ *m,* bib, feeder

babear /baβe'ar/ *vi* to dribble, slaver; *Fig. Inf.* slobber over, be sloppy

babel /ba'βel/ *m,* babel

babélico /ba'βeliko/ *a* Babelian, Babel-like confusion; unintelligible

Babia, estar en /'baβia, es'tar en/ to be daydreaming

bable /'baβle/ *m,* Asturian (language)

babor /ba'βor/ *m, Naut.* larboard, port

babosa /ba'βosa/ *f,* slug; young onion

baboso /ba'βoso/ *a.* slavering; *Fig. Inf.* "sloppy"; *Inf.* incompetent, useless

babucha /ba'βutʃa/ *f,* heelless slipper, babouche

babuino /ba'βuino/ *m, Zool.* baboon

baca /'baka/ *f,* luggage carrier (on roof of bus, etc.)

bacalao /baka'lao/ *m,* codfish

baceta /ba'θeta; ba'seta/ *f,* pool (in card games)

bache /'batʃe/ *m,* rut (in road); pothole

bacheo /ba'tʃeo/ *m,* repairing of streets

bachiller /batʃi'ʎer; batʃi'yer/ *mf* high-school graduate *m, Inf.* babbler. *f.* **bachillera,** *Inf.* blue-stocking; garrulous woman

bachillerarse /batʃiʎe'rarse; batʃiye'rarse/ *vr* to graduate as a bachelor

bachillerato /batʃiʎe'rato; batʃiye'rato/ *m,* baccalaureate, bachelor's degree

bacía /ba'θia; ba'sia/ *f,* bowl; barber's circular shaving-dish; barber's trade sign

bacilo /ba'θilo; ba'silo/ *m,* bacillus

bacterial, bacteriano /bakte'rial, bakte'riano/ *a* bacterial

báculo /'bakulo/ *m,* staff; walking-stick; *Fig.* support. **b. episcopal,** bishop's crozier

badajo /ba'ðaho/ *m,* clapper (of a bell); chatterbox, gossip

badana /ba'ðana/ *f,* cured sheepskin, chamois leather, washleather; sweat band; *Inf.* **zurrar** (*a uno*) **la b.,** to take the hide off; insult

badén /ba'ðen/ *m,* channel made by rain, furrow; conduit

badil /ba'ðil/ *m,* fire-shovel

badulaque /baðu'lake/ *m, Inf.* good-for-nothing

bagaje /ba'gahe/ *m, Mil.* baggage; beast of burden, transport animal; luggage

bagatela /baga'tela/ *f,* trifle, oddment, bagatelle

bagazo /ba'gaθo; ba'gaso/ *m,* oilcake, bagasse

bagual /ba'gual/ *a West. Hem.* untamed, wild; doltish, dull. *m,* untamed horse, wild horse

bahía /ba'ia/ *f,* bay, harbor

bailable /bai'laβle/ *a* dance (of music). *m, Theat.* dance number

bailador /baila'ðor/ **(-ra)** *n* dancer

bailar /bai'lar/ *vi* to dance; spin around. **b. al son que le toca,** to adapt oneself to circumstances

bailarín /baila'rin/ *a* dancing. *m,* professional dancer. **b. de cuerda, bailarín de la cuerda floja,** tightrope dancer

bailarina /baila'rina/ *f,* ballerina

baile /'baile/ *m,* dance; ball; ballet. **b. de máscaras,** masked ball. **b. de trajes,** fancy-dress ball. **b. de San Vito,** St. Vitus' dance. **b. ruso,** ballet

bailotear /bailote'ar/ *vi* to jig about; dance

baja /'baha/ *f,* drop, diminution; fall (in price, etc.); *Mil.* casualty; discharge. *Inf.* **darse de b.,** to leave an employment

bajada /ba'haða/ *f,* descent, fall; slope, incline; hollow, depression. **b. de aguas,** roof gutter

bajamar /baha'mar/ *f,* low tide

bajar /ba'har/ *vi* to descend; go down; get off; drop; fall, decrease; —*vt* lower, take down, bring down; let down; dismount, alight; bend, droop; drop; reduce (price); *Fig.* lower (voices); humiliate, humble; **b. a tierra,** to step ashore; **b. la cabeza ante,** to submit to (e.g. a judgment) *vr* alight, dismount; humble oneself

bajeza /ba'heθa; ba'hesa/ *f,* base action; meanness; *Fig.* humble estate, lowliness. **b. de ánimo,** timorousness

bajío /ba'hio/ *m, Naut.* shallows, shoal; depression, hollow

bajista /ba'hista/ *mf* speculator, bear (Stock Exchange)

bajo /'baho/ *a* low; short, not tall; downcast; under; subordinate; pale (of colors); humble (origin); base; coarse, vulgar; cheap (price); low (sounds). *m,* depth; shoal, sand bank; *Mus.* bass; *pl* petticoats, skirts; horses' hoofs —*adv* beneath, below —*prep* under, beneath. **b. juramento,** upon oath. **bajo relieve,** bas relief. **en voz baja,** in a low voice. **planta baja,** ground floor. **por lo b.,** in a whisper; in secret, on the sly

bajón /ba'hon/ *m, Mus.* bassoon; bassoon player; *Fig. Inf.* downfall

bajonista /baho'nista/ *mf* bassoon player

bala /'bala/ *f,* bullet, ball; bale. **b. fría,** spent bullet. **b. luminosa,** tracer bullet. **b. perdida,** stray bullet. *Inf.* **como una b.,** like a shot

balada /ba'laða/ *f,* ballad, song

baladí /bala'ði/ *a* worthless, insignificant

baladro /ba'laðro/ *m,* yell, outcry, shout

baladrón /bala'ðron/ *a* braggart

baladronada /balaðro'naða/ *f,* bravado, bragging

balagar /bala'gar/ *m,* straw rick

bálago /'balago/ *m,* straw; soap-ball; straw rick

balance /ba'lanθe; ba'lanse/ *m,* balance; swinging, oscillation; rolling, rocking (of a ship, etc.); doubt, insecurity, *Com.* balance; balance sheet

balancear /balanθe'ar; balanse'ar/ *vi* to

swing; oscillate; vacillate, hesitate; —*vt* balance; —*vr* balance oneself; rock or swing oneself

balanceo /balan'θeo; balan'seo/ *m*, balancing; rocking; swinging; rolling (of a ship, etc.)

balancín /balan'θin; balan'sin/ *m*, swingbar; whipple-tree; balance beam; tightrope dancer's pole; minting-mill; yoke (for carrying pails); *pl Naut*. lifts

balandra /ba'landra/ *f*, *Naut*. sloop, cutter

balanza /ba'lanθa; ba'lansa/ *f*, balance; scale; judgment; comparison. **b. de comercio**, balance of trade. **en balanzas**, in doubt or danger, in the balance

balar /ba'lar/ *vi* to bleat (sheep)

balasto /ba'lasto/ *m*, *Rail*. ballast

balaustrada /balaus'traða/ *f*, balustrade

balaustre /bala'ustre/ *m*, baluster

balazo /ba'laθo; ba'laso/ *m*, shot, bullet wound

balbuceo /balβu'θeo; balβu'seo/ *m*, stammering; babbling; lisping; **balbuceos** *Fig*. beginnings, early stages (e.g. *los b. de la literatura yídica*, the beginnings of Yiddish literature)

balbuciente /balβu'θiente; balβu'siente/ *a* stammering; babbling; lisping

balbucir /balβu'θir; balβu'sir/ *vi irr defective* to stammer; lisp; babble; read hesitantly. See **lucir**

Balcanes, los /bal'kanes, los/ the Balkans

balcánico /bal'kaniko/ *a* Balkan

balcón /bal'kon/ *m*, balcony

baldaquín /balda'kin/ *m*, canopy, baldachin

baldar /bal'dar/ *vt* to cripple; impede, obstruct

balde /'balde/ *m*, bucket

balde /'balde/ **(en)** *adv* in vain. **de b.**, gratis, free of charge

baldear /balde'ar/ *vt Naut*. to wash the decks

baldío /bal'dio/ *a* untilled; fallow; useless, worthless; vagrant

baldón /bal'don/ *m*, insult; dishonor

baldonar /baldo'nar/ *vt* to insult

baldosa /bal'dosa/ *f*, paving stone; tile

Baleares, las Islas /bale'ares, las 'islas/ the Balearic Islands

baleárico /bale'ariko/ *a* Balearic

baliza /ba'liθa; ba'lisa/ *f*, *Naut*. buoy, beacon

balizamiento /baliθa'miento; balisa'miento/ *m*, marking with beacons, marking with buoys; traffic signs and signals

ballena /ba'ʎena; ba'yena/ *f*, whale; whalebone

balneario /balne'ario/ *a* pertaining to public baths; bathing; holiday; spa. *m*, watering place, spa

balompié /balom'pie/ *m*, football (game)

balón /ba'lon/ *m*, large ball; football;

Chem. balloon; bundle; bale. **b. de ensayo**, *Fig*. feeler

baloncesto /balon'θesto; balon'sesto/ *m*, *Sports*. basketball

balota /ba'lota/ *f*, ballot

balotaje /balo'tahe/ *m*, balloting; run-off election

balotar /balo'tar/ *vi* to ballot

balsa /'balsa/ *f*, pond; raft

balsadera /balsa'ðera/ *f*, ferry

balsámico /bal'samiko/ *a* balmy

bálsamo /'balsamo/ *m*, balm

balsero /bal'sero/ *m*, ferryman; rafter (person fleeing a country by raft, rowboat, etc.)

báltico /'baltiko/ *a* Baltic. **el Mar Báltico** the Baltic Sea

baluarte /ba'luarte/ *m*, bulwark; bastion; protection, defense

bambolearse /bambole'arse/ *vr* to sway; swing; totter; be shaky; stagger

bamboleo /bambo'leo/ *m*, rocking; swinging; tottering; staggering; reeling

bambolla /bam'βoʎa; bam'βoya/ *f*, *Inf*. ostentation, swank

bambú /bam'βu/ *m*, bamboo

banal /ba'nal/ *a* banal, commonplace

banana /ba'nana/ *f*, banana

banasta /ba'nasta/ *f*, big basket

banasto /ba'nasto/ *m*, big round basket

banca /'banka/ *f*, bench; card game; stall; *Com*. banking

bancada /ban'kaða/ *f*, rowing seat

bancal /ban'kal/ *m*, oblong garden plot; terrace

bancario /ban'kario/ *a* banking, bank

bancarrota /banka'rrota/ *f*, bankruptcy. **hacer b.**, to go bankrupt

banco /'banko/ *m*, form, bench; rowing seat; settle; seat; bench; *Com*. bank; *Naut*. bar, shoal; school (of fish). **b. azul**, government benches in Spanish Parliament. **b. de arena**, sand-bank. **b. de descuento**, discount bank. **b. de emisión**, banco emisor, bank of issue. **b. de hielo**, iceberg. **b. de nivel**, benchmark

banda /'banda/ *f*, wide ribbon; sash; ribbon, insignia; strip; border; party, group; gang; flock (of birds); zone, belt; side (of ship); *Mus*. band; cushion (billiards); *Herald*. bar, bend. **b. elástica**, rubber band. *Naut*. **dar a la b.**, to lie along

bandada /ban'daða/ *f*, flock (of birds)

bandeja /ban'deha/ *f*, tray, salver

bandera /ban'dera/ *f*, banner, flag; colors, standard. **b. de popa**, ensign. **jurar la b.**, (*Mil. Nav.*) to take the oath of allegiance

banderilla /bande'riʎa; bande'riya/ *f*, banderilla (bullfighting)

banderillero /banderi'ʎero; banderi'yero/ *m*, man who puts banderillas on bulls

banderín /bande'rin/ *m*, *dim* small flag; recruiting post

banderizo /bande'riθo; bande'riso/ *a* factious; vehement, excitable

banderola /bande'rola/ f, banderole, pennon; bannerole

bandido /ban'diðo/ **(-da)** a and n outlaw, fugitive. m, bandit; highwayman; rogue, desperado

bando /'bando/ m, proclamation, order; faction, group, party

bandolerismo /bandole'rismo/ m, brigandage

bandolero /bando'lero/ m, robber, footpad, brigand

bandolín /bando'lin/ m, mandolin

bandurria /ban'durria/ f, Mus. mandolin

banjo /'banho/ m, banjo

banquero /ban'kero/ m, banker

banqueta /ban'keta/ f, three-legged stool; seat; footstool

banquete /ban'kete/ m, banquet, feast

banquetear /bankete'ar/ vt and vi to banquet

banqueteo /banke'teo/ m, banqueting, feasting

bañado /ba'ɲaðo/ m, chamber pot; West. Hem. marshy land, marsh; **bañados** pl marsh

bañador /baɲa'ðor/ **(-ra)** a bathing —n bather. m, bathing dress; bath, vat

bañar /ba'ɲar/ vt to bathe; coat, cover; dip; lave, wash; Fig. bathe (of sunlight, etc.) —vr take a bath; bathe

bañera /ba'ɲera/ f, bath attendant; bathtub

bañista /ba'ɲista/ mf bather; one who takes spa waters

baño /'baɲo/ m, bathing; bath; bathroom; bathtub; bagnio, Turkish prison; covering, coat; pl mineral baths, spa. **b. de mar**, sea bath. **b. de María**, double saucepan. **b. de sol**, sunbath. **casa de baños**, public baths. **cuarto de b.**, bathroom

baptisterio /baptis'terio/ m, baptistery; Eccl. font

baquelita /bake'lita/ f, bakelite

baqueta /ba'keta/ f, ramrod; pl drumsticks; Mil. gauntlet

bar /bar/ m, bar; café

barahúnda /bara'unda/ f. See baraúnda

baraja /ba'raha/ f, pack (of cards); game of cards

barajar /bara'har/ vt to shuffle (cards); jumble, mix; —vi quarrel

baranda /ba'randa/ f, handrail, banister; cushion (of billiard table)

barandilla /baran'diʎa; baran'diya/ f, dim railing

baratija /bara'tiha/ f, (gen. pl) trifle, oddment

baratillo /bara'tiʎo; bara'tiyo/ m, second-hand article, frippery; second-hand shop or stall; bargain counter

barato /ba'rato/ a cheap; easy. m, bargain sale —adv cheaply

baratura /bara'tura/ f, cheapness

baraúnda /bara'unda/ f, uproar, confusion

barba /'barβa/ f, chin; beard; whiskers;

fin; barb (of a feather); m, actor who plays old men. f pl, fibers of plants. **b. bien poblada**, a thick beard. **barbas de ballena**, whalebone. Fig. Inf. **echar a las barbas**, to throw in a person's face. **en la barba, en las barbas**, to ones face (e.g. Me lo dijeron en las barbas. They told me so to my face). **hacer la b.**, to shave; Inf. annoy

barbacoa /barβa'koa/ f, West Hem. barbecue; trellis (for climbing plants)

barbado /bar'βaðo/ a bearded. m, shoot; sucker; transplanted plant

barbárico /bar'βariko/ a barbarian; barbaric

barbaridad /barβari'ðað/ f, barbarity; blunder; atrocity; outrage; Inf. huge amount. **¡Qué b.!** How awful! You don't say so!

barbarie /bar'βarie/ f, barbarism; barbarity, cruelty

barbarismo /barβa'rismo/ m, barbarism; cruelty; barbarians

bárbaro /'barβaro/ **(-ra)** a and n barbarian —a fierce; headstrong; uncivilized. **como un b.**, like crazy (e.g. estudiar como un b., to study like crazy)

barbechar /barβe'tʃar/ vt to plow; leave fallow

barbecho /bar'βetʃo/ m, Agr. fallow; first plowing

barbería /barβe'ria/ f, barber shop

barbero /bar'βero/ m, barber

barbihecho /barβi'etʃo/ a fresh-shaved

barbilampiño /barβilam'piɲo/ a smooth-faced, beardless, clean-shaven

barbilindo /barβi'lindo/ a dandified, dappy; m, dandy

barbilla /bar'βiʎa; bar'βiya/ f, point of the chin; chin. **acariciar la b. (de)**, to chuck under the chin

barbiquejo /barβi'keho/ m, Naut. bobstay; hat-guard

barbudo /bar'βuðo/ a heavily bearded

barbulla /bar'βuʎa; bar'βuya/ f, Inf. babble, chatter, murmur of voices

barca /'barka/ f, small boat, bark; barge. **b. de pasaje**, ferryboat. **b. plantaminas**, minelayer

barcada /bar'kaða/ f, boat-load; ferry crossing

barcaza /bar'kaθa; bar'kasa/ f, Naut. lighter; barge. **b. de desembarco**, landingcraft

barco /'barko/ m, boat; ship; hollow, rut. **b. barredero**, trawler. **b. siembraminas**, minelayer

barda /'barða/ f, horse armor; thatch; shingle; (Mexico) cement fence, cement wall

bardal /bar'ðal/ m, thatched wall; mud wall

bardar /bar'ðar/ vt to thatch

bario /'bario/ m, barium

barítono /ba'ritono/ m, baritone

barlovento /barlo'βento/ m, Naut. windward

barnacla /bar'nakla/ *m*, barnacle

barniz /bar'niθ; bar'nis/ *m*, varnish; glaze; smattering, veneer

barnizar /barni'θar; barni'sar/ *vt* to varnish; glaze

barométrico /baro'metriko/ *a* barometric

barómetro /ba'rometro/ *m*, barometer

barquero /bar'kero/ *m*, boatman; bargee; *Ent.* water-boatman

barquillo /bar'kiʎo; bar'kiyo/ *m*, wafer, cornet

barra /'barra/ *f*, bar; ingot; railing (in courtroom); sandbank; fault (in cloth); lever, crossbar; (in cricket) bail; *Mus.* bar. **b. de jabón de afeitar**, shaving-stick. **a barras derechas**, without deceit

barraca /ba'rraka/ *f*, cabin, hut; stall; sideshow. **b. de tiro**, shooting gallery

barranca /ba'rranka,/ *f*, **barranco** *m*, furrow, channel, rut; gorge; difficulty, the

barredor /barre'δor/ **(-ra)** *n* sweeper

barredura /barre'δura/ *f*, sweeping; *pl* sweepings; rubbish

barrena /ba'rrena/ *f*, borer, gimlet, drill, auger. *Aer.* **b. de cola**, tail-spin

barrenar /barre'nar/ *vt* to drill, bore; blast (in quarries)

barrenero /barre'nero/ *m*, driller; blaster

barreno /ba'rreno/ *m*, blast hole; bore, drill; vanity

barreño /ba'rreno/ *m*, earthenware bowl (for dish washing, etc.)

barrer /ba'rrer/ *vt* to sweep; *Fig.* clear, make a clean sweep

barrera /ba'rrera/ *f*, barrier; barricade; *Fig.* obstacle. **b. de golpe**, automatic gate (at level crossings, etc.). **b. de minas**, minefield

barriada /barria'δa/ *f*, district; quarter (of a city)

barricada /barri'kaδa/ *f*, barricade

barriga /ba'rriga/ *f*, *Inf.* belly

barrigón /barri'gon, barri'guδo/ *a* pot-bellied

barril /ba'rril/ *m*, barrel; cask; water-butt

barrilero /barri'lero/ *m*, cooper

barrio /'barrio/ *m*, district, quarter; suburb. **barrios bajos**, slums, back streets. **el otro b.**, the other world, Eternity

barrizal /barri'θal; barri'sal/ *m*, muddy place; claypit

barro /'barro/ *m*, mud; clay; earthenware drinking vessel; *Inf.* money

barroco /ba'rroko/ *a* baroque

barrote /ba'rrote/ *m*, thick iron bar; stave, bond

barruntar /barrun'tar/ *vt* to conjecture; suspect

barrunto /ba'rrunto/ *m*, conjecture; indication, sign

bártulos /'bartulos/ *m pl*, household goods; *Fig.* means, wherewithal

barullo /ba'ruʎo; ba'ruyo/ *m*, *Inf.* confusion, disorder; mob

basar /ba'sar/ *vr* to base, place on a base; *Fig.* found, base; —*vr* (*with en*) rely upon, base oneself on

basca /'baska/ *f*, (gen. *pl*) nausea; retching; wave of anger

báscula /'baskula/ *f*, weighing-machine, platform-scale; weigh-bridge

base /'base/ *f*, base; (*Chem. Geom. Mil.*) base; basis; *Archit.* pedestal; *Mus.* root. **sin b.**, baseless

básico /'basiko/ *a* basic

Basilea /basi'lea/ Basel, Basle

basílica /ba'silika/ *f*, palace; church, basilica

basquear /baske'ar/ *vi* to retch; feel squeamish

bastante /bas'tante/ *a* sufficient, enough —*adv* sufficiently; enough; fairly; a good deal; somewhat. **Hace b. calor**, It is quite hot. **Tengo b.**, I have enough. **Tenemos b. tiempo**, We have sufficient time

bastar /bas'tar/ *vi* to suffice. **¡Basta!** Enough! No more! Stop! **¡Basta de...!** Enough of...! **Basta decir que...,** Suffice it to say that...

bastardía /bastar'δia/ *f*, bastardy, illegitimacy; baseness, meanness

bastardilla /bastar'δiʎa; bastar'δiya/ *f*, *Print.* italics

bastardo /bas'tarδo/ **(-da)** *a* bastard; spurious —*n* bastard

bastear /baste'ar/ *vt* *Sew.* to baste

bastidor /basti'δor/ *m*, embroidery frame; *Art.* stretcher (for canvas), *Theat.* wing; *Mech.* underframe; chassis, carriage; frame (of a window). *Fig.* **entre bastidores**, behind the scenes

bastilla /bas'tiʎa; bas'tiya/ *f*, *Sew.* hem; bastille

bastimentar /bastimen'tar/ *vt* to provision; supply

bastimento /basti'mento/ *m*, supplies; provisioning

bastión /bas'tion/ *m*, bastion

basto /'basto/ *m*, pack-saddle; ace of clubs; clubs (cards) —*a* rude; tough; *Fig.* unpolished, rough

bastón /bas'ton/ *m*, cane, walking-stick; rod (of office); truncheon. **b. de junquillo**, Malacca cane. **empuñar el b.**, to take control, take over. **meter el b.**, to mediate

basura /ba'sura/ *f*, rubbish, refuse; dung; sweepings

basurero /basu'rero/ *m*, dustman; dunghill, rubbish dump; kitchen middens; dust-bin

bata /'bata/ *f*, dressing-gown; smoking-jacket; old-fashioned dress; overall, smock

batacazo /bata'kaθo; bata'kaso/ *m*, bump, noise of a fall; *Polit.* dark horse

batahola /bata'ola/ *f*, *Inf.* hurly-burly, hubbub

batalla /ba'taʎa; ba'taya/ *f*, battle; *Fig.* struggle, conflict; tournament; *Art.* battle-piece. **b. campal**, pitched battle

batallador /bataʎa'δor; bataya'δor/ *a* fighting, warlike

batallar /bata'ʎar; bata'yar/ *vi* to battle, fight; dispute, argue; hesitate

batallón /bata'ʎon; bata'yon/ *m*, battalion

batanero /bata'nero/ *m*, fuller

batata /ba'tata/ *f*, sweet potato

batea /ba'tea/ *f*, wooden tray; punt

batería /bate'ria/ *f*, (*Mil. Elec. Naut.*) battery. **b. de cocina**, kitchen utensils. **b. de pilas secas**, dry battery. **b. de teatro**, stage lights. **b. eléctrica**, electric battery

batida /ba'tiða/ *f*, game drive; attack; *Metall.* beating

batido /ba'tiðo/ *a* beaten (of metals); shot (of silk); trodden, worn (roads, etc.). *m*, *Cul.* batter; hunting party

batidor /bati'ðor/ *m*, beater; scout; outrider; hair comb; *Cul.* whisk. **b. de oro** (*or* **de plata**), gold (*or* silver) beater

batiente /ba'tiente/ *m*, jamb (of door, etc.); damper (piano); leaf (of door); place where sea beats against cliffs, etc.

batihoja /bati'oha/ *m*, gold beater; metal worker

batimiento /bati'miento/ *m*, beating

batín /ba'tin/ *m*, smoking-jacket; man's dressing-gown

batir /ba'tir/ *vt* to beat, slap; demolish; dismantle, take down (stall, etc.); hammer, flatten; batter; *Fig.* beat (of sun, etc.); stir; pound; churn; comb (hair); vanquish, defeat; coin; reconnoiter, beat; throw down or drop; —*vr* fight; swoop (birds of prey). **b. palmas**, to clap, applaud

batista /ba'tista/ *f*, cambric, batiste

baturrillo /batu'rriʎo; batu'rriyo/ *m*, hotchpotch (gen. food); *Inf.* farrago, medley

batuta /ba'tuta/ *f*, baton, conductor's wand. **llevar la b.**, *Inf.* boss the show, call the music; be in charge, to rule the roost

baúl /ba'ul/ *m*, trunk; *Inf.* belly. **b. escaparate** *or* **b. mundo**, wardrobe trunk

bausán /bau'san/ **(-ana)** *n* guy, strawman; puppet; fool, idiot; lazybones

bautismo /bau'tismo/ *m*, baptism

bautista /bau'tista/ *m*, baptizer, baptist. **San Juan B.**, St. John the Baptist

bautisterio /bautis'terio/ *m*, baptistery

bautizar /bauti'θar; bauti'sar/ *vt* to baptize, christen; *Inf.* nickname; *Inf.* water (wine); accidentally shower with water

bautizo /bau'tiθo; bau'tiso/ *m*, baptism; christening party

baya /'baia/ *f*, berry

bayeta /ba'yeta/ *f*, baize; flannel

bayo /'bayo/ **(-ya)** *a* bay (of horses)

bayoneta /bayo'neta/ *f*, bayonet. **b. calada**, fixed bayonet

bayonetazo /bayone'taθo; bayone'taso/ *m*, bayonet thrust

baza /'baθa; 'basa/ *f*, tricks taken (playing cards). *Fig. Inf.* **meter b.**, to stick one's oar in

bazar /ba'θar; ba'sar/ *m*, bazaar; shop, store; department store

bazo /'baθo; 'baso/ *m*, *Anat.* spleen —*a* yellow-brown

bazucar, bazuquear /baθu'kar, baθuke'ar; basu'kar, basuke'ar/ *vt* to shake or stir (liquids)

bazuqueo /baθu'keo; basu'keo/ *m*, shaking or stirring of liquids

be /be/ *f*, letter B. *m*, baa

beata /be'ata/ *f*, devout woman; *Inf.* pious hypocrite, prude; Sister of Mercy; over-religious woman

beatería /beate'ria/ *f*, sanctimoniousness; bigotry

beatificación /beatifika'θion; beatifika'sion/ *f*, beatification

beatificar /beatifi'kar/ *vt* to make happy; sanctify; beatify

beatitud /beati'tuð/ *f*, blessedness, beatitude; happiness

beato /be'ato/ **(-ta)** *a* happy; blessed, beatified; devout; prudish —*n* devout person; over-pious person

bebé /be'βe/ *m*, baby

bebedero /beβe'ðero/ *a* drinkable. *m*, drinking trough or place

bebedizo /beβe'ðiθo; beβe'ðiso/ *a* drinkable. *m*, draught of medicine; love-potion; poisonous drink

bebedor /beβe'ðor/ **(-ra)** *a* drinkable —*n* drinker; toper

beber /be'βer/ *vt* to drink; absorb; —*vi* toast, drink to the health (of); tipple. *m*, drinking; drink

bebida /be'βiða/ *f*, drink; beverage; alcoholic liquor

beca /'beka/ *f*, academic scarf or sash; scholarship, exhibition

becado, becario /be'kaðo, be'kario/ *m*, exhibitioner, scholarship holder

becerro /be'θerro; be'serro/ *m*, bullock; bull calf; calf-skin. **b. marino**, *Zool.* seal

bedel /be'ðel/ *m*, beadle; servitor, university porter

befar /be'far/ *vt* to mock, ridicule

befo /'befo/ *a* thick-lipped; knock-kneed. *m*, animal's lip

bejín /be'hin/ *m*, *Bot.* puff-ball; spoiled child

beldad /bel'dað/ *f*, beauty; belle

beldar /bel'dar/ *vt* *Agr.* to winnow

Belén /be'len/ Bethlehem

belén /be'len/ *m*, nativity, manager; *Inf.* bedlam; *Inf.* gossip

belfo /'belfo/ *a* thick-lipped

belga /'belga/ *a* and *mf* Belgian

Bélgica /'belhika/ Belgium

bélgico /'belhiko/ *a* Belgian

Belice /be'liθe; be'lise/ Belize

belicista /beli'θista; beli'sista/ *adj* war, militaristic; *mf* warmonger

bélico /'beliko/ *a* warlike, military

belicosidad /belikosi'ðað/ *f*, bellicosity

belicoso /beli'koso/ *a* bellicose, aggressive; warlike

beligerancia /belihe'ranθia; belihe'ransia/ f, belligerency

beligerante /belihe'rante/ a and mf belligerent

belitre /be'litre/ a Inf. knavish, cunning

bellaco /be'ʎako; be'yako/ **(-ca)** a artful, cunning —n knave

bellaquería /beʎake'ria; beyake'ria/ f, roguery, knavery, cunning

bellasombra /beʎa'sombra; beya'sombra/ f, umbra tree

belleza /be'ʎeθa; be'yesa/ f, beauty, loveliness, fairness

bello /'beʎo; 'beyo/ a beautiful

bellota /be'ʎota; be'yota/ f, acorn; carnation bud; ornamental button, knob

bemol /be'mol/ a and m, Mus. flat. Inf. **tener bemoles,** to be thorny, be difficult

bencina /ben'θina; ben'sina/ f, benzine; gasoline

bendecir /bende'θir, bendo'oir/ vt irr to praise, extol; bless; dedicate, consecrate. See **decir**

bendición /bendi'θion; bendi'sion/ f, benediction; blessing; consecration; pl marriage ceremony. **b. de la mesa,** grace before meals

bendito /ben'dito/ a holy, blessed; fortunate; simple. **ser un b.,** to be a simpleton; be a good soul. **¡Benditos los ojos que te ven!** It's so nice to see you!

beneficencia /benefi'θenθia; benefi-'sensia/ f, beneficence; charitable institutions

beneficiación /benefiθia'θion; benefisia-'sion/ f, benefaction

beneficiado /benefi'θiaðo; benefi'siaðo/ **(-da)** n beneficiary. m, incumbent of a benefice

beneficiador /benefiθia'ðor; benefisia-'ðor/ **(-ra)** n benefactor

beneficiar /benefi'θiar; benefi'siar/ vt to benefit; improve; cultivate (land); exploit (mine); purchase (directorship, etc.); sell at a loss (bonds, etc.)

beneficiario /benefi'θiario; benefi'siario/ **(-ia)** n beneficiary

beneficiencia /benefi'θienθia; benefi-'siensia/ f, beneficence, charity

beneficio /bene'fiθio; bene'fisio/ m, benefit; profit; cultivation (land, etc.); working (mine); Eccl. benefice; Theat. benefit

beneficioso /benefi'θioso; benefi'sioso/ a beneficial; useful

benéfico /be'nefiko/ a beneficent; kind, helpful; charitable

benemérito /bene'merito/ a benemeritus, worthy, meritorious

beneplácito /bene'plaθito; bene'plasito/ m, approbation; consent

benevolencia /beneβo'lenθia; beneβo'lensia/ f, benevolence, goodwill

benévolo /be'neβolo/ a benevolent, kind

benignidad /benigni'ðað/ f, kindness; mildness (of the weather, etc.)

benigno /be'nigno/ a kind; benign; mild; balmy

beodo /be'oðo/ **(-da)** a drunk, intoxicated —n drunkard

berenjena /beren'hena/ f, eggplant

bergante /ber'gante/ m, rascal, rogue

Berlín /ber'lin/ Berlin

berlinés /ber'lines/ **(-esa)** a and n of or from Berlin

bermejear /bermehe'ar/ vi to be or look reddish

bermejo /ber'meho/ a reddish; red; red-gold; carroty (of hair)

bermellón /berme'ʎon; berme'yon/ m, vermilion

Berna /'berna/ Berne

bernardina /bernar'ðina/ f, lie; boast; gibberish

bernardo /ber'narðo/ **(-da)** a and n Eccl. Bernardine (Order of St. Bernard)

berquelio /ber'kelio/ m, berkelium

berrear /berre'ar/ vi to low, bellow; yell, squall; shriek; —vr reveal, confess

berrido /be'rriðo/ m, lowing, bellowing, Inf. yell

berrinche /be'rrintʃe/ m, Inf. tantrum, fit, fit of sulks

berro /'berro/ m, watercress

berroqueña /berro'keɲa/ f, granite

berza /'berθa; 'bersa/ f, cabbage

besamanos /besa'manos/ m, ceremony of kissing royal hand, levee; kissing fingers (in salute)

besar /be'sar/ vt to kiss; Inf. brush against, touch (of things); —vr kiss one another; Inf. bang into, knock against one another

beso /'beso/ m, kiss; knock, collision

bestia /'bestia/ f, quadruped (especially horses or mules); beast. mf Inf. nasty piece of work. **b. de carga,** beast of burden. **como una b.,** like a dog (e.g. Trabajo como una b. I work like a dog)

bestial /bes'tial/ a bestial; brutal; beastly

bestialidad /bestiali'ðað/ f, brutality; bestiality; beastliness

bestialismo /bestia'lismo/ m, bestiality (sexual orientation)

besuquear /besuke'ar/ vt Inf. to cover with kisses; —vr Inf. spoon, make love

besuqueo /besu'keo/ m, Inf. kissing and spooning

betún /be'tun/ m, bitumen; shoe blacking; kind of cement. **b. de Judea** or **b. judaico,** asphalt

bezo /'beθo; 'beso/ m, blubber lip; proud flesh (of a wound)

bezudo /be'θuðo; be'suðo/ a thick-lipped

biberón /biβe'ron/ m, feeding bottle

Biblia /'biβlia/ f, Bible

bíblico /'biβliko/ a biblical

bibliófilo /biβli'ofilo/ m, bibliophile

bibliografía /biβliogra'fia/ f, bibliography

bibliográfico /biβlio'grafiko/ a bibliographical

biblioteca /biβlio'teka/ f, library; book series. **b. por subscripción,** circulating library

bibliotecario /biβliote'kario/ **(-ia)** n librarian

bibliotecnia, bibliotecología, biblioteconomía /biβlio'teknia, biβlioteko'lohia, biβliotekono'mia/ f, library science

bicarbonato /bikarβo'nato/ m, bicarbonate

bíceps /'biθeps; 'biseps/ m, biceps

bicho /'bitʃo/ m, any small animal or reptile; quadruped; fighting bull; scarecrow, sight. **b. viviente,** Inf. living soul. **mal b.,** rogue

bicicleta /biθi'kleta; bisi'kleta/ f, bicycle, bike. **ir** (or **andar** or **montar**) **en b.,** to bicycle, bike, go by bicycle, go by bike

bicoca /bi'koka/ f, Inf. trifle, bagatelle

bicolor /biko'lor/ a bicolored

bidé /bi'ðe/ m, bidet

bien /bien/ m, ideal goodness, perfection; benefit, advantage; welfare; pl property, wealth —adv well; willingly; happily; perfectly; easily; enough, sufficient; all right! very well! **b. que,** although. **b. de equipo,** capital good. **bienes muebles,** movables, goods and chattels. **bienes raíces,** real estate. **el B. y el Mal,** Good and Evil. **¡Está b.!** All right! **no b.,** scarcely, as soon as. **si b.,** although, even if. **¿Y b.?** And so what? Well, then; What next?

bienal /bie'nal/ a biennial

bienamado /biena'maðo/ a dearly beloved

bienandante /bienan'dante/ a prosperous; happy

bienandanza /bienan'danθa; bienan'dansa/ f, happiness, welfare; prosperity

bienaventurado /bienaβentu'raðo/ a blessed, holy; happy; Inf. over-simple, innocent, foolish

bienaventuranza /bienaβentu'ranθa; bienaβentu'ransa/ f, blessedness

bienestar /bienes'tar/ m, wellbeing; ease; comfort

bienhablado /biena'βlaðo/ a wellspoken; civil, polite

bienhadado /biena'ðaðo/ a fortunate, happy

bienhechor /biene'tʃor/ **(-ra)** a kind, helpful —n benefactor

bienintencionado /bienintenθio'naðo; bienintensio'naðo/ a well-meaning

bienio /'bienio/ m, biennium, space of two years, period of two years

bienquisto /bien'kisto/ a respected; generally esteemed

bienvenida /biembe'niða/ f, safe or happy arrival; welcome. **dar la b.,** to welcome

bienvivir /biembi'βir/ vi to live comfortably; live decently or uprightly

bies /bies/ m, bias, cross; slant

biftec /bif'tek/ m, beefsteak

bifurcación /bifurka'θion; bifurka'sion/ f, bifurcation; fork, branch, junction

bifurcarse /bifur'karse/ vr to fork, branch

bigamia /bi'gamia/ f, bigamy

bígamo /'bigamo/ **(-ma)** a bigamous —n bigamist

bigote /bi'gote/ m, moustache; pl whiskers

bigotudo /bigo'tuðo/ a moustached, whiskered

bikini /bi'kini/ m, bikini

bilateral /bilate'ral/ a bilateral

bilingüe /bi'lingue/ a bilingual

bilioso /bi'lioso/ a bilious

bilis /'bilis/ f, bile

billar /bi'ʎar; bi'yar/ m, billiards; billiard table

billete /bi'ʎete; bi'yete/ m, note, short letter; ticket; banknote. **b. circular,** excursion ticket. **b. de abono,** season ticket. **b. de andén,** platform ticket. **b. de banco,** banknote. **b. de favor,** free ticket. **b. de ida y vuelta,** round trip ticket. **b. entero,** full fare. **b. kilométrico,** tourist ticket. **b. sencillo,** oneway. **medio b.,** half-fare

billón /bi'ʎon; bi'yon/ m, billion

bimestral /bimes'tral/ a bimonthly

bimestre /bi'mestre/ a bimonthly. m, two months' duration; money paid or received at two-monthly intervals

bimotor /bimo'tor/ a two-motor. m, twin-engined aircraft

binario /bi'nario/ a binary

binóculo /bi'nokulo/ m, opera glasses

binomio /bi'nomio/ a and m, binomial

biodiversidad f, biodiversity

biofísica /bio'fisika/ f, biophysics

biografía /biogra'fia/ f, biography

biográfico /bio'grafiko/ a biographical

biógrafo /'biografo/ **(-fa)** n biographer; (Chile) movie theater (e.g. ¡Vamos al biógrafo! Let's go to the movies!)

biología /biolo'hia/ f, biology

biológico /bio'lohiko/ a biological

biólogo /'biologo/ m, biologist

biombo /'biombo/ m, screen

bioquímica /bio'kimika/ f, biochemistry

bioquímico /bio'kimiko/ m, biochemist

bipartido /bipar'tiðo/ a bipartite

biplano /bi'plano/ m, biplane

biplaza /bi'plaθa; biplasa/ a two-seater

birlar /bir'lar/ vt to bowl from where the bowl stopped; Inf. knock down; snatch away; Inf. rob

Birmania /bir'mania/ Burma

birmano /bir'mano/ **(-na)** a and n Burmese

bis /bis/ adv twice; repeat; encore —a duplicate; **B** (in addresses, e.g., Calle de Alcalá 18bis, 18b Alcalá St.)

bisabuela /bisa'βuela/ f, greatgrandmother

bisabuelo /bisa'βuelo/ m, greatgrandfather

bisagra /bi'sagra/ f, hinge; shoemaker's polisher

bisbís /bis'βis/ m, game of chance

bisbisar /bisβi'sar/ *vt Inf.* to mutter; whisper

bisbiseo /bisβi'seo/ *m, Inf.* muttering; murmuring; whispering

bisecar /bise'kar/ *vt* to bisect

bisectriz /bisek'triθ; bisek'tris/ *f*, bisector

bisel /bi'sel/ *m*, bevel, chamfer

bisiesto /bi'siesto/ *a* leap and *m*, leap (year)

bisnieto /bis'nieto/ **(-ta)** *n* great-grandchild

bisonte /bi'sonte/ *m*, bison

bisoño /bi'soɲo/ **(-ña)** *a* inexperienced, raw —*n* recruit; *Inf.* greenhorn

bistec /bis'tek/ *m*, beef steak

bisturí /bistu'ri/ *m*, surgical knife

bisunto /bi'sunto/ *a* grubby, greasy

bisutería /bisute'ria/ *f*, imitation jewelry

bizantino /biθan'tino; bisan'tino/ *a* Byzantine

bizarría /biθa'rria; bisa'rria/ *f*, handsomeness; dash; verve; gallantry, courage; magnificence; liberality; whim, caprice

bizarro /bi'θarro; bi'sarro/ *a* handsome; dashing; gallant, courageous; liberal; splendid, magnificent

bizco /'biθko; 'bisko/ *a* squint-eyed, cross-eyed

bizcocho /biθ'kotʃo; bis'kotʃo/ *m*, biscuit; spongecake; bisque

bizma /'biθma; 'bisma/ *f*, poultice. **poner bizmas**, to poultice

biznieto /biθ'nieto; bis'nieto/ *n* See **bisnieto**

blanca /'blanka/ *f*, old Spanish coin; *Inf.* penny; *Mus.* minim. **sin b.**, penniless

blanco /'blanko/ *a* white; fair-skinned; blank, vacant; *Inf.* cowardly. *m*, target; blank left in writing; white person; interval. **b. de España**, whiting. **b. de la uña**, half-moon of the nail. **dar en el b.**, to hit the mark. **en b.**, blank, unused; *Inf.* in vain; uncomprehendingly; (of nights) sleepless

blancor, /blan'kor,/ *m.* **blancura** *f*, whiteness; fairness (of skin)

blandear /blande'ar/ *vt* to moderate, soothe; brandish; —*vi Fig.* give way, yield

blandir /blan'dir/ *vt* to brandish, wield, flourish

blando /'blando/ *a* soft; mild (weather); delicate; kind; peaceable; delicate, effeminate; *Inf.* cowardly

blandón /blan'don/ *m*, wax taper

blandura /blan'dura/ *f*, softness; poultice; blandishment, compliment; mildness (of weather); gentleness, affability; luxury

blanquear /blanke'ar/ *vt* to bleach; whitewash; whiten; —*vi* appear white; show white

blanquecino /blanke'θino; blanke'sino/ *a* whitish

blanqueo /blan'keo/ *m*, whitening; whitewashing; bleaching

blasfemador /blasfema'ðor/ **(-ra)** *a* blaspheming —*n* blasphemer

blasfemar /blasfe'mar/ *vi* to blaspheme; curse, swear

blasfemia /blas'femia/ *f*, blasphemy; insult

blasfemo /blas'femo/ **(-ma)** *n* blasphemer —*a* blasphemous

blasón /bla'son/ *m*, heraldry; escutcheon; glory, honor. **una familia con antiguos blasones**, a family of ancient lineage

blasonar /blaso'nar/ *vt* to blazon; —*vi* boast, brag, blazon abroad

bledo /'bleðo/ *m*, blade, leaf. **no importar un b.**, not to matter a straw

blindado /blin'daðo/ *a Nav.* armored, ironclad

blindaje /blin'dahe/ *m, Nav.* armor-plating; *Mil.* blindage

blindar /blin'dar/ *vt* to plate with armor, to case with steel

blondo /'blondo/ *a* fair, blond, flaxen-haired

bloque /'bloke/ *m*, block, slab

bloquear /bloke'ar/ *vt* to blockade; besiege

bloqueo /blo'keo/ *m*, blockade; siege; blocking; freezing (of assets). **violar el b.**, to run the blockade

blusa /'blusa/ *f*, blouse

boa /'boa/ *f*, boa, large snake. *m*, boa (fur)

boato /bo'ato/ *m*, outward show, ostentation

bobería /boβe'ria/ *f*, foolishness, stupidity

bóbilis, bóbilis /'boβilis, 'boβilis/ **(de)** *adv Inf.* free of charge; without effort

bobina /bo'βina/ *f*, bobbin, spool, reel; *Elec.* coil; spool (of fishing rod)

bobo /'boβo/ **(-ba)** *a* stupid, idiotic; simple, innocent —*n* fool. *m*, clown, jester

boca /'boka/ *f*, mouth; pincers (of crustaceans); entrance or exit; mouth (of a river); gulf, inlet; orifice, opening; muzzle (of guns); cutting edge (of tools); taste (of wine, etc.). **b. abajo**, face down, prone. **b. arriba**, on one's back, face up, supine. **b. del estómago**, pit of the stomach. **b. rasgada**, large mouth. **a b.**, verbally. **a b. de jarro**, point-blank. **a pedir de b.**, just as one would wish. **de b.**, by word of mouth. *Inf.* **sin decir esta b. es mía**, without a word, in silence

bocacalle /boka'kaʎe; boka'kaye/ *f*, entrance (to a street); street junction

bocadillo /boka'ðiʎo; boka'ðiyo/ *m*, narrow ribbon; sandwich

bocado /bo'kaðo/ *m*, mouthful. **b. de reyes**, delicacy, exquisite dish (of food); snack; bite; (horse's) bit; bridle; *pl* preserved fruit cut up

bocamanga /boka'manga/ *f*, wrist (of sleeve)

bocanada /boka'naða/ *f*, mouthful (of liquid); cloud (of smoke). **b. de aire**, gust of wind

boceto /bo'θeto; bo'seto/ *m*, sketch; outline; rough-cast model

bocha /'botʃa/ f, *Sports.* bowl; *pl* bowls

bochorno /bo'tʃorno/ m, sultry weather; heat, stuffiness; blush, hot flush; shame

bochornoso /botʃor'noso/ a sultry; shameful

bocina /bo'θina; bo'sina/ f, trumpet; megaphone; foghorn; hooter; *Auto.* horn; horn (of gramophone); *Astron.* Ursa Minor

bocio /'boθio; 'bosio/ m, *Med.* goiter

boda /'boða/ f, wedding, marriage. **bodas de oro,** fiftieth (golden) anniversary. **bodas de plata,** silver wedding anniversary

bodega /bo'ðega/ f, wine-cellar; storeroom; stockroom; granary; *West Hem.* grocery store; *Naut.* hold (of ship)

bodegón /boðe'gon/ m, eating-house; tavern; *Art.* still-life; genre picture

bofes /'bofes/ m pl, lungs, lights. *Inf.* **echar los b.,** to work oneself to death

bofetada /bofe'taða/ f. **bofetón** m, blow, slap; box on the ear

boga /'boga/ f, rowing; fashion, vogue; *Mech.* bogie. mf oarsman, rower. **estar en b.,** to be fashionable

bogador /boga'ðor/ **(-ra)** n rower, oarsman

bogar /bo'gar/ vi to row

bogavante /boga'βante/ m, lobster

bohemio /bo'emio/ **(-ia)** a and n gipsy; bohemian; Bohemian. m, archer's short cloak

boicot, boicoteo /boi'kot, boiko'teo/ m, boycott

boicotear /boikote'ar/ vt to boycott

boina /'boina/ f, Basque cap; beret

boj /box/ m, box tree; boxwood, box oak; shoemaker's tool

bola /'bola/ f, globe; ball; *Sports.* bowl; *Archit.* balloon; *Inf.* trick, lie; (Cuba) rumor. **b. de nieves,** snowball. *Inf.* **dejar rodar la b.,** to let things slide

bolea /bo'lea/ f, (tennis) volley; throw

bolera /bo'lera/ f, bowling alley

bolero /bo'lero/ m, bolero; dancer; *Inf.* top hat

boleta /bo'leta/ f, admission ticket; billet ticket; warrant, voucher; summons, ticket, traffic ticket

boletín /bole'tin/ m, bulletin; admission ticket; pay warrant; *Com.* price list; learned periodical. **b. de noticias,** news bulletin. **b. meteorológico,** weather report

boliche /bo'litʃe/ m, jack (in bowls); cup-and-ball toy; small oven (for charcoal); dragnet. **juego de b.,** bowls

bólido /'boliðo/ m, *Astron.* bolide, meteor

boliviano /boli'βiano/ **(-na)** a and n Bolivian. m, silver coin

bollo /'boʎo; 'boyo/ m, bread roll; bun; bulge, bruise (in metal); *Med.* lump

bollón /bo'ʎon; bo'yon/ m, round-headed or brass-headed nail; *Bot.* bud (especially vines)

bolo /'bolo/ m, skittle, ninepin; pillow (for lace making); Cuban coin; *Med.* large pill; *Fig. Inf.* blockhead; *pl* skittles (game of)

bolsa /'bolsa/ f, purse; bag; footmuff; fold, pucker; pouch; exchange, stock exchange, capital, money; prize money; *Med.* sac; *Mineral.* pocket. **b. de estudio,** scholarship grant. **b. de trabajo,** labor exchange. **b. de valores,** stock exchange. **bajar** (or **subir**) **la b.,** to fall (or rise) (of stock exchange quotations). **jugar a la b.,** to speculate on the stock exchange

bolsillo /bol'siʎo; bol'siyo/ m, pocket; purse; money

bolsista /bol'sista/ mf stock-broker; speculator (on the stock exchange)

bomba /'bomba/ f, *Mech.* pump; pumping engine; bomb; *Mil.* shell; lamp globe; *Inf.* improvised verses; *Inf.* drinking bout. **¡B.!** Listen! Here goes! **b. de incendios,** fire-engine. **b. marina,** waterspout. **b. de mecha atrasada,** time bomb. **b. volante,** flying-bomb. **a prueba de b.,** bombproof. **arrojar bombas,** to bomb. *Inf.* **caer como una b.,** to be a bombshell

bombachos /bom'βatʃos/ a baggy, loosefitting; m pl, plus fours

bombardear /bombarðe'ar/ vt to bombard; bomb; shell

bombardeo /bombar'ðeo/ m, bombardment, bombing; shelling

bombástico /bom'βastiko/ a bombastic, high sounding

bombazo /bom'βaθo; bom'βaso/ m, bombshell; bomb crater; noise of an exploding bomb

bombear /bombe'ar/ vt to pump; bombard, shell; praise

bombero /bom'βero/ m, worker of a pressure pump; fireman; mortar, howitzer

bombilla /bom'βiʎa; bom'βiya/ f, *Naut.* lantern; (*Elec. Phys.*) bulb; small pump; straw for drinking maté *West Hem.*

bombillo /bom'βiʎo; bom'βiyo/ m, w.c. siphon; handpump

bombo /'bombo/ m, big drum or player of it; *Naut.* barge, ferry; ballot box; exaggerated praise

bombón /bom'βon/ m, bonbon, sweet

bombonera /bombo'nera/ f, box for toffee, etc.

bonachón /bona'tʃon/ a *Inf.* genial, good-natured

bonaerense /bonae'rense/ a and mf of or from the Province of Buenos Aires

bonancible /bonan'θiβle; bonan'siβle/ a calm (of weather, sea)

bonanza /bo'nanθa; bo'nansa/ f, fair weather; prosperity

bondad /bon'dað/ f, goodness; kindness, helpfulness. **Tenga la b. de...,** Be good enough to..., Please...

bondadoso /bonda'ðoso/ a good, kind

bonete /bo'nete/ m, academic cap; *Zool.* reticulum (ruminants); *Eccl.* biretta. **gran b.,** important person. *Inf.* **a tente b.,** insistently

bonificación /bonifika'θion; bonifika'sion/ f, bonus; allowance, discount

bonito /bo'nito/ *a* pretty; graceful; (ironical) fine. *m*, *Ichth.* bonito

bono /'bono/ *m*, voucher; *Com.* bond, certificate. **b. postal**, postal money order. **bono del gobierno**, government bond

boñiga /bo'ɲiɣa/ *f*, cow-dung, animal manure

boqueada /boke'aða/ *f*, gasp, opening of the mouth. **dar las boqueadas, estar en las últimas boqueadas**, to be at the last gasp

boquear /boke'ar/ *vi* to gasp; be dying; *Inf.* be at last gasp (of things); —*vt* say, utter

boquerón /boke'ron/ *m*, large opening; *Ichth.* anchovy (fish); whitebait

boquete /bo'kete/ *m*, narrow entrance, aperture; gap, breach; hole

boquiabierto /bokia'βierto/ *a* open-mouthed; amazed

boquiancho /bo'kiantʃo/ *a* wide-mouthed

boquilla /bo'kiʎa; bo'kiya/ *f*, *dim* small mouth; mouthpiece (of wind instruments, etc.); cigar- or cigarette-holder; gas-burner; nozzle; tip (of cigarettes)

boquirroto /boki'rroto/ *a Inf.* loquacious, indiscreet

borbollar /borβo'ʎar; borβo'yar/ *vi* to bubble, foam, froth

borbollón, borbotón /borβo'ʎon, borβo'ton; borβo'yon, borβo'ton/ *m*, gushing, bubbling, welling up. **a borbollones**, in a torrent; hastily, impetuously

borbotar /borβo'tar/ *vi* to gush out, well up

bordado /bor'ðaðo/ *m*, embroidery

bordador /borða'nðor/ **(-ra)** *n* embroiderer

bordar /bor'ðar/ *vt* to embroider; *Fig.* perform perfectly

borde /'borðe/ *m*, edge; fringe; verge; rim; mount (of a picture); brim (of a hat); side (of ship) —*a* wild (of plants); illegitimate. **estar lleno hasta los bordes**, to be full to the brim

bordear /borðe'ar/ *vt* to border, trim with a bordear; line (a street, e.g. *Diez mil personas bordearon las calles durante el desfile*, Ten thousand people lined the streets during the parade)

bordillo /bor'ðiʎo; bor'ðiyo/ *m*, curbstone, curb.

bordo /'borðo/ *m*, side (of ships); border, edge. **a b.**, on board

bordón /bor'ðon/ *m*, pilgrim's staff; monotonous repetition; refrain; *Mus.* bass string; *Fig.* guide, stay

borgoña /bor'goɲa/ *m*, Burgundy wine

bórico /'boriko/ *a* boric

borla /'borla/ *f*, tassel; puff (for powder). *Fig.* **tomar la b.**, to take one's doctorate, graduate

bornear /borne'ar/ *vt* to bend, twist; *Archit.* hoist into position; —*vr* warp (wood)

borra /'borra/ *f*, yearling ewe; thickest wool; wad-stuffing; lees, sediment; fluff, dust; *Inf.* trash. **b. de algodón**, cotton-waste

borrachera /borra'tʃera/ *f*, drunkenness; orgy, carousal; *Inf.* blunder

borrachín /borra'tʃin/ **(-ina)** *n* tippler, toper

borrachito /borra'tʃito/ *a* high (on liquor), tipsy

borracho /bo'rratʃo/ **(de)** *a* drunk (on), intoxicated (with); *Inf.* blind (with rage, etc.) —*n* tippler, drunkard

borrador /borra'ðor/ *m*, rough draft. **en borrador**, in the works (e.g. *Tiene dos ensayos en borrador*, She has two essays in the works). **estar en borrador**, to be in the works

borradura /borra'ðura/ *f*, erasure

borrajear /borrahe'ar/ *vt* to scribble

borrar /bo'rrar/ *vt* to erase; cross out; blot out; *Fig.* obliterate

borrasca /bo'rraska/ *f*, storm, tempest; peril, danger; *Inf.* orgy

borrascoso /borras'koso/ *a* stormy; disordered, turbulent

borrego /bo'rrego/ **(-ga)** *n* lamb; *Inf.* nincompoop, simpleton; *m pl*, fleecy clouds; white horses (waves)

borrico /bo'rriko/ **(-ca)** *n* donkey; fool. *m*, sawing-horse

borrón /bo'rron/ *m*, blot; rough draft; defect; *Fig.* stigma

borroso /bo'rroso/ *a* blurred, indistinct; full of dregs, muddy

bosque /'boske/ *m*, wood, forest

bosquejar /boske'har/ *vt Art.* to sketch; sketch out, draft; model in rough (sculpture); outline

bosquejo /bos'keho/ *m*, outline, sketch; rough plan or idea; unfinished work. **en bosquejo**, grosso modo

bostar /bos'tar/ *m*, ox barn

bostezar /boste'θar; boste'sar/ *vi* to yawn

bostezo /bos'teθo; bos'teso/ *m*, yawning, yawn

bota /'bota/ *f*, small wineskin; barrel; butt; boot. **b. de montar**, riding boot. **botas de campaña**, top-boots. **botas de vadear**, waders

botada, botadura /bo'taða, bota'ðura/ *f*, launching (of a ship)

botador /bota'ðor/ *m*, thrower; boating-pole; nail-puller

botánica /bo'tanika/ *f*, botany

botánico /bo'taniko/ **(-ca)** *a* botanical —*n* botanist

botar /bo'tar/ *vt* to fling; launch (boat); *Naut.* shift the helm; —*vi* jump; bounce, rebound; rear, prance (horses)

botarate /bota'rate/ *m*, *Inf.* madcap, devil-may-care

botarel, botarete /bota'rel, bota'rete/ *m*, *Archit.* abutment, buttress, flying buttress

bote /'bote/ *m*, thrust (with lance, etc.);

rearing (of horse); rebound; *Aer.* bump; open boat; small bottle, jar. **b. salvavidas,** lifeboat. *Inf.* **de b. en b.,** chockfull

botella /bo'teʎa/ bo'teya/ *f,* bottle; bottleful; flask

botica /bo'tika/ *f,* chemist's shop; medicines, remedies; physic; store, shop; medicine chest

boticario /boti'kario/ *m,* apothecary, chemist

botija /bo'tiha/ *f,* earthen jug; *Slang* chunky person

botijo /bo'tiho/ *m,* earthenware jar with spout and handle

botillería /botiʎe'ria/ botiye'ria/ *f,* ice-cream bar

botín /bo'tin/ *m,* gaiter; buskin; booty

botiquín /boti'kin/ *m,* first-aid kit; medicine chest

botón /bo'ton/ *m,* bud; button; knob, handle; switch (electric); press button (bell); *Bot.* center; button (on a foil); *Mech.* stud

bóveda /b'oβeða/ *f, Archit.* vault, arch; crypt; cavern. **b. celeste,** sky

boxeador /boksea'ðor/ *m,* boxer

boxear /bokse'ar/ *vi Sports.* to box

boxeo /bok'seo/ *m, Sports.* boxing

boya /'boya/ *f, Naut.* buoy; float

boyante /bo'yante/ *a* floating; light, buoyant; prosperous

boyar /bo'yar/ *vi Naut.* to float

boyero /bo'yero/ *m,* cowherd

boza /'boθa; 'bosa/ *f,* painter (of a boat)

bozal /bo'θal; bo'sal/ *m,* muzzle; nosebag; harness bells. *mf Inf.* greenhorn; —*a* wild, untamed (horses)

bozo /'boθo; 'boso/ *m,* down which precedes beard; muzzle; headstall; lips, snout

bracero /bra'θero; bra'sero/ *m,* one who offers his arm (to a lady); day laborer; strong man. **de b.,** arm-in-arm

bracete /bra'θete; bra'sete/ *m,* small arm. **de b.,** arm-in-arm

braga /'braga/ *f,* (gen. *pl*) breeches; knickerbockers; hoist or pulley rope

bragazas /bra'gaθas; bra'gasas/ *m, Inf.* weak-willed, fellow, soft specimen

braguero /bra'gero/ *m, Med.* truss

bragueta /bra'geta/ *f,* fly (of breeches)

bramante /bra'mante/ *a* roaring. *m,* twine, pack-thread

bramar /bra'mar/ *vi* to roar; rage; *Fig.* howl (of the wind, etc.)

bramido /bra'miðo/ *m,* bellowing; roaring; yell of rage; *Fig.* howling (wind, sea, etc.)

brancada /bran'kaða/ *f,* drag net

branquia /'brankia/ *f,* (gen. *pl*) *Ichth.* gill

brasa /'brasa/ *f,* live coal. **estar como en brasas,** to be like a cat on hot bricks

brasero /bra'sero/ *m,* brazier

Brasil /bra'sil/ Brazil

brasileño /brasi'leɲo/ **(-ña)** *a* and *n* Brazilian

bravata /bra'βata/ *f,* bravado; threat

braveza /bra'βeθa; bra'βesa/ *f,* ferocity, savageness; valor; violence, fury (of elements)

bravío /bra'βio/ *a* savage, untamed; wild (plants); uncultured

bravo /'braβo/ *a* valiant; surly, rude; independent, strong-minded, good, excellent; savage (animals); stormy (sea); rough, rugged; violent, angry; *Inf.* sumptuous, magnificent

bravura /bra'βura/ *f,* ferocity (animals); courage (persons); boastful threat

braza /'braθa; 'brasa/ *f, Naut.* fathom; stroke (in swimming)

brazado /bra'θaðo; bra'saðo/ *m,* armful

brazal /bra'θal; bra'sal/ *m,* armlet, brassard

brazalete /braθa'lete; brasa'lete/ *m,* bracelet; brassard

brazo /'braθo; 'braso/ *m,* arm; upper arm; front paw; *Mech.* arm; branch (of chandelier, etc.); bough; arm (of chair); power, courage; *pl* protectors; workmen, hands. **b. de mar,** firth, arm of the sea. **a b. partido,** in unarmed fight, man to man. **con los brazos abiertos,** welcomingly; willingly, gladly. **dar los brazos (a),** to embrace. *Inf.* **hecho un b. de mar,** dressed up to the nines

brea /'brea/ *f,* pitch, tar; sacking, canvas

brebaje /bre'βahe/ *m,* beverage; unpleasant drink; *Naut.* draft (of beer, grog, etc.)

brecha /'bretʃa/ *f, Mil.* breach; opening; *Fig.* impression (on mind). **morir en la b.,** to fight to the last ditch; die in harness

brécol /'brekol/ *m, Bot.* broccoli

brega /'brega/ *f,* fight; quarrel; disappointment, trick. **andar a la b.,** to work hard. **dar b.,** to play a trick

bregar /bre'gar/ *vi* to fight; work hard; *Fig.* struggle; **bregarse con,** to tackle (a problem)

breña /'breɲa/ *f,* rough ground, bramble patch

breñoso /bre'ɲoso/ *a* rugged, rocky

brete /'brete/ *m,* fetters, shackles; *Fig.* fix, squeeze, tight spot, tight squeeze (e.g. *Estoy en un brete.* I'm in a tight spot)

breva /'breβa/ *f,* early fig; early acorn; *Fig.* advantage, "plum"; *Inf.* peach (girl); *Inf.* windfall, piece of luck; Havana cigar

breve /'breβe/ *a* brief; concise. *m,* papal brief. *f, Mus.* breve. **en b.,** shortly, concisely; in a short while, soon

brevedad /breβe'ðað/ *f,* brevity

breviario /bre'βiario/ *m,* breviary

brezal /bre'θal; bre'sal/ *m,* heath, moor

brezo /'breθo; 'breso/ *m, Bot.* heath

bribón /bri'βon/ **(-ona)** *n* rogue, ruffian —*a* knavish, dishonest; lazy

bribonada /briβo'naða/ *f,* knavery, mischievous trick

bribonear /briβone'ar/ *vi* to idle; play tricks, be a rogue

bribonería /briβone'ria/ *f,* rascality, vagrant life

brida /'briða/ f, bridle

brigada /bri'gaða/ f, Mil. brigade; Naut. division of fleet; beasts of burden. **brigada millonaria,** (Castroist Cuba) team of thirty sugarcane cutters who cut a million or more arrobas in one harvest

brigadier /briga'ðier/ m, brigadier-general

brillante /bri'ʎante; bri'yante/ a sparkling, brilliant; Fig. outstanding. m, diamond

brillantez /briʎan'teθ; briyan'tes/ f, brightness, luster; fame; Fig. brilliance

brillantina /briʎan'tina; briyan'tina/ f, brilliantine

brillar /bri'ʎar; bri'yar/ vi to shine, sparkle, gleam, glisten; Fig. be brilliant or outstanding

brillo /'briʎo; 'briyo/ m, brilliancy, brightness, shine; fame, glory; distinction, brilliance, splendor

brincar /brin'kar/ vi to spring, leap, skip, frisk; Fig. Inf. skip, omit; Inf. grow angry; —vt jump a child up and down

brinco /'brinko/ m, leap, spring; skip, frolicking

brindar /brin'dar/ vi to invite, provoke (of things); (with prep a or por) drink the health of, toast; —vt and vi give, present; offer; —vr offer one's services

brindis /'brindis/ m, toast (drink)

brío /'brio/ m, vigor; spirit, courage; gusto, verve

brioso /'brioso/ a vigorous, enterprising; spirited, courageous; dashing, lively

briqueta /bri'keta/ f, briquette

brisa /'brisa/ f, breeze; grape pressings

británico /bri'taniko/ a British

brizna /'briθna; 'brisna/ f, shred, paring; blade (grass); filament, fiber; string (of bean-pod, etc.); splinter, chip

brocado /bro'kaðo/ m, brocade —a brocade or embroidered like brocade

brocal /bro'kal/ m, puteal (of a well); mouthpiece (of wineskin); metal ring (of sword-sheath)

brocha /'brotʃa/ f, brush. **b. de afeitar,** shaving brush. **de b. gorda,** crudely painted. **pintor de b. gorda,** decorator

brochada /bro'tʃaða/ f, stroke (of the brush)

broche /'brotʃe/ m, clasp, fastening; brooch; hooks and eyes

broma /'broma/ f, merriment; joke, jest; ship-worm. **b. literaria,** literary hoax

bromear /brome'ar/ (se) vi and vr to joke, make fun

bromista /bro'mista/ a joking, jesting; mischievous; mf genial person; prankster, tease

bronca /'bronka/ f, Inf. shindy

bronce /'bronθe; 'bronse/ m, bronze; brass; Poet. gun, bell, trumpet; bronze statue; sunburn

bronceado /bronθe'aðo; bronse'aðo/ a bronzed; sunburned. m, sunburn

broncear /bronθe'ar; bronse'ar/ vt to bronze; sunburn

bronco /'bronko/ a rough, coarse; brittle; (of metals); harsh (voice, musical instruments); rigid, stiff; surly

bronconeumonía /,bronkoneumo'nia/ f, bronchopneumonia

bronquial /bron'kial/ a bronchial

bronquio /'bronkio/ m, (gen. pl) bronchi

bronquitis /bron'kitis/ f, bronchitis

broquel /bro'kel/ m, shield; Fig. protection

broqueta /bro'keta/ f, skewer

brotadura /brota'ðura/ f, budding

brotar /bro'tar/ vi to germinate, sprout; gush forth (water); issue forth, burst out; Fig. appear (of rash); Fig. begin to appear; —vt to bring forth; produce (of earth)

brote /'brote/ m, bud, sprout; Fig. germ, genesis; iota, jot, atom

broza /'broθa, 'brosa/ f, garden rubbish; debris; thicket

bruces /'bruθes; 'bruses/ **(a or de)** adv face downwards. **caer de b.,** to fall flat. Also with other verbs: **dar, echarse,** etc.

bruja /'bruha/ f, witch; owl; Inf. hag

brujería /bruhe'ria/ f, witchcraft

brujo /'bruho/ m, magician, wizard

brújula /'bruhula/ f, magnetic needle; compass; mariner's compass. **b. de bolsillo,** pocket compass. **b. giroscópica,** gyrocompass

brumoso /bru'moso/ a misty, hazy

bruno /'bruno/ a dark brown

bruñidor /bruɲi'ðor/ **(-ra)** a polishing —n burnisher. m, polisher (instrument)

bruñir /bru'ɲir/ vt to polish, burnish; Inf. apply make up

brusco /'brusko/ a brusque, rude; blunt; sudden, unexpected; sharp (of bends)

Bruselas /bru'selas/ Brussels

brusquedad /bruske'ðað/ f, brusquerie, rudeness; bluntness; suddenness, unexpectedness; sharpness (of a bend)

brutal /bru'tal/ a brutal

brutalidad /brutali'ðað/ f, brutality; Fig. brutishness; viciousness

bruto /'bruto/ a stupid, unreasonable; vicious; unpolished, rough. m, animal (gen. quadruped). **en b.,** in the rough; Com. in bulk. **diamante en b.,** an uncut diamond

bruza /'bruθa; 'brusa/ f, strong brush; scrubbing brush

Bs. As. /,buenos 'aires/ abbrev. of Buenos Aires

bu /bu/ m, Inf. bogey man

buba /'buβa/ f, pustule; pl buboes

bubónico /bu'βoniko/ a bubonic

buceador /buθea'ðor; busea'ðor/ m, diver

bucear /buθe'ar; buse'ar/ vi to work as a diver; swim under water; Fig. investigate

buceo /bu'θeo; bu'seo/ m, diving; dive; Fig. investigation

buche /'butʃe/ m, craw or crop; mouth-

ful; wrinkle, pleat; *Inf.* stomach, belly.
Fig. Inf. inmost heart

bucle /'bukle/ *m,* ringlet, curl

bucólico /bu'koliko/ *a* bucolic

budín /bu'ðin/ *m,* pudding

budismo /bu'ðismo/ *m,* Buddhism

budista /bu'ðista/ *a* and *mf* Buddhist

buen /buen/ *a Abbr.* of **bueno,** good.
Used before *m,* singular nouns and infinitives used as nouns, e.g. *un b. libro,* a
good book. *el b. cantar,* good singing

buenaventura /buenaßen'tura/ *f,* good
luck; fortune told from hand

bueno /'bueno/ (see **buen**) *a* good; kind;
useful; convenient; pleasant; healthy;
large (drink, etc.); simple, innocent; suitable; sufficient; opportune. ¡**B.!** Good!;
Enough!; All right! **a buenas,** willingly.
de buenas a primeras, at first sight, from
the beginning. **hacer bueno,** to prove,
justify (a claim)

buey /buei/ *m,* ox. **b. suelto,** *Inf.* freelance; bachelor

búfalo /'bufalo/ **(-la)** *n* buffalo

bufanda /bu'fanda/ *f,* scarf

bufar /bu'far/ *vi* to bellow; snort; *Inf.*
snort with rage

bufete /bu'fete/ *m,* desk, writing table;
lawyer's office or practice; sideboard

bufo /'bufo/ *a* comic. *m,* clown, buffoon

bufón /bu'fon/ *m,* buffoon, clown; jester
—*a* comical, clownish

bufonada /bufo'naða/ *f,* buffoonery,
clowning; raillery, taunt

bufonear /bufone'ar/ **(se)** *vr* and *vi* to
joke, jest, parody

bufonería. /bufone'ria/ See **bufonada**

buhardilla /buar'ðiʎa; buar'ðiya/ *f,* garret; skylight

búho /'buo/ *m,* owl; *Inf.* hermit, unsociable person

buhonería /buone'ria/ *f,* peddling, hawking; peddler's wares

buhonero /buo'nero/ *m,* pedler

buido /'buiðo/ *a* sharp-pointed; sharp

buitre /'buitre/ *m,* vulture

bujía /bu'hia/ *f,* candle; candlestick; *Elec.*
candle-power; *Auto.* sparking plug

bulbo /'bulßo/ *m, Bot.* bulb. **b. dentario,**
pulp (of teeth)

bulevar /bule'ßar/ *m,* boulevard, promenade

búlgaro /'bulgaro/ **(-ra)** *a* and *n* Bulgarian

bulla /'buʎa; 'buya/ *f,* noise; bustle; confusion; fuss. *Inf.* **meter a b.,** to throw
into great confusion

bullebulle /buʎe'ßuʎe; buye'ßuye/ *mf*
busybody; madcap

bullente /bu'ʎente; bu'yente/ *adj* boiling,
bubbling; frothy (beer); swarming, teeming. **b. de sol,** drenched in sunlight, sundrenched

bullicio /bu'ʎiθio; bu'yisio/ *m,* noise, bustle; rioting; uproar

bullicioso /buʎi'θioso; buyi'sioso/ *a*

noisy, merry, boisterous; rebellious;
lively, restless

bullir /bu'ʎir; bu'yir/ *vi* to boil; foam,
bubble; *Fig.* seethe; *Fig.* swarm (insects);
bustle; —*vt* move, stir; —*vr* stir, give
signs of life

bulto /'bulto/ *m,* bulk, mass, size; form
of person, etc., seen indistinctly; swelling;
bust, statue; bundle, package, piece of
luggage; pillowcase. *Fig. Inf.* **poner de
b.,** to put clearly, emphasize. **ser de b.,**
to be obvious

bumerang /bume'raŋ/ *m,* boomerang

buñuelo /bu'ɲuelo/ *m,* bun; waffle, fritter; *Fig.* botch

buque /'buke/ *m,* ship, vessel; capacity
of ship; ship's hull. **b. barreminas,** minesweeper. **b. de guerra,** battleship, manof-war. **b. de vapor,** steamer. **b. de vela,**
sailing ship. **b. escuela,** trainingship. **b.
mercante,** merchant vessel. **b. submarino,** submarine. **b. transbordador,**
train-ferry

burbuja /bur'ßuha/ *f,* bubble

burbujear /burßuhe'ar/ *vi* to bubble

burdel /bur'ðel/ *m,* brothel; *Inf.* untidy,
noisy place —*a* lascivious

burdo /'burðo/ *a* coarse, tough

burgo /'burgo/ *m,* borough, burgh

burgués /bur'ges/ **(-esa)** *a* and *n* bourgeois

burguesía /burge'sia/ *f,* bourgeoisie

buriel /bu'riel/ *a* dark red

buril /bu'ril/ *m,* burin, engraver's tool

burla /'burla/ *f,* mockery; joke, jest; trick.
b. burlando, without effort; negligently.
de burlas, in fun. **entre burlas y veras,**
half-jokingly

burlador /burla'ðor/ *a* mocking. *m,* libertine, rake; deceiver

burlar /bur'lar/ *vt* to play a trick on; deceive; disappoint; —*vr* and *vi* (*with de*)
make fun of, laugh at, ridicule

burlesco /bur'lesko/ *a* jocular, comic,
burlesque

burlón /bur'lon/ **(-ona)** *a* joking; mocking, scoffing —*n* joker; scoffer

buró /bu'ro/ *m,* bureau, writing-desk

burocracia /buro'kraθia; buro'krasia/ *f,*
bureaucracy

burócrata /bu'rokrata/ *mf* bureaucrat

burocrático /buro'kratiko/ *a* bureaucratic

burocratismo /burokra'tismo/ *m,* bureaucracy, red tape

burrajo /bu'rraho/ *m,* dry stable dung
used as fuel

burro /'burro/ *m,* ass, donkey; sawing-horse; card game

bursátil /bur'satil/ *a Com.* relating to the
stock exchange; financial

busca /'buska/ *f,* search; hunting party;
research; pursuit

buscado /bus'kaðo/ *adj* deliberate, intentional (negligence, etc.)

buscador /buska'ðor/ **(-ra)** *n* searcher;
investigator. *m,* finder (of a camera, etc.)

buscapié /buska'pie/ *m*, hint or suggestion; *Fig*. feeler

buscapiés /buska'pies/ *m*, squib, cracker

buscar /bus'kar/ *vt* to search, look for; pursue. **ir a b.**, to go to look for, go and get; bring, fetch

buscarruidos /buska'rruiðos/ *mf Inf*. quarrel maker

buscavidas /buska'βiðas/ *mf Inf*. busybody; *Inf*. go-getter

buscón /bus'kon/ **(-ona)** *n* searcher; pickpocket, thief, swindler, rogue

buscona /bus'kona/ *f*, prostitute

busilis /bu'silis/ *m*, *Inf*. knotty problem, snag; **ahí está el b.,** there's the rub; core, main point

búsqueda /'buskeða/ **(de)** *f*, search (for)

busto /'busto/ *m*, *Art*. bust, head and shoulders

butaca /bu'taka/ *f*, armchair; *Theat*. orchestra stall; seat (in movies, etc.)

buz /buθ/ *m*, respectful kiss

buzo /'buθo; 'buso/ *m*, diver

buzón /bu'θon; bu'son/ *m*, mailbox; letter-box; canal, channel; sluice

C

C. /k/ abbrev. of ciudadano

cábala /'kaβala/ *f.* cabala; divination; *Inf.* intrigue. **hacer cábalas,** to venture a guess

cabalgar /kaβal'gar/ *vi* to ride a horse; ride in procession

caballa /ka'βaʎa; ka'βaya/ *f.* mackerel

caballeresco /kaβaʎe'resko; kaβaye'resko/ *a* gentlemanly; knightly; chivalrous

caballería /kaβaʎe'ria; kaβaye'ria/ *f.* riding animal; cavalry; knightly deed or quest; any of Spanish Military Orders; knight-errantry; knighthood; chivalry; share of the spoils of war; horsemanship. **c. andante,** knight-errantry. **c. ligera,** *Mil.* light horse. **c. mayor,** horses, mares, mules. **c. menor,** asses, donkeys

caballeriza /kaβaʎe'riθa; kaβaye'risa/ *f.* stable; stud of horses; staff of a stable

caballerizo /kaβaʎe'riθo; kaβaye'riso/ *m.* head stable-groom. **c. mayor del rey,** Master of the King's Horse

caballero /kaβa'ʎero; kaβa'yero/ *m.* gentleman; cavalier; knight. **c. andante,** knight-errant. *Inf.* **c. de industria,** adventurer, sharper. **el C. de la Mancha,** the Knight of La Mancha. **el C. Sin Miedo y Sin Tacha,** the Seigneur of Bayart. **c. del hábito,** knight of one of the Spanish Military Orders. **c. novel,** untried knight. **armar c.,** to dub a knight

caballerosidad /kaβaʎerosi'ðað; kaβayerosi'ðað/ *f.* gentlemanliness; nobility; generosity; chivalry

caballeroso /kaβaʎe'roso; kaβaye'roso/ *a* gentlemanly; noble; generous; chivalrous

caballete /kaβa'ʎete; kaβa'yete/ *m.* ridge (of a roof); *Mil.* wooden horse; brake (for flax and hemp); *Agr.* furrow; easel; sawing-frame; trestle; bridge (of the nose)

caballito /kaβa'ʎito; kaβa'yito/ *m.* dim little horse; *pl* merry-go-round; automatic horse gambling game; circus equestrian act. **c. del diablo,** dragonfly

caballo /ka'βaʎo; ka'βayo/ *m.* horse; (chess) knight; (Spanish cards) queen; sawing-frame; *pl* cavalry. **c. balancín,** rocking horse. **c. de batalla,** war-horse; *Fig.* hobby-horse; forte; crux. **c. de cartón,** hobby-horse; rocking horse. **c. de carrera,** racehorse. **c. de tiro,** draft-horse. **c. de vapor,** horsepower. **c. marino,** sea-horse. **a c.,** on horseback. **A c. regalado no le mires el diente,** Never look a gift horse in the mouth. **caer bien a c.,** to have a good seat (on a horse). **ser un c. loco en una cacharrería,** to be like a bull in a china shop

cabaña /ka'βaɲa/ *f.* hut, cabin, cottage; flock (of sheep); drove (of mules); *Art.* pastoral scene; balk (billiards)

cabaret /kaβa'ret/ *m.* cabaret, nightclub

cabaretero /kaβare'tero/ *m.* nightclub owner

cabecear /kaβeθe'ar; kaβese'ar/ *vi* to nod; shake the head in disapproval; move the head from side to side; toss the head (horses); (*Aer. Naut.*) pitch; sway (of a carriage); lean; —*vt* refoot (socks); head (wine)

cabeceo /kaβe'θeo; kaβe'seo/ *m.* nod, shake (of head); (*Naut. Aer.*) pitching; lurching (of a carriage, etc.); bight (of river)

cabecera /kaβe'θera; kaβe'sera/ *f.* top, upper portion, head; seat of honor; bedhead; river source; capital (country or county); illustrated chapter heading; pillow; inscription, heading

cabellera /kaβe'ʎera; kaβe'yera/ *f.* head of long hair; hair-switch; tail (of comet)

cabello /ka'βeʎo; ka'βeyo/ *m.* hair; head of hair; silk (of maize). *Fig. Inf.* **asirse de un c.,** to clutch at a straw

cabelludo /kaβe'ʎuðo; kaβe'yuðo/ *a* hairy; *Bot.* fibrous

caber /ka'βer/ *vi irr* to be room for, contain; fit into, go into (e.g. *No cabemos todos en este coche,* There isn't room for all of us in this car); happen, befall, have (e.g. *No les cupo tal suerte,* They did not have such luck—Such luck did not befall them); be possible (e.g. *Todo cabe en Dios,* All things are possible with God). **No cabe más,** There's no room for anything else; *Fig.* That's the limit. *Fig.* **no c. en sí,** to be beyond oneself (with joy, pride, etc.). **No cabe duda de que,** There's no doubt that —*Pres. Indic.* **quepo, cabes,** etc —*Fut.* **cabré,** etc —*Conditional* **cabría,** etc —*Preterite* **cupe, cupiste,** etc —*Pres. Subjunc.* **quepa, quepas,** etc —*Imperf. Subjunc.* **cupiese,** etc.

cabestrillo /kaβes'triʎo; kaβes'triyo/ *m.* sling; thin chain (for ornament). **en c.,** in a sling (e.g. *Tenía el brazo en c.,* His arm was in a sling)

cabeza /ka'βeθa; ka'βesa/ *f.* head; top, upper end; nail-head; brain; mind; judgment; self-control; edge (of book); peak, summit; source, origin; individual, person; head of cattle; capital city. *m.* leader, chief, head. *Mech.* **c. de biela,** big-end. *Inf.* **c. de chorlito,** scatterbrain (person). **c. de hierro,** blockhead. *Mil.* **de puente,** bridgehead. **c. de partido,** principal town of a region. **c. de turco,** scapegoat. *Fig. Inf.* **meter a uno en la c.,** to put into someone's head. *Inf.* **quebrarse la c.,** to rack one's brains. *Inf.* **quitar a uno de la c.** (**una cosa),** to dissuade; get an idea out of someone's head

cabezada /kaβe'θaða; kaβe'saða/ *f.* blow with or on the head; nod; headsale; headstall; *Naut.* pitching. **dar cabezadas,** to nod, go to sleep

cabezal /kaβe'θal; kaβe'sal/ *m.* small head pillow; *Surg.* pad; bolster; narrow mattress; *Mech.* head

cabezudo /kaβe'θuðo; kaβe'suðo/ *a* large-headed; *Inf.* obstinate; *Inf.* heady (of wine). *m,* carnival grotesque

cabida /ka'βiða/ *f,* space, capacity; extent, area

cabildear /kaβilde'ar/ *vi* to canvass votes, lobby

cabildo /ka'βildo/ *m, Eccl.* chapter; municipal council; meeting, or meeting place of council. **c. abierto,** town meeting

cabina /ka'βina/ *f,* cabin. **c. telefónica** phone booth

cabizbajo /kaβiθ'βaho; kaβis'βaho/ *a* crestfallen; pensive, melancholy

cable /'kaβle/ *m,* cable; string (of bridge); cable's length; **c. aéreo,** overhead cable. **c. alimentario,** feed line. **c. eléctrico,** electric cable

cabo /'kaβo/ *m,* end, extremity; stump, stub; handle, shaft, haft; leader; *Geog.* cape; end, conclusion; *Naut.* rope; ply (of wool, etc.); *Mil.* corporal; *pl* accessories (clothes); horse's tail and mane. **c. de maestranza,** foreman. **c. de mar,** naval quartermaster. **c. furriel,** *Mil.* quartermaster. **al c.,** in the end. **llevar a c.,** to finish

Cabo de Hornos /'kaβo de 'ornos/ Cape Horn

cabra /'kaβra/ *f,* nanny-goat; goat. **c. montesa,** wild goat

cabrerizo /kaβre'riθo; kaβreriso/ **(-za)** *a* goatish. *m,* goatherd

cabrero /ka'βrero/ **(-ra)** *m,* goatherd

cabria /'kaβria/ *f,* winch, hoist

cabrilla /ka'βriʎa; ka'βriya/ *f,* saw-horse; *pl Astron.* Pleiades; burn marks on legs from sitting too near fire; white crests (of waves)

cabrillear /kaβriʎe'ar; kaβriye'ar/ *vi* to foam, froth (the sea)

cabrío /ka'βrio/ *a* goatish. *m,* herd of goats. **macho c.,** male goat, he-goat

cabriola /ka'βriola/ *f,* fouetté (in dancing); spin in the air (acrobats); curvet (horses); caper

cabriolar /kaβrio'lar/ *vi* to curvet; caper, skip

cabritilla /kaβri'tiʎa; kaβri'tiya/ *f,* dressed kid; lambskin, etc.

cabrito /ka'βrito/ *m, Zool.* kid; *pl* toasted maize, popcorn

cabrón /ka'βron/ *m,* billy goat, buck, he-goat; *Inf.* complaisant husband, cuckold; *Chile* owner or operator of a brothel

cabrona /ka'βrona/ *f, Chile* bawd, madam

cabujón /kaβu'hon/ *m, Mineral.* uncut gem; unpolished ruby; *pl* vignettes

cacahuete /kaka'uete/ *m, Bot.* peanut, monkey nut

cacao /ka'kao/ *m, Bot.* cacao tree; cacaonut

cacarear /kakare'ar/ *vi* to crow, cackle; —*vt Inf.* boast

cacatúa /kaka'tua/ *f,* cockatoo

cacería /kaθe'ria; kase'ria/ *f,* hunting party; hunting bag, booty; *Art.* hunting scene

cacerola /kaθe'rola; kase'rola/ *f,* stewpot, casserole

cachalote /katʃa'lote/ *m,* sperm whale

cachar /ka'tʃar/ *vt* to break in fragments; split (wood)

cacharro /ka'tʃarro/ *m,* coarse earthenware vessel; *Inf.* decrepit, worthless object

cachazudo /katʃa'θuðo; katʃa'suðo/ *a* phlegmatic, slow

cachear /katʃe'ar/ *vt* to search (a person) for weapons

Cachemira /katʃe'mira/ Kashmir

cachemira /katʃe'mira/ *f,* cashmere

cacheo /ka'tʃeo/ *m,* search (of persons) for weapons

cachete /ka'tʃete/ *m,* blow on the head or face with one's fist; cheek (especially fat one)

cachiporra /katʃi'porra/ *f,* club, bludgeon

cachivache /katʃi'βatʃe/ *m. Inf.* (gen. *pl*) trash; pots, pans, utensils

cacho /'katʃo/ *m,* small slice (gen. of bread or fruit)

cachón /ka'tʃon/ *m,* breaker, wave; small waterfall

cachorro /ka'tʃorro/ **(-rra)** *n* puppy; cub. *m,* small pistol

cacillo /ka'θiʎo; ka'siyo/ *m,* ladle; basting spoon

cacique /ka'θike; ka'sike/ *m,* Indian chief, cacique; *Inf.* political "boss"

caciquismo /kaθi'kismo; kasi'kismo/ *m,* political "bossism"

caco /'kako/ *m,* pickpocket, thief; *Inf.* poltroon

cacofonía /kakofo'nia/ *f,* cacophony

cacografía /kakogra'fia/ *f,* cacography

cacto /'kakto/ *m,* cactus

cacumen /ka'kumen/ *m, Inf.* brains, acumen

cada /'kaða/ *a* every, each. **c. cual,** each. **c. que,** whenever; every time that. **c. y cuando que,** whenever

cadalso /ka'ðalso/ *m,* scaffold; platform, stand

cadáver /ka'ðaβer/ *m,* corpse

cadena /ka'ðena/ *f,* chain; link, tie; *Fig.* bond; *Fig.* sequence (of events); *Law.* imprisonment; *Archit.* buttress; grand chain (dancing); **c. de montañas,** range of mountains. **c. perpetua,** life imprisonment

cadencia /ka'ðenθia; ka'ðensia/ *f,* cadence; rhythm; *Mus.* measure, time; *Mus.* cadenza

cadencioso /kaðen'θioso; kaðen'sioso/ *a* rhythmic

cadente /ka'ðente/ *a* falling, declining; decaying, dying; rhythmic

cadera /ka'ðera/ *f,* hip; flank

caderillas /kaðe'riʎas; kaðe'riyas/ *f pl,* bustle, panniers

cadete /ka'ðete/ *m, Mil.* cadet

cadi /'kaði/ *mf* caddy

caducar /kaðu'kar/ *vi* to become senile;

become invalid, be annulled; expire, lapse; *Fig.* be worn out

caducidad /kaðuθiˈðað; kaðusiˈðað/ *f,* decrepitude; lapse, expiry

caduco /kaˈðuko/ *a* senile; decrepit; perishable; lapsed; obsolete

caduquez /kaðuˈkeθ; kaðuˈkes/ *f,* senility

caedizo /kaeˈðiθo; kaeˈðiso/ *a* ready to fall; timid, cowardly, weak

caer /kaˈer/ *vi irr* to fall, drop; drop out or off; suit, fit, become; fail; fade (colors); *Fig.* drop (voice); (*with sobre*) attack, fall upon; (*with en*) fall in or on to; decay, collapse; understand; (*with preps. a, hacia*) *Fig.* look on to; face; (*with por, en*) *Fig.* fall on, occur on; —*vr Aer.* crash; fly off (buttons, etc.). **c. de cabeza,** to fall head foremost. **c. en conflicto (con),** to come into conflict (with) **c. en las manos de uno,** to come into somebody's possession (come to be owned by somebody). **c. en gracia,** to make a good impression, arouse affection. **caerse de suyo,** to be self-evident. **c. por tierra,** (plan, etc.) to fall through. **Cayó enfermo,** He was taken ill. **cayendo y levantado,** dying *Pres. Indic.* **caigo, caes,** etc —*Pres. Part.* **cayendo.** *Preterite* **cayó cayeron.** *Pres. Subjunc.* **caiga,** etc.

café /kaˈfe/ *m,* coffee (tree, berry, drink); café, coffeehouse. **c. con leche,** café au lait

cafeína /kafeˈina/ *f,* caffeine

cafetal /kafeˈtal/ *m,* coffee plantation

cafetera /kafeˈtera/ *f,* coffeepot; *Peru* cab, taxi

cafeto /kaˈfeto/ *m,* coffee tree

cafiche /kaˈfitʃe/ *m, Argentina, Chile* pimp

caficultor /kafikulˈtor/ *m,* coffee-grower

caficultura /kafikulˈtura/ *f,* coffee-growing

cafúa /kaˈfua/ *f, Argentina* clink, slammer

cagar /kaˈgar/ **(se)** *vi vt vr* to evacuate (bowels); —*vt Inf.* spoil, make a botch of

cagarruta /kagaˈrruta/ *f,* dung of sheep, deer, rabbits, etc.

caída /kaˈiða/ *f,* falling; fall; ruin; failure; close of day; *Fig.* falling off; hanging (curtains, etc.); diminution; incline; *pl* coarse wool; *Inf.* repartee. **a la c. de la tarde,** at the end of the afternoon. **a la c. del sol,** at sunset

caído /kaˈiðo/ **(-da)** *a* debilitated, languid; lapsed; (of a shoulder) sloping. **los caídos,** the fallen, the dead (in war, etc.)

caimán /kaiˈman/ *m,* alligator; *Inf.* shark, astute person

caja /ˈkaha/ *f,* box; safe, cash box; coffin; (of a vehicle) body; *Mus.* drum; case (of piano, watch, etc.); cavity; well (of a stair); *Com.* cash; cash-desk; cashier's office; *Bot.* sheath. **c. de ahorros,** savings bank. **c. de caudales,** strong-box. *Print.* **c. de imprenta,** type case. **c. de música,** musical box. **c. de reclutamiento,** recruiting office. **c. de velocidades,** gear-

box. **c. registradora,** cash register. **c. torácica,** rib cage, thoracic cage

cajero /kaˈhero/ **(-ra)** *m,* boxmaker; —*n Com.* cashier; pedler **c. automático,** automatic teller, automatic teller machine, bank machine, money machine

cajetilla /kaheˈtiʎa; kaheˈtiya/ *f,* packet (cigarettes, etc.)

cajón /kaˈhon/ *m,* chest, locker, case; drawer. **c. de municiones,** ammunition-box

cal /kal/ *f,* lime. **c. muerta,** slaked lime. **c. viva,** quicklime. *Fig. Inf.* **de c. y canto,** tough, strong

cala /ˈkala/ *f,* sample slice (of fruit); *Naut.* hold; *Surg.* probe; cove, small bay; *Bot.* iris

calabacera /kalaβaˈθera; kalaβaˈsera/ *f, Bot.* pumpkin or gourd plant

calabaza /kalaˈβaθa; kalaˈβasa/ *f, Bot.* pumpkin (plant and fruit); gourd; *Inf.* dolt. **dar calabazas,** to refuse (suitor); flunk (an examinee). *Inf.* **llevar calabazas,** to get the sack; be jilted

calabobos /kalaˈβoβos/ *m, Inf.* drizzle

calabozo /kalaˈβoθo; kalaˈβoso/ *m,* dungeon; prison cell; pruning knife

calada /kaˈlaða/ *f,* soaking, wetting through; flight of bird of prey; swoop. **dar una c.,** *Fig. Inf.* to dress down

calado /kaˈlaðo/ *a* soaked, wet through. *m, Sew.* open-work; fretwork; *Naut.* draft of a ship; water level; *pl* lace. **c. hasta los huesos,** soaked to the skin; madly in love

calador /kalaˈðor/ *m,* one who does open or fretwork; caulking iron; borer; *Surg.* probe

calafatear /kalafateˈar/ *vt Naut.* to caulk

calamar /kalaˈmar/ *m, Zool.* squid, calamari

calambre /kaˈlambre/ *m,* cramp. **c. del escribiente,** writer's cramp

calamidad /kalamiˈðað/ *f,* misfortune, calamity

calamina /kalaˈmina/ *f, Mineral.* calamine

calamitoso /kalamiˈtoso/ *a* calamitous; unfortunate, unhappy

cálamo /ˈkalamo/ *m,* ancient flute; stalk (of grass); *Poet.* pen

calandria /kaˈlandria/ *f, Ornith.* calender, lark; *Mech.* calender; treadmill. *mf Inf.* malingerer

calaña /kaˈlaɲa/ *f,* sample; model; pattern; kind, quality; temperament; cheap fan

calar /kaˈlar/ *vt* to permeate, soak through; pierce; do openwork (in cloth, paper, metal); cut a sample slice from fruit; pull (hat, etc.) well down on head; put down (an eyeshade or visor); fix (bayonets, etc.); *Inf.* understand (persons); *Inf.* guess, realize; *Naut.* let down; —*vi Naut.* draw (water); —*vr* be drenched, wet through; swoop (birds of prey); *Inf.* sneak in —*a* calcareous

calar /kaˈlar/ *m,* limestone deposit or region

calavera /kala'βera/ f, skull. m, daredevil, madcap; roué

calaverada /kalaβe'raða/ f, Inf. daredevilment, foolishness; escapade

calcañar /kalka'ɲar/ m, heel (of foot)

calcar /kal'kar/ vt to trace (drawing); press with foot; copy servilely, imitate

calce /'kalθe; 'kalse/ m, rim of a wheel; wedge; tire

calceta /kal'θeta; kal'seta/ f, stocking; fetter. Inf. **hacer c.,** to knit

calcetería /kalθete'ria; kalsete'ria/ f, hosiery shop; hosiery trade

calcetero /kalθe'tero; kalse'tero/ (-ra) n hosier; hose maker or darner

calcetín /kalθe'tin; kalse'tin/ m, sock

calcificación /kalθifika'θion; kalsifika-'sion/ f, Med. calcification

calcio /'kalθio; 'kalsio/ m, calcium

calco /'kalko/ m, tracing (drawing)

calcografiar /kalkoɣra'fiar/ vt to transfer; make chalcographies of

calcomanía /kalkoma'nia/ f, transfer

calculación /kalkula'θion; kalkula'sion/ f, calculation

calculado /kalku'laðo/ a calculated

calculador /kalkula'ðor/ a calculating. m, calculating machine; comptometer

calcular /kalku'lar/ vt to calculate

cálculo /'kalkulo/ m, calculation; Math. estimate; investigation; conjecture, (Math Med.) calculus. **c. hepático,** Med. gallstone

calda /'kalda/ f, heating; pl hot mineral baths

caldear /kalde'ar/ vt to heat

caldeo /kal'deo/ (-ea) a and n Chaldean

caldeo /kal'deo/ m, heating

caldera /kal'dera/ f, cauldron; cauldron full; West Hem. teapot; Engin. boiler. **c. de vapor,** steam-boiler

caldería /kalde're'ria/ f, coppersmith's trade and shop

calderero /kalde'rero/ m, boiler maker; coppersmith; tinker

calderilla /kalde'riʎa; kalde'riya/ f, holy water stoup; any copper coin

caldero /kal'dero/ m, small cauldron; casserole; kettle

calderón /kalde'ron/ m, large cauldron; Mus. rest; Mus. trill; pause

caldo /'kaldo/ m, broth; salad dressing; pl Agr. oil, wine, vegetable juices

calefacción /kalefak'θion; kalefak'sion/ f, heating. **c. central,** central heating

calendario /kalen'dario/ m, calendar. **c. deportivo,** fixture card. **c. gregoriano,** Gregorian calendar

calendas /ka'lendas/ f pl, calends. **en las c. griegas,** at the Greek calends

caléndula /ka'lendula/ f, marigold

calentador /kalenta'ðor/ a heating, warming. m, heater; warming-pan

calentamiento /kalenta'miento/ m, heating, warming

calentar /kalen'tar/ vt irr to heat, warm; rev-up (an engine); hasten; Inf. spank;

—vr warm oneself; be in heat (animals); grow excited. See **acertar**

calentura /kalen'tura/ f, fever

calera /ka'lera/ f, lime-pit; lime-kiln; fishing smack

calesa /ka'lesa/ f, calash, calèche, chaise (two-wheeled carriage)

caleta /ka'leta/ f, cove, creek

caletre /ka'letre/ m, Inf. discernment, head, sense

calibrar /kali'βrar/ vt to calibrate; gauge

calibre /ka'liβre/ m, Mech. gauge; bore, caliber; diameter (tubes, pipes, etc.)

calidad /kali'ðað/ f, quality; role; character, temperament; condition, requisite; importance, gravity, personal particulars; nobility; pl qualities of the mind. **c. originaria,** rank and birth. **c. de oficio,** justification for action. **en c. de,** in the capacity of

cálido /'kaliðo/ a warm, hot; warming, heating; vehement, ardent; Art. warm

calidoscópico /kaliðos'kopiko/ a kaleidoscopic

calidoscopio /kaliðos'kopio/ m, kaleidoscope

calientalibros /kalienta'liβros/ m, bookworm (person)

calientapiés /kalienta'pies/ m, footwarmer

calientaplatos /kalienta'platos/ m, hot plate, plate-warmer

caliente /ka'liente/ a warm, hot; excited; Art. warm

calientito /kalien'tito/ a piping hot

calificable /kalifi'kaβle/ a classifiable; qualifiable

calificación /kalifika'θion; kalifika'sion/ f, classification; qualification; judgment; mark, place (examinations)

calificar /kalifi'kar/ vt to class; authorize; judge (qualities); Fig. ennoble; —vr prove noble descent

californio /kali'fornio/ (-ia) a and n Californian

caliginoso /kalihi'noso/ a murky, dark

caligrafía /kaligra'fia/ f, calligraphy

calígrafo /ka'ligrafo/ m, calligraphist

calinoso /kali'noso/ a hazy

calistenia /kalis'tenia/ f, callisthenics

caliza /ka'liθa; ka'lisa/ f, limestone

callado /ka'ʎaðo; ka'yaðo/ a silent; reserved; secret

callar /ka'ʎar; ka'yar/ (se) vi and vr to say nothing, keep silent; stop speaking; stop making any sound (persons, animals, things); —vt conceal, keep secret; omit, leave out; Inf. interj ¡Calle! You don't say so! **Quien calla otorga,** Silence gives consent

calle /'kaʎe; 'kaye/ f, street. Inf. **abrir c.,** to clear the way. Inf. **dejar en la c.,** to leave destitute. Inf. **echar a la c.,** put out of the house, to throw out of the house; make known, publish. **ponerse en la c.,** to go out

calleja, callejuela /ka'ʎeha, kaʎe'huela/

ka'yeha, kaye'huela/ f, small street, alley, side street

callejear /kaʎehe'ar; kayehe'ar/ vi to walk the streets, wander about the streets, loaf around the streets

callejero /kaʎe'hero; kaye'hero/ a fond of gadding. m, street directory

callejón /kaʎe'hon; kaye'hon/ m, alley, lane. **c. sin salida,** cul-de-sac; Fig. impasse

callicida /kaʎi'θiða; kayi'siða/ m, corn cure

callista /ka'ʎista; ka'yista/ mf chiropodist

callo /'kaʎo; 'kayo/ m, corn, callosity; Med. callus; pl tripe

calloso /ka'ʎoso; ka'yoso/ a callous, horny

calma /'kalma/ f, calm, airlessness; serenity, composure; quiet, tranquillity, peace. **c. chicha,** dead calm. **en c.,** at peace; tranquil; calm (of the sea)

calmante /kal'mante/ a calming, soothing. Med. a and m, sedative, tranquilizer

calmar /kal'mar/ vt to soothe, calm; moderate, mitigate; pacify; quench (thirst); —vi grow calm; moderate; be becalmed

calmoso /kal'moso/ a calm, tranquil; Inf. sluggish, lazy; imperturbable

calor /ka'lor/ m, heat; ardor, vehemence; cordiality; Fig. heat (of battle); excitement

caloría /kalo'ria/ f, Phys. calorie

calórico /ka'loriko/ a Phys. caloric, thermic

calorífero /kalo'rifero/ a heat-giving. m, heater, radiator

calorífico /kalo'rifiko/ a calorific

calumnia /ka'lumnia/ f, calumny; Law. slander

calumniador /kalumnia'ðor/ (**-ra**) a slandering —n calumniator, slanderer

calumniar /kalumni'ar/ vt to calumniate; Law. slander

calumnioso /kalum'nioso/ a calumnious, slanderous

caluroso /kalu'roso/ a hot, warm; cordial, friendly; enthusiastic; ardent, impassioned; excited

calva /'kalβa/ f, bald patch on head; worn place (cloth, etc.); bare spot, clearing (trees, etc.)

Calvario /kal'βario/ m, Calvary; Inf. series of disasters; Inf. debts

calvicie /kal'βiθie; kalβisie/ f, baldness

calvinista /kalβi'nista/ mf Calvinist —a Calvinistic

calvo /'kalβo/ a bald; bare, barren (land); worn (cloth, etc.)

calza /'kalθa; 'kalsa/ f, breeches (gen. pl); wedge; Inf. stocking. Inf. **tomar calzas,** to beat it

calzada /kal'θaða; kal'saða/ f, roadway. **c. romana,** Roman road

calzado /kal'θaðo; kal'saðo/ m, footwear, shoes

calzador /kalθa'ðor; kalsa'ðor/ m, shoehorn

calzadura /kalθa'ðura; kalsa'ðura/ f,

wedging (of a wheel); act of putting on shoes; felloe of a wheel

calzar /kal'θar; kal'sar/ vt to put on shoes; wear (spurs, gloves, etc.); wedge, block (wheel); scotch (a wheel). Fig. Inf. **c. el coturno,** don the buskin; write in the sublime style; write a tragedy, write tragedies. **calzarse a una persona,** to have a person in one's pocket

calzón /kal'θon; kal'son/ m, breeches (gen. pl). Fig. Inf. **ponerse los calzones,** to wear the breeches (of a woman)

calzonazos /kalθo'naθos; kalso'nasos/ m, Inf. weak-willed, easily led fellow

calzoncillos /kalθon'θiʎos; kalson'siyos/ m pl, drawers, pants

cama /'kama/ f, bed; bedstead; bedhanging; lair, form; floor (of a cart); check (of bridle) (gen. pl). **c. de campaña,** camp bed. **c. de matrimonio,** double bed. **c. de monja,** single bed. **c. de operaciones,** operating table. **c. turca,** settee-bed. **guardar c.,** to stay in bed

camafeo /kama'feo/ m, cameo

camaleón /kamale'on/ m, chameleon; Inf. changeable person

cámara /'kamara/ f, chamber; hall; house (of deputies); granary; Naut. state room; chamber (firearms, mines); Phys. camera; human excrement; Auto. inner tube. **c. acorazada,** strong-room. **c. alta,** Upper House. **c. baja** or **c. de los comunes,** lower house, house of commons. **c. de comercio,** chamber of commerce. **c. oscura,** (optics) dark room

camarada /kama'raða/ mf pal, companion, comrade

camaradería /kamaraðe'ria/ f, comradeship, companionship

camarera /kama'rera/ f, waiting-maid; waitress; chambermaid; stewardess

camarero /kama'rero/ m, waiter; papal chamberlain; chamberlain; steward; valet. **c. mayor,** lord chamberlain

camarilla /kama'riʎa; kama'riya/ f, palace or other clique, coterie; Inf. backscratch

camarín /kama'rin/ m, Theat. dressingroom; closet; boudoir; cage (of a lift); niche

camarón /kama'ron/ m, prawn, shrimp; tip, reward

camarote /kama'rote/ m, cabin; berth

cambalachear /kambalatʃe'ar/ vt Inf. to barter

cambiable /kam'βiaβle/ a exchangeable; changeable

cambiante /kam'βiante/ a exchanging; changing. m, sheen, luster (gen. pl); money changer

cambiar /kam'βiar/ vt to exchange; convert —vt and vi change, alter; —vi and vr to veer (wind). **c. de aguas,** Poet. to move (change one's residence). **c. de aire,** get a change of scenery. **c. de frente,** to face about; Fig. change front

cambio /'kambio/ m, exchange; change; Com. rate of exchange; money change;

Com. premium on bills of exchange. **a c. de, en c. de**, in exchange for; instead of. **en c.**, instead, on the other hand. **c. de velocidad**, *Auto.* gear-changing. **letra de c.**, bill of exchange. **libre c.**, free trade

cambista /kam'/βista/ *mf* money changer. *m*, banker

camelar /kame'lar/ *vt Inf.* to woo; seduce

camello /ka'meʎo; ka'meyo/ *m*, camel. **c. pardal**, giraffe

camellón /kame'ʎon; kame'yon/ *m*, furrow; drinking trough; *Mexico* island, traffic island, median strip

camilla /ka'miʎa; ka'miya/ *f*, couch; small round skirted table with brazier underneath; stretcher, litter

caminador /kamina'ðor/ *a* in the habit of walking a great deal

caminante /kami'nante/ *mf* walker, traveler

caminar /kami'nar/ *vi* to travel; walk; *Fig.* move on, go (inanimate things). *Fig. Inf.* **c. derecho**, to walk uprightly

caminata /kami'nata/ *f*, long, tiring walk; excursion

caminejo /kami'neho/ *m*, worn path

camino /ka'mino/ *m*, road; route; journey; way, means; **c. de hierro**, railway. **c. de mesa**, table-runner. **c. de sirga**, towpath. **c. real**, highway, main road. **de c.**, on the way, in passing. **ponerse en c.**, to set out

camión /ka'mion/ *m*, truck. **c. de volteo, c. volquete** dump truck; *Mexico* bus

camioneta /kamio'neta/ *f*, light truck, pick-up truck; *West. Hem.* station wagon

camisa /ka'misa/ *f*, shirt; stiff shirt; thin skin (of fruit); sloughed skin of snakes; coat (of whitewash, etc.); *Mech.* jacket; mantle (gas). **c. de fuerza**, straitjacket. **dejar sin c.**, *Inf.* to leave penniless

camisería /kamise'ria/ *f*, shirt shop or factory

camiseta /kami'seta/ *f*, vest, T-shirt. **c. de fútbol**, soccer player's jersey

camisón /kami'son/ *m*, large wide shirt; night shirt

camomila /kamo'mila/ *f*, chamomile

camorra /ka'morra/ *f*, *Inf.* brawl, shindy. **armar c.**, to start a row

campamento /kampa'mento/ *m*, camping; *Mil.* encampment; camp; jamboree

campana /kam'pana/ *f*, bell; anything bell-shaped; church, parish. **c. de chimenea**, mantelpiece. **c. de hogar**, hood, shutter (of a fireplace)

campanario /kampa'nario/ *m*, belfry, bell tower

campaneo /kampa'neo/ *m*, bell-ringing; chime

campanilla /kampa'niʎa; kampa'niya/ *f*, hand-bell; bubble; any bell-shaped flower

campanillazo /kampani'ʎaθo; kampani'yaso/ *m*, loud peal of a bell

campante /kam'pante/ *a* outstanding; *Inf.* proud, satisfied

campanudo /kampa'nuðo/ *a* bell-shaped;

sonorous (of words); pompous (of speech)

campaña /kam'paɲa/ *f*, level country; campaign. *Naut.* voyage, cruise. **correr la c.**, to reconnoiter. **la C. del Desierto**, the War against the Gauchos (in Argentina)

campar /kam'par/ *vi* to camp. *Inf.* **c. por sus respetos**, to stand on one's own feet

campeador /kampea'ðor/ *a* mighty in battle

campear /kampe'ar/ *vi* to go out to graze; grow green (crops); excel; *Mil.* be engaged in a campaign, reconnoiter

campechano /kampe'tʃano/ *a Inf.* hearty; frank; cheerful; generous

campeón /kampe'on/ *m*, champion; advocate, defender

campeonato /kampeo'nato/ *m*, championship

campesino /kampe'sino/ **(-na)** *a* rural, rustic —*n* country dweller

campestre /kam'pestre/ *a* rural

campiña /kam'piɲa/ *f*, expanse of cultivated land; countryside, landscape

campo /'kampo/ *m*, country (as opposed to urban areas); field; *Fig.* sphere, province; (*Phys. Herald. Mil.*) field; *Art.* ground; *Mil.* camp, army; plain ground (of silks, etc.). «C. Abierto», "Miscellaneous" (e.g. as the title of a section in a book catalog). **c. de aterrizaje**, *Aer.* landing-field. **c. de batalla**, battlefield. **c. de concentración**, concentration camp. **c. de experimentación**, testing ground. **c. de golf**, golf course. **c. de prisioneros** *Mil.* prison camp. **c. de tiro**, rifle-range. **c. santo**, graveyard. **c. visual**, field of vision. **a c. abierto**, in the open air. **a c. travieso**, cross-country

camuflaje /kamu'flahe/ *m*, camouflage

camuflar /kamu'flar/ *vt* to camouflage

cana /'kana/ *f*, gray hair

Canadá /kana'ða/ Canada

canadiense /kana'ðiense/ *a* and *mf* Canadian

canal /ka'nal/ *m*, canal. *mf*, *Geol.* subterranean waterway; channel; *Anat.* canal, duct; defile, narrow valley; gutter; drinking trough; animal carcass. **abrir en c.**, to open up, split open

Canal de la Mancha /ka'nal de la 'mantʃa/ English Channel

canalera /kana'lera/ *f*, roof gutter

canaleta /kana'leta/ *f*, (wooden) trough; gutter (on roof)

canalete /kana'lete/ *m*, paddle

canalización /kanaliθa'θion; kanalisa'sion/ *f*, canalization; *Elec.* main, mains; piping, tubing

canalizar /kanali'θar; kanali'sar/ *vt* to make canals or channels; regulate waters of rivers, etc.; canalize

canalla /ka'naʎa; ka'naya/ *f*, *Inf.* mob, rabble. *m*, *Inf.* scoundrel

canallesco /kana'ʎesko; kana'yesko/ *a* scoundrelly, knavish; despicable

canalón /kana'lon/ *m*, gutter, spout; shovel hat; pantile

canapé /kana'pe/ *m*, sofa

Canarias, las Islas /ka'narias, las 'islas/ the Canary Islands

canario /ka'nario/ **(-ia)** *m*, canary —*a* and *n* pertaining to or native of the Canary Islands.

canasta /ka'nasta/ *f*, hamper, basket; card game

canastilla /kanas'tiʎa; kanas'tiya/ *f*, small basket; layette

canastillo /kanas'tiʎo; kanas'tiyo/ *m*, basket-work tray

cáncamo /'kankamo/ *m*, ring-bolt

cancamusa /kanka'musa/ *f*, *Inf.* trick, deception

cancel /kan'θel; kan'sel/ *m*, draftscreen; *Eccl.* screen

cancela /kan'θela; kan'sela/ *f*, wrought-iron door

cancelación /kanθela'θion; kansela'sion/ *f*, cancellation; expunging

cancelar /kanθe'lar; kanse'lar/ *vt* to cancel; expunge, annul; abolish, blot out; pay off, clear (a mortgage)

cáncer /'kanθer; 'kanser/ *m*, cancer

cancerar /kanθe'rar; kanse'rar/ *vt* to consume; weaken; mortify; —*vr* suffer from cancer; become cancerous

canceroso /kanθe'roso; kanse'roso/ *a* cancerous

cancha /'kantʃa/ *f*, *Sports.* fronton; (tennis) court; cockpit; yard; hippodrome; widest part of a river; road; toasted maize

canciller /kanθi'ʎer; kansi'yer/ *m*, chancellor; foreign minister; assistant vice-consul

cancillería /kanθiʎe'ria; kansiye'ria/ *f*, chancellorship; chancellery; foreign ministry

canción /kan'θion; kan'sion/ *f*, song; lyric poem; musical accompaniment; old name for any poetical composition. **volver a la misma c.,** *Fig.* to be always harping on the same theme

cancionero /kanθio'nero; kansio'nero/ *m*, collection of songs and verses; songbook

cancionista /kanθio'nista; kansio'nista/ *mf* singer; song writer

candado /kan'daðo/ *m*, padlock; earring

candela /kan'dela/ *f*, candle; horse-chestnut flower; candlestick; *Inf.* fire. **en c.,** *Naut.* vertical (of masts, etc.)

candelabro /kande'laβro/ *m*, candelabrum

candelero /kande'lero/ *m*, candlestick; lamp; candle maker or seller; *Naut.* stanchion

candente /kan'dente/ *a* candescent, red-hot

candidatear /kandiðate'ar/ *vi* to run (for office)

candidato /kandi'ðato/ **(-ta)** *n* candidate

candidatura /kandiða'tura/ *f*, candidature

candidez /kandi'ðeθ; kandi'ðes/ *f*, simplicity, ingenuousness; candidness

cándido /'kandiðo/ *a* white; simple, ingenuous; candid, frank

candil /kan'dil/ *m*, oil lamp; Greek lamp; tips of stag's horns; *Inf.* cock of a hat

candileja /kandi'leha/ *f*, oil reservoir of lamp; *pl* footlights, floats

candor /kan'dor/ *m*, extreme whiteness; sincerity, candor; simplicity, innocence

candoroso /kando'roso/ *a* candid, open; simple, honest

canela /ka'nela/ *f*, *Bot.* cinnamon; *Fig.* anything exquisitely perfect

canelo /ka'nelo/ *m*, cinnamon tree —*a* cinnamon-colored

cangilón /kanhi'lon/ *m*, pitcher, jar; bucket (for water); dredging bucket

cangreja /kaŋ'greha/ *f*, *Naut.* gaffsail. **c. de mesana,** *Naut.* jigger

cangrejo /kaŋ'greho/ *m*, crab. **c. de mar,** sea-crab. **c. ermitaño,** hermit crab

canguro /kaŋ'guro/ *m*, kangaroo

caníbal /ka'niβal/ *a* and *mf* cannibal

canibalismo /kaniβa'lismo/ *m*, cannibalism

canica /ka'nika/ *f*, marble (for playing with)

canícula /ka'nikula/ *f*, dog days; *Astron.* Dog star

caniculares /kaniku'lares/ *m pl* dog days

canijo /ka'niho/ *a* *Inf.* delicate, sickly; anemic, stunted

canilla /ka'niʎa; ka'niya/ *f*, long bone of leg or arm; any principal bones in bird's wing; tap, faucet; spool, reel; fault (in cloth)

canino /ka'nino/ *a* canine

canje /'kanhe/ *m*, (diplomacy, *Mil.*, *Com.*) exchange, substitution. **c. de prisioneros,** exchange of prisoners

canjear /kanhe'ar/ *vt* to exchange

cano /'kano/ *a* white-haired, hoary; ancient; *Poet.* white

canoa /ka'noa/ *f*, canoe; launch. **c. automóvil,** motor launch

canoero /kano'ero/ **(-ra)** *n* canoeist

canon /'kanon/ *m*, rule; (*Eccl. Print.*) canon; catalog; part of the Mass; *Mus.* canon, catch; tax *pl* canon law

canonizar /kanoni'θar; kanoni'sar/ *vt* to canonize; extol, exalt; approve, acclaim

canoso /ka'noso/ *a* white-haired, hoary

cansado /kan'saðo/ **(-da)** *a* tired; weary; exhausted; decadent; tiresome; *Inf.* fed up —*n* bore, tedious person

cansancio /kan'sanθio; kan'sansio/ *m*, fatigue, weariness

cansar /kan'sar/ *vt* to tire, weary; *Agr.* exhaust soil; bore; badger, annoy; —*vr* be tired; grow weary

cantante /kan'tante/ *a* singing. *mf* professional singer

cantar /kan'tar/ *vi* to sing; twitter, chirp; extol; *Inf.* squeak, creak; *Fig.* call (cards); *Inf.* squeal, confess. *m*, song. **C. de los**

Cantares, Song of Songs. **cantarlas claras,** to call a spade a spade

cántara /'kantara/ f, pitcher, jug

cantárida /kan'tariða/ f, Spanish fly

cántaro /'kantaro/ m, pitcher, jug; jugful; varying wine measure; ballot box; tax on spirits and oil

cantata /kan'tata/ f, cantata

cantatriz /kanta'triθ; kanta'tris/ f, singer, prima donna

cante /'kante/ m, song; singing

cantera /kan'tera/ f, Mineral. quarry; capacity, talent

cantería /kante'ria/ f, stone-cutting; quarrying; building made of hewn stone

cantidad /kanti'ðað/ f, quantity; large part; portion; sum of money; quantity (prosody). **c. llovida,** rainfall

cantil /kan'til/ m, cliff; steep rock

cantimplora /kantim'plora/ f, water cooler; canteen (of water); siphon

cantina /kan'tina/ f, wine cellar; canteen; refreshment room

cantinero /kanti'nero/ m, sutler; owner of a canteen

canto /'kanto/ m, singing; song; canto; epic or other poem; end, rim, edge; noncutting edge (knives, swords); pebble, stone; angle (of a building). Mus. **c. llano,** plain-song. **al c. del gallo,** at cockcrow. **de c.,** on edge

cantón /kan'ton/ m, province, region; corner (of a street); cantonment; Herald. canton, quartering

cantonera /kanto'nera/ f, corner-piece (books, furniture, etc., as ornament); angle-iron; bracket, small shelf

cantor /kan'tor/ **(-ra)** a singing —n singer; song-bird

canturía /kantu'ria/ f, singing exercise; vocal music; monotonous song; droning; Mus. execution, technique

canturreo, /kantu'rreo,/ m, **canturria** f, humming; droning

canturriar /kantu'rriar/ vi Inf. to hum, sing under one's breath

caña /'kaɲa/ f, stalk; reed; bone of arm or leg; leg (of a trouser, stocking, boot, etc.); marrow; Bot. cane; tumbler, glass; wine measure; gallery (of mine); pl mock joust on horseback using **cañas** as spears. **c. de azúcar,** sugar-cane. **c. de pescar,** fishing rod. **c. del timón,** tiller Naut.

cañada /ka'ɲaða/ f, glen, gulch, gully, hollow, ravine, vale, cattle path; West. Hem. brook, cattle track

cañamazo /kaɲa'maθo; kaɲa'maso/ m, hempen canvas; embroidery canvas; embroidered canvas

cáñamo /'kaɲamo/ m, hemp

cañar /ka'ɲar/ m, canebrake; growth of reeds; fishgarth made of reeds

cañavalera /kaɲaβa'lera/ f, canefield

cañaveral /kaɲaβe'ral/ m, cane-brake; West Hem. bamboo field

cañazo /ka'ɲaθo; ka'ɲaso/ m, blow with a cane

cañería /kaɲe'ria/ f, conduit; pipe; piping

cañero /ka'ɲero/ m, pipe layer

caño /'kaɲo/ m, pipe, tube, sewer; organ pipe; jet (of water); mine gallery

cañón /ka'ɲon/ m, pipe, cylindrical tube; flue; quill (of birds); cannon; soft down; Archit. shaft (of column); stack (of a chimney). **c. antiaéreo,** A.A. gun. **c. antitanque,** anti-tank gun. **c. de escalera,** well of a staircase; Slang. terrific-looking, absolutely gorgeous (e.g. mujer cañón)

cañonazo /kaɲo'naθo; kaɲo'naso/ m, cannon shot; roar of a cannon

cañonear /kaɲone'ar/ vt to bombard

cañonería /kaɲone'ria/ f, Mil. group of cannon; Mus. set of organ pipes

cañonero /kaɲo'nero/ m, gunboat

cañuto /ka'ɲuto/ m, Bot. internode; small pipe or tube; Inf. tale-bearer

caoba /ka'oβa/ f, Bot. mahogany

caos /'kaos/ m, chaos; confusion

caótico /ka'otiko/ a chaotic

capa /'kapa/ f, cloak; cape; Eccl. cope; coating; layer; cover; coat (animals); Fig. cloak, disguise; Geol. stratum. **la c. del cielo,** the canopy of heaven. Fig. Inf. **echar la c. al toro,** to throw one's cap over the windmill. Naut. **estarse** (or **ponerse) a la c.,** to lie to

capacete /kapa'θete; kapa'sete/ m, helmet

capacidad /kapaθi'ðað; kapasi'ðað/ f, capacity; extension, space; mental capacity, talent; opportunity, means; Law. capacity. **c. de compra,** buying power, purchasing power. **c. de producción,** output

capacitación /kapaθita'θion; kapasita'sion/ f, qualification, (act of) qualifying; (act of) training

capacitar /kapaθi'tar; kapasi'tar/ vt to capacitate, qualify, enable

capar /ka'par/ vt to castrate, geld; Inf. diminish, reduce

caparazón /kapara'θon; kapara'son/ m, caparison, horse blanket; waterproof cover; hood (of carriages); nosebag; shell (insects, crustaceans)

capataz /kapa'taθ; kapa'tas/ m, foreman; steward; overseer

capaz /ka'paθ; ka'pas/ a capacious; large, spacious; capable, competent; Law. able

capcioso /kapˈθioso; kapˈsioso/ a deceitful, artful; captious, carping

capear /kape'ar/ vt to steal a cape; play the bull with a cape (bullfighting); Inf. put off with excuses, deceive; Naut. lie to

capellán /kape'ʎan; kape'yan/ m, chaplain; any ecclesiastic

capeo /ka'peo/ m, playing the bull with a cape (bullfighting)

caperuza /kape'ruθa; kape'rusa/ f, hood, pointed cap; Archit. coping-stone

capigorrón /kapigo'rron/ a Inf. loafing. m, loafer, idler

capilar /kapi'lar/ a capillary

capilla /ka'piʎa; ka'piya/ f, cowl, hood; chapel; Eccl. chapter; Eccl. choir. **c. ar-**

diente, chapelle ardente. **estar en c.,** to await execution (criminals); *Inf.* be in suspense, await anxiously

capillo /ka'piʎo; ka'piyo/ *m,* baby's bonnet; cocoon of silkworm; flowerbud

capirote /kapi'rote/ *m,* academic hood and cap; hood (falconry); tall pointed cap. **ser tonto de c.,** *Inf.* to be a complete fool

capitación /kapita'θion; kapita'sion/ *f,* poll-tax, capitation

capital /kapi'tal/ *a* relating to the head; capital (sins, etc.); main, principal. *m,* capital, patrimony; *Com.* capital stock. *f,* capital (city). **c. pagado,** paid-in capital stock

capitalismo /kapita'lismo/ *m,* capitalism

capitalista /kapita'lista/ *a* capitalistic. *mf* capitalist

capitalización /kapitaliθa'θion; kapitalisa'sion/ *f,* capitalization

capitalizar /kapitali'θar; kapitali'sar/ *vt* to capitalize

capitán /kapi'tan/ *m,* captain, skipper; chief, leader; ringleader. *Aer.* **c. de aviación,** group captain. **c. de fragata,** *Nav.* commander. **c. de puerto,** harbor master. **c. general de ejército,** field-marshal

capitana /kapi'tana/ *f,* admiral's ship; *Inf.* captain's wife

capitanear /kapitane'ar/ *vt* to captain, command; *Fig.* guide, lead

capitolio /kapi'tolio/ *m,* dignified building; *Archit.* acropolis; Capitol

capitulación /kapitula'θion; kapitula'sion/ *f,* agreement, pact; capitulation; *pl* marriage articles

capitular /kapitu'lar/ *a* capitulary, belonging to a Chapter. *m,* capitular, member of a Chapter —*vi* to make an agreement; capitulate; sing prayers; arrange order

capítulo /ka'pitulo/ *m, Eccl.* Chapter; meeting of town council, etc.; chapter (of book); item (in a budget); determination, decision

capó /ka'po/ *m, Auto.* hood

capón /ka'pon/ *a* castrated; gelded. *m,* capon; bundle of firewood or vines

caponera /kapo'nera/ *f,* coop for fattening capons; *Inf.* jail; *Inf.* place where one lives well free of charge

capota /ka'pota/ *f, Bot.* head of teasel; bonnet; hood (of vehicles)

capote /ka'pote/ *m,* short, brightly colored cape (used by bullfighters); cape coat; (cards) slam; *Inf.* scowl

capricho /ka'pritʃo/ *m,* caprice, fancy; strong desire

caprichoso /kapri'tʃoso/ *a* capricious; whimsical

Capricornio /kapri'kornio/ *m,* Capricorn

cápsula /'kapsula/ *f,* cartridge-case; bottlecap; (*Bot. Med. Chem. Zool.*) capsule

captar /kap'tar/ *vt* gain, attract (goodwill, attention, etc.); *Mech.* collect; monitor (foreign broadcasts)

captor /kap'tor/ *m,* capturer

captura /kap'tura/ *f, Law.* capture; seizing, arrest

capturar /kaptu'rar/ *vt* to capture; arrest, apprehend

capucha /ka'putʃa/ *f,* hood; cowl; *Print.* circumflex accent

capullo /ka'puʎo; ka'puyo/ *m,* cocoon; flower bud; acorn cup; *Anat.* prepuce

caqui /'kaki/ *m,* khaki; khaki color

cara /'kara/ *f,* face; likeness, aspect; façade, front; surface; side (of metal, etc.); mien. **c. a c.,** face to face; frankly; openly. *Inf.* **c. de juez,** severe face. *Inf.* **c. de pascua,** smiling face. *Inf.* **c. de vinagre,** sour face. **c. o cruz,** heads or tails. **de c.,** opposite. **hacer a dos caras,** to be deceitful, be two-faced. **hacer c. (a),** to stand up to

carabina /kara'βina/ *f,* carbine; rifle

caracol /kara'kol/ *m,* snail; snail's shell; cure; *Zool.* cochlea; winding stair. **c. marino,** periwinkle. **¡Caracoles!** Fancy!

caracola /kara'kola/ *f,* conch shell used as a horn

caracolear /karakole'ar/ *vi* to prance from side to side (horses)

carácter /ka'rakter/ *m,* sign, mark; character, writing (gen. *pl*); style of writing; brand (animals); nature, temperament; character, individuality, strong-mindedness, energy, firmness; condition, state, capacity. **comedia de c.,** psychological play. **en su c. de,** as in one's capacity as. **caracteres de imprenta,** printing types

característica /karakte'ristika/ *f,* quality, characteristic; *Math.* characteristic; actress who plays the part of an old woman

característico /karakte'ristiko/ *a* characteristic, distinctive. *m,* actor who plays roles of old men

caracterización /karakteriθa'θion; karakterisa'sion/ *f,* characterization; *Theat.* make-up

caracterizar /karakteri'θar; karakteri'sar/ *vt* to characterize; confer an office, honor, dignity, on; *Theat.* create a character; —*vr Theat.* to make up, dress as, a character

¡caramba! /ka'ramba/ *interj* gosh!; blast!

carámbano /ka'rambano/ *m,* icicle

carambola /karam'βola/ *f,* cannon (billiards); *Inf.* double effect; *Inf.* trick, deception

caramelo /kara'melo/ *m,* caramel; toffee

caramillo /kara'miʎo; kara'miyo/ *m,* flageolet; small flute, pipe; gossip, intrigue

carapacho /kara'patʃo/ *m,* carapace, shell

carátula /ka'ratula/ *f,* mask; *Fig.* dramatic art, the theater

caravana /kara'βana/ *f,* caravan, group of traders, pilgrims, etc. (especially in East); *Inf.* crowd of excursionists, picnickers, etc.

¡caray! /ka'rai/ *interj* blast!; gosh!

carbón /kar'βon/ *m,* coal; charcoal; **black chalk,** crayon. **c. bituminoso,** soft coal. **c. de coque,** coke. **c. de leña,** charcoal. **c. mineral,** coal, anthracite. **mina de c.,** coal-mine

carbonear /karβone'ar/ *vt* to turn into charcoal; *Naut.* coal

carboneo /karβo'neo/ *m,* coaling

carbonera /karβo'nera/ *f,* coal-cellar, coal-house, etc.; coal-scuttle; woman who sells charcoal or coal; charcoal burner

carbonería /karβone'ria/ *f,* coal or charcoal merchant's office

carbonero /karβo'nero/ *a* relating to coal or charcoal. *m,* collier; charcoal maker; coal merchant; *Naut.* coal-ship

carbónico /kar'βoniko/ *a Chem.* carbonic

carbonizar /karβoni'θar; karβoni'sar/ *vt* to carbonize

carbono /kar'βono/ *m, Chem.* carbon

carbunco /kar'βunko/ *m, Med.* carbuncle

carbúnculo /kar'βunkulo/ *m,* carbuncle, ruby

carburador /karβura'ðor/ *m,* carburetor

carcaj /kar'kah/ *m,* quiver (for arrows)

carcajada /karka'haða/ *f,* burst of laughter, guffaw. **reírse a carcajadas,** to roar with laughter

carcajearse /karkahe'arse/ *vi* to guffaw

carcamal /karka'mal/ *m, Inf.* dotard

cárcel /'karθel; 'karsel/ *f,* prison, jail

carcelario /karθe'lario; karse'lario/ *a* prison, jail

carcelero /karθe'lero; karse'lero/ **(-ra)** *a* jail —*n* jailer

cárcola /'karkola/ *f,* treadle (of a loom)

carcoma /kar'koma/ *f,* wood-worm; dry rot; *Fig.* gnawing care; spendthrift

carcomer /karko'mer/ *vt* to gnaw wood (worms); *Fig.* undermine (health, etc.); —*vr* be worm-eaten

carda /'karða/ *f,* card, carding; teasel head; card brush; *Inf.* reprimand

cardador /karða'ðor/ **(-ra)** *n* carder, comber

cardadura /karða'ðura/ *f,* carding; carding frame

cardar /kar'ðar/ *vt* to card, tease; brush up (felt, etc.)

cardenal /karðe'nal/ *m,* cardinal; cardinal bird; bruise

cárdeno /'karðeno/ *a* livid

cardíaco /kar'ðiako/ *a Med.* cardiac

cardinal /karði'nal/ *a* principal; cardinal (point); *Gram.* cardinal (number)

cardiógrafo /kar'ðiografo/ *m, Med.* cardiograph

cardiograma /karðio'grama/ *m, Med.* cardiogram

cardizal /karði'θal; karði'sal/ *m,* waste land covered with thistles and weeds

cardo /'karðo/ *m, Bot.* thistle

carear /kare'ar/ *vt* to confront; compare; —*vi* turn towards, face; —*vr* meet; come together

carecer /kare'θer; kare'ser/ *vi irr* to be short; lack, need (e.g. *Carece de las con-*

diciones necesarias, It lacks the necessary conditions). See **conocer**

carena /ka'rena/ *f, Naut.* bottom; careening

carenar /kare'nar/ *vt* to careen

carencia /ka'renθia; ka'rensia/ *f,* shortage, lack

carestía /kares'tia/ *f,* shortage, scarcity; famine; dearness, high price

careta /ka'reta/ *f,* mask; beekeeper's veil; fencing mask. *Fig.* **quitar la c. (a),** to unmask

carey /ka'rei/ *m, Zool.* shell turtle; tortoise-shell

carga /'karga/ *f,* loading; *Elec.* charging, charge; load; burden, weight; cargo; explosive charge; *Fig.* imposition; tax; duty, obligation. *Naut.* **c. de profundidad,** depth charge

cargadero /karga'ðero/ *m,* place where goods are loaded or unloaded

cargado /kar'gaðo/ *a* loaded; heavy, sultry; strong (tea, coffee). **c. de cadenas,** (prisoner, etc.) in chains. **c. de espaldas,** round-shouldered

cargador /karga'ðor/ *m,* loader; porter; dockhand; pitchfork; rammer; *Mech.* stoker; *Elec.* charger

cargamento /karga'mento/ *m, Naut.* cargo, freight, shipload

cargar /kar'gar/ *vt* to load; charge (guns, etc.); stoke; overburden; tax, impose; blame for, charge with; *Inf.* annoy, bore; *Argentina Inf.* to kid, tease; *Com.* charge, book; *Mil.* attack; (football) tackle; —*vi* tip, slope; (*with con*) carry away; be loaded with (fruit); assume responsibility; (*with sobre*) importune, urge; lean against; —*vr* turn (head, etc.); lower, grow darker (sky); (*with de*) be abundant (in or with); load oneself with

cargazón /karga'θon; karga'son/ *f,* cargo; loading; heaviness; darkness (of the sky)

cargo /'kargo/ *m,* loading; load, weight; post, office; duty, obligation; management, charge; care; *Com.* debit; accusation. *Com.* **el c. y la data,** debit and credit. **hacerse c. de,** to take charge of; understand; consider carefully. **ser en c. (a),** to be debtor (to)

cariarse /ka'riarse/ *vr* to become carious

caribe /ka'riβe/ *a* Caribbean. *mf* cannibal, savage

caricatura /karika'tura/ *f,* caricature

caricaturesco /karikatu'resko/ *a* caricaturish

caricaturista /karikatu'rista/ *mf* caricaturist

caricaturizar /karikaturi'θar; karikaturi'sar/ *vt* to caricature

caricia /ka'riθia; ka'risia/ *f,* caress

caridad /kari'ðað/ *f,* charity; charitableness; alms

caries /'karies/ *f,* caries

carilargo /kari'largo/ *a Inf.* long-faced

carilleno /kari'ʎeno; kari'yeno/ *a Inf.* plump-faced, round-faced

cariño /ka'riɲo/ *m*, affection; love; caress affectionately (gen. *pl*); fondness, inclination. **con c.**, affectionately

cariñoso /kari'ɲoso/ *a* affectionate; loving; kind

carismático /karis'matiko/ *a* charismatic

caritativo /karita'tiβo/ *a* charitable

cariz /ka'riθ; ka'ris/ *m*, appearance of the sky; look, face; aspect; *Inf.* outlook (for a business deal, etc.)

carmen /'karmen/ *m*, country house and garden (Granada); song; poem

carmesí /karme'si/ *a* crimson. *m*, crimson color; cramoisy

carmín /kar'min/ *m*, red, carmine color; red wild rose-tree and flower

carnada /kar'naða/ *f*, bait

carnaje /kar'nahe/ *m*, salted meat

carnal /kar'nal/ *a* carnal; lascivious; materialistic, worldly; related by blood

carnaval /karna'βal/ *m*, carnival. **martes de c.**, Shrove Tuesday

carnavalesco /karnaβa'lesko/ *a* carnival

carne /'karne/ *f*, flesh; meat; pulpy part of fruit; carnality. **c. concentrada**, meat extract. **c. congelada**, frozen meat. **c. de gallina** *Fig.* gooseflesh. **c. de membrillo**, quince cheese or conserve. **c. y hueso**, *Fig.* flesh and blood. *Inf.* **cobrar carnes**, to put on weight. **poner toda la c. en el asador**, *Inf.* to put all one's eggs in one basket

carnero /kar'nero/ *m*, sheep; mutton; mortuary; charnel-house; family burial vault. **c. marino**, *Zool.* seal

carnet /kar'net/ *m*, notebook, diary; identity card; membership card, pass. **c. de chófer**, driving license

carnicería /karniθe'ria; karnise'ria/ *f*, butcher's shop; carnage, slaughter

carnicero /karni'θero; karni'sero/ *a* carnivorous; inhuman, cruel. *m*, butcher

carnívoro /kar'niβoro/ *a* carnivorous. *m*, carnivore

carnosidad /karnosi'ðað/ *f*, proud flesh; local fat; fatness

carnoso /kar'noso/ *a* meaty; fleshy; full of marrow; *Bot.* pulpy, juicy

caro /'karo/ *a* beloved; expensive; dear —*adv* expensively; dear

carótida /ka'rotiða/ *f*, carotid artery

carpa /'karpa/ *f*, *Ichth.* carp. **c. dorada**, goldfish

carpanta /kar'panta/ *f*, *Inf.* violent hunger

carpeta /kar'peta/ *f*, table or chest cover, doily; writing case; portfolio; docket, letter file

carpetazo, dar /karpe'taθo, dar; karpe'taso, dar/ *vt* to shelve (a project, etc.)

carpintear /karpinte'ar/ *vi* to carpenter

carpintería /karpinte'ria/ *f*, carpenter's shop; carpentry

carpintero /karpin'tero/ *m*, carpenter, joiner; *Theat.* scene-shifter. **c. de carretas**, wheelwright. **c. de ribera**, shipwright

carraca /ka'rraka/ *f*, rattle; ratchet-drill

carraspear /karraspe'ar/ *vi* to clear one's throat, cough

carraspera /karras'pera/ *f*, *Inf.* hoarseness

carrera /ka'rrera/ *f*, run; race; racing; racecourse; *Astron.* course; high road; route; *Mas.* layer, course; line, row; *Fig.* ladder (in stockings, etc.); course; duration (of life); career, profession; conduct; girder. **c. de fondo**, long-distance race. **c. de relevos, c. de equipos**, relay race. **a c. abierta, a c. tendida**, at full speed

carrerista /karre'rista/ *mf* racing enthusiast; professional racer

carreta /ka'rreta/ *f*, long, narrow two-wheeled cart; wagon; tumbril

carretada /karre'taða/ *f*, cart-load; *Inf.* great deal, mass

carretaje /karre'tahe/ *m*, cartage; carriage, transport

carrete /ka'rrete/ *m*, spool, reel, bobbin; fishing reel; *Elec.* coil; *Photo.* film spool

carretera /karre'tera/ *f*, high road

carretería /karrete'ria/ *f*, number of carts; carting trade; cartwright's yard

carretero /karre'tero/ *m*, cartwright; carter, driver

carretilla /karre'tiʎa; karre'tiya/ *f*, wheelbarrow; hand cart; railway truck; squib. **de c.**, *Inf.* mechanically, without thought; (*with saber, repetir*, etc.) by rote

carretón /karre'ton/ *m*, truck, trolley; hand cart

carril /ka'rril/ *m*, wheel mark; furrow, rut; cart road, narrow road; rail (railways, etc.)

carrillera /karri'ʎera; karri'yera/ *f*, jaw (of some animals); chin strap; *pl* bonnet strings, etc.

carrillo /ka'rriʎo; ka'rriyo/ *m*, cheek; jowl

carriola /ka'rriola/ *f*, truckle bed; curricle

carro /'karro/ *m*, cart; cartload; car, chariot; carriage (of a typewriter, etc.); chassis; *Astron.* Plow, Great Bear. *Mil.* **c. blindado**, armored car. *Mil.* **c. de asalto**, tank. **c. de mudanzas**, moving van. **c. de regar**, watercart

carrocería /karroθe'ria; karrose'ria/ *f*, place where carriages are made, sold, repaired; *Auto.* coachwork, body shop

carrocha /ka'rrotʃa/ *f*, eggs (of insects)

carromato /karro'mato/ *m*, road wagon; covered wagon

carroña /ka'rroɲa/ *f*, putrid flesh, carrion

carroza /ka'rroθa; ka'rrosa/ *f*, elegant coach; state coach; carriage; float (for tableaux, etc.); *Naut.* awning

carruaje /ka'rruahe/ *m*, carriage; any vehicle

carta /'karta/ *f*, letter; charter; royal order; playing card; chart, map. **c. certificada**, registered letter. **c. de amparo**, safe-conduct. **c. de crédito**, *Com.* letter of credit. **c. de marear**, sea chart. **c. de naturaleza**, naturalization papers. **c. de pé-**

same, letter of condolence.•**c. de venta**, *Com.* bill of sale. **c. ejecutoria de hidalguía**, letters patent of nobility. **carta-poder**, letter of proxy, proxy. **cartas rusas**, (game of) consequences. **poner las cartas boca arriba**, *Fig.* to lay one's cards on the table

cartabón /karta'βon/ *m*, set-square; shoemaker's slide; quadrant

cartaginés /kartahi'nes/ **(-esa)** *a* and *n* Carthaginian

cartapacio /karta'paθio; karta'pasio/ *m*, note-book; schoolbag, satchel; file, batch of papers

cartear /karte'ar/ *vi Cards.* to play low; —*vr* to correspond by letter

cartel /kar'tel/ *m*, placard, poster; cartel; pasquinade, lampoon. **fijar carteles**, to placard

cartela /kar'tela/ *f*, tablet (for writing); slip (of paper, etc.); *Archit.* console, bracket

cartelera /karte'lera/ *f*, billboard

cartelero /karte'lero/ *m*, billpaster, billsticker

carteo /kar'tco/ *m*, correspondence (by letter)

cartera /kar'tera/ *f*, pocketbook; wallet; dispatch-case; portfolio; notebook; pocket flap; office of a cabinet minister; *Com.* shares

cartería /karte'ria/ *f*, sorting room (in a post-office)

carterista /karte'rista/ *mf* pickpocket

cartero /kar'tero/ *m*, mail carrier, postman

Cartesio /kar'tesio/ Descartes

carteta /kar'teta/ *f*, lansquenet (card game)

cartilaginoso /kartilahi'noso/ *a* cartilaginous

cartílago /kar'tilago/ *m*, cartilage

cartilla /kar'tiʎa; kar'tiya/ *f*, first reading book; primer; certificate of ordination; note-book; liturgical calendar. **c. de racionamiento**, ration book

cartógrafo /kar'tografo/ *m*, map maker

cartón /kar'ton/ *m*, pasteboard, cardboard; *Archit.* bracket; *Art.* cartoon, design

cartuchera /kartu't ʃera/ *f*, cartridge-pouch; cartridge-belt

cartucho /kar'tut ʃo/ *m*, cartridge; paper cone

cartuja /kar'tuha/ *f*, Carthusian Order or monastery

cartujo /kar'tuho/ *m*, Carthusian monk; *Inf.* taciturn, reserved man

cartulina /kartu'lina/ *f*, Bristol board, oaktag, pasteboard, card

carúncula /ka'runkula/ *f*, caruncle, comb of cock, etc.

casa /'kasa/ *f*, house; home; household; residence, dwelling; family house; *Com.* firm. **c. consistorial**, town hall. **c. cuna**, crèche. **c. de campo**, country-house. **c. de empeño**, pawnshop. **c. de**

huéspedes, boarding house, lodging-house. **c. de los sustos**, haunted house (at amusement park). **c. de moneda**, mint. **c. de socorro**, First Aid Post. **c. de vecindad**, tenement. **c. mala**, house of ill repute. **c. solar** *or* **c. solariega**, family seat. **en c.**, at home (also sport usage). **poner c.**, to set up house

casaca /ka'saka/ *f*, dress coat. **volver la c.**, to become a turncoat, change one's allegiance

casación /kasa'θion; kasa'sion/ *f*, *Law.* cassation

casadero /kasa'ðero/ *a* marriageable

casadoro /kasa'ðoro/ *m*, *Costa Rica* bus

casamiento /kasa'miento/ *m*, marriage; wedding

casar /ka'sar/ *vt* to marry (of a priest); *Law.* repeal; *Inf.* marry off; join; match, harmonize; —*vi* and *vr* (*with con*) to get married

casar /ka'sar/ *m*, group of houses

casca /'kaska/ *f*, grape skin; tan (bark); shell, peel, rind

cascabel /kaska'βel/ *m*, small bell (for harness, etc.). **serpiente de c.**, rattlesnake. *Inf.* **ser un c.**, to be featherbrained

cascabeleo /kaska'βeleo/ *m*, jingling of bells

cascabillo /kaska'βiʎo; kaska'βiyo/ *m*, husk (of cereals)

cascada /kas'kaða/ *f*, cascade; waterfall

cascadura /kaska'ðura/ *f*, cracking, crack

cascajo /kas'kaho/ *m*, gravel, shingle; *Inf.* broken, old things; junk; nuts

cascanueces /kaska'nueθes; kaska'nueses/ *m*, nutcrackers

cascar /kas'kar/ *vt* to crack, split, break; *Inf.* beat; *Fig. Inf.* break down (of health); —*vi Inf.* talk, chatter

cáscara /'kaskara/ *f*, shell; peel, rind; bark. *Med.* **c. sagrada**, cascara

cascarón /kaska'ron/ *m*, eggshell; *Archit.* vault

cascarrabias /kaska'rraβias/ *mf Inf.* spitfire

casco /'kasko/ *m*, cranium; broken fragment of china, glass, etc.; crown of hat; helmet; tree of saddle; bottle; tank, pipe; barrel; *Naut.* hull; hoof; quarter (of fruit); *pl Inf.* head. **c. colonial**, sunhelmet. **c. respiratorio**, smoke-helmet

caserío /kase'rio/ *m*, group of houses; country house

casero /ka'sero/ *a* home made; home bred; familiar; informa; *Inf.* domesticated, home-loving; domestic. *m*, *landlord*; caretaker; tenant

caserón /kase'ron/ *m*, large tumbledown house, mansion, hall

caseta /ka'seta/ *f*, hut; cottage; booth, stall. **c. de baños**, bathing van

casi /'kasi/ *adv* almost, nearly. **c. c.**, very nearly

casilla /ka'siʎa; ka'siya/ *f*, hut; cabin;

lodge; ticket office; pigeon-hole. *Aer.* **c. del piloto,** cockpit

casillero /kasi'ʎero; kasi'yero/ *m,* file cabinet, filing cabinet; locker (as in a locker room); set of pigeonholes; *Sports.* scoreboard; *Rail.* crossing guard

casino /ka'sino/ *m,* casino; club

caso /'kaso/ *m,* happening, event; chance, hazard; occasion, opportunity; case, matter; (*Med. Gram.*) case. **en el c. de,** in a position to (e.g. *No estamos en el c. de pagar tanto dinero.* We are in no position to pay so much money). **en tal c.,** in such a case. **en todo c.,** in any case. **no hacer c. de,** to take no notice of. **venir al c.,** to be opportune

caspa /'kaspa/ *f,* dandruff; scab

caspio /'kaspio/ *a* Caspian

casquillo /kas'kiʎo; kas'kiyo/ *m,* tip, cap, ferrule; socket; arrow-head; metal cartridge-case

casta /'kasta/ *f,* race; caste; breed (animals); kind, species, quality. **de buena c.,** pedigree (e.g. *perros de buena c.,* pedigree dogs)

castaña /kas'taɲa/ *f, Bot.* chestnut; knot, bun (of hair)

castañar /kasta'ɲar/ *m,* chestnut plantation or grove

castañetear /kastaɲete'ar/ *vi* to play the castanets; snap one's fingers; chatter (of teeth); knock together (of knees)

castaño /kas'taɲo/ *a* chestnut-colored. *m,* chestnut tree; chestnut wood. **c. de Indias,** horse-chestnut tree

castañuela /kasta'ɲuela/ *f,* castanet. **tocar las castañuelas,** to play the castanets

castellano /kaste'ʎano; kaste'yano/ **(-na)** *n* Castilian; Spaniard. *m,* Spanish (language); castellan —*a* Castilian; Spanish

casticismo /kasti'θismo; kasti'sismo/ *m,* purity (of language); Spanish spirit; traditionalism

castidad /kasti'ðað/ *f,* chastity

castigador /kastiga'ðor/ *a* punishing. *m,* punisher; *Inf.* lady-killer

castigadora /kastiga'ðora/ *f, Inf.* manhunter

castigar /kasti'gar/ *vt* to punish; chastise; chasten, advise; pain, grieve; correct, edit; decrease (expenses); *Com.* allow a discount

castigo /kas'tigo/ *m,* punishment; emendation, correction

Castilla /kas'tiʎa; kas'tiya/ Castile

castillo /kas'tiʎo; kas'tiyo/ *m,* castle; howdah. **c. de naipes,** house of cards. **c. de proa,** *Naut.* forecastle. **c. fuerte,** fortified castle. *Inf.* **hacer castillos en el aire,** to build castles in the air or in Spain

castizo /kas'tiθo; kas'tiso/ *a* pureblooded; prolific; pure (of language); typically Spanish; traditional

casto /'kasto/ *a* chaste; pure, unsullied

castor /kas'tor/ *m, Zool.* beaver (animal and fur); soft, woollen cloth

castración /kastra'θion; kastra'sion/ *f,* castration, gelding

castrar /kas'trar/ *vt* to castrate, geld; prune; remove honeycomb from hives; weaken

castrense /kas'trense/ *a* military

castrista /kas'trista/ *v* and *mf* Castroite

casual /ka'sual/ *a* accidental, casual

casualidad /kasuali'ðað/ *f,* chance, coincidence. **por c.,** by chance. **ser mucha c. que...,** to be too much of a coincidence that...

casucha /ka'sutʃa/ *f, Inf.* tumbledown hut

casuista /ka'suista/ *a* casuistic. *mf* casuist

cata /'kata/ *f,* tasting; taste, sample

catabolismo /kataβo'lismo/ *m,* catabolism

cataclismo /kata'klismo/ *m,* cataclysm

catacumbas /kata'kumbas/ *f pl,* catacombs

catador /kata'ðor/ *m,* taster, sampler

catadura /kata'ðura/ *f,* tasting; look, countenance (gen. qualified)

catafalco /kata'falko/ *m,* catafalque

catalán /kata'lan/ **(-ana)** *a* and *n* Catalan, Catalonian. *m,* Catalan (language)

cataléptico /kata'leptiko/ *a* cataleptic

catalogar /katalo'gar/ *vt* to catalog, list

catálogo /ka'talogo/ *m,* catalog, list

Cataluña /kata'luɲa/ Catalonia

cataplasma /kata'plasma/ *f,* cataplasm

catapulta /kata'pulta/ *f,* catapult

catar /ka'tar/ *vt* to taste, sample; see, examine; inspect; regard

catarata /kata'rata/ *f,* cataract, waterfall; *Med.* cataract (of the eyes)

catarral /kata'rral/ *a* catarrhal

catarro /ka'tarro/ *m,* catarrh; common cold

catástrofe /ka'tastrofe/ *f, Lit.* tragic climax; catastrophe

catastrófico /katas'trofiko/ *a* catastrophic

catavinos /kata'βinos/ *m,* professional wine taster; *Inf.* tippler, tavern haunter

catecismo /kate'θismo; kate'sismo/ *m,* catechism

cátedra /'kateðra/ *f,* university chair; chair in a Spanish *instituto;* professorship; university lecture room; subject taught by professor; reading desk, lectern; *Eccl.* throne; *Eccl.* see. **c. del espíritu santo,** pulpit. **c. de San Pedro,** Holy See

catedral /kate'ðral/ *f,* and *a* cathedral

catedrático /kate'ðratiko/ **(-ca)** *n* professor

categoría /katego'ria/ *f, Philos.* category; class, rank

categórico /kate'goriko/ *a* categorical, downright

cateo /ka'teo/ *m, West. Hem.* sampling; prospecting; house search (by the police)

catequismo /kate'kismo/ *m,* catechism; question and answer method of teaching

catequista /kate'kista/ *mf* catechist

catequizar /kateki'θar; kateki'sar/ *vt* to catechize; persuade, induce

caterva /ka'terβa/ *f.* crowd, throng; jumble, collection

catéter /ka'teter/ *m, Surg.* probe; catheter

catódico /ka'toðiko/ *a Elec.* cathodic

cátodo /'katoðo/ *m,* cathode

catolicismo /katoli'θismo; katoli'sismo/ *m,* Catholicism

católico /ka'toliko/ **(-ca)** *a* universal, catholic; infallible —*a* and *n* Catholic (by religion)

catorce /ka'torθe; ka'torse/ *a* fourteen; fourteenth. *m,* number fourteen; fourteenth (of days of month)

catre /'katre/ *m,* camp-bed; truckle-bed; cot

Cáucaso, el /'kaukaso, el/ the Caucasus

cauce /'kauθe; 'kause/ *m,* river or stream bed; ditch, irrigation canal

cauchal /kau'tʃal/ *m,* rubber plantation

cauchera /kau'tʃera/ *f,* rubber tree

caucho /'kautʃo/ *m,* caoutchouc, rubber

caución /kau'θion; kau'sion/ *f,* caution, precaution; surety; security

caucional /kauθio'nal; kausio'nal/ *a* See **libertad**

caudal /kau'ðal/ *m,* wealth, capital; flow, volume (of water); plenty, abundance (e.g. *un c de conocimientos,* a wealth of knowledge)

caudaloso /kauða'loso/ *a* carrying much water; wealthy; abundant

caudillo /kau'ðiʎo; kau'ðiyo/ *m,* head, leader; chief tain. **el C.,** (title of Francisco Franco)

causa /'kausa/ *f,* cause; reason, motive; lawsuit; *Law.* trial. **c. final,** *Philos.* final cause. **c. pública,** public welfare. **ser c. bastante para...,** to be reason enough to...

causador /kausa'ðor/ **(-ra)** *a* motivating —*n* occasioner, originator

causalidad /kausali'ðað/ *f,* causality

causante /kau'sante/ *a* causative, causing. *m, Law.* principal; *Mexico* taxpayer

causar /kau'sar/ *vt* to cause; occasion

causticidad /kaustiθi'ðað; kaustisi'ðað/ *f,* causticity; mordacity

cáustico /'kaustiko/ *a* burning, caustic; scathing; mordant; *Surg.* caustic

cautela /kau'tela/ *f,* caution; astuteness, cunning

cauteloso /kaute'loso/ *a* cautious; cunning

cauterio /kau'terio/ *m,* cautery

cauterización /kauteriθa'θion; kauterisa'sion/ *f,* cauterization

cauterizar /kauteri'θar; kauteri'sar/ *vt* to cauterize

cautivar /kauti'βar/ *vt* to capture; captivate, charm; attract; —*vi* become a prisoner

cautiverio /kauti'βerio/ *m,* captivity

cautivo /kau'tiβo/ **(-va)** *a* and *n* captive

cauto /'kauto/ *a* cautious; prudent; sly

cava /'kaβa/ *f,* digging (especially vines); wine cellar in royal palaces

cavador /kaβa'ðor/ **(-ra)** *n* digger, hoer

cavadura /kaβa'ðura/ *f,* digging, hoeing; sinking (wells)

cavar /ka'βar/ *vt* to dig, hoe; sink (wells); —*vi* hollow; *Fig.* go deeply into a thing

caverna /ka'βerna/ *f,* cavern, cave; *Med.* cavity (generally in the lung)

cavernícola /kaβer'nikola/ *a* cave. **hombre c.,** cave-man

cavernoso /kaβer'noso/ *a* cavernous; caverned; *Fig.* hollow (cough, etc.); deaf

cavidad /kaβi'ðað/ *f,* cavity; sinus; cell

cavilación /kaβila'θion; kaβila'sion/ *f,* caviling

cavilar /kaβi'lar/ *vt* to cavil; criticize

caviloso /kaβi'loso/ *a* captious

caza /'kaθa; 'kasa/ *f,* hunting; hunt, chase; game. *m, Aer.* fighter. *Aer.* **c. lanzacohetes,** rocket-launching aircraft. **c. nocturno,** night fighter. *Naut.* **dar c.,** to pursue

cazaautógrafos /ˌkaθaau'tografos; ˌkasaau'tografos/ *m,* autograph hunter

cazadero /kaθa'ðero; kasa'ðero/ *m,* hunting ground

cazador /kaθa'ðor; kasa'ðor/ *a* hunting. *m, Mil.* chasseur; huntsman

cazadora /kaθa'ðora; kasa'ðora/ *f,* huntress; jacket; forage cap

cazafortunas /kaθafor'tunas; kasafor'tunas/ *mf* fortune hunter

cazar /ka'θar; ka'sar/ *vt* to hunt; chase; *Fig. Inf.* run to earth; *Fig. Inf.* catch out; *Inf.* overcome by flattery

cazo /'kaθo; 'kaso/ *m,* ladle; dipper

cazoleta /kaθo'leta; kaso'leta/ *f,* small pan; bowl (of pipe, etc.); sword guard; boss of a shield; pan (of a firelock)

cazuela /ka'θuela; ka'suela/ *f,* earthenware cooking dish; stew-pot; part of theater formerly reserved for women; *Theat.* gallery

cazurro /ka'θurro; ka'surro/ *a Inf.* unsociable; surly, boorish

ce /θe; se/ *f,* name of the letter C —*interj* Look! Chist! **ce por be,** in detail

cebada /θe'βaða; se'βaða/ *f,* barley (plant and grain). **c. perlada,** pearl barley

cebado /θe'βaðo; se'βaðo/ *a* on the prowl; having tasted human flesh (animal) -

cebar /θe'βar; se'βar/ *vt* to feed or fatten (animals); fuel, feed (furnace, etc.); prime, charge (fire-arms, etc.); start up (machines); bait (fish hook); stimulate (passion, etc.); —*vi* stick in, penetrate (nails, screws, etc.); —*vr* put one's mind to; grow angry. **cebarse en vanas esperanzas,** to nurture vain hopes

cebo /'θeβo; 'seβo/ *m,* fodder; detonator; encouragement; food; bait

cebolla /θe'βoʎa; se'βoya/ *f,* onion; onion bulb; any bulbous stem; oil bulb (of lamp). **c. escalonia,** shallot

cebollana /θeβoˈʎana; seβoˈyana/ f,
chive

cebollero /θeβoˈʎero; seβoˈyero/ **(-ra)** n
onion seller

cebolleta /θeβoˈʎeta; seβoˈyeta/ f, leek;
young onion

cebollino /θeβoˈʎino; seβoˈyino/ m, onion seed; onion bed; chive

cebra /ˈθeβra; ˈseβra/ f, zebra

ceca /ˈθeka; ˈseka/ f, mint (for coining
money); name of mosque in Cordova. **de
C. en Meca,** from pillar to post, hither
and thither

cecear /θeθeˈar; seseˈar/ vi to lisp

ceceo /θeˈθeo; seˈseo/ m, lisping

cedazo /θeˈðaθo; seˈðaso/ m, sieve,
strainer

ceder /θeˈðer; seˈðer/ vt to cede, give up;
transfer; —vi give in, yield; diminish, decrease (fever, storm, etc.); fail, end; happen, turn out; sag, give, stretch. **No c. la
fama a,** to be no less famous than

cedro /ˈθeðro; ˈseðro/ m, cedar tree; cedar wood. **c. dulce,** red cedar

cédula /ˈθeðula; ˈseðula/ f, document,
certificate, card. Eccl. **c. de comunión,**
Communion card. **c. personal,** identity
card. **c. real,** royal letters patent

céfiro /ˈθefiro; ˈsefiro/ m, west wind;
Poet. zephyr

cegajoso /θegaˈhoso; segaˈhoso/ a blear-
eyed

cegar /θeˈgar; seˈgar/ vi irr to become
blind; —vt to put out the eyes; Fig. blind;
wall up, close up, stop up; infatuate
—Pres. Indic. **ciego, ciegas, ciega, cie-
gan.** Pres. Subjunc. **ciegue, ciegues,
ciegue, cieguen**

cegato /θeˈgato; seˈgato/ a Inf. short-
sighted

ceguedad, ceguera /θegeˈðað, θeˈgera;
segeˈðað, seˈgera/ f, blindness; delusion;
ignorance

ceja /ˈθeha; ˈseha/ f, eyebrow; cloud cap;
mountain peak; Mus. bridge (of stringed
instruments). Fig. **quemarse las cejas,** to
burn the midnight oil

cejar /θeˈhar; seˈhar/ vi to go backwards;
give way, hesitate

cejijunto /θehiˈhunto; sehiˈhunto/ a having eyebrows that almost meet, beetle-
browed

cejo /ˈθeho; ˈseho/ m, river mist

cejudo /θeˈhuðo; seˈhuðo/ a having long
thick eyebrows

celada /θeˈlaða; seˈlaða/ f, helmet; ambush; fraud, trick

celador /θelaˈðor; selaˈðor/ **(-ra)** a
watchful, zealous —n supervisor; caretaker; guard (at a museum, etc.)

celaje /θeˈlahe; seˈlahe/ m, sky with scud-
ding clouds (gen. pl); skylight, window;
promising sign, presage

celar /θeˈlar; seˈlar/ vt to be zealous in
discharge of duties; spy upon; watch;
oversee, superintend; conceal; engrave

celda /ˈθelda; ˈselda/ f, cell

celebración /θeleβraˈθion; seleβraˈsion/ f,
celebration; applause

celebrador /θeleβraˈðor; seleβraˈðor/
(-ra) n celebrator; applauder

celebrante /θeleˈβrante; seleˈβrante/ a
celebrating. m, Eccl. celebrant

celebrar /θeleˈβrar; seleˈβrar/ vt to celebrate; applaud; praise; venerate; hold,
conduct; **c. que** + subj, to be happy that,
be glad that —vt and vi Eccl. officiate;
—vr take place

célebre /ˈθeleβre; ˈseleβre/ a famous

celebridad /θeleβriˈðað; seleβriˈðað/ f,
fame, celebrity; magnificence, show,
pomp

celeridad /θeleriˈðað; seleriˈðað/ f, celerity

celeste /θeˈleste; seˈleste/ a celestial,
heavenly

celestial /θelesˈtial; selesˈtial/ a celestial,
heavenly; perfect, delightful; Inf. foolish
(ironical)

celestina /θelesˈtina; selesˈtina/ f, procuress (allusion to Tragicomedia de Calixto y
Melibea)

celibato /θeliˈβato; seliˈβato/ m, celibacy;
Inf. bachelor

célibe /ˈθeliβe; ˈseliβe/ a celibate, unmarried. mf unmarried person

celo /ˈθelo; ˈselo/ m, enthusiasm, ardor;
religious zeal; devotion; jealousy; heat,
rut; pl jealousy, suspicion. **dar celos (a),**
to make jealous

celosía /θeloˈsia; seloˈsia/ f, lattice; Venetian blind

celoso /θeˈloso; seˈloso/ a zealous; jealous; suspicious

celta /ˈθelta; ˈselta/ a Celtic. mf Celt

célula /ˈθelula; ˈselula/ f, cell

celular /θeluˈlar; seluˈlar/ a cellular —m,
cellular phone

celulosa /θeluˈlosa; seluˈlosa/ f, cellulose

cementar /θemenˈtar; semenˈtar/ vt to
cement

cementerio /θemenˈterio; semenˈterio/
m, cemetery

cemento /θeˈmento; seˈmento/ m, cement

cena /ˈθena; ˈsena/ f, evening meal; supper; Last Supper

cenáculo /θeˈnakulo; seˈnakulo/ m, cena-
cle

cenador /θenaˈðor; senaˈðor/ m, diner
out; arbor, pergola

cenagal /θenaˈgal; senaˈgal/ m, quagmire;
Fig. impasse

cenar /θeˈnar; seˈnar/ vi to dine, sup;
—vt eat for evening meal, sup off

cenceño /θenˈθeɲo; senˈseɲo/ a slim,
thin

cencerrada /θenθeˈrraða; senseˈrraða/ f,
noisy mock serenade given to widows or
widowers on the first night of their new
marriage

cencerrear /θenθerreˈar; senserreˈar/ vi
to jingle; Inf. play out of tune; bang in
the wind, rattle; squeak

cencerreo /θenθe'rreo; sense'rreo/ *m*, jingling; jangle; rattling; squeaking

cencerro /θen'θerro; sen'serro/ *m*, cowbell

cendal /θen'dal; sen'dal/ *m*, gauze; *Eccl.* stole; barbs of a feather

cenicero /θeni'θero; seni'sero/ *m*, ashpan; ash-pit; ash-tray

ceniciento /θeni'θiento; seni'siento/ *a* ash colored, ashen. **la Cenicienta,** Cinderella

cenit /'θenit; 'senit/ *m*, *Astron.* zenith; *Fig.* peak, summit

ceniza /θe'niθa; se'nisa/ *f*, ash, cinders

cenotafio /θeno'tafio; seno'tafio/ *m*, cenotaph

censo /'θenso; 'senso/ *m*, census; agreement for settlement of an annuity; annual ground rent; leasehold

censor /θen'sor; sen'sor/ *m*, censor; censorious person; *Educ.* proctor

censual /θen'sual; sen'sual/ *a* pertaining to census, annuity, rents

censualista /θensua'lista; sensua'lista/ *mf* annuitant

censura /θen'sura; sen'sura/ *f*, censorship; criticism; blame, reproach; scandal, gossip; *Psychol.* censorship

censurable /θensu'raβle; sensu'raβle/ *a* reprehensible; censorable

censurar /θensu'rar; sensu'rar/ *vt* to judge; censure; criticize

centauro /θen'tauro; sen'tauro/ *m*, *Myth.* centaur

centavo /θen'taβo; sen'taβo/ *m*, hundredth part; cent

centella /θen'teʎa; sen'teya/ *f*, lightning; spark; flash; *Fig.* spark (of anger, affection, etc.)

centellear /θenteʎe'ar; senteye'ar/ *vi* to flash; twinkle; sparkle

centelleo /θente'ʎeo; sente'yeo/ *m*, scintillation; sparkle; flash

centén /θen'ten; sen'ten/ *m*, Spanish gold coin once worth 100 reals and later 25 pesetas

centena /θen'tena; sen'tena/ *f*, hundred

centenal, centenar /θente'nal, θente'nar; sente'nal, sente'nar/ *m*, hundred; centenary; rye field. **a centenares,** by the hundred, in crowds

centenario /θente'nario; sente'nario/ **(-ia)** *a* centenary —*n* centenarian. *m*, centenary

centeno /θen'teno; sen'teno/ *m*, *Bot.* rye

centésimo /θen'tesimo; sen'tesimo/ *a* and *m*, hundredth

centígrado /θen'tiɣraðo; sen'tiɣraðo/ *a* centigrade

centigramo /θenti'ɣramo; senti'ɣramo/ *m*, centigram

centilitro /θenti'litro; senti'litro/ *m*, centiliter

centímetro /θenti'metro; senti'metro/ *m*, centimeter. **c. cúbico,** cubic centimeter, milliliter

céntimo /'θentimo; 'sentimo/ *a* hundredth. *m*, centime (coin)

centinela /θenti'nela; senti'nela/ *mf* *Mil.* sentry, sentinel; person on watch. **estar de c.,** to be on sentry duty; be on guard

central /θen'tral; sen'tral/ *a* central; centric. *f*, head office; central depot; mother house. **c. de fuerza,** power-house. **c. telefónica,** telephone exchange

centralilla, centralita /θentra'liʎa, θentra'lita; sentra'liya, sentra'lita/ *f*, local exchange, private exchange

centralización /θentraliθa'θion; sentralisa'sion/ *f*, centralization

centralizador /θentraliθa'ðor; sentralisa'ðor/ *a* centralizing

centralizar /θentrali'θar; sentrali'sar/ *vt* to centralize

centrar /θen'trar; sen'trar/ *vt* to center

céntrico /'θentriko; 'sentriko/ *a* central, centric; centrally located; downtown

centrífugo /θen'trifuɣo; sen'trifuɣo/ *a* centrifugal

centrípeto /θen'tripeto; sen'tripeto/ *a* centripetal

centro /'θentro; 'sentro/ *m*, center; headquarters, meeting place, club; center, hub; middle; core (of a rope); *Fig.* focus. *Phys.* **c. de gravedad,** center of gravity. **c. de mesa,** table center-piece. *Anat.* **centro nervioso,** nerve center

centroamericano /θentroameri'kano; sentroameri'kano/ **(-na)** *a* and *n* Central American

ceñidamente /θeɲiða'mente; seɲiða'mente/ tightly (e.g. *un argumento c. organizado,* a tightly organized plot)

ceñido /θe'ɲiðo; se'ɲiðo/ *a* thrifty; waspwaisted, slender waisted; fitting (of garments)

ceñir /θe'ɲir; se'ɲir/ *vt irr* to girdle; surround; shorten, abbreviate; —*vr* be moderate (speech, expenditure, etc.); conform, confine oneself (to). **ceñirse a las reglas,** to abide by the rules —*Pres. Indic.* ciño, ciñes, ciñen. *Pres. Part.* ciñendo. *Preterite* ciñó, ciñeron. *Pres. Subjunc.* ciña, etc —*Imperf. Subjunc.* ciñese, etc.

ceño /'θeɲo; 'seɲo/ *m*, band, hoop; frown; *Fig.* dark outlook

ceñudo /θe'ɲuðo; se'ɲuðo/ *a* frowning

cepa /'θepa; 'sepa/ *f*, stump; vine-stock; root (tails, antlers, etc.); *Fig.* origin, trunk (of a family); *Biol.* strain. **de la más pura c.,** of the best quality

cepillar /θepi'ʎar; sepi'yar/ *vt* to brush; plane; smooth

cepillo /θe'piʎo; se'piyo/ *m*, brush; plane; poor-box, offertory-box. **c. para los dientes,** toothbrush. **c. para ropa,** clothes-brush. **c. para el suelo,** scrubbing-brush. **c. para las uñas,** nailbrush

cepo /'θepo; 'sepo/ *m*, bough; wooden stocks; snare; trap; poor-box; collecting-box

cera /'θera; 'sera/ *f*, beeswax; wax; wax

candles, etc., used at a function. *Inf.* **ser como una c.**, to be like wax (in the hands of)

cerador /θera'ðor; sera'ðor/ *m*, floor waxer (person)

ceradora /θera'ðora; sera'ðora/ *f*, floor waxer (machine)

cerámica /θe'ramika; se'ramika/ *f*, ceramics; ceramic art, pottery

cerámico /θe'ramiko; se'ramiko/ *a* ceramic

cerbatana /θerβa'tana; serβa'tana/ *f*, blow-pipe, popgun; pea-shooter; ear-trumpet

cerca /'θerka; 'serka/ *f*, fence, wall

cerca /'θerka; 'serka/ *adv* near. **c. de**, near to; almost, nearly (e.g. *c. de las once*, nearly eleven o'clock)

cercado /θer'kaðo; ser'kaðo/ *m*, enclosure, fenced in place; fence

cercanía /θerka'nia; serka'nia/ *f*, nearness, proximity; (*gen. pl*) outskirts, surroundings

cercano /θer'kano; ser'kano/ *a* near, neighboring; impending; early

cercar /θer'kar; ser'kar/ *vt* to enclose; build a wall or fence round; to lay siege to; crowd round; *Mil.* surround

cercenamiento /θerθena'miento; sersena'miento/ **(a)** *m*, curtailment (of)

cercenar /θerθe'nar; serse'nar/ *vt* to lop off the ends, clip; curtail, diminish; abridge; whittle

cerciorar /θerθio'rar; sersio'rar/ *vt* to assure, confirm; —*vr* make sure

cerco /'θerko; 'serko/ *m*, ring, hoop; fence; siege; small conversational circle; spin, circling; halo (sun, moon); frame; sash (of a window). **poner c.** (**a**), to lay siege to, blockade

cerda /'θerða; 'serða/ *f*, sow; bristle

Cerdeña /θer'ðeɲa; ser'ðeɲa/ Sardinia

cerdo /'θerðo; 'serðo/ *m*, pig, hog

cereal /θere'al; sere'al/ *a* and *m*, cereal

cerebelo /θere'βelo; sere'βelo/ *m*, *Anat.* cerebellum

cerebro /θe'reβro; se'reβro/ *m*, cerebrum; brain; intelligence

ceremonia /θere'monia; sere'monia/ *f*, ceremony; function, display; formality. **de c.**, ceremonial; formally. **por c.**, for politeness' sake

ceremonial /θeremo'nial; seremo'nial/ *a* ceremonial. *m*, ceremony; rite; protocol (rules of behavior)

ceremonioso /θeremo'nioso; seremo'nioso/ *a* ceremonious; formal, over-courteous

cereza /θe'reθa; se'resa/ *f*, cherry

cerezal /θere'θal; sere'sal/ *m*, cherry orchard

cerezo /θe'reθo; se'reso/ *m*, cherry tree; cherry wood

cerilla /θe'riʎa; se'riya/ *f*, wax taper; match; ear wax

cerner /θer'ner; ser'ner/ *vt irr* to sieve; watch, observe; *Fig.* sift, clarify; —*vi* bolt

(of plants); drizzle; —*vr* waddle; hover; threaten (of evil, etc.) —*Pres. Indic.* **cierno, ciernes, cierne, ciernen.** *Pres. Subjunc.* **cierna, ciernas, cierna, ciernan**

cernidillo /θerni'ðiʎo; serni'ðiyo/ *m*, drizzle; teetering walk

cernido /θer'niðo; ser'niðo/ *m*, sifting, sieving; sifted flour

cerniduras /θerni'ðuras; serni'ðuras/ *f pl*, siftings

cero /'θero; 'sero/ *m*, *Math.* zero; naught; (tennis) love. *Fig. Inf.* **ser un c.**, to be a mere cipher

cerote /θe'rote; se'rote/ *m*, cobbler's wax. *Inf.* fear

cerquita /θer'kita; ser'kita/ *adv* very near, hard by

cerradero, /θerra'ðero; serra'ðero,/ *m*, **cerradera** *f*, bolt staple; catch of a lock; clasp or strings of a purse

cerradizo /θerra'ðiθo; serra'ðiso/ *a* closable, lockable

cerrado /θe'rraðo; se'rraðo/ *a* closed; compact; incomprehensible, obscure; overcast, cloudy; *Inf.* taciturn; secretive. *m*, enclosure

cerradura /θerra'ðura; serra'ðura/ *f*, fastening, lock; closing, locking

cerraja /θe'rraha; se'rraha/ *f*, lock (of a door); bolt

cerrajería /θerrahe'ria; serrahe'ria/ *f*, locksmith's craft; locksmith's workshop or shop

cerrajero /θerra'hero; serra'hero/ *m*, locksmith

cerramiento /θerra'miento; serra'miento/ *m*, closing, locking up; fence; enclosure, shooting preserve; partition wall

cerrar /θe'rrar; se'rrar/ *vt irr* to close; lock, fasten, bolt; shut up; *Mech.* shut off, turn off; fold up; block or stop up; seal (letters, etc.); close down; terminate; obstruct; (*with con*) attack; —*vi* close; close in (of night, etc.); —*vr* heal up (wounds); close (flowers); *Radio.* close down; crowd together; *Fig.* stand firm. *Inf.* **cerrarse la espuela**, to take a nightcap, have a last drink. **c. la marcha**, to bring up the rear. **al c. la edición**, stop press. See **acertar**

cerrazón /θerra'θon; serra'son/ *f*, dark, overcast sky heralding a storm

cerril /θe'rril; se'rril/ *a* rough, rocky; wild, untamed (cattle, horses); *Inf.* boorish

cerrillar /θerri'ʎar; serri'yar/ *vt* to mill coins

cerro /'θerro; 'serro/ *m*, neck of an animal; spine, backbone; hill. *Fig.* **irse por los cerros de Úbeda**, to go off the track, indulge in irrelevancies

cerrojo /θe'rroho; se'rroho/ *m*, bolt (of a door, etc.); lock (of a door, gun, etc.)

certamen /θer'tamen; ser'tamen/ *m*, contest; competition; match

certero /θer'tero; ser'tero/ *a* well-aimed; sure, well-timed; knowledgeable, sure

certeza, certidumbre /θer'teθa, θerti'ðumbre; ser'tesa, serti'ðumbre/ f, certitude, assurance

certificación /θertifika'θion; sertifika-'sion/ f, certification; certificate; affidavit

certificado /θertifi'kaðo; sertifi'kaðo/ a certified; registered. m, registered letter; certificate

certificar /θertifi'kar; sertifi'kar/ vt to certify; register (letter, etc.)

certificatorio /θertifika'torio; sertifika-'torio/ a certifying or serving to certify

certísimo /θer'tisimo; ser'tisimo/ a learned form of the superlative of **cierto** (see **certísimo**)

certitud /θerti'tuð; serti'tuð/ f, certitude

cervantino /θerβan'tino; serβan'tino/ a Cervantine

cervecería /θerβeθe'ria; serβese'ria/ f, brewery; ale-house

cervecero /θerβe'θero; serβe'sero/ (**-ra**) n brewer; beer seller

cerveza /θer'βeθa; ser'βesa/ f, beer, ale. **c. negra**, stout

cerviz /θer'βiθ; ser'βis/ f, cervix, nape (of neck). **doblar** (or **bajar**) **la c.**, to humble oneself

cesación /θesa'θion; sesa'sion/ f, cessation, stopping

cesante /θe'sante; se'sante/ a dismissed; pensioned off. **declarar c.** (a), to dismiss (a person from a post). **estar c.**, to be out of a job

cesantía /θesan'tia; sesan'tia/ f, status of dismissed or retired official; retirement pension

cesar /θe'sar; se'sar/ vi to cease, stop, end; leave an employment; desist; retire

cesáreo /θe'sareo; se'sareo/ a Cesarean; imperial

cese /'θese; 'sese/ m, stopping of payment for an employment

cesión /θe'sion; se'sion/ f, cession; transfer; resignation; Law. release

césped /'θespeð; 'sespeð/ m, grass, sward; sod, lawn

cesta /'θesta; 'sesta/ f, basket, hamper; Sports. racket; cradle (for a wine bottle)

cestada /θes'taða; ses'taða/ f, basketful

cestería /θeste'ria; seste'ria/ f, basket-making, basketweaving; basket factory; basket shop; basketwork

cestero /θes'tero; ses'tero/ (**-ra**) n basket maker or seller

cesto /'θesto; 'sesto/ m, basket, hamper, skip

cesura /θe'sura; se'sura/ f, cesura

cetrino /θe'trino; se'trino/ a greenish-yellow; sallow; citrine; melancholy; reserved, aloof

cetro /'θetro; 'setro/ m, scepter; verge; reign

chabacanería /tʃaβakane'ria/ f, bad taste; vulgarity

chabacano /tʃaβa'kano/ a vulgar, common; rude, uncouth

chacal /tʃa'kal/ m, Zool. jackal

cháchara /'tʃatʃara/ f, Inf. empty chatter; verbiage

chacharear /tʃatʃare'ar/ vi to chatter; gabble, cackle

chacharero /tʃatʃa'rero/ a Inf. chattering; talkative

chacolotear /tʃakolote'ar/ vi to clatter, clink (loose horseshoe)

chacota /tʃa'kota/ f, merriment, mirth

chacotear /tʃakote'ar/ vi Inf. to be merry, have fun

chacotón /tʃako'ton/ a of a boisterous humor

chafado /tʃa'faðo/ a taken aback; disappointed

chafallar /tʃafa'ʎar; tʃafa'yar/ vt Inf. to mend carelessly, botch

chafar /tʃa'far/ vt to flatten; crumple, crease (clothes); Inf. heckle

chal /tʃal/ m, shawl

chalanear /tʃalane'ar/ vt to bargain; indulge in sharp practice

chalar /tʃa'lar/ vt to drive mad; enamor

chaleco /tʃa'leko/ m, waistcoat; cardigan

Chalo /'tʃalo/ pet form of the male given name Carlos "Charles", hence = English Chuck; Bud, Mac (in direct address to a male whose name one does not know)

chalote /tʃa'lote/ m, shallot

chalupa /tʃa'lupa/ f, shallop; launch; canoe; long boat, ship's boat

chamar /tʃa'mar/ vt Inf. to palm off, barter

chamarasca /tʃama'raska/ f, brushwood, tinder

chamarilero /tʃamari'lero/ (**-ra**) n secondhand dealer

chamarreta /tʃama'rreta/ f, sheepskin jacket; Mexico jacket

chambón /tʃam'βon/ a Inf. awkward, clumsy; lucky

chambonada /tʃambo'naða/ f, Inf. blunder; fluke, chance

chambra /'tʃambra/ f, dressing-jacket, peignoir, negligee

chamicera /tʃami'θera; tʃami'sera/ f, piece of scorched earth (woodland, etc.)

chamorro /tʃa'morro/ a close-cropped, shorn (hair)

champán /tʃam'pan/ m, champagne. **c. obrero**, humorous cider

champaña /tʃam'paɲa/ m, champagne

champar /tʃam'par/ vt Inf. to cast in a person's face, remind

champú /tʃam'pu/ m, shampoo

chamuscar /tʃamus'kar/ vt to scorch; singe

chanada /tʃa'naða/ f, Inf. trick, mischievous act

chancearse /tʃanθe'arse; tʃanse'arse/ vr to joke

chancero /tʃan'θero; tʃan'sero/ a joking, facetious

chanchollada /tʃantʃo'ʎaða; tʃantʃo-'yaða/ f, dirty trick, foul play, trick

chanchullo /tʃan'tʃuʎo; tʃan'tʃuyo/ m, Inf. fraud

chanciller /tʃanθiʎer; tʃansi'yer/ m,
chancellor

chancillería /tʃanθiʎe'ria; tʃansiye'ria/ f,
chancery

chancla /'tʃankla/ f, down at heel shoe;
heelless slipper

chancleta /tʃan'kleta/ f, heelless slipper,
babouche. mf Inf. ninny

chancleteo /tʃankle'teo/ m, clicking of
heelless slippers

chanclo /tʃanklo/ m, overshoe; Welling-
ton

chanfaina /tʃan'faina/ f, Cul. savory fric-
assee

chanflón /tʃan'flon/ a tough, coarse; ungainly

chantaje /tʃan'tahe/ m, blackmail

chantajista /tʃanta'hista/ mf blackmailer

chantar /tʃan'tar/ vt to put on, clothe;
Inf. tell plainly. Inf. **c. sus verdades,** to
tell hometruths

chanza /tʃanθa; 'tʃansa/ f, joke, jest

chapa /'tʃapa/ f, plate, sheet; veneer;
clasp; Inf. prudence, common sense;
rouge. **c. de hierro,** sheet-iron. **c. de
identidad,** number plate

chapado a la antigua /tʃa'paðo a la
an'tigua/ a old-fashioned

chapalear /tʃapale'ar/ vi to dabble in water; splash; clatter (of a horseshoe)

chapaleo /tʃapa'leo/ m, dabbling, paddling; splash; clattering, clink (of a horseshoe)

chapaleteo /tʃapale'teo/ m, lapping of
water; splashing (of rain)

chaparrear /tʃaparre'ar/ vi to pour with
rain

chaparrón /tʃapa'rron/ m, heavy shower
of rain, downpour

chapear /tʃape'ar/ vt to veneer; —vi
clatter (loose horseshoe)

chaperón /tʃape'ron/ m, hood

chapeta /tʃa'peta/ f, dim clasp; red flush
or spot on cheek

chapetón /tʃape'ton/ (-ona) n West
Hem. recently arrived European, especially Spaniard

chapino /tʃa'pino/ a and m, Mexico contemptuous Guatemalan

chapitel /tʃapi'tel/ m, Archit. capital;
spire

chapodar /tʃapo'ðar/ vt to prune, lop off
branches; cut down, reduce

chapotear /tʃapote'ar/ vt to sponge,
moisten, damp; —vi paddle, splash; dabble or trail the hands (in water)

chapoteo /tʃapo'teo/ m, moistening,
sponging; paddling, splashing; dabbling

chapucear /tʃapuθe'ar; tʃapuse'ar/ vt to
botch, do badly; bungle

chapuceramente /tʃapuθera'mente;
tʃapusera'mente/ adv awkwardly. **hablar
el japonés c.,** to speak broken Japanese

chapucería /tʃapuθe'ria; tʃapuse'ria/ f,
roughness, poor workmanship; botch

chapucero /tʃapu'θero; tʃapu'sero/ a
rough, badly finished; bungling, clumsy,
awkward

chapurrado /tʃapu'rraðo/ a broken (e.g.
hablar un italiano c., to speak broken Italian)

chapurrar, chapurrear /tʃapu'rrar,
tʃapurre'ar/ vt to speak badly (a language); jabber; Inf. mix (drinks)

chapuz /tʃa'puθ; tʃa'pus/ m, ducking,
submerging; plunge; unimportant job;
clumsiness

chapuzar /tʃapu'θar; tʃapu'sar/ vt to
duck, submerge; plunge

chaqueta /tʃa'keta/ f, jacket; Mech. casing

chaquetilla /tʃake'tiʎa; tʃake'tiya/ f,
short jacket; coatee; blazer

chaquetón /tʃake'ton/ m, short coat. **c.
de piloto,** Aer. pea-jacket

charca /'tʃarka/ f, pond, pool; reservoir

charco /'tʃarko/ m, puddle; Inf. sea

charla /'tʃarla/ f, Inf. chatter; conversation; talk, informal lecture

charlar /'tʃarlar/ vi Inf. to prattle, chatter;
chat, converse; give a talk (on)

charlatán /tʃarla'tan/ (-ana) a loquacious, garrulous; indiscreet; fraudulent,
false —n charlatan; chatterer

charlatanería /tʃarlatane'ria/ f, loquac-
ity, garrulity; quackery

charlatanismo /tʃarlata'nismo/ m, charlatanism, quackery

charnela /tʃar'nela/ f, hinge; hinged joint

charol /tʃa'rol/ m, japan, varnish; patent
leather

charolar /tʃaro'lar/ vt to japan, varnish

charpa /'tʃarpa/ f, pistol-belt; sling

charrán /tʃa'rran/ (-ana) n rogue, trickster

charranada /tʃarra'naða/ f, roguery,
knavery

charrería /tʃarre'ria/ f, tawdriness; gaud-
iness

charro /'tʃarro/ a churlish, coarse; flashy,
tawdry

chasca /'tʃaska/ f, brushwood, firewood

chascar /tʃas'kar/ vi to creak, crack;
clack (the tongue); swallow

chascarrillo /tʃaska'rriʎo; tʃaska'rriyo/
m, Inf. amusing anecdote, good story

chasco /'tʃasko/ m, trick, practical joke;
disappointment. **llevarse un c.,** to meet
with a disappointment

chasis /'tʃasis/ m, Auto. chassis; Photo.
plate-holder; Mech. underframe

chasquear /tʃaske'ar/ vt to play a trick
on; wag (one's tongue); crack (a whip,
one's knuckles); break a promise, disappoint; —vi creak, crack; meet with a disappointment

chasquido /tʃas'kiðo/ m, crack (of
whip); creaking (of wood); click (of the
tongue)

chatarra /tʃa'tarra/ f, scrap iron; junk

chato /'tʃato/ a flat-nosed; flat

chauvinismo /tʃauβi'nismo/ m, chauvinism

chaval /tʃa'βal/ *a Inf.* young. *m*, lad

chaveta /tʃa'βeta/ *f, Mech.* bolt, pin, peg, cotter, key

checo /'tʃeko/ **(-ca)** *a* and *n* Czech. Czech (language)

Chejov /tʃe'hoβ/ Chekov

Chengis-Jan /tʃenhis-'han/ Genghis Khan

chepa /'tʃepa/ *f, Inf.* hunch (back); hump

cheque /'tʃeke/ *m*, check. **c. cruzado**, crossed check

chica /'tʃika/ *f,* girl; *Inf.* dear

chicana /tʃi'kana/ *f,* chicanery

chicano /tʃi'kano/ *a* and *n* Chicano, American of Mexican ancestry

chícharo /'tʃitʃaro/ *m*, pea

chicharrón /tʃitʃa'rron/ *m, Cul.* crackling; burnt meat; *Inf.* sunburnt person

chichón /tʃi'tʃon/ *m*, bruise, bump

chichonera /tʃitʃo'nera/ *f,* child's protective hat (something like a straw crashhelmet)

chicle /'tʃikle/ *m*, chewing gum

chico /'tʃiko/ *a* little, small; young. *m*, little boy; youth; *Inf.* old boy, dear. **Es un buen c.**, He's a good fellow

chicoleo /tʃiko'leo/ *m, Inf.* compliment

chicote /tʃi'kote/ *mf* sturdy child. *m, Inf.* cigar

chifla /'tʃifla/ *f,* whistling, whistle; tanner's paring knife

chiflado /tʃi'flaðo/ *a Inf.* cracked, daft; crack-brained

chifladura /tʃifla'ðura/ *f,* whistling; *Inf.* whim, mania, hobby

chiflar /tʃi'flar/ *vi* to whistle; —*vt* to make fun of, hiss; pare or scrape leather; *Inf.* swill, tipple; —*vr Inf.* have a slate loose; be slightly mad; *Inf.* lose one's head over, adore

chifle /'tʃifle/ *m*, whistle, whistling; decoy call (birds)

chile /'tʃile/ *m, Bot.* red pepper, chili

chileno /tʃi'leno/ **(-na)** *a* and *n* Chilean

chillador /tʃiʎa'ðor/ tʃiya'ðor/ *a* screaming, shrieking

chillar /tʃi'ʎar; tʃi'yar/ *vi* to scream, shriek; creak; squeak; jabber (monkeys, etc.); *Art.* be strident (of colors)

chillería /tʃiʎe'ria; tʃiye'ria/ *f,* shrieking, screaming

chillido /tʃi'ʎiðo; tʃi'yiðo/ *m*, scream, shriek; squeak (of mice, etc.); jabber (of monkeys, etc.)

chillón /tʃi'ʎon; tʃi'yon/ *a Inf.* screaming, yelling; strident, piercing; crude, loud (colors)

chimenea /tʃime'nea/ *f,* chimney; funnel; fireplace; kitchen range

chimpancé /tʃimpan'θe; tʃimpan'se/ *m*, chimpanzee

china /'tʃina/ *f,* pebble; porcelain, china; Chinese silk

chinche /'tʃintʃe/ *f,* bedbug; thumbtack, drawing-pin. *mf Inf.* bore

chinchona /tʃin'tʃona/ *f,* quinine

chinchorrería /tʃintʃorre'ria/ *f, Inf.* impertinence, tediousness; gossip

chinero /tʃi'nero/ *m*, china cupboard

chino /'tʃino/ **(-na)** *a* and *n* Chinese. *m*, Chinese (language)

Chipre /'tʃipre/ Cyprus

chipriota /tʃi'priota/ *a* and *mf* Cypriot

chiquillada /tʃiki'ʎaða; tʃiki'yaða/ *f,* childishness, puerility

chiquillería /tʃikiʎe'ria; tʃikiye'ria/ *f, Inf.* crowd of children

chiquillo /tʃi'kiʎo; tʃi'kiyo/ **(-lla)** *n* small boy

chiquito /tʃi'kito/ **(-ta)** *a dim* chico, tiny, very small —*n* little one, small boy

chiripa /tʃi'ripa/ *f,* (billiards) fluke; *Inf.* happy coincidence, stroke of luck; lucky guess

chirlar /tʃir'lar/ *vi Inf.* to gabble, talk loudly

chirlo /'tʃirlo/ *m*, knife wound, sabre cut; knife scar

chirona /tʃi'rona/ *f, Inf.* jail

chirriador /tʃirria'ðor/ *a* sizzling, crackling; creaking, squeaking

chirriar /tʃi'rriar/ *vi* to sizzle, crackle; creak, squeak; squawk; *Inf.* croak, sing out of tune

chirrido /tʃi'rriðo/ *m*, squawk; croaking; noise of grasshoppers; squeaking; creaking, creak

¡chis! /tʃis/ *interj* Shh! Silence!

chisme /'tʃisme/ *m*, gossip, tale; small household utensil, trifle

chismear /tʃisme'ar/ *vt* to tell tales, gossip

chismero /tʃismero/ **(-ra), chismoso** **(-sa)** *a* gossiping, talebearing —*n* gossip, tale bearer

chispa /'tʃispa/ *f,* spark; ember; *Elec.* spark; tiny diamond; small particle; wit; quickwittedness; *Inf.* drunkenness. **c. del encendido**, ignition spark

chispazo /tʃis'paθo; tʃis'paso/ *m*, flying out of a spark, sparking; damage done by spark; *Inf.* gossip, rumor

chispeante /tʃispe'ante/ *a* sparking; sparkling; *Fig.* scintillating (with wit etc.)

chispear /tʃispe'ar/ *vi* to throw out sparks, spark; sparkle, gleam; *Fig.* scintillate; drizzle gently

chisporrotear /tʃisporrote'ar/ *vi Inf.* to sputter; fizz

chisporroteo /tʃisporro'teo/ *m, Inf.* sputtering; fizz

chisposo /tʃis'poso/ *a* sputtering, throwing out sparks

chistar /tʃis'tar/ *vi* to speak, break silence (gen. used negatively)

chiste /'tʃiste/ *m*, witticism, bon mot; amusing incident; joke

chistera /tʃis'tera/ *f,* creel (for fish); *Inf.* top-hat, tile

chistoso /tʃis'toso/ *a* joking; amusing, funny

chiticallando /tʃitika'ʎando; tʃitika-'yando/ *adv* quietly, stealthily; *Inf.* on the quiet, in secret

¡chito! ¡chitón! /'tʃito; tʃi'ton/ *interj* Hush! Sh!

chiva /'tʃiβa/ *f, Panama* bus

chivo /'tʃiβo/ *n Zool.* kid. **c. expiatorio,** scapegoat

chocante /tʃo'kante/ *a* colliding; provoking; shocking; surprising

chocar /tʃo'kar/ *vi* to collide; strike (against); run into; fight, clash; —*vt* clink (glasses); provoke, annoy; surprise, shock. **¡Choca cinco!** Clasp five!, Gimme five!, Put it there!, Give some skin! (invitation to shake hands)

chocarrería /tʃokarre'ria/ *f,* coarse joke

chochear /tʃotʃe'ar/ *vi* to be senile; *Fig. Inf.* dote (on)

chocho /'tʃotʃo/ *a* senile; *Fig. Inf.* doting

choco /'tʃoko/ *m,* small hump, hunchback

chocolate /tʃoko'late/ *m,* chocolate; drinking chocolate. **c. a la española,** thick chocolate. **c. a la francesa,** French drinking chocolate

chófer /'tʃofer/ *m,* chauffeur; driver

choque /'tʃoke/ *m,* collision; shock; jar; *Med.* concussion; fight; clink (of glasses); clash; *Mil.* skirmish

choricera /tʃori'θera; tʃori'sera/ *f,* sausage-making machine

choricero /tʃori'θero; tʃori'sero/ **(-ra)** *n* sausage maker

chorizo /tʃo'riθo; tʃo'riso/ *m,* kind of pork sausage; counterweight

chorrear /tʃorre'ar/ *vi* to spout, jet; drip; *Fig. Inf.* trickle, arrive slowly

chorreo /tʃo'rreo/ *m,* drip, dripping; spouting, gushing

chorrera /tʃo'rrera/ *f,* spout; drip; jabot, lace front

chorro /'tʃorro/ *m,* jet; stream (of water, etc.); *Fig.* shower. **a chorros,** in a stream; in abundance, plentifully

choza /'tʃoθa; 'tʃosa/ *f,* hut, cabin; cottage

chubasco /tʃu'βasko/ *m,* squall, downpour; storm; transitory misfortune

chuchería /tʃutʃe'ria/ *f,* gewgaw, trinket; savory titbit; snaring, trapping

chucruta /tʃu'kruta/ *f,* sauerkraut

chueca /'tʃueka/ *f,* round head of a bone; small ball; game like shinty; *Inf.* practical joke

chufa /'tʃufa/ *f, Bot.* chufa; *Inf.* joke, trick

chufería /tʃufe'ria/ *f,* place where drink made of **chufas** is sold

chufla /'tʃufla/ *f,* flippant remark

chufleta /tʃu'fleta/ *f, Inf.* joke; taunt

chulada /tʃu'laða/ *f,* mean trick, base action; drollery

chulería /tʃule'ria/ *f,* drollness; attractive personality

chuleta /tʃu'leta/ *f, Cul.* cutlet, chop; mutton-chop; *Inf.* slap

chulo /'tʃulo/ *a* droll, amusing; attractive. *m,* slaughterhouse worker; bullfighter's assistant; pimp; rogue

chumbera /tʃum'βera/ *f,* prickly pear; Indian fig

chunga /'tʃuŋga/ *f, Inf.* banter, teasing

chupada /tʃu'paða/ *f,* sucking; suck; suction

chupado de cara, c. de mofletes /tʃu'paðo de 'kara; mof'letes/ *a* lantern-jawed

chupador /tʃupa'ðor/ *a* sucking. *m,* baby's comforter or dummy

chupar /tʃu'par/ *vt* to suck; absorb (of plants); *Fig. Inf.* drain, rob; —*vr* grow thin. **chuparse los dedos,** *Inf.* to lick one's lips; be delighted

churdón /tʃur'ðon/ *m,* raspberry cane; raspberry; raspberry vinegar

churrigueresco /tʃurrige'resko/ *a* Churrigueresque

churro /'tʃurro/ *a* coarse (of wool). *m, Cul.* a kind of fritter eaten with chocolate, coffee, etc.

churumbela /tʃurum'βela/ *f, Mus.* pipe; reed for drinking mate *West Hem.*

chusma /'tʃusma/ *f,* galley hands, crew; rabble, mob

chuzón /tʃu'θon; tʃu'son/ *a* wily, suspicious, cunning

cianuro /θia'nuro; sia'nuro/ *m,* cyanide

ciar /θiar; siar/ *vi* to go backwards; *Naut.* row backwards; *Fig.* make no headway (negotiations)

ciática /'θiatika; 'siatika/ *f,* sciatica

ciático /'θiatiko; 'siatiko/ *a* sciatic

ciberespacio *m,* cyberspace

cicatero /θika'tero; sika'tero/ *a* avaricious, niggardly, mean

cicatriz /θika'triθ; sika'tris/ *f,* cicatrice; *Fig.* scar, mark, impression

cicatrización /θikatriθa'θion; sikatrisa'sion/ *f,* cicatrization

cicatrizar /θikatri'θar; sikatri'sar/ *vt* to cicatrize, heal; —*vr* scar over

cíclico /'θikliko; 'sikliko/ *a* cyclic, cyclical

ciclismo /θi'klismo; si'klismo/ *m,* bicycling

ciclista /θi'klista; si'klista/ *mf* cyclist

ciclo /'θiklo; 'siklo/ *m,* cycle (of time). **c. artúrico, c. de Artús,** Arthurian Cycle. **c. de conferencias,** series of lectures

ciclón /θi'klon; si'klon/ *m,* cyclone

ciclópeo /θi'klopeo; si'klopeo/ *a* cyclopean

cicuta /θi'kuta; si'kuta/ *f,* hemlock

cidra /'θiðra; 'siðra/ *f,* citron

cidro /'θiðro; 'siðro/ *m,* citron tree

ciego /'θiego; 'siego/ *a* blind; dazed, blinded; choked up. *m,* blind man; *Anat.* cæcum. **a ciegas,** blindly; heedlessly

cielo /'θielo; 'sielo/ *m,* sky, firmament; atmosphere; climate; paradise; Providence; bliss, glory; roof, canopy; *Inf.* darling. **a c. abierto,** in the open air. **parecer un c.,** to be heavenly

ciempiés /θiem'pies; siem'pies/ *m,* centipede

cien /θien; sien/ *a* abb. **ciento,** hundred.

Used always before substantives (e.g. *c. hombres,* 100 men)

ciénaga /'θienaga; 'sienaga/ *f,* swamp; morass

ciencia /'θienθia; 'siensia/ *f,* science; knowledge; erudition, ability. **ciencias naturales,** natural science. **a c. cierta,** for certain, without doubt (gen. with *saber*)

cieno /'θieno; 'sieno/ *m,* slime, mud); silt

científico /θien'tifiko; sien'tifiko/ *a* scientific. *m,* scientist

ciento /'θiento; 'siento/ (cf. **cien**) *a* hundred; hundredth. *m,* hundred. **por c.,** per cent.

cierne, en /'θierne,∙en; 'sierne, en/ in flower; *Fig.* in the early stages, in embryo

cierre /'θierre; 'sierre/ *m,* closing, shutting; closing time of shops, etc.; fastening; fastener; clasp (of a necklace, handbag, etc.). **c. cremallera,** zip fastener. **c. metálico,** doorshutter

ciertamente /θierta'mente; sierta'mente/ *adv* certainly; undoubtedly; indeed

cierto /'θierto; 'sierto/ *a* certain, sure; true, particular (e.g. *c. hombre,* a certain man (note no *def. art.*)). **un c. sabor,** a special flavor. **una cosa cierta,** something certain. **no, por c.,** no, certainly not. **por c.,** truly, indeed

cierva /'θierβa; 'sierβa/ *f,* hind

ciervo /'θierβo; 'sierβo/ *m,* stag. **c. volante,** stagbeetle

cifra /'θifra; 'sifra/ *f,* number; figure; sum total; cipher, code; monogram; abbreviation

cifrar /θi'frar; si'frar/ *vt* to write in cipher; summarize, abridge; (*with en*) be dependent on; depend on

cigarra /θi'garra; si'garra/ *f, Ent.* cicada, harvest fly

cigarral /θiga'rral; siga'rral/ *m,* (Toledo) countryhouse and garden or orchard

cigarrera /θiga'rrera; siga'rrera/ *f,* woman who makes or sells cigars; cigar-cabinet; cigar-case

cigarrillo /θiga'rriʎo; siga'rriyo/ *m,* cigarette

cigarro /θi'garro; si'garro/ *m,* cigar

cigüeña /θi'gueɲa; si'gueɲa/ *f, Ornith.* stork; *Mech.* crank

cilindrero /θilin'drero; silin'drero/ *m,* organ grinder

cilíndrico /θi'lindriko; si'lindriko/ *a* cylindrical

cilindro /θi'lindro; si'lindro/ *m,* cylinder; roller

cima /'θima; 'sima/ *f,* summit; top of trees; apex; *Archit.* coping; head (thistle, etc.); *Fig.* aim, goal, end

cimbalero /θimba'lero; simba'lero/ **(-ra)** *n* cymbalist

címbalo /'θimbalo; 'simbalo/ *m,* cymbal

cimborrio /θim'βorrio; sim'βorrio/ *m, Archit.* cupola; cimborium

cimbrar, cimbrear /θim'βrar, θimbre'ar; sim'βrar, simbre'ar/ *vt* to bend; brandish; —*vr* sway (in walking)

cimbreño /θim'βreɲo; sim'βreɲo/ *a* graceful, lithe, willowy

cimbreo /θim'βreo; sim'βreo/ *m,* swaying, bending

cimentar /θimen'tar; simen'tar/ *vt irr* to lay foundations; refine (gold, metals, etc.); found; *Fig.* ground (in virtue, etc.). See **acertar**

cimera /θi'mera; si'mera/ *f,* crest of helmet

cimiento /θi'miento; si'miento/ *m,* foundation (of a building); bottom; groundwork; origin, base. **abrir los cimientos,** to lay the foundations

cinc /θink; sink/ *m,* zinc

cincel /θin'θel; sin'sel/ *m,* chisel; burin, engraver

cincelador /θinθela'ðor; sinsela'ðor/ **(-ra)** *n* engraver; chiseler

cincelar /θinθe'lar; sinse'lar/ *vt* to chisel; carve; engrave

cincha /'θintʃa; 'sintʃa/ *f,* girth of a saddle

cincho /'θintʃo; 'sintʃo/ *m,* belt, girdle; iron hoop

cinco /'θinko; 'sinko/ *a* and *m,* five; fifth. **a las c.,** at five o'clock

cincuenta /θin'kuenta; sin'kuenta/ *a* and *m,* fifty; fiftieth

cincuentavo /θinkuen'taβo; sin-kuen'taβo/ *a* fiftieth

cincuentenario /θinkuente'nario; sinkuente'nario/ *m,* fiftieth anniversary

cincuentón /θinkuen'ton; sinkuen'ton/ **(-ona)** *a* and *n* fifty years old (person)

cine, cinema /'θine, θi'nema; 'sine, si'nema/ *m,* cinema, movies. **c. sonoro,** sound film

cinemática /θine'matika; sine'matika/ *f, Phys.* kinematics

cinematografía /θinematogra'fia; sinematogra'fia/ *f,* cinematography

cinematográfico /θinemato'grafiko; sinemato'grafiko/ *a* cinematographic

cinematógrafo /θinema'tografo; sinema'tografo/ *m,* motion-picture camera; cinema

cínico /'θiniko; 'siniko/ *a* cynical; impudent; untidy. *m,* cynic

cinismo /θi'nismo; si'nismo/ *m,* cynicism

cinta /'θinta; 'sinta/ *f,* ribbon; tape; strip; film (cinematograph). **c. métrica,** tape-measure

cintillo /θin'tiʎo; sin'tiyo/ *m,* hatband; small ring set with gems

cinto /'θinto; 'sinto/ *m,* belt, girdle. **c. de pistolas,** pistol-belt

cintoteca /θinto'teka; sinto'teka/ *f,* tape library

cintura /θin'tura; sin'tura/ *f,* waist; belt; girdle

cinturón /θintu'ron; sintu'ron/ *m,* large waist; belt girdle; sword-belt; that which encircles or surrounds. **c. de seguridad,** seat belt

ciprés /θi'pres; si'pres/ *m, Bot.* cypress tree or wood

circo /'θirko; 'sirko/ *m*, circus; amphitheater

circón /θir'kon; sir'kon/ *m*, zircon

circuir /θir'kuir; sir'kuir/ *vt. irr* to surround, encircle. See **huir**

circuito /θir'kuito; sir'kuito/ *m*, periphery; contour; (*Elec. Phys.*) circuit. **corto c.**, short circuit

circulación /θirkula'θion; sirkula'sion/ *f*, circulation; traffic. **c. de la sangre**, circulation of the blood. **calle de gran c.**, busy street

circular /θirku'lar; sirku'lar/ *a* circular. *f*, circular —*vt* to pass round; —*vi* circle; circulate; move in a circle; move about; run, travel (traffic)

circulatorio /θirkula'torio; sirkula'torio/ *a* circulatory

círculo /'θirkulo; 'sirkulo/ *m*, circle; circumference; circuit; casino, social club

circuncidar /θirkunθi'ðar; sirkunsi'ðar/ *vt* to circumcise; modify, reduce

circuncisión /θirkunθi'sion; sirkunsi'sion/ *f*, circumcision

circunciso /θirkun'θiso; sirkun'siso/ *a* circumcised

circundar /θirkun'dar; sirkun'dar/ *vt* to surround

circunferencia /θirkunfe'renθia; sirkunfe'rensia/ *f*, circumference

circunflejo /θirkun'fleho; sirkun'fleho/ *a* circumflex. **acento c.**, circumflex accent

circunnavegación /θirkunnaβega'θion; sirkunnaβega'sion/ *f*, circumnavigation

circunnavegar /θirkunnaβe'gar; sirkunnaβe'gar/ *vt* to circumnavigate

circunscribir /θirkunskri'βir; sirkunskri-'βir/ *vt* to circumscribe —*Past Part.* **circunscrito**

circunscripción /θirkunskrip'θion; sirkunskrip'sion/ *f*, circumscription

circunspección /θirkunspek'θion; sirkunspek'sion/ *f*, circumspection; seriousness, dignity

circunspecto /θirkuns'pekto; sirkuns'pekto/ *a* circumspect; serious, dignified

circunstancia /θirkuns'tanθia; sirkuns'tansia/ *f*, circumstance; incident, detail; condition. **c. agravante**, aggravating circumstance. **c. atenuante**, extenuating circumstance. **bajo las circunstancias**, in the circumstances. **de circunstancias**, occasional (e.g. *poesías de circunstancias*, occasional verse). **estar al nivel de las circunstancias**, to rise to the occasion

circunstanciado /θirkunstan'θiaðo; sirkunstan'siaðo/ *a* circumstantiated, detailed

circunstancial /θirkunstan'θial; sirkunstan'sial/ *a* circumstantial; occasional (e.g. *poesías circunstanciales*, occasional verse)

circunstante /θirkuns'tante; sirkuns'tante/ *a* surrounding; present. *mf* person present, bystander

circunvecino /θirkumbe'θino; sirkumbe'sino/ *a* adjacent, neighboring

cirial /θi'rial; si'rial/ *m*, processional candlestick

cirio /'θirio; 'sirio/ *m*, wax candle

cirrosis /θi'rrosis; si'rrósis/ *f*, cirrhosis

ciruela /θi'ruela; si'ruela/ *f*, plum; prune. **c. claudia, c. veidal**, greengage. **c. damascena**, damson

ciruelo /θi'ruelo; si'ruelo/ *m*, plum tree

cirugía /θiru'hia; siru'hia/ *f*, surgery

cirujano /θiru'hano; siru'hano/ *m*, surgeon

cisma /'θisma; 'sisma/ *m*, or *f*, schism; disagreement, discord. **el C. de Occidente**, the Western Schism

cismático /θis'matiko; sis'matiko/ *a* schismatic; discordant, inharmonious

cisne /'θisne; 'sisne/ *m*, swan

cisterna /θis'terna; sis'terna/ *f*, watertank, cistern

cístico /'θistiko; 'sistiko/ *a* cystic

cita /'θita; 'sita/ *f*, appointment; quotation, citation

citación /θita'θion; sita'sion/ *f*, quotation; *Law.* summons

citar /θi'tar; si'tar/ *vt* to make an appointment; cite, quote; *Law.* summon. **c. en comparecencia**, to summon to appear in court

cítara /'θitara; 'sitara/ *f*, *Mus.* zither

citatorio /θita'torio; sita'torio/ *m*, summons

citerior /θite'rior; site'rior/ *a* hither, nearer

cítrico /'θitriko; 'sitriko/ *a* citric

ciudad /θiu'ðað; siu'ðað/ *f*, city; municipal body. **la c. señorial**, the Aristocratic City (Ponce, Puerto Rico)

ciudadanía /θiuðaða'nia; siuðaða'nia/ *f*, citizenship

ciudadano /θiuða'ðano; siuða'ðano/ **(-na)** *a* city; civic, born in or belonging to a city —*n* citizen; burgess; bourgeois. **c. de honor**, freeman (of a city)

ciudadela /θiuða'ðela; siuða'ðela/ *f*, citadel

cívico /'θiβiko; 'siβiko/ *a* civic; patriotic

civicultura /θiβikul'tura; siβikul'tura/ *f*, raising of civets

civil /θi'βil; si'βil/ *a* civil; civilian; polite

civilidad /θiβili'ðað; siβili'ðað/ *f*, politeness, civility

civilización /θiβiliθa'θion; siβilisa'sion/ *f*, civilization

civilizador /θiβiliθa'ðor; siβilisa'ðor/ *a* civilizing

civilizar /θiβili'θar; siβili'sar/ *vt* to civilize; educate; —*vr* grow civilized; be educated

civismo /θi'βismo; si'βismo/ *m*, civism; patriotism; civics

cizalla /θi'θaʎa; si'saya/ *f*, shears, shearing machine; metal filings

cizaña /θi'θaɲa; si'saɲa/ *f*, *Bot.* darnel, tare; vice, evil; dissension, discord (gen. with *meter* and *sembrar*)

clamar /kla'mar/ *vi* to cry out; *Fig.* de-

mand (of inanimate things); vociferate; speak solemnly

clamor /kla'mor/ *m*, outcry, shouting; shriek, complaint; knell, tolling of bells

clamorear /klamore'ar/ *vt* to implore, clamor (for); —*vi* toll (of bells)

clamoroso /klamo'roso/ *a* noisy, clamorous

clandestino /klandes'tino/ *a* clandestine, secret

clara /'klara/ *f*, white of egg; bald patch (in fur). *Inf*. fair interval on a rainy day

claraboya /klara'βoya/ *f*, skylight; *Archit*. clerestory

clarear /klare'ar/ *vt* to clear; give light to; —*vi* to dawn; grow light; —*vr* be transparent. *Inf*. reveal secrets unwittingly

clarete /kla'rete/ *m*, claret (wine); claret color —*a* claret; claret-colored

claridad /klari'ðað/ *f*, clearness; transparency; lightness, brightness; distinctness; clarity; good reputation, renown; plain truth, home truth (gen. *pl*)

clarificación /klarifika'θion; klarifika'sion/ *f*, clarification; purifying, refining

clarificar /klarifi'kar/ *vt* to illuminate; clarify, purify; refine (sugar, etc.)

clarín /kla'rin/ *m*, bugle; clarion; organ stop; bugler

clarinete /klari'nete/ *m*, clarinet; clarinet player

clarión /kla'rion/ *m*, white chalk, crayon

clarividencia /klariβi'ðenθia; klariβi'ðensia/ *f*, perspicuity, clear-sightedness

clarividente /klariβi'ðente/ *a* perspicacious, clear-sighted

claro /'klaro/ *a* clear; light, bright; distinct; pure, clean; transparent, translucent; light (of colors); easily understood; evident, obvious; frank; cloudless; shrewd, quick-thinking; famous. *m*, skylight; space between words; break in a speech; space in procession, etc.; *Art*. (gen. *pl*) high lights —*interj* ¡C.! or ¡C. está! Of course! **a las claras**, openly, frankly

claroscuro /klaros'kuro/ *m*, chiaroscuro; monochrome

clase /'klase/ *f*, class, group; kind, sort, quality; class (school, university); lecture room; lecture, lesson; order, family. **c. dirigente**, ruling class. **c. media**, middle class. **c. social**, social class

clasicismo /klasi'θismo; klasi'sismo/ *m*, classicism

clasicista /klasi'θista; klasi'sista/ *a* and *mf* classicist

clásico /'klasiko/ *a* classic; notable; classical. *m*, classic

clasificación /klasifika'θion; klasifika'sion/ *f*, classification

clasificador /klasifika'ðor/ (**-ra**) *n* classifier. **c. de billetes**, ticket-punch

clasificar /klasifi'kar/ *vt* to classify, arrange. **c. correspondencia**, to file letters

claudicación /klauðika'θion; klauðika'sion/ *f*, limping; negligence; hesitancy, weakness; backing down

claudicar /klauði'kar/ *vi* to limp; be negligent; hesitate, give way

claustro /'klaustro/ *m*, cloister; council, faculty, senate (of university); monastic rule

claustrofobia /klaustro'foβia/ *f*, claustrophobia

cláusula /'klausula/ *f*, clause. **c. de negación implícita**, contrary-to-fact clause. **c. principal**, main clause. **c. subordinada**, dependent clause, subordinate clause. **c. sustantiva**, noun clause

clausura /klau'sura/ *f*, sanctum of convent; claustration; solemn ending ceremony of tribunal, etc. **la vida de c.**, monastic or conventual life

clava /'klaβa/ *f*, club, truncheon; *Naut*. scupper

clavadizo /klaβa'ðiθo; klaβa'ðiso/ *a* nail-studded (doors, etc.)

clavar /kla'βar/ *vt* to nail; fasten with nails; pierce, prick; set gems (jeweler); spike (cannon, gun); *Fig*. fix (eyes, attention, etc.); *Inf*. cheat

clave /'klaβe/ *m*, clavichord. *f*, code, key; *Mus*. clef; *Archit*. keystone; plug (telephones); **c. (de)**, key to. *Mus*. **c. de sol**, treble clef

clavel /kla'βel/ *m*, *Bot*. carnation plant and flower

clavetear /klaβete'ar/ *vt* to stud with nails; *Fig*. round off (business affairs)

clavicordio /klaβi'korðio/ *m*, clavichord

clavícula /kla'βikula/ *f*, clavicle

clavija /kla'βiha/ *f*, peg, pin; plug; peg of stringed instrument; axle-pin

clavo /'klaβo/ *m*, nail, spike, peg; corn (on foot); anguish. **c. de especia**, clove. **c. de herradura**, hob-nail

clemencia /kle'menθia; kle'mensia/ *f*, mildness; clemency; mercy

clemente /kle'mente/ *a* mild; clement; merciful

cleptomanía /kleptoma'nia/ *f*, kleptomania

cleptómano /klep'tomano/ (**-na**) *a* and *n* kleptomaniac

clerecía /klere'θia; klere'sia/ *f*, clergy

clerical /kleri'kal/ *a* belonging to the clergy; clerical

clericalismo /klerika'lismo/ *m*, clericalism

clérigo /'klerigo/ *m*, cleric, clergyman; clerk (in Middle Ages)

clero /'klero/ *m*, clergy

cliente /'kliente/ *mf* client, customer; protégé, ward

clientela /klien'tela/ *f*, patronage, protection; clientele

clima /'klima/ *m*, climate, clime

clímax /'klimaks/ *m*, climax

clínica /'klinika/ *f*, clinic, nursing home; department of medicine or surgery

clínico /'kliniko/ *a* clinical

cloaca /klo'aka/ f, sewer, drain; Zool. cloaca

cloquear /kloke'ar/ vi to go broody (hen); cluck

cloqueo /klo'keo/ m, cluck, clucking

clorato /klo'rato/ m, chlorate

cloro /'kloro/ m, chlorine

cloroformizar /kloroformi'θar; kloroformi'sar/ vt to chloroform

cloroformo /kloro'formo/ m, chloroform

club /kluβ/ m, club

clueca /'klueka/ f, broody hen

clueco /'klueko/ a broody (hens); Inf. doddering

C.N.T. /knt/ initialism of Confederación Nacional de Trabajo

coacción /koak'θion; koak'sion/ f, coercion

coactivo /koak'tiβo/ a coercive

coadjutor /koaðhu'tor/ m, co-worker, assistant

coadunar /koaðu'nar/ vt to join or mingle together

coagulación /koagula'θion; koagula'sion/ f, coagulation

coagular /koagu'lar/ vt to coagulate; clot; curdle

coágulo /ko'agulo/ m, clot; coagulation; congealed blood

coalición /koali'θion; koali'sion/ f, coalition

coartada /koar'taða/ f, alibi. **probar la c.,** to prove an alibi

coartar /koar'tar/ vt to limit, restrict

cobarde /ko'βarðe/ a cowardly; irresolute. m, coward

cobardía /koβar'ðia/ f, cowardice

cobayo /ko'βayo/ m, guinea-pig

cobertera /koβer'tera/ f, lid, cover

cobertizo /koβer'tiθo; koβer'tiso/ m, overhanging roof; shack, shed, hut. **c. de aeroplanos,** Aer. hangar

cobertura /koβer'tura/ f, covering; coverlet; wrapping

cobija /ko'βiha/ f, imbrex tile; cover

cobijar /koβi'har/ vt to cover; shelter

cobra /'koβra/ f, Zool. cobra; rope or thong for yoking oxen; retrieval (of game)

cobradero /koβra'ðero/ a that which can be collected, recoverable

cobrador /koβra'ðor/ m, collector, receiver —a collecting. **c. de tranvía,** tram conductor

cobranza /ko'βranθa; ko'βransa/ f, receiving, collecting; collection of fruit or money

cobrar /ko'βrar/ vt to collect (what is owed); charge; earn; regain, recover; feel, experience (emotions); wind, pull in (ropes, etc.); gain, acquire; retrieve (game); —vr recuperate. **c. ánimo,** to take courage. **c. cariño (a),** to grow fond of. **c. fuerzas,** to gather strength. **c. importancia,** to gain importance. **¿Cuánto cobra Vd.?** How much do you charge?; How much do you earn?

cobre /'koβre/ m, Mineral. copper; copper kitchen utensils; pl Mus. brass

cobrizo /ko'βriθo; ko'βriso/ a containing copper; copper-colored

cocacolismo /kokako'lismo/ n Inf. economic dependence on the United States and adoption of its pop culture

cocacolonización /kokakoloniθa'θion; kokakolonisa'sion/ f, economic domination by the United States and introduction of its pop culture

cocacolonizar /kokakoloni'θar; kokakoloni'sar/ vt (United States) to gain economic control of... and introduce into its pop culture

cocaína /koka'ina/ f, cocaine

coceador /koθea'ðor; kosea'ðor/ a inclined to kick; kicking (animals)

coceadura /koθea'ðura; kosea'ðura/ f, kicking

cocear /koθe'ar; kose'ar/ vi to kick; Inf. kick against, oppose

cocedero /koθe'ðero; kose'ðero/ a easily cooked

cocer /ko'θer; ko'ser/ vt. irr to boil; cook; bake (bricks, etc.); digest; Surg. suppurate; —vl boil (of a liquid); ferment; —vr suffer pain or inconvenience over a long period —Pres. Indic. **cuezo, cueces, cuece, cuecen.** Pres. Subjunc. **cueza, cuezas, cueza, cuezan**

coche /'kotʃe/ m, carriage, car. **c. camas,** sleeping car. **c. -camioneta,** station wagon. **c. cerrado,** Auto. sedan. **c. de muchos caballos,** high-powered car. **c. de plaza,** hackney-carriage. **c. fúnebre,** hearse. **c. -línea,** intercity bus. f, Ecuador puddle

cochera /ko'tʃera/ f, coach house; tramway depot

cochero /ko'tʃero/ m, coachman; driver —a easily cooked

cochina /ko'tʃina/ f, sow

cochinería /kotʃine'ria/ f, Inf. filthiness; mean trick

cochinilla /kotʃi'niʎa; kotʃi'niya/ f, wood louse; cochineal insect; cochineal

cochinillo /kotʃi'niʎo; kotʃi'niyo/ m, sucking-pig. **c. de Indias,** guinea-pig

cochino /ko'tʃino/ m, pig; Inf. filthy person —a filthy

cocido /ko'θiðo; ko'siðo/ a boiled, cooked, baked. m, dish of stewed meat, pork, chicken, with peas, etc.

cociente /ko'θiente; ko'siente/ m, quotient

cocimiento /koθi'miento; kosi'miento/ m, cooking; decoction

cocina /ko'θina; ko'sina/ f, kitchen; pottage; broth; cookery. **c. de campaña,** field-kitchen. **c. económica,** cooking range

cocinar /koθi'nar; kosi'nar/ vt to cook; —vi Inf. meddle, interfere

cocinería /koθine'ria; kosine'ria/ f, Naut. galley

cocinero /koθi'nero; kosi'nero/ **(-ra)** *n* cook, chef

cocinilla /koθi'niʎa; kosi'niya/ *f*, spirit-stove

coco /'koko/ *m*, *Bot.* coconut tree and fruit; coconut shell; grub, maggot; bogeyman; hobgoblin; *Inf.* grimace. *Inf.* **ser un c.**, to be hideously ugly

cocodrilo /koko'ðrilo/ *m*, crocodile

cócora /'kokora/ *mf Inf.* bore, nosy Parker

cocotero /koko'tero/ *m*, coconut palm

coctel /kok'tel/ *m*, cocktail

cocuyo /ko'kuyo/ *m*, firefly

codal /ko'ðal/ *a* cubital. *m*, shoot of a vine; prop, strut; frame of a hand-saw

codazo /ko'ðaθo; ko'ðaso/ *m*, blow or nudge of the elbow. **dar codazos**, to elbow, shoulder out of the way

codear /koðe'ar/ *vi* to jostle; elbow, nudge; —*vr* be on terms of equality with

codeína /koðe'ina/ *f*, codeine

codelincuente /koðelin'kuente/ *mf* partner in crime, accomplice

codera /ko'ðera/ *f*, elbow rash; elbow-piece or patch

códice /'koðiðe; 'koðise/ *m*, codex

codicia /ko'ðiθia; ko'ðisia/ *f*, covetousness; greed

codiciar /koðiθi'ar; koðisi'ar/ *vt* to covet

codicilo /koðiˈθilo; koðiˈsilo/ *m*, codicil

codicioso /koðiˈθioso; koðiˈsioso/ **(-sa)** *a* covetous; *Inf.* hardworking —*n* covetous person

codificación /koðifikaˈθion, koðifikaˈsion/ *f*, codification

codificar /koðifiˈkar/ *vt* to codify, compile

código /'koðigo/ *m*, code of laws. **c. civil**, civil laws. **c. de la circulación, c. de la vía pública**, highway code, traffic code. *Naut.* **c. de señales**, signal code. **c. penal**, criminal laws. **c. postal**, zip code

codillo /ko'ðiʎo; ko'ðiyo/ *m*, knee (of quadrupeds); shaft (of branch); bend (pipe, tube); stirrup

codo /'koðo/ *m*, elbow; angle, bend (pipe, tube); cubit. *Inf.* **hablar por los codos**, to chatter

codorniz /koðor'niθ; koðor'nis/ *f*, *Ornith.* quail

coeficiente /koefiˈθiente; koefiˈsiente/ *m*, coefficient

coercer /koer'θer; koer'ser/ *vt* to restrain, coerce

coercitivo /koerθiˈtiβo; koersiˈtiβo/ *a* coercive

coetáneo /koe'taneo/ **(-ea)** *a* contemporaneous —*n* contemporary

coevo /ko'eβo/ *a* coeval

coexistencia /koeksis'tenθia; koeksis'tensia/ *f*, co-existence

coexistir /koeksis'tir/ *vi* to co-exist

cofradía /kofra'ðia/ *f*, confraternity, brotherhood or sisterhood **c. de gastronomía**, eating club (US), dining society (UK)

cofre /'kofre/ *m*, trunk, chest (for clothes); coffer

cogedor /kohe'ðor/ *m*, collector, gatherer; dustpan; coal-shovel

coger /ko'her/ *vt* to seize, hold; catch; take, collect, gather; have room for; take up or occupy space; find; catch in the act; attack, surprise; reach; **c. un berrinche**, have a fit, have a tantrum —*vi* have room, fit

cogida /ko'hiða/ *f*, gathering, picking; *Inf.* fruit harvest; toss (bullfighting)

cogido /ko'hiðo/ *m*, pleat, fold; crease. **estar c. de tiempo** to be pressed for time.

cogitabundo /kohita'βundo/ *a* very pensive

cognación /kogna'θion; kogna'sion/ *f*, cognation; kinship

cogollo /ko'goʎo; ko'goyo/ *m*, heart (of lettuce, etc.); shoot; topmost branches of pine tree

cogote /ko'gote/ *m*, nape (of neck)

cohabitación /koaβita'θion; koaβita'sion/ *f*, cohabitation

cohabitar /koaβi'tar/ *vt* to cohabit

cohechar /koe'tʃar/ *vt* to bribe, corrupt; suborn

cohecho /koe'tʃo/ *m*, bribing; bribe

coherencia /koe'rɛnθia; koe'rensia/ *f*, coherence, connection

coherente /koe'rente/ *a* coherent

cohesión /koe'sion/ *f*, cohesion

cohesivo /koe'siβo/ *a* cohesive

cohete /ko'ete/ *m*, rocket

cohibir /koi'βir/ *vt* to restrain; repress. See **Prohibir.**

cohombro /ko'ombro/ *m*, cucumber

cohonestar /koones'tar/ *vt Fig.* to gloss over, cover up; make appear decent (actions, etc.)

cohorte /ko'orte/ *f*, cohort

coincidencia /koinθi'ðenθia; koinsi'ðensia/ *f*, coincidence

coincidir /koinθi'ðir; koinsi'ðir/ *vt* to coincide; (two or more people) be in the same place at the same time. **c. con que...** to agree that...

coito /'koito/ *m*, coitus

cojear /kohe'ar/ *vi* to limp; wobble, be unsteady (of furniture); *Fig. Inf.* go wrong or astray; *Inf.* suffer from (vice, bad habit)

cojera /ko'hera/ *f*, lameness, limp

cojijoso /kohi'hoso/ *a* peevish

cojín /ko'hin/ *m*, cushion; pad; pillow (for lace-making)

cojinete /kohi'nete/ *m*, small cushion; *Mech.* bearing. **c. de bolas**, ball-bearing

cojo /'koho/ *a* lame; unsteady, wobbly (of furniture, etc.)

col /kol/ *f*, cabbage. **c. de Bruselas**, Brussels sprouts

cola /'kola/ *f*, tail; train (of gown); shank (of a button); queue; tailpiece (of a violin, etc.); appendage; glue. **c. de milano,**

dovetail. **c. de pescado,** isinglass. **formar c.,** to line up, queue up

colaboración /kolaβora'θion; kolaβora-'sion/ f, collaboration. **en c.,** joint (e.g. *obra en colaboración,* joint work)

colaboracionista /kolaβoraθio'nista; kolaβorasio'nista/ mf collaborationist

colaborador /kolaβora'ðor/ **(-ra)** n collaborator

colaborar /kolaβo'rar/ vt to collaborate

colación /kola'θion; kola'sion/ f, conferment of a degree; collation (of texts); light repast; cold supper; area of a parish

colada /ko'laða/ f, wash; bleaching; mountain path; *Metall.* casting; *Inf.* trusty sword (allusion to name of one of the Cid's swords)

coladero /kola'ðero/ m, colander, sieve, strainer; narrow path

colador /kola'ðor/ m, colander

coladura /kola'ðura/ f, straining, filtration; *Inf.* untruth; *Inf.* howler, mistake

colapso /ko'lapso/ m, *Med.* prostration, collapse

colar /ko'lar/ vt irr to filter, strain; bleach; *Metall.* cast; —vi go through a narrow place; *Inf.* drink wine; —vr thread one's way; *Inf.* enter by stealth, steal in; *Inf.* tell untruths —*Pres. Indic.* **cuelo, cuelas, cuela, cuelan.** *Pres. Subjunc.* **cuele, cueles, cuele, cuelen**

colcha /'koltʃa/ f, bedspread, counterpane, quilt

colchadura /koltʃa'ðura/ f, quilting

colchón /kol'tʃon/ m, mattress. **c. de muelles,** spring-mattress. **c. de viento,** air-bed

colección /kolek'θion; kolek'sion/ f, collection

coleccionador /kolekθiona'ðor; koleksiona'ðor/ **(-ra)** n collector

coleccionar /kolekθio'nar; koleksio'nar/ vt to collect

coleccionista /kolekθio'nista; koleksio'nista/ mf collector

colecta /ko'lekta/ f, assessment; collection (of donations); *Eccl.* collect; voluntary offering

colectivero /kolekti'βero/ m, bus driver

colectividad /kolektiβi'ðað/ f, collectivity; body of people

colectivismo /kolekti'βismo/ m, collectivism

colectivo /kolek'tiβo/ a collective; *Argentina* (local) bus

colector /kolek'tor/ m, gatherer; collector; tax-collector; water-pipe; waterconduit; *Elec.* commutator, collector

colega /ko'lega/ m, colleague

colegial /kole'hial/ **(-la)** a college, collegiate —n student; pupil; *Fig. Inf.* novice.

colegiarse /kole'hiarse/ vr to meet as an association (professional, etc.)

colegiata /kole'hiata/ f, college church

colegiatura /kolehia'tura/ f, scholarship, fellowship (money granted a student); tuition (fee paid by a student), tuition fee, tuition fees

colegio /ko'lehio/ m, college; school; academy; association (professional); council, convocation; college or school buildings. **c. de abogados,** bar association. **c. de cardenales,** College of Cardinals. **c. electoral,** polling-booth. **c. militar,** military academy

colegir /kole'hir/ vt irr to collect, gather; deduce, infer. See **elegir**

cólera /'kolera/ f, bile, anger. m, cholera. **montar en c.,** to fly into a rage

colérico /ko'leriko/ a angry; choleric; suffering from cholera

colesterina /koleste'rina/ f, *Chem.* cholesterol

coletazo /kole'taθo; kole'taso/ m, blow with one's tail, lash with one's tail; lash of a dying fish; *Fig.* last hurrah

colgadero /kolga'ðero/ a able to be hung up. m, coat-hanger, hook

colgadizo /kolga'ðiθo; kolga'ðiso/ a hanging. m, overhanging roof

colgadura /kolga'ðura/ f, hangings, drapery, tapestries. **c. de cama,** bedhangings

colgajo /kol'gaho/ m, tatter; bunch (of grapes, etc.); *Surg.* skin lap

colgar /kol'gar/ vt irr to hang up; decorate with hangings; *Inf.* hang, kill; —vi hang, be suspended; *Fig.* be dependent. See **contar**

colibrí /koli'βri/ m, hummingbird

cólico /'koliko/ m, colic

coliflor /koli'flor/ f, cauliflower

coligarse /koli'garse/ vr to confederate, unite

colilla /ko'liʎa; ko'liya/ f, stub (of a cigar or cigarette)

colina /ko'lina/ f, hill; cabbage seed; *Chem.* choline

colindante /kolin'dante/ a adjacent, contiguous

coliseo /koli'seo/ m, coliseum; theater

colisión /koli'sion/ f, collision; abrasion, bruise; *Fig.* clash (of ideas)

colitis /ko'litis/ f, colitis

collado /ko'ʎaðo; ko'yaðo/ m, hill, hillock

collar /ko'ʎar; ko'yar/ m, necklace; chain of office or honor; collar (dogs, etc.)

colmado /kol'maðo/ a abundant. m, provision shop

colmar /kol'mar/ vt to fill to overflowing; bestow generously, heap upon

colmena /kol'mena/ f, beehive

colmenero /kolme'nero/ **(-ra)** n beekeeper

colmillo /kol'miʎo; kol'miyo/ m, canine tooth; tusk; fang

colmo /'kolmo/ m, overflow; highest point; completion, limit, end. **ser el c.,** *Inf.* to be the last straw. **el c. de los colmos,** the absolute limit

colocación /koloka'θion; koloka'sion/ f, placing, putting; situation, place; employment; *Sports.* placing; order, arrangement; *Ling.* collocation

colocar /kolo'kar/ *vt* to place, put, arrange; place in employment. **c. bajo banderas,** to draft (into the armed forces) —*vr* place oneself

colofonia /kolo'fonia/ *f,* solid resin (for bows of stringed instruments, etc.)

colombiano /kolom'biano/ **(-na)** *a* and *n* Colombian

colonia /ko'lonia/ *f,* colony; plantation

colonial /kolo'nial/ *a* colonial

colonización /koloniθa'θion; kolonisa'sion/ *f,* colonization

colonizador /koloniθa'ðor; kolonisa'ðor/ **(-ra)** *a* colonizing —*n* colonizer

colonizar /koloni'θar; koloni'sar/ *vt* to colonize; settle

colono /ko'lono/ *m,* settler, colonist; farmer

coloquio /ko'lokio/ *m,* colloquy, conversation, talk; colloquium

color /ko'lor/ *m,* color; dye; paint; rouge; coloring; pretext, excuse; character, individuality; *pl* natural colors. **c. estable, c. sólido,** fast color. **mudar de c.,** to change color. **de c.,** colored. **so c.,** under the pretext. **ver las cosas c. de rosa,** to see things through rose-colored glasses

coloración /kolora'θion; kolora'sion/ *f,* coloration, painting

colorado /kolo'raðo/ *a* colored. *West Hem.* red, reddish; *Inf.* blue, obscene; specious

colorante /kolo'rante/ *a* coloring. *m,* dyestuff; coloring (substance)

colorar /kolo'rar/ *vt* to color; dye

colorear /kolore'ar/ *vt* to color; pretext; *Fig.* whitewash, excuse; —*vi* show color; be reddish; grow red, ripe (tomatoes, cherries, etc.)

colorete /kolo'rete/ *m,* rouge

colorido /kolo'riðo/ *m,* coloring, color

colosal /kolo'sal/ *a* colossal, enormous; extraordinary, excellent

coloso /ko'loso/ *m,* colossus; *Fig.* outstanding person or thing, giant; **el C. del Norte, el Gran C. del Norte,** (contemptuous epithet for the United States of America)

columbrar /kolum'brar/ *vt* to discern in the distance, glimpse; conjecture, guess

columna /ko'lumna/ *f, Mil. Archit. Print.* column; *Fig.* protection, shelter; *Naut.* stanchion. **c. cerrada,** *Mil.* etc. mass formation. **c. de los suspiros,** agony column (in a newspaper)

columnata /kolum'nata/ *f,* colonnade

columpiar /kolum'piar/ *vt* to swing; dangle (one's feet); —*vr Inf.* sway in walking; swing

columpio /ko'lumpio/ *m,* swing

colusión /kolu'sion/ *f,* collusion

coma /'koma/ *f, Gram.* comma. *m, Med.* coma

comadre /ko'maðre/ *f,* midwife; *Inf.* procuress, go-between; *Inf.* pal, gossip

comadrear /komaðre'ar/ *vi Inf.* to gossip

comadrón /koma'ðron/ *m,* accoucheur

comadrona /koma'ðrona/ *f,* midwife

comandancia /koman'danθia; koman'dansia/ *f, Mil.* command; commandant's H.Q.

comandante /koman'dante/ *m,* commandant; commander; major; squadron-leader —*a Mil.* commanding. **c. en jefe,** commanding officer

comandita /koman'dita/ *f, Com.* sleeping partnership; private company

comando /ko'mando/ *m, Mil.* commando

comarca /ko'marka/ *f,* district, region

comatoso /koma'toso/ *a* comatose

comba /'komba/ *f,* bend, warping; jump rope, skipping-rope; camber (of road)

combadura /komba'ðura/ *f,* curvature; warping; camber (of a road)

combar /kom'bar/ *vt* to bend; twist; warp; camber

combate /kom'bate/ *m,* fight, combat; mental strife; contradiction, opposition. **c. judicial,** trial by combat. **dejar fuera de c., (a)** (boxing) to knock out

combatiente /komba'tiente/ *m,* combatant, soldier

combatir /komba'tir/ *vi* to fight; —*vt* attack; struggle against (winds, water, etc.); contradict, oppose; *Fig.* disturb, trouble (emotions)

combinación /kombina'θion; kombina'sion/ *f,* combination; list of words beginning with same letter; project; concurrence; underskirt, petticoat. **estar en c.** (**con**), to be in cahoots (with), connive (with)

combinar /kombi'nar/ *vt* to combine; (*Mil. Nav.*) join forces; arrange, plan; *Chem.* combine; **combinar para + inf.** (two or more people) to make arrangements to + inf.

combustible /kombus'tiβle/ *a* combustible. *m,* fuel

combustión /kombus'tion/ *f,* combustion. **c. activa,** rapid combustion. **c. espontánea,** spontaneous combustion

comedia /ko'meðia/ *f,* comedy; play; theater; comic incident; *Fig.* play-acting, theatricalism. **c. alta,** art theater. **c. de costumbres,** comedy of manners. **c. de enredo,** play with very involved plot. *Inf.* **hacer la c.,** to play-act, pretend

comedianta /kome'ðianta/ *f,* actress

comediante /kome'ðiante/ *m,* actor; *Inf.* dissembler

comedido /kome'ðiðo/ *a* courteous; prudent; moderate

comedimiento /komeði'miento/ *m,* courtesy; moderation; prudence

comedir /kome'ðir/ *vt irr* to prepare, premeditate; —*vr* restrain oneself, be moderate; offer one's services. See **pedir**

comedor /kome'ðor/ *a* voracious. *m,* dining-room

comensal /komen'sal/ *mf* table companion

comentador /komenta'ðor/ **(-ra)** *n* commentator

comentar /komen'tar/ *vt* explain (document); *Inf.* comment

comentario /komen'tario/ **(a)** *m*, commentary (on)

comento /ko'mento/ *m*, comment; commentary

comenzante /komen'θante; komen'sante/ *mf* beginner, novice —*a* initial

comenzar /komen'θar; komen'sar/ *vt vi irr* to begin, commence. See **empezar**

comer /ko'mer/ *m*, eating; food —*vi* to eat; feed; dine —*vt* eat; *Inf.* enjoy an income; waste (patrimony); consume, exhaust; fade (of colors); —*vr* be troubled, uneasy, remorseful. **ser de buen c.**, to have a good appetite; taste good. **tener que c.**, to be obliged to eat; have to eat; have enough to eat

comerciable /komer'θiaβle; komer'siaβle/ *a* marketable; sociable, pleasant (of persons)

comercial /komer'θial; komer'sial/ *a* commercial

comerciante /komer'θiante; komer'siante/ *a* trading. *mf* merchant, trader

comerciar /komer'θiar; komer'siar/ *vt* to trade; have dealings (with)

comercio /ko'merθio; ko'mersio/ *m*, trade, commerce; intercourse, traffic; illicit sexual intercourse; shop, store; tradesmen; commercial quarter of town

comestible /komes'tiβle/ *a* edible, eatable. *m*, (gen. *pl*) provisions

cometa /ko'meta/ *m*, *Astron.* comet. *f*, kite (toy). **c. celular**, box-kite

cometer /kome'ter/ *vt* to entrust, hand over to; commit (crime, sins, etc.); *Com.* order

cometido /kome'tiðo/ *m*, charge, commission; moral obligation; function

comezón /kome'θon; kome'son/ *f*, itching, irritation; hankering, longing

comicidad /komiθi'ðað; komisi'ðað/ *f*, comic element; comic spirit

cómico /'komiko/ *a* comic; funny, comical. *m*, actor; comedian. **c. de la legua**, strolling player

comida /ko'miða/ *f*, food; meal; dinner; eating. **c. de gala**, state banquet. **c. de prueba**, *Med.* test meal

comienzo /ko'mienθo; ko'mienso/ *m*, beginning, origin

comillas /ko'miʎas; ko'miyas/ *f pl*, *Gram.* inverted commas

comilón /komi'lon/ **(-ona)** *a Inf.* gluttonous —*n* glutton

comisar /komi'sar/ *vt* to confiscate, sequestrate

comisaría /komisa'ria/ *f*, commissaryship; commissariat. **c. de policía**, police station

comisario /komi'sario/ *m*, deputy, agent; commissary, head of police; commissioner. **alto c.**, high commissioner. **c. propietario**, stockholders' representative

comisión /komi'sion/ *f*, perpetration, committal; commission; committee; *Com.* commission

comisionado /komisio'naðo/ **(-da)** *a* commissioned. *m*, commissary

comisionar /komisio'nar/ *vt* to commission

comité /komi'te/ *m*, committee

comitiva /komi'tiβa/ *f*, retinue, following

como /'komo/ *adv* like, as; in the same way; thus, accordingly; in the capacity of; so that; since —*conjunc* if (*followed by subjunc.*); because. **c. no**, unless. **¿Cómo?** How? In what way? Why? Pardon? What did you say? *interj* **¡Cómo!** What! You don't say! **¡Cómo no!** Why not! Of course! Surely! **¿Cómo que...?** What do you mean that...?

cómo /'komo/ *m*, the wherefore. **no saber el porqué ni el c.**, not to know the why or wherefore

cómoda /'komoða/ *f*, chest of drawers

comodidad /komoði'ðað/ *f*, comfort; convenience; advantage; utility, interest

comodín /komo'ðin/ *m*, (in cards) joker

cómodo /'komoðo/ *a* comfortable; convenient; opportune

comoquiera que /komo'kiera ke/ *adv* by any means that, anyway; whereas, given that

compacto /kom'pakto/ *a* compact, dense; close (type)

compadecer /kompaðe'θer; kompaðe'ser/ *vt irr* to pity; —*vr* (*with* **de**) sympathize with; pity; harmonize, agree with. See **conocer**

compadre /kom'paðre/ *m*, *Inf.* pal

compaginar /kompahi'nar/ *vt* to fit together; join, put in order; harmonize, square (e.g. *compaginé una cuenta con la otra*, I squared one account with the other); *Print.* make up

compañero /kompa'ɲero/ **(-ra)** *n* companion, comrade; fellow-member; partner (games); *Fig.* pair, fellow, mate (things). **c. de armas**, brother-in-arms, companion-at-arms. **c. de cabina**, boothmate. **c. de exilio**, companion in exile, fellow exile. **c. de generación**, contemporary, person of the same generation. **c. de viaje**, traveling companion; *Polit.* fellow traveler (communist sympathizer)

compañía /kompa'ɲia/ *f*, company; society, association; theatrical company (*Com. Mil.*) company. **C. de Jesús**, Order of Jesus. **c. de la zarza**, guild of guards and woodcutters for autos de fe. **c. de navegación**, shipping company. **c. por acciones**, joint stock company

comparación /kompara'θion; kompara'sion/ *f*, comparison

comparar /kompa'rar/ *vt* to compare; collate

comparativo /kompara'tiβo/ *a* comparative

comparecencia /kompare'θenθia; kompare'sensia/ *f,* (gen. *Law.*) appearance

comparecer /kompare'θer; kompare'ser/ *vi irr Law.* to appear (before tribunal, etc.); present oneself. See **conocer**

comparendo /kompa'rendo/ *m, Law.* summons

comparsa /kom'parsa/ *f,* retinue; *Theat.* chorus; troop of carnival revelers dressed alike. *mf Theat.* supernumerary actor

compartimiento /komparti'miento/ *m,* share, division; railway carriage. *Naut.* **c. estanco,** compartment

compartir /kompar'tir/ *vt* to share out, divide; participate

compás /kom'pas/ *m,* compasses; callipers; size; compass, time; range of voice; (*Naut. Mineral.*) compass; *Mus.* time, rhythm, bar, marking time. **c. de mar,** mariner's compass. **c. de puntas,** dividers, callipers. **fuera de c.,** *Mus.* out of time, out of joint (of the times). *Mus.* **llevar el c.,** to beat time

compasar /kompa'sar/ *vt* to measure with compasses; arrange or apportion accurately; *Mus.* put into bars

compasivo /kompa'siβo/ *a* compassionate; tender-hearted

compatibilidad /kompatiβili'ðað/ *f,* compatibility

compatriota /kompa'triota/ *mf* compatriot

compeler /kompe'ler/ *vt* to compel, force

compendiar /kompen'diar/ *vt* to abridge, summarize

compendio /kom'pendio/ *m,* compendium. **en c.,** briefly

compendioso /kompen'dioso/ *a* summary, condensed; compendious

compenetración /kompenetra'θion; kompenetra'sion/ *f,* co-penetration; intermingling

compenetrado /kompene'traðo/ **(de)** *a* thoroughly convinced (of)

compenetrarse /kompene'trarse/ *vr* to co-penetrate; intermingle

compensación /kompensa'θion; kompensa'sion/ *f,* compensating; compensation

compensar /kompen'sar/ *vt* to equalize, counterbalance; compensate

compensatorio /kompensa'torio/ *a* compensatory; equalizing

competencia /kompe'tenθia; kompe'tensia/ *f,* competition, contest; rivalry; competence; aptitude; *Law.* jurisdiction

competente /kompe'tente/ *a* adequate, opportune; rightful, correct; apt, suitable; learned, competent

competer /kompe'ter/ *vi irr* to belong to; devolve on; concern. See **pedir**

competición /kompeti'θion; kompeti'sion/ *f,* competition

competidor /kompeti'ðor/ **(-ra)** *n* competitor

competir /kompe'tir/ *vi irr* to compete, contest; be equal (to), vie (with). See **pedir**

compilar /kompi'lar/ *vt* to compile

compinche /kom'pintʃe/ *mf Inf.* pal, chum

complacencia /kompla'θenθia; kompla'sensia/ *f,* satisfaction, pleasure

complacer /kompla'θer; kompla'ser/ *vt irr* to oblige, humor; —*vr* (*with en*) be pleased or satisfied with; delight in, like to. See **nacer**

complaciente /kompla'θiente; kompla'siente/ *a* pleasing; obliging, helpful

complejo /kom'pleho/ *a* complex; intricate. *m,* complex. **c. de inferioridad,** inferiority complex

complemento /komple'mento/ *m,* complement (all meanings)

completar /komple'tar/ *vt* to complete; perfect

completo /kom'pleto/ *a* full; finished; perfect

complexión /komplek'sion/ *f,* physical constitution

complexo /kom'plekso/ *a* complex; intricate

complicación /komplika'θion; komplika'sion/ *f,* complication

complicar /kompli'kar/ *vt* to complicate; muddle, confuse; —*vr* be complicated; be muddled or confused

cómplice /'kompliθe; 'komplise/ *mf* accomplice

complot /kom'plot/ *m, Inf.* conspiracy, plot, intrigue

componedor /kompone'ðor/ **(-ra)** *n* repairer; arbitrator; bone-setter; *Mus.* composer; writer, author, compiler; *Print.* compositor

componenda /kompo'nenda/ *f,* mending, repair; *Inf.* settlement; compromise, arbitration; *Inf.* shady business

componente /kompo'nente/ *a and m,* component

componer /kompo'ner/ *vt irr* to construct, form; *Mech.* resolve; compose, create; *Print.* compose; prepare, concoct, mend, repair; settle (differences); remedy; trim; correct, adjust; *Lit. Mus.* compose; add up to, amount to; —*vi* write (verses); *Mus.* compose; —*vr* dress oneself up. **c. el semblante,** to compose one's features; *Inf.* **componérselas,** to fix matters, use one's wits. See **poner**

componible /kompo'niβle/ *a* reparable, mendable; able to be arranged or adjusted

comportamiento /komporta'miento/ *m,* conduct; deportment

comportar /kompor'tar/ *vt* to tolerate; —*vr* behave, comport oneself

composición /komposi'θion; komposi'sion/ *f,* composition; repair; arrangement, compromise; *Print.* composition; *Gram.* compound; *Chem.* constitution; *Mech.* resolution

compositor /komposi'tor/ **(-ra)** *n Mus.* composer; *Print.* compositor

compostura /kompos'tura/ *f,* composition, structure; repair; neatness (of person); adulteration; arrangement, agreement; discretion, modesty

compota /kom'pota/ f. fruit preserve, compote; thick sauce

compra /'kompra/ f. buying; marketing, shopping; purchase. **estar de compras,** Euph. to be in the family way. **ir de compras,** to go shopping

comprador /kompra'ðor/ **(-ra)** a purchasing —n purchaser; buyer; shopper

comprar /kom'prar/ vt to buy; bribe

comprender /kompren'der/ vt to encircle, surround; include, comprise, contain; understand

comprensible /kompren'siβle/ a comprehensible

comprensión /kompren'sion/ f. comprehension, understanding

comprensivo /kompren'siβo/ a understanding; comprehensive

compresa /kom'presa/ f. Med. compress, swab; pack (for the face, etc.)

compresión /kompre'sion/ f. compression; squeeze

compresivo /kompre'siβo/ a compressive

compresor /kompre'sor/ m. compressor; Auto. Aer. supercharger

comprimido /kompri'miðo/ m. tablet, pill

comprimir /kompri'mir/ vt to compress; squeeze; restrain; —vr restrain oneself

comprobación /komproβa'θion; komproβa'sion/ f. verification; checking; proof

comprobante /kompro'βante/ a verifying; confirmatory

comprobar /kompro'βar/ vt irr to verify, check; confirm, prove. See **probar**

comprobatorio /komproβa'torio/ a confirmatory; verifying; testing

comprometedor /kompromete'ðor/ a Inf. compromising; jeopardizing

comprometer /komprome'ter/ vt to submit to arbitration; compromise; imperil, jeopardize; —vr pledge oneself; Inf. compromise oneself

comprometido /komprome'tiðo/ a awkward, embarrassing; (e.g. literature of a writer) committed, engagé

compromiso /kompro'miso/ m, compromise, agreement, arbitration, commitment, obligation; appointment, engagement; jeopardy; difficulty

compuesto /kom'puesto/ a and past part made-up, built-up; composite; circumspect; Bot. Gram. compound. m, composite; preparation, compound

compulsar /kompul'sar/ vt to collate; Law. make a transcript of

compulsivo /kompul'siβo/ a compelling

compunción /kompun'θion; kompun'sion/ f, compunction

compungir /kompun'hir/ vt to cause remorse or pity; —vr repent; sympathize with, pity

computación /komputa'θion; kom-puta'sion/ f, **cómputo** m, calculation, computation

computador /komputa'ðor/ **(-ra)** n computer

computar /kompu'tar/ vt to compute

cómputo /'komputo/ m, computation; estimate

comulgar /komul'gar/ vt to administer Holy Communion; —vi receive Holy Communion

comulgatorio /komulga'torio/ m, communion rail, altar rail

común /ko'mun/ a general, customary, ordinary; public, communal; universal, common; vulgar, low. m, community, population; water-closet. **en c.,** in common; generally. **por lo c.,** generally. **sentido c.,** common sense

comunicable /komuni'kaβle/ a communicable; communicative, sociable

comunicación /komunika'θion; komunika'sion/ f, communication; (telephone) call, message; letter (to the press); Mil. communiqué; pl lines of communication, transport

comunicado /komuni'kaðo/ m, official communication, communiqué; letter (to the press)

comunicar /komuni'kar/ vt to communicate; transmit; impart, share; —vr comunicarse con, (door) to open onto (e.g. Esta puerta se comunica con el jardín. This door opens onto the garden); communicate, converse, correspond with each other

comunidad /komuni'ðað/ f, the common people; community; generality, majority; pl Hist. Commune

comunión /komu'nion/ f, communion; intercourse, fellowship; Eccl. Communion

comunismo /komu'nismo/ m, communism

comunista /komu'nista/ a and mf communist

con /kon/ prep with; by means of; in the company of; towards, to; although (followed by infin., but generally translated by an inflected verb, e.g. C. ser almirante, no le gusta el mar, Although he is an admiral, he doesn't like the sea); by (followed by infin. and generally translated by a gerund, e.g. c. hacer todo esto, by doing all this). **c. bien,** safe and sound, safely (e.g. Llegamos con bien. We arrived safely.) **c. cuentagotas,** sparingly; stingily. **c. que,** so, then. **c. tal que,** provided that, on condition that. **c. todo,** nevertheless. **¿Con...?** Is this...? (on the telephone, e.g. ¿Con el Sr. Piñangos? Is this Mr. Piñangos?)

conato /ko'nato/ m, effort, endeavor; tendency; Law. attempted crime

concatenación /konkatena'θion; konkatena'sion/ f, concatenation

concavidad /konkaβi'ðað/ f, concavity; hollow

cóncavo /'konkaβo/ a concave. m, concavity; hollow

concebible /konθe'βiβle; konse'βiβle/ *a* conceivable

concebir /konθe'βir; konse'βir/ *vi irr* to become pregnant; conceive, imagine; understand; —*vt* conceive, acquire (affection, etc.). See **pedir**

conceder /konθe'ðer; konse'ðer/ *vt* to confer, grant; concede; agree to

concejal /konθe'hal; konse'hal/ *m,* councillor; alderman

concejo /kon'θeho; kon'seho/ *m,* town council; town hall; council meeting

concentración /konθentra'θion; konsentra'sion/ *f,* concentration

concentrado /konθen'traðo; konsen'traðo/ *a* concentrated; (of persons) reserved

concentrar /konθen'trar; konsen'trar/ *vt* to concentrate

concéntrico /kon'θentriko; kon'sentriko/ *a* concentric

concepción /konθep'θion; konsep'sion/ *f,* conception; idea, concept; *Eccl.* Immaculate Conception

concepto /kon'θepto; kon'septo/ *m,* idea, concept; epigram; opinion. **en mi c.,** in my opinion; judgment. **por c. de,** in payment of

conceptualismo /konθeptua'lismo; konseptua'lismo/ *m,* conceptualism

conceptuar /konθep'tuar; konsep'tuar/ *vt* to judge, take to be; believe; imagine

conceptuoso /konθep'tuoso; konsep'tuoso/ *a* witty, ingenious

concernencia /konθer'nenθia; konser'nensia/ *f,* respect, relation

concerniente /konθer'niente; konser'niente/ *a* concerning

concernir /konθer'nir; konser'nir/ *vi irr defective* to concern. See **discernir**

concertadamente /konθertaða'mente; konsertaða'mente/ *adv* methodically, orderly; by arrangement, or agreement

concertar /konθer'tar; konser'tar/ *vt irr* to arrange, settle, adjust; bargain; conclude (business deal); harmonize; compare, correlate; tune instruments; —*vi* reach an agreement. See **acertar**

concertina /konθer'tina; konser'tina/ *f,* concertina

concertista /konθer'tista; konser'tista/ *mf Mus.* performer, soloist; *Mus.* manager. **c. de piano,** concert pianist

concesión /konθe'sion; konse'sion/ *f,* conceding, grant; concession; lease

concesionario /konθesio'nario; konsesio'nario/ *m, Law.* concessionaire, leaseholder

concha /'kontʃa/ *f,* shell; turtle-shell; prompter's box; cove, creek; anything shell-shaped. *Fig.* **meterse en su c.,** to retire into one's shell. *Inf.* **tener más conchas que un galápago,** to be very cunning

conciencia /kon'θienθia; kon'siensia/ *f,* consciousness; conscience; conscientiousness. **c. doble,** dual personality. **ancho de c.,** broad-minded. **a c.,** conscientiously

concienzudo /konθien'θuðo; konsien'suðo/ *a* of a delicate conscience, scrupulous; conscientious

concierto /kon'θierto; kon'sierto/ *m,* methodical arrangement; agreement; *Mus.* concert; *Mus.* concerto. **de c.,** by common consent

conciliábulo /konθi'liaβulo; konsi'liaβulo/ *m,* conclave, private meeting; secret meeting

conciliación /konθilia'θion; konsilia'sion/ *f,* conciliation; similarity, affinity; protection, favor

conciliador /konθilia'ðor; konsilia'ðor/ *a* conciliatory

conciliar /konθi'liar; konsi'liar/ *m,* concilor —*vt* to conciliate; *Fig.* reconcile (opposing theories, etc.). **c. el sueño,** to induce sleep, woo sleep —*vr* win liking (or sometimes dislike)

concilio /kon'θilio; kon'silio/ *m,* council; *Eccl.* assembly; conciliary decree; findings of council

concisión /konθi'sion; konsi'sion/ *f,* conciseness, brevity

conciso /kon'θiso; kon'siso/ *a* concise

concitar /konθi'tar; konsi'tar/ *vt* to stir up, foment

conciudadano /konθiuða'ðano; konsiuða'ðano/ **(-na)** *n* fellow citizen; fellow countryman

cónclave /'konklaβe/ *m,* conclave; meeting

concluir /kon'kluir/ *vt irr* to conclude, finish; come to a conclusion, decide; infer, deduce; convince by reasoning; *Law.* close legal proceedings; —*vr* expire, terminate. **c. con,** to put an end to. See **huir**

conclusión /konklu'sion/ *f,* finish, end; decision; close, denouement; theory, proposition (gen. *pl*); deduction, inference; *Law.* close. **en c.,** in conclusion

conclusivo /konklu'siβo/ *a* final; conclusive

concluyente /konklu'yente/ *a* concluding; convincing; conclusive

concomer /konko'mer/ *vi Inf.* to give a shrug, shrug one's shoulders; fidget with an itch. **c. de placer,** to itch with pleasure

concomitante /konkomi'tante/ *a and m,* concomitant

concordador /konkorða'ðor/ **(-ra)** *a* peacemaking —*n* peacemaker

concordancia /konkor'ðanθia; konkor'ðansia/ *f,* harmony, agreement; (*Mus. Gram.*) concord; *pl* concordance

concordar /konkor'ðar/ *vt irr* to bring to agreement; —*vi* agree. See **acordar**

concorde /kon'korðe/ *a* agreeing; harmonious

concordia /kon'korðia/ *f,* concord, agreement, harmony; written agreement

concreción /konkre'θion; konkre'sion/ *f,* concretion

concretar /konkre'tar/ *vt* to combine, bring together; make concise; resume;

—*vr Fig.* confine oneself (to a subject) to hammer out, work out (an agreement)

concreto /kon'kreto/ *a* concrete, real, not abstract. **en c.,** in definite terms; finally, to sum up

concubina /konku'βina/ *f,* concubine, mistress

conculcar /konkul'kar/ *vt* to trample under foot, tread on; break, violate

concupiscente /konkupis'θente; konkupis'sente/ *a* concupiscent, lustful; greedy

concurrencia /konku'rrenθia; konku'rrensia/ *f,* assembly; coincidence; attendance; help, influence

concurrido /konku'rriðo/ *a* crowded; busy; frequented

concurrir /konku'rrir/ *vi* to coincide; contribute; meet together; agree, be of same opinion; compete (in an examination, etc.)

concurso /kon'kurso/ *m,* crowd, concourse; conjunction, coincidence; help; competition; (tennis) tournament; competitive examination; invitation to offer tenders. **c. de acreedores,** creditors' meeting. **c. interno,** competitive examination for a position open to staff members only

concusión /konku'sion/ *f,* concussion; shock; extortion

condado /kon'daðo/ *m,* earldom; county

condecir /konde'θir; konde'sir/ **(con)** *vi* to agree (with)

condecoración /kondekora'θion; kondekora'sion/ *f,* conferment of an honor, decoration; medal

condecorar /kondeko'rar/ *vt* to confer a decoration or medal

condena /kon'dena/ *f, Law.* sentence; punishment; penalty

condenable /konde'naβle/ *a* culpable, guilty; worthy of damnation

condenado /konde'naðo/ **(-da)** *a* damned; wicked, harmful —*n Law.* convicted criminal

condenador /kondena'ðor/ *a* condemning; incriminating; blaming

condenar /konde'nar/ *vt Law.* to pronounce sentence (on), convict; condemn; disapprove; wall or block or close up. **c. a galeras,** to condemn to the gallies —*vr* blame oneself; be eternally damned

condenatorio /kondena'torio/ *a* condemnatory; incriminating

condensación /kondensa'θion; kondensa'sion/ *f,* condensation

condensador /kondensa'ðor/ *a* condensing. *m,* (*Elec. Mech. Chem.*) condenser

condensante /konden'sante/ *a* condensing

condensar /konden'sar/ *vt* to condense; thicken; abridge

condescendencia /kondesθen'denθia; kondessen'densia/ *f,* affability, graciousness

condescender /kondesθen'der; kon-

dessen'der/ *vi irr* to be obliging, helpful, agreeable. See **entender**

condescendiente /kondesθen'diente; kondessen'diente/ *a* affable, gracious

condestable /kondes'taβle/ *m, Hist.* constable, commander-in-chief

condición /kondi'θion; kondi'sion/ *f,* condition; quality; temperament; character; (social) position; rank, family; nobility, circumstance; stipulation, condition, requirement. **estar en condiciones de,** to be in a position to. **no estar en condiciones de,** to be in no condition to

condicional /kondiθio'nal; kondisio'nal/ *a* conditional

condicionar /kondiθio'nar; kondisio'nar/ *vi* to come to an agreement, arrange; —*vt* impose conditions

condimentación /kondimenta'θion; kondimenta'sion/ *f, Cul.* seasoning

condimentar /kondimen'tar/ *vt* to flavor, season (food)

condimento /kondi'mento/ *m,* condiment, flavoring

condiscípulo /kondis'θipulo; kondis'sipulo/ *m,* schoolfellow

condolencia /kondo'lenθia; kondo'lensia/ *f,* compassion; condolence

condolerse /kondo'lerse/ *vr* (*with de*) to sympathize with, be sorry for. See **doler**

condonar /kondo'nar/ *vt* to condone

conducción, conducencia /konduk'θion; konduk'sion, konduθenθia; kondusensia/ *f,* transport, conveyance, carriage; guiding; direction, management; *Phys.* conduction; *Mech.* control-gear. *Auto.* **c. a izquierda,** left-hand drive

conducente /kondu'θente; kondu'sente/ *a* conducting, conducive

conducir /kondu'θir; kondu'sir/ *vt irr* to transport, convey, carry; *Phys.* conduct; guide, lead; manage, direct; *Auto.* drive; conduce; —*vi* be suitable; —*vr* behave, conduct oneself —*Pres. Indic.* **conduzco, conduces,** etc —*Preterite* **conduje, condujiste,** etc —*Pres. Subjunc.* **conduzca, conduzcas,** etc —*Imperf. Subjunc.* **condujese,** etc.

conducta /kon'dukta/ *f,* transport, conveyance; management, conduct, direction; behavior

conductivo /konduk'tiβo/ *a* conductive

conducto /kon'dukto/ *m,* pipe, conduit, drain, duct; *Fig.* channel, means; *Anat.* tube

conductor /konduk'tor/ **(-ra)** *n* guide; leader; driver (vehicles); *m, Phys.* conductor. **c. de caballos,** teamster. **c. de entrada,** *Radio.* lead-in. **c. del calor,** heat-conductor. **c. eléctrico,** electric wire or cable

conectar /konek'tar/ *vt Elec.* to connect, switch on; couple; attach, join

conejillo de Indias /kone'hiλo de 'indias; kone'hiyo de 'indias/ *m,* guineapig

conejo /ko'neho/ *m,* rabbit

conexión /konek'sion/ *f,* connection;

Elec. switching on, connection; joint; joining; *pl* friends, connections; *Elec.* wiring

conexo /ko'nekso/ *a* connected

confabulación /konfaβula'θion; konfaβula'sion/ *f,* confabulation, conspiracy

confabular /konfaβu'lar/ *vi* to confer; —*vr* scheme, plot

confalón /konfa'lon/ *m,* standard, banner

confección /konfek'θion; konfek'sion/ *f,* making; confection; making-up; concoction, remedy; ready-made garment

confeccionador /konfekθiona'ðor; konfeksiona'ðor/ **(-ra)** *n* maker (of clothes, etc.)

confeccionar /konfekθio'nar; konfeksio'nar/ *vt* to make; prepare; make up (pharmaceuticals)

confederación /konfeðera'θion; konfeðera'sion/ *f,* alliance, pact; confederacy, federation

confederarse /konfeðe'rarse/ *vr* to confederate, be allied

conferencia /konfe'renθia; konfe'rensia/ *f,* conference, meeting; lecture; (telephone) long-distance call (US), trunk call (UK)

conferenciante /konferen'θiante; konferen'siante/ *mf* lecturer

conferenciar /konferen'θiar; konferen'siar/ *vi* to confer

conferir /konfe'rir/ *vt irr* to grant, concede; consider, discuss; compare, correlate. See **herir**

confesable /konfe'saβle/ *a* acknowledgeable, avowable

confesar /konfe'sar/ *vt irr* to avow, declare; acknowledge, admit; *Eccl.* hear confession; —*vr Eccl.* confess —*Pres. Indic.* **confieso, confiesas, confiesa, confiesan.** *Pres. Subjunc.* **confiese, confieses, confiese, confiesen**

confesión /konfe'sion/ *f,* confession

confesionario, confesonario, confesorio /konfesio'nario, konfeso'nario, konfe'sorio/ *m, Eccl.* confessional

confesor /konfe'sor/ *m,* confessor

confeti /kon'feti/ *m,* confetti

confianza /kon'fianθa; kon'fiansa/ *f,* confidence, trust; assurance, courage; over-confidence, conceit; intimacy; familiarity. **de c.,** reliable (e.g. *persona de c.,* reliable person); informal (e.g. *reunión de c.,* informal meeting). **en c.,** in confidence, confidentially

confianzudo /konfian'θuðo; konfian'suðo/ *a Inf.* overconfident

confiar /kon'fiar/ *vi* (*with en*) to trust in, hope; —*vt* (*with prep a* or *en*) entrust, commit to the care of; confide in

confidencia /konfi'ðenθia; konfi'ðensia/ *f,* trust; confidence; confidential information

confidente /konfi'ðente/ **(-ta)** *a* trustworthy, true. *m,* seat for two —*n* confidant(e); spy

configuración /konfigura'θion; konfigura'sion/ *f,* configuration, form, lie

configurar /konfigu'rar/ *vt* to shape

confín /kon'fin/ *m,* boundary, frontier; limit —*a* boundary

confinar /konfi'nar/ *vi* (*with con*) to be bounded by, contiguous to; —*vt* banish; place in confinement

confirmación /konfirma'θion; konfirma'sion/ *f,* corroboration; *Eccl.* confirmation

confirmar /konfir'mar/ *vt* to corroborate; uphold; *Eccl.* confirm

confirmatorio /konfirma'torio/ *a* confirmatory

confiscación /konfiska'θion; konfiska'sion/ *f,* confiscation

confiscar /konfis'kar/ *vt* to confiscate

confitar /konfi'tar/ *vt* to candy, crystallize or preserve (fruit, etc.); *Fig.* sweeten

confite /kon'fite/ *m,* bonbon, sugared almond, etc.

confitería /konfite'ria/ *f,* confectionery

confitura /konfi'tura/ *f,* preserve, jam

conflagración /konflagra'θion; konflagra'sion/ *f,* conflagration, blaze; uprising, rebellion

conflicto /kon'flikto/ *m,* strife, struggle; spiritual conflict; *Fig.* difficult situation

confluencia /kon'fluenθia; kon'fluensia/ *f,* confluence; crowd

confluir /kon'fluir/ *vi irr* to meet, flow together (rivers); run together (roads); crowd. See **huir**

conformación /konforma'θion; konforma'sion/ *f,* conformation; make-up, structure (*e.g.* of an organization)

conformar /konfor'mar/ *vt* to fit, adjust; —*vr* agree, be of the same opinion; submit, comply; to make up (e.g. *los grupos sociales que conforman este país,* the social groups who make up this country)

conforme /kon'forme/ *a* similar, alike; consistent; in agreement; long-suffering, resigned —*adv* according (to), in proportion (to)

conformidad /konformi'ðað/ *f,* conformity; similarity; resignation; agreement, harmony; proportion, symmetry. **de c.,** by common consent. **en c.,** according to

confort /kon'fort/ *m,* comfort

confortante /konfor'tante/ *a* comforting; consoling; strengthening (of beverages)

confortar /konfor'tar/ *vt* to comfort, reassure; encourage; console

confrontación /konfronta'θion; konfronta'sion/ *f,* confrontment; comparison (of texts, etc.)

confrontar /konfron'tar/ *vt* to bring face to face; compare, correlate; —*vi* face; (*with con*) be contiguous to, border on

confundir /konfun'dir/ *vt* to mix, confuse; jumble together; mistake; *Fig.* confound (in argument); humble; bewilder, perplex; —*vr* be mixed together; mistake, confuse; be ashamed; be bewildered

confusión /konfu'sion/ *f,* confusion; perplexity; shame; jumble

confuso /kon'fuso/ *a* mixed, upset; jumbled; obscure; indistinct; blurred; bewildered

confutar /konfu'tar/ vt to confute

congelación /konhela'θion; konhela'sion/ f, freezing; congealment. **punto de c.,** freezing point

congelar /konhe'lar/ vt to congeal; freeze

congénito /kon'henito/ a congenital

congestión /konhes'tion/ f, Med. congestion

congestionar /konhestio'nar/ vt to congest; —vr Med. be overcharged (with blood)

conglomeración /konglomera'θion; konglomera'sion/ f, conglomeration

conglomerar /konglome'rar/ vt to conglomerate

congoja /kon'goha/ f, anguish, anxiety, grief

congraciarse /kongra'θiarse; kongra'siarse/ (con), vr to ingratiate oneself (with), get into the good graces (of)

congratulación /kongratula'θion; kongratula'sion/ f, congratulation

congratular /kongratu'lar/ vt to congratulate; —vr congratulate oneself

congratulatorio /kongratula'torio/ a congratulatory

congregación /kongrega'θion; kongrega'sion/ f, gathering, meeting, congregation; brotherhood, guild

congregar /kongre'gar/ **(se)** vt and vr to meet, assemble

congreso /kon'greso/ m, congress; conference, meeting; sexual intercourse

congrio /'kongrio/ m, conger eel

congruencia /kon'gruenθia; kon'gruensia/ f, suitability, convenience; Math. congruence

congruente /kon'gruente/ a convenient, opportune; Math. congruent

cónico /'koniko/ a conical, tapering Math. conic

conjetura /konhe'tura/ f, conjecture

conjeturar /konhetu'rar/ vt to conjecture, surmise

conjugación /konhuga'θion; konhuga'sion/ f, conjugation

conjugar /konhu'gar/ vt to conjugate

conjunción /konhun'θion; konhun'sion/ f, connection, union association; (Astron. Gram.) conjunction

conjuntivitis /konhunti'βitis/ f, conjunctivitis

conjunto /kon'hunto/ a united, associated adjoining; mingled, mixed (with) bound, affiliated. m, whole; combo, ensemble (of musicians). **c. habitacional,** housing complex, housing project

conjura, conjuración /kon'hura, konhura'θion; kon'hura, konhura'sion/ f, conspiracy, plot

conjurador /konhura'ðor/ **(-ra)** n conspirator, plotter; exorcist

conjurar /konhu'rar/ vi to conspire, plot vt swear, take an oath; exorcise; implore, beg; ward off (danger)

conjuro /kon'huro/ m, plot, conspiracy, spell, incantation; entreaty

conllevar /konʎe'βar; konye'βar/ vt to share (troubles) bear, put up with; endure

conmemoración /komemora'θion; komemora'sion/ f, commemoration

conmemorar /komemo'rar/ vt to commemorate

conmemorativo /komemora'tiβo/ a commemorative

conmensurable /komensu'raβle/ a commensurable

conmigo /ko'migo/ pers pron 1st pers. sing. mf, with myself, with me

conminar /komi'nar/ vt to threaten

conmiseración /komisera'θion; komisera'sion/ f, commiseration, compassion, pity

conmoción /komo'θion; komo'sion/ f, disturbance (mind or body); upheaval, commotion. **c. eléctrica,** electric shock

conmovedor /komoβe'ðor/ a moving, pitiful; stirring, thrilling

conmover /komo'βer/ vt irr to perturb, stir; move to pity. **c. los cimientos de,** to shake the foundations of; —vr be emotionally moved. See **mover**

conmutador /komuta'ðor/ m, Elec. commutator; change-over switch

conmutar /komu'tar/ vt to commute; Elec. switch, convert

connato /kon'nato/ a contemporary

connatural /konnatu'ral/ a innate, inborn

connivencia /konni'βenθia; konni'βensia/ f, connivance

connotar /konno'tar/ vt to connote

cono /'kono/ m, (Geom. Bot.) cone. **el C. Sur,** the Southern Cone

conocedor /konoθe'ðor; konose'ðor/ **(-ra)** n one who knows; connoisseur; expert

conocer /kono'θer; kono'ser/ vt irr to know; understand; observe, perceive; be acquainted (with); conjecture; confess, acknowledge; know carnally; —vr know oneself; know one another. **conocerle a uno la voz,** to recognize somebody's voice (e.g. Le conozco la voz. I recognize her by her voice.) **conocerle a uno en su manera de andar,** to recognize somebody by his gait, recognize somebody by his walk —Pres. Indic. **conozco, conoces,** etc —Pres. Subjunc. **conozca,** etc.

conocido /kono'θiðo; kono'siðo/ **(-da)** a illustrious, distinguished —n acquaintance

conocimiento /konoθi'miento; konosi'miento/ m, knowledge; understanding; intelligence; acquaintance (not friend); consciousness; Com. bill of lading; pl knowledge, learning

conque /'konke/ conjunc so, so that (e.g. ¿C. Juan se va? So John's going away?)

conquista /kon'kista/ f, conquest

conquistar /konkis'tar/ vt to conquer; Fig. captivate, win

consagración /konsagra'θion; konsagra'sion/ f, consecration; dedication

consagrar /konsa'grar/ vt to consecrate; dedicate, devote; deify; —vr (with prep a) dedicate oneself to, engage in

consciente /kons'θiente; kons'siente/ a conscious; aware; sane. m, Psychol. conscious

conscripción /konskrip'θion; konskrip'sion/ f, conscription

conscripto /kons'kripto/ m, conscript

consecuencia /konse'kuenθia; konse'kuensia/ f, consequence, outcome; logical consequence, conclusion; importance; consistence (of people)

consecuente /konse'kuente/ a consequent, resultant; consistent. **c. consigo mismo,** self-consistent m, consequence; Math. consequent

consecutivo /konseku'tiβo/ a consecutive, successive

conseguir /konse'gir/ vt irr to obtain, achieve. See **seguir**

consejero /konse'hero/ **(-ra)** n adviser; member of council. m. **c. de estado,** counselor of state

consejo /kon'seho/ m, advice; council; commission, board; council chamber or building. **c. de administración,** board of directors. **c. de guerra,** council of war. **c. del reino,** council of the realm. **c. privado,** privy council

consenso /kon'senso/ m, consensus of opinion, unanimity

consentido /konsen'tiðo/ a complaisant (of husband); spoiled, over-indulged

consentimiento /konsenti'miento/ m, consent; assent

consentir /konsen'tir/ vt irr to permit, allow; believe; tolerate, put up with; overindulge, spoil; —vr crack, give way (furniture, etc.). **c. en,** to consent to; to agree to. See **sentir**

conserje /kon'serhe/ m, concierge, porter; warden or keeper (of castle, etc.)

conserjería /konserhe'ria/ f, conciergerie, porter's lodge; warden's dwelling (in castles, etc.)

conserva /kon'serβa/ f, jam; preserve; pickles; Naut. convoy. **en c.,** preserved, tinned

conservación /konserβa'θion; konserβa'sion/ f, upkeep; preservation, maintenance; Cul. preserving; conservation. **c. refrigerada,** cold storage

conservador /konserβa'ðor/ **(-ra)** a keeping, preserving —a and n preserver; Polit. conservative; traditionalist. m, curator

conservadurismo /konserβaðu'rismo/ m, conservatism

conservar /konser'βar/ vt to keep, maintain, preserve; keep up (custom, etc.); guard; Cul. preserve. **c. en buen estado,** to keep in repair

conservatorio /konserβa'torio/ m, conservatoire; academy. **c. de música,** academy of music, conservatoire

considerable /konsiðe'raβle/ a considerable; worthy of consideration, powerful; numerous; large; important

consideración /konsiðera'θion; konsiðera'sion/ f, consideration, attention; reflection, thought; civility; importance. **en c. de,** considering

considerado /konsiðe'raðo/ a considerate; prudent; distinguished; important

considerar /konsiðe'rar/ vt to consider, reflect upon; treat with consideration (persons); judge, estimate, feel (e.g. Considero que... I feel that...)

consigna /kon'signa/ f, Mil. watchword; left luggage office

consignar /konsig'nar/ vt to assign, lay aside; deposit; Com. consign; entrust, commit; put in writing; Law. deposit in trust; book (a suspect)

consignatario /konsigna'tario/ m, Law. trustee; mortgagee; Com. consignee. **c. de buques,** shipping agent

consigo /kon'sigo/ pers pron 3rd sing. and pl. mf with himself, herself, oneself, yourself, yourselves, themselves

consiguiente /konsi'giente/ a consequent, resulting. m, consequence. **por c.,** in consequence

consistencia /konsis'tenθia; konsis'tensia/ f, solidity; consistence, density; consistency, congruity, relevance

consistente /konsis'tente/ a of a certain consistency; solid

consistir /konsis'tir/ vi (with en) to consist in; be comprised of; be the result of

consola /kon'sola/ f, console table; piertable; Mech. bracket

cónsola /'konsola/ f, radio cabinet

consolación /konsola'θion; konsola'sion/ f, consolation

consolador /konsola'ðor/ **(-ra)** n comforter, consoler

consolar /konso'lar/ vt irr to comfort, console. **consolarse de + inf.,** to console oneself for + pp. See **contar**

consolidación /konsoliða'θion; konsoliða'sion/ f, consolidation; stiffening

consolidar /konsoli'ðar/ vt to consolidate; strengthen; combine, unite; —vr Law. unite

consomé /konso'me/ m, consommé

consonancia /konso'nanθianb; konso'nansia/ f, harmony; agreement

consonante /konso'nante/ a consonant, consistent. m, rhyme. f, Gram. consonant

consorcio /kon'sorθio; kon'sorsio/ m, partnership; trust; intimacy, common life

consorte /kon'sorte/ mf consort; companion, associate, partner; spouse

conspicuo /kons'pikuo/ a outstanding, distinguished; conspicuous

conspiración /konspira'θion; konspira'sion/ f, conspiracy

conspirador /konspira'ðor/ **(-ra)** n conspirator

conspirar /konspi'rar/ vi to conspire; plot, scheme; tend, combine

constancia /kons'tanθia; kons'tansia/ *f,* constancy, steadfastness; stability, steadiness; transcript (of grades). **c. de estudios,** transcript (of grades)

constante /kons'tante/ *a* constant; durable; *Mech.* steady, non-oscillating. *m,* constant

constar /kons'tar/ *vi* to be evident, be clear; (*with de*) be composed of, consist of, comprise

constelación /konstela'θion; konstela-'sion/ *f, Astron.* constellation; climate

consternación /konsterna'θion; konsterna'sion/ *f,* dismay, alarm

consternarse /konster'narse/ *vr* to be dismayed or alarmed

constipado /konsti'paðo/ *m, Med.* cold; chill

constiparse /konsti'parse/ *vr* to catch a cold or chill

constitución /konstitu'θion; konstitu'sion/ *f,* constitution; composition, make-up (e.g. *la c. del suelo,* the make-up of the soil)

constituir /konsti'tuir/ *vt irr* to constitute, form; found, establish; (*with en*) appoint, nominate; *Fig.* place in (a difficult situation, etc.); —*vr* (*with en* or *por*) be appointed or authorized; be under (an obligation). See **huir**

constituyente, constitutivo /konstitu'yente, konstitu'tiβo/ *a* and *m,* constituent

constreñir /konstre'ɲir/ *vt irr* to constrain, oblige; constrict; constipate. See **ceñir**

constricción /konstrik'θion; konstrik'sion/ *f,* constriction; contraction, shrinkage

construcción /konstruk'θion; konstruk'sion/ *f,* construction; art or process of construction; fabric, structure; *Gram.* construction; building, erection. **c. de caminos,** road making. **c. naval,** shipbuilding

constructor /konstruk'tor/ **(-ra)** *a* building, constructive —*n* builder; constructor

construir /kons'truir/ *vt irr* to construct; build, make; *Gram.* construct. See **huir**

consuelo /kon'suelo/ *m,* consolation; comfort, solace; joy, delight

cónsul /'konsul/ *m,* consul

consulado /konsu'laðo/ *m,* consulate. **c. general,** consulate general

consulta /kon'sulta/ *f,* deliberation, consideration; advice; reference; conference, consultation

consultar /konsul'tar/ *vt* to discuss, consider; seek advice, consult. **consultarlo con la almohada,** *Fig.* to sleep on it, think it over, mull it over

consultor /konsul'tor/ **(-ra)** *a* consultative, advisory; consulting —*n* consultant; adviser. **c. externo,** outside consultant

consultorio /konsul'torio/ *m, Med.* consulting rooms; surgery; technical information bureau

consumación /konsuma'θion; konsuma'sion/ *f,* consummation; completion, attainment; extinction, end

consumar /konsu'mar/ *vt* to consummate; complete, accomplish, perfect

consumido /konsu'miðo/ *a Inf.* emaciated, wasted away; timid, spiritless

consumidor /konsumi'ðor/ **(-ra)** *a* consuming —*n* consumer, user

consumir /konsu'mir/ *vt* to destroy; consume, use; waste away, wear away; *Eccl.* take communion; *Inf.* grieve; —*vr* be destroyed; *Inf.* be consumed with grief

consumo /kon'sumo/ *m,* consumption; demand. **c. de combustible,** fuel consumption

contabilidad /kontaβili'ðað/ *f,* bookkeeping; accounts; accounting

contable /kon'taβle/ *m,* bookkeeper

contacto /kon'takto/ *m,* contact (also *Elec. Mil.*). **en c.,** in common (e.g. *Los dos libros tienen mucho en c.* The two books have much in common.)

contado /kon'taðo/ *a* few; infrequent; rare. **al c.,** *Com.* cash down. **por de c.,** presumably; of course, naturally

contador /konta'ðor/ *a* counting. *m,* accountant; *Law.* auditor; counter (in banks); *Elec.* meter, counter; *Naut.* purser. **c. oficial,** *Argentina* certified public accountant. **c. público titulado,** certified public accountant

contagiar /konta'hiar/ *vt* to infect; corrupt, pervert; —*vr* (*with con, de* or *por*) be infected by or through

contagio /kon'tahio/ *m,* infection; contagious disease; *Fig.* contagion, perversion, corruption

contagioso /konta'hioso/ *a* infectious; *Fig.* catching, contagious

contaminación /kontamina'θion; kontamina'sion/ *f,* contamination; pollution

contaminar /kontami'nar/ *vt* to pollute, contaminate; infect; *Fig.* corrupt

contante /kon'tante/ *a* ready (of money)

contar /kon'tar/ *vt irr* to count; recount, tell; place to account; include, count among; —*vi* calculate, compute. **contarle a uno las cuarenta,** *Inf.* to give someone a piece of one's mind. **c. con,** to rely upon; reckon upon —*Pres. Indic.* **cuento, cuentas, cuenta, cuenta.** *Pres. Subjunc.* **cuente, cuentes, cuente, cuenten**

contemplación /kontempla'θion; kontempla'sion/ *f,* meditation, contemplation; consideration

contemplar /kontem'plar/ *vt* to consider, reflect upon; look at, contemplate; indulge, please

contemporáneo /kontempo'raneo/ **(de)** *a* contemporaneous (to *or* with) *n* contemporary

contemporizar /kontempori'θar; kontempori'sar/ *vi* to temporize, gain time

contencioso /konten'θioso; konten'sioso/ *a* contentious, argumentative; *Law.* litigious

contender /konten'der/ *vi irr* to contain;

restrain, hold back; comprise; —*vr* control oneself. See **entender**

contendiente /konten'diente/ *mf* contestant

contener /konte'ner/ *vt irr* to contain; include; comprise; hold back; restrain; check, repress; hold down, subdue; suppress, put down; —*vr* contain oneself; keep one's temper; keep quiet; refrain. See **tener**

contenido /konte'nido/ *m*, contents —*a* contained; *Fig.* restrained; reserved (of persons)

contentar /konten'tar/ *vt* to satisfy, please; *Com.* endorse; —*vr* be pleased or satisfied

contento /kon'tento/ *a* happy; content; satisfied; pleased. *m*, pleasure; contentment. **no caber de c.,** to be overjoyed

contestación /kontesta'θion; kontesta'sion/ *f*, reply, answer; discussion, argument, dispute

contestar /kontes'tar/ *vt* to reply, answer; confirm, attest; —*vi* accord, harmonize

contexto /kon'teksto/ *m*, context

contienda /kon'tienda/ *f*, struggle, fight; quarrel, dispute; discussion

contigo /kon'tigo/ *pers pron* 2nd sing. *mf* with thee, with you

contiguo /kon'tiguo/ *a* adjacent, near

continoncia /konti'nenθia; konti'nensia/ *f*, moderation, self-restraint; continence; chastity; containing

continental /konti'nental/ *a* continental. *m*, express messenger service; *Puerto Rico* person from the mainland United States

continente /konti'nente/ *a* continent. *m*, container; demeanor, bearing; *Geog.* continent; mainland

contingente /kontin'hente/ *a* incidental; fortuitous; dependent; *m*, *Mil.* taskforce, contingent

continuación /kontinua'θion; kontinua'sion/ *f*, continuation; prolongation; sequel (of a story, etc.)

continuar /konti'nuar/ *vt* to continue; —*vi* continue; last, remain, go on; —*vr* be prolonged

continuidad /kontinui'daθ/ *f*, continuity

continuo /kon'tinuo/ *a* continuous, steady, uninterrupted; persevering, tenacious; persistent, lasting, unremitting. *m*, a united whole. **de c.,** continuously

contonearse /kontone'arse/ *vr* to swing the hips (in walking); strut

contorno /kon'torno/ *m*, contour, outline; (gen. *pl*) environs, surrounding district

contra /'kontra/ *prep* against, counter, athwart; opposed to, hostile to; in front of, opposite; toward. *m*, opposite view or opinion. *f*, *Inf.* difficulty, trouble. **c. la corriente,** upstream. **el pro y el c.,** the pros and cons. **en c.,** in opposition, against

contrabalancear /kontraβalanθe'ar;

kontraβalanse'ar/ *vt* to counterbalance; *Fig.* compensate

contrabandista /kontraβan'dista/ *a* smuggling. *mf* smuggler

contrabando /kontra'βando/ *m*, contraband; smuggling

contracción /kontrak'θion; kontrak'sion/ *f*, contraction; shrinkage; abridgment; abbreviation

contradanza /kontra'danθa; kontra'dansa/ *f*, square dance

contradecir /kontrade'θir; kontrade'sir/ *vt irr* to contradict; —*vr* contradict oneself. See **decir**

contradicción /kontradik'θion; kontradik'sion/ *f*, contradiction

contradictorio /kontradik'torio/ *a* contradictory

contraer /kontra'er/ *vt irr* to shrink, reduce in size, shorten; abridge; contract (matrimony, obligations); *Fig.* acquire (diseases, habits); —*vr* shorten, contract, shrink. See **traer**

contrahacer /kontraa'θer; kontraa'ser/ *vt irr* to forge, counterfeit; mimic; imitate. See **hacer**

contrahecho /kontra'etʃo/ *a* deformed

contralto /kon'tralto/ *m*, contralto (voice)

contramarcha /kontra'martʃa/ *f*, retrogression; *Mil.* countermarch

contramedida /kontrame'dida/ *f*, counter-measure

contraorden /kontra'orden/ *f*, countermand

contrapedalear /kontrapedale'ar/ *vi* to backpedal

contrapelo /kontra'pelo/ *a adv* the wrong way of the hair, against the grain; *Inf.* reluctantly, distastefully

contrapeso /kontra'peso/ *m*, counterpoise, counterweight; balancing-pole (acrobats); *Fig.* counterbalance; makeweight

contraponer /kontrapo'ner/ *vt irr* to compare; place opposite; oppose. See **poner**

contraproducente /kontraprodu'θente; kontraprodu'sente/ *a* counteractive, counterproductive, unproductive, self-deceiving; self-defeating

contrapuesto /kontra'puesto/ *a* opposing, divergent

contrapunto /kontra'punto/ *m*, counterpoint

contrariar /kontra'riar/ *vt* to counter, oppose; impede; vex, annoy

contrariedad /kontrarie'daθ/ *f*, contrariety, opposition; obstacle; vexation, trouble

contrario /kon'trario/ **(-ia)** *a* opposite; hostile, opposed; harmful; adverse, contrary —*n* adversary; opponent. *m*, obstacle. *f.* **contraria,** contrary, opposite. **al contrario,** on the contrary. **llevar la contraria** (a), to oppose; contradict

contrasentido /kontrasen'tido/ *m*, wrong sense, opposite sense (of words);

contradiction of initial premise; self-contradiction; nonsense

contraseña /kontra'seɲa/ f, countersign; *Mil.* password

contrastar /kontras'tar/ vt to contrast; oppose, resist; check (weights and measures); assay; *Mech.* calibrate, gauge; —vi contrast

contraste /kon'traste/ m, contrast; opposition, difference; weights and measures inspector; dispute, clash. **en c. a,** in contrast to

contrata /kon'trata/ f, **contrato,** m, contract. **contrato de arrendamiento,** lease

contratación /kontrata'θion; kontrata'sion/ f, hiring; *Com.* transaction; commerce, trade

contratar /kontra'tar/ vt to contract, enter into an agreement; make a bargain (with), deal (with); hire, contract

contratiempo /kontra'tiempo/ m, mishap, accident

contratista /kontra'tista/ mf contractor

contravención /kontraβen'θion; kontraβen'sion/ f, contravention; violation. **en c. a,** in violation of

contraveneno /kontraβe'neno/ m, *Med.* antidote; remedy, precaution

contravenir /kontraβe'nir/ vt irr to infringe, contravene. See **venir**

contraventana /kontraβen'tana/ f, shutter (for windows)

contravidriera /kontraβið'riera/ f, storm window

contrayente /kontra'yente/ a contracting. mf contracting party (used of matrimony)

contribución /kontriβu'θion; kontriβu'sion/ f, contribution; tax. **c. sobre la propiedad,** property tax

contribuir /kontri'βuir/ vt irr to pay (taxes); contribute. See **huir**

contribuyente /kontriβu'yente/ a contributing; contributory. mf contributor; taxpayer

contrincante /kontrin'kante/ m, competitor, candidate (public examinations); rival, opponent

control /kon'trol/ m, control; checking. **c. de precios,** price control

controlar /kontro'lar/ vt to control

controversia /kontro'βersia/ f, controversy

controvertir /kontroβer'tir/ vi and vt irr to dispute, argue against, deny. See **sentir**

contumacia /kontu'maθia; kontu'masia/ f, obstinacy; *Law.* contumacy

contumaz /kontu'maθ; kontu'mas/ a stubborn; impenitent; *Law.* contumacious; *Med.* obstinate, resistant (to cure)

conturbar /kontur'βar/ vt to perturb, make anxious, disturb; —vr be perturbed

contuso /kon'tuso/ a contused, bruised

convalecencia /kombale'θenθia; kombale'sensia/ f, convalescence; convalescent home

convalecer /kombale'θer; kombale'ser/ vi irr to convalesce, get better; *Fig.* recover, regain (influence, etc.). See **conocer**

convaleciente /kombale'θiente; kombale'siente/ a and mf convalescent

convalidar /kombali'ðar/ vt to ratify, confirm

convencer /komben'θer; komben'ser/ vt to convince; prove beyond doubt, demonstrate to (persons); be convincing (e.g. *No convence,* It's not convincing; He's not convincing.) vr be convinced

convencimiento /kombenθi'miento; kombensi'miento/ m, conviction, belief, assurance

convención /komben'θion; komben'sion/ f, pact, formal agreement; harmony, conformity; convention

convencionalismo /kombenθiona'lismo; kombensiona'lismo/ m, conventionality

convenido /kombe'niðo/ a agreed

conveniencia /kombe'nienθia; kombe'niensia/ f, conformity, harmony, adjustment; experience, suitability, convenience; advantage; agreement, pact; post as domestic; ease, comfort; pl income; social conventions

conveniente /kombe'niente/ a convenient, opportune; suitable, fitting; profitable; useful; decorous. **tener por c. + inf,** to think it fitting to + inf, find it appropriate to + *Inf.*

convenio /kom'benio/ m, pact, treaty; *Com.* agreement, contract

convenir /kombe'nir/ vi irr to agree; assemble, congregate; belong; be suitable; —vr agree; suit oneself. **No me conviene salir esta tarde,** It does not suit me to go out this afternoon. **Me convendría pasar un mes allí,** It would be a good idea (or a wise thing) for me to spend a month there. See **venir**

convento /kom'bento/ m, convent; monastery; religious community

conventual /komben'tual/ a conventual; monastic. m, *Eccl.* conventual

convergencia /komber'henθia; komber'hensia/ f, convergence

convergir /komber'hir/ vi to converge; *Fig.* coincide (views, etc.)

conversación /kombersa'θion; kombersa'sion/ f, conversation; intercourse, company; *Law.* criminal conversation

conversar /komber'sar/ vi to converse; chat; live with others; know socially

conversión /komber'sion/ f, conversion; change, transformation; *Com.* conversion; *Mil.* wheel; wheeling

convertible /komber'tiβle/ a convertible

convertir /komber'tir/ vt irr to change, transform; convert; reform; —vr be transformed; be converted; be reformed. See **sentir**

convexo /kom'bekso/ a convex

convicción /kombik'θion; kombik'sion/ f, conviction; certitude; *Law.* conviction

convicto /kom'bikto/ (**-ta**) a and n *Law.* convict

convidado /kombi'ðaðo/ **(-da)** n guest

convidar /kombi'ðar/ vt to invite (persons); encourage, provoke; entice, attract; —vr invite oneself; offer one's services

convincente /kombin'θente; kombin'sente/ a convincing

convite /kom'bite/ m, invitation; banquet; party

convivencia /kombi'βenθia; kombi'βensia/ f, coexistence, common life, life together. **c. pacífica,** peaceful coexistence

convivir /kombi'βir/ vi to live together, live under the same roof

convocación /komboka'θion; komboka'sion/ f, convocation

convocar /kombo'kar/ vt to convene, convoke

convoy /kom'boi/ m, convoy; escort; following; cruet-stand

convulsión /kombul'sion/ f, convulsion

convulsivo /kombul'siβo/ a convulsive

conyugal /konyu'gal/ a conjugal

cónyuge /'konyuhe/ mf husband or (and) wife (used gen. in pl)

coñac /ko'nak/ m, brandy

cooperación /koopera'θion; koopera'sion/ f, cooperation

cooperador /koopera'ðor/ **(-ra)** a cooperative —n cooperator, collaborator

cooperar /koope'rar/ vi to cooperate

cooperativa /koopera'tiβa/ f, cooperative society

cooperativo /koopera'tiβo/ a cooperative

coordenada /koorðe'naða/ f, coordinate

coordinación /koorðina'θion; koorðina'sion/ f, coordination

coordinar /koorði'nar/ vt to coordinate, classify

copa /'kopa/ f, wineglass, goblet; glassful; top branches (of trees); crown (of hat); *Cards.* heart; gill (liquid measure); *Inf.* drink, glass; pl *Cards.* hearts (in Spanish pack, goblets)

copartícipe /kopar'tiθipe; kopar'tisipe/ mf co-partner, partaker, participant

copec /'kopek/ m, kopeck

Copenhague /kope'nage/ Copenhagen

copero /ko'pero/ m, cupbearer; sideboard; cocktail cabinet

copete /ko'pete/ m, lock, tress (hair); tuft, crest; forelock (horses); head, top (ice-cream, drinks); *Inf.* **de alto c.,** aristocratic; socially prominent

copia /'kopia/ f, abundance, plenty; copy, reproduction; transcript; imitation

copiador /kopia'ðor/ **(-ra)** a copying —n copier; transcriber. m, copybook

copiar /ko'piar/ vt to copy

copioso /ko'pioso/ a abundant, plentiful

copla /'kopla/ f, couplet; popular four-line poem; couple, pair; pl *Inf.* verses

coplero /kop'lero/ **(-ra)** n balladmonger; poetaster

copo /'kopo/ m, cop (of a spindle); snowflake

copón /ko'pon/ m, large goblet; *Eccl.* ciborium, chalice

cópula /'kopula/ f, connection; coupling; joining; copulation

copularse /kopu'larse/ vr to copulate

coque /'koke/ m, coke

coqueluche /koke'lutʃe/ f, whooping cough

coqueta /ko'keta/ f, coquette, flirt

coquetear /kokete'ar/ vi to flirt

coqueteo /koke'teo/ m, coquetry; flirtation

coquetería /kokete'ria/ f, coquetry

coquetón /koke'ton/ a coquettish

coraje /ko'rahe/ m, courage, valor; anger

coral /ko'ral/ m, coral. f, coral snake. m, *Bot.* coral tree; pl coral beads

coral /ko'ral/ a choral

coraza /ko'raθa; ko'rasa/ f, cuirass; shell (of tortoise); armor-plate, armor (ships, etc.)

corazón /kora'θon; kora'son/ m, heart; courage, spirit; love, tenderness; good will, benevolence; core (of a fruit); *Fig.* pith. **de c.,** sincerely. **tener el c. en la mano,** to wear one's heart on one's sleeve

corazonada /koraθo'naða; koraso'naða/ f, feeling, instinct; presentiment, apprehension

corbata /kor'βata/ f, necktie; scarf; ribbon (insignia)

corbatería /korβate'ria/ f, necktie shop

corbatero /korβa'tero/ m, necktie maker; necktie dealer; tie rack

corbeta /kor'βeta/ f, corvette

corcel /kor'θel; kor'sel/ m, charger or battle horse

corchea /kor'tʃea/ f, *Mus.* quaver

corchete /kor'tʃete/ m, *Sew.* hook and eye; hook

corcho /'kortʃo/ m, *Bot.* cork, cork bark; stopper, cork; cork mat; bee hive

corcova /kor'koβa/ f, hump, abnormal protuberance

corcovado /korko'βaðo/ **(-da)** a hunchbacked, crooked —n hunchback

cordaje /kor'ðahe/ m, *Naut.* cordage, tackling, rope

cordel /kor'ðel/ m, cord; *Naut.* line. **a c.,** in a straight line

cordero /kor'ðero/ m, lamb; dressed lambskin; peaceable, mild man; Jesus (gen. **Divino C.**)

cordial /kor'ðial/ a warming, invigorating; affectionate, loving, friendly. m, *Med.* cordial

cordialidad /korðiali'ðað/ f, cordiality, friendliness

cordillera /korði'ʎera; korði'yera/ f, mountain range

cordobán /korðo'βan/ m, cured goatskin; Cordovan leather; Spanish leather

cordobés /korðo'βes/ **(-esa)** a and n Cordovan

cordón /kor'ðon/ m, cord; cordon; *Eccl.* rope girdle; *Archit.* string-course

cordoncillo /korðon'θiʎo; korðon'siyo/

m, rib (in cloth); ridge, milling (of coins);
Sew. piping

cordura /kor'ðura/ *f,* good sense, prudence

Corea /ko'rea/ Korea

coreografía /koreogra'fia/ *f,* choreogra-
phy; art of dancing

coreógrafo /kore'ografo/ *m,* choreographer

corista /ko'rista/ *m, Eccl.* chorister. *mf
Theat.* member of the chorus

cornada /kor'naða/ *f,* horn thrust or
wound (bulls, etc.)

córnea /'kornea/ *f,* cornea

corneja /kor'neha/ *f,* carrion or black
crow

córneo /'korneo/ *a,* horny, corneous

corneta /kor'neta/ *f, Mus.* bugle; *Mus.*
cornet; swineherd's horn; *Mil.* pennon.
m, bugler; *Mil.* cornet. **c. de monte,**
hunting horn

cornetín /korne'tin/ *m, dim* **corneta,**
Mus. cornet; cornet player

cornezuelo /korne'θuelo; korne'suelo/ *m,
dim* little horn; *Med.* ergot; *Bot.* variety
of olive

cornisa /kor'nisa/ *f,* cornice

cornucopia /kornu'kopia/ *f,* cornucopia,
horn of plenty; sconce; mirror

cornudo /kor'nuðo/ *a* horned. *m,* cuckold. **el C.,** the Devil

coro /'koro/ *m,* choir; chorus; *Archit.*
choir. **hacer c.** (**a),** to listen to, support.
saber de c., to know by heart

corolario /koro'lario/ *m,* corollary

corona /ko'rona/ *f,* garland, wreath; halo;
(*Astron. Archit.*) corona; crown (of
tooth); crown (of head); tonsure; crown
(coin); royal power; kingdom; triumph;
reward; summit, height, peak; circlet (for
candles)

coronación /korona'θion; korona'sion/ *f,*
coronation; coping stone

coronamiento /korona'miento/ *m,* coronation; coping stone; *Fig.* crowning
touch; *Naut.* taffrail

coronar /koro'nar/ *vt* to crown; crown
(in draughts); complete, round off; —*vr*
be crowned; crown oneself; be tipped or
capped

coronel /koro'nel/ *m,* colonel

coronela /koro'nela/ *f, Inf.* colonel's wife

coronelía /korone'lia/ *f,* colonelcy

coronilla /koro'niʎa; koro'niya/ *f, dim*
small crown; crown of head; *Fig. Inf.* **estar hasta la c.,** to be fed up

coroza /ko'roθa; ko'rosa/ *f,* dunce's cap

corpiño /kor'piɲo/ *m,* bodice

corporación /korpora'θion; korpora'sion/
f, corporation, body, association

corporal /korpo'ral/ *a* and *m, Eccl.* corporal

corporativo /korpora'tiβo/ *a* corporate,
corporative

corpóreo /kor'poreo/ *a* corporeal

corporizar /korpori'θar; korpori'sar/ *vt* to
embody

corpulento /korpu'lento/ *a* corpulent,
stout

Corpus /'korpus/ *m,* Corpus Christi

corpúsculo /kor'puskulo/ *m,* corpuscle

corral /ko'rral/ *m,* yard; pen, enclosure,
corral; old-time theater. **c. de madera,**
timber yard. *Inf.* **hacer corrales,** to play
truant

correa /ko'rrea/ *f,* leather strap or thong;
flexibility; *Mech.* belt, band

corrección /korrek'θion; korrek'sion/ *f,*
correction; correctness; punishment;
emendation. **c. de pruebas,** proofreading,
proofing, reading proof

correcional /korre'θional; korre'sional/ *a*
correctional. *m,* reformatory

correcto /ko'rrekto/ *a* correct; well-bred;
unexceptionable, irreproachable; regular
(of features)

corredera /korre'ðera/ *f,* link (engines);
Mech. slide; *Naut.* log; racecourse; *Inf.*
procuress

corredizo /korre'ðiθo; korre'ðiso/ *a* easy
to untie; running (of knots); sliding

corredor /korre'ðor/ **(-ra)** *n* runner. *m,
Com.* broker; corridor; *Inf.* meddler; *Inf.*
procurer, pimp —*a* running. **c. de bolsa,**
stockbroker

corregible /korre'hiβle/ *a* corrigible

corregir /korre'hir/ *vt irr* to correct;
scold, punish; moderate, counteract;
Mech. adjust; —*vr* mend one's ways. **c.
pruebas,** to read proof —*Pres. Indic.*
corrijo, corriges, corrige, corrigen. *Pres.
Part.* **corrigiendo.** *Pres. Subjunc.* **corrija,
corrijas,** etc —*Imperf. Subjunc.*
corrigiese, etc.

correlación /korrela'θion; korrela'sion/ *f,*
correlation

correligionario /korrelihio'nario/ **(-ia)** *n*
coreligionist; fellow-supporter or believer

correo /ko'rreo/ *m,* courier; mail; post-
office; letters. **c. aéreo,** air-mail. **c. certificado,** registered mail. **c. electrónico,** e-
mail. **a vuelta de c.,** by return of mail.
tren c., mail train

correr /ko'rrer/ *vi* to run; race; sail;
steam; flow; blow; flood; extend, stretch;
pass (of time); fall due (salary, etc.); be
current or general; (*with con*) be in
charge of or responsible for; —*vt* draw (a
horse); fasten, slide (bolts, etc.); draw
(curtains); undergo, suffer; sell, auction;
Inf. steal; *Fig.* embarrass; spread (a rumor, etc.); catch, make (bus, train, etc.);
—*vr* slide, glide, slip; run (of colors); *Inf.*
spread oneself, talk too much. **c. cañas,**
to participate in a mock joust using reeds
as spears

correspondencia /korrespon'denθia;
korrespon'densia/ *f,* relationship, connection; intercourse, communication; correspondence, letters; equivalence, exact
translation

corresponder /korrespon'der/ *vi* to requite, repay; be grateful; belong to, concern; devolve upon, fall to; suit, harmo-

nize (with); fit; —*vr* correspond by
letters; like or love each other

correspondiente /korrespon'diente/ *a*
suitable; proportionate; corresponding. *mf*
correspondent

corresponsal /korrespon'sal/ *mf* correspondent (especially professional); *Com.*
agent

correveidile /korreβei'ðile/ *mf Inf.* tale-
bearer, gossip

corrida /ko'rriða/ *f,* race, run; *Aer.* taxi-
ing; bull fight (abb. for **c. de toros**)

corrido /ko'rriðo/ *a* extra, over (of
weight); embarrassed; experienced

corriente /ko'rriente/ *a* current, present;
well-known; usual, customary; fluent
(style); ordinary, average; easy. *f,* flow,
stream; *Fig.* course (of events, etc.); *Elec.*
current —*adv* quite, exactly. *Elec.* **c. alterna,** alternating current. **c. continua,**
direct current. **c. de aire,** draft. **estar al
c.,** to be informed (of something)

Corriente del Golfo /ko'rriente del
'golfo/ Gulf Stream

corro /'korro/ *m,* circle, group; ring (for
children's games)

corroboración /korroβora'θion; korroβo-
ra'sion/ *f,* corroboration, confirmation

corroborar /korroβo'rar/ *vt* to fortify;
corroborate, support

corroborativo /korroβora'tiβo/ *a* corroborative

corroer /korro'er/ *vt irr* to corrode, waste
away; *Fig.* gnaw. See **roer**

corromper /korrom'per/ *vt* to rot; mar;
spoil, ruin; seduce; corrupt (texts); bribe;
Fig. contaminate, corrupt; —*vi* stink; —*vr*
putrefy, rot; be spoiled; *Fig.* be corrupted

corrosión /korro'sion/ *f,* corrosion

corrosivo /korro'siβo/ *a* corrosive

corrugación /korruga'θion; korruga'sion/
f, corrugation, wrinkling

corrupción /korrup'θion; korrup'sion/ *f,*
rot, putrefaction; corruption, depravity;
decay; stink; bribery; falsification (of
texts); corruption (of language, etc.)

corrupto /ko'rrupto/ *a* corrupt

corruptor /korrup'tor/ **(-ra)** *n* corrupter

corsé /kor'se/ *m,* corset

corsetería /korsete'ria/ *f,* corset shop or
manufactory

cortacircuitos /kortaθir'kuitos; korta-
sir'kuitos/ *m, Elec.* circuit breaker, cut-
out; disconnecting switch

cortado /kor'taðo/ *a* fitting, proportioned;
disjointed (style); confused, shamefaced

cortador /korta'ðor/ *m,* cutter; cutter-out
(dresses, etc.); butcher

cortadura /korta'ðura/ *f,* cut, wound;
cutting (from periodicals); defile; *pl* clippings, cuttings

cortalápices /korta'lapiθes; korta'lapises/
m, pencil sharpener

cortante /kor'tante/ *a* cutting; sharp;
piercing (of wind, etc.); trenchant

cortapapel /kortapa'pel/ *m,* paper-knife

cortapisa /korta'pisa/ *f,* condition, stipulation

cortaplumas /korta'plumas/ *m,* penknife

cortar /kor'tar/ *vt* to cut; cut out
(dresses, etc.); switch off, shut off (water,
electricity, etc.); cleave, divide; cut
(cards); pierce (wind, etc.); interrupt, impede; omit, cut; *Fig.* interrupt (conversation); decide, determine; —*vr* be confused
or shamefaced; curdle, turn sour (e.g. *Se
cortó la leche,* The milk turned sour);
split, fray; chap

cortavidrios /korta'βiðrios/ *m,* diamond,
glasscutter

corte /'korte/ *f,* court (royal); retinue;
yard; *pl* Spanish parliament. *m,* cutting,
cut; blade, cutting edge; cutting out,
dressmaking; length, material required for
garment, shoes, etc.; cut, fit; style; book
edge; *Archit.* section; means, expedient;
counting of money (in a till). **c. de caja,**
counting of money (in a till). **c. trasversal,** side view

cortedad /korte'ðað/ *f,* shortness, brevity; smallness; stupidity, dullness; timidity, shyness. **c. de fuerzas,** lack of
strength

cortejar /korte'har/ *vt* to accompany, escort; woo, court

cortejo /kor'teho/ *m,* courtship, wooing;
suite, accompaniment; gift, present; homage, attention; *Inf.* lover, beau

cortés /kor'tes/ *a* polite, attentive, courteous, civil

cortesía /korte'sia/ *f,* politeness, courtesy; attentiveness; civility; gift, present;
favor. **c. internacional,** courtesy of nations. **c. de boca mucho vale y poco
cuesta.** Courtesy is worth much and costs
little

corteza /kor'teθa, kor'tesa/ *f, Bot.* bark;
Anat. cortex; skin, peel, crust; aspect, appearance; roughness. **c. terrestre,** Earth's
crust, crust of the Earth. **de c.,** superficial
(e.g. explanation)

cortijo /kor'tiho/ *m,* farmhouse and land

cortina /kor'tina/ *f,* curtain; *Fig.* veil; *Inf.*
heel taps; *Mil.* curtain, screen. **c. de
fuego de artillería,** anti-aircraft barrage.
c. de globos de intercepción, balloon
barrage. **c. de humo,** smoke screen. **c.
metálica,** metal shutter

corto /'korto/ *a* short, brief; timid, bashful; concise; defective; stupid, dull;
tongue-tied, inarticulate. **c. circuito,** *Elec.*
short-circuit. **c. de alcances,** dull-witted.
c. de vista, short-sighted

coruscar /korus'kar/ *vi* to glitter, shine

corvadura /korβa'ðura/ *f,* bend; curvature

cosa /'kosa/ *f,* thing. **c. rara,** strange to
relate; an extraordinary thing. **como si
tal c.,** as though nothing had happened.
Inf. **poquita c.,** a person of no account

cosecha /ko'setʃa/ *f,* harvest; harvest
time; reaping, gathering, lifting; yield,
produce; crop, shower (of honors, etc.).
c. de vino, vintage

cosechar /kose'tʃar/ vi and vt to harvest, reap

coseno /ko'seno/ m, cosine

coser /ko'ser/ vt to sew, stitch; join, unite; press together (lips, etc.). **c. a puñaladas**, to stab repeatedly

cosmético /kos'metiko/ a and m, cosmetic

cósmico /'kosmiko/ a cosmic

cosmografía /kosmogra'fia/ f, cosmography

cosmonave /kosmo'naβe/ f, spaceship

cosmopolita /kosmopo'lita/ a and mf cosmopolitan

cosmopolitismo /kosmopoli'tismo/ m, cosmopolitanism

cosmos /'kosmos/ m, cosmos

cospel /kos'pel/ m, blank (from which to stamp coins); to ken; subway to ken

cosquillas /kos'kiʎas; kos'kiyas/ f pl, tickling. **hacer c.** (a), to tickle

cosquillear /koskiʎe'ar; koskiye'ar/ vt to tickle

cosquilleo /koski'ʎeo; koski'yeo/ m, tickle, tickling

cosquilloso /koski'ʎoso; koski'yoso/ a ticklish; hypersensitive, touchy

costa /'kosta/ f, cost; expense; coast; pl Law. costs. **a c. de**, by dint of; at the cost of. **a toda c.**, at all costs

Costa de Marfil /'kosta de mar'fil/ Ivory Coast

costado /kos'taðo/ m, Anat. side; Mil. flank; side; pl line of descent, genealogy. Naut. **dar el c.**, to be broadside on

costal /kos'tal/ m, sack, bag

costanero /kosta'nero/ a sloping; coast, coastal

costar /kos'tar/ vi irr to cost; cause. See contar

costarriqueño /kostarri'keɲo/ **(-ña)** a and n Costa Rican

coste /'koste/ m, cost, price

costear /koste'ar/ vt to pay for, defray the expense of; Naut. coast; —vr pay (for itself)

costilla /kos'tiʎa; kos'tiya/ f, (Anat. Aer. Naut. Archit.) rib; Fig. Inf. better half, wife; pl Inf. back, behind

costillaje, costillar /kosti'ʎahe, kosti'ʎar; kosti'yahe, kosti'yar/ m, Anat. ribs; Naut. ship's frame

costoso /kos'toso/ a expensive, costly; valuable; dear, costly, difficult

costra /'kostra/ f, crust; scab; rind (of cheese)

costumbre /kos'tumbre/ f, habit; custom

costumbrista /kostum'brista/ mf writer on everyday life and customs —a (of literary work) dealing with life and customs

costura /kos'tura/ f, sewing; seam; needlework; joint; riveting

costurera /kostu'rera/ f, seamstress

cota /'kota/ f, Surv. elevation, height; coat of mail); quota. **c. de malla**, chainmail

cotangente /kotan'hente/ f, cotangent

cotejar /kote'har/ vt to compare; collate

cotejo /ko'teho/ m, comparison; collation

cótel /'kotel/ m, cocktail, drink

cotelera /kote'lera/ f, cocktail shaker

cotidiano /koti'ðiano/ a daily

cotizable /koti'θaβle; koti'saβle/ a valued at; (of prices, shares) quoted

cotización /kotiθa'θion; kotisa'sion/ f, Com. quotation; Com. rate. **boletín de c.**, price list (of shares, etc.)

cotizar /koti'θar; koti'sar/ vt Com. to quote (prices, rates)

coto /'koto/ m, enclosed ground; boundary stone; preserve, covert; hand's breadth; end, stop, limit. **c. de caza**, game preserve

cotorra /ko'torra/ f, small green parrot; magpie; Inf. chatterbox

coyote /ko'yote/ m, coyote, prairie wolf; Mexico fixer (anyone who can pull strings to cut red tape or achieve something illegally); smuggler (of goods or people)

coyuntura /koyun'tura/ f, Anat. joint; juncture, occasion

coz /koθ; kos/ f, kick, recoil (of gun); butt (of a rifle); Inf. slap in the face, unprovoked rudeness. **dar coces**, to kick

cráneo /'kraneo/ m, cranium, skull

crápula /'krapula/ f, drunkenness; depravity, immorality, debauchery

craso /'kraso/ a fat, greasy; thick; unpardonable, crass (often with ignorancia). m, fatness; ignorance

creación /krea'θion; krea'sion/ f, creation; universe, world; foundation, establishment; appointment (dignitaries)

creador /krea'ðor/ **(-ra)** n creator, originator. m, God —a creative

crear /kre'ar/ vt to create; found, institute, establish; make, appoint

crecer /kre'θer; kre'ser/ vi irr to grow; grow up; increase in size; grow longer; wax (moon); come in (of the tide); increase in value (money); —vr become more sure of oneself; swell with pride; grow in authority. See nacer

creces /'kreθes; 'kreses/ f pl, increase, interest. **con c.**, fully, amply. **pagar con c.**, Fig. to pay with interest

crecida /kre'θiða; kre'siða/ f, swollen river or stream; food; rising (of the tide)

crecido /kre'θiðo; kre'siðo/ a grown up; considerable; abundant, plentiful; large; full; serious, important

crecidos /kre'θiðos; kre'siðos/ m pl, widening stitches (knitting)

creciente /kre'θiente; kre'siente/ a growing; rising (of the tide); crescent (moon). m, Herald. crescent. f, rising of the tide; crescent moon

crecimiento /kreθi'miento; kresi'miento/ m, growing; growth, development; increase (in value, money); waxing (of moon)

credencial /kreðen'θial; kreðen'sial/ a accrediting

credenciales /kreðen'θiales; kreðen'siales/ *f pl*, credentials

credibilidad /kreðiβili'ðað/ *f*, credibility

crédito /'kreðito/ *m*, belief, credence; assent, acquiescence; reputation, name; favor, popularity, acceptance; *Com.* credit; *Com.* letter of credit. **créditos activos**, assets. **créditos pasivos**, liabilities. **a c.**, on credit

credo /'kreðo/ *m*, creed. *Inf.* **en un c.**, in a jiffy

credulidad /kreðuli'ðað/ *f*, credulity

crédulo /'kreðulo/ *a* credulous

creencia /kre'enθia; kre'ensia/ *f*, belief; religion, sect, faith

creer /kre'er/ *vt irr* to believe; think, consider, opine; think likely or probable. **¡Ya lo creo!** I should just think so! Rather! **creerse la divina garza**, *Mexico* to think one is God's gift to the world. **creerse descender del sobaco de Jesucristo**, to think one is God's gift to the world —*Pres. Part.* **creyendo**. *Preterite* **creyó**, **creyeron**. *Imperf. Subjunc.* **creyese**, etc.

creíble /kre'iβle/ *a* credible

crema /'krema/ *f*, cream (off milk); custard mold, cream, shape; face cream; cold cream; elect, flower (of society, etc.)

cremallera /krema'ʎera; krema'yera/ *f*, *Mech.* rack, ratch; zip fastener. **colgar la c.**, to give a house-warming

crematorio /krema'torio/ *m*, crematorium —*a* burning; cremating

cremoso /kre'moso/ *a* creamy

crencha /'krentʃa/ *f*, parting (of the hair); each side of parting

crepitación /krepita'θion; krepita'sion/ *f*, crackling, sputtering; hissing; roar (of a fire); *Med.* crepitation

crepitar /krepi'tar/ *vi* to crackle; sputter; hiss; roar (of a fire); *Med.* crepitate

crepuscular /krepusku'lar/ *a* twilight

crepúsculo /kre'puskulo/ *m*, twilight, half light

Creso /'kreso/ Croesus

crespo /'krespo/ *a* curly, frizzy (hair); rough (of animal's fur); curled (leaves); artificial, involved (style)

crespón /kres'pon/ *m*, crape

cresta /'kresta/ *f*, comb (of cock, etc.); tuft, topknot (birds); plume; summit, top (of mountains); crest (of a wave); *Herald.* crest

Creta /'kreta/ Crete

creta /'kreta/ *f*, chalk

creyente /kre'yente/ *a* believing; religious. *mf* believer

cría /'kria/ *f*, rearing; bringing up; nursing; suckling; breeding; brood; litter

criada /kri'aða/ *f*, servant, maid

criadero /kria'ðero/ *m*, *Mineral.* vein, deposit; tree nursery, plantation; breeding farm or place —*a* prolific

criado /kri'aðo/ *m*, servant —*a* bred, brought up (used with *bien* or *mal*, well or badly brought up)

criador /kria'ðor/ **(-ra)** *n* breeder, keeper,

raiser —*a* creating; rearing; creative; fertile, rich

crianza /kri'anθa; kri'ansa/ *f*, feeding, suckling; lactation; manners. **buena (or mala) c.**, good (or bad) breeding or upbringing

criar /kri'ar/ *vt* to create; procreate; rear, educate, bring up; feed, nurse, suckle; raise (birds, animals); inspire, give rise to. **Me crié raquítico,** I grew up delicate

criatura /kria'tura/ *f*, being, creature; man, human being; infant; small child; fetus; *Fig.* puppet, tool

criba /'kriβa/ *f*, sieve, cribble

cribar /kri'βar/ *vt* to sieve; riddle (earth, etc.)

crimen /'krimen/ *m*, crime. **c. pasional**, crime of passion

criminal /krimi'nal/ *a* and *m*, criminal

criminalidad /kriminali'ðað/ *f*, guilt; crime ratio; delinquency

criminalista /krimina'lista/ *mf* criminal lawyer; criminologist

criminología /kriminolo'hia/ *f*, criminology

crin /krin/ *f*, horsehair; (gen. *pl*) mane

crinolina /krino'lina/ *f*, crinoline

crío /'krio/ *m*, *Inf.* kid, brat

criollo /'krioʎo; 'krioyo/ **(-lla)** *a* and *n* creole —*a* indigenous, native

cripta /'kripta/ *f*, crypt

criptografía /kriptogra'fia/ *f*, cryptography

crisis /'krisis/ *f*, crisis. **c. de desarrollo**, growing pains. **c. de vivienda**, housing shortage

crisma /'krisma/ *m*, or *f*, chrism

crisol /kri'sol/ *m*, crucible; melting pot

crispado /kris'paðo/ *a* stiffened

crispar /kris'par/ *vt* to cause to contract or twitch; —*vr* twitch. *Inf.* **Se me crispan los nervios,** My nerves are all on edge

cristal /kris'tal/ *m*, crystal; glass; windowpane; mirror; water. **c. tallado,** cut glass

cristalería /kristale'ria/ *f*, glassware; glass manufacture; glass panes; glass and china shop

cristalino /krista'lino/ *a* crystalline. *m*, lens (of the eye)

cristalización /kristaliθa'θion; kristalisa'sion/ *f*, crystallization

cristalizar /kristali'θar; kristali'sar/ *vi* to crystallize; *Fig.* take shape; —*vt* cause to crystallize

cristalografía /kristalogra'fia/ *f*, crystallography

cristiandad /kristian'dað/ *f*, Christendom

cristianismo /kristia'nismo/ *m*, Christianity; Christendom

cristianizar /kristiani'θar; kristiani'sar/ *vt* to convert to Christianity, christianize

cristiano /kris'tiano/ **(-na)** *a* and *n* Christian —*a Inf.* watered (of wine). *m*, *Inf.* Spanish (contrasted with other languages); *Inf.* soul, person

cristo /'kristo/ *m*, Christ; crucifix. *Inf.*

donde C. dio las tres voces, in the middle of nowhere

cristus /'kristus/ *m*, Christ-cross; alphabet. **no saber el c.,** to be extremely ignorant

criterio /kri'terio/ *m*, criterion, standard; judgment, discernment; opinion. **a c. de,** in the opinion of. **según mi c.,** in my opinion

crítica /'kritika/ (a) *f*, criticism (of)

criticar /kriti'kar/ *vt* to criticize; censure, find fault with, blame

crítico /'kritiko/ *a* critical; censorious; dangerous, difficult; *Med.* critical. *m*, critic; fault-finder

criticón /kriti'kon/ **(-ona)** *a* censorious, hyper-critical —*n* fault-finder

Croacia /kro'aθia; kro'asia/ Croatia

croar /kro'ar/ *vi* (frog) to croak

croata /kro'ata/ *a* and *mf* Croatian

croché /kro'tʃe/ *m*, crochet work

cromado /kro'maðo/ *a* chromium-plated

crónica /'kronika/ *f*, chronicle; diary of events

crónico /'kroniko/ *a* chronic; inveterate

cronología /kronolo'hia/ *f*, chronology

cronológico /krono'lohiko/ *a* chronological

cronómetro /kro'nometro/ *m*, stopwatch

croqueta /kro'keta/ *f*, croquette

croquis /'krokis/ *m*, sketch, outline, drawing. **c. de nivel,** (optical) foresight

crótalo /'krotalo/ *m*, rattlesnake; snapper (kind of castanet)

cruce /'kruθe; 'kruse/ *m*, crossing; point of intersection; crossroads

crucero /kru'θero; kru'sero/ *m*, *Eccl.* cross-bearer; crossroads; *Archit.* transept; *Astron.* Cross; *Naut.* cruiser

crucificar /kruθifi'kar; krusifi'kar/ *vt* to crucify; *Fig. Inf.* torment, torture

crucifijo /kruθi'fiho; krusi'fiho/ *m*, crucifix

crucifixión /kruθifik'sion; krusifik'sion/ *f*, crucifixion

cruciforme /kruθi'forme; krusi'forme/ *a* cruciform

crucigrama /kruθi'grama; krusi'grama/ *m*, crossword puzzle

cruda /'kruða/ *f*, *Mexico* hangover

crudeza /kru'ðeθa; kru'ðesa/ *f*, rawness, uncookedness; unripeness; rawness (silk, etc.); crudeness; harshness; *Inf.* boasting

crudo /'kruðo/ *a* uncooked, raw; green, unripe; indigestible; raw, natural, unbleached; harsh, cruel; cold, raw; *Inf.* boastful. **crudos de petróleo,** *m pl* crude oil

crueldad /kruel'daθ/ *f*, cruelty; harshness

cruento /'kruento/ *a* bloody

crujía /kru'hia/ *f*, passage, corridor; *Naut.* midship gangway

crujidero /kruhi'ðero/ *a* crackling; creaking; crispy; clattering; rustling; chattering

crujido /kru'hiðo/ *m*, creak, crack, crackling, rustle

crujir /kru'hir/ *vi* to creak, crackle, rustle

crup /krup/ *m*, croup

crustáceo /krus'taθeo; krus'taseo/ *a* and *m*, crustacean

cruzada /kru'θaða; kru'saða/ *f*, crusade; crossroads; campaign

cruzado /kru'θaðo; kru'saðo/ *a* cross; double-breasted (of coats). *m*, crusader; member of military order

cruzamiento /kruθa'miento; krusa'miento/ *m*, crossing; intersection

cruzar /kru'θar; kru'sar/ *vt* to cross; intersect; interbreed; bestow a cross upon; *Naut.* cruise; —*vr* take part in a crusade; cross one another; coincide; *Geom.* intersect

cu /ku/ *f*, name of the letter Q

cuaderna /kua'ðerna/ *f*, *Naut.* ship's frame, timber; double fours (backgammon)

cuaderno /kua'ðerno/ *m*, notebook, jotter, account book; *Inf.* card pack. *Naut.* **c. de bitácora,** logbook

cuadra /'kuaðra/ *f*, stable; ward, dormitory; hall, large room; quarter of a mile

cuadrado /kua'ðraðo/ *a* square; perfect, exact. *m*, square; (*Mil. Math.*) square; window-frame; clock (of a stocking)

cuadragenario /kuaðrahe'nario/ *a* forty years old

cuadragésima /kuaðra'hesima/ *f*, Quadragesima

cuadrángulo /kua'ðraŋgulo/ *m*, quadrangle

cuadrante /kua'ðrante/ *m*, quadrant; dial, face

cuadrar /kua'ðrar/ *vt* (*Math.*) to square; make square; —*vi* correspond, tally; fit, be appropriate —*vr Mil.* stand at attention; *Fig. Inf.* dig one's heels in

cuadrática /kua'ðratika/ *f*, quadratic equation

cuadrático /kua'ðratiko/ *a* quadratic

cuadratura /kuaðra'tura/ *f*, squareness; (*Math. Astron.*) quadrature

cuadrilátero /kuaðri'latero/ *m*, quadrilateral; boxing ring —*a* quadrilateral

cuadrilla /kua'ðriʎa; kua'ðriya/ *f*, gang; company, band, group; police patrol; quadrille (dance); matadors and their assistants (at a bull fight). **c. carrillana,** track gang

cuadro /'kuaðro/ *m*, square; picture-frame; frame (of bicycle); flowerbed; *Theat.* tableau, scene; spectacle, sight; board (of instruments); description (in novel, etc.); *Mil.* command, officers; square (of troops). **c. de distribución,** *Elec.* main switchboard. **c. enrejado,** play pen. **cuadro de costumbres,** word-picture of everyday life and customs. **cuadro vivo,** tableau vivant. **a cuadros,** checked, in squares

cuadrúpedo /kua'ðrupeðo/ **(-da)** *a* and *n* quadruped

cuádruple /kua'ðruple/ *a* quadruple

cuajada /kua'haða/ *f*, curd (of milk)

cuajar /kua'har/ *m*, maw (of a ruminant)

cuajar /kua'har/ *vt* to coagulate; curdle; —*vi Inf.* achieve, get away with; —*vr* be coagulated or curdled; *Inf.* be packed or chock full; get stuck (e.g. a piece of food in one's throat)

cuajarón /kuaha'ron/ *m*, clot (of blood, etc.)

cuajo /'kuaho/ *m*, rennet; coagulation; curdling; *Anat.* abomasum

cual /kual/ *rel pron sing. mf* and *neut pl* **cuales**, which; who; such as (e.g. *Le detuvieron sucesos cuales suelen ocurrir*, He was detained by events such as usually happen). **a c. mas**, vying (with) (e.g. *Los dos canónigos a c. más grueso*, The two canons each fatter (vying in fatness) than the other). **c.** is used with *def art* **el (la, lo, los, las) cual(es)**; who; which, when the antecedent is a noun (e.g. *Juan saltó en el barco, el c. zarpó en seguida*, John jumped into the boat which sailed at once). **por lo c.**, for which reason —*adv* like (gen. literary or poet.). **¿cuál?** *interr. pron* (no article) which? what? e.g. *Aquí tienes dos cuadros, ¿cuál de ellos te gusta?* Here are two pictures, which one do you like? Also expresses an implicit question, e.g. *No sé cuál te guste*, I don't know which you will like. **¡cuál!** *adv interj* how! **c.... c.** *indef pron* some... some

cualesquier /kuales'kier/ *a pl* of **cualquier**

cualesquiera /kuales'kiera/ *a pl* of **cualquiera**

cualidad /kuali'ðað/ *f*, quality; characteristic; talent

cualitativo /kualita'tiβo/ *a* qualitative

cualquier /kual'kier/ *Abbr.* **of cualquiera**, any; *pl* **cualesquier.** Only used as abb. *before* noun

cualquiera /kual'kiera/ *a mf* any, e.g. *una canción c.*, any song —*pron* anybody, each, anyone whatsoever, whoever (e.g. *¡C. diría que no te gusta!* Anyone would say you don't like it!) *Inf.* a nobody

cuán /ku'an/ *adv* how (e.g. *¡C. bello es!* How beautiful it is). Used only before *a* or *adv.* Abb. of **cuánto**

cuando /'kuando/ *adv* when; if —*interr* **¿cuándo?** *conjunc* although; since; sometimes; —*prep* during (e.g. *c. la guerra*, during the war) **c. más**, at most, at best. **c. menos**, at the least. **c. no**, if not (e.g. *Es agnóstica cuando no atea*, She's an agnostic, if not an atheist) **de c. en c.**, from time to time

cuandoquiera /kuando'kiera/ *adv* whenever

cuantía /kuan'tia/ *f*, quantity, amount; importance, rank, distinction

cuantiar /kuan'tiar/ *vt* to value, estimate; tax

cuantioso /kuan'tioso/ *a* large, considerable; numerous; plentiful, abundant

cuantitativo /kuantita'tiβo/ *a* quantitative

cuanto /'kuanto/ *a* as much as, all the; *pl* as many as, all the (e.g. *Te daré cuantas muñecas veas allí*, I'll give you all the dolls you see there) —*a correlative* the... the, as... as (e.g. *C. más tanto, mejor*, The more the better). **cuánto**, *a* and *pron interr* and *interj* how much; *pl* how many (e.g. *¡Cuánto tiempo sin verla!* How long without seeing her!) *pron neut* **cuanto**, as much as, all that (e.g. *Te daré c. quieras*, I shall give you all that you wish) —*adv* **cuanto**, as soon as. **c. antes**, as soon as possible. **c. a** or **en c. a**, concerning —*adv* and *conjunc* **c. más**, all the more (e.g. *Se lo diré c. más que tenía esa intención*, I shall tell him all the more because I meant to do so) —*adv* **en c.**, as soon as, immediately (e.g. *Lo haré en c. venga*, I shall do it immediately he comes). **en c. a**, with regard to. **por c.**, inasmuch, for this reason —*adv interj* **¿Cuánto?** How much? How long? *adv interj* How! How much! (e.g. *¡Cuánto me gustaría ir!* How much I should like to go!)

cuáquero /'kuakero/ **(-ra)** *n* Quaker

cuarenta /kua'renta/ *a* and *m*, forty; fortieth

cuarentena /kuaren'tena/ *f*, fortieth; period of forty days, months or years; Lent; quarantine

cuarentón /kuaren'ton/ **(-ona)** *n* person forty years old

cuaresma /kua'resma/ *f*, Lent

cuarta /'kuarta/ *f*, quarter, fourth; hand's breadth; *Mus.* fourth; *Astron.* quadrant

cuartear /kuarte'ar/ *vt* to quarter, divide into quarters; cut or divide into pieces

cuartel /kuar'tel/ *m*, barracks; *Naut.* hatch; quarter, fourth; *Herald.* quarter; district, ward; flowerbed; *Inf.* house, accommodation; *Mil.* quarter, mercy; *Mil.* billet, station. *Mil.* **c. general**, general headquarters

cuartelada /kuarte'laða/ *f*, *Naut.* quarter; military rebellion, military uprising, mutiny

cuartelar /kuarte'lar/ *vt Herald.* to quarter

cuartelazo /kuarte'laθo; kuarte'laso/ *m*, military rebellion, military uprising, mutiny

cuarto /'kuarto/ *m*, room; quarter, fourth; point (of compass); watch (on battleships); *Astron.* quarter, phase; portion, quarter; joint (of meat); *pl* quarters (of animals); *Inf.* penny, farthing —*a* quarter, fourth. **c. creciente**, first phase (of moon). **c. de hora**, quarter of an hour. **en c.**, *Print.* in quarto. *Inf.* **no tener un c.**, to be broke

cuarzo /'kuarθo; 'kuarso/ *m*, quartz

cuasidelito /kuasiðe'lito/ *m*, *Law.* technical offense

cuatrillón /kuatri'ʎon; kuatri'yon/ *m*, quadrillion

cuatrimestre /kuatri'mestre/ *a* of four months' duration. *m*, space of four months

cuatrimotor /kuatrimo'tor/ *m*, *Aer.* four-engine airplane

cuatrisílabo /kuatri'silaβo/ *a* quadrisyllabic

cuatro /'kuatro/ *a* four; fourth. *m*, figure four; fourth (of days of months); playing-card with four spots; *Mus.* quartet. **el c. de mayo**, the fourth of May. **Son las c.**, It is four o'clock

cuatrocientos /kuatro'θientos; kuatro'sientos/ *a* four hundred; four hundredth

cuba /'kuβa/ *f*, barrel, cask; tub, vat; *Inf.* pot-bellied person; *Inf.* drunkard, toper

cubano /ku'βano/ **(-na)** *a* and *n* Cuban

cubería /kuβe'ria/ *f*, cooperage

cubeta /ku'βeta/ *f*, *dim* keg, small cask; bucket, pail; *Photo.* developing dish

cubicar /kuβi'kar/ *vt Math.* to cube; *Geom.* measure the volume of

cúbico /'kuβiko/ *a* cubic

cubículo /ku'βikulo/ *m*, cubicle

cubierta /ku'βierta/ *f*, cover; envelope; casing; deck (of ship); tire cover; book-jacket; pretext, excuse. **c. de escotilla**, *Naut.* companion-hatch. **c. de paseo**, promenade deck

cubierto /ku'βierto/ *m*, cover, place at table; course (of a meal); table d'hôte, complete meal; roof. **un c. de doscientas pesetas**, a two hundred peseta meal

cubil /ku'βil/ *m*, lair, den (of animals)

cubilete /kuβi'lete/ *m*, *Cul.* mold; dice box; conjurer's cup

cubismo /ku'βismo/ *m*, cubism

cubista /ku'βista/ *mf* cubist —*a* cubistic

cubo /'kuβo/ *m*, bucket, pail; *Mech.* socket; *Math.* cube; hub (of a wheel); mill-pond

cubrecama /kuβre'kama/ *m*, bedspread

cubrir /ku'βrir/ *vt* to cover; *Mil.* defend; spread over, extend over; conceal, hide; *Com.* cover; dissemble; *Archit.* roof; —*vr* cover one's head; pay, meet (debts, etc.); cover or protect oneself (by insurance, etc.) —*Past Part.* **cubierto**

cucaracha /kuka'ratʃa/ *f*, cockroach

cuchara /ku'tʃara/ *f*, spoon; ladle; *Naut.* boat scoop; scoop, dipper. *Fig.* **meter c.**, to stick one's oar in

cucharada /kutʃa'raða/ *f*, spoonful; ladleful

cuchichear /kutʃitʃe'ar/ *vi* to whisper

cuchicheo /kutʃi'tʃeo/ *m*, whisper; whispering; murmur

cuchillada /kutʃi'ʎaða; kutʃi'yaða/ *f*, knife thrust or wound; *pl* (in sleeves, etc.) slashes; fight, blows

cuchillo /ku'tʃiʎo; ku'tʃiyo/ *m*, knife; *Sew.* gore, gusset (gen. *pl*); authority, power; anything triangular in shape. **pasar a c.**, to put to the sword

cuclillas, en /ku'kliʎas, en; ku'kliyas, en/ *adv* in a squatting position

cuculla /ku'kuʎa; ku'kuya/ *f*, cowl, hood

cucurucho /kuku'rutʃo/ *m*, paper cornet

cuello /'kueʎo; 'kueyo/ *m*, *Anat.* neck; neck (of bottle, etc.); *Sew.* neck; collar; necklet (of fur, etc.)

cuenca /'kuenka/ *f*, socket (of eye); *Geog.* catchment-basin; gorge, deep valley. **c. de un río**, river-basin

cuenta /'kuenta/ *f*, count, counting; calculation; account; bead; charge, responsibility; reckoning; explanation, reason; *Com.* bill. **c. a cero, c. a la inversa, c. atrás**, countdown. **c. corriente**, current account. **cuentas alegres, cuentas galanas**, *Inf.* idle dreams, illusions. **c. pendiente**, outstanding account. *Inf.* **caer en la c.**, to tumble to; realize. **llevar la c.**, to reckon, keep account. **sin c.**, countless. **tener en c.**, to bear in mind

cuentacorrentista /kuentakorren'tista/ *mf* one who has a bank account

cuentagotas /kuenta'gotas/ *m*, dropper, dropping tube

cuentakilómetros /kuentaki'lometros/ *m*, speedometer

cuentapasos /kuenta'pasos/ *m*, pedometer

cuentista /kuen'tista/ *mf* storyteller; *Inf.* gossip

cuento /'kuento/ *m*, story, tale; narrative; calculation; *Inf.* gossip, fairytale; *Math.* million. **c. de viejas**, old wives' tale. *Fig. Inf.* **dejarse de cuentos**, to go straight to the point. *Inf.* **Va de c.**, It is told, they say

cuerda /'kuerða/ *f*, rope; cord; string; *Geom.* chord; *Mus.* string; catgut; chain (of clock); *Mus.* chord; vocal range. **dar c. (a)**, to wind up (a watch); lead on, make talk. **de cuerdas cruzadas**, overstrung (of a piano)

cuerdo /'kuerðo/ *a* sane; prudent; level-headed

cuerno /'kuerno/ *m*, *Anat.* horn; feeler, antenna; *Mus.* horn; horn (of the moon). **c. de abundancia**, horn of plenty. *Inf.* **poner en los cuernos de la luna**, to praise to the skies

cuero /'kuero/ *m*, hide, pelt; leather. **c. charolado**, patent leather. **en cueros**, stark naked

cuerpo /'kuerpo/ *m*, *Anat.* body or trunk; flesh (as opposed to spirit); bodice; volume, book; main portion; collection; size, volume; physical appearance; corpse; group, assembly; corporation, association; *Geom.* solid; *Chem.* element; thickness, density; *Mil.* corps. **c. de bomberos**, fire brigade. **c. de guardia**, guardhouse. **c. de la vida**, staff of life; *Inf.* **dar con el c. en tierra**, to fall flat. **de c. entero**, *Art.* full-length (portrait). **en c.**, without a coat, lightly clad. **un c. a c.**, a clinch (in wrestling)

cuervo /'kuerβo/ *m*, raven; crow

cuesta /'kuesta/ *f*, slope, incline, gradient. **c. abajo (arriba)**, down (up) hill. **a cuestas**, on one's back; having the responsibility of

cuestión /kues'tion/ *f*, problem, question;

quarrel, disagreement; affair, matter; torture

cuestionar /kuestio'nar/ vt to discuss, debate

cuestionario /kuestio'nario/ m, questionnaire

cueva /'kueβa/ f, cave, cavern; basement, cellar. *Fig.* **c. de ladrones,** den of thieves

cuidado /kui'ðaðo/ m, carefulness, pains; attention; charge, care, responsibility; anxiety, fear —*interj* **¡C.!** Careful! Look out! **Me tiene sin c. su opinión,** I am not interested in his (your) opinion. *Inf.* **estar al c. de,** to be under the direction of. **estar de c.,** to be dangerously ill

cuidadoso /kuiða'ðoso/ **(de)** a careful (about *or* with); anxious (about); concerned (with); watchful; conscientious

cuidar /kui'ðar/ vt to care for; tend; take care of, look after; mind, be careful of; —*vr* look after oneself

cuita /'kuita/ f, misfortune, anxiety, trouble

cuitado /kui'taðo/ a unfortunate, worried; timid, bashful, humble

culata /ku'lata/ f, *Anat.* haunch; butt (of fire-arms); back, rear; *Auto.* sump

culebra /ku'leβra/ f, snake; *Inf.* trick, joke; *Inf.* sudden uproar. **hacer c.,** to stagger along

culebrear /kuleβre'ar/ vi to wriggle; grovel; meander, wind

culí /ku'li/ m, coolie

culinario /kuli'nario/ a culinary

culminación /kulmina'θion; kulmina'sion/ f, culmination, peak; *Astron.* zenith

culminante /kulmi'nante/ a culminating; *Fig.* outstanding

culminar /kulmi'nar/ vi to culminate (in)

culo /'kulo/ m, buttocks, seat; rump; anus; base, bottom. **c. de lámpara,** *Archit.* pendant; *Print.* tail-piece

culpa /'kulpa/ f, fault; blame. **echar la c.** (a), to blame. **por c. de,** through the fault of. **tener la c.,** to be to blame

culpabilidad /kulpaβili'ðað/ f, guilt

culpable /kul'paβle/ a culpable

culpado /kul'paðo/ **(-da)** n culprit

culpar /kul'par/ vt to blame, accuse; criticize, censure

cultígeno /kul'tiheno/ m, cultigen

cultivable /kulti'βaβle/ a cultivable

cultivación /kultiβa'θion; kultiβa'sion/ f, cultivation; culture

cultivador /kultiβa'ðor/ **(-ra)** n cultivator; planter

cultivar /kulti'βar/ vt to cultivate; develop; exercise, practice (professions); culture (bacteriology)

cultivo /kul'tiβo/ m, cultivation; farming; culture (bacteriological)

culto /'kulto/ a cultivated; educated; cultured; elegant, artificial (style). m, worship; cult; religion, creed; homage

cultura /kul'tura/ f, cultivation; culture. **de c. universitaria,** college-educated

cultural /kultu'ral/ a cultural

cumbre /'kumbre/ f, peak, crest, summit; *Fig.* zenith, acme

cumpleaños /kumple'aɲos/ m, birthday

cumplido /kum'pliðo/ a complete; thorough; long; plentiful; courteous, punctilious; fulfilled. m, courtesy, attention; formality. **gastar cumplidos,** to stand on ceremony; be formal

cumplimentar /kumplimen'tar/ vt to congratulate; perform, carry out

cumplimentero /kumplimen'tero/ a over-complimentary; *Inf.* gushing

cumplimiento /kumpli'miento/ m, fulfillment, performance; courtesy, formality; completion; complement

cumplir /kum'plir/ vt to perform, carry into effect; reach (of age); keep (promises). **c. su palabra,** to keep one's word; —vi perform a duty; expire, fall due; serve the required term of military service; be necessary, behove; —vr be fulfilled, come true. **por c.,** as a matter of form

cumulativo /kumula'tiβo/ a cumulative

cúmulo /'kumulo/ m, heap, pile; great many, host, mass, myriad; (cloud) cumulus, thunderhead

cuna /'kuna/ f, cradle; foundling hospital; birthplace; origin, genesis; *pl* cat's cradle (game)

cundir /kun'dir/ vi to extend, spread (gen. liquids); be diffused (news); expand, grow

cuneiforme /kunei'forme/ a wedge-shaped, cuneiform

cuña /'kuɲa/ f, wedge; *Mech.* quoin. *Mil.* **practicar una c.,** to make a wedge

cuñada /ku'ɲaða/ f, sister-in-law

cuñado /ku'ɲaðo/ m, brother-in-law

cuño /'kuɲo/ m, die, stamp; *Fig.* impression; mark on silver, hallmark. **de viejo c.,** old-guard (e.g. socialites)

cuota /'kuota/ f, quota; share; subscription; fee

Cupido /ku'piðo/ m, Cupid; philanderer

cupo /'kupo/ m, quota; share; tax rate; *Mil.* contingent

cupón /ku'pon/ m, coupon

cúpula /'kupula/ f, *Archit.* dome, cupola; *Bot.* cup

cura /'kura/ m, parish priest; *Inf.* Roman Catholic priest. f, cure (e.g. *La enfermedad tiene c.,* The illness can be cured); healing; remedy. **c. de almas,** cure of souls. **primera c.,** first aid. *Inf.* **c. de misa y olla,** ignorant priest

curable /ku'raβle/ a curable

curación /kura'θion; kura'sion/ f, cure, remedy; healing

curador /kura'ðor/ **(-ra)** n curer, salter. m, (*Scots law*) curator —a curing; healing

curaduría /kuraðu'ria/ f, *Law.* guardianship

curanderismo /kurande'rismo/ m, quackery, charlatanism; quack medicine

curandero /kuran'dero/ **(-ra)** n quack doctor; charlatan

curar /ku'rar/ *vi* to heal, cure; (*with de*) take care of; care about, mind; —*vt* cure, salt; treat medically (bandage, give medicines, etc.); cure (leather); bleach (cloth); season (timber); *Fig.* remedy (an evil)

curativo /kura'tiβo/ *a* curative

curato /ku'rato/ *m, Eccl.* parish, cure

Curazao /kura'θao; kura'sao/ Curaçao

curdo, /'kurðo,/ **(-da)** *a* Kurdish —*n* Kurd

curia /'kuria/ *f, Law.* bar; tribunal; *Eccl.* curia; care, attention

curiana /ku'riana/ *f,* cockroach

curiosamente /kuriosa'mente/ *adv* curiously; carefully, attentively; neatly

curiosear /kuriose'ar/ *vi* to pry; be curious (about); meddle, be a busybody

curiosidad /kuriosi'ðað/ *f,* curiosity; inquisitiveness, meddlesomeness; neatness, carefulness, conscientiousness; curio

curioso /ku'rioso/ *a* curious; inquisitive; interesting, odd; neat, clean; conscientious, careful

Curita /ku'rita/ *f, trademark* Band-Aid

cursado /kur'saðo/ *a* experienced, versed

cursante /kur'sante/ *m,* student

cursar /kur'sar/ *vt* to frequent, visit; do repeatedly; study, attend classes, take courses (e.g. *¿En qué escuela cursan?* At what school are you studying?); expedite (public admin.)

cursi /'kursi/ *a Inf.* vulgar, in bad taste; loud, crude

cursilería /kursile'ria/ *f, Inf.* vulgarity, bad taste

cursillo /kur'siʎo; kursiyo/ *m,* minicourse, short course; short series of lectures

cursiva /kur'siβa/ *f,* italics. **en c.,** in italics, italicized

cursivo /kur'siβo/ *a* cursive

curso /'kurso/ *m,* course, direction; duration, passage (time); progress; route; course of study; academic year; succession, series; *Com.* tender

curtido /kur'tiðo/ *m,* tanning; leather; tanned leather (gen. *pl*)

curtidor /kurti'ðor/ *m,* tanner

curtiduría /kurtiðu'ria/ *f,* tannery

curtimiento /kurti'miento/ *m,* tanning; effect of weather on the complexion; toughening-up; hardening

curtir /kur'tir/ *vt* to tan; *Fig.* bronze (complexions); make hardy, harden up; —*vr* be weatherbeaten; be hardy. *Inf.* **estar curtido en,** to be experienced in; be expert at

curul /ku'rul/ *a* **curule** *m,* seat (in parliament)

curva /'kurβa/ *f,* curve; bend. *Surv.* **c. de nivel,** contour line

curvatura, curvidad /kurβa'tura, kurβi'ðað/ *f,* curvature

curvo /'kurβo/ *a* curved; bent. *m,* curve

custodia /kus'toðia/ *f,* custody; guardianship, care; *Eccl.* monstrance; custodian, keeper; guardian; guard

custodiar /kusto'ðiar/ *vt* to watch, guard; look after, care for; *Naut.* convoy

custodio /kus'toðio/ *a* guardian; guarding; custodial. *m,* custodian; guard. **angel c.,** guardian angel

cutáneo /ku'taneo/ *a* cutaneous, skin

cutícula /ku'tikula/ *f,* cuticle

cutis /'kutis/ *m,* complexion; skin (sometimes *f*)

cuyo /'kuyo/ (**cuya, cuyos, cuyas**) *rel pron poss* whose, of which (e.g. *el viejo cuya barba era más blanca que la nieve,* the old man whose beard was whiter than snow) —*interr* **¿Cúyo?** Whose? (e.g. *¿Cúyos son estos lápices?* Whose pencils are these?) (gen. **de quién** or **de quiénes** is used rather than **cúyo**). *m,* beau, lover

D

daca /'daka/ Give me!

dádiva /'daðiβa/ f, gift, present

dadivosidad /daðiβosi'ðað/ f, generosity

dadivoso /daði'βoso/ a generous, liberal

dado /'daðo/ m, die; *Archit.* dado —*conjunc* **d. que,** given that, supposing that. **cargar los dados,** to load the dice

dador /da'ðor/ **(-ra)** n giver, donor. m, Com. bearer; Com. drawer (of a bill of exchange)

daguerrotipo /dagerro'tipo/ m, daguerreotype

¡dale! /'dale/ interj Stop! No more about...!

dalia /'dalia/ f. Bot. dahlia

dallar /da'ʎar; da'yar/ vt to scythe (grass)

dalle /'daʎe/ m, scythe

dalmática /dal'matika/ f, dalmatic, loose tunic or vestment

daltoniano /dalto'niano/ a color-blind

daltonismo /dalto'nismo/ m, color-blindness

dama /'dama/ f, lady; noblewoman; lady-in-waiting; lady-love; mistress, concubine; queen (chess); king (checkers); *Theat.* **d. primera,** leading lady

damas /'damas/ f pl, checkers (game)

Damasco /da'masko/ Damascus

damasco /da'masko/ m, damask

damería /dame'ria/ f, prudery, affectation

damnificar /damnifi'kar/ vt to injure

danés /da'nes/ **(-esa)** a Danish —n Dane. m, Danish (language)

danta /'danta/ f, Zool. tapir

Danubio, el /da'nuβio, el/ the Danube

danza /'danθa; 'dansa/ f, dance; set (of dancers); Fig. Inf. dirty business. **d. de arcos,** dance of the arches. **d. de cintas,** maypole dance. **d. de monos,** amusing spectacle

danzador /danθa'ðor; dansa'ðor/ **(-ra)** n dancer; —a dancing

danzar /dan'θar; dan'sar/ vt and vi to dance; —vi jump up and down, rattle; Inf. interfere, meddle

danzarín /danθa'rin; dansa'rin/ **(-ina)** n good dancer; Inf. meddler; Inf. playboy

danzón /dan'θon; dan'son/ m, Cuban dance

dañado /da'ɲaðo/ a evil, perverse; damned; spoiled, damaged

dañador /daɲa'ðor/ **(-ra)** a harmful —n injurer, offender

dañar /da'ɲar/ vt to hurt, harm; damage, spoil; —vr spoil, deteriorate

dañino /da'ɲino/ a destructive (often of animals); hurtful, harmful. **animales dañinos,** vermin, pests

daño /'daɲo/ m, hurt; damage; loss. Law. **daños y perjuicios,** damages. **hacerse d.,** to hurt oneself

dañoso /da'ɲoso/ a hurtful, harmful

dar /dar/ vt irr to give; wish, express (congratulations, etc.); hand over, concede; grant; inspire; produce, yield; cause, create; sacrifice; propose, put forward; take (a walk); believe, consider; deliver (blows, etc.); administer (medicine); provide with; apply, coat with; occasion; perform (plays); propose (a toast); give forth, emit; set (norms), render (thanks, etc.); hold (banquets, etc.); proffer, hold out; —vi to strike (clocks); (with prep a) overlook, look on to (e.g. Su ventana da a la calle, His window looks on to the street); (with con) find, meet (things, persons); (with de) fall on, fall down (e.g. Dio de cabeza, He fell head first. Dio de espaldas, He fell on his back); (with en) fall into, incur; insist on or persist in (doing something); acquire the habit of (e.g. Dieron en no venir a vernos, They took to not coming to see us); solve, guess (riddles, etc.); strike, wound, hurt (e.g. La bala le dio en el brazo, The bullet struck him in the arm); (with por) decide on (e.g. Di por no hacerlo, I decided not to do it) —vr to yield, give in; (with prep a) engage in, devote oneself to; (with por) think or consider oneself (e.g. Me di por muerto, I gave myself up for dead). **d. alas a,** to propagate, spread (a belief). **darse a la vela,** to set sail. **darse la mano,** to shake hands. **darse por buenos,** to make up a quarrel, be friends. **darse prisa,** to hurry up, make haste. **darse uno a conocer,** to make oneself known. **darse uno por entendido,** to show that one understands; be grateful. **No se me da un bledo,** I don't care a straw. **d. abajo,** to fall down. **d. bien por mal,** to return good for evil. **d. a conocer,** to make known. **d. a entender,** to suggest, hint. **d. a luz,** to give birth; publish, issue. **d. cuenta de,** to give an account of. **d. de baja,** Mil. to muster out, discharge. **d. de comer,** to feed. **d. de sí,** to stretch, expand; produce, yield; give of itself (oneself, himself, themselves) (either in good or bad sense). **d. diente con diente,** to chatter (of teeth), shiver. **d. el pésame,** to tender condolences. **d. en cara,** Fig. Inf. to throw in one's face. **d. en el clavo,** Fig. to hit the mark. **d. en qué pensar,** to make suspicious, cause to think. **d. fe,** to certify, attest. **d. fiado,** to give on credit. **d. fianza,** to give security. **d. fin a,** to finish. **d. licencia,** to permit, allow. **d. los buenos días,** to wish good day or good morning. **d. mal,** to have bad luck at cards. **d. parte de,** to announce; issue a communiqué about (e.g. Dieron parte de la pérdida del buque, They announced the loss of the ship). **d. prestado,** to lend. **d. qué decir,** to cause a scandal. **d. qué hacer,** to cause trouble. **d. razón de,** to give an account of. **d. sobre uno,** to assault a person. **d. un abrazo,** to embrace. **d. voces,** to shriek; call out. Inf. **Donde las dan las toman,** It's only tit-for-tat. Inf. **No me da la real**

gana, I darn well don't want to —*Pres. Indic.* **doy, das,** etc —*Preterite* **di, diste,** etc —*Pres. Subjunc.* **dé,** etc —*Imperf. Subjunc.* **diese,** etc.

dardo /'darðo/ *m,* (*Mil. Sports.*) dart; *Ichth.* dace; lampoon

dares y tomares /dares i tomares/ *m, pl* give and take; *Inf.* back-chat. Generally used with *andar, haber* or *tener*

dársena /'darsena/ *f, Naut.* dock

data /'data/ *f,* date (calendar); *Com.* credit

datar /'datar/ *vt* to date; —*vi* (*with de*) date from; —*vr Com.* credit

dátil /'datil/ *m, Bot.* date

dato /'dato/ *m,* datum; basis, fact

de /de/ *f,* name of letter D —*prep* of (possessive) (e.g. *Este cuadro es de Vd.,* This picture is yours); from (place and time) (e.g. *Vengo de Madrid,* I come from Madrid. *de vez en cuando,* from time to time); with, of, from, as the result of (e.g. *Lloraban de miedo,* They were crying with fright. *Murió de un ataque del corazón,* He died from a heart attack); for, to (e.g. *Es hora de marchar,* It is time to leave); with (of characteristics) (e.g. *el señor de los lentes,* the gentleman with the eyeglasses. *el cuarto de la alfombra azul,* the room with the blue carpet); when, as (e.g. *De niños nos gustaban los juguetes,* When we were children we liked toys); by (e.g. *Es un ensayo del mismo autor,* It is an essay by the same author. *Fue amado de todos,* He was loved by all. *Es hidalgo de nacimiento,* He is a gentleman by birth). Indicates the material of which a thing is made (e.g. *La mesa es de mármol,* The table is marble). Indicates contents of a thing (e.g. *un vaso de leche,* a glass of milk). Shows manner in which an action is performed (e.g. *Lo hizo de prisa,* He did it hurriedly). Shows the use to which an article is put (e.g. *una mesa de escribir,* a writing-table. *una máquina de coser,* a sewing-machine. *un caballo de batalla,* a war-horse). Sometimes used for emphasis (e.g. *El tonto de tu secretario,* That fool of a secretary of yours). Used by Spanish married women before husband's family name (e.g. *Señora Martínez de Cabra,* Mrs. Cabra (née Martínez)). Used after many adverbs (generally of time or place) to form prepositional phrases (e.g. *detrás de,* behind. *enfrente de,* opposite to; in front of. *de acá para allá,* here and there. *de allí a poco,* shortly afterward. *de allí a pocos días,* a few days later. *de bamba,* by chance. *de cabo a rabo,* from cover to cover. *además de,* besides, etc.). Used at beginning of various adverbial phrases (e.g. *de noche,* at night. *de día,* by day. *de antemano,* previously, *la persona de mi derecha* the person at my right, etc.). Used partitively before nouns, pronouns, adjectives (e.g. *Estas historias tienen algo de verdad,* These stories have some truth in them. *¿Qué hay de nuevo?* What's the

news?) Forms many compound words (e.g. *deponer, denegar,* etc.). With **"uno"** means "at" (e.g. *Lo cogió de un salto,* He caught it at one bound). **de a** is used before expressions of price, weight, etc. (e.g. *un libro de a cinco pesetas,* a five-peseta book)

debajo /de'βaho/ *adv* underneath; below

debate /de'βate/ *m,* discussion, debate; dispute

debatible /deβa'tiβle/ *a* debatable

debatir /deβa'tir/ *vt* to discuss, debate, argue

debe /'deβe/ *m, Com.* debtor

debelar /deβe'lar/ *vt* to conquer, overthrow

deber /de'βer/ *vt* to owe (e.g. *Le debo mil pesetas,* I owe him one thousand pesetas). Used as auxiliary verb followed by infinitive, ought to, be obliged to (e.g. *Debía haberlo hecho,* I ought to have done it. *Deberá hacerlo,* He will have to do it); be destined to (e.g. *La princesa que más tarde debió ser reina,* The princess who later was destined to be queen); be essential, must (e.g. *La cuestión debe ser resuelta,* The question must be settled); (*with de* + *infin.*) be probable (indicates supposition) (e.g. *Debe de tener cincuenta años,* He is probably about fifty. *Debía de sufrir del corazón,* He probably suffered from heart trouble); (preceded by a negative *with de* + *infin.*) be impossible (e.g. *No debe de ser verdad,* It can't be true)

deber /de'βer/ *m,* duty, obligation; debt. **hacer su d.,** to do one's duty

debidamente /deβiða'mente/ *adv* justly, rightly; duly

debido /de'βiðo/ *a* correct, due. **d. a,** owing to, because of

débil /'deβil/ *a* weak; *Fig.* spineless; frail

debilidad /deβili'ðað/ *f,* weakness; feebleness

debilitación /deβilita'θion/ *m;* deβilitasión/ *f,* debilitation

debilitante /deβili'tante/ *a* weakening

debilitar /deβili'tar/ *vt* to weaken; —*vr* become weak

débito /'deβito/ *m,* debit, debt; duty

debutar /deβu'tar/ *vi* to appear for the first time, make one's début

decadencia /deka'ðenθia; dekaðensia/ *f,* decadence, decline

decadente /deka'ðente/ *a* decadent, decaying

decaer /deka'er/ *vi irr* to fail (persons); decay, decline. See **caer**

decagramo /deka'gramo/ *m,* decagram

decaimiento /dekai'miento/ *m,* decadence; *Med.* prostration

decalaje /deka'lahe/ *m, Aer.* stagger

decalitro /deka'litro/ *m,* decaliter

decálogo /de'kalogo/ *m,* decalogue, the Ten Commandments

decampar /de'kampar/ *vi Mil.* to decamp

decano /de'kano/ *m,* senior member; *Educ.* dean

decantación /dekanta'θion; dekantasion/ f, decantation

decantar /dekan'tar/ vt to decant (wines); praise

decapitación /dekapita'θion; dekapitasion/ f, decapitation

decapitar /dekapi'tar/ vt to decapitate, behead

decena /de'θena; de'sena/ f, ten; Mus. tenth

decenario /deθe'nario; dese'nario/ m, decade

decencia /de'θenθia; de'sensia/ f, propriety, decency; decorum, modesty

decenio /de'θenio; de'senio/ m, decade

deceno /de'θeno; de'seno/ a tenth

decentar /deθen'tar; desen'tar/ vt irr to begin, cut (loaves, etc.); Fig. undermine (health, etc.); —vr suffer from bedsores. See **acertar**

decente /de'θente; de'sente/ a decent, honest; respectable; suitable; tidy

decepción /deθep'θion; desep'sion/ f, disillusionment, disappointment

dechado /de'tʃaðo/ m, model, ideal; Sew. sampler; exemplar, ideal

decible /de'θiβle; de'siβle/ a expressible

decidero /de'θiðero; de'siðero/ a that which can be safely said

decidido /deθi'ðiðo; desi'ðiðo/ a decided; resolute, determined

decidir /deθi'ðir; desi'ðir/ vt to resolve, decide; —vr make up one's mind

decidor /deθi'ðor; desi'ðor/ (-ra) a talkative, fluent, eloquent —n good talker

decimal /deθi'mal; desi'mal/ a decimal; pertaining to tithes. **sistema d.,** metric system

décimo /'deθimo; 'desimo/ a tenth. m, tenth part; tenth of a lottery ticket

decimoctavo /deθimok'taβo; desimok'taβo/ a eighteenth

decimocuarto /deθimo'kuarto; desimo'kuarto/ a fourteenth

decimonono /deθimo'nono; desimo'nono/ a nineteenth

decimoquinto /deθimo'kinto; desimo'kinto/ a fifteenth

decimoséptimo /deθimo'septimo; desimo'septimo/ a and m, seventeenth

decimosexto /deθimo'seksto; desimo'seksto/ a sixteenth

decimotercio /deθimoter'θio; desimoter'sio/ a thirteenth

decir /de'θir; de'sir/ vt irr to say; name; indicate, show; tell. **d. bien,** to go with, suit; speak the truth; be eloquent. **d. entre** (or **para**) **sí,** to say to oneself. Inf. **d. nones,** to refuse. **¡Diga!** Hello! (telephone). Inf. **el que dirán,** public opinion (what will people say!). **Es d.,** That is to say. **Se dice,** It is said, people say —Pres. Ind. **digo, dices,** etc —Pres. Part. **diciendo.** Past Part. **dicho.** Fut. **diré,** etc —Condit. **diría,** etc —Preterite **dije,** etc —Pres. Subjunc. **diga,** etc —Imperf. Subjunc. **dijese,** etc.

decir /de'θir; de'sir/ m, saying, saw; maxim, witticism (often pl.)

decisión /deθi'sion; desi'sion/ f, decision, resolution; Law. judgment; firmness, strength (of character)

decisivo /deθi'siβo; desi'siβo/ a decisive

declamación /deklama'θion; deklama'sion/ f, declamation, oration; Theat. delivery; recitation

declamar /dekla'mar/ vi to make a speech, declaim; recite

declamatorio /deklama'torio/ a declamatory, rhetorical

declaración /deklara'θion; deklara'sion/ f, declaration; exposition, explanation; confession; statement; Law. deposition. **d. jurada,** affidavit, sworn statement

declaradamente /deklaraða'mente/ adv avowedly

declarante /dekla'rante/ a declaring. mf Law. deponent

declarar /dekla'rar/ vt to declare; make clear, explain; Law. find; —vi Law. give evidence; —vr avow, confess (one's sentiments, etc.), show, reveal itself

declinación /deklina'θion; deklina'sion/ f, fall, descent; decadence, decay; Astron. declination; Gram. declension. Inf. **no saber las declinaciones,** not to know one's ABC, be very ignorant

declinar /dekli'nar/ vi to slope; diminish, fall, decline, deteriorate; Fig. near the end; —vt Gram. decline

declive /de'kliβe,/ m. **declividad** f, slope, incline; gradient

decomisar /dekomi'sar/ vt to confiscate, seize

decoración /dekora'θion; dekora'sion/ f, decoration; ornament, embellishment; Theat. scenery

decorado /deko'raðo/ m, Theat. scenery, décor

decorador /dekora'ðor/ m, decorator

decorar /deko'rar/ vt to adorn, ornament; Poet. decorate, honor

decorativo /dekora'tiβo/ a decorative

decoro /de'koro/ m, respect, reverence; prudence, circumspection; decorum, propriety; integrity, decency; Archit. decoration

decoroso /deko'roso/ a decorous, honorable, decent

decrecer /dekre'θer; dekre'ser/ vi irr to decrease, grow less. See **conocer**

decreciente /dekre'θiente; dekre'siente/ a decreasing

decrépito /de'krepito/ a decrepit

decretar /dekre'tar/ vt to decree, decide; Law. give a judgment (in a suit)

decreto /de'kreto/ m, decree, order; judicial decree

decuplar, decuplicar /dekup'lar, dekupli'kar/ vt to multiply by ten

decurso /de'kurso/ m, course, lapse (of time)

dedada /de'ðaða/ f, thimbleful, finger; pinch

dedal /de'ðal/ m, thimble; finger-stall

dédalo /'deðalo/ m, labyrinth

dedeo /de'ðeo/ m, Mus. touch

dedicación /deðika'θion; deðika'sion/ f, dedication (all meanings)

dedicar /deði'kar/ vt to dedicate; devote; consecrate; —vr (with prep a) dedicate oneself to, engage in

dedicatoria /deðika'toria/ f, dedication (of a book, etc.)

dedicatorio /deðika'torio/ a dedicatory

dedillo, saber al /de'ðiʎo, saβer al; de'ðiyo, saβer al/ Fig. to have at one's fingertips, know perfectly

dedo /'deðo/ m, finger; toe; finger's breadth. **d. anular**, third (ring) finger. **d. de en medio** or **del corazón**, middle finger. **d. índice**, forefinger. **d. meñique**, little finger. **d. pulgar**, thumb or big toe. Fig. Inf. **a dos dedos de**, within an inch of. Fig. Inf. **chuparse los dedos**, to smack one's lips over. Inf. **estar unidos como los dedos de la mano**, to be as thick as thieves

deducción /deðuk'θion; deðuk'sion/ f, inference, deduction; derivation; (Mus. Math.) progression

deducir /deðu'θir; deðu'sir/ vt irr to deduce, infer; deduct, subtract; Law. plead, allege in pleading. See **conducir**

defecación /defeka'θion; defeka'sion/ f, purification; defecation

defecar /defe'kar/ vt to clarify, purify; defecate

defección /defek'θion; defek'sion/ f, defection

defectible /defek'tiβle/ a deficient; imperfect

defecto /de'fekto/ m, defect, fault; imperfection

defectuoso /defek'tuoso/ a imperfect, defective

defender /defen'der/ vt irr to defend, protect; maintain, uphold; forbid; hinder; —vr defend oneself. See **entender**

defendible /defen'diβle/ a defensible

defensa /de'fensa/ f, defence; protection; (hockey) pad; Law. defense; Sports. back; pl Mil. defenses; Naut. fenders. **d. química**, chemical warfare. Mil. **defensas costeras**, coastal defenses

defensiva /defen'siβa/ f, defensive

defensivo /defen'siβo/ a defensive: m, safeguard

defensor /defen'sor/ (-ra) n defender. m, Law. counsel for the defense

deferencia /defe'renθia; deferensia/ f, deference

deferente /defe'rente/ a deferential

deferir /defe'rir/ vi irr to defer, yield; —vt delegate —Pres. Indic. **defiero**, **defieres**, **defiere**, **defieren**. Pres. Part. **defiriendo**. Preterite **defirió**, **defirieron**. Pres. Subjunc. **defiera**, etc —Imperf. Subjunc. **defiriese**, etc.

deficiencia /defi'θienθia; defi'siensia/ f, defect, deficiency

deficiente /defi'θiente; defi'siente/ a faulty, deficient

déficit /'defiθit; 'defisit/ m, deficit

definible /defi'niβle/ a definable

definición /defini'θion; defini'sion/ f, definition; decision

definido /defi'niðo/ a definite

definir /defi'nir/ vt to define; decide

definitivo /ðefini'tiβo/ a definitive. **en definitiva**, definitely; in short

deflagración /deflagra'θion; deflagra'sion/ f, sudden blaze, deflagration

deflagrar /defla'grar/ vi to go up in flames

deformado /defor'maðo/ a deformed; misshapen

deformador /deforma'ðor/ (-ra) a disfiguring, deforming —n disfigurer

deformar /defor'mar/ vt to deform; —vr become deformed or misshapen

deformidad /deformi'ðað/ f, deformity; gross error; vice, lapse

defraudación /defrauða'θion; defrauða'sion/ f, defrauding; deceit

defraudador /defrauða'ðor/ (-ra) n defrauder

defraudar /defrau'ðar/ vt to defraud; usurp; frustrate, disappoint; impede

defunción /defun'θion; defun'sion/ f, decease, death

degeneración /dehenera'θion; dehenera'sion/ f, degeneration. **d. grasienta**, fatty degeneration

degenerado /dehene'raðo/ (-da) a and n degenerate

degenerar /dehene'rar/ vi to degenerate

deglución /deglu'θion; deglu'sion/ f, swallowing, deglutition

deglutir /deglu'tir/ vi and vt to swallow

degollación /degoʎa'θion; degoya'sion/ f, decollation, throat slitting

degolladero /degoʎa'ðero; degoya'ðero/ m, slaughterhouse; execution block

degollar /dego'ʎar; dego'yar/ vt irr to behead; slit the throat; Fig. destroy; (Fig. Theat.) murder; Inf. annoy, bore —Pres. Indic. **degüello**, **degüellas**, **degüella**, **degüellan**. Pres. Subjunc. **degüelle**, **degüelles**, **degüelle**, **degüellen**

degradación /degraða'θion; degraða'sion/ f, degradation; humiliation, debasement; Art. gradation, shading (colors, light)

degradante /degra'ðante/ a degrading, humiliating

degradar /degra'ðar/ vt to degrade; humiliate; Art. grade, blend; —vr degrade oneself

degustación /degusta'θion; degusta'sion/ f, act of tasting or sampling

dehesa /de'esa/ f, pasture, meadow

deificación /deifika'θion; deifika'sion/ f, deification

deificar /deifi'kar/ vt to deify; overpraise

dejadez /deha'ðeθ; deha'ðes/ f, slovenliness; neglect; laziness; carelessness

dejado /de'haðo/ *a* lazy; neglectful; slovenly; discouraged, depressed

dejamiento /deha'miento/ *m,* relinquishment; negligence; lowness of spirits; indifference

dejar /de'har/ *vt* to leave; omit, forget, allow, permit (e.g. *Déjame salir,* Let me go out); yield, produce, entrust, leave in charge; believe, consider; intend, appoint; cease, stop; forsake, desert; renounce, relinquish; bequeath; give away; —*vr* neglect oneself; engage (in); lay oneself open to, allow oneself; abandon oneself (to), fling oneself (into); *Fig.* be depressed or languid; (*with de* + *infin.*) cease to (e.g. *Se dejó de hacerlo,* He stopped doing it); —*vi* (*with de* + *adjective*) be none the less, be rather (e.g. *No deja de ser sorprendente,* It isn't any the less surprising). **d. aparte,** to omit, leave out. **d. atrás,** to overtake; *Fig.* leave behind, beat. **d. caer,** to let fall. **dejarse caer,** to let oneself fall; *Fig. Inf.* to let fall, utter; appear suddenly. **dejarse vencer,** to give way, allow oneself to be persuaded

dejo /'deho/ *m,* relinquishment; end; accent (of persons); savor, after-taste; negligence; *Fig.* touch, flavor

del /del/ contraction of **de** + **el,** (*def. art. m*) of the (e.g. *del perro,* of the dog)

delación /dela'θion; dela'sion/ *f,* accusation, denunciation

delantal /delan'tal/ *m,* apron

delante /de'lante/ *adv* before, in front, in the presence (of)

delantera /delan'tera/ *f,* front, front portion; *Theat.* orchestra stall, front seat; front (of garment). **tomar la d.,** to take the lead; *Inf.* steal a march on

delantero /delan'tero/ *a* fore, front. *m,* postilion; *Sports.* forward. **d. centro,** *Sports.* centerforward

delatable /dela'taβle/ *a* impeachable; blameworthy

delatar /dela'tar/ *vt* to inform against, accuse; impeach

delator /dela'tor/ **(-ra)** *a* denunciatory, accusing —*n* denouncer, informer

delegación /delega'θion; delega'sion/ *f,* delegation; proxy

delegado /dele'gaðo/ **(-da)** *n* delegate; proxy

delegar /dele'gar/ *vt* to delegate

deleitable /delei'taβle/ *a* delightful

deleitar /delei'tar/ *vt* to delight, charm, please; —*vr* delight (in)

deleite /de'leite/ *m,* delight; pleasure

deleitoso /delei'toso/ *a* delightful, pleasant

deletrear /deletre'ar/ *vi* to spell; *Fig.* decipher

deletreo /dele'treo/ *m,* spelling; *Fig.* decipherment

deleznable /deleθ'naβle; deles'naβle/ *a* fragile, brittle; slippery; brief, fugitive, transitory

delfín /del'fin/ *m,* (*Ichth. Astron.*) dolphin; dauphin

delgadez /delga'ðeθ; delga'ðes/ *f,* thinness; slenderness, leanness

delgado /del'gaðo/ *a* slim; thin; scanty; poor (of land); sharp, perspicacious

delgaducho /delga'ðutʃo/ *a* slenderish, somewhat thin

deliberación /deliβera'θion; deliβera'sion/ *f,* deliberation; consideration; discussion

deliberadamente /deliβeraða'mente/ *adv* deliberately

deliberante /deliβe'rante/ *a* deliberative, considering

deliberar /deliβe'rar/ *vi* to deliberate, consider; —*vt* decide after reflection; discuss

delicadez /delika'ðeθ; delika'ðes/ *f,* weakness; delicacy; hypersensitiveness; amiability

delicadeza /delika'ðeθa; delika'ðesa/ *f,* delicacy; fastidiousness; refinement, subtlety; sensitiveness; consideration, tact; scrupulosity

delicado /deli'kaðo/ *a* courteous; tactful; fastidious; weak, delicate; fragile, perishable; delicious, tasty; exquisite; difficult, embarrassing; refined, discriminating, sensitive; scrupulous; subtle; hypersensitive, suspicious. **d. de salud,** in poor health

delicia /deli'θia; deli'sia/ *f,* pleasure, delight; sensual pleasure

delicioso /deli'θioso; deli'sioso/ *a* delightful, agreeable, pleasant

delincuencia /delin'kuenθia; delin'kuensia/ *f,* delinquency

delincuente /delin'kuente/ *a* and *mf* delinquent

delineación /delinea'θion; delinea'sion/ *f,* delineation; diagram, design, plan

delineador /delinea'ðor/ **(-ra),** *n* **delineante** *m,* draftsman, designer

delineamiento /delinea'miento/ *m,* delineation

delinear /deline'ar/ *vt* to delineate; sketch; describe

delirante /deli'rante/ *a* delirious

delirar /deli'rar/ *vi* to be delirious; act or speak foolishly

delirio /de'lirio/ *m,* delirium; frenzy; foolishness, nonsense. **d. de grandezas,** illusions of grandeur

delito /de'lito/ *m,* delict, offense against the law, crime

delta /'delta/ *f,* fourth letter of Greek alphabet. *m,* delta (of a river)

delusorio /delu'sorio/ *a* deceptive

demacrado /dema'kraðo/ *a* emaciated

demacrarse /dema'krarse/ *vr* to become emaciated

demagogia /dema'gohia/ *f,* demagogy

demagogo /dema'gogo/ **(-ga)** *n* demagogue

demanda /de'manda/ *f,* petition, request; collecting (for charity); collecting box; want ad; question; search; undertaking; *Com.* order or demand; *Law.* claim

demandadero /demanda'ðero/ **(-ra)** n
convent or prison messenger; errandboy

demandado /deman'daðo/ **(-da)** n Law.
defendant; Law. respondent

demandante /deman'dante/ mf Law.
plaintiff

demandar /deman'dar/ vt to ask, request; desire, yearn for; question; Law.
claim

demarcar /demar'kar/ vt to fix boundaries, demarcate

demás /de'mas/ a other —adv besides. **lo
d.,** the rest. **los (las) d.,** the others. **por
d.,** useless; superfluous. **por lo d.,** otherwise; for the rest

demasía /dema'sia/ f, excess; daring; insolence; guilt, crime. **en d.,** excessively

demasiado /dema'siaðo/ a too; too
many; too much —adv excessively

demencia /de'menθia; de'mensia/ f, madness, insanity

demencial /demen'θial; demen'sial/ a insane

dementar /demen'tar/ vt to render insane; —vr become insane

demente /de'mente/ a insane, mad. mf
lunatic

demérito /de'merito/ m, demerit, fault

demisión /demi'sion/ f, submission, acquiescence

democracia /demo'kraθia; demo'krasia/
f, democracy

demócrata /de'mokrata/ mf democrat

democrático /demo'kratiko/ a democratic

democratizar /demokrati'θar; demokra-
ti'sar/ vt to make democratic

demoledor /demole'ðor/ **(-ra)** a demolition —n demolisher

demoler /demo'ler/ vt irr to demolish,
destroy, dismantle. See **moler**

demolición /demoli'θion; demoli'sion/ f,
demolition, destruction, dismantling

demoníaco /demo'niako/ a devilish; possessed by a demon

demonio /de'monio/ m, devil; evil spirit
—interj ¡Demonios! Deuce take it! Inf.
tener el d. en el cuerpo, to be always on
the move, be very energetic

demora /de'mora/ f, delay; Naut. bearing; Com. demurrage

demorar /demo'rar/ vt to delay; —vi
stay, remain, tarry; Naut. bear

demostración /demostra'θion; de-
mostra'sion/ f, demonstration; proof

demostrador /demostra'ðor/ **(-ra)** a
demonstrating —n demonstrator

demostrar /demos'trar/ vt irr to demonstrate, explain; prove; teach. See **mostrar**

demostrativo /demostra'tiβo/ a demonstrative. Gram. **pronombre d.,** demonstrative pronoun

demudación /demuða'θion; demuða'sion/
f, change; alteration

demudar /demu'ðar/ vt to change, vary;
alter, transform; —vr change suddenly
(color, facial expression, etc.); grow angry

denario /de'nario/ a denary. m, denarius

denegación /denega'θion; denega'sion/ f,
denial; refusal

denegar /dene'gar/ vt irr to deny, refuse.
See **acertar**

dengue /'dengue/ m, affectation, faddi-
ness, fastidiousness

denigrable /deni'graβle/ a odious

denigración /denigra'θion; denigra'sion/
f, slander, defamation (of character)

denigrante /deni'grante/ a slanderous

denigrar /deni'grar/ vt to slander; insult

denodado /deno'ðaðo/ a valiant, daring

denominar /denomi'nar/ vt to name,
designate

denostar /denos'tar/ vt irr to revile, insult. See **acordar**

denotar /deno'tar/ vt to denote, indicate

densidad /densi'ðað/ f, density; closeness, denseness; Phys. specific gravity;
obscurity

denso /'denso/ a compact, close; thick,
dense; crowded; dark, confused

dentado /den'taðo/ a toothed; pronged;
dentate

dentadura /denta'ðura/ f, set of teeth
(real or false). **d. de rumiante,** teeth like
an ox. **d. postiza,** false teeth

dental /den'tal/ a dental

dentar /den'tar/ vt irr to provide with
teeth, prongs, etc.; —vi cut teeth. See
sentar

dentellada /dente'ʎaða; dente'yaða/ f,
gnashing or chattering of teeth; bite;
toothmark

dentellar /dente'ʎar; dente'yar/ vt to
chatter, grind, gnash (teeth)

dentellear /denteʎe'ar; denteye'ar/ vt to
bite, sink the teeth into

dentera /den'tera/ f, **(dar)** to set one's
teeth on edge; Fig. Inf. make one's mouth
water

dentición /denti'θion; denti'sion/ f, teething, dentition

dentífrico /den'tifriko/ m, toothpaste

dentista /den'tista/ mf dentist

dentro /'dentro/ adv within, inside. **d.
de poco,** soon, shortly. **por d.,** from the
inside; on the inside

denudación /denuða'θion; denuða'sion/
f, denudation; Geol. erosion

denudar /denu'ðar/ vt to denude

denuesto /de'nuesto/ m, insult

denuncia /de'nunθia; de'nunsia/ f, denunciation, accusation

denunciante /denun'θiante; denun'siante/ a accusing. mf Law. denouncer

denunciar /denun'θiar; denun'siar/ vt to
give notice, inform; herald, presage; declare, proclaim; denounce; Law. accuse

denunciatorio /denunθia'torio; denun-
sia'torio/ a denunciatory

deparar /depa'rar/ vt to furnish, offer,
present

departamental /departamen'tal/ a departmental

departamento /departa'mento/ *m*, department; compartment (railway); branch, section. **d. de lactantes,** nursery (in a hospital)

depauperar /depaupe'rar/ *vt* to impoverish; —*vr.Med.* grow weak, become emaciated

dependencia /depen'denθia; depen'densia/ *f*, dependence; subordination; dependency; *Com.* branch; firm, agency; business affair; kinship or affinity; *pl Archit.* offices; *Com.* staff; accessories

depender /depen'der/ *vi* (*with de*) to be subordinate to; depend on; be dependent on, need

dependiente /depen'diente/ **(-ta)** *a* and *n* dependent, subordinate. *m*, employee; shop assistant

depilación /depila'θion; depila'sion/ *f*, depilation

depilar /depi'lar/ *vt* to depilate

depilatorio /depila'torio/ *m*, depilatory

deplorar /deplo'rar/ *vt* to deplore, lament

deponente /depo'nente/ *a* deposing; affirming. *mf* deponent. *Gram.* **verbo d.,** deponent verb

deponer /depo'ner/ *vt irr* to lay aside; depose, oust; affirm, testify; remove, take from its place; *Law.* depose. See **poner**

deportación /deporta'θion; deporta'sion/ *f*, deportation

deportar /depor'tar/ *vt* to exile; deport

deporte /de'porte/ *m*, sport; *pl* games. **d. de vela,** sailing, boating

deportismo /depor'tismo/ *m*, sport

deportista /depor'tista/ *a* sporting. *mf* sportsman (sportswoman)

deportivo /depor'tiβo/ *a* sporting

deposición /deposi'θion; deposi'sion/ *f*, affirmation, statement; *Law.* deposition; degradation, removal (from office, etc.)

depositador /deposita'ðor/ **(-ra)** *a* depositing —*n* depositor

depositar /deposi'tar/ *vt* to deposit; place in safety; entrust; lay aside, put away; —*vr Chem.* settle

depositario /deposi'tario/ **(-ia)** *a* pertaining to a depository —*n* depositary, trustee

depósito /de'posito/ *m*, deposit; depository; *Com.* depot, warehouse; *Chem.* deposit, sediment; tank, reservoir; *Mil.* depot. **d. de bencina, d. de gasolina,** gas tank; service station. **d. de municiones,** munitions dump. *Com.* **en d.,** in bond. **Queda hecho el d. que marca la ley,** Copyright reserved

depravación /depraβa'θion; depraβa-'sion/ *f*, depravity

depravar /depra'βar/ *vt* to deprave, corrupt; —*vr* become depraved

deprecación /depreka'θion; depreka'sion/ *f*, supplication, petition; deprecation

deprecar /depre'kar/ *vt* to supplicate, petition; deprecate

depreciación /depreθia'θion; depre-sia'sion/ *f*, depreciation, fall in value

depreciar /depre'θiar; depre'siar/ *vt* to depreciate, reduce the value (of)

depredar /depre'ðar/ *vt* to pillage

depresión /depre'sion/ *f*, depression. **d. nerviosa,** nervous breakdown

deprimir /depri'mir/ *vt* to depress, compress, press down; depreciate, belittle; —*vr* be compressed

depuración /depura'θion; depura'sion/ *f*, cleansing, purification; *Polit.* purge

depurar /depu'rar/ *vt* to cleanse, purify; *Polit.* purge

derecha /de'retʃa/ *f*, right hand; *Polit.* (gen. *pl*) Right. *Mil.* **¡D.!** Right Turn! **a la d.,** on the right

derechamente /deretʃa'mente/ *adv* straight, directly; prudently, justly; openly, frankly

derechista /dere'tʃista/ *mf Polit.* rightist

derecho /de'retʃo/ *a* straight; upright; right (not left); just, reasonable; *Sports.* forehand —*adv* straightaway. *m*, right; law; just claim; privilege; justice, reason; exemption; right side (cloth, etc.); *pl* dues, taxes; fees. **d. a la vía,** right of way. **d. de apelación,** right to appeal. **d. de visita,** (international law) right of search. **derechos de aduana,** custom-house duties. **derechos de entrada,** import duties. **según d.,** according to law. **usar de su d.,** to exercise one's right

derechura /dere'tʃura/ *f*, directness; straightness; uprightness

derivación /deriβa'θion; deriβa'sion/ *f*, origin, derivation; inference, consequence; *Gram.* derivation

derivar /deri'βar/ *vi* to originate; *Naut.* drift; —*vt* conduct, lead; *Gram.* derive; *Elec.* tap

dermatología /dermatolo'hia/ *f*, dermatology

derogación /deroga'θion; deroga'sion/ *f*, repeal, annulment; deterioration

derogar /dero'gar/ *vt* to annul, repeal; destroy, suppress

derramado /derra'maðo/ *a* extravagant, wasteful

derramamiento /derrama'miento/ *m*, pouring out; spilling; scattering

derramar /derra'mar/ *vt* to pour out; spill; scatter; apportion (taxes); publish abroad, spread; —*vr* be scattered; overflow

derrame /de'rrame/ *m*, spilling; leakage; overflow; scattering; slope

derredor /derre'ðor/ *m*, circumference. **al (or en) d.,** round about

derrelicto /derre'likto/ *a* abandoned; derelict. *m, Naut.* derelict

derrengado /derreŋ'gaðo/ *a* crooked; crippled

derretimiento /derreti'miento/ *m*, melting; thaw; liquefaction; *Inf.* burning passion

derretir /derre'tir/ *vt irr* to melt, liquefy; waste, dissipate; —*vr* be very much in love; *Inf.* be susceptible (to love); *Inf.* long, be impatient. See **pedir**

derribar /derri'βar/ vt to demolish; knock down; fell; throw down; Aer. shoot down; throw (in wrestling); Fig. overthrow; demolish, explode (a myth); control (emotions); —vr fall down; prostrate oneself; throw oneself down. **d. el chapeo,** humorous to doff one's hat

derribo /de'rriβo/ m, demolition; debris, rubble; throw (in wrestling)

derrocadero /derroka'ðero/ m, rocky precipice

derrocar /derro'kar/ vt to throw down from a rock; demolish (buildings); overthrow, oust

derrochador /derrotʃa'ðor/ **(-ra)** a wasteful, extravagant —n spendthrift

derrochar /derro'tʃar/ vt to waste, squander

derrota /de'rrota/ f, road; route, path; Naut. course; Mil. defeat

derrotar /derro'tar/ vt to squander; destroy, harm; Mil. defeat; —vr Naut. drift, lose course

derrotero /derro'tero/ m, Naut. course; Naut. ship's itinerary; number of sea charts; means to an end, course of action

derrotista /derro'tista/ mf defeatist

derruir /de'rruir/ vt irr to demolish (a building). See **huir**

derrumbadero /derrumba'ðero/ m, precipice; risk, danger

derrumbar /derrum'bar/ vt to precipitate; —vr throw oneself down, collapse, tumble down (buildings, etc.)

derrumbe /de'rrumbe/ m, collapse; subsidence

desabarrancar /desaβarran'kar/ vt to pull out of a ditch or rut; extricate (from a difficulty)

desabor /desa'βor/ m, insipidity

desabotonar /desaβoto'nar/ vt to unbutton; —vi open (flowers)

desabrido /desa'βriðo/ a insipid, poortasting; inclement (weather); disagreeable; unsociable; homely, plain (woman)

desabrigar /desaβri'gar/ vt to uncover; leave without shelter

desabrigo /desa'βrigo/ m, want of clothing or shelter; poverty, destitution

desabrimiento /desaβri'miento/ m, insipidity; harshness, disagreeableness; melancholy, depression

desabrir /desa'βrir/ vt to give a bad taste (to food); annoy, trouble

desabrochar /desaβro'tʃar/ vt to unbutton, untie; open; —vr Inf. confide, open up

desacatar /desaka'tar/ vt to behave disrespectfully (towards); lack reverence

desacato /desa'kato/ m, irreverence; disrespect

desacertar /desaθer'tar/ vi desaser'tar/ vi irr to be wrong; act imprudently. See **acertar**

desacierto /desa'θierto; desa'sierto/ m, mistake, miscalculation, blunder

desacomodado /desakomo'ðaðo/ a lacking means of subsistence; poor; unemployed (servants); troublesome

desacomodar /desakomo'ðar/ vt to incommode, make uncomfortable, inconvenience; dismiss, discharge

desaconsejar /desakonse'har/ vt to advise against, dissuade

desacoplar /desakop'lar/ vt to disconnect

desacordar /desakor'ðar/ vt irr Mus. to put out of tune; —vr (with de) forget. See **acordar**

desacostumbrado /desakostum'braðo/ a unaccustomed; unusual

desacotar /desako'tar/ vt to remove (fences); refuse, deny; —vi withdraw (from agreement, etc.)

desacreditar /desakreði'tar/ vt to discredit

desacuerdo /desa'kuerðo/ m, disagreement, discord; mistake; forgetfulness; swoon, loss of consciousness

desadornar /desaðor'nar/ vt to denude of ornaments

desadorno /desa'ðorno/ m, lack of ornaments; bareness

desafecto /desa'fekto/ a disaffected; hostile. m, disaffection

desaferrar /desafe'rrar/ vt irr to untie, unfasten; Fig. wean from; Naut. weigh anchor. See **acertar**

desafiador /desafia'ðor/ **(-ra)** a challenging —n challenger. m, duelist

desafiar /desa'fiar/ vt to challenge; compete with; oppose

desafinar /desafi'nar/ vi Mus. to go out of tune; Fig. Inf. speak out of turn

desafío /desa'fio/ m, challenge; competition; duel

desaforado /desafo'raðo/ a lawless; outrageous; enormous

desaforar /desafo'rar/ vt to infringe (laws, etc.); —vr be disorderly

desaforrar /desafo'rrar/ vt to remove the lining of or from

desafortunado /desafortu'naðo/ a unfortunate

desagarrar /desaga'rrar/ vt Inf. to release, loosen; unhook

desagraciado /desagra'θiaðo; desagra'siaðo/ a ugly, unsightly

desagraciar /desagra'θiar; desagra'siar/ vt to disfigure, make ugly

desagradable /desagra'ðaβle/ a disagreeable; unpleasant

desagradar /desagra'ðar/ vi to be disagreeable, displease (e.g. Me desagráda su voz, I find his voice unpleasant)

desagradecer /desagraðe'θer; desagraðe'ser/ vt irr to be ungrateful (for). See **conocer**

desagradecido /desagraðe'θiðo; desagraðe'siðo/ a ungrateful

desagrado /desa'graðo/ m, displeasure, dislike, dissatisfaction

desagraviar /desagra'βiar/ vt to make amends, apologize; indemnify

desagravio /desa'graβio/ *m*, satisfaction, reparation; compensation

desagregar /desagre'gar/ **(se)** *vt* and *vr* to separate

desaguar /desa'guar/ *vt* to drain off; dissipate; —*vi* flow (into sea, etc.)

desagüe /de'sague/ *m*, drainage; outlet; drain; catchment

desaguisado /desagi'saðo/ *a* outrageous, lawless. *m*, offense, insult

desahogado /desao'gaðo/ *a* brazen, insolent; clear, unencumbered; in comfortable circumstances

desahogar /desao'gar/ *vt* to ease, relieve; —*vr* unburden oneself; recover (from illness, heat, etc.); get out of debt; speak one's mind

desahogo /desa'ogo/ *m*, relief, alleviation; ease; comfort, convenience; freedom, frankness; unburdening (of one's mind). *Inf.* **vivir con d.**, to be comfortably off

desahuciar /desau'θiar; desau'siar/ *vt* to banish all hope; give up, despair of the life of; put out (tenants). When the third syllable of this verb is stressed, it is spelled with **ú**: *Pres. Indic.* **desahúcio, desahúcias, desahúcia, desahúcian.** *Pres. Subj.* **desahúcie, desahúcies, desahúcie, desahúcien.** *Imperf.* **desahúcia, desahúcie, desahúcien**

desahúcio /desa'uθio; desa'usio/ *m*, ejection, dispossession (of tenants)

desahumar /desau'mar/ *vt* to clear of smoke

desairado /desai'raðo/ *a* unattractive, graceless, ugly; unsuccessful, crestfallen; slighted

desairar /desai'rar/ *vt* to disdain, slight, disregard; underrate (things)

desaire /des'aire/ *m*, gracelessness, ugliness; insult, slight

desalabanza /desala'βanθa; desala'βansa/ *f*, disparagement; criticism

desalación /desala'θion; desala'sion/ *f*, desalinization

desalado /desa'laðo/ *a* anxious, precipitate, hasty

desalar /desa'lar/ *vt* to remove the salt from; take off wings; —*vr* walk or run at great speed; long for, yearn

desalentar /desalen'tar/ *vt irr* to make breathing difficult (work, fatigue); discourage; —*vr* be depressed or sad. See **sentar**

desaliento /desa'liento/ *m*, depression, discouragement, dismay

desalinear /desaline'ar/ *vt* to throw out of the straight

desaliñar /desali'ɲar/ *vt* to disarrange, make untidy, crumple

desaliño /desa'liɲo/ *m*, untidiness, slovenliness; negligence, carelessness

desalmado /desal'maðo/ *a* soulless, conscienceless; cruel

desalmamiento /desalma'miento/ *m*, inhumanity, consciencelessness; cruelty

desalmidonar /desalmiðo'nar/ *vt* to remove starch from

desalojamiento /desaloha'miento/ *m*, dislodgement, ejection

desalojar /desalo'har/ *vt* to dislodge, remove, eject; —*vi* move out, remove

desalquilado /desalki'laðo/ *a* untenanted, vacant

desalquilar /desalki'lar/ *vt* to leave, or cause to leave, rented premises

desalterar /desalte'rar/ *vt* to soothe, calm

desamarrar /desama'rrar/ *vt* to untie; separate; *Naut.* unmoor

desamor /desa'mor/ *m*, indifference; lack of sentiment or affection; hatred

desamotinarse /desamoti'narse/ *vr* to cease from rebellion; submit

desamparar /desampa'rar/ *vt* to abandon, forsake; leave (a place)

desamparo /desam'paro/ *m*, desertion; need

desamueblado /desamue'βlaðo/ *a* unfurnished

desamueblar /desamue'βlar/ *vt* to empty of furniture

desangrar /desaŋ'grar/ *vt Med.* to bleed; drain (lake, etc.); impoverish, bleed; —*vr* lose much blood

desanidar /desani'ðar/ *vi* to leave the nest; —*vt* eject, expel

desanimado /desani'maðo/ *a* downhearted; (of places) dull, quiet

desanimar /desani'mar/ *vt* to discourage, depress

desanublar, /desanu'βlar,/ *vt* **desanublarse** *vr* to clear up (weather)

desanudar /desanu'ðar/ *vt* to untie; disentangle

desapacibilidad /desapaθiβili'ðað; desapasiβili'ðað/ *f*, disagreeableness, unpleasantness

desapacible /desapa'θiβle; desapa'siβle/ *a* disagreeable; unpleasant; unsociable

desaparecer /desapare'θer; desapare'ser/ *vt irr* to cause to disappear; —*vi* and *vr* disappear. See **conocer**

desaparecido /desapare'θiðo; desapare'siðo/ *a* late (deceased); *Mil.* missing

desaparejar /desapare'har/ *vt* to unharness

desaparición /desapari'θion; desapari'sion/ *f*, disappearance

desapegar /desape'gar/ *vt* to unstick, undo; —*vr* be indifferent, cast off a love or affection

desapego /desa'pego/ *m*, lack of affection or interest, coolness

desapercibido /desaperθi'βiðo; desapersi'βiðo/ *a* unnoticed; unprovided, unprepared

desapercibimiento /desaperθiβi'miento; desapersiβi'miento/ *m*, unpreparedness

desapiadado /desapia'ðaðo/ *a* merciless

desaplicación /desaplika'θion; desaplika'sion/ *f*, laziness, lack of application; carelessness, negligence

desaplicado /desapli'kaðo/ *a* lazy; careless

desapoderado /desapoðe'raðo/ *a* precipitate, uncontrolled; furious, violent

desapoderar /desapoðe'rar/ *vt* to dispossess, rob; remove from office

desapolillar /desapoli'ʎar; desapoli'yar/ *vt* to free from moths; —*vr Inf.* take an airing

desaposentar /desaposen'tar/ *vt* to evict; drive away

desapreciar /desapre'θiar; desapre'siar/ *vt* to scorn

desaprensivo /desapren'siβo/ *a* unscrupulous

desapretar /desapre'tar/ **(se)** *vt* and *vr irr* to slacken. See **acertar**

desaprisionar /desaprisio'nar/ *vt* to release from prison

desaprobación /desaproβa'θion; desaproβa'sion/ *f*, disapproval

desaprobar /desapro'βar/ *vt irr* to disapprove; disagree with. See **probar**

desapropiamiento /desapropia'miento/ *m*, renunciation or transfer of property

desapropiarse /desapropi'arse/ *vr* to renounce or transfer (property)

desaprovechado /desaproβe't ʃaðo/ *a* unprofitable; backward; unintelligent

desaprovechar /desaproβe't ʃar/ *vt* to take no advantage of, waste; —*vi Fig.* lose ground, lose what one has gained

desarmar /desar'mar/ *vt* to disarm; dismantle, dismount; appease

desarme /de'sarme/ *m*, disarming; disarmament

desarraigar /desarrai'gar/ *vt* to pull up by root (plants); extirpate, suppress; eradicate (opinion, etc.); exile

desarraigo /desa'rraigo/ *m*, uprooting; extirpation; eradication; exile

desarreglado /desarre'glaðo/ *a* disarranged; untidy; intemperate, immoderate

desarreglar /desarre'glar/ *vt* to disarrange

desarreglo /desa'rreglo/ *m*, disorder; disarrangement; irregularity

desarrendar /desarren'dar/ *vt irr* to unbridle a horse; end a tenancy or lease. See **recomendar**

desarrollar /desarro'ʎar; desarro'yar/ *vt* to unroll; increase, develop, grow, unfold; explain (theory); —*vr* develop, grow

desarrollo /desa'rroʎo; des'arroyo/ *m*, unrolling; development; growth; explanation

desarropar /desarro'par/ *vt* to uncover, remove the covers, etc. from

desarticular /desartiku'lar/ *vt* to disarticulate; *Mech.* disconnect

desaseado /desase'aðo/ *a* dirty; unkempt, slovenly

desaseo /desa'seo/ *m*, dirtiness; slovenliness

desasosegar /desasose'gar/ *vt irr* to disturb, make anxious. See **cegar**

desasosiego /desaso'siego/ *m*, uneasiness, disquiet

desastre /de'sastre/ *m*, disaster, calamity

desastroso /desas'troso/ *a* unfortunate, calamitous

desatacar /desata'kar/ *vt* to unfasten, undo, unbutton

desatadura /desata'ðura/ *f*, untying

desatar /desa'tar/ *vt* to untie; melt, dissolve; elucidate, explain; —*vr* loosen the tongue; lose self control; lose all reserve; unbosom oneself

desatascar /desatas'kar/ *vt* to pull out of the mud; free from obstruction; extricate from difficulties

desatavío /desata'βio/ *m*, carelessness in dress, slovenliness

desatención /desaten'θion; desaten'sion/ *f*, inattention, abstraction; incivility

desatender /desaten'der/ *vt irr* to pay no attention to; disregard, ignore. See **entender**

desatentado /desaten'taðo/ *a* imprudent, ill-advised; excessive, immoderate

desatento /desa'tento/ *a* inattentive, abstracted; discourteous

desatinado /desati'naðo/ *a* foolish, imprudent, wild

desatinar /desati'nar/ *vt* to bewilder; —*vi* behave foolishly; lose one's bearings

desatino /desa'tino/ *m*, folly, foolishness, imprudence, rashness; blunder, faux pas, mistake

desatrancar /desatran'kar/ *vt* to unbar the door; remove obstacles

desaturdir /desatur'ðir/ *vt* to rouse (from torpor, etc.)

desautorizar /desautori'θar; desautori'sar/ *vt* to remove from authority; discredit

desavenencia /desaβe'nenθia; desaβe'nensia/ *f*, disharmony, disagreement

desavenido /desaβe'niðo/ *a* disagreeing, discordant

desavenir /desaβe'nir/ *vt irr* to upset. See **venir**

desaventajado /desaβenta'haðo/ *a* disadvantageous; unfavorable, inferior

desaviar /desa'βiar/ *vt* to lead astray; deprive of a necessity; —*vr* lose one's way

desavisado /desaβi'saðo/ *a* unaware, unprepared

desavisar /desaβi'sar/ *vt* to take back one's previous advice

desayunador /desayuna'ðor/ *m*, breakfast nook

desayunarse /desayu'narse/ *vr* to have breakfast, eat breakfast

desayuno /desa'yuno/ *m*, breakfast

desazón /desa'θon; desa'son/ *f*, insipidity, lack of flavor; poorness (soil); anxiety, trouble; vexation

desazonar /desaθo'nar; desaso'nar/ *vt* to make insipid; make anxious, worry; vex; —*vr* feel out of sorts

desbandada /desβan'daða/ *f*, dispersal, rout. **a la d.,** in confusion or disorder

desbandarse /desβan'darse/ *vr* to disband, retreat in disorder; *Mil.* desert

desbaratado /desβara'taðo/ *a Inf.* corrupt, vicious

desbaratar /desβara'tar/ *vt* to spoil, destroy; dissipate, waste; foil, thwart (a plot); *Mil.* rout; —*vi* talk foolishly; —*vr* go too far, behave badly

desbastar /desβas'tar/ *vt* to plane, dress; polish, refine, civilize

desbocar /desβo'kar/ *vt* to break the spout or neck (of jars, etc.); —*vi* run (into) (of streets, etc.); —*vr* bolt (horses); curse, swear

desboquillar /desβoki'ʎar/ desβoki'yar/ *vt* to remove or break a stem or mouthpiece

desbordamiento /desβorða'miento/ *m*, overflowing, flood

desbordarse /desβor'ðarse/ *vr* to overflow; lose self-control. **d. en alabanzas para,** to heap praise on

desbravar /desβra'βar/ *vt* to break in (horses, etc.); —*vi* grow less savage; lose force, decrease

descabalgadura /deskaβalga'ðura/ *f*, alighting (from horses, etc.)

descabalgar /deskaβal'gar/ *vi* to alight (from horse); —*vt* dismantle (gun)

descabellado /deskaβe'ʎaðo; deskaβe'yaðo/ *a* disheveled; ridiculous, foolish

descabellar /deskaβe'ʎar; deskaβe'yar/ *vt* to disarrange, ruffle (hair)

descabezado /deskaβe'θaðo; deskaβe'saðo/ *a* headless; rash, impetuous

descabezar /deskaβe'θar; deskaβe'sar/ *vt* to behead; cut the top off (trees, etc.); *Fig. Inf.* break the back of (work); —*vi* abut, join; —*vr* (*with con* or *en*) rack one's brains about

descalabazarse /deskalaβa'θarse; deskalaβa'sarse/ *vr Inf.* to rack one's brains

descalabradura /deskalaβra'ðura/ *f*, head wound or scar

descalabrar /deskala'βrar/ *vt* to wound in the head; wound; harm

descalabro /deska'laβro/ *m*, misfortune, mishap

descalzar /deskal'θar; deskal'sar/ *vt* to remove the shoes and stockings; undermine; —*vr* remove one's shoes and stockings; lose a shoe (horses)

descalzo /des'kalθo; des'kalso/ *a* barefoot

descaminar /deskami'nar/ *vt* to lead astray; pervert, corrupt

descamisado /deskami'saðo/ **(-da)** *a Inf.* shirtless; ragged, poor —*n Inf.* down and out, outcast; vagabond

descansado /deskan'saðo/ *a* rested, refreshed; tranquil

descansar /deskan'sar/ *vi* to rest, repose oneself; have relief (from anxiety, etc.); sleep; *Agr.* lie fallow; sleep in death; (*with en*) trust, have confidence in; (*with sobre*) lean on or upon; —*vt* (*with sobre*) rest (a thing) on another. **¡Que en paz descanse!** May he rest in peace!

descanso /des'kanso/ *m*, rest, repose; relief (from care); landing of stairs; *Mech.* bench, support; *Mil.* stand easy

descarado /deska'raðo/ *a* impudent, brazen

descararse /deska'rarse/ *vr* to behave impudently

descarga /des'karga/ *f*, unloading; *Naut.* discharge of cargo; *Elec.* discharge; *Mil.* volley. **d. cerrada,** dense volley, fusillade

descargadero /deskarga'ðero/ *m*, wharf

descargador /deskarga'ðor/ *m*, unloader, docker; *Elec.* discharger

descargar /deskar'gar/ *vt* to unload; *Mil.* fire; unload (fire-arms); *Elec.* discharge; rain (blows) upon; *Fig.* free, exonerate; —*vi* disembogue (of rivers); burst (clouds); —*vr* relinquish (employment); shirk responsibility; *Law.* clear oneself

descargo /des'kargo/ *m*, unloading; *Com.* acquittance; *Law.* answer to an impeachment

descargue /des'karge/ *m*, unloading

descarnado /deskar'naðo/ *a* fleshless; scraggy; spare, lean

descarnador /deskarna'ðor/ *m*, dental scraper; tanner's scraper

descarnar /deskar'nar/ *vt* to scrape off flesh; corrode; inspire indifference to earthly things

descaro /des'karo/ *m*, impudence

descarriar /deska'rriar/ *vt* to lead astray; —*vr* be lost, be separated (from others); *Fig.* go astray

descarrilamiento /deskarrila'miento/ *m*, derailment

descarrilar /deskarri'lar/ *vi* to run off the track, be derailed

descarrío /deska'rrio/ *m*, losing one's way

descartar /deskar'tar/ *vt* to put aside; —*vr* discard (cards); shirk, make excuses

descascarar /deskaska'rar/ *vt* to peel; shell; —*vr* peel off

descendencia /desθen'denθia; dessen'densia/ *f*, descendants, offspring; lineage, descent

descender /desθen'der; dessen'der/ *vi irr* to descend; flow (liquids); (*with de*) descend from, derive from; —*vt* lower, let down. See **entender**

descendiente /desθen'diente; dessen'diente/ *mf* descendant, offspring —*a* descending

descenso /des'θenso; des'senso/ *m*, descent; lowering, letting down; degradation

descentralizar /desθentrali'θar; dessentrali'sar/ *vt* to decentralize

desceñir /desθe'ɲir; desse'ɲir/ **(se)** *vt* and *vr irr* to ungird, remove a girdle, etc. See **ceñir**

descepar /desθe'par; desse'par/ *vt* to tear up by the roots; *Fig.* extirpate

descercado /desθer'kaðo; desser'kaðo/ *a* unfenced, open

descifrable /desθi'fraβle; dessi'fraβle/ *a* decipherable

descifrador /desθifra'ðor; dessifra'ðor/ *m*, decipherer, decoder

descifrar /desθi'frar; dessi'frar/ *vt* to decipher; decode

descinchar /desθin't ʃar; dessin't ʃar/ *vt* to loosen or remove girths (of horse)

desclavar /deskla'βar/ *vt* to remove nails; unnail, unfasten

descoagular /deskoagu'lar/ *vt* to liquefy, dissolve, melt

descocado /desko'kaðo/ *a Inf.* brazen, saucy

descogollar /deskogo'ʎar; deskogo'yar/ *vt* to prune a tree of shoots; remove hearts (of lettuces, etc.)

descolar /desko'lar/ *vt irr* to cut off or dock an animal's tail. See **colar**

descolgar /deskol'gar/ *vt irr* to unhang; lower; —*vr* lower oneself (by rope, etc.); come down, descend; *Inf.* come out (with), utter. See **volcar**

descollar /desko'ʎar; desko'yar/ *vi irr* to excel, be outstanding. See **degollar**

descoloramiento /deskolora'miento/ *m*, discoloration

descolorar /deskolo'rar/ *vt* to discolor; —*vr* be discolored

descolorido /deskolo'riðo/ *a* discolored; pale-colored; pallid

descomedido /deskome'ðiðo/ *a* excessive, disproportionate; rude

descomedimiento /deskomeði'miento/ *m*, disrespect, lack of moderation, rudeness

descomedirse /deskome'ðirse/ *vr irr* to be disrespectful or rude. See **pedir**

descomponer /deskompo'ner/ *vt irr* to disorder, disarrange; *Chem.* decompose; unsettle; —*vr* go out of order; rot, putrefy; be ailing; lose one's temper. See **poner**

descomposición /deskomposi'θion; deskomposi'sion/ *f*, disorder, confusion; discomposure; *Chem.* decomposition; putrefaction

descompostura /deskompos'tura/ *f*, decomposition; slovenliness, dirtiness, untidiness; impudence, rudeness

descompuesto /deskom'puesto/ *a* rude, impudent

descomunal /deskomu'nal/ *a* enormous, extraordinary

desconcertar /deskonθer'tar; deskonser'tar/ *vt irr* to disorder, disarrange; dislocate (bones); disconcert, embarrass; —*vr* disagree; be impudent. See **acertar**

desconcierto /deskon'θierto; deskon'sierto/ *m*, disorder, disarrangement; dislocation; embarrassment; disagreement; impudence

desconectar /deskonek'tar/ *vt* to disconnect; switch off

desconfianza /deskon'fianθa; deskon'fiansa/ *f*, lack of confidence

desconfiar /deskon'fiar/ *vi* to lack confidence

desconocer /deskono'θer; deskono'ser/ *vt irr* to forget; be unaware of; deny, disown; pretend ignorance; not to understand (persons, etc.). See **conocer**

desconocido /deskono'θiðo; deskono-'siðo/ **(-da)** *a* unknown; ungrateful —*n* stranger; ingrate

desconocimiento /deskonoθi'miento; deskonosi'miento/ *m*, unawareness; ignorance; ingratitude

desconsiderado /deskonsiðe'raðo/ *a* inconsiderate; discourteous; rash

desconsolación /deskonsola'θion; deskonsola'sion/ *f*, affliction, trouble

desconsolar /deskonso'lar/ *vt irr* to afflict, make disconsolate; —*vr* grieve, despair. See **colar**

desconsuelo /deskon'suelo/ *m*, anguish, affliction, despair

descontar /deskon'tar/ *vt irr Com.* to make a discount; ignore, discount; take for granted, leave aside. See **contar**

descontentadizo /deskontenta'ðiθo; deskontenta'ðiso/ *a* discontented, difficult to please; fastidious, finicky

descontentar /deskonten'tar/ *vt* to displease; —*vr* be dissatisfied

descontento /deskon'tento/ *m*, discontent, dissatisfaction

descontextualizar /deskontekstuali'θar; deskontekstuali'sar/ *vt* to take out of context

descontrolarse /deskontro'larse/ *vr* to lose control, lose control of oneself

desconveniencia /deskombe'nienθia; deskombe'niensia/ *f*, inconvenience, unsuitability, disagreement

desconvenir /deskombe'nir/ *vi irr* to disagree; be unsuitable, unsightly or odd (things). See **venir**

descorazonamiento /deskoraθona-'miento; deskorasona'miento/ *m*, depression, despair

descorazonar /deskoraθo'nar; deskoraso'nar/ *vt* to tear out the heart; depress, discourage

descorchar /deskor't ʃar/ *vt* to take the cork from cork tree; draw a cork (bottles); force, break into (safes)

descorrer /desko'rrer/ *vt* to re-run (race, etc.); draw back (curtains, etc.); —*vi* run, flow (liquids)

descortés /deskor'tes/ *a* impolite

descortesía /deskorte'sia/ *f*, impoliteness, discourtesy

descoser /desko'ser/ *vt Sew.* to unpick; —*vr* be unpicked; be indiscreet or tactless

descosido /desko'siðo/ *a* tactless, talkative; *Fig.* disjointed; desultory; unsewn. *m*, *Sew.* rent, hole

descoyuntamiento /deskoyunta'miento/ *m*, dislocation (bones); irritation, bore; ache, pain

descoyuntar /deskoyun'tar/ *vt* to dislocate (bones); bore, annoy; —*vr* be dislocated

descrédito /des'kreðito/ *m,* fall in value (things); discredit (persons)

descreer /deskre'er/ *vt irr* to disbelieve; depreciate, disparage (persons). See **creer**

descreído /deskre'iðo/ **(-da)** *a* unbelieving —*n* unbeliever; infidel

describir /deskri'βir/ *vt* to describe; outline, sketch —*Past Part.* **descrito**

descripción /deskrip'θion; deskrip'sion/ *f,* description; *Law.* inventory

descuajar /deskua'har/ *vt* to liquefy; *Inf.* discourage; *Agr.* pull up by the root

descuartizar /deskuarti'θar; deskuarti'sar/ *vt* to quarter; joint (meat); *Inf.* carve, cut into pieces, break up

descubierto /desku'βierto/ *a* bareheaded; exposed. *m,* deficit. **al d.,** openly; in the open, without shelter. **girar en d.,** to overdraw (a bank account)

descubridor /deskuβri'ðor/ **(-ra)** *n* discoverer; inventor; explorer. *m, Mil.* scout

descubrimiento /deskuβri'miento/ *m,* find; discovery; revelation; newly discovered territory

descubrir /desku'βrir/ *vt* to reveal; show; discover; learn; unveil (memorials, etc.); —*vr* remove one's hat; show oneself, reveal one's whereabouts —*Past Part.* **descubierto**

descuento /des'kuento/ *m,* reduction; *Com.* rebate, discount

descuidado /deskui'ðaðo/ *a* negligent; careless; untidy; unprepared

descuidar /deskui'ðar/ *vt* to relieve (of responsibility, etc.); distract, occupy (attention, etc.); —*vi* and *vr* be careless; —*vr* (*with de* or *en*) neglect

descuido /des'kuiðo/ *m,* carelessness, negligence; oversight, mistake; incivility; forgetfulness; shameful act

desde /'desðe/ *prep* since, from (time or space); after (e.g. *d. hoy,* from today). **d. la ventana,** from the window. **d. allá,** from the other world. **d. aquella época,** since that time

desdecir /desðe'θir; desðe'sir/ *vi irr* (*with de*) to degenerate, be less good than; be discordant, clash; be unworthy of; —*vr* unsay one's words, retract. See **decir**

desdén /des'ðen/ *m,* indifference, coldness; disdain, scorn

desdeñar /desðe'ɲar/ *vt* to scorn; —*vr* (*with de*) dislike, be reluctant

desdeñoso /desðe'ɲoso/ *a* disdainful, scornful

desdibujado /desðiβu'haðo/ *a* badly drawn; blurred, confused

desdicha /des'ðitʃa/ *f,* misfortune; extreme poverty, misery. **por d.,** unfortunately

desdichado /desði'tʃaðo/ *a* unfortunate; *Inf.* timid, weak-kneed

desdicharse /desði'tʃarse/ *vr* to bewail one's fate

desdinerarse una fortuna /des-

ðine'rarse 'una for'tuna/ *vr* to spend a fortune

desdoblar /desðo'βlar/ *vt* to unfold

desdoro /des'ðoro/ *m,* discredit, dishonor

deseable /dese'aβle/ *a* desirable

desear /dese'ar/ *vt* to desire; yearn or long for

desechar /dese.t'tʃar/ *vt* to reject, refuse; scorn; cast out, expel; put away (thoughts, etc.); cast off (old clothes); turn (key); give up

desecho /de'setʃo/ *m,* residue, rest, remains; cast-off; scorn

desembalar /desemba'lar/ *vt* to unpack

desembarazar /desembara'θar; desembara'sar/ *vt* to clear of obstruction; disembarrass, free; vacate; —*vr Fig.* rid oneself of obstacles

desembarazo /desemba'raθo; desemba'raso/ *m,* freedom, insouciance, naturalness

desembarcadero /desembarka'ðero/ *m,* landing-stage

desembarcar /desembar'kar/ *vt* to unload; —*vt* disembark; alight from vehicle

desembarco /desem'barko/ *m,* disembarkation, landing; staircase landing

desembargar /desembar'gar/ *vt* to free of obstacles or impediments; *Law.* remove an embargo

desembargo /desem'bargo/ *m, Law.* removal of an embargo

desembarque /desem'barke/ *m,* disembarkation, landing

desembocadero /desemboka'ðero/ *m,* exit, way out; mouth (rivers, etc.)

desembocadura /desemboka'ðura/ *f,* mouth (rivers, etc.); street opening

desembocar /desembo'kar/ *vi* (*with en*) to lead to, end in; flow into (rivers)

desembolsar /desembol'sar/ *vt* to take out of a purse; pay, spend

desembolso /desem'bolso/ *m,* disbursement; expenditure

desemboscarse /desembos'karse/ *vr* to get out of the wood; extricate oneself from an ambush

desembozo /desem'boθo; desem'boso/ *m,* uncovering of the face

desembragar /desembra'gar/ *vt Mech.* to disengage (the clutch, etc.)

desembravecer /desembraβe'θer; desembraβe'ser/ *vt irr* to tame, domesticate. See **conocer**

desembriagar /desembria'gar/ **(se)** *vt* and *vr* to sober up (after a drinking bout)

desembrollar /desembro'ʎar; desembro'yar/ *vt Inf.* to disentangle, unravel

desemejanza /deseme'hanθa; deseme-'hansa/ *f,* unlikeness

desemejar /deseme'har/ *vi* to be unlike; —*vt* disfigure, deform

desempacar /desempa'kar/ *vt* to unpack

desempapelar /desempape'lar/ *vt* to unwrap, remove the paper from; remove wallpaper

desempaquetar /desempake'tar/ vt to unpack

desemparentado /desemparen'taðo/ a without relatives

desempedrar /desempe'ðrar/ vt irr to take up the flags (of a pavement). See **acertar**

desempeñar /desempe'ɲar/ vt to redeem (pledges); free from debt; fulfil (obligations, etc.); take out of pawn; hold, fill (an office); extricate (from difficulties, etc.); perform, carry out; *Theat.* act

desempeño /desempe'ɲo/ m, redemption of a pledge; fulfillment (of an obligation, etc.); performance, accomplishment; *Theat.* acting of a part

desempolvar /desempol'βar/ vt to free from dust, dust

desencadenar /desenkaðe'nar/ vt to unchain, unfetter; *Fig.* unleash, let loose; —vr *Fig.* break loose

desencajamiento /desenkaha'miento/ m, disjointedness, dislocation; ricketiness, broken-down appearance

desencajar /desenka'har/ vt to disconnect, disjoint; dislocate; —vr be out of joint; be contorted (of the face); be tired looking

desencantar /desenkan'tar/ vt to disenchant

desencanto /desen'kanto/ m, disenchantment; disillusionment

desencerrar /desenθe'rrar; desense'rrar/ vt irr to set at liberty; unlock; disclose, reveal. See **acertar**

desenchufar /desentʃu'far/ vt to disconnect, unplug (electric plugs, etc.)

desenclavijar /desenklaβi'har/ vt to remove the pegs or pins; disconnect, disjoint

desencolerizar /desenkoleri'θar; desenkoleri'sar/ vt to placate; —vr lose one's anger, grow calm

desenconar /desenko'nar/ vt to reduce (inflammation); appease (anger, etc.); —vr become calm

desencono /desen'kono/ m, reduction of inflammation; appeasement (of anger, etc.)

desenfadado /desenfa'ðaðo/ a expeditious; natural, at ease; gay; forward, bold; wide, spacious

desenfadar /desenfa'ðar/ vt to appease, make anger disappear

desenfado /desen'faðo/ m, freedom; ease; unconcern, frankness

desenfardar /desenfar'ðar/ vt to unpack bales

desenfrailar /desenfrai'lar/ vi to leave the cloister, become secularized; *Inf.* emancipate oneself

desenfrenar /desenfre'nar/ vt to unbridle (horses); —vr give rein to one's passions, etc.; break loose (storms, etc.)

desenfreno /desen'freno/ m, license, lasciviousness; complete freedom from restraint

desenganchar /desengan'tʃar/ vt to unhook; uncouple; unfasten; unharness

desengañador /desengaɲa'ðor/ a undeceiving

desengañar /desenga'ɲar/ vt to undeceive, disillusion

desengaño /desen'gaɲo/ m, undeceiving, disabuse; disillusionment

desengarzar /desengar'θar; desengar'sar/ vt to loosen from its setting; unlink, unhook, unclasp

desengastar /desengas'tar/ vt to remove from its setting (jewelry, etc.)

desengrasar /desengra'sar/ vt to remove the grease from, clean; —vi *Inf.* grow thin

desenlace /desen'laθe; desen'lase/ m, loosening, untying; *Lit.* denouement, climax (of play, etc.)

desenlazar /desenla'θar; desenla'sar/ vt to untie, unloose; *Lit.* unravel (a plot)

desenmarañar /desenmara'ɲar/ vt to disentangle; *Fig.* straighten out

desenmascarar /desenmaska'rar/ vt to remove the mask from; *Fig.* unmask

desenmudecer /desenmuðe'θer; desenmuðe'ser/ vi irr to be freed of a speech impediment; break silence, speak. See **conocer**

desenojar /deseno'har/ vt to soothe, appease; —vr distract oneself, amuse oneself

desenredar /desenre'ðar/ vt to disentangle; *Fig.* set right; straighten out; —vr extricate oneself, get out of a difficulty

desenredo /desen'reðo/ m, disentanglement; *Lit.* climax

desentablar /desenta'βlar/ vt to tear up planks or boards; disorder, disrupt

desentenderse /desenten'derse/ vr irr (with de) to pretend to be ignorant of; take no part in. See **entender**

desenterramiento /desenterra'miento/ m, disinterment; *Fig.* unearthing, recollection

desenterrar /desente'rrar/ vt irr to unbury, disinter; rummage out; *Fig.* unearth, bring up, recall. See **acertar**

desentoldar /desentol'dar/ vt to take away an awning; *Fig.* strip of ornament

desentonar /desento'nar/ vt to humiliate; —vi *Mus.* be out of tune; speak rudely; —vr be inharmonious; raise the voice (anger, etc.), behave badly

desentono /desen'tono/ m, bad behavior, rudeness; *Mus.* discord; grating quality or harshness (of voice)

desentorpecer /desentorpe'θer; desentorpe'ser/ vt irr to restore feeling to (numbed limbs); free from torpor; —vr become bright and intelligent. See **conocer**

desentramparse /desentram'parse/ vr *Inf.* free oneself from debt

desentrañar /desentra'ɲar/ vt to disembowel; *Fig.* unravel, penetrate; —vr give away one's all

desentumecer /desentume'θer; desentume'ser/ vt irr to free from numbness (limbs); —*vr* be restored to feeling (numb limbs). See **conocer**

desenvainar /desembai'nar/ *vt* to unsheath; *Inf.* reveal, bring into the open

desenvoltura /desembol'tura/ *f,* naturalness, ease, freedom; eloquence, facility (of speech); effrontery, audacity, shamelessness (especially in women)

desenvolver /desembol'βer/ *vt irr* to unroll; unfold; *Fig.* unravel, explain; *Fig.* develop, work out (theories, etc.); —*vr* unroll; unfold; lose one's timidity, blossom out; be over-bold; extricate oneself (from a difficulty). See **resolver**

desenvuelto /desem'buelto/ *a* natural, easy; impudent, bold

deseo /de'seo/ *m,* desire, will, wish

deseoso /dese'oso/ *a* desirous, wishful

desequilibrar /desekili'βrar/ **(se)** *vt* and *vr* to unbalance

desequilibrio /deseki'liβrio/ *m,* lack of balance; confusion, disorder; mental instability

deserción /deser'θion; deser'sion/ *f, Mil.* desertion. **d. estudiantil,** school dropout

desertar /deser'tar/ *vt Mil.* to desert; *Inf.* quit

desertor /deser'tor/ *m, Mil.* deserter; *Inf.* quitter

desesperación /desespera'θion; desespera'sion/ *f,* desperation, despair; frenzy, violence

desesperado /desespe'raðo/ *a* desperate, hopeless; frenzied

desesperanza /desespe'ranθa; desespe'ransa/ *f,* despair; hopelessness

desesperanzar /desesperan'θar; desesperan'sar/ *vt* to render hopeless; —*vr* despair, lose hope

desesperar /desespe'rar/ *vt* to make hopeless; *Inf.* annoy, make furious; —*vr* lose hope, despair; be frenzied

desestimación /desestima'θion; desestima'sion/ *f,* disrespect, lack of esteem; rejection

desestimar /desesti'mar/ *vt* to scorn; reject

desfachatado /desfatʃa'taðo/ *a Inf.* impudent, brazen

desfachatez /desfatʃa'teθ; desfatʃa'tes/ *f, Inf.* effrontery, cheek

desfalcador /desfalka'ðor/ **(-ra)** *a* embezzling —*n* embezzler

desfalcar /desfal'kar/ *vt* to remove a part of; embezzle

desfalco /des'falko/ *m,* diminution, reduction; embezzlement

desfallecer /desfaʎe'θer; desfaye'ser/ *vt irr* to weaken; —*vi* grow weak; faint, swoon. See **conocer**

desfallecimiento /desfaʎeθi'miento; desfayesi'miento/ *m,* weakness, languor; depression, discouragement; faint, swoon

desfavorable /desfaβo'raβle/ *a* unfavorable; hostile, contrary

desfavorecer /desfaβore'θer; des-

faβore'ser/ *vt irr* to withdraw one's favor, scorn; disfavor; oppose. See **conocer**

desfiguración /desfigura'θion; desfigura'sion/ *f,* deformation; disfigurement

desfigurar /desfigu'rar/ *vt* to deform, misshape; disfigure; *Fig.* disguise, mask; obscure, darken; distort, misrepresent; —*vr* be disfigured (by rage, etc.)

desfiladero /desfila'ðero/ *m,* defile, gully

desfilar /desfi'lar/ *vi* to walk in file; *Inf.* file out; *Mil.* file or march past

desfile /des'file/ *m, Mil.* march past; parade; walk past; procession

desflorar /desflo'rar/ *vt* to tarnish, stain; deflower, violate; *Fig.* touch upon, deal lightly with

desfortalecer /desfortale'θer; desfortale'ser/ *vt irr Mil.* to dismantle a fortress. See **conocer**

desgaire /des'gaire/ *m,* untidiness, slovenliness; affectation of carelessness (in dress); scornful gesture. **al d.,** with an affectation of carelessness, negligently

desgajar /desga'har/ *vt* to tear off a tree branch; break; —*vr* break off; dissociate oneself (from)

desgana /des'gana/ *f,* lack of appetite; lack of interest, indifference; reluctance

desganar /desga'nar/ *vt* to dissuade; —*vr* lose one's appetite; become bored or indifferent, lose interest

desgarbado /desgar'βaðo/ *a* slovenly, slatternly; gawky, graceless

desgarrado /desga'rraðo/ *a* dissolute, vicious; impudent, brazen

desgarrar /desga'rrar/ *vt* to tear; —*vr* leave, tear oneself away

desgarro /des'garro/ *m,* tearing, rent, breach; boastfulness, impudence, effrontery

desgastar /desgas'tar/ *vt* to corrode, wear away; spoil, corrupt; —*vr* lose one's vigor, grow weak; wear away

desgaste /des'gaste/ *m,* attrition; wearing down or away; corrosion; wear and tear

desgobernar /desgoβer'nar/ *vt irr* to upset or rise against the government; dislocate (bones); *Naut.* neglect the tiller; —*vr* affect exaggerated movements in dancing. See **recomendar**

desgobierno /desgo'βierno/ *m,* misgovernment; mismanagement; maladministration; disorder, tumult

desgoznar /desgoθ'nar; desgos'nar/ *vt* to unhinge; —*vr Fig.* lose one's self-control

desgracia /des'graθia; des'grasia/ *f,* misfortune, adversity; mishap, piece of bad luck; disgrace, disfavor; disagreeableness, brusqueness; ungraciousness. **por d.,** unhappily, unfortunately

desgraciado /desgra'θiaðo; desgra'siaðo/ *a* unfortunate, unhappy; unlucky; dull, boring; disagreeable

desgraciar /desgra'θiar; desgra'siar/ *vt* to displease; spoil the development (of), destroy; maim; —*vr* fall out of friendship;

be out of favor; turn out badly, fail; be destroyed or spoiled; be maimed

desgranar /desgra'nar/ *vt Agr.* to thresh, flail; —*vr* break (string of beads, etc.)

desgrasante /desgra'sante/ *m*, grease remover

desgreñar /desgre'ɲar/ *vt* to dishevel the hair; —*vr Inf.* pull each other's hair, come to blows

desguarnecer /desguarne'θer; desguarne'ser/ *vt irr* to strip of trimming; *Mil.* demilitarize; *Mil.* disarm; dismantle; unharness. See **conocer**

deshabitado /desaβi'taðo/ *a* uninhabited, empty

deshabituar /desaβi'tuar/ *vt* to disaccustom; —*vr* lose the habit, become unaccustomed

deshacer /desa'θer; desa'ser/ *vt irr* to undo; destroy; *Mil.* rout, defeat; take to pieces; melt; pulp (paper); untie (knots, etc.); open (parcels); diminish, decrease; break in pieces, smash; *Fig.* obstruct, spoil; —*vr* be wasted or spoiled; be full of anxiety; vanish; try or work very hard; injure oneself; be emaciated, grow extremely thin; (*with de*) part with. **d. agravios**, to right wrongs. See **hacer**

desharrapado /desarra'paðo/ *a* tattered, shabby

deshebillar /deseβi'ʎar; deseβi'yar/ *vt* to unbuckle

deshecha /des'etʃa/ *f*, pretense, evasion; courteous farewell; obligatory departure

deshelar /dese'lar/ *vt irr* to thaw, melt. See **acertar**

desherbar /deser'βar/ *vt irr* to pull up weeds. See **acertar**

desheredar /desere'ðar/ *vt* disinherit; —*vr Fig.* lower oneself

desherrar /dese'rrar/ *vt irr* to unfetter, unchain; strike off horseshoes; —*vr* lose a shoe (horses). See **acertar**

deshidratación /desiðrata'θion; desiðrata'sion/ *f*, dehydration

deshidratar /desiðra'tar/ *vt* to dehydrate

deshielo /des'ielo/ *m*, thaw

deshilado /desi'laðo/ *a* in single file. *m*, *Sew.* drawn-thread work (gen. *pl*). **a la deshilada**, *Mil.* in file formation; secretly

deshiladura /desila'ðura/ *f*, unraveling

deshilar /desi'lar/ *vt* to unravel; *Sew.* draw threads; *Cul.* shred, grate

deshilvanado /desilβa'naðo/ *a Fig.* disjointed, disconnected

deshilvanar /desilβa'nar/ *vt Sew.* to remove the tacking threads

deshincar /desin'kar/ *vt* to pull out, remove, draw out

deshinchar /desin'tʃar/ *vt* to remove a swelling; deflate; lessen the anger of; —*vr* decrease, subside (swellings); deflate; *Inf.* grow humble

deshollejar /desoʎe'har; desoye'har/ *vt* to skin, peel (fruit); shell (peas, etc.)

deshollinador /desoʎina'ðor; desoyina-

'ðor/ *m*, chimney-sweep; wall-brush; chemical chimney cleaner

deshollinar /desoʎi'nar; desoyi'nar/ *vt* to sweep chimneys; clean down walls; *Inf.* examine closely

deshonestidad /desonesti'ðað/ *f*, immodesty, shamelessness; indecency

deshonesto /deso'nesto/ *a* shameless, immodest; dissolute, vicious; indecent

deshonor /deso'nor/ *m*, dishonor; disgrace, insult

deshonrabuenos /desonra'βuenos/ *mf Inf.* slanderer; degenerate

deshonrador /desonra'ðor/ **(-ra)** *a* dishonorable —*n* dishonorer

deshonrar /deson'rar/ *vt* to dishonor; insult; seduce (women)

deshonroso /deson'roso/ *a* dishonorable, insulting, indecent

deshora /de'sora/ *f*, inconvenient time. **a d.,** *or* **a deshoras,** at an inconvenient time, unseasonably; extempore

deshuesar /desue'sar/ *vt* to bone, remove the bone (from meat); stone (fruit)

deshumedecer /desumeðe'θer; desumeðe'ser/ *vt irr* to dry; —*vr* become dry. See **conocer**

desidia /de'siðia/ *f*, negligence; laziness

desidioso /desi'ðioso/ *a* negligent; lazy

desierto /de'sierto/ *a* deserted, uninhabited, solitary. *m*, desert; wilderness

designación /designa'θion; designa'sion/ *f*, designation; appointment

designar /desig'nar/ *vt* to plan, intend; designate; appoint

designio /de'signio/ *m*, intention, idea

desigual /desi'gual/ *a* unequal; uneven (ground); rough; arduous, difficult; changeable

desigualar /desigua'lar/ *vt* to make unequal; —*vr* prosper

desigualdad /desigual'dað/ *f*, inequality; unevenness, rockiness; *Fig.* changeability; variability

desilusión /desilu'sion/ *f*, disillusionment; disappointment

desilusionar /desilusio'nar/ *vt* to disillusion; —*vr* become disillusioned; be undeceived

desinclinar /desinkli'nar/ *vt* to dissuade

desinfección /desinfek'θion; desinfek'sion/ *f*, disinfection

desinfectante /desinfek'tante/ *a* and *m*, disinfectant

desinfectar /desinfek'tar/ *vt* to disinfect

desinflación /desinfla'θion; desinfla'sion/ *f*, deflation

desinflar /desin'flar/ *vt* to deflate

desinterés /desinte'res/ *m*, disinterestedness

desinteresado /desintere'saðo/ *a* disinterested; generous

desinteresarse /desintere'sarse/ *vr* to lose interest, grow indifferent

desistencia, /desis'tenθia,; desis'tensia/ *f*, **desistimiento** *m*, desistance, ceasing

desistir /desis'tir/ *vi* to desist; cease; *Law.* renounce

desjuntar /deshun'tar/ **(se)** *vt* and *vr* to separate; divide

deslavar /desla'βar/ *vt* to wash superficially; spoil by washing, take away the body of (cloth, etc.)

desleal /desle'al/ *a* disloyal, treacherous

deslealtad /desleal'taδ/ *f*, disloyalty

deslenguado /desleŋ'guaδo/ *a* shameless, foulmouthed

desliar /des'liar/ *vt* to untie, undo, unloose

desligadúra /desliga'δura/ *f*, untying, loosening

desligar /desli'gar/ *vt* to unfasten, unbind; *Fig.* solve, unravel; relieve of an obligation; *Mus.* play staccato; —*vr* come unfastened, grow loose. **desligarse de,** to weasel out of, wiggle out of (a promise)

deslindar /deslin'dar/ *vt* to fix the boundaries (of); limit, circumscribe

desliz /des'liθ; des'lis/ *m*, slipping, slip, slide; skid; indiscretion, slip; peccadillo, trifling fault

deslizadizo /desliθa'δiθo; deslisa'δiso/ *a* slippery

deslizar /desli'θar; desli'sar/ *vt* to slip, slide; skid; —*vr* commit an indiscretion; speak or act unwisely; escape, slip away; slip; skid

deslucido /des'luθiδo; des'lusiδo/ *a* fruitless, vain; stupid, clumsy, awkward; discolored; tarnished, dull; unsuccessful

deslucimiento /desluθi'miento; deslusi'miento/ *m*, clumsiness, gracelessness; failure, lack of success

deslucir /deslu'θir; deslu'sir/ *vt irr* to fade; discolor, stain; tarnish; spoil; sully the reputation of; —*vr* do a thing badly, fail at. See **lucir**

deslumbrador /deslumbra'δor/ *a* dazzling

deslumbrar /deslumb'rar/ *vt* to dazzle; confuse, bewilder; *Fig.* daze (with magnificence)

deslustrar /deslus'trar/ *vt* to dull, dim, tarnish; frost (glass); discredit, sully (reputation)

deslustre /des'lustre/ *m*, dullness, tarnish; frosting (of glass); disgrace, stigma

deslustroso /deslus'troso/ *a* ugly, unsuitable, unbecoming

desmadejar /desmaδe'har/ *vt* to debilitate, enervate

desmán /des'man/ *m*, outrageous behavior; disaster, misfortune

desmandado /desman'daδo/ *a* disobedient

desmandar /desman'dar/ *vt* to cancel, revoke (orders); withdraw (an offer) —*vr* behave badly; stray

desmantelado /desmante'laδo/ *a* dismantled, dilapidated

desmantelamiento /desmantela'miento/ *m*, dismantling; dilapidation

desmantelar /desmante'lar/ *vt* to dismantle; abandon, forsake

desmaña /des'maɲa/ *f*, lack of dexterity, clumsiness, awkwardness

desmañado /desma'ɲaδo/ *a* clumsy, awkward, unhandy

desmayar /desma'yar/ *vt* to cause to faint; —*vi* grow discouraged, lose heart; —*vr* swoon, faint

desmayo /des'mayo/ *m*, depression, discouragement; faint, swoon

desmedido /desme'δiδo/ *a* disproportionate; excessive

desmedirse /desme'δirse/ *vr* to misbehave, go too far

desmedrado /desme'δraδo/ *a* thin, emaciated; deteriorated, spoiled

desmedrar /desme'δrar/ *vt* to spoil, ruin; —*vi* deteriorate; decline

desmedro /des'meδro/ *m*, impairment; decline, deterioration. **en d, de,** to the detriment of

desmejorar /desmeho'rar/ *vt* to spoil, impair, cause to deteriorate; —*vr* deteriorate; —*vt* and *vr* decline in health; lose one's beauty

desmelenar /desmele'nar/ *vt* to ruffle or dishevel the hair

desmembrar /desmem'brar/ *vt* to dismember; separate, divide

desmentida /desmen'tiδa/ *f*, action of giving the lie to

desmentir /desmen'tir/ *vt irr* to give the lie to; contradict, deny; lower oneself; behave unworthily; —*vi* deviate (from right direction, etc.). See **sentir**

desmenuzar /desmenu'θar; desmenu'sar/ *vt* to crumble, break into small pieces; *Fig.* examine in detail; —*vr* be broken up

desmerecedor /desmereθe'δor; desmerese'δor/ *a* unworthy

desmerecer /desmere'θer; desmere'ser/ *vt irr* to become undeserving of; —*vi* deteriorate; be inferior to. See **conocer**

desmesura /desme'sura/ *f*, insolence; disproportion; excess

desmesurado /desmesu'raδo/ *a* disproportionate; excessive; enormous; insolent, uncivil

desmesurar /desmesu'rar/ *vt* to disarrange, disorder; —*vr* be insolent

desmigajar /desmiga'har/ **(se)** *vt* and *vr* to crumble

desmilitarizar /desmilitari'θar; desmilitari'sar/ *vt* to demilitarize

desmonetización /desmonetiθa'θion; desmonetisa'sion/ *f*, demonetization; conversion of coin into bullion

desmontable /desmon'taβle/ *a* movable; sectional

desmontadura /desmonta'δura/ *f*, clearing; deforestation; leveling; demounting; dismounting

desmontar /desmon'tar/ *vt* to clear wholly or partly of trees or shrubs; clear up (rubbish); level (ground); dismantle;

dismount; uncock (firearms); —*vi* and *vr* dismount (from horse, etc.)

desmonte /des'monte/ *m*, clearing of trees and shrubs; clearing, cleared ground; timber remaining

desmoralización /desmoraliθa'θion; desmoralisa'sion/ *f*, demoralization, corruption

desmoralizador /desmoraliθa'ðor; desmoralisa'ðor/ *a* demoralizing

desmoralizar /desmorali'θar; desmorali-'sar/ *vt* to demoralize, corrupt

desmoronamiento /desmorona'miento/ *m*, crumbling; decay, ruin

desmoronar /desmoro'nar/ *vt* to destroy, decay; crumble; —*vr* crumble away, fall into ruin; decline, decay; wane, fade (power, etc.)

desmovilizar /desmoβili'θar; desmoβili-'sar/ *vt* to demobilize

desnacificación /desnaθifika'θion; desnasifika'sion/ *f*, denazification

desnatar /desna'tar/ *vt* to skim; *Fig.* take the cream or best

desnaturalización /desnaturaliθa'θion; desnaturalisa'sion/ *f*, denaturalization

desnaturalizar /desnaturali'θar; desnaturali'sar/ *vt* to denaturalize; exile; deform, disfigure, pervert; —*vr* give up one's country

desnivel /desni'βel/ *m*, unevenness; slope, drop

desnivelar /desniβe'lar/ **(se)** *vi* and *vr* to become uneven

desnudar /desnu'ðar/ *vt* to undress; *Fig.* despoil, strip, denude; —*vr* undress oneself; deprive oneself

desnudez /desnu'ðeθ; desnu'ðes/ *f*, nudity; nakedness; bareness; plainness

desnudo /des'nuðo/ *a* nude; ill-clad; bare, naked; clear, patent; *Fig.* destitute (of grace, etc.). *m*, *Art.* nude

desnutrición /desnutri'θion; desnutri-'sion/ *f*, malnutrition

desobedecer /desoβeðe'θer; desoβeðe'ser/ *vt irr* to disobey. See **conocer**

desobediencia /desoβe'ðienθia; desoβe-'ðiensia/ *f*, disobedience

desobediente /desoβe'ðiente/ *a* disobedient

desobligar /desoβli'gar/ *vt* to free from obligation; offend, hurt

desocupación /desokupa'θion; desokupa'sion/ *f*, lack of occupation; leisure

desocupado /desoku'paðo/ *a* idle; vacant, unoccupied

desocupar /desoku'par/ *vt* to empty; vacate; —*vr* give up an employment or occupation

desodorante /desoðo'rante/ *a* and *m*, deodorant

desojar /deso'har/ *vt* to break the eye of (needles, etc.); —*vr* gaze intently

desolación /desola'θion; desola'sion/ *f*, destruction, desolation; affliction

desolador /desola'ðor/ *a* desolate; grievous

desolar /deso'lar/ *vt irr* to lay waste, destroy; —*vr* grieve, be disconsolate. See **contar**

desollado /deso'ʎaðo; deso'yaðo/ *a* Inf. impertinent, barefaced. *m*, carcass

desolladura /desoʎa'ðura; desoya'ðura/ *f*, flaying, skinning; *Irif.* slander

desollar /deso'ʎar; deso'yar/ *vt irr* to flay, skin; harm, discredit. **d. vivo,** *Inf.* to extort an exorbitant price; slander. See **contar**

desopinado /desopi'naðo/ *a* discredited

desopinar /desopi'nar/ *vt* to discredit, defame

desorden /de'sorðen/ *m*, disorder, disarray; confusion; excess

desordenado /desorðe'naðo/ *a* disordered; vicious; licentious

desordenar /desorðe'nar/ *vt* to disorder; confuse; —*vr* go beyond the just limits; behave badly; be impertinent

desorganización /desorganiθa'θion; desorganisa'sion/ *f*, disorganization

desorientación /desorienta'θion; desorienta'sion/ *f*, disorientation, loss of bearings; lack of method, confusion

desorientar /desorien'tar/ *vt* to disorient; perplex, confuse; —*vr* lose one's way; be disoriented

desove /de'soβe/ *m*, spawning; spawning season

desovillar /desoβi'ʎar; desoβi'yar/ *vt* to unwind; uncoil; uncurl; explain, clarify

despabilado /despaβi'laðo/ *a* alert, wideawake; watchful, vigilant

despabilar /despaβi'lar/ *vt* to snuff (a candle); trim (lamps); hasten, expedite; finish quickly; steal, rob; *Fig.* quicken (intelligence, etc.); *Inf.* kill; —*vr* rouse oneself, wake up

despachador /despatʃa'ðor/ **(-ra)** *n* dispatcher, sender

despachar /despa'tʃar/ *vt* to expedite; dispatch, conclude; forward, send; attend to correspondence; sell; dismiss; *Inf.* serve in a shop; *Inf.* kill; —*vi* hasten; carry letters to be signed (in offices, etc.); —*vr* get rid of

despacho /despa'tʃo/ *m*, transaction, execution; study; office, room; department; booking-office; dispatch, shipment; expedient; commission, warrant; dispatch (diplomatic); telegram; telephone message. **d. particular,** private office

despachurrar /despa'tʃurrar/ *vt* Inf. to crush, squash; recount in a muddled fashion; *Fig.* squash flat, confound

despacio /des'paθio; des'pasio/ *adv* slowly, little by little; deliberately, leisurely —*interj* Careful! Gently now!

despacito /despa'θito; despa'sito/ *adv* Inf. very slowly

despalmar /despal'mar/ *vt* Naut. to careen, caulk

despampanar /despampa'nar/ *vt* Agr. to prune vines; Inf. amaze, stun, astound;

—*vi Inf.* relieve one's feelings; —*vr Inf.* receive a serious injury (through falling)

desparpajar /despar'paɣar/ *vt* to spoil; —*vi Inf.* chatter

desparpajo /despar'paxo/ *m, Inf.* loquaciousness, pertness; disorder, muddle

desparramar /desparra'mar/ *vt* to disperse, scatter; squander, waste (money, etc.); —*vr* amuse oneself; be dissipated

despavorido /despaβo'riðo/ *a* terrified, panicstricken

despechar /despe't ʃar/ *vt* to anger; make despair; *Inf.* wean; —*vr* be angry; be in despair

despecho /des'pet ʃo/ *m,* rancor, malice; despair. **a d. de,** in spite of

despechugar /despet ʃu'ɣar/ *vt* to cut off the breast (fowls); —*vr Inf.* show the bosom

despectivo /despek'tiβo/ *a* contemptuous, depreciatory

despedazar /despeða'θar; despeða'sar/ *vt* to cut or break into pieces; *Fig.* break (heart, etc.)

despedida /despe'ðiða/ *f,* dismissal, discharge; seeing off (a visitor, etc.); farewell, good-by

despedir /despe'ðir/ *vt irr* to throw out, emit, cast up; dismiss, discharge; see off (on a journey or after a visit); banish (from the mind); get rid of; —*vr* say good-by; leave (employment). See **pedir**

despegado /despe'ɣaðo/ *a Inf.* indifferent, unconcerned, cold

despegar /despe'ɣar/ *vt* to unstick; unglue; separate, detach; —*vr* become estranged; come apart or unstuck; —*vi Aer.* take off. **sin d. los labios,** without saying a word

despegue /des'peɣe/ *m, Aer.* take-off

despeinar /despei'nar/ *vt* to disarrange the hair; undo the coiffure

despejado /despe'haðo/ *a* lively, sprightly; logical, clear-cut; cloudless; spacious, unobstructed, clear

despejar /despe'har/ *vt* to clear, free of obstacles; **d. el camino de,** to clear the way for; *Fig.* elucidate, solve; *Math.* find the value of; —*vr* smarten up, grow gay; amuse oneself; clear up (weather, sky, etc.); improve (a patient)

despejo /des'peho/ *m,* freeing of obstacles; smartness, gaiety; grace, elegance; perkiness; clear-sightedness, intelligence

despeluzar /despelu'θar; despelu'sar/ *vt* to disorder the hair; cause the hair to stand on end; horrify; —*vr* stand on end (hair); be horrified or terrified

despeluznante /despeluθ'nante; despelus'nante/ *a* hair-raising, terrifying

despender /despen'der/ *vt* to spend; waste

despensa /des'pensa/ *f,* larder, pantry; store (of food); *Naut.* steward's room; stewardship

despeñadero /despeɲa'ðero/ *m,* precipice, crag; dangerous undertaking, risk —*a* steep, precipitous

despeñar /despe'ɲar/ *vt* to precipitate, fling down from a height, hurl down; —*vr* fling oneself headlong; throw oneself into (vices, etc.)

despeño /des'peɲo/ *m,* precipitation; headlong fall; *Fig.* collapse, ruin

desperdiciador /desperði'θiaðor; desperði'siaðor/ (**-ra**) *a* squandering, wasting —*n* squanderer

desperdiciar /desperði'θiar; desperði'siar/ *vt* to squander; *Fig.* misspend, waste

desperdicio /desper'ðiθio; desper'ðisio/ *m,* waste; remains, leftovers (gen. *pl*)

desperdigar /desperði'ɣar/ *vt* to separate, sever; scatter

desperecerse /despere'θerse; despere'serse/ *vr irr* to crave, yearn (for). See **conocer**

desperezarse /despere'θarse; despere'sarse/ *vr* to stretch oneself

desperfecto /desper'fekto/ *m,* imperfection, flaw; slight deterioration

despernado /desper'naðo/ *a* weary, footsore

despertador /desperta'ðor/ (**-ra**) *a* awakening —*n* awakener. *m,* alarm clock; incentive; stimulus

despertar /desper'tar/ *vt irr* to awaken; bring to mind, recall; stimulate; —*vi* waken; *Fig.* wake up, become more intelligent. See **acertar**

despiadado /despia'ðaðo/ *a* cruel, merciless

despicar /despi'kar/ *vt* to satisfy, content; —*vr* revenge oneself

despierto /des'pierto/ *a* wide-awake, clever

despilfarrar /despilfa'rrar/ *vt* to squander, waste

despilfarro /despil'farro/ *m,* slovenliness; waste, extravagance; mismanagement, maladministration

despintar /despin'tar/ *vt* to paint out; wash off the paint; efface, blot out; disfigure, deform; —*vi* be unlike or unworthy (of); —*vr* fade (colors); forget

despiojar /despio'har/ *vt* to remove lice, delouse; *Inf.* rescue from misery

despique /des'pike/ *m,* vengeance, revenge

despistar /despis'tar/ *vt* to throw off the scent; mislead

desplacer /despla'θer; despla'ser/ *vt irr* to displease, m, disgust, displeasure, sorrow. See **placer**

desplantar /desplan'tar/ (**se**) *vt* and *vr* to deviate from the vertical

desplazamiento /desplaθa'miento; desplasa'miento/ *m, Naut.* displacement

desplegadura /desplega'ðura/ *f,* unfolding

desplegar /desple'ɣar/ *vt irr* to unfold; spread open; *Fig.* reveal, disclose, explain; evince, display; *Mil.* deploy troops; —*vr* unfold, open (flowers, etc.); *Mil.* deploy. See **cegar**

despliegue /des'pliege/ *m*, unfolding; spreading out; evincing, demonstration; *Mil.* deployment

desplomar /desplo'mar/ *vt* to put out of the straight, cause to lean (walls, buildings); —*vr* lean, tilt (buildings); topple, fall down (walls, etc.); collapse (people); be ruined

desplome /des'plome/ *m*, collapse

despoblación /despoβla'θion; despoβla-'sion/ *f*, depopulation. **d. forestal**, deforestation

despoblado /despo'βlaðo/ *m*, wilderness; deserted place

despojar /despo'har/ *vt* to plunder, despoil; dispossess; —*vr* (*with de*) remove (garments, etc.); relinquish, give up

despojo /des'poho/ *m*, pillaging, spoliation; booty, plunder; butcher's offal; *pl* remains, leavings; debris, rubble; corpse

despolvorear /despolβore'ar/ *vt* to remove dust; *Fig.* shake off

desposado /despo'saðo/ *a* recently married; fettered, handcuffed. **los desposados**, the newlyweds

desposeer /despose'er/ *vt* to dispossess; —*vr* renounce one's possessions. See **creer**

desposorio /despo'sorio/ *m*, betrothal, promise of marriage; (*gen. pl*) wedding, marriage

déspota /'despota/ *m*, despot, tyrant

despótico /des'potiko/ *a* tyrannical

despotricarse /despotri'karse/ *vr* to rave (against), rail (against)

despreciable /despre'θiaβle; despre'siaβle/ *a* worthless, contemptible

despreciar /despre'θiar; despre'siar/ *vt* to scorn, despise; —*vr* despise oneself

despreciativo /despre'θia'tiβo; despre-sia'tiβo/ *a* contemptuous, scornful

desprecio /des'preθio; des'presio/ *m*, contempt, scorn

desprender /despren'der/ *vt* to loosen, remove, unfix; give off (gases, etc.); —*vr* work loose, give way; deduce, infer; give away, deprive oneself (of)

desprendido /despren'diðo/ *a* disinterested; generous

desprendimiento /desprendi'miento/ *m*, loosening; removal, separation; emission; indifference, lack of interest; generosity; impartiality

despreocupación /despreokupa'θion; despreokupa'sion/ *f*, fair mindedness, impartiality; lack of interest

despreocupado /despreoku'paðo/ *a* unprejudiced, broadminded; indifferent, uninterested

despreocuparse /despreoku'parse/ *vr* to shake off prejudice; (*with de*) pay no attention to; set aside

desprestigiar /despresti'hiar/ *vt* to discredit; —*vr* lose prestige; lose caste

desprestigio /despres'tihio/ *m*, loss of prestige, discredit

desprevenido /despreβe'niðo/ *a* unprepared, improvident

desproporción /despropor'θion; despropor'sion/ *f*, disproportion

desproporcionado /desproporθio'naðo; desproporsio'naðo/ *a* disproportionate; out of proportion

despropósito /despro'posito/ *m*, nonsense, absurdity

después /des'pues/ *adv* afterwards, after, next (of time and place) (e.g. *Vendrá d. de Pascua*, He will come after Easter. *Zaragoza viene d. de Madrid*, Saragossa comes after Madrid)

despuntar /despun'tar/ *vt* to blunt the point; *Naut.* double, sail round; —*vi* show green, sprout; appear (the dawn); grow clever; *Fig.* stand out, excel

desquiciamiento /deskiθia'miento; deskisia'miento/ *m*, unhinging; disconnecting; *Fig.* upsetting, throwing out of gear; downfall, fall from favor

desquiciar /deski'θiar; deski'siar/ *vt* to unhinge; disconnect; *Fig.* throw out of gear, upset; banish from favor; —*vr* become unhinged; *Fig.* be disordered; upset

desquitar /deski'tar/ **(se)** *vt* and *vr* to retrieve a loss; take revenge, retaliate

desquite /des'kite/ *m*, compensation; revenge

destacamento /destaka'mento/ *m*, *Mil.* detachment

destacar /desta'kar/ *vt Mil.* to detach; —*vr* excel; be prominent; be conspicuous; *Art.* stand out

destajista /desta'hista/ *mf* pieceworker; jobber (worker)

destajo /des'taho/ *m*, piecework; job. **a d.**, quickly and diligently. *Inf.* **hablar a d.**, to chatter, talk too much

destapar /desta'par/ *vt* to remove the cover or lid; reveal, uncover; —*vr* be uncovered; reveal oneself. **no destaparse**, to keep quiet, be mum

destartalado /destarta'laðo/ *a* tumble-down, rickety; poverty-stricken

destello /des'teλo; deste'yo/ *m*, gleam, sparkle, brilliance; flash, beam, ray; *Fig.* gleam (of talent)

destemplado /destem'plaðo/ *a* out of tune; inharmonious; intemperate; *Art.* inharmonious; *Inf.* out of sorts, indisposed

destemplanza /destem'planθa; destem-'plansa/ *f*, inclemency, rigor (weather); intemperance, excess, abuse; *Inf.* indisposition; lack of moderation (actions, speech)

destemplar /destem'plar/ *vt* to disturb, upset, alter; *Mus.* put out of tune; put to confusion; —*vr* be unwell; *Fig.* go too far, behave badly; lose temper (metals)

destemple /des'temple/ *m*, *Mus.* being out of tune; *Med.* indisposition; uncertainty (weather); lack of temper (metals); disturbance, disorder; intemperance, excess, confusion

desternillarse de risa /desterni'λarse

de 'rrisa; **desterni'yarse de 'rrisa/** to shake with laughter

desterrado /deste'rraðo/ **(-da)** *a* exiled —*n* exile

desterrar /deste'rrar/ *vt irr* to exile; shake off the soil; *Fig.* discard, lay aside; extirpate (an error). See **recomendar**

destetar /deste'tar/ *vt* to wean

destiempo, a /des'tiempo, a/ *adv* untimely, inopportunely

destierro /des'tierro/ *m,* banishment, exile; place of exile; remote place

destilación /destila'θion; destila'sion/ *f,* distillation

destilador /destila'ðor/ **(-ra)** *n* distiller. *m,* still

destilar /desti'lar/ *vt* to distill; filter; —*vi* to drip

destilatorio /destila'torio/ *a* distilling. *m,* distillery; still

destilería /destile'ria/ *f,* distillery

destinar /desti'nar/ *vt* to destine; appoint; assign

destino /des'tlno/ *m,* fate, destiny; post, appointment; destination. **con d. a,** going to, bound for

destitución /destitu'θion; destitu'sion/ *f,* destitution; discharge, dismissal

destituir /destitu'ir/ *vt irr* (*with de*) to dismiss or discharge from (employment); deprive of. See **huir**

destorcer /destor'θer; destor'ser/ *vt irr* to untwist; straighten out; —*vr Naut.* drift. See **torcer**

destornillado /destorni'ʎaðo; destorni-'yaðo/ *a* reckless; *Fig. Inf.* with a screw loose

destornillador /destorniʎa'ðor; destorni-ya'ðor/ *m,* screwdriver

destornillar /destorni'ʎar; destorni'yar/ *vt* to unscrew; —*vr* act rashly

destrenzar /destren'θar; destren'sar/ *vt* to unplait. **destrenzarse las cintas,** to unlace one's shoes

destreza /des'treθa; des'tresa/ *f,* dexterity; agility

destrón /des'tron/ *m,* blind person's guide

destronamiento /destrona'miento/ *m,* dethronement

destronar /destro'nar/ *vt* to dethrone; depose; oust

destroncamiento /destronka'miento/ *m,* detruncation

destroncar /destron'kar/ *vt* to lop; detruncate (trees); dislocate, disjoint; mutilate; *Fig.* ruin, seriously harm; tire out; —*vr* be exhausted or tired

destrozar /destro'θar; destro'sar/ *vt* to destroy; break in pieces, shatter; *Mil.* wipe out, annihilate; squander, dissipate

destrozo /des'troθo; des'troso/ *m,* destruction, ruin; shattering; *Mil.* rout; dissipation, waste

destrozón /destro'θon; destro'son/ *a* hard on wearing apparel, shoes, etc.

destrucción /destruk'θion; destruk'sion/ *f,* destruction; ruin, irreparable loss

destructor /destruk'tor/ **(-ra)** *a* destructive —*n* destroyer. *m, Nav.* destroyer

des'truir /destruir/ *vt irr* to destroy, ruin, annihilate; frustrate, blast, disappoint; deprive of means of subsistence; squander, waste; —*vr Math.* cancel. See **huir**

desuello /desue'ʎo; desue'yo/ *m,* flaying, skinning; forwardness, impertinence; extortion, fleecing. *Fig. Inf.* **¡Es un d.!** It's highway robbery!

desunión /desu'nion/ *f,* disunion, separation; *Fig.* discord, disharmony

desunir /desu'nir/ *vt* to disunite, separate; *Fig.* cause discord or disharmony

desvaído /desβa'iðo/ *a* gaunt, lanky; pale, faded, dull (of colors)

desvalido /des'βaliðo/ *a* unprotected, helpless

desvalimiento /desβali'miento/ *m,* defenselessness, lack of protection; lack of favor; desertion, abandonment

desvalorización /desβaloriθa'θion; desβalorisa'sion/ *f,* devaluation

desván /des'βan/ *m,* garret

desvanecer /desβane'θer; desβane'ser/ *vt irr* to cause to disappear; disintegrate; make vain; remove; —*vr* evaporate; faint, swoon; grow vain or conceited. See **conocer**

desvanecimiento /desβaneθi'miento; desβanesi'miento/ *m,* faintness, loss of consciousness; vanity, conceit

desvariar /desβa'riar/ *vi* to be delirious; rave, talk wildly

desvarío /desβa'rio/ *m,* foolish action, absurdity; delirium; monstrosity; whim, caprice

desvelar /desβe'lar/ *vt* to keep awake; —*vr* be sleepless; (*with por*) take great care over

desvelo /des'βelo/ *m,* sleeplessness, vigil; care, attention, vigilance; anxiety. **con d.,** watchfully

desvencijar /desβenθi'har; desβensi'har/ *vt* to loosen, disconnect, disjoint; —*vr* work loose, become disjointed

desventaja /desβen'taha/ *f,* disadvantage. **estar en d.,** to be at a disadvantage

desventajoso /desβenta'hoso/ *a* disadvantageous

desventura /desβen'tura/ *f,* misfortune

desventurado /desβentu'raðo/ *a* unfortunate; timid, faint-hearted; miserly

desvergonzado /desβergon'θaðo; desβergonsaðo/ *a* shameless, brazen, impudent

desvergonzarse /desβergon'θarse; desβergon'sarse/ *vr irr* to be brazen, be impudent. See **avergonzar**

desvergüenza /desβer'guenθa; desβer'guensa/ *f,* insolence; shamelessness

desvestir /desβes'tir/ **(se)** *vt and vr irr* to undress. See **pedir**

desviación /desβia'θion; desβia'sion/ *f*, deviation, deflection

desviar /des'βiar/ *vt* to divert, deflect; dissuade

desvío /des'βio/ *m*, deviation; indifference, coldness; repugnance

desvirtuar /desβir'tuar/ *vt* to decrease in strength or merit

desvivirse /desβi'βirse/ *vr* (*with por*) to adore, love dearly; yearn for, be dying to; do one's best to please, (e.g. *Juan se desvive por servirme,* John does his best to help me)

detallar /deta'ʎar; deta'yar/ *vt* to tell in detail; relate

detalle /de'taʎe; de'taye/ *m*, detailed account; detail, particular

detallismo /deta'ʎismo; deta'yismo/ *m*, meticulous attention to details

detective /de'tektiβe/ *mf* detective

detector /detek'tor/ *m*, detector; *Radio.* catwhisker

detención /deten'θion; deten'sion/ *f*, stop, halt; delay; prolixity; arrest, detention. **con d.,** carefully, meticulously

detener /dete'ner/ *vt irr* to detain, stop; arrest; retain, keep; —*vr* go slowly; tarry; halt, stop; (*with en*) pause over, stop at. See **tener**

detenido /dete'niðo/ *a* timid, irresolute; miserable, mean

deterioración /deteriora'θion; deteriora-'sion/ *f*, deterioration

deteriorar /deterio'rar/ **(se)** *vt* and *vr* to deteriorate

determinación /determina'θion; determina'sion/ *f*, determination; daring; decision

determinado /determi'naðo/ *a* resolute, determined

determinar /determi'nar/ *vt* to determine, limit; discern, distinguish; specify, appoint; decide, resolve; *Law.* define, judge; —*vr* make up one's mind

detersorio /deter'sorio/ *a* and *m,* detergent

detestable /detes'taβle/ *a* detestable

detestar /detes'tar/ *vt* to abominate, detest

detonación /detona'θion; detona'sion/ *f*, detonation

detonar /deto'nar/ *vi* to detonate

detracción /detrak'θion; detrak'sion/ *f*, detraction

detractor /detrak'tor/ **(-ra)** *a* slandering *n* detractor, slanderer

detraer /detra'er/ *vt irr* to detract, take away; separate; slander. See **traer**

detrás /de'tras/ *adv* behind, after (place). **por d.,** in the rear; *Fig.* behind one's back

detrimento /detri'mento/ *m,* detriment; moral harm. **en d. de,** to the detriment of

deuda /'deuða/ *f,* debt; fault, offense; sin. **d. exterior,** foreign debt. **estar en d. con,** to be indebted to. **Perdónanos nuestras deudas,** Forgive us our trespasses

deudo /'deuðo/ *m,* relative, kinsman; kinship, relationship

deudor /deu'ðor/ **(-ra)** *a* indebted —*n* debtor. **d. hipotecario,** mortgagor

devanadera /deβana'ðera/ *f,* bobbin, reel, spool; winder (machine)

devanador /deβana'ðor/ **(-ra)** *n* winder (person). *m,* spool, bobbin

devanar /deβa'nar/ *vt* to reel, wind. *Inf.* **devanarse los sesos,** to rack one's brains

devanear /deβane'ar/ *vi* to rave, talk nonsense

devaneo /deβa'neo/ *m,* delirium; foolishness, nonsense; dissipation; love affair

devastación /deβasta'θion; deβasta'sion/ *f,* devastation

devastar /deβas'tar/ *vt* to devastate, lay waste; *Fig.* destroy, ruin

develador /deβela'ðor/ *m,* betrayer

devengar /deβeŋ'gar/ *vt* to have a right to, earn (salary, interest, etc.)

devoción /deβo'θion; deβo'sion/ *f,* piety; affection, love; pious custom; prayer

devocionario /deβoθio'nario; deβosio-'nario/ *m,* prayer book

devolver /deβol'βer/ *vt irr* to restore to original state; return, give back; repay. See **resolver**

devorador /deβora'ðor/ **(-ra)** *a* devouring —*n* devourer

devorar /deβo'rar/ *vt* to devour; destroy, consume

devoto /de'βoto/ **(-ta)** *a* devout, pious; devoted, fond —*n* devotee. *m,* object of devotion

día /dia/ *m,* day; daylight; *pl* name or saint's day; birthday (e.g. *Hoy son los días de María,* This is Mary's saint's day (or birthday)). **d. de Año Nuevo,** New Year's Day. **d. de asueto,** day off. **d. de ayuno** or **de vigilia,** fast day. **d. del cura,** *humorous* wedding day. **d. del juicio,** Day of Judgment. **d. de los difuntos,** All Souls' Day. **d. de recibo,** at home day. **d. de Reyes,** Epiphany (when Spanish children receive their Christmas presents). **d. de trabajo** or **d. laborable,** working day. **d. por medio,** every other day. **días caniculares,** dog days. **d. por d.,** day by day. **al d.,** up to date; per day. **al otro d.,** next day. **¡Buenos días!** Good morning! Good day! **de d.,** by day. **de d. en d.,** from day to day. **de un d. a otro,** any time now, very soon. **el d. de mañana,** tomorrow, the near future. **un d. sí y otro no,** every other day. **vivir al d.,** to live up to one's income

diabético /dia'βetiko/ *a* diabetic

diablo /'diaβlo/ *m,* devil; Satan; *Fig.* fiend. *Inf.* **d. cojuelo,** mischievous devil; *Fig. Inf.* **Anda el d. suelto,** The Devil's abroad, there's trouble. *Inf.* **tener el d. en el cuerpo,** to be as clever as the Devil; be mischievous

diablura /dia'βlura/ *f,* mischief, prank; devilry

diabólico /dia'βoliko/ *a* diabolical, devilish; *Inf.* fiendish, iniquitous

diadema /dia'ðema/ *f*, diadem; crown; tiara

diafanidad /diafani'ðað/ *f*, transparency

diáfano /'diafano/ *a* transparent, diaphanous

diafragma /dia'fragma/ *m*, *Anat. Mech.* diaphragm; sound-box (of a phonograph)

diagnosticar /diagnosti'kar/ *vt Med.* to diagnose

diagnóstico /diag'nostiko/ *a* diagnostic. *m*, diagnosis. **d. precoz**, early diagnosis

diagonal /diago'nal/ *a* diagonal; oblique

diagrama /dia'grama/ *m*, diagram

diagramación /diagrama'θion; diagrama'sion/ *f*, layout (of a publication)

dialecto /dia'lekto/ *m*, dialect

dialogar /dialo'gar/ *vi* to hold dialogue, converse; —*vt* write dialogue

diálogo /'dialogo/ *m*, dialogue

diamante /dia'mante/ *m*, diamond; miner's lamp; glass-cutting diamond. **d. bruto**, rough diamond

diamantista /diaman'tista/ *mf* diamond-cutter; diamond merchant

diametral /diame'tral/ *a* diametrical

diámetro /di'ametro/ *m*, diameter

diana /'diana/ *f*, *Mil.* reveille; bull's-eye (of a target); the moon

¡diantre! /'diantre/ *interj Inf.* the deuce!

diapasón /diapa'son/ *m*, *Mus.* tuning fork; diapason; neck (of violins, etc.). **d. normal**, tuning fork. **d. vocal**, pitch-pipe

diapositiva /diaposi'tiβa/ *f*, *Photo.* diapositive; (lantern) slide

diario /'diario/ *a* daily. *m*, diary; daily paper; daily expenses. **d. de navegación**, ship's log. **d. de viaje**, travel diary, trip journal

diarrea /dia'rrea/ *f*, diarrhea

diatriba /dia'triβa/ *f*, diatribe

dibujante /diβu'hante/ *m*, sketcher; draftsman; designer

dibujar /diβu'har/ *vt Art.* to draw; describe, depict; —*vr* appear, be revealed; be outlined, stand out

dibujo /di'βuho/ *m*, drawing; sketch, design, pattern; depiction, description. **d. a la pluma**, pen-and-ink drawing. **d. a pulso**, freehand drawing. **d. del natural**, drawing from life

dicción /dik'θion; dik'sion/ *f*, word; diction, language, style

diccionario /dikθio'nario; diksio'nario/ *m*, dictionary

díceres /'diθeres; 'diseres/ *m pl West. Hem.* news

dicha /'ditʃa/ *f*, happiness; good fortune. **por d.**, by chance; fortunately

dicharacho /ditʃa'ratʃo/ *m*, *Inf.* vulgar expression, slangy expression

dicho /'ditʃo/ *m*, saying, phrase, expression; witty remark; *Law.* declaration; *Inf.* insult —*a* said, aforementioned —*past part* decir, "said." **D. y hecho**, No sooner said than done. **Del d. al hecho hay muy gran trecho**, There's many a slip

'twixt the cup and the lip. **Lo d. d.**, The agreement stands

dichoso /di'tʃoso/ *a* happy; lucky; *Inf.* blessed, wretched, darn

diciembre /di'θiembre; di'siembre/ *m*, December

dictado /dik'taðo/ *m*, title of honor; dictation; *pl* promptings (of heart, etc.). **escribir al d.**, to write to dictation

dictador /dikta'ðor/ *m*, dictator

dictadura /dikta'ðura/ *f*, dictatorship

dictáfono /dik'tafono/ *m*, dictaphone

dictamen /dik'tamen/ *m*, judgment, opinion

dictaminar /diktami'nar/ *vi* to give judgment or opinion

dictar /dik'tar/ *vt* to dictate; suggest, inspire. **dictar fallo**, to hand down a decision, render judgment

dictatorial, dictatorio /diktato'rial, dikta'torio/ *a* dictatorial

dicterio /dik'terio/ *m*, taunt, insult

didáctica /di'ðaktika/ *f*, didactics

didáctico /di'ðaktiko/ *a* didactic

diecinueve /dieθi'nueβe; diesi'nueβe/ *a* and *m*, nineteen

dieciocho /die'θiotʃo; die'siotʃo/ *a* and *m*, eighteen

dieciséis /dieθi'seis; diesi'seis/ *a* and *m*, sixteen

diecisiete /dieθi'siete; diesi'siete/ *a* and *m*, seventeen

diente /diente/ *m*, tooth; tooth (of saw, etc.); tusk; cog (of wheel), prong (of fork); tongue (of a buckle). **d. de leche**, milk-tooth. *Bot.* **d. de león**, dandelion. **d. de perro**, *Sew.* feather-stitch. *Inf.* **dar d. con d.**, to chatter (teeth). *Fig. Inf.* **enseñar** (*or* mostrar) **los dientes**, to show one's teeth; threaten. *Inf.* **estar a d.**, to be famished. **hablar entre dientes**, to mutter; fume, grumble. *Inf.* **tener buen d.**, to have a good appetite. **traer a uno entre dientes**, to loathe someone; speak scandal of

diestra /'diestra/ *f*, right hand; protection

diestro /'diestro/ *a* right (hand); skillful, dextrous; astute, shrewd; cunning; favorable, happy. *m*, expert fencer; bullfighter; halter; bridle

dieta /'dieta/ *f*, *Med.* diet; *Inf.* fast, abstinence; legislative assembly; travel allowance (gen. *pl*); day's journey of ten leagues; daily fee (gen. *pl*)

dietario /die'tario/ *m*, household accounts' book

dietética /die'tetika/ *f*, dietetics

dietista /die'tista/ *mf* dietician

diez /dieθ; dies/ *a* ten; tenth. *m*, ten; decade of rosary

diezmar /dieθ'mar; dies'mar/ *vt* to tithe; decimate; punish every tenth person

diezmo /'dieθmo; 'diesmo/ *m*, ten per cent tax; tithe

difamación /difama'θion; difama'sion/ *f*, defamation, libel

difamador /difama'ðor/ **(-ra)** a libeling —n libeler

difamar /difa'mar/ vt to libel; denigrate

difamatorio /difama'torio/ a libelous, defamatory

diferencia /dife'renθia; dife'rensia/ f, unlikeness, dissimilarity; Math. difference; dissension, disagreement. **a d. de,** unlike; in contrast to

diferenciación /diferenθia'θion; diferensia'sion/ f, differentiation. **d. del trabajo,** division of labor

diferencial /diferen'θial; diferen'sial/ a differential

diferenciar /diferen'θiar; diferen'siar/ vt to differentiate; change the function (of); —vi dissent, disagree; —vr be different, differ; distinguish oneself

diferente /dife'rente/ a different, various

diferir /dife'rir/ vt irr to delay, retard; postpone; suspend, interrupt; —vi be different. See **discernir**

difícil /di'fiθil; di'fisil/ a difficult

dificultad /difikul'taθ/ f, difficulty; impediment, obstacle; objection

dificultar /difikul'tar/ vt to raise difficulties; put obstacles in the way; —vi think difficult (of achievements)

dificultoso /difikul'toso/ a difficult; Inf. ugly (face, figure, etc.)

difidencia /difi'ðenθia; difi'ðensia/ f, mistrust; lack of faith, doubt

difidente /difi'ðente/ a mistrustful

difracción /difrak'θion; difrak'sion/ f, diffraction

difteria /dif'teria/ f, diphtheria

difundir /difun'dir/ vt to diffuse (fluids); spread, publish, divulge; Radio. broadcast

difunto /di'funto/ **(-ta)** a and n deceased. m, corpse

difusión /difu'sion/ f, diffusion; prolixity; Radio. broadcasting

difusivo /difu'siβo/ a diffusive

difuso /di'fuso/ a widespread, diffuse; prolix, wordy

digerible /dihe'riβle/ a digestible

digerir /dihe'rir/ vt irr to digest; bear patiently; consider carefully; Chem. digest. See **sentir**

digestivo /dihes'tiβo/ a digestive

digitación /dihita'θion; dihita'sion/ f, Mus. fingering

digital /dihi'tal/ a digital. f, Bot. foxglove, digitalis

dígito /'dihito/ a digital. m, (Astron. Math.) digit

dignarse /dig'narse/ vr to deign, condescend

dignatario /digna'tario/ m, dignitary

dignidad /digni'ðað/ f, dignity, stateliness; serenity, loftiness; high office or rank; high repute, honor; Eccl. dignitary

dignificar /dignifi'kar/ vt to dignify

digno /'digno/ a worthy, deserving; upright, honorable; fitting, suitable, appropriate

digresión /digre'sion/ f, digression

dije /'dihe/ m, charm; trinket, any small piece of jewelry; Inf. person of excellent qualities, jewel

dilacerar /dilaθe'rar; dilase'rar/ vt to lacerate, tear flesh; Fig. discredit

dilación /dila'θion; dila'sion/ f, delay

dilapidación /dilapiða'θion; dilapi'ðasion/ f, waste, dissipation, squandering

dilapidar /dilapi'ðar/ vt to waste, squander

dilatación /dilata'θion; dilata'sion/ f, expansion; enlargement, widening; prolongation; Surg. dilatation; respite (in trouble)

dilatar /dila'tar/ vt to dilate, enlarge; expand; delay, postpone; spread, publish abroad; prolong; —vr expand; be prolix, spread oneself

dilatorio /dila'torio/ a procrastinating, dilatory

dilección /dilek'θion; dilek'sion/ f, affection, love

dilema /di'lema/ m, dilemma

diletantismo /diletan'tismo/ m, dilettantism

diligencia /dili'henθia; dili'hensia/ f, care, conscientiousness, industry; haste, briskness; diligence (coach); Inf. business, occupation. **hacer sus diligencias,** to try one's best

diligenciar /dilihen'θiar; dilihen'siar/ vt to set on foot, put into motion

diligente /dili'hente/ a diligent, conscientious, industrious; speedy, prompt

dilucidación /diluθiða'θion; dilusiða'sion/ f, elucidation, clarification

dilucidar /diluθi'ðar; dilusi'ðar/ vt to elucidate, clarify

dilución /dilu'θion; dilu'sion/ f, dilution

diluir /dili'uir/ vt irr to dilute. See **huir**

diluviar /dilu'βiar/ vi to teem with rain

diluvio /di'luβio/ m, flood, inundation; Inf. very heavy rain, deluge; overabundance

dimanación /dimana'θion; dimana'sion/ f, emanation, source

dimanar /dima'nar/ vi (with de) to rise in (rivers); proceed from, originate in

dimensión /dimen'sion/ f, dimension; size, extent

dimes y diretes /'dimes i di'retes/ m pl, Inf. back-chat

diminuto /dimi'nuto/ a defective, incomplete; minute, very small

dimisión /dimi'sion/ f, resignation (of office, etc.)

dimisorias /dimi'sorias/ f pl, Eccl. letter dimissory. Inf. **dar d. a uno,** to give a person his marching orders, dismiss

dimitente /dimi'tente/ a resigning; retiring. mf resigner (of a post)

dimitir /dimi'tir/ vt to resign (office, post, etc.)

Dinamarca /dina'marka/ Denmark

dinamarqués /dinamar'kes/ **(-esa)** a Danish —n Dane

dinámica /di'namika/ f, dynamics

dinámico /di'namiko/ *a* dynamic

dinamita /dina'mita/ *f,* dynamite

dinamo /'dinamo/ *f,* dynamo

dinastía /dinas'tia/ *f,* dynasty

dineral /dine'ral/ *m,* large amount of money, fortune

dinero /di'nero/ *m,* money; Peruvian coin; wealth, fortune; currency. **d. contante, d. junto,** ready cash, **Poderoso caballero es Don D.,** Money talks

dinosauro /dino'sauro/ *m,* dinosaur

dintel /'dintel/ *m,* lintel

diocesano /dioθe'sano; diose'sano/ *a* diocesan

diócesis /'dioθesis; 'diosesis/ *f,* diocese

Dios /dios/ *m,* God; deity. **¡D. le guarde!** God keep you! **¡D. lo quiera!** God grant it! **D. mediante,** God willing (D.V.). **¡D. mío!** Good gracious! **De menos nos hizo D.,** Nothing is impossible, Never say die. *Inf.* **haber (*or* armarse) la de D. es Cristo,** to be the deuce of a row. **¡No lo quiera D.!** God forbid! **¡Plegue a D.!** Please God! **¡Por D.!** For goodness sake! Heavens! **¡Válgame D.!** Bless me! **¡Vaya Vd. con D.!** Goodbye! Off with you! Depart! **¡Vive D.!** By God!

diosa /'diosa/ *f,* goddess

diploma /di'ploma/ *m,* license, bull; diploma. **d. de suficiencia,** general diploma

diplomacia /diplo'maθia; diplo'masia/ *f,* diplomacy; tactfulness; *Inf.* astuteness

diplomático /diplo'matiko/ *a* diplomatic; tactful; *Inf.* astute. *m,* diplomat. **cuerpo d.,** diplomatic corps

dipsomanía /dipsoma'nia/ *f,* dipsomania

dipsómano /dip'somano/ **(-na)** *n* dipsomaniac

diputación /diputa'θion; diputa'sion/ *f,* deputation; mission

diputado /dipu'taðo/ **(-da)** *n* deputy, delegate. **d. a Cortes,** member of the Spanish Parliament, congressman

diputar /dipu'tar/ *vt* to appoint, depute; delegate; empower

dique /'dike/ *m,* dike; dam; dry dock; *Fig.* bulwark, check; **d. flotante,** floating dock

dirección /direk'θion; direk'sion/ *f,* direction; management, control, guidance; directorate; instruction; information; order, wish, command; editorial board; directorship, managership; (postal) address; managerial office. **d. cablegráfica,** cable address. **d. particular,** home address

directiva /direk'tiβa/ *f,* board, governing body

directivo /direk'tiβo/ *a* directive, controlling, guiding, managing

directo /di'rekto/ *a* direct; straight

director /direk'tor/ **(-ra)** *a* directing, controlling —*n* director; manager; principal, head (schools, etc.); editor. **d. del ceremonial,** chief of protocol. **d. de escena,** stagemanager. **d. espiritual,** *Eccl.* father confessor. **d. gerente,** managing director

directorio /direk'torio/ *a* directory, advising. *m,* directory; directorate, board of directors

dirigir /diri'hir/ *vt* to direct; regulate; govern; supervise; guide; *Mus.* conduct; address (an envelope, etc.); keep (a shop, etc.); edit; put (a question); point (a gun); cast (a glance); —*vr* go; wend one's way. **d. la palabra (a),** to speak to, address. **d. la vista a,** to look towards, look in the direction of, turn towards, turn in the direction of. **dirigirse a,** to go towards; make one's way to

dirimir /diri'mir/ *vt* to annul, make void; break, dissolve; settle (disputes, etc.)

discernimiento /disθerni'miento; disserni'miento/ *m,* discernment; judgment; discrimination

discernir /disθer'nir; disser'nir/ *vt irr* to discern, distinguish —*Pres. Indic.* **discierno, disciernes, discierne, disciernen.** *Pres. Subjunc.* **discierna, disciernas, discierna, disciernan**

disciplina /disθi'plina; dissi'plina/ *f,* discipline; system, philosophy, education; submission, obedience; subject (arts or science); *pl* scourge

disciplinar /disθipli'nar; dissipli'nar/ *vt* to train; educate; scourge, beat; discipline; —*vr* scourge oneself

disciplinario /disθipli'nario; dissipli'nario/ *a* disciplinary

discipulado /disθipu'laðo; dissipu'laðo/ *m,* pupilship, studentship; education, teaching; discipleship; body of pupils (of a school, etc.)

discípulo /dis'θipulo; dis'sipulo/ **(-la)** *n* pupil, student; disciple, follower

disco /'disko/ *m,* discus; disk; phonograph record; *Astron.* disk. **d. compacto,** compact disc. **d. de señales,** railway signal. **d. giratorio,** turntable (of a phonograph)

discontinuo /diskon'tinuo/ *a* intermittent, discontinuous

discordancia /diskor'ðanθia; diskor'ðansia/ *f,* discord, disagreement

discordar /diskor'ðar/ *vi* to be discordant; disagree; *Mus.* be out of tune

discreción /diskre'θion; diskre'sion/ *f,* discretion; circumspection; prudence, good sense; shrewdness; pithy or clever saying. **a d.,** at discretion; at will; voluntarily. *Mil.* **darse (*or* entregarse) a d.,** to surrender unconditionally

discrecional /diskreθio'nal; diskresio'nal/ *a* optional, voluntary

discrepancia /diskre'panθia; diskre'pansia/ *f,* discrepancy; disagreement

discrepar /diskre'par/ *vi* to be discrepant; differ; disagree

discreto /dis'kreto/ *a* discreet; ingenious; witty

disculpa /dis'kulpa/ *f,* excuse

disculpable /diskul'paβle/ *a* excusable

disculpar /diskul'par/ *vt* to excuse; forgive, pardon; —*vr* apologize; excuse oneself

discurrir /disku'rrir/ *vi* to wander, roam;

flow, run (rivers, etc.); (*with en*) consider, think about; (*with sobre*) discourse on; —*vt* invent; conjecture

discursivo /diskur'siβo/ *a* discursive; thoughtful, reflective

discurso /dis'kurso/ *m*, reasoning power; oration, discourse; consideration, reflection; speech, conversation; dissertation. **d. aceptatorio,** acceptance speech

discusión /disku'sion/ *f*, discussion

discutible /disku'tiβle/ *a* debatable; disputable

discutir /disku'tir/ *vt* to discuss, debate, consider

disecar /dise'kar/ *vt Anat.* to dissect; stuff animals; mount plants

diseminación /disemina'θion; disemina-'sion/ *f*, dissemination

diseminar /disemi'nar/ *vt* to disseminate; spread

disensión /disen'sion/ *f*, dissension

disentería /disente'ria/ *f*, dysentery

disentimiento /disenti'miento/ *m*, dissent

diseñador /disena'ðor/ *m*, delineator, drawer

diseñar /dise'nar/ *vt* to outline, sketch

diseño /di'seno/ *m*, outline, sketch; plan; description

disertación /diserta'θion; diserta'sion/ *f*, dissertation

disertar /diser'tar/ *vi* (*with sobre*) to discourse on, discuss, treat of

disfavor /disfa'βor/ *m*, disfavor, discourtesy, slight

disfraz /dis'fraθ; dis'fras/ *m*, disguise; mask; fancy dress; pretense

disfrazar /disfra'θar; disfra'sar/ *vt* to disguise; dissemble, misrepresent; —*vr* disguise oneself; wear fancy dress

disfrutar /disfru'tar/ *vt* to enjoy (health, comfort, friendship, etc.); reap the benefit of; —*vi* take pleasure in, enjoy

disfrute /dis'frute/ *m*, enjoyment, use, benefit

disgustado /disgus'taðo/ *a* annoyed; discontented, dissatisfied; melancholy, depressed

disgustar /disgus'tar/ *vt* to displease, dissatisfy; annoy; *Fig.* depress; —*vr* quarrel, fall out. **Me disgusta la idea de marcharme,** I don't like the idea of going away

disgusto /dis'gusto/ *m*, displeasure, dissatisfaction; discontent; annoyance; affliction, sorrow, trouble; quarrel; boredom; repugnance

disidente /disi'ðente/ *a* dissenting. *mf* dissenter, nonconformist

disímil /di'simil/ *a* dissimilar, different, unlike

disimulación /disimula'θion; disimula-'sion/ *f*, dissimulation, pretense

disimulado /disimu'laðo/ *a* feigned, pretended

disimular /disimu'lar/ *vt* to dissemble;

pretend, feign; put up with, tolerate; misrepresent, misinterpret

disimulo /di'simulo/ *m*, pretense, dissimulation; tolerance, patience

disipación /disipa'θion; disipa'sion/ *f*, dispersion; dissipation, frivolity; immorality

disipado /disi'paðo/ *a* spendthrift; dissipated, frivolous

disipar /disi'par/ *vt* to disperse; squander; —*vr* evaporate; vanish, fade, disappear

dislate /di'slate/ *m*, absurdity, nonsense

dislocar /dislo'kar/ *vt* to dislocate; —*vr* dislocate; sprain

disminución /disminu'θion; disminu'sion/ *f*, diminution. **ir (una cosa) en d.,** to diminish, decrease; taper, grow to a point

disminuido físico /dismi'nuiðo 'fisiko/ *m*, physically impaired person, physically handicapped person

disminuir /dismi'nuir/ *vt and vi irr* to diminish, decrease. See **huir**

disociación /disoθia'θion; disosia'sion/ *f*, dissociation. **d. nuclear,** nuclear fission

disociar /diso'θiar; diso'siar/ *vt* to dissociate, separate; *Chem.* dissociate

disolución /disolu'θion; disolu'sion/ *f*, dissolution; immorality, laxity; disintegration; loosening, relaxation

disoluto /diso'luto/ *a* dissolute, vicious

disolvente /disol'βente/ *m*, dissolvent, solvent

disolver /disol'βer/ *vt irr* to loosen, undo; *Chem.* dissolve; separate, disintegrate; annul. See **resolver**

disonancia /diso'nanθia; diso'nansia/ *f*, dissonance; disagreement; *Mus.* dissonant

disonante /diso'nante/ *a* dissonant; discordant, inharmonious

disonar /diso'nar/ *vi irr* to be inharmonious; disagree. See **sonar**

dispar /dis'par/ *a* unequal; unlike, different

disparador /dispara'ðor/ *m*, shooter, firer; trigger (of firearms); ratchet (of watch)

disparar /dispa'rar/ *vt* to shoot, fire; throw or discharge with violence; —*vr* run precipitately; rush (towards); bolt (horses); race (of a machine); explode, go off; *Inf.* go too far, misbehave

disparatado /dispara'taðo/ *a* foolish; absurd, unreasonable

disparatar /dispara'tar/ *vi* to act or speak foolishly

disparate /dispa'rate/ *m*, foolishness, nonsense

disparidad /dispari'ðað/ *f*, disparity, dissimilarity

disparo /dis'paro/ *m*, shooting; explosion; racing (of an engine); discharge; foolishness

dispendio /dis'pendio/ *m*, squandering, extravagance

dispensa /dis'pensa/ *f*, dispensation; privilege

dispensación /dispensa'θion; dispensa'sion/ f, dispensation; exemption

dispensar /dispen'sar/ vt to grant, concede, distribute; exempt; excuse, forgive

dispepsia /dis'pepsia/ f, dyspepsia

dispersar /disper'sar/ vt to disperse, scatter, separate; Mil. rout

dispersión /disper'sion/ f, dispersion

disperso /dis'perso/ a dispersed, scattered; Mil. separated from regiment

displicencia /displi'θenθia; displi'sensia/
f, disagreeableness, coldness; hesitation,
lack of enthusiasm

displicente /displi'θente; displi'sente/ a
unpleasant, disagreeable; difficult, peevish

disponer /dispo'ner/ vt irr to arrange,
dispose; direct, order; decide; prepare,
get ready, —vi (with de) dispose of, make
free with; possess; have at one's disposal;
—vr prepare oneself to die; make one's
will, get ready. See **poner**

disponible /dispo'niβle/ a disposable;
available

disposición /disposi'θion; disposi'sion/ f,
arrangement; order, instruction; decision,
preparation; aptitude, talent; disposal;
condition of health; temperament; grace
of bearing; promptitude, competence;
measure, step, preliminary; Archit. plan;
proviso, stipulation; symmetry. **A la d.
de Vd,** I (we, he, it, etc.) am at your disposal. **hallarse en d. de hacer una cosa,**
to be ready to do something. **última d.,**
last will and testament

dispuesto /dis'puesto/ a ready, prepared;
handsome, gallant; clever, wide-awake.
bien d., well-disposed; well, healthy. **mal
d.,** ill-disposed; disinclined; out of sorts,
indisposed

disputa /dis'puta/ f, dispute. **sin d.,** undoubtedly

disputar /dispu'tar/ vt to argue, debate;
dispute, question; Fig. fight for

distancia /dis'tanθia; dis'tansia/ f, distance; interval of time; difference, dissimilarity; unfriendliness, coolness

distanciar /distan'θiar; distan'siar/ vt to
separate, place farther apart

distante /dis'tante/ a separated; distant;
far off

distar /dis'tar/ vi to be distant (time and
place); be different, unlike

distender /disten'der/ **(se)** vt and vr
Med. to distend, swell

distinción /distin'θion; distin'sion/ f, distinction, differentiation; difference, individuality; privilege, honor; clarity, order;
distinction (of bearing or mind). **a d. de,**
unlike, different from

distinguible /distiŋ'guiβle/ a distinguishable

distinguido /distiŋ'guido/ a distinguished, illustrious

distinguir /distiŋ'guir/ vt to distinguish,
discern; differentiate; characterize; esteem, honor, respect; discriminate; see
with difficulty; make out; —vr be different; excel, distinguish oneself

distintivo /distin'tiβo/ a distinguishing;
distinctive. m, distinguishing mark

distinto /dis'tinto/ a different; distinct;
clear

distracción /distrak'θion; distrak'sion/ f,
distraction; abstraction, heedlessness; ab-
sentmindedness; pleasure, amusement; licentiousness

distraer /distra'er/ vt irr to lead astray;
distract (attention); influence for bad;
amuse —vr be absentminded; amuse oneself. See **traer**

distraído /distra'ido/ a abstracted, absentminded; inattentive; licentious

distribución /distriβu'θion; distriβu'sion/
f, distribution; (gen. pl) share

distribuidor /distriβui'ðor/ **(-ra)** a distributing —n distributor

distribuir /distri'βuir/ vt irr to distribute;
share out, divide. See **huir**

distributivo /distriβu'tiβo/ a distributive

distrito /dis'trito/ m, district

disturbio /dis'turβio/ m, disturbance

disuadir /disua'ðir/ vt to dissuade

disuasión /disua'sion/ f, dissuasion

disuasivo /disua'siβo/ a dissuasive

diurético /diu'retiko/ a diuretic

divagación /diβaga'θion; diβaga'sion/ f,
wandering, roaming; digression

divagar /diβa'gar/ vi to wander; roam;
digress

diván /di'βan/ m, divan (Turkish supreme
council); divan, sofa; collection of Arabic,
Persian or Turkish poems

divergencia /diβer'henθia; diβer'hensia/
f, divergence; disagreement

divergente /diβer'hente/ a divergent;
conflicting, dissentient

divergir /diβer'hir/ vi to diverge; dissent

diversidad /diβersi'ðað/ f, diversity, unlikeness, difference; variety

diversificar /diβersifi'kar/ vt to differentiate; vary

diversión /diβer'sion/ f, pastime, amusement; Mil. diversion

diverso /di'βerso/ a diverse, unlike; pl
various, many

divertido /diβer'tiðo/ a amusing, funny,
entertaining

divertir /diβer'tir/ vt irr to lead astray;
turn aside; entertain; Mil. create a diversion —vr amuse oneself. See **sentir**

dividendo /diβi'ðendo/ m, dividend.
Com. **d. activo,** dividend

dividir /diβi'ðir/ vt to divide; distribute;
stir up discord; —vr (with de) part company with, leave

divieso /di'βieso/ m, Med. boil

divinamente /diβina'mente/ adv di-
vinely; excellently, admirably, perfectly

divinidad /diβini'ðað/ f, divinity, Godhead; person or thing of great beauty

divinizar /diβini'θar; diβini'sar/ vt to deify; sanctify; extol

divino /di'βino/ a divine; excellent, admirable, superb

divisa /di'βisa/ f. badge, emblem; *Herald.* motto

divisar /diβi'sar/ vt to glimpse, descry

división /diβi'sion/ f. division, partition; discord; (*Math. Mil.*) division; hyphen; apportionment; district, ward

divisor /diβi'sor/ **(-ra)** a dividing, separating. m, *Math.* divisor —n divider, separator

divisoria /diβi'soria/ f. dividing line

divorciar /diβor'θiar; diβor'siar/ vt to divorce; separate; —vr be divorced, be separated

divorcio /di'βorθio; di'βorsio/ m. divorce

divulgación /diβulga'θion; diβulga'sion/ f. spreading, publication, propagation

divulgar /diβul'gar/ **(se)** vt and vr to spread abroad, publish

dobladillo /doβla'ðiλo; doβla'ðiyo/ m, *Sew.* hem; turn-up (of a trouser)

doblado /do'βlaðo/ a stocky, thickset, sturdy; rocky, rough, uneven; dissembling. m, garret

dobladura /doβla'ðura/ f. fold, crease; crease mark

doblamiento /doβla'miento/ m, doubling; folding

doblar /do'βlar/ vt to double, multiply by two; fold, double; bend; persuade, induce; *Naut.* double, sail round; turn, walk round; —vi *Eccl.* ring the passing bell; *Theat.* double a role; —vr fold, double; bend; bow; stoop; allow oneself to be persuaded

doble /'doβle/ a double, twofold; duplicate; insincere, false; thick (cloth); *Bot.* double (flowers); hardy, robust. m, fold, crease; *Eccl.* passing-bell; Spanish dance step —adv double, twice. *Eccl.* **rito d.,** full rites

doblegar /doβle'gar/ vt to fold; bend; brandish; dissuade in favor of another proposition; —vr submit, give way, acquiesce

doblete /do'βlete/ a of medium thickness. m, imitation jewel

doblez /do'βleθ; do'βles/ m, fold, crease; fold mark. mf, double dealing, treachery

doce /'doθe; 'dose/ a twelve. m, twelve; twelfth (of the month). **las d.,** twelve o'clock

docena /do'θena; do'sena/ f, dozen. **la d. del fraile,** baker's dozen

docente /do'θente; do'sente/ a teaching

dócil /'doθil; 'dosil/ a docile; obedient; flexible, easily worked (metals, etc.)

docilidad /doθili'ðað; dosili'ðað/ f, docility; obedience; flexibility

docto /'dokto/ a learned, erudite

doctor /dok'tor/ **(-ra)** n doctor; physician; teacher. f, *Inf.* blue-stocking

doctorado /dokto'raðo/ m, doctorate

doctorarse /dokto'rarse/ vr to get one's doctorate

doctrina /dok'trina/ f, doctrine; instruction, teaching; theory, conception; *Eccl.* sermon

documentación /dokumenta'θion; dokumenta'sion/ f, documentation; collection of documents, papers

documental /dokumen'tal/ a documental. m, documentary film

documentar /dokumen'tar/ vt to document

dogal /do'gal/ m, halter; noose; slipknot. *Fig.* **estar con el d. a la garganta,** to be in a fix

dogma /'dogma/ m, dogma

dogmático /dog'matiko/ a dogmatic

dólar /'dolar/ m, dollar

dolencia /do'lenθia; do'lensia/ f, ailment; pain; ache

doler /do'ler/ vi irr to be in pain; be reluctant; —vr be sorry, regretful; grieve; sympathize, be compassionate; complain —*Pres. Indic.* **duelo, dueles, duele, duelen.** *Pres. Subjunc.* **duela, duelas, duela, duelan**

doliente /do'liente/ a suffering; ill; afflicted, sad. mf sufferer, ill person. m, chief mourner

dolo /'dolo/ m, fraud; deception; deceit; *Law.* premeditation

dolor /do'lor/ m, pain, ache; mental suffering. **d. sordo,** dull pain

dolorido /dolo'riðo/ a painful; afflicted, sad

doloroso /dolo'roso/ a sad, regrettable; mournful, sorrowful; pitiful; painful

doloso /do'loso/ a deceitful, fraudulent

domable /do'maβle/ a tamable; controllable

domadura /doma'ðura/ f, taming, breaking in; controlling (emotions)

domar /do'mar/ vt to tame, break in; control, repress (emotions)

domesticable /domesti'kaβle/ a tamable; domesticable

domesticar /domesti'kar/ vt to tame; domesticate; —vr grow tame; become domesticated

doméstico /do'mestiko/ **(-ca)** a domestic, domesticated; tame —n domestic worker

domiciliar /domiθi'liar; domisi'liar/ vt to domicile; —vr become domiciled, settle down

domicilio /domi'θilio; domi'silio/ m, domicile; house

dominación /domina'θion; domina'sion/ f, domination; power, authority; command (of a military position, etc.); *Mil.* high ground; pl dominions, angels

dominador /domina'ðor/ a dominating; overbearing

dominante /domi'nante/ a dominating; overbearing, domineering; dominant. f, *Mus.* dominant

dominar /domi'nar/ vt to dominate; repress, subdue; *Fig.* master (branch of knowledge); —vi stand out; —vr control oneself

domingo /do'mingo/ m, Sunday. **d. de Cuasimodo,** Low Sunday. **d. de Pente-**

costés, Whitsuntide Sunday. **d. de Ra-mos,** Palm Sunday. **d. de Resurrección,** Easter Sunday

dominicano /domini'kano/ **(-na)** *a* and *n* Dominican; native of Santo Domingo

dominio /'dominio/ *m,* authority, power; rule, sovereignty; dominion (country); domain

dominó /domi'no/ *m,* domino; game of dominoes

don /don/ *m,* gift; quality, characteristic; talent. **d. de gentes,** the human touch; charm

don /don/ *m,* title of respect equivalent to English Mr. or Esquire. Used only before given name and *not* before a family name, e.g. *don Juan Martínez,* or *don Juan*

donación /dona'θion; dona'sion/ *f,* donation, gift, grant

donador /dona'ðor/ **(-ra)** *a* donating —*n* donor

donaire /do'naire/ *m,* discretion, wit; witticism; gracefulness, elegance

donar /do'nar/ *vt* to bestow, give; transfer; grant

donativo /dona'tiβo/ *m,* gift, present, donation

donde /'donde/ *adv* where, wherein. Sometimes used as relative pronoun "in which" (e.g. *La casa d. estaba.* The house in which I was) —*interr* **¿dónde? ¿A dónde va Vd.?** Where are you going to? **¿De dónde viene Vd.?** Where do you come from? **¿Por dónde se va a Madrid?** Which is the way to Madrid?

dondequiera /donde'kiera/ *adv* wherever, anywhere, everywhere

donoso /do'noso/ *a* witty; graceful

donosura /dono'sura/ *f,* wit; grace; dash, verve

doña /'dona/ *f,* feminine equivalent of **don** (e.g. *D. Catalina Palacios*)

dorado /do'raðo/ *a* golden, gilded; fortunate, happy. *m,* gilding

dorador /dora'ðor/ *m,* gilder

doradura /dora'ðura/ *f,* gilding

dorar /do'rar/ *vt* to gild; make golden; *Fig.* gild the pill; *Cul.* toast lightly; —*vr* become golden

dormidero /dormi'ðero/ *a* soporiferous, narcotic

dormilón /dormi'lon/ **(-ona)** *a Inf.* sleepy —*n* sleepyhead

dormir /dor'mir/ *vi irr* to sleep; spend the night; *Fig.* grow calm; sleep (tops); (*with sobre*) sleep on, consider; —*vt* put to sleep; —*vr* go to sleep; go slow over, neglect; be dormant; go numb (limbs). **d. como un lirón,** to sleep like a top. *Inf.* **d. la mona,** to sleep oneself sober. *entre* **duerme y vela,** half-awake —*Pres. Indic.* **duermo, duermes, duerme, duermen.** *Pres. Part.* **durmiendo.** *Preterite* **durmió, durmieron.** *Pres. Subjunc.* **duerma, duermas, duerma, duerman**

dormitar /dormi'tar/ *vi* to doze

dormitivo /dormi'tiβo/ *a* and *m,* sedative

dormitorio /dormi'torio/ *m,* dormitory; bedroom

dorso /'dorso/ *m,* back; dorsum

dos /dos/ *a* two. *m,* two; second (of the month). **las d.,** two o'clock. **d. a d.,** two against two. **de d. en d.,** two by two. *Inf.* **en un d. por tres,** in a twinkling

doscientos /dos'θientos; dos'sientos/ *a* and *m,* two hundred; two hundredth

dosel /do'sel/ *m,* canopy; dais

dosis /'dosis/ *f,* dose; quantity

dotación /dota'θion; dota'sion/ *f,* endowment; *Naut.* crew; staff, workers; equipment

dotar /do'tar/ *vt* to give as dowry; endow, found; *Fig.* endow (with talents, etc.); equip; apportion (salary)

dote /'dote/ *mf,* dowry. *f,* (gen. *pl*) gifts, talents. **dotes de mando,** capacity for leadership

draga /'draga/ *f,* dredger

dragado /dra'gaðo/ *m,* dredging

dragaminas /draga'minas/ *m, Nav.* minesweeper

dragar /dra'gar/ *vt* to dredge

dragón /dra'gon/ *m,* dragon; *Bot.* snapdragon; *Mil.* dragoon; *Zool.* dragon, giant lizard; *Astron.* Draco

dragona /dra'gona/ *f,* female dragon; *Mil.* shoulder-strap

drama /'drama/ *m,* play; drama. **d. lírico,** opera

dramática /dra'matika/ *f,* dramatic art

dramático /dra'matiko/ *a* dramatic; vivid, unexpected, moving

dramaturgo /drama'turgo/ *m,* dramatist, playwright

drenaje /dre'nahe/ *m,* drainage (of land and wounds)

dril /dril/ *m,* drill, cotton cloth

droga /'droga/ *f,* drug; falsehood, deception; nuisance

droguería /droge'ria/ *f,* chemist's shop; drug trade

droguero /dro'gero/ **(-ra)** *n* chemist, druggist

ducado /du'kaðo/ *m,* dukedom; duchy; ducat

ducha /'dutʃa/ *f,* shower-bath; douche; stripe in cloth; furrow

ducho /'dutʃo/ *a* experienced, skillful

dúctil /'duktil/ *a* ductile (metals); adaptable, docile, flexible

ductilidad /duktili'ðað/ *f,* ductility; adaptability

duda /'duða/ *f,* doubt, hesitation; problem. **sin d.,** doubtless

dudable /du'ðaβle/ *a* doubtful

dudar /du'ðar/ *vi* to be in doubt; —*vt* doubt, disbelieve

dudoso /du'ðoso/ *a* doubtful; uncertain, not probable

duela /'duela/ *f,* hoop, stave

duelista /due'lista/ *mf* dueler; duelist

duelo /'duelo/ *m,* sorrow, grief; mourning; mourners; duel; (gen. *pl*) troubles, trials. **duelos y quebrantos,** *Cul.* fried offal. **sin d.,** in abundance

duende /'duende/ *m,* imp, elf, sprite, ghost

dueña /'dueɲa/ *f,* owner, proprietress, mistress; duenna; married lady *Obs.*

dueño /'dueɲo/ *m,* owner, proprietor; master (of servants). **d. de sí mismo,** self-controlled

dula /'dula/ *f,* common pasture ground or herds

dulce /'dulθe; dulse/ *a* sweet; fresh, pure; fresh, not salty; fragrant; melodious; pleasant, agreeable; tender, gentle; soft (metals). *m,* sweetmeat, bonbon. **d. de almíbar,** preserved fruit.

dulcedumbre /dulθe'ðumbre; dulse'ðumbre/ *f,* sweetness; softness

dulcémele /dulθe'mele; dulse'mele/ *m,* dulcimer

dulcera /dul'θera; dul'sera/ *f,* preserve dish, fruit dish

dulcería /dulθe'ria; dulse'ria/ *f,* See **confitería**

dulcificar /dulθifi'kar; dulsifi'kar/ *vt* to make sweet; alleviate, sweeten

dulcinea /dul'θinea; dul'sinea/ *f, Inf.* sweetheart; ideal

dulzaina /dul'θaina; dul'saina/ *f, Mus.* flageolet

dulzura /dul'θura; dul'sura/ *f,* sweetness; gentleness; pleasure; meekness; agreeableness

duna /'duna/ *f,* (gen. *pl*) sand dune

dúo /'duo/ *m, Mus.* duet

duodécimo /duo'ðeθimo; duoðesimo/ *a* twelfth

duodeno /duo'ðeno/ *a* twelfth. *m, Anat.* duodenum

duplicación /duplika'θion; duplika'sion/ *f,* duplication

duplicado /dupli'kaðo/ *m,* duplicate

duplicar /dupli'kar/ *vt* to duplicate; double

duplicidad /dupliθi'ðað; duplisi'ðað/ *f,* duplicity, falseness

duque /'duke/ *m,* duke

duquesa /du'kesa/ *f,* duchess

duración /dura'θion; dura'sion/ *f,* duration; durability

duradero /dura'ðero/ *a* lasting; durable

durante /du'rante/ *adv* during

durar /du'rar/ *vi* to continue; endure, last

dureza /du'reθa; du'resa/ *f,* hardness; *Med.* callosity; severity, harshness

durmiente /dur'miente/ *a* sleeping. *mf* sleeper; *m, Archit.* dormant

duro /'duro/ *a* hard; firm, unyielding; vigorous, robust; severe, inclement; exacting, cruel; *Mus.* metallic, harsh; *Art.* crude, too sharply defined; miserly, avaricious; obstinate; self-opinionated; unbearable, intolerable; merciless, hard; harsh (style). *m,* Spanish coin worth five pesetas

E

¡ea! /'ea/ *interj* Well!; Come on!; Let's see! (often used with **pues**)

ebanista /eβa'nista/ *mf* cabinetmaker

ebanistería /eβaniste'ria/ *f.* cabinetmaker's shop; cabinetmaking or work

ébano /'eβano/ *m,* ebony

ebrio /'eβrio/ *a* intoxicated, inebriated

ebullición /eβuʎi'θion; eβuyi'sion/ *f,* boiling, ebullition

echada /e'tʃaða/ *f,* throw, cast; pitch; fling; length of a man

echador /etʃa'ðor/ **(-ra)** *n* thrower. *m, Inf.* chucker-out

echadura /etʃa'ðura/ *f,* sitting on eggs to hatch them; (gen. *pl*) gleanings

echamiento /etʃa'miento/ *m,* throw, fling; throwing, casting; expulsion; rejection

echar /e'tʃar/ *vt* to throw, fling; eject, drive away; cast out, expel; put forth, sprout; emit, give forth; cut (teeth); dismiss, discharge; couple (animals); pour (liquids); place, apply; put into, fill; turn (keys, locks); impute; attribute; impose (penalty, taxes, etc.); play (game); try one's luck; distribute; publish, make known; perform (plays); (*with por*) go in direction of; (*with prep a + infin.*) begin to (e. **a andar**, to begin to walk); —*vr* throw oneself down, lie down; sit on eggs (birds); abate, calm (wind); apply oneself, concentrate on; rush (towards), fling oneself (upon). **e. abajo,** to overthrow; demolish. **e. aceite al fuego,** to add fuel to the flames. *Naut.* **e. a pique,** to sink. **e. a vuelo,** to ring (bells). **e. carnes,** to put on weight, grow fat. **e. cuentas,** to reckon up. **e. de menos,** to miss; mourn absence of. **e. de ver,** to notice. *Fig.* **e. en cara,** to throw in one's face, reproach. **echarla de majo,** to play the gallant. **e. las cartas al correo,** to post the letters. **e. las cartas,** to tell fortunes. **e. el pie atrás,** *Fig.* to climb down; *Fig.* back out. **e. raíces,** to take root; **e. las bases de, e. los cimientos de,** to lay the foundation of, lay the foundation for. *Fig.* become established. **e. rayos por la boca,** to fly into a rage. **e. suertes,** to draw lots. **echarlo todo a rodar,** to spoil everything. **e. una mano,** to lend a hand

ecléctico /e'klektiko/ **(-ca)** *a* and *n* eclectic

eclesiástico /ekle'siastiko/ *a* ecclesiastical. *m,* ecclesiastic, clergyman; Ecclesiasticus

eclipsar /eklip'sar/ *vt Astron.* to eclipse; surpass, outvie; —*vr Astron.* be in eclipse; disappear

eclipse /e'klipse/ *m, Astron.* eclipse; retirement, withdrawal

eco /'eko/ *m,* echo; verse-echo; muffled sound; slavish imitation or imitator

economato /ekono'mato/ *m,* trusteeship; cooperative store

economía /ekono'mia/ *f,* economy, thrift; structure, organization; poverty, shortage;

saving (of time, labor, etc.); *pl* savings. **e. dirigida,** planned economy. **e. doméstica,** domestic economy. **e. política,** political economy

económico /eko'nomiko/ *a* economic; thrifty; avaricious; cheap

economista /ekono'mista/ *mf* economist

economizar /ekonomi'θar; ekonomi'sar/ *vt* to economize; save

ecónomo /e'konomo/ *m,* trustee, guardian

ecuación /ekua'θion; ekua'sion/ *f,* (*Math.* and *Astron.*) equation. **e. personal,** personal equation

ecuador /ekua'ðor/ *m,* equator

ecuánime /ekua'nime/ *a* calm, unruffled; impartial

ecuanimidad /ekuanimi'ðað/ *f,* calmness, serenity; impartiality

ecuatorial /ekuato'rial/ *a* equatorial

ecuatoriano /ekuato'riano/ **(-na)** *a* and *n* Ecuadorian

ecuestre /e'kuestre/ *a* equestrian

ecuménico /eku'meniko/ *a* ecumenical

eczema /'ekθema; 'eksema/ *m,* eczema

edad /e'ðað/ *f,* age; epoch; period. **e. de piedra,** Stone Age. **e. media,** Middle Ages. **de cierta e.,** middle-aged. **ser mayor de e.,** to have attained one's majority. **ser menor de e.,** to be a minor

edema /e'ðema/ *m,* edema

Edén /e'ðen/ *m,* Eden; *Fig.* paradise

edición /eði'θion; eði'sion/ *f,* edition. **e. diamante,** miniature edition. **e. príncipe,** first edition

edicto /e'ðikto/ *m,* edict, decree; public notice

edificación /eðifika'θion; eðifika'sion/ *f,* building, construction; edification

edificador /eðifika'ðor/ **(-ra)** *a* uplifting, edifying; building —*n* builder

edificar /eðifi'kar/ *vt* to build, construct; edify

edificio /eði'fiθio; eði'fisio/ *m,* building, structure, fabric

editar /eði'tar/ *vt* (of a publisher) to publish; edit

editor /eði'tor/ **(-ra)** *n* publisher; editor

editorial /eðito'rial/ *a* publishing; editorial. *m,* editorial, leading article

edredón /eðre'ðon/ *m,* down of an eiderduck; eiderdown, quilt

educación /eðuka'θion; eðuka'sion/ *f,* upbringing; education; good breeding, good manners

educado /eðu'kaðo/ *a* educated. **ser mal e.,** to be badly brought up; be ill-mannered

educador /eðuka'ðor/ **(-ra)** *a* educating —*n* educator

educar /eðu'kar/ *vt* to educate; bring up, train, teach, develop

educativo /eðuka'tiβo/ *a* educational, educative

efe /'efe/ *f*, name of letter F

efectivo /efek'tiβo/ *a* effective; real. *m*, cash. **hacer e.**, to put into effect

efecto /e'fekto/ *m*, effect, result; purpose, intent; impression; *pl* assets; goods, chattels. **efectos de escritorio,** stationery. **efectos públicos,** public securities. **en e.**, in fact, actually. **llevar a e.,** to put into effect; make effective

efectuación /efektua'θion; efektua'sion/ *f*, accomplishment, execution

efectuar /efek'tuar/ *vt* to accomplish, effect; make (a payment); —*vr* be effected; happen, take place

eferente /efe'rente/ *a* efferent

efervescencia /eferβes'θenθia; eferβes'sensia/ *f*, effervescence; excitement, enthusiasm

efervescente /eferβes'θente; eferβes'sente/ *a* effervescent

eficacia /efi'kaθia; efi'kasia/ *f*, efficacy; effectiveness

eficaz /efi'kaθ; efi'kas/ *a* efficacious; effective

eficiencia /efi'θienθia; efi'siensia/ *f*, efficiency

eficiente /efi'θiente; efi'siente/ *a* efficient, effective

efigie /e'fihie/ *f*, effigy; image, representation, symbol

efímero /e'fimero/ *a* ephemeral; brief

eflorescencia /eflores'θenθia; eflores'sensia/ *f*, *Chem.* efflorescence

efusión /efu'sion/ *f*, effusion; *Fig.* spate (of words, etc.)

efusivo /efu'siβo/ *a* effusive, expansive

Egeo, Mar /e'heo, mar/ Aegean Sea

égida /'ehiða/ *f*, shield; egis, protection

egipcíaco /ehip'θiako; ehip'siako/ **(-ca), egipcio (-ia)** *a* and *n* Egyptian

Egipto /e'hipto/ Egypt

egoísmo /ego'ismo/ *m*, egoism

egoísta /ego'ista/ *a* egoistic. *mf* egoist

egotismo /ego'tismo/ *m*, egotism

egotista /ego'tista/ *a* egotistical. *mf* egotist

egregio /e'grehio/ *a* distinguished, celebrated

egresado /egre'saðo/ *m*, graduate (of a certain school)

eje /'ehe/ *m*, axis; axle-tree; shaft; pivot, fundamental idea. **e. trasero,** rear-axle

ejecución /eheku'θion; eheku'sion/ *f*, accomplishment, performance; execution, technique; death penalty

ejecutable /eheku'taβle/ *a* feasible, practicable

ejecutante /eheku'tante/ *mf* *Mus.* executant, performer

ejecutar /eheku'tar/ *vt* to discharge, perform; put to death; (*Art. Mus.*) execute; serve (a warrant, etc.); *Law.* seize (property)

ejecutivo /eheku''tiβo/ *a* executive; urgent

ejecutor /eheku'tor/ *m*, executor

ejecutoria /eheku'toria/ *f*, letters patent of nobility; *Law.* judgment, sentence

ejecutoría /ehekuto'ria/ *f*, executorship

ejemplar /ehem'plar/ *a* exemplary. *m*, copy, specimen; precedent; example; warning

ejemplificar /ehemplifi'kar/ *vi* to exemplify

ejemplo /e'hemplo/ *m*, example, precedent; illustration, instance; specimen. **dar e.,** to set an example. **por e.,** for example

ejercer /eher'θer; eher'ser/ *vt* to practice (a profession); perform, fulfill; exercise, use

ejercicio /eher'θiθio; eher'sisio/ *m*, exercise; practice; performance; exertion, effort; *Mil.* exercises (gen. *pl*). **ejercicios espirituales,** spiritual exercises. **ejercicios físicos,** physical training

ejercitar /eherθi'tar; ehersi'tar/ *vt* to exercise; train, teach; —*vr* exercise; practice

ejército /e'herθito; e'hersito/ *m*, army

el /el/ *def art m*, sing the

él /el/ *pers pron sing m*, he; it (*f*. **ella.** *neut* **ello**) (e.g. *Lo hizo él,* He did it). Also used with prep. (e.g. *Lo hicimos por él,* We did it for him)

elaboración /elaβora'θion; elaβora'sion/ *f*, elaboration, working out

elaborado /elaβo'raðo/ *a* elaborate

elaborar /elaβo'rar/ *vt* to elaborate; produce, work out

elasticidad /elastiθi'ðað; elastisi'ðað/ *f*, elasticity; adaptability

elástico /e'lastiko/ *a* elastic; adaptable. *m*, elastic tape; elastic material

ele /'ele/ *f*, name of letter L

elección /elek'θion; elek'sion/ *f*, choice; election; selection; discrimination

electivo /elek'tiβo/ *a* elective

electo /e'lekto/ *m*, elect, candidate elect

elector /elek'tor/ **(-ra)** *n* elector, voter. *m*, German prince *Obs.*

electorado /elekto'raðo/ *m*, electorate

electoral /elekto'ral/ *a* electoral

electricidad /elektriθi'ðað; elektrisi'ðað/ *f*, electricity

electricista /elektri'θista; elektri'sista/ *mf* electrician

eléctrico /e'lektriko/ *a* electric; electrical

electrificar /elektrifi'kar/ *vt* to electrify

electrizar /elektri'θar; elektri'sar/ *vt* to electrify; startle; —*vr* be electrified

electrocución /elektroku'θion; elektroku'sion/ *f*, electrocution

electrocutar /elektroku'tar/ *vt* to electrocute

electroimán /elektroi'man/ *m*, electromagnet

electrólisis /elek'trolisis/ *f*, electrolysis

electromotriz /elektro'motriθ; elektro'motris/ *a* electromotive. **fuerza e.,** electromotive force

electrón /elek'tron/ *m*, electron

electrotecnia /elektro'teknia/ *f*, electrical engineering

electroterapia /elektrote'rapia/ f, Med. electrotherapy

elefante /ele'fante/ **(-ta)** n elephant

elefantino /elefan'tino/ a elephantine

elegancia /ele'ganθia; ele'gansia/ f, elegance, grace; fashionableness; Lit. beauty of style

elegante /ele'gante/ a elegant; graceful, lovely; fashionable, stylish

elegía /ele'hia/ f, elegy

elegibilidad /elehiβili'ðað/ f, eligibility

elegible /ele'hiβle/ a eligible

elegir /ele'hir/ vt irr to select, prefer; elect —Pres. Indic. **elijo, eliges, elige, eligen.** Pres. Part. **eligiendo.** Preterite **eligió, eligieron.** Pres. Subj. **elija,** etc.

elemental /elemen'tal/ a elemental; fundamental; elementary

elemento /ele'mento/ m, element; component, constituent; Elec. element; pl rudimente. Mil. **elementos de choque,** shock troops

elevación /eleβa'θion; eleβa'sion/ f, lifting, raising; height, high ground; elevation; altitude; Fig. eminence; elevation, advancement; ecstasy; raising (of the voice)

elevado /ele'βaðo/ a sublime, lofty

elevar /ele'βar/ vt to raise, lift; Fig. exalt; —vr be in ecstasy, be transported. **elevarse de categoría,** to rise in status

elfo /'elfo/ m, elf

eliminación /elimina'θion; elimina'sion/ f, elimination

eliminador /elimina'ðor/ a eliminatory. m, eliminator

eliminar /elimi'nar/ vt to eliminate

elipse /e'lipse/ f, ellipse

elipsis /e'lipsis/ f, ellipsis

elíptico /e'liptiko/ a elliptic

elíseo /e'liseo/ m, Elysium —a Elysian. **campos elíseos,** Elysian fields

ella /'eʎa; 'eya/ pers pron 3rd sing f she; it. See **él**

ello /'eʎo; 'eyo/ pers pron 3rd sing neut that, the fact, it. **Ello es que...,** The fact is that... **No tengo tiempo para ello,** I have no time for that

ellos, ellas /'eʎos, 'eʎas; 'eyos, 'eyas/ pers pron 3rd pl m and f, they. See **él**

elocución /eloku'θion; eloku'sion/ f, elocution; style of speech

elocuencia /elo'kuenθia; elo'kuensia/ f, eloquence

elocuente /elo'kuente/ a eloquent

elogiador /elohia'ðor/ **(-ra)** a eulogistic —n eulogist

elogiar /elo'hiar/ vt to eulogize, praise

elogio /e'lohio/ m, eulogy, praise. **«Elogio de la Locura»,** "In Praise of Folly"

elucidar /eluθi'ðar; elusi'ðar/ vt to elucidate, clarify

eludible /elu'ðiβle/ a escapable, avoidable

eludir /elu'ðir/ vt to elude, avoid

emaciación /emaθia'θion; emasia'sion/ f, emaciation

emanación /emana'θion; emana'sion/ f, emanation; effluvium

emanar /ema'nar/ vi to emanate (from), originate (in)

emancipación /emanθipa'θion; emansipa'sion/ f, emancipation; enfranchisement

emancipador /emanθipa'ðor; emansipa'ðor/ **(-ra)** a emancipatory —n emancipator

emancipar /emanθi'par; emansi'par/ vt to emancipate, free; enfranchise; —vr emancipate oneself; become independent; free oneself

emascular /emasku'lar/ vt to emasculate

embadurnar /embaður'nar/ vt to smear, smudge, daub

embajada /emba'haða/ f, embassy; ambassadorship; embassy building; Inf. message

embajador /embaha'ðor/ m, ambassador; emissary

embajadora /embaha'ðora/ f, wife of ambassador; woman ambassador

embalaje /emba'lahe/ m, packing; bale; wrapper; packing charge

embalar /emba'lar/ vt to pack

embaldosado /embaldo'saðo/ m, tiled pavement or floor

embaldosar /embaldo'sar/ vt to tile, pave with tiles

embalsamar /embalsa'mar/ vt to embalm; perfume

embalse /em'balse/ m, dam; damming, impounding (of water)

embanastar /embanas'tar/ vt to place in a basket; crowd, squeeze

embarazada /embara'θaða; embara'saða/ a f, pregnant

embarazar /embara'θar; embara'sar/ vt to impede, hinder, embarrass; —vr be hindered or embarrassed; be pregnant

embarazo /emba'raθo; emba'raso/ m, difficulty, impediment; pregnancy; timidity, embarrassment

embarazoso /embara'θoso; embara'soso/ a embarrassing; inconvenient; difficult, troublesome

embarcación /embarka'θion; embarka'sion/ f, ship, vessel; embarkation

embarcadero /embarka'ðero/ m, wharf, dock; quay; pier; jetty

embarcar /embar'kar/ vt to embark, ship; board (boat, train, etc.); —vr embark; board

embarco /em'barko/ m, embarking, embarkation

embargar /embar'gar/ vt to obstruct, impede; Law. seize; suspend, paralyse

embargo /em'bargo/ m, Law. seizure; embargo. **sin e.,** nevertheless, however

embarque /em'barke/ m, loading, embarkation (goods)

embarrancar /embarran'kar/ vi Naut. to run aground; —vr Naut. be stuck on a reef or in the mud

embarrilar /embarri'lar/ *vt* to barrel

embarullar /embaru'ʎar; embaru'yar/ *vt Inf.* to mix up, muddle; do hastily and badly

embastar /embas'tar/ *vt Sew.* to baste; tack

embaste /em'baste/ *m, Sew.* basting; tacking stitch

embate /em'bate/ *m,* beating of the waves; sudden attack; unexpected misfortune

embaucar /embau'kar/ *vt* to deceive, hoodwink

embaular /embau'lar/ *vt* to pack in a trunk; *Inf.* stuff with food

embazar /emba'θar; emba'sar/ *vt* to dye brown; hinder; amaze; —*vr* be amazed; be tired or bored; be satiated

embebecer /embeβe'θer; embeβe'ser/ *vt irr* to entertain, amuse; engross, fascinate; —*vr* be dumbfounded. See **conocer**

embebecimiento /embeβeθi'miento; embeβesi'miento/ *m,* astonishment; absorption, engrossment

embeber /embe'βer/ *vt* to absorb; contain; shrink, contract; saturate; insert, introduce; incorporate; —*vi* shrink; —*vr* be amazed; master or absorb (a subject). **embebido en sus pensamientos,** absorbed in thought

embelecar /embele'kar/ *vt* to dupe, deceive, trick

embelesar /embele'sar/ *vt* to astonish; fascinate, enchant; —*vr* be astonished or fascinated

embeleso /embe'leso/ *m,* astonishment; fascination; charm

embellecer /embeʎe'θer; embeye'ser/ *vt irr* to embellish; —*vr* beautify oneself. See **conocer**

embellecimiento /embeʎeθi'miento; embeyesi'miento/ *m,* beautifying, embellishment

embestida /embes'tiða/ *f,* assault, attack, onrush; *Inf.* importunity

embestir /embes'tir/ *vt irr* to rush upon, assault; *Inf.* importune, be a nuisance to; —*vi Fig. Inf.* clash, be inharmonious. See **pedir**

emblema /em'blema/ *m,* emblem; symbol; badge

emblemático /emble'matiko/ *a* emblematic; symbolical

embobar /embo'βar/ *vt* to entertain, fascinate; —*vr* be dumbfounded

embobecer /emboβe'θer; emboβe'ser/ *vt irr* to make stupid. See **conocer**

embocadero /emboka'ðero/ *m,* narrow entrance, bottleneck; mouth of a channel

embocadura /emboka'ðura/ *f,* entrance by a narrow passage; *Mus.* mouthpiece; flavor (of wine); estuary, mouth of a river; *Theat.* proscenium

embocar /embo'kar/ *vt* to put in the mouth; go through a narrow passage; deceive; *Inf.* devour, wolf; initiate a business deal

embolia /em'bolia/ *f,* embolism

émbolo /'embolo/ *m, Mech.* piston, plunger

embolsar /embol'sar/ *vt* to place money in a purse; collect (a debt, etc.)

emborrachar /emborra't ʃar/ *vt* to intoxicate; daze, stupefy; —*vr* become intoxicated; run (of dyes)

emborrascarse /emborras'karse/ *vr* to be furious; become stormy (weather); *Fig.* go downhill (business concern)

emborronar /emborro'nar/ *vt* to blot; scribble, write hastily

emboscar /embos'kar/ *vt Mil.* to set an ambush; —*vr* lie in ambush

embotar /embo'tar/ *vt* to blunt (cutting edge); —*vi Fig.* weaken; —*vr* become blunt

embotellado /embote'ʎaðo; embote-'yaðo/ *m,* bottling; *Fig.* bottleneck

embotellador /embote'ʎaðor; embote-'yaðor/ **(-ra)** *n* bottler. *f.* **embotelladora,** bottling outfit

embotellar /embote'ʎar; embote'yar/ *vt* to bottle; bottle up, prevent from escaping

embozar /embo'θar; embo'sar/ *vt Fig.* to cloak, dissemble; muffle; —*vr* muffle oneself up

embozo /em'boθo; em'boso/ *m,* anything used to cover or muffle the face; pretense, pretext; facings (gen. *pl*); yashmak

embragar /embra'gar/ *vt* to sling, lift; *Mech.* let in the clutch

embrague /em'brage/ *m;* hoisting, slinging; *Mech.* clutch

embravecer /embraβe'θer; embraβe'ser/ *vt irr* to infuriate; —*vr* be enraged; be boisterous (sea). See **conocer**

embrazadura /embraθa'ðura; embrasa'ðura/ *f,* grasping, clasping; handle, clasp

embrear /embre'ar/ *vt* to tar, paint with pitch

embriagador /embriaga'ðor/ *a* intoxicating

embriagar /embria'gar/ *vt* to intoxicate; enrapture; —*vr* become inebriated

embriaguez /embria'geθ; embria'ges/ *f,* intoxication, inebriation; rapture

embrión /em'brion/ *m,* embryo; germ, rough idea

embrionario /embrio'nario/ *a* embryonic

embrocación /embroka'θion; embroka-'sion/ *f, Med.* embrocation

embrollar /embro'ʎar; embro'yar/ *vt* to entangle; embroil

embrollo /em'broʎo; em'broyo/ *m,* tangle; falsehood; difficult situation

embromar /embro'mar/ *vt* to tease, chaff; trick, deceive; waste the time of; annoy; harm

embrujar /embru'har/ *vt* to bewitch

embrutecer /embrute'θer; embrute'ser/ *vt irr* to make brutish or stupid; —*vr* become brutish. See **conocer**

embudo /em'buðo/ *m, Chem.* funnel

embuste /em'buste/ *m*, lie, fraud; *pl* trinkets

embustero /embus'tero/ **(-ra)** *a* deceitful, knavish —*n* liar, cheat, trickster

embutido /embu'tiðo/ *m*, inlaid work; *Cul.* sausage

embutir /embu'tir/ *vt* to inlay; stuff full, cram; —*vt* and *vr Inf.* stuff with food

eme /'eme/ *f*, name of letter M

emergencia /emer'henθia; emer'hensia/ *f*, emergence; accident, emergency

emerger /emer'her/ *vi* to emerge; have its source (rivers, etc.)

emérito /e'merito/ *a* emeritus

emético /e'metiko/ *a* and *m*, emetic

emigración /emigra'θion; emigra'sion/ *f*, emigration; migration; number of emigrants

emigrado /emi'graðo/ *m*, emigrant, emigré

emigrante /emi'grante/ *a* and *mf* emigrant

emigrar /emi'grar/ *vi* to emigrate; migrate

eminencia /emi'nenθia; emi'nensia/ *f*, highland; importance, prominence; outstanding personality, genius; title given to cardinals

eminente /emi'nente/ *a* high, elevated; prominent, illustrious

emisión /emi'sion/ *f*, emission; *Radio.* broadcast; *Com.* issue (bonds, etc.); floating (of a loan)

emisor /emi'sor/ *m*, *Elec.* transmitter.

emisora /emi'sora/ *f*, *Radio.* broadcasting station

emitir /emi'tir/ *vt* to emit; *Radio.* broadcast; *Com.* issue (bonds, paper money, etc.); utter, give voice to

emoción /emo'θion; emo'sion/ *f*, emotion

emocional /emo'θional; emo'sional/ *a* emotional; emotive

emocionante /emoθio'nante; emosio'nante/ *a* moving, causing emotion; thrilling

emocionar /emoθio'nar; emosio'nar/ *vt* to cause emotion, move; —*vr* be stirred by emotion; be thrilled

emolumento /emolu'mento/ *m*, emolument (gen. *pl*)

emotivo /emo'tiβo/ *a* emotive

empachado /empa't∫aðo/ *a* awkward, clumsy

empachar /empa't∫ar/ *vt* to hinder, impede; disguise, dissemble; —*vr* overeat, stuff; be bashful

empacho /em'pat∫o/ *m*, bashfulness, timidity; embarrassment, impediment; indigestion, satiety

empadronamiento /empaðrona'miento/ *m*, census

empadronar /empaðro'nar/ *vt* to take the census

empalagoso /empala'goso/ *a* sickly, oversweet; cloying; *Fig.* sugary, honeyed

empalar /empa'lar/ *vt* to impale

empalizada /empali'θaða; empali'saða/ *f*, stockade, fencing

empalmar /empal'mar/ *vt* to dovetail; splice (ropes); clamp; *Fig.* combine (plans, actions, etc.); —*vi* join (railroad lines); couple (railroad trains); —*vr* palm (as in conjuring)

empalme /em'palme/ *m*, connection; splicing; *Fig.* combination (of plans, etc.); railroad junction; continuation; palming, secreting

empanada /empa'naða/ *f*, savory turnover or pie; secret negotiations, intrigue

empanar /empa'nar/ *vt* to bread; *Cul.* cover with breadcrumbs; *Agr.* sow grain

empañar /empa'ɲar/ *vt* to swaddle; tarnish, dim; blur; *Fig.* sully (fame, etc.)

empapar /empa'par/ *vt* to saturate; absorb; impregnate; —*vr* be saturated; absorb; *Fig.* be imbued

empapelador /empapela'ðor/ *m*, paperhanger

empapelar /empape'lar/ *vt* to wrap in paper; paper (a room, etc.)

empaque /em'pake/ *m*, packing; paneling; *Inf.* mien, air; pomposity

empaquetador /empaketa'ðor/ **(-ra)** *n* packer

empaquetar /empake'tar/ *vt* to pack; make up parcels or packages; overcrowd

emparedado /empare'ðaðo/ **(-da)** *a* cloistered, reclusive —*n* recluse. *m*, *Cul.* sandwich

emparejar /empare'har/ *vt* to pair, match; equalize, make level; —*vi* come abreast (of); be equal

emparentar /emparen'tar/ *vi irr* to become related by marriage. See **acertar**

empastadura /empasta'ðura/ *f*, filling (of teeth)

empastar /empas'tar/ *vt* to cover with glue or paste; bind in boards (books); fill (teeth). **empastado en tela**, clothbound

empaste /em'paste/ *m*, pasting, gluing; filling (teeth)

empatar /empa'tar/ *vt* to equal, tie with

empate /em'pate/ *m*, tie, draw; dead heat

empecatado /empeka'taðo/ *a* willful; evil-minded, wicked; incorrigible, impenitent; extremely unlucky

empecer /empe'θer; empe'ser/ *vt irr* to harm, damage; —*vi* hinder. See **conocer**

empedernido /empeðer'niðo/ *a* stonyhearted, cruel

empedrado /empe'ðraðo/ *a* dappled (horses); *Fig.* flecked (with clouds). *m*, paving; pavement

empedrar /empe'ðrar/ *vt irr* to pave with stones. See **acertar**

empegadura /empega'ðura/ *f*, coat of pitch

empegar /empe'gar/ *vt* to coat with pitch; mark with pitch (sheep)

empeine /em'peine/ *m*, groin; instep

empellar /empe'ʎar; empe'yar/ *vt* to push, jostle

empellón /empe'ʎon; empe'yon/ *m*, hard push. *Inf.* **a empellones**, by pushing and shoving

empeñado /empe'ɲaðo/ *a* violent, heated (of disputes)

empeñar /empe'ɲar/ *vt* to pledge, leave as surety; pawn; oblige, compel; appoint as mediator; —*vr* bind oneself, be under an obligation; (*with en*) insist on; persist in; —*vr* intercede; mediate; *Mil.* begin (a battle). **empeñado en**, determined to, intent on

empeño /em'peɲo/ *m*, pledge, surety; obligation, engagement; fervent desire; purpose, intention; determination, resolve; guarantor; *Inf.* influence, favor

empeoramiento /empeora'miento/ *m*, worsening; deterioration

empeorar /empeo'rar/ *vt* to make worse; —*vi* and *vr* deteriorate, grow worse

empequeñecer /empekeɲe'θer; empekeɲe'ser/ *vt irr* to diminish, lessen; make smaller; belittle. See **conocer**

emperador /empera'ðor/ *m*, emperor

emperatriz /empera'triθ; empera'tris/ *f*, empress

emperezar /empere'θar; empere'sar/ *vt* to obstruct, hinder; —*vr* be lazy

empezar /empe'θar; empe'sar/ *vt irr* to begin, commence; initiate; —*vi* begin —*Pres. Indic.* **empiezo, empiezas, empieza, empiezan.** *Preterite* **empecé, empezaste**, etc —*Pres. Subjunc.* **empiece, empieces, empiece, empecemos, empecéis, empiecen**

empinado /empi'naðo/ *a* steep; lofty; arrogant; exalted

empinar /empi'nar/ *vt* to raise; tip, tilt (drinking vessels); —*vr* stand on tiptoe; rear, prance; tower, rise; *Aer.* zoom, climb steeply. *Inf.* **e. el codo**, to lift the elbow, tipple

empírico /em'piriko/ **(-ca)** *a* empiric —*n* quack, charlatan

empizarrado /empiθa'rraðo; empisa'rraðo/ *m*, slate roof

emplastar /emplas'tar/ *vt Med.* to apply plasters; make up; paint; *Inf.* hinder, obstruct; —*vr* be smeared

emplasto /em'plasto/ *m*, *Med.* plaster; poultice; *Inf.* put-up job, fraud

emplazamiento /emplaθa'miento; emplasa'miento/ *m*, placing, location; site; *Law.* summons; *Naut.* berth

emplazar /empla'θar; empla'sar/ *vt* to convene, arrange a meeting; *Law.* summon

empleado /emple'aðo/ **(-da)** *n* employee; clerk. **e. público**, civil servant

emplear /em'plear/ *vt* to employ; lay out, invest (money); use; —*vr* be employed or occupied

empleo /em'pleo/ *m*, employment; investment, laying out (of money); occupation; post, office

emplomar /emplo'mar/ *vt* to lead, solder or cover with lead; affix lead seals on or to; weight (a stick, etc.)

emplumecer /emplume'θer; emplume'ser/ *vi irr* to fledge, grow feathers. See **conocer**

empobrecer /empoβre'θer; empoβre'ser/ *vt* to impoverish; —*vi* and *vr* become poor; decay. See **conocer**

empobrecimiento /empoβreθi'miento; empoβresi'miento/ *m*, impoverishment

empollar /empo'ʎar; empo'yar/ *vt* to hatch; —*vi* produce a brood (of bees); *Inf.* brood on, consider; *Inf.* grind, cram, swot (of students)

empollón /empo'ʎon; empo'yon/ **(-ona)** *n Inf.* plodder, grind, swot

empolvar /empol'βar/ *vt* to cover with dust; powder

emponzoñar /emponθo'ɲar; emponso'ɲar/ *vt* to poison; pervert, corrupt

emporio /em'porio/ *m*, emporium

empotrar /empo'trar/ *vt* to embed, implant; fix down

emprendedor /emprende'ðor/ *a* capable, efficient, enterprising

emprender /empren'der/ *vt* to undertake; (*with prep a or con*) *Inf.* accost, tackle, buttonhole

empresa /em'presa/ *f*, undertaking, task; motto, device; intention, design; management; firm; enterprise, deal

empresarial /empresa'rial/ *a* entrepreneurial

empresario /empre'sario/ *m*, contractor; theatrical manager

empréstito /em'prestito/ *m*, loan

empujar /empu'har/ *vt* to push; *Fig.* exert pressure, influence

empuje /em'puhe/ *m*, push; *Archit.* pressure; energy; power, influence

empujón /empu'hon/ *m*, violent thrust or push. *Inf.* **a empujones**, by pushing and shoving; intermittently

empuñar /empu'ɲar/ *vt* to grasp; grip; clutch

emulación /emula'θion; emula'sion/ *f*, emulation, competition, rivalry

emulador /emula'ðor/ *a* emulative

emular /emu'lar/ *vt* to emulate, rival, compete with

émulo /'emulo/ **(-la)** *a* emulative, rival —*n* competitor, rival

emulsivo /emul'siβo/ *a* emulsive

en /en/ *prep* in; into; on, upon; at; by. **en Madrid**, in Madrid. **en junio**, in June. **Se echó en un sillón**, He threw himself into an armchair. **Se transformó en mariposa**, It turned into a butterfly. **Hay un libro en la mesa**, There is a book on the table. **María está en casa**, Mary is at home. **en un precio muy alto**, at a very high price. **El número de candidatos ha disminuido en un treinta por ciento**, The number of candidates has decreased by thirty percent. **En** appears in a number of adverbial phrases, e.g. *en particular*, in particular, *en secreto*, in secret, *en seguida*, immediately. When it is used with a gerund, it means after, as soon as, when, e.g. *En llegando a la puerta llamó*, When he arrived at the door, he knocked. *En todas partes se cuecen habas,* That happens everywhere; It happens in the best of families

enagua /e'nagua/ *f.* slip, crinoline, petticoat

enajenación /enahena'θion; enahena-'sion/ *f.* transference, alienation (property); abstraction, absent-mindedness. **e. mental,** lunacy

enajenar /enahe'nar/ *vt* to transfer (property)

enaltecer /enalte'θer; enalte'ser/ *vt irr* to elevate, raise; exalt. See **conocer**

enamoradizo /enamora'ðiθo; enamora-'ðiso/ *a* susceptible, easily enamored; fickle

enamorado /enamo'raðo/ *a* in love, lovesick; easily enamored

enamorar /enamo'rar/ *vt* to arouse love in; court, make love to; —*vr* fall in love; (with *de*) become fond of (things)

enano /e'nano/ **(-na)** *a* small, dwarf —*n* dwarf

enarbolar /enarβo'lar/ *vt* to hoist (flags); —*vr* prance (horses); become angry

enardecer /enarðe'θer; enarðe'ser/ *vt irr* to kindle, stimulate (passion, quarrel, etc.); —*vr* be afire (with passion); *Med.* be inflamed. See **conocer**

encabezamiento /enkaβeθa'miento; enkaβesa'miento/ *m,* census taking; tax register; tax assessment; heading, inscription, running head

encabezar /enkaβe'θar; enkaβe'sar/ *vt* to take the census of; put on the tax register; open a subscription list; put a heading or title to; lead, head; —*vr* compound, settle by agreement (taxes, etc.)

encadenamiento /enkaðena'miento/ *m,* fettering, chaining; connection, link, relation

encadenar /enkaðe'nar/ *vt* to chain, fetter; *Fig.* link up, connect; *Fig.* paralyze. **encadenar el interés de,** to capture the interest of

encajar /enka'har/ *vt* to insert, fit one thing inside another; force in; fit tightly; *Inf.* be opportune, fit in (often with *bien*); —*vr* squeeze or crowd in; *Inf.* butt in, interfere

encaje /en'kahe/ *m,* fitting, insertion; socket, groove; joining; lace; inlay, mosaic

encalar /enka'lar/ *vt* to whitewash

encallar /enka'ʎar; enka'yar/ *vi Naut.* to run aground; *Fig.* be held up (negotiations, etc.)

encalvecer /enkalβe'θer; enkalβe'ser/ *vi irr* to grow bald. See **conocer**

encamado /enka'maðo/ *a* bedridden, confined to one's bed; *m,* person confined to his bed

encamarse /enka'marse/ *vr* to go to bed (gen. illness); be laid flat (grain, etc.); crouch

encaminadura /enkamina'ðura/ *f,* en-

caminamiento *m,* directing, forwarding, routing

encaminar /enkami'nar/ *vt* to guide; direct; regulate; manage; promote, advance; —*vr* (with prep *a*) make for, go in the direction of

encandecer /enkande'θer; enkande'ser/ *vt irr* to make incandescent. See **conocer**

encandilar /enkandi'lar/ *vt* to dazzle; mislead; *Inf.* poke (the fire); —*vr* be bloodshot (eyes)

encanecer /enkane'θer; enkane'ser/ *vi irr* to grow gray- or white-haired; grow mold; grow old. See **conocer**

encanijar /enkani'har/ *vt* to make weak, sickly (gen. of babies); —*vr* be delicate or ailing

encantado /enkan'taðo/ *a Inf.* daydreaming, abstracted; haunted; rambling (of houses)

encantador /enkanta'ðor/ *a* captivating, bewitching, delightful. *m,* sorcerer, magician. **e. de serpientes,** snake charmer

encantamiento /enkanta'miento/ *m,* enchantment, spell, charm

encantar /enkan'tar/ *vt* to enchant, weave a spell; delight, captivate, charm

encañada /enka'naða/ *f,* gorge, ravine

encañado /enka'naðo/ *m,* trellis; pipeline

encañar /enka'nar/ *vt* to run water through a pipe; stake plants; wind thread on a spool

encañonar /enkano'nar/ *vt* to run into pipes; pleat, fold

encapotarse /enkapo'tarse/ *vr.* to muffle oneself in a cloak; scowl; be overcast; lower (sky)

encapricharse /enkapri'tʃarse/ *vr* to take a fancy (to); insist on having one's own way, be stubborn

encaramar /enkara'mar/ *vt* to raise, lift; climb; praise, extol. **e. al poder,** to put in power (e.g. a dictator). **encaramarse por,** to climb up

encarar /enka'rar/ *vt* to place face to face; aim (at); —*vt* and *vr* face; come face to face

encarcelación /enkarθela'θion; enkarsela'sion/ *f,* incarceration

encarcelar /enkarθe'lar; enkarse'lar/ *vt* to imprison, jail; clamp

encarecer /enkare'θer; enkare'ser/ *vt irr* to raise the price; overpraise, exaggerate; recommend strongly; —*vi* and *vr* increase in price. See **conocer**

encarecimiento /enkareθi'miento; enkaresi'miento/ *m,* increase (in price); enhancement; exaggeration. **con e.,** insistently, earnestly

encargado /enkar'gaðo/ *m,* person in charge; manager; agent, representative. **e. de negocios,** chargé d'affaires

encargar /enkar'gar/ *vt* to enjoin; commission; recommend; advise; *Com.* order

encargo /en'kargo/ *m,* charge, commission; order; office, employ; responsibility

encariñarse /enkari'ɲarse/ (con), vi to become fond (of)

encarnación /enkarna'θion; enkarna'sion/ f, incarnation

encarnar /enkar'nar/ vi to incarnate; pierce the flesh; Fig. leave a strong impression; —vt symbolize, personify; —vr mingle, blend

encarnizado /enkarni'θaðo; enkarni'saðo/ a bloodshot (eyes); flesh-colored; bloody, cruel (gen. of battles)

encarnizamiento /enkarniθa'miento; enkarnisa'miento/ m, cruelty, fury

encarnizar /enkarni'θar; enkarni'sar/ vt to infuriate; —vr devour flesh (animals); persecute, ill-treat

encarrilar /enkarri'lar/ vt to set on the track or rails (vehicles); Fig. put right, set on the right track

encartar /enkar'tar/ vt to proscribe, outlaw; place on the tax register; Law. summon, cite

encartonar /enkarto'nar/ vt to cover with cardboard; bind in boards (books)

encasar /enka'sar/ vt Surg. to set (a bone)

encasquetar /enkaske'tar/ (se) vt and vr to pull a hat well down on the head; —vr get a fixed idea

encastillar /enkasti'ʎar; enkasti'yar/ vt to fortify with castles; —vr retire to a castle; be headstrong, obstinate

encauzar /enkau'θar; enkau'sar/ vt to channel; Fig. direct, guide

encefalitis /enθefa'litis; ensefa'litis/ f, encephalitis. **e. letárgica**, encephalitis lethargica, sleeping sickness

encendedor /enθende'ðor; ensende'ðor/ a lighting. m, lighter. **e. de bolsillo**, pocket lighter

encender /enθen'der; ensen'der/ vt irr to light; switch on; set fire to, kindle; arouse (emotions); inflame, incite; —vr blush. See **entender**

encendido /enθen'diðo; ensen'diðo/ a high-colored; inflamed; ardent. m, Auto. ignition

encerado /enθe'raðo; ense'raðo/ a waxcolored. m, oilskin; sticking plaster; blackboard; tarpaulin

encerar /enθe'rar; ense'rar/ vt to wax, varnish with wax; stain with wax; inspissate (lime)

encerrar /enθe'rrar; ense'rrar/ vt irr to shut up, imprison; include, contain; —vr go into seclusion. See **acertar**

enchufar /entʃu'far/ vt to connect tubes; Fig. combine (jobs, etc.); Elec. plug, connect

enchufe /en'tʃufe/ m, joint, fitting together (of tubes); Elec. wall socket, plug; part-time post; Inf. cushy job. **e. de reducción**, Elec. adapter

encía /en'θia; en'sia/ f, gum (of the mouth)

enciclopedia /enθiklo'peðia; ensiklo-'peðia/ f, encyclopedia

enciclopédico /enθiklo'peðiko; ensiklo-'peðiko/ a encyclopedic

encierro /en'θierro; en'sierro/ m, act of closing or shutting up; prison; retreat, confinement

encima /en'θima; en'sima/ adv over; above; at the top; besides; (with de) on, on top of. **por e. de esto**, over and above this, besides this

encinta /en'θinta; en'sinta/ a f, pregnant

encintar /enθin'tar; ensin'tar/ vt to decorate with ribbons

enclavar /enkla'βar/ vt to nail; pierce; embed; Inf. deceive

enclenque /en'klenke/ a ailing, weak; puny, anemic

encoger /enko'her/ vt to shrink, contract, recoil; discourage; —vi shrink (wood, cloth, etc.); —vr shrink from, recoil; be discouraged; be timid or bashful

encogimiento /enkohi'miento/ m, shrinkage; contraction; depression, discouragement; timidity; bashfulness

encolerizar /enkoleri'θar; enkoleri'sar/ vt to anger; —vr be angry

encomendar /enkomen'dar/ vt irr to charge with, entrust; recommend, commend; —vr (with prep a) put one's trust in; send greetings to. See **acertar**

encomiar /enko'miar/ vt to eulogize, praise

encomienda /enko'mienda/ f, commission, charge; knight commandership; insignia of knight commander; land formerly granted in America to conquistadores; recommendation, commendation; protection, defense; pl greetings, compliments, messages

encomio /en'komio/ m, eulogy; strong recommendation

enconar /enko'nar/ vt to irritate, exasperate; —vr Med. be inflamed; be exasperated; (with en) burden one's conscience with

encono /en'kono/ m, rancor, resentment, ill will

encontrado /enkon'traðo/ a facing, opposite, in front; hostile, inimical, opposed (to)

encontrar /enkon'trar/ vt irr to meet; find; —vi meet; encounter unexpectedly; (with con) run into, collide with; —vr be antagonistic; find; feel, be; differ, disagree (opinions); (with con) meet, come across. **e. eco**, to strike a responsive chord. **encontrarse con el cura de su pueblo**, to find someone who knows all about, meet someone who knows all about. **¿Cómo se encuentra Vd?** How are you? Pres. Indic. **encuentro**, etc —Pres. Subjunc. **encuentre**, etc.

encontrón /enkon'tron/ m, collision, violent impact

encopetado /enkope'taðo/ a conceited, proud; of noble descent; prominent, important

encorajar /enkora'har/ vt to encourage, inspire, hearten; —vr be angry

encorvadura /enkorβa'ðura/ f. bending, curving

encorvar /enkor'βar/ vt to bend, curve; —vr have a leaning toward, favor

encostrar /enkos'trar/ vt to cover with a crust; —vr form a crust

encrespar /enkres'par/ vt to curl (hair); enrage; —vr be curly (hair); stand on end (hair, feathers, from fright); be angry; grow rough (sea); become complicated, entangled

encrestado /enkres'taðo/ a crested; haughty, arrogant

encrestarse /enkres'tarse/ vr to stiffen the comb or crest (birds)

encrucijada /enkruθi'haða; enkrusi'haða/ f. crossroad, intersection; ambush

encrudecer /enkruðe'θer; enkruðe'ser/ vt irr to make raw-looking; annoy; —vr be annoyed. See **conocer**

encuadernación /enkuaðerna'θion; enkuaðerna'sion/ f. bookbinding; binding (of a book); bookbinder's workshop. **e. en tela**, cloth binding

encuadernador /enkuaðerna'ðor/ (**-ra**) n bookbinder

encuadernar /enkuaðer'nar/ vt to bind (a book)

encuadrar /enkuað'rar/ vt to frame; fit one thing into another, insert; limit; Mil. enlist

encubierto /enku'βierto/ a concealed; secret

encubridor /enkuβri'ðor/ (**-ra**) a concealing, hiding —n hider; harborer; accomplice; receiver (of stolen goods); Law. accessory after the fact

encubrimiento /enkuβri'miento/ m. hiding, concealment; Law. accessory before (after) the fact; receiving (of stolen goods)

encubrir /enkuβ'rir/ vt to conceal; receive (stolen goods); Law. prosecute as an accessory. Past. Part. **encubierto**

encuentro /en'kuentro/ m. collision; meeting, encounter; opposition, hostility; Mil. fight, skirmish; Archit. angle. **ir al e. de**, to go in search of. **salir al e.** (**de**), to go to meet; resist

encuesta /en'kuesta/ f. investigation, examination

encumbrado /enkum'braðo/ a elevated, high

encumbramiento /enkumbra'miento/ m. act of elevating; height; aggrandizement; advancement

encumbrar /enkum'brar/ vt to raise, elevate; exalt, promote; ascend, climb to the top; —vr be proud; be lofty, tower

encurtir /enkur'tir/ vt to pickle

ende /'ende/ adv Obs. there. **por e.**, therefore

endeble /en'deβle/ a weak, frail

endeblez /ende'βleθ; ende'βles/ f. weakness

endecha /en'detʃa/ f. dirge

endémico /en'demiko/ a Med. endemic

endemoniado /endemo'niaðo/ a devil-possessed; Inf. fiendish, malevolent

endemoniar /endemo'niar/ vt to possess with a devil; Inf. enrage

endentar /enden'tar/ vt irr Mech. to cut the cogs (of a wheel); engage, interlock (gears, wheels, etc.). See **regimentar**

endentecer /endente'θer; endente'ser/ vi irr to cut teeth. See **conocer**

enderezamiento /endereθa'miento; enderesa'miento/ m. straightening; directing, guiding; putting right, correction

enderezar /endere'θar; endere'sar/ vt to straighten; direct, guide; put right, correct; —vt take the right road; —vr straighten oneself; prepare to

endeudarse /endeu'ðarse/ vr to contract debts; be under an obligation

endiablado /endia'βlaðo/ a ugly, monstrous; Inf. fiendish

endiosar /endio'sar/ vt to deify; —vr be puffed up with pride; be abstracted or lost in ecstasy

endomingarse /endomiŋ'garse/ vr to put on one's Sunday best

endosante /endo'sante/ m. endorser

endosar /endo'sar/ vt Com. to endorse; transfer, pass on

endoso /en'doso/ m. Com. endorsement

endulzar /endul'θar; endul'sar/ vt to sweeten; soften, mitigate

endurecer /endure'θer; endure'ser/ vt irr to harden; toughen, inure; make severe or cruel; —vr grow hard; become hardened or robust; be harsh or cruel. **endurecerse al trabajo**, to become hardened to work. See **conocer**

endurecimiento /endureθi'miento; enduresi'miento/ m. hardness; obstinacy, tenacity

ene /'ene/ f. name of letter N

enemigo /ene'migo/ (**-ga**) a hostile —n enemy; antagonist. m. devil

enemistad /enemis'taθ/ f. enmity, hostility

enemistar /enemis'tar/ vt to make enemies of; —vr (with con) become an enemy of; cease to be friendly with

energía /ener'hia/ f. energy, vigor

enérgico /e'nerhiko/ a energetic, vigorous

enero /e'nero/ m. January

enervar /ener'βar/ vt to enervate, weaken; Fig. take the force out of (reasons, etc.)

enfadar /enfa'ðar/ vt to make angry; —vr become angry

enfado /en'faðo/ m. anger; annoyance; trouble, toil

enfadoso /enfa'ðoso/ a vexatious; troublesome, wearisome

enfaldar /enfal'dar/ vt to tuck up the skirts; lop off lower branches (of trees)

enfangarse /enfaŋ'garse/ vr to cover oneself with mud; Inf. dirty one's hands, sully one's reputation; wallow in vice

énfasis /'enfasis/ m, or f, emphasis

enfático /en'fatiko/ a emphatic

enfermar /enfer'mar/ vi to fall ill; —vt cause illness; Fig. weaken. **Enfermó del corazón,** He fell ill with heart trouble.

enfermedad /enferme'ðað/ f, illness; Fig. malady, distemper. **e. del sueño,** sleeping sickness

enfermera /enfer'mera/ f, nurse

enfermería /enferme'ria/ f, infirmary; hospital; first-aid station

enfermero /enfer'mero/ m, nurse

enfermizo /enfer'miθo/ enfer''miso/ a ailing, delicate; unhealthy, unwholesome

enfermo /en'fermo/ a ill; Fig. corrupt, diseased; delicate, sickly —n patient. **e. venéreo,** person with a venereal disease

enfilar /enfi'lar/ vt to place in line; string; Mil. enfilade

enflaquecer /enflake'θer; enflake'ser/ vt irr to make thin; weaken, enervate; —vi grow thin; lose heart. See **conocer**

enfocar /enfo'kar/ vt to focus; envisage

enfoque /en'foke/ m, focus

enfoscado /enfos'kaðo/ a ill-humored; immersed in business matters

enfrascar /enfras'kar/ vt to bottle; —vr (with en) plunge into, entangle oneself in (undergrowth, etc.); become engrossed or absorbed in

enfrenar /enfre'nar/ vt to bridle; curb (a horse); restrain, repress; check

enfrente /en'frente/ adv in front, opposite, facing; in opposition

enfriadero /enfria'ðero/ m, cooling place, cold cellar, root cellar

enfriar /enf'riar/ vt to cool; Fig. chill, make indifferent; —vr grow cold; Fig. grow stormy (weather)

enfurecer /enfure'θer; enfure'ser/ vt irr to enrage. See **conocer**

enfurruñarse /enfurru'narse/ vr Inf. to fume, be angry; be disgruntled

engalanar /engala'nar/ vt to decorate, embellish. **engalanado como nunca,** dressed to the nines, dressed to kill

enganchar /engan'tʃar/ vt to hook; couple, connect; hitch, harness, yoke; Inf. seduce, hook; Mil. bribe into army; —vr be hooked or caught on a hook; Mil. enlist

enganche /en'gantʃe/ m, hooking; coupling (of railroad trains, etc.); connection; yoke, harness; hook; Inf. enticement; Mil. enlistment

engañadizo /engana'ðiθo; enganaðiso/ a easily deceived, simple

engañador /engana'ðor/ **(-ra)** a deceiving; deceptive —n deceiver, impostor

engañar /enga'nar/ vt to deceive; defraud, cheat; beguile, while away; hoax, humbug; —vr be mistaken; deceive oneself. **e. como a un chino,** Inf. to pull the wool over a person's eyes. **Las apariencias engañan,** Appearances are deceptive

engañifa /enga'nhook;ifa/ f, Inf. swindle, fraud

engaño /en'gano/ m, deceit; deception; illusion; fraud; falsehood

engañoso /enga'noso/ a deceitful, false; fraudulent; deceptive, misleading

engarce /en'garθe/ engarse/ m, hooking; coupling; setting (of jewels)

engarzar /engar'θar; engar'sar/ vt to link, couple, enchain; hook; curl; set (jewels)

engastar /engas'tar/ vt to set (jewels)

engaste /en'gaste/ m, setting (of jewels)

engatusar /engatu'sar/ vt Inf. to wheedle, coax, flatter

engendrar /enhen'drar/ vt to procreate; engender, produce, cause

engendro /en'hendro/ m, fetus; abnormal embryo; literary monstrosity

englobar /englo'βar/ vt to include, comprise, embrace

engolfarse /engol'farse/ vr to sail out to sea; (with en) Fig. be absorbed in

engomar /engo'mar/ vt to gum

engordar /engor'ðar/ vt to fatten; —vi grow fat; Inf. prosper, grow rich

engorro /en'gorro/ m, impediment, obstacle, difficulty

engorroso /engo'rroso/ a difficult, troublesome

engranaje /engra'nahe/ m, Mech. gearing, gear; Fig. connection, link

engrandecer /engrande'θer; engrande-'ser/ vt irr to enlarge; augment; eulogize; promote, exalt. See **conocer**

engrandecimiento /engrandeθi'miento; engrandesi'miento/ m, enlargement; increase; exaggeration, eulogization; advancement, promotion

engrasado /engra'saðo/ m, oiling; greasing

engrasar /engra'sar/ vt to grease; lubricate, oil; manure; stain with grease

engreír /engre'ir/ vt irr to make conceited; —vr become vain or conceited. See **reír**

engrescar /engres'kar/ **(se)** vt and vr to start a quarrel

engrosar /engro'sar/ vt irr to fatten, thicken; Fig. increase, swell; manure; —vi put on weight, grow fat. See **contar**

engrudar /engru'ðar/ vt to paste, glue

engullir /engu'ʎir; engu'yir/ vt to gobble, swallow

enhebrar /ene'βrar/ vt to thread (needles); string

enhestar /enes'tar/ vt irr to erect; set upright; —vr rise; rear up; straighten oneself up. See **acertar**

enhiesto /en'iesto/ a upright, erect

enhorabuena /enora'βuena/ f, congratulation —adv well and good. **dar la e.,** to congratulate

enhoramala /enora'mala/ adv in an evil hour. Inf. **¡Vete e.!** Go to the devil!

enhorquetado /enorke'taðo/ a in the saddle

enigma /e'nigma/ m, enigma

enigmático /enig'matiko/ a enigmatical

enjabonar /enhaβo'nar/ vt to soap; Inf. soap down, flatter

enjalbegar /enhalβe'gar/ vt to whitewash

enjambrar /enhamb'rar/ vt to hive bees; —vi multiply, increase

enjambre /en'hambre/ m, swarm (of bees); crowd

enjaular /enhau'lar/ vt to cage; Inf. jail

enjoyar /enho'yar/ vt to adorn with jewels; beautify; set with precious stones

enjuagadura /enhuaga'ðura/ f, rinsing (the mouth); rinse water; mouthwash

enjuagar /enhua'gar/ vt to rinse; —vr rinse the mouth

enjuague /en'huage/ m, rinse; rinsing; mouthwash; tooth mug; scheme, plan

enjugar /enhu'gar/ vt to dry; cancel, write off; wipe, mop (perspiration, tears, etc.); —vr grow lean

enjuiciar /enhui'θiar; enhui'siar/ vt to submit a matter to arbitration; Law. prosecute; Law. render judgment; Law. adjudicate (a case)

enjundia /en'hundia/ f, animal fat or grease; Fig. substance, meat; strength, vigor; constitution, temperament

enjuto /en'huto/ a dry; lean. m pl, brushwood; Cul. canapés, savories

enlace /en'laθe; en'lase/ m, connection; link, tie; Chem. bond; alliance, relationship; marriage

enlazar /enla'θar; enla'sar/ vt to tie, bind; join, link; lasso; —vr marry; be allied, related. **e. con,** to connect with (of trains); link up with

enlentecerse /enlente'θerse; enlente-'serse/ vr to decelerate, go slow, slow down

enlodar /enlo'ðar/ vt to muddy; Fig. smirch, sully

enloquecer /enloke'θer; enloke'ser/ vt irr to drive insane; —vi go mad. See **conocer**

enlosado /enlo'saðo/ m, tile floor

enlucir /enlu'θir; enlu'sir/ vt irr to plaster (walls); polish (metals). See **lucir**

enlutar /enlu'tar/ vt to put in mourning, drape with crepe; darken, obscure; sadden; —vr go into mourning; become dark

enmarañar /emara'ɲar/ vt to tangle, disorder (hair, etc.); complicate, confuse; —vr be tangled; be sprinkled with clouds

enmascarar /emaska'rar/ vt to mask; disguise, dissemble; —vr be masked

enmendar /emen'dar/ vt irr to correct, improve; reform; compensate, indemnify; Law. repeal; —vr be improved or corrected; mend one's ways. See **acertar**

enmienda /e'mienda/ f, correction; reform; indemnity; compensation; amendment; pl Agr. fertilizers

enmohecer /emoe'θer; emoe'ser/ vt irr to rust; —vr become moldy. See **conocer**

enmudecer /emuðe'θer; emuðe'ser/ vt irr to silence; —vi become dumb; be silent. See **conocer**

enmugrecer /emugre'θer; emugre'ser/ vt irr to cover with grime; —vr be grimy, dirty. See **conocer**

ennegrecer /ennegre'θer; ennegre'ser/ vt irr to dye black; make black; —vr become black; become dark or cloudy. See **conocer**

ennoblecer /ennoβle'θer; ennoβle'ser/ vt irr to ennoble; enrich, embellish; adorn, befit. See **conocer**

ennoblecimiento /ennoβleθi'miento; ennoβlesi'miento/ m, ennoblement; enrichment

enojadizo /enoha'ðiθo; enoha'ðiso/ a irritable, peevish

enojar /eno'har/ vt to anger; annoy, irritate; —vr be angry; rage, be rough (wind, sea)

enojo /e'noho/ m, anger; resentment; vexations, troubles, trials (gen. pl). **con gran e. de,** much to the annoyance of

enojoso /ono'hoso/ a annoying; troublesome, tiresome

enorgullecer /enorguʎe'θer; enorguye-'ser/ vt irr to make proud; —vr be proud. See **conocer**

enorme /e'norme/ a enormous, huge; monstrous, heinous

enormidad /enormi'ðað/ f, hugeness; enormity; wickedness

enramar /enra'mar/ vt to intertwine branches; embower; —vi branch (trees)

enrarecer /enrare'θer; enrare'ser/ vt irr to rarefy; —vr become rarefied; grow rare. See **conocer**

enredador /enreða'ðor/ **(-ra)** a mischievous, willful; intriguing, scheming; Inf. gossiping, meddlesome —n intriguer; Inf. meddler

enredar /enre'ðar/ vt to catch in a net; put down nets or snares; entangle; sow discord; compromise, involve (in difficulties); —vi be mischievous; —vr be entangled; be involved (in difficulties)

enredo /en'reðo/ m, tangle; mischief, prank; intrigue, malicious falsehood; difficult situation; plot

enredoso /enre'ðoso/ a tangled; fraught with difficulties

enrejado /enre'haðo/ m, railing, paling; trellis or latticework; Sew. openwork

enriquecer /enrike'θer; enrike'ser/ vt irr to enrich; exalt, aggrandize; —vi grow rich; prosper, flourish. See **conocer**

enriscado /enris'kaðo/ a craggy, rocky

enrojecer /enrohe'θer; enrohe'ser/ vt irr to redden; make blush; —vr grow red; blush. See **conocer**

enroscar /enros'kar/ vt to twist, twine; —vr turn (screw); twist; coil

ensaimada /ensai'maða/ f, Spanish pastry cake

ensalada /ensa'laða/ f, salad; hodgepodge

ensaladera /ensala'ðera/ f, salad bowl

ensalmo /en'salmo/ m, spell, charm. **por e.,** as if by magic, rapidly

ensalzar /ensal'θar; ensal'sar/ vt to exalt, promote; praise

ensamblador /ensambla'ðor/ m, joiner, assembler

ensambladura /ensambla'ðura/ f, assemblage, joinery; joining; dovetailing

ensamblar /ensam'blar/ vt to assemble; join, dovetail, mortise

ensanchador /ensantʃa'ðor/ m, glove stretcher

ensanchar /ensan'tʃar/ vt to widen, enlarge, extend; Sew. let out, stretch; —vr put on airs

ensanche /en'santʃe/ m, dilatation, widening; stretch; extension; Sew. turnings, letting out; (city) extension

ensangrentar /ensaŋgren'tar/ vt irr to stain with blood; —vr be bloodstained; be overhasty. See **regimentar**

ensañar /ensa'ɲar/ vt to irritate, infuriate; —vr be merciless (with vanquished)

ensartar /ensar'tar/ vt to string (beads); thread (needles); spit, pierce; tell a string (of falsehoods)

ensayar /ensa'yar/ vt to try out; Chem. test; Theat. rehearse; assay

ensayista /ensa'yista/ mf essayist

ensayo /ensa'yo/ m, test, trial; Lit. essay; assay; experiment; rehearsal. **e. general,** dress rehearsal

ensenada /ense'naða/ f, cove, inlet

enseña /en'seɲa/ f, ensign, standard

enseñanza /ense'ɲanθa; ense̯ansa/ f, teaching; education; example, experience. **e. primaria,** elementary education. **e. secundaria,** secondary education. **e. superior,** higher education

enseñar /ense'ɲar/ vt to teach, instruct; train; point out; exhibit, show; —vr become accustomed. **e. la oreja,** Fig. to show the cloven hoof

enseñorearse /enseɲore'arse/ vr to take possession (of)

enseres /en'seres/ m pl, household goods; utensils; equipment

ensillar /ensi'ʎar; ensi'yar/ vt to saddle

ensimismarse /ensimis'marse/ vr to be lost in thought

ensoberbecer /ensoβerβe'θer; ensoβerβe''ser/ vt irr to make haughty; —vr become arrogant; grow rough (sea). See **conocer**

ensordecedor /ensorðeθe'ðor; ensorðese'ðor/ a deafening

ensordecer /ensorðe'θer; ensorðe'ser/ vt irr to deafen; —vi become deaf; keep silent, refuse to reply. See **conocer**

ensuciar /ensu'θiar; ensu'siar/ vt to soil, dirty; Fig. sully; —vr be dirty; Inf. accept bribes

ensueño /en'sueɲo/ m, dream; illusion; fancy

entablado /enta'βlaðo/ m, stage, dais; wooden floor; planking

entablar /enta'βlar/ vt to plank, floor with boards; board up; Surg. splint; undertake, initiate (negotiations, etc.); begin

(conversations, etc.); —vr settle (winds). **e. acción judicial,** to take legal action

entalladura /entaʎa'ðura; entaya'ðura/ f, carving; sculpture; mortise, notch

entallar /enta'ʎar; enta'yar/ vt to carve; sculpture; engrave; notch, groove; tap (trees); fit (well or ill) at the waist

entallecer /entaʎe'θer; entaye'ser/ vi irr to sprout (plants). See **conocer**

entapizar /entapi'θar; entapi'sar/ vt to hang with tapestry; upholster; Fig. cover, carpet

entarimado /entari'maðo/ m, wooden floor; dais

ente /'ente/ m, entity, being; Inf. object, individual

enteco /en'teko/ a sickly, ailing, delicate

entendederas /entende'ðeras/ f pl, Inf. understanding

entendedor /entende'ðor/ **(-ra)** a understanding, comprehending —n one who understands. **A buen e. pocas palabras,** A word to the wise is sufficient

entender /enten'der/ vt to comprehend, understand; know; deduce, infer; intend; believe; (with de) be familiar with or knowledgeable about; (with en) have as a profession or trade; be engaged in; have authority in; —vr understand oneself; have a reason (for behavior); understand each other; have an amatory understanding; be meant, signify; (with con) have an understanding with. **a mi e.,** in my opinion, as I see it —Pres. Indic. entiendo, entiendes, entiende, entienden. Pres. Subjunc. entienda, entiendas, entienda, entiendan

entendido /enten'diðo/ a learned, knowledgeable

entendimiento /entendi'miento/ m, understanding; mind, reason, intelligence

enteramente /entera'mente/ adv completely, entirely, wholly

enterar /ente'rar/ vt to inform, advise

entereza /ente'reθa; entere̯sa/ f, entirety; completeness; impartiality, integrity; fortitude, constancy; strictness, rigor

enternecer /enterne'θer; enterne'ser/ vt irr to soften, make tender; move to pity; —vr be touched by compassion. See **conocer**

enternecimiento /enterneθi'miento; enternesi'miento/ m, compassion, pity; tenderness

entero /en'tero/ a entire; whole; robust, healthy; upright, just; constant, loyal; virgin; pure; Inf. strong, tough (cloth); Math. integral

enterrador /enterra'ðor/ m, gravedigger

enterrar /ente'rrar/ vt irr to inter; outlive; bury, forget. See **acertar**

entibiar /enti'βiar/ vt to make lukewarm; Fig. cool, temper

entidad /enti'ðað/ f, entity; value, importance

entierro /en'tierro/ m, interment, burial; grave; funeral; buried treasure

entoldar /entol'dar/ vt to cover with an

awning; hang with tapestry, etc., drape; cover (sky, clouds)

entonación /entona'θion; entona'sion/ *f,* intonation; modulation (voice); conceit

entonado /ento'naðo/ *m,* haughty, conceited

entonar /ento'nar/ *vt* to modulate (voice); intone; blow (organ bellows); lead (song); *Med.* tone up; *Art.* harmonize; —*vr* become conceited; *Com.* improve, harden (stock, etc.)

entonces /en'tonθes; entonses/ *adv* then, at that time; in that case, that being so

entontecer /entonte'θer; entonteser/ *vt irr* to make stupid or foolish; —*vr* become stupid. See **conocer**

entornar /entor'nar/ *vt* to leave ajar; half-close; upset, turn upside down

entorpecer /entorpe'θer; entorpe'ser/ *vt irr* to numb, make torpid; confuse, daze; obstruct, delay; —*vr* go numb; be confused. See **conocer**

entorpecimiento /entorpeθi'miento; entorpesi'miento/ *m,* numbness, torpidity; stupidity, dullness; delay, obstruction

entrada /en'traða/ *f,* entrance; door, gate; admission; *Cul.* entree; admission ticket; *Theat.* house; takings, gate; *Mil.* entry; beginnings (of month, etc.); intimacy; right of entry. **entradas y salidas,** comings and goings; collusion; *Com.* ingoing and outgoing

entrampar /entram'par/ *vt* to trap (animals); swindle; *Fig. Inf.* entangle (business affairs); *Inf.* load with debts; —*vr* be bogged down; *Inf.* be in debt

entrante /en'trante/ *a* incoming, entrant; next, coming (month)

entraña /en'traɲa/ *f,* entrail; *pl* heart; *Fig.* center, core; humaneness; temperament. *Inf.* **no tener entrañas,** to be heartless, be without feeling

entrañable /entra'ɲaβle/ *a* intimate; dearly loved

entrar /en'trar/ *vi* (*with en*) to enter, go into, come in; flow into; *Fig.* have access to; join, become a member; *Fig.* be taken by (fever, panic, etc.); *Mil.* enter; be an ingredient of; (*with por, en*) penetrate, pierce; (*with de*) embrace (professions, etc.); (*with prep a* + *infin*) begin to; (*with en* + *noun*) begin to be (e.g. *e. en calor,* begin to be hot) or begin to take part in (e.g. *e. en lucha,* begin to fight); —*vt* introduce, make enter; *Mil.* (*with en*) occupy; —*vr* (*with en*) squeeze in. **e. en apetito,** to work up an appetite, get an appetite. *Inf.* **no e. ni salir en,** to take no part in. *Inf.* **No me entra,** I don't understand it

entre /'entre/ *prep* between; among; to. **e. joyas,** among jewels. **E. las dos se escribió la carta,** Between them, they wrote the letter. **Dije e. mí,** I said to myself. **los días de e. semana,** weekdays. **e. tanto,** in the meanwhile.

entreabrir /entrea'βrir/ *vt* to leave ajar; half-open —*Past Part.* **entreabierto**

entreacto /entre'akto/ *m,* interval, entr'acte; small cigar

entrecoger /entreko'her/ *vt* to intercept, catch; constrain, compel

entrecortado /entrekor'taðo/ *a* intermittent (sounds); faltering, broken (voice)

entredicho /entre'ðitʃo/ *m,* prohibition; *Eccl.* interdiction

entredós /en'treðos/ *m, Sew.* insertion

entrefino /entre'fino/ *a* middling, fairly fine

entrega /en'trega/ *f,* handing over; delivery; *Lit.* part, serial; installment. **por entregas,** as a serial, serial (of stories)

entregar /entre'gar/ *vt* to hand over; deliver; surrender; —*vr* give oneself up; surrender; submit; (*with prep a*) engage in, be absorbed in; (*with prep a* or *en*) give oneself over to (vice, etc.)

entreguista /entre'gista/ *mf* defeatist

entrelazar /entrela'θar; entrela'sar/ *vt* to interlace, intertwine; interweave

entrelistado /entrelis'taðo/ *a* striped

entrelucir /entrelu'θir; entrelu'sir/ *vi irr* to show through, be glimpsed. See **lucir**

entremedias /entre'meðias/ *adv* in between, halfway; in the meantime

entremés /entre'mes/ *m,* hors d'oeuvres (gen. *pl*); interlude, one-act farce

entremeter /entreme'ter/ *vt* to place between or among, —*vr* intrude; meddle, pry

entremetido /entreme'tiðo/ (**-da**) *a* meddlesome —*n* busybody, meddler

entremetimiento /entremeti'miento/ *m,* meddlesomeness

entremezclar /entremeθ'klar; entremes- 'klar/ *vt* to intermingle

entrenador /entrena'ðor/ (**-ra**) *n* trainer; *Sports.* coach

entrenamiento /entrena'miento/ *m,* training, exercise

entrenar /entre'nar/ (**se**) *vt* and *vr* to train; exercise; *Sports.* coach

entreoír /entreo'ir/ *vt* to overhear; hear imperfectly

entrepaño /entre'paɲo/ *m, Archit.* panel; pier (between windows, etc.)

entrepiernas /entre'piernas/ *f pl,* crotch

entrepuente /entre'puente/ *m, Naut.* between decks; steerage quarters

entresacar /entresa'kar/ *vt* to choose or pick out; thin out (plants); thin (hair)

entresuelo /entre'suelo/ *m,* mezzanine, entresol; ground floor

entresueño /entre'sueɲo/ *m,* daydream

entretejer /entrete'her/ *vt* to interweave; interlace; *Lit.* insert

entretela /entre'tela/ *f, Sew.* interlining

entretener /entrete'ner/ *vt irr* to keep waiting; make more bearable; amuse, entertain; delay, postpone; maintain, upkeep; —*vr* amuse oneself. See **tener**

entretenido /entrete'niðo/ *a* amusing, entertaining

entretenimiento /entreteni'miento/ *m,*

amusement; pastime, diversion; upkeep, maintenance

entretiempo /entre'tiempo/ *m*, between seasons, spring or autumn

entreverar /entreβe'rar/ *vt* to intermingle

entrevista /entre'βista/ *f*, meeting, interview

entristecer /entriste'θer; entriste'ser/ *vt irr* to sadden; —*vr* grieve. See **conocer**

entroncar /entron'kar/ *vt* to prove descent; —*vi* be related, or become related (by marriage)

entronque /entron'ke/ *m*, blood relationship, cognation; junction

entumecer /entume'θer; entume'ser/ *vt irr* to numb; —*vr* go numb; swell, rise (sea, etc.). See **conocer**

enturbiar /entur'βiar/ *vt* to make turbid or cloudy; confuse, disorder; —*vr* become turbid; be in disorder

entusiasmar /entusias'mar/ *vt* to inspire enthusiasm; —*vr* be enthusiastic

entusiasmo /entu'siasmo/ *m*, enthusiasm

entusiasta /entu'siasta/ *a* enthusiastic. *mf* enthusiast

enumerar /enume'rar/ *vt* to enumerate

enunciación /enunθia'θion; enunsia'sion/ *f*, statement, declaration, enunciation

enunciar /enun'θiar; enun'siar/ *vt* to state clearly, enunciate

envalentonamiento /embalentona-'miento/ *m*, boldness; braggadocio, bravado

envalentonar /embalento'nar/ *vt* to make bold (gen. in a bad sense); —*vr* strut, brag; take courage

envanecer /embane'θer; embane'ser/ *vt irr* to make vain or conceited; —*vr* be vain; be conceited

envanecimiento /embaneθimiento; embanesi'miento/ *m*, conceit, vanity

envasador /embasa'ðor/ (**-ra**) *n* packer. *m*, funnel

envasar /emba'sar/ *vt* to bottle; barrel; sack (grain, etc.); pack in any container; pierce (with sword)

envase /em'base/ *m*, bottling; filling; container; packing

envejecer /embehe'θer; embehe'ser/ *vt irr* to make old, wear out; —*vi* grow old. See **conocer**

envenenamiento /embenena'miento/ *m*, poisoning

envenenar /embene'nar/ *vt* to poison; corrupt, pervert; put a malicious interpretation on; embitter; —*vr* take poison

envergadura /emberga'ðura/ *f*, wingspan

envés /em'bes/ *m*, wrong side of anything; *Inf.* back. **al e.,** wrong side out

enviado /em'biaðo/ *m*, messenger; envoy. **e. extraordinario,** special envoy

enviar /em'biar/ *vt* to send, dispatch

enviciar /embi'θiar; embi'siar/ *vt* to corrupt, make vicious; —*vr* (*with con, en*) take to (drink, etc.)

envidia /em'biðia/ *f*, envy; emulation; desire (to possess)

envidiable /embi'ðiaβle/ *a* enviable

envidiar /embi'ðiar/ *vt* to envy, grudge; emulate

envidioso /embi'ðioso/ *a* envious

envilecer /embile'θer; embile'ser/ *vt irr* to debase; —*vr* degrade oneself. See **conocer**

envío /em'bio/ *m*, *Com.* remittance; consignment

enviudar /embiu'ðar/ *vi* to become a widow or widower

envoltura /embol'tura/ *f*, swaddling clothes; covering; wrapping

envolver /embol'βer/ *vt irr* to enfold; envelop; wrap up, parcel; *Fig.* contain, enshrine; swaddle, swathe; roll into a ball; confound (in argument); *Mil.* outflank; implicate (person). See **mover**

enyesado /enye'saðo/ *m*, plastering; stucco

enyesar /enye'sar/ *vt* to plaster; *Surg.* apply a plaster bandage

enzarzar /enθar'θar; ensar'sar/ *vt* to fill or cover with brambles; —*vr* be caught on brambles; set one person against another; get in difficulties; quarrel

eñe /'eɲe/ *f*, name of letter Ñ

épica /'epika/ *f*, epic

épico /'epiko/ *a* epic

epicúreo /epi'kureo/ (**-ea**) *a* epicurean; sensual, voluptuous —*n* epicure

epidemia /epi'ðemia/ *f*, epidemic

epidémico /epi'ðemiko/ *a* epidemic

epifanía /epifa'nia/ *f*, Epiphany, Twelfth Night

epiglotis /epi'glotis/ *f*, epiglottis

epígrafe /epi'grafe/ *m*, epigraph, inscription; title, motto

epigrama /epi'grama/ *m*, inscription; epigram

epilepsia /epi'lepsia/ *f*, epilepsy

epiléptico /epi'leptiko/ (**-ca**) *a* and *n* epileptic

epílogo /e'pilogo/ *m*, recapitulation; summary, digest; epilogue

episodio /epi'soðio/ *m*, episode; digression

epístola /e'pistola/ *f*, epistle

epitafio /epi'tafio/ *m*, epitaph

epíteto /e'piteto/ *m*, epithet

epítome /e'pitome/ *m*, epitome; summary, abstract

época /'epoka/ *f*, epoch, period; space of time. **é. de celo,** mating season. **é. de lluvias,** rainy season. **é. de secas,** dry season. **en aquella é.,** at that time

epopeya /epo'peya/ *f*, epic poem; *Fig.* epic

equidad /eki'ðað/ *f*, fairness; reasonableness; equity

equidistante /ekiðis'tante/ *a* equidistant

equilibrar /ekili'βrar/ *vt* to balance; *Fig.* maintain in equilibrium, counterbalance

equilibrio /eki'liβrio/ *m*, equilibrium; equanimity; *Fig.* balance

equilibrista /ekili'βrista/ *mf* equilibrist, tightrope walker

equipaje /eki'pahe/ *m,* luggage, baggage; *Naut.* crew

equipar /eki'par/ *vt* to equip, furnish

equipo /e'kipo/ *m,* outfitting, furnishing; equipment; team; trousseau

equis /'ekis/ *f,* name of letter X

equitación /ekita'θion; ekita'sion/ *f,* · horsemanship, riding

equitativo /ekita'tiβo/ *a* equitable, just, fair

equivalencia /ekiβa'lenθia; ekiβalensia/ *f,* equivalence, equality

equivalente /ekiβa'lente/ *a* equivalent

equivaler /ekiβa'ler/ *vi irr* to be equivalent; *Geom.* be equal. See **valer**

equivocación /ekiβoka'θion; ekiβoka-'sion/ *f,* error, mistake

equivocadamente /ekiβokaða'mente/ *adv* mistakenly, by mistake

equivocar /ekiβo''kar/ *vt* to mistake; —*vr* be mistaken or make a mistake. **equivocarse de medio a medio,** to be off by a long shot

equívoco /e'kiβoko/ *a* equivocal, ambiguous. *m,* equivocation

era /'era/ *f,* era; threshing floor; vegetable or flower bed

erario /e'rario/ *m,* public treasury, exchequer

erección /erek'θion; erek'sion/ *f,* raising; erection, elevation; foundation, institution

erguir /er'gir/ *vt irr* to raise; straighten; lift up; —*vr* straighten up; tower; grow proud —*Pres. Indic.* **irgo** (or **yergo**), **irgues, irguen.** *Pres. Part.* **irguiendo.** *Preterite* **irguió, irguieron.** *Pres. Subjunc.* **irga** or **yerga,** etc.

erial /e'rial/ *m,* uncultivated land

erigir /eri'hir/ *vt* to found, establish; promote, exalt. **erigirse contra,** to rise up against

erisipela /erisi'pela/ *f,* erysipelas

erizado /eri'θaðo; eri'saðo/ *a* standing on end (of hair); prickly, covered with bristles or quills. **e. de espinas,** bristling with thorns; covered with bristles or quills

erizar /eri'θar; eri'sar/ *vt* to set on end (hair); beset with difficulties; —*vr* stand on end, bristle (hair, quills, etc.)

erizo /e'riθo; e'riso/ *m,* hedgehog; husk (of some fruits); *Inf.* touch-me-not, unsociable person; *Mech.* sprocket wheel. **e. de mar,** sea urchin

ermitaño /ermi'taɲo/ *m,* hermit

erosión /ero'sion/ *f,* erosion

erótico /e'rotiko/ *a* erotic

errabundo /erra'βundo/ *a* wandering, errant, vagrant

erradamente /erraði'mente/ *adv* erroneously

erradicable /erraði'kaβle/ *a* eradicable

erradicación /erraðika'θion; erraðika-'sion/ *f,* eradication

erradicar /erraði'kar/ *vt* to eradicate

errante /e'rrante/ *a* wandering; erring; errant

errar /e'rrar/ *vi irr* to err, fail; rove, roam; wander (attention, etc.); —*vr* be mistaken. *Auto.* **e. el encendido,** to misfire —*Pres. Indic.* **yerro, yerras, yerra, yerran.** *Pres. Subjunc.* **yerre, yerres, yerre, yerren**

errata /e'rrata/ *f,* misprint

errático /e'rratiko/ *a* wandering, vagrant; *Med.* erratic

erre /'erre/ *f,* name of letter R

erróneo /e'rroneo/ *a* erroneous, mistaken

error /e'rror/ *m,* error. **error de más,** an overestimate. **error de menos,** an underestimate

eructar /eruk'tar/ *vi* to eructate, belch

erudición /eruði'θion; eruði'sion/ *f,* erudition

erudito /eru'ðito/ *a* learned, erudite. *m,* scholar. **e. a la violeta,** pseudo-learned

erupción /erup'θion; erup'sion/ *f,* *Med.* rash; eruption

es /es/ *irr 3rd pers. sing Pres. Indic.* of ser, is

esa /'esa/ *f, dem a* that. **ésa,** *f, dem. pron* that one; the former; the town in which you are (e.g. Iré a é. mañana, I shall come to your town tomorrow). Used generally in letters. See **ése**

esbeltez /esβel'teθ; esβel'tes/ *f,* slenderness

esbelto /es'βelto/ *a* tall and slim and graceful, willowy

esbozar /esβo'θar; esβo'sar/ *vt* to sketch, outline

esbozo /es'βoθo; es'βoso/ *m,* sketch; outline, rough plan, first draft

escabechar /eskaβe'tʃar/ *vt* to pickle; dye (the hair, etc.); *Inf.* kill in anger; *Inf.* fail (an examination)

escabeche /eska'βetʃe/ *m,* *Cul.* pickle; hair dye

escabechina /eskaβe'tʃina/ *f,* *Inf.* heavy failure (in an examination)

escabel /eska'βel/ *m,* footstool; small backless chair; *Fig.* steppingstone

escabioso /eska'βioso/ *a* scabby, scabious

escabro /es'kaβro/ *m,* scab, mange

escabroso /eska'βroso/ *a* rough; rocky; uneven; rude, unpolished, uncivil; risqué, improper

escabullirse /eskaβu'ʎirse; eskaβu'yirse/ *vr irr* to escape; run away; slip out unnoticed. See **mullir**

escafandra /eska'fandra/ *f,* diving suit, diving outfit

escala /es'kala/ *f,* ladder; (*Mus. Math.*) scale; dial (of machines); proportion, ratio; stage, stopping place; measuring rule; *Naut.* port of call. **e. de toldilla,** companion ladder. *Mus.* **e. mayor,** major scale. **e. menor,** minor scale. *Naut.* **hacer e. en un puerto,** to call at a port

escalada /eska'laða/ *f,* escalade

escalafón /eskala'fon/ *m*, salary scale; roll, list

escalamiento /eskala'miento/ *m*, scaling, climbing; storming

escalar /eska'lar/ *vt* to scale; climb, ascend; storm, assail, enter or leave violently

escaldadura /eskalda'ðura/ *f*, scalding; scald

escaldar /eskal'dar/ *vt* to scald; make red-hot; —*vr* scald or burn oneself. **Gato escaldado del agua fría huye,** Once bitten, twice shy

escalera /eska'lera/ *f*, staircase; stair. **e. abajo,** below stairs. **e. de caracol,** spiral staircase. **e. de mano,** ladder. **e. de tijera,** stepladder. **e. móvil,** escalator

escalfar /eskal'far/ *vt* to poach (eggs); burn (bread)

escalinata /eskali'nata/ *f*, outside staircase or flight of steps, perron

escalofrío /eskalo'frio/ *m*, (gen. *pl*) shiver, shudder

escalón /eska'lon/ *m*, step, stair; rung (of a ladder); *Fig.* steppingstone; grade, rank. **en escalones,** in steps

escalpar /eskal'par/ *vt* to scalp

escalpelo /eskal'pelo/ *m*, scalpel

escama /es'kama/ *f*, *Zool.* scale; anything scale-shaped; flake; suspicion, resentment

escamar /eska'mar/ *vt* to scale (fish); make suspicious —*vr Inf.* be suspicious or disillusioned

escamoso /eska'moso/ *a* scaly

escamotear /eskamote'ar/ *vt* to make disappear; palm (in conjuring); steal

escamoteo /eskamo'teo/ *m*, disappearance; stealing

escampada /eskam'paða/ *f*, *Inf.* clear interval on a rainy day

escampar /eskam'par/ *vi* to cease raining; clear up (of the weather, sky); stop (work, etc.)

escandalizar /eskandali'θar; eskandali'sar/ *vt* to shock, scandalize; disturb with noise; —*vr* be vexed or irritated

escándalo /es'kandalo/ *m*, scandal; commotion, uproar; bad example; viciousness; astonishment

escandaloso /eskanda'loso/ *a* disgraceful, scandalous; turbulent

Escandinavia /eskandi'naβia/ Scandinavia

escandinavo /eskandi'naβo/ **(-va)** *a* and *n* Scandinavian

escantillón /eskanti'ʎon; eskanti'yon/ *m*, template, pattern; rule

escaño /es'kaɲo/ *m*, bench with a back

escapada /eska'paða/ *f*, escape; escapade

escapar /eska'par/ *vt* to spur on (a horse); —*vi* escape; flee; avoid, evade; —*vr* escape; leak (gas, etc.). **Se me escapó su nombre,** His name escaped me. **e. por un pelo,** to have a narrow escape

escaparate /eskapa'rate/ *m*, showcase, cabinet; shop window

escapatoria /eskapa'toria/ *f*, escape, flight; *Inf.* loophole

escape /es'kape/ *m*, flight; evasion; escape (gas, etc.); *Auto.* exhaust. **a e.,** at full speed

escápula /es'kapula/ *f*, scapula

escara /es'kara/ *f*, scar

escarabajo /eskara'βaho/ *m*, beetle, scarab; *Fig. Inf.* dwarf; *pl Inf.* scrawl

escaramuza /eskara'muθa; eskara'musa/ *f*, skirmish

escaramuzar /eskaramu'θar; eskaramu'sar/ *vi* to skirmish

escarapela /eskara'pela/ *f*, cockade, rosette; brawl

escarbadientes /eskarβa'ðientes/ *m*, toothpick

escarbar /eskar'βar/ *vt* to scratch, scrabble (fowls); root, dig; rake out (the fire); inquire into

escarcha /es'kartʃa/ *f*, hoarfrost

escarchar /eskar'tʃar/ *vt Cul.* to frost, ice; spread with frosting; —*vi* freeze lightly

escardar /eskar'ðar/ *vt* to weed; *Fig.* separate good from bad

escarlata /eskar'lata/ *f*, scarlet; scarlet cloth

escarlatina /eskarla'tina/ *f*, scarlet fever

escarmentar /eskarmen'tar/ *vt irr* to reprehend or punish severely; —*vi* learn from experience, be warned. See **acertar**

escarmiento /eskar'miento/ *m*, disillusionment, experience; warning; punishment, fine

escarnecedor /eskarneθe'ðor; eskarnese'ðor/ **(-ra)** *a* mocking —*n* mocker

escarnecer /eskarne'θer; eskarne'ser/ *vt irr* to mock. See **conocer**

escarnio /es'karnio/ *m*, gibe, jeer

escarola /eska'rola/ *f*, endive; frilled ruff

escarpa /es'karpa/ *f*, steep slope, declivity; escarpment

escasear /eskase'ar/ *vt* to dole out, give grudgingly; save, husband; —*vi* be scarce or short; grow less

escasez /eska'seθ; eska'ses/ *f*, meanness, frugality; want; shortage, scarcity

escaso /es'kaso/ *a* scarce; short; bare; parsimonious

escatimar /eskati'mar/ *vt* to cut down, curtail

escatimoso /eskati'moso/ *a* malicious, guileful

escayola /eska'yola/ *f*, plaster of Paris

escena /es'θena; es'sena/ *f*, *Theat.* stage; scene; scenery; theater, drama; spectacle, sight; episode, incident. **director de e.,** producer. **poner en e.,** *Theat.* to produce

escenario /esθe'nario; esse'nario/ *m*, *Theat.* stage; scenario

escénico /es'θeniko; es'seniko/ *a* scenic

escenografía /esθenogra'fia; essenogra'fia/ *f*, scenography

escepticismo /esθepti'θismo; essepti'sismo/ *m*, scepticism

escéptico /es'θeptiko; es'septiko/ **(-ca)** *a* sceptical —*n* sceptic

escindir /esθin'dir; essin'dir/ *vt* to split

escisión /esθi'sion; essi'sion/ *f*, cleavage, split; splitting; schism; disagreement

esclarecer /esklare'θer; esklare'ser/ *vt irr* to illuminate; ennoble, make illustrious; *Fig.* enlighten; elucidate; —*vi* dawn. See **conocer**

esclarecido /esklare'θiðo; esklare'siðo/ *a* distinguished, illustrious

esclavitud /esklaβi'tuð/ *f*, slavery; fraternity

esclavizar /esklaβi'θar; esklaβi'sar/ *vt* to enslave

esclavo /es'klaβo/ **(-va)** *n* slave; member of a brotherhood —*a* enslaved. *f*, slave bracelet; ID bracelet

esclerosis /eskle'rosis/ *f*, sclerosis

esclerótica /eskle'rotika/ *f*, sclerotic

esclusa /es'klusa/ *f*, lock; sluice gate; weir

escoba /es'koβa/ *f*, broom, brush; *Bot.* yellow broom

escobada /esko'βaða/ *f*, sweep, stroke (of a broom)

escobar /esko'βar/ *vt* to sweep with a broom

escocer /esko'θer; esko'ser/ *vi irr* to smart; *Fig.* sear; —*vr* hurt, smart; be chafed. See **mover**

escocés /esko'θes; esko'ses/ **(-esa)** *a* Scots, Scottish —*n* Scot

Escocia /es'koθia; eskosia/ Scotland

escofina /esko'fina/ *f*, rasp, file

escoger /esko'her/ *vt* to choose, select

escogido /esko'hiðo/ *a* choice, select

escolar /esko'lar/ *a* school; pupil. *m*, pupil

escollera /esko'ʎera; esko'yera/ *f*, breakwater, sea wall, jetty

escollo /es'koʎo; es'koyo/ *m*, reef; danger, risk; difficulty, obstacle

escolta /es'kolta/ *f*, escort, guard

escoltar /eskol'tar/ *vt* to escort; guard, conduct

escombrar /eskom'brar/ *vt* to remove obstacles, free of rubbish; *Fig.* clean up

escombro /es'kombro/ *m*, debris, rubble, rubbish; mackerel

esconder /eskon'der/ *vt* to hide, conceal; *Fig.* contain, embrace; —*vr* hide

escondidas, a /eskon'diðas, a/ *adv* secretly

escondite, escondrijo /eskon'dite, eskon'driho/ *m*, hiding place. **jugar al escondite**, to play hide-and-seek

escopeta /esko'peta/ *f*, shotgun. **e. de aire comprimido**, air gun, popgun. **e. de pistón**, repercussion gun. **e. de viento**, air gun

escopetazo /eskope'taθo; eskope'taso/ *m*, gunshot; gunshot wound; *Fig.* bombshell

escopetear /eskopete'ar/ *vt* to shoot repeatedly

escopetero /eskope'tero/ *m*, musketeer; gunsmith; man with a gun

escoplo /es'koplo/ *m*, chisel

escorbuto /eskor'βuto/ *m*, scurvy

escoria /es'koria/ *f*, dross, slag; scoria, volcanic ash; *Fig.* dregs

escorial /esko'rial/ *m*, slag heap

escorpión /eskor'pion/ *m*, scorpion; Scorpio

escorzo /es'korθo; es'korso/ *m*, *Art.* foreshortening

escotado /eskota'ðo/ *a* low-cut (of dresses)

escotadura /eskota'ðura/ *a* low neck (of a dress); piece cut out of something; *Theat.* large trapdoor; recess

escotar /esko'tar/ *vt* to cut low in the neck (of dresses); pay one's share (of expenses)

escote /es'kote/ *m*, low neck (of a dress); shortness (of sleeves); share (of expenses), lace yoke

escotilla /esko'tiʎa; esko'tiya/ *f*, *Naut.* hatch

escozor /esko'θor; esko'sor/ *m*, smart, pricking pain; irritation, prickle; heartache

escriba /es'kriβa/ *m*, (*Jewish hist.*) scribe

escribanía /eskriβa'nia/ *f*, secretaryship; notaryship; bureau, office; writing case; inkstand

escribano /eskri'βano/ *m*, notary public; secretary

escribiente /eskri'βiente/ *mf* clerk

escribir /eskri'βir/ *vt* to write; —*vr* enlist; enroll; correspond by writing —*Past Part.* **escrito**

escrito /es'krito/ *m*, writing, manuscript; literary or scientific work; *Law.* writ. **por e.**, in writing

escritor /eskri'tor/ **(-ra)** *n* writer, author

escritorio /eskri'torio/ *m*, escritoire; office

escritura /eskri'tura/ *f*, writing; handwriting; *Law.* deed; literary work. **Sagrada E.**, Holy Scripture

escrófula /es'krofula/ *f*, scrofula

escroto /es'kroto/ *m*, scrotum

escrúpulo /es'krupulo/ *m*, scruple, qualm; conscientiousness; scruple (pharmacy)

escrupulosidad /eskrupulosi'ðað/ *f*, conscientiousness, scrupulousness

escrupuloso /eskrupu'loso/ *a* scrupulous; exact, accurate

escrutador /eskruta'ðor/ **(-ra)** *n* scrutinizer —*a* examining, inspecting

escrutar /eskru'tar/ *vt* to scrutinize, examine; count (votes)

escrutinio /eskru'tinio/ *m*, scrutiny, examination; count (votes)

escuadra /es'kuaðra/ *f*, carpenter's square; architect's square; *Nav.* fleet; *Aer.* squadron; *Mil.* squad. **e. de agrimensor**, *Surv.* cross-staff

escuadrar /eskuað'rar/ *vt* (and *Mas.*) to square

escuadrilla /eskuaðˈriʎa; eskuaðˈriya/ *f*, squadron (airplanes, small ships)

escuálido /esˈkualiðo/ *a* filthy, squalid; sordid; thin

escucha /esˈkutʃa/ *f*, listening; peephole; *Mil.* sentinel

escuchar /eskuˈtʃar/ *vt* to listen; attend to, heed; —*vr* like the sound of one's own voice

escudero /eskuˈðero/ *m*, squire, page; gentleman; shield maker

escudete /eskuˈðete/ *m*, escutcheon; shield; gusset; white water lily

escudilla /eskuˈðiʎa; eskuˈðiya/ *f*, bowl

escudo /esˈkuðo/ *m*, shield; escudo; escutcheon; protection, defense; ward (of a keyhole)

escudriñador /eskuðriɲaˈðor/ **(-ra)** *a* searching; curious, prying —*n* scrutinizer; pryer

escudriñar /eskuðriˈɲar/ *vt* to scrutinize; scan; investigate; pry into

escuela /esˈkuela/ *f*, school; school building; style; (*Lit.* and *Art.*) school. **e. de artes y oficios**, industrial school. **e. industrial**, technical school. **e. normal**, normal school

escueto /esˈkueto/ *a* dry, bare, unadorned; simple, exact; unencumbered

esculpir /eskulˈpir/ *vt* to sculpture; engrave

escultor /eskulˈtor/ **(-ra)** *n* sculptor

escultura /eskulˈtura/ *f*, sculpture; carving; modeling

escupir /eskuˈpir/ *vi* to expectorate; —*vt* *Fig.* spit out; cast away, throw out

escurreplatos /eskurreˈplatos/ *m*, dishrack, draining rack

escurrido /eskuˈrriðo/ *a* narrow-hipped; skintight (of skirts)

escurridor /eskurriˈðor/ *m*, colander, sieve; dishrack; drainingboard

escurriduras /eskurriˈðuras/ *f pl*, lees, dregs

escurrir /eskuˈrrir/ *vt* to drain to the dregs; wring, press out; drain; —*vi* trickle, drip; slip, slide; —*vr* slip away, edge away; escape, slip out; skid

esdrújulo /esˈðruhulo/ *a Gram.* of words where the accent falls on the antepenultimate syllable

ese /ˈese/ *f*, name of letter S; S-shaped link (in a chain). *Inf.* **andar haciendo eses**, to reel about drunkenly

ese /ˈese/ *m, dem a* (*f*, **esa**. *pl* **esos, esas**) that; those. **ése**, *m, dem pron* (*f*, **ésa**. *neut* **eso**. *pl* **ésos, ésas**) that one; the former (e.g. *Me gusta éste, pero ése no me gusta*, I like this one, but I do not like that one

esencia /esˈenθia; esˈensia/ *f*, essence, nature, character; extract; *Chem.* essence

esencial /esenˈθial; esenˈsial/ *a* essential

esfera /esˈfera/ *f*, *Geom.* sphere, globe, ball; sky; rank; face, dial; province, scope

esférico /esˈferiko/ *a* spherical

esfinge /esˈfinhe/ *f*, sphinx

esforzado /esforˈθaðo; esforˈsaðo/ *a* valiant, courageous; spirited

esforzar /esforˈθar; esforˈsar/ *vt irr* to encourage; invigorate; —*vr* make an effort. See **contar**

esfuerzo /esˈfuerθo; esˈfuerso/ *m*, effort; courage; spirit; vigor; exertion, strain; *Mech.* stress. **sin e.**, effortless

esfumar /esfuˈmar/ *vt Art.* shade; *Art.* stump; dim; —*vr* disappear

esgrima /esˈgrima/ *f*, (art of) fencing

esgrimidor /esgrimiˈðor/ *m*, fencer, swordsman

esgrimir /esgriˈmir/ *vt* to fence; fend off

esguince /esˈginθe; esˈginse/ *m*, dodging, twist; expression or gesture of repugnance; *Med.* sprain

eslabón /eslaˈβon/ *m*, link (in a chain); steel for producing fire. **e. perdido**, *Fig.* missing link

eslabonar /eslaβoˈnar/ *vt* to link; connect, unite

eslavo /esˈlaβo/ **(-va)** *a* Slavic —*n* Slav

esloveno /esloˈβeno/ **(-na)** *a* and *n* Slovene

esmaltar /esmalˈtar/ *vt* to enamel; decorate, adorn

esmalte /esˈmalte/ *m*, enamel; enamelwork; smalt; brilliance

esmerado /esmeˈraðo/ *a* careful, painstaking

esmeralda /esmeˈralda/ *f*, emerald

esmerar /esmeˈrar/ *vt* to polish; —*vr* (*with en*) take great pains with (or to)

esmeril /esmeˈril/ *m*, emery

esmero /esˈmero/ *m*, great care, conscientiousness

esnob /esˈnoβ/ *a* snobbish. *mf* snob

eso /ˈeso/ *neut dem pron* that; the fact that; that idea, affair, etc.; about (of time) (e.g. *Vendrá a e. de las nueve*, He will come about nine o'clock). **Eso** refers to an abstraction, never to one definite object. **No me gusta e.**, I don't like that kind of thing. **e. es**, that's it. **por e.**, therefore, for that reason

esófago /esˈofago/ *m*, esophagus

esotérico /esoˈteriko/ *a* esoteric

espaciar /espaˈθiar; espaˈsiar/ *vt* to space; *Print.* lead; —*vr* spread oneself, enlarge (upon)

espacio /esˈpaθio; esˈpasio/ *m*, space; capacity; interval, duration; slowness; *Print.* lead

espada /esˈpaða/ *f*, sword; matador; swordsman; (cards) spade. **entre la e. y la pared**, *Fig.* between a rock and a hard place; between undesirable alternatives.

espadachín /espaðaˈtʃin/ *m*, good swordsman; bully, quarrelsome fellow

espalda /esˈpalda/ *f*, *Anat.* back (often *pl*); rear, back portion; *Mil.* rear guard. **de espaldas**, with one's (its, his, etc.) back turned; on one's (its, etc.) back

espaldar /espalˈdar/ *m*, backpiece of a

cuirass; back (of chair); garden trellis, espalier

espaldarazo /espalda'raθo; espalda'raso/ m, accolade

espaldera /espal'dera/ f, espalier, trellis

espantadizo /espanta'ðiθo; espanta'ðiso/ a easily frightened

espantapájaros /espanta'paharos/ m, scarecrow

espantar /espan'tar/ vt to frighten, terrify; chase off; —vr be amazed; be scared

espanto /es'panto/ m, terror, panic; dismay; amazement; threat

espantoso /espan'toso/ a horrible, terrifying, awesome; amazing

España /es'paɲa/ Spain

español /espa'ɲol/ (**-la**) a Spanish —n Spaniard. m, Spanish (language). **a la española,** in Spanish fashion

españolía /espaɲo'lia/ f, Spanish colony, Spanish community (outside Spain)

españolismo /espaɲo'lismo/ m, love of things Spanish; Hispanism

españolizar /espaɲoli'θar; espaɲoli'sar/ vt to hispanize; —vr adopt Spanish customs

esparadrapo /espara'ðrapo/ m, court plaster

esparcimiento /esparθi'miento; esparsi'miento/ m, scattering; naturalness, frankness; geniality

esparcir /espar'θir; espar'sir/ vt to scatter, sprinkle, disperse; spread, publish abroad; entertain; —vr be scattered; amuse oneself

espárrago /es'parrago/ m, asparagus

esparraguera /esparra'gera/ f, asparagus plant; asparagus bed; asparagus dish

Esparta /es'parta/ Sparta

espartano /espar'tano/ (**-na**) a and n Spartan

esparto /es'parto/ m, esparto grass

espasmo /es'pasmo/ m, spasm

espasmódico /espas'moðiko/ a spasmodic

espátula /es'patula/ f, spatula; palette knife

especia /es'peθia; es'pesia/ f, spice. **nuez de e.,** nutmeg

especial /espe'θial; espe'sial/ a special; particular

especialidad /espeθiali'ðað; espesiali'ðað/ f, specialty; branch (of learning)

especialista /espeθia'lista; espesia'lista/ mf specialist

especialización /espeθialiθa'θion; espesialisa'sion/ f, specialization

especializarse /espeθiali'θarse; espesiali'sarse/ vr to specialize

especie /es'peθie; es'pesie/ f, class, kind; species; affair, matter, case; idea, image; news; pretext, appearance

especiería /espeθie'ria; espesie'ria/ f, spice trade; spice shop

especiero /espe'θiero; espe'siero/ (**-ra**) n spice merchant; spice rack

especificación /espeθifika'θion; espesi-

fika'sion/ f, specification. **e. normalizada,** standard specification

especificar /espeθifi'kar; espesifi'kar/ vt to specify, particularize

específico /espe'θifiko; espe'sifiko/ a and m, specific patent medicine

espécimen /es'peθimen; es'pesimen/ m, specimen, sample

especioso /espe'θioso; espe'sioso/ a lovely, perfect; specious

espectacular /espektaku'lar/ a spectacular

espectáculo /espek'takulo/ m, spectacle, sight; show, display

espectador /espekta'ðor/ (**-ra**) n spectator

espectral /espek'tral/ a spectral; faint, dim

espectro /es'pektro/ m, phantom, specter; *Phys.* spectrum

especulación /espekula'θion; espekula'sion/ f, conjecture; *Com.* speculation

especulador /espekula'ðor/ (**-ra**) n speculator

especular /espeku'lar/ vt to examine, look at; (*with en*) reflect on, consider; —vi *Com.* speculate

especulativo /espekula'tiβo/ a speculative; thoughtful, meditative

espejismo /espe'hismo/ m, mirage; illusion

espejo /es'pecho/ m, mirror; *Fig.* model. **e. de cuerpo entero,** full-length mirror. **e. retrovisor,** rearview mirror

espejuelo /espe'huelo/ m, small mirror; *Mineral.* selenite; *Mineral.* sheet of talc; pl lenses, eyeglasses

espeluznante /espeluθ'nante; espelus'nante/ a hair-raising

espeluznar /espeluθ'nar; espelus'nar/ vt to dishevel; untidy (hair, etc.); —vr stand on end (hair)

espera /es'pera/ f, waiting; expectation; *Law.* adjournment; caution, restraint; *Law.* respite

esperantista /esperan'tista/ mf Esperantist

esperanto /espe'ranto/ m, Esperanto

esperanza /espe'ranθa; espe'ransa/ f, hope

esperanzar /esperan'θar; esperan'sar/ vt to inspire hope in

esperar /espe'rar/ vt to hope; expect; await; (*with en*) have faith in. **e. sentado,** *Fig. Inf.* to whistle for

esperma /es'perma/ f, sperm, semen. **e. de ballena,** spermaceti

esperpento /esper'pento/ m, *Inf.* scarecrow, grotesque; folly, madness; fantastic dramatic composition

espesar /espe'sar/ vt to thicken; make closer; tighten (fabrics); —vr thicken; grow denser or thicker

espeso /es'peso/ a thick; dense; greasy, dirty

espesor /espe'sor/ m, thickness; density

espesura /espe'sura/ f, thickness; density; thicket; filth

espetar /espe'tar/ vt Cul. to spit, skewer; pierce; Inf. utter, give; —vr be stiff or affected; Inf. push oneself in, intrude

espía /es'pia/ mf spy. f, Naut. warp

espiar /es'piar/ vt to spy upon, watch; —vi Naut. warp

espiga /es'piga/ f, Bot. spike, ear; sprig; peg; tang, shank (of sword); tenon, dowel; Naut. masthead; Herald. garb

espigar /espi'gar/ vt to glean; tenon; —vi Bot. begin to show the ear or spike; —vr Bot. bolt; shoot up, grow (persons)

espigón /espi'gon/ m, sting; sharp point; breakwater; bearded spike (corn, etc.)

espigueo /espi'geo/ m, gleaning

espín /es'pin/ m, porcupine

espina /es'pina/ f, thorn; prickle; splinter; fish bone; Anat. spine; suspicion, doubt

espinaca /espi'naka/ f, spinach

espinal /espi'nal/ a spinal

espinar /espi'nar/ m, thorn brake; Fig. awkward position —vt to prick, wound, hurt

espinazo /espi'naθo; espi'naso/ m, backbone

espinilla /espi'niʎa; espi'niya/ f, shinbone; blackhead

espinoso /espi'noso/ a thorny; difficult, intricate

espionaje /espio'nahe/ m, espionage; spying

espira /es'pira/ f, (Geom. Archit.) helix; turn, twist (of winding stairs); whorl (of a shell)

espiración /espira'θion; espira'sion/ f, expiration; respiration

espiral /espi'ral/ a spiral. f, Geom. spiral; spiral watchspring

espirar /espi'rar/ vt to exhale, breathe out; inspire; encourage; —vi breathe; breathe out; Poet. blow (wind)

espiritisimo /espiri'tisimo/ m, spiritualism

espiritista /espiri'tista/ a spiritualist. mf spiritualist

espiritoso /espiri'toso/ a lively, active, spirited; spirituous

espíritu /es'piritu/ m, spirit; apparition; specter; soul; intelligence; mind; mood, temper, outlook; underlying principle, spirit; devil (gen. pl) vigor, ardor, vivacity; Chem. essence; Chem. spirits; turn of mind. **E. Santo,** Holy Ghost

espiritual /espiri'tual/ a spiritual

espiritualidad /espirituali'ðað/ f, spirituality

esplendidez /esplendi'ðeθ; esplendiðes/ f, liberality, abundance; splendor, pomp

espléndido /es'plendiðo/ a magnificent; liberal; resplendent (gen. pl)

esplendor /esplen'dor/ m, splendor, brilliance; distinction, nobility

esplendoroso /esplendo'roso/ a splendid, brilliant; radiant

espliego /es'pliego/ m, lavender

esplín /es'plin/ m, spleen, melancholy

espolear /espole'ar/ vt to prick with the spur; encourage, stimulate

espoleta /espo'leta/ f, fuse (of explosives); breastbone (of fowls); wishbone. **e. de tiempo, e. graduada,** time fuse. **e. de seguridad,** safety fuse

espolón /espo'lon/ m, spur (of a bird or mountain range); Naut. ram; breakwater; buttress; Naut. fender

espolvorear /espolßore'ar/ vt to sprinkle with powder

esponja /es'ponha/ f, sponge

esponjadura /esponha'ðura/ f, sponging

esponjar /espon'har/ vt to make spongy; sponge; —vr swell with pride; Inf. bloom with health

esponjoso /espon'hoso/ a spongy, porous

esponsales /espon'sales/ m pl, betrothal; marriage contract

espontaneidad /espontanei'ðað/ f, spontaneity

espontáneo /espon'taneo/ a spontaneous

espora /es'pora/ f, spore

esporádico /espo'raðiko/ a sporadic

esposa /es'posa/ f, wife; pl handcuffs

esposo /es'poso/ m, husband; pl husband and wife

espuela /es'puela/ f, spur; stimulus; (Ornith. Bot.) spur. **e. de caballero,** larkspur

espulgar /espul'gar/ vt to delouse; examine carefully

espuma /es'puma/ f, froth, foam; Cul. scum; Fig. the best of anything, flower; Fig. Inf. **crecer como la e.,** to flourish like weeds

espumadera /espuma'ðera/ f, skimming ladle

espumajear /espumahe'ar/ vi to foam at the mouth

espumajoso /espuma'hoso/ a frothy, foaming

espumar /espu'mar/ vt to skim (soup, etc.); —vi foam; increase rapidly

espumoso /espu'moso/ a frothy, foaming

espurio /es'purio/ a bastard; spurious

esputo /es'puto/ m, sputum

esquela /es'kela/ f, note; (printed) card

esqueleto /eske'leto/ m, skeleton; Inf. skinny person; framework

esquema /es'kema/ f, diagram, layout sketch; scheme, plan. **e. de una máquina,** drawing of a machine

esquemático /eske'matiko/ a schematic; diagrammatic

esquematizar /eskemati'θar; eskemati'sar/ vt to plan, outline

esquí /es'ki/ m, ski, snowshoe

esquiador /eskia'ðor/ m, skier

esquiar /es'kiar/ vi to ski

esquife /es'kife/ m, skiff

esquila /es'kila/ f, cattle bell; small bell,

hand bell; sheep shearing; (*Ichth. Bot.*) squill

esquiladora /eskila'ðora/ *f.* shearing machine

esquilar /eski'lar/ *vt* to shear, clip (sheep, etc.)

esquilmar /eskil'mar/ *vt* to harvest; impoverish

esquimal /eski'mal/ *a* and *mf* Eskimo

esquina /es'kina/ *f.* corner

esquinado /eski'naðo/ *a* having corners; *Fig.* difficult to approach (people)

esquirla /es'kirla/ *f.* splinter (of a bone); shrapnel

esquirol /eski'rol/ *m. Inf.* strikebreaker, blackleg

esquivar /eski'βar/ *vt* to avoid; —*vr* slip away, disappear; excuse oneself

esquivez /eski'βeθ; eskiβes/ *f.* unsociableness; unfriendliness, aloofness

esquivo /es'kiβo/ *a* unsociable, elusive, aloof

esquizado /eski'θaðo; cskisaðo/ *a* mottled (of marble)

estabilidad /estaβili'ðað/ *f.* stability; fastness (of colors)

estabilizar /estaβili'θar; estaβili'sar/ *vt* to stabilize

estable /es'taβle/ *a* stable; fast (of colors)

establecer /estaβle'θer; estaβle'ser/ *vt irr* to establish, found, institute; decree; —*vr* take up residence; open (a business firm). See *conocer*

establecimiento /estaβleθi'miento; estaβlesi'miento/ *m.* law, statute; foundation, institution; establishment

establo /es'taβlo/ *m.* stable

estaca /es'taka/ *f.* stake, pole; *Agr.* cutting; cudgel

estacada /esta'kaða/ *f.* fence; *Mil.* palisade; place fixed for a duel

estacar /esta'kar/ *vt* to stake; fence; tie to a stake; —*vr Fig.* be as still as a post

estación /esta'θion; esta'sion/ *f.* position, situation; season; station (railroad, etc.); depot; time, period; stop, halt; building, headquarters; *Bot.* habitat; (*Surv. Geom. Eccl.*) station

estacionamiento /estaθiona'miento; estasiona'miento/ *m.*, stationariness; *Auto.* parking

estacionar /estaθio'nar; estasio'nar/ *vt* to station, place; *Auto.* park (a car); —*vr* remain stationary; place oneself

estacionario /estaθio'nario; estasio'nario/ *a* motionless; *Astron.* stationary. *m,* stationer

estadía /esta'ðia/ *f.* stay, sojourn; *Art.* sitting (of a model)

estadio /es'taðio/ *m.* racetrack; stadium; furlong

estadista /esta'ðista/ *mf.* statistician; statesman, stateswoman

estadística /esta'ðistika/ *f.* statistics

estadístico /esta'ðistiko/ *a* statistical

estadizo /esta'ðiθo; estaðiso/ *a* stagnant

estado /es'taðo/ *m,* state; condition; rank, position; *Polit.* state; profession; status; *Com.* statement. **e. de guerra,** state of war; martial law. **e. mayor central,** (*Nav. Mil.*) general staff. **e. tapón,** *Polit.* buffer state. **tomar e.,** to marry; *Eccl.* profess; be ordained a priest

Estados Unidos de América /es'taðos u'niðos de a'merika/ United States of America

estadounidense /estaðouni'ðense/ *a* United States

estafa /es'tafa/ *f.* swindle

estafador /estafa'ðor/ **(-ra)** *n* swindler

estafar /esta'far/ *vt* to swindle

estafeta /esta'feta/ *f.* courier, messenger; branch post office; diplomatic pouch

estagnación /estagna'θion; estagna'sion/ *f.* stagnation

estallar /esta'ʎar; esta'yar/ *vi* to explode; burst; *Fig.* break out

estallido /esta'ʎiðo; esta'yiðo/ *m,* explosion, report; crash, crack; *Fig.* outbreak; *Auto.* **e. de un neumático,** blowout (of a tire)

estambre /es'tambre/ *m,* woolen yarn, worsted; stamen

estameña /esta'meɲa/ *f.* serge

estampa /es'tampa/ *f.* illustration, picture; print; aspect; printing press; track, step; *Metall.* boss, stud

estampación /estampa'θion; estampa'sion/ *f.* stamping; printing; imprinting. **e. en seco,** tooling (of a book)

estampado /estam'paðo/ *a* printed (of textiles). *m,* textile printing; printed fabric

estampar /estam'par/ *vt* to print, stamp; leave the print (of); bestow, imprint. **e. en relieve,** to emboss. **e. en seco,** to tool (a book)

estampería /estampe'ria/ *f.* print or picture shop; trade in prints

estampero /estam'pero/ *m,* print dealer, picture dealer

estampido /estam'piðo/ *m,* report, bang, detonation; crash

estampilla /estam'piʎa; estam'piya/ *f.* rubber stamp; seal

estampillar /estampi'ʎar; estampi'yar/ *vt* to stamp, imprint

estancado /estan'kaðo/ *a* stagnant; blocked, held up

estancar /estan'kar/ *vt* to check, stem; set up a monopoly; *Fig.* hold up (negotiations, etc.); —*vr* be stagnant

estancia /es'tanθia; es'tansia/ *f.* stay, residence; dwelling; lounge, livingroom; stanza; *West Hem.* farm

estanciero /estan'θiero; estan'siero/ *m, West Hem.* farmer

estanco /es'tanko/ *a Naut.* watertight. *m,* monopoly; shop selling government monopoly goods; archive

estandarte /estan'darte/ *m,* standard, flag. **e. real,** royal standard

estanque /es'tanke/ *m,* tank; pool; reservoir

estanquero /estanˈkero/ **(-ra)** n seller of government monopoly goods (tobacco, matches, etc.)

estante /esˈtante/ a present; extant; permanent. m, shelf; bookcase; bin (for wine)

estantería /estanteˈria/ f, shelving; shelves, bookcase

estañar /estaˈɲar/ vt to tin; solder

estaño /esˈtaɲo/ m, tin

estaquilla /estaˈkiʎa; estaˈkiya/ f, peg, cleat

estar /esˈtar/ vi irr to be. Indicates: 1. Position or place (e.g. Está a la puerta, He is at the door). 2. State (e.g. Las flores están marchitas, The flowers are faded). 3. Used to form the continuous or progressive tense (e.g. Siempre está (estaba) escribiendo, He is (was) always writing). 4. In contrast to verb ser, indicates impermanency (e.g. Está enfermo, He is ill). 5. Estar forms an apparent passive where no action is implied (e.g. El cuadro está pintado al óleo, The picture is painted in oils). 6. Used in some impersonal expressions (e.g. ¡Bien está! All right! ¡Claro está! Of course! etc.). e. de, to be in, or on, or acting as (e.g. e. de prisa, to be in a hurry. e. de capitán, to be acting as a captain). e. para, to be on the point of; to be nearly; to be in the mood for. e. para llover, to be on the point of raining. e. por, to remain to be done; have a mind to (e.g. La historia está por escribir, The story remains to be written). e. bien, to be well (healthy). Mech. e. bajo presión, to have the steam up. Polit. e. en el poder, to be in office. e. en una cuenca, Dominican Republic to be broke. ¿A cómo (or A cuántos) estamos? What is the date? Pres. Ind. estoy, estás, está, estamos, estáis, están. Preterite estuve, etc —Pres. Subjunc. esté, estés, esté, estén. Imperf. Subjunc. estuviese, etc.

estatal /estaˈtal/ a state

estático /esˈtatiko/ a static

estatua /esˈtatua/ f, statue

estatuaria /estaˈtuaria/ f, statuary

estatuir /estaˈtuir/ vt irr to establish, order. See **huir**

estatura /estaˈtura/ f, stature, height (of persons)

estatuto /estaˈtuto/ m, statute, law

este /ˈeste/ m, east

este /ˈeste/ m, dem a this (f, esta, pl estos, estas, these). éste, m, dem pron this one; the latter. (f, ésta, neut esto, pl éstos, éstas, these ones; the latter) (e.g. Aquel cuadro no es tan hermoso como éste, That picture is not as beautiful as this one)

estela /esˈtela/ f, wake, track (of a ship)

estenografía /estenograˈfia/ f, shorthand

estenográfico /estenoˈgrafiko/ a shorthand

estenógrafo /esteˈnografo/ **(-fa)** n stenographer

estentóreo /estenˈtoreo/ a stentorian

estepa /esˈtepa/ f, steppe, arid plain

estera /esˈtera/ f, matting

esterar /esteˈrar/ vt to cover with matting; —vi Inf. muffle oneself up

estercolar /esterkoˈlar/ vt to manure

estercolero /esterkoˈlero/ m, manure pile; driver of a dung cart

estereoscopio /estereoˈskopio/ m, stereoscope

estéril /esˈteril/ a sterile, barren; unfruitful, unproductive

esterilidad /esteriliˈðað/ f, sterility; barrenness, unfruitfulness

esterilización /esteriliθaˈθion; esterilisaˈsion/ f, sterilization

esterilizador /esteriliθaˈðor; esterilisaˈðor/ a sterilizing. m, sterilizer

esterilizar /esteriliˈθar; esteriliˈsar/ vt to make barren; Med. sterilize

esterilla /esteˈriʎa; esteˈriya/ f, mat, matting

esterlina /esterˈlina/ a f, sterling. **libra e.**, pound sterling

esternón /esterˈnon/ m, sternum

estertor /esterˈtor/ m, stertorous breathing, rattle

estética /esˈtetika/ f, aesthetics —a aesthete

estético /esˈtetiko/ a aesthetic m, aesthete

estetoscopio /estetoˈskopio/ m, stethoscope

esteva /esˈteβa/ f, plow handle

estevado /esteˈβaðo/ a bandy-legged

estibador /estiβaˈðor/ m, stevedore, dock worker

estibar /estiˈβar/ vt Naut. to stow

estiércol /esˈtierkol/ m, dung; manure

estigio /esˈtihio/ a Stygian; (Fig. Poet.) infernal

estigma /esˈtigma/ m, stigma

estigmatizar /estigmatiˈθar; estigmatiˈsar/ vt to brand; stigmatize; insult

estilar /estiˈlar/ vi to be accustomed; —vt draw up (document)

estilete /estiˈlete/ m, stiletto, dagger; needle, hand, pointer; Med. stylet

estilista /estiˈlista/ mf stylist

estilística /estiˈlistika/ f, stylism, stylistics

estilo /esˈtilo/ m, (Art. Archit. Lit.) style, writing instrument; gnomon, pointer; manner, way; Bot. style. **por el e.**, in some such way, like that

estilográfico /estiloˈgrafiko/ a stylographic. **pluma estilográfica**, fountain pen

estima /esˈtima/ f, appreciation, esteem, consideration

estimable /estiˈmaβle/ a estimable

estimación /estimaˈθion; estimaˈsion/ f, valuation, estimate; regard, esteem. **e. prudente**, conservative estimate

estimar /estiˈmar/ vt to value, estimate; esteem, judge

estimulante /estimuˈlante/ m, Med. stimulant —a stimulating

estimular /estimu'lar/ vt to stimulate, excite; goad on, encourage, incite

estímulo /es'timulo/ m, stimulus; incitement, encouragement

estío /es'tio/ m, summer

estipendio /esti'pendio/ m, stipend, pay, remuneration

estipulación /estipula'θion; estipula'sion/ f, stipulation; Law. clause, condition

estipular /estipu'lar/ vt to stipulate; arrange terms; Law. covenant

estirado /esti'raðo/ a stretched out; tight, stiff; wire-drawn (metals); stiff, pompous; parsimonious

estirar /esti'rar/ vt to stretch; iron roughly (clothes); Metall. wire-draw; dole out (money); Fig. stretch, go beyond the permissible; —vr stretch oneself

estirpe /es'tirpe/ f, race, stock, lineage

esto /'esto/ dem pron neut this, this matter, this idea, etc. Always refers to abstractions, never to a definite object. **e. de,** the matter of. **e. es,** that's it; namely. **por e.,** for this reason. **a todo e.,** meanwhile

Estocolmo /esto'kolmo/ Stockholm

estofa /es'tofa/ f, Sew. quilting; kind, quality

estofado /esto'faðo/ m, stew —a Sew. quilted; stewed

estofar /esto'far/ vt Sew. to quilt; make a stew

estoicismo /estoi'θismo; estoi'sismo/ m, stoicism

estoico /es'toiko/ **(-ca)** n stoic —a stoical

estólido /es'toliðo/ **(-da)** a idiotic —a idiot

estomacal /estoma'kal/ a stomach

estómago /es'tomago/ m, stomach

estomático /esto'matiko/ a pertaining to the mouth, oral

estomatitis /estoma'titis/ f, stomatitis

estonio /es'tonio/ **(-ia)** a and n Estonian. m, Estonian (language)

estopa /es'topa/ f, tow; oakum

estopilla /esto'piʎa; esto'piya/ f, batiste, lawn; calico, cotton cloth

estopín /esto'pin/ m, Mil. quick march

estoque /es'toke/ m, rapier; narrow sword

estoquear /estoke'ar/ vt to wound or kill with a rapier

estorbador /estorβa'ðor/ **(-ra)** a obstructive —n obstructer

estorbar /estor'βar/ vt to obstruct, impede; hinder

estorbo /es'torβo/ m, obstruction; hindrance, nuisance

estornudar /estornu'ðar/ vi to sneeze

estornudo /estor'nuðo/ m, sneezing; sneeze

estrabismo /estra'βismo/ m, Med. strabismus, squint, cast

estrada /es'traða/ f, road, highway

estrado /es'traðo/ m, dais

estrafalario /estrafa'lario/ a Inf. slovenly, untidy; Inf. eccentric, odd

estragar /estra'gar/ vt to corrupt, spoil, vitiate; ruin, destroy

estrago /es'trago/ m, devastation, destruction, ruin, havoc

estrambótico /estram'botiko/ a Inf. eccentric

estrangulación /estraŋgula'θion; estraŋgula'sion/ f, strangulation; Auto. throttling

estrangulador /estraŋgula'ðor/ **(-ra)** a strangling —n strangler. m, Auto. throttle

estrangular /estraŋgu'lar/ vt to strangle

estraperlista /estraper'lista/ mf black marketeer

estraperlo /estra'perlo/ m, black market

estratagema /estrata'hema/ f, stratagem, trick

estrategia /estra'tehia/ f, strategy

estratégico /estra'tehiko/ a strategic

estratego /estra'tego/ m, strategist

estrato /es'trato/ m, Geol. stratum

estratosfera /estratos'fera/ f, stratosphere

estrechar /estre'tʃar/ vt to make narrower, tighten; hold tightly, clasp; compel, oblige; —vr tighten oneself up; reduce one's expenses; Fig. tighten the bonds (of friendship, etc.). **e. la mano,** to shake hands

estrechez /estre'tʃeθ; estre'tʃes/ f, narrowness; tightness; scantiness; poverty, want. **e. de miras,** narrowmindedness

estrecho /es'tretʃo/ a narrow; tight; intimate, close; austere, rigid; meanspirited. m, Geog. strait

estregar /estre'gar/ vt irr to rub, scour, scrub, scrape, scratch. See **cegar**

estrella /es'treʎa; es'treya/ f, star; fortune, fate; anything star-shaped; Fig. star. **e. de la pantalla,** movie star. **e. de mar,** starfish. **e. de rabo,** comet. **e. fugaz,** shooting star. **tener e.,** to be born under a lucky star

estrellado /estre'ʎaðo; estre'yaðo/ a star-shaped; full of stars, starry; shattered, broken; fried (eggs)

estrellamar /estreʎa'mar; estreya'mar/ f, starfish

estrellar /estre'ʎar; estre'yar/ vt Inf. to shatter, break into fragments; fry (eggs); —vr be starry or sprinkled with stars; be dashed against; fail in, come up against

estrellón /estre'ʎon; estre'yon/ m, large, artificial star (painted or otherwise); starlike firework

estremecer /estreme'θer; estreme'ser/ vt irr to cause to tremble; perturb; —vr shudder, tremble. See **conocer**

estremecimiento /estremeθi'miento; estremesi'miento/ m, shudder, trembling; agitation

estrenar /estre'nar/ vt to use or do for the first time; inaugurate; give the first performance of (plays, etc.); —vr do for the first time; *Com.* make the first sale of the day

estreno /es'treno/ *m,* commencement, inauguration; first appearance; *Theat.* first performance, opening night, premiere

estrenuo /es'trenuo/ *a* strong, energetic, agile

estreñimiento /estreɲi'miento/ *m,* constipation

estreñir /estre'ɲir/ *vt* to constipate

estrépito /es'trepito/ *m,* clamor, din, great noise; fuss, show

estrepitoso /estrepi'toso/ *a* noisy, clamorous

estreptococo /estrepto'koko/ *m,* streptococcus

estreptomicina /estreptomi'θina; estreptomi'sina/ *f,* streptomycin

estribar /estri'βar/ *vi* (*with en*) to lean on, rest on, be supported by; *Fig.* be based on

estribillo /estri'βiʎo; estri'βiyo/ *m,* refrain

estribo /es'triβo/ *m,* stirrup; footboard, step, running board (of vehicles); *Archit.* buttress or pier; *Fig.* stay, support; *Anat.* stapes; *Mech.* stirrup piece. **perder los estribos,** to lose patience, forget oneself

estribor /estri'βor/ *m,* starboard

estricnina /estrik'nina/ *f,* strychnine

estricto /es'trikto/ *a* strict, exact; unbending, severe

estridente /estri'ðente/ *a* strident, shrill

estridor /estri'ðor/ *m,* strident or harsh sound; screech; creak

estro /'estro/ *m,* inspiration

estrofa /es'trofa/ *f,* strophe; verse, stanza

estropajo /estro'paho/ *m,* scourer, dishcloth; worthless person or thing

estropajoso /estropa'hoso/ *a Inf.* indistinct, stammering; dirty and ragged; tough (meat, etc.)

estropear /estrope'ar/ *vt* to spoil, damage; ruin, undo, spoil (plans, effects, etc.); ill-treat, maim; —*vr* hurt oneself, be maimed; spoil, deteriorate

estructura /estruk'tura/ *f,* fabric, structure; *Fig.* construction

estructural /estruktu'ral/ *a* structural

estruendo /es'truendo/ *m,* din, clatter; clamor, noise; ostentation

estruendoso /estruen'doso/ *a* noisy

estrujar /estru'har/ *vt* to squeeze, crush (fruit); hold tightly, press, squeeze, bruise; *Fig. Inf.* squeeze dry

estrujón /estru'hon/ *m,* squeeze, pressure; final pressing (grapes)

estuario /es'tuario/ *m,* estuary

estuche /es'tutʃe/ *m,* case; casket, box; cover; sheath

estuco /es'tuko/ *m,* stucco; plaster

estudiante /estu'ðiante/ *mf* student

estudiantil /estuðian'til/ *a Inf.* student

estudiantina /estuðian'tina/ *f,* strolling band of students playing and singing, generally in aid of charity

estudiar /estu'ðiar/ *vt* to study. **e. de,** study to be a (e.g. *e. de rabino,* study to be a rabbi); learn; *Art.* copy

estudio /es'tuðio/ *m,* study; sketch; disquisition, dissertation; studio; diligence; *Art.* study; reading room, den

estudiosidad /estuðiosi'ðað/ *f,* studiousness

estudioso /estu'ðioso/ *a* studious

estufa /es'tufa/ *f,* heating stove; hothouse; hot room (in bathhouses); drying chamber; *Elec.* heater

estufador /estufa'ðor/ *m,* stewpot or casserole

estulto /es'tulto/ *a* foolish

estupefacción /estupefak'θion; estupefak'sion/ *f,* stupefaction

estupefacto /estupe'fakto/ *a* stupefied, stunned, amazed

estupendo /estu'pendo/ *a* wonderful, marvelous

estupidez /estupi'ðeθ; estupi'ðes/ *f,* stupidity

estúpido /es'tupiðo/ *a* stupid

estupor /estu'por/ *m, Med.* stupor; astonishment

estupro /es'tupro/ *m, Law.* rape

estuque /es'tuke/ *m,* stucco

estuquería /estuke'ria/ *f,* stuccowork

esturión /estu'rion/ *m,* sturgeon

esvástica /es'βastika/ *f,* swastika

etapa /e'tapa/ *f, Mil.* field ration; *Mil.* halt, camp; stage, juncture. **a pequeñas etapas,** by easy stages (of a journey)

etcétera /et'θetera; et'setera/ etcetera

éter /'eter/ *m,* ether; *Poet.* sky

eternidad /eterni'ðað/ *f,* eternity

eternizar /eterni'θar; eterni'sar/ *vt* to drag out, prolong; eternize, perpetuate

eterno /e'terno/ *a* eternal, everlasting; lasting, enduring

ética /'etika/ *f,* ethics

ético /'etiko/ *a* ethical. *m,* moralist

etimología /etimolo'hia/ *f,* etymology

etimológico /etimo'lohiko/ *a* etymological

etiología /etiolo'hia/ *f,* etiology

etíope /e'tiope/ *a and mf* Ethiopian

Etiopía /etio'pia/ Ethiopia

etiqueta /eti'keta/ *f,* etiquette; label

etiquetero /etike'tero/ *a* ceremonious, stiff; prim

étnico /'etniko/ *a* ethnic; heathen

etrusco /e'trusko/ (**-ca**) *a and n* Etruscan

eucalipto /euka'lipto/ *m,* eucalyptus

Eucaristía /eukaris'tia/ *f,* Eucharist

eufemismo /eufe'mismo/ *m,* euphemism

eufonía /eufo'nia/ *f,* euphony

eufónico /eu'foniko/ *a* euphonious

euforia /eu'foria/ *f,* resistance to disease; buoyancy, well-being

eunuco /eu'nuko/ *m,* eunuch

Europa /eu'ropa/ Europe

europeo /euro'peo/ (**-ea**) *a and n* European

éuscaro /'euskaro/ *a* Basque. *m,* Basque (language)

evacuación /eβakua'θion; eβakua'sion/ f, evacuation

evacuar /eβa'kuar/ vt to vacate; evacuate, empty; finish, conclude (a business deal, etc.)

evadir /eβa'ðir/ vt· to avoid, elude; —vr escape; elope

evaluación /eβalua'θion; eβalua'sion/ f, valuation; estimation

evaluar /eβa'luar/ vt to evaluate, estimate; gauge; value

evangélico /eβan'heliko/ a evangelical

evangelio /eβan'helio/ m, Gospel; Christianity; Inf. indisputable truth

evangelizar /eβanheli'θar; eβanheli'sar/ vt to evangelize

evaporación /eβapora'θion; eβapora-'sion/ f, evaporation

evaporar /eβapo'rar/ **(se)** vt and vr to evaporate; disappear, vanish

evasión, evasiva /eβa'sion, eβa'siβa/ f, subterfuge, evasion; flight, escape

evasivo /eβa'siβo/ a evasive

evento /e'βento/ m, happening, event; contingency

eventual /eβen'tual/ a possible, fortuitous; accidental (expenses); extra (emoluments)

eventualidad /eβentuali'ðað/ f, eventuality

evicción /eβik'θion; eβik'sion/ f, Law. eviction

evidencia /eβi'ðenθia; eβiðensia/ f, proof, evidence. **ponerse en e.,** to put oneself forward

evidenciar /eβiðen'θiar; eβiðen'siar/ vt to show, make obvious

evidente /eβi'ðente/ a obvious, evident

evitable /eβi'taβle/ a avoidable

evitación /eβita'θion; eβita'sion/ f, avoidance

evitar /eβi'tar/ vt to avoid; shun, eschew

evocación /eβoka'θion; eβoka'sion/ f, evocation

evocador /eβoka'ðor/ a evocative

evocar /eβo'kar/ vt to evoke

evolución /eβolu'θion; eβolu'sion/ f, evolution; development; (Mil. Nav.) maneuver; change; Geom. involution

evolucionar /eβoluθio'nar; eβolusio'nar/ vi to evolve; (Nav. Mil.) maneuver; change, alter

evolutivo /eβolu'tiβo/ a evolutional

exacerbación /eksaθerβa'θion; eksaserβa'sion/ f, exacerbation

exacerbar /eksáθer'βar; eksaser'βar/ vt to exasperate; exacerbate

exactitud /eksakti'tuð/ f, exactitude; correctness; punctuality

exacto /ek'sakto/ a exact; correct; punctual

exageración /eksahera'θion; eksahera-'sion/ f, exaggeration

exagerador /eksahera'ðor/ **(-ra)** a given to exaggerating —n exaggerater

exagerar /eksahe'rar/ vt to exaggerate

exaltación /eksalta'θion; eksalta'sion/ f, exaltation

exaltar /eksal'tar/ vt to exalt, elevate; extol; —vr grow excited or agitated

examen /ek'samen/ m, inquiry; investigation, research; examination; Geol. survey. **e. parcial,** quiz (at school)

examinador /eksamina'ðor/ **(-ra)** n examiner

examinando /eksami'nando/ **(-da)** n candidate, examinee

examinar /eksami'nar/ vt to inquire into; investigate; inspect; examine; —vr take an examination

exangüe /ek'sangue/ a bloodless, pale; exhausted, weak; dead

exánime /eksa'nime/ a lifeless; spiritless, weak

exasperación /eksaspera'θion; eksaspera'sion/ f, exasperation

exasperador, exasperante /eksaspera-'ðor, eksaspe'rante/ a exasperating

exasperar /eksaspe'rar/ vt to exasperate; irritate, annoy

excarcelar /ekskarθe'lar; ekskarse'lar/ vt to release from jail

excavación /ekskaβa'θion; ekskaβa'sion/ f, excavation

excavador /ekskaβa'ðor/ **(-ra)** n excavator. f, Mech. excavator

excavar /ekska'βar/ vt to hollow; excavate; Agr. hoe (roots of plants)

excedente /eksθe'ðente; eksse'ðente/ a exceeding; excessive; surplus

exceder /eksθe'ðer; eksse'ðer/ vt to exceed; —vr forget oneself, go too far

excelencia /eksθe'lenθia; eksse'lensia/ f, excellence, superiority; Excellency (title)

excelente /eksθe'lente; eksse'lente/ a excellent; Inf. first-rate

excelso /eks'θelso; eks'selso/ a lofty, high; eminent, mighty; sublime

excentricidad /eksθentriθi'ðað; ekssentrisi'ðað/ f, eccentricity

excéntrico /ek'θentriko; eks'sentriko/ a unconventional; erratic; Geom. eccentric

excepción /eksθep'θion; ekssep''sion/ f, exception

exceptuar /eksθep'tuar; ekssep'tuar/ vt to except

excerpta, excerta /eks'θerpta, eks'θerta; eks'serpta, eks'serta/ f, excerpt, extract

excesivo /eksθe'siβo; eksse'siβo/ a excessive

exceso /eks'θeso; eks'seso/ m, excess; Com. surplus; pl crimes, excesses. **e. de peso** or **e. de equipaje,** excess baggage

excipiente /eksθi'piente; ekssi'piente/ m, excipient

excisión /eksθi'sion; ekssi'sion/ f, excision

excitable /eksθi'taβle; ekssi'taβle/ a excitable, high-strung

excitación /eksθita'θion; ekssita'sion/ f, excitation; excitement

excitador /eksθita'ðor; ekssita'ðor/ *a* exciting, stimulating. *m, Phys.* exciter

excitar /eksθi'tar; ekssi'tar/ *vt* to excite, stimulate, provoke; *Elec.* energize; —*vr* become agitated or excited

exclamación /eksklama'θion; eksklama'sion/ *f,* exclamation, interjection

exclamar /ekskla'mar/ *vi* to exclaim

exclamatorio /eksklama'torio/ *a* exclamatory

excluir /eksk'luir/ *vt irr* to exclude, keep out; reject, bar. See **huir**

exclusiva /eksklu'siβa/ *f,* exclusion; special privilege, sole right

exclusive /eksklu'siβe/ *adv* exclusively; excluded

exclusivo /eksklu'siβo/ *a* exclusive

excomulgado /ekskomul'gaðo/ **(-da)** *a* and *n Eccl.* excommunicate; *Inf.* wicked (person)

excomulgar /ekskomul'gar/ *vt* to excommunicate

excomunión /ekskomu'nion/ *f,* excommunication

excoriar /eksko'riar/ *vt* to flay, excoriate; —*vr* graze oneself

excremento /ekskre'mento/ *m,* excrement

excretar /ekskre'tar/ *vi* to excrete

exculpación /ekskulpa'θion; ekskulpa'sion/ *f,* exoneration

exculpar /ekskul'par/ **(se)** *vt* and *vr* to exonerate

excursión /ekskur'sion/ *f,* excursion, trip; *Mil.* incursion

excursionismo /ekskursio'nismo/ *m,* sightseeing; hiking

excursionista /ekskursio'nista/ *mf* excursionist; hiker

excusa /eks'kusa/ *f,* excuse

excusabaraja /ekskusaβa'raha/ *f,* basket with a lid

excusado /eksku'saðo/ *a* excused; exempt; unnecessary, superfluous; reserved, private. *m,* lavatory, toilet

excusar /eksku'sar/ *vt* to excuse; avoid, ward off, prevent; exempt; —*vr* excuse oneself

execración /eksekra'θion; eksekra'sion/ *f,* execration

execrar /ekse'krar/ *vt* to execrate; denounce; loathe

exención /eksen'θion; eksen'sion/ *f,* exemption

exentar /eksen'tar/ *vt* to exempt

exento /ek'sento/ *a* exempt; free, liberated; open (of buildings, etc.)

exequias /ekse'kias/ *f pl,* obsequies

exhalación /eksala'θion; eksala'sion/ *f,* exhalation; shooting star; lightning; emanation, effluvium

exhalar /eksa'lar/ *vt* to exhale, give off; *Fig.* give vent to

exhausto /ek'sausto/ *a* exhausted

exhibición /eksiβi'θion; eksiβi'sion/ *f,* exhibition

exhibicionismo /eksiβiθio'nismo; eksiβisio'nismo/ *m,* exhibitionism

exhibicionista /eksiβiθio'nista; eksiβisio'nista/ *mf* exhibitionist

exhibir /eksi'βir/ *vt* to exhibit, show

exhortación /eksorta'θion; eksorta'sion/ *f,* exhortation

exhortar /eksor'tar/ *vt* to exhort

exhumar /eksu'mar/ *vt* to exhume, disinter

exigencia /eksi'henθia; eksi'hensia/ *f,* exigency; demand

exigente /eksi'hente/ *a* exigent

exigir /eksi'hir/ *vt* to exact, collect; need, require; demand

exiguo /ek'siguo/ *a* exiguous, meager

eximio /ek'simio/ *a* most excellent; illustrious

eximir /eksi'mir/ *vt* to exempt

existencia /eksis'tenθia; eksis'tensia/ *f,* existence; *pl Com.* stock on hand

existir /eksis'tir/ *vi* to exist, be; live

éxito /'eksito/ *m,* success; result, conclusion

éxodo /'eksoðo/ *m,* Exodus; exodus, emigration. **é. rural,** rural depopulation

exoneración /eksonera'θion; eksonera'sion/ *f,* exoneration

exonerar /eksone'rar/ *vt* to exonerate; discharge (from employment)

exorbitancia /eksorβi'tanθia; eksorβi'tansia/ *f,* exorbitance

exorbitante /eksorβi'tante/ *a* exorbitant, excessive

exorcista /eksor'θista; eksor'sista/ *m,* exorcist

exorcizar /eksorθi'θar; eksorsi'sar/ *vt* to exorcize

exornar /eksor'nar/ *vt* to adorn; embellish (*Lit.* style)

exótico /ek'sotiko/ *a* exotic, rare

expandir /ekspan'dir/ *vt* to expand

expansión /ekspan'sion/ *f,* expansion; recreation, hobby

expansivo /ekspan'siβo/ *a* expansive; communicative, frank

expatriación /ekspatria'θion; ekspatria'sion/ *f,* expatriation

expatriarse /ekspa'triarse/ *vr* to emigrate, leave one's country

expectación /ekspekta'θion; ekspekta'sion/ *f,* expectation; expectancy

expectante /ekspek'tante/ *a* expectant

expectativa /ekspekta'tiβa/ *f,* expectancy; expectation

expectoración /ekspektora'θion; ekspektora'sion/ *f,* expectoration

expectorar /ekspekto'rar/ *vt* to expectorate

expedición /ekspeði'θion; ekspeði'sion/ *f,* expedition; speed, promptness; *Eccl.* bull, dispensation; excursion; forwarding, dispatch

expediente /ekspe'ðiente/ *m, Law.* proceedings; file of documents; expedient, device, means; expedition; promptness; motive, reason; provision

expedir /ekspe'ðir/ *vt irr* to expedite; forward, send, ship; issue, make out (checks, receipts, etc.); draw up (documents); dispatch, deal with. See **pedir**

expedito /ekspe'ðito/ *a* expeditious, speedy

expeler /ekspe'ler/ *vt* to expel, discharge, emit

expendedor /ekspende'ðor/ **(-ra)** *a* spending —*n* spender; agent; retailer; seller; *Law.* **e. de moneda falsa,** distributor of counterfeit money

expendeduría /ekspendeðu'ria/ *f,* shop where government monopoly goods are sold (tobacco, stamps, etc.)

expender /ekspen'der/ *vt* to spend (money); *Com.* retail; *Com.* sell on commission; *Law.* distribute counterfeit money

expensas /ek'spensas/ *f pl,* costs, charges

experiencia /ekspe'rienθia; ekspe'riensia/ *f,* experience; practice, experiment

experimentación /eksperimenta'θion; eksperimenta'sion/ *f,* experiencing

experimentar /eksperimen'tar/ *vt* to test, try; experience; feel

experimento /eksperi'mento/ *m,* experiment

experto /ek'sperto/ **(-ta)** *a* practiced, expert —*n* expert

expiación /ekspia'θion; ekspia'sion/ *f,* expiation

expiar /eks'piar/ *vt* to expiate, atone for; pay the penalty of; *Fig.* purify

expiatorio /ekspia'torio/ *a* expiatory

expiración /ekspira'θion, ekspira'sion/ *f,* expiration

expirar /ekspi'rar/ *vi* to die; *Fig.* expire; die down; exhale, expire

explanación /eksplana'θion; eksplana'sion/ *f,* leveling; explanation, elucidation

explanar /ekspla'nar/ *vt* to level; explain

explayar /ekspla'yar/ *vt* to extend, enlarge; —*vr* spread oneself, enlarge (upon); enjoy an outing; confide (in)

explicación /eksplika'θion; eksplika'sion/ *f,* explanation; elucidation

explicar /ekspli'kar/ *vt* to explain; expound; interpret, elucidate; —*vr* explain oneself

explicativo /eksplika'tiβo/ *a* explanatory

explícito /eks'pliðito; eksplisito/ *a* explicit, clear

exploración /eksplora'θion; eksplorasion/ *f,* exploration

explorador /eksplora'ðor/ *a* exploring. *m,* explorer; prospector; boy scout; *Mil.* scout

explorar /eksplo'rar/ *vt* to explore; investigate; *Med.* probe

exploratorio /eksplora'torio/ *a* exploratory

explosión /eksplo'sion/ *f,* explosion; outburst, outbreak. **hacer falsas explosiones,** *Mech.* to misfire

explosivo /eksplo'siβo/ *a* and *m,* explosive. **e. violento,** high explosive

explotación /eksplota'θion; eksplota'sion/ *f,* development, exploitation

explotar /eksplo'tar/ *vt* to work (mines); *Fig.* exploit

expoliación /ekspolia'θion; ekspolia'sion/ *f,* spoliation

expoliar /ekspo'liar/ *vt* to despoil

exponente /ekspo'nente/ *a* and *mf* exponent. *m, Math.* index

exponer /ekspo'ner/ *vt irr* to show, expose; expound, interpret; risk, jeopardize; abandon (child). See **poner**

exportación /eksporta'θion; eksporta'sion/ *f,* exportation; export

exportador /eksporta'ðor/ **(-ra)** *a* export —*n* exporter

exportar /ekspor'tar/ *vt* to export

exposición /eksposi'θion; eksposi'sion/ *f,* exposition, demonstration; petition; exhibition; *Lit.* exposition; *Photo.* exposure; orientation, position

expósito /eks'posito/ **(-ra)** *a* and *n* foundling

expositor /eksposi'tor/ **(-ra)** *a* and *n* exponent —*n* exhibitor

exprés /eks'pres/ *a* express. *m,* messenger or delivery service; express train; transport office

expresar /ekspre'sar/ *vt* to express (all meanings)

expresión /ekspre'sion/ *f,* statement, utterance; phrase, wording; expression; presentation; manifestation; gift, present; squeezing; pressing (of fruits, etc.)

expresivo /ekspre'siβo/ *a* expressive; affectionate

expreso /eks'preso/ *a* express; clear, obvious. *m,* courier, messenger

exprimir /ekspri'mir/ *vt* to squeeze, press (fruit); press, hold tightly; express, utter

expropiación /ekspropia'θion; ekspropia'sion/ *f,* expropriation

expropiar /ekspro'piar/ *vt* to expropriate; commandeer

expugnar /ekspug'nar/ *vt Mil.* to take by storm

expulsar /ekspul'sar/ *vt* to expel, eject, dismiss

expulsión /ekspul'sion/ *f,* expulsion

expurgar /ekspur'gar/ *vt* to cleanse, purify; expurgate

exquisito /eks'kisito/ *a* exquisite, choice; delicate, delicious

extasiarse /eksta'siarse/ *vr* to fall into ecstasy; marvel (at), delight (in)

éxtasis /'ekstasis/ *m,* ecstasy; rapture

extático /eks'tatiko/ *a* ecstatic

extemporáneo /ekstempo'raneo/ *a* untimely; inopportune, inconvenient

extender /eksten'der/ *vt irr* to spread; reach, extend; elongate; enlarge, amplify; unfold, open out, stretch; draw up (documents); make out (checks, etc.); —*vr* stretch out; lie down; spread, be generalized; extend; last (of time); record; stretch, open out. **extenderse en,** to expatiate on. See **entender**

extensión /eksten'sion/ f. extension; expanse; length; extent; duration; extension (logic)

extensivo /eksten'siβo/ a extensive, spacious; extensible

extenso /eks'tenso/ a extensive, vast

extensor /eksten'sor/ a extensor, m, chest expander

extenuación /ekstenua'θion; ekstenua-'sion/ f, emaciation, weakness; extenuation

extenuar /ekste'nuar/ vt to exhaust, weaken; —vr become weak

exterior /ekste'rior/ a external; foreign (trade, etc.). m, outside, exterior; outward appearance

exterioridad /eksteriori'ðað/ f, outward appearance; outside, externality; pl ceremonies, forms; ostentation

exteriorizar /eksteriori'θar; eksteriori-'sar/ vt to exteriorize, reveal

exterminador /ekstermina'ðor/ (**-ra**) a exterminating —n exterminator

exterminar /ekstermi'nar/ vt to exterminate; devastate

exterminio /ekster'minio/ m, extermination; devastation

externado /ekster'naðo/ m, day school

externo /eks'terno/ (**-na**) a external —n day

extinción /ekstin'θion; ekstin'sion/ f, extinction; extinguishment; abolition, cancellation

extinguir /ekstiŋ'guir/ vt to extinguish; destroy

extintor /ekstin'tor/ m, fire extinguisher

extirpación /ekstirpa'θion; ekstirpa'sion/ f, extirpation

extirpador /ekstirpa'ðor/ (**-ra**) a extirpating —n extirpator

extirpar /ekstir'par/ vt to extirpate; Fig. eradicate

extorsión /ekstor'sion/ f, extortion

extorsionar /ekstorsio'nar/ vt to extort

extra /'ekstra/ prefix outside, without, beyond —prep besides —a extremely, most. m, Inf. extra

extracción /ekstrak'θion/ f, extraction; drawing (lottery); origin, lineage; exportation

extractar /ekstrak'tar/ vt to abstract, summarize

extracto /eks'trakto/ m, abstract, summary; Chem. extract

extractor /ekstrak'tor/ a extracting. m, extractor

extradición /ekstraði'θion; ekstraði'sion/ f, extradition

extraer /ekstra'er/ vt irr to extract; draw out; export; Chem. extract. See **traer**

extranjero /ekstran'hero/ (**-ra**) a alien, foreign —n foreigner. m, abroad, foreign country

extrañar /ekstra'ɲar/ vt to exile; alienate, estrange; wonder at; miss, feel the loss of; —vr be exiled; be estranged; be amazed (by); refuse (to do a thing)

extrañeza /ekstra'ɲeθa; ekstra'ɲesa/ f, strangeness; estrangement; surprise

extraño /eks'traɲo/ a strange, unusual; foreign, extraneous

extraoficial /ekstraofi'θial; ekstraofi'sial/ a unofficial

extraordinario /ekstraorði'nario/ a extraordinary; special. m, Cul. extra course

extravagancia /ekstraβa'ganθia; ekstraβa'gansia/ f, eccentricity; queerness; folly

extravagante /ekstraβa'gante/ a eccentric; queer, strange; absurd

extravertido /ekstraβer'tiðo/ m, extrovert

extraviar /ekstra'βiar/ vt to mislead; mislay; —vr lose one's way; be lost (of things); Fig. go astray

extravío /ekstra'βio/ m, deviation, divergence; error; aberration, lapse

extremado /ekstre'maðo/ a extreme

extremar /ekstre'mar/ vt to take to extremes; —vr do one's best

extremidad /ekstremi'ðað/ f, end; extremity; remotest part; edge; limit; pl extremities

extremista /ekstre'mista/ a and mf extremist

extremo /eks'tremo/ a last, ultimate; extreme; furthest; great, exceptional; utmost. m, end, extreme; highest degree; extreme care; pl excessive emotional display

extremoso /ekstre'moso/ a immoderate, exaggerated; very affectionate

exuberante /eksuβe'rante/ a abundant, copious; exuberant

exudar /eksu'ðar/ vi and vt to exude

exultación /eksulta'θion; eksulta'sion/ f, exultation; rejoicing

exultar /eksul'tar/ vi to exult

F

fabada /fa'βaða/ *f*, dish of broad beans with pork, sausage or bacon

fábrica /'faβrika/ *f*, manufacture; making; factory, works; fabric, structure; building; creation; invention. **f. de papel**, paper mill. **marca de f.**, trademark

fabricación /faβrika'θion; faβrika'sion/ *f*, make; making; construction. **f. en serie**, mass production

fabricador /faβrika'ðor/ **(-ra)** *a* creative, inventive —*n* fabricator; maker

fabricante /faβri'kante/ *a* manufacturing. *m*, manufacturer; maker

fabricar /faβri'kar/ *vt* to manufacture; make; construct, build; devise; invent, create

fabril /fa'βril/ *a* manufacturing

fábula /'faβula/ *f*, rumor, gossip; fiction; fable; story, plot; mythology; myth; laughingstock; falsehood.

fabuloso /faβu'loso/ *a* fabulous; fictitious; incredible, amazing

faca /'faka/ *f*, jackknife

facción /fak'θion; fak'sion/ *f*, rebellion; faction, party, band; feature (of the face) (gen. *pl*); military exploit; any routine military duty

faccioso /fak'θioso; fak'sioso/ **(-sa)** *a* factional; factious; seditious —*n* rebel

faceta /fa'θeta; fa'seta/ *f*, facet (gems); aspect, view

facha /'fatʃa/ *f*, *Inf.* countenance, look; face; guy, scarecrow. *Naut.* **ponerse en f.**, to lie to

fachada /fa'tʃaða/ *f*, facade, front (of a building, ship, etc.); *Inf.* build, presence (of a person); frontispiece (of a book)

fachenda /fa'tʃenda/ *f*, *Inf.* boastfulness, vanity

fácil /'faθil; 'fasil/ *a* easy; probable; easily led; docile; of easy virtue (women) —*adv* easy

facilidad /faθili'ðað; fasili'ðað/ *f*, easiness; facility, aptitude; ready compliance; opportunity

facilitar /faθili'tar; fasili'tar/ *vt* to facilitate, expedite; provide, deliver

facineroso /faθine'roso; fasine'roso/ *a* criminal, delinquent. *m*, criminal; villain

facsímile /fak'simile/ *m*, facsimile

factible /fak'tiβle/ *a* feasible, practicable

facticio /fak'tiθio; fak'tisio/ *a* factitious, artificial

factor /fak'tor/ *m*, *Com.* factor, agent; *Math.* factor; element; consideration

factótum /fak'totum/ *m*, *Inf.* factotum, handyman; *Inf.* busybody; confidential agent or deputy

factura /fak'tura/ *f*, *Com.* invoice, bill, account; *Art.* execution; workmanship; making

facturar /faktu'rar/ *vt* *Com.* to invoice, register (luggage on a railroad)

facultad /fakul'tað/ *f*, faculty; mental or physical aptitude, capability; authority, right; science, art; *Educ.* faculty; license

facultar /fakul'tar/ *vt* to authorize, permit

facultativo /fakulta'tiβo/ *a* belonging to a faculty; optional, permissive. *m*, physician

facundia /fa'kundia/ *f*, eloquence

facundo /fa'kundo/ *a* eloquent

faena /fa'ena/ *f*, manual labor; mental work; business affairs (gen. *pl*)

fagot /fa'got/ *m*, bassoon

fagotista /fago'tista/ *mf* bassoon player

faisán /fai'san/ **(-ana)** *Ornith.* cock (hen) pheasant

faja /'faha/ *f*, belt; sash, scarf; corset, girdle; *Geog.* zone; newspaper wrapper; *Archit.* fascia; swathing band

fajar /fa'har/ *vt* to swathe; swaddle (a child)

fajero /fa'hero/ *m*, swaddling band

fajín /fa'hin/ *m*, ceremonial ribbon or sash worn by generals, etc.

fajina /fa'hina/ *f*, stack; brushwood; (*fort.*) fascine

fajo /'faho/ *m*, bundle, sheaf; *pl* swaddling clothes

falacia /fa'laθia; fa'lasia/ *f*, fraud, deceit; deceitfulness; fallacy

falange /fa'lanhe/ *f*, *Mil.* phalanx; *Anat.* phalange; (*Spanish pol.*) Falange

falaz /fa'laθ; fa'las/ *a* deceitful; fallacious

falda /'falda/ *f*, skirt; lap, flap, panel (of a dress); slope (of a hill); the lap; loin (of beef, etc.); brim of a hat; *pl Inf.* petticoats, women. **f. escocesa**, kilt. **f.-pantalón**, divided skirt, culottes.

faldero /fal'dero/ *a* lap (dog); fond of the company of women

faldón /fal'don/ *m*, long, flowing skirt; shirttail; coattail

falibilidad /faliβili'ðað/ *f*, fallibility

falible /fa'liβle/ *a* fallible

falla /'faʎa; faya/ *f*, deficiency, defect; failure; *Geol.* displacement; bonfire (Valencia); *Mineral.* slide

fallar /fa'ʎar; fa'yar/ *vt Law.* to pass sentence; —*vi* be deficient

falleba /fa'ʎeβa; fa'yeβa/ *f*, shutter bolt

fallecer /faʎe'θer; faye'ser/ *vi irr* to die; fail. See **conocer**

fallecimiento /faʎeθi'miento; fayesi'miento/ *m*, death, decease

fallido /fa'ʎiðo; fa'yiðo/ *a* frustrated; bankrupt

fallo /'faʎo; 'fayo/ *m*, *Law.* verdict; judgment

falsario /fal'sario/ *a* falsifying, forging, counterfeiting; deceiving, lying. *m*, falsifier, forger, counterfeiter

falseamiento /falsea'miento/ *m*, falsifying; forging

falsear /false'ar/ *vt* to falsify; forge; counterfeit; penetrate; —*vi* weaken; *Mus.* be out of tune (strings)

falsedad /false'ðað/ *f,* falseness; false-hood

falsete /fal'sete/ *m,* spigot; *Mus.* falsetto voice

falsificación /falsifika'θion; falsifika-'sion/ *f,* falsification; forgery

falsificador /falsifika'ðor/ *a* falsifying; forging. *m,* falsifier; forger

falsificar /falsifi'kar/ *vt* to forge, counter-feit; falsify

falso /'falso/ *a* false; forged, counterfeit; treacherous, untrue, deceitful; incorrect; sham; vicious (horses). **de f.,** falsely; de-ceitfully

falta /'falta/ *f,* lack, shortage; defect; mistake; *Sports.* fault; shortcoming; non-appearance, absence; deficiency in legal weight of coin; *Law.* offense. **f. de éxito,** failure. **hacer f.,** to be necessary. **sin f.,** without fail

faltar /fal'tar/ *vi* to be lacking; fail, die; fall short; be absent from an appoint-ment; not to fulfill one's obligations. **f. a,** to be unfaithful to, break (e.g. *Faltó a su palabra,* He broke his promise). *Inf.* **¡No faltaba más!** I should think not!; That's the limit!

falto /'falto/ *a* lacking, wanting; defec-tive; wretched, mean, timid. **f. de per-sonal,** short-handed

faltriquera /faltri'kera/ *f,* pocket; hip pocket

fama /'fama/ *f,* rumor, report; reputation; fame

famélico /fa'meliko/ *a* ravenous

familia /fa'milia/ *f,* family; household; kindred. **ser de f.,** to run in the family

familiar /fami'liar/ *a* familiar; familiar; well known; unceremonious; plain, sim-ple; colloquial (language). *m, Eccl.* famil-iar; servant; intimate friend; familiar spirit

familiaridad /familiari'ðað/ *f,* familiarity

familiarizar /familiari'sar/ *vt* to familiarize; —*vr* become familiar; accustom oneself

familiarmente /familiar'mente/ *adv* fa-miliarly

famoso /fa'moso/ *a* famous; notorious; *Inf.* excellent, perfect; *Inf.* conspicuous

fámula /'famula/ *f, Inf.* female servant

fámulo /'famulo/ *m,* servant of a college; *Inf.* servant

fanal /fa'nal/ *m,* lantern (of a lighthouse); *Naut.* poop lantern; lantern; lamp glass

fanático /fa'natiko/ **(-ca)** *a* fanatical —*n* fanatic; *Inf.* fan, enthusiast

fanatismo /fana'tismo/ *m,* fanaticism

fanatizar /fanati'θar; fanati'sar/ *vt* to make fanatical; turn into a fanatic

fandango /fan'daŋgo/ *m,* lively Andalu-sian dance

fanega /fa'nega/ *f,* grain measure about the weight of 1.60 bushel; land measure (about 1½ acres)

fanfarrón /fanfa'rron/ **(-ona)** *a Inf.* boastful; swaggering —*n* swashbuckler; boaster

fanfarronear /fanfarrone'ar/ *vi* to swag-ger; brag

fanfarronería /fanfarrone'ria/ *f,* brag-ging

fango /'faŋgo/ *m,* mud, mire; degrada-tion

fangoso /faŋ'goso/ *a* muddy, miry

fantasear /fantase'ar/ *vi* to let one's fancy roam; boast

fantasía /fanta'sia/ *f,* fancy, imagination; fantasy; caprice; fiction; *Inf.* presump-tion; *Mus.* fantasia

fantasma /fan'tasma/ *m,* ghost, phan-tom; vision; image, impression; presump-tuous person. *f, Inf.* scarecrow; apparition

fantasmagórico /fantasma'goriko/ *a* phantasmagoric

fantástico /fan'tastiko/ *a* fanciful, imagi-nary; fantastic, imaginative; presumptu-ous, conceited

fantoche /fan'totʃe/ *m,* puppet; *Inf.* yes-man, mediocrity

faquín /fa'kin/ *m,* porter, carrier

farándula /fa'randula/ *f,* profession of low comedian; troupe of strolling players; cunning trick

fardel /far'ðel/ *m,* bag, knapsack; bundle

fardo /far'ðo/ *m,* bundle, bale, package

farfulla /far'fuʎa; far'fuya/ *f, Inf.* mum-bling; gibbering. *mf Inf.* mumbler

farfullar /farfu'ʎar; farfu'yar/ *vt Inf.* to mumble; gibber; *Inf.* act in haste

faringe /fa'rinhe/ *f,* pharynx

faringitis /farin'hitis/ *f,* pharyngitis

farisaico /fari'saiko/ *a* pharisaical

farmacéutico /farma'θeutiko; farma-'seutiko/ *a* pharmaceutical. *m,* pharmacist

farmacia /far'maθia; far'masia/ *f,* phar-macy

farmacólogo /farma'kologo/ *m,* pharma-cologist

faro /'faro/ *m,* lighthouse; beacon, guide; *Auto.* headlight

farol /fa'rol/ *m,* lantern, lamp; streetlamp; cresset

farola /fa'rola/ *f,* lamppost (generally with several branches); lantern

farolero /faro'lero/ *m,* lantern maker; lamplighter; lamp tender —*a Inf.* swag-gering, braggart

fárrago /'farrago/ *m,* hodgepodge

farsa /'farsa/ *f,* old name for a play; farce; theatrical company; poor, badly constructed play; sham, trick, deception

farsante /far'sante/ *m,* comedian; *Obs.* actor; *Fig. Inf.* humbug

fascinación /fasθina'θion; fassina'sion/ *f,* evil eye; enchantment, fascination

fascinador /fasθina'ðor; fassina'ðor/ **(-ra)** *a* bewitching; fascinating —*n* charmer

fascinante /fasθi'nante; fassi'nante/ *a* fascinating

fascinar /fasθi'nar; fassi'nar/ *vt* to bewitch, place under a spell; deceive, impose upon; attract, fascinate

fascismo /fas'θismo; fas'sismo/ *m*, fascism

fascista /fas'θista; fas'sista/ *a and mf* fascist

fase /'fase/ *f*, phase; aspect

fastidiar /fasti'ðiar/ *vt* to disgust, bore; annoy; —*vr* be bored

fastidio /fasti'ðio/ *m*, sickness, squeamishness; annoyance, boredom, dislike, repugnance

fastidioso /fasti'ðioso/ *a* disgusting, sickening; annoying; boring, tiresome

fastuoso /fas'tuoso/ *a* ostentatious; pompous

fatal /fa'tal/ *a* fatal, mortal; predetermined, inevitable; ill-fated, unhappy, disastrous; evil

fatalidad /fatali'ðað/ *f*, fatality; inevitability; disaster, ill-fatedness

fatalista /fata'lista/ *a* fatalistic. *mf* fatalist

fatalmente /fatal'mente/ *adv* inevitably, unavoidably; unhappily, unfortunately; extremely badly

fatídico /fa'tiðiko/ *a* prophetic (gen. of evil)

fatiga /fa'tiga/ *f*, fatigue; toil; difficult breathing; hardship, troubles (gen. *pl*)

fatigar /fati'gar/ *vt* to tire; annoy; —*vr* be tired

fatigoso /fati'goso/ *a* tired; tiring; tiresome, annoying

fatuidad /fatui'ðað/ *f*, fatuousness, inanity, foolishness; conceit; priggishness

fatuo /fa'tuo/ *a* fatuous, foolish; conceited; priggish. *m*, self-satisfied fool. **fuego f.**, will o' the-wisp

fauces /'fauθes; 'fauses/ *f pl*, gullet

fauna /'fauna/ *f*, fauna

fausto /'fausto/ *m*, pomp, magnificence, ostentation —*a* fortunate, happy

fautor /fau'tor/ *m*, protector, helper; accomplice. **f. de guerra,** warmonger

favor /fa'βor/ *m*, aid, protection, support; favor, honor, service; love favor, sign of favor. **a f. de,** in favor of; on behalf of

favorable /faβo'raβle/ *a* kind, helpful; favorable

favorecedor /faβoreθe'ðor; faβorese'ðor/ **(-ra)** *a* favoring, helping —*n* helper; protector

favorecer /faβore'θer; faβore'ser/ *vt irr* to aid, protect, support; favor; do a service, grant a favor. See **conocer**

favorito /faβo'rito/ **(-ta)** *a and n* favorite

fayenza /fa'yenθa; fa'yensa/ *f*, faience

faz /faθ; fas/ *f*, face; external surface of a thing, side; frontage

fe /fe/ *f*, faith; confidence, trust, good opinion; belief; solemn promise; assertion; certificate, attestation; faithfulness. **f. de erratas,** *Print.* errata. **dar f.,** *Law.* to testify. **de buena f.,** in good faith. **en f.,** in proof

fealdad /feal'ðað/ *f*, ugliness; base action

febrero /fe'βrero/ *m*, February

febril /fe'βril/ *a* feverish; ardent, violent; passionate

fecal /fe'kal/ *a* fecal

fecha /'fetʃa/ *f*, date. **a la f.,** at present, now. **hasta la f.,** up to the present (day)

fechar /fe'tʃar/ *vt* to date, write the date

fecundar /fekun'dar/ *vt* to fertilize; fecundate

fecundizar /fekundi'θar; fekundi'sar/ *vt* to fertilize; make fruitful

fecundo /fe'kundo/ *a* fertile, fecund, prolific; abundant

federación /feðera'θion; feðera'sion/ *f*, federation, league

federal /feðe'ral/ *a* federal. *mf* federalist

fehaciente /fea'θiente; fea'siente/ *a* *Law.* authentic, attested

felicidad /feliθi'ðað; felisi'ðað/ *f*, happiness; contentment, satisfaction; good fortune

felicitación /feliθita'θion; felisita'sion/ *f*, congratulation

felicitar /feliθi'tar; felisi'tar/ *vt* to congratulate; wish well; —*vr* congratulate oneself

feligrés /feli'gres/ **(-esa)** *n* parishioner

feligresía /feligre'sia/ *f*, parish

feliz /fe'liθ; fe'lis/ *a* happy; fortunate; skillful, felicitous (of phrases, etc.)

felón /fe'lon/ **(-ona)** *n* felon

felonía /felo'nia/ *f*, felony

felpa /'felpa/ *f*, plush; *Inf.* drubbing, beating

felpudo /fel'puðo/ *a* plush

femenino /feme'nino/ *a* feminine; female; *Fig.* weak

fementido /femen'tiðo/ *a* sly, false, treacherous, unfaithful

feminismo /femi'nismo/ *m*, feminism

feminista /femi'nista/ *a* feminist. *mf* feminist

fémur /'femur/ *m*, femur, thigh bone

fenecer /fene'θer; fene'ser/ *vt irr* to conclude, finish; —*vi* die; be ended. See **conocer**

fenecimiento /feneθi'miento; fenesi'miento/ *m*, end; death

fenomenal /fenome'nal/ *a* phenomenal; *Inf.* terrific

fenómeno /fe'nomeno/ *m*, phenomenon; *Inf.* something of great size

feo /'feo/ *a* ugly; alarming, horrid; evil. *m*, *Inf.* slight, insult

feraz /fe'raθ; 'feras/ *a* fruitful, fertile

féretro /'feretro/ *m*, coffin; bier

feria /'feria/ *f*, fair, market; workday; holiday; rest

feriar /fe'riar/ *vt* to buy at a fair; bargain —*vi* cease work, take a holiday

fermentación /fermenta'θion; fermenta-'sion/ *f*, fermentation

fermentar /fermen'tar/ *vi* to ferment; be agitated; —*vt* cause to ferment

fermento /fer'mento/ *m*, ferment; leaven; *Chem.* enzyme

ferocidad /feroθi'ðað; ferosi'ðað/ f, ferocity, cruelty

feroz /fe'roθ; fe'ros/ a ferocious, cruel

férreo /'ferreo/ a ferrous; hard, tenacious. **línea férrea**, railroad

ferretería /ferrete'ria/ f, ironworks; ironmonger's shop; ironware, hardware

ferrocarril /ferroka'rril/ m, railroad, railway; railroad train. **f. de cremallera**, rack railroad. **f. funicular**, funicular railway

ferroviario /ferro'βiario/ a railroad, railway. m, railroad employee

fértil /'fertil/ a fertile; fruitful, productive

fertilidad /fertili'ðað/ f, fertility

fertilizar /fertili'θar; fertili'sar/ vt to fertilize, make fruitful

férula /'ferula/ f, ferule; Surg. splint; Fig. yoke, rule

fervor /fer'βor/ m, intense heat; fervor, devotion; zeal

fervoroso /ferβo'roso/ a fervent, zealous, devoted

festejar /feste'har/ vt to feast, entertain; woo; celebrate; —vr amuse oneself

festejo /feste'ho/ m, feast, entertainment; courtship, wooing; pl public celebrations

festín /fes'tin/ m, private dinner or party; sumptuous banquet

festival /festi'βal/ m, musical festival; festival

festividad /festiβi'ðað/ f, festivity; Eccl. celebration, solemnity; witticism

festivo /fes'tiβo/ a joking, witty; happy, gay; solemn, worthy of celebration. **día f.**, holiday

festón /fes'ton/ m, garland, wreath; festoon; border; scalloped edging

festonear /festone'ar/ vt to garland, festoon; border

fetal /fe'tal/ a fetal

fetiche /fe'titʃe/ m, fetish

fétido /'fetiðo/ a stinking, fetid

feto /'feto/ m, fetus

feudal /feu'ðal/ a feudal; despotic

feudo /'feuðo/ m, fief; fee. **f. franco**, freehold

fiado, al /'fiaðo, al/ adv on credit. **en f.**, on bail

fiador /fia'ðor/ (-ra) n guarantor; bail. m, fastener, loop (of a coat, clock, etc.); safety catch, bolt. **salir f.**, to be surety (for); post bail

fiambre /'fiambre/ m, cold meat, cold dish; Inf. stale, out-of-date news, etc.; Inf. corpse

fiambrera /fiam'brera/ f, lunchbox, lunchpail

fianza /'fianθa; 'fiansa/ f, guarantee, bail; surety; security. Law. **dar f.**, to guarantee; post bail

fiar /fi'ar/ vt to go surety for, post bail; sell on credit; trust; confide; —vr (with de) confide in; trust

fibra /'fiβra/ f, fiber; filament; energy, strength; Mineral. vein; grain (of wood)

fibroso /fi'βroso/ a fibrous; fibroid

ficción /fik'θion; fik'sion/ f, falsehood; invention; fiction, imaginative creation; pretense

ficha /'fitʃa/ f, chip, counter; domino; index card, filing card. **f. antropométrica**, personal particulars card

fichar /fi'tʃar/ vt to record personal particulars on a filing card; file, index

fichero /fi'tʃero/ m, filing cabinet; card catalog

ficticio /fik'tiθio; fik'tisio/ a fictitious

fidedigno /fiðe'ðigno/ a trustworthy, bona fide

fidelidad /fiðeli'ðað/ f, fidelity, honesty; loyalty; punctiliousness

fideos /fi'ðeos/ m pl, vermicelli. m, Inf. scraggy person

fiduciario /fiðu'θiario; fiðu'siario/ a Law. fiduciary. m, Law. trustee

fiebre /'fieβre/ f, fever; great agitation, excitement. **f. de oro**, gold fever. **f. palúdica**, malarial fever. **f. puerperal**, puerperal fever. **f. tifoidea**, typhoid fever

fiel /fiel/ a faithful, loyal; true, exact. m, axis; pointer (of a scale or balance)

fieltro /'fieltro/ m, felt

fiera /'fiera/ f, wild beast; cruel person

fiereza /fie'reθa; fie'resa/ f, savageness, wildness; cruelty, fierceness; deformity

fiero /'fiero/ a wild, savage; ugly; huge, enormous; horrible, alarming; haughty

fiesta /'fiesta/ f, merriment, gaiety; entertainment, feast; Inf. joke; festivity, celebration; public holiday; caress, cajolery (gen. pl); pl holidays. **f. fija** Eccl. immovable feast. Inf. **estar de f.**, to be making merry. **hacer f.**, to take a holiday. Inf. **Se acabó la f.**, It's all over and done with

figón /fi'gon/ m, eating house, diner

figura /fi'gura/ f, shape, form; face; Art. image, figure; Law. form; court card; Mus. note; Theat. character, role; (Geom. Gram. Dance.) figure. **f. de nieve**, snowman. Naut. **f. de proa**, figurehead. Fig. **f. decorativa**, figurehead. Fig. **hacer f.**, to cut a figure

figurado /fi'guraðo/ a figurative; rhetorical

figurar /figu'rar/ vt to shape, mold; simulate, pretend; represent; —vi be numbered among; cut a figure; —vr imagine

figurativo /figura'tiβo/ a figurative; symbolical

figurilla /figu'riʎa; figu'riya/ mf Inf. ridiculous, dwarfish figure. f, Art. statuette

figurín /figu'rin/ m, fashion plate or model

fijación /fiha'θion; fiha'sion/ f, fixing; nailing; sticking, posting; attention, fixity; Chem. fixation; firmness, stability

fijador /fiha'ðor/ m, (Med. Photo.) fixative; setting lotion; Art. varnish —a fixing

fijamente /fiha'mente/ adv firmly; attentively

fijar /fi'har/ vt to fix; glue, stick; nail; make firm; settle, appoint (a date); fix, concentrate (attention, gaze); (Photo.

Med.) fix; —*vr* decide; notice (e.g. *No me había fijado,* I hadn't noticed). **f. anuncios,** to post bills

fijeza /fi'heθa; fi'hesa/ *f,* fixedness; firmness, stability; constancy, steadfastness

fijo /'fiho/ *a* firm; fixed; stable; steadfast; permanent; exact. **de f.,** certainly, without doubt

fila /'fila/ *f,* line, row; *Mil.* rank; antipathy, hatred. **en f.,** in a line

filacteria /filak'teria/ *f,* phylactery

filamento /fila'mento/ *m,* filament

filantropía /filantro'pia/ *f,* philanthropy

filantrópico /filan'tropiko/ *a* philanthropic

filántropo /fi'lantropo/ *m,* philanthropist

filarmónico /filar'moniko/ *a* philharmonic

filatelia /fila'telia/ *f,* philately, stamp collecting

filatélico /fila'teliko/ *a* philatelic

filatelista /filate'lista/ *mf* philatelist, stamp collector

filete /fi'lete/ *m, Archit.* filet; *Cul.* small spit; filet (of meat or fish); thread of a screw; *Sew.* hem

filiación /filia'θion; filia'sion/ *f,* filiation; affiliation, relationship; *Mil.* regimental register

filial /fi'lial/ *a* filial; affiliated

filibustero /filiβus'tero/ *m,* filibuster

filigrana /fili'grana/ *f,* filigree; watermark (of paper); *Fig.* delicate creation

Filipinas, las /fili'pinas, las/ the Philippines

filipino /fili'pino/ **(-na)** *a* and *n* Philippine

filmar /fil''mar/ *vt* to film

filme /'filme/ *m,* (cinema) film

filo /'filo/ *m,* cutting edge; dividing line

filólogo /fi'lologo/ *m,* philologist

filón /fi'lon/ *m, Mineral.* vein, lode; *Fig.* gold mine

filosofar /filoso'far/ *vi* to philosophize

filosofía /filoso'fia/ *f,* philosophy. **f. moral,** moral philosophy. **f. natural,** natural philosophy

filosófico /filo'sofiko/ *a* philosophic

filósofo /fi'losofo/ *m,* philosopher —*a* philosophic

filtrar /fil'trar/ *vt* to filter; —*vi* filter through, percolate; —*vr Fig.* disappear (of money, etc.)

filtro /'filtro/ *m,* filter, strainer; love potion, philter

fin /fin/ *m,* finish, end, conclusion; purpose, goal, aim; limit, extent. **a f. de,** in order to, so that. **a fines de,** toward the end of (with months, years, etc.) (e.g. *a fines de octubre,* toward the end of October). **en f.,** at last; in fine; well then! **por f.,** finally

finado /fi'nado/ **(-da)** *n* deceased, dead person

final /fi'nal/ *a* final. *m,* end, finish; *Sports.* final (gen. *pl*)

finalidad /finali'ðað/ *f,* finality; purpose

finalista /fina'lista/ *mf Sports.* finalist

finalizar /finali'θar; finali'sar/ *vt* to conclude, finish; —*vi* be finished; close (stock exchange)

financiar /finan'θiar; finan'siar/ *vt* to finance

financiero /finan'θiero; finan'siero/ *a* financial. *m,* financier

finanzas /fi'nanθas; fi'nansas/ *f pl,* finance

finar /fi'nar/ *vi* to die; —*vr* desire, long for a thing

finca /'finka/ *f,* land, real estate; house property, country house, ranch

fineza /fi'neθa; fi'nesa/ *f,* fineness; excellence, goodness; kindness, expression of affection; good turn, friendly act; gift; beauty, delicacy

fingido /fin'hido/ *a* pretended; assumed; feigned; sham

fingimiento /finhi'miento/ *m,* pretense; affectation, assumption

fingir /fin'hir/ *vt* to pretend, feign; imagine

finiquitar /finiki'tar/ *vt* to close and pay up an account; *Inf.* end

finiquito /fini'kito/ *m,* closing of an account; final receipt, quittance; quietus

finito /fi'nito/ *a* finite

finlandés /finlan'des/ **(-esa)** *a* Finnish —*n* Finn. *m,* Finnish (language)

Finlandia /fin'landia/ Finland

fino /'fino/ *a* fine; excellent, good; slim, slender, thin; delicate, subtle; dainty (of people); cultured, polished; constant, loving; sagacious, shrewd; *Mineral.* refined

finura /fi'nura/ *f,* fineness; excellence; delicacy; courtesy

fiordo /'fiorðo/ *m,* fjord

firma /'firma/ *f,* signature; act of signing; *Com.* firm name, firm

firmamento /firma'mento/ *m,* firmament

firmante /fir'mante/ *a* signing. *mf* signatory

firmar /fir'mar/ *vt* to sign

firme /'firme/ *a* firm; hard; steady, solid; constant, resolute, loyal. *m,* foundation, base. *Mil.* **¡Firmes!** Attention! **batir de f.,** to strike hard

firmeza /fir'meθa; fir'mesa/ *f,* stability, firmness; constancy, resoluteness, loyalty

fiscal /fis'kal/ *a* fiscal. *m,* attorney general; public prosecutor; meddler. **f. de quiebras,** official receiver

fiscalizar /fiskali'θar; fiskali'sar/ *vt* to prosecute; pry into; meddle with; censure, criticize

fisco /'fisko/ *m,* national treasury, exchequer, revenue

fisgar /fis'gar/ *vt* to harpoon; pry; —*vi* mock, make fun of

fisgón /fis'gon/ **(-ona)** *a* prying; mocking —*n* pryer; mocker; eavesdropper

fisgoneo /fisgo'neo/ *m,* prying; eavesdropping

física /'fisika/ *f,* physics

físico /'fisiko/ *a* physical. *m*, physicist; physician; physique

fisioterapia /fisiote'rapia/ *f*, physiotherapy

fisonomía /fisono'mia/ *f*, physiognomy

fístula /'fistula/ *f*, pipe, conduit; *Mus.* pipe; *Surg.* fistula

fisura /fi'sura/ *f*, fissure

fláccido /'flakθiðo; 'flaksiðo/ *a* flaccid, soft, flabby

flaco /'flako/ *a* thin; weak, feeble; *Fig.* weak-minded; dispirited. *m*, failing, weakness. *Inf.* **hacer un f. servicio,** to do an ill turn. **estar f. de memoria,** to have a weak memory

flagelar /flahe'lar/ *vt* to scourge; *Fig.* lash

flagelo /fla'helo/ *m*, whip; scourge

flagrante /fla'grante/ *a Poet.* refulgent; present; actual. **en f.,** in the very act, flagrante delicto

flagrar /fla'grar/ *vi Poet.* to blaze, be refulgent

flamante /fla'mante/ *a* resplendent; brand-new; fresh, spick-and-span

flamenco /fla'menko/ **(-ca)** *m*, *Ornith.* flamingo —*a* and *n* Flemish —*a* Andalusian; gypsy; buxom, fresh

flan /flan/ *m*, baked custard, creme caramel. **estar como un f.,** to shake like a leaf, be nervous

flanco /'flanko/ *m*, side; *Mil.* flank

flanquear /flanke'ar/ *vt Mil.* to flank

flanqueo /flan'keo/ *m*, *Mil.* outflanking

flaquear /flake'ar/ *vi* to grow weak; weaken; totter (buildings, etc.); be disheartened, flag

flaqueza /fla'keθa; fla'kesa/ *f*, weakness; thinness; faintness, feebleness; frailty, fault; loss of zeal

flato /'flato/ *m*, flatulence, gas

flatulento /flatu'lento/ *a* flatulent, gassy

flauta /'flauta/ *f*, flute

flautín /flau'tin/ *m*, piccolo

flautista /flau'tista/ *mf* flutist

flebitis /fle'βitis/ *f*, phlebitis

flebotomía /fleβoto'mia/ *f*, phlebotomy; bloodletting

flecha /'fletʃa/ *f*, arrow, dart

flechar /fle'tʃar/ *vt* to shoot an arrow or dart; wound or kill with arrows; *Inf.* inspire love; —*vi* bend a bow to shoot

flechazo /fle'tʃaθo; fle'tʃaso/ *m*, wound with an arrow; *Inf.* love at first sight

flechero /fle'tʃero/ *m*, archer; arrow maker

fleco /'fleko/ *m*, fringe; fringe (of hair)

flema /'flema/ *f*, phlegm; sluggishness

flemático /fle'matiko/ *a* phlegmatic; sluggish

flemón /fle'mon/ *m*, gumboil; abscess

flequillo /fle'kiʎo; fle'kiyo/ *m*, fringe (of hair)

fletamento /fleta'mento/ *m*, chartering (a ship)

fletar /fle'tar/ *vt* to charter a ship; embark merchandise or people

flete /'flete/ *m*, freightage; cargo, freight

flexibilidad /fleksiβili'ðað/ *f*, flexibility; suppleness, adaptability

flexible /fle'ksiβle/ *a* pliant, supple; flexible, adaptable. *m*, *Elec.* flex

flexión /fle'ksion/ *f*, flexion; bend, bending; deflection

flirtear /flirte'ar/ *vi* to flirt

flirteo /flir'teo/ *m*, flirtation

flojedad /flohe'ðað/ *f*, flabbiness; weakness, feebleness; laziness, negligence

flojo /'floho/ *a* flabby; slack, loose; weak, feeble; lazy, slothful; poor (of a literary work, etc.)

floqueado /floke'aðo/ *a* fringed

flor /flor/ *f*, flower; best (of anything); bloom (on fruit); virginity; grain (of leather); compliment (gen. *pl*); menstruation (gen. *pl*). **f. de especia,** mace. **f. de la edad,** prime, youth. **f. del cuclillo,** mayflower. **f. del estudiante,** French marigold. **flores de mano,** artificial flowers. **flores de oblón,** hops. **a f. de,** on the surface of, level with. **andarse en flores,** *Fig.* to beat about the bush. **echar flores,** to pay compliments. **en f.,** in bloom

flora /'flora/ *f*, flora

floral /flo'ral/ *a* floral. **juegos florales,** poetry contest

florear /flore'ar/ *vt* to adorn with flowers; —*vi* execute a flourish on the guitar

florecer /flore'θer; flore'ser/ *vi irr* to flower, bloom; flourish, prosper; —*vr* grow mold (of cheese, etc.). See **conocer**

floreciente /flore'θiente; flore'siente/ *a* flowering; prosperous

florecimiento /floreθi'miento; floresi'miento/ *m*, flowering; prosperity

Florencia /flo'renθia; flo'rensia/ Florence

floreo /flo'reo/ *m*, witty conversation; flourish (on the guitar or in fencing)

florero /flo'rero/ *m*, vase; flower pot; *Art.* flower piece

florescencia /flores'θenθia; flores'sensia/ *f*, flowering; flowering season, florescence

floresta /flo'resta/ *f*, grove, wooded park, woodland; *Fig.* collector of beautiful things; anthology

florido /flo'riðo/ *a* flowery; best, most select; florid, ornate

florilegio /flori'lehio/ *m*, anthology, collection

florista /flo'rista/ *mf* artificial-flower maker; florist; flower seller

florón /flo'ron/ *m*, large flower; *Archit.* fleuron; honorable deed

flota /'flota/ *f*, fleet of merchant ships. **f. aérea,** air force

flotación /flota'θion; flota'sion/ *f*, floating. *Naut.* **línea de f.,** water line

flotador /flota'ðor/ *a* floating. *m*, float

flotamiento /flota'miento/ *m*, floating

flotante /flo'tante/ *a* floating

flotar /flo'tar/ *vi* to float on water or in air

flote /'flote/ *m*, floating. **a f.,** afloat; independent, solvent

flotilla /flo'tiʎa; flo'tiya/ *f*, flotilla; fleet of small ships. **f. aérea,** air fleet

fluctuación /fluktua'θion; fluktua'sion/ *f*, fluctuation; hesitation, vacillation

fluctuante /fluk'tuante/ *a* fluctuating

fluctuar /fluktu'ar/ *vi* to fluctuate; be in danger (things); vacillate, hesitate; undulate; oscillate

fluidez /flui'ðeθ; flui'ðes/ *f*, fluidity

flúido /'fluiðo/ *a* fluid; fluent. *m*, fluid; *Elec.* current

fluir /flu'ir/ *vi irr* to flow. See **huir**

flujo /'fluho/ *m*, flow, flux; rising tide. **f. de sangre,** hemorrhage

fluorescente /fluores'θente; fluores'sente/ *a* fluorescent

flux /fluks/ *m*, flush (in cards)

foca /'foka/ *f*, *Zool.* seal

foco /'foko/ *m*, focus; center; origin; source, *Theat.* spotlight, core (of an abscess)

fofo /'fofo/ *a* spongy, soft; flabby

fogata /fo'gata/ *f*, bonfire

fogón /fo'gon/ *m*, fire, cooking area, kitchen range, kitchen stove; furnace of a steamboiler; vent of a firearm

fogonazo /fogo'naθo; fogo'naso/ *m*, powder flash

fogonero /fogo'nero/ *m*, stoker

fogosidad /fogosi'ðað/ *f*, enthusiasm; vehemence; ardor

fogoso /fo'goso/ *a* ardent; vehement; enthusiastic

folclórico /fol'kloriko/ *a* pertaining to folklore

folclorista /folklo'rista/ *mf* folklorist

folículo /fo'likulo/ *m*, follicle

folio /'folio/ *m*, leaf of a book or manuscript, folio. **en f.,** in folio

follaje /fo'ʎahe; fo'yahe/ *m*, foliage; leafy ornamentation; crude, unnecessary decoration; verbosity

folletín /foʎe'tin; foye'tin/ *m*, feuilleton, literary article; serial story; *Inf.* dime novel, potboiler

folleto /fo'ʎeto; fo'yeto/ *m*, pamphlet, leaflet

follón /fo'ʎon; fo'yon/ *a* lazy; caddish; craven

fomentación /fomenta'θion; fomenta'sion/ *f*, *Med.* fomentation, poultice

fomentador /fomenta'ðor/ *a* fomenting. *m*, fomenter

fomentar /fomen'tar/ *vt* to warm, foment; incite, instigate; *Med.* apply poultices

fomento /fo'mento/ *m*, heat, shelter; fuel; protection, encouragement; *Med.* fomentation

fonda /'fonda/ *f*, inn; restaurant

fondear /fonde'ar/ *vt Naut.* to sound; search a ship; examine carefully; —*vi Naut.* anchor

fondillos /fon'diʎos; fon'diyos/ *m pl*, seat (of the trousers)

fondista /fon'dista/ *mf* owner of an inn or restaurant

fondo /'fondo/ *m*, bottom (of a well, etc.); bed (of the sea, etc.); depth; rear, portion at the back; ground (of fabrics); background; *Com.* capital; *Com.* stock; *Fig.* fund (of humor, etc.); character, nature; temperament; *Fig.* substance, core, essence; *Naut.* bottom; *pl Com.* resources, funds. **f. de amortización,** sinking fund. **f. doble** *or* **f. secreto,** false bottom. **f. muerto, f. perdido** *or* **f. vitalicio,** life annuity. *Com.* **fondos inactivos,** idle capital. **a fondo,** completely, thoroughly. **artículo de f.,** editorial, lead article. *Sports.* **carrera de f.,** long-distance race. *Naut.* **irse a f.,** to sink, founder

fonética /fo'netika/ *f*, phonetics

fonético /fo'netiko/ *a* phonetic

fontanero /fonta'nero/ *m*, pipe layer; plumber

forajido /fora'hiðo/ (**-da**) *a* fugitive, outlawed —*n* robber, fugitive

forastero /foras'tero/ (**-ra**) *a* strange, foreign; alien, exotic —*n* stranger

forcejear /forθehe'ar; forsehe'ar/ *vi* to struggle; try, strive; oppose, contradict

forcejo /for'θeho; for'seho/ *a*, struggle; endeavor; opposition, hostility

forense /fo'rense/ *a* forensic

forillo /fo'riʎo; fo'riyo/ *m*, *Theat.* backdrop

forja /'forha/ *f*, forge

forjador /forha'ðor/ *m*, smith, ironworker

forjar /for'har/ *vt* to forge; fabricate; create; counterfeit

forma /'forma/ *f*, shape, form; arrangement; method; style; manifestation, expression; formula, formulary; ceremonial; *Print.* form; manner; means, way; mold, matrix; style of handwriting. *Law.* **en debida f.,** in due form

formación /forma'θion; forma''sion/ *f*, formation; form, contour, shape; (*Mil. Geol.*) formation. **f. del censo,** census taking

formador /forma'ðor/ *a* forming, shaping

formal /for'mal/ *a* apparent, formal; serious, punctilious, steady; truthful, reliable; sedate; orderly, regular, methodical

formaldehído /formalde'iðo/ *m*, formaldehyde

formalidad /formali'ðað/ *f*, orderliness, propriety; formality; requirement, requisite; ceremony; seriousness, sedateness; punctiliousness

formalismo /forma'lismo/ *m*, formalism; bureaucracy, red tape

formalizar /formali'θar; formali'sar/ *vt* to put into final form; legalize; formulate, enunciate; —*vr* take seriously (a joke)

formar /for'mar/ *vt* to shape; form; educate, mold; *Mil.* form. **formarle causa a uno,** to bring charges against someone —*vr* develop, grow

formato /for'mato/ *m*, *Print.* format; *Chem.* formate

formidable /formi'ðaβle/ *a* formidable, awe-inspiring; huge, enormous

fórmula /'formula/ *f*, formula; prescription; mode of expression. (*Math. Chem.*) **f. clásica**, standard formula

formular /formu'lar/ *vt* to formulate; prescribe

formulario /formu'lario/ *m, Law.* formulary; handbook

formulismo /formu'lismo/ *m*, formulism; bureaucracy, red tape

fornicador /fornika'ðor/ **(-ra)** *a* and *n* fornicator

fornicar /forni'kar/ *vi* to fornicate

fornido /for'niðo/ *a* stalwart, muscular, strong

foro /'foro/ *m*, forum; law courts; law, bar, legal profession; *Theat.* back scenery; leasehold

forraje /fo'rrahe/ *m*, forage, fodder; foraging

forrajear /forrahe'ar/ *vt* to gather forage, go foraging

forrar /fo'rrar/ *vt Sew.* to line; cover, encase, make a cover for

forro /'forro/ *m*, lining, inner covering; cover (of a book)

fortalecedor /fortaleθe'ðor; fortalese'ðor/ *a* fortifying

fortalecer /fortale'θer; fortale'ser/ *vt irr* to fortify. See **conocer**

fortaleza /forta'leθa; forta'lesa/ *f*, vigor; fortitude; fortress; natural defense. *Aer.* **f. volante**, flying fortress

fortificación /fortifika'θion; fortifika'sion/ *f*, fortification

fortificador /fortifika'ðor/ *a* fortifying

fortificar /fortifi'kar/ *vt* to fortify

fortísimo /for'tisimo/ *a superl* **fuerte** extremely strong

fortuito /for'tuito/ *a*, fortuitous, chance

fortuna /for'tuna/ *f*, fate, destiny; fortune, capital, estate; tempest. **por f.**, fortunately. **probar f.**, to try one's luck

forzado /for'θaðo; for'saðo/ *a* forced, obliged. *m*, convict condemned to the galleys

forzador /forθa'ðor; forsa'ðor/ *m*, violator, seducer

forzar /for'θar; for'sar/ *vt irr* to force, break open; take by force; rape, ravish; oblige, compel —*Pres. Indic.* **fuerzo, fuerzas, fuerza, fuerzan** —*Preterite* **forcé, forzaste**, etc —*Pres. Subjunc.* **fuerce, fuerces, fuerce, forcemos, forcéis, fuercen**

forzoso /for'θoso; for'soso/ *a* obligatory, unavoidable, necessary

forzudo /for'θuðo; for'suðo/ *a* brawny, stalwart

fosa /'fosa/ *f*, grave; socket (of a joint). **f. común**, potter's field.

fosar /fo'sar/ *vt* to undermine; dig a trench around

fosforecer /fosfore'θer; fosfore'ser/ *vi irr* to phosphoresce. See **conocer**

fosforera /fosfo'rera/ *f*, matchbox

fosforescente /fosfores'θente; fosfores'sente/ *a* phosphorescent

fósforo /'fosforo/ *m*, phosphorus; match; morning star

fósil /'fosil/ *a* and *m*, fossil; *Inf.* antique

fosilizarse /fosili'θarse; fosili'sarse/ *vr* to become fossilized

foso /'foso/ *m*, hole, hollow, pit; trench; pit (in garages); *Theat.* room under the stage.

foto /'foto/ *f*, snapshot, photo

fotocopia /foto'kopia/ *f*, photocopy

fotogénico /foto'heniko/ *a* photogenic

fotograbado /fotogra'βaðo/ *m*, photogravure

fotografía /fotogra'fia/ *f*, photography; photograph

fotografiar /fotogra'fiar/ *vt* to photograph

fotográfico /foto'grafiko/ *a* photographic

fotógrafo /fo'tografo/ *m*, photographer

fotostato /foto'stato/ *m*, photostat

frac /frak/ *m*, tail coat

fracasar /fraka'sar/ *vi* to break, crumble, be shattered; collapse (of plans, etc.); fail; be disappointed

fracaso /fra'kaso/ *m*, shattering; collapse (of plans, etc.); disaster; failure, disappointment, downfall

fracción /frak'θion; frak'sion/ *f*, division into parts; fraction. **f. impropia**, *Math.* improper fraction

fractura /frak'tura/ *f*, fracture. **f. conminuta**, compound fracture

fracturar /fraktu'rar/ *vt* to fracture

fragancia /fra'ganθia; fra'gansia/ *f*, fragrance, perfume; renown, good name

fragante /fra'gante/ *a* fragrant; perfumed; flagrant

frágil /'frahil/ *a* fragile, brittle; perishable, frail; weak, sinful

fragilidad /frahili'ðað/ *f*, fragility; frailty, sinfulness

fragmentario /fragmen'tario/ *a* fragmentary

fragmento /frag'mento/ *m*, fragment

fragor /fra'gor/ *m*, noise, crash

fragosidad /fragosi'ðað/ *f*, roughness, rockiness, unevenness

fragoso /fra'goso/ *a* craggy, rocky; rough; noisy, clamorous

fragua /'fragua/ *f*, forge

fraguado /fra'guaðo/ *m*, forging; *Mas.* setting

fraguar /fra'guar/ *vt* to forge, work; plot, scheme; —*vi* set (concrete, etc.)

fraile /'fraile/ *m*, friar, monk. *Inf.* **f. de misa y olla**, ignorant friar

frambuesa /fram'buesa/ *f*, raspberry

francachela /franka'tʃela/ *f, Inf.* binge

francés /fran'θes; fran'ses/ **(-esa)** *a* French —*n* Frenchman (-woman). *m*, French (language). **a la francesa**, in French fashion

francesilla /franθe'siʎa; franse'siya/ *f, Cul.* French roll

Francia /'franθia; 'fransia/ France

francmasón /frankma'son/ **(-ona)** n Freemason

francmasonería /frankmasone'ria/ f, freemasonry

franco /'franko/ a generous, liberal; exempt; sincere, genuine, frank; duty-free; Frank; Franco (in compound words). m, franc (coin). **f. de porte**, post-free; prepaid

francotirador /frankotira'ðor/ m, sharpshooter, franc tireur

franela /fra'nela/ f, flannel

frangir /fran'hir/ vt to divide, quarter

frangollar /fraŋgo'ʎar; fraŋgo'yar/ vt to scamp, skimp (work); botch, bungle

franja /'franha/ f, fringe; border, trimming; stripe. Radio. **f. undosa**, wave band

franjar /fran'har/ vt Sew. to fringe, trim

franqueadora /frankea'ðora/ f, postage meter

franquear /franke'ar/ vt to exempt; make free, make a gift of; clear the way; stamp, prepay; free (slaves); —vr fall in easily with others' plans; make confidences

franqueo /fran'keo/ m, exemption; bestowal, making free; postage, stamping; enfranchisement (of slaves)

franqueza /fran'keθa; fran'kesa/ f, exemption, freedom; generosity, liberality; sincerity, frankness

franquicia /fran'kiθia; fran'kisia/ f, exemption from excise duties

frasco /'frasko/ m, bottle, flask; powder flask or horn. **f. cuentagotas**, drop bottle

frase /'frase/ f, sentence; phrase; epigram; idiom, style. **f. hecha**, cliché

fraseología /fraseolo'hia/ f, phraseology; wording

fraternal /frater'nal/ a brotherly

fraternidad /fraterni'ðað/ f, fraternity, brotherhood

fraternizar /fraterni'θar; fraterni'sar/ vi to fraternize

fratricidio /fratri'θiðio; fratri'siðio/ m, fratricide (act)

fraude /'frauðe/ m, fraud, deception

fraudulento /frauðu'lento/ a fraudulent

fray /frai/ m, Abbr. **fraile**. Always followed by a proper name (e.g. F. Bartolomé, Friar Bartholomew)

frazada /fra'θaða; fra'saða/ f, blanket

frecuencia /fre'kuenθia; fre'kuensia/ f, frequency. **f. radioeléctrica**, radiofrequency

frecuentación /frekuenta'θion; frekuenta'sion/ f, frequenting, visiting

frecuentador /frekuenta'ðor/ **(-ra)** n frequenter

frecuentar /frekuen'tar/ vt to frequent

frecuente /fre'kuente/ a frequent

fregadero /frega'ðero/ m, kitchen sink

fregado /fre'gaðo/ m, scrubbing; rubbing; scouring; washing; Inf. murky business

fregador /frega'ðor/ m, kitchen sink; scrub brush; dishcloth. **f. mecánico de platos**, dishwasher

fregar /fre'gar/ vt irr to rub; scour; wash (dishes). See **cegar**

fregotear /fregote'ar/ vt Inf. to clean or scour inefficiently

freír /fre'ir/ vt irr Cul. to fry. See **reír**

fréjol /'frehol/ m, kidney bean

frenar /fre'nar/ vt to restrain, hold back; bridle, check; Mech. brake

frenesí /frene'si/ m, madness, frenzy; vehemence, exaltation

frenético /fre'netiko/ a mad, frenzied; vehement, exalted

freno /'freno/ m, bridle; Mech. brake; restraint, check. **f. de pedal**, foot brake. **f. neumático**, vacuum brake, pneumatic brake

frente /'frente/ f, brow, forehead; front portion; countenance; head; heading; beginning (of a letter, etc.). m, Mil. front. mf facade; front; obverse (of coins) —adv in front, opposite. **f. a f.**, face to face. **con la f. levantada**, with head held high; proudly; insolently. **de f.**, abreast

fresa /'fresa/ f, strawberry plant and fruit (especially small or wild varieties); Mech. milling cutter, miller

fresadora /fresa'ðora/ f, milling machine

fresal /fre'sal/ m, strawberry bed

fresca /'freska/ f, cool air; fresh air; Inf. home truth

fresco /'fresko/ a cool; fresh, new; recent; buxom, fresh-colored; calm, serene; Inf. impudent, cheeky, bold; thin (cloths). m, coolness; fresh air; Art. fresco. **al f.**, in the open air. **hacer f.**, to be cool or fresh

frescote /fres'kote/ a Inf. ruddy and corpulent

frescura /fres'kura/ f, coolness; freshness; pleasant verdure and fertility; Inf. cheek, nerve; piece of insolence; unconcern, indifference; calmness, serenity

fresón /fre'son/ m, strawberry (large, cultivated varieties)

fresquera /fres'kera/ f, meat locker; cool place

fresquista /fres'kista/ mf fresco painter

friable /'friaβle/ a brittle; friable, powdery

frialdad /frial'dað/ f, coldness, chilliness; Med. frigidity; indifference, lack of interest; foolishness; negligence

fríamente /fria'mente/ adv coldly; coolly, with indifference; dully, flatly

fricción /frik'θion; frik'sion/ f, friction

friccionar /frikθio'nar; friksio'nar/ vt to rub; give a massage

friega /'friega/ f, friction, massage

frigidez /frihi'ðeθ; frihi'ðes/ f, See **frialdad**

frígido /'frihiðo/ a frigid

frigorífico /frigo'rifiko/ a refrigerative. m, refrigerator, cold-storage locker

frío /'frio/ a cold; Med. frigid; indifferent,

uninterested; dull, uninteresting; inefficient. *m*, coldness, chill; cold

friolero /frio'lero/ *a* sensitive to cold

frisa /'frisa/ *f*, frieze cloth

frisar /fri'sar/ *vt* to frizz, curl (cloth); scrub, rub; —*vi* approach, be nearly (e.g. *Frisa en los setenta años,* He's nearly seventy)

friso /'friso/ *m*, frieze; dado, border

fritada /fri'taða/ *f*, *Cul.* fry, fried food

frito /'frito/ *a* fried

fritura /fri'tura/ *f*, frying; fried food

frivolidad /friβoli'ðað/ *f*, frivolity

frivolité /friβoli'te/ *m*, *Sew.* tatting

frívolo /'friβolo/ *a* frivolous, superficial; futile, unconvincing

fronda /'fronda/ *f*, *Bot.* leaf; frond (of ferns); *pl* foliage

frondosidad /frondosi'ðað/ *f*, luxuriance of foliage

frondoso /fron'doso/ *a* leafy

frontera /fron'tera/ *f*, frontier; facade

fronterizo /fronte'riðo; fronte'riso/ *a* frontier; facing, opposite

frontero /fron'tero/ *a* facing, opposite. *m*, (*Obs. Mil.*) frontier commander

frontispicio /frontis'piðio; frontis'pisio/ *m*, frontispiece; facade; *Fig. Inf.* face, dial

frontón /fron'ton/ *m*, pelota court; jai alai court; *Archit.* pediment

frotamiento, frote /frota'miento, 'frote/ *m*, rubbing, friction

frotar /fro'tar/ *vt* to rub

frotis /'frotis/ *m*, *Med.* smear

fructífero /fruk'tifero/ *a* fruitful, fructiferous

fructuoso /fruk'tuoso/ *a* fruitful, fertile; useful

frufrú /fru'fru/ *m*, rustle (of silk, etc.)

frugal /fru'gal/ *a* frugal; saving, economical

frugalidad /frugali'ðað/ *f*, frugality, abstemiousness, moderation

fruición /frui'θion; frui'sion/ *f*, enjoyment; fruition; satisfaction

fruir /fruir/ *vi irr* to enjoy what one has long desired. See **fruir**

frunce /'frunθe; 'frunse/ *m*, *Sew.* shirring; gather; ruffling; tuck; pucker; wrinkle

fruncimiento /frunθi'miento; frunsi'miento/ *m*, wrinkling; puckering; *Sew.* shirring

fruncir /frun'θir; frun'sir/ *vt* to frown; purse (the lips); pucker; *Sew.* shirr, pleat, gather; reduce in size; conceal the truth; —*vr* pretend to be prudish. **f. el ceño,** to knit one's brow, scowl

fruslería /frusle'ria/ *f*, trifle, nothing

frustración /frustra'θion; frustra'sion/ *f*, frustration

frustrar /frus'trar/ *vt* to disappoint; frustrate, thwart

fruta /'fruta/ *f*, fruit; *Inf.* consequence, result. **f. de hueso,** stone fruit. *Cul.* **f. de sartén,** fritter

frutal /fru'tal/ *a* fruit-bearing. *m*, fruit tree

frutería /frute'ria/ *f*, fruit

frutero /fru'tero/ (**-ra**) *a* fruit —*n* fruit seller. *m*, fruit dish; *Art.* painting of fruit; basket of imitation fruit

fruticultura /frutikul'tura/ *f*, fruit farming

fruto /'fruto/ *m*, fruit; product, result; profit, proceeds; *Agr.* grain

fu /fu/ spitting (of cats) —*interj* expression of scorn. *Inf.* **ni f. ni fa,** neither one thing nor the other

fuego /'fuego/ *m*, fire; conflagration; firing (of firearms); beacon; hearth, home; rash; ardor; heat (of an argument, etc.); —*interj* ¡F.! *Mil.* Fire! **fuegos artificiales,** fireworks. **a sangre y f.,** by fire and sword. *Mil.* **hacer f.,** to fire (a weapon). **pegar f.,** to set on fire

fuelle /'fueʎe; 'fueye/ *m*, bellows; bag (of a bagpipe); *Sew.* pucker, wrinkle; hood (of a carriage, etc.); wind cloud; *Inf.* talebearer. **f. de pie,** foot pump

fuente /'fuente/ *f*, stream, spring; fountain; meat dish; genesis, origin; source, headwaters; tap

fuera /'fuera/ *adv* outside, out —*interj* get out! **f. de,** besides, in addition to. **f. de alcance,** out of reach. **f. de sí,** beside oneself (with rage, etc.). **de f.,** from the outside. **por f.,** on the outside, externally

fuero /'fuero/ *m*, municipal charter; jurisdiction; compilation of laws; legal right or privilege; *pl Inf.* arrogance. **los fueros de León,** the laws of León

fuerte /'fuerte/ *a* strong, resistant; robust; spirited, vigorous; hard (of diamonds, etc.); rough, uneven; impregnable; terrible, tremendous; overweight (of coins); active; efficacious, effective; expert, knowledgeable; *Gram.* strong; intense; loud; tough. *m*, fort; talent, strong point; *Mus.* forte —*adv* strongly; excessively. **tener genio f.,** to be quick-tempered

fuerza /'fuerθa; 'fuersa/ *f*, strength; power, might; force; efficacy; fortress; *Sew.* stiffening; *Mech.* power; violence; toughness, durability, solidity; potency; authority; courage; vigor; *pl Fig. Inf.* livewires, influential people. **a f. de,** by means of, by dint of. **a la f.,** forcibly. **en f. de,** because of, on account of. **por f. mayor,** by main force. **ser f.,** to be necessary

fuga /'fuga/ *f*, flight, escape, running away; leak (gas, etc.); elopement; *Mus.* fugue; ardor, strength. **f. de cerebros,** brain drain

fugarse /fu'garse/ *vr* to run away; elope, escape

fugaz /fu'gaθ; fu'gas/ *a* fugitive; fleeting, brief

fugitivo /fuhi'tiβo/ (**-va**) *a* fugitive; runaway, escaping; transient —*n* fugitive

fulano /fu'lano/ (**-na**) *n* so-and-so, such a person **f.,** **zutano, y mengano,** *Inf.* Tom, Dick, and Harry

fulcro /'fulkro/ *m*, fulcrum

fulgente, fúlgido /ful'hente, 'fulhiðo/ *a* brilliant, shining

fulgor /ful'gor/ *m*, brilliance, brightness

fullero /fu'ʎero/ fu'yero/ **(-ra)** *a* cheating; crafty, astute —*n* cheat, cardsharper

fulminante /fulmi'nante/ *a Med.* fulminant; fulminating; thundering. *m*, percussion cap

fulminar /fulmi'nar/ *vt* to fulminate (all meanings)

fulmíneo, fulminoso /ful'mineo, fulmi'noso/ *a* fulminous, pertaining to lightning

fumadero /fuma'ðero/ *m*, smoking room

fumador /fuma'ðor/ **(-ra)** *a* smoking —*n* smoker. «No fumadores», "Nonsmoking" (area)

fumar /fu'mar/ *vi* to smoke; —*vr Inf.* dissipate, waste

fumigación /fumiga'θion; fumiga'sion/ *f*, fumigation

fumigador /fumiga'ðor/ **(-ra)** *n* fumigator

fumigar /fumi'gar/ *vt* to fumigate

funámbulo /fu'nambulo/ *n* tightrope walker, acrobat

función /fun'θion; fun'sion/ *f*, function; working, operation; *Theat.* performance; activity, duty; ceremony; celebration; *Math.* function; *Mil.* battle

funcional /funθio'nal; funsio'nal/ *a* functional

funcionamiento /funθiona'miento; funsiona'miento/ *m*, functioning

funcionar /funθio'nar; funsio'nar/ *vi* to function, work. «No funciona», "Out of order"

funcionario /funθio'nario; funsio'nario/ *m*, functionary, official; civil servant

funda /'funda/ *f*, case, cover, sheath; hold-all. **f. de almohada,** pillowcase

fundación /funda'θion; funda'sion/ *f*, foundation

fundadamente /fundaða'mente/ *adv* with reason, on good evidence

fundador /funda'ðor/ **(-ra)** *n* founder, creator; originator

fundamental /funda'mental/ *a* fundamental

fundamento /funda'mento/ *m, Mas.* foundation; basis; basic principle, reason; origin, root

fundar /fun'dar/ *vt* to build, erect; base; found, institute; create, establish; —*vr* (with *en*) found, base upon. **f. una compañía,** *Com.* to float a company

fundición /fundi'θion; fundi'sion/ *f*, foundry; smelting, founding, casting; cast iron; *Print.* font

fundido fotográfico /fun'diðo foto'grafiko/ *m*, composite photograph

fundidor /fundi'ðor/ *m*, founder, smelter.

fundir /fun'dir/ *vt* to melt; found, smelt;

cast (metals); —*vr* join together, unite; *Elec.* blow (fuses)

fúnebre /'funeβre/ *a* funeral; dismal, lugubrious, mournful

funeral /fune'ral/ *a* funeral

funerales /fune'rales/ *m pl*, funeral; *Eccl.* memorial masses

funeraria /fune'raria/ *f*, funeral home, undertaker

funesto /fu'nesto/ *a* unlucky, unfortunate; mournful, melancholy, sad

fungoso /fuŋ'goso/ *a* spongy, fungous

furgón /fur'gon/ *m*, wagon; van; guard's van, baggage car, luggage cart. **f. postal,** mail truck

furia /'furia/ *f, Myth.* fury; rage, wrath; fit of madness; raging, violence (of the elements); speed, haste

furibundo /furi'βundo/ *a* frantic, furious; raging

fúrico /'furiko/ *a* stark raving mad

furioso /fu'rioso/ *a* furious, enraged; mad, insane; violent, terrible; enormous, excessive

furor /fu'ror/ *m*, fury, rage; poetic frenzy; violence; furor

furtivo /fur'tiβo/ *a* furtive; covert, clandestine; pirate (editions)

fuselado /fuse'laðo/ *a* streamlined

fuselaje /fuse'lahe/ *m*, fuselage

fusible /fu'siβle/ *a* fusible. *m, Elec.* fuse; fuse wire

fusil /fu'sil/ *m*, rifle

fusilamiento /fusila'miento/ *m*, execution by shooting

fusilar /fusi'lar/ *vt* to execute by shooting; *Inf.* plagiarize

fusilazo /fusi'laθo; fusi'laso/ *m*, rifle shot

fusión /fu'sion/ *f*, melting, liquefying; fusion, blending; mixture, union; *Com.* merger, amalgamation

fusionar /fusio'nar/ *vt* to blend, fuse, merge; —*vr Com.* combine, form a merger

fusta /'fusta/ *f*, brushwood; whip

fuste /'fuste/ *m*, wood, timber; *Poet.* saddle; *Fig.* core, essence; importance, substance; shaft of a lance; *Archit.* shaft. **hombre de buen f.,** a man with a good (physical) constitution

fustigar /fusti'gar/ *vt* to whip, lash; rebuke harshly

fútbol /'futβol/ *m*, football; soccer

futbolista /futβo'lista/ *mf* football player; soccer player

fútil /'futil/ *a* futile, ineffectual, worthless

futilidad /futili'ðað/ *f*, futility, worthlessness

futura /fu'tura/ *f, Law.* reversion (of offices); *Inf.* fiancée

futurista /futu'rista/ *mf* futurist

futuro /fu'turo/ **(-ra)** *a* future. *m*, future —*n Inf.* betrothed

G

gabán /ga'βan/ *m*, overcoat; cloak

gabardina /gaβar'ðina/ *f*, gabardine; weatherproof coat

gabarro /ga'βarro/ *m*, flaw (in cloth); knot (in stone); snag, drawback; slip, error (in accounts)

gabinete /gaβi'nete/ *m*, study, library; sitting room; den; *Polit.* cabinet; collection, museum, gallery; laboratory; boudoir; studio; display cabinet. **g. de lectura**, reading room

gaceta /ga'θeta; ga'seta/ *f*, bulletin, review, record; newspaper; gazette (official Spanish government organ); *Inf.* newshound

gacetero /gaθe'tero; gase'tero/ **(-ra)** *n* newsdealer. *m*, news reporter

gacetilla /gaθe'tiʎa; gase'tiya/ *f*, news in brief, miscellany column, society news; gossip column; *Inf.* newshound

gacha /'gatʃa/ *f*, unglazed crock; *pl* pap; porridge

gaché /ga'tʃe/ *m*, (among the Romany) Andalusian; *Inf.* fellow

gacho /'gatʃo/ *a* drooping, bent downward; slouch (hat); (of ears) lop

gachón /ga'tʃon/ *a Inf.* attractive, charming

gafar /ga'far/ *vt* to claw; seize with a hook, hook; mend with a bracket (pottery)

gafas /'gafas/ *f pl*, spectacles; goggles; spectacle earhooks; grapplehooks

gafete /ga'fete/ *m*, hook and eye; clasp

gaita /'gaita/ *f*, bagpipe; hand organ; kind of clarinet; *Inf.* neck. **g. gallega**, bagpipe

gaitería /gaite'ria/ *f*, crude, gaudy garment or ornament

gaitero /gai'tero/ *a Inf.* overmerry; loud, crude. *m*, piper

gajes /'gahes/ *m pl*, salary; emoluments; perquisites

gajo /'gaho/ *m*, branch, bough (gen. cut); little cluster (of grapes); bunch (of fruit); quarter (of oranges, etc.); prong (of forks, etc.)

gala /'gala/ *f*, evening or full dress; grace, wit; flower, cream, best; gala; *pl* finery; trappings; wedding presents. **de g.**, full dress. **hacer g. de**, to glory in, boast of

galán /ga'lan/ *m*, handsome, well-made man; lover, wooer, gallant; *Theat.* leading man or one of leading male roles

galancete /galan'θete; galan'sete/ *m*, handsome little man; *Theat.* male juvenile lead

galano /ga'lano/ *a* smart, well-dressed; agreeable, pleasing; beautiful; ornamented; *Fig.* elegant (speech, style, etc.)

galante /ga'lante/ *a* gallant, courtly, attentive; flirtatious (of women); licentious

galanteador /galantea'ðor/ *a* flirtatious. *m*, philanderer; wooer

galantear /galante'ar/ *vt* to court; flirt with; make love to; *Fig.* procure assiduously

galanteo /galan'teo/ *m*, courtship; flirtation; love-making; wooing

galantería /galante'ria/ *f*, courtesy; attention, compliment; elegance, grace; gallantry; generosity, liberality

galanura /gala'nura/ *f*, showiness, gorgeousness; elegance, grace; prettiness

galápago /ga'lapago/ *m*, freshwater tortoise; cleat

galardón /galar'ðon/ *m*, reward, recompense, prize

galardonar /galarðo'nar/ *vt* to reward, recompense

galbanoso /galβa'noso/ *a Inf.* slothful

galera /ga'lera/ *f*, van, wagon, cart; *Naut.* galley; prison for women; *Print.* galley. **echar a galeras**, to condemn to the galleys

galerada /gale'raða/ *f*, galley proof

galería /gale'ria/ *f*, gallery; corridor, passage; collection of paintings; *Mineral.* gallery, drift; *Theat.* gallery

galerna /ga'lerna/ *f*, tempestuous northwest wind (gen. on Spanish north coast)

Gales /'gales/ Wales

galés /ga'les/ **(-esa)** *a* Welsh —*n* Welshman. *m*, Welsh (language)

galga /'galga/ *f*, boulder, rolling stone; greyhound bitch

galgo /'galgo/ *m*, greyhound. **g. ruso**, borzoi

gálibo /'galiβo/ *m*, *Naut.* mold; elegance

galicado /gali'kaðo/ *a* gallicized

galicismo /gali'θismo; gali'sismo/ *m*, gallicism

gálico /'galiko/ *m*, syphilis —*a* gallic

Galilea /gali'lea/ Galilee

galimatías /galima'tias/ *m*, *Inf.* gibberish, nonsense

gallardear /gaʎarðe'ar; gayarðe'ar/ *vi* to behave with ease and grace

gallardete /gaʎar'ðete; gayar'ðete/ *m*, pennant; bunting

gallardía /gaʎar'ðia; gayar'ðia/ *f*, grace, dignity; spirit, dash; courage; liveliness

gallardo /ga'ʎarðo; ga'yarðo/ *a* handsome, upstanding; gallant; spirited; fine, noble; lively

gallear /gaʎe'ar; gaye'ar/ *vi Inf.* to put on airs; be a bully; shout, bawl (with anger, etc.); *Fig. Inf.* stand out

gallego /ga'ʎego; ga'yego/ **(-ga)** *a* and *n* Galician. *m*, Galician (language)

galleta /ga'ʎeta; ga'yeta/ *f*, biscuit; *Inf.* slap; anthracite, lump coal; small jar or vessel

gallina /ga'ʎina; ga'yina/ *f*, hen. *mf Inf.* coward. **gallina ciega**, blindman's buff. **acostarse con las gallinas**, to go to bed early

gallinaza /gaʎi'naθa; gayi'nasa/ *f*, hen dung

gallinero /gaʎi'nero; gayi'nero/ **(-ra)** n poultry dealer. m, henhouse; brood of hens; Theat. gallery; babel, noisy place

gallito /ga'ʎito; ga'yito/ m, small cock; cock of the walk; bully

gallo /ga'ʎo; ga'yo/ m, Ornith. cock; Inf. false note (in singing); Inf. boss, chief. **g. de viento**, weathercock. Inf. **alzar el g.**, to put on airs, boast. **Cada g. canta en su muladar**, Every man is boss in his own house. Inf. **Otro g. nos cantara**, Our lot (or fate) would have been very different

galón /ga'lon/ m, galloon, braid; Mil. stripe; gallon (measure)

galoneadura /galonea'ðura/ f, braiding, trimming

galonear /galone'ar/ vt to trim with braid

galopante /galo'pante/ a galloping (of consumption, etc.)

galopar /galo'par/ vi to gallop; Mech. wobble

galope /ga'lope/ m, gallop. **a or de g.**, at the gallop; on the run, quickly. **andar a g. corto**, to canter

galopín /galo'pin/ m, ragamuffin, urchin; rogue, knave; Inf. clever rogue; Naut. cabin boy

galvanizar /galβani'θar; galβani'sar/ vt Elec. to galvanize; electroplate; Fig. shock into life

gama /'gama/ f, Mus. scale; gamut, range; doe

gambito /gam'bito/ m, gambit (in chess)

gamella /ga'meʎa; ga'meya/ f, trough (for washing, feeding animals, etc.)

gamo /'gamo/ m, buck (of the fallow deer)

gamuza /ga'muθa; ga'musa/ f, chamois; chamois leather

gana /'gana/ f, appetite; wish, desire. **de buena g.**, willingly. **de mala g.**, reluctantly. **tener g.** (**de**), to wish, desire, want. **no tener g.**, to have no appetite, not be hungry. **No me da la g.**, I don't want (to), I won't

ganable /ga'naβle/ a attainable; earnable

ganadería /ganaðe'ria/ f, livestock; strain (of cattle); cattle raising; stock farm; cattle dealing

ganadero /gana'ðero/ m, cattle raiser or dealer; herdsman

ganado /ga'naðo/ m, livestock, herd; flock; hive (of bees); Inf. mob. **g. mayor**, cattle, mules, horses. **g. menor**, sheep, goats, etc. **g. moreno**, hogs, swine. **g. vacuno**, cattle

ganador /gana'ðor/ **(-ra)** a winning —n winner

ganancia /ga'nanθia; ga'nansia/ f, winning; gain, profit

ganancial, gananancioso /ganan'θial, ga-nan'θioso; ganan'sial, ganan'sioso/ a gainful, profitable; lucrative

ganapán /gana'pan/ m, laborer; porter; Inf. boor

ganar /ga'nar/ vt to gain; win; conquer;

arrive at; earn; surpass, beat; achieve; acquire; —vi prosper

ganchero /gan'tʃero/ m, lumberjack

ganchillo /gan'tʃiʎo; gan'tʃiyo/ m, cro-chet hook; crochet. **hacer g.**, to crochet

gancho /'gantʃo/ m, hook; stump (of a branch); shepherd's crook; crochet hook; Inf. trickster, pimp; Inf. scribble

ganchoso /gan'tʃoso/ a hooked; bent; curved

gandujar /gandu'har/ vt Sew. to pleat, tuck, shirr

gandul /gan'dul/ **(-la)** a Inf. lazy —n lazybones, loafer

ganga /'ganga/ f, Mineral. gangue, ma-trix; bargain, cinch

ganglio /'ganglio/ m, ganglion

gangoso /gaŋ'goso/ a nasal; with a twang (of speech)

gangrena /gaŋ'grena/ f, gangrene

gangrenoso /gaŋgre'noso/ a gangrenous

ganoso /ga'noso/ a wishful, desirous, anxious

gansada /gàn'saða/ f, Inf. impertinence, foolishness

ganso /'ganso/ **(-sa)** n goose, gander; slow-moving person; yokel, bumpkin

ganzúa /gan'θua; gan'sua/ f, skeleton key; Inf. picklock, burglar; Inf. pumper, inquisitive person

gañán /ga'nan/ m, farm worker; day la borer; brawny fellow

gañir /ga'nir/ vi irr to yowl, yelp, howl (of dogs, etc.); crow, croak; Inf. talk hoarsely. See **mullir**

garabatear /garaβatc'ar/ vi to hook, catch with hooks; scribble; Fig. Inf. beat around the bush

garabato /gara'βato/ m, hook; Agr. weed clearer; scrawl, scribble; Inf. charm, sex appeal; pothook; boat hook; pl ges-tures, movements (with the hands)

garaje /ga'rahe/ m, garage

garante /ga'rante/ mf guarantor; refer-ence (person) —a responsible, guarantee-ing

garantía /garan'tia/ f, guarantee; secu-rity, pledge; Law. warranty

garantir /garan'tir/ vt to guarantee; war-rant, vouch for

garapiñar /garapi'nar/ vt to ice, freeze (drinks, syrups, etc.); Cul. candy, coat with sugar

garbanzo /gar'βanθo; gar'βanso/ m, chickpea. **g. negro**, Fig. black sheep

garbo /'garβo/ m, jaunty air; grace, ele-gance; frankness; generosity, liberality

garboso /gar'βoso/ a attractive; hand-some, sprightly, gay; graceful; munificent

garduño /gar'ðuɲo/ **(-ña)** n Inf. sneak thief

garete /ga'rete/ **(ir** or **irse al)** Naut. to be adrift

garfear /garfe'ar/ vi to catch with a hook, hook

garfio /'garfio/ m, grappling iron, hook, drag hook, cramp; gaff

gargajear /gargahe'ar/ *vi* to expectorate

gargajo /gar'gaho/ *m*, phlegm

garganta /gar'ganta/ *f*, throat; gullet; instep; defile; neck, shaft, narrowest part

gargantear /gargante'ar/ *vi* to warble, trill

gárgara /'gargara/ *f*, gargling (gen. *pl*). **hacer gárgaras**, to gargle

gargarismo /garga'rismo/ *m*, gargling; gargle

gárgol /'gargol/ *a* rotten (eggs). *m*, groove, mortise

garita /ga'rita/ *f*, sentry box; porter's lodge; hut; cabin. **g. de señales**, (railroad) signal box

garitero /gari'tero/ *m*, gambling house keeper; gambler

garito /ga'rito/ *m*, gambling house; profits of a gambling house

garra /'garra/ *f*, paw with claws; talon; hand; *Mech.* clamp, claw. *Fig.* **caer en las garras de**, to fall into the clutches (of)

garrafa /ga'rrafa/ *f*, decanter, carafe; carboy

garrapata /garra'pata/ *f*, *Ent.* tick

garrapatear /garrapate'ar/ *vi* to scribble

garrapato /garra'pato/ *m*, scribble, scrawl

garrido /ga'rriðo/ *a* handsome; gallant; elegant; graceful

garroba /ga'rroβa/ *f*, carob bean

garrocha /ga'rrotʃa/ *f*, goad. **salto a la g.**, pole jumping

garrotazo /garro'taθo; garro'taso/ *m*, blow with a truncheon or cudgel. **dar garrotazos de ciego**, to lay about one

garrote /ga'rrote/ *m*, truncheon, club; *Med.* tourniquet; garrote. **dar g. (a)**, to strangle

garrotillo /garro'tiʎo; garro'tiyo/ *m*, croup

garrucha /ga'rrutʃa/ *f*, pulley; *Mech.* gin block

garrulidad /garruli'ðað/ *f*, garrulity, loquaciousness

gárrulo /'garrulo/ *a* twittering, chirping (birds); garrulous; murmuring, babbling (wind, water, etc.)

garza /'garθa; 'garsa/ *f*, heron

garzo /'garθo; 'garso/ *a* blue (gen. of eyes)

gas /gas/ *m*, gas; fumes. **g. asfixiante**, poison gas. **cámara de g.**, gasbag, gas chamber

gasa /'gasa/ *f*, gauze. **tira de g.**, black mourning band

gaseosa /gase'osa/ *f*, aerated water

gaseoso /gase'oso/ *a* gaseous

gasista /ga'sista/ *mf* gas fitter; gasman

gasolina /gaso'lina/ *f*, gasoline, petrol

gasómetro /ga'sometro/ *m*, gas meter; gasometer

gastado /gas'taðo/ *a* worn; worn-out; exhausted

gastador /gasta'ðor/ **(-ra)** *a* extravagant, wasteful —*n* spendthrift. *m*, *Mil.* sapper; convict condemned to hard labor

gastar /gas'tar/ *vt* to spend (money); wear out; exhaust; ruin, destroy; display or have habitually; possess, use, wear; —*vr* wear out; run down (of a battery)

gasto /'gasto/ *m*, spending; expenditure; consumption (of gas, etc.); expense, cost, charge; wear (and tear). **g. suplementario**, extra charge

gástrico /'gastriko/ *a* gastric

gastritis /gas'tritis/ *f*, gastritis

gastronomía /gastrono'mia/ *f*, gastronomy

gastrónomo /gas'tronomo/ **(-ma)** *n* gastronome

gata /'gata/ *f*, she-cat; wreath of mist; *Inf.* Madrilenian woman. **a gatas**, on all fours

gatear /gate'ar/ *vi* to climb like a cat; *Inf.* crawl on all fours; —*vt Inf.* scratch (of a cat); steal, pinch

gatillo /ga'tiʎo; ga'tiyo/ *m*, *dim* small cat; dental forceps; trigger (of gun); *Inf.* juvenile petty thief

gato /'gato/ *m*, cat; tomcat; moneybag or its contents; *Inf.* jack; mousetrap; *Inf.* cat burglar, sneak thief; *Inf.* Madrilenian; clamp. **g. atigrado**, tiger cat. **g. de algalia**, civet cat. **g. de Angora**, Persian cat. **g. montés**, wildcat. **g. romano**, tabby cat. **dar g. por liebre**, to serve cat for hare, to deceive; misrepresent. *Inf.* **Hay g. encerrado**, There's more to this than meets the eye

gaucho /'gautʃo/ **(-cha)** *n* gaucho; cowboy, rider

gaveta /ga'βeta/ *f*, drawer (of a desk)

gavia /'gaβia/ *f*, main topsail; *pl* topsails; crow's-nest

gavilla /ga'βiʎa; ga'βiya/ *f*, sheaf (of corn, etc.); gang, rabble

gaviota /ga'βiota/ *f*, seagull

gazapo /ga'θapo; ga'sapo/ *m*, young rabbit; *Inf.* cunning fellow; fib, lie; slip, blunder

gazmoño /gaθ'moɲo; gas'moɲo/ *a* hypocritical, prudish; priggish

gaznápiro /gaθ'napiro; gas'napiro/ **(-ra)** *n* ninny, simpleton

gaznate /gaθ'nate; gas'nate/ *m*, windpipe

gazpacho /gaθ'patʃo; gas'patʃo/ *m*, cold soup containing bread, onions, vinegar, olive oil, garlic, etc.

ge /he/ *f*, name of the letter G

gehena /he'ena/ *m*, gehenna, hell

géiser /'heiser/ *m*, geyser

gelatina /hela'tina/ *f*, gelatin. **g. incendiaria**, napalm. **g. seca**, cooking gelatin

gelatinoso /helati'noso/ *a* gelatinous

gemelo /he'melo/ **(-la)** *a* and *n* twin. *m pl*, field or opera glasses, binoculars; cuff links; *Astron.* Gemini

gemido /he'miðo/ *m*, groan, lament, moan

gemidor /hemi'ðor/ *a* groaning, moaning; wailing (of the wind, etc.)

gemir /he'mir/ *vi irr* to moan, groan, lament; *Fig.* wail, howl. See **pedir**

gene /'hene/ *m,* gene

genealogía /henealo'hia/ *f,* genealogy

genealógico /henea'lohiko/ *a* genealogical

genealogista /henealo'hista/ *mf* genealogist

generación /henera'θion; henera'sion/ *f,* generation, reproduction; species; generation

generador /henera'ðor/ *a* generative. *m, Mech.* generator

general /hene'ral/ *a* general; universal; widespread; common, usual. *m,* (*Mil. Eccl.*) general. **g. de división,** *Mil.* major general. **en** *or* **por lo g.,** generally

generalidad /henerali'ðað/ *f,* majority, bulk; generality

generalísimo /henera'lisimo/ *m,* generalissimo, commander in chief

generalización /heneraliθa'θion; heneralisa'sion/ *f,* generalization

generalizar /henerali'θar; henerali'sar/ *vt* to generalize; —*vr* become widespread or general

generar /hene'rar/ *vt* to generate

genérico /he'neriko/ *a* generic

género /'henero/ *m,* kind; class; way, mode; *Com.* goods; species; genus; *Gram.* gender; cloth, material. **g. chico,** short theatrical pieces (gen. one act). **g. humano,** humankind

generosidad /henerosi'ðað/ *f,* hereditary nobility; generosity; magnanimity; liberality, munificence; courage

generoso /hene'roso/ *a* noble (by birth); magnanimous; generous (of wine); munificent; courageous; excellent

genésico /he'nesiko/ *a* genetic

génesis /'henesis/ *m,* Genesis. *f,* beginning, origin

genial /he'nial/ *a* of genius; highly talented; brilliant; characteristic, individual; pleasant; cheerful

genialidad /heniali'ðað/ *f,* genius; talent; brilliance; eccentricity, oddity

genio /'henio/ *m,* nature, individuality, temperament; temper; character; talent; genius; genie, spirit. **corto de g.,** unintelligent. **mal g.,** bad temper

genital /heni'tal/ *a* genital. *m,* testicle (gen. *pl*)

genitivo /heni'tiβo/ *a* reproductive, generative. *m, Gram.* genitive

Génova /'henoβa/ Genoa

gente /'hente/ *f,* people, a crowd; nation; army; *Inf.* family; followers, adherents. **g. baja,** rabble. **g. de bien,** honest folk; respectable people. **g. de paz,** friends (reply to sentinel's challenge). **g. fina,** nice, cultured people. **g. menuda,** children, small fry

gentecilla /hente'θiʎa; hente'siya/ *f, dim Inf.* rabble; contemptible people

gentil /hen'til/ *a* pagan, idolatrous; spirited, dashing, handsome; notable, extraordinary; graceful, charming

gentileza /henti'leθa; henti'lesa/ *f,* grace; elegance; beauty; verve, sprightliness; courtesy; show, ostentation

gentilhombre /hentil'ombre/ *m,* gentleman; handsome man; kind sir! **gentileshombres de cámara,** gentlemen-in-waiting

gentilicio /henti'liθio; henti'lisio/ *a* national; family

gentilidad /hentili'ðað/ *f,* idolatry, paganism; heathendom

gentío /hen'tio/ *m,* crowd, throng

gentualla, gentuza /hen'tuaʎa, hen'tuθa; hen'tuaya, hen'tusa/ *f,* canaille, rabble

genuflexión /henuflek'sion/ *f,* genuflection

genuino /he'nuino/ *a* pure; authentic, genuine

geografía /heogra'fia/ *f,* geography

geográfico /heo'grafiko/ *a* geographical

geógrafo /he'ografo/ *m,* geographer

geología /heolo'hia/ *f,* geology

geológico /heo'lohiko/ *a* geological

geólogo /he'ologo/ *m,* geologist

geometría /heome'tria/ *f,* geometry. **g. del espacio,** solid geometry

geométrico /heo'metriko/ *a* geometrical

geranio /he'ranio/ *m,* geranium

gerencia /he'renθia; he'rensia/ *f, Com.* managership; manager's office; management

gerente /he'rente/ *m, Com.* manager

germanía /herma'nia/ *f,* thieves' slang; association of thieves; sixteenth-century political brotherhood

germen /'hermen/ *m,* germ, sprout; *Bot.* embryo; genesis, origin

germinación /hermina'θion; hermina'sion/ *f,* germination

germinar /hermi'nar/ *vi* to germinate, sprout; develop, grow

gerundio /he'rundio/ *m, Gram.* gerund; *Inf.* pompous ass; *Inf.* tub-thumper

gesta /'hesta/ *f,* heroic deed. **cantar de g.,** epic or heroic poem

gestación /hesta'θion; hesta'sion/ *f,* gestation

gestear /heste'ar/ *vi* to gesture, grimace

gesticulación /hestikula'θion; hestikula'sion/ *f,* gesticulation; grimace

gesticular /hestiku'lar/ *vi* to grimace, gesticulate —*a* gesticulatory

gestión /hes'tion/ *f,* negotiation; management, conduct; effort, exertion; measure

gestionar /hestio'nar/ *vt* to negotiate; conduct; undertake; take steps to attain

gesto /'hesto/ *m,* gesture; facial expression; grimace; face, visage

gestor /hes'tor/ *a* (**-ra**) *n* manager; partner; promoter —*a* managing

Getsemaní /hetsema'ni/ Gethsemane

giba /'hiβa/ *f,* hump, hunchback; *Inf.* nuisance, inconvenience

gibón /hi'βon/ *m,* gibbon

giboso /hi'βoso/ a hunchbacked

gibraltareño /hiβralta'reɲo/ a Gibraltarian

giganta /hi'ganta/ f. giantess

gigante /hi'gante/ a gigantic. m. giant.

gigantesco /higan'tesko/ a giant, gigantic; Fig. outstanding

gigantez /higan'teθ; higan'tes/ f. gigantic size

gigantón /higan'ton/ (-ona) n enormous giant; carnival grotesque

gimnasia /him'nasia/ f. gymnastics

gimnasio /him'nasio/ m. gymnasium; school, academy

gimnasta /him'nasta/ mf gymnast

gimnástico /him'nastiko/ a gymnastic

gimotear /himote'ar/ vi Inf. to whine (often used scornfully)

gimoteo /himo'teo/ m. Inf. whining, whimpering

ginebra /hi'neβra/ f. gin (drink); confusion; babble, din

ginecología /hinekolo'hia/ f. gynecology

ginecológico /hineko'lohiko/ a gynecological

ginecólogo /hine'kologo/ (-ga) n gynecologist

girado /hi'raðo/ m. Com. drawee

girador /hira'ðor/ m. Com. drawer

giralda /hi'ralda/ f. weathercock in the shape of a person or animal; tower at Seville

girar /hi'rar/ vi to revolve; deal (with), concern; turn, branch (streets, etc.); Com. trade; Mech. turn on, revolve; —vt and vi Com. draw, cash. **g. en descubierto,** Com. to overdraw

girasol /hìra'sol/ m. sunflower

giratorio /hira'torio/ a revolving, gyrating; swiveling

giro /'hiro/ m. revolution, turn; revolving; trend; course (of affairs); style, turn (of phrase); threat; knife gash; Com. draft, drawing; Com. line of business, specialty. **g. postal,** postal order

giroscopio /hiros'kopio/ m. gyroscope

gitanería /hitane'ria/ f. cajolery, wheedling; gypsies; gypsy saying or action

gitanesco /hita'nesko/ a gypsy, gypsylike

gitano /hi'tano/ (-na) a gypsy; gypsylike; seductive, attractive; sly —n gypsy

glaciar /gla'θiar; gla'siar/ m. glacier

glándula /'glandula/ f. gland

glicerina /gliθe'rina; glise'rina/ f. glycerin, glycerol

globo /'gloβo/ m. Geom. sphere; globe, world; globe (Elec. Gas.); balloon. **g. aerostático,** air balloon. **g. terrestre,** world; geographical globe

glóbulo /'gloβulo/ m. globule.

gloria /'gloria/ f. heavenly bliss; fame, glory; delight, pleasure; magnificence, splendor; Art. apotheosis, glory. m. Eccl. doxology

gloriar /glo'riar/ vt to praise; —vr (with de or en) boast about; be proud of, rejoice in

glorieta /glo'rieta/ f. bower, arbor; open space in a garden; street square

glorificación /glorifika'θion; glorifika'sion/ f. glorification

glorificador /glorifika'ðor/ a glorifying

glorificar /glorifi'kar/ vt to exalt, raise up; glorify, extol; —vr (with de or en) be proud of; glory in; boast of

glorioso /glo'rioso/ a glorious; Eccl. blessed; boastful, bragging

glosa /'glosa/ f. gloss; explanation, note

glosar /glo'sar/ vt Lit. to gloss

glosario /glo'sario/ m. glossary

glosopeda /gloso'peða/ f. foot-and-mouth disease

glotón /glo'ton/ (-ona) a greedy, gluttonous —n glutton

glotonería /glotone'ria/ f. gluttony, greed

glucosa /glu'kosa/ f. glucose

gn- /gn-/ For words so beginning, see spellings without **g.**

gobernación /goβerna'θion; goβerna'sion/ f. government; governor's office or building; ministry of the interior, home office (abb. for **ministerio de G.**)

gobernador /goβerna'ðor/ (-ra) a governing, n governor

gobernalle /goβer'naʎe; goβer'naye/ m. helm

gobernante /goβer'nante/ a governing. m. Inf. self-appointed director or manager

gobernar /goβer'nar/ vt irr to govern, rule; lead, conduct; manage; steer; control; —vi govern; Naut. obey the tiller. See **recomendar**

gobierno /go'βierno/ m. government (all meanings); Naut. helm; control (of machines, business, etc.)

goce /'goθe; 'gose/ m. enjoyment; possession

gol /gol/ m. Sports. goal

gola /'gola/ f. throat; gullet; gorget; tucker, bib

golf /golf/ m. golf. **palo de g.,** golf club

golfear /golfe'ar/ vi to loaf

golfería /golfe'ria/ f. loafing; vagabondage; loafers

golfo /'golfo/ (-fa) m. Geog. gulf; sea, ocean —n ragamuffin, urchin. m. Inf. loafer; lounge lizard, wastrel

Golfo Pérsico /'golfo 'persiko/ Persian Gulf

golilla /go'liʎa; go'liya/ f. ruff; m. Inf. magistrate

gollería /goʎe'ria; goye'ria/ f. dainty, tidbit; Inf. affectation, persnicketiness

gollete /go'ʎete; go'yete/ m. gullet; neck (of a bottle, etc.); Mech. nozzle

golondrina /golon'drina/ f. Ornith. swallow. **g. de mar,** tern

golosina /golo'sina/ f. tidbit, delicacy; desire, caprice; pleasant useless thing

goloso /go'loso/ a fond of sweet things; greedy, desirous; appetizing

golpe /'golpe/ *m*, blow, knock; pull (at the oars); ring (of a bell); *Mech.* stroke; crowd; fall (of rain, etc.); mass, torrent; misfortune; shock, collision; spring lock; beating (of the heart); flap (of a pocket); *Sew.* passementerie; surprise; point, wit; bet. **g. de estado**, coup d'état. **g. de fortuna**, stroke of fortune. **g. de mano**, rising, insurrection. **g. en vago**, blow in the air; disappointment. **g. franco**, *Sports.* free kick. **de g.**, suddenly; quickly

golpeadura /golpea'ðura/ *f*, **golpeo** /gol'peo/ *m*, knocking, striking; beating, throbbing

golpear /golpe'ar/ *vt* and *vi* to knock, strike; beat, throb

goma /'goma/ *f*, gum, rubber; India rubber; rubber band

gomería /gome'ria/ *f*, tire store

gomero /go'mero/ *a* gum; rubber. *m*, *West Hem.* rubber planter

gomoso /go'moso/ *a* gummy; gum

góndola /'gondola/ *f*, gondola

gondolero /gondo'lero/ *m*, gondolier

gonorrea /gono'rrea/ *f*, gonorrhea

gordo /'gorðo/ *a* fat, stout; greasy, oily, thick (thread, etc.). *m*, animal fat, suet. *Inf.* **ganar el g.**, to win first prize (in a lottery, etc.)

gorgojo /gor'goho/ *m*, weevil; *Fig.* dwarf

gorgorito /gorgo'rito/ *m*, *Inf.* quaver, tremolo, trill (gen. *pl*)

gorgoteo /gorgo'teo/ *m*, gurgle

gorjear /gorhe'ar/ *vi* to trill, warble; twitter; —*vr* crow (of a baby)

gorjeo /gor'heo/ *m*, trill, shake; warbling, twitter; crowing, lisping (of a child)

gorra /'gorra/ *f*, cap; bonnet; *Mil.* busby; hunting cap. **vivir de g.**, *Inf.* to sponge

gorrista /go'rrista/ *mf Inf.* parasite; sponger

gorro /'gorro/ *m*, cap; bonnet

gorrón /go'rron/ *m*, smooth, round pebble; *Mech.* pivot, gudgeon; sponger, waster —*a* parasitical

gota /'gota/ *f*, drop (of liquid); gout

gotear /gote'ar/ *vi* to drop, trickle, drip; leak; drizzle; give or receive in driblets

gótico /'gotiko/ *a* Gothic; noble, illustrious

gotoso /go'toso/ **(-sa)** *a* gouty —*n* sufferer from gout

gozar /go'θar/ go'sar/ *vt* to enjoy, have; take pleasure (in), delight (in); know carnally; —*vi* (*with de*) enjoy; have, possess

gozne /'goθne/ 'gosne/ *m*, hinge

gozo /'goθo/ 'goso/ *m*, enjoyment, possession; gladness, joy; *pl* couplets in honor of the Virgin Mary or a saint. *Inf.* **¡Mi g. en el pozo!** I'm sunk! All is lost!

gozoso /go'θoso/ go'soso/ *a* glad, happy —*adv* gladly; with pleasure

grabado /gra'βaðo/ *m*, engraver's art; engraving; illustration, picture. **g. al agua fuerte**, etching. **g. al agua tinta**, aquatint

grabador /graβa'ðor/ **(-ra)** *n* engraver

grabar /gra'βar/ *vt* to engrave; *Fig.* leave a deep impression

gracejo /gra'θeho/ gra'seho/ *m*, humor, wit; cheerfulness

gracia /'graθia/ 'grasia/ *f*, grace; attraction, grace; favor; kindness; jest, witticism; pardon, mercy; pleasant manner; obligingness, willingness; *pl* thanks, thank you. **gracias a**, thanks to. **¡Gracias a Dios!** Thank God! Thank goodness! **las Gracias**, the Three Graces

grácil /'graθil/ 'grasil/ *a* slender; small

graciosidad /graθiosi'ðað/ grasiosi'ðað/ *f*, beauty, perfection, grace

gracioso /gra'θioso/ gra'sioso/ **(-sa)** *a* attractive, graceful, elegant; witty, humorous; free, gratis —*n Theat.* comic role; *m*, *Theat.* fool

grada /'graða/ *f*, step, stair; gradin, seat; stand, gallery; *Agr.* harrow; *Naut.* runway; *pl* perron, flight of stairs

gradación /graða'θion/ graða'sion/ *f*, gradation; climax

grado /'graðo/ *m*, step, stair; degree (of relationship); university degree; grade, class (in schools), (*Fig. Geom. Phys.*) degree; will, desire. **de buen g.**, willingly. **en sumo g.**, in the highest degree

graduación /graðua'θion/ graðua'sion/ *f*, graduation; *Mil.* rank; rating (of a ship's company). **g. de oficial**, *Mil.* commission

graduado /gra'ðuaðo/ *a* graded; *Mil.* brevet. *m*, graduate

gradual /gra'ðual/ *a* gradual

graduar /gra'ðuar/ *vt* to classify; *Mil.* grade; confer a degree on; measure; test; *Com.* standardize; *Mech.* calibrate; —*vr* graduate, receive a degree. **g. la vista**, to test the eyes. **graduarse de oficial**, *Mil.* to get one's commission

gráfica /'grafika/ *f*, graph

gráfico /'grafiko/ *a* graphic; vivid

grafología /grafolo'hia/ *f*, graphology

grajear /grahe'ar/ *vi* to caw; gurgle, burble (of infants)

grajo /'graho/ *m*, *Ornith.* rook

gramática /gra'matika/ *f*, grammar. *Inf.* **g. parda**, horse sense

gramático /gra'matiko/ *a* grammatical. *m*, grammarian

gramo /'gramo/ *m*, gram

gran /gran/ *a Abbr.* See **grande**. Used before a singular noun. big; great; grand

grana /'grana/ *f*, grain, seed; seed time; cochineal; kermes; red

granada /gra'naða/ *f*, *Mil.* grenade, shell; pomegranate

granadero /grana'ðero/ *m*, grenadier; *Inf.* very tall person

granar /gra'nar/ *vi Agr.* to seed; run to seed

granate /gra'nate/ *m*, garnet; dark red

Gran Bretaña /gran bre'taɲa/ Great Britain

grande /'grande/ *a* big, large; great, illustrious; grand. *m*, great man; grandee. **en**

g., in a large size; as a whole; in style, lavishly

grandeza /gran'deθa; gran'desa/ f. largeness; greatness, magnificence; grandeeship; vastness, magnitude

grandílocuo /gran'dilokuo/ a grandiloquent

grandioso /gran'dioso/ a grandiose, magnificent

grandor /gran'dor/ m, size

granear /grane'ar/ vt Agr. to sow; grain (of leather)

granero /gra'nero/ m, granary; grain-producing country

granito /gra'nito/ m, dim small grain; granite; small pimple

granizar /grani'θar; grani'sar/ vi to hail, sleet; —vi and vt Fig. shower down, deluge

granizo /gra'niθo; gra'niso/ m, hail, sleet; hailstorm; Fig. shower, deluge

granja /'granha/ f, farm; farmhouse; dairy farm, dairy

granjear /granhe'ar/ vt to trade, profit, earn; obtain, acquire; —vr gain, win

granjería /granhe'ria/ f, farming; agricultural profits; earnings, profits

granjero /gran'hero/ (-ra) n farmer

grano /'grano/ m, Agr. grain; seed; bean (coffee, etc.); particle; markings, grain (of wood, etc.); pimple; grain (measure). Fig. Inf. **ir al g.,** to go to the root of the matter; come to the point

granuja /gra'nuha/ f, grape pit. m, Inf. urchin, scamp; knave, rogue

granujiento /granu'hiento/ a pimply

gránulo /'granulo/ m, granule

granuloso /granu'loso/ a granulous

grapa /'grapa/ f, cramp, dowel, clamp; block hook; Elec. cleat; staple

grasa /'grasa/ f, fat; grease; oil; dripping, suet

grasiento /gra'siento/ a greasy; grubby, dirty

gratificación /gratifika'θion; gratifika'sion/ f, monetary reward; fee, remuneration; gratuity

gratificar /gratifi'kar/ vt to recompense; please, gratify

gratis /'gratis/ a and adv gratis

gratitud /grati'tuð/ f, gratitude

grato /'grato/ a pleasing, agreeable; free, gratuitous

gratuito /gra'tuito/ a gratuitous, free; baseless, unfounded

gravamen /gra'βamen/ m, obligation; burden; tax

gravar /gra'βar/ vt to burden, weigh upon; tax

grave /'graβe/ a heavy; important, momentous, grave; dignified, serious; sedate; tiresome; low-pitched, low; Gram. grave accent

gravedad /graβe'ðað/ f, Phys. gravity

gravitación /graβita'θion; graβita'sion/ f, Phys. gravitation; seriousness; sedateness; importance; enormity, gravity

gravitar /graβi'tar/ vi to gravitate; lean or rest (upon)

gravoso /gra'βoso/ a grievous, oppressive; onerous; costly

graznar /graθ'nar; gras'nar/ vi to caw; cackle; quack; croak; sing stridently, screech

Grecia /'greθia; 'gresia/ Greece

gregario /gre'gario/ a gregarious

gregüescos /gre'gueskos/ m pl, wide breeches (sixteenth and seventeenth centuries)

gremial /gre'mial/ a pertaining to a guild, union, or association. m, member of a guild, union, or association

gremio /'gremio/ m, guild, corporation, union; society, association; (univ.) general council

greña /'greɲa/ f, tangled lock (of hair) (gen. pl); tangle, confused mass

gresca /'greska/ f, uproar, tumult; fight, row

grey /grei/ f, flock, drove, herd; Eccl. flock, company; people, nation

grial /grial/ m, grail

griego /'griego/ (-ga) a and n Greek. m, Greek (language); Inf. gibberish

grieta /'grieta/ f, fissure; crevice; chink; split; flaw; vein (in stone, etc.); Mech. leak

grifo /'grifo/ m, griffin; tap; cock

grillo /'griʎo; 'griyo/ m, cricket; Bot. shoot; pl fetters, irons, chains; Fig. shackles

grima /'grima/ f, revulsion, horror

gringo /'gringo/ (-ga) n Inf. foreigner (scornful)

gripe /'gripe/ f, influenza; grippe

gris /gris/ a and m, gray

grisú /gri'su/ m, firedamp

gritador /grita'ðor/ (-ra) a shouting —n shouter

gritar /gri'tar/ vi to shout, yell, scream; howl down; hoot

gritería /grite'ria/ f, shouting, yelling, clamor

grito /'grito/ m, shout, yell, shriek, scream. Inf. **poner el g. en el cielo,** to cry to high heaven, complain

Groenlandia /groen'landia/ Greenland

grosería /grose'ria/ f, rudeness; roughness (of workmanship); ignorance; rusticity

grosero /gro'sero/ a coarse; rough; thick; unpolished, rude

grotesco /gro'tesko/ a grotesque, absurd

grúa /'grua/ f, Mech. crane, hoist, derrick. **g. de pescante,** jib crane. **g. móvil,** traveling crane

gruesa /'gruesa/ f, twelve dozen, gross

grueso /'grueso/ a stout, corpulent; large. m, bulk, body; major portion, majority; thick stroke (of a letter); thickness, density. **en g.,** in bulk

grulla /'gruʎa; 'gruya/ f, Ornith. crane

grumo /'grumo/ m, clot; heart (of vegetables); bunch, cluster; bud

gruñido /gru'niðo/ *m*, grunt; growl

gruñir /gru'nir/ *vi* to grunt; growl; grumble; squeak, creak (doors, etc.) —*Pres. Part.* gruñendo. *Pres. Indic.* gruño, gruñes, etc.

grupo /'grupo/ *m*, knot, cluster; band, group; *Art.* group; *Mech.* set

gruta /'gruta/ *f*, cavern, grotto

guacamayo /guaka'mayo/ *m*, macaw

guadameci /guaðame'θi; guaðame'si/ *m*, embossed decorated leather

guadaña /gua'ðaɲa/ *f*, scythe

guagua /'guagua/, *f Caribbean* bus

gualdo /'gualdo/ *a* yellow, golden

gualdrapa /gual'drapa/ *f*, saddlecloth, trappings; *Inf.* tatter, rag

guante /'guante/ *m*, glove. **g. con puño,** gauntlet glove. **g. de boxeo,** boxing glove. **g. de cabritilla,** kid glove. **arrojar el g.,** to throw down the gauntlet; challenge, defy

guapear /guape'ar/ *vi Inf* to make the best of a bad job; *Inf.* pride oneself on being well dressed

guapeza /gua'peθa; gua'pesa/ *f*, prettiness; *Inf.* resolution, courage; *Inf.* smartness or showiness of dress; boastful act or behavior

guapo /'guapo/ *a* pretty; handsome; *Inf.* daring, enterprising; *Inf.* smart, well-dressed, foppish; *Inf.* handsome. *m*, braggart, brawler; beau, lover; *Inf.* fine fellow, son of a gun

guarda /'guarða/ *mf* keeper, guard. *f*, guarding, keeping, custodianship, preservation; guardianship; observance, fulfillment; flyleaf, end page (books); warder (of locks or keys); *Mech.* guard; guard (of a fan)

guardabarrera /guarðaβa'rrera/ *mf* gatekeeper at a level crossing (railroad)

guardabarro /guarða'βarro/ *m*, mudguard

guardabosque /guarða'βoske/ *mf* gamekeeper

guardabrisa /guarða'βrisa/ *m*, *Auto.* windshield; glass candle shield

guardacostas /guarða'kostas/ *m*, coast guard; *Naut.* revenue cutter

guardalmacén /guarðalma'θen; guarðalma'sen/ *mf* storekeeper

guardameta /guarða'meta/ *mf* goalkeeper

guardamuebles /guarða'mueβles/ *m*, furniture warehouse

guardapolvo /guarða'polβo/ *m*, dustcover; light overcoat; inner case of a pocket watch

guardar /guar'ðar/ *vt* to keep; preserve, retain; maintain, observe; save, put aside, lay away; defend, protect; guard; —*vr* (*with de*) avoid, guard against. **g. compás con,** to be in tune with. **guardarse mucho,** to think twice before. **g. silencio,** to keep silent. **¡Guarda!** Take care! **¡Guárdate del agua mansa!** Still waters run deep!

guardarropa /guarða'rropa/ *m*, cloakroom. *mf* cloakroom attendant; keeper of the wardrobe. *m*, wardrobe, clothes closet

guardarropía /guarðarro'pia/ *f*, theatrical wardrobe

guardería /guarðe'ria/ *f*, day nursery, day-care center

guardia /'guarðia/ *f*, guard, escort; protection; (*Mil. Naut.*) watch; regiment, body (of troops); guard (fencing). *m*, guardsman; policeman. **g. de asalto,** armed police. **g. de corps,** royal bodyguard. **g. civil,** civil guard. **g. marina,** midshipman. **g. municipal,** city police. *Mil.* **montar la g.,** to mount guard

guardián /guar'ðian/ (**-ana**) *n* keeper; custodian; warden. *m*, watchman; jailer

guardilla /guar'ðiʎa; guar'ðiya/ *f*, attic, garret

guarecer /guare'θer; guare'ser/ *vt irr* to shelter, protect, aid; preserve, keep; cure; —*vr* take shelter. See **conocer**

guarida /gua'riða/ *f*, lair, den, refuge, shelter; haunt, resort

guarismo /gua'rismo/ *m*, *Math.* figure; number, numeral

guarnecer /guarne'θer; guarne'ser/ *vt irr* to decorate, adorn; *Sew.* trim, face, border; *Mil.* garrison; *Mas.* plaster. See **conocer**

guarnecido /guarne'θiðo; guarne'siðo/ *m*, *Mas.* plastering

guarnición /guarni'θion; guarni'sion/ *f*, *Sew.* trimming, ornament, border, fringe; *Mech.* packing; *Mil.* garrison; setting (of jewels); guard (of a sword, etc.); *pl* harness; fittings

guasa /'guasa/ *f*, *Inf.* dullness, boringness; joke. **de g.,** jokingly

guasón /gua'son/ *a Inf.* dull, tedious; humorous, jocose

guatemalteco /guatemal'teko/ (**-ca**) *a* and *n* Guatemalan

guayaba /gua'yaβa/ *f*, guava; guava jelly

Guayana /gua'yana/ Guiana

gubernamental /guβernamen'tal/ *a* governmental

gubernativo /guβerna'tiβo/ *a* governmental; administrative

guedeja /ge'ðeha/ *f*, long tress or lock of hair; forelock; lion's mane

guerra /'gerra/ *f*, war; struggle; fight; *Fig.* hostility. *Inf.* **dar g.,** to give trouble, annoy. **en g. con,** at war with. **la g. de Cuba,** the Spanish-American War

guerrear /gerre'ar/ *vi* to make war, fight; oppose

guerrero /ge'rrero/ (**-ra**) *a* war, martial; warrior; *Inf.* troublesome, annoying —*n* fighter. *m*, warrior, soldier

guerrillear /gerriʎe'arr gerriye'ar/ *vi* to wage guerrilla warfare; fight as a guerrilla

guerrillero /gerri'ʎero; gerri'yero/ *m*, guerrilla fighter

guía /'gia/ *mf* guide, conductor; adviser; director. *f*, guide, aid; guidebook; *Mech.* guide, slide; directory; signpost. **g. de**

ferrocarriles, train schedule, railroad timetable. **g. de teléfonos,** telephone directory

guiar /giar/ *vt* to guide; lead, conduct; *Mech.* work, control; *Auto.* drive; pilot; teach, direct, govern

guija /'giha/ *f,* pebble

guijarro /gi'harro/ *m,* smooth, round pebble; boulder; cobblestone

guijarroso /giha'rroso/ *a* pebbly, cobbled

guijo /'giho/ *m,* gravel; granite chips; pebble

guillotina /giʎo'tina; giyo'tina/ *f,* guillotine; paper-cutting machine

guillotinar /giʎoti'nar; giyoti'nar/ *vt* to guillotine, decapitate

guinga /'giŋga/ *f,* gingham

guiñada /gi'naða/ *f,* wink; blink; *Naut.* yaw

guiñapo /gi'napo/ *m,* rag, tatter; sloven, ragamuffin

guiñar /gi'nar/ *vt* to wink; blink; *Naut.* yaw; —*vr* wink at each other

guiño /'gino/ *m,* wink

guión /gi'on/ *m,* royal standard; banner; summary; leader of a dance; *Gram.* hyphen; subtitle (in films). **g. mayor,** *Gram.* dash

guirigay /giri'gai/ *m,* *Inf.* gibberish; uproar, babble

guirnalda /gir'nalda/ *f,* garland, wreath

guisa /'gisa/ *f,* way, manner; will, desire. **a g. de,** in the manner or fashion of

guisado /gi'saðo/ *m,* *Cul.* stew; cooked dish

guisante /gi'sante/ *m,* *Agr.* pea; pea plant. **g. de olor,** sweetpea

guisar /gi'sar/ *vt* to cook; stew; *Cul.* prepare, dress; adjust, arrange

guiso /'giso/ *m,* cooked dish

guitarra /gi'tarra/ *f,* guitar

guitarrista /gita'rrista/ *mf* guitar player

guito /'gito/ *a* vicious (horses, mules)

gula /'gula/ *f,* greed, gluttony

gusaniento /gusa'niento/ *a* worm-eaten; maggoty

gusano /gu'sano/ *m,* worm; caterpillar; maggot; meek, downtrodden person. **g. de seda,** silkworm

gusanoso /gusa'noso/ *a* wormy

gustar /gus'tar/ *vt* to taste, savor; try; —*vi* be pleasing, give pleasure; like. **Me gusta el libro,** I like the book. **La película no me gustó,** I didn't like the film. **g. de,** to like, is used only when a person is the subject

gusto /'gusto/ *m,* taste; flavor; savor; pleasure, delight; will, desire; discrimination, taste, style, fashion, manner; whim, caprice. **a g.,** to taste; according to taste. **con mucho g.,** with great pleasure. **dar g.,** to please. **de buen g.,** in good taste

gustoso /gus'toso/ *a* savory, palatable; willingly, with pleasure; pleasant, agreeable

Habana, la /a'βana, la/ Havana
habanero /aβa'nero/ **(-ra), habano**
(-na) *a* and *n* Havanese, from Havana.
m. **habano,** Havana cigar
haber /a'βer/ *m,* estate, property (gen.
pl); income; *Com.* credit balance. **h.
monedado,** specie
haber /a'βer/ *vt irr* to have; catch, lay
hands on (e.g. *El reo fue habido,* The
criminal was caught) —*v aux* (e.g. *Hemos
escrito la carta,* We have written the letter) —*v impers* to happen, take place; be
—*3rd pers. sing Pres. Indic.* **ha** is replaced
by **hay,** meaning there is or there are
(e.g. *No hay naranjas en las tiendas,*
There are no oranges in the shops). In
certain weather expressions, **hay** means it
is (e.g. *Hay luna,* It is moonlight). Used of
expressions of time, **haber** means to
elapse and **ha** (*3rd pers. sing Pres. Indic.*)
has adverbial force of "ago" (e.g. *muchos
días ha,* many days ago) **h. de,** to be
necessary (less strong than **h. que**) (e.g.
Hemos de verle mañana, We must see
him tomorrow. *He de hacer el papel de
Manolo,* I am to play the part of Manolo).
h. que, to be unavoidable, be essential.
With this construction the form **hay** is
used (e.g. *Hay que darse prisa,* We (or
one) must hurry. **No hay que enojarse,**
There's no need to get annoyed). **no h.,
más que pedir,** to leave nothing to be desired. **no h. tal,** to be no such thing. *Inf.*
habérselas con, to quarrel or fall out
with. **Hubo una vez...,** Once upon a
time... **¡No hay de qué!,** Don't mention
it!; Not at all!; You're welcome! **No hay
para que...,** There's no point in.... **poco
tiempo ha,** a little while ago. **¿Qué hay?**
What's the matter?; What's new? **¿Qué
hay de nuevo?** What's new? *Pres. Indic.*
he, has, ha, hemos, habéis, han. *Fut.*
habré, etc —*Condit.* **habría,** etc
—*Preterite* **hube, hubiste, hubo, hubi-
mos, hubisteis, hubieron.** *Pres. Subjunc.*
haya, etc —*Imperf. Subjunc.* **hubiese,** etc.
habichuela /aβi't∫uela/ *f,* kidney bean
hábil /'aβil/ *a* clever; skillful; able; lawful
habilidad /aβili'ðað/ *f,* ability; skill; accomplishment; craftsmanship, workmanship
habilidoso /aβili'ðoso/ *a* accomplished;
able; skillful
habilitación /aβilita'θion; aβilita'sion/ *f,*
habilitation; paymastership; equipment;
furnishing
habilitar /aβili'tar/ *vt* to qualify; equip;
furnish; habilitate; enable; *Com.* capitalize
habitable /aβi'taβle/ *a* habitable
habitación /aβita'θion; aβita'sion/ *f,* habitation, dwelling; room in a house; residence; (*Bot. Zool.*) habitat; caretaking
habitante /aβi'tante/ *m,* inhabitant
hábito /'aβito/ *m,* attire; *Eccl.* habit; use,
custom; skill, facility; *pl* vestments;
gown, robe. **tomar el h.,** to become a
monk or nun

habitual /aβi'tual/ *a* habitual, usual
habituar /aβi'tuar/ *vt* to accustom; —*vr*
accustom oneself; grow used (to)
habitud /aβi'tuð/ *f,* habit, custom; connection, relationship
habla /'aβla/ *f,* speech; language; dialect;
discourse. **al h.,** within speaking distance
hablado /a'βlaðo/ *a* spoken. **bien h.,**
well-spoken; courteous. **mal h.,** ill-
spoken; rude
hablador /aβla'ðor/ **(-ra)** *a* talkative;
gossipy —*n* chatterbox; gossip
habladuría /aβlaðu'ria/ *f,* gossip; impertinent chatter
hablanchín /aβlan't∫in/ *a Inf.* chattering,
gossiping
hablar /a'βlar/ *vi* to speak; converse; express oneself; arrange; (*with de*) speak
about, discuss; gossip about, criticize;
(*with por*) intercede on behalf of; —*vt*
speak (a language); say, speak; —*vr*
speak to one another. **no hablarse,** to
not be on speaking terms. **h. a gritos,** to
shout. **h. alto,** to speak loudly or in
strong terms. **h. bien** (*or* **mal),** to be
well- (or ill-) spoken; be polite (or rude).
h. claro, to speak frankly. **h. consigo** *or*
h. entre sí, to talk to oneself. *Inf.* **h. cristiano, h. en cristiano,** to speak clearly or
intelligibly; speak frankly. **hablarlo todo,**
to talk too much. **h. por h.,** to talk for
talking's sake. *Inf.* **h. por los codos,** to
chatter. **h. sin ton ni son,** to speak foolishly
habilla /a'βli∆a; a'βliya/ *f,* rumor, tittle-
tattle, gossip
hacecillo /aθe'θi∆o; ase'siyo/ *m,* small
sheaf; small bundle; *Bot.* fascicle; beam
(of light)
hacedero /aθe'ðero; ase'ðero/ *a* feasible,
practicable
hacedor /aθe'ðor; ase'ðor/ *m,* maker;
steward, manager; Creator
hacendado /aθen'daðo; asen'daðo/ **(-da)**
a landed —*n* landowner; *West Hem.* cattle rancher
hacendoso /aθen'doso; asen'doso/ *a* diligent, hard-working
hacer /a'θer; a'ser/ *vt irr* to make; fashion, form, construct; do, perform; cause,
effect; arrange, put right; contain; accustom, harden; pack (luggage); imagine, invent, create; improve, perfect; compel,
oblige; deliver (speeches); compose;
earn; *Math.* add up to; suppose, imagine
(e.g. *Sus padres hacían a María en casa,*
Her parents imagined that Mary was at
home); put into practice, execute; play
the part of or act like (e.g. *h. el gracioso,*
to play the buffoon); shed, cast (e.g. *El
roble hace sombra,* The oak casts a
shadow); assemble, convoke (meetings,
gatherings); give off, produce (e.g. *La chimenea hace humo,* The chimney is smok-

ing); perform (plays); (*with el, la, lo, and some nouns*) pretend to be (e.g. *Se hizo el desconocido,* He pretended to be ignorant). (**h.** followed by infin. is sometimes translated by a past participle in English (e.g. *Lo hice h.,* I had it done).) *vi* to matter, be important, signify (e.g. *Su llegada no hace nada al caso,* His arrival makes no difference to the case. *Se me hace muy poco...,* It matters to me very little...); be fitting or suitable; concern, be pertinent; match, go with; agree, be in harmony; (*with de*) act as, discharge duties of temporarily (e.g. *h. de camarero,* to be a temporary waiter); (*with por*) try to, attempt to (e.g. *Haremos por decírselo,* We shall try to tell him) —*vi impers* Used in expressions concerning: 1. the weather. 2. lapse of time. English uses the verb "to be' in both cases, e.g.:

1. **hace** buen (or mal) **tiempo,** it is fine (or bad) weather. **hace mucho frío,** it is very cold. **hace sol,** it is sunny. **hace viento,** it is windy. **¿Qué tiempo hace?** What is the weather like?

2. **hace** + an expression of time is followed by **que** introducing a clause (e.g. *Hace dos horas que llegamos,* It is two hours since we arrived) or **hace** + an expression of time may be followed by **desde** + a noun (e.g. *Hace dos años desde aquel día,* It is two years since that day)

When an action or state that has begun in the past is still continuing in the present, the Spanish verb is in the Pres. Ind., whereas the English verb is in the Perfect (e.g. *Hace un mes que la veo todos los días,* I have been seeing her every day for a month). This rule holds good with other tenses. English Pluperfect, Future Perfect, Conditional Perfect become in Spanish Imperfect, Future, Conditional, respectively. *Naut.* **h. agua,** to leak. **h. aguas,** to pass water, urinate. **h. alarde de,** to boast of. **h. América,** to strike it rich. **h. el amor a,** to make love to, court, woo. **h. autoridad,** to be authoritative. **h. a todo,** to have many uses; be adaptable. **h. bancarrota,** to go bankrupt. **h. un berrinche, hacerse un berrinche,** to have a fit, have a tantrum. *Fig. Inf.* **h. buena,** to justify. **h. calceta,** to knit. **h. cara** or **frente a,** to face; resist. **h. caso,** to take notice, mind (e.g. *¡No hagas caso!* Never mind!). **h. causas,** to bring charges, institute proceedings. **h. cuentas,** to reckon up. **h. daño,** to harm. *Inf.* **h. de las suyas,** to behave in his usual manner or play one of his usual tricks. **h. diligencias por,** to endeavor to. **h. fiesta,** to take a holiday. **h. fuerza,** to struggle. **h. fuerza a,** *Fig.* to do violence to (e.g. *Hizo fuerza a sus creencias,* He did violence to his beliefs). **h. h.,** to cause to be made (e.g. *He hecho hacer un vestido,* I have had a dress made). **h. juego,** to make a set, match (e.g. *El sombrero hace juego con el traje,* The hat goes with the dress). **h. la corte**

(a), to court, woo. *Fig. Inf.* **h. la vista gorda,** to turn a blind eye. **h. la vida del claustro,** to lead a cloistered existence. **h. mal,** to do wrong; be harmful (food, etc.). **h. pedazos,** to break. **h. pinos** (or **pinitos**) to totter; toddle; stagger. *Aer.* **h. rizos,** to loop the loop. **h. saber,** to make known; notify. **h. seguir,** to forward (letters). **h. señas,** to make signs (wave, beckon, etc.). *Inf.* **h. una que sea sonada,** to cause a big scandal. **¡Hágame el favor!** Please! *Pres. Indic.* **hago, haces,** etc —*Fut.* **haré,** etc —*Condit.* **haría,** etc —*Imperat.* **haz, haga, hagamos, haced, hagan.** *Preterite* **hice, hiciste, hizo, hicimos, hicisteis, hicieron.** *Pres. Subjunc.* **haga,** etc —*Imperf. Subjunc.* **hiciese,** etc.

hacerse /a'θerse; a'serse/ *vr irr* to become (e.g. *Se ha hecho muy importante,* It (or he) has become very important); grow up (e.g. *Miguel se ha hecho hombre,* Michael has grown up (become a man)); develop, mature; pass oneself off as, pretend to be; (*with prep a*) become accustomed to or used to (e.g. *Me haré a este clima,* I shall grow used to this climate); withdraw or retire to (of places); (*with de or con*) provide oneself with. **h. a la vela,** to set sail. **h. a (uno),** to seem (e.g. *Eso que me cuentas se me hace increíble,* What you tell me seems incredible). *Inf.* **h. chiquito,** to be modest. **h. tarde,** to grow late; *Fig.* be too late. See **hacer**

hacha /'atʃa/ *f,* large candle; torch; ax. **h. pequeña,** hatchet

hachazo /a'tʃaθo; a'tʃaso/ *m,* stroke of an ax

hache /'atʃe/ *f,* name of the letter H

hacia /'aθia; 'asia/ *prep* toward, near, about. **h. adelante,** forward, onward

hacienda /a'θienda; a'sienda/ *f,* country estate, land; property; *pl* domestic tasks; cattle. **h. pública,** public funds. **ministerio de h.,** national treasury, exchequer

hacina /a'θina; a'sina/ *f, Agr.* stack; heap, pile

hacinamiento /aθina'miento; asina'miento/ *m,* stacking, piling; accumulation

hacinar /aθi'nar; asi'nar/ *vt Agr.* to stack sheaves; accumulate, amass; pile up, heap

hada /'aða/ *f,* fairy

hado /'aðo/ *m,* fate; destiny

Haití /ai'ti/ Haiti

haitiano /ai'tiano/ (**-na**) *a* and *n* Haitian

halagar /ala'gar/ *vt* to caress; flatter; coax; please, delight

halago /a'lago/ *m,* flattery; coaxing; caress; source of pleasure, delight

halagüeño /ala'gueɲo/ *a* flattering; pleasing; caressing; hopeful, promising

hálito /'alito/ *m,* breath; vapor; *Poet.* breeze

hallado /a'ʎaðo; a'ʃaðo/ *a* and *Past Part.* found, met. **bien h.,** welcome; happy, contented. **mal h.,** unwelcome; uneasy, discontented

hallar /a'ʎar; a'yar/ *vt* to find; meet; observe; discover; find out; —*vr* be present; be, find oneself

hallazgo /a'ʎaθgo; a'yasgo/ *m,* finding; thing found; finder's reward

halo /'alo/ *m,* halo

halterofilia /altero'filia/ *f,* weightlifting

hamaca /a'maka/ *f,* hammock

hambre /'ambre/ *f,* hunger; famine; desire, yearning. **tener h.,** to be hungry

hambriento /am'briento/ *a* hungry; famished; *Fig.* starved (of affection, etc.)

hamo /'amo/ *m,* fishhook

hampa /'ampa/ *f,* rogue's life; gang of rogues; underworld, slum

hangar /aŋ'gar/ *m,* hangar

haragán /ara'gan/ **(-ana)** *a* lazy, idle —*n* idler, lazybones

harapiento /ara'piento/ *a* ragged

harapo /a'rapo/ *m,* tatter, rag

harina /a'rina/ *f,* flour; powder; farina. *Inf.* **ser h. de otro costal,** to be a horse of another color

harnero /ar'nero/ *m,* sieve

harón /a'ron/ *a* slothful, slow; lazy, idle

harpillera /arpi'ʎera; arpi'yera/ *f,* sackcloth, sacking

hartar /ar'tar/ *vt* to satiate; tire, annoy; satisfy the appetite; shower (with blows, etc.)

hartazgo /ar'taθgo; ar'tasgo/ *m,* satiety

harto /'arto/ *a* satiated; tired (of), *adv* enough

hartura /ar'tura/ *f,* satiety; abundance

hasta /'asta/ *prep* until; as far as; down or up to —*conjunc* also, even. **h. la vista,** See you! Ciaio! Au revoir! **h. mañana,** until tomorrow

hastío /as'tio/ *m,* loathing; distaste; nausea

hato /'ato/ *m,* personal clothing; herd of cattle; gang (of suspicious characters); crowd, mob; *Inf.* group, party. *Inf.* **liar el h.,** to pack up

hay /ai/ there is; there are. See **haber**

haya /'aya/ *f,* beech tree; beechwood

Haya, La /'aya, la/ The Hague

haz /aθ; as/ *m,* bundle, sheaf; *Mil.* file; *pl* fasces; *f,* visage; surface; face. **h. de la tierra,** face of the earth. **h. de luz,** beam of light. *Fig.* **ser de dos haces,** to be two-faced

haz /aθ; as/ *2nd pers imperat* **hacer**

hazaña /a'θaɲa; a'saɲa/ *f,* exploit, prowess

hazmerreír /aθmerre'ir; asmerre'ir/ *m,* *Inf.* laughingstock

he /e/ *interj* and *adv* Hallo! Hist!; Behold! **¡Heme aquí!** Here I am. **he aquí,** here is...

hebilla /e'βiʎa; e'βiya/ *f,* buckle

hebra /'eβra/ *f,* thread; fiber; flesh; *Mineral.* vein, streak; filament (textiles); grain (of wood); *pl Poet.* hair. *Inf.* **pegar la h.,** to start a conversation

hebreo /e'βreo/ **(-ea)** *a* Hebraic, Jewish —*n* Jew. *m,* Hebrew (language)

hechicería /etʃiθe'ria; etʃise'ria/ *f,* sorcery; spell, enchantment

hechicero /etʃi'θero; etʃi'sero/ *a* bewitching, magic; charming, attractive

hechizar /etʃi'θar; etʃi'sar/ *vt* to bewitch; charm, attract, delight

hechizo /e'tʃiθo; e'tʃiso/ *m,* magic spell; fascination, charm; delight, pleasure

hecho /'etʃo/ *a* developed, mature; accustomed, used; perfected, finished; ready-made. **h. una furia,** like a fury, very angry. **bien h.,** well-made, well-proportioned; well or rightly done

hecho /etʃo/ *m,* deed, action; fact; happening, event. **los Hechos de los Apóstoles,** the Acts of the Apostles

hechura /e'tʃura/ *f,* making, make; creation; form; figure, statue; *Lit.* composition; build (of body); *Fig.* puppet, creature; *pl* price paid for work done. **de h. sastre,** *a* tailor-made

hectárea /ekta'rea/ *f,* hectare

heder /e'ðer/ *vi irr* to stink; be intolerable. See **entender**

hediondez /eðion'deθ; eðion'des/ *f,* stink, stench

hediondo /e'ðiondo/ *a* stinking; intolerable, pestilential; obscene

hegemonía /ehemo'nia/ *f,* hegemony

helada /e'laða/ *f,* frost. **h. blanca,** hoar frost

heladera /ela'ðera/ *f,* refrigerator

helado /e'laðo/ *a* frozen; ice-cold; astounded, disdainful. *m,* iced drink; sherbet, ice cream

helar /e'lar/ *vt irr* to freeze; ice, chill; astound; discourage; —*vr* become iced; freeze; become ice-cold —*v impers* to freeze. See **acertar**

helecho /e'letʃo/ *m,* fern

hélice /'eliθe; 'elise/ *f,* spiral, helical line; screw, propeller; *Geom.* helix; *Astron.* Ursa Major

helicóptero /eli'koptero/ *m,* *Aer.* helicopter

helio /'elio/ *m,* helium

helvecio /el'βeθio; el'βesio/ **(-ia)** *a* and *n* Helvetian

hembra /'embra/ *f,* female; *Inf.* woman; nut of a screw; eye of a hook. *Inf.* **una real h.,** a fine figure of a woman

hemiciclo /emi'θiklo; emi'siklo/ *m,* hemicycle; floor (of a legislative building)

hemisférico /emis'feriko/ *a* hemispherical

hemisferio /emis'ferio/ *m,* hemisphere

hemofilia /emo'filia/ *f,* hemophilia.

hemoglobina /emoglo'βina/ *f,* hemoglobin

hemorragia /emo'rrahia/ *f,* hemorrhage

hemorroides /emo'rroiðes/ *f,* hemorrhoids

henchido /en'tʃiðo/ *a* swollen

henchimiento /entʃi'miento/ *m,* swelling; inflation; filling

henchir /en'tʃir/ vt irr to fill; stuff; swell —Pres. Indic. hincho, hinches, hinche, hinchen. Pres. Part. hinchiendo. Pres. Subjunc. hincha, etc —Imperf. Subjunc. hinchiese, etc —Imperat. hinche, hincha, hinchamos, henchid, hinchan

hendedura /ende'ðura/ f, fissure; rift

hender /en'der/ vt irr to split, crack; Fig. cleave (air, water, etc.); make one's way through. See **entender**

hendidura /endi'ðura/ f, split, fissure, crack, chink

heno /'eno/ m, hay

hepático /e'patiko/ a hepatic

heráldica /e'raldika/ f, heraldry

heraldo /e'raldo/ m, herald; harbinger

herbaje /er'βahe/ m, herbage; pasture, grass; thick woolen cloth

herbario /er'βario/ m, herbalist, botanist; herbarium —a herbal

herbívoro /er'βiβoro/ a herbivorous

hercúleo /er'kuleo/ a herculean

heredad /ere'ðað/ f, landed property; country estate

heredar /ere'ðar/ vt to inherit; make a deed of gift to; inherit characteristics, etc.; take as heir

heredera /ere'ðera/ f, heiress

heredero /ere'ðero/ m, heir; inheritor. **h. aparente**, heir apparent. **presunto h.**, heir presumptive

hereditario /ereði'tario/ a hereditary

hereje /e'rehe/ mf heretic

herejía /ere'hia/ f, heresy

herencia /e'renθia; e'rensia/ f, inheritance; heredity; heritage

herético /e'retiko/ a heretical

herida /e'riða/ f, wound; insult; anguish. **h. contusa**, contusion. **h. penetrante**, deep wound

herir /e'rir/ vt irr to wound; strike, harm; Fig. pierce (of sun's rays); Fig. pluck (strings of a musical instrument); impress (the senses); affect (the emotions); offend (gen. of words) —Pres. Part. hiriendo. Pres. Indic. hiero, hieres, hiere, hieren. Preterite hirió, hirieron. Pres. Subjunc. hiera, hieras, hiera, hiramos, hiráis, hieran. Imperf. Subjunc. hiriese, etc.

hermafrodita /ermafro'ðita/ a and mf hermaphrodite

hermana /er'mana/ f, sister; twin, pair (of things). **h. de leche**, foster sister. **h. política**, sister-in-law

hermanar /erma'nar/ vt to join; mate; harmonize; —vt and vr be the spiritual brother of, be compatible

hermanastra /erma'nastra/ f, stepsister

hermanastro /erma'nastro/ m, stepbrother

hermandad /erman'dað/ f, brotherhood; friendship, intimacy; relationship (of one thing to another); confraternity. **Santa H.**, Spanish rural police force instituted in the fifteenth century

hermano /er'mano/ m, brother; pair; twin (of things); Eccl. brother. **h. de**

raza, member of the same race. **h. político**, brother-in-law

hermético /er'metiko/ a hermetic

hermosear /ermose'ar/ vt to embellish, beautify, adorn

hermoso /er'moso/ a beautiful; shapely; handsome; fine, wonderful (weather, view, etc.)

hermosura /ermo'sura/ f, beauty; pleasantness, attractiveness, perfection of form; belle

hernia /'ernia/ f, hernia

héroe /'eroe/ m, hero

heroicidad /eroiθi'ðað; eroisi'ðað/ f, heroism

heroico /e'roiko/ a heroic

heroína /ero'ina/ f, heroine

heroismo /ero'ismo/ m, heroism

herpes /'erpes/ m pl, or f pl, herpes

herrada /e'rraða/ f, pail

herrador /erra'ðor/ m, blacksmith

herradura /erra'ðura/ f, horseshoe

herraje /e'rrahe/ m, ironwork

herramienta /erra'mienta/ f, tool; set of tools

herrar /e'rrar/ vt irr to shoe horses; brand (cattle); decorate with iron. See **acertar**

herrería /erre'ria/ f, forge; ironworks; blacksmith's shop; clamor, tumult, confusion

herrero /e'rrero/ m, smith

herrete /e'rrete/ m, ferrule, tag

herrumbre /e'rrumbre/ f, rust; taste of iron

herrumbroso /errum'broso/ a rusty

hervidero /erβi'ðero/ m, boiling, bubbling; Fig. ebullition; swarm, crowd

hervir /er'βir/ vi irr to boil; foam and froth (sea); seethe (emotions); surge (crowds); (with en) abound in, swarm with. See **sentir**

hervor /er'βor/ m, boiling; ebullition, vigor, zest; seething, agitation

hesitación /esita'θion; esita'sion/ f, hesitation, doubt, uncertainty

hesitar /esi'tar/ vi to hesitate, vacillate

heteo /e'teo/ (-ea) a and n Hittite

heterodina /etero'ðina/ a f, Radio. heterodyne

heterodoxia /etero'ðoksia/ f, heterodoxy

heterodoxo /etero'ðokso/ a heterodox

heterogeneidad /eterohenei'ðað/ f, heterogeneity

heterogéneo /etero'heneo/ a heterogeneous

hético /'etiko/ a hectic, consumptive

hexagonal /eksago'nal/ a hexagonal

hexágono /e'ksagono/ m, hexagon

hez /eθ; es/ f, (gen. pl heces) lees, dregs

hiato /'iato/ m, hiatus

hibridación /iβriða'θion; iβriða'sion/ f, hybridization

híbrido /'iβriðo/ a and m, hybrid

hidalgo /i'ðalgo/ (-ga) n noble, aristocrat —a noble; illustrious; generous

hidalguía /iðal'gia/ *f.* nobility; generosity, nobility of spirit

hidrato /i'ðrato/ *m.* hydrate. **h. de carbono,** carbohydrate

hidráulica /i'ðraulika/ *f.* hydraulics

hidráulico /i'ðrauliko/ *a* hydraulic

hidroavión /iðroa'βion/ *m.* flying boat

hidrocéfalo /iðro'θefalo; iðro'sefalo/ *a* hydrocephalic

hidrodinámica /iðroði'namika/ *f.* hydrodynamics

hidroeléctrico /iðroe'lektriko/ *a* hydroelectric

hidrofobia /iðro'foβia/ *f.* hydrophobia; rabies

hidrógeno /i'ðroheno/ *m.* hydrogen

hidropesía /iðrope'sia/ *f.* dropsy

hidroplano /iðro'plano/ *m.* seaplane

hidroterapia /iðrote'rapia/ *f.* hydrotherapy

hiedra /'ieðra/ *f.* ivy

hiel /iel/ *f.* gall, bile, bitterness, affliction; *pl* troubles

hielo /'ielo/ *m.* ice, frost; freezing, icing; stupefaction; indifference, coldness. *Inf.* estar hecho un h., to be as cold as ice

hiena /'iena/ *f.* hyena

hierba /'ierβa/ *f.* grass; small plant; herb. **h. cana,** groundsel. **mala h.,** weed

hierbabuena /ierβa'βuena/ *f. Bot.* mint

hierra /'ierra/ *f.* branding time

hierro /'ierro/ *m.* iron; brand with hot iron; iron or steel head of a lance, etc.; instrument or shape made of iron; weapon of war *pl* fetters. **h. colado,** cast iron. **h. dulce,** wrought iron. **h. en planchas,** sheet iron. **h. viejo,** scrap iron

hígado /'igaðo/ *m.* liver; courage

higiene /i'hiene/ *f.* hygiene; cleanliness, neatness. **h. privada,** personal hygiene. **h. pública,** public health

higiénico /i'hieniko/ *a* hygienic

higo /'igo/ *m.* fig. **h. chumbo,** prickly pear

higuera /i'gera/ *f.* fig tree

hija /'iha/ *f.* daughter; native of a place; offspring

hijastro /i'hastro/ **(-ra)** *n* stepchild

hijo /'iho/ *m.* son; child; native of a place; offspring; shoot, sprout; *pl* descendants. **h. de la cuna,** foundling. **h. de leche,** foster child. **h. natural,** natural child. **h. político,** son-in-law

hijuela /i'huela/ *f.* little daughter; small mattress; small drain; side road; accessory, subordinate thing; piece of material for widening a garment; *Law.* part of an inheritance

hila /'ila/ *f.* row, line; gut; *Surg.* lint (gen. *pl*)

hilacha /i'latʃa/ *f.* thread raveled from cloth; fiber, filament. **h. de vidrio,** spun glass

hilado /i'laðo/ *m.* spinning; thread, yarn

hilandería /ilande'ria/ *f.* spinning; spinning mill; mill. **h. de algodón,** cotton mill

hilandero /ilan'dero/ **(-ra)** *n* spinner

hilar /i'lar/ *vt* to spin; reason, infer, discourse

hilaridad /ilari'ðað/ *f.* hilarity; quiet happiness

hilaza /i'laθa; i'lasa/ *f.* yarn

hilera /i'lera/ *f.* line, file, row; fine yarn; *Mil.* file, rank; *Metall.* wire drawer; *Mas.* course (of bricks)

hilo /'ilo/ *m.* thread; linen; wire; mesh (spiders, silkworm's web, etc.); edge (of a blade); thin stream (of liquid); thread (of discourse)

hilván /il'βan/ *m. Sew.* basting; tack

hilvanar /ilβa'nar/ *vt Sew.* to baste

himalayo /ima'layo/ *a* Himalayan

himen /'imen/ *m.* hymen

himeneo /ime'neo/ *m.* marriage, wedding

himno /'imno/ *m.* hymn

hincapié /inka'pie/ *m.* foothold. **hacer h.,** to insist, make a stand

hincar /in'kar/ *vt* to thrust in; drive in, sink; —*vr* kneel. **h. el diente,** to bite. **h. la uña,** to scratch. **hincarse de rodillas,** to kneel down

hinchado /in'tʃaðo/ *a* puffed up, vain; pompous, high-flown, redundant (style)

hinchar /in'tʃar/ *vt* to inflate; puff out (the chest); swell (of a river, etc.); exaggerate (events); —*vr* swell; grow vain, be puffed up

hinchazón /intʃa'θon; intʃa'son/ *f.* swelling; vanity, presumption; pomposity, euphuism (style)

hinojo /i'noho/ *m. Bot.* fennel; knee. **de hinojos,** on bended knee

hipar /i'par/ *vi* to hiccup; pant (of dogs); be overanxious; be overtired; sob, cry

hipérbole /i'perβole/ *f.* hyperbole

hiperbólico /iper'βoliko/ *a* hyperbolical

hipertrofiarse /ipertro'fiarse/ *vr* to hypertrophy

hipnosis /ip'nosis/ *f.* hypnosis

hipnótico /ip'notiko/ *a* hypnotic. *m.* hypnotic drug

hipnotismo /ipno'tismo/ *m.* hypnotism

hipnotización /ipnotiθa'θion; ipnotisa'sion/ *f.* hypnotization

hipnotizar /ipnoti'θar; ipnoti'sar/ *vt* to hypnotize

hipo /'ipo/ *m.* hiccup; sob; longing, desire; dislike, disgust

hipocondría /ipokon'dria/ *f.* hypochondria

hipocondríaco /ipokon'driako/ **(-ca)** *a* hypochondriacal —*n* hypochondriac

hipocresía /ipokre'sia/ *f.* hypocrisy

hipócrita /i'pokrita/ *a* hypocritical. *mf* hypocrite

hipodérmico /ipo'ðermiko/ *a* hypodermic

hipódromo /i'poðromo/ *m.* hippodrome, racetrack

hipopótamo /ipo'potamo/ *m.* hippopotamus

hipoteca /ipo'teka/ *f.* mortgage

hipotecable /ipote'kaβle/ *a* mortgageable

hipotecar /ipote'kar/ *vt* to mortgage

hipótesis /i'potesis/ *f*, hypothesis

hipotético /ipo'tetiko/ *a* hypothetical

hirsuto /ir'suto/ *a* hirsute, hairy

hirviente /ir'βiente/ *a* boiling

hispánico /is'paniko/ *a* Spanish

hispanismo /ispa'nismo/ *m*, Hispanism

hispanista /ispa'nista/ *mf* Hispanist

hispanoamericano /ispanoameri'kaño/ **(-na)** *a* and *n* Spanish-American, Hispano-American

histeria /is'teria/ *f*, hysteria

histérico /is'teriko/ *a* hysterical; hysteric

histerismo /iste'rismo/ *m*, Med. hysteria

historia /is'toria/ *f*, history; narrative, story; tale; *Inf*. gossip (gen. *pl*); *Art*. historical piece. **h. natural**, natural history. **h. sagrada**, biblical history. *Fig. Inf.* dejarse de historias, to stop beating around the bush

historiador /istoria'ðor/ **(-ra)** *n* historian

historiar /isto'riar/ *vt* to narrate, relate; record, chronicle

histórico /is'toriko/ *a* historical; historic

historieta /isto'rieta/ *f*, short story; anecdote

historiografía /istoriogra'fia/ *f*, historiography

histriónico /ist'rioniko/ *a* histrionic

hitlerismo /itle'rismo/ *m*, Hitlerism

hito /'ito/ *m*, milestone; boundary mark; *Fig*. mark, target. **de h. en h.**, from head to foot

hocico /o'θiko; o'siko/ *m*, snout; *Inf*. face, mug; *Inf*. angry gesture; *Naut*. prow. **meter el h.**, to stick one's nose into other people's business

hogaño /o'gaño/ *adv Inf.* during this year; at the present time

hogar /o'gar/ *m*, hearth, fireplace; home, house; family life; firebox (of a locomotive)

hoguera /o'gera/ *f*, bonfire

hoja /'oha/ *f*, *Bot*. leaf; petal; sheet (metal, paper, etc.); page (of book); blade (sharp instruments); leaf (door, window); sword. **h. de cálculo**, spreadsheet. **h. de servicios**, service or professional record. **h. de tocino**, side of bacon. **h. extraordinaria**, extra, special edition (of a newspaper). **h. volante**, handbill, supplement. **volver la h.**, to turn over (pages); change one's opinion; turn the conversation

hojalata /oha'lata/ *f*, tin plate

hojalatería /ohalate'ria/ *f*, tinware; tin shop

hojalatero /ohala'tero/ *m*, tinsmith

hojaldre /o'haldre/ *m*, or *f*, puff pastry

hojarasca /oha'raska/ *f*, withered leaves; excessive foliage; rubbish, trash

hojear /ohe'ar/ *vt* to turn the leaves of a book; skip, skim, read quickly; —*vi* exfoliate

hojuela /o'huela/ *f*, *dim* little leaf; *Bot*. leaflet; pancake

¡hola! /'ola/ *interj* Hallo! Goodness!

Holanda /o'landa/ Holland

holandés /olan'des/ **(-esa)** *a* and *n* Dutchman (-woman) *m*, Dutch (language)

holgado /ol'gaðo/ *a* leisured, free; loose, wide; comfortable; well-off, rich

holganza /ol'ganθa; ol'gansa/ *f*, repose, leisure, ease; idleness; pleasure

holgar /ol'gar/ *vi irr* to rest; be idle; be glad; be unused or unnecessary (things) —*vr* enjoy oneself, amuse oneself; be glad. See **contar**

holgazán /olga'θan; olga'san/ **(-ana)** *a* idle —*n* idler

holgazanería /olgaθane'ria; olgasane'ria/ *f*, idleness, sloth

holgorio /ol'gorio/ *m*, rejoicing, festivity, merriment

holgura /ol'gura/ *f*, enjoyment, merrymaking; width; comfort, ease; *Mech*. free play

hollar /o'ʎar; o'yar/ *vt irr* to trample under foot; humiliate. See **degollar**

hollejo /o'ʎeho; o'yeho/ *m*, peel, thin skin (of fruit); *Agr*. chaff

hollín /o'ʎin; o'yin/ *m*, soot

holocausto /olo'kausto/ *m*, holocaust

hológrafo /o'lografo/ *m*, holograph

hombradía /ombra'ðia/ *f*, manliness; courage

hombre /'ombre/ *m*, man; adult; omber (cards) —*interj* ¡**h**.! *Inf*. Old fellow! You don't say so! **¡h. al agua!** Man overboard! **h. de bien**, honest, honorable man. **h. de estado**, statesman. **h. de muchos oficios**, jack-of-all-trades. **h. de negocios**, businessman; man of affairs. **h. de pro**, worthy man; famous man. **ser muy h.**, to be a real man, be very manly

hombrera /om'brera/ *f*, epaulette; shoulderpad

hombro /'ombro/ *m*, shoulder. **echar al h.**, to shoulder; undertake, take the responsibility of. **encogerse de hombros**, to shrug one's shoulders; be indifferent or uninterested

homenaje /ome'nahe/ *m*, allegiance; homage; veneration, respect

homeópata /ome'opata/ *a* homeopathic. *mf* homeopath

homicida /omi'θiða; omi'siða/ *a* murderous, homicidal. *mf* murderer (-ess)

homicidio /omi'θiðio; omi'siðio/ *m*, homicide (act)

homilía /omi'lia/ *f*, homily

homogéneo /omo'heneo/ *a* homogeneous

homólogo /o'mologo/ *a* homologous

homónimo /o'monimo/ *a* homonymous. *m*, homonym

homosexual /omose'ksual/ *a* and *mf* homosexual

honda /'onda/ *f*, sling, catapult

hondear /onde'ar/ *vt Naut*. to sound, plumb; *Naut*. unload

hondo /'ondo/ *a* deep; low; *Fig*. profound; deep, intense (emotion). *m*, depth

hondón /on'don/ *m*, depth, recess

hondonada /ondo'naða/ f. hollow; glen; valley

hondura /on'dura/ f. depth

hondureño /ondu'reɲo/ (-ña) a and n Honduran

honestidad /onesti'ðað/ f. honorableness; virtue; respectability; modesty; courtesy

honesto /o'nesto/ a honorable, virtuous; modest; honest, just

hongo /'oŋgo/ m. fungus; toadstool; bowler hat

honor /o'nor/ m. honor; fame; reputation (women); modesty (women); praise; pl rank, position; honors

honorable /ono'raβle/ a honorable

honorario /ono'rario/ a honorary. m, honorarium, fee

honorífico /ono'rifiko/ a honorary; honorable

honra /'onra/ f. self-respect, honor, personal dignity; reputation; chastity and modesty (women); pl obsequies

honradez /onra'ðeθ; onra'ðes/ f. honesty; honorableness, integrity; respectability

honrado /on'raðo/ a honest; honorable

honrar /on'rar/ vt to respect; honor; —vr to be honored

honroso /on'roso/ a honor-giving, honorable

hora /'ora/ f. hour; opportune moment; pl book of hours. **horas hábiles,** working hours. **horas muertas,** wee hours; wasted time. **a última h.,** at the last minute. **dar la h.,** to strike the hour. ¿Qué h. es? What time is it?

horadar /ora'ðar/ vt to bore, pierce

horario /o'rario/ a hourly. m, timetable; hour hand of a clock; watch

horca /'orka/ f. gibbet, gallows; Agr. pitchfork; fork; prop for trees

horcajadas /orka'haðas/ (a) adv astride

horcajadura /orkaha'ðura/ f. crotch

horchata /or'tʃata/ f. drink made of chufas or crushed almonds

horda /'orða/ f. horde

horizontal /oriθon'tal; orison'tal/ a horizontal

horizonte /ori'θonte; ori'sonte/ m, horizon. **nuevos horizontes,** new opportunities

horma /'orma/ f. mold; cobbler's last; stone wall. Fig. Inf. hallar la h. de su zapato, to find what suits one; meet one's match

hormiga /or'miga/ f. ant

hormigón /ormi'gon/ m, concrete. **h. armado,** ferro-concrete

hormiguear /ormige'ar/ vi to itch; crowd, swarm

hormiguero /ormi'gero/ m, anthill; crowd, swarm

hormona /or'mona/ f. hormone

hornero /or'nero/ (-ra) n baker

horno /'orno/ m, oven; furnace; kiln; bakery. **h. alfarero,** firing oven (for pottery). **h. de cocina,** kitchen stove. **h. de**

cuba, blast furnace. **h. de ladrillo,** brick kiln. **alto h.,** iron-smelting furnace

horóscopo /o'roskopo/ m, horoscope

horquilla /or'kiʎa; or'kiya/ f, forked stick; hairpin; hatpin; Agr. fork; hook. **viraje en h.,** hairpin turn

horrendo /o'rrendo/ a horrible, frightful

horrible /o'rriβle/ a horrible

horrífico /o'rrifiko/ a horrific

horripilante /orripi'lante/ a hair-raising, horrifying

horrísono /o'rrisono/ a Poet. horrid-sounding, terrifying

horror /o'rror/ m, horror; horribleness; atrocity, enormity

horrorizar /orrori'θar; orrori'sar/ vt to horrify; —vr be horrified, be terrified

horroroso /orro'roso/ a dreadful, horrible; horrid; Inf. hideous, most ugly

hortaliza /orta'liθa; orta'lisa/ f, green vegetable, garden produce

hortelano /orte'lano/ m, market gardener

horticultor /ortikul'tor/ (-ra) n horticulturalist

horticultura /ortikul'tura/ f, horticulture

hosco /'osko/ a dark brown; unsociable, sullen; crabbed

hospedaje /ospe'ðahe/ m, lodging; board, payment

hospedar /ospe'ðar/ vt to lodge, receive as a guest; —vr and vi lodge, stay

hospicio /os'piθio; os'pisio/ m, hospice; almshouse, workhouse; lodging; orphanage

hospital /ospi'tal/ m, hospital; hospice. **h. de sangre,** field hospital

hospitalario /ospita'lario/ a hospitable

hospitalidad /ospitali'ðað/ f, hospitality; hospitableness; hospital

hostelero /oste'lero/ (-ra) n innkeeper

hostería /oste'ria/ f, hostelry; inn

hostia /'ostia/ f, Eccl. wafer, Host; sacrificial victim

hostigamiento /ostiga'miento/ m, harassment. **h. sexual,** sexual harassment

hostigar /osti'gar/ vt to chastise; harass; tease, annoy

hostil /os'til/ a hostile

hostilidad /ostili'ðað/ f, hostility

hotel /'otel/ m, hotel; villa

hotelero /ote'lero/ (-ra) n hotelkeeper

hoy /oi/ adv today; at present. **h. día** or **h. en día,** today. **h. por h.,** day by day; at the present time. **de h. en adelante,** from today forward

hoya /'oya/ f, hole; grave; valley, glen; bed (of a river)

hoyo /'oyo/ m, hole; pockmark; grave; hollow

hoyuelo /o'yuelo/ m, dim little hole; dimple

hoz /oθ; os/ f, sickle; defile

hozar /o'θar; o'sar/ vt to root (pigs, etc.)

hucha /'utʃa/ f, large chest; strongbox; savings

hueco /'ueko/ a empty; hollow; vain; hollow (sound); pompous (style); spongy, soft; inflated. *m*, hollow; interval of time or place; *Inf.* vacancy; gap in a wall, etc.

huelga /'uelga/ *f*, strike; leisure; lying fallow; merrymaking. **h. de brazos caídos**, sit-down strike. **h. patronal**, lockout strike

huelguista /uel'gista/ *mf* striker

huella /'ueʎa; 'ueya/ *f*, footprint, track; footstep; tread (of stairs); *Print.* impression; vestige, trace. **h. digital**, fingerprint

huérfano /'uerfano/ **(-na)** *n* orphan —*a* unprotected, uncared for

huero /'uero/ *a* addled; empty, hollow

huerta /'uerta/ *f*, kitchen garden; orchard; irrigation land

huerto /'uerto/ *m*, orchard; kitchen garden

hueso /'ueso/ *m*, bone; stone (of fruit); kernel, core; drudgery; cheap, useless thing of poor quality. *Inf.* **no dejar un h. sano**, to tear (a person) to pieces. **tener los huesos molidos**, to be tired out; be bruised

huésped /'uespeð/ **(-da)** *n* guest; host; innkeeper

hueste /'ueste/ *f*, (gen. *pl*) army on the march; host; party, supporters

huesudo /ue'suðo/ *a* bony

huevo /'ueβo/ *m*, egg. **h. duro**, hard-boiled egg. **h. estrellado**, fried egg. **h. pasado por agua**, soft-boiled egg. **huevos revueltos**, scrambled eggs

huida /'uiða/ *f*, flight, escape; bolting (of a horse); outlet

huir /uir/ *vi irr* to flee; fly (of time); elope; run away, bolt; (*with de*) avoid —*Pres. Part.* **huyendo**. *Pres. Indic.* **huyo, huyes, huyen**. *Preterite* **huyó, huyeron**. *Pres. Subjunc.* **huya**, etc —*Imperf. Subjunc.* **huyese**, etc.

hule /'ule/ *m*, oilcloth; rubber

hulla /'uʎa; 'uya/ *f*, coal mine, coal, soft coal

hullera /u'ʎera; u'yera/ *f*, colliery, coal mine

humanidad /umani'ðað/ *f*, humanity; human nature; human weakness; compassion; affability; *Inf.* stoutness; *pl* study of humanities

humanismo /uma'nismo/ *m*, humanism

humanista /uma'nista/ *mf* humanist —*a* humanistic

humanitario /umani'tario/ *a* humanitarian

humanizar /umani'θar; umani'sar/ *vt* to humanize

humano /u'mano/ *a* human; understanding, sympathetic. *m*, human being

humareda /uma'reða/ *f*, cloud of smoke

humear /ume'ar/ *vi* to give forth smoke; give oneself airs

humedad /ume'ðað/ *f*, humidity; dampness; moisture

humedecer /umeðe'θer; umeðe'ser/ *vt irr* to moisten, wet, damp; —*vr* grow moist. See **conocer**

húmedo /'umeðo/ *a* humid; damp; wet

húmero /'umero/ *m*, humerus

humildad /umil'dað/ *f*, humility; lowliness; humbleness

humilde /u'milde/ *a* meek; lowly; humble

humillación /umiʎa'θion; umiya'sion/ *f*, humiliation

humillante /umi'ʎante; umi'yante/ *a* humiliating; debasing; mortifying

humillar /umi'ʎar; umi'yar/ *vt* to humble; humiliate; —*vr* humble oneself

humo /'umo/ *m*, smoke; vapor, fume; vanity, airs

humor /u'mor/ *m*, *Med.* humor; temperament, disposition; mood. **de buen h.**, good-tempered. **de mal h.**, ill-tempered

humorada /umo'raða/ *f*, humorous saying, extravagance, witticism

humorista /umo'rista/ *mf* humorist

humorístico /umo'ristiko/ *a* humorous

humoso /u'moso/ *a* smoky, reeky

hundible /un'diβle/ *a* sinkable

hundido /un'diðo/ *a* sunken (of cheeks, etc.); hollow, deep-set (of eyes)

hundimiento /undi'miento/ *m*, sinking; collapse; subsidence (of earth)

hundir /un'dir/ *vt* to sink; oppress; confound; destroy, ruin; —*vr* collapse (building); sink; *Fig. Inf.* disappear

húngaro /'uŋgaro/ **(-ra)** *a* and *n* Hungarian. *m*, Hungarian (language)

Hungría /uŋ'gria/ Hungary

huracán /ura'kan/ *m*, hurricane

huraña /ura'ɲia/ *f*, shyness, unsociableness; diffidence; wildness (of animals, etc.)

huraño /u'raɲo/ *a* shy, unsociable; diffident; wild (of animals, etc.)

hurgar /ur'gar/ *vt* to stir; poke, rake; touch; rouse, incite —*vr* pick one's nose

hurgón /ur'gon/ *m*, fire rake, poker; *Inf.* sword

hurgonada /urgo'naða/ *f*, raking (of the fire, etc.)

hurón /u'ron/ **(-ona)** *n* ferret —*a* shy, unsociable

¡hurra! /'urra/ *interj* Hurrah!

hurtadillas /urta'ðiʎas; urta'ðiyas/ **(a)** *adv* by stealth, secretly

hurtar /ur'tar/ *vt* to steal; encroach (sea, river); plagiarize; —*vr* hide oneself

hurto /'urto/ *m*, theft. **coger con el h. en las manos**, *Fig.* to catch red-handed

husmear /usme'ar/ *vt* to sniff out; *Inf.* pry; —*vi* smell bad (of meat)

huso /'uso/ *m*, spindle; bobbin

¡huy! /'ui/ *interj* (denoting pain or surprise) Oh!

icnografía /iknogra'fia/ f. ichnography
icnográfico /ikno'grafiko/ a ichnographical
icono /i'kono/ m. icon
iconoclasta /ikono'klasta/ a iconoclastic. mf iconoclast
iconografía /ikonogra'fia/ f. iconography
ictericia /ikte'riθia; ikte'risia/ f. jaundice
ida /'iða/ f. setting out, departure, going; impetuous action; precipitancy; track, trail (of animals). **de i. y vuelta**, round trip (of tickets)
idea /i'ðea/ f. idea. *Inf.* ¡**Qué ideas tienes!** What (odd) ideas you have!
ideal /i'ðeal/ a ideal; perfect. m, model; ideal
idealidad /iðeali'ðað/ f. ideality
idealismo /iðea'lismo/ m. idealism
idealista /iðea'lista/ a idealistic. mf idealist
idealización /iðealiθa'θion; iðealisa'sion/ f. idealization
idealizar /iðeali'θar; iðeali'sar/ vt to idealize
idear /iðe'ar/ vt to imagine; devise; plan; design; draft, draw up
ídem /'iðem/ adv idem
idéntico /i'ðentiko/ a identical
identidad /iðenti'ðað/ f. identity
identificable /iðentifi'kaβle/ a identifiable
identificación /iðentifika'θion; iðentifika'sion/ f. identification
identificar /iðentifi'kar/ vt to identify; recognize; —vr (with con) identify oneself with
ideología /iðeolo'hia/ f. ideology. **i. racista**, racial ideology
ideológico /iðeo'lohiko/ a ideological
ideólogo /iðe'ologo/ **(-ga)** n ideologist; dreamer, planner
idioma /i'ðioma/ m. language, tongue
idiomático /iðio'matiko/ a idiomatic
idiosincrásico /iðiosin'krasiko/ a idiosyncratic
idiota /i'ðiota/ a idiot; idiotic. mf idiot
idiotez /iðio'teθ; iðio'tes/ f. idiocy
idiotismo /iðio'tismo/ m, *Gram.* idiom; ignorance
idólatra /i'ðolatra/ a idolatrous; adoring. mf idolater, heathen
idolatrar /iðola'trar/ vt to idolize; worship, love excessively
idolatría /iðola'tria/ f. idolatry; adoration, idolization
ídolo /'iðolo/ m, idol
idóneo /i'ðoneo/ a suitable; competent, fit
iglesia /i'glesia/ f. church. **i. colegial**, collegiate church. **cumplir con la i.**, to discharge one's religious duties. **llevar a una mujer a la i.**, to lead a woman to the altar
ignición /igni'θion; igni'sion/ f. ignition
ignominioso /ignomi'nioso/ a ignominious
ignorancia /igno'ranθia; igno'ransia/ f.

ignorance. **pretender i.**, to plead ignorance
ignorante /igno'rante/ a ignorant; unaware, uninformed. mf ignoramus
ignorar /igno'rar/ vt to be unaware of, not to know
ignoto /ig'noto/ a unknown, undiscovered
igual /i'gual/ a equal; level; even, smooth; very similar; alike; uniform; proportionate; unchanging; constant; indifferent; same. mf equal. m, *Math.* equal sign. **al i.**, equally. **sin i.**, peerless, without equal. **Me es completamente i.**, It's all the same to me
igualación /iguala'θion; iguala'sion/ f, equalization; leveling; arrangement, agreement; matching; *Math.* equation
igualar /igua'lar/ vt to equalize, make equal; match; pair; level, flatten; smooth; adjust; arrange, agree upon; weigh, consider; *Math.* equate; —vi be equal
igualdad /igual'dað/ f, equality; uniformity, harmony; evenness; smoothness; identity, sameness. **i. de ánimo**, equability, equanimity
igualmente /igual'mente/ adv equally; the same, likewise
ijada /i'haða/ f, side, flank; pain in the side
ilación /ila'θion; ila'sion/ f. connection, reference
ilegal /ile'gal/ a illegal
ilegalidad /ilegali'ðað/ f, illegality
ilegible /ile'hiβle/ a illegible, unreadable
ilegítimo /ile'hitimo/ a illegitimate; false
íleon /'ileon/ m, ilium
ileso /i'leso/ a unharmed, unhurt
iletrado /ile'traðo/ a unlettered, uncultured
iliberal /iliβe'ral/ a illiberal; narrow-minded
iliberalidad /iliβerali'ðað/ f, illiberality; narrow-mindedness
ilícito /i'liθito; i'lisito/ a illicit
ilimitado /ilimi'taðo/ a unlimited, boundless
iliterato /ilite'rato/ a illiterate, uncultured
ilógico /i'lohiko/ a illogical
iluminación /ilumina'θion; ilumina'sion/ f, illumination; lighting. **i. intensiva**, floodlighting
iluminador /ilumina'ðor/ **(-ra)** a lighting; illuminating —n *Art.* illuminator
iluminar /ilumi'nar/ vt to illuminate; light; *Art.* illuminate; enlighten
ilusión /ilu'sion/ f, illusion; illusoriness; hope; dream
ilusionarse /ilusio'narse/ vr to harbor illusions
ilusivo /ilu'siβo/ a deceptive, illusive

iluso /i'luso/ *a* deceived, deluded; dreamy; visionary

ilusorio /ilu'sorio/ *a* illusory; deceptive; null

ilustración /ilustra'θion; ilustra'sion/ *f*, illustration, picture; enlightenment; explanation; illustrated newspaper or magazine; erudition, knowledge; example, illustration

ilustrado /ilu'straðo/ *a* erudite, learned; knowledgeable, well-informed

ilustrador /ilustra'ðor/ **(-ra)** *a* illustrative —*n* illustrator

ilustrar /ilus'trar/ *vt* to explain, illustrate; enlighten, instruct; illustrate (books); make illustrious; inspire with divine light

ilustrativo /ilustra'tiβo/ *a* illustrative

ilustre /i'lustre/ *a* illustrious, distinguished

imagen /i'mahen/ *f*, image; effigy, statue; idea; metaphor, simile. **i. nítida,** sharp image

imaginable /imahi'naβle/ *a* imaginable

imaginación /imahina'θion; imahina'sion/ *f*, imagination

imaginar /imahi'nar/ *vi* to imagine; —*vt* suppose, conjecture; discover, invent; imagine. **¡Imagínese!** Just imagine!

imaginario /imahi'nario/ *a* imaginary

imaginativa /imahina'tiβa/ *f*, imagination; common sense

imaginativo /imahina'tiβo/ *a* imaginative

imaginería /imahine'ria/ *f*, imagery

imán /i'man/ *m*, magnet; attraction, charm; imam

imanar /ima'nar/ *vt* to magnetize

imbécil /im'beθil; im'besil/ *a* imbecile; stupid, idiotic. *mf* imbecile

imbecilidad /imbeθili'ðað; imbesili'ðað/ *f*, imbecility; folly, stupidity

imberbe /im'berβe/ *a* beardless. *Inf.* **joven i.,** stripling

imborrable /imbo'rraβle/ *a* ineffaceable

imbuir /im'buir/ *vt irr* to imbue. See **huir**

imitable /imi'taβle/ *a* imitable

imitación /imita'θion; imita'sion/ *f*, imitation; reproduction, copy

imitado /imi'taðo/ *a* imitation; imitated

imitador /imita'ðor/ **(-ra)** *a* imitation; imitative —*n* imitator

imitar /imi'tar/ *vt* to imitate; counterfeit

imitativo /imita'tiβo/ *a* imitative

impacción /impak'θion; impak'sion/ *f*, impact

impaciencia /impa'θienθia; impa'siensia/ *f*, impatience

impacientar /impaθien'tar; impasien'tar/ *vt* to make impatient, annoy; —*vr* grow impatient

impaciente /impa'θiente; impa'siente/ *a* impatient

impacto /im'pakto/ *m*, impact. **i. de lleno,** direct hit

impalpable /impal'paβle/ *a* impalpable

impar /im'par/ *a* odd; unpaired; single, uneven. **número impar,** odd number

imparcial /impar'θial; impar'sial/ *a* impartial

imparcialidad /imparθiali'ðað; imparsiali'ðað/ *f*, impartiality

impartible /impar'tiβle/ *a* indivisible

impasibilidad /impasiβili'ðað/ *f*, impassivity, indifference

impasible /impa'siβle/ *a* impassive

impavidez /impaβi'ðeθ; impaβi'ðes/ *f*, dauntlessness; serenity in the face of danger

impávido /im'paβiðo/ *a* dauntless; calm, composed, imperturbable

impecabilidad /impekaβili'ðað/ *f*, impeccability, perfection

impecable /impe'kaβle/ *a* impeccable, perfect

impedido /impe'ðiðo/ *a* disabled

impedimento /impeði'mento/ *m*, obstacle; hindrance; *Law.* impediment

impedir /impe'ðir/ *vt irr* to impede; obstruct; prevent; thwart; disable; delay; *Poet.* amaze. See **pedir**

impeler /impe'ler/ *vt* to push; incite; drive; urge

impender /impen'der/ *vt* to spend money

impenetrabilidad /impenetraβili'ðað/ *f*, impenetrability; imperviousness; obscurity, difficulty

impenetrable /impene'traβle/ *a* impenetrable, dense; impervious; *Fig.* unfathomable; obscure

impenitencia /impeni'tenθia; impeni'tensia/ *f*, impenitence

impenitente /impeni'tente/ *a* impenitent

impensado /impen'saðo/ *a* unexpected, unforeseen

imperante /impe'rante/ *a* ruling, dominant

imperar /impe'rar/ *vi* to rule; command

imperativo /impera'tiβo/ *a* commanding —*a* and *m*, *Gram.* imperative

imperdible /imper'ðiβle/ *m*, safety pin

imperdonable /imperðo'naβle/ *a* unpardonable, inexcusable

imperecedero /impereθe'ðero; imperese'ðero/ *a* undying, eternal, everlasting

imperfección /imperfek'θion; imperfek'sion/ *f*, imperfection, inadequacy; fault, blemish; weakness

imperfecto /imper'fekto/ *a* imperfect; inadequate; faulty —*a* and *m*, *Gram.* imperfect

imperial /impe'rial/ *a* imperial. *f*, upper deck of a bus or streetcar

impericia /impe'riθia; impe'risia/ *f*, inexpertness; unskillfulness, unhandiness

imperio /im'perio/ *m*, empire; rule, reign; command, sway; imperial dignity; arrogance, haughtiness. *Fig. Inf.* **valer un i.,** to be priceless

imperioso /impe'rioso/ *a* imperious

imperito /impe'rito/ *a* inexpert; clumsy, unskilled

impermeabilizar /impermeaβili'θar; impermeaβili'sar/ *vt* to waterproof

impermeable /imperme'aβle/ *a* watertight, impermeable; impervious. *m*, raincoat, mackintosh

imperterrito /imper'territo/ *a* unafraid, dauntless

impertinencia /impertinen'θia; impertinen'sia/ *f*, impertinence, insolence; peevishness; fancy, whim; overexactness, meticulousness; interference, intrusion

impertinente /imperti'nente/ *a* impertinent; irrelevant; inopportune; officious, interfering

imperturbabilidad /imperturβaβili'ðað/ *f*, imperturbability

imperturbable /impertur'βaβle/ *a* calm, imperturbable

impetrar /impe'trar/ *vt* to obtain by entreaty; implore

ímpetu /'impetu/ *m*, impetus, momentum; speed, swiftness; violence

impetuosidad /impetuosi'ðað/ *f*, impetuosity

impetuoso /impe'tuoso/ *a* impetuous; precipitate

impiedad /impie'ðað/ *f*, cruelty, harshness, irreligion

impío /im'pio/ *a* impious, wicked; irreverent, irreligious

implacabilidad /implakaβili'ðað/ *f*, implacability; relentless

implantación /implanta'θion; implanta'sion/ *f*, inculcation, implantation

implantar /implan'tar/ *vt* to inculcate, implant (ideas, etc.)

implicación /implika'θion; implika'sion/ *f*, implication; contradiction (in terms); complicity

implicar /impli'kar/ *vt* to implicate; imply, infer; involve, entangle; —*vi* imply contradiction (gen. with negatives)

implicatorio /implika'torio/ *a* contradictory; implicated (in crime)

implícito /im'pliθito; im'plisito/ *a* implicit; implied

implorante /implo'rante/ *a* imploring

implorar /implo'rar/ *vt* to implore, entreat

impolítico /impo'litiko/ *a* impolitic; unwise, inexpedient; tactless

impoluto /impo'luto/ *a* unpolluted, spotless, pure

imponderable /imponde'raβle/ *a* imponderable, immeasurable; most excellent

imponente /impo'nente/ *a* imposing; awe-inspiring

imponer /impo'ner/ *vt irr* to exact; impose; malign, accuse falsely; instruct, acquaint; *Fig.* impress (with respect, etc.); invest or deposit (money); *Print.* impose; give, bestow (a name) —*vr* assert oneself. See **poner**

imponible /impo'niβle/ *a* taxable; ratable

impopular /impopu'lar/ *a* unpopular

importación /importa'θion; importa'sion/ *f*, *Com.* importation; import

importador /importa'ðor/ (**-ra**) *a* import, importing —*n* importer

importancia /impor'tanθia; impor'tansia/ *f*, importance; magnitude

importante /impor'tante/ *a* important

importar /impor'tar/ *vi* to matter; be important; concern, interest; —*vt* amount to; import; include, comprise. **¡No importa!** It doesn't matter! Never mind!

importe /im'porte/ *m*, amount; value, cost. **i. bruto**, gross or total amount. **i. líquido** or **neto**, net amount

importunación /importuna'θion; importuna'sion/ *f*, importuning; importunity

importunadamente /importunaða'mente/ *adv* importunately

importunar /importu'nar/ *vt* to importune, pester

importunidad /importuni'ðað/ (*also* **importunación**) *f*, importunity

importuno /impor'tuno/ *a* importunate, inopportune, ill-timed; persistent; tedious

imposibilidad /imposiβili'ðað/ *f*, impossibility

imposibilitado /imposiβili'taðo/ *a* disabled, crippled; incapable, unable

imposibilitar /imposiβili'tar/ *vt* to disable; render unable; make impossible

imposible /impo'siβle/ *a* impossible

imposición /imposi'θion; imposi'sion/ *f*, imposition; exaction; tax, duty, tribute; *Print.* makeup **i. de manos**, *Eccl.* laying on of hands

impostor /impos'tor/ (**-ra**) *n* impostor

impostura /impos'tura/ *f*, swindle, imposture; aspersion, slur, imputation

impotable /impo'taβle/ *a* undrinkable

impotencia /impo'tenθia; impo'tensia/ *f*, impotence

impotente /impo'tente/ *a* impotent; powerless

impracticable /imprakti'kaβle/ *a* impracticable; impossible; impassable (roads, etc.)

imprecar /impre'kar/ *vt* to imprecate, curse

impregnación /impregna'θion; impregna'sion/ *f*, impregnation, permeation, saturation

impregnar /impreg'nar/ *vt* impregnate; to permeate; —*vr* become impregnated

impremeditado /impremeði'taðo/ *a* unpremeditated

imprenta /im'prenta/ *f*, printing; printing house or office; print; letterpress

impreparación /imprepara'θion; imprepara'sion/ *f*, unpreparedness

imprescindible /impresθin'diβle; impressin'diβle/ *a* indispensable, essential

impresión /impre'sion/ *f*, printing; impression; effect; influence; imprint, stamp; *Print.* impression; print. **impresión digital**, fingerprint

impresionable /impresio'naβle/ *a* impressionable, susceptible

impresionante /impresio'nante/ *a* imposing; moving, affecting

impresionar /impresio'nar/ *vt* to impress; affect; fix in the mind; *Fig.* move deeply, stir; (*Radio.* cinema) record

impreso /im'preso/ *m*, (gen. *pl*) printed matter

impresor /impre'sor/ *m*, printer

imprevisión /impreβi'sion/ *f*, lack of foresight; improvidence

imprevisto /impre'βisto/ *a* unforeseen, unexpected, sudden

imprevistos /impre'βistos/ *m pl*, incidental expenses

imprimar /impri'mar/ *vt* to prime (of paint)

imprimir /impri'mir/ *vt* to print; stamp; impress upon (the mind)

improbable /impro'βaβle/ *a* improbable

improbo /im'proβo/ *a* vicious, corrupt, dishonest; hard, arduous

improductivo /improðuk'tiβo/ *a* unproductive; unprofitable, fruitless

impronta /im'pronta/ *f, Art.* cast, mold

impronunciable /impronun'θiaβle; impronun'siaβle/ *a* unpronounceable; ineffable

improperio /impro'perio/ *m*, insult, affront

impropiedad /impropie'ðað/ *f*, inappropriateness; unsuitableness; impropriety

impropio /im'propio/ *a* unsuitable; inappropriate; inadequate; improper

improporcionado /improporθio'naðo; improporsio'naðo/ *a* disproportionate, out of proportion

impróvido /im'proβiðo/ *a* improvident, heedless

improvisación /improβisa'θion; improβisa'sion/ *f*, improvisation

improvisador /improβisa'ðor/ (**-ra**) *n* improviser

improvisamente /improβisa'mente/ *adv* unexpectedly, suddenly

improvisar /improβi'sar/ *vt* to improvise

improviso, improvisto /impro'βiso, impro'βisto/ *a* unexpected, unforeseen. **al** (*or* **de**) **improviso,** unexpectedly

imprudencia /impru'ðenθia; impru-'ðensia/ *f*, imprudence, rashness, indiscretion

imprudente /impru'ðente/ *a* imprudent, unwise, rash

impúbero /im'puβero/ *a* below the age of puberty

impudencia /impu'ðenθia; impu'ðensia/ *f*, impudence, impertinence

impudente /impu'ðente/ *a* brazen, impudent

impudicia /impu'ðiθia; impu'ðisia/ *f*, immodesty, brazenness

impúdico /im'puðiko/ *a* immodest, brazen

impuesto /im'puesto/ *m*, tax; duty. **i. de utilidades,** income tax. **i. sucesorio,** inheritance tax

impugnable /impug'naβle/ *a* impugnable, refutable

impugnación /impugna'θion; impugna-'sion/ *f*, refutation; contradiction

impugnar /impug'nar/ *vt* to refute, contradict; oppose; criticize

impulsar /impul'sar/ *vt* to impel; prompt; cause; drive, operate, propel

impulsión /impul'sion/ *f*, impulse; impetus; *Mech.* operation, driving; propulsion

impulsivo /impul'siβo/ *a* impulsive; irreflexive, precipitate

impulso /im'pulso/ *m*, stimulus, incitement; impulse, desire; *Mech.* drive, impulse

impulsor /impul'sor/ (**-ra**) *a* driving, impelling —*n* driver, operator

impune /im'pune/ *a* unpunished

impunemente /impune'mente/ *adv* with impunity

impureza /impu'reθa; impu'resa/ *f*, impurity; lack of chastity; obscenity, indecency

impurificar /impurifi'kar/ *vt* to defile; make impure; adulterate

impuro /im'puro/ *a* impure; adulterated; polluted; immoral, unchaste

imputar /impu'tar/ *vt* to impute; attribute

inacabable /inaka'βaβle/ *a* endless, interminable, ceaseless; wearisome

inaccesible /inakθe'siβle; inakse'siβle/ *a* inaccessible; incomprehensible

inacción /inak'θion; inak'sion/ *f*, inaction

inaceptable /inaθep'taβle; inasep'taβle/ *a* unacceptable

inactivo /inak'tiβo/ *a* inactive; idle; unemployed; *Naut.* laid-up

inadecuado /inaðe'kuaðo/ *a* inadequate, insufficient

inadvertencia /inaðβer'tenθia; inaðβer-'tensia/ *f*, inadvertence; oversight, mistake, slip

inadvertido /inaðβer'tiðo/ *a* unnoticed; inattentive; inadvertent, unintentional; negligent

inafectado /inafek'taðo/ *a* unaffected, natural

inagotable /inago'taβle/ *a* inexhaustible, unfailing; abundant

inaguantable /inaguan'taβle/ *a* unbearable, intolerable

inajenable /inahe'naβle/ *a* inalienable

inalterable /inalte'raβle/ *a* unalterable

inamovibilidad /inamoβiβili'ðað/ *f*, immovability

inamovible /inamo'βiβle/ *a* immovable

inanición /inani'θion; inani'sion/ *f*, inanition

inanimado /inani'maðo/ *a* inanimate

inapagable /inapa'gaβle/ *a* inextinguishable

inapelable /inape'laβle/ *a* unappealable; irremediable, inevitable

inapetencia /inape'tenθia; inape'tensia/ *f*, lack of appetite

inaplazable /inapla'θaβle; inapla'saβle/ *a* undeferable, unable to be postponed

inaplicación /inaplika'θion; inaplika'sion/ *f*, laziness, inattention, negligence

inaplicado /inapli'kaðo/ *a* lazy; inattentive; careless

inapreciable /inapre'θiaβle; inapre'siaβle/ *a* inappreciable; invaluable

inarticulado /inartiku'laðo/ *a* inarticulate; out of reach

inasequible /inase'kiβle/ *a* unattainable; out of reach

inaudito /inau'ðito/ *a* unheard of, unprecedented; extraordinary, strange

inauguración /inaugura'θion; inaugura-'sion/ *f*, inauguration; induction; inception, commencement

inaugurar /inaugu'rar/ *vt* to inaugurate; induct

inaveriguable /inaβeri'guaβle/ *a* unascertainable

inca /'inka/ *mf* Inca

incaico /in'kaiko/ *a* Incan

incalificable /inkalifi'kaβle/ *a* indescribable, unclassable; vile

incandescencia /inkandes'θenθia; inkandes'sensia/ *f*, incandescence, white heat

incandescente /inkandes'θente; inkandes'sente/ *a* incandescent

incansable /inkan'saβle/ *a* indefatigable; unflagging; unwearying

incapacidad /inkapaθi'ðað; inkapasi'ðað/ *f*, incapacity; incompetence

incapacitar /inkapaθi'tar; inkapasi'tar/ *vt* to incapacitate; disable

incapaz /inka'paθ; inka'pas/ *a* incapable, incompetent; inefficient

incasable /inka'saβle/ *a* unmarriageable; antimarriage

incautarse /inkau'tarse/ *vr* to seize, take possession (of)

incauto /in'kauto/ *a* incautious; unwary

incendiar /inθen'diar/ *vt* to set on fire, set alight

incendiario /inθen'diario; insen'diario/ (-ia) *a* and *n* incendiary

incendio /in'θendio; in'sendio/ *m*, conflagration, fire; consuming passion

incensar /inθen'sar; insen'sar/ *vt irr Eccl.* to cense, incense; flatter. See **acertar**

incensario /inθen'sario; insen'sario/ *m*, incense burner, incensory

incentivo /inθen'tiβo; insen'tiβo/ *m*, incentive; encouragement

incertidumbre /inθerti'ðumbre; inserti'ðumbre/ *f*, uncertainty, incertitude

incesable, incesante /inθe'saβle, inθe-'sante; inse'saβle, inse'sante/ *a* incessant, continuous

incesto /in'θesto; in'sesto/ *m*, incest

incestuoso /inθes'tuoso; inses'tuoso/ *a* incestuous

incidencia /inθi'ðenθia; insi'ðensia/ *f*, incidence

incidente /inθi'ðente; insi'ðente/ *a* incidental. *m*, incident, event, occurrence

incidir /inθi'ðir; insi'ðir/ *vi* (*with en*) to incur, fall into (e.g. *Incidió en el pecado*, He fell into sin)

incienso /in'θienso; in'sienso/ *m*, incense; flattery

incierto /in'θierto; in'sierto/ *a* untrue, false; uncertain; unknown

incinerador /inθinera'ðor; insinera'ðor/ *m*, incinerator

incinerar /inθine'rar; insine'rar/ *vt* incinerate, reduce to ashes

incipiente /inθi'piente; insi'piente/ *a* incipient

incircunciso /inθirkun'θiso; insirkun'siso/ *a* uncircumcised

incisión /inθi'sion; insi'sion/ *f*, incision

incisivo /inθi'siβo; insi'siβo/ *a* sharp, keen; incisive, sarcastic, caustic

inciso /in'θiso; in'siso/ *m*, clause; comma

incitación /inθita'θion; insita'sion/ *f*, incitement; *Fig.* spur, stimulus

incitar /inθi'tar; insi'tar/ *vt* to incite; stimulate, encourage

incivil /inθi'βil; insi'βil/ *a* rude, discourteous, uncivil

incivilidad /inθiβili'ðað; insiβili'ðað/ *f*, rudeness, incivility

inclasificable /inklasifi'kaβle/ *a* unclassifiable

inclemencia /inkle'menθia; inkle'mensia/ *f*, harshness, severity; inclemency (of the weather). **a la i.,** at the mercy of the elements

inclemente /inkle'mente/ *a* inclement

inclinación /inklina'θion; inklina'sion/ *f*, inclination; slope; slant; tendency, propensity; predilection, fondness; bow (in greeting); *Geom.* inclination

inclinar /inkli'nar/ *vt* to incline, tilt, slant; bow; bend; influence; persuade; —*vi* resemble; —*vr* lean; stoop; tilt; tend, incline (to); view favorably (e.g. *Me inclino a creerlo*, I am inclined to believe it)

ínclito /in'klito/ *a* famous, celebrated

incluir /in'kluir/ *vt irr* to comprise, embrace, contain; include; take into account. See **huir**

inclusa /in'klusa/ *f*, foundling home

inclusión /inklu'sion/ *f*, inclusion; relationship, intercourse, friendship

inclusive /inklu'siβe/ *adv* including

inclusivo /inklu'siβo/ *a* inclusive

incluso /in'kluso/ *adv* including, inclusive —*prep* even

incoar /inko'ar/ *vt* to begin (especially lawsuits)

incoativo /inkoa'tiβo/ *a* inceptive

incobrable /inko'βraβle/ *a* irrecoverable; irredeemable

incógnita /in'kognita/ *f*, *Math.* X; unknown quantity; secret motive; unknown lady

incógnito /in'kognito/ *a* unknown. *m*, incognito, assumed name, disguise

incoherente /inkoe'rente/ *a* incoherent, disconnected; illogical

íncola /'inkola/ *mf* resident, dweller, inhabitant

incoloro /inko'loro/ *a* colorless, uncolored

incólume /in'kolume/ *a* unharmed, unscathed; untouched, undamaged

incombustibilidad /inkombustiβili'ðað/ *f*, incombustibility

incommutable /inkommu'taβle/ *a* unalterable, immutable, unchangeable

incomodar /inkomo'ðar/ *vt* to disturb, incommode, inconvenience; annoy; —*vr* disturb oneself, put oneself out; grow angry. ¡No se incomode! Please don't move!; Please don't be angry!

incomodidad /inkomoði'ðað/ *f*, discomfort; inconvenience; trouble, upset; annoyance

incómodo /in'komoðo/ *a* uncomfortable; inconvenient; troublesome, tiresome. *m*, discomfort; inconvenience

incompartible /inkompar'tiβle/ *a* indivisible

incompasivo /inkompa'siβo/ *a* unsympathetic, hard

incompetencia /inkompe'tenθia; inkompe'tensia/ *f*, incompetence

incomplejo, incomplexo /inkom'pleho, inkom'plekso/ *a* noncomplex, simple

incomponible /inkompo'niβle/ *a* unrepairable, unmendable

incomprensible /inkompren'siβle/ *a* incomprehensible

incomprensión /inkompren'sion/ *f*, incomprehension

incomunicado /inkomuni'kaðo/ *a* in solitary confinement (of a prisoner)

incomunicar /inkomuni'kar/ *vt* to sentence to solitary confinement; isolate, deprive of means of communication; —*vr* become a recluse

inconcebible /inkonθe'βiβle; inkonse-'βiβle/ *a* inconceivable

inconciliable /inkonθi'liaβle; inkonsi-'liaβle/ *a* irreconcilable

incondicional /inkondiθio'nal; inkondisio'nal/ *a* unconditional

inconexión /inkone'ksion/ *f*, disconnectedness

inconexo /inkone'kso/ *a* unconnected; incoherent

inconfeso /inkon'feso/ *a* unconfessed

incongruencia /inkoŋgru'enθia; inkoŋgru'ensia/ *f*, incongruity

incongruente /inkoŋgru'ente/ *a* incongruous, inappropriate

inconmovible /inkomo'βiβle/ *a* immovable; unflinching, unshakable

inconquistable /inkonkis'taβle/ *a* unconquerable; *Fig.* resolute, inflexible

inconsciencia /inkon'sθienθia; inkons'siensia/ *f*, unconsciousness; subconscious

inconsciente /inkon'sθiente; inkons-'siente/ *a* unconscious, involuntary; subconscious

inconsecuencia /inkonse'kuenθia; inkonse'kuensia/ *f*, inconsequence; inconsistency

inconsecuente /inkonse'kuente/ *a* inconsequential; inconsistent

inconsideración /inkonsiðera'θion; inkonsiðera'sion/ *f*, thoughtlessness

inconsiderado /inkonsiðe'raðo/ *a* thoughtless; heedless; selfish

inconsiguiente /inkonsi'giente/ *a* illogical, inconsistent

inconsistente /inkonsis'tente/ *a* inconsistent

inconstancia /inkons'tanθia; inkons'tansia/ *f*, inconstancy, infidelity

inconstante /inkons'tante/ *a* inconstant, fickle

inconstitucional /inkonstituθio'nal; inkonstitusio'nal/ *a* unconstitutional

incontaminado /inkontami'ñaðo/ *a* uncontaminated

incontestable /inkontes'taβle/ *a* undeniable, unquestionable

incontinencia /inkonti'nenθia; inkonti'nensia/ *f*, incontinence

incontinente /inkonti'nente/ *a* incontinent

incontrastable /inkontras'taβle/ *a* insuperable, invincible; undeniable, unanswerable; *Fig.* unshakable, inconvincible

incontrovertible /inkontroβer'tiβle/ *a* undeniable, incontrovertible

inconvencible /inkomben'θiβle; inkomben'siβle/ *a* inconvincible

inconveniencia /inkombe'nienθia; inkombe'niensia/ *f*, discomfort; inconvenience; unsuitability

inconveniente /inkombe'niente/ *a* awkward, inconvenient; uncomfortable; inappropriate. *m*, inconvenience; obstacle, impediment; disadvantage

incorporar /inkorpo'rar/ *vt* to incorporate; cause to sit up, lift up; —*vr* sit up, raise oneself; become a member, join (associations); be incorporated; blend, mix

incorpóreo /inkor'poreo/ *a* incorporeal; immaterial

incorrección /inkorrek'θion; inkorrek'sion/ *f*, incorrectness; indecorum, impropriety

incorrecto /inko'rrekto/ *a* incorrect; indecorous, unbecoming, improper

incorregible /inkorre'hiβle/ *a* incorrigible

incorrupción /inkorrup'θion; inkorrup'sion/ *f*, incorruption; purity; integrity; wholesomeness

incorrupto /inko'rrupto/ *a* incorrupt; pure; chaste

incredulidad /inkreðuli'ðað/ *f*, incredulity, scepticism

incrédulo /in'kreðulo/ **(-la)** *a* incredulous; atheistic; unbelieving. —*n* atheist; unbeliever, sceptic

increíble /inkre'iβle/ *a* incredible; marvelous, extraordinary

incremento /inkre'mento/ *m*, increment, increase

increpación /inkrepa'θion; inkrepa'sion/ *f*, scolding, harsh rebuke

increpar /inkre'par/ *vt* to scold, rebuke harshly

incriminante /inkrimi'nante/ *a* incriminating

incriminar /inkrimi'nar/ *vt* to incriminate, accuse; exaggerate (a charge, etc.)

incrustación /inkrusta'θion; inkrusta-'sion/ f, incrustation; *Art.* inlay

incubación /inkuβa'θion; inkuβa'sion/ f, hatching; *Med.* incubation

incubadora /inkuβa'ðora/ f, incubator (for chickens)

incubar /inku'βar/ vi to sit on eggs (of hens); —vt hatch; *Med.* incubate

inculcar /inkul'kar/ vt to press one thing against another; instill, inculcate; —vr grow more fixed in one's views

inculpable /inkul'paβle/ a blameless, innocent

inculpar /inkul'par/ vt to blame; accuse

incultivable /inkulti'βaβle/ a uncultivatable; untillable

inculto /in'kulto/ a uncultivated, untilled; uncultured; uncivilized

incultura /inkul'tura/ f, lack of cultivation; lack of culture

incumbencia /inkum'benθia; inkumben-sia/ f, obligation, moral responsibility, duty

incumbir /inkum'bir/ vi to be incumbent on; concern

incurable /inku'raβle/ a incurable; inveterate, hopeless

incuria /in'kuria/ f, negligence, carelessness

incurrir /inku'rrir/ vi (*with en*) to fall into (error, etc.); incur (dislike, etc.)

incursión /inkur'sion/ f, incursion; inroad

indagación /indaga'θion; indaga'sion/ f, investigation, inquiry

indagar /inda'gar/ vt to investigate, examine; inquire. **i. precios,** to inquire about prices

indebido /inde'βiðo/ a undue, immoderate improper; illegal, illicit

indecencia /inde'θenθia; inde'sensia/ f, indecency; obscenity; impropriety

indecente /inde'θente; inde'sente/ a indecent; obscene; improper

indecible /inde'θiβle; inde'siβle/ a unutterable, ineffable, unspeakable

indeciso /inde'θiso; inde'siso/ a undecided; hesitant, irresolute; vague; noncommittal

indeclinable /indekli'naβle/ a obligatory; unavoidable; *Gram.* indeclinable, uninflected

indecoro /inde'koro/ m, impropriety, indecorum

indecoroso /indeko'roso/ a indecorous, unbecoming; base, mean

indefectible /indefek'tiβle/ a unfailing; perfect

indefectiblemente /indefektiβle'mente/ adv invariably

indefendible /indefen'diβle/ a indefensible

indefenso /inde'fenso/ a unprotected, defenseless

indefinible /indefi'niβle/ a indefinable, vague; indescribable

indefinido /indefi'niðo/ a indefinite, vague; undefined; *Gram.* indefinite

indeleble /inde'leβle/ a indelible

indeliberado /indeliβe'raðo/ a unpremeditated; unconsidered

indemme /in'demme/ a unharmed, undamaged

indemnidad /indemni'ðað/ f, indemnity

indemnización /indemniθa'θion; indemnisa'sion/ f, compensation, indemnification; indemnity

indemnizar /indemni'θar; indemni'sar/ vt to indemnify, compensate

indemostrable /indemo'straβle/ a indemonstrable, incapable of demonstration

independencia /indepen'denθia; indepen'densia/ f, independence

independiente /indepen'diente/ a independent; self-contained

indescifrable /indesθi'fraβle; indessi'fraβle/ a undecipherable; illegible

indeterminado /indetermi'naðo/ a indeterminate; vague, doubtful, uncertain; hesitant, irresolute; *Math.* indeterminate

indiano /in'diano/ (**-na**) a and n Indian; East Indian; West Indian. m, nouveau riche, one who returns rich from the Western Hemisphere

indicación /indika'θion; indika'sion/ f, indication; sign, evidence; intimation, hint

indicador /indika'ðor/ a indicative. m, indicator. **i. del nivel de gasolina,** gas gauge

indicar /indi'kar/ vt to indicate; show; point out; simply, suggest; intimate

indicativo /indika'tiβo/ a indicative —a and m, *Gram.* indicative

índice /'indiθe; 'indise/ m, index; indication, sign; library catalog; catalog room; hand (of a clock); pointer, needle (of instruments); gnomon (of a sundial); *Math.* index; foretinger. **I. expurgatorio,** the Index

indicio /in'diθio; in'disio/ m, indication; sign; evidence. **indicios vehementes,** circumstantial evidence

indiferencia /indife'renθia; indife'rensia/ f, indifference

indiferente /indife'rente/ a indifferent

indígena /in'dihena/ a native, indigenous. mf native

indigencia /indi'henθia; indi'hensia/ f, destitution, indigence; impecuniosity

indigente /indi'hente/ a destitute, indigent; impecunious

indigestión /indihes'tion/ f, indigestion

indigesto /indi'hesto/ a indigestible; *Lit.* muddled, confused; unsociable, brusque

indignación /indigna'θion; indigna'sion/ f, indignation, anger

indignado /indig'naðo/ a indignant

indignar /indig'nar/ vt to anger, make indignant; —vr grow angry

indignidad /indigni'ðað/ f, unworthiness; indignity; personal affront

indigno /in'digno/ a unworthy; base, despicable

indio /'indio/ (**-ia**) a Indian; blue —n Indian. m, indium

indirecta /indi'rekta/ f, hint, covert suggestion, innuendo. *Inf.* **i. del padre Cobos**, strong hint

indirecto /indi'rekto/ a indirect

indisciplinado /indisθipli'naðo; indissipli'naðo/ a undisciplined

indiscreción /indiskre'θion; indiskre'sion/ f, indiscretion

indiscreto /indis'kreto/ a indiscreet

indiscutible /indisku'tiβle/ a unquestionable, undeniable

indisoluble /indiso'luβle/ a indissoluble

indispensable /indispen'saβle/ a indispensable

indisponer /indispo'ner/ *vt irr* to make unfit or incapable; indispose, make ill; (*with con or contra*) set against, make trouble with; —*vr* be indisposed; (*with con or contra*) quarrel with. See **poner**

indisposición /indisposi'θion; indisposi'sion/ f, reluctance, disinclination; indisposition, brief illness

indisputable /indispu'taβle/ a indisputable

indistinguible /indistiŋ'guiβle/ a undistinguishable

indistinto /indis'tinto/ a indistinct; indeterminate; vague

individual /indiβi'ðual/ a individual; peculiar, characteristic, m, (tennis) single

individuo /indi'βiðuo/ (**-ua**) a individual; indivisible. m, individual; member, associate; *Inf.* self —*n Inf.* person

indiviso /indi'βiso/ a undivided

indócil /in'doθil; in'dosil/ a unmanageable; disobedient; brittle, unpliable (of metals)

indocilidad /indoθili'ðað; indosili'ðað/ f, indocility; disobedience; brittleness (of metals)

índole /'indole/ f, temperament, nature; kind, sort

indolencia /indo'lenθia; indo'lensia/ f, idleness, indolence

indolente /indo'lente/ a nonpainful; indifferent, insensible; idle, indolent

indoloro /indo'loro/ a painless

indomable /indo'maβle/ a untamable; invincible; indomitable; ungovernable, unmanageable

indómito /in'domito/ a untamed; untamable; unmanageable, unruly; indomitable

indubitable /induβi'taβle/ a unquestionable

inducción /induk'θion; induk'sion/ f, persuasion; *Phys.* induction

inducir /indu'θir; indu'sir/ *vt irr* to persuade, prevail upon; induce; infer, conclude. See **conducir**

indudable /indu'ðaβle/ a indubitable

indulgente /indul'hente/ a indulgent, tender; tolerant

indultar /indul'tar/ *vt* to pardon; exempt

indulto /in'dulto/ m, amnesty; exemption; forgiveness; *Eccl.* indult

indumentaria /indumen'taria/ f, clothing; outfit (of clothes)

industria /in'dustria/ f, assiduity, industriousness; pains, effort, ingenuity; industry. **i. pesada**, heavy industry. **i. cárnica**, meat industry. **i. extractivos**, mining industry

industrial /indus'trial/ a industrial. m, industrialist

industrialismo /industria'lismo/ m, industrialism

industriar /indus'triar/ *vt* to teach, train; —*vr* find a way, manage, succeed in

industrioso /indus'trioso/ a industrious; diligent, assiduous

inédito /i'neðito/ a unpublished; unedited

inefable /ine'faβle/ a ineffable

ineficacia /inefi'kaθia; inefi'kasia/ f, inefficiency; ineffectiveness

ineficaz /inefi'kaθ; inefi'kas/ a ineffective; inefficient

ineludible /inelu'ðiβle/ a unavoidable

ineptitud /inepti'tuð/ f, ineptitude

inepto /i'nepto/ a inept, incompetent; unfit, unsuitable

inequívoco /ine'kiβoko/ a unequivocal

inercia /i'nerθia; i'nersia/ f, inertia

inerme /i'nerme/ a defenseless, unprotected; (*Bot. Zool.*) unarmed

inerte /i'nerte/ a inert

inescrutable /ineskru'taβle/ a inscrutable, unfathomable

inesperado /inespe'raðo/ a unexpected, sudden

inestable /ines'taβle/ a unstable

inestimable /inesti'maβle/ a inestimable

inevitable /ineβi'taβle/ a inevitable

inexactitud /ineksakti'tuð/ f, inexactitude, inaccuracy; error, mistake

inexacto /ine'ksakto/ a inexact, inaccurate; erroneous

inexcusable /ineksku'saβle/ a inexcusable, unforgivable; indispensable

inexhausto /ineks'austo/ a inexhaustible

inexistente /ineksis'tente/ a nonexistent

inexorable /inekso'raβle/ a inexorable

inexperiencia /inekspe'rienθia; inekspe'riensia/ f, inexperience

inexperto /ineks'perto/ a inexperienced; inexpert

inexplorado /ineksplo'raðo/ a unexplored

inexplosible /ineksplo'siβle/ a inexplosive

inexpresivo /inekspre'siβo/ a inexpressive; reticent

inexpugnable /inekspug'naβle/ a impregnable; *Fig.* unshakable, firm; obstinate

inextinguible /inekstiŋ'guiβle/ a inextinguishable; everlasting, perpetual

infalibilidad /infaliβili'ðað/ f, infallibility

infalible /infa'liβle/ a infallible

infamación /infama'θion; infama'sion/ f, defamation

infamador /infama'ðor/ (**-ra**) a slandering —*n* slanderer

infamar /infa'mar/ *vt* to defame, slander

infame /in'fame/ *a* infamous, vile

infamia /in'famia/ *f,* infamy; baseness, vileness

infancia /in'fanθia; in'fansia/ *f,* infancy, babyhood; childhood

infantería /infante'ria/ *f,* infantry

infantil /infan'til/ *a* infantile, babyish; innocent, candid

infatigable /infati'gaβle/ *a* unwearying, indefatigable

infatuación /infatua'θion; infatua'sion/ *f,* infatuation

infatuar /infa'tuar/ *vt* to infatuate; —*vr* become infatuated

infausto /in'fausto/ *a* unlucky, unfortunate

infección /infek'θion; infek'sion/ *f,* infection

infeccioso /infek'θioso; infek'sioso/ *a* infectious

infectar /infek'tar/ *vt* to infect; corrupt, pervert; —*vr* become infected; be corrupted

infecto /in'fekto/ *a* infected; corrupt, perverted; tainted

infecundo /infe'kundo/ *a* sterile, barren

infelice /infe'liθe; infe'lise/ *a* *Poet.* unhappy, unfortunate

infelicidad /infeliθi'ðað; infelisi'ðað/ *f,* unhappiness

infeliz /infe'liθ; infe'lis/ *a* unhappy; unfortunate; *Inf.* simple, good-hearted

inferencia /infe'renθia; infe'rensia/ *f,* inference, connection

inferior /infe'rior/ *a* inferior; lower; second-rate; subordinate. *mf* inferior, subordinate

inferioridad /inferiori'ðað/ *f,* inferiority

inferir /infe'rir/ *vt irr* to infer, deduce; involve, imply; occasion; inflict. See **sentir**

infernáculo /infer'nakulo/ *m,* hopscotch

infernal /infer'nal/ *a* infernal; devilish, fiendish; wicked, inhuman; *Inf.* confounded

inferno /in'ferno/ *a* *Poet.* infernal

infértil /in'fertil/ *a* infertile

infestación /infesta'θion; infesta'sion/ *f,* infestation

infestar /infes'tar/ *vt* to infest, swarm in; infect; injure, damage

infesto /in'festo/ *a* *Poet.* harmful, dangerous

inficionar /infiθio'nar; infisio'nar/ *vt* to infect; pervert, corrupt

infidelidad /infiðeli'ðað/ *f,* faithlessness, infidelity; disbelief in Christian religion; unbelievers, infidels

infidencia /infi'ðenθia; infi'ðensia/ *f,* disloyalty, faithlessness

infiel /in'fiel/ *a* unfaithful, disloyal; inaccurate, incorrect; infidel, unbelieving. *mf* infidel, nonbeliever

infierno /in'fierno/ *m,* hell; hades (gen. *pl*); *Fig. Inf.* inferno. **en el quinto i.,** very far off, at the end of the world. **en los quintos infiernos,** at the end of nowhere

infiltración /infiltra'θion; infiltra'sion/ *f,* infiltration; inculcation, implantation

infiltrar /infil'trar/ *vt* to infiltrate; imbue, inculcate

ínfimo /'infimo/ *a* lowest; meanest, vilest, most base; cheapest, poorest (in quality)

infinidad /infini'ðað/ *f,* infinity; infinitude; great number

infinitivo /infini'tiβo/ *a and m, Gram.* infinitive

infinito /infi'nito/ *a* infinite; endless; boundless; countless. *m, Math.* infinite —*adv* excessively, immensely

inflación /infla'θion; infla'sion/ *f,* inflation; distension; pride, vanity

inflamable /infla'maβle/ *a* inflammable

inflamación /inflama'θion; inflama'sion/ *f,* inflammation; *Engin.* ignition

inflamador /inflama'ðor/ *a* inflammatory

inflamar /infla'mar/ *vt* to set on fire; *Fig.* inflame, excite; —*vr* take fire; *Med.* become inflamed; grow hot or excited

inflamatorio /inflama'torio/ *a Med.* inflammatory

inflar /in'flar/ *vt* to inflate; blow up, distend; throw out (one's chest); exaggerate; make haughty or vain; —*vr* be swollen or inflated; be puffed up with pride

inflexibilidad /infleksiβili'ðað/ *f,* inflexibility; rigidity; immovability, constancy

inflexión /infle'ksion/ *f,* bending, flexion; diffraction (optics); inflection

infligir /infli'hir/ *vt* to impose, inflict (penalties)

influencia /influ'enθia; influ'ensia/ *f,* influence; power, authority; *Elec.* charge

influir /in'fluir/ *vt irr* to influence; affect; (*with en*) cooperate in, assist with. See **huir**

influjo /in'fluho/ *m,* influence; flux, inflow of the tide

influyente /influ'yente/ *a* influential

información /informa'θion; informa'sion/ *f,* information; legal inquiry; report; research, investigation

informador /informa'ðor/ **(-ra)** *a* informing, acquainting —*n* informant

informal /infor'mal/ *a* informal, irregular; unreliable (of persons); unconventional

informalidad /informali'ðað/ *f,* irregularity; unconventionality; unreliability

informar /infor'mar/ *vt* to inform, acquaint with; —*vi Law.* plead; —*vr* (*with de, en, or sobre*) find out about, investigate

informática /infor'matika/ *f,* information sciences

informativo /informa'tiβo/ *a* informative

informe /in'forme/ *a* formless, shapeless. *m,* report, statement; information; *Law.* plea; *pl* data, particulars; references

infortificable /infortifi'kaβle/ *a* unfortifiable

infortuna /infor'tuna/ *f, Astrol.* evil influence

infortunado /infortu'naðo/ a unfortunate

infortunio /infor'tunio/ m, misfortune; unhappiness, adversity; mischance, ill luck

infracción /infrak'θion; infrak'sion/ f, transgression, infringement

infracto /in'frakto/ a imperturbable

infrangible /infran'hiβle/ a unbreakable

infranqueable /infranke'aβle/ a insuperable, unsurmountable

infrarrojo /infra'rroho/ a infrared

infrascrito /infras'krito/ a undersigned; undermentioned

infringir /infrin'hir/ vt to infringe, transgress, break

infructífero /infruk'tifero/ a unfruitful; worthless, useless

infructuosidad /infruktuosi'ðað/ f, unfruitfulness; worthlessness, uselessness

infructuoso /infruk'tuoso/ a fruitless; useless, worthless

infundado /infun'daðo/ a unfounded, groundless

infundio /in'fundio/ m, Inf. nonsense, untruth

infundir /infun'dir/ vt to infuse, imbue with

infusión /infu'sion/ f, infusion

ingeniar /inhe'niar/ vt to devise, concoct, plan; —vr contrive, find a way, manage

ingeniería /inhenie'ria/ f, engineering

ingeniero /inhe'niero/ m, engineer. **i. agrónomo,** agricultural engineer. **i. de caminos, canales y puertos,** civil engineer. **i. radiotelegrafista,** radio engineer. **cuerpo de ingenieros,** royal engineers

ingenio /in'henio/ m, mind; inventive capacity; imaginative talent; man of genius; talent, cleverness; ingeniousness; machine; guillotine (bookbinding)

ingeniosidad /inheniosi'ðað/ f, ingeniousness; witticism, clever remark

ingenioso /inhe'nioso/ a talented, clever; ingenious

ingénito /in'henito/ a unengendered, unconceived; innate, inborn

ingente /in'hente/ a huge, enormous

ingenuidad /inhenui'ðað/ f, ingenuousness, naiveté

ingenuo /in'henuo/ a ingenuous, naive, artless, unaffected

Inglaterra /ingla'terra/ England

ingle /'ingle/ f, groin

inglés /in'gles/ (**-esa**) a English; British —n Englishman; Briton. m, English (language); Inf. creditor. **a la inglesa,** in English fashion. **marcharse a la inglesa,** Inf. to take French leave

ingobernable /ingoβer'naβle/ a ungovernable, unruly

ingratitud /ingrati'tuð/ f, ingratitude

ingrato /in'grato/ a ungrateful; irksome, thankless; disagreeable

ingrávido /in'graβiðo/ a light weight

ingrediente /ingre'ðiente/ m, ingredient

ingresar /ingre'sar/ vi to return, come in

(money); (with en) join, become a member of, enter

ingreso /in'greso/ m, joining, entering, admission; Com. money received; opening, commencement; pl earnings, takings, revenue

inhábil /in'aβil/ a unskillful; unpracticed; incompetent, unfit; unsuitable, ill-chosen

inhabilidad /inaβili'ðað/ f, unskillfulness; incompetence; unsuitability; inability

inhabilitación /inaβilita'θion; inaβilita'sion/ f, incapacitation; disqualification; disablement

inhabilitar /inaβili'tar/ vt to make ineligible; disqualify; incapacitate, make unfit; —vr become ineligible; be incapacitated

inhabitable /inaβi'taβle/ a uninhabitable

inhabitado /inaβi'taðo/ a uninhabited, deserted

inhalación /inala'θion; inala'sion/ f, inhalation

inhalador /inala'ðor/ m, Med. inhaler

inhalar /ina'lar/ vt to inhale

inhallable /ina'ʎaβle; ina'yaβle/ a nowhere to be found, unfindable

inhereditable /inhereði'taβle/ a uninheritable

inherencia /ine'renθia; ine'rensia/ f, inherency

inherente /ine'rente/ a inherent, innate

inhestar /ines'tar/ vt irr to raise, lift up; erect. See **acertar**

inhibición /iniβi'θion; iniβi'sion/ f, inhibition

inhibir /ini'βir/ vt Law. to inhibit; —vr inhibit or restrain oneself. See **prohibir**

inhibitorio /iniβi'torio/ a Law. inhibitory

inhonesto /ino'nesto/ a indecent, obscene; immodest

inhospedable, inhospitalario /inospe'ðaβle, inospita'lario/ a inhospitable; bleak, uninviting; exposed

inhospitalidad /inospitali'ðað/ f, inhospitality

inhumación /inuma'θion; inuma'sion/ f, inhumation, burial

inhumadora /inuma'ðora/ f, crematory

inhumanidad /inumani'ðað/ f, inhumanity; brutality

inhumano /inu'mano/ a inhuman; brutal, barbarous

inhumar /inu'mar/ vt to bury, inter

iniciación /iniθia'θion; inisia'sion/ f, initiation

iniciador /iniθia'ðor; inisia'ðor/ (**-ra**) a initiating; —n initiator

inicial /ini'θial; ini'sial/ a and f, initial

iniciar /ini'θiar; ini'siar/ vt to initiate; admit, introduce; originate; —vr be initiated; Eccl. take minor or first orders

iniciativa /iniθia'tiβa; inisia'tiβa/ f, initiative

inicuo /ini'kuo/ a iniquitous, most unjust, wicked

inimaginable /inimahi'naβle/ a inconceivable

inimicísimo /inimi'θisimo; inimi'sisimo/ *a superl* **enemigo** most hostile

ininteligible /ininteli'hiβle/ *a* unintelligible

iniquidad /iniki'ðað/ *f*, iniquity, wickedness

injerir /inhe'rir/ *vt irr* to insert, place within, introduce; interpolate; —*vr* meddle. See **sentir**

injertar /inher'tar/ *vt Agr.* to graft

injerto /in'herto/ *m*, *Agr.* graft; grafting; grafted plant, briar, or tree

injuria /in'huria/ *f*, insult; slander; outrage; wrong, injustice; harm, damage

injuriador /inhuria'ðor/ **(-ra)** *a* insulting —*n* offender, persecutor

injuriar /inhu'riar/ *vt* to insult; slander; outrage; wrong, persecute; harm, damage

injurioso /inhu'rioso/ *a* insulting; slanderous; offensive, abusive; harmful

injusticia /inhus'tiθia; inhus'tisia/ *f*, injustice; lack of justice; unjust action

injustificable /inhustifi'kaβle/ *a* unjustifiable

injustificado /inhustifi'kaðo/ *a* unjustified

injusto /in'husto/ *a* unjust; unrighteous

inllevable /inʎe'βaβle; inye'βaβle/ *a* unbearable, intolerable

inmaculado /imaku'laðo/ *a* immaculate, pure

inmarcesible, inmarchitable /imarθe'siβle, imartʃi'taβle; imarsesiβle, imartʃitaβle/ *a* unfading, imperishable

inmaterial /imate'rial/ *a* incorporeal; immaterial

inmaturo /ima'turo/ *a* immature; unripe

inmediación /imeðia'θion; imeðia'sion/ *f*, nearness, proximity; contact; *pl* outskirts, neighborhood, environs

inmediatamente /imeðiata'mente/ *adv* near; immediately, at once

inmediato /ime'ðiato/ *a* adjoining, close, nearby; immediate, prompt

inmejorable /imeho'raβle/ *a* unsurpassable, unbeatable

inmemorable, inmemorial /imemo'raβle, imemo'rial/ *a* immemorial

inmensidad /imensi'ðað/ *f*, vastness, huge extent; infinity; infinite space; immensity; huge number

inmenso /i'menso/ *a* vast; infinite; immense; innumerable

inmensurable /imensu'raβle/ *a* immeasurable, incalculable

inmerecido /imere'θiðo; imere'siðo/ *a* undeserved, unmerited

inmérito /i'merito/ *a* wrongful, unjust

inmeritorio /imeri'torio/ *a* unmeritorious, unpraiseworthy

inmersión /imer'sion/ *f*, immersion; dip

inmigración /imigra'θion; imigra'sion/ *f*, immigration

inmigrante /imi'grante/ *a and mf* immigrant

inmigrar /imi'grar/ *vi* to immigrate

inminente /imi'nente/ *a* imminent

inmiscuir /imis'kuir/ *vt* to mix; —*vr* meddle. May be conjugated regularly or like **huir**

inmobiliario /imoβi'liario/ *a* concerning real estate

inmoble /i'moβle/ *a* immovable; motionless, immobile, stationary; *Fig.* unshakable, unflinching

inmoderación /imoðera'θion; imoðera'sion/ *f*, immoderateness, excess

inmoderado /imoðe'raðo/ *a* immoderate; unrestrained, excessive

inmodestia /imo'ðestia/ *f*, immodesty

inmodesto /imo'ðesto/ *a* immodest

inmolar /imo'lar/ *vt* to immolate; *Fig.* sacrifice, give up; —*vr Fig.* sacrifice oneself

inmoral /imo'ral/ *a* immoral

inmortal /imor'tal/ *a* immortal

inmortalizar /imortali'θar; imortali'sar/ *vt* to immortalize

inmotivado /imoti'βaðo/ *a* unfounded, without reason

inmoto /i'moto/ *a* motionless, stationary

inmóvil /i'moβil/ *a* immovable, fixed; motionless; steadfast, constant

inmovilizar /imoβili'θar; imoβili'sar/ *vt* to immobilize

inmueble /i'mueβle/ *m*, *Law.* immovable estate

inmundicia /imun'diθia; imun'disia/ *f*, filth, nastiness; dirt; rubbish, refuse; obscenity, indecency

inmundo /i'mundo/ *a* dirty, filthy; obscene, indecent; unclean

inmune /i'mune/ *a* exempt; *Med.* immune

inmunidad /imuni'ðað/ *f*, exemption; immunity

inmunizar /imuni'θar; imuni'sar/ *vt* to immunize

inmutable /imu'taβle/ *a* immutable, unchangeable; imperturbable

inmutación /imuta'θion; imuta'sion/ *f*, change, alteration, difference

inmutar /imu'tar/ *vt* to change, alter, vary; —*vr* change one's expression (through fear, etc.)

innato /in'nato/ *a* innate; inherent; instinctive, inborn

innatural /innatu'ral/ *a* unnatural

innavegable /innaβe'gaβle/ *a* unnavigable; unseaworthy (of ships)

innecesario /inneθe'sario; innese'sario/ *a* unnecessary

innegable /inne'gaβle/ *a* undeniable; indisputable, irrefutable

innocuo /inno'kuo/ *a* harmless, innocuous

innovación /innoβa'θion; innoβa'sion/ *f*, innovation

innovador /innoβa'ðor/ **(-ra)** *a* innovatory —*n* innovator

innovar /inno'βar/ *vt* to introduce innovations

innumerable /innume'raβle/ *a* innumerable, countless

innúmero /in'numero/ a countless, innumerable

inobediente /inoβe'ðiente/ a disobedient

inobservable /inoβser'βaβle/ a unobservable

inobservante /inoβser'βante/ a unobservant

inocencia /ino'θenθia; ino'sensia/ f, innocence; simplicity, candor; harmlessness

inocentada /inoθen'taða; inosen'taða/ f, Inf. naïve remark or action; fool's trap; practical joke

inocente /ino'θente; ino'sente/ a innocent; candid, simple; harmless; easily deceived

inocentón /inoθen'ton; inosen'ton/ a Inf. extremely credulous and easily taken in

inoculación /inokula'θion; inokula'sion/ f, inoculation

inoculador /inokula'ðor/ m, inoculator

inocular /inoku'lar/ vt to inoculate; pervert, corrupt; contaminate

inodoro /ino'ðoro/ a odorless. m, toilet, lavatory

inofensivo /inofen'siβo/ a inoffensive, harmless

inolvidable /inolβi'ðaβle/ a unforgettable

inoperable /inope'raβle/ a inoperable

inopia /i'nopia/ f, poverty; scarcity

inopinado /inopi'naðo/ a unexpected, sudden

inoportunidad /inoportuni'ðað/ f, inopportuneness, unseasonableness; unsuitability

inoportuno /inopor'tuno/ a inopportune, untimely

inorgánico /inor'ganiko/ a inorganic

inoxidable /inoksi'ðaβle/ a rustless

inquebrantable /inkeβran'taβle/ a unbreakable; final, irrevocable

inquietador /inkieta'ðor/ **(-ra)** a disturbing —n disturber

inquietar /inkie'tar/ vt to disturb; trouble, make anxious, worry; —vr be disquieted, worry

inquieto /in'kieto/ a restless; unquiet; fidgety; disturbed, anxious, worried, uneasy

inquietud /inkie'tuð/ f, restlessness; uneasiness; worry; trouble, care, anxiety

inquilinato /inkili'nato/ m, tenancy; rent; Law. lease; (rental) rates

inquilino /inki'lino/ **(-na)** n tenant; lessee

inquina /in'kina/ f, dislike, grudge

inquinar /inki'nar/ vt to contaminate, corrupt, infect

inquiridor /inkiri'ðor/ **(-ra)** a inquiring, examining —n investigator

inquirir /inki'rir/ vt irr to inquire; examine, look into. See **adquirir**

inquisición /inkisi'θion; inkisi'sion/ f, inquiry, investigation; Eccl. Inquisition

inquisidor /inkisi'ðor/ **(-ra)** a inquiring, investigating —n investigator. m, Eccl. inquisitor; judge

insaciable /insa'θiaβle; insa'siaβle/ a insatiable

insalubre /insa'luβre/ a unhealthy

insanable /insa'naβle/ a incurable

insania /in'sania/ f, insanity

insano /in'sano/ a insane, mad

inscribir /inskri'βir/ vt to inscribe; record; enter (a name on a list, etc.), register, enroll; engrave; Geom. inscribe —Past Part. inscrito

inscripción /inskrip'θion; inskrip'sion/ f, inscription; record, enrollment; registration; government bond

insecticida /insekti'θiða; insekti'siða/ a insecticide

insectívoro /insek'tiβoro/ a insectivorous

insecto /in'sekto/ m, insect

inseguridad /inseguri'ðað/ f, insecurity

inseguro /inse'guro/ a insecure; unsafe; uncertain

insensatez /insensa'teθ; insensa'tes/ f, folly, foolishness

insensato /insen'sato/ a foolish, stupid, mad

insensibilidad /insensiβili'ðað/ f, insensibility; imperception; callousness, hardheartedness

insensibilizar /insensiβili'θar; insensiβili-'sar/ vt to make insensible (to sensations)

insensible /insen'siβle/ a insensible; imperceptive, insensitive; unconscious, senseless; imperceptible, inappreciable; callous

inserción /inser'θion; inser'sion/ f, insertion; interpolation; grafting

insertar /inser'tar/ vt to insert; introduce; interpolate; —vr (Bot. Zool.) become attached

inservible /inser'βiβle/ a useless; unfit; unsuitable

insidia /in'siðia/ f, insidiousness; snare, ambush

insidiar /insi'ðiar/ vt to waylay, ambush; set a trap for; scheme against

insidioso /insi'ðioso/ a insidious; treacherous; scheming, guileful

insigne /in'signe/ a illustrious, famous; distinguished

insignia /in'signia/ f, symbol; badge; token; banner, standard; Naut. pennant; pl insignia

insignificancia /insignifi'kanθia; insignifi'kansia/ f, meaninglessness; unimportance, triviality; insignificance, insufficiency

insignificante /insignifi'kante/ a meaningless; unimportant; insignificant, small

insinuación /insinua'θion; insinua'sion/ f, insinuation; hint; implication; suggestion

insinuador /insinua'ðor/ a insinuating; suggestive, implicative

insinuar /insi'nuar/ vt to insinuate; suggest, hint; —vr ingratiate oneself; creep in

insipidez /insipi'ðeθ; insipi'ðes/ f, tastelessness, insipidity; Fig. dullness

insípido /in'sipiðo/ a tasteless, insipid; dull, uninteresting, boring

insistencia /insis'tenθia; insis'tensia/ f, insistence

insistente /insis'tente/ a insistent

insistir /insis'tir/ vi (with en or sobre) to lay stress upon, insist on; persist in

ínsito /'insito/ a inherent, innate

insociable /inso'θiaβle; inso'siaβle/ a unsociable

insolación /insola'θion; insola'sion/ f, insolation, exposure to the sun; sunstroke

insolar /inso'lar/ vt to expose to the sun's rays; —vr contract sunstroke

insolencia /inso'lenθia; inso'lensia/ f, insolence; impudence, impertinence

insolentarse /insolen'tarse/ vr to grow insolent; be impudent

insolente /inso'lente/ a insolent; impudent, impertinent

insólito /in'solito/ a unaccustomed; infrequent; unusual; unexpected

insoluble /inso'luβle/ a insoluble

insoluto /inso'luto/ a unpaid, outstanding

insolvente /insol'βente/ a insolvent

insomne /in'somne/ a sleepless

insomnio /in'somnio/ m, insomnia

insondable /inson'daβle/ a unfathomable, bottomless; inscrutable, secret

insoportable /insopor'taβle/ a intolerable, unbearable

insostenible /insoste'niβle/ a indefensible; arbitrary, baseless

inspección /inspek'θion; inspek'sion/ f, inspection; supervision; examination; inspectorship; inspector's office

inspeccionar /inspekθio'nar; inspeksio'nar/ vt to inspect; survey, examine. **i. una casa**, to view a house

inspector /inspek'tor/ (-ra) a inspecting, examining —n supervisor. m, inspector; surveyor

inspiración /inspira'θion; inspira'sion/ f, inspiration; inhalation

inspirador /inspira'ðor/ (-ra) a inspiring —n inspirer

inspirar /inspi'rar/ vt to breathe in, inhale; blow (of the wind); inspire; —vr be inspired; (with en) find inspiration in, imitate

instabilidad /instaβili'ðað/ f, instability; unsteadiness; shakiness; unreliability, inconstancy

instable /ins'taβle/ a unstable

instalación /instala'θion; instala'sion/ f, plant, apparatus; erection, fitting; induction; installment, settling in

instalador /instala'ðor/ (-ra) n fitter; one who installs (electricity, etc.)

instalar /insta'lar/ vt to appoint, induct; erect (a plant, etc.); install, put in; lay on; Elec. wire; —vr install oneself, settle down

instancia /ins'tanθia; ins'tansia/ f, instance; argument; suggestion; supplication; request; formal petition. **de primera i.**, in the first instance, firstly

instantánea /instan'tanea/ f, Photo. snapshot

instantáneo /instan'taneo/ a instantaneous

instante /ins'tante/ a urgent. m, second; instant, moment. **a cada i.**, every minute; frequently. **al i.**, at once, immediately. **por instantes**, continually; immediately

instar /ins'tar/ vt to press; persuade; insist upon; —vi be urgent, press

instauración /instaura'θion; instaura-'sion/ f, restoration; renewal; renovation

instaurador /instaura'ðor/ (-ra) a renovating, renewing —n restorer, renovator

instaurar /instau'rar/ vt to restore; repair; renovate, renew

instigación /instiga'θion; instiga'sion/ f, instigation, incitement

instigar /insti'gar/ vt to instigate, incite; induce

instilación /instila'θion; instila'sion/ f, instillment, pouring drop by drop; inculcation, implantation

instintivo /instin'tiβo/ a instinctive

instinto /ins'tinto/ m, instinct. **por i.**, by instinct, naturally

institución /institu'θion; institu'sion/ f, setting up, establishment; institution; teaching, instruction; pl institutes, digest

instituir /insti'tuir/ vt irr to found, establish; institute; instruct, teach. See **huir**

instituto /insti'tuto/ m, institute; secondary school. **i. de belleza**, beauty parlor, beauty salon

instrucción /instruk'θion; instruk'sion/ f, teaching, instruction; knowledge, learning; education; pl orders; rules; instruction. **i. primaria**, primary education. **i. pública**, public education

instructivo /instruk'tiβo/ a instructive

instructor /instruk'tor/ (-ra) a instructive —n instructor

instruido /ins'truiðo/ a cultured, well-educated; knowledgeable

instruir /ins'truir/ vt irr to teach, instruct; train; inform, acquaint with; Law. formulate. See **huir**

instrumentar /instrumen'tar/ vt Mus. to score

instrumentista /instrumen'tista/ mf Mus. instrumentalist; instrument maker

instrumento /instru'mento/ m, tool, implement; machine, apparatus; Mus. instrument; means, medium; legal document. **i. de cuerda**, string instrument. **i. de percusión**, percussion instrument. **i. de viento**, wind instrument

insuave /in''suaβe/ a unpleasant (to the senses); rough

insubordinación /insuβorðina'θion; insuβorðina'sion/ f, insubordination, rebellion

insubordinado /insuβorði'naðo/ a insubordinate, unruly

insubordinar /insuβorði'nar/ vt to rouse to rebellion; —vr become insubordinate, rebel

insubsistente /insuβsis'tente/ a unstable; groundless, unfounded

insubstancial /insuβstan'θial; insuβstan-'sial/ a insubstantial, unreal, illusory; pointless, worthless, superficial

insubstancialidad /insuβstanθiali'ðað; insuβstansiali'ðað/ f. superficiality, worthlessness

insuficiencia /insufi'θienθia; insufi-'siensia/ f. insufficiency, shortage; incompetence, inefficiency

insuficiente /insufi'θiente; insufi'siente/ a insufficient, scarce, inadequate

insufrible /insu'friβle/ a insufferable, unbearable, intolerable

insulina /insu'lina/ f. insulin

insulsez /insul'seθ; insul'ses/ f. insipidity, tastelessness; dullness; tediousness

insulso /in'sulso/ a insipid, tasteless; tedious; dull

insultante /insul'tante/ a insulting

insultar /insul'tar/ vt to insult; call names; —vr take offense

insulto /in'sulto/ m. insult; sudden attack; sudden illness, fit

insumable /insu'maβle/ a incalculable; excessive, exorbitant

insumergible /insumer'hiβle/ a unsinkable

insumiso /insu'miso/ a rebellious

insurgente /insur'hente/ a insurgent, rebellious. m, rebel

insurrección /insurrek'θion; insurrek-'sion/ f. insurrection

insurreccionar /insurrekθio'nar; insurreksio'nar/ vt to incite to rebellion; —vr rise in rebellion

insurrecto /insu'rrekto/ **(-ta)** n rebel

insustituible /insusti'tuiβle/ a indispensable

intachable /inta'tʃaβle/ a irreproachable; impeccable, perfect

intacto /in'takto/ a untouched; intact, uninjured; whole, entire; complete; pure

integración /integra'θion; integra'sion/ f, integration

integral /inte'gral/ a integral

integrar /inte'grar/ vt to integrate; Com. repay

integridad /integri'ðað/ f. wholeness; completeness; integrity, probity, honesty; virginity

íntegro /'integro/ a integral, whole; upright, honest

integumento /integu'mento/ m. integument; pretense, simulation

intelectiva /intelek'tiβa/ f, understanding

intelecto /inte'lekto/ m, intellect

intelectual /intelek'tual/ a intellectual

intelectualidad /intelektuali'ðað/ f, understanding, intellectuality; intelligentsia

inteligencia /inteli'henθia; inteli'hensia/ f, intelligence; intellect; mental alertness; mind; meaning, sense; experience, skill; understanding, secret agreement; information, knowledge; Intelligence, Secret Service

inteligente /inteli'hente/ a intelligent; clever; skillful; capable, competent

inteligible /inteli'hiβle/ a intelligible; understandable; able to be heard

intemperancia /intempe'ranθia; intempe'ransia/ f, intemperance, lack of moderation

intemperante /intempe'rante/ a intemperate

intemperie /intem'perie/ f, stormy weather. **a la i.,** at the mercy of the elements; in the open air

intempestivo /intempes'tiβo/ a inopportune, ill-timed

intención /inten'θion; inten'sion/ f, intention; determination, purpose; viciousness (of animals); caution. Inf. **con segunda i.,** with a double meaning, slyly

intencionado /intenθio'naðo; intensio-'naðo/ a intentioned, disposed

intencional /intenθio'nal; intensio'nal/ a intentional, designed, premeditated

intendencia /inten'denθia; inten'densia/ f, management; supervision; administration; Polit. intendancy. Mil. **cuerpo de i.,** quartermaster corps, army supply corps

intensar /inten'sar/ vt to intensify

intensidad /intensi'ðað/ f, intensity; ardor; vehemence

intensificar /intensifi'kar/ vt to intensify

intensivo /inten'siβo/ a intensive

intenso /in'tenso/ a intense; ardent; fervent, vehement

intentar /inten'tar/ vt to intend, mean; propose; try, endeavor; initiate. **i. fortuna,** to try one's luck

intento /in'tento/ m, intention, determination; purpose. **de i.,** on purpose; knowingly

interacción /interak'θion; interak'sion/ f, interaction; reciprocal effect; Chem. reaction

intercalar /interka'lar/ vt to intercalate; interpolate, include, insert

intercambiable /interkam'biaβle/ a interchangeable

intercambio /inter'kambio/ m, interchange

interceder /interθe'ðer; interse'ðer/ vi to intercede, plead for

interceptación /interθepta'θion; intersepta'sion/ f,, interception

interceptar /interθep'tar; intersep'tar/ vt to intercept; interrupt; hinder

intercesor /interθe'sor; interse'sor/ **(-ra)** a interceding —n intercessor

intercutáneo /interku'taneo/ a intercutaneous

interdecir /inter'ðeθir; inter'ðesir/ vt irr to forbid, prohibit. See **decir**

interdicción /interðik'θion; interðik'sion/ f, interdiction, prohibition

interdicto /inter'ðikto/ m, interdict

interés /inte'res/ m, interest; yield, profit; advantage; Com. interest; inclination, fondness; attraction, fascination; pl money matters. **i. compuesto,** compound interest. **intereses creados,** bonds of interest; vested interests

interesado /intere'saðo/ a involved, concerned; biased; selfish

interesante /intere'sante/ a interesting

interesar /intere'sar/ **(se)** vi and vr to be interested; —vt Com. invest; interest

interfecto /inter'fekto/ **(-ta)** n Law. victim (of murder)

interferencia /interfe'renθia; interfe'rensia/ f, Phys. interference

ínterin /'interin/ m, interim —adv meanwhile, in the meantime

interinamente /interina'mente/ adv in the interim; provisionally

interinar /interi'nar/ vt to discharge (duties) provisionally, act temporarily as

interino /inte'rino/ a acting, provisional, temporary

interior /inte'rior/ a interior; inner; inside; indoor; inland; internal, domestic (policies, etc.); inward, spiritual. m, interior, inside; mind, soul; pl entrails

interjección /interhek'θion; interhek-'sion/ f, Gram. interjection, exclamation

interlocución /interloku'θion; interloku'sion/ f, dialogue, conversation

interlocutorio /interloku'torio/ a Law. interlocutory

intérlope /in'terlope/ a interloping. mf interloper

interludio /inter'luðio/ m, interlude

intermediario /interme'ðiario/ **(-ia)** a and n intermediary. m, Com. middleman

intermedio /inter'meðio/ a intermediate. m, interim; Theat. interval. **por i. de,** through, by the mediation of

intermisión /intermi'sion/ f, intermission, interval

intermitente /intermi'tente/ a intermittent

intermitir /intermi'tir/ vt to interrupt, suspend, discontinue

internación /interna'θion; interna'sion/ f, going inside; penetration; taking into

internacional /internaθio'nal; internasio'nal/ a international

internado /inter'naðo/ m, boarding school

internamiento /interna'miento/ m, internment

internar /inter'nar/ vt to take or send inland; —vi penetrate; —vr (with en) go into the interior of (a country); get into the confidence of; study deeply (a subject)

Internet m, **el,** the Internet.

interno /in'terno/ **(-na)** a interior; internal; inner; inside; boarding (student) —n boarding school student; Med. intern

interpelación /interpela'θion; interpela'sion/ f, Law. interpellation; appeal

interpelar /interpe'lar/ vt Law. to interpellate; appeal to, ask protection from

interpolación /interpola'θion; interpola'sion/ f, interpolation, insertion; interruption

interpolar /interpo'lar/ vt to interpolate; interject

interponer /interpo'ner/ vt irr to interpose, insert, intervene; designate as an arbitrator; —vr intervene. See **poner**

interposición /interposi'θion; interposi'sion/ f, interposition; intervention; mediation, arbitration

interpretación /interpreta'θion; interpreta'sion/ f, interpretation; translation

interpretador /interpreta'ðor/ **(-ra)** a interpretative —n interpreter

interpretar /interpre'tar/ vt to interpret; translate; attribute; expound, explain. **i. mal,** to misconstrue; translate wrongly

interpretativo /interpreta'tiβo/ a interpretative

intérprete /in'terprete/ mf interpreter

interregno /inte'rregno/ m, interregnum. **i. parlamentario,** parliamentary recess

interrogación /interroga'θion; interroga'sion/ f, interrogation; question; Gram. question mark

interrogador /interroga'ðor/ **(-ra)** n questioner

interrogante /interro'gante/ a interrogating. m, Print. question mark

interrogar /interro'gar/ vt to interrogate, question

interrogativo /interroga'tiβo/ a interrogative

interrumpir /interrum'pir/ vt to interrupt; hinder, obstruct; Elec. break contact

interrupción /interrup'θion; interrup'sion/ f, interruption; stoppage (of work); Elec. break

interruptor /interrup'tor/ **(-ra)** a interrupting —n interrupter. m, Elec. switch, interruptor. **i. de dos direcciones,** Elec. two-way switch

intersecarse /interse'karse/ vr Geom. to intersect

intersección /intersek'θion; intersek-'sion/ f, Geom. intersection

intersticio /inter'stiθio; inter'stisio/ m, interstice, crack, crevice; interval, intervening space

intervalo /inter'βalo/ m, interval

intervención /interβen'θion; interβen'sion/ f, intervention; mediation, intercession; auditing (of accounts)

intervenir /interβe'nir/ vi irr to take part (in); intervene, interfere; arbitrate, mediate; happen, occur; —vt Com. audit. See **venir**

interventor /interβen'tor/ **(-ra)** a intervening —n one who intervenes. m, auditor; inspector

intestado /intes'taðo/ **(-da)** a and n Law. intestate

intestino /intes'tino/ a intestinal. m, intestine

íntima, intimación /'intima, intima-'θion; 'intima, intima'sion/ f, intimation, notification

intimar /inti'mar/ vt to intimate; inform,

notify; —*vr* penetrate; —*vr* and *vi* become intimate or friendly

intimidación /intimiða'θion; intimiða'sion/ *f*, intimidation, terrorization

intimidad /intimi'ðað/ *f*, intimacy

intimidar /intimi'ðar/ *vt* to intimidate, terrorize, cow

íntimo /'intimo/ *a* intimate; deep-seated, inward; private, personal

intitular /intitu'lar/ *vt* to give a title to, entitle, call; —*vr* call oneself

intolerable /intole'raβle/ *a* intolerable; unbearable

intolerancia /intole'ranθia; intole'ransia/ *f*, narrow-mindedness, intolerance, bigotry

intolerante /intole'rante/ *a* narrow-minded, illiberal; *Med.* intolerant

intonso /in'tonso/ *a* long-haired, unshorn; boorish, ignorant

intoxicación /intoksika'θion; intoksika'sion/ *f*, poisoning

intoxicar /intoksi'kar/ *vt* to poison

intraducible /intraðu'θiβle; intraðu'siβle/ *a* untranslatable

intramuros /intra'muros/ *adv* within the town walls, within the city

intranquilizar /intrankili'θar; intrankili'sar/ *vt* to disquiet, make uneasy, worry

intranquilo /intran'kilo/ *a* uneasy, anxious

intransferible /intransfe'riβle/ *a* untransferable, not transferable

intransigencia /intransi'henθia; intransi'hensia/ *f*, intolerance, intransigence

intransigente /intransi'hente/ *a* intolerant, intransigent

intransitable /intransi'taβle/ *a* impassable; unsurmountable

intransitivo /intransi'tiβo/ *a* intransitive

intratable /intra'taβle/ *a* intractable; impassable; rough; unsociable, difficult

intrauterino /intrawte'rino/ *a* intrauterine

intravenoso /intraβe'noso/ *a* intravenous

intrepidez /intrepi'ðeθ; intrepi'ðes/ *f*, trepidity, dauntlessness, gallantry

intrépido /in'trepiðo/ *a* intrepid, dauntless, gallant

intriga /in'triga/ *f*, scheme, intrigue; entanglement; *Lit.* plot

intrigante /intri'gante/ *mf* intriguer, schemer

intrigar /intri'gar/ *vi* to intrigue, scheme, plot

intrincación /intrinka'θion; intrinka'sion/ *f*, intricacy

intrincado /intrin'kaðo/ *a* intricate

intrincar /intrin'kar/ *vt* to complicate, obscure, confuse

intríngulis /in'triŋgulis/ *m*, *Inf.* ulterior motive

intrínseco /in'trinseko/ *a* intrinsic, inherent; essential

introducción /introðuk'θion; introðuk'sion/ *f*, introduction

introducir /introðu'θir; introðu'sir/ *vt irr* to introduce; insert; fit in; drive in; pres-

ent, introduce; bring into use; cause, occasion; show in, bring in; —*vr* interfere, meddle; enter. See **conducir**

intromisión /intromi'sion/ *f*, intromission; interference; *Geol.* intrusion

introspección /introspek'θion; introspek'sion/ *f*, introspection

introverso /intro'βerso/ *a* introvert

intruso /in'truso/ **(-sa)** *a* intruding, intrusive —*n* intruder

intuición /intui'θion; intui'sion/ *f*, intuition

intuir /in'tuir/ *vt irr* to know by intuition. See **huir**

intuitivo /intui'tiβo/ *a* intuitive

intuito /in'tuito/ *m*, glance, look, view

inundación /inunda'θion; inunda'sion/ *f*, flood; flooding; excess, superabundance

inundar /inun'dar/ *vt* to flood; swamp; *Fig.* inundate, overwhelm

inurbano /inur'βano/ *a* discourteous, uncivil, impolite

inusitado /inusi'taðo/ *a* unusual, unaccustomed; rare

inútil /i'nutil/ *a* useless

inutilidad /inutili'ðað/ *f*, uselessness

inutilizar /inutili'θar; inutili'sar/ *vt* to render useless; disable, incapacitate; spoil, damage

invadir /imba'ðir/ *vt* to invade

invalidación /imbaliða'θion; imbaliða'sion/ *f*, invalidation

invalidar /imbali'ðar/ *vt* to invalidate

invalidez /imbali'ðeθ; imbali'ðes/ *f*, invalidity; disablement; infirmity

inválido /im'baliðo/ **(-da)** *a* weak, infirm; invalid, null; disabled —*m* invalid; disabled soldier

invariable /imba'riaβle/ *a* invariable

invariación /imbaria'θion; imbaria'sion/ *f*, invariableness

invariante /imba'riante/ *m*, invariant

invasión /imba'sion/ *f*, invasion, encroachment, incursion

invasor /imba'sor/ **(-ra)** *a* invading; *Med.* attacking —*n* invader

invectiva /imbek'tiβa/ *f*, invective

invencible /imben'θiβle; imben'siβle/ *a* invincible

invención /imben'θion; imben'sion/ *f*, invention, discovery; deception, fabrication, lie; creative imagination; finding (e.g. *i. de la Santa Cruz*, Invention of the Holy Cross)

invendible /imben'diβle/ *a* unsalable

inventar /imben'tar/ *vt* to invent; create; imagine; concoct, fabricate (lies, etc.)

inventariar /imbenta'riar/ *vt* to make an inventory of; *Com.* take stock of

inventario /imben'tario/ *m*, inventory; *Com.* stock taking

inventiva /imben'tiβa/ *f*, inventiveness, ingenuity; creativeness

inventivo /imben'tiβo/ *a* inventive

invento /im'bento/ *m*, See **invención**

inventor /imben'tor/ **(-ra)** *n* inventor, discoverer; liar, storyteller

inverecundo /imbere'kundo/ *a* shameless, brazen

inverisímil /imberi'simil/ *a* See **inverosímil**

invernáculo /imber'nakulo/ *m*, greenhouse; conservatory

invernadero /imberna'ðero/ *m*, winter quarters; greenhouse

invernal /imber'nal/ *a* wintry; winter

invernar /imber'nar/ *vi irr* to winter; hibernate; be wintertime. See **acertar**

inverosímil /imbero'simil/ *a* unlikely, improbable

inverosimilitud /imberosimili'tuð/ *f*, improbability

inverso /im'berso/ *a* inverse; inverted

invertebrado /imberte'βraðo/ *a and m*, invertebrate

invertir /imber'tir/ *vt irr* to invert, transpose; reverse; *Com*. invest; spend (time). See **sentir**

investigación /imbestiga'θion; imbestiga'sion/ *f*, investigation, examination; research; inquiry

investigador /imbestiga'ðor/ **(-ra)** *a* investigating —*n* investigator; researcher

investigar /imbesti'gar/ *vt* to investigate, examine; research on

investir /imbes'tir/ *vt irr* to confer upon, decorate with; invest, appoint. See **pedir**

inveterado /imbete'raðo/ *a* inveterate

invicto /im'bikto/ *a* invincible; unconquered

invierno /im'bierno/ *m*, winter; rainy season

inviolabilidad /imbiolaβili'ðað/ *f*, inviolability. **i. parlamentaria**, parliamentary immunity

inviolable /imbio'laβle/ *a* inviolable; infallible

inviolado /imbio'laðo/ *a* inviolate

invisibilidad /imbisiβili'ðað/ *f*, invisibility

invisible /imbi'siβle/ *a* invisible

invitación /imbita'θion; imbita'sion/ *f*, invitation

invitado /imbi'taðo/ **(-da)** *n* guest

invitar /imbi'tar/ *vt* to invite; urge, request; allure, attract

invocación /imboka'θion; imboka'sion/ *f*, invocation

invocador /imboka'ðor/ **(-ra)** *n* invoker

invocar /imbo'kar/ *vt* to invoke

involucro /imbo'lukro/ *m*, involucre

involuntario /imbolun'tario/ *a* involuntary

invulnerable /imbulne'raβle/ *a* invulnerable

inyección /inyek'θion; inyek'sion/ *f*, injection

inyectado /inyek'taðo/ *a* bloodshot (of eyes)

inyectar /inyek'tar/ *vt* to inject

ir /ir/ *vi irr* to go; bet (e.g. *Van cinco pesetas que no lo hace*, I bet five pesetas he doesn't do it); be different, be changed (e.g. *¡Qué diferencia va entre esto y aquello!* What a difference there is between this and that!); suit, be becoming, fit (e.g. *El vestido no te va bien*, The dress doesn't suit you); extend; lead, go in the direction of (e.g. *Este camino va a Lérida*, This road leads to Lerida); get along, do, proceed, be (e.g. *¿Cómo te va estos días?* How are you getting along these days?); come (e.g. *Ahora voy*, I'm coming now); *Math*. carry (e.g. *siete y van cuatro*, seven, and four to carry); *Math*. leave (e.g. *De quince a seis van nueve*, Six from fifteen leaves nine). With a gerund, **ir** indicates the continuation of the action, or may mean to become or to grow (e.g. *Iremos andando hacia el mar*, We shall go on walking toward the sea, or *Entre tanto iba amaneciendo*, In the meanwhile it was growing light). With a past participle, **ir** means "to be" (e.g. *Voy encantado de lo que he visto*, I am delighted with what I have seen). With **a** + *infin*, **ir** means to prepare (to do) or to intend (to do) or to be on the point of doing (e.g. *Van a cantar la canción que te gusta*, They are going (or preparing) to sing the song you like). With **prep a** + *noun*, **ir** indicates destination (e.g. *Voy al cine*, I'm going to the cinema. *¿A dónde vamos?* Where are we going to?). **ir** + **con** means to go in the company of, or to do a thing in a certain manner (e.g. *Hemos de ir con cuidado*, We must go carefully). **ir** + **en** means to concern, interest (e.g. *¿Qué le va a él en este asunto?* What has this affair to do with him?). **ir** + **por** means to follow the career of, become (e.g. *Juan va por abogado*, John is going to be a lawyer). It also means to go and bring, or to go for (e.g. *Iré por agua*, I shall go and bring (or for) water) —*vr* to go away, leave, depart; die; leak (of liquids); evaporate; overbalance, slip (e.g. *Se le fueron los pies*, He slipped (and lost his balance)); be worn out, grow old, deteriorate; be incontinent; *Fig*. *Inf*. **írsele a uno una cosa**, not to notice or not to understand a thing. *Naut*. **irse a pique**, to founder, sink. **Se le fueron los ojos tras María**, He couldn't keep his eyes off Mary. **i. a caballo**, to ride, go on horseback. **i. adelante**, to go on ahead, lead; *Fig*. *Inf*. forge ahead, go ahead. **i. al cuartel**, to go into the army. **i. a una**, to cooperate in. **i. bien** *Fig*. *Inf*. to go on well; be well. **i. de brazo**, to walk arm in arm. **i. de compras**, to go shopping. **i. de juerga** *Inf*. to go on a binge. **i. de bicicleta** *or* **en coche**, to go by bicycle or to ride (in a car or carriage). **i. por**, to do things in order, take one thing at a time. *Fig*. *Inf*. **i. tirando**, to carry on, manage. **¿Cómo le va?** How are things with you? How are you getting along? *Inf*. **no irle ni venirle a uno nada en un asunto**, to be not in the least concerned in (an affair). **¡Qué va!** Rubbish! Nothing of the sort! **¿Quién va?** *Mil*. Who goes there? **Vamos**, Let's go (also used as an exclamation:

Good gracious! You don't say so! Well!)
Vamos a ver..., Let's see.... **¡Vaya!** What
a...!; Come now! Never mind! **¡Vaya a
paseo!** or **¡Vaya con su música a otra
parte!** Take yourself off! Get out! **¡Vaya
con Dios!** God keep you! Good-bye! *Pres.
Ind.* **voy, vas, va, vamos, váis, van.** *Pres.
Part.* **yendo.** *Preterite* **fui, fuiste, fue, fuimos, fuisteis, fueron.** *Imperf.* **iba,** etc
—*Pres. Subjunc.* **vaya,** etc —*Imperf. Subjunc.* **fuese,** etc —*Imperat.* **vé**

ira /'ira/ *f,* wrath, anger; vengeance; raging, fury (of elements); *pl* cruelties, acts
of vengeance

iracundia /ira'kundia/ *f,* irascibility, irritability; anger

iracundo /ira'kundo/ *a* irascible, irritable,
choleric; angry; raging, tempestuous

iranio /i'ranio/ **(-ia)** *a* and *n* Iranian

irascibilidad /irasθiβili'ðað; irassiβili'ðað/
f, irascibility; petulance

iridiscencia /iriðis'θenθia; iriðis'sensia/ *f,*
iridescence

iridiscente /iriðis'θente; iriðis'sente/ *a* iridescent

iris /'iris/ *m,* rainbow; *Anat.* iris (of the
eye)

Irlanda /ir'landa/ Ireland

irlandés /irlan'des/ **(-esa)** *a* and *n* Irish-
man (woman)

ironía /iro'nia/ *f,* irony

irónico /i'roniko/ *a* ironical

irracional /irraθio'nal; irrasio'nal/ *a* irrational; illogical, unreasonable; *Math.* irrational, absurd

irradiación /irraðia'θion; irraðia'sion/ *f,*
radiation, irradiation

irradiar /irra'ðiar/ *vt* to radiate, irradiate

irrazonable /irraθo'naβle; irraso'naβle/ *a*
unreasonable

irreal /irre'al/ *a* unreal

irrealidad /irreali'ðað/ *f,* unreality

irrealizable /irreali'θaβle; irreali'saβle/ *a*
unachievable, unattainable

irrebatible /irreβa'tiβle/ *a* irrefutable, evident

irreconciliable /irrekonθi'liaβle; irrekon-
si'liaβle/ *a* irreconcilable, intransigent

irrecuperable /irrekupe'raβle/ *a* irretrievable

irredimible /irreði'miβle/ *a* irredeemable

irreemplazable /irreempla'θaβle; irreem-
pla'saβle/ *a* irreplaceable

irreflexivo /irreflek'siβo/ *a* thoughtless;
rash, impetuous

irreformable /irrefor'maβle/ *a* unreform-
able

irrefragable /irrefra'gaβle/ *a* indisputable, unquestionable

irrefrenable /irrefre'naβle/ *a* unmanageable, uncontrollable

irrefutable /irrefu'taβle/ *a* irrefutable

irregular /irregu'lar/ *a* irregular; infrequent, rare

irregularidad /irregulari'ðað/ *f,* irregularity; abnormality; *Inf.* moral lapse

irreligión /irreli'hion/ *f,* irreligion

irreligiosidad /irrelihiosi'ðað/ *f,* impiety,
godlessness

irreligioso /irreli'hioso/ *a* irreligious, impious

irremediable /irreme'ðiaβle/ *a* irremediable

irremediablemente /ir-
remeðiaβle'mente/ *adv* unavoidably;
hopelessly

irremisible /irremi'siβle/ *a* unpardonable,
inexcusable

irremunerado /irremune'raðo/ *a* unre-
munerated, gratuitous

irreparable /irrepa'raβle/ *a* irreparable

irreprensible /irrepren'siβle/ *a* blameless, unexceptionable

irreprochable /irrepro'tʃaβle/ *a* irreproachable

irresistible /irresis'tiβle/ *a* irresistible;
ravishing

irresolución /irresolu'θion; irresolu'sion/
f, vacillation, indecision

irresoluto /irreso'luto/ *a* hesitant, irresolute

irrespetuoso /irrespe'tuoso/ *a* disrespectful

irresponsabilidad /irresponsaβili'ðað/ *f,*
irresponsibility

irresponsable /irrespon'saβle/ *a* irresponsible

irreverencia /irreβe'renθia; irreβe'rensia/
f, irreverence

irreverente /irreβe'rente/ *a* irreverent

irrevocabilidad /irreβokaβili'ðað/ *f,* ir-
revocability, finality

irrevocable /irreβo'kaβle/ *a* irrevocable

irrigación /irriga'θion; irriga'sion/ *f,* irrigation

irrigador /irriga'ðor/ *m,* spray, sprinkler;
Med. syringe, spray

irrigar /irri'gar/ *vt* (*Med. Agr.*) to irrigate

irrisible /irri'siβle/ *a* ridiculous, laughable, absurd

irrisión /irri'sion/ *f,* derision; laughingstock

irrisorio /irri'sorio/ *a* ridiculous; derisive

irritabilidad /irritaβili'ðað/ *f,* irritability,
petulance, irascibility

irritable /irri'taβle/ *a* irritable

irritación /irrita'θion; irrita'sion/ *f, Med.*
irritation; petulance, exasperation

irritador /irrita'ðor/ *a* irritating; exasperating. *m,* irritant

irritante /irri'tante/ *a* irritating; exasperating

irritar /irri'tar/ *vt* to exasperate, annoy;
provoke, inflame; (*Med. Law.*) irritate

írrito /'irrito/ *a Law.* null, void

irrogar /irro'gar/ *vt* to occasion (damage,
harm)

irrompible /irrom'piβle/ *a* unbreakable

irrumpir /irrum'pir/ *vi* to enter violently,
break in

irrupción /irrup'θion; irrup'sion/ *f,* irruption, incursion, invasion

irruptor /irrup'tor/ *a* invading, attacking

isabelino /isaβe'lino/ *a* Isabelline (pertaining to Spanish Queen Isabella II (reigned 1830–68)); bay (of horses)

isla /'isla/ f, island; block (of houses)

islámico /is'lamiko/ a Islamic

islamismo /isla'mismo/ m, Islam

islandés /islan'des/ (**-esa**), **islándico** (**-ca**) a Icelandic —n Icelander. m, Icelandic (language)

Islandia /is'landia/ Iceland

isleño /is'leɲo/ (**-ña**) a island —n islander; native of the Canary Islands

isleta /is'leta/ f, islet

islote /is'lote/ m, barren islet

isótope, isótopo /i'sotope, i'sotopo/ m, isotope

israelita /israe'lita/ mf Israelite —a Israeli

ístmico /'istmiko/ a isthmian

istmo /'istmo/ m, isthmus

Italia /i'talia/ Italy

italiano /ita'liano/ (**-na**) a and n Italian. m, Italian (language)

itálico /i'taliko/ a italic

iteración /itera'θion; itera'sion/ f, iteration, repetition

iterar /ite'rar/ vt to repeat, reiterate

iterativo /itera'tiβo/ a iterative, repetitive

itinerario /itine'rario/ a and m, itinerary

izar /i'θar; i'sar/ vt Naut. to hoist

izquierda /iθ'kierða; is'kierða/ f, left, left-hand side; Polit. left. ¡I.! Mil. Left face! **a la i.**, on the left

izquierdo /iθ'kierðo; is'kierðo/ a left, left-hand; left-handed; bent, twisted, crooked

JK

¡ja, ja, ja! /ha, ha, ha/ *interj* Ha! ha! ha!

jabalina /haβa'lina/ *f*, sow of wild boar; javelin

jabón /ha'βon/ *m*, soap. **j. blando**, soft soap. **j. de olor** *or* **j. de tocador**, toilet soap. **j. de sastre**, French chalk, steatite

jabonadura /haβona'ðura/ *f*, soaping; *pl* soapsuds, lather

jabonar /haβo'nar/ *vt* to soap; wash; *Inf.* dress down, scold

jabonera /haβo'nera/ *f*, soapdish or box; soapwort

jabonoso /haβo'noso/ *a* soapy

jaca /'haka/ *f*, pony; filly

jácara /'hakara/ *f*, gay, roguish ballad; song and dance

jacinto /ha'θinto; ha'sinto/ *m*, hyacinth; jacinth. **j. de ceilán**, zircon. **j. occidental**, topaz. **j. oriental**, ruby

jaco /'hako/ *m*, short coat of mail; hack, jade

jactancia /hak'tanθia; hak'tansia/ *f*, bragging, boasting

jactancioso /haktan'θioso; haktan'sioso/ **(-sa)** *a* boastful —*n* braggart

jactarse /hak'tarse/ *vr* to brag, boast

jaculatoria /hakula'toria/ *f*, ejaculatory prayer

jade /'haðe/ *m*, *Mineral.* jade

jadeante /haðe'ante/ *a* panting

jadear /haðe'ar/ *vi* to pant

jadeo /ha'ðeo/ *m*, pant; panting; hard breathing

jaez /ha'eθ; ha'es/ *m*, harness (gen. *pl*); kind, sort; *pl* trappings

jaguar /ha'guar/ *m*, jaguar

jalbegar /halβe'gar/ *vt* to whitewash; make up the face

jalbegue /hal'βege/ *m*, whitewash

jalde /'halde/ *a* bright yellow

jalea /ha'lea/ *f*, jelly. **j. de membrillo**, quince jelly

jalear /hale'ar/ *vt* to encourage, urge on (by shouts, etc.)

jaleo /ha'leo/ *m*, act of encouraging dancers by clapping, shouting, etc.; Andalusian song and dance, *Inf.* uproar

jamaicano /hamai'kano/ **(-na)** *a* and *n* Jamaican

jamás /ha'mas/ *adv* never. **nunca j.**, never. **por siempre j.**, for always, forever

jamba /'hamba/ *f*, jamb (of a door or window)

jamón /ha'mon/ *m*, ham

jamona /ha'mona/ *f*, *Inf.* plumpish middle-aged woman

Japón /ha'pon/ Japan

japonés /hapo'nes/ **(-esa)** *a* and *n* Japanese. *m*, Japanese (language)

jaque /'hake/ *m*, check (in chess); braggart. **j. mate**, checkmate. **en j.**, at bay

jaquear /hake'ar/ *vt* to check (in chess); *Mil.* harass the enemy

jaqueca /ha'keka/ *f*, migraine, sick headache. *Inf.* **dar una j.**, to annoy

jarabe /ha'raβe/ *m*, syrup. **j. tapatío**, Mexican hat dance

jarana /ha'rana/ *f*, roundhouse; *Inf.* revelry; fight, roughhouse; trick, deception

jarcia /'harθia; 'harsia/ *f*, equipment; *Naut.* tackle, rigging (gen. *pl*); fishing tackle; *Inf.* heap, mixture, medley

jardín /har'ðin/ *m*, garden

jardinar /harði'nar/ *vt* to landscape

jardinera /harði'nera/ *f*, plant stand, jardiniere; open streetcar

jardinería /harðine'ria/ *f*, gardening

jardinero /harði'nero/ **(-ra)** *n* gardener

jareta /ha'reta/ *f*, *Sew.* running hem; *Naut.* netting

jarra /'harra/ *f*, jar, jug. **en jarras**, arms akimbo

jarrete /ha'rrete/ *m*, calf (of the leg)

jarretera /harre'tera/ *f*, garter. **Orden de la J.**, Order of the Garter

jarro /'harro/ *m*, pitcher; jug; jar; vase

jarrón /ha'rron/ *m*, garden urn; vase

jaspe /'haspe/ *m*, jasper

jaspeado /haspe'aðo/ *a* marbled, mottled; dappled; frosted (of glass)

jauja /'hauha/ *f*, *Fig.* paradise, land of milk and honey

jaula /'haula/ *f*, cage; crate; miner's cage

jazmín /haθ'min; has'min/ *m*, jasmine. **j. amarillo**, yellow jasmine. **j. de la India**, gardenia

jefa /'hefa/ *f*, forewoman; manager; leader, head

jefatura /hefa'tura/ *f*, chieftainship; managership; leadership. **j. de policía**, police station or headquarters

jefe /'hefe/ *m*, chief; head, leader; manager; *Mil.* commanding officer. *Mil.* **j. de estado mayor**, chief of staff. **j. del tren**, railroad guard

jengibre /hen'hiβre/ *m*, ginger

jeque /'heke/ *m*, sheik

jerarca /he'rarka/ *m*, hierarch

jerarquía /herar'kia/ *f*, hierarchy

jerárquico /he'rarkiko/ *a* hierarchical

jeremiada /here'miaða/ *f*, lamentation

jerez /he'reθ; he'res/ *m*, sherry

jerga /'herga/ *f*, thick frieze cloth; jargon

jergón /her'gon/ *m*, straw or hay mattress, pallet; misfit (garments); *Inf.* fat, lazy person

Jericó /heri'ko/ Jericho

jerigonza /heri'gonθa; heri'gonsa/ *f*, jargon; gibberish

jeringa /he'ringa/ *f*, syringe

jeringar /herin'gar/ *vt* to inject; syringe; *Inf.* annoy

jeringuilla /herin'guiʎa; herin'guiya/ *f*, small syringe; mock orange

jeroglífico /hero'glifiko/ *a* hieroglyphic. *m*, hieroglyph

jersey /her'sei/ *m*, jersey, sweater

Jerusalén /herusa'len/ Jerusalem

jesuita /he'suita/ *m*, Jesuit

jesuita, jesuítico /he'suita, he'suitiko/ *a* jesuitical

Jesús /he'sus/ *m*, Jesus —*interj* Goodness!; Bless you! (said to someone after sneezing). **¡ay J.!** Alas! *Inf.* **en un decir J.**, in a trice

jeta /'heta/ *f*, hog's snout; blubber lip; *Inf.* face, mug

jinete /hi'nete/ *m*, horseman, rider; horse soldier, cavalryman

jingoísmo /hingo'ismo/ *m*, jingoism

jip /hip/ *m*, jeep

jipijapa /hipi'hapa/ *f*, very fine straw. **sombrero de j.**, panama hat

jira /'hira/ *f*, strip of cloth; picnic; tour

jirafa /hi'rafa/ *f*, giraffe

jirón /hi'ron/ *m*, rag; piece of a dress, etc.; portion of a whole

jocosidad /hokosi'ðað/ *f*, pleasantry, jocularity; joke

jocoso /ho'koso/ *a* waggish; jocose, joyous

jocundidad /hokundi'ðað/ *f*, jocundity

jocundo /ho'kundo/ *a* jocund

jofaina /ho'faina/ *f*, washbowl

Jordán /hor'ðan/ Jordan (river)

Jordania /hor'ðania/ Jordan (country)

jornada /hor'naða/ *f*, day's journey; journey, trip; *Mil.* expedition; duration of a working day; opportunity; span of life; act of a drama. **a grandes jornadas**, by forced marches, rapidly

jornal /hor'nal/ *m*, day's wages or labor

jornalear /hornale'ar/ *vi* to work by the day

jornalero /horna'lero/ **(-ra)** *n* day laborer; wage earner

joroba /ho'roβa/ *f*, hump; *Inf.* impertinence, nuisance

jorobado /horo'βaðo/ **(-da)** *a* humpbacked —*n* hunchback

jota /'hota/ *f*, name of letter J; popular Spanish dance; jot, tittle (always used negatively). **no saber j.**, to be completely ignorant

joven /'hoβen/ *a* young. *mf* young man or woman

jovenzuelo /hoβen'θuelo/ **(-la)** *n* youngster, boy

jovialidad /hoβiali'ðað/ *f*, joviality, cheerfulness

joya /'hoia/ *f*, jewel; present; *Archit.* astragal; *Fig.* a jewel of a person

joyería /hoie'ria/ *f*, jeweler's shop or workshop

joyero /ho'iero/ *m*, jeweler; jewel box

juanete /hua'nete/ *m*, bunion; prominent cheekbone; *Naut.* topgallant sail

jubilación /huβila'θion; huβila'sion/ *f*, retirement; pensioning off; pension

jubilado /huβi'laðo/ *a* retired

jubilar /huβi'lar/ *vt* to pension off; excuse from certain duties; *Inf.* put aside as useless (things); —*vr* rejoice; retire or be pensioned off

jubileo /huβi'leo/ *m*, jubilee

júbilo /'huβilo/ *m*, rejoicing, merriment. **j. de vivir**, joie de vivre

jubiloso /huβi'loso/ *a* jubilant, happy

judaísmo /huða'ismo/ *m*, Judaism

judería /huðe'ria/ *f*, Jewry

judesmo /hu'ðesmo/ *m*, Judezmo (Romance language of Jews)

judía /hu'ðia/ *f*, Jew (female); Jewish quarter, Jewish neighborhood; haricot bean. **judías verdes**, string beans

judicatura /huðika'tura/ *f*, judicature; judgeship; judiciary

judío /hu'ðio/ **(-ía)** *a* Jewish —*n* Jew. **j. errante**, wandering Jew

juego /'huego/ *m*, play, sport; gambling; hand (of cards); set; suite; *Mech.* play, working. **j. de café**, coffee set. **j. de los cientos**, piquet. **j. de manos**, sleight of hand, conjuring. **j. de naipes**, game of cards. **j. limpio**, fair play. **j. sencillo**, single (at tennis). **j. sucio**, foul play. **juegos florales**, floral games, poetry contest. **juegos malabares**, juggling. **en j.**, in operation; at stake. **entrar en j.**, to come into play. **hacer j.**, to match. **hacer juegos malabares**, to juggle

juerga /'huerga/ *f*, *Inf.* spree, binge. **ir de j.**, *Inf.* to go on a binge

jueves /'hueβes/ *m*, Thursday. **¡No es cosa del otro j.!** *Inf.* It's no great shakes! It's nothing to write home about!

juez /hueθ; hues/ *m*, judge. **j. arbitrador**, arbitrator; referee. **j. municipal**, magistrate

jugada /hu'gaða/ *f*, play; playing; move, throw; *Fig.* bad turn

jugador /huga'ðor/ **(-ra)** *a* gambling; playing —*n* gambler; player. **j. de manos**, conjurer

jugar /hu'gar/ *vi irr* to play; frolic; take part in a game; gamble; make a move (in a game); *Mech.* work; handle (a weapon); *Com.* intervene; —*vt* play (a match); bet; handle (a weapon); risk. **j. el lance**, *Fig.* to play one's cards well. **j. limpio**, to play fair; *Fig. Inf.* be straightforward. **j. sucio**, to play foul. **jugarse el todo por el todo**, to stake everything —*Pres. Indic.* **juego, juegas, juega, juegan**. *Pres. Subjunc.* **juegue, juegues, juegue, jueguen**

juglar /hug'lar/ *m*, entertainer; buffoon; juggler; minstrel

juglaresco /hugla'resko/ *a* pertaining to minstrels

jugo /'hugo/ *m*, sap; juice; *Fig.* essence. **j. de muñeca**, elbow grease

jugosidad /hugosi'ðað/ *f*, juiciness, succulence; *Fig.* pithiness

jugoso /hu'goso/ *a* juicy, succulent; *Fig.* pithy

juguete /hu'gete/ *m*, toy; plaything; *Fig.* puppet

juguetear /hugete'ar/ *vi* to frolic, gambol

jugueteo /huge'teo/ *m*, gamboling; play, dalliance

juguetería /hugete'ria/ *f*, toy trade; toy shop

juguetón /huge'ton/ *a* playful

juicio /'huiθio; 'huisio/ *m,* judgment; wisdom, prudence; sanity, right mind; opinion; horoscope. **j. final,** Last Judgment. **j. sano,** right mind. **asentar el j.,** to settle down, become sensible. **estar fuera de j.,** to be insane. **pedir en j.,** to sue at law

juicioso /hui'θioso; hui'sioso/ *a* judicious; prudent

julio /'hulio/ *m,* July; *Elec.* joule

jumento /hu'mento/ *m,* ass; beast of burden

junco /'hunko/ *m, Bot.* rush, reed; *Naut.* junk

junio /'hunio/ *m,* June

junta /'hunta/ *f,* joint; assembly, council; committee; union, association; session, sitting; entirety, whole; board, management. **j. de comercio,** board of trade. **j. directiva,** managerial board

juntar /hun'tar/ *vt* to join, unite (*with prep a or con*); couple; assemble; amass; leave ajar (door); —*vr* (*with con*) frequent company of; meet; join; copulate

junto /'hunto/ *a* united, together —*adv* (*with prep a*) near; —*adv* together, simultaneously. **en j.,** altogether, in all

jura /'hura/ *f,* solemn oath; swearing

jurado /hu'raðo/ *m,* jury; jury

juramentar /huramen'tar/ *vt* to swear in; —*vr* take an oath

juramento /hura'mento/ *m,* oath; curse, imprecation. **j. falso,** perjury, **prestar j.,** to take an oath

jurar /hu'rar/ *vt* to swear an oath; swear allegiance; —*vi* curse, be profane

jurídico /hu'riðiko/ *a* juridical, legal

jurisconsulto /huriskon'sulto/ *m,* jurisconsult

jurisdicción /hurisðik'θion; hurisðik'sion/ *f. Law.* jurisdiction; boundary; authority

jurisprudencia /hurispru'ðenθia; hurispru'ðensia/ *f,* jurisprudence

jurista /hu'rista/ *mf* jurist

justar /hus'tar/ *vi* to joust

justicia /hus'tiθia; hus'tisia/ *f,* justice; equity, right; penalty, punishment; righteousness; court of justice; *Inf.* death penalty, execution. **administrar j.,** to dispense justice

justiciero /husti'θiero; husti'siero/ *a* just

justificable /hustifi'kaβle/ *a* justifiable

justificación /hustifika'θion; hustifika'sion/ *f,* justification, impartiality, fairness; convincing proof

justificar /hustifi'kar/ *vt* to justify, vindicate; adjust, regulate; prove innocent; —*vr* justify oneself; prove one's innocence

justipreciar /hustipre'θiar; hustipre'siar/ *vt* to appraise, value

justiprecio /husti'preθio; husti'presio/ *m,* appraisement, valuation

justo /'husto/ *a* just; righteous, virtuous; exact, accurate; tight-fitting, close —*adv* justly; exactly; tightly

juvenil /huβe'nil/ *a* young

juventud /huβen'tuð/ *f,* youthfulness, youth; younger generation

juzgado /huθ'gaðo; hus'gaðo/ *m,* court of law; jurisdiction; judgeship

juzgar /huθ'gar; hus'gar/ *vt* to judge, pass sentence on; decide, consider

kerosén /kero'sen/ *m,* kerosene

kilo /'kilo/ *prefix* meaning a thousand. *m, Abbr.* kilogram

kilogramo /kilo'gramo/ *m,* kilogram (2.17 lb.)

kilometraje /kilome'trahe/ *m,* number of kilometers; mileage

kilométrico /kilo'metriko/ *a* kilometric. **billete k.,** tourist ticket

kilómetro /ki'lometro/ *m,* kilometer (about ⅝ mile)

kilovatio /kilo'βatio/ *m, Elec.* kilowatt

kiosco /'kiosko/ *m,* kiosk

laberinto /laβe'rinto/ *m,* labyrinth; *Fig.* tangle, complication; *Anat.* labyrinth of the ear

labia /'laβia/ *f, Inf.* blarney, gab

labihendido /laβien'diðo/ *a* harelipped

labio /'laβio/ *m,* lip; rim, edge. **l. leporino,** harelip. **cerrar los labios,** to close one's lips; keep silent

labor /la'βor/ *f,* work, toil; sewing; needlework; husbandry, farming; silkworm egg; *Mineral.* working; trimming; plowing, harrowing

laborable /laβo'raβle/ *a* workable; cultivable, tillable. **día l.,** workday

laborar /laβo'rar/ *vt* to work; till; plow; construct; —*vi* scheme, plot, plan

laboratorio /laβora'torio/ *m,* laboratory

laborear /laβore'ar/ *vt* to work; till, cultivate; *Naut.* reeve

laboreo /laβo'reo/ *m,* tilling, cultivation; working, development (of mines, etc.)

laborioso /laβo'rioso/ *a* industrious, diligent; laborious, tedious, hard

laborista /laβo'rista/ *a* and *mf* belonging to the Labor Party

labra /'laβra/ *f,* stonecutting; carving or working (metal, stone, or wood)

labrada /la'βraða/ *f,* fallow land ready for sowing

labradero /laβra'ðero/ *a* workable; cultivable, tillable

labrado /la'βraðo/ *a* and *past part* worked; fashioned; carved; embroidered; figured, patterned. *m,* (gen. *pl*) cultivated ground

labrador /laβra'ðor/ *m,* laborer, worker; farmer; peasant

labradora /laβra'ðora/ *f,* peasant girl; farm girl

labrandera /laβran'dera/ *f,* seamstress

labrantío /labran'βtio/ *a* tillable, cultivable. *m,* farming

labranza /la'βranθa; la'βransa/ *f,* tillage, cultivation; farm; farmland; farming; employment, work

labrar /la'βrar/ *vt* to work, do; carve; fashion, construct, make; *Agr.* cultivate, till; plow; embroider; sew; bring about, cause; —*vi Fig.* impress deeply, leave a strong impression

labriego /la'βriego/ **(-ga)** *n* agricultural laborer; peasant

laca /'laka/ *f,* lac; lacquer, varnish; *Art.* lake (pigment)

lacayo /la'kaio/ *m,* groom; lackey, footman

lacear /laθe'ar; lase'ar/ *vt Sew.* to trim with bows; tie, lace; snare, trap

laceración /laθera'θion; lasera'sion/ *f,* laceration

lacerado /laθe'raðo; lase'raðo/ *a* unhappy, unfortunate; leprous

lacerar /laθe'rar; lase'rar/ *vt* to lacerate, mangle, tear; distress, wound the feelings of

lacería /laθe'ria; lase'ria/ *f,* poverty, misery; toil, drudgery; trouble, affliction

lacero /la'θero; la'sero/ *m,* cowboy, one who uses a lasso; poacher

lacio /'laθio; 'lasio/ *a* drooping, limp; withered, faded; straight (hair)

lacónico /la'koniko/ *a* laconic; concise; Laconian

lacra /'lakra/ *f,* aftereffect, trace (of illness); vice; fault

lacrar /la'krar/ *vt* to impair the health; infect with an illness; injure, prejudice (the interests, etc.); seal with sealing wax

lacre /'lakre/ *m,* sealing wax —*a* red

lacrimoso /lakri'moso/ *a* tearful, lachrymose

lactancia /lak'tanθia; lak'tansia/ *f,* lactation

lactar /lak'tar/ *vt* to suckle; feed with milk; —*vi* take or drink milk

lácteo /'lakteo/ *a* lacteal; milky

ladear /laðe'ar/ *vt* to incline; tilt; turn aside, twist; skirt, pass close to; reach by a roundabout way, go indirectly to, —*vr* tilt; be in favor of, incline to; be equal to

ladeo /la'ðeo/ *m,* tilt; sloping; turning aside

ladera /la'ðera/ *f,* slope, incline; hillside

ladería /laðe'ria/ *f,* terrace on a hillside

ladero /la'ðero/ *a* lateral

ladilla /la'ðiʎa; la'ðiya/ *f,* crab louse

ladino /la'ðino/ *a* eloquent; versatile linguistically; wily, crafty; *m,* Ladino (variety of Judezmo)

lado /'laðo/ *m,* side; edge, margin; slope, declivity; faction, party; side, flank; face (of a coin); *Fig.* aspect, view; line of descent; means, way; favor, protection; *pl* helpers, protectors; advisers. **al l.,** near at hand. *Inf.* **dar de l.** (a), to cool off, fall out with. **dejar a un l. (una cosa),** to omit, pass over (a thing). **mirar de l.** or **de medio l.,** to look upon with disapproval; steal a look at

ladrador /laðra'ðor/ *a* barking

ladrar /la'ðrar/ *vi* to bark; *Inf.* threaten without hurting

ladrido /la'ðriðo/ *m,* bark, barking; slander, gossip

ladrillar /laðri'ʎar; laðri'yar/ *vt* to floor or pave with bricks. *m,* brickyard; brickkiln

ladrillo /la'ðriʎo; la'ðriyo/ *m,* brick; tile

ladrón /la'ðron/ **(-ona)** *a* robbing, thieving —*n* thief, robber; burglar. *m,* **l. de corazones,** ladykiller

ladronera /laðro'nera/ *f,* thieves' den; thieving, pilfering; strongbox

lagar /la'gar/ *m,* wine or olive press

lagarta /la'garta/ *f,* female lizard; *Inf.* she-serpent, cunning female

lagartija /lagar'tiha/ *f,* wall lizard, small lizard

lagarto /la'garto/ *m,* lizard; *Inf.* sly, artful person, fox; *Inf.* insignia of Spanish Military Order of Santiago

lago /'lago/ m, lake

lagotear /lagote'ar/ vi Inf. to wheedle, play up to

lagotería /lagote'ria/ f, wheedling, coaxing, flattery

lágrima /'lagrima/ f, tear; drop (of liquid); exudation, oozing (from trees)

lagrimal /lagri'mal/ a lachrymal

lagrimear /lagrime'ar/ vi to shed tears

lagrimeo /lagri'meo/ m, weeping, crying; watering of the eyes

lagrimoso /lagri'moso/ a tearful; watery (of eyes); sad, tragic

laguna /la'guna/ f, small lake, lagoon; lacuna; gap, hiatus

laical /lai'kal/ a lay, secular

laicismo /lai'θismo; lai'sismo/ m, secularism

laico /'laiko/ a lay, secular

lama /'lama/ f, ooze, slime. m, lama, Buddhist priest

lameculos /lame'kulos/ mf Inf. toady

lamedura /lame'ðura/ f, licking; lapping

lamentable /lamen'taβle/ a lamentable

lamentación /lamenta'θion; lamenta'sion/ f, lamentation; lament

lamentador /lamenta'ðor/ (-ra) a lamenting, wailing —n wailer, mourner

lamentar /lamen'tar/ vt to mourn, lament, bewail; —vr bemoan, bewail

lamento /la'mento/ m, lament

lamentoso /lamen'toso/ a lamenting, afflicted; lamentable

lamer /la'mer/ vt to lick; pass the tongue over; touch lightly; lap

lámina /'lamina/ f, sheet (of metal); lamina; engraving; illustration, picture; engraving plate

laminación /lamina'θion; lamina'sion/ f, lamination, rolling (of metals)

laminar /lami'nar/ a laminate; laminated —vt to roll (metals); laminate; lick

lámpara /'lampara/ f, lamp; radiance, light, luminous body; grease spot. **l. de los mineros** or **l. de seguridad,** safety lamp. **l. de soldar,** blowpipe. **l. termiónica,** Radio. thermionic valve. **atizar la l.,** to trim the lamp; Inf. refill drinking glasses

lampiño /lam'piɲo/ a beardless, cleanshaven; smooth-faced; Bot. nonhirsute

lana /'lana/ f, wool; fleece; woolen garments or cloth; woolen trade (gen. pl)

lanar /la'nar/ a wool; wool-bearing. **ganado l.,** sheep

lance /'lanθe; 'lanse/ m, throw, cast; casting a fishing line; catch of fish; crisis, difficult moment; Lit. episode; quarrel; move (in a game). Fig. **l. apretado,** difficult position, tight corner. **l. de fortuna,** chance, fate. **l. de honor,** affair of honor; duel

lancear /lanθe'ar/ lanse'ar/ vt to wound with a lance; lance

lanceta /lan'θeta; lan'seta/ f, lancet

lancha /'lantʃa/ f, Naut. launch; lighter; ship's boat; small boat; flagstone. **l.**

bombardera or **l. cañonera,** gunboat. **l. de salvamento,** ship's lifeboat. **l. escampavía,** patrol boat

landa /'landa/ f, lande

lanero /la'nero/ a woolen. m, wool merchant; wool warehouse

langosta /laŋ'gosta/ f, locust; lobster. **l. migratoria,** locust

langostín /laŋgos'tin/ m, crayfish

languidecer /laŋgiðe'θer; laŋgiðe'ser/ vi irr to languish, pine. See **conocer**

languidez /laŋgui'ðeθ; laŋgui'ðes/ f, lassitude, inertia; languor

lánguido /'laŋgiðo/ a listless, weak, languid; halfhearted; languishing, languorous

lanolina /lano'lina/ f, lanolin

lanosidad /lanosi'ðað/ f, woolliness; down (on leaves, etc.)

lanoso, lanudo /la'noso, la'nuðo/ a woolly

lanza /'lanθa; 'lansa/ f, lance, spear; lancer; nozzle (of a hosepipe). **correr lanzas,** to joust (in a tournament). **estar con la l. en ristre,** to have the lance in rest; be prepared or ready. Inf. **ser una l.,** to be very clever

lanzadera /lanθa'ðera; lansa'ðera/ f, weaver's shuttle; sewing machine shuttle. Inf. **parecer una l.,** to be constantly on the go

lanzallamas /lanθa'ʎamas; lansa'yamas/ m, flamethrower

lanzamiento /lanθa'miento; lansa'miento/ m, throwing; cast, throw; Law. dispossession; Naut. launching

lanzaminas /lanθa'minas; lansa'minas/ m, minelayer

lanzar /lan'θar; lan'sar/ vt to throw, cast, hurl; Naut. launch; vomit; Law. dispossess; Agr. take root; —vr hurl oneself, rush; take (to), embark (upon)

lanzatorpedos /lanθator'peðos; lansator'peðos/ (**tubo**) m, torpedo tube

lañar /la'ɲar/ vt to clamp; clean fish (for salting)

lapa /'lapa/ f, barnacle, limpet

lapicero /lapi'θero; lapi'sero/ m, pencil holder, pencil case; mechanical pencil

lápida /'lapiða/ f, memorial tablet; gravestone

lapidación /lapiða'θion; lapiða'sion/ f, lapidation, stoning

lapidar /lapi'ðar/ vt to stone, lapidate; throw stones at

lapislázuli /lapis'laθuli; lapis'lasuli/ m, lapis lazuli

lápiz /'lapiθ; 'lapis/ m, graphite; pencil; crayon. **l. para los labios,** lipstick

lapizar /lapi'θar; lapi'sar/ m, graphite mine —vt to pencil

lapón /la'pon/ (**-ona**) a Lappish —n Laplander. m, Sami (language)

lapso /'lapso/ m, lapse, period, passage; slip, error, failure

laquear /lake'ar/ vt to lacquer, paint

lar /lar/ m, home; pl lares

lardear /larðe'ar/ vt Cul. to baste

lardo /'larðo/ *m*, lard; animal fat

lardoso /lar'ðoso/ *a* greasy; fat; oily

larga /'larga/ *f*, longest billiard cue; delay (gen. *pl*). **a la l.**, in the long run

largamente /larga'mente/ *adv* fully, at length; generously; widely, extensively; comfortably

largar /lar'gar/ *vt* to slacken, loosen; *Naut.* unfurl; set at liberty; *Fig. Inf.* let fly (oaths, etc.); administer (blows, etc.); —*vr Inf.* quit, leave (in a hurry or secretly); *Naut.* set sail

largo /'largo/ *a* long; generous, liberal; abundant, plentiful; protracted; prolonged; expeditious; *pl* many long (e.g. *por largos años*, for many long years). *m*, *Mus.* largo; length. *Inf.* **¡L. de aquí!** Get out! **a la larga**, in length; eventually; finally; slowly; with many digressions. **a lo l.**, lengthwise; along the length (of); in the distance, far off; along the length (of). *Fig.* **ponerse de l.**, to make one's debut in society; come of age

largor /lar'gor/ *m*, **largura** *f*, length

largueza /lar'geθa/ lar'gesa/ *f*, length; generosity, munificence

largura /lar'gura/ *f*, length

laringe /la'rinhe/ *f*, larynx

laringitis /larin'hitis/ *f*, laryngitis

larva /'larβa/ *f*, larva; worm, grub; specter, phantom

las /las/ *def art. f pl*, of **la** the —*pers pron acc f pl*, of **la**, them

lascivia /las'θiβia; las'siβia/ *f*, lasciviousness

lascivo /las'θiβo; las'siβo/ *a* lascivious, lewd; wanton

lasitud /lasi'tuð/ *f*, lassitude, weariness, exhaustion

laso /'laso/ *a* weary, exhausted; weak; untwisted (of silk, etc.)

lástima /'lastima/ *f*, compassion, pity; pitiful sight; complaint, lamentation. **dar l.**, to cause pity. **Es l.**, It's a pity. **tener l.** (a *or* de) to be sorry for (persons)

lastimador /lastima'ðor/ *a* harmful, injurious; painful

lastimar /lasti'mar/ *vt* to hurt, harm, injure; pity; *Fig.* wound, distress; —*vr* (*with de*) be sorry for or about; complain, lament

lastimero /lasti'mero/ *a* pitiful; mournful; injurious, harmful

lastimoso /lasti'moso/ *a* pitiful, heart-breaking; mournful

lastre /'lastre/ *m*, ballast; good sense, prudence

lata /'lata/ *f*, can, tin; tin plate; can of food. **en l.**, canned, tinned (of food). *Inf.* **Es una l.**, It's a bore, It's an awful nuisance

latamente /lata'mente/ *adv* extensively, at length; broadly

latente /la'tente/ *a* latent

lateral /late'ral/ *a* lateral

látex /'lateks/ *m*, latex

latido /la'tiðo/ *m*, yelp, bark; beat; throb; palpitation

latifundios /lati'fundios/ *m pl*, latifundia (large agricultural estates)

latigazo /lati'gaθo; lati'gaso/ *m*, lash; crack of a whip; sudden blow of fate; *Inf.* draft (of wine, etc.); harsh scolding; *Naut.* jerk or flapping (of sails)

látigo /'latigo/ *m*, whip, lash; cinch, girth of a saddle

latín /la'tin/ *m*, Latin. **bajo l.**, low Latin. *Inf.* **saber l.**, to know the score; be smart

latinajo /lati'naho/ *m*, *Inf.* bad Latin

latinizar /latini'θar; latini'sar/ *vt* to latinize; —*vi Inf.* use Latin phrases

latino /la'tino/ *a* Latin; lateen sail

latinoamericano /latinoameri'kano/ **(-na)** *a* and *n* Latin-American

latir /la'tir/ *vi* to yelp, howl; bark; throb, palpitate, beat

latitud /lati'tuð/ *f*, latitude; area, extent; breadth

latitudinario /lati,tuði'nario/ *a* latitudinarian

lato /'lato/ *a* extensive; large; broad (of word meanings)

latón /la'ton/ *m*, brass

latoso /la'toso/ *a* boring, troublesome, annoying

latrocinio /latro'θinio; latro'sinio/ *m*, larceny

latvio /'latβio/ **(-ia)** *a* and *n* Latvian

laúd /la'uð/ *m*, lute

laudable /lau'ðaβle/ *a* praiseworthy, laudable

láudano /'lauðano/ *m*, laudanum

laudatorio /lauða'torio/ *a* laudatory

laurear /laure'ar/ *vt* to crown with laurel; honor, reward

laurel /lau'rel/ *m*, bay tree. **l. cerezo**, laurel. **l. rosa**, rosebay, oleander

láureo /'laureo/ *a* laurel

lauréola /lau'reola/ *f*, laurel wreath

lauro /'lauro/ *m*, bay tree; glory, triumph

lava /'laβa/ *f*, lava

lavable /la'βaβle/ *a* washable

lavabo /la'βaβo/ *m*, washstand; cloak-room, lavatory

lavada /la'βaða/ *f*, load of wash, load

lavadedos /laβa'ðeðos/ *m*, fingerbowl

lavadero /laβa'ðero/ *m*, washing place; laundry

lavado /la'βaðo/ *m*, washing; cleaning; wash. **l. al seco**, dry cleaning

lavadura /laβa'ðura/ *f*, washing

lavamanos /laβa'manos/ *m*, washstand; lavatory

lavamiento /laβa'miento/ *m*, washing, cleansing, ablution

lavanda /la'βanda/ *f*, lavender

lavandera /laβan'dera/ *f*, laundress; washerwoman

lavandería /laβande'ria/ *f*, laundry

lavandero /laβan'dero/ *m*, laundry; laundryman

lavaplatos /laβa'platos/ *m*, dishwasher

lavar /la'βar/ *vt* to wash; *Fig.* wipe out,

purify; paint in watercolors. **l. al seco,** to dry-clean

lavativa /laβa'tiβa/ f, enema; syringe, clyster; *Inf.* nuisance, bore

lavatorio /laβa'torio/ m, washing, lavation; *Eccl.* lavabo; lavatory, washing place; *Eccl.* maundy

lavazas /la'βaθas; la'βasas/ f pl, dirty soapy water

laxante /lak'sante/ a and m, laxative

laxar /lak'sar/ vt to loosen, relax; soften

laxitud /laksi'tuð/ f, laxity

laxo /'lakso/ a lax; slack

lazar /la'θar; la'sar/ vt to lasso

lazarillo /laθa'riʎo; lasa'riyo/ m, boy who guides a blind person

lazo /'laθo; 'laso/ m, bow; knot of ribbons; tie; ornamental tree; figure (in dancing); lasso; rope, bond; lace (of a shoe); *Fig.* trap, snare; bond, obligation; slipknot. **l. corredizo,** running knot. *Fig. Inf.* **armar l.,** to set a trap. *Inf.* **caer en el l.,** to fall into the trap, be deceived

le /le/ pers pron dat m, or f, 3rd pers sing to him, to her, to it, to you (e.g. *María le dio el perro,* Mary gave him (her, you) the dog). Clarity may require the addition of a **él, a ella, a usted** (e.g. *Le dio el perro a ella,* etc.) —pers pron acc m, 3rd pers sing him (e.g. *Le mandé a casa,* I sent him home)

leal /le'al/ a loyal; faithful (animals)

lealtad /leal'tað/ f, loyalty; faithfulness; sincerity, truth

lección /lek'θion; lek'sion/ f, reading; lesson; oral test; warning, example. **l. práctica,** object lesson. **dar l.,** to give a lesson. **tomar la l.,** to hear a lesson

lechas /'letʃas/ f pl, soft roe; milt

leche /'letʃe/ f, milk; milky fluid of some plants and seeds. *Inf.* **estar con la l. en los labios,** to be young and inexperienced

lechera /le'tʃera/ f, milkmaid; milk can or jug

lechería /letʃe'ria/ f, dairy; dairy shop

lechero /le'tʃero/ (**-ra**) a dairy, milk; milky; milch, milk-giving —n milk seller. **industria lechera,** dairy farming

lecho /'letʃo/ m, bed; couch; animal's bed, litter; riverbed; bottom of the sea; layer; *Geol.* stratum

lechón /le'tʃon/ m, suckling pig; hog; *Inf.* slovenly man

lechoso /le'tʃoso/ a milky

lechuga /le'tʃuga/ f, lettuce; frill, flounce. *Inf.* **como una l.,** as fresh as a daisy

lechuguina /letʃu'gina/ f, *Inf.* affected, overdressed young woman

lechuguino /letʃu'gino/ m, lettuce plant; *Inf.* young blood, gallant; *Inf.* foppish young man

lechuza /le'tʃuθa; le'tʃusa/ f, barn owl

lector /lek'tor/ (**-ra**) n reader; lecturer

lectura /lek'tura/ f, reading; lecture; culture, knowledge

ledo /'leðo/ a happy, content

leer /le'er/ vt irr to read; explain, interpret; teach; take part in an oral test. See **creer**

legación /lega'θion; lega'sion/ f, *Eccl.* legateship; legation

legado /le'gaðo/ m, legacy; legate

legajo /le'gaho/ m, bundle, docket; file

legal /le'gal/ a legal; legitimate; upright, trustworthy

legalidad /legali'ðað/ f, legality

legalizar /legali'θar; legali'sar/ vt to legalize

legamente /lega'mente/ adv ignorantly, stupidly

légamo /'legamo/ m, mud, slime

legañoso /lega'noso/ a bleary-eyed

legar /le'gar/ vt to bequeath; send as a legate

legatario /lega'tario/ (**-ia**) n legatee, one to whom a legacy is bequeathed

legendario /lehen'dario/ a legendary

legible /le'hiβle/ a legible

legión /le'hion/ f, legion

legionario /lehio'nario/ a and m, legionary

legislación /lehisla'θion; lehisla'sion/ f, legislation

legislador /lehisla'ðor/ (**-ra**) a legislative —n legislator

legislar /lehis'lar/ vi to legislate

legislativo /lehisla'tiβo/ a legislative

legislatura /lehisla'tura/ f, legislature

legista /le'hista/ mf jurist; student of law

legítima /le'hitima/ f, portion of a married man's estate that cannot be willed away from his wife and children

legitimación /lehitima'θion; lehitima'sion/ f, legitimation

legitimar /lehiti'mar/ vt to legitimize

legitimidad /lehitimi'ðað/ f, legitimacy

legítimo /le'hitimo/ a legitimate; real, true

lego /'lego/ a lay, secular. m, layman

legua /'legua/ f, league (approximately 5.573 meters). **a la l., de cien leguas, desde media l.,** from afar

legumbre /le'gumbre/ f, pulse; vegetable

leguminoso /legumi'noso/ a leguminous

leído /le'iðo/ a well-read

lejanía /leha'nia/ f, distance

lejano /le'hano/ a distant, remote, far off

lejía /le'hia/ f, lye; bleaching solution; *Inf.* dressing-down, scolding

lejos /'lehos/ adv far off, far, distant. m, perspective, view from afar; *Art.* background. **a lo l.,** far off, in the distance. **de** or **desde l.,** from afar, from a distance

lelo /'lelo/ a stupid; fatuous, inane

lema /'lema/ m, chapter heading; argument, summary; motto; theme, subject

lencería /lenθe'ria; lense'ria/ f, linen goods; linen merchant's shop; linen closet

lene /'lene/ a smooth, soft; kind, sweet, gentle; lightweight

lengua /'lengua/ f, *Anat.* tongue; mother tongue, language; clapper of a bell; information. *mf* spokes. **l. de escorpión** *or* **mala l.,** scandalmonger, backbiter. **l. de fuego,** *Eccl.* tongue of fire, flame. **l. del agua,** waterline, timberline. **l. de oc,** langue d'oc. **l. de oil,** langue d'oil. **l. de tierra,** neck of land, promontory. **l. viva,** modern language. *Inf.* **andar en lenguas,** to be on every lip, to be famous. *Inf.* **hacerse lenguas de,** to praise it, to the skies. *Inf.* **irse (a uno) la l.,** to be indiscreet, talk too much. **poner l.** *or* **lenguas en,** to gossip about. *Inf.* **tener mucha l.,** to be very talkative. **tomar l.** *or* **lenguas,** to find out about, inform oneself on

lenguado /leŋ'guaðo/ *m., Ichth.* sole

lenguaje /leŋ'guahe/ *m.,* language; style; speech, idiom. **l. vulgar,** common speech

lengüeta /leŋ'gueta/ *f, dim* little tongue; *Mus.* tongue (of wind instruments); barb (of an arrow); needle (of a balance)

lenitivo /leni'tiβo/ *a* lenitive; soothing. *m., Med.* lenitive; *Fig.* balm (of sorrow, etc.)

lente /'lente/ *m,* lens; *pl* eyeglasses. **l. de aumento,** magnifying glass

lenteja /len'teha/ *f,* lentil; lentil plant

lentejuela /lente'huela/ *f,* sequin

lentitud /lenti'tuð/ *f,* lentitude; slowness, deliberation

lento /'lento/ *a* slow, deliberate; sluggish, heavy; *Med.* glutinous, adhesive

leña /'leɲa/ *f,* firewood; *Inf.* beating, birching. *Fig.* **echar l. al fuego,** to add fuel to the flame. *Fig.* **llevar l. al monte,** to carry coals to Newcastle

leñador /leɲa'ðor/ **(-ra)** *n* woodcutter; firewood dealer

leñera /le'ɲera/ *f,* woodpile; woodshed

leño /'leɲo/ *m,* wooden log; wood, timber; *Poet.* ship; *Inf.* blockhead

leñoso /le'ɲoso/ *a* woody, ligneous

león /le'on/ *m,* lion. *Astron.* Leo; valiant man. **l. marino,** sea lion

leona /le'ona/ *f,* lioness

leonés /leo'nes/ **(-esa)** *a* and *n* Leonese

leopardo /leo'parðo/ *m,* leopard

lepra /'lepra/ *f,* leprosy

leproso /le'proso/ *a* leprous

lerdo /'lerðo/ *a* slow, lumbering (gen. horses); stupid, slow-witted, dull

les /les/ *pers pron dat 3rd pers pl mf,* to them (e.g. *Les dimos las flores,* We gave them flowers. *Les hablé del asunto,* I spoke to them about the matter)

lesbio /'lesβio/ **(-ia)** *a* and *n* lesbian

lesión /le'sion/ *f,* lesion, wound; *Fig.* injury

lesionar /lesio'nar/ *vt* to wound; *Fig.* injure

leso /'leso/ *a* wounded, hurt; offensive, injurious; *Fig.* unbalanced, perturbed (of the mind). **crimen de lesa majestad,** crime of lèse-majesté

letal /le'tal/ *a* lethal; deadly

letanía /leta'nia/ *f, Eccl.* litany

letargia /le'tarhia/ *f, Med.* lethargy

letárgico /le'tarhiko/ *a* lethargic

letargo /le'targo/ *m,* lethargy; indifference, apathy

Letonia /le'tonia/ Latvia

letra /'letra/ *f,* letter (of alphabet); *Print.* type; penmanship, hand; *Fig.* letter, literal meaning; words (of a song); inscription; *Com.* bill, draft; cunning, shrewdness; *pl* learning, knowledge. **l. abierta,** *Com.* open credit. **l. de cambio,** *Com.* bill of exchange. **l. gótica,** Gothic characters. **l. itálica,** italics. **l. mayúscula,** capital letter. **l. paladial,** palatal. **facultad de letras,** faculty of arts. **La l. con sangre entra,** Learning is acquired with pain. **primeras letras,** early education, first letters

letrado /le'traðo/ *a* learned, educated; *Inf.* presumptuous; pedantic. *m,* lawyer

letrero /le'trero/ *m,* label; inscription; poster, bill; sign, indicator. **l. luminoso,** illuminated sign

letrilla /le'triʎa/ le'triya/ *f,* short poem, often set to music

letrina /le'trina/ *f,* latrine

leva /'leβa/ *f, Naut.* weighing anchor; *Mil.* levy, forced enrollment; tappet; *Mech.* lever; *Mech.* cam; *Inf.* **irse a l. y a monte,** to flee, beat it, quit

levadizo /leβa'ðiθo; leβa'ðiso/ *a* able to be raised or lowered (bridges). **puente l.,** drawbridge

levadura /leβa'ðura/ *f,* leaven, yeast; rising (of bread)

levantada /leβan'taða/ *f,* act of rising from bed

levantamiento /leβanta'miento/ *m,* raising, lifting; rebellion, revolt; ennoblement, elevation; settlement of accounts

levantar /leβan'tar/ *vt* to raise, lift; pick up; build; cancel, remove; encourage, rouse; recruit, enlist; cut (cards); leave, abandon; survey; disturb (game); produce, increase (prices); raise (the voice); *Fig.* ennoble, elevate; cause, occasion; libel, accuse falsely; *—vr* rise; get up; stand up; stand out, be prominent; rebel; leave one's bed after an illness. **l. bandera,** to rebel. **l. el campo,** to break camp. **levantarse del izquierdo,** *Inf.* to get out of bed on the wrong side

levante /le'βante/ *m,* east; Levant; east wind

levar /le'βar/ *vt Naut.* to weigh anchor; *—vr* set sail

leve /'leβe/ *a* light (in weight); unimportant, trifling

levedad /leβe'ðað/ *f,* lightness (in weight); unimportance, levity, flippancy

levita /le'βita/ *m,* Levite; deacon. *f,* frock coat

levitación /leβita'θion; leβita'sion/ *f,* levitation

levítico /le'βitiko/ *a* Levitical. *m,* Leviticus

levitón /leβi'ton/ *m,* frock coat

léxico /'leksiko/ *m,* lexicon

ley /lei/ *f,* law; precept; regulation, rule;

doctrine; loyalty, faithfulness; affection, love; legal standard (weights, measures, quality); ratio of gold or silver in coins, jewelry; statute, ordinance; *pl* the Law. **l. de préstamo y arriendo,** Lend-Lease Act.

ley suntuaria, sumptuary law. *Inf.* **a la l.,** with care and decorum. **a l. de caballero,** on the word of a gentleman. **de buena l.,** *a* excellent; —*adv* genuinely; in good faith. **de mala l.,** *a* disreputable, base; —*adv* in bad faith

leyenda /le'ienda/ *f,* legend; inscription; story, tale

leyente /le'iente/ *a* reading. *mf* reader

lezna /'leθna; 'lesna/ *f,* awl

lía /'lia/ *f,* plaited esparto rope; *pl* lees, dregs

liar /li'ar/ *vt* to fasten or tie up; wrap up, parcel; roll (a cigarette); *Inf.* entangle, embroil; —*vr* take a lover, enter on a liaison. *Inf.* **liarlas,** to quit, sneak off; *Inf.* kick the bucket, die

Líbano, el /'liβano, el/ Lebanon

libar /li'βar/ *vt* to suck; perform a libation; sip, taste; sacrifice

libelo /li'βelo/ *m,* libel; *Law.* petition

libélula /li'βelula/ *f,* dragonfly

liberación /liβera'θion; liβera'sion/ *f,* liberation, freeing; receipt, quittance; *Law.* reconveyance (of mortgages)

liberador /liβera'ðor/ **(-ra)** *a* liberating, freeing —*n* liberator

liberal /liβe'ral/ *a* generous, openhanded; liberal, tolerant; learned (of professions) —*a* and *mf Polit.* liberal

liberalidad /liβerali'ðað/ *f,* generosity, magnanimity

liberalismo /liβera'lismo/ *m,* liberalism

liberalizar /liβerali'θar; liβerali'sar/ *vt* to liberalize, make liberal

liberar /liβe'rar/ *vt* to liberate

libertad /liβer'tað/ *f,* liberty, freedom; independence; privilege, right (gen. *pl*); exemption; licentiousness; forwardness, familiarity; naturalness, ease of manner; facility, capacity; immunity. **l. caucional,** freedom on bail, release on bail. **l. de cultos,** freedom of worship; religious toleration. **l. vigilada,** *Law.* probation. **poner en l.,** to set at liberty; (*with de*) *Fig.* free from

libertador /liβerta'ðor/ **(-ra)** *a* liberating, freeing —*n* liberator, deliverer

libertinaje /liβerti'nahe/ *m,* libertinage, licentiousness

libertino /liβer'tino/ **(-na)** *a* debauched, licentious. *m,* libertine —*n* child of a freed slave

libídine /li'βiðine/ *f,* lust

libidinoso /liβiði'noso/ *a* libidinous, lustful

libra /'liβra/ *f,* pound (measure, coinage); *Astron.* Libra. **l. esterlina,** pound sterling. **l. medicinal,** pound troy

librador /liβra'ðor/ **(-ra)** *a* freeing, liberating —*n* deliverer, liberator. *m, Com.* drawer (of bill of exchange, etc.)

libramiento /liβra'miento/ *m,* liberation, deliverance; *Com.* delivery; order of payment

libranza /li'βranθa; li'βransa/ *f, Com.* draft

librar /li'βrar/ *vt* to liberate, free; protect (from misfortune); *Com.* draw (a draft); *Com.* deliver; place confidence in; issue, enact; —*vi* bring forth children; —*vr* (*with de*) escape from; get rid of

libre /'liβre/ *a* free; at liberty, disengaged; unhampered, untrammeled; independent; bold, brazen; dissolute, vicious; exempt; vacant, unoccupied; unmarried; clear, free; mutinous, rebellious; isolated, remote; innocent; unharmed. **l. cambio,** free trade

librea /li'βrea/ *f,* livery

librecambio /liβre'kambio/ *m,* free trade

librepensador /liβrepensa'ðor/ **(-ra)** *a* freethinking —*n* freethinker

librería /liβre'ria/ *f,* bookshop; book trade, bookselling; bookcase

librero /li'βrero/ *m,* bookseller. **l. anticuario,** antiquarian bookseller; rare-book dealer

libreta /li'βreta/ *f, Cul.* 1-lb. loaf; notebook; passbook, bankbook

libretista /liβre'tista/ *mf* librettist

libreto /li'βreto/ *m,* libretto

libro /'liβro/ *m,* book; *Mus.* libretto; *Zool.* omasum. **l. copiador,** *Com.* letter book. **l. de actas,** minute book. **l. de caja,** *Com.* cash book. **l. de cheques,** checkbook. **l. de facturas,** *Com.* invoice book. **l. de reclamaciones,** complaint book. **l. de texto,** textbook. **l. diario,** *Com.* daybook. **l. mayor,** ledger. **l. talonario,** receipt book. *Fig. Inf.* **hacer l. nuevo,** to turn over a new leaf; introduce innovations

licencia /li'θenθia; li'sensia/ *f,* permission, license; licentiousness; boldness, insolence; *Educ.* bachelor's degree, licentiate. **l. absoluta,** *Mil.* discharge

licenciado /liθen'θiaðo; lisen'siaðo/ **(-da)** *a* pedantic; free, exempt; licensed —*n Educ.* bachelor; licentiate. *m,* discharged soldier

licenciar /liθen'θiar; lisen'siar/ *vt* to allow, permit; license; dismiss, discharge; confer degree of bachelor or licentiate; *Mil.* discharge; —*vr* become licentious; receive bachelor's degree or licentiate

licenciatura /liθenθia'tura; lisensia'tura/ *f,* degree of licentiate or bachelor; graduation as such; licentiate course of study

licencioso /liθen'θioso; lisen'sioso/ *a* licentious, dissolute

liceo /li'θeo; li'seo/ *m,* lyceum

licitación /liθita'θion; lisita'sion/ *f,* bidding (at auction)

licitador /liθita'ðor; lisita'ðor/ *m,* bidder (at auction)

licitar /liθi'tar; lisi'tar/ *vt* to bid for (at auction)

lícito /'liθito; 'lisito/ *a* permissible, lawful

licor /li'kor/ *m,* liquor, alcoholic drink; liquid

licoroso /liko'roso/ *a* aromatic, generous (of wines)

licuadora /likua'ðora/ *f*, blender

licuar /li'kuar/ *vt* to liquefy

licuefacción /likuefak'θion; likuefak'sion/ *f*, liquefaction

lid /lið/ *f*, combat, fight; dispute, controversy. **en buena l.**, in fair fight; by fair means

líder /'liðer/ *m*, leader; chief

lidia /'liðia/ *f*, fighting; bullfight

lidiador /liðia'ðor/ **(-ra)** *n* combatant, fighter

lidiar /li'ðiar/ *vi* to fight; *Fig*. struggle; (*with contra or con*) oppose, fight against; —*vt* fight (a bull). **¡Cuánto tienen que l. con...!** *Fig*. What a struggle they have with...!

liebre /'lieβre/ *f*, hare

liendre /'liendre/ *f*, nit

lienza /'lienθa; liensa/ *f*, narrow strip (of cloth)

lienzo /'lienθo; 'lienso/ *m*, linen; cotton; cambric; hemp cloth; *Art*. canvas

liga /'liga/ *f*, garter, bandage; birdlime; mixture, blend; *Metall*. alloy; alliance, coalition; league (football, etc.)

ligación /liga'θion; liga'sion/ *f*, tying; binding; union

ligado /li'gaðo/ *m*, *Mus*. legato; *Mus*. tie

ligadura /liga'ðura/ *f*, bond, tie; binding, fastening; *Fig*. shackle, link; (*Surg*. *Mus*.) ligature; *Naut*. lashing

ligamento /liga'mento/ *m*, tie, bond; mixture; *Anat*. ligament

ligar /li'gar/ *vt* to tie, bind; *Metall*. alloy; join, connect; render impotent by sorcery; *Mus*. slur (notes); —*vr* ally, join together; *Fig*. bind oneself. **l. cabos**, to put two and two together

ligereza /lihe'reθa; lihe'resa/ *f*, lightness (of weight); swiftness; nimbleness, fickleness; tactless remark, indiscretion

ligero /li'hero/ *a* light (in weight); swift, nimble; light (sleep); unimportant, insignificant; easily digested (food); thin (fabrics, etc.); fickle, changeable. **l. de cascos**, frivolous, gay. **a la ligera**, lightly; quickly; without fuss. **de l.**, impetuously, thoughtlessly; easily, with ease

lija /'liha/ *f*, dogfish; sandpaper

lila /'lila/ *f*, lilac bush and flower; lilac color —*a Inf*. foolish, vain

lima /'lima/ *f*, sweet lime, citron fruit; lime tree; file (tool); filing, polishing

limadura /lima'ðura/ *f*, filing; polishing; *pl* filings

limar /li'mar/ *vt* to file, smooth with a file; *Fig*. touch up, polish

limazo /li'maθo; li'maso/ *m*, slime, viscosity (especially of snails, etc.)

limbo /'limbo/ *m*, limbo; edge, hem; (*Astron. Bot*.) limb; limb (of a quadrant, etc.). *Inf*. **estar en el l.**, to be bewildered or abstracted

limeño /li'meɲo/ **(-ña)** *a* and *n* native of or belonging to Lima (Peru)

limitación /limita'θion; limita'sion/ *f*, limitation; limit, extent, bound; district, area

limitar /limi'tar/ *vt* to limit; curb, restrict; bound

límite /'limite/ *m*, limit, extent; boundary, border; end, confine

limítrofe /li'mitrofe/ *a* bordering, contiguous

limo /'limo/ *m*, mud, mire, slime

limón /li'mon/ *m*, lemon; lemon tree

limonada /limo'naða/ *f*, lemonade. **l. seca**, lemonade powder

limonar /limo'nar/ *m*, lemon grove

limonero /limo'nero/ **(-ra)** *n* lemon seller. *m*, lemon tree

limosna /li'mosna/ *f*, alms

limosnear /limosne'ar/ *vi* to beg, ask alms

limoso /li'moso/ *a* slimy, muddy

limpiabotas /limpia'βotas/ *m*, bootblack (person)

limpiador /limpia'ðor/ **(-ra)** *a* cleaning —*n* cleaner

limpiadura /limpia'ðura/ *f*, cleaning; *pl* rubbish

limpiamente /limpia'mente/ *adv* cleanly; dexterously, neatly; sincerely, candidly; generously, charitably

limpiaparabrisas /limpiapara'βrisas/ *m*, windshield wiper

limpiapipas /limpia'pipas/ *m*, pipe cleaner

limpiar /lim'piar/ *vt* to clean; *Fig*. cleanse, clear; empty, free (from); *Agr*. thin out; *Inf*. steal, pinch; *Inf*. win (gambling); —*vr* clean oneself

limpiauñas /limpia'uɲas/ *m*, orange stick (for fingernails)

limpidez /limpi'ðeθ; limpi'ðes/ *f*, *Poet*. limpidity

límpido /'limpiðo/ *a Poet*. limpid

limpieza /lim'pieθa; lim'piesa/ *f*, cleanliness; cleaning; chastity; purity; altruism; uprightness, integrity; neatness, tidiness; dexterity, skill, precision; fair play

limpio /'limpio/ *a* clean; pure, unalloyed, unmixed; neat, tidy; pure-blooded; unharmed, free. **en l.**, in substance; as a fair copy; clearly; *Com*. net

linaje /li'nahe/ *m*, lineage, family; offspring; kind; sort, quality

linajudo /lina'huðo/ **(-da)** *a* highborn —*n* noble, aristocrat; one who alleges his noble descent

linaza /li'naθa; li'nasa/ *f*, linseed

lince /'linθe; 'linse/ *m*, lynx; fox, crafty person

linchamiento /lintʃa'miento/ *m*, lynching

linchar /lin'tʃar/ *vt* to lynch

lindar /lin'dar/ *vi* to run together, be contiguous

linde /'linde/ *mf* limit, extent; boundary

lindero /lin'dero/ *a* bordering, contiguous. *m*, boundary. *Inf*. **con linderos y arrabales**, with many digressions

lindeza /lin'deθa; lin'desa/ f. beauty, loveliness; witticism; pl (Inf. ironical) insults

lindo /'lindo/ a lovely, beautiful; perfect, exquisite. m, Inf. fop (gen. **lindo don Diego**)

línea /'linea/ f. line; kind, class; ancestry, lineage; limit, extent; Mil. file; equator. **l. aérea**, airline. Naut. **l. de flotación**, waterline. **l. de toque**, touchline (in soccer). **l. recta**, direct line (of descent)

linear /line'ar/ a linear —vt to line, mark with lines; Art. sketch

linfa /'linfa/ f, Med. lymph; vaccine; Poet. water

linfático /lin'fatiko/ a lymphatic

lingote /lin'gote/ m, ingot; bar (of iron). **l. de fundición**, pig iron

lino /'lino/ m, Bot. flax; linen; Poet. ship's sail, canvas

linóleo /li'noleo/ m, linoleum

linterna /lin'terna/ f, lantern; lighthouse; lamp. **l. sorda**, dark lantern

lío /'lio/ m, bundle; Inf. muddle, imbroglio; Inf. liaison, amour. Inf. **armar un l.**, to make a muddle, cause trouble. Inf. **hacerse un l.**, to get in a fix; get in a muddle

liquidable /liki'ðaβle/ a liquefiable

liquidación /likiða'θion; likiða'sion/ f, liquefaction; Com. clearance, sale; Com. settlement

liquidar /liki'ðar/ vt to liquefy; Com. settle; Com. liquidate; finish; —vr liquefy

liquidez /liki'ðeθ; liki'ðes/ f, liquidness

líquido /'likiðo/ a liquid; Com. net. m, liquid; Com. net profit

lira /'lira/ f, Mus. lyre; Astron. Lyra; lira (coin)

lírica /'lirika/ f, lyrical verse, lyric

lírico /'liriko/ a lyrical

lirio /'lirio/ m, lily. **l. cárdeno**, yellow flag (iris). **l. de los valles**, lily of the valley

Lisboa /lis'βoa/ Lisbon

lisbonense /lisβo'nense/ a and mf **lisbonés** (**-esa**) a and n Lisboan

lisiado /li'siaðo/ a lame, crippled

lisiar /li'siar/ vt to cripple, lame; —vr be disabled; be lame

liso /'liso/ a smooth; sleek; unadorned, plain; unicolored

lisonja /li'sonha/ f, flattery, adulation

lisonjear /lisonhe'ar/ vt to flatter; fawn upon; Fig. delight (the ear). **lisonjearse de...**, to flatter oneself on...

lisonjero /lison'hero/ (**-ra**) a flattering; sweet, pleasant (sounds) —n flatterer

lista /'lista/ f, strip of cloth; streak; rib; stripe; catalog, list. **l. de correos**, general delivery, poste restante. **l. de platos**, bill of fare. **pasar l.**, to call the roll; check the list

listado /lis'taðo/ a streaked; striped; ribbed

listo /'listo/ a clever; expeditious, diligent; ready, prepared

listón /lis'ton/ m, ribbon; strip (of wood)

lisura /li'sura/ f, smoothness; sleekness; flatness; sincerity

litera /li'tera/ f, litter; Naut. berth

literal /lite'ral/ a literal

literario /lite'rario/ a literary

literato /lite'rato/ (**-ta**) a literary —n writer, litterateur

literatura /litera'tura/ f, literature

litigación /litiga'θion; litiga'sion/ f, litigation

litigante /liti'gante/ mf litigant

litigar /liti'gar/ vt to litigate; —vi dispute, argue

litigio /li'tihio/ m, lawsuit; dispute, argument

litigioso /liti'hioso/ a litigious; quarrelsome, disputatious

litisexpensas /litiseks'pensas/ f pl, Law. costs of a suit; legal expenses

litoral /lito'ral/ a and m, littoral

litro /'litro/ m, liter

Lituania /li'tuania/ Lithuania

lituano /li'tuano/ (**-na**) a and n Lithuanian. m, Lithuanian (language)

liturgia /li'turhia/ f, liturgy

litúrgico /li'turhiko/ a liturgical

liviandad /liβian'daδ/ f, lightness (of weight); fickleness; unimportance; frivolity; lewdness; act of folly, indiscretion

liviano /li'βiano/ a light weight; fickle; unimportant, trifling, frivolous; lascivious

lívido /'liβiðo/ a livid

llaga /'ʎaga; 'yaga/ f, ulcer; sore; grief, affliction; Fig. thorn in the flesh

llagar /ʎa'gar; ya'gar/ vt to ulcerate; make or produce sores; Fig. wound; —vr be covered with sores

llama /'ʎama; 'yama/ f, flame; ardor, vehemence; marsh; Zool. llama

llamada /ʎa'maða; ya'maða/ f, call; Mil. call-to-arms, call. **l. molestosa**, annoyance call, nuisance call

llamado /ʎa'maðo; ya'maðo/ a called; so-called

llamador /ʎama'ðor; yama'ðor/ (**-ra**) n caller. m, door knocker; doorbell

llamamiento /ʎama'miento; yama'miento/ m, calling; call; divine summons, inspiration; invocation, appeal; summons, convocation

llamar /ʎa'mar; ya'mar/ vt to call; invoke, call upon; summon, convoke; name; attract; —vi knock (at a door); ring (a bell); —vr be named, be called; Naut. veer (wind). **Se llama Pedro**, His name is Peter

llamarada /ʎama'raða; yama'raða/ f, flame, flash; blaze, flare (of anger, etc.)

llamativo /ʎama'tiβo; yama'tiβo/ a striking, showy; provocative

llamear /ʎame'ar; yame'ar/ vi to throw out flames, blaze

llana /'ʎana; 'yana/ f, mason's trowel; plain; surface of a page

llanada /ʎa'naða; ya'naða/ f, plain

llanamente /ʎana'mente; yana'mente/

adv frankly, plainly; naturally, simply; candidly, sincerely

llanero /ʎa'nero; ya'nero/ **(-ra)** *n* plain dweller

llaneza /ʎa'neθa; ya'nesa/ *f,* naturalness; candor; familiarity; simplicity (of style)

llano /'ʎano; 'yano/ *a* flat, level; smooth, even; shallow (of receptacles); unaffected, homely, natural; plain (of dresses); manifest, evident; easy; straightforward, candid; informal; simple (of style). *m,* plain; level stretch of ground

llanta /'ʎanta; 'yanta/ *f, Auto.* tire; rim, felloe. **l. de rueda,** wheel, rim

llanto /'ʎanto; 'yanto/ *m,* weeping, flood of tears

llanura /ʎa'nura; ya'nura/ *f,* smoothness, evenness, levelness; plain

llave /'ʎaβe; 'yaβe/ **(de)** *f,* key (to); spigot (of), faucet (of), tap (of); spanner, wrench; *Elec.* switch; clock winder; *Mus.* key, clef; *Archit.* keystone; *Print.* brace; *Mech.* wrench; lock (of a gun); tuning key; piston (of musical instruments); lock (in wrestling); *Fig.* key (of a problem or a study). **l. de transmisión,** sender (telegraphy). **l. inglesa,** monkey-wrench, spanner. **l. maestra,** master key, skeleton key. **echar la l.,** to lock. **torcer la l.,** to turn the key

llavero /ʎa'βero; ya'βero/ **(-ra)** *n* keeper of the keys. *m,* key ring. **l. de cárcel,** turnkey

llegada /ʎe'gaða; ye'gaða/ *f,* arrival, advent

llegar /ʎe'gar; ye'gar/ *vi* to arrive; last, endure; reach; achieve a purpose; be sufficient, suffice; amount (to); make; —*vt* bring near, draw near; gather; —*vr* come near, approach; adhere. **l. a ser,** to become. **l. a un punto muerto,** to reach a deadlock. **l. hasta...,** to stretch as far as...

llena /'ʎena; 'yena/ *f,* spate, overflow

llenar /ʎe'nar; ye'nar/ *vt* to fill; occupy (a post); satisfy, please; fulfill; satiate; pervade; fill up (a form); —*vi* be full (of the moon); —*vr Inf.* stuff, overeat; *Fig. Inf.* be fed-up

lleno /'ʎeno; 'yeno/ *a* full; replete; abundant; complete. *m,* full moon; *Theat.* full house; *Inf.* glut, abundance; perfection. **de l., de l. en l.,** entirely, completely

llevadero /ʎeβa'ðero; yeβa'ðero/ *a* tolerable, bearable

llevar /ʎe'βar; ye'βar/ *vt* to carry, transport; charge (a price); yield, produce; carry off, take away; endure, bear; persuade; guide, take; direct; wear (clothes); carry (a handbag, etc.); introduce, present; gain, achieve; manage (a horse); pass, spend (of time); (*with past part*) have (e.g. *Llevo escrita la carta,* I have written the letter); *Math.* carry; (*with prep. a*) surpass, excel. **l. a cabo,** to accomplish. **l. a cuestas,** to carry on one's back; support. **l. la correspondencia,** to look after the correspondence. **l. la de-**

lantera, to take the lead. **l. luto,** to be in mourning. **llevarse bien,** to get on well, agree

llorar /ʎo'rar; yo'rar/ *vi* to weep, cry; drip; water (eyes); —*vt* lament, mourn; bewail one's troubles

lloriquear /ʎorike'ar; yorike'ar/ *vi* to whine, snivel

lloriqueo /ʎori'keo; yori'keo/ *m,* whining, sniveling

llorón /ʎo'ron; yo'ron/ *a* weeping; sniveling, whining. *m,* long plume. **niño llorón,** crybaby

lloroso /ʎo'roso; yo'roso/ *a* tearful; grievous, sad; sorrowful

llover /ʎo'βer; yo'βer/ *vi impers irr* to rain; come in abundance (of troubles, etc.); —*vr* leak (roofs, etc.). **l. a cántaros,** to rain in torrents, rain cats and dogs. **l. sobre mojado,** to add insult to injury. **como llovido,** unexpectedly. See *mover*

llovizna /ʎo'βiθna; yo'βisna/ *f,* drizzle, fine rain

lloviznar /ʎoβiθ'nar; yoβis'nar/ *vi* to drizzle

lluvia /'ʎuβia; 'yuβia/ *f,* rain; rainwater; *Fig.* shower; rose (of watering can)

lluvioso /ʎu'βioso; yu'βioso/ *a* rainy, showery

lo /lo/ *def art. neut* the thing, part, fact, what, that which. Used before adjectives, past participles, sometimes before nouns and adverbs (e.g. *Lo barato es caro,* Cheap things are dear (in the long run).) Lo **mío es mío, pero lo tuyo es de ambos,** What's mine is mine, but what is yours belongs to both of us. **Juan siente mucho lo ocurrido,** John is very sorry for what has happened. **a lo lejos,** in the distance). **lo... que,** how (e.g. *No sabes lo bueno que es,* You don't know how good he is) —*pers pron acc m,* or *neut* him; it; that, it (e.g. *Lo harán mañana,* They will do it tomorrow). Means some, any, one, as substitute for noun already mentioned (e.g. *Carecemos de azúcar; no lo hay,* We are short of sugar; there isn't any). **Lo cortés no quita lo valiente,** One can be courteous and still insistent

loa /'loa/ *f,* praise, eulogy; *Theat.* prologue; short dramatic piece; *Obs.;* dramatic eulogy

loable /lo'aβle/ *a* praiseworthy

loar /lo'ar/ *vt* to praise; commend

lobo /'loβo/ **(-ba)** *n* wolf. *m, (Bot. Anat.)* lobe; *Inf.* drinking fit. **l. marino,** *Zool.* seal. *Inf.* **pillar un l.,** to get drunk

lóbrego /'loβrego/ *a* murky, dark; dismal; mournful, lugubrious

lobreguez /loβre'geθ; loβre'ges/ *f,* obscurity, gloom, darkness

lóbulo /'loβulo/ *m,* lobe

local /lo'kal/ *a* local. *m,* premises; place, spot, scene

localidad /lokali'ðað/ *f,* location; locality; place, spot; seat (in theaters, etc.).

localización /lokaliθa'θion; lokalisa'sion/ f, localization, placing; place

localizar /lokali'θar; lokali'sar/ vt to localize

loción /lo'θion; lo'sion/ f, lotion

loco /'loko/ (-ca) a insane, mad; rash, foolish, crazy; excessive, enormous; amazing; extraordinary; infatuated —n lunatic; rash person. Fig. Inf. **Es un l. de atar,** He's completely crazy!

locomoción /lokomo'θion; lokomo'sion/ f, locomotion

locomotor /lokomo'tor/ a locomotive

locomotora /lokomo'tora/ f, locomotive

locuaz /lo'kuaθ; lo'kuas/ a loquacious

locución /loku'θion; loku'sion/ f, style of speech; phrase, idiom; Gram. locution

locura /lo'kura/ f, insanity, lunacy; madness, fury; folly, foolishness

locutor /loku'tor/ (-ra) n (radio) announcer; commentator

locutorio /loku'torio/ m, locutory; phone booth

lodo /'loðo/ m, mud

lodoso /lo'ðoso/ a muddy

logarítmico /loga'ritmiko/ a logarithmic

logaritmo /loga'ritmo/ m, logarithm

logia /'lohia/ f, (Freemason's) lodge

lógica /'lohika/ f, logic. Inf. **l. parda,** common sense

lógico /'lohiko/ (-ca) a logical —n logician

logística /lo'histika/ f, logistics

lograr /lo'grar/ vt to achieve, attain, obtain; enjoy; (with infin) succeed in; —vr succeed in, achieve; reach perfection

logro /'logro/ m, achievement, attainment; profit, gain; usury, money-lending

loma /'loma/ f, knoll, hill

lombarda /lom'βarða/ f, red cabbage

lombardo /lom'βarðo/ (-da) a from or of Lombardy (Italy). —n native of Lombardy (Italy). m, mortgage bank

lombriz /lom'βriθ; lom'βris/ f, earthworm, common worm. **l. intestinal,** intestinal worm. **l. solitaria,** tapeworm

lomo /'lomo/ m, loin, back of a book; ridge between furrows; pl ribs; loins

lona /'lona/ f, canvas, sailcloth

londinense /londi'nense/ a London. mf Londoner

Londres /'londres/ London

longanimidad /longanimi'ðað/ f, longanimity, fortitude

longaniza /longa'niθa; longa'nisa/ f, Cul. pork sausage

longevidad /lonheβi'ðað/ f, longevity

longitud /lonhi'tuð/ f, length; longitude. **l. de onda,** Radio. wavelength

lonja /'lonha/ f, slice, rasher; Com. exchange; market; grocery store; woolen warehouse

lonjista /lon'hista/ mf provision merchant, grocer

lontananza /lonta'nanθa; lonta'nansa/ f, distance (also Art.). **en l.,** in the distance, far off

loor /lo'or/ m, praise

loquear /loke'ar/ vi to play the fool; romp

lord /lorð/ m, lord; pl **lores,** lords

loro /'loro/ m, Ornith. parrot

los /los/ def art m pl, the (e.g. **l. sombreros,** the hats) —pers pron acc 3rd pers m pl, them. **Tus cigarrillos no están sobre la mesa; los tengo en mi bolsillo,** Your cigarettes are not on the table; I have them in my pocket. Means some, any, ones, as substitution for noun already stated (e.g. Los cigarros están en la caja si los hay, The cigars are in the box, if there are any). Used demonstratively followed by de or que introducing relative clause, those of; those which, those who; the ones that (who) (e.g. Estaba leyendo algunos libros de los que tienes en tu cuarto, I was reading some books from among those which you have in your room)

losa /'losa/ f, flagstone; slab; tombstone

lote /'lote/ m, lot, portion, share

lotería /lote'ria/ f, lottery; lotto (game); lottery office

lotero /lo'tero/ (-ra) n seller of lottery tickets

loto /'loto/ m, lotus; lotus flower or fruit

loza /'loθa; 'losa/ f, porcelain, china

lozanía /loθa'nia; losa'nia/ f, luxuriance (of vegetation); vigor, lustiness; arrogance

lozano /lo'θano; lo'sano/ a luxuriant, exuberant; vigorous, lusty; arrogant

lubricación /luβrika'θion; luβrika'sion/ f, lubrication

lubricante /luβri'kante/ a lubricant

lubricar /luβri'kar/ vt to lubricate

lúbrico /'luβriko/ a slippery, smooth; lascivious, lustful

lucera /lu'θera; lu'sera/ f, skylight

lucero /lu'θero; lu'sero/ m, evening star; any bright star; white star (on a horse's head); brilliance, radiance; pl Poet. eyes, orbs. **l. del alba,** morning star

lucha /'lutʃa/ f, fight; struggle; wrestling match; argument, disagreement. **l. grecorromana,** wrestling. **l. igualada,** close fight. **l. libre,** catch-as-catch-can fight

luchador /lutʃa'ðor/ (-ra) n fighter; struggler

luchar /lu'tʃar/ vi to fight hand to hand; wrestle; fight; struggle; argue

lucidez /luθi'ðeθ; lusi'ðes/ f, brilliance, shine; lucidity, clarity

lucido /lu'θiðo; lu'siðo/ a splendid, brilliant; sumptuous; fine, elegant

lúcido /'luθiðo; 'lusiðo/ a Poet. brilliant; lucid; clear

luciente /lu'θiente; lu'siente/ a bright, shining

lucimiento /luθi'miento; lusi'miento/ m, brilliance, luster; success, triumph; elegance; display, ostentation

lucir /lu'θir; lu'sir/ vi irr to shine, scintillate; excel, outshine; be successful; —vt illuminate; display, show off; show; —vr dress elegantly; be successful; excel, be brilliant —*Pres. Indic.* **luzco, luces,** etc —*Pres. Subjunc.* **luzca,** etc.

lucrativo /lukra'tiβo/ *a* lucrative

lucro /'lukro/ *m,* gain, profit

luctuoso /luk'tuoso/ *a* lugubrious, mournful

lucubración /lukuβra'θion; lukuβra'sion/ *f,* lucubration

ludibrio /lu'ðiβrio/ *m,* mockery, ridicule

luego /'luego/ *adv* immediately; afterward, later; then; soon, presently —*conjunc* therefore. **l. que,** as soon as. **desde l.,** immediately, at once; of course, naturally; in the first place. **hasta l.,** au revoir, good by for the present

lugar /lu'gar/ *m,* place; spot; village, town, city; region, locality; office, post; passage, text; opportunity, occasion; cause, motive; place on a list; room, space; seat. **l. común,** commonplace. **en l. de,** instead of. **en primer l.,** firstly, in the first place. **hacer l.,** to make room, make way. *Law.* **No ha l.,** The petition is refused **tener l.,** to take place; have the time or opportunity (to)

lugareño /luga'reɲo/ **(-ña)** *a* peasant, regional —*n* villager, peasant

lugarteniente /lugarte'niente/ *m,* lieutenant; substitute, deputy

lúgubre /'luguβre/ *a* lugubrious, dismal, mournful

lujo /'luho/ *m,* luxury; abundance, profusion. **artículos de l.,** luxury goods

lujoso /lu'hoso/ *a* luxurious; abundant, profuse

lujuria /lu'huria/ *f,* lasciviousness; excess, intemperance

lujuriante /luhu'riante/ *a* luxuriant, abundant, profuse

lujurioso /luhu'rioso/ *a* lascivious, voluptuous

lumbago /lum'βago/ *m,* lumbago

lumbre /'lumbre/ *f,* fire; light; splendor, lustre; transom window, opening, skylight; *pl* tinderbox

lumbrera /lum'βrera/ *f,* luminary; skylight; dormer window; eminent authority

luminar /lumi'nar/ *m,* luminary (also *Fig.*)

luminaria /lumi'naria/ *f,* illumination;

fairy lamp, small light; lamp burning before the Sacrament in Catholic churches

luminosidad /luminosi'ðað/ *f,* luminosity

luminoso /lumi'noso/ *a* luminous; bright

luna /'luna/ *f,* moon; mirror; satellite; sheet of plate glass. **l. creciente,** new or rising moon. **l. de miel,** honeymoon. **l. llena,** full moon. **l. menguante,** waning moon. **media l.,** crescent moon

lunado /lu'naðo/ *a* half-moon, crescent

lunar /lu'nar/ *m,* beauty spot; *Fig.* stain, blot (on reputation, etc.); blemish, slight imperfection —*a* lunar

lunático /lu'natiko/ **(-ca)** *a* and *n* lunatic

lunes /'lunes/ *m,* Monday

luneta /lu'neta/ *f,* lens (of eyeglasses), *Theat.* orchestra stall; (*Archit. Mil.*) lunette

lupa /'lupa/ *f,* magnifying glass

lupanar /lupa'nar/ *m,* brothel

lustrador /lustra'ðor/ *m,* polisher. **l. de piso,** floor polisher

lustrar /lus'trar/ *vt* to lustrate, purify; polish, burnish; roam, journey

lustre /'lustre/ *m,* polish, sheen, gloss; glory, luster

lustro /'lustro/ *m,* lustrum, period of five years; chandelier

lustroso /lus'troso/ *a* shining, glossy; brilliant; glorious, noble

luteranismo /lutera'nismo/ *m,* Lutheranism

luterano /lute'rano/ **(-na)** *a* and *n* Lutheran

luto /'luto/ *m,* mourning; grief, affliction; *pl* mourning draperies. **estar de l.,** to be in mourning

luxación /luksa'θion; luksa'sion/ *f,* *Surg.* luxation, dislocation

luz /luθ; lus/ *f,* light; glow; brightness, brilliance; information, news; *Fig.* luminary; day, daylight; *pl* culture, learning; windows. **luces de estacionamiento,** parking lights. **a buena l.,** in a good light; in a favorable light; after due consideration. **a primera l.,** at dawn. **dar a l.,** to publish (a book); bring forth (children); reveal. **entre dos luces,** in the dawn light; in the twilight; *Inf.* tipsy. **media l.,** half-light, twilight

M

macabro /ma'kaβro/ *a* macabre

macadán /maka'ðan/ *m*, macadam

macagua /ma'kagua/ *f*, *Ornith*. macaw

macanudo /maka'nuðo/ *a* (*Inf. West. Hem.*) extraordinary; enormous; robust; fine, excellent

macarrones /maka'rrones/ *m pl*, macaroni; *Naut.* stanchions

macarse /ma'karse/ *vr* to go bad, rot (fruit)

maceración /maθera'θion; masera'sion/ *f*, maceration; steeping, soaking; mortification of the flesh

macerar /maθe'rar; mase'rar/ *vt* to macerate; steep, soak; mortify

maceta /ma'θeta; ma'seta/ *f*, *dim* small mace; handle, haft (of tools); stonecutter's hammer; flowerpot

machaca /ma'tʃaka/ *f*, pestle; pulverizer. *mf Inf.* bore, tedious person

machacador /matʃaka'ðor/ (**-ra**) *a* crushing, pounding —*n* beater, crusher, pounder

machacar /matʃa'kar/ *vt* to crush, pound; —*vi* importune; harp on a subject

machacón /matʃa'kon/ *a* tiresome, prolix

machado /ma'tʃaðo/ *m*, hatchet, ax

macho /'matʃo/ *m*, male; male animal (he-goat, stallion, etc.); male plant; hook (of hook and eye); screw; *Metall*. core; tap (tool); *Inf.* dunderhead, fool; *Archit.* buttress —*a* male; stupid, ignorant; vigorous, strong. **m. cabrío**, he-goat

machacadura /matʃuka'ðura/ *f*, **machucamiento** *m*, pounding, crushing; bruising

machucar /matʃu'kar/ *vt* to crush, pound; bruise

machucho /ma'tʃutʃo/ *a* prudent, sensible; adult, mature

macicez /maθi'θeθ; masi'ses/ *f*, solidity; massiveness; thickness

maciento /maθi'lento; masi'lento/ *a* thin, lean, emaciated

macizar /maθi'θar; masi'sar/ *vt* to block up, fill up

macizo /ma'θiθo; ma'siso/ *a* massive, compact, solid; *Fig.* well-founded, unassailable; thick; strong. *m*, solidity, compactness; bulk, volume; flowerbed; solid tire

macrocosmo /makro'kosmo/ *m*, macrocosm

mácula /'makula/ *f*, stain, spot; *Fig.* blot, blemish; *Inf.* trick, deception; *Astron.* macula

madeja /ma'ðeha/ *f*, skein, hank; lock of hair; *Inf.* dummy, useless person

madera /ma'ðera/ *f*, wood; timber; *Inf.* kind, sort; *Mus.* wind instruments. **m. contrachapada**, plywood. **m. de construcción**, timber. **maderas de sierra,**

lumber wood. *Inf.* **ser de mala m.**, to be a ne'er-do-well

maderada /maðe'raða/ *f*, lumber wood

maderaje /maðe'rahe/ *m*, woodwork, timber work

maderero /maðe'rero/ *m*, timber merchant; lumberjack; carpenter

madería /maðe'ria/ *f*, timber yard

madero /ma'ðero/ *m*, wooden beam; log, piece of lumber; ship, vessel; *Inf.* blockhead or insensible person

madrastra /ma'ðrastra/ *f*, stepmother; anything unpleasant

madraza /ma'ðraθa; ma'ðrasa/ *f*, *Inf.* overindulgent mother

madre /'maðre/ *f*, mother; matron; cause, genesis; *fm*. dame, mother; riverbed; dam; womb; main sewer; chief irrigation channel. **m. de familia,** mother; housewife. **m. de leche,** wet nurse. **m. política,** mother-in-law; stepmother. *Inf.* **sacar de m. (a),** to provoke, irritate (a person)

madreperla /maðre'perla/ *f*, mother-of-pearl

madreselva /maðre'selβa/ *f*, honeysuckle

madrigado /maðri'gaðo/ *a* twice-married (women); *Fig.* experienced, wide-awake

madrileño /maðri'leɲo/ (**-ña**) *a* and *n* Madrilenian

madrina /ma'ðrina/ *f*, godmother; matron of honor or bridesmaid; sponsor; patroness; prop; stanchion

madrugada /maðru'gaða/ *f*, dawn, daybreak; early rising. **de m.,** at dawn

madrugador /maðruga'ðor/ (**-ra**) *a* early rising —*n* early riser

madrugar /maðru'gar/ *vi* to get up early; gain time; anticipate, be beforehand

maduración /maðura'θion; maðura'sion/ *f*, ripening; mellowing; preparation; ripeness; maturity

madurador /maðura'ðor/ *a* ripening; maturing

maduramente /maðura'mente/ *adv* maturely; sensibly

madurar /maðu'rar/ *vt* to ripen; mature; think out; —*vi* ripen; grow mature, learn wisdom

madurez /maðu'reθ; maðu'res/ *f*, ripeness; maturity; mellowness; wisdom

maduro /ma'ðuro/ *a* ripe; mature; mellow; adult; wise

maestra /ma'estra/ *f*, schoolmistress; teacher, instructor; queen bee; guide, model

maestral /maes'tral/ *a* referring to the grand master of one of the Spanish military orders; teaching, pedagogic, *m*, mistral (wind); cell of a queen bee

maestrear /maestre'ar/ *vt* to direct, control, manage; prune vines; —*vi Inf.* bully, domineer

maestría /maes'tria/ *f*, mastery, skill; *Educ.* master's degree

maestro /ma'estro/ *a* masterly; excellent; chief, main; midship. *m*, master, expert;

teacher; instructor; master craftsman; *Educ.* master; *Mus.* composer; *Naut.* mainmast. **m. de armas,** fencing master. **m. de capilla,** *Eccl.* choirmaster. **m. de obras,** building contractor; master builder. **El ejercicio hace m.,** Practice makes perfect

Magallanes, Estrecho de /maga'ʎanes, es'tretʃo de; maga'yanes, es'tretʃo de/ Straits of Magellan

magdalena /magða'lena/ *f,* madeleine (cake); magdalen, penitent. *Inf.* **estar hecha una M.,** to be inconsolable

magia /'mahia/ *f,* magic

mágica /'mahika/ *f,* magic; enchantress, sorceress

mágico /'mahiko/ *a* magic; marvelous, wonderful. *m,* magician; enchanter, wizard

magín /ma'hin/ *m, Inf.* imagination; head, mind

magisterio /mahis'terio/ *m,* teaching profession; teaching diploma; teaching post; pedantry, pompousness. **ejercer su m. en,** to be employed as a teacher in

magistrado /mahis'traðo/ *m,* magistrate; magistracy

magistral /mahis'tral/ *a* magistral; authoritative, magisterial; pedantic, pompous

magnanimidad /magnanimi'ðað/ *f,* magnanimity; generosity, liberality

magnánimo /mag'nanimo/ *a* magnanimous, generous, noble

magnate /mag'nate/ *m,* magnate

magnesia /mag'nesia/ *f,* magnesia

magnesio /mag'nesio/ *m,* magnesium

magnético /mag'netiko/ *a* magnetic

magnetismo /magne'tismo/ *m,* magnetism

magnetizar /magneti'θar; magneti'sar/ *vt* to magnetize; mesmerize

magneto /mag'neto/ *m,* magneto

magnificar /magnifi'kar/ *vt* to magnify, enlarge; praise, extol

magnificencia /magnifi'θenθia; magnifi'sensia/ *f,* magnificence, pomp, splendor

magnífico /mag'nifiko/ *a* magnificent; splendid, wonderful, fine; excellent

magnitud /magni'tuð/ *f,* magnitude; quantity; importance

magno /'magno/ *a* great; famous. **Alejandro M.,** Alexander the Great

magnolia /mag'nolia/ *f,* magnolia

mago /'mago/ *m,* magician; *pl* magi

magro /'magro/ *a* lean; scraggy. *m, Inf.* lean pork

magullar /magu'ʎar; magu'yar/ *vt* to bruise

mahonesa /mao'nesa/ *f,* mayonnaise

maíz /ma'iθ; ma'is/ *m,* corn

maja /'maha/ *f,* belle

majada /ma'haða/ *f,* sheepfold; dung

majadería /mahaðe'ria/ *f,* impertinence, insolence

majadero /maha'ðero/ *a* persistent, tedi-

ous. *m,* bobbin (for lace making); pestle —*n* fool, bore

majador /maha'ðor/ *m,* pestle

majar /ma'har/ *vt* to pound, crush; *Inf.* importune, annoy

majestad /mahes'tað/ *f,* majesty (title); dignity; stateliness

majestuosidad /mahestuosi'ðað/ *f,* majesty; dignity

majestuoso /mahes'tuoso/ *a* majestic; stately; dignified

majo /'maho/ *a* arrogant, aggressive; gaudily attired, smart; dashing, handsome; attractive, pretty; elegant, well-dressed. *m,* beau, gallant, man about town

majuelo /ma'huelo/ *m,* new vine; species of white hawthorn

mal /mal/ *a Abbr.* **malo.** Used only before *m sing* nouns (e.g. *un m. cuarto de hora,* a bad quarter of an hour). *m,* evil; damage; harm; misfortune; illness, disease; trouble (e.g. *El m. es,* The trouble is). **m. de altura,** air sickness. **m. de ojo,** evil eye. **m. de pledra,** lithiasis, stone. **m. francés,** syphilis. **el m. menor,** the lesser of two evils —*interj* ¡**M. haya!** A curse upon! **echar a m.,** to scorn (things); waste, squander. **llevar a m.** (una cosa), to take (a thing) badly, complain. **No hay m. que por bien no venga,** It's an ill wind that blows no one any good, Every cloud has a silver lining. **parar en m.,** to come to a bad end

mal /mal/ *adv* badly; unfavorably; wrongly; wickedly; with difficulty; scarcely, barely. **m. que bien,** willingly or unwillingly; rightly or wrongly. **de m. en peor,** from bad to worse

malabarista /malaβa'rista/ *mf* juggler

malaconsejado /malakonse'haðo/ *a* ill-advised; imprudent

malacostumbrado /malakostum'βraðo/ *a* badly trained, spoiled; having bad habits

malagueña /mala'geɲa/ *f,* popular song of lament

malandanza /malan'danθa; malan'dansa/ *f,* evildoing; misfortune, misery; poverty

malandrín /malan'drin/ *a* wicked, ill-disposed. *m,* scoundrel, miscreant

malaria /ma'laria/ *f,* malaria

malaventura /malaβen'tura/ *f,* misfortune, adversity, bad luck

malaventurado /malaβentu'raðo/ *a* unfortunate, unlucky

malbaratador /malβarata'ðor/ **(-ra)** *a* wasteful, spendthrift —*n* squanderer, spendthrift

malbaratar /malβara'tar/ *vt* to squander, waste; sell at a loss

malcasado /malka'saðo/ *a* adulterous, unfaithful

malcasar /malka'sar/ **(se)** *vt* and *vr* to marry badly

malcomido /malko'miðo/ *a* underfed

malcontento /malkon'tento/ **(-ta)** *a* dissatisfied, discontented; rebellious —*n* malcontent, rebel

malcriado /mal'kriaðo/ *a* badly brought up; ill-bred; spoiled, peevish

maldad /mal'daθ/ *f*, badness; depravity, wickedness

maldecidor /maldeθi'ðor; maldesi'ðor/ **(-ra)** *a* slanderous —*n* scandalmonger, slanderer

maldecir /malde'θir; malde'sir/ *vt irr* to curse; —*vt* and *vi* slander, backbite. See decir

maldiciente /maldi'θiente; maldi'siente/ *a* defamatory, slanderous; cursing, reviling. *m*, slanderer; curser

maldición /maldi'θion; maldi'sion/ *f*, malediction; curse, imprecation

maldispuesto /maldis'puesto/ *a* indisposed, ill; reluctant

maldita /mal'dita/ *f*, *Inf*. tongue. *Inf*. **soltar la m.**, to say too much, go too far

maldito /mal'dito/ *a* accursed; wicked; damned; poor (of quality); *Inf*. not a...

maleabilidad /maleaβili'ðaθ/ *f*, malleability, flexibility

maleable /male'aβle/ *a* malleable, flexible

maleante /male'ante/ *a* rascally, villainous. *mf* evildoer

malecón /male'kon/ *m*, breakwater

maledicencia /maleði'θenθia; maleði'sensia/ *f*, slander, abuse, backbiting; cursing

maleficencia /malefi'θenθia; malefi'sensia/ *f*, wrongdoing

maleficio /male'fiθio; male'fisio/ *m*, (magic) curse; spell; charm

maléfico /ma'lefiko/ *a* malefic, harmful. *m*, sorcerer

malestar /males'tar/ *m*, indisposition; slight illness; discomfort

maleta /ma'leta/ *f*, suitcase, valise, grip; *m*, *Inf*. clumsy matador; duffer (at games, etc.). **hacer la m.**, to pack a suitcase; *Inf*. prepare for a journey, get ready to leave

maletín /male'tin/ *m*, small suitcase or valise

malevolencia /maleβo'lenθia; maleβo'lensia/ *f*, malevolence, hatred, malice

malévolo /ma'leβolo/ *a* malevolent, malicious

maleza /ma'leθa; ma'lesa/ *f*, weeds; undergrowth; thicket

malgastador /malgasta'ðor/ **(-ra)** *a* thriftless, wasteful —*n* squanderer

malgastar /malgas'tar/ *vt* to waste (time); squander, throw away (money)

malhablado /mala'βlaðo/ *a* foul-tongued, indecent

malhadado /mala'ðaðo/ *a* ill-fated, unhappy

malhecho /mal'etʃo/ *a* deformed, twisted (persons). *m*, evil deed, wrongdoing

malhechor /male'tʃor/ **(-ra)** *n* malefactor; evildoer

malhumorado /malumo'raðo/ *a* ill-humored, bad-tempered

malicia /ma'liθia; ma'lisia/ *f*, wickedness, evil; malice, maliciousness; acuteness, subtlety, shrewdness; craftiness, guile; *Inf*. suspicion

maliciar /mali'θiar; mali'siar/ *vt* to suspect; spoil, damage; hurt, harm

malicioso /mali'θioso; mali'sioso/ *a* malicious; vindictive; wicked; shrewd, clever; *Inf*. suspicious; artful

malignidad /maligni'ðaθ/ *f*, malignancy, spite, ill will

maligno /ma'ligno/ *a* malignant, spiteful; wicked; *Med*. malignant

malintencionado /malintenθio'naðo; malintensio'naðo/ *a* ill-intentioned, badly disposed

malla /'maʎa; 'maya/ *f*, mesh (of a net); coat of mail; *pl Theat*. tights. **m. de alambre**, wire netting. **cota de m.**, coat of mail

Mallorca /ma'ʎorka; ma'yorka/ Majorca

malmandado /malman'daðo/ *a* disobedient; reluctant, unwilling

malo /'malo/ *a* bad; wicked; evil; injurious; harmful; illicit; licentious; ill; difficult; troublesome, annoying; *Inf*. mischievous; knavish; rotten, decaying —*interj* **¡M.!** That's bad!; You shouldn't have done that!; That's a bad sign! **de malas**, unluckily, unhappily. **el M.**, the Evil One, the Devil. **estar m.**, to be ill. **Lo m. es**, The trouble is, The worst of it is. **por malas o por buenas**, willy-nilly, willingly or unwillingly. **ser m.**, to be wicked; be evil; behave badly (children)

malograr /malo'grar/ *vt* to lose (time); waste, throw away (opportunities); —*vr* fall through, fail; wither, fade; die early, come to an untimely end

malogro /ma'logro/ *m*, loss, waste (time, opportunity); frustration; decline, fading; untimely death

malparar /malpa'rar/ *vt* to ill-treat; damage. **quedar malparado**, to get the worst of

malparir /malpa'rir/ *vt Med*. to miscarry

malparto /mal'parto/ *m*, miscarriage; abortion

malquerencia /malke'renθia; malke'rensia/ *f*, ill will, aversion, dislike

malquistar /malkis'tar/ *vt* to stir up trouble; make unpopular; estrange; —*vr* make oneself disliked

malquisto /mal'kisto/ *a* unpopular, disliked

malsano /mal'sano/ *a* unhealthy

malta /'malta/ *m*, malt

maltraer /maltra'er/ *vt irr* to ill-treat; insult. See traer

maltratamiento /maltrata'miento/ *m*, abuse, ill usage; damage, deterioration

maltratar /maltra'tar/ *vt* to ill-treat; abuse, insult; misuse, spoil, damage

maltrato /mal'trato/ *m*, maltreatment; misuse

maltrecho /mal'tretʃo/ *a* ill-treated, bruised; abused, insulted; damaged

manga

malucho /ma'lutʃo/ *a Inf.* off-color, below par, not well

malva /'malβa/ *f,* mallow. **m. real, m. rosa,** *or* **m. loca,** hollyhock. **ser como una m.,** *Fig. Inf.* to be a clinging vine

malvado /mal'βaðo/ *a* evil, malevolent, fiendish —*n* villain, fiend

malvavisco /malβa'βisko/ *m, Bot.* marshmallow

malversación /malβersa'θion; malβersa'sion/ *f,* malversation, maladministration; misappropriation (of funds)

malversador /malβersa'ðor/ **(-ra)** *n* bad or corrupt administrator

malversar /malβer'sar/ *vt* to misappropriate (funds)

mama /'mama/ *f, Inf.* mamma, mommy; breast; udder

mamá /ma'ma/ *f,* mamma

mamar /ma'mar/ *vt* to suck (the breast); *Inf* wolf, swallow; learn from an early age; enjoy, obtain unfairly; —*vr* get drunk

mamarracho /mama'rratʃo/ *m, Inf.* scarecrow, dummy; anything grotesque looking

mamífero /ma'mifero/ *a* mammalian. *m,* mammal

mamotreto /mamo'treto/ *m,* notebook, memorandum; *Inf.* large book or bulky file of papers

mampara /mam'para/ *f,* folding screen; screen; partition

mamparo /mam'paro/ *m,* bulkhead

mampostería /mamposte'ria/ *f,* masonry, stonemasonry

mamut /ma'mut/ *m,* mammoth

maná /ma'na/ *m,* manna

manada /ma'naða/ *f,* handful; herd, flock; group, drove, crowd

manadero /mana'ðero/ *m,* herdsman, drover; spring, stream

manantial /manan'tial/ *m,* fountain, source, spring; head (of a river)

manar /ma'nar/ *vi* to flow, stream; be plentiful

manatí /mana'ti/ *m,* sea cow, manatee

mancar /man'kar/ *vt* to injure, maim; —*vi* grow calm (elements)

manceba /man'θeβa; man'seβa/ *f,* concubine; girl

mancebo /man'θeβo; man'seβo/ *m,* youth, stripling; bachelor; shop assistant

mancha /'mantʃa/ *f,* spot, smear, stain; blotch; plot of ground; patch of vegetation; stigma, disgrace

manchar /man'tʃar/ *vt* to stain; smear; spot, speckle; disgrace; tarnish

mancilla /man'θiʎa; man'siya/ *f,* stain; slur

mancillar /manθi'ʎar; mansi'yar/ *vt* to stain; *Fig.* smirch

manco /'manko/ **(-ca)** *a* maimed, disabled; one-handed; one-armed; armless; handless; incomplete, faulty —*n* disabled person

mancomunidad /mankomuni'ðað/ *f,* association, society; community, union; commonwealth; regional legislative assembly

manda /'manda/ *f,* offer, suggestion, proposition; legacy

mandadero /manda'ðero/ **(-ra)** *n* convent or prison messenger; errand boy (girl)

mandado /man'daðo/ *m,* order, command; errand

mandamiento /manda'miento/ *m,* order, command; *Eccl.* commandment; *Law.* writ; *pl Inf.* one's five fingers

mandar /man'dar/ *vt* to order, command; bequeath, will; send; control, drive; promise, offer; order (e.g. *Mandó hacerse un traje,* He ordered a suit to be made); —*vr* walk unaided (convalescents, etc.); lead into one another (rooms, etc.); **¿Quién manda aquí?** Who is in charge here?

mandarina /manda'rina/ *f,* mandarin (classical Chinese); mandarin orange

mandatario /manda'tario/ *m,* mandatary

mandato /man'dato/ *m,* mandate; command; *Eccl.* maundy. *Polit.* mandate. **cuarto m.,** fourth term (of President, Governor, etc.)

mandíbula /man'diβula/ *f,* jaw; jawbone; mandible

mandilón /mandi'lon/ *m, Inf.* coward, nincompoop

mandioca /man'dioka/ *f,* manioc, cassava; tapioca

mando /'mando/ *m,* authority, power; (*Mil. Nav.*) command; *Engin.* regulation; controls (of a machine, etc.). **m. a distancia,** remote control. *Aer.* **m. de dos pilotos,** dual-controlled. **mandos gemelos,** dual control. **al m. de,** under the command of; under the direction of

mandolín /mando'lin/ *m,* **mandolina** *f,* mandolin

mandón /man'don/ *a* domineering, bossy

manear /mane'ar/ *vt* to hobble (a horse); manage, control

manecilla /mane'θiʎa; mane'siya/ *f, dim* little hand; hand of a clock; *Print.* fist

manejable /mane'haβle/ *a* manageable, controllable

manejar /mane'har/ *vt* to handle; use, wield; control; manage, direct; ride (horses); —*vr* manage to move around (after an accident, illness)

manejo /ma'neho/ *m,* handling; use, wielding; control; management, direction; horsemanship; intrigue

maneota /mane'ota/ *f,* hobble, shackle

manera /ma'nera/ *f,* manner, way, means; behavior, style (gen. *pl*); class (of people); *Art.* style, manner. **a la m. de,** like, in the style of. **de esa m.,** in that way; according to that, in that case. **de m. que,** so that. **en gran m.,** to a great extent. **sobre m.,** exceedingly

manga /'manga/ *f,* sleeve; bag; grip; handle; pipe (of a hose); strainer; waterspout; body of troops; beam, breadth of a ship; *pl* profits. **m. de viento,** whirlwind.

echar de m. a, to make use of a person. *Inf.* estar de m., to be in league. tener m. ancha, to be broad-minded. *Fig. Inf.* traer (una cosa) en la m., to have (something) up one's sleeve

mangana /maŋ'gana/ *f*, lasso

manganilla /maŋga'niʎa; maŋga'niya/ *f*, sleight of hand; hoax, trick

mangle /'maŋgle/ *m*, mangrove tree

mango /'maŋgo/ *m*, handle, haft, stock; mango. m. de cuchillo, knife handle

mangonear /maŋgone'ar/ *vi Inf.* to loaf, roam about; interfere, meddle

mangonero /maŋgo'nero/ *a Inf.* meddlesome

mangosta /maŋ'gosta/ *f*, mongoose

mangote /maŋ'gote/ *m, Inf.* long, wide sleeve; black oversleeve

manguera /maŋ'guera/ *f*, hose; sleeve, tube; airshaft; waterspout

manguito /maŋ'guito/ *m*, muff; black oversleeve; wristlet, cuff; *Mech.* bush, sleeve

manía /ma'nia/ *f*, mania, obsession; whim, fancy

maníaco /ma'niako/ (**-ca**) *a* maniacal; capricious, extravagant —*n* maniac

maniático /ma'niatiko/ (**-ca**) *a* maniacal; capricious; faddy, fussy —*n* crank

manicomio /mani'komio/ *m*, insane asylum, mental hospital

manicura /mani'kura/ *f*, manicure

manicuro /mani'kuro/ (**-ra**) *n* manicurist

manida /ma'niða/ *f*, lair, den; dwelling, habitation

manifestación /manifesta'θion; manifesta'sion/ *f*, declaration, statement; exhibition; demonstration; *Eccl.* exposition (of the Blessed Sacrament)

manifestante /manifes'tante/ *mf* demonstrator

manifestar /manifes'tar/ *vt irr* to declare, make known, state; exhibit, show; *Eccl.* to expose (the Blessed Sacrament). See **acertar**

manifiesto /mani'fiesto/ *a* obvious, evident. *m*, manifesto; *Naut.* manifest; *Eccl.* exposition of the Blessed Sacrament. poner de m., to show; make public; reveal

manija /ma'niha/ *f*, handle, stock, haft; hand lever; clamp; tether (for horses, etc.)

manilla /ma'niʎa; ma'niya/ *f*, bracelet; handcuff, manacle

maniobra /ma'nioβra/ *f*, operation, process; *Mil.* maneuver; intrigue; tackle, gear; handling, management; *Naut.* working of a ship; *pl* shunting (trains)

maniobrar /manio'βrar/ *vi Mil.* to maneuver; *Naut.* handle, work (ships)

manipulación /manipula'θion; manipula-'sion/ *f*, handling; manipulation; control, management

manipulador /manipula'ðor/ *a* manipulative. *m*, sending key (telegraphy)

manipular /manipu'lar/ *vt* to handle; manipulate; manage, direct

maniquí /mani'ki/ *m*, mannequin; dummy; *Inf.* puppet, weak person

manirroto /mani'rroto/ (**-ta**) *a* wasteful, extravagant —*n* spendthrift

manivela /mani'βela/ *f, Mech.* crank, lever

manjar /man'har/ *m*, dish, food; pastime, recreation, pleasure. m. blanco, blancmange

mano /'mano/ *f*, hand; coat, coating; quire (of paper); front paw (animals); elephant's trunk; side, hand; hand (of a clock); game (of cards, etc.); lead (at cards); way, means; ability; power; protection, favor; compassion; aid, help; scolding; *Mus.* scale; pestle; workers. *Inf.* editing, correction of a literary work (gen. by a person more skilled than the author). m. de mortero, pestle. m. de obra, (manual) labor. manos muertas, *Law.* mortmain. m. sobre m., with folded hands; lazily, indolently. a la m., at hand, nearby; within one's grasp. a manos llenas, in abundance, abundantly. bajo m., in an underhand manner, secretly. buenas manos, cleverness, ability; dexterity. de primera m., first-hand, new. estar dejado de la m. de Dios, to be very unlucky; be very foolish. poner la m. en, to ill-treat; slap, buffet. Si a m. viene..., If by chance... tender la m., to put out one's hand, shake hands. traer entre manos, to have on hand, be engaged in

manojo /ma'noho/ *m*, bunch, handful. a manojos, in handfuls; plentifully, in abundance

manosear /manose'ar/ *vt* to handle; paw, touch repeatedly; finger

manoseo /mano'seo/ *m*, handling; fingering; *Inf.* pawing, feeling

manotada /mano'taða/ *f*, slap, cuff

manotear /manote'ar/ *vt* to slap, cuff; —*vi* gesticulate, gesture with the hands

manoteo /mano'teo/ *m*, gesticulation with the hands

mansalva /man'salβa/ (**a**) *adv* without danger

mansedumbre /manse'ðumbre/ *f*, meekness; kindness; gentleness

mansión /man'sion/ *f*, stay, visit; dwelling, abode; mansion

manso /'manso/ *a* soft, gentle; meek, mild; tame; peaceable, amiable; calm

manta /'manta/ *f*, blanket; horse blanket; traveling rug; *Inf.* hiding, thrashing. m. de viaje, traveling rug. *Inf.* a m. de Dios, in abundance. dar una m., to toss in a blanket. *Fig. Inf.* tirar de la m., to let the cat out of the bag

mantear /mante'ar/ *vt* to toss in a blanket

manteca /man'teka/ *f*, lard; cooking fat; grease; *Argentina* butter. como m., as mild as milk, as soft as butter

mantecada /mante'kaða/ f. buttered toast

mantecoso /mante'koso/ a greasy

mantel /man'tel/ m. tablecloth; altar cloth

mantelería /mantele'ria/ f. table linen

mantener /mante'ner/ vt irr to maintain; keep, feed; support; continue, persevere with; uphold, affirm; keep up; —vr support oneself; remain in a place; (with en) continue to uphold (views, etc.), persevere in. **mantenerse firme**, Fig. to stand one's ground. See **tener**

mantenimiento /manteni'miento/ m. maintenance; support; sustenance, nourishment; affirmation; upkeep; livelihood

mantequera /mante'kera/ f. churn; dairymaid; butter dish

mantequero /mante'kero/ m. dairyman; butter dish

mantequilla /mante'kiʎa; mante'kiya/ f. butter

mantilla /man'tiʎa; man'tiya/ f. mantilla; saddlecloth pl baby's long clothes. **estar en mantillas**, to be in swaddling clothes; Fig. be in early infancy

manto /'manto/ m. cloak, cover, disguise; Zool. mantle; Mineral. layer

mantón /man'ton/ m. shawl. **m. de Manila**, Manila shawl

manuable /ma'nuaβle/ a easy to handle or use, handy

manual /ma'nual/ a manual; handy, easy to use; docile, peaceable. m. manual, textbook; Eccl. book of ritual; notebook

manubrio /ma'nuβrio/ m. handle, crank

manufactura /manufak'tura/ f. manufacture; manufactured article; factory

manufacturar /manufaktu'rar/ vt to manufacture

manufacturero /manufaktu'rero/ a manufacturing

manuscrito /manus'krito/ a and m. manuscrito

manutención /manuten'θion; manuten'sion/ f. maintenance; upkeep; protection

manzana /man'θana; man'sana/ f. apple; block (of houses); city square; Adam's apple

manzanal /manθa'nal; mansa'nal/ m. apple orchard; apple tree

manzanar /manθa'nar; mansa'nar/ m. apple orchard

manzanilla /manθa'niʎa; mansa'niya/ f. white sherry wine; Bot. chamomile; chamomile tea; knob, ball (on furniture); pad (on an animal's foot)

manzano /man'θano; man'sano/ m. apple tree

maña /'maɲa/ f. skill, dexterity; craftiness, guile; vice, bad habit (gen. pl). **darse m. para**, to contrive to

mañana /ma'ɲana/ f. morning; tomorrow. m. future, tomorrow —adv tomorrow; in time to come; soon. ¡M.! Tomorrow! Another day! Not now! (gen-

erally to beggars). **de m.**, early in the morning. **muy de m.**, very early in the morning. **pasado m.**, the day after tomorrow

mañanica /maɲa'nika/ f. early morning

mañear /maɲe'ar/ vt to arrange cleverly; —vi behave shrewdly

mañero /ma'ɲero/ a shrewd, clever; easily worked; handy

mañoso /ma'ɲoso/ a clever, skillful; crafty; vicious, with bad habits

mañuela /ma'ɲuela/ f. low guile

mapa /'mapa/ m. map; card. **m. en relieve**, relief map. **m. del estado mayor**, ordnance map. Inf. **no estar en el m.**, to be off the map; be most unusual (of things)

mapache /ma'patʃe/ m. raccoon

maqueta /ma'keta/ f. (Art. Archit.) model

maquiavélico /makia'βeliko/ a Machiavellian

maquillaje /maki'ʎahe; maki'yahe/ m. makeup, cosmetics; making up (of the face)

maquillar /maki'ʎar; maki'yar/ (se) vt and vr to make up (the face, etc.)

máquina /'makina/ f. machine, mechanism; engine; apparatus; plan, scheme; machine, puppet; Inf. mansion, palace; plenty; locomotive; fantasy, product of the imagination. **m. de vapor**, steam engine. **m. de arrastre**, traction engine; tractor. **m. de coser**, sewing machine. **m. de escribir**, typewriter. **m. fotográfica**, camera. **m. de impresionar**, movie camera. **m. de imprimir**, printing machine. **m. herramienta**, machine tool. **m. neumática**, air pump

maquinación /makina'θion; makina'sion/ f. intrigue, machination

maquinador /makina'ðor/ **(-ra)** n intriguer, schemer

maquinar /maki'nar/ vt to intrigue, scheme, plot

maquinaria /maki'naria/ f. machinery; applied mechanics; mechanism

maquinista /maki'nista/ mf driver, enginer; mechanic; machinist; locomotive driver

mar /mar/ mf sea; great many, abundance. **m. bonanza** or **m. en calma**, calm sea. **m. de fondo** or **m. de leva**, swell. **alta m.**, high seas. **a mares**, plentifully. **arar en el m.**, to labor in vain. Naut. **hacerse a la m.**, to put out to sea. **la m. de historias**, a great number of stories

maraña /ma'raɲa/ f. undergrowth; tangle; Fig. difficult position; intrigue; silk waste

marasmo /ma'rasmo/ m. Med. marasmus, atrophy; inactivity, paralysis

maravilla /mara'βiʎa; mara'βiya/ f. marvel, wonder; admiration; amazement; marigold. **a m.**, wonderfully. **a las mil maravillas**, to perfection, excellently. **por m.**, by chance; occasionally

maravillar /maraβi'ʎar; maraβi'yar/ vt to amaze, cause admiration; —vr (with de) marvel at, admire; be amazed by

maravilloso /maraβi'ʎoso; maraβi'yoso/ a marvelous, wonderful

marbete /mar'βete/ m, label, tag; edge, border

marca /'marka/ f, mark, sign; brand; frontier zone, border country; standard, norm (of size); make, brand; measuring rule; Sports. record. **m. de fábrica**, brand, trademark. **m. de ley**, hallmark. **m. registrada**, registered name. **de m.**, excellent, of excellent quality

marcado /mar'kaðo/ a marked; pronounced; strong (of accents)

marcador /marka'ðor/ a marking. m, marker; scoreboard; bookmark

marcar /mar'kar/ vt to mark; brand; embroider initials on linen; tell the time (watches); show the amount (cash register, etc.); dial (telephone); Sports. score (a goal); notice, observe; set aside, earmark; —vr Naut. check the course. **m. el compás** to beat time

marcha /'martʃa/ f, departure; running, working; Mil. march; speed (of trains, ships, etc.); Mus. march; progress, course (of events). **m. atrás**, backing, reversing. **m. de ensayo**, trial run. **m. forzada**, Mil. forced march. **a largas marchas**, with all speed. **a toda m.**, at top speed; full speed ahead; by forced marches; Mil. **batir la m.**, to strike up a march. **en m.**, underway; working; in operation

marchar /mar'tʃar/ vi to run; work; function; go; leave, depart; progress, proceed; Mil. march; go (clocks); —vr leave, go away

marchitable /martʃi'taβle/ a perishable, fragile

marchitar /martʃi'tar/ vt to wither, fade; blight, spoil; weaken; —vr wither; be blighted

marchito /mar'tʃito/ a withered; faded; blighted, frustrated

marcial /mar'θial; mar'sial/ a martial, courageous, militant

marcialidad /marθiali'ðað; marsiali'ðað/ f, war-like spirit, militancy

marco /'marko/ m, mark (German coin); boundary mark; frame (of a picture, etc.). **m. de ventana**, window frame

marea /ma'rea/ f, tide; strand, water's edge; light breeze; drizzle; dew; street dirt. **m. creciente**, flood tide. **m. menguante**, ebb tide. **m. muerta**, neap tide

mareaje /ma'reahe/ m, seamanship; ship's course

marear /mare'ar/ vt to navigate; sell; sell publicly; Inf. annoy; —vr be seasick; feel faint; feel giddy; be damaged at sea (goods)

marejada /mare'haða/ f, surge, swell; high sea; tidal wave; commotion, uproar

mareo /ma'reo/ m, seasickness; nausea; dizziness; Inf. irritation, tediousness

mareta /ma'reta/ f, movement of the waves; sound, noise (of a crowd)

marfil /mar'fil/ m, ivory

marfileño /marfi'leɲo/ a ivory; ivory-like

marfuz /mar'fuθ; mar'fus/ a spurned, rejected; deceitful

margarina /marga'rina/ f, margarine

margarita /marga'rita/ f, pearl; marguerite, oxeye daisy; daisy; periwinkle

margen /'marhen/ mf edge, fringe, border, verge; margin (of a book); opportunity; marginal note. **dar m. para**, to provide an opportunity for; give rise to

marginal /marhi'nal/ a marginal

margoso /mar'goso/ a loamy, marly

marica /ma'rika/ f, magpie. m, (offensive) homosexual; milksop

maricón /mari'kon/ m, (offensive) homosexual

maridable /mari'ðaβle/ a marital, matrimonial

maridaje /mari'ðahe/ m, conjugal union and harmony; intimate relationship (between things)

maridar /mari'ðar/ vi to get married; mate, live as husband and wife; —vt unite, link, join together

marido /ma'riðo/ m, husband

marihuana /mari'uana/ f, marijuana

marimacho /mari'matʃo/ m, Inf. mannish woman

marina /ma'rina/ f, coast, seashore; Art. seascape; seamanship; navy, fleet. **m. de guerra**, navy. **m. mercante**, merchant navy

marinera /mari'nera/ f, sailor's blouse

marinería /marine'ria/ f, profession of a sailor; seamanship; crew of a ship; sailors (as a class)

marinero /mari'nero/ m, sailor, seaman. **m. de agua dulce**, freshwater sailor (a novice). **m. práctico**, able seaman. **a la marinera**, in a seaman-like fashion

marinesco /mari'nesko/ a seamanly

marino /ma'rino/ a marine, sea; seafaring; shipping. m, sailor, mariner

marioneta /mario'neta/ f, marionette, puppet

mariposa /mari'posa/ f, butterfly; nightlight

mariposear /maripose'ar/ vi to flutter, flit, fly about; flirt, be fickle; follow about, dance attendance on

mariquita /mari'kita/ f, Ent. ladybird; parakeet.

marisabidilla /marisaβi'ðiʎa; mari-saβi'ðiya/ f, Inf. blue-stocking, know-it-all

mariscal /maris'kal/ m, Mil. marshal; field marshal; blacksmith

marisco /ma'risko/ m, shellfish

marisma /ma'risma/ f, bog, morass, swamp

marital /mari'tal/ a marital

marítimo /ma'ritimo/ a maritime, sea

marmita /mar'mita/ f, stewpot; copper, boiler

mármol /'marmol/ *m*, marble; work executed in marble

marmóreo /mar'moreo/ *a* marble; *Poet.* marmoreal

marmota /mar'mota/ *f*, *Zool.* marmot; sleepyhead, dormouse

Mar Muerto /mar 'muerto/ Dead Sea

marquesina /marke'sina/ *f*, marquee

marquetería /markete'ria/ *f*, marquetry

marrana /ma'rrana/ *f*, sow; *Inf.* slattern, slut

marrano /ma'rrano/ *m*, pig, hog; Marrano

marras /'marras/ **(de)** *adv* long ago, in the dim past

marrasquino /marras'kino/ *m*, maraschino liqueur

marro /'marro/ *m*, tick, tag (game)

Mar Rojo /mar 'rroho/ Red Sea

marrón /ma'rron/ *a* maroon; brown. *m*, brown color, maroon color; quoit

marroquí /marro'ki/ *a* and *mf* Moroccan. *m*, Morocco leather

Marruecos /ma'rruekos/ Morocco

marrullería /marruʎe'ria; marruye'ria/ *f*, flattery, cajolery

marrullero /marru'ʎero; marru'yero/ **(-ra)** *a* wheedling, flattering —*n* wheedler, cajoler

Marsella /mar'seʎa; mar'seya/ Marseilles

marsellés /marse'ʎes; marse'yes/ **(-esa)** *a* and *n* of or from Marseilles. *f*. **la Marsellesa**, the Marseillaise

marsopa /mar'sopa/ *f*, porpoise

marta /'marta/ *f*, sable; marten

Marte /'marte/ *m*, Mars

martes /'martes/ *m*, Tuesday. **m. de carnaval**, mardi gras

martillar /marti'ʎar; marti'yar/ *vt* to hammer; oppress

martillazo /marti'ʎaθo; marti'yaso/ *m*, hammer blow

martilleo /marti'ʎeo; marti'yeo/ *m*, hammering; noise of the hammer; clink, clatter

martillo /mar'tiʎo; mar'tiyo/ *m*, hammer; oppressor, tyrant; auction rooms. **a m.**, by hammering. **de m.**, wrought (of metals)

martinete /marti'nete/ *m*, hammer (of a pianoforte); pile driver; drop hammer. **m. de báscula**, tilt hammer

Martinica /marti'nika/ Martinique

martín pescador /mar'tin peska'ðor/ *m*, kingfisher

mártir /'martir/ *mf* martyr

martirio /mar'tirio/ *m*, martyrdom

martirizar /martiri'θar; martiri'sar/ *vt* to martyr; torture, torment, martyrize; tease, annoy

marzo /'marθo; 'marso/ *m*, March

mas /mas/ *conjunc* but; yet

más /mas/ *adv compar* more; in addition, besides; rather, preferably. *Math.* plus. **el (la, etc.) más,** *adv superl* the most, etc. **m. bien,** more; rather, preferably. **m. que,** only; but; more than; although,

even if. **a lo m.,** at the most; at the worst. **a m.,** besides, in addition. **de m.,** superfluous, unnecessary, unwanted. **no... m. que,** only. **por m. que,** however; even if. **sin m. ni m.,** without further ado. **M. vale un mal arreglo que un buen pleito,** A bad peace is better than a good war

masa /'masa/ *f*, mass; dough; whole, aggregate; majority (of people); mortar. **en la m. de la sangre,** *Fig.* in the blood, in a person's nature

masada /ma'saða/ *f*, farmhouse and stock

masaje /ma'sahe/ *m*, massage

masajista /masa'hista/ *mf* masseur; masseuse

mascar /mas'kar/ *vt* to chew; masticate; *Inf.* mumble, mutter

máscara /'maskara/ *f*, mask; fancy dress; pretext, excuse. *mf* masquerader, reveler; *pl* masquerade. **m. para gases,** gas mask

mascarada /maska'raða/ *f*, masquerade; company of revelers

mascarón /maska'ron/ *m*, large mask; *Archit.* gargoyle. **m. de proa,** *Naut.* figurehead

mascota /mas'kota/ *f*, mascot

masculinidad /maskulini'ðað/ *f*, masculinity

masculino /masku'lino/ *a* masculine; male; manly, vigorous

mascullar /masku'ʎar; masku'yar/ *vt* *Inf.* to chew; mutter, mumble

masera /ma'sera/ *f*, kneading bowl; cloth for covering dough

masilla /ma'siʎa; ma'siya/ *f*, mastic, putty

masón /ma'son/ **(-ona)** *n* Freemason

masonería /masone'ria/ *f*, freemasonry

masónico /ma'soniko/ *a* masonic

masoquismo /maso'kismo/ *m*, masochism

masticación /mastika'θion; mastika'sion/ *f*, mastication

masticar /masti'kar/ *vt* to masticate, eat; *Inf.* chew upon, consider

mástil /'mastil/ *m*, *Naut.* mast; upright, stanchion; pole (of a tent); stem, trunk; neck (of a guitar, etc.)

mastín /mas'tin/ *m*, mastiff

mastodonte /masto'ðonte/ *m*, mastodon

mastoides /mastoi'ðes/ *a* mastoid

mastuerzo /mas'tuerθo; mas'tuerso/ *m*, watercress; fool, blockhead

masturbación /masturßa'θion; masturßa'sion/ *f*, masturbation

masturbarse /mastur'ßarse/ *vr* to masturbate

mata /'mata/ *f*, plant, shrub; stalk, sprig; grove, copse. **m. de pelo,** mat of hair

matachín /mata'tʃin/ *m*, mummer; butcher; *Inf.* swashbuckler

matadero /mata'ðero/ *m*, slaughterhouse, abattoir

matafuego /mata'fuego/ *m*, fire extinguisher; fireman

matalotaje /matalo'tahe/ *m*, ship's supplies, stores; *Inf.* hodgepodge

matamoros /mata'moros/ *a* swashbuckling, swaggering

matamoscas /mata'moskas/ *m*, fly swatter

matanza /ma'tanθa; ma'tansa/ *f*, killing, massacre, slaughter; butchery (animals); *Inf.* persistence, determination

matar /ma'tar/ *vt* to kill; quench (thirst); put out (fire, light); slake (lime); tarnish (metal); bevel (corners, etc.); pester, importune; suppress; compel; *Art.* tone down; —*vr* kill oneself; be disappointed, grieve; overwork. **estar a m.**, to be at daggers drawn. **matarse por,** to try hard to; work hard for

matasanos /mata'sanos/ *m*, *Inf.* quack (doctor); bad doctor

matasellos /mata'seʎos; mata'seyos/ *m*, cancellation, postmark

mate /'mate/ *a* matte, unpolished, dull. *m*, checkmate (chess); maté, Paraguayan tea; gourd; vessel made from gourd, coconut, etc.

maté /ma'te/ *m*, maté, Paraguayan tea

matemáticas /mate'matikas/ *f pl*, mathematics. **m. prácticas,** applied mathematics. **m. teóricas,** pure mathematics

matemático /mate'matiko/ *a* mathematical; exact. *m*, mathematician

materia /ma'teria/ *f*, matter; theme, subject matter; subject (of study); matter, stuff, substance; pus, matter; question, subject; reason, occasion. **m. colorante,** dye. **materias plásticas,** plastics. **materias primas,** raw materials. **en m. de,** concerning; in the matter of

material /mate'rial/ *a* material; dull, stupid, limited. *m*, material; ingredient; plant, factory; equipment. **m. móvil ferroviario,** rolling stock (railroads)

materialista /materia'lista/ *a* materialistic. *mf* materialist

materializar /materiali'θar; materiali'sar/ *vt* to materialize; —*vr* materialize; grow materialistic, grow less spiritual

maternidad /materni'ðað/ *f*, maternity, motherhood

materno /ma'terno/ *a* maternal

matiz /ma'tiθ; ma'tis/ *m*, combination of colors; tone, hue; shade (of meaning, etc.)

matizar /mati'θar; mati'sar/ *vt* to combine, harmonize (colors); tint, shade; tinge (words, etc.)

matojo /ma'toho/ *m*, shrub, bush

matorral /mato'rral/ *m*, thicket, bush, undergrowth

matraca /ma'traka/ *f*, rattle; *Inf.* scolding, dressing-down; insistence, importunity

matraquear /matrake'ar/ *vi* to make a noise with a rattle; *Inf.* scold

matriarcado /matriar'kaðo/ *m*, matriarchy

matricida /matri'θiða; matri'siða/ *mf* matricide (person)

matricidio /matri'θiðio; matri'siðio/ *m*, matricide (crime)

matrícula /ma'trikula/ *f*, list, register; matriculation; registration number (of a car, etc.). **m. de buques,** maritime register. **m. de mar,** mariner's register; maritime register

matriculación /matrikula'θion; matrikula'sion/ *f*, matriculation; registration

matricular /matriku'lar/ *vt* to matriculate; enrol; *Naut.* register; —*vr* matriculate; enroll, register

matrimonial /matrimo'nial/ *a* matrimonial

matrimonio /matri'monio/ *m*, marriage, matrimony; married couple. **m. a yuras,** secret marriage. **m. de la mano izquierda** *or* **m. morganático,** morganatic marriage. **contraer m.,** to get married

matritense /matri'tense/ *a* and *mf* Madrilenian

matriz /ma'triθ; ma'tris/ *f*, uterus, womb; matrix, mold; *Mineral.* matrix; nut, female screw

matrona /ma'trona/ *f*, married woman; matron; midwife; female customs officer

matusalén /matusa'len/ *m*, Methuselah, very old man

matute /ma'tute/ *m*, smuggling; contraband; gambling den

matutero /matu'tero/ **(-ra)** *n* smuggler, contrabandist

matutino /matu'tino/ *a* matutinal, morning

maula /'maula/ *f*, trash; remnant; deception, fraud, trick. *mf Inf.* good-for-nothing; lazybones. *Inf.* **ser buena m.,** to be a trickster or a fraud

maulería /maule'ria/ *f*, remnant stall; trickery

maullar /mau'ʎar; mau'yar/ *vi* to meow, mew (cats)

mausoleo /mauso'leo/ *m*, mausoleum

maxilar /maksi'lar/ *a* maxillary. *m*, jaw

máxima /'maksima/ *f*, maxim, rule, precept, principle

máxime /'maksime/ *adv* principally, chiefly

máximo /'maksimo/ *a superl* **grande** greatest, maximum, top. *m*, maximum

maya /'maya/ *f*, common daisy; May queen

mayo /'mayo/ *m*, May; maypole; bouquet, wreath of flowers; *pl* festivities on eve of May Day

mayonesa /mayo'nesa/ *f*, mayonnaise

mayor /ma'yor/ *a compar* **grande** bigger; greater; elder; main, principal; older; high (mass, etc.); *Mus.* major. *mf* major (of full age) —*a superl* **grande. el, la, lo mayor, los (las) mayores,** the biggest, greatest; eldest; chief, principal. **por m.,** in short, briefly; *Com.* wholesale

mayor /ma'yor/ *m*, head, director; chief clerk; *Mil.* major; *pl* ancestors

mayoral /mayo'ral/ *m*, head shepherd; coachman, driver; foreman, overseer, supervisor, steward

mayorazgo /mayo'raθgo; mayo'rasgo/ *m*,

Law. entail; entailed estate; heir (to an entail); eldest son; right of primogeniture

mayoría /mayo'ria/ *f.* majority

mayormente /mayor'mente/ *adv* chiefly; especially

mayúscula /ma'yuskula/ *f.* capital letter, upper-case letter

mayúsculo /ma'yuskulo/ *a* large; capital (letters). **letra mayúscula**, capital letter, upper-case letter

maza /'maθa; 'masa/ *f.* mallet; club, bludgeon; mace; bass drum stick; pile driver; bone, stick, etc., tied to dog's tail in carnival; *Inf.* pedant, bore; important person, authority. **m. de polo**, polo mallet

mazamorra /maθa'morra; masa'morra/ *f.* dish made of cornmeal; biscuit crumbs; broken fragments, remains

mazapán /maθa'pan; masa'pan/ *m.* marzipan

mazmorra /maθ'morra; mas'morra/ *f.* dungeon

mazo /'maθo; 'maso/ *m.* mallet; bundle, bunch; importunate person; clapper (of a bell)

mazonería /maθone'ria; masone'ria/ *f.* stonemasonry

mazonero /maθo'nero; maso'nero/ *m.* stonemason

mazorca /ma'θorka; ma'sorka/ *f.* spindleful; spike, ear (of corn); cocoa berry; camarilla, group

me /me/ *pers pron acc or dat 1st sing mf* me; to me

meandro /me'andro/ *m.* meandering, twisting, winding; wandering

Meca, la /'meka, la/ Mecca

mecánica /me'kanika/ *f.* mechanics; mechanism, machinery; *Inf.* worthless thing; mean action

mecánico /me'kaniko/ *a* mechanical; power-operated; base, ill-bred. *m,* engineer; mechanic

mecanismo /meka'nismo/ *m.* mechanism; works, machinery

mecanizar /mekani'θar; mekani'sar/ *vt* to mechanize

mecanografía /mekanogra'fia/ *f.* typewriting

mecanografiar /mekanografi'ar/ *vt* to typewrite, type

mecanografista /mekanogra'fista/ *mf* **mecanógrafo (-fa)** *n* typist

mecedor /meθe'ðor; mese'ðor/ *a* rocking, swaying. *m,* swing

mecedora /meθe'ðora; mese'ðora/ *f.* rocking chair

mecenas /me'θenas; me'senas/ *m,* Maecenas, patron

mecer /me'θer; me'ser/ *vt* to stir, mix; shake; rock; swing

mecha /'metʃa/ *f.* wick; bit, drill; fuse (of explosives); match (for cannon, etc.); fat bacon (for basting); lock of hair; skein, twist

mechar /me'tʃar/ *vt* *Cul.* to baste, lard

mechero /me'tʃero/ *m,* gas burner; pocket lighter; socket of a candlestick

medalla /me'ðaʎa; me'ðaya/ *f.* medal; medallion; plaque, round panel; *Inf.* piece of eight (coin)

medallón /meða'ʎon; me'ðayon/ *m,* large medal; medallion; locket

médano /'meðano/ *m,* sand dune

media /'meðia/ *f.* stocking

mediación /meðia'θion; meðia'sion/ *f.* mediation, arbitration; intercession

mediado /me'ðiaðo/ *a* half-full. **a mediados (del mes,** etc.**),** toward the middle (of the month, etc.)

mediador /meðia'ðor/ **(-ra)** *n* mediator, arbitrator; intercessor

medianamente /meðiana'mente/ *adv* moderately; passably, fairly well

medianero /meðia'nero/ **(-ra)** *a* middle; intervening, intermediate; mediatory —*n* mediator. *m,* owner of a semidetached house or of one in a row

mediano /me'ðiano/ *a* medium, average; moderate; *Inf.* middling, passable, fair

medianoche /meðia'notʃe/ *f.* midnight

mediante /me'ðiante/ *a* mediatory —*adv* by means of, by, through

mediar /me'ðiar/ *vi* to reach the middle; get halfway; elapse half a given time; intercede, mediate; arbitrate; be in between or in the middle; intervene, take part

medicación /meðika'θion; meðika'sion/ *f.* medication

medicamento /meðika'mento/ *m,* medicament, medicine, remedy

medicastro /meði'kastro/ *m,* unskilled physician; quack, charlatan

medicina /meði'θina; meði'sina/ *f.* medicine; medicament

medicinar /meðiθi'nar; meðisi'nar/ *vt* to attend; treat (patients)

médico /'meðiko/ **(-ca)** *a* medical —*n* doctor of medicine. **m. de cabecera,** family doctor. **m. general,** general practitioner

medida /me'ðiða/ *f.* measurement; measuring stick; measure, precaution (gen. with *tomar, adoptar,* etc.); gauge; judgment, wisdom; meter; standard. **a m. que,** while, at the same time as. **tomar las medidas (a),** *Fig.* to take a person's measure, sum him up. **tomar sus medidas,** to take his (their) measurements; take the necessary measures. **un traje hecho a m.,** a suit made to measure

medieval /meðie'βal/ *a* medieval

medio /'meðio/ *a* half; middle; intermediate; halfway. *m,* half; middle; *Art.* medium; spiritualist medium; proceeding, measure, precaution; environment, medium; middle way, mean; *Sports.* half-back. **m. galope,** canter. **m. tiempo,** *Sports.* halftime. **a medias,** by halves; half, partly. **de por m.,** by halves; in between; in the way. **estar de por m.,** to be in the way; take part in. *Inf.* **quitar de en m.,** to get rid of. **quitarse de en m.,** to go away, remove oneself

mediocre /me'ðiokre/ *a* mediocre

mediocridad /meðiokri'ðað/ *f.* mediocrity; insignificance

mediodía /meðio'ðia/ *m,* noon, meridian; south

mediopelo /meðio'pelo/ *m,* lower middle class

medir /me'ðir/ *vt irr* to measure; (metrics) scan; survey (land); compare; —*vr* measure one's words; act with restraint. See **pedir**

meditabundo /meðita'βundo/ *a* pensive, meditative, thoughtful

meditación /meðita'θion; meðita'sion/ *f,* meditation; consideration; reflection

meditador /meðita'ðor/ *a* meditative, thoughtful

meditar /meði'tar/ *vt* to meditate, consider, muse

mediterráneo /meðite'rraneo/ *a* mediterranean; inland, landlocked

medra /'meðra/ *f,* progress; improvement, betterment; growth; prosperity

medrar /me'ðrar/ *vi* to flourish, grow; become prosperous or improve one's position

medro /'meðro/ *m,* improvement, progress. See **medra**

medroso /me'ðroso/ *a* timid, frightened; frightful, horrible

médula /'meðula/ *f,* marrow; *Bot.* pith; *Fig.* essence, core

medusa /me'ðusa/ *f,* jellyfish

megáfono /me'gafono/ *m,* megaphone

megalómano /mega'lomano/ **(-na)** *n* megalomaniac

mejicano /mehi'kano/ **(-na)** *a* and *n* Mexican

Méjico /'mehiko/ Mexico

mejilla /me'hiʎa; me'hiya/ *f, Anat.* cheek

mejor /me'hor/ *a compar* **bueno** better —*adv* better; rather; sooner; preferably —*a superl* bueno. el, la, lo mejor; los, las mejores, the best; most preferable. m. que m., better and better. *Inf.* a lo m., probably, in all probability. tanto m., so much the better

mejora /me'hora/ *f,* improvement; bettering; progress; higher bid (at auctions)

mejorable /meho'raβle/ *a* improvable

mejoramiento /mehora'miento/ *m,* betterment, improvement

mejorar /meho'rar/ *vt* to improve; better; outbid; —*vi* grow better (in health); improve (weather); make progress; rally (of markets). Mejorando lo presente, Present company excepted

mejoría /meho'ria/ *f,* improvement, progress; betterment; superiority; advantage, profit

mejunje /me'hunhe/ *m, Inf.* brew, potion, cure-all, stuff

melancolía /melanko'lia/ *f,* melancholia; sadness, depression, melancholy

melancólico /melan'koliko/ *a* melancholy, sad; depressing

melaza /me'laθa; me'lasa/ *f,* molasses

melena /me'lena/ *f,* long side whiskers; loose, flowing hair (in women); overlong hair (in men); lion's mane. *Inf.* andar a la m., to start a fight or quarrel. *Inf.* traer a la m., to drag by the hair, force

melifluo /me'lifluo/ *a* mellifluous, sweet-voiced; honeyed

melindre /me'lindre/ *m,* honey fritter; affectation, scruple, fastidiousness; narrow ribbon

melindroso /melin'droso/ *a* overfastidious, affected, prudish

mella /'meʎa; 'meya/ *f,* nick, notch; dent; gap; harm, damage (to reputation, etc.). hacer m., *Fig.* to make an impression (on the mind); *Mil.* breach, drive a wedge

mellar /me'ʎar; me'yar/ *vt* to nick, notch; dent; damage

mellizo /me'ʎiθo; me'yiso/ **(-za)** *a* and *n* twin

melocotón /meloko'ton/ *m,* peach; peach tree

melodía /melo'ðia/ *f,* melody; tune; melodiousness

melódico /me'loðiko/ *a* melodic, melodious

melodioso /melo'ðioso/ *a* melodious, tuneful, sweet-sounding

melodrama /melo'ðrama/ *m,* melodrama

melodramático /meloðra'matiko/ *a* melodramatic

melón /me'lon/ *m,* melon

meloso /me'loso/ *a* honeyed; sweet; gentle; mellifluous

membrana /mem'brana/ *f,* membrane

membrete /mem'brete/ *m,* note, memorandum; note or card of invitation; superscription, heading; address (of person)

membrillo /mem'briʎo; mem'briyo/ *m,* quince tree; quince; quince jelly

membrudo /mem'bruðo/ *a* brawny, strong, muscular

memo /'memo/ *a* silly, stupid

memorándum /memo'randum/ *m,* notebook, jotter; memorandum

memorar /memo'rar/ **(se)** *vt* and *vr* to remember, recall

memoria /me'moria/ *f,* memory; remembrance, recollection; monument; memorial; report; essay, article; codicil; memorandum; record, chronicle; *pl* regards, compliments, greetings; memoirs; memoranda. *Inf.* m. de grillo, poor memory. de m., by heart. flaco de m., forgetful. hacer m., to remember

memorial /memo'rial/ *m,* notebook; memorial, petition

memorioso /memo'rioso/ *a* mindful, unforgetful

mención /men'θion; men'sion/ *f,* mention. m. honorífica, honorable mention. hacer m. de, to mention

mencionar /menθio'nar; mensio'nar/ *vt* to mention

mendacidad /mendaθi'ðað; mendasi'ðað/ *f,* mendacity, untruthfulness

mendaz /men'daθ; men'das/ *a* mendacious, untruthful

mendicante /mendi'kante/ *a* begging; *Eccl.* mendicant. *mf* beggar

mendigar /mendi'gar/ *vt* to beg for alms; entreat, supplicate

mendigo /men'digo/ **(-ga)** *n* beggar

mendoso /men'doso/ *a* mendacious, untruthful; mistaken

mendrugo /men'drugo/ *m,* crust of bread

menear /mene'ar/ *vt* to sway, move; wag; shake; manage, control, direct; —*vr* *Inf.* get a move on; sway, move; wriggle

meneo /me'neo/ *m,* swaying movement; wagging; shaking; wriggling; management, direction; *Aer.* bump; *Inf.* spanking

menester /menes'ter/ *m,* lack, shortage; necessity; occupation, employment; *pl* physical necessities; *Inf.* tools, implements, equipment. **haber m.,** to need, require. **ser m.,** to be necessary or requisite

menesteroso /meneste'roso/ *a* indigent, poverty-stricken, needy

menestra /me'nestra/ *f,* vegetable soup; dried vegetable (gen. *pl*)

mengano /meŋ'gano/ **(-na)** *n* so-and-so (used instead of the name of the person)

mengua /'meŋgua/ *f,* decrease; lack, shortage; waning (of the moon, etc.); dishonor, disgrace; poverty

menguado /meŋ'guaðo/ **(-da)** *a* timid, cowardly; silly, stupid; mean, avaricious —*n* coward; fool; skinflint. *m,* narrowing stitch when knitting socks

menguante /meŋ'guante/ *a* ebb; waning; decreasing. *f,* ebb tide; decadence, decline. **m. de la luna,** waning of the moon

menguar /meŋ'guar/ *vi* to decrease; decline, decay; wane; ebb; narrow (socks); —*vt* diminish; disgrace, discredit

menopausia /meno'pausia/ *f,* menopause

menor /me'nor/ *a compar* less, smaller; younger, minor; *Mus.* minor. *m,* minor. *f,* (logic) minor —*a superl* **el, la, lo m.; los, las menores,** the least; smallest; youngest. **m. de edad,** minor (in age). **por m.,** at retail; in detail

Menorca /me'norka/ Minorca

menoría /meno'ria/ *f,* subordination, dependence; inferiority; minority (underage); childhood, youth

menos /'menos/ *adv* less; minus; least; except. **m. de** or **m. que,** less than. **al m., por lo m.,** at least. **a m. que,** unless. **De m. nos hizo Dios,** Never say die, Nothing is impossible. **poco más o m.,** more or less, about

menoscabar /menoska'βar/ *vt* to lessen, diminish, decrease; deteriorate; damage; disgrace, discredit

menoscabo /menos'kaβo/ *m,* decrease, diminishment; harm, damage, loss

menospreciable /menospre'θiaβle; menospre'siaβle/ *a* despicable, contemptible

menospreciador /menospreθia'ðor;

menospresia'ðor/ (-ra) *a* scornful —*n* scorner, despiser

menospreciar /menospre'θiar; menospre'siar/ *vt* to despise, scorn; underestimate, have a poor opinion of

menosprecio /menos'preθio; menos'presio/ *m,* scorn, derision; underestimation

mensaje /men'sahe/ *m,* message; official communication

mensajería /mensahe'ria/ *f,* carrier service; steamship line

mensajero /mensa'hero/ **(-ra)** *n* messenger; errand boy

menstruación /menstrua'θion; menstrua'sion/ *f,* menstruation

menstruar /menstru'ar/ *vi* to menstruate

mensual /men'sual/ *a* monthly

mensualidad /mensuali'ðað/ *f,* monthly salary, monthly payment

mensurar /mensu'rar/ *vt* to measure

menta /'menta/ *f,* menthe, mint; peppermint

mentado /men'taðo/ *a* celebrated, distinguished, famous

mental /men'tal/ *a* mental

mentalidad /mentali'ðað/ *f,* mentality

mentar /men'tar/ *vt irr* to mention. See **sentar**

mente /'mente/ *f,* mind; intelligence, understanding; will, intention

mentecatería /mentekate'ria/ *f,* folly, stupidity

mentecato /mente'kato/ **(-ta)** *a* foolish, silly; feeble-minded, simple —*n* fool, idiot

mentir /men'tir/ *vi irr* to lie; be untruthful; deceive, mislead; falsify; *Poet.* belie; disagree, be incompatible; —*vt* break a promise, disappoint. **m. como un bellaco,** to lie like a trooper See **sentir**

mentira /men'tira/ *f,* lie, falsehood; error (in writing); *Inf.* white spot (on a fingernail); cracking (of fingerjoints). **m. oficiosa,** white lie. **Parece m.,** It seems incredible

mentiroso /menti'roso/ *a* lying; false; full of errors (literary works); deceptive

mentís /men'tis/ *m,* giving the lie (literally, you lie); proof, demonstration (of error)

mentol /'mentol/ *m,* menthol

menú /me'nu/ *m,* menu

menudamente /menuða'mente/ *adv* minutely; in detail, circumstantially

menudear /menuðe'ar/ *vt* to do frequently; do repeatedly; —*vi* happen frequently; describe in detail; *Com.* sell by retail

menudencia /menu'ðenθia; menu'ðensia/ *f,* minuteness, smallness; exactness, care, accuracy; trifle, worthless object; small matter; *pl* offal; pork sausages

menudeo /menu'ðeo/ *m,* repetition; description in detail; *Com.* retail. **al m.,** at retail

menudillos /menu'ðiʎos; menu'ðiyos/ *m pl,* giblets; offal

menudo /menu'ðo/ *a* minute, tiny; despicable; thin; small; vulgar; meticulous, exact; small (money). *m*, small coal; *m pl*, offal, entrails; small change (money). **a m.**, often, frequently. **por m.**, in detail, carefully; *Com.* in small lots

meñique /me'ɲike/ *a Inf.* very small. *m*, little finger (in full, **dedo m.**)

meollo /me'oλo; me'oyo/ *m*, brain; *Anat.* marrow; *Fig.* essence, core, substance; understanding; *Inf.* **no tener m. (una cosa)**, to be worthless, unsubstantial (things)

mequetrefe /meke'trefe/ *m, Inf.* coxcomb, whippersnapper

mercadeo /merka'ðeo/ *m*, marketing (study of markets)

mercader /merka'ðer/ *m*, dealer, merchant, trader. **m. de grueso**, wholesaler

mercado /mer'kaðo/ *m*, market; marketplace

mercancía /merkan'θia; merkan'sia/ *f*, goods, merchandise; commerce, trade, traffic

mercante /mer'kante/ *a* trading; commercial. *m*, merchant, dealer, trader

mercantil /merkan'til/ *a* mercantile, commercial

merced /mer'θeð; mer'seð/ *f*, salary, remuneration; favor, benefit, kindness; will, desire, pleasure; mercy, grace; courtesy title given to untitled person (e.g. *vuestra m.*, your honor. Has now become *usted* and is universally used). **m. a**, thanks to. **estar uno a m. de**, to live at someone else's expense, be dependent on

mercenario /merθe'nario; merse'nario/ **(-ia)** *n Eccl.* member of the Order of la Merced. *m, Mil.* mercenary; day laborer —*a* mercenary

mercería /merθe'ria; merse'ria/ *f*, haberdashery, mercery

mercerizar /merθeri'θar; merseri'sar/ *vt* to mercerize

mercero /mer'θero; mer'sero/ *m*, haberdasher, mercer

mercurio /mer'kurio/ *m*, mercury, quicksilver; *Astron.* Mercury

merecedor /mereθe'ðor; merese'ðor/ *a* deserving, worthy

merecer /mere'θer; mere'ser/ *vt irr* to deserve, be worthy of; attain, achieve; be worth; —*vi* deserve, be deserving. **m. bien de**, to deserve well of; have a claim on the gratitude of. See **conocer**

merecido /mere'θiðo; mere'siðo/ *m*, due reward

merecimiento /mereθi'miento; meresi-'miento/ *m*, desert; merit

merendar /meren'dar/ *vi irr* to have lunch; pry into another's affairs; —*vt* have (a certain food) for lunch. *Inf.* **merendarse (una cosa)**, to obtain (a thing), have it in one's pocket. See **recomendar**

merendero /meren'dero/ *m*, lunchroom; tearoom

merengue /me'reŋge/ *m, Cul.* meringue

meretriz /mere'triθ; mere'tris/ *f*, prostitute

meridiana /meri'ðiana/ *f*, daybed, chaise longue; siesta

meridiano /meri'ðiano/ *a* meridian. *m*, meridian. **a la meridiana**, at noon

meridional /meriðio'nal/ *a* meridional, southern

merienda /me'rienda/ *f*, tea, snack; lunch; *Inf.* hunchback. *Inf.* **juntar meriendas**, to join forces, combine interests

merino /me'rino/ *a* merino. *m*, merino wool; shepherd of merino sheep

mérito /'merito/ *m*, merit; desert; worth, excellence. **de m.**, excellent, notable. **hacer m. de**, to mention

meritorio /meri'torio/ *a* meritorious. *m*, unpaid worker, learner

merluza /mer'luθa; mer'lusa/ *f*, hake; *Inf.* drinking bout. *Inf.* **pescar una m.**, to get drunk

merma /'merma/ *f*, decrease, drop; loss, waste, reduction; leakage

mermar /mer'mar/ *vi* to diminish, waste away, decrease; evaporate; leak; —*vt* filch, pilfer; reduce, decrease

mermelada /merme'laða/ *f*, conserve, preserve; jam; marmalade

mero /'mero/ *a* mere; simple; plain

merodear /meroðe'ar/ *vi* to maraud, raid

merodeo /mero'ðeo/ *m*, raiding, marauding

mes /'mes/ *m*, month; menses, menstruation

mesa /'mesa/ *f*, table; board, directorate; meseta, tableland; staircase landing; flat (of a sword, etc.); game of billiards. **m. de batalla**, post office sorting table. **m. de caballete**, trestle table. **m. de noche**, bedside table. **m. de tijeras**, folding table. **m. giratoria**, turntable. **alzar** (*or* **levantar) la m.**, to clear the table. **cubrir** (*or* **poner) la m.**, to set the table

mesada /me'saða/ *f*, monthly wages, monthly payment

meseta /me'seta/ *f*, staircase landing; plateau, tableland

mesiánico /me'sianiko/ *a* Messianic

Mesías /me'sias/ *m*, Messiah

mesilla /me'siλa; me'siya/ *f*, small table; laughing admonition; landing (of a stair)

mesón /me'son/ *m*, inn, tavern

mesonero /meso'nero/ **(-ra)** *n* innkeeper

mesta /'mesta/ *f*, ancient order of sheep farmers; *pl* confluence, meeting (of rivers)

mester /'mester/ *m*, craft, occupation. **m. de clerecía**, learned poetic meter of the Spanish Middle Ages. **m. de juglaría**, popular poetry and troubadour songs

mestizo /mes'tiθo; mes'tiso/ *a* half-breed; hybrid; cross-breed

mesura /me'sura/ *f*, sedateness; dignity; courtesy; moderation

mesurado /mesu'raðo/ *a* sedate; dignified; moderate, restrained, temperate

meta /'meta/ *f*, goalpost *Fig.* aim, end; goal; goalkeeper

metabolismo /metaβo'lismo/ *m*, metabolism

metáfora /me'tafora/ *f*, metaphor

metafórico /meta'foriko/ *a* metaphorical

metal /me'tal/ *m*, metal; brass; timbre of the voice; state, condition; quality, substance; *Herald.* gold or silver; *Mus.* brass (instruments)

metálico /me'taliko/ *a* metallic. *m*, metalworker; coin, specie; bullion

metalizar /metali'θar; metali'sar/ *vt* to metallize, make metallic; —*vr* become metallized; grow greedy for money

metalurgia /metalur'hia/ *f*, metallurgy

metalúrgico /meta'lurhiko/ *a* metallurgical. *m*, metallurgist

metamorfosis /metamor'fosis/ *f*, metamorphosis

metedor /mete'ðor/ **(-ra)** *n* placer, inserter; smuggler, contrabandist

metemuertos /mete'muertos/ *Inf.* meddler, Nosy Parker

meteórico /mete'oriko/ *a* meteoric

meteorito /meteo'rito/ *m*, meteorite

meteoro /mete'oro/ *m*, meteor

meteorología /meteorolo'hia/ *f*, meteorology

meteorologista /meteorolo'hista/ *mf* meteorologist; weather forecaster

meter /me'ter/ *vt* to place; put; introduce, insert; stake (gambling); smuggle; cause, occasion; place close together; persuade to take part in; *Sew.* take in fullness; deceive, humbug; cram in, pack tightly; *Naut.* take in sail; —*vr* interfere, butt in; meddle (with); take up, follow (occupations); be overfamiliar; disembogue, empty itself (rivers, etc.); attack with the sword; (*with prep a*) follow (occupations); become, turn (e.g. *meterse a predicar*, to turn preacher); (*with con*) pick a quarrel with. **meterse en precisiones**, to go into details. *Inf.* **meterse en todo**, to be very meddlesome

metesillas y sacamuertos /mete'siʎas i saka'muertos; mete'siyas i saka'muertos/ *m*, scene shifter, stagehand

meticulosidad /metikulosi'ðað/ *f*, meticulosity; timorousness

meticuloso /metiku'loso/ *a* meticulous, fussy; timid, nervous

metido /me'tiðo/ *a* tight; crowded; crabbed (of handwriting). *m*, *Sew.* material for letting out (seams). **m. en años**, quite old (person)

metimiento /meti'miento/ *m*, insertion, introduction; influence; sway

metódico /me'toðiko/ *a* methodical

metodismo /meto'ðismo/ *m*, Methodism

metodista /meto'ðista/ *a* methodistic. *mf* Methodist

método /'metoðo/ *m*, method

metodología /metoðolo'hia/ *f*, methodology

metralla /me'traʎa; me'traya/ *f*, *Mil.* grapeshot, shrapnel

métrico /'metriko/ *a* metric; metrical

metro /'metro/ *m*, (verse) meter; meter (measurement); subway, underground railway

metrónomo /me'tronomo/ *m*, metronome

metrópoli /me'tropoli/ *f*, metropolis, capital; see of a metropolitan bishop; mother country

metropolitano /metropoli'tano/ *a* metropolitan. *m*, metropolitan bishop

México /'mehiko/ Mexico

mezcla /'meθkla; 'meskla/ *f*, mixture; blend, combination; mixed cloth, tweed; mortar

mezclar /meθ'klar; mes'klar/ *vt* to mix, blend, combine; —*vr* mix, mingle; take part; interfere, meddle; intermarry

mezcolanza /meθko'lanθa; mesko'lansa/ *f*, *Inf.* hodgepodge

mezquindad /meθkin'dað; meskin'dað/ *f*, poverty; indigence; miserliness; paltriness; meanness; poorness

mezquino /meθ'kino; mes'kino/ *a* needy, impoverished; miserly, stingy; small, diminutive; unhappy; mean, paltry

mezquita /meθ'kita; mes'kita/ *f*, mosque

mi /'mi/ *poss pron* my. *m*, *Mus.* mi, E

mí /'mi/ *pers pron acc gen dat 1st pers sing* me. Used only after prepositions (e.g. *Lo hicieron por mí*, They did it for me)

miaja /'miaha/ *f*, See **migaja**

mica /'mika/ *f*, *Mineral.* mica; coquette, flirt

micción /mik'θion; mik'sion/ *f*, micturition

micho /'mitʃo/ **(-cha)** *n Inf.* puss, pussycat

micra /'mikra/ *f*, micron, thousandth part of a millimeter

microbio /mi'kroβio/ *m*, microbe

microbiología /mikroβiolo'hia/ *f*, microbiology

microbrigada /mikroβri'gaða/ *f*, team of volunteer workers (Castroist Cuba)

microcosmo /mikro'kosmo/ *m*, microcosm

micrófono /mi'krofono/ *m*, microphone

microonda /mikro'onda/ *f*, microwave

microscópico /mikros'kopiko/ *a* microscopic

microscopio /mikros'kopio/ *m*, microscope

miedo /'mieðo/ *m*, fear, apprehension, terror. **m. al público**, stagefright. **tener m.**, to be afraid

miedoso /mie'ðoso/ *a Inf.* fearful, nervous

miel /miel/ *f*, honey. **m. de caña**, sugarcane syrup. *Inf.* **quedarse a media m.**, to see one's pleasure snatched away. *Inf.* **ser de mieles**, to be most pleasant or agreeable

mielitis /mie'litis/ *f*, myelitis

miembro /mi'embro/ *m*, *Anat.* limb; penis; member, associate; part, portion, section; *Math.* member

miente /'miente/ *f*, thought, imagination,

mind. **parar** or **poner mientes en,** to consider, think about. **venírsele a las mientes,** to occur to one's mind

mientras /'mientras/ *adv* while. **m. más...,** the more.... **m. que,** while (e.g. *m. que esperaba en el jardín,* while he was waiting in the garden). **m. tanto,** in the meanwhile

miércoles /'mierkoles/ *m,* Wednesday. **m. de ceniza,** Ash Wednesday

mierda /'mierða/ *f, (vulgar)* shit; *Inf.* filth

mies /'mies/ *f,* cereal plant, grain; harvest time; *pl* grain fields

miga /'miga/ *f,* breadcrumb; crumb; *Inf.* essence, core; substance; bit, scrap; *pl* fried breadcrumbs. *Inf.* **hacer buenas** (or **malas**) **migas,** to get on well (or badly) together

migaja /mi'gaha/ *f,* breadcrumb; bit, scrap; trifle, mere nothing; *pl* crumbs (from the table); remains, remnants

migajón /miga'hon/ *m,* crumb (of a loaf): *Fig. Inf.* essence, substance, core

migración /migra'θion; migra'sion/ *f,* migration; emigration

migraña /mi'graɲa/ *f,* migraine

migratorio /migra'torio/ *a* migratory

mijo /'miho/ *m,* millet; maize

mil /mil/ *a* thousand; thousandth; many, large number. *m,* thousand; thousandth. *Inf.* **Son las m. y quinientas,** It's extremely late (of the hour)

milagrero /mila'grero/ *a Inf.* miraculous

milagro /mi'lagro/ *m,* miracle; marvel, wonder. **¡M.!** Amazing! Just fancy!

milagroso /mila'groso/ *a* miraculous, marvelous, wonderful

mildeu /'mildeu/ *m,* mildew

milenario /mile'nario/ *a* millenary; millennial. *m,* millenary; millennium

milésimo /mi'lesimo/ *a* thousandth

milicia /mi'liθia; mi'lisia/ *f,* militia; military; art of war; military profession

miligramo /mili'gramo/ *m,* milligram

mililitro /mili'litro/ *m,* milliliter

milímetro /mi'limetro/ *m,* millimeter

militante /mili'tante/ *a* militant

militar /mili'tar/ *a* military. *m,* soldier —*vi* to fight in the army; struggle (for a cause); *Fig.* militate (e.g. *Las circunstancias militan en favor de* (or *contra*) *sus ideas,* Circumstances militate against his ideas)

militarismo /milita'rismo/ *m,* militarism

militarista /milita'rista/ *a* militaristic. *mf* militarist

militarizar /militari'θar; militari'sar/ *vt* to militarize; make war-like

milla /'miʎa; 'miya/ *f,* mile

millar /mi'ʎar; mi'yar/ *m,* thousand; vast number (gen. *pl*)

millón /mi'ʎon; mi'yon/ *m,* million

millonario /miʎo'nario; miyo'nario/ **(-ia)** *a* and *n* millionaire

mimar /mi'mar/ *vt* to spoil, overindulge; caress, fondle

mimbre /'mimbre/ *mf* osier; willow tree. *m,* wicker

mimbrear /mimbre'ar/ *vi* to sway, bend

mimbrera /mim'brera/ *f,* osier; osier bed; willow

mímica /'mimika/ *f,* mimicry; mime

mímico /'mimiko/ *a* mimic

mimo /'mimo/ *m,* mimic, buffoon; mime; caress, expression of affection, tenderness; overindulgence

mimoso /mi'moso/ *a* affectionate, demonstrative

mina /'mina/ *f,* mine; excavation, mining; underground passage; lead (in a pencil); (*Mil. Nav.*) mine; *Fig.* gold mine. *Mil.* **m. terrestre,** landmine

minador /mina'ðor/ *m,* excavator; *Nav.* minelayer; *Mil.* sapper

minar /mi'nar/ *vt* to excavate, mine; *Fig.* undermine; (*Mil. Nav.*) mine; work hard for

minarete /mina'rete/ *m,* minaret

mineral /mine'ral/ *a* and *m,* mineral

mineralogía /mineralo'hia/ *f,* mineralogy

mineralógico /minera'lohiko/ *a* mineralogical

minería /mine'ria/ *f,* mining, mineworking; mineworkers

minero /mi'nero/ *a* mining. *m,* miner, mineworker; source, origin

miniatura /minia'tura/ *f,* miniature

miniaturista /miniatu'rista/ *mf* miniaturist

mínima /'minima/ *f, Mus.* minim; very small thing or portion

mínimo /'minimo/ *a superl* **pequeño** smallest; minimum; meticulous, precise. *m,* minimum; (meteorological) trough

ministerial /ministe'rial/ *a* ministerial

ministerio /minis'terio/ *m,* office, post; *Polit.* cabinet; ministry; government office; government department

ministrar /minis'trar/ *vt* and *vi* to fill; administer (an office); —*vt* minister to; give, provide

ministro /mi'nistro/ *m,* instrument, agency; minister of state, cabinet minister; clergyman, minister; minister plenipotentiary; policeman. **m. de estado,** secretary of state. **m. de gobernación,** secretary of the interior. **m. de hacienda,** treasurer. **m. de relaciones extranjeras,** foreign secretary. **primer m.** prime minister

minorar /mino'rar/ *vt* to diminish, decrease

minoría /mino'ria/ *f,* minority, smaller number; minority (of age)

minoridad /minori'ðað/ *f,* minority (of age)

minucia /mi'nuθia; minu'sia/ *f,* smallness; morsel, mite; *pl* details, trifles, minutiae

minuciosidad /minuθiosi'ðað; minusiosi'ðað/ *f,* meticulousness, minuteness, precision

minucioso /minu'θioso; minu'sioso/ *a* meticulous, precise, minute

minúsculo /mi'nuskulo/ *a* minute, very small

minuta /mi'nuta/ *f*, memorandum, minute; note; list, catalog

minutero /minu'tero/ *m*, minute hand (of a clock)

minuto /mi'nuto/ *a* minute, very small. *m*, minute

mío /'mio/ *m*. **mía**, *f*, (*m pl*. **míos**, *f pl*. **mías**) *poss pron* mine (e.g. *Las flores son mías*, The flowers are mine). **Mi** is used before nouns, not **mío**. Also used with article (e.g. *Este sombrero no es el mío*, This hat is not mine (my one)). **de mío**, by myself, without help. *Inf.* **¡Esta es la mía!** This is my chance!

miope /mi'ope/ *a* myopic. *mf* myopic person

miopía /mio'pia/ *f*, shortsightedness

mira /'mira/ *f*, sight (optical instruments, guns); intention, design; *Mil.* watchtower; care, precaution. **andar, estar** *or* **quedar a la m.**, to be vigilant, be on the lookout

mirada /mi'raða/ *f*, look; gaze. **lanzar miradas de carnero degollado (a)**, to cast sheep's eyes at

miradero /mira'ðero/ *m*, object of attention, cynosure; observation post, lookout

mirador /mira'ðor/ (**-ra**) *n* spectator. *m*, *Archit.* oriel; enclosed balcony; observatory

miramiento /mira'miento/ *m*, observation, gazing; scruple, consideration; precaution, care; thoughtfulness

mirar /mi'rar/ *vt* to look at, gaze at; observe, behold; watch; consider, look after; value, appreciate; concern; believe, think; (*with prep a*) overlook, look on to; face; (*with por*) care for, protect; look after, consider. **m. contra el gobierno**, *Inf.* to be squint-eyed. **m. de hito en hito**, to look over, stare at. **mirarse en (una cosa)**, to consider (a matter) carefully

miríada /mi'riaða/ *f*, myriad, huge number

mirilla /mi'riʎa; mi'riya/ *f*, peephole

miriñaque /miri'ɲake/ *m*, trinket, ornament; crinoline

mirlarse /mir'larse/ *vr Inf.* to give oneself airs

mirón /mi'ron/ *a* inquisitive, curious

mirto /'mirto/ *m*, myrtle

misa /'misa/ *f*, (*Eccl. Mus.*) mass. **m. de difuntos**, requiem mass. **m. del gallo**, midnight mass. **m. mayor**, high mass. **m. rezada**, low mass. **como en m.**, in profound silence. **oír m.**, to attend mass

misal /mi'sal/ *m*, missal

misantropía /misantro'pia/ *f*, misanthropy

misantrópico /misan'tropiko/ *a* misanthropic

miscelánea /misθe'lanea; misse'lanea/ *f*, medley, assortment, miscellany

misceláneo /misθe'laneo; misse'laneo/ *a* assorted, miscellaneous, mixed

miserable /mise'raβle/ *a* miserable, un-

happy; timid, pusillanimous; miserly, mean; despicable

miseria /mi'seria/ *f*, misery; poverty, destitution; avarice, miserliness; *Inf.* poor thing, trifle

misericordia /miseri'korðia/ *f*, mercy, compassion

misericordioso /miserikor'ðioso/ *a* merciful, compassionate

mísero /'misero/ *a Inf.* fond of churchgoing

misión /mi'sion/ *f*, mission; vocation; commission, duty, errand

misionar /misio'nar/ *vi* to missionize, act as a missionary; *Eccl.* conduct a mission

misionero /misio'nero/ *m*, missioner; missionary

mismo /'mismo/ *a* same; similar; self (e.g. *ellos mismos*, they themselves); very, same (e.g. *Ahora m. voy*, I'm going this very minute). **Me da lo m.**, It makes no difference to me. **por lo m.**, for that selfsame reason

misógino /mi'sohino/ *m*, misogynist

misterio /mis'terio/ *m*, mystery

misterioso /miste'rioso/ *a* mysterious

mística /'mistika/ *f*, **misticismo** *m*, mysticism

místico /'mistiko/ *a* mystic

mistificación /mistifika'θion; mistifika-'sion/ *f*, mystification; mystery; deception

mistificar /mistifi'kar/ *vt* to mystify; deceive

mitad /mi'taθ/ *f*, half; middle, center. *Fig. Inf.* **cara m.**, better half. *Inf.* **mentir por la m. de la barba**, to lie barefacedly

mítico /'mitiko/ *a* mythical

mitigación /mitiga'θion; mitiga'sion/ *f*, mitigation

mitigar /miti'gar/ *vt* to mitigate, moderate, alleviate; appease

mitin /'mitin/ *m*, mass meeting

mito /'mito/ *m*, myth

mitología /mitolo'hia/ *f*, mythology

mitológico /mito'lohiko/ *a* mythological

mitón /mi'ton/ *m*, mitten

mixto /'miksto/ *a* mixed, blended; hybrid; composite; mongrel. *m*, mixed train (carrying freight and passengers); sulphur match

mixtura /miks'tura/ *f*, mixture, blend; compound; mixture (medicine)

¡miz, miz! /miθ, miθ; mis, mis/ puss, puss!

mobiliario /moβi'liario/ *a* movable (goods). *m*, furniture

moblaje /mo'βlahe/ *m*, household goods and furniture

mocasín /moka'sin/ *m*, moccasin

mocedad /moθe'ðað; mose'ðað/ *f*, youth, adolescence; mischief, prank. *Fig. Inf.* **correr sus mocedades**, to sow one's wild oats

mochila /mo't ʃila/ *f*, knapsack; nosebag; military rations for a march

mocho /'motʃo/ *a* blunted, topless,

lopped; *Inf.* shorn, cropped. *m*, butt, butt end

moción /mo'θion; mo'sion/ *f*, motion, movement; impulse, tendency; divine inspiration; motion (of a debate)

moco /'moko/ *m*, mucus; candle drips; snuff of a candle. *Inf.* **caérsele el m.,** to be very simple, be easily deceived

mocoso /mo'koso/ **(-sa)** *a* running of the nose, sniffling; unimportant, insignificant —*n* coxcomb, stripling

moda /'moða/ *f*, fashion. **estar** *or* **ser de m.,** to be fashionable, be in fashion. **la última m.,** the latest fashion

modales /mo'ðales/ *m pl*, manners, behavior

modalidad /moðali'ðað/ *f*, form, nature; *Mus.* modality

modelado /moðe'laðo/ *m*, *Art.* modeling

modelar /moðe'lar/ *vt Art.* to model; —*vr* model oneself (on), copy

modelo /mo'ðelo/ *m*, example, pattern; model. *mf Art.* life model

módem *m*, modem

moderación /moðera'θion; moðerasion/ *f*, moderation; restraint, temperance, equability

moderado /moðe'raðo/ *a* moderate; restrained, temperate

moderador /moðera'ðor/ **(-ra)** *a* moderating —*n* moderator

moderar /moðe'rar/ *vt* to moderate; temper, restrain; —*vr* regain one's self-control; behave with moderation

modernista /moðer'nista/ *a* modernistic; modern. *mf* modernist

modernización /moðerniθa'θion; moðernisa'sion/ *f*, modernization

modernizar /moðerni'θar; moðerni'sar/ *vt* to modernize

moderno /mo'ðerno/ *a* modern. *m*, modern. **a la moderna,** in modern fashion

modestia /mo'ðestia/ *f*, modesty

modesto /mo'ðesto/ *a* modest

módico /'moðiko/ *a* moderate (of prices, etc.)

modificable /moðifi'kaβle/ *a* modifiable

modificación /moðifika'θion; moðifika'sion/ *f*, modification

modificador, modificante /moðifika'-ðor, moðifi'kante/ *a* modifying, moderating

modificar /moðifi'kar/ *vt* to modify; moderate

modismo /mo'ðismo/ *m*, idiom, idiomatic expression

modista /mo'ðista/ *mf* dressmaker; couturier; milliner

modo /'moðo/ *m*, mode, method, style; manner, way; moderation, restraint; civility, politeness (often *pl*); *Mus.* mode; *Gram.* mood. **m. de ser,** nature, temperament. **de m. que,** so that. **de ningún m.,** not at all, by no means. **de todos modos,** in any case

modorra /mo'ðorra/ *f*, deep sleep, stupor

modorro /mo'ðorro/ *a* drowsy, heavy

modoso /mo'ðoso/ *a* demure; well-behaved

modulación /moðula'θion; moðula'sion/ *f*, modulation

modulador /moðula'ðor/ **(-ra)** *a* modulative —*n* modulator, *m*, *Mus.* modulator

modular /moðu'lar/ *vt* and *vi* to modulate

mofa /'mofa/ *f*, mockery, ridicule, jeering

mofador /mofa'ðor/ **(-ra)** *a* jeering —*n* scoffer, mocker

mofarse /mo'farse/ *vr* (*with de*) to make fun of, jeer at

mofeta /mo'feta/ *f*, noxious gas; damp (gas); *Zool.* skunk

moflete /mo'flete/ *m*, *Inf.* plump cheek

mofletudo /mofle'tuðo/ *a* plump-cheeked

mohín /mo'in/ *m*, grimace

mohína /mo'ina/ *f*, grudge, rancor; sullenness; sulkiness

mohíno /mo'ino/ *a* depressed, gloomy; sulky; black or black-nosed (of animals)

moho /'moo/ *m*, mold, fungoid growth; moldiness; moss. *Inf.* **no criar m.,** to be always on the move

mohoso /mo'oso/ *a* mossy; moldy

mojada /mo'haða/ *f*, wetting; *Inf.* stab; sop of bread

mojador /moha'ðor/ **(-ra)** *n* wetter. *m*, stamp moistener

mojar /mo'har/ *vt* to wet; moisten; *Inf.* stab, wound with a dagger; —*vi* take part in; meddle, interfere; —*vr* get wet

mojicón /mohi'kon/ *m*, kind of sponge-cake; *Inf.* slap in the face

mojiganga /mohi'ganga/ *f*, masquerade, mummer's show; farce; funny sight, figure of fun

mojigatería /mohigate'ria/ *f*, hypocrisy; sanctimoniousness; prudery

mojigato /mohi'gato/ **(-ta)** *a* hypocritical; sanctimonious; prudish —*n* hypocrite; bigot; prude

mojón /mo'hon/ *m*, boundary marker; milestone; heap. **m. kilométrico,** milestone

molar /mo'lar/ *a* molar

molde /'molde/ *m*, mold, matrix; *Fig.* model, pattern. **de m.,** printed; suitably, conveniently; perfectly. **letra de m.,** printed letters, print

moldear /molde'ar/ *vt* to mold, cast

moldura /mol'dura/ *f*, molding

moldurar /moldu'rar/ *vt* to mold

molécula /mo'lekula/ *f*, molecule

moler /mo'ler/ *vt irr* to grind, crush; tire, exhaust; ill-treat; pester, annoy. **m. a palos,** to beat black and blue —*Pres. Indic.* **muelo, mueles, muele, muelen.** *Pres. Subjunc.* **muela, muelas, muela, muelan**

molestia /mo'lestia/ *f*, inconvenience, trouble; annoyance; discomfort, pain; bore, nuisance. **Es una m.,** It's a nuisance

molesto /mo'lesto/ *a* inconvenient, troublesome; annoying; painful; uncomfortable; boring, tedious

moletón /mole'ton/ *m*, flannelet

molicie /mo'liθie; mo'lisie/ *f*, softness, smoothness; effeminacy, weakness

molienda /mo'lienda/ *f*, milling; grinding; mill; portion ground at one time; *Inf.* exhaustion, fatigue; *Inf.* nuisance

molificar /molifi'kar/ *vt* to mollify, appease

molimiento /moli'miento/ *m*, milling; grinding; exhaustion, fatigue

molinero /moli'nero/ *a* mill. *m*, miller

molinillo /moli'niʎo; moli'niyo/ *m*, hand mill, small grinder; mincing machine; beater. **m. de café**, coffee mill

molino /mo'lino/ *m*, mill; harum-scarum, rowdy; bore, tedious person; *Inf.* mouth. **m. de rueda de escalones**, treadmill. **m. de viento**, windmill

molleja /mo'ʎeha; mo'yeha/ *f*, gizzard

mollera /mo'ʎera; mo'yera/ *f*, crown of the head; brains, sense. *Inf.* **ser duro de m.**, to be obstinate; be stupid

molusco /mo'lusko/ *m*, mollusk

momentáneo /momen'taneo/ *a* momentary, brief; instantaneous, immediate

momento /mo'mento/ *m*, moment, minute; importance; *Mech.* moment. **al m.**, immediately. **a cada m.**, all the time; frequently. **por momentos**, continually; intermittently

momería /mome'ria/ *f*, mummery

momero /mo'mero/ **(-ra)** *n* mummer

momia /'momia/ *f*, mummy

momificar /momifi'kar/ *vt* to mummify; —*vr* become mummified

mona /'mona/ *f*, female monkey; *Inf.* imitator; drinking bout; drunk. *Inf.* **ser la última m.**, to be of no account, be unimportant

monacal /mona'kal/ *a* monkish, monastic

monacillo /mona'θiʎo; mona'siyo/ *m*, *Eccl.* acolyte

monada /mo'naða/ *f*, mischievous prank; affected gesture or grimace; small, pretty thing; childish cleverness; flattery; rash act; *pl* monkey shines

monaguillo /mona'giʎo; mona'giyo/ *m*, *Eccl.* acolyte

monarca /mo'narka/ *mf* monarch

monarquía /monar'kia/ *f*, monarchy

monasterio /mona'sterio/ *m*, monastery; convent

monástico /mo'nastiko/ *a* monastic

mondadientes /monda'ðientes/ *m*, toothpick

mondar /mon'dar/ *vt* to skin, peel; *Agr.* prune; cut the hair; cleanse; free of rubbish; *Inf.* deprive of possessions; —*vr* pick one's teeth

mondo /'mondo/ *a* simple, plain; bare; unadulterated, pure

moneda /mo'neða/ *f*, coin, piece of money; coinage; *Inf.* wealth; cash. **m. corriente**, currency. **m. metálica**, specie. **pagar en buena m.,** to give entire satisfaction. **pagar en la misma m.,** to pay back in the same coin, return like for like.

Inf. **ser m. corriente,** to be usual or very frequent

monedero /mone'ðero/ *m*, coiner, minter; handbag; purse

monería /mone'ria/ *f*, mischievous trick; unimportant trifle; pretty thing; childish cleverness, pretty ways

monetario /mone'tario/ *a* monetary. *m*, collection of coins and medals

monigote /moni'gote/ *m*, *Inf.* boor; grotesque, puppet

monitor /moni'tor/ *m*, monitor

monja /'monha/ *f*, nun; *pl* sparks

monje /'monhe/ *m*, monk

monjil /mon'hil/ *a* nun-like. *m*, nun's habit

mono /'mono/ *a Inf.* pretty, attractive; amusing, funny. *m*, monkey; person given to grimacing; rash youth; coverall. *Inf.* **estar de monos**, to be on bad terms

monogamia /mono'gamia/ *f*, monogamy

monógamo /mo'nogamo/ *a* monogamous —*n* monogamist

monografía /monogra'fia/ *f*, monograph

monograma /mono'grama/ *m*, monogram

monolítico /mono'litiko/ *a* monolithic

monolito /mono'lito/ *m*, monolith

monólogo /mo'nologo/ *m*, monologue

monomaníaco /monoma'niako/ **(-ca)** *a n* monomaniac

monopatín /monopa'tin/ *m*, scooter

monoplano /mono'plano/ *m*, monoplane

monopolio /mono'polio/ *m*, monopoly

monopolista /monopo'lista/ *mf* monopolist

monopolizar /monopoli'θar; monopoli'sar/ *vt* to monopolize

monoteísmo /monote'ismo/ *m*, monotheism

monoteísta /monote'ista/ *mf* monotheist

monotonía /monoto'nia/ *f*, monotony; monotone

monótono /mo'notono/ *a* monotonous

monseñor /monse'ɲor/ *m*, monsignor

monserga /mon'serga/ *f*, *Inf.* rigmarole; jargon

monstruo /'monstruo/ *m*, monster; freak, monstrosity; cruel person

monstruosidad /monstruosi'ðað/ *f*, monstrousness, monstrosity

monstruoso /mon'struoso/ *a* monstrous, abnormal; enormous; extraordinary; atrocious, outrageous

monta /'monta/ *f*, mounting a horse; total; *Mil.* mounting signal; breeding station (horses)

montacargas /monta'kargas/ *m*, hoist, lift; freight elevator

montador /monta'ðor/ *m*, mounter; mounting block

montadura /monta'ðura/ *f*, mounting; mount, setting (of jewels)

montaje /mon'tahe/ *m*, assembling, setting up (machines); presentation (of a book); (cinema) montage

montano /mon'tano/ *a* hilly, mountainous

montante /mon'tante/ *m,* upright, stanchion; tent pole

montaña /mon'taɲa/ *f,* mountain; mountainous country. **montañas rusas,** roller coaster (at an amusement park)

montañés /mon'taɲes/ **(-esa)** *a* mountain —*n* mountain dweller; native of Santander

montañoso /monta'ɲoso/ *a* mountainous; hilly

montar /mon'tar/ *vi* to ascend, climb up, get on top; mount (a horse); ride (a horse); be important; —*vt* get on top of; ride (a horse); total, amount to; set up (apparatus, machinery); *Naut.* sail around, double; set, mount (gems); cock (firearms); fine for trespassing; wind (a clock); command (a ship); *Naut.* carry, be fitted with (guns, etc.). **m. a horcajadas en,** to mount astride; straddle. **montarse en cólera,** to fly into a rage

montaraz /monta'raθ/ **monta'ras** *a* mountain-dwelling; wild, savage; rude, uncivilized, uncouth. *m,* gamekeeper, forester

montazgo /mon'taθgo; mon'tasgo/ *m,* toll payable for cattle moving from one province to another

monte /'monte/ *m,* mount, hill; woodland; obstacle, impediment. **m. de piedad,** pawnshop. **m. pío,** savings fund

montería /monte'ria/ *f,* hunt, chase; art of hunting

montés /mon'tes/ *a* wild, savage, untamed

montículo /mon'tikulo/ *m,* mound, hill

montón /mon'ton/ *m,* heap, pile; *Inf.* abundance, lot. *Inf.* **a, de** *or* **en m.,** all jumbled up together. **a montones,** in abundance

montuoso /mon'tuoso/ *a* mountainous

montura /mon'tura/ *f,* riding animal, mount; horse trappings; setting up, mounting (artillery, etc.)

monumental /monumen'tal/ *a* monumental

monumento /monu'mento/ *m,* monument; document, record; tomb

monzón /mon'θon; mon'son/ *mf,* monsoon

moña /'moɲa/ *f,* doll; dressmaker's model; bow for the hair; bullfighter's black bow; baby's bonnet; *Inf.* drinking bout

moño /'moɲo/ *m,* bun, chignon; topknot (birds); bunch of ribbons; *pl* tawdry trimmings

moqueta /mo'keta/ *f,* moquette

moquete /mo'kete/ *m,* slap in the face

mora /'mora/ *f,* blackberry; mulberry; bramble; Moorish girl, Moorish woman

morada /mo'raða/ *f,* dwelling, abode; sojourn, stay

morado /mo'raðo/ *a* purple

morador /mora'ðor/ **(-ra)** *n* dweller; sojourner

moral /mo'ral/ *a* moral, ethical. *f,* morality, ethics; morale. *m,* blackberry bush

moraleja /mora'leha/ *f,* moral, lesson

moralidad /morali'ðað/ *f,* morality

moralista /mora'lista/ *mf* moralist

moralización /moraliθa'θion; moralisa-'sion/ *f,* moralization

moralizador /moraliθa'ðor; moralisa'ðor/ **(-ra)** *a* moralizing —*n* moralizer

moralizar /morali'θar; morali'sar/ *vt* to reform, correct; —*vi* moralize

moratoria /mora'toria/ *f,* moratorium

morbidez /mor'βiðeθ; mor'βiðes/ *f, Art.* morbidezza; softness

mórbido /'morβiðo/ *a* morbid, diseased; *Art.* delicate (of flesh tones); soft

morbo /'morβo/ *m,* illness. **m. gálico,** syphilis

morboso /mor'βoso/ *a* ill; morbid, unhealthy

morcilla /mor'θiʎa; mor'siya/ *f, Cul.* black pudding; (*Inf. Theat.*) gag

morcillero /morθi'ʎero; morsi'yero/ **(-ra)** *n* seller of black puddings; (*Inf. Theat.*) actor who gags

mordacidad /morðaθi'ðað; morðasi'ðað/ *f,* corrosiveness; mordacity, sarcasm; *Cul.* piquancy

mordaz /mor'ðaθ; mor'ðas/ *a* corrosive; sarcastic, caustic, mordant; *Cul.* piquant

mordaza /mor'ðaθa; mor'ðasa/ *f,* gag

mordedor /morðe'ðor/ *a* biting; scandalmongering

mordedura /morðe'ðura/ *f,* bite, biting

morder /mor'ðer/ *vt irr* to bite; nibble, nip; seize, grasp; corrode, eat away; slander; etch —*Pres. Indic.* **muerdo, muerdes, muerde, muerden.** *Pres. Subjunc.* **muerda, muerdas, muerda, muerdan**

mordiente /mor'ðiente/ *m,* fixative (for dyeing); mordant —*a* mordant (of acid)

mordiscar /morðis'kar/ *vt* to nibble, bite gently; bite

mordisco /mor'ðisko/ *m,* nibble; nibbling; bite; biting; piece bitten off

moreno /mo'reno/ **(-na)** *a* dark brown; swarthy complexioned; dark (of people) —*n Inf.* negro, mulatto

morfina /mor'fina/ *f,* morphine

morfinómano /morfi'nomano/ **(-na)** *n* morphine addict

moribundo /mori'βundo/ **(-da)** *a* moribund, dying —*n* dying person

morillo /mo'riʎo; mo'riyo/ *m,* andiron, fire-dog

morir /mo'rir/ *vi irr* to die; fade, wither; decline, decay; disappear; yearn (for); long (to); go out (lights, fire); —*vr* die; go numb (limbs); (*with por*) adore, be mad about. *Inf.* **m. vestido,** to die a violent death. **¡Muera!** Down with! *Past Part.* **muerto.** For other tenses see **dormir**

morisco /mo'risko/ **(-ca)** *a* Moorish —*n* Morisco, Moor converted to Christianity

mormón /mor'mon/ **(-ona)** *n* Mormon

mormónico /mor'moniko/ *a* Mormon

moro /'moro/ **(-ra)** *a* Moorish —*n* Moor; Mohammedan. *Inf.* **haber moros y cristianos,** to be the deuce of a row. *Inf.* **Hay moros en la costa,** The coast is not clear; There's trouble in the offing

morosidad /morosi'ðað/ *f,* slowness, delay; sluggishness, sloth

moroso /mo'roso/ *a* slow, dilatory; sluggish, lazy

morra /'morra/ *f,* crown of the head

morral /mo'rral/ *m,* nose-bag; knapsack; game-bag; *Inf.* lout

morriña /mo'rriɲa/ *f,* cattle plague, murrain; *Inf.* depression, blues; homesickness

morro /'morro/ *m,* anything round; hummock, hillock; round pebble; headland, cliff

morsa /'morsa/ *f,* walrus

mortaja /mor'taha/ *f,* shroud, winding sheet

mortal /mor'tal/ *a* mortal; fatal, deadly; on the point of death; great, tremendous; certain, sure. *mf* mortal

mortalidad /mortali'ðað/ *f,* humanity, human race; mortality, death-rate

mortandad /mortan'dað/ *f,* mortality, number of deaths

mortecino /morte'θino; morte'sino/ *a* dead from natural causes (animals); weak; fading; dull, dead (of eyes); flickering; on the point of death or extinction

mortero /mor'tero/ *m,* mortar (for building); *Mil.* mortar; pounding mortar

mortífero /mor'tifero/ *a* deadly, mortal

mortificación /mortifika'θion; mortifika'sion/ *f, Med.* gangrene; humiliation, wounding; mortification (of the flesh)

mortificar /mortifi'kar/ *vt Med.* to mortify; humiliate, wound, hurt; mortify (the flesh); —*vr* become gangrenous

mortuorio /mor'tuorio/ *a* mortuary. *m,* funeral, obsequies

mosaico /mo'saiko/ *a* and *m,* mosaic

mosca /'moska/ *f,* fly; *Inf.* nuisance; bore, pest; cash; *pl* sparks. *Inf.* **m. muerta,** underhanded person. *Inf.* **papar moscas,** to gape, be dumbfounded. *Inf.* **soltar la m.,** to give or spend money unwillingly

moscardón /moskar'ðon/ *m,* gadfly

moscatel /moska'tel/ *a* muscatel. *m,* muscatel (grapes and wine); *Inf.* pest, tedious person

Moscú /mos'ku/ Moscow

mosquear /moske'ar/ *vt* to drive off flies; reply crossly; whip; —*vr* be exasperated; brush aside obstacles

mosquero /mos'kero/ *m,* flypaper

mosquitero /moski'tero/ *m,* mosquito net

mosquito /mos'kito/ *m,* mosquito; midge, gnat; *Inf.* tippler, drunkard

mostacho /mos'tatʃo/ *m,* mustache, whiskers; *Inf.* smudge on the face

mostaza /mos'taθa; mos'tasa/ *f,* mustard plant or seed; *Cul.* mustard

mostrador /mostra'ðor/ **(-ra)** *n* one who shows, exhibitor. *m,* shop counter; face of a watch

mostrar /mos'trar/ *vt irr* to show; indicate, point out; demonstrate, prove; manifest, reveal; —*vr* show oneself, be (e.g. *Se mostró bondadoso,* He showed himself to be kind) —*Pres. Indic.* **muestro, muestras, muestra, muestran.** *Pres. Subjunc.* **muestre, muestres, muestre, muestren**

mostrenco /mos'trenko/ *a Inf.* stray, vagrant, homeless; *Inf.* dull, ignorant; *Inf.* fat, heavy

mota /'mota/ *f,* fault in cloth; mote, defect, fault; mound, hill; thread of cotton, speck of dust, etc.; fleck (of the sun, etc.); spot

mote /'mote/ *m,* maxim, saying; motto, device; catchword, slogan; nickname

motejar /mote'har/ *vt* to nickname, call names, dub

motete /mo'tete/ *m,* motet

motín /mo'tin/ *m,* mutiny, riot

motivar /moti'βar/ *vt* to motivate, cause; explain one's reasons

motivo /mo'tiβo/ *a* motive. *m,* cause, motive; *Mus.* motif. **con m. de,** on account of, because of. **de m. propio,** of one's own free will

motocicleta /motoθi'kleta; motosi'kleta/ *f,* motorcycle

motociclista /motoθi'klista; motosi'klista/ *mf* motorcyclist

motor /mo'tor/ **(-ra)** *a* motive, driving. *m,* motor, engine —*n* (person) mover, motive force. **m. de combustión interna,** internal combustion engine. **m. de retroacción,** jet engine

motorista /moto'rista/ *mf* motorist, driver

movedizo /moβe'ðiθo; moβe'ðiso/ *a* movable; insecure, unsteady; shaky; changeable, vacillating

mover /mo'βer/ *vt irr* to move; operate, drive; sway; wag; persuade, induce; excite; move (to pity, etc.); (*with prep a*) cause; —*vi* sprout (plants); —*vr* move —*Pres. Indic.* **muevo, mueves, mueve, mueven.** *Pres. Subjunc.* **mueva, muevas, mueva, muevan**

movible /mo'βiβle/ *a* movable; insecure, shaky. *m,* motive, cause, incentive

movilizar /moβili'θar; moβili'sar/ *vt* to mobilize

movimiento /moβi'miento/ *m,* movement; perturbation, excitement; *Mus.* movement; *Lit.* fire, spirit; *Mech.* motion, movement. *Mil.* **m. envolvente,** encircling movement

moza /'moθa; 'mosa/ *f,* maid; girl; waitress. **m. de partido,** party girl, prostitute. **buena m.,** fine, upstanding young woman

mozo /'moθo; 'moso/ *a* young, unmarried. *m,* boy, youth; bachelor; waiter; porter. **m. de cordel** *or* **m. de esquina,**

street porter, message boy. **m. de estación,** railroad porter. **buen m.,** fine, upstanding young man

muaré /mua're/ *m,* moiré silk

muceta /mu'θeta; mu'seta/ *f, Educ.* hood, short cape (of a graduate's gown)

muchacha /mu'tʃatʃa/ *f,* girl, lass; female servant

muchachada /mutʃa'tʃaða/ *f,* childish prank

muchachez /mutʃa'tʃeθ; mutʃa'tʃes/ *f,* boyhood; girlhood

muchachil /mutʃa'tʃil/ *a* boyish; girlish

muchacho /mu'tʃatʃo/ *m,* boy, youth; male servant

muchedumbre /mutʃe'ðumbre/ *f,* abundance, plenty; crowd, multitude; mass, mob

muchísimo /mu'tʃisimo/ *a superl* very much —*adv* very great deal, very much

mucho /'mutʃo/ *a* much; plenty of; very; long (time); *pl* many, numerous —*adv* a great deal; much; very much; yes, certainly; frequently; often; very (e.g. *Me alegro m.,* I am very glad); to a great extent; long (time). **con m.,** by far, easily. **ni con m.,** nor anything like it, very far from it. **ni m. menos,** and much less. **por m. que,** however much

mucílago /mu'θilago; mu'silago/ *m,* mucilage, gum

muda /'muða/ *f,* change, transformation; change of clothes; molting season; molt, sloughing of skin (snakes, etc.); change of voice (in boys)

mudable /mu'ðaβle/ *a* changeable, inconstant

mudanza /mu'ðanθa; muðansa/ *f,* change; furniture removal; step, figure (in dancing); changeability, inconstancy

mudar /mu'ðar/ *vt* to change; alter, transform; exchange; remove; dismiss (from employment); molt; slough the skin (snakes, etc.); change the voice (boys); —*vr* alter one's behavior; change one's residence; change one's expression; *Inf.* go away, depart

mudéjar /mu'ðehar/ *m, Archit.* style containing Moorish and Christian elements. *mf* Moor who remained in Spain under Christian rule

mudez /mu'ðeθ; mu'ðes/ *f,* dumbness; silence, muteness

mudo /'muðo/ *a* dumb; silent, mute, quiet

mueblaje /mue'βlahe/ *m,* household goods and furniture

mueble /'mueβle/ *m,* piece of furniture; furnishing

mueblería /mueβle'ria/ *f,* furniture store or factory

mueca /'mueka/ *f,* grimace

muela /'muela/ *f,* grindstone; molar (tooth); millstone; flat-topped hill. **m. del juicio,** wisdom tooth. **dolor de muelas,** toothache

muelle /'mueʎe; 'mueʝe/ *a* soft, smooth; voluptuous, sensuous; luxurious. *m,*

spring (of a watch, etc.); wharf, quay; freight platform (railroad). **m. real,** mainspring (of a watch). **m. del volante,** hairspring.

muérdago /'muerðago/ *m,* mistletoe

muerte /'muerte/ *f,* death; destruction, annihilation; end, decline. *Inf.* una **m. chiquita,** a nervous shudder. **a m.,** to the death, with no quarter. **de m.,** implacably, inexorably (of hatred); very seriously (of being ill). **dar m. (a),** to kill. **estar a la m.,** to be on the point of death. **a cada m. de un obispo,** once in a blue moon

muerto /'muerto/ **(-ta)** *a* dead; slaked (lime); *Mech.* neutral; faded, dull (colors); languid, indifferent. **m.** is used in familiar speech as *past part* **matar** (e.g., *Le ha muerto,* He has killed him) —*n* corpse. *Inf.* **desenterrar los muertos,** to speak ill of the dead. *Inf.* **echarle a uno el m.,** to pass the buck. *Inf.* **estar m. por,** to be dying, yearning for. **ser el m.,** to be dummy (at cards)

muesca /'mueska/ *f,* notch, mortise, groove

muestra /'muestra/ *f,* shop sign; sample, specimen; pattern, model; demeanor; watch or clock face; sign, indication; poster, placard; *Mil.* muster roll. **hacer m.,** to show

mugido /mu'hiðo/ *m,* mooing or lowing (of cattle)

mugir /mu'hir/ *vi* to low or moo (cattle); bellow, shout; rage (elements)

mugre /'mugre/ *f,* grease, grime, dirt

mugriento /mu'griento/ *a* grimy, greasy

mujer /mu'her/ *f,* woman; wife. **m. de la vida airada** *or* **m. del partido** *or* **m. pública,** prostitute. **m. de la luna,** man in the moon. **m. de su casa,** good housewife. **tomar m.,** to take a wife

mujeriego /muhe'riego/ *a* womanly, feminine; (of men) dissolute, given to philandering. **cabalgar a mujeriegas,** to ride sidesaddle

mujeril /muhe'ril/ *a* womanly, feminine

mula /'mula/ *f,* female mule; mule (heelless slipper). *Inf.* **Se me fue la m.,** My tongue ran away with me

muladar /mula'ðar/ *m,* refuse heap, junkpile, dunghill

mular /mu'lar/ *a* mule; mulish

mulato /mu'lato/ **(-ta)** *a* and *n* mulatto

muleta /mu'leta/ *f,* crutch; bullfighter's red flag; support, prop

mullir /mu'ʎir; mu'ʝir/ *vt irr* to make soft, shake out (wool, down, etc.); *Fig.* prepare the way; *Agr.* hoe the roots (of vines, etc.) —*Pres. Part.* **mullendo.** *Preterite* **mulló, mulleron.** *Imperf. Subjunc.* **mullese,** etc.

mulo /'mulo/ *m,* mule

multa /'multa/ *f,* fine

multar /mul'tar/ *vt* to impose a fine on

multicolor /multiko'lor/ *a* multicolored

multilátero /multi'latero/ *a* multilateral

multimillonario /multimiʎo'nario; multimiyo'nario/ **(-ia)** a and n multimillion-aire

multiplicación /multiplika'θion; multi-plika'sion/ f. multiplication

multiplicador /multiplika'ðor/ **(-ra)** n multiplier. m, Math. multiplier

multiplicar /multipli'kar/ **(se)** vt and vr to multiply; reproduce

múltiplo /'multiplo/ a and m, multiple

multisecular /multiseku'lar/ a age-old, many centuries old

multitud /multi'tuð/ f, multitude, great number; crowd; rabble, masses, mob

mundanal, mundano /munda'nal, mun'dano/ a worldly, mundane

mundial /mun'dial/ a world, worldwide

mundo /'mundo/ m, world, universe; human race; earth; human society; world (of letters, science, etc.); secular life; Eccl. vanities of the flesh; geographical globe. **echar al m.,** to give birth to; produce; bring forth. **el Nuevo M.,** the New World, America. Inf. **medio m.,** half the earth, a great crowd. Inf. **ponerse el m. por montera,** to treat the world as one's oyster. **ser hombre del m.,** to be a man of the world. Inf. **tener m. or mucho m.,** to be very experienced, know the world. **todo el m.,** everyone. **venir al m.,** to be born. **ver m.,** to travel, see the world

mundología /mundolo'hia/ f, worldliness, experience of the world

munición /muni'θion; muni'sion/ f, Mil. munition; small shot. Mil. **m. de boca,** fodder and food supplies

municipal /muniθi'pal; munisi'pal/ a municipal. m, policeman

municipalidad /muniθipali'ðað; munisipali'ðað/ f, municipality

municipio /muni'θipio; muni'sipio/ m, municipality, town council

munificencia /munifi'θenθia; munifi'sensia/ f, munificence, generosity

munífico /mu'nifiko/ a munificent, generous

muñeca /mu'ɲeka/ f, Anat. wrist; doll; puppet; dressmaker's dummy; polishing pad; mannequin; boundary marker; Inf. flighty young woman

muñeco /mu'ɲeko/ m, boy doll; puppet; Inf. playboy

muñir /mu'ɲir/ vt irr to summon, convoke; arrange, dispose. See **mullir**

mural /mu'ral/ a mural

muralla /mu'raʎa; mu'raya/ f, town wall; rampart, fortification

murar /mu'rar/ vt to surround with a wall, wall in

murciélago /mur'θielago; mur'sielago/ m, Zool. bat

murmullo /mur'muʎo; mur'muyo/ m, whisper; whispering; rustling; purling, lapping, splashing; mumbling, muttering

murmuración /murmura'θion; murmura-'sion/ f, slander, backbiting, gossip

murmurador /murmura'ðor/ **(-ra)** a gossiping, slanderous —n gossip, backbiter

murmurar /murmu'rar/ vi to rustle (leaves, etc.); purl, lap, splash (water); whisper; mumble, mutter; —vi and vt Inf. slander, backbite

murmurio /mur'murio/ m, rustling; lapping (of water); whispering; murmur; Inf. slander

muro /'muro/ m, wall; defensive wall, rampart

musaraña /musa'raɲa/ f, Zool. shrew; any small animal; Inf. ridiculous effigy, guy. Inf. **mirar a las musarañas,** to be absent-minded

musculatura /muskula'tura/ f, musculature

músculo /'muskulo/ m, muscle; strength, brawn

musculoso /musku'loso/ a muscular; strong, brawny

muselina /muse'lina/ f, muslin

museo /mu'seo/ m, museum. **m. de pintura,** art gallery, picture gallery

musgo /'musgo/ m, moss

música /'musika/ f, music; melody, harmony; musical performance; musical composition; group of musicians; sheet music. Inf. **m. celestial,** vain words, moonshine. Inf. **m. ratonera,** badly played music. Inf. **¡Vaya con su m. a otra parte!** Get out! Go to hell!

musical /musi'kal/ a musical

músico /'musiko/ **(-ca)** a music —n musician. **m. ambulante,** strolling musician. **m. mayor,** bandleader

musitar /musi'tar/ vi to mutter, mumble

muslo /'muslo/ m, thigh

musulmán /musul'man/ **(-ana)** a and n Muslim

mutación /muta'θion; muta'sion/ f, change, mutation; sudden change in the weather; Theat. change of scene

mutilación /mutila'θion; mutila'sion/ f, mutilation; damage; defacement

mutilar /muti'lar/ vt to mutilate; spoil, deface, damage; cut short; reduce

mutis /'mutis/ m, Theat. exit. **hacer m.** Theat. to exit; keep quiet, say nothing

mutismo /mu'tismo/ m, mutism, dumbness; silence, speechlessness

mutualidad /mutuali'ðað/ f, reciprocity, mutuality, interdependence; principle of mutual aid; mutual aid society

mutualista /mutua'lista/ mf member of a mutual aid society

mutuo /'mutuo/ a reciprocal, mutual, interdependent

muy /'mui/ adv very; very much; much. Used to form absolute superlative (e.g., **m. rápidamente,** very quickly). Can modify adjectives, nouns used adjectivally, adverbs, participles (e.g. **María es m. mujer,** Mary is very much a woman (very womanly)). **m. temprano,** very early. **M. señor mío,** Dear Sir (in letters)

N Ñ

nabo /'naβo/ *m*, turnip; turnip root; any root stem; *Naut*. mast; stock (of a horse's tail)

nácar /'nakar/ *m*, mother-of-pearl

nacer /na'θer; na'ser/ *vi irr* to be born; rise (rivers, etc.); sprout; grow (plumage, fur, leaves, etc.); descend (lineage); appear (stars, etc.); originate; *Fig*. issue forth; appear suddenly; (*with prep a* or *para*) be destined for, have a natural leaning toward. **n. con pajitas de oro en la cuna**, to be born with a silver spoon in one's mouth —*vr* grow; sprout; *Sew*. split at the seams —*Pres. Indic*. **nazco, naces,** etc —*Pres. Subjunc*. **nazca,** etc.

nacido /na'θiðo; na'siðo/ *a* and *past part* born; suitable, fit. *m*, (gen. *pl*) the living and the dead. **bien n.,** noble, well-born; well-bred. **mal n.,** base-born; ill-bred

naciente /na'θiente; na'siente/ *a* growing; nascent. *m*, east

nacimiento /naθi'miento; nasi'miento/ *m*, birth; source (of rivers, etc.); birthplace; origin; lineage; *Astron*. rising; nativity crib, manger. **de n.,** from birth; by birth; born

nación /na'θion; na'sion/ *f*, nation; country; *Inf*. birth

nacional /naθio'nal; nasio'nal/ *a* national; native. *mf* citizen, national

nacionalidad /naθionali'ðað; nasionali'ðað/ *f*, nationality

nacionalismo /naθiona'lismo; nasiona'lismo/ *m*, nationalism

nacionalización /naθionaliθa'θion; nasionalisa'sion/ *f*, naturalization; nationalization; acclimatization

nacionalizar /naθionali'θar; nasionali'sar/ *vt* to naturalize; nationalize

nada /'naða/ *f*, void, nothingness —*pron indef* nothing —*adv* by no means. **casi n.,** very little, practically nothing. **¡De n.!** Not at all! Don't mention it! You're welcome! **No vale para n.,** He (it, she) is of no use

nadaderas /naða'ðeras/ *f pl*, water wings (for swimming)

nadador /naða'ðor/ (**-ra**) *n* swimmer —*a* swimming

nadar /na'ðar/ *vi* to swim; float; have an abundance (of); *Inf*. be too large (of garments, etc.). **n. y guardar la ropa,** *Fig*. to sit on the fence

nadería /naðe'ria/ *f*, trifle

nadie /'naðie/ *pron indef* no one. *m*, *Fig*. a nobody

nadir /na'ðir/ *m*, nadir

nado /'naðo/ *a* by swimming; afloat

nafta /'nafta/ *f*, naphtha

naftalina /nafta'lina/ *f*, naphthalene

naipe /'naipe/ *m*, playing card; pack of cards

nalga /'nalga/ *f*, (gen. *pl*) buttock(s)

nana /'nana/ *f*, *Inf*. grandma; lullaby

nao /'nao/ *f*, ship

napoleónico /napole'oniko/ *a* Napoleonic

Nápoles /'napoles/ Naples

napolitano /napoli'tano/ (**-na**) *a* and *n* Neapolitan

naranja /na'ranha/ *f*, orange. **n. dulce,** blood orange. **n. mandarina,** tangerine. *Inf*. **media n.,** better half

naranjada /naran'haða/ *f*, orangeade

naranjo /na'ranho/ *m*, orange tree; *Inf*. lout, blockhead

narciso /nar'θiso; nar'siso/ *m*, narcissus; dandy, fop. **n. trompón,** daffodil

narcótico /nar'kotiko/ *a* and *m*, narcotic

narcotraficante /narkotrafi'kante/ *mf* drug dealer

nardo /'narðo/ *m*, tuberose, spikenard, nard

narigudo /nari'guðo/ *a* large-nosed; nose-shaped

nariz /na'riθ; na'ris/ *f*, nose; nostril; snout; nozzle; sense of smell; bouquet (of wine). **n. perfilada,** well-shaped nose. **n. respingona,** snub nose. *Inf*. **meter las narices,** to meddle, interfere

narración /narra'θion; narra'sion/ *f*, narration, account

narrador /narra'ðor/ (**-ra**) *a* narrative —*n* narrator

narrar /na'rrar/ *vt* to narrate, tell, relate

narrativa /narra'tiβa/ *f*, narrative; account; narrative skill

narrativo, narratorio /narra'tiβo, na-rra'torio/ *a* narrative

nata /'nata/ *f*, cream; *Fig*. the flower, elite; *pl* whipped cream with sugar

natación /nata'θion; nata'sion/ *f*, swimming. **n. a la marinera,** trudgen stroke

natal /na'tal/ *a* natal; native. *m*, birth; birthday

natalicio /nata'liθio; nata'lisio/ *a* natal —*a* and *m*, birthday

natalidad /natali'ðað/ *f*, birth rate

natatorio /nata'torio/ *a* swimming. *m*, swimming pool

natillas /na'tiλas; na'tiyas/ *f pl*, custard

natividad /natiβi'ðað/ *f*, nativity; birth; Christmas

nativo /na'tiβo/ *a* indigenous; native; innate

nato /'nato/ *a* born; inherent; ex officio

natura /na'tura/ *f*, nature; *Mus*. major scale

natural /natu'ral/ *a* natural; native; indigenous; spontaneous; sincere, candid; physical; usual, ordinary; *Mus*. natural; unadulterated, pure; *Herald*. proper. *mf* native, citizen. *m*, temperament; disposition; instinct (of animals); natural inclination. **al n.,** naturally, without art. **del n.,** *Art*. from life

naturaleza /natura'leθa; natura'lesa/ *f*, nature; character; disposition; instinct; temperament; nationality, origin; naturalization; kind, class; constitution, physique. **n. humana**, humankind. **n. muerta**, *Art.* still life

naturalizar /naturali'θar; naturali'sar/ *vt* to naturalize; acclimatize; **—vr** become naturalized; become acclimatized

naufragar /naufra'gar/ *vi* to be shipwrecked; fail, be unsuccessful

naufragio /nau'frahio/ *m*, shipwreck; disaster, loss

náufrago /'naufrago/ **(-ga)** *n* shipwrecked person. *m*, shark

náusea /'nausea/ *f*, nausea (*pl* more usual); repugnance

nauseabundo, nauseoso /nausea'βundo, nause'oso/ *a* nauseous; nauseating, repugnant

náutica /'nautika/ *f*, navigation; yachting; seamanship

náutico /'nautiko/ *a* nautical

navaja /na'βaha/ *f*, razor; clasp knife; boar tusk; sting; *Inf.* slanderous tongue. **n. de afeitar**, (shaving) razor

navajada /naβa'haða/ *f*, slash with a razor

naval /na'βal/ *a* naval

navarro /na'βarro/ **(-ra)** *a* and *n* Navarrese

nave /'naβe/ *f*, ship; *Archit.* nave. **n. aérea**, airship. *Archit.* **n. lateral**, aisle. **n. principal**, *Archit.* nave

navegable /naβe'gaβle/ *a* navigable

navegación /naβega'θion; naβega'sion/ *f*, navigation; sea voyage

navegante /naβe'gante/ *a* voyaging; navigating. *m*, navigator

navegar /naβe'gar/ *vi* to navigate; sail; fly

navidad /naβi'ðað/ *f*, nativity; Christmas; *pl* Christmastime

naviero /na'βiero/ *a* shipping. *m*, ship owner

navío /na'βio/ *m*, warship; ship. **n. de transporte**, transport. **n. de tres puentes**, three-decker

nazismo /na'θismo; na'sismo/ *m*, nazism

neblina /ne'βlina/ *f*, fog; mist

nebuloso /neβu'loso/ *a* foggy; misty; cloudy; somber, melancholy; confused, nebulous

necedad /neθe'ðað; nese'ðað/ *f*, silliness

necesario /neθe'sario; nese'sario/ *a* necessary; unavoidable

neceser /neθe'ser; nese'ser/ *m*, dressing case. *Sew.* **n. de costura**, workbox

necesidad /neθesi'ðað; nesesi'ðað/ *f*, necessity; poverty, want; shortage, need; emergency. **de n.**, necessarily

necesitado /neθesi'taðo; nesesi'taðo/ **(-da)** *a* needy, poor **—n** poor person

necesitar /neθesi'tar; nesesi'tar/ *vt* to necessitate; compel, oblige; **—vi** be necessary, need

necio /'neθio; 'nesio/ *a* stupid; senseless; unreasonable

necrología /nekrolo'hia/ *f*, necrology, obituary

neerlandés /neerlan'des/ *a* Dutch

nefando /ne'fando/ *a* iniquitous

nefario /ne'fario/ *a* nefarious

nefasto /ne'fasto/ *a* disastrous, ill-omened

nefritis /ne'fritis/ *f*, nephritis

negable /ne'gaβle/ *a* deniable

negación /nega'θion; nega'sion/ *f*, negation; privation; negative; nay; *Gram.* negative particle; *Law.* traverse

negado /ne'gaðo/ *a* inept, unfitted; stupid

negar /ne'gar/ *vt irr* to deny; refuse; prohibit; disclaim; dissemble; disown; *Law.* traverse; **—vr** refuse, avoid; decline (to receive visitors). See **acertar**

negativa /nega'tiβa/ *f*, denial; refusal; *Photo.* negative

negativo /nega'tiβo/ *a* negative

negligencia /negli'henθia; negli'hensia/ *f*, negligence; omission; carelessness; forgetfulness

negligente /negli'hente/ *a* negligent; careless; neglectful

negociable /nego'θiaβle; nego'siaβle/ *a* negotiable

negociación /negoθia'θion; negosia'sion/ *f*, negotiation; business affair, deal

negociado /nego'θiaðo; nego'siaðo/ *m*, department, section (of a ministry, etc.); business

negociante /nego'θiante; nego'siante/ *m*, businessman **—a** negotiating; trading

negociar /nego'θiar; nego'siar/ *vi* to trade, traffic; negotiate

negocio /ne'goθio; ne'gosio/ *m*, occupation; trade; business; employment; transaction; *pl* business affairs. **hombre de negocios**, businessman

negra /'negra/ *f*, black girl, black woman; *Inf.* honey, *West Hem.* sweetheart

negro /'negro/ *a* black; dark; melancholy; disastrous; *Herald.* sable. *m*, black; black (color). **n. de humo**, lampblack

negruzco /ne'gruθko; ne'grusko/ *a* blackish

nemotécnica /nemo'teknika/ *f*, mnemonics

nene /'nene/ **(-na)** *n Inf.* baby; darling

nenúfar /ne'nufar/ *m*, white water lily

neo /'neo/ *m*, neon

neocelandés /neoθelan'des; neoselan'des/ **(-esa)** *a* New Zealand **—n** New Zealander

neófito /ne'ofito/ **(-ta)** *n* neophyte

neoyorquino /neoior'kino/ **(-na)** *a* New York **—n** New Yorker

nepotismo /nepo'tismo/ *m*, nepotism

Neptuno /nep'tuno/ *m*, *Astron.* Neptune; *Poet.* sea

nervio /'nerβio/ *m*, nerve; sinew; *Bot.* vein; vigor; *Mus.* string. **n. ciático**, sciatic nerve

nervioso /ner'βioso/ *a* nervous; overwrought, agitated; vigorous; neural; sinewy; jerky (of style, etc.)

nervosidad /nerβosi'ðað/ *f*, nervousness;

nervosity; flexibility (metals); jerkiness (of style, etc.); force, efficacy

nervudo /ner'βuðo/ *a* strong-nerved, vigorous

nesga /'nesga/ *f*, *Sew.* gore

neto /'neto/ *a* neat; clean; pure; *Com.* net. *m*, *Archit.* dado

neumático /neu'matiko/ *a* pneumatic. *m*, rubber tire

neumococo /neumo'koko/ *m*, pneumococcus

neurálgico /neu'ralhiko/ *a* neuralgic

neurastenia /neuras'tenia/ *f*, neurasthenia

neurasténico /neuras'teniko/ **(-ca)** *a* and *n* neurasthenic

neurólogo /neu'rologo/ *m*, neurologist

neurosis /neu'rosis/ *f*, neurosis. **n. de guerra**, war neurosis; shell shock

neurótico /neu'rotiko/ **(-ca)** *a* and *n* neurotic

neutral /neu'tral/ *a* neutral; indifferent

neutralidad /neutrali'ðað/ *f*, neutrality; impartiality, indifference

neutralizar /neutrali'θar; neutrali'sar/ *vt* to neutralize; counteract, mitigate

neutro /'neutro/ *a* neuter; *Chem.* neutral; *Mech.* neuter; sexless

nevada /ne'βaða/ *f*, snowfall

nevar /ne'βar/ *vi* and *vt impers* to snow —*Pres. Indic.* **nieva**. *Pres. Subjunc.* **nieve**

nevera /ne'βera/ *f*, refrigerator; icehouse

nevoso /ne'βoso/ *a* snowy

nexo /'nekso/ *m*, nexus; connection, union

ni /ni/ *conjunc* neither, nor. **ni bien ni mal**, neither good nor bad. **ni siquiera**, not even. **¡Ni creas!**, **¡Ni creas!** Nonsense!

niara /'niara/ *f*, haystack, rick

nicaragüeño /nikara'gueno/ **(-ña)** *a* and *n* Nicaraguan

nicho /'nitʃo/ *m*, niche; recess (in a wall)

nicotina /niko'tina/ *f*, nicotine

nidada /ni'ðaða/ *f*, nest full of eggs; brood, clutch

nidal /ni'ðal/ *m*, nest; nest egg; haunt; cause, foundation

nido /'niðo/ *m*, nest; den; hole; dwelling; haunt. **n. de ametralladoras**, *Mil.* pillbox

niebla /'nieβla/ *f*, fog; mist; cloud; mildew; haze

nieto /'nieto/ **(-ta)** *n* grandchild; descendant

nieve /'nieβe/ *f*, snow; whiteness. **deportes de n.**, winter sports

Nilo, el /'nilo, el/ the Nile

nimbo /'nimbo/ *m*, halo, nimbus

nimiedad /nimie'ðað/ *f*, prolixity; *Inf.* fussiness; fastidiousness, delicacy

nimio /'nimio/ *a* prolix; *Inf.* fussy; fastidious; *Inf.* parsimonious

ninfa /'ninfa/ *f*, nymph; *Ent.* chrysalis

ningún /niŋ'gun/ *a* *Abbr.* of **ninguno**. Used before *m*, *sing* nouns only. **De n. modo**, In no way! Certainly not!

niña /'niɲa/ *f*, girl. **n. del ojo**, pupil (of the eye). **n. de los ojos**, apple of one's eye, darling

niñada /ni'ɲaða/ *f*, childishness, foolish act

niñera /ni'ɲera/ *f*, nursemaid

niñería /niɲe'ria/ *f*, childish act; trifle; childishness, folly

niñez /ni'ɲeθ; ni'ɲes/ *f*, childhood; beginning, early days; *Fig.* cradle

niño /'niɲo/ **(-ña)** *a* childish; young; inexperienced; imprudent —*n* child; young or inexperienced person. **n. de la doctrina**, charity child. **n. terrible**, enfant terrible. **desde n.**, from childhood

nipón /ni'pon/ **(-ona)** *a* and *n* Japanese

níquel /'nikel/ *m*, *Chem.* nickel

niquelar /nike'lar/ *vt* to chrome-plate

nirvana /nir'βana/ *m*, nirvana

níspero /'nispero/ *m*, medlar tree; medlar

níspola /'nispola/ *f*, medlar

nitidez /niti'ðeθ; niti'ðes/ *f*, brightness, neatness, cleanliness

nítido /'nitiðo/ *a* bright, neat, clean (often *Poet.*)

nitrato /ni'trato/ *m*, nitrate

nítrico /'nitriko/ *a* nitric

nitrógeno /ni'troheno/ *m*, nitrogen

nivel /ni'βel/ *m*, level; levelness. **n. de albañil**, plummet. **n. de burbuja**, spirit level. **a n.**, on the level. **estar al n. de las circunstancias**, to rise to the occasion; save the day

nivelación /niβela'θion; niβela'sion/ *f*, leveling

nivelador /niβela'ðor/ **(-ra)** *a* leveling —*n* leveler

nivelar /niβe'lar/ *vt* to level; *Fig.* make equal

níveo /'niβeo/ *a* snowy; snow-white

Niza /'niθa; 'nisa/ Nice

no /no/ *adv* no; not. **no bien**, no sooner. **no sea que**, unless. **no tal**, no such thing

noble /'noβle/ *a* noble, illustrious; generous; outstanding, excellent; aristocratic. *mf* nobleman (-woman)

nobleza /no'βleθa; no'βlesa/ *f*, nobility

noche /'notʃe/ *f*, night; darkness; confusion, obscurity. *Inf.* **n. toledana**, restless night. **¡Buenas noches!** Good night! **de n.**, by night. **esta n.**, tonight

nochebuena /notʃe'βuena/ *f*, Christmas Eve

nochebueno /notʃe'βueno/ *m*, yule log; Christmas cake

noción /no'θion; no'sion/ *f*, notion, idea; *pl* elementary knowledge

nocividad /noθiβi'ðað; nosiβi'ðað/ *f*, noxiousness

nocivo /no'θiβo; no'siβo/ *a* noxious

nocturno /nok'turno/ *a* nocturnal; melancholy. *m*, *Mus.* nocturne

nodriza /no'ðriθa; no'ðrisa/ *f*, wet nurse

nogal /no'gal/ *m*, walnut tree; walnut wood

nómada /'nomaða/ *a* nomadic

nombradía /nom'βraðia/ *f*, renown

nombramiento /nombra'miento/ *m,* naming; appointment; nomination

nombrar /nom'βrar/ *vt* to name; nominate; appoint; mention (in dispatches, etc.)

nombre /'nombre/ *m,* name; title; reputation; proxy; *Gram.* noun; *Mil.* password. **n. de pila,** Christian name. **por n.,** called; by name. **Su n. anda puesto en el cuerno de la Luna,** He (she) is praised to the skies

nomenclatura /nomenkla'tura/ *f,* nomenclature

nómina /'nomina/ *f,* list, register; payroll; amulet

nominación /nomina'θion; nomina'sion/ *f,* nomination, appointment

nominador /nomina'ðor/ **(-ra)** *a* nominating —*n* nominator

nominal /nomi'nal/ *a* nominal

nomo /'nomo/ *m,* gnome

non /non/ *a* odd (of numbers)

nonada /no'naða/ *f,* nothing, practically nothing

nonagenario /nonahe'nario/ **(-ia)** *a* and *n* nonagenarian

nones /'nones/ *m, pl* certainly not, definitely not, nope

nopal /no'pal/ *m,* nopal, prickly pear tree

noquear /noke'ar/ *vt (Boxing)* to knock out, K.O.

norabuena /nora'βuena/ *f,* congratulation

nordeste /nor'ðeste/ *m,* northeast

nórdico /'norðiko/ **(-ca)** *a* and *n* Nordic

noria /'noria/ *f,* water well; chain pump; *Inf.* hard, monotonous work

norma /'norma/ *f,* square (used by builders, etc.); *Fig.* norm, standard, model

normal /nor'mal/ *a* normal, usual; standard, average. *f,* normal school, teacher's college (also **escuela n.**)

normalidad /normali'ðað/ *f,* normality

normalista /norma'lista/ *mf* student at a teacher's college

normalización /normaliθa'θion; normalisa'sion/ *f,* normalization; standardization

normalizar /normali'θar; normali'sar/ *vt* to make normal; standardize

noroeste /noro'este/ *m,* northwest

norte /'norte/ *m,* north pole; north; north wind; polestar; *Fig.* guide

norteamericano /norteameri'kano/ **(-na)** *a* and *n* North American; *(U.S.A.)* American

norteño /nor'teɲo/ *a* northerly, northern

Noruega /no'ruega/ Norway

noruego /no'ruego/ **(-ga)** *a* and *n* Norwegian. *m,* Norwegian (language)

nos /nos/ *pers pron pl mf acc* and *dat* (direct and indirect object) of **nosotros,** us; to us (e.g. *Nos lo dio,* He gave it to us)

nosotros, nosotras /no'sotros, no'sotras/ *pers pron pl mf* we; us. Also used with preposition (e.g. *Lo hicieron por nosotros,* They did it for us)

nostalgia /nos'talhia/ *f,* nostalgia

nostálgico /nos'talhiko/ *a* nostalgic; melancholy; homesick

nota /'nota/ *f,* mark, sign; annotation, comment; *Mus.* note; memorandum; *Com.* bill, account; criticism, imputation; mark (in exams); repute, renown; note (diplomatic)

notable /no'taβle/ *a* notable, remarkable; outstanding, prominent; with distinction (examination mark). *m pl,* notabilities

notación /nota'θion; nota'sion/ *f, (Mus. Math.)* notation; annotation

notar /no'tar/ *vt* to mark, indicate; observe, notice; note down; annotate; dictate, read out; criticize, reproach; discredit

notaría /nota'ria/ *f,* profession of a notary; notary's office

notarial /nota'rial/ *a* notarial

notario /no'tario/ *m,* notary public

noticia /no'tiθia; no'tisia/ *f,* rudiment, elementary knowledge; information; news (gen. *pl*); *pl* knowledge. **atrasado de noticias,** *Fig.* behind the times

noticiar /noti'θiar; noti'siar/ *vt* to inform, give notice

noticiario /noti'θiario; noti'siario/ *m,* news bulletin, newsreel.

noticiero /noti'θiero; noti'siero/ *m,* newspaper

noticioso /noti'θioso; noti'sioso/ *a* informed; learned; newsy

notificación /notifika'θion; notifika'sion/ *f, Law.* notification. **n. de reclutamiento,** draft notice

notificar /notifi'kar/ *vt* to notify officially; inform; warn

noto /'noto/ *a* known. *m,* south wind

notoriedad /notorie'ðað/ *f,* notoriety, publicity; flagrancy; fame, renown

notorio /no'torio/ *a* well-known; notorious, obvious; flagrant

novatada /noβa'taða/ *f, Inf.* ragging (of a freshman); blunder

novato /no'βato/ **(-ta)** *a* new, inexperienced —*n* novice, beginner

novecientos /noβe'θientos; noβe'sientos/ *a* and *m,* nine hundred

novedad /noβe'ðað/ *f,* newness, novelty; change, alteration; latest news; surprise; *pl* novelties. **sin n.,** no change; all well (or as usual); safely, without incident

novel /no'βel/ *a* new; inexperienced

novela /no'βela/ *f,* novel; tale; falsehood. **n. caballista,** western, cowboy story. **n. por entregas,** serial (story)

novelero /noβe'lero/ **(-ra)** *a* fond of novelty and change; fond of novels; fickle —*n* newshound, gossip

novelesco /noβe'lesko/ *a* novelistic; imaginary

novelista /noβe'lista/ *mf* novelist

novelística /noβe'listika/ *f,* art of novel writing

novena /no'βena/ *f, Eccl.* novena, religious services spread over nine days

noveno /no'βeno/ *a* and *m,* ninth

noventa /no'βenta/ *a* and *m*, ninety; ninetieth

novia /'noβia/ *f*, bride; fiancée

noviazgo /no'βiaθgo; no'βiasgo/ *m*, engagement, betrothal

novicio /no'βiθio; no'βisio/ **(-ia)** *n Eccl.* novice; beginner, apprentice; unassuming person

noviembre /no'βiembre/ *m*, November

novillo /no'βiλo; no'βiyo/ *m*, bullock. **hacer novillos**, to play truant

novio /'noβio/ *m*, bridegroom; fiancé; novice, beginner

nubada /nu'βaða/ *f*, cloudburst, rainstorm; abundance, plenty

nubarrón /nuβa'rron/ *m*, dense, lowering cloud, storm cloud

nube /'nuβe/ *f*, cloud; *Fig.* screen, impediment. **n. de verano**, summer cloud; passing annoyance

nublado /nu'βlaðo/ *a* cloudy; overcast. *m*, storm cloud; menace, threat; multitude, crowd

nublarse /nu'βlarse/ *vr* to cloud over

nubloso /nu'βloso/ *a* cloudy; unfortunate, unhappy

nuca /'nuka/ *f*, nape

núcleo /'nukleo/ *m*, kernel; stone, pip (of fruit); nucleus; *Fig.* core, essence

nudillo /nu'ðiλo; nu'ðiyo/ *m*, knuckle; *Mas.* plug

nudo /'nuðo/ *m*, knot; (*Bot. Med.*) node; joint; *Naut.* knot; *Fig.* bond, tie; *Fig.* crux, knotty point. **n. al revés**, granny knot. **n. de comunicaciones**, communication center. **n. de marino**, reef knot. **n. de tejedor**, sheet bend (knot). **n. en la garganta**, *Fig.* lump in the throat (from emotion)

nudoso /nu'ðoso/ *a* knotted, knotty; gnarled

nuera /'nuera/ *f*, daughter-in-law

nuestro, nuestra /'nuestro, 'nuestra/ *poss pron* 1st *pers pl mf* our; ours. **los nuestros**, our friends, supporters, party, profession, etc.

nueva /'nueβa/ *f*, news

nuevamente /nueβa'mente/ *adv* again

Nueva Orleans /'nueβa orle'ans/ New Orleans

Nueva York /'nueβa york/ New York

Nueva Zelanda, Zelandia /'nueβa θe'landa, θe'landia; 'nueβa se'landa, se'landia/ New Zealand

nueve /'nueβe/ *a* nine; ninth. *m*, number nine; ninth (of the month) (e.g. *el nueve*

de marzo, March 9th). **a las nueve**, at nine o'clock

nuevo /'nueβo/ *a* new; fresh; newly arrived; inexperienced; unused, scarcely worn. **de n.**, again. ¿**Qué hay de n.?** What's the news? What's new?

nuez /nueθ; nues/ *f*, walnut; *Anat.* Adam's apple. **n. moscada**, nutmeg

nulidad /nuli'ðað/ *f*, nullity; incompetence, ineptitude; worthlessness

nulo /'nulo/ *a* null, void; incapable; worthless

numeración /numera'θion; numera'sion/ *f*, calculation; numbering

numerar /nume'rar/ *vt* to number; enumerate; calculate

numerario /nume'rario/ *a* numerary. *m*, cash

numérico /nu'meriko/ *a* numerical

número /'numero/ *m*, number; figure; numeral; size (of gloves, etc.); quantity; issue, copy; rhythm; *Gram.* number; item (of a program); *pl Eccl.* Numbers. **n. del distrito postal**, ZIP code. **n. quebrado**, *Math.* fraction. **sin n.**, numberless

numeroso /nume'roso/ *a* numerous; harmonious

numismática /numis'matika/ *f*, numismatics

nunca /'nunka/ *adv* never. **n. jamás**, nevermore. **N. digas «De esta agua no beberé!»** Never say "Never!"

nuncio /'nunθio; 'nunsio/ *m*, messenger; papal nuncio; *Fig.* harbinger

nupcial /nup'θial; nup'sial/ *a* nuptial

nupcialidad /nupθiali'ðað; nupsiali'ðað/ *f*, marriage rate

nupcias /'nupθias; 'nupsias/ *f pl*, nuptials, marriage

nutrición /nutri'θion; nutri'sion/ *f*, nourishment; nutrition

nutrido /nu'triðo/ *a* abundant; numerous

nutrimento /nutri'mento/ *m*, nutriment; nourishment; nutrition, *Fig.* food, encouragement

nutrir /nu'trir/ *vt* to nourish; encourage; *Fig.* fill

nutritivo /nutri'tiβo/ *a* nourishing, nutritive

ñiquiñaque /ɲikiɲ'nake/ *m*, *Inf.* good-for-nothing, wastrel; *Inf.* trash

ñoñería /ɲoɲe'ria/ *f*, *Inf.* drivel; folly, stupidity

ñoño /'ɲoɲo/ **(-ña)** *a Inf.* sentimental; foolish, idiotic —*n* fool.

O

o /o/ f, letter O —*conjunc* or, either. **o** becomes **u** before words beginning with **o** or **ho** (e.g. *gloria u honor*)

oasis /o'asis/ m, oasis; *Fig.* refuge, haven

obduración /oβðura'θion; oβðura'sion/ f, obstinacy, stubbornness, obduracy

obedecer /oβeðe'θer; oβeðe'ser/ *vt irr* to obey; *Fig.* respond; bend, yield (metals, etc.); —*vi* result (from), arise (from). See **conocer**

obedecimiento /oβeðeθi'miento; oβeðesi'miento/ m, **obediencia** f, obedience

obediente /oβe'ðiente/ a obedient; docile

obertura /oβer'tura/ f, *Mus.* overture

obeso /o'βeso/ a obese

óbice /'oβiθe; 'oβise/ m, obstacle, impediment

obispo /o'βispo/ m, bishop. **o. sufragáneo,** suffragan bishop

óbito /'oβito/ m, death, demise

obituario /oβi'tuario/ m, obituary; obituary column

objeción /oβhe'θion; oβhe'sion/ f, objection

objetar /oβhe'tar/ *vt* to object to, oppose

objetivar /oβheti'βar/ *vt* to view objectively

objetividad /oβhetiβi'ðað/ f, objectivity

objetivo /oβhe'tiβo/ a objective. m, *Opt.* eyepiece; object finder; aim, goal

objeto /oβ'heto/ m, object; subject, theme; purpose; aim, goal. **sin o.,** without object; aimlessly

oblicuo /o'βlikuo/ a slanting, oblique

obligación /oβliga'θion; oβliga'sion/ f, obligation; *Com.* bond; *Com.* debenture; *pl* responsibilities; *Com.* liabilities

obligacionista /oβligaθio'nista; oβligasio'nista/ mf *Com.* bond holder, debenture holder

obligado /oβli'gaðo/ m, contractor (to a borough, etc.); *Mus.* obbligato

obligar /oβli'gar/ *vt* to compel, oblige, constrain; lay under an obligation; *Law.* mortgage; —*vr* bind oneself, promise

obligatorio /oβliga'torio/ a obligatory

oboe /o'βoe/ m, oboe; oboe player, oboist

óbolo /'oβolo/ m, obol, ancient Greek coin

obra /'oβra/ f, work; anything made; literary, artistic, scientific production; structure, construction; repair, alteration (to buildings, etc.); means, influence, power; labor, or time spent; action, behavior. **o. de caridad,** charitable act. **o. maestra,** masterpiece. **obras públicas,** public works. **poner por o.,** to put into effect; to set to work on. **o. de,** about, approximately

obrar /o'βrar/ *vt* to work; make, do; execute, perform; affect; construct, build; —*vi* be, exist (things); act, behave. **o. mal,** to behave badly, do wrong

obrero /o'βrero/ **(-ra)** a working —n worker; *pl* workers

obscenidad /oβsθeni'ðað; oβsseni'ðað/ f, obscenity

obsceno /oβs'θeno; oβs'seno/ a obscene

obsequiar /oβse'kiar/ *vt* to entertain, be attentive (to); give presents (to); court, make love to. **Me obsequia con un reloj,** He is presenting me with a watch

obsequio /oβ'sekio/ m, attention; gift; deference. **en o. de,** as a tribute to

obsequioso /oβse'kioso/ a obliging, courteous, attentive

observable /oβser'βaβle/ a observable

observación /oβserβa'θion; oβserβa'sion/ f, observation; remark

observador /oβserβa'ðor/ **(-ra)** a observing —n observer

observancia /oβser'βanθia; oβser'βansia/ f, observance; respect, reverence

observar /oβser'βar/ *vt* to notice; inspect, examine; fulfill; remark; watch, spy upon; *Astron.* observe

observatorio /oβserβa'torio/ m, observatory

obsesión /oβse'sion/ f, obsession

obsesionar /oβsesio'nar/ *vt* to obsess

obseso /oβ'seso/ a obsessed

obsolecer /oβsole'θer; oβsole'ser/ *vi* to obsolesce, become obsolete

obsoleto /oβso'leto/ a obsolete

obstáculo /oβs'takulo/ m, impediment; obstacle

obstante, no /oβs'tante, no/ *adv* in spite of; nevertheless

obstar /oβs'tar/ *vi* to impede, hinder

obstetra /oβs'tetra/ mf obstetrician

obstetricia /oβste'triθia; oβste'trisia/ f, obstetrics

obstinación /oβstina'θion; oβstina'sion/ f, obstinacy

obstinado /oβsti'naðo/ a obstinate, stubborn

obstinarse /oβsti'narse/ *vr* (*with en*) to persist in, insist on, be stubborn about

obstinaz /oβsti'naθ; oβsti'nas/ a obstinate

obstrucción /oβstruk'θion; oβstruk'sion/ f, obstruction

obstruir /oβs'truir/ *vt irr* to obstruct; block; hinder; —*vr* become choked or stopped up (pipes, etc.). See **huir**

obtención /oβten'θion; oβten'sion/ f, obtainment; attainment, realization

obtener /oβte'ner/ *vt irr* to obtain; attain; maintain, preserve. See **tener**

obturador /oβtura'ðor/ m, stopper; shutter (of a camera)

obturar /oβtu'rar/ *vt* to stopper, plug; block, obstruct

obtuso /oβ'tuso/ a blunt, dull; (*Geom. and Fig.*) obtuse

obviar /oβ'βiar/ *vt* to obviate

obvio /'oββio/ a obvious, evident, apparent

ocasión /oka'sion/ f. occasion; opportunity; motive, cause; danger, risk; *Inf.* **asir la o. por la melena,** to take time by the forelock. **de o.,** second-hand

ocasional /okasio'nal/ a chance, fortuitous; occasional

ocasionar /okasio'nar/ vt to cause, occasion; excite, provoke; risk, endanger

ocaso /o'kaso/ m. sunset; west; dusk; decadence, decline

occidental /okθiðen'tal; oksiðen'tal/ a Western

occidente /okθi'ðente; oksi'ðente/ m, West, Occident

occiso /ok'θiso; ok'siso/ a murdered; killed

oceánico /oθe'aniko; ose'aniko/ a oceanic

océano /o'θeano; o'seano/ m, ocean; immensity, abundance

ochenta /o'tʃenta/ a and m, eighty; eightieth

ochentón /otʃen'ton/ (-ona) n octogenarian

ocho /'otʃo/ a eight; eighth. m, figure eight; playing card with eight pips; eight; eighth day (of the month). **las o.,** eight o'clock

ochocientos /otʃo'θientos; otʃo'sientos/ a and m, eight hundred; eight-hundredth

ocio /'oθio; 'osio/ m, leisure, idleness; pl pastimes; leisure time

ociosidad /oθiosi'ðað; osiosi'ðað/ f, idleness, laziness; leisure

ocioso /o'θioso; o'sioso/ (-sa) a idle; useless, worthless; unprofitable, fruitless —n idle fellow

octava /ok'taβa/ f, octave

octavo /ok'taβo/ a eighth. m, eighth. **en o.,** in octavo

octogenario /oktohe'nario/ (-ia) a and n octogenarian

octubre /ok'tuβre/ m, October

ocular /oku'lar/ a ocular. m, eyepiece

oculista /oku'lista/ mf oculist

ocultación /okulta'θion; okulta'sion/ f, hiding, concealment

ocultar /okul'tar/ vt to hide, conceal; disguise; keep secret

oculto /o'kulto/ a hidden; secret; occult. **en o.,** secretly, quietly

ocupación /okupa'θion; okupa'sion/ f, occupancy; occupation, pursuit; employment, office, trade

ocupado /oku'paðo/ a occupied; busy

ocupante /oku'pante/ m, occupant

ocupar /oku'par/ vt to take possession of; obtain or hold (job); occupy, fill; inhabit; employ; hinder, embarrass; hold the attention (of); —vr (*with en*) be engaged in, be occupied with; (*with con*) concentrate on (a business affair, etc.)

ocurrencia /oku'rrenθia; oku'rrensia/ f, occurrence, incident; bright idea; witty remark

ocurrir /oku'rrir/ vi to anticipate; happen, take place; occur, strike (ideas)

oda /'oða/ f, ode

odiar /o'ðiar/ vt to hate

odio /'oðio/ m, hatred; malevolence

odioso /o'ðioso/ a hateful, odious

odisea /oði'sea/ f, odyssey

odorífero /oðo'rifero/ a odoriferous, fragrant

odre /'oðre/ m, goatskin, wineskin; *Inf.* wine bibber

oeste /o'este/ m, west

ofender /ofen'der/ vt to ill-treat, hurt; offend, insult; anger, annoy; —vr be offended

ofendido /ofen'diðo/ a offended; resentful

ofensa /o'fensa/ f, injury, harm; offense, crime

ofensiva /ofen'siβa/ f, *Mil.* offensive. **tomar la o.,** to take the offensive

ofensivo /ofen'siβo/ a offensive

ofensor /ofen'sor/ (-ra) n offender

oferta /o'ferta/ f, offer; gift; proposal; *Com.* tender. **o. y demanda,** supply and demand

oficial /ofi'θial; ofi'sial/ a official. m, official; officer; clerk; executioner; worker

oficiala /ofi'θiala; ofi'siala/ f, trained female worker

oficialidad /ofiθiali'ðað; ofisiali'ðað/ f, officialdom; officers

oficiar /ofi'θiar; ofi'siar/ vt *Eccl.* to celebrate or serve (mass); communicate officially, inform; *Inf.* (*with de*) act as

oficina /ofi'θina; ofi'sina/ f, workshop; office; pharmaceutical laboratory; pl cellars, basement (of a house)

oficinesco /ofiθi'nesko; ofisi'nesko/ a bureaucratic, red-tape

oficinista /ofiθi'nista; ofisi'nista/ mf clerk, office employee, office worker

oficio /o'fiθio; o'fisio/ m, occupation, employment; office, function, capacity; craft; operation; trade, business; official communication; office, bureau; *Eccl.* office. **Santo O.,** Holy Office. *Fig.* **buenos oficios,** good offices

oficiosidad /ofiθiosi'ðað; ofisiosi'ðað/ f, diligence, conscientiousness; helpfulness, friendliness; officiousness

oficioso /ofi'θioso; ofi'sioso/ a conscientious; helpful, useful; officious; meddlesome; unofficial, informal

ofrecer /ofre'θer; ofre'ser/ vt irr to offer; present; exhibit; consecrate, dedicate; —vr occur, suggest itself; volunteer. **¿Qué se le ofrece?** What do you require? What would you like? See **conocer**

ofrecimiento /ofreθi'miento; ofresi'miento/ m, offer, offering

ofrenda /o'frenda/ f, *Eccl.* offering; gift; present

oftalmología /oftalmolo'hia/ f, ophthalmology

oftalmólogo /oftal'mologo/ m, oculist, ophthalmologist

ofuscación /ofuska'θion; ofuska'sion/ f, **ofuscamiento** m, obfuscation, dazzle, dimness of sight; mental confusion, bewilderment

ofuscar /ofus'kar/ *vt* to dazzle, daze; dim, obfuscate; confuse, bewilder

ogro /'ogro/ *m*, ogre

oídas, de /o'iðas, de/ *adv* by hearsay

oído /o'iðo/ *m*, sense of hearing; ear. **de o.**, by ear. **decir al o.**, to whisper in a person's ear. *Mus.* **duro de o.**, hard of hearing; having a bad ear (for music). **estar sordo de un o.**, to be deaf in one ear

oidor /oi'ðor/ *m*, hearer; judge, *Obs.* magistrate

oír /o'ir/ *vt irr* to hear; give ear to, listen; understand —*Pres. Part* **oyendo**. *Pres. Indic.* **oigo, oyes, oye, oyen**. *Preterite* **oyó, oyeron**. *Pres. Subjunc.* **oiga**, etc. —*Imperf. Subjunc.* **oyese**, etc.

ojal /o'hal/ *m*, buttonhole; slit, hole

¡ojalá! /oha'la/ *interj* If only that were so! God grant!

ojeada /ohe'aða/ *f*, glance

ojear /ohe'ar/ *vt* to look at, stare at; bewitch; scare, startle

ojera /o'hera/ *f*, dark shadow (under the eye); eye bath

ojeriza /ohe'riθa; ohe'risa/ *f*, ill-will, spite

ojeroso /ohe'roso/ *a* having dark shadows under the eyes, wan, haggard

ojete /o'hete/ *m*, eyelet

ojo /'oho/ *m*, eye; hole; slit; socket; keyhole; eye (of a needle); span (of a bridge); core (of a corn); attention, care; mesh; spring, stream, well (of a staircase); *pl* darling. **¡ojo!** Take care! **o. avizor**, sharp watch; lynx eye. **Ojos que no ven, corazón que no siente**, Out of sight, out of mind. **o. saltón**, prominent, bulging eye. **o. vivo**, bright eye. **a o. de buen cubero**, at a guess. **a ojos vistas**, visibly; patently

ola /'ola/ *f*, billow; wave (atmospheric)

ole /'ole/ *m*, Andalusian dance

¡olé! /o'le/ *interj* Bravo!

oleada /ole'aða/ *f*, big wave, breaker; swell (of the sea); *Fig.* surge (of a crowd)

oleaje /ole'ahe/ *m*, swell, surge, billowing

olear /ole'ar/ *vt* to administer extreme unction

óleo /'oleo/ *m*, oil; *Eccl.* holy oil (gen.*pl*). **al ó.**, in oils

oleoducto /oleo'ðukto/ *m*, oil pipeline

oler /o'ler/ *vt irr* to smell; guess, discover; pry, smell out; —*vi* smell; (*with prep a*) smell of; smack of, be reminiscent of —*Pres. Indic.* **huelo, hueles, huele, huelen**. *Pres. Subjunc.* **huela, huelas, huela, huelan**

olfatear /olfate'ar/ *vt* to sniff, snuff, smell; *Inf.* pry into

olfativo, olfatorio /olfa'tiβo, olfa'torio/ *a* olfactory

olfato /ol'fato/ *m*, sense of smell; shrewdness

olfatorio /olfa'torio/ *a* olfactory

oliente /o'liente/ (**mal**) *a* evil-smelling

oligarquía /oligar'kia/ *f*, oligarchy

oligárquico /oli'garkiko/ *a* oligarchic

olímpico /o'limpiko/ *a* Olympic; Olympian

oliva /o'liβa/ *f*, olive tree; olive; barn owl; peace

olivar /oli'βar/ *m*, olive grove

olivo /o'liβo/ *m*, olive tree

olla /'oʎa; 'oya/ *f*, stew pot; Spanish stew; whirlpool. **o. podrida**, rich Spanish stew containing bacon, fowl, meat, vegetables, ham, etc. **las ollas de Egipto**, the fleshpots of Egypt

olmo /'olmo/ *m*, elm tree

olor /o'lor/ *m*, odor, scent, smell; hope, promise; suspicion, hint; reputation. **o. de santidad**, odor of sanctity

oloroso /olo'roso/ *a* fragrant, perfumed

olvidadizo /olβiða'ðiθo; olβiða'ðiso/ *a* forgetful

olvidar /olβi'ðar/ (**se**) *vt* and *vr* to forget; neglect, desert. **Se me olvidó el libro**, I forgot the book. **Me olvidé de lo pasado**, I forgot the past

olvido /ol'βiðo/ *m*, forgetfulness; indifference, neglect; oblivion

ombligo /om'βligo/ *m*, navel; *Fig.* core, center

ominoso /omi'noso/ *a* ominous

omisión /omi'sion/ *f*, omission; carelessness, negligence; neglect

omiso /o'miso/ *a* omitted; remiss; careless. **hacer caso o. de**, to set aside, ignore

omitir /omi'tir/ *vt* to omit

ómnibus /'omniβus/ *m*, bus

omnímodo /om'nimoðo/ *a* all-embracing

omnipotencia /omnipo'tenθia; omnipo'tensia/ *f*, omnipotence

omnipotente /omnipo'tente/ *a* omnipotent, all-powerful

omnisciencia /omnis'θienθia; omnis'siensia/ *f*, omniscience

omniscio /om'nisθio; om'nissio/ *a* omniscient

omnívoro /om'niβoro/ *a* omnivorous

omoplato /omo'plato/ *m*, scapula, shoulder blade

once /'onθe; 'onse/ *a* eleven; eleventh. *m*, eleven; eleventh (of the month). **las o.**, eleven o'clock

onceno /on'θeno; on'seno/ *a* eleventh

onda /'onda/ *f*, wave; *Fig.* flicker (of flames); *Sew.* scallop; *Phys.* wave; ripple; *pl* waves (in hair). *Radio.* **o. corta**, short wave. **o. etérea**, ether wave. **o. sonora**, sound wave

ondeante /onde'ante/ *a* waving; flowing

ondear /onde'ar/ *vi* to wave; ripple; undulate; roll (of the sea); float, flutter, stream; *Sew.* scallop; —*vr* swing, sway

ondeo /on'deo/ *m*, waving; undulation

ondulación /ondula'θion; ondula'sion/ *f*, undulation; wave; wriggling; twisting. **o. permanente**, permanent wave, perm

ondulado /ondu'laðo/ *a* wavy; undulating; scalloped

ondular /ondu'lar/ *vi* to writhe, squirm, wriggle; twist; coil; —*vt* wave (in hair)

oneroso /one'roso/ *a* onerous, heavy; troublesome

ónice /'oniθe; 'onise/ *m,* onyx

onomástico /ono'mastiko/ *a* onomastic. **día o.,** saint's day

onza /'onθa; 'onsa/ *f,* ounce. **por onzas,** by ounces; sparingly

onzavo /on'θaβo; on'saβo/ *a* and *m,* eleventh

opacidad /opaθi'ðað; opasi'ðað/ *f,* opacity; obscurity; gloom

opaco /o'pako/ *a* opaque; dark; gloomy, sad

ópalo /'opalo/ *m,* opal

opción /op'θion; op'sion/ *f,* option; choice, selection; *Law.* option

ópera /'opera/ *f,* opera

operación /opera'θion; opera'sion/ *f, Surg.* operation; execution, performance; *Com.* transaction

operar /ope'rar/ *vt Surg.* to operate; —*vi* act, have an effect; operate, control; *Com.* transact

operario /ope'rario/ **(-ia)** *n* worker, hand; operator; mechanic

opereta /ope'reta/ *f,* operetta, light opera

opinar /opi'nar/ *vi* to have or form an opinion, think; judge, consider

opinión /opi'nion/ *f,* opinion, view; reputation

opio /'opio/ *m,* opium. **fumadero de o.,** opium den

opíparo /o'piparo/ *a* magnificent, sumptuous (banquets, etc.)

oponer /opo'ner/ *vt irr* to oppose; resist, withstand; protest against; —*vr* oppose; be contrary or hostile (to); face, be opposite; object (to), set oneself against; compete (in public exams). See **poner**

oporto /o'porto/ *m,* port (wine)

oportunidad /oportuni'ðað/ *f,* opportunity, occasion

oportunista /oportu'nista/ *a* and *mf* opportunist

oportuno /opor'tuno/ *a* opportune; timely

oposición /oposi'θion; oposi'sion/ *f,* opposition; resistance; antagonism; public competitive exam for a post; (*Astron. Polit.*) opposition

opositor /oposi'tor/ **(-ra)** *n* opponent; competitor

opresión /opre'sion/ *f,* oppression; hardship; pressure. **o. de pecho,** difficulty in breathing

opresor /opre'sor/ **(-ra)** *a* oppressive —*n* oppressor

oprimir /opri'mir/ *vt* to oppress; treat harshly; press, crush; choke

oprobio /o'proβio/ *m,* opprobrium

optar /op'tar/ *vt* to take possession of; (*with por*) choose

óptica /'optika/ *f, Phys.* optics; peepshow

óptico /'optiko/ *a* optic, optical. *m,* optician

optimismo /opti'mismo/ *m,* optimism

optimista /opti'mista/ *mf* optimist —*a* optimistic

óptimo /'optimo/ *a superl* **bueno** best, optimal, optimum

opugnar /opug'nar/ *vt* to resist violently; *Mil.* assault, attack; impugn, challenge

opulencia /opu'lenθia; opu'lensia/ *f,* opulence, riches; excess, superabundance

opulento /opu'lento/ *a* opulent, rich

opúsculo /o'puskulo/ *m,* monograph, opuscule

oración /ora'θion; ora'sion/ *f,* oration, speech; prayer; *Gram.* sentence

oráculo /o'rakulo/ *m,* oracle

orador /ora'ðor/ **(-ra)** *n* orator; speech maker. *m,* preacher

oral /o'ral/ *a* oral; verbal; buccal

orar /o'rar/ *vi* to harangue, make an oration; pray; —*vt* request, beg

orate /o'rate/ *mf* lunatic

oratoria /ora'toria/ *f,* oratory, eloquence

oratorio /ora'torio/ *a* oratorical. *m,* oratory, chapel; *Mus.* oratorio

órbita /'orβita/ *f, Astron.* orbit; *Fig.* sphere; *Anat.* orbit, eye socket

orden /'orðen/ *mf* order, mode of arrangement; succession, sequence; group; system; orderliness, neatness; coherence; plan; *Eccl.* order, brotherhood; (*Zool. Bot.*) group, class; *Archit.* order; *Math.* degree. *f,* precept, command; *Com.* order; *pl Eccl.* ordination. (*Mil. Naut.*) **o. de batalla,** battle array. **o. de caballería,** order of knighthood. **o. del día,** order of the day. *Eccl.* **dar órdenes,** to ordain. **en o.,** in order; with regard to (to). **por su o.,** in its turn; successively

ordenación /orðena'θion; orðena'sion/ *f,* order, orderly arrangement, disposition; ordinance, precept; *Eccl.* ordination

ordenador /orðena'ðor/ *m Spain* computer

ordenancista /orðenan'θista; orðenan-'sista/ *mf Mil.* martinet; disciplinarian

ordenanza /orðe'nanθa; orðe'nansa/ *f,* order, method; command, instruction; ordinance, regulation (gen. *pl*). *m, Mil.* orderly

ordenar /orðe'nar/ *vt* to put in order, arrange; command, give instructions to; decree; direct, regulate; *Eccl.* ordain; —*vr* (*with de*) *Eccl.* be ordained as

ordeñar /orðe'ɲar/ *vt* to milk

ordinal /orði'nal/ *a* ordinal. *m,* ordinal number

ordinario /orði'nario/ *a* ordinary, usual; vulgar, coarse, uncultured; rude; commonplace, average, mediocre. *m, Eccl.* ordinary; carrier; courier. **de o.,** usually, ordinarily

orégano /o'regano/ *m,* wild marjoram

oreja /o'reha/ *f,* external ear; lug; tab, flap; tongue (of a shoe). *Inf.* **con las orejas caídas,** down in the mouth, depressed

orejera /ore'hera/ *f,* earflap; mold board (of a plow)

orejudo /ore'huðo/ a large- or long-eared

oreo /o'reo/ m, zephyr; ventilation; airing

orfanato /orfa'nato/ m, orphanage, orphan asylum

orfandad /orfan'dað/ f, orphanhood; defenselessness, lack of protection

orfebre /or'feβre/ mf gold- or silversmith

orfebrería /orfeβre'ria/ f, gold- or silverwork

orfeón /orfe'on/ m, choral society

organdí /organ'di/ m, organdy

orgánico /or'ganiko/ a organic; harmonious; Fig. organized

organillero /organi'ʎero; organi'yero/ (-ra) n organ grinder

organillo /orga'niʎo; orga'niyo/ m, barrel organ

organismo /orga'nismo/ m, organism; organization, association

organista /orga'nista/ mf organist

organización /organiθa'θion; organisa'sion/ f, organization; order, arrangement

organizador /organiθa'ðor; organisa'ðor/ (-ra) a organizing —n organizer

organizar /organi'θar; organi'sar/ vt to organize; regulate; constitute

órgano /'organo/ m, Mus. organ; (Anat. Bot.) organ; means, agency. **o. de manubrio**, barrel organ

orgasmo /or'gasmo/ m, orgasm

orgía /or'hia/ f, orgy

orgullo /or'guʎo; or'guyo/ m, pride; arrogance

orgulloso /orgu'ʎoso; orgu'yoso/ a proud; haughty

orientación /orienta'θion; orienta'sion/ f, orientation; exposure, prospect; bearings

oriental /orien'tal/ a Oriental, Eastern. mf Oriental

orientar /orien'tar/ vt to orientate; —vr find one's bearings; familiarize oneself (with)

oriente /o'riente/ m, Orient, the East; luster (of pearls); youth, childhood; origin, source

origen /o'rihen/ m, origin, source, root; stock, extraction; reason, genesis. **dar o. a**, to give rise to. **país de o.**, native land

original /orihi'nal/ a original; earliest, primitive; new, first-hand; novel, fresh; inventive, creative; eccentric; quaint. m, original manuscript; original; sitter (for portraits); eccentric

originalidad /orihinali'ðað/ f, originality

originar /orihi'nar/ vt to cause, originate; invent; —vr spring from, originate (in)

originario /orihi'nario/ a original, primary; primitive; native (of)

orilla /o'riʎa; o'riya/ f, limit, edge; hem, border; selvage; shore, margin; bank (of a river, etc.); sidewalk; brink, edge. **a la o.**, on the brink; nearly

orillar /ori'ʎar; ori'yar/ vt to settle, arrange, conclude; —vi reach the shore or bank; Sew. leave a hem; Sew. border; leave a selvage on cloth

orín /o'rin/ m, rust; pl urine

orinar /ori'nar/ vi to urinate

oriundo /o'riundo/ a native (of); derived (from)

orla /'orla/ f, border, fringe; selvage (of cloth, garments); ornamental border (on diplomas, etc.)

orlar /or'lar/ vt to border; edge, trim

ornamentación /ornamenta'θion; ornamenta'sion/ f, ornamentation

ornamental /ornamen'tal/ a ornamental

ornamentar /ornamen'tar/ vt to ornament; embellish

ornamento /orna'mento/ m, ornament; decoration; gift, virtue, talent; pl Eccl. vestments

ornar /or'nar/ vt to ornament, adorn, embellish

ornato /or'nato/ m, decoration, ornament

oro /'oro/ m, gold; gold coins or jewelery; Fig. riches, pl diamonds (cards). **o. batido**, gold leaf. **o. en polvo**, gold dust. Fig. **como un o.**, shining with cleanliness. **el as de oros**, the ace of diamonds

orondo /o'rondo/ a hollow; Inf. pompous; Inf. swollen, spongy

oropel /oro'pel/ m, brass foil; showy, cheap thing; trinket; tinsel

orquesta /or'kesta/ f, orchestra

orquestación /orkesta'θion; orkesta'sion/ f, orchestration

orquestal /orkes'tal/ a orchestral

orquestar /orkes'tar/ vt to orchestrate

orquídea /or'kiðea/ f, orchid

ortiga /or'tiga/ f, Bot. nettle

orto /'orto/ m, rising (of sun, stars)

ortodoxia /orto'ðoksia/ f, orthodoxy

ortodoxo /orto'ðokso/ a orthodox

ortografía /ortogra'fia/ f, orthography

ortográfico /orto'grafiko/ a orthographical

ortopedia /orto'peðia/ f, orthopedics

ortopédico /orto'peðiko/ (-ca) a orthopedic —n orthopedist

ortopedista /ortope'ðista/ mf orthopedist

oruga /o'ruga/ f, caterpillar

orzuelo /or'θuelo; or'suelo/ m, Med. sty; trap (for wild animals)

os /os/ pers pron 2nd pl mf dat and acc of **vos** and **vosotros** you, to you

osa /'osa/ f, she-bear; Astron. **O. mayor**, Big Bear; **O. menor**, Little Bear

osadía /osa'ðia/ f, boldness, audacity

osado /o'saðo/ a daring, bold

osamenta /osa'menta/ f, skeleton; bones (of a skeleton)

osar /o'sar/ vi to dare; risk, venture

oscilante /osθi'lante; ossi'lante/ a oscillating

oscilar /osθi'lar; ossi'lar/ vi to oscillate, sway; hesitate, vacillate

ósculo /'oskulo/ m, kiss, osculation

oscurecer /oskure'θer; oskure'ser/ vt irr to darken; Fig. tarnish, dim, sully; confuse, bewilder; express obscurely; Art. shade; —vr grow dark; —vr cloud over (sky); *Inf.* disappear (things, gen. by theft). See **conocer**

oscuridad /oskuri'ðað/ *f,* darkness; gloom, blackness; humbleness; obscurity, abstruseness

oscuro /os'kuro/ *a* dark; humble, unknown; abstruse, involved; obscure; uncertain, dangerous. **a oscuras,** in the dark; ignorant

osificarse /osifi'karse/ *vr* to ossify

ósmosis /'osmosis/ *f,* osmosis

oso /'oso/ *m,* bear. **o. blanco,** polar bear

ostensible /osten'siβle/ *a* ostensible; obvious

ostensión /osten'sion/ *f,* show, display, manifestation

ostensivo /osten'siβo/ *a* ostensive

ostentación /ostenta'θion; ostenta'sion/ *f,* manifestation; ostentation

ostentar /osten'tar/ *vt* to exhibit, show; boast, show off

ostentoso /osten'toso/ *a* magnificent, showy, ostentatious

osteópata /oste'opata/ *mf* osteopath

osteopatía /osteopa'tia/ *f,* osteopathy

ostra /'ostra/ *f,* oyster. **vivero de ostras,** oyster bed

ostracismo /ostra'θismo; ostra'sismo/ *m,* ostracism

otear /ote'ar/ *vt* to observe; look on at

otero /o'tero/ *m,* hill, height, eminence

otomana /oto'mana/ *f,* ottoman, couch

otomano /oto'mano/ *a* Ottoman

otoñal /oto'ɲal/ *a* autumnal, autumn, fall

otoño /o'toɲo/ *m,* autumn, fall

otorgamiento /otorga'miento/ *m,* granting; consent, approval; license, award

otorgar /otor'gar/ *vt* to grant; concede, approve; *Law.* grant, stipulate, execute

otro /'otro/ **(-ra)** *a* other, another —*n* another one

otrosí /otro'si/ *adv* besides, moreover

ovación /oβa'θion; oβa'sion/ *f,* ovation, triumph; applause

ovacionar /oβaθio'nar; oβasio'nar/ *vt* to applaud

oval /o'βal/ *a* oval

óvalo /'oβalo/ *m,* oval

ovario /o'βario/ *m,* ovary

oveja /o'βeha/ *f,* ewe

ovejuno /oβe'huno/ *a* relating to ewes or sheep, sheep-like

ovillar /oβi'ʎar; oβi'yar/ *vi* to wind thread into a ball; —*vr* curl up; huddle

OVNI /'oβni/ *m,* UFO

ovulación /oβula'θion; oβula'sion/ *f,* ovulation

óxido /'oksiðo/ *m,* oxide. **ó. de carbono,** carbon monoxide. **ó. de cinc,** zinc oxide

oxígeno /ok'siheno/ *m,* oxygen

oyente /o'iente/ *mf* hearer; *pl* audience

ozono /o'θono; o'sono/ *m,* ozone

P

pábulo /'paβulo/ *m*, food; *Fig*. pabulum

pacedero /paθe'ðero; pase'ðero/ *a Agr.* grazing, meadow

pacer /pa'θer; pa'ser/ *vi irr Agr.* to graze; —*vt* nibble away; eat away. See **nacer**

paciencia /pa'θienθia; pa'siensia/ *f*, patience

paciente /pa'θiente; pa'siente/ *a* patient; long-suffering; complacent. *mf Med.* patient

pacienzudo /paθien'θuðo; pasien'suðo/ *a* extremely patient or long-suffering

pacificación /paθifika'θion; pasifika'sion/ *f*, pacification; serenity, peace of mind

pacificador /paθifika'ðor; pasifika'ðor/ **(-ra)** *a* peace making; pacifying —*n* peace maker

pacificar /paθifi'kar; pasifi'kar/ *vt* to pacify; —*vi* make peace; —*vr* grow quiet, become calm (sea, etc.)

pacífico /pa'θifiko; pa'sifiko/ *a* pacific, meek, mild; peace-loving, peaceful. **el Océano P.**, the Pacific Ocean

pacifista /paθi'fista; pasi'fista/ *a* and *mf* pacifist

pacotilla /pako'tiʎa; pako'tiya/ *f*, goods. *Inf.* **hacer su p.**, to make one's packet or fortune. **ser de p.**, to be poor stuff; be jerry-built (of houses)

pactar /pak'tar/ *vt* to stipulate, arrange; contract

pacto /'pakto/ *m*, agreement, contract; pact

padecer /paðe'θer; paðe'ser/ *vt irr* to suffer; feel keenly; experience, undergo; tolerate. **p. desnudez**, to go unclothed. **p. hambre**, to go hungry. See **conocer**

padrastro /pa'ðrastro/ *m*, stepfather; cruel father; *Fig*. impediment, obstacle; hangnail

padrazo /pa'ðraθo; pa'ðraso/ *m*, *Inf.* indulgent father

padre /'paðre/ *m*, father; stallion; head (of the family, etc.); *Eccl.* genesis, source; author, creator; *pl* parents; ancestors. **p. adoptivo**, foster father. **p. de familia**, paterfamilias. **P. Eterno**, Eternal Father. **p. nuestro**, Lord's Prayer. **P. Santo**, Holy Father, the Pope

padrear /paðre'ar/ *vi* to take after one's father; *Zool.* reproduce, breed

padrino /pa'ðrino/ *m*, godfather; sponsor; second (in duels, etc.); patron; best man

padrón /pa'ðron/ *m*, census; pattern; model; memorial stone

paella /pa'eʎa; pa'eya/ *f*, *Cul.* savory rice dish of shellfish, chicken, and meat

paga /'paga/ *f*, payment; amends, restitution; pay; payment of fine; reciprocity (in love, etc.)

pagadero /paga'ðero/ *a* payable. *m*, date and place when payment is due

pagador /paga'ðor/ **(-ra)** *n* payer. *m*, teller; wages clerk; paymaster

pagaduría /pagaðu'ria/ *f*, pay office

pagano /pa'gano/ **(-na)** *a* and *n* pagan; heathen

pagar /pa'gar/ *vt* to pay; make restitution, expiate; return, requite (love, etc.); —*vr* (*with de*) become fond of; be proud of. **p. adelantado**, to prepay. *Com.* **p. al contado**, to pay cash. **p. la casa**, to pay the rent (for one's residence)

pagaré /paga're/ *m*, *Com.* promissory note, I.O.U.

página /'pahina/ *f*, page (of a book); episode, occurrence

paginar /pahi'nar/ *vt* to paginate

pago /'pago/ *m*, payment; recompense, reward; region of vineyards, olive groves, etc.

pagoda /pa'goða/ *f*, pagoda, temple; idol

país /pa'is/ *m*, country, nation; region; *Art.* landscape. **del p.**, typical of the country of origin (gen. of food)

paisaje /pai'sahe/ *m*, countryside; landscape, scenery

paisajista, paisista /paisa'hista, pai'sista/ *mf* landscape painter

paisano /pai'sano/ **(-na)** *n* compatriot; peasant; civilian

Países Bajos, los /pa'ises 'bahos, los/ the Low Countries, the Netherlands

paja /'paha/ *f*, straw; chaff; trash; *Fig*. padding. **ver la p. en el ojo del vecino y no la viga en el nuestro**, to see the mote in our neighbor's eye and not the beam in our own

pájara /'pahara/ *f*, hen (bird); kite (toy); *Inf.* jay; prostitute. **p. pinta**, game of forfeits

pajarear /pahare'ar/ *vt* to snare birds; loaf, idle about

pajarero /paha'rero/ *m*, bird catcher or seller —*a Inf.* frivolous, giddy; *Inf.* gaudy (colors)

pajarita /paha'rita/ *f*, bow tie

pájaro /'paharo/ *m*, bird. **p. bobo**, penguin. **p. carpintero**, woodpecker. *Fig. Inf.* **p. gordo**, big gun. **p. mosca**, hummingbird

paje /'pahe/ *m*, page; *Naut.* cabin boy

pajizo /pa'hiθo; pa'hiso/ *a* made of straw; covered or thatched with straw; strawcolored

pala /'pala/ *f*, paddle; blade (of an oar); shovel; spade; baker's peel (long-handled shovel); cutting edge of a spade, hoe, etc.; *Sports.* racket; vamp, upper (of a shoe); pelota or jai alai racket; tanner's knife; *Inf.* guile, cunning; cleverness, dexterity. **p. de hélice**, propeller blade. **p. para pescado**, fish server. *Inf.* **corta p.**, ignoramus; blockhead

palabra /pa'laβra/ *f*, word; power of speech; eloquence; offer, promise; *pl* magic formula, spell. **p. de clave**, code word. **p. de matrimonio**, promise of marriage. **p. de rey**, inviolable promise.

palabras cruzadas, crossword puzzle. **bajo p. de**, under promise of. **cuatro palabras**, a few words; short conversation. **de p.**, verbally, by word of mouth. **dirigir la p. a**, to address, speak to. **faltar a su p.**, to break one's promise. **llevar la p.**, to be spokesperson. **medias palabras**, half-words; hint, insinuation. **su p. empeñada**, one's solemn word. **tener la p.**, to have the right to speak (in meetings, etc.) (e.g. *El señor Martínez tiene la p.*, Mr. Martínez has the floor)

palabrería /pala'βre'ria/ *f*, verbosity, wordiness

palabrota /pala'βrota/ *f*, *Inf.* coarse language; long word

palaciego /pala'θiego; pala'siego/ **(-ga)** *a* pertaining to palaces; *Fig.* courtesan —*n* courtier

palacio /pa'laθio; pa'lasio/ *m*, palace; mansion

paladar /pala'ðar/ *m*, *Anat.* palate; taste; discernment, sensibility

paladear /palaðe'ar/ *vt* to taste with pleasure, savor; enjoy, relish

paladino /pala'ðino/ *a* public, clear, open

palanca /pa'lanka/ *f*, *Mech.* lever; handle; bar; (high) diving board. **p. de arranque**, starting gear. **p. de cambio de velocidad**, gear-changing lever. **p. de mando**, control stick

palangana /palaŋ'gana/ *f*, washbasin

palanganero /palaŋga'nero/ *m*, washstand

palastro /pa'lastro/ *m*, sheet iron or steel

palazón /pala'θon; pala'son/ *f*, woodwork

palco /'palko/ *m*, *Theat.* box; stand, raised platform, enclosure. **p. de platea**, orchestra

palenque /pa'lenke/ *m*, enclosure; stand; platform; palisade

paleografía /paleogra'fia/ *f*, paleography

paleógrafo /pale'ografo/ *m*, paleographer

Palestina /pales'tina/ Palestine

paleta /pa'leta/ *f*, *dim* little shovel; trowel; *Art.* palette; fireplace shovel; mason's trowel; *Anat.* shoulder blade; blade (of a propeller, ventilator, etc.); *Chem.* spatula

paliación /palia'θion; palia'sion/ *f*, palliation; excuse

paliar /pa'liar/ *vt* to dissemble, excuse; palliate, mitigate

paliativo /palia'tiβo/ *a* palliative; extenuating

palidecer /paliðe'θer; paliðe'ser/ *vi irr* to turn pale. See **conocer**

palidez /pali'ðeθ; pali'ðes/ *f*, pallor, paleness

pálido /'paliðo/ *a* pale, pallid

palillo /pa'liʎo; pa'liyo/ *m*, *dim* small stick; toothpick; bobbin (for lacemaking); drumstick; *Fig.* chatter; *pl* castanets

palinodia /pali'noðia/ *f*, *Lit.* palinode. **cantar la p.**, to eat one's words, recant

palio /'palio/ *m*, Greek mantle; cape; *Eccl.* pallium; canopy, awning

palique /pa'like/ *m*, *Inf.* chat. **estar de p.**, to be having a chat

paliquear /palike'ar/ *vi* to chat

paliza /pa'liθa; pa'lisa/ *f*, caning, beating

palizada /pali'θaða; pali'saða/ *f*, paling, fence; palisade, stockade. **p. de tablas**, hoarding

palma /'palma/ *f*, palm tree; palm leaf; date palm; palm (of the hand); hand; triumph. **llevarse la p.**, to bear away the palm; take the cake

palmada /pal'maða/ *f*, slap; *pl* handclapping

palmado /pal'maðo/ *a* web (of feet); palmy

palmar /pal'mar/ *a* palmaceous; palmar; clear, obvious. *m*, palm grove

palmatoria /palma'toria/ *f*, ferule, ruler; candlestick

palmear /palme'ar/ *vi* to clap hands

palmera /pal'mera/ *f*, palm tree

palmetazo /palme'taθo; palme'taso/ *m*, slap on the hand with a ruler; *Fig.* slap in the face

palmo /'palmo/ *m*, span; hand's breadth. **p. a p.**, inch by inch, piecemeal

palmotear /palmote'ar/ *vt* to applaud, clap

palo /'palo/ *m*, stick; rod; pole; timber, wood; wooden log; *Naut.* mast; blow with a stick; execution by hanging; suit (of playing cards); fruit stalk; *Herald.* pale. **p. de Campeche**, logwood. **p. de hule**, rubber tree. **p. de rosa**, tulipwood. *Naut.* **p. mayor**, mainmast. *Naut.* **a p. seco**, under bare poles. **de tal p., tal astilla**, a chip off the old block; like father like son. **estar del mismo p.**, to be of the same mind, agree

paloma /pa'loma/ *f*, dove; pigeon; gentle person; *pl Naut.* white horses. **p. buchona**, pouter pigeon. **p. mensajera**, carrier pigeon. **p. torcaz**, wood pigeon

palomar /palo'mar/ *m*, dovecote; pigeon loft

palomero /palo'mero/ **(-ra)** *n* pigeon fancier; pigeon dealer

palomino /palo'mino/ *m*, young pigeon

palomo /pa'lomo/ *m*, male pigeon; wood pigeon

palotes /pa'lotes/ *m pl*, drumsticks; pothooks (in writing)

palpabilidad /palpaβili'ðað/ *f*, palpability

palpable /pal'paβle/ *a* palpable, tangible

palpar /pal'par/ *vt* to palpate, examine by touch; grope, walk by touch; *Fig.* see clearly

palpitación /palpita'θion; palpita'sion/ *f*, beating (of a heart); *Med.* palpitation; convulsive movement

palpitante /palpi'tante/ *a* palpitating; quivering; beating; (of a question) burning

palpitar /palpi'tar/ *vi* to beat (heart);

throb, palpitate; shudder, move convulsively; *Fig.* manifest itself (passions, etc.)

palpo /'palpo/ *m.* palp, feeler

palúdico /pa'luðiko/ *a* marshy, swampy; malarial

paludismo /palu'ðismo/ *m.* malaria; paludism

palurdo /pa'lurðo/ **(-da)** *a Inf.* gross, rude, boorish —*n* boor

palustre /pa'lustre/ *m.* mason's trowel —*a* marshy, swampy

pamela /pa'mela/ *f.* wide-brimmed straw sailor (woman's hat)

pamema /pa'mema/ *f. Inf.* unimportant trifle, *Inf.* caress

pampa /'pampa/ *f.* pampa, treeless plain

pámpano /'pampano/ *m.* young vine shoot; vine leaf

pamplina /pam'plina/ *f. Inf.* nonsense, rubbish

pan /pan/ *m.* bread; loaf; *Cul.* piecrust; *Fig.* food; wheat; gold leaf; *pl* cereals. **p. ázimo,** unleavened bread. **p. de oro,** gold leaf. **llamar al p. p. y al vino vino,** to call a spade a spade. **venderse como p. bendito,** to sell like hot cakes

pana /'pana/ *f.* velveteen, velours

panacea /pana'θea; pana'sea/ *f.* panacea; cure-all

panadería /panaðe'ria/ *f.* bakery trade or shop; bakery

panadero /pana'ðero/ **(-ra)** *n* baker. *m pl.* Spanish dance

panadizo /pana'ðiθo; pana'ðiso/ *m. Med.* whitlow; *Inf.* ailing person, crock

panal /pa'nal/ *m.* honeycomb; wasp's nest

Panamá /pana'ma/ Panama

panameño /pana'meɲo/ **(-ña)** *a* and *n* Panamanian

panamericanismo /panamerika'nismo/ *m.* pan-Americanism

panarra /pa'narra/ *m. Inf.* simpleton

páncreas /'pankreas/ *m.* pancreas

pancreático /pankre'atiko/ *a* pancreatic

panda /'panda/ *f.* gallery of a cloister. *mf Zool.* panda

pandereta /pande'reta/ *f.* tambourine

pandero /pan'dero/ *m.* tambourine; *Inf.* windbag

pandilla /pan'diʎa; pan'diya/ *f.* league, group; gang (of burglars, etc.); party, crowd, band

pane /'pane/ *f.* breakdown

panecillo /pane'θiʎo; pane'siyo/ *m. dim* roll (of bread)

panegírico /pane'hiriko/ *a* and *m,* panegyric

panel /pa'nel/ *m.* panel

panetela /pane'tela/ *f.* panada

pánfilo /'panfilo/ **(-la)** *a* sluggish, phlegmatic, slow-moving —*n* sluggard

panfleto /pan'fleto/ *m.* pamphlet

paniaguado /pania'guaðo/ *m.* servant; favorite, protégé

pánico /'paniko/ *a* and *m,* panic

panoli /pa'noli/ *a Inf.* doltish, stupid

panoplia /pa'noplia/ *f.* panoply; collection of arms

panorama /pano'rama/ *m.* panorama; view

panorámico /pano'ramiko/ *a* panoramic

pantalla /pan'taʎa; pan'taya/ *f.* lampshade; face screen; movie screen; shade, reflector

pantalón /panta'lon/ *m.* pant, trouser (gen. *pl*); knickers. **p. de corte,** striped trousers. **pantalones bombachos,** plus fours

pantano /pan'tano/ *m.* marsh, swamp; impediment; artificial pool

pantanoso /panta'noso/ *a* marshy, swampy; *Fig.* awkward, full of pitfalls

panteón /pante'on/ *m.* pantheon

pantera /pan'tera/ *f.* panther

pantomima /panto'mima/ *f.* pantomime; mime

pantorrilla /panto'rriʎa; panto'rriya/ *f.* calf (of the leg)

pantuflo /pan'tuflo/ *m.* house slipper

panza /'panθa; 'pansa/ *f.* paunch, stomach; belly (of jugs, etc.). *Inf.* **un cielo de p. de burra,** a dark gray sky

pañal /pa'ɲal/ *m.* diaper; shirttail; *pl* long clothes, swaddling clothes; infancy

pañería /paɲe'ria/ *f.* drapery stores; drapery

paño /'paɲo/ *m.* woolen material; cloth; fabric; drapery, hanging; tapestry; linen; bandage; tarnish or other mark; *Naut.* canvas; *Sew.* breadth, width (of cloth); panel (in a dress); floor cloth, duster; livid mark on the face; *pl* garments. **p. de lágrimas,** consoler, sympathizer. **p. mortuorio,** pall (on a coffin). **paños menores,** underwear. **p. verde,** gambling table. **al p.,** *Theat.* from the wings, from without. *Inf.* **poner el p. al púlpito,** to hold forth, spread oneself

pañoleta /paɲo'leta/ *f.* kerchief, triangular scarf; fichu

pañuelo /pa'ɲuelo/ *m.* kerchief; handkerchief

papa /'papa/ *m.* pope; *Inf.* papa, daddy. *f, Inf.* potato; stupid rumor; nonsense; *pl* pap; *Cul.* sop; food

papá /pa'pa/ *m, Inf.* papa, daddy

papada /pa'paða/ *f,* double chin; dewlap

papado /pa'paðo/ *m,* papacy

papagayo /papa'gaio/ *m,* parrot

papanatas /papa'natas/ *m, Inf.* simpleton

papar /pa'par/ *vt* to sip, take soft food; *Inf.* eat; neglect, be careless about

papel /pa'pel/ *m,* paper; document; manuscript; *Theat.* role, part; pamphlet; sheet of paper; paper, monograph, essay; guise, role; *Theat.* character. **p. carbón, p. carbónico,** carbon paper. **p. celofán,** cellophane. **p. cuadriculado,** graph paper, cartridge paper. **p. de calcar,** carbon paper; tracing paper. **p. de escribir,** writing paper. **p. de estaño,** tinfoil. **p. de estraza,** brown paper. **p. de fumar,** cigarette paper. **p. de lija,** emery- or sandpaper. **p.**

de paja de arroz, rice paper. **p. de seda,** tissue paper. **p. de tornasol,** litmus paper. **p. del estado,** government bonds. **p. higiénico,** toilet paper. **p. moneda,** paper money. **p. pintado,** wallpaper. **p. secante,** blotting paper. **p. sellado,** official stamped paper. **hacer buen (mal) p.,** to do well (badly). **hacer el p. (de),** *Theat.* to act the part (of); feign, pretend

papelear /papele'ar/ *vi* to turn over papers, search among them; *Inf.* cut a dash

papeleo /pape'leo/ *m,* bureacracy, red tape

papelera /pape'lera/ *f,* mass of papers; desk (for keeping papers)

papelería /papele'ria/ *f,* heap of papers; stationer's shop; stationery

papelero /pape'lero/ **(-ra)** *a* paper, stationery —*n* paper maker; stationer

papeleta /pape'leta/ *f,* slip or scrap of paper

papelista /pape'lista/ *mf* paper maker; stationer; paperhanger

papelucho /pape'lutʃo/ *m,* old or dirty piece of paper; trash, worthless writing; *Inf.* rag (newspaper)

papera /pa'pera/ *f,* mumps

papilla /pa'piʎa; pa'piya/ *f,* pap; guile, wiliness

papiro /pa'piro/ *m,* papyrus

papo /'papo/ *m,* dewlap; gizzard (of a bird); goiter. **p. de cardo,** thistledown

paquete /pa'kete/ *m,* packet; parcel, package

par /par/ *a* equal; alike; corresponding. *m,* pair, couple; team (of oxen, mules); peer (title); rafter (of a roof); *Mech.* torque, couple; *Elec.* cell. *f,* par. **a la p.,** jointly; simultaneously; *Com.* at par. **a pares,** two by two. **de p. en p.,** wide-open (doors, etc.). **sin p.,** peerless, excellent

para /'para/ *prep* in order to; for; to; for the sake of (e.g., *Lo hice p. ella,* I did it for her sake); enough to (gen. with *bastante,* etc.); in the direction of, toward; about to, on the point of (e.g., *Está p. salir,* He is on the point of going out). Expresses:
1. *Purpose* (e.g., *La educan p. bailarina,* They are bringing her up to be a dancer. *Lo dije p. ver lo que harías,* I said it to (in order to) see what you would do)
2. *Destination* (e.g., *Salió p. Londres,* He left for London)
3. *Use* (e.g., *seda p. medias,* silk for stockings. *un vaso p. flores,* a vase for flowers)
4. *An appointed time* (e.g., *Lo pagaré p. Navidad,* I will pay it at Christmas).
p. con, toward (a person) (e.g., *Ha obrado muy bien p. con mi hermano,* He has behaved very well toward my brother)
p. coneretar, to be exact, to wit
p. que, in order to, so that (e.g., *Lo puse en la mesa p. que lo vieses,* I put it on the table so that you would see it)
¿P. qué? Why? For what reason?

p. siempre, forever. **decir p. sí,** to say to oneself. **sin qué ni p. qué,** without rhyme or reason

parábola /pa'raβola/ *f,* parable; *Geom.* parabola

parabrisas /para'βrisas/ *m,* windshield

paracaídas /paraka'iðas/ *m,* parachute

paracaidista /parakai'ðista/ *mf* parachutist

parada /pa'raða/ *f,* stopping, halting; stop; stoppage, suspension; halt; *Mil.* review; interval, pause; cattle stall; dam; gambling stakes; parry (in fencing); relay (of horses). **p. de coches,** taxi rank. **p. de tranvía,** streetcar stop. **p. discrecional,** request stop (buses, etc.)

paradero /para'ðero/ *m,* railroad station; stopping place; end, conclusion; whereabouts

parado /pa'raðo/ *a* still; indolent, lazy; unoccupied, leisured; silent, reserved; timid; unemployed

paradoja /para'ðoha/ *f,* paradox

paradójico /para'ðohiko/ *a* paradoxical

parador /para'ðor/ *m,* inn, tavern, hostelry

paráfrasis /pa'rafrasis/ *f,* paraphrase

paraguas /pa'raguas/ *m,* umbrella

paraguayo /para'guayo/ **(-ya)** *a* and *n* Paraguayan

paraíso /para'iso/ *m,* paradise; garden of Eden; heaven; (*Inf. Theat.*) gallery, gods

paraje /pa'rahe/ *m,* place, locality, spot; state, condition

paralela /para'lela/ *f,* *Mil.* parallel; *pl* parallel bars (for gymnastic exercises)

paralelo /para'lelo/ *a* parallel; analogous; similar. *m,* parallel, similarity; *Geog.* parallel

parálisis /pa'ralisis/ *f,* paralysis

paralítico /para'litiko/ **(-ca)** *a* and *n* paralytic

paralización /paraliθa'θion; paralisa'sion/ *f,* paralysis; cessation; *Com.* dullness, quietness

paralizar /parali'θar; parali'sar/ *vt* to paralyze; stop

paramento /para'mento/ *m,* ornament; trappings (of a horse); face (of a wall); facing (of a building). **paramentos sacerdotales,** liturgical vestments or ornaments

páramo /'paramo/ *m,* paramo, treeless plain; desert, wilderness

parangón /paraŋ'gon/ *m,* comparison; similarity

parangonar /paraŋgo'nar/ *vt* to compare

paraninfo /para'ninfo/ *m,* *Archit.* paranymph, university hall; best man (weddings); messenger of good

paranoico /para'noiko/ *m,* paranoiac

parapetarse /parape'tarse/ *vr* to shelter behind a parapet; take refuge behind

parapoco /para'poko/ *mf Inf.* ninny, numskull

parar /pa'rar/ *vi* to stop, halt; end, finish; lodge; come into the hands of; —*vt* stop; detain; prepare; bet, stake; point (hunting dogs); parry (fencing); —*vr* halt; be interrupted **p. mientes en**, to notice; consider. **sin p.**, immediately, at once; without stopping

pararrayos /para'rraios/ *m*, lightning conductor

parasitario, parasítico /parasi'tario, para'sitiko/ *a* parasitic

parásito /pa'rasito/ *m*, parasite; *Fig.* sponger; *pl Radio.* interference —*a* parasitic

parasol /para'sol/ *m*, sunshade; *Bot.* umbel

paratifoidea /paratifoi'ðea/ *f*, paratyphoid

parca /'parka/ *f*, Fate; *Poet.* death. **las Parcas**, the Three Fates

parcela /par'θela/ *f*, plot, parcel (of land); atom, particle

parche /'partʃe/ *m*, *Med.* plaster; *Auto.* patch; drum, drumhead, parchment of drum; patch, mend

parcial /par'θial/ *a* partial, incomplete; biased, prejudiced; factional, party; participatory

parcialidad /parθiali'ðað/ *f*, partiality, bias, prejudice; party, faction, group; intimacy, friendship

parco /'parko/ *a* scarce, scanty; temperate, moderate; frugal

pardo /'parðo/ *a* brown; gray, drab, dun-colored; cloudy, dark; husky (voices). *m*, leopard

parear /pare'ar/ *vt* to pair, match; put in pairs; compare

parecer /pare'θer/ *vi irr* to appear; look, seem; turn up (be found) —*impers* believe, think (e.g. *me parece*, it seems to me, I think, my opinion is); —*vr* look alike, resemble one another. See **conocer**

parecer /pare'θer/ *m*, opinion, belief; appearance, looks

parecido /pare'θiðo/ *a* (*with bien* or *mal*) good- or bad-looking. *m*, resemblance

pared /pa'reð/ *f*, wall; partition wall; side, face. **p. maestra**, main wall. **p. medianera**, party wall. **Las paredes oyen**, The walls have ears. *Inf.* **pegado a la p.**, confused, taken aback

pareja /pa'reha/ *f*, pair; dance partner; couple. **p. desparejada**, mismatched pair. **parejas mixtas**, mixed doubles (in tennis). **correr parejas** *or* **correr a las parejas**, to be equal; go together, happen simultaneously; be on a par

parejo /pa'reho/ *a* equal; similar; smooth, flat; even, regular

parentela /paren'tela/ *f*, relatives, kindred; parentage

parentesco /paren'tesko/ *m*, kinship; relationship; affinity; *Inf.* connection, link

paréntesis /pa'rentesis/ *m*, parenthesis; digression. **entre p.**, incidentally

paria /'paria/ *mf* pariah; outcast

parida /pa'riða/ *a f*, newly delivered of a child

paridad /pari'ðað/ *f*, parity; analogy, similarity

pariente /pa'riente/ **(-ta)** *n* relative, relation; *Inf.* husband (wife)

parir /pa'rir/ *vt* to give birth to; *Fig.* bring forth; reveal, publish; —*vi* lay eggs

París /pa'ris/ Paris

parla /'parla/ *f*, speech; loquaciousness, eloquence; verbiage

parlamentar /parlamen'tar/ *vi* to converse; discuss (contracts, etc.); *Mil.* parley

parlamento /parla'mento/ *m*, legislative assembly; parliament; discourse, speech; *Theat.* long speech; *Mil.* parley

parlanchín /parlan'tʃin/ *a Inf.* talkative, chattering, loquacious

parlar /par'lar/ *vt* and *vi* to speak freely or easily; chatter; reveal, speak indiscreetly; babble (of streams, etc.)

parlero /par'lero/ *a* talkative; gossiping, indiscreet; talking (birds); *Fig.* expressive (eyes, etc.); prattling, babbling (brook, etc.)

parlotear /parlote'ar/ *vi Inf.* to chatter, gossip

paro /'paro/ *m*, *Inf.* work stoppage; lockout; *Ornith.* tit. **p. forzoso**, unemployment

parodia /pa'roðia/ *f*, parody

parótida /pa'rotiða/ *f*, parotid gland; parotitis, mumps

parotiditis /paroti'ðitis/ *f*, parotitis, mumps

paroxismo /parok'sismo/ *m*, *Med.* paroxysm; frenzy, ecstasy, fit

parpadear /parpaðe'ar/ *vi* to blink

párpado /'parpaðo/ *m*, eyelid

parque /'parke/ *m*, park; depot, park; paddock, pen. **p. de atracciones**, pleasure ground. **p. de (*or* para) automóviles**, car park, parking lot

parquedad /parke'ðað/ *f*, scarcity; moderation, temperance; parsimony, frugality

parra /'parra/ *f*, vine. **hoja de p.**, *Fig.* fig leaf

párrafo /'parrafo/ *m*, paragraph; *Gram.* paragraph sign. **p. aparte**, new paragraph. **echar un p.**, to chat, gossip

parranda /pa'rranda/ *f*, *Inf.* binge; strolling band of musicians. **ir de p.**, to go on a binge

parrilla /pa'rriʎa; pa'rriya/ *f*, *Cul.* griller, broiler; grill, gridiron; *Engin.* grate. *Cul.* **a la p.**, grilled

párroco /'parroko/ *m*, parish priest; parson

parroquia /pa'rrokia/ *f*, parish church; parish; clergy of a parish; clientele, customers

parroquiano /parro'kiano/ **(-na)** *a* parochial —*n* parishioner; client, customer

parsimonia /parsi'monia/ *f*, frugality, thrift; prudence, moderation

parsimonioso /parsimo'nioso/ *a* parsimonious

parte /'parte/ *f*, part; share; place; portion; side, faction; *Law.* party; *Theat.* part, role. *m*, communication, message; telegraph or telephone message; (*Mil. Nav.*) communiqué. *f pl*, parts, talents. **p. actora,** *Law.* prosecution. **p. de la oración,** part of speech. **partes litigantes,** *Law.* contending parties. **dar p.,** to notify; (*Mil. Naut.*) report; give a share (in a transaction). **de algún tiempo a esta p.,** for some time past. **de p. de,** in the name of, from. **en p.,** partly. **por todas partes,** on all sides, everywhere. **ser p. a** *or* **ser p. para que,** to contribute to. **tener de su p. (a),** to count on the favor of. **la quinta p.,** one-fifth, etc.

partera /par'tera/ *f*, midwife

partero /par'tero/ *m*, accoucheur

partición /parti'θion; parti'sion/ *f*, partition, distribution; (*Aer. Naut.*) accommodation

participación /partiθipa'θion; partisipa'sion/ *f*, participation; notice, warning; announcement (of an engagement, etc.); *Com.* share

participante /partiθi'pante; partisi'pante/ *a* and *mf* participant

participar /partiθi'par; partisi'par/ *vi* to participate, take part (in), share; —*vt* inform; announce (an engagement, etc.)

partícipe /par'tiθipe; par'tisipe/ *a* sharing. *mf* participant

participio /parti'θipio; parti'sipio/ *m*, participle

partícula /par'tikula/ *f*, particle, grain; *Gram.* particle

particular /partiku'lar/ *a* private; peculiar; special, particular; unusual; individual. *mf* private individual. *m*, matter, subject. **en p.,** especially; privately

particularidad /partikulari'ðað/ *f*, individuality; specialty; rareness, unusualness; detail, circumstance; intimacy, friendship

particularizar /partikulari'θar; partikulari'sar/ *vt* to detail, particularize; single out, choose; —*vr* (*with en*) be characterized by

partida /par'tiða/ *f*, departure; entry, record (of birth, etc.); certificate (of marriage, etc.); *Com.* item; *Com.* lot, allowance; *Mil.* guerrilla; armed band; expedition, excursion; game (of cards, etc.); rubber (at bridge, etc.); *Inf.* conduct, behavior; place, locality; death. *Com.* **p. doble,** double entry. **Las siete Partidas,** code of Spanish laws compiled by Alfonso X (1252–84)

partidario /parti'ðario/ **(-ia)** *a* partisan —*n* adherent, disciple. *m*, partisan, guerrilla

partidarismo /partiða'rismo/ *m*, partisanship

partido /par'tiðo/ *m*, party, group, faction; profit; *Sports.* match; team; agreement, pact. **p. conservador,** *Polit.* conservative party. **p. obrero** *or* **p. laborista,** *Polit.* labor party. **buen p.,** *Fig.* good match, catch. **sacar p. de,** to take advantage of, make the most of. **tomar p.,** to enlist; join, become a supporter (of)

partidor /parti'ðor/ *m*, divider, apportioner; cleaver, chopper; hewer

partir /par'tir/ *vt* to divide; split; crack, break; separate; *Math.* divide; —*vi* go, depart; start (from). **p. como el rayo,** be off like a flash —*vr* disagree, become divided; leave, depart

partitura /parti'tura/ *f*, *Mus.* score

parto /'parto/ *m*, parturition, birth; newborn child; *Fig.* creation, offspring; important event

parturienta /partu'rienta/ *a f*, parturient

parva /'parβa/ *f*, light breakfast; threshed or unthreshed grain; heap, mass

parvedad /parβe'ðað/ *f*, smallness; scarcity; light breakfast (taken on fast days)

parvo /'parβo/ *a* little, small

párvulo /'parβulo/ **(-la)** *n* child —*a* small; innocent, simple; lowly, humble

pasa /'pasa/ *f*, raisin; *Naut.* channel; passage, flight (of birds). **p. de Corinto,** currant

pasada /pa'saða/ *f*, passing, passage; money sufficient to live on; passage, corridor. **dar p.,** to let pass, put up with. *Inf.* **mala p.,** bad turn, dirty trick

pasadero /pasa'ðero/ *a* passable, traversable; fair (health); tolerable, passable. *m*, steppingstone

pasadizo /pasa'ðiθo; pasa'ðiso/ *m*, narrow corridor or passage; alley, narrow street; *Naut.* alleyway

pasado /pa'saðo/ *m*, past; *pl* ancestors. **Lo p.,** What's past is past, **p. de moda,** out of fashion, unfashionable

pasador /pasa'ðor/ *m*, bolt, fastener; *Mech.* pin, coupler; pin (of brooches, etc.); colander; *Naut.* marlin spike; shirt stud

pasaje /pa'sahe/ *m*, passing; passage; fare; passage money; *Naut.* complement of passengers; channel, strait; (*Mus. Lit.*) passage; modulation, transition (of voice); voyage; passage; covered way; road

pasajero /pasa'hero/ **(-ra)** *a* crowded public (thoroughfare); transitory, fugitive; passing; temporary —*n* passenger

pasamanería /pasamane'ria/ *f*, passementerie work, industry or shop

pasamano /pasa'mano/ *m*, passementerie; banister, handrail; *Naut.* gangway

pasante /pa'sante/ *a Herald.* passant. *m*, student teacher; articled clerk; apprentice; student. **p. de pluma,** law clerk

pasaporte /pasa'porte/ *m*, passport; license, permission. **dar el p. (a),** *Inf.* to give the sack (to)

pasar /pa'sar/ *vt* to pass; carry, transport; cross over; send; go beyond, overstep; run through, pierce; upset; overtake; transfer; suffer, undergo; sieve; study; dry (grapes, etc.); smuggle; surpass; omit; swallow (food); approve; dissemble; transform; spend (time); —*vi* pass; be transferred; be infectious; have enough to live on; cease; last; die; pass away; pass (at cards); be transformed; be current (money); be salable (goods); (*with prep a + infin*) begin to; (*with por*) pass as; have a reputation as; visit; (*with sin*) do without —*impers* happen, occur —*vr* end; go over to another party; forget; go stale or bad; *Fig.* go too far, overstep the mark; permeate. **p. contrato**, to draw up a contract; sign a contract. **p. la voz**, to pass the word along. **p. por alto (de)**, to omit, overlook. **p. de largo**, to go by without stopping. **pasarse de listo**, to be too clever. **¡No pases cuidado!** Don't worry!

pasarela /pasa'rela/ *f*, gangplank

pasatiempo /pasa'tiempo/ *m*, pastime, hobby, amusement

pascua /'paskua/ *f*, Passover; Easter; Christmas; Twelfth Night; Pentecost; *pl* twelve days of Christmas. **P. florida**, Easter Sunday. **dar las pascuas**, to wish a merry Christmas. **¡Felices pascuas!** Merry Christmas!

pase /'pase/ *m*, pass (with the hands and in football, etc.); safe conduct; free pass; thrust (in fencing)

paseante /pase'ante/ *mf* stroller, promenader, passerby

pasear /pase'ar/ *vt* to take a walk; parade up and down, display; —*vi* take a walk; go for a drive; go for a ride (on horseback, etc.); stroll up and down; —*vr* touch upon lightly, pass over; loaf, be idle; drift; float

paseo /pa'seo/ *m*, walk, stroll; drive; outing, expedition; promenade; boulevard. **p. a caballo**, ride on horseback

pasillo /pa'siʎo; pa'siyo/ *m*, gallery; corridor; lobby; railway corridor; *Sew.* basting stitch

pasión /pa'sion/ *f*, suffering; passivity; passion; desire; *Eccl.* passion. **con p.**, passionately

pasivo /pa'siβo/ *a* passive; inactive; *Com.* sleeping (partner); *Gram.* passive. *m*, *Com.* liabilities

pasmar /pas'mar/ *vt* to freeze to death (plants); dumbfound, amaze, stun; chill; —*vr* be stunned or amazed

pasmo /'pasmo/ *m*, amazement, astonishment; wonder, marvel; *Med.* tetanus, lockjaw

pasmoso /pas'moso/ *a* astounding, amazing; wonderful

paso /'paso/ *a* dried (of fruit)

paso /'paso/ *m*, step; pace; passage, passing; way; footstep; progress, advancement; passage (in a book); *Sew.* tacking stitch; occurrence, event; *Theat.* short play; gait, walk; strait, channel; migratory flight (birds); *Mech.* pitch; event or scene from the Passion; armed combat; death; *pl* measures, steps —*adv* softly, in a low voice; gently. **p. a nivel**, level crossing. **p. a p.**, step by step. **p. doble**, quick march; Spanish dance. **p. volante**, (gymnastics) giant stride. **a cada p.**, at

every step; often. **al p.**, without stopping; on the way, in passing. **ceder el p.**, to allow to pass. **de p.**, in passing; incidentally. **llevar el p.**, to keep in step. **marcar el p.**, to mark time. **salir al p. (a)**, to waylay, confront; oppose. **seguir los pasos (a)**, to follow; spy upon

pasta /'pasta/ *f*, *Cul.* dough; paste; pastry; piecrust; batter; *Cul.* noodle paste; paper pulp; board (bookbinding). **ser de buena p.**, to be good-natured

pastar /pas'tar/ *vt* to take to pasture; —*vi* graze, pasture

pastel /pas'tel/ *m*, cake; *Art.* pastel; pie; *Inf.* plot, secret understanding; cheating (at cards); *Print.* pie; *Inf.* fat, stocky person

pastelear /pastele'ar/ *vi Inf.* to indulge in shady business (especially in politics)

pastelería /pastele'ria/ *f*, cake bakery; cake shop; confectioner's art; confectionery

pastelillo /paste'liʎo; paste'liyo/ *m*, *Cul.* turnover

pastelón /paste'lon/ *m*, meat or game pie

pasteurizar /pasteuri'θar; pasteuri'sar/ *vt* to pasteurize

pastilla /pas'tiʎa; pas'tiya/ *f*, tablet; cake; lozenge; pastille, drop; tread (of a tire)

pasto /'pasto/ *m*, grazing land, pasture; fodder; *Fig.* fuel, food; spiritual food. **a p.**, in plenty, abundantly. **de p.**, of daily use

pastor /pas'tor/ **(-ra)** *n* shepherd. *m*, *Eccl.* pastor

pastoral /pasto'ral/ *a* rustic, country; *Eccl.* pastoral. *f*, pastoral poem; *Eccl.* pastoral letter

pastorear /pastore'ar/ *vt* to graze, put to grass; *Eccl.* have charge of souls

pastoso /pas'toso/ *a* doughy; mealy; pasty; mellow

pata /'pata/ *f*, paw and leg (animals); foot (of table, etc.); duck; *Inf.* leg. **p. de gallo**, blunder; crow's-foot, wrinkle. **meter la p.**, to interfere, put one's foot in it. *Inf.* **tener mala p.**, to be unlucky

patada /pa'taða/ *f*, kick, stamp; *Inf.* step, pace

patagón /pata'gon/ **(-ona)** *a* and *n* Patagonian

patalear /patale'ar/ *vi* to stamp (with the feet)

pataleo /pata'leo/ *m*, kicking; stamping

patán /pa'tan/ *m*, *Inf.* yokel; boor, churl

patanería /patane'ria/ *f*, *Inf.* boorishness, churlishness

patata /pa'tata/ *f*, potato

patatús /pata'tus/ *m*, *Inf.* petty worry; mishap; *Med.* stroke, fit

patear /pate'ar/ *vt Inf.* to stamp; *Fig.* walk on, treat badly; —*vi Inf.* stamp the feet; be furiously angry; (*Golf*) putt

patena /pa'tena/ *f*, engraved medal worn by country women; *Eccl.* paten

patentar /paten'tar/ *vt* to issue a patent; take out a patent, patent

patente /pa'tente/ *a* obvious, patent; *f.* patent; warrant, commission; letters patent. **p. de invención,** patent. **p. de sanidad,** clean bill of health

patentizar /patenti'θar; patenti'sar/ *vt* to make evident

paternidad /paterni'ðað/ *f,* paternity

paterno /pa'terno/ *a* paternal

patético /pa'tetiko/ *a* pitiable; pathetic, moving

patibulario /patiβu'lario/ *a* heartrending, harrowing

patíbulo /pa'tiβulo/ *m,* scaffold

paticojo /pati'koho/ *a Inf.* lame; wobbly; unsteady

patilla /pa'tiʎa; pa'tiya/ *f,* side whisker (gen. *pl*); *pl* old Nick, the Devil

patín /pa'tin/ *m,* skate; runner (of a sled); (*Aer.* and of vehicles) skid; *Mech.* shoe. **p. del diablo,** scooter. **p. de ruedas,** roller skate

patinador /patina'ðor/ **(-ra)** *n* skater

patinar /pati'nar/ *vi* to skate; slip, lose one's footing; skid (vehicles and planes)

patinazo /pati'naθo; pati'naso/ *m,* skid (of a vehicle)

patinete /pati'nete/ *m,* child's scooter

patio /'patio/ *m,* courtyard; *Theat.* pit

patitieso /pati'tieso/ *a Inf.* paralyzed in the hands or feet; open-mouthed, amazed; stiff, unbending, proud

patituerto /pati'tuerto/ *a* crooked-legged; pigeon-toed; *Inf.* lopsided

pato /'pato/ *m,* duck; *Inf.* **pagar el p.,** to be a scapegoat

patojo /pa'toho/ *a* waddling

patología /patolo'hia/ *f,* pathology

patoso /pa'toso/ *a Fig.* heavy, pedestrian, tedious

patraña /pa'traɲa/ *f,* nonsense, rubbish, fairy tale

patria /'patria/ *f,* motherland, native country; native place. **p. chica,** native region

patriarca /pa'triarka/ *m,* patriarch

patricio /pa'triθio; pa'trisio/ **(-ia)** *a* and *n* patrician

patrimonio /patri'monio/ *m,* patrimony

patriota /pa'triota/ *mf* patriot

patriótico /pa'triotiko/ *a* patriotic

patriotismo /patrio'tismo/ *m,* patriotism

patrocinar /patroθi'nar; patrosi'nar/ *vt* to protect, defend; favor, sponsor; patronize

patrocinio /patro'θinio; patro'sinio/ *m,* protection, defense; sponsorship; patronage

patrón /pa'tron/ **(-ona)** *n* patron, sponsor; patron saint; landlord; employer. *m,* coxswain; *Naut.* master, skipper; pattern, model; standard. **p. de oro,** gold standard

patronato /patro'nato/ *m,* patronage, protection; employers' association; charitable foundation. **p. de turismo,** tourist bureau

patrono /pa'trono/ **(-na)** *n* protector; sponsor; patron; patron saint; employer

patrulla /pa'truʎa; pa'truya/ *f,* Mil. patrol; group, band

patrullar /patru'ʎar; patru'yar/ *vi* Mil. patrol; march about

pauperismo /paupe'rismo/ *m,* destitution, pauperism

pausa /'pausa/ *f,* pause, interruption; delay; *Mus.* rest; *Mus.* pause. **a pausas,** intermittently

pausado /pau'saðo/ *a* deliberate, slow —*adv* slowly, deliberately

pausar /pau'sar/ *vi* to pause

pauta /'pauta/ *f,* standard, norm, design; *Fig.* guide, model

pavada /pa'βaða/ *f,* flock of turkeys

pavana /pa'βana/ *f,* pavane, stately dance

pavero /pa'βero/ **(-ra)** *a* vain; strutting —*n* turkey keeper or vendor. *m,* broad-brimmed Andalusian hat

pavimentación /paβimenta'θion; paβimenta'sion/ *f,* paving, flagging

pavimento /paβi'mento/ *m,* pavement

pavo /'paβo/ **(-va)** *n Ornith.* turkey. **p. real,** peacock. *Inf.* **pelar la pava,** to serenade, court

pavón /pa'βon/ *m, Ornith.* peacock; peacock butterfly; preservative paint (for steel, etc.); gunmetal

pavonear /paβone'ar/ *vi* to strut, peacock (also *vr*); *Inf.* hoodwink, dazzle

pavor /pa'βor/ *m,* terror, panic

pavoroso /paβo'roso/ *a* fearful, awesome, dreadful

payasada /paia'saða/ *f,* clowning, practical joke; clown's patter

payaso /pa'iaso/ *m,* clown

paz /paθ; pas/ *f,* peace; harmony, concord; peaceableness. **¡P. sea en esta casa!** Peace be upon this house! (salutation). **estar en p.,** to be at peace; be quits, be even. **poner** (*or* meter) **p.,** to make peace (between dissentients). **venir de p.,** to come with peaceful intentions

pazguato /paθ'guato; pas'guato/ **(-ta)** *n* simpleton, booby

pazpuerca /paθ'puerka; pas'puerka/ *f,* slattern

pe /pe/ *f,* name of the letter P. *Inf.* **de pe a pa,** from A to Z, from beginning to end

peaje /pe'ahe/ *m,* toll (on bridges, roads, etc.)

peatón /pea'ton/ *m,* pedestrian; walker; country postman

peca /'peka/ *f,* mole, freckle

pecado /pe'kaðo/ *m,* sin; fault; excess; defect; *Inf.* the Devil. **p. capital,** mortal sin

pecador /peka'ðor/ *a* sinful. *m,* sinner. **¡P. de mí!** Poor me!

pecadora /peka'ðora/ *f,* sinner; *Inf.* prostitute

pecaminoso /pekami'noso/ *a* sinful

pecar /pe'kar/ *vi* to sin; trespass, transgress; (*with de*) be too,... (e.g. *El libro peca de largo,* The book is too long)

peceño /pe'θeɲo; pe'seɲo/ *a* pitch-black (horses, etc.); tasting of pitch

pechera /pe'tʃera/ f, shirt front; chest protector; bib, tucker; shirt frill; Inf. bosom

pecho /'petʃo/ m, Anat. chest; breast; bosom; mind, conscience; courage, endurance; Mus. quality (of voice); incline, slope. **p. arriba**, uphill. **abrir su p.** (or **con**), to unbosom oneself to. **dar el p.** (a), to suckle. **de pechos**, leaning on. **echar el p. al agua**, Fig. to embark courageously upon. **tomar a pechos** (**una cosa**), to take (a thing) very seriously; take to heart

pechuga /pe'tʃuga/ f, breast (of a bird); Inf. breast, bosom; slope, incline

pecoso /pe'koso/ a freckled; spotted (with warts)

pecuario /pe'kuario/ a Agr. stock; cattle

peculiar /peku'liar/ a peculiar, individual

peculiaridad /pekuliari'ðað/ f, peculiarity

peculio /pe'kulio/ m, private money or property

pecunia /pe'kunia/ f, Inf. cash

pecuniario /peku'niario/ a pecuniary

pedagogía /peðago'hia/ f, education, pedagogy

pedagogo /peða'gogo/ m, schoolmaster; educationalist; Fig. mentor

pedal /pe'ðal/ m, Mech. treadle, lever, Mus. pedal; Mus. sustained harmony. Auto. **p. de embrague**, clutch pedal

pedalear /peðale'ar/ vi to pedal

pedante /pe'ðante/ a pedantic. mf pedant

pedantería /peðante'ria/ f, pedantry

pedazo /pe'ðaθo; pe'ðaso/ m, bit, piece; lump; fragment, portion. Inf. **p. del alma**, **p. del corazón**, **p. de las entrañas**, loved one, dear one. **a pedazos** or **en pedazos**, in pieces, in bits. **hacer pedazos**, to break into fragments

pedernal /peðer'nal/ m, flint; anything very hard

pedestal /peðes'tal/ m, pedestal; base; stand; Fig. foundation

pedestre /pe'ðestre/ a pedestrian; dull, uninspired

pediatra /pe'ðiatra/ mf pediatrician

pedicuro /peði'kuro/ m, chiropodist

pedido /pe'ðiðo/ m, Com. order; request, petition

pedigüeño /peði'gueɲo/ a importunate, insistent

pedimento /peði'mento/ m, petition, demand; Law. claim; Law. motion

pedir /pe'ðir/ vt irr to ask, request; Com. order; demand; necessitate; desire; ask in marriage. **p. en juicio**, Law. to bring an action against. Inf. **pedírselo** (a uno) **el cuerpo**, to desire (something) ardently. **a p. de boca**, according to one's wish —Pres. Part. **pidiendo**. Pres. Indic. **pido**, **pides**, **pide**, **piden**. Preterite **pidió**, **pidieron**. Pres. Subjunc. **pida**, etc —Imperf. Subjunc. **pidiese**, etc.

pedo /'peðo/ m, fart

pedrada /pe'ðraða/ f, casting a stone; blow with a stone; innuendo

pedrea /pe'ðrea/ f, stone throwing; fight with stones; shower of hailstones

pedregal /peðre'gal/ m, stony ground

pedrería /peðre'ria/ f, precious stones

pedrisco /pe'ðrisko/ m, hailstone; shower of stones; pile of stones

pega /'pega/ f, sticking; cementing; joining; pitch; varnish; Inf. joke; beating; Ornith. magpie

pegadizo /pega'ðiθo; pega'ðiso/ a sticky, gummy, adhesive; detachable, removable; Fig. clinging, importunate (of people)

pegado /pe'gaðo/ m, sticking plaster; patch

pegajoso /pega'hoso/ a sticky, gluey; viscid; contagious, catching; Inf. oily, unctuous; Fig. Inf. cadging, sponging

pegar /pe'gar/ vt to stick; cement; join, fasten; press (against); infect with (diseases); hit, strike; give (a shout, jump, etc.); patch; —vi spread, catch (fire, etc.); Fig. make an impression, have influence; be opportune; —vr Cul. stick, burn; meddle; become enthusiastic about; take root in the mind. **p. un tiro (a)**, to shoot

pegote /pe'gote/ m, sticking plaster; Fig. Inf. sponger; Inf. patch

peinado /pei'naðo/ m, hairdressing or style; headdress —a Inf. effeminate, overelegant (men); overcareful (style). **un p. al agua**, a finger wave

peinador /peina'ðor/ **(-ra)** m, peignoir, dressing gown —n hairdresser

peinadura /peina'ðura/ f, brushing or combing of hair; pl hair combings

peinar /pei'nar/ vt to comb, dress the hair; card (wool); cut away (rock)

peine /'peine/ m, comb; Mech. hackle, reed; instep; Inf. crafty person

peladilla /pela'ðiʎa; pela'ðiya/ f, sugared almond; smooth, small pebble

pelado /pe'laðo/ a plucked; bare, unadorned; needy, poor; hairless; skinned; peeled; without shell; treeless

peladura /pela'ðura/ f, peeling; shelling; skinning; plucking (feathers)

pelafustán /pelafus'tan/ m, Inf. good-fornothing, scamp

pelagra /pe'lagra/ f, pellagra

pelaje /pe'lahe/ m, fur, wool

pelamesa /pela'mesa/ f, brawl, fight; lock, tuft (of hair)

pelapatatas /pelapa'tatas/ m, potato peeler

pelar /pe'lar/ vt to tear out or cut the hair; pluck; skin; peel; shell; rob, fleece; —vr lose one's hair

peldaño /pel'daɲo/ m, step, stair, tread, rung

pelea /pe'lea/ f, battle; quarrel, dispute; fight (among animals); effort, exertion; Fig. struggle

peleador /pelea'ðor/ a fighting; quarrelsome, aggressive

pelear /pele'ar/ vi to fight; quarrel; struggle, strive. **p. como perro y gato,** to fight like cat and mouse —*vr* come to blows; fall out, become enemies

pelechar /pele't ʃar/ *vi* to get a new coat (of animals); grow new feathers (of birds); *Inf.* prosper, flourish; grow well

pelele /pe'lele/ *m,* effigy; *Inf.* nincompoop

peletería /pelete'ria/ *f,* furrier; fur shop

pelícano /pe'likano/ *m,* pelican

película /pe'likula/ *f,* film. **p. fotográfica,** roll of film. **p. sonora,** sound film

peligrar /peli'grar/ *vi* to be in danger

peligro /pe'ligro/ *m,* danger, peril. **correr p.** *or* **estar en p.,** to be in danger

peligroso /peli'groso/ *a* dangerous, perilous, risky

pelirrojo /peli'rroho/ *a* red-haired

pelleja /pe'ʎeha; pe'yeha/ *f,* hide, skin (of animals); sheepskin

pellejo /pe'ʎeho; pe'yeho/ *m,* hide; pelt; skin; wineskin; *Inf.* drunkard; peel, skin (of fruit)

pelliza /pe'ʎiθa; pe'yisa/ *f,* fur or fur-trimmed coat

pellizcar /peʎiθ'kar; peyis'kar/ *vt* to pinch, tweak, nip; pilfer

pellizco /pe'ʎiθko; pe'yisko/ *m,* pinch, nip, tweak; nipping, pinching; bit, pinch

pelmazo /pel'maθo; pel'maso/ *m,* squashed mass; *Inf.* idler, sluggard; *Inf.* bore

pelo /'pelo/ *m,* hair; down (on birds and fruit); fiber, filament; hair trigger (firearms); hairspring (watches); kiss (in billiards); nap (of cloth), grain (of wood); flaw (in gems); raw silk. **p. de camello,** camel's hair. **a p.,** in the nude; without a hat; opportunely. **en p.,** bareback (of horses). **hacerse el p.,** to do one's hair; have one's hair cut. *Inf.* **no tener p. de tonto,** to be smart, clever. *Inf.* **no tener pelos en la lengua,** to be outspoken. *Inf.* **tomar el p.** (a), to pull a person's leg. **venir a p.,** to be apposite; come opportunely

pelón /pe'lon/ *a* hairless; *Fig. Inf.* broke, fleeced

pelonería /pelone'ria/ *f, Inf.* poverty, misery

pelota /pe'lota/ *f,* ball; ball game. **p. base,** baseball. **p. vasca,** pelota. **en p.,** stark naked

pelotari /pelo'tari/ *m,* professional pelota player

pelotazo /pelo'taθo; pelo'taso/ *m,* knock or blow with a ball

pelotear /pelote'ar/ *vt* to audit accounts; —*vi* play ball; throw, cast; quarrel; argue

pelotera /pelo'tera/ *f, Inf.* brawl

pelotón /pelo'ton/ *m,* big ball; lump of hair; crowd, multitude; *Mil.* platoon. **p. de ejecución,** firing squad

peluca /pe'luka/ *f,* wig; periwig; *Inf.* scolding

peludo /pe'luðo/ *a* hairy. *m,* long-haired rug

peluquería /peluke'ria/ *f,* hairdressing establishment; hairdressing trade

peluquero /pelu'kero/ **(-ra)** *n* hairdresser; barber

pelusa /pe'lusa/ *f,* down, soft hair; fluff, nap

pena /'pena/ *f,* punishment, penalty; grief; pain, suffering; difficulty, trouble; mourning veil; hardship; anxiety; embarrassment; tail feather. **p. capital** *or* **p. de la vida,** capital punishment. **a duras penas,** with great difficulty. **so p. de,** under penalty of. **valer** (*or* **merecer**) **la p.,** to be worth while

penable /pe'naβle/ *a* punishable

penacho /pe'natʃo/ *m,* topknot, crest (of birds); plume, panache; *Inf.* pride, arrogance

penado /pe'naðo/ **(-da)** *a* difficult, laborious; painful, troubled, afflicted —*n* convict

penal /pe'nal/ *a* penal; punitive

penalidad /penali'ðað/ *f,* trouble, labor, difficulty; *Law.* penalty

penar /pe'nar/ *vt* to penalize; punish; —*vi* suffer; undergo purgatorial pains; —*vr* suffer anguish. **p. por,** to long for

pendejo /pen'deho/ *m,* pubic hair; *Inf.* coward; jerk

pendencia /pen'denθia; pen'densia/ *f,* fight; quarrel

pendenciar /penden'θiar; penden'siar/ *vi* to fight; quarrel

pendenciero /penden'θiero; penden'siero/ *a* quarrelsome, aggressive

pender /pen'der/ *vi* to hang; depend; be pending

pendiente /pen'diente/ *a* pending; hanging; *Com.* outstanding. *m,* earring; pendant. *f,* slope, incline; gradient

péndola /'pendola/ *f,* feather, plume; quill pen; pendulum (of a clock)

pendón /pen'don/ *m,* pennon, banner; *Bot.* shoot; *Inf.* lanky, slatternly woman; *pl* reins

péndulo /'pendulo/ *a* pendulous, hanging. *m,* pendulum

pene /'pene/ *m,* penis

penetración /penetra'θion; penetra'sion/ *f,* penetration; understanding, perspicuity; sagacity, shrewdness

penetrador /penetra'ðor/ *a* penetrating, perspicacious; sagacious, acute

penetrante /pene'trante/ *a* penetrating; deep; piercing (of sounds); acute, shrewd

penetrar /pene'trar/ *vt* to penetrate; permeate; master, comprehend; (*with en*) enter

penicilina /peniθi'lina; penisi'lina/ *f,* penicillin

península /pe'ninsula/ *f,* peninsula. **la P.** the Iberian Peninsula

Península Ibérica, la /pe'ninsula i'βerika, la/ the Iberian Peninsula

penique /pe'nike/ *m,* penny

penitencia /peni'tenθia; peni'tensia/ *f,* penitence, repentance; penance

penitenciaría /peniten θia'ria; penitensia-'ria/ f, penitentiary

penitente /peni'tente/ a penitent, repentant. mf penitent

penoso /pe'noso/ a laborious, difficult; grievous; painful; troublesome; *Inf.* foppish

pensado /pen'saðo/ a premeditated, deliberate. **de p.,** intentionally. **mal p.,** malicious, evil-minded

pensador /pensa'ðor/ a thinking; pensive. m, thinker

pensamiento /pensa'miento/ m, mind; thought; idea; suspicion, doubt; heartsease pansy; maxim; intention, project

pensar /pen'sar/ vt irr to think; purpose, intend; (*with en, sobre*) reflect upon; think about; —vt feed (animals). **p. entre sí, p. para consigo** or **p. para sí,** to think to oneself. See **acertar**

pensativo /pensa'tiβo/ a reflective, pensive

pensión /pen'sion/ f, pension, allowance; boarding house, private hotel; scholarship grant; cost of board; trouble, drudgery

pensionado /pensio'naðo/ **(-da)** a pensioned; retired —n scholarship holder. m, boarding school

pensionar /pensio'nar/ vt to pension, grant a pension to; charge a pension on

pensionista /pensio'nista/ mf pensioner; boarder

pentágono /pen'tagono/ m, pentagon —a pentagonal

Pentateuco /penta'teuko/ m, Pentateuch

Pentecostés /pentekos'tes/ m, Pentecost, Whitsuntide

penúltimo /pe'nultimo/ a next to the last, penultimate

penuria /pe'nuria/ f, scarcity; want, penury

peña /'peɲa/ f, crag, rock; boulder; group of friends; club. **ser una p.,** to be stony-hearted

peñasco /pe'ɲasko/ m, craggy peak

peñón /pe'ɲon/ m, rock; cliff; peak

peón /pe'on/ m, pedestrian; laborer; *South American* farmhand; top (toy); piece (chess, checkers); *Mech.* axle; infantryman. **p. caminero,** road mender. **p. de ajedrez,** pawn (in chess)

peonza /pe'onθa; pe'onsa/ f, top; teetotum

peor /pe'or/ a *compar* **malo** worse —adv *compar* **mal,** worse —a *superl* **el (la, lo) peor; los (las) peores,** the worst. **o que p.,** worse and worse. **tanto p.,** so much the worse

pepino /pe'pino/ m, cucumber plant; cucumber; *Fig.* pin, straw

pepita /pe'pita/ f, *Mineral.* nugget; pip, seed (of fruit)

péptico /'peptiko/ a peptic

pequeñez /peke'neθ; peke'nes/ f, littleness, smallness; pettiness; childhood; infancy; trifle, insignificant thing; meanness, baseness

pequeño /pe'keɲo/ a little, small; petty; very young; short, brief; humble, lowly

pera /'pera/ f, pear; goatee; *Fig.* plum, sinecure

perca /'perka/ f, *Ichth.* perch

percal /per'kal/ m, percale, calico

percalina /perka'lina/ f, percaline, binding cloth

percance /per'kanθe; per'kanse/ m, perquisite, attribute (gen. pl); disaster, mischance

percepción /perθep'θion; persep'sion/ f, perception; idea, conception

perceptible /perθep'tiβle; persep'tiβle/ a perceptible

perceptivo /perθep'tiβo; persep'tiβo/ a perceptive

perceptor /perθep'tor; persep'tor/ **(-ra)** a perceptive —n observer

percha /'pertʃa/ f, stake, pole; coat hanger; perch (for birds); rack (for hay); hall stand, coat and hat stand, coatrack

perchero /per'tʃero/ m, hall stand; clothes rack; row of perches (for fowl, etc.)

percibir /perθi'βir; persi'βir/ vt to collect, draw, receive; perceive; understand, grasp

percibo /per'θiβo; per'siβo/ m, perceiving; collecting, drawing, receiving

percolador /perkola'ðor/ m, percolator (coffee)

percusión /perku'sion/ f, percussion; shock, vibration

percutir /perku'tir/ vt to percuss, strike

perdedor /perðe'ðor/ **(-ra)** a losing —n loser

perder /per'ðer/ vt to lose; throw away, squander; spoil, destroy; —vi fade (of colors); —vr lose one's way, be lost; be confused or perplexed; be shipwrecked; take to vice, become dissolute; be spoiled or destroyed; disappear; love madly. **p. la chaveta (por),** to go out of one's head (for), be wild (about). **p. los estribos,** to let the chance slip. **p. los estribos,** to lose patience. **p. terreno,** to lose ground. **perderse de vista,** to be lost to sight. **echarse a p.,** to spoil, be damaged. See **entender**

perdición /perði'θion; perði'sion/ f, loss; perdition, ruin; damnation; depravity, viciousness

pérdida /'perðiða/ f, loss; waste. **p. cuantiosa,** heavy losses

perdidamente /perðiða'mente/ adv ardently, desperately; uselessly

perdigón /perði'ɣon/ m, young partridge; decoy partridge; hailstone, pellet, shot

perdiz /per'ðiθ; per'ðis/ f, partridge. **p. blanca,** ptarmigan

perdón /per'ðon/ m, pardon, forgiveness; remission. **con p.,** with your permission; excuse me

perdonable /perðo'naβle/ a pardonable, excusable

perdonar /perðo'nar/ vt to pardon, for-

give; remit, excuse; exempt; waste, lose;
give up (a privilege)

perdulario /perðu'lario/ a careless, negligent; slovenly; vicious, depraved

perdurable /perðu'raβle/ a perpetual, everlasting; enduring, lasting

perdurar /perðu'rar/ vi to last, endure

perecedero /pereθe'ðero; perese'ðero/ a
brief, fugitive, transient; perishable. m,
Inf. poverty, want

perecer /pere'θer; pere'ser/ vi irr to end,
finish; perish, die; suffer (damage, grief,
etc.); be destitute; —vr (with por) long
for, crave; desire ardently. See **conocer**

peregrinación /peregrina'θion; peregri-
na'sion/ f, journey, peregrination; pilgrimage

peregrinamente /peregrina'mente/ adv
rarely, not often; beautifully, perfectly

peregrino /pere'grino/ (-na) a and n pilgrim —a migratory (birds); rare, unusual;
extraordinary, strange; beautiful, perfect

perejil /pere'hil/ m, parsley; Inf. ornament or apparel (gen. pl); pl honors, titles

perengano /pereŋ'gano/ (-na) n
so-and-so, such a one

perenne /pe'renne/ a incessant, constant;
Bot. perennial

perentorio /peren'torio/ a peremptory;
conclusive, decisive; urgent, pressing

pereza /pe'reθa; pe'resa/ f, laziness; languor, inertia; slowness, deliberateness

perezoso /pere'θoso; pere'soso/ a lazy;
languid; slothful; slow, deliberate. m,
Zool. sloth

perfección /perfek'θion; perfek'sion/ f,
perfection; perfecting, perfect thing, virtue, grace

perfeccionamiento /perfek-
θiona'miento; perfeksiona'miento/ m,
perfecting; progress, improvement

perfeccionar /perfekθio'nar; perfeksio-
'nar/ vt to perfect; complete

perfecto /per'fekto/ a perfect; excellent,
very good; complete; whole; Gram. perfect

perfidia /per'fiðia/ f, perfidy, treachery

pérfido /'perfiðo/ a perfidious, treacherous

perfil /per'fil/ m, ornament, decoration;
outline, contour; profile; section (of
metal); fine stroke of letters); pl finishing touches; politeness, attention, courtesy. **de p.**, in profile; sideways

perfilado /perfi'laðo/ a long, elongated
(of faces, etc.)

perfilar /perfi'lar/ vt to draw in profile;
outline; —vr place oneself sideways, show
one's profile; Inf. dress up, titivate

perforación /perfora'θion; perfora'sion/
f, perforation, boring; hole

perforador /perfora'ðor/ a perforating,
boring. m, Mech. drill

perforar /perfo'rar/ vt to perforate,
pierce; bore, drill, make a hole in

perfumador /perfuma'ðor/ (-ra) a perfuming —n perfumer. m, perfume burner

perfumar /perfu'mar/ vt to perfume; —vi
give off perfume

perfume /per'fume/ m, perfume; scent,
fragrance

perfumería /perfume'ria/ f, scent factory; perfumery; perfume shop

perfunctorio /perfunk'torio/ a perfunctory

pergamino /perga'mino/ m, parchment,
vellum; document; diploma; pl aristocratic descent

pericia /pe'riθia; pe'risia/ f, expertness;
skilled workmanship

pericial /peri'θial; peri'sial/ a expert,
skillful

perico /pe'riko/ m, parakeet

periferia /peri'feria/ f, periphery

periférico /peri'feriko/ a peripheral

perilla /pe'riʎa; pe'riya/ f, pear-shaped
ornament; goatee; imperial. **p. de la
oreja,** lobe of the ear. **venir de p.,** to be
most opportune

perímetro /pe'rimetro/ m, perimeter;
precincts

perínclito /pe'rinklito/ a distinguished, illustrious; heroic

periodicidad /perioðiθi'ðað; perioðisi-
'ðað/ f, periodicity

periódico /pe'rioðiko/ a periodic. m,
newspaper; periodical publication

periodicucho /perioði'kutʃo/ m, rag
(bad newspaper)

periodismo /perio'ðismo/ m, journalism

periodista /perio'ðista/ mf journalist

periodístico /perio'ðistiko/ a journalistic

período /pe'rioðo/ m, period; Phys. cycle; menstruation period; Gram. clause;
age, era

peripatético /peripa'tetiko/ a peripatetic

peripecia /peri'peθia; peri'pesia/ f, sudden change of fortune, vicissitude

peripuesto /peri'puesto/ a Inf. overelegant, spruce, too well-dressed; smart

periquete /peri'kete/ m, Inf. jiffy, trice

periquito /peri'kito/ m, parakeet; budg-
erigar

periscopio /peris'kopio/ m, periscope

perito /pe'rito/ (-ta) a expert; skillful,
experienced —n expert

perjudicador /perhuðika'ðor/ (-ra) a injurious, prejudicial —n injurer

perjudicar /perhuði'kar/ vt to harm,
damage, injure; prejudice

perjudicial /perhuði'θial; perhuði'sial/ a
injurious, noxious, harmful; prejudicial

perjuicio /per'huiθio; per'huisio/ m, injury, damage; harm; Law. prejudice

perjurador /perhura'ðor/ (-ra) n perjurer

perjurar /perhu'rar/ vi to perjure oneself,
commit perjury; swear, curse

perjurio /per'hurio/ m, perjury

perjuro /per'huro/ (-ra) a perjured, for-
sworn —n perjurer

perla /'perla/ f, pearl; Archit. bead; Fig.
treasure, jewel, dear. **de perlas,** excellent;
exactly right

perlero /per'lero/ a pearl

perlesía /perle'sia/ f. paralysis; palsy

permanecer /permane'θer; permane'ser/ *vi irr* to stay, remain. **p. en posición de firme,** to stand at attention. See **conocer**

permanencia /perma'nenθia; perma'nensia/ f. stay, sojourn; permanence

permanente /perma'nente/ a permanent; lasting, enduring

permisible /permi'siβle/ a permissible, allowable

permisivo /permi'siβo/ a permissive

permiso /per'miso/ m. permission, leave; permit; (*Mil.* etc.) pass. **¡Con p.!** Excuse me!; Allow me!

permitir /permi'tir/ vt to permit, allow

permuta /per'muta/ f. exchange

permutación /permuta'θion; permuta-'sion/ f. permutation, interchange

permutar /permu'tar/ vt to exchange

pernear /perne'ar/ vi to kick; *Inf.* bustle, fret, be impatient

pernetas, en /per'netas, en/ adv barelegged

perniciosidad /perniθiosi'ðað; pernisio-si'ðað/ f. perniciousness

pernicioso /perni'θioso; perni'sioso/ a pernicious

pernil /per'nil/ m. *Anat.* hock; ham; leg of pork; leg (of trousers)

pernio /'pernio/ m. hinge (of doors, windows)

perniquebrar /pernike'βrar/ vt irr to break the legs of. See **quebrar**

perno /'perno/ m. bolt, pin, spike

pernoctar /pernok'tar/ vi to spend the night (away from home)

pero /'pero/ conjunc but. m. *Inf.* defect; difficulty, snag

perogrullada /perogru'ʎaða; perogru-'yaða/ f. *Inf.* truism

perol /pe'rol/ m. *Cul.* pan

peroración /perora'θion; perora'sion/ f. peroration

perorar /pero'rar/ vi to make a speech; *Inf.* speak pompously; ask insistently

peróxido /pe'roksiðo/ m. peroxide

perpendicular /perpendiku'lar/ a perpendicular. f. perpendicular

perpetración /perpetra'θion; perpetra-'sion/ f. perpetration

perpetrar /perpe'trar/ vt to perpetrate

perpetua /per'petua/ f. *Bot.* immortelle, everlasting

perpetuación /perpetua'θion; perpetua-'sion/ f. perpetuation

perpetuar /perpe'tuar/ vt to perpetuate; —vr last, endure

perpétuo /per'petuo/ a everlasting; lifelong

perplejidad /perplehi'ðað/ f. perplexity, bewilderment, doubt

perplejo /per'pleho/ a perplexed, bewildered, doubtful

perquirir /perki'rir/ vt irr to search carefully. See **adquirir**

perra /'perra/ f. bitch; *Inf.* sot, drunkard; tantrums. **p. chica,** five-cent coin. **p. gorda,** ten-cent coin

perrada /pe'rraða/ f. pack of dogs; *Inf.* dirty trick

perrera /pe'rrera/ f. dog kennel; useless toil; *Inf.* tantrums

perrería /perre'ria/ f. pack of dogs; *Inf.* dirty trick; fit of anger

perro /'perro/ m. dog. **p. caliente** hot dog. **p. danés,** Great Dane. **p. de aguas,** poodle; spaniel. **p. de casta,** thoroughbred dog. **p. de lanas** poodle. **p. de muestra,** pointer. **p. de presa,** bulldog. **p. de San Bernardo,** St. Bernard (dog). **p. de Terranova,** Newfoundland (dog). **p. del hortelano,** dog in the manger. **p. dogo** bulldog. **p. esquimal** husky. **p. faldero,** lap dog. **p. lobo,** wolfhound. **p. pachón,** dachshund. **p. pastor alemán** or **p. policía,** German shepherd. **p. pequinés,** Pekingese. **p. perdiguero,** retriever. **p. pomerano,** spitz, Pomeranian (dog). **p. sabueso español,** spaniel. **p. zorrero,** foxhound. *Inf.* **A p. viejo no hay tus tus,** You can't fool an old dog. **vivir como perros y gatos,** *Inf.* to live like cat and dog

persa /'persa/ a and mf Persian. m. Persian (language)

persecución /perseku'θion; perseku'sion/ f. pursuit; persecution; annoyance, importuning

perseguidor /persegi'ðor/ (**-ra**) a pursuing; tormenting —n pursuer; tormentor, persecutor

perseguimiento /persegi'miento/ m. pursuit

perseguir /perse'gir/ vi irr to pursue; persecute, torment; importune. See **seguir**

perseverancia /perseβe'ranθia; perseβe-'ransia/ f. perseverance

perseverante /perseβe'rante/ a persevering; constant

perseverar /perseβe'rar/ vi to persevere; last, endure

persiana /per'siana/ f. Venetian blind; flowered silk material

persignar /persig'nar/ vt to sign; make the sign of the cross over; —vr cross oneself

persistencia /persis'tenθia; persis'tensia/ f. persistence

persistente /persis'tente/ a persistent

persistir /persis'tir/ vi to persist

persona /per'sona/ f. person; personage; character (in a play, etc.); (*Gram. Eccl.*) person. **de p. a p.,** in private, face to face

personaje /perso'nahe/ m. important person, personage; character (in a play, etc.)

personal /perso'nal/ a personal. m. staff, personnel

personalidad /personali'ðað/ f. personality

personalismo /persona'lismo/ m. personality; personal question

personalizar /personali'θar; personali-'sar/ vt to become personal, be offensive

personarse /perso'narse/ *vr* to present oneself, call, appear

personificar /personifi'kar/ *vt* to personify

perspectiva /perspek'tiβa/ *f*, perspective; view; outlook; aspect, appearance. **p. aérea**, bird's-eye view

perspicacia /perspi'kaθia; perspi'kasia/ *f*, perspicacity, shrewdness

perspicaz /perspi'kaθ; perspi'kas/ *a* perspicacious, clear-sighted

perspicuo /pers'pikuo/ *a* lucid, clear

persuadir /persua'ðir/ *vt* to persuade

persuasible /persua'siβle/ *a* persuadable

persuasión /persua'sion/ *f*, persuasion; belief, conviction, opinion

persuasivo /persua'siβo/ *a* persuasive

pertenecer /pertene'θer; pertene'ser/ *vi irr* to belong; relate, concern. See **conocer**

perteneciente /pertene'θiente; pertene-'siente/ *a* belonging (to), pertaining (to)

pertenencia /perte'nenθia; perte'nensia/ *f*, ownership, proprietorship; property, accessory

pértiga /'pertiga/ *f*, long rod; pole. **salto de p.**, pole vaulting

pertinacia /perti'naθia; perti'nasia/ *f*, pertinacity, doggedness

pertinaz /perti'naθ; perti'nas/ *a* pertinacious, stubborn, dogged

pertinencia /perti'nenθia; perti'nensia/ *f*, relevance, appropriateness

pertinente /perti'nente/ *a* relevant, apposite; appropriate

pertrechar /pertre'tʃar/ *vt* to supply, equip; prepare, make ready

pertrechos /per'tretʃos/ *m pl, Mil.* armaments, stores; equipment, appliances

perturbación /perturβa'θion; perturβa-'sion/ *f*, disturbance; agitation

perturbar /pertur'βar/ *vt* to disturb; agitate

Perú /pe'ru/ Peru

peruano /pe'ruano/ **(-na)** *a and n* Peruvian

perversidad /perβersi'ðað/ *f*, wickedness, depravity

perversión /perβer'sion/ *f*, perversion; wickedness, evil

perverso /per'βerso/ *a* wicked, iniquitous, depraved

pervertir /perβer'tir/ *vt irr* to pervert, corrupt; distort. See **sentir**

pesa /'pesa/ *f*, weight; clock weight; gymnast's weight. **pesas y medidas**, weights and measures

pesacartas /pesa'kartas/ *m*, letter scale, letter balance

pesadez /pesa'ðeθ; pesa'ðes/ *f*, heaviness; obesity; tediousness, tiresomeness; slowness; fatigue

pesadilla /pesa'ðiʎa; pesa'ðiya/ *f*, nightmare

pesado /pe'saðo/ *a* heavy; obese; deep (of sleep); oppressive (of weather); slow;

unwieldy; tedious; impertinent; dull, boring; offensive

pesadumbre /pesa'ðumbre/ *f*, heaviness; grief, sorrow; trouble, anxiety

pésame /'pesame/ *m*, expression of condolence. **dar el p.**, to present one's condolences

pesantez /pesan'teθ; pesan'tes/ *f*, weight, heaviness; seriousness, gravity

pesar /pe'sar/ *m*, grief, sorrow; remorse. **a p. de**, in spite of

pesar /pe'sar/ *vi* to weigh; be heavy; be important; grieve, cause regret (e.g., *Me pesa mucho*, I am very sorry); influence, affect; —*vt* weigh; consider. **Mal que me** (te, etc.) **pese...**, Much as I regret...

pesaroso /pesa'roso/ *a* regretful, remorseful; sorrowful

pesca /'peska/ *f*, fishery; angling, fishing; catch of fish. **p. a la rastra**, trawling. **p. deportiva** sport fishing. **p. mayor**, deep-sea fishing

pescadería /peskaðe'ria/ *f*, fishery; fish store; fish market

pescado /pes'kaðo/ *m*, fish (out of the water); salt cod

pescador /peska'ðor/ **(-ra)** *n* fisherman; angler

pescar /pes'kar/ *vt* to fish; *Inf.* catch in the act; acquire. **p. a la rastra**, to trawl

pescuezo /pes'kueθo; pes'kueso/ *m*, neck; throat; haughtiness, arrogance. **torcer el p.**, to wring the neck (of chickens, etc.)

pesebre /pe'seβre/ *m*, manger, stable; feeding trough

pesimismo /pesi'mismo/ *m*, pessimism

pesimista /pesi'mista/ *a* pessimistic. *mf* pessimist

pésimo /'pesimo/ *a superl* **malo** extremely bad

peso /'peso/ *m*, weighing; weight; heaviness; gravity; importance; influence; load; peso (coin); scale, balance. **p. bruto**, gross weight. **p. de joyería**, troy weight. **p. específico**, *Phys.* specific gravity. **p. pluma**, (*Boxing*) featherweight

pespunte /pes'punte/ *m*, backstitch

pesquera /pes'kera/ *f*, fishing ground, fishery

pesquería /peske'ria/ *f*, fishing, angling; fisherman's trade; fishing ground, fishery

pesquisa /pes'kisa/ *f*, investigation, examination; search

pesquisar /peski'sar/ *vt* to investigate, look into; search

pestaña /pes'taɲa/ *f*, eyelash; *Sew.* edging, fringe; ear, lug; *Naut.* fluke

pestañear /pestaɲe'ar/ *vi* to wink; blink; flutter the eyelashes

peste /'peste/ *f*, plague, pestilence; nauseous smell; epidemic; pest; vice; *pl* oaths, curses. **p. bubónica**, bubonic plague. **p. roja** syphilis. **p. de las abejas**, foul brood. **echar pestes**, to swear; fume

pestífero /pes'tifero/ *a* noxious

pestilencia /pesti'lenθia; pesti'lensia/ *f*, plague, pestilence

pestilente /pesti'lente/ *a* pestilential

pestillo /pes'tiʎo; pes'tiyo/ *m*, latch; lock bolt. **p. de golpe**, safety latch

petaca /pe'taka/ *f*, cigarette or cigar case; tobacco pouch

pétalo /'petalo/ *m*, petal

petardo /pe'tarðo/ *m*, detonator; torpedo; firecracker; fraud

petición /peti'θion; peti'sion/ *f*, petition, request

petimetra /peti'metra/ *f*, stylish and affected young woman

petimetre /peti'metre/ *m*, fop

petitorio /peti'torio/ *a* petitionary. *m*, *Inf*. importunity

peto /'peto/ *m*, breastplate; front (of a shirt); bib

pétreo /'petreo/ *a* petrous

petrificación /petrifika'θion, petrifika 'sion/ *f*, petrifaction

petrificar /petrifi'kar/ *vt* to petrify; —*vr* become petrified

petróleo /pe'troleo/ *m*, petroleum; oil, mineral oil. **p. bruto**, crude oil. **p. de lámpara**, kerosene

petrolero /petro'lero/ **(-ra)** *a* oil, petroleum —*n* petroleum seller; incendiarist. *m*, oil tanker

petrolífero /petro'lifero/ *a* oil-bearing

petulancia /petu'lanθia; petu'lansia/ *f*, insolence; vanity

petulante /petu'lante/ *a* insolent; vain

pez /peθ; pes/ *m*, fish; *pl* Pisces. *f*, *Chem*. pitch. **p. sierra**, swordfish

pezón /pe'θon; pe'son/ *m*, *Bot*. stalk; nipple; axle pivot; point (of land, etc.)

piadoso /pia'ðoso/ *a* compassionate; kind, pitiful; pious, religious

piafar /pia'far/ *vi* to stamp, paw the ground (horses)

pianista /pia'nista/ *mf* piano maker; piano dealer; pianist

piano /'piano/ *m*, pianoforte. **p. de cola**, grand piano. **p. de media cola**, baby grand. **p. vertical**, upright piano

piante /'piante/ *a* chirping, twittering

piar /piar/ *vi* to chirp, twitter

piara /'piara/ *f*, herd of swine; pack (of horses, etc.)

pica /'pika/ *f*, *Mil*. pike; bullfighter's goad; pike soldier; stonecutter's hammer. **a p. seca**, in vain. **pasar por las picas**, to suffer hardship. **poner una p. en Flandes**, to triumph over great difficulties

picada /pi'kaða/ *f*, prick; bite; peck; *Aer*. dive

picado /pi'kaðo/ *a* *Sew*. pinked. *m*, *Cul*. hash

picador /pika'ðor/ *m*, horse trainer; meat chopper; horseman armed with a goad (bullfights)

picadura /pika'ðura/ *f*, puncture; prick; sting; *Sew*. pinking; peck (of birds); cut tobacco; black tobacco; beginning of caries in teeth

picajoso /pika'hoso/ *a* hypersensitive, touchy, peevish

picante /pi'kante/ *a* piquant; mordant; hot, highly seasoned. *m*, mordancy; pungency

picapleitos /pika'pleitos/ *m*, *Inf*. shady lawyer, pettifogger

picaporte /pika'porte/ *m*, latch, door catch; door knocker

picar /pi'kar/ *vt* to prick; sting; peck; bite; chop fine; mince; nibble (of fishing); irritate (the skin); *Sew*. pink; burn (the tongue); eat (grapes); goad; spur; stipple (walls); stimulate, encourage; split, cleave; *Mil*. harass; vex; *Mus*. play staccato; —*vi* burn (of the sun); smart (of cuts, etc.); eat sparingly; *Auto*. knock; (*with en*) knock at (doors, etc.); —*vr* be moth-eaten; go rotten (fruit, etc.); grow choppy (of the sea); be piqued; boast

picardear /pikarðe'ar/ *vi* to play the rogue; behave mischievously

picardía /pikar'ðia/ *f*, knavery, roguery; mischievousness; practical joke; wantonness

picaresco /pika'resko/ *a* roguish, picaresque, knavish

pícaro /'pikaro/ **(-ra)** *a* knavish; base, vile; astute; mischievous —*n* rogue

picatoste /pika'toste/ *m*, kind of fritter

picazo /pi'kaθo; pi'kaso/ *m*, blow with a pike or anything pointed; peck, tap with a beak (of birds); sting

picazón /pika'θon; pika'son/ *f*, itch, irritation; annoyance

pichel /pi'tʃel/ *m*, tankard

pichón /pi'tʃon/ **(-ona)** *m*, male pigeon —*n Inf*. darling

pico /'piko/ *m*, beak (of birds); peak; woodpecker; odd amount (e.g. *treinta y p.*, thirty-odd); sharp point; spout (of a jug, etc.); *Inf*. mouth; blarney, gab. **p. de cigüeña**, crane's-bill. **p. de oro**, silver-tongued orator

picor /pi'kor/ *m*, burning sensation in the mouth; smarting, itching, irritation

picoso /pi'koso/ *a* pitted, marked by smallpox

picota /pi'kota/ *f*, pillory; peak; spire

picotazo /piko'taθo; piko'taso/ *m*, peck; dab; sting, bite

picoteado /pikote'aðo/ *a* peaked, having points

picotear /pikote'ar/ *vt* to peck (of a bird); —*vi* toss the head (of horses); *Inf*. chatter senselessly; —*vr Inf*. slang each other

picotero /piko'tero/ *a Inf*. chattering, talkative; indiscreet

pictografía /piktogra'fia/ *f*, picture writing

pictórico /pik'toriko/ *a* pictorial

picudo /pi'kuðo/ *a* pointed, peaked; having a spout; *Inf*. chattering

pie /pie/ *m*, foot; stand, support; stem (of a glass, etc.); standard (of a lamp); *Bot*. trunk, stem; sapling; lees, sediment;

Theat. cue; foot (measure); custom; (metrics) foot; motive, cause; pretext; (metrics) meter. **p. de cabra,** crowbar. **p. de imprenta,** printer's mark, printer's imprint. **p. de piña,** clubfoot. **p. de rey,** calliper. **p. palmado,** webfoot. **al p. de la letra,** punctiliously. *Inf.* **andar con pies de plomo,** to walk warily. **a p.,** on foot. **a p. firme,** without budging; steadfastly. *Inf.* **buscar tres pies al gato,** to look for something that isn't there; twist a person's words. **de a p.,** on foot. **en p. de guerra,** on a wartime footing. *Inf.* **poner pies en polvorosa,** to quit

piedad /pie'ðað/ *f,* piety; pity, compassion; *Art.* pietà

piedra /'pieðra/ *f,* stone; tablet; *Med.* gravel. **p. de amolar,** whetstone, grindstone. **p. angular,** cornerstone (also *Fig.*). **p. caliza,** limestone. **p. clave,** keystone. **p. de construcción,** building stone; child's block. **p. de toque,** touchstone, test. **p. filosofal,** philosopher's stone. **p. fundamental,** foundation stone. **p. miliaria,** milestone. **p. mortuoria,** tombstone. *Fig. Inf.* **no dejar p. sin remover,** to leave no stone unturned. **no dejar p. sobre p.,** to demolish, destroy completely

piel /piel/ *f,* skin; fur; hide; leather; peel (of some fruits); rind (of bacon). **p. de gallina,** *Fig.* goose flesh. **p. de rata,** horse blanket. **p. de Rusia,** Russian leather.

piélago /'pielago/ *m,* high seas; sea, ocean; glut, superabundance

pienso /'pienso/ *m,* *Agr.* fodder

pierna /'pierna/ *f,* *Anat.* leg; *Mech.* shank; leg of a compass. *Inf.* **a p. suelta,** at one's ease. **en piernas,** barelegged

pietismo /pie'tismo/ *m,* pietism

pietista /pie'tista/ *a* pietistic. *mf* pietist

pieza /'pieθa/ 'piesa/ *f,* portion; piece; component part; room; *Theat.* play; roll (of cloth); piece (in chess, etc.); coin; piece (of music). **p. de recambio** *or* **p. de repuesto,** spare part. **p. de recibo,** reception room. *Inf.* **quedarse en una p.,** to be struck dumb

pigmentación /pigmenta'θion; pigmenta'sion/ *f,* pigmentation

pigmento /pig'mento/ *m,* pigment

pignoración /pignora'θion; pignora'sion/ *f,* hypothecation; pawning; mortgage

pignorar /pigno'rar/ *vt* to hypothecate; pawn; mortgage

pigre /'pigre/ *a* lazy; negligent, careless

pigricia /pi'griθia; pi'grisia/ *f,* laziness; negligence

pijama /pi'hama/ *m,* pajamas

pila /'pila/ *f,* trough, basin; heap, pile; *Elec.* battery; *Eccl.* parish; pier, pile; *Phys.* cell. **p. atómica,** atomic pile. **p. bautismal,** *Eccl.* font

pilar /pi'lar/ *m,* fountain basin; milestone; pillar

pilastra /pi'lastra/ *f,* pier, pile; pilaster

píldora /'pildora/ *f,* *Med.* pill; *Inf.* disagreeable news

pillador /piʎa'ðor; piya'ðor/ **(-ra)** *a* pillaging, plundering —*n* plunderer

pillaje /pi'ʎahe; pi'yahe/ *m,* pillaging, looting; robbery, theft

pillar /pi'ʎar; pi'yar/ *vt* to pillage; steal, rob; seize, snatch; *Inf.* surprise, find out (in a lie, etc.). **pillarse el dedo,** to get one's finger caught (in a door, etc.)

pillear /piʎe'ar; piye'ar/ *vi Inf.* to lead a rogue's life

pillería /piʎe'ria; piye'ria/ *f, Inf.* gang of rogues; *Inf.* rogue's trick

pillo /'piʎo; 'piyo/ *m,* rogue, knave

pilón /pi'lon/ *m,* fountain basin; pestle; loaf sugar; pylon

pilotar /pilo'tar/ *vt* to pilot

pilotear /pilote'ar/ *vt* to pilot

piloto /pi'loto/ *m,* pilot; mate (in merchant ships). **p. de pruebas,** test pilot

pimentero /pimen'tero/ *m,* pepper plant; pepper shaker

pimentón /pimen'ton/ *m,* red pepper, cayenne

pimienta /pi'mienta/ *f,* pepper. **p. húngara,** paprika. *Inf.* **ser como una p.,** to be sharp as a needle

pimiento /pi'miento/ *m,* pimento; capsicum; red pepper; pepper plant. **p. de cornetilla,** chili pepper

pina /'pina/ *f,* conical stone; felloe (of a wheel)

pinacoteca /pinako'teka/ *f,* art gallery, picture gallery

pináculo /pi'nakulo/ *m,* pinnacle, summit; climax, culmination; *Archit.* finial

pincel /pin'θel; pin'sel/ *m,* paintbrush; artist, painter; painting technique. **p. para las cejas,** eyebrow pencil

pincelada /pinθe'laða; pinse'laða/ *f,* brushstroke. **dar la última p.,** to add the finishing touch

pincelero /pinθe'lero; pinse'lero/ **(-ra)** *m* seller or maker of paintbrushes; brush box

pinchadura /pintʃa'ðura/ *f,* prick, puncture, piercing; sting; nipping, biting

pinchar /pin'tʃar/ *vt* to prick; puncture; pierce; sting; nip, bite. **no p. ni cortar,** to be ineffective (of persons)

pinchazo /pin'tʃaθo; pin'tʃaso/ *m,* prick; puncture; sting; incitement

pinche /'pintʃe/ *m,* scullion

pineda /pi'neða/ *f,* pinewood

pingajo /piŋ'gaho/ *m, Inf.* tatter, rag

pingo /'piŋgo/ *m, Inf.* tatter, rag; *pl Inf.* cheap clothes

pingüe /'piŋgue/ *a* fat, greasy; fertile, rich

pingüino /piŋ'guino/ *m,* penguin

pino /'pino/ *a* steep. *m, Bot.* pine, deal; *Poet.* ship. **p. de tea,** pitch pine. **p. silvestre,** red fir

pinta /'pinta/ *f,* spot; marking; mark; fleck; look, appearance; pint (measure); drop, drip; spot ball (in billiards)

pintamonas /pinta'monas/ *mf Inf.* dauber

pintar /pin'tar/ vt to paint; describe, picture; exaggerate; —vi show, manifest itself; —vr make up (one's face). Inf. **pintarse solo para,** to be very good at, excel at

pintiparado /pintipa'raðo/ a most similar, very alike; fitting, apposite

pintiparar /pintipa'rar/ vt Inf. to compare

pintor /pin'tor/ **(-ra)** n painter, artist. **p. callejero,** sidewalk artist, pavement artist. **p. de brocha gorda,** house painter

pintoresco /pinto'resko/ a picturesque, quaint, pretty

pintorrear /pintorre'ar/ vt Inf. to daub, paint badly

pintura /pin'tura/ f, painting; paint, pigment; picture, painting; description. **p. a la aguada,** watercolor painting. **p. al fresco,** fresco. **p. al látex,** latex paint. **p. al óleo,** oil painting. **p. al pastel,** pastel drawing

pinturero /pintu'rero/ a Inf. affected, conceited; dandified, overdressed

pinza /'pinθa; 'pinsa/ f, clamp. **p. de la ropa,** clothes peg

pinzas /'pinθas; 'pinsas/ f pl, pincers; pliers; tweezers; forceps. **p. hemostáticas,** arterial forceps

piña /'pina/ f, pineapple; cluster, knot (of people, etc.); pinecone

piñón /pi'non/ m, pine nut; Mech. pinion, chain wheel

pío /'pio/ a pious; compassionate; good; piebald. m, chirping, cheep; Inf. longing

piojo /'pioho/ m, louse

piojoso /pio'hoso/ a lousy; avaricious, stingy

pionero /pio'nero/ m, pioneer

pipa /'pipa/ f, barrel, cask; tobacco pipe; pip (of fruits)

pipar /pi'par/ vi to smoke a pipe

pipiar /pi'piar/ vi to chirp, twitter

pique /'pike/ m, pique, resentment. **a p. de,** on the verge of, about to. **echar a p.,** Naut. to sink; destroy. **irse a p.,** to sink, founder

piquete /pi'kete/ m, puncture, small wound; Mil. picket; pole, stake; small hole (in garments); picket (in strikes)

pira /'pira/ f, funeral pyre; bonfire

piragua /pi'ragua/ f, piragua, canoe

pirámide /pi'ramiðe/ f, pyramid

pirarse /pi'rarse/ vr Inf. to slip away

pirata /pi'rata/ a piratical mf pirate; savage, cruel person

piratear /pirate'ar/ vi to play the pirate

piratería /pirate'ria/ f, piracy; plunder, robbery

pirático /pi'ratiko/ a piratical

pirenaico, pirineo /pire'naiko, piri'neo/ a Pyrenean

Pirineos, los /piri'neos, los/ the Pyrenees

piromancia /piro'manθia; piro'mansia/ f, pyromancy

piropear /pirope'ar/ vt Inf. to pay compliments to

piropo /pi'ropo/ m, carbuncle; Inf. compliment. **echar piropos,** to pay compliments

pirotecnia /piro'teknia/ f, pyrotechnics

pirotécnico /piro'tekniko/ a pyrotechnical. m, pyrotechnist

pirrarse /pi'rrarse/ vr Inf. to desire ardently

pírrico /'pirriko/ a Pyrrhic

pirueta /pi'rueta/ f, pirouette, twirl

pisada /pi'saða/ f, treading, stepping; footprint, footstep; stepping on a person's foot. **seguir las pisadas de alguien,** Fig. to follow in someone's footsteps, imitate someone

pisapapeles /pisapa'peles/ m, paperweight

pisar /pi'sar/ vt to tread upon; trample upon; crush; Mus. press (strings); trespass upon

picaverde /pisa'βerðe/ m, Inf. fop, dandy

piscicultura /pisθikul'tura; pissikul'tura/ f, pisciculture, fish farming

piscina /pis'θina; pis'sina/ f, fishpond; swimming pool; Eccl. piscina

piscolabis /pisko'laβis/ m, Inf. snack, light meal

piso /'piso/ m, treading, trampling; story; floor; flooring; apartment. **p. bajo,** ground floor

pisón /pi'son/ m, rammer, ram

pisotear /pisote'ar/ vt to trample; crush under foot; tread on; step on; humiliate, treat inconsiderately

pisoteo /piso'teo/ m, trampling under foot; treading

pista /'pista/ f, track, trail (of animals); circus ring; racetrack, racecourse. **p. de patinar,** skating rink. **p. de vuelo,** Aer. landing field. Inf. **seguir la p. a,** to spy upon

pistacho /pis'tatʃo/ m, pistachio

pistar /pis'tar/ vt to pestle, pound

pistero /pis'tero/ m, feeding cup

pistilo /pis'tilo/ m, pistil

pistola /pis'tola/ f, pistol. **p. ametralladora,** machine gun.

pistolera /pisto'lera/ f, holster; pistol case

pistolero /pisto'lero/ m, gangster

pistoletazo /pistole'taθo; pistole'taso/ m, pistol shot; pistol wound

pistón /pis'ton/ m, Mus. piston; Mil. percussion cap; Mech. piston

pitada /pi'taða/ f, blast on a whistle, whistling; impertinence

pitanza /pi'tanθa; pi'tansa/ f, alms, charity; Inf. daily food; pittance, scanty remuneration

pitar /pi'tar/ vi to play the whistle; —vt pay (debts); smoke; give alms to

pitido /pi'tiðo/ m, blast on a whistle; whistling (of birds)

pitillera /piti'ʎera; piti'yera/ f, cigarette case; female cigarette maker

pito /'pito/ m, whistle; Mus. fife. Inf. **Cuando pitos flautas, cuando flautas**

pitos, It's always the unexpected that happens. *Inf.* **no valer un p.**, to be not worth a straw

pitoflero /pito'flero/ **(-ra)** *n* mediocre performer (gen. on a wind instrument); *Inf.* talebearer, gossip

pitón /pi'ton/ *m*, *Zool.* python; nascent horn (of goats, etc.); spout; protuberance; *Bot.* sprout

pitorrearse /pitorre'arse/ *vr* to ridicule, mock

pivote /pi'βote/ *m*, pivot, swivel, gudgeon

piyama /pi'yama/ *m*, pajamas

pizarra /pi'θarra; pi'sarra/ *f*, slate; blackboard

pizarrero /piθa'rrero; pisa'rrero/ *m*, slater

pizarrín /piθa'rrin; pisa'rrin/ *m*, slate pencil

pizca /'piθka; 'piska/ *f*, *Inf.* atom, speck, crumb; jot, whit. **¡Ni p.!** Not a scrap!

pizpireta /piθpi'reta; pispi'reta/ *a f*, *Inf.* coquettish; smart; dressed up

placa /'plaka/ *f*, plate, disk; *Art.* plaque; *Photo.* plate; star (insignia). **p. recordatorio**, commemorative plaque

pláceme /'plaθeme; 'plaseme/ *m*, congratulation

placentero /plaθen'tero; plasen'tero/ *a* agreeable, pleasant

placer /pla'θer; pla'ser/ *vt irr* to please, give pleasure to, gratify. *m*, *Naut.* reef, sandbank; pleasure; wish, desire; permission, consent; entertainment, diversion. **a p.**, at one's convenience; at leisure —*Pres. Indic.* **plazco**, **places**, etc —*Preterite* **plugo**, **pluguieron**. *Pres. Subjunc.* **plazca**, etc —*Imperf. Subjunc.* **pluguiese**, etc.

placible /pla'θiβle; pla'siβle/ *a* agreeable, pleasant

plácido /'plaθido; 'plasido/ *a* placid, calm, serene

placiente /pla'θiente; pla'siente/ *a* pleasing, attractive

plácito /'plaθito; 'plasito/ *m*, decision, judgment, opinion

plaga /'plaga/ *f*, plague; disaster, calamity; epidemic; glut; pest; grief

plagar /pla'gar/ *vt* (*with de*) to infect with; —*vr* (*with de*) be covered with; be overrun by; be infested with

plagiar /pla'hiar/ *vt* to plagiarize, copy; kidnap, hold for ransom

plagiario /pla'hiario/ **(-ia)** *n* plagiarist

plagio /'plahio/ *m*, plagiary; kidnapping

plan /plan/ *m*, plan; scheme; plane. **p. quinquenal**, five-year plan

plana /'plana/ *f*, sheet, page; mason's trowel; plain. **p. mayor**, (*Mil. Nav.*) staff

planadora /plana'δora/ *f*, steamroller

plancha /'plantʃa/ *f*, sheet, slab, plate; flatiron; horizontal suspension (in gymnastics); *Naut.* gangway, gangplank; *Inf.* howler

planchado /plan'tʃaδo/ *m*, ironing; ironing to be done or already finished

planchador /plantʃa'δor/ **(-ra)** *n* ironer

planchar /plan'tʃar/ *vt* to iron, press with an iron

planeador /planea'δor/ *m*, *Aer.* glider

planear /plane'ar/ *vt* to plan out; make plans for; —*vi Aer.* glide

planeta /pla'neta/ *m*, planet

planetario /plane'tario/ *a* planetary. *m*, planetarium

planicie /pla'niθie; pla'nisie/ *f*, levelness, evenness; plain

plano /'plano/ *a* flat, level; plane. *m*, *Geom.* plane; plan, map; *Aer.* aileron, wing

planta /'planta/ *f*, *Bot.* plant; sole (of the foot); plantation; layout, plan; position of the feet (in dancing, fencing); scheme, project. **p. baja**, ground floor. **p. vivaz**, perennial plant. *Inf.* **buena p.**, good appearance

plantación /planta'θion; planta'sion/ *f*, planting; plantation; nursery

plantador /planta'δor/ **(-ra)** *n* planter. *m*, *Agr.* dibble. *f*, **plantadora**, mechanical planter

plantar /plan'tar/ *vt* to plant; erect; place; found, set up; pose (a problem); raise (a question, etc.); *Inf.* leave in the lurch; —*vr* take up one's position; jib (of horses); oppose

planteamiento /plantea'miento/ *m*, execution; putting into practice; planning; statement (of problems)

plantel /plan'tel/ *m*, nursery garden; training school, nursery

plantilla /plan'tiʎa; plan'tiya/ *f*, young plant; insole (of shoes); *Mech.* template, jig

plantío /plan'tio/ *m*, plantation, afforestation; planting —*a* planted or ready for planting (ground)

plantón /plan'ton/ *m*, plant or sapling ready for transplanting; *Bot.* cutting; doorkeeper, porter. **dar un p. (a)**, to keep (a person) waiting a long time

plañidero /plaɲi'δero/ *a* mournful, piteous, anguished

plañido /pla'ɲiδo/ *m*, lament, weeping, wailing

plañir /pla'ɲir/ *vi and vt irr* to lament, wail, weep. See **tañer**

plasma /'plasma/ *m*, plasma

plasmar /plas'mar/ *vt* to mold, throw (pottery)

plástica /'plastika/ *f*, art of clay modeling; plastic

plástico /'plastiko/ *a* plastic; flexible, malleable, soft

plata /'plata/ *f*, silver; silver (coins); money; white. **p. labrada**, silverware

plataforma /plata'forma/ *f*, platform; running board (of a train); *Rail.* turntable

plátano /'platano/ *m*, banana tree, banana; plantain; plane tree

platea /pla'tea/ *f*, *Theat.* pit. **butaca de p.**, pit stall

plateado /plate'aðo/ *a* silvered; silver-plated; silvery

platear /plate'ar/ *vt* to electroplate, silver

platería /plate'ria/ *f*, silversmith's art or trade; silversmith's shop or workshop

platero /pla'tero/ *m*, silversmith; jeweler

plática /'platika/ *f*, conversation; exhortation, sermon; address, discourse

platicar /plati'kar/ *vt and vi* to converse (about)

platillo /pla'tiʎo; pla'tiyo/ *m*, saucer; kitty (in card games); pan (of a scale); *pl* cymbals

platinado /plati'naðo/ *m*, plating

platino /pla'tino/ *m*, platinum

platívolo /pla'tiβolo/ *m*, flying saucer

plato /'plato/ *m*, plate; dish; *Cul.* course, dish; pan (of a scale). **p. sopero,** soup plate. **p. trinchero,** meat dish. *Inf.* **comer en un mismo p.,** to be on intimate terms. **nada entre dos platos,** much ado about nothing

platónico /pla'toniko/ *a* Platonic

plausible /plau'siβle/ *a* plausible, reasonable

playa /'plaia/ *f*, beach, seashore, strand

plaza /'plaθa; 'plasa/ *f*, square (in a town, etc.); marketplace; fortified town; space; duration; employment, post.; *Com.* market. **p. de armas,** garrison town; military camp. **p. de toros,** bullring. **p. fuerte,** strong place, fortress. **sentar p.,** to enlist in the army

plazo /'plaθo; 'plaso/ *m*, term, duration; expiration of term, date of payment; installment. **a plazos,** *Com.* by installments, on the installment system

plazoleta /plaθo'leta; plaso'leta/ *f*, small square (in gardens, etc.)

pleamar /plea'mar/ *f*, *Naut.* high water

plebe /'pleβe/ *f*, common people; rabble, mob

plebeyo /ple'βeio/ **(-ya)** *a* plebeian —*n* commoner, plebeian

plebiscito /pleβis'θito; pleβis'sito/ *m*, plebiscite

plegable /ple'gaβle/ *a* foldable

plegadera /plega'ðera/ *f*, folder; folding knife; paper folder

plegadizo /plega'ðiθo; plega'ðiso/ *a* folding; collapsible; jointed

plegado /ple'gaðo/ *m*, pleating; folding

plegador /plega'ðor/ *a* folding. *m*, folding machine

plegadura /plega'ðura/ *f*, folding, doubling; fold, pleat

plegar /ple'gar/ *vt irr* to fold; pleat; *Sew.* gather; —*vr* submit, give in. See **acertar**.

plegaria /ple'garia/ *f*, fervent prayer

pleitear /pleite'ar/ *vt* to go to court about; indulge in litigation

pleitista /plei'tista/ *a* quarrelsome, litigious

pleito /'pleito/ *m*, action, lawsuit; dispute, quarrel; litigation. **p. de familia,** family squabble. **ver el p.,** *Law.* to try a case

plenario /ple'nario/ *a* full, complete; *Law.* plenary

plenipotencia /plenipo'tenθia; plenipo'tensia/ *f*, full powers (diplomatic, etc.)

plenipotenciario /plenipoten'θiario; plenipoten'siario/ *a and m*, plenipotentiary

plenitud /pleni'tuð/ *f*, fullness, completeness; plenitude, abundance

pleno /'pleno/ *a* full. *m*, general meeting

pleuresía /pleure'sia/ *f*, pleurisy

pliego /'pliego/ *m*, sheet (of paper); letter, packet of papers

pliegue /'pliege/ *m*, fold, pleat; *Sew.* gather

plisar /pli'sar/ *vt* to pleat; fold

plomada /plo'maða/ *f*, plummet; sounding lead; plumb, lead

plomería /plome'ria/ *f*, plumbing; plumbing business; lead roofing

plomero /plo'mero/ *m*, plumber

plomizo /plo'miθo; plo'miso/ *a* lead-like; lead-colored, gray

plomo /'plomo/ *m*, lead (metal); plummet; bullet; *Inf.* bore, tedious person

pluma /'pluma/ *f*, feather; pen; plumage; quill; penmanship; writer; writing profession. **p. estilográfica,** fountain pen. **a vuela p.,** as the pen writes, written in a hurry

plumado /plu'maðo/ *a* feathered

plumaje /plu'mahe/ *m*, plumage, feathers; plume

plúmeo /'plumeo/ *a* feathered, plumed

plumero /plu'mero/ *m*, feather duster; plume, feather; plumage

plumón /plu'mon/ *m*, down; feather bed

plural /plu'ral/ *a and m*, plural

pluralidad /plurali'ðað/ *f*, plurality; multitude, number

plurilingüe /pluri'lingue/ *a* multilingual

plusmarquista /plusmar'kista/ *mf* *Sports.* recordholder

plutocracia /pluto'kraθia; pluto'krasia/ *f*, plutocracy

plutócrata /plu'tokrata/ *mf* plutocrat

pluviómetro /plu'βiometro/ *m*, rain gauge

poblacho /po'βlatʃo/ *m*, miserable town or village

población /poβla'θion; poβla'sion/ *f*, peopling; population; town

poblado /po'βlaðo/ *m*, inhabited place; town; village

poblador /poβla'ðor/ **(-ra)** *a* populating —*n* colonist, settler

poblar /po'βlar/ *vt irr* to colonize; people, populate; breed fast; stock, supply; —*vr* put forth leaves (of trees). See **contar**

pobre /'poβre/ *a* poor; indigent, needy; mediocre; unfortunate; humble, meek. *mf* beggar, pauper, needy person. *Inf.* **ser p. de solemnidad,** to be down and out

pobretón /poβre'ton/ *a* extremely needy

pobreza /po'βreθa; po'βresa/ *f*, poverty, need; shortage; timidity; *Mineral.* baseness; poorness (of soil, etc.)

pocilga /po'θilga; po'silga/ *f*, pigsty; *Inf.* filthy place

poción /po'θion; po'sion/ *f*, potion, drink; mixture, dose

poco /'poko/ *a* little, scanty; *pl* few. *m*, small amount, a little —*adv* little; shortly, in a little while. **p. a p.**, by degrees, little by little; slowly. **p. más o menos**, more or less, approximately. **por p.**, almost, nearly (always used with the present tense, e.g., *Por p. me caigo*, I almost fell). **tener en p. (a)**, to have a poor opinion of; undervalue

podadera /poða'ðera/ *f*, pruning knife

podar /po'ðar/ *vt Agr.* to prune, trim

poder /po'ðer/ *m*, power; authority, jurisdiction; *Law.* power of attorney; strength; ability; proxy; efficacy; possession; *pl* authority; power of attorney. **los poderes constituidos**, the established authorities; the powers that be. **p. de adquisición**, purchasing power. **casarse por poderes**, to be married by proxy

poder /po'ðer/ *vt irr* to be able to (e.g., *Podemos comprar estas naranjas*, We can (are able to) buy these oranges). *Dice que la calamidad podía haberse evitado*, He says that the disaster could have been averted). **p.** also expresses possibility (e.g., *Pueden haber ido a la ciudad*, They may have gone to the city. *¡Qué distinta pudo haber sido su vida!* How different his life might have been!) —*impers* to be possible. **a más no p.**, of necessity, without being able to help it; to the utmost. **no p. con**, to be unable to control or manage. **no p. hacer más**, to have no alternative, have to; be unable to do more. **no p. menos de**, to be obliged to, have no alternative but. **no p. contener su emoción**, to be overcome with emotion. **no p. ver a**, to hate (persons) —*impers* **Puede que venga esta tarde**, He may come (perhaps he will come) this afternoon —*Pres. Part.* **pudiendo**. *Pres. Indic.* **puedo, puedes, puede, pueden.** *Fut.* **podré**, etc —*Condit.* **podría**, etc —*Preterite* **pude, pudiste**, etc —*Pres. Subjunc.* **pueda, puedas, pueda, puedan.** *Imperf. Subjunc.* **pudiese**, etc.

poderío /poðe'rio/ *m*, power, authority; sway, rule; dominion; wealth

poderoso /poðe'roso/ *a* powerful; opulent; effective, efficacious; mighty, magnificent

podredumbre /poðre'ðumbre/ *f*, decay; pus; *Fig.* canker, anguish

podredura, podrición /poðre'ðura, po-ðri'θion; poðre'ðura, poðri'sion/ *f*, putrefaction; decay

podrido /po'ðriðo/ *a* rotten; putrid; corrupt; decayed

podrir /po'ðrir/ *vt* See **pudrir**

poema /po'ema/ *m*, poem. **p. sinfónico**, tone poem

poesía /poe'sia/ *f*, poetry, verse; lyric, poem

poeta /po'eta/ *m*, poet

poética /po'etika/ *f*, poetics

poético /po'etiko/ *a* poetical

poetisa /poe'tisa/ *f*, poetess

poetizar /poeti'θar; poeti'sar/ *vi* to write verses; —*vt* poeticize

polaco /po'lako/ **(-ca)** *a* Polish —*n* Pole. *m*, Polish (language)

polainas /po'lainas/ *f pl*, leggings, puttees, gaiters

polar /po'lar/ *a* polar

polarización /polariθa'θion; polarisa'sion/ *f*, polarization

polarizar /polari'θar; polari'sar/ *vt* to polarize

polca /'polka/ *f*, polka

polea /po'lea/ *f*, pulley; *Naut.* block

polémica /po'lemika/ *f*, polemic, controversy, dispute

polémico /po'lemiko/ *a* polemical

polemista /pole'mista/ *mf* disputant, controversialist

polen /'polen/ *m*, pollen

polichinela /politʃi'nela/ *m*, Punchinello

policía /poli'θia; poli'sia/ *f*, police; government, polity, administration; civility, courtesy; cleanliness, tidiness. *m*, policeman. **p. urbana**, city police

policíaco /poli'θiako; poli'siako/ *a* police; detective

polifacético /polifa'θetiko; polifa'setiko/ *a* many-sided

polifónico /poli'foniko/ *a* polyphonic

poligamia /poli'gamia/ *f*, polygamy

polígamo /po'ligamo/ **(-ma)** *a* polygamous —*n* polygamist

políglota /poli'glota/ **(-ta)** *n* polyglot. *f*, polyglot Bible

polígono /po'ligono/ *a* polygonal. *m*, polygon

polilla /po'liʎa; po'liya/ *f*, moth; moth grub; destroyer, ravager

polinesio /poli'nesio/ **(-ia)** *a* and *n* Polynesian

polinización /poliniθa'θion; polinisa'sion/ *f*, pollination

poliomielitis /poliomie'litis/ *f*, poliomyelitis, polio

pólipo /'polipo/ *m*, *Zool.* polyp; octopus; *Med.* polyp

polista /po'lista/ *mf* polo player

politécnico /poli'tekniko/ *a* polytechnic

politeísta /polite'ista/ *a* polytheistic. *mf* polytheist

política /po'litika/ *f*, politics; civility, courtesy; diplomacy; tact; policy

politicastro /politi'kastro/ *m*, corrupt politician

político /po'litiko/ *a* political; civil, courteous; in-law, by marriage (relationships). *m*, politician

politiquear /politike'ar/ *vi Inf.* to dabble in politics, talk politics

póliza /'poliθa; 'polisa/ *f*, *Com.* policy; *Com.* draft; share certificate; revenue stamp; admission ticket; lampoon. **p. a prima fija**, fixed-premium policy. **p. de**

seguros, insurance policy. **p. dotal,** endowment policy

polizón /poli'θon; poli'son/ *m,* loafer, tramp; stowaway; bustle (of a dress)

polla /'poʎa; 'poya/ *f,* pullet; *Inf.* flapper, young woman

pollastro /po'ʎastro; po'yastro/ **(-ra)** *n* pullet.

pollera /po'ʎera; po'yera/ *f,* female poultry breeder or seller; chicken coop; go-cart

pollería /poʎe'ria; poye'ria/ *f,* poultry market or shop

pollero /po'ʎero; po'yero/ *n* poultry breeder; poulterer. *m,* hen coop

pollo /'poʎo; 'poyo/ *m,* chicken; *Inf.* youth, stripling; *Fig. Inf.* downy bird. *Inf.* **p. pera,** young blood, lad. **sacar pollos,** to hatch chickens

polo /'polo/ *m,* pole (all meanings); *Fig.* support; popular Andalusian song; *Sports.* polo. **de p. a p.,** from pole to pole

polonés /polo'nes/ **(-esa)** *a* Polish —*n* Pole

Polonia /po'lonia/ Poland

poltrón /pol'tron/ *a* lazy, idle

poltronería /poltrone'ria/ *f,* idleness, laziness

polución /polu'θion; polu'sion/ *f, Med.* ejaculation

poluto /po'luto/ *a* filthy, unclean

polvareda /polβa'reða/ *f,* dust cloud; storm, agitation

polvera /pol'βera/ *f,* powder bowl; powder puff; powder compact

polvo /'polβo/ *m,* dust; powder; pinch (of snuff, etc.); *pl* face or dusting powder. **Se hizo como por polvos de la madre celestina,** It was done as if by magic. *Inf.* **limpio de p. y paja,** gratis, for nothing; net (of profit)

pólvora /'polβora/ *f,* gunpowder; bad temper. **p. de algodón,** guncotton.

polvoriento /polβo'riento/ *a* dusty; powdery, covered with powder

polvorín /polβo'rin/ *m,* very fine powder; powder magazine; powder flask

pomada /po'maða/ *f,* pomade; salve, ointment

pómez /'pomeθ; 'pomes/ *f,* pumice stone (piedra p.)

pomo /'pomo/ *m, Bot.* pome; pomander; nosegay; pommel, hilt (of a sword); handle; rose (of watering can)

pompa /'pompa/ *f,* pomp, splendor; ceremonial procession; air bubble; peacock's outspread tail; *Naut.* pump; billowing of clothes in the wind

Pompeya /pom'peia/ Pompeii

pomposo /pom'poso/ *a* stately, ostentatious, magnificent; inflated, pompous; florid, bombastic

pómulo /'pomulo/ *m,* cheekbone

ponche /'pontʃe/ *m,* punch, toddy

ponchera /pon'tʃera/ *f,* punch bowl

poncho /'pontʃo/ *a* lazy, negligent. *m,* military cloak; poncho, cape

ponderación /pondera'θion; pondera-'sion/ *f,* weighing; reflection, consideration; exaggeration

ponderador /pondera'ðor/ *a* reflective, deliberate; exaggerated

ponderar /ponde'rar/ *vt* to weigh; consider, ponder; exaggerate; overpraise

ponderoso /ponde'roso/ *a* heavy; ponderous; circumspect

ponencia /po'nenθia; po'nensia/ *f,* clause, section; office of referee or arbitrator; report, referendum

poner /po'ner/ *vt irr* to place, put; arrange; set (the table); bet, stake; appoint (to an office); call, name; lay (eggs); set down (in writing); calculate, count; suppose; leave to a person's judgment; risk; contribute; prepare; need, take; cause, inspire (emotions); make, cause; adapt; add; cause to become (angry, etc.); insult, praise; (with *prep a* + *infin*) begin to. **p. a contribución,** to lay under contribution, turn to account, utilize. **ponerle el cascabel al gato** *or* **el collar al gato,** to bell the cat. **p. los cuernos (a),** to cuckold. **p. al corriente,** to bring up to date, inform. **p. a prueba,** to test. **p. casa,** to set up house. *Inf.* **p. colorado a,** to make blush. **p. coto a,** to put a stop to, check. **p. en comparación,** to compare. **p. conato en,** to put a great deal of effort into. **p. en cotejo,** to collate. **p. en limpio,** to make a fair copy (of). **p. en marcha,** to start, set in motion. **p. en práctica,** to put into effect. **p. por caso,** to take as an example (e.g. *Pongamos por caso...* For example,...). **p. por encima (de),** to prefer —*vr* to place oneself; become; put on (garments, etc.); dirty or stain oneself; set (of the sun, stars); oppose; deck oneself, dress oneself up; arrive; (with *prep a* + *infin*) begin to. **ponerse al corriente,** to bring oneself up to date. **ponerse bien,** to improve; get better (in health). **ponerse colorado,** to blush, flush. **p. una base racional a la fe,** to give faith a rational foundation. **p. los cimientos de,** lay the foundation of, lay the foundations for. **p. una conferencia,** to make a long-distance call —*Pres. Indic.* **pongo, pones,** etc —*Fut.* **pondré,** etc —*Condit.* **pondría,** etc —*Imperat.* **pon.** *Past Part.* **puesto.** *Preterite* **puse, pusiste,** etc —*Pres. Subjunc.* **ponga,** etc —*Imperf. Subjunc.* **pusiese,** etc.

poniente /po'niente/ *m,* west; west wind

pontazgo /pon'taθgo; pon'tasgo/ *m,* bridge toll

pontificado /pontifi'kaðo/ *m,* pontificate, papacy

pontífice /pon'tifiθe; pon'tifise/ *m,* pontifex; pope, pontiff; archbishop; bishop

ponzoña /pon'θoɲa; pon'soɲa/ *f,* poison, venom

ponzoñoso /ponθo'ɲoso; ponso'ɲoso/ *a* poisonous, venomous; noxious; harmful

popa /'popa/ *f, Naut.* stern, poop. **en p.,** abaft, astern, aft

populachería /populat∫e'ria/ f, cheap popularity with the rabble

populachero /popula't∫ero/ a mob, vulgar

populacho /popu'lat∫o/ m, mob, rabble

popular /popu'lar/ a popular

popularidad /populari'ðað/ f, popularity

popularizar /populari'θar; populari'sar/ vt to popularize; —vr grow popular

populoso /popu'loso/ a populous, crowded

popurrí /popu'rri/ m, Cul. stew; potpourri; miscellany

poquedad /poke'ðað/ f, paucity, scarcity; timidity, cowardice; trifle, mere nothing

poquísimo /po'kisimo/ a superl poco very little

poquito /po'kito/ m, very little

por /por/ prep for; by; through, along; during; because, as (e.g. Lo desecharon p. viejo, They threw it away because it was old); however (e.g. p. bonito que sea, however pretty it is); during; in order to (e.g. Lo hice p. no ofenderla, I did it in order not to offend her); toward, in favor of, for; for the sake of; on account of, by reason of (e.g. No pudo venir p. estar enfermo, He could not come on account of his illness); via, by (e.g. p. correo aéreo, by airmail); as for (e.g. P. mí, lo rechazo, As for me, I refuse it. p. mi cuenta, to my way of thinking; on my own); in exchange for (e.g. Me vendió dos libros p. seis dólares, He sold me two books for six dollars); in the name of; as a substitute for, instead of (e.g. Hace mi trabajo p. mí, He is doing my work for me); per. **Por** has several uses: 1. Introduces the agent ⋯ ⋯ssive (e.g. La novela fue escrita ⋯ ⋯ novel was written by him). 2. ⋯ ⋯vement through, along or ⋯ ⋯laban p. la calle, They ⋯ ⋯ong (or down) the street). 3. Deno⋯ ⋯ at or during which an action occurs (e.g. Ocurrió p. entonces un acontecimiento de importancia, About that time an important event occurred). 4. Expresses rate or proportion (e.g. seis por ciento, six percent). 5. With certain verbs, means "to be' and expresses vague futurity (e.g. El libro queda p. escribir, The book remains to be written). **p. cortesía,** by courtesy, out of politeness. **p. cortesía de,** by courtesy of. **p. escrito,** in writing. **p. fas or p. nefas,** by fair means or foul; at any cost. **p. mucho que,** however great, however much; in spite of, notwithstanding. **¿P. qué?** Why? **p. si acaso,** in case, if by chance. **estar p.,** to be about to; be inclined to. **P. un clavo se pierde la herradura,** For want of a nail, the shoe was lost.

porcelana /porθe'lana; porse'lana/ f, porcelain, china; chinaware

porcentaje /porθen'tahe; porsen'tahe/ m, percentage

porción /por'θion; por'sion/ f, portion; Com. share; Inf. crowd; allowance, pittance

porcionista /porθio'nista; porsio'nista/ mf shareholder; sharer; boarding school student

pordiosear /porðiose'ar/ vi to ask alms, beg

pordioseo /porðio'seo/ m, asking alms, begging

pordiosero /porðio'sero/ (-ra) a begging —n beggar

porfía /por'fia/ f, obstinacy; importunity; tenacity. **a p.,** in competition

porfiado /por'fiaðo/ a obstinate, obdurate, persistent

porfiar /por'fiar/ vi to be obstinate, insist; persist

pórfido /'porfiðo/ m, porphyry

pormenor /porme'nor/ m, particular, detail (gen. pl); secondary matter

pormenorizar /pormenori'θar; pormenori'sar/ vt to describe in detail

pornografía /pornogra'fia/ f, pornography

pornográfico /porno'grafiko/ a pornographic, obscene

poro /'poro/ m, pore

poroso /po'roso/ a porous, leaky

porque /'porke/ conjunc because, for; in order that

porqué /por'ke/ m, reason, wherefore, why; Inf. money. **el cómo y el p.,** the why and the wherefore

porquería /porke'ria/ f, Inf. filth, nastiness; dirty trick; rudeness, gross act; trifle, thing of no account

porra /'porra/ f, club, bludgeon; last player (in children's games); Inf. vanity, boastfulness; bore, tedious person

porrada /po'rraða/ f, blow with a club; buffet, knock, fall; Inf. folly; glut, abundance

porrazo /po'rraθo; po'rraso/ m, blow with a club; buffet, knock, fall

porrear /porre'ar/ vi to insist, harp on

porrería /porre'ria/ f, Inf. folly; obduracy, persistence

porreta /po'rreta/ f, green leaves of leeks, onions, and cereals. Inf. **en p.,** stark-naked

portaaviones /portaa'βiones/ m, aircraft carrier

portacartas /porta'kartas/ m, mailbag

portachuelo /porta't∫uelo/ m, defile, narrow mountain pass

portada /por'taða/ f, front, facade; frontispiece, title page; portal, doorway

portado /por'taðo/ (**bien** or **mal**) a well- or ill-dressed or behaved

portador /porta'ðor/ (**-ra**) n carrier. m, Com. bearer; Mech. carrier

portaestandarte /ˌportaestan'darte/ m, standard-bearer

portafolio /porta'folio/ m, portfolio

portafusil /porta'fusil/ m, rifle sling

portal /por'tal/ *m*, entrance, porch; portico; city gate

portalámpara /porta'lampara/ *f*, lamp holder; *Elec.* socket

portalibros /porta'liβros/ *m*, bookstrap

portalón /porta'lon/ *m*, gangway

portamanteo /portaman'teo/ *m*, traveling bag

portamonedas /portamo'neðas/ *m*, pocketbook; handbag, purse

portanuevas /porta'nueβas/ *mf* bringer of news, newsmonger

portaobjetos /portaoβ'hetos/ *m*, stage (of a microscope)

portar /por'tar/ *vt* to retrieve (of dogs); carry (arms); —*vr* behave (well or badly); bear oneself, act; be well, or ill (in health)

portátil /por'tatil/ *a* portable

portavoz /porta'βoθ; porta'βos/ *m*, megaphone; spokesman, mouthpiece

portazgo /por'taθgo; por'tasgo/ *m*, toll; tollbooth

portazguero /portaθ'gero; portas'gero/ *m*, toll collector

portazo /por'taθo; por'taso/ *m*, bang of the door; slamming the door in a person's face

porte /'porte/ *m*, transport; *Com.* carriage; postage; freight, transport cost; porterage; behavior, conduct; bearing; looks; capacity, volume; size, dimension; nobility (of descent); *Naut.* tonnage. **p. pagado**, charges prepaid

porteador /portea'ðor/ *m*, carrier; porter; carter

portear /porte'ar/ *vt* to carry, transport; —*vr* migrate (of birds)

portento /por'tento/ *m*, marvel, prodigy, portent

portentoso /porten'toso/ *a* marvelous, portentous

portería /porte'ria/ *f*, porter's lodge; porter's employment; *Sports.* goal

portero /por'tero/ **(-ra)** *n* doorman, doorkeeper; porter; concierge; janitor; *Sports.* goalkeeper. **p. eléctrico**, door buzzer

portezuela /porte'θuela; porte'suela/ *f*, *dim* small door; carriage door; pocket flap

pórtico /'portiko/ *m*, portico, piazza; porch; vestibule, hall

portillo /por'tiλo; por'tiyo/ *m*, breach, opening; defile, narrow pass; *Fig.* loophole

portón /por'ton/ *m*, hall door, inner door

portorriqueño /portorri'keɲo/ **(-ña)** *a* and *n* Puerto Rican

portuario /por'tuario/ *a* dock, port

portugués /portu'ges/ **(-esa)** *a* and *n* Portuguese. *m*, Portuguese (language)

portuguesada /portuge'saða/ *f*, exaggeration

porvenir /porβe'nir/ *m*, future time

¡porvida! /por'βiða/ *interj* By the saints! By the Almighty!

pos /pos/ *prefix* after; behind. Also *adv* **en p.**, with the same meanings

posa /'posa/ *f*, tolling bell; *pl* buttocks

posada /po'saða/ *f*, dwelling; inn, tavern; lodging; hospitality

posaderas /posa'ðeras/ *f pl*, buttocks

posadero /posa'ðero/ **(-ra)** *n* innkeeper; boardinghouse keeper

posar /po'sar/ *vi* to lodge, live; rest; alight, perch; —*vt* set down (a burden); —*vr* settle (liquids); (*with en* or *sobre*) perch upon

posdata /pos'ðata/ *f*, P.S., postscript

pose /'pose/ *f*, *Photo.* time exposure; *Inf.* pose

poseedor /posee'ðor/ **(-ra)** *n* possessor, holder

poseer /pose'er/ *vt irr* to own, possess; know (a language, etc.); —*vr* restrain oneself. **estar poseído por**, to be possessed by (passion, etc.); be thoroughly convinced of. See **creer**

posesión /pose'sion/ *f*, ownership, occupancy; possession; property, territory (often *pl*)

posesionarse /posesio'narse/ *vr* to take possession; lay hold (of)

posesivo /pose'siβo/ *a* possessive

posesor /pose'sor/ **(-ra)** *n* owner, possessor

posfecha /pos'fetʃa/ *f*, postdate

posguerra /pos'gerra/ *f*, postwar period

posibilidad /posiβili'ðað/ *f*, possibility; probability; opportunity, means, chance; *pl* property, wealth

posibilitar /posiβili'tar/ *vt* to make possible, facilitate

posible /po'siβle/ *a* possible. *m pl*, property, personal wealth. **hacer lo p.** *or* **hacer todo lo p.**, to do everything possible; do one's best

posición /posi'θion; posi'sion/ *f*, placing; position; situation; status

positivo /posi'tiβo/ *a* positive; certain, definite; (*Math. Elec.*) plus; true, real

posma /'posma/ *f*, *Inf.* sluggishness, sloth

posmeridiano /posmeri'ðiano/ *a* and *m*, postmeridian

poso /'poso/ *m*, sediment; lees, dregs; repose, quietness

posponer /pospo'ner/ *vt irr* (*with prep a*) to place after; make subordinate to; value less than. See **poner**

posta /'posta/ *f*, post horse; stage, post; stake (cards)

postal /pos'tal/ *a* postal. *f*, postcard, postal card

poste /'poste/ *m*, post, stake

postema /pos'tema/ *f*, tumor, abscess; bore, tedious person

postergación /posterga'θion; posterga'sion/ *f*, delay; delaying; relegation; disregard of seniority (in promotion)

postergar /poster'gar/ *vt* to delay; disregard a senior claim to promotion

posteridad /posteri'ðað/ *f*, descendants; posterity

posterior /poste'rior/ *a* back, rear; hind; subsequent

posterioridad /posteriori'ðað/ *f*, posteriority

posteriormente /posterior'mente/ *adv* later, subsequently

postigo /pos'tiɣo/ *m*, secret door; grating, hatch; postern; shutter (of a window)

postizo /pos'tiθo; pos'tiso/ *a* false, artificial, not natural. *m*, switch of false hair

postor /pos'tor/ *m*, bidder (at an auction)

postración /postra'θion; postra'sion/ *f*, prostration; exhaustion; depression, distress

postrar /pos'trar/ *vt* to cast down, demolish; prostrate, exhaust; —*vr* kneel down; be prostrated or exhausted

postre /'postre/ *a* last (in order). *m*, *Cul.* dessert. **a la p.**, at last, finally

postrero /pos'trero/ *a* last (in order); rearmost, hindmost

postrimeramente /postrimera'mente/ *adv* lastly, finally

postulación /postula'θion; postula'sion/ *f*, entreaty, request

postulado /postu'laðo/ *m*, assumption; supposition; working hypothesis; *Geom.* postulate

postulante /postu'lante/ **(-ta)** *n Eccl.* postulant, applicant, candidate

postular /postu'lar/ *vt* to postulate

póstumo /'postumo/ *a* posthumous

postura /pos'tura/ *f*, posture, bearing; laying (of an egg); bid (at an auction); position; agreement, pact; bet, stake; planting; transplanted tree. **p. de vida**, way of life

potable /po'taβle/ *a* drinkable. **agua p.**, drinking water

potaje /po'tahe/ *m*, stew, potage; dried vegetables; mixed drink; hotchpotch

potasa /po'tasa/ *f*, potash

potasio /po'tasio/ *m*, potassium

pote /'pote/ *m*, pot; jar; flowerpot; *Cul.* cauldron; *Cul.* stew

potencia /po'tenθia; po'tensia/ *f*, power; potency; *Mech.* performance, capacity; strength, force; *Math.* power; rule, dominion

potencial /poten'θial; poten'sial/ *a* potential

potente /po'tente/ *a* potent; powerful; *Inf.* enormous

potestad /potes'tað/ *f*, authority, power; podesta, Italian magistrate; potentate; *Math.* power; *pl* angelic powers

potestativo /potesta'tiβo/ *a Law.* facultative

potingue /po'tiŋgue/ *m*, *Inf.* brew; mixture; lotion; medicine; filthy place, pigsty

potra /'potra/ *f*, filly

potrada /po'traða/ *f*, herd of colts

potrear /potre'ar/ *vt Inf.* to tease, annoy

potro /'potro/ *m*, colt, foal; rack (for torture); vaulting horse. **p. mesteño**, mustang

pozo /'poθo; 'poso/ *m*, well; shaft (in a mine). *Auto.* **p. colector**, crankcase

práctica /'praktika/ *f*, practice; custom, habit; method; exercise

practicabilidad /praktikaβili'ðað/ *f*, feasibility

practicable /prakti'kaβle/ *a* feasible, practicable

practicante /prakti'kante/ *m*, medical practitioner; medical student; *Med.* intern; first-aid practitioner

practicar /prakti'kar/ *vt* to execute, perform; practice; make

práctico /'praktiko/ *a* practical; experienced, expert; workable. *m*, *Naut.* pilot

pradera /pra'ðera/ *f*, meadow, field; lawn

prado /'praðo/ *m*, meadow; grassland; field; lawn; walk (in cities)

Praga /'praga/ Prague

pragmatista /pragma'tista/ *a* pragmatic. *mf* pragmatist

pravedad /praβe'ðað/ *f*, wickedness, immorality, depravity

pravo /'praβo/ *a* wicked, immoral, depraved

pre /pre/ *m*, *Mil.* daily pay —*prep insep* pre-

preámbulo /pre'ambulo/ *m*, preamble, preface; importunate digression

precario /pre'kario/ *a* precarious, uncertain, insecure

precaución /prekau'θion; prekau'sion/ *f*, precaution, safeguard

precaucionarse /prekauθio'narse; prekausio'narse/ *vr* to take precautions, safeguard oneself

precautelar /prekaute'lar/ *vt* to forewarn; take precautions

precaver /preka'βer/ *vt* to prevent, avoid; —*vr* (*with de or contra*) guard against

precavido /preka'βiðo/ *a* cautious, forewarned

precedencia /preθe'ðenθia; prese'ðensia/ *f*, priority, precedence; superiority; preference, precedence

precedente /preθe'ðente; prese'ðente/ *a* preceding. *m*, antecedent; precedent

preceder /preθe'ðer; prese'ðer/ *vt* to precede; have precedence over, be superior to

preceptivo /preθep'tiβo; presep'tiβo/ *a* preceptive; didactic

precepto /pre'θepto; pre'septo/ *m*, precept; order, injunction; rule, commandment. **de p.**, obligatory

preceptor /preθep'tor; presep'tor/ **(-ra)** *n* teacher, instructor, tutor, preceptor

preciado /pre'θiaðo; pre'siaðo/ *a* excellent, esteemed, precious; boastful

preciar /pre'θiar; pre'siar/ *vt* to esteem, value; valuate, price; —*vr* boast

precintar /preθin'tar; presin'tar/ *vt* to seal; rope, string, tie up

precinto /pre'θinto; pre'sinto/ *m*, sealing; roping, tying up; strap

precio /'preθio; 'presio/ *m*, price, cost;

recompense, reward; premium; rate; reputation, importance; esteem. **p. de tasa,** controlled price

preciosidad /preθiosi'ðað; presiosi'ðað/ f, preciousness; exquisiteness, fineness; richness; wittiness; *Inf.* loveliness, beauty; thing of beauty

precioso /pre'θioso; pre'sioso/ a precious; exquisite, fine, rare; rich; witty; *Inf.* lovely, delicious, attractive

precipicio /preθi'piθio; presi'pisio/ m, precipice; heavy fall; ruin, disaster

precipitación /preθipita'θion; presipita'sion/ f, precipitancy, haste; rashness; *Chem.* precipitation

precipitadamente /preθipitaða'mente; presipitaða'mente/ adv precipitately, in haste; rashly, foolishly

precipitado /preθipi'taðo; presipi'taðo/ a precipitate, rash, thoughtless m. *Chem.* precipitate

precipitar /preθipi'tar; presipi'tar/ vt to precipitate, hurl headlong; hasten; *Chem.* precipitate; —vr hurl oneself headlong; hasten, rush

precipitoso /preθipi'toso; presipi'toso/ a precipitous; rash, heedless

precisamente /preθisa'mente; presisa'mente/ adv exactly, precisely, just; necessarily. **Y p. en aquel instante llegó,** And just at that moment he arrived

precisar /preθi'sar; presi'sar/ vt to fix, arrange; set forth, draw up, state; compel, force, oblige

precisión /preθi'sion; presi'sion/ f, accuracy, precision; necessity, conciseness, clarity; compulsion, obligation

preciso /pre'θiso; pre'siso/ a necessary, unavoidable; concise, clear; precise, exact

precitado /preθi'taðo; presi'taðo/ a aforementioned

preclaro /pre'klaro/ a illustrious, distinguished, celebrated

precocidad /prekoθi'ðað; prekosi'ðað/ f, precocity

precognición /prekogni'θion; prekogni'sion/ f, foreknowledge

preconcebido /prekonθe'βiðo; prekonse'βiðo/ a preconceived

preconcepto /prekon'θepto; prekon'septo/ m, preconceived idea, preconceived notion

preconizar /prekoni'θar; prekoni'sar/ vt to eulogize, praise publicly

preconocer /prekono'θer; prekono'ser/ vt irr to know beforehand; foresee. See **conocer**

precoz /pre'koθ; pre'kos/ a precocious

precursor /prekur'sor/ **(-ra)** a precursory; preceding, previous —n precursor

predecesor /preðeθe'sor; preðese'sor/ **(-ra)** n predecessor

predecir /preðe'θir; preðe'sir/ vt irr to foretell, prophesy. See **decir**

predestinación /preðestina'θion; preðestina'sion/ f, predestination

predestinado /preðesti'naðo/ **(-da)** a predestined; foreordained —n one of the predestined

predestinar /preðesti'nar/ vt to predestine, foreordain

prédica /'preðika/ f, *Inf.* (contemptuous) sermon

predicación /preðika'θion; preðika'sion/ f, preaching; homily, sermon

predicado /preði'kaðo/ m, (*Gram. Philos.*) predicate

predicador /preðika'ðor/ **(-ra)** a preaching —n preacher

predicamento /preðika'mento/ m, predicament; reputation

predicar /preði'kar/ vt to publish; manifest; preach; —vi overpraise; *Inf.* lecture, scold. **p. en el desierto,** to preach to the wind

predicción /preðik'θion; preðik'sion/ f, prediction, prophecy

predilección /preðilek'θion; preðilek'sion/ f, predilection, preference, partiality

predilecto /preði'lekto/ a favorite, preferred

predisponer /preðispo'ner/ vt irr to predispose. See **poner**

predisposición /preðisposi'θion; preðisposi'sion/ f, predisposition; tendency, prejudice

predominación /preðomina'θion; preðomina'sion/ f, predominance

predominante /preðomi'nante/ a predominant; prevailing

predominar /preðomi'nar/ vi and vt to predominate; prevail; tower above; overlook

predominio /preðo'minio/ m, predominance, ascendancy, preponderance

preeminencia /preemi'nenθia; preemi'nensia/ f, preeminence

preeminente /preemi'nente/ a preeminent

preexistente /preeksis'tente/ a preexistent

preexistir /preeksis'tir/ vi to preexist, exist before

prefacio /pre'faθio; pre'fasio/ m, introduction, preface, prologue; *Eccl.* preface

prefecto /pre'fekto/ m, prefect

preferencia /prefe'renθia; prefe'rensia/ f, preference; superiority. **de p.,** preferred, favorite; preferably

preferente /prefe'rente/ a preferable; preferential; preferred (of stock)

preferible /prefe'riβle/ a preferable

preferir /prefe'rir/ vt irr to prefer; excel, exceed —*Pres. Part.* **prefiriendo.** *Pres. Indic.* **prefiero, prefieres, prefiere, prefieren.** *Preterite* **prefirió, prefirieron.** *Pres. Subjunc.* **prefiera, prefieras, prefiera, prefieran.** *Imperf. Subjunc.* **prefiriese,** etc.

prefijo /pre'fiho/ m, prefix

pregón /pre'gon/ m, public proclamation; marriage banns

pregonar /prego'nar/ vt to proclaim publicly; cry one's wares; publish abroad;

eulogize, praise; proscribe, outlaw. **p. a los cuatro vientos,** *Inf.* to shout from the rooftops

preguerra /pre'gerra/ *f*, prewar period

pregunta /pre'gunta/ *f*, question; *Com.* inquiry; questionnaire, interrogation. *Inf.* **andar** (*or* **estar) a la cuarta p.,** to be very hard up, be on the rocks. **hacer una p.,** to ask a question

preguntador /pregunta'ðor/ **(-ra)** *a* questioning; inquisitive; —*n* questioner; inquisitive person

preguntar /pregun'tar/ *vt* to question, ask; (*with por*) inquire for; —*vr* ask oneself, wonder

prehistoria /preis'toria/ *f*, prehistory

prehistórico /preis'toriko/ *a* prehistoric

prejuicio /pre'huiθio; pre'huisio/ *m*, prejudice

prejuzgar /prehuθ'gar; prehus'gar/ *vt* to prejudge, judge hastily

prelación /prela'θion; prela'sion/ *f*, preference

preliminar /prelimi'nar/ *a* preliminary, prefatory. *m*, preliminary

preludiar /prelu'ðiar/ *vi* and *vt Mus.* to play a prelude (to); —*vt* prepare, initiate

preludio /pre'luðio/ *m*, introduction; prologue; *Mus.* prelude; *Mus.* overture

prematuro /prema'turo/ *a* premature, untimely; unseasonable; immature, unripe

premeditar /premeði'tar/ *vt* to premeditate, plan in advance

premiador /premia'ðor/ **(-ra)** *a* rewarding —*n* rewarder

premiar /pre'miar/ *vt* to reward, requite

premio /'premio/ *m*, prize; reward; premium; *Com.* interest. **p. en metálico,** cash prize. *Inf.* **p. gordo,** first prize (in a lottery)

premioso /pre'mioso/ *a* tight; troublesome, annoying; stern, strict; slow-moving; burdensome, hard; labored (of speech or style)

premisa /pre'misa/ *f*, premise; sign, indication

premonitorio /premoni'torio/ *a* premonitory

premura /pre'mura/ *f*, urgency, haste

prenda /'prenda/ *f*, pledge; token, sign; jewel; article of clothing; talent, gift; loved one; *pl* game of forfeits

prendar /pren'dar/ *vt* to pawn; charm, delight; —*vr* (*with de*) take a liking to

prender /pren'der/ *vt* to seize; arrest; capture, catch —*vi* take root (plants); catch fire; be infectious

prendería /prende'ria/ *f*, second-hand shop

prenombre /pre'nombre/ *m*, given name, praenomen

prensa /'prensa/ *f*, press; printing press; newspapers, the press. **dar a la p.,** to publish

prensado /pren'saðo/ *m*, **prensadura** *f*, pressing; flattening; squeezing

preñado /pre'naðo/ *a* pregnant; bulging, sagging (walls, etc.); swollen. *m*, pregnancy

preñez /pre'neθ; pre'nes/ *f*, pregnancy; suspense

preocupación /preokupa'θion; preokupa'sion/ *f*, anxiety, preoccupation; prejudice

preocupar /preoku'par/ *vt* to preoccupy; make anxious; bias, prejudice; —*vr* be anxious; be prejudiced

preordinar /preorði'nar/ *vt Eccl.* to predestine

preparación /prepara'θion; prepara'sion/ *f*, preparation; treatment; compound, specific

preparado /prepa'raðo/ *a* ready, prepared. *m*, preparation, patent food, etc.

preparar /prepa'rar/ *vt* to prepare; —*vr* prepare oneself; qualify

preparativo /prepara'tiβo/ *a* preparatory. *m*, preparation

preparatorio /prepara'torio/ *a* preparatory

preponderancia /preponde'ranθia; preponde'ransia/ *f*, preponderance

preponderante /preponde'rante/ *a* preponderant; dominant

preponderar /preponde'rar/ *vi* to preponderate; dominate; outweigh

preposición /preposi'θion; preposi'sion/ *f*, preposition

prepósito /pre'posito/ *m*, chairman, head, president; *Eccl.* provost

prerrogativa /prerroga'tiβa/ *f*, prerogative

presa /'presa/ *f*, hold, grasp; seizure, capture; booty; dam; lock (on rivers, canals); weir; ditch, trench; embankment; slice, bit. **hacer p.,** to seize; take advantage of (circumstances)

presagiar /presa'hiar/ *vt* to prophesy, presage, bode

presagio /pre'sahio/ *m*, presage, sign; presentiment, foreboding

présbita /'presβita/ *a* long-sighted, far-sighted

presbiteriano /presβite'riano/ **(-na)** *a* and *n* Presbyterian

presciencia /pres'θienθia; pres'siensia/ *f*, prescience, foresight

presciente /pres'θiente; pres'siente/ *a* prescient, farsighted

prescindible /presθin'diβle; pressin'diβle/ *a* nonessential, able to be dispensed with

prescindir /presθin'dir; pressin'dir/ *vi* (*with de*) to pass over, omit; do without. **Prescindiendo de esto...,** Leaving this aside....

prescribir /preskri'βir/ *vt* to prescribe, order

prescripción /preskrip'θion; preskrip'sion/ *f*, prescription

presencia /pre'senθia; pre'sensia/ *f*, presence, attendance; appearance; looks; ostentation. **p. de ánimo,** presence of mind

presenciar /presen'θiar; presen'siar/ *vt* to be present at; witness, behold

presentación /presenta'θion; presenta'sion/ *f*, presentation; introduction

presentar /presen'tar/ *vt* to show; present, make a gift of; introduce (persons); —*vr* occur; present oneself; offer one's services

presente /pre'sente/ *a* present. *m*, gift; present time. *Law*. **Por estas presentes...,** By these presents.... **tener p.,** to remember

presentimiento /presenti'miento/ *m*, presentiment, apprehension

presentir /presen'tir/ *vt irr* to have a presentiment of. See **sentir**

preservación /preserβa'θion; preserβa-'sion/ *f*, preservation, protection, saving

preservar /preser'βar/ *vt* to preserve, protect, save

preservativo /preserβa'tiβo/ *a* preservative. *m*, preservative, safeguard, protection

presidencia /presi'ðenθia; presi'ðensia/ *f*, presidency; chairmanship; presidential seat or residence

presidencial /presiðen'θial; presiðen'sial/ *a* presidential

presidenta /presi'ðenta/ *f*, female president; president's wife; chairwoman

presidente /presi'ðente/ *m*, president; chairman; head, director; presiding judge

presidiar /presi'ðiar/ *vt* to garrison

presidiario /presi'ðiario/ *m*, convict

presidio /pre'siðio/ *m*, garrison; garrison town; fortress; penitentiary; imprisonment; *Law*. hard labor; assistance, protection

presidir /presi'ðir/ *vt* to preside over; act as chairperson for; influence, determine

presión /pre'sion/ *f*, pressure

preso /'preso/ **(-sa)** *n* prisoner, captive; convict

prestador /presta'ðor/ **(-ra)** *a* lending, loan —*n* lender

prestamista /presta'mista/ *mf* moneylender; pawnbroker

préstamo /'prestamo/ *m*, loan; lending. **casa de préstamos,** pawnshop

prestar /pres'tar/ *vt* to lend; assist; pay (attention); give; —*vi* be useful; give, expand; —*vr* be suitable; lend itself; offer oneself. **tomar prestado,** to borrow

presteza /pres'teθa; pres'tesa/ *f*, speed; promptness, dispatch

prestidigitador /prestiðihita'ðor/ **(-ra)** *n* juggler, conjurer

prestigio /pres'tihio/ *m*, magic spell, sorcery; trick, illusion (of conjurers, etc.); influence, prestige

prestigioso /presti'hioso/ *a* illusory; influential

presumido /presu'miðo/ *a* conceited, vain; presumptuous

presumir /presu'mir/ *vt* to suppose, presume; —*vi* be conceited

presunción /presun'θion; presun'sion/ *f*,

supposition, presumption; vanity, presumptuousness

presuntuoso /presun'tuoso/ *a* presumptuous, vain

presuponer /presupo'ner/ *vt irr* to presuppose, assume; budget, estimate. See **poner**

presuposición /presuposi'θion; presuposi'sion/ *f*, presupposition

presupuesto /presu'puesto/ *m*, motive, reason; supposition, assumption; estimate; *Com.* tender; national budget

presuroso /presu'roso/ *a* swift, speedy

pretencioso /preten'θioso; preten'sioso/ *a* pretentious, vain

pretender /preten'der/ *vt* to seek, solicit; claim; apply for; attempt, try; woo, court

pretendiente /preten'diente/ **(-ta)** *n* pretender; candidate; petitioner; suitor

pretensión /preten'sion/ *f*, pretension; claim; *pl* ambitions

pretérito /pre'terito/ *a* past. *m*, preterite

pretextar /preteks'tar/ *vt* to allege as a pretext or excuse

pretexto /pre'teksto/ *m*, pretext, excuse

prevalecer /preβale'θer; preβale'ser/ *vi irr* to prevail; be dominant; take root (plants). See **conocer**

prevaleciente /preβale'θiente; preβale'siente/ *a* prevailing; prevalent

prevaricación /preβarika'θion; preβarika'sion/ *f*, prevarication

prevaricador /preβarika'ðor/ **(-ra)** *n* prevaricator

prevaricar /preβari'kar/ *vi* to prevaricate

prevención /preβen'θion; preβen'sion/ *f*, prevention; precaution; prejudice; police station; *Mil.* guard room; foresight, prevision; preparation. **de p.,** as a precaution

prevenido /preβe'niðo/ *a* prepared; cautious, forewarned

prevenir /preβe'nir/ *vt irr* to prepare; prevent, avoid; warn; prejudice; occur, happen; *Fig.* overcome (obstacles); —*vr* be ready; be forewarned. See **venir**

preventivo /preβen'tiβo/ *a* preventive

prever /pre'βer/ *vt irr* to foresee, forecast, anticipate. See **ver**

previamente /preβia'mente/ *adv* previously, in advance

previo /'preβio/ *a* previous, advance

previsión /preβi'sion/ *f*, forecast; foresight, prevision, prescience. **p. social,** social insurance

previsor /preβi'sor/ *a* farsighted, provident

prieto /'prieto/ *a* almost black, blackish; tight; mean, avaricious

prima /'prima/ *f*, *Eccl.* prime; *Com.* premium; female cousin

primacía /prima'θia; prima'sia/ *f*, supremacy, preeminence; primacy; primateship

primada /pri'maða/ *f*, *Inf.* act of sponging on, taking advantage of

primario /pri'mario/ *a* primary. *m*, professor who gives the first lecture of the day

primavera /primaˈβera/ *f*, springtime; primrose; figured silk material; beautifully colored thing; youth; prime

primerizo /primeˈriθo; primeˈriso/ **(-za)** *n* novice; beginner; apprentice; firstborn

primero /priˈmero/ *a* first; former; excellent, first-rate —*adv* first; in the first place. **primera enseñanza,** primary education. **primera materia,** raw material. **primer plano,** *Art.* foreground. **primera cura,** first aid. **de buenas a primeras,** all at once, suddenly

primicia /priˈmiθia; priˈmisia/ *f*, first fruits; offering of first fruits; *pl* first effects

primitivo /primiˈtiβo/ *a* original, early; primitive

primo /ˈprimo/ **(-ma)** *a* first; excellent, fine —*n* cousin; *Inf.* simpleton; *Inf.* pigeon, dupe. **p. carnal,** first cousin. *Inf.* **hacer el p.,** to be a dupe. *Inf.* **ser prima hermana de,** to be the twin of (of things)

primogénito /primoˈhenito/ **(-ta)** *a* and *n* firstborn

primor /priˈmor/ *m*, exquisite care; beauty, loveliness; thing of beauty

primoroso /primoˈroso/ *a* beautiful; exquisitely done; dexterous, skillful

princesa /prinˈθesa; prinˈsesa/ *f*, princess

principal /prinθiˈpal; prinsiˈpal/ *a* chief, principal; illustrious; fundamental, first. *m*, head, principal (of a firm); *Com.* capital, principal; first floor

principalmente /prinθipalˈmente; prinsipalˈmente/ *adv* principally, chiefly

príncipe /ˈprinθipe; ˈprinsipe/ *m*, leader; prince. **p. de Asturias,** prince of Asturias. **p. de la sangre,** prince of the blood royal

principiante /prinθiˈpiante; prinsiˈpiante/ **(-ta)** *n* beginner, novice; apprentice

principiar /prinθiˈpiar; prinsiˈpiar/ *vt* to begin, commence

principio /prinˈθipio; prinˈsipio/ *m*, beginning; principle; genesis, origin; rudiment; axiom; constituent **al p.,** at first. **a principios,** at the beginning (of the month, year, etc.). **en p.,** in principle

pringar /prinˈgar/ *vt Cul.* to soak in fat; stain with grease; *Inf.* wound; take part in a business deal; slander; —*vr Inf.* appropriate, misuse (funds, etc.)

pringoso /prinˈgoso/ *a* greasy

pringue /ˈpringue/ *mf*, animal fat, lard; grease spot

prioridad /prioriˈðað/ *f*, priority

prisa /ˈprisa/ *f*, haste, speed; skirmish, foray. **a toda p.,** with all speed. **correr p.,** to be urgent. **dar p.,** to hasten, speed up. **darse** (*or* **estar de**) **p.,** to hurry

prisión /priˈsion/ *f*, prison, jail; seizure; captivity, imprisonment; *Fig.* bond; obstacle, shackle; *pl* fetters

prisma /ˈprisma/ *m*, prism

prismáticos /prisˈmatikos/ *m pl*, field glasses

pristino /prisˈtino/ *a* pristine

privación /priβaˈθion; priβaˈsion/ *f*, privation; lack, shortage; deprivation; degradation

privada /priˈβaða/ *f*, toilet, privy, water closet

privadamente /priβaðaˈmente/ *adv* privately; individually, separately

privado /priˈβaðo/ *a* private; individual, personal. *m*, favorite; confidant

privanza /priˈβanθa; priˈβansa/ *f*, court favor, intimacy of princes

privar /priˈβar/ *vt* to deprive; dismiss (from office); interdict, forbid; —*vi* prevail, be in favor; —*vr* swoon; deprive oneself

privilegiar /priβileˈhiar/ *vt* to privilege; bestow a favor on

privilegio /priβiˈlehio/ *m*, privilege; prerogative; concession; copyright; patent

pro /pro/ *mf* advantage, benefit. **el p. y el contra,** the pros and cons. **en p.,** in favor

proa /ˈproa/ *f*, prow, bow

probabilidad /proβaβiliˈðað/ *f*, probability

probable /proˈβaβle/ *a* probable; likely; provable

probación /proβaˈθion; proβaˈsion/ *f*, proof, test; novitiate, probation

probado /proˈβaðo/ *a* tried, tested, proved

probar /proˈβar/ *vt irr* to prove; test; taste; try on (clothes); —*vi* suit; (*with prep a* + *infin*) try to. **p. fortuna,** to try one's luck —*Pres. Indic.* **pruebo, pruebas, prueba, prueban.** *Pres. Subjunc.* **pruebe, pruebes, prueben**

probidad /proβiˈðað/ *f*, probity, trustworthiness, honesty

problema /proˈβlema/ *m*, problem

problemático /proβleˈmatiko/ *a* problematical, uncertain

probo /ˈproβo/ *a* honest, trustworthy

procaz /proˈkaθ; proˈkas/ *a* insolent, pert, brazen

procedencia /proθeˈðɔnθia; proseˈðensia/ *f*, origin, source; parentage, descent; port of sailing or call

procedente /proθeˈðente; proseˈðente/ *a* arriving or coming from

proceder /proθeˈðer; proseˈðer/ *vi* to proceed; behave; originate, arise; continue, go on; act. *Law.* **p. contra,** to proceed against (a person)

procedimiento /proθeðiˈmiento; proseðiˈmiento/ *m*, proceeding, advancement; procedure; legal practice; process

proceloso /proθeˈloso; proseˈloso/ *a* tempestuous

prócer /ˈproθer; ˈproser/ *a* exalted, eminent; lofty. *m*, exalted personage

procesado /proθeˈsaðo; proseˈsaðo/ **(-da)** *n* defendant

procesamiento /proθesaˈmiento; prosesaˈmiento/ *m*, suing, suit; indictment. **p. de textos,** word processing.

procesar /proθeˈsar; proseˈsar/ *vt Law.* to proceed against, sue

procesión /proθeˈsion; proseˈsion/ *f*, proceeding, emanating; procession; *Inf.* train, string. **andar** (*or* **ir) por dentro la p.,** to feel keenly without betraying one's emotion

proceso /pro'θeso; pro'seso/ *m,* process; progress, advancement; lapse of time; lawsuit

proclamación /proklama'θion; proklama'sion/ *f,* proclamation; acclaim, applause

proclamar /prokla'mar/ *vt* to proclaim; acclaim; publish abroad; reveal, show

proclividad /prokliβi'ðað/ *f,* proclivity, tendency

procreación /prokrea'θion; prokrea'sion/ *f,* procreation

procreador /prokrea'ðor/ **(-ra)** *a* procreative —*n* procreator

procrear /prokre'ar/ *vt* to procreate, beget, engender

procuración /prokura'θion; prokura'sion/ *f,* procurement; assiduity, care; *Law.* power of attorney; *Law.* attorneyship

procurador /prokura'ðor/ **(-ra)** *m,* proxy; *Law.* attorney; proctor —*n* procurer

procurar /proku'rar/ *vt* to try, attempt; procure, get; exercise the profession of a lawyer

prodigalidad /proðigali'ðað/ *f,* prodigality, lavishness; waste, extravagance

prodigar /proði'gar/ *vt* to waste, squander; lavish, bestow freely; —*vr* make oneself cheap

prodigio /pro'ðihio/ *m,* marvel, wonder; prodigy; monster; miracle

prodigioso /proði'hioso/ *a* wonderful; prodigious; monstrous; miraculous

pródigo /'proðigo/ **(-ga)** *a* wasteful, extravagant; lavish, generous —*n* spendthrift, wastrel, prodigal

producción /proðuk'θion; proðuk'sion/ *f,* production; output, yield; generation (of heat, etc.); crop

producir /proðu'θir; proðu'sir/ *vt irr* to produce; generate; yield, give; cause, occasion; publish; —*vr* explain oneself; arise, appear, be produced. **p. efecto,** to have effect; take effect. See **conducir**

productividad /proðuktiβi'ðað/ *f,* productivity

productivo /proðuk'tiβo/ *a* productive; fertile; profitable

producto /pro'ðukto/ *m,* produce; product; profit; yield, gain; *Math.* product. *Chem.* **p. derivado,** by-product

productor /proðuk'tor/ **(-ra)** *a* productive —*n* producer

proeza /pro'eθa; pro'esa/ *f,* prowess, gallantry; skill

profanación /profana'θion; profana'sion/ *f,* profanation

profanar /profa'nar/ *vt* to profane

profano /pro'fano/ *a* profane; dissolute; pleasure-loving, worldly; immodest; lay, ignorant

profecía /profe'θia; profe'sia/ *f,* proph-

ecy; *Eccl.* Book of the Prophets; opinion, view

proferir /profe'rir/ *vt irr* to utter, pronounce. See **herir**

profesar /profe'sar/ *vt* to exercise, practice (professions); *Eccl.* profess; believe in; teach

profesión /profe'sion/ *f,* profession; trade, occupation; avowal, admission

profesional /profesio'nal/ *a* professional

profeso /pro'feso/ **(-sa)** *a Eccl.* professed —*n* professed monk

profesor /profe'sor/ **(-ra)** *n* teacher; professor

profesorado /profeso'raðo/ *m,* teaching staff; teaching profession; professorship; professorate

profeta /pro'feta/ *m,* prophet; seer

profetisa /profe'tisa/ *f,* prophetess

profetizar /profeti'θar; profeti'sar/ *vt* to prophesy; imagine, suppose

proficiente /profi'θiente; profi'siente/ *a* proficient

profiláctico /profi'laktiko/ *a* and *m,* prophylactic

prófugo /'profugo/ **(-ga)** *a* and *n* fugitive from justice. *m, Mil.* one who evades military service

profundidad /profundi'ðað/ *f,* depth; profundity, obscurity; *Geom.* depth; concavity; intensity (of feeling); vastness (of knowledge, etc.)

profundizar /profundi'θar; profundi'sar/ *vt* to deepen; hollow out; *Fig.* go into deeply, fathom

profundo /pro'fundo/ *a* deep; low; *Fig.* intense, acute; abstruse, profound; *Fig.* vast, extensive; high. *m,* depth, profundity; *Poet.* ocean, the deep; *Poet.* hell

profuso /pro'fuso/ *a* profuse, abundant; extravagant, wasteful

progenie /pro'henie/ *f,* descendants

prognosis /prog'nosis/ *f,* prognosis; forecast

programa /pro'grama/ *m,* program; edict, public notice; plan, scheme; *Educ.* calendar; syllabus; timetable

progresar /progre'sar/ *vt* and *vi* to make progress; progress, advance

progresión /progre'sion/ *f,* progression; advancement, progress

progresista /progre'sista/ *a Polit.* progressive. *mf* progressive

progresivo /progre'siβo/ *a* progressive; advancing

progreso /pro'greso/ *m,* progress, advancement; growth; improvement, development

prohibición /proiβi'θion; proiβi'sion/ *f,* forbidding, prohibition

prohibir /proi'βir/ *vt* to forbid, prohibit. «**Prohibido el paso,**» "No thoroughfare"

prohijamiento /proiha'miento/ *m,* child adoption; fathering (of a bill, etc.)

prohijar /proi'har/ *vt* to adopt (children, ideas); *Fig.* father

prohombre /pro'ombre/ *m*, master of a guild; respected, wellliked man

prójimo /'prohimo/ *m*, fellow man, brother, neighbor.

prole /'prole/ *f*, progeny, young offspring

proletariado /proleta'riaðo/ *m*, proletariat

proletario /prole'tario/ *a* poor; common, vulgar. *m*, plebeian; pauper; proletarian

prolífico /pro'lifiko/ *a* prolific; abundant, fertile

prolijo /pro'liho/ *a* verbose, prolix; fussy, fastidious; tedious, importunate

prologar /prolo'gar/ *vt* to prologue; provide with a preface

prólogo /'prologo/ *m*, preface; prologue; introduction

prolongación /prolonga'θion; prolonga'sion/ *f*, lengthening; prolongation, protraction; extension

prolongar /prolon'gar/ *vt* to lengthen; *Geom.* produce; prolong, spin out

promediar /prome'ðiar/ *vt* to distribute or divide into two equal portions; average; —*vi* arbitrate; place oneself between two people; reach half-time

promedio /pro'meðio/ *m*, average; middle, center

promesa /pro'mesa/ *f*, promise; augury, favorable sign

prometer /prome'ter/ *vt* to promise; attest, certify; —*vi* promise well, look hopeful; —*vr* devote oneself to service of God; anticipate confidently, expect; become engaged (marriage). *Inf.* **prometérselas muy felices,** to have high hopes

prometido /prome'tiðo/ **(-da)** *n* betrothed. *m*, promise

prominencia /promi'nenθia; promi'nensia/ *f*, prominence, protuberance; eminence, hill

prominente /promi'nente/ *a* prominent, protuberant; eminent, elevated

promiscuar /promis'kuar/ *vi* to eat meat and fish on fast days

promiscuo /pro'miskuo/ *a* indiscriminate, haphazard, promiscuous; ambiguous

promoción /promo'θion; promo'sion/ *f*, promotion; batch, class, year (of recruits, students, etc.)

promontorio /promon'torio/ *m*, headland; promontory; cumbersome object

promotor /promo'tor/ **(-ra)** *a* promotive —*n* promoter; supporter

promover /promo'βer/ *vt irr* to promote, further, advance; promote (a person). **p. un proceso (a),** to bring a suit (against). See **mover**

promulgación /promulga'θion; promulga'sion/ *f*, promulgation

promulgar /promul'gar/ *vt* to publish officially, proclaim; promulgate. *Law.* **p. sentencia,** to pass judgment

pronombre /pro'nombre/ *m*, pronoun

pronosticar /pronosti'kar/ *vt* to prognosticate, forecast; presage

pronóstico /pro'nostiko/ *m*, omen, prediction; almanac; prognosis; sign, indication. **p. del tiempo,** weather forecast

prontitud /pronti'tuð/ *f*, quickness, promptness; quick-wittedness; *Fig.* sharpness, liveliness; celerity, dispatch

pronto /'pronto/ *a* quick, speedy; prompt; ready, prepared. *m*, *Inf.* sudden decision —*adv* immediately; with all speed; soon. **de p.,** suddenly; without thinking. **por lo p.,** temporarily, provisionally

prontuario /pron'tuario/ *m*, compendium, handbook; summary

pronunciación /pronunθia'θion; pronunsia'sion/ *f*, pronunciation

pronunciamiento /pronunθia'miento; pronunsia'miento/ *m*, military uprising; political manifesto; *Law.* pronouncement of sentence

pronunciar /pronun'θiar; pronun'siar/ *vt* to pronounce, articulate; decide, determine; *Law.* pronounce judgment; give or make (a speech)

propagación /propaga'θion; propaga'sion/ *f*, propagation; dissemination; transmission

propaganda /propa'ganda/ *f*, propaganda organization; propaganda

propagandista /propagan'dista/ *mf* propagandist

propagar /propa'gar/ *vt* to reproduce; propagate, disseminate; —*vr* reproduce, multiply; propagate, spread

propalar /propa'lar/ *vt* to disseminate, spread abroad

propasarse /propa'sarse/ *vr* to go too far, forget oneself; overstep one's authority

propender /propen'der/ *vi* to be inclined, have a leaning toward

propensión /propen'sion/ *f*, propensity, inclination; tendency

propenso /pro'penso/ *a* inclined, disposed; liable

propiciación /propiθia'θion; propisia'sion/ *f*, propitiation

propiciar /propi'θiar; propi'siar/ *vt* to propitiate, appease

propicio /pro'piθio; pro'pisio/ *a* propitious, auspicious; kind, favorable

propiedad /propie'ðað/ *f*, estate, property; ownership; landed property; attribute, quality, property; *Art.* resemblance, naturalness

propietario /propie'tario/ **(-ia)** *a* proprietary —*n* proprietor, owner

propina /pro'pina/ *f*, gratuity, tip. *Inf.* **de p.,** in addition, extra

propinar /propi'nar/ *vt* to treat to a drink; administer (medicine); *Inf.* give (slaps, etc.)

propincuo /pro'pinkuo/ *a* near, contiguous, adjacent

propio /'propio/ *a* own, one's own; typical, characteristic; individual, peculiar; suitable, apt; natural, real; same. *m*, messenger; *pl* public lands

proponente /propo'nente/ *a* proposing. *m,* proposer; *Com.* tenderer

proponer /propo'ner/ *vt irr* to propose, suggest; make a proposition; propose (for a post, office, etc.); *Math.* state; —*vr* intend, purpose. **proponerse para un empleo,** to apply for a post. See **poner**

proporción /propor'θion; propor'sion/ *f,* proportion; chance, opportunity; size; *Math.* proportion

proporcionado /proporθio'naðo; proporsio'naðo/ *a* fit, suitable; proportionate; symmetrical

proporcionar /proporθio'nar; proporsio'nar/ *vt* to allot, proportion; supply, provide, give; adapt

proposición /proposi'θion; proposi'sion/ *f,* proposition; motion (in a debate)

propósito /pro'posito/ *m,* proposal; intention, aim; subject, question, matter. **a p.,** suitable, apropos, by the way, incidentally. **de p.,** with the intention, proposing. **fuera de p.,** irrelevant

propuesta /pro'puesta/ *f,* proposal, tender

propugnar /propug'nar/ *vt* to defend, protect

propulsar /propul'sar/ *vt* to repulse, throw back; propel, drive

propulsión /propul'sion/ *f,* repulse; propulsion

prorrata /pro'rrata/ *f,* quota, share, apportionment. **a p.,** in proportion

prorratear /prorrate'ar/ *vt* to apportion, distribute proportionately, prorate

prorrogación /prorroga'θion; prorroga'sion/ *f,* prorogation, adjournment; extension (of time); renewal (of a lease, etc.)

prorrogar /prorro'gar/ *vt* to extend, prolong; defer, suspend, prorogue; renew (leases, etc.)

prorrumpir /prorrum'pir/ *vt* (*with en*) to burst out; utter, give vent to, burst into

prosa /'prosa/ *f,* prose; prosaism, prosaic style; *Inf.* dull verbosity; monotony, tediousness

prosaico /pro'saiko/ *a* prosaic; prosy; monotonous, tedious; matter-of-fact

prosapia /pro'sapia/ *f,* family, lineage, descent

proscribir /proskri'βir/ *vt* to proscribe, outlaw; forbid, prohibit —*Past Part.* proscrito

proscrito /pros'krito/ (**-ta**) *n* outlaw, exile

prosecución /proseku'θion; proseku'sion/ *f,* prosecution, performance; pursuit

proseguir /prose'gir/ *vt irr* to continue, proceed with. See **pedir**

prosélito /pro'selito/ *m,* convert, proselyte

prosista /pro'sista/ *mf* prose writer

prospecto /pros'pekto/ *m,* prospectus

prosperar /prospe'rar/ *vt* to prosper; protect; —*vi* flourish, prosper

prosperidad /prosperi'ðað/ *f,* prosperity; wealth; success

próspero /'prospero/ *a* favorable, propitious, fortunate; prosperous

próstata /'prostata/ *f,* prostate

prostitución /prostitu'θion; prostitu'sion/ *f,* prostitution

prostituir /prosti'tuir/ *vt irr* to prostitute; —*vr* become a prostitute; sell oneself, debase oneself. See **huir**

prostituta /prosti'tuta/ *f,* prostitute

protagonista /protago'nista/ *mf* hero or heroine, principal character; leading figure, protagonist

protección /protek'θion; protek'sion/ *f,* protection, defense; favor, aid

protector /protek'tor/ *a* protective. *m,* protector; guard

protectorado /protekto'raðo/ *m,* protectorate

protectriz /protek'triθ; protek'tris/ *f,* protectress

proteger /prote'her/ *vt* to protect, defend; favor, assist

protegido /prote'hiðo/ (**-da**) *n* protégé

proteína /prote'ina/ *f,* protein

protervia /pro'terβia/ *f,* depravity, perversity

protervo /pro'terβo/ *a* depraved, perverse

protesta, protestación /pro'testa, pro'testa'θion; pro'testa, protesta'sion/ *f,* protest; protestation, declaration

protestante /protes'tante/ *a and mf* Protestant

protestantismo /protestan'tismo/ *m,* Protestantism

protestar /protes'tar/ *vt* to declare, attest; (*with contra*) protest against; (*with de*) affirm vigorously

protesto /pro'testo/ *m, Com.* protest; objection

protocolo /proto'kolo/ *m,* protocol

prototipo /proto'tipo/ *m,* model, prototype

protuberancia /protuβe'ranθia; protuβe'ransia/ *f,* protuberance, projection, swelling

provecho /pro'βetʃo/ *m,* gain, benefit; profit; advantage; progress, proficiency. **¡Buen p.!** Enjoy your food! Enjoy your meal! **ser de p.,** to be advantageous or useful

provechoso /proβe'tʃoso/ *a* beneficial; profitable; advantageous; useful

provecto /pro'βekto/ *a* ancient, venerable; mature, experienced

proveer /proβe'er/ *vt irr* to provide; furnish; supply; confer (an honor or office); transact, arrange. **p. de,** to furnish or supply with; fit with. See **creer**

provenir /proβe'nir/ *vi irr* (*with de*) to originate in, proceed from. See **venir**

Provenza /pro'βenθa; pro'βensa/ Provence

proverbio /pro'βerβio/ *m,* proverb; omen; *pl* Book of Proverbs

providencia /proβi'ðenθia; proβi'ðensia/ f. precaution, foresight; provision, furnishing; measure, preparation. **la Divina P.**, Providence

próvido /'proβiðo/ a provident, thrifty, careful; kind, favorable

provincia /pro'βinθia; pro'βinsia/ f. province; Fig. sphere

provincial /proβin'θial; proβin'sial/ a provincial. m, Eccl. provincial

provinciano /proβin'θiano; proβin'siano/ (-na) a provincial —n provincial, rustic, countryman; native of Biscay

provisión /proβi'sion/ f. stock, store; provision; supply; food supply (gen. pl); catering; means, way

provisional /proβisio'nal/ a temporary, provisional

provisor /proβi'sor/ m, purveyor, supplier; Eccl. vicar general

provocador /proβoka'ðor/ (-ra) a provocative —n provoker; instigator

provocar /proβo'kar/ vt to provoke; incite; irritate; help, assist; Inf. vomit

provocativo /proβoka'tiβo/ a provocative

próximamente /'proksimamente/ adv proximately; soon; approximately

proximidad /proksimi'ðað/ f, nearness, proximity (in time or space)

próximo /'proksimo/ a near, neighboring; next; not distant (of time)

proyección /proiek'θion; proiek'sion/ f, projection (all meanings)

proyectar /proiek'tar/ vt to throw; cast; plan, contrive; design; project; —vr jut out; be cast (a shadow, etc.)

proyectil /proyek'til/ m, projectile

proyecto /pro'iekto/ a placed in perspective. m, project, plan, scheme; planning; intention, idea

proyector /proiek'tor/ (-ra) n designer, planner. m, searchlight; spotlight; projector

prudencia /pru'ðenθia; pru'ðensia/ f, prudence, sagacity, caution; moderation

prudencial /pruðen'θial; pruðen'sial/ a prudent, discreet; safe

prudente /pru'ðente/ a prudent, cautious; provident

prueba /'prueβa/ f, proof; test; testing; trial; fitting (of garments); sample; taste; Law. evidence; (Photo. Print.) proof. Law. **p. de indicios** or **p. indiciaria**, circumstantial evidence. Photo. **p. negativa**, negative. Com. **a p.**, on approval; on trial; up to standard, perfect. **a p. de**, proof against (water, etc.). **poner a p.**, to put to the test, try out

prurito /pru'rito/ m, pruritus; desire, longing

ps- /ps-/ For words so beginning (e.g. psicología, psiquiatría), see spellings without p

púa /'pua/ f, prong; tooth (of a comb); quill (of a porcupine); Agr. graft; plectrum (for playing the mandolin, etc.);

anxiety, grief; pine needle; Inf. crafty person

pubertad /puβer'tað/ f, puberty

púbico /'puβiko/ a pubic

publicación /puβlika'θion; puβlika'sion/ f, publication; announcement, proclamation; revelation; publishing of marriage banns

publicador /puβlika'ðor/ (-ra) a publishing —n publisher; announcer

publicar /puβli'kar/ vt to publish; reveal; announce, proclaim; publish (marriage banns)

publicidad /puβliθi'ðað; puβlisi'ðað/ f, publicity; advertising, propaganda

publicista /puβli'θista; puβli'sista/ mf publicist; publicity agent

público /'puβliko/ a well-known, universal; common, general; public. m, public; audience; gathering, attendance. **dar al p.** or **sacar al p.**, to publish

puchero /pu'tʃero/ m, Cul. kind of stew; stew pot; Inf. daily food; puckering of the face preceding tears

pudicia /pu'ðiθia; pu'ðisia/ f, modesty; bashfulness; chastity

púdico /'puðiko/ a modest; bashful; chaste

pudiente /pu'ðiente/ a rich, wealthy; powerful

pudín /pu'ðin/ m, pudding

pudor /pu'ðor/ m, modesty; bashfulness, shyness

pudoroso /puðo'roso/ a modest; shy

pudrir /pu'ðrir/ vt to rot, putrefy; irritate, worry, provoke; —vi rot in the grave; —vr rot; be consumed with anxiety

puebla /'pueβla/ f, town; population; gardener's seed setting

pueblo /'pueβlo/ m, town; village, hamlet; people, population, inhabitants; common people; working classes; nation

puente /'puente/ mf bridge; Mus. bridge (of stringed instruments); Naut. bridge; crossbeam, transom. **p. colgante**, suspension bridge. **p. levadizo**, drawbridge. **hacer p. de plata** (a), to remove obstacles for, make plain sailing

puerco /'puerko/ m, pig; wild boar —a filthy; rough, rude; low, mean. **p. espín** or **p. espino**, porcupine. **p. marino**, dolphin. **p. montés** or **p. salvaje**, wild boar

puericultura /puerikul'tura/ f, child care

pueril /pue'ril/ a childish, puerile; foolish, silly; trivial

puerilidad /puerili'ðað/ f, puerility; foolishness; triviality

puerro /'puerro/ m, leek

puerta /'puerta/ f, door; gate; goal (football, soccer, hockey); means, way. **p. batiente**, swinging door. **p. caediza**, trapdoor. **p. corrediza**, sliding door. **p. de servicio**, tradesman's entrance. **p. falsa** or **p. secreta**, secret door; side door. **p. trasera**, back door. **a p. cerrada**, in camera; in secret. Inf. **dar con la p. en las narices** (de), to slam the door in a person's face; offend, insult. **llamar a la p.,** to knock at the door; be on the verge of happening. **tomar la p.,** to depart, go away

puerto /'puerto/ *m,* harbor; port; defile, narrow pass; refuge, haven. **p. fluvial,** river port. **p. franco,** free port. **tomar p.,** to put into port; take refuge

pues /pues/ *conjunc* then; since, as; for, because; well —*adv* yes, certainly —*conjunc* **p. que,** since, as

puesta /'puesta/ *f, Astron.* setting, sinking; stake (in gambling). **p. al día,** aggiornamento; updating; modernization. **p. de largo,** coming of age; coming-out party. **p. del sol,** sunset

puesto /'puesto/ *m,* post, job; booth, stall; beat, pitch; place, position; state, condition; *Mil.* encampment, barracks; office, position. **p. de los testigos,** witness box. **p. de mando,** command, position of authority.

puesto /'puesto/ *a (with bien or mal)* well-or badly dressed —*conjunc* **p. que,** since, as; although

pugilista /puhi'lista/ *mf* boxer

pugna /'pugna/ *f,* fight, struggle; rivalry, conflict

pugnante /pug'nante/ *a* hostile, conflicting, rival

pugnar /pug'nar/ *vi* to fight; quarrel; *(with con, contra)* struggle against, oppose; *(with por, para)* strive to

pugnaz /pug'naθ; pug'nas/ *a* pugnacious

puja /'puha/ *f,* outbidding (at an auction); higher bid; push, thrust

pujador /puha'ðor/ **(-ra)** *n* bidder or outbidder (at an auction)

pujante /pu'hante/ *a* strong, powerful, vigorous

pujanza /pu'hanθa; pu'hansa/ *f,* strength, vigor

pujar /pu'har/ *vt* to push on; bid or outbid (at an auction); —*vi* stutter; hesitate, falter; *Inf.* show signs of weeping

pujo /'puho/ *m,* irresistible impulse; desire; will; purpose, intention

pulcritud /pulkri'tuð/ *f,* beauty, loveliness, delicacy; fastidiousness, subtlety

pulcro /'pulkro/ *a* beautiful, lovely; delicate, fine; fastidious, subtle

pulga /'pulga/ *f,* flea; small top (toy). **el juego de la p.,** tiddlywinks. *Inf.* **tener malas pulgas,** to be irritable

pulgada /pul'gaða/ *f,* inch

pulgar /pul'gar/ *m,* thumb

pulidez /puli'ðeθ; puli'ðes/ *f,* elegance, fineness; polish, smoothness; neatness

pulido /pu'liðo/ *a* elegant, fine; polished, smooth; neat

pulimentar /pulimen'tar/ *vt* to polish, burnish

pulir /pu'lir/ *vt* to polish, burnish; give the finishing touch to; beautify, decorate; *Fig.* polish up, civilize; —*vr* beautify oneself; become polished and polite

pulla /'puʎa; 'puya/ *f,* lewd remark; strong hint; witty comment

pulmón /pul'mon/ *m,* lung

pulmonía /pulmo'nia/ *f,* pneumonia

pulpa /'pulpa/ *f,* fleshy part of fruit; *Anat.* pulp; wood pulp

pulpería /pulpe'ria/ *f, West Hem.* grocery, grocery store, general store

púlpito /'pulpito/ *m,* pulpit

pulpo /'pulpo/ *m,* octopus. *Inf.* **poner como un p.,** to beat to a pulp

pulposo /pul'poso/ *a* pulpy, pulpous

pulsación /pulsa'θion; pulsa'sion/ *f,* pulsation; throb, beat

pulsar /pul'sar/ *vt* to touch, feel; take the pulse of; *Fig.* explore (a possibility); —*vi* beat (the heart, etc.)

pulsera /pul'sera/ *f,* bracelet; wrist bandage. **p. de pedida,** betrothal bracelet

pulso /'pulso/ *m,* pulse; steadiness of hand; tact, diplomacy, circumspection. **a p.,** freehand (drawing). **tomar a p.** (**una cosa),** to try a thing's weight. **tomar el p.** (**a),** to take a person's pulse

pulular /pulu'lar/ *vi* to pullulate, sprout; abound, be plentiful; swarm, teem; multiply (of insects)

pulverización /pulβeriθa'θion; pulβerisa'sion/ *f,* pulverization; atomization

pulverizador /pulβeriθa'ðor; pulβerisa'ðor/ *m,* atomizer, sprayer; scent spray

pulverizar /pulβeri'θar; pulβeri'sar/ *vt* to pulverize, grind, make into powder; atomize; spray

pundonor /pundo'nor/ *m,* **(punto de honor)** point of honor, sense of honor

pundonoroso /pundono'roso/ *a* careful of one's honor; honorable, punctilious

pungir /pun'hir/ *vt* to prick, pierce; revive an old sorrow; *Fig.* wound, sting (passions)

punitivo /puni'tiβo/ *a* punitive, punitory

punta /'punta/ *f,* sharp end, point; butt (of a cigarette); end, point, tip; cape, headland; trace, touch, suspicion; nib (of a pen); pointing (pointer dogs); *Herald.* point; *pl* point lace. **p. de París,** wire nail. **p. seca,** drypoint, engraving needle. **sacar p.,** to sharpen; *Inf.* twist (a remark)

puntada /pun'taða/ *f, Sew.* stitch; innuendo, hint

puntal /pun'tal/ *m, Naut.* draft, depth; stanchion, prop, brace, pile; *Fig.* basis, foundation

puntapié /punta'pie/ *m,* kick

punteado /punte'aðo/ *m,* plucking the strings of a guitar, etc.; sewing

puntear /punte'ar/ *vt* to make dots; *Mus.* pluck the strings of; play the guitar; sew; *Art.* stipple; —*vi Naut.* tack

puntera /pun'tera/ *f,* mend in the toe of a stocking; toe cap; new piece on the toe of shoe; *Inf.* kick

puntería /punte'ria/ *f,* aiming (of a firearm); aim, sight (of a firearm); marksmanship

puntiagudo /puntia'guðo/ *a* pointed, sharp-pointed

puntilla /pun'tiʎa; pun'tiya/ *f,* narrow lace edging; headless nail, wire nail; brad, tack. **de puntillas,** on tiptoe

puntilloso /punti'ʎoso; punti'yoso/ *a* punctilious; overfastidious, fussy

punto /'punto/ *m* dot; point; pen nib; gun sight; *Sew.* stitch; dropped stitch, hole; weaving stitch, mesh; *Gram.* full stop, period; hole (in belts for adjustment); place, spot; point, mark; subject matter; *Mech.* cog; degree, extent; taxi stand; instant; infinitesimal amount; opportunity, chance; vacation, recess; aim, goal; point of honor. **p. de congelación,** freezing point. **p. de ebullición,** boiling point. **p. de fuga,** vanishing point. **p. de fusión,** melting point. **p. de partida,** starting point. **p. de vista,** point of view. **p. final,** *Gram.* period, full stop. **p. interrogante,** question mark. **p. menos,** a little less. **p. y coma,** semicolon. **p. cardinal,** cardinal point. **p. suspensivo,** *Gram.* ellipsis point, suspension point, leader, dot. **a p.,** in readiness; immediately. **en p.,** sharp, prompt (e.g. *a las seis en p.,* at six o'clock sharp)

puntuación /puntua'θion; puntua'sion/ *f,* punctuation; *Sports.* score

puntual /pun'tual/ *a* punctual; punctilious; certain, indubitable; suitable, convenient

puntualidad /puntuali'ðað/ *f,* punctuality; punctiliousness; certainty; exactitude, accuracy

puntualizar /puntuali'θar; puntuali'sar/ *vt* to describe in detail; give the finishing touch to, perfect; impress on the mind

puntuar /pun'tuar/ *vt* to punctuate

punzada /pun'θaða; pun'saða/ *f,* prick, sting; puncture, piercing; sudden pain, twinge, stitch; *Fig.* anguish, pain

punzar /pun'θar; pun'sar/ *vt* to pierce, puncture; prick; punch, perforate; —*vi* revive, make itself felt (pain or sorrow)

puñado /pu'ɲaðo/ *m,* handful; a few, some, a small quantity. **a puñados,** in handfuls; liberally, lavishly

puñal /pu'ɲal/ *m,* dagger

puñalada /puɲa'laða/ *f,* dagger thrust; stab, wound; *Fig.* unexpected blow (of fate). **p. por la espalda,** stab in the back

puñetazo /puɲe'taθo; puɲe'taso/ *m,* blow with the fist

puño /'puɲo/ *m,* fist; handful; cuff (of a sleeve); wristband; handle, head, haft; hilt (of a sword); *pl Inf.* guts, courage. **p. de amura,** *Naut.* tack. **p. de un mani-**

llar, handlebar grip. *Inf.* **meter en un p.,** to overawe. *Inf.* **ser como un p.,** to be tightfisted; be small (in stature)

pupila /pu'pila/ *f,* female child ward; *Anat.* pupil; *Inf.* cleverness, talent

pupilaje /pupi'lahe/ *m,* pupilage, minority; boarding house, guesthouse; boarding school; price of board residence; dependence, bondage

pupilo /pu'pilo/ **(-la)** *n* ward, minor; boarder; boarding school student

pupitre /pu'pitre/ *m,* desk, school desk

pureza /pu'reθa; pu'resa/ *f,* purity; perfection, excellence; chastity; disinterestedness, genuineness; clearness

purga /'purga/ *f,* laxative, purge; waste product

purgación /purga'θion; purga'sion/ *f,* purging; menstruation; gonorrhea

purgante /pur'gante/ *a* purgative. *m,* purge, cathartic

purgar /pur'gar/ *vt* to cleanse, purify; expiate, atone for; (*Med. Law.*) purge; suffer purgatorial pains; clarify, refine; —*vr* rid oneself, purge oneself

purgatorio /purga'torio/ *m,* purgatory —*a* purgatorial

puridad /puri'ðað/ *f,* purity; secrecy, privacy. **en p.,** openly, without dissembling; secretly, in private

purificación /purifika'θion; purifika'sion/ *f,* purification; cleansing

purificar /purifi'kar/ *vt* to purify; cleanse; —*vr* be purified

puritano /puri'tano/ **(-na)** *a* puritanical —*n* Puritan

puro /'puro/ *a* pure; undiluted; unalloyed; unmixed; disinterested, honest; virgin; absolute, sheer; mere, simple. *m,* cigar. **de p.,** by sheer..., by dint of

púrpura /'purpura/ *f,* purple; *Poet.* blood; purpura; *Herald.* purpure; purple (cloth); dignity of an emperor, cardinal, consul

purpurear /purpure'ar/ *vi* to look like purple; be tinged with purple

pus /pus/ *m,* pus, matter

pusilánime /pusi'lanime/ *a* pusillanimous, timid, cowardly

pústula /'pustula/ *f,* pustule

puta /'puta/ *f,* whore

putativo /puta'tiβo/ *a* putative

puto /'puto/ *m,* male prostitute

putrefacción /putrefak'θion/ *f,* putrefak'sion/ *f,* putrefaction; rottenness, putrescence

putrefacto /putre'fakto/ *a* rotten, decayed

pútrido /'putriðo/ *a* putrid, rotten

quebrada /ke'βraða/ f, mountain gorge; *Com.* bankruptcy

quebradizo /keβra'ðiθo; keβra'ðiso/ a brittle, fragile; ailing, infirm; delicate, frail

quebrado /ke'βraðo/ **(-da)** m, *Math.* fraction; —n *Com.* bankrupt —a rough, uneven (ground); *Med.* ruptured; bankrupt; ailing, broken-down

quebradura /keβra'ðura/ f, snap, breaking; gap, crevice; hernia

quebrantamiento /keβranta'mjento/ m, crushing; splitting, cleaving; fracture, rupture; profanation, desecration; burglary; violation, breaking, infringement; fatigue; *Law.* annulment; exhaustion

quebrantanueces /keβranta'nweθes; keβranta'nueses/ m, nutcrackers

quebrantar /keβran'tar/ vt to break, shatter; crush, pound; transgress, infringe; break out, force; tone down, soften; moderate, lessen; bore, exhaust; move to pity; *Inf.* break in (horses); profane; overcome (difficulties); assuage, placate, *Law.* revoke (wills); —vr be shaken or bruised, suffer from aftereffects

quebranto /ke'βranto/ m, breaking, shattering; crushing, pounding; infringement; breaking out (from prison); weakness, exhaustion; compassion, pity; loss, damage; pain, suffering

quebrar /ke'βrar/ vt irr to break, shatter; crush; impede, hinder; make pale (color, gen. of complexion); mitigate, moderate; bend, twist; overcome (difficulties); —vi break off (a friendship); weaken, give way; go bankrupt; —vr *Med.* suffer from hernia; be interrupted (of mountain ranges). **quebrarse los ojos**, to strain one's eyes —*Pres. Indic.* **quiebro, quiebras, quiebra, quiebran.** *Pres. Subjunc.* **quiebre, quiebres, quiebre, quiebren**

queda /'keða/ f, curfew; curfew bell

quedada /ke'ðaða/ f, stay, sojourn

quedar /ke'ðar/ vi to stay, sojourn; remain; be left over; (*with por + infin.*) remain to be (e.g. *Queda por escribir*, It remains to be written); (*with por*) be won by or be knocked down to; be, remain in a place; end, cease; (*with en*) reach an agreement (e.g. *Quedamos en no ir*, We have decided not to go). **q. en esta alternativa...**, to face this alternative:... —vr remain; abate (wind); grow calm (sea); (*with con*) keep, retain possession of. **q. bien o mal**, to behave well or badly, come off well or badly (in business affairs, etc.). **quedarse muerto**, to be astounded

quedo /'keðo/ a still, motionless; quiet, tranquil —adv in a low voice; quietly, noiselessly. **de q.**, slowly, gradually —*interj* **¡Q.!** Quiet!

quehacer /kea'θer; kea'ser/ m, odd job; task; business (gen. *pl*)

queja /'keha/ f, lamentation, grief; complaint, grudge; quarrel

quejarse /ke'harse/ vr to lament; complain, grumble; *Law.* lodge an accusation (against)

quejido /ke'hiðo/ m, complaint, moan

quejoso /ke'hoso/ a querulous, complaining

quejumbre /ke'humbre/ f, complaint, whine; querulousness

quema /'kema/ f, burn; burning; fire, conflagration

quemado /ke'maðo/ m, burned patch of forest; *Inf.* anything burned or burning

quemador /kema'ðor/ **(-ra)** m, jet, burner —n incendiary

quemadura /kema'ðura/ f, burn; scald; burning

quemajoso /kema'hoso/ a smarting, burning, pricking

quemar /ke'mar/ vt to burn; dry up, parch; scorch; tan, bronze; scald; throw away, sell at a loss; —vi burn, be excessively hot; —vr be very hot; be dried up with the heat; burn with (passions); *Inf.* be near the attainment of a desired end. **quemarse las cejas**, to burn the midnight oil, study too hard

quemazón /kema'θon; kema'son/ f, burning; conflagration; intense heat; *Inf.* smarting; *Inf.* hurtful remark; *Inf.* vexation, soreness

querella /ke'reʎa; ke'reya/ f, complaint; quarrel, fight

querellarse /kere'ʎarse; kere'yarse/ vr to complain; lament, bemoan; *Law.* lodge an accusation; *Law.* contest a will

querelloso /kere'ʎoso; kere'yoso/ a complaining, grumbling, querulous

querencia /ke'renθia; ke'rensia/ f, love, affection; homing instinct; lair; natural inclination or desire

querer /ke'rer/ vt irr to desire, wish; want, will; attempt, endeavor; (*with a*) love —*impers* be on the point of. **q. decir**, to mean. ¿**Qué quiere decir esto?** What does this mean? **sin q.**, unintentionally. See **entender**

querer /ke'rer/ m, affection, love

querido /ke'riðo/ **(-da)** n lover; beloved; darling —a dear

querub, querube /ke'ruβ, ke'ruβe/ *Poet.* **querubín** m, cherub

quesera /ke'sera/ f, dairymaid; dairy; cheese vat; cheese board; cheese dish

queso /'keso/ m, cheese. **q. de bola**, Dutch cheese. **q. rallado**, grated cheese

¡quia! /kia/ *interj Inf.* You don't say so!

quianti /'kianti/ m, chianti

quicio /'kiθio; 'kisio/ m, threshold; hinge; *Mech.* bushing. **fuera de q.**, out of order; unhinged. **sacar de q.**, to displace (things); annoy, irritate; drive crazy

quiebra /'kieβra/ f, breach, crack; rut, fissure; loss; bankruptcy

quiebro /'kieβro/ m. twisting of the body, dodging; Mus. trill

quien /kien/ rel pron mf pl **quienes.** interr **quién, quiénes** who; whom; he (she, etc.) who, anyone who, whoever; which; whichever (e.g. mis padres a quienes respeto, my parents whom I respect. Quien te quiere te hará llorar, Whoever (he, those, who) love(s) you will make you weep. ¿Quién está a la puerta? Who is at the door? ¿De quién es? Whose is it? To whom does it belong?) —indef pron one (pl some)

quienquiera /kien'kiera/ indef pron mf pl **quienesquiera,** whosoever, whichever, whomsoever

quietador /kieta'ðor/ **(-ra)** a tranquilizing, soothing —n soother

quieto /'kieto/ a quiet, still; peaceful, tranquil; virtuous, respectable

quietud /kie'tuð/ f. stillness, repose; peacefulness; rest, quietness

quijada /ki'haða/ f. jawbone, jaw; Mech. jaw

quijotada /kiho'taða/ f. quixotic action, quixotism

quijote /ki'hote/ m. cuisse; thigh guard; quixotic person

quijotesco /kiho'tesko/ a quixotic

quilate /ki'late/ m. carat; degree of excellence (gen. pl). Inf. **por quilates,** in small bits, parsimoniously

quillotrar /kiʎo'trar; kiyo'trar/ vt Inf. to encourage, incite; woo, make love to; consider; —vr Inf. fall in love; dress up; whine, complain

quillotro /ki'ʎotro; ki'yotro/ m. Inf. incentive; indication, sign; love affair; puzzle, knotty point; compliment; dressing up

quimera /ki'mera/ f. chimera, fancy, vision; quarrel, dispute

quimérico /ki'meriko/ a chimerical, fanciful

química /'kimika/ f. chemistry

químico /'kimiko/ a chemical. m. chemist. **productos químicos,** chemicals

quimono /ki'mono/ m. kimono

quina /'kina/ f. cinchona; quinine; pl Arms of Portugal. Inf. **tragar q.,** to suffer in patience, put up with

quinario /ki'nario/ a quinary

quincalla /kin'kaʎa; kin'kaya/ f. cheap jewelery; fancy goods

quincallería /kinkaʎe'ria; kinkaye'ria/ f. cheap jewelry shop; hardware factory or industry; cheap jewelry; fancy goods

quince /'kinθe; 'kinse/ a and m. fifteen; fifteenth

quinceañero /kinθea'ɲero; kinsea'ɲero/ f. sweet sixteen party, sweet sixteen (in Spanish-speaking areas, held at age fifteen)

quincena /kin'θena; kin'sena/ f. fortnight, two weeks; bimonthly pay; Mus. fifteenth

quincenal /kinθe'nal; kinse'nal/ a fort-

nightly; lasting a fortnight, lasting two weeks

quinceno /kin'θeno; kin'seno/ a fifteenth

quinientos /ki'nientos/ a five hundred; five-hundredth. m, five hundred

quinina /ki'nina/ f. quinine

quinqué /kin'ke/ m. oil lamp, student's lamp, table lamp; perspicuity, talent

quinquenio /kin'kenio/ m. period of five years, lustrum

quinta /'kinta/ f. country house; Mus. fifth; conscripting men into army by drawing lots; Mil. draft

quintaesencia /kintae'senθia; kintae'sensia/ f. quintessence

quintar /kin'tar/ vt to draw one out of every five; draw lots for conscription into the army; —vi reach the fifth (day, etc., gen. of the moon)

quintería /kinte'ria/ f. farm

quintero /kin'tero/ m. farmer; farmworker

quinteto /kin'teto/ m. quintet

Quintín, San. armarse /kin'tin, san ar'marse/ (or **haber) la de San Q.** to quarrel, make trouble; be a row

quinto /'kinto/ a a fifth. m, one-fifth; Mil. conscript; duty of twenty percent; Law. fifth part of an estate. **quinta columna,** fifth column. **quinta esencia,** quintessence

quintuplicar /kintupli'kar/ vt to quintuplicate

quintuplo /'kintuplo/ a fivefold, quintuple

quiñón /ki'ɲon/ m. share of land owned jointly, share of the profits

quiosco /'kiosko/ m, kiosk, stand; pavilion, pagoda. **q. de música,** bandstand

quiquiriquí /kikiri'ki/ m, cock-a-doodledoo; Fig. Inf. cock of the walk

quiromancia /kiro'manθia; kiro'mansia/ f. chiromancy, palmistry

quiromántico /kiro'mantiko/ **(-ca)** n chiromancer, palmist

quirúrgico /ki'rurhiko/ a surgical

quirurgo /ki'rurgo/ m, surgeon

quisicosa /kisi'kosa/ f. Inf. riddle, puzzle, enigma

quisquilla /kis'kiʎa; kis'kiya/ f. trifle, quibble, scruple; prawn, shrimp

quisquilloso /kiski'ʎoso; kiski'yoso/ a quibbling, overscrupulous, fastidious; hypersensitive; irascible, touchy

quistarse /kis'tarse/ vr to make oneself well-liked or loved

quiste /'kiste/ m. Med. cyst

quita /'kita/ f. Law. discharge (of part of a debt)

quitaesmalte /kitaes'malte/ m. nail polish remover (for fingernails)

quitamanchas /kita'mantʃas/ mf, dry cleaner, clothes cleaner

quitamotas /kita'motas/ mf Inf. flatterer, adulator

quitanieve /kita'nieβe/ m, snowplow

quitanza /ki'tanθa; ki'tansa/ *f*, quittance; quietus

quitapesares /kitape'sares/ *m*, *Inf*. consolation, solace, comfort

quitar /ki'tar/ *vt* to remove; take off or away; clear (the table); rob, steal; prevent, impede; parry (in fencing); separate; redeem (pledges); forbid; annul, repeal (laws, etc.); free from (obligations); —*vr* shed, take off, remove; get rid of; leave, quit. **quitarse de encima (a)**, to get rid of someone or something. **q. el**

polvo, to dust. **de quita y pon**, detachable, removable; adjustable

quitasol /kita'sol/ *m*, parasol, sunshade

quitasueño /kita'sueɲo/ *m*, *Inf*. sleep banisher, anxiety

quite /'kite/ *m*, hindering, impeding; obstruction; parry (in fencing). **estar al q.**, to be ready to protect someone

quizá, quizás /ki'θa, ki'θas; ki'sa, ki'sas/ *adv* perhaps. **q. y sin q.**, without doubt, certainly

R

rábano /'rraβano/ *m,* radish. **r. picante,** horseradish

rabel /rra'βel/ *m, Mus.* rebec; *Inf.* backside, seat

rabera /rra'βera/ *f,* tail-end; chaff, siftings

rabí /rra'βi/ *m,* rabbi

rabia /'rraβia/ *f,* rabies, hydrophobia; anger, fury. *Inf.* **tener r.** (a), to hate

rabiar /rra'βiar/ *vi* to suffer from hydrophobia; groan with pain; be furious; (*with por*) yearn for, desire. **a r.,** excessively

rabicorto /rraβi'korto/ *a* short-tailed

rabieta /rra'βieta/ *f, Inf.* tantrum

rabilargo /rraβi'largo/ *a* long-tailed

rabínico /rra'βiniko/ *a* rabbinical

rabinismo /rraβi'nismo/ *m,* rabbinism

rabino /rra'βino/ *m,* rabbi. **gran r.,** chief rabbi

rabioso /rra'βioso/ *a* rabid; furious, angry; vehement. **perro r.,** mad dog

rabo /'rraβo/ *m,* tail; *Bot.* stalk; *Inf.* train (of a dress); shank (of a button). **r. del ojo,** corner of the eye. *Fig. Inf.* **ir r. entre piernas,** to have one's tail between one's legs

rabón /rra'βon/ *a* tailless, docked; bobtailed

rabudo /rra'βuðo/ *a* big-tailed

racimo /rra'θimo; rra'simo/ *m,* bunch (of grapes or other fruits); cluster; raceme

raciocinar /rraθioθi'nar; rrasiosi'nar/ *vi* to reason

raciocinio /rraθio'θinio; rrasio'sinio/ *m,* reasoning; ratiocination; discourse, speech

ración /rra'θion; rra'sion/ *f,* ration; portion (in a restaurant); meal allowance; *Eccl.* prebendary. *Inf.* **r. de hambre,** starvation diet; pittance, starvation wages

racional /rraθio'nal; rrasio'nal/ *a* reasonable, logical; rational

racionalidad /rraθionali'ðað; rrasionali'ðað/ *f,* reasonableness; rationality

racionamiento /rraθiona'miento; rrasiona'miento/ *m,* rationing. *f.* **cartilla de r.,** ration book

racionar /rraθio'nar; rrasio'nar/ *vt* to ration

rada /'rraða/ *f,* bay, cove; *Naut.* road, roadstead

radar /rra'ðar/ *m,* radar

radiación /rraðia'θion; rraðia'sion/ *f,* radiation; *Radio.* broadcasting

radiactividad /rraðiaktiβi'ðað/ *f,* radioactivity

radiactivo /rraðiak'tiβo/ *a* radioactive

radiador /rraðia'ðor/ *m,* radiator (for heating); *Auto.* radiator

radiante /rra'ðiante/ *a Phys.* radiating; brilliant, shining; *Fig.* beaming (with satisfaction)

radiar /rra'ðiar/ *vi Phys.* to radiate; —*vt* broadcast (by radio)

radical /rraði'kal/ *a* radical; fundamental; *Polit.* radical. *m, Gram.* root; (*Math. Chem.*) radical. *mf Polit.* radical

radicar /rraði'kar/ **(se)** *vi* and *vr* to take root. **r. una solicitud,** file an application, submit an application —*vi* be (in a place)

radio /'rraðio/ *m,* (*Geom. Anat.*) radius; radium. *f,* radio

radioaficionado /rraðioafiθio'naðo; rraðioafisio'naðo/ **(-da)** *n* radio amateur; *Inf.* ham, wireless fan or enthusiast

radioaudición /rraðioauði'θion; rraðioauði'sion/ *f,* radio broadcast

radiocomunicación /rraðiokomunika'θion; rraðiokomunika'sion/ *f,* radio transmission

radiodifundir /rraðioðifun'dir/ *vt Radio.* to broadcast

radiodifusión, radioemisión /rraðioðifu'sion, rraðioemi'sion/ *f, Radio.* broadcast; broadcasting

radioemisora /rraðioemi'sora/ *f,* radio station

radioescucha /rraðioes'kutʃa/ *mf* radio listener

radiofotografía /rraðiofotogra'fia/ *f,* radiophotography; x-ray photograph. **tomar una r. de,** to x-ray

radiografía /rraðiogra'fia/ *f,* radiography

radiografiar /rraðiogra'fiar/ *vt* to x-ray, radiograph

radiología /rraðiolo'hia/ *f,* radiology

radiólogo /rra'ðiologo/ *mf* radiologist

radiorreceptor /rraðiorreθep'tor; rraðiorresep'tor/ *m,* receiver, wireless set

radioscopia /rraðio'skopia/ *f,* radioscopy

radioterapia /rraðiote'rapia/ *f,* radiotherapy, radiotherapeutics

radiotransmisor /rraðiotransmi'sor/ *m,* (radio) transmitter

radioyente /rraðio'yente/ *mf* radio listener

raedera /rrae'ðera/ *f,* scraper

raedor /rrae'ðor/ *a* scraping; abrasive

raedura /rrae'ðura/ *f,* scraping; rubbing; fraying

raer /rra'er/ *vt irr* to scrape; abrade; fray; *Fig.* extirpate. See **caer**

ráfaga /'rrafaga/ *f,* gust or blast of wind; light cloud; flash (of light)

rafe /'rrafe/ *m,* eaves

rafia /'rrafia/ *f,* raffia

raído /'rraiðo/ *a* frayed, threadbare; brazen, barefaced

raíz /rra'iθ; rra'is/ *f,* root. **r. amarga,** horseradish. **r. cuadrada** (cúbica), square (cube) root. **r. pivotante,** tap root. **a r.,** close to the root, closely. **a r. de,** as a result of; after. **de r.,** from the root, entirely. **echar raíces,** to take root

raja /'rraha/ *f,* split, crack; chip, splinter (of wood); slice (of fruit, etc.)

rajá /rra'ha/ *m,* rajah

rajadura /rraha'ðura/ *f,* splitting; crack, split, crevice; *Geol.* break

rajar /rra'har/ vt to crack, split; slice; —vi Inf. boast; chatter; —vr crack, split; Inf. take back one's words

ralea /rra'lea/ f, kind, quality; (Inf. scornful) race, lineage

ralear /rrale'ar/ vi to grow thin (cloth, etc.); behave true to type (gen. in a bad sense)

rallador /rraʎa'ðor; rraya'ðor/ m, Cul. grater

rallar /rra'ʎar; rra'yar/ vt Cul. to grate; Inf. bother, annoy

rallo /'rraʎo; 'rrayo/ m, Cul. grater; rasp

ralo /'rralo/ a sparse, thin

rama /'rrama/ f, bough, branch; Fig. branch (of family). Fig. Inf. **andarse por las ramas**, to beat around the bush. **en r.**, Com. raw; unbound (of books)

ramaje /rra'mahe/ m, thickness of branches, denseness of foliage

ramal /rra'mal/ m, strand (of rope); halter; branch line (of a railroad); fork (of a road, etc.); ramification, division

ramalazo /rrama'laθo, rrama'laso/ m, blow with a rope; mark left by this; bruise

rambla /'rrambla/ f, bed, channel, course; avenue, boulevard (in Catalonia)

ramera /rra'mera/ f, whore

ramificación /rramifika'θion; rramifika'sion/ f, ramification; Anat. bifurcation

ramificarse /rramifi'karse/ vr to branch, fork; Fig. spread

ramillete /rrami'ʎete; rrami'yete/ m, bouquet; table centerpiece; Bot. cluster

ramo /'rramo/ m, Bot. branch; twig, spray; bouquet, bunch; wreath; Fig. branch (of learning, etc.); Com. line (of business); Fig. touch, slight attack. **Domingo de Ramos**, Palm Sunday

ramoso /rra'moso/ a branchy, thick with branches

rampa /'rrampa/ f, gradient, incline; Mil. ramp; launching site

ramplón /rram'plon/ a stout, heavy (of shoes); coarse; vulgar; bombastic

rana /'rrana/ f, frog. **r. de San Antonio**, tree frog

ranchero /rran'tʃero/ m, Mil. cook; small farmer; West Hem. rancher

rancho /'rrantʃo/ m, mess, rations; settlement, camp; hut, cabin; Inf. group, huddle; West Hem. ranch; Naut. gang. **hacer r.**, Inf. to make room

rancidez /rranθi'ðeθ; rransi'ðes/ f, rancidness; staleness; rankness; antiquity

ranciedad /rranθie'ðað; rransie'ðað/ f, rancidness; antiquity, oldness; mustiness

rancio /'rranθio; 'rransio/ a rancid, rank; mellow (of wine); ancient; traditional; musty

rango /'rraŋgo/ m, grade, class; range (Mil. Nav. and social) rank; file, line

ranura /rra'nura/ f, groove; rabbet; slot, notch

rapacidad /rrapaθi'ðað; rrapasi'ðað/ f, rapacity, avidity, greed

rapador /rrapa'ðor/ a scraping. m, Inf. barber

rapapolvo /rrapa'polβo/ m, Inf. severe scolding, dressing-down

rapar /rra'par/ (se) vt and vr to shave; —vt crop, cut close (hair); Inf. steal, pinch

rapaz /rra'paθ; rra'pas/ a rapacious. m, young boy. **ave r.**, bird of prey

rapaza /rra'paθa; rra'pasa/ f, young girl

rape /'rrape/ m, Inf. hasty shave or haircut. **al r.**, close-cropped

rapé /rra'pe/ m, snuff

rapidez /rrapi'ðeθ; rrapi'ðes/ f, speed, swiftness, rapidity

rápido /'rrapiðo/ a quick, swift; express (trains). m, torrent, rapid; express train

rapiña /rra'piɲa/ f, robbery, plundering, sacking

rapiñar /rrapi'ɲar/ vt Inf. to steal, pinch

raposa /rra'posa/ f, vixen, fox; Inf. wily person

raposo /rra'poso/ m, (male) fox

rapsodia /rrap'soðia/ f, rhapsody

raptar /rrap'tar/ vt to abduct; rob

rapto /'rrapto/ m, abduction, rape; snatching, seizing; ecstasy, trance; Med. loss of consciousness

raptor /rrap'tor/ m, kidnapper, abductor

raqueta /rra'keta/ f, racket (tennis, badminton, squash rackets); croupier's rake. **r. de nieve**, snowshoe

raquítico /rra'kitiko/ a Med. rachitic; small, minute; weak, feeble, rickety

raquitismo /rraki'tismo/ m, rickets

rarefacer /rrarefa'θer; rrarefa'ser/ (se) vt and vr irr to rarefy. See **satisfacer**

rareza /rra'reθa; rra'resa/ f, rareness, unusualness; eccentricity, whim; oddity, curio

raridad /rrari'ðað/ f, rarity; thinness; scarcity

raro /'rraro/ a rare, unusual, uncommon; notable, outstanding; odd, eccentric, queer; rarefied (gases, etc.). **rara vez**, seldom. **lo r. de**, the strange thing about (e.g. Lo r. del caso es..., the strange thing about the case is...)

ras /rras/ m, level. **a r.**, flush (with), nearly touching

rasa /'rrasa/ f, worn place in cloth; clearing, glade

rasar /rra'sar/ vt to level with a strickle; graze, brush, touch lightly; —vr grow clear (of the sky, etc.)

rascacielos /rraska'θielos; rraska'sielos/ m, skyscraper

rascadura /rraska'ðura/ f, scraping; scratching

rascar /rras'kar/ vt to scratch; claw; scrape; twang (a guitar, etc.). Inf. ¡Que se rasque! Let him put up with it! Let him lump it!

rascón /rras'kon/ a sour, tart

rasgadura /rrasga'ðura/ f, tearing; tear, rip, rent

rasgar /rras'gar/ **(se)** vt and vr to tear, rip; —vt strum the guitar

rasgo /'rrasgo/ m, flourish (of the pen); felicitous expression; characteristic, quality; pl features (of the face)

rasgón /rras'gon/ m, rip, tear

rasguear /rrasge'ar/ vt to strum, twang (the guitar); —vi write with a flourish

rasgueo /rras'geo/ m, flourish (on a guitar); scratch (of a pen)

rasguñar /rrasgu'ɲar/ vt to scratch, scrape; claw; Art. sketch

rasguño /rras'guɲo/ m, scratch; Art. sketch, outline

raso /'rraso/ a flat; free of obstacles; glossy; clear (sky, etc.); plain; undistinguished; backless (chairs). m, satin. **al r.,** in the open air

raspa /'rraspa/ f, Bot. beard (of cereals); fishbone; bunch of grapes; Bot. husk; scraper

raspador /rraspa'ðor/ m, eraser; scraper, rasp

raspadura /rraspa'ðura/ f, scraping; erasing; shavings, filings

raspar /rras'par/ vt to scrape; erase; rob, steal; burn, bite (wine, etc.)

rastra /'rrastra/ f, trace, sign; sled; string of onions, etc.; anything dragging; Agr. harrow; Agr. rake. **a la r.,** dragging; reluctantly. **pescar a la r.,** to trawl

rastrear /rrastre'ar/ vt to trace, trail; drag, trawl; surmise, conjecture, investigate; —vi Agr. rake; fly low

rastrero /rras'trero/ a dragging, trailing; low-flying; servile, abject; Bot. creeping. m, slaughterhouse employee

rastrillar /rrastri'ʎar; rrastri'yar/ vt to rake; dress, comb (flax)

rastrillo /rras'triʎo; rras'triyo/ m, Agr. rake; hackle; portcullis; Agr. rack

rastro /'rrastro/ m, Agr. rake; track, trail; wholesale meat market; slaughterhouse; trace, vestige; second-hand market (in Madrid)

rasurar /rrasu'rar/ **(se)** vt and vr to shave

rata /'rrata/ f, rat. m, Inf. pickpocket. **r. almizclera,** muskrat. Inf. **más pobre que las ratas,** poorer than a church mouse

ratear /rrate'ar/ vt to rebate pro rata; apportion; thieve on a small scale, filch; —vi crawl, creep

ratería /rrate'ria/ f, filching, petty theft, picking pockets; meanness, parsimony

ratero /rra'tero/ **(-ra)** n pilferer, petty thief, pickpocket

ratificación /rratifika'θion; rratifika'sion/ f, ratification

ratificar /rratifi'kar/ vt to ratify

rato /'rrato/ m, short interval of time, while. **buen (mal) r.,** pleasant (unpleasant) time. **r. perdido,** leisure moment. **a ratos,** sometimes, occasionally. **de r. en**

r., from time to time. **pasar el r.,** Inf. to while away the time

ratón /rra'ton/ **(-ona)** n mouse

ratonera /rrato'nera/ f, mousetrap; mousehole; mouse nest. Fig. **caer en la r.,** to fall into a trap

raudal /rrau'ðal/ m, torrent, cascade; Fig. flood, abundance

raudo /'rrauðo/ a swift, rapid

ravioles /rra'βioles/ m pl, ravioli

raya /'rraya/ f, stripe, streak; limit, end; part (of the hair); boundary; Gram. dash; score (some games). m, Ichth. ray. **pasar de r.,** to go too far; misbehave

rayadillo /rraya'ðiʎo; rraya'ðiyo/ m, striped cotton

rayano /rra'yano/ a neighboring; border; almost identical, very similar

rayar /rra'yar/ vt to draw lines; streak; stripe; cross out; underline; rifle (a gun); —vi verge (on), border (on); appear (of dawn, daylight); excel; be similar. **Raya en los catorce años,** He is about fourteen

rayo /'rrayo/ m, Phys. beam, ray; thunderbolt; flash of lightning; spoke; quickwitted person; capable, energetic person; sudden pain; disaster, catastrophe. **r. de sol,** sunbeam. **r. catódico,** cathode ray. **r. x,** x-ray. Fig. **echar rayos,** to breathe forth fury

rayón /rra'yon/ m, rayon

raza /'rraθa; 'rrasa/ f, race; breed; lineage, family; kind, class; crack, crevice. **de r.,** purebred

razón /rra'θon; rra'son/ f, reason; reasoning; word, expression; speech, argument; motive, cause; order, method; justice, equity; right, authority; explanation; Math. ratio, proportion. **r. de estado,** raison d'état, reasons of state. Com. **r. social,** firm, trade name. **a r. de,** at a rate of. **dar la r. (a),** to agree with. **estar puesto en r.,** to stand to reason. **tener r.,** to be in the right

razonable /rraθo'naβle; rraso'naβle/ a reasonable; moderate

razonamiento /rraθona'miento; rrasona'miento/ m, reasoning

razonar /rraθo'nar; rraso'nar/ vi to reason; speak; —vt attest, confirm

razzia /'rraθθia; 'rrassia/ f, foray; pillaging, sacking; police raid

re /rre/ m, Mus. re, D

reabsorción /rreaβsor'θion; rreaβsor'sion/ f, reabsorption

reacción /rreak'θion; rreak'sion/ f, reaction. **r. de Bayardo,** quick reaction of someone always ready to help those in distress

reaccionar /rreakθio'nar; rreaksio'nar/ vi to react

reaccionario /rreakθio'nario; rreaksio'nario/ **(-ia)** a and n reactionary

reacio /rre'aθio; rre'asio/ a recalcitrant

reactivo /rreak'tiβo/ m, reagent —a reactive; reacting

readmitir /rreaðmi'tir/ vt to readmit

reajustar /rreahus'tar/ *vt* to readjust

real /rre'al/ *a* actual, real; kingly; royal; royalist; *Fig.* regal; *Inf.* fine, handsome. *m*, silver coin, real; *m pl*, encampment, camp. **alzar el r.**, *Mil.* to strike camp. **asentar el r.**, *Mil.* to encamp. **r. decreto**, royal decree. **sitio r.**, royal residence. **un r., sobre otro**, *Inf.* cash in full

realce /rre'alθe; rre'alse/ *m*, raised or embossed work; renown, glory; *Art.* high light

realeza /rrea'leθa; rrea'lesa/ *f*, royalty, royal majesty

realidad /rreali'ðað/ *f*, reality; sincerity, truth. **en r.**, in fact, actually

realismo /rrea'lismo/ *m*, realism; regalism; royalism

realista /rrea'lista/ *a* realistic; royalist. *mf* realist; royalist; regalist

realizable /rreali'θaβle; rreali'saβle/ *a* realizable; practicable

realización /rrealiθa'θion; rrealisa'sion/ *f*, realization; performance; execution

realizar /rreali'θar; rreali'sar/ *vt* to perform, execute, carry out; *Com.* realize. **r. beneficio**, to make a profit

realmente /rreal'mente/ *adv* really, truly; actually

realzar /rreal'θar; rreal'sar/ *vt* to heighten, raise; emboss; exalt; enhance; *Art.* intensify (colors, etc.)

reanimar /rreani'mar/ *vt* to reanimate; revive, restore, resuscitate; encourage

reanudación /rreanuða'θion; rreanuða'sion/ *f*, resumption, renewal

reanudar /rreanu'ðar/ *vt* to resume, continue

reaparecer /rreapare'θer; rreapare'ser/ *vi irr* to reappear. See **conocer**

rearmar /rrear'mar/ *vi* to rearm

reaseguro /rrease'guro/ *m*, reinsurance, underwriting

reasumir /rreasu'mir/ *vt* to reassume; resume

reata /rre'ata/ *f*, string of horses or mules. **de r.**, in single file; *Inf.* blindly, unquestioningly; *Inf.* at once

rebaja /rre'βaha/ *f*, diminution; *Com.* discount, rebate; remission

rebajar /rreβa'har/ *vt* to lower; curtail, lessen; remit; *Com.* reduce in price; *Mech.* file; *Elec.* step down; humble, humiliate; —*vr* cringe, humble oneself

rebanada /rreβa'naða/ *f*, slice, piece (of bread, etc.)

rebanar /rreβa'nar/ *vt* to cut into slices; split

rebaño /rre'βaɲo/ *m*, flock, drove, herd; *Eccl.* flock

rebasar /rreβa'sar/ *vt* to exceed, go beyond; *Mil.* bypass

rebate /rre'βate/ *m*, altercation, dispute, quarrel

rebatir /rreβa'tir/ *vt* to repulse, repel; fight again; fight hard; oppose, resist; *Com.* deduct; refuse, reject

rebato /rre'βato/ *m*, alarm, tocsin; *Mil.* surprise attack; panic, dismay

rebeca /rre'βeka/ *f*, cardigan, jersey

rebelarse /rreβe'larse/ *vr* to mutiny, rebel; oppose, resist

rebelde /rre'βelde/ *a* mutinous, rebellious; wilful, disobedient; stubborn. *mf* rebel

rebeldía /rreβel'dia/ *f*, rebelliousness; willfulness; stubbornness; *Law.* nonappearance

rebelión /rreβe'lion/ *f*, insurrection, revolt

reblandecer /rreβlande'θer; rreβlande'ser/ *vt irr* to soften; —*vr* become soft. See **conocer**

reblandecimiento /rreβlandeθi'miento; rreβlandesi'miento/ *m*, softening; *Med.* flabbiness

reborde /rre'βorðe/ *m*, rim, edge; *Mech.* flange. **r. de acera**, curb

rebordear /rreβorðe'ar/ *vt* to flange

rebosar /rreβo'sar/ *vt* to overflow, run over, *Fig.* abound in, express one's feelings

rebotar /rreβo'tar/ *vi* to rebound; clinch (nails, etc.); refuse; —*vr* change color; *Inf.* be vexed

rebote /rre'βote/ *m*, rebounding; rebound

rebozar /rreβo'θar; rreβo'sar/ *vt* to muffle up; coat with batter

rebozo /rre'βoθo; rre'βoso/ *m*, muffling up, hiding the face; head shawl; pretense, excuse. *Fig.* **sin r.**, openly

rebueno /rre'βueno/ *a Inf.* extremely good, fine

rebullir /rreβu'ʎir; rreβu'yir/ *vi* to stir, show signs of movement; *Fig.* swarm, seethe

rebusca /rre'βuska/ *f*, close search; gleaning; remains

rebuscado /rreβus'kaðo/ *a* affected, unnatural (of style)

rebuznar /rreβuθ'nar; rreβus'nar/ *vi* to bray

recadero /rreka'ðero/ **(-ra)** *n* messenger, errand boy

recado /rre'kaðo/ *m*, message; greeting, note; gift, present; daily marketing; outfit, implements; precaution, safeguard

recaer /rreka'er/ *vi irr* to fall again; *Med.* relapse; lapse, backslide; devolve, fall upon. See **caer**

recaída /rreka'iða/ *f*, falling again; *Med.* relapse; lapse

recalar /rreka'lar/ *vt* to impregnate; *Naut.* call at (a port), come within sight of land

recalcada /rrekal'kaða/ *f*, pressing down, squeezing; emphasis; *Naut.* list

recalcar /rrekal'kar/ *vt* to press down; squeeze; pack tight; stress, emphasize; —*vi Naut.* list; —*vr Inf.* say over and over, savor one's words

recalcitrante /rrekalθi'trante; rrekalsi'trante/ *a* obdurate, recalcitrant

recalentar /rrekalen'tar/ *vt irr* to overheat; superheat; reheat. See **sentar**

recamado /rreka'maðo/ *m*, raised embroidery

recámara /rre'kamara/ *f*, dressing room; explosives chamber; breech of a gun; *Inf.* caution

recambio /rre'kambio/ *m*, spare, spare part; *Com.* re-exchange

recapacitar /rrekapaθi'tar; rrekapasi'tar/ *vi* to search one's memory; think over

recapitulación /rrekapitula'θion; rrekapitula'sion/ *f*, summary, résumé

recapitular /rrekapitu'lar/ *vt* to recapitulate, summarize

recargar /rrekar'gar/ *vt* to recharge; load again; reaccuse; overcharge; overdress or overdecorate; —*vr Med.* become more feverish. **r. acumuladores,** to recharge batteries

recargo /rre'kargo/ *m*, charge; new load; *Law.* new accusation; overcharge, extra cost; *Med.* temperature increase

recatado /rreka'taðo/ *a* prudent, discreet, circumspect; modest, shy

recatar /rreka'tar/ *vt* to hide, conceal; —*vr* be prudent or cautious

recato /rre'kato/ *m*, caution, prudence; modesty, shyness, reserve

recauchutar /rrekautʃu'tar/ *vt* to retread (tires)

recaudación /rrekauða'θion; rrekauða-'sion/ *f*, collecting; collection (of taxes, etc.); tax collector's office

recaudador /rrekauða'ðor/ *m*, tax collector

recaudar /rrekau'ðar/ *vt* to collect, recover (taxes, debts, etc.); deposit, place in custody

recaudo /rre'kauðo/ *m*, collecting; collection (of taxes, etc.); precaution, safeguard; *Law.* surety

recelar /rreθe'lar; rrese'lar/ *vt* to suspect, fear, mistrust; —*vr (with de)* be afraid or suspicious of

recelo /rre'θelo; rre'selo/ *m*, suspicion, mistrust, doubt, fear

receloso /rreθe'loso; rrese'loso/ *a* suspicious, distrustful, doubtful

recepción /rreθep'θion; rresep'sion/ *f*, receiving, reception; admission, acceptance; reception, party; *Law.* cross-examination

receptáculo /rreθep'takulo; rresep'takulo/ *m*, receptacle, container; *Fig.* refuge; *Bot.* receptacle

receptador /rreθepta'ðor; rresepta'ðor/ **(-ra)** *n* receiver (of stolen goods); accomplice

receptor /rreθep'tor; rresep'tor/ **(-ra)** *a* receiving —*n* recipient. *m, Elec.* receiver; wireless set. **r. de galena,** crystal set. **r. telefónico,** telephone receiver

receta /rre'θeta; rre'seta/ *f, Med.* prescription; *Cul.* recipe

recetar /rreθe'tar; rrese'tar/ *vt Med.* to prescribe; *Inf.* demand

rechapear /rretʃape'ar/ *vt* to replate

rechazar /rretʃa'θar; rretʃa'sar/ *vt* to repulse; resist; refuse; oppose, deny (the truth of); contradict

rechazo /rre'tʃaθo; rre'tʃaso/ *m*, recoil; rebound; refusal

rechinamiento, rechino /rretʃina-'miento, rre'tʃino/ *m*, squeaking, creaking; gnashing (of teeth)

rechinar /rretʃi'nar/ *vi* to squeak, creak; gnash (teeth); chatter (teeth); do with a bad grace

rechoncho /rre'tʃontʃo/ *a* squat, stocky

recibí /rreθi'βi; rresi'βi/ *m, Com.* receipt

recibidor /rreθiβi'ðor; rresiβi'ðor/ **(-ra)** *a* receiving —*n* recipient. *m*, reception room

recibimiento /rreθiβi'miento; rresiβi'miento/ *m*, reception; welcome; greeting; reception room, waiting room; hall, vestibule

recibir /rreθi'βir; rresi'βir/ *vt* to obtain, receive; support, bear; suffer, experience (attack, injury); approve; accept, receive; entertain; stand up to (attack); —*vr (with de)* graduate, take office as

recibo /rre'θiβo; rre'siβo/ *m*, reception; *Com.* receipt; reception room, waiting room; hall, vestibule. *Com.* **acusar r.,** to acknowledge receipt

recidiva /rreθi'ðiβa; rresi'ðiβa/ *f, Med.* relapse

recién /rre'θien; rre'sien/ *adv* recently, newly. Shortened form of **reciente** before a past participle (e.g. *r. llegado,* newly arrived)

reciente /rre'θiente; rre'siente/ *a* recent; new; fresh

recinto /rre'θinto; rre'sinto/ *m*, precincts; neighborhood; premises, place

recio /'rreθio; 'rresio/ *a* strong; robust; bulky, thick; rough, uncouth; grievous, hard; severe (weather); impetuous, precipitate

recipiente /rreθi'piente; rresi'piente/ *a* receiving. *m*, receptacle, container, vessel

reciprocar /rreθipro'kar; rresipro'kar/ to reciprocate

recíproco /rre'θiproko; rre'siproko/ *a* reciprocal

recitación /rreθita'θion; rresita'sion/ *f*, recitation

recitar /rreθi'tar; rresi'tar/ *vt* to recite, declaim

reclamación /rreklama'θion; rreklama'sion/ *f*, reclamation; objection, opposition; *Com.* claim

reclamar /rrekla'mar/ *vi* to oppose, object to; *Poet.* resound; —*vt* call repeatedly; *Com.* claim; decoy (birds)

reclamo /rre'klamo/ *m*, decoy bird; enticement, allurement; *Law.* reclamation; advertisement. **objeto de r.,** advertising sample. **venta de r.,** bargain sale

recluir /rre'kluir/ *vt irr* to immure, shut up; detain, arrest. See **huir**

reclusión /rreklu'sion/ *f*, confinement, seclusion; prison

recluso /rre'kluso/ **(-sa)** *n* recluse

recluta /rre'kluta/ f. recruiting. *mf Mil.* recruit

reclutamiento /rrekluta'miento/ m. recruiting

reclutar /rreklu'tar/ vt to enlist recruits, recruit

recobrar /rreko'βrar/ vt to recover, regain; —vr recuperate; regain consciousness

recobro /rre'koβro/ m. recovery; *Mech.* pick-up

recocer /rreko'θer; rreko'ser/ vt irr to reboil; recook; overboil; overcook; anneal (metals); —vr *Fig.* be tormented (by emotion), be all burned up. See **cocer**

recodo /rre'koδo/ m. bend, turn, loop

recogedor /rrekohe'δor/ a sheltering. m, *Agr.* gleaner

recoger /rreko'her/ vt to gather, pick; pick up; retake; collect (letters from a mailbox, etc.); amass; shrink, narrow; keep; hoard; shelter; reap, pick; —vr withdraw, retire; go home; go to bed; retrench, economize; give oneself to meditation

recogida /rreko'hiδa/ f. collection (of letters from a mailbox); withdrawal; retirement; harvest

recogido /rreko'hiδo/ a recluse; cloistered, confined

recogimiento /rrekohi'miento/ m, gathering, picking; collection, accumulation; seclusion; shelter; women's reformatory

recolección /rrekolek'θion; rrekolek'sion/ f, summary, résumé; harvest; collection (of taxes, etc.); *Eccl.* convent of a reformed order; mystic ecstasy

recomendación /rrekomenda'θion; rrekomenda'sion/ f, recommendation (all meanings)

recomendar /rrekomen'dar/ vt irr to recommend (all meanings); entrust, commend —*Pres. Indic.* **recomiendo, recomiendas, recomienda, recomiendan.** *Pres. Subjunc.* **recomiende, recomiendes, recomiende, recomienden**

recompensa /rrekom'pensa/ f, compensation; recompense, reward

recompensar /rrekompen'sar/ vt to compensate; requite; reward, recompense

recomposición /rrekomposi'θion; rrekomposi'sion/ f, recomposition

recomprar /rrekom'prar/ vt to repurchase

reconcentrar /rrekonθen'trar; rrekonsen'trar/ vt to concentrate; dissemble; —vr withdraw into oneself, meditate

reconciliable /rrekonθi'liaβle; rrekonsi'liaβle/ a reconcilable

reconciliación /rrekonθilia'θion; rrekonsilia'sion/ f, reconciliation

reconciliar /rrekonθi'liar; rrekonsi'liar/ vt to reconcile; *Eccl.* reconsecrate; *Eccl.* hear a short confession; —vr become reconciled; *Eccl.* make an additional confession

recondicionar /rrekondiθio'nar; rrekondisio'nar/ vt to rebuild, overhaul, recondition

recóndito /rre'kondito/ a recondite

reconocer /rrekono'θer; rrekono'ser/ vt irr to examine, inspect; recognize; admit, acknowledge; own, confess; search; *Polit.* recognize; *Mil.* reconnoiter; (with por) adopt as (a son, etc.); recognize as; —vr be seen, show; acknowledge, confess; know oneself. **Bien se reconoce que no está aquí,** It's easy to see he's not here. See **conocer**

reconocido /rrekono'θiδo; rrekono'siδo/ a grateful

reconocimiento /rrekonoθi'miento; rrekonosi'miento/ m, examination, inspection; recognition; acknowledgement, admission; search; *Mil.* reconnoitering; adoption; gratitude

reconstruir /rrekons'truir/ vt irr to reconstruct, rebuild; recreate. See **huir**

reconvención /rrekomben'θion; rrekomben'sion/ f, rebuke, reproof; recrimination; *Law.* countercharge

recopilación /rrekopila'θion; rrekopila'sion/ f, summary, compendium; collection (of writings); digest (of laws)

recopilar /rrekopi'lar/ vt to compile, collect

recordar /rrekor'δar/ vt irr to cause to remember, remind; remember; —vi remember; awake. See **acordar**

recordatorio /rrekorδa'torio/ m, reminder —a commemorative (e.g. a plaque)

recorrer /rreko'rrer/ vt to travel over; pass through; wander around; examine, inspect; read hastily; overhaul, renovate

recorrido /rreko'rriδo/ m, journey, run; *Mech.* stroke; overhaul. **r. de despegue,** *Aer.* take-off run

recortar /rrekor'tar/ vt to clip, trim, pare; cut out; *Art.* outline; —vr stand out (against), be outlined (against)

recorte /rre'korte/ m, clipping, paring; cutting; cutout; *Art.* outline; pl snippets, clippings. **r. de periódico,** newspaper cutting, newspaper clipping

recostar /rrekos'tar/ vt irr (with en or contra) to lean, rest against; —vr (with en or contra) lean against, rest on; lean back; recline. See **contar**

recreación /rrekrea'θion; rrekrea'sion/ f, recreation, hobby

recrear /rrekre'ar/ vt to entertain, amuse; —vr amuse oneself; delight (in), enjoy

recreo /rre'kreo/ m, recreation, hobby; playtime, recess (in schools); place of amusement. **salón de r.,** recreation room

recriminador /rrekrimina'δor/ a recriminatory

recriminar /rrekrimi'nar/ vt to recriminate

recrudecer /rrekruδe'θer; rrekruδe'ser/ **(se)** vi and vr irr to recur, return. See **conocer**

rectángulo /rrek'taŋgulo/ m, rectangle —a rectangular

rectificable /rrektifi'kaβle/ a rectifiable

rectificación /rrektifika'θion; rrekti-fika'sion/ *f*, rectification; *Mech.* grinding

rectificar /rrektifi'kar/ *vt* to rectify; *Mech.* grind; —*vr* mend one's ways; *Mil.* **r. el frente**, to straighten the line

rectitud /rrekti'tuð/ *f*, straightness; rectitude, integrity; exactness; righteousness

recto /'rrekto/ *a* straight; upright; erect; literal (meaning); just, fair; single-breasted (of coats); *m*, right angle; rectum

rector /rrek'tor/ **(-ra)** *n* director; principal, headmaster. *m*, *Eccl.* rector

rectorado /rrekto'raðo/ *m*, principalship, headmaster- (mistress-) ship, directorship; *Eccl.* rectorship

recua /'rrekua/ *f*, drove of beasts of burden; *Inf.* string or line (of things)

recubrir /rreku'βrir/ *vt* to re-cover; coat; plate —*Past Part.* recubierto

recuento /rre'kuento/ *m*, calculation; recount; inventory

recuerdo /rre'kuerðo/ *m*, memory, remembrance; memento; *pl* greetings, regards

recular /rreku'lar/ *vi* to recoil, draw back; *Inf.* go back on, give up

recuperable /rrekupe'raβle/ *a* recoverable, recuperable

recuperación /rrekupera'θion; rrekupera'sion/ *f*, recovery, recuperation; *Chem.* recovery

recurrir /rreku'rrir/ *vi* to recur; (*with prep a*) have recourse to; appeal to

recurso /rre'kurso/ *m*, recourse, resort; choice, option; reversion; petition; *Law.* appeal; *pl* means of livelihood; *Fig.* way out, last hope

recusar /rreku'sar/ *vt* to refuse; challenge the authority (of)

red /rreð/ *f*, net; network; hairnet; railing, grating; *Fig.* snare; system (of communications, etc.); *Fig.* combination (of events, etc.); *Elec.* mains. **r. de arrastre**, trawl net. *Fig. Inf.* **caer en la r.**, to fall into the trap

redacción /rreðak'θion; rreðak'sion/ *f*, phrasing; editorial office; editing; editorial board

redactar /rreðak'tar/ *vt* to write, phrase; draw up; edit

redactor /rreðak'tor/ **(-ra)** *a* editorial —*n* editor

redención /rreðen'θion; rreðen'sion/ *f*, redemption; ransom; deliverance, salvation; redeeming, paying off (a mortgage, etc.)

redentor /rreðen'tor/ **(-ra)** *a* redeeming, redemptive —*n* redeemer

redil /rre'ðil/ *m*, sheepfold

redimible /rreði'miβle/ *a* redeemable

redimir /rreði'mir/ *vt* to ransom; redeem, buy back; pay off (a mortgage, etc.); deliver, free; *Eccl.* redeem

rédito /'rreðito/ *m*, *Com.* income, revenue, interest; profit

redoblamiento /rreðoβla'miento/ *m*, re-doubling; bending back (of nails, etc.); rolling (of a drum)

redoblar /rreðo'βlar/ *vt* to redouble; repeat; bend back (nails, etc.); —*vi* roll (a drum)

redoble /rre'ðoβle/ *m*, doubling; redoubling; repetition; roll (of a drum)

redonda /rre'ðonda/ *f*, district; pasture ground; *Naut.* square sail; *Mus.* semibreve. **a la r.**, around

redondear /rreðonde'ar/ *vt* to make round; round; free (from debt, etc.); —*vr* acquire a fortune; clear oneself (of debts, etc.)

redondel /rreðon'del/ *m*, traffic circle, rotary, roundabout

redondo /rre'ðondo/ *a* round; circular; unequivocal, plain. *m*, round, circle; *Inf.* cash

reducción /rreðuk'θion; rreðuk'sion/ *f*, reduction; *Mil.* defeat, conquest; decrease; *Com.* rebate; (*Math. Chem.*) reduction

reducir /rreðu'θir; rreðu'sir/ *vt irr* to reduce; decrease, cut down; break up; *Art.* scale down; *Elec.* step down; subdue; (*Chem. Math. Surg.*) reduce; exchange; divide into small fragments; persuade; —*vr* be obliged to, have to; live moderately. See **conducir**

redundancia /rreðun'danθia; rreðun'dansia/ *f*, redundance

redundante /rreðun'dante/ *a* redundant

redundar /rreðun'dar/ *vi* to overflow; be excessive or superfluous; (*with en*) redound to

reduplicar /rreðupli'kar/ *vt* to reduplicate

ree /rree/ For words so beginning (e.g. *re-editar, reexportar*), see spellings with one *e*

refacción /rrefak'θion; rrefak'sion/ *f*, refection, light meal; compensation, reparation

refajo /rre'faho/ *m*, skirt, underskirt

refección /rrefek'θion; rrefek'sion/ *f*, refection, light meal

refectorio /rrefek'torio/ *m*, refectory

referencia /rrefe'renθia; rrefe'rensia/ *f*, report, account; allusion; regard, relation; *Com.* reference (gen. *pl*); consideration

referente /rrefe'rente/ *a* concerning, related (to)

referir /rrefe'rir/ *vt irr* to narrate; describe; direct, guide; relate, refer, concern; —*vr* allude (to); refer (to); concern. See **sentir**

refinación /rrefina'θion; rrefina'sion/ *f*, refining

refinado /rrefi'naðo/ *a* refined; polished; cultured; crafty

refinamiento /rrefina'miento/ *m*, refinement, subtlety, care

refinar /rrefi'nar/ *vt* to refine, purify; polish, perfect

refinería /rrefine'ria/ *f*, refinery

reflector /rreflek'tor/ *a* reflecting. *m*, reflector; searchlight; shade (for lamps, etc.)

reflejar /rrefle'har/ vi *Phys.* to reflect; —vt consider; show, mirror; —vr *Fig.* be reflected, be seen

reflejo /rre'fleho/ m, reflection; image; glare —a reflex; considered, judicious

reflexión /rreflek'sion/ f, *Phys.* reflection; consideration, thought

reflexionar /rrefleksio'nar/ vt (with *en* or *sobre*) to consider, reflect upon

reflexivo /rreflek'siβo/ a *Phys.* reflective; thoughtful

reflorecer /rreflore'θer; rreflore'ser/ vi *irr* to flower again; return to favor (ideas, etc.). See **conocer**

reflujo /rre'fluho/ m, reflux, refluence; ebb tide

refocilar /rrefoθi'lar; rrefosi'lar/ vt to warm up, brace up, give pleasure to; —vr enjoy oneself

reforma /rre'forma/ f, reform; improvement; reformation; *Hist.* Reformation

reformación /rreforma'θion; rreforma'sion/ f, reform, improvement

reformador /rreforma'ðor/ **(-ra)** a reformatory, reforming —n reformer

reformar /rrefor'mar/ vt to remake; reshape; repair, mend, restore; improve, correct; *Eccl.* reform; reorganize; —vr mend one's ways, improve; control oneself

reformatorio /rreforma'torio/ m, reformatory —a reforming, reformatory

reformista /rrefor'mista/ mf reformist, reformer —a reformatory

reforzador /rreforθa'ðor; rreforsa'ðor/ m, *Photo.* reinforcing bath; *Elec.* booster

reforzamiento /rreforθa'miento; rreforsa'miento/ m, stiffening, reinforcing

reforzar /rrefor'θar; rrefor'sar/ vt *irr* to reinforce, strengthen, stiffen; encourage, inspirit. See **forzar**

refractar /rrefrak'tar/ vt to refract

refractario /rrefrak'tario/ a stubborn; (*Phys. Chem.*) refractory; unmanageable, unruly; fireproof

refrán /rre'fran/ m, proverb

refranero /rrefra'nero/ m, collection of proverbs

refregar /rrefre'gar/ vt *irr* to rub; scrub, scour; *Fig. Inf.* rub in, insist on. See **cegar**

refrenar /rrefre'nar/ vt to curb, check (horses); control, restrain

refrendar /rrefren'dar/ vt to countersign, endorse, legalize

refrescante /rrefres'kante/ a refreshing, cooling

refrescar /rrefres'kar/ vt to cool, chill; repeat; *Fig.* brush up, revise; —vi be rested or refreshed; grow cooler; take the air; freshen (wind); take a cool drink; —vr grow cooler; take the air; take a cool drink

refresco /rre'fresko/ m, refreshment; cool drink

refriega /rre'friega/ f, affray, scuffle, rough-and-tumble

refrigeración /rrefrihera'θion; rrefrihera-'sion/ f, refrigeration

refrigerador /rrefrihera'ðor/ m, refrigerator

refrigerante /rrefrihe'rante/ a refrigerative; chilling; cooling. m, cooling chamber, cooler

refrigerar /rrefrihe'rar/ vt to chill; cool; freeze, refrigerate; refresh

refrigerio /rrefri'herio/ m, coolness; consolation; refreshment, food

refuerzo /rre'fuerθo; rre'fuerso/ m, reinforcement, strengthening; aid, help

refugiado /rrefu'hiaðo/ **(-da)** a and n refugee

refugiar /rrefu'hiar/ vt to protect, shelter; —vr take refuge

refugio /rre'fuhio/ m, refuge, shelter, protection; traffic island. **r. antiaéreo,** air raid shelter. **r. para peatones,** traffic island

refulgencia /rreful'henθia; rreful'hensia/ f, resplendence, splendor, brilliance

refulgente /rreful'hente/ a resplendent, refulgent, dazzling

refulgir /rreful'hir/ vi to shine, be dazzling

refundición /rrefundi'θion; rrefundi'sion/ f, recasting (of metals); adaptation; rehash, refurbishing

refundir /rrefun'dir/ vt to recast (metals); include, comprise; adapt; rehash, refurbish; —vi *Fig.* promote, contribute to

refunfuñador /rrefunfuɲa'ðor/ a grumbling, fuming

refunfuñar /rrefunfu'ɲar/ vi to grumble, growl, fume

refunfuño /rrefun'fuɲo/ m, grumble, fuming; snort

refutar /rrefu'tar/ vt to refute

regadera /rrega'ðera/ f, watering can; irrigation canal; sprinkler

regadío /rrega'ðio/ m, irrigated land; irrigation, watering —a irrigated

regajal, regajo /rrega'hal, rre'gaho/ m, pool, puddle; stream, brook

regalado /rrega'laðo/ a delicate, highly bred; luxurious, delightful

regalar /rrega'lar/ vt to make a gift of, give; caress, fondle; indulge, cherish; entertain, regale; —vr live in luxury

regalía /rrega'lia/ f, royal privilege; right, exemption; perquisite, emolument

regaliz /rrega'liθ; rrega'lis/ m, **regaliza** f, licorice

regalo /rre'galo/ m, gift, present; satisfaction, pleasure; entertainment, regalement; luxury, comfort

regalón /rrega'lon/ a *Inf.* pampered

regañadientes, a /rregaɲa'ðientes/ adv unwillingly, grumblingly

regañar /rrega'ɲar/ vi to snarl (dogs); crack (skin of fruits); grumble, mutter; *Inf.* quarrel; —vt *Inf.* scold

regaño /rre'gaɲo/ *m*, angry look or gesture; *Inf.* scolding

regañón /rrega'ɲon/ **(-ona)** *a Inf.* grumbling, complaining; scolding —*n Inf.* grumbler

regar /rre'gar/ *vt irr* to water, sprinkle with water; flow through, irrigate; spray; *Fig.* shower (with), strew. See **cegar**

regata /rre'gata/ *f*, regatta; small irrigation channel (for gardens, etc.)

regate /rre'gate/ *m*, twist of the body, sidestep; dribbling; (in soccer); *Inf.* dodging, evasion

regatear /rregate'ar/ *vt* to haggle over, beat down (prices); resell, retail; dribble (a ball); *Fig. Inf.* dodge, avoid; —*vi* bargain, haggle; *Naut.* take part in a regatta, race

regateo /rrega'teo/ *m*, haggling, bargaining

regatero /rrega'tero/ **(-ra)** *a* retail —*n* retailer

regatón /rrega'ton/ **(-ona)** *m*, ferrule, tip —*a* haggling, bargaining —*n* haggler; retailer

regatonear /rregatone'ar/ *vt* to resell at retail

regazo /rre'gaθo; rre'gaso/ *m*, lap, knees; *Fig.* heart, bosom

regenerador /rrehenera'ðor/ **(-ra)** *n* regenerator —*a* regenerative, reforming

regenerar /rrehene'rar/ *vt* to regenerate, reform

regenta /rre'henta/ *f*, wife of the president of a court of session

regentar /rrehen'tar/ *vt* to fill temporarily (offices); rule, govern; manage, run (businesses)

regente /rre'hente/ *a* ruling. *mf* regent. *m*, president of a court of session; manager

regidor /rrehi'ðor/ *a* ruling, governing. *m*, magistrate, alderman

régimen /'rrehimen/ *m*, administration, management; reglme; (*Med. Gram.*) regimen; *Mech.* rating

regimentar /rrehimen'tar/ *vt irr* to form into regiments; regiment —*Pres. Indic.* **regimiento, regimientas, regimienta, regimientan.** *Pres. Subjunc.* **regimiente, regimientes, regimiente, regimienten**

regimiento /rrehi'miento/ *m*, *Mil.* regiment; administration, rule

regio /'rrehio/ *a* royal; magnificent, regal

región /rre'hion/ *f*, region, country; area, tract, space. **r. industrial**, industrial area

regir /rre'hir/ *vt irr* to govern, rule; administer, conduct; *Gram.* govern; —*vi* be in force (laws, etc.); work, function; *Naut.* obey the helm. See **pedir**

registrador /rrehistra'ðor/ *a* recording. *m*, registrar, keeper of records; recorder. **caja (registradora),** (cash) register

registrar /rrehis'trar/ *vt* to examine, inspect; search; copy, record; mark the place (in a book); observe, note; (of thermometers, etc.) record, show; look on to (houses, etc.); —*vr* register (hotels, etc.)

registro /rre'histro/ *m*, search; registration, entry; record; recording; reading (of a thermometer, etc.); *Mech.* damper; registry; register (book); *Mus.* range, compass (voice); *Mus.* register (organ); (*Mech. Print.*) register; bookmark. **r. civil,** register of births, marriages, and deaths

regla /'rregla/ *f*, ruler, measuring stick; rule, principle, guide, precept; system, policy; *Med.* period; moderation; method, order. **r. de cálculo,** slide rule. **r. T,** T-square. **en r.,** in due form. **por r.,** general, generally, as a rule

reglamentación /rreglamenta'θion; rreglamenta'sion/ *f*, regulation; rules and regulations

reglamento /rregla'mento/ *m*, bylaw; regulation, ordinance

reglar /rre'glar/ *vt* to rule (lines); regulate; govern; control; —*vr* restrain oneself, mend one's ways

regocijar /rregoθi'har; rregosi'har/ *vt* to cheer, delight; —*vr* enjoy oneself, rejoice

regocijo /rrego'θiho; rrego'siho/ *m*, happiness, joy; cheer, merriment

regordete /rregor'ðete/ *a Inf.* chubby

regresar /rregre'sar/ *vi* to return

regresión /rregre'sion/ *f*, return; retrogression; regression

regreso /rre'greso/ *m*, return

reguera /rre'gera/ *f*, irrigation channel, ditch

regulación /rregula'θion; rregula'sion/ *f*, regulation; *Mech.* control, timing

regulador /rregula'ðor/ *m*, *Mech.* governor, regulator —*a* regulating, controlling

regular /rregu'lar/ *vt* to adjust, regulate; *Mech.* govern —*a* methodical, ordered; moderate; average, medium; (*Eccl. Mil. Geom. Gram.*) regular; so-so, not bad; probable. **por lo r.,** generally

regularidad /rregulari'ðað/ *f*, regularity

regularizar /rregulari'θar; rregulari'sar/ *vt* to regularize; regulate

regurgitar /rregurhi'tar/ *vi* to regurgitate

rehabilitar /rreaβili'tar/ *vt* to rehabilitate; —*vr* rehabilitate oneself

rehacer /rrea'θer; rrea'ser/ *vt irr* to remake; repair, mend; —*vr* recover one's strength; control one's emotions; *Mil.* rally. See **hacer**

rehén /rre'en/ *m*, hostage (gen. *pl*); *Mil.* pledge, security

rehenchir /rreen't ʃir/ *vt irr* to restuff; refill, recharge. See **henchir**

reherir /rree'rir/ *vt irr* to repulse. See **herir**

rehilar /rrei'lar/ *vt* to spin too much or twist the yarn; —*vi* totter, stagger; whizz (arrows, etc.). See **prohibir**

reimponer /rreimpo'ner/ *vt irr* to reimpose. See **poner**

reimpresión /rreimpre'sion/ *f*, reprint

reimprimir /rreimpri'mir/ *vt* to reprint

reina /'rreina/ *f*, queen; queen (in chess); queen bee; peerless beauty, belle

reinado /rrei'naðo/ *m,* reign; heyday, fashion

reinante /rrei'nante/ *a* reigning; prevalent

reinar /rrei'nar/ *vi* to reign; influence; endure, prevail

reincidencia /rreinθi'ðenθia; rreinsi-'ðensia/ *f,* relapse (into crime, etc.), recidivism

reincidente /rreinθi'ðente; rreinsi'ðente/ *mf* backslider

reincidir /rreinθi'ðir; rreinsi'ðir/ *vi* to relapse (into crime, etc.)

reincorporar /rreinkorpo'rar/ *vt* to reincorporate; —*vr* join again, become a member again

reino /'rreino/ *m,* kingdom

reinstalación /rreinstala'θion; rreinstala-'sion/ *f,* reinstatement

reinstalar /rreinsta'lar/ *vt* to reinstate; —*vr* be reinstalled

reintegrar /rreinte'grar/ *vt* to reintegrate; —*vr* be reinstated, recuperate, recover

reir /rre'ir/ *vi irr* to laugh; sneer, jeer; *Fig.* smile (nature); —*vt* laugh at; —*vr* *Inf.* (with *de*) scorn. **reírse a carcajadas,** to shout with laughter —*Pres. Part.* **riendo.** *Pres. Indic.* **río, ríes, ríe, ríen.** *Preterite* **rió, rieron.** *Pres. Subjunc.* **ría,** etc —*Imperf. Subjunc.* **riese.**

roiteración /rreitera'θion; rreitera'sion/ *f,* reiteration, repetition

reiteradamente /rreiteraða'mente/ *adv* repeatedly, reiteratively

reiterar /rreite'rar/ *vt* to reiterate, repeat

reivindicar /rreiβindi'kar/ *vt Law.* to recover

reja /'rreha/ *f,* colter, plowshare; plowing, tilling; grating, grille

rejado /rre'haðo/ *m,* railing, grating

rejilla /rre'hiʎa; rre'hiya/ *f,* grating; grille, lattice; luggage rack (in a train); cane (for chairs, seats, etc.); wire mesh; small brazier; *Elec.* grid; *Mech.* grate

rejuntar /rrehun'tar/ *vt* to point (a wall)

rejuvenecer /rrehuβene'θer; rrehuβene'ser/ *vt irr* to rejuvenate; *Fig.* revive; bring up to date; —*vi* and *vr* be rejuvenated, grow young again, rejuvenesce. See **conocer**

relación /rrela'θion; rrela'sion/ *f,* relation; connection (of ideas); report, statement; narrative, account; *Math.* ratio; *Law.* brief; intercourse, association, dealings (gen. *pl*); list; analogy, relation. **tener relaciones con,** to have dealings with; be engaged or betrothed to; woo, court

relacionar /rrelaθio'nar; rrelasio'nar/ *vt* to recount, narrate, report; connect, relate; —*vr* be connected

relajación /rrelaha'θion; rrelaha'sion/ *f,* relaxation; recreation; laxity, dissoluteness

relajar /rrela'har/ *vt* to relax; recreate, amuse; make less rigorous; *Law.* remit; —*vr* become relaxed; be dissolute, lax, or vicious

relamer /rrela'mer/ *vt* to lick again; —*vr* lick one's lips; *Fig.* overpaint, make up too much; ooze satisfaction, brag

relamido /rrela'miðo/ *a* overdressed; affected

relámpago /rre'lampago/ *m,* lightning; flash, gleam; streak of lightning (of quick persons or things); flash of wit, witticism

relampaguear /rrelampage'ar/ *vi* to lighten (of lightning); flash, gleam

relapso /rre'lapso/ *a* relapsed, lapsed (into error, vice)

relativo /rrela'tiβo/ *a* relevant, pertinent; relative, comparative; *Gram.* relative

relato /rre'lato/ *m,* narration, account, report

relator /rrela'tor/ **(-ra)** *a* narrating —*n* narrator. *m, Law.* reporter

relección /rrelek'θion; rrelek'sion/ *f,* reelection

releer /rrele'er/ *vt irr* to reread; revise. See **creer**

relegar /rrele'gar/ *vt* to banish; relegate; set aside

relegir /rrele'hir/ *vt irr* to reelect. See **elegir**

relente /rre'lente/ *m,* night dew, dampness; *Inf.* cheek, impudence

relevación /rreleβa'θion; rreleβa'sion/ *f,* *Art.* relief; release; remission, exemption

relevar /rrele'βar/ *vt Art.* to work in relief; emboss; relieve, free; dismiss; excuse, pardon; aid, succor; *Fig.* aggrandize; *Mil.* relieve; —*vi* carve in relief

relevo /rre'leβo/ *m,* relay; *Mil.* relief

relieve /rre'lieβe/ *m, Art.* relief; *pl* leftovers, remains (of food). **alto r.,** high relief. **bajo r.,** low relief

religar /rreli'gar/ *vt* to retie, fasten again; fasten more securely; solder

religión /rreli'hion/ *f,* religion; creed, faith, philosophy; devotion, religious practice. **r. reformada,** Protestantism. **entrar en r.,** *Eccl.* to profess

religionario /rrelihio'nario/ *m,* Protestant

religiosidad /rrelihiosi'ðað/ *f,* religiosity; religiousness; conscientiousness, punctiliousness

religioso /rreli'hioso/ **(-sa)** *a* religious; punctilious, conscientious; moderate —*n* religious

relinchar /rrelin'tʃar/ *vi* to whinny, neigh

reliquia /rre'likia/ *f,* residue (gen. *pl*); *Eccl.* relic; vestige, remnant, memento; permanent disability or ailment

rellanar /rreʎa'nar; rreʎyanar/ *vt* to make level again; —*vr* stretch oneself at full length

rellano /rre'ʎano; rre'yano/ *m,* landing (of a staircase); level stretch (of ground)

rellenar /rreʎe'nar; rreye'nar/ *vt* to refill, replenish; fill up; *Mas.* plug, point; *Cul.* stuff; *Inf.* cram with food (gen —*vr*)

relleno /rre'ʎeno; rre'yeno/ *m, Cul.* stuffing; replenishing; filling; *Fig.* padding (of speeches, etc.)

reloj /rre'loh/ *m,* clock; watch. **r. de**

arena, hourglass. **r. de bolsillo,** watch. **r. de la muerte,** deathwatch beetle. **r. de péndulo,** grandfather clock. **r. de pulsera,** wristwatch. **r. de repetición,** repeater. **r. de sol** *or* **r. solar,** sundial

relojería /rrelohe'ria/ *f,* watch or clock making; jeweler, watch maker's shop

relojero /rrelo'hero/ **(-ra)** *n* watch maker, watch repairer

reluciente /rrelu'θiente; rrelu'siente/ *a* shining, sparkling; shiny

relucir /rrelu'θir; rrelu'sir/ *vi irr* to glitter, sparkle, gleam; *Fig.* shine, excel. See **lucir**

relumbrar /rrelum'βrar/ *vi* to be resplendent, shine, glitter

remache /rre'matʃe/ *m,* riveting; rivet

remanso /rre'manso/ *m,* backwater; stagnant water; sloth, dilatoriness

remar /rre'mar/ *vi* to row, paddle, scull; toil, strive

rematadamente /rremataða'mente/ *adv* completely, entirely, absolutely

rematado /rrema'taðo/ *a* beyond hope, extremely ill; utterly lost; *Law.* convicted

rematar /rrema'tar/ *vt* to end, finish; finish off, kill; knock down at auction; *Sew.* finish; —*vi* end; —*vr* be ruined or spoiled

remate /rre'mate/ *m,* end, conclusion; extremity; *Archit.* coping; *Archit.* terminal; highest bid; auction. **de r.,** utterly hopeless

rembarcar /rrembar'kar/ *vt* to reembark, reship

rembolsable /rrembol'saβle/ *a* repayable

rembolsar /rrembol'sar/ *vt* to recover (money); refund, return (money)

rembolso /rrem'βolso/ *m,* repayment. **contra r.,** cash on delivery, C.O.D.

remedar /rreme'ðar/ *vt* to copy, imitate; mimic

remediar /rreme'ðiar/ *vt* to remedy; aid, help; save from danger; prevent (trouble)

remedio /rre'meðio/ *m,* remedy; emendation, correction; help; refuge, protection; *Med.* remedy. **No hay más r.,** There's nothing else to do, It's the only way open. **no tener más r.,** to be unable to help (doing something), be obliged to

remedo /rre'meðo/ *m,* imitation; poor copy

remendar /rremen'dar/ *vt irr* to mend, patch; darn; repair; correct. See **recomendar**

remendón /rremen'don/ **(-ona)** *n* cobbler; mender of old clothes

remero /rre'mero/ **(-ra)** *n* oarsman, rower; sculler

remesa /rre'mesa/ *f,* remittance; consignment, shipment

remiendo /rre'miendo/ *m, Sew.* patch; mend, darn; emendation; *Inf.* insignia of one of the Spanish military orders. **a remiendos,** *Inf.* piecemeal

remilgo /rre'milgo/ *m,* affectation; mannerism; prudery, squeamishness

reminiscencia /rreminis'θenθia; reminis-'sensia/ *f,* reminiscence; memory, recollection

remirado /rremi'raðo/ *a* wary, cautious, prudent, circumspect

remirar /rremi'rar/ *vt* to revise, go over again; —*vr* take great care over; behold with pleasure

remisión /rremi'sion/ *f,* sending; remission; pardon, forgiveness; foregoing, relinquishment; abatement, diminution; *Lit.* reference, allusion

remiso /rre'miso/ *a* timid, spiritless; languid, slow

remitente /rremi'tente/ *mf* sender —*a* sending

remitir /rremi'tir/ *vt* to remit, send; pardon, forgive; defer, postpone; abate, diminish; relinquish, forgo; *Lit.* refer; —*vr* remit, submit, consult; refer (to), cite

remo /'rremo/ *m,* oar, scull, paddle; arm or leg (of men or animals, gen. *pl*); wing (gen. *pl*); hard, continuous toil; galleys. **al r.,** by dint of rowing; *Inf.* struggling with hardships

remojar /rremo'har/ *vt* to soak, steep; celebrate by drinking

remolacha /rremo'latʃa/ *f,* beet

remolcador /rremolka'ðor/ *m, Naut.* tow, tug —*a Naut.* towing, riot

remolcar /rremol'kar/ *vt* (*Naut. Auto.*) to tow; *Fig.* press into service, use

remolino /rremo'lino/ *m,* whirlwind; eddy, swirl; whirlpool; crowd, throng, swarm; disturbance, riot

remolonear /rremolone'ar/ *vi Inf.* to loiter, lag; avoid work; be lax or dilatory

remolque /rre'molke/ *m,* towage, towing; towline; barge; *Auto.* trailer. **a r.,** on tow

remontar /rremon'tar/ *vt* to scare off (game); *Mil.* supply with fresh horses; resole (shoes); *Fig.* rise to great heights (of oratory, etc.); —*vr* soar (of birds); (*with prep a*) date from, go back to; originate in

remoquete /rremo'kete/ *m,* blow with the fist; witticism; *Inf.* flirtation, courtship

remorder /rremor'ðer/ *vt irr* to bite again or repeatedly; *Fig.* gnaw, nag, cause uneasiness or remorse; —*vr* show one's feelings. See **morder**

remordimiento /rremorði'miento/ *m,* remorse

remoto /rre'moto/ *a* distant, remote; unlikely, improbable

remover /rremo'βer/ *vt irr* to remove, move; stir; turn over; dismiss, discharge. See **mover**

remozar /rremo'θar; rremo'sar/ *vt* to cause to appear young; freshen up, bring up to date; —*vr* look young

remplazar /rrempla'θar; rrempla'sar/ *vt* to replace; exchange, substitute; succeed, take the place of

remplazo /rrem'plaθo; rrem'plaso/ *m,* replacement; exchange, substitute; successor; *Mil.* replacement

remudar /rremu'ðar/ *vt* to replace

remuneración /rremunera'θion; rremunera'sion/ *f.* remuneration; reward

remunerador /rremunera'ðor/ **(-ra)** *a* remunerative, recompensing —*n* remunerator

remunerar /rremune'rar/ *vt* to recompense, reward

remusgar /rremus'gar/ *vi* to suspect, imagine

renacer /rrena'θer; rrena'ser/ *vi irr* to be reborn. See **nacer**

renacimiento /rrenaθi'miento; rrenasi'miento/ *m,* rebirth; Renaissance

renacuajo /rrena'kuaho/ *m,* tadpole; *Mech.* frog; *Inf.* twerp

rencarnación /rrenkarna'θion; rrenkarna'sion/ *f,* reincarnation

rencarnar /rrenkar'nar/ **(se)** *vi* and *vr* to be reincarnated

rencilla /rren'θiʎa; rren'siʎa/ *f,* grudge, grievance, resentment

rencilloso /rrenθi'ʎoso; rrensi'yoso/ *a* peevish, easily offended, touchy

rencor /rren'kor/ *m,* rancor, spite, old grudge. **guardar r.,** to bear malice

rencoroso /rrenko'roso/ *a* rancorous, malicious, spiteful

rencuentro /rren'kuentro/ *m,* collision; *Mil.* encounter, clash

rendición /rrendi'θion; rrendi'sion/ *f,* surrender; yield, profit

rendido /rren'diðo/ *a* submissive, obsequious

rendija /rren'diha/ *f,* crevice, cleft, crack, fissure

rendimiento /rrendi'miento/ *m,* weariness, fatigue; submissiveness, obsequiousness; yield, profit; *Mech.* efficiency

rendir /rren'dir/ *vt irr Mil.* to cause to surrender; defeat; overcome, conquer; give back, return; yield, provide; tire, exhaust; vomit; pay, render; —*vr* be exhausted, be worn out; surrender. *Mil.* **r. el puesto,** to retire from or give up a post. See **pedir**

renegado /rrene'gaðo/ **(-da)** *n* renegade, apostate; turncoat; *Inf.* malignant person —*a* renegade

renegador /rrenega'ðor/ **(-ra)** *n* blasphemer; foul-mouthed person

renegar /rrene'gar/ *vt irr* to deny, disown; loathe, hate; —*vi (with de)* apostatize; blaspheme; *Inf.* curse. See **cegar**

renganchar /rrengan'tʃar/ **(se)** *vt* and *vr Mil.* to reenlist

renganche /rren'gantʃe/ *m, Mil.* reenlistment

renglón /rren'glon/ *m, Print.* line; *pl* writing, composition

reniego /rre'niego/ *m,* blasphemy; *Inf.* foul language, cursing

renitencia /rreni'tenθia; rreni'tensia/ *f,* repugnance

reno /'rreno/ *m,* reindeer

renombrado /rrenom'braðo/ *a* illustrious, famous

renombre /rre'nombre/ *m,* surname; renown, reputation, fame

renovable /rreno'βaβle/ *a* renewable, replaceable

renovación /rrenoβa'θion; rrenoβa'sion/ *f,* replacement; renewal; renovation; transformation, reform

renovador /rrenoβa'ðor/ **(-ra)** *n* reformer; renovator —*a* renovating; reforming

renovar /rreno'βar/ *vt irr* to renew; renovate; replace; exchange; reiterate, repeat. See **contar**

renta /'rrenta/ *f,* yield, profit; income; revenue; government securities; rent; tax

rentero /rren'tero/ **(-ra)** *n* tenant farmer. *m,* one who farms out land

rentista /rren'tista/ *mf* financier; bondholder; person who lives on a private income, rentier

renuente /rre'nuente/ *a* refractory, willful

renuncia, renunciación /rre'nunθia, rrenunθia'θion; rre'nunsia, rrenunsia'sion/ *f,* renunciation; resignation; abandonment, relinquishment

renunciar /rrenun'θiar; rrenun'siar/ *vt* to renounce; refuse; scorn; abandon, relinquish; resign; revoke (at cards). **r. a,** to give up

renuncio /rre'nunθio; rre'nunsio/ *m,* revoke (cards); *Inf.* falsehood

reñidamente /rreniða'mente/ *adv* strongly, stubbornly, fiercely

reñir /rre'ɲir/ *vi irr* to quarrel, dispute; fight; be on bad terms, fall out; —*vt* scold; fight (battles, etc.). See **ceñir**

reo /'rreo/ *mf* criminal; offender, guilty party; *Law.* defendant

reojo /rre'oho/ *m,* **(mirar de)** to look out of the corner of the eye; *Fig.* look askance

reorganizar /rreorgani'θar; rreorgani'sar/ *vt* to reorganize

repantigarse /rrepanti'garse/ *vr* to stretch out one's legs, make oneself comfortable

reparable /rrepa'raβle/ *a* remediable, reparable; worthy of note

reparación /rrepara'θion; rrepara'sion/ *f,* repair, mending; reparation, satisfaction; indemnity, compensation

reparador /rrepara'ðor/ *a* repairing, mending; faultfinding; restoring; satisfying, compensating

reparar /rrepa'rar/ *vt* to repair; restore; consider; correct, remedy; atone for, expiate; indemnify; hold up, detain; protect, guard; *(with en)* notice; —*vi* halt, be detained; —*vr* control oneself

reparo /rre'paro/ *m,* repair; restoration; remedy; note, reflection; warning; doubt, scruple; guard; protection; parry (at fencing)

repartición /rreparti'θion; rreparti'sion/ *f,* distribution

repartidor /rreparti'ðor/ **(-ra)** *a* distributing —*n* distributor; tax assessor

repartimiento /rreparti'miento/ *m*, distribution, allotment; assessment

repartir /rrepar'tir/ *vt* to distribute; share out; allot; deal (cards); assess; *Com.* deliver

reparto /rre'parto/ *m*, distribution; assessment; delivery (of letters, etc.); *Theat.* cast; deal (at cards)

repasar /rrepa'sar/ *vt* to pass by again; peruse, reexamine; brush up, revise; skim, glance over; mend, repair (garments); edit, revise; hone

repaso /rre'paso/ *m*, second passage through; reexamination, perusal; revision, editing; brushing up, revision; repair, mending; *Inf.* dressing-down, scolding

repatriado /rrepa'triaðo/ **(-da)** *n* repatriate

repatriar /rrepa'triar/ *vt* to repatriate; —*vi* and *vr* return to one's own country

repecho /rre'petʃo/ *m*, steep slope. **a r.,** uphill

repelar /rrepe'lar/ *vt* to pull by the hair; put through its paces (of a horse); clip, cut; remove, diminish

repeler /rrepe'ler/ *vt* to repel, throw back; reject, refute

repelo /rre'pelo/ *m*, anything against the grain; *Inf.* skirmish; reluctance, repugnance

repente /rre'pente/ *m*, *Inf.* sudden or unexpected movement. **de r.,** suddenly

repentino /rrepen'tino/ *a* sudden, unexpected

repentizar /rrepenti'θar; rrepenti'sar/ *vi* *Mus.* to sight-read

repercusión /rreperku'sion/ *f*, repercussion; vibration

repercutir /rreperku'tir/ *vi* to recoil, rebound; —*vr* reverberate; reecho; *Fig.* have repercussions; —*vt Med.* repel

repertorio /rreper'torio/ *m*, repertory

repetición /rrepeti'θion; rrepeti'sion/ *f*, repetition; *Art.* replica, copy; repeater (in clocks); recital

repetidamente /rrepetiða'mente/ *adv* repeatedly

repetir /rrepe'tir/ *vt irr* to repeat, do over again; reiterate; *Art.* copy, make a replica of; recite. See **pedir**

repicar /rrepi'kar/ *vt* to chop, mince; peal (of bells); prick again; —*vr* pride oneself (on), boast

repique /rre'pike/ *m*, chopping, mincing; peal, pealing (of bells); disagreement, grievance

repisa /rre'pisa/ *f*, *Archit.* bracket; ledge; shelf. **r. de chimenea,** mantelpiece

replegar /rreple'gar/ *vt irr* to refold, fold many times; —*vr Mil.* retreat in good order. See **cegar**

repleto /rre'pleto/ *a* replete

réplica /'rreplika/ *f*, reply, answer; replica

replicar /rrepli'kar/ *vi* to contradict, dispute; answer, reply. **¡No me repliques!** *Inf.* Don't answer back!

repliegue /rre'pliege/ *m*, double fold, crease; doubling, folding; *Mil.* withdrawal

repoblación /rrepoβla'θion; rrepoβla-'sion/ *f*, repeopling, repopulation

repoblar /rrepo'βlar/ *vt* to repeople, repopulate

repollo /rre'poʎo; rre'poyo/ *m*, white cabbage; heart (of lettuce, etc.)

reponer /rrepo'ner/ *vt irr* to replace; reinstate; restore; reply; —*vr* recover, regain (possessions); grow well again; grow calm. See **poner**

reportación /rreporta'θion; rreporta'sion/ *f*, serenity, moderation

reportaje /rrepor'tahe/ *m*, journalistic report

reportar /rrepor'tar/ *vt* to restrain, moderate; achieve, obtain; carry; bring; —*vr* control oneself

reporte /rre'porte/ *m*, report, news; rumor

reportero /rrepor'tero/ **(-ra)** *a* news, report —*n* reporter

reposado /rrepo'saðo/ *a* quiet, peaceful, tranquil

reposar /rrepo'sar/ *vi* to rest, repose oneself; sleep, doze; lie in the grave; settle (liquids); rest (on)

reposición /rreposi'θion; rreposi'sion/ *f*, replacement; restoration; renewal; recovery (of health); *Theat.* revival

repositorio /rreposi'torio/ *m*, repository

reposo /rre'poso/ *m*, rest, repose; peace, tranquility; sleep

repostería /rreposte'ria/ *f*, confectioner's shop; pantry; butler's pantry

repostero /rrepos'tero/ *m*, confectioner, pastry cook

repregunta /rrepre'gunta/ *f*, cross-examination

repreguntar /rrepregun'tar/ *vt* to cross-examine

reprender /rrepren'der/ *vt* to scold, reprimand, rebuke

reprensible /rrepren'siβle/ *a* reprehensible, censurable

reprensión /rrepren'sion/ *f*, scolding, reprimand, rebuke

represa /rre'presa/ *f*, damming, holding back (water); dam, lock; restraining, controlling

represalia /rrepre'salia/ *f*, reprisal (gen. *pl*); retaliation

represar /rrepre'sar/ *vt* to dam, harness (water); *Naut.* retake, recapture; *Fig.* restrain, control

representación /rrepresenta'θion; rrepresenta'sion/ *f*, representation; *Theat.* performance; authority; dignity; *Com.* agency; portrait, image; depiction, expression; petition

representante /rrepresen'tante/ *a* representative. *mf* representative; actor; performer

representar /rrepresen'tar/ *vt* to represent; *Theat.* perform; depict, express; describe, portray; —*vr* imagine, picture to oneself

representativo /rrepresenta'tiβo/ *a* representative

represión /rrepre'sion/ *f*, repression; recapture

represivo /rrepre'siβo/ *a* repressive

reprimenda /rrepri'menda/ *f*, rebuke, reprimand

reprimir /rrepri'mir/ *vt* to repress, restrain, control; —*vr* restrain oneself

reprobación /rreproβa'θion; rreproβa'sion/ *f*, censure; reprobation

reprobar /rrepro'βar/ *vt irr* to reprove; censure; fail (in an exam). See **probar**

reproche /rre'protʃe/ *m*, reproaching; rebuke, reproach

reproducción /rreproðuk'θion; rreproðuk'sion/ *f*, reproduction. **r. a gran escala**, large-scale model

reproducir /rreproðu'θir; rreproðu'sir/ *vt irr* to reproduce. See **conducir**

reproductor /rreproðuk'tor/ **(-ra)** *a* reproductive —*n* breeding animal

reps /rreps/ *m*, rep (fabric)

reptil /rrep'til/ *a* reptilian; crawling. *m*, reptile

república /rre'puβlika/ *f*, republic; state, commonwealth. **la r. de las letras,** the republic of letters

República Dominicana /rre'puβlika domini'kana/ Dominican Republic

republicano /rrepuβli'kano/ **(-na)** *a* and *n* republican

repudiación /rrepuðia'θion; rrepuðia'sion/ *f*, repudiation

repudiar /rrepu'ðiar/ *vt* to cast off (a wife); repudiate, renounce

repuesto /rre'puesto/ *a* retired, hidden. *m*, stock, provision; serving table; pantry; stake (at cards, etc.). **de r.,** spare, extra

repugnancia /rrepug'nanθia; rrepug'nansia/ *f*, inconsistency, contradiction; aversion, dislike; reluctance; repugnance

repugnante /rrepug'nante/ *a* repugnant, loathsome

repugnar /rrepug'nar/ *vt* to contradict, be inconsistent with; hate, be averse to (e.g. *La idea me repugna,* I hate the idea)

repujar /rrepu'har/ *vt* to work in repoussé

repulir /rrepu'lir/ *vt* to repolish, reburnish; —*vt and vr* make up too much, overdress

repulsa /rre'pulsa/ *f*, snub, rebuff; rejection; repulse

repulsar /rrepul'sar/ *vt* to decline, reject; repulse; deny, refuse; rebuff

repulsión /rrepul'sion/ *f*, repulsion; rebuff; aversion, dislike

repulsivo /rrepul'siβo/ *a* repellent

reputación /rreputa'θion; rreputa'sion/ *f*, reputation

reputar /rrepu'tar/ *vt* to believe, consider (e.g. *Le reputo por honrado,* I believe him

to be an honorable man); appreciate, esteem

requebrar /rreke'βrar/ *vt irr* to break into smaller pieces; make love to, woo; compliment, flatter. See **quebrar**

requemar /rreke'mar/ *vt* to burn again; overcook; dry up, parch (of plants, etc.); burn (the mouth) (of spicy foods, etc.); —*vr Fig.* suffer inwardly

requerir /rreke'rir/ *vt irr* to inform, notify; examine; need, necessitate; require; summon; woo; persuade. See **sentir**

requesón /rreke'son/ *m*, cream cheese; curd

requetebién /rrekete'βien/ *adv Inf.* exceedingly well

requiebro /rre'kieβro/ *m*, compliment, expression of love; wooing, flirtation

requisito /rreki'sito/ *m*, requisite

res /rres/ *f*, animal, beast; head of cattle

resabiar /rresa'βiar/ *vt* to make vicious, cause bad habits; —*vr* contract bad habits or vices; be discontented; relish

resabio /rre'saβio/ *m*, disagreeable aftertaste; bad habit, vice

resaca /rre'saka/ *f*, surf, undertow, surge; *Com.* redraft

resalado /rresa'laðo/ *a Inf.* very witty; most attractive

resaltar /rresal'tar/ *vi* to rebound; project, jut out; grow loose, fall out; *Fig.* stand out, be prominent

resalto /rre'salto/ *m*, rebound; projection

resbaladizo /rresβala'ðiθo; rresβala'ðiso/ *a* slippery; difficult, delicate (of a situation)

resbalar /rresβa'lar/ *vi* to slip; slide; skid; err, fall into sin

resbalón /rresβa'lon/ *m*, slip; slide; skid; temptation, error

rescatador /rreskata'ðor/ **(-ra)** *n* ransomer; rescuer

rescatar /rreska'tar/ *vt* to ransom; redeem, buy back; barter; free, rescue; *Fig.* redeem (time, etc.)

rescate /rres'kate/ *m*, ransom; redemption; barter; amount of ransom

rescisión /rresθi'sion; rressi'sion/ *f*, annulment, abrogation

rescoldo /rres'koldo/ *m*, ember, cinder; scruple, qualm, doubt

resentimiento /rresenti'miento/ *m*, deterioration, impairment; animosity, resentment

resentirse /rresen'tirse/ *vr irr* to deteriorate, be impaired; be hurt or offended. See **sentir**

reseña /rre'seɲa/ *f*, *Mil.* review; short description; review (of a book)

reseñar /rrese'ɲar/ *vt Mil.* to review; describe briefly, outline

reserva /rre'serβa/ *f*, store, stock; exception, qualification; reticence; restraint, moderation; (*Eccl. Law.*) reservation; (*Mil. Naut.*) reserve. **sin r.,** frankly, without reserve

reservación /rreserβa'θion; rreserβa'sion/ f, reservation; scruple

reservado /rreser'βaðo/ a reserved, reticent; prudent, moderate; kept, reserved. m, reserved compartment; private apartment, private garden, etc.

reservar /rreser'βar/ vt to keep, hold; postpone; reserve (rooms, etc.); exempt; keep secret; withhold (information); Eccl. reserve; —vr await a better opportunity; be cautious

reservista /rreser'βista/ a (Mil. Nav.) reserved. mf reservist

resfriado /rres'friaðo/ m, Med. cold, chill

resfriar /rres'friar/ vt to chill; Fig. cool, moderate; —vi grow cold; —vr catch a cold; Fig. cool off (of love, etc.)

resguardar /rresguar'ðar/ vt to protect; shelter; —vr take refuge; (with de) guard against; (with con) shelter by

resguardo /rres'guarðo/ m, protection, guard; Com. guarantee, security; Com. voucher; preservation; vigilance (to prevent smuggling, etc.); contraband guards

residencia /rresi'ðenθia; rresi'ðensia/ f, stay, residence; home, domicile; Eccl. residence

residencial /rresiðen'θial; rresiðen'sial/ a residential; resident, residentiary

residente /rresi'ðente/ a resident. mf inhabitant. m, resident, minister resident (diplomatic)

residir /rresi'ðir/ vi to live, inhabit; reside officially; be found, be, exist

residuo /rre'siðuo/ m, residuum, remainder; Math. remainder; Chem. residue

resignación /rresigna'θion; rresigna'sion/ f, resignation; fortitude, submission

resignar /rresig'nar/ vt to resign, relinquish; —vr submit; resign oneself

resina /rre'sina/ f, resin

resistencia /rresis'tenθia; rresis'tensia/ f, resistance, opposition; endurance; (Phys. Mech. Psychol.) resistance

resistente /rresis'tente/ a resistant; tough; hardy (of plants)

resistir /rresis'tir/ vi to resist, oppose; reject; —vt endure, bear; resist; —vr fight, resist

resolución /rresolu'θion; rresolu'sion/ f, decision; boldness, daring; determination, resolution; decree

resoluto /rreso'luto/ a resolute, bold; brief, concise; able, expert

resolver /rresol'βer/ vt irr to determine, decide; summarize; solve; dissolve; analyze; (Phys. Med.) resolve; —vr decide, determine; be reduced to, become; Med. resolve —Pres. Indic. **resuelvo, resuelves, resuelve, resuelven.** Past Part. **resuelto.** Pres. Subjunc. **resuelva, resuelvas, resuelva, resuelvan**

resonancia /rreso'nanθia; rreso'nansia/ f, resonance, sonority, ring; fame, reputation

resonante /rreso'nante/ a resonant; resounding

resonar /rreso'nar/ vi irr to resound, echo. See **tronar**

resoplido, resoplo /rreso'pliðo, rre'soplo/ m, heavy breathing, pant, snort

resorte /rre'sorte/ m, Mech. spring; elasticity; Fig. means, instrument

respaldo /rres'paldo/ m, back (of chairs, etc.); reverse side (of a piece of paper)

respecto /rres'pekto/ m, relation, regard, reference. **con r. a,** or **r. a,** with regard to, with respect to, concerning

respetabilidad /rrespetaβili'ðað/ f, respectability; worthiness

respetable /rrespe'taβle/ a worthy of respect; respectable; Fig. considerable, large

respetar /rrespe'tar/ vt to respect, revere

respeto /rres'peto/ m, respect, honor; consideration, reason. **de r.,** spare, extra; special, ceremonial

respetuoso /rrespe'tuoso/ a venerable, worthy of honor; respectful, courteous

respingo /rres'pingo/ m, wincing; jerk, shake; Inf. gesture of reluctance or dislike

respirable /rrespi'raβle/ a breathable

respiración /rrespira'θion; rrespira'sion/ f, breathing, respiration; ventilation

respirador /rrespira'ðor/ a breathing; respiratory. m, respirator

respirar /rrespi'rar/ vi to breathe; exhale, give off; take courage; have a breathing space, rest; Inf. speak. **sin r.,** continuously, without stopping for breath

respiratorio /rrespira'torio/ a respiratory

respiro /rres'piro/ m, breathing; breathing space, respite

resplandecer /rresplande'θer; rresplande'ser/ vi irr to glitter, gleam; shine, excel. See **conocer**

resplandeciente /rresplande'θiente; rresplande'siente/ a glittering, resplendent, shining

resplandor /rresplan'dor/ m, radiance, brilliance; glitter, gleam; majesty, splendor

responder /rrespon'der/ vt to reply; satisfy, answer; —vi reecho; requite, return; produce, provide; Fig. answer, have the desired effect; Com. (with de) answer for, guarantee; Com. correspond

respondón /rrespon'don/ a Inf. pert, impudent, cheeky, given to answering back

responsabilidad /rresponsaβili'ðað/ f, responsibility

responsable /rrespon'saβle/ a responsible

respuesta /rres'puesta/ f, answer, reply; response; refutation; repartee

resquebrajarse /rreskeβra'harse/ vr to crack, split

resquicio /rres'kiθio; rres'kisio/ m, crack, chink, slit; opportunity

restablecer /rrestaβle'θer; rrestaβle'ser/ vt irr to reestablish; restore; —vr recover one's health; reestablish oneself. See **conocer**

restablecimiento /rrestaβleθi'miento;

rrestaβlesi'miento/ *m*, reestablishment; restoration

restar /rres'tar/ *vt Math.* to subtract; deduct; return (a ball); —*vi* remain. **No me resta más que decir adiós,** It only remains for me to say good-by

restauración /rrestaura'θion; rrestaura'sion/ *f*, restoration; renovation

restaurante /rrestau'rante/ *m*, restaurant

restaurantero /rrestauran'tero/ *m*, restaurant operator; restaurant owner; restaurateur

restaurar /rrestau'rar/ *vt* to recover, recuperate; renovate, repair; restore

restaurativo /rrestaura'tiβo/ *a* and *m*, restorative

restitución /rrestitu'θion; rrestitu'sion/ *f*, restitution

restituible /rresti'tuiβle/ *a* returnable, replaceable

restituir /rresti'tuir/ *vt irr* to return, give back; restore; reestablish; —*vr* return to one's place of departure. See **huir**

resto /'rresto/ *m*, rest, balance; *Math.* remainder; *pl* remains

restorán /rresto'ran/ *m*, restaurant

restricción /rrestrik'θion; rrestrik'sion/ *f*, limitation, restriction

restrictivo /rrestrik'tiβo/ *a* restrictive; restraining

restringir /rrestriŋ'gir/ *vt* to limit, restrict; contract

resucitar /rresuθi'tar; rresusi'tar/ *vt* to raise from the dead; *Fig. Inf.* revive; —*vi* resuscitate

resuello /rre'sueʎo; rre'sueyo/ *m*, breathing; panting, hard breathing

resuelto /rre'suelto/ *a* audacious, daring; resolute, capable

resulta /rre'sulta/ *f*, consequence, result; decision, resolution; vacant post. **de resultas de,** as the result of; in consequence of

resultado /rresul'taðo/ *m*, result, consequence, outcome

resultar /rresul'tar/ *vi* to result, follow; turn out, happen; result (in); *Inf.* turn out well. **El vestido no me resulta,** The dress isn't a success on me

resumen /rre'sumen/ *m*, summary. **en r.,** in short

resumir /rresu'mir/ *vt* to summarize, abridge; sum up, recapitulate; —*vr* be contained; be included

resurgimiento /rresurhi'miento/ *m*, resurgence, revival

resurgir /rresur'hir/ *vi* to reappear, rise again, revive; resuscitate

resurrección /rresurrek'θion; rresurrek'sion/ *f*, resurrection

retablo /rre'taβlo/ *m*, *Archit.* altarpiece, retable; frieze; series of pictures

retaguardia /rreta'guarðia/ *f*, rear guard. **a r.,** in the rear. **picar la r.,** to harass the rear guard

retajar /rreta'har/ *vt* to cut in the round; circumcise

retama /rre'tama/ *f*, *Bot.* broom. **r. común** *or* **r. de olor,** Spanish broom. **r. de escobas,** common broom

retar /rre'tar/ *vt* to challenge; *Inf.* reproach, accuse

retardar /rretar'ðar/ *vt* to retard, delay

retardo /rre'tarðo/ *m*, delay, retardment

retazo /rre'taθo; rre'taso/ *m*, remnant, cutting; excerpt, fragment

retén /rre'ten/ *m*, stock, reserve, provision; *Mil.* reserve

retención /rreten'θion; rreten'sion/ *f*, retention

retener /rrete'ner/ *vt irr* to keep, retain; recollect, remember; keep back; *Law.* detain; deduct. See **tener**

retentiva /rreten'tiβa/ *f*, retentiveness, memory

retentivo /rreten'tiβo/ *a* retentive

reticencia /rreti'θenθia; rreti'sensia/ *f*, reticence

reticente /rreti'θente; rreti'sente/ *a* reticent

retina /rre'tina/ *f*, retina

retintín /rretin'tin/ *m*, ringing; tinkling; *Inf.* sarcastic tone

retiñir /rreti'ɲir/ *vi* to tinkle, clink; jingle

retirada /rreti'raða/ *f*, withdrawal; retirement; seclusion, refuge; *Mil.* retreat

retirado /rreti'raðo/ *a* remote, secluded; *Mil.* retired

retirar /rreti'rar/ *vt* to withdraw; remove; repel, throw back; hide, put aside; —*vr* withdraw; retire; *Mil.* retreat

retiro /rre'tiro/ *m*, withdrawal; removal; seclusion, privacy; *Mil.* retreat; retirement; *Eccl.* retreat. **dar el r. (a),** to place on the retired list

reto /'rreto/ *m*, challenge; threat

retocar /rreto'kar/ *vt* to touch again or repeatedly; *Photo.* retouch; restore (pictures); *Fig.* put the finishing touch to

retoñar /rreto'ɲar/ *vi* to sprout, shoot; *Fig.* revive, resuscitate

retoño /rre'toɲo/ *m*, sprout, shoot

retoque /rre'toke/ *m*, frequent touching; finishing touch; touch, slight attack

retorcer /rretor'θer; rretor'ser/ *vt irr* to twist; contort; confound with one's own argument; misconstrue, distort; —*vr* contort; writhe. See **torcer**

retórica /rre'torika/ *f*, rhetoric; *pl Inf.* quibbling

retórico /rre'toriko/ **(-ca)** *a* rhetorical —*n* rhetorician

retornar /rretor'nar/ *vt* to return, give back; turn, twist; turn back; —*vi* and *vr* return, go back

retorno /rre'torno/ *m*, return, going back; recompense, repayment; exchange; return journey

retortijón /rretorti'hon/ *m*, twisting, curling. **r. de tripas,** stomachache

retozar /rreto'θar; rreto'sar/ *vi* to skip, frisk, frolic, gambol; romp; *Fig.* be aroused (passions)

retracción /rretrak'θion; rretrak'sion/ f, drawing back, retraction

retractar /rretrak'tar/ vt to retract, recant, withdraw

retráctil /rre'traktil/ a retractile

retraer /rretra'er/ vt irr to bring back again; dissuade; buy back, redeem; —vr take refuge; retire; withdraw; go into seclusion. See **traer**

retraído /rretra'iðo/ a fugitive, refugee; retired, solitary; timid, nervous, unsociable

retrasar /rretra'sar/ vt to postpone, delay; turn back (the clock); —vi be slow (of clocks); —vr be behind time, be late; be backward (persons)

retraso /rre'traso/ m, lateness; delay, dilatoriness; loss of time (clocks); setting back (of the clock) (e.g. *El reloj lleva cinco minutos de r.*, The clock is five minutes slow)

retratar /rretra'tar/ vt to paint or draw the portrait of; portray, describe; photograph; copy, imitate

retrato /rre'trato/ m, portrait; portrayal; *Fig.* image, likeness

retrechería /rretretʃe'ria/ f, *Inf.* craftiness, evasiveness

retrete /rre'trete/ m, toilet, water closet

retribución /rretriβu'θion; rretriβu'sion/ f, recompense, reward

retribuir /rretri'βuir/ vt irr to recompense, reward. See **huir**

retroactivo /rretroak'tiβo/ a retroactive

retroceder /rretroθe'ðer; rretrose'ðer/ vi to withdraw, move back, draw back; recede

retroceso /rretro'θeso; rretro'seso/ m, retrocedence, withdrawal; *Med.* retrogression

retrogradación /rretrograða'θion; rretrograða'sion/ f, retrogression

retrógrado /rre'troˈgraðo/ a retrogressive, retrograde; *Polit.* reactionary

retronar /rretro'nar/ vi irr to bang, thunder, resound with noise. See **tronar**

retrospectivo /rretrospek'tiβo/ a retrospective

retruécano /rre'truekano/ m, antithesis; play on words, pun

retumbante /rretum'βante/ a resounding; pompous, high-flown

retumbar /rretum'βar/ vi to resound, echo, reverberate; roll (of thunder); roar (of a cannon)

retumbo /rre'tumbo/ m, reverberation, echo; rumble; roll (of thunder); roar (of a cannon, etc.)

reumático /rreu'matiko/ a rheumatic

reumatismo /rreuma'tismo/ m, rheumatism

reunión /rreu'nion/ f, reunion, union; meeting; assembly, gathering

reunir /rreu'nir/ vt to reunite; unite; join; gather, assemble; —vr meet, assemble; unite

revacunar /rreβaku'nar/ vt to revaccinate

revalidación /rreβaliða'θion; rreβaliða-'sion/ f, ratification, confirmation

revalidar /rreβali'ðar/ vt to ratify, confirm; —vr pass a final examination

revejido /rreβe'hiðo/ a prematurely old

revelación /rreβela'θion; rreβela'sion/ f, revelation; *Photo.* developing

revelador /rreβela'ðor/ a revealing. m, *Photo.* developer

revelar /rreβe'lar/ vt to reveal; *Photo.* develop

revendedor /rreβende'ðor/ **(-ra)** a reselling, retail —n retailer

revender /rreβen'der/ vt to resell; retail (goods)

reventa /rre'βenta/ f, resale; retail

reventar /rreβen'tar/ vi irr to burst, explode; break in foam (waves); burst forth; *Fig.* burst (with impatience, etc.); *Inf.* explode (with anger, etc.); —vt break, crush; *Fig.* wear out, exhaust; *Inf.* irritate, vex; —vr burst; *Fig.* be exhausted. See **sentar**

reventón /rreβen'ton/ a bursting. m, explosion, bursting; steep hill; hole, fix, difficulty; uphill work, heavy toil

reverberación /rreβerβera'θion; rreβerβera'sion/ f, reflection (of light); reverberation, resounding

reverberar /rreβerβe'rar/ vi to reflect; resound, reverberate

reverbero /rreβer'βero/ m, reverberation; reflector

reverdecer /rreβerðe'θer; rreβerðe'ser/ vi irr to grow green again; revive, acquire new vigor. See **conocer**

reverencia /rreβeren'θia; rreβeren'sia/ f, respect, veneration; bow; curtsy; *Eccl.* reverence (title)

reverencial /rreβeren'θial; rreβeren'sial/ a reverential, respectful

reverenciar /rreβeren'θiar; rreβeren'siar/ vt to revere; honor; respect

reverendo /rreβe'rendo/ a reverend; venerable; *Inf.* overprudent

reversión /rreβer'sion/ f, reversion

reverso /rre'βerso/ m, wrong side, back; reverse side (of coins)

reverter /rreβer'ter/ vi irr to overflow. See **entender**

revertir /rreβer'tir/ vi *Law.* to revert

revés /rre'βes/ m, wrong side, back, reverse; cuff, slap; backhand (in ballgames); check, setback, reverse; disaster, misfortune. **al r.,** on the contrary; wrong side out. **de r.,** from left to right, counterclockwise

revesado /rreβe'saðo/ a complicated, difficult; willful

revestimiento /rreβesti'miento/ m, *Mas.* lining, coating

revestir /rreβes'tir/ vt irr to dress; *Mas.* coat, line; *Fig.* cover, clothe; —vr be dressed or dress oneself; *Fig.* be captivated (by an idea); become haughty or full of oneself; rise to the occasion, develop qualities necessary. See **pedir**

reviejo /rre'βieho/ *a* very old. *m*, dead branch (of trees)

revisar /rreβi'sar/ *vt* to revise; examine

revisión /rreβi'sion/ *f*, revision; reexamination; *Law.* retrial

revisor /rreβi'sor/ *a* revising, examining. *m*, reviser; ticket inspector

revista /rre'βista/ *f*, reexamination, revision; review, periodical; *Theat.* revue; reinspection; review (of a book, etc.); *Law.* new trial; *Mil.* review. **pasar r.,** to inspect; review

revivir /rreβi'βir/ *vi* to resuscitate; revive

revocación /rreβoka'θion; rreβoka'sion/ *f*, revocation, cancellation, annulment

revocar /rreβo'kar/ *vt* to revoke, annul; dissuade; repel, throw back; wash (walls); *Law.* discharge

revolcar /rreβol'kar/ *vt irr* to knock down, trample underfoot; lay flat (in an argument); —*vr* wallow; dig one's heels in, be obstinate. See **volcar**

revolotear /rreβolote'ar/ *vi* to flutter, fly around; twirl; —*vt* hurl, toss

revoltillo /rreβol'tiλo; rreβol'tiyo/ *m*, jumble, hodgepodge; confusion, tangle

revoltoso /rreβol'toso/ *a* rebellious; mischievous, willful; intricate

revolución /rreβolu'θion; rreβolu'sion/ *f*, turn, revolution, rebellion, uprising; revolution

revolucionar /rreβoluθio'nar; rreβolusio'nar/ *vt* to revolutionize

revolucionario /rreβoluθio'nario; rreβolusio'nario/ **(-ia)** *a* and *n* revolutionary

revolver /rreβol'βer/ *vt irr* to turn over; turn upside down; wrap up; revolve; stir; reflect upon, consider; upset, cause disharmony; search through, disorder (papers, etc.); —*vr* move from side to side; change (in the weather). See **resolver**

revólver /rre'βolβer/ *m*, revolver

revuelco /rre'βuelko/ *m*, wallowing

revuelo /rre'βuelo/ *m*, second flight (of birds); irregular course of flight; disturbance, upset

revuelta /rre'βuelta/ *f*, second turn or revolution; revolt, rebellion; quarrel, fight; turning point; change of direction, turn; change (of opinions, posts, etc.)

revueltamente /rreβuelta'mente/ *adv* in confusion, higgledy-piggledy

revulsión /rreβul'sion/ *f*, revulsion

rexaminar /rreksami'nar/ *vt* to reexamine

rexpedir /rrekspe'ðir/ *vt* to forward, send on

rexportación /rreksporta'θion; rrekspor-ta'sion/ *f*, reexport

rexportar /rrekspor'tar/ *vt Com.* to reexport

rey /rrei/ *m*, king (in cards, chess); queen bee; *Inf.* swineherd; *Fig.* king, chief. *Herald.* **r. de armas**, king-of-arms. **reyes magos**, magi. **día de Reyes**, Twelfth Night. **servir al r.**, to fight for the king

reyerta /rre'yerta/ *f*, quarrel, row, rumpus

rezagar /rreθa'gar; rresa'gar/ *vt* to leave behind; postpone, delay; —*vr* lag behind, straggle

rezar /rre'θar; rre'sar/ *vt* to pray, say prayers; say mass; *Inf.* state, say; —*vi* pray; *Inf.* fume, grumble. **El edicto reza así**, The edict runs like this, The edict reads like this

rezo /'rreθo; 'rreso/ *m*, prayer; devotions

rezongar /rreθoŋ'gar; rreson'gar/ *vi* to grouse, grumble

rezumar /rreθu'mar; rresu'mar/ **(se)** *vr* and *vi* to percolate, ooze through; *Inf.* leak out, be known

ría /'rria/ *f*, estuary, river mouth, firth

riachuelo /rria'tʃuelo/ *m*, rivulet, stream

ribaldería /rriβalde'ria/ *f*, ribaldry

ribazo /rri'βaθo; rri'βaso/ *m*, slope, incline

ribera /rri'βera/ *f*, bank, margin, shore, strand

ribereño /rriβe're.ɲo/ **(-ña)** *a* and *n* riparian

ribete /rri'βete/ *m*, binding, border, trimming; stripe; increase, addition; dramatic touch, exaggeration; *pl* indications, signs

ribetear /rriβete'ar/ *vt Sew.* to bind, trim, edge

ricacho /rri'katʃo/ **(-cha)** *n Inf.* newly rich person, nouveau riche

ricamente /rrika'mente/ *adv* richly, opulently; beautifully, splendidly; luxuriously

ricino /rri'θino; rri'sino/ *m*, castor oil plant

rico /'rriko/ *a* wealthy, rich; abundant; magnificent, splendid; delicious. **r. como Creso**, rich as Croesus

ricura /rri'kura/ *f*, *Inf.* richness, wealth

ridiculez /rriðiku'leθ; rriðiku'les/ *f*, absurd action or remark; ridiculousness; affectation; folly

ridículo /rri'ðikulo/ *a* ridiculous, absurd; grotesque; preposterous, outrageous. *m*, reticule

riego /'rriego/ *m*, watering, spraying; irrigation

riel /'rriel/ *m*, ingot; rail (of a train or streetcar)

rienda /'rrienda/ *f*, rein (gen. *pl*); restraint; *pl* administration, government. **a r. suelta**, swiftly; without restraint

riesgo /'rriesgo/ *m*, risk, danger

rifa /'rrifa/ *f*, raffle; quarrel, disagreement

rifar /rri'far/ *vt* to raffle; —*vi* quarrel, fall out

rifle /'rrifle/ *m*, rifle

rigidez /rrihi'ðeθ; rrihi'ðes/ *f*, stiffness; rigidity; harshness

rígido /'rrihiðo/ *a* stiff; rigid; inflexible; severe, harsh

rigor /rri'gor/ *m*, severity, sternness; rigor; hardness; inflexibility; *Med.* rigor. **en r.**, strictly speaking. **ser de r.**, to be essential, be indispensable

rigorista /rrigo'rista/ *mf* martinet

riguroso /rrigu'roso/ *a* rigorous; harsh, cruel; austere, rigid; strict, exact, scrupulous

rijoso /rri'hoso/ *a* quarrelsome; lascivious

rima /'rrima/ *f*, rhyme, rime; heap; *pl* lyrics

rimador /rrima'ðor/ **(-ra)** *a* rhyming, rimer —*n* rhymer, rimer

rimar /rri'mar/ *vi* to compose verses; —*vi* and *vt* rhyme, rime

rimbombo /rrim'ɓombo/ *m*, reverberation (of a sound)

rimero /rri'mero/ *m*, heap, pile

Rin, el /rrin, el/ the Rhine

rincón /rrin'kon/ *m*, corner, angle; retreat, hiding place; *Inf.* home, nest, nook

rinconera /rrinko'nera/ *f*, corner cupboard; corner table

ringlera /rriŋ'glera/ *f*, file, line, row

ringlero /rriŋ'glero/ *m*, guiding line for writing

ringorrangos /rriŋgo'rraŋgos/ *m pl*, *Inf.* exaggerated flourishes in writing; *Inf.* unnecessary frills or ornaments

rinoceronte /rrinoθe'ronte; rrinose'ronte/ *m*, rhinoceros

riñón /rri'ɲon/ *m*, kidney; *Fig.* center, heart; *pl Anat.* back

río /'rrio/ *m*, river; *Fig.* stream, flood

rioja /'rrioha/ *m*, red wine from Rioja

ripio /'rripio/ *m*, remains, rest; debris, rubbish; *Lit.* padding; verbiage, prolixity. **no perder r.,** to lose no occasion or opportunity

riqueza /rri'keθa; rri'kesa/ *f*, riches, wealth; abundance; richness, magnificence

risa /'rrisa/ *f*, laugh; laughter; cause of amusement, joke

risco /'rrisko/ *m*, crag

riscoso /rris'koso/ *a* craggy

risible /rri'siβle/ *a* laughable

risoles /rri'soles/ *m pl*, rissoles

risotada /rriso'taða/ *f*, loud laugh

ristra /'rristra/ *f*, string (of onions, etc.); file, line, row

risueño /rri'sueɲo/ *a* smiling; cheerful; pleasant, agreeable; favorable, hopeful

rítmico /'rritmiko/ *a* rhythmic

ritmo /'rritmo/ *m*, rhythm

rito /'rrito/ *m*, rite

rivalidad /rriβali'ðað/ *f*, rivalry, competition; hostility

rivalizar /rriβali'θar; rriβali'sar/ *vi* to compete, rival

rizado /rri'θaðo; rri'saðo/ *m*, curling; pleating, crimping; rippling, ruffling

rizar /rri'θar; rri'sar/ *vt* to curl (hair); ripple, ruffle (of water); pleat, crimp; —*vr* be naturally wavy (of hair)

rizo /'rriθo; 'rriso/ *m*, curl, ringlet; cut velvet. *Aer.* **hacer el r.,** to loop the loop; *Naut.* to take in reefs

rizoso /rri'θoso; rri'soso/ *a* naturally curly or wavy (hair)

robador /rroβa'ðor/ **(-ra)** *a* robbing —*n* robber, thief. *m*, abductor

robar /rro'βar/ *vt* to rob; abduct; wash away, eat away (rivers, sea); remove honey from the hive; draw (in cards, dominoes); *Fig.* capture (love, etc.)

roblar /rro'βlar/ *vt* to reinforce, strengthen; clinch

roble /'rroβle/ *m*, oak tree; oak; *Fig.* bulwark, tower of strength

roblón /rro'βlon/ *m*, rivet

robo /'rroβo/ *m*, theft, robbery; booty

robustecer /rroβuste'θer; rroβuste'ser/ *vt irr* to strengthen. See **conocer**

robustez /rroβus'teθ; rroβus'tes/ *f*, strength, robustness

robusto /rro'βusto/ *a* vigorous, robust, hearty, strong

roca /'rroka/ *f*, rock; *Fig.* tower of strength

roce /'rroθe; 'rrose/ *m*, rubbing, brushing, touching, friction; social intercourse

rociada /rro'θiaða; rro'siaða/ *f*, dewing; sprinkling; dew-wet grass given as medicine to horses and mules; *Fig.* shower; general slander; harsh rebuke

rociar /rro'θiar; rro'siar/ *vi* to fall as dew; drizzle; —*vt* sprinkle, spray; *Fig.* shower (with)

rocín /rro'θin; rro'sin/ *m*, sorry nag; hack; *Inf.* ignoramus, boor

rocinante /rroθi'nante; rrosi'nante/ *m*, poor nag (alluding to Don Quixote's horse)

rocío /rro'θio; 'rrosio/ *m*, dew; dewdrop; drizzle, light shower; *Fig.* sprinkling, spray

rocoso /rro'koso/ *a* rocky

rodaballo /rroða'βaʎo; rroða'βayo/ *m*, turbot; *Inf.* crafty man

rodada /rro'ðaða/ *f*, wheel mark or track

rodado /rro'ðaðo/ *a* dappled (of horses)

rodaje /rro'ðahe/ *m*, wheeling; shooting (of a film)

rodante /rro'ðante/ *a* rolling

rodar /rro'ðar/ *vi* to roll; revolve, turn; run on wheels; wander, roam; be moved about; be plentiful, abound; happen successively; (*with por*) fall down, roll down

Rodas /'rroðas/ Rhodes

rodear /rroðe'ar/ *vi* to walk around; go by a roundabout way; *Fig.* beat around the bush; —*vt* encircle, surround; besiege; *West Hem.* round up (cattle)

rodeno /rro'ðeno/ *a* red (of rocks, earth, etc.)

rodeo /rro'ðeo/ *m*, encirclement; indirect and longer way; trick to evade pursuit; *West Hem.* rodeo, roundup; stockyard, cattle enclosure; *Fig.* beating around the bush; evasive reply

rodera /rro'ðera/ *f*, rail, track, line; cart rut or track

rodilla /rro'ðiʎa; rro'ðiya/ *f*, knee; floor cloth. **de rodillas,** on one's knees. **ponerse de rodillas,** *or* **hincar las rodillas,** to kneel down

rodillera /rroði'ʎera; rroði'yera/ *f*, kneecap, kneepad; mend at the knee of garments; bagginess of trouser knees

rodillo /rro'ðiʎo; rro'ðiyo/ *m*, roller; traction engine; *Print*. inking roller; garden roller. **r. de pastas**, *Cul*. rolling pin

rododendro /rroðo'ðendro/ *m*, rhododendro

rodrigón /rroðri'gon/ *m*, stake, prop (for plants); *Inf*. old retainer who serves as a ladies' escort

roedor /rroe'ðor/ *a* gnawing; *Fig*. nagging; biting —*a* and *m*, rodent

roedura /rroe'ðura/ *f*, biting, gnawing; corrosion

roer /rro'er/ *vt irr* to gnaw, nibble, eat; corrode, wear away; trouble, afflict —*Pres. Indic.* **roigo, roes**, etc —*Preterite* **royó, royeron**. *Imperf. Subjunc.* **royese**, etc.

rogación /rroga'θion/ *f*, request, supplication, entreaty; *Eccl.* rogation

rogar /rro'gar/ *vt irr* to request; beseech, beg. See **contar**

rogativo /rroga'tiβo/ *a* supplicatory, petitioning

roído /rroi'ðo/ *a* gnawed, eaten; *Inf*. miserable, stingy

rojal /rro'hal/ *a* red (of soil, etc.). *m*, red earth

rojear /rrohe'ar/ *vi* to appear red; be reddish

rojete /rro'hete/ *m*, rouge

rojez /rro'heθ; rro'hes/ *f* ', redness

rojizo /rro'hiθo; rro'hiso/ *a* reddish

rojo /'rroho/ *a* red; fair; red-gold (of hair); *Polit.* radical, red

rol /rrol/ *m*, roll, list

roldana /rrol'dana/ *f*, pulley wheel

rollizo /rro'ʎiθo; rro'yiso/ *a* round; plump, sturdy. *m*, log

rollo /'rroʎo; 'rroyo/ *m*, roll; *Cul.* rolling pin; log; town cross or pillar; anything rolled (paper, etc.); twist (of tobacco)

Roma /'rroma/ Rome

romance /rro'manθe; rro'manse/ *a* and *m*, romance (language). *m*, Spanish; ballad; romance of chivalry; *pl Fig.* fairy tales, excuses. **en buen r.**, *Fig.* in plain words

romano. /rro'mano/ **(-na)** *a* and *n* Roman. **a la romana**, in the Roman way. **cabello a la romana**, *Inf.* bobbed hair

romántico /rro'mantiko/ **(-ca)** *a* romantic; emotional; fanciful —*n* romantic; romanticist

romería /rrome'ria/ *f*, pilgrimage; excursion, picnic (made on a saint's day)

romero /rro'mero/ **(-ra)** *m*, rosemary —*n* pilgrim

romo /'rromo/ *a* blunt, dull, unsharpened; flat (of noses)

rompecabezas /rrompeka'βeθas; rrompeka'βesas/ *m*, bludgeon; knuckleduster; *Inf.* teaser, puzzle, riddle; jigsaw puzzle

rompeimágenes /rrompei'mahenes/ *mf* iconoclast

rompeolas /rrompe'olas/ *m*, jetty, breakwater

romper /rrom'per/ *vt* to break; shatter, break into fragments; spoil, ruin; break up, plow; *Fig.* cut, divide (of water, etc.); *Fig.* end, break; interrupt; infringe, break; —*vi* break; break (of waves); sprout, flower; (*with prep a*) begin to. **Rompió a hablar**, He broke into speech —*Past Part.* **roto**

rompiente /rrom'piente/ *a* breaking. *m*, reef, shoal

rompimiento /rrompi'miento/ *m*, break, rupture; crack, split; breakage; infringement; plowing up; *Fig.* dividing (water, etc.); spoiling, ruining; opening (of buds, etc.)

ron /rron/ *m*, rum

roncar /rron'kar/ *vi* to snore; *Fig.* roar, howl (of the sea, wind, etc.); *Inf.* brag

roncear /rronθe'ar; rronse'ar/ *vi* to be dilatory or unwilling; *Inf.* flatter, cajole; *Naut.* lag behind, sail slowly

roncero /rron'θero; rron'sero/ *a* dilatory, slow; grumbling, complaining; cajoling, flattering

roncha /'rrontʃa/ *f*, wheal; bruise, bump; *Inf.* money lost through trickery; thin, round slice

ronco /'rronko/ *a* hoarse, husky

ronda /'rronda/ *f*, round, beat, patrol; serenading party; *Inf.* round (of drinks)

rondador /rronda'ðor/ *m*, watchman; roundsman; serenader; night wanderer

rondalla /rron'daʎa; rron'daya/ *f*, tale, fairy tale

rondar /rron'dar/ *vi* to patrol, police; walk the streets by night; serenade; —*vt* haunt; hover about; *Inf.* overcome (of sleep, etc.)

rondó /rron'do/ *m*, rondo

ronquear /rronke'ar/ *vi* to be hoarse

ronquera /rron'kera/ *f*, hoarseness

ronquido /rron'kiðo/ *m*, snore; hoarse sound

ronronear /rronrone'ar/ *vi* to purr (of cats)

ronzar /rron'θar; rron'sar/ *vt* to munch, crack with the teeth

roña /'rroɲa/ *f*, mange (in sheep); grime, filth; mold; moral corruption; *Inf.* stinginess; *Inf.* trick, deception

roñería /rroɲe'ria/ *f*, *Inf.* meanness, stinginess

roñoso /rro'ɲoso/ *a* scabby; filthy; rusty; *Inf.* mean, stingy

ropa /'rropa/ *f*, fabric, material, stuff; clothes, wearing apparel; garment, outfit; robe (of office). **r. blanca**, underclothes; (domestic) linen. **r. hecha**, ready-made clothing. **r. talar**, long gown; cassock

ropaje /rro'pahe/ *m*, clothes, garments; vestments; drapery; *Fig.* form, outline

ropavejería /rropaβehe'ria/ *f*, old-clothes shop

ropavejero /rropaβe'hero/ **(-ra)** *n* old-clothes dealer

ropería /rrope'ria/ f. clothier's shop or trade; wardrobe; cloakroom.

ropero /rro'pero/ **(-ra)** n clothier; keeper of the wardrobe. m. wardrobe; charitable organization

ropón /rro'pon/ m. a loose-fitting gown generally worn over clothes

roque /'rroke/ m. rook (in chess)

roqueño /rro'keɲo/ a rocky; hard as rock

rorro /'rrorro/ m. Inf. infant, baby

rosa /'rrosa/ f. rose; anything rose-shaped; artificial rose; red spot on the body; Archit. rose window; pl rosettes. m. rose color. **r. de los vientos**, mariner's compass. **r. laurel**, oleander

rosado /rro'saðo/ a rose-colored; rosé (wines)

rosal /rro'sal/ m. rose tree. **r. de tallo**, standard rose tree

rosaleda, rosalera /rrosa'leða, rrosa-'lera/ f. rose garden

rosario /rro'sario/ m. rosary; Fig. string; chain pump; Inf. backbone

rosbif /rros'βif/ m. roast beef

rosca /'rroska/ f. screw and nut; Cul. twist (of bread or cake); spiral

roscado /rros'kaðo/ a twisted, spiral

rosear /rrose'ar/ vi to turn to rose, become rose-colored

róseo /'rroseo/ a rose-colored

roseta /rro'seta/ f. dim small rose; rosette; rose of a watering can; rosette copper; pl toasted maize. **r. de fiebre**, rush of fever

rosetón /rrose'ton/ m. large rosette; Archit. rose window

roso /'rroso/ a bald, worn; red

rosquilla /rros'kiʎa/ rros'kiya/ f. ring-shaped cake

rostro /'rrostro/ m. bird's beak; face, visage. **conocer de r.**, to know by sight. **dar en r.**, Fig. to throw in one's face

rotación /rrota'θion/ rrota'sion/ f. rotation. **r. de cultivos**, rotation of crops

rotativo /rrota'tiβo/ a rotary

roto /'rroto/ a shabby, ragged; vicious, debauched

rotonda /rro'tonda/ f. rotunda

rótula /'rrotula/ f. rotula, patella

rotular /rrotu'lar/ vt to label; give a title or heading to

rótulo /'rrotulo/ m. title; poster, placard; label

rotundamente /rrotunda'mente/ adv tersely, roundly, plainly

rotundidad /rrotundi'ðað/ f. rotundity; roundness; finality (of words, etc.)

rotundo /rro'tundo/ a round; rotund; sonorous; final, plain (of words, etc.)

rotura /rro'tura/ f. breaking, shattering; plowing up; breakage; rupture

roya /'rroya/ f. rust, mildew; tobacco

roza /'rroθa; 'rrosa/ f. Agr. clearing (of weeds, etc.); ground ready for sowing. **de r. abierta**, open cast (of mining)

rozadura /rroθa'ðura; rrosa'ðura/ f. rubbing, friction; abrasion, chafing

rozagante /rroθa'gante; rrosa'gante/ a long and elaborate (dresses); upstanding; handsome; strapping, fine

rozamiento /rroθa'miento; rrosa'miento/ m. grazing, brushing, rubbing; discord, disharmony, disagreement; Mech. friction

rozar /rro'θar; rro'sar/ vt Agr. to clear of weeds; crop, nibble; scrape; brush against, touch; —vi brush, rub, touch; —vr have dealings with, know; stammer; be like, resemble

rubeola /rruβe'ola/ f. rubella

rubí /rru'βi/ m. ruby; jewel (of a watch)

rubia /'rruβia/ f. Bot. madder; blonde (girl, woman)

rubicundez /rruβikun'deθ; rruβikun'des/ f. rubicundity, ruddiness, redness

rubicundo /rruβi'kundo/ a red-gold; ruddy-complexioned; reddish

rubio /'rruβio/ a red-gold, gold; fair, blond

rublo /'rruβlo/ m. ruble

rubor /rru'βor/ m. blush, flush; bashfulness

ruborizarse /rruβori'θarse; rruβori'sarse/ vr to blush; be shamefaced

ruboroso /rruβo'roso/ a shamefaced; blushing

rúbrica /'rruβrika/ f. rubric; personal mark, flourish added to one's signature

rubricar /rruβri'kar/ vt to sign and seal; sign with an X or other symbol; sign with a flourish

rucio /'rruθio; 'rrusio/ a fawn, light-gray (of animals); Inf. going gray, gray-haired

rudamente /rruða'mente/ adv rudely, abruptly, churlishly; roughly

rudeza /rru'ðeθa; rru'ðesa/ f. roughness; rudeness, uncouthness; stupidity

rudimentario /rruðimen'tario/ a rudimentary

rudimento /rruði'mento/ m. embryo; pl rudiments

rudo /'rruðo/ a rough; unfinished; uncouth, boorish, rude; stupid

rueca /'rrueka/ f. distaff (in spinning); spinning wheel; curve, twist

rueda /'rrueða/ f. wheel; group, circle; spread of a peacock's tail; roller, castor; round piece or slice; turn, chance; succession (of events); wheel (used for torture). **r. libre**, freewheeling. Inf. **hacer la r. (a)**, to flatter, make a fuss of

ruedo /'rrueðo/ m. turning, rotation; circumference; lined hem of a cassock; circuit

ruego /'rruego/ m. request, entreaty

rufián /rru'fian/ m. ruffian; pimp

rufo /'rrufo/ a fair; red-haired; curly-haired

rugido /rru'hiðo/ m. roaring, roar; creaking; gnashing; rumbling

rugir /rru'hir/ vi to roar; squeak, creak; gnash (the teeth)

ruibarbo /rrui'βarβo/ m. rhubarb

ruido /'rruiðo/ *m.* noise, din; disturbance; rumor. **hacer** (*or* **meter**) **r.,** to cause a sensation. *Inf.* **ser más el r. que las nueces,** to be much ado about nothing

ruidoso /rrui'ðoso/ *a* noisy; notable

ruin /rru'in/ *a* base, vile; despicable; mean; puny

ruina /'rruina/ *f.* ruin, downfall; financial ruin; fall, decline; *pl* ruins

ruinar /rrui'nar/ *vt* to ruin

ruindad /rruin'daδ/ *f.* baseness; meanness; pettiness, unworthiness; mean trick, despicable action

ruinoso /rrui'noso/ *a* half-ruined; ruinous; useless, worthless

ruiseñor /rruise'nor/ *m.* nightingale

ruleta /rru'leta/ *f.* roulette

rumano /rru'mano/ **(-na)** *a* and *n* Romanian. *m.* Romanian (language)

rumbo /'rrumbo/ *m.* *Naut.* course, way, route; direction; *Inf.* swank. **con r. a,** headed for, in the direction of. **hacer r. a,** to sail for; make for

rumboso /rrum'βoso/ *a* *Inf.* pompous, dignified; open-handed, generous

rumia /'rrumia/ *f.* rumination; cud

rumiante /rru'miante/ *a* and *mf* *Zool.* ruminant —*a Inf.* reflective, meditative

rumiar /rru'miar/ *vt* *Zool.* to ruminate; *Inf.* reflect upon, chew on; *Inf.* fume, rage

rumor /rru'mor/ *m.* noise; rumor; murmur, babble; dull sound

rupia /'rrupia/ *f.* rupee

ruptura /rrup'tura/ *f.* *Fig.* rupture; *Surg.* hernia

rural /rru'ral/ *a* rustic, rural

Rusia /'rrusia/ Russia

ruso /'rruso/ **(-sa)** *a* and *n* Russian. *m,* Russian (language)

rusticar /rrusti'kar/ *vi* to rusticate

rusticidad /rrustiθi'ðaδ; rrustisi'ðaδ/ *f.* rusticity; boorishness, coarseness

rústico /'rrustiko/ *a* rustic, country; boorish, uncouth. *m.* countryman; yokel; peasant. **en rústica,** in paper covers (of books)

ruta /'rruta/ *f.* route; *Fig.* way. **r. de evitación,** bypass, detour

rutilante /rruti'lante/ *a* *Poet.* sparkling, glowing

rutilar /rruti'lar/ *vi* *Poet.* to gleam, sparkle

rutina /rru'tina/ *f.* routine

rutinario /rruti'nario/ *a* routine

rutinero /rruti'nero/ **(-ra)** *a* routinistic —*n* routinist

S

sábalo /'saβalo/ *m. Ichth.* shad

sabana /sa'βana/ *f.* savannah

sábana /'saβana/ *f.* bed sheet; altar cloth. *Inf.* pegársele (a uno) las sábanas, to be tied to the bed, get up late

sabandija /saβan'diha/ *f.* any unpleasant insect or reptile; *Fig.* vermin

sabanero /saβa'nero/ **(-ra)** *n* savannah dweller —*a* savannah

sabanilla /saβa'niʎa; saβa'niya/ *f.* small piece of linen (kerchief, towel, etc.); altar cloth

sabático /sa'βatiko/ *a* sabbatical

sabedor /saβe'ðor/ *a* aware; knowledgeable, knowing

sabelotodo /saβelo'toðo/ *mf Inf.* know-it-all

saber /sa'βer/ *m.* learning; wisdom

saber /sa'βer/ *vt irr* to know; be able to, know how; —*vi* know; be shrewd, be well aware of; (*with prep a*) taste of; be like or similar to. **s. al dedillo,** *Fig.* to have at one's fingertips. **a s.,** viz.; namely. *Inf.* no s. cuántas son cinco, not to know how many beans make five. **no s. dónde meterse,** to be overcome by shame; have the jitters. **No sé cuántos,** I don't know how many. **No sé quién,** I don't know who (which person). **No sé qué,** I don't know what. **un no sé qué,** a certain something; a touch (of). **¡Quién sabe!** Who knows!; Time will tell —*Pres. Indic.* sé, sabes, etc —*Fut.* sabré, etc —*Condit.* sabría, etc —*Preterite* supe, etc —*Pres. Subjunc.* sepa, etc —*Imperf. Subjunc.* supiese, etc.

sabidillo /saβi'ðiʎo; saβi'ðiyo/ **(-lla)** *a* and *n Inf.* know-it-all

sabiduría /saβiðu'ria/ *f.* prudence, wisdom; erudition, learning; knowledge, awareness. **Libro de la S. de Salomón,** Book of Wisdom

sabiendas, a /sa'βiendas, a/ *adv* knowingly, consciously

sabihondo /sa'βiondo/ **(-da)** *n Inf.* know-it-all

sabio /'saβio/ **(-ia)** *a* wise; learned, erudite; prudent, sagacious; knowing (of animals); performing (of animals) —*n* wise person; scholar, erudite person

sablazo /sa'βlaθo; sa'βlaso/ *m,* saber thrust or wound; *Inf.* sponging, taking advantage of. **dar un s. (a),** *Inf.* to sponge on; touch for money

sable /'saβle/ *m,* saber; *Herald.* sable; *Inf.* talent for sponging on people —*a Herald.* sable

sablear /saβle'ar/ *vi Inf.* to touch for invitations, loans, etc.; cadge

sablista /sa'βlista/ *mf Inf.* sponger, cadger

saboneta /saβo'neta/ *f.* hunting case watch, hunter

---

sabor /sa'βor/ *m,* taste, flavor; impression, effect. **a s.,** to taste; at pleasure

saboreamiento /saβorea'miento/ *m,* savoring, relishing, enjoyment

saborear /saβore'ar/ *vt* to flavor, season; relish, savor; appreciate, enjoy; —*vr* relish, savor; enjoy

saboreo /saβo'reo/ *m,* tasting; savoring; relishing

sabotaje /saβo'tahe/ *m,* sabotage

saboteador /saβotea'ðor/ *m,* saboteur

sabroso /sa'βroso/ *a* tasty, savory, well-seasoned; delightful, delicious; *Inf.* piquant, racy

sabueso /sa'βueso/ *m,* cocker spaniel. **s. de artois,** hound

saburra /sa'βurra/ *f,* fur (on the tongue)

saca /'saka/ *f,* drawing out, removing; export, transport, shipping; removal, extraction; legal copy (of a document). **estar de s.,** to be on sale; *Inf.* be marriageable (of women)

sacabocados /sakaβo'kaðos/ *m,* punch (tool); *Inf.* cinch, easy matter

sacabuche /saka'βutʃe/ *m, Mus.* sackbut; sackbut player; *Inf.* insignificant little man; *Naut.* hand pump

sacacorchos /saka'kortʃos/ *m,* corkscrew

sacacuartos /saka'kuartos/ *m, Inf.* catchpenny

sacada /sa'kaða/ *f,* territory cut off from a province

sacamanchas /saka'mantʃas/ *mf.* See quitamanchas

sacamiento /saka'miento/ *m,* removing, taking out

sacamuelas /saka'muelas/ *mf* dentist; charlatan, quack; *Inf.* windbag

sacapotras /saka'potras/ *m, Inf.* unskilled surgeon

sacar /sa'kar/ *vt* to draw out; extract; pull out; take out; remove; dispossess, turn out; free from, relieve; examine, investigate; extort (the truth); extract (sugar, etc.); win (prizes, games); copy; discover, find out; elect by ballot; obtain, achieve; exclude; show, exhibit; quote, mention; produce, invent; manufacture; note down; put forth; unsheath (swords); bowl (in cricket); serve (in tennis). **s. a bailar,** to invite to dance. **s. a luz,** to publish, print; reveal, bring out. **s. a paseo,** to take for a walk. **s. de pila,** to be a godfather or godmother to. **s. en claro** *or* **s. en limpio,** to copy; conclude, infer, gather. **sacarse en conclusión que...,** the conclusion is that...

sacarina /saka'rina/ *f,* saccharin

sacasillas /saka'siʎas; saka'siyas/ *m, Inf. Theat.* stagehand

sacerdocio /saθer'ðoθio; saser'ðosio/ *m,* priesthood

sacerdotal /saθerðo'tal; saserðo'tal/ *a* priestly

sacerdote /saθer'ðote; saser'ðote/ *m,* priest

sacerdotisa /saθerðo'tisa; saserðo'tisa/ f,
priestess. **sumo s.**, high priestess

sachar /sa't∫ar/ vt to weed

saciable /sa'θiaβle; sa'siaβle/ a satiable

saciar /sa'θiar; sa'siar/ vt to satisfy; satiate; —vr be satiated

saciedad /saθie'ðað; sasie'ðað/ f, satiety,
surfeit

saco /'sako/ m, handbag; sack, bag; sackful; sack coat; Biol. sac; Mil. sack, plundering. **s. de noche**, dressing case, week-
end case. Inf. **no echar en s. roto**, not to
forget, to remember

sacramentalmente /sakramental'mente/
adv sacramentally; in confession

sacramentar /sakramen'tar/ vt to consecrate; administer the Blessed Sacrament;
hide, conceal

sacramentario /sakramen'tario/ **(-ia)** n
sacramentalist; sacramentarian

sacramento /sakra'mento/ m, sacrament;
Eccl. Host; Eccl. mystery. **s. del altar**, Eucharist. **con todos los sacramentos**, with
all the sacraments; done in order, complete with all formalities. **recibir los sacramentos**, to receive the last sacraments

sacrificador /sakrifika'ðor/ **(-ra)** a sacri-
ficing —n sacrificer

sacrificar /sakrifi'kar/ vt to sacrifice;
slaughter; —vr consecrate oneself to God;
sacrifice oneself; devote or dedicate oneself (to)

sacrificio /sakri'fiθio; sakri'fisio/ m, sacrifice; offering, dedication; surrendering,
forgoing; compliance, submission. **s. del
altar**, sacrifice of the mass

sacrilegio /sakri'lehio/ m, sacrilege

sacrílego /sa'krilego/ a sacrilegious

sacristán /sakris'tan/ m, sacristan; sexton; hoop (for dresses). Inf. **s. de amén**,
yes-man. Inf. **ser gran s.**, to be very
crafty

sacristana /sakris'tana/ f, wife of a sacristan or sexton; nun in charge of a convent sacristy

sacristanía /sakrista'nia/ f, office of a
sacristan or sexton

sacristía /sakris'tia/ f, sacristy; vestry;
office of a sacristan or sexton

sacro /'sakro/ a sacred; Anat. sacral

sacrosanto /sakro'santo/ a sacrosanct

sacudida /saku'ðiða/ f, shake, shaking;
jerk, jar, jolt; twitch, pull; Aer. bump

sacudido /saku'ðiðo/ a unsociable; difficult, wayward; determined, bold

sacudidor /sakuði'ðor/ **(-ra)** a shaking;
jerking —n shaker. m, carpet beater;
duster

sacudidura /sakuði'ðura/ f, shaking (especially to remove dust); jerking

sacudimiento /sakuði'miento/ m, shake,
shaking; jerk; twitch, pull; jolt

sacudir /saku'ðir/ vt to shake; flap, wave;
jerk, twitch; beat, bang; shake off; —vr
shake off, avoid

sadismo /sa'ðismo/ m, sadism

sadista /sa'ðista/ mf sadist

sadístico /sa'ðistiko/ a sadistic

saeta /sa'eta/ f, arrow, dart; clock hand,
watch hand; magnetic needle; short sung
expression of religious ecstasy; Astron.
Sagitta

saga /'saga/ f, saga

sagacidad /sagaθi'ðað; sagasi'ðað/ f, sagacity

sagaz /sa'gaθ; sa'gas/ a sagacious,
shrewd; farseeing; quick on the scent
(dogs)

sagrado /sa'graðo/ a sacred; holy; sacrosanct, venerable; accursed, detestable. m,
sanctuary, refuge; haven

Sáhara, el /'saara, el/ the Sahara

sahornarse /saor'narse/ vr to chafe,
grow sore

sahorno /sa'orno/ m, chafing, abrasion

sahumado /sau'maðo/ a improved, rendered more excellent; perfumed; fumi-
gated

sahumador /sauma'ðor/ m, perfumer;
fumigating vessel

sahumar /sau'mar/ vt to perfume; fumigate. See **desahuciar**

sahumerio /sau'merio/ m, perfuming; fumigation; fume, smoke

saín /sa'in/ m, fat, grease; sardine oil (for
lamps); grease spot (on clothes)

sainar /sai'nar/ vt to fatten up (animals)

sainete /sai'nete/ m, Cul. sauce; Theat.
one-act parody or burlesque; farce; delicacy, tidbit; delicate taste (of food)

sainetero /saine'tero/ m, writer of sai-
netes

sajar /sa'har/ vt Surg. to scarify

sal /sal/ f, salt; wit; grace, gracefulness.
s. de cocina, common kitchen salt. **s. de
la Higuera**, Epsom salts. **s. gema**, rock
salt. **s. marina**, sea salt. **sales inglesas**,
smelling salts. Inf. **estar hecho de s.**, to
be full of wit. Inf. **hacerse s. y agua**, to
melt away, disappear (of riches, etc.)

sala /'sala/ f, drawing room; large room,
hall; Law. courtroom; Law. bench; **s. de
apelación**, court of appeal. **s. de hospital**, hospital ward. **s. de justicia**, court of
justice. **s. de lectura**, reading room. Law.
guardar s., to respect the court

salacidad /salaθi'ðað; salasi'ðað/ f, lewdness, salaciousness

saladero /sala'ðero/ m, salting or curing
place; West Hem. meat packing factory

saladillo /sala'ðiʎo; sala'ðiyo/ m, salt
pork

salado /sa'laðo/ a salty, briny; brackish;
witty; attractive, amusing

salador /sala'ðor/ **(-ra)** a salting, curing
—n salter, curer. m, curing place

saladura /sala'ðura/ f, salting, curing

salamandra /sala'mandra/ f, salamander;
fire sprite

salar /sa'lar/ vt to salt; season with salt;
oversalt; cure, pickle (meat, etc.)

salario /sa'lario/ m, salary

salaz /sa'laθ; sa'las/ a lewd, lecherous

salazón /sala'θon; sala'son/ *f*, salting, curing; salt meat or fish trade

salazonero /salaθo'nero; salaso'nero/ *a* salting, curing

salchicha /sal'tʃitʃa/ *f*, sausage

salchichería /saltʃitʃe'ria/ *f*, sausage shop

salchichón /saltʃi'tʃon/ *m*, *Cul.* salami, kind of sausage

saldar /sal'dar/ *vt Com.* to settle, pay in full; sell out cheap; balance

saldo /'saldo/ *m*, *Com.* balance; closing of an account; bargain sale. **s. acreedor,** credit balance. **s. deudor,** debit balance. **s. líquido,** net balance

salero /sa'lero/ *m*, saltshaker, saltcellar; salt storage warehouse; *Inf.* wit

salida /sa'liða/ *f*, going out; leaving; departure; sailing; exit, way out; projection, protrusion; *Fig.* escape, way out; outcome, result; witty remark; *Mil.* sally; *Com.* outlay, expense; *Com.* opening, sale, salability; environs, outskirts. **s. de dólares,** dollar drain. **s. de tono,** *Inf.* an impertinent remark. **dar s.,** *Com.* to enter on the credit side

salidero /sali'ðero/ *a* fond of going out; *m*, exit, way out

salidizo /sali'ðiθo; sali'ðiso/ *m*, *Archit.* projection —*a* projecting

saliente /sa'liente/ *a* outgoing; salient, projecting. *m*, east; projection; salient. **s. continental,** continental shelf

salina /sa'lina/ *f*, salt mine; saltworks

salinero /sali'nero/ *m*, salt merchant; salter; salt worker

salino /sa'lino/ *a* saline. *m*, *Med.* saline

salir /sa'lir/ *vi irr* to go out; depart, leave; succeed in getting out; escape; appear (of the sun, etc.); sprout, show green; fade, come out (of stains); project, stand out; grow, develop; turn out, result; happen, take place; cost; sail; end (of seasons, time); lead off, start (some games); be published (books); do (well or badly), succeed or fail; appear, show oneself; be drawn, win (lottery tickets); balance, come out right (accounts); be elected; become; give up (posts); lead to (of streets, etc.); *Naut.* overtake; (*with prep a*) guarantee, be surety for; resemble, be like; (*with con*) utter, come out with; commit, do inopportunely; succeed in, achieve (e.g. *Salió con la suya,* He got his own way); (*with de*) originate in; break away from (traditions, conventions); get rid of; (*with por*) stand up for, protect; go surety for, guarantee —*vr* leak; boil over; overflow; (*with con*) achieve, get; (*with de*) *Fig.* break away from. *Theat.* **s. a la escena,** to enter, come on to the stage. **s. de,** to recover from (an illness). **no acabar de s. de,** to not be completely recovered from. **s. del apuro,** to get out of trouble. **s. de estampía,** to stampede (of animals). **s. pitando,** *Inf.* to get out in a hurry. **Esta idea no salió de Juan,** This wasn't John's idea. **salga lo que saliere,**

Inf. come what may... —*Pres. Indic.* **salgo, sales,** etc —*Fut.* **saldré,** etc —*Condit.* **saldría,** etc —*Pres. Subjunc.* **salga,** etc.

salitre /sa'litre/ *m*, saltpeter

saliva /sa'liβa/ *f*, saliva. *Inf.* **tragar s.,** to put up with; be unable to speak through emotion

salivación /saliβa'θion; saliβa'sion/ *f*, salivation

salivar /sali'βar/ *vi* to salivate; spit

sallar /sa'ʎar; sa'yar/ *vt* to weed

salmear /salme'ar/ *vi* to intone psalms

salmista /sal'mista/ *mf* psalmist; psalmodist, psalm chanter

salmo /'salmo/ *m*, psalm

salmodia /sal'moðia/ *f*, psalmody; *Inf.* drone; psalter

salmodiar /salmo'ðiar/ *vi* to chant psalms; —*vt* drone

salmón /sal'mon/ *m*, salmon

salmonete /salmo'nete/ *m*, red mullet

salmuera /sal'muera/ *f*, brine

salobre /sa'loβre/ *a* salt, salty; brackish

salón /sa'lon/ *m*, drawing room; large room or hall; reception room; salon, reception, social gathering. **s. de muestras,** showroom

salpicadura /salpika'ðura/ *f*, sprinkling, spattering, splashing

salpicar /salpi'kar/ *vt* to sprinkle, scatter; bespatter, splash

salpicón /salpi'kon/ *m*, *Cul.* kind of salmagundi; *Inf.* hodgepodge; spattering

salpimentar /salpimen'tar/ *vt irr* to season with pepper and salt; sprinkle; *Fig.* leaven, enliven (a speech, etc.). See **regimentar**

salpullido /salpu'ʎiðo; salpu'yiðo/ *m*, rash, skin eruption

salsa /'salsa/ *f*, sauce; gravy. **s. mahonesa** or **s. mayonesa,** mayonnaise sauce. **s. mayordoma,** sauce maître d'hôtel

salsera /sal'sera/ *f*, sauce boat, gravy boat

saltabanco /salta'βanko/ *m*, mountebank; street entertainer, juggler

saltabarrancos /saltaβa'rrankos/ *mf Inf.* madcap, harum-scarum

saltador /salta'ðor/ **(-ra)** *a* jumping —*n* jumper; acrobat. *m*, jump rope, skip rope

saltamontes /salta'montes/ *m*, grasshopper

saltaparedes /saltapa'reðes/ *mf Inf.* madcap, romp

saltar /sal'tar/ *vi* to jump, leap, spring; prance; frisk, gambol; rebound; blow up; burst, break asunder; pop (of corks); fly off, come off (buttons, etc.); gush out, shoot up (liquids); break apart, be shattered; be obvious, stand out; come to mind, suggest itself; show anger; *Fig.* let slip, come out with (remarks); —*vt* leap or jump over; poke out (eyes); cover (the female); omit, pass over; blow up, explode. **s. a la cuerda,** to jump rope, play with a skip rope. **s. a la vista,** to be obvious, leap to the eye. **s. diciendo,** *Inf.* to come out with, say

saltarín /salta'rin/ **(-ina)** *a* dancing —*n* dancer

saltatriz /salta'triθ; salta'tris/ *f,* ballet dancer, female acrobat

saltatumbas /salta'tumbas/ *m,* (*Inf.* contemptuous) cleric who makes his living off funerals

salteador /saltea'ðor/ '*m,* highwayman

salteamiento /saltea'miento/ *m,* highway robbery, holdup; assault, attack

saltear /salte'ar/ *vt* to hold up and rob; assault, attack; jump from one thing to another, do intermittently; forestall; surprise, amaze

salterio /sal'terio/ *m,* psaltery

saltimbanco, saltimbanqui /saltim'βanko, saltim'βanki/ *m,* *Inf.*. See **saltabanco**

salto /'salto/ *m,* jump, leap, bound; leapfrog (game); precipice, ravine; waterfall; assault; important promotion; omission (of words). **s. de agua,** waterfall. **s. de cama,** peignoir, bathrobe. **s. de campana,** overturning. *Inf.* **s. de mal año,** sudden improvement in circumstances. **s. de mata,** flight, escape. **s. mortal,** leap of death; somersault. **s. de pie,** spillway. **dar un s.,** to leap. **en un s.,** at one jump; swiftly

saltón /sal'ton/ *a* jumping, leaping; prominent (teeth, eyes). *m,* grasshopper

salubre /sa'luβre/ *a* salubrious, healthful

salubridad /saluβri'ðað/ *f,* healthfulness

salud /sa'luð/ *f,* health; salvation; welfare, well-being; *Eccl.* state of grace; *pl* civilities, greetings. **¡S. y pesetas!** Here's to your good health and prosperity! (on drinking). **gastar s.,** to enjoy good health. *Inf.* **vender (** *or* **verter) s.,** to look full of health

saludable /salu'ðaβle/ *a* healthy, wholesome

saludador /saluða'ðor/ **(-ra)** *a* greeting, saluting —*n* greeter. *m,* charlatan, quack

saludar /salu'ðar/ *vt* to greet, salute; hail (as king, etc.); send greetings to; bow; *Mil.* fire a salute

saludo /sa'luðo/ *m,* greeting, salutation; bow; (*Mil. Nav.*) salute

salutación /saluta'θion; saluta'sion/ *f,* greeting, salutation; Ave Maria

salva /'salβa/ *f,* salutation, greeting; (*Mil. Nav.*) salvo, volley; salute (of guns); salver; ordeal (to establish innocence); solemn assurance, oath; sampling, tasting (of food, drink). **s. de veintiún cañonazos,** twenty-one–gun salute

salvación /salβa'θion; salβa'sion/ *f,* liberation, deliverance; salvation

salvado /sal'βaðo/ *m,* bran

salvador /salβa'ðor/ **(-ra)** *a* saving, redeeming —*n* deliverer. *m,* redeemer

salvadoreño /salβaðore'ɲo/ **(-ña)** *a* and *n* Salvadorean

salvaguardia /salβa'guarðia/ *m,* guard,

watch. *f,* safeguard; protection, defense; safe conduct, passport

salvajada /salβa'haða/ *f,* savagery, brutal action

salvaje /sal'βahe/ *a* wild (plants, animals); rough, uncultivated; uncultured, uncivilized. *mf* savage

salvajismo /salβa'hismo/ *m,* savagery

salvamano, a /salβa'mano, a/ *adv* safely

salvamente /salβa'mente/ *adv* safely, securely

salvamento /salβa'mento/ *m,* salvation; deliverance, security, safety; place of safety; salvage

salvante /sal'βante/ *adv Inf.* except, save

salvar /sal'βar/ *vt* to save; *Eccl.* redeem; avoid (difficulty, danger); exclude, except; leap, jump; pass over, clear; *Law.* prove innocent; *Naut.* salve. **s. la diferencia,** to bridge the gap —*vi* taste, sample (food, drink); —*vr* be saved from danger; *Eccl.* be redeemed

salvavidas /salβa'βiðas/ *m,* life belt; safety belt; life preserver; traffic island

salvedad /salβe'ðað/ *f,* qualification, reservation

salvo /'salβo/ *a* safe, unharmed; excepting, omitting —*adv* except. **a s.,** safely, without harm. **a su s.,** to his (her, their) satisfaction; at his (her, etc.) pleasure. **dejar a s.,** to exclude, leave aside. **en s.,** in safety

salvoconducto /salβokon'dukto/ *m,* safe conduct, pass

samarita /sama'rita/ *a* and *mf* **samaritano (-na)** *a* and *n* Samaritan

sambenito /sambe'nito/ *m,* penitent's gown (Inquisition); disgrace, dishonor

san /san/ *a Abbr.* of **santo.** Used before masculine singular names of saints except **Santos Tomás (** *or* **Tomé), Domingo, Toribio**

sanable /sa'naβle/ *a* curable

sanador /sana'ðor/ **(-ra)** *a* healing, curing —*n* healer

sanalotodo /sanalo'toðo/ *m, Inf.* cure-all, universal remedy

sanar /sa'nar/ *vt* to cure, heal; —*vi* recover, get well; heal

sanatorio /sana'torio/ *m,* sanatorium; convalescent home

sanchopancesco /santʃopan'θesko; santʃopan'sesko/ *a* like or pertaining to Sancho Panza

sanción /san'θion; san'sion/ *f,* authorization, consent; sanction; penalty

sancionable /sanθio'naβle; sansio'naβle/ *a* sanctionable

sancionar /sanθio'nar; sansio'nar/ *vt* to authorize, approve; sanction

sancochar /sanko'tʃar/ *vt Cul.* to parboil, half-cook

sandalia /san'dalia/ *f,* sandal

sandez /san'deθ; san'des/ *f,* foolishness, stupidity; folly

sandía /san'dia/ *f,* watermelon

sandio /'sandio/ *a* foolish, inane

sandunga /san'duŋga/ f, Inf. attractiveness, winsomeness, grace

sandunguero /sanduŋ'guero/ a Inf. attractive, appealing, winsome

saneado /sane'aðo/ a unencumbered, nontaxable, free

saneamiento /sanea'miento/ m, guarantee, security; indemnity; stabilization (of currency); drainage

sanear /sane'ar/ vt Com. to guarantee, secure; indemnify; stabilize (currency); drain (land, etc.)

Sanedrín /sane'ðrin/ m, Sanhedrin

sangradura /saŋgra'ðura/ f, inner bend of the arm; Surg. bleeding; draining off

sangrar /saŋ'grar/ vt Surg. to bleed; drain off; Inf. extort money, bleed; Print. indent; draw off resin (from pines, etc.); —vi bleed; —vr bleed; have oneself bled; run (of colors)

sangre /'saŋgre/ f, blood; lineage, family. **s. fría,** sang-froid. **a s. fría,** in cold blood, premeditated. **a s. y fuego,** by fire and sword, without quarter. Inf. **bullir la s.,** to have youthful blood in one's veins. **llevar en la s.,** Fig. to be in the blood. **subírsele la s. a la cabeza,** to grow excited. Fig. Inf. **tener s. de horchata,** to have milk and water in one's veins

sangría /saŋ'gria/ f, Surg. bloodletting; resin cut (on pines, etc.)

sangriento /saŋ'griento/ a bloody, bloodstained; bloodthirsty, cruel; mortal (insults, etc.); Poet. blood-colored

sangüesa /saŋ'guesa/ f, raspberry

sanguijuela /saŋgi'huela/ f, leech; Fig. Inf. sponger

sanguina /saŋ'gina/ f, red crayon drawing, sanguine

sanguinario /saŋgi'nario/ a vengeful, bloody, cruel

sanguíneo /saŋ'gineo/ a blood; sanguineous; sanguine, fresh-complexioned; blood-colored

sanidad /sani'ðað/ f, safety, security; healthiness; health department. **s. interior,** Public Health. **S. militar,** army medical corps

sanitario /sani'tario/ a sanitary, hygienic. m, Mil. medical officer

sano /'sano/ a healthy; safe, secure; healthful, wholesome; unhurt, unharmed; upright, honest; sincere; Inf. entire, undamaged; sane. **s. y salvo,** safe and sound. Inf. **cortar por lo s.,** to cut one's losses

santa /'santa/ f, female saint

santamente /santa'mente/ adv in a saintly manner; simply

santero /san'tero/ (-ra) a given to image worship —n accomplice (of a burglar); caretaker (of a hermitage); beggar

santiamén /santia'men/ m, Inf. trice, twinkling

santidad /santi'ðað/ f, sanctity; saintliness; godliness. **Su S.,** His Holiness

santificador /santifika'ðor/ (-ra) a sanctifying —n sanctifier

santificar /santifi'kar/ vt to sanctify, make holy; consecrate; dedicate; keep (feast days)

santiguada /santi'guaða/ f, crossing oneself; rough treatment, harsh reproof

santiguar /santi'guar/ vt to make the sign of the cross over; Inf. beat, rain blows on; —vr cross oneself; Inf. be dumbfounded

santo /'santo/ a holy; saintly; saint (see **san**); consecrated; inviolate, sacred; Inf. simple, sincere, ingenuous. m, image of a saint; saint's day, name day (of a person); Mil. password. **Santa Hermandad,** Holy Brotherhood (former name of the Spanish rural police force). **S. Oficio,** Holy Office, Inquisition. **S. y bueno,** Well and good, All right! Inf. **alzarse con el s. y la limosna,** to take the lot, make off with everything. **llegar y besar el s.,** to do in a trice. Inf. **No es s. de mi devoción,** I'm not very keen on him. Inf. **todo el s. día,** the whole blessed day

santón /san'ton/ m, dervish, santon. Inf. hypocrite, sham saint

santoral /santo'ral/ m, book of saints; calendar of saints; choir book

santuario /santu'ario/ m, sanctuary

santurrón /santu'rron/ (-ona) a sanctimonious; hypocritical; prudish —n hypocrite

santurronería /santurrone'ria/ f, sanctimoniousness

saña /'saɲa/ f, fury, blind rage; lust for revenge, cruelty

sañoso, sañudo /sa'ɲoso, sa'ɲuðo/ a furious, blind with rage; cruel

sapidez /sapi'ðeθ; sapi'ðes/ f, flavor, sapidity

sápido /'sapiðo/ a tasty, savory

sapiencia /sa'pienθia; sa'piensia/ f, wisdom; knowledge; erudition

sapo /'sapo/ m, toad

saque /'sake/ m, Sports. serve, service; service or bowling line; Sports. server; Sports. bowler; bowling (in cricket)

saqueador /sakea'ðor/ (-ra) a looting, pillaging —n pillager, plunderer

saquear /sake'ar/ vt to pillage, plunder, sack

saqueo /sa'keo/ m, plundering, pillage, sacking

saquilada /saki'laða/ f, small sackful (especially of grain)

sarampión /saram'pion/ m, measles

sarasa /sa'rasa/ m, (Inf. and contemptuous) pansy, faggot

sarcasmo /sar'kasmo/ m, sarcasm

sarcástico /sar'kastiko/ a sarcastic

sarcia /'sarθia; 'sarsia/ f, load, cargo

sarcófago /sar'kofago/ m, sarcophagus

sarda /'sarða/ f, mackerel

sardana /sar'ðana/ f, traditional Catalonian dance

sardina /sar'ðina/ f, sardine. **s. arenque,** herring. **como sardinas en banasta,** Fig. packed like sardines

sardinero /sarði'nero/ **(-ra)** *a* sardine —*n* sardine seller or dealer. *m*, famous district of Santander

sardo /'sarðo/ **(-da)** *a* and *n* Sardinian

sardónico /sar'ðoniko/ *a* sardonic

sarga /'sarga/ *f*, (silk) serge; willow

sargenta /sar'henta/ *f*, sergeant's wife; -*Inf.* mannish, overbearing woman

sargentear /sarhente'ar/ *vt* to be in charge as a sergeant; command, captain; *Inf.* boss

sargento /sar'hento/ *m*, sergeant

sarna /'sarna/ *f*, scabies. **s. perruna**, mange. **más viejo que la s.,** *Inf.* older than the plague

sarnoso /sar'noso/ *a* itchy; mangy

sarraceno /sarra'θeno; sarra'seno/ **(-na)** *a* Saracen —*n* Saracen; Moor

sarracina /sarra'θina; sarra'sina/ *f*, scuffle

sarro /'sarro/ *m*, furry encrustation, scale; film; tartar (on teeth)

sarta /'sarta/ *f*, string, link (of pearls, etc.); file, line

sartén /sar'ten/ *f*, frying pan. **tener la s. por el mango,** *Inf.* to be top dog

sastra /'sastra/ *f*, female tailor; tailor's wife

sastre /'sastre/ *m*, tailor. **ser buen s.,** *Inf.* to be an expert (in)

sastrería /sastre'ria/ *f*, tailoring; tailor's shop

Satanás /sata'nas/ *m*, Satan; devil

satánico /sa'taniko/ *a* satanic

satélite /sa'telite/ *m*, satellite; follower, admirer, sycophant

satén /sa'ten/ *m*, sateen

satinar /sati'nar/ *vt* to calender; glaze; satin (paper)

sátira /'satira/ *f*, satire

satírico /sa'tiriko/ *a* satiric

satisfacción /satisfak'θion; satisfak'sion/ *f*, settlement, payment; atonement, expiation; satisfaction; gratification; amends; complacency, conceit; contentment; apology. **tomar s.,** to avenge oneself

satisfacer /satisfa'θer; satisfa'ser/ *vt irr* to pay, settle; atone for, expiate; gratify; quench; fulfill, observe; compensate, indemnify; discharge, meet; convince, persuade; allay, relieve; reward; explain; answer, satisfy; —*vr* avenge oneself; satisfy oneself —*Pres. Indic.* **satisfago, satisfaces,** etc —*Fut.* **satisfaré,** etc —*Condit.* **satisfaría,** etc —*Preterite* **satisfice,** etc —*Past Part.* **satisfecho.** *Pres. Subjunc.* **satisfaga,** etc —*Imperf. Subjunc.* **satisficiese,** etc.

satisfactorio /satisfak'torio/ *a* satisfactory

satisfecho /satis'fetʃo/ *a* self-satisfied, complacent; happy, contented

saturar /satu'rar/ *vt* to satiate, fill; saturate

saturnino /satur'nino/ *a* saturnine, melancholy, morose

Saturno /sa'turno/ *m*, Saturn

sauce /'sauθe; 'sause/ *m*, willow. **s. llorón,** weeping willow

savia /'saβia/ *f*, sap; energy, zest

saxófono /sak'sofono/ *or* **saxofón** *m*, saxophone

saya /'saya/ *f*, skirt; long tunic

sayal /sa'yal/ *m*, thick woolen material

sayo /'sayo/ *m*, loose smock; *Inf.* any garment. **cortar un s. (a),** *Inf.* to gossip behind a person's back

sayón /sa'yon/ *m*, executioner; *Inf.* hideous-looking man

sazón /sa'θon; sa'son/ *f*, ripeness, maturity; season; perfection, excellence; opportunity; taste, flavor; seasoning. **a la s.,** at that time, then. **en s.,** in season; opportunely

sazonador /saθona'ðor; sasona'ðor/ **(-ra)** *a* seasoning —*n* seasoner

sazonar /saθo'nar; saso'nar/ *vt Cul.* to season; mature; —*vr* mature, ripen

se /se/ *object pron reflexive 3rd sing* and *pl mf* 1. Used as accusative (direct object) himself, herself, yourself, themselves, yourselves (e.g. *Juan se ha cortado,* John has cut himself). 2. Used as dative or indirect object to himself, at himself, herself, themselves, etc. (e.g. *María se mira al espejo,* Mary looks at herself in the mirror). Reciprocity is also expressed by reflexive (e.g. *No se hablan,* They do not speak to one another). When a direct object pron. (accusative) and an indirect object pron., both in the 3rd pers. (sing. or pl.), are used together, the indirect object pron. becomes **se** (instead of **le** or **les**) (e.g. *Se lo doy,* I give it to him). Many Spanish reflexive verbs have English equivalents that are not reflexive (e.g. *desayunarse,* to breakfast, *arrepentirse,* to repent, *quejarse,* to complain). Some intransitive (neuter) verbs have a modified meaning when used reflexively (e.g. *marcharse,* to go away, *dormirse,* to fall asleep). The passive may be formed by using **se** + 3rd pers. sing. of verb (e.g. *se dice,* it is said, people say). A number of impersonal phrases are also formed in this way (e.g. «*Se alquila,*» "To Let," «*Se vende,*» "For Sale"). The imperative is used in the same way (e.g. *Véase la página dos,* See page two)

sebáceo /se'βaθeo; se'βaseo/ *a* sebaceous

sebo /'seβo/ *m*, tallow; candle grease; fat, grease

seboso /se'βoso/ *a* tallowy; fat, greasy

seca /'seka/ *f*, drought; *Naut.* unsubmerged sandbank

secadora /seka'ðora/ *f*, dryer, drying machine, clothesdryer. **s. de cabello,** hairdryer

secamente /seka'mente/ *adv* tersely, brusquely, curtly; dryly

secamiento /seka'miento/ *m*, drying

secano /se'kano/ *m*, nonirrigated land; *Naut.* unsubmerged sandbank; anything very dry

secante /se'kante/ *a* drying —*a* and *f*, *Geom*. secant. **papel s.**, blotting paper

secar /se'kar/ *vt* to dry; desiccate; annoy, bore; —*vr* dry; dry up (of streams, etc.); wilt, fade (of plants); become parched; grow thin, become emaciated; be very thirsty; become hard-hearted

sección /sek'θion; sek'sion/ *f*, act of cutting; section, part, portion; *Geom. Mil.* section. **s. cónica**, conic section. **s. de amenidades**, entertainment section (of a newspaper). **s. de reserva**, *Mil.* reserve list

seccionar /sekθio'nar; seksio'nar/ *vt* to divide into sections, section

secesión /seθe'sion; sese'sion/ *f*, secession

seco /'seko/ *a* dry; dried up, parched; faded, wilted; dead (plants); thin, emaciated; unadorned; barren, arid; brusque, curt; severe, strict; indifferent, unenthusiastic; sharp (sounds); dry (wines). **a secas**, only; solely; simply, just. **en s.**, on dry land; curtly. *Inf.* **dejar s.** (a), to dumbfound, petrify

secreción /sekre'θion; sekre'sion/ *f*, segregation, separation; *Med.* secretion

secretaría /sekreta'ria/ *f*, secretaryship; secretary's office, secretariat

secretario /sekre'tario/ **(-ia)** *n* secretary; amanuensis, clerk. *m*, actuary; registrar. **s. de asuntos exteriores** *or* **s. de asuntos extranjeros**, foreign secretary. **s. particular**, private secretary

secretear /sekrete'ar/ *vi Inf.* to whisper, have secrets

secreto /se'kreto/ *m*, secret; secrecy, silence; confidential information; mystery; secret drawer —*a* secret; private, confidential. **en s.**, in secret, confidentially. **s. a voces**, open secret

secta /'sekta/ *f*, sect

sectario /sek'tario/ **(-ia)** *a* and *n* sectarian —*n* fanatical believer

sector /sek'tor/ *m*, sector

secuaz /se'kuaθ; se'kuas/ *mf* follower, disciple

secuela /se'kuela/ *f*, sequel, result

secuencia /se'kuenθia; se'kuensia/ *f*, *Eccl.* sequence; (cinema) sequence

secuestrador /sekuestra'ðor/ **(-ra)** *a* sequestrating —*n* sequestrator

secuestrar /sekues'trar/ *vt* to sequester; kidnap

secuestro /se'kuestro/ *m*, sequestration; kidnapping; *Surg.* sequestrum

secular /seku'lar/ *a* secular, lay; centennial; age-old, ancient; *Eccl.* secular

secularizar /sekulari'θar; sekulari'sar/ *vt* to secularize; —*vr* become secularized

secundar /sekun'dar/ *vt* to second, aid

secundario /sekun'dario/ *a* secondary; accessory, subordinate; *Geol.* mesozoic

sed /seð/ *f*, thirst; desire, yearning, appetite. **apagar** (or **matar**) **la s.**, to quench one's thirst. **tener s.**, to be thirsty

seda /'seða/ *f*, silk; bristle (boar, etc.). **s.**
cordelada, twist silk. **s. ocal**, floss silk. **s. vegetal** *or* **s. artificial**, artificial silk. *Inf.* **como una s.**, as smooth as silk; sweet-tempered; achieved without any trouble

sedación /seða'θion; seða'sion/ *f*, calming, soothing

sedar /se'ðar/ *vt* to soothe, calm

sedativo /seða'tiβo/ *a* and *m*, *Med.* sedative

sede /'seðe/ *f*, *Eccl.* see; bishop's throne; *Fig.* seat (of government, etc.); Holy See (also **Santa S.**)

sedentario /seðen'tario/ *a* sedentary

sedición /seði'θion; seði'sion/ *f*, sedition

sedicioso /seði'θioso; seði'sioso/ *a* seditious

sediento /se'ðiento/ *a* thirsty; parched, dry (land); eager (for), desirous (of)

sedimentación /seðimenta'θion; seðimenta'sion/ *f*, sedimentation

sedimentar /seðimen'tar/ *vt* to leave a sediment; —*vr* settle, form a sediment

sedimento /seði'mento/ *m*, sediment; dregs, lees; scale (on boilers)

sedoso /se'ðoso/ *a* silky, silk-like

seducción /seðuk'θion; seðuk'sion/ *f*, seduction; temptation, blandishment, wile; charm, allurement

seducir /seðu'θir; seðu'sir/ *vt irr* to seduce; tempt, lead astray; charm, attract; corrupt, bribe. See **conducir**

seductivo /seðuk'tiβo/ *a* tempting; seductive, charming

seductor /seðuk'tor/ **(-ra)** *a* tempting; charming —*n* seducer; charming person

sefardí /sefar'ði/ *mf* Iberian Jew or Jewess; *pl* Sephardim —*a* Sephardic

segadera /sega'ðera/ *f*, sickle

segador /sega'ðor/ *m*, reaper, harvester

segadora /sega'ðora/ *f*, mowing machine, harvester; woman harvester

segar /se'gar/ *vt irr* to scythe, cut down; reap, harvest; mow. See **cegar**

seglar /se'glar/ *a* secular, lay. *mf* layman

segmento /seg'mento/ *m*, segment; *Geom.* segment. **s. de émbolo**, piston ring

segoviano /sego'βiano/ **(-na)** *a* and *n* Segovian

segregación /segrega'θion; segrega'sion/ *f*, segregation

segregar /segre'gar/ *vt* to segregate, separate; *Med.* secrete

seguida /se'giða/ *f*, continuation, prolongation. **de s.**, continuously; immediately. **en s.**, at once, immediately

seguidamente /segiða'mente/ *adv* continuously; immediately

seguidilla /segi'ðiʎa; segi'ðiya/ *f*, popular Spanish tune and dance and verse sung to them; *Inf.* diarrhea

seguido /se'giðo/ *a* continuous, successive; direct, straight

seguidor /segi'ðor/ **(-ra)** *a* following —*n* follower, disciple

seguimiento /segi'miento/ m, following, pursuit; continuation, resumption

seguir /se'gir/ vt irr to follow; go after, pursue, prosecute, execute; continue, go on; accompany, go with; exercise (a profession); subscribe to, believe in; agree with; persecute; pester, annoy; imitate; *Law.* institute (a suit); handle, manage; —vr result, follow as a consequence; follow in order, happen by turn; originate —*Pres. Part.* **siguiendo.** *Pres. Indic.* **sigo, sigues, sigue, siguen.** *Pres. Subjunc.* **siga,** etc —*Imperf. Subjunc.* **siguiese**

según /se'gun/ adv according to; as. **s. parece,** as it seems. **s. y como,** as, according to

segundar /segun'dar/ vt to repeat, do again; —vi be second, follow the first

segundero /segun'dero/ a Agr. of the second flowering or fruiting. m, second hand (of a watch)

segundo /se'gundo/ a second. m, second in command, deputy head; *Astron. Geom.* second. **segunda intención,** double meaning. **segunda velocidad,** *Auto.* second gear. **de segunda mano,** secondhand. **sin s.,** without peer or equal

segundogénito /segundo'henito/ **(-ta)** a and n secondborn

segurador /segura'ðor/ m, surety, security (person)

seguramente /segura'mente/ adv securely, safely; surely, of course, naturally

seguridad /seguri'ðað/ f, security; safety; certainty; trustworthiness; *Com.* surety. **con toda s.,** with complete safety, surely, absolutely. **de s.,** a safety

seguro /se'guro/ a secure; safe; certain, sure; firm, fixed; reliable, trustworthy, unfailing. m, certainty; haven, place of safety; *Com.* insurance; permit; *Mech.* ratchet. **s. contra incendio, accidentes, robo,** fire, accident, burglary insurance. **s. sobre la vida,** life insurance. **de s.,** surely, certainly. **en s.,** in safety

seis /seis/ a six; sixth. m, six; sixth (of the month); playing card or domino with six spots. **Son las s.,** It is six o'clock

seiscientos /seis'θientos; seis'sientos/ a six hundred; six-hundredth. m, six hundred

selección /selek'θion; selek'sion/ f, selection, choice. **s. natural,** natural selection

selectivo /selek'tiβo/ a selective

selecto /se'lekto/ a choice, select, excellent

sellar /se'ʎar; se'yar/ vt to seal; stamp; end, conclude; close

sello /'seʎo; 'seyo/ m, seal; stamp. **s. fiscal,** stamp duty. **s. postal,** postage stamp

selva /'selβa/ f, forest, wood; jungle

selvático /sel'βatiko/ a sylvan, wood, forest; wild

selvoso /sel'βoso/ a wooded, sylvan

semáforo /se'maforo/ m, semaphore, traffic light

semana /se'mana/ f, week; week's salary. **S. Mayor** or **S. Santa,** Holy Week.

entre s., during the week, on weekdays; weekdays

semanal /sema'nal/ a weekly; of a week's duration

semanario /sema'nario/ a weekly. m, weekly periodical

semanero /sema'nero/ a employed by the week

semblante /sem'βlante/ m, facial expression, countenance; face; appearance, look, aspect. **componer el s.,** to pull oneself together, straighten one's face. **mudar de s.,** to change color, change one's expression; alter (of circumstances)

semblanza /sem'βlanθa; sem'βlansa/ f, biographical sketch. **s. literaria,** short literary biography

sembrado /sem'βraðo/ m, sown land

sembrador /sembra'ðor/ **(-ra)** a sowing —n sower

sembradura /sembra'ðura/ f, Agr. sowing

sembrar /sem'βrar/ vt irr Agr. to sow; scatter, sprinkle; spread, disseminate. See **sentar**

semeja /se'meha/ f, resemblance, similarity; indication, sign (gen. pl)

semejante /seme'hante/ a like, similar; such a; *Math.* similar. m, similarity, imitation. mf fellow man

semejanza /seme'hanθa; seme'hansa/ f, similarity, likeness. **a s. de,** in the likeness of; like

semejar /seme'har/ **(se)** vi and vr to resemble

semen /'semen/ m, semen; *Bot.* seed

semental /semen'tal/ a Agr. seed; breeding (of male animals). m, stallion

sementera /semen'tera/ f, Agr. sowing; sown land; seedbed; seedtime; *Fig.* hotbed, nursery, genesis

semestral /semes'tral/ a biannual, half-yearly; lasting six months

semestre /se'mestre/ a biannual. m, half-year, period of six months; six months' salary; semester

semicírculo /semi'θirkulo; semi'sirkulo/ m, semicircle

semidifunto /semiði'funto/ a half-dead

semidormido /semiðor'miðo/ a half-asleep

semiesférico /semies'feriko/ a hemispherical

semilla /se'miʎa; se'miya/ f, Bot. seed; *Fig.* germ, genesis

semillero /semi'ʎero; semi'yero/ m, seedbed; nursery; *Fig.* hotbed, origin

semilunio /semi'lunio/ m, Astron. half-moon

seminario /semi'nario/ m, seedbed; nursery; genesis, origin; seminary; tutorial. **s. conciliar,** theological seminary

seminarista /semina'rista/ mf seminarist

semiótica /semi'otika/ f, Med. symptomatology; semiotics

semita /se'mita/ mf Semite —a Semitic

semítico /se'mitiko/ a Semitic

semivivo /semi'βiβo/ a half-alive

sémola /'semola/ f, semolina

sempiterna /sempi'terna/ f, everlasting flower; thick woolen material

sempiterno /sempi'terno/ a eternal

Sena, el /'sena, el/ the Seine

sena /'sena/ f, Bot. senna; six-spotted die

senado /se'naðo/ m, senate; senate house; any grave assembly

senador /sena'ðor/ m, senator

senario /se'nario/ a senatorial

senatorio /sena'torio/ a senatorial

sencillez /senθi'ʎeθ; sensi'yes/ f, simplicity; naturalness; easiness; ingenuousness, candor

sencillo /sen'θiʎo; sen'siyo/ a simple; unmixed; natural; thin, light (fabric); easy; ingenuous, candid; unadorned, plain; single; sincere

senda /'senda/ f, path, footpath; way; means

senderear /sendere'ar/ vt to conduct along a path; make a pathway; —vi attain by tortuous means

sendero /sen'dero/ m, footpath, path

sendos, sendas /'sendos, 'sendas/ a m, and f pl, one each (e.g. Les dio sendos lápices, He gave them each a pencil)

senectud /senek'tuð/ f, old age

senil /se'nil/ a senile

senilidad /senili'ðað/ f, senility

seno /'seno/ m, hollow; hole; concavity; bosom, breast; chest; uterus, womb; any internal cavity of the body; bay, cove; lap (of a woman); interior (of anything), heart; gulf; Math. sine; Anat. sinus

sensación /sensa'θion; sensa'sion/ f, sensation

sensacional /sensaθio'nal; sensasio'nal/ a sensational

sensacionalista /sensaθiona'lista; sensasiona'lista/ a sensationalist

sensatez /sensa'teθ; sensa'tes/ f, prudence, good sense

sensato /sen'sato/ a prudent, wise

sensibilidad /sensiβili'ðað/ f, sensibility

sensibilizar /sensiβili'θar; sensiβili'sar/ vt Photo. to sensitize

sensible /sen'siβle/ a sensible, sensitive; tender, feeling; perceptible; noticeable; definite; sensitive; sad, regrettable

sensiblemente /sensiβle'mente/ adv appreciably; perceptibly; painfully, sadly

sensiblería /sensiβle'ria/ f, sentimentality, sentimentalism

sensiblero /sensi'βlero/ a oversentimental

sensitivo /sensi'tiβo/ a sensuous; sensitive, sensible

sensorio /sen'sorio/ a sensory. m, sensorium

sensual /sen'sual/ a sensual; sensitive, sensible; carnal, voluptuous

sensualidad /sensuali'ðað/ f, sensuality; sensualism

sensualismo /sensua'lismo/ m, sensualism; Philos. sensationalism

sensualista /sensua'lista/ mf Philos. sensationalist; sensualist

sentadero /senta'ðero/ m, resting place, improvised seat

sentado /sen'taðo/ a prudent, circumspect

sentar /sen'tar/ vt irr to seat; —vi Inf. suit, agree with (e.g. No me sienta este clima (este plato), This climate (dish) doesn't suit me); fit, become; Inf. please, satisfy, be agreeable to; —vr sit down; Inf. leave a mark on the skin —Pres. Ind. siento, sientas, sienta, sientan. Pres. Subjunc. siente, sientes, siente, sienten

sentencia /sen'tenθia; sen'tensia/ f, opinion, belief; maxim; Law. verdict, sentence; decision, judgment. Law. fulminar (or pronunciar) la s., to pass sentence

sentenciador /sentenθia'ðor; sentensia'ðor/ a Law. sentencing

sentenciar /senten'θiar; senten'siar/ vt Law. to sentence; Inf. destine, intend

sentencioso /senten'θioso; senten'sioso/ a sententious

sentidamente /sentiða'mente/ adv feelingly; sadly, regretfully

sentido /sen'tiðo/ m, sense (hearing, seeing, touch, smell, taste); understanding, sense; meaning, interpretation, signification; perception, discrimination; judgment; direction, way —a and past part felt; expressive; hypersensitive, touchy. s. común, common sense. costar un s., Fig. Inf. to cost a fortune. perder el s., to lose consciousness

sentimental /sentimen'tal/ a emotional; sentimental; romantic

sentimentalismo /sentimenta'lismo/ m, emotional quality; sentimentalism

sentimiento /senti'miento/ m, feeling, sentiment; sensation, impression; grief, sorrow. Le acompaño a usted en su s., I sympathize with you in your sorrow (bereavement)

sentina /sen'tina/ f, well (of a ship); Naut. bilge; cesspool; sink of iniquity

sentir /sen'tir/ vt irr to feel, experience; hear; appreciate; grieve, regret; believe, consider; envisage, foresee; —vr complain; suffer; think or consider oneself; crack; feel, be; go rotten, decay (gen. with estar + Past Part.). m, view, opinion; feeling. sin s., without feeling; without noticing —Pres. Part. sintiendo. Pres. Indic. siento, sientes, siente, sienten. Preterite sintió, sintieron. Pres. Subjunc. sienta, sientas, sienta, sintamos, sintáis, sientan. Imperf. Subjunc. sintiese, etc.

seña /'sena/ f, sign, mark; gesture; Mil. password; signal; pl address, domicile. s. mortal, definite or unmistakable sign. dar señas, to show signs, manifest. hablar por señas, to converse by signs

señal /se'nal/ f, mark, sign; boundary stone; landmark; scar; signal; trace, vestige; indication, symptom, token; symbol, sign; image, representation; prodigy, mar-

vel; deposit, advance payment. **s. de
aterrizaje,** *Aer.* landing signal. **s. de niebla,** fog signal. **señales horarias,** *Radio.*
time signal. **en s.,** as a sign, in proof of.
s. luminosa de la circulación, traffic
light, traffic robot

señaladamente /seɲalaða'mente/ *adv*
especially, particularly, notably

señalado /seɲa'laðo/ *a* famous, distinguished; important, notable

señalador /seɲala'ðor/ *m, Argentina*
bookmark

señalamiento /seɲala'miento/ *m,* marking; pointing out; appointment, designation

señalar /seɲa'lar/ *vt* to mark; indicate,
point out; fix, arrange; wound; signal;
stamp; appoint (to office); —*vr* excel

señero /se'ɲero/ *a* solitary, isolated

señor /se'ɲor/ *a Inf.* gentlemanly. *m,*
owner, master; mister, esquire; **(S.)** the
Lord; lord, sire. **s. de horca y cuchillo,**
feudal lord, lord of life and death

señora /se'ɲora/ *f,* lady, owner, mistress;
madam; wife. **s. de compañía,** chaperon;
lady companion. **Nuestra S.,** Our Lady

señorear /seɲore'ar/ *vt* to control, run,
manage; master; domineer; appropriate,
seize; dominate, overlook; restrain (emotions); —*vr* behave with dignity

señoría /seɲo'ria/ *f,* lordship (title and
person); lordship, jurisdiction; area, territory; control, restraint

señoría /seɲo'ria/ *f,* dignity, sedateness;
self-control

señorial /seɲo'rial/ *a* manorial; noble,
dignified, lordly

señoril /seɲo'ril/ *a* lordly, noble, aristocratic

señorío /seɲo'rio/ *m,* lordship; jurisdiction, dominion

señorita /seɲo'rita/ *f,* young lady; miss;
Inf. mistress of the house

señorito /seɲo'rito/ *m,* young gentleman;
Inf. master of the house; master (address); *Inf.* young man about town

señuelo /se'ɲuelo/ *m,* decoy; bait; allurement, attraction. **caer en el s.,** *Fig.
Inf.* to fall into the trap

sepancuantos /sepan'kuantos/ *m, Inf.*
scolding, rebuke; spanking

separación /separa'θion; separa'sion/ *f,*
separation

separado /sepa'raðo/ *a* separate

separador /separa'ðor/ **(-ra)** *a* separating
—*n* separator. *m,* filter. **s. de aceite,** oil
filter

separar /sepa'rar/ *vt* to separate; divide;
dismiss (from a post); lay aside; —*vr*
retire, resign; separate

separatismo /separa'tismo/ *m,* separatism

separatista /separa'tista/ *a* and *mf* separatist

septentrión /septen'trion/ *m, Astron.*
Great Bear; north

septentrional /septentrio'nal/ *a* north;
northern

septicemia /septi'θemia; septi'semia/ *f,*
septicemia

séptico /'septiko/ *a* septic

septiembre /sep'tiembre/ *m,* September

séptimo /'septimo/ *a* and *m,* seventh

septuagenario /septuahe'nario/ **(-ia)** *a*
and *n* septuagenarian

sepulcro /se'pulkro/ *m,* sepulcher

sepultador /sepulta'ðor/ **(-ra)** *a* burying
—*n* gravedigger; burier

sepultar /sepul'tar/ *vt* to inter, bury;
hide, cover up

sepultura /sepul'tura/ *f,* interment;
grave; tomb

sepulturero /sepultu'rero/ *m,* gravedigger

sequedad /seke'ðað/ *f,* dryness, barrenness; acerbity, sharpness

sequía /se'kia/ *f,* drought

séquito /'sekito/ *m,* following, suite, retinue; general approval, popularity

ser /ser/ *m,* essence, nature; being; existence, life. **El S. Supremo,** The Supreme
Being, God

ser /ser/ *vi irr* to be (e.g. *El sombrero es
azul,* The hat is blue). **Ser** may agree
with either subject or complement,
though when latter is *pl* the verb tends to
be so too (e.g. *Son las once,* (*horas*), It is
eleven o'clock. *Cien libras son poco dinero,* A hundred pounds is a small
amount). If verbal complement is pers.
pron., **ser** agrees with it both in number
and person (e.g. *Son ellos,* It is they. *Soy
yo,* It is I). In impers. phrases the pron. is
not expressed (e.g. *Es difícil,* It is difficult.
Es sorprendente, It is surprising). **ser**
means to exist (e.g. *Pienso luego soy,* I
think, therefore I am). **ser** (also **ser de**
with nouns or obj. prons.) means to belong to, be the property of (e.g. *Este gato
es mío,* This cat is mine. *El libro es de
Juan,* The book belongs to John). Signifies to happen, occur (e.g. *¿Cómo fue eso?*
How did that happen?). Means to be suitable or fitting (e.g. *Este vestido no es para
una señora mayor,* This dress is not suitable for an elderly lady). Expresses price,
to be worth (e.g. *¿A cuánto es la libra?*
How much is it a pound?; How much is
the pound (sterling) worth?). Means to be
a member of, belong to (e.g. *Es de la Academia Española,* He is a member of the
Spanish Academy). Means to be of use,
be useful for (e.g. *Esta casa no es para
una familia numerosa,* This house is no
use for a large family). **Ser** expresses nationality (e.g. *Son francesas,* They are
French. *Somos de Londres,* We are from
London) —*Auxiliary verb* used to form
passive voice (e.g. *Esta historia ha sido
leída por muchos,* This story has been
read by many. *Fueron mandados al
Japón,* They were sent to Japan. **s. de ver,**
to be worth seeing. **s. para poco,** to be of
little use, amount to little. **s. testigo de,** to

witness. *¡Cómo es eso!* How can that be! Surely not! *¡Cómo ha de s.!* How should it be!; One must resign oneself. *Érase una vez or que érase,* Once upon a time. *es a saber, viz.,* that is to say. *un sí es no es,* a touch of, a suspicion of) —*Pres. Part.* **siendo.** *Pres. Indic.* **soy, eres, es, somos, sois, son.** *Fut.* **seré,** etc —*Condit.* **sería,** etc —*Preterite* **fui, fuiste, fue, fuimos, fuisteis, fueron.** *Imperf.* **era,** etc —*Past Part.* **sido.** *Pres. Subjunc.* **sea,** etc —*Imperf. Subjunc.* **fuese,** etc —*Imperat.* **sé**

seráfico /se'rafiko/ *a* seraphic

serafín /sera'fin/ *m,* seraphim

serenar /sere'nar/ *vt* to calm; soothe; clear; —*vr* grow calm; clear up (weather); clear (liquids); be soothed or pacified

serenata /sere'nata/ *f,* serenade

serenidad /sereni'ðað/ *f,* serenity, composure, tranquility; Serene Highness (title)

sereno /se'reno/ *a* cloudless, fair; composed, serene. *m,* dew; night watchman

serie /'serie/ *f,* series, sequence, succession; *Math.* progression; (*Biol. Elec.*) series; break (in billiards)

seriedad /serie'ðað/ *f,* seriousness, earnestness; gravity; austerity; sternness; importance; sincerity; solemnity

serigrafía /serigra'fia/ *f,* silkscreen printing

serio /'serio/ *a* serious, earnest; grave; austere; stern; important; sincere, genuine; solemn. **en s.,** seriously

sermón /ser'mon/ *m,* sermon; scolding. **dar un s.,** to give a sermon; scold

sermonear /sermone'ar/ *vi* to preach sermons; —*vt* scold

serpear /serpe'ar/ *vi* to wind, twist; wriggle, squirm; coil

serpentear /serpente'ar/ *vi* to wind, twist, meander; stagger along; wriggle; coil; *Aer.* yaw

serpenteo /serpen'teo/ *m,* winding, twisting; wriggling; coiling; *Aer.* yaw

serpentina /serpen'tina/ *f, Mineral.* serpentine; paper streamer

serpentino /serpen'tino/ *a* serpentine; *Poet.* winding, sinuous

serpiente /ser'piente/ *f,* snake, serpent; Satan, the Devil; *Astron.* Serpent. **s. de anteojos,** cobra. **s. de cascabel,** rattlesnake

serranía /serra'nia/ *f,* mountainous territory

serrano /se'rrano/ **(-na)** *a* mountain, highland —*n* highlander, mountain dweller

serrucho /se'rrutʃo/ *m,* handsaw. **s. de calar,** fretsaw

Servia /'serβia/ Serbia

servible /ser'βiβle/ *a* serviceable; useful

servicial /serβi'θial; serβi'sial/ *a* useful, serviceable; obliging, obsequious

servicio /ser'βiθio; ser'βisio/ *m,* service; domestic service; cult, devotion; care, attendance; military service; set, service; department, section; present of money; cover (cutlery, etc., at table); domestic staff, servants. **s. informativo,** news service. **s. nocturno permanente,** all-night service. **hacer un flaco s.** (a), *Inf.* to do someone an ill turn. **prestar servicios,** to render service, serve

servidor /serβi'ðor/ **(-ra)** *n* servant, domestic; name by which one refers to oneself (e.g. *Un s. lo hará con mucho gusto,* I (your servant) will do it with much pleasure). *m,* wooer, lover; bowler (in cricket). **los servidores de una ametralladora,** the crew (of a gun). **Quedo de Vd. atento y seguro s.,** I remain your obedient servant (in letters), Yours faithfully

servidumbre /serβi'ðumbre/ *f,* serfdom; servitude; servants, domestic staff; obligation, duty; enslavement (by passions); right of way; use, service

servil /ser'βil/ *a* servile; humble

servilismo /serβi'lismo/ *m,* servility; abjectness; absolutism (Spanish history)

servilleta /serβi'ʎeta; serβi'yeta/ *f,* table napkin. **s. higiénica,** sanitary napkin

servio /'serβio/ **(-ia)** *a* and *n* Serbian

servir /ser'βir/ *vi irr* to be employed (by), be in the service (of); serve (as), perform the duties (of); be of use; wait (on), be subject to. *Mil.* serve in the armed forces; wait at table; be suitable or favorable; *Sports.* serve; perform a service; follow the lead (cards); (*with de*) act as, be a deputy for; be a substitute for; —*vt* serve; worship; do a favor to; woo, court; serve (food, drink); —*vr* be pleased or willing, deign; help oneself to (food); (*with de*) make use of. **no s. para nada,** to be good for nothing, be useless. **No sirves para tales cosas,** You are no good at this sort of thing. **Para s. a Vd,** At your service. **¡Sírvase de...!** (followed by infin.), Please! **s. de,** to serve as (e.g. *s. de base a,* to serve as a basis for). See **pedir**

sésamo /'sesamo/ *m,* sesame

sesenta /se'senta/ *a* and *m,* sixty; sixtieth

sesentón /sesen'ton/ **(-ona)** *n Inf.* person of sixty

sesga /'sesga/ *f, Sew.* gore

sesgado /ses'gaðo/ *a* oblique, slanting

sesgar /ses'gar/ *vt Sew.* to cut on the bias; slant, slope; place askew, twist to one side

sesgo /'sesgo/ *a* slanting, oblique; serious-faced. *m,* slope, slant, obliquity; compromise, middle way. **al s.,** on the slant

sesión /se'sion/ *f,* session, meeting; conference, consultation; *Law.* sitting; term. **abrir la s.,** to open the meeting. **levantar la s.,** to adjourn the meeting

seso /'seso/ *m,* brain; prudence; *pl* brains. **perder el s.,** to go mad; *Fig.* lose one's head

sestear /seste'ar/ *vi* to take an afternoon nap; rest; settle

sesudez /sesu'ðeθ; sesu'ðes/ *f,* prudence, shrewdness

sesudo /se'suðo/ *a* sensible, prudent

seta /'seta/ *f*, mushroom. **s. venenosa**, poisonous toadstool

setal /se'tal/ *m*, mushroom bed, patch, or field

setecientos /sete'θientos; sete'sientos/ *a* and *m*, seven hundred; seven-hundredth

setenta /se'tenta/ *a* and *m*, seventy; seventieth

setentón /seten'ton/ **(-ona)** *n* septuagenarian

seter /'seter/ *m*, setter (dog)

setiembre /se'tiembre/ *m*. See **septiembre**

seto /'seto/ *m*, fence; hedge

seudo /'seuðo/ *a* pseudo

seudónimo /seu'ðonimo/ *m*, pseudonym

severidad /seβeri'ðað/ *f*, severity; harshness; strictness, rigor; austerity; seriousness

severo /se'βero/ *a* severe; harsh; strict, rigid, scrupulous, exact; austere; serious

sevillano /seβi'ʎano; seβi'yano/ **(-na)** *a* and *n* of or from Seville, Sevillian

sexagenario /seksahe'nario/ **(-ia)** *n* sexagenarian

sexo /'sekso/ *m*, sex; (sexual) organ

sexología /seksolo'hia/ *f*, sexology

sexólogo /sck'sologo/ **(-ga)** *n* sexologist

sexto /'seksto/ *a* sixth

sexualidad /seksuali'ðað/ *f*, sexuality

si /si/ *m*, Mus. B, seventh note of the scale —*conjunc* if; whether; even if, although. In conditional clause, **si**, meaning if, is followed by indicative tense unless statement be contrary to fact (e.g. *Si pierdes el tren, volverás a casa*, If you miss your train you will return home, *but Si hubieran venido habríamos ido al campo*. If they had come (but they didn't) we would have gone to the country). **Si** is used at the beginning of a clause to make expressions of doubt, desire, or affirmation more emphatic (e.g. *¡Si lo sabrá él, con toda su experiencia!* Of course he knows it, with all his experience. *¿Si será falsa la noticia?* Can the news be false?) **Si** also means whether (e.g. *Me preguntaron si era médico o militar*, They asked me whether I was a doctor or a soldier). Sometimes means even if, although (e.g. *Si viniesen no lo harían*, Even if they came they would not do it. *como si*, as if. *por si acaso*, in case, in the event of. *si bien*, although.

sí /si/ *pers pron reflexive 3rd pers m*, and *f*, *sing* and *pl* himself, herself, itself, themselves. Always used with prep. (e.g. *para sí*, for himself, herself, etc. *de por sí*, separately, on its own. *decir para sí*, to say to oneself)

sí /si/ *adv* yes. **sí** or **si que** is frequently used to emphasize a verb generally in contrast to a previous negative (e.g. *Ellos no lo harán, pero yo sí*, They won't do it but I will). Often translated by "did" (e.g. *No lo vi todo, pero lo que sí vi*, I didn't see it all, but what I did see...). *m*, as-

sent; yes; consent. **dar el sí**, to say yes; agree; accept an offer of marriage

siberiano /siβe'riano/ **(-na)** *a* and *n* Siberian

sicario /si'kario/ *m*, paid assassin

Sicilia /si'θilia; si'silia/ Sicily

siciliano /siθi'liano; sisi'liano/ **(-na)** *a* and *n* Sicilian

sicoanálisis /sikoa'nalisis/ *m*, psychoanalysis

sicoanalista /sikoana'lista/ *mf* psychoanalyst

sicoanalizar /sikoanali'θar; sikoanali'sar/ *vt* to psychoanalyze

sicofanta, sicofante /siko'fanta, siko'fante/ *m*, sycophant

sicología /sikolo'hia/ *f*, psychology

sicológico /siko'lohiko/ *a* psychological

sicólogo /si'kologo/ **(-ga)** *n* psychologist

sicomoro /siko'moro/ *m*, sycamore

sicopático /siko'patiko/ *a* psychopathic

sicosis /si'kosis/ *f*, Med. psychosis

sicoterapia /sikote'rapia/ *f*, psychotherapy

SIDA /'siða/ *m*, AIDS

sidra /'siðra/ *f*, cider

siega /'siega/ *f*, reaping, harvesting; harvest time; harvest, crop

siembra /'siembra/ *f*, Agr. sowing; seedtime; sown field

siempre /'siempre/ *adv* always. **s. que**, provided that; whenever. **para s.**, for ever. **por s. jamás**, for always, for ever and ever

siempreviva /siempre'βiβa/ *f*, Bot. everlasting flower. **s. mayor**, houseleek

sien /sien/ *f*, Anat. temple

sierpe /'sierpe/ *f*, serpent, snake; anything that wriggles; kite (toy); Bot. sucker; hideous person

sierra /'sierra/ *f*, saw; ridge of mountains; sawfish; slope; hillside. **s. de cerrojero**, hacksaw. **s. de cinta**, handsaw

siervo /'sierβo/ **(-va)** *n* slave; servant; serf

siesta /'siesta/ *f*, noonday heat; afternoon nap

siete /'siete/ *a* seven; seventh. *m*, seven; seventh (days of the month); playing card with seven spots; number seven. **las s.**, seven o'clock. Inf. **más que s.**, more than somewhat, extremely

sífilis /'sifilis/ *f*, syphilis

sifilítico /sifi'litiko/ **(-ca)** *a* and *n* syphilitic

sifón /si'fon/ *m*, siphon; siphon bottle; soda water; Mech. trap

sigilo /si'hilo/ *m*, seal; secrecy, concealment; silence, reserve

sigiloso /sihi'loso/ *a* secret, silent

sigla /'sigla/ *f*, acronym

siglo /'siglo/ *m*, century; long time, age; social intercourse, society, world. **s. de oro**, golden age. **en** *or* **por los siglos de los siglos**, for ever and ever

signar /sig'nar/ *vt* to sign; make the sign of the cross over; —*vr* cross oneself

signatura /signa'tura/ f, Print. signature; mark, sign; Mus. signature

significación /signifika'θion; signi-fika'sion/ f, **significado** m, meaning; importance, significance

significar /signifi'kar/ vt to signify, indi-cate; mean; publish, make known; —vi represent, mean; be worth

significativo /signifika'tiβo/ a significant

signo /'signo/ m, sign, indication, token; sign, character; Math. symbol; sign of the zodiac; Mus. sign; Med. symptom; Eccl. gesture of benediction; destiny, fate

siguiente /si'giente/ a following; next, subsequent. **el día s.,** the next day

sílaba /'silaβa/ f, syllable

silabear /silaβe'ar/ vi and vt to pro-nounce by syllables, syllabize

silabeo /silaβe'o/ m, pronouncing syllable by syllable, syllabication

silabo /'silaβo/ m, syllabus, list

silba /'silβa/ f, hissing (as a sign of disap-proval)

silbador /silβa'ðor/ **(-ra)** a whistling; hissing —n whistler; one who hisses

silbar /sil'βar/ vi to whistle; whizz, rush through the air; —vi and vt Theat. hiss

silbato /sil'βato/ m, whistle; air hole

silbido, silbo /sil'βiðo, 'silβo/ m, whis-tle, whistling; hiss, hissing

silenciar /silen'θiar; silen'siar/ vt to si-lence; keep secret

silencio /si'lenθio; si'lensio/ m, silence; noiselessness, quietness; omission, disre-gard; Mus. rest. **en s.,** in silence; quietly; uncomplainingly. **pasar en s. (una cosa),** to pass over (something) in silence, omit. **s. de muerte,** deathly silence

silencioso /silen'θioso; silen'sioso/ a si-lent; noiseless; tranquil, quiet. m, (Auto. firearms) silencer

silla /'siʎa, 'siya/ f, chair; riding saddle; Mech. rest, saddle; Eccl. see. **s. de ma-nos,** sedan chair. **s. de montar,** riding saddle. **s. de posta,** post chaise. **s. de ruedas,** wheelchair. **s. de tijera,** deck chair; campstool. **s. giratoria,** swivel chair. **s. poltrona,** easy chair. Inf. **pegár-sele la s.,** to overstay one's welcome

sillar /si'ʎar; si'yar/ m, ashlar, quarry stone; horseback

sillería /siʎe'ria; siye'ria/ f, set of chairs; pew, choir stalls; chair factory; shop where chairs are sold; chair making; Mas. ashlar masonry

silleta /si'ʎeta; si'yeta/ f, bedpan; fire-man's lift

sillín /si'ʎin; si'yin/ m, light riding saddle; seat, saddle (of bicycles, etc.)

sillón /si'ʎon; si'yon/ m, armchair; side-saddle. **s.-cama,** reclining chair. **s. de mimbres,** cane chair

silo /'silo/ m, Agr. silo; dark cavern, dark cave

silogismo /silo'hismo/ m, syllogism

silueta /si'lueta/ f, silhouette; figure

siluro /si'luro/ m, catfish; Nav. self-propelling torpedo

silva /'silβa/ f, literary miscellany; metri-cal form

silvestre /sil'βestre/ a Bot. wild; sylvan; uncultivated; savage

silvicultor /silβikul'tor/ m, forester

silvicultura /silβikul'tura/ f, forestry

sima /'sima/ f, abyss, chasm

simbiosis /sim'biosis/ f, symbiosis

simbólico /sim'boliko/ a symbolical

simbolismo /simbo'lismo/ m, symbolism

simbolista /simbo'lista/ mf symbolist

simbolizar /simboli'θar; simboli'sar/ vt to symbolize, represent

símbolo /'simbolo/ m, symbol. **s. de la fe,** Eccl. Creed

simetría /sime'tria/ f, symmetry

simétrico /si'metriko/ a symmetric; sym-metrical

simetrizar /simetri'θar; simetri'sar/ vt to make symmetrical

simiente /si'miente/ f, seed; semen; germ, genesis, origin

simiesco /si'miesko/ a apish, ape-like

símil /'simil/ a similar. m, comparison; simile

similar /simi'lar/ a similar

similitud /simili'tuð/ f, similarity

simio /'simio/ **(-ia)** n ape

simpatía /simpa'tia/ f, liking, understand-ing, affection; fellow feeling; sympathy

simpático /sim'patiko/ a friendly, nice, decent, congenial; sympathetic. **gran s.,** Anat. sympathetic

simpatizar /simpati'θar; simpati'sar/ vi to get on well, be congenial

simple /'simple/ a simple; single, not double; insipid; easy; plain, unadorned; stupid, silly; pure, unmixed; easily de-ceived, simple; naïve, ingenuous; mere; mild, meek. mf simpleton; fool

simpleza /sim'pleθa; sim'plesa/ f, foolish-ness, stupidity; simplicity

simplicidad /simpliθi'ðað; simplisi'ðað/ f, simplicity; candor, ingenuousness

simplicísimo /simpli'θisimo; simpli-'sisimo/ a superl most simple, exceedingly simple

simplificable /simplifi'kaβle/ a simplifi-able

simplificación /simplifika'θion; simpli-fika'sion/ f, simplification, simplifying

simplificador /simplifika'ðor/ a simplify-ing

simplificar /simplifi'kar/ vt to simplify

simplista /sim'plista/ mf herbalist

simulación /simula'θion; simula'sion/ f, pretense, simulation

simulacro /simu'lakro/ m, image, simula-crum; vision, fancy; Mil. mock battle

simuladamente /simulaða'mente/ adv pretendedly

simulador /simula'ðor/ **(-ra)** a feigned —n dissembler

simular /simu'lar/ vt to feign, pretend

simultanear /simultane'ar/ vt to perform simultaneously

simultaneidad /simultanei'ðað/ f, simultaneousness

simultáneo /simul'taneo/ a simultaneous

simún /si'mun/ m, sandstorm

sin /sin/ prep without (e.g. Lo hizo s. hablar, He did it without speaking). **s. embargo**, nevertheless. **s. fin**, endless. **s. hilos**, radio, wireless

sinagoga /sina'goga/ f, synagogue

sinapismo /sina'pismo/ m, Med. mustard plaster; Inf. pest, bore

sincerarse /sinθe'rarse; sinse'rarse/ vr to justify oneself; vindicate one's actions

sinceridad /sinθeri'ðað; sinseri'ðað/ f, sincerity

sincero /sin'θero; sin'sero/ a sincere

síncope /'sinkope/ m, syncope

sincronizar /ʌinkroni'θarι; ʋinkroni'sar/ vt to synchronize; Radio. tune in

sindéresis /sin'deresis/ f, discretion, good sense

sindicación /sindika'θion; sindika'sion/ f, syndication

sindicado /sindi'kaðo/ m, syndicate

sindical /sindi'kal/ a syndical

sindicalismo /sindika'lismo/ m, syndicalism, trade unionism

sindicalista /sindika'lista/ mf syndicalist, trade unionist —a syndicalistic, trade unionist

sindicar /sindi'kar/ vt to accuse, charge; censure; syndicate

sindicato /sindi'kato/ m, syndicate; trade union. **s. gremial**, trade union. **S. Internacional de Trabajadoras de la Aguja**, International Ladies' Garment Workers' Union

sindicatura /sindika'tura/ f, (official) receivership

síndico /'sindiko/ m, Com. receiver, trustee

síndrome /'sindrome/ m, syndrome

sinecura /sine'kura/ f, sinecure

sinergia /si'nerhia/ f, synergy

sinfín /sin'fin/ m, countless number

sinfonía /sinfo'nia/ f, symphony

sinfónico /sin'foniko/ a symphonic

sinfonista /sinfo'nista/ mf composer of symphonies, player in a symphony orchestra

sinfonola /sinfo'nola/ f, jukebox

Singapur /siŋa'pur/ Singapore

singladura /siŋgla'ðura/ f, Naut. day's sailing; nautical twenty-four hours (beginning at midday)

singlar /siŋ'glar/ vi Naut. to sail a given course

singular /siŋgu'lar/ a singular, single; individual; extraordinary, remarkable —a and m, Gram. singular

singularidad /siŋgulari'ðað/ f, individuality, peculiarity; strangeness, remarkableness; oddness, eccentricity

singularizar /siŋgulari'θar; siŋgulari'sar/ vt to particularize, single out; Gram.

make singular, singularize; —vr distinguish oneself, stand out; be distinguished (by)

sinhueso /sin'ueso/ f, Inf. tongue (organ of speech)

sínico /'siniko/ a Chinese

siniestra /si'niestra/ f, left, lefthand

siniestro /si'niestro/ a left (side); vicious, perverse; sinister; unlucky. m, viciousness, depravity (gen. pl); shipwreck, sinking; disaster, catastrophe; Com. damage, loss

sinnúmero /sin'numero/ m, countless number

sino /'sino/ m, fate, destiny —conjunc but; except (e.g. No lo hicieron ellos s. yo, They didn't do it, I did. no... s., not..., but); only (e.g. No sólo lo dijo él s. ella, Not only he said it, but she did too)

sinónimo /si'nonimo/ a synonymous. m, synonym

sinopsis /si'nopsis/ f, synopsis

sinóptico /si'noptiko/ a synoptic

sinrazón /sinra'θon; sinra'son/ f, injustice, wrong

sinsabor /sinsa'βor/ m, unpleasantness, trouble; grief, anxiety

sintaxis /sin'taksis/ f, syntax

síntesis /'sintesis/ f, synthesis

sintético /sin'tetiko/ a synthetic

sintetizar /sinteti'θar; sinteti'sar/ vt to synthesize

síntoma /'sintoma/ m, symptom

sintomático /sinto'matiko/ a symptomatic

sintonización /sintoniθa'θion; sintonisa'sion/ f, Radio. tuning in

sintonizador /sintoniθa'ðor; sintonisa'ðor/ m, Radio. tuner

sintonizar /sintoni'θar; sintoni'sar/ vt Radio. to tune in

sinuosidad /sinuosi'ðað/ f, sinuosity

sinuoso /si'nuoso/ a sinuous, winding

sinvergüenza /simber'guenθa; simber'guensa/ mf rascal, knave, rogue

Sión /'sion/ Zion

sionismo /sio'nismo/ m, Zionism

sionista /sio'nista/ a and mf Zionist

siquiatra /si'kiatra/ m, psychiatrist

siquiatría /sikia'tria/ f, psychiatry

síquico /'sikiko/ a psychic

siquiera /si'kiera/ conjunc although, even if. **s.... s.**, whether... or —adv at least; even (e.g. Hay que pedir mucho para tener s. la mitad, One must ask a great deal to get even half). **ni s.**, not even (e.g. No había nadie, ni s. un perro, There was no one, not even a dog)

Siracusa /sira'kusa/ Syracuse

sirena /si'rena/ f, mermaid, siren; siren; foghorn

sirga /'sirga/ f, towline

Siria /'siria/ Syria

sirio /'sirio/ (-ia) a and n Syrian. m, Sirius

sirte /'sirte/ f, sandbank, submerged rock

sirvienta /sir'βienta/ f, female servant

sirviente /sir'βiente/ a serving. m, servant

sisa /'sisa/ f, pilfering; Sew. dart. **s. dorada**, gold lacquer

sisador /sisa'ðor/ (**-ra**) n filcher, pilferer

sisar /si'sar/ vt to pilfer, filch, steal; Sew. take in, make darts in

sisear /sise'ar/ vi and vt to hiss (disapproval); sizzle

sísmico /'sismiko/ a seismic

sismógrafo /sis'mografo/ m, seismograph

sismología /sismolo'hia/ f, seismology

sismológico /sismo'lohiko/ a seismological

sistema /sis'tema/ m, system. **s. ferroviario**, railroad system. **s. métrico**, metric system

sistemático /siste'matiko/ a systematic

sistematizar /sistemati'θar; sistemati-'sar/ vt to systematize

sístole /'sistole/ f, systole

sitiador /sitia'ðor/ a besieging. m, besieger

sitial /si'tial/ m, ceremonial chair

sitiar /si'tiar/ vt Mil. to lay siege to; surround, besiege

sitio /'sitio/ m, place, spot; room, space; site; locality; Mil. siege, blockade. **No hay s.**, There's no room

sito /'sito/ past part situated, located

situación /situa'θion; situa'sion/ f, situation; position; circumstances; condition, state; location

situado /si'tuaðo/ past part situated, placed. m, income, interest

situar /si'tuar/ vt to situate, locate, place; assign funds; —vr place oneself

smoking /'smoking/ m, tuxedo, tux, dinner jacket

snobismo /sno'βismo/ m, snobbery

so /so/ prep under (used only with **color, pena, pretexto, capa**) (e.g. so color de, under the pretext of) —interj ¡**So!** Whoa! (to horses)

soba /'soβa/ f, rubbing; kneading; massaging; drubbing, beating; handling, touching

sobaco /so'βako/ m, armpit; Bot. axil

sobajar /soβa'har/ vt to squeeze, press

sobaquera /soβa'kera/ f, Sew. armhole; dress shield

sobar /so'βar/ vt to rub; knead; massage; beat, thrash; handle, touch, paw (persons); soften

soberanear /soβerane'ar/ vi to tyrannize, domineer

soberanía /soβera'nia/ f, sovereignty; dominance, sway, rule; dignity, majesty

soberano /soβe'rano/ (**-na**) a sovereign; superb; regal, majestic —n ruler, lord. m, sovereign (coin)

soberbia /so'βerβia/ f, arrogance, haughtiness; conceit, presumption; ostentation, pomp; rage, anger

soberbio /so'βerβio/ a haughty, arrogant; conceited; superb, magnificent; lofty, soaring; spirited (of horses)

sobón /so'βon/ a Inf. overdemonstrative, mushy; Inf. lazy

sobordo /so'βordo/ m, Naut. manifest, freight list

sobornador /soβorna'ðor/ (**-ra**) a bribing —n briber

sobornar /soβor'nar/ vt to bribe

soborno /so'βorno/ m, bribing; bribe; inducement

sobra /'soβra/ f, excess, surplus; insult, outrage; pl leftovers (from a meal); remains, residue; rubbish, trash. **de s.**, in abundance; in excess, surplus; unnecessary, superfluous; too well

sobradamente /soβraða'mente/ adv abundantly; in excess

sobrado /so'βraðo/ a excessive; brazen, bold; wealthy, rich. m, garret

sobrante /so'βrante/ a surplus, leftover, remaining. m, remainder, surplus, excess

sobrar /so'βrar/ vt to exceed; have too much of (e.g. Me sobran mantas, I have too many blankets); —vi be superfluous; remain, be left. Inf. **Aquí sobro yo**, I am in the way here, My presence is superfluous

sobrasada /soβra'saða/ f, spicy sausage

sobre /'soβre/ prep upon, on; above, over; concerning, about; apart from, besides; about (e.g. s. las nueve, at about nine o'clock) (indicates approximation); toward; after. m, envelope; address, superscription. **s. cero**, above freezing (Fahrenheit); above zero (Centigrade). **s. el nivel del mar**, above sea level. **s. manera**, excessively, extremely. **s. todo**, especially

sobreabundancia /soβreaβun'danθia; soβreaβun'dansia/ f, superabundance, excess

sobreabundante /soβreaβun'dante/ a superabundant

sobreabundar /soβreaβun'dar/ vi to be superabundant

sobrealiento /soβrea'liento/ m, heavy, painful breathing

sobrealimentación /soβrealimenta'θion; soβrealimenta'sion/ f, overfeeding; Auto. supercharge

sobrealimentar /soβrealimen'tar/ vt Auto. to supercharge

sobrecama /soβre'kama/ f, bedspread, quilt

sobrecarga /soβre'karga/ f, overload; rope, etc., for securing bales and packs; additional trouble or anxiety

sobrecargar /soβrekar'gar/ vt to overload; weigh down; Sew. oversew, fell

sobrecargo /soβre'kargo/ m, Naut. purser; flight attendant

sobrecejo /soβre'θeho; soβre'seho/ m, frown

sobrecoger /soβreko'her/ vt to take by surprise; —vr be frightened or apprehensive

sobrecogimiento /soβrekohi'miento/ *m.* fright, apprehension

sobrecomida /soβreko'miða/ *f.* dessert

sobrecoser /soβreko'ser/ *vt Sew.* to oversew, whip

sobrecrecer /soβrekre'θer; soβrekre'ser/ *vi irr* to grow too much. See **conocer**

sobrecubierta /soβreku'βierta/ *f.* second lid or cover; dust jacket (of a book); *Naut.* upper deck

sobrecuello /soβre'kueʎo; soβre'kueyo/ *m.* overcollar; loose collar

sobredicho /soβre'ðit∫o/ *a* aforementioned, aforesaid

sobreexcitar /soβreeksθi'tar; soβreekssi-'tar/ *vt* to overexcite

sobrefaz /soβre'faθ; soβre'fas/ *f.* surface, exterior

sobreganar /soβrega'nar/ *vt* to make an excess profit

sobreguarda /soβre'guarða/ *m.* head guard; extra or second guard

sobrehilar /soβrei'lar/ *vt* to oversew or overcast. See **prohibir**

sobrehumano /soβreu'mano/ *a* superhuman

sobrellevar /soβreʎe'βar; soβreye'βar/ *vt* to help in the carrying of a burden; endure, bear; make excuses for, overlook; help

sobremesa /soβre'mesa/ *f.* tablecloth; after-dinner conversation. **de s.**, *Fig.* at the dinner table

sobrenatural /soβrenatu'ral/ *a* supernatural; extraordinary, singular

sobrenombre /soβre'nombre/ *m.* additional surname; nickname

sobrentender /soβrenten'der/ *vt irr* to take for granted, understand as a matter of course; —*vr* go without saying. See **entender**

sobrepaga /soβre'paga/ *f.* overpayment; extra pay

sobreparto /soβre'parto/ *m.* time after parturition; afterbirth

sobrepasar /soβrepa'sar/ *vt* to exceed; outdo, excel

sobreponer /soβrepo'ner/ *vt irr* to place over; overlap; —*vr* rise above (circumstances); dominate (persons). See **poner**

sobreprecio /soβre'preθio; soβre'presio/ *m.* extra charge, rise in price

sobreproducción /soβreproðuk'θion; soβreproðuk'sion/ *f.* overproduction

sobrepujar /soβrepu'har/ *vt* to excel, surpass, outdo

sobrerrealismo /soβrerrea'lismo/ *m.* surrealism

sobrerrealista /soβrerrea'lista/ *a* and *mf* surrealist

sobresaliente /soβresa'liente/ *a* overhanging; projecting; distinctive, outstanding; excellent, remarkable. *m.* "excellent" (mark in examinations). *mf Theat.* understudy

sobresalir /soβresa'lir/ *vi irr* to overhang,

project; stand out; be conspicuous or noticeable; excel; distinguish oneself. See **salir**

sobresaltar /soβresal'tar/ *vt* to assail, rush upon; startle, frighten suddenly; —*vi Art.* stand out, be striking; —*vr* be startled or frightened

sobresalto /soβre'salto/ *m.* sudden attack; unexpected shock; agitation; sudden fear. **de s.**, unexpectedly

sobresanar /soβresa'nar/ *vi* to heal superficially but not deeply; conceal, dissemble

sobrescribir /soβreskri'βir/ *vt* to label; address, superscribe —*Past Part.* **sobrescrito**

sobrescrito /soβres'krito/ *m.* address, superscription

sobrestante /soβres'tante/ *m.* overseer; supervisor; foreman; inspector

sobresueldo /soβre'sueldo/ *m.* additional salary, bonus

sobretarde /soβre'tarðe/ *f.* early evening, late afternoon

sobretodo /soβre'toðo/ *m.* overcoat

sobrevenida /soβreβe'niða/ *f.* sudden arrival

sobrevenir /soβreβe'nir/ *vi irr* occur, take place; supervene. See **venir**

sobrevidriera /soβreβi'ðriera/ *f.* storm window; wire-mesh window guard

sobrevienta /soβre'βienta/ *f.* gust of wind; fury, violence; shock, surprise. **a s.**, suddenly

sobreviviente /soβreβi'βiente/ *a* surviving. *mf* survivor

sobrevivir /soβreβi'βir/ *vi* to survive

sobriedad /soβrie'ðað/ *f.* sobriety, moderation

sobrina /so'βrina/ *f.* niece

sobrino /so'βrino/ *m.* nephew

sobrio /'soβrio/ *a* sober, moderate, temperate

socaliña /soka'liɲa/ *f.* cunning, craft

socaliñero /sokali'ɲero/ **(-ra)** *a* cunning —*n* trickster

socapa /so'kapa/ *f.* blind, pretext. **a s.**, secretly; cautiously

socarra /so'karra/ *f.* scorching, singeing; craftiness

socarrón /soka'rron/ *a* cunning, deceitful; malicious, sly (of humor, etc.)

socarronería /sokarrone'ria/ *f.* cunning, craftiness; slyness (of humor, etc.); knavish action

socava /so'kaβa/ *f.* undermining; *Agr.* hoeing round tree roots

socavar /soka'βar/ *vt* to undermine

sociabilidad /soθiaβili'ðað; sosiaβili'ðað/ *f.* sociability

sociable /so'θiaβle; so'siaβle/ *a* sociable; social

social /so'θial; so'sial/ *a* social

socialismo /soθia'lismo; sosia'lismo/ *m.* socialism

socialista /soθia'lista; sosia'lista/ *mf* socialist —*a* socialistic

sociedad /soθie'ðað; sosie'ðað/ *f*, society; association; *Com.* partnership; *Com.* company. *Com.* **s. anónima**, incorporated company, limited company. **S. de las Naciones**, League of Nations. **s. de socorros mutuos**, mutual aid society. **s. en comandita**, private company

socio /'soθio; 'sosio/ **(-ia)** *n* associate, partner; member. **s. comanditario**, *Com.* silent partner

sociología /soθiolo'hia; sosiolo'hia/ *f*, sociology

sociológico /soθio'lohiko; sosio'lohiko/ *a* sociological

sociólogo /so'θiologo; so'siologo/ **(-ga)** *n* sociologist

socolor /soko'lor/ *m*, pretext —*adv* (also **so c.**) under pretext

socorredor /sokorre'ðor/ **(-ra)** *a* aiding, succoring —*n* helper

socorrer /soko'rrer/ *vt* to aid, succor, assist; pay on account

socorrido /soko'rriðo/ *a* helpful, generous, prompt to assist; well-equipped, well-furnished; well-supplied

socorro /so'korro/ *m*, aid, help, assistance; payment on account; *Mil.* relief (provisions or arms)

socrático /so'kratiko/ *a* socratic

sodio /'soðio/ *m*, sodium

sodomía /soðo'mia/ *f*, sodomy

sodomita /soðo'mita/ *mf* sodomite —*a* sodomitic

soez /so'eθ; so'es/ *a* base, vile; vulgar

sofá /so'fa/ *m*, sofa, couch

sofisma /so'fisma/ *m*, sophism, fallacy

sofista /so'fista/ *a* sophistic. *mf* sophist, quibbler

sofistería /sofiste'ria/ *f*, sophistry

sofístico /so'fistiko/ *a* sophistic, fallacious

soflama /so'flama/ *f*, thin flame; glow; flush, blush; specious promise, deception

soflamar /sofla'mar/ *vt* to shame, make blush; promise with intent to deceive, swindle; —*vr Cul.* burn

sofocación /sofoka'θion; sofoka'sion/ *f*, suffocation, smothering; shame; anger

sofocador, sofocante /sofoka'ðor, sofo'kante/ *a* suffocating; stifling

sofocar /sofo'kar/ *vt* to suffocate, smother; extinguish; dominate, oppress; pester, importune; shame, make blush, make angry; agitate; —*vr* be ashamed; be angry

sofoco /so'foko/ *m*, mortification, chagrin; shame; anger; suffocation, smothering; hot flush

sofrenada /sofre'naða/ *f*, sudden check, pulling up short (of horses); harsh scolding; moral restraint

sofrenar /sofre'nar/ *vt* to pull up, check suddenly (horses); scold harshly; restrain, repress (emotions)

soga /'soga/ *f*, rope; land measure (varies in length). *m*, *Inf.* rogue, knave

soja /'soha/ *f*, soybean

sojuzgador /sohuθga'ðor; sohusga'ðor/ **(-ra)** *a* conquering, oppressive —*n* conqueror, oppressor

sojuzgar /sohuθ'gar; sohus'gar/ *vt* to conquer, oppress, subdue

sol /sol/ *m*, sun; sunlight; day; Peruvian coin; *Mus.* G, fifth note of the scale, sol. **de s. a s.**, from sunrise to sunset. **hacer s.**, to be sunny. **morir uno sin s. sin luz y sin moscas**, *Inf.* to die abandoned by all. **no dejar a s. ni a sombra**, *Inf.* to follow everywhere; pester constantly. **tomar el s.**, to bask in the sun

solado /so'laðo/ *m*, paving; tile floor

solamente /sola'mente/ *adv* only; exclusively; merely, solely. **s. que**, only that; nothing but

solana /so'lana/ *f*, sunny corner; Solarium

solanera /sola'nera/ *f*, sunburn; sunny spot

solapa /so'lapa/ *f*, lapel; excuse, pretext. **de s.**, *Inf.* secretly

solapado /sola'paðo/ *a* cunning, sly

solapar /sola'par/ *vt Sew.* to provide with lapels; *Sew.* cause to overlap; dissemble; —*vi Sew.* overlap

solapo /so'lapo/ *m*, lapel; *Inf.* slap, buffet. **a s.**, *Inf.* secretly, slyly

solar /so'lar/ *vt irr* to pave; sole (shoes). *m*, family seat, manor house; building site; lineage, family —*a* solar. See **color**

solariego /sola'riego/ *a* memorial; of an old and noble family

solas, a /'solas, a/ *adv* alone, in private

solaz /so'laθ; so'las/ *m*, consolation; pleasure; relief, relaxation. **a s.**, enjoyably, pleasantly

solazar /sola'θar; sola'sar/ *vt* to solace, comfort; amuse, entertain; rest; —*vr* be comforted; find pleasure (in)

soldada /sol'daða/ *f*, salary, wages, emoluments; (*Nav. Mil.*) pay

soldadesca /solda'ðeska/ *f*, soldiering, military profession; troops. **a la s.**, in a soldier-like way

soldadesco /solda'ðesko/ *a* military, soldier

soldado /sol'daðo/ *m*, soldier; defender, partisan. **s. raso**, *Mil.* private

soldador /solda'ðor/ *m*, solderer, welder; soldering iron

soldadura /solda'ðura/ *f*, welding, soldering; correction, emendation

soldar /sol'dar/ *vt irr* to weld; mend by welding; correct, put right; *Mil.* wipe out, liquidate. See **contar**

solecismo /sole'θismo; sole'sismo/ *m*, solecism

soledad /sole'ðað/ *f*, solitude; loneliness; homesickness; *pl* melancholy Andalusian song and dance (also *f pl.* **soleares**)

solemne /so'lemne/ *a* solemn; magnificent; formal; serious, grave, important; pompous; *Inf.* downright, complete

solemnidad /solemni'ðað/ *f*, solemnity; magnificence; formality; gravity, seriousness; solemn ceremony; religious ceremony; legal formality

solemnización /solemniθa'θion; solemnisa'sion/ f, solemnization

solemnizar /solemni'θar; solemni'sar/ vt to solemnize, celebrate; extol

soler /so'ler/ vi irr defective to be in the habit, be used; happen frequently (e.g. Solía hacerlo los lunes, I generally did it on Mondays. Suele llover mucho aquí, It rains a great deal here). See **moler**

solercia /so'lerθia; so'lersia/ f, shrewdness, ability, astuteness

solevantado /soleβan'taðo/ a agitated; restless

solevantar /soleβan'tar/ vt to raise, push up; incite to rebellion. **s. con gatos,** Mech. to jack up

solfeo /sol'feo/ m, Mus. sol-fa; Inf. spanking, drubbing

solicitación /soliθita'θion; solisita'sion/ f, request; application; solicitation; wooing; search (for a post); attraction, inducement

solicitador /soliθita'ðor, solisita'ðor/ **(-ra)** a soliciting —n solicitor. m, agent; applicant

solicitante /soliθi'tante; solisi'tante/ mf applicant, candidate

solicitar /soliθi'tar, solisi'tar/ vt to solicit; request; apply for; make love to, court; seek (posts, etc.); try to, attempt to; manage (business affairs); Phys. attract; appeal to

solícito /so'liθito; so'lisito/ a solicitous; conscientious; careful

solicitud /soliθi'tuð; solisi'tuð/ f, diligence, conscientiousness; solicitude; request; application; appeal, entreaty; petition; Com. demand. **a s.,** on request

solidaridad /soliðari'ðað/ f, solidarity

solidario /soli'ðario/ a Law. jointly responsible or liable

solidez /soli'ðeθ; soli'ðes/ f, solidity; Fig. force, weight (of arguments, etc.)

solidificar /soliðifi'kar/ **(se)** vt and vr to solidify

sólido /'soliðo/ a compact, solid; thick; fast or lasting (of colors); indisputable, convincing. m, (Geom. Phys.) solid; solidus (ancient coin)

soliloquiar /solilo'kiar/ vi Inf. to soliloquize, talk to oneself

soliloquio /soli'lokio/ m, soliloquy

solista /so'lista/ mf soloist

solitario /soli'tario/ **(-ia)** a abandoned; deserted; solitary; secluded; solitude-loving —n recluse. m, solitaire diamond; hermit; solitaire (card game). **hacer solitarios,** to play solitaire (card game)

sólito /'solito/ a accustomed, wonted; customary, habitual

soliviantar /soliβian'tar/ vt to rouse, incite, excite

soliviar /soli'βiar/ vt to help to lift up; —vr half get up, raise oneself

sollastre /so'ʎastre; so'yastre/ m, scullion; brazen rogue

sollozante /soʎo'θante; soyo'sante/ a sobbing

sollozar /soʎo'θar; soyo'sar/ vi to sob

sollozo /so'ʎoθo; so'yoso/ m, sob

solo /'solo/ a sole, only; alone; lonely; deserted, forsaken. m, solo performance; (cards) solo; solitaire (card game). **a solas,** alone; without help, unaided

sólo /'solo/ or **solo** adv only; merely, solely; exclusively

solomillo /solo'miʎo; solo'miyo/ m, sirloin; filet (of meat)

solsticio /sols'tiθio; sols'tisio/ m, solstice. **s. hiemal,** winter solstice. **s. vernal,** summer solstice

soltar /sol'tar/ vt irr to loosen; let go; disengage; untie; release; let drop; let out (a laugh, etc.); solve; Inf. utter; turn on (taps); set free; —vr work loose; grow skillful; (with prep. a + infin.) begin to do (something). See **contar**

soltera /sol'tera/ f, spinster

soltería /solte'ria/ f, bachelorhood; spinsterhood

soltero /sol'tero/ a unmarried, single. m, bachelor

solterón /solte'ron/ m, confirmed bachelor

solterona /solte'rona/ f, confirmed old maid

soltura /sol'tura/ f, loosening; untying; freedom from restraint; ease, independence; impudence; immorality, viciousness; facility of speech; Law. release

soluble /so'luβle/ a soluble, dissolvable; solvable

solución /solu'θion; solu'sion/ f, dissolution, loosening; (Math. Chem.) solution; answer, solution; payment, satisfaction; Lit. climax; conclusion, end (of negotiations)

solucionar /soluθio'nar; solusio'nar/ vt to solve, find a solution for

solvencia /sol'βenθia; sol'βensia/ f, Com. solvency

solventar /solβen'tar/ vt to pay or settle accounts; solve (problems, difficulties)

solvente /sol'βente/ a Com. solvent

somático /so'matiko/ a somatic, corporeal

somatología /somatolo'hia/ f, somatology

sombra /'sombra/ f, shadow; shade; darkness, dimness; specter, phantom; defense, refuge, protection; resemblance, likeness; defect; Inf. luck; gaiety, charm; trace, vestige; Art. shading, shadow. **sombras chinescas,** shadow show. **a la s.,** in the shade; Inf. in jail. **hacer s.,** to shade; Fig. stand in the light, be an obstacle; protect. **ni por s.,** by no means; without warning. **no tener s. de,** to have not a trace of.... **tener buena s.,** Inf. to be witty or amusing and agreeable. **tener mala s.,** Inf. to bring bad luck, exert an evil influence upon; be dull and disagreeable

sombrear /sombre'ar/ vt to shadow,

shade; *Art.* shade; —*vi* begin to show (of mustaches, beards)

sombrerera /sombre'rera/ *f*, milliner; hatbox

sombrero /som'ßrero/ *m*, hat; *Mech.* cap, cowl; sounding board; head (of mushrooms, toadstools). **s. calañés**, Andalusian hat. **s. chambergo**, broad-brimmed plumed hat. **s. de canal** *or* **teja**, shovel hat (worn by clergymen). **s. de copa**, top hat. **s. de jipijapa**, Panama hat. **s. de tres picos**, three-cornered hat, cocked hat. **s. flexible**, soft felt hat. **s. hongo**, bowler (hat)

sombría /som'ßria/ *f*, shady spot

sombrilla /som'ßriʎa/ som'ßriya/ *f*, sunshade

sombrío /som'ßrio/ *a* dark; shadowy; overcast; *Art.* shaded; gloomy, melancholy

someramente /somera'mente/ *adv* superficially; briefly, summarily

somero /so'mero/ *a* superficial, shallow; summary, rudimentary, brief

someter /some'ter/ *vt* to put down, defeat; submit, place before; subject. **s. a votación**, to put to a vote —*vr* yield, surrender; (*with prep a*) undergo

sometimiento /someti'miento/ *m*, defeat; submission (to arbitration, etc.); subjection

somnambulismo /somnambu'lismo/ *m*, somnambulism, sleepwalking

somnámbulo /som'nambulo/ **(-la)** *a* somnambulistic —*n* somnambulist

son /son/ *m*, sound; rumor; reason, motive; means, way; guise, manner. **al s. de**, to the sound of; to the music of. **en s. de**, in the manner of, as, like, under pretext of

sonado /so'naðo/ *a* famous; much admired or talked of. **hacer una que sea sonada**, *Inf.* to cause a great scandal; do something noteworthy

sonaja /so'naha/ *f*, metal jingles on a tambourine; baby's rattle

sonajero /sona'hero/ *m*, baby's rattle

sonar /so'nar/ *vi irr* to sound; be quoted, be mentioned; ring; *Inf.* be familiar, remember (e.g. *No me suena el nombre*, I don't remember the name); (*with prep a*) be reminiscent of; —*vt* sound; ring; play on; clink; —*vr* be rumored, be reported; blow one's nose —*Pres. Indic.* **sueno, suenas, suena, suenan**. *Pres. Subjunc.* **suene, suenes, suena, suenen**

sonata /so'nata/ *f*, sonata

sonda /'sonda/ *f*, *Naut.* taking of soundings, heaving the lead; sound, plummet, lead; dragrope; probe, sound

sondar /son'dar/ *vt Naut.* to take soundings; probe; *Inf.* sound, try to find out; bore, drill

sondeo /son'deo/ *m*, *Naut.* sounding; *Mineral.* drilling; probing

soneto /so'neto/ *m*, sonnet

sonido /so'niðo/ *m*, sound; literal meaning; rumor, report

sonoro, sonero /so'noro/ *a* sounding; resonant, loud; sonorous

sonreir, sonreirse /son'reir, sone-'reirse/ *vi and vr irr* to smile; —*vi* look pleasant (landscape, etc.); look favorable (of circumstances). **sonreir tras la barba**, to laugh to oneself. See **reir**

sonriente /son'riente/ *a* smiling

sonrisa /son'risa/ *f*, smile

sonrojar /sonro'har/ *vt* to cause to blush; —*vr* blush

sonrosado /sonro'saðo/ *a* rosy, rose-colored, pink

sonrosar /sonro'sar/ *vt* to make rose-colored; —*vr* blush, flush

sonroseo /sonro'seo/ *m*, blush, flush

sonsaca /son'saka/ *f*, removal by stealth; pilfering; enticement; *Fig.* pumping (of a person for information)

sonsacar /sonsa'kar/ *vt* to remove by stealth; steal, pilfer; entice away; *Fig.* pump (a person for information), draw out

sonsonete /sonso'nete/ *m*, rhythmic tapping or drumming; monotonous sound (gen. unpleasant); sarcastic tone of voice

soñador /sona'ðor/ **(-ra)** *a* dreamy, sleepy —*n* dreamer

soñar /so'nar/ *vt* to dream; imagine, conjure up; (*with con*) dream of; (*with prep a*) fear (of persons)

soñoliento /sono'liento/ *a* sleepy, drowsy; soothing; slow, leisurely

sopa /'sopa/ *f*, sop, piece of bread; soup. **s. boba**, beggar's portion; life of ease at others' expense. **andar a la s.**, to beg one's way. **hecho una s.**, *Inf.* wet through

sopera /so'pera/ *f*, soup tureen

sopero /so'pero/ *m*, soup plate, soup bowl —*a* fond of soup

sopesar /sope'sar/ *vt* to try the weight of

sopetón /sope'ton/ *m*, blow, cuff. **de s.**, suddenly

soplada /so'plaða/ *f*, puff of wind

soplado /so'plaðo/ *a Inf.* overelegant; haughty, stiff. *m*, fissure, chasm

soplador /sopla'ðor/ **(-ra)** *a* instigatory. *m*, blower, fan —*n* instigator; blower

soplar /so'plar/ *vi* to blow; —*vt* blow; blow away; inflate, blow up; filch, steal; instigate, inspire; accuse; fan; prompt, help out; —*vr Inf.* eat and drink too much; *Inf.* be puffed up, grow haughty —*interj* ¡**Sopla**! *Inf.* You don't say so!

soplo /'soplo/ *m*, blow; blowing; instant, trice; *Inf.* hint, tip; *Inf.* accusation; *Inf.* tale-bearer; puff, breath (of wind)

soplón /so'plon/ **(-ona)** *a Inf.* tale-bearing, backbiting —*n* tale-bearer. *m*, *Auto.* scavenger

soponcio /so'ponθio/ so'ponsio/ *m*, *Inf.* fainting fit

sopor /so'por/ *m*, stupor; deep sleep

soporífero /sopo'rifero/ *a* soporiferous

soportable /sopor'taßle/ *a* bearable

soportar /sopor'tar/ *vt* to bear; carry, support; put up with, tolerate

soporte /so'porte/ *m*, rest, support; *Mech.* bearing; *Mech.* bracket, support

sorbedor /sorβe'ðor/ **(-ra)** *a* supping, sipping —*n* sipper

sorber /sor'βer/ *vt* to suck; imbibe; swallow; *Fig.* absorb eagerly (ideas); sip

sorbete /sor'βete/ *m*, sherbet, iced drink; French ice cream

sorbo /'sorβo/ *m*, sucking; imbibition; swallow; sip; mouthful, gulp

sordamente /sorða'mente/ *adv* secretly, quietly

sordera /sor'ðera/ *f*, deafness

sórdido /'sorðiðo/ *a* dirty, squalid; mean, niggardly; sordid

sordina /sor'ðina/ *f*, *Mus.* sordine, mute; *Mus.* damper. **a la s.**, on the quiet, in secret

sordo /'sorðo/ *a* deaf; silent, quiet; dull, muted (of sounds), insensible, inanimate; obdurate, uncompliant. **a la sorda** *or* **a lo s.** *or* **a sordas**, in silence, quietly

sordomudez /sorðomu'ðeθ; sorðomu-'ðes/ *f*, deaf-muteness, deaf-mutism

sordomudo /sorðo'muðo/ **(-da)** *a* and *n* deaf-mute

sorna /'sorna/ *f*, slowness, sluggishness; craftiness, guile, knavery; malice

sorprendente /sorpren'dente/ *a* surprising, amazing

sorprender /sorpren'der/ *vt* to surprise, amaze

sorpresa /sor'presa/ *f*, surprise; amazement; shock

sortear /sorte'ar/ *vt* to raffle; draw lots for; avoid artfully (difficulties, etc.); fight (bulls)

sorteo /sor'teo/ *m*, raffle; casting lots

sortija /sor'tiha/ *f*, ring (for a finger); ring (for a curtain, etc.); curl

sortilegio /sorti'lehio/ *m*, sorcery, magic

sortílego /sor'tilego/ **(-ga)** *a* magic —*m* sorcerer, fortuneteller

sosa /'sosa/ *f*, sodium carbonate, soda ash. **s. cáustica**, sodiumhydroxide, caustic soda, soda

sosegado /sose'gaðo/ *a* tranquil, peaceful, calm

sosegador /sosega'ðor/ **(-ra)** *a* soothing, calming —*n* appeaser, soother

sosegar /sose'gar/ *vt irr* to soothe, quiet; reassure; appease, moderate; —*vi* grow still; rest, sleep; —*vr* grow quiet; calm down, be appeased; grow still. See **cegar**

sosia /'sosia/ *m*, double, exact likeness (of persons)

sosiego /so'siego/ *m*, calm; peace, tranquility

soslayar /sosla'yar/ *vt* to slant, place in an oblique position; *Fig.* go around (a difficulty)

soslayo /sos'layo/ *a* slanting. **al s.**, obliquely, on the slant; askance

soso /'soso/ *a* saltless, insipid; dull, uninteresting; heavy (of people)

sospecha /sos'petʃa/ *f*, suspicion

sospechar /sospe'tʃar/ *vt* and *vi* to suspect

sospechoso /sospe'tʃoso/ *a* suspicious. *m*, suspect

sostén /sos'ten/ *m*, support; *Mech.* stand, support; brassiere, bra, bustier; steadiness (of a ship)

sostenedor /sostene'ðor/ **(-ra)** *a* supporting —*n* supporter

sostener /soste'ner/ *vt irr* to support; defend, uphold; bear, tolerate; help, aid; maintain, support. **s. una conversación**, to carry on a conversation. See **tener**

sostenido /soste'niðo/ *a Mus.* sostenuto, sustained —*a* and *m*, *Mus.* sharp

sostenimiento /sosteni'miento/ *m*, support; defense; toleration, endurance; maintenance, sustenance

sota /'sota/ *f*, jack, knave (in cards); *Inf.* baggage, hussy. *m*, foreman, supervisor —*prep* deputy, substitute (e.g. *sotamontero*, deputy huntsman)

sótano /'sotano/ *m*, basement, cellar

sotavento /sota'βento/ *m*, leeward. **a s.**, on the lee

sotechado /sote'tʃaðo/ *m*, hut, shed

soterrar /sote'rrar/ *vt irr* to bury in the ground; hide, conceal. See **acertar**

sotileza /soti'leθa; soti'lesa/ *f*, fine cord for fishing (in Santander province)

soto /'soto/ *m*, thicket, grove, copse

soviético /so'βietiko/ *a* soviet

sovoz, a /so'βoθ, a; so'βos, a/ *adv* in a low voice

su, sus /su, sus/ *poss pron 3rd pers mf sing* and *pl* his, her, its, one's, your, their

suasorio /sua'sorio/ *a* suasive, persuasive

suave /'suaβe/ *a* soft, smooth; sweet; pleasant, harmonious, quiet; slow, gentle; meek; delicate, subtle

suavidad /suaβi'ðað/ *f*, softness, smoothness; sweetness; pleasantness; quietness; gentleness; meekness; delicacy

suavizador /suaβiθa'ðor; suaβisa'ðor/ *a* softening, smoothing; soothing, quietening. *m*, razor strop

suavizar /suaβi'θar; suaβi'sar/ *vt* to soften; smooth; strop (a razor); moderate, temper; *Mech.* steady; quieten; ease

subalternar /suβalter'nar/ *vt* to put down, subdue

subalterno /suβal'terno/ *a* subordinate. *m*, subordinate; *Mil.* subaltern

subarrendar /suβarren'dar/ *vt irr* to sublet. See **recomendar**

subarrendatario /suβarrenda'tario/ **(-ia)** *n* sublessee

subarriendo /suβa'rriendo/ *m*, sublease, sublet

subasta /su'βasta/ *f*, auction sale. **sacar a pública s.**, to sell by auction

subastar /suβas'tar/ *vt* to auction

subcentral /suβθen'tral; suβsen'tral/ *f*, substation

subclase /suβ'klase/ *f*, subclass

subcomisión /suβkomi'sion/ *f*, subcommittee

subconsciencia /suβkons'θienθia; suβkons'siensia/ *f*, subconscious

subcutáneo /suβku'taneo/ *a* subcutaneous

subdirector /suβðirek'tor/ **(-ra)** *n* deputy, assistant director

súbdito /'suβðito/ **(-ta)** *a* dependent, subject —*n* subject (of a state)

subdividir /suβðiβi'ðir/ *vt* to subdivide

subgobernador /suβɡoβerna'ðor/ *m*, deputy governor, lieutenant governor

subibaja /suβi'βaha/ *f*, seesaw, teetertotter

subida /su'βiða/ *f*, ascension, ascent; upgrade; rise; carrying up; raising (of a theater curtain)

subidero /suβi'ðero/ *m*, uphill road; mounting block; way up (to a higher level)

subido /su'βiðo/ *a* strong (of scents); deep (of colors); expensive, high-priced; best, finest

subidor /suβi'ðor/ *m*, porter, carrier; elevator

subintendente /suβinten'dente/ *m*, deputy or assistant intendant

subir /su'βir/ *vi* to ascend, climb, go up; mount; rise; *Com.* amount (to), reach; prosper, advance, be promoted; grow more acute (of illnesses); intensify; *Mus.* raise the pitch (of an instrument or voice); —*vt* ascend, climb; pick up, take up; raise up; place higher; build up, make taller; straighten up, place in a vertical position; increase, raise (in price or value); —*vr* ascend, climb. **s. a caballo**, to mount a horse. **subirse a la cabeza**, *Inf.* to go to one's head (of alcohol, etc.)

subitáneo /suβi'taneo/ *a* sudden

súbito /'suβito/ *a* unexpected, unforeseen; sudden; precipitate, impulsive —*adv* suddenly (also **de s.**)

subjefe /suβ'hefe/ *m*, deputy chief, second in command

subjetivo /suβhe'tiβo/ *a* subjective

subjuntivo /suβhun'tiβo/ *a* and *m*, subjunctive

sublevación /suβleβa'θion; suβleβa'sion/ *f*, **sublevamiento** *m*, rebellion, mutiny, uprising

sublevar /suβle'βar/ *vt* to rouse to rebellion; excite (indignation, etc.); —*vr* rebel

sublimación /suβlima'θion; suβlima'sion/ *f*, sublimation

sublimado /suβli'maðo/ *m*, *Chem.* sublimate

sublimar /suβli'mar/ *vt* to exalt, raise up; *Chem.* sublimate

sublime /su'βlime/ *a* sublime

sublimidad /suβlimi'ðað/ *f*, sublimity, majesty, nobility

submarino /suβma'rino/ *a* submarine. *m*, submarine. **s. de bolsillo** *or* **s. enano**, midget submarine

suboficial /suβofi'θial; suβofi'sial/ *m*, *Mil.* subaltern; *Nav.* petty officer

subordinación /suβorðina'θion; suβorðina'sion/ *f*, dependence, subordination

subordinado /suβorði'naðo/ **(-da)** *a* and *n* subordinate

subordinar /suβorði'nar/ *vt* to subordinate

subproducto /suβpro'ðukto/ *m*, by-product

subrayar /suβra'yar/ *vt* to underline; emphasize

subrepción /suβrep'θion; suβrep'sion/ *f*, underhand dealing; *Law.* subreption

subrepticio /suβrep'tiθio; suβrep'tisio/ *a* surreptitious; clandestine

subrogar /suβro'ɡar/ *vt* *Law.* to surrogate, elect as a substitute

subs /suβs/ -- For words so beginning not found here, see **sus-**

subsanar /suβsa'nar/ *vt* to make excuses for; remedy, put right; indemnify

subscriptor /suβskrip'tor/ **(-ra)** *n* subscriber

subsecretario /suβsekre'tario/ **(-ia)** *n* assistant secretary

subsecuente /suβse'kuente/ *a* subsequent

subsidiario /suβsi'ðiario/ *a* subsidized; subsidiary

subsidio /suβ'siðio/ *m*, subsidy

subsiguiente /suβsi'ɡiente/ *a* subsequent; next

subsistencia /suβsis'tenθia; suβsis'tensia/ *f*, permanence; stability; subsistence, maintenance; livelihood

subsistir /suβsis'tir/ *vi* to last, endure; subsist, live; make a livelihood

subsuelo /suβ'suelo/ *m*, subsoil, substratum

subterfugio /suβter'fuhio/ *m*, subterfuge, trick

subterráneo /suβte'rranco/ *a* underground, subterranean. *m*, subterranean place

subtítulo /suβ'titulo/ *m*, subtitle; caption

suburbano /suβur'βano/ **(-na)** *a* suburban —*n* suburbanite

suburbio /su'βurβio/ *m*, suburb

subvención /suββen'θion; suββen'sion/ *f*, subsidy, subvention, grant

subvencionar /suββenθio'nar; suββensio'nar/ *vt* to subsidize

subvenir /suββe'nir/ *vt irr* to help, succor; subsidize. See **venir**

subversivo /suββer'siβo/ *a* subversive

subvertir /suββer'tir/ *vt irr* to subvert, overturn, ruin. See **sentir**

subyugación /suβyuɡa'θion; suβyuɡa'sion/ *f*, subjugation

subyugador /suβyuɡa'ðor/ **(-ra)** *a* subjugating —*n* conqueror

subyugar /suβyu'ɡar/ *vt* to subjugate, overcome

succión /suk'θion; suk'sion/ *f*, suction

suceder /suθe'ðer; suse'ðer/ *vi* to follow,

come after; inherit, succeed —*impers* happen, occur

sucedido /suθe'δiδo; suse'δiδo/ *m, Inf.* event, occurrence

sucesión /suθe'sion; suse'sion/ *f,* succession; series; offspring, descendants; *Law.* estate

sucesivo /suθe'siβo; suse'siβo/ *a* successive. **en lo s.,** in future

suceso /su'θeso; su'seso/ *m,* happening, occurrence; course (of time); outcome, result

sucesor /suθe'sor; suse'sor/ **(-ra)** *a* succeeding —*n* successor

suciedad /suθie'δaδ; susie'δaδ/ *f,* dirt; filth, nastiness; obscenity

sucinto /su'θinto; su'sinto/ *a* succinct, brief, concise

sucio /'suθio; 'susio/ *a* dirty, unclean; stained; easily soiled; *Fig.* sullied, spotted; obscene; dirty (of colors); *Fig.* tainted, infected. **jugar s.,** *Sports.* to play in an unsporting manner

suco /'suko/ *m,* juice

sucoso /su'koso/ *a* juicy

suculencia /suku'lenθia; suku'lensia/ *f,* succulence; juiciness

suculento /suku'lento/ *a* succulent; juicy

sucumbir /sukum'βir/ *vi* to yield, give in; die, succumb; lose a lawsuit

sucursal /sukur'sal/ *a* branch. *f, Com.* branch (of a firm)

sud /suδ/ *m,* south (gen. **sur**). Used in combinations like **sudamericano**

sudadero /suδa'δero/ *m,* horse blanket; sudatorium, sweating bath

sudafricano /suδafri'kano/ **(-na)** *a* and *n* South African

sudamericano /suδameri'kano/ **(-na)** *a* and *n* South American

sudante /su'δante/ *a* sweating, perspiring

sudar /su'δar/ *vi* and *vt* to perspire, sweat; ooze; —*vi Inf.* toil; —*vt* bathe in sweat; *Inf.* give reluctantly. **s. frío,** to break out in a cold sweat. **s. la gota gorda,** *Fig. Inf.* to be in a stew

sudario /su'δario/ *m,* shroud

sudeste /su'δeste/ *m,* southeast; southeast wind

sudoeste /suδo'este/ *m,* southwest; southwest wind

sudor /su'δor/ *m,* sweat, perspiration; toil; juice, moisture, sap, gum

sudoroso /suδo'roso/ *a* sweaty

Suecia /'sueθia; 'suesia/ Sweden

sueco /'sueko/ **(-ca)** *a* Swedish —*n* Swede. *m,* Swedish (language)

suegra /'suegra/ *f,* mother-in-law

suegro /'suegro/ *m,* father-in-law

suela /'suela/ *f,* sole (of a shoe). *Ichth.* sole; tanned leather; base. **no llegarle a uno a la s. del zapato,** *Inf.* to be not fit to hold a candle to.

sueldo /'sueldo/ *m,* salary, wages; *Obs.* Spanish coin. **a s.,** for a salary, salaried

suelo /'suelo/ *m,* ground, earth; soil; bottom, base; sediment, dregs; site, plot;

floor; flooring; story; land, territory; hoof (of horses); earth, world; *pl* chaff of grain. **s. natal,** native land; *Inf.* to fall flat. **dar consigo en el s.,** to fall down. **dar en el s. con,** to throw down; damage, spoil. *Inf.* **estar (una cosa) por los suelos,** to be dirt cheap

suelta /'suelta/ *f,* loosening, unfastening; hobble (for horses); relay of oxen. **dar s. a,** to let loose, allow to go out for a time

suelto /'suelto/ *a* swift; competent, efficient; odd, separate; licentious; flowing, easy (style); loose, unbound. *m,* single copy (of a newspaper); loose change; newspaper paragraph

sueño /'sueno/ *m,* dream; sleep; drowsiness, desire for sleep; vision, fancy. **s. pesado,** deep sleep. **conciliar el s.,** to court sleep. **echar un s.,** *Inf.* to take a nap. **en sueños,** in a dream; while asleep. **entre sueños,** between sleeping and waking. **¡Ni por sueño!** *Inf.* Certainly not! I wouldn't dream of it!

suero /'suero/ *m,* serum. **s. de la leche,** whey

suerte /'suerte/ *f,* chance, luck; good luck; destiny, fate; condition, state; kind, species, sort; way, manner; bullfighter's maneuver; parcel of land. **de s. que,** so that; as a result. **echar suertes,** to draw lots. **tener buena s.,** to be lucky

suéter /'sueter/ *m,* sweater

suficiencia /sufi'θienθia; sufi'siensia/ *f,* sufficiency; talent, aptitude; pedantry. **a s.,** enough

suficiente /sufi'θiente; sufi'siente/ *a* sufficient, enough; suitable

sufijo /su'fiho/ *m,* suffix

sufragar /sufra'gar/ *vt* to assist, aid; favor; pay, defray

sufragio /su'frahio/ *m,* aid, assistance; *Eccl.* suffragium, pious offering; vote; suffrage

sufragista /sufra'hista/ *f,* suffragette

sufrible /su'friβle/ *a* bearable, endurable

sufrido /su'friδo/ *a* long-suffering, resigned; complaisant (of husbands); dirt-resistant (colors)

sufrimiento /sufri'miento/ *m,* suffering, pain; affliction; tolerance

sufrir /su'frir/ *vt* to suffer, undergo, experience; bear, endure; tolerate, put up with; allow, permit; resist, oppose; expiate; —*vi* suffer

sugerir /suhe'rir/ *vt irr* to suggest. See **sentir**

sugestión /suhes'tion/ *f,* suggestion

sugestionable /suhestio'naβle/ *a* easily influenced, open to suggestion

sugestionador /suhestiona'δor/ *a* suggestive

sugestionar /suhestio'nar/ *vt* to suggest hypnotically; dominate, influence

sugestivo /suhes'tiβo/ *a* suggestive, stimulating

suicida /sui'θiδa; sui'siδa/ *a* suicidal, fatal. *mf* suicide (person)

suicidarse /suiθi'δarse; suisi'δarse/ vr to commit suicide

suicidio /sui'θiδio; sui'siδio/ m, suicide (act)

Suiza /'suiθa; 'suisa/ Switzerland

suiza /'suiθa; 'suisa/ f, row, rumpus, scrap

suizo /'suiθo; 'suiso/ (-za) a and n Swiss

sujeción /suhe'θion; suhe'sion/ f, subjection, domination; fastening, fixture; obedience, conformity

sujetador /suheta'δor/ m, clamp; clip

sujetar /suhe'tar/ vt to fasten; fix; hold down; grasp, clutch; subdue; —vr (with prep a) conform to, obey. **s. con alfileres**, to pin up. **s. con tornillos**, to screw down

sujeto /su'heto/ a liable, subject. m, topic, subject; person, individual; Gram. Philos. subject

sulfurar /sulfu'rar/ vt to sulphurate; —vr grow irritated, become angry

sulfúrico /sul'furiko/ a sulphuric

sultán /sul'tan/ m, sultan

suma /'suma/ f, total; amount, sum; Math. addition; summary, digest; computation. **en s.**, in brief, in short, finally

sumador /suma'δor/ (-ra) n summarizer; computator, adder

sumamente /suma'mente/ adv extremely, most

sumar /su'mar/ vt to sum up, summarize; Math. add up

sumaria /su'maria/ f, written indictment

sumariamente /sumaria'mente/ adv concisely, in brief; Law. summarily

sumario /su'mario/ a brief, concise, abridged; Law. summary. m, summary, résumé, digest

sumergible /sumer'hiβle/ a sinkable; submergible. m, submarine

sumergir /sumer'hir/ vt to dip, immerse; sink, submerge; Fig. overwhelm (with grief, etc.); —vr sink; dive; be submerged

sumersión /sumer'sion/ f, immersion, dive, submersion

sumidero /sumi'δero/ m, cesspool; drain; sink; pit, gully

suministrar /suminis'trar/ vt to purvey, supply, provide

suministro /sumi'nistro/ m, purveyance; provision; supply

sumir /su'mir/ vt to sink; submerge; Eccl. consummate; Fig. overwhelm (with grief, etc.); —vr fall in, become sunken (of cheeks, etc.); sink; be submerged

sumisión /sumi'sion/ f, submission, obedience; Com. estimate, tender

sumiso /su'miso/ a submissive, docile

sumista /su'mista/ mf quick reckoner, computator. m, condenser, summarizer; abridger

sumo /'sumo/ a supreme; high; tremendous, extraordinary. **a lo s.**, at the most; even if, although. **en s. grado**, in the highest degree

suntuoso /sun'tuoso/ a magnificent, luxurious, sumptuous

supeditar /supeδi'tar/ vt to oppress; overcome, conquer; subordinate

superabundante /superaβun'dante/ a superabundant, excessive

superádito /supe'raδito/ a superadded

superar /supe'rar/ vt to overcome, conquer; surpass; do better than

superávit /supe'raβit/ m, Com. balance, surplus

superchería /supertʃe'ria/ f, trickery, guile

supereminencia /superemi'nenθia; peremi'nensia/ f, supereminence, greatest eminence

supereminente /superemi'nente/ a supereminent

superentender /superenten'der/ vt irr to supervise, superintend. See **entender**

superestructura /superestruk'tura/ f, superstructure

superficial /superfi'θial; superfi'sial/ a surface, shallow; superficial, rudimentary; futile

superficialidad /superfiθiali'δaδ; superfisiali'δaδ/ f, superficiality; futility; shallowness

superficie /super'fiθie; super'fisie/ f, area; surface; outside, exterior. **s. de rodadura**, tire tread

superfino /super'fino/ a superfine

superfluo /su'perfluo/ a superfluous, redundant

superhombre /super'ombre/ m, superman

superintendencia /superinten'denθia; superinten'densia/ f, supervision; superintendentship; higher administration

superintendente /superinten'dente/ mf superintendent; supervisor

superior /supe'rior/ a higher, upper; excellent, fine; superior; higher (education, etc.). m, head, director; superior

superiora /supe'riora/ f, mother superior

superioridad /superiori'δaδ/ f, superiority

superlativo /superla'tiβo/ a and m, superlative

superproducción /superproδuk'θion; superproδuk'sion/ f, overproduction; superproduction

superrealismo /superrea'lismo/ m, surrealism

superrealista /superrea'lista/ a surrealist

superstición /supersti'θion; supersti'sion/ f, superstition

supersticioso /supersti'θioso; supersti'sioso/ a superstitious

supervivencia /superβi'βenθia; superβi'βensia/ f, survival

superviviente /superβi'βiente/ a surviving. mf survivor

supino /su'pino/ a supine; foolish, stupid. m, Gram. supine

suplantación /suplanta'θion; suplanta'sion/ f, supplanting

suplantar /suplan'tar/ *vt* to forge, alter (documents); supplant

suplefaltas /suple'faltas/ *mf Inf.* scapegoat

suplementario /suplemen'tario/ *a* supplementary, additional

suplemento /suple'mento/ *m,* supplement; supply, supplying; newspaper supplement; *Geom.* supplement

suplente /su'plente/ *m,* substitute, proxy; *Fig.* makeweight

súplica /'suplika/ *f,* supplication, prayer; request

suplicación /suplika'θion; suplika'sion/ *f,* entreaty, supplication; *Law.* petition

suplicante /supli'kante/ *a* supplicatory; *Law.* petitioning. *mf* supplicator; *Law.* petitioner

suplicar /supli'kar/ *vt* to beg, supplicate; request; *Law.* appeal

suplicio /su'pliθio; su'plisio/ *m,* torment, torture; execution; place of torture or execution; affliction; anguish. **último s.,** capital punishment

suplir /su'plir/ *vt* to supply, furnish; substitute, take the place of; overlook, forgive

suponer /supo'ner/ *vt irr* to suppose, take for granted; simulate; comprise, include; —*vi* carry weight, wield authority. See **poner**

suposición /suposi'θion; suposi'sion/ *f,* supposition; conjecture, assumption; distinction, talent, importance; falsity, falsehood

supositorio /suposi'torio/ *m,* suppository

supremacía /suprema'θia; suprema'sia/ *f,* supremacy

supremo /su'premo/ *a* supreme; matchless, incomparable; last

supresión /supre'sion/ *f,* suppression; destruction, eradication; omission

suprimir /supri'mir/ *vt* to suppress; destroy, eradicate; omit, leave out. **s. una calle al tráfico,** to close a street to traffic, ban traffic from a street

supuesto /su'puesto/ *a* supposed; so-called; reputed. *m,* supposition, hypothesis. **por s.,** presumably; doubtless

supurar /supu'rar/ *vi* to suppurate

sur /sur/ *m,* south; south wind

surcar /sur'kar/ *vt* to plow furrows; furrow, line; cut, cleave (water, etc.)

surco /'surko/ *m,* furrow; wrinkle, line; groove, channel; rut

surgidero /surhi'ðero/ *m, Naut.* road, roadstead

surgir /sur'hir/ *vi* to spout, gush, spurt; *Naut.* anchor; appear, show itself; come forth, turn up

surrealismo /surrea'lismo/ *m,* surrealism

surrealista /surrea'lista/ *a* and *mf* surrealist

surtida /sur'tiða/ *f,* hidden exit; false door; *Naut.* slipway

surtidero /surti'ðero/ *m,* outlet, drain; jet, fountain

surtido /sur'tiðo/ *a* mixed, assorted. *m,* variety, assortment; stock, range. **de s.,** in everyday use

surtidor /surti'ðor/ **(-ra)** *n* purveyor, supplier. *m,* fountain, jet. **s. de gasolina,** gasoline pump, gas pump

surtimiento /surti'miento/ *m,* assortment; stock

surtir /sur'tir/ *vt* to provide, supply, furnish; —*vi* spurt, gush

surto /'surto/ *a* calm, reposeful; *Naut.* anchored

¡sus! /sus/ *interj* Come on! Hurry up!

susceptibilidad /susθeptiβili'ðað; susseptiβili'ðað/ *f,* susceptibility

susceptible /susθep'tiβle; sussep'tiβle/ *a* susceptible, open to; touchy, oversensitive

suscitar /susθi'tar; sussi'tar/ *vt* to cause, originate; provoke, incite; —*vr* arise, take place

suscribir /suskri'βir/ *vt* to sign; agree to; —*vr* subscribe, contribute; take out a subscription (to a periodical, etc.) —*Past Part.* **suscrito**

suscripción /suskrip'θion; suskrip'sion/ *f,* subscription; agreement, accession

susodicho /suso'ðitʃo/ *a* aforesaid

suspender /suspen'der/ *vt* to suspend, hang up; postpone, defer, stop; amaze, dumbfound; suspend (from employment); fail (an exam); adjourn (meetings); —*vr* rear (of horses)

suspensión /suspen'sion/ *f,* suspension; postponement, stoppage, deferment; amazement; failure (in an exam); adjournment (of a meeting); springs (of a car). *Com.* **s. de pagos,** suspension of payments. **con mala s.,** badly sprung (of a car)

suspensivos /suspen'siβos/ *m, pl* suspension points, ellipsis points

suspenso /sus'penso/ *a* amazed, bewildered. *m,* failure slip (in an exam). **en s.,** in suspense

suspicacia /suspi'kaθia; suspi'kasia/ *f,* suspiciousness; mistrust, uneasiness

suspicaz /suspi'kaθ; suspi'kas/ *a* suspicious, mistrustful

suspirado /suspi'raðo/ *a* eagerly desired, longed for

suspirar /suspi'rar/ *vt* and *vi* to sigh. **s. por,** to long for

suspiro /sus'piro/ *m,* sigh; breath; glass whistle; *Mus.* brief pause, pause sign. **último s.,** *Inf.* last kick, end

sustancia /sus'tanθia; sus'tansia/ *f,* substance, juice, extract, essence; *Fig.* core, pith; *Fig.* meat; wealth, estate; worth, importance; nutritive part; *Inf.* common sense. *Anat.* **s. gris,** gray matter. **en s.,** in short

sustanciación /sustanθia'θion; sustansia'sion/ *f,* substantiation

sustancial /sustan'θial; sustan'sial/ *a* substantial, real; important, essential; nutritive; solid

sustanciar /sustan'θiar; sustan'siar/ *vt* to substantiate; summarize, extract, abridge

sustancioso /sustan'θioso; sustan'sioso/ *a* substantial; nutritive

sustantivo /sustan'tiβo/ *a* and *m*, *Gram.* substantive, noun

sustentable /susten'taβle/ *a* arguable, defensible

sustentación /sustenta'θion; sustenta'sion/ *f*, maintenance; defense

sustentar /susten'tar/ *vt* to sustain, keep; support, bear; nourish, feed; uphold, advocate. **s. un ciclo de conferencias,** to give a series of lectures

sustento /sus'tento/ *m*, maintenance, preservation; nourishment, sustenance; support

sustitución /sustitu'θion; sustitu'sion/ *f*, substitution

sustituible /susti'tuiβle/ *a* substitutive, replaceable

sustituir /susti'tuir/ *vt irr* to substitute. See **huir**

sustituto /susti'tuto/ **(-ta)** *n* substitute

susto /'susto/ *m*, fright, shock; apprehension. **dar un s. (a),** to scare

sustracción /sustrak'θion; sustrak'sion/ *f*, subtraction

sustraer /sustra'er/ *vt irr* to remove, separate; rob, steal; *Math.* subtract; —*vr* depart, remove oneself; avoid. See **traer**

susurrador /susurra'ðor/ **(-ra)** *a* whispering; murmuring; rustling —*n* whisperer

susurrante /susu'rrante/ *a* whispering; murmuring; rustling

susurrar /susu'rrar/ *vi* to whisper; murmur; rustle; babble, purl, prattle (of water); —*vi* and *vr* be whispered abroad

susurro /su'surro/ *m*, whispering, whisper; murmur; rustle; lapping

sutil /'sutil/ *a* fine, thin; penetrating, subtle, keen

sutileza, sutilidad /suti'leθa, sutili'ðað; suti'lesa, sutili'ðað/ *f*, fineness, thinness; subtlety, penetration. **sutileza de manos,** dexterity; light-fingeredness; sleight of hand

sutilizaciones /sutiliθa'θiones; sutilisa'siones/ *f*, *pl* casuistry, hairsplitting, quibbling

sutilizar /sutili'θar; sutili'sar/ *vt* to make thin, refine; *Fig.* finish, perfect; *Fig.* split hairs, make subtle distinctions

sutura /su'tura/ *f*, suture

suyo, suya /'suyo, 'suya/ *m*, and *f*, *pl* **suyos, suyas,** *poss pron* and *a* 3rd *pers* his; hers; its; yours; theirs; of his, of hers, etc. (e.g. *Este libro es suyo,* This book is his (hers, yours, theirs). **Este libro es uno de los suyos,** This book is one of his (hers, etc.). (**suyo** is often used with def. art. **el, la,** etc.) **los suyos,** his (hers, yours, etc.) family, following, adherents, etc. **de suyo,** of its very nature, of itself; spontaneously. **salirse con la suya,** to get one's own way. *Inf.* **ver la suyo,** to see one's opportunity

tabalear /taβale'ar/ **(se)** *vt* and *vr* to rock, sway, swing; —*vi* drum with the fingers

tabaleo /taβa'leo/ *m*, swaying, rocking; drumming with the fingers

tábano /'taβano/ *m*, *Ent.* horsefly

tabanque /ta'βanke/ *m*, potter's wheel

tabaque /ta'βake/ *m*, small osier basket (for fruit, sewing, etc.); large tack

tabaquera /taβa'kera/ *f*, tobacco jar, tobacco tin; bowl of pipe tobacco; tobacco pouch; snuffbox

tabaquería /taβake'ria/ *f*, tobacconist's shop

tabaquero /taβa'kero/ **(-ra)** *n* worker in a tobacco factory; tobacconist

tabardillo /taβar'ðiλo; taβarðiyo/ *m*, fever. **t. de tripas**, typhoid. **t. pintado**, typhus

taberna /ta'βerna/ *f*, public house, tavern

tabernáculo /taβer'nakulo/ *m*, tabernacle

tabicar /taβi'kar/ *vt* to wall or board up; hide, cover up

tabique /ta'βike/ *m*, partition wall, inside wall; thin wall

tabla /'taβla/ *f*, plank of wood, board; *Metall.* plate; slab; flat side, face (of wood); *Sew.* box pleat; table (of contents, etc.); *Art.* panel, vegetable garden; butcher's slab; butcher's stall; *pl* tablets (for writing); (*Math.* etc.) tables; stalemate (chess, checkers); draw (in an election); *Theat.* boards, stage. **t. de armonía,** sounding board (of musical instruments). **t. de lavar,** washboard. **t. de materias,** table of contents. **t. de multiplicación,** multiplication table. **t. rasa,** clean sheet (of paper, etc.); complete ignorance. **T. Redonda,** Round Table (of King Arthur). **escapar** *or* **salvarse en una t.,** to have a narrow escape, escape in the nick of time

tablado /ta'βlaðo/ *m*, flooring; platform; *Theat.* stage; scaffold, gibbet. **sacar al t.,** to produce, put on the stage; to make known, publish

tablear /taβle'ar/ *vt* to saw into planks; *Sew.* make box pleats in; hammer iron into sheets

tablero /ta'βlero/ *m*, board (of wood); paneling; boarding; slab; shop counter; board (checkers, chess). **t. de instrumentos,** dashboard; instrument panel

tableta /ta'βleta/ *f*, tablet; pastille, lozenge

tablilla /ta'βliλa; ta'βliya/ *f*, small board; tablet; bulletin board, notice board

tablón /ta'βlon/ *m*, thick plank; wooden beam; *Inf.* drinking bout

tabú /ta'βu/ *m*, taboo

taburete /taβu'rete/ *m*, stool; tabouret

tacañería /takaɲe'ria/ *f*, miserliness, niggardliness; craftiness

tacaño /ta'kaɲo/ *a* miserly, niggardly; crafty

tacha /'tatʃa/ *f*, imperfection, defect; spot, stain; fault; large tack. **poner t.,** to criticize, object to

tachable /ta'tʃaβle/ *a* censurable, blameworthy

tachar /ta'tʃar/ *vt* to criticize, blame; cross out, erase; charge, accuse

tacho de basura /'tatʃo de ba'sura/ *m*, *Argentina* garbage can

tachón /ta'tʃon/ *m*, round-headed ornamental nail; *Sew.* gold or silver studs, trimming; crossing out, erasure

tachonar /tatʃo'nar/ *vt* to stud with round-headed nails; *Sew.* trim with gold or silver studs or trimming

tachoso /ta'tʃoso/ *a* imperfect, defective, faulty; spotted, stained

tachuela /ta'tʃuela/ *f*, tack

tácito /'taθito; 'tasito/ *a* silent, unexpressed; tacit, implied

taciturno /taθi'turno; tasi'turno/ *a* taciturn; reserved; dismal, gloomy, melancholy

taco /'tako/ *m*, stopper, plug; billiard cue; rammer; wad, wadding (in a gun); pop gun; taco (food); tear-off calendar; *Inf.* snack; obscenity, oath. **t. de papel,** writing tablet

tacón /ta'kon/ *m*, heel (of a shoe)

taconear /takone'ar/ *vi* to stamp with one's heels; walk heavily on one's heels; walk arrogantly

táctica /'taktika/ *f*, method, technique; *Mil.* tactics; policy, means

táctico /'taktiko/ *a* tactical. *m*, *Mil.* tactician

táctil /'taktil/ *a* tactile

tacto /'takto/ *m*, sense of touch; touch, feel; touching; skill; tact

tafetán /tafe'tan/ *m*, taffeta; *pl* flags, standards. **t. de heridas** *or* **t. inglés,** court plaster

tafilete /tafi'lete/ *m*, morocco leather

tahúr /ta'ur/ *m*, gambler; cardsharper

Tailandia /tai'landia/ Thailand

taimado /tai'maðo/ *a* knavish, crafty; obstinate, headstrong

taimería /taime'ria/ *f*, cunning, craftiness

taita /'taita/ *m*, daddy

taja /'taha/ *f*, cut, cutting; slice; washboard

tajada /ta'haða/ *f*, slice; strip, portion; steak, filet; *Inf.* cough; drinking bout; hoarseness

tajadera /taha'ðera/ *f*, cheese knife; chisel; *pl* sluice gate

tajado /ta'haðo/ *a* steep, sheer (of cliffs, etc.)

tajadura /taha'ðura/ *f*, cutting, dividing, dissection

tajamar /taha'mar/ *m*, cutwater; breakwater; raft

tajar /ta'har/ *vt* to cut, chop; sharpen, trim (quill pens)

Tajo, el /'taho, el/ the Tagus

tajo /'taho/ *m*, cut, incision; task; cutting (in a mountain, etc.); cut, thrust (of sword); executioner's block; chopping board; washboard; steep cliff, precipice

tajón /ta'hon/ *m*, butcher block; chopping board

tal /tal/ *a pl* **tales,** such; said (e.g. *el t. Don Juan,* the said Don Juan). **tal** is always used before nouns and (except when meaning "the said") without def. art. **un t.,** a certain (e.g. *un t. hombre,* a certain man) —*pron* some, some people; someone; such a thing —*adv* so, thus. **t. para cual,** two of a kind, a well-matched pair; tit for tat. **con t. que,** *conjunc* on condition that, provided that. **No hay t.,** There is no such thing. *Inf.* **¿Qué t.?** How are you? What's the news? What's new?

tala /'tala/ *f*, felling or cutting down (of trees); cropping of grass (ruminants)

talador /tala'ðor/ **(-ra)** *a* felling, cutting; destructive —*n* feller, cutter; destroyer

taladrar /tala'ðrar/ *vt* to drill, bore, gouge holes; pierce, perforate; punch (a ticket); assail or hurt the ear (sounds); *Fig.* go into deeply (a subject)

taladro /ta'laðro/ *m*, drill, gimlet, gouge; drill hole, bore; puncher (for tickets, etc.)

tálamo /'talamo/ *m*, marriage bed; (*Bot. Anat.*) thalamus

talante /ta'lante/ *m*, mode of execution, technique; personal appearance, mien; disposition, temperament; wish, desire; aspect, appearance. **de buen (mal) t.,** willingly (unwillingly)

talar /ta'lar/ *a* full-length, long (of gowns, robes, etc.)

talar /ta'lar/ *vt* to fell, chop down (trees); ravage, lay waste; prune (gen. olive trees)

talco /'talko/ *m*, *Mineral.* talc; sequin, tinsel

talcualillo /talkua'liʎo; talkua'liyo/ *a Inf.* not too bad, fairly good; slightly better (of health)

taled /ta'leð/ *m*, prayer shawl, tales, tallit

talega /ta'lega/ *f*, sack, bag; sackful; money bag; *pl Inf.* cash wealth

talego /ta'lego/ *m*, narrow sack; *Inf.* dumpy person

talento /ta'lento/ *m*, talent (Greek coin); talent, gift, quality; intelligence, understanding; cleverness

talentoso /talen'toso/ *a* talented

talión /ta'lion/ *m*, **(ley de)** law of retaliation

talismán /talis'man/ *m*, talisman

talla /'taʎa; 'taya/ *f*, carving (especially wood); cutting (of gems); reward for apprehension of a criminal; ransom; stature, height, size; height measuring rod

tallado /ta'ʎaðo; ta'yaðo/ *a* **bien (** or **mal),** well (or badly) carved; well (or badly) proportioned, of a good (or bad) figure

tallado /ta'ʎaðo; ta'yaðo/ *m*, carving

tallador /taʎa'ðor; taya'ðor/ *m*, metal engraver; die sinker

tallar /ta'ʎar; ta'yar/ *vt Art.* to carve; engrave; cut (gems); value, estimate; measure height (of persons)

tallarín /taʎa'rin; taya'rin/ *m*, (gen. *pl*) *Cul.* noodle

talle /'taʎe; 'taye/ *m*, figure, physique; waist; fit (of clothes); appearance, aspect. *Inf.* **largo de t.,** long-waisted; long drawn out, overlong. **tener buen t.,** to have a good figure

taller /ta'ʎer; ta'yer/ *m*, workshop; factory; mill; workroom, atelier; industrial school; school of arts and crafts; studio

tallista /ta'ʎista; ta'yista/ *mf* engraver; wood carver; sculptor

tallo /'taʎo; 'tayo/ *m*, *Bot.* stalk; shoot; slice of preserved fruit; cabbage. **t. rastrero,** *Bot.* runner

talludo /ta'ʎuðo; ta'yuðo/ *a* long-stalked; lanky, overgrown; no longer young, aging (of women); habit-ridden

talmúdico /tal'muðiko/ *a.* Talmudic

talón /ta'lon/ *m*, heel; heel (of a shoe); *Com.* counterfoil; luggage receipt; *Com.* sight draft; coupon; heel (of a violin bow). *Inf.* **apretar los talones,** to take to one's heels. *Inf.* **pisarle (a uno) los talones,** to follow on a person's heels; rival successfully

talonario /talo'nario/ *m*, stub book

tamaño /ta'maɲo/ *a compar* so big; so small (e.g. *La conocí tamaña,* I knew her when she was so high) (indicating her size with a gesture)); so great, so large (e.g. *tamaña empresa,* so great an undertaking). *m*, size

tamarindo /tama'rindo/ *m*, tamarind

tambalear /tambale'ar/ **(se)** *vi* and *vr* to totter, sway, shake; reel, stagger

tambaleo /tamba'leo/ *m*, swaying; tottering; rocking; shaking; staggering, reeling

también /tam'bien/ *adv* also, too; in addition, as well

tambor /tam'bor/ *m*, *Mus.* drum; drummer; embroidery frame; *Mech.* drum, cylinder; roaster (for coffee, chestnuts, etc.). **t. mayor,** drum major. **a t. (or con t.) batiente,** with drums beating; triumphantly, with colors flying

tamborear /tambore'ar/ *vi* to totter, sway; stagger, reel

tamboril /tambo'ril/ *m*, tabor

tamborilear /tamborile'ar/ *vi* to play the tabor; —*vt* eulogize, extol

tamborín /tambo'rin/ *m*, tabor

Támesis, el /'tamesis, el/ the Thames

tamiz /ta'miθ; ta'mis/ *m*, sieve

tamizar /tami'θar; tami'sar/ *vt* to sieve

tampoco /tam'poko/ *adv* neither, not... either, nor... either; no more (e.g. *No lo ha hecho María t.,* Mary hasn't done it either)

tampón /tam'pon/ *m*, stamp moistener; *Surg.* tampon

tan /tan/ *adv Abbr.* **tanto.** so, as. Used

before adjectives and adverbs, excepting **más, mejor, menos, peor,** which need **tanto. t....** como, as... as. **t. siquiera,** even (see **siquiera**). **t. sólo,** only, solely (e.g. *No vengo t. sólo para saludarte,* I do not come merely to greet you). **qué... t.,** what a... (e.g. *¡Qué día t. hermoso!* What a lovely day!)

tanda /'tanda/ *f,* turn; opportunity; task; shift, relay; game (of billiards); bad habit; collection, batch, group; round (of a game); (*Dance.*) set

tándem /'tandem/ *m,* tandem

tandeo /tan'deo/ *m,* allowance of irrigation water, turn for using water

tangente /tan'hente/ *a* and *f, Geom.* tangent

tanque /'tanke/ *m, Mil.* tank; cistern, tank, reservoir; ladle, dipper

tanteador /tantea'ðor/ *m, Sports.* scorer, marker; scoreboard

tantear /tante'ar/ *vt* to measure, compare; consider fully; test, try out; *Fig.* probe, pump (persons); estimate roughly; *Art.* sketch, block in; *—vt* and *vi Sports.* keep the score of

tanteo /tan'teo/ *m,* measurement, comparison; test; rough estimate; *Sports.* score

tanto /'tanto/ *a* so much; as much; very great; as great; *pl* **tantos,** so many; as many (e.g. *Tienen tantas flores como nosotros,* They have as many flowers as we). In comparisons **tanto** is used before **más, mejor, menos, peor,** but generally **tan** is used before adjectives and adverbs (e.g. *¡Tanto peor!* So much the worse!) *—pron dem* that (e.g. *por lo t.,* therefore, on that account). *m,* so much, a certain amount; copy of a document; man, piece (in games); point (score in games); *Com.* rate (e.g. *el t. por ciento,* the percentage, the rate); *pl* approximation, odd (e.g. *Llegaron cien hombres y tantos,* A hundred-odd men arrived) *—adv* so much; as much; so, in such a way. **t.... como,** the same as, as much as. **t.... cuanto,** as much as. **t. más,** the more. **t. menos,** the less (e.g. *Cuanto más* (*menos*) *dinero tiene* **t.** *más* (*menos*) **quiere,** The more (less) money he has, the more (less) he wants). **t. más** (*menos*)... **cuanto que,** all the more (less)... because. **algún t.,** a certain amount, somewhat. **al t. de** (**una cosa),** aware of, acquainted with (a thing). **en t. or entre t.,** meanwhile. **las tantas,** *Inf.* late hour, wee hours. **No es para t.,** *Inf.* It's not as bad as that, there's no need to make such a fuss; he (she, it) isn't equal to it. **otro t.,** the same, as much; as much more. **un t.,** a bit, somewhat

tañedor /tañe'ðor/ **(-ra)** *n Mus.* player

tañer /ta'ñer/ *vt irr Mus.* to play; *—vi* sway, swing. **t. la occisa,** to sound the death (in hunting) *—Pres. Part.* tañendo. *Preterite* tañó, tañeron. *Imperf. Subjunc.* tañese, etc.

tañido /ta'ɲiðo/ *m,* tune, sound, note; toll, peal; ring

tapa /'tapa/ *f,* lid; cover; cover (of books)

tapaboca /tapa'βoka/ *m,* blow on the mouth; *f,* scarf, muffler; *Inf.* remark that silences someone

tapada /ta'paða/ *f,* veiled woman, one whose face is hidden

tapadera /tapa'ðera/ *f,* loose lid, top, cover

tapadero /tapa'ðero/ *m,* stopper

tapador /tapa'ðor/ **(-ra)** *a* covering *—n* coverer. *m,* stopper; lid; cover

tapagujeros /tapagu'heros/ *m, Inf.* unskilled mason or bricklayer; *Fig. Inf.* stopgap (person)

tapar /ta'par/ *vt* to cover; cover with a lid; muffle up, veil; hide, keep secret; close up, stop up

taparrabo /tapa'rraβo/ *m,* loincloth; swimming trunks

tapete /ta'pete/ *m,* rug; tablecover. *Inf.* **t. verde,** gaming table. *Fig.* **estar sobre el t.,** to be on the carpet, be under consideration

tapia /'tapia/ *f,* adobe; mud wall; fence. *Inf.* **más sordo que una t.,** as deaf as a post

tapiar /ta'piar/ *vt* to wall up; put a fence around, fence in

tapicería /tapiθe'ria; tapise'ria/ *f,* set of tapestries; tapestry work; art of tapestry making; upholstery; tapestry storehouse or shop

tapicero /tapi'θero; tapi'sero/ *m,* tapestry weaver or maker; upholsterer; carpet layer; furnisher

tapiz /ta'piθ; ta'pis/ *m,* tapestry; carpet

tapizar /tapi'θar; tapi'sar/ *vt* to cover with tapestry; cover, clothe; upholster; carpet; hang with tapestry; furnish with hangings or drapes

tapón /ta'pon/ *m,* stopper; cork (of a bottle); plug; *Surg.* tampon

taponar /tapo'nar/ *vt* to stopper, cork; plug; *Surg.* tampon; *Mil.* seal off

taponazo /tapo'naθo; tapo'naso/ *m,* pop (of a cork)

tapujarse /tapu'harse/ *vr* to wrap oneself up, muffle oneself

tapujo /ta'puho/ *m,* scarf, muffler, face covering; disguise; *Inf.* pretense, subterfuge

taquera /ta'kera/ *f,* rack (for billiard cues)

taquería /take'ria/ *f,* taco stand

taquígrafo /ta'kigrafo/ **(-fa)** *n* shorthand writer, stenographer

taquilla /ta'kiʎa; ta'kiya/ *f,* booking office; box office; grille, window (in banks, etc.); rolltop desk, cupboard for papers; *Theat.* takings, cash

tara /'tara/ *f,* tally stick; *Com.* tare

taracea /tara'θea; tara'sea/ *f,* inlaid work, marquetry

taracear /taraθe'ar; tarase'ar/ *vt* to inlay

tarambana /taram'bana/ *mf Inf.* madcap

tarántula /ta'rantula/ *f,* tarantula

tararear /tarare'ar/ *vt* to hum a tune

tarareo /tara'reo/ *m,* humming, singing under one's breath

tarasca /ta'raska/ *f,* figure of a dragon (carried in Corpus Christi processions); *Inf.* hag, trollop

tarascada /taras'kaða/ *f,* bite, nip; *Inf.* insolent reply

tarascar /taras'kar/ *vt* to bite; wound with the teeth

tardanza /tar'ðanθa; tar'ðansa/ *f,* delay, tardiness; slowness

tardar /tar'ðar/ *vi* to delay; be tardy, arrive late; take a long time. **a más t.,** at the latest

tarde /'tarðe/ *f,* afternoon —*adv* late. **¡Buenas tardes!** Good afternoon! **de t. en t.,** from time to time, sometimes. **hacerse t.,** to grow late. **Más vale t. que nunca,** Better late than never

tardecer /tarðe'θer; tarðe'ser/ *vi impers irr* to grow dusk. See **conocer**

tardecita, tardecita /tarðe'θika, tarðe-'θita; tarðe'sika, tarðe'sita/ *f,* dusk, late afternoon

tardiamente /tar'ðiamente/ *adv* late; too late

tardío /tar'ðio/ *a* late; backward; behind; slow, deliberate

tardo /'tarðo/ *a* slow, slothful, tardy; late; dilatory; stupid, slow-witted; badly spoken, inarticulate

tarea /ta'rea/ *f,* task, work

tarifa /ta'rifa/ *f,* price list; tariff

tarifar /tari'far/ *vt* to put a tariff on

tarima /ta'rima/ *f,* stand, raised platform

tarín barín /ta'rin ba'rin/ *adv Inf.* more or less, about

tarja /'tarha/ *f,* large shield; ancient coin; tally stick. *Inf.* **beber sobre t.,** to drink on credit

tarjar /tar'har/ *vt* to reckon by tally

tarjeta /tar'heta/ *f,* buckler, small shield; *Archit.* tablet bearing an inscription; title (of maps and charts); visiting card; invitation (card). **t. de visita,** visiting card. **t. postal,** postcard. **t. telefónica,** calling card (phone)

tarro /'tarro/ *m,* jar, pot

tarso /'tarso/ *m, Anat.* tarsus, ankle; *Zool.* hock; *Ornith.* shank

tarta /'tarta/ *f,* cake pan; cake; tart

tártago /'tartago/ *m,* spurge; *Inf.* misfortune, disappointment

tartajear /tartahe'ar/ *vi* to stammer; stutter

tartajeo /tarta'heo/ *m,* stammering; stuttering

tartajoso /tarta'hoso/ **(-sa)** *a* stammering; stuttering —*n* stutterer

tartalear /tartale'ar/ *vi Inf.* to stagger, totter; be speechless, be dumbfounded

tartamudear /tartamuðe'ar/ *vi* to stammer, stutter

tartamudeo /tartamu'ðeo/ *m.* **tartamudez** *f,* stammering; stuttering

tártaro /'tartaro/ **(-ra)** *m,* cream of tartar; tartar (on teeth); *Poet.* hell, hades —*a* and *n* Tartar

tartufo /tar'tufo/ *m,* hypocrite

tarugo /ta'rugo/ *m,* thick wooden peg; stopper; wooden block

tasa /'tasa/ *f,* assessment, valuation; valuation certificate; fixed price; standard rate; measure, rule

tasación /tasa'θion; tasa'sion/ *f,* valuation; assessment

tasador /tasa'ðor/ *m,* public assessor; valuer

tasajo /ta'saho/ *m,* salt meat; piece of meat

tasar /ta'sar/ *vt* to value; price; fix remuneration; tax; regulate; rate; dole out sparingly

tasca /'taska/ *f,* gambling den; tavern

tascar /tas'kar/ *vt* to dress (hemp, etc.); graze, crop the grass

tasquera /tas'kera/ *f, Inf.* quarrel, row, rumpus

tasquil /tas'kil/ *m,* wood splinter, chip

tata /'tata/ *m, Inf. West Hem.* daddy

tatarabuela /tatara'βuela/ *f,* great-great-grandmother

tatarabuelo /tatara'βuelo/ *m,* great-great-grandfather

tataranieta /tatara'nieta/ *f,* great-great-granddaughter

tataranieto /tatara'nieto/ *m,* great-great-grandson

tatas, andar a /'tatas, an'dar a/ *vt* to walk on all fours

¡tate! /'tate/ *interj* Stop!; Be careful!; Go slowly!; Now I understand!, Of course!

tatuaje /ta'tuahe/ *m,* tattooing

tatuar /tatu'ar/ *vt* to tattoo

taumaturgo /tauma'turgo/ *m,* thaumaturge, magician

taurino /tau'rino/ *a* taurine; pertaining to bullfights

tauromaquia /tauro'makia/ *f,* bullfighting, tauromachy

tautología /tautolo'hia/ *f,* tautology

taxi /'taksi/ *m,* taxi

taxista /tak'sista/ *m,* taxi driver

taza /'taθa; 'tasa/ *f,* cup; cupful; basin (of a fountain)

tazar /ta'θar; ta'sar/ **(se)** *vt* and *vr* to fray (of cloth)

taz a taz /taθ a taθ; tas a tas/ *adv* in exchange, without payment; even

tazón /ta'θon; ta'son/ *m,* large cup; bowl

te /te/ *f,* name of the letter T. *mf* dat. and acc. of *pers pron 2nd pers sing* thee; you; to thee, to you. Never used with a preposition

té /te/ *m,* tea

tea /tea/ *f,* torch; firebrand

teatral /tea'tral/ *a* theatrical

teatro /te'atro/ *m,* theater; stage; dramatic works; dramatic art; drama, plays. **t. de variedades,** music hall. **t. por ho-**

ras, theater where short, one-act plays are staged hourly

teca /'teka/ *f*, teak

techado /te'tʃaðo/ *m*, ceiling; roof

techador /tetʃa'ðor/ *m*, roofer

techar /te'tʃar/ *vt* to roof

techo /'tetʃo/ *m*, roof; ceiling; dwelling, habitation

techumbre /te'tʃumbre/ *f*, ceiling; roof

tecla /'tekla/ *f*, key (of keyed instruments); typewriter, linotype, or calculating machine key; *Fig.* difficult or delicate point. *Inf.* **dar en la t.,** to hit on the right way of doing a thing

teclado /te'klaðo/ *m*, keyboard

teclear /tekle'ar/ *vi* to finger the keyboard; run one's fingers over the keyboard; *Inf.* drum or tap with the fingers; —*vt* tap (the keys, etc.); *Inf.* try out various schemes

tecleo /te'kleo/ *m*, fingering the keys; *Inf.* drumming with the fingers; scheme, means

técnica /'teknika/ *f*, technique

tecnicismo /tekni'θismo; tekni'sismo/ *m*, technical jargon; technicality, technical term

técnico /'tekniko/ *a* technical. *m*, technician

tecnicolor /tekniko'lor/ *m*, technicolor

tecnología /teknolo'hia/ *f*, technology

tecnológico /tekno'lohiko/ *a* technological

tecnólogo /tek'nologo/ *m*, technologist

tedio /'teðio/ *m*, tedium, boredom, ennui

tedioso /te'ðioso/ *a* tedious, boring

tegumento /tegu'mento/ *m*, integument, tegument

teja /'teha/ *f*, tile, slate. *Inf.* **de tejas abajo,** in the normal way; in the world of men. **de tejas arriba,** in a supernatural way; in heaven

tejado /te'haðo/ *m*, roof

tejar /te'har/ *m*, tile works —*vt* to roof with tiles

tejavana /teha'βana/ *f*, penthouse, open shed

tejedor /tehe'ðor/ **(-ra)** *a* weaving; *Inf.* scheming —*n* weaver; *Inf.* schemer

tejedura /tehe'ðura/ *f*, weaving; fabric; texture

tejemaneje /tehema'nehe/ *m*, *Inf.* cleverness, knack

tejer /te'her/ *vt* to weave; plait; spin a cocoon; arrange, regulate; concoct, hatch (schemes); wind in and out (in dancing)

tejido /te'hiðo/ *m*, texture, weaving; textile; *Anat.* tissue; fabric, material

tejo /'teho/ *m*, quoit, discus; metal disk; yew tree

tela /'tela/ *f*, fabric, material, cloth; membrane; film (on liquids); spiderweb, cobweb; inner skin (of fruit, vegetables); film over the eye; matter, subject; scheme, plot. **t. metálica,** wire gauze. **en t. de juicio,** under consideration, in doubt. **lle-**

garle a uno a las telas del corazón, to hurt deeply, cut to the quick

telar /te'lar/ *m*, loom, weaving machine; *Theat.* gridiron

telaraña /tela'raɲa/ *f*, cobweb; mere trifle, bagatelle. *Inf.* **mirar las telarañas,** to be absent-minded

telarañoso /telara'ɲoso/ *a* cobwebby

telecomunicación /telekomunika'θion; telekomunika'sion/ *f*, telecommunication

telefonear /telefone'ar/ *vt* to telephone, call

telefonía /telefo'nia/ *f*, telephony. **t. sin hilos,** wireless telephony, broadcasting

telefónico /tele'foniko/ *a* telephonic

telefonista /telefo'nista/ *mf* telephone operator

teléfono /te'lefono/ *m*, telephone. **t. automático,** dial telephone. **llamar por t. (a),** to telephone, call, ring up

telefundir /telefun'dir/ *vt* to telecast

telegrafía /telegra'fia/ *f*, telegraphy. **t. sin hilos,** wireless telegraphy

telegrafiar /telegra'fiar/ *vt* to telegraph

telegráfico /tele'grafiko/ *a* telegraphic

telegrafista /telegra'fista/ *mf* telegraph operator

telégrafo /te'legrafo/ *m*, telegraph. **t. sin hilos,** wireless telegraph. *Inf.* **hacer telégrafos,** to talk by signs

telegrama /tele'grama/ *m*, telegram

telepatía /telepa'tia/ *f*, telepathy

telepático /tele'patiko/ *a* telepathic

telescópico /teles'kopiko/ *a* telescopic

telescopio /teles'kopio/ *m*, telescope

telespectador /telespekta'ðor/ *m*, TV viewer, member of the television audience

televisión /teleβi'sion/ *f*, television

telilla /te'liʎa; te'liya/ *f*, film (on liquids); thin fabric

telón /te'lon/ *m*, *Theat.* curtain; drop scene. **t. contra incendios, t. de seguridad,** *Theat.* safety curtain. **t. de boca,** drop curtain. **t. de foro,** drop scene

tema /'tema/ *m*, theme, subject; *Mus.* motif, theme; thesis, argument. *f*, obstinacy; obsession, mania; hostility, grudge, rancor

temático /te'matiko/ *a* thematic; pigheaded, obstinate

temblador /tembla'ðor/ **(-ra)** *a* trembling, shaking —*n* Quaker

temblante /tem'blante/ *a* shaking; quivering. *m*, bracelet

temblar /tem'blar/ *vi* *irr* to tremble, shake; wave, quiver; shiver with fear. See **acértar**

temblequear, templetear /tembleke'ar, templete'ar/ *vi* *Inf.* tremble; shake with fear

temblón /tem'blon/ *a* *Inf.* trembling, shaking. *m*, *Inf.* aspen

temblor /tem'blor/ *m*, shake, trembling, shiver. **t. de tierra,** earthquake

tembloroso, tembloso /temblo'roso, tem'bloso/ *a* trembling, shaking, shivering, quivering

temedero /teme'ðero/ a fearsome, dread

temer /te'mer/ vt to fear, dread; suspect, imagine; —vi be afraid

temerario /teme'rario/ a reckless, impetuous; thoughtless, hasty

temeridad /temeri'ðað/ f, recklessness, impetuosity, temerity; thoughtlessness; act of folly; rash judgment

temerón /teme'ron/ a Inf. swaggering, bombastic

temeroso /teme'roso/ a frightening, dread; fearful, timid; afraid, suspicious

temible /te'miβle/ a dread, awesome

temor /te'mor/ m, fear

temoso /te'moso/ a obstinate, headstrong

témpano /'tempano/ m, tabor; drumhead; block, flat piece; side of bacon. **t. de hielo**, iceberg, ice floe

temperación /tempera'θion; tempera'sion/ f, tempering

temperamento /tempera'mento/ m, temperament, nature; compromise, agreement

temperar /tempe'rar/ vt to temper

temperatura /tempera'tura/ f, temperature

temperie /tem'perie/ f, weather conditions

tempestad /tempes'taθ/ f, storm

tempestivo /tempes'tiβo/ a opportune, seasonable

tempestuoso /tempes'tuoso/ a stormy

templa /'templa/ f, tempera; pl Anat. temples

templado /tem'plaðo/ a moderate; temperate (of regions); lukewarm; Mus. in tune; restrained (of style); Inf. brave, long-suffering. **estar bien** (or **mal**) **templado**, Inf. to be well (or badly) tuned (of musical instruments); be in a good (or bad) temper; be good- (or ill-) natured

templanza /tem'planθa; tem'plansa/ f, moderation; sobriety; mildness of climate

templar /tem'plar/ vt to tune; Metall. temper; moderate; warm; allay, appease; anneal; Art. harmonize, blend; Naut. trim the sails; —vr control oneself, be moderate; —vi grow warm

temple /'temple/ m, weather conditions; temperature; temper (of metals, etc.); nature, disposition; bravery; mean, average; Mus. tuning. **al t.**, in tempera

templete /tem'plete/ m, dim shrine; niche (for statues); kiosk, pavilion

templo /'templo/ m, temple

temporada /tempo'raða/ f, space of time, season, while. **de t.**, seasonal; temporary. **estar de t.**, to be out of town, on holiday

temporal /tempo'ral/ a temporal; temporary; secular, lay; transient, fugitive. m, storm, tempest; rainy period; seasonal laborer

temporáneo, temporario /tempo'raneo, tempo'rario/ a temporary, impermanent, fleeting

temporejar /tempore'har/ vt Naut. to lie to in a storm

temporizar /tempori'θar; tempori'sar/ vi to while away the time; temporize

tempranero /tempra'nero/ a early

temprano /tem'prano/ a early —adv in the early hours; prematurely, too soon

temulento /temu'lento/ a intoxicated, drunken

tenacidad /tenaθi'ðað; tenasi'ðað/ f, adhesiveness; resistance, toughness; obstinacy, tenacity

tenacillas /tena'θiʎas; tena'siyas/ f pl, dim small tongs; candle snuffers; sugar tongs; curling irons; tweezers

tenaz /te'naθ; te'nas/ a adhesive; hard, resistant, unyielding; tenacious, obstinate

tenaza /te'naθa; te'nasa/ f, claw (of a lobster, etc.); pl tongs; pincers; pliers; dental forceps

tenazada /tena'θaða; tena'saða/ f, seizing with tongs; strong bite, snap; rattle of tongs

tenazón /tena'θon; tena'son/ (**a** or **de**) adv without taking aim, wildly; unexpectedly

tención /ten'θion; ten'sion/ f, retention, holding; grip

ten con ten /ten kon ten/ m, Inf. tact, diplomacy

tendencia /ten'denθia; tenden'sia/ f, tendency

tendencioso /tenden'θioso; tenden'sioso/ a tendentious, biased

tender /ten'der/ vt irr to hang out; unfold, spread out; extend, hold out; Mas. plaster; —vi tend, incline; —vr lie down at full length; place one's cards on the table; gallop hard (of horses). See **entender**

tendero /ten'dero/ (**-ra**) n shopkeeper; retailer. m, tent maker

tendido /ten'diðo/ m, row of seats in a bullfight arena; clothes hung out to dry; clear sky; Mas. plaster

tendón /ten'don/ m, tendon

tenebroso /tene'βroso/ a dark, gloomy

tenedor /tene'ðor/ m, table fork; possessor, retainer; Com. holder; payee. **t. de libros**, bookkeeper

teneduría /teneðu'ria/ f, employment of a bookkeeper. **t. de libros**, bookkeeping

tenencia /te'nenθia; te'nensia/ f, possession; tenancy, occupation; lieutenancy

tener /te'ner/ vt irr to have; hold; grasp; possess, own; uphold, maintain; contain; include; hold fast, grip; stop; keep (promises); lodge, accommodate; (with en) value, estimate (e.g. Le tengo en poco, I have a poor opinion of him); (with para) be of the opinion that (e.g. tengo para mí, my opinion is); (with por) believe, consider; —vi be wealthy; —vr steady oneself; hold on to; lean (on); rest (on); defend oneself; uphold; rely on; (with por) consider oneself as. **tener** is used to express: 1. Age (e.g. ¿Cuántos años tiene Vd? How old are you?). 2. Pos-

session (e.g. *Tenemos muchos sombreros,*
We have a great many hats). 3. *Measurements* (e.g. *El cuarto tiene dieciocho metros de largo,* The room is eighteen meters long). Translated by "be" when describing some physical and mental states (e.g. *Tenemos miedo,* We are afraid. *Tengo sueño,* I am sleepy. *Tienen frío (calor),* They are cold (hot)). Used as *auxiliary verb* replacing *haber* in compound tenses of transitive verbs (e.g. *Tengo escritas las cartas,* I have written the letters). **t. a bien,** to think fit, please, judge convenient. **t. algo en cuenta a uno,** to hold something against someone. **t. a menos de hacer (una cosa),** to scorn to do (a thing). **t. cruda,** to have a hangover. **t. curiosidad por,** to be curious about. **t. curiosidad por que + *subj*** to be interested that. **t. en aprecio,** to appreciate, esteem, value. **t. en cuenta,** to bear in mind. **t. en lugar,** to take place, occur. **t. en menos (a),** to despise (a person). **t. gana,** to want, wish; feel disposed; have an appetite. **t. lugar,** to take place, occur. **t. muchas partes cruzadas,** to be well-traveled. **t. mucho colegio,** to be well-educated. **t. muy en cuenta,** to certainly bear in mind. **t. poco colegio,** to have had little education. **t. presente,** to remember. **t. que,** to have to (e.g. *tengo que hacerlo,* I must do it). **t. que ver (con),** to have something to do (with), be related to. **no tenerlas todas consigo,** *Inf.* to have the jitters —*Pres. Ind.* tengo, tienes, tiene, tenemos, tenéis, tienen. *Preterite* tuve, etc —*Fut.* tendré, etc —*Condit.* tendría, etc —*Pres. Subjunc.* tenga, etc —*Imperf. Subjunc.* tuviese, etc.

tenguerengue, en /teŋgueˈreŋgue, en/ *adv Inf.* rickety, insecure

tenia /ˈtenia/ *f,* tapeworm; *Archit.* fillet, narrow molding

teniente /teˈniente/ *a* owning, holding; unripe (of fruit); *Inf.* slightly deaf; stingy, mean. *m,* deputy, substitute; *Mil.* first lieutenant, lieutenant. **t. coronel,** lieutenant colonel. **t. de navío,** naval lieutenant. **t. general,** *Mil.* lieutenant general. **t. general de aviación,** air marshal

tenis /ˈtenis/ *m,* tennis

tenor /teˈnor/ *m,* import, contents (of a letter, etc.); constitution, composition; *Mus.* tenor

tenorio /teˈnorio/ *m,* rake, Don Juan, philanderer

tensión /tenˈsion/ *f,* tautness; tension; strain, stress; *Elec.* tension

tenso /ˈtenso/ *a* taut; tight; tense

tentación /tentaˈθion; tentaˈsion/ *f,* temptation; attraction, inducement

tentáculo /tenˈtakulo/ *m,* tentacle; feeler

tentadero /tentaˈðero/ *m,* yard for trying out young bulls for bullfighting

tentador /tentaˈðor/ **(-ra)** *a* tempting; attractive —*n* tempter. *m,* the Devil

tentalear /tentaleˈar/ *vt* to examine by touch

tentar /tenˈtar/ *vt irr* to touch, feel; examine by touch; incite, encourage; try, endeavor; test; tempt; *Surg.* probe. See **sentar**

tentativa /tentaˈtiβa/ *f,* endeavor, attempt; preliminary exam (at some univs.)

tentempié /tentemˈpie/ *m, Inf.* snack, bite

tenue /ˈtenue/ *a* thin; slender, delicate; trivial, worthless, insignificant; pale; faint

tenuidad /tenuiˈðað/ *f,* slenderness; delicacy; triviality, insignificance; paleness; faintness

teñir /teˈɲir/ *vt irr* to dye; *Art.* darken; color, tinge; —*vr* be dyed; be tinged or colored. See **ceñir**

teocracia /teoˈkraθia; teoˈkrasia/ *f,* theocracy

teocrático /teoˈkratiko/ *a* theocratic

teologal /teoloˈɣal/ *a* theological

teología /teoloˈhia/ *f,* theology, divinity

teológico /teoˈlohiko/ *a* theological

teólogo /teˈologo/ *a* theological. *m,* theologian, divine; student of theology

teorema /teoˈrema/ *m,* theorem

teoría /teoˈria/ *f,* theory

teórica /teˈorika/ *f,* theory

teórico /teˈoriko/ *a* theoretical, speculative. *m,* theorist

teorizar /teoriˈθar; teoriˈsar/ *vt* to consider theoretically, theorize about

teoso /teˈoso/ *a* resinous, gummy

teosofía /teosoˈfia/ *f,* theosophy

tepe /ˈtepe/ *m,* sod, cut turf

terapéutico /teraˈpeutiko/ *a* therapeutic

terapia /teˈrapia/ *f,* therapy

tercer /terˈθer; terˈser/ *a Abbr.* of **tercero** third. Used before *m, sing* nouns

tercera /terˈθera; terˈsera/ *f,* procuress; *Mus.* third

tercería /terθeˈria; terseˈria/ *f,* arbitration, mediation; temporary occupation of a fortress, etc.

tercero /terˈθero; terˈsero/ **(-ra)** *a* third; mediatory —*n* third; mediator. *m,* pimp; *Eccl.* tertiary; tithes collector; third person. **¡A la tercera va la vencida!** Third time lucky!

terceto /terˈθeto; terˈseto/ *m,* tercet, triplet

tercia /ˈterθia; ˈtersia/ *f,* one-third; *Eccl.* tierce, third hour; storehouse for tithes. **tercias reales,** royal share of ecclesiastical tithes

terciana /terˈθiana; terˈsiana/ *f,* tertian fever

terciar /terˈθiar; terˈsiar/ *vt* to slant; sling sideways; divide into three; equalize weight (on beasts of burden); plow or dig for the third time; *Agr.* prune; —*vr* be opportune, come at the right time —*vi* mediate, arbitrate; make up a number (for cards, etc.); reach the third day (of the moon); take part, participate

terciario /terˈθiario; terˈsiario/ *a* third, tertiary; *Geol.* tertiary. *m, Eccl.* tertiary

tercio /ˈterθio; ˈtersio/ *a* third. *m,* one-third; *Mil.* infantry regiment; *Obs.*, body of foreign volunteers; fishermen's association; *pl* brawny limbs of a man. **hacer t.,** to take part in; make up the number of. **hacer buen** (*or* **mal) t. a alguien,** to do someone a good (or bad) turn

terciopelo /terθio'pelo; tersio'pelo/ *m,* velvet; velveteen

terco /'terko/ *a* pigheaded, obstinate; hard, tough

tergiversación /terhiβersa'θion; terhiβersa'sion/ *f,* tergiversation, vacillation

tergiversar /terhiβer'sar/ *vt* to tergiversate, shuffle, vacillate

termal /ter'mal/ *a* thermal

termas /'termas/ *f pl,* thermal springs, hot mineral baths; thermal

térmico /'termiko/ *a* thermic

terminación /termina'θion; termina'sion/ *f,* conclusion, termination; end, finish; ending of a word; *Gram.* termination

terminador /termina'ðor/ **(-ra)** *a* concluding —*n* finisher

terminal /termi'nal/ *a* terminal; final. *m, Elec.* terminal. **t. de carga,** cargo terminal

terminante /termi'nante/ *a* conclusive, definite; categorical

terminar /termi'nar/ *vt* to end, conclude; complete; —*vr* and *vi* end

término /'termino/ *m,* limit, end; term, expression; boundary marker; district, suburb; space, period; state, condition; boundary; object, aim; appearance, demeanor, behavior (gen. *pl*); completion; *Mus.* tone; (*Math. Law. Logic.*) term. **t. medio,** *Math.* average; medium; compromise, middle way. **correr el t.,** to lapse (of time). **en primer t.,** *Art.* in the foreground. **medios términos,** evasions, excuses. **primer t.,** (cinema) closeup

terminología /terminolo'hia/ *f,* terminology

termita /ter'mita/ *f,* thermite. *m,* termite

termodinámica /termoði'namika/ *f,* thermodynamics

termómetro /ter'mometro/ *m,* thermometer

termos /'termos/ *m,* thermos, vacuum bottle

termóstato /ter'mostato/ *m,* thermostat

terna /'terna/ *f,* triad, trio; set of dice

terne /'terne/ *a Inf.* bullying, braggartly; persistent, obstinate; robust. *mf* bully

ternera /ter'nera/ *f,* female calf; veal

ternero /ter'nero/ *m,* male calf

terneza /ter'neθa; ter'nesa/ *f,* tenderness, kindness; softness; softheartedness; endearment, caress, compliment (gen. *pl*)

ternilla /ter'niʎa; ter'niya/ *f,* cartilage, gristle

ternísimo /ter'nisimo/ *a superl* **tierno** most tender

terno /'terno/ *m,* triad; suit of clothes, three-piece suit; oath, curse

ternura /ter'nura/ *f,* softness; softheartedness; tenderness, kindness, sweetness

terquedad, terquería, terqueza

/terke'ðað, terke'ria, ter'keθa; ter'kesa/ *f,* obstinacy, obduracy

terracota /terra'kota/ *f,* terra cotta

terrado /te'rraðo/ *m,* flat roof

Terranova /terra'noβa/ Newfoundland

terraplén /terra'plen/ *m,* embankment; *Mil.* terreplein

terraplenar /terraple'nar/ *vt* to fill up with earth; fill in (a hollow); make into an embankment; terrace

terrateniente /terrate'niente/ *mf* landowner

terraza /te'rraθa; te'rrasa/ *f,* terrace; flat roof; flower border (of a garden)

terregoso /terre'goso/ *a* lumpy, full of clods (of soil)

terremoto /terre'moto/ *m,* earthquake

terrenal /terre'nal/ *a* terrestrial

terreno /te'rreno/ *a* terrestrial. *m,* ground, land; *Fig.* sphere; region; soil; plot of land. **ganar t.,** *Fig.* to win ground, make progress. **medir el t.,** *Fig.* to feel one's way

térreo /'terreo/ *a* earthy

terrero /te'rrero/ *a* earthly; low-flying, almost touching the ground; humble. *m,* flat roof; pile or mound of earth; deposit of earth, alluvium; target; mineral refuse

terrestre /te'rrestre/ *a* terrestrial, earthly

terrezuela /terre'θuela; terre'suela/ *f,* poor soil

terribilidad /terriβili'ðað/ *f,* terribleness, horribleness; rampancy

terribilísimo /terriβi'lisimo/ *a superl* most terrible

terrible /te'rriβle/ *a* terrible, horrible; rude, unsociable, ill-humored; enormous, huge

terrífico /te'rrifiko/ *a* terrible, frightful

territorial /territo'rial/ *a* territorial

territorialidad /territoriali'ðað/ *f,* territoriality

territorio /terri'torio/ *m,* territory; jurisdiction. **t. bajo mandato,** mandated territory

terrizo /te'rriθo; te'rriso/ *a* earthen

terrón /te'rron/ *m,* clod (of earth); lump; *pl* lands, landed property. **t. de azúcar,** lump of sugar

terrorismo /terro'rismo/ *m,* terrorism

terrorista /terro'rista/ *mf* terrorist

terrosidad /terrosi'ðað/ *f,* earthiness

terroso /te'rroso/ *a* earthy; earthen

terruño /te'rruɲo/ *m,* plot of ground; native earth; country; soil

terso /'terso/ *a* smooth, shiny, glossy; *Lit.* elegant, polished (style)

tersura /ter'sura/ *f,* smoothness, glossiness; elegance (of style)

tertulia /ter'tulia/ *f,* regular social meeting (gen. in cafés); conversational group; party; part of Spanish cafés set apart for players of chess, etc. **hacer t.,** to meet for conversation

tertuliano /tertu'liano/ **(-na)** *n* **tertuliante,** *mf* **tertulio (-ia),** *n* member of a tertulia

tesar /te'sar/ *vt Naut.* to make taut; —*vi* step backward, back (oxen)

tesela /te'sela/ *f,* tessera, square used in mosaic work

tesina /te'sina/ *f,* master's essay, thesis

tesis /'tesis/ *f,* thesis

teso /'teso/ *a* tight, taut, tense. *m,* hilltop; bulge, lump

tesón /te'son/ *m,* persistence, obstinacy, tenacity

tesorería /tesore'ria/ *f,* treasury; treasuryship

tesorero /teso'rero/ **(-ra)** *n* treasurer

tesoro /te'soro/ *m,* treasure; public treasury; hoard; *Fig.* gem, excellent person; thesaurus. **t. de duende,** fairy gold

testa /'testa/ *f,* head; face, front; *Inf.* sense, acumen. **t. coronada,** crowned head

testaclón /testa'θion, testa'sion/ *f,* erasure, crossing out

testado /tes'taðo/ *a* testate

testador /testa'ðor/ **(-ra)** *n* testator

testaferro /testa'ferro/ *m, Fig.* figurehead, proxy

testamentar /testamen'tar/ *vt* to bequeath

testamentaria /testamen'taria/ *f,* execution of a will; *Law.* estate; executors' meeting

testamentario /testamen'tario/ *a* testamental, testamentary

testamento /testa'mento/ *m, Law.* will; testament. **Antiguo T.,** Old Testament. **ordenar** (*or* **otorgar) su t.,** to make one's will

testar /tes'tar/ *vi* to make a will; —*vt* erase, cross out

testarrón /testa'rron/ *a Inf.* pigheaded

testarudez /testaru'ðeθ; testaru'ðes/ *f,* obstinacy, obduracy

testarudo /testa'ruðo/ *a* stubborn, obstinate

testera /tes'tera/ *f,* front, face; front seat (in a vehicle); upper half of an animal's face; tester, canopy

testículo /tes'tikulo/ *m,* testicle

testificar /testifi'kar/ *vt* to testify; affirm, assert; attest, prove

testigo /tes'tigo/ *mf* witness. *m,* proof, evidence. *Law.* **t. de cargo,** witness for the prosecution. *Law.* **t. de descargo,** witness for the defense. **t. de vista,** eyewitness. *Law.* **hacer testigos,** to bring forward witnesses

testimonial /testimo'nial/ *a* confirmatory, proven

testimoniar /testimo'niar/ *vt* to attest, confirm, bear witness to

testimoniero /testimo'niero/ **(-ra)** *a* slanderous; hypocritical —*n* slanderer, hypocrite

testimonio /testi'monio/ *m,* testimony, proof; slander; affidavit

testuz /tes'tuθ; tes'tus/ *m,* front of the head (of some animals); nape (of animals)

teta /'teta/ *f,* mammary gland, breast; teat, dug, udder. **dar la t.** (**a),** to suckle

tétano, tétanos /'tetano, 'tetanos/ *m,* tetanus

tetera /te'tera/ *f,* teapot; teakettle

tetilla /te'tiʎa; te'tiya/ *f, dim* rudimentary teat or nipple; nipple (of a nursing bottle)

tétrico /'tetriko/ *a* gloomy; somber

textil /teks'til/ *a* and *m,* textile

texto /'teksto/ *m,* text; quotation, citation; textbook

textura /teks'tura/ *f,* texture; weaving; structure (of a novel, etc.); animal structure

tez /teθ; tes/ *f,* complexion, skin

ti /ti/ *pers pron 2nd sing mf dat acc abl* thee, you. Always used with prep. (e.g. *por ti,* by thee (you))

tía /'tia/ *f,* aunt; *Inf.* wife, mother, dame; *Inf.* coarse creature. **t. abuela,** grandaunt, great-aunt. *Inf.* **quedarse para t.,** to be left an old maid

tiara /'tiara/ *f,* ancient Persian headdress; papal tiara; coronet; dignity and power of the papacy

tibetano /tiβe'tano/ **(-na)** *a* and *n* Tibetan. *m,* Tibetan (language)

tibia /'tiβia/ *f,* flute; tibia

tibieza /ti'βieθa; ti'βiesa/ *f,* tepidity; indifference, lack of enthusiasm

tibio /'tiβio/ *a* tepid, warm; indifferent, unenthusiastic

tiburón /tiβu'ron/ *m,* shark

ticket /'tikket/ *m,* ticket; pass, membership card

tictac /tik'tak/ *m,* ticktock (of a clock)

tiempo /'tiempo/ *m,* time; season; epoch, period; chance, opportunity; leisure, free time; weather; *Mus.* tempo; *Gram.* tense; *Naut.* storm. **t. ha,** many years ago, long ago. **t. medio** *or* **medio t.,** *Sports.* halftime. **abrir el t.,** to clear up (of the weather). **ajustar los tiempos,** to fix the date (chronology). **a largo t.,** after a long time. **andando el t.,** in the course of time. **a su t.,** in due course, at the proper time. **a t.,** in time, at the right time. **a un t.,** simultaneously, at the same time. **cargarse el t.,** to cloud over (of the sky). **con t.,** in advance, with time; in time. **correr el t.,** to pass, move on (of time). **de t. en t.,** from time to time. **engañar** (*or* **entretener) el t.,** to kill time, while away the hours. *Inf.* **en t., de Maricastaña** *or* **del rey Perico,** long, long ago. **fuera de t.,** unseasonably, inopportunely; out of season. **ganar t.,** to gain time; *Inf.* hurry. **hacer t.,** to wait, cool one's heels; *Fig.* mark time. **perder el t.,** to waste time; misspend or lose time. **sentarse el t.,** to clear up (of the weather). **tomarse t.** (**para),** to postpone, take time for (or to)

tienda /'tienda/ *f,* tent; *Naut.* awning, canopy; shop, store. **t. de antigüedades,** antique shop. **t. de campaña,** bell tent, pavilion. **t. oxígena,** oxygen tent

tienta /'tienta/ *f.* astuteness; cleverness; *Surg.* probe; trying out young bulls for the bullring. **a tientas,** by touch, gropingly

tiento /'tiento/ *m.* touching, feeling; touch, feel; blind person's cane; tightrope walker's pole; manual control, steady hand; caution, care, tact; *Mus.* preliminary flourish; *Inf.* slap buffet; tentacle. **a t.,** by touch; unsurely, gropingly

tierno /'tierno/ *a* soft; tender; kind; sweet; delicate; softhearted; fresh, recent; affectionate

tierra /'tierra/ *f.* world, planet; earth; soil; ground; cultivated ground, land; homeland, native land; region; district, territory. **t. adentro,** inland. **t. de batán,** fuller's earth. **t. de Promisión,** Promised Land. **t. de Siena,** sienna. **besar la t.,** *Inf.* to fall down. **dar en t. con,** to throw down; demolish. **echar en t.,** *Naut.* to put ashore, land. **echar por t.,** *Fig.* to overthrow, destroy. **echar t. a,** *Fig.* to bury, forget. *Inf.* **la t. de María Santísima,** Andalusia. **por t.,** overland. **saltar en t.,** to land, disembark. **venir** (*or* **venirse) a t.,** to fall down, topple over

Tierra Santa /'tierra 'santa/ Holy Land

tieso /'tieso/ *a* hard, rigid, stiff; healthy, robust; taut; spirited, courageous; obstinate, stiff-necked; distant, formal —*adv* firmly, strongly

tiesto /'tiesto/ *m.* flowerpot; broken piece of earthenware

tiesura /tie'sura/ *f.* hardness, rigidity, stiffness; physical fitness; courageousness; obstinacy; formality, stiffness

tifoidea /tifoi'ðea/ *f.* typhoid

tifón /ti'fon/ *m.* typhoon

tifus /'tifus/ *m.* typhus. **t. exantemático,** trench fever

tigre /'tigre/ *m.* tiger; ferocious person

tigresa /ti'gresa/ *f.* tigress

tijera /ti'hera/ *f.* scissors (gen. *pl*); any scissor-shaped instrument; shears; drainage channel; carpenter's horse; scandalmonger, gossip

tijeretear /tiherete'ar/ *vt* to cut with scissors; *Inf.* interfere arbitrarily

tijereteo /tihere'teo/ *m.* scissor cut; click of the scissors

tila /'tila/ *f.* lime tree or flower; linden tree or flower; infusion made of lime flowers

tildar /til'dar/ *vt* to cross out, erase; stigmatize; place a tilde over a letter

tilde /'tilde/ *mf.* bad reputation; tilde; *f.* jot, iota

timar /ti'mar/ *vt* to swindle, cheat, deceive; —*vr Inf.* exchange looks or winks

timba /'timba/ *f.* *Inf.* casino, gambling den; game of chance

timbal /tim'bal/ *m.* kettledrum

timbalero /timba'lero/ *m.* kettledrum player

timbrador /timbra'ðor/ *m.* stamper; stamping machine; rubber stamp

timbrar /tim'brar/ *vt* to stamp; place the crest over a coat of arms

timbre /'timbre/ *m.* postage stamp; heraldic crest; excise stamp; bell, push-button; *Mus.* timbre; noble deed; personal merit

timidez /timi'ðeθ; timi'ðes/ *f.* timidity, nervousness

tímido /'timiðo/ *a* timid, nervous

timo /'timo/ *m.* *Inf.* swindling, trick; thymus

timón /ti'mon/ *m.* *Naut.* helm; rudder; management, direction; stick of a rocket. **t. de dirección,** *Aer.* tailfin

timonear /timone'ar/ *vi Naut.* to steer

timonel, timonero /timo'nel, timo'nero/ *m.* helmsman, coxswain

timorato /timo'rato/ *a* godfearing; timid, vacillating

tímpano /'timpano/ *m.* *Anat.* eardrum, tympanum; *Mus.* kettledrum; *Archit.* tympanum; *Print.* tympan

tina /'tina/ *f.* vat; flour bin; large earthenware jar; wooden tub; bath

tinaja /ti'naha/ *f.* large earthenware jar; jarful

tinglado /tiŋ'glaðo/ *m.* overhanging roof; open shed; penthouse; intrigue

tiniebla /ti'nieβla/ *f.* gloom, darkness (gen. *pl*); *pl* profound ignorance; confusion of mind; *Eccl.* tenebrae

tino /'tino/ *m.* skilled sense of touch; good eye, accurate aim; judgment, shrewdness; vat. **sacar de t.** (a), to bewilder, confuse; irritate, exasperate. **sin t.,** without limit, excessively

tinta /'tinta/ *f.* color, tint; ink; staining, dyeing; dye, stain; *pl* shades, colors; *Art.* mixed colors ready for painting. **t. china,** India ink. **t. simpática,** invisible ink. **recargar las tintas,** *Fig.* to overpaint, lay the colors on too thick. *Inf.* **saber de buena t.** (una cosa), to learn (a thing) from a reliable source

tintar /tin'tar/ *vt* to dye; color, tinge, stain

tinte /'tinte/ *m.* dyeing, staining; color; dye; stain; dye house; pretext, disguise

tintero /tin'tero/ *m.* inkwell. *Inf.* **dejar** (*or* **quedársele a uno) en el t.,** to forget, omit (to say, write)

tintín /tin'tin/ *m.* ring, peal; clink; chink

tintinar /tinti'nar/ *vi* to ring, tinkle; clink; jingle

tintineo /tinti'neo/ *m.* ringing, tinkling; clinking; jingle

tinto /'tinto/ *a* red (of wine). *m.* red wine; dark red

tintorería /tintore'ria/ *f.* dyeing industry; dyeing and dry-cleaning shop

tintorero /tinto'rero/ **(-ra)** *n* dyer; dry cleaner

tintura /tin'tura/ *f.* dyeing, staining; color, tint; dye; stain; tincture; smattering, slight knowledge

tinturar /tintu'rar/ *vt* to dye; color, tinge, stain; give a superficial notion of

tiña /'tiɲa/ f, ringworm; *Inf.* meanness, stinginess

tiñoso /ti'ɲoso/ a mangy; afflicted with ringworm; *Inf.* mean, stingy

tío /'tio/ m, uncle; gaffer; fellow, chap; fool; stepfather; father-in-law. **t. abuelo,** granduncle, great-uncle

tiovivo /tio'βiβo/ m, merry-go-round

típico /'tipiko/ a typical

tiple /'tiple/ m, soprano or treble voice. *mf* soprano

tipo /'tipo/ m, model, pattern; type; print, type; species, group (of animals, etc.); *Inf.* guy, chap

tipografía /tipogra'fia/ f, typography

típula /'tipula/ f, daddy-longlegs

tiquismiquis /tikis'mikis/ m pl, ridiculous scruples; affected courtesies —a *Inf.* faddy, fussy

tira /'tira/ f, strip, band, ribbon, stripe, rib. **t. cómica,** comic strip

tirabuzón /tiraβu'θon; tiraβu'son/ m, corkscrew; ringlet, curl; hair curler

tirada /ti'raða/ f, throwing; drawing, pulling; cast, throw; distance, space; *Print.* edition, issue; circulation (of a newspaper, etc.); stroke (in golf); lapse, interval (of time). **t. aparte,** reprint (of an article, etc.)

tirado /ti'raðo/ a *Inf.* dirt-cheap. m, wire drawing

tirador /tira'ðor/ **(-ra)** n thrower, caster; drawer, puller, marksman. m, handle, knob; *Mech.* trigger; bell rope, bell pull; *Print.* pressman. **t. de bota,** boot tag. **t. de gomas,** catapult. **t. de oro,** gold wire drawer

tiramiento /tira'miento/ m, pulling; stretching

tiramira /tira'mira/ f, long, narrow mountain range; long line of persons or things; distance

tiranía /tira'nia/ f, tyranny, despotism

tiránico /ti'raniko/ a tyrannical

tiranizar /tirani'θar; tirani'sar/ vt to tyrannize over

tirano /ti'rano/ **(-na)** a tyrannous, tyrannical; *Fig.* overwhelming, dominating —n tyrant

tirante /ti'rante/ a taut; tense, strained. m, trace (of a harness); shoulderstrap; suspender (gen. pl); *Archit.* tie

tirantez /tiran'teθ; tiran'tes/ f, tautness; tension, strain; straight distance between two points. **estado de t.,** *Polit.* strained relations

tiranuelo /tira'nuelo/ m, petty tyrant

tirar /ti'rar/ vt to throw, cast; fling, aim, toss; throw down, overthrow; pull; draw; discharge, shoot; stretch, pull out; rule, draw (lines); squander, waste; *Print.* print; —vi attract; pull; (*with prep* a) turn to, turn in the direction of; incline, tend to; incline toward, have a tinge of (colors); try, aspire to; (*with de*) wield, unsheath, draw out (firearms, arms); —vr cast oneself, precipitate oneself; throw

oneself on. *Inf.* **ir tirando,** to carry on, get along somehow

tirilla /ti'riʎa; ti'riya/ f, *Sew.* shirt neckband

tiritaña /tiri'taɲa/ f, thin silk material; *Inf.* mere nothing, trifle

tiritar /tiri'tar/ vi to shiver with cold

tiritón /tiri'ton/ m, shiver, shudder

Tiro /'tiro/ Tyre

tiro /'tiro/ m, throwing; throw, cast; toss, fling; try (in football); shooting; piece of artillery; report, shot (of a gun); discharge (firearms); shooting range or gallery; team (of horses); range (of firearms, etc.); hoisting cable; flight (of stairs); *Mineral.* shaft; *Inf.* trick; robbery, theft; innuendo, insinuation; grave harm or injury; pl sword belt. **t. de pichón,** pigeon shooting. **t. par,** four-in-hand. **a t.,** within firing range; within reach. **de tiros largos,** *Inf.* in full regalia

tiroides /ti'roiðes/ f, thyroid gland

tirón /ti'ron/ m, novice, beginner; pull, tug, heave. **de un t.,** with one tug; at one stroke, at one blow

tiroriro /tiro'riro/ m, *Inf.* sound of a wind instrument; pl *Inf.* wind instruments

tirotearse /tirote'arse/ vr *Mil.* to exchange fire; indulge in repartee

tiroteo /tiro'tco/ m, shooting, exchange of shots; crackle (of rifle fire)

tirria /'tirria/ f, *Inf.* hostility, grudge, dislike

tirulato /tiru'lato/ a dumbfounded, stupefied

tisana /ti'sana/ f, tisane

tísico /'tisiko/ **(-ca)** a tuberculous —n sufferer from tuberculosis, consumptive

tisis /'tisis/ f, tuberculosis

tisú /ti'su/ m, silver or gold tissue

titánico /ti'taniko/ a titanesque; colossal, huge

títere /'titere/ m, puppet; *Fig. Inf.* dummy, grotesque; *Inf.* fool; obsession, fixed idea; pl *Inf.* circus; Punch and Judy show. *Inf.* **echar los títeres a rodar,** to upset the whole show; quarrel, fall out with. *Inf.* **no dejar t. con cabeza,** to destroy entirely, smash up completely; leave no one

titerero /tite'rero/ **(-ra), tititiretero (-ra),** n titerista *mf* puppet showman; acrobat; juggler

titilación /titila'θion; titila'sion/ f, quiver, tremor; twinkling, winking, gleam

titilador, titilante /titila'ðor, titi'lante/ a quivering, trembling; twinkling

titilar /titi'lar/ vi to quiver, tremble; twinkle

titiritaina /titiri'taina/ f, *Inf.* muffled strains of musical instruments; merrymaking, uproar

titiritar /titiri'tar/ vi to tremble, shiver, shudder

titubear /tituβe'ar/ vi to totter, sway, rock; stutter, stammer; toddle; hesitate, vacillate

titubeo /titu'βeo/ *m*, tottering, swaying; stuttering; hesitation

titulado /titu'laðo/ *m*, titled person; one who holds an academic title

titular /titu'lar/ *a* titular —*vt* to entitle, call; —*vi* obtain a title (of nobility); —*vr* style oneself, call oneself

título /'titulo/ *m*, title; heading; inscription; pretext, excuse; diploma, certificate; claim, right; noble title and its owner; section, clause; (univ.) degree; *Com.* stock certificate, bond; *Com.* title; caption; qualification, right, merit; basis of a claim or privilege; *pl Com.* securities, stocks. **t. de la columna**, *Print.* running title. **títulos de propiedad**, title deeds. **t. del reino**, title of nobility. **a t.**, under pretext

tiza /'tiθa; 'tisa/ *f*, chalk; whiting; calcined stag's antler

tiznar /tiθ'nar; tis'nar/ *vt* to make sooty; dirty, stain, begrime; *Fig.* sully, tarnish

tizne /'tiθne; 'tisne/ *m*, (sometimes *f*) soot; charcoal; stain (on one's honor, etc.); *Agr.* blight

tizón /ti'θon; ti'son/ *m*, firebrand; *Agr.* blight; *Fig.* stain (on one's honor, etc.)

tizona /ti'θona; ti'sona/ *f*, *Inf.* sword (by allusion to name of that of the Cid)

tizonear /tiθone'ar; tisone'ar/ *vi* to poke or rake the fire

toalla /to'aʎa; to'aya/ *f*, towel. **t. continua**, roller towel. **t. rusa**, Turkish towel

tobillera /toβi'ʎera; toβi'yera/ *f*, *Inf.* girl, flapper

tobillo /to'βiʎo; to'βiyo/ *m*, ankle

tobogán /toβo'gan/ *m*, toboggan; chute (in apartment buildings or amusement parks)

toca /'toka/ *f*, headdress; toque; wimple; coif

tocable /to'kaβle/ *a* touchable

tocado /to'kaðo/ *a Fig.* touched, half-crazy. *m*, headdress; coiffure, hairdressing

tocador /toka'ðor/ **(-ra)** *n Mus.* player. *m*, dressing table; kerchief; boudoir; cloakroom; dressing room; dressing case

tocamiento /toka'miento/ *m*, touching, feeling; touch; *Fig.* inspiration

tocante /to'kante/ *a* touching. **t. a**, concerning, with regard to

tocar /to'kar/ *vt* to touch, feel; *Mus.* play; knock, rap; summon; ring, peal; brush against; discover by experience; persuade, inspire; mention, touch upon; *Naut.* touch bottom; *Art.* retouch, touch up —*vi* belong; stop (at); touch at; be one's turn; concern, interest; be one's lot; adjoin, be near to; be opportune; be allied or closely related to; find the scent (of dogs). **t. en un puerto**, *Naut.* to touch at a port. **Ahora me toca a mí**, Now it's my turn. **Es un problema que me toca de cerca**, It is a problem that touches me very nearly. **a toca teja**, *Inf.* in ready cash

tocayo /to'kayo/ **(-ya)** *n* namesake

tocho /'totʃo/ *a* boorish, loutish, countrified. *m*, iron bar

tocino /to'θino; to'sino/ *m*, bacon; salt pork

tocón /to'kon/ *m*, stump (of a tree or an amputated limb)

todavía /toða'βia/ *adv* still; even; nevertheless; yet. **No han venido t.**, They have not come yet. **Queda mucho que hacer t.**, There is still much to be done.

todo /'toðo/ *a* all; whole, entire; every, each. *m*, whole, entirety; whole word (in charades); all; *pl* all; everyone —*adv* wholly, entirely. **t. lo posible**, everything possible; all one can, one's best. **t. lo que**, all that which. **ante t.**, in the first place; especially, particularly. **así y t.**, nevertheless. **a t. esto**, in the meanwhile. **con t. or con t. esto or con t. y esto**, nevertheless, in spite of this. **del t.**, wholly, completely. **jugar el t. por el t.**, to risk everything on the outcome. **sobre t.**, especially. **y t.**, in addition, as well. **Todos somos hijos de Adán y Eva, sino que nos diferencia la lana y la seda**, We are all equal, but some of us are more equal than others

todopoderoso /toðopoðe'roso/ *a* all-powerful, almighty. *m*, the Almighty, God

toga /'toga/ *f*, toga; robe, gown

toldadura /tolda'ðura/ *f*, awning; canopy; hanging; curtain

toldillo /tol'diʎo; tol'diyo/ *m*, covered litter or sedan chair; *West Hem.* mosquito net

toldo /'toldo/ *m*, awning; canopy; pomp, show

tole /'tole/ *m*, outcry, uproar, tumult

tolerable /tole'raβle/ *a* bearable, tolerable

tolerancia /tole'ranθia; tole'ransia/ *f*, tolerance, forbearance; permission

tolerante /tole'rante/ *a* tolerant, broad-minded

tolerantismo /toleran'tismo/ *m*, religious toleration

tolerar /tole'rar/ *vt* to put up with, bear, tolerate; overlook, allow, forgive

tolla /'toʎa; 'toya/ *f*, marsh, bog

tollina /to'ʎina; to'yina/ *f*, *Inf.* spanking, whipping

tolmo /'tolmo/ *m*, tor

tolondro /to'londro/ *a* stupid, heedless, reckless. *m*, bump, bruise

tolva /'tolβa/ *f*, chute (for grain, etc.)

toma /'toma/ *f*, taking; receiving; conquest, capture; dose (of medicine)

tomadura /toma'ðura/ *f*, taking, receiving; dose (of medicine). *Inf.* **t. de pelo**, leg-pull, joke

tomar /to'mar/ *vt* to take; pick up; conquer; eat; drink; adopt, employ; contract (habits); engage (employees); rent; understand; steal; remove; buy; suffer; *Fig.* overcome (by laughter, sleep, etc.); choose; possess physically; —*vi* (with *por*) go in the direction of; —*vr* grow rusty; go moldy; (with *con*) quarrel with.

t. a chacota, to take as a joke. **t. a pechos,** to take to heart. **t. el fresco,** to take the air. **tomarla con,** to contradict, oppose; bear a grudge. **t. la delantera,** to take the lead; excel, beat. **t. las de Villadiego,** *Inf.* to quit, show one's heels. **t. por su cuenta,** to undertake, take charge of; take upon oneself. **t. su desquite con,** to get even with. **Más vale un toma que dos te daré,** A little help is worth a lot of promises. **¡Toma!** *Inf.* Fancy! You don't say!; Of course! There's nothing new about that!

tomate /to'mate/ *m,* tomato; tomato plant; *Inf.* hole, potato (in stockings, etc.)

tomatera /toma'tera/ *f,* tomato plant

tómbola /'tombola/ *f,* raffle (gen. for charity); jumble sale

tomillo /to'miʎo; to'miyo/ *m,* thyme

tomo /'tomo/ *m,* volume, book; importance, worth

ton /ton/ *m, Abbr.* **tono.** **sin t. ni son,** *Inf.* without rhyme or reason

tonada /to'naða/ *f,* words of a song and its tune

tonadilla /tona'ðiʎa; tona'ðiya/ *f,* dim short song; comic song; *Theat.* musical interlude *Obs.*

tonalidad /tonali'ðað/ *f,* tonality

tonar /to'nar/ *vi Poet.* to thunder or lightning

tonel /to'nel/ *m,* barrel; cask; butt

tonelada /tone'laða/ *f,* ton

tonga, tongada /'tonga, ton'gaða/ *f,* layer, stratum; *Inf.* task

tónico /'toniko/ *a* tonic. *m, Med.* tonic; pick-me-up

tonificador, tonificante /tonifika'ðor, tonifi'kante/ *a* strengthening, invigorating tonic

tonillo /to'niʎo; to'niyo/ *m, dim* monotonous singsong voice; regional accent

tonina /to'nina/ *f,* tuna; dolphin

tono /'tono/ *m,* inflection, modulation; (*Mus. Med. Art.*) tone; pitch, resonance; energy, strength; style; manner, behavior; *Mus.* key; mode of speech. **bajar el t.,** *Fig. Inf.* to change one's tune. *Inf.* **darse t.,** to put on side, give oneself airs. **de buen (mal) t.,** in good (bad) taste

tonsila /ton'sila/ *f,* tonsil

tonsilitis /tonsi'litis/ *f,* tonsillitis

tonsura /ton'sura/ *f,* shearing; hair cutting; *Eccl.* tonsure

tonsurar /tonsu'rar/ *vt* to shear, clip; cut the hair off; *Eccl.* tonsure

tontaina /ton'taina/ *mf Inf.* ninny, fool

tontear /tonte'ar/ *vi* to behave foolishly; play the fool

tontería /tonte'ria/ *f,* foolishness, stupidity; piece of folly; trifle, bagatelle

tontiloco /tonti'loko/ *a Inf.* crazy, daft

tontivano /tonti'βano/ *a* vain, conceited

tonto /'tonto/ (**-ta**) *a* silly, stupid, simple; foolish, absurd —*n* fool, idiot. *m,* short coat, stroller. **t. de capirote,** *Inf.* an utter fool. **a tontas y a locas,** without rhyme or reason, topsy-turvy. **volver t. (a),** *Fig. Inf.* to drive crazy

topacio /to'paθio; to'pasio/ *m,* topaz

topar /to'par/ *vt* (*with con*) to run into, collide with, hit; meet unexpectedly; come across, find; —*vi* butt (of horned animals); take a bet (in cards); consist in (of obstacles); meet with (difficulties); *Inf.* be successful

tope /'tope/ *m,* projection, part that juts out; obstacle, impediment; collision, bump; crux, difficult point; quarrel, fight; *Mech.* stop; *Naut.* masthead; *Rail.* buffer. **hasta el t.,** completely full, full to the brim

topetada /tope'taða/ *f,* butt (of horned animals); *Inf.* knock, bang

topetar /tope'tar/ *vt* and *vi* to butt (of horned animals); —*vt* meet, run into

topetón /tope'ton/ *m,* butt; collision, impact, bump; blow on the head

tópico /'topiko/ *a* topical. *m,* topic, theme

topo /'topo/ *m, Zool.* mole; *Inf.* clumsy or shortsighted person; dolt, ninny

topografía /topogra'fia/ *f,* topography

toque /'toke/ *m,* touch, touching; pealing, ringing (of bells); crux, essence; test, proof; touchstone; *Metall.* assay; warning; *Inf.* tap (on the shoulder, etc.); *Art.* touch. **t. de luz,** *Art.* light (in a picture). **t. de obscuro,** *Art.* shade (in a picture). **t. de queda,** curfew. **t. de tambor,** beating of a drum. **dar un t. a,** *Inf.* to put to the test; pump (for information)

toquetear /tokete'ar/ *vt* to keep touching, handle repeatedly

toquilla /to'kiʎa; to'kiya/ *f,* hatband, hat trimming; kerchief; small shawl

torácico /to'raθiko; to'rasiko/ *a* thoracic

toral /to'ral/ *a* principal, chief, main

tórax /'toraks/ *m,* thorax

torbellino /torβe'ʎino; torβe'yino/ *m,* whirlwind; spate of things; *Inf.* madcap

torcedero /torθe'ðero; torse'ðero/ *a* twisted, crooked

torcedor /torθe'ðor; torse'ðor/ *a* twisting. *m,* twister; cause of continual anxiety

torcedura /torθe'ðura; torse'ðura/ *f,* twisting; sprain, wrench

torcer /tor'θer; tor'ser/ *vt irr* to twist; bend; turn, bear (of roads, etc.); slant, slope, incline; misconstrue, pervert; dissuade; wrench, sprain (muscles); corrupt (justice). **t. el gesto,** to make a wry face —*vr* turn sour (of wine, milk); *Fig.* go astray; turn out badly (of negotiations) —*Pres. Indic.* **tuerzo, tuerces,** etc —*Pres. Subjunc.* **tuerza, tuerzas, tuerza, tuerzan**

torcido /tor'θiðo; tor'siðo/ *a* bent, crooked, sloping, inclined; curved; dishonest, tortuous. *m,* silk twist

torcijón /torθi'hon; torsi'hon/ *m,* stomachache

torcimiento /torθi'miento; torsi'miento/ *m,* twisting; twist, turn; circumlocution; digression

toreador /torea'ðor/ *m,* bullfighter

torear /tore'ar/ *vi* and *vt* to fight bulls; —*vt* ridicule; exasperate, provoke; *Inf.* string along, deceive

toreo /to'reo/ *m,* bullfighting

torero /to'rero/ *a Inf.* bullfighting. *m,* bullfighter

torete /to'rete/ *m, dim* small bull; *Inf.* problem, difficult question; engrossing topic of conversation

tormenta /tor'menta/ *f,* storm; misfortune, calamity; indignation, agitation

tormento /tor'mento/ *m,* torment; torture; pain; anxiety, anguish. **dar t.** (a), to torture; inflict pain (on)

tormentoso /tormen'toso/ *a* stormy, tempestuous; *Naut.* pitching, rolling

torna /'torna/ *f,* return; restitution; backwater

tornaboda /torna'βoða/ *f,* day after a wedding; rejoicings of this day

tornada /tor'naða/ *f,* return home; return visit, revisit; *Poet.* envoy

tornadizo /torna'ðiθo; torna'ðiso/ **(-za)** *a Inf.* changeable; —*n* turncoat

tornamiento /torna'mjento/ *m,* return; change, transformation

tornar /tor'nar/ *vt* to return, give back; change, transform; —*vi* return, go back; continue

tornasol /torna'sol/ *m,* sunflower; sheen, changing light; *Chem.* litmus

tornasolar /tornaso'lar/ *vt* to look iridescent; change the color of, cause to appear variegated

tornátil /tor'natil/ *a* turned (in a lathe); inconstant, changeable; *Poet.* spinning, revolving

tornavoz /torna'βoθ; torna'βos/ *m,* soundboard, sounding board

torneador /tornea'ðor/ *m,* turner; jouster, fighter in a tournament

tornear /torne'ar/ *vt Sports.* to put a spin on (balls); turn in a lathe; —*vi* turn around, spin; fight in a tournament; turn over in the mind

torneo /tor'neo/ *m,* tournament

tornillero /torni'ʎero; torni'yero/ *m,* (*Inf. Mil.*) deserter

tornillo /tor'niʎo; tor'niyo/ *m,* screw; (*Inf. Mil.*) desertion

torniquete /torni'kete/ *m,* turnstile; tourniquet. **dar t.** (a), to pervert, misinterpret (meanings)

torniscón /tornis'kon/ *m, Inf.* slap, buffet, blow; pinch

torno /'torno/ *m,* lathe; turntable (of a convent, etc.); turn, rotation; windlass; dumbwaiter; axletree; spinning wheel; bend, loop (in a river). **en t.,** round about, around; in exchange

toro /'toro/ *m,* bull; Taurus; *pl* bullfight. *Inf.* **t. corrido,** tough nut to crack, wise guy. *Inf.* **Ciertos son los toros,** So it's true (gen. of bad news)

toronja /to'ronha/ *f,* grapefruit

toroso /to'roso/ *a* strong, vigorous, robust

torpe /'torpe/ *a* heavy, slow, encumbered; torpid; clumsy, unskilled; stupid, dull-witted; obscene, indecent; base, infamous; ugly

torpedear /torpeðe'ar/ *vt* to torpedo

torpedero /torpe'ðero/ *m,* torpedo boat

torpedo /tor'peðo/ *m, Ichth.* torpedo fish, electric ray; torpedo; sports car. **t. automóvil,** self-propelling torpedo

torpeza /tor'peθa; tor'pesa/ *f,* slowness, heaviness; torpidity; stupidity; lack of skill, clumsiness; indecency; ugliness; baseness, infamy

tórpido /'torpiðo/ *a* torpid

torrar /to'rrar/ *vt* to toast, brown

torre /'torre/ *f,* tower; belfry, steeple; turret; rook (in chess); *Naut.* gun turret; stack, pile (of chairs, etc.); country house with a garden. **t. del tráfico,** traffic light. **t. de viento,** castle in the air, castle in Spain

torrefacción /torrefak'θion; torrefak-'sion/ *f,* toasting (of coffee, etc.)

torrencial /torren'θial; torren'sial/ *a* torrential

torrente /to'rrente/ *m,* torrent; *Fig.* spate, rush; crowd

torreznero /torreθ'nero; torres'nero/ **(-ra)** *n Inf.* lazybones, idler

tórrido /'torriðo/ *a* torrid

torsión /tor'sion/ *f,* twisting, torsion

torta /'torta/ *f,* cake; pastry, tart; *Inf.* slap. **t. de reyes,** traditional Twelfth Night cake

tortada /tor'taða/ *f,* meat pie, game pie

tortera /tor'tera/ *f,* cake pan; baking dish; whorl (of a spindle)

tortícolis /tor'tikolis/ *m,* crick (in the neck)

tortilla /tor'tiʎa; tor'tiya/ *f,* omelet. **t. a la española,** potato omelet. **hacer t.,** to smash to atoms. **Se volvió la t.,** *Inf.* The tables are turned

tórtolo /'tortolo/ *m,* male turtledove; *Inf.* devoted lover

tortuga /tor'tuga/ *f,* turtle; tortoise. **a paso de t.,** at a snail's pace

tortuosidad /tortuosi'ðað/ *f,* tortuousness; winding; indirectness; deceitfulness

tortuoso /tor'tuoso/ *a* tortuous; winding; disingenuous, deceitful

tortura /tor'tura/ *f,* twistedness; torture, torment; anguish, grief. **una t. china,** excruciating torture

torturar /tortu'rar/ *vt* to torture

torva /'torβa/ *f,* squall of rain or snow

tos /tos/ *f,* cough. **t. ferina,** whooping cough

tosco /'tosko/ *a* rough, unpolished; coarse; boorish, uncouth

toser /to'ser/ *vi* to cough

tósigo /'tosigo/ *m,* poison, venom; anguish; affliction

tosigoso /tosi'goso/ *a* poisoned, venomous

tosquedad /toske'ðað/ *f,* roughness, lack

of polish; coarseness; boorishness, uncouthness

tostada /tos'taða/ *f, Cul.* toast

tostado /tos'taðo/ *a* golden brown, tanned. *m,* roasting (of coffee, etc.)

tostador /tosta'ðor/ **(-ra)** *n* toaster (of peanuts, etc.). *m,* toaster (utensil); coffee or peanut roaster

tostadura /tosta'ðura/ *f,* toasting; roasting (of coffee, etc.)

tostón /tos'ton/ *m,* buttered toast; anything overtoasted; roast pig; *Inf.* nuisance, bore

total /to'tal/ *a* total, entire, whole; general. *m,* total —*adv* in short; so, therefore

totalidad /totali'ðað/ *f,* whole; aggregate, entirety

totalitario /totali'tario/ *a* totalitarian

tótem /'totem/ *m,* totem

tóxico /'toksiko/ *a* toxic. *m,* toxic substance

toxicología /toksikolo'hia/ *f,* toxicology

toxina /tok'sina/ *f,* toxin

tozo /'toθo; 'toso/ *a* dwarfish, small

tozudo /to'θuðo; to'suðo/ *a* obstinate, obdurate

tozuelo /to'θuelo; to'suelo/ *m,* scruff, fat nape (of animals)

traba /'traβa/ *f,* setting (of a saw's teeth); tether (for horses); difficulty, obstacle; fastening; bond, tie; shackle; *Law.* distraint

trabacuenta /traβa'kuenta/ *f,* mistake in accounts; argument, difference of opinion

trabajado /traβa'haðo/ *a* and *past part* wrought; fashioned; labored, exhausted, weary

trabajador /traβaha'ðor/ **(-ra)** *a* working; conscientious —*n* worker

trabajar /traβa'har/ *vi* to work; function; stand the strain, resist (of machines, etc.); exert oneself, strive; toil, labor; operate, work; produce, yield (the earth fruits, etc.); —*vt* work; till, cultivate; exercise (a horse); worry, annoy, weary; operate, drive; —*vr* make every effort, work hard

trabajo /tra'βaho/ *m,* work; toil, labor; operation, working; difficulty, obstacle; literary work; hardship, trouble; process; *pl* poverty; hardship. **t. a destajo,** piecework. **t. al ralentí,** go-slow tactics. **trabajos forzados** (*or* **forzosos),** *Law.* hard labor. **pasar trabajos,** to undergo hardships

trabajosamente /traβahosa'mente/ *adv* painstakingly

trabajoso /traβa'hoso/ *a* difficult, hard; ailing, delicate; needy; afflicted

trabalenguas /traβa'lenguas/ *m, Inf.* tongue twister, jawbreaker

trabamiento /traβa'miento/ *m,* joining, fastening; uniting; initiation, commencement; shackling; hobbling (of horses)

trabar /tra'βar/ *vt* to join, unite, fasten; grasp, seize; set the teeth (of a saw); thicken; begin, initiate; hobble (of horses); reconcile, bring together, harmo-

nize; shackle; *Law.* distrain; —*vr* speak with an impediment; stutter, hesitate. **t. amistad,** to make friends. **t. conversación,** to get into conversation. **Se me trabó la lengua,** I began to stutter

trabazón /traβa'θon; traβa'son/ *f,* join, union, fastening; connection; thickness, consistency

trabilla /tra'βiʎa; tra'βiya/ *f,* vest strap; dropped stitch (in knitting)

trabuca /tra'βuka/ *f,* squib, Chinese firecracker, riprap

trabucar /traβu'kar/ *vt* to turn upside down, upset; confuse, bewilder; mix up, confuse (news, etc.); pronounce or write incorrectly

trabucazo /traβu'kaθo; traβu'kaso/ *m,* shot or report of a blunderbuss; *Inf.* calamity, unexpected misfortune

trabuco /tra'βuko/ *m, Mil.* catapult; blunderbuss

trabuquete /traβu'kete/ *m,* catapult

tracamundana /trakamun'dana/ *f, Inf.* barter, exchange of trash; hubbub, uproar

tracción /trak'θion; trak'sion/ *f,* pulling; traction

tracoma /tra'koma/ *f,* trachoma

tracto /'trakto/ *m,* tract, area, expanse; lapse of time

tractor /trak'tor/ *m,* tractor. **t. de orugas,** caterpillar tractor

tradición /traði'θion; traði'sion/ *f,* tradition

tradicional /traðiθio'nal; traðisio'nal/ *a* traditional

traducción /traðuk'θion; traðuk'sion/ *f,* translation; interpretation, explanation

traducible /traðu'θiβle; traðu'siβle/ *a* translatable

traducir /traðu'θir; traðu'sir/ *vt irr* to translate; interpret, explain; express. See **conducir**

traductor /traðuk'tor/ **(-ra)** *n* translator; interpreter

traedizo /trae'ðiθo; trae'ðiso/ *a* portable, movable

traer /tra'er/ *vt irr* to bring; attract; cause, occasion; wear, have on; quote, cite (as proof); compel, force; persuade; conduct, lead (persons); be engaged in; —*vr* dress (well *or* badly). **t. consigo,** to bring with it; have or carry or bring with one. **t. entre manos,** to have on hand —*Pres. Indic.* **traigo, traes,** etc —*Pres. Part.* **trayendo.** *Preterite* **traje, trajiste,** etc —*Pres. Subjunc.* **traiga,** etc —*Imperf. Subjunc.* **trajese,** etc.

trafagador /trafaga'ðor/ *m,* dealer, trafficker, merchant

tráfago /'trafago/ *m,* traffic, trade; toil, drudgery

trafalmejas /trafal'mehas/ *a Inf.* rowdy, crazy, *mf Inf.* rowdy

traficante /trafi'kante/ *mf* dealer, merchant, trader

traficar /trafi'kar/ *vi* to trade; travel

tráfico /'trafiko/ *m*, traffic; trade, commerce

tragaderas /traga'ðeras/ *f pl*, throat, gullet. *Inf.* **tener buenas t.**, to be very credulous; be tolerant (of evil)

tragadero /traga'ðero/ *m*, throat, gullet; sink, drain; hole, plug

tragador /traga'ðor/ **(-ra)** *n* glutton, guzzler

tragahombres /traga'ombres/ *mf Inf.* braggart, bully

tragaleguas /traga'leguas/ *mf Inf.* fast walker

tragaluz /traga'luθ; traga'lus/ *m*, skylight; fan light

tragantón /tragan'ton/ **(-ona)** *a Inf.* guzzling, greedy. —*n* glutton

tragantona /tragan'tona/ *f. Inf.* spread, large meal; swallowing with difficulty; *Fig. Inf.* hard pill to swallow

tragaperras /traga'perras/ *m, Inf.* vending machine, catchpenny

tragar /tra'gar/ *vt* to swallow; eat ravenously, devour; engulf, swallow up; believe, take in; tolerate, put up with; dissemble; consume, absorb

tragedia /tra'heðia/ *f*, tragedy

trágico /'trahiko/ **(-ca)** *a* tragic —*n* tragedian; writer of tragedies

tragicómico /trahi'komiko/ *a* tragicomic

trago /'trago/ *m*, swallow, gulp, draft; *Fig. Inf.* bitter pill. **a tragos**, *Inf.* little by little, slowly

tragón /tra'gon/ **(-ona)** *a Inf.* greedy, gluttonous —*n* glutton

tragonear /tragone'ar/ *vt Inf.* to devour, eat avidly

traición /trai'θion; trai'sion/ *f*, treason, treachery. **a t.**, treacherously

traicionar /traiθio'nar; traisio'nar/ *vt* to betray

traicionero /traiθio'nero; traisio'nero/ **(-ra)** *a* treacherous —*n* traitor

traída /tra'iða/ *f*, conduction. **t. de aguas**, water supply

traidor /trai'ðor/ **(-ra)** *a* treacherous —*n* traitor

traílla /tra'iʎa; tra'iya/ *f*, lead, leash (for animals)

traje /'trahe/ *m*, dress, apparel; outfit, costume; suit. **t. de americana**, lounge suit. **t. de ceremonia** or **t. de etiqueta**, full-dress uniform; evening dress (men). **t. de luces**, bullfighter's gala outfit. **t. de montar**, riding habit. **t. de noche**, evening dress (women). **t. paisano**, civilian dress; lounge suit

trajín /tra'hin/ *m*, carriage, transport; busyness, moving around; bustle; clatter

trajinar /trahi'nar/ *vt* to carry, transport; —*vi* be busy, go about one's business

tralla /'traʎa; 'traya/ *f*, rope, cord; lash (of a whip); whip

trama /'trama/ *f*, woof, texture (of cloth); twisted silk; intrigue, scheme; *Lit.* plot; olive flower

tramar /tra'mar/ *vt* to weave; prepare,

hatch (plots); *Fig.* prepare the way for; —*vi* flower (of trees, especially olive)

tramitación /tramita'θion; tramita'sion/ *f*, transaction, conduct; procedure, method

tramitar /trami'tar/ *vt* to transact, conduct, settle

trámite /'tramite/ *m*, transit; negotiation; phase of a business deal; requirement, condition

tramo /'tramo/ *m*, plot of ground; flight of stairs, staircase; stretch, expanse, reach, tract

tramontana /tramon'tana/ *f*, north wind; arrogance, haughtiness

tramoya /tra'moya/ *f, Theat.* stage machinery; trick, deception, hoax

tramoyista /tramo'yista/ *mf* stage carpenter; stagehand; scene-shifter; trickster, impostor, swindler

trampa /'trampa/ *f*, trap, snare; trapdoor; flap of a shop counter; trouser fly; trick, swindle; overdue debt. *Fig. Inf.* **caer en la t.**, to fall into the trap. *Inf.* **coger en la t.**, to catch in a trap; catch in the act

trampantojo /trampan'toho/ *m, Inf.* optical illusion, swindle

trampeador /trampea'ðor/ *a Inf.* swindling —*n* trickster, swindler

trampear /trampe'ar/ *vi Inf.* to obtain money on false pretenses; struggle on (against illness, etc.); keep oneself alive, make shift; —*vt* defraud, swindle

trampolín /trampo'lin/ *m*, springboard; diving board; *Fig.* jumping-off place

tramposo /tram'poso/ **(-sa)** *n* debtor; cardsharper; swindler

tranca /'tranka/ *f*, thick stick, cudgel; bar (of a window, etc.)

trancada /tran'kaða/ *f*, stride

trancar /tran'kar/ *vt* to bar the door; —*vi Inf.* oppose, resist

trancazo /tran'kaθo; tran'kaso/ *m*, blow with a stick; influenza, flu

trance /'tranθe; 'transe/ *m*, crisis, difficult juncture; danger, peril. **t. de armas**, armed combat. **a todo t.**, at all costs, without hesitation

tranco /'tranko/ *m*, stride; threshold. *Inf.* **en dos trancos**, in a trice

tranquilar /tranki'lar/ *vt Com.* to check off

tranquilidad /trankili'ðað/ *f*, tranquility, peace, quietness; composure, serenity

tranquilizador /trankiliθa'ðor/ trankilisa'ðor/ *a* tranquilizing, soothing

tranquilizar /trankili'θar; trankili'sar/ *vt* to calm, quiet; soothe

tranquilo /tran'kilo/ *a* tranquil, quiet, peaceful; serene, composed

transacción /transak'θion; transak'sion/ *f*, compromise, arrangement; transaction, negotiation, deal

transandino /transan'dino/ *a* transandean

transatlántico /transa'tlantiko/ *a* transatlantic. *m*, (transatlantic) liner

transbordar /transβor'ðar/ *vt* to transship; transfer, remove goods from one vehicle to another

transbordo /trans'βorðo/ *m*, transshipment, transshipping; transfer, removal

transcendencia /transθen'denθia; transsen'densia/ *f* See **trascendencia**

transcendental /transθenden'tal; transsenden'tal/ *a*. See **trascendental**

transcribir /transkri'βir/ *vt* to transcribe; copy —*Past Part.* **transcrito**

transcripción /transkrip'θion; transkrip-'sion/ *f*, transcription; copy, transcript

transcurrir /transku'rrir/ *vi* to elapse, pass (time)

transcurso /trans'kurso/ *m*, passage, lapse, course (of time)

transepto /tran'septo/ *m*, transept

transeúnte /tran'seunte/ *a* transient, temporary. *mf* passerby; visitor, sojourner

transferencia /transfe'renθia; transfe-'rensia/ *f*, transfer (from one place to another); *Law.* conveyance, transference. **t. bancaria,** bank draft

transferidor /transferi'ðor/ **(-ra)** *a* transferring —*n* transferrer; *Law.* transferor

transferir /transfe'rir/ *vt irr* to transfer, move from one place to another; *Law.* convey (property, etc.); postpone. See **sentir**

transfigurar /transfigu'rar/ *vt* to transfigure

transfijo /trans'fiho/ *a* transfixed

transformación /transforma'θion; transforma'sion/ *f*, transformation

transformador /transforma'ðor/ *a* transformative. *m*, *Elec.* transformer

transformar /transfor'mar/ *vt* to transform, reform (persons); —*vr* be transformed; reform, mend one's ways

tránsfuga /'transfuga/ *mf* **tránsfugo** *m*, fugitive; political turncoat

transfusor /transfu'sor/ *a* transfusive

transgredir /transgre'ðir/ *vt* to transgress, infringe

transgresión /transgre'sion/ *f*, infringement, violation, transgression

transgresor /transgre'sor/ **(-ra)** *a* infringing —*n* transgressor, violator

transición /transi'θion; transi'sion/ *f*, transition, change

transido /tran'siðo/ *a* exhausted, worn-out, spent; niggardly, mean

transigencia /transi'henθia; transi-'hensia/ *f*, tolerance, forbearance, indulgence

transigente /transi'hente/ *a* tolerant, forbearing

transigir /transi'hir/ *vi* to be tolerant; be broad-minded —*vt* put up with, tolerate

transitable /transi'taβle/ *a* passable, traversable

transitar /transi'tar/ *vi* to cross, pass through; travel

tránsito /'transito/ *m*, passage, crossing; transit; stopping place; transition, change; gallery of a cloister; *Eccl.* holy death. **de t.,** temporarily; in transit (of goods). **hacer tránsitos,** to break one's journey, stop

transitorio /transi'torio/ *a* transitory, fugitive, fleeting

translimitación /translimita'θion; translimita'sion/ *f*, trespass; bad behavior; armed intervention in a neighboring state

translimitar /translimi'tar/ *vt* to overstep the boundaries (of a state, etc.); overstep the limits (of decency, etc.)

translúcido /trans'luθiðo; trans'lusiðo/ *a* translucent, semitransparent

transmigrar /transmi'grar/ *vi* to migrate; transmigrate (of the soul)

transmisión /transmi'sion/ *f*, transmission. **t. del pensamiento,** thought transference

transmisor /transmi'sor/ *a* transmitting. *m*, *Elec.* transmitter, sender

transmitir /transmi'tir/ *vt* to transmit; *Mech.* drive

transoceánico /transoθe'aniko; transose'aniko/ *a* transoceanic

transparencia /transpa'renθia; transpa'rensia/ *f*, transparency; obviousness

transparentarse /transparen'tarse/ *vr* to be transparent; show through; *Fig.* reveal, give away (secrets)

transparente /transpa'rente/ *a* transparent; translucent; evident, obvious. *m*, windowshade, blind

transpiración /transpira'θion; transpira'sion/ *f*, transpiration; perspiration

transpirar /transpi'rar/ *vi* to perspire; transpire

transponer /transpo'ner/ *vt irr* to move, transfer; transplant; transpose; —*vr* hide behind; sink behind the horizon (of the sun, stars); be half-asleep. See **poner**

transportador /transporta'ðor/ **(-ra)** *a* transport —*n* transporter. *m*, *Geom.* protractor

transportar /transpor'tar/ *vt* to transport; *Mus.* transpose; carry; —*vr Fig.* be carried away by (anger, rapture)

transporte /trans'porte/ *m*, transport, carriage; cartage; *Naut.* transport; strong emotion, transport, ecstasy

transversal, transverso /transβer'sal, trans'βerso/ *a* transverse

tranvía /tram'bia/ *m*, street railway; streetcar. **t. de sangre,** horse-drawn streetcar.

trapacear /trapaθe'ar; trapase'ar/ *vi* to cheat, swindle

trapacete /trapa'θete; trapa'sete/ *m*, *Com.* daybook

trapacista /trapa'θista; trapa'sista/ *mf* trickster, swindler, knave

trapajoso /trapa'hoso/ *a* ragged, shabby, tattered

trápala /'trapala/ *f*, noise, confusion, hubbub; noise of horse's hoofs, gallop; *Inf.* trick, swindle; prattling, babbling. *mf Inf.* babbler, prattler; trickster

trapalear /trapale'ar/ *vi* to walk noisily, tramp; *Inf.* chatter, babble

trapatiesta /trapa'tiesta/ *f, Inf.* brawl, row, quarrel

trapaza /tra'paθa; tra'pasa/ *f,* hoax, swindle

trapecio /tra'peθio; tra'pesio/ *m,* trapeze; *Geom.* trapezium, trapezoid

trapería /trape'ria/ *f,* old-clothes shop; old clothes, rags, trash, frippery

trapero /tra'pero/ **(-ra)** *n* old-clothes seller; rag merchant; ragpicker

trapezoide /trape'θoiðe; trape'soiðe/ *m,* trapezium, trapezoid

trapichear /trapitʃe'ar/ *vi Inf.* to make shift, endeavor

trapiento /tra'piento/ *a* ragged, shabby

trapillo /tra'piʎo; tra'piyo/ *m, Inf.* poverty-stricken lover; nest egg, savings. *Inf.* **de t.,** in a state of undress, in négligé

trapío /tra'pio/ *m, Inf.* spirit of a fighting bull; verve, dash, independent air (of women)

trapisonda /trapi'sonda/ *f, Inf.* uproar, brawl; hubbub, bustle; snare, fix

trapisondear /trapisonde'ar/ *vi Inf.* to be given to brawling; scheme, intrigue

trapisondista /trapison'dista/ *mf* brawler; schemer, trickster

trapo /'trapo/ *m,* rag; *Naut.* canvas; bullfighter's cape; *pl* garments, bits and pieces. *Inf.* **poner como un t.** (a), to dress down, scold. *Inf.* **soltar el t.,** to burst out crying or laughing

trapujo /tra'puho/ *m, Inf.* trick; subterfuge

traque /'trake/ *m,* report, bang (of a rocket, etc.); fuse (of a firework)

tráquea /'trakea/ *f,* trachea

traqueotomía /trakeoto'mia/ *f,* tracheotomy

traquetear /trakete'ar/ *vi* to crack, bang, go off with a report; rattle; jolt (of trains, etc.) —*vt* shake, stir; *Inf.* paw, handle too much

traqueteo /trake'teo/ *m,* banging (of fireworks); creaking; rattling; jolting (of trains, etc.)

traquido /tra'kiðo/ *m,* report (of a gun); crack (of a whip); creak

tras /tras/ *prep* after; behind; following, in pursuit of; trans- (in compounds). *m, Inf.* buttock; sound of a blow, bang, bump. **t. t.,** knocking (at a door); banging

trasalcoba /trasal'koβa/ *f,* dressing room

trasbarrás /trasβa'rras/ *m,* bang, bump, noise

trascendencia /trasθen'denθia; trassen'densia/ *f,* transcendence, excellence; consequence, result

trascendental /trasθenden'tal; trassenden'tal/ *a* transcendental; important, far-reaching

trascender /trasθen'der; trassen'der/ *vi irr* to spread to, influence; become

known, leak out; exhale a scent; —*vt* investigate, discover. See **entender**

trascolar /trasko'lar/ *vt irr* to filter, strain; cross over, traverse. See **colar**

trascordarse /traskor'ðarse/ *vr irr* to mix up, make a muddle of, forget. See **acordar**

trasechar /trase'tʃar/ *vt* to ambush, waylay

trasegar /trase'gar/ *vt irr* to upset, turn upside down; transfer, move from one place to another; empty, pour out, upset (liquids). See **cegar**

traseñalar /traseɲa'lar/ *vt* to re-mark, mark again

trasera /tra'sera/ *f,* rear, back, rear portion

trasero /tra'sero/ *a* rear, back. *m,* hindquarters, rump; buttocks, seat; *pl Inf.* ancestors

trasgo /'trasgo/ *m,* imp, sprite, puck

trashumar /trasu'mar/ *vi* to go from winter to summer pasture (or vice versa) (of flocks)

trasiego /tra'siego/ *m,* emptying, pouring out, upsetting (of liquids); decanting (of wines)

traslación /trasla'θion; trasla'sion/ *f,* removal, transfer; alteration (of the date for a meeting); metaphor

trasladable /trasla'ðaβle/ *a* removable, movable, transferable

trasladar /trasla'ðar/ *vt* to remove, transfer; move from one place to another; alter (the date of a meeting); translate; copy, transcribe; —*vr* remove (from a place)

traslado /tras'laðo/ *m,* removal; transfer; transcription

traslapar /trasla'par/ *vt* to cover, overlap

traslapo /tras'lapo/ *m,* overlap, overlapping

traslucirse /traslu'θirse; traslu'sirse/ *vr irr* to be transparent or translucent; shine through; come out (of secrets); infer, gather. See **lucir**

traslumbramiento /traslumbra'miento/ *m,* dazzle, glare, brilliance

traslumbrar /traslum'βrar/ *vt* to dazzle; —*vr* flicker, glimmer; fade quickly, disappear

trasluz /tras'luθ; tras'lus/ *m,* reflected light. **al t.,** against the light

trasmañanar /trasmaɲa'nar/ *vt* to put off from day to day

trasminar /trasmi'nar/ *vt* to undermine, excavate; —*vi* percolate, ooze; penetrate, spread

trasnochada /trasno'tʃaða/ *f,* previous night, last night; night's vigil; sleepless night; *Mil.* night attack

trasnochado /trasno'tʃaðo/ *a* stale, old; weary; hackneyed; drawn, pinched

trasnochador /trasnotʃa'ðor/ **(-ra)** *n* one who watches by night or stays up all night; *Inf.* night owl, reveler

trasnochar /trasno'tʃar/ *vi* to stay up all

night; watch through the night; spend the night; **—vt** sleep on, leave for the following day

trasnoche, trasnocho /tras'notʃe, tras-'notʃo/ m, Inf. night out; night vigil

trasoir /traso'ir/ vt irr to hear incorrectly, misunderstand. See **oir**

trasojado /traso'haðo/ a haggard, tired-eyed

trasoñar /traso'ɲar/ vt irr to imagine, mistake a dream for reality. See **contar**

traspalar /traspa'lar/ vt to fork (grain); shovel; transfer, move

trasparencia /traspa'renθia; traspa-'rensia/ f. See **transparencia**

traspasar /traspa'sar/ vt to transfer, move; cross; Law. convey, make over to; pierce; transgress, flout; exceed one's authority; Fig. go too far; reexamine, go over again; give intolerable pain (of illness, grief). **se traspasa**, to be disposed of (houses, etc.)

traspaso /tras'paso/ m, transport, transfer; Law. conveyance; property transferred; price agreed upon

traspié /tras'pie/ m, slip, catching of the foot, stumble; heel of the foot. **dar traspiés**, Inf. to blunder

trasplantación /trasplanta'θion; trasplanta'sion/ f, **trasplante** m, transplantation; emigration

trasplantar /trasplan'tar/ vt Agr. to transplant; **—vi** emigrate

trasplante /tras'plante/ m, planting out

traspuesta /tras'puesta/ f, transposition; back quarters; rear (of a house); back yard

trasquilar /traski'lar/ vt to cut the hair unevenly; shear (sheep); Inf. cut down, diminish

trastada /tras'taða/ f, Inf. dirty trick, mean act

traste /'traste/ m, fret (of stringed instruments); tasting cup. **dar al t. con**, to spoil, upset, damage. Inf. **sin trastes**, topsy-turvy, without method

trastear /traste'ar/ vt to play well (on the mandolin, etc.); Inf. manage tactfully; **—vi** move around, change (furniture, etc.); discuss excitedly

trastejar /traste'har/ vt to repair the roof; renew slates; overhaul

trastienda /tras'tienda/ f, back of a shop; room behind a shop; Inf. wariness, caution

trasto /'trasto/ m, piece of furniture; (household) utensil; lumber, useless furniture; Theat. wing or set piece; Inf. useless person, ne'er-do-well; oddment, thing; pl implements, equipment

trastornar /trastor'nar/ vt to turn upside down; perturb, disturb; Fig. overpower (of scents, etc.); disorder, upset; dissuade; make mad; derange the mind

trastorno /tras'torno/ m, upset; perturbation, anxiety; disorder; mental derangement; confusion (of the senses)

trastrabillar /trastraβi'ʎar; trastraβi'yar/

vi to stumble, slip; totter, sway; hesitate; stutter, be tongue-tied

trastrocamiento /trastroka'miento/ m, alteration, change; disarrangement

trastrocar /trastro'kar/ vt irr to alter, change, disarrange; change the order of. See **contar**

trasudar /trasu'ðar/ vt to perspire

trasuntar /trasun'tar/ vt to copy, transcribe; summarize

trasunto /tra'sunto/ m, copy, transcript; imitation

trasver /tras'βer/ vt irr to see through or between, glimpse; see incorrectly. See **ver**

trata /'trata/ f, slave trade. **t. de blancas**, white slave traffic

tratable /tra'taβle/ a easily accessible, sociable, unpretentious

tratadista /trata'ðista/ mf writer of a treatise; expert, writer on special subjects

tratado /tra'taðo/ m, pact, agreement; treaty; treatise

tratador /trata'ðor/ (**-ra**) n arbitrator

tratamiento /trata'miento/ m, treatment; courtesy title; address, style, Med. treatment; process. **t. de textos**, word processing

tratante /tra'tante/ m, merchant, dealer

tratar /tra'tar/ vt to handle, use; conduct, manage, have dealings with, meet, know (e.g. Yo no le trato, I don't know him); behave well or badly toward; care for, treat; discuss, deal with (e.g. ¿De qué trata el libro? What is the book about?); propose, suggest; Chem. treat; (with de) address as, call; **—vi** have amorous relations; (with de) try to, endeavor to; (with en) trade in; **—vr** look after oneself, treat oneself; conduct oneself

trato /'trato/ m, use, handling; management; conduct, behavior; manner, demeanor; appellation, title; commerce, traffic; dealings, intercourse; treatment; agreement, arrangement. **t. colectivo**, collective bargaining

traumático /trau'matiko/ a traumatic

través /tra'βes/ m, slant, slope; mishap; (Mil. Archit.) traverse. **a t. or al t.**, across; through. **de t.**, athwart; through

travesaño /traβe'saɲo/ m, crossbar; bolster; rung (of a ladder); traverse

travesear /traβese'ar/ vi to run about, romp, be mischievous; lead a vicious life; speak wittily; move ceaselessly (of water, etc.)

travesía /traβe'sia/ f, crossing; traverse; crossroad; side road or street; distance, space; sea crossing; crosswise position; stretch of road within a town

travestido /traβes'tiðo/ a disguised, dressed up

travesura /traβe'sura/ f, romping, frolic; mischief; prank; quick-wittedness

traviesa /tra'βiesa/ f, sleeping car, sleeper (railroad); Archit. rafter; distance between two points

travieso /tra'βieso/ a transverse, crosswise; mischievous, willful; debauched;

clever, subtle; ever-moving (of streams, etc.)

trayecto /tra'yekto/ *m*, run, distance, journey; stretch, expanse, tract; fare stage

trayectoria /trayek'toria/ *f*, trajectory; journey

traza /'traθa; 'trasa/ *f*, plan, design, draft; scheme, project; idea, proposal; aspect, appearance; means, manner. **Hombre pobre todo es trazas,** A poor man is full of schemes (for bettering himself)

trazado /tra'θaðo; tra'saðo/ *m*, designing, drawing; design, draft, model, plan; course, direction (of a canal, etc.)

trazar /tra'θar; tra'sar/ *vt* to plan, draft, design; make a drawing of; trace; describe; map out, arrange

trazo /'traθo; 'traso/ *m*, line, stroke; outline, contour, form, line; *Art.* fold in drapery; stroke of the pen

trebejar /treβe'har/ *vi* to frolic, skip, play

trebejo /tre'βeho/ *m*, chessman, chess piece; utensil, article (gen. *pl*); plaything

trébol /'treβol/ *m*, clover

trece /'treθe; 'trese/ *a* and *m*, thirteen, thirteenth. *m*, thirteenth (day of the month)

trecho /'tretʃo/ *m*, distance, space; interval (of time). **a trechos,** at intervals. **de t. en t.,** from time to time

trefe /'trefe/ *a* pliable, flexible; light; spurious (of coins)

tregua /'tregua/ *f*, truce, respite, rest. **dar treguas,** to afford relief, give a respite; give time

treinta /'treinta/ *a* and *m*, thirty; thirtieth. *m*, thirtieth (day of the month)

tremebundo /treme'βundo/ *a* fearsome, dread

tremedal /treme'ðal/ *m*, bog; quagmire

tremendo /tre'mendo/ *a* fearful, formidable; awesome; *Inf.* tremendous, enormous

trementina /tremen'tina/ *f*, turpentine

tremolar /tremo'lar/ *vt* and *vi* to wave, fly (of banners); *Fig.* make a show of

tremolina /tremo'lina/ *f*, noise of the wind; *Inf.* hubbub, confusion

trémulo /'tremulo/ *a* trembling, tremulous

tren /tren/ *m*, supply, provision; outfit; equipment; pomp, show; railroad train; following, train. **t. ascendente,** up train (from coast to interior). *Inf.* **t. botijo,** excursion train. **t. con coches corridos,** corridor train. **t. correo,** mail train. **t. descendente,** down train (from interior to coast). **t. mixto,** train carrying passengers and freight. **t. ómnibus,** accommodation train, slow, stopping train. **t. rápido,** express

trencilla /tren'θiʎa; tren'siya/ *f*, braid, trimming

trenza /'trenθa; 'trensa/ *f*, plait, braid; plait of hair; bread twist. **en t.,** in plaits, plaited (of hair)

trenzar /tren'θar; tren'sar/ *vt* to plait, braid; —*vi* curvet, prance

trepa /'trepa/ *f*, perforation, boring, piercing; climbing; creeping; *Inf.* half-somersault; grain, surface (of wood); craftiness, slyness; deception, fraud; beating, drubbing

trepador /trepa'ðor/ *a* climbing; crawling; *Bot.* creeping, climbing. *m*, climbing place

trepanación /trepana'θion; trepana'sion/ *f*, trepanning

trepanar /trepa'nar/ *vt* to trepan

trepante /tre'pante/ *a* creeping; *Bot.* twining, climbing

trepar /tre'par/ *vi* to climb, ascend; *Bot.* climb or creep; bore, perforate

trepatrepa /trepa'trepa/ *m*, jungle gym, monkey bars

trepidación /trepiða'θion; trepiða'sion/ *f*, trepidation, dread; vibration; jarring, shaking

trepidar /trepi'ðar/ *vi* to shiver, shudder; vibrate; shake; jar

trépido /'trepiðo/ *a* shuddering, shivering; vibrating

tres /tres/ *a* three; third. *m*, figure three; third (day of the month); three (of playing cards); trio. *Inf.* **como t. y dos son cinco,** as sure as two and two make four

trescientos /tres'θientos; tres'sientos/ *a* and *m*, three hundred; three-hundredth

treta /'treta/ *f*, scheme; trick, hoax; feint (in fencing)

tría /'tria/ *f*, selection, choice; worn place (in cloth)

triangulación /triangula'θion; triangula'sion/ *f*, triangulation

triángulo /tri'angulo/ *a* triangular. *m*, (*Geom. Mus.*) triangle. **t. acutángulo,** acute triangle. **t. obtusángulo,** obtuse triangle. **t. rectángulo,** right-angled triangle

triar /triar/ *vt* to select, pick out; —*vi* fly in and out of the hive (of bees); —*vr* grow threadbare, become worn

tribu /'triβu/ *f*, tribe, species, family

tribulación /triβula'θion; triβula'sion/ *f*, tribulation, suffering

tribuna /tri'βuna/ *f*, tribune; platform, rostrum, pulpit; spectators' gallery; stand. **t. de la prensa,** press gallery. **t. del jurado,** jury box. **t. del órgano,** organ loft

tribunado /triβu'naðo/ *m*, tribunate

tribunal /triβu'nal/ *m*, law court; *Law.* bench; judgment seat; tribunal; board of examiners. **t. de menores,** children's court, juvenile court. *Naut.* **t. de presas,** prize court. **t. de primera instancia,** *Law.* petty sessions. **t. militar,** court-martial

tribuno /tri'βuno/ *m*, tribune; political speaker

tributar /triβu'tar/ *vt* to pay taxes; offer, render (thanks, homage, etc.)

tributario /triβu'tario/ **(-ia)** *a* tributary; tax-paying, contributive —*n* taxpayer. *m*, tributary (of a river)

tributo /tri'βuto/ *m*, contribution; tax; tribute, homage; census

triciclo /tri'θiklo; tri'siklo/ *m*, tricycle

tricolor /triko'lor/ *a* three-colored

tricorne /tri'korne/ *a Poet*. three-cornered, three-horned

tricornio /tri'kornio/ *a* three-cornered. *m*, three-cornered hat

tricotomía /trikoto'mia/ *f*, trichotomy, division into three

tridente /tri'ðente/ *a* tridentate, three-pronged. *m*, trident

trienio /'trienio/ *m*, space of three years

trigo /'trigo/ *m*, wheat plant; ear of wheat; wheat field (gen. *pl*); wealth, money. **t. sarraceno**, buckwheat. **t. tremés** or **t. trechel** or **t. tremesino** or **t. de marzo**, summer wheat

trigonometría /trigonome'tria/ *f*, trigonometry

trigueño /tri'geɲo/ *a* brunette, dark

triguero /tri'gero/ *a* wheat; wheat-growing. *m*, grain sieve; grain merchant

trilátero /tri'latero/ *a* three-sided, trilateral

trilingüe /tri'liŋgue/ *a* trilingual

trilla /'triʎa; 'triya/ *f*, red mullet; *Agr*. harrow; threshing; threshing season

trillado /tri'ʎaðo; tri'yaðo/ *a* frequented, trodden, worn (of paths); hackneyed

trilladora /triʎa'ðora; triya'ðora/ *f*, threshing machine

trillar /tri'ʎar; tri'yar/ *vt* to thresh; *Inf*. frequent; ill-treat

trillo /'triʎo; 'triyo/ *m*, threshing machine; harrow

trillón /tri'ʎon; tri'yon/ *m*, trillion

trilogía /trilo'hia/ *f*, trilogy

trimestral /trimes'tral/ *a* quarterly; terminal (in schools, etc.)

trimestre /tri'mestre/ *a* quarterly; terminal. *m*, quarter, three months; term (in schools, etc.); quarterly payment; quarterly rent

trinado /tri'naðo/ *m*, *Mus*. trill; twittering, shrilling (of birds)

trinar /tri'nar/ *vi Mus*. to trill; twitter, shrill; *Inf*. get in a temper, be furious

trincapiñones /trinkapi'ɲones/ *m*, *Inf*. scatterbrained youth

trincar /trin'kar/ *vt* to fasten securely; tie tightly; pinion; *Naut*. lash, make fast; cut up, chop; *Inf*. tipple; —*vi Naut*. sail close to the wind

trincha /'trintʃa/ *f*, vest strap

trinchante /trin'tʃante/ *m*, table carver; carving fork; stonecutter's hammer

trinchar /trin'tʃar/ *vt* to carve (at table); *Inf*. decide, dispose

trinchera /trin'tʃera/ *f*, *Mil*. trench; cutting (for roads, etc.); trench coat

trinchero /trin'tʃero/ *m*, platter, trencher; serving table, side table

trineo /tri'neo/ *m*, sled, sledge, sleigh

trinidad /trini'ðað/ *f*, trinity

trinomio /tri'nomio/ *m*, trinomial

trinquete /trin'kete/ *m*, *Naut*. mainmast; mainsail; *Sports*. rackets; *Mech*. ratchet

trinquis /'trinkis/ *m*, *Inf*. draft, drink

trío /'trio/ *m*, trio

tripa /'tripa/ *f*, entrail, gut; *Inf*. belly; inside (of some fruits). **hacer de tripas corazón**, *Inf*. to take heart, buck up. **revolver las tripas** (a), *Fig*. *Inf*. to make one sick

tripartición /triparti'θion; triparti'sion/ *f*, tripartition

tripartir /tripar'tir/ *vt* to divide into three

tripartito /tripar'tito/ *a* tripartite

tripicallos /tripi'kaʎos; tripi'kayos/ *m pl*, *Cul*. tripe

triple /'triple/ *a* triple; three-ply (of yarn)

triplicar /tripli'kar/ *vt* to treble

trípode /'tripoðe/ *m*, (sometimes *f*) three-legged stool or table; tripod; trivet

tripulación /tripula'θion; tripula'sion/ *f*, crew (ships and aircraft)

tripulante /tripu'lante/ *m*, crew member

tripular /tripu'lar/ *vt* to provide with a crew, man; equip, furnish; serve in, work as the crew of

trique /'trike/ *m*, crack, creak. *Inf*. **a cada t.**, at every moment

triquiñuela /triki'ɲuela/ *f*, *Inf*. evasion, subterfuge

triquitraque /triki'trake/ *m*, tap, rap; crack; firework

tris /tris/ *m*, crack, noise of glass, etc., cracking; *Inf*. instant, trice. **estar en un t.** (de), to be on the verge (of), within an inch (of)

trisar /tri'sar/ *vt* to crack, break, splinter (of glass); —*vi* chirp, twitter (especially of swallows)

trisca /'triska/ *f*, cracking, crushing, crackling (of nuts, etc.); noise, tumult

triscar /tris'kar/ *vi* to make a noise with the feet; gambol, frolic; creak, crack; —*vt* blend, mingle; set the teeth of a saw

trisecar /trise'kar/ *vt* to trisect

trisección /trisek'θion; trisek'sion/ *f*, trisection

trisemanal /trisema'nal/ *a* three times weekly; every three weeks

trisílabo /tri'silaβo/ *a* trisyllabic

trismo /'trismo/ *m*, lockjaw, trismus

triste /'triste/ *a* unhappy, sorrowful; melancholy, gloomy; sad; piteous, unfortunate; useless, worthless

tristeza, tristura /tris'teθa, tris'tura; tris'tesa, tris'tura/ *f*, unhappiness; melancholy, gloom; sadness; piteousness

tritón /tri'ton/ *m*, merman

triturar /tritu'rar/ *vt* to crumble, crush; chew; masticate; ill-treat, bruise; refute, contradict

triunfada /triun'faða/ *f*, trumping (at cards)

triunfador /triunfa'ðor/ **(-ra)** *a* triumphant —*n* victor

triunfal /triun'fal/ *a* triumphal

triunfante /triun'fante/ *a* triumphant

triunfar /triun'far/ *vi* to triumph; be victorious, win; trump (at cards); spend ostentatiously

triunfo /'triunfo/ *m*, triumph; victory; trump card; success; booty, spoils of war; conquest

triunvirato /triumbi'rato/ *m*, triumvirate

trivial /tri'βial/ *a* well-known, hackneyed; frequented, trodden; commonplace, mediocre; trivial, unimportant

trivialidad /triβiali'ðað/ *f*, banality, triteness; mediocrity; triviality

trivio /'triβio/ *m*, road junction

triza /'triθa; 'trisa/ *f*, fragment, bit; *Naut.* rope. **hacer trizas**, to smash to bits

trizar /tri'θar; tri'sar/ *vt* to smash up, destroy

trocada, a la /tro'kaða, a la/ *adv* contrariwise; in exchange

trocar /tro'kar/ *vt irr* to exchange; vomit; distort, misconstrue, mistake; —*vr* change, alter one's behavior; change places with another; be transferred. See **contar**

trocear /troθe'ar; trose'ar/ *vt* to divide into pieces

trocha /'trotʃa/ *f*, short cut; trail, path, track

trochemoche, a /trotʃe'motʃe, a/ *adv* *Inf.* without rhyme or reason, pell-mell

trofeo /tro'feo/ *m*, trophy; victory; military booty

troglodita /troglo'ðita/ *a* and *mf* troglodyte. *m*, *Fig.* savage, barbarian. *mf* glutton

troj /troh/ *f*, granary

trola /'trola/ *f*, *Inf.* lie, nonsense, hoax

trole /'trole/ *m*, trolley

trolebús /trole'βus/ *m*, trolley car

trolero /tro'lero/ *a* *Inf.* deceiving, lying

tromba /'tromba/ *f*, waterspout

trombón /trom'bon/ *m*, trombone; trombone player. **¡Trombones y platillos!** Great Scot!

trombosis /trom'bosis/ *f*, thrombosis

trompa /'trompa/ *f*, elephant's trunk; *Mus.* horn; proboscis (of insects); waterspout; humming top. **t. de Falopio**, fallopian tube

trompada /trom'paða/ *f*, *Inf.* bang, bump; blow, buffet, slap; collision

trompazo /trom'paθo; trom'paso/ *m*, heavy blow, knock, bang

trompear /trompe'ar/ *vi* to play with a top; —*vt* knock about

trompero /trom'pero/ *m*, top maker —*a* deceiving, swindling

trompeta /trom'peta/ *f*, trumpet; bugle. *m*, trumpeter; bugler; *Inf.* ninny. **t. de amor**, sunflower

trompetada /trompe'taða/ *f*, *Inf.* stupid remark, piece of nonsense

trompetazo /trompe'taθo; trompe'taso/ *m*, bray of a trumpet; bugle blast; *Inf.* stupid remark

trompetear /trompete'ar/ *vi Inf.* to play the trumpet or bugle

trompeteo /trompe'teo/ *m*, trumpeting, trumpet call; sound of the bugle

trompetería /trompete'ria/ *f*, collection of trumpets; metal organ pipes

trompetero /trompe'tero/ *m*, trumpet or bugle maker or player

trompetilla /trompe'tiʎa; trompe'tiya/ *f*, *dim* little trumpet; ear trumpet

trompicar /trompi'kar/ *vt* to make stumble, trip —*vi* stumble, trip up

trompo /'trompo/ *m*, humming or spinning top; *Inf.* dolt, idiot

tronada /tro'naða/ *f*, thunderstorm

tronado /tro'naðo/ *a* worn-out; threadbare, old; poor, poverty-stricken; down at the heels

tronar /tro'nar/ *v impers irr* to thunder; —*vi* growl, roar (of guns); *Inf.* go bankrupt, be ruined; *Inf.* protest against, attack; (*with con*) quarrel with —*Pres. Indic.* **trueno, truenas, truena, truenan.** *Pres. Subjunc.* **truene, truenes, truene, truenen**

troncal /tron'kal/ *a* trunk; main, principal

tronchar /tron'tʃar/ *vt* to break off, lop off (branches)

troncho /'trontʃo/ *m*, *Bot.* stem, stalk, branch

tronco /'tronko/ *m*, *Anat. Bot.* trunk; main body or line (of communications); trunk line; common origin, stock; *Inf.* blockhead, dolt; callous person. *Fig.* **estar hecho un t.**, to lie like a log; sleep like a log

tronera /tro'nera/ *f*, *Naut.* porthole; embrasure; slit window; pocket of a billiards table. *mf Inf.* madcap, harumscarum

trono /'trono/ *m*, throne; *Eccl.* tabernacle; shrine; kingly might; *pl* thrones, hierarchy of angels

tronzador /tronθa'ðor; tronsa'ðor/ *m*, two-handled saw

tronzar /tron'θar; tron'sar/ *vt* to smash, break into bits; *Sew.* pleat; exhaust, overtire

tropa /'tropa/ *f*, crowd (of people); troops, military; *Mil.* call to arms; *pl* army. **t. de línea**, regiment of the line. **tropas de asalto**, storm troopers. **tropas de refresco**, fresh troops. **en t.**, in a crowd; in groups

tropel /tro'pel/ *m*, rush, surge (of crowds, etc.); bustle, confusion; crowd, multitude; heap, jumble (of things). **en t.**, in a rush; in a crowd

tropelía /trope'lia/ *f*, rush, dash; violence; outrage

tropezar /trope'θar; trope'sar/ *vi irr* to stumble, slip; (*with con*) meet unexpectedly or accidentally come up against, be faced with (difficulties); quarrel with or oppose; fall into (bad habits). See **empezar**

tropezón /trope'θon; trope'son/ *m*, stumbling, slipping; stumbling block, obstacle. **a tropezones**, *Inf.* stumblingly; by fits and starts

tropical /tropi'kal/ *a* tropical

trópicos /'tropikos/ *m pl.* tropics

tropiezo /tro'pieθo; tro'pieso/ *m,* stumble; stumbling block, obstacle; hitch; impediment; slip, peccadillo, fault; difficulty, embarrassment; fight, skirmish; quarrel

tropo /'tropo/ *m,* trope, figure of speech

troquel /tro'kel/ *m,* die, mold

trotamundos /trota'mundos/ *m. Inf.* globetrotter

trotar /tro'tar/ *vi* to trot; *Inf.* hurry, get a move on

trote /'trote/ *m,* trot; toil, drudgery. **t. corto,** jog-trot. **al t.,** with all speed

trotón /tro'ton/ **(-ona)** *a* trotting. *m,* horse. *f,* chaperone

trova /'troβa/ *f,* verse; song, lay, ballad; love song

trovador /troβa'ðor/ **(-ra)** *m,* troubadour, minstrel —*n* poet

trovadoresco /troβaðo'resko/ *a* pertaining to minstrels, troubadour

trovar /tro'βar/ *vi* to compose verses; write ballads; misconstrue, misinterpret

trozo /'troθo; 'troso/ *m,* part, fragment; piece, portion; *Lit.* selection. **t. de abordaje,** *Nav.* landing party

trucha /'trutʃa/ *f,* trout. **t. asalmonada,** salmon trout

truco /'truko/ *m,* trick, deception

truculencia /truku'lenθia; truku'lensia/ *f,* harshness, cruelty, truculence

truculento /truku'lento/ *a* fierce, harsh, truculent

trueco /'trueko/ *m,* exchange. **a t. de,** in exchange for; on condition that

trueno /'trueno/ *m,* thunder; report, noise (of firearms); *Inf.* rake, scapegrace

trueque /'trueke/ *m,* exchange. **a. (** *or* **en) t.,** in exchange

trufa /'trufa/ *f, Bot.* truffle; nonsense, idle talk

trufar /tru'far/ *vt Cul.* to stuff with truffles; —*vi Inf.* lie, tell fibs

truhán /tru'an/ **(-ana)** *a* knavish, roguish, comic —*n* knave, rogue; clown, buffoon

truhanería /truane'ria/ *f,* knavery, act of a rogue; clowning, buffoonery; collection of rogues

trujar /tru'har/ *vt* to partition off

trulla /'truʎa/ 'truya/ *f,* uproar, tumult; crowd, throng

truncar /trun'kar/ *vt* to shorten, truncate; decapitate, mutilate; omit, cut out (words, etc.); curtail, abridge; mutilate, deform (texts, etc.)

tú /tu/ *pers pron 2nd sing mf* thou, you. **tratar de t. (a),** to address familiarly; be on intimate terms with

tu /tu/ *poss pron mf* thy, your. Used only before nouns

tubería /tuβe'ria/ *f,* piping, tubing; pipe system; pipe factory

tubo /'tuβo/ *m,* pipe, tube; lamp chimney; flue; *Anat.* duct, canal. **t. acústico,**

speaking tube. **t. de ensayo,** test tube. **t. de escape,** exhaust pipe. **t. lanzatorpedos,** torpedo tube. **t. termiónico,** *Radio.* thermionic valve

tucán /tu'kan/ *m,* toucan

tuerca /'tuerka/ *f,* nut (of a screw)

tuerto /'tuerto/ *a* one-eyed. *m, Law.* tort; *pl* afterpains. **a t.,** unjustly

tueste /'tueste/ *m,* toasting

tuétano /'tuetano/ *m,* marrow. *Inf.* **hasta los tuétanos,** to the depths of one's being

tufillas /tu'fiʎas; tu'fiyas/ *mf Inf.* easily irritated person

tufo /'tufo/ *m,* strong smell, poisonous vapor; *Inf.* stink; side, airs, conceit (often *pl*); lock of hair over the ears

tugurio /tu'gurio/ *m,* shepherd's hut; miserable little room; *Inf.* haunt, low dive

tulipán /tuli'pan/ *m,* tulip

tullido /tu'ʎiðo, tu'yiðo/ *a* partially paralyzed; maimed, crippled

tullir /tu'ʎir; tu'yir/ *vt irr* to maim, cripple; paralyze; —*vr* become paralyzed; be crippled. See **mullir**

tumba /'tumba/ *f,* tomb; tumble, overbalancing; somersault; Catherine wheel

tumbar /tum'bar/ *vt* to knock down; kill, drop; *Inf.* overpower, overcome (of odors, wine) —*vi* fall down; *Naut.* run aground; —*vr Inf.* lie down, stretch oneself out

tumbo /'tumbo/ *m,* tumble, overbalancing; undulation (of ground); rise and fall of sea waves; imminent danger; book containing deeds and privileges of monasteries and churches

tumbón /tum'bon/ *a Inf.* crafty, sly; idle, lazy. *m,* trunk with an arched lid

tumefacción /tumefak'θion; tumefak'sion/ *f,* swelling

tumefacto, túmido /tume'fakto, 'tumiðo/ *a* swollen

tumor /tu'mor/ *m,* tumor

tumulto /tu'multo/ *m,* riot, uprising; tumult, commotion, disturbance

tumultuario, tumultuoso /tumul'tuario, tumul'tuoso/ *a* noisy, tumultuous, confused

tuna /'tuna/ *f,* prickly pear tree or fruit; vagrant life; strolling student musicians (playing to raise money for charity)

tunante /tu'nante/ *a* rascally, roguish. *mf* rascal, scoundrel

tunantuelo /tunan'tuelo/ **(-la)** *n Inf.* imp, little rascal

tunda /'tunda/ *f,* shearing of cloth; *Inf.* sound beating, hiding

tundear /tunde'ar/ *vt* to beat, drub, buffet

tundidora /tundi'ðora/ *f,* woman who shears cloth; cloth-shearing machine; lawn mower

tundir /tun'dir/ *vt* to shear (cloth); mow (grass); *Inf.* beat, wallop

túnel /'tunel/ *m,* tunnel

túnica /'tunika/ *f,* tunic, chiton; tunicle; robe

tuno /'tuno/ **(-na)** *a* knavish, rascally
—*n* rascal, scoundrel

tupido /tu'piðo/ *a* thick, dense; obtuse,
dull, stupid

tupir /tu'pir/ *vt* to thicken, make dense;
press tightly; —*vr* stuff oneself with food
or drink

turba /'turβa/ *f*, crowd, multitude; peat

turbación /turβa'θion; turβa'sion/ *f*, disturbance; upset; perturbation; bewilderment, confusion; embarrassment

turbador /turβa'ðor/ **(-ra)** *a* disturbing,
upsetting —*n* disturber, upsetter

turbamulta /turβa'multa/ *f*, *Inf.* mob,
rabble

turbante /tur'βante/ *a* upsetting, perturbing. *m*, turban

turbar /tur'βar/ *vt* to disturb, upset;
make turbid, muddy; bewilder, confuse;
embarrass

turbina /tur'βina/ *f*, turbine

turbio /'turβio/ *a* turbid, muddy; trou-
blous; turbulent, disturbed; obscure, confused (style); indistinct, blurred, *m pl*,
lees, sediment (of oil)

turbión /tur'βion/ *m*, brief storm, squall;
Fig. shower, rush

turbulencia /turβu'lenθia; turβu'lensia/ *f*,
turbidity, muddiness; turbulence, commotion; disturbance, confusion

turbulento /turβu'lento/ *a* muddy, turbid; turbulent, disturbed; confused

turca /'turka/ *f*, *Inf.* drinking bout

turco /'turko/ **(-ca)** *a* Turkish —*n* Turk.
m, Turkish (language)

turgencia /tur'henθia; tur'hensia/ *f*,
swelling, turgidity

turgente /tur'hente/ *a* *Med.* turgescent;
Poet. turgid, prominent, swollen

turismo /tu'rismo/ *m*, touring, tourist industry. **coche de t.,** touring car

turista /tu'rista/ *mf* tourist

turno /'turno/ *m*, turn. **por t.,** in turn

turquesa /tur'kesa/ *f*, turquoise

Turquía /tur'kia/ Turkey

turrón /tu'rron/ *m*, kind of nougat; almond paste; *Inf.* soft job, sinecure; civil
service job

turulato /turu'lato/ *a* *Inf.* dumbfounded,
speechless, inarticulate

¡tus! /tus/ *interj* word for calling dogs.
sin decir t. ni mus, *Inf.* without saying
anything

tutear /tute'ar/ *vt* to address as tú (instead of the formal usted); treat familiarly

tutela /tu'tela/ *f*, guardianship; tutelage;
protection, defense

tuteo /tu'teo/ *m*, the use in speaking to a
person of the familiar tú instead of the
formal usted

tutor /tu'tor/ **(-ra)** *n* guardian. *m*, stake
(for plants); protector, defender

tuyo, tuya, tuyos, tuyas /'tuyo, 'tuya,
'tuyos, 'tuyas/ *poss pron 2nd sing* and *pl*
mf thine, yours. Used sometimes with
def. art. (e.g. *Este sombrero es el tuyo,*
This hat is yours)

u /u/ *f,* letter U —*conjunc* Used instead of **o** or before words beginning with **o** or **ho** (e.g. *fragante u oloroso*)

ubérrimo /u'βerrimo/ *a superl* most fruitful; very abundant

ubicación /uβika'θion; uβika'sion/ *f,* situation, position, location

ubicar /uβi'kar/ *vt* to place, situate; —*vi* and *vr* be situated

ubicuo /u'βikuo/ *a* omnipresent; ubiquitous

ubre /'uβre/ *f,* udder

ucelele /uθe'lele; use'lele/ *m,* ukulele

Ucrania /u'krania/ Ukraine

ucranio /u'kranio/ **(-ia)** *a* and *n* Ukrainian

¡uf! /uf/ *interj* ugh!

ufanarse /ufa'narse/ *vr* to pride oneself, put on airs

ufanía /ufa'nia/ *f,* pride, conceit

ufano /u'fano/ *a* conceited, vain; satisfied, pleased; expeditious, masterly

ujier /u'hier/ *m,* usher

úlcera /'ulθera; 'ulsera/ *f,* ulcer

ulceración /ulθera'θion; ulsera'sion/ *f,* ulceration

ulcerar /ulθe'rar; ulse'rar/ **(se)** *vt* and *vr* to ulcerate

ulterior /ulte'rior/ *a* farther, ulterior; subsequent

ulteriormente /ulterior'mente/ *adv* subsequently, later

ultimación /ultima'θion; ultima'sion/ *f,* ending, finishing

ultimar /ulti'mar/ *vt* to end, conclude

ultimátum /ulti'matum/ *m,* ultimatum

último /'ultimo/ *a* last; farthermost; ultimate; top; final, definitive; most valuable, best; latter; recent. **«Última Hora.»** "Stop Press." **a última hora,** *Fig.* at the eleventh hour. **en estos últimos años,** in recent years. **a últimos de mes,** towards the end of the month. **el ú. piso,** the top floor. **por ú.,** finally. *Inf.* **estar en las últimas,** to be at the end, be finishing

ultra /'ultra/, *adv* besides; (with words like *mar*) beyond; (as prefix) excessively

ultrajar /ultra'har/ *vt* to insult; scorn, despise

ultraje /ul'trahe/ *m,* insult, outrage

ultrajoso /ultra'hoso/ *a* offensive, insulting, abusive

ultramar /ultra'mar/ *m,* overseas, abroad

ultramarino /ultrama'rino/ *a* oversea; ultramarine. *m,* foreign produce (gen. *pl*)

ultrarrojo /ultra'rroho/ *a* infrared

ultratumba /ultra'tumba/ *adv* beyond the grave

ultravioleta /ultraβio'leta/ *a* ultraviolet

ululación /ulula'θion; ulula'sion/ *f,* screech, howl; hoot of an owl

ulular /ulu'lar/ *vi* to howl, shriek, screech; hoot (of an owl)

umbral /um'bral/ *m,* threshold; *Fig.* starting point; *Archit.* lintel. **atravesar** (*or* **pisar**) **los umbrales,** to cross the threshold

umbría /um'bria/ *f,* shady place

umbrío /um'brio/ *a* shady, dark

umbroso /um'broso/ *a* shady

un /un/ *Abbr.* of **uno, a,** one. Used before *m, sing f,* **una,** *indef art* a, an; a; one

unánime /u'nanime/ *a* unanimous

unanimidad /unanimi'ðað/ *f,* unanimity. **por u.,** unanimously

unción /un'θion; un'sion/ *f,* anointing; *Eccl.* Extreme Unction; unction, fervor

undécimo /un'deθimo; un'desimo/ *a* eleventh

undulación /undula'θion; undula'sion/ *f,* undulation; *Phys.* wave

undular /undu'lar/ *vi* to undulate; wriggle; float, wave (flags, etc.)

undulatorio /undula'torio/ *a* undulatory

ungir /un'hir/ *vt* to anoint

ungüento /uŋ'guento/ *m,* ointment; lotion; *Fig.* balm, unguent

único /'uniko/ *a* unique; sole, solitary, only. **Lo ú. que se puede hacer es...,** The only thing one can do is...

unicolor /uniko'lor/ *a* of one color

unidad /uni'ðað/ *f,* unity; unit; (*Math. Mil.*) unit. **u. de bagaje,** piece of baggage. (of drama) **u. de lugar,** unity of place. **u. de tiempo,** unity of time

unidamente /uniða'mente/ *adv* jointly; harmoniously

unificación /unifika'θion; unifika'sion/ *f,* unification

unificar /unifi'kar/ **(se)** *vt* and *vr* to unify, unite

uniformación /uniforma'θion; uniforma-'sion/ *f,* standardization

uniformar /unifor'mar/ *vt* to make uniform, standardize; put into uniform; —*vr* become uniform

uniforme /uni'forme/ *a* uniform; same, similar. *m,* uniform

uniformidad /uniformi'ðað/ *f,* uniformity

unilateral /unilate'ral/ *a* one-sided, unilateral

unión /u'nion/ *f,* union; correspondence, conformity; agreement; marriage; alliance, federation; composition; mixture; combination; proximity, nearness; (mystic) union

unionista /unio'nista/ *mf Polit.* unionist

unir /u'nir/ *vt* to unite, join; mix, combine; bind, fasten; connect, couple; bring together; marry; *Fig.* harmonize, conciliate; —*vr* join together, unite; be combined; marry; (*with prep* **a** or **con**) be near to; associate with

unísono /u'nisono/ *a* unisonant. **al u.,** in unison; unanimously

universal /uniβer'sal/ *a* universal; well-informed; widespread

universidad /uniβersi'ðað/ *f,* university; universality; universe

universitario /uniβersi'tario/ *a* university

universo /uni'βerso/ a universal. m, universe

uno /'uno/ (f, **una**) a a, one; single, only; same; pl some; about, nearly. m, one (number). **Tiene unos doce años,** He is about twelve. **unas pocas manzanas,** a few apples —pron someòne; one thing, same thing; pl some people. **No sabe uno qué creer,** One doesn't know what to believe. **Unos dicen que no, otros que sí,** Some (people) say no, others yes. **Juan no tiene libros y le voy a dar uno,** John has no books and I am going to give him one. **Todo es uno,** It's all the same. **u. a u.,** one by one. **u. que otro,** a few. **u. y otro,** both. **unos cuantos,** a few, some. **Es la una,** It is one o'clock

untar /un'tar/ vt to anoint; grease, oil; Inf. bribe; —vr smear oneself with grease or similar thing; Fig. Inf. line one's pockets. **u. el carro,** Fig. to grease the wheels

unto /'unto/ m, grease; animal fat; Fig. balm

untuoso /un'tuoso/ a fat, greasy

uña /'uɲa/ f, nail (of fingers or toes); hoof, trotter, claw; stinging tail of scorpion; thorn; stump of tree branch; Naut. fluke; Fig. Inf. light fingers (gen. pl). **afilarse las uñas,** to sharpen one's claws, prepare for trouble. **comerse las uñas,** to bite one's nails. **caer en las uñas de,** to fall into the clutches of. **hincar la u. (en),** to stick the claws into; to defraud, overcharge. **ser u. y carne,** to be devoted friends

uñero /u'ɲero/ m, ingrowing nail, ingrown nail

¡upa! /'upa/ interj Up you get! Up you go! Upsy daisy! (gen. to children)

uranio /u'ranio/ m, uranium

urbanidad /urβani'ðað/ f, civility, good manners, urbanity

urbanismo /urβa'nismo/ m, town planning; housing scheme

urbanizar /urβani'θar; urβani'sar/ vt to civilize, polish; urbanize

urbano /ur'βano/ a urban, city; urbane

urbe /'urβe/ f, city, metropolis

urbícola /ur'βikola/ mf city dweller

urdemalas /urðe'malas/ m, schemer, intriguer

urdidera /urði'ðera/ f, warping-frame

urdimbre /ur'ðimbre/ f, warp; scheming, plotting

urdir /ur'ðir/ vt to warp; weave; scheme, intrigue

uretra /u'retra/ f, urethra

urgencia /ur'henθia; ur'hensia/ f, urgency; necessity; compulsion

urgente /ur'hente/ a urgent

urgir /ur'hir/ vi to be urgent; be valid, be in force (laws)

urinario /uri'nario/ a urinary. m, urinal

urna /'urna/ f, urn; ballot box; glass case

urraca /u'rraka/ f, magpie

uruguayo /uru'guayo/ **(-ya)** a and n Uruguayan

usado /u'saðo/ a worn out; accustomed, efficient. Com. **al u.,** in the usual form. **ropa usada,** second-hand clothing, worn clothing

usanza /u'sanθa; usansa/ f, custom, usage

usar /u'sar/ vt to use; wear, make use of; follow (trade, occupation); —vi be accustomed

uso /'uso/ m, use; custom; fashion; habit; wear and tear. **al u.,** according to custom. **al u. de,** in the manner of

usted /us'teð/ mf you pl **ustedes.** Often abbreviated to **Vd, V, Vds, VV** or **Ud, Uds**

usual /u'sual/ a usual; general, customary; sociable

usufructo /usu'frukto/ m, Law. usufruct; life-interest; profit

usura /u'sura/ f, usury; profiteering. **pagar con u.,** to pay back a thousandfold

usurario /usu'rario/ a usurious

usurear /usure'ar/ vi to lend or borrow with usury; profiteer, make excess profits

usurero /usu'rero/ **(-ra)** n usurer; profiteer

usurpador /usurpa'ðor/ **(-ra)** a usurping —n usurper

usurpar /usur'par/ vt to usurp

utensilio /uten'silio/ m, utensil; tool, implement (gen. pl)

uterino /ute'rino/ a uterine

útero /'utero/ m, uterus

útil /'util/ a useful; profitable; Law. lawful (of days, etc.). m, usefulness, profit; pl **útiles,** utensils, tools

utilidad /utili'ðað/ f, utility; usefulness; profit

utilitario /utili'tario/ a utilitarian

utilizar /utili'θar; utili'sar/ vt to utilize

utillaje /uti'ʎahe; uti'yahe/ m, machinery

utópico /u'topiko/ a Utopian

uva /'uβa/ f, grape. **u. espina,** kind of gooseberry. **u. moscatel,** muscatel grape. Inf. **hecho una u.,** dead-drunk

uvero /u'βero/ **(-ra)** a pertaining or relating to grapes, grape —n grape seller

v /be/ f, letter V. **v doble** or **doble v**, letter W. **V** or **Vd, VV**, *Abbr.* **vuestra (s) merced (es)**, *mf sing and pl* you

vaca /ˈbaka/ f, cow. **v. de San Antón**, *Ent.* ladybug

vacación /baka'θion; baka'sion/ f, vacation, holiday (gen. *pl*); vacancy; act of vacating (employment). **vacaciones retribuidas**, paid vacation

vacada /ba'kaða/ f, herd of cows

vacancia /ba'kanθia; ba'kansia/ f, vacancy

vacante /ba'kante/ a vacant. f, vacancy

vacar /ba'kar/ vi to be vacant; take a holiday; retire temporarily; (*with prep a*) dedicate oneself to, engage in

vaciado /ba'θiaðo; ba'siaðo/ m, plaster cast; *Archit.* excavation

vaciamiento /baθia'miento; basia'miento/ m, emptying; molding, casting; depletion

vaciar /ba'θiar; ba'siar/ vt to empty; drain, drink; mold, cast; *Archit.* excavate; hone; copy; —vi flow (into) (rivers); —vr *Inf.* blurt out

vaciedad /baθie'ðað; basie'ðað/ f, emptiness; foolishness, inanity

vacilación /baθila'θion; basila'sion/ f, swaying; tottering; staggering; hesitation, perplexity

vacilante /baθi'lante; basi'lante/ a swaying; tottering; staggering; hesitating, vacillating

vacilar /baθi'lar; basi'lar/ vi to sway; totter; stagger; flicker; hesitate

vacío /ba'θio; ba'sio/ a empty, void; fruitless, vain; unoccupied, vacant, deserted; imperfect; hollow, empty; conceited, immature. m, hollow; *Anat.* flank; vacancy; shortage; *Phys.* vacuum. **v. de aire**, air-pocket. **de v.**, unloaded (carts, etc.). **en v.**, in vacuo. *Inf.* **hacer el v. (a)**, to send to Coventry

vacuidad /bakui'ðað/ f, emptiness; vacuity

vacuna /ba'kuna/ f, cowpox; vaccine. **v. antivariolosa**, smallpox vaccine

vacunación /bakuna'θion; bakuna'sion/ f, vaccination

vacunar /baku'nar/ vt to vaccinate; inoculate

vacuo /ˈbakuo/ a empty; vacant. m, void; vacuum

vadeable /baðe'aβle/ a fordable (rivers, etc.); *Fig.* surmountable

vadear /baðe'ar/ vt to ford, wade; *Fig.* overcome (obstacles); *Fig.* sound, find out the opinion (of); —vr behave

vademécum /baðe'mekum/ m, vade mecum; school satchel

vado /ˈbaðo/ m, ford; expedient, help

vagabundear /bagaβunde'ar/ vi to wander, roam, loiter

vagabundeo /bagaβun'deo/ m, vagabondage

vagabundo /baga'βundo/ (**-da**) a roving, wandering; vagrant —n tramp, vagabond

vagar /ba'gar/ m, leisure; interval, pause —vi be idle or at leisure; wander, roam

vagido /ba'hiðo/ m, cry, wail (infants)

vago /ˈbago/ (**-ga**) a vagrant, idle; vague; *Art.* indefinite, blurred —n idler. m, tramp; loafer. **en v.**, unsuccessfully, vainly

vagón /ba'gon/ m, wagon; (railway) coach. **v. comedor**, dining car

vagoneta /bago'neta/ f, open truck (railways, mines, etc.)

vaguear /bage'ar/ vi to roam, wander; loaf

vaguedad /bage'ðað/ f, vagueness; vague remark

vaharada /baa'raða/ f, whiff, exhalation

vahído /ba'iðo/ m, vertigo

vaho /ˈbao/ m, vapor, fume

vaina /ˈbaina/ f, scabbard; *Bot.* sheath, pod; case (scissors, etc.)

vainilla /bai'niʎa; bai'niya/ f, *Bot.* vanilla; *Sew.* drawn-thread work

vaivén /bai'βen/ m, swing, sway, seesaw; instability, fluctuation

vajilla /ba'hiʎa; ba'hiya/ f, china; dinner service

vale /ˈbale/ m, *Com.* bond, I.O.U., promissory note; voucher; valediction

valedero /bale'ðero/ a valid, binding

valedor /bale'ðor/ (**-ra**) n protector, sponsor

valentía /balen'tia/ f, bravery; heroic deed; boast; (*Art. Lit.*) dash, imagination, fire; superhuman effort

valentón /balen'ton/ a boastful, blustering

valer /ba'ler/ vt irr to protect; defend; produce (income, etc.); cost; —vi be worth; deserve; have power or authority; be of importance or worth; be a protection; be current (money); be valid; —vr (*with de*) make use of. m, value, worth. **v. la pena**, to be worthwhile. **v. tanto como cualquiera**, to be as good as the next guy, be as good as the next fellow. **¡Válgame Dios!** Heavens! Bless me! **Más vale así**, It's better thus. **Vale más ser cola de león que cabeza de ratón**. Better a big frog in a small puddle than a small frog in a big puddle —*Pres. Indic.* **valgo, vales**, etc —*Fut.* **valdré**, etc —*Condit.* **valdría**, etc —*Pres. Subjunc.* **valga**, etc.

valeroso /bale'roso/ a active, energetic; courageous; powerful

valía /ba'lia/ f, value, price; influence, worth; faction, party. **a las valías**, at the highest price

validación /baliða'θion; baliða'sion/ f, validation; force, soundness

validar /bali'ðar/ vt to make strong; validate

validez /bali'ðeθ; bali'ðes/ f, validity

valido /ba'liðo/ *a* favorite, esteemed. *m*, court favorite; prime minister

válido /'baliðo/ *a* firm, sound, valid; strong, robust

valiente /ba'liente/ *a* strong, robust; courageous; active; excellent; excessive; enormous (gen. *iron*); boastful

valija /ba'liha/ *f*, valise, suitcase, grip; mail bag; mail

valimiento /bali'miento/ *m*, value; favor; protection, influence

valioso /ba'lioso/ *a* valuable; powerful; wealthy

valisoletano /balisole'tano/ **(-na)** *a* and *n* of or from Valladolid

valla /'baʎa; 'baya/ *f*, barricade, paling; stockade; *Fig.* obstacle. **v. publicitaria,** billboard

vallado /ba'ʎaðo; ba'yaðo/ *m*, stockade; enclosure

valle /'baʎe; 'baye/ *m*, valley; vale; river-basin

valor /ba'lor/ *m*, worth, value; price; courage; validity; power; yield; income; insolence; *pl Com.* securities

valoración /balora'θion; balora'sion/ *f*, valuation; appraisement

valorar /balo'rar/ *vt* to value; appraise

valorización /baloriθa'θion; balorisa'sion/ *f*, valuation

vals /bals/ *m*, waltz

valsar /bal'sar/ *vi* to waltz

valuación /balua'θion; balua'sion/ *f*. See **valoración**

valuar /balu'ar/ *vt* to value; appraise; assess

válvula /'balβula/ *f*, *Mech.* valve. *Auto.* **v. de cámara (del neumático),** tire-valve. **v. de seguridad,** safety-valve

vampiro /bam'piro/ *m*, vampire; *Fig.* bloodsucker

vanagloria /bana'gloria/ *f*, vaingloriousness, conceit

vanagloriarse /banaglo'riarse/ *vr* to be conceited

vanaglorioso /banaglo'rioso/ **(-sa)** *a* conceited —*n* boaster

vanamente /bana'mente/ *adv* vainly; without foundation; superstitiously; arrogantly

vandalismo /banda'lismo/ *m*, vandalism; destructiveness

vanguardia /baŋ'guarðia/ *f*, vanguard; *pl* outerworks. **a v.,** in the forefront

vanidad /bani'ðað/ *f*, vanity; ostentation; empty words; illusion. *Inf.* **ajar la v. de,** to take (a person) down a peg

vanidoso /bani'ðoso/ **(-sa)** *a* vain; ostentatious —*n* conceited person

vano /'bano/ *a* vain; hollow, empty; useless, ineffectual; unsubstantial, illusory. *m*, span (bridge). **v. único,** single span. **en v.,** uselessly, in vain

vapor /ba'por/ *m*, steam, vapor; fainting fit; steamboat; *pl* hysterics. **v. de ruedas, v. de paleta,** paddle steamer. **v. volan-**

dero, tramp steamer. **al v.,** full steam ahead; *Inf.* with all speed

vaporación /bapora'θion; bapora'sion/ *f*, evaporation

vaporización /baporiθa'θion; baporisa-'sion/ *f*, vaporization

vaporizador /baporiθa'ðor; baporisa'ðor/ *m*, vaporizer; spray, sprayer

vaporizar /bapori'θar; bapori'sar/ *vt* to vaporize; spray

vaporoso /bapo'roso/ *a* vaporous; ethereal; gauzy

vapular /bapu'lar/ *vt* to whip

vapuleo /bapu'leo/ *m*, whipping, spanking

vaquería /bake'ria/ *f*, herd of cattle; dairy; dairy farm

vaquero /ba'kero/ **(-ra)** *n* cowboy; **vaqueros,** *m*, *pl* jeans

vara /'bara/ *f*, staff; rod; wand (of authority); vara (nearly one yard); shaft (of cart). **v. de aforar,** water gauge

varar /ba'rar/ *vi Naut.* to run aground; *Fig.* be held up (negotiations, etc.); —*vt Naut.* put in dry dock

varear /bare'ar/ *vt* to knock down (fruit from tree); beat (with a rod); measure with a rod; sell by the rod; —*vr* grow thin

variabilidad /bariaβili'ðað/ *f*, variableness

variable /ba'riaβle/ *a* variable; changeable, inconsistent

variación /baria'θion; baria'sion/ *f*, variation

variado /ba'riaðo/ *a* varied; variegated

variante /ba'riante/ *a* varying. *f*, variant; discrepancy

variar /ba'riar/ *vt* to vary; change; —*vi* change; be different

varicela /bari'θela; bari'sela/ *f*, chicken pox

varicoso /bari'koso/ *a* varicose

variedad /barie'ðað/ *f*, variety; change; inconstancy, instability; alteration; variation; *Biol.* variety

varilla /ba'riʎa; ba'riya/ *f*, *dim* rod; rib (fan, umbrella). **v. de virtudes,** conjurer's wand. *Mech.* **v. percusora,** tappet rod

vario /'bario/ *a* different, diverse; inconstant, changeable; variegated; *pl* some, a few

varón /ba'ron/ *m*, male; man

varonil /baro'nil/ *a* male; manly

Varsovia /bar'soβia/ Warsaw

vasallaje /basa'ʎahe; basa'yahe/ *m*, vassalage; dependence; tribute money

vasallo /ba'saʎo; ba'sayo/ **(-lla)** *n* vassal —*a* vassal; dependent

vasco /'basko/ **(-ca), vascongado (-da)** *a* and *n* Basque

vascuence /bas'kuenθe; bas'kuense/ *m*, Basque (language); *Inf.* gibberish

vaselina /base'lina/ *f*, vaseline

vasija /ba'siha/ *f*, vessel, receptacle, jar

vaso /'baso/ *m*, receptacle; glass, tankard,

mug; glassful; (*Naut. Anat. Bot.*) vessel; garden-urn; vase

vástago /'bastago/ *m,* stem, shoot; offspring, descendant; piston rod

vastedad /baste'ðað/ *f,* extensiveness, largeness, vastness

vasto /'basto/ *a* vast, extensive

vate /'bate/ *m,* bard; seer

vaticano /bati'kano/ *a* and *m,* Vatican

vaticinar /batiθi'nar; batisi'nar/ *vt* to prophesy, foretell

vaticinio /bati'θinio; bati'sinio/ *m,* prediction

vatio /'batio/ *m,* watt.. **v. hora,** watt hour

ve /be/ *f,* name of the letter V. **v. doble** *or* **doble v.,** name of the letter W

vecinal /beθi'nal; besi'nal/ *a* neighboring

vecindad /beθin'dað; besin'dað/ *f,* neighborhood. **buena v.,** good neighborliness. **hacer mala v.,** to be a nuisance to one's neighbors

vecindario /beθin'dario; besin'dario/ *m,* neighborhood; population of a district

vecino /be'θino; be'sino/ **(-na)** *a* neighboring; near; similar —*n* neighbor; citizen; inhabitant

vector /bek'tor/ *m,* carrier (of disease)

veda /'beða/ *f,* close season; prohibition

vedamiento /beða'miento/ *m,* prohibition

vedar /be'ðar/ *vt* to forbid; prevent

vedija /be'ðiha/ *f,* tangled lock of hair; piece of matted wool; curl (of smoke)

vega /'bega/ *f,* fertile lowland plain; meadow

vegada /be'gaða/ *f.* See **vez**

vegetal /behe'tal/ *a* vegetal; plant. *m,* vegetable, plant

vegetar /behe'tar/ *vi* to flourish, grow (plants); *Fig.* vegetate

vegetariano /beheta'riano/ **(-na)** *a* and *n* vegetarian

vehemencia /bee'menθia; bee'mensia/ *f,* vehemence

vehemente /bee'mente/ *a* vehement; vivid

vehículo /be'ikulo/ *m,* vehicle; means, instrument

veinte /'beinte/ *a* and *m,* twenty; twentieth

veintena /bein'tena/ *f,* a score

veinticinco /beinti'θinko; beinti'sinko/ *a* and *m,* twenty-five; twenty-fifth

veinticuatro /beinti'kuatro/ *a* and *m,* twenty-four; twenty-fourth

veintidós /beinti'ðos/ *a* and *m,* twenty-two; twenty-second

veintinueve /beinti'nueβe/ *a* and *m,* twenty-nine; twenty-ninth

veintiocho /beinti'otʃo/ *a* and *m,* twenty-eight; twenty-eighth

veintiséis /beinti'seis/ *a* and *m,* twenty-six; twenty-sixth

veintisiete /beinti'siete/ *a* and *m,* twenty-seven; twenty-seventh

veintitrés /beinti'tres/ *a* and *m,* twenty-three; twenty-third

veintiuno /bein'tiuno/ *a* and *m,* twenty-one; twenty-first. Abbreviates to **veintiún** before a noun (even if one or more adjectives intervene)

vejación /beha'θion; beha'sion/ *f,* illtreatment, persecution

vejamen /be'hamen/ *m,* irritation, provocation; taunt; lampoon

vejar /be'har/ *vt* to ill-treat, persecute; plague

vejatorio /beha'torio/ *a* vexing, annoying

vejete /be'hete/ *m, Inf.* silly old man

vejez /be'heθ; be'hes/ *f,* oldness; old age; platitude. **vejeces,** *pl* ailments of old age.

vejiga /be'higa/ *f,* bladder; blister. **v. natatoria,** float (of a fish)

vela /'bela/ *f,* vigil; watch; pilgrimage; sentinel, watchman; candle; *Naut.* sail; awning; night work, overtime. **v. de cangreja,** boom sail. **v. de mesana,** mizzen sail. **v. de trinquete,** foresail. **v. latina,** lateen sail. **a toda v.,** with all speed. **alzar velas,** to hoist sail. **en v.,** wakeful, without sleep. *Inf.* **estar entre dos velas,** to be tipsy

velación /bela'θion; bela'sion/ *f,* vigil; watch; marriage ceremony of veiling (gen. *pl*)

velada /be'laða/ *f,* vigil; watch; evening party

velado /be'laðo/ *a* veiled; dim; (of voice) thick, indistinct

velador /bela'ðor/ **(-ra)** *a* watchful; vigilant. *m,* candlestick; small round table —*n* watcher, guard

velar /be'lar/ *vt* to watch, be wakeful; work overtime or at night; *Eccl.* watch; *Fig.* (with *por*) watch over, defend; —*vt* veil; conceal; *Photo.* blur; (with *prep a*) wake (corpse); sit with (patient at night)

veleidad /belei'ðað/ *f,* velleity; fickleness

veleidoso /belei'ðoso/ *a* inconstant, changeable

velero /be'lero/ **(-ra)** *m,* sailing ship; sailmaker —*n* candlemaker

veleta /be'leta/ *f,* weathercock; float, quill (fishing). *mf* changeable person

vello /'beʎo; 'beyo/ *m,* down, soft hair

vellocino /beʎo'θino; beyo'sino/ *m,* wool; fleece

vellón /be'ʎon; be'yon/ *m,* fleece; copper and silver alloy formerly used in sense of "sterling"; *Obs.* copper coin

vellosidad /beʎosi'ðað; beyosi'ðað/ *f,* downiness, hairiness

velloso /be'ʎoso; be'yoso/ *a* downy, hairy

velludo /be'ʎuðo; be'yuðo/ *a* hairy, downy. *m,* plush, velvet

velo /'belo/ *m,* veil; curtain; *Eccl.* humeral veil; excuse, pretext; *Zool.* velum. **v. del paladar,** soft palate. **correr el v.,** to disclose a secret. **tomar el v.,** to take the veil, become a nun

velocidad /beloθi'ðað; belosi'ðað/ *f,*

speed; *Mech.* velocity. *Aer.* **v. ascensio-nal**, rate of climb. *Mech.* **v. del choque**, speed of impact. **en gran v.**, by passenger train. **en pequeña v.**, by goods train

velocípedo /belo'θipeðo; belo'sipeðo/ *m*, velocipede

velódromo /be'loðromo/ *m*, velodrome

velón /be'lon/ *m*, oil lamp

veloz /be'loθ; be'los/ *a* swift; quick-thinking or acting

vena /'bena/ *f*, (*Bot. Anat.*) vein; streak, veining (in wood or stone); *Mineral.* seam; underground spring; inspiration. **estar de v.**, to be in the mood; be inspired

venablo /be'naβlo/ *m*, javelin

venado /be'naðo/ *m*, venison; deer

venal /be'nal/ *a* venous; saleable; venal

venalidad /benali'ðað/ *f*, saleableness; venality

vencedor /benθe'ðor; bense'ðor/ **(-ra)** *a* conquering —*n* conqueror

vencer /ben'θer; ben'ser/ *vt* to conquer; defeat; overcome, rise above; outdo, excel; restrain, control (emotions); convince, persuade; —*vi* succeed, triumph; *Com.* fall due, mature; *Com.* expire; —*vr* control oneself; twist, incline

vencible /ben'θiβle; ben'siβle/ *a* conquerable; superable

vencimiento /benθi'miento; bensi'miento/ *m*, defeat; conquest, victory; bend, twist (of things); *Com.* expiration; *Com.* maturity (of a bill)

venda /'benda/ *f*, bandage; fillet. **tener una v. en los ojos**, to be blind (to the truth)

vendaje /ben'dahe/ *m*, bandage

vendar /ben'dar/ *vt* to bandage; *Fig.* blind (generally passions)

vendaval /benda'βal/ *m*, strong wind

vendedor /bende'ðor/ **(-ra)** *a* selling —*n* seller

vender /ben'der/ *vt* to sell; betray; —*vr* sell oneself; be sold; risk all (for someone); *Fig.* give away (secret); (*with por*) sell under false pretences. **v. al contado**, to sell for cash. **v. al por mayor**, to sell wholesale. **v. al por menor**, to sell retail. **venderse caro**, to be unsociable

vendí /ben'di/ *m*, *Com.* certificate of sale

vendible /ben'diβle/ *a* purchasable; saleable

vendimia /ben'dimia/ *f*, vintage; profit, fruits

vendimiador /bendimia'ðor/ **(-ra)** *n* vintager

vendimiar /bendi'miar/ *vt* to harvest the grapes; take advantage of; *Inf.* kill

Venecia /be'neθia; be'nesia/ Venice

veneciano /bene'θiano; bene'siano/ **(-na)** *a* and *n* Venetian

veneno /be'neno/ *m*, poison; venom; danger (to health or soul); evil passion

venenosidad /benenosi'ðað/ *f*, poisonousness

venenoso /bene'noso/ *a* poisonous, venomous

venera /be'nera/ *f*, scallop-shell (pilgrim's badge); badge, decoration

veneración /benera'θion; benera'sion/ *f*, respect, veneration

venerador /benera'ðor/ **(-ra)** *a* venerating —*n* venerator, respector

venerar /bene'rar/ *vt* to venerate; worship

venéreo /be'nereo/ *a* venereal

venero /be'nero/ *m*, spring of water; horary line on sundial; origin, genesis; *Mineral.* bed

venezolano /beneθo'lano; beneso'lano/ **(-na)** *a* and *n* Venezuelan

vengador /benga'ðor/ **(-ra)** *a* avenging —*n* avenger

venganza /ben'ganθa; ben'gansa/ *f*, revenge

vengar /ben'gar/ *vt* to avenge; —*vr* avenge oneself

vengativo /benga'tiβo/ *a* vindictive

venia /'benia/ *f*, pardon, forgiveness; permission; inclination of head (in greeting); *Law.* license issued to minors to manage their own estate

venial /be'nial/ *a* venial

venialidad /beniali'ðað/ *f*, veniality

venida /be'niða/ *f*, arrival, coming; return; attack (fencing); precipitancy

venidero /beni'ðero/ *a* future

venideros /beni'ðeros/ *m pl*, successors; posterity

venir /be'nir/ *vi irr* to come; arrive; turn up (at cards); fit, suit, consent, agree; *Agr.* grow; follow, come after, succeed; result, originate; occur (to the mind); feel, experience; (*with prep a* + *infin.*) happen finally, come to pass; (*with en*) decide, resolve; —*vr* ferment. **v. a menos**, to deteriorate, decline; come upon evil days. **v. a pelo**, to come opportunely, be just right. **v. a ser**, to become. **venirse abajo**, to fall, collapse. **¿A qué viene este viaje?** What is the purpose of this journey? **el mes que viene**, next month. **El vestido te viene muy ancho**, The dress is too wide for you. **Me vino la idea de marcharme**, It occurred to me to leave. **en lo por venir**, in the future —*Pres. Indic.* **vengo, vienes, viene, venimos, venís, vienen.** *Pres. Part.* **viniendo.** *Fut.* **vendré**, etc —*Condit.* **vendría**, etc —*Preterite* **vine, viniste, vino, vinimos, vinisteis, vinieron.** *Pres. Subjunc.* **venga**, etc —*Imperf. Subjunc.* **viniese**, etc.

venoso /be'noso/ *a* veined; venous

venta /'benta/ *f*, selling; sale; inn; *Inf.* wilderness; *pl Com.* turnover. **v. pública**, auction. **a la v.**, on sale. **la V. de la Mesilla**, the Gadsden Purchase

ventada /ben'taða/ *f*, gust of wind

ventaja /ben'taha/ *f*, advantage; profit

ventajoso /benta'hoso/ *a* advantageous

ventana /ben'tana/ *f*, window. **v. de guillotina**, sash window. **v. salediza**, bay window. **echar algo por la v.,** to waste a thing

ventanal /benta'nal/ *m,* large window

ventanilla /benta'niʎa; benta'niya/ *f,* small window (as in railway compartments); grill (ticket office, bank, etc.); nostril

ventarrón /benta'rron/ *m,* high wind

ventear /bente'ar/ *v impers* to blow (of the wind); —*vt* sniff air (animals); air, dry; investigate; —*vr* be spoiled by air (tobacco, etc.)

ventero /ben'tero/ **(-ra)** *n* innkeeper

ventilación /bentila'θion; bentila'sion/ *f,* ventilation; ventilator; current of air

ventilador /bentila'ðor/ *m,* ventilating fan; ventilator

ventilar /benti'lar/ *vt* to ventilate; shake, winnow; air; discuss

ventisca /ben'tiska/ *f,* snowstorm

ventiscar, ventisquear /bentis'kar, bentiske'ar/ *v impers* to snow with a high wind

ventisquero /bentis'kero/ *m,* glacier; snowfield, snowdrift; snowstorm

ventolera /bento'lera/ *f,* gust of wind; *Inf.* boastfulness; whim, caprice

ventor /ben'tor/ **(-ra)** *n* pointer (dog)

ventosa /ben'tosa/ *f,* vent (pipes, etc.); *Zool.* sucker; *Surg.* cupping glass

ventosidad /bentosi'ðað/ *f,* flatulence

ventoso /ben'toso/ *a* windy; flatulent

ventrículo /ben'trikulo/ *m,* ventricle

ventrílocuo /ben'trilokuo/ **(-ua)** *a* ventriloquial —*n* ventriloquist

ventriloquia /bentri'lokia/ *f,* ventriloquism

ventrudo /ben'truðo/ *a* big-bellied

ventura /ben'tura/ *f,* happiness; chance, hazard; risk, danger. **a la v.,** at a venture. **buena v.,** good luck. **por v.,** perhaps; by chance; fortunately

venturoso /bentu'roso/ *a* fortunate

Venus /'benus/ *m,* Venus. *f,* beautiful woman, beauty

ver /ber/ *vt irr* to see; witness, behold; visit; inspect, examine; consider; observe; know, understand; (*with de + infin.*) try to; —*vr* be seen; show oneself, appear; experience, find oneself; exchange visits; meet. **v. mundo,** to travel. **V. y creer,** Seeing is believing. **A mi v.,** In my opinion. **¡A v.!** Let's see!; Wait and see! **no tener nada que v. con,** to have no connection with, nothing to do with. **Veremos,** Time will tell. **Verse en la casa,** to be a stay-at-home. **Ya se ve,** Of course, Naturally —*Pres. Indic.* **veo, ves,** etc —*Imperf.* **veía,** etc —*Past Part.* **visto.** *Pres. Subjunc.* **vea,** etc —*Imperf. Subjunc.* **viese,** etc

vera /'bera/ *f,* edge; border; shore. **a la v.,** on the edge, on the verge

veracidad /beraθi'ðað; berasi'ðað/ *f,* truthfulness, veracity

veraneante /berane'ante/ *mf* summer

resident, summer vacationist, holiday-maker

veranear /berane'ar/ *vi* to spend the summer

veraneo /bera'neo/ *m,* summer vacation, summer holidays, summering

veraniego /bera'niego/ *a* summer; light, unimportant

verano /be'rano/ *m,* summer; dry season *West Hem.*

veras /'beras/ *f pl,* reality, truth; fervor, earnestness. **de v.,** really; in earnest

veraz /be'raθ; be'ras/ *a* truthful, veracious

verbal /ber'ßal/ *a* verbal; oral

verbena /ber'ßena/ *f, Bot.* verbena, vervain; fair held on eve of a saint's day

verbigracia /berßi'graθia; berßi'grasia/ *adv* for instance. *m,* example

verbo /'berßo/ *m,* word; vow; *Gram.* verb. **v. activo** *or* **v. transitivo,** active or transitive verb. **v. auxiliar,** auxiliary verb. **v. intransitivo** *or* **v. neutro,** intransitive or neuter verb. **v. reflexivo** *or* **v. recíproco,** reflexive verb

verbosidad /berßosi'ðað/ *f,* verbosity

verboso /ber'ßoso/ *a* verbose, prolix

verdad /ber'ðað/ *f,* truth, veracity; reality. **a la v.,** indeed; without doubt. **en v.,** in truth; indeed. **cantar cuatro verdades a alguien,** to tell someone a few home truths. **la pura v.,** the plain truth

verdadero /berða'ðero/ *a* true; real; sincere; truthful

verdal /ber'ðal/ *a* green. **ciruela v.,** greengage

verde /'berðe/ *a* green; unripe; fresh (vegetables); youthful; immature, undeveloped; obscene, dissolute. *m,* green (color); verdure, foliage

verdear /berðe'ar/ *vi* to look green; be greenish; grow green

verdecer /berðe'θer; berðe'ser/ *vi irr* to grow green, be verdant. See **conocer**

verdín /ber'ðin/ *m,* verdure; mold; verdigris

verdinegro /berði'negro/ *a* dark green

verdor /ber'ðor/ *m,* verdure; greenness; strength; youth (also *pl*)

verdoso /ber'ðoso/ *a* greenish

verdugo /ber'ðugo/ *m,* hangman, executioner; wale, mark; shoot of tree; switch; whip; *Fig.* scourge; tyrant

verdulera /berðu'lera/ *f,* greengrocer; market woman; *Inf.* harridan

verdulería /berðule'ria/ *f,* greengrocer's shop

verdulero /berðu'lero/ *m,* greengrocer

verdura /ber'ðura/ *f,* verdure; green garden produce, vegetables (gen. *pl*); *Art.* foliage; obscenity

verecundo /bere'kundo/ *a* bashful

vereda /be'reða/ *f,* footpath; sheep track

veredicto /bere'ðikto/ *m, Law.* verdict; judgment, considered opinion

verga /'berga/ *f,* steel bow of crossbow; *Naut.* yard; *Inf.* penis

vergel /ber'hel/ *m,* orchard

vergonzoso /bergon'θoso; bergon'soso/ **(-sa)** *a* shameful; bashful, shamefaced —*n* shy person

vergüenza /ber'gwenθa; ber'gwensa/ *f.* shame; self-respect; bashfulness, timidity; shameful act; public punishment

vericueto /beri'kueto/ *m.* narrow, stony path

verídico /be'riðiko/ *a* veracious; true, exact

verificación /berifika'θion; berifika'sion/ *f.* verification, checking; *Law.* **v. de un testamento**, probate

verificador /berifika'ðor/ **(-ra)** *a* verifying, checking —*n* inspector, checker

verificar /berifi'kar/ *vt* to prove; verify; —*vr* take place, happen; check; come true. *Elec.* **v. las conexiones,** to check the connections

verisímil /beri'simil/ *a* credible, probable

verja /'berha/ *f.* grating, grill; railing

vermut /ber'mut/ *m.* vermouth

vernáculo /ber'nakulo/ *a* native, vernacular

verosímil /bero'simil/ *a* credible, probable

verosimilitud /berosimili'tuð/ *f.* verisimilitude, probability

verruga /be'rruga/ *f.* *Med.* wart; *Inf.* bore; defect

versar /ber'sar/ *vi* to revolve; *(with sobre)* concern, deal with (book, etc.); —*vr* become versed (in)

versátil /ber'satil/ *a* *Zool.* versatile; changeable; fickle

versatilidad /bersatili'ðað/ *f.* *Zool.* versatility; changeableness; fickleness

versículo /ber'sikulo/ *m.* versicle; verse (of the Bible)

versificar /bersifi'kar/ *vi* to write verses; —*vt* put into verse, versify

versión /ber'sion/ *f.* translation; version; account

verso /'berso/ *m.* poetry, verse; stanza; line (of a poem). **v. suelto,** blank verse

vertedor /berte'ðor/ *m.* drain, sewer; chute

verter /ber'ter/ *vt irr* to pour; spill; empty; translate; —*vi* flow. See **entender**

vertical /berti'kal/ *a* and *f.*, vertical

vertiente /ber'tiente/ *a* emptying. *mf.* slope, incline; watershed

vertiginoso /bertihi'noso/ *a* giddy; vertiginous

vértigo /'bertigo/ *m.* giddiness, faintness

vesícula /be'sikula/ *f.* blister; *(Anat. Bot.)* vesicle

vespertino /besper'tino/ *a* evening

vestíbulo /bes'tiβulo/ *m.* hall, vestibule foyer

vestido /bes'tiðo/ *m.* dress; clothes

vestidura /besti'ðura/ *f.* garment; *pl* vestments

vestigio /bes'tihio/ *m.* footprint, trace, mark; remains; *Fig.* vestige

vestir /bes'tir/ *vt irr* to clothe, dress; adorn; embellish (ideas); *Fig.* disguise (truth); simulate, pretend; —*vi* be dressed; —*vr* dress oneself; *Fig.* be covered. See **pedir**

vestuario /bes'tuario/ *m.* clothing, dress; *Theat.* wardrobe or dressing room; *Eccl.* vestry; *Mil.* uniform

veta /'beta/ *f.* vein; stripe, rib (fabric)

veterano /bete'rano/ **(-na)** *a* and *n* veteran

veterinaria /beteri'naria/ *f.* veterinary science

veterinario /beteri'nario/ *a* veterinary. *m.* veterinary surgeon

veto /'beto/ *m.* veto; prohibition

vetusto /be'tusto/ *a* ancient, very old

vez /beθ/ *f.* time, occasion; turn; *pl* proxy, deputy, substitute. **a la v.,** simultaneously. **alguna v.,** sometime. **a su v.,** in its (her, his, their) turn. **a veces,** sometimes. **de una v.,** at the one time. **de v. en cuando,** from time to time. **en v. de,** instead of. **hacer las veces de,** to be a substitute for. **otra v.,** again. **Su cuarto es dos veces más grande que éste,** His room is twice as large as this one

vía /'bia/ *f.* way; road; railway track or gauge; *Anat.* tract; (mystic) way; route; conduct; *pl* procedure. **v. ancha,** broad gauge (railway). **v. angosta,** narrow gauge. **v. de agua,** *Naut.* leak. *Law.* **v. ejecutiva,** seizure, attachment. **v. férrea,** railway. **v. láctea,** Milky Way. **v. muerta,** railway siding. **v. principal,** main line. **v. pública,** public thoroughfare. **v. romana,** Roman road. **v. secundaria,** *Rail.* side line. **por v. aérea,** by air, by airplane

viable /'biaβle/ *a* viable; practicable; workable; passable

viaducto /bia'ðukto/ *m.* viaduct

viajante /bia'hante/ *mf* traveling salesman, commercial traveler

viajar /bia'har/ *vi* to travel, journey, voyage

viaje /'biahe/ *m.* journey; voyage; water-supply; travel journal; *Naut.* **v. de ensayo,** trial trip. **v. redondo,** circular tour. **¡Buen v.!** Have a good trip! Bon voyage!

viajero /bia'hero/ **(-ra)** *a* traveling —*n* traveler; passenger

víbora /'biβora/ *f.* viper

vibración /biβra'θion; biβra'sion/ *f.* vibration; jar, jolt; thrill

vibrante /bi'βrante/ *a* shaking; vibrant; thrilling

vibrar /bi'βrar/ *vt* to shake, oscillate; —*vi* vibrate; jar, jolt; quiver, thrill

vibratorio /biβra'torio/ *a* vibratory, vibrative

vicario /bi'kario/ *a* vicarious. *m.*, vicar; curate; deputy

vicepresidente /biθepresi'ðente; bisepresi'ðente/ **(-ta)** *n* vice president

viciar /bi'θiar; bi'siar/ *vt* to corrupt; adulterate; forge; annul; interpret maliciously, misconstrue; —*vr* become vicious

vicio /'biθio; 'bisio/ *m.* vice; defect; error, fraud; bad habit; excess, exaggerated desire; viciousness (animals); overgrowth (plants); peevishness (children). **tener el v. de,** to have the bad habit of. **el v. del juego,** fondness for gambling

vicioso /bi'θioso; bi'sioso/ *a* vicious; vigorous, overgrown; abundant; *Inf.* spoiled (children)

vicisitud /biθisi'tuð; bisisi'tuð/ *f,* vicissitude

víctima /'biktima/ *f,* victim

¡víctor! /'biktor/ *interj* Victor!; Long live!; Hurrah!

victoria /bik'toria/ *f,* victory, triumph; victoria

victoriano /bikto'riano/ **(-na)** *a* and *n* Victorian

victorioso /bikto'rioso/ *a* victorious

vid /bið/ *f,* vine

vida /'biða/ *f,* life; livelihood; human being; biography; vivacity. **v. airada,** dissolute life. **la v. allende la muerte,** life after death. **de por v.,** for life. **darse buena v.,** to live comfortably; enjoy one's life. **dar mala v.,** to ill-treat. **en la v.,** in life; never. **ganarse la v.,** to make one's living

vidente /bi'ðente/ *m,* clairvoyant; seer

videograbación /biðeograβa'θion; biðeograβa'sion/ *f,* videotape

vidriar /bi'ðriar/ *vt* to glaze (earthenware)

vidriera /bi'ðriera/ *f,* glass window (gen. stained or colored)

vidriero /bi'ðriero/ *m,* glazier —*a* made of glass

vidrio /'biðrio/ *m,* glass; anything made of glass; fragile thing; touchy person. **v. inastillable,** safety-glass. **v. jaspeado,** frosted glass. **v. pintado** or **v. de color,** stainedglass. **v. plano,** plate glass. **v. soplado,** blown glass

vidrioso /bi'ðrioso/ *a* brittle; slippery; fragile; hypersensitive; *Fig.* glazed (eyes)

vieja /'bieha/ *f,* old woman

viejo /'bieho/ *a* old; ancient; former; oldfashioned; worn out. *m,* old man

Viena /'biena/ Vienna

vienés /bie'nes/ **(-esa)** *a* and *n* Viennese

viento /'biento/ *m,* wind; scent (of game, etc.); guy (rope); upheaval; vanity. **v. en popa,** *Naut.* following wind; without a hitch, prosperously. **vientos alisios,** trade-winds. **v. terral,** land wind. **a los cuatro vientos,** in all directions. **contra v. y marea,** *Fig.* against all obstacles. **correr malos vientos,** to be unfavorable (of circumstances). **refrescar el v.,** to stiffen (of the breeze)

vientre /'bientre/ *m,* stomach; belly; vitals; *Law.* venter

viernes /'biernes/ *m,* Friday. **V. Santo,** Good Friday

viga /'biga/ *f,* beam, rafter; girder; joist; mill beam. **v. maestra,** main beam or girder

vigente /bi'hente/ *a* valid; in force (laws, customs)

vigésimo /bi'hesimo/ *a* twentieth

vigía /bi'hia/ *f,* watch tower; (gen. *m*) look-out, watch

vigilancia /bihi'lanθia; bihi'lansia/ *f,* watchfulness, vigilance; watch patrol

vigilante /bihi'lante/ *a* watchful. *m,* watcher; watchman. **v. escolar,** truant officer

vigilar /bihi'lar/ *vi* to watch over; supervise

vigilia /bi'hilia/ *f,* vigil; wakefulness; night study; *Eccl.* vigil, eve; wake; *Mil.* watch. **día de v.,** fast-day

vigor /bi'gor/ *m,* strength; activity; vigor, efficiency; validity

vigorizar /bigori'θar; bigori'sar/ *vt* to invigorate; exhilarate; encourage

vigorosidad /bigorosi'ðað/ *f,* vigorousness

vigoroso /bigo'roso/ *a* strong, vigorous

vihuela /bi'uela/ *f,* lute

vil /bil/ *a* vile, infamous; base, despicable; untrustworthy

vileza /bi'leθa; bi'lesa/ *f,* baseness; vileness, infamy

vilipendiar /bilipen'diar/ *vt* to revile

vilipendio /bili'pendio/ *m,* vilification; contempt

villa /'biʎa; 'biya/ *f,* villa; country house; town

villancico /biʎan'θiko; biyan'siko/ *m,* carol

villanesco /biʎa'nesko; biya'nesko/ *a* peasant; rustic, country

villanía /biʎa'nia; biya'nia/ *f,* humbleness of birth; vileness; villainy

villano /bi'ʎano; bi'yano/ **(-na)** *n* peasant —*a* rustic, country; boorish; base

vinagre /bi'nagre/ *m,* vinegar

vinagreta /bina'greta/ *f,* vinegar sauce

vinagroso /bina'groso/ *a* vinegary; *Inf.* bad-tempered, acid

vincular /binku'lar/ *vt Law.* to entail; *Fig.* base; —*vr* perpetuate —*a Law.* entail

vínculo /'binkulo/ *m,* tie, bond; *Law.* entail

vindicación /bindika'θion; bindika'sion/ *f,* vindication; justification; excuse

vindicador /bindika'ðor/ **(-ra)** *n* vindicator —*a* vindicative

vindicar /bindi'kar/ *vt* to avenge; vindicate; justify; excuse

vindicativo /bindika'tiβo/ *a* avenging; vindicatory

vinícola /bi'nikola/ *a* wine-growing; wine

vinicultor /binikul'tor/ **(-ra)** *n* wine grower, viniculturalist

vinicultura /binikul'tura/ *f,* wine-growing, viniculture

vino /'bino/ *m,* wine; fermented fruit juice. **v. de Oporto,** port wine. **v. generoso,** well-matured wine. **v. tinto,** red wine

vinoso /bi'noso/ *a* vinous; fond of wine

viña /'biɲa/ *f,* vineyard

viñador /biɲa'ðor/ *m,* vineyard-keeper; vine-cultivator

viñedo /bi'ɲeðo/ *m,* vineyard

viñeta /bi'ɲeta/ f, vignette

viola /'biola/ f, Mus. viola; Bot. viola, pansy. mf viola player

violación /biola'θion; biola'sion/ f, violation; infringement

violado /bio'laðo/ a violet

violador /biola'ðor/ (**-ra**) n violator. m, seducer

violar /bio'lar/ vt to violate; infringe; rape; spoil, harm

violencia /bio'lenθia; bio'lensia/ f, violence; outrage; rape

violentar /biolen'tar/ vt to force; falsify, misinterpret; force an entrance; —vr force oneself

violento /bio'lento/ a violent; repugnant; impetuous, hasty-tempered; unnatural, false; unreasonable

violeta /bio'leta/ f, Bot. violet. m, violet color. **v. de febrero,** snowdrop

violín /bio'lin/ m, violin

violinista /bioli'nista/ mf violinist

violón /bio'lon/ m, double-bass, bass viol; double-bass player

violoncelista /biolonθe'lista; biolon-se'lista/ mf cellist

violoncelo /biolon'θelo; biolon'selo/ m, cello

vira /'bira/ f, welt (of a shoe); dart

viraje /bi'rahe/ m, Auto. change of direction; bend, turn

virar /bi'rar/ vt Naut. to put about; Photo. tone; —vi Naut. tack; Auto. change direction. **v. de bordo,** Naut. to lay off

virgen /bir'hen/ mf virgin. f, Astron. Virgo

virginal /birhi'nal/ a virginal; pure, unspotted

virginidad /birhini'ðað/ f, virginity

virgulilla /birgu'liʎa; birgu'liya/ f, comma; cedilla; accent; apostrophe; fine line

viril /bi'ril/ a manly, virile. m, clear glass screen

virilidad /birili'ðað/ f, virility

virote /bi'rote/ m, arrow; shaft; Inf. young blood

virrey /bi'rrei/ m, viceroy

virtual /bir'tual/ a virtual; implicit

virtualidad /birtuali'ðað/ f, virtuality

virtualmente /birtual'mente/ adv virtually; tacitly

virtud /bir'tuð/ f, virtue; power; strength, courage; efficacy. **en v. de,** in virtue of

virtuosidad /birtuosi'ðað/ f, virtuosity

virtuoso /bir'tuoso/ a virtuous; powerful, efficacious. m, virtuoso, artist

viruela /bi'ruela/ f, smallpox (gen. pl)

virulencia /biru'lenθia; biru'lensia/ f, virulence

virulento /biru'lento/ a virulent

virus /'birus/ m, virus

viruta /bi'ruta/ f, wood-shaving

visaje /bi'sahe/ m, grimace

visar /bi'sar/ vt to visa; endorse

vis cómica /bis 'komika/ f, the comic spirit

viscoso /bis'koso/ a viscous, sticky

visera /bi'sera/ f, visor; eye-shade; peak (of a cap)

visibilidad /bisiβili'ðað/ f, visibility

visillo /bi'siʎo; bi'siyo/ m, window-blind

visión /bi'sion/ f, seeing, sight; queer sight; vision; hallucination; Inf. scarecrow, sight

visionario /bisio'nario/ (**-ia**) a and n visionary

visir /bi'sir/ m, vizier. **gran v.,** grand vizier

visita /bi'sita/ f, visit; visitor; inspection. **v. de cumplido,** formal call. **v. de sanidad,** health inspection. **hacer una v.,** to pay a call

visitación /bisita'θion; bisita'sion/ f, visitation; visit

visitador /bisita'ðor/ (**-ra**) n regular visitor. m, inspector —a visiting; inspecting

visitar /bisi'tar/ vt to visit; inspect; Med. attend; Eccl. examine. **v. los monumentos,** to see the sights, go sightseeing

visiteo /bisi'teo/ m, receiving or paying of visits

vislumbrar /bislum'βrar/ vt to glimpse; surmise, conjecture

vislumbre /bis'lumbre/ f, glimmer, glimpse; surmise, glimmering (gen. pl); semblance, appearance

viso /'biso/ m, view point, elevation; glare; shimmer, gleam; colored slip under transparent dress; semblance. **de v.,** prominent (persons)

visón /bi'son/ m, mink

víspera /'bispera/ f, eve; Eccl. day before festival; prelude, preliminary pl Eccl. vespers. **en vísperas de,** on the eve of

vista /'bista/ f, vision, sight; view; eyes; eyesight; meeting, interview; Law. hearing (of a case); apparition; picture of a view; clear idea; connection (of things); proposition, intention; glance; pl window, door, skylight, opening for light. **v. corta,** short sight. **v. de lince,** sharp eyes. **a primera v.,** at first sight. **a v. de,** in sight of; in the presence of. **conocer de v.,** to know by sight. **dar una v.,** to take a look. **doble v.,** second sight; clairvoyance. **en v. de,** in view of, considering. **estar a la v.,** to be evident. Inf. **hacer la v. gorda,** to turn a blind eye. **¡Hasta la v.!** Good-bye! **perder de v.** (**a**), to lose sight of

vistazo /bis'taθo; bis'taso/ m, glance. **echar un v.,** to cast a glance

visto /'bisto/ past part irr **ver.** Law. whereas. **bien v.,** approved. **mal v.,** disapproved. **V. Bueno** (**V° B°**) Approved, Passed. **v. que,** since, inasmuch as

vistoso /bis'toso/ a showy, gaudy; beautiful

visual /bi'sual/ a visual

vital /bi'tal/ a vital; essential

vitalicio /bita'liθio; bita'lisio/ a lifelong. m, life-insurance

vitalidad /bitali'ðað/ f, vitality

vitamina /bita'mina/ *f*, vitamin

vitando /bi'tando/ *a* odious; bad; vital

vitela /bi'tela/ *f*, vellum

vitícola /bi'tikola/ *a* viticultural. *mf* viti-culturist

viticultura /bitikul'tura/ *f*, viticulture

¡vítor! /'bitor/ *interj* Victor!; Hurrah!; Long live!

vitorear /bitore'ar/ *vt* to cheer; applaud, acclaim

vítreo /'bitreo/ *a* glassy, vitreous

vitrina /bi'trina/ *f*, show-case; display cabinet

vitriólico /bi'trioliko/ *a* vitriolic

vitriolo /bi'triolo/ *m*, vitriol

vitualla /bi'tuaʎa; bi'tuaya/ *f*, (gen. *pl*) victuals, provisions

vituperable /bitupe'raβle/ *a* blamewor-thy, vituperable

vituperar /bitupe'rar/ *vt* to censure, blame, vituperate

vituperio /bitu'perio/ *m*, vituperation

viuda /'biuða/ *f*, widow

viudo /'biuðo/ *m*, widower

¡viva! /'biβa/ *interj* Long live!; Hurrah!

vivacidad /biβaθi'ðað; biβasi'ðað/ *f*, vivacity, gaiety; ardor, warmth; brightness

vivamente /biβa'mente/ *adv* quickly, lively

vivaque /bi'βake/ *m*, bivouac

vivar /bi'βar/ *m*, warren; aquarium; breeding ground; well (of a fishing boat)

vivaracho /biβa'ratʃo/ *a* Inf. sprightly, cheery, lively

vivaz /bi'βaθ; bi'βas/ *a* vigorous; quick-witted; sprightly; Bot. perennial; vivid, bright

víveres /'biβeres/ *m pl*, provisions; Mil. stores

vivero /bi'βero/ *m*, Bot. nursery; vivar-ium; small marsh

viveza /bi'βeθa; bi'βesa/ *f*, quickness, briskness; vehemence; perspicuity; witti-cism; resemblance; brightness (eyes, colors); thoughtless word or act

vividero /biβi'ðero/ *a* habitable

vívido /bi'βiðo/ *a* Poet. vivid

vividor /biβi'ðor/ (**-ra**) *a* frugal, thrifty; dissolute —*n* liver; long-liver; libertine, rake

vivienda /bi'βienda/ *f*, dwelling

viviente /bi'βiente/ *a* living

vivificar /biβifi'kar/ *vt* to vivify; comfort

vivir /bi'βir/ *vi* to be alive, live; last, en-dure; (*with* en) inhabit. *m*, life. **¿Quién vive?** Mil. Who goes there? **v. a costillas ajenas,** to live at someone else's expense, live off someone else

vivisección /biβisek'θion; biβisek'sion/ *f*, vivisection

vivo /'biβo/ *a* alive; intense, strong; bright; Mil. active; subtle, ingenious; pre-cipitate; Fig. lasting, enduring; diligent; hasty; impetuous, expressive. *m*, edge. **al v., a lo v.,** to the life; vividly

vizcaíno /biθ'kaino; bis'kaino/ (**-na**) *a* and *n* Biscayan

Vizcaya, el Golfo de /biθ'kaya, el 'golfo de; bis'kaya, el 'golfo de/ the Bay of Biscay

vocablo /bo'kaβlo/ *m*, word

vocabulario /bokaβu'lario/ *m*, vocabu-lary

vocación /boka'θion; boka'sion/ *f*, voca-tion; trade, profession

vocal /bo'kal/ *a* vocal; oral. *f*, Gram. vowel. *mf* voting member

vocear /boθe'ar; bose'ar/ *vi* to cry out, shout; —*vt* proclaim; call for; acclaim

vocerío /boθe'rio; bose'rio/ *m*, shouting; clamor, outcry

vociferación /boθifera'θion; bosifera-'sion/ *f*, vociferation, outcry

vociferar /boθife'rar; bosife'rar/ *vt* to boast (of); —*vi* shout, vociferate

vocinglería /boθiŋgle'ria; bosiŋgle'ria/ *f*, clamor; babble, chatter

vocinglero /boθiŋ'glero; bosiŋ'glero/ *a* vociferous; prattling, babbling

vodca /'boðka/ *m*, vodka

volada /bo'laða/ *f*, short flight. Mech. **v. de grúa,** jib

voladura /bola'ðura/ *f*, explosion; blast-ing

volandas (en), volandillas (en) /bo'landas, bolan'diʎas; bo'landas, bo-lan'diyas/ *adv* in the air, as though flying; Inf. in a trice

volante /bo'lante/ *a* flying; wandering, restless. *m*, frill, flounce; screen; fan (of a windmill); Mech. flywheel; Mech. balance wheel (watches); coiner's stamp mill; shuttle-cock. Auto. **v. de dirección,** steer-ing-wheel

volantón /bolan'ton/ (**-ona**) *n* fledgling

volar /bo'lar/ *vi irr* to fly (birds, insects, aviation); float in the air; hurry; disap-pear suddenly; burst, explode; jut out (buttresses, etc.); cleave (air) (arrows, etc.); Fig. spread (rumors); —*vt* explode; blast; anger. See **contar**

volatería /bolate'ria/ *f*, fowling; fowls; poultry; flock of birds; Fig. crowd (of ideas)

volátil /bo'latil/ *a* volatile; inconstant

volcán /bol'kan/ *m*, volcano; violent pas-sion. **v. extinto,** extinct volcano

volcar /bol'kar/ *vt irr* to overturn, cap-size; make dizzy; cause a change (of opinion); annoy; —*vi* overturn —*Pres. Indic.* **vuelco, vuelcas, vuelca, vuelcan.** *Preterite* **volqué, volcaste,** etc —*Pres. Subjunc.* **vuelque, vuelques, vuelque, vuelquen**

volear /bole'ar/ *vt* to strike in the air, vol-ley; Agr. sow broadcast

voleo /bo'leo/ *m*, volley (tennis, etc.); high kick; straight punch

volición /boli'θion; boli'sion/ *f*, volition

volquete /bol'kete/ *m*, tip-cart

voltaje /bol'tahe/ *m*, voltage

voltario /bol'tario/ *a* versatile; capri-cious, headstrong

voltear /bolte'ar/ *vt* to whirl; turn; overturn; change place (of); *Archit.* construct an arch or vault; —*vi* revolve; tumble, twirl (acrobats)

volteo /bol'teo/ *m,* turning, revolution; whirl; overturning; twirling; *Elec.* voltage

voltereta /bolte'reta/ *f,* somersault

voltio /'boltio/ *m,* volt

volubilidad /boluβili'ðað/ *f,* inconstancy, fickleness

voluble /bo'luβle/ *a* easily turned; inconstant, changeable; *Bot.* twining

volumen /bo'lumen/ *m,* bulk, size; volume, book

voluminoso /bolumi'noso/ *a* voluminous, bulky

voluntad /bolun'tað/ *f,* will, volition; wish; decree; free will; intention; affection; free choice; consent. **a v.,** at will; by choice. **de buena v.,** of good will; willingly, with pleasure. **de su propia v.,** of one's own free will. **mala v.,** hostility, ill-will

voluntario /bolun'tario/ **(-ia)** *a* voluntary; strong-willed —*n* volunteer

voluntarioso /bolunta'rioso/ *a* self-willed

voluptuoso /bolup'tuoso/ *a* voluptuous

volver /bol'βer/ *vt irr* to turn; turn over; return; pay back; direct, aim; translate; restore; change, alter; close (doors, etc.); vomit; reflect, reverberate; —*vi* come back; continue (speech, etc.); bend, turn (roads); (*with prep a + infin.*) do something again (e.g. *v. a leer,* to read over again); (*with por + noun*) protect; —*vr* become; go sour; turn. **v. a las filas,** *Mil.* to reduce to the ranks. **v. en sí,** to regain consciousness. **v. la cabeza,** to turn one's head. **volverse atrás,** *Fig.* to back out. **volverse loco,** to go mad. See **resolver**

vomitar /bomi'tar/ *vt* to vomit; *Fig.* vomit forth; *Fig.* spit out (curses, etc.); *Inf.* burst into confidences

vomitivo /bomi'tiβo/ *a and m,* emetic

vómito /'bomito/ *m,* vomit

vorágine /bo'rahine/ *f,* vortex, whirlpool

voraz /bo'raθ; bo'ras/ *a* voracious

vórtice /'bortiθe; 'bortise/ *m,* whirlpool; *Fig.* vortex

vortiginoso /bortihi'noso/ *a* vortical

vos /bos/ *pers pron 2nd pers sing* and *pl* you.

vosotros, vosotras /bo'sotros, bo'sotras/ *pers pron 2nd pers pl mf* you

votación /bota'θion; bota'sion/ *f,* voting

votador /bota'ðor/ **(-ra)** *n* voter; swearer

votar /bo'tar/ *vi* and *vt* to vote; make a vow; curse, swear. **v. una proposición de confianza,** to pass a vote of confidence

votivo /bo'tiβo/ *a* votive

voto /'boto/ *m,* vote; vow; voter; prayer; curse; desire; opinion. **v. de calidad,** casting vote. **v. de confianza,** vote of confidence

voz /boθ; bos/ *f,* voice; sound, noise; cry, shout (gen. *pl*); word; expression; *Mus.* singer or voice; *Gram.* mood; vote; rumor; instruction, order. **v. común,** general opinion. **a voces,** in a shout, loudly. **llevar la v. cantante,** *Inf.* to have the chief say

vuelco /'buelko/ *m,* overturning

vuelo /'buelo/ *m,* flight; wing; *Sew.* skirtfullness; ruffle, frill; *Archit.* buttress. **v. a ciegas,** *Aer.* blind flying. **v. de distancia,** long-distance flight. **v. de patrulla,** patrol or reconnaissance flight. **v. de reconocimento,** reconnaissance flight. **v. nocturno,** *Aer.* night flying. **v. sin parar,** non-stop flight. **al v.,** on the wing; in passing; quickly. **alzar (** or **levantar) el v.,** to take flight

vuelta /'buelta/ *f,* revolution, turn; bend, curve; return; restitution; recompense; repetition; wrong side; beating; *Sew.* facing, cuff; change (money); conning (lessons, etc.); stroll, walk, change; vault, ceiling; *Sports.* round; *Mech.* **vueltas por minuto,** revolutions per minute. **a v. de correo,** by return mail, by return of post. **a la v.,** on returning; overleaf. **dar la v.,** to turn round, make a détour. **dar una v.,** to take a stroll. **dar vueltas,** to revolve; search (for); consider. **media v.,** half turn

vuestro, vuestra, vuestros, vuestras /'buestro, 'buestra, 'buestros, 'buestras/ *poss pron 2nd pl mf* your, yours

vulgar /bul'gar/ *a* popular; general, common; vernacular; mediocre

vulgaridad /bulgari'ðað/ *f,* vulgarity

vulgarismo /bulga'rismo/ *m,* vulgarism

vulgarización /bulgariθa'θion; bulgarisa'sion/ *f,* vulgarization; popularization

vulgarizar /bulgari'θar; bulgari'sar/ *vt* to vulgarize; popularize; translate into the vernacular; —*vr* grow vulgar

vulgo /'bulgo/ *m,* mob

vulnerable /bulne'raβle/ *a* vulnerable

wáter /'water/ *m*, toilet, water-closet

whisky /'wiski/ *m*, whiskey

xenofobia /seno'foθia/ *f*, xenophobia, hatred of foreigners

xilófono /si'lofono/ *m*, xylophone

y /i/ *conjunc* and. See **e**

ya /ya/ *adv* already; formerly; soon; now; finally; immediately; well, yes, quite. Used of past, present and future time, and in various idiomatic ways. **Ha venido ya**, He has already come. **¡Ya caerá!** His time will come!, He will get his comeuppance! **Ya vendrá**, He will come soon. **¡Ya voy!** Coming! **¡Ya lo creo!** Of course!; I should think so! **¡Ya!** Quite!; I understand. **ya no**, no longer. **ya que**, since

yacente /ya'θente; ya'sente/ *a* recumbent, reclining (statues, etc.)

yacer /ya'θer; ya'ser/ *vi irr* to be lying at full length; lie (in the grave); be situated, be; lie (with), sleep (with); graze by night —*Pres. Indic.* **yazgo** *or* **yazco**, **yaces**, etc —*Pres. Subjunc.* **yazga** *or* **yazca**, etc.

yaciente /ya'θiente; ya'siente/ *a* recumbent

yacija /ya'θiha; ya'siha/ *f*, bed; couch; tomb

yacimiento /yaθi'miento; yasi'miento/ *m*, *Geol.* deposit

yanqui /'yanki/ *a* and *mf* *contemptuous and offensive* North American (gen. U.S.A.)

yarda /'yarða/ *f*, yard (English measure)

yate /'yate/ *m*, *Naut.* yacht

ye /ye/ *f*, name of the letter Y

yegua /'yegua/ *f*, mare

yelmo /'yelmo/ *m*, helmet

yema /'yema/ *f*, bud; yolk (of egg); sweetmeat; *Fig.* best of anything. **y. del dedo**, finger-tip

yermo /'yermo/ *a* uninhabited, deserted; uncultivated. *m*, wilderness, desert

yerno /'yerno/ *m*, son-in-law

yerro /'yerro/ *m*, error; mistake; fault

yerto /'yerto/ *a* stiff, rigid

yesca /'yeska/ *f*, tinder; fuel; stimulus

yeso /'yeso/ *m*, gypsum, calcium sulphate; plaster; plaster cast

yídish /'yiðis/ *n* and *a* Yiddish

yo /yo/ *pers pron 1st sing mf* I. **el yo**, the ego

yodo /'yoðo/ *m*, iodine

yuca /'yuka/ *f*, yucca

yucateco /yuka'teko/ *(-ca)* *a* and *n* from or pertaining to Yucatan

yugo /'yugo/ *m*, yoke; nuptial tie; oppression; *Naut.* transom; *Fig.* **sacudir el y.**, to throw off the yoke

Yugo /'yugo/ *(e)* **slavia** Yugoslavia

yugo /'yugo/ *(e)* **slavo** *(-va)* *a* and *n* Yugoslav

yugular /yugu'lar/ *a* *Anat.* jugular. *m*, jugular vein

yunque /'yunke/ *m*, anvil; patient, undaunted person; hard worker; *Anat.* incus

WXYZ

yunta /'yunta/ *f*, yoke (of oxen, etc.)

yute /'yute/ *m*, jute fiber or fabric

yuxtaponer /yukstapo'ner/ *vt irr* to juxtapose. See **poner**

yuxtaposición /yukstaposi'θion; yukstaposi'sion/ *f*, juxtaposition

zafar /θa'far; sa'far/ *vt* to embellish, garnish, adorn; *Naut.* lighten (a ship); —*vr* escape, hide oneself; *(with de)* excuse oneself, avoid; get rid of

zafarrancho /θafa'rrantʃo; safa'rrantʃo/ *m*, *Naut.* clearing the decks; *Inf.* damage; *Inf.* scuffle

zafiedad /θafie'ðað; safie'ðað/ *f*, rudeness, ignorance, boorishness

zafio /'θafio; 'safio/ *a* rude, unlettered, boorish

zafiro /θa'firo; sa'firo/ *m*, sapphire

zafra /'θafra; 'safra/ *f*, olive oil container; sugar crop or factory; *Mineral.* waste

zaga /'θaga; 'saga/ *f*, rear. *m*, last player. **en z.**, behind. *Inf.* **no quedarse en z.**, not to be left behind; be not inferior

zagal /θa'gal; sa'gal/ *m*, youth; strong, handsome lad; young shepherd; full skirt

zagala /θa'gala; sa'gala/ *f*, maiden, girl; young shepherdess

zagual /θa'gual; sa'gual/ *m*, paddle

zaguán /θa'guan; sa'guan/ *m*, entrance hall; vestibule

zaguero /θa'gero; sa'gero/ *a* loitering, straggling. *m*, *Sports.* back

zahareño /θaa'reɲo; saa'reɲo/ *a* untamable, wild (birds); unsociable, disdainful

zaherir /θae'rir; sae'rir/ *vt irr* to upbraid, reprehend; nag. See **herir**

zahorí /θao'ri; sao'ri/ *m*, soothsayer; waterfinder; sagacious person

zahúrda /θa'urða; sa'urða/ *f*, pigsty

zaino /'θaino; 'saino/ *a* treacherous; vicious (horses); chestnut (horses); black (cows)

zalagarda /θala'garða; sala'garða/ *f*, ambush; skirmish; snare, trap; *Inf.* trick, ruse; *Inf.* mock battle

zalamería /θalame'ria; salame'ria/ *f*, adulation, flattery

zalamero /θala'mero; sala'mero/ *(-ra)* *a* wheedling, flattering —*n* flatterer

zalea /θa'lea; sa'lea/ *f*, sheepskin

zamacuco /θama'kuko; sama'kuko/ *m*, *Inf.* oaf, dolt; *Inf.* drinking bout

zamarra /θa'marra; sa'marra/ *f*, sheepskin jacket

zamarrear /θamarre'ar; samarre'ar/ *vt* to worry, shake (prey); *Fig. Inf.* beat up; *Inf.* floor, confound

zambo /'θambo; 'sambo/ *a* knock-kneed

zambullida /θambu'ʎiða; sambu'yiða/ *f*, plunge, submersion; thrust (in fencing)

zambullir /θambu'ʎir; sambu'yir/ *vt* to plunge in water, submerge; —*vr* dive; hide oneself, cover oneself

zampar /θam'par; sam'par/ *vt* to conceal (one thing in another); eat greedily; (*with en*) arrive suddenly

zampatortas /θampa'tortas; sampa- 'tortas/ *mf Inf.* glutton

zampoña /θam'poɲa; sam'poɲa/ *f,* rustic flute; *Inf.* unimportant work

zanahoria /θana'oria; sana'oria/ *f,* carrot

zanca /'θanka; 'sanka/ *f,* long leg (birds); *Inf.* long thin leg; *Archit.* stringboard (of stairs)

zancada /θan'kaða; san'kaða/ *f,* swift stride

zancadilla /θanka'ðiʎa; sanka'ðiya/ *f,* trip (wrestling); *Inf.* trick, deceit. **echar la z.** (**a**), to trip up

zancajear /θankahe'ar; sankahe'ar/ *vi* to stride about

zancajo /θan'kaho; san'kaho/ *m,* heel-bone; torn heel (stocking, shoe); *Inf.* ill-shaped person. *Inf.* **no llegarle al z.,** to be immensely inferior to someone

zancajoso /θanka'hoso; sanka'hoso/ *a* flatfooted; slovenly

zanco /'θanko; 'sanko/ *m,* stilt. *Fig. Inf.* **andar** (*or* **estar**) **en zancos,** to have gone up in the world

zancudo /θan'kuðo; san'kuðo/ *a* long-legged

zangandungo /θaŋgan'duŋgo; saŋgan- 'duŋgo/ **(-ga)** *n Inf.* loafer

zanganear /θaŋgane'ar; saŋgane'ar/ *vi Inf.* to loaf

zángano /'θaŋgano; 'saŋgano/ *m, Ent.* drone; *Inf.* idler, parasite

zangolotear /θaŋgolote'ar; saŋgolote'ar/ *vt Inf.* to shake violently; —*vi* fuss about, bustle; —*vr* rattle (windows, etc.)

zangoloteo /θaŋgolo'teo; saŋgolo'teo/ *m,* shaking; rattling

zanguango /θaŋ'guaŋgo; saŋ'guaŋgo/ *m, Inf.* lazybones

zanja /'θanha; 'sanha/ *f,* trench, ditch; drain; furrow

zanjar /θan'har; san'har/ *vt* to excavate; *Fig.* remove (obstacles)

zapa /'θapa; 'sapa/ *f,* shovel, spade; *Mil.* sap; sandpaper

zapador /θapa'ðor; sapa'ðor/ *m, Mil.* sapper

zapapico /θapa'piko; sapa'piko/ *m,* pick-ax; mattock

zapaquilda /θapa'kilda; sapa'kilda/ *f, Inf.* she-cat

zapar /θa'par; sa'par/ *vi Mil.* to sap

zaparrastrar /θaparras'trar; saparras'trar/ *vi Inf.* to trail along the floor (dresses)

zapata /θa'pata; sa'pata/ *f,* half-boot; piece of leather used to stop creaking of a hinge; *Archit.* lintel; (*Naut. Mech.*) shoe

zapatazo /θapa'taθo; sapa'taso/ *m,* blow with a shoe; fall, thud; stamping (horses); flap (of sail)

zapateado /θapate'aðo; sapate'aðo/ *m,* dance in which rhythmic drumming of heels plays important part

zapatear /θapate'ar; sapate'ar/ *vt* to hit with a shoe; stamp feet; drum heels (in dancing); *Inf.* ill-treat; thump ground (rabbits); —*vi* stamp (horses); *Naut.* flap (sails); —*vr Fig.* stand one's ground

zapateo /θapa'teo; sapa'teo/ *m,* stamping; rhythmic drumming of heels

zapatera /θapa'tera; sapa'tera/ *f,* cobbler's wife; woman who makes or sells shoes

zapatería /θapate'ria; sapate'ria/ *f,* shoe-making; shoe shop

zapatero /θapa'tero; sapa'tero/ *m,* shoe-maker; shoe seller. **z. remendón,** cobbler

zapatilla /θapa'tiʎa; sapa'tiya/ *f,* slipper; trotter, hoof

zapato /θa'pato; sa'pato/ *m,* shoe

¡zape! /'θape; 'sape/ *interj Inf.* shoo! Used for frightening away cats; exclamation of surprise or warning

zapear /θape'ar; sape'ar/ *vt* to scare away cats; *Inf.* frighten off

zaque /'θake; 'sake/ *m,* leather bottle, wineskin; *Inf.* drunkard, sot

zaquizamí /θaki'ða'mi; sakisa'mi/ *m,* garret; dirty little house or room

zarabanda /θara'βanda; sara'βanda/ *f,* saraband; *Inf.* racket, row

zaragata /θara'gata; sara'gata/ *f, Inf.* fight, brawl

Zaragoza /θara'goθa; sara'gosa/ Saragossa

zaragüelles /θara'gueʎes; sara'gueyes/ *m, pl* wide pleated breeches

zaranda /θa'randa; sa'randa/ *f,* sieve, strainer, colander

zarandajas /θaran'dahas; saran'dahas/ *f, pl Inf.* odds and ends

zarandar /θaran'dar; saran'dar/ *vt* to sieve (grapes, grain); strain; *Inf.* pick out the best; —*vr Inf.* move quickly

zarandillo /θaran'diʎo; saran'diyo/ *m,* small sieve, strainer; *Inf.* a live wire, energetic person; Spanish dance

zaraza /θa'raθa; sa'rasa/ *f,* chintz

zarcillo /θar'θiʎo; sar'siyo/ *m,* earring; *Bot.* tendril; *Agr.* trowel

zarco /'θarko; 'sarko/ *a* light blue (generally eyes or water)

zarpa /'θarpa; 'sarpa/ *f, Naut.* weighing anchor; paw

zarpada /θar'paða; sar'paða/ *f,* blow with a paw

zarpar /θar'par; sar'par/ *vt and vi Naut.* to weigh anchor, sail

zarza /'θarθa; 'sarsa/ *f, Bot.* bramble, blackberry bush

zarzal /θar'θal; sar'sal/ *m,* bramble patch

zarzamora /θarθa'mora; sarsa'mora/ *f,* blackberry

zarzo /'θarθo; 'sarso/ *m,* hurdle; wattle

zarzoso /θar'θoso; sar'soso/ *a* brambly

zarzuela /θar'θuela; sar'suela/ *f,* comic opera; musical comedy

¡zas! /θas; sas/ *m,* sound of a bang or blow

zascandil /θaskan'dil; saskan'dil/ *m, Inf.* busybody

zatara /θa'tara; sa'tara/ *f,* raft

zeda /'θeða; 'seða/ *f,* name of the letter Z

zenit /'θenit; 'senit/ *m.* See **cenit**

zeta /'θeta; 'seta/ *f.* See **zeda**

zigzag /θig'θag; sig'sag/ *m,* zigzag

zigzaguear /θigθage'ar; sigsage'ar/ *vi* to zigzag

zinc /θink; sink/ *m,* zinc

zipizape /θipi'θape; sipi'sape/ *m, Inf.* row, quarrel

zoca /'θoka; 'soka/·*f,* square

zoclo /'θoklo; 'soklo/ *m,* clog, sabot

zoco /'θoko; 'soko/ *m,* square; market; clog, sabot

zodiaco /θo'ðiako; so'ðiako/ *m,* zodiac

zona /'θona; 'sona/ *f,* girdle, band; strip (of land); zone; *Med.* shingles. **z. de depresión,** air pocket. **z. templada,** temperate zone. **z. tórrida,** torrid zone

zonal /θo'nal; so'nal/ *a* zonal

zoologia /θoolo'hia; soolo'hia/ *f,* zoology

zopenco /θo'penko; so'penko/ *a Inf* oafish

zopo /'θopo; 'sopo/ *a* maimed, deformed (hands, feet)

zoquete /θo'kete; so'kete/ *m,* block; dowel; hunk of bread; *Inf* short, ugly man; *Inf.* dunderhead

zorcico /θor'θiko; sor'siko/ *m,* Basque song and dance

zorra /'θorra; 'sorra/ *f,* vixen; fox; *Inf.* cunning person; *Inf.* prostitute; *Inf.* drinking bout; truck, dray

zorrera /θo'rrera; so'rrera/ *f,* foxhole

zorro /'θorro; 'sorro/ *m,* fox; fox-skin; *Inf.* knave

zóster /'θoster; 'soster/ *f, Med.* shingles

zote /'θote; 'sote/ *a* dull, ignorant

zozobra /θo'θoβra; so'soβra/ *f, Naut.* foundering, capsizing; anxiety

zozobrar /θoθo'βrar; soso'βrar/ *vi Naut.* to founder, sink; *Naut.* plunge, shiver; be anxious, vacillate

zueco /'θueko; 'sueko/ *m,* sabot, clog

zulú /θu'lu; su'lu/ *a* and *mf* Zulu

zumbar /θum'βar; sum'βar/ *vi* to buzz, hum; ring (of the ears); whizz; twang (of a guitar, etc.); *Fig. Inf.* be on the brink

zumbido /θum'βiðo; sum'βiðo/ *m,* buzzing, humming; ringing (in the ears); whizz; twanging (of a guitar, etc.); *Inf.* slap, blow

zumbón /θum'βon; sum'βon/ *a* waggish, jocose

zumo /'θumo; 'sumo/ *m,* sap; juice; profit, advantage

zumoso /θu'moso; su'moso/ *a* succulent, juicy

zurcido /θur'θiðo; sur'siðo/ *m, Sew.* darn; mend

zurcidor /θurθi'ðor; sursi'ðor/ **(-ra)** *n* darner, mender. **z. de voluntades,** *humorous* pimp

zurcidura /θurθi'ðura; sursi'ðura/ *f,* darning; mending; darn

zurcir /θur'θir; sur'sir/ *vt* to darn; mend, repair; join; *Fig.* concoct, weave

zurdo /'θurðo; 'surðo/ *a* left-handed

zurra /'θurra; 'surra/ *f, Tan.* currying; *Inf.* spanking; *Inf.* quarrel

zurrapa /θu'rrapa; su'rrapa/ *f,* (gen. *pl*) sediment, lees, dregs

zurrar /θu'rrar; su'rrar/ *vt* to curry (leather); *Inf.* spank; *Inf.* dress down, scold

zurriago /θu'rriago; su'rriago/ *m,* whip

zurribanda /θurri'βanda; surri'βanda/ *f, Inf.* whipping; fight, quarrel

zurriburri /θurri'βurri; surri'βurri/ *m, Inf.* ragamuffin; mob; uproar

zurrido /θu'rriðo; su'rriðo/ *m, Inf.* blow; dull noise

zurrir /θu'rrir; su'rrir/ *vi* to have a confused sound, hum, rattle

zurrón /θu'rron; su'rron/ *m,* shepherd's pouch; leather bag; *Bot.* husk

zutano /θu'tano; su'tano/ **(-na)** *n Inf.* so-and-so, such a one

English-Spanish
Dictionary

a /eɪ/ *n* (letter) a, *f*; *Mus.* la, *m.* **symphony in A major,** sinfonía en la mayor, *f*. **A1,** de primera clase; de primera calidad, excelente

a, an /ə, ən; *when stressed* eɪ:, æn/ *indef art.* (one) un, *m*; una, *f*; (with weights, quantities) el, *m*; la, *f*; (with weeks, months, years, etc.) por, al, *m*; a la, *f*. The indef. art. is omitted in Spanish before nouns expressing nationality, profession, rank, and generally before a noun in apposition. It is omitted also before certain words such as **mil, ciento, otro, semejante, medio,** etc. Not translated in book titles, e.g., *A History of Spain*, Historia de España. *prep* a. In phrases such as *to go hunting*, ir a cazar. As prefix, see *abed, ashore*, etc. *Madrid, a Spanish city*, Madrid, ciudad de España. *three times a month*, tres veces al mes. *ten dollars an hour*, diez dólares por hora. *thirty miles an hour*, treinta millas por hora. *a certain Mrs. Brown*, una tal Sra. Brown. *a thousand soldiers*, mil soldados. *half an hour later*, media hora después

aback /ə'bæk/ *adv Naut.* en facha; *Fig.* sorprendido, desconcertado. **to take a.,** desconcertar, coger desprevenido (a)

abandon /ə'bændən/ *vt* abandonar; dejar; desertar, desamparar; renunciar; entregar. *—n* entusiasmo, fervor, *m*; naturalidad, *f*. **to a. oneself to,** (despair, vice, etc.) entregarse a

abandonment /ə'bændənmənt/ *n* abandono, *m*; renunciación, *f*; deserción, *f*

abase /ə'beɪs/ *vt* humillar; degradar; abatir

abasement /ə'beɪsmənt/ *n* humillación, degradación, *f*; abatimiento, *m*

abash /ə'bæʃ/ *vt* avergonzar; confundir; desconcertar

abate /ə'beɪt/ *vt* disminuir, reducir; (a price) rebajar; (suppress) suprimir, abolir; (remit) condonar, remitir; (annul) anular; (moderate) moderar; (of pride, etc.) humillar; (of pain) aliviar. *—vi* disminuir; moderarse; (of the wind and *Fig.*) amainar; cesar; apaciguarse, calmarse

abatement /ə'beɪtmənt/ *n* disminución, *f*; reducción, *f*; mitigación, *f*; (of price) rebaja, *f*; supresión, *f*; remisión, *f*; (annulment) anulación, *f*; (of pride) humillación, *f*; (of the wind and of enthusiasm, etc.) amaine, *m*; (of pain, etc.) alivio, *m*

abbreviate /ə'brivi,eɪt/ *vt* abreviar; condensar, resumir

abbreviation /ə,brivi'eɪʃən/ *n* abreviación, *f*; resumen, *m*, condensación, *f*; (of a word) abreviatura, *f*

abdicate /'æbdɪ,keɪt/ *vt* renunciar; (a throne) abdicar

abdication /,æbdɪ'keɪʃən/ *n* renuncia, *f*; abdicación, *f*

abdomen /'æbdəmən/ *n* abdomen, *m*

abduct /æb'dʌkt/ *vt* raptar, secuestrar

abduction /æb'dʌkʃən/ *n* rapto, *m*; (*Anat., Philos.*) abducción, *f*

A

aberration /,æbə'reɪʃən/ *n* aberración (also *Astron., Phys., Biol.*), *f*

abet /ə'bɛt/ *vt* ayudar, apoyar, favorecer; incitar, alentar; (in bad sense) ser cómplice de

abeyance /ə'beɪəns/ *n* suspensión, *f*; expectativa, esperanza, *f*. **in a.,** en suspenso; vacante; latente

abhor /æb'hɔr/ *vt* detestar, odiar, aborrecer; repugnar

abhorrence /æb'hɔrəns/ *n* detestación, *f*, odio, aborrecimiento, *m*; repugnancia, *f*

abhorrent /æb'hɔrəpt/ *a* detestable, odioso, aborrecible; repugnante

abide /ə'baɪd/ *vi* morar, quedar. *—vt* aguardar, *Inf.* aguantar, sufrir. **to a. by,** atenerse a, cumplir; sostener

abiding /ə'baɪdɪŋ/ *a* permanente, constante, perenne

ability /ə'bɪlɪti/ *n* habilidad, facultad, *f*, poder, *m*; talento, *m*, capacidad, *f*. **to the best of my a.,** lo mejor que yo pueda

abject /'æbdʒɛkt/ *a* abyecto, miserable; despreciable; vil; servil

abjure /æb'dʒʊr/ *vt* abjurar; renunciar; retratar

ablaze /ə'bleɪz/ *adv* en llamas, ardiendo. *—a* brillante; (with, of anger, etc.) dominado por

able /'eɪbəl/ *a* capaz (de); (clever) hábil; competente; en estado (de); *Law.* apto legalmente, capaz; bueno, excelente. **to be a. to,** poder; ser capaz de; (know how) saber. **a.-bodied,** fuerte, fornido. **a.-bodied seaman,** marinero práctico, *m*

ably /'eɪbli/ *adv* hábilmente; competentemente

abnormal /æb'nɔrməl/ *a* anormal; irregular

aboard /ə'bɔrd/ *adv* a bordo. *—prep* a bordo de. **to go a.,** embarcarse, ir a bordo. **All a.!** ¡Viajeros a bordo!; (a train) ¡Viajeros al tren!

abode /ə'boud/ *n* morada, habitación, *f*; residencia, *f*; (stay) estancia, *f*

abolish /ə'bɒlɪʃ/ *vt* abolir, suprimir, anular

abominable /ə'bɒmənəbəl/ *a* abominable, aborrecible; repugnante, execrable; *Inf.* horrible

abominate /ə'bɒmə,neɪt/ *vt* abominar, aborrecer, detestar

abomination /ə,bɒmə'neɪʃən/ *n* abominación, *f*; aborrecimiento, *m*; horror, *m*

aboriginal /,æbə'rɪdʒənl/ *a* aborigen; primitivo

aborigines /,æbə'rɪdʒə,niz/ *n pl* aborígenes, *m pl*

abort /ə'bɔrt/ *vi* abortar, malparir; *Fig.* malograrse

abortion /ə'bɔrʃən/ *n* aborto, *m*; *Fig.* fracaso, malogro, *m*

abound /ə'baund/ vi abundar (en)

about /ə'baut/ adv (around) alrededor; (round about) a la redonda, en torno; (all over) por todas partes; (up and down) acá y acullá; por aquí, por ahí; en alguna parte; por aquí; (in circumference) en circunferencia; (almost) casi, aproximadamente; (by turns) por turnos, en rotación. —prep alrededor de; en torno; por; (near to) cerca de; (on one's person) sobre; (on the subject of) sobre; (concerning) acerca de; (over) por, a causa de; en; (of) de; (with time by the clock) a eso de, sobre; (towards) hacia; (engaged in) ocupado en; (on the point of) a punto de. **a. here,** por aquí. **a. nothing,** por nada. **a. supper time,** hacia la hora de cenar. **a. three o'clock,** a eso de las tres. **A. turn!** ¡Media vuelta! (a la izquierda o a la derecha). **He wandered a. the streets,** Vagaba por las calles. **somewhere a.,** en alguna parte. **to be a. to,** estar para, estar a punto de. **to bring a.,** ocasionar. **to come a.,** suceder. **to know a.,** saber de. **to set a.,** empezar, iniciar; (a person) acometer. **What are you thinking a.?** ¿En qué piensas?

above /ə'bʌv/ adv arriba; en lo alto; encima; (superior) superior; (earlier) antes; (higher up on a page, etc.) más arriba; (in heaven) en el cielo. —prep encima de; por encima de; sobre; (beyond) fuera de; fuera del alcance de; (superior to) superior a; (more than) más de; (too proud to) demasiado orgulloso para; (too good to) demasiado bueno para; (in addition to) además de, en adición a; (with degrees of temperature) sobre. —a anterior; (with past participles) antes. **from a.,** desde arriba. **a. all,** sobre todo. **over and a.,** además de. **a. board,** adv abiertamente, con las cartas boca arriba. —a franco y abierto. **a. mentioned,** supradicho, susodicho, antes citado

abrasion /ə'breiʒən/ n abrasión, f; rozadura, f; Geol. denudación, f

abreast /ə'brest/ adv de frente, al lado uno de otro; Naut. por el través. **to keep a. of the times,** mantenerse al día. **to ride six a.,** cabalgar a seis de frente. **a. with,** al nivel de, a la altura de

abridge /ə'brɪdʒ/ vt abreviar; resumir; condensar, compendiar; disminuir; reducir

abridgment /ə'brɪdʒmənt/ n abreviación, f; resumen, m, sinopsis, f; disminución, f; reducción, f

abroad /ə'brɔd/ adv (out) fuera, afuera; (gone out) salido; ausente; (everywhere) en todas partes; (in foreign lands) en el extranjero. **to go a.,** salir de casa, echarse a la calle; ir al extranjero; (of rumors, etc.) propagarse, rumorearse

abrogation /,æbrə'geiʃən/ n abrogación, anulación, f

abrupt /ə'brʌpt/ a (precipitous) escarpado, precipitado, abrupto; (unexpected) repentino, inesperado; (of persons) brusco, descortés; (of style) seco

abscess /'æbses/ n absceso, m

abscond /æb'skɒnd/ vi evadirse; huir, escaparse; (with money) desfalcar

absence /'æbsəns/ n ausencia, f; alejamiento, m; (of mind) abstracción, f, ensimismamiento, m; (lack) falta, f. **leave of a.,** permiso para ausentarse, m; Mil. licencia, f, permiso, m

absent /a 'æbsənt; v æb'sent/ a ausente; alejado (de); (in mind) abstraído, ensimismado, distraído. —vt ausentarse; alejarse. **the a.,** los ausentes. **a.-mindedness,** ensimismamiento, m, abstracción, f

absentee /,æbsən'ti/ n ausente, mf

absently /'æbsəntli/ adv distraídamente

absolute /'æbsə,lut/ a absoluto; perfecto; puro; (unconditional) incondicional; (downright) categórico; completo; (true) verdadero; (unlimited) ilimitado. **the a.,** lo absoluto

absolve /æb'zɒlv, -'sɒlv/ vt absolver; (free) exentar, eximir; librar; exculpar

absorb /æb'sɔrb, -'zɔrb/ vt absorber; (drink) beber; (use up) gastar; (of shocks) amortiguar; (Fig. digest) asimilar; (engross) ocupar (el pensamiento, etc.). **to be absorbed in,** Fig. enfrascarse en, engolfarse en, estar entregado a

absorbent /æb'sɔrbənt, -'zɔr-/ a and n absorbente, m. **a. cotton,** algodón hidrófilo, m

absorbing /æb'sɔrbɪŋ, -'zɔr-/ a absorbente; Fig. sumamente interesante

absorption /æb'sɔrpʃən, -'zɔrp-/ n absorción, f; (Fig. digestion) asimilación, f; (engrossment) enfrascamiento, m, preocupación, f, abstracción, f

abstain /æb'stein/ vi abstenerse (de); evitar

abstemious /æb'stimiəs/ a abstemio, abstinente; sobrio; moderado

abstention /æb'stenʃən/ n abstención, f; abstinencia, f; privación, f

abstinence /'æbstənəns/ n abstinencia, f. **day of a.,** día de ayuno, m

abstract /a, v æb'strækt, 'æbstrækt; n 'æbstrækt/ a abstracto. —n extracto, resumen, m; abstracción, f. —vt abstraer; separar; extraer; (précis) resumir; (steal) substraer. **in the a.,** en abstracto

abstracted /æb'stræktɪd/ a distraído, desatento, absorto, ensimismado

abstraction /æb'strækʃən/ n abstracción, f; (of mind) preocupación, desatención, f; (stealing) substracción, f

abstruse /æb'strus/ a abstruso, ininteligible; obscuro; recóndito

absurd /æb'sɜrd/ a absurdo, grotesco; ridículo, disparatado; cómico

absurdity /æb'sɜrdɪti/ n absurdidad, ridiculez, f; disparate, m, tontería, f

abundance /ə'bʌndəns/ n abundancia, copia, f; muchedumbre (de), multitud (de), f; riqueza, f; prosperidad, f

abundant /ə'bʌndənt/ a abundante, copioso; rico. **to be a. in,** abundar en

abuse /n ə'byus; v ə'byuz/ n abuso, m; (bad language) insulto, m, injuria, f. —vt (ill-use) maltratar; (misuse) abusar (de); (revile) insultar, injuriar; (deceive) engañar

abuser /ə'byuzər/ n abusador (-ra); injuriador (-ra); (defamer) denigrante, mf

abusive /ə'byusɪv/ a abusivo; (scurrilous) insultante, injurioso, ofensivo

abut (on) /ə'bʌt/ vi lindar con; terminar en; estar adosado a

abysmal /ə'bɪzməl/ a abismal

abyss /ə'bɪs/ n abismo, m, sima, f; (hell) infierno, m

academic /,ækə'dɛmɪk/ a académico

academy /ə'kædəmi/ n academia, f; conservatorio, m; (school) colegio, m; (of riding, etc.) escuela, f. **A. of Music,** Conservatorio de Música, m

accede /æk'sid/ vi (to a throne) ascender (al trono); tomar posesión (de); (join) hacerse miembro (de); aceptar; (agree) acceder (a), consentir (en), convenir (en)

accelerate /æk'sɛlə,reit/ vt acelerar; apresurar; (shorten) abreviar

accelerator /æk'sɛlə,reitər/ n (of a vehicle) acelerador, m

accent /'æksɛnt/ n acento (all meanings), m. —vt acentuar

accentuate /æk'sɛntʃu,eit/ vt acentuar; dar énfasis a

accept /æk'sɛpt/ vt aceptar; (believe) creer; recibir; admitir; (welcome) acoger

acceptable /æk'sɛptəbəl/ a aceptable; admisible; agradable; (welcome) bien acogido

acceptance /æk'sɛptəns/ n aceptación, f. **a. speech** discurso aceptatorio; (approval) aprobación, f; (welcome) buena acogida, f; Com. aceptación, f

access /'æksɛs/ n acceso, m; entrada, f; (way) camino, m; Med. ataque, m; (fit) transporte, m; (advance) avance, m. **easy of a.,** accesible; fácil de encontrar

accessible /æk'sɛsəbəl/ a accesible; asequible

accession /æk'sɛʃən/ n (to the throne, etc.) advenimiento, m; aumento, m; (acquisition) adición, f; adquisición, f; Law. accesión, f

accessory /æk'sɛsəri/ a accesorio; secundario; suplementario, adicional. —n accesorio, m; Law. cómplice, mf. **a. before the fact,** instigador (-ra). **a. after the fact,** encubridor (-ra)

accident /'æksɪdənt/ n accidente, m; (chance) casualidad, f; (mishap) contratiempo, m. **by a.,** por casualidad, accidentalmente. **a. insurance,** seguro contra accidentes

accidental /,æksɪ'dɛntl/ a accidental, casual, fortuito. —n Mus. accidente, m

accidentally /,æksɪ'dɛntli/ adv accidentalmente; por casualidad; sin querer

acclaim /ə'kleim/ vt aclamar; proclamar; vitorear, aplaudir

acclamation /,æklə'meiʃən/ n aclamación, f; aplauso, vítor, m

acclimatize /ə'klaimə,taiz/ vt aclimatar

accolade /'ækə,leid/ n acolada, f, espaldarazo, m

accommodate /ə'kɒmə,deit/ vt acomodar; ajustar; adaptar; (reconcile) reconciliar; (provide) proveer, proporcionar; (oblige) complacer; (fit) poner, instalar; (lodge) hospedar; (lend) prestar; (hold) tener espacio para, contener; (give a seat to) dar un sitio a. **to a. oneself to,** adaptarse a

accommodating /ə'kɒmə,deitɪŋ/ a acomodadizo; (obliging) servicial

accommodation /ə,kɒmə'deiʃən/ n acomodación, f; ajuste, m; adaptación, f; (arrangement) arreglo, m; (reconciliation) reconciliación, f; (lodging) alojamiento, m; (Aer. Naut.) partición, f; (space, room or seat) sitio, m; (loan) préstamo, m. **We found the accommodations good in this hotel,** Estuvimos muy bien en este hotel. **a. ladder,** escalera real, f

accompaniment /ə'kʌmpənimənt/ n acompañamiento, m

accompanist /ə'kʌmpənist/ n acompañante (-ta)

accompany /ə'kʌmpəni/ vt acompañar

accompanying /ə'kʌmpəniɪŋ/ a anexo n acompañamiento, m

accomplice /ə'kɒmplɪs/ n cómplice, comparte, mf

accomplish /ə'kɒmplɪʃ/ vt llevar a cabo, efectuar; terminar; (fulfil) cumplir; perfeccionar; (achieve) conseguir, lograr

accomplished /ə'kɒmplɪʃt/ a consumado; perfecto; culto; (talented) talentoso

accomplishment /ə'kɒmplɪʃmənt/ n efectuación, f; realización, f, logro, m; (fulfilment) cumplimiento, m; (gift) prenda, f, talento, m; pl **accomplishments,** partes, dotes, f pl; conocimientos, m pl

accord /ə'kɔrd/ n acuerdo, m; unión, f; consentimiento, m; concierto, m, concordia, f; voluntad, f. —vt otorgar, conceder. —vi estar de acuerdo (con); armonizar (con). **of one's own a.,** espontáneamente. **with one a.,** unánimemente

accordance /ə'kɔrdns/ n acuerdo, m, conformidad, f; arreglo, m. **in a. with,** de acuerdo con, según, con arreglo a

according /ə'kɔrdɪŋ/ adv según, conforme. **a. as,** conforme a, a medida que. **a. to,** según

accordingly /ə'kɔrdɪŋli/ adv en consecuencia, por consiguiente; pues

accordion /ə'kɔrdiən/ n acordeón, m. **to a.-pleat,** vt plisar

accost /ə'kɔst/ vt abordar, acercarse a; dirigirse a, hablar

account /ə'kaunt/ vt (judge) considerar, creer, juzgar, tener por. —vi (for) explicar; (understand) comprender; (be responsible) responder de, dar razón de; justificar

account /ə'kaunt/ *n* (bill) cuenta, *f;* factura, *f;* (narrative) narración, relación, *f;* (description) descripción, *f;* historia, *f;* versión, *f;* (list) enumeración, *f;* (reason) motivo, *m,* causa, *f;* (importance) importancia, *f;* (weight) peso, *m;* (news) noticias, *f pl;* (advantage) provecho, *m,* ventaja, *f.* **by all accounts,** según lo que se oye, según voz pública. **current a.,** cuenta corriente, *f.* **outstanding a.,** cuenta pendiente, *f.* **on a.,** a cuenta. **on a. of,** a causa de, por motivo de. **on no a.,** de ninguna manera. **on that a.,** por lo tanto. **to be of no a.,** ser insignificante; ser de poca importancia; *Inf.* ser la última mona. **to give an a.,** contar, hacer una relación (de). **to give an a. of oneself,** explicarse. **to keep a.,** llevar la cuenta. **to settle accounts,** ajustar cuentas. **to take into a.,** considerar. **to turn to a.,** sacar provecho de. **a. book,** libro de cuentas, *m*

accountability /ə,kauntə'biliti/ *n* responsabilidad, *f*

accountable /ə'kauntəbəl/ *a* responsable

accountancy /ə'kauntṇsi/ *n* contabilidad, *f*

accountant /ə'kauntṇt/ *n* contador, *m.* **chartered a.,** contador autorizado, *m.* **accountant's office,** contaduría, *f*

accouterment /ə'kutərmənt/ *n* atavío, *m;* equipo, *m*

accredit /ə'krɛdɪt/ *vt* acreditar

accretion /ə'kriʃən/ *n* acrecentamiento, aumento, *m;* *Law.* accesión, *f*

accrue /ə'kru/ *vi* resultar (de), proceder (de); originarse (en); aumentar

accumulate /ə'kyumyə,leit/ *vt* acumular; amontonar, atesorar. —*vi* acumularse; aumentarse, crecer

accumulation /ə,kyumyə'leiʃən/ *n* acumulación, *f;* amontonamiento, *m*

accumulative /ə'kyumyə,leitɪv/ *a* acumulador; adquisitivo, ahorrador

accuracy /'ækyərəsi/ *n* exactitud, corrección

accurate /'ækyərɪt/ *a* exacto, correcto, fiel; (of persons) exacto, minucioso; (of apparatus) de precisión

accurately /'ækyərɪtli/ *adv* con exactitud, correctamente; con precisión

accursed /ə'kɜrsɪd, ə'kɜrst/ *a* maldito

accusation /,ækyu'zeiʃən/ *n* acusación, *f.* **to lodge an a.,** querellarse ante el juez

accusatory /ə'kyuzə,tɔri/ *a* acusatorio

accuse /ə'kyuz/ *vt* acusar

accused /ə'kyuzd/ *n* *Law.* acusado (-da)

accuser /ə'kyuzər/ *n* acusador (-ra)

accustom /ə'kʌstəm/ *vt* acostumbrar (a), habituar (a)

accustomed /ə'kʌstəmd/ *a* acostumbrado, usual; general; característico

ace /eis/ *n* as, *m;* *Fig.* pelo, *m.* **to be within an ace of,** estar a dos dedos de

acerbity /ə'sɜrbɪti/ *n* acerbidad, *f;* *Fig.* aspereza, *f;* severidad, *f;* sequedad, *f*

acetylene /ə'sɛtḷ,in/ *n* acetileno, *m.* **a. lamp,** lámpara de acetileno, *f*

ache /eik/ *n* dolor, *m;* pena, *f.* —*vi* doler. **My head aches,** Me duele la cabeza, Tengo dolor de cabeza

achievable /ə't ʃivəbəl/ *a* alcanzable, asequible; factible

achieve /ə'tʃiv/ *vt* conseguir, lograr; (reach) alcanzar; (obtain) obtener, ganar

achievement /ə'tʃivmənt/ *n* logro, *m,* realización, obtención, *f;* (deed) hazaña, *f;* (work) obra, *f;* (success) éxito, *m;* (discovery) descubrimiento, *m;* (victory) victoria, *f*

aching /'eikɪŋ/ *n* dolor, *m;* pena, angustia, *f.* —*a* doliente; afligido

acid /'æsɪd/ *a* and *n* ácido, *m.* **fatty a.,** ácido graso, *m*

acknowledge /æk'nɒlɪdʒ/ *vt* reconocer; confesar; (reply to) contestar a; (appreciate) agradecer. **to a. receipt,** *Com.* acusar recibo

acknowledgment /æk'nɒlɪdʒmənt/ *n* reconocimiento, *m;* confesión, *f;* (appreciation) agradecimiento, *m;* (reward) recompensa, *f;* (of a letter) acuse de recibo, *m*

acme /'ækmi/ *n* cumbre, *f;* *Fig.* auge, apogeo, *m*

acne /'ækni/ *n* acné, *m*

acolyte /'ækə,lait/ *n* acólito, monacillo (male) *m,* acólita, monacilla *f,* (female)

acorn /'eikɔrn/ *n* bellota, *f.* **a. cup,** capullo de bellota, *m.* **a.-shaped,** en forma de bellota, abellotado

acoustic /ə'kustɪk/ *a* acústico

acoustics /ə'kustɪks/ *n pl* acústica, *f*

acquaint /ə'kweint/ *vt* dar a conocer, comunicar, informar (de), dar parte (de); familiarizar (con). **to be acquainted with,** conocer; saber. **to make oneself acquainted with,** familiarizarse con; entablar amistad con

acquaintance /ə'kweintṇs/ *n* conocimiento, *m;* (person) conocido (-da); *pl* **acquaintances,** amistades, *f pl.* **to make their a.,** conocer (a), llegar a conocer (a)

acquiesce /,ækwi'ɛs/ *vi* asentir (en), consentir (a)

acquiescence /,ækwi'ɛsəns/ *n* acquiescencia, *f,* consentimiento, *m*

acquire /ə'kwai°r/ *vt* adquirir, obtener; (diseases, habits) contraer; ganar; (learn) aprender

Acquired Immune Deficiency Syndrome /ə'kwai°rd/ *n* el síndrome de Inmunodeficiencia Adquirida, *m*

acquirement /ə'kwai°rmənt/ *n* adquisición, *f;* (learning) conocimiento, *m;* (talent) talento, *m*

acquisition /,ækwə'zɪʃən/ *n* adquisición, *f*

acquisitive /ə'kwɪzɪtɪv/ *a* adquisitivo

acquit /ə'kwɪt/ *vt* (a debt) pagar; exonerar; *Law.* absolver; (a duty) cumplir. **to a. oneself well (badly),** portarse bien (mal); salir bien (mal)

acquittal /ə'kwɪtḷ/ *n* (of a debt) pago, *m;*

Law. absolución, *f;* (of a duty) cumplimiento, *m*

acre /'eikər/ *n* (measure) acre, *m; pl* **acres,** terrenos, campos, *m pl*

acreage /'eikərɪdʒ/ *n* acres, *m pl*

acrimonious /ˌækrəˈmouniəs/ *a* acrimonioso, áspero; mordaz, sarcástico

acrobat /'ækrəˌbæt/ *n* acróbata, *mf*

acrobatic /ˌækrəˈbætɪk/ *a* acrobático

acronym /'ækrənɪm/ *n* sigla, *f*

across /əˈkrɔs/ *adv* a través, de través, transversalmente; (on the other side) al otro lado; de una parte a otra; (of the arms, etc.) cruzados, *m pl. —prep* a través de; al otro lado de; (upon) sobre; por. **He went a. the road,** Cruzó la calle. **to run a.,** correr por; tropezar con; dar con. **a. country,** a campo travieso. **a. the way,** en frente

act /ækt/ *n* acción, obra, *f,* hecho, *m;* acto, *m; Law.* ley, *f. Theat.* acto, *m.* **in the act,** en el acto. **in the act (of doing),** en acto de (hacer algo). **in the very act,** en flagrante. **the Acts of the Apostles,** los Actos de los Apóstoles. **act of God,** fuerza mayor, *f.* **act of indemnity,** bill de indemnidad, *m*

act /ækt/ *vt* (a play) representar, hacer; (a part) desempeñar, hacer (un papel); (pretend) simular, fingir. *—vi* obrar, actuar; (behave) portarse, conducirse; (function) funcionar; producir su efecto; (feign) fingir; (as a profession) ser actor. **to act as,** hacer de; cumplir las funciones de. **to act as a second,** (in a duel) apadrinar. **to act for,** representar; ser el representante de. **to act upon,** obrar sobre; afectar; influir en

acting /'æktɪŋ/ *n* (of a play) representación (de una comedia), *f;* (of an actor) interpretación (de un papel), *f;* (as a hobby) el hacer comedia; (dramatic art) arte dramática, *f. —a* interino, suplente; comanditario. **He is a. captain,** Está de capitán. **a. partner,** socio (-ia) comanditario (-ia)

action /'ækʃən/ *n* acción, *f;* función, *f;* operación, *f;* (movement) movimiento, *m;* (effect) efecto, *m;* influencia, *f; Law.* proceso, *m; Mil.* batalla, acción, *f; Lit.* acción, *f.* **in a.,** en actividad; en operación; *Mil.* en el campo de batalla. **man of a.,** hombre de acción, *m.* **to be killed in a.,** morir en el campo de batalla. **to bring an a. against,** pedir en juicio, entablar un pleito contra. **to put into a.,** hacer funcionar; introducir. **to take a.,** tomar medidas (para). **to take a. against,** prevenirse contra; *Law.* proceder contra

actionable /'ækʃənəbəl/ *a* procesable, punible

active /'æktɪv/ *a* activo; ágil; diligente; *Mil.* vivo; enérgico; *Gram.* activo. **to make a.,** activar, estimular

activity /æk'tɪvɪti/ *n* actividad, *f*

actor /'æktər/ *n* actor, *m;* (in comedy) comediante, *m*

actress /'æktrɪs/ *n* actriz, *f;* (in comedy) comediante, *f*

actual /'æktʃuəl/ *a* actual, existente; real, verdadero

actuality /ˌæktʃuˈælɪti/ *n* realidad, *f*

actually /'æktʃuəli/ *adv* en efecto, realmente, en realidad

actuary /'æktʃuˌɛri/ *n* actuario de seguros, *m*

actuate /'æktʃuˌeit/ *vt* mover, animar, excitar

acumen /əˈkyumən/ *n* cacumen, *m,* agudeza, sagacidad, *f*

acute /əˈkyut/ *a* agudo; (shrewd) perspicaz; (of a situation) crítico. **a. accent,** acento agudo, *m.* **a.-angled,** acutángulo

acuteness /əˈkyutnɪs/ *n* agudeza, *f;* (shrewdness) perspicacia, penetración, *f*

ad /æd/ *n* anuncio, *m.* See **advertisement**

Adam /'ædəm/ *n* Adán, *m.* **Adam's apple,** nuez de la garganta, *f*

adamant /'ædəmənt/ *a* firme, duro, inexorable

adapt /əˈdæpt/ *vt* adaptar; ajustar, acomodar; aplicar; (a play, etc.) refundir, arreglar; *Mus.* arreglar

adaptability /əˌdæptəˈbɪlɪti/ *n* adaptabilidad, *f*

adaptable /əˈdæptəbəl/ *a* adaptable

adaptation /ˌædəpˈteiʃən/ *n* adaptación, *f;* (of a play, etc.) refundición, *f;* (Mus. etc.) arreglo, *m*

adapter /əˈdæptər/ *n* (of a play, etc.) refundidor (-ra); *Elec.* enchufe de reducción, *m*

add /æd/ *vt* añadir; juntar; (up) sumar. **add insult to injury,** al mojado echarle agua, añadir a una ofensa otra mayor. **to add to,** añadir a; (increase) aumentar, acrecentar. **to add up,** sumar. **to add up to,** subir a; (mean) querer decir.

adder /'ædər/ *n* víbora, serpiente, *f*

addict /'ædɪkt/ *n* adicto (-ta).

addicted /əˈdɪktɪd/ *a* aficionado (a), amigo (de), dado (a); adicto (a); adicto (a)

addiction /əˈdɪkʃən/ *n* afición, propensión, *f;* adicción, *f*

addition /əˈdɪʃən/ *n* añadidura, *f; Math.* adición, suma, *f.* **in a.** (**to),** además (de), también

address /*n* əˈdrɛs, ˈædrɛs; *v* əˈdrɛs/ *n* (on a letter) sobrescrito, *m;* (of a person) dirección, *f,* señas, *f pl;* (speech) discurso, *m;* (petition) memorial, *m,* petición, *f;* (dedication) dedicatoria, *f;* (invocation) invocación, *f;* (deportment) presencia, *f;* (tact) diplomacia, habilidad, *f; pl* **addresses,** corte, *f. —vt* (a ball) golpear; (a letter) dirigir, poner el sobrescrito a; (words, prayers) dirigir (a); hablar, hacer un discurso. **to a. oneself to a task,** dedicarse a (or entregarse a or emprender) una tarea. **to deliver an a.,** pronunciar un discurso. **to pay one's addresses to,** cortejar, hacer la corte (a), galantear

addressee /ˌædrɛˈsi/ *n* destinatario (-ia)

adduce /əˈdus/ *vt* aducir, alegar; aportar

adenoids /'ædn,ɔidz/ n pl amígdalas, f pl

adept /a ə'dept/ n 'ædept/ a adepto, versado, consumado. —n adepto, m

adequacy /'ædɪkwəsi/ n adecuación, f; suficiencia, f; competencia, f

adequate /'ædɪkwɪt/ a adecuado; proporcionado; suficiente; competente; a la altura (de)

adhere /æd'hɪər/ vi adherirse; pegarse; ser fiel (a); persistir (en)

adherence /æd'hɪərəns/ n Fig. adhesión, f

adherent /æd'hɪərənt/ n partidario (-ia)

adhesion /æd'hiʒən/ n adherencia, f; (to a party, etc.) adhesión, f

adhesive /æd'hisɪv/ a adhesivo; (sticky) pegajoso. **a. tape,** esparadrapo, m; Elec. cinta aisladora adherente, f

adjacent /ə'dʒeisənt/ a próximo, contiguo, adyacente, vecino

adjective /'ædʒɪktɪv/ n adjetivo, m

adjoin /ə'dʒɔin/ vt estar contiguo a, lindar con; juntar. —vi colindar

adjoining /ə'dʒɔinɪŋ/ a vecino, de al lado, adyacente; cercano

adjourn /ə'dʒɜrn/ vt aplazar, diferir; (a meeting, etc.) suspender, levantar. —vi retirarse. **The debate was adjourned,** Se suspendió el debate. **to a. a meeting,** levantar la sesión

adjournment /ə'dʒɜrnmənt/ n aplazamiento, m; (of a meeting) suspensión (de la sesión), f

adjudicate /ə'dʒudɪ,keit/ vt adjudicar; Law. declarar; juzgar. —vi ejercer las funciones del juez; fallar, dictar sentencia

adjudication /ə,dʒudɪ'keiʃən/ n adjudicación, f; Law. fallo, m, sentencia, f; (of bankruptcy) declaración (de quiebra), f; concesión, f, otorgamiento, m

adjunct /'ædʒʌŋkt/ n atributo, m; accesorio, m; adjunto, m; Gram. adjunto, m

adjure /ə'dʒʊr/ vt conjurar; rogar encarecidamente

adjust /ə'dʒʌst/ vt ajustar; regular; arreglar; (correct) corregir; adaptar

adjustable /ə'dʒʌstəbəl/ a ajustable; regulable; desmontable; de quita y pon

adjustment /ə'dʒʌstmənt/ n ajuste, m; regulación, f; arreglo, m; (correction) corrección, f; adaptación, f; Com. prorrateo, m

administer /æd'mɪnəstər/ vt administrar; (laws) aplicar; (blows, etc.) dar; (an office) ejercer; (govern) regir, gobernar; (provide) suministrar; (an oath) tomar; (justice) hacer; (the sacraments) administrar; (with to) contribuir a. **to a. an oath,** tomar juramento (a)

administration /æd,mɪnə'streiʃən/ n administración, f; (government) gobierno, m; dirección, f; (of laws) aplicación, f; distribución, f

administrative /æd'mɪnə,streitɪv/ a administrativo; gubernativo

administrator /æd'mɪnə,streitər/ n administrador, m

admirable /'ædmərəbəl/ a admirable

admiral /'ædmərəl/ n almirante, m. **A. of the Fleet,** almirante supremo, m. **admiral's ship,** capitana, f

admiration /,ædmə'reiʃən/ n admiración, f

admire /æd'maiər/ vt sentir admiración por; (love) amar; (like) gustar; (respect) respetar

admirer /æd'maiərər/ n admirador (-ra); (amateur) aficionado (-da), apasionado (-da); (partisan) satélite, m; (lover) enamorado, amante, m

admiring /æd'maiərɪŋ/ a admirativo, de admiración

admissible /æd'mɪsəbəl/ a admisible; aceptable; lícito, permitido

admission /æd'mɪʃən/ n admisión, f; recepción, f; entrada, f; confesión, f, reconocimiento, m. **No a.!** Entrada prohibida. **right of a.,** derecho de entrada, m. **A. free,** Entrada libre. **a. ticket,** entrada, f

admit /æd'mɪt/ vt admitir; recibir; dejar entrar; hacer entrar, introducir; (hold) contener; (concede) conceder; (acknowledge) reconocer, confesar. **to a. of,** permitir; sufrir

admittance /æd'mɪtns/ n admisión, f; entrada, f. **No a.!** Prohibida la entrada. **to gain a.,** lograr entrar

admittedly /æd'mɪtɪdli/ adv según opinión general; sin duda

admonish /æd'mɒnɪʃ/ vt (advise) aconsejar; amonestar, advertir; (reprimand) reprender

admonition /,ædmə'nɪʃən/ n amonestación, f; advertencia, f; admonición, f

admonitory /æd'mɒnɪ,tɔri/ a amonestador

ad nauseam /'æd nɔziəm/ adv hasta la saciedad

ado /ə'du/ n (noise) ruido, m; (trouble) trabajo, m, dificultad, f; (fuss) barahúnda, f. **much ado about nothing,** mucho ruido y pocas nueces, nada entre dos platos. **without more ado,** sin más ni más

adolescence /,ædl'ɛsəns/ n adolescencia, f

adolescent /,ædl'ɛsənt/ a and n adolescente, mf

adopt /ə'dɒpt/ vt adoptar

adopted /ə'dɒptɪd/ a adoptivo

adoption /ə'dɒpʃən/ n adopción, f; (choice) elección, f

adore /ə'dɔr/ vt adorar

adoringly /ə'dɔrɪŋli/ adv con adoración

adorn /ə'dɔrn/ vt adornar, embellecer; (Fig. of persons) adornar con su presencia

adornment /ə'dɔrnmənt/ n adorno, m; ornamento, m; embellecimiento, m

adrenalin /ə'drɛnlɪn/ n adrenalina, f

adrift /ə'drɪft/ a and adv a merced de las olas; a la ventura. **to turn a.,** Inf. poner de patitas en la calle

adroit /ə'drɔit/ a hábil

adult /ə'dʌlt/ *a* and *n* adulto (-ta)

adult education *n* educación de los adultos, *f*

adulterate /v ə'dʌltə,reit; *a* ə'dʌltə,reit; -tərɪt/ *vt* adulterar; falsificar; contaminar. —*a* adulterado; falsificado; impuro

adulteration /ə,dʌltə'reiʃən/ *n* adulteración, *f*; falsificación, *f*; impureza, *f*; contaminación, *f*

adulterer /ə'dʌltərər/ *n* adúltero, *m*

adultery /ə'dʌltəri/ *n* adulterio, *m*. **to commit a.,** cometer adulterio, adulterar

advance /æd'væns/ *n* avance, *m*; (progress) progreso, adelantamiento, *m*; (improvement) mejora, *f*; (of shares) alza, *f*; (of price) subida, *f*; (loan) préstamo, *m*; (in rank) ascenso, *m*; *pl* **advances,** (overtures) avances, *m pl*; (proposals) propuestas, *f pl*; (of love) requerimientos amorosos, *m pl.* **in a.,** de antemano, con anticipación, con tiempo, previamente, (of money) por adelantado. **a. guard,** *Mil.* avanzada, *f.* **a. payment,** anticipo, *m*, paga por adelantado, *f*

advance /æd'væns/ *vt* avanzar; (suggest) sugerir, proponer; (encourage) fomentar; (a person) ascender; (improve) mejorar; (of events, dates) adelantar; (of prices, stocks) hacer subir; (money) anticipar; (of steps) tomar. —*vi* avanzar; (progress) progresar; (in rank, studies, etc.) adelantar; (of prices) subir

advanced /æd'vænst/ *a* avanzado; (developed) desarrollado; (mentally, of children) precoz; (course) superior. **a. research,** investigaciones superiores. **a. standing,** equivalencias, *f pl.* **a. views,** ideas avanzadas, *f pl*

advancement /æd'vænsmənt/ *n* adelantamiento, *m*; progreso, *m*; (encouragement) fomento, *m*; (in employment) promoción, *f*; prosperidad, *f*

advancing /æd'vænsɪŋ/ *a* que avanza; (of years) que pasan

advantage /æd'væntɪdʒ/ *n* ventaja, *f*; superioridad, *f*; (benefit) provecho, beneficio, *m*; interés, *m*; ocasión favorable, oportunidad, *f*; (tennis) ventaja, *f.* **to have the a. of,** tener la ventaja de. **to show to a.,** embellecer, realzar; aumentar la belleza (etc.) de. **to take a. of,** sacar ventaja de, aprovecharse de; (deceive) engañar. **to take a. of the slightest pretext,** asirse de un cabello

advantageous /,ædvən'teidʒəs/ *a* ventajoso, provechoso. **to be a.,** ser de provecho

adventure /æd'vɛntʃər/ *n* aventura, *f*; riesgo, *m*; (chance) casualidad, *f*; *Com.* especulación, *f.* —*vt* aventurar, arriesgar. —*vi* arriesgarse, osar

adventurer /æd'vɛntʃərər/ *n* aventurero, *m*; (one living by his wits) caballero de industria, *m*; (in commerce) especulador, *m*

adventuresome /æd'vɛntʃərsəm/ *a* de aventura

adventurous /æd'vɛntʃərəs/ *a* aven-

turero; osado, audaz; (dangerous) peligroso, arriesgado

adversary /'ædvər,sɛri/ *n* adversario (-ia)

adverse /æd'vɜrs/ *a* adverso; hostil (a); malo; desfavorable; (opposite) opuesto

advertise /'ædvər,taiz/ *vt* anunciar. —*vi* poner un anuncio; (oneself) llamar la atención

advertisement /,ædvər'taizmənt, æd'vɜrtɪsmənt/ *n* anuncio, *m*; (poster) cartel, *m*; (to attract attention) reclamo, *m.* **to put an a. in the paper,** poner un anuncio en el periódico. **a. hoarding,** cartelera, *f*

advertiser /'ædvər,taizər/ *n* anunciante, *mf*

advertising /'ædvər,taizɪŋ/ *n* anuncios, *m pl*; publicidad, propaganda, *f*; medios publicitarios, *m pl*

advice /æd'vais/ *n* consejo, *m*; (warning) advertencia, amonestación, *f*; (news) noticia, *f*, aviso, *m*; *Com.* comunicación, *f*; (belief) parecer, *m*, opinión, *f*. **piece of a.,** consejo, *m.* **to follow the a. of,** seguir los consejos de. **to give a.,** dar consejos

advisable /æd'vaizəbəl/ *a* conveniente, aconsejable; prudente

advise /æd'vaiz/ *vt* aconsejar; (inform) avisar, informar

advised /æd'vaizd/ *a* avisado; premeditado. **ill-a.,** mal aconsejado; imprudente. **well-a.,** bien aconsejado; prudente

adviser /æd'vaizər/ *n* consejero (-ra)

advocacy /'ædvəkəsi/ *n* defensa, *f*; apología, *f*; abogacía, intercesión, *f*

advocate /*n* 'ædvəkɪt; *v* -,keit/ *n Law.* abogado (-da); defensor (-ra); (champion) campeón, *m.* —*vt* abogar, defender; sostener, apoyar; recomendar

aegis /'idʒɪs/ *n* égida, *f*; protección, *f*

aerial /'ɛəriəl/ *a* aéreo, de aire; etéreo; fantástico. —*n* (radio) antena, *f.* **indoor a.,** antena interior, *f*

aerobics /ɛə'roubɪks/ *n* aerobismo *m*

aeronautics /,ɛərə'nɔtɪks/ *n* aeronáutica, *f*

afar /ə'fɑr/ *adv* a lo lejos, en la distancia. **from a.,** desde lejos

affable /'æfəbəl/ *a* afable, condescendiente

affair /ə'fɛər/ *n* asunto, *m*, cosa, *f*; cuestión, *f*; (business) negocio, *m*; (Fam. applied to a machine, carriage, etc.) artefacto, *m*; (of the heart) amorío, *m.* **a. of honour,** lance de honor, *m*

affect /ə'fɛkt/ *vt* afectar; influir; *Med.* atacar; (move) impresionar, conmover; enternecer; (harm) perjudicar; (frequent) frecuentar; (like) gustar de; (love) amar; (wear) vestir; (use) gastar, usar; (feign) aparentar; (boast) hacer alarde de

affected /ə'fɛktɪd/ *a* afectado; influido; *Med.* atacado; (moved) conmovido, impresionado; enternecido; (inclined) dispuesto, inclinado; (artificial) artificioso; amanerado, afectado; (of style) rebuscado, artificial

affection /ə'fɛkʃən/ n afecto, cariño, m; amor, m; apego, m; simpatía, f; (emotion) emoción, f, sentimiento, m; Med. afección, enfermedad, f

affectionate /ə'fɛkʃənɪt/ a afectuoso, cariñoso; mimoso; (tender) tierno; expresivo

affectionately /ə'fɛkʃənɪtli/ adv afectuosamente. **Yours a.,** tu cariñoso..., tu..., que te quiere

affidavit /,æfɪ'deɪvɪt/ n declaración jurada, declaración jurídica f, atestiguación, f

affiliate /ə'fɪli,eɪt/ vt afiliar; adoptar; Law. imputar; Law. legitimar

affiliation /ə,fɪli'eɪʃən/ n afiliación, f; adopción, f; legitimación de un hijo, f

affirm /ə'fɜrm/ vt afirmar, aseverar, declarar; confirmar. —vi Law. declarar ante un juez

affirmation /,æfər'meɪʃən/ n afirmación, f; aserción, f; confirmación, f; Law. declaración, deposición, f

affix /v ə'fɪks; n 'æfɪks/ vt fijar; pegar; añadir; (seal, one's signature) poner. —n Gram. afijo, m

afflict /ə'flɪkt/ vt afligir, atormentar, aquejar

affliction /ə'flɪkʃən/ n aflicción, f; tribulación, pesadumbre, f; calamidad, f; miseria, f; (ailment) achaque, m

affluence /'æfluəns/ n afluencia, f; abundancia, f; riqueza, f; opulencia, f

affluent /'æfluənt/ a abundante; rico; opulento

afford /ə'fɔrd/ vt dar, proporcionar; producir; ofrecer; (bear) soportar; poder con; (financially) tener medios para; permitirse el lujo de; (be able) poder. **I could not a. to pay so much,** No puedo (podía) pagar tanto

afforestation /ə,fɔrə'steɪʃən/ n conversión en bosque, f; plantación de un bosque, f

affront /ə'frʌnt/ n afrenta, f, insulto, agravio, m. —vt insultar, ultrajar, afrentar; (offend) ofender

afield /ə'fild/ adv en el campo; lejos. **to go far a.,** ir muy lejos

afire /ə'faɪʳr/ adv en fuego, en llamas. Fig. ardiendo

aflame /ə'fleɪm/ adv en llamas; Fig. encendido

afloat /ə'flout/ adv a flote; Naut. a bordo; (solvent) solvente; en circulación; (floating) flotante; (swamped) inundado; (in full swing) en marcha, en movimiento

afoot /ə'fut/ adv a pie; en marcha, en movimiento; en preparación. **to set a.,** iniciar, poner en marcha

aforesaid /ə'fɔr,sɛd/ a consabido, dicho, susodicho

afraid /ə'freid/ a espantado; temeroso, miedoso. **I'm a. that...,** Me temo que.... **to be a.,** tener miedo. **to make a.,** dar miedo (a)

afresh /ə'frɛʃ/ adv de nuevo, otra vez

African /'æfrɪkən/ a and n africano (-na)

aft /æft/ adv en popa; a popa. **fore and aft,** de proa a popa

after /'æftər/ prep (of place) detrás de; (of time) después de; (behind) en pos de; (following) tras; (in spite of) a pesar de; (in consequence of) después de, a consecuencia de; (in accordance with) según; (in the style of) al estilo de, en imitación de. —adv (later) después, más tarde; (subsequently) después (que); (when) cuando. —a futuro, venidero. **day a. day,** día tras día. **on the day a.,** al día siguiente. **soon a.,** poco después. **to look a.,** cuidar de. **to go a.,** ir a buscar; seguir. **the day a. tomorrow,** pasado mañana. **What are you a.?** ¿Qué buscas? **a. all,** después de todo. **a. the manner of,** a la moda de, según la moda de; al estilo de. **a.-dinner conversation,** conversación de sobremesa, f. **a. glow,** resplandor crepuscular, reflejo del sol poniente en el cielo, m. **a. life,** vida futura, f. **a. pains,** dolores de sobreparto, m pl. **a. taste,** dejo, resabio, m

afterbirth /'æftər,bɜrθ/ n placenta, f

aftermath /'æftər,mæθ/ n consecuencias, f pl, resultado, m

afternoon /'æftər'nun/ n tarde, f. **Good a.!** ¡Buenas tardes! **a. nap,** siesta, f. **a. tea,** el té de las cinco

afterthought /'æftər,θɔt/ n reflexión tardía, f; segunda intención, f. **to have an a.,** pensar en segundo lugar

afterwards /'æftərwərdz/ adv después; más tarde

again /ə'gɛn/ adv (once more) otra vez, de neuvo; por segunda vez, dos veces; (on the other hand) por otra parte; (moreover) además; (likewise) también; (returned) de vuelta. Sometimes translated by prefix re in verbs. **as much a.,** otro tanto. **never a.,** nunca más. **not a.,** no más. **now and a.,** de vez en cuando. **to do a.,** volver a hacer, hacer de nuevo. **a. and a.,** repetidas veces

against /ə'gɛnst/ prep (facing) enfrente de; contra; (in preparation for) para; (contrary to) contrario a; (opposed to) opuesto a; (near) cerca de. **a. the grain,** a contrapelo

age /eɪdʒ/ n edad, f; (generation) generación, f; (epoch) siglo, período, m; época, f; (old age) vejez, f; (majority) mayoría de edad, f, vi envejecer. **at any age,** a cualquier edad. **the golden age,** la edad de oro; (in literature, etc.) el siglo de oro. **from age to age,** por los siglos de los siglos. **to be of age,** ser mayor de edad. **to be under age,** ser menor de edad. **to come of age,** llegar a la mayoría de edad. **She is six years of age,** Ella tiene seis años. **age-old,** secular

aged /eɪdʒd; 'eɪdʒɪd/ a de la edad de; (old) anciano, viejo. **a girl a. four,** una niña de cuatro años

ageless /'eɪdʒlɪs/ a siempre joven; eterno

agency /'eɪdʒənsi/ n órgano, m, fuerza, f;

acción, f; influencia, f; intervención, f; mediación, f; *Com.* agencia, f. **through the a. of,** por la mediación (or influencia) de

agenda /ə'dʒɛndə/ n agenda, f

agent /'eidʒənt/ n agente, m; *Com.* representante, mf; *Law.* apoderado (-da). **business a.,** agente de negocios, m

agglomeration /ə,glɒmə'reiʃən/ n aglomeración, f

aggrandizement /ə'grændɪzmənt/ n engrandecimiento, m

aggravate /'ægrə,veit/ vt agravar, hacer peor; intensificar; (annoy) irritar, exasperar

aggravating /'ægrə,veitɪŋ/ a agravante, agravador; (tiresome) molesto; (annoying) irritante. **a. circumstance,** circunstancia agravante, f

aggravation /,ægrə'veiʃən/ n agravación, f, intensificación, f; (annoyance) irritación, f

aggregate /'ægrɪgɪt, -,geit/ a total. —n agregado, conjunto, m. **in the a.,** en conjunto

aggression /ə'grɛʃən/ n agresión, f

aggressive /ə'grɛsɪv/ a agresivo

aggrieved /ə'grivd/ a afligido; ofendido; lastimero

aghast /ə'gæst/ a horrorizado, espantado; (amazed) estupefacto

agile /'ædʒəl/ a ágil; ligero; vivo

agility /æ'dʒɪlɪti/ n agilidad, f; ligereza, f

agitate /'ædʒɪ,teit/ vt agitar; excitar; inquietar, perturbar; discutir. **to a. for,** luchar por; excitar la opinión pública en favor de

agitation /,ædʒɪ'teiʃən/ n agitación, f; perturbación, f; discusión, f

aglow /ə'glou/ a and adv brillante, fulgente; encendido

ago /ə'gou/ adv hace. **a short while ago,** hace poco. **How long ago?** ¿Cuánto tiempo hace? **long ago,** hace mucho. **many years ago,** hace muchos años. **I last saw him ten years ago,** La última vez que le vi fue hace diez años

agog /ə'gɒg/ a agitado; ansioso; excitado; impaciente; curioso. —adv con agitación; con ansia; con curiosidad

agonize /'ægə,naiz/ vt atormentar. —vi sufrir intensamente; retorcerse de dolor

agonizing /'ægə,naizɪŋ/ a (of pain) intenso; atormentador

agony /'ægəni/ n agonía, f; angustia, f; paroxismo, m. **a. column,** columna de los suspiros, f

agree /ə'gri/ vi estar de acuerdo. **Do you a. or disagree?** ¿Coincides o discrepas?; convenir (en); acordar; ponerse de acuerdo, entenderse; (suit) sentar bien, probar; (consent) consentir (en); *Gram.* concordar, (get on well) llevarse bien; (correspond) estar conforme (con). **to a. to,** convenir en, consentir en. **to a. with,** estar de acuerdo con, apoyar; dar la razón a; (suit) sentar bien; *Gram.* concordar

agreeable /ə'griəbəl/ a agradable; afable,

amable; (pleasant) ameno, grato; conforme; dispuesto a (hacer algo); conveniente

agreeableness /ə'griəbəlnɪs/ n (of persons) afabilidad, amabilidad, f; amenidad, f; deleite, m; conformidad, f

agreeably /ə'griəbli/ adv agradablemente; de acuerdo (con), conforme (a)

agreed /ə'grid/ a convenido, acordado; (approved) aprobado. —interj ¡convenido! ¡de acuerdo!

agreement /ə'grimənt/ n acuerdo, m; pacto, m; acomodamiento, concierto, m; contrato, m; *Com.* convenio, m; conformidad, f; consentimiento, m; *Gram.* concordancia, f. **in a.,** conforme. **in a. with,** de acuerdo con; según. **to reach an a.,** ponerse de acuerdo

agricultural /,ægri'kʌltʃərəl/ a agrícola. **a. engineer,** ingeniero agrónomo, m. **a. laborer,** labriego, m. **a. show,** exposición agrícola, f

agriculture /'ægri,kʌltʃər/ n agricultura, f

agronomist /ə'grɒnəmɪst/ n agrónomo, m

agronomy /ə'grɒnəmi/ n agronomía, f

aground /ə'graund/ adv *Naut.* varado, encallado. **running a.,** varada, f. **to run a.,** varar

ague /'eigyu/ n fiebre intermitente, f; *Fig.* escalofrío, m

ahead /ə'hɛd/ adv delante; enfrente; al frente (de); a la cabeza (de); adelante; hacia delante; *Naut.* por la proa. **Go a.!** ¡Adelante! **It is straight a.,** Está directamente enfrente. **to go straight a.,** ir hacia delante; seguir (haciendo algo)

aid /eid/ n ayuda, f; socorro, auxilio, m; subsidio, m, vt ayudar; socorrer, auxiliar. **in aid of,** pro, en beneficio de. **first aid,** primera cura, f. **first aid post,** puesto de socorro, m. **to come or go to the aid of,** acudir en defensa de

AIDS /eidz/ n el SIDA, m

ail /eil/ vt afligir; doler; pasar. —vi estar indispuesto (or enfermo). **What ails you?** *Inf.* ¿Qué te pasa?

ailing /'eilɪŋ/ a enfermizo, enclenque, achacoso

ailment /'eilmənt/ n enfermedad, f, achaque, m

aim /eim/ n (of firearms) puntería, f; (mark) blanco, m; *Fig.* objeto, fin, m; *Fig.* intención, f, propósito, m, vt (a gun) apuntar; dirigir; (throw) lanzar; (a blow) asestar. —vi apuntar (a); (a remark at) decir por; aspirar (a); intentar, proponerse. **Is your remark aimed at me?** ¿Lo dices por mí? **to aim high,** apuntar alto; *Inf.* picar alto. **to miss one's aim,** errar el tiro. **to take aim,** apuntar. **with the aim of,** con objeto de, a fin de

aimless /'eimlɪs/ a **aimlessly,** adv sin objeto, a la ventura

air /ɛər/ n aire, m, (all meanings). **by air,** en avión; (of mail) por avión; (of goods) por vía aérea. **in the air,** al aire; al aire libre; (as though flying) en volandas. **in the open air**, al aire libre, al fresco, a la intemperie. **to be on the air**, *Radio*. hablar por radio. **to give oneself airs**, darse tono, tener humos. **to take the air**, tomar el fresco; despegar. **air balloon**, globo aerostático, *m*; (toy) globo, *m*. **air-base**, base aérea, *f*. **air-bed**, colchón de aire, *m*. **air-borne (to become)**, levantar el vuelo, despegar. **air-brake**, *Mech*. freno neumático, *m*. **air-chamber**, cámara de aire, *f*. **air chief marshal**, general del ejército del aire, *m*. **air-cock**, válvula de escape de aire, *f*. **air commodore**, general de brigada de aviación, *m*. **air conditioning**, purificación de aire, *f*. **air-cooled**, enfriado por aire. **air crash**, accidente de avicación, *m*. **air current**, corriente de aire, *m*. **air-cushion**, almohadilla neumática, *f*. **air-field**, campo de aviación, *m*. **air fleet**, flotilla aérea, *f*. **air force**, fuerza aérea, flota aérea, *f*. **air-gun**, escopeta de viento, *f*. **air-hole**, respiradero, *m*. **air-hostess**, azafata, *f*. **air-lift**, puente aéreo, *m*. **air-liner**, avión de pasajeros, *m*. **airline** línea aérea, aerolínea, *f*. **airmail**, correo aéreo, *m*. **by airmail**, por avión. **air marshal**, teniente general de aviación, *m*. **air-pocket**, bolsa (or vacío, *m*) de aire, *f*. **air pollution** contaminación atmosférica, *f*. **air pump**, bomba neumática, *f*. **air raid**, bombardeo aéreo, *m*. **air-raid shelter**, refugio antiaéreo, *m*. **air-raid warning**, alarma aérea, *f*. **air-route**, vía aérea, *f*. **air-screw**, hélice de avión, *f*. **air-shaft**, respiradero de mina, *m*. **air shuttle**, puente aéreo, *m*. **air squadron**, escuadrilla aérea, *f*. **air stream**, chorro de aire, *m*. **air taxi**, avión taxi, *m*. **air-tight**, herméticamente cerrado. **air valve**, válvula de aire, *f*. **air vice-marshal**, general de división de aviación, *m*

air /ɛər/ *vt* airear, orear; secar al aire; ventilar; *Fig*. sacar a lucir, emitir; *Fig*. ostentar

aircraft /'ɛər,kræft/ *n* aparato, avión, *m*. **a. barrage**, cortina de fuego de artillería, *f*. **a.-carrier**, porta-aviones, *m*. **a. factory**, fábrica de aeroplanos, *f*

airing /'ɛərɪŋ/ *n* aireación, *f*; ventilación, *f*; secamiento, *m*; (walk) vuelta, *f*, paseo, *m*. **to take an a.**, dar una vuelta

airplane /'ɛər,pleɪn/ *n* aeroplano, avión, *m*. **jet-propelled a.**, aeroplano de reacción, *m*. **model a.**, aeroplano en miniatura, *m*

airport /'ɛər,pɔrt/ *n* aeropuerto, *m*

airsick /'ɛər,sɪk/ *a* mareado en el aire, mareado

airy /'ɛəri/ *a* aéreo; (breezy) airoso; ligero; vaporoso; alegre; (vain) vano; (flippant) frívolo

aisle /aɪl/ *n* nave lateral, ala, *f*

ajar /ə'dʒɑr/ *a* entreabierto, entornado. **to leave a.**, dejar entreabierto, entornar

akimbo /ə'kɪmbou/ *adv* en jarras. **with arms a.**, con los brazos en jarras

akin /ə'kɪn/ *a* consanguíneo, emparentado; análogo, relacionado; semejante

alarm /ə'lɑrm/ *n* alarma, *f*, toque de alarma, *m*; (tocsin) rebato, *m*; sobresalto, *m*, alarma, *f*. —*vt* alarmar; *Mil*. dar la alarma (a); asustar. **to give the a.**, dar la alarma. **a. bell**, timbre de alarma, *m*. **a. clock**, despertador, *m*. **a. signal**, señal de alarma, *f*

alarming /ə'lɑrmɪŋ/ *a* alarmante

alarmingly /ə'lɑrmɪŋli/ *adv* de un modo alarmante; espantosamente

alarmist /ə'lɑrmɪst/ *n* alarmista, *mf*

alas! /ə'læs/ *interj* ¡ay!

albeit /ɔl'biːt/ *conjunc* aunque, si bien; sin embargo

album /'ælbəm/ *n* álbum, *m*

albumin /æl'byumən/ *n* albúmina, *f*

alcohol /'ælkə,hɔl/ *n* alcohol, *m*. **industrial a.**, alcohol desnaturalizado, *m*. **wood a.**, alcohol metílico, alcohol de madera, *m*

alcoholic /,ælkə'hɔlɪk/ *a* alcohólico

alcove /'ælkouv/ *n* alcoba, *f*; nicho, *m*

alderman /'ɔldərmən/ *n* concejal, *m*

ale /eɪl/ *n* cerveza, *f*. **ale-house**, cervecería, *f*

alert /ə'lɜrt/ *a* alerto; vigilante; despierto; vivo. —*n* sirena, *f*. **to be on the a.**, estar sobre aviso; estar vigilante

alertly /ə'lɜrtli/ *adv* alertamente

alertness /ə'lɜrtnɪs/ *n* vigilancia, *f*; viveza, *f*; prontitud, *f*

algebra /'ældʒəbrə/ *n* álgebra, *f*

algebraic /,ældʒə'breɪk/ *a* algebraico

Algeria /æl'dʒɪəriə/ Argelia, *f*

Algerian /æl'dʒɪəriən/ *a and n* argelino (-na)

alias /'eɪliəs/ *adv* alias, por otro nombre. —*n* nombre falso, seudónimo, *m*

alibi /'ælə,baɪ/ *n Law*. coartada, *f*. **to prove an a.**, probar la coartada

alien /'eɪliən/ *a* ajeno; (foreign) extranjero; extraño; contrario. —*n* extranjero (-ra). **a. to**, ajeno a; repugnante a. **Aliens Department**, Sección de Extranjeros, *f*

alienable /'eɪliənəbəl/ *a* enajenable

alienate /'eɪliə,neɪt/ *vt* alejar, hacer indiferente; (property) enajenar, traspasar

alienation /,eɪliə'neɪʃən/ *n* desvío, *m*; enajenación, *f*; traspaso, *m*; enajenación mental, *f*

alight /ə'laɪt/ *vi* apearse (de), bajar (de); desmontar (de); (of birds, etc.) posarse (sobre)

alight /ə'laɪt/ *a* encendido, iluminado; en llamas

align /ə'laɪn/ *vt* alinear

alignment /ə'laɪnmənt/ *n* alineación, *f*

alike /ə'laɪk/ *a* semejante; igual. —*adv* del mismo modo; igualmente

alimentary /,ælə'mɛntəri/ *a* nutritivo; alimenticio. **a. canal**, tubo digestivo, *m*

alimony /'ælə,mouni/ *n Law*. alimentos, *m pl*, pensión alimenticia, *f*

alive /ə'laɪv/ *a* viviente; vivo; del mundo;

(busy) animado, concurrido; (aware) sensible; (alert) lleno de vida, enérgico, despierto. **He is still a.,** Aún vive. **He is the best man a.,** Es el mejor hombre que existe, Es el mejor hombre del mundo. **half-a.,** semivivo. **while a.,** en vida. **a. to,** consciente de, sensible de. **a. with,** plagado de, lleno de

all /ɔl/ a todo, m; toda, f; todos, m pl; todas, f pl; (in games) iguales. —adv enteramente, completamente; del todo; absolutamente. **after all,** después de todo; sin embargo. **at all,** nada; de ninguna manera; en absoluto. **fifteen all,** (tennis) quince iguales. **for good and all,** para siempre. **if that's all,** si no es más que eso. **in all,** en conjunto. **It is all one to me,** Me da igual. **not at all,** de ningún modo, nada de eso; nada; (never) jamás; (as a polite formula) No hay de qué. **once for all,** una vez por todas; por última vez. **That is all,** Eso es todo. **all along,** (of time) siempre, todo el tiempo; (of place) a lo largo de, de un extremo a otro de. **all but,** (almost) casi, por poco; (except) todo menos. **all joking aside,** fuera de burla. **all of them,** todos ellos, m pl; todas ellas, f pl. **All right!** ¡Bien! ¡Está bien! ¡Entendido! **all that,** todo eso; (as much as) cuanto. **all that which,** todo lo que. **all those who,** todos los que, m pl; todas las que, f pl. **all the more,** cuanto más. **all the same,** sin embargo, a pesar de todo. **all the worse,** tanto peor

all /ɔl/ n todo, m; todos, m pl; todas, f pl; (everyone, all men) todo el mundo. **to lose one's all,** perder todo lo que se tiene. **All is lost,** Todo se ha perdido. **all told,** en conjunto

all /ɔl/ (in compounds) **all-absorbing,** que todo lo absorbe; sumamente interesante. **all-bountiful,** de suma bondad. **all-conquering,** invicto. **all-consuming,** que todo lo consume; irresistible; ardiente. **all-enduring,** resignado a todo. **All Fools' Day,** Día de los Inocentes, m, (December 28). **all-fours,** a cuatro patas; a gatas. **to go on all fours,** andar a gatas. **All hail!** ¡Salud! ¡Bienvenido! **all-important,** suma importancia importante. **all-in insurance,** seguro contra todo riesgo, m. **all-in wrestling,** lucha libre, f. **all-loving,** de un amor infinito. **all-merciful,** de una compasión infinita, sumamente misericordioso. **all-powerful,** omnipotente, todo poderoso. **all-round,** completo, cabal; universal. **an all-round athlete,** un atleta completo. **All Souls' Day,** Día de las Ánimas, Día de los difuntos, m. **all-wise,** omniscio

Allah /ˈælə/ n Alá, m

allay /əˈlei/ vt calmar; (relieve) aliviar; apaciguar

allegation /ˌæliˈgeiʃən/ n alegación, f

allege /əˈledʒ/ vt afirmar, declarar; alegar

allegiance /əˈlidʒəns/ n lealtad, f; fidelidad, f; obediencia, f

alleluia /ˌæləˈluyə/ n aleluya, mf

allergic /əˈlɔrdʒɪk/ a alérgico

allergist /ˈælərdʒɪst/ n alergólogo, m

allergy /ˈælərdʒi/ n alergia, f

alleviate /əˈliviˌeit/ vt aliviar

alleviation /əˌliviˈeiʃən/ n alivio, m; mitigación, f

alley /ˈæli/ n callejuela, f, callejón, m; avenida, f; (skittle a.) pista de bolos, f. **a.-way,** Naut. pasadizo, m

alliance /əˈlaiəns/ n alianza, f; parentesco, m

allied /ˈælaid/ a aliado; allegado

alligator /ˈæliˌgeitər/ n caimán, m. **a. pear,** avocado, m

allocate /ˈæləˌkeit/ vt asignar, destinar; distribuir, repartir

allocation /ˌæləˈkeiʃən/ n asignación, f; distribución, f, repartimiento, m

allotment /əˈlotmənt/ n repartimiento, m, distribución, f; porción, f; lote, m; parcela de tierra, huerta, f

allow /əˈlau/ vt permitir; autorizar; dejar; tolerar, sufrir; (provide) dar; conceder, otorgar; (acknowledge) admitir; confesar; (discount) descontar; (a pension) hacer; deducir. **to a. for,** tener en cuenta; ser indulgente con; deducir; dejar (espacio, etc.) para

allowable /əˈlauəbəl/ a admisible, permisible; lícito, legítimo

allowance /əˈlauəns/ n ración, f; (discount) descuento, m; pensión, f; concesión, f; excusa, f; (subsidy) subsidio, m; (bonus) abono, m; (monthly) mesada, f. **to make a. for,** tener presente; hacer excusas para, ser indulgente con

alloy /n ˈæloi, v əˈlɔi/ n aleación, f; liga, f; mezcla, f. —vt alear, ligar; mezclar

all-star game /ˈɔlˌstar/ n juego de estrellas, m

allude /əˈlud/ vi aludir (a), referirse (a)

allure /əˈlur/ vt convidar, provocar; atraer; seducir, fascinar

allurement /əˈlurmənt/ n (snare) añagaza, f; atracción, f; tentación, seducción, f

alluring /əˈlurɪŋ/ a atractivo, seductor, tentador; (promising) halagüeño

allusion /əˈluʒən/ n alusión, referencia, f; insinuación, f

ally /n ˈælai, v əˈlai/ n aliado (-da), allegado (-da); asociado (-da); (state) aliado, m. —vt unir. **to become allies,** aliarse

almanac /ˈɔlməˌnæk/ n almanaque, m

almighty /ɔlˈmaiti/ a omnipotente

almond /ˈamənd/ n almendra, f; (tree) almendro, m. **bitter a.,** almendra amarga, f. **green a.,** almendruco, m. **milk of almonds,** horchata de almendras, f; (for the hands) loción de almendras, f. **sugar a.,** almendra garapiñada, f. **a.-eyed,** con, or de, ojos rasgados. **a. paste,** pasta de almendras, f. **a.-shaped,** en forma de almendra, almendrado

almost /ˈɔlmoust/ adv casi; por poco

alms /amz/ n limosna, f. **to ask a.,** pedir

limosna, mendigar. **to give a.,** dar limosna. **a.-box,** cepillo de limosna, *m*

almsgiving /'ɑmz,gɪvɪŋ/ *n* caridad, *f*

aloft /ə'lɔft/ *adv* arriba, en alto

alone /ə'loun/ *a* solo; solitario. —*adv* a solas, sin compañía; solamente; únicamente. **to leave a.,** dejar solo; dejar en paz

along /ə'lɔŋ/ *adv* adelante; a lo largo; todo el tiempo. —*prep* a lo largo de; por; al lado (de); en compañía (de). **Come a.l** ¡Ven! **all a.,** todo el tiempo, desde el principio; a lo largo de. **a. with,** junto con; en compañía de

alongside /ə'lɔŋ'said/ *adv* al lado; *Naut.* al costado. —*prep* junto a, al lado de; *Naut.* al costado de. **to bring a.,** *Naut.* abarloar. **to come a.,** *Naut.* acostarse

aloof /ə'luf/ *adv* a distancia; lejos. —*a* altanero, esquivo; reservado. **to keep a.,** mantenerse alejado

aloud /ə'laud/ *adv* en alta voz, alto

alpaca /æl'pækə/ *n* alpaca, *f*

alphabet /'ælfə,bɛt/ *n* alfabeto, *m*; abecedario, *m*

alphabetical /,ælfə'bɛtɪkəl/ *a* alfabético

already /ɔl'rɛdi/ *adv* ya; previamente

also /'ɔlsou/ *adv* también, igualmente, además

altar /'ɔltər/ *n* altar, *m*. **high a.,** altar mayor, *m*. **to lead a woman to the a.,** llevar a una mujer a la iglesia. **a.-cloth,** mantel del altar, *m*. **a.-piece,** retablo, *m*. **a.-rail,** mesa del altar, *f*

altar boy *n* acólito, monaguillo, *m*

altar girl *n* acólita, monaguilla, *f*

altar server *n* acólito, monaguillo, *m* (male), acólita, monaguilla, *f* (female)

alter /'ɔltər/ *vt* cambiar; alterar; modificar; corregir; transformar; (clothes) arreglar. —*vi* cambiar

alteration /,ɔltə'reɪʃən/ *n* cambio, *m*, alteración, *f*; modificación, *f*; corrección, *f*; innovación, *f*; (to buildings, etc.) reforma, *f*; renovación, *f*; arreglo, *m*

alternate /a 'ɔltərnɪt; *v* -,neit/ *a* alternativo; (*Bot.* and of rhymes) alterno. —*vt* and *vi* alternar

alternating /'ɔltər,neitɪŋ/ *a* alternador. **a. current,** *Elec.* corriente alterna, *f*

alternation /,ɔltər'neiʃən/ *n* alternación, *f*; (of time) transcurso, *m*; turno, *m*

alternative /ɔl'tɜrnətɪv/ *n* alternativa, *f*, *a* alternativo, alterno. **to have no a. but,** no poder menos de

alternative medicine /ɔl'tɜrnətɪv 'mɛdəsɪn/ *n* medicina alternativa *f*

alternator /'ɔltər,neitər/ *n* *Elec.* alternador, *m*

although /ɔl'ðou/ *conjunc* aunque, bien que; si bien; no obstante, a pesar de

altitude /'ælti,tud/ *n* altitud, elevación, *f*; altura, *f*

alto /'æltou/ *n* (voice) contralto, *m*; (singer) contralto, *mf*; viola, *f*

altogether /,ɔltə'gɛðər/ *adv* completamente; del todo; en conjunto

altruism /'æltru,ɪzəm/ *n* altruísmo, *m*

altruist /'æltruɪst/ *n* altruista, *mf*

aluminum /ə'lumənəm/ *n* aluminio, *m*

aluminum foil *n* hoja de aluminio, *f*

always /'ɔlweiz/ *adv* siempre

amalgam /ə'mælgəm/ *n* amalgama, *f*; mezcla, *f*

amalgamate /ə'mælgə,meit/ *vt* amalgamar; combinar, unir. —*vi* amalgamarse; combinarse, unirse

amalgamation /ə,mælgə'meiʃən/ *n* amalgamación, *f*; combinación, *f*; mezcla, *f*

amass /ə'mæs/ *vt* acumular, amontonar

amateur /'æmə,tʃʊr/ *a* and *n* aficionado (-da), (sports) no profesional. **a. theatricals,** función de aficionados, *f*

amateurish /'æmə,tʃʊrɪʃ/ *a* no profesional; de aficionado; superficial; (clumsy) torpe

amaze /ə'meiz/ *vt* asombrar, sorprender; pasmar; confundir

amazed /ə'meizd/ *a* asombrado; sorprendido; admirado; asustado

amazement /ə'meizmənt/ *n* asombro, pasmo, *m*; sorpresa, *f*; (wonderment) admiración, *f*; estupor, *m*

amazing /ə'meizɪŋ/ *a* asombroso, pasmoso; sorprendente

amazingly /ə'meizɪŋli/ *adv* asombrosamente

Amazon River, the el (Río de las) Amazonas, *m*

ambassador /æm'bæsədər/ *n* embajador, *m*

ambassadress /æm'bæsədrɪs/ *n* embajadora, *f*

amber /'æmbər/ *n* ámbar, *m*, *a* ambarino

ambidextrous /,æmbɪ'dɛkstrəs/ *a* ambidextro

ambiguity /,æmbɪ'gyuɪti/ *n* ambigüedad, *f*

ambiguous /æm'bɪgyuəs/ *a* ambiguo, equívoco

ambition /æm'bɪʃən/ *n* ambición, *f*

ambitious /æm'bɪʃəs/ *a* ambicioso. **to be a. to,** ambicionar

amble /'æmbəl/ *n* (of a horse) paso de andadura, *m*; paso lento, *m*. —*vi* (of a horse) andar a paso de andadura; andar lentamente

ambulance /'æmbyələns/ *n* ambulancia, *f*. **a. corps,** cuerpo de sanidad, *m*. **a. man,** sanitario, *m*

ambulatory /'æmbyələ,tɔri/ *n* paseo, *m*; claustro, *m*, *a* ambulante

ambush /'æmbʊʃ/ *n* acecho, *m*, asechanza, *f*; *Mil.* emboscada, *f*. —*vt* acechar, asechar; *Mil.* emboscar; sorprender. **to be in a.,** emboscarse, estar en acecho

ameba /ə'mibə/ *n* amiba, *f*

amelioration /ə,milyə'reiʃən/ *n* mejora, *f*

amen /'ei'mɛn, 'ɑ'mɛn/ *n* amén, *m*

amenable /ə'minəbəl/ *a* sujeto (a); responsable; dócil; fácil de convencer, dispuesto a ser razonable; dispuesto a escuchar. **to make a. to reason,** hacer razonable

amend /ə'mɛnd/ vt enmendar; modificar. —vi reformarse

amendment /ə'mɛndmənt/ n enmienda, f; modificación, f

amends /ə'mɛndz/ n pl reparación, f; satisfacción, f; compensación, f. **to make a.,** dar satisfacción

amenity /ə'mɛniti/ n amenidad, f

America /ə'mɛrɪkə/ América, f

American /ə'mɛrɪkən/ n americano (-na); (U.S.A.) norteamericano (-na). —a americano, de América; norteamericano, de los Estados Unidos. **Central A.,** a and n centroamericano (-na). **A. bar,** bar americano, m

Americanize /ə'mɛrɪkə,naiz/ vt americanizar

amethyst /'æməθɪst/ n amatista, f

amiability /,eimiə'bɪliti/ n amabilidad, afabilidad, cordialidad, f

amiable /'eimiəbəl/ a amable, afable, cordial

amiably /'eimiəbli/ adv amablemente, con afabilidad

amicable /'æmɪkəbəl/ a amigable, amistoso

amid, amidst /ə'mɪd; ə'mɪdst/ prep en medio de; entre; rodeado por

amidships /ə'mɪd,ʃɪps/ adv en el centro del buque, en medio del navío

amiss /ə'mɪs/ adv mal; de más; (ill) indispuesto, enfermo; (inopportunely) inoportunamente. —a malo. **It would not come a.,** No vendría mal. **to take a.,** llevar a mal

ammeter /'æm,mitər/ n Elec. amperímetro, m

ammonia /ə'mounyə/ n amoníaco, m

ammunition /,æmyə'nɪʃən/ n munición, f. **a. box,** cajón de municiones, m

amnesia /æm'niʒə/ n amnesia, f

amnesty /'æmnəsti/ n amnistía, f. **to concede an a. to,** amnistiar

amok /ə'mʌk/ (**to run a.**) atacar a ciegas

among /ə'mʌŋ/ prep en medio de; entre; con

amoral /ei'mɔrəl/ a amoral

amorality /,eimə'ræliti/ n amoralidad, f

amorous /'æmərəs/ a amoroso; (tender) tierno

amorousness /'æmərəsnɪs/ n erotismo, m; galantería, f

amorphous /ə'mɔrfəs/ a amorfo

amortization /,æmərtə'zeiʃən/ n amortización, f

amortize /'æmər,taiz/ vt amortizar

amount /ə'maunt/ n importe, m, suma, f; cantidad, f. vi (to) subir a, ascender a, llegar a; valer; reducirse a. **gross a.,** importe bruto, m. **net a.,** importe líquido, importe neto, m. **It amounts to the same thing, then,** Es igual entonces, Viene a ser lo mismo pues. **What he says amounts to this,** Lo que dice se reduce a esto

ampere /'æmpiər/ n amper, amperio, m

amphibian /æm'fɪbiən/ n anfibio, m

amphibious /æm'fɪbiəs/ a anfibio

amphitheater /'æmfə,θiətər/ n anfiteatro, m

amphora /'æmfərə/ n ánfora, f

ample /'æmpəl/ a amplio; abundante; extenso, vasto; (sufficient) bastante, suficiente

amplification /,æmpləfɪ'keiʃən/ n amplificación, f

amplifier /'æmplə,faiər/ n amplificador, m

amplify /'æmplə,fai/ vt amplificar; aumentar, ampliar

amplitude /'æmplɪ,tud/ n amplitud, f; abundancia, f; extensión, f

amply /'æmpli/ adv ampliamente; abundantemente; suficientemente

amputate /'æmpyu,teit/ vt amputar

amputation /,æmpyu'teiʃən/ n amputación, f

amulet /'æmyəlɪt/ n amuleto, m

amuse /ə'myuz/ vt divertir, entretener, distraer. **to a. oneself,** divertirse; pasarlo bien

amusement /ə'myuzmənt/ n diversión, f, entretenimiento, m; (hobby) pasatiempo, m. **a. park,** parque de atracciones, m

amusing /ə'myuzɪŋ/ a divertido, entretenido; (of people) salado

amusingly /ə'myuzɪŋli/ adv de un modo divertido, entretenidamente

an /ən/ See a

anachronism /ə'nækrə,nɪzəm/ n anacronismo, m

anachronistic /ə,nækrə'nɪstɪk/ a anacrónico

anagram /'ænə,græm/ n anagrama, m

analgesia /,ænl'dʒiziə/ n analgesia, f

analgesic /,ænl'dʒizɪk/ a and n analgésico, m.

analogous /ə'næləgəs/ a análogo

analogy /ə'nælədʒi/ n analogía, f

analysis /ə'næləsɪs/ n análisis, m

analyst /'ænlɪst/ n analista, mf

analytical /,ænl'ɪtɪkəl/ a analítico

anarchic /æn'ɔrkɪk/ a anárquico

anarchism /'ænər,kɪzəm/ n anarquismo, m

anarchist /'ænərkɪst/ n anarquista, mf

anarchy /'ænərki/ n anarquía, f

anastigmatic /,ænəstɪg'mætɪk/ a anastigmático

anathema /ə'næθəmə/ n anatema, mf

anatomically /,ænə'tɒmɪkli/ adv anatómicamente; físicamente

anatomist /ə'nætəmɪst/ n anatomista, mf

anatomy /ə'nætəmi/ n anatomía, f

ancestor /'ænsɛstər/ n antepasado, abuelo, m

ancestral /æn'sɛstrəl/ a de sus antepasados; de familia; hereditario. **a. home,** casa solariega, f

ancestry /'ænsɛstri/ n antepasados, m pl;

linaje, abolengo, *m;* estirpe, *f;* nacimiento, *m;* origen, *m*

anchor /'æŋkɑr/ *n* ancla, *f. Fig.* áncora, *f.*
—*vt* sujetar con el ancla. —*vi* anclar,
echar anclas, fondear. **at a.,** al ancla.
drag a., ancla flotante, ancla de arrastre,
f. **sheet a.,** ancla de la esperanza, *f; Fig.*
ancla de salvación, *f.* **to drop a.,** anclar.
to ride at a., estar al ancla. **to weigh a.,**
levar el ancla

anchorage /'æŋkərɪdʒ/ *n* anclaje, *m;* an-
cladero, fondeadero, *m;* derechos de anclaje, *m pl*

anchorite /'æŋkəˌrait/ *n* anacoreta, *mf*

anchovy /'æntʃouvi/ *n* anchoa, *f,* boquerón, *m*

ancient /'einʃənt/ *a* anciano; antiguo.
—*n pl* **ancients,** los antiguos. **from a.
times,** de antiguo. **most a.,** antiquísimo

and /ænd, ənd/ *conjunc* y; (before
stressed i or hi) e; (after some verbs and
before infin.) de, a; que; (with) con; (often not translated before infins.) **Better
and better,** Mejor que mejor. **I shall try
and do it,** Trataré de hacerlo. **to come
and see,** venir a ver. **We shall try and
speak to him,** Procuraremos hablar con
él

Andalusia /ˌændlˈuʒə/ Andalucía, *f*

Andalusian /ˌændlˈuʒən/ *a* andaluz. —*n*
andaluz (-za). **A. hat,** sombrero calañés,
m

Andean /'ændiən/ *a* andino

Andes, the /'ændiz/ los Andes, *f*

andiron /'ændˌaiᵊrn/ *n* morillo, *m*

Andorran /æn'dɔrən/ *a* and *n* andorrano
(-na)

anecdote /'ænɪkˌdout/ *n* anécdota, *f*

anemia /ə'nimiə/ *n* anemia, *f*

anemic /ə'nimɪk/ *a* anémico

anesthesia /ˌænəs'θiʒə/ *n* anestesia, *f*

anesthetic /ˌænəs'θɛtɪk/ *a* and *n* acólito,
monaguillo, *m*

anesthetist /ə'nɛsθɪtɪst/ *n* anestesiador
(-ra)

anesthetize /ə'nɛsθɪˌtaiz/ *vt* anestesiar

aneurism /'ænyəˌrɪzəm/ *n* aneurisma, *mf*

angel /'eindʒəl/ *n* ángel, *m*

angelic /æn'dʒɛlɪk/ *a* angélico

anger /'æŋgər/ *n* cólera, ira, *f,* enojo, *m,*
vt enojar, encolerizar; hacer rabiar

angina /æn'dʒainə/ *n* angina, *f.* **a. pectoris,** angina de pecho, *f.*

angle /'æŋgəl/ *n* ángulo, *m;* rincón, *m;*
esquina, *f;* (of a roof) caballete, *m; Fig.*
punto de vista, *m, vi* pescar con caña. **at
an a.,** a un lado. **a.-iron,** hierro angular,
m. **to a. for,** pescar; *Fig.* procurar obtener

Angle /'æŋgəl/ *a* and *n* anglo (-la)

angler /'æŋglər/ *n* pescador (-ra) de caña

Anglican /'æŋglɪkən/ *a* and *n* anglicano
(-na)

Anglicism /'æŋgləˌsɪzəm/ *n* anglicismo,
inglesismo, *m*

angling /'æŋglɪŋ/ *n* pesca con caña, *f*

Anglo- (in compounds) anglo-. **A.-**

American, *a* and *n* angloamericano (-na).
A.-Indian, *a* and *n* angloindio (-ia). **A.-
Saxon,** *a* and *n* anglosajón (-ona); (lan-
guage) anglosajón, *m*

angora /æŋ'gɔrə/ *n* angora, *f.* **a. cat,**
gato de angora, *m.* **a. rabbit,** conejo de
angora, *m*

angrily /'æŋgrəli/ *adv* airadamente

angry /'æŋgri/ *a* (of persons) enfadado,
enojado, airado; (of waves, etc.) furioso;
Med. inflamado; (red) rojo; (scowling)
ceñudo; (dark) obscuro. **to be a.,** estar
enojado. **to grow a.,** enojarse, enfadarse;
(of waves) encresparse; (of the sky) obscurecerse. **to make a.,** enojar

anguish /'æŋgwɪʃ/ *n* agonía, *f,* dolor, *m;*
angustia, *f.* —*vt* angustiar

angular /'æŋgyələr/ *a* angular; (of
features, etc.) anguloso

animal /'ænəməl/ *a* and *n* animal *m.* **a.
fat,** grasa animal, *f.* **a. kingdom,** reino
animal, *m.* **a. spirits,** *Philos.* espíritus animales, *m pl;* brío, *m,* energía, *f*

animate /*v* 'ænəˌmeit; *a* -mɪt/ *vt* animar;
inspirar. —*a* animado; viviente

animated /'ænəˌmeitɪd/ *a* animado; vivo,
lleno de vida

animation /ˌænə'meiʃən/ *n* animación, *f;*
vivacidad, *f;* calor, fuego, *m*

animosity /ˌænə'mɒsɪti/ *n* animosidad, *f,*
hostilidad, *f*

aniseed /'ænəˌsid/ *n* anís, *m*

anisette /ˌænə'sɛt/ *n* (liqueur) anisete, *m*

ankle /'æŋkəl/ *n* tobillo, *m.* **a. bone,**
hueso del tobillo, *m.* **a. sock,** calcetín
corto, *m*

anklet /'æŋklɪt/ *n* brazalete para el tobillo, *m;* (support) tobillera, *f*

annals /'ænlz/ *n pl* anales, *m pl*

annex /*v* ə'nɛks; 'æneks; *n* 'æneks/ *vt*
unir, juntar; anexar. —*n* anexo, *m*

annexation /ˌænɪk'seiʃən/ *n* anexión, *f*

annihilate /ə'naiəˌleit/ *vt* aniquilar

annihilation /əˌnaiə'leiʃən/ *n* aniquilación,

anniversary /ˌænə'vɜrsəri/ *a* and *n*
aniversario, *m.*

annotate /'ænəˌteit/ *vt* anotar, acotar,
comentar, hacer anotaciones a

annotation /ˌænə'teiʃən/ *n* anotación, *f;*
nota, *f*

annotator /'ænəˌteitər/ *n* anotador (-ra),
comentador (-ra)

announce /ə'nauns/ *vt* proclamar; declarar; publicar; anunciar

announcement /ə'naunsmənt/ *n* proclama, *f;* declaración, *f;* publicación, *f;*
anuncio, *m;* (of a betrothal) participación,
f

announcer /ə'naunsər/ *n* anunciador
(-ra); (radio or TV) locutor (-ra)

annoy /ə'nɔi/ *vt* exasperar, irritar, disgustar; molestar, incomodar

annoyance /ə'nɔiəns/ *n* disgusto, *m,*
exasperación, *f;* molestia, *f,* fastidio, *m*

annoying /ə'nɔiɪŋ/ *a* enojoso, molesto,
fastidioso

annual /'ænyuəl/ *a* anual. —*n* anuario, *m;* calendario, *m;* planta anual, *f*

annually /'ænyuəli/ *adv* anualmente, cada año

annuity /ə'nuɪti/ *n* anualidad, pensión vitalicia, *f*

annul /ə'nʌl/ *vt* anular

annulment /ə'nʌlmənt/ *n* anulación, *f*

annunciation /ə,nʌnsi'eiʃən/ *n* anunciación, *f.* **the A.,** la Anunciación

anoint /ə'nɔint/ *vt* untar; (before death) olear; (a king, etc.) ungir

anointing /ə'nɔintɪŋ/ *n* unción, *f*

anomalous /ə'nɒmələs/ *a* anómalo

anomaly /ə'nɒməli/ *n* anomalía, *f*

anonymity /,ænə'nɪmɪti/ *n* anónimo, *m*

anonymous /ə'nɒnəməs/ *a* anónimo. **a. letter,** anónimo, *m*

anonymously /ə'nɒnəməsli/ *adv* anónimamente

another /ə'nʌðər/ *a* otro; (different) distinto. —*n* otro, *m;* otra, *f.* **For one thing... and for a.,** En primer lugar..., y además (y por otra cosa). **one after a.,** uno después de otro. **They love one a.,** Ellos se aman. **They sent it from one to a.,** Lo mandaron de uno a otro

answer /'ænsər, 'an-/ *n* contestación, respuesta, *f;* (refutation) refutación, *f;* (pert reply) réplica, *f;* (solution) solución, *f; Math.* resultado, *m; Law.* contestación a la demanda, *f*

answer /'ænsər, 'an-/ *vt* responder, contestar; (a letter, etc.) contestar a; (refute) refutar; (reply pertly) replicar; (write) escribir; (return) devolver; (suit) servir; (a bell, etc.) acudir a; (the door) abrir. —*vi* contestar; (succeed) tener éxito; dar resultado. **to a. by return,** contestar a vuelta de correo, **to a. back,** replicar. **to a. for,** ser responsable por; ser responsable de; (speak for) hablar por; (guarantee) garantizar, responder de

answerable /'ænsərəbəl/ *a* responsable; refutable; (adequate) adecuado. **to make a. for,** hacer responsable de

answering machine *n* contestador telefónico, contestador, *m*

ant /ænt/ *n* hormiga, *f.* **ant-eater,** oso hormiguero, *m.* **ant-hill,** hormiguero, *m*

antagonism /æn'tægə,nizəm/ *n* antagonismo, *m;* hostilidad, oposición, *f*

antagonist /æn'tægənist/ *n* antagonista, *mf*

antagonistic /æn,tægə'nistik/ *a* antagónico, hostil

antagonize /æn'tægə,naiz/ *vt* contender; hacer hostil (a)

antarctic /ænt'ɑrktik/ *a* antártico. —*n* polo antártico, *m*

antecedent /,æntə'sidnt/ *a* and *n* antecedente, *m.*

antedate /'ænti,deit/ *vt* antedatar; anticipar

antelope /'ænti,oup/ *n* antílope, *m*

antenna /æn'tenə/ *n* antena, *f*

anterior /æn'tiəriər/ *a* anterior

anthem /'ænθəm/ *n* antífona, *f*

anthology /æn'θɒlədʒi/ *n* antología, floresta, *f*

anthracite /'ænθrə,sait/ *n* antracita, *f,* carbón mineral, *m*

anthropologist /,ænθrə'pɒlədʒist/ *n* antropólogo, *m*

anthropology /,ænθrə'pɒlədʒi/ *n* antropología, *f*

anti-aircraft /,ænti'eər,kræft, ,æntai-/ *a* antiaéreo. **A.A. gun,** cañon antiaéreo, *m*

antibody /'ænti,bɒdi/ *n* anticuerpo, *m*

antic /'æntik/ *n* travesura, *f*

anticipate /æn'tisə,peit/ *vt* (foresee) prever; anticipar; adelantarse a; (hope) esperar; (frustrate) frustrar; (enjoy) disfrutar con anticipación de

anticipation /æn,tisə'peiʃən/ *n* anticipación, *f;* adelantamiento, *m;* esperanza, expectación, *f.* **in a. of,** en espera de

anticipatory /æn'tisəpə,tɔri/ *a* anticipador

anticlimax /,ænti'klaimæks, ,æntai / *n* anticlímax, *m*

antidote /'ænti,dout/ *n* antídoto, contraveneno, *m*

antifreeze /'ænti,friz/ *n* anticongelante, *m*

Antilles, the /æn'tiliz/ las Antillas, *f*

antimony /'æntə,mouni/ *n* antimonio, *m*

antipathetic /,æntipə'θetik/ *a* antipático

antipathy /æn'tipəθi/ *n* antipatía, *f*

antipode /'ænti,poud/ *n pl* antípodas, *mf pl*

antiquarian /,ænti'kwɛəriən/ *a* anticuario

antiquary /'ænti,kweri/ *n* anticuario, *m*

antiquated /'ænti,kweitid/ *a* anticuado

antique /æn'tik/ *a* antiguo. —*n* antigüedad, antigualla, *f.* **a. dealer,** anticuario, *m.* **a. shop,** tienda de antigüedades, *f*

antiquity /æn'tikwiti/ *n* antigüedad, *f;* ancianidad, *f*

anti-Semitic /,æntisə'mitik, ,æntai-/ *a* antisemita

anti-Semitism /,ænti'semi,tizəm, ,æntai-/ *n* antisemitismo, *m*

antiseptic /,æntə'septik/ *a* and *n* antiséptico, *m*

antisocial /,ænti'souʃəl, ,æntai-/ *a* antisocial

antithesis /æn'tiθəsis/ *n* antítesis, *f*

antithetic /,ænti'θetik/ *a* antitético

antitoxin /,ænti'tɒksin/ *n* antitoxina, *f*

antler /'æntlər/ *n* asta, *f*

antrum /'æntrəm/ *n* antro, *m*

Antwerp /'æntwərp/ Amberes, *m*

anus /'einəs/ *n* ano, *m*

anvil /'ænvil/ *n* yunque, *m,* bigornia, *f*

anxiety /æŋ'zaiiti/ *n* inquietud, intranquilidad, *f;* preocupación, *f;* ansiedad, *f;* curiosidad, *f;* impaciencia, *f;* (wish) deseo, afán, *m*

anxious /'æŋkʃəs, 'æŋʃəs/ *a* inquieto, intranquilo; preocupado; ansioso; impaciente; deseoso. **to be a.,** estar inquieto;

apurarse. **to be a. to,** ansiar, tener deseos de. **to make a.,** preocupar, inquietar, intranquilizar

anxiously /'æŋkʃəsli, 'æŋʃəs-/ adv con inquietud; ansiosamente; impacientemente

any /'ɛni/ a cualquiera; (before the noun only) cualquier; (some) algún, m; alguna, f; (every) todo; (expressing condition or with interrogatives or negatives, following the noun) alguno, m; alguna, f, (is often not translated in a partitive sense) *Have you any butter?* ¿Tienes mantequilla?) —pron algo; (with the relevant noun) algún, etc.; lo, m, and neut; la, f; los, m pl; las, f pl. **He hasn't any pity,** No tiene piedad alguna. **at any rate,** de todos modos; por lo menos. **If there is any,** Si lo (la, etc.) hay. **in any case,** venga lo que venga. **not any,** ninguno, m; ninguna, f. **Whether any of them...,** Si alguno de ellos... **any further,** más lejos. **any longer,** más largo; (of time) más tiempo. **any more,** nada más; nunca más

anybody /'ɛni,bɒdi/ n and pron (someone) alguien; cualquiera, mf; (everyone) todo el mundo; (with a negative) nadie; (of importance) persona de importancia, f. **hardly a.,** casi nadie

anyhow /'ɛni,hau/ adv de cualquier modo; (with a negative) de ningún modo; de cualquier manera; (at least) por lo menos, en todo caso; (carelessly) sin cuidado

anyone /'ɛni,wʌn/ n. See anybody

anything /'ɛni,θɪŋ/ n algo, m, alguna cosa, f; (negative) nada; cualquier cosa, f; todo (lo que). **a. but,** todo menos

anyway /'ɛni,wei/ adv de todos modos, con todo; venga lo que venga; (anyhow) de cualquier modo

anywhere /'ɛni,wɛər/ adv en todas partes, dondequiera; en cualquier parte; (after a negative) en (or a) ninguna parte

aorta /ei'ɔrtə/ n aorta, f

apart /ə'pɑrt/ adv aparte; a un lado; separadamente; separado (de); apartado (de). **a. from,** aparte de, dejando a un lado. **to keep a.,** mantener aislado; distinguir (entre). **to take a.,** desarmar. **wide a.,** muy distante

apartment /ə'pɑrtmənt/ n cuarto, m, habitación, f; (flat) piso, m

apathetic /,æpə'θɛtɪk/ a apático; indiferente

apathy /'æpəθi/ n apatía, f; indiferencia, f

ape /eip/ n simio, m

aperture /'æpərtʃər/ n abertura, f; agujero, m; orificio, m

apiece /ə'pis/ adv cada uno; por persona

apish /'eipɪʃ/ a simiesco, de simio; (affected) afectado; (foolish) tonto

aplomb /ə'plɒm/ n confianza en sí, f, aplomo, m

apocalyptic /ə,pɒkə'lɪptɪk/ a apocalíptico

Apocrypha /ə'pɒkrəfə/ n libros apócrifos, m pl

apocryphal /ə'pɒkrəfəl/ a apócrifo

apologetic /ə,pɒlə'dʒɛtɪk/ a apologético

apologize /ə'pɒlə,dʒaiz/ vi presentar sus excusas; disculparse, excusarse; (regret) sentir

apology /ə'pɒlədʒi/ n excusa, disculpa, f; defensa, apología, f; (makeshift) substituto, m

apoplexy /'æpə,plɛksi/ n apoplegía, f

apostasy /ə'pɒstəsi/ n apostasía, f

apostate /ə'pɒsteit/ n apóstata, mf. renegado (-da)

apostle /ə'pɒsəl/ n apóstol, m. **Apostles' Creed,** el Credo de los Apóstoles

apostolic /,æpə'stɒlɪk/ a apostólico

apostrophe /ə'pɒstrəfi/ n apóstrofe, mf; (punctuation mark) apóstrofo, m

Apothecaries' weight peso de boticario, m

apothegm /'æpə,θɛm/ n apotegma, m

appalling /ə'pɒlɪŋ/ a espantoso, horrible

apparatus /,æpə'rætəs/ n aparato, m; máquina, f; instrumentos, m pl

apparel /ə'pærəl/ n ropa, f; vestiduras, f pl; ornamento, m. —vt vestir

apparent /ə'pærənt/ a aparente; visible; evidente, manifiesto; (of heirs) presunto. **to become a.,** manifestarse

apparently /ə'pærəntli/ adv al parecer, aparentemente

apparition /,æpə'rɪʃən/ n aparición, f, fantasma, espectro, m

appeal /ə'pil/ n súplica, f; llamamiento, m; (charm) atracción, f, encanto, m; Law. apelación, alzada, f. —vi (to) suplicar (a); hacer llamamiento (a); poner por testigo (a); recurrir a; llamar la atención de; interesar (a); (attract) atraer, encantar; Law. apelar. **It doesn't a. to him,** No le atrae, No le gusta. **to allow an a.,** revocar una sentencia apelada. **without a.,** inapelable

appealing /ə'pilɪŋ/ a suplicante; atrayente

appealingly /ə'pilɪŋli/ adv de un modo suplicante

appear /ə'pɪər/ vi (of persons and things) aparecer; (seem) parecer; (before a judge) comparecer, presentarse (ante el juez); (of books) publicarse; (of lawyers) representar; (of the dawn) rayar; (of the sun, etc.) salir; (show itself) manifestarse. **to cause to a.,** hacer presentarse; (show) hacer ver; (prove) demonstrar, probar

appearance /ə'pɪərəns/ n aparición, f; (show, semblance or look, aspect) apariencia, f; presencia, f; aspecto, m; (in court of law) comparecencia, f; (of a book) publicación, f; (arrival) llegada, f; (view) perspectiva, f; (ghost) aparición, f, fantasma, m. **first a.,** (of an actor, etc.) debut, m; (of a play) estreno, m. **to all appearances,** según las apariencias. **to make one's first a.,** aparecer por primera vez; Theat. debutar. **Appearances are deceptive,** Las apariencias engañan

appease /ə'piz/ vt apaciguar, aplacar, pacificar; satisfacer

appeasement /ə'pizmənt/ *n* apaciguamiento, aplacamiento, *m,* pacificación, *f;* satisfacción, *f*

appellant /ə'pɛlənt/ *a* and *n Law.* apelante, *mf*

appellation /,æpə'leiʃən/ *n* nombre, *m;* título, *m*

append /ə'pɛnd/ *vt* añadir; (a seal) poner; (enclose) incluir, anexar

appendage /ə'pɛndidʒ/ *n* accesorio, *m;* (*Bot. Zool.*) apéndice, *m*

appendicitis /ə,pɛndə'saitis/ *n* apendicitis, *f*

appendix /ə'pɛndiks/ *n* apéndice, *m*

appetite /'æpɪ,tait/ *n* apetito, *m; Fig.* hambre, *f;* deseo, *m.* **to have a bad a.,** no tener apetito, estar desganado. **to have a good a.,** tener buen apetito. **to whet the a.,** abrir el apetito

appetizer /'æpɪ,taizər/ *n* aperitivo, *m*

appetizing /'æpɪ,taiziŋ/ *a* apetitoso

applaud /ə'plɔd/ *vt* and *vi* aplaudir; aclamar, ovacionar; celebrar

applause /ə'plɔz/ *n* aplauso, *m;* ovación, *f;* aprobación, alabanza, *f*

apple /'æpəl/ *n* manzana, *f.* **the a. of one's eye,** la niña de los ojos. **a. orchard,** manzanar, *m.* **a. sauce,** compota de manzanas, *f.* **a. tart,** pastel de manzanas, *m.* **a. tree,** manzano, *m*

appliance /ə'plaiəns/ *n* aparato, *m;* instrumento, *m;* utensilio, *m;* máquina, *f*

applicant /'æplɪkənt/ *n* candidato, *m;* aspirante, *m;* solicitante, *mf*

application /,æplɪ'keiʃən/ *n* aplicación, *f;* solicitud, *f;* petición, *f;* empleo, *m.* **on a.,** a solicitar

appliqué /,æplɪ'kei/ *a* aplicado. —*n* aplicación, *f*

apply /ə'plai/ *vt* aplicar; (use) emplear; (place) poner; (give) dar; (the brakes) frenar; *vi* ser aplicable; ser a propósito; dirigirse (a); acudir (a); (for a post) proponerse para. **a. for,** solicitar, pedir; (a post) proponerse para. **a. for admission (to...),** solicitar el ingreso (en...). **a. oneself to,** ponerse a; dedicarse a, consagrarse a

appoint /ə'pɔint/ *vt* (prescribe) prescribir, ordenar; señalar; asignar; (furnish) amueblar; equipar; (create) crear, establecer; (to a post) nombrar, designar; (manage) gobernar; organizar. **at the appointed hour,** a la hora señalada. **well-appointed,** bien amueblado; bien equipado

appointive /ə'pɔintɪv/ *a* por nombramiento

appointment /ə'pɔintmənt/ *n* (assignation) cita, *f;* (to a post) nombramiento, *m;* (post, office) cargo, *m;* creación, *f.* **By Royal A.,** Proveedor de la Real Casa. **to make an a. with,** citar

apportion /ə'pɔrʃən/ *vt* dividir; distribuir; prorratear; (taxes) derramar

apportionment /ə'pɔrʃənmənt/ *n* repartimiento, *m,* distribución, *f;* división, *f;* prorrateo, *m*

apposite /'æpəzɪt/ *a* a propósito, pertinente, oportuno; justo

appraisal /ə'preizəl/ *n* valoración, valuación, *f;* estimación, *f*

appraise /ə'preiz/ *vt* valorar, tasar; estimar

appreciable /ə'priʃiəbəl/ *a* apreciable, perceptible

appreciably /ə'priʃiəbli/ *adv* sensiblemente

appreciate /ə'priʃi,eit/ *vt* (understand) darse cuenta de, comprender; estimar; apreciar; (distinguish) distinguir. —*vi* encarecer, aumentar en valor; (of shares) subir, estar en alza

appreciation /ə,priʃi'eiʃən/ *n* (understanding) comprensión, *f;* apreciación, *f;* (recognition, etc.) aprecio, reconocimiento, *m;* (in value) aumento (en valor), *m,* subida de precio, *f*

appreciatively /ə'priʃətivli/ *adv* con aprecio

apprehend /,æprɪ'hɛnd/ *vt* aprehender, prender; comprender, aprehender; (fear) temer

apprehension /,æprɪ'hɛnʃən/ *n* aprehensión, comprensión, *f;* (fear) aprensión, *f;* (seizure) aprehensión, presa, *f*

apprehensive /,æprɪ'hɛnsɪv/ *a* aprehensivo; (fearful) aprensivo

apprehensiveness /,æprɪ'hɛnsɪvnɪs/ *n* aprehensión, *f;* (fear) aprensión, *f,* temor, *m*

apprentice /ə'prɛntɪs/ *n* aprendiz (-za). **to bind a.,** poner de aprendiz

apprenticeship /ə'prɛntɪs,ʃip/ *n* aprendizaje, *m.* **to serve an a.,** hacer el aprendizaje

apprise /ə'praiz/ *vt* dar parte (de), informar (de)

approach /ə'proutʃ/ *vt* acercarse a; aproximarse a; (pull, etc. nearer) acercar, aproximar; (resemble) parecerse a, ser semejante a; (speak to) hablar con; entablar negociaciones con. —*vi* acercarse, aproximarse. —*n* acercamiento, *m;* (arrival) llegada, *f;* aproximación, *f;* (of night, etc.) avance, *m;* (entrance) entrada, *f;* avenida, *f;* vía, *f;* (step) paso, *m;* (to a subject) punto de vista (sobre), concepto (de), *m;* (introduction) introducción, *f;* *pl* **approaches,** (environs) alrededores, *m pl,* inmediaciones, *f pl;* (seas) mares, *m pl;* (overtures) avances, *m pl*

approachable /ə'proutʃəbəl/ *a* accesible

approaching /ə'proutʃɪŋ/ *a* venidero, próximo, cercano

approbation /,æprə'beiʃən/ *n* asentimiento, *m;* aprobación, *f*

appropriate /*a* ə'proupriit; *v* -,eit/ *a* apropiado; conveniente; *vt* adueñarse de, tomar posesión de, apropiar

appropriately /ə'proupriitli/ *adv* propiamente; convenientemente; justamente

appropriateness /ə'proupriitnɪs/ *n* conveniencia, *f;* justicia, *f*

appropriation /ə,proupri'eiʃən/ *n* apropiación, *f;* aplicación, *f;* empleo, *m*

approval /ə'pruvəl/ n aprobación, f; consentimiento, m. **on a.**, a prueba

approve /ə'pruv/ vt aprobar; confirmar; (sanction) autorizar, sancionar; ratificar; estar contento (de); (oneself) demostrarse. —vi aprobar

approved /ə'pruvd/ a aprobado; bien visto; (on documents) Visto Bueno (V° B°)

approximate /a ə'prɒksəmɪt; v -,meit/ a aproximado. —vt acercar. —vi aproximarse (a)

approximately /ə'prɒksəmɪtli/ adv aproximadamente, poco más o menos

approximation /ə,prɒksə'meiʃən/ n aproximación, f

apricot /'æprɪ,kɒt/ n albaricoque, m. **a. tree**, albaricoquero, m

April /'eiprəl/ n abril, m, a abrileño. **A. Fool's Day**, el 1° de abril; (in Spain) el Día de los Inocentes (December 28)

apron /'eiprən/ n delantal, m; (of artisans and freemasons) mandil, m. **to be tied to a mother's a.-strings**, estar cosido a las faldas de su madre. **a.-stage**, proscenio, m. **a.-string**, cinta del delantal, f

apse /æps/ n ábside, mf

apt /æpt/ a apto, listo; propenso (a), inclinado (a); expuesto (a); (suitable) apropiado, oportuno

aptitude /'æptɪ,tud/ n aptitud, disposición, facilidad, f

aptly /'æptli/ adv apropiadamente; justamente, bien

aquarelle /,ækwə'rɛl/ n acuarela, f

aquarium /ə'kwɛəriəm/ n acuario, m

aquatic /ə'kwætɪk/ a acuático

aqueduct /'ækwɪ,dʌkt/ n acueducto, m

aqueous /'ækwiəs/ a ácueo, acuoso

aquiline /'ækwə,lain/ a aguileño

Arab /'ærəb/ a árabe. —n árabe, mf

arabesque /,ærə'bɛsk/ n arabesco, m

Arabian /ə'reibiən/ a árabe, arábigo. **The A. Nights**, Las Mil y Una Noches

Arabic /'ærəbɪk/ a arábigo. —n (language) arábigo; árabe, m

arable /'ærəbəl/ a cultivable, labrantío

arbiter /'ɑrbɪtər/ n árbitro (-ra), arbitrador (-ra)

arbitrariness /'ɑrbɪ,trerinɪs/ n arbitrariedad, f

arbitrary /'ɑrbɪ,treri/ a arbitrario

arbitrate /'ɑrbɪ,treit/ vi arbitrar, juzgar como árbitro; someter al arbitraje

arbitration /,ɑrbɪ'treiʃən/ n arbitraje, m

arbitrator /'ɑrbɪ,treitər/ See **arbiter**

arc /ɑrk/ n arco, m. **arc-light**, lámpara de arco, f

arcade /ɑr'keid/ n arcada, f; galería, f; pasaje, m

arch /ɑrtʃ/ n arco, m; (vault) bóveda, f. —vt abovedar; arquear; encorvar

arch /ɑrtʃ/ a (roguish) socarrón; (coy) coquetón

arch- /ɑrtʃ/ prefix archi-

archaic /ɑr'keiɪk/ a arcaico

archangel /'ɑrk,eindʒəl/ n arcángel, m

archbishop /'ɑrtʃ'bɪʃəp/ n arzobispo, m

archenemy /'ɑrtʃ'ɛnəmi/ n mayor enemigo (-ga); Demonio, m

archeological /,ɑrkɪə'lodʒɪkəl/ a arqueológico

archeologist /,ɑrki'ɒlədʒɪst/ n arqueólogo, m

archeology /,ɑrki'ɒlədʒi/ n arqueología, f

archer /'ɑrtʃər/ n flechero, saltero, m; Mil. arquero, f

archery /'ɑrtʃəri/ n ballestería, f

archery range n campo de tiro con arco, m

archipelago /,ɑrkə'pelə,gou/ n archipiélago, m

architect /'ɑrkɪ,tɛkt/ n arquitecto, m

architectural /,ɑrkɪ'tɛktʃərəl/ n arquitectónico

architecture /'ɑrkɪ,tɛktʃər/ n arquitectura, f

archive /'ɑrkaiv/ n archivo, m

archivist /'ɑrkəvɪst/ n archivero, m

archness /'ɑrtʃnɪs/ n coquetería, f; malicia, f

archway /'ɑrtʃ,wei/ n arcada, f, pasaje abovedado, m; arco, m

arctic /'ɑrktɪk, 'ɑrtɪk/ a ártico; muy frío. **A. Circle**, Círculo ártico, m

ardent /'ɑrdnt/ a ardiente; apasionado, vehemente; fogoso

ardently /'ɑrdntli/ adv ardientemente; con vehemencia, apasionadamente

ardor /'ɑrdər/ n ardor, m

arduous /'ɑrdʒuəs/ a arduo, difícil

are /ɑr/ pl of present indicative of **be**. See **be. There are**, Hay

area /'ɛəriə/ n área, f; superficie, f; (extent) extensión, f; espacio, m; región, f; (of a house) patio, m; (of a concert hall, etc.) sala, f

area code n característica, f, (Chile), código territorial (Spain), prefijo (Spain), código interurbano, código (Argentina), m

arena /ə'rinə/ n arena, f

Argentinian /,ɑrdʒən'tɪniən/ a and n argentino (-na)

argonaut /'ɑrgə,nɒt/ n (Zool. and Myth.) argonauta, m

argot /'ɑrgou, -gət/ n jerga, f; (thieves') germanía, f

arguable /'ɑrgyuəbəl/ a discutible

argue /'ɑrgyu/ vt discutir; persuadir; (prove) demostrar. —vi argüir, discutir; sostener. **to a. against**, hablar en contra de, oponer

arguing /'ɑrgyuiŋ/ n razonamiento, m; argumentación, f; discusión, f

argument /'ɑrgyəmənt/ n argumento, m

argumentative /,ɑrgyə'mɛntətɪv/ a argumentador; contencioso

arid /'ærɪd/ a árido, seco

aridity /ə'rɪdɪti/ n aridez, f

arise /ə'raiz/ vi levantarse; (appear) surgir, aparecer; ofrecerse, presentarse; (of sound) hacerse oír; provenir (de); proceder (de); (result) hacerse sentir; (rebel) sublevarse

aristocracy /ˌærə'stɒkrəsi/ n aristocracia, f

aristocrat /ə'rɪstə,kræt/ n aristócrata, mf

aristocratic /ə,rɪstə'krætɪk/ a aristocrático

arithmetic /ə'rɪθmətɪk/ n aritmética, f

arithmetical /,ærɪθ'mɛtɪkəl/ a aritmético

ark /ɑrk/ n arca, f. **Noah's ark,** arca de Noé, f. **Ark of the Covenant,** arca de la alianza, f

arm /ɑrm/ n (*Anat. Geog. Mech.* of a chair, a cross, and *Fig.*) brazo, m; (lever) palanca, f; (of a tree) rama, f, brazo, m; (sleeve) manga, f; *Naut.* cabo de una verga, m; (weapon) arma, f; (of army, navy, etc.) ramo, m pl. **arms,** *Herald.* armas, f pl, escudo, m. **in arms,** en brazos; armado; en oposición. **To arms!** ¡A las armas! **to keep at arm's length,** guardar las distancias; tratar fríamente. **to lay down arms,** rendir las armas. **to present arms,** presentar las armas. **to receive with open arms,** recibir con los brazos abiertos. **to take up arms,** alzarse en armas, empuñar las armas. **under arms,** sobre las armas. **with folded arms,** con los brazos cruzados. **arm in arm,** del bracete, de bracero. **arm of the sea,** brazo de mar, m. **arm-rest,** brazo, m

arm /ɑrm/ vt armar; proveer (de); (*Fig.* fortify) fortificar. —vi armarse

armada /ɑr'mɑdə/ n armada, f

armament /'ɑrməmənt/ n armamento, m

armchair /'ɑrm,tʃɛər/ n sillón, m, silla poltrona, f

armed /ɑrmd/ a armado

armful /ɑrm,fʊl/ n brazado, m

armistice /'ɑrməstɪs/ n armisticio, m

armor /'ɑrmər/ n armadura, f; (for ships, etc.) blindaje, m. —vt blindar, acorazar. **(to) a.-plate,** vt blindar. —n coraza, plancha blindada, f

armored /'ɑrmərd/ a blindado, acorazado. **a. car,** carro blindado, m. **a. cruiser,** crucero acorazado, m

armory /'ɑrməri/ n armería, f

army /'ɑrmi/ n ejército, m; multitud, muchedumbre, f. **to be in the a.,** ser del ejército. **to go into the a.,** alistarse. **a. corps,** cuerpo del ejército, m. **a. estimates,** presupuesto del ejército, m. **a. list,** escalafón del ejército, m. **A. Medical Corps,** Sanidad Militar, f. **A. Supply Corps,** Cuerpo de Intendencia, m

aroma /ə'roumə/ n aroma, m

aromatic /,ærə'mætɪk/ a aromático

around /ə'raund/ prep alrededor de; por todas partes de; cerca de; (with words like corner) a la vuelta de. —adv alrededor; a la redonda, en torno; por todas partes; de un lado para otro

arouse /ə'rauz/ vt despertar; excitar. **a. (someone's) suspicions,** despertar las sospechas (de fulano)

arraign /ə'rein/ vt acusar; *Law.* procesar

arraignment /ə'reinmənt/ n acusación, f; *Law.* procesamiento, m

arrange /ə'reindʒ/ vt arreglar; acomo-

dar; poner en orden, clasificar; (place) colocar; (order) ordenar, disponer; (contrive) agenciar; organizar; preparar; *Mus.* adaptar; (of differences) concertar, ajustar. —vi convenir, concertarse; arreglar; hacer preparativos

arrangement /ə'reindʒmənt/ n arreglo, m; clasificación, f; disposición, f; (agreement) acuerdo, m; *Mus.* adaptación, f; pl **arrangements,** preparativos, m pl

array /ə'rei/ n (of troops) orden de batalla, mf; formación, f; colección, f; (dress) atavío, m, vt poner en orden de batalla; formar (las tropas, etc.); ataviar, adornar

arrears /ə'rɪərz/ n pl atrasos, m pl. **in a.,** atrasado

arrest /ə'rɛst/ vt detener, impedir; (the attention) atraer; (capture) arrestar, prender; (judgment) suspender. —n (stop) interrupción, parada, f; (hindrance) estorbo, m; (detention) arresto, m, detención, f; (of a judgment) suspensión, f. **under a.,** bajo arresto

arresting /ə'rɛstɪŋ/ a que llama la atención, notable, muy interesante; asombroso, chocador

arrival /ə'raivəl/ n llegada, venida, f, advenimiento, m; *Naut.* arribada, f; entrada, f; el, m, (la, f), que llega. **on a.,** al llegar, a la llegada. **the new arrivals,** los recién llegados

arrive /ə'raiv/ vi llegar; aparecer; (happen) suceder; *Naut.* arribar; entrar. **to a. at,** (a place or conclusion) llegar a

arrogance /'ærəgəns/ n arrogancia altivez, soberbia, f

arrogant /'ærəgənt/ a altivo, arrogante, soberbio

arrogate /'ærə,geit/ vt arrogar

arrow /'ærou/ n saeta, flecha, f. **a.-head,** punta de flecha, f. **a.-shaped,** en forma de flecha, sagital. **a. wound,** flechazo, saetazo, m

arsenal /'ɑrsənl/ n arsenal, m

arsenic /'ɑrsənɪk/ n arsénico, m

arson /'ɑrsən/ n incendio premeditado, m

art /ɑrt/ n arte, mf; (cleverness) habilidad, f; (cunning) artificio, m. **Faculty of Arts,** Facultad de Letras, f; **fine arts,** bellas artes, f pl. **art exhibition,** exposición de pinturas, f. **art gallery,** museo de pinturas, m. **art school,** colegio de arte, m

arterial /ɑr'tɪəriəl/ a arterial; (of roads) de primera clase. **a. forceps,** pinzas hemostáticas, f pl

artery /'ɑrtəri/ n arteria, f

artful /'ɑrtfəl/ a hábil, ingenioso; (crafty) astuto

artfulness /'ɑrtfəlnɪs/ n habilidad, ingeniosidad, f; astucia, maña, f

arthritic /ɑr'θrɪtɪk/ a artrítico

arthritis /ɑr'θraitɪs/ n artritis, f

artichoke /'ɑrtɪ,tʃouk/ n alcachofa, f. **Jerusalem a.,** aguaturma, f

article /'ɑrtɪkəl/ n artículo, m; (object) objeto, m, cosa, f; pl **articles,** escritura, f; contrato, m; estatutos, m pl. —vt escriturar; contratar. **leading a.**, artículo de fondo, *m*. **articles of apprenticeship**, contrato de aprendizaje, *m*. **articles of association**, estatutos de asociación, *m pl*. **articles of war**, código militar, *m*

articulate /v ar'tıkyə,leit/ *a* -lıt/ *vt* articular; pronunciar, articular. —*vi* estar unido por articulación; articular. —*a* articulado; claro; expresivo

articulation /ar,tıkyə'leiʃən/ *n* articulación, *f*, (all meanings)

artifice /'artəfıs/ *n* artificio, *m*; arte, *m*, or *f*, habilidad, *f*

artificial /,artə'fıʃəl/ *a* artificial; falso, fingido; afectado. **a. flowers**, flores de mano, *f pl*. **a. silk**, seda artificial, seda vegetal, *f*

artificial intelligence /artə'fıʃəl ın'tɛlıdʒəns/ *n* inteligencia artificial, *f*

artificiality /,artə,fıʃi'ælıti/ *n* artificialidad, *f*; falsedad, *f*; afectación, *f*

artillery /ar'tıləri/ *n* artillería, *f*. **field a.**, artillería volante (or ligera or montada), *f*. **a. practice**, ejercicio de cañón, *m*

artisan /'artəzən/ *n* artesano (-na)

artist /'artıst/ *n* artista, *mf*; (painter) pintor (-ra)

artistic /ar'tıstık/ *a* artístico

artistry /'artıstri/ *n* habilidad artística, *f*, arte, *mf*

artless /'artlıs/ *a* natural; sencillo, cándido, inocente

artlessly /'artlısli/ *adv* con naturalidad; con inocencia

artlessness /'artlısnıs/ *n* naturalidad, *f*; sencillez, candidez, inocencia, *f*

as /æz/ *adv conjunc rel pron* como; así como; (followed by infin.) de; (in comparisons) tan... como; (while) mientras; a medida que; (when) cuando, al (followed by infin.); (since) puesto que, visto que; (because) porque; (although) aunque; por; (according to) según; en; (in order that) para (que). **as a rule**, por regla general. **Once as he was walking**, Una vez mientras andaba. **as... as**, tan... como. **as far as**, hasta; en cuanto a. **as from**, desde. **as good as**, tan bueno como. **as if**, como si. **as it were**, por decirlo así, en cierto modo. **as many**, otros tantos (e.g. *six embassies in as many countries*, seis embajadas en otros tantos países). **as many as**, tanto... como; todos los que. **as soon as**, en cuanto, luego que, así que. **as soon as possible**, cuanto antes. **as sure as can be**, sin duda alguna. **as to**, en cuanto a. **as usual**, como de costumbre. **as well**, también. **as well as**, (besides) además de; tan bien como. **as yet**, todavía.

asbestos /æs'bɛstəs/ *n* asbesto, amianto, *m*

ascend /ə'sɛnd/ *vt and vi* subir; (on, in) subir a; ascender; (rise) elevarse; (a river) remontar. **to a. the stairs**, subir las escaleras. **to a. the pulpit**, subir al púlpito. **to a. the throne**, subir al trono

ascendancy /ə'sɛndənsi/ *n* ascendiente, influjo, *m*

ascendant /ə'sɛndənt/ *n* elevación, *f*. —*a* ascendente; predominante. **to be in the a.**, *Fig.* ir en aumento; predominar

ascension /ə'sɛnʃən/ *n* subida, ascensión, *f*; (of the throne) advenimiento (al trono), *m*. **The A.**, La Ascensión

ascent /ə'sɛnt/ *n* subida, *f*, ascenso, *m*; elevación, *f*; (slope) cuesta, pendiente, *f*

ascertain /,æsər'tein/ *vt* averiguar, descubrir

ascertainable /,æsər'teinəbəl/ *a* averiguable, descubrible

ascetic /ə'sɛtık/ *a* ascético. —*n* asceta, *mf*

ascribe /ə'skraib/ *vt* atribuir, adscribir, imputar

aseptic /ə'sɛptık/ *a* aséptico

ash /æʃ/ *n* ceniza, *f*; cenizas, *f pl*; (tree and wood) fresno, *m*; *pl* ashes, cenizas, *f pl*; restos mortales, *m pl*. **mountain ash**, serbal, *m*. **ash-bin**, basurero, *m*. **ash-coloured**, ceniciento. **ash grove**, fresneda, *f*. **ashtray**, cenicero, *m*. **Ash Wednesday**, miércoles de ceniza, *m*

ashamed /ə'ʃeimd/ *a* avergonzado. **to be a. of**, avergonzarse de. **to be a. of oneself**, avergonzarse, tener vergüenza de sí mismo

ashore /ə'ʃɔr/ *adv* a tierra; en tierra. **to go or put a.**, desembarcar

Asiatic /,eiʒi'ætık/ *a and n* asiático (-ca)

aside /ə'said/ *adv* a un lado; aparte. —*n Theat.* aparte, *m*. **to set a.**, poner a un lado; (omit) dejar aparte; descontar; abandonar; (a judgment) anular. **to take a.**, llevar aparte

asinine /'æsə,nain/ *a* asnal

ask /æsk/ *vt* (a question; enquire) preguntar; (request; demand) pedir; (beg) rogar; (invite) invitar. **to ask a question**, hacer una pregunta. **to ask about**, preguntar acerca de. **to ask after**, preguntar por. **to ask down**, invitar a bajar; invitar a visitar (a alguien). **to ask for**, pedir; preguntar por. **ask for the moon**, pedir cotofas en el golfo. **to ask in**, invitar (a alguien) a entrar

askance /ə'skæns/ *adv* al (or de) soslayo, de reojo; con recelo

askew /ə'skyu/ *adv* oblicuamente; al lado; a un lado; sesgadamente

aslant /ə'slænt/ *prep* a través de

asleep /ə'slip/ *a and adv* dormido. **to be a.**, estar dormido. **to fall a.**, dormirse

asparagus /ə'spærəgəs/ *n* espárrago, *m*. **a. bed**, esparraguera, *f*

aspect /'æspɛkt/ *n* aspecto, *m*; vista, *f*; apariencia, *f*, semblante, *m*. **to have a southern a.**, dar (mirar) al sur

asperity /ə'spɛrıti/ *n* aspereza, *f*

aspersion /ə'spərʒən/ *n Eccl.* aspersión, *f*; calumnia, *f*; insinuación, *f*

asphalt /'æsfɔlt/ *n* asfalto, *m*, *vt* asfaltar

asphyxia /æs'fıksiə/ *n* asfixia, *f*

asphyxiate /æs'fıksi,eit/ *vt* asfixiar

aspirant /'æspərənt/ *n* aspirante, candidato, *m*

aspire /ə'spai³r/ *vi* aspirar (a), pretender, ambicionar; alzarse

aspirin /'æspərɪn/ *n* aspirina, *f*

ass /æs/ *n* asno, *m*

assail /ə'seil/ *vt* atacar, acometer, arremeter

assailant /ə'seilənt/ *n* asaltador (-ra)

assassin /ə'sæsɪn/ *n* asesino, *mf*

assassinate /ə'sæsə͵neit/ *vt* asesinar

assassination /ə͵sæsə'neiʃən/ *n* asesinato, *m*

assault /ə'sɔlt/ *n* asalto, *m*; acometida, embestida, *f*; *Fig.* ataque, *m.* —*vt* asaltar; acometer, embestir; atacar. **to take by a.,** tomar por asalto

assemblage /ə'semblɪdʒ/ *n* reunión, *f*; (of a machine) montaje, *m*; (of people) muchedumbre, *f* concurso, *m*; (of things) colección, *f*, grupo, *m*

assemble /ə'sembəl/ *vt* (persons) reunir, convocar; (things and persons) juntar; (a machine, etc.) armar, ensamblar. —*vi* reunirse, congregarse; acudir

assembly /ə'sembli/ *n* asamblea, *f*; reunión, *f*; *Eccl.* concilio, *m.* **a. line,** cadena de montaje, línea de montaje, *f.* **a. room,** sala de reuniones, *f*; sala de baile, *f*

assent /ə'sent/ *n* asentimiento, consentimiento, *m*; aprobación, *f*; (parliamentary, *Law.*) sanción, *f.* —*vi* asentir (a), consentir (en); aprobar

assert /ə'sɜrt/ *vt* mantener, defender; declarar, afirmar; hacer valer, reclamar. **to a. oneself,** imponerse, hacerse sentir; hacer valer sus derechos

assertion /ə'sɜrʃən/ *n* aserción, afirmación, *f*; defensa, *f*; reclamación, *f*

assertive /ə'sɜrtɪv/ *a* afirmativo; dogmático

assess /ə'ses/ *vt* tasar, valorar; fijar, señalar; repartir (contribuciones, etc.)

assessment /ə'sesmənt/ *n* tasación, *f*; fijación, *f*; repartimiento, *m*

assessor /ə'sesər/ *n Law.* asesor (-ra); (of taxes) repartidor (-ra); (valuer) tasador, *m.* **public a.,** tasador, *m*

asset /'æset/ *n* ventaja, *f*; adquisición, *f*; cualidad, *f*; *pl* **assets,** fondos, *m pl*; *Com.* activo, *m*, créditos activos, *m pl*

assiduous /ə'sɪdʒuəs/ *a* asiduo

assign /ə'sain/ *vt Law.* ceder; señalar, asignar; (appoint) destinar; fijar; atribuir, imputar. —*n* cesionario (-ia)

assignation /͵æsɪg'neiʃən/ *n* asignación, *f*; cita, *f*; *Law.* cesión, *f*

assignment /ə'sainmənt/ *n Law.* cesión, *f*; escritura de cesión, *f*; atribución, *f*; parte, porción, *f*

assimilate /ə'sɪmə͵leit/ *vt* asimilar; incorporarse. —*vi* mezclarse

assist /ə'sɪst/ *vt* ayudar; auxiliar, socorrer; (uphold) apoyar; (further) promover, fomentar. —*vi* (be present) asistir (a)

assistance /ə'sɪstəns/ *n* ayuda, *f*; auxilio, socorro, *m*; apoyo, *m*; (furtherance) fomento, *m.* **public a.,** asistencia pública, *f*

assistant /ə'sɪstənt/ *n* ayudante, *m*; *Eccl.* asistente, *m*; (in a shop) dependiente (-ta); colaborador (-ra); (university) auxiliar, *m*; sub-. **a. secretary,** subsecretario (-ia). **a. secretaryship,** subsecretaría, *f*

associate /*n* ə'souʃiɪt; *v* -si͵eit/ *n* asociado (-da); miembro, *m*; socio (-ia); compañero (-ra), amigo (-ga); colega, *m*; colaborador (-ra); (confederate) cómplice, *mf* a asociado; auxiliar. —*vt* asociar; unir, juntar. **to a. oneself with,** asociarse con; asociarse a. **to a. with,** frecuentar la compañía de, ir con

association /ə͵sousi'eiʃən/ *n* asociación, *f*; unión, *f*; sociedad, *f*; compañía, corporación, *f*; (connection) relación, *f.* **a. football,** fútbol, *m*

assort /ə'sɔrt/ *vt* clasificar; mezclar

assorted /ə'sɔrtɪd/ *a* surtido, mezclado. **They are a well-a. pair,** Son una pareja bien avenida

assortment /ə'sɔrtmənt/ *n* clasificación, *f*, arreglo, *m*; surtido, *m*, mezcla, *f*

assuage /ə'sweidʒ/ *vt* mitigar; suavizar; calmar; aliviar

assume /ə'sum/ *vt* asumir; tomar; apropiarse; (wear) revestir; (suppose) suponer; poner por caso

assumed /ə'sumd/ *a* fingido, falso; supuesto

assumption /ə'sʌmpʃən/ *n* asunción, *f*; apropiación, arrogación, *f*; suposición, *f.* **Feast of the A.,** Fiesta de la Asunción, *f*

assurance /ə'ʃurəns/ *n* garantía, *f*; promesa, *f*; confianza, seguridad, *f*; (in a good sense) aplomo, *m*, naturalidad, *f*; (in a bad sense) presunción frescura, *f*, descaro, *m*; *Com.* seguro, *m*

assure /ə'ʃur/ *vt* asegurar

assured /ə'ʃurd/ *a* aseguardo; seguro

asterisk /'æstərɪsk/ *n* asterisco, *m*

asthma /'æzmə/ *n* asma, *f*

asthmatic /æz'mætɪk/ *a* asmático

astigmatic /͵æstɪg'mætɪk/ *a* astigmático

astir /ə'stɜr/ *adv* en movimiento; (out of bed) levantado; excitado

astonish /ə'stɒnɪʃ/ *vt* sorprender, asombrar

astonished /ə'stɒnɪʃt/ *a* atónito, estupefacto

astonishing /ə'stɒnɪʃɪŋ/ *a* sorprendente, asombroso

astonishment /ə'stɒnɪʃmənt/ *n* asombro, *m*, sorpresa, estupefacción, *f*

astound /ə'staund/ *vt* aturdir, pasmar. **to be astounded,** *Inf.* quedarse muerto

astounding /ə'staundɪŋ/ *a* asombroso

astray /ə'strei/ *adv* desviado, extraviado; por el mal camino. **to go a.,** errar el camino, perderse; *Fig.* descarriarse

astride /ə'straid/ *adv* a horcajadas. —*prep* a horcajadas sobre; a ambos lados de

astringent /ə'strɪndʒənt/ *a* astringente

astrologer /ə'strɒlədʒər/ n astrólogo (-ga)

astrological /ˌæstrə'lɒdʒɪkəl/ a astrológico

astrology /ə'strɒlədʒɪ/ n astrología, f

astronaut /'æstrəˌnɔt/ n astronauta, mf

astronomer /ə'strɒnəmər/ n astrónomo, m

astronomical /ˌæstrə'nɒmɪkəl/ a astronómico

astronomy /ə'strɒnəmɪ/ n astronomía, f

astute /ə'stut/ a astuto, sagaz; (with knave, etc.) redomado, pícaro

astuteness /ə'stutnɪs/ n astucia, sagacidad, f

asunder /ə'sʌndər/ adv en dos; separadamente; lejos uno de otro

asylum /ə'sailəm/ n asilo, m; (for the insane) manicomio, m

asymmetrical /ˌeɪsɪ'mɛtrɪkəl/ a asimétrico

asymmetry /eɪ'sɪmɪtrɪ/ n asimetría, f

at /æt/ prep a; en casa de; en; de; con; por; (before) delante de. Sometimes forms part of verb, e.g. to aim at, apuntar. to look at, mirar. May be translated by using pres. part., e.g. They were at play, Estaban jugando. at a bound, de un salto. at peace, en paz. at the doctor's, en casa del médico. at the crack of dawn, al rayar el alba, al romper el alba. at the head, a la cabeza. John is at Brighton, Juan está en Brighton. at first, al principio. at last, por fin. at no time, jamás. at once, en seguida. at most, a lo más. at all events, en todo caso. What is he getting at? ¿Qué quiere saber? at home, en casa. at-home day, día de recibo, m

atheism /'eɪθɪˌɪzəm/ n ateísmo, m

atheist /'eɪθɪɪst/ n ateo (-ea)

atheistic /ˌeɪθɪ'ɪstɪk/ a ateo

Athens /'æθɪnz/ Atenas, f

athlete /'æθlit/ n atleta, m

athletic /æθ'lɛtɪk/ a atlético

athletics /æθ'lɛtɪks/ n atletismo, m

Atlantic /æt'læntɪk/ a and n atlántico m. A. Charter, Carta del Atlántico, f. A. liner, transatlántico, m

Atlantis /æt'læntɪs/ Atlántida, f

atlas /'ætləs/ n atlas, m

atmosphere /'ætməsˌfɪər/ n aire, m; atmósfera, f; Fig. ambiente, m

atmospheric /ˌætməs'fɛrɪk/ a atmosférico

atoll /'ætɒl/ n atolón, m

atom /'ætəm/ n átomo, m. splitting of the a., escisión del átomo, f

atomic /ə'tɒmɪk/ a atómico. a. bomb, bomba atómica, f. a. pile, pila atómica, f. a. theory, teoría atómica, f

atomize /'ætəˌmaɪz/ vt pulverizar

atomizer /'ætəˌmaɪzər/ n pulverizador, m

atone /ə'toun/ vi (for) expiar

atonement /ə'tounmənt/ n expiación, f

atrocious /ə'trouʃəs/ a atroz; horrible

atrocity /ə'trɒsɪtɪ/ n atrocidad, f

atrophy /'ætrəfɪ/ n atrofia, f, vi atrofiarse

attach /ə'tætʃ/ vt (Law. of goods) embargar; (Law. of persons) arrestar; (fix) fijar; (tie) atar; (join) juntar; (stick) pegar; (connect) conectar; (hook) enganchar; (with a brooch, etc.) prender; (blame, etc.) imputar; (importance, etc.) dar, conceder; (assign) asignar; (attract) atraer; (enclose) adjuntar, incluir. —vi pertenecer (a), ser indivisible (de). to a. oneself to, pegarse a; adherirse a, asociarse con; acompañar; hacerse inseparable de

attaché /ætæ'ʃeɪ/ n agregado, m. a. case, maletín, m

attachment /ə'tætʃmənt/ n (Law. of goods) embargo, m, vía ejecutiva, f; (Law. of persons) arresto, m; unión, f; conexión, f; (hooking) enganche, m; (with a brooch, etc.) prendimiento, m; (tying) atadura, f; (fixing) fijación, f; (affection) apego, cariño, m; (friendship) amistad, f

attack /ə'tæk/ n ataque, m; Mil. ofensiva, f; (access) acceso, m. —vt atacar

attacker /ə'tækər/ n atacador (-ra), asaltador (-ra)

attain /ə'teɪn/ vt alcanzar, conseguir, lograr. —vi llegar a; alcanzar

attainable /ə'teɪnəbəl/ a asequible, realizable; accesible

attainment /ə'teɪnmənt/ n consecución, obtención, f; logro, m; pl attainments, prendas, dotes, f pl

attempt /ə'tɛmpt/ vt (try) procurar, tratar de, intentar; ensayar; querer; Law. hacer una tentativa (de), atentar. —n tentativa, prueba, f; esfuerzo, ensayo, m; (criminal) atentado, m, tentativa, f

attend /ə'tɛnd/ vt prestar atención (a); escuchar; (look after) cuidar (de); (serve) servir; (accompany) acompañar; (await) esperar. —vi (be present) asistir (a); (of a doctor) visitar; (accompany) acompañar; (bring) acarrear, traer; (follow) seguir. to be attended with, traer consigo, acarrear

attendance /ə'tɛndəns/ n asistencia, presencia, f; (those present) público, m, concurrencia, f; servicio, m; (train) acompañamiento, m; Med. asistencia, f, tratamiento médico, m. to be in a., acompañar (a)

attendant /ə'tɛndənt/ a que acompaña; que sigue; concomitante. —n criado (-da); (keeper) guardián (-ana); (nurse) enfermero (-ra); (in a cloakroom) guardarropa, f; (in a theater) acomodador (-ra); (on a train) mozo, m; (waiter) camarero, m; (at baths) bañero f

attention /ə'tɛnʃən/ n atención, f; cuidado, m. A.! ¡Atención!; Mil. ¡Firmes! to pay a., prestar atención. to stand to a., cuadrarse, permanecer en posición de firmes

attentive /ə'tɛntɪv/ a atento; solícito; cortés, obsequioso

attentively /ə'tɛntɪvlɪ/ adv con atención, atentamente; solícitamente

attentiveness /ə'tɛntɪvnɪs/ n cuidado, m; cortesía, f

attenuate /ə'tɛnyu,eit/ *vt* atenuar
attenuating /ə'tɛnyu,eitɪŋ/ *a* atenuante.
  a. circumstance, circunstancia atenuante,
  f
attest /ə'tɛst/ *vt* atestar. —*vi* atestiguar,
  deponer, dar fe
attestation /ˌætɛ'steiʃən/ *n* atestación,
  deposición, *f*; (certificate) certificado, *m*,
  fe, *f*
attic /'ætɪk/ *n* buhardilla, guardilla, *f*, desván, sotabanco, *m*
Attic /'ætɪk/ *a* ático
attire /ə'taiər/ *n* atavío, *m*; (dress) traje,
  m; (finery) galas, *f pl, vt* ataviar, vestir;
  engalanar
attitude /'ætɪ,tud/ *n* actitud, *f*; postura,
  f; posición, *f*
attorney /ə'tɜrni/ *n* (solicitor) abogado
  (-da); (agent) apoderado (-da); (public)
  procurador, *m*. **power of a.,** poderes, *m*
  pl procuración, *f*. **A.-general,** fiscal, *m*
attract /ə'trækt/ *vt* atraer; (charm) seducir, cautivar, apetecer; (invite) convidar;
  (goodwill, etc.) captar
attraction /ə'trækʃən/ *n* atracción, *f*;
  atractivo, aliciente, encanto, *m*
attractive /ə'træktɪv/ *a* atrayente; atractivo, seductivo; apetecible; encantador
attributable /ə'trɪbyutəbəl/ *a* imputable,
  atribuible
attribute /*v* ə'trɪbyut; *n* 'ætrə,byut/ *vt*
  atribuir (a), achacar (a), imputar (a). —*n*
  atributo, *m*
attribution /ˌætrə'byuʃən/ *n* atribución,
  imputación, *f*; atributo, *m*
attrition /ə'trɪʃən/ *n* atrición, *f*
auburn /'ɔbərn/ *a* castaño, rojizo
auction /'ɔkʃən/ *n* subasta, almoneda, *f*;
  venta pública, pública subasta, *f, vt* subastar. **to put up to a.,** sacar a pública
  subasta
auctioneer /ˌɔkʃə'nɪər/ *n* subastador
  (-ra)
audacious /ɔ'deiʃəs/ *a* atrevido, audaz,
  osado, temerario; (shameless) descarado,
  impudente
audaciously /ə'deiʃəsli/ *adv* osadamente;
  descaradamente
audacity /ɔ'dæsɪti/ *n* audacia, osadía,
  temeridad, *f*, atrevimiento, *m*; (shamelessness) descaro, *m*, desvergüenza, *f*
audible /'ɔdəbəl/ *a* audible, oíble
audibly /'ɔdəbli/ *adv* en forma audible,
  perceptiblemente, en alta voz
audience /'ɔdiəns/ *n* (interview and
  Law.) audiencia, *f*; oyentes, *m pl*, auditorio, público, *m*. **to give a.,** dar audiencia. **a. chamber,** sala de recepción, *f*
audit /'ɔdɪt/ *vt* intervenir, examinar
  (cuentas). —*n* intervención, *f*, ajuste (de
  cuentas), *m*
audition /ɔ'dɪʃən/ *n* audición, *f*
auditor /'ɔdɪtər/ *n* (hearer) oyente, *mf*;
  interventor, contador, *m*
auditorium /ˌɔdɪ'tɔriəm/ *n* sala de espec-
  táculos, *f*

aught /ɔt/ *n* algo. **For a. I know,** Por lo
  que yo sepa
augment /ɔg'mɛnt/ *vt* aumentar, acrecentar. —*vi* aumentarse, acrecentarse
augmentation /ˌɔgmɛn'teiʃən/ *n* aumento, acrecentamiento, *m*; añadidura, *f*
augur /'ɔgər/ *n* agorero (-ra). —*vt* and *vi*
  presagiar, anunciar; pronosticar, agorar
augury /'ɔgyəri/ *n* predicción, *f*; agüero,
  presagio, pronóstico, *m*
August /'ɔgəst/ *n* agosto, *m*
august /ɔ'gəst/ *a* augusto
aunt /ænt, ɑnt/ *n* tía, *f*. **great-a.,** tía
  abuela, *f*. **A. Sally,** el pim, pam, pum
aura /'ɔrə/ *n* exhalación, *f*; influencia
  psíquica, *f*; *Med.* aura, *f*
auricle /'ɔrɪkəl/ *n* (of the heart) aurícula,
  ala del corazón, *f*; oreja, *f*, pabellón de la
  oreja, *m*
auspicious /ɔ'spɪʃəs/ *a* propicio, favorable, feliz
austere /ɔ'stɪər/ *a* severo, austero, adusto; ascético; (of style) desnudo
austerity /ɔ'stɛrɪti/ *n* austeridad, severidad, *f*; ascetismo, *m*; (of style) desnudez,
  f
Australian /ɔ'streilyən/ *a* and *n* australiano (-na)
Austrian /'ɔstriən/ *a* and *n* austríaco
  (-ca)
authentic /ɔ'θɛntɪk/ *a* auténtico
authenticate /ɔ'θɛntɪ,keit/ *vt* autenticar
authenticity /ˌɔθɛn'tɪsɪti/ *n* autenticidad,
  f
author /'ɔθər/ *n* autor, *m*
authoritarian /əˌθɔrɪ'tɛəriən/ *a* autoritario
authoritative /ə'θɔrɪ,teitɪv/ *a* autoritario
authority /ə'θɔrɪti/ *n* autoridad, *f*; poder,
  m. **to have on the best a.,** tener de muy
  buena fuente
authorization /ˌɔθərə'zeiʃən/ *n* autorización, *f*
authorize /'ɔθə,raiz/ *vt* autorizar
autobiographical /ˌɔtə,baiə'græfɪkəl/ *a*
  autobiográfico
autobiography /ˌɔtəbai'ɒgrəfi/ *n* autobiografía, *f*
autocracy /ɔ'tɒkrəsi/ *n* autocracia, *f*
autocrat /'ɔtə,kræt/ *n* autócrata, *mf*
autocratic /ˌɔtə'krætɪk/ *a* autocrático
autograph /'ɔtə,græf/ *n* autógrafo, *m*
automatic /ˌɔtə'mætɪk/ *a* automático. **a.
  gate,** (at level crossings, etc.) barrera de
  golpe, *f*. **a. machine,** máquina automática, *f*; *Inf.* tragaperras, *m*. **a. pencil,** lapicero, *m*
automobile /ˌɔtəmə'bil/ *n* automóvil, *m*
autonomous /ɔ'tɒnəməs/ *a* autónomo
autonomy /ɔ'tɒnəmi/ *n* autonomía, *f*
autopsy /'ɔtɒpsi/ *n* autopsia, *f*
autumn /'ɔtəm/ *n* otoño, *m*
autumnal /ɔ'tʌmnl/ *a* otoñal, de otoño
auxiliary /ɔg'zɪlyəri/ *a* auxiliar. —*n*
  auxiliador, *m*
avail /ə'veil/ *vi* servir; valer; importar.

—*vt* aprovechar. **to a. oneself of,** valerse de, aprovecharse de. **to no a.,** en balde

availability /ə,veilə'bɪlɪti/ *n* utilidad, *f;* disponibilidad, *f;* provecho, *m;* (validity) validez, *f*

available /ə'veiləbəl/ *a* útil; disponible; aprovechable; válido

avalanche /'ævə,læntʃ/ *n* alud, lurte, *m*

avarice /'ævərɪs/ *n* avaricia, *f*

avaricious /,ævə'rɪʃəs/ *a* avaro, avaricioso

avenge /ə'vendʒ/ *vt* vengar; vindicar. **to a. oneself for,** vengarse de

avenger /ə'vendʒər/ *n* vengador (-ra)

avenging /ə'vendʒɪŋ/ *a* vengador

avenue /'ævə,nyu/ *n* avenida, *f*

aver /ə'vɜr/ *vt* afirmar, asegurar

average /'ævərɪdʒ/ *n* promedio, término medio, *m;* (marine insurance) avería, *f, a* de promedio; típico; corriente; normal.
—*vt* hallar el término medio (de); prorratear, proporcionar; ser por término medio. **general a.,** (marine insurance) avería gruesa, *f.* **on the a.,** por término medio

averse /ə'vɜrs/ *a* opuesto (a); desinclinado (a); enemigo (de); repugnante. **to be a. to,** no gustar de; oponerse a; estar desinclinado a; ser enemigo de; repugnar

aversion /ə'vɜrʒən/ *n* aversión, *f;* repugnancia, *f*

avert /ə'vɜrt/ *vt* apartar; (avoid) evitar

aviary /'eivi,ɛri/ *n* avería, pajarera, *f*

aviation /,eivi'eiʃən/ *n* aviación, *f*

aviator /'eivi,eitər/ *n* aviador (-ra)

avid /'ævɪd/ *a* ávido

avocation /,ævə'keiʃən/ *n* pasatiempo, *m,* distracción, *f;* ocupación, *f;* profesión, *m*

avoid /ə'vɔid/ *vt* evitar; (pursuit) evadir, eludir; guardarse (de), rehuir; *Law.* anular

avoidable /ə'vɔidəbəl/ *a* evitable, eludible

avow /ə'vau/ *vt* confesar; declarar

avowal /ə'vauəl/ *n* confesión, admisión, *f*

avowedly /ə'vaudli/ *adv* por confesión propia

await /ə'weit/ *vt* aguardar, esperar

awake /ə'weik/ *vt* despertar. —*vi* despertarse. —*a* despierto; vigilante; consciente (de); atento (a)

awakening /ə'weikəniŋ/ *n* despertamiento, *m*

award /ə'wɔrd/ *n* sentencia, decisión, *f;* adjudicación, *f;* (prize) premio, *m.* —*vt* adjudicar; otorgar, conceder. **She was awarded a professorship in Greek,** Ganó unas oposiciones para una cátedra de griego

aware /ə'wɛər/ *a* consciente, sabedor. **to be well a. of,** saber muy bien. **to make a. of,** hacer saber

awash /ə'wɒʃ/ *adv* a flor de agua

away /ə'wei/ *adv* a distancia, a lo lejos, lejos; (absent) ausente; (out) fuera; (unceasingly) sin parar, continuamente; (wholly) completamente; (visibly) a ojos vistas. In verbs of motion **a.** is rendered by the reflexive, e.g. *to go a.,* marcharse. Sometimes not translated, e.g. *to take a.,* quitar. —*interj* ¡fuera de aquí! ¡márchese Vd.!; ¡vámonos! ¡adelante! *nine miles a.,* a nueve millas de distancia. *a. in the distance,* allá a lo lejos. *She sang a.,* Ella seguía cantando

awe /ɔ/ *n* temor reverente, *m;* horror, *m;* respeto, *m;* reverencia, *f, vt* intimidar, aterrar; infundir respeto (a). **to stand in awe of,** tener respeto (a), reverenciar

awesome /'ɔsəm/ *a* pavoroso, temible, aterrador; terrible; (august) augusto; (imposing) imponente

awestruck /'ɔ,strʌk/ *a* espantado, aterrado

awful /'ɔfəl/ *a* terrible, pavoroso; horrible; temible; atroz; *Inf.* enorme. **How a.!** *Inf.* ¡Qué barbaridad!

awfully /'ɔfəli, 'ɔfli/ *adv* terriblemente; horriblemente; *Inf.* muy

awfulness /'ɔfəlnɪs/ *n* lo terrible; lo horrible; atrocidad, *f;* (of a crime, etc.) enormidad, *f*

awkward /'ɔkwərd/ *a* difícil; peligroso; delicado; embarazoso; (of time, etc.) inconveniente, inoportuno; (of things) incómodo; (clumsy) torpe, desmañado; desagradable; (ungraceful) sin gracia. **the a. age,** la edad difícil

awkwardly /'ɔkwərdli/ *adv* torpemente; incómodamente; con dificultad; sin gracia. **He is a. placed,** Se encuentra en una situación difícil

awkwardness /'ɔkwərdnɪs/ *n* dificultad, *f;* peligro, *m;* delicadeza, *f;* inconveniencia, inoportunidad, *f;* (clumsiness) torpeza, desmaña, *f;* (ungracefulness) falta de gracia, *f*

awl /ɔl/ *n* lezna, *f,* punzón, *m*

awning /'ɔniŋ/ *n* toldo, palio, *m; Naut.* toldilla, *f*

awry /ə'rai/ *adv* a un lado; oblicuamente; *Fig.* mal. —*a* torcido; *Fig.* descarriado

ax /æks/ *n* hacha, *f*

axiom /'æksiəm/ *n* axioma, *m*

axiomatic /,æksiə'mætɪk/ *a* axiomático

axis /'æksɪs/ *n* eje, *m; Zool.* axis, *m.* **A. power,** potencia del Eje

axle /'æksəl/ *n* eje, *m;* peón, árbol (de una rueda), *m.* **back a.,** eje trasero, *m.* **differential a.,** eje diferencial, *m.* **front a.,** eje delantero, *m*

aye /ai/ *interj* sí. —*n* voto afirmativo, *m*

Aztec /'æztɛk/ *a* and *n* azteca, *mf*

azure /'æʒər/ *n* azul celeste, *m*

b /bi/ *n* (letter) be, *f;* Mus. si, *m*
babble /'bæbəl/ *n* (chatter) charla, *f;* (of a child) gorjeo, *m;* (confused sound) vocinglería, barbulla, *f,* rumor, *m;* (of water) murmullo, susurro, *m.* —*vi* charlar; (of children) gorjearse; (incoherently) balbucir; (water) murmurar, susurrar; (a secret) descubrir
babbling /'bæbliŋ/ *n* garrulería, locuacidad, *f;* (incoherent speech) balbuceo, *m.* (of water) murmullo, *m.* —*a* gárrulo, locuaz; balbuciente; murmurante
baboon /bæ'bun/ *esp.* Brit. bə-/ *n* babuíno, *m*
baby /'beibi/ *n* bebé, crío, *m;* niño (-ña) de pecho, *Fig.* gran bebé, *m;* niño mimado, *m, a* infantil. **b. blue,** azul claro, *m.* **b. doll,** muñeca bebé, *f.* **b. grand piano,** piano de media cola, *m*
baby carriage *n* coche de niños, *m*
babyish /'beibiiʃ/ *a* infantil, aniñado, pueril
babysitter /'beibi,sitər/ *n* cuidaniños, *mf*
baccalaureate /,bækə'lɔriit, -'lɒr-/ *n* bachillerato, *m*
bachelor /'bætʃələr/ *n* soltero, célibe, *m;* (of a university) licenciado, bachiller, *m;* (as a title) caballero, *m.* **confirmed b.,** solterón, *m.* **degree of b.,** licenciatura, *f.* **to receive the degree of b.,** licenciarse, bachillerarse
back /bæk/ *n* Anat. espalda, *f;* (of an animal) lomo, espinazo, *m;* (reins, loins) riñones, *m pl;* (of chairs, sofas) respaldo, *m;* (of a book) lomo, *m;* (back, bottom) fondo, *m;* parte posterior, parte de atrás, *f;* (of a hand, brush and many other things) dorso, *m;* (of a coin) reverso, *m;* el otro lado de alguna cosa; (in football, hockey) defensa, *m;* Theat. foro, *m;* (of fire-arms) culata, *f;* (of a knife) canto, *m;* (upper portion) parte superior, *f.* —*a* posterior, trasero; de atrás; (remote) alejado, apartado; inferior; (overdue) past; out of date) atrasado; (earlier) anterior; Anat. dorsal. **at the b.,** detrás, *m;* en el fondo; en la última fila. **at the b. of one's mind,** por sus adentros, en el fondo del pensamiento. **behind one's b.,** a espaldas de uno, en ausencia de uno. **half-b.,** medio, *m.* **on one's b.,** boca arriba; a cuestas. **to see the b. of,** *Inf.* ver por última vez, desembarazarse de. **to turn one's b. on,** volver la espalda (a). **with one's b. to the engine,** de espaldas a la máquina. **b. to b.,** espalda con espalda
back /bæk/ *vt* empujar hacia atrás; (a vehicle) dar marcha atrás; hacer retroceder; (line) reforzar; (support) apoyar; (sign) endosar; (bind) forrar; (bet on) apostar a; (a sail) fachear. —*vi* retroceder; dar marchar atrás; (of the wind) girar; (with on to) dar sobre, dominar; (with down) abandonar (una pretensión, etc.). **to b. out,** salir, marcharse; volverse atrás; (retract) desdecirse
back /bæk/ *adv* detrás; atrás; otra vez, de nuevo; (returned) de vuelta; a alguna distancia; (at home) en casa. —*interj* ¡atrás! **A few weeks b.,** Hace unas semanas, Unas semanas atrás. **It stands b. from the road,** Está a alguna distancia del camino. **to go b. to,** (of families, etc.) remontar a. **to come b.,** regresar. **to come b. again,** regresar de nuevo, regresar por segunda vez
back axle *n* eje trasero, *m*
backbite /'bæk,bait/ *vt* cortar (a uno) un sayo, desollarle (a uno) vivo, murmurar de
backbone /'bæk,boun/ *n* espinazo, *m,* columna vertebral, *f.* **to the b.,** hasta la médula
backed /bækt/ *a* (lined) forrado; (in compounds: of persons) de espalda; (of chairs) de respaldo
backfire /'bæk,faiər/ *n* contrafuego *m,* falsa explosión, *f*
background /'bæk,graund/ *n* fondo, *m;* Art. último término, *m.* **in the b.,** en el fondo; Art. en último término; *Fig.* en las sombras; alejado, a distancia
backhanded /'bæk,hændid/ *a* de revés, dado con el revés de la mano; *Fig.* ambiguo, equívoco
backing /'bækiŋ/ *n* forro, *m;* (lining) refuerzo, *m;* (of a vehicle) marcha atrás, *f,* retroceso, *m;* (betting) el apostar (a); (wagers) apuestas, *f pl;* (Fig. support) apoyo, *m,* ayuda, *f;* garantía, *f*
backlog /'bæk,lɒg/ *n* Com. rezago de pedidos, *m*
backroom /'bæk'rum/ *n* cuarto interior, *m,* habitación trasera, *f.* **b. boy,** investigador ocupado en trabajos secretos para el gobierno, *m*
back seat *n* asiento trasero, *m;* fondo, *m.* **to take a b.-s.,** permanecer en el fondo, ceder el paso
backside /'bæk,said/ *n* trasero, *m,* posaderas, nalgas, *f pl*
backslide /'bæk,slaid/ *vi* recaer, reincidir
backstage /'bæk'steidʒ/ *n* foro, fondo del escenario, *m, adv* hacia el foro; detrás de bastidores
backstairs /'bæk'stɛərz/ *n* escalera de servicio, *f; Fig.* vías secretas, *f pl, a* de cocina; *Fig.* secreto
backstitch /'bæk,stitʃ/ *n* Sew. pespunte, *m, vt* and *vi* pespuntar
backstroke /'bæk,strouk/ *n* reculada, *f; Sports.* revés, *m*
backward /'bækwərd/ *a* hacia atrás; vuelto hacia atrás; (in development) atrasado, poco avanzado; lento; negligente; (shy) modesto; (late) tardío; atrasado; retrógrado; (dull) torpe; retrospectivo. —*adv* hacia atrás; atrás; al revés; (of falling) de espaldas; (of time) al pasado. **to go b. and forward,** ir y venir. **b. and forward,** de acá para allá

backwardness /'bækwǝrdnɪs/ n atraso, m; lentitud, f; negligencia, f; modestia, f; (lateness) tardanza, f; atraso, m; (dullness) torpeza, f; falta de progreso, f

backwards /'bækwǝrdz/ adv See **backward**

backwater /'bæk,wɔtǝr/ n remanso, m

backwoods /'bæk'wʊdz/ n monte, m, selva, f

bacon /'beikǝn/ n tocino, m

bacteria /bæk'tɪɪǝriǝ/ n bacteria, f

bacteriologist /,bæktɪǝri'plǝdʒɪst/ n bacteriólogo, m

bacteriology /,bæktɪǝri'plǝdʒi/ n bacteriología, f

bad /bæd/ a malo; (wicked) perverso; (ill) enfermo, malo (with estar); (naughty, undutiful) malo (with ser); (of coins) falso; (of debts) incobrable; (rotten) podrido; (harmful) nocivo; (dangerous) peligroso; (of pains, a cold) fuerte; intenso; (of a shot) errado; (mistaken) equivocado; (unfortunate) desgraciado. —n el mal, lo malo; (persons) los malos. **extremely bad,** pésimo. **from bad to worse,** de mal en peor. **It's too bad!** ¡Esto es demasiado! **to go bad,** (fruit) macarse; (food) estropearse. **bad habit,** mala costumbre, f, vicio, m. **to have the bad habit of,** tener el vicio de. **bad temper,** malhumor, mal genio, m. **bad tempered,** malhumorado. **bad turn,** flaco servicio, m, mala pasada, f

badge /bædʒ/ n insignia, f; (decoration) condecoración, f; símbolo, emblema, m; (mark) marca, f

badger /'bædʒǝr/ n tejón, m, vt cansar, molestar

Bad Lands (of Nebraska and South Dakota) Tierras malas f pl; (of Argentina) la Travesía, f

badly /'bædli/ adv mal. **extremely b.,** pésimamente. **to want something b.,** necesitar algo con urgencia. **b. done,** mal hecho. **b. disposed,** malintencionado

badminton /'bædmɪntn/ n el juego del volante, m

badness /'bædnɪs/ n maldad, f; mala calidad, f; lo malo

bad-smelling /'bæd ,smɛlɪŋ/ a maloliente

baffle /'bæfǝl/ vt desconcertar; (bewilder) tener perplejo (a); contrariar, frustrar; (obstruct) impedir; (avoid) evitar. **to b. description,** no haber palabras para describir

baffling /'bæflɪŋ/ a desconcertante; difícil; confuso; perturbador; (of people) enigmático

bag /bæg/ n saco, m; talega, f; (hand) bolsa, f, saco (de mano), m; (for tools) capacho, m; (for sewing) costurero, m; (of bagpipes) fuelle, m; (saddle) alforja, f; (briefcase) cartera, f; (suitcase) maleta, f; (under the eye) ojera, f; (game shot) caza, f. —vt entalegar; coger, cazar; matar; tomar. —vi (of garments) arrugarse. **to clear out bag and baggage,** liar el

petate. **a bag of bones,** (person) un manojo de huesos. **bag wig,** peluquín, m

bagatelle /,bægǝ'tɛl/ n bagatela, friolera, f; (game) billar romano, m

bagful /'bægfʊl/ n saco, m; bolsa, f

baggage /'bægɪdʒ/ n equipaje, m; Mil. bagaje, m; (madcap) pícara, f; (jade) mujerzuela, f. **b. master,** (railway) factor, m. **b. car,** furgón de equipaje, m

baggage rack n (of automobile) portaequipajes, m

baggy /'bægi/ a (creased, of trousers) con rodilleras, arrugado; (wide) bombacho

bagpipe /'bæg,paip/ n gaita, f

bagpiper /'bæg,paipǝr/ n gaitero, m

bah /ba/ interj ¡bah!

Bahamas, the /bǝ'hɑmǝz/ las Islas Bahamas, las Islas Lucayas, f

bail /beil/ n Law. fianza, caución, f; (person) fiador (-ra); (cricket) travesaño, m, barra, f. —vt Law. poner en libertad bajo fianza; salir fiador (por); (a boat) achicar. **on b.,** en fiado. **to go b.,** dar fianza, fiar.

bailiff /'beilɪf/ n Law. agente ejecutivo, m; alguacil, m; mayordomo, m; capataz, m

bait /beit/ n cebo, m; anzuelo, m; (fodder) pienso, m, vt cebar; (feed) dar pienso (a); azuzar; atormentar; (attract) atraer

baiting /'beitɪŋ/ n cebadura, f; combate, m; tormenta, f

baize /beiz/ n bayeta, f. **green b.,** tapete verde, m

bake /beik/ vt cocer; hacer (pan, etc.). **I like to bake cakes,** Me gusta hacer pasteles; Fig. endurecer. —vi cocerse

baker /'beikǝr/ n panadero, hornero, m. **a baker's dozen,** la docena del fraile

bakery /'beikǝri, 'beikri/ n panadería, f

baking /'beikɪŋ/ n cocimiento, m, cocción, f; (batch) hornada, f; el hacer (pan, etc.) a Inf. abrasador. **b.-dish,** tortera, f. **b.-powder,** levadura química, f

balance /'bælǝns/ n balanza, f; equilibrio, m; Com. balance, saldo, m; (in a bank) saldo (a favor del cuentacorrentista), m; Math. resto, m; Astron. Libra, f; (pendulum) péndola, f; (counterweight) contrapeso, m. **credit b.,** saldo acreedor, m. **debit b.,** saldo deudor, m. **net b.,** saldo líquido, m. **to lose one's b.,** perder el equilibrio. **to strike a b.,** hacer balance. **b. of power,** equilibrio político, m. **b. of trade,** balanza de comercio, f. **b.-sheet,** balance, avanzo, m. **b. wheel,** (of watches) volante, m

balance /'bælǝns/ vt balancear, abalanzar; contrapesar; (accounts) saldar; equilibrar; comparar; considerar, examinar. —vi balancearse; ser de igual peso; equilibrarse; (accounts) saldarse

balancing /'bælǝnsɪŋ/ n balanceo, m; Com. balance, m. **b.-pole,** balancín, m

balcony /'bælkǝni/ n balcón, m; galería, f; Theat. anfiteatro, m

bald /bɔld/ a calvo; (of style) seco, pobre; Fig. desnudo, árido, pelado; sin adorno;

(simple) sencillo. **to grow b.,** ponerse calvo, encalvecer

baldly /'bɔldli/ adv secamente; sencillamente

baldness /'bɔldnɪs/ n calvicie, f; (of style) sequedad, pobreza, f; (bareness) desnudez, aridez, f

bale /beil/ n (bundle) fardo, m; (of cotton, paper, etc.) bala, f

Balearic Islands, the las Islas Baleares, f

baleful /'beilfəl/ a malicioso, siniestro, maligno

balk /bɔk/ n obstáculo, m; (beam) viga, f; (billiards) cabaña, f. —vt frustrar; impedir. —vi resistirse, rehusar

Balkan /'bɔlkən/ a balcánico

Balkans, the los Balcanes, m

ball /bɔl/ n globo, m, esfera, f; (plaything) pelota, f; (as in billiards, cricket, croquet) bola, f; (in football, basket ball) balón, m; (shot) bala, f; (of wool, etc.) ovillo, m; (of the eye) globo (del ojo), m; (of the thumb) yema (del pulgar), f; (of the foot) planta (del pie), f; (dance) baile, m. —vt apelotonarse. **red b.,** (in billiards) mingo, m. **to play b.,** jugar a la pelota. **to roll oneself into a b.,** aovillarse, hacerse un ovillo. **b.-and-socket joint,** articulación esférica, f. **b.-bearing,** cojinete de bolas, m

ballad /'bæləd/ n romance, m; (song) balada, f

ballast /'bæləst/ n (Naut. and Fig.) lastre, m; Rail. balasto, m. —vt lastrar; llenar de balasto

ballerina /ˌbælə'rinə/ n bailarina, f

ballet /bæ'lei/ n baile ruso, ballet, m; baile, m. **b. master,** director de ballet, m

balloon /bə'lun/ n globo aerostático, m; Chem. balón, m; (toy) globo, m; Archit. bola, f. **captive b.,** globo cautivo, m. **barrage,** cortina de globos de intercepción, f. **b.-tyre,** neumático balón, m

ballot /'bælət/ n votación, f; papeleta para votar, cédula de votación, f. —vi votar, balotar. **b. box,** urna electoral, f

ballpoint pen /'bɔl,pɔint/ n pluma esférica, f, birome, m (Argentina), puntobola, m (Bolivia), esfero, m (Colombia)

ballroom /'bɔl,rum/ n salón de baile, m; salón de fiestas, m

balm /bam/ n bálsamo, m; Fig. ungüento, m

balminess /'bamɪnɪs/ n fragancia, f; aroma, m; (gentleness) suavidad, f

balmy /'bami/ a balsámico; fragante; aromático; (soft) suave; (soothing) calmante

Baltic /'bɔltɪk/ the el (Mar) Báltico, m

baluster /'bæləstər/ n balaustre, m

balustrade /'bælə,streid/ n balaustrada, barandilla, f, antepecho, m

bamboo /bæm'bu/ n bambú, m

bamboozle /bæm'buzəl/ vt engatusar, embaucar

bamboozling /bæm'buzlɪŋ/ n embaucamiento, engaño, m

ban /bæn/ n interdicción, f; prohibición, f; bando, m. —vt prohibir; proscribir

banal /bə'næl/ a banal, vulgar, trivial

banality /bə'nælɪti/ n banalidad, vulgaridad, trivialidad, f

banana /bə'nænə/ n (tree and fruit) plátano, m; (fruit) banana, f. **b. plantation,** platanar, m

band /bænd/ n lista, tira, f; zona, f; (black mourning) tira de gasa, f; (sash) faja, f; (ribbon) banda; cinta, f; (bandage) venda, f; Mech. correa, f; Archit. listón, m; Mus. banda, f; (group) pandilla, f, grupo, m. —vt congregar, reunir. —vi reunirse, asociarse. **b.-saw,** sierra de cinta, f

bandage /'bændɪdʒ/ n venda, f, vendaje, m, vt vendar, poner un vendaje en (limbs, etc. or persons)

bandit /'bændɪt/ n bandido, bandolero, m

bandmaster /'bænd,mæstər/ n músico mayor, m; director de orquesta, m

bandsman /'bændzmən/ n músico, m

bandstand /'bænd,stænd/ n quiosco de música, m

bandy /'bændi/ vt cambiar, trocar; pasar de uno a otro

bandy-legged /'bændi ˌlegid/ a estevado, zanquituerto

bane /bein/ n (poison) veneno, m; perdición, ruina, f; (nuisance) plaga, f

baneful /'beinfəl/ a pernicioso, funesto; dañino; maligno

bang /bæŋ/ n golpe, golpazo, m; (of an explosive, fire-arm) estallido, m, detonación, f; (of a firework) traque, m; (of a door) portazo, m; (with the fist) puñetazo, m; (noise) ruido, m; (fringe) flequillo, m. —vt golpear; (beat) sacudir; (throw) lanzar, arrojar con violencia; (a door, etc.) cerrar de golpe, cerrar con violencia. —vi golpear; estallar; (thunder) retronar; (in the wind) cencerrear. —interj ¡pum! ¡zas!

banging /'bæŋɪŋ/ n golpeadura, f; sacudidura, f; detonación, f; ruido, m

bangle /'bæŋgəl/ n (slave b.) esclava, f; pulsera, f; brazalete, m; (for ankles) ajorca, f

banish /'bænɪʃ/ vt desterrar; apartar; (from the mind) despedir, ahuyentar; (suppress) suprimir

banishment /'bænɪʃmənt/ n destierro, m; expulsión, f; relegación, f; (suppression) supresión, f

banister /'bænəstər/ n baranda, f, pasamano, m

banjo /'bændʒou/ n banjo, m

bank /bæŋk/ n (of rivers, etc.) ribera, orilla, f, margen, m; (of clouds) banda, capa, f; (of sand, fog, snow) banco, m; (embankment) terraplén, m; Com. banco, m; (gaming) banca, f; (for foreign exchange) casa de cambio, f. **b. account,** cuenta corriente, f. **b. book,** libreta de banco, f. **b. clerk,** empleado del banco, m. **b. holiday,** fiesta oficial, f, **b.-note,**

billete de banco, *m*. **b. stock,** acciones de un banco, *f pl*

bank /bæŋk/ *vt* estancar, represar; amontonar; poner (dinero) en un banco, depositar en un banco; —*vi* tener cuenta corriente en un banco; (gaming) tener la banca; ser banquero; *Aer.* inclinarse al virar

banker /'bæŋkər/ *n* banquero, *m,* (also at cards); (money-changer) cambista, *mf*

banking /'bæŋkɪŋ/ *n Com.* banca, *f; Aer.* vuelo inclinado, *m, a Com.* bancario. **b. house,** casa de banca, *f*

bankrupt /'bæŋkrʌpt/ *a* insolvente, quebrado. —*n* quebrado (-da). **to go b.,** declararse en quiebra, hacer bancarrota

bankruptcy /'bæŋkrʌptsi/ *n* bancarrota, quiebra, *f; Fig.* pobreza, decadencia, *f.* **fraudulent b.,** quiebra fraudulenta, *f.* **b. court,** tribunal de quiebras, *m*

banner /'bænər/ *n* bandera, *f*

banquet /'bæŋkwɪt/ *n* banquete, *m, vt* and *vi* banquetear

banqueting /'bæŋkwɪtɪŋ/ *a* de banquetes. **b. hall,** sala de banquetes, *f*

bantam /'bæntəm/ *n* gallina enana, *f.* **b. weight,** (Sports.) *a* de peso gallo. —*n* peso gallo, *m*

banter /'bæntər/ *vt* and *vi* tomar el pelo (a). —*n* chistes, *m pl,* burlas, *f pl*

baptism /'bæptɪzəm/ *n* bautismo, *m; Fig.* bautizo, *m*

baptist /'bæptɪst/ *n* bautista, *m.* **St. John the B.,** San Juan Bautista

baptize /bæp'taiz, 'bæptaiz/ *vt* bautizar

bar /bar/ *n* barra, *f;* (of chocolate, soap) pastilla, *f; Herald.* banda, *f;* (on a window) reja, *f;* (of a door) tranca, *f,* barrote, *m;* (bar lever) palanca, *f;* (of a balance) astil, *m; Mus.* barra, *f;* (in the sea, etc.) banco, alfaque, *m;* (barrier) barrera, *f;* (barrister's profession) foro, *m,* curia, *f; Fig.* tribunal, *m;* (in a court) barra, *f; Fig.* impedimento, *m;* (of light) rayo, *m;* (stripe) raya, *f;* (for refreshments) bar, *m;* mostrador del bar, *m.* —*vt* atrancar, abarrotar; impedir, obstruir; prohibir; exceptuar, excluir; (streak) rayar. **the b.,** el cuerpo de abogados. **to be called to the b.,** ser recibido como abogado en los tribunales. **b.-tender,** camarero del bar, *m*

bar association *n* colegio de abogados, *m*

barb /barb/ *n* púa, *f;* (of an arrow, fishhook, etc.) lengüeta, *f;* (of a lance) roquete, *m;* (of fish) barbilla, *f;* (of a feather) barba, *f;* (horse) caballo berberisco, *m.* —*vt* proveer de púas; armar de lengüetas

barbarian /bar'bɛəriən/ *a* bárbaro, barbárico. —*n* bárbaro (-ra)

barbaric /bar'bærɪk/ *a* barbárico, salvaje

barbarism /'barbə,rɪzəm/ *n* barbarismo, salvajismo, *m;* crueldad, *f;* (of style) barbarismo, *m*

barbarous /'barbərəs/ *a* feroz, cruel, salvaje; inculto

barbecue /'barbɪ,kyu/ *n* barbacoa, *f*

barbed wire /'barbd/ *n* alambre de púas, alambre espinoso, *m*

barber /'barbər/ *n* barbero, *m.* **barber shop,** barbería, *f*

bard /bard/ *n* bardo, vate, *m*

bare /bɛər/ *a* desnudo; descubierto; vacío; (mere) mero, solo; (worn) raído; pelado, raso; (unadorned) sencillo; (unsheathed) desnudo; (arid) árido; (curt) seco; (unprotected) desabrigado; pobre. —*vt* desnudar; descubrir; revelar. **He bared his head,** Se descubrió. **to lay b.,** dejar al desnudo; revelar

bareback /'bɛər,bæk/ *a* que monta en pelo. —*adv* en pelo

barefaced /'bɛər,feist/ *a* descarado, desvergonzado, cínico

barefoot /'bɛər,fʊt/ *a* descalzo

bareheaded /'bɛər,hɛdɪd/ *a* sin sombrero, descubierto

barelegged /'bɛər,lɛgɪd/ *a* en pernetas, en piernas

barely /'bɛərli/ *adv* apenas; escasamente; meramente, solamente

bareness /'bɛərnɪs/ *n* desnudez, *f;* desadorno, *m;* (aridity) aridez, *f;* pobreza, *f*

bargain /'bargən/ *n* contrato, *m;* pacto, acuerdo, *m;* (purchase) ganga, *f.* —*vi* negociar; (haggle) regatear; (expect) esperar. **It is a b.,** Es una ganga; Trato hecho. **to get the best of the b.,** salir ganando. **to strike a b.,** cerrar un trato. **b. counter,** sección de saldos, *f.* **b. sale,** venta de saldos, *f*

bargainer /'bargənər/ *n* negociador (-ra); regatón (-ona)

bargaining /'bargənɪŋ/ *n* negociación, gestión, *f;* (haggling) regateo, *m*

barge /bardʒ/ *n* (for freight) barcaza, gabarra, *f;* falúa, *f;* lancha, *f.* —*vi* (into) tropezar con; dar empujones

baritone /'bærɪ,toun/ *n* barítono, *m*

bark /bark/ *n* (of a tree) corteza, *f;* (quinine) quina, *f;* (boat, Poet.) barca, *f; Naut.* buque de tres palos, *m;* (of a dog) ladrido, *m;* (of a fox) aullido, *m;* (of a gun) ruido, *m.* —*vi* (of a dog) ladrar; (of a fox) aullar; (of a gun) tronar

barking /'barkɪŋ/ *n* ladrido, *m;* (of stags) rebramo, *m;* (of foxes) aullidos, *m pl;* (of guns) trueno, *m*

barley /'barli/ *n* cebada, *f, a* de cebada. **pearl b.,** cebada perlada, *f.* **b.-bin,** cebadera, *f.* **b. dealer,** cebadero, *m.* **b. field,** cebadal, *m.* **b.-water,** hordiate, *m*

barm /barm/ *n* (froth on beer) giste, *m;* (leaven) levadura, *f*

barmaid /'bar,meid/ *n* moza de bar, camarera, *f*

barn /barn/ *n* pajar, granero, hórreo, *m.* **b.-owl,** lechuza, *f*

barometer /bə'rɒmɪtər/ *n* barómetro, *m*

baroque /bə'rouk/ *a* barroco. **the b.,** lo barroco

barrack /'bærək/ *n Mil.* cuartel, *m,* caserna, *f, vt* acuartelar

barrage /bə'raʒ/ *n* presa de contención,

f; Mil. cortina de fuego, *f;* (barrier) barrera, *f;* (of questions) lluvia, *f.* **b. balloon,** globo de intercepción, *m*

barrel /'bærəl/ *n* barril, *m;* tonel, *m,* cuba, *f;* (of a gun) cañón, *m; Mech.* cilindro, *m;* (of an animal) cuerpo, *m.* —*vt* embarrilar, entonelar. **b.-organ,** organillo, órgano de manubrio, *m*

barrelled /'bærəld/ *a* embarrilado; (of guns, generally in compounds) dé... cañones. **double-b. gun,** escopeta de dos cañones, *f*

barren /'bærən/ *a* estéril; (of ground) árido; (fruitless) infructuoso

barrenness /'bærən,nɪs/ *n* esterilidad, *f;* aridez, sequedad, *f;* (fruitlessness) inutilidad, *f*

barricade /'bærɪ,keɪd/ *n* barricada, *f;* barrera, *f, vt* cerrar con barricadas; obstruir

barricading /'bærɪ,keɪdɪŋ/ *n* el cerrar con barricadas; la defensa con barricadas (de)

barrier /'bæriər/ *n* barrera, *f;* impedimento, *m;* (for customs duties) portazgo, *m*

barring /'bɑrɪŋ/ *prep* salvo, excepto, con la excepción de, menos

barrister /'bærəstər/ *n* abogado (-da)

barter /'bɑrtər/ *n* cambio, trueque, *m;* tráfico, *m, vt and vi* cambiar, trocar; traficar

barterer /'bɑrtərər/ *n* traficante, *mf*

base /beɪs/ *a* bajo, vil, ruin; soez; indigno; impuro; (of metals) de mala ley. —*n* base, *f;* fundamento, *m;* pie, *m; Archit.* pedestal, *m;* (Mil. Chem. Geom.) base, *f;* (of a vase) asiento, *m, vt* basar; fundar. **b. action,** bajeza, *f.* **b. line,** *Sports.* línea de base, *f.* **b. metal,** metal común, *m*

baseball /'beɪsbɔl/ *n* pelota base, *f*

baseless /'beɪslɪs/ *a* sin base; sin fundamento; insostenible

basement /'beɪsmənt/ *n* sótano, *m*

baseness /'beɪsnɪs/ *n* bajeza, vileza, ruindad, *f*

bashful /'bæʃfəl/ *a* vergonzoso, ruboroso; tímido, corto; (unsociable) huraño, esquivo

bashfulness /'bæʃfəlnɪs/ *n* vergüenza, *f;* rubor, *m;* encogimiento, *m;* timidez, cortedad, *f;* (unsociableness) huraña, esquivez, *f*

basic /'beɪsɪk/ *a* básico; fundamental

basilica /bə'sɪlɪkə/ *n* basílica, *f*

basilisk /'bæsəlɪsk/ *n* basilisco, *f*

basil (sweet) /'bæzəl, 'beɪ-/ *n Bot.* albahaca, *f*

basin /'beɪsən/ *n* vasija, *f;* (for washing) jofaina, *f;* (barber's) bacía, *f;* (of a fountain) taza, *f; Anat.* bacinete, *m;* (of a harbor) concha, *f;* (of a river) cuenca, *f;* (in the earth) hoya, *f;* (dock) dársena, *f*

basis /'beɪsɪs/ *n* base, *f;* fundamento, *m;* elemento principal, *m*

bask /bæsk/ *vi* calentarse; (in the sun) tomar el sol

basket /'bæskɪt/ *n* cesta, *f;* canasta, *f;*

(frail) espuerta, *f.* **flat b.,** azafate, *m.* **large b.,** banasta, *f.* **b. with a lid,** excusabaraja, *f.* **b. ball,** baloncesto, *m.* **b. maker** or **dealer,** banastero, cestero, *m.* **b. work** or **shop** or **factory,** cestería, *f.* **b. work chair,** sillón de mimbres, *m*

basketful /'bæskɪt,fʊl/ *n* cesta, cestada, *f*

Basle /bɑl/ Basilea, *f*

Basque /bæsk/ *a* and *n* vasco (-ca), vascongado (-da). —*n* (language) vascuence, *m*

bas-relief /,bɑrɪ'lif, ,bæs-/ *n* bajo relieve, *m*

bass /beɪs/ *n Mus.* bajo, *m;* (for tying) esparto, *m, a Mus.* bajo. **double b.,** contrabajo, *m.* **figured b.,** bajo cifrado, *m.* **b. clef,** clave de fa, *f.* **b. string,** bordón, *m.* **b. voice,** voz baja, *f*

bassinet /,bæsə'nɛt/ *n* cochecito de niño, *m*

bastard /'bæstərd/ *n* bastardo (-da), hijo (-ja) natural. —*a* bastardo, ilegítimo; espurio

baste /beɪst/ *vt Sew.* bastear, hilvanar, embastar; *Cul.* enlardar, lardear

basting /'beɪstɪŋ/ *n Sew.* embaste, *m; Cul.* lardeamiento, *m.* **b. spoon,** cacillo, *m.* **b. stitch,** pasillo, *m*

bastion /'bæstʃən/ *n* bastión, baluarte, *m.* **to fortify with bastions,** abastionar

bat /bæt/ *n Zool.* murciélago, *m;* (in cricket) paleta, *f;* (in table tennis) pala, *f.* —*vi* (cricket) golpear con la paleta. See **without**

batch /bætʃ/ *n* (of loaves, etc.) hornada, *f;* lote, *m;* (of recruits) promoción, *f*

bath /bæθ/ *n* baño, *m;* (room) cuarto de baño, *m;* (vat) bañador, *f;* (for swimming) piscina cubierta, *f;* (in the open air) piscina al aire libre, *f; Photo.* baño, *m,* solución, *f.* —*vt* bañar, lavar. **hot mineral baths,** termas, *f pl.* **Order of the B.,** Orden del Baño, *f.* **public baths,** casa de baños, *f.* **reinforcing b.,** *Photo.* reforzador, *m.* **to take a b.,** bañarse, tomar un baño. **b.-chair,** cochecillo de inválido, *m.* **b.-robe,** bata de baño, *f,* albornoz, *m.* **b. room,** cuarto de baño, *f.* **b. towel,** toalla del baño, *f.* **b. tub,** bañera, *f,* baño, *m*

bathe /beɪð/ *vt* bañar, lavar; (of light, etc.) bañar, envolver. —*vi* bañarse. —*n* baño, *m.* **to go for a b.,** ir a bañarse

bather /'beɪðər/ *n* bañista, *mf;* bañador (-ra)

bathing /'beɪðɪŋ/ *a* de baño; balneario, *n* baño, *m.* **b. cap,** gorro de baño, *m.* **b. dress,** traje de baño, *m.* **b. gown,** albornoz, *m,* bata de baño, *f.* **b. machine,** caseta de baños, *f.* **b.-pool,** piscina, *f.* **b.-resort,** estación balnearia, *f.* **b.-shoes,** calzado de baño, *m*

bathos /'beɪθɒs/ *n* paso de lo sublime a lo ridículo, *m;* anticlímax, *m*

baton /bə'tɒn/ *n* bastón de mando, *m; Mus.* batuta, *f;* (policeman's) porra, *f*

batten /'bætŋ/ *vi* engordar (de); medrar,

prosperar. **to b. down,** cerrar las escotillas

batter /'bætər/ *n Cul.* batido, *m;* pasta, *f; Sports.* lanzador, *m.* —*vt* apalear, golpear; (demolish) derribar, demoler; (with artillery) cañonear; batir. **to coat with b.,** rebozar. **to b. down,** derribar

battery /'bætəri/ *n* (*Mil. Nav.*) batería, *f; Elec.* pila, batería, *f; Law.* agresión, *f.* **dry b.,** batería de pilas, *f.* **storage b.,** acumulador, *m.* **b. cell,** pila de batería eléctrica, *f*

battle /'bætl/ *n* batalla, *f;* pelea, *f,* combate, *m;* (struggle) lucha, *f.* —*vi* batallar, pelear; luchar. **b.-array,** orden de batalla, *f.* **b.-axe,** hacha de combate, *f.* **b.-cruiser,** acorazado, *m.* **b.-field,** campo de batalla, *m.* **b.-front,** frente de combate, *m.* **b.-piece,** *Art.* batalla, *f.* **b.-ship,** buque de guerra, *m*

bauble /'bɔbəl/ *n* (trifle) chuchería, fruslería, *f;* (fool's) cetro de bufón, *m*

bawdy /'bɔdi/ *a* obsceno, indecente, escabroso

bawl /bɔl/ *vi* chillar, vocear

bay /bei/ *n Geog.* bahía, *f;* (small) abra, *f; Bot.* laurel, *m;* (horse) bayo, *m;* (howl) aullido, *m; Archit.* abertura, *f; Rail.* andén, *m.* —*a* (of horses) bayo, isabelino. —*vi* aullar. **at bay,** en jaque, acorralado. **sick-bay,** enfermería, *f.* **to keep at bay,** tener a distancia; tener alejado; entretener. **bay rum,** ron de malagueta, *m.* **bay window,** ventana salediza, *f*

bayonet /'beiənɛt/ *n* bayoneta, *f, vt* herir o matar con bayoneta. **fixed b.,** bayoneta calada, *f.* **b. charge,** carga de bayoneta, *f.* **b. thrust,** bayonetazo, *m*

bazaar /bə'zɑr/ *n* bazar, *m*

be /bi/ *vi* ser; (of position, place, state, temporariness) estar; (exist) existir; (in impersonal expressions) haber; (of expressions concerning the weather and time) hacer; (remain) quedar; (leave alone) dejar; (do) hacer; (of one's health) estar; (of feeling cold, hot, afraid, etc. and of years of one's age) tener; (live) vivir; (belong) ser (de), pertenecer (a); (matter, concern) importar (a); (happen) ocurrir, suceder; (find oneself) hallarse, encontrarse, estar; (arrive) llegar (a); (cost) costar; (be worth) valer; (celebrate, hold) celebrarse, tener lugar; (forming continuous tense with present participle active or passive) estar; (with past participle forming passive) ser (this construction is often replaced by reflexive form when no ambiguity is entailed); (with infinitive expressing duty, intention) haber de; (must) tener que. **He is a soldier (doctor, etc.),** Es soldado (médico, etc.). **He is on guard,** Está de guardia. **They were at the door (in the house, etc.),** Estaban a la puerta (en la casa, etc.). **I am writing a letter,** Estoy escribiendo una carta (but this form is often replaced by a simple tense, e.g. escribo...). **It remains to be written,** Queda por escribir. **What is**

to be done? ¿Qué hay que hacer? **Woe is me!** ¡Ay de mí! **to be hot (cold),** (of things) estar caliente (frío); (of weather) hacer calor (frío); (of persons) tener calor (frío). **How is John? He is well,** ¿Cómo está Juan? Está bien de salud. **It is daylight,** Es de día. **It is cloudy,** Está nublado. **She is 10,** Tiene diez años. **They are afraid,** Tienen miedo. **I am to go there tomorrow,** He de ir allí mañana. **What is to be will be,** Lo que tiene que ser será. **If John were to come we could go into the country,** Si viniera Juan podríamos ir al campo. **Be that as it may,** Sea como sea. **It is seven years since we saw him,** Hace siete años que no le vemos. **We have been here for three years,** Hace tres años que estamos aquí, Llevamos tres años aquí. **There is** or **there are,** Hay. **There will be many people,** Habrá mucha gente. **There were many people,** Había mucha gente. **There are many people,** Hay mucha gente. **It is three miles to the next village,** Estamos a tres millas del pueblo próximo. **So be it!** ¡Así sea. **Your pen is not to be seen,** Tu pluma no se ve. **It is to be hoped that...,** Se espera que...; ¡Ojalá que...! **The door is open,** La puerta está abierta. **The door was opened by Mary,** La puerta fue abierta por María. **He was accused of being a fascist,** Lo acusaron de fascista. **to be about to,** estar por; (of a more imminent action) estar para, estar a punto de. **to be in,** estar dentro; estar en casa. **to be off,** marcharse, irse. **Be off!** ¡Márchate! ¡Vete!; ¡Fuera! **to be out,** estar fuera; haber salido; no estar en casa; (of a light, etc.) estar apagado. **to be up,** estar levantado. **to be up to,** proyectar, traer entre manos; urdir, maquinar

beach /bitʃ/ *n* playa, *f;* costa, *f.* —*vt* (a boat) encallar en la costa. **b. shoes,** playeras, *f pl.* **b. suit,** vestido de playa, *m*

beach club *n* club de playa, *m*

beacon /'bikən/ *n* (lighthouse) faro, *m;* (buoy) baliza, *f,* fanal, *m;* (watch-tower) atalaya, *f; Fig.* guía, *f.* —*vt* iluminar. **b. fire,** almenara, *f*

bead /bid/ *n* cuenta, *f;* (of glass) abalorio, *m;* (drop) gota, *f; Archit.* perla, *f;* (bubble) burbuja, *f;* (foam) espuma, *f; pl* **beads,** rosario, *m, vt* adornar con abalorios. **to tell one's beads,** rezar el rosario. **b. work,** abalorio, *m*

beak /bik/ *n* pico, *m;* punta, *f; Naut.* espolón, *m.* **to tap with the b.,** picotear

beaker /'bikər/ *n* copa, *f; Chem.* vaso de precipitado, *m*

beam /bim/ *n Archit.* madero, *m,* viga, *f;* (width of a ship) manga, *f;* (of a balance) palanca, *f;* (of a plough) cama, *f;* (of light) rayo, destello, *m; Phys.* rayo, *m;* (smile) sonrisa brillante, *f; pl* **beams,** (of a building) envigado, *m;* (of a ship) baos, *m pl.* **main b.,** *Archit.* viga maestra, *f.* **b. feather,** astil, *m.* **b. of light,** rayo de luz, haz de luz, *m*

beam /bim/ vt lanzar, emitir; difundir. —vi brillar, fulgurar, destellar; estar radiante, estar rebosando de alegría

beaming /'bimɪŋ/ a brillante; radiante

bean /bin/ n haba, f; judía, alubia, f; (of coffee) grano, m. **broad b.,** haba, f. **French, haricot, kidney b.,** judía, f. **string b.,** judía verde, f. **b. field,** habar, m

bear /beər/ n Zool. oso, m; (she-bear) osa, f; (Stock Exchange) bajista, mf. **Great B.,** Astron. Osa Mayor, f, Septentrión, m. **Little B.,** Astron. Osa Menor, f. **polar b.,** oso blanco, m. **b.-cub,** osezno, m. **bear's den,** osera, f. **b.-garden,** patio de osos, m; Inf. merienda de negros, pl. **b.-hunting,** caza de osos, f. **b.-like,** osuno. **b.-pit,** recinto de los osos, m

bear /beər/ vt and vi (carry) llevar; (show) ostentar; (company, etc.) hacer; (profess) profesar; (of spite, etc. and of relation) guardar; (have) tener; (fruit) dar; (give birth to) parir; (support) sostener; (endure) aguantar; (suffer) padecer, sufrir; (tolerate) tolerar, sufrir; (a strain, an operation, etc.) resistir; (lean on) apoyarse en; (experience) experimentar; (produce) producir, dar; (enjoy) disfrutar de; (use) usar; (impel) empujar; (occupy, hold) ocupar; (go) dirigirse. **It was suddenly borne in on them that...,** De pronto vieron claro que... **I cannot b. any more,** No puedo más. **We cannot b. him,** No le aguantamos, No le sufrimos. **His language won't b. repeating,** Su lenguaje no puede repetirse. **to bring to b.,** ejercer (presión, etc.). **to b. a grudge,** guardar rencor (a), tener ojeriza (a). **to b. arms,** llevar armas; servir en el ejército o la milicia. **to b. company,** hacer compañía (a), acompañar (a). **to b. in mind,** tener en cuenta, tener presente; acordarse de. **to b. oneself,** conducirse, portarse. **to b. to the right,** ir hacia la derecha. **to b. witness,** atestiguar. **to b. false witness,** levantar falso testimonio. **to b. away,** llevarse; ganar. **to b. down,** hundir; derribar; bajar. **to b. down on,** avanzar rápidamente hacia; correr hacia; Naut. arribar sobre; (attack) caer sobre. **to b. in,** llevar adentro. **to b. off,** llevarse; ganar; Naut. apartarse de la costa. **to b. on, upon,** apoyarse en; (refer to) referirse a. **to b. out,** llevar fuera; confirmar; apoyar; justificar. **to b. up,** llevar arriba; llevar a la cumbre (de); (sostener); (recover) cobrar ánimo; (against) resistir; hacer frente a. **to b. with,** soportar; sufrir; aguantar; llevar con paciencia; ser indulgente con

bearable /'beərəbəl/ a soportable; aguantable; tolerable

beard /bɪərd/ n barba, f; (of cereals) raspa, arista, f, vt desafiar. **thick b.,** barba bien poblada, f

beardless /'bɪərdlɪs/ a barbilampiño, desbarbado, imberbe, lampiño

bearer /'beərər/ n llevador (-ra), portador

(-ra); (of a bier) andero, m; Com. dador, portador, m. **good b.,** Agr. árbol fructífero, m. **to b.,** Com. al portador

bearing /'beərɪŋ/ n porte, m; postura, f; presencia, f; conducta, f; aspecto, m; relación, f; (meaning) significación, f; Naut. demora, orientación, f; Mech. cojinete, soporte, m; (endurance) tolerancia, f; pl **bearings,** (way) camino, m; Herald. escudo de armas, m. **to get one's bearings,** orientarse; encontrar el camino. **to lose one's bearings,** desorientarse; perderse. **to have a b. on,** tener relación con; tener que ver con; influir en

beast /bist/ n animal, bruto, m; cuadrúpedo, m; (cattle) res, f; bestia, f. **wild b.,** fiera, f. **b. of burden,** acémila, bestia de carga, f. **b. of prey,** animal de rapiña, m

beastly /'bistli/ a bestial, brutal, obsceno; Inf. horrible

beat /bit/ n latido, m, pulsación, f; golpe, m; (of a drum) toque (de tambor), m; (of a clock) tictac, m; sonido repetido, m; vibración, f

beat /bit/ vt and vi batir; golpear; (thrash) pegar, dar una paliza (a); (to remove dust, etc.) sacudir; (shake) agitar; (the wings) aletear; (hunting) batir; (excel) exceder, superar; ganar; (defeat) vencer; (of the rain, etc.) azotar; (a drum) tocar; (of the sun) batir, dar (en); (throb) latir, palpitar, pulsar. **to b. about the bush,** andarse por las ramas. **to stop beating about the bush,** dejarse de historias. **to b. a retreat,** Mil. emprender la retirada; huir. **to b. black and blue,** moler a palos. **to b. hollow,** vencer completamente; ganar fácilmente; aventajar con mucho. **to b. it,** Inf. escaparse corriendo. **to b. time,** Mus. llevar el compás; triunfar sobre la vejez. **to b. to it,** Inf. tomar la delantera. **to b. against,** golpear contra; chocar contra. **to b. back,** rechazar; (sobs, etc.) ahogar; reprimir. **to b. down,** (prices) regatear; (of the sun) caer de plomo, caer de plano; reducir; suprimir; destruir. **to b. off,** rechazar; echar a un lado. **to b. out,** hacer salir; (metals) batir; (a tune) llevar el compás (de). **to b. up,** Cul. batir; (a mattress) mullir; asaltar; maltratar

beaten /'bitn/ a (of paths) trillado; (conquered) vencido; (of metals) batido; (dejected) deprimido; (trite) trivial, vulgar

beater /'bitər/ n batidor, m; (for carpets) sacudidor (de alfombras), m; Cul. batidor, m

beating /'bitɪŋ/ n batimiento, m; vencimiento, m; (thrashing) paliza, f; (of the heart, etc.) palpitación, f, latido, m; (of metals) batida, f; (of a drum) rataplán, toque de tambor, m; (of waves) embate, m; (of wings) aleteo, aletazo, m

beau /bou/ n galán, m; (fop) petimetre, m

beautiful /'byutəfəl/ a bello, lindo, hermoso; magnífico; excelente; exquisito; elegante; encantador, delicioso

beautify /'byutə,fai/ vt embellecer; hermosear; adornar. **to b.** oneself, arreglarse, ponerse elegante

beauty /'byuti/ n belleza, hermosura, lindeza, f; magnificencia, f; excelencia, f; elegancia, f; encanto, m; (belle) beldad, Venus, f. **to lose one's b.**, desmejorarse, perder su hermosura. **b. contest**, concurso de belleza, m. **b. parlor**, salón de belleza, instituto de belleza, m. **b. sleep**, el primer sueño de la noche. **b. spot**, lunar, m; lunar postizo, m; (place) sitio hermoso, m. **b. treatment**, masaje facial, m

beaver /'bivər/ n castor, m; (hat) sombrero de copa, m; (of helmet) babera, f

because /bɪ'kɔz/ conjunc porque. **b. of**, debido a, a causa de

beckon /'bɛkən/ vt and vi hacer señas (a); llamar por señas, llamar con la mano

become /bɪ'kʌm/ vi volverse; llegar a ser, venir a ser; convertirse en; ponerse; hacerse; (befit) convenir; (suit) ir bien (a), favorecer. **He became red**, Se enrojeció. **The hat becomes you**, El sombrero te va bien. **He became king**, Llegó a ser rey. **What has b. of her?** ¿Qué es de ella?; (Where is she?) ¿Qué se ha hecho de ella? **b. binding**, adquirir carácter de compromiso

becoming /bɪ'kʌmɪŋ/ a propio; correcto; decoroso; (suitable) conveniente; (of dress) que favorece, que va bien. **This dress is b. to you**, Este vestido te favorece

bed /bɛd/ n cama, f, lecho, m; (of sea) fondo, m; (of river) cauce, m; Geol. yacimiento, m; (in a garden) cuadro, macizo (de jardín), m; (of a machine) asiento, m; (of a building) cimiento, m; Fig. fundamento, m, base, f, vt (plants) plantar; (fix) fijar, poner. **double bed**, cama de matrimonio, f. **single bed**, cama de monja, f. **in bed**, en cama. **to be gone to bed**, haber ido a la cama. **to be in bed**, estar acostado. **to get into bed**, meterse en cama. **to get out of bed**, levantarse de la cama. **to go to bed**, acostarse, ir a la cama. **to make the beds**, hacer las camas. **to put to bed**, acostar. **to stay in bed**, quedarse en cama, guardar cama. **bed-bug**, chinche, f. **bed-clothes**, ropa de cama, f. **bedcover**, cubrecama, colcha, f. **bed-head**, cabecera, f. **bed-pan**, silleta, f. **bed-sore**, úlcera de decúbito, f

bedchamber /'bɛd,tʃeimbər/ n dormitorio, m, alcoba, f

bedded /'bɛdɪd/ a con... cama(s). **a double-b. room**, un cuarto con dos camas; un cuarto con cama de matrimonio

bedding /'bɛdɪŋ/ n ropa de cama, f; cama para el ganado, f

bedeck /bɪ'dɛk/ vt embellecer, adornar, engalanar

bedlam /'bɛdləm/ n belén, manicomio, m; Fig. babel, m

bedraggled /bɪ'drægəld/ a mojado y sucio

bedridden /'bɛd,rɪdn/ a postrado en cama, inválido

bedrock /'bɛd,rɒk/ n lecho de roca, m; Fig. principios fundamentales, fundamentos, m pl

bedroom /'bɛd,rum/ n cuarto de dormir, dormitorio, m, habitación, f

bedside /'bɛd,said/ n lado de cama, m; cabecera, f. **b. manner**, mano izquierda, diplomacia, f. **b.-table**, mesa de noche, f

bedspread /'bɛd,sprɛd/ n colcha, cubrecama, sobrecama, f

bedstead /'bɛd,stɛd/ n cama, f

bedtime /'bɛd,taim/ n hora de acostarse, f

bee /bi/ n abeja, f; (meeting) reunión, f, a abejuno. **queen bee**, rey, m, abeja maestra, f. **to have a bee in one's bonnet**, tener una manía (or idea fija). **to make a bee-line for**, ir directamente a. **bee-eater**, Ornith. abejaruco, m. **bee hive**, colmena, f; abejar, m. **bee-keeper**, apicultor (-ra), colmenero (-ra), abejero (-ra). **bee's wax**, cera de abeja, f

beech /bitʃ/ n haya, f. **plantation of b. trees**, hayal, m. **b.-nut**, hayuco, m

beef /bif/ n carne de vaca, f; (flesh) carne, f; (strength) fuerza, f. **roast b.**, rosbif, m. **b.-tea**, caldo, m

beefsteak /'bif,steik/ n biftec, bistec, m

beer /bɪər/ n cerveza, f. **b. barrel**, barril de cerveza, m. **b.-house**, cervecería, f. **b. mug**, jarro para la cerveza, m

beet /bit/ n remolacha, f. **b. sugar**, azúcar de remolacha, m

beetle /'bitl/ n escarabajo, m. **b.-browed**, cejijunto

beetroot /'bit,rut/ n remolacha, f

befall /bɪ'fɔl/ vi acontecer, suceder, ocurrir. —vt ocurrir (a), acontecer (a)

befit /bɪ'fɪt/ vt convenir (a), ser digno de

befitting /bɪ'fɪtɪŋ/ a conveniente, apropiado; digno; oportuno

before /bɪ'fɔr/ adv delante; al frente; (of time) antes, anteriormente; (of space) antes; (already) ya. —prep delante de; en frente de; (of time, order) ante; (in the presence of) ante, en presencia de; (rather than) antes de. **b. going**, antes de marcharse. **B. I did it**, Antes de que lo hiciera; Antes de hacerlo. **as never b.**, como nunca. **b. long**, en breve, dentro de poco. **b.-mentioned**, antes citado. **b. the mast**, al pie del mástil, e.g. *two years b. the mast*, dos años al pie del mástil.

beforehand /bɪ'fɔr,hænd/ adv previamente, de antemano

befoul /bɪ'faul/ vt ensuciar; Fig. manchar, difamar

befriend /bɪ'frɛnd/ vt proteger, ayudar, favorecer, amparar

beg /bɛg/ vt pedir, implorar, suplicar. —vi mendigar, pordiosear; vivir de limosna. **I beg to propose**, Me permito proponer; Tengo el gusto de proponer; (the health of) Brindo a la salud de. **I beg your pardon!** ¡Vd. dispense!; (when passing in front of anyone, etc.) Con permiso; (in conversation for repetition of a word) ¿Cómo? **to beg the question,** dar por sentado lo mismo que se trata de probar. **His conduct begs description,** No hay palabras para su comportamiento

beget /bɪ'gɛt/ vt procrear, engendrar; causar; suscitar

beggar /'bɛgər/ n mendigo (-ga), pordiosero (-ra). **beggars can't be choosers,** a falta de pan, se conforma con tortillas (Mexico); vt empobrecer; arruinar. **to b. description,** no haber palabras para describir

beggarly /'bɛgərli/ a miserable, pobre

begging /'bɛgɪŋ/ a mendicante, pordiosero. —n mendicidad, f, pordioseo, m. **to go b.,** andar mendigando. **b. letter,** carta pidiendo dinero, f

begin /bɪ'gɪn/ vt and vi empezar; comenzar; iniciar; (a conversation) entablar; (open) abrir; inaugurar; tener su principio; nacer. **to b. to,** empezar a; (start on) ponerse a; (with laughing, etc.) romper a. **to b. with,** empezar por; para empezar, en primer lugar

beginner /bɪ'gɪnər/ n principiante (-ta); (novice) novato (-ta), iniciador (-ra); autor (-ra)

beginning /bɪ'gɪnɪŋ/ n principio, comienzo, m; origen, m. **at the b.,** al principio; (of the month) a principios (de). **from the b. to the end,** desde el principio hasta el fin, Inf. de pe a pa. **in the b.,** al principio. **to make a b.,** comenzar, empezar

begone /bɪ'gɔn/ interj ¡fuera! ¡márchate! ¡vete!

begrudge /bɪ'grʌdʒ/ vt envidiar

beguile /bɪ'gail/ vt engañar; defraudar; (time) entretener; (charm) encantar, embelesar

beguilement /bɪ'gailmənt/ n engaño, m; (of time) entretenimiento, m; (charm) encanto, m

behalf /bɪ'hæf/ n (preceded by on or upon) por; (from) de parte (de); a favor (de); en defensa (de)

behave /bɪ'heiv/ vi (oneself) conducirse, portarse; (act) obrar, proceder. **to b. badly,** portarse mal; obrar mal. **B.!** ¡Pórtate bien!

behavior /bɪ'heivyər/ n conducta, f; comportamiento, m; proceder, m; (manner) modales, m pl; Biol. reacción, f

behead /bɪ'hɛd/ vt decapitar, descabezar

behest /bɪ'hɛst/ n precepto, mandato, m

behind /bɪ'haind/ adv detrás; por detrás; atrás; hacia atrás; en pos; (of time and order) después; (late and in arrears) con retraso; (old-fashioned) atrasado. —prep detrás de; por detrás de; inferior a; menos avanzado que. —n Inf. trasero, m. **from b.,** por detrás. **to be b. time,** retrasarse; llegar tarde. **b. the back of,** a espaldas de. **b. the scenes,** entre bastidores. **b. the times,** Fig. atrasado de noticias; pasado de moda. **the ideology b. the French Revolution,** la ideología que informó la Revolución Francesa.

behold /bɪ'hould/ vt ver, mirar, contemplar; presenciar. —interj ¡he aquí! ¡mira!

beholden /bɪ'houldən/ a obligado, agradecido

beholder /bɪ'houldər/ n espectador (-ra). **the beholders,** los que lo presenciaban

beige /beiʒ/ n beige, color arena, m

being /'biɪŋ/ n existencia, f; operación, f; ser, m; (spirit) alma, f, espíritu, m; esencia, f. **human b.,** ser humano, m, alma viviente, f. **for the time b.,** por ahora, por el momento

bejewel /bɪ'dʒuəl/ vt enjoyar, adornar con joyas

belabor /bɪ'leibər/ vt apalear, golpear

belated /bɪ'leitid/ a tardío

belay /bɪ'lei/ vt amarrar

belch /bɛltʃ/ n eructo, m; detonación, f; (of a volcano) erupción, f. —vi eructar. —vt vomitar; (curses, etc.) escupir; despedir, arrojar

belching /'bɛltʃɪŋ/ n eructación, f; (of smoke, etc.) vómito, m, emisión, f

beleaguer /bɪ'ligər/ vt sitiar

Belgium /'bɛldʒəm/ Bélgica, f

belie /bɪ'lai/ vt desmentir, contradecir; defraudar

belief /bɪ'lif/ n creencia, f; fe, f; opinión, f, parecer, m; (trust) confianza, f. **in the b. that,** creyendo que, en la creencia de que

believable /bɪ'livəbəl/ a creíble

believe /bɪ'liv/ vt and vi creer; opinar, ser de la opinión, parecer (a uno); confiar, tener confianza. **I b. not,** Creo que no, Me parece que no. **I b. so,** Creo que sí, Me parece que sí. **to make (a person) b.,** hacer (a uno) creer. **to b. in,** creer en; confiar en, tener confianza en

believer /bɪ'livər/ n persona que cree, f; creyente, mf

belittle /bɪ'lɪtl/ vt achicar; conceder poca importancia a

bell /bɛl/ n campana, f; (hand-bell) campanilla, f; (small, round) cascabel, m; (on cows, etc.) cencerro, m, esquila, f; (electric, push, or bicycle) timbre, m; (jester's) cascabeles, m pl; (cry of stag) bramido, m. —vt poner un cascabel (a). —vi (stags) bramar, roncar. **To bear away the b.,** Fig. llevarse la palma. **to ring the b.,** tocar el timbre; agitar la campanilla. **to ring the bells,** tocar las campanas. **to b. the cat,** ponerle el cascabel al gato, ponerle el collar al gato. **b.-boy,** botones, mozo de hotel, m. **b.-clapper,** badajo, m. **b.-flower,** campanilla, f. **b.-founder,** campanero, m. **b.-mouthed,** abocinado. **b.-pull,** tirador de campanilla, m. **b.-ringer,** campanero, m. **b.-shaped,** campanudo. **b.-tent,** pabellón, m. **b. tower,** campanario, m

belle /bɛl/ n beldad, f

belles-lettres /bɛl ˈlɛtrə/ n pl bellas letras, f pl

bellicose /ˈbɛlɪˌkous/ a belicoso, agresivo

belligerent /bəˈlɪdʒərənt/ a beligerante; belicoso, guerrero. —n beligerante, mf

bellow /ˈbɛlou/ n (shout) grito, m; rugido, bramido, m; (of guns) trueno, m. —vi gritar, vociferar; rugir, bramar; tronar

bellows /ˈbɛlouz/ n fuelle, m

belly /ˈbɛli/ n vientre, m, barriga, f; (of a jug, etc.) panza, f; estómago, m; (womb) seno, m. —vt hinchar. —vi hincharse

belong /bɪˈlɔŋ/ vi pertenecer (a); tocar (a), incumbir (a); (to a place) ser de; residir en

belongings /bɪˈlɔŋɪŋz/ n pl efectos, m pl; posesiones, f pl; (luggage) equipaje, m

beloved /bɪˈlʌvɪd/ a muy amado, muy querido. —n querido (-da)

below /bɪˈlou/ adv abajo; (under) debajo; (further on) más abajo; (in hell) en el infierno; (in this world) en este mundo, aquí abajo. —prep bajo; (underneath) debajo de; (after) después de; (unworthy of) indigno de; inferior a. **The valley lay b. us,** El valle se extendía a nuestros pies. **b. zero,** bajo cero

belt /bɛlt/ n cinturón, m; (of a horse) cincha, f; (corset) faja, f; Geog. zona, f; (of a machine) correa (de transmisión), f

beltway /ˈbɛltˌwei/ n anillo periférico, m

bemoan /bɪˈmoun/ vt deplorar, lamentar

bemuse /bɪˈmyuz/ vt confundir, desconcertar

bench /bɛntʃ/ n banco, m; (with a back) escaño, m; mesa de trabajo, f; (carpenter's, shoemaker's, in a boat, in parliament) banco, m; (judges) tribunal, m

bend /bɛnd/ n corvadura, f; curva, vuelta, f; (in a river, street) recodo, m; (on a road) codo viraje, m; (of the knee) corva, f; (in a pipe) codo, m; Naut. nudo, m; Herald. banda, f. **sheet b.,** (knot) nudo de tejedor, m

bend /bɛnd/ vt encorvar; doblegar; torcer; (the head) bajar; (the body) inclinar; (steps) dirigir, encaminar; (the mind) aplicarse, dedicarse. —vi encorvarse; doblegarse; torcerse; (arch) arquear; inclinarse. **to b. the knee,** arrodillarse. **on bended knee,** de rodillas. **to b. back,** vt redoblar. —vi redoblarse; inclinarse hacia atrás. **to b. down,** agacharse; inclinarse. **to b. forward,** inclinarse hacia delante. **to b. over,** inclinarse encima de

bendable /ˈbɛndəbəl/ a que puede doblarse; plegadizo; flexible

bending /ˈbɛndɪŋ/ n doblamiento, m; flexión, f; inclinación, f. —a doblado; inclinado

beneath /bɪˈniθ/ adv abajo; debajo; (at one's feet) a los pies de uno. —prep bajo; debajo de; al pie de; (unworthy, inferior) indigno. **He married b. him,** Se casó fuera de su clase

benediction /ˌbɛnɪˈdɪkʃən/ n bendición, f; gracia divina, merced, f

benefaction /ˈbɛnəˌfækʃən/ n beneficiación, f; buena obra, f; beneficio, favor, m

benefactor /ˈbɛnəˌfæktər/ n bienhechor, m; protector, m; patrono, m; fundador, m

beneficence /bəˈnɛfəsəns/ n beneficiencia, caridad, f, buenas obras, f pl

beneficial /ˌbɛnəˈfɪʃəl/ a beneficioso; provechoso, útil

beneficiary /ˌbɛnəˈfɪʃiˌeri/ n beneficiado (-da), beneficiario (-ia)

benefit /ˈbɛnəfɪt/ n beneficio, bien, m; provecho, m, utilidad, f; (favor) favor, m; Theat. beneficio, m; (help) ayuda, f, servicio, m. —vt beneficiar; aprovechar; (improve) mejorar. —vi (with by) sacar provecho de; ganar. **for the b. of,** para; en pro de, a favor de. **b. society,** sociedad benéfica, f

benevolence /bəˈnɛvələns/ n benevolencia, bondad, f; liberalidad, f; caridad, f; favor, m

benevolent /bəˈnɛvələnt/ a benévolo; bondadoso; caritativo. **b. society,** sociedad de beneficencia, f

benighted /bɪˈnaitɪd/ a sorprendido por la noche; Fig. ignorante

bent /bɛnt/ n talento, m; inclinación, afición, f, a torcido, encorvado; resuelto

benumb /bɪˈnʌm/ See **numb**

benzine /ˈbɛnzin/ n bencina, f

bequeath /bɪˈkwið/ vt legar, dejar (en el testamento); transmitir

bequest /bɪˈkwɛst/ n legado, m

bereave /bɪˈriv/ vt privar (de), quitar; arrebatar; afligir. **the bereaved parents,** los padres afligidos

bereavement /bɪˈrivmənt/ n privación, f; (by death) pérdida, f; aflicción, f

bereft /bɪˈrɛft/ a privado (de); desamparado; indefenso. **utterly b.,** completamente solo

beret /bəˈrei/ n boina, f

berry /ˈbɛri/ n baya, f; (of coffee, etc.) fruto, m, vi dar bayas; coger bayas

berth /bɜrθ/ n (bed) litera, f; (cabin) camarote, m; (anchorage) anclaje, fondeadero, m; (job) empleo, m, vt (a ship) fondear. **to give a wide b. to,** Naut. ponerse a resguardo de; apartarse mucho de; evitar

beseech /bɪˈsitʃ/ vt suplicar, rogar, implorar; (ask for) pedir con ahinco

beseeching /bɪˈsitʃɪŋ/ a suplicante, implorante. —n súplica, f; ruego, m

beseechingly /bɪˈsitʃɪŋli/ adv suplicantemente

beset /bɪˈsɛt/ vt atacar, acosar; aquejar, acosar, perseguir. **beset by personal misfortune,** acosado por las desgracias personales; (block) obstruir; (surround) rodear, cercar

besiege /bɪˈsidʒ/ vt sitiar; (assail) asaltar, asediar; (surround) rodear; importunar

besieging /bɪˈsidʒɪŋ/ a sitiador. —n sitio, asalto, m; asedio, m, importunación, f

besmear /bɪ'smɪər/ vt embadurnar, ensuciar

besotted /bɪ'sɒtɪd/ a estúpido; embrutecido; atontado

bespatter /bɪ'spætər/ vt manchar; derramar; salpicar

bespeak /bɪ'spik/ vt reservar; (goods) encargar; (signify) demostrar, indicar, significar; *Poet.* hablar

best /bɛst/ a superl of **good** and **well,** mejor; el (la) mejor, *m, f.,* los (las) mejores, *m pl, f pl.* —adv mejor; el mejor; (most) más. **as b. I can,** como mejor pueda. **at the b.,** cuando más, en el mejor caso. **He did it for the b.,** Lo hizo con la mejor intención. **the b.,** lo mejor. **to be at one's b.,** brillar; lucirse. **to do one's b.,** hacer todo lo posible. **to get the b. of,** llevar la mejor parte de; triunfar de (or sobre). **to make the b. of,** sacar el mayor provecho de. **The next b. thing to do is...,** Lo mejor que queda ahora por hacer es... **b. man,** padrino de boda, *m.* **to be b. man to,** apadrinar, ser padrino de. **b. seller,** libro que se vende más, libro favorito, *m*

bestial /'bɛstʃəl/ a bestial

bestiality /ˌbɛstʃɪ'ælɪti/ n bestialidad, *f*

bestir (oneself) /bɪ'stər/ vr menearse, moverse; preocuparse; (hurry) darse prisa

bestow /bɪ'stoʊ/ vt (place) poner; (with upon) conferir, conceder, otorgar; (a present) regalar

bestowal /bɪ'stoʊəl/ n puesta, *f;* otorgamiento, *m,* concesión, *f;* (of a present) regalo, *m,* dádiva, *f*

bestride /bɪ'straɪd/ vt montar a horcajadas en; poner una pierna en cada lado de; cruzar de un tranco

bestseller /'bɛst'sɛlər/ n campeón de venta, *m;* éxito editorial, triunfo de librería, *m*

bet /bɛt/ n apuesta, postura, *f, vi* apostar; (gamble) jugar. **What do you bet?** ¿Qué apuesta Vd.?

betake (oneself) /bɪ'teɪk/ vr acudir (a); darse (a); marcharse

bethink (oneself) /bɪ'θɪŋk/ vr pensar, reflexionar; (remember) recordar, hacer memoria; ocurrirse

Bethlehem /'bɛθlɪˌhɛm/ Belén, *m*

betimes /bɪ'taɪmz/ adv pronto; de buena hora, temprano; con tiempo

betoken /bɪ'toʊkən/ vt presagiar, prometer; indicar

betray /bɪ'treɪ/ vt traicionar; revelar, descubrir; (a woman) seducir; (show) dejar ver

betrayal /bɪ'treɪəl/ n traición, *f;* (of confidence) abuso (de confianza), *m;* (of a woman) seducción, *f*

betrayer /bɪ'treɪər/ n traidor (-ra)

betroth /bɪ'troʊð/ vt desposar(se) con, prometer(se). **to be betrothed to,** estar desposado con

betrothal /bɪ'troʊðəl/ n desposorio, *m,* esponsales, *m pl;* (duration) noviazgo, *m*

betrothed /bɪ'troʊð/ n desposado (-da), futuro (-ra)

better /'bɛtər/ a compar of **good,** mejor; superior. —adv mejor; más. —vt mejorar; exceder. —n apostador (-ra). **He has bettered himself,** Ha mejorado su situación. **It is b. to...,** Es mejor..., Vale más... (followed by infin.). **little b.,** poco mejor; algo mejor; poco más. **much b.,** mucho mejor. **our betters,** nuestros superiores. **so much the b.,** tanto mejor. **the b. to,** para mejor. **to be b.,** ser mejor; (of health) estar mejor. **to get b.,** mejorar. **to get the b. of,** triunfar sobre, vencer. **b. half,** *Inf.* media naranja, *f.* **b. off,** mejor situado, más acomodado

betterment /'bɛtərmənt/ n mejora, *f,* mejoramiento, *m;* adelantamiento, avance, *m*

betting /'bɛtɪŋ/ n apuesta, *f*

bettor /'bɛtər/ n apostador (-ra)

between /bɪ'twin/ prep entre; en medio de; de. **the break b. Mr. X and Mrs. Y,** el rompimiento del Sr. X y la Sra. Y. —adv en medio; entre los dos. **far b.,** a grandes intervalos. **b. now and then,** desde ahora hasta entonces. **b. one thing and another,** entre una cosa y otra. **b. ourselves,** entre nosotros

beverage /'bɛvərɪdʒ/ n brebaje, *m,* bebida, *f*

bevy /'bɛvi/ n grupo, *m;* (of birds) bandada, *f;* (of roes) manada, *f*

bewail /bɪ'weɪl/ vt lamentar, llorar

beware /bɪ'wɛər/ vi guardarse (de); cuidar (de); desconfiar (de). —interj ¡cuidado! ¡atención! **B. of imitations!** ¡Desconfiad de las imitaciones!

bewilder /bɪ'wɪldər/ vt aturdir, abobar; dejar perplejo (a); confundir

bewildered /bɪ'wɪldərd/ a aturdido, abobado; perplejo; confuso

bewildering /bɪ'wɪldərɪŋ/ a incomprensible; complicado

bewilderment /bɪ'wɪldərmənt/ n aturdimiento, *m;* perplejidad, *f;* confusión, *f*

bewitch /bɪ'wɪtʃ/ vt hechizar; fascinar, encantar

bewitching /bɪ'wɪtʃɪŋ/ a encantador, hechicero, fascinante. —n embrujamiento, encantamiento, *m*

beyond /bɪ'ɒnd/ prep más allá de; más lejos que; (behind) tras, detrás de; (of time) después de; *Fig.* fuera del alcance de; (without) fuera de; (above) encima de; (not including) aparte. —adv más allá; más lejos; detrás. **b. doubt,** fuera de duda. **b. question,** indiscutible. **b. the sea,** allende el mar. **That is b. me,** Eso es demasiado para mí; Eso no está en mi mano; Eso está fuera de mi alcance. **the back of b.,** donde Cristo dio las tres voces, las quimbambas. **the B.,** la otra vida

bias /'baɪəs/ n sesgo, bies, través, *m; Fig.* prejuicio, *m;* parcialidad, *f, vt* influir; predisponer. **to cut on the b.,** cortar al sesgo

biassed /'baiəst/ a parcial; tendencioso

bib /bɪb/ n babero, m; pechera, f, vi beber mucho, empinar el codo

Bible /'baibəl/ n Biblia, f

biblical /'bɪblɪkəl/ a bíblico. **b. history,** historia sagrada, f

bibliography /,bɪbli'ɒgrəfi/ n bibliografía, f

bibulous /'bɪbyələs/ a bebedor, borrachín

bicarbonate /bai'kɑrbənɪt/ n bicarbonato, m

bicentenary /,baisɛn'tɛnəri/ n segundo centenario, m

biceps /'baisɛps/ n bíceps, m

bicker /'bɪkər/ vi disputar, altercar; (of stream, etc.) murmurar, susurrar; (of flame) bailar, centellear

bickering /'bɪkərɪŋ/ n altercado, argumento, m

bicycle /'baisɪkəl/ n bicicleta, f, vi andar en bicicleta, ir de bicicleta

bicycling /'baisɪklɪŋ/ n ciclismo; m

bicyclist /'baisɪklɪst/ n biciclista, mf

bid /bɪd/ n (at auction) postura, f; (bridge) puja, f; oferta, f, vt mandar, ordenar, invitar a; (at an auction) pujar, licitar. **to make a bid for,** (attempt) hacer un esfuerzo para; procurar. **to bid fair,** prometer; dar indicios de; dar esperanzas de. **to bid goodbye to,** decir adiós (a), despedirse de. **to bid welcome,** dar la bienvenida (a)

biddable /'bɪdəbəl/ a obediente, dócil; manso

bidder /'bɪdər/ n postor, m, pujador (-ra). **the highest b.,** el mejor postor

bidding /'bɪdɪŋ/ n (order) orden, f; instrucción, f; invitación, f; (at an auction) postura, licitación, f. **to do a person's b.,** hacer lo que se le manda

bide /baid/ vt aguardar, esperar. **to b. by,** (fulfil) cumplir con

bidet /bi'dei/ n bidé, m

biennial /bai'ɛniəl/ a bianual, bienal

bier /bɪər/ n andas, f pl; féretro, ataúd, m

bifocal /bai'foukəl/ a bifocal

bifurcate /'baifər,keit/ vt and vi bifurcar(se)

big /bɪg/ a grande; grueso; (grown up) mayor; (tall) alto; voluminoso; (vast) extenso, vasto; (full) lleno (de); (with young) preñada; importante. **to talk big,** echarla de importante. **big-boned,** huesudo. **big-end,** Auto. biela, f. **big game,** caza mayor, f. **big gun,** Inf. pájaro gordo, m

bigamist /'bɪgəmɪst/ n bígamo (-ma)

bight /bait/ n (in a rope) vuelta (de un cabo), f; (bay) ensenada, f

bigness /'bɪgnɪs/ n grandor, m; gran tamaño, m; altura, f; (tallness of a person) gran talle, m; (vastness) extensión, f; importancia, f

bigot /'bɪgət/ n fanático (-ca)

bigoted /'bɪgətɪd/ a fanático, intolerante

bigotry /'bɪgətri/ n fanatismo, m, intolerancia, f

bikini /bɪ'kini/ n bikini, m

bile /bail/ n bilis, hiel, f; mal humor, m, cólera, f

bilingual /bai'lɪŋgwəl/ a bilingüe

bilious /'bɪlyəs/ a bilioso

bill /bɪl/ n (parliamentary) proyecto de ley, m; Law. escrito, m; Com. cuenta, f; (poster) cartel, m; (program) programa, m; (cast) repertorio, m; (bank note) billete de banco, m; (of a bird) pico, m; (for pruning) podadera, f. **due b.,** Com. abonaré, m. **Post no bills!** Se prohíbe fijar carteles. **b. of exchange,** letra de cambio, f. **b. of fare,** lista de platos, f; Fig. programa, m. **b. of health,** patente de sanidad, f. **b. of rights,** declaración de derechos, f. **b. of sale,** contrato de venta, m, carta de venta, f. **b.-poster,** fijador de carteles, cartelero, m

bill /bɪl/ vt anunciar; publicar; poner en el programa; fijar carteles en. **to bill and coo,** (doves) arrullar; Inf. besuquearse

billboard /'bɪl,bɔrd/ n tablero publicitario, m

billed /bɪld/ a (in compounds) de pico

billet /'bɪlɪt/ n alojamiento, m; (of wood) pedazo (de leña), m; (job) empleo, destino, m, vt alojar (en or con)

billiards /'bɪlyərdz/ n pl billar, m. **billiard ball,** bola de billar, f. **billiard cue,** taco, m. **billiard cushion,** baranda de la mesa de billar, f. **billiard marker,** marcador, m. **billiard match,** partida de billar, f. **billiard player,** jugador (-ra) de billar. **billiard room,** sala de billar, f. **billiard table,** mesa de billar, f

billing /'bɪlɪŋ/ n facturación, f

billion /'bɪlyən/ n billón, m; (U.S.A. and France) mil millones, m pl

bill of particulars n relación detallada, f

billow /'bɪlou/ n oleada, f; Poet. ola, f; Fig. onda, f. —vi hincharse, encresparse; ondular

billowy /'bɪloui/ a ondulante, ondeante

bimonthly /bai'mʌnθli/ a bimestral

bin /bɪn/ n hucha, f; arcón, m; recipiente, m; depósito, m; cajón, m; (for wine) estante, m

binary /'bainəri/ a binario

bind /baind/ vt atar; unir, ligar; amarrar; (in sheaves) agavillar; (bandage) vendar; sujetar; fijar; aprisionar; (a book) encuadernar; Sew. ribetear; (oblige) obligar; comprometer; (constipate) estreñir; contratar (como aprendiz). **I feel bound to,** Me siento obligado a. **to b. over,** obligar a comparecer ante el juez

binder /'baindər/ n encuadernador (-ra); Agr. agavilladora, f

binding /'baindɪŋ/ a válido, valedero; obligatorio; **become b.,** adquirir carácter de compromiso; Med. constrictivo. —n atadura, ligación, f; (of books) encuadernación, f; Sew. ribete, m

binge /bɪndʒ/ n parranda, juerga, f. **to go on the b.,** ir de parranda, ir de picos pardos, ir de juerga

binocular /bə'nɒkyələr/ a binocular. —n pl **binoculars**, binóculos, gemelos, m pl
biodiversity /,baioudɪ'vɜrsɪti/ n biodiversidad, f
biography /bai'ɒgrəfi/ n biografía, vida, f
biologist /bai'ɒlədʒɪst/ n biólogo, m
biology /bai'ɒlədʒi/ n biología, f
biped /'baipɛd/ n bípedo, m, a bípedo, bípede
birch /bɜrtʃ/ n Bot. abedul, m; (rod) vara, f. —a de abedul. —vt pegar con una vara, dar una paliza (a)
bird /bɜrd/ n pájaro, m; ave, f. **Birds of a feather flock together,** Cada cual se arrima a su cada cual. **hen b.,** pájara, f. **b.-call,** voz del pájaro, f, canto del ave, m. **b. catcher or vendor,** pajarero, m. **bird's-eye view,** vista de pájaro, perspectiva aérea, f. **b.-fancier,** aficionado (-da) a las aves; criador (-ra) de pájaros. **b.-like,** como un pájaro; de pájaro. **b.-lime,** liga, f. **to go b.-nesting,** ir a coger nidos de pájaros. **b. of paradise,** ave del paraíso, f. **b. of passage,** ave de paso, f. **b. of prey,** ave rapaz, f. **b.-seed,** alpiste, m
birth /bɜrθ/ n nacimiento, m; (act of) parto, m; origen, m; (childhood) infancia, f; (family) linaje, m, familia, f; Fig. creación, f. **from b.,** de nacimiento. **to give b. to,** dar a luz, echar al mundo, parir. **b. certificate,** partida de nacimiento, certificación de nacimiento, f. **b. control,** anticoncepcionismo, m, regulación de la fecundidad, f. **b.-mark,** antojos, m pl. **b.-place,** lugar de nacimiento, m. **b.-rate,** natalidad, f
birthday /'bɜrθ,dei/ n cumpleaños, m
birthright /'bɜrθ,rait/ n derecho de nacimiento, m; herencia, f
Biscay, the Bay of /bɪs'kei/ el Golfo de Vizcaya, m
biscuit /'bɪskɪt/ n galleta, f; bizcocho, m. **b. box or maker,** galletero, m. **b.-like,** abizcochado
bisect /bai'sɛkt/ vt dividir en dos partes iguales; Geom. bisecar
bishop /'bɪʃəp/ n obispo, m; (in chess) alfil, m. **bishop's crozier,** báculo episcopal, cayado, m
bison /'baisən/ n bisonte, m
bit /bɪt/ n pedazo, m; (of grass, etc.) brizna, f; (moment) instante, m; (quantity) cantidad, f; (of a drill) mecha, f; (part) parte, f; (passage) trozo, m; (horse's) bocado, m; Inf. miga, f. **a bit,** un tanto, algo, un poco. **in bits,** en pedazos. **Not a bit!** ¡Nada!; ¡Ni pizca!; ¡Claro que no! **bit by bit,** poco a poco, gradualmente. **to take the bit between one's teeth,** desbocarse; Fig. rebelarse. **Wait a bit!** ¡Espera un momento!
bitch /bɪtʃ/ n (female dog) perra, f; (fox) zorra, f; (wolf) loba, f
bite /bait/ n mordedura, f; mordisco, m; (mouthful, snack) bocado, m; (of fish and insects) picada, f; (hold) asimiento, m;

(sting, pain) picadura, f; (pungency) resquemor, m; (offer) oferta, f; (Fig. mordancy) mordacidad, acritud, f. —vt and vi morder; (gnaw) roer; (of fish, insects) picar; (of hot dishes) resquemar; (of acids) corroer; (deceive) engañar, defraudar; (of wheels, etc.) agarrar; (hurt, wound) herir. **to b. one's tongue,** morderse la lengua. **to b. the dust,** caer al suelo
biting /'baitɪŋ/ a (stinging) picante; (mordant) mordaz, acre; (of winds, etc.) penetrante; satírico. —n mordedura, f; roedura, f
bitter /'bɪtər/ a amargo; (sour) agrio, ácido; (of winds) penetrante; (of cold) intenso; cruel. **to the b. end,** hasta la muerte; hasta el último extremo. **b.-sweet,** agridulce
bitterness /'bɪtərnɪs/ n amargura, f; (sourness) acidez, f; (of cold) intensidad, f; crueldad, f
bitters /'bɪtərz/ n pl (drink) bíter, m, angostura, f
bitumen /bai'tumən/ n betún, m
bizarre /bɪ'zɑr/ a raro, extravagante; grotesco
black /blæk/ a negro; obscuro; (sad) triste, melancólico; funesto; (wicked) malo, perverso; (sullen) malhumorado. —n (color) negro, m; (mourning) luto, m; (negro) negro, m; (negress) negra, f; (stain) mancha, f; (dirt) tizne, m. —vt ennegrecer; tiznar. **in b. and white,** por escrito. **to look on the b. side,** verlo todo negro. **b. art,** nigromancia, f. **b.-currant,** grosella negra, f. **b.-eyed,** ojinegro, con ojos negros. **b.-haired,** pelinegro, de pelo negro. **b.-lead,** plombagina, f. **b.-list,** lista negra, f. **b.-market,** estraperlo, mercado negro, m. **b.-marketeer,** estraperlista, mf. **b.-out,** obscurecimiento, apagamiento, m. **b.-pudding,** morcilla, f. **b. sheep,** oveja negra, f; Fig. oveja descarriada, f; (of a family) garbanzo negro, m. **b.-water fever,** melanuria, f
blackberry /'blæk,bɛri/ n mora, zarzamora, f; (bush) zarza, f, moral, m
blackbird /'blæk,bɜrd/ n mirlo, m
blackboard /'blæk,bɔrd/ n encerado, m, pizarra, f
blacken /'blækən/ vt ennegrecer; tiznar; Fig. manchar, desacreditar. —vi ennegrecerse
black eye n ojo como un tomate, ojo morado, m
blackguard /'blægɑrd/ n tipo de cuidado, perdido, m
blackhead /'blæk,hɛd/ n espinilla, f
blackmail /'blæk,meil/ n chantaje, m, vt hacer víctima de un chantaje; arrancar dinero por chantaje (a)
blackmailer /'blæk,meilər/ n chantajista, mf
blackness /'blæknɪs/ n negrura, f; obscuridad, f; (wickedness) maldad, perversidad, f

blacksmith /'blæk,smıθ/ *n* herrero, *m*.
blacksmith's forge, herrería, *f*

bladder /'blædər/ *n Anat.* vejiga, *f;* ampolla, *f;* (of sea-plants) vesícula, *f;* (of fish) vejiga natatoria, *f*

blade /bleid/ *n* (leaf) hoja, *f;* (of grass, etc.) brizna, *f;* (of sharp instruments) hoja, *f;* (of oar) pala, *f;* (of propeller) paleta, ala, *f*

bladed /'bleidıd/ *a* de... hojas. **a two-b. knife,** un cuchillo de dos hojas

blame /bleim/ *n* culpa, *f;* responsabilidad, *f;* censura, *f.* —*vt* culpar, echar la culpa (a); tachar, censurar, criticar; acusar. **You are to b. for this,** Vd. tiene la culpa de esto

blameless /'bleimlıs/ *a* inculpable; inocente; intachable; elegante

blamelessness /'bleimlısnıs/ *n* inculpabilidad, inocencia, *f;* elegancia, *f*

blameworthy /'bleim,wзrðı/ *a* culpable, digno de censura, vituperable

blanch /blæntʃ/ *vt Cul.* mondar; hacer palidecer. —*vi* palidecer, perder el color

bland /blænd/ *a* afable, cortés; dulce, agradable

blandish /'blændıʃ/ *vt* adular, halagar, acariciar

blank /blæŋk/ *a* en blanco; (empty) vacío; desocupado; pálido; (confused) confuso, desconcertado; (expressionless) sin expresión; (of verse) suelto; sin adorno. —*n* blanco, hueco, *m;* papel en blanco, *m;* laguna, *f.* **b. cartridge,** cartucho para salvas, cartucho de fogueo, *m.* **b. verse,** verso suelto, *m*

blanket /'blæŋkıt/ *n* manta, frazada, *f;* (of a horse) sudadero *m; Fig.* capa, *f.* —*vt* cubrir con una manta. **to toss in a b.,** mantear. **wet b.,** aguafiestas, *mf.* **b. maker or seller,** mantero, *m.* **b. vote,** voto colectivo, *m*

blankly /'blæŋkli/ *adv* con indiferencia; sin comprender; (flatly) categóricamente

blankness /'blæŋknıs/ *n* confusión, *f,* desconcierto, *m;* (emptiness) vaciedad, *f;* indiferencia, *f;* incomprensión, *f*

blare /blɛər/ *n* sonido de la trompeta o del clarín, *Poet.* clangor, *m;* (of a car horn) ruido, *m.* —*vi* sonar

blarney /'blɑrni/ *n* labia, *f.* —*vt* lisonjear

blaspheme /blæs'fim/ *vi* blasfemar. —*vt* renegar de, maldecir

blasphemous /'blæsfəməs/ *a* blasfemo, blasfematorio

blasphemy /'blæsfəmi/ *n* blasfemia, *f*

blast /blæst/ *n* (of wind) ráfaga (de viento), *f;* (of a trumpet, etc.) trompetazo, son, *m;* (of a whistle) pitido, *m;* (draft) soplo, *m;* explosión, *f; Fig.* influencia maligna, *f.* —*vt* (rock) barrenar, hacer saltar; (wither) marchitar, secar; *Fig.* destruir; (curse) maldecir. **in full b.,** en plena marcha. **b.-furnace,** alto horno, horno de cuba, *m.* **b. hole,** barreno, *m*

blasting /'blæstıŋ/ *n* (of rock) voladura, *f;* (withering) marchitamiento, *m; Fig.* destrucción, ruina, *f;* (cursing) maldic-

iones, *f pl.* **a.** destructor; *Fig.* funesto. **b. charge,** carga explosiva, *f*

blatant /'bleitnt/ *a* ruidoso; agresivo; llamativo; (boastful) fanfarrón

blaze /bleiz/ *n* llama, *f;* fuego, *m;* conflagración, *f;* luz brillante, *f;* (of anger, etc.) acceso, *m.* —*vi* llamear, encenderse en llamas; brillar, resplandecer. **a b. of color,** una masa de color. **Go to blazes!** ¡Vete al infierno!

blazon /'bleizən/ *n Herald.* blasón, *m; Fig.* proclamación, *f, vt* blasonar; adornar; proclamar

bleach /blitʃ/ *n* lejía, *f.* —*vt* blanquear; descolorar. —*vi* ponerse blanco; descolorarse

bleaching /'blitʃıŋ/ *n* blanqueo, *m.* **b. powder,** hipoclorito de cal, *m*

bleak /blik/ *a* yermo, desierto; frío; expuesto; (sad) triste; severo

bleakness /'bliknıs/ *n* situación expuesta, *f;* desnudez, *f;* frío, *m;* (sadness) tristeza, *f;* severidad, *f*

bleary-eyed /'blıəri ,aid/ *a* legañoso, cegajoso

bleat /blit/ *n* balido, *m, vt* and *vi* balar, dar balidos

bleed /blid/ *vi* sangrar, echar sangre; sufrir. —*vt* sangrar; arrancar dinero a

bleeding /'blidıŋ/ *n* hemorragia, *f;* sangría, *f*

blemish /'blɛmıʃ/ *n* imperfección, *f,* defecto, *m;* (on fruit) maca, *f;* (stain) mancha, *f;* deshonra, *f*

blend /blɛnd/ *n* mezcla, mixtura, *f;* combinación, *f;* fusión, *f.* —*vt* mezclar; combinar. —*vi* mezclarse; combinarse

bless /blɛs/ *vt* bendecir; consagrar; (praise) alabar, glorificar; hacer feliz (a). **B. me!** ¡Válgame Dios!

blessed /'blɛsıd/ *a* bendito; *Eccl.* beato, bienaventurado; (dear) querido; feliz; *Inf.* maldito

blessing /'blɛsıŋ/ *n* bendición, *f;* (grace) bendición de la mesa, *f;* (mercy) merced, gracia, *f;* favor, *m;* (good) bien, *m.* **He gave them his b.,** Les echó su bendición **Bless you!** (to someone who has sneezed) ¡Jesús!

blight /blait/ *n Agr.* tizne, tizón, *m;* (of cereals) añublo, *m;* (mould) roña, *f;* (greenfly) pulgón, *m; Fig.* influencia maligna, *f;* (frustration) desengaño, *m;* (spoil-sport) aguafiestas, *mf vt* atizonar; anublar; (wither) marchitar, secar; *Fig.* frustrar, destruir; malograr

blind /blaind/ *a* ciego; (secret) secreto; (of a door, etc.) falso; (closed) cerrado, sin salida; (unaware) ignorante; sin apreciación (de). **to be b.,** ser ciego; *Fig.* tener una venda en los ojos. **to be b. in one eye,** ser tuerto. **to turn a b. eye,** hacer la vista gorda. **b. alley,** callejón sin salida, *m.* **b. as a bat,** más ciego que un topo. **b. flying,** *Aer.* vuelo a ciegas, *m.* **b. man,** ciego, hombre ciego, *m.* **b. obedience,** obediencia ciega, *f.* **b. side,** (of persons) lado débil, *m*. **b. woman**, ciega, mujer ciega, *f*

blind /blaind/ *vt* cegar; poner una venda en los ojos (de); (dazzle) deslumbrar; hacer cerrar los ojos a; hacer ignorar

blind /blaind/ *n* persiana, *f*; (Venetian) celosía, *f*; (deception) pretexto, *m*; velo, *m*

blindfold /'blaind,fould/ *vt* vendar los ojos (a); *Fig.* poner una venda en los ojos (de). —*a* and *adv* con los ojos vendados; a ciegas; con los ojos cerrados

blindman's buff /'blaind,mænz 'bʌf/ *n* gallina ciega, *f*

blindness /'blaindnis/ *n* ceguedad, *f*; ofuscación, *f*; ignorancia, *f*

blink /blɪŋk/ *n* parpadeo, *m*, guiñada, *f*; (of light) destello, *m*; reflejo, *m*; *vi* parpadear, pestañear; (of lights) destellar

bliss /blɪs/ *n* felicidad, *f*; deleite, placer, *m*; *Eccl.* gloria, *f*

blissful /'blɪsfəl/ *a* feliz

blister /'blɪstər/ *n* *Med.* vesícula, *f*; ampolla, *f*; (bubble) burbuja, *f* —*vt* ampollar; *Fig.* herir

blithe /blaið/ *a* alegre

blizzard /'blɪzərd/ *n* ventisca, nevasca, *f*

bloated /'bloutid/ *a* abotagado, hinchado; orgulloso; indecente

blob /blɒb/ *n* masa, *f*; mancha, *f*; gota, *f*

block /blɒk/ *n* bloque, *m*; (log) leño, *m*; *Naut.* polea, *f*; (for beheading and of a butcher) tajo, *m*; (for mounting) apeadero, *m*; (of shares, etc.) lote, *m*; (of houses) manzana, *f*; (jam) atasco, *m*; (obstruction) obstrucción, *f*; (for hats) forma, *f*. **A chip off the old b.**, De tal palo tal astilla. **b. and tackle**, *Naut.* polea con aparejo. **b.-hook**, grapa, *f*. **b.-house**, *Mil.* blocao, *m*

block /blɒk/ *vt* bloquear; cerrar (el paso); (stop up) atarugar, atascar; (a wheel) calzar; (a bill, etc.) obstruir; (hats) poner en forma. **to b. the way**, cerrar el paso.

blockade /blɒ'keid/ *n* bloqueo, *m*, *vt* bloquear. **to run the b.**, violar el bloqueo

blockhead /'blɒk,hɛd/ *n* leño, zoquete, imbécil, *m*

blond(e) /blɒnd/ *a* (of hair) rubio; (of complexion) de tez blanca. —*n* hombre rubio, *m*; (woman) rubia, mujer rubia, *f*. **peroxide b.**, rubia oxigenada, *f*. **b. lace**, blondina, *f*

blood /blʌd/ *n* sangre, *f*; (relationship) parentesco, *m*; (family) linaje, *m*, prosapia, *f*; (life) vida, *f*; (sap) savia, *f*; jugo, *m*; (horse) caballo de pura raza, *m*; (dandy) galán, *m*. —*vt* sangrar. **bad b.**, mala sangre, *f*; odio, *m*; mala leche, *f* **blue b.**, sangre azul, *f*. **in cold b.**, a sangre fría, *f*. **My b. is up**, Se me enciende la sangre. **My b. runs cold**, Se me hiela la sangre. **to be in the b.**, llevar en la sangre. **b.-bank**, banco de sangre, *m*. **b.-bath**, matanza, *f*. **b.-colored**, de color de sangre, sanguíneo. **b.-feud**, venganza de sangre, *f*. **b.-guilt**, culpabilidad de homicidio, *m*. **b.-heat**, calor de sangre, *m*. **b.-**

letting, sangría, *f*. **b. orange**, naranja dulce, *f*. **b.-plasma**, plasma sanguíneo, *m*. **b.-poisoning**, septicemia, *f*; infección, *f*. **b.-pressure**, presión sanguínea, *f*. **b. purity**, limpieza de sangre, *f*. **b.-red**, rojo como la sangre. **b.-relation**, pariente (-ta) consanguíneo(a). **b.-relationship**, consanguinidad, *f*. **b.-stain**, mancha de sangre, *f*. **b.-stained**, ensangrentado, manchado de sangre. **b.-stone**, sanguinaria, *f*. **b.-sucker**, sanguijuela, *f*; *Fig.* vampiro, *m*; (usurer) avaro (-ra). **b.-vessel**, vaso sanguíneo, *m*

bloodhound /'blʌd,haund/ *n* sabueso, *m*

bloodiness /'blʌdinis/ *n* estado sangriento, *m*; crueldad, ferocidad, *f*

bloodless /'blʌdlis/ *a* exangüe; pálido; incruento; anémico; indiferente

bloodshed /'blʌd,ʃɛd/ *n* efusión de sangre, *f*; matanza, carnicería, *f*

bloodshot /'blʌd,ʃɒt/ *a* (of the eye) inyectado

bloodthirsty /'blʌd,θɜrsti/ *a* sanguinario, carnicero

bloody /'blʌdi/ *a* sangriento; (of battles) encarnizado; (cruel) sanguinario, cruel

bloom /blum/ *n* flor, *f*; florecimiento, *m*; (on fruit) flor, *f*; (prime) lozanía, *f*; (on the cheeks) color sano, *m*. —*vi* florecer. **in b.**, en flor

blooming /'blumɪŋ/ *a* florido; en flor; fresco; lozano; brillante

blossom /'blɒsəm/ *n* flor, *f* —*vi* florecer. **to b. out into**, hacerse, llegar a ser; (wear) lucir; (buy) comprarse

blot /blɒt/ *n* borrón, *m*; mancha, *f*. —*vt* manchar; (erase) tachar; (dry) secar. **to b. out**, borrar; destruir; secar con papel secante

blotch /blɒtʃ/ *n* (on the skin, or stain) mancha, *f*

blotter /'blɒtər/ *n* *Com.* libro borrador, *m*; teleta, *f*

blouse /blaus/ *n* blusa, *f*

blow /blou/ *n* golpe, *m*; bofetada, *f*; (with the fist) puñetazo, *m*; (with the elbow) codazo, *m*; (with a club) porrazo, *m*; (with a whip) latigazo, *m*; (blossoming) floración, *f*; (disaster) desastre, *m*, tragedia, *f*. **to come to blows**, venirse a las manos. **at a b.**, con un solo golpe; de una vez. **We are going for a b.**, Vamos a tomar el fresco. **b. below the belt**, golpe bajo, *m*. **b. in the air**, golpe en vago, *m*. **b. of fate**, latigazo de la fortuna, *m*

blow /blou/ *vi* (of wind) soplar (el viento), hacer viento, correr aire; (pant) jadear, echar resoplidos; (of fuses) fundirse. —*vt* (wind instruments) tocar; soplar; (inflate) inflar; (swell) hinchar. **to b. a kiss**, tirar un beso. **to b. one's nose**, sonarse las narices. **to b. away**, disipar; ahuyentar; llevar (el viento). **to b. down**, echar por tierra, derribar (el viento). **to b. in**, llevar adentro, hacer entrar (el viento); (windows, etc.) quebrar (el viento). **to b. off**, quitar (el viento). **to**

b. open, abrir (el viento). **to b. out,** hacer salir (el viento); llevar afuera (el viento); (a light) matar de un soplo, apagar soplando. **to b. over,** pasar por (el viento); soplar por; disiparse; olvidarse. **to b. up,** (inflate) inflar; (the fire) avivar (el fuego); (explode) volar; (swell) hinchar

blowing /'blouɪŋ/ n soplo, m; violencia, f; (blossoming) florecimiento, m. **b. up,** voleo, m; explosión, f

blow-up /'blou ,ʌp/ n (photograph) fotografía ampliada, f

blubber /'blʌbər/ vi gimotear; berrear. —n (of the whale) grasa de ballena, f. **b.-lip,** bezo, m. **b.-lipped,** bezudo

bludgeon /'blʌdʒən/ n cachiporra, porpa, f; garrote, m; estaca, f. —vt golpear con una porra, dar garrotazos (a)

blue /blu/ a azul; (with bruises) amoratado; (sad) deprimido, melancólico; (obscene) verde; (dark) sombrío; (traditionalist) conservador. —n azul, m; (sky) cielo, m; (for clothes) añil de lavandera, m; pl **blues,** melancolía, depresión, f; (homesickness) morriña, f. —vt (laundry) añilar. **to look b.,** parecer deprimido; (of prospects, etc.) ser poco halagüeño. **b. black,** azul negro, m; (of hair) azabache, m. **b.-bottle,** Ent. moscón, m. **b.-eyed,** con ojos azules. **b. gum,** eucalipto, m. **B. Peter,** bandera de salida, f. **b. print,** fotocopia, f; plan, m

bluestocking /'blu,stɒkɪŋ/ n marisabidilla, doctora, f

bluff /blʌf/ a (of cliffs, etc.) escarpado; (of persons) franco, campechano, brusco

bluish /'bluɪʃ/ a azulado

blunder /'blʌndər/ n desacierto, desatino, m; equivocación, f; (in a translation, etc.) falta, f. —vi tropezar (con); desacertar; equivocarse; Inf. meter la pata. —vt manejar mal; estropear

blundering /'blʌndərɪŋ/ a desacertado; equivocado; imprudente n. See **blunder**

blunt /blʌnt/ a romo, embotado; obtuso; (abrupt) brusco; franco; descortés; (plain) claro. —vt enromar, embotar; (the point) despuntar; Fig. hacer indiferente; (pain) mitigar

bluntly /'blʌntli/ adv sin filo; sin punta; bruscamente, francamente; claramente

bluntness /'blʌntnɪs/ n embotamiento, m; Fig. brusquedad, franqueza, f; claridad, f

blur /blɜr/ n borrón, m; mancha, f; imagen indistinta, f. —vt borrar; manchar; Photo. velar

blurred /blɜrd/ a borroso; indistinto, turbio

blurt (out) /blɜrt/ vt proferir bruscamente; revelar sin querer

blush /blʌʃ/ n rubor, m; rojo, m. —vi enrojecerse, ruborizarse, ponerse colorado; avergonzarse (por)

blushing /'blʌʃɪŋ/ a ruboroso; púdico

bluster /'blʌstər/ vi (of the wind) soplar con furia; (of waves) encresparse, embravecerse; (of persons) bravear, fanfarronear. —n furia, violencia, f; tumulto, m; fanfarronería, f

blustering /'blʌstərɪŋ/ a (of wind) violento, fuerte; (of waves) tumultuoso; (of people) fanfarrón, valentón

board /bɔrd/ n tabla, f; (for notices) tablón, m; (b. residence) pensión, f; (table) mesa, f; (food) comida, f; (for chess, checkers) tablero, m; (sign) letrero, m; (of instruments) cuadro, m; (bookbinding) cartón, m; Naut. bordo, m; (committee) junta, dirección, f; tribunal, m; pl **boards** Theat. tablas, f pl. **above b.,** abiertamente, sin disimulo. **free on b.,** (f. o.b.) franco a bordo. **in boards,** (of books) encartonado. **managerial b.,** junta directiva, f. **on b.,** a bordo. **on the boards,** Theat. en las tablas. **to go on b.,** ir a bordo. **b. and lodging,** pensión completa, casa y comida, f. **b. of directors,** consejo de administración, m. **b. of examiners,** tribunal de exámenes, m. **b. of trade,** junta de comercio, f; ministerio de comercio, m

board /bɔrd/ vt entablar, enmaderar; embarcar en; (Nav. a ship) abordar; (lodge) alojar, tomar a pensión

boarder /'bɔrdər/ n huésped (-da); (at school) pensionista, mf alumno (-na) interno (-na)

boarding /'bɔrdɪŋ/ n entablado, m; (planking) tablazón, f; (of a ship) abordaje, m; (of a train) subida (al tren), f. **b.-house,** casa de huéspedes, pensión, f. **b.-school,** pensionado, m

boarding gate n puerta de embarque, f

boast /boust/ n jactancia, f; ostentación, f; (honor) gloria, f. —vi jactarse, vanagloriarse; alabarse; ostentar. **to b. about,** jactarse de; hacer gala de; gloriarse en

boaster /'boustər/ n vanaglorioso (-sa), jactancioso (-sa)

boastful /'boustfəl/ a vanaglorioso, jactancioso; ostentador

boastfulness /'boustfəlnɪs/ n vanagloria, jactancia, f; fanfarronería, f; ostentación, f

boat /bout/ n barco, m; bote, m; (in a fun fair) columpio, m, lancha, f; (for sauce or gravy) salsera, f. —vi ir en barco; (row) remar; navegar. **to b. down,** bajar en barco. **to b. up,** subir en barco. **b. building,** construcción de barcos, f. **b. club,** club náutico, m. **b. crew,** tripulación de un barco, f. **b.-hook,** bichero, garabato, m. **b.-house,** cobertizo de las lanchas, m. **b.-load,** barcada, f. **b.-race,** regata, f. **b.-scoop,** achicador, m. **b.-shaped,** en forma de barco. **b.-train,** tren que enlaza con un vapor, m

boating /'boutɪŋ/ n pasear en bote, m; manejo de un bote, m; (rowing) remo, m. **b.-pole,** botador, m

boatswain /'bousən/ n contramaestre, m. **boatswain's mate,** segundo contramaestre, m

bob /bɒb/ n (curtsey) reverencia, f;

(woman's hair) pelo a la romana, m; (of bells) toque (de campana), m. —vi saltar; moverse. —vt cortar corto. **long bob**, (hair) melena, f. **to bob up**, ponerse de pie; surgir. **to bob up and down**, subir y bajar; bailar. **bob-tail**, rabo corto, m. **bob-tailed**, rabón

Bob /bɒb/ (pet form of *Robert*) Beto (Mexico)

bobbin /'bɒbɪn/ n carrete, huso, m; (of wool, etc.) ovillo, m; (of looms, sewing machines) bobina, f; (in lace-making) bolillo, palillo, m

bode /boud/ vt presagiar, prometer. **to b. ill**, prometer mal. **to b. well**, prometer bien

bodily /'bɒdɪli/ a del cuerpo; físico; corpóreo; real; material; (of fear) de su persona. —adv corporalmente; en persona, personalmente; en conjunto, enteramente; en una pieza

boding /'boudɪŋ/ a ominoso, amenazador. —n presagio, m; agüero, m

body /'bɒdi/ n Anat. cuerpo, m; (trunk) tronco, m; (corpse) cadáver, m; (of a vehicle) caja, f; (of a motor-car) carrocería, f; (of a ship) casco, m; (of a church) nave, f; (centre) centro, m; (of a book, persons, consistency and Astron.) cuerpo, m; (person) persona, f; corporación, f; grupo, m; (of an army) grueso (de ejercito), m; organismo, m. **in a b.**, en masa, juntos (juntas); en corporación. **to have enough to keep b. and soul together**, tener de que vivir. **b.-snatcher**, junta cadáveres mf ladrón de cadáveres, m. **b.-snatching**, robo de cadáveres, m

bodyguard /'bɒdi,gɑrd/ n guardia de corps, f; guardia, f; (escort) escolta, f

body language n el lenguaje del cuerpo, m

bog /bɒg/ n pantano, marjal, m, marisma, f

bogey /'bougi; 'bugi/ n duende, m; (to frighten children) coco, m; (nightmare) pesadilla, f

bogus /'bougəs/ a postizo, falso

boil /bɔil/ vi bullir, hervir; (cook) cocer. —vt hervir; cocer. —n ebullición, f; Med. divieso, m. **to b. away**, consumirse hirviendo; Chem. evaporar a seco. **to b. over**, rebosar

boiler /'bɔilər/ n Cul. marmita, olla, f; (of a furnace) caldera, f. **double-b.**, baño de María, m. **steam-b.**, caldera de vapor, f. **b.-maker**, calderero, m. **b. room**, cámara de la caldera, f. **b.-suit**, mono, m

boiling /'bɔilɪŋ/ n ebullición, f, hervor, m; (cooking) cocción, f, a hirviente. **b. point**, punto de ebullición, m

boisterous /'bɔistərəs/ a (of persons) exuberante, impetuoso; (stormy) tempestuoso, borrascoso; violento

boisterously /'bɔistərəsli/ adv impetuosamente, ruidosamente; tempestuosamente; con violencia

boisterousness /'bɔistərəsnɪs/ n exube-

rancia, impetuosidad, f; violencia, f; tempestuosidad, borrascosidad, f

bold /bould/ a intrépido, audaz; (determined) resuelto; (forward) atrevido; (showy) llamativo; (clear) claro. **b.-faced**, descarado, desvergonzado. **b.-faced type**, letra negra, f

boldly /'bouldli/ adv intrépidamente; descaradamente; resueltamente; claramente

boldness /'bouldnɪs/ n intrepidez, valentía, f; resolución, f; (forwardness) osadía, f, descaro, atrevimiento, m; claridad, f

Bolivian /bou'lɪviən/ a and n boliviano (-na)

bolster /'boulstər/ n travesaño, m. —vt apuntalar; Fig. apoyar

bolt /boult/ n pasador, cerrojo, m; (pin) perno, m; (knocker) aldaba, f; (roll) rollo, m; (flight) huida, f; (of a crossbow) flecha, f; (from the blue) rayo, m. —adv (upright) recto como una flecha; enhiesto; rígido. **b. and nut**, perno y tuerca, m

bolt /boult/ vt echar el cerrojo (a); (empernar; (Fam. eat) zampar. —vi huir; (horses) desbocarse, dispararse; (plants) cerner. **to b. down**, cerrar con cerrojo. **to b. in**, entrar corriendo, entrar de repente. **to b. off**, marcharse corriendo. **to b. out**, vi salir de golpe. —vt cerrar fuera

bomb /bɒm/ n bomba, f, vt bombardear. **to be a b.-shell**, Fig. caer como una bomba. **b.-carrier**, portabombas, m. **b. crater**, bombazo, m. **b.-release**, (Aer. Nav.) lanzabombas, m. **b.-sight**, mira de avión de bombardeo, f

bombard /bɒm'bard/ vt bombardear, bombear; Fig. llover (preguntas, etc.) sobre

bombardment /bɒm'bardmənt/ n bombardeo, m

bombast /'bɒmbæst/ n ampulosidad, pomposidad, f

bombastic /bɒm'bæstɪk/ a bombástico, altisonante, pomposo

bomber /'bɒmər/ n avión de bombardeo, bombardero, m. **dive b.**, bombardero en picado, m. **heavy b.**, bombardero pesado, m. **light b.**, bombardero ligero, m. **b. command**, servicio de bombardeo, m

bonafide /'bounə,faid/ a fidedigno

bond /bɒnd/ n lazo, vínculo, m; Chem. enlace, m; (financial) obligación, f; (security) fianza, f; (Customs) depósito, m; pl **bonds**, cadenas, f pl, a esclavo. **in b.**, en depósito. **bonds of interest**, intereses creados, m pl. **b.-holder**, obligacionista, mf

bondage /'bɒndɪdʒ/ n esclavitud, f; servidumbre, f; cautiverio, m; prisión, f

bone /boun/ n hueso, m; (of fish) espina (de pez), f; (whale b.) ballena, f; pl **bones**, cuerpo, m, vt deshuesar; poner ballenas (a or en). **to be all skin and bones**, estar en los huesos. **to have a b. to pick with**, tener que arreglar las cuentas con. **b.-ash**, cendra, f

boner /'bounǝr/ n gazapo, m, patochada, plancha, f

bonfire /'bɒn,faiǝr/ n fogata, hoguera, f

bonnet /'bɒnit/ n capota, f; (of babies) gorra, f; (of men) boina, f; (of chimney and of machines) sombrerete, m

bonus /'bounǝs/ n paga extraordinaria, bonificación, f; sobresueldo, m; (of food, etc.) ración extraordinaria, f

bon vivant /bō vi'vā/ n alegre, vividor, m

bony /'bouni/ a huesudo; (of fish-bones) lleno de espinas; óseo

booby /'bubi/ n pazguato, bobo, m. **b.-prize**, último premio, m. **b.-trap**, trampa, f; Mil. mina, f

book /buk/ n libro, m; volumen, tomo, m; (of an opera) libreto, m. —vt anotar en un libro; apuntar; (seats) tomar (localidades); (tickets) sacar (billetes); (of the issuing clerk) dar; (reserve) reservar; inscribir; consignar (a suspect); (engage) contratar; (invite) comprometer. **to turn the pages of a b.**, hojear un libro. **b.-ends**, sostén para libros, sujetalibros, m. **b.-keeper**, tenedor de libros, m. **b.-keeping**, teneduría de libros, f. **b.-maker**, apostador de profesión, m. **b. of reference**, libro de consulta, m. **b.-plate**, exlibris, m. **b.-post**, tarifa de impresos, f. **b.-shop**, librería, f. **b.-trade**, venta de libros, f; comercio de libros, m

bookbinder /'buk,baindǝr/ n encuadernador (-ra) de libros

bookbinding /'buk,baindiŋ/ n encuadernación de libros, f

bookcase /'buk,keis/ n armario de libros, m

booking /'bukiŋ/ n (of rooms, etc.) reservación, f; (of tickets) toma, f; Com. asiento, m; (engagement) contratación, f. **b.-clerk**, vendedor (-ra) de billetes. **b.-office**, despacho de billetes, m; taquilla, f

bookish /'bukiʃ/ a aficionado a los libros; docto, erudito

bookmark /'buk,mɑrk/ n marcador, m

bookseller /'buk,selǝr/ n librero, m

bookshelf /'buk,ʃelf/ n estante para libros, m

bookworm /'buk,wɜrm/ n polilla que roe los libros, f; Fig. ratón de biblioteca, m

boom /bum/ n Naut. botavara, f; (of a crane) aguilón, m; (noise) ruido, m; (of the sea) bramido, m; (thunder) trueno, m; (in a port) cadena de puerto, f; Com. actividad, f; (Fig. peak) auge, m, vi sonar; bramar; tronar; Com. subir; ser famoso. **b. sail**, vela de cangreja, f

boomerang /'bumǝ,ræŋ/ n bumerang, m

boon /bun/ n favor, m, merced, f; bien, m, ventaja, f; don, m; privilegio, m, a (of friends) íntimo

boor /bur/ n monigote, patán, palurdo, m

boorish /'buriʃ/ a rudo, zafio, rústico, cerril

boost /bust/ vt Elec. aumentar la fuerza de; Inf. empujar; subir; (advertise) dar bombo (a)

boot /but/ n bota, f; (of a car) compartimiento para equipaje, m. **button-boots**, botas de botones, f pl. **riding-boots**, botas de montar, f pl. **to b.**, además, de añadidura. **b.-maker**, zapatero, m. **b.-tag**, tirador de bota, m. **b.-tree**, horma de bota, f

bootblack /'but,blæk/ n limpiabotas, m

booth /buθ/ n puesto, m, barraca, f

bootlegger /'but,legǝr/ n contrabandista de alcohol, m

booty /'buti/ n botín, m; tesoro, m

booze /buz/ vi emborracharse. —n alcohol, m; borrachera, f

boozer /'buzǝr/ n borracho (-cha)

boracic /bǝ'ræsik/ a bórico. —n ácido bórico, m

borax /'boræks/ n bórax, m

bordello /bɔr'dɛlou/ n burdel, m

border /'bɔrdǝr/ n borde, m; (of a lake, etc.) orilla, f; (edge) margen, m; (of a diploma, etc.) orla, f; Sew. ribete, m, orla, f; (fringe) franja, f; (garden) arriate, m; (territory) frontera, f; límite, confín, m. —vt Sew. orlar, ribetear; ornar (de); (of land) lindar con. **to b. on**, (of land) tocar, lindar con; (approach) rayar en. **b. country**, región fronteriza, f

borderland /'bɔrdǝr,lænd/ n zona fronteriza, f; lindes, m pl

borderline /'bɔrdǝr,lain/ n frontera, f; límite, m; margen, m, a fronterizo; lindero; (uncertain) dudoso, incierto

bore /bɔr/ n taladro, barreno, m; perforación, f; (hole) agujero, m; (of guns) calibre, m; (wave) oleada, f; (nuisance) fastidio, m; (dullness) aburrimiento, tedio, m; (person) pelmazo, m, machaca, mf vt taladrar, barrenar, horadar; perforar; hacer un agujero (en); (exhaust) aburrir; fastidiar. **It's a b.**, Es una lata. **to be bored**, aburrirse, fastidiarse

boredom /'bɔrdǝm/ n aburrimiento, m; tedio, hastío, m

boring /'bɔriŋ/ a aburrido, pesado, tedioso; molesto, fastidioso. —n taladro, m; horadación, f; sondeo, m; perforación, f

born /bɔrn/ a nacido; (by birth) de nacimiento; (b. to be) destinado a; natural (de). **He was b. in 1870**, Nació en 1870. **to be b.**, nacer, venir al mundo. **to be b. again**, renacer, volver a nacer. **well-b.**, bien nacido. **b. with a silver spoon in one's mouth**, Nacido de pie, Nacido un domingo

borough /'bɜrou/ n burgo, m; villa, f; ciudad, f. **b. surveyor**, arquitecto municipal, m

borrow /'bɒrou/ vt pedir prestado; apropiarse, adoptar; copiar; (arithmetic) restar; (a book from a library) tomar prestado. **May I b. your pencil?** ¿Quieres prestarme tu lápiz?

borrower /'bɒrouǝr/ n el (la) que pide o toma prestado

borrowing /'bɒrouiŋ/ n el pedir prestado, acto de pedir prestado, m

bosh /bɒʃ/ *n* patrañas, tonterías, *f pl;* palabrería, *f*

Bosnian /'bɒznɪən/ *a* bosnio

bosom /'buzəm/ *n* pecho, *m;* (heart) corazón, *m;* (of the earth, etc.) seno, *m.* **b. friend,** amigo (-ga) del alma, amigo (-ga) íntimo (-ma)

boss /bɒs/ *n* (of a shield) corcova saliente, *f;* tachón, *m; Archit.* pinjante, *m. Inf.* amo, *m;* jefe, *m.* —*vt* mandar; dominar. **political b.,** cacique, *m*

bossism /'bɒsɪzəm/ *n* caudillaje, *m*

bossy /'bɒsɪ/ *a* mandón, autoritario

botanical /bə'tænɪkəl/ *a* botánico. **b. garden,** jardín botánico, *m*

botany /'bɒtn̩i/ *n* botánica, *f*

botch /bɒtʃ/ *n* (clumsy work) chapucería, *f;* remiendo, *m.* —*vt* chapucear, chafallar; (patch) remendar

both /bouθ/ *a* and *pron* ambos, *m pl;* ambas, *f pl;* los dos, *m pl;* las dos, *f pl, adv* tan(to)... como; (and) y; a la vez, al mismo tiempo. **It appealed both to the young and the old,** Gustó tanto a los jóvenes como a los viejos. **b. of you,** ustedes dos, vosotros dos. **b. pretty and useful,** bonito y útil a la vez

bother /'bɒðər/ *n* molestia, *f,* fastidio, *m;* (worry) preocupación, *f;* dificultad, *f;* (fuss) alboroto, *m.* —*vt* molestar, fastidiar; preocupar. —*vi* preocuparse

bottle /'bɒtl/ *n* botella, *f;* (smaller) frasco, *m;* (babies) biberón, *m;* (for water) cantimplora, *f,* vt embotellar, envasar, enfrascar. **to b. up,** (liquids, capital, armies, navies) embotellar; (feelings) refrenar. **to bring up on the b.,** criar con biberón. **b.-green,** verde botella, *m.* **b.-neck,** (in an industry) embotellado, *m;* (in traffic) atascadero, *m.* **b.-washer,** fregaplatos, *mf;* (machine) máquina para limpiar botellas, *f*

bottle cap *n* corchalata, *f*

bottled /'bɒtl̩d/ *a* en botella; (of fruit, vegetables) conservado

bottling /'bɒtlɪŋ/ *n* embotellado, *m;* envase, *m.* **b. outfit,** embotelladora, *f;* (for fruit, etc.) aparato para conservar frutas o legumbres, *m*

bottom /'bɒtəm/ *n* base, *f;* (deepest part) fondo, *m;* (last place) último lugar, *m;* fundamento, *m;* (of a chair) asiento, *m;* (of a page, table, mountain, etc.) pie, *m;* (posterior) culo, *m;* (of a river) lecho, *m;* (of the sea) fondo, *m;* (of a ship) casco, *m;* (of a skirt) orilla, *f;* (truth) realidad, verdad, *f;* (basis) origen, *m,* causa, *f.* **at b.,** en realidad. **at the b.,** en el fondo. **false b.,** fondo doble, fondo secreto, *m.* **to be at the b. of,** ocupar el último lugar en; ser el causante de. **to get to the b. of,** descubrir la verdad de; profundizar en, analizar. **to sink to the b.,** (of ships) irse a pique

bottomless /'bɒtəmlɪs/ *a* sin fondo; (of chairs, etc.) sin asiento; (unfathomable) insondable

bough /bau/ *n* rama, *f,* brazo (de un árbol) *m*

boulder /'bouldər/ *n* roca, peña, *f;* canto rodado, *m;* bloque de roca, *m*

boulevard /'buləˌvard/ *n* bulevar, *m*

bounce /bauns/ *n* bote, rebote, *m;* salto, *m;* (boasting) fanfarronería, *f, vi* rebotar; saltar, brincar. —*vt* hacer botar o saltar

bound /baund/ *n* límite, *m;* (jump) salto, brinco, *m, vt* limitar, confinar. —*vi* saltar, brincar; (bounce) botar. **within bounds,** dentro del límite. **b. for,** con destino a; (of ships) con rumbo a

boundary /'baundəri/ *n* límite, lindero, *m;* término, *m;* frontera, *f;* raya, *f.* **b. stone,** mojón, *m*

boundless /'baundlɪs/ *a* sin límites, infinito; inmenso

bounty /'baunti/ *n* generosidad, munificencia, *f;* don, *m;* (subsidy) subvención, *f*

bouquet /bou'kei, bu-/ *n* ramo, ramillete (de flores), *m;* perfume, *m;* (of wine) nariz, *f*

bourgeois /bʊr'ʒwa/ *a* and *n* burgués (-esa)

bourgeoisie /ˌbʊrʒwa'zi/ *n* burguesía, mesocracia, *f*

bout /baut/ *n* turno, *m;* (in fencing, boxing, wrestling) asalto, *m;* (of illness, coughing) ataque, *m;* (fight) lucha, *f,* combate, *m;* (of drinking) borrachera, *f*

bow /bou/ *n* (weapon) arco, *m;* (of a saddle) arzón (de silla), *m; Mus.* arco, *m;* (knot) lazo, *m;* (greeting) saludo, *m;* reverencia, inclinación, *f;* (of a boat) proa, *f.* **to tie a bow,** hacer un lazo. **bow and arrows,** arco y flechas, *m.* **bow-legged,** patizambo. **bow window,** ventana saliente, *f*

bow /bau/ *vi* inclinarse; hacer una reverencia, saludar; (remove the hat) descubrirse; *Fig.* inclinarse (ante); (submit) someterse (a), reconocer; agobiarse; *Mus.* manejar el arco. —*vt* (usher in) introducir en, conducir a; doblar; inclinar. **to bow down (to),** humillarse ante; obedecer; (worship) reverenciar, adorar. **to bow out,** despedir con una inclinación del cuerpo

bowel /'bauəl/ *n* intestino, *m; pl* **bowels,** *Fig.* seno, *m,* entrañas, *f pl*

bower /'bauər/ *n* (arbor) enramada, *f;* glorieta, *f;* (boudoir) tocador de señora, *m*

bowing /'bauɪŋ/ *n Mus.* arqueada, *f;* saludo, *m, a* (of acquaintance) superficial

bowl /boul/ *n* receptáculo, *m;* (of a fountain) taza, *f;* (of a pipe) cazoleta, *f;* (barber's) bacía, *f;* (for washing) jofaina, *f;* (for punch) ponchera, *f;* (goblet) copa, *f;* (for soup) escudilla, *f;* (for fruit) frutero, *m;* (of a spoon) paleta, *f;* (ball) boliche, *m.* —*vt* tirar; (in cricket) sacar; (a hoop) jugar con; (in ninepins) tumbar con una bola. **to b. along,** recorrer; ir en coche o carruaje (por). **to b. over,** *Fig.* dejar consternado (a), desconcertar

bowler /'boulər/ *n* (in cricket) servidor,

m; (hat) sombrero hongo, *m;* (skittle player) jugador de bolos, *m*

bowling /'boulıŋ/ *n* (in cricket) saque, *m;* (skittles) juego de bolos, *m;* juego de boliche, *m.* **b. alley,** bolera, pista de bolos, *f,* salón de boliche, *m.* **b.-green,** bolera en cesped, *f*

bow tie /bou/ *n* pajarita, *f*

box /bɒks/ *n* caja, *f;* (case) estuche, *m;* (luggage) baúl, *m,* maleta, *f;* (for a hat) sombrerera, *f; Bot.* boj, *m; Theat.* palco, *m;* (for a sentry, signalman, etc.) garita, *f,* casilla, *f;* (on a carriage) pescante, *m;* (blow) cachete, *m,* bofetada, *f;* (for a horse) vagón, *m.* **post office box,** apartado de correos, *m.* **box-kite,** cometa celular, *f.* **box-maker,** cajero, *m.* **box office,** taquilla, *f.* **box-pleat,** *Sew.* tabla, *f*

box /bɒks/ *vt* encajonar, meter en una caja. —*vi* boxear. **to box the ears of,** calentar las orejas de. **to box up,** encerrar

boxer /'bɒksər/ *n Sports.* boxeador, pugilista, *m*

boxing /'bɒksıŋ/ *n* encajonamiento, *m;* envase, *m; Sports.* boxeo, pugilato, *m.* **B. Day,** Día de San Esteban, *m,* (A Spanish child receives its Christmas presents on the Día de Reyes (Twelfth Night).) **b.-gloves,** guantes de boxeo, *m pl.* **b.-ring,** cuadrilátero de boxeo, *m*

box-office success /'bɒks ,ɔfıs/ *n* éxito de taquilla, *m*

boy /bɔi/ *n* muchacho, niño, rapaz, *m;* (older) chico, joven, *m.* **new boy,** nuevo alumno, *m.* **old boy** (of a school) antiguo alumno, *m;* (Fam. address) chico. **small boy,** chiquillo, pequeño, crío, *m.* **b. doll,** muñeco, *m.* **boy scout,** muchacho explorador, *m*

boycott /'bɔikɒt/ *vt* boicotear. —*n* boicot, *m*

boyhood /'bɔihʊd/ *n* muchachez, mocedad, *f;* (childhood) niñez, *f*

boyish /'bɔiıʃ/ *a* muchachil; pueril; de niñez

brace /breis/ *n* (prop) puntal, barrote, *m;* abrazadera, *f;* berbiquí, *m;* viento, tirante, *m;* freno (for the teeth), *m,* (pair) par, *m; pl* **braces,** tirantes, *m pl.* —*vt* apuntalar; asegurar; ensamblar; *Naut.* bracear; (trousers) tirar; *Fig.* fortalecer, refrescar

bracelet /'breislıt/ *n* pulsera, *f,* brazalete, *m,* ajorca, *f*

bracing /'breisıŋ/ *a* (of air, etc.) fortificante, tónico; estimulador

bracket /'brækıt/ *n* consola, *f; Archit.* repisa, *f;* soporte, *m;* (on furniture, etc.) cantonera, *f; Print.* paréntesis angular, *m;* (for a light) brazo (de alumbrado), *m.* —*vt Print.* poner entre paréntesis; juntar. **in brackets,** entre paréntesis. **They were bracketed equal,** Fueron juzgados iguales

brackish /'brækıʃ/ *a* salobre

brag /bræg/ *vi* jactarse, fanfarronear. —*n* jactancia, *f.* **to b. about,** hacer alarde de

braggart /'brægərt/ *a* baladrón, jactancioso. —*n* jactancioso, fanfarrón, *m*

braid /breid/ *n* trencilla, *f,* cordoncillo, *m;* (for trimming) galón, *m;* (plait) trenza, *f.* —*vt* (hair) trenzar; (trim) galonear; acordonar, trencillar

brain /brein/ *n* cerebro, *m;* entendimiento, *m,* inteligencia, *f;* talento, *m;* (common sense) sentido común, *m; pl* **brains,** sesos, *m pl,* (animal and human); cacumen, *m.* —*vt* romper la crisma (a). **to blow one's brains out,** levantarse la tapa de los sesos. **to rack one's brains,** devanarse los sesos. **Brains Trust,** masa cefálica, *f;* consorcio de inteligencias, *m.* **b.-box,** cráneo, *m.* **b.-fever,** fiebre cerebral, *f.* **b.-storm,** crisis nerviosa, *f.* **b.-wave,** idea luminosa, *f.* **b.-work,** trabajo intelectual, *m*

brainchild /'brein,tʃaild/ *n* engendro, *m*

brain drain *n* fuga de cerebros, *f*

brainless /'breinlıs/ *a* sin seso; tonto

brainy /'breini/ *a* sesudo, inteligente, talentudo

braise /breiz/ *vt Cul.* asar

brake /breik/ *n* (of vehicles and *Fig.*) freno, *m;* (flax and hemp) caballete, *m;* (carriage) break, *m;* (thicket) matorral, *m.* —*vt* (vehicles) frenar; (hemp, etc.) rastrillar. **foot-b.,** freno de pedal, *m.* **hand-b.,** freno de mano, *m.* **to b. hard,** frenar de repente. **to release the b.,** quitar el freno

bran /bræn/ *n* salvado, *m*

branch /bræntʃ, brɑntʃ/ *n* (of a tree, a family) rama, *f;* (of flowers, of learning) ramo, *m;* (of a river) tributario, afluente, *m;* (of roads, railways) ramal, *m;* (of a firm) sucursal, dependencia, *f.* —*a* sucursal, dependiente; (of roads, railways) secundario. —*vi* echar ramas; bifurcarse, dividirse; ramificarse. **to b. off,** bifurcarse, ramificarse. **to b. out,** extenderse; emprender cosas nuevas

branching /'bræntʃıŋ/ *n* ramificación, *f;* división, *f.* **b. off,** bifurcación, *f*

brand /brænd/ *n* tizón, *m;* (torch) tea, *f;* (on cattle, etc.) hierro, *m;* (trademark) marca de fábrica, *f;* marca, *f;* (stigma) estigma, *m.* —*vt* marcar con el hierro, herrar; marcar; estigmatizar, tildar. **b.-new,** flamante

branding /'brændıŋ/ *n* (of livestock) herradero, *m;* (of slaves, criminals) estigmatización, *f;* difamación, *f.* **b.-iron,** hierro de marcar, *m*

brandish /'brændıʃ/ *vt* blandir

brandy /'brændi/ *n* coñac, *m*

brass /bræs/ *n* latón, *m; Mus.* metal, *m;* (tablet) placa conmemorativa, *f; Inf.* dinero, *m.* **the b.,** *Mus.* el metal. **b. band,** banda de instrumentos de viento, *f.* **b.-neck,** *Inf.* cara dura, *f.* **b. works** or **shop,** latonería, *f*

brassiere /brə'zıər/ *n* sostén, *m*

brat /bræt/ *n* crío, *m*

bravado /brə'vɑdou/ *n* bravata, *f*

brave /breiv/ *a* valiente, animoso, intrépido; espléndido, magnífico; bizarro.

—*n* valiente, *m.* —*vt* desafiar, provocar; arrostrar

bravery /'breivəri/ *n* valentía, *f,* valor, *m,* intrepidez, *f,* coraje, *m;* esplendidez, suntuosidad, *f;* bizarría, *f*

bravo /'brɑvou/ *n* bandido, *m;* asesino pagado, *m, interj* ¡bravo! ¡ole!

brawl /brɔl/ *n* camorra, reyerta, pelotera, *f.* —*vi* alborotar; (of streams) murmurar. **to start a b.,** armar camorra

brawler /'brɔlər/ *n* camorrista, *mf*

brawn /brɔn/ *n* Cul. embutido, *m;* músculo, *m;* (strength) fuerza, *f*

brawny /'brɔni/ *a* membrudo, musculoso, forzudo

brazen /'breizən/ *a* de latón; (of voice) bronca; desvergonzado, descarado

brazier /'breizər/ *n* (fire) brasero, *m;* latonero, *m*

Brazil /brə'zɪl/ el Brasil, *m*

Brazilian /brə'zɪlyən/ *a* and *n* brasileño (-ña)

breach /britʃ/ *n* violación, contravención, *f;* (gap) abertura, *f; Mil.* brecha, *f.* —*vt Mil.* hacer brecha (en); (in a line of defence) hacer mella (en). **b. of confidence,** abuso de confianza, *m.* **b. of promise,** incumplimiento de la palabra de casamiento, *m.* **b. of the peace,** alteración del orden público, *f,* quebrantamiento de la paz, *m*

bread /brɛd/ *n* pan, *m.* **to earn one's b. and butter,** ganarse el pan. **brown b.,** pan moreno, *m.* **unleavened b.,** pan ázimo, *m.* **b. and butter,** pan con mantequilla, *m; Fig.* sustento diario, *m.* **b.-basket,** cesta de pan, *f; Inf.* estómago, *m.* **b.-bin,** caja del pan, *f.* **b.-crumb,** miga, *f;* migaja, *f.* **b.-knife,** cuchillo para cortar el pan, *m.* **b. poultice,** cataplasma de miga de pan, *f.* **b.-winner,** ganador (-ra) de pan, trabajador (-ra)

breadth /brɛdθ/ *n* anchura, *f;* latitud, *f;* liberalidad, *f; Sew.* ancho de una tela, *m*

break /breik/ *n* rotura, *f;* (opening) abertura, *f; Geol.* rajadura, *f;* (fissure) grieta, *f;* solución de continuidad, *f;* interrupción, *f;* (billiards) serie, *f;* (change) cambio, *m;* (in a boy's voice) muda (de la voz), *f;* (blank) vacío, *m;* (in the market) baja, *f;* intervalo, *m;* descanso, *m;* pausa, *f;* (truce) tregua, *f;* (clearing) clara, *f; Mus.* quiebra (de la voz), *f;* (carriage) break, *m; (Fam.* folly) disparate, *m.* **with a b. in one's voice,** con voz entrecortada. **b. of day,** aurora, alba, *f.* **at the b. of day,** al despuntar el alba

break /breik/ *vt* romper; quebrar; quebrantar, fracturar; (breach) abrir brecha en; (in two) partir, dividir; (into pieces) hacer pedazos, despedazar; (into small pieces) desmenuzar; (into crumbs) desmigajar; (destroy) destrozar; (a blow) parar; (a law) infringir, violar; (the bank in gambling) quebrar; (a journey, etc.) interrumpir; (of a habit) desacostumbrar, hacer perder el vicio de; (a promise) no cumplir, faltar a; (a record) superar;

(plow ground) roturar; (spoil) estropear; arruinar; *Com.* ir a la quiebra; (an official) degradar; (an animal) domar, amansar; (Fig. crush) subyugar; (betray) traicionar; (Fig. of silence, a spell, a lance, peace, the ranks) romper; (cushion) amortiguar; (lessen) mitigar; (disclose) revelar; *Elec.* interrumpir. **to b. one's promise,** faltar a su palabra. **to b. the ice,** Fig. romper el hielo. **to b. asunder,** romper en dos (partes); dividir. **to b. down,** derribar; echar abajo; destruir; (suppress) suprimir; subyugar; abolir; disolver. **to b. in,** (animals) domar, amaestrar; (persons) disciplinar; (new shoes) ahormar, romper. **to b. in two,** partir; dividir en dos; (split) hender. **to b. off,** separar, quitar; (a branch) desgajar; *Fig.* romper; interrumpir; cesar. **to b. open,** forzar, abrir a la fuerza. **to b. up,** hacer pedazos; (scatter) poner en fuga, dispersar; hacer levantar la sesión; (the ground) roturar; (parliament) disolver; (a ship) desguazar, deshacer (un buque)

break /breik/ *vi* romperse; quebrarse; quebrantarse; (of beads) desgranarse; (burst) reventar, estallar; (of abscesses) abrirse; (of a boy's voice) mudar; (Fig. and of clouds, etc.) romperse; desaparecer; (of the dawn) despuntar (el alba), amanecer; (sprout) brotar; (of a ball) torcerse; (of fine weather) terminar; (change) cambiar; (of a storm) estallar. **to b. loose,** desasirse; *Fig.* desencadenarse. **to b. away,** escaparse, fugarse; (from a habit) romper con, independizarse de (another country); disiparse. **to b. down,** (of machinery, cars) averiarse; (fail) frustrarse, malograrse; (weep) deshacerse en lágrimas; (lose one's grip) perder la confianza en sí; (in health) sufrir una crisis de salud. **The car broke down,** El auto tuvo una avería. **to b. in,** (of burglars) forzar la entrada; irrumpir (en), penetrar (en); exclamar. **to b. in on,** sorprender; entrar de sopetón; invadir; interrumpir; caer sobre; molestar. **to b. into,** (force) forzar; (utter) romper a, prorrumpir en; empezar (a); pasar de repente a; (of time, etc.) ocupar; hacer perder. **to b. off,** (of speech) interrumpirse; cesar; (detach) desprenderse, separarse; (of branches) desgajarse. **to b. out,** huir, escaparse; *Fig.* estallar; aparecer; declararse; (of fire) tomar fuego; derramarse; (of an eruption) salir. **to b. over,** derramarse por; bañar. **to b. through,** abrirse paso (por); abrirse salida (por); atravesar; *Fig.* penetrar; (of the sun, etc.) romper (por). **to b. up,** (depart) separarse; (of meetings) levantarse la sesión; dispersarse; (smash) hacerse pedazos; disolverse; (of a school) cerrarse, empezar las vacaciones; (melt) fundir; desbandarse; (of a camp) levantar (el campo); (grow old) hacerse viejo; (be ill) estar agotado. **to b. with,** romper con; cesar; reñir con

breakable /'breikəbəl/ *a* quebradizo, frágil

breakage /'breikɪdʒ/ *n* rompimiento, quebrantamiento, *m;* cosa rota, *f;* fractura, *f*

breakdown /'breik,daun/ *n* accidente, *m;* (of a machine) avería, *f; Auto.* pane, *f;* (failure) fracaso, *m*, falta de éxito, *f;* deterioración, *f;* (in health) crisis de salud, *f.* **b. gang,** pelotón de reparaciones, *m*

breaker /'breikər/ *n* oleada, *f*

breakfast /'brɛkfəst/ *n* desayuno, *m.* —*vi* desayunar(se), tomar el desayuno. **to have a good b.,** desayunar bien. **b.-cup,** tazón, *m.* **b.-time,** hora del desayuno, *f*

breaking /'breikɪŋ/ *n* rompimiento, *m;* quebrantamiento, *m;* fractura, *f;* ruptura, *f;* (in two) división, *f;* (into pieces) despedazamiento, *m;* (into small pieces) desmenuzamiento, *m;* (destruction) destrozo, *m;* (of a blow) parada, *f;* (of a law, etc.) violación, *f;* (of one's word) no cumplimiento, *m;* (of a journey, of sleep, etc.) interrupción, *f;* (escape) escape, *m*, huida, *f;* (of an animal) domadura, *f;* (of a boy's voice) muda (de la voz), *f;* (of news) revelación, *f.* **b. down,** demolición, *f;* (of negotiations) suspensión, *f.* **b. in,** irrupción, *f;* (of an animal) domadura, *f;* (training) entrenamiento, *m.* **b. open,** forzamiento, *m;* quebranto, *f.* **b. out,** huida, *f*, escape, *m; Fig.* estallido, *m;* aparición, *f;* declaración, *f;* (scattering) derramamiento, *m;* (of a rash) erupción, *f.* **b. up,** dispersión, *f;* disolución, *f;* fin, *m;* ruina, *f;* (of a school) cierre, *m;* (change in weather) cambio, *m;* (of a meeting) levantamiento (de una sesión), *m;* (of the earth) roturación, *f*

breakneck /'breik,nɛk/ *a* rápido, veloz, precipitado

bream /brɪm/ *n Ichth.* sargo, *m.* **sea-b.,** besugo, *m*

breast /brɛst/ *n* pecho, *m;* (of birds) pechuga, *f;* (of female animals) teta, mama, *f;* (heart) corazón, *m*, *vt* (the waves) cortar (las olas); luchar con; *Fig.* arrostrar, hacer frente a. **b.-bone,** esternón, *m.* **b. high,** alto hasta el pecho. **b.-pin,** alfiler de pecho, *m.* **b.-pocket,** bolsillo de pecho, *m.* **b.-stroke,** estilo pecho, *m*

breast cancer *n* el cáncer del seno, *m*

breath /brɛθ/ *n* aliento, *m;* suspiro, *m;* (phonetics) aspiración, *f;* (breeze) soplo (de aire), *m;* (of scandal, etc.) murmurio, *m;* (fragrance) perfume, *m*, fragancia, *f;* (life) vida, *f.* **in a b.,** de un aliento. **in the same b.,** sin respirar. **out of b.,** sin aliento. **under one's b.,** por lo bajo, entre dientes. **to draw b.,** tomar aliento. **to get one's b. back,** cobrar aliento. **to hold one's b.,** contener el aliento. **to take one's b. away,** *Fig.* dejar consternado (a)

breathe /brið/ *vi* respirar; vivir; (of air, etc.) soplar; (take the air) tomar el fresco; (rest) tomar aliento. —*vt* respirar; exha-

lar; dar aire (a); (whisper) murmurar; (convey) expresar, revelar; (infuse) infundir. **to b. forth fury,** echar rayos. **to b. hard,** jadear. **to b. one's last,** exhalar el último suspiro. **to b. in,** inspirar

breathing /'briðɪŋ/ *n* respiración, *f;* (of the air, etc.) soplo, *m;* (phonetics) aspiración, *f.* —*a* que respira; viviente. **hard** or **heavy b.,** jadeo, resuello, resoplido, *m.* **b.-space,** *Fig.* respiro, *m*

breathless /'brɛθlɪs/ *a* jadeante, sin aliento; (dead) muerto; (sultry) sin un soplo de aire; intenso, profundo; (of haste) precipitado

breathlessness /'brɛθlɪsnɪs/ *n* falta de aliento, *f;* respiración difícil, *f;* (death) muerte, *f;* (of weather) falta de aire, *f*

bred /brɛd/ *a* criado. **ill (well) b.,** mal (bien) criado. **pure-b.,** de raza

breeches /'brɪtʃɪz/ *n* calzones, *m pl;* pantalones, *m pl.* **riding-b.,** pantalones de montar, *m pl.* **to wear the b.,** *Fig.* ponerse los calzones

breed /brid/ *n* casta, raza, *f;* tipo, *m;* clase, *f*, *vt* procrear; engendrar, crear; (bring up) educar; criar. —*vi* reproducirse; sacar cría; multiplicarse. **to b. in-and-in,** procrear sin mezclar razas

breeding /'bridɪŋ/ *n* reproducción, *f;* cría, *f;* (upbringing) crianza, *f;* educación, *f;* instrucción, *f;* producción, *f;* creación, *f*, *a* de cría; (of male animals) semental; prolífico. **bad b.,** mala crianza, *f.* **good b.,** buena crianza, *f.* cruzamiento de razas, *m.* **B. will out,** Aunque la mona se vista de seda, mona se queda. **b. farm,** criadero, *m*

breeze /briz/ *n* brisa, *f*, vientecillo, soplo de aire, *m;* (argument) altercación, *f*, argumento, *m;* (of coke) cisco de coque, *m.* **fresh b.,** brisa fresca, *f.* **light b.,** brisa floja, *f.* **strong b.,** viento fuerte, viento muy fresco, *m*

breezy /'brizi/ *a* con brisa, fresco; expuesto a la brisa; oreado; (of manner) animado, jovial

brethren /'brɛðrɪn/ *n pl* hermanos, *m pl*

brevet /brə'vɛt/ *n Mil.* graduación honoraria, *f;* nombramiento honorario, *m.* —*vt Mil.* graduar

brevity /'brɛvɪti/ *n* brevedad, *f;* concisión, *f*

brew /bru/ *n* mezcla, *f;* brebaje, *m.* —*vt* hacer (cerveza, té, etc.); preparar, mezclar; *Fig.* urdir, tramar. —*vi* prepararse; urdirse; (storm) gestarse

brewery /'bruəri/ *n* cervecería, fábrica de cerveza, *f*

bribe /braib/ *n* soborno, cohecho, *m*, *vt* sobornar, cohechar. **to take bribes,** dejarse sobornar

bribery /'braibəri/ *n* soborno, *m*

brick /brɪk/ *n* ladrillo, *m;* (for children) piedra de construcción, *f;* bloque, *m; Inf.* buen chico, *m*, joya, *f*, *a* de ladrillo. —*vt* enladrillar. **b.-floor,** ladrillado, *m;* **b.-kiln,** horno de ladrillo, *m.* **b.-maker,** ladrillero, *m.* **b.-yard,** ladrillar, *m*

bricklayer /'brɪk,leɪər/ n albañil, m

bridal /'braɪdl/ a nupcial; de la boda; de la novia. **b. bed,** tálamo, m. **b. cake,** torta de la boda, f. **b. shop,** tienda para novias, f. **b. shower,** despedida de soltera, despedida de soltería, f. **b. song,** epitalamio, m. **b. veil,** velo de la novia, velo nupcial, m. **b. wreath,** corona de azahar, f

bride /braɪd/ n novia, desposada, f; (after marriage) recién casada, f

bridegroom /'braɪd,grum/ n novio, m; (after marriage) recién casado, m

bridesmaid /'braɪdz,meɪd/ n madrina de boda, f; niña encargada de sostener la cola de la novia, f

bridge /brɪdʒ/ n (engineering, Mus. Naut.) puente, m; lomo (de la nariz), m; (game) bridge, m, vt construir un puente (sobre); pontear; (obstacles) salvar; evitar; (fill in) ocupar, llenar. **auction b.,** bridge por subasta, m. **contract b.,** bridge por contrato, m. **suspension-b.,** puente colgante, m. **b. toll,** pontazgo, m

bridle /'braɪdl/ n brida, f; freno, m. —vt embridar, enfrenar; Fig. reprimir. —vi (of horses) levantar la cabeza; (of persons) erguirse; hacer un gesto despreciativo. **snaffle b.,** bridón, m. **b. path,** camino de herradura, m

brief /brif/ a breve, corto; conciso; lacónico, seco; rápido; fugaz, pasajero. —n (papal) breve, m; Law. relación, f; escrito, m. —vt (a barrister) instruir. **to hold a b. for,** defender, abogar por. **b.-case,** portapapeles, m; cartera (grande), f

briefly /'brifli/ adv brevemente; en pocas palabras; sucintamente; (tersely) secamente

brigand /'brɪɡənd/ n bandolero, bandido, m

bright /braɪt/ a brillante, reluciente; vivo; cristalino; subido; claro; optimista; alegre; inteligente; (quick-witted) agudo; ilustre; (smiling) risueño; (of future, etc.) halagüeño. **to be as b. as a new pin,** estar como una ascua de oro. **b. blue,** azul subido, m. **b.-eyed,** con ojos vivos, con ojos chispeantes, ojialegre

brighten /'braɪtn/ vt hacer brillar; (polish) pulir; (make happy) alegrar; (improve) mejorar. —vi (of the weather) aclarar, despejarse (el cielo); sentirse más feliz; mejorar

brightness /'braɪtnɪs/ n brillo, m; claridad, f; esplendor, m; (of colors) brillantez, f; vivacidad, f; inteligencia, f; agudeza de ingenio, f

Bright's disease /braɪts/ n enfermedad de Bright, glomerulonefritis, f

brilliance /'brɪlyəns/ n fulgor, brillo, m, refulgencia, f; esplendor, m; lustre, m; talento, m; brillantez, gloria, f

brilliant /'brɪlyənt/ a brillante. —n (gem) brillante, m. **to be b.,** (in conversation, etc.) brillar; (be clever) ser brillante

brilliantine /'brɪlyən,tin/ n brillantina, f

brim /brɪm/ n (of a glass, etc.) borde, m; (of a hat) ala, f; margen, m, orilla, f. **to be full to the b.,** estar lleno hasta los bordes; Fig. rebosar. **eyes brimming with tears,** ojos arrasados de lágrimas

brine /braɪn/ n salmuera, f; mar, m; Poet. lágrimas, f pl

bring /brɪŋ/ vt traer; llevar; transportar; (take a person or drive a vehicle) conducir; Fig. acarrear, traer; causar, ocasionar; producir; crear; (induce) persuadir; hacer (ver, etc.); (be worth) valer; (sell for) vender por; Law. entablar (un pleito, etc.): (before a judge) hacer comparecer (ante); (present) presentar; (attract) atraer; (place) poner. **to b. home,** llevar a casa; Fig. hacer ver, hacer sentir; demostrar; (a crime) probar contra. **to b. near,** acercar. **to b. about,** efectuar, poner por obra; causar, ocasionar; (achieve) lograr, conseguir. **to b. again,** traer otra vez, llevar de nuevo. **to b. away,** llevarse. **to b. back,** devolver; traer; (of memories) recordar. **to b. down,** llevar abajo, bajar; (of persons) hacer bajar; (humble) humillar; hacer caer; (of prices) hacer bajar; arruinar; destruir. **to b. down the house,** Theat. hacer venirse el teatro abajo. **to b. forth,** (give birth to) dar a luz; producir; causar; sacar a luz. **to b. forward,** hacer adelantarse; empujar hacia adelante; Fig. avanzar; (allege) alegar; Com. llevar a nueva cuenta; presentar, producir. **brought forward,** Com. suma y sigue. **to b. in,** (things) llevar adentro; (persons) hacer entrar; introducir; aparecer con, presentarse con; (meals) servir; producir; declarar; (a verdict) dictar (sentencia de), fallar. **to b. into being,** poner en práctica; dar origen (a). **to b. off,** (a ship) poner a flote; (rescue) salvar, rescatar; (carry out) efectuar, poner en práctica; (achieve) conseguir, lograr. **B. me the glass off the table,** Tráeme el vaso que hay en la mesa. **to b. on,** causar, inducir; acarrear; iniciar. **He brought a book on to the stage,** Entró en escena llevando un libro (o con un libro). **to b. out,** sacar; poner afuera; (a person) hacer salir; publicar; (a play) poner en escena; sacar a luz; (an idea, jewels, etc.) sacar a relucir; revelar; demostrar; hacer aparecer; (a girl in society) poner de largo (a). **to b. over,** llevar al otro lado; hacer venir; traer; conducir; hacer cruzar; (convert) convertir. **to b. round,** traer; llevar; (from a swoon) sacar de un desmayo; curar; persuadir; conciliar. **to b. through,** hacer atravesar; llevar a través de; ayudar a salir de (un apuro); (an illness) curar de. **to b. to,** traer a; llevar a; (from a swoon) hacer volver en sí; Naut. ponerse a la capa. **He cannot b. himself to,** No puede persuadirse a. **to b. together,** reunir; (things) juntar, amontonar; reconciliar, poner en paz. **to b. under,** someter; sojuzgar; incluir. **to b. up,** llevar arriba, subir; (a person) hacer subir; hacer avanzar; (a price) hacer subir; ir (a); andar;

(breed) criar; (educate) educar, criar; (in a discussion) hacer notar; vomitar. **to b. up the rear,** ir al fin (de); *Mil.* ir a la retaguardia. **well** (or **badly**) **brought up,** bien (o mal) educado. **to b. upon oneself,** buscarse, incurrir (en). **to b. up-to-date,** poner al día; refrescar; rejuvenecer

bringing /'brɪŋɪŋ/ *n* acción de llevar o traer, *f;* conducción, *f;* transporte, *m.* **b. forth,** producción, *f.* **b. in,** introducción, *f.* **b. out,** producción, *f;* publicación, *f;* (of a girl in society) puesta de largo, *f.* **b. under,** reducción, *f;* subyugación, *f.* **b. up,** educación, crianza, *f*

brink /brɪŋk/ *n* borde, margen, *m;* (of water) orilla, *f; Fig.* margen, *m.* **on the b.,** al margen; a la orilla. **to be on the b. of,** (doing something) estar para, estar a punto de

briny /'braini/ *a* salado

briquette /brɪ'kɛt/ *n* briqueta, *f,* aglomerado de carbón, *m*

brisk /brɪsk/ *a* activo; vivo; animado; rápido, acelerado; enérgico

briskness /'brɪsknɪs/ *n* actividad, *f;* viveza, *f;* animación, *f;* rapidez, *f;* energía, *f*

bristle /'brɪsəl/ *n* cerda, seda, *f, vi* erizarse

bristly /'brɪsli/ *a* erizado, cerdoso; espinoso; hirsuto

British /'brɪtɪʃ/ *a* británico. **the B.,** el pueblo británico; los ingleses

brittle /'brɪtl/ *a* frágil, quebradizo, delezable, friable

broach /broutʃ/ *n Cul.* espetón, asador, *m.* —*vt* espitar (un barril); abrir; *Fig.* introducir

broad /brɔd/ *a* ancho; grande; (extensive) vasto, extenso; a **b. confession,** una confesión amplia; (full) pleno; (of accents) marcado; (of words) lato; (clear) claro; (of the mind) liberal, tolerante; (of humor, etc.) grosero; (general) general, comprensivo. **in b. daylight,** en pleno día. **b.-brimmed,** de ala ancha. **b.-faced,** cariancho. **b.-minded,** tolerante, liberal, ancho de conciencia, abierto al mundo. **b.-mindedness,** tolerancia, liberalidad, *f.* **to be b.-minded,** ser tolerante, tener manga ancha. **b.-shouldered,** ancho de espaldas

broadcast /'brɔd,kæst/ *n Agr.* siembra al vuelo, *f; Radio.* radiodifusión, radiotransmisión, emisión, *f,* a radiado. —*adv* por todas partes; extensamente. —*vt Agr.* sembrar a vuelo; *Radio.* radiodifundir, radiar, transmitir por radio; (news, etc.) diseminar

broadcaster /'brɔd,kæstər/ *n* (lecturer) conferenciante, *mf;* radiodifusor (-ra) (announcer) locutor (-ra)

broadcasting /'brɔd,kæstɪŋ/ *n* radiación, radiodifución, *f;* radio, *f.* **b.-station,** estación de radio, emisora, *f.* **b.-studio,** estudio de emisión, *m*

broaden /'brɔdn/ *vt* ampliar, ensanchar. —*vi* ampliarse, ensancharse

broadly /'brɔdli/ *adv* anchamente; con

marcado acento dialectal; de una manera general

broadness /'brɔdnɪs/ *n* anchura, *f;* extensión, vastedad, *f;* tolerancia, *f;* liberalidad, *f;* grosería, *f;* (of accent) acento marcado, *m*

broadside /'brɔd,said/ *n* (of a ship) costado, *m;* (of guns) andanada, *f; Fig.* batería, *f; Print.* cara de un pliego, *f.* **to be b. on,** dar el costado

brocade /brou'keid/ *a* and *n* brocado *m.* —*vt* decorar con brocado. **imitation b.,** brocatel, *m*

broccoli /'brɒkəli/ *n* bróculi, brécol, *m*

brochure /brou'ʃur/ *n* folleto, *m*

broil /brɔil/ *vt* emparrillar, asar. —*vi* asarse

broke /brouk/ *a* quebrado

broken /'broukən/ *a* roto; quebrado; (spiritless) abatido, desalentado; (infirm) agotado, debilitado; (ruined) arruinado; (of ground) desigual, escabroso; (of a language) chapucero; (spoilt) estropeado; imperfecto; incompleto; (loose) suelto; (of a horse, etc.) domado; (of the weather) variable; (of sleep) interrumpido; (of the heart, of shoes, etc.) roto; (of the voice, sobs, sighs) entrecortado; (of the voice through old age, etc.) cascada; (incoherent) incoherente. **b.-down,** (tired) rendido, agotado; arruinado; (not working) estropeado. **b.-hearted,** roto el corazón, angustiado. **b.-winged,** aliquebrado. **I speak broken Spanish,** Hablo el español chapuceramente

broker /'broukər/ *n* corredor, *m;* (stock) corredor de bolsa, *m*

brokerage /'broukərɪdʒ/ *n* corretaje, *m*

bronchi /'brɒŋki/ *n pl* bronquios, *m pl*

bronchitis /brɒŋ'kaitɪs/ *n* bronquitis, *f*

bronze /brɒnz/ *n* bronce, *m;* objeto de bronce, *m,* a de bronce. —*vt* broncear. **B. Age,** Edad de Bronce, *f*

brooch /broutʃ/ *n* broche, *m;* alfiler de pecho, *m*

brood /brud/ *n* (of birds) nidada, *f;* (of chickens) pollada, *f;* (other animals) cría, *f;* prole, *f, vi* empollar. **to b. over,** meditar sobre, rumiar; (of mountains, etc.) dominar

brook /bruk/ *n* arroyo, riachuelo, *m, vt* tolerar, sufrir, permitir

broom /brum/ *n* escoba, *f; Bot.* retama, *f;* hiniesta, *f.* **common b.,** retama de escobas, *f.* **Spanish b.,** retama común, retama de olor, hiniesta, *f.* **b.-handle,** palo de escoba, *m*

broth /brɔθ/ *n* caldo, *m*

brothel /'brɒθəl/ *n* burdel, lupanar, *m,* casa de trato, *f*

brother /'brʌðər/ *n* hermano, *m;* (colleague) colega, *m; Inf.* compañero, *m.* **foster-b.,** hermano de leche, *m.* **half-b.,** medio hermano, *m.* **step-b.,** hermanastro, *m.* **b.-in-law,** hermano político, cuñado, *m.* **b.-officer,** compañero de promoción, *m*

brotherhood /'brʌðər,hʊd/ n fraternidad, f; Eccl. cofradía, f; hermandad, f
brotherliness /'brʌðərlinɪs/ n fraternidad, f
brotherly /'brʌðərli/ a fraterno
brow /brau/ n frente, f; ceja, f; (of a hill) cresta, cumbre, f; (edge) borde, m. **to knit one's b.,** fruncir el ceño
browbeat /'brau,bit/ vt intimidar, amenazar
brown /braun/ a castaño; (gallicism often used of shoes, etc.) marrón; pardo; (of complexion, eyes, hair) moreno; (dark brown) bruno; (blackish) negruzco; (toasted) tostado; (burnt) quemado. —n color moreno, m; color pardo, m; castaño, m; (from the sun) bronce, m. —vt (toast) tostar; (a person) volver moreno, broncear; (meat) asar. —vi tostarse; volverse moreno, broncearse; asarse. **b. bear,** oso pardo, m. **b. owl,** autillo, m. **b. paper,** papel de estraza, m. **b. study,** ensimismamiento, m, meditación, f. **b. sugar,** azúcar moreno (or quebrado), m
brownish /'braunɪʃ/ a morenucho; que tira a castaño o a bruno; parduzco; trigueño
browse /brauz/ vi pacer; (through a publication) hojear (un libro)
browsing /'brauzɪŋ/ n apacentamiento, m; hojeo (de un libro), m; lectura, f, estudio, m
bruise /bruz/ n cardenal, m; abolladura, f; (in metal) bollo, m; (on fruit) maca, f. —vt acardenalar, magullar; abollar; (fruit) macar
bruising /'bruzɪŋ/ n magullamiento, m; (of metal) abolladura, f; (crushing) machacadura, f; (boxing) boxeo, pugilato, m
brunette /bru'nɛt/ n trigueña, morena, f
brunt /brʌnt/ n peso, m; golpe, m; choque, m; esfuerzo, m. **to bear the b.,** soportar el peso; sufrir el choque; Inf. pagar el pato
brush /brʌʃ/ n cepillo, m; (broom) escoba, f; (for whitewashing, etc.) brocha, f; (for painting) pincel, m; (of a fox) cola (de zorro), f; (undergrowth) breñal, matorral, m; (fight) escaramuza, f; (argument) altercación, f. **scrubbing-b.,** cepillo para fregar, m. **shoe-b.,** cepillo para limpiar los zapatos, m. **stroke of the b.,** brochada, f; pincelada, f. **whitewash-b.,** brochón, m. **b. maker** or **seller,** escobero (-ra); pincelero (-ra)
brush /brʌʃ/ vt cepillar; (sweep) barrer; frotar; (touch) rozar; (touch lightly) acariciar. **to b. against,** rozar, tocar. **to b. aside,** echar a un lado; Fig. no hacer caso de; ignorar. **to b. off,** sacudir(se); quitar(se); (sweep) barrer. **to b. up,** cepillar; (wool) cardar; (tidy) asear; (a subject) refrescar, repasar
brushing /'brʌʃɪŋ/ n acepilladura, f; (sweeping) barredura, f; (touching) roce, rozamiento, m; (of hair) peinadura, f

brushwood /'brʌʃ,wʊd/ n enjutos, m pl, chamarasca, f; matorral, m
brusque /brʌsk/ a brusco, seco
brusqueness /'brʌsknɪs/ n brusquedad, f
Brussels /'brʌsəlz/ a bruselense; de Bruselas. **B. lace,** encaje de Bruselas, m
brutal /'brutl/ a bestial, brutal; salvaje, inhumano
brutality /bru'tælɪti/ n brutalidad, bestialidad, f; barbaridad, ferocidad, f
brutalize /'brutl,aiz/ vt embrutecer
brute /brut/ n bruto, animal, m; salvaje, bárbaro, m. **b. force,** la fuerza bruta
brutish /'brutɪʃ/ a bruto; sensual, bestial; grosero; salvaje; estúpido; ignorante. **to become b.,** embrutecerse
bubble /'bʌbəl/ n burbuja, f; borbollón, m, vi burbujear; borbollar, bullir, hervir
bubbling /'bʌbəlɪŋ/ n burbujeo, m; hervidero, m; (of brooks) murmullo, m, a burbujeante; hirviente; (of brooks) parlero; (of wine) espumoso, efervescente
buccaneer /,bʌkə'nɪər/ n corsario, m; aventurero, m
buck /bʌk/ n Zool. gamo, m; (male) macho, m; (fop) galán, petimetre, m, vi (of a horse) caracolear; fanfarronear. **to pass the b.,** Inf. echarle a uno el muerto. **b.-rabbit,** conejo, m. **to b. up,** hacer de tripas corazón
bucket /'bʌkɪt/ n cubo, balde, m, cubeta, f
buckle /'bʌkəl/ n hebilla, f. —vt enhebillar, abrochar con hebilla. —vi doblarse. **to b. to,** ponerse a hacer algo con ahínco
buckskin /'bʌk,skɪn/ n ante, m
buckwheat /'bʌk,wit/ n alforfón, trigo sarraceno, m
bucolic /byu'kɒlɪk/ a bucólico, pastoril
bud /bʌd/ n brote, m; botón, capullo, m; (of vines) bollón, m; (of vegetables) gema, f. —vt brotar, germinar. —vt injertar de escudete
Buddhism /'budɪzəm/ n budismo, m
Buddhist /'budɪst/ n budista, mf
budding /'bʌdɪŋ/ n brotadura, f; (of roses, etc) injerto de escudete, m; Fig. germen, m
budge /bʌdʒ/ vi moverse, menearse. —vt mover
budget /'bʌdʒɪt/ n presupuesto, f; (of news, etc.) colección, f. —vi presuponer
buffalo /'bʌfə,lou/ n búfalo, f
buffer /'bʌfər/ n (railway) parachoques, m; (of cars) amortiguador, m. **b. state,** estado tapón, m
buffet /bə'fei/ n bofetón, m; bofetada, f; bar, m. —vt abofetear; golpear; luchar con las olas
buffoon /bə'fun/ n bufón, m
bug /bʌg/ n chinche, m
bugle /'byugəl/ n corneta, trompeta, f; (bead) abalorio, m. **b. blast,** trompetazo, m
build /bɪld/ vt edificar; (engines, ships, organs, etc.) construir; (a nest and Fig.)

hacer; (have built) hacer, edificar; crear;
formar; fundar. —*n* estructura, *f;* (of the
body) hechura, *f;* talle, *m.* **to b. castles
in Spain,** hacer castillos en el aire.

built-up area, zona urbana, *f.* **to b. up,**
construir, levantar; (block) tapar; (business, reputation) establecer, crear. **to b.
upon,** *Fig.* contar con, confiar en; esperar
de

builder /'bɪldər/ *n* constructor, *m;* maestro de obras, *m;* (laborer) albañil, *m;*
creador (-ra), fundador (-ra); arquitecto,
m

building /'bɪldɪŋ/ *n* edificación, *f;* construcción, *f;* edificio, *m;* fundación, *f;*
creación, *f.* **b. contractor,** maestro de
obras, *m.* **b. material,** material de construcción, *m.* **b. site,** solar, terreno, *m.* **b.
timber,** madera de construcción, *f*

built-in /'bɪlt ,ɪn/ *a* empotrado. **b. closet,**
armario empotrado, *m*

bulb /bʌlb/ *n Bot.* bulbo, *m;* (*Elec. Phys.*)
bombilla, *f;* (of an oil lamp) cebolla, *f*

bulge /bʌldʒ/ *n* bulto, *m;* hinchazón, *f;*
protuberancia, *f; Mil.* bolsa (en el frente),
f. —*vi* hincharse; estar lleno (de)

bulging /'bʌldʒɪŋ/ *a* lleno (de); con bultos; hinchado (de)

bulk /bʌlk/ *n* volumen, tamaño, *m;* bulto,
m; (larger part) grueso, *m;* mayor parte,
f; (of people) mayoría, *f;* (of a ship) capacidad, *f.* **in b.,** *Com.* en bruto, en
grueso. **to b. large,** tener mucha importancia

bulkhead /'bʌlk,hɛd/ *n Naut.* mamparo,
m

bulkiness /'bʌlkɪnɪs/ *n* abultamiento, *m;*
volumen, tamaño, *m*

bulky /'bʌlki/ *a* voluminoso, grande,
grueso

bull /bʊl/ *n* toro, *m; Astron.* Tauro, *m;*
(of some animals) macho, *m;* (Stock Exchange) alcista, *mf;* (of the Pope) bula
(del Papa), *f.* **a b. in a china shop,** un
caballo loco en una cacharrería. **to fight
bulls,** torear. **b.-calf,** ternero, *m.* **bull's
eye,** blanco, *m;* acierto, *m.* **b. fight,** corrida de toros, *f.* **b. fighter's gala uniform,** traje de luces, *m.* **b.-ring,** plaza de
toros, *f*

bulldog /'bʊl,dɔg/ *n* perro dogo, perro de
presa, *m*

bulldozer /'bʊl,douzər/ *n* (excavator) tozodora, *f*

bullet /'bʊlɪt/ *n* bala, *f.* **spent b.,** bala
fría, *f.* **stray b.,** bala perdida, *f.* **b.-proof,**
a prueba de bala, blindado

bulletin /'bʊlɪtɪn/ *n* boletín, *m*

bulletin board *n* tablero de anuncios,
tablero de avisos, tablón, *m*

bulletproof vest /'bʊlɪt,pruf/ *n* chaleco
blindado, *m*

bullfighter /'bʊl,faɪtər/ *n* torero, *m* (on
foot), toreador, *m* (on horseback)

bullion /'bʊlyən/ *n Com.* metálico, *m;*
oro (or plata) en barras, *m, f*

bullpen /'bʊl,pɛn/ *n* toril, *m* (bullfighting); calentador, *m* (baseball)

bully /'bʊli/ *n* valentón, perdonavidas,
gallito, *m;* rufián, *m.* —*vt* intimidar; tratar mal. **b. beef,** vaca en lata, *f*

bulwark /'bʊlwərk/ *n* baluarte, *m; Naut.*
antepecho, *m*

bumblebee /'bʌmbəl,bi/ *n* abejorro, *m*

bump /bʌmp/ *n* golpe, *m;* ruido, *m;* choque, *m;* (bruise) chichón, *m,* roncha, *f;*
Aer. sacudida, *f,* meneo, *m.* —*vi* (into,
against) tropezar con; (along) saltar en.
—*vt* chocar (contra)

bumper /'bʌmpər/ *n* copa llena hasta los
bordes, *f,* vaso lleno, *m;* (of a car)
parachoques, *m.* **a b. harvest,** una cosecha abundante

bumpkin /'bʌmpkɪn/ *n* patán, villano, *m*

bumptious /'bʌmpʃəs/ *a* fatuo, presuntuoso, presumido

bumpy /'bʌmpi/ *n* (of surface) desigual,
escabroso; (of a vehicle) incómodo, con
mala suspensión

bun /bʌn/ *n* buñuelo, bollo, *m;* (hair)
moño, *m*

bunch /bʌntʃ/ *n* (of fruit) racimo, *m;*
manojo, *m;* (of flowers) ramo, *m;* (tuft)
penacho, *m;* (gang) pandilla, *f, vi* arracimarse; agruparse

bundle /'bʌndl/ *n* atado, lío, *m;* (of
papers) legajo, *m;* (of sticks) haz, *m;*
(sheaf) fajo, *m;* (package) paquete, *m;*
fardo, hatillo, *m;* (roll) rollo, *m, vt* atar,
liar; envolver; empaquetar; (stuff) meter,
introducir. **to b. in,** meter dentro (de). **to
b. out,** despachar sin ceremonia, poner
de patitas en la calle

bungalow /'bʌngə,lou/ *n* casa de un solo
piso, *f*

bungle /'bʌngəl/ *vt* estropear; hacer mal.
—*n* equivocación, *f,* yerro, *m;* cosa (o
obra) mal hecha, *f*

bungling /'bʌnglɪŋ/ *a* chapucero, torpe

bunion /'bʌnyən/ *n* juanete (del pie), *m*

bunk /bʌŋk/ *n* litera, *f, vi Inf.* poner pies
en polvorosa, pirarse

bunker /'bʌŋkər/ *n Naut.* pañol, *m;* (for
coal) carbonera, *f;* (golf) hoya de arena, *f*

bunkum /'bʌŋkəm/ *n* patrañas, *f pl*

bunting /'bʌntɪŋ/ *n* gallardete, *m*

buoy /'bui/ *n* boya, baliza, *f, vt* boyar;
abalizar; *Fig.* sostener. **light b.,** boya
luminosa, *f*

buoyancy /'bɔiənsi/ *n* flotación, *f; Fig.*
optimismo, *m,* alegría, *f*

buoyant /'bɔiənt/ *a* boyante; ligero

burden /'bɜrdn/ *n* carga, *f,* peso, *m;* (of a
ship) tonelaje, *m,* capacidad, *f;* (of a
song) estribillo, *m;* (gist) esencia, *f.* —*vt*
cargar. **to be a b. on,** pesar sobre

burdensome /'bɜrdnsəm/ *a* pesado,
oneroso, gravoso; abrumador

bureau /'byʊrou/ *n* buró, secreter, *m;* escritorio, *m;* (office) dirección, oficina, *f;*
departamento, *m*

bureaucracy /byʊ'rɒkrəsi/ *n* burocracia,
f

bureaucrat /'byʊrə,kræt/ *n* burócrata,
mf; Inf. mandarín, *m*

bureaucratic /ˌbyurə'krætɪk/ a burocrático

burglar /'bɜrglər/ n ladrón de casas, escalador, m. **cat b.,** gato, m. **b. alarm,** alarma contra ladrones, f. **b. insurance,** seguro contra robo, m

burglary /'bɜrgləri/ n robo nocturno de una casa, m

burgle /'bɜrgəl/ vi robar una casa de noche. —vt robar

burial /'bɛriəl/ n entierro, m. **b.-ground,** campo santo, cementerio, m. **b. service,** misa de difuntos, f. **b. society,** sociedad de entierros, f

burlap /'bɜrlæp/ n arpillera, f

burlesque /bər'lɛsk/ a burlesco. —n parodia, f. —vt parodiar

burly /'bɜrli/ a corpulento, fornido

Burma /'bɜrmə/ Birmania, f

Burmese /bər'miz/ a and n birmano (-na)

burn /bɜrn/ vt quemar; calcinar; (bricks) cocer; cauterizar; (the tongue) picar; (dry up) secar; (the skin by sun or wind) tostar. —vi quemar; arder; Fig. abrasarse (en). **b. at the stake,** vt quemar en la hoguera. **to b. to ashes,** reducir a cenizas. **to b. away,** consumir(se). **to b. oneself,** quemarse. **to b. up,** quemar del todo, consumir. **to b. with,** Fig. abrasarse en

burn /bɜrn/ n quemadura, f; (stream) arroyo, m

burner /'bɜrnər/ n quemador (-ra); mechero, m

burning /'bɜrnɪŋ/ n quema, f; incendio, m; fuego, m; (inflammation) inflamación, f; (pain) quemazón, f; abrasamiento, m. —a en llamas; ardiente; intenso; (notorious) notorio, escandaloso; abrasador; palpitante. **b. question,** cuestión palpitante, f

burnish /'bɜrnɪʃ/ n bruñido, m; lustre, brillo, m, vt bruñir; pulir, pulimentar, dar brillo a; (weapons) acicalar. —vi tomar lustre

burr /bɜr/ n Bot. cáliz de flor con espinas, m; Mech. rebaba, f; sonido fuerte de la erre, m

burrow /'bɜrou/ n madriguera, f, vivar, m; (for rabbits) conejera, f. —vt amadrigar; minar

bursar /'bɜrsər/ n tesorero, m; becario, m

burst /bɜrst/ n estallido, m, explosión, f; (in a pipe) avería, f, (fit) acceso, m; transporte, m; (effort) esfuerzo, m; (expanse) extensión, f, panorama, m. **b. of applause,** salva de aplausos, f

burst /bɜrst/ vi estallar; reventar; quebrarse; romperse; (overflow) desbordar; (of seams) nacerse; derramarse (por); (into laughter) romper a; (into tears) deshacerse en. —vt quebrar; romper; hacer estallar. **to b. upon the view,** aparecer de pronto. **to b. into,** irrumpir en; (exclamations, etc.) prorrumpir en. **to b. into tears,** romper a llorar, deshacerse en lágrimas. **to b. open,** abrir con violencia; forzar

bursting /'bɜrstɪŋ/ n estallido, m; quebrantamiento, m; (overflowing) desbordamiento, m

bury /'bɛri/ vt enterrar, sepultar; sumergir; (hide) esconder, ocultar; (forget) echar tierra a

bus /bʌs/ n autobús, ómnibus, Mexico camión, Caribbean guagua, m. **to travel by bus,** ir en autobús. **bus station,** estación de autobuses, f

bush /buʃ/ n arbusto, matojo, m; (undergrowth) maleza, f; tierra virgen, f; Mech. manguito, m

bushel /'buʃəl/ n medida de áridos, f, (In England 8 gallons or 36.37 liters)

bushy /'buʃi/ a lleno de arbustos; denso; espeso; grueso; (eyebrows, etc.) poblado

busily /'bɪzəli/ adv diligentemente, solícitamente; afanosamente, laboriosamente. **He was b. occupied in...,** Estaba muy ocupado en...

business /'bɪznɪs/ n ocupación, f; quehaceres, m pl; (matter) asunto, m, cosa, f; empleo, oficio, m; Com. negocio(s), m, pl; casa comercial, f; (trade) comercio, m; (clients, connection) clientela, f; (right) derecho, m; Theat. juego escénico, m, pantomima, f. **He had no b. to do that,** No tenía derecho a hacer eso. **Mind your own b.!** ¡No te metas donde no te llaman! **on b.,** por negocios. **to be in b. for oneself,** tener negocios por su propia cuenta. **to mean b.,** hacer algo en serio; estar resuelto. **to send about his b.,** mandar a paseo (a). **to set up in b.,** establecer un negocio. **b. affairs,** negocios, m pl. **b. agent,** agente de negocios, m. **b. hours,** horas de trabajo, f pl. **b.-like,** formal, práctico, sistemático. **b. man,** hombre de negocios, negociante, m

business administration n administración de empresas, f

bust /bʌst/ n Art. busto, bulto, m; pecho, m. **b. bodice,** sostén, m

bustle /'bʌsəl/ n actividad, animación, f; confusión, f; (of a dress) polizón, tontillo, m. —vi menearse, darse prisa. —vt dar prisa (a)

bustling /'bʌslɪŋ/ a activo; ocupado; atareado; animado; bullicioso, ruidoso

busy /'bɪzi/ a ocupado; atareado; activo, diligente; (of places) animado, bullicioso; (of streets) de gran circulación; (officious) entremetido. **to b. oneself,** ocuparse (en, con); dedicarse (a), entregarse (a); (interfere) entrometerse (con). **to be b.,** estar ocupado; estar atareado, tener mucho que hacer. **b.-body,** bullebulle, mf. entremetido (-da), chismoso (-sa)

but /bʌt/ conjunc prep adv pero; sino; (only) solamente; (except) menos; excepto; (almost) casi; que no; si no; (that) que; (nevertheless) sin embargo, empero, no obstante; (without) sin, sin que; (of time recently passed) no más que, tan recientemente. —n pero, m. **He cannot choose but go,** No puede hacer otra cosa que marcharse. **to do nothing but...,**

hacer únicamente..., no hacer más que...
but for, a no ser por. **but yesterday,**
solamente ayer. **but then (or but yet),**
pero

butcher /'butʃər/ n carnicero, m. —vt
matar reses; hacer una carnicería en.
butcher's boy, mozo del carnicero, m.
butcher's shop, carnicería, f

butchery /'butʃəri/ n carnicería, f; matanza, f

butler /'bʌtlər/ n mayordomo, m. **butler's pantry,** despensa, repostería, f

butt /bʌt/ n (cask) tonel, m, pipa, f; (for
water) barril, m; (of a cigarette, etc.)
colilla, f; (of fire-arms) culata, f; (handle)
mango, cabo, m; (billiards) mocho, m;
(earthwork) terrero, m; (Fig. object) objeto (de), m; (of bulls, etc.) topetada, f;
pl **butts,** campo de tiro, m; (target)
blanco, m. —vt (toss) topar, acornear;
(meet) tropezar (con). **to b. in,** Inf. entrometerse, meter baza; encajarse

butter /'bʌtər/ n mantequilla, f, vt untar
con mantequilla. **b.-dish,** mantequera, f.
b.-fingers, torpe, m. **b.-knife,** cuchillo
para mantequilla, m. **b.-milk,** suero de
mantequilla, m. **b.-print,** molde para
mantequilla, m. **b.-sauce,** mantequilla
fundida, f

butterfly /'bʌtər,flai/ n mariposa, f

butterscotch /'bʌtər,skɒtʃ/ n dulce de
azúcar y mantequilla, m

buttocks /'bʌtəks/ n pl nalgas, posaderas, f pl

button /'bʌtn/ n botón, m; pl **buttons,**
botones, paje, m. —vt abotonar, abrochar.
—vi abotonarse, abrocharse. **to press the
b.,** apretar el botón. **b.-hook,** abotonador,
m

buttonhole /'bʌtn,houl/ n ojal, m; flor
que se lleva en el ojal, f. —vt Sew. hacer
ojales; (embroidery) hacer el festón; Inf.
importunar

buttress /'bʌtrɪs/ n estribo, macho, con-
trafuerte, m; Fig. apoyo, sostén, m. —vt
afianzar, estribar; Fig. apoyar, sostener.
flying-b., arbotante, m

buxom /'bʌksəm/ a (of a woman) fresca,
guapetona, frescachona

buy /bai/ vt comprar; obtener; (achieve)
lograr; (bribe) sobornar. **to buy on
credit,** comprar al fiado. **to buy back,**
comprar de nuevo; redimir; (ransom) rescatar. **to buy for,** (a price) comprar por;
(purpose or destination) comprar para. **to
buy in,** (at an auction) comprar por
cuenta del dueño. **to buy off,** librarse de
uno con dinero. **to buy out,** (of a business) comprar la parte de un socio. **to
buy up,** comprar todo, acaparar

buyer /'baiər/ n comprador (-ra)

buying /'baiɪŋ/ n compra, f. **b. back,** rescate, m. **b. up,** acaparamiento, m

buzz /bʌz/ n zumbido, m; (whisper) susurro, murmullo, m; (of a bell) sonido
(del timbre), m, vi zumbar; susurrar

buzzer /'bʌzər/ n zumbador, m; sirena, f;
(bell) timbre, m

by /bai/ prep por; de; en; a; con; (of
place) cerca de, al lado de; (according to)
según, de acuerdo con; (in front of, past)
delante (de); (at the latest) antes de, al
más tardar; (expressing agency) por; (by
means of) mediante; (through, along) por;
(upon) sobre; (for) para; (under) bajo.
He will be here by Wednesday, Estará
aquí para el miércoles; (not later than)
Estará aquí antes del miércoles (or el
miércoles al más tardar). **How did he
come by it?** ¿Cómo llegó a su poder? **He
will come by train,** Vendrá en tren. **I
know her by sight,** La conozco de vista.
**There are three children by the first
marriage,** Hay tres niños del primer
matrimonio. **He goes by the name of
Pérez,** Se le conoce por (or bajo) el nombre de Pérez. **six feet by eight,** seis pies
por ocho. **They called her by her name,**
La llamaron por su nombre. **two by two,**
dos por dos. **The picture was painted
by Cézanne,** El cuadro fue pintado por
Cézanne. **drop by drop,** gota a gota. **by
a great deal,** con mucho. **by all means,**
naturalmente; de todos modos; cueste lo
que cueste. **by chance,** por ventura. **by
day (night),** de día (noche). **by daylight,**
a la luz del día. **by doing it,** con hacerlo.
by myself, solo; sin ayuda. **"By Appointment"** «Cita Previa». **by chance or
by mischance,** por ventura o por desdicha. **an hour away by car,** a una hora
de automóvil. **music by Brahms,** música
de Brahms. **pull by the hair,** tirar por el
pelo. **take by the hand,** llevar de la
mano.

by /bai/ adv (near) cerca; (before) delante; al lado; a un lado; aparte; (of
time) pasado. **to put by,** (keep) guardar;
(throw away) desechar; (accumulate)
acumular; (put out of the way) arrinconar. **to pass by,** pasar; pasar delante
(de). **by and by,** luego; pronto; más
tarde. **by now,** ya, antes de ahora. **by
the way,** entre paréntesis, a propósito; de
paso; al lado del camino. **by-election,**
elección parcial, f. **by-law,** reglamento,
m. **by-pass,** ruta de evitación, f, desvío,
m; (Mech. Elec.) derivación, f. —vi
desviarse de; Mil. rebasar. **by-product,**
derivado, m; Chem. producto derivado,
m; Fig. consecuencia, f; resultado, m

bye /bai/ n (in cricket) meta, f. **by the
bye,** a propósito, entre paréntesis

bygone /'bai,gɒn/ a pasado. **Let
bygones be bygones,** Lo pasado pasado

bystander /'bai,stændər/ n espectador
(-ra); pl **bystanders,** los circunstantes

byway /'bai,wei/ n camino desviado, m;
Fig. senda indirecta, f; pl **byways,** andurriales, m pl

byword /'bai,wɜrd/ n proverbio, m; objeto de burla o escándalo, m

Byzantium /bɪ'zænʃiəm/ Bizancio, m

c /si/ n (letter) c, f; Mus. do, m
cab /kæb/ n (horse-drawn) simón, m; (taxi) coche de alquiler, m; (of a locomotive) cabina del conductor, f. **cab-rank**, punto de coches, m
cabaret /ˌkæbəˈrei/ n cabaret, m; taberna, f
cabbage /ˈkæbɪdʒ/ n col, berza, f. **red c.**, lombarda, f. **c. butterfly**, mariposa de col, f
cabin /ˈkæbɪn/ n cabaña, choza, f; Naut. camarote, m; (railway) garita, f; Aer. cabina, f. **c. boy**, grumete, galopín, mozo de cámara, m. **c. trunk**, baúl mundo, m
cabinet /ˈkæbənɪt/ n (piece of furniture) vitrina, f; colección, exposición, f; Polit. gabinete, m; (of a radio) cónsola, f. **c.-maker**, ebanista, m. **c.-making**, ebanistería, f. **c. meeting**, consejo de ministros, m. **c. minister**, ministro, m
cable /ˈkeibəl/ n amarra, maroma, f; cable, m; cable(grama), m, vt cablegrafiar. **electric c.**, cable eléctrico, m. **overhead c.**, cable aéreo, m
cabman /ˈkæbmən/ n cochero de punto, simón, m
cache /kæʃ/ n escondite, escondrijo, m
cackle /ˈkækəl/ vi (of a hen) cacarear; (of a goose) graznar; (of humans) chacharear. —n cacareo, m; graznido, m; cháchara, f
cacophony /kəˈkɒfəni/ n cacofonía, f
cactus /ˈkæktəs/ n cacto, m
cad /kæd/ n sinvergüenza, m; tipo de cuidado, m
caddish /ˈkædɪʃ/ a mal educado, grosero
caddy /ˈkædi/ n (for tea) cajita para té, f; (golf) cadi, mf
cadger /ˈkædʒər/ n sablista, mf; mendigo, m; (loafer) golfo, m
cadmium /ˈkædmiəm/ n cadmio, m
café /kæˈfei/ n café, m
cafeteria /ˌkæfɪˈtɪəriə/ n bar automático, m
caffeine /ˈkæfiːn/ n cafeína, f
cage /keidʒ/ n (animal's, bird's) jaula, f; (of a lift) camarín, m; (for transporting miners) jaula, f. —vt enjaular; encerrar
Cain /kein/, **to raise** armar lo de Dios es Cristo
cajole /kəˈdʒoul/ vt lisonjear; engatusar; embromar; instar
cake /keik/ n Cul. pastel, m, torta, f; (of chocolate, etc.) pastilla, f. —vt and vi cuajar; formar costra; (with mud) enlodar. **to sell like hot cakes**, venderse como pan bendito. **to take the c.**, llevarse la palma. **c. of soap**, pastilla de jabón, f. **c.-shop**, pastelería, f
calamine /ˈkæləmain/ n calamina, f
calamitous /kəˈlæmɪtəs/ a calamitoso, desastroso
calamity /kəˈlæmɪti/ n calamidad, f; desastre, m
calcium /ˈkælsiəm/ n calcio, m
calculate /ˈkælkyəˌleit/ vt calcular; adaptar. **to c. on**, contar con

---

calculated /ˈkælkyəˌleitɪd/ a premeditado. **to be c. to**, conducir a; ser a propósito para
calculating /ˈkælkyəˌleitɪŋ/ n cálculo, m, a calculador; (of persons) interesado; (shrewd) perspicaz; atento. **c. machine**, máquina de calcular, f, calculador, m
calculation /ˌkælkyəˈleiʃən/ n cálculo, m; calculación, f
calculus /ˈkælkyələs/ n cálculo, m
calendar /ˈkæləndər/ n calendario, m; almanaque, m; (university, etc.) programa, m
calf /kæf/ n becerro (-rra), ternero (-ra), m; (young of other animals) hijuelo, m; (of the leg) pantorrilla, f; (leather) cuero de becerro, m; piel, f; calf's-foot, pie de ternera, m. **c. love**, amor de muchachos, m
calibrate /ˈkæləˌbreit/ vt calibrar
calico /ˈkælɪˌkou/ n indiana, f; percal, m. **c.-printer**, fabricante de estampados, m
Californian /ˌkæləˈfɔrnyən/ a californio. —n californio (-ia)
calk /kɔk/ See **caulk**
call /kɔl/ n llamada, f; (shout) grito, m; (of a bird) canto, m; (signal) señal, f; (visit) visita, f; (by a ship) escala, f; Mil. toque, m; (need) necesidad, f; (of religion, etc.) vocación, f; invitación, f; (demand) demanda, f; exigencia, f. **They came at my c.**, Acudieron a mi llamada. **c. to arms**, llamada, llamada a filas, f. **port of c.**, puerto de escala, m. **telephone c.**, llamada telefónica, f. **to pay a c.**, hacer una visita. **within c.**, al alcance de la voz. **c.-box**, cabina del teléfono, f. **c.-boy**, ayudante del traspunte, m
call /kɔl/ vi llamar; gritar, dar voces; (visit) visitar, hacer una visita (a); venir; (stop) parar; (of a ship) hacer escala. —vt llamar; (a meeting, etc.) convocar; (awaken) despertar, llamar; (say) decir; (appoint) nombrar; (at cards) declarar. **She is called Dorothy**, Se llama Dorotea. **Madrid calling!** ¡Aquí Radio Madrid! **Will you c. me at eight o'clock, please?** Haga el favor de despertarme (llamarme) a las ocho. **to c. at a port**, hacer escala en un puerto. **to c. a halt**, hacer alto. **to c. a strike**, declarar una huelga. **to c. names**, vituperar, injuriar. **to c. to account**, pedir cuentas (a). **to c. to arms**, tocar el arma; alarmar. **to c. to mind**, acordarse (de), recordar. **to c. to witness**, hacer testigo (de). **to c. back**, vi llamar; hacer volver; (unsay) desdecir. —vi (return) volver; venir a buscar; ir a buscar. **I called back for the parcel**, Volví a buscar el paquete. **to c. for**, pedir a gritos; llamar; (demand) pedir; exigir; (collect a person) pasar a buscar; (parcels, etc.) ir (o venir) a recoger. **He called for help**, Pidió socorro a gritos. **to**

c. forth, producir; provocar; inspirar; revelar; (bring together) reunir. **to c. in,** hacer entrar; invitar; (a specialist, etc.) llamar; (worn coin) retirar de la circulación; recoger. **to c. in question,** poner en duda. **to c. off,** (dogs, etc.) llamar; (a strike) cancelar; parar; terminar; (a person) disuadir (de); (postpone) aplazar; suspender; (refrain) desistir de). **to c. on,** (visit) hacer una visita (a), ir a ver, visitar; (of a doctor) visitar; (a person to do something) recurrir (a); (for a speech) invitar (a hablar); (invoke) invocar. **I shall now c. on Mr. Martínez,** Doy la palabra al señor Martínez. **to c. out,** vt hacer salir; provocar; inspirar; (challenge) desafiar, retar. —vi gritar. **c. the roll,** pasar lista. **to c. over,** (names) pasar lista (de). **to c. up,** hacer subir; (to the army) llamar a filas (a); (telephone) llamar por teléfono (a); (memories) evocar. **to c. upon.** See to c. on

caller /'kɔlər/ n visita, f

calligraphist /kə'lɪgrəfɪst/ n calígrafo, m

calling /'kɔlɪŋ/ n llamamiento, m; (occupation) profesión, f; empleo, m; vocación, f; (of a meeting) convocación, f

calling card /'kɔlɪŋ ,kɑrd/ n (telephone) tarjeta telefónica, f

callisthenics /,kæləs'θɛnɪks/ n pl calistenia, f

callous /'kæləs/ a (of skin) calloso; Fig. insensible, duro, inhumano

callousness /'kæləsnɪs/ n falta de piedad, inhumanidad, dureza, f

callow /'kælou/ a (of birds) implume; (inexperienced) bisoño, inexperto, novato

callus /'kæləs/ n callo, m

calm /kɑm/ n calma, f; paz, tranquilidad, f; sosiego, m; serenidad, f. —a (of the sea) en calma; tranquilo; sereno; sosegado. —vt calmar; tranquilizar; apaciguar. —vi calmarse; tranquilizarse; sosegarse. **dead c.,** calma chicha, f

calming /'kɑmɪŋ/ a calmante

calmness /'kɑmnɪs/ n calma, tranquilidad, f; ecuanimidad, serenidad, f

calorie /'kæləri/ n caloría, f

calumny /'kæləmni/ n calumnia, f

calve /kæv/ vi (of a cow, etc.) parir

cam /kæm/ n Mech. leva, f. **camshaft,** árbol de levas, m

camaraderie /,kɑmə'rɑdəri/ n compañerismo, m

camcorder /'kæm,kɔrdər/ n videocámara, f, camcórder, m

camel /'kæməl/ n camello (-lla). **c.-driver,** camellero, m. **camel's hair,** pelo de camello, m

cameo /'kæmi,ou/ n camafeo, m

camera /'kæmərə/ n Photo. máquina fotográfica, f. **folding c.,** máquina fotográfica plegable, f. **in c.,** a puerta cerrada. **c. obscura,** cámara obscura, f

camouflage /'kæmə,flɑʒ/ n camuflaje, m, vt camuflar

camp /kæmp/ n campamento, m; campo, m; Fig. vida de cuartel, f; (for school children, etc.) colonia, f; (party) partido, m. —vi acampar; vivir en tiendas de campaña. **to break c.,** levantar el campo. **c.-bed,** cama de campaña, f. **c.-stool,** silla de campaña, f

campaign /kæm'pein/ n campaña, f. —vi hacer una campaña

campaigner /kæm'peinər/ n veterano, m; propagandista, mf

campaigning /kæm'peinɪŋ/ n campañas, f pl

camphor /'kæmfər/ n alcanfor, m

camphorated /'kæmfə,reitɪd/ a alcanforado

campus /'kæmpəs/ n recinto, m (Puerto Rico), ciudad universitaria, f

can /kæn/ v aux poder; (know how to) saber. **You can go to the village when you like,** Puedes ir al pueblo cuando quieras. **I cannot allow that,** No puedo permitir eso. **What can they mean?** ¿Qué quieren decir? **If only things could have been different!** ¡Si solamente las cosas hubiesen sido distintas! **Can you come to dinner on Saturday?** ¿Puede Vd. venir a cenar el sábado? **I can come later if you like,** Puedo (or Podría) venir más tarde si Vd. quiere. **Mary can** (knows how to) **play the piano,** María sabe tocar el piano **You can't have your cake and eat it too.** No hay rosa sin espinas

can /kæn/ n lata, f; (for carrying sandwiches, etc.) fiambrera, f. —vt conservar en latas. **canopener,** abrelatas, m

Canada /'kænədə/ el Canadá, m

Canadian /kə'neidiən/ a canadiense. —n canadiense, mf

canaille /kə'nai/ n gentualla, gentuza, f

canal /kə'næl/ n canal, m

canalization /,kænl̩ə'zeiʃən/ n canalización, f

canalize /'kænl̩,aiz/ vt canalizar

canary /kə'nɛəri/ n canario (-ia); color de canario, m; vino de Canarias, m. **roller c.,** canario de raza flauta, m. **c.-seed,** alpiste, m

Canary Islands, the /kə'nɛəri/ las Islas Canarias, m

cancel /'kænsəl/ vt cancelar; revocar; borrar; anular. **to c. out,** Math. anular

cancellation /,kænsə'leiʃən/ n cancelación, f; revocación, f; anulación, f

cancer /'kænsər/ n Med. cáncer, m; Astron. Cáncer, m

cancerous /'kænsərəs/ a canceroso. **to become c.,** cancerarse

candelabrum /,kændl̩'ɑbrəm/ n candelabro, m

candid /'kændɪd/ a franco; sincero. **If I am to be c.,** Si he de decir la verdad, Si he de ser franco

candidate /'kændɪ,deit/ n candidato (-ta); aspirante, m

candidature /'kændɪdə,tʃʊr/ n candidatura, f

candidness /'kændɪdnɪs/ n franqueza, f; sinceridad, f

candied /'kændɪd/ a (of peel, etc.) almibarado, garapiñado

candle /'kændl/ n vela, candela, f. **wax c.,** cirio, m. **You cannot hold a c. to him,** No llegas a la suela de su zapato, Ni llegas a sus pies, Ni le llegas a los pies. **The game is not worth the c.,** La cosa no vale la pena. **to burn the c. at both ends,** consumir la vida. **c.-grease,** sebo, m. **c.-light,** luz de las velas, f; luz artificial, f. **c.-maker,** candelero, m. **c.-power,** Elec. potencia luminosa, bujía, f. **c.-snuffer,** apagavelas, matacandelas, m

candlestick /'kændl͵stɪk/ n candelero, m, palmatoria, f; (processional) cirial, m

candor /'kændər/ n franqueza, f; sinceridad, f; candor, m

candy /'kændi/ n caramelo, bombón, m, vt garapiñar, almibarar

cane /kein/ n Bot. caña, f; (for chair seats, etc.) rejilla, f; (walking stick) bastón, m; (for punishment) vara, f. —vt apalear, pegar. **sugar-c.,** caña de azúcar, f. **c.-break,** cañaveral, m. **c. chair,** sillón de mimbres, m. **c.-sugar,** azúcar de caña, m. **c.-syrup,** miel de caña, f

canine /'keinain/ a canino. —n (tooth) diente canino, m

canister /'kænəstər/ n bote, m, cajita, f

canker /'kæŋkər/ n úlcera, f; (in trees) cancro, m; Fig. cáncer, m, vt roer; Fig. corromper

canned /kænd/ a en lata

cannibal /'kænəbəl/ n caníbal, mf antropófago (-ga). —a caníbal, antropófago

cannibalism /'kænəbə͵lɪzəm/ n canibalismo, m, antropofagía, f

canning /'kænɪŋ/ n conservación en latas, f. **c. factory,** fábrica de conservas alimenticias, f

cannon /'kænən/ n (fire-arm) cañón, m; (billiards) carambola, f, vi carambolear. **to c. into,** chocar con. **c.-ball,** bala de cañón, f. **c.-shot,** cañonazo, m

canny /'kæni/ a cuerdo, sagaz

canoe /kə'nu/ n canoa, f; piragua, f, vi ir en canoa

canoeist /kə'nuɪst/ n canoero (-ra)

canon /'kænən/ n (Eccl. Mus. Print.) canón, m; (dignitary) canónigo, m; (criterion) criterio, m. **c. law,** derecho canónico, m

canonize /'kænə͵naiz/ vt canonizar

canopy /'kænəpi/ n dosel, toldo, m; palio, m; Fig. capa, bóveda, f. **the c. of heaven,** la capa (or bóveda) del cielo

cant /kænt/ vt inclinar; ladear. —vi inclinarse; (be a hypocrite) camandulear. —n (slope) inclinación, f; sesgo, desplomo, m; (hypocrisy) gazmoñería, f

cantankerous /kæn'tæŋkərəs/ a irritable, intratable, malhumorado

cantata /kən'tɑtə/ n cantata, f

canteen /kæn'tin/ n cantina, f; (water bottle) cantimplora, f. **c. of cutlery,** juego de cubiertos, m

canter /'kæntər/ n medio galope, m, vi andar a galope corto

canting /'kæntɪŋ/ a hipócrita

canto /'kæntou/ n canto, m

canton /'kæntn/ n (province and Herald.) cantón, m, vt (of soldiers) acantonar

cantor /'kæntər/ n Eccl. chantre, m

canvas /'kænvəs/ n lona, f; Art. lienzo, m; Naut. vela, f, paño, m. **under c.,** en tiendas de campaña; (of ships) a toda vela

canvass /'kænvəs/ vt (votes, etc.) solicitar

canvasser /'kænvəsər/ n solicitador (-ra) (de votos, etc.)

canvassing /'kænvəsɪŋ/ n solicitación (de votos, etc.), f

canyon /'kænyən/ n cañón, m

cap /kæp/ n gorra, f; (with a peak) montera, f; (type of military headgear with brim at front) quépis, m; (cardinal's) birrete, m; Educ. bonete, m; (pointed) caperuza, f; (woman's old-fashioned) cofia, f; (jester's) gorro de bufón, m; (on a bottle) cápsula, tapa, f. —vt Educ. conferir el grado (a). **cap and bells,** gorro de bufón, m. **cap and gown,** birrete y muceta, toga y birrete, toga y bonete. **to throw one's cap over the windmill,** echar la capa al toro. **to cap it all,** ser el colmo

capability /͵keipə'bɪlɪti/ n capacidad, f; aptitud, f

capable /'keipəbəl/ a capaz; competente; (of improvement) susceptible; (full of initiative) emprendedor

capably /'keipəbli/ adv competentemente

capacious /kə'peiʃəs/ a espacioso; grande; extenso

capacitate /kə'pæsɪ͵teit/ vt capacitar

capacity /kə'pæsɪti/ n capacidad, f; calidad, f; aptitud, f. **in one's c. as,** en calidad de. **seating c.,** número de asientos, m; (in aircraft) número de plazas, m

caparison /kə'pærəsən/ n caparazón, m

cape /keip/ n (cloak) capa, f; (short) capotillo, m, capeta, f; (fur) cuello, m; Geog. cabo, promontorio, m. **c. coat,** capote, m

Cape Horn /'keip 'hɔrn/ Cabo de Hornos, m

caper /'keipər/ vi (gambol) brincar, saltar; cabriolar, corcovear; (play) juguetear. —n travesura, f; zapateta, f; cabriola, f; (whim) capricho, m; Bot. alcaparra, f. **to c. about,** dar saltos, brincar; juguetear

capillary /'kæpə͵lɛri/ a capilar. —n vaso capilar, m

capital /'kæpɪtl/ a capital; mortal; de muerte; de vida; principal; (of letters) mayúscula; (very good) excelente. —n (city) capital, f; (letter) (letra) mayúscula, f; Com. capital, m; Archit. capitel, chapitel, m. **floating c.,** capital fluctuante, m. **idle c.,** fondos inactivos, m pl. **c. punishment,** pena de muerte, pena capital, pena de la vida, f. **C.!** ¡Estupendo! ¡Excelente! **to make c. out of,** aprovecharse de, sacar ventaja de

capitalism /'kæpɪtl̩,ɪzəm/ *n* capitalismo, *m*

capitalist /'kæpɪtl̩ɪst/ *n* capitalista, *mf*

capitalistic /,kæpɪtl̩'ɪstɪk/ *a* capitalista

capitalization /,kæpɪtl̩ə'zeɪʃən/ *n* capitalización, *f*

capitalize /'kæpɪtl̩,aiz/ *vt* capitalizar

Capitol /'kæpɪtl̩/ *n* Capitolio, *m*

capitulate /kə'pɪtʃə,leɪt/ *vi* capitular

capitulation /kə,pɪtʃə'leɪʃən/ *n* capitulación, *f*

capon /'keipɒn/ *n* capón, *m*

caprice /kə'pris/ *n* capricho, *m*

capricious /kə'prɪʃəs/ *a* caprichoso

capriciousness /kə'prɪʃəsnɪs/ *n* carácter inconstante, *m*; lo caprichoso

capsize /'kæpsaiz/ *vt Naut.* hacer zozobrar; volcar. —*vi Naut.* zozobrar; volcarse

capsule /'kæpsəl/ *n* (*Bot. Med. Chem. Zool.*) cápsula, *f*

captain /'kæptən/ *n* (*Mil. Nav. Aer.* and *Sports.*) capitán, *m, vt* capitanear. **to c. a team,** ser el capitán de un equipo. **group c.,** *Aer.* capitán de aviación, *m*

captaincy /'kæptənsi/ *n* capitanía, *f*

caption /'kæpʃən/ *n* (arrest) arresto, *m*; (heading) encabezamiento, título, pie, *m*; (cinema) subtítulo, *m*

captious /'kæpʃəs/ *a* capcioso, caviloso

captivate /'kæptə,veit/ *vt* cautivar, seducir

captivating /'kæptə,veitɪŋ/ *a* encantador, seductor

captive /'kæptɪv/ *a* cautivo, *n* cautivo (-va), prisionero (-ra), preso (-sa). **c. balloon,** globo cautivo, globo de observación, *m*

captivity /kæp'tɪvɪti/ *n* cautiverio, *m*

captor /'kæptər/ *n* el, *m*, (*f*, la) que hace prisionero (-ra)

capture /'kæptʃər/ *n* captura, *f*; presa, toma, *f*; *Law.* captura, *f.* —*vt* prender, capturar; tomar

car /kɑr/ *n* (chariot) carro, *m*; (tram) tranvía, *m*; (motor) automóvil, coche, *m*; (on a train) coche vagón, *m*. **sleeping car,** coche camas, *m*. **car park,** parque de automóviles, *m*

carafe /kə'ræf/ *n* garrafa, *f*

caramel /'kærəməl/ *n* caramelo, *m*; azúcar quemado, *m*

carat /'kærət/ *n* quilate, *m*

caravan /'kærə,væn/ *n* caravana, *f*; coche de gitanos, *m*; coche habitación, *m*

caraway /'kærə,wei/ *n* alcaravea, *f*

carbarn /'kɑr,bɑrn/ *n* encierro, *m* (Mexico), cochera, cochera de tranvías, *f,* cobertizo, cobertizo para tranvías, *m*

carbohydrate /,kɑrbou'haidreit/ *n* hidrato de carbono, *m*

carbolic /kɑr'bɒlɪk/ *a* carbólico. **c. acid,** ácido fénico, *m*

carbon /'kɑrbən/ *n* carbono, *m*. **c. copy,** copia en papel carbón, *f*. **c. dioxide,** anhídrido carbónico, *m*. **c. monoxide,** óxide

de carbono, *m*. **c. paper,** papel carbón, papel de calcar, *m*

carbonated /'kɑrbə,neitɪd/ *a* (beverage) carbónico (formal), con gas (informal)

carbonize /'kɑrbə,naiz/ *vt* carbonizar

carboy /'kɑrbɔi/ *n* damajuana, garrafa, *f*

carbuncle /'kɑrbʌŋkəl/ *n Med.* carbunco, *m*; (stone) carbúnculo, *m*

carburetor /'kɑrbə,reitər/ *n* carburador, *m*

carcass /'kɑrkəs/ *n* (animal) res muerta, *f*; (corpse) cadáver, *m*; (body) cuerpo, *m*; (of a ship) casco, *m*

card /kɑrd/ *n* (playing) naipe, *m*; (pasteboard) cartulina, *f*; (visiting, postal, etc.) tarjeta, *f*; (index) ficha, *f*; (for wool, etc.) carda, *f.* —*vt* (wool, etc.) cardar. **I still have a c. up my sleeve,** Me queda todavía un recurso. **to lay one's cards on the table,** poner las cartas boca arriba. **to play one's cards well,** *Fig.* jugar el lance. **admission c.,** billete de entrada, *m*. **post c.,** tarjeta postal, *f*. **visiting c.,** tarjeta de visita, *f*. **c.-case,** tarjetero, *m*. **c.-index,** fichero, *m.* —*vt* poner en el fichero. **c.-sharper,** fullero, *m*. **c.-table,** mesa de juego, *f*. **c. trick,** juego de manos con cartas, *m*

cardboard /'kɑrd,bɔrd/ *n* cartón, *m, a* de cartón

cardiac /'kɑrdi,æk/ *a* cardíaco

cardigan /'kɑrdɪgən/ *n* rebeca, chaqueta de punto, *f*

cardinal /'kɑrdn̩l/ *a* cardinal. —*n* cardenal, *m*. **c. number,** número cardinal, *m*. **c. points,** puntos cardinales, *m pl*

carding /'kɑrdɪŋ/ *n* (of wool, etc.) cardadura, *f*. **c. machine,** carda mecánica, *f*

cardiogram /'kɑrdiə,græm/ *n* cardiograma, *m*

care /kɛər/ *n* cuidado, *m*; atención, *f*; inquietud, ansia, *f*; (charge) cargo, *m.* —*vi* preocuparse; tener interés; (suffer) sufrir. **I don't c.,** Me es igual; No me importa. **I don't c. a straw,** No se me da un bledo. **They don't c. for eggs,** No les gustan los huevos. **We don't c. what his opinion is,** Su opinión nos tiene sin cuidado (or no nos importa). **to c. for,** cuidar, mirar por; (love) querer (a); (like) gustar. **Take c.!** ¡Cuidado! ¡Ojo! **Take c. not to spoil it!** ¡Ten cuidado que no lo estropees! **Would you c. to...?** ¿Le gustaría...? ¿Tendría inconveniente en...? **c. of,** (on a letter, etc.) en casa de. **c.-free,** *a* libre de cuidados

careen /kə'rin/ *vt* carenar. —*vi* dar a la banda

career /kə'rɪər/ *n* carrera, *f*; curso, *m.* —*vi* correr a carrera tendida; galopar

careful /'kɛərfəl/ *a* cuidadoso (de); atento (a); prudente. **Be c.!** ¡Cuidado! **to be c.,** tener cuidado

carefully /'kɛərfəli/ *adv* con cuidado. **drive c.,** manejar con cuidado; cuidadosamente; prudentemente; atentamente

carefulness /'kɛərfəlnɪs/ *n* cuidado, *m*; atención, *f*; prudencia, *f*

careless /'kɛərlıs/ a sin cuidado; indiferente (a); insensible (a); negligente; (of mistakes, etc.) de (or por) negligencia

carelessly /'kɛərlısli/ adv indiferentemente; negligentemente; descuidadamente

carelessness /'kɛərlısnıs/ n indiferencia, f; negligencia, f; descuido, m; omisión, f

caress /kə'rɛs/ n caricia, f, vt acariciar

caretaker /'kɛər,teikər/ n (of museums, etc.) guardián (-ana); (of flats, etc.) portero (-ra)

careworn /'kɛər,wɔrn/ a devorado de inquietud, ansioso

cargo /'kɑrgou/ n cargamento, m, carga, f. **c.-boat,** barco de carga, m

Caribbean Sea, the el Mar Caribe, m

caricature /'kærıkətʃər/ n caricatura, f, vt caricaturizar

caricaturist /'kærıkə,tʃurıst/ n caricaturista, mf

carles /'kɛəriz/ n caries, f

carious /'kɛəriəs/ a cariado. **to become c.,** cariarse

carnage /'kɑrnıdʒ/ n carnicería, f

carnal /'kɑrnl/ a carnal; sensual

carnation /kɑr'neiʃən/ n clavel, m

carnival /'kɑrnəvəl/ n carnaval. m. a de carnaval, carnavalesco

carnivore /'kɑrnə,vɔr/ n carnívoro, m

carnivorous /kɑr'nıvərəs/ a carnívoro

carol /'kærəl/ n villancico, m; canto, m. —vi cantar alegremente; (of birds) trinar, gorjear

carotid /kə'rɒtıd/ n carótida, f

carousal /kə'rauzəl/ n borrachera, f; holgorio, m, jarana, f

carouse /kə'rauz/ vi emborracharse. —n borrachera, orgía, f

carp /kɑrp/ n carpa, f, vi criticar, censurar

carpenter /'kɑrpəntər/ n carpintero, m, vi carpintear. **carpenter's bench,** banco de carpintero, m. **carpenter's shop,** carpintería, f

carpentry /'kɑrpəntri/ n carpintería, f

carpet /'kɑrpıt/ n alfombra, f; Fig. tapete, m. —vt cubrir de una alfombra, alfombrar; entapizar. **to be on the c.,** estar sobre el tapete. **c.-beater,** sacudidor de alfombras, m. **c. merchant,** alfombrista, m. **c. slippers,** zapatillas de fieltro, f pl. **c.-sweeper,** aspirador de polvo, m

carpeting /'kɑrpıtıŋ/ n alfombrado, m

carping /'kɑrpıŋ/ a capcioso, criticón

carriage /'kærıdʒ/ n (carrying) transporte, porte, m; (deportment) porte, continente, m, presencia, f; (vehicle) carruaje, m; carroza, f; coche, m; (railway) departamento, m; (chassis) chasis, bastidor, m; (of a typewriter, etc.) carro, m. **hackney c.,** coche de plaza, m. **c. and pair,** carroza de dos caballos, f. **c. door,** portezuela, f. **c.-forward,** porte debido. **c.-free,** franco de porte. **c.-paid,** porte pagado

carrier /'kæriər/ n el, m, (f, la) que lleva; portador (-ra); Com. mensajero, m; (on a car, bicycle) portaequipajes, m; (of a disease) vector, m; (aircraft) porta-aviones, m. **c.-pigeon,** paloma mensajera, f

carrion /'kæriən/ n carroña, f. **c.-crow,** chova, f

carrot /'kærət/ n zanahoria, f

carry /'kæri/ vt llevar; transportar; traer; conducir; (Mil. of arms) portar; (have with one) tener consigo; (an enemy position) tomar, ganar; (a motion) aprobar; (oneself) portarse; (one's point, etc.) ganar; (in the mind) retener; (conviction) convencer; (involve) implicar; (influence) influir; (send) despachar, enviar; (contain) incluir, comprender. —vi (of the voice, etc.) alcanzar, llegar. **The noise of the guns carried a long way,** El ruido de los cañones se oía desde muy lejos. **to fetch and c.,** traer y llevar. **to c. all before one,** vencer todos los obstáculos. **to c. into effect,** poner en efecto. **to c. one's audience with one,** captar (or cautivar) su auditorio. **to c. oneself well,** tener buena presencia. **to c. on one's back,** llevar a cuestas. **to c. the day,** quedar victorioso, quedar señor del campo. **to c. weight,** Fig. ser de peso. **to c. along,** llevar; (drag) arrastrar; conducir; acarrear. **to c. away,** llevar; llevarse, llevar consigo; (kidnap) robar, secuestrar; (of emotions) dominar; (by enthusiasm) entusiasmar; (inspire) inspirar. **to c. forward,** llevar a cabo; avanzar; fomentar; (bookkeeping) pasar a cuenta nueva. **to c. off,** (things) llevarse; (persons) llevar consigo (a); (abduct or steal) robar; (kill) matar; (a prize) ganar. **to c. (a thing) off well,** llevar la mejor parte, salir vencedor. **to c. on,** vt (a discussion, etc.) seguir, continuar. **c. on a conversation,** llevar una conversación; mantener; (a business, etc.) tener; dirigir. —vi ir tirando; seguir trabajando. **to c. out,** realizar, llevar a cabo; hacer, ejecutar, efectuar; (a promise) cumplir. **to c. through,** llevar a cabo

cart /kɑrt/ n carro, m. —vt acarrear; llevar. **c.-horse,** caballo de tiro, m. **c.-load,** carretada, f, carro, m. **c.-wheel,** rueda de carro, f; (somersault) voltereta, f

carte blanche /'kɑrt 'blɑntʃ/ n carta blanca, f

cartel /kɑr'tɛl/ n cartel, m

cartilage /'kɑrtlıdʒ/ n cartílago, m

carton /'kɑrtn/ n caja de cartón, f

cartoon /kɑr'tun/ n (design for tapestry, etc.) cartón, m; caricatura, f

cartoonist /kɑr'tunıst/ n caricaturista, mf

cartridge /'kɑrtrıdʒ/ n cartucho, m. **blank c.,** cartucho sin bala, m. **c.-belt,** cartuchera, canana, f. **c.-case,** cápsula de proyectil, f

carve /kɑrv/ vt tallar, labrar; grabar; cortar; (meat, etc.) trinchar; (a career, etc.) hacer, forjarse

carver /'kɑrvər/ n tallador, m; (at table) trinchador, m; (implement) trinchante, m

carving /'kɑrvıŋ/ n talla, f; (design) tallado, m. **c.-knife,** trinchante, m

cascade /kæs'keid/ n cascada, catarata, f,
salto de agua, m; Fig. chorro, m. —vi
chorrear

case /keis/ n caso, m; Law. proceso, m,
causa, f; Gram. caso, m; Med. caso, m;
enfermo (-ma); (box) caja, f; (for scissors, etc.) vaina, f; (for a cushion, etc.)
funda, f; (for jewels, manicure implements, etc.) estuche, m; (of a piano,
watch and Print.) caja, f; (for documents)
carpeta, f; (glass) vitrina, f; (for a book)
sobrecubierta, f; (dressing) neceser, m.
—vt cubrir; forrar; resguardar. **pack-
ing-c.**, caja de embalaje, f. **c. of goods**,
caja de mercancías, f; bulto, m. **in any
c.**, en todo caso; venga lo que venga. **in
c.**, por si acaso. **in c. of emergency**, en
caso de urgencia. **in such a c.**, en tal
caso. **in the c. of**, en el caso de; respecto
a. **lower c.**, Print. caja baja, f. **upper c.**,
Print. caja alta, f. **c.-hardened**, (of iron)
templado; Fig. endurecido, indiferente

case closed! ¡asunto concluido!

cash /kæʃ/ n efectivo, metálico, m; dinero
contante, m; Inf. dinero, m; Com. caja, f.
—vt cobrar; pagar, hacer efectivo. **hard
or ready c.**, dinero contante, m. **to pay
c.**, pagar al contado. **c. on delivery**, (C.
O.D.) contra reembolso. **c. on hand**, efectivo en caja, m. **c.-book**, libro de caja, m.
c.-box, caja, f. **c.-desk**, caja, f. **c. down**,
pago al contado, m. **c. prize**, premio en
metálico, m. **c.-register**, caja registradora,
f

cashew /kæʃu/ n anacardo, m

cashier /kæ'ʃɪər/ n cajero (-ra). —vt
degradar. **cashier's desk**, caja, f

cash machine n cajero automático, m

cashmere /'kæʒmɪər/ n cachemira, f

casino /kə'sinou/ n casino, m

cask /kæsk/ n pipa, barrica, f, tonel, m;
cuba, f

casket /'kæskɪt/ n cajita, arquilla, f, co-
frecito, m

casserole /'kæsəˌroul/ n cacerola, f

cast /kæst/ vt arrojar, tirar; (in fishing,
the anchor, dice, darts, lots, a net,
glances, blame, etc.) echar; (skin) mudar;
(lose) perder; (a shadow, etc.) proyectar;
(a vote) dar; (mold) vaciar; (accounts)
echar, calcular; (a horoscope) hacer; (the
parts in a play) repartir; (an actor for a
part) dar el papel de; (metals) colar,
fundir. **the shadow by the wall**, la
sombra proyectada por el muro. **to c. anchor**, echar anclas, anclar. **to c. in one's
lot with**, compartir la suerte de. **to c.
something in a person's teeth**, echar en
cara (a). **to c. lots**, echar suertes. **to c.
about**, meditar, considerar; imaginar;
(devise) inventar. **to c. aside**, desechar;
poner a un lado; abandonar. **to c. away**,
tirar lejos; desechar; (money) derrochar,
malgastar. **to be c. away**, Naut. naufragar. **to c. down**, (overthrow) derribar,
destruir; (eyes) bajar; (depress) desanimar, deprimir; (humiliate) humillar. **to
be c. down**, estar deprimido. **c. iron**, n

hierro colado, hierro fundido, m. **c.-iron**,
a de hierro colado; Fig. inflexible. **to c.
off**, quitarse; desechar; (a wife) repudiar;
(desert) abandonar; (free oneself) librarse
(de). **c.-off**, n desecho, m. **c.-off clothing**, ropa de desecho, f. **to c. out**, echar
fuera; hacer salir; excluir. **to c. up**,
echar; vomitar; (a sum) sumar; (something at a person) reprochar

cast /kæst/ n (of dice, fishing-line)
echada, f; (of a net) redada, f; (worm)
molde, m; (of a play) reparto, m; (of
mind) inclinación, f; (in the eye) defecto
en la mirada, m; (of colour) matiz, tinte,
m. **c. of features**, facciones, f pl, fisonomía, f. **plaster c.**, vaciado, m.

castanets /ˌkæstə'nɛts/ n pl castañuelas,
f pl

castaway /'kæstəˌwei/ n náufrago (-ga);
Fig. perdido (-da)

caste /kæst/ n casta, f; clase social, f. **to
lose c.**, desprestigiarse

castigate /'kæstɪˌgeit/ vt castigar

Castile /kæ'stil/ Castilla, f

Castilian /kæ'stɪlyən/ a castellano. —n
castellano (-na); (language) castellano, m

casting /'kæstɪŋ/ n lanzamiento, m; (of
metals) fundición, colada, f; obra de
fundición, f. **c.-net**, esparavel, m. **c.-
vote**, voto de calidad, m

castle /'kæsəl/ n castillo, m; (in chess)
torre, f, roque, m. **to build castles in
Spain**, hacer castillos en el aire

castor /'kæstər/ n Zool. castor, m; (for
sugar) azucarero, m; (cruet) convoy, m;
(on chairs, etc.) ruedecilla, roldana, f. **c.-
oil**, aceite de ricino, m. **c.-sugar**, azúcar
en polvo, m

castrate /'kæstreit/ vt castrar, capar

casual /'kæʒuəl/ a fortuito, accidental;
ligero, superficial; Inf. despreocupado. **c.
worker**, jornalero, m

casually /'kæʒuəli/ adv por casualidad;
de paso; negligentemente

casualness /'kæʒuəlnɪs/ n Inf. negligencia, despreocupación, f

casualty /'kæʒuəlti/ n víctima, f; herido,
m; Mil. baja, f; pl **casualties**, heridos, m
pl; muertos, m pl. **c.-list**, lista de vícti-
mas, f; Mil. lista de bajas, f

cat /kæt/ n gato (-ta). **She is an old cat**,
Ella es una vieja chismosa. **to be like a
cat on hot bricks**, estar como en brasas,
to let the cat out of the bag, tirar de la
manta. **to lead a cat-and-dog life**, vivir
como perros y gatos. **cat's-cradle**, (game)
cunas, f pl. **cat's paw**, (person) hombre
de paja, m; Naut. bocanada de viento, f.
cat o' nine tails, gato de siete colas, m,
penca, f. **catwhisker**, Radio. detector, m

cataclysm /'kætəˌklɪzəm/ n cataclismo,
m

catacombs /'kætəˌkoumz/ n pl catacumbas, f pl

Catalan /'kætlˌæn/ a catalán (-ana). —n
catalán; (language) catalán, m

catalogue /'kætlˌɔg/ n catálogo, m, vt catalogar

Catalonia /ˌkæt·l'ouniə/ Cataluña, f

cat-and-mouse /'kæt ŋ 'maus/ n el juego de ratón, m

catapult /'kætə,pʌlt/ n Mil. catapulta, f; Aer. catapulta (para lanzar aviones), f; (toy) tirador de gomas, m. —vt tirar con una catapulta (or con un tirador de gomas); (throw) lanzar

cataract /'kætə,rækt/ n catarata, cascada, f, salto de agua, m; (of the eye) catarata, f

catarrh /kə'tɑr/ n catarro, m; constipado, resfriado, m

catastrophe /kə'tæstrəfi/ n catástrofe, f, desastre, m; (in drama) desenlace, m

catastrophic /ˌkætəs'trofɪk/ a catastrófico

catch /kætʃ/ vt coger; agarrar, asir; (capture) prender, haber; (a disease) contraer; (habit) tomar; (on a hook, etc.) enganchar; (surprise) sorprender, (understand) comprender; (hear) oír; (with blows, etc.) dar. —vi (of a lock) encajarse; (become entangled) engancharse; (of a fire) encenderse. **to c. a glimpse of,** ver por un instante (a); alcanzar a ver, entrever. **to c. at,** asir; agarrarse (a); echar mano de; procurar asir; alargar la mano hacia; (an idea, etc.) adoptar con entusiasmo. **to c. on,** (be popular) tener éxito; (understand) comprender. **to c. out,** coger en el acto; coger en un error; Sports. coger. **to c. up,** coger; interrumpir. **to c. up with,** (a person) alcanzar; (news) ponerse al corriente de

catch /kætʃ/ n presa, f; (of fish) redada, pesca, f; (of a window, etc.) cerradura, f; (latch) pestillo, m; (trick) trampa, f; Mus. canon, m. **a good c.,** (matrimonial) un buen partido. **to have a c. in one's voice,** hablar con voz entrecortada. **c.-as-c.-can,** lucha libre, f

catching /'kætʃɪŋ/ a contagioso

catchment /'kætʃmənt/ n desagüe, m

catchword /'kætʃ,wərd/ n reclamo, m; (theater cue) pie, apunte, m; (slogan) mote, m

catchy /'kætʃi/ a atractivo. **It's a c. tune,** Es una canción que se pega

catechism /'kæti,kizəm/ n catequismo, m

categorical /ˌkæti'gorikəl/ a categórico

category /'kæti,gori/ n categoría, f

cater /'keitər/ vi proveer, abastecer. **to c. for all tastes,** atender a todos los gustos

caterer /'keitərər/ n despensero (-ra)

catering /'keitərɪŋ/ n provisión, f

caterpillar /'kætə,pilər/ n oruga, f. **c. tractor,** tractor de orugas, m

caterwaul /'kætər,wɔl/ vi (of a cat) maullar

catharsis /kə'θɑrsis/ n Med. purga, f; Fig. catarsis, f

cathedral /kə'θidrəl/ n catedral, f

catheter /'kæθɪtər/ n catéter, m

cathode /'kæθoud/ n cátodo, m. **c. rays,** rayos catódicos, m pl. **c. ray tube,** tubo de rayos catódicos, m

catholic /'kæθəlɪk/ a católico

Catholicism /kə'θolə,sɪzəm/ n catolicismo, m

cattle /'kætl/ n ganado vacuno, m; ganado, m; animales, m pl. **c.-dealer,** ganadero, m. **c.-lifter,** hurtador de ganado, m. **c.-pen,** corral, m. **c.-raiser,** criador de ganado, m. **c.-raising,** ganadería, f. **c.-ranch,** hacienda de ganado, estancia, f. **c.-show,** exposición de ganado, f. **c.-truck,** vagón de ferrocarril para ganado, m

cattle rustler n abigeo, cuatrero, ladrón de ganado, m

cattle rustling n abigeato, m

catty /'kæti/ a gatuno; malicioso, chismoso

Caucasian /kɔ'keiʒən/ a and n caucáseo (-ea)

Caucasus, the /'kɔkəsəs/ el Cáucaso

cauldron /'kɔldrən/ n caldera, f

cauliflower /'kɔlə,flauər/ n coliflor, f

caulk /kɔk/ vt calafatear

causality /kɔ'zælɪti/ n causalidad, f

cause /kɔz/ n causa, f; (reason) motivo, m, razón, f; (lawsuit) proceso, m. —vt causar; ocasionar, suscitar; (oblige) hacer, obligar (a). **final c.,** Philos. causa final, f. **to have good c. for,** tener buen motivo para

causeway /'kɔz,wei/ n dique, m; acera, f

caustic /'kɔstɪk/ a cáustico; Fig. mordaz. **c. soda,** sosa cáustica, f

cauterization /ˌkɔtərə'zeiʃən/ n cauterización, f

cauterize /'kɔtə,raiz/ vt cauterizar

cautery /'kɔtəri/ n cauterio, m

caution /'kɔʃən/ n prudencia, cautela, f; (warning) amonestación, f; aviso, m. —vt amonestar. **to proceed with c.,** ir con prudencia; ir despacio

"Caution" /'kɔʃən/ (road sign) «Precaución»

cautionary /'kɔʃə,nɛri/ a (of tales) de escarmiento

cautious /'kɔʃəs/ a cauteloso, cauto; prudente, circunspecto

cautiously /'kɔʃəsli/ adv cautamente; prudentemente. **to go c.,** Inf. ir con pies de plomo

cavalcade /ˌkævəl'keid/ n cabalgata, f

cavalier /ˌkævə'liər/ n jinete, m; caballero, m; galán, m, a arrogante, altanero

cavalry /'kævəlri/ n caballería, f. **c.-man,** jinete, soldado de a caballo, m

cave /keiv/ n cueva, caverna, f. **to c. in,** hundirse; desplomarse; Fig. rendirse. **c.-man,** hombre cavernícola, m

cavern /'kævərn/ n caverna, f

cavernous /'kævərnəs/ a cavernoso

caviar /'kævi,ɑr/ n caviar, m

cavil /'kævəl/ vi cavilar

cavity /'kævɪti/ n cavidad, f; hoyo, m; hueco, m; (in a lung) caverna, f

cavy /'keivi/ n cobayo (-ya), conejillo (-lla) de las Indias

caw /kɔ/ n graznido, m, vi graznar, grajear

cayenne /kai'en/ n pimentón, m

cease /sis/ vi cesar (de), dejar de; parar. —vt cesar de; parar de; (payments, etc.) suspender; discontinuar. **C. fire!** ¡Cesar fuego!

ceaseless /'sislıs/ a incesante,continuo, sin cesar

ceaselessly /'sislısli/ adv sin cesar, incesantemente

ceasing /'sisɪŋ/ n cesación, f. **without c.,** sin cesar

cedar /'sidər/ n (tree and wood) cedro, m. **red c.,** cedro dulce, m

cede /sid/ vt ceder, traspasar; (admit) conceder

cedilla /sɪ'dılə/ n zedilla, f

ceiling /'silɪŋ/ n techo, m; Aer. altura máxima, f. **c. price,** máximo precio, m

celebrate /'selə,breit/ vt celebrar; solemnizar. **Their marriage was celebrated in the autumn,** Su casamiento se solemnizó en el otoño

celebrated /'selə,breitıd/ a célebre, famoso

celebration /,selə'breiʃən/ n celebración, f; festividad, f

celebrity /sə'lɛbrıti/ n celebridad, f

celerity /sə'lɛrıti/ n celeridad, f

celery /'sɛləri/ n apio, m

celestial /sə'lɛstʃəl/ a celestial

celibacy /'sɛləbəsi/ n celibato, m

celibate /'sɛləbıt/ a célibe. —n célibe, mf

cell /sɛl/ n celda, f; (Bot. Biol.) célula, f; (bees, wasps) celdilla, f; Elec. elemento, m

cellar /'sɛlər/ n sótano, m; (wine) bodega, f

cellist /'tʃɛlıst/ n violoncelista, mf

cello /'tʃɛlou/ n violoncelo, m

cellophane /'sɛlə,fein/ n (papel) celofán, m

cellular /'sɛlyələr/ a celular, celuloso

cellular phone /'sɛlyələr 'foun/ n móvil, m, celular, m (West. Hem.)

celluloid /'sɛlyə,lɔid/ n celuloide, f

cellulose /'sɛlyə,lous/ n celulosa, f

Celt /kɛlt, sɛlt/ n celta, mf

Celtic /'kɛltık, 'sɛl-/ a celta

cement /sɪ'mɛnt/ n cemento, m, vt cementar

cemetery /'sɛmɪ,tɛri/ n cementerio, m

censor /'sɛnsər/ n censor, m, vt censurar. **banned by the c.,** prohibido por la censura

censorious /sɛn'sɔriəs/ a severo; crítico

censorship /'sɛnsər,ʃıp/ n censura, f

censure /'sɛnʃər/ vt censurar, culpar, criticar

census /'sɛnsəs/ n censo, m. **to take the c.,** formar el censo, levantar el censo, tomar el censo, empadronar

census-taking /'sɛnsəs ,teikıŋ/ n la formación del censo, la formación de los censos, f, el levantamiento del censo, el levantamientos de los censos, m

cent /sɛnt/ n (coin) centavo, m. **per c.,** por ciento. **not to have a c.,** not to **have a c. to one's name,** no tener donde caer muerto

centenarian /,sɛntn̩'ɛəriən/ a and n centenario (-ia)

centenary /sɛn'tɛnəri/ n centenario, m, a centenario

center /'sɛntər/ n centro, m; medio, m. —a central; centro. —vt centrar; concentrar (en). **nervous centers,** centros nerviosos, m pl. **c.-forward,** Sports. delantero centro, m. **c.-half,** Sports. medio centro, m. **c. of gravity,** centro de gravedad, m. **c.-piece,** centro, m

centerfold /'sɛntər,fould/ n páginas centrales, f pl

centigrade /'sɛntɪ,greid/ a centígrado

centimeter /'sɛntə,mitər/ n centímetro, m. **cubic c.,** centímetro cúbico, m

centipede /'sɛntə,pid/ n ciempiés, m

central /'sɛntrəl/ a central; céntrico. **The house is very c.,** La casa es muy céntrica. **C. American,** a and n centroamericano (-na). **c. depot,** central, f. **c. heating,** calefacción central, f

centralize /'sɛntrə,laiz/ vt centralizar

centrifugal /sɛn'trıfyəgəl/ a centrífugo

centripetal /sɛn'trıpıtl/ a centrípeto

century /'sɛntʃəri/ n siglo, m, centuria, f

ceramic /sə'ræmık/ a cerámico

ceramics /sə'ræmıks/ n cerámica, f

cereal /'sıəriəl/ a cereal. —n cereal, m

cerebellum /,sɛrə'bɛləm/ n cerebelo, m

cerebral /sə'ribrəl/ a cerebral

cerebrum /sə'ribrəm/ n cerebro, m

ceremonial /,sɛrə'mouniəl/ a ceremonial; de ceremonia. —n ceremonial, m

ceremonially /,sɛrə'mouniəli/ adv ceremonialmente; con ceremonia

ceremonious /,sɛrə'mouniəs/ a ceremonioso

ceremoniousness /,sɛrə'mouniəsnıs/ n ceremonia, formalidad, f

ceremony /'sɛrə,mouni/ n ceremonia, f. **to stand on c.,** gastar cumplidos. **without c.,** sin cumplidos

cerise /sə'ris/ a de color cereza

certain /'sɜrtn/ a (sure) seguro; cierto; (unerring) certero. **a c. man,** cierto hombre. **I am c. that...,** Estoy seguro de que... **to know for c.,** saber con toda seguridad, saber a ciencia cierta. **to make c. of,** asegurarse de

certainly /'sɜrtn̩li/ adv seguramente; ciertamente; (as a reply) sin duda; naturalmente. **c. not,** no, por cierto; claro que no

certainty /'sɜrtn̩ti/ n certidumbre, f; seguridad, f; convicción, f. **of a c.,** seguramente

certificate /n sər'tıfıkıt; v –,keit/ n certificado, m; fe, f; partida, f; Com. bono, título, m; diploma, m. —vt certificar. **birth c.,** partida de nacimiento, f. **death c.,** partida de defunción, f. **marriage c.,** partida de casamiento, f

certify /'sɜrtə,fai/ vt certificar; atestiguar; declarar

certitude /'sɜrtɪ,tyud/ n certeza, certidumbre, f

Cervantine /sər'væntɪn/ a cervantino

cervix /'sɜrvɪks/ n Anat. cerviz, f

Cesarean /sə'zɛəriən/ a cesáreo

cessation /sɛ'seifən/ n cesación, f

cession /'sefən/ n cesión, f

cesspool /'sɛs,pul/ n sumidero, m

cf. cfr.

chafe /tʃeif/ vt (rub) frotar; (make sore) escocer, rozar. —vi raerse, desgastarse; escocerse; Fig. impacientarse; Fig. irritarse, enojarse

chaff /tʃæf/ n (of grain) ahechadura, f; (in a general sense and Fig.) paja, f; tomadura de pelo, burla, f. —vt (a person) tomar el pelo (a), burlarse de

chafing /'tʃeifɪŋ/ n frotación, f; (soreness) excoriación, f, Fig. impaciencia, f. **c.-dish**, escalfador, m

chagrin /ʃə'grɪn/ n mortificación, decepción, f, disgusto, m. vt mortificar

chain /tʃein/ n cadena, f, vt encadenar. **c. of mountains**, cadena de montañas, cordillera, f. **c.-gang**, cadena de presidiarios, f. **c.-mail**, cota de malla, f. **c.-stitch**, cadeneta, f. **c.-stores**, empresa con sucursales, f. **in chains**, cargado de cadenas (e.g., prisoners in chains, prisioneros cargados de cadenas)

chair /tʃɛər/ n silla, f; Educ. cátedra, f; (of a meeting) presidencia, f. —vt llevar en hombros (a). **C.!** ¡Orden! **easy-c.**, (silla) poltrona, f. **to be in the c.**, ocupar la presidencia; presidir. **to take a c.**, sentarse, tomar asiento. **to take the c.**, presidir. **swivel-c.**, silla giratoria, f. **wheel-c.**, silla de ruedas, f. **c.-back**, respaldo de una silla, m

chairman /'tʃɛərmən/ n presidente (-ta). **to act as c.**, presidir

chairmanship /'tʃɛərmən,ʃɪp/ n presidencia, f

chaise longue /'ʃeiz 'lɔŋ/ n meridiana, tumbona, f

chalet /ʃæ'lei/ n chalet, m

chalice /'tʃælɪs/ n cáliz, m

chalk /tʃɔk/ n creta, f; (for writing, etc.) tiza, f, yeso, m. —vt marcar con tiza; dibujar con tiza. **to c. up**, apuntar. **not by a long c.**, no con mucho

chalky /'tʃɔki/ a cretáceo; cubierto de yeso; (of the complexion) pálido

challenge /'tʃælɪndʒ/ n provocación, f; (of a sentry) quién vive, m; (to a duel, etc.) desafío, reto, m; Law. recusación, f; concurso, m. —vt (of a sentry) dar el quién vive (a); desafiar; provocar; Law. recusar

challenger /'tʃælɪndʒər/ n desafiador (-ra)

challenging /'tʃælɪndʒɪŋ/ a desafiador, provocador

chamber /'tʃeimbər/ n cuarto, m; sala, f; (bed-) dormitorio, m, alcoba, f; cámara, f;

Mech. cilindro, m; (in a gun) cámara, f. **c. concert**, concierto de música de cámara, m. **c.-maid**, camarera, f. **c. music**, música de cámara, f. **c. of commerce**, cámara de comercio, f. **c.-pot**, orinal, m

chameleon /kə'miliən/ n camaleón, m

chamois /'ʃæmi/ n gamuza, f, rebeco, m. **c. leather**, piel de gamuza, f

chamomile /'kæmə,mail/ n camomila, manzanilla, f

champ /tʃæmp/ vt mascar; morder. —vi Fig. impacientarse

champagne /ʃæm'pein/ n (vino de) champaña, m

champion /'tʃæmpiən/ n campeón, m; defensor (-ra)

championship /'tʃæmpiən,ʃɪp/ n campeonato, m; (of a cause) defensa, f

chance /tʃæns/ n casualidad, f; suerte, fortuna, f; posibilidad, f; probabilidad, f; esperanza, f; (opportunity) ocasión, oportunidad, f. —a fortuito; accidental. —vi impers suceder, acontecer. —vt Inf. arriesgar; probar. **by c.**, por casualidad; por ventura. **if by c.**, si acaso. **If it chances that...**, Si sucede que; Si a mano viene que... **The chances are that...**, Las probabilidades son que... **There is no c.**, No hay posibilidad; No hay esperanza. **to let the c. slip**, perder la ocasión. **to take a c.**, aventurarse, arriesgarse. **to c. to do**, hacer algo por casualidad. **to c. upon**, encontrar por casualidad.

chancellor /'tʃænsələr/ n canciller, m; Educ. cancelario, m. **C. of the Exchequer**, Ministro de Hacienda, m

chandelier /,ʃændḷ'iər/ n araña de luces, f

chandler /'tʃændlər/ n velero, m

change /tʃeindʒ/ vt cambiar; transformar; modificar; (clothes) mudarse (de); (one thing for another) trocar; sustituir (por). —vi cambiar; (clothes) mudarse. **All c.!** ¡Cambio de tren! **to c. a check**, cambiar un cheque. **to c. color**, cambiar de color; (of persons) mudar de color. **to c. countenance**, demudarse. **to c. front**, Fig. cambiar de frente. **to c. hands**, (of shops, etc.) cambiar de dueño. **to c. one's clothes**, cambiar de ropa, mudarse de ropa. **to c. one's mind**, cambiar de opinión. **to c. one's tune**, cambiar de tono. **to c. the subject**, cambiar de conversación. **to c. trains**, cambiar de trenes

change /tʃeindʒ/ n cambio, m; transformación, f; modificación, f; variedad, f; (of clothes, feathers) muda, f; (Theat. of scene) mutación, f; (money) cambio, m; (small coins) suelto, m; (stock) bolsa, f; lonja, f; vicisitud, f; (of bells) toque (de campanas), m. **for a c.**, para cambiar, como un cambio; para variar. **small c.**, suelto, m, moneda suelta, f. **c. for the better**, cambio para mejor, m. **c. for the worse**, cambio para peor, m. **c. of clothes**, cambio de ropa, m; **c. of front**, Fig. cambio de frente, m. **c. of heart**, cambio de sentimientos, m; conversión, f.

c. **of life,** menopausia, *f.* **c.-over,** cambio, *m*

changeability /ˌtʃeɪndʒəˈbɪlɪti/ *n* mutabilidad, *f;* inconstancia, volubilidad, *f*

changeable /ˈtʃeɪndʒəbəl/ *a* voluble; variable; cambiable

changeless /ˈtʃeɪndʒlɪs/ *a* immutable; constante

changeling /ˈtʃeɪndʒlɪŋ/ *n* niño (-ña) cambiado (-da) por otro

changing /ˈtʃeɪndʒɪŋ/ *a* cambiante. **c.-room,** vestuario, *m*

channel /ˈtʃænl/ *n* (of a river, etc.) cauce, *m;* canal, *m;* (irrigation) acequia, *f;* (strait) estrecho, *m; Fig.* conducto, *m;* (furrow) surco, *m,* estría, *f;* (of information, etc.) medio, *m.* —*vt* acanalar; (furrow) surcar; (conduct) encauzar

chant /tʃænt/ *n* canto llano, *m;* salmo, *m.* —*vt* salmodiar; cantar; recitar

chaos /ˈkeɪɒs/ *n* caos, *m*

chaotic /keɪˈɒtɪk/ *a* caótico, desordenado

chap /tʃæp/ *vt* agrietar. —*vi* agrietarse. —*n Inf.* chico, *m*

chapbook /ˈtʃæpˌbʊk/ *n* librito de cordel, *m*

chapel /ˈtʃæpəl/ *n* capilla, *f;* templo disidente, *m*

chaperon /ˈʃæpəˌroʊn/ *n* dama de compañía, señora de compañía, dueña, *f, vt* acompañar

chaplain /ˈtʃæplɪn/ *n* capellán, *m*

chaplet /ˈtʃæplɪt/ *n* guirnalda, *f;* rosario, *m;* (necklace) collar, *m*

chapter /ˈtʃæptər/ *n* (in a book) capítulo, *m; Eccl.* cabildo, capítulo, *m.* **a c. of accidents,** una serie de desgracias. **c. house,** sala capitular, *f*

char /tʃɑr/ *vt* (a house, etc.) fregar, hacer la limpieza de; (of fire) carbonizar. —*n Inf.* fregona, asistenta, *f*

character /ˈkærɪktər/ *n* carácter, *m;* (of a play) personaje, *m;* (role) papel, *m;* (eccentric) tipo, *m.* **Gothic characters,** caracteres góticos, *m pl.* **in c.,** característico; apropiado. **in the c. of,** en el papel de. **out of c.,** nada característico; no apropiado. **principal c.,** protagonista, *mf.* **c. actor,** actor de carácter, *m.* **c. actress,** actriz de carácter

characteristic /ˌkærɪktəˈrɪstɪk/ *a* característico, típico. —*n* característica, peculiaridad, *f,* rasgo, *m*

characterize /ˈkærɪktəˌraɪz/ *vt* caracterizar

characterless /ˈkærɪktərlɪs/ *a* sin carácter; insípido, soso

charade /ʃəˈreɪd/ *n* charada, *f*

charcoal /ˈtʃɑrˌkoʊl/ *n* carbón de leña, *m;* (for blacking the face, etc.) carbón, *m; Art.* carboncillo, *m.* **c. burner,** carbonera, *f.* **c. crayon,** carboncillo, *m.* **c. drawing,** dibujo al carbón, *m*

charge /tʃɑrdʒ/ *vt* cargar; (enjoin) encargar; (accuse) acusar (de); (with price) cobrar; (with a mission, etc.) encomendar, confiar; *Mil.* acometer, atacar. —*vi Mil.* atacar; (a price) cobrar, pedir. **How**

much do you c.? ¿Cuánto cobra Vd.? **to c. with a crime,** acusar de un crimen

charge /tʃɑrdʒ/ *n* (load) carga, *f;* (price) precio, *m;* gasto, *m;* (on an estate, etc.) derechos, *m pl;* (task) encargo, *m;* (office or responsibility) cargo, *m;* (guardianship) tutela, *f;* (care) cuidado, *m;* exhortación, *f; Law.* acusación, *f; Mil.* ataque, *m.* **He is in c. of...,** Está encargado de...; Es responsable de... **The diamonds are in the c. of...,** Los diamantes están a cargo de. **depth c.,** carga de profundidad, *f.* **extra c.,** gasto suplementario, *m;* (on a train) suplemento, *m.* **free of c.,** gratis. **c. for admittance,** entrada, *f.* **to bring a c. against,** acusar de. **to give (someone) in c.,** entregar (una persona) a la policía. **to take c. of,** encargarse de

chargé d'affaires /ʃɑrˈʒeɪ dəˈfɛər/ *n* encargado de negocios, *m*

charger /ˈtʃɑrdʒər/ *n* caballo de guerra, corcel, *m*

chariness /ˈtʃɛərɪnɪs/ *n* cautela, *f*

chariot /ˈtʃærɪət/ *n* carro, *m*

charioteer /ˌtʃærɪəˈtɪər/ *n* auriga, *m*

charitable /ˈtʃærɪtəbəl/ *a* caritativo; benéfico

charitableness /ˈtʃærɪtəbəlnɪs/ *n* caridad, *f*

charity /ˈtʃærɪti/ *n* caridad, *f;* beneficencia, *f;* (alms) limosna, *f.* **c. child,** niño (-ña) de la doctrina

charlatan /ˈʃɑrlətn/ *n* charlatán (-ana); (quack) curandero, *m*

charlatanism /ˈʃɑrlətnˌɪzəm/ *n* charlatanismo, *m;* curanderismo, *m*

charm /tʃɑrm/ *n* hechizo, *m;* ensalmo, *m;* (amulet) amuleto, *m;* (trinket) dije, *m;* (general sense) encanto, atractivo, *m.* —*vt* encantar, hechizar, fascinar

charming /ˈtʃɑrmɪŋ/ *a* encantador; atractivo, seductor, fascinador

charm school *n* academia de buenos modales, *f*

chart /tʃɑrt/ *n Naut.* carta de marear, *f;* (graph) gráfica, *f.* —*vt* poner en una carta

charter /ˈtʃɑrtər/ *n* carta, *f;* (of a city, etc.) fuero, *m;* cédula, *f.* —*vt* (a ship) fletar; (hire) alquilar. **royal c.,** cédula real, *f*

charwoman /ˈtʃɑrˌwʊmən/ *n* fregona, asistenta; mujer de hacer faenas, *f*

chary /ˈtʃɛəri/ *a* cauteloso; desinclinado; frugal

chase /tʃeɪs/ *n* caza, *f;* seguimiento, *m.* —*vt* cazar; dar caza (a); perseguir; (drive off) ahuyentar; *Fig.* dispar, hacer desaparecer; (engrave) cincelar. **to give c. to,** dar caza (a). **to go on a wild goose c.,** buscar pan de trastrigo

chasm /ˈkæzəm/ *n* sima, *f,* precipicio, *m; Fig.* abismo, *m*

chassis /ˈtʃæsi/ *n* chasis, *m*

chaste /tʃeɪst/ *a* casto

chasten /ˈtʃeɪsən/ *vt* castigar; corregir; humillar, mortificar

chastened /ˈtʃeɪsənd/ *a* sumiso, dócil

chastise /tʃæsˈtaɪz/ *vt* castigar

chastisement /tʃæs'taizmənt/ n castigo, m

chastity /'tʃæstɪti/ n castidad, f

chat /tʃæt/ vi charlar, conversar. —n conversación, charla, f. **They are having a c.,** Están charlando, Están de palique

chattels /'tʃætəlz/ n pl bienes muebles, efectos, m pl

chatter /'tʃætər/ vi charlar; hablar por los codos, chacharear; (of water) murmurar; (of birds) piar; (of monkeys, etc.) chillar; (of teeth) rechinar; (of a person's teeth) dar diente con diente. —n charla, f; cháchara, parla, f; (of water) murmurio, m; (of birds) gorjeo, m; (of monkeys, etc.) chillidos, m pl

chatterbox /'tʃæt,ər bɒks/ n badajo, m, cotorra, f

chatterer /'tʃætərər/ n hablador (-ra)

chattering /'tʃætərɪŋ/ n charla, cháchara, f; (of teeth) rechinamiento, m, a gárrulo, chacharero, locuaz

chauffeur /'ʃoufər/ n chófer, m

chauvinism /'ʃouvə,nɪzəm/ n chauvinismo, m

cheap /tʃip/ a barato; (of works of art) cursi. —adv barato. **dirt c.,** baratísimo. **to be dirt c.,** estar por los suelos. **to hold** (something) **c.,** tener en poco, estimar en poco

cheapen /'tʃipən/ vt disminuir el valor de; reducir el precio de

cheaply /'tʃipli/ adv barato; a bajo precio

cheapness /'tʃipnɪs/ n baratura, f; precio módico, m; mal gusto, m, vulgaridad, f

cheat /tʃit/ n engaño, fraude, m, estafa, f; (person) fullero (-ra), trampista, mf embustero (-ra). —vt engañar; defraudar; (at cards) hacer trampas. **He cheated me out of my property,** Me defraudó de mi propiedad

cheating /'tʃitɪŋ/ n engaño, m; fraude, m; (at cards) fullerías, f pl

check /tʃɛk/ n (chess) jaque, m; revés, m; impedimento, m; contratiempo, m; (of a bridle) cama, f; (control) freno, m; control, m; (checking) verificación, f; (ticket) papeleta, f; (counterfoil) talón, m; (square) cuadro, m; (bill) cuenta, f; (bank) cheque, m. —vt (chess) jaquear; (hamper) refrenar; detener; contrarrestar; (test) verificar. —vi detenerse. **to c. off,** marcar. **to c. oneself,** detenerse; contenerse. **to c. up,** comprobar. **crossed c.,** cheque cruzado, m. **c. book,** libro de cheques, m

checked /tʃɛkt/ a (cloth) a cuadros

checker /'tʃɛkər/ vt escaquear; (variegate) motear, salpicar; diversificar. **a checkered career,** una vida accidentada

checking /'tʃɛkɪŋ/ n represión, f; control, m; verificación, f; comprobación, f

checkmate /'tʃɛk,meit/ n mate, jaque, mate, m. —vt dar mate (a); (plans, etc.) frustrar

checks and balances n pl frenos y contrapesos, m pl

cheek /tʃik/ n mejilla, f; Inf. descaro, m;

insolencia, f. **They have plenty of c.,** Tienen mucha cara dura. **c. by jowl,** cara a cara; al lado de. **c.-bone,** pómulo, m

cheekiness /'tʃikinɪs/ n cara dura, insolencia, f

cheeky /'tʃiki/ a insolente, descarado; (pert) respondón

cheep /tʃip/ n pío, m, vi piar

cheer /tʃiər/ n alegría, f, regocijo, m; vítor, m; aplauso, m. —vt animar; alegrar, regocijar; vitorear, aplaudir. **to be of good c.,** estar alegre; ser feliz. **C. up!** ¡Ánimo! **to c. up,** animarse, cobrar ánimo

cheerful /'tʃiərfəl/ a alegre; jovial; de buen humor. **It is a c. room,** Es un cuarto alegre

cheerfully /'tʃiərfəli/ adv alegremente; (willingly) con mucho gusto, de buena gana

cheerfulness /'tʃiərfəlnɪs/ n alegría, f; jovialidad, f; buen humor, m

cheering /'tʃiərɪŋ/ n vítores, m pl, aclamaciones, f pl, a animador

cheerleader /'tʃiər,lidər/ n porro, m

cheerless /'tʃiərlɪs/ a triste; sin alegría; (dank) obscuro, lóbrego

cheese /tʃiz/ n queso, m. **cream c.,** queso de nata, m. **grated c.,** queso rallado, m. **c.-dish,** quesera, f. **c.-mite,** cresa, f. **c.-paring,** n corteza de queso, f. —a Inf. tacaño. **c.-vat,** quesera, f

cheesy /'tʃizi/ a caseoso

chemical /'kɛmɪkəl/ a químico. **c. warfare,** defensa química, f

chemicals /'kɛmɪkəlz/ n pl productos químicos, m pl

chemise /ʃə'miz/ n camisa (de mujer), f

chemist /'kɛmɪst/ n químico, m. **chemist's shop,** farmacia, f; droguería, f

chemistry /'kɛməstri/ n química, f

cherish /'tʃɛrɪʃ/ vt amar, querer; (a hope, etc.) abrigar, acariciar

cherry /'tʃɛri/ n (fruit) cereza, f; (tree and wood) cerezo, m. **c. brandy,** aguardiente de cerezas, m. **c. orchard,** cerezal, m

cherub /'tʃɛrəb/ n querub(e), querubín, m

chess /tʃɛs/ n ajedrez, m. **c.-board,** tablero de ajedrez, m

chessman /'tʃɛs,mæn/ n pieza de ajedrez, f

chest /tʃɛst/ n arca, f, cofre, m; cajón, m; Anat. pecho, m. **to throw out one's c.,** inflar el pecho. **c.-expander,** extensor, m. **c. of drawers,** cómoda, f

chestnut /'tʃɛs,nʌt/ n (tree) castaño, m; (fruit) castaña, f; (color) castaño, color castaño, m; (horse) caballo castaño, m; (joke) chiste del tiempo de Maricastaña, m, a castaño. **horse-c. tree,** castaño de Indias, m

chew /tʃu/ vt mascar, mascullar; (ponder) masticar

chewing /'tʃuɪŋ/ n masticación, f. **c.-gum,** chicle, m

chianti /ki'anti/ n (wine) quianti, m

chiaroscuro /kɪˌɑrə'skyʊrou/ *n* claroscuro, *m*

chic /ʃik/ *n* chic, *m*, elegancia, *f*

chicanery /ʃɪ'keinəri/ *n* sofistería, *f*

chicken /'tʃɪkən/ *n* pollo, *m*. **c.-hearted,** medroso, cobarde, timorato. **c.-pox,** varicela, *f*

chickenwire /'tʃɪkən,waiᵊr/ *n* alambrillo, *m*

chickpea /'tʃɪk,pi/ *n* garbanzo, *m*

chickweed /'tʃɪk,wid/ *n* pamplina, *f*

chicory /'tʃɪkəri/ *n* achicoria, *f*

chide /tʃaid/ *vt* reprender, reñir

chidingly /'tʃaidɪŋli/ *adv* en tono de reprensión

chief /tʃif/ *n* jefe, *m*, *a* principal; primero; en jefe; mayor. **c.-of-staff,** jefe de estado mayor, *m*

chiefly /'tʃifli/ *adv* principalmente; sobre todo

chieftain /'tʃiftən/ *n* caudillo, *m;* (of a clan) cabeza, jefe, *m*

chiffon /ʃɪ'fɒn/ *n* chifón, *m*, gasa, *f*

chiffonier /ˌʃɪfə'nɪər/ *n* cómoda, *f*

chignon /'ʃinyɒn/ *n* moño, *m*

child /tʃaild/ *n* niño (-ña); hijo (-ja). **from a c.,** desde niño, desde la niñez. **with c.,** encinta, embarazada. **How many children do you have?** ¿Cuántos hijos tiene Vd.? **child's play,** juegos infantiles, *m pl; Fig.* niñerías, *f pl.* **c. welfare,** puericultura, *f*

childbirth /'tʃaild,bɜrθ/ *n* parto, *m*

childhood /'tʃaildhʊd/ *n* niñez, infancia, *f.* **from his c.,** desde su niñez, desde niño

childish /'tʃaildɪʃ/ *a* de niño; aniñado; pueril; fútil. **to grow c.,** chochear

childishly /'tʃaildɪʃli/ *adv* como un niño

childishness /'tʃaildɪʃnɪs/ *n* puerilidad, *f;* futilidad, *f*

child labor *n* trabajo de menores, trabajo infantil, *m*

childless /'tʃaildlɪs/ *a* sin hijos; sin niños

childlike /'tʃaild,laik/ *a* de niño, aniñado; pueril

children /'tʃɪldrən/ See **child**

Chilean /'tʃɪliən/ *a and n* chileno (-na)

chili /'tʃɪli/ *n* chile, pimento de cornetilla, *m*

chill /tʃɪl/ *n* frío, *m;* (of fear, etc.) estremecimiento, *m;* (illness) resfriado, *m;* (unfriendliness) frialdad, frigidez, *f*, *a* frío; (unfriendly) frígido. —*vt* enfriar; helar; (with fear, etc.) dar escalofríos (de); (discourage) desalentar. —*vi* tener frío; tener escalofríos. **to take the c. off,** templar, calentar un poco

chilliness /'tʃɪlinɪs/ *n* frío, *m;* (unfriendliness) frialdad, frigidez, *f*

chilly /'tʃɪli/ *a* frío; (sensitive to cold) friolero; (of politeness, etc.) glacial, frígido

chime /tʃaim/ *n* juego de campanas, *m;* repique, campaneo, *m;* armonía, *f.* —*vi* (of bells) repicar; *Fig.* armonizar. **to c. the hour,** dar la hora

chimera /kɪ'mɪərə/ *n* quimera, *f*

chimerical /kɪ'mɛrɪkəl/ *a* quimérico

chimney /'tʃɪmni/ *n* chimenea, *f;* (of a lamp) tubo (de lámpara), *m*. **c.-corner,** rincón de chimenea, *m*. **c.-pot,** sombrerete de chimenea, *m*. **c.-stack,** chimenea, *f*. **c.-sweep,** limpiador de chimeneas, deshollinador, *m*

chimpanzee /ˌtʃɪmpæn'zi, tʃɪm'pænzi/ *n* chimpancé, *m*

chin /tʃɪn/ *n* barbilla, barba, *f*, mentón, *m*. **c.-rest,** mentonera, *f*. **c.-strap,** barboquejo, *m;* venda para la barbilla, *f*

china /'tʃainə/ *n* china, porcelana, *f;* loza, *f*. **—a** de porcelana; de loza. **c. cabinet,** chinero, *m*

chinchilla /tʃɪn'tʃɪlə/ *n* (animal and fur) chinchilla, *f*

Chinese /tʃai'niz/ *a and n* chino (-na); (language) chino, *m*. **C. lantern,** farolillo de papel, *m*. **C. white,** óxido blanco de cinc, *m*

chink /tʃɪŋk/ *n* resquicio, *m*, grieta, hendidura, *f;* (clink) retintín, tintineo, *m*. **—vi** tintinar

chintz /tʃɪnts/ *n* zaraza, *f*

chip /tʃɪp/ *n* astilla, *f;* (counter) ficha, *f*. **—vt** picar; cincelar. **a c. off the old block,** de tal palo tal astilla. **c. potatoes,** patatas fritas, *f pl*

chiropodist /kɪ'rɒpədɪst/ *n* pedicuro, *m*, callista, *mf*

chiropractor /'kairəˌpræktər/ *n* quiropráctico, *m*

chirp /tʃɜrp/ *vi* piar, gorjear. **—n** pío, gorjeo, *m*

chirping /'tʃɜrpɪŋ/ *n* pïada, *f*, *a* gárrulo, piante

chisel /'tʃɪzəl/ *n* escoplo, cincel, *m*, *vt* cincelar. **cold c.,** cortafrío, *m*

chitchat /'tʃɪt,tʃæt/ *n* charla, *f*

chivalrous /'ʃɪvəlrəs/ *a* caballeroso

chivalry /'ʃɪvəlri/ *n* caballería, *f;* caballerosidad, *f*. **novel of c.,** novela de caballería, *f*

chive /tʃaiv/ *n Bot.* cebollana, *f*, cebollino, *m*

chlorine /'klɔrin/ *n* cloro, *m*

chloroform /'klɔrəˌfɔrm/ *n* cloroformo, *m*, *vt* cloroformizar

chock-full /'tʃɒk 'fʊl/ *a* lleno de bote en bote

chocolate /'tʃɔkəlɪt/ *n* chocolate, *m*, *a* de chocolate. **thick drinking-c.,** chocolate a la española, *m*. **thin drinking-c.,** chocolate a la francesa, *m*. **c. shop,** chocolatería, *f*

choice /tʃɔis/ *n* selección, *f;* preferencia, *f;* elección, *f;* opción, *f;* alternativa, *f;* lo más escogido. **—a** escogido, selecto; excelente. **for c.,** con preferencia

choir /kwaiᵊr/ *n* coro, *m*. **c.-boy,** niño del coro, *m*. **c.-master,** maestro de capilla, *m*

choke /tʃouk/ *vi* ahogarse; atragantarse; obstruirse. **—vt** ahogar; estrangular. **to c. with laughter,** ahogarse de risa. **to c. back,** (words) tragar. **to c. off,** (a person) disuadir (de); quitarse de encima(a).

to c. up, obstruir, cerrar, obturar; (hide) cubrir, tapar

choking /'tʃoukiŋ/ a asfixiante, sofocante. —n ahogamiento, m, sofocación, f

cholera /'kɒlərə/ n cólera, m

cholesterol /kə'lɛstə,roul/ n colesterina, f

choose /tʃuz/ vt escoger; elegir; optar por; (wish) querer, gustar. **They will do it when they c.,** Lo harán cuando les parezca bien. **If you c.,** Si Vd. quiere; Si Vd. gusta. **He was chosen as Mayor,** Fue elegido alcalde. **There is nothing to c. between them,** No hay diferencia entre ellos; Tanto vale el uno como el otro. **You cannot c. but love her,** No puedes menos de quererla

choosing /'tʃuziŋ/ n selección, f; (for an office, etc.) elección, f

chop /tʃɒp/ vt cortar; (mince) picar; (split) hender, partir. —n (meat) chuleta, f; (jaw) quijada, f. **to c. about, round,** (of the wind) girar, virar. **to c. down,** (trees) talar. **to c. off,** separar; cortar; tajar. **to c. up,** cortar en pedazos

choppy /'tʃɒpi/ a picado, agitado

chopstick /'tʃɒp,stɪk/ n palillo chino, m

choral /'kɔrəl/ a coral

chord /kɔrd/ n cuerda, f; Mus. acorde, m; **the right c.,** Fig. la cuerda sensible

choreographer /,kɔri'ɒgrəfər/ n coreógrafo, m

chorus /'kɔrəs/ n coro, m; (in revues) comparsa, f, acompañamiento, m; (of a song) refrán, m. **to sing in c.,** cantar a coro. **c. girl,** corista, f

chosen /'tʃouzən/ a escogido; elegido. **the c.,** los elegidos

Christ /kraist/ n Cristo, Jesucristo, m

christen /'krɪsən/ vt bautizar

christening /'krɪsəniŋ/ n bautizo, m, a bautismal, de bautizo

Christian /'krɪstʃən/ a cristiano. —n cristiano (-na). **C. name,** nombre de pila, m

Christianity /,krɪstʃi'ænɪti/ n cristianismo, m

Christmas /'krɪsməs/ n Navidad, f. **A Merry C.!** ¡Felices Pascuas (de Navidad)! **Father C.,** Padre Noel, m; (Sp. equivalent) Los Reyes Magos. **C. box,** regalo de Navidad, m. **C. card,** felicitación de Navidad, f. **C. carol,** villancico de Navidad, m. **C. Day,** día de Navidad, m. **C. Eve,** Nochebuena, f. **C.-tide,** Navidades, f pl. **C. tree,** árbol de Navidad, m

Christopher Columbus /'krɪstəfər kə'lʌmbəs/ Cristóbal Colón, m

chrome /kroum/ n cromo, m. **c. yellow,** amarillo de cromo, m

chromosome /'kroumə,soum/ n cromosoma, m

chronic /'krɒnɪk/ a crónico; inveterado

chronicle /'krɒnɪkəl/ n crónica, f, vt narrar

chronicler /'krɒnɪklər/ n cronista, mf

chronological /,krɒnl'ɒdʒɪkəl/ a

cronológico. **in c. order,** por orden cronológico

chronology /krə'nɒlədʒi/ n cronología, f

chrysanthemum /krɪ'sænθəməm/ n crisantemo, m

chubbiness /'tʃʌbinɪs/ n gordura, f

chubby /'tʃʌbi/ a regordete, gordito. **c.-cheeked,** mofletudo

chuck /tʃʌk/ vt (throw) lanzar, arrojar; (discontinue) abandonar, dejar. —n (in a lathe) mandril, m. **to c. under the chin,** acariciar la barbilla (a). **to c. away,** derrochar; malgastar, perder. **to c. out,** echar, poner en la calle

chuckle /'tʃʌkəl/ vi reír entre dientes. —n risa ahogada, f; risita, f

chum /tʃʌm/ n compinche, camarada, mf. **to c. up with,** ser camarada de

chunk /tʃʌŋk/ n pedazo, trozo, m

church /tʃɜrtʃ/ n Iglesia, f; (Protestant) templo, m, vt (a woman) purificar. **poor as a c. mouse,** más pobre que las ratas. **the C. of England,** la iglesia anglicana. **to go to c.,** ir a misa; ir al templo. **c. music,** música sagrada, f

churchyard /'tʃɜrtʃ,yard/ n cementerio, m

churl /tʃɜrl/ n patán, m

churlish /'tʃɜrlɪʃ/ a grosero, cazurro; (mean) tacaño, ruin

churn /tʃɜrn/ n mantequera, f. —vt (cream) batir; Fig. azotar, agitar

chute /ʃut/ n (for grain, etc.) manga de tolva, f; vertedor, m; (in flats and fun fairs) tobogán, deslizadero, m

cicada /sɪ'keidə/ n cigarra, f

cicatrize /'sɪkə,traiz/ vt cicatrizar. —vi cicatrizarse

cider /'saidər/ n sidra, f

cigar /sɪ'gɑr/ n cigarro, m. **c.-box,** cigarrera, f. **c.-case,** petaca, f, cigarrera, f. **c.-cutter,** corta-puros, m

cigarette /,sɪgə'rɛt/ n cigarrillo, pitillo, m. **c.-butt,** colilla, f. **c.-case,** pitillera, f. **c.-holder,** boquilla, f. **c.-lighter,** encendedor de cigarrillos, m. **c.-paper,** papel de fumar, m

cinch /sɪntʃ/ n (of a saddle) cincha, f; Inf. ganga, f; Inf. seguridad, f. **c.-strap,** látigo, m

cinder /'sɪndər/ n ceniza, f; carbonilla, f. **red-hot c.,** rescoldo, m. **c.-track,** pista de ceniza, f

cinematography /,sɪnəmə'tɒgrəfi/ n cinematografía, f

cinnamon /'sɪnəmən/ n (spice) canela, f; (tree) canelo, m; color de canela, m

cipher /'saifər/ n Math. cero, m; Fig. nulidad, f; (code) cifra, f; monograma, m. **to be a mere c.,** ser un cero

circle /'sɜrkəl/ n círculo, m; (revolution) vuelta, f; (group) grupo, m; (club, etc.) centro, m; (cycle) ciclo, m. —vt dar vueltas alrededor de; rodear; ceñir; an application, examination, etc.) en un círculo. —vi dar vueltas; volar en círculo; (of a hawk, etc.)

cernerse. **dress-c.,** *Theat.* anfiteatro, *m.*
the family c., el círculo de la familia. **to
come full c.,** dar la vuelta. **upper c.,**
Theat. segundo piso, *m.* **vicious c.,** círculo vicioso, *m*

circuit /'sɜrkɪt/ *n* circuito, *m;* (tour) gira,
f; (revolution) vuelta, *f;* (radius) radio,
m. **short c.,** corto circuito, *m.* **c.-breaker,**
corta-circuitos, *m*

circuit court of appeals *n* tribunal
colegial de circuito, *m*

circuitous /sər'kyuɪtəs/ *a* indirecto; tortuoso

circular /'sɜrkyələr/ *a* circular; redondo.
—*n* carta circular, *f;* circular, *f.* **c. tour,**
viaje redondo, *m*

circularize /'sɜrkyələ,raiz/ *vt* enviar circulares (a)

circulate /'sɜrkyə,leit/ *vi* circular. —*vt*
hacer circular; poner en circulación;
(news, etc.) divulgar, diseminar

circulating library /'sɜrkyə,leitɪŋ/ *n* biblioteca por subscripción, *f*

circulation /,sɜrkyə'leifən/ *n* circulación,
f; (of a newspaper, etc.) tirada, circulación, *f.* **c. of the blood,** circulación de la
sangre, *f*

circulatory /'sɜrkyələ,tɔri/ *a* circulatorio

circumcise /'sɜrkəm,saiz/ *vt* circuncidar

circumcised /'sɜrkəm,saizd/ *a* circunciso

circumcision /,sɜrkəm'sɪʒən/ *n* circuncisión, *f*

circumference /sər'kʌmfərəns/ *n* circunferencia, *f*

circumlocution /,sɜrkəmlou'kyufən/ *n*
circumlocución, *f*

circumnavigate /,sɜrkəm'nævɪ,geit/ *vt*
circumnavegar

circumscribe /'sɜrkəm,skraib/ *vt* circunscribir; *Fig.* limitar

circumscribed /'sɜrkəm,skraibd/ *a* circunscripto; *Fig.* limitado

circumscription /,sɜrkəm'skrɪpfən/ *n*
circunscripción, *f;* *Fig.* limitación, restricción, *f*

circumspect /'sɜrkəm,spɛkt/ *a* circunspecto; discreto, correcto; prudente

circumspection /,sɜrkəm'spɛkfən/ *n* circunspección, *f;* prudencia, *f*

circumspectly /'sɜrkəm,spɛktli/ *adv* con
circunspección; prudentemente

circumstance /'sɜrkəm,stæns/ *n* circunstancia, *f;* detalle, *m.* **aggravating c.,** circunstancia agravante, *f.* **attenuating c.,**
circunstancia atenuante, *f.* **in the
circumstances,** en las circunstancias. **in
easy circumstances,** en buena posición,
acomodado. **Do you know what his
circumstances are?** ¿Sabes cuál es su situación económica? **under the
circumstances,** bajo las circunstancias

circumstantial /,sɜrkəm'stænfəl/ *a* circunstancial; detallado. **c. evidence,**
prueba de indicios, *f*

ircumvent /,sɜrkəm'vɛnt/ *vt* frustrar;
ɳpedir

circumvention /,sɜrkəm'vɛnfən/ *n*
frustración, *f*

circus /'sɜrkəs/ *n* circo, *m;* plaza redonda, *f;* (traffic) redondel, *m*

cirrhosis /sɪ'rousɪs/ *n* cirrosis, *f*

cistern /'sɪstərn/ *n* tanque, *m;* cisterna, *f,*
aljibe, *m*

citation /sai'teifən/ *n* *Law.* citación, *f;*
cita, *f*

cite /sait/ *vt* citar

citizen /'sɪtəzən/ *n* ciudadano (-na); vecino (-na); natural, *mf.* **fellow c.,** conciudadano, *m;* compatriota, *mf*

citizenship /'sɪtəzən,fɪp/ *n* ciudadanía, *f*

citric /'sɪtrɪk/ *a* cítrico

citron /'sɪtrən/ *n* (fruit) cidra, *f;* (tree) cidro, *m*

city /'sɪti/ *n* ciudad, *f,* *a* municipal

civic /'sɪvɪk/ *a* cívico; municipal

civics /'sɪvɪks/ *n* civismo, *m*

civil /'sɪvəl/ *a* civil; doméstico; (polite)
cortés, atento; (obliging) servicial. **C.
Aeronautics Board,** Dirección general de
aeronáutica civil, *f.* **c. defense,** defensa
pasiva, *f.* **c. engineer,** ingeniero de
caminos, canales y puertos, *m.* **C. Service,** cuerpo de empleados del Estado, *m*

civilian /sɪ'vɪlyən/ *a* civil. —*n* ciudadano
(-na). **c. dress,** traje paisano, *m*

civility /sɪ'vɪlɪti/ *n* civilidad, cortesía, *f*

civilization /,sɪvələ'zeifən/ *n* civilización,
f

civilize /'sɪvə,laiz/ *vt* civilizar

civilly /'sɪvəli/ *adv* civilmente, cortésmente

clad /klæd/ *a* vestido

claim /kleim/ *vt* reclamar; pretender
exigir; *Law.* demandar; (assert) afirmar.
—*vi* *Law.* pedir en juicio. —*n*
reclamación, *f;* pretensión, *f;* *Law.* demanda, *f;* (in a gold-field, etc.) concesión,
f; (right) derecho, *m.* **to lay c. to,** pretender a; exigir. **to put in a c. for,** reclamar

claimant /'kleimənt/ *n* *Law.* demandante,
mf; pretendiente (-ta); *Com.* acreedor
(-ra)

clairvoyance /klɛr'vɔiəns/ *n* doble
vista, *f*

clairvoyant /klɛr'vɔiənt/ *n* vidente, *m*

clam /klæm/ *n* almeja, chirla, *f*

clamber /'klæmbər/ *vi* trepar, encaramarse. —*n* subida difícil, *f*

clamminess /'klæmɪnɪs/ *n* viscosidad,
humedad, *f*

clammy /'klæmi/ *a* viscoso; húmedo, mojado

clamor /'klæmər/ *n* clamor, estruendo, *m;*
gritería, vocería, *f.* —*vi* gritar, vociferar.
to c. against, protestar contra. **to c. for,**
pedir a voces

clamorous /'klæmərəs/ *a* clamoroso, ruidoso, estrepitoso

clamp /klæmp/ *n* grapa, *f;* abrazadera, *f;*
tornillo, *m;* (pile) montón, *m.* —*vt*
empalmar; sujetar, lañar

clan /klæn/ n clan, m; familia, f; partido, grupo, m

clandestine /klæn'dɛstɪn/ a clandestino, furtivo

clang /klæŋ/ vi sonar; (of a gate, etc.) rechinar. —vt hacer sonar. —n sonido metálico, m; estruendo, m

clank /klæŋk/ vi dar un ruido metálico; crujir. —vt hacer sonar; (glasses) hacer chocar. —n ruido metálico, m; el crujir

clannish /'klænɪʃ/ a exclusivista

clap /klæp/ vt (hands) batir; (spurs, etc.) poner rápidamente; (one's hat on) encasquetarse (el sombrero); (shut) cerrar apresuradamente. —vi aplaudir. —n (of the hands) palmada, f; (of thunder) trueno, m; (noise) ruido, m. **to c. eyes on,** echar la vista encima de. **to c. someone on the back,** dar una palmada en la espalda (a). **to c. the hands,** batir las palmas

clapper /'klæpər/ n (of a bell) badajo, m

clapping /'klæpɪŋ/ n aplausos, m pl

claret /'klærɪt/ n clarete, m

clarification /,klærəfə'keɪʃən/ n clarificación, f; elucidación, f

clarify /'klærə,faɪ/ vt clarificar; elucidar, aclarar

clarinet /,klærə'nɛt/ n clarinete, m

clarinettist /,klærə'nɛtɪst/ n clarinete, m

clarity /'klærɪti/ n claridad, f; lucidez, f

clash /klæʃ/ vi chocar; encontrarse; (of events) coincidir; (of opinions, etc.) oponerse, estar en desacuerdo; (of colors) desentonar, chocar. —n estruendo, fragor, m; choque, m; Mil. encuentro, m; (of opinions, etc.) desacuerdo, m; disputa, f

clasp /klæsp/ vt (a brooch, etc.) abrochar, enganchar; (embrace) abrazar; (of plants, etc.) ceñir. —n (brooch) broche, m; (of a belt) hebilla, f; (of a necklace, handbag, book) cierre, m; (for the hair) pasador, m. **to c. someone in one's arms,** tomar en los brazos (a), abrazar. **c.-knife,** navaja, f

class /klæs/ n clase, f; (kind) especie, f; (of exhibits, etc.) categoría, f. —vt clasificar. **in a c. by itself,** único en su línea. **the lower classes,** las clases bajas. **the middle classes,** la clase media. **the upper classes,** la clase alta. **c.-mate,** condiscípulo (-la). **c.-room,** sala de clase, f; salón de clase, f. **c. war,** lucha de clases, f

classic /'klæsɪk/ a clásico. —n clásico, m

classical /'klæsɪkəl/ a clásico

classifiable /'klæsə,faɪəbəl/ a clasificable

classification /,klæsəfɪ'keɪʃən/ n clasificación, f

classified /'klæsə,faɪd/ a (secreto) reservado, secreto; (advertisement) por palabras

classified advertisement n anuncio por palabras, m

classify /'klæsə,faɪ/ vt clasificar

clatter /'klætər/ vi hacer ruido; (knock) golpear; (of loose horseshoes) chacolotear. —vt hacer ruido con; chocar (una

cosa contra otra). —n ruido, m; (hammering) martilleo, m; (of horseshoes) chacoloteo, m; (of a crowd) estruendo, m, bulla, f. **John clattered along the street,** Los pasos de Juan resonaban por la calle

clause /klɔz/ n Gram. cláusula, f; Law. condición, estipulación, cláusula, f

claustrophobia /,klɔstrə'foubiə/ n claustrofobia, f

clavicle /'klævɪkəl/ n clavícula, f

claw /klɔ/ n garra, f; (of a lobster, etc.) tenaza, f; (hook) garfio, gancho, m. —vt arañar, clavar las uñas en; (tear) desgarrar. **c.-hammer,** martillo de orejas, m

clay /kleɪ/ n arcilla, f; barro, m; (pipe) pipa de barro, f. **c.-pit,** barrizal, m

clean /klin/ a limpio; puro, casto. —adv limpio; completamente; exactamente. **to make a c. sweep (of),** no dejar títere con cabeza. **to make a c. breast of,** confesar sin tormento, no quedarse con nada en el pecho. **to show a c. pair of heels,** tomar las de Villadiego. **c. bill of health,** patente de sanidad, m. **c.-cut,** bien definido; claro. **c.-limbed,** bien proporcionado, gallardo. **c.-shaven,** lampiño; sin barba, bien afeitado

clean /klin/ vt limpiar; (streets) barrer; (a floor) fregar; (dry)clean) lavar al seco. **to c. one's hands (teeth),** limpiarse las manos (los dientes). **to c. up,** limpiar; (tidy) asear; poner en orden

cleaner /'klinər/ n limpiador (-ra); (charwoman) fregona, f; (stain remover) sacamanchas, m; (drycleaner, person) tintorero (-ra)

cleaning /'klinɪŋ/ n limpieza, f, a de limpiar. **dry-c.,** lavado al seco, m. **c. rag,** trapo de limpiar, m

cleanliness /'klɛnlɪnɪs/ n limpieza, f; aseo, m

cleanse /klɛnz/ vt limpiar; lavar; purgar; purificar

cleansing /'klɛnzɪŋ/ n limpieza, f; lavamiento, m; purgación, f; purificación, f

clear /klɪər/ a claro; (of the sky) sereno, despejado; transparente; (free (from)) libre (de); (open) abierto; (of profit, etc.) neto; (of thoughts, etc.) lúcido; (apparent) evidente, explícito; (of images) distinto; absoluto; (whole) entero, completo. **c. majority,** mayoría absoluta, f. **c. profit,** beneficio neto, m. **c.-cut,** bien definido. **c.-headed,** perspicaz; inteligente. **c.-sighted,** clarividente

clear /klɪər/ vt aclarar; despejar; limpiar; librar (de); quitar; (one's throat) carraspear; (Com. stock) liquidar; (of a charge) absolver; (one's character) vindicar; (avoid, miss) evitar; (jump) salvar, saltar; (a court, etc.) desocupar; (a debt) satisfacer; (an account) saldar; (a mortgage) cancelar; (win) ganar; hacer un beneficio de; (through customs) despachar en la aduana. —vi (of sky, etc.) serenarse; escampar; (of wine, etc.) aclararse; despacharse en la aduana. **to c. the table,**

levantar la mesa, levantar los manteles.
to c. the way, abrir calle; *Fig.* abrir paso.
to c. away, *vt* quitar; disipar. —*vi*
disiparse. **to c. off,** *vt* (finish) terminar;
(debts) pagar; (discharge) despedir. —*vi*
(of rain) despejarse, escampar; marcharse. **to c. out,** *vt* limpiar; (a drain,
etc.) desatascar; vaciar; echar. —*vi*
marcharse, escabullirse. **C. out!** ¡Fuera! **c.
the decks,** hacer zafarrancho. **c. the
decks for action,** hacer zafarrancho. **to
c. up,** *vt* poner en orden; (a mystery,
etc.) aclarar, resolver, *vi* (of weather)
serenarse, escampar, despejarse

clearance /'klɪərəns/ *n* (of trees, etc.)
desmonte, *m;* eliminación, *f;* expulsión, *f;*
Mech. espacio muerto, *m;* despacho de
aduana, *m.* **to make a c. of,** deshacerse
de. **c. sale,** liquidación, venta de saldos, *f*

clearing /'klɪərɪŋ/ *n* (in a wood) claro,
m; desmonte, *m;* (*Com.* of goods) liquidación, *f;* (of one's character) vindicación, *f.*
c.-house, casa de compensación, *f*

cleavage /'klividʒ/ *n* hendimiento, *m;* (in
views, etc.) escisión, *f*

cleave /kliv/ *vt* partir; abrir; (air, water,
etc.) surcar, hender. —*vi* partirse; (stick)
pegarse, adherirse

cleaver /'klivər/ *n* partidor, *m;* hacha, *f*

cleft /kleft/ *n* hendedura, fisura, rendija, *f;*
abertura, *f.* **c.-palate,** paladar hendido, *m*

clemency /'klɛmənsi/ *n* (of weather)
benignidad, *f;* (of character, etc.) clemencia, *f*

clement /'klɛmənt/ *a* (of weather)
benigno; (of character, etc.) clemente,
benévolo

clench /klɛntʃ/ *vt* agarrar; (teeth, etc.)
apretar; (a bargain) cerrar, concluir

clergy /'klɜrdʒi/ *n* clero, *m,* clérigos, *m pl*

clergyman /'klɜrdʒimən/ *n* clérigo, *m*

cleric /'klɛrɪk/ *n* eclesiástico, *m*

clerical /'klɛrɪkəl/ *a* clerical; de oficina.
c. error, error de oficina, *m.* **c. work,** trabajo de oficina, *m*

clerk /klɜrk/ *n* (clergyman) clérigo, *m;* (in
an office) oficinista, escribiente, *m;* oficial, *m;* secretario, *m*

clever /'klɛvər/ *a* listo, inteligente; ingenioso; hábil; (dexterous) diestro

cleverly /'klɛvərli/ *adv* hábilmente;
diestramente, con destreza

cleverness /'klɛvərnɪs/ *n* talento, *m;* inteligencia, *f;* habilidad, *f;* (dexterity)
destreza, *f*

cliché /kli'ʃei/ *n* frase hecha, frase de cajón, *f*

click /klɪk/ *vi* (of the tongue) dar un
chasquido; (of a bolt, etc.) cerrarse a
golpe; hacer tictac. —*vt* (one's tongue)
chascar; (a bolt, etc.) cerrar a golpe. —*n*
golpe seco, *m;* tictac, *m;* (of the tongue)
chasquido, *m.* **to c. one's heels together,** hacer chocar los talones

client /'klaɪənt/ *n* cliente, *mf;* (customer)
parroquiano (-na)

clientele /,klaɪən'tɛl/ *n* clientela, *f*

cliff /klɪf/ *n* acantilado, *m,* roca, escarpa,
f

climate /'klaɪmɪt/ *n* clima, *m*

climax /'klaɪmæks/ *n* culminación, *f;*
(rhetoric) gradación, *f;* (of a play,
etc.) desenlace, *m*

climb /klaɪm/ *vt* and *vi* trepar; escalar;
montar; subir; ascender. **rate of c.,** *Aer.*
velocidad ascensional, *f.* **to c. down,** bajar; *Fig.* echar el pie atrás. **to c. over,**
(obstacles) salvar. **to c. up,** encaramarse
por; subir por; montar

climber /'klaɪmər/ *n* alpinista, *mf;* (plant)
trepadera, enredadera, *f;* (social) arribista,
mf

clinch /klɪntʃ/ *vt* (nails, etc.) remachar,
rebotar; (a bargain, etc.) cerrar; (an argument, etc.) remachar. —*n* (wrestling)
cuerpo a cuerpo, *m*

cling /klɪŋ/ *vi* pegarse (a); agarrarse (a);
(of scents) pegarse; (follow) seguir. **They
clung together for an instant,** Quedaron
abrazados un instante

clinging /'klɪŋɪŋ/ *a* tenaz; (of plants,
etc.) trepador; (of persons) manso, dócil.
to be a c. vine, *Inf.* ser una malva

clinic /'klɪnɪk/ *n* clínica, *f*

clink /klɪŋk/ *vi* retiñir; (of glasses) cho-
carse. —*vt* hacer sonar; (glasses) chocar.
—*n* retintín, *m;* (of a hammer) martilleo,
m; sonido metálico, *m;* (of glasses) choque, *m*

clip /klɪp/ *vt* (grasp) agarrar; (sheep, etc.)
esquilar; (trim) recortar, cercenar;
(prune) podar; (a ticket) taladrar. —*n*
pinza, *f;* (paper-clip) sujetapapeles, *m;*
Mech. grapa, escarpia, *f;* (for ornament)
sujetador, *m.* **to c. a person's wings,**
Fig. cortar (or quebrar) las alas (a)

clipper /'klɪpər/ *n* (person) esquilador
(-ra); (*Naut.* and *Aer.*) clíper, *m; pl*
clippers, tenazas de cortar, *f pl;* (for
pruning) podaderas, *f pl;* (punch) taladro,
m

clipping /'klɪpɪŋ/ *n* (of sheep, etc.) esquileo, *m;* (of a newspaper, etc.) recorte,
m

clique /klik/ *n* camarilla, *f*

cloak /klouk/ *n* capa, *f;* manto, *m; Fig.*
velo, *m.* —*vt* encapotar; embozar; (conceal) ocultar, encubrir. **c. and sword
play,** comedia de capa y espada, *f.* **c.-
room,** guardarropa, *m;* (ladies') tocador,
m; (on a station) consigna, *f*

clock /klɒk/ *n* reloj, *m;* (of a stocking)
cuadrado, *m.* **It is six o'clock,** Son las
seis. **c.-face,** esfera de reloj, *f.* **c.-maker,**
relojero, *m.* **c.-making,** relojería, *f.* **c.-
work,** aparato de relojería, *m.* **to go like
c.-work,** ir como un reloj. **c.-work train,**
tren de cuerda, *m*

clockwise /'klɒk,waiz/ *a* and *adv* en el
sentido de las agujas del reloj; de derecha
a izquierda

clod /klɒd/ *n* (of earth) terrón, *m;*
(corpse) tierra, *f;* (person) zoquete, *m.* **c.-
hopper,** patán, *m*

clog /klɒg/ n (shoe) zueco, zoclo, m; (obstacle) estorbo, obstáculo, m. —vt embarazar; estorbar, impedir; (block) obturar, cerrar; Fig. paralizar

cloister /'klɔistər/ n claustro, m; convento, m. —vt enclaustrar

close /klous/ a estrecho; (of a prisoner) incomunicado; (reticent) reservado; (niggardly) tacaño, avaro; (scarce) escaso; (of friends) íntimo; (equal) igual; (lacking space) apretado; (dense) denso; (thick) tupido; compacto; (of a copy, etc.) fiel, exacto; (thorough) concienzudo; (careful) cuidadoso; (attentive) atento; (to the roots) a raíz; (of shaving) bueno; (of weather) pesado, sofocante; (of rooms) mal ventilado. **at c. quarters,** de cerca. **It is c. to eight o'clock,** Son casi las ocho. **to press c.,** perseguir de cerca; fatigar. **c. at hand, c. by,** cerca; al lado; a mano. **c. -cropped,** (of hair) al rape. **c. fight,** lucha igualada, f. **c.-fisted,** tacaño, apretado. **c.-fitting,** ajustado, ceñido al cuerpo; pequeño. **c. season,** veda, f. **c. -up,** n (cinema) primer plano, m

close /klouz/ n (end) fin, m, conclusión, f; (of day) caída, f; Mus. cadencia, f; (enclosure) cercado, m; (square) plazoleta, f; (alley) callejón, m; (of a cathedral) patio, m. **at the c. of day,** a la caída de la tarde. **to bring to a c.,** terminar; llevar a cabo. **to draw to a c.,** tocar a su fin; estar terminando

close /klouz/ vt cerrar; (end) concluir, terminar; poner fin a. —vi cerrar(se); (of a wound) cicatrizarse, cerrarse; (end) terminar(se), acabar, concluir. **to c. the ranks,** cerrar filas. **to c. about,** (surround) rodear, cercar; (envelop) envolver. **to c. down,** vt cerrar. —vi cerrar; Radio. cerrarse. **to c. in,** (surround) cercar; (of night) cerrar; caer; (envelop) envolver; (of length of days) acortarse. **to c. in on,** cercar. **to c. round,** envolver; (of water) tragar. **to c. up,** vt cerrar; cerrar completamente; obstruir. —vi (of persons) acercarse; (of a wound) cicatrizarse; cerrarse

closed /klouzd/ a cerrado. **"Road C.,"** Paso Cerrado. **to have a c. mind,** ser cerrado de mollera; sufrir de estrechez de miras

closely /'klousli/ adv estrechamente; de cerca; (carefully) cuidadosamente; (exactly) exactamente; (attentively) con atención, atentamente

closeness /'klousnɪs/ n estrechez, f; densidad, f; (nearness) proximidad, f; (of a copy, etc.) fidelidad, exactitud, f; (stuffiness), falta de aire, f; (of friendship) intimidad, f; (stinginess) tacañería, f; (reserve) reserva

closet /'klɒzɪt/ n camarín, m; (cupboard) alacena, f; (water) excusado, m

closing /'klouzɪŋ/ n cerramiento, m; (of an account) saldo, m. **c. time,** cierre, m, hora de cerrar, f

clot /klɒt/ n coágulo, grumo, m. —vt coagular. —vi coagularse, cuajarse

cloth /klɔθ/ n tela, f; paño, m; (table) mantel, m; (clergy) clero, m. **She cleaned the books with a c.,** Ella limpió los libros con un paño. **in c.,** (of books) en tela

clothe /klouð/ vt vestir; cubrir; (with authority, etc.) revestir. **to c. oneself,** vestirse

clothes /klouz/ n pl vestidos, m pl, ropa, f. **a suit of c.,** un traje. **old c. shop,** ropavejería, f. **c.-basket,** cesta de la colada, f. **c.-brush,** cepillo para ropa, m. **c.-hanger,** percha, f. **c.-horse,** enjugador, m. **c.-line,** cuerda de la ropa, f. **c.-peg,** pinza de la ropa, f. **c.-prop,** palo para sostener la cuerda de la colada, m

clothing /'klouðɪŋ/ n vestidos, m pl, ropa, f. **article of c.,** prenda de vestir, f

cloud /klaud/ n nube, f. —vt anublar, oscurecer; empañar; (blot out) borrar. —vi anublarse. **to be under a c.,** estar bajo sospecha. **summer c.,** nube de verano, f. **storm-c.,** nubarrón, m. **c.-burst,** nubada, f, chaparrón, m. **c.-capped,** coronado de nubes

cloudiness /'klaudinɪs/ n nebulosidad, f; obscuridad, f; (of liquids) turbiedad, f

cloudless /'klaudlɪs/ a sin nubes, despejado; sereno, claro

cloudy /'klaudi/ a nublado, nubloso; obscuro; (of liquids) turbio

clove /klouv/ n clavo de especia, m; (of garlic) diente de ajo, m. **c.-tree,** clavero, m

cloven /'klouvən/ a hendido. **to show the c. hoof,** enseñar la oreja. **c. hoof,** pezuña, f

clover /'klouvər/ n trébol, m. **to be in c.,** nadar en la abundancia

clown /klaun/ n patán, m; bufón, tonto, m; (in a circus) payaso, m. —vi hacer el tonto, hacer el payaso

cloying /'klɔiɪŋ/ a empalagoso

club /klʌb/ n porra, cachiporra, clava, f; (gymnastic) maza, f; (hockey) bastón de hockey, m; (golf) palo de golf, m; (in cards) basto, m; (social) club, m. —vt golpear. **to c. together,** asociarse, unirse. **We clubbed together to buy him a present,** Entre todos le compramos un regalo. **c.-house,** club, m

clubfoot /'klʌb,fut/ n pie calcáneo, pie contrahecho, pie de piña, pie equino, pie talo, pie zambo, m

clue /klu/ n indicio, m; (to a problem) clave, f; (of a crossword) indicación, f; idea, f

clump /klʌmp/ n bloque, pedazo, m; (of trees) grupo, m; (of feet) ruido, m

clumsiness /'klʌmzinɪs/ n torpeza, f; falta de maña, f; pesadez, f

clumsy /'klʌmzi/ a torpe; desmañado; chapucero, sin arte; (lumbering) pesado; (in shape) disforme

cluster /'klʌstər/ n (of currants, etc.) racimo, m; (of flowers) ramillete, m; grupo, *m.* —*vi* arracimarse; agruparse. **They clustered round him,** Se agrupaban a su alrededor

clutch /klʌtʃ/ *vt* agarrar; sujetar, apretar. —*n Mech.* embrague, *m;* (of eggs) nidada, *f; Fig.* garras, *f pl.* **to fall into the clutches of,** caer en las garras de. **to make a c. at,** procurar agarrar. **to throw in the c.,** *Mech.* embragar. **to throw out the c.,** *Mech.* desembragar. **c. pedal,** pedal de embrague, *m*

clutter /ˈklʌtər/ *n* desorden, *m,* confusión, *f, vt* desordenar

coach /koutʃ/ *n* carroza, *f;* charabán, *m; Rail.* vagón, coche, *m;* (hackney) coche de alquiler, *m; Sports.* entrenador, *m;* (tutor) profesor particular, *m.* —*vt Sports.* entrenar; (teach) preparar, dar lecciones particulares (a). **through c.,** coche directo, *m.* **c.-box,** pescante, *m.* **c.-house,** cochera, *f*

coaching /ˈkoutʃɪŋ/ *n Sports.* entrenamiento, *m;* lecciones particulares, *f pl*

coagulate /kouˈægyə‚leit/ *vi* coagularse. —*vt* coagular, cuajar

coal /koul/ *n* carbón, *m;* pedazo de carbón, *m;* (burning) brasa, *f.* —*vi* carbonear, hacer carbón. —*vt* proveer de carbón; carbonear. **to carry coals to Newcastle,** llevar leña al monte, elevar aqua al mar. **to haul a person over the coals,** reprender a alguien. **c.-barge,** (barco) carbonero, *m.* **c.-black,** negro como el azabache. **c.-cellar, house,** carbonera, *f.* **c.-dust,** cisco, *m.* **c.-field,** yacimiento de carbón, *m.* **c.-gas,** gas de hulla, *m.* **c.-heaver,** cargador de carbón, *m.* **c.-merchant,** carbonero, *m.* **c.-mine,** mina de carbón, *f.* **c.-miner,** minero de carbón, *m.* **c.-scuttle,** carbonera, *f.* **c.-tar,** alquitrán mineral, *m*

coalesce /‚kouəˈles/ *vi* fundirse; unirse; incorporarse

coalition /‚kouəˈlɪʃən/ *n* coalición, *f*

coarse /kɔrs/ *a* (in texture) basto, burdo; tosco; (gross) grosero; vulgar. **c.-grained,** de fibra gruesa; (of persons) vulgar, poco fino

coarsen /ˈkɔrsən/ *vt* (of persons) embrutecer. —*vi* embrutecerse; (of the skin) curtirse

coarseness /ˈkɔrsnɪs/ *n* basteza, *f;* tosquedad, *f;* (of persons) grosería, indelicadeza, *f;* vulgaridad, *f*

coast /koust/ *n* costa, *f;* litoral, *m.* —*vi* costear; deslizarse en un tobogán; dejar muerto el motor. **The c. is not clear,** Hay moros en la costa. **c.-guard,** guardacostas, *m.* **c.-line,** litoral, *m*

coastal /ˈkoustl/ *a* costanero, costero. **c. defences,** defensas costeras, *f pl*

coat /kout/ *n* abrigo, *m;* gabán, *m;* chaqueta, *f;* (animal's) capa, *f;* (of paint) mano, *f.* —*vt* recubrir; (with paint, etc.) dar una mano de. **fur c.,** abrigo de pieles, *m.* **sports c.,** Americana sport, *f.* **c. of arms,** escudo de armas, *m.* **c. of mail,** cota de malla, *f.* **c.-hanger,** percha, *f*

coating /ˈkoutɪŋ/ *n* (of paint, etc.) capa, mano, *f*

coax /kouks/ *vt* instar; halagar; persuadir (a)

coaxing /ˈkouksɪŋ/ *n* ruegos, *m pl;* mimos, *m pl,* caricias, *f pl;* persuasión, *f.* —*a* mimoso, zalamero; persuasivo

cobbler /ˈkɒblər/ *n* zapatero remendón, *m.* **cobbler's last,** horma, *f.* **cobbler's wax,** cerote, *m*

cobblestone /ˈkɒbəl‚stoun/ *n* guijarro, *m,* piedra, *f*

cobweb /ˈkɒb‚web/ *n* telaraña, *f*

cocaine /kouˈkein/ *n* cocaína, *f*

cochlea /ˈkɒklia/ *n* caracol (del oído), *m*

cock /kɒk/ *n* gallo, *m;* (male) macho, *m;* (tap) grifo, *m,* espita, *f;* (of a gun) martillo, *m;* (weather-vane) veleta, *f;* (of hay) montón, *m.* —*vt* (a gun) amartillar; (a hat) ladear; (raise) erguir, enderezar. **a cocked hat,** un sombrero de tres picos. **at half c.,** (of a gun) desamartillada *f.* **He cocked his head,** Erguió la cabeza. **The dog cocked its ears,** El perro aguzó las orejas. **to c. one's eye at,** lanzar una mirada (a). **c.-a-doodle-doo,** quiquiriquí, *m.* **c.-a-hoop,** triunfante, jubiloso; arrogante. **c.-crow,** canto del gallo, *m.* **c.-fight,** riña de gallos, *f.* **c.-of-the-walk,** gallito, *m.* **c.-sure,** pagado de sí mismo; completamente convencido

cockpit /ˈkɒk‚pɪt/ *n* gallería, *f; Aer.* casilla del piloto, *f; Fig.* arena, *f*

cockroach /ˈkɒk‚routʃ/ *n* cucaracha, *f*

cocktail /ˈkɒk‚teil/ *n* (drink) cótel, coctel, *m.* **to shake a c.,** mezclar un coctel. **c. party,** coctel *m.* **c. shaker,** cotelera, *f*

cocky /ˈkɒki/ *a* fatuo, presuntuoso

cocoa /ˈkoukou/ *n* cacao, *m*

coconut /ˈkoukə‚nʌt/ *n* coco, *m; Inf.* cabeza, *f.* **c. milk,** agua de coco, *f.* **c. shy,** pim, pam, pum, *m.* **c. tree,** cocotero, *m*

cocoon /kəˈkun/ *n* capullo, *m*

cod /kɒd/ *n* bacalao, *m.* **cod-liver oil,** aceite de hígado de bacalao, *m*

coddle /ˈkɒdl/ *vt* criar con mimo, mimar, consentir

code /koud/ *n* código, *m;* clave, *f;* (secret) cifra, *f.* —*vt* poner en cifra. **signal c.,** *Naut.* código de señales, *m.* **c. word,** palabra de clave, *f*

codeine /ˈkoudin/ *n* codeína, *f*

codex /ˈkoudeks/ *n* códice, *m*

codicil /ˈkɒdəsəl/ *n* codicilio, *m*

codify /ˈkɒdə‚fai/ *vt* codificar

coefficient /‚kouəˈfɪʃənt/ *n* coeficiente, *m*

coerce /kouˈɜrs/ *vt* forzar, obligar; constreñir

coercion /kouˈɜrʃən/ *n* coerción, coacción, *f*

coercive /kouˈɜrsɪv/ *a* coercitivo, coactivo

coeval /kouˈivəl/ *a* coevo

coexist /‚kouɪgˈzɪst/ *vi* coexistir

coexistence /‚kouɪgˈzɪstəns/ *n* coexistencia, *f*

coffee /'kɔfi/ *n* café, *m.* **black c.**, café solo, *m.* **white c.**, café con leche, *m.* **c.-bean**, grano de café, *m.* **c.-cup**, taza para café, *f.* **c.-house**, café, *m.* **c.-mill**, molinillo de café, *m.* **c.-plantation**, cafetal, *m.* **c.-pot**, cafetera, *f.* **c.-set**, juego de café, *m.* **c.-tree**, cafeto, *m*

coffer /'kɔfər/ *n* cofre, *m;* arca, caja, *f*

coffin /'kɔfɪn/ *n* ataúd, féretro, *m;* caja, *f*

cog /kɔg/ *n Mech.* diente (de rueda), *m*

cogency /'koudʒənsi/ *n* fuerza, *f*

cogent /'koudʒənt/ *a* convincente, fuerte; urgente

cogitate /'kɔdʒɪ,teit/ *vi* pensar, considerar, meditar

cogitation /,kɔdʒɪ'teiʃən/ *n* reflexión, meditación, consideración, *f*

cognac /'kounyæk/ *n* coñac, *m*

cognate /'kɔgneit/ *a* (of stock) consanguíneo; afín; análogo; semejante

cognizance /'kɔgnəzəns/ *n* conocimiento, *m;* jurisdicción, *f*

cogwheel /'kɔg,wil/ *n* rueda dentada, *f*

cohabit /kou'hæbɪt/ *vi* cohabitar

cohere /kou'hɪər/ *vi* pegarse, adherirse; unirse

coherent /kou'hɪərənt/ *a* coherente; consecuente

cohesion /kou'hiʒən/ *n* cohesión, *f;* coherencia, *f*

cohort /'kouhɔrt/ *n* cohorte, *f*

coiffure /kwa'fyur/ *n* peinado, *m;* tocado, *m*

coil /kɔil/ *vt* arrollar; (*Naut.* of ropes) adujar. —*vi* arrollarse; enroscarse; serpentear. —*n* rollo, *m;* (of a serpent and ropes) anillo, *m;* (of hair) trenza, *f; Elec.* carrete, *m.* **coil of smoke,** nube de humo, *f.* **to c. up,** hacerse un ovillo

coin /kɔin/ *n* moneda, *f; Inf.* dinero, *m.* —*vt* acuñar; (a new word) inventar. **to pay back in the same c.,** pagar en la misma moneda

coinage /'kɔinidʒ/ *n* acuñación, *f;* moneda, *f;* sistema monetario, *m;* invención, *f;* (new word) neologismo, *m*

coincide /,kouin'said/ *vi* coincidir (con); estar conforme, estar de acuerdo

coincidence /kou'ɪnsɪdəns/ *n* coincidencia, *f;* (chance) casualidad, *f*

coiner /'kɔinər/ *n* acuñador de moneda, *m;* monedero falso, *m;* (of phrases, etc.) inventor, *m*

coitus /'kouitəs/ *n* coito, *m*

colander /'kɔləndər/ *n* colador, *m*

cold /kould/ *a* frío. —*n* frío, *m; Med.* catarro, constipado, *m.* **I am c.,** Tengo frío. **It is c.,** Está frío; (weather) Hace frío. **to catch a c.,** acatarrarse, resfriarse. **to grow c.,** enfriarse; (of the weather) empezar a hacer frío. **in c. blood,** a sangre fría. **c.-blooded,** (fishes, etc.) de sangre fría; (chilly, of persons) friolero; (pitiless) insensible, sin piedad; (of actions) a sangre fría, premeditado. **c.-chisel,** cortafrío, *m.* **c. cream,** crema (para el cutis), *f.* **c.-hearted,** seco, insensible. **c.-shoulder,** *n*

frialdad, *f.* —*vt* tratar con frialdad (a). **c.-storage,** conservación refrigerada, *f*

coldness /'kouldnɪs/ *n* frío, *m;* (of one's reception, etc.) frialdad, *f;* (of heart) inhumanidad, *f*

colic /'kɔlɪk/ *n* cólico, *m*

coliseum /,kɔlɪ'siəm/ *n* coliseo, *m*

colitis /kə'laitɪs/ *n* colitis, *f*

collaborate /kə'læbə,reit/ *vi* colaborar (con)

collaborator /kə'læbə,reitər/ *n* colaborador (-ra); (quisling) colaboracionista, *mf*

collapse /kə'læps/ *n* derrumbamiento, *m;* desplome, *m; Med.* colapso, *m;* (of buildings and *Fig.*) hundimiento, *m;* (of plans) frustración, *f;* (failure) fracaso, *m.* —*vi* derrumbarse; (of buildings, etc.) hundirse, venirse abajo; (of persons, fall) desplomarse; *Med.* sufrir colapso; (of plans, etc.) frustrarse, venirse abajo. **George came to us after the c. of France,** Jorge vino a quedarse con nosotros después del hundimiento de Francia

collapsible /kə'læpsəbəl/ *a* plegable

collar /'kɔlər/ *n* (of a garment and of fur) cuello, *m;* (of a dog, etc., and necklace) collar, *m.* —*vt* (seize) agarrar. **detachable c.,** cuello suelto, *m.* **high c.,** alzacuello, *m.* **c.-bone,** clavícula, *f*

collate /kou'leit/ *vt* cotejar; (to a benefice) colacionar

collateral /kə'lætərəl/ *a* colateral

collation /kə'leiʃən/ *n* colación, *f*

colleague /'kɔlig/ *n* colega, *m;* compañero (-ra)

collect /'kɔlɛkt/ *vt* (assemble) reunir; (catch) coger; acumular; (call for) pasar a buscar, ir (or venir) a buscar; (pick up) recoger; (taxes, etc.) recaudar; coleccionar; (one's strength, etc. and debts, etc.) cobrar; (letters) recoger. —*vi* reunirse, congregarse; acumularse. —*n Eccl.* colecta, *f.* **to c. oneself,** reponerse

collected /kə'lɛktɪd/ *a* (of persons) seguro de sí.

collection /kə'lɛkʃən/ *n* reunión, *f;* (of data, etc.) acumulación, *f;* (of pictures, stamps, etc.) colección, *f;* (of a debt, etc.) cobranza, *f;* (of taxes, etc.) recaudación, *f;* (from a mail box) recogida, *f;* (of laws, etc.) compilación, *f; Eccl.* ofertorio, *m;* (of donations) colecta, *f*

collection agency *n* agencia de cobros de cuentas, *f*

collective /kə'lɛktɪv/ *a* colectivo. **c. bargaining,** regateo colectivo, trato colectivo, *m*

collector /kə'lɛktər/ *n* (of pictures, etc.) coleccionador (-ra), coleccionista, *mf;* cobrador, *m; Elec.* colector, *m*

college /'kɔlidʒ/ *n* colegio, *m;* escuela, *f;* universidad, *f.* **C. of Cardinals,** Colegio de Cardenales, *m*

collegiate /kə'lidʒɪt/ *a* colegial, colegiado. **c. church,** iglesia colegial, *f*

collide /kə'laid/ *vi* chocar (contra), topar

(con); estar en conflicto (con). **c. head-on,** chocar frontalmente

collie /'kɒli/ n perro de pastor escocés, m

collier /'kɒlyər/ n minero de carbón, m; (barco) carbonero, m

collision /kə'lɪʒən/ n choque, m, colisión, f; (of interests, etc.) antagonismo, conflicto, m. **to come into c. with,** chocar con

colloquial /kə'loukwiəl/ a familiar

colloquy /'kɒləkwi/ n coloquio, m

collusion /kə'luʒən/ n colusión, f. **to be in c.,** Law. coludir; conspirar, estar de manga

Cologne /kə'loun/ Colonia, f

Colombia /kə'lʌmbiə/ Colombia, f

Colombian /kə'lʌmbiən/ a colombiano. —n colombiano (-na)

colon /'koulən/ n Anat. colon, m; (punctuation) dos puntos, m pl

colonel /'kɜrnl/ n coronel, m

colonial /kə'louniəl/ a colonial. —n habitante de las colonias, m. **C. Office,** Ministerio de Asuntos Coloniales, m

colonnade /ˌkɒlə'neid/ n columnata, f

colony /'kɒləni/ n colonia, f

color /'kʌlər/ n color, m; colorido, m; tinta, f; materia colorante, f, insignia, f; bandera, f, estandarte, m; pl colors, m Naut. pabellón, m. —vt colorar; pintar; iluminar; (influence) influir, afectar. —vi colorarse; ruborizarse; encenderse. **fast c.,** color estable, color sólido, m. **regimental colors,** bandera del regimiento, f. **with colors flying,** con tambor batiente, a banderas desplegadas. **to be off c.,** estar malucho, estar indispuesto. **to change c.,** (of persons) mudar de color, mudar de semblante. **to give c. to,** (a story, etc.) hacer verosímil. **to lay the colors on too thick,** recargar las tintas. **to pass with flying colors,** salir triunfante. **under c. of,** so color de, a pretexto de. **c.-blind,** daltoniano. **c.-blindness,** daltonismo, m

colored /'kʌlərd/ a colorado; de color

coloring /'kʌlərɪŋ/ n (substance) colorante, m; (act of) coloración, f; Art. colorido, m; (of complexion) colores, m pl

colorist /'kʌlərɪst/ n colorista, mf

colorless /'kʌlərlɪs/ a sin color, incoloro; Fig. insípido

colossal /kə'lɒsəl/ a colosal, gigantesco; enorme; Inf. estupendo

colossus /kə'lɒsəs/ n coloso, m

colt /koult/ n potro, m; (boy) muchacho alegre, m

colter /'koultər/ n reja, reja del arado, f

column /'kɒləm/ n columna, f. **Fifth C.,** quinta columna, f

columned /'kɒləmd/ a con columnas

columnist /'kɒləmnɪst/ n periodista, m

coma /'koumə/ n coma, m

comatose /'kɒmə,tous/ a comatoso

comb /koum/ n peine, m; (for flax) carda, f; (curry) almohaza, f; (of cock) cresta, carúncula, f; (of a wave) cima, cresta, f; (honey) panal, m, vt (hair) pei-

nar; (flax) rastrillar, cardar. **c. and brush,** cepillo y peine. **high c.,** peineta, f. **to c. one's hair,** peinarse

combat / v kəm'bæt; n 'kɒmbæt/ vt luchar contra, combatir, resistir. —vi combatir, pelear. —n combate, m; lucha, batalla, f. **in single c.,** cuerpo a cuerpo

combatant /kəm'bætnt/ n combatiente, m, a combatiente

combative /kəm'bætɪv/ a belicoso, pugnaz

combination /ˌkɒmbə'neiʃən/ n combinación, f; mezcla, f; unión, f; asociación, f; pl combinations. camisa pantalón, f. **c. lock,** cerradura de combinación, f

combine / v kəm'bain; n 'kɒmbain/ vt combinar; reunir, juntar; Chem. combinar. —vi combinarse; asociarse (con); Com. fusionarse. —n asociación, f; Com. monopolio, m

combings /'koumɪŋz/ n pl peinaduras, f pl

combustible /kəm'bʌstəbəl/ a combustible. —n combustible, m

combustion /kəm'bʌstʃən/ n combustión, f. **rapid c.,** combustión rápida, f. **spontaneous c.,** combustión espontánea, f

come /kʌm/ vi venir; llegar; avanzar; acercarse; (happen) suceder, acontecer; (result) resultar; (find oneself) encontrarse, hallarse; (become) llegar a ser; (begin to) ponerse (a), empezar (a). **Coming!** ¡Voy! ¡Allá voy! **C., c.!** ¡Vamos! ¡No es para tanto! ¡Ánimo! **I am ready whatever comes,** Estoy preparado venga lo que venga. **He comes of a good family,** Es (Viene) de buena familia. **I came to know him well,** Llegué a conocerle bien. **I don't know what came over me,** No sé lo que me pasó. **When I came to consider it,** Cuando me puse a considerarlo. **The bill comes to six thousand pesetas,** La cuenta sale a seis mil pesetas. **He comes up before the judge tomorrow,** Ha de comparecer ante el juez mañana. **What you say comes to this,** Lo que dice Vd. se reduce a esto. **What is the world coming to?** ¿A dónde va parar el mundo? **It does not c. within my scope,** No está dentro de mi alcance. **to c. apart,** deshacerse; romperse; dividirse. **to c. home to,** Fig. impresionar hondo, tocar en lo más íntimo; hacer comprender (a). **to c. into bloom,** empezar a tener flores, florecer. **to c. into one's head,** venir a las mientes. **to c. into the world,** venir al mundo. **to c. near,** acercarse; aproximarse, estar próximo. **to c. next,** venir después; suceder luego. **to c. to an end,** terminar, acabarse. **to c. to blows,** venir a las manos. **to c. to grief,** salir mal parado; (of schemes, etc.) malograrse. **to c. to hand,** venir a mano; (of letters) llegar a las manos (de). **to c. to life,** despertar; animarse; resucitarse. **to c. to nothing,** frustrarse; no quedar en nada. **to c. to pass,** suceder; realizarse. **to c. to terms,** ponerse de acuerdo. **to c. true,** cumplirse, verificarse. **to c. about,** suceder, acontecer, tener lugar; (of the wind) girar. **to c. across,** dar con, encontrar por casualidad; tropezar con. **to c. after,** (a situation) solicitar; (follow) seguir (a); venir más tarde (que); (succeed) suceder. **to c. again,** volver. **to c. along,** caminar (por); andar (por); (arrive) llegar. **C. along!** ¡Ven! ¡Vamos! ¡Andamos! **to c. at,** alcanzar; (attack) embestir, atacar; (gain) obtener, adquirir. **to c. away,** irse, marcharse; (break) deshacerse. **to c. back,** volver. **c.-back,** n Inf. respuesta, f; contraataque, m. **to c. before,** llegar antes; preceder (a). **to c. between,** interponerse (entre), intervenir. **to c. by,** pasar por, pasar junto a; (acquire) obtener, adquirir; (achieve) conseguir. **to c. down,** bajar, descender; (in the world) venir a menos; (be demolished) demolerse; (collapse) derrumbarse, hundirse; (of prices) bajar; (of traditions, etc.) llegar e.g. *This work has c. down to us in two fifteenth-century manuscripts* Esta obra nos ha llegado en dos manuscritos del siglo quince; (fall) caer. **c.-down,** n caída, f; frustración, f; desengaño, m; desprestigio, m; pérdida de posición, f. **to c. down on a person,** cantar la cartilla (a). **to c. forward,** avanzar, adelantarse; (offer) ofrecerse; presentarse. **to c. in,** entrar; (of money) ingresar; (of trains, etc.) llegar; (of the tide) crecer; (of the new year) empezar; (of fashion) ponerse de moda; (be useful) servir (para). **C. in!** ¡Adelante! ¡Pase Vd.! **to c. into,** (a scheme) asociarse con; (property) heredar; (the mind) presentarse a la imaginación, ocurrirse (a). **to c. off,** (happen) tener lugar; realizarse, efectuarse; (be successful) tener éxito; (break off) separarse (de); romperse. **to c. off well,** tener éxito; (of persons) salir bien. **c. off the press,** salir de prensas. **to c. on,** avanzar; (of actors) salir a la escena; (progress) hacer progresos; (develop) desarrollarse; (of pain, etc.) acometer (a); (arrive) llegar; (of a lawsuit) verse. **C. on!** ¡Vamos! ¡En marcha! **to c. out,** salir; (of stars) nacer; (of buds, etc.) brotar; (of the moon, etc.) asomarse;-(of stains) borrarse, salir; (of a book) ver la luz, publicarse; (of secrets) divulgarse, saberse; (of a girl, in society) ponerse de largo; (on strike) declararse en huelga; (of fashions, etc.) aparecer. **to c. out with,** (a remark) soltar; (oaths, etc.) prorrumpir (en); (disclose) revelar, hacer público. **to c. round,** (to see someone) venir a ver (a); (coax) engatusar; (after a faint, etc.) volver en sí; (after illness) reponerse; (to another's point of view) aceptar, compartir. **to c. through,** pasar por; (trials, etc.) subir; salir de; (of liquids) salirse. **to c. to,** volver en sí. **to c. together,** reunirse, juntarse; venir juntos; unirse. **to c. under,** venir (o estar) bajo la jurisdicción de; (the influence of) estar dominado por; (figure among) figurar entre, estar comprendido en. **to c. up,** subir; (of sun, moon) salir; (of plants) brotar; (of problems, etc.) surgir; (in conversation) discutirse; (before a court) comparecer. **to c. up to,** (equal) igualar, ser igual (a); rivalizar con; (in height) llegar hasta. **He came up to them in the street,** Les abordó (o se les acercó) en la calle. **We have c. up against many difficulties,** Hemos tropezado con muchas dificultades. **This novel does not c. up to his last,** Esta última novela no es tan buena como la anterior. **The party did not c. up to their expectations,** La reunión no fue tan divertida como esperaban. **to c. up with,** (a person) alcanzar (a). **to c. upon,** encontrar, hallar; tropezar con; encontrar por casualidad. **to c. upon evil days,** venir a menos

comedian /kəˈmidiən/ n actor cómico, comediante, m

comedy /ˈkɒmɪdɪ/ n comedia, f. **c. of manners,** comedia de costumbres, f

comeliness /ˈkʌmlɪnɪs/ n hermosura, f

comely /ˈkʌmli/ a hermoso

comer /ˈkʌmər/ n el, m, (f, la) que viene. **all comers,** todo el mundo. **first c.,** primer (-ra) venido (-da)

comet /ˈkɒmɪt/ n cometa, m

comfort /ˈkʌmfərt/ vt consolar, confortar; (encourage) animar; (reassure) alegrar; —n consuelo, m; satisfacción, f; comodidad, f; bienestar, m. **He lives in great c.,** Vive con mucha comodidad. **c.-loving,** comodón

comfortable /ˈkʌmftəbəl/ a cómodo; (with income) suficiente; (consoling) consolador. **to make oneself c.,** ponerse cómodo

comfortably /ˈkʌmftəbli/ adv cómodamente; suficientemente; fácilmente; con facilidad; (well) bien. **He is c. off,** Está bien de dinero

comforter /ˈkʌmfərtər/ n consolador (-ra); (baby's) chupador, m; (scarf) bufanda, f

comforting /ˈkʌmfərtɪŋ/ a consolador

comfortless /ˈkʌmfərtlɪs/ a incómodo, sin comodidad; desconsolador; (of persons) inconsolable, desconsolado

comic /ˈkɒmɪk/ a cómico; bufo; satírico. —n cómico, m; pl **comics,** (printed) historietas cómicas, f pl. **c. opera,** ópera cómica, f. **c. paper,** periódico satírico, m

comical /ˈkɒmɪkəl/ a cómico; divertido, gracioso

coming /ˈkʌmɪŋ/ a (with year, etc.) próximo, que viene; (promising) de porvenir; (approaching) que se acerca. —n venida, f; llegada, f; advenimiento, m. **c.-out party,** puesta de largo, f. **comings and goings,** entradas y salidas, f pl

comma /ˈkɒmə/ n coma, f. **inverted commas,** comillas, f pl

command /kəˈmænd/ vt mandar, ordenar; (silence, respect, etc.) imponer; (an army, fleet, etc.) comandar; capitanear; (one's emotions) dominar; (have at one's disposal) disponer de; (a military position, view) dominar; (sympathy, etc.) despertar, merecer; (of price) venderse por. —*vi* mandar. —*n* orden, *f;* (*Mil. Nav.*) mando, *m;* (of an army, etc.) comandancia, *f;* (of one's emotions, etc.) dominio, *m;* (of a military position, etc.) dominación, *f;* disposición, *f.* **By Royal C.,** Por Real Orden; (of shops, etc.) Proveedor de la Real Casa. **The house commands lovely views of the mountains,** La casa tiene hermosas vistas de las montañas. **word of c.,** orden, *f.* **Yours to c.,** A la disposición de Vd.

commandant /ˌkɒmənˈdænt/ *n* comandante, *m*

commandeer /ˌkɒmənˈdɪər/ *vt* (conscript) reclutar; *Mil.* requisar; expropiar

commander /kəˈmændər/ *n Mil.* comandante, *m; Nav.* capitán de fragata, *m;* (of order of Knighthood) comendador, *m.* **c.-in-chief,** generalísimo, *m.* **C. of the Faithful,** Comendador de los creyentes, *m*

commanding /kəˈmændɪŋ/ *a Mil.* comandante; imponente; (of manner) imperioso; dominante. **c. officer,** comandante en jefe, *m*

commandment /kəˈmændmənt/ *n* precepto, mandamiento, *m.* **the Ten Commandments,** los diez mandamientos

commando /kəˈmændou/ *n Mil.* comando, *m*

commemorate /kəˈmɛməˌreit/ *vt* conmemorar

commence /kəˈmɛns/ *vt* comenzar, empezar, principiar. —*vi* comenzar. **He commenced to eat,** Empezó a comer

commencement /kəˈmɛnsmənt/ *n* principio, comienzo, *m*

commend /kəˈmɛnd/ *vt* (entrust) encomendar; recomendar; alabar

commendable /kəˈmɛndəbəl/ *a* loable; recomendable

commendation /ˌkɒmənˈdeiʃən/ *n* aprobación, alabanza, *f,* aplauso, *m*

commensurable /kəˈmɛnsərəbəl/ *a* conmensurable

commensurate /kəˈmɛnsərɪt/ *a* proporcionado (a); conforme (a)

comment /ˈkɒmɛnt/ *n* observación, *f;* (on a work) comento, *m;* explicación, nota, *f.* —*vi* hacer una observación (sobre); (a work) comentar, anotar. **to c. unfavorably on,** criticar

commentary /ˈkɒmənˌtɛri/ *n* comentario, *m;* (on a person, etc.) comentos, *m pl,* observaciones, *f pl*

commentator /ˈkɒmənˌteitər/ *n* comentador (-ra); (of a work) comentarista, *mf*

commerce /ˈkɒmərs/ *n* comercio, *m;* negocios, *m pl;* (social) trato, *m*

commercial /kəˈmɜrʃəl/ *a* comercial; mercantil. **c. traveler,** viajante, *mf*

commercialism /kəˈmɜrʃəˌlɪzəm/ *n* mercantilismo, *m*

commercialize /kəˈmɜrʃəˌlaiz/ *vt* hacer objeto de comercio

commingle /kəˈmɪŋɡəl/ *vt* mezclar. —*vi* mezclarse

commiserate /kəˈmɪzəˌreit/ *vi* compadecerse (de), apiadarse (de)

commiseration /kəˌmɪzəˈreiʃən/ *n* conmiseración, compasión, *f*

commission /kəˈmɪʃən/ *n* comisión, *f; Mil.* graduación de oficial, *f.* —*vt* comisionar; (a ship) poner en servicio activo, armar; (appoint) nombrar. **in c.,** en servicio, activo. **out of c.,** (of ships) inutilizado; inservible. **c. agent,** comisionista, *mf* **to gain one's c.,** *Mil.* graduarse de oficial. **to put out of c.,** retirar del servicio; poner fuera de combate; estropear

commissioner /kəˈmɪʃənər/ *n* comisario, *m.* **High C.,** alto comisario, *m.* **c. for oaths,** notario, *m.* **c. of police,** jefe de policía, *m*

commit /kəˈmɪt/ *vt* entregar (a); (a crime) cometer; (to prison) encarcelar; (for trial) remitir. **to c. oneself,** comprometerse. **to c. to memory,** aprender de memoria. **to c. to writing,** poner por escrito

commitment /kəˈmɪtmənt/ *n* (financial, etc.) obligación, responsabilidad, *f;* compromiso, *m*

committal /kəˈmɪtl/ *n* (of an offence) comisión, *f;* (placing, entrusting) entrega, *f;* (to prison) encarcelamiento, *m;* (legal procedure) auto de prisión, *m.*

committee /kəˈmɪti/ *n* comité, *m;* comisión, junta, *f;* consejo, *m.* **They decided in c.,** Tomaron la resolución en comité. **c. of management,** consejo de administración, *m*

commodious /kəˈmoudiəs/ *a* espacioso, grande

commodity /kəˈmɒditi/ *n* artículo, *m,* mercancía, *f*

common /ˈkɒmən/ *a* común; general, corriente; universal; vulgar; (disparaging) cursi; (elementary) elemental. —*n* pastos comunes, *m pl.* **He is not a c. man,** No es un hombre cualquiera; No es un hombre vulgar. **in c.,** en común. **the c. man,** el hombre medio. **the c. people,** el pueblo. **c. sense,** sentido común, *m.* **c. soldier,** soldado raso, *m.* **c. speech,** lenguaje vulgar, *m.* **c. usage,** uso corriente, *m*

commoner /ˈkɒmənər/ *n* plebeyo (-ya)

commonly /ˈkɒmənli/ *adv* comúnmente, por lo general

commonplace /ˈkɒmənˌpleis/ *n* lugar común, *m;* trivialidad, *f.* —*a* trivial

commons /ˈkɒmənz/ *n* el pueblo; (House of) Cámara de los Comunes, *f;* (food) provisiones, *f pl.* **to be on short c.,** comer mal, estar mal alimentado

Commonwealth /ˈkɒmənˌwɛlθ/ *n* estado, *m;* república, *f;* comunidad (de naciones), *f;* mancomunidad, *f.* **the Commonwealth of Puerto Rico,** el Estado Libre Asociado de Puerto Rico, *m*

commotion /kə'mouʃən/ n confusión, f; conmoción, perturbación, f; tumulto, m

communal /kə'myunl/ a comunal

commune /'komyun/ n comuna, f; comunión, f, vi conversar (con). **to c. with oneself,** hablar consigo

communicant /kə'myunɪkənt/ n Eccl. comulgante, mf; (of information) informante, mf

communicate /kə'myunɪˌkeit/ vt comunicar; (diseases) transmitir. —vi comunicarse (con); Eccl. comulgar

communication /kəˌmyunɪ'keiʃən/ n comunicación, f. **lines of c.,** comunicaciones, f pl. **to get into c. with,** ponerse en comunicación con. **c.-cord,** (in a railway carriage) timbre de alarma, m

communicative /kə'myunɪˌkeitɪv/ a comunicativo; expansivo

communicativeness /kə'myunɪˌkeitɪvnɪs/ n carácter expansivo, m; locuacidad, f

communion /kə'myunyən/ n comunión, f. **Holy c.,** comunión, f. **to take c.,** comulgar. **c. card,** cédula de comunión, f. **c. cup,** cáliz, f. **c. table,** sagrada mesa, f; altar, m

communiqué /kəˌmyunɪ'kei/ n comunicación, parte, f. **to issue a c.,** dar parte

communism /'komyəˌnɪzəm/ n comunismo, m

communist /'komyənɪst/ n comunista, mf a comunista

community /kə'myunɪti/ n comunidad, f. **the c.,** la nación; el público. **c. center,** centro social, m

commute /kə'myut/ vt conmutar; reducir

compact / n 'kompækt; v kəm'pækt/ n (pact) acuerdo, pacto, m; (powder) polvorera, f. —a compacto; firme; sólido; apretado, cerrado; (of persons) bien hecho; (of style) conciso, sucinto

compact disc /'kompækt 'dɪsk/ n disco compacto, m

compactness /kəm'pæktnɪs/ n compacidad, f; (of style) concisión, f

companion /kəm'pænyən/ n compañero (-ra); camarada, mf; (of an Order) caballero, m, (or dama, f). —vt acompañar. **lady c.,** señora de compañía, f. **c.-hatch,** cubierta de escotilla, f. **c.-ladder,** escala de toldilla, f

companionable /kəm'pænyənəbəl/ a sociable, amistoso

companionship /kəm'pænyənˌʃɪp/ n compañía, f; compañerismo, m

company /'kompəni/ n (Com. Mil. etc.) compañía, f; (ship's) tripulación, f. **I will keep you c.,** Te haré compañía. **to part c. with,** separarse de. **Present c. excepted!** ¡Mejorando lo presente! **They are not very good c.,** No son muy divertidos

compare /kəm'pɛər/ vt comparar. —vi compararse; poder compararse. ser comparable. **beyond c.,** sin comparación; sin igual. **to c. favorably with,** no perder

por comparación con. **to c. notes,** cambiar impresiones

comparison /kəm'pærəsən/ n comparación, f. **in c. with,** comparado con

compartment /kəm'pɑrtmənt/ n compartimiento, m; Rail. departamento, m

compass /'kʌmpəs/ n circuito, m; límites, m pl; alcance, m; (of a voice) gama, f; Naut. brújula, f; pl **compasses,** compás, m. —vt (achieve) conseguir; (plan) idear, **mariner's c.,** compás de mar. m, rosa de los vientos, f. **pocket c.,** brújula de bolsillo, f. **to c. about,** cercar, rodear

compassion /kəm'pæʃən/ n compasión, f. **to have c. on,** apiadarse de, compadecerse de

compassionate /kəm'pæʃənɪt/ a compasivo, piadoso. **c. leave,** permiso, m

compatriot /kəm'peitriət/ n compatriota, mf

compel /kəm'pɛl/ vt obligar (a), forzar (a); exigir; imponer. **His attitude compels respect,** Su actitud impone el respeto

compelling /kəm'pɛlɪŋ/ a compulsivo

compendious /kəm'pɛndiəs/ a compendioso, sucinto

compendium /kəm'pɛndiəm/ n compendio, m; resumen, m

compensate /'kompənˌseit/ vt compensar; (reward) recompensar; (for loss, etc.) indemnizar. **to c. for,** compensar; indemnizar contra

compensation /ˌkompən'seiʃən/ n compensación, f; (reward) recompensa, f; (for loss, etc.) indemnización, f

compensatory /kəm'pɛnsəˌtori/ a compensatorio

compete /kəm'pit/ vi competir (con); rivalizar; ser rivales; (in a competition) concurrir

competence /'kompɪtəns/ n aptitud, f; capacidad, f; competencia, f

competent /'kompɪtənt/ a competente; capaz

competition /ˌkompɪ'tɪʃən/ n competencia, competición, rivalidad, f; emulación, f; (contest, etc.) concurso, m. **spirit of c.,** espíritu de competencia, m

competitive /kəm'petɪtɪv/ a competidor; de competición. **c. examination,** oposición, f

competitor /kəm'petɪtər/ n competidor (-ra)

compilation /ˌkompə'leiʃən/ n compilación, f

compile /kəm'pail/ vt compilar

complacence /kəm'pleisəns/ n complacencia, satisfacción, f; contento de sí mismo, m

complacent /kəm'pleisənt/ a satisfecho; pagado de sí mismo

complain /kəm'plein/ vi quejarse; lamentarse; Law. querellarse. **He complains about everything,** Se queja de todo

complaint /kəm'pleint/ n queja, f; lamento, m; Law. demanda, f; (illness) enfermedad, f. **to lodge a c. (against),** quejarse (de)

complaisant /kəm'pleisənt/ a complaciente, cortés, afable; (of husbands) consentido, sufrido

complement / n 'kɒmpləmənt; v -,ment/ n complemento, m; total, número completo, m. —vt completar

complementary /,kɒmplə'mentəri/ a complementario

complete /kəm'plit/ a entero; completo; perfecto; acabado. —vt completar; acabar; (happiness, etc.) coronar, poner el último toque (a); (years) cumplir; (forms) llenar

completion /kəm'plifən/ n terminación, f, fin, m

complex / a kəm'plɛks; n 'kɒmplɛks/ a complejo. —n complejo, m. **inferiority c.,** complejo de inferioridad, m

complexion /kəm'plɛkfən/ n tez, f, cutis, m; Fig. carácter, m

complexity /kəm'plɛksiti/ n complejidad, f

compliance /kəm'plaiəns/ n condescendencia, f; (subservience) sumisión, f; obediencia, f. **in c. with,** de acuerdo con, en conformidad con

compliant /kəm'plaiənt/ a condescendiente; sumiso, dócil; obediente

complicate /'kɒmpli,keit/ vt complicar

complicated /'kɒmpli,keitid/ a complejo; complicado; enredado

complicity /kəm'plisiti/ n complicidad, f. **c. in a crime,** complicidad en un crimen

compliment / n 'kɒmpləmənt; v -,ment/ n cumplido, m, cortesía, f; requiebro, Inf. piropo, m; favor, m; honor, m; (greeting) saludo, m; (congratulation) felicitación, f. —vt cumplimentar; requebrar; (flatter) adular, lisonjear; (congratulate) felicitar. **They did him the c. of reading his book,** Le hicieron el honor de leer su libro. **to pay compliments,** hacer cumplidos; Inf..echar piropos

complimentary /,kɒmplə'mentəri/ a lisonjero; galante. **c. ticket,** billete gratuito, m

comply /kəm'plai/ vi (with) cumplir, obedecer; conformarse (con); consentir

component /kəm'pounənt/ a componente. —n componente, m

comport /kəm'pɔrt/ vt **(oneself),** comportarse

comportment /kəm'pɔrtmənt/ n comportamiento, m, conducta, f

compose /kəm'pouz/ vt (all meanings) componer. **to c. oneself,** serenarse, calmarse. **to c. one's features,** componer el semblante

composed /kəm'pouzd/ a sereno, tranquilo, sosegado

composite /kəm'pɒzit/ a compuesto; mixto. —n compuesto, m; Bot. planta compuesta, f

composition /,kɒmpə'zifən/ n (all meanings) composición, f

composure /kəm'pouʒər/ n tranquilidad,

serenidad, calma, f; sangre fría, f, aplomo, m

compote /'kɒmpout/ n compota, f

compound /'kɒmpaund/ vt mezclar, componer; concertar. —a compuesto. —n compuesto, m; mixtura, f. **c. interest,** interés compuesto, m

comprehend /,kɒmprɪ'hend/ vt comprender

comprehensible /,kɒmprɪ'hensəbəl/ a comprensible

comprehension /,kɒmprɪ'henʃən/ n comprensión, f

comprehensive /,kɒmprɪ'hensɪv/ a comprensivo

compress / v kəm'pres; n 'kɒmpres/ vt comprimir; condensar; reducir, abreviar. —n compresa, f

compression /kəm'preʃən/ n compresión, f

compressor /kəm'presər/ n compresor, m

comprise /kəm'praiz/ vt .comprender, abarcar, incluir

compromise /'kɒmprə,maiz/ n compromiso, m, transacción, f; componenda, f. —vt (settle) componer, arreglar; (jeopardize) arriesgar; comprometer. —vi transigir. **to c. oneself,** comprometerse

compromising /'kɒmprə,maiziŋ/ a comprometedor

compulsion /kəm'pʌlʃən/ n compulsión, fuerza, f. **under c.,** a la fuerza

compulsory /kəm'pʌlsəri/ a obligatorio. **c. measures,** medidas obligatorias, f pl. **c. powers,** poderes absolutos, m pl

compunction /kəm'pʌŋkʃən/ n compunción, f, remordimiento, m; escrúpulo, m. **without c.,** sin escrúpulo

computation /,kɒmpyu'teiʃən/ n computación, f, cómputo, m

compute /kəm'pyut/ vt computar, calcular.

computer /kəm'pyutər/ m computador, m (Western Hemisphere), ordenador, m (Spain)

computer center n centro calculador, centro de computación, m

comrade /'kɒmræd/ n camarada, mf compañero (-ra)

con /kɒn/ vt estudiar; leer con atención; Naut. gobernar (el buque)

concave /kɒn'keiv/ a cóncavo

conceal /kən'sil/ vt esconder, ocultar; (the truth, etc.) encubrir, callar; disimular

concealed /kən'sild/ a oculto; escondido; disimulado. **c. lighting,** iluminación indirecta, f. **c. turning,** (on a road) viraje oculto, m

concealment /kən'silmənt/ n ocultación, f; encubrimiento, m; (place of) escondite, m; secreto, m

concede /kən'sid/ vt conceder

conceit /kən'sit/ n presunción, vanidad, fatuidad, f, envanecimiento, m. **to have a good c. of oneself,** estar pagado de sí mismo

conceited /kən'siːtɪd/ *a* presumido, fatuo, vanidoso

conceivable /kən'siːvəbəl/ *a* concebible, imaginable

conceive /kən'siːv/ *vt* concebir; (affection, etc.) tomar; (an idea, etc.) formar; (plan) formular, idear. —*vi* concebir; (understand) comprender; (suppose) imaginar, suponer

concentrate /'kɒnsən,treɪt/ *vt* concentrar. —*vi* concentrarse; (on, upon) dedicarse (a), entregarse (a); prestar atención (a), concentrar atención (en)

concentration /,kɒnsən'treɪʃən/ *n* concentración, *f*. **c. camp**, campo de concentración, *m*

concentric /kən'sɛntrɪk/ *a* concéntrico

concept /'kɒnsɛpt/ *n* concepto, *m*

conception /kən'sɛpʃən/ *n* concepción, *f*; conocimiento, *m*; idea, *f*, concepto, *m*. **to have not the remotest c. of**, no tener la menor idea de

concern /kən'sɜrn/ *vt* tocar, tener que vercon, importar, concernir; interesar; referirse (a); tratar (de); (trouble) preocupar, inquietar; (take part in) ocuparse (de or con). —*n* asunto, *m*, cosa, *f*; (share) interés, *m*; (anxiety) inquietud, *f*; solicitud, *f*; (business) casa comercial, firma, *f*. **as concerns...,** en cuanto a..., respecto a... **It concerns the date of the next meeting,** Es cuestión de la fecha de la próxima reunión. **It is no c. of yours,** No tiene nada que ver contigo. **The book is concerned with the adventures of two boys,** El libro trata de las aventuras de dos muchachos

concerned /kən'sɜrnd/ *a* ocupado (en); afectado; (in a crime) implicado (en); (troubled) preocupado; inquieto, agitado

concerning /kən'sɜrnɪŋ/ *prep* tocante a, con respecto a, referente a, sobre

concert /'kɒnsɜrt/ *n* acuerdo, concierto, *m*, armonía, *f*; *Mus.* concierto, *m*, *vt* concertar, acordar. **in c. with,** de acuerdo con. **c. hall,** sala de conciertos, *f*

concerted /kən'sɜrtɪd/ *a* concertado

concerto /kən'tʃɛrtou/ *n* concierto, *m*

concession /kən'sɛʃən/ *n* concesión, *f*; privilegio, *m*

concessionaire /kən,sɛʃə'nɛər/ *n* concesionario, *m*

conciliate /kən'sɪli,eɪt/ *vt* conciliar

conciliatory /kən'sɪliə,tɔri/ *a* conciliador

concise /kən'saɪs/ *a* conciso, breve, sucinto

conclude /kən'kluːd/ *vt* concluir. —*vi* concluirse

conclusion /kən'kluːʒən/ *n* conclusión, *f*. **in c.,** en conclusión, para terminar. **to come to the c. that...,** concluir que...

conclusive /kən'kluːsɪv/ *a* conclusivo, concluyente, decisivo

concoct /kɒn'kɒkt/ *vt* confeccionar; inventar

concomitant /kɒn'kɒmɪtənt/ *a* concomitante. —*n* concomitante, *m*

concord /'kɒnkɔrd/ *n* concordia, buena inteligencia, armonía, *f*; (*Mus. Gram.*) concordancia, *f*; (of sounds) armonía, *f*

concordance /kɒn'kɔrdns/ *n* concordia, armonía, *f*; (book) concordancias, *f pl*

concrete /'kɒnkrit/ *a* concreto; de hormigón. —*n* hormigón, *m*. —*vt* concretar; cubrir de hormigón. **reinforced c.,** hormigón armado, *m*

concur /kən'kɜr/ *vi* coincidir, concurrir; estar de acuerdo, convenir (en)

concurrence /kən'kɜrəns/ *n* (agreement) acuerdo, consentimiento, *m*, aprobación, *f*

concurrent /kən'kɜrənt/ *a* concurrente; unánime; coincidente

concussion /kən'kʌʃən/ *n* concusión, *f*; *Med.* concusión cerebral, *f*

condemn /kən'dɛm/ *vt* condenar; censurar, culpar; (forfeit) confiscar. **condemned cell,** celda de los condenados a muerte, *f*

condemnation /,kɒndɛm'neɪʃən/ *n* condenación, *f*; censura, *f*

condense /kən'dɛns/ *vt* condensar. —*vi* condensarse

condenser /kən'dɛnsər/ *n* (*Elec. Mech. Chem.*) condensador, *m*

condescend /,kɒndə'sɛnd/ *vi* dignarse; (in a bad sense) consentir (en); (with affability) condescender

condescending /,kɒndə'sɛndɪŋ/ *a* condescendiente

condescendingly /,kɒndə'sɛndɪŋli/ *adv* con condescendencia

condescension /,kɒndə'sɛnʃən/ *n* condescendencia, *f*; afabilidad, *f*

condign /kən'daɪn/ *a* condigno

condiment /'kɒndəmənt/ *n* condimento, *m*

condition /kən'dɪʃən/ *n* condición, *f*; estado, *m*; *pl* **conditions,** condiciones, *f pl*; circunstancias, *f pl*. **on c. that,** con tal que; siempre que, dado que. **to be in no c. to,** no estar en condiciones de. **to change one's c.,** cambiar de estado. **to keep oneself in c.,** mantenerse en buena forma

conditional /kən'dɪʃənl/ *a* condicional. **to be c. on,** depender de

conditioned /kən'dɪʃənd/ *a* acondicionado. **c. reflex,** reflejo acondicionado, *m*

condole /kən'doul/ *vi* condolerse (de); (on a bereavement) dar el pésame

condolence /kən'douləns/ *n* condolencia, *f*. **to present one's condolences,** dar el pésame

condom /'kɒndəm/ *n* condón, *m*

condone /kən'doun/ *vt* condonar, perdonar

conduce /kən'dus/ *vi* contribuir, conducir

conducive /kən'dusɪv/ *a* que contribuye, conducente; favorable

conduct /*n* 'kɒndʌkt; *v* kən'dʌkt/ *n* conducta, *f*. —*vt* conducir; guiar; *Mus.* dirigir; (oneself) portarse, conducirse; *Phys.* conducir. —*vi Mus.* dirigir (una orquesta, etc.); *Phys.* ser conductor. **con-**

ducted tour, excursión acompañada, f; viaje acompañado, m

conductor /kən'dʌktər/ n (guide) guía, mf; (of an orchestra) director, m; (on a tram, etc.) cobrador, m; Phys. conductor, m

conduit /'kɒnduɪt/ n conducto, m; cañería, f; canal, m

cone /koun/ n (Bot. Geom. etc.) cono, m

confection /kən'fɛkʃən/ n confección, f, vt confeccionar

confectionery /kən'fɛkʃə,nɛri/ n confitería, pastelería, repostería, f

confederate / a, n kən'fedərɪt; v -'fedə,reit/ a confederado; aliado. —n confederado, m; (in crime) cómplice, mf. —vt confederar. —vi confederarse; aliarse

confer /kən'fɜr/ vt conceder, conferir; (an honor, etc.) otorgar, investir (con). —vi consultar (con); deliberar, considerar

conference /'kɒnfərəns/ n conferencia, consulta, f; conversación, f

conferment /kən'fɜrmənt/ n otorgamiento, m; concesión, f

confess /kən'fɛs/ vt confesar, reconocer; Inf. admitir; (of a priest) confesar; (of a penitent) confesarse. —vi hacer una confesión; (one's sins) confesarse. **I c. that I was surprised**, No puedo negar que me sorprendió

confessed /kən'fɛst/ a confesado, declarado

confession /kən'fɛʃən/ n confesión, f; reconocimiento, m; declaración, f; religión, f; (creed) credo, m. **to go to c.**, confesarse. **to hear a c.**, confesar (a)

confessional /kən'fɛʃənļ/ n confesionario, m

confessor /kən'fɛsər/ n confesor, m

confetti /kən'fɛti/ n pl confeti, papel picado m, serpentina, f

confidant /'kɒnfɪ,dænt/ n confidente, m

confidante /,kɒnfɪ'dænt/ n confidenta, f

confide /kən'faid/ vi confiar (a or en). —vt confiar

confidence /'kɒnfɪdəns/ n confianza, f; seguridad, f; (revelation) confidencia, f. **in c.**, en confianza. **over-c.**, presunción, f. **to have c. in**, tener confianza en. **c. man**, caballero de industria, estafador, m. **c. trick**, timo, m

confident /'kɒnfɪdənt/ a confiado; seguro; (conceited) presumido

confidential /,kɒnfɪ'dɛnʃəl/ a confidencial; de confianza. **c. clerk**, empleado (-da) de confianza. **c. letter**, carta confidencial, f

confidentially /,kɒnfɪ'dɛnʃəli/ adv en confianza, confidencialmente

confidently /'kɒnfɪdəntli/ adv confiadamente

confiding /kən'faidɪŋ/ a confiado

confine /kən'fain/ vt limitar; (imprison) encerrar. **confined space**, espacio limitado, m. **to be confined**, (of a woman) estar de parto, parir. **to be con-**

fined to one's room, no poder dejar su cuarto. **to c. oneself to**, limitarse a

confinement /kən'fainmənt/ n encierro, m, prisión, f; reclusión, f; (of a woman) parto, m. **to suffer solitary c.**, estar incomunicado

confines /'kɒnfainz/ n pl límites, m pl; confines, m pl; fronteras, f pl

confirm /kən'fɜrm/ vt confirmar; corroborar; Eccl. confirmar

confirmation /,kɒnfər'meiʃən/ n confirmación, f; (of a treaty) ratificación, f; Eccl. confirmación, f

confirmed /kən'fɜrmd/ a inveterado

confiscate /'kɒnfə,skeit/ vt confiscar

conflagration /,kɒnflə'greiʃən/ n conflagración, f, incendio, m

conflict / n 'kɒnflɪkt; v kən'flɪkt/ n conflicto, m; lucha, f. —vi estar opuesto (a), estar en contradicción (con)

conflicting /kən'flɪktɪŋ/ a opuesto; incompatible; (of evidence) contradictorio

conform /kən'fɔrm/ vt ajustar, conformar. —vi ajustarse (a), amoldarse (a); conformarse (a); adaptarse (a)

conformity /kən'fɔrmɪti/ n conformidad, f. **in c. with**, en conformidad con, con arreglo a

confound /kɒn'faund/ vt confundir. **C. it!** ¡Demonio!

confounded /kɒn'faundɪd/ a perplejo; Inf. maldito

confront /kən'frʌnt/ vt hacer frente (a), afrontar; salir al paso; confrontar

confuse /kən'fyuz/ vt turbar, aturdir; confundir (con); (the issue) obscurecer; (disconcert) desconcertar, dejar confuso (a); dejar perplejo (a). **You have confused one thing with another**, Has confundido una cosa con otra. **My mind was confused**, Mis ideas eran confusas; Tenía la cabeza trastornada

confused /kən'fyuzd/ a confuso

confusing /kən'fyuzɪŋ/ a turbador; desconcertante. **It is all very c.**, Todo ello es muy difícil de comprender

confusion /kən'fyuʒən/ n confusión, f. **covered with c.**, confuso, avergonzado. **to be in c.**, estar confuso; estar en desorden

confute /kən'fyut/ vt (a person) confundir; (by evidence) refutar, confutar

congeal /kən'dʒil/ vt congelar; (blood) coagular. —vi congelarse, helarse; coagularse

congenial /kən'dʒinyəl/ a (of persons) simpático; propicio, favorable; agradable

congenital /kən'dʒɛnɪtļ/ a congénito

congest /kən'dʒɛst/ vt atestar; amontonar; Med. congestionar

congested /kən'dʒɛstɪd/ a Med. congestionado; (of places) atestado de gente; de mayor población; concurrido. **c. area**, área de mayor densidad de población, f

congestion /kən'dʒɛstʃən/ n Med. congestión, f; densidad del tráfico, f; mayor densidad de población, f

congratulate /kən'grætʃə,leit/ vt felicitar, dar la enhorabuena (a); congratular

congratulation /kən,grætʃə'leiʃən/ n felicitación, enhorabuena, f; congratulación, f

congratulatory /kən'grætʃələ,tɔri/ a de felicitación, congratulatorio

congregate /'kɒŋgrı,geit/ vi congregarse, reunirse, juntarse

congregation /,kɒŋgrı'geiʃən/ n congregación, f; asamblea, reunión, f; (in a church) fieles, m pl; (parishioners) feligreses, m pl

congress /'kɒŋgrıs/ n congreso, m. **C.-man,** miembro del Congreso, m

conjecture /kən'dʒɛktʃər/ n conjetura, f, vt conjeturar

conjoint /kən'dʒɔint/ a asociado, conjunto

conjugal /'kɒndʒəgəl/ a conyugal

conjugate /'kɒndʒə,geit/ vt conjugar. —vi conjugarse

conjugation /,kɒndʒə'geiʃən/ n conjugación, f

conjunction /kən'dʒʌŋkʃən/ n conjunción, f. **in c. with,** de acuerdo con

conjunctivitis /,kən,dʒʌŋktə'vaitıs/ n conjuntivitis, f

conjure /'kɒndʒər/ vt (implore) rogar, suplicar. —vi (juggle) hacer juegos de manos. **a name to c. with,** un nombre todopoderoso. **to c. up,** (spirits) conjurar; Fig. evocar

conjuring /'kɒndʒərıŋ/ n prestidigitación, f, juegos de manos, m pl. **c. trick,** juego de manos, m. **c. up,** evocación, f

connect /kə'nɛkt/ vt juntar, unir; (relate) relacionar; asociar; (Elec. and Mech.) conectar. —vi juntarse, unirse; relacionarse; asociarse; (of events) encadenarse; (of trains) enlazar. **This train connects with the Madrid express,** Este tren enlaza con el expreso de Madrid. **They are connected with the Borgia family,** Están emparentados con los Borgia, Son parientes de los Borgia

connected /kə'nɛktıd/ a conexo; (coherent) coherente; relacionado; asociado; (in a crime) implicado; (by marriage, etc.) emparentado

connecting /kə'nɛktıŋ/ a que une; (Mech. and Elec.) conectivo; (of doors, etc.) comunicante. **c.-link,** Mech. varilla de conexión, f; Fig. lazo, m. **c.-rod,** biela, f

connivance /kə'naivəns/ n consentimiento, m; complicidad, f

connive (at) /kə'naiv/ vi hacer la vista gorda, ser cómplice (en)

connotation /,kɒnə'teiʃən/ n connotación, f

connote /kə'nout/ vt connotar

conquer /'kɒŋkər/ vt conquistar; vencer. —vi triunfar

conquering /'kɒŋkərıŋ/ a conquistador, vencedor; triunfante, victorioso

conqueror /'kɒŋkərər/ n conquistador, m; vencedor, m

conquest /'kɒnkwɛst/ n conquista, f. **to make a c. of,** conquistar

conscience /'kɒnʃəns/ n conciencia, f. **in all c.,** en verdad. **with a clear c.,** con la conciencia limpia. **c.-stricken,** lleno de remordimientos

conscientious /,kɒnʃi'ɛnʃəs/ a concienzudo; diligente. **c. objector,** objetor de conciencia, m

conscientiously /,kɒnʃi'ɛnʃəsli/ adv concienzudamente

conscientiousness /,kɒnʃi'ɛnʃəsnıs/ n conciencia, diligencia, f; rectitud, f

conscious /'kɒnʃəs/ a consciente. —n Psychol. consciente, m. **to become c.,** (after unconsciousness) volver en sí. **to become c. of,** darse cuenta de

consciously /'kɒnʃəsli/ adv conscientemente, a sabiendas

consciousness /'kɒnʃəsnıs/ n conciencia, f; conocimiento, sentido, m. **to lose c.,** perder el conocimiento, perder el sentido. **to recover c.,** recobrar el sentido, volver en sí

consecrate /'kɒnsı,kreit/ vt consagrar; bendecir

consecration /,kɒnsı'kreiʃən/ n consagración, f; dedicación, f

consecutive /kən'sɛkyətıv/ a consecutivo

consensus /kən'sɛnsəs/ n consenso, m, unanimidad, f. **c. of opinion,** opinión general, f

consent /kən'sɛnt/ vi consentir. —n consentimiento, m; permiso, m, aquiescencia, f. **by common c.,** de común acuerdo

consequence /'kɒnsı,kwɛns/ n consecuencia, f; resultado, m; importancia, f, **in c.,** por consiguiente. **of no c.,** de resultas de. **of no c.,** sin importancia

consequent /'kɒnsı,kwɛnt/ a consecuente, consiguiente

consequential /,kɒnsı'kwɛnʃəl/ a consecuente; (of persons) fatuo, engreído

consequently /'kɒnsı,kwɛntli/ adv por consiguiente, en consecuencia

conservation /,kɒnsər'veiʃən/ n conservación, f. **c. of energy,** conservación de energía, f

conservative /kən'sɜrvətıv/ a preservativo; conservador. —n conservador (-ra). **c. party,** partido conservador, m

conservatoire /kən,sɜrvə'twar/ n conservatorio de música, m

conservatory /kən'sɜrvə,tɔri/ n invernáculo, invernadero, m

conserve /kən'sɜrv/ vt conservar

consider /kən'sıdər/ vt considerar, pensar meditar; tomar en cuenta; examinar; (deem) juzgar; (believe) creer, estar convencido de (que); (of persons) considerar. **all things considered,** considerando todos los puntos, después de considerarlo todo

considerable /kən'sıdərəbəl/ a considerable

considerate /kən'sɪdərɪt/ *a* considerado, solícito

considerately /kən'sɪdərtli/ *adv* con consideración, solícitamente

consideration /kən,sɪdə'reɪʃən/ *n* consideración, *f;* reflexión, deliberación, *f;* remuneración, *f.* **out of c. for,** en consideración de; por consideración a. **to take into c.,** tomar en cuenta, tomar en consideración

considered /kən'sɪdərd/ *a* considerado

considering /kən'sɪdərɪŋ/ *prep* en consideración de, considerando, en vista de

consign /kən'saɪn/ *vt* consignar; *Fig.* enviar. **to c. to oblivion,** sepultar en el olvido

consignee /,kɒnsaɪ'niː/ *n* consignatario, *m*

consignment /kən'saɪnmənt/ *n* consignación, *f;* envío, *m*

consist /kən'sɪst/ *vi* consistir (en); ser compatible (con). **to c. of,** componerse de, consistir de

consistent /kən'sɪstənt/ *a* compatible; lógico; (of persons) consecuente

consistently /kən'sɪstəntli/ *adv* conformemente (a); consecuentemente

consolation /,kɒnsə'leɪʃən/ *n* consuelo, *m,* consolación, *f*

console /'kɒnsoul/ *vt* consolar; confortar. —*n Archit.* cartela, *f.* **c. table,** consola, *f*

consolidate /kən'sɒlɪ,deɪt/ *vt* consolidar. —*vi* consolidarse

consoling /kən'soulɪŋ/ *a* consolador; confortador

consonant /'kɒnsənənt/ *a* consonante

consort /*n* 'kɒnsɔrt, *v* kən'sɔrt/ *n* consorte, *mf.* **to c. with,** frecuentar la compañía de; ir con; acompañar (a). **prince c.,** príncipe consorte, *m*

conspicuous /kən'spɪkyuəs/ *a* conspicuo; prominente; notable. **to be c.,** destacarse; llamar la atención. **to make oneself c.,** ponerse en evidencia, llamar la atención

conspicuously /kən'spɪkyuəsli/ *adv* visiblemente; muy en evidencia

conspiracy /kən'spɪrəsi/ *n* conspiración, *f;* complot, *m*

conspirator /kən'spɪrətər/ *n* conspirador (-ra)

conspire /kən'spaɪər/ *vi* conspirar

constancy /'kɒnstənsi/ *n* constancia, *f*

constant /'kɒnstənt/ *a* constante; incesante. —*n* constante, *m*

constellation /,kɒnstə'leɪʃən/ *n* constelación, *f*

consternation /,kɒnstər'neɪʃən/ *n* consternación, *f;* espanto, terror, *m*

constipate /'kɒnstɪ,peɪt/ *vt* estreñir

constipation /,kɒnstɪ'peɪʃən/ *n* estreñimiento, *m,* constipación de vientre, *f*

constituency /kən'stɪtʃuənsi/ *n* distrito electoral, *m*

constituent /kən'stɪtʃuənt/ *a* constituyente. —*n* constituyente, *m;* componente, *m;* elector (-ra)

constitute /'kɒnstɪ,tut/ *vt* constituir; nombrar; autorizar

constitution /,kɒnstɪ'tuʃən/ *n* constitución, *f*

constitutional /,kɒnstɪ'tuʃənl/ *a* constitucional

constrain /kən'streɪn/ *vt* obligar, forzar. **I felt constrained to help them,** Me sentí obligado a ayudarles

constrained /kən'streɪnd/ *a* (of smiles, etc.) forzado; (of silences) violento; (of persons) avergonzado

constraint /kən'streɪnt/ *n* fuerza, compulsión, *f;* (of atmosphere) tensión, *f;* (reserve) reserva, *f;* vergüenza, *f*

constrict /kən'strɪkt/ *vt* apretar, estrechar

construct /kən'strʌkt/ *vt* edificar; construir

construction /kən'strʌkʃən/ *n* construcción, *f;* interpretación, *f.* **to put a wrong c. on,** interpretar mal

constructive /kən'strʌktɪv/ *a* constructor

constructor /kən'strʌktər/ *n* constructor, *m*

construe /kən'stru/ *vt* construir; (translate) traducir; *Fig.* interpretar

consul /'kɒnsəl/ *n* cónsul, *m*

consular fees *n pl* derechos consulares, *m pl*

consulate /'kɒnsəlɪt/ *n* consulado, *m.* **c. general,** consulado general, *m*

consult /kən'sʌlt/ *vt* consultar. —*vi* consultar (con), aconsejarse (con)

consultant /kən'sʌltənt/ *n* (*Med.* and other uses) especialista, *m*

consultation /,kɒnsəl'teɪʃən/ *n* consulta, *f*

consulting /kən'sʌltɪŋ/ *a* consultor. **c. hours,** horas de consulta, *f pl.* **c. rooms,** consultorio, *m*

consume /kən'sum/ *vt* consumir; (eat) comerse, tragarse. —*vi* consumirse. **to be consumed by envy,** estar consumido por la envidia. **to be consumed by thirst,** estar muerto de sed

consumer /kən'sumər/ *n* consumidor (-ra)

consummate /*a* 'kɒnsəmɪt; *v* -,meɪt/ *a* consumido, perfecto. —*vt* consumar

consumption /kən'sʌmpʃən/ *n* consumo, *m;* gasto, *m; Med.* tuberculosis, *f.* **fuel c.,** consumo de combustible, *m*

consumptive /kən'sʌmptɪv/ *a* destructivo; *Med.* tísico, hético. —*n* tísico (-ca)

contact /'kɒntækt/ *n* contacto, *m, vt* ponerse en contacto con. **to be in c. with,** estar en contacto con

contagious /kən'teɪdʒəs/ *a* contagioso

contain /kən'teɪn/ *vt* contener; incluir; *Geom.* encerrar; (arithmetic) ser divisible por; (oneself) dominarse. **I could not c. myself,** No pude dominarme

container /kən'teɪnər/ *n* recipiente, *m;* envase, *m;* (box) caja, *f*

contaminate /kən'tæmə,neɪt/ *vt* contaminar; corromper

contemplate /'kɒntəm,pleɪt/ *vt* contemplar; meditar, considerar; (plan) tener intención de, pensar, proponerse

contemplation /,kɒntəm'pleiʃən/ n contemplación, f; meditación, f; expectación, esperanza, f; (plan) proyecto, m. **to have something in c.,** proyectar algo

contemplative /kən'templətɪv/ a contemplativo

contemporary /kən'tempə,reri/ a contemporáneo; (of persons) coetáneo; (of events, etc.) actual. —n contemporáneo (-ea)

contempt /kən'tempt/ n desprecio, menosprecio, m; desdén, m. **c. of court,** falta de respeto a la sala, f

contemptible /kən'temptəbəl/ a menospreciable, despreciable; vil

contempt of court n rebeldía a la corte, f

contemptuous /kən'temptʃuəs/ a desdeñoso; despectivo; de desprecio. **to be c. of,** desdeñar; menospreciar, tener en poco (a)

contemptuously /kən'temptʃuəsli/ adv con desprecio, desdeñosamente

contend /kən'tend/ vi contender; (affirm) sostener, mantener. **He contended that...,** Sostuvo que...; **contending party,** Law. parte litigante, f

content / n 'kɒntent; a, v kən'tent/ n contenido, m; capacidad, f; (emotion) contento, m; satisfacción, f. —a contento; satisfecho (de). —vt contentar; satisfacer. **to one's heart's c.,** a pedir de boca; a gusto de uno; cuanto quisiera

contented /kən'tentid/ a satisfecho, contento

contention /kən'tenʃən/ n disputa, controversia, discusión, f; argumento, m, opinión, f

contentious /kən'tenʃəs/ a contencioso

contentment /kən'tentmənt/ n contentamiento, m; contento, m

contest / v kən'test; n 'kɒntest/ vt disputar; (a suit) defender; (a match, an election, etc.) disputar. —n disputa, f; combate, m, lucha, f; (competition) concurso, m

contestant /kən'testənt/ n contendiente, mf

context /'kɒntekst/ n contexto, m

contiguous /kən'tɪgyuəs/ a contiguo, lindero, adyacente

continence /'kɒntɪnəns/ n continencia, f

continent /'kɒntɪnənt/ a continente. —n continente, m

continental /,kɒntɪn'entl/ a continental

continental shelf n plataforma continental, f

contingency /kən'tɪndʒənsi/ n contingencia, f

contingent /kən'tɪndʒənt/ a contingente. —n Mil. contingente, m. **to be c. on,** (of events) depender de

continual /kən'tɪnyuəl/ a continuo

continuation /kən,tɪnyu'eiʃən/ n continuación, f; prolongación, f

continue /kən'tɪnyu/ vt continuar; seguir; prolongarse; durar. —vi continuar;

seguir; proseguir; perpetuar; (in an office) retener. **to be continued,** se continuará, continuará, seguirá

continuity /,kɒntn'uiti/ n continuidad, f

continuous /kən'tɪnyuəs/ a continuo. **c. performance,** sesión continua, f

continuously /kən'tɪnyuəsli/ adv de continuo, continuamente

contort /kən'tɔrt/ vt retorcer

contortion /kən'tɔrʃən/ n contorsión, f

contour /'kɒntʊr/ n contorno, m; curva de nivel, f. **c. map,** mapa con curvas de nivel, m

contraband /'kɒntrə,bænd/ n contrabando, m

contraception /,kɒntrə'sepʃən/ n anticoncepción, f

contraceptive /,kɒntrə'septɪv/ n anticonceptivo, m

contract /n 'kɒntrækt; v kən'trækt/ n pacto, m; (Com. and Law.) contrato, m; (betrothal) esponsales, m pl; (marriage) capitulaciones, f pl: (cards) "Bridge," m. —vt contraer; (acquire) adquirir, contraer; (a marriage, etc.) contraer; (be betrothed to) desposarse con; (by formal contract) contratar; pactar. —vi (shrink) contraerse, encogerse; comprometerse por contrato. **breach of c.,** no cumplimiento de contrato, m. **c. party,** (of matrimony) contrayente, mf

contraction /kən'trækʃən/ n contracción, f (act or process); forma contracta, f (like isn't or can't)

contractor /'kɒntræktər/ n contratista, mf

contradict /,kɒntrə'dɪkt/ vt contradecir; desmentir

contradiction /,kɒntrə'dɪkʃən/ n contradicción, f; negación, f

contradictory /,kɒntrə'dɪktəri/ a contradictorio; opuesto (a), contrario (a)

contraption /kən'træpʃən/ n Inf. artefacto, m

contrariness /'kɒntrerinis/ n Inf. testarudez, terquedad, f

contrariwise /'kɒntreri,waiz/ adv al contrario; al revés

contrary /'kɒntreri/ a contrario; opuesto (a); desfavorable, poco propicio; (of persons) difícil, terco. —n contraria, f; (logic) contrario, m, adv en contra, contrariamente. **on the c.,** al contrario. **to be c.,** (of persons) llevar la contraria

contrast /n 'kɒntræst; v kən'træst/ n contraste, m. —vt contrastar (con). —vi contrastar (con), hacer contraste (con)

contravene /,kɒntrə'vin/ vt contravenir; atacar, oponerse (a)

contribute /kən'trɪbyut/ vt contribuir; (an article) escribir

contribution /,kɒntrə'byuʃən/ n contribución, f; (to a review, etc.) artículo, m

contributor /kən'trɪbyətər/ n contribuyente, mf; (to a journal) colaborador (-ra)

contrite /kən'trait/ a penitente, arrepentido, contrito

contrition /kən'trɪʃən/ n contrición, penitencia, f; arrepentimiento, m

contrivance /kən'traɪvəns/ n invención, f; (scheme) treta, idea, estratagema, f; (machine) aparato, mecanismo, artefacto, m

contrive /kən'traɪv/ vt inventar; idear, proyectar. —vi (succeed in) lograr, conseguir; (manage) arreglárselas

control /kən'troul/ n autoridad, f; dominio, m; gobierno, m; dirección, f; regulación, f; (restraint) freno, m; (Biol. and Spirit.) control, m; (of a vehicle) conducción, f; manejo, m, manipulación, f; pl **controls**, Mech. mando, m. —vt dirigir, regir; regular; usar, manejar, manipular; controlar; (dominate) dominar; (curb) refrenar, reprimir; (command) mandar. **He lost c. of the car**, Perdió el mando (or control) del automóvil. **out of c.**, fuera de mando, fuera de control. **remote c.**, mando a distancia, m. **to c. oneself**, dominarse, contenerse. **to lose c. of oneself**, no lograr dominarse, perder el control. **c. stick**, Aer. palanca de mando, f. **c. tower**, Aer. torre de mando, f

controller /kən'troulər/ n interventor, m; (device) regulador, m

controlling /kən'troulɪŋ/ n See **control**. a regulador

controversial /ˌkɒntrə'vɜrʃəl/ a debatible, discutible

controversy /'kɒntrə,vɜrsi/ n controversia, f; argumento, m; altercación, disputa, f

contumacious /ˌkɒntʊ'meɪʃəs/ a contumaz

contumely /'kɒntʊməli/ n contumelia, f

contusion /kən'tuʒən/ n herida contusa, f

conundrum /kə'nʌndrəm/ n acertijo, rompecabezas, m; problema, m

convalesce /ˌkɒnvə'lɛs/ vi convalecer, estar convaleciente

convalescence /ˌkɒnvə'lɛsəns/ n convalecencia, f

convalescent /ˌkɒnvə'lɛsənt/ a convaleciente. —n convaleciente, mf. **c. home**, casa de convalecencia, f

convene /kən'vin/ vt (a meeting) convocar; (person) citar. —vi reunirse

convenience /kən'vinyəns/ n conveniencia, f; (comfort) comodidad, f; utilidad, f; (advantage) ventaja, f; (public) retretes, m pl. **at one's c.**, cuando le sea conveniente a uno. **to make a c. of**, abusar de. **with all modern conveniences**, con todo el confort moderno

convenient /kən'vinyənt/ a conveniente; apropiado; cómodo. **I shall make it c. to see him at 6 p.m.**, Arreglaré mis asuntos para verle a las seis

conveniently /kən'vinyəntli/ adv cómodamente; oportunamente; sin inconveniente

convent /'kɒnvɛnt/ n convento, m

convention /kən'vɛnʃən/ n convención, f

conventional /kən'vɛnʃənl/ a convencional

conventual /kən'vɛntʃuəl/ a conventual. —n conventual, m

converge /kən'vɜrdʒ/ vi convergir

convergence /kən'vɜrdʒəns/ n convergencia, f

convergent /kən'vɜrdʒənt/ a convergente

conversance /kən'vɜrsəns/ n familiaridad, f; conocimiento, m

conversant /kən'vɜrsənt/ a familiar, versado, conocedor. **c. with**, versado en

conversation /ˌkɒnvər'seɪʃən/ n conversación, f. **to engage in c. with**, entablar conversación con

conversational /ˌkɒnvər'seɪʃənl/ a de conversación; (talkative) locuaz

converse /kən'vɜrs/ vi conversar. **to c. by signs**, hablar por señas

conversion /kən'vɜrʒən/ n conversión, f

convert /v kən'vɜrt, n 'kɒnvɜrt/ vt convertir; transformar. —n converso (-sa). **to become a c.**, convertirse

convertible /kən'vɜrtəbəl/ a convertible; transformable

convex /a kɒn'vɛks; n 'kɒnvɛks/ a convexo

convey /kən'veɪ/ vt transportar; conducir, llevar; (a meaning, etc.) comunicar, dar a entender; expresar; Law. traspasar

conveyance /kən'veɪəns/ n transporte, m; conducción, f; medio de transporte, m; vehículo, m; carruaje, m; (of property) traspaso, m; (document) escritura de traspaso, f. **public c.**, coche de alquiler, m; ómnibus, m

convict /n 'kɒnvɪkt; v kən'vɪkt/ n convicto, m; presidiario, m. —vt Law. condenar; culpar. **c. settlement**, colonia penal, f

conviction /kən'vɪkʃən/ n (of a prisoner) condenación, f; (belief) convencimiento, m, convicción, f

convince /kən'vɪns/ vt convencer

convincing /kən'vɪnsɪŋ/ a convincente

conviviality /kən,vɪvi'ælɪti/ n jovialidad, f

convocation /ˌkɒnvə'keɪʃən/ n convocación, f

convoke /kən'vouk/ vt convocar

convolution /ˌkɒnvə'luʃən/ n circunvolución, f; espira, f

convoy /'kɒnvɔɪ/ vt convoyar, escoltar. —n convoy, m. **to sail in a c.**, navegar en convoy

convulse /kən'vʌls/ vt agitar; sacudir; estremecer. **to be convulsed with laughter**, desternillarse de risa, morirse de risa

convulsion /kən'vʌlʃən/ n convulsión, f; conmoción, f

convulsive /kən'vʌlsɪv/ a convulsivo

cook /kʊk/ n cocinero (-ra). —vt guisar, cocer, cocinar; (falsify) falsear

cooker /'kʊkər/ n cocina, f. **gas c.**, cocina de gas, f

cooking /'kʊkɪŋ/ n arte de guisar, m, or

f; cocina, *f;* (of accounts, etc.) falsificación, *f.* **c. range,** cocina económica, *f.* **c.-stove,** cocina, *f.* **c. utensils,** batería de cocina, *f*

cool /kul/ *a* fresco; bastante frío; (not ardent and of receptions, etc.) frío; (calm) sereno, imperturbable. —*n* fresco, *m.* —*vi* enfriarse; (of love, etc.) resfriarse; (of the weather) refrescar; (of persons) refrescarse. —*vt* refrescar; enfriar. **to grow cooler,** (of weather) refrescarse; (of persons) tener menos calor. **It is c.,** Hace fresco. **to be as c. as a cucumber,** tener sangre fría. **c. drink,** bebida fría, *f.* **c.-headed,** sereno, imperturbable

cooling /'kulɪŋ/ *n* enfriamiento, *m,* a refrescante

coolly /'kuli/ *adv* frescamente; fríamente, con frialdad; imperturbablemente; (impudently) descaradamente

coolness /'kulnɪs/ *n* frescura, *f;* (of a welcome, etc.) frialdad, *f;* (sangfroid) sangre fría, serenidad, *f;* aplomo, *m*

coop /kup/ *n* gallinero, *m;* caponera, *f, vt* enjaular; encerrar. **to keep** (someone) **cooped up,** tener encerrado (a)

cooper /'kupər/ *n* tonelero, barrilero, *m, vt* hacer barriles

cooperate /kou'ɒpəˌreit/ *vi* cooperar; colaborar

cooperation /kou,ɒpə'reiʃən/ *n* cooperación, *f*

cooperative /kou'ɒpərətɪv/ *a* cooperativo. **c. society,** cooperativa, *f*

coopt /kou'ɒpt/ *vt* elegir por votación

coordinate /*v* kou'ɔrdəˌeit; *n, a* kou'ɔrdnɪt/ *vt* coordinar. —*n Math.* coordenada, *f.* —*a* coordenado

coordination /kou,ɔrdn'eiʃən/ *n* coordinación, *f*

cop /kɒp/ *n* (police officer) chapa (Ecuador), polizonte, *mf*

cope /koup/ *n Eccl.* capa, *f;* (of heaven) dosel, *m,* bóveda, *f.* **to c. with,** contender con; (a difficulty) hacer cara a, arrostrar

Copenhagen /,koupən'heigən, -'hɑgən/ Copenhague, *m*

copier /'kɒpiər/ *n* copiador (-ra)

coping /'koupɪŋ/ *n Archit.* albardilla, *f.* **c.-stone,** teja cumbrera, *f; Fig.* coronamiento, *m*

copious /'koupiəs/ *a* copioso, abundante

copiously /'koupiəsli/ *adv* en abundancia

copper /'kɒpər/ *n* cobre, *m;* (coin) calderilla, *f;* (vessel) caldera, *f.* —*a* de cobre. **c.-colored,** cobrizo. **c.-smith,** calderero, *m.* **c.-sulphate,** sulfato de cobre, *m*

copulate /'kɒpyəˌleit/ *vi* copularse

copy /'kɒpi/ *n* copia, *f;* (of a book) ejemplar, *m;* (of a paper) número, *m;* manuscrito, *m;* (subject-matter) material, *m.* —*vt* copiar; imitar; tomar como modelo (a). **rough c.,** borrador, *m.* **c.-book,** cuaderno de escritura, *m*

copying /'kɒpiɪŋ/ *n* imitación, *f;* transcripción, *f.* **c. ink,** tinta de copiar, *f*

copyist /'kɒpiɪst/ *n* copiador (-ra); (plagiarist) copiante, *mf*

copyright /'kɒpiˌrait/ *n* derechos de autor, *m pl;* propiedad literaria, *f.* —*a* protegido por los derechos de autor. —*vt* registrar como propiedad literaria. **C. reserved,** Derechos reservados, Queda hecho el depósito que marca la ley

copywriter /'kɒpiˌraitər/ *n* escritor de anuncios, *m*

coquetry /'koukɪtri/ *n* coquetería, *f*

coquette /kou'ket/ *n* coqueta, *f*

coquettish /kou'ketɪʃ/ *a* coquetón; atractivo

coral /'kɔrəl/ *n* coral, *m;* (polyp) coralina, *f.* —*a* de coral, coralino. **white c.,** madrépora, *f.* **c. beads,** corales, *m pl.* **c.-island,** atalón, *m.* **c.-reef,** escollo de coral, *m.* **c. snake,** coral, *f*

cord /kɔrd/ *n* cuerda, *f;* cordel, *m;* cordón, *m.* —*vt* encordelar. **spinal c.,** médula espinal, *f.* **umbilical c.,** cordón umbilical, *m*

cordial /'kɔrdʒəl/ *a* cordial; sincero, fervoroso. —*n* cordial, *m*

cordiality /kɔr'dʒælɪti/ *n* cordialidad, *f*

cordon /'kɔrdn/ *n* cordón, *m;* cinto, *m.* **to c. off,** acordonar

cordovan /'kɔrdəvən/ *a* cordobés. —*n* (leather) cordobán, *m*

corduroy /'kɔrdəˌrɔi/ *n* pana de cordoncillo, *f*

core /kɔr/ *n* (of a fruit) corazón, *m;* (of a rope) alma, *f,* centro, *m;* (of an abscess) foco, *m;* (of a corn) ojo, *m; Fig.* núcleo, *m;* esencia, *f;* lo esencial

coreligionist /,kɔri'lɪdʒənɪst/ *n* correligionario (-ia)

cork /kɔrk/ *n* corcho, *m;* (of a bottle) tapón, *m,* a de corcho. —*vt* tapar con corcho, taponar; (wine) encorchar; (the face) tiznar con corcho quemado. **pop of a c.,** taponazo, *m.* **to draw a c.,** descorchar. **c.-jacket,** chaleco salvavidas, *m.* **c. tree,** cornoque, *m*

corkscrew /'kɔrk,skru/ *n* sacacorchos, *m*

corn /kɔrn/ *n* grano, cereal, *m;* (wheat) trigo, *m;* (maize) maíz, *m;* (single seed) grano, *m;* (on the foot, etc.) callo, *m.* **Indian c.,** maíz, *m.* **c. cure,** callicida, *m.* **c.-exchange,** bolsa de granos, *f.* **c.-field,** campo de trigo, *m.* **c.-flower,** aciano, *m*

cornea /'kɔrniə/ *n* córnea, *f*

corner /'kɔrnər/ *n* ángulo, *m;* (of a street or building) esquina, *f;* (of a room) rincón, *m; Auto.* viraje, *m; Com.* monopolio, *m;* (of the eye) rabo, *m;* (Assoc. football) "corner," *m.* —*vt* arrinconar; acorralar; *Com.* acaparar. **the four corners of the earth,** las cinco partes del mundo. **a tight c.,** un lance apretado, un apuro. **to drive into a c.,** *Fig.* poner entre la espada y la pared. **to look out of the c. of the eye,** mirar de reojo. **to turn the c.,** doblar la esquina; *Fig.* pasar la crisis. **c.-cupboard,** rinconera, *f.* **c. seat,** asiento del rincón, *m.* **c.-stone,** piedra angular, *f*

cornered /'kɔrnərd/ *a* (of a person) aco-

rralado, en aprieto; (of hats) de... picos.
three-c. hat, sombrero de tres picos, *m*
cornet /kɔr'net/ *n* (musical instrument)
corneta, *f; Mil.* corneta, *m;* (paper)
cucurucho, *m.* **c. player,** cornetín, *m*
cornflour /'kɔrn,flauər/ *n* harina de
maíz, *f*
cornucopia /,kɔrnə'koupiə/ *n* cornucopia, *f*
corollary /'kɔrə,leri/ *n* corolario, *m*
coronation /,kɔrə'neiʃən/ *n* coronación, *f*
coroner /'kɔrənər/ *n* juez de guardia, *mf,*
médico forense, *m*
corporal /'kɔrpərəl/ *a* corporal, *n Mil.*
cabo, *m;* (altar-cloth) corporal, *m.* **c.
punishment,** castigo corporal, *m*
corporation /,kɔrpə'reiʃən/ *n* corporación, *f;* concejo, cabildo municipal, *m;*
(*Com. U.S.A.*) sociedad anónima, *f*
corporeal /kɔr'pɔriəl/ *a* corpóreo
corps /kɔr/ *n* cuerpo, *m*
corpse /kɔrps/ *n* cadáver, *m*
corpulence /'kɔrpyələns/ *n* gordura, obesidad, *f*
corpulent /'kɔrpyələnt/ *a* corpulento,
grueso, gordo
corpus /'kɔrpəs/ *n* cuerpo, *m.* **C. Christi,**
Corpus, *m.* **c. delicti,** cuerpo del delito, *m*
corpuscle /'kɔrpəsəl/ *n* corpúsculo, *m*
correct /kə'rekt/ *a* correcto; exacto, justo.
—*vt* corregir; rectificar; amonestar, reprender
correction /kə'rekʃən/ *n* corrección, *f;*
rectificación, *f*
corrective /kə'rektɪv/ *a* correctivo. —*n*
correctivo, *m*
correctness /kə'rektnɪs/ *n* corrección, *f;*
exactitud, *f;* justicia, *f*
correlate /'kɔrə,leit/ *vt* poner en correlación. —*vi* tener correlación
correlation /,kɔrə'leiʃən/ *n* correlación, *f*
correspond /,kɔrə'spɒnd/ *vi* corresponder (a); (by letter) escribirse, co-
rresponderse
correspondence /,kɔrə'spɒndəns/ *n* correspondencia, *f; Com.* correo, *m.* **c.
course,** curso por correspondencia, *m*
correspondent /,kɔrə'spɒndənt/ *n* correspondiente, *mf;* (*Com.* and journalist)
corresponsal, *mf.* **special c.,** corresponsal
extraordinario, *m*
corresponding /,kɔrə'spɒndɪŋ/ *a* correspondiente. **c. member,** miembro correspondiente, *m*
corridor /'kɔridər/ *n* corredor, pasillo, *m;*
(railway) pasillo, *m; Polit.* corredor, *m.* **c.
train,** tren con coches corridos, *m*
corroborate /kə'rɒbə,reit/ *vt* corroborar,
confirmar
corroboration /kə,rɒbə'reiʃən/ *n* corroboración, confirmación, *f*
corroborative /kə'rɒbə,reitɪv/ *a* corroborativo, confirmatorio
corrode /kə'roud/ *vt* corroer, morder; *Fig.*
roer
corrosion /kə'rouʒən/ *n* corrosión, *f*

corrosive /kə'rousɪv/ *a* corrosivo; mordaz
corrugate /'kɔrə,geit/ *vt* arrugar. —*vi*
arrugarse
corrugated /'kɔrə,geitɪd/ *a* arrugado;
ondulado. **c. iron,** chapa canaleta, *f*
corrugation /,kɔrə'geiʃən/ *n* corrugación, *f,* arrugamiento, *m*
corrupt /kə'rʌpt/ *a* corrompido; vicioso,
desmoralizado. —*vt* corromper. —*vi*
corromperse
corruption /kə'rʌpʃən/ *n* corrupción, *f*
corsage /kɔr'sɑʒ/ *n* corpiño, *m*
corset /'kɔrsit/ *n* corsé, *m, vt* encorsetar.
c. shop, corsetería, *f*
cortege /kɔr'teʒ/ *n* séquito, acompañamiento, *m;* desfile, *m*
cortex /'kɔrteks/ *n Bot. Anat.* corteza, *f*
cortisone /'kɔrtə,zoun/ *n* (drug) corti-
sona, *f*
coruscation /,kɔrə'skeiʃən/ *n* brillo, *m*
cosignatory /kou'signə,tɔri/ *n* cosigna-
tario (-ia)
cosine /'kousain/ *n* coseno, *m*
cosiness /'kouzinis/ *n* comodidad, *f*
cosmetic /kɒz'metik/ *a* cosmético. —*n*
afeite, cosmético, *m*
cosmic /'kɒzmik/ *a* cósmico
cosmopolitanism /,kɒzmə'pɒlitņ,izəm/
n cosmopolitismo, *m*
cosmos /'kɒzməs/ *n* cosmos, universo, *m*
Cossack /'kɒsæk/ *a* cosaco. —*n* cosaco
(-ca)
cosset /'kɒsit/ *vt* mimar, consentir
cost /kɒst/ *vi* costar. —*n* costa, *f,* coste,
precio, *m; Fig.* costa, *f; pl* costs, *Law.*
costas, *f pl.* **at all costs,** cueste lo que
cueste, a toda costa. **to my c.,** a mi costa.
c. of living, coste de la vida, *m.* **to c. a
fortune,** costar un sentido
Costa-Rican /'kɒstə'rikən/ *a* costarriqueño. —*n* costarriqueño (-ña)
coster /'kɔstər/ *n* vendedor (-ra) ambulante
costliness /'kɒstlinis/ *n* alto precio, *m;*
suntuosidad, *f*
costly /'kɒstli/ *a* costoso; suntuoso, magnífico
costume /'kɒstum/ *n* traje, *m;* (fancy-
dress) disfraz, *m;* (tailored) traje sastre,
m; **"Costume,"** (among credits in films
and plays) «Vestuario»
cot /kɒt/ *n* (hut) choza, cabaña, *f;*
(child's) camita, *f*
coterie /'koutəri/ *n* círculo, grupo, *m;*
(clique) camarilla, *f*
cotillion /kə'tilyən/ *n* cotillón, *f*
cottage /'kɒtidʒ/ *n* cabaña, choza, *f;* casita, *f;* hotelito, *m;* torre, villa, *f*
cotton /'kɒtņ/ *n* algodón, *m, a* de algodón. **I don't c. to the idea at all,** No me
gusta nada la idea; La idea no me seduce.
sewing-c., hilo de coser, *m.* **c. goods,**
géneros de algodón, *m pl.* **c. mill,** hilandería de algodón, algodonería, *f.* **c.
plantation,** algodonal, *m.* **c.-seed oil,**
aceite de semilla de algodón, *m.* **c.-**

spinner, hilandero (-ra) de algodón. **c.-wool,** algodón en rama, *m.* **c.-yarn,** hilo de algodón, *m*

couch /kautʃ/ *n* sofá, canapé, *m;* (bed) lecho, *m;* (lair) cama, *f.* —*vt* (lay down) acostar, echar; (a lance) enristrar; (express) expresar, redactar. —*vi* acostarse; (crouch) agacharse; estar en acecho

cough /kɔf/ *vi* toser. —*n* tos, *f.* **to c. up,** escupir, expectorar. **c.-drop,** pastilla para la tos, *f*

coughing /'kɔfɪŋ/ *n* tos, *f*

could /kud/. See **can**

council /'kaunsəl/ *n* consejo, *m;* junta, *f; Eccl.* concilio, *m.* **Privy C.,** consejo privado, *m.* **C. of the Realm,** Concejo del Reino, *m.* **to hold c.,** celebrar un consejo; aconsejarse (con); consultarse. **town c.,** ayuntamiento, *m.* **c. chamber,** sala consistorial, *f;* sala de actos, *f.* **c. houses,** casas baratas, *f pl.* **c. of war,** consejo de guerra, *m*

councilor /'kaunsələr/ *n* concejal, *m;* miembro de la junta, *m*

counsel /'kaunsəl/ *n* consultación, *f;* deliberación, *f;* consejo, *m; Law.* abogado, *m.* —*vt* aconsejar. **a c. of perfection,** un ideal imposible. **to keep one's own c.,** no decir nada, callarse, guardar silencio. **to take c. with,** consultar (a), aconsejarse con

counselor /'kaunsələr/ *n* consejero, *m.* **c. of state,** consejero de estado, *m*

count /kaunt/ *vt* contar; calcular; (consider) creer, considerar. —*vi* contar. —*n* cuenta, *f;* (of votes) escrutinio, *m; Law.* capítulo, *m.* **John simply doesn't c.,** Juan no cuenta para nada. **Erudition alone counts for very little,** La mera erudición sirve para muy poco. **to keep c. of,** tener cuenta de. **to lose c. of,** perder cuenta de. **to c. on,** contar con; (doing something) esperar. **to c. up,** contar

count /kaunt/ *n* (title) conde, *m*

countenance /'kauntnəns/ *n* semblante, *m;* expresión de la cara, *f;* aspecto, *m;* (favor) apoyo, *m,* ayuda, *f.* —*vt* autorizar, aprobar; apoyar, ayudar. **to put (a person) out of c.,** desconcertar (a)

counter /'kauntər/ *n* (in a bank) contador, *m;* (in a shop) mostrador, *m;* (in games) ficha, *f, adv* contra, al contrario; al revés. —*a* opuesto (a), contrario (a). —*vt* parar; contestar. **to run c. to my inclinations,** oponerse a mis deseos. **to c. with the left,** (boxing) contestar con la izquierda. **c.-attack,** contraataque, *m.* **c.-attraction,** atracción contraria, *f.* **c.-offensive,** contraofensiva, *f.* **c.-reformation,** contrarreforma, *f.* **c.-revolution,** contrarrevolución, *f*

counteract /ˌkauntərˈækt/ *vt* neutralizar; frustrar

counterbalance /'kauntər,bæləns/ *n* contrapeso, *m, vt* contrabalancear; compensar, igualar

counterblast /'kauntər,blæst/ *n* denunciación, *f;* respuesta, *f*

countercharge /'kauntər,tʃardʒ/ *n* recriminación, *f.* —*vt* recriminar; *Law.* reconvenir

counterfeit /'kauntər,fɪt/ *a* falso, espurio; fingido. —*n* falsificación, *f;* imitación, *f;* moneda falsa, *f;* (person) impostor (-ra). —*vt* imitar; (pretend) fingir; (coins, handwriting, etc.) falsificar

counterfeiter /'kauntər,fɪtər/ *n* falsario (-ia)

counterfoil /'kauntər,fɔil/ *n* talón, *m*

countermand /*v* ˌkauntərˈmænd; *n* 'kauntər,mænd/ *vt* contramandar; (an order) revocar, cancelar. —*n* contraorden, *f;* revocación, *f*

countermarch /'kauntər,martʃ/ *n* contramarcha, *f*

countermeasure /'kauntər,mɛʒər/ *n* contramedida, *f*

counterpart /'kauntər,part/ *n* contraparte, *f;* (of a document) duplicado, *m*

counterplot /'kauntər,plot/ *n* contratreta, *f*

counterpoint /'kauntər,point/ *n Mus.* contrapunto, *m*

counterpoise /'kauntər,pɔiz/ *n* contrapeso, *m;* equilibrio, *m, vt* contrabalancear, contrapesar

countersign /'kauntər,sain/ *n* contraseña, *f, vt* refrendar

counting /'kauntɪŋ/ *n* cuenta, *f;* numeración, *f;* (of votes) escrutinio, *m.* **c.-house,** contaduría, *f*

countless /'kauntlıs/ *a* innumerable. **a c. number,** un sinfín, un sinnúmero

countrified /'kʌntrə,faid/ *a* rústico, campesino

country /'kʌntri/ *n* país, *m;* (fatherland) patria, *f;* región, campiña, tierra, *f;* (as opposed to town) campo, *m.* —*a* del campo; campesino, campestre, rústico. **He lives in the c.,** Vive en el campo. **c. club,** club campestre, *m.* **c. cousin,** provinciano (-na). **c.-dance,** baile campestre, *m.* **c. gentleman,** hacendado, *m.* **c. girl,** campesina, *f;* aldeana, *f.* **c.-house,** finca, *f;* casa de campo, *f.* **c. life,** vida del campo, *f.* **c.-seat,** finca, *f*

countryman /'kʌntrimən/ *n* campesino, *m;* hombre del campo, *m;* compatriota, *m*

countryside /'kʌntri,said/ *n* campo, *m;* campiña, *f*

countrywoman /'kʌntri,wumən/ *n* campesina, *f;* compatriota, *f*

county /'kaunti/ *n* condado, *m;* provincia, *f.* **c. council,** diputación provincial, *f.* **c. town,** cabeza de partido, *f;* ciudad provincial, *f*

county seat *n* cabecera municipal, cabeza de partido, *f*

coup /ku/ *n* golpe, *m.* **c. d'état,** golpe de estado, *m*

coupe /kup/ *n* cupé, *m*

couple /'kʌpəl/ *n* par, *m;* (in a dance, etc.) pareja, *f.* —*vt* enganchar, acoplar; (in marriage) casar; (animals) aparear; (ideas) asociar; (names) juntar. **the young (married) c.,** el matrimonio joven

couplet /'kʌplɪt/ n copla, f

coupling /'kʌplɪŋ/ n enganche, acoplamiento, m; (of railway carriages) enganche, m; (of ideas) asociación, f

coupon /'kupɒn/ n talón, m; cupón, f

courage /'kɜrɪdʒ/ n valor, m. **C.!** ¡Ánimo! **to muster up c.,** cobrar ánimo

courageous /kə'reɪdʒəs/ a valiente

courier /'kɜriər/ n correo, m, estafeta, f; (guide) guía, m; (newspaper) estafeta, f

course /kɔrs/ n curso, m; (of time) transcurso, m; (of events) marcha, f; (of a river, etc.) cauce, m; (of stars) carrera, f, curso, m; (of a ship) derrota, f, rumbo, m; (way) camino, m, ruta, f; (of conduct) línea de conducta, f; actitud, f; (of study) curso, m; (of a meal) plato, m; (of an illness) desarrollo, m; Med. tratamiento, m. **He took it as a matter of c.,** Lo tomó sin darle importancia. **in due c.,** a su tiempo debido. **in the c. of time,** andando el tiempo, en el transcurso de los años. **of c.,** claro está; naturalmente. **Are you coming tomorrow? Of c.!** ¿Vienes mañana? ¡Ya lo creo! **the best c. to take,** lo mejor que se puede hacer, el mejor planteamiento, m

course /kɔrs/ vt cazar, perseguir; Poet. correr por, cruzar. —vi (of blood, etc.) correr; cazar

court /kɔrt/ n (yard) patio, m; (tennis) campo de tenis, m; (fives, racquets) cancha, f; (royal) corte, f; (of justice) tribunal, m; (following) séquito, acompañamiento, m. —vt hacer la corte (a); cortejar, pretender; solicitar; (sleep) conciliar. **to pay c. to,** (a woman) galantear, pretender; (a person) hacer la rueda (a). **to respect the c.,** Law. guardar sala. **c. of appeal,** sala de apelación, f. **c. of justice,** sala de justicia, f; tribunal de justicia, m. **supreme c.,** tribunal supremo, m. **c.-card,** figura, f. **c.-dress,** traje de corte, m. **c. house,** palacio de justicia, m. **c. jester,** bufón, m. **c.-martial,** tribunal militar, m. **c.-plaster,** tafetán inglés, tafetán de heridas, m. **c.-room,** sala de justicia, f

courteous /'kɜrtiəs/ a cortés

courtesy /'kɜrtəsi/ n cortesía, f; favor, m, merced, f; permiso, m

courtier /'kɔrtiər/ n cortesano, palaciego, m

courtliness /'kɔrtlɪnɪs/ n cortesía, urbanidad, f; dignidad, f; elegancia, f

courtly /'kɔrtli/ a cortés, galante; digno; elegante

courtship /'kɔrtʃɪp/ n noviazgo, m; galanteo, m

courtyard /'kɔrt,yɑrd/ n patio, m

cousin /'kʌzən/ n primo (-ma). **first c.,** primo (-ma) carnal. **second c.,** primo (-ma) segundo (-da)

cove /kouv/ n cala, abra, ensenada, f

covenant /'kʌvənənt/ n contrato, m; estipulación, f; pacto, m; alianza, f. —vt prometer; estipular

cover /'kʌvər/ vt cubrir; abrigar; (dissemble) disimular; (a distance) recorrer; (comprise) comprender, abarcar; (with confusion, etc.) llenar (de); (with a revolver, etc.) amenazar (con); (an overdraft, etc.) garantizar; (of stallions) cubrir; (of a hen and eggs) empollar; (a story, journalism) investigar. —n cubierta, f; (for a chair, umbrella, etc.) funda, f; (of a saucepan, jar, etc.) tapa, f; (dishcover) tapadera, f; (of a book) cubierta, tapa, f; (of a letter) sobre, m; (shelter) abrigo, m; protección, f; (undergrowth) maleza, f; Fig. velo, manto, m; (pretence) pretexto, m; Com. garantía, f. **outer c.,** (of tire) cubierta de neumático, f. **to c. oneself with glory,** cubrirse de gloria. **to c. up,** cubrir completamente; (with clothes) arropar; (wrap up) envolver. **to c. with a revolver,** amenazar con un revólver. **to read a book from c. to c.,** leer un libro del principio al fin. **to take c.,** refugiarse, tomar abrigo. **under c.,** bajo tejado; al abrigo

cover charge n consumo mínimo, precio del cubierto, m

covering /'kʌvərɪŋ/ n cubrimiento, m; cubierta, f; envoltura, f; capa, f; abrigo, m. **c. letter,** carta adjunta, f

covert /a 'kouvərt; n 'kʌvərt/ a oculto; furtivo. —n guardia f

covertly /'kouvərtli/ adv secretamente, furtivamente

covet /'kʌvɪt/ vt codiciar; ambicionar, suspirar por

covetous /'kʌvɪtəs/ a codicioso; ávido; ambicioso

covetousness /'kʌvɪtəsnɪs/ n codicia, avaricia, f; avidez, f; ambición, f

cow /kau/ vt intimidar, acobardar

cow /kau/ n vaca, f; (of other animals) hembra, f. **c.-bell,** cencerro, m, zumba, f. **c.-catcher,** Auto. salvavidas, m. **c.-hide,** cuero, cuero de vaca, zurriago, m; penca, f. **c.-house,** establo, m, boyera, f. **c.-pox,** vacuna, f

coward /'kauərd/ n cobarde, m, a cobarde

cowardice /'kauərdɪs/ n cobardía, f

cowardly /'kauərdli/ a cobarde

cowboy /'kau,bɔɪ/ n vaquero, m; gaucho, "cowboy," m

cower /'kauər/ vi no saber dónde meterse; temblar, acobardarse

cowl /kaul/ n capucha, f; (of a chimney) sombrerete, m

coworker /'kou,wɜrkər, kou'wɜr-/ n colaborador (-ra)

cowshed /'kau,ʃed/ n establo, m

coxcomb /'kɒks,koum/ n (of a jester) gorra de bufón, f; mequetrefe, m

coy /kɔɪ/ a modoso, tímido; coquetón

coyness n timidez, modestia, f; coquetería, f

cozy /'kouzi/ a cómodo; agradable; caliente. **You are very c. here,** Estás muy bien aquí

crab /kræb/ n (sea) cangrejo de mar, cámbaro, m; (river) cangrejo, m; Astron. Cáncer, m. —vt (thwart) frustrar. **hermit c.,**

cangrejo ermitaño, m. **c.-apple,** manzana silvestre, f. **c.-louse,** ladilla, f

crabbed /'kræbɪd/ a áspero, hosco, desabrido, arisco; (of handwriting) apretado, metido

crack /kræk/ vt hender; quebrantar, romper; (nuts) cascar; (a whip and fingers) chasquear; (a bottle of wine) abrir. —vi (of earth, skin, etc.) agrietarse; romperse, quebrarse; (of the voice) romper; (of the male voice) mudar. —n hendedura, rendija, f; quebraja, f; (of a whip) chasquido, m; (of a rifle) estallido, m; (blow) golpe, garrotazo, m, a excelente, de primera categoría; estupendo. **to c. a joke,** decir un chiste. **to c. up,** vt dar bombo (a), alabar. —vi (in health) quebrantarse; (airplane) cuartearse, estrellarse. **c.-brained,** chiflado; estúpido, loco

cracked /krækt/ a grietado; (of a bell, etc.) hendido; (of the voice) cascada; (of a person) chiflado

cracker /'krækər/ n (firework) petardo, m; buscapiés, m

crackle /'krækəl/ vi (of burning wood, etc.) crepitar; (rustle) crujir; (of rifle fire) tirotear. —n crepitación, f; crujido, m; (of rifle fire) tiroteo, m

crackling /'kræklɪŋ/ n. See crackle; Cul. chicharrón, m

Cracow /'krækau/ Cracovia, f

cradle /'kreɪdl/ n cuña, f; Fig. niñez, infancia, f; (for a limb) arco de protección, m; (for winebottle) cesta, f. —vt mecer. **c.-song,** canción de cuna, f

craft /kræft/ n (guile) astucia, f; (skill) habilidad, f; arte, mf; (occupation) oficio manual, m; profesión, f; (guild) gremio, m; (boat) barco, m, embarcación, f

craftiness /'kræftinɪs/ n astucia, f

craftsman /'kræftsmən/ n artífice, m; arte sano, m; artista, m

craftsmanship /'kræftsmən,ʃɪp/ n arte, m, or f; habilidad, f; artificio, m

crafty /'kræfti/ a astuto, taimado

crag /kræg/ n peña, f, risco, despeñadero, m

craggy /'krægi/ a escabroso, escarpado; peñascoso, riscoso

cram /kræm/ vt henchir; atestar; (one's mouth) llenar (de); (poultry) cebar; (a pupil) preparar para un examen; (a subject) empollar. —vi (with food) atracarse. **The room was crammed with people.** La sala estaba atestada de gente

cramp /kræmp/ n Med. calambre, m; (numbness) entumecimiento, m; (rivet) grapa, f. —vt dar calambre (a); (numb) entumecer; (fasten) lañar; (Fig. hamper) estorbar. **to c. someone's style,** cortar los vuelos (a). **writer's c.,** calambre del escribiente, m

cramped /kræmpt/ a (of space) apretado, estrecho; (of writing) menuda

cranberry /'kræn,bɛri/ n arándano, m

crane /kreɪn/ n Ornith. grulla, f; (machine) grúa, f. **jib c.,** grúa de pescante, f. **travelling c.,** grúa móvil, f. **to c. one's**

neck, estirar el cuello. **crane's bill,** pico de cigüeña, m

cranium /'kreɪniəm/ n cráneo, m

crank /kræŋk/ n (handle) manivela, f; (person) maniático (-ca). —vt poner en marcha (un motor) con la manivela

crankiness /'kræŋkinɪs/ n (crossness) irritabilidad, f, mal humor, m; (eccentricity) excentricidad, f

cranky /'kræŋki/ a (cross) irritable, mal humorado; (eccentric) chiflado, maniático, excéntrico

cranny /'kræni/ n hendedura, grieta, f

crape /kreɪp/ n crespón, m

crash /kræʃ/ n caer estrepitosamente; romperse; estallarse; (of aircraft, cars) estrellarse; Fig. hundirse, arruinarse. —n estrépito, estruendo, m; estallido, m; (of aircraft) accidente de aviación, m; (car) accidente, m, (or choque, m) de automóviles; (financial) ruina, f; Fig. hundimiento, m. **to c. into,** estrellarse contra, chocar con. **c. helmet,** casco, m. **c.-landing,** aterrizaje violento, m

crass /kræs/ a craso

crate /kreɪt/ n (box) caja de embalaje, f; (basket) canasto, m, banasta, f

crater /'kreɪtər/ n cráter, m

cravat /krə'væt/ n corbata, f

crave /kreɪv/ vt suplicar, implorar. **to c. for,** perecer por, suspirar por, anhelar

craven /'kreɪvən/ a cobarde, pusilánime. —n poltrón, cobarde, m

craving /'kreɪvɪŋ/ n deseo vehemente, m, sed, f

crawfish /'krɔ,fɪʃ/ n cangrejo de río, m; cigala, f

crawl /krɔl/ vi arrastrarse; andar a gatas; andar a paso de tortuga; (abase oneself) humillarse; (be full of) abundar (en). —n paso de tortuga, m; (swimming) arrastne, m

crayfish /'kreɪ,fɪʃ/ n cangrejo de río, m; cigala, f

crayon /'kreɪɒn/ n carbón, m; pastel, m; (pencil) lápiz de color, m. —vt dibujar con pastel, etc. **c. drawing,** dibujo al carbón, m

craze /kreɪz/ vt enloquecer, volver loco (a). —n manía, f, capricho, entusiasmo, m; (fashion) moda, f

craziness /'kreɪzinɪs/ n locura, f

crazy /'kreɪzi/ a loco; chiflado; (of structure) dilapidado. **He is c. about music,** Está loco por la música. **to be completely c.,** (of persons) ser un loco de atar; ser completamente loco. **to drive c.,** volver loco (a)

creak /krik/ vi (of shoes, chairs, etc.) crujir; (of gates, etc.) rechinar, chirriar. —n crujido, m; chirrido, m

creaky /'kriki/ a crujiente, que cruje; chirriador

cream /krim/ n crema, f; nata, f; Fig. flor, nata, f. —a de nata. **whipped c.,** nata batida, f. **c. cake,** pastel de nata, m. **c.-cheese,** queso de nata, m. **c.-colored,**

de color crema. **c.-jug,** jarro para crema, *m.* **c. of tartar,** cremor, tártaro, *m*

creamy /'krimi/ *a* cremoso

crease /kris/ *n* (wrinkle) arruga, *f;* (fold) pliegue, *m;* (in trousers) raya, *f;* (in cricket) línea de la meta, *f.* —*vt* (wrinkle) arrugar; (fold) plegar; (trousers) poner la raya en. —*vi* arrugarse

create /kri'eit/ *vt* crear; (appoint) nombrar; (produce) suscitar, producir

creation /kri'eiʃən/ *n* creación, *f;* establecimiento, *m;* (appointment) nombramiento, *m*

creative /kri'èitɪv/ *a* creador; de la creación

creativeness /kri'eitɪvnɪs/ *n* facultad creativa, inventiva, *f*

creator /kri'eitər/ *n* creador (-ra)

creature /'kritʃər/ *n* criatura, *f;* animal, *m.* **c. comforts,** bienestar material, *m*

credence /'kridns/ *n* crédito, *m,* fe, creencia, *f; Eccl.* credencia, *f.* **to give c. to,** dar crédito (a), creer

credentials /krɪ'dɛnʃəlz/ *n pl* credenciales, *f pl*

credibility /,krɛdə'bɪlɪti/ *n* credibilidad, verosimilitud, *f*

credible /'krɛdəbəl/ *a* creíble, verosímil; (of persons) digno de confianza

credit /'krɛdɪt/ *n* caleta, abra, *f.* honor, *m;* (Com. and banking) crédito, *m;* (in bookkeeping) data, *f.* —*vt* dar fe (a), dar crédito (a); creer; atribuir; (bookkeeping) acreditar. **It does them c.,** Les hace honor. **on c.,** a crédito, al fiado. **open c.,** *Com.* letra abierta, *f.* **to give on c.,** dar fiado. **c. balance,** haber, *m*

creditable /'krɛdɪtəbəl/ *a* loable, honroso, digno de alabanza

creditor /'krɛdɪtər/ *n* acreedor (-ra); (bookkeeping) haber, *m*

credulous /'krɛdʒələs/ *a* crédulo

credulously /'krɛdʒələsli/ *adv* con credulidad, crédulamente

creed /krid/ *n* credo, *m*

creek /krik/ *n* caleta, abra, *f*

creep /krip/ *vi* arrastrarse; (of plants and birds) trepar; (of infants) andar a gatas; (totter) hacer pinitos; (slip) deslizarse; (cringe) lisonjear, rebajarse; (of one's flesh) sentir hormigueo. **to c. about on tiptoe,** andar de puntillas. **to c. into a person's favor,** insinuarse en el favor de. **to c. in,** entrar sin ser notado (en); deslizarse en. **to c. on,** (of time) avanzar lentamente; (of old age, etc.) acercarse insensiblemente. **to c. out,** salir sin hacer ruido; escurrirse. **to c. up,** trepar por; subir a gatas

cremate /'krimeit/ *vt* incinerar

cremation /krɪ'meiʃən/ *n* cremación, *f*

creole /'krioul/ *a* criollo. —*n* criollo (-lla)

crescent /'krɛsənt/ *n* media luna, *f; Herald.* creciente, *m;* calle en forma de semicírculo, *f.* —*a* en forma de media luna; *Poet.* creciente

cress /krɛs/ *n Bot.* berro, *m*

crest /krɛst/ *n* (of a cock, etc.) cresta, *f;* (plume) penacho, *m;* (of a helmet) cimera, *f;* (of a hill) cumbre, cima, *f;* (of a wave) cresta, *f.* **family c.,** blasón, escudo, *m*

crestfallen /'krɛst,fɔlən/ *a* cabizbajo, cariacontecido

crevice /'krɛvɪs/ *n* intersticio, *m,* rendija, grieta, *f*

crew /kru/ *n* (of ships, boats, aircraft) tripulación, *f;* (of a gun) servidores de una ametralladora, *m pl;* (gang) pandilla, cuadrilla, *f*

crib /krɪb/ *n* pesebre, *m;* (child's) camita de niño, *f;* (plagiary) plagio, *m.* —*vt* (plagiarize) plagiar; (steal) hurtar

crick /krɪk/ *n* (in the neck) tortícolis, *m*

cricket /'krɪkɪt/ *n Ent.* grillo, *m;* (game) cricquet, *m.* **c. ball,** pelota de cricquet, *f.* **c. bat,** paleta de cricquet, *f.* **c. ground,** campo de cricquet, *m.* **c. match,** partido de cricquet, *m*

crime /kraim/ *n* crimen, *m;* ofensa, *f,* delito, *m*

criminal /'krɪmənl/ *a* criminal. —*n* criminal, *m;* reo, *mf* **C. Investigation Department,** (nearest equivalent) policía secreta, *f.* **c. laws,** código penal, *m*

criminologist /,krɪmə'nɒlədʒɪst/ *n* criminalista, *m*

criminology /,krɪmə'nɒlədʒi/ *n* criminología, *f*

crimp /krɪmp/ *vt* (hair) rizar

crimson /'krɪmzən, -sən/ *n* carmesí, *m.* —*a* de carmesí. —*vt* teñir de carmesí. —*vi* enrojecerse

cringe /krɪndʒ/ *vi* temblar; asustarse, acobardarse; inclinarse (ante)

cringing /'krɪndʒɪŋ/ *a* servil, humilde; adulador

crinkle /'krɪŋkəl/ *vi* arrugarse; rizarse. —*vt* arrugar. —*n* arruga, *f*

cripple /'krɪpəl/ *n* tullido (-da); cojo (-ja). —*vt* lisiar, tullir, estropear; *Fig.* paralizar

crisis /'kraisɪs/ *n* crisis, *f*

crisp /krɪsp/ *a* (of hair and of leaves) crespo; (fresh) fresco; (stiff) tieso; (of style) nervioso, vigoroso; (of manner) decidido; (of repartee) chispeante; (of tone) incisivo

crisscross /'krɪs,krɒs/ *vt* (a body of water or land) surcar

criterion /krai'tɪəriən/ *n* criterio, *m*

critic /'krɪtɪk/ *n* crítico, *m;* censor, *m*

critical /'krɪtɪkəl/ *a* crítico

criticism /'krɪtə,sɪzəm/ *n* crítica, *f*

criticize /'krɪtə,saiz/ *vt* criticar; censurar

critique /krɪ'tik/ *n* crítica, *f*

croak /krouk/ *vi* (of frogs) croar; (of ravens) graznar; (of persons) lamentarse, gruñir

Croat /'krouæt/ *a* croata. —*n* croata, *mf*

Croatia /krou'eiʃə/ Crocia, *f*

crochet /krou'ʃei/ *n* ganchillo, *m, vi* hacer ganchillo. —*vt* hacer (algo) en ganchillo. **c. hook,** aguja de gancho, *f,* ganchillo, *m.* **c. work,** croché, ganchillo, *m*

crockery /'krɒkəri/ *n* loza, *f,* cacharros, *m pl.* **c. store,** cacharrería, *f*

crocodile /'krɒkə,dail/ *n* cocodrilo, *m.* **c. tears,** lágrimas de cocodrilo, *f pl*

crony /'krouni/ *n* compinche, *mf*

crook /krʊk/ *n* curva, *f;* (staff) cayado, *m;* (swindler) caballero de industria, estafador, *m, vt* doblar, encorvar

crooked /'krʊkid/ *a* curvo; encorvado; torcido; ladeado; (deformed) contrahecho; (of paths, etc.) tortuoso; (dishonest) torcido, tortuoso

crookedly /'krʊkidli/ *adv* torcidamente; de través

crookedness /'krʊkidnis/ *n* encorvadura, *f,* tortuosidad, *f;* sinuosidad, *f*

croon /krun/ *vt* and *vi* canturrear; cantar

crooner /'krunər/ *n* cantante, *mf*

crop /krɒp/ *n* (of birds) buche, *m;* (whip) látigo, *m,* fusta, *f;* (handle) mango, *m;* (harvest) cosecha, *f;* (of the hair) cortadura, *f.* —*vt* cortar; (nibble) rozar; (hair) rapar. **Eton c.,** pelo a la garçonne, *m.* **to c. up,** aparecer, surgir

crop rotation *n* la rotación de cultivos, *f*

croquette /krou'kɛt/ *n* Cul. croqueta, *f*

cross /krɒs/ *n* cruz, *f;* Biol. cruzamiento, *m;* (Sew. bias) bies, *m.* **in the shape of a c.,** en cruz. **the Red C.,** la Cruz Roja. **c.-bearer,** Eccl. crucero, *m*

cross /krɒs/ *vt* cruzar; atravesar; pasar por; (a check and animals) cruzar; (thwart) contrariar. **It did not c. my mind,** No se me ocurrió. **Our letters must have crossed,** Nuestras cartas deben haberse cruzado. **to c. oneself,** Eccl. persignarse. **to c. out,** tachar, rayar. **to c. over,** *vt* atravesar, cruzar. —*vi* ir al otro lado

cross /krɒs/ *a* transversal; cruzado; oblicuo; (contrary) opuesto (a); (bad-tempered) malhumorado. **c.-breed,** *a* mestizo, atravesado. **c.-country,** *a* a campo travieso. **c.-examination,** Law. repregunta, *f,* contrainterrogatorio, *m.* **c.-examine,** *vt* Law. repreguntar; interrogar. **c.-eyed,** bizco. **c.-fire,** Mil. fuego cruzado, *m sing* fuegos cruzados, *m pl;* Fig. tiroteo, *m.* **c.-grained,** (of wood) vetiseségado; (of persons) áspero, intratable, desabrido. **c.-legged,** con las piernas cruzadas. **c.-purpose,** despropósito, *m.* **at c.-purposes,** a despropósito. **c.-question,** *vt* Law. repreguntar; interrogar. **c. reference,** contrarreferencia, *f.* **c. section,** sección transversal, *f.* **c.-stitch,** punto cruzado, *m.* **c.-word puzzle,** crucigrama, *m*

crossbred /'krɒs,brɛd/ *a* cruzado, mestizo; híbrido

crossbreed /'krɒs,brid/ *n* mestizo (-za); híbrido, *m*

crossing /'krɒsiŋ/ *n* cruzamiento, *m;* (of the sea) travesía, *f;* (intersection) cruce, *m;* paso, *m.* **level c.,** paso a nivel, *m.* **pedestrian c.,** paso para peatones, *m.* **c.-sweeper,** barrendero, *m*

crossly /'krɒsli/ *adv* con mal humor, con displicencia, irritablemente

crossroad /'krɒs,roud/ *n* travesía, *f;* cruce, *m; pl* **crossroads,** cruce, cruce de caminos, *m sing* encrucijada, *f sing*

crosswise /'krɒs,waiz/ *adv* en cruz; a través

crotch /krɒtʃ/ *n* (of a tree) bifurcación, *f;* Anat. horcajadura, *f;* (of breeches) entrepiernas, *f pl*

crotchet /'krɒtʃit/ *n* Mus. semínima, *f;* (fad) capricho, *m;* extravagancia, excentricidad, *f*

crotchety /'krɒtʃiti/ *a* caprichoso; raro, excéntrico; difícil

crouch /krautʃ/ *vi* acurrucarse, agacharse, acuclillarse

croup /krup/ *n* (disease) crup, garrotillo, *m;* (of a horse) grupa, anca, *f*

croupier /'krupiər/ *n* coime, crupié, *m*

crow /krou/ *n* Ornith. cuervo, *m;* Ornith. grajo, *m;* (of a cock) canto del gallo, cácareo, *m;* (of an infant) gorjeo, *m.* —*vi* (of a cock) cantar, cacarear; (of an infant) gorjearse. **as the c. flies,** en línea recta **to c. over,** gallear, cantar victoria

crow's-foot, pata de gallo, *f.* **crow's-nest,** Naut. gavias, *f pl*

crowbar /'krou,bar/ *n* alzaprima, palanca, *f*

crowd /kraud/ *n* multitud, muchedumbre, *f;* concurso, *m;* vulgo, *m;* (majority) mayoría, *f;* Theat. acompañamiento, *m.* —*vi* reunirse, congregarse; agolparse, remolinarse, apiñarse. —*vt* (fill) llenar, atestar. **in a c.,** en tropel. **So many ideas crowded in on me,** Se me ocurrieron tantas ideas a la vez. **to follow the c.,** seguir la multitud; Fig. ir con la mayoría. **to c. in,** entrar en tropel. **to c. round,** cercar, agruparse alrededor de. **to c. together,** apiñarse. **to c. up,** subir en masa, subir en tropel

crowded /'kraudid/ *a* lleno; atestado; apiñado; (weighed down) agobiado; (of hours, etc.) lleno

crowing /'krouiŋ/ *n* cacareo, canto del gallo, *m;* (of an infant) gorjeos, *m pl;* (boasting) jactancia, *f*

crown /kraun/ *n* corona, *f;* (of the head) coronilla, corona, *f;* (of a hat) copa, *f;* Archit. coronamiento, *m.* —*vt* coronar. **c. prince,** príncipe heredero, *m*

crowning /'krauniŋ/ *n* coronamiento, *m;* Archit. remate, *m, a* final; supremo

crucial /'kruʃəl/ *a* decisivo, crítico; difícil

crucible /'krusəbəl/ *n* crisol, *m*

crucifix /'krusəfiks/ *n* crucifijo, *m*

crucifixion /,krusə'fikʃən/ *n* crucifixión, *f*

crude /krud/ *a* crudo; (of colors) chillón, llamativo; (uncivilized) cerril, inculto; (vulgar) cursi; (of truth, etc.) desnudo

crudity /'kruditi/ *n* crudeza, *f*

cruel /'kruəl/ *a* cruel

cruelty /'kruəlti/ *n* crueldad, *f*

cruet /'kruit/ *n* ánfora, vinagrera, *f;* (stand) angarillas, *f pl,* convoy, *m*

cruise /kruz/ *vi* cruzar, navegar; (of cars) correr. —*n* viaje por mar, *m*

cruiser /'kruzər/ *n* crucero, *m*

crumb /krʌm/ *n* miga, *f*; (spongy part of bread) migaja, *f*. —*vt* (bread) desmigajar; desmenuzar. **c. brush,** recogemigas, *m*

crumble /'krʌmbəl/ *vt* desmigajar, desmenuzar. —*vi* desmoronarse, desmigajarse; *Fig.* hundirse, derrumbarse; *Fig.* desaparecer

crumbling /'krʌmblɪŋ/ *n* (of buildings, etc.) desmoronamiento, *m*; *Fig.* destrucción, *f*

crumple /'krʌmpəl/ *vt* arrugar, ajar. —*vi* arrugarse. **to c. up,** *vt* (crush) estrujar; (persons) dejar aplastado. —*vi* (collapse) hundirse, derrumbarse; (of persons) desplomarse; (despair) desalentar

crunch /krʌntʃ/ *vt* mascar; hacer crujir. —*vi* crujir

crusade /kru'seid/ *n* cruzada, *f*

crusader /kru'seidər/ *n* cruzado, *m*

crush /krʌʃ/ *vt* aplastar; (to powder) moler, triturar; (grapes, etc.) exprimir; (crease) arrugar; (opposition, etc.) vencer; (annihilate) aniquilar, destruir; (abash) humillar, confundir; (hope, etc.) matar; (of sorrow, etc.) agobiar. **We all crushed into his diningroom,** Fuimos en tropel a su comedor. **to c. up,** machacar, moler; (paper, etc.) estrujar

crushing /'krʌʃɪŋ/ *a* (of defeats and replies) aplastante; (of sorrow, etc.) abrumador

crust /krʌst/ *n* (of bread, pie) corteza, *f*; (scab) costra, *f*; (of the earth, snow) capa, *f*. —*vt* encostrar. —*vi* encostrarse. **c. of bread,** mendrugo de pan, *m*

crusty /'krʌsti/ *a* costroso; (of persons) malhumorado, irritable; áspero

crutch /krʌtʃ/ *n* muleta, *f*; (fork) horquilla, *f*; (crotch) horcajadura, *f*

crux /krʌks/ *n* problema, *m*; (knotty point) nudo, *m*

cry /krai/ *vi* (weep) llorar; (shout) gritar; (exclaim) exclamar. —*vt* (one's wares) pregonar. —*n* grito, *m*. **to cry for help,** pedir socorro a voces. **to cry to high heaven,** poner el grito en el cielo. **to cry one's eyes out,** llorar a mares. **to cry down,** desacreditar. **to cry off,** desdecirse; volverse atrás. **to cry out,** *vi* gritar. —*vi* dar gritos; gritar; *Fig.* clamar. **cry-baby,** niño (-ña) llorón (-ona)

crying /'kraiɪŋ/ *a* urgente; notorio. —*n* gritos, *m pl*; (weeping) llanto, *m*, lamentaciones, *f pl*; (tears) lágrimas, *f pl*

crypt /krɪpt/ *n* cripta, *f*

cryptic /'krɪptɪk/ *a* secreto, oculto

crystal /'krɪstl/ *n* cristal, *m*. **c. set,** *Radio.* receptor de galena, *m*

cub /kʌb/ *n* cachorro (-rra)

Cuban /'kyubən/ *a* cubano. —*n* cubano (-na)

cubbyhole /'kʌbi,houl/ *n* refugio, *m*; garita, *f*; cuarto pequeño, *m*; chiribitil, *m*

cube /kyub/ *n* cubo, *m*; (of sugar) terrón, *m*. —*vt* cubicar. **c. root,** raíz cúbica, *f*

cubic /'kyubɪk/ *a* cúbico

cubicle /'kyubɪkəl/ *n* cubículo, *m*

cuckold /'kʌkəld/ *n* cornudo, *m*

cuckoo /'kuku/ *n* cuclillo, *m*; (cry) cucú, *m*. **c.-clock,** reloj de cuclillo, *m*

cucumber /'kyukʌmbər/ *n* cohombro *m*

cuddle /'kʌdl/ *vt* abrazar. —*n* abrazo, *m*. **to c. up together,** estar abrazados

cudgel /'kʌdʒəl/ *n* porra, estaca, tranca, *f*, *vt* aporrear, apalear. **to c. one's brains,** devanarse los sesos. **to take up the cudgels for,** salir en defensa de

cue /kyu/ *n* *Theat.* pie, *m*; (lead) táctica, *f*; (hint) indicación, *f*; (of hair) coleta, *f*; (billiard) taco (de billar), *m*. **to take one's cue from,** tomar como modelo (a); seguir el ejemplo de

cuff /kʌf/ *n* abofetear. —*n* (blow) bofetón, *m*; (of sleeve) puño, *m*, bocamanga, valenciana, *f*. **c.-links,** gemelos, *m pl*

cuisine /kwɪ'zin/ *n* cocina, *f*

culinary /'kyulə,neri/ *a* culinario

culminate /'kʌlmə,neit/ *vi* culminar (en), terminar (en). **culminating point,** punto culminante, *m*

culmination /,kʌlmə'neiʃən/ *n* culminación, *f*; *Fig.* apogeo, punto culminante, *m*

culprit /'kʌlprɪt/ *n* culpado (-da)

cult /kʌlt/ *n* culto, *m*

cultivable /'kʌltəvəbəl/ *a* cultivable, labradero

cultivate /'kʌltə,veit/ *vt* cultivar

cultivated /'kʌltə,veitɪd/ *a* cultivado; (of persons) culto, fino

cultivation /,kʌltə'veiʃən/ *n* cultivación, *f*; (of the land) cultivo, *m*; (of persons, etc.) cultura, *f*

cultivator /'kʌltə,veitər/ *n* cultivador (-ra); (machine) cultivador, *m*

cultural /'kʌltʃərəl/ *a* cultural

culture /'kʌltʃər/ *n* cultura, *f*; (bacteriology) cultivo, *m*, *vt* (bacteriology) cultivar

cultured /'kʌltʃərd/ *a* culto

cumbersome /'kʌmbərsəm/ *a* pesado; incómodo

cumulative /'kyumyələtɪv/ *a* cumulativo

cunning /'kʌnɪŋ/ *a* astuto, taimado. —*n* (skill) habilidad, *f*; astucia, *f*

cup /kʌp/ *n* taza, *f*; (*Eccl.* and *Bot.*) cáliz, *m*; *Sports.* copa, *f*; (hollow) hoyo, *m*, hondonada, *f*. **c.-final,** *Sports.* final de la copa, *m*. **c.-tie,** *Sports.* partido eliminatorio, *m*

cupboard /'kʌbərd/ *n* armario, *m*; (in the wall) alacena, *f*. **c. love,** amor interesado, *m*

cupful /'kʌpfʊl/ *n* taza, *f*

cupidity /kyu'pɪditi/ *n* avaricia, codicia, *f*

cup of sorrow *n* ramito de amargura, *m*

cupola /'kyupələ/ *n* cúpula, *f*

cur /kɜr/ *n* perro mestizo, *m*; canalla, *m*

curable /'kyʊrəbəl/ *a* curable

curative /'kyʊrətɪv/ *a* curativo, terapéutico

curator /kyu'reitər/ n (of a museum) director, m; (Scots law) curador, m

curb /kɜrb/ n (of a bridle) barbada, f; *Fig.* freno, m; (stone) bordillo, m, guarnición, f. —vt (a horse) enfrenar; *Fig.* refrenar, reprimir; (limit) limitar

curd /kɜrd/ n requesón, m; cuajada, f

curdle /'kɜrdl/ vi coagularse; (of blood) helarse. —vt coagular; (blood) helar

cure /kyur/ n cura, f; *Eccl.* curato, m. —vt curar; (salt) salar; *Fig.* remediar. **to take a c.,** tomar una cura. **c.-all,** panacea, f. **c. of souls,** cura de almas, f

curer /'kyurər/ n (of fish, etc.) salador, m; (of evils, etc.) remediador, m

curfew /'kɜrfyu/ n toque de queda, m

curio /'kyuri,ou/ n curiosidad, antigüedad, f

curiosity /,kyuri'ɒsiti/ n curiosidad, f

curious /'kyuriəs/ a (all meanings) curioso

curl /kɜrl/ n (of hair) rizo, bucle, m; (of smoke) penacho, m. —vt rizar. —vi rizarse; *Sports.* jugar al curling **in c.,** rizado. **to c. one's lip,** hacer una mueca de desdén. **to c. up,** vt arrollar; *Fig.* dejar fuera de combate (a). —vi hacerse un ovillo, enroscarse; (of leaves) abarquillarse; *Fig.* desplomarse; desanimarse. **c.-paper,** papillote, m

curling /'kɜrliŋ/ n (game) curling, m, a rizado. **c.-tongs,** encrespador, m

curly /'kɜrli/ a rizado, crespo

currant /'kɜrənt/ n (dry) pasa de Corinto, f; (fresh) grosella, f. **black c.,** grosella negra, f; (bush) grosellero negro, m. **c.-bush,** grosellero, m

currency /'kɜrənsi/ n uso corriente, m; moneda corriente, f, dinero, m; dinero en circulación, m; valor corriente, m; estimación, f

current /'kɜrənt/ a corriente; presente, de actualidad; (of money) en circulación. —n (of water, etc., *Fig. Elec.*) corriente, f. **alternating c.,** *Elec.* corriente alterna, f. **direct c.,** *Elec.* corriente continua, f. **the c. number of a magazine,** el último número de una revista. **c. events,** actualidades, f pl

curriculum /kə'rikyələm/ n plan de estudios, m; curso, m

curriculum vitae /'vaiti/ n hoja de vida, f

curry /'kɜri/ vt (leather) zurrar; (a horse) almohazar; *Cul.* condimentar con cari. **to c. favor with,** insinuarse en el favor de. **c.-comb,** almohaza, f

curse /kɜrs/ n maldición, f; blasfemia, f; (ruin) azote, castigo, m. —vt maldecir; (afflict) castigar. —vi blasfemar, echar pestes

cursed /'kɜrsid, kɜrst/ a maldito; abominable, odioso

cursing /'kɜrsiŋ/ n maldición, f; blasfemias, f pl

cursorily /'kɜrsərəli/ adv rápidamente; de prisa; superficialmente

cursory /'kɜrsəri/ a rápido; apresurado; superficial

curt /kɜrt/ a seco, brusco; corto

curtail /kər'teil/ vt abreviar; reducir; disminuir

curtailment /kər'teilmənt/ n abreviación, f; reducción, f; disminución, f

curtain /'kɜrtn/ n cortina, f; *Theat.* telón, m. —vt poner cortinas (a) **drop c.,** telón de boca, m. **iron c.,** *Polit.* telón de acero, m. **to c. off,** separar por cortinas. **c.-lecture,** reprimenda conyugal, f. **c.-raiser,** entremés, m. **c.-ring,** anilla, f

curtness /'kɜrtnis/ n brusquedad, sequedad, f

curtsey /'kɜrtsi/ n reverencia, cortesía, f, vi hacer una reverencia

curve /kɜrv/ n curva, f; *Mech.* codo, m; (*Auto.* of a road) viraje, m. —vt encorvar, torcer. —vi encorvarse, torcerse; (of a road) hacer un viraje.

curved /kɜrvd/ a curvo

curvet /'kɜrvit/ n corveta, cabriola, f, vi corvetear, corcovear, cabriolar

cushion /'kuʃən/ n almohada, f; cojín, m; (billiards) banda, f; (of fingers, etc.) pulpejo, m. —vt proveer de almohadas; (a shock) amortiguar; suavizar

custard /'kʌstərd/ n flan, m, natillas, f pl

custodian /kʌ'stoudiən/ n custodio, m; guardián, m; (of a museum, etc.) director, m

custody /'kʌstədi/ n custodia, f; guarda, f; prisión, f; *in safe c.,* en lugar seguro. **to take (a person) into c.,** arrestar

custom /'kʌstəm/ n costumbre, f; uso, m; *Com.* parroquia, clientela, f (sales) ventas, f pl; pl **Customs,** aduana, f. **to go through the Customs,** pasar por la aduana. **Customs duty,** derechos de aduana, m pl. **Customs officer,** aduanero, m. **c.-house,** aduana, f

customarily /,kʌstə'merəli/ adv habitualmente, por lo general

customary /'kʌstə,meri/ a acostumbrado, usual, habitual

customer /'kʌstəmər/ n cliente, mf parroquiano (-na). **He is a queer c.,** Es un tipo raro

cut /kʌt/ vt cortar; (diamonds) tallar; (hay, etc.) segar; (carve) labrar, tallar; (engrave) grabar; (a lecture, etc.) no asistir a; (cards) destajar, cortar; (*Fig.* wound) herir; (reduce) reducir; abreviar; (teeth) echar; (of lines) cruzar. —vi cortar; cortar bien; (*Fam.* go) marcharse a prisa y corriendo. **I must get my hair cut,** He de hacerme cortar el pelo. **That cuts both ways,** Es una arma de dos filos. **His opinion cuts no ice,** Su opinión no cuenta. **Mary cut him dead,** María hizo como si no le reconociera. **to cut a caper,** dar saltos; hacer cabriolas. **to cut a person short,** echar el tablacho (a). **to cut and run,** poner los pies en polvorosa. **to cut for deal,** (cards) cortar para ver quién da las cartas. **to cut short,** (a career) terminar. **to cut to the quick,** herir en lo más vivo. **to cut across,** cortar al través; (fields, etc.) atravesar; tomar por un atajo. **to cut away,** *vt* quitar. —*vi Inf.* poner pies en polvorosa. **to cut down,** derribar; (by the sword) acuchillar; (by death, etc.) segar, malograr; (expenses, etc.) reducir; (abbreviate) cortar, abreviar. **to cut off,** cortar, separar; amputar; (on a telephone) cortar la comunicación; (gas, water, etc.) cortar; (supply of food, etc.) interrumpir; (of death) llevarse. **to cut off with a shilling,** desheredar (a). **to cut out,** (dresses, etc.) cortar; (oust) suplantar. **He is not cut out for medicine,** No tiene la disposición para la medicina. **to cut up,** trinchar, cortar en pequeños trozos; (afflict) entristecer, afligir. **to cut up rough,** *Inf.* ponerse furioso

cut /kʌt/ *a* cortado. **well-cut features,** facciones regulares, *f pl.* **cut and dried opinion,** opinión hecha, idea fija, *f;* ideas cerradas, *f pl.* **cut glass,** cristal tallado, *m*

cut /kʌt/ *n* corte, *m;* (with a whip) latigazo, *m;* (with a sword) cuchillada, *f;* (with a sharp instrument) tajo, *m;* cortadura, *f;* (in prices, etc.) reducción, *f;* (engraving) grabado, *m;* clisé, *m;* (of cards) corte, *m.* **short cut,** atajo, *m.* **the cut of a coat,** el corte de un abrigo. **to give (someone) the cut direct,** pasar cerca de (una persona) sin saludarle. **cut-out,** *n* (paper) recortado, *m; Elec.* cortacircuitos, *m.* **cut-throat,** *n* asesino, *m*

cute /kyut/ *a* cuco, listo; mono

cuticle /'kyutɪkəl/ *n* cutícula, *f*

cutlery /'kʌtləri/ *n* cuchillería, *f*

cutlet /'kʌtlɪt/ *n* chuleta, *f*

cutting /'kʌtɪŋ/ *n* corte, *m;* (of diamonds) talla, *f;* (in a mountain, etc.) tajo, *m; Agr.* plantón, *m;* (of cloth) retazo, *m;* (newspaper) recorte, *m.* —*a* cortante; (of remarks) mordaz. **newspaper c.,** recorte de periódico. **c. down,** (of trees) tala, *f;* reducción, *f*

cyberspace /'saibər,speis/ *n* ciberespacio, *m*

cycle /'saikəl/ *n* ciclo, *m;* período, *m;* (bicycle) bicicleta, *f.* —*vi* ir en bicicleta

cyclic /'saiklɪk/ *a* cíclico

cycling /'saiklɪŋ/ *n* ciclismo, *m*

cyclist /'saiklɪst/ *n* ciclista, *mf*

cyclone /'saikloun/ *n* ciclón, *m*

Cyclopean task *n* obra ciclopéa, *f*

cylinder /'sɪlɪndər/ *n* cilindro, *m; Mech.* tambor, *m.* **c. head,** culata, *f*

cylindrical /sɪ'lɪndrɪkəl/ *a* cilíndrico

cymbal /'sɪmbəl/ *n* címbalo, platillo, *m*

cymbalist /'sɪmbəlɪst/ *n* cimbalero (-ra)

cynic /'sɪnɪk/ *n* cínico, *m*

cynical /'sɪnɪkəl/ *a* cínico

cynicism /'sɪnə,sɪzəm/ *n* cinismo, *m*

cynosure /'sainə,ʃʊr/ *n Astron.* Osa Menor, *f;* blanco, *m*

cypress /'saiprəs/ *n* (tree and wood) ciprés, *m.* **c. grove,** cipresal, *m*

Cypriot /'sɪpriət/ *a* chipriota. —*n* chipriota, *mf*

Cyprus /'saiprəs/ Isla de Chipre, *f*

cyst /sɪst/ *n* quiste, *m*

Czech /tʃɛk/ *a* checo. —*n* checo (-ca); (language) checo, *m*

D

d /di/ n (letter) de, f; Mus. re, m
dab /dæb/ vt golpear suavemente, tocar; (sponge) esponjar; (moisten) mojar. —n golpecito, golpe blando, m; (small piece) pedazo pequeño, m; (blob) borrón, m; (peck) picotazo, m; Inf. experto (-ta). **to dab at one's eyes,** secarse los ojos
dabble /'dæbəl/ vt mojar (en). —vi chapotear; (engage in) entretenerse en; (meddle in) meterse en; (speculate in) especular en. **to d. in politics,** meterse en política
dabbler /'dæblər/ n aficionado (-da)
daddy /'dædi/ n papaíto, m. **d.-longlegs,** típula, f
daft /dæft/ a bobo, tonto, chiflado; loco
dagger /'dægər/ n daga, f, puñal, m; Print. cruz, f. **to be at daggers drawn,** estar a matar. **to look daggers (at),** lanzar miradas de odio (hacia), mirar echando chispas. **d. thrust,** puñalada, f
daily /'deili/ a diario, de todos los días; cotidiano. —adv diariamente, cada día, todos los días; cotidianamente. —n (paper) diario, m. **d. bread,** pan cotidiano, pan de cada día, m. **d. help,** (person) asistenta, f. **d. pay,** jornal, m; Mil. pre, m
daintiness /'deintinis/ n delicadeza, f; elegancia, f; (beauty) primor, m
dainty /'deinti/ a delicado; elegante; primoroso, exquisito; (fastidious) melindroso, difícil. —n bocado exquisito, m, golosina, f
dairy /'dɛəri/ n lechería, f. **d. cattle,** vacas lecheras, f pl. **d.-farm,** granja, f. **d.-farmer,** granjero (-ra). **d.-farming,** industria lechera, f
dairyman /'dɛərimən/ n lechero, m
dais /'deiɪs/ n estrado, m
daisy /'deizi/ n margarita, f
dale /deil/ n valle, m
dalliance /'dæliəns/ n (delay) tardanza, f; (play) jugueteo, m; diversiones, f pl; (caresses) caricias, f pl, abrazos, m pl
dally /'dæli/ vi tardar, perder el tiempo; entretenerse, divertirse; (make love) holgar (con); (with an idea) entretenerse con, jugar con
dam /dæm/ n (of animals) madre, f; (of a river, etc.) presa, f, embalse, m; (mole) dique, m; pared de retención, f. —vt represar, embalsar; cerrar; (restrain) contener, reprimir
damage /'dæmɪdʒ/ n daño, perjuicio, m; mal, m; avería, f; pérdida, f; (Fam. price) precio, m; pl **damages,** Law. daños y perjuicios, m pl. —vt dañar, perjudicar; estropear; deteriorar; (reputation, etc.) comprometer
damaging /'dæmɪdʒɪŋ/ a perjudicial; comprometedor
Damascus /də'mæskəs/ Damasio, m
damask /'dæməsk/ n (cloth) damasco, m; (steel) acero damasquino, m. —a de damasco; damasquino. —vt (metals) damasquinar; (cloth) adamascar. **d.-like,** adamascado. **d. rose,** rosa de Damasco, f

dame /deim/ n dama, señora, f; Inf. madre, f; (schoolmistress) amiga, f
damming /'dæmɪŋ/ n embalse, m, represa, f; retención, f; represión, f
damn /dæm/ vt condenar al infierno; maldecir; vituperar. **D. it!** ¡Maldito sea!
damnable /'dæmnəbəl/ a detestable, infame; Inf. horrible
damnation /dæm'neiʃən/ n condenación, perdición, f; maldición, f; vituperación, f
damned /dæmd/ a condenado; maldito; detestable, odioso
damning /'dæmɪŋ/ a que condena; irresistible
damp /dæmp/ a húmedo. —n humedad, f; (mist) niebla, f; exhalación, f; (gas) mofeta, f; Fig. tristeza, depresión, f. —vt humedecer, mojar; apagar, amortiguar; (depress) deprimir, entristecer; (stifle) ahogar; (lessen) moderar; (trouble) turbar. **d.-proof,** impermeable
damper /'dæmpər/ n (of a chimney) registro de humos, m; (of a piano) batiente, m; (for stamps) mojador, m; (gloom) depresión, tristeza, f; (restraint) freno, m
dampness /'dæmpnis/ n humedad, f
damsel /'dæmzəl/ n chica, muchacha, f; damisela, f
damson /'dæmzən/ n ciruela damascena, f. **d. tree,** ciruelo damasceno, m
dance /dæns/ n danza, f; baile, m. —vi bailar, danzar; saltar, brincar. —vt bailar; hacer saltar. **to d. attendance on,** servir humildemente; hacer la rueda (a). **to lead someone a d.,** hacer bailar. **d. band,** orquestina, f; orquesta de jazz, f. **d. floor,** pista de baile, f. **d. hall,** salón de baile, m. **d. music,** música bailable, f. **d.-number,** (in a theater) bailable, m. **d. of death,** danza de la muerte, f
dancer /'dænsər/ n bailarín (-ina); danzador (-ra), bailador (-ra); pl **dancers,** (partners) parejas de baile, f pl
dancing /'dænsɪŋ/ n baile, m, danza, f. **d.-girl,** bailarina, f; (Indian) bayadera, f. **d.-master,** maestro de baile, m. **d. school,** academia de baile, f. **d. slipper,** zapatilla de baile, f
dandle /'dændl/ vt mecer, hacer saltar sobre las rodillas, hacer bailar
dandruff /'dændrəf/ n caspa, f
dandy /'dændi/ n dandi, petimetre, barbilindo, m
Dane /dein/ n danés (-esa). **Great D.,** perro danés, m
danger /'deindʒər/ n peligro, m; riesgo, m. **out of d.,** fuera de peligro. **to be in d.,** correr peligro, peligrar, estar en peligro
dangerous /'deindʒərəs/ a peligroso; arriesgado; nocivo
dangle /'dæŋgəl/ vi colgar, pender. —vt dejar colgar; oscilar; (show) mostrar

Danish /'deɪnɪʃ/ a danés, de Dinamarca. —n (language) danés, m

dank /dæŋk/ a húmedo

Danube, the /'dænyub/ el (Río) Danubio, m

dapper /'dæpər/ a apuesto, aseado; activo, vivaz

dapple /'dæpəl/ vt motear, salpicar, manchar. **d.-grey**, a rucio

dare /dɛər/ vi atreverse, osar. —vt arriesgar; desafiar, provocar; hacer frente a, arrostrar. —n reto, m. **I d. say!** ¡Ya lo creo! ¡No lo dudo! **I d. say that...**, No me sorprendería que...; Supongo que... **d.-devil**, calavera, m; atrevido (-da), valeroso (-sa)

daring /'dɛərɪŋ/ a intrépido, audaz; atrevido; (dangerous) arriesgado, peligroso. —n audacia, osadía, f, atrevimiento, m; peligro, m

dark /dɑrk/ a oscuro; (of complexion, etc.) moreno; negro; lóbrego; (of colours) oscuro; misterioso; enigmático; secreto, escondido; (sad) funesto, triste; (evil) malo, malévolo; (ignorant) ignorante, supersticioso. —n oscuridad, f; (shade) sombra, f; ignorancia, f. **after d.**, a nocturno. —adv después del anochecer. **in the d.**, a oscuras; de noche; Fig. be in the d., quedarse en la luna. **to become d.**, oscurecerse; (cloud over) anublarse; (become night) anochecer. **to keep d.**, vt tener secreto. —vi esconderse. **d. ages**, los siglos de la ignorancia y de la superstición. **d.-eyed**, de ojos negros, ojinegro. **d. horse**, caballo desconocido, m; Polit. batacazo, m. **d. lantern**, linterna sorda, f. **d. room**, cuarto oscuro, m; Photo. laboratorio fotográfico, m; (optics) cámara oscura, f

darken /'dɑrkən/ vt obscurecer; sombrear; (of color) hacer más oscuro; (sadden) entristecer. —vi obscurecerse; (of the sky) anublarse; (of the face with emotion) inmutarse.

darkly /'dɑrkli/ adv oscuramente; misteriosamente; con malevolencia; secretamente; (archaic) indistintamente

darkness /'dɑrknɪs/ n oscuridad, f, tinieblas, f pl; sombra, f; (of color) oscuro, m; (of the complexion) color moreno, m; (of eyes, hair) negrura, f; (night) noche, f; (ignorance) ignorancia, f; (privacy) secreto, m. **Prince of d.**, el príncipe de las tinieblas

darling /'dɑrlɪŋ/ a querido, amado; (greatest) mayor. —n querido (-da); (favorite) el predilecto, la predilecta, la favorito, la favorita. **My d.!** ¡Amor mío! ¡Vida mía! ¡Pichoncito mío!

darn /dɑrn/ vt zurcir, remendar. —n zurcido, remiendo, m

darner /'dɑrnər/ n zurcidor (-ra); (implement) huevo de zurcir, m

darning /'dɑrnɪŋ/ n zurcidura, f; zurcido, recosido, m. **d.-needle**, aguja de zurcir, f. **d. wool**, lana de zurcir, f

dart /dɑrt/ n dardo, m; movimiento rápido, m; avance rápido, m; Sew. sisa, f. —vi lanzarse, abalanzarse (sobre); volar; correr, avanzar rápidamente. —vt lanzar, arrojar; dirigir. **to make darts in**, Sew. sisar

dash /dæʃ/ n (spirit) fogosidad, f, brío, m; energía, f; (impact) choque, golpe, m; (mixture) mezcla, f; (of a liquid) gota, f; (of the pen) rasgo, m; (attack) ataque, m; avance rápido, m; (a little) algo, un poco (de); Gram. raya, f; (show) ostentación, f. **He made a d. for the door**, Se precipitó a la puerta, Corrió hacia la puerta. **to cut a d.**, hacer gran papel. **d.-board**, tablero de instrumentos, m

dash /dæʃ/ vt arrojar con violencia; (break) quebrar, estrellar; (sprinkle) rociar (con), salpicar (con); (mix) mezclar; (knock) golpear; (disappoint) frustrar, destruir; (confound) confundir; (depress) desanimar. —vi (rush) precipitarse; quebrarse, estrellarse; chocar (contra); (of waves) romperse. **to d. to pieces**, hacer añicos, estrellar. **to d. along**, avanzar rápidamente; correr. **to d. away**, vi marcharse apresuradamente. **to d. apart** bruscamente. **to d. down**, vi bajar aprisa. —vt derribar; (overturn) volcar; (throw) tirar. **to d. off**, vi marcharse rápidamente. —vt hacer apresuradamente; (a letter, etc.) escribir de prisa; (sketch) bosquejar rápidamente. **to d. out**, vi salir precipitadamente; lanzarse a la calle. —vt (erase) borrar; hacer saltar. **to d. through**, atravesar rápidamente; hacer de prisa.

dashing /'dæʃɪŋ/ a valiente; (spirited) fogoso, gallardo; majo, brillante. —n choque, m; (breaking) quebrantamiento, m; (of the waves) embate, m

dastardly /'dæstərdli/ a cobarde

data /'deɪtə/ n pl datos, m pl

database /'deɪtə,beɪs/ n base de datos, f

data processing n elaboración electrónica de datos, f, recuento de datos, m

date /deɪt/ n fecha, f; (period) época, f; (term) plazo, m; (duration) duración, f; (appointment) cita, f; Bot. dátil, m. —vt fechar, datar; poner fecha a; asignar. —vi datar (de), remontar (a). **out of d.**, anticuado; pasado de moda; (of persons) atrasado de noticias. **to be up to d.**, ser nuevo; ser de última moda; (of persons) estar al día. **to bring up to d.**, renovar; (of persons) poner al corriente. **to fix the d.**, señalar el día; (chronologically) ajustar los tiempos. **to d.**, hasta la fecha. **under d. (of)**, con fecha (de). **up to d.**, hasta hoy, hasta ahora. **What is the d.?** ¿Qué fecha es? ¿A cómo estamos hoy? ¿A cuántos estamos hoy? **d. palm**, datilera, f

date of expiry n fecha de caducidad, f

daub /dɔb/ vt barrar, embadurnar; manchar, ensuciar; untar; (paint) pintorrear. —n embadurnamiento, m; (picture) aleluya, f

daughter /'dɔtər/ n hija, f. **adopted d.**,

hija adoptiva, *f.* **little d.,** hijuela, *f.* **d.-in-law,** nuera, *f*

daunt /dɔnt, dɑnt/ *vt* intimidar, acobardar; dar miedo (a), espantar; (dishearten) desanimar

dauntless /'dɔntlɪs/ *a* impávido, intrépido

dawdle /'dɔdl/ *vi* perder el tiempo; haraganear, gandulear

dawdler /'dɔdlər/ *n* gandul (-la)

dawn /dɔn/ *n* alba, madrugada, primera luz, *f; Fig.* aurora, *f.* —*vi* amanecer, alborear, romper el día; (appear) mostrarse, asomar. **at d.,** a primera luz, al amanecer, de madrugada, al alba. **It had not dawned on me,** No me había ocurrido

day /dei/ *n* día, *m;* luz del día, *f;* (day's work) jornada, *f;* (battle) batalla, *f;* (victory) victoria, *f; pl* **days,** (time) tiempos, *m pl,* época, *f;* (life) vida, *f;* (years) años, *m pl, a* diario. **all day long,** durante todo el día. **any day,** cualquier día. **by day,** de día. **by the day,** al día. **every day,** todos los días, cada día. **every other day,** un día sí y otro no, cada dos días. **from this day forward,** desde hoy en adelante. **from day to day,** de día en día. **Good day!** ¡Buenos días! **in these days,** en estos días. **in olden days,** en la antigüedad; *Inf.* en tiempos de Maricastaña. **in the days of,** en los tiempos de; durante los años de; durante la vida de. **next day,** el día siguiente. **(on) the next day,** al día siguiente, al otro día. **one of these days,** un día de éstos. **some fine day,** el mejor día, de un día a otro. **the day after tomorrow,** pasado mañana. **the day before yesterday,** anteayer. **the day before,** la víspera. **to win the day,** ganar el día, salir victorioso. **day after day,** cada día, día tras día. **day by day,** día por día. **day in, day out,** sin cesar, día tras día. **day-book,** *Com.* libro diario, *m.* **day's holiday,** día de asueto, *m;* día libre, *m.* **day laborer,** jornalero, *m.* **day nursery,** guardería de niños, *f.* **day-pupil,** alumno (-na) externo (-na). **day-school,** externado, *m.* **day shift,** turno de día, *m.* **day-star,** lucero del alba, *m.* **day ticket,** billete de excursión, *m*

daybreak /'dei,breik/ *n* alba, *f,* amanecer, *m.* **at d.,** al romper el día, al amanecer

daydream /'dei,drim/ *n* ensueño, *m;* ilusión, *f;* fantasía, visión, *f.* —*vi Lit.* soñar despierto, dejar volar sus pensamientos; *Fig.* hacerse ilusiones

daydreamer /'dei,drimər/ *n* soñador (-ra); visionario (-ia)

daylight /'dei,lait/ *n* luz del día, *f,* día, *m;* (contrasted with artificial light) luz natural, *f.* **in broad d.,** a plena calle, a plena luz, en plena luz del día. **It's d. robbery!** ¡Es un desuello! **d.-saving,** hora de verano, *f*

daytime /'dei,taim/ *n* día, *m.* **in the d.,** durante el día

daze /deiz/ *vt* aturdir, confundir; (dazzle)

deslumbrar. —*n* aturdimiento, *m,* confusión, *f;* perplejidad, *f*

dazzle /'dæzəl/ *vt* (camouflage) disfrazar; deslumbrar, ofuscar. —*n* deslumbramiento, *m;* brillo, *m,* refulgencia, *f*

dazzling /'dæzlɪŋ/ *a* deslumbrador; brillante

dead /dɛd/ *a and past part* muerto; inanimado; (withered) marchito; (deep) profundo; (unconscious) inerte; inmóvil; insensible; (numb) entumecido; (complete) absoluto, completo; (sure) certero, excelente; (useless) inútil; (of color and human character) apagado; sin espíritu; inactivo; (of eyes) mortecino; (of sound) sordo, opaco; (of villages, etc.) desierto, despoblado; (quiet) silencioso; (empty) vacío; (monotonous) monótono; (of fire) apagado; (with weight, language) muerto; *Elec.* interrumpido; *Law.* muerto civilmente. —*adv* completamente, enteramente; del todo; directamente; exactamente; profundamente. **the d.,** los muertos. **in the d. of night,** en las altas horas de la noche. **to be d.,** estar muerto; haber muerto. **to be d. against,** estar completamente opuesto a. **to drop d.,** caer muerto; morir de repente. **to go d. slow,** ir muy lentamente. **to rise from the d.,** resucitar. **to sham d.,** hacer la mortecina, fingirse muerto. **to speak ill of the d.,** hablar mal de los muertos; *Inf.* desenterrar los muertos. **d. ball,** pelota fuera de juego, *f.* **d.-beat,** muerto de cansancio. **d. body,** cadáver, cuerpo muerto, *m.* **d. calm,** calma profunda, *f; Naut.* calma chicha, *f.* **d. certainty,** seguridad completa, *f.* **d.-drunk,** hecho una uva. **d. end,** callejón sin salida, *m.* **d. heat,** empate, *m.* **d. language,** lengua muerta, *f.* **d.-letter,** letra muerta, *f;* carta devuelta o no reclamada, *f.* **d.-lock,** punto muerto, *m.* **to reach a d.-lock,** llegar a un punto muerto. **d. march,** marcha fúnebre, *f.* **d. season,** temporada de calma, *f.* **d. set,** empeñado (en). **d. shot,** (person) tirador (-ra) certero (-ra) (shot) tiro certero, *m.* **d. silence,** silencio profundo, *m.* **d. stop,** parada en seco, *f.* **d. tired,** rendido. **d. weight,** peso muerto, *m.* **d. wood,** leña seca, *f;* material inútil, *m*

deaden /'dɛdn/ *vt* amortiguar; (of pain) calmar; (remove) quitar; (of colours) apagar

deadening /'dɛdnɪŋ/ *n* amortiguamiento, *m*

deadly /'dɛdli/ *a* mortal; implacable; *Inf.* insoportable. —*adv* mortalmente. **He was d. pale,** Estaba pálido como un muerto. **the seven d. sins,** los siete pecados mortales. **d. nightshade,** belladona, *f*

deadness /'dɛdnɪs/ *n* falta de vida, *f;* inercia, *f;* marchitez, *f;* (numbness) entumecimiento, *m;* desanimación, *f;* parálisis, *f*

Dead Sea, the el mar Muerto, *m*

deaf /dɛf/ *a* sordo. **d. people,** los sordos.

to be d., ser sordo; padecer sordera. **to be as d. as a post**, ser más sordo que una tapia. **to become d.**, ensordecer, volverse sordo. **to fall on d. ears**, caer en saco roto. **to turn a d. ear**, hacerse el sordo. **d. aid**, audífono, *m*. **d.-and-dumb**, sordomudo. **d.-and-dumb alphabet**, alfabeto manual, abecedario manual, *m*. **d.-mute**, sordomudo (-da). **d.-mutism**, sordomudez, *f*

deafen /'dɛfən/ *vt* asordar, ensordecer

deafening /'dɛfənɪŋ/ *a* ensordecedor

deafness /'dɛfnɪs/ *n* sordera, *f*

deal /dil/ *n* (transaction) negocio, trato, *m*; (at cards) reparto, *m*; (wood) pino, *m*; (plank) tablón de pino, *m*. **a d.**, mucho. **a very great d.**, muchísimo. **to conclude a d.**, cerrar un trato

deal /dil/ *vt* repartir; (a blow) asestar, dar; (cards) dar; (justice) dispensar. **to d. a blow at**, asestar un golpe; *Fig.* herir (en); *Fig.* destruir de un golpe. **to d. in**, comerciar en, traficar en; ocuparse en; meterse en. **to d. out**, dispensar. **to d. with**, (buy from) comprar de; tener relaciones con, tratar; entenderse con; portarse con; (of affairs) ocuparse en, arreglar, dirigir; (contend) luchar con; (discuss) discutir, tratar de; (of books) versar sobre

dealer /'dilər/ *n* traficante, *m*& mercader, *m*; (at cards) el que da las cartas

dealing /'dilɪŋ/ *n* conducta, *f*; proceder, *m*; trato, *m*; tráfico, *m*; *pl* **dealings**, relaciones, *f pl*; transacciones, *f pl*

dean /din/ *n Eccl.* deán, *m*; *Educ.* decano, *m*

dear /dɪər/ *a* (beloved) querido, amado; (charming) encantador, simpático; (in letters) estimado, querido; (favorite) predilecto; (expensive) caro. —*n* querido (-da); persona querida, *f*, bien amado (-da). —*adv* caro. **Oh d.!** ¡Dios mío! ¡Ay!

dearly /'dɪərli/ *adv* tiernamente, entrañablemente; caro

dearness /'dɪərnɪs/ *n* cariño, afecto, *m*, ternura, *f*; (of price) precio alto, *m*

dearth /dɜrθ/ *n* carestía, *f*; (of news, etc.) escasez, *f*

death /dɛθ/ *n* muerte, *f*; (*Law.* and in announcements) fallecimiento, *m*, defunción, *f*. **to be at death's door**, estar a la muerte. **to put to d.**, ajusticiar. **to the d.**, a muerte. **untimely d.**, muerte repentina, *f*; malogro, *m*. **death's head**, calavera, *f*. **d. certificate**, partida de defunción, *f*. **d.-duties**, derechos de herencia, *m pl*. **d.-like**, cadavérico. **d.-mask**, mascarilla, *f*. **d. penalty**, pena de muerte, *f*. **d.-rate**, mortalidad, *f*. **d.-rattle**, sarrillo, *m*. **d.-trap**, lugar peligroso, *m*; *Fig.* trampa, *f*. **d.-warrant**, sentencia de muerte, *f*. **d.-watch bettle**, reloj de la muerte, *m*

deathbed /'dɛθ,bɛd/ *n* lecho mortuorio, lecho de muerte, *m*. **on one's d.**, en su lecho de muerte

deathblow /'dɛθ,bloʊ/ *n* golpe mortal, *m*

deathly /'dɛθli/ *a* mortal

death toll *n* (of a bell) doble, toque de difuntos, *m*; (casualties) número de muertos, saldo de muertos, *m*

debacle /də'bɑkəl/ *n Fig.* ruina, *f*

debar /dɪ'bɑr/ *vt* excluir, privar

debase /dɪ'beɪs/ *vt* degradar, humillar, envilecer; (the coinage) alterar (la moneda)

debasement /dɪ'beɪsmənt/ *n* degradación, humillación, *f*, envilecimiento, *m*; (of the coinage) alteración (de la moneda), *f*

debasing /dɪ'beɪsɪŋ/ *a* degradante, humillante

debatable /dɪ'beɪtəbəl/ *a* discutible

debate /dɪ'beɪt/ *n* debate, *m*; discusión, *f*; disputa, *f*. —*vt* and *vi* debatir; discutir; disputar; considerar

debating /dɪ'beɪtɪŋ/ *n* discusión, *f*; argumentación, *f*

debauch /dɪ'bɔtʃ/ *vt* corromper, pervertir; (a woman) seducir, violar. —*n* libertinaje, *m*; borrachera, *f*

debauched /dɪ'bɔtʃt/ *a* vicioso, licencioso

debauchery /dɪ'bɔtʃəri/ *n* libertinaje, mal vivir, *m*, viciosidad, licencia, *f*

debenture /dɪ'bɛntʃər/ *n* obligación, *f*. **d. holder**, obligacionista, *mf*

debilitate /dɪ'bɪlɪ,teɪt/ *vt* debilitar

debit /'dɛbɪt/ *n* débito, cargo, *m*; saldo deudor, *m*; "debe" de una cuenta, *m*. —*vt* adeudar. **d. and credit**, el cargo y la data. **d. balance**, saldo deudor, *m*

debonair /ˌdɛbə'nɛər/ *a* gallardo, gentil, donairoso; alegre

débris /deɪ'bri/ *n* escombros, desechos, *m pl*; ruinas, *f pl*; *Geol.* despojos, *m pl*

debt /dɛt/ *n* deuda, *f*. **a bad d.**, una deuda incobrable. **to be in the d. of**, ser en cargo a; deber dinero a; *Fig.* sentirse bajo una obligación. **to get into d.**, adeudarse, contraer deudas

debtor /'dɛtər/ *n* deudor (-ra); *Com.* debe, *m*

debunk /deɪ'bʌŋk/ *vt* demoler

debut /deɪ'byu/ *n* (of a debutante) puesta de largo, *f*; (of a play, etc.) estreno, *m*. **to make one's d.**, ponerse de largo, presentarse en sociedad

debutante /'dɛbyuˌtɑnt/ *n* debutante, *f*

decade /'dɛkeɪd/ *n* década, *f*, decenio, *m*; (of the rosary) decena, *f*

decadence /'dɛkədəns/ *n* decadencia, *f*

decadent /'dɛkədənt/ *a* decadente

decamp /dɪ'kæmp/ *vi Mil.* decampar; escaparse, fugarse

decant /dɪ'kænt/ *vt* decantar

decanter /dɪ'kæntər/ *n* garrafa, *f*

decapitate /dɪ'kæpɪˌteɪt/ *vt* decapitar, descabezar

decay /dɪ'keɪ/ *vi* (rot) pudrirse; degenerar; marchitarse; (of teeth) cariarse; (crumble) desmoronarse, caer en ruinas; decaer, declinar; (come down in the world) venir a menos, arruinarse. —*n* pudrición, putrefacción, *f*; (of teeth) caries, f; (withering) marchitez, f; degeneración, f; desmoronamiento, m; ruina, f; (oldness) vejez, f; decadencia, declinación, f; (fall) caída, f

decease /dɪ'sis/ n fallecimiento, m, defunción, f, vi fallecer

deceased /dɪ'sist/ n finado (-da), difunto (-ta). —a difunto

deceit /dɪ'sit/ n engaño, fraude, m; duplicidad, f

deceitful /dɪ'sitfəl/ a engañoso, falso; embustero, mentiroso; ilusorio

deceitfulness /dɪ'sitfəlnɪs/ n falsedad, duplicidad, f

deceivable /dɪ'sivəbəl/ a fácil a engañar, engañadizo

deceive /dɪ'siv/ vt engañar; (disappoint) decepcionar, desilusionar; frustrar. **If my memory does not d. me,** Si la memoria no me engaña, Si mal no me acuerdo

deceiver /dɪ'sivər/ n engañador (-ra); seductor, m

deceiving /dɪ'sivɪŋ/ a engañador

December /dɪ'sɛmbər/ n diciembre, m

decency /'disənsi/ n decoro, f, decencia, f; pudor, m, modestia, f; conveniencias, f pl; Inf. bondad, f; (manners) cortesía, f, buenos modales, m pl

decent /'disənt/ a decente; decoroso, honesto; púdico; (likable) simpático; (of things) bastante bueno; (honorable) honrado

decentralize /di'sɛntrə,laiz/ vt descentralizar

deception /dɪ'sɛpʃən/ n engaño, m; ilusión, f

deceptive /dɪ'sɛptɪv/ a engañoso, mentiroso, ilusorio

decide /dɪ'said/ vt decidir; Law. determinar. —vi decidir, resolver; acordar, quedar en; juzgar; Law. dictar sentencia, fallar

decided /dɪ'saidɪd/ a decidido; (downright) categórico, inequívoco; resuelto; positivo; definitivo

decidedly /dɪ'saidɪdli/ adv decididamente; categóricamente; definitivamente

decimal /'dɛsəməl/ a decimal. **d. fraction,** fracción decimal, f. **d. point,** punto decimal, m. **d. system,** sistema métrico, m

decimate /'dɛsə,meit/ vt diezmar

decipher /dɪ'saifər/ vt descifrar; deletrear

decision /dɪ'sɪʒən/ n decisión, determinación, f; Law. sentencia, f, fallo, m; (agreement) acuerdo, m; (of character) firmeza, resolución, f

decisive /dɪ'saisɪv/ a decisivo; terminante, conclusivo; crítico

decisiveness /dɪ'saisɪvnɪs/ n carácter decisivo, m; firmeza, resolución, f; decisión, f

deck /dɛk/ n cubierta, f; (of cards) baraja (de naipes), f. —vt adornar, ataviar; decorar. **between decks,** entrecubiertas, f pl. **lower d.,** cubierta, f. **promenade d.,** cubierta de paseo, f. **upper d.,** cubierta

superior, f. **d.-cabin,** camarote de cubierta, m. **d.-chair,** silla de cubierta, silla de tijera, silla extensible, f. **d.-hand,** marinero, estibador, m

declaim /dɪ'kleim/ vt recitar. —vi perorar, declamar

declamation /,dɛklə'meiʃən/ n declamación, f

declamatory /dɪ'klæmə,tɔri/ a declamatorio

declaration /,dɛklə'reiʃən/ n declaración, f; manifiesto, m; proclamación, f

declare /dɪ'klɛər/ vt declarar; proclamar; afirmar; manifestar; confesar. —vi declarar; Law. deponer, testificar. **to d. war (on)** declarar la guerra (a)

declaredly /dɪ'klɛərɪdli/ adv declaradamente, explícitamente, abiertamente

decline /dɪ'klain/ n declinación, decadencia, f; disminución, f; debilitación, f; (of the day) caída, f; (of stocks, shares) depresión, f; (illness) consunción, f; (Fig. setting) ocaso, m, vi declinar; inclinarse; decaer, disminuir; debilitarse; (refuse) negarse (a). —vt (refuse) rechazar, rehusar; Gram. declinar; (avoid) evitar

declining /dɪ'klainɪŋ/ a declinante. **in one's d. years,** en sus últimos años

declutch /di'klʌtʃ/ vi desembragar

decode /di'koud/ vt descifrar

décolletee /deiknlə'tei/ a escotado

decompose /,dikəm'pouz/ vt descomponer. —vi descomponerse

decontaminate /,dikən'tæmə,neit/ vt descontaminar

decontrol /,dikən'troul/ vt suprimir las restricciones sobre

decorate /'dɛkə,reit/ vt adornar (con), embellecer; (by painting, etc.) decorar, pintar; (honor) investir (con), condecorar

decoration /,dɛkə'reiʃən/ n decoración, f; Theat. decorado, m; (honor) condecoración, f; ornamento, m

decorative /'dɛkərətɪv/ a decorativo

decorator /'dɛkə,reitər/ n decorador, m; (interior) adornista, m

decorous /'dɛkərəs/ a decoroso, decente; correcto

decorum /dɪ'kɔrəm/ n decoro, m; corrección, f

decoy /n 'dikɔi; v dɪ'kɔi/ n señuelo, m; añagaza, f; (trap) lazo, m, trampa, f; Fig. añagaza, f. —vt (birds) reclamar, atraer con señuelo; Fig. tentar (con), seducir (con). **d. bird,** pájaro de reclamo, m

decrease /n 'dikris; v dɪ'kris/ n disminución, f; baja, f; reducción, f; (of the moon, waters) mengua, f, vi decrecer, disminuir; bajar; menguar. —vt disminuir; reducir

decreasingly /dɪ'krisɪŋli/ adv de menos en menos

decree /dɪ'kri/ n decreto, m; edicto, m. —vi and vt decretar, mandar

decrepit /dɪ'krɛpɪt/ a decrépito

decry /dɪ'krai/ vt desacreditar, rebajar

dedicate /v 'dɛdɪ,keit; a -kɪt/ vt dedicar;

consagrar; destinar; aplicar; (a book, etc.) dedicar. **to d. oneself to,** dedicarse a, consagrarse a, entregarse a

dedication /ˌdɛdɪˈkeɪʃən/ n dedicación, f; consagración, f; (of a book, etc.) dedicatoria, f

deduce /dɪˈdus/ vt derivar; deducir, inferir

deduct /dɪˈdʌkt/ vt deducir; descontar

deduction /dɪˈdʌkʃən/ n deducción, f; descuento, m

deed /did/ n acción, f; hecho, acto, m; hazaña, f; (reality) realidad, f; Law. escritura, f; Law. contrato, m. **d. of gift,** escritura de donación, f

deem /dim/ vt juzgar, creer, estimar

deep /dip/ a profundo; (wide) ancho; (low) bajo; (thick) espeso; (of colours) subido; (of sounds) grave, profundo; (immersed (in)) absorto (en); (of the mind) penetrante; (secret) secreto; (intense) intenso, hondo; (cunning) astuto, artero; (dark) oscuro; (of mourning) riguroso. —n Poet. piélago, mar, m; profundidad, f; abismo, m, adv profundamente; a una gran profundidad. **to be in d. waters,** Fig. estar con el agua al cuello. **to be three feet d.,** tener tres pies de profundidad. **to be d. in,** estar absorto en; (of debt) estar cargado de. **three d.,** tres de fondo. **d. into the night,** hasta las altas horas de la noche. **d.-felt,** hondamente sentido. **d. mourning,** luto riguroso, m. **d.-rooted,** arraigado. **d.-sea fishing,** pesca mayor, f. **d.-sea lead,** escandallo, m. **d.-seated,** íntimo, profundo; arraigado. **d.-set,** hundido

deepen /ˈdipən/ vt profundizar, ahondar; (broaden) ensanchar; (intensify) intensificar; (increase) aumentar; (of colors) aumentar el tono de, intensificar. —vi hacerse más profundo, hacerse más hondo; intensificarse; aumentarse; (of sound) hacerse más grave

deeply /ˈdipli/ adv profundamente; intensamente; fuertemente

deer /dɪər/ n ciervo (-va), venado, m, a cervuno. **d.-hound,** galgo de cazar venados, m. **d.-skin,** piel de venado, f. **d.-stalking,** caza del ciervo, f

deface /dɪˈfeɪs/ vt desfigurar, mutilar; estropear; (erase) borrar

defamation /ˌdɛfəˈmeɪʃən/ n difamación, denigración, f

defamatory /dɪˈfæməˌtɔri/ a difamatorio, denigrante

defame /dɪˈfeɪm/ vt difamar, denigrar, calumniar

default /dɪˈfɔlt/ n omisión, f, descuido, m; falta, f; ausencia, f; Law. rebeldía, f. —vi dejar de cumplir; faltar; no pagar. —vt Law. condenar en rebeldía. **in d. of,** en la ausencia de

defaulter /dɪˈfɔltər/ n el, m, (f, la) que no cumple sus obligaciones; delincuente, mf; desfalcador (-ra); Law. rebelde, mf

defeat /dɪˈfit/ vt vencer, derrotar; frustrar; (reject) rechazar; (elude) evitar; Fig.

vencer, triunfar sobre. —n derrota, f; vencimiento, m; frustración, f; rechazamiento, m. **to d. one's own ends,** defraudar sus intenciones

defeatist /dɪˈfitɪst/ n derrotista, mf

defecate /ˈdɛfɪˌkeɪt/ vt defecar

defect /n ˈdifɛkt, dɪˈfɛkt; v dɪˈfɛkt/ n defecto, m; imperfección, f; falta, f

defection /dɪˈfɛkʃən/ n defección, f; deserción, f; (from a religion) apostasía, f

defective /dɪˈfɛktɪv/ a defectuoso; Gram. defectivo; falto; imperfecto; (mentally) anormal. —n persona anormal, f, anormal, m

defend /dɪˈfɛnd/ vt defender; proteger; preservar; sostener; (a thesis) sustentar

defendant /dɪˈfɛndənt/ n Law. acusado (-da), procesado (-da), demandado (da)

defender /dɪˈfɛndər/ n defensor (-ra); (of a thesis) sustentante, mf

defense /dɪˈfɛns/ n defensa, f; justificación, f; pl **defenses,** defensas, f pl; obras de fortificación, f pl. **for the d.,** (of witnesses) de descargo; (of counsel) para la defensa. **in d. of,** en defensa de. **in one's own d.,** en su propia defensa. **d. in depth,** Mil. defensa en fondo, f

defenseless /dɪˈfɛnslɪs/ a indefenso, sin defensa

defensible /dɪˈfɛnsəbəl/ a defendible; justificable

defensive /dɪˈfɛnsɪv/ a defensivo. —n defensiva, f. **to be on the d.,** estar a la defensiva

defer /dɪˈfɜr/ vt (postpone) diferir, aplazar; suspender. —vi (yield) deferir, ceder; (delay) tardar, aguardar. **deferred payment,** pago a plazos, m

deference /ˈdɛfərəns/ n deferencia, f, respeto, m; consideración, f

deferential /ˌdɛfəˈrɛnʃəl/ a deferente, respetuoso

deferment /dɪˈfɜrmənt/ n aplazamiento, m; suspensión, f

defiance /dɪˈfaɪəns/ n desafío, m; provocación, f; oposición, f; insolencia, f. **in d. of,** en contra de

defiant /dɪˈfaɪənt/ a provocativo; insolente

defiantly /dɪˈfaɪəntli/ adv de un aire provocativo; insolentemente

deficiency /dɪˈfɪʃənsi/ n falta, deficiencia, f; imperfección, f; defecto, m; omisión, f; (scarcity) carestía, f; (in accounts) déficit, m

deficient /dɪˈfɪʃənt/ a deficiente; falto, incompleto; imperfecto; pobre; defectuoso; (not clever at) débil (en); (mentally) anormal. **to be d. in,** carecer de; ser pobre en

deficit /ˈdɛfəsɪt/ n déficit, m; descubierto, m

defile /dɪˈfaɪl/ n desfiladero, m. —vt contaminar; profanar; manchar; deshonrar. —vi Mil. desfilar

define /dɪˈfaɪn/ vt definir; (throw into relief) destacar; fijar; Law. determinar

definite /'dɛfənɪt/ a definido; positivo; categórico; exacto; concreto. **d. article,** artículo definido, m

definitely /'dɛfənɪtli/ adv positivamente; claramente. **definitely not!** ¡definitivamente no!

definition /ˌdɛfə'nɪʃən/ n definición, f

definitive /dɪ'fɪnɪtɪv/ a definitivo

deflate /dɪ'fleɪt/ vt desinflar. —vi desinflarse, deshincharse

deflation /dɪ'fleɪʃən/ n desinflación, f

deflect /dɪ'flɛkt/ vt desviar; apartar. —vi desviarse; apartarse

deforestation /dɪˌfɔrɪ'steɪʃən/ n desforestación, desmontadura, despoblación forestal, f

deform /dɪ'fɔrm/ vt deformar, desfigurar; afear

deformation /ˌdifɔr'meɪʃən/ n deformación, f

deformity /dɪ'fɔrmɪti/ n deformidad, f

defraud /dɪ'frɔd/ vt defraudar

defrauder /dɪ'frɔdər/ n defraudador (-ra)

defray /dɪ'freɪ/ vt sufragar, costear, pagar

defrayal /dɪ'freɪəl/ n pago, m

defrost /dɪ'frɔst/ vt deshelar

deft /dɛft/ a diestro; hábil

deftly /'dɛftli/ adv con destreza; hábilmente

defunct /dɪ'fʌŋkt/ a and n difunto (-ta)

defy /dɪ'faɪ/ vt desafiar; (face) arrostrar; (violate) contravenir

degeneracy /dɪ'dʒɛnərəsi/ n degeneración, f; depravación, degradación, f

degenerate /a, n dɪ'dʒɛnərɪt; v -ˌreɪt/ a and n degenerado (-da). —vi degenerar

degeneration /dɪˌdʒɛnə'reɪʃən/ n degeneración, f

degradation /ˌdɛgrɪ'deɪʃən/ n degradación, f; abyección, f

degrade /dɪ'greɪd/ vt degradar; envilecer, deshonrar

degrading /dɪ'greɪdɪŋ/ a degradante

degree /dɪ'gri/ n grado, m; punto, m; clase social, f. **by degrees,** poco a poco, gradualmente, **five degrees below zero,** cinco grados bajo cero. **in the highest d.,** en sumo grado, en grado superlativo. **to a certain d.,** hasta cierto punto. **to receive a d.,** graduarse

degree-granting institution /dɪ'gri ˌgræntɪŋ/ n plantel habilitado para expedir títulos, m

dehydrate /di'haidreɪt/ vt deshidratar

de-ice /di'ais/ vt deshelar

deify /'diə,fai/ vt deificar, endiosar

deign /dein/ vi dignarse. —vt conceder

deity /'diiti/ n deidad, divinidad, f; dios, m

dejected /dɪ'dʒɛktɪd/ a abatido, desanimado, deprimido

dejection /dɪ'dʒɛkʃən/ n abatimiento, desaliento, m, melancolía, f

delay /dɪ'lei/ n retraso, m, dilación, tardanza, demora, f. —vt retrasar, demorar; (a person) entretener; (postpone) aplazar;

(obstruct) impedir. —vi tardar; entretenerse. **without more d.,** sin más tardar

delectable /dɪ'lɛktəbəl/ a deleitoso, delicioso

delegacy /'dɛlɪgəsi/ n delegación, f

delegate /n 'dɛlɪgɪt; v -ˌgeɪt/ n delegado (-da). —vt delegar, diputar

delegation /ˌdɛlɪ'geɪʃən/ n delegación, f

delete /dɪ'lit/ vt suprimir, borrar

deleterious /ˌdɛlɪ'tɪəriəs/ a deletéreo

deletion /dɪ'liʃən/ n supresión, borradura, f

deliberate /a dɪ'lɪbərɪt; v -ˌreɪt/ a premeditado, intencionado; (slow) pausado, lento. —vi and vt deliberar, discurrir, considerar

deliberately /dɪ'lɪbərɪtli/ adv (intentionally) con premeditación, a sabiendas; (slowly) pausadamente, lentamente

deliberation /dɪˌlɪbə'reɪʃən/ n reflexión, f, deliberación, consideración, f; (slowness) lentitud, pausa, f

deliberative /dɪ'lɪbərətɪv/ a deliberativo, de liberante

delicacy /'dɛlɪkəsi/ n delicadeza, f; fragilidad, f; suavidad, f; sensibilidad, f; escrupulosidad, f; (of health) debilidad, delicadez, f; (difficulty) dificultad, f; (food) manjar exquisito, m, golosina, f

delicate /'dɛlɪkɪt/ a delicado; fino; frágil; suave; exquisito; delicado (de salud); (of situations) difícil

delicatessen /ˌdɛlɪkə'tɛsən/ n (store) fiambrería, f

delicious /dɪ'lɪʃəs/ a delicioso

deliciousness /dɪ'lɪʃəsnɪs/ n deleite, m, lo delicioso; excelencia, f; delicias, f pl

delight /dɪ'lait/ n deleite, regocijo, m; encanto, m, delicia, f; placer, gozo, m. —vt deleitar, encantar; halagar. —vi deleitarse, complacerse. **to be delighted with,** estar encantado con. **to d. in,** deleitarse en, complacerse en; tomar placer en

delightful /dɪ'laitfəl/ a delicioso, precioso, encantador

delimit /dɪ'lɪmɪt/ vt delimitar

delimitation /dɪˌlɪmɪ'teɪʃən/ n delimitación, f

delineate /dɪ'lɪni,eɪt/ vt delinear, diseñar; Fig. pintar, describir

delinquency /dɪ'lɪŋkwənsi/ n delincuencia, f; criminalidad, f; culpa, f; delito, m

delinquent /dɪ'lɪŋkwənt/ a delincuente. —n delincuente, mf

delirious /dɪ'lɪəriəs/ a delirante; desvariado; Inf. loco. **to be d.,** delirar, desvariar

delirium /dɪ'lɪəriəm/ n delirio, desvarío, m. **d. tremens,** delírium tremens, m

deliver /dɪ'lɪvər/ vt librar (de); (distribute) repartir; (hand over) entregar; (recite) recitar, decir; (a speech) pronunciar; comunicar; (send) despachar, expedir; (a blow) asestar; (give) dar; (bring) traer; (battle, a lecture) dar; (a woman, of a doctor) asistir en el parto (a); (a child) traer al mundo; (a judgmént) pronunciar. **to be delivered (of a child),** dar a luz. **to d. oneself up,** entregarse. **delivered free,** porte pagado.

deliverance /dı'lıvərəns/ n libramiento, rescate, m; redención, salvación, f; (of a judgment) pronuncia, f

deliverer /dı'lıvərər/ n libertador (-ra); salvador (-ra); (distributor) repartidor (-ra); entregador (-ra)

delivery /dı'lıvəri/ n (distribution) reparto, m, distribución, f; entrega, f; Law. cesión, f; (of a judgment) pronuncia, f; (of a speech) pronunciación, f; (manner of speaking) declamación, f; dicción, f; (of a child) parto, m. **on d.,** al entregarse. **The letter came by the first d.,** La carta llegó en el primer reparto. **d. man,** mozo de reparto, m. **d. note,** nota de entrega, f. **d. van,** camión de reparto, m

delivery truck n camioneta de reparto, furgoneta, f, sedán de reparto, m

dell /dɛl/ n hondonada, f; pequeño valle, m

delouse /di'laus/ vt despiojar, espulgar

delta /'dɛltə/ n (Greek letter) delta, f; (of a river) delta, m

delude /dı'lud/ vt engañar; ilusionar. **to d. oneself,** engañarse

deluded /dı'ludıd/ a iluso, engañado, ciego

deluge /'dɛlyudʒ/ n diluvio, m. —vt diluviar; inundar (con)

delusion /dı'luʒən/ n engaño, m, ceguedad, f; error, m; ilusión, f

delve /dɛlv/ vt and vi cavar; Fig. ahondar (en), penetrar (en), investigar

demagogic /,dɛmə'gɒdʒɪk/ a demagógico

demagogue /'dɛmə,gɒg/ n demagogo (-ga)

demagogy /'dɛmə,goudʒi/ n demagogia, f

demand /dı'mænd/ n exigencia, f; Com. demanda, f; petición, f; Polit. Econ. consumo, m. —vt exigir; requerir; pedir; (claim) reclamar. **in d.,** en demanda. **on d.,** al solicitarse. **to be in d.,** ser popular. **d. note,** apremio, m

demanding /dı'mændıŋ/ a exigente

demarcate /dı'mɑrkeit/ vt demarcar

demean (oneself) /dı'min/ vr degradarse, rebajarse

demeanor /dı'minər/ n conducta, f; continente, porte, aire, m; (manners) modales, m pl

demented /dı'mɛntıd/ a demente, loco

demerit /dı'mɛrıt/ n demérito, m

demi- prefix semi; casi. **d.-tasse,** taza cafetera, jícara, f

demijohn /'dɛmı,dʒɒn/ n damajuana, f

demilitarize /di'mılıtə,raiz/ vt desmilitarizar

demise /dı'maiz/ n Law. traslación de dominio, f; sucesión de la corona, f; (death) óbito, fallecimiento, m

demobilization /di,moubələ'zeiʃən/ n desmovilización, f

demobilize /di'moubə,laiz/ vt desmovilizar

democracy /dı'mɒkrəsi/ n democracia, f

democrat /'dɛmə,kræt/ n demócrata, mf

democratic /,dɛmə'krætık/ a democrático. **to make d.,** democratizar

demolish /dı'mɒlıʃ/ vt demoler, derribar; Fig. destruir; (eat) engullir, devorar

demolisher /dı'mɒlıʃər/ n demoledor, m; Fig. destructor (-ra)

demolition /,dɛmə'lıʃən/ n demolición, f; derribo, m, a demoledor; de demolición. **d. squad,** pelotón de demolición, m

demon /'dimən/ n demonio, diablo, m

demoniacal /,dimə'naikəl/ a demoníaco

demonstrate /'dɛmən,streit/ vt demostrar; mostrar, probar. —vi hacer una demostración

demonstration /,dɛmən'streiʃən/ n demostración, f; manifestación, f

demonstrative /də'mɒnstrətıv/ a demostrativo; (of persons) expresivo, mimoso. **d. pronoun,** pronombre demostrativo, m

demoralization /dı,mɔrələ'zeiʃən/ n desmoralización, f

demoralize /dı'mɔrə,laiz, -'mɒr-/ vt desmoralizar

demoralizing /dı'mɔrə,laizıŋ/ a desmoralizador

demur /dı'mɜr/ vi dudar, vacilar; objetar, protestar; poner dificultades. —n objeción, protesta, f

demure /dı'myʊr/ a serio, modoso recatado; púdico; de una coquetería disimulada

demurely /dı'myʊrli/ adv modestamente; con recato; con coquetería disimulada

demureness /dı'myʊrnıs/ n seriedad, f, recato, m; modestia fingida, coquetería disimulada, f

demy /də'mai/ n papel marquilla, m; becario de Magdalen College, Oxford, m

den /dɛn/ n madriguera, guarida, f; (of thieves) cueva, f; (in a zoo) cercado, recinto, m; (study) gabinete, m; (squalid room) cuartucho, m

denaturalize /di'nætʃərə,laiz/ vt desnaturalizar

denial /dı'naiəl/ n negación, f; rechazo, m; contradicción, f; negativa, f

denizen /'dɛnəzən/ n habitante, m; ciudadano (-na)

Denmark /'dɛnmɑrk/ Dinamarca, f

denominate /dı'nɒmə,neit/ vt denominar, nombrar

denomination /dı,nɒmə'neiʃən/ n denominación, f; secta, f; clase, f

denominational /dı,nɒmə'neiʃənl/ a sectario

denominator /dı'nɒmə,neitər/ n Math. denominador, m

denote /dı'nout/ vt denotar, indicar; significar

dénouement /,deinu'mɑ̃/ n desenlace, desenredo, m; solución, f

denounce /dɪ'nauns/ *vt* denunciar; delatar, acusar

denouncer /dɪ'naunsər/ *n* denunciante, *mf* delator (-ra)

dense /dɛns/ *a* denso; espeso, compacto; tupido; impenetrable; *Inf.* estúpido

densely /'dɛnsli/ *adv* densamente; espesamente. **d. populated,** con gran densidad de población

density /'dɛnsɪti/ *n* densidad, *f;* espesor, *m;* consistencia, *f; Inf.* estupidez, *f*

dent /dɛnt/ *n* mella, *f;* (in metal) abolladura, *f, vt* mellar; abollar

dental /'dɛntl/ *a* dental. —*n* letra dental, *f.* **d. forceps,** gatillo, *m.* **d. mechanic,** mecánico dentista, *m.* **d. surgeon,** odontólogo, *m*

dental floss *n* seda dental, *f*

dentist /'dɛntɪst/ *n* dentista, *mf;* odontólogo, *m*

dentistry /'dɛntəstri/ *n* odontología, *f*

denture /'dɛntʃər/ *n* dentadura, *f*

denude /dɪ'nud/ *vt* denudar, despojar, privar (de)

denunciation /dɪ,nʌnsi'eiʃən/ *n* denuncia, *f;* acusación, delación, *f*

denunciatory /dɪ'nʌnsiə,tori/ *a* denunciatorio

Denver boot /'dɛnvər/ *n* cepo, *m*

deny /dɪ'nai/ *vt* negar; desmentir; rehusar; rechazar; renegar (de); (give up) renunciar, sacrificar. **to d. oneself,** privarse (de); sacrificar; negarse

deodorant /di'oudərənt/ *a* and *n* desodorante, *m*

deodorize /di'oudə,raiz/ *vt* desinfectar, destruir el olor de

depart /dɪ'part/ *vi* marcharse, irse, partir; (of trains, etc., and meaning go out) salir; (deviate) desviarse (de), apartarse (de); (go away) alejarse; (leave) dejar; (disappear) desaparecer; (alter) cambiar; (die) morir

departed /dɪ'partɪd/ *a* (past) pasado; desaparecido; (dead) difunto, muerto. —*n* difunto (-ta)

department /dɪ'partmənt/ *n* departamento, *m;* sección, *f;* (of learning) ramo, *m;* (in France) distrito administrativo, *m.* **d. store,** grandes tiendas, *f pl,* (Argentina), grandes almacenes, *m pl*

departmental /dɪ,part'mɛntl/ *a* departamental

departure /dɪ'partʃər/ *n* partida, ida, *f;* (going out, and of trains, etc.) salida, *f;* (deviation) desviación, *f,* el apartarse. **d. from the rules,** el apartarse de las reglas, *f;* (disappearance) desaparición, *f;* (change) cambio, *m;* (giving up) renuncia, *f;* (death) muerte, *f.* **to take one's d.,** marcharse

depend /dɪ'pɛnd/ *vi* depender. **to d. on,** depender de; (rest on) apoyarse en; (count on) contar con; (trust) fiarse de; tener confianza en, estar seguro de. **That depends!** ¡Eso depende!

dependable /dɪ'pɛndəbəl/ *a* digno de confianza; seguro

dependent /dɪ'pɛndənt/ *a* dependiente; subordinado; condicional. —*n* dependiente, *m.* **to be d. on,** depender de

depict /dɪ'pɪkt/ *vt* representar; pintar; dibujar; *Fig.* describir, retratar

depiction /dɪ'pɪkʃən/ *n* representación, *f;* pintura, *f;* dibujo, *m; Fig.* descripción, *f*

depilate /'dɛpə,leit/ *vt* depilar

depilatory /dɪ'pɪlə,tori, -,touri/ *a* and *n* depilatorio *m.*

deplete /dɪ'plit/ *vt* agotar; disipar

depletion /dɪ'pliʃən/ *n* agotamiento, *m*

deplorable /dɪ'plorəbəl/ *a* lamentable, deplorable

deplore /dɪ'plor/ *vt* deplorar, lamentar

deploy /dɪ'ploi/ *vt* desplegar. —*vi* desplegarse. —*n* despliegue, *m*

deployment /dɪ'ploimənt/ *n* despliegue, *m*

depopulate /di'popyə,leit/ *vt* despoblar

deport /dɪ'port/ *vt* deportar

deportation /,dipor'teiʃən/ *n* deportación, *f*

deportment /dɪ'portmənt/ *n* comportamiento, *m;* porte, aire, *m;* conducta, *f*

depose /dɪ'pouz/ *vt* destronar; (give evidence) testificar, declarar

deposit /dɪ'pozit/ *n* depósito, *m; Geol.* yacimiento, filón, *m;* sedimento, *m.* —*vt* depositar. **to leave a d.,** dejar un depósito. **d. account,** cuenta corriente, *f*

deposition /,dɛpə'zɪʃən/ *n* deposición, *f; Law.* testimonio, *m,* declaración, *f;* (from the Cross) descendimiento, *m,* (de la Cruz)

depositor /dɪ'pozitər/ *n* depositador (-ra)

depository /dɪ'pozi,tori/ *n* depositaría, *f,* almacén, *m;* (of knowledge, etc.) pozo, *m*

depot /'dipou/ *n* almacén, *m;* (military headquarters) depósito, *m;* (for army vehicles, etc.) parque, *m;* (for buses, etc.) estación, *f*

depravation /,dɛprə'veiʃən/ *n* depravación, *f*

depraved /dɪ'preivd/ *a* depravado, perverso, vicioso

depravity /dɪ'prævɪti/ *n* corrupción, maldad, perversión, *f*

deprecate /'dɛprɪ,keit/ *vt* desaprobar, criticar; lamentar, deplorar

deprecatingly /'dɛprɪ,keitɪŋli/ *adv* con desaprobación, críticamente

deprecation /,dɛprɪ'keiʃən/ *n* deprecación, *f;* desaprobación, crítica, *f*

deprecatory /'dɛprɪkə,tori/ *a* deprecativo; de desaprobación, de crítica

depreciate /dɪ'priʃi,eit/ *vt* depreciar, rebajar; *Fig.* tener en poco, menospreciar. —*vi* depreciarse, deteriorarse; bajar de precio

depreciation /dɪ,priʃi'eiʃən/ *n* (in value) amortización, depreciación, *f; Fig.* desprecio, *m*

depredation /,dɛprə'deiʃən/ *n* depredación, *f*

depress /dɪ'prɛs/ *vt* deprimir; (weaken)

debilitar; (humble) humillar; (dispirit) abatir, entristecer; (trade) desanimar, paralizar

depressed /dɪˈprɛst/ a deprimido, desalentado, melancólico, triste; (of an area) necesitado

depressing /dɪˈprɛsɪŋ/ a melancólico, triste; pesimista

depression /dɪˈprɛʃən/ n depresión, f; (hollow) hoyo, m; (sadness) desaliento, abatimiento, m, melancolía, f; (in prices) baja, f; (in trade) desanimación, parálisis, f; Astron. depresión, f

deprivation /ˌdɛprəˈveɪʃən/ n privación, f; pérdida, f

deprive /dɪˈpraɪv/ vt privar (de), despojar (de); defraudar (de); Eccl. destituir (de)

depth /dɛpθ/ n profundidad, f; (thickness) espesor, m, fondo, m; (of night, winter, the country) medio, m; (of sound) gravedad, f; (of colour, feeling) intensidad, f; (abstruseness) dificultad, f; (sagacity) sagacidad, f; pl **depths**, profundidades, f pl; abismo, m; lo más hondo; lo más íntimo. **to be 4 feet in d.**, tener cuatro pies de profundidad. **to the depths of one's being**, hasta lo más íntimo de su ser; hasta los tuétanos. **d. charge**, carga de profundidad, f

deputize (for) /ˈdɛpyəˌtaɪz/ vi desempeñar las funciones de, substituir

deputy /ˈdɛpyəti/ n (substitute) lugarteniente, m; (agent) representante, m; apoderado, m; (parliamentary) diputado, m; (in compounds) sub, vice. **d.-governor**, subgobernador, m. **d.-head**, subjefe, m; (of a school) subdirector (-ra)

derail /dɪˈreɪl/ vt (hacer) descarrilar

derailment /dɪˈreɪlmənt/ n descarrilamiento, m

derange /dɪˈreɪndʒ/ vt desordenar; desorganizar; turbar; (mentally) trastornar, hacer perder el juicio (a)

derangement /dɪˈreɪndʒmənt/ n desorden, m; turbación, f; (mental) trastorno, m, locura, f

derby /ˈdɜrbi/ n carrera del Derby, f; (hat) sombrero hongo, m

deregulate /dɪˈrɛgyəˌleɪt/ vt desregular

derelict /ˈdɛrəlɪkt/ a abandonado, derrelicto. —n derrelicto, m

dereliction /ˌdɛrəˈlɪkʃən/ n abandono, m; omisión, negligencia, f; descuido, m

deride /dɪˈraɪd/ vt burlarse de, mofarse de; ridiculizar

derision /dɪˈrɪʒən/ n irrisión, f, menosprecio, m

derisive /dɪˈraɪsɪv/ a irrisorio; irónico

derivation /ˌdɛrəˈveɪʃən/ n derivación, f

derivative /dɪˈrɪvətɪv/ a derivativo. —n derivado, m

derive /dɪˈraɪv/ vt derivar; obtener; extraer; Fig. sacar, hallar. —vi (from) derivar de; proceder de; remontar a

dermatologist /ˌdɜrməˈtɒlədʒɪst/ n dermatólogo, m

derogatory /dɪˈrɒgəˌtɔri/ a despectivo, despreciativo; deshonroso

derrick /ˈdɛrɪk/ n grúa, machina, f; abanico, m

descant /n ˈdɛskænt; v dɛsˈkænt/ n Mus. discante, m. —vi Mus. discantar; discurrir (sobre), disertar (sobre)

descend /dɪˈsɛnd/ vi descender, bajar; (be inherited) pasar a; (fall) caer; (of the sun) ponerse. —vt bajar. **to d. from**, descender de. **to d. to**, (lower oneself) rebajarse; (consider) venir a, considerar. **to d. upon**, caer sobre; (arrive unexpectedly) llegar inesperadamente, invadir

descendant /dɪˈsɛndənt/ n descendiente, mf; pl **descendants**, descendencia, f

descent /dɪˈsɛnt/ n descenso, m; bajada, f; (slope) pendiente, cuesta, f; (attack) invasión, f, ataque, m; (lineage) descendencia, alcurnia, procedencia, f; (inheritance) herencia, f; transmisión, f. **D. from the Cross**, Descendimiento de la Cruz, m

describe /dɪˈskraɪb/ vt describir; pintar

description /dɪˈskrɪpʃən/ n descripción, f

descriptive /dɪˈskrɪptɪv/ a descriptivo

descry /dɪˈskraɪ/ vt divisar, descubrir; Poet. ver

desecrate /ˈdɛsɪˌkreɪt/ vt profanar

desert /dɪˈzɜrt/ vt abandonar; dejar; (Mil. etc.) desertar. —vi desertar

desert /ˈdɛzərt/ n desierto, m

desert /dɪˈzɜrt/ n (merit) mérito, m **to receive one's deserts**, llevar su merecido

deserted /dɪˈzɜrtɪd/ a abandonado; desierto; solitario; inhabitado, despoblado

deserter /dɪˈzɜrtər/ n desertor, m

desertion /dɪˈzɜrʃən/ n abandono, m, deserción, f; (Mil. etc.) deserción, f

deserve /dɪˈzɜrv/ vt and vi merecer

deserving /dɪˈzɜrvɪŋ/ a merecedor; meritorio. **to be d. of**, merecer

design /dɪˈzaɪn/ n proyecto, m; plan, m; intención, f, propósito, m; objeto, m; modelo, m; (pattern) diseño, dibujo, m; arte del dibujo, mf vt idear; proyectar; (destine) destinar, dedicar; diseñar, dibujar, delinear; planear. **by d.**, expresamente, intencionalmente

designate /v ˈdɛzɪgˌneɪt; a -nɪt/ vt señalar; designar; (appoint) nombrar. —a electo

designation /ˌdɛzɪgˈneɪʃən/ n designación, f; nombramiento, m

designer /dɪˈzaɪnər/ n inventor (-ra), autor (-ra); delineador (-ra); dibujante, mf; (of public works, etc.) proyectista, mf

designing /dɪˈzaɪnɪŋ/ a intrigante, astuto

desirability /dɪˌzaɪ³rəˈbɪlɪti/ n lo deseable; conveniencia, f; ventaja, f

desirable /dɪˈzaɪ³rəbəl/ a deseable; conveniente; ventajoso; agradable; apetecible

desire /dɪˈzaɪ³r/ vt desear; querer; ansiar, ambicionar; (request) rogar, pedir; (order) mandar. —n deseo, m; ansia, aspiración, f; ambición, f; impulso, m; (will) voluntad, f. **to d. ardently**, perecerse por; suspirar por

desirous /dɪˈzaɪ³rəs/ a deseoso (de); ambicioso (de); ansioso (de); impaciente (a); curioso (de)

desist /dɪ'sɪst/ *vi* desistir; dejar (de)

desk /desk/ *n* pupitre, *m*; escritorio, buró, *m*; mesa de trabajo, *f*; (cashier's) caja, *f*; (teacher's, lecturer's; pulpit) cátedra, *f*

desolate /a 'desəlɪt/ *v* -,leɪt/ *a* solitario; desierto; deshabitado; abandonado; arruinado; árido; (afflicted) desolado, angustiado. —*vt* desolar; despoblar

desolation /,desə'leɪʃən/ *n* desolación, *f*; aflicción, angustia, *f*; desconsuelo, *m*

despair /dɪ'speər/ *n* desesperación, *f*; *vi* perder toda esperanza. **His life is despaired of,** Se ha perdido la esperanza de salvarle (la vida). **to be in d.,** estar desesperado

despairing /dɪ'speərɪŋ/ *a* desesperado

despairingly /dɪ'speərɪŋli/ *adv* sin esperanza

desperate /'despərɪt/ *a* desesperado; sin esperanza; irremediable; furioso; violento; (dangerous) arriesgado, peligroso; terrible

desperately /'despərɪtli/ *adv* desesperadamente; furiosamente; terriblemente

desperation /,despə'reɪʃən/ *n* desesperación, *f*; furia, violencia, *f*

despicable /'despɪkəbəl/ *a* vil, despreciable; insignificante

despise /dɪ'spaɪz/ *vt* despreciar; desdeñar

despite /dɪ'spaɪt/ *prep* a pesar de

despoil /dɪ'spɔɪl/ *vt* despojar, desnudar

despoliation /dɪ,spouli'eɪʃən/ *n* despojo, *m*

despondency /dɪ'spɒndənsi/ *n* abatimiento, desaliento, *m*, desesperación, *f*

despondent /dɪ'spɒndənt/ *a* abatido, desanimado, deprimido

despot /'despət/ *n* déspota, *m*

despotic /des'pɒtɪk/ *a* despótico

dessert /dɪ'zɜrt/ *n* postre, *m*, a de postre. **d. plate,** plato para postre, *m*. **d.-spoon,** cuchara de postre, *f*

destination /,destə'neɪʃən/ *n* destinación, *f*

destine /'destɪn/ *vt* destinar; dedicar; predestinar

destiny /'destəni/ *n* destino, *m*

destitute /'destɪ,tut/ *a* indigente, menesteroso; desnudo (de); privado (de); desprovisto (de), falto (de); desamparado

destitution /,destɪ'tuʃən/ *n* destitución, indigencia, miseria, *f*; privación, falta, *f*; desamparo, *m*

destroy /dɪ'strɔɪ/ *vt* destruir; demoler; deshacer; (kill) matar; exterminar; (finish) acabar con

destroyer /dɪ'strɔɪər/ *n* destructor (-ra); *Nav.* destructor, cazatorpedero, *m*

destruction /dɪ'strʌkʃən/ *n* destrucción, *f*; demolición, *f*; ruina, *f*; pérdida, *f*; muerte, *f*; exterminio, *m*; perdición, *f*

destructive /dɪ'strʌktɪv/ *a* destructivo, destructor; (of animals) dañino. **d. animal,** animal dañino, *m*, alimaña, *f*

destructiveness /dɪ'strʌktɪvnɪs/ *n* destructividad, *f*; instinto destructor, *m*

desultory /'desəl,tɔri/ *a* inconexo; sin método, descosido; irregular

detach /dɪ'tætʃ/ *vt* separar, desprender; (unstick) despegar; *Mil.* destacar

detachable /dɪ'tætʃəbəl/ *a* separable, de quita y pon

detached /dɪ'tætʃt/ *a* suelto, separado; (*Fig.* with outlook, etc.) imparcial; indiferente, despegado. **d. house,** hotelito, *m*

detachment /dɪ'tætʃmənt/ *n* separación, *f*; *Mil.* destacamento, *m*; (*Fig.* of mind) imparcialidad, *f*; independencia (de espíritu, etc.), *f*; indiferencia, *f*

detail /dɪ'teɪl/ *n* detalle, *m*; pormenor, *m*, particularidad, *f*; circunstancia, *f*; *Mil.* destacamento, *m*. —*vt* detallar; particularizar, referir con pormenores; *Mil.* destacar. **in d.,** detalladamente; al por menor; *Inf.* ce por be. **to go into details,** entrar en detalles

detain /dɪ'teɪn/ *vt* detener; (arrest) arrestar, prender; (withhold) retener; (prevent) impedir

detect /dɪ'tekt/ *vt* descubrir; averiguar; (discern) discernir, percibir; *Elec.* detectar

detection /dɪ'tekʃən/ *n* descubrimiento, *m*; averiguación, *f*; percepción, *f*

detective /dɪ'tektɪv/ *n* detective, *m*, a de detectives, policíaco. **d. novel,** novela policíaca, *f*

detector /dɪ'tektər/ *n* descubridor, *m*; *Elec.* detector, *m*; *Mech.* indicador, *m*

detention /dɪ'tenʃən/ *n* detención, *f*; (arrest) arresto, *m*; (confinement) encierro, *m*

deter /dɪ'tɜr/ *vt* desanimar, desalentar; acobardar; (dissuade) disuadir; (prevent) impedir

detergent /dɪ'tɜrdʒənt/ *a* detersorio. —*n* detersorio, *m*

deteriorate /dɪ'tɪəriə,reɪt/ *vt* deteriorar. —*vi* deteriorarse; empeorar

deterioration /dɪ,tɪəriə'reɪʃən/ *n* deterioración, *f*; empeoramiento, *m*

determination /dɪ,tɜrmə'neɪʃən/ *n* determinación, *f*; definición, *f*; resolución, decisión, *f*; *Law.* fallo, *m*; *Med.* congestión, *f*

determine /dɪ'tɜrmɪn/ *vt* determinar; definir; decidir, resolver; concluir; (fix) señalar; *Law.* sentenciar. —*vi* resolverse, decidirse; (insist (on)) empeñarse en, insistir en

determined /dɪ'tɜrmɪnd/ *a* determinado; resuelto, decidido; (of price) fijo

deterrent /dɪ'tɜrənt/ *a* disuasivo. —*n* freno, *m*. **to act as a d.,** servir como un freno

deterrent capability *n* poder de disuasión, *m*

detest /dɪ'test/ *vt* detestar, abominar, aborrecer

detestable /dɪ'testəbəl/ *a* detestable, aborrecible, abominable

detestation /,dite'steɪʃən/ *n* detestación, abominación, *f*, aborrecimiento, *m*

detonate /'dɛtn̩,eit/ vt hacer detonar. —vi detonar, estallar

detonation /,dɛtn̩'eiʃən/ n detonación, f

detour /'ditur/ n rodeo, m; desvío, m, desviación, f

detract /dɪ'trækt/ vt quitar; (diminish) disminuir; (slander) detraer, denigrar

detriment /'dɛtrəmənt/ n detrimento, m; perjuicio, m; daño, m

detrimental /,dɛtrə'mɛntl̩/ a perjudicial

Deuteronomy /,dutə'rɒnəmi/ n Deuteronomio, m

devaluation /di,vælyu'eiʃən/ n desvalorización, f

devalue /di'vælyu/ vt rebajar el valor de

devastate /'dɛvə,steit/ vt devastar, asolar

devastation /,dɛvə'steiʃən/ n devastación, f

develop /dɪ'vɛləp/ vt desarrollar; (make progress) avanzar, fomentar; perfeccionar; Photo. revelar. '—vi desarrollarse; crecer; avanzar, progresar; evolucionar

developer /dɪ'vɛləpər/ n Photo. revelador, m

development /dɪ'vɛləpmənt/ n desarrollo, m; evolución, f; progreso, avance, m; (encouragement) fomento, m; (event) acontecimiento, suceso, m; (product) producto, m; (working) explotación, f; Photo. revelación, f

deviate /'divi,eit/ vi desviarse (de); (disagree) disentir (de)

deviation /,divi'eiʃən/ n desviación, f

device /dɪ'vais/ n (contrivance) aparato, artefacto, mecanismo, m; (invention) invento, m; (trick) expediente, artificio, m; (scheme) proyecto, m; (design) dibujo, emblema, m; (motto) divisa, leyenda, f; pl **devices,** placeres, caprichos, m pl

devil /'dɛvəl/ n diablo, Satanás, m; demonio, m; (printer's) aprendiz de impresor, m. **Go to the d.!** ¡Vete enhoramala! **He is a poor d.,** Es un pobre diablo. **little d.,** diablillo, m. **The devil's abroad,** Anda el diablo suelto. **The d. take it!** ¡Lléveselo el diablo! **to play the d. with,** arruinar por completo. **What the d.!** ¡Qué diablos! **d.-possessed,** endemoniado

devilish /'dɛvəlɪʃ/ a diabólico, demoníaco; infernal

devious /'diviəs/ a desviado; tortuoso

devise /dɪ'vaiz/ vt idear, inventar; fabricar; Law. legar

deviser /dɪ'vaizər/ n inventor (-ra)

devitalize /di'vait,aiz/ vt restar vitalidad, privar de vitalidad

devoid /dɪ'vɔid/ a desprovisto (de), privado (de); libre (de), exento (de)

devolve /dɪ'vɒlv/ vt traspasar, transmitir. —vi (on, upon) incumbir (a), corresponder (a), tocar (a)

devote /dɪ'vout/ vt dedicar; consagrar. **to d. oneself to,** darse a, dedicarse a; consagrarse a

devoted /dɪ'voutɪd/ a fervoroso, apasionado; (faithful) fiel, leal

devotedly /dɪ'voutɪdli/ adv con devoción

devotee /,dɛvə'ti/ n devoto (-ta), admirador (-ra); aficionado (-da)

devotion /dɪ'vouʃən/ n devoción, f; dedicación, f; (zeal) celo, m; afición, f; (loyalty) lealtad, f; pl **devotions,** rezos, m pl, oraciones, f pl

devotional /dɪ'vouʃənl̩/ a devoto, religioso, de devoción. **devotional literature,** literatura de devoción, f

devour /dɪ'vaur/ vt devorar; consumir

devouring /dɪ'vauriŋ/ a devorador; absorbente

devout /dɪ'vaut/ a devoto, piadoso, practicante (e.g., a d. Catholic, un católico practicante)

devoutly /dɪ'vautli/ adv piadosamente

dew /du/ n rocío, sereno, relente, m; Fig. rocío, m, vt rociar; humedecer; (refresh) refrescar. **d.-drop,** aljófar, m, gota de rocío, f

dexterity /dɛk'stɛriti/ n destreza, f

dextrine /'dɛkstrɪn/ n dextrina, f

dextrose /'dɛkstrous/ n dextrosa, glucosa, f

dextrous /'dɛkstrəs/ a diestro; hábil, listo

diabetes /,daiə'bitɪs/ n diabetes, f

diabetic /,daiə'bɛtɪk/ a diabético

diabolical /,daiə'bɒlɪkəl/ a diabólico

diagnose /'daiəg,nous/ vt diagnosticar

diagnosis /,daiəg'nousɪs/ n diagnóstico, m, diagnosis, f

diagnostician /,daiəgnɒ'stiʃən/ n diagnóstico, m

diagonal /dai'ægənl̩/ n diagonal, f

diagram /'daiə,græm/ n diagrama, m; esquema, f; gráfico, m

dial /'daiəl/ n (sundial) reloj de sol, m; (of clocks, gas-meter) esfera, f; (of machines) indicador, m; (of a wireless set) cuadrante graduado, m; (of a telephone) marcador, disco, m. —vt (a telephone number) marcar. **d. telephone,** teléfono automático, m

dialect /'daiə,lɛkt/ n dialecto, m, habla, f, a dialectal

dialogue /'daiə,lɔg/ n diálogo, m. **to hold a d.,** dialogar

dialysis /dai'æləsɪs/ n diálisis, f

diameter /dai'æmɪtər/ n diámetro, m

diametrical /,daiə'mɛtrɪkəl/ a diametral

diamond /'daimənd/ n diamante, m; brillante, m; (tool) cortavidrios, m; (cards) oros (de baraja), m pl. **rough d.,** diamante bruto, m. **d.-bearing,** diamantífero. **d. cutter,** diamantista, mf **d. cutting,** talla de diamantes, f. **d. edition,** edición diamante, f. **d.-like,** adiamantado. **d. wedding,** bodas de diamante, f pl

diaper /'daipər/ n lienzo adamascado, m; (baby's) pañal, m; (woman's) servilleta higiénica, f

diaphanous /dai'æfənəs/ a diáfano, transparente

diaphragm /'daiə,fræm/ n diafragma, m

diarrhea /,daiə'riə/ n diarrea, f

diary /'daɪərɪ/ n diario, m

diastole /daɪ'æstl/ n diástole, f

diatribe /'daɪə,traɪb/ n diatriba, denunciación violenta, f

dice /daɪs/ n pl dados, m pl. **to load the d.,** cargar los dados

dicky /'dɪkɪ/ n (front) pechera postiza, f; (seat) trasera, f; (apron) delantal, m. **d. seat,** Inf. ahí te pudras, sm

dictaphone /'dɪktə,foʊn/ n dictáfono, m

dictate /'dɪkteɪt/ vt dictar; mandar. —n (order) dictamen, m; Fig. dictado, m

dictation /dɪk'teɪʃən/ n dictado, m. **to write from d.,** escribir al dictado

dictator /'dɪkteɪtər/ n dictador, m

dictatorial /,dɪktə'tɔrɪəl/ a dictatorial, dictatorio, imperioso

dictatorship /dɪk'teɪtər,ʃɪp/ n dictadura, f

diction /'dɪkʃən/ n dicción, f

dictionary /'dɪkʃə,neɪ/ n diccionario, m

didactic /daɪ'dæktɪk/ a didáctico

die /daɪ/ vi morir; fallecer, finar; (wither) marchitarse; (disappear) desvanecerse, desaparecer; (of light) palidecer; extinguirse; (end) cesar; (desire) ansiar, perecerse (por). **Never say die!** ¡Mientras hay vida, hay esperanza! **to die early,** morir temprano; malograrse. **to die a violent death,** tener una muerte violenta, Inf. morir mal vestido. **to die from natural causes,** morir por causas naturales; Inf. morir en la cama. **to die hard,** luchar contra la muerte; tardar en morir; tardar en desaparecer. **to die of a broken heart,** morir con el corazón destrozado, morir de pena. **to die away,** desaparecer gradualmente; extinguirse poco a poco; dejar de oírse poco a poco; cesar; pasar. **to die down,** extinguirse gradualmente; palidecer; dejar de oírse; desaparecer; (of the wind) amainar; perder su fuerza. **to die out,** desaparecer; olvidarse; dejar de existir; pasarse de moda

die /daɪ/ n dado, m; Fig. suerte, f; (stamp) cuño, troquel, m; Archit. cubo, m. **The die is cast,** La suerte está echada.

die-sinker /daɪ'dæktɪk/ a grabador en hueco, m

diehard /'daɪ,hɑrd/ n valiente, m; tradicionalista empedernido, m; partidario (-ia) entusiasta

diesel /'dizəl, -səl/ a Diesel. **d. engine,** motor Diesel, m

diet /'daɪɪt/ n dieta, f, régimen dietario, m; (assembly) dieta, f. —vi estar a dieta, hacer régimen

dietetic /,daɪɪ'tɛtɪk/ a dietético

dietician /,daɪɪ'tɪʃən/ n dietista, mf

differ /'dɪfər/ vi diferenciarse; (contradict) contradecir; (disagree) no estar de acuerdo; disentir

difference /'dɪfərəns/ n diferencia, f; disparidad, f; contraste, m; (of opinion) disensión, f; controversia, disputa, f. **to make no d.,** no hacer diferencia alguna; no afectar; dar lo mismo, no importar

different /'dɪfərənt/ a distinto; diferente; vario, diverso

differential /,dɪfə'rɛnʃəl/ a diferencial. **d. calculus,** cálculo diferencial, m

differentiate /,dɪfə'rɛnʃɪ,eɪt/ vt diferenciar, distinguir. —vi diferenciarse, distinguirse

differentiation /,dɪfə,rɛnʃɪ'eɪʃən/ n diferenciación, f

difficult /'dɪfɪ,kʌlt/ a difícil. **to make d.,** dificultar

difficulty /'dɪfɪ,kʌlti/ n dificultad, f. **d. in breathing,** opresión de pecho, f

diffidence /'dɪfɪdəns/ n modestia, timidez, f; huraña, f; falta de confianza en sí mismo, f

diffident /'dɪfɪdənt/ a modesto, tímido; huraño; sin confianza en sí mismo

diffract /dɪ'frækt/ vt difractar

diffuse /v dɪ'fyuz; a -'fyus/ vt difundir. —a difuso; (long-winded) prolijo

diffusion /dɪ'fyuʒən/ n difusión, f; esparcimiento, m; diseminación, f

dig /dɪg/ vt and vi cavar; excavar; (of animals) escarbar; (mine) zapar, minar; (into a subject) ahondar (en); (with the spurs) aguijonear, dar con las espuelas; (poke) clavar. **to dig in,** enterrarse; Mil. abrir trincheras; Inf. arreglarse las cosas. **to dig out,** excavar; sacar cavando, sacar con azadón; extraer. **to dig up,** desenterrar; descubrir

digest /v dɪ'dʒɛst, daɪ-; n 'daɪdʒɛst/ vt clasificar; codificar; (food, also chem. and Fig. tolerate and think over) digerir; (of knowledge and territory) asimilar. —vi digerir. —n compendio, resumen, m; Law. digesto, m; recopilación, f. **This food is easy to d.,** Este alimento es fácil de digerir; Este alimento es muy ligero

digestible /dɪ'dʒɛstəbəl, daɪ-/ a digerible, digestible

digestion /dɪ'dʒɛstʃən, daɪ-/ n digestión, f; (of ideas) asimilación, f; Chem. digestión, f

digestive /dɪ'dʒɛstɪv, daɪ-/ a digestivo

digger /'dɪgər/ n cavador (-ra)

digging /'dɪgɪŋ/ n cavadura, f; excavación, f; pl diggings, minas, f pl; excavaciones, f pl; Inf. alojamiento, m, posada, f

digit /'dɪdʒɪt/ n dígito, m

digital /'dɪdʒɪtl/ a digital, dígito

digitalin /,dɪdʒɪ'tælɪn/ n digitalina, f

digitalis /,dɪdʒɪ'tælɪs/ n digital, f

dignified /'dɪgnə,faɪd/ a serio, grave; majestuoso; (worthy) digno; solemne; altivo; noble

dignify /'dɪgnə,faɪ/ vt dignificar, honrar; exaltar; dar dignidad (a); ennoblecer

dignitary /'dɪgnɪ,tɛrɪ/ n dignatario, m; dignidad, f

dignity /'dɪgnɪtɪ/ n dignidad, f; (rank) rango, m; (post) cargo, puesto, m; (honor) honra, f; (stateliness) majestad, f; mesura, seriedad, f; (haughtiness) altivez, f; (nobility) nobleza, f. **to stand on one's d.,** darse importancia

digress /dɪ'grɛs, daɪ-/ vi divagar

digression /dɪ'greʃən, dai-/ n digresión, divagación, f

dike /daik/ n dique, m; (ditch) acequia, f; canal, m; (embankment) zanja, f, vt represar

dilapidated /dɪ'læpɪ,deitɪd/ a arruinado, destartalado; (of fortune) dilapidado; (of persons, families) venido a menos; (shabby) raído

dilate /dai'leit/ vt dilatar; ensanchar. —vi dilatarse. **to d. upon,** extenderse sobre, dilatarse en

dilatory /'dɪlə,tɔri/ a dilatorio, tardo; (slow) lento

dilemma /dɪ'lɛmə/ n dilema, m

dilettante /'dɪlɪ,tant/ n diletante, m; aficionado (-da)

dilettantism /'dɪlɪtən,tɪzəm/ n diletantismo, m

diligence /'dɪlɪdʒəns/ n diligencia, f; asiduidad, f; (care) cuidado, m; (coach) diligencia, f

diligent /'dɪlɪdʒənt/ a diligente, asiduo, aplicado, industrioso; (painstaking) concienzudo

dilute /dɪ'lut, dai-/ vt diluir; Fig. adulterar. —a diluido

dilution /dɪ'luʃən, dai-/ n dilución, f; Fig. adulteración, f

dim /dɪm/ a (of light) apagado, débil, tenue; (of sight) turbio; (dark) sombrío, oscuro; (blurred, etc.) empañado; indistinto, confuso. —vt obscurecer; empañar; (dazzle) ofuscar; (eclipse) eclipsar; reducir la intensidad (de una luz); (of memories) borrar. **dim intelligence,** de brumoso seso

dimension /dɪ'mɛnʃən/ n dimensión, f; (size) tamaño, m; (scope) extensión, f, alcance, m

diminish /dɪ'mɪnɪʃ/ vt disminuir; reducir; debilitar, atenuar. —vi disminuir; reducirse; debilitarse, atenuarse

diminishing /dɪ'mɪnɪʃɪŋ/ a menguante

diminution /,dɪmə'nuʃən/ n disminución, f; reducción, f; atenuación, f

diminutive /dɪ'mɪnyətɪv/ a diminutivo. —n diminutivo, m

dimly /'dɪmli/ adv obscuramente; vagamente; indistintamente. **dimly lit,** apenas alumbrado

dimness /'dɪmnɪs/ n oscuridad, f; deslustre, m; (of light) tenuidad (de la luz), f; confusión, f

dimple /'dɪmpəl/ n hoyuelo, m

dimpled /'dɪmpəld/ a con hoyuelos, que tiene hoyuelos

din /dɪn/ n estrépito, estruendo, ruido, m; algarabía, barahúnda, f, vt ensordecer

dine /dain/ vi (in the evening) cenar; (at midday) comer. —vt convidar a cenar o a comer. **to d. out,** cenar o comer fuera

diner /'dainər/ n (on a train) coche comedor, coche restaurante, m; cenador, m; comedor, m

dinghy /'dɪŋgi/ n lancha, f; canoa, f; bote, m. **rubber d.,** canoa de goma, f

dingy /'dɪndʒi/ a deslucido, empañado; sucio; oscuro; (of persons) desaseado

dining car /'dainɪŋ/ n coche comedor, vagón restaurante, m

dining room n comedor, m; refectorio, m

dining table n mesa del comedor, f

dinner /'dɪnər/ n (in the evening) cena, f; (at midday) comida, f. **over the d. table,** de sobremesa. **d.-jacket,** smoking, m. **d. party,** cena, f. **d. plate,** plato, m. **d. roll,** panecillo, m. **d. service,** vajilla, f

dinosaur /'dainə,sɔr/ n dinosauro, m

dint /dɪnt/ **(by d. of)** a fuerza de, a costa de

diocese /'daiəsɪs/ n diócesis, f

dip /dɪp/ n inmersión, f; baño, m; (in the ground) declive, m; (in the road) columpio, m, depresión, f; (slope) pendiente, f; (candle) vela de sebo, f; (of the horizon) depresión (del horizonte), f; (of the needle) inclinación (de la aguja), f. —vt sumergir; bañar; (put) poner. —vi inclinarse hacia abajo. **to dip into a book,** hojear un libro. **to dip the colors,** saludar con la bandera. **to dip the headlights,** bajar los faros

diphtheria /dɪf'θɪəriə/ n difteria, f

diploma /dɪ'ploumə/ n diploma, m

diplomacy /dɪ'plouməsi/ n diplomacia, f; tacto, m

diploma mill n fábrica de títulos académicos, f

diplomat /'dɪplə,mæt/ n diplomático, m

diplomatic /,dɪplə'mætɪk/ a diplomático. **d. bag,** valija diplomática, f. **d. corps,** cuerpo diplomático, m

dipper /'dɪpər/ n (ladle) cazo, m; Astron. Osa Mayor, f

dipsomaniac /,dɪpsə'meiniæk/ n dipsómano (-na)

dire /daiər/ a espantoso, horrible; cruel; funesto

direct /dɪ'rɛkt, dai-/ a directo; claro, inequívoco; (of descent) recto; (of electric current) continuo; exacto. —adv directamente. —vt dirigir; (command) ordenar, encargar; dar instrucciones. **d. action,** acción directa, f. **d. current,** corriente continua, f. **d. line,** línea directa, f; (of descent) línea recta, f. **d. object,** acusativo, m. **d. speech,** oración directa, f

direct dialing n discado directo, m

direction /dɪ'rɛkʃən, 'dai-/ n dirección, f; rumbo, m; instrucción, f; (on a letter) sobrescrito, m; señas, f pl. **in the d. of,** en la dirección de; hacia; Naut. con rumbo a. **in all directions,** por todas partes; a los cuatro vientos. **to go in the d. of,** ir en la dirección de; tomar por. **Directions for use,** Direcciones para el uso. **d. indicator, d. signal,** (on car) indicador de dirección, m

directive /dɪ'rɛktɪv, dai-/ a directivo, director

directness /dɪ'rɛktnɪs, dai-/ n derechura, f

director /dɪ'rektər, daɪ-/ n director (-triz, -ora), **managing d.,** director gerente, m

directory /dɪ'rektəri, daɪ-/ n directorio, m, guía, f. **telephone d.,** guía de teléfonos, f

dirge /dɜrdʒ/ n endecha, f, lamento, m; canto fúnebre, m

dirigible /'dɪrɪdʒəbəl/ n dirigible, m

dirt /dɜrt/ n mugre, suciedad, f; (mud) lodo, m; (earth) tierra, f; (dust) polvo, m; Fig. inmundicia, f. **d.-cheap,** sumamente barato. **to be d. cheap,** (of goods) estar por los suelos. **d.-track,** pista de ceniza, f. **d.-track racing,** carreras en pista de ceniza, f pl

dirtiness /'dɜrtɪnɪs/ n suciedad, f; (untidiness) desaseo, m; sordidez, f; (meanness) bajeza, f

dirty /'dɜrti/ a sucio; (untidy) desaseado; (muddy) enlodado; (dusty) polvoriento; (of weather) borrascoso; (sordid) sórdido; (base, mean) vil; (indecent) indecente, verde, obsceno. —vt ensuciar. **d. trick,** mala pasada, f

disability /,dɪsə'bɪlɪti/ n incapacidad, f; impotencia, f; desventaja, f

disable /dɪs'eɪbəl/ vt (cripple) estropear, tullir; hacer incapaz (de), incapacitar; imposibilitar; (destroy) destruir; Law. incapacitar legalmente

disabled /dɪs'eɪbəld/ a inválido; impedido, lisiado; (in the hand) manco; incapacitado; (of ships, etc.) fuera de servicio, estropeado. **d. soldier,** inválido, m

disablement /dɪs'eɪbəlmənt/ n (physical) invalidez, f; inhabilitación, f; Law. impedimento, m

disabuse /dɪsə'byuz/ vt desengañar, sacar de un error

disadvantage /,dɪsəd'væntɪdʒ/ n desventaja, f. **to be under the d. of,** sufrir la desventaja de

disadvantaged /,dɪsəd'væntɪdʒd/ a (financially) de escasos recursos

disadvantageous /dɪs,ædvən'teɪdʒəs/ a desventajoso

disaffection /,dɪsə'fekʃən/ n desafecto, descontento, m

disagree /,dɪsə'gri/ vi no estar de acuerdo; diferir; (quarrel) reñir; (not share the opinion of) no estar de la opinión (de); (of food, etc.) sentar mal; no probar. **The meat disagreed with me,** La carne me sentó mal

disagreeable /,dɪsə'griəbəl/ a desagradable; repugnante; (of persons) antipático, displicente

disagreeableness /,dɪsə'griəbəlnɪs/ n lo desagradable; (of persons) displicencia, f

disagreement /,dɪsə'grimənt/ n desacuerdo, m; diferencia, f; desavenencia, f; discordia, f; (quarrel) riña, disputa, f; discrepancia, f

disallow /,dɪsə'laʊ/ vt negar; rechazar

disappear /,dɪsə'pɪər/ vi desaparecer. **to cause to d.,** hacer desaparecer

disappearance /,dɪsə'pɪərəns/ n desaparición, f

disappoint /,dɪsə'pɔɪnt/ vt desilusionar; frustrar; (hopes) defraudar; (deprive) privar de; (annoy) contrariar; (break a promise) faltar (a la palabra)

disappointing /,dɪsə'pɔɪntɪŋ/ a desengañador; pobre; triste; poco halagüeño

disappointment /,dɪsə'pɔɪntmənt/ n desengaño, m, decepción, f; frustración, f; desilusión, f; (vexation) contrariedad, f; contratiempo, m. **to suffer a d.,** sufrir un desengaño; Inf. llevarse un chasco

disapproval /,dɪsə'pruvəl/ n desaprobación, f

disapprove /,dɪsə'pruv/ vt desaprobar

disapproving /,dɪsə'pruvɪŋ/ a de desaprobación, severo

disarm /dɪs'ɑrm/ vt desarmar. —vi desarmarse; deponer las armas

disarmament /dɪs'ɑrməmənt/ n desarme, m

disarrange /,dɪsə'reɪndʒ/ vt desarreglar; descomponer, desajustar; (hair) despeinar

disarrangement /,dɪsə'reɪndʒmənt/ n desarreglo, m; desajuste, m; desorden, m

disarray /,dɪsə'reɪ/ n desorden, desarreglo, m; confusión, f. —vt desordenar, desarreglar

disaster /dɪ'zæstər/ n desastre, m; catástrofe, m; infortunio, m

disastrous /dɪ'zæstrəs/ a desastroso; funesto, trágico

disavow /,dɪsə'vaʊ/ vt repudiar; retractar

disavowal /,dɪsə'vaʊəl/ n repudiación, f

disband /dɪs'bænd/ vt licenciar. —vi desbandarse, dispersarse

disbelief /,dɪsbɪ'lif/ n incredulidad, f; desconfianza, f

disbelieve /,dɪsbɪ'liv/ vt and vi descreer, no creer; desconfiar (de)

disburse /dɪs'bɜrs/ vt desembolsar, pagar

disbursement /dɪs'bɜrsmənt/ n desembolso, m

disc /dɪsk/ n disco, m

discard /v dɪ'skɑrd; n 'dɪskɑrd/ vt desechar, arrinconar; despedir; (at cards) descartar. —n (at cards) descarte, m

discern /dɪ'sɜrn/ vt discernir, distinguir, percibir

discernible /dɪ'sɜrnəbəl/ a distinguible, perceptible

discerning /dɪ'sɜrnɪŋ/ a perspicaz, discernidor

discernment /dɪ'sɜrnmənt/ n discernimiento, m

discharge /v dɪs'tʃɑrdʒ/ vt descargar; (a gun) disparar, tirar; (an arrow) lanzar; Elec. descargar; emitir; (dismiss) destituir; despedir; arrojar; Mil. licenciar; (exempt) dispensar (de); (exonerate) absolver, exonerar; (free) dar libertad (a); (from hospital) dar de baja (a); Law. revocar; (perform) cumplir, ejecutar; (pay) pagar, saldar; (of an abscess, etc.) supurar.

discharge /n 'dɪstʃɑrdʒ/ n (of firearms) disparo, tiro, m; (of artillery) descarga, f; (of goods, cargo) descargue, m; Elec. descarga, f; (from a wound, etc.) pus, m, supuración, *f*; (from the intestine) flujo, *m*; (of a debt) pago, m.; *Com.* descargo, *m*; (receipt) carta de pago, quitanza, *f*; *Mil.* licencia absoluta, *f*; (dismissal) despedida, destitución, *f*; (exoneration) exoneración, *f*; (freeing) liberación, *f*; (from hospital) baja, *f*; (performance) cumplimiento, *m*; ejecución, *f*

disciple /dɪˈsaipəl/ *n* discípulo (-la)

disciplinarian /ˌdɪsəpləˈnɛəriən/ *n* disciplinario (-ia)

disciplinary /ˈdɪsəpləˌnɛri/ *a* disciplinario

discipline /ˈdɪsəplɪn/ *n* disciplina, *f*, *vt* disciplinar

disclaim /dɪsˈkleim/ *vt* renunciar (a); (repudiate) rechazar, repudiar

disclaimer /dɪsˈkleimər/ *n* *Law.* renunciación, *f*; repudiación, *f*

disclose /dɪsˈklouz/ *vt* descubrir, revelar

disclosure /dɪsˈklouʒər/ *n* descubrimiento, *m*, revelación, *f*

discolor /dɪsˈkʌlər/ *vt* descolorar. —*vi* descolorarse

discoloration /dɪsˌkʌləˈreiʃən/ *n* descoloramiento, *m*

discomfit /dɪsˈkleim/ *vt* desconcertar

discomfort /dɪsˈkʌmfərt/ *n* falta de comodidades, *f*; incomodidad, *f*; malestar, *m*; molestia, *f* inquietud, *f*; dolor, *m*

discomposure /ˌdɪskəmˈpouʒər/ *n* confusión, agitación, inquietud, *f*

disconcert /ˌdɪskənˈsɜrt/ *vt* desconcertar, turbar; (of plans, etc.) frustrar

disconnect /ˌdɪskəˈnɛkt/ *vt* separar; (of railway engines, etc.) desacoplar; desconectar; (of electric plugs) desenchufar

disconnected /ˌdɪskəˈnɛktɪd/ *a* inconexo; incoherente, deshilvanado

disconsolate /dɪsˈkɒnsəlɪt/ *a* desconsolado, triste

disconsolately /dɪsˈkɒnsəlɪtli/ *adv* desconsoladamente, tristemente

discontent /ˌdɪskənˈtɛnt/ *n* descontento, disgusto, *m*, *vt* descontentar, desagradar

discontented /ˌdɪskənˈtɛntɪd/ *a* descontentadizo, descontento, disgustado

discontinuance /ˌdɪskənˈtɪnyuəns/ *n* descontinuación, cesación, *f*; interrupción, *f*

discontinue /ˌdɪskənˈtɪnyu/ *vt* descontinuar; cesar; interrumpir; (of payments, etc.) suspender. —*vi* cesar

discontinuous /ˌdɪskənˈtɪnyuəs/ *a* descontinuo; interrumpido; intermitente

discord /ˈdɪskɔrd/ *n* discordia, *f*; *Mus.* disonancia, *f*, desentono, *m*

discordant /dɪsˈkɔrdənt/ *a* discorde, poco armonioso; incongruo; *Mus.* disonante, desentonado, *f*. **to be d.,** discordar; ser incongruo; *Mus.* disonar

discount /ˈdɪskaunt/ *n* *also* dɪsˈkaunt/ *n* descuento, *f*; rebaja, *f*. —*vt* descontar; rebajar; balancear; (disconsider) desechar. **at a d.,** al descuento; bajo la par; fácil de obtener; superfluo; *Fig.* en disfavor, en descrédito. **rate of d.,** tipo de descuento, *m*. **d. for cash,** descuento por venta al contado, *m*

discourage /dɪsˈkɜrɪdʒ/ *vt* desalentar, desanimar; oponerse a; disuadir; frustrar

discouragement /dɪsˈkɜrɪdʒmənt/ *n* desaliento, *m*; desaprobación, oposición, *f*; disuasión, *f*; (obstacle) estorbo, *m*

discouraging /dɪsˈkɜrɪdʒɪŋ/ *a* poco animador, que ofrece pocas esperanzas; (with prospect, etc.) nada halagüeño

discourse /*n* ˈdɪskɔrs; *v* dɪsˈkɔrs/ *n* discurso, *m*; plática, *f*; (treatise) disertación, *f*. —*vi* (converse) platicar, conversar; (with on, upon) disertar sobre, discurrir sobre; tratar de

discourteous /dɪsˈkɜrtiəs/ *a* descortés, desconsiderado

discover /dɪsˈkʌvər/ *vt* descubrir; (see) ver; (realize) darse cuenta de; (show) manifestar; revelar

discoverer /dɪsˈkʌvərər/ *n* descubridor (-ra); revelador (-ra)

discovery /dɪsˈkʌvəri/ *n* descubrimiento, *m*; revelación, *f*

discredit /dɪsˈkrɛdɪt/ *n* descrédito, *m*; deshonra, *f*; duda, *f*. —*vt* dudar (de), no creer (en); desacreditar; deshonrar

discreditable /dɪsˈkrɛdɪtəbəl/ *a* deshonroso, ignominioso, vergonzoso

discreet /dɪsˈkrit/ *a* discreto; prudente, circunspecto

discreetly /dɪsˈkritli/ *adv* discretamente; prudentemente

discrepancy /dɪsˈkrɛpənsi/ *n* discrepancia, diferencia, *f*; contradicción, *f*

discretion /dɪsˈkrɛʃən/ *n* discreción, *f*; prudencia, circunspección, *f*; juicio, *m*; voluntad, *f*. **at d.,** a discreción. **at one's own d.,** a voluntad (de uno). **years of d.,** edad de discreción, *f*

discriminate /dɪsˈkrɪmˌneit/ *vi* distinguir (entre); hacer una distinción (en favor de or en perjuicio de). —*vt* distinguir

discriminating /dɪsˈkrɪməˌneitɪŋ/ *a* discerniente, que sabe distinguir, juicioso; culto; diferencial

discrimination /dɪsˌkrɪməˈneiʃən/ *n* discernimiento, *m*; gusto, *m*; distinción, *f*; discriminación, *f*

discursive /dɪsˈkɜrsɪv/ *a* discursivo; digresivo

discus /ˈdɪskəs/ *n* disco, *m*. **d. thrower,** discóbolo, *m*

discuss /dɪsˈkʌs/ *vt* discutir; hablar de; debatir; (deal with) tratar; (*Fam.* a dish) probar; (a bottle of wine) vaciar

discussion /dɪsˈkʌʃən/ *n* discusión, *f*; debate, *m*

disdain /dɪsˈdein/ *n* desdén, *m*; altivez, *f*. —*vt* desdeñar, desairar, despreciar. **to d. to,** desdeñarse de

disdainful /dɪsˈdeinfəl/ *a* desdeñoso; altivo

disease /dɪˈziz/ *n* enfermedad, *f*; *Fig.* mal, *m*. **infectious d.,** enfermedad contagiosa, *f*

diseased /dɪˈzizd/ *a* enfermo; (of fruit, etc.) malo

disembark /ˌdɪsɛm'bɑrk/ vt and vi desembarcar

disembarkation /dɪsˌɛmbɑr'keɪʃən/ n desembarque, m; Mil. desembarco (de tropas), m

disembodied /ˌdɪsɛm'bɒdid/ a incorpóreo

disembowel /ˌdɪsɛm'bauəl/ vt desentrañar, destripar

disenchant /ˌdɪsɛn'tʃænt/ vt desencantar; deschechizar; desilusionar

disenchantment /ˌdɪsɛn'tʃæntmənt/ n desencanto, m; desilusión, f

disengage /ˌdɪsɛn'geɪdʒ/ vt desasir; soltar; (gears) desembragar; (uncouple) desacoplar; (free) librar

disentangle /ˌdɪsɛn'tæŋgəl/ vt (undo) desatar, desanudar; separar; (of threads, etc., and Fig.) desenredar, desenmarañar. —vi desenredarse

disfavor /dɪs'feɪvər/ n disfavor, m; (disapproval) desaprobación, f. —vt desaprobar

disfigure /dɪs'fɪgyər/ vt desfigurar, afear; deformar; (mar) estropear

disfigurement /dɪs'fɪgyərmənt/ n desfiguración, f; deformidad, f; defecto, m

disfranchise /dɪs'fræntʃaiz/ vt privar de los derechos civiles (a)

disgorge /dɪs'gɔrdʒ/ vt and vi vomitar; (of a river) desembocar (en); hacer restitución (de lo robado)

disgrace /dɪs'greɪs/ n vergüenza, ignominia, f; deshonra, f; (insult) afrenta, f; (scandal) escándalo, m; disfavor, m. —vt deshonrar; despedir con ignominia. **in d.,** fuera de favor; desacreditado; (of children and animals) castigado

disgraceful /dɪs'greɪsfəl/ a deshonroso; ignominioso; escandaloso

disgruntled /dɪs'grʌntl̩d/ a refunfuñador, enfurruñado, malhumorado

disguise /dɪs'gaɪz/ n disfraz, m; (mask) máscara, f. —vt disfrazar; cubrir, tapar; (Fig. conceal) ocultar. **in d.,** disfrazado

disgust /dɪs'gʌst/ n repugnancia, aversión, f; aborrecimiento, m; asco, m. —vt repugnar, inspirar aversión; disgustar; dar asco (a)

disgusted /dɪs'gʌstɪd/ a asqueado; disgustado; furioso; (bored) aburrido

disgusting /dɪs'gʌstɪŋ/ a repugnante; odioso, horrible; asqueroso

dish /dɪʃ/ n (for meat, vegetables, fruit, etc.) fuente, f; (food) plato, m; pl **dishes,** platos, m pl, vajilla, f. —vt servir; Inf. frustrar. **cooked d.,** guiso, m. **special d. for today,** plato del día, m. **to wash the dishes,** fregar los platos. **d.-cloth,** (for washing) fregador, m; (for drying) paño de los platos, m. **d.-cover,** cubre-platos, m. **d.-rack,** escurre-platos, m. **d.-washer,** lavaplatos, lavavajillas, m. **d.-water,** agua de lavar los platos, f

disharmony /dɪs'harmənɪ/ n falta de armonía, f; (disagreement) discordia, desavenencia, f; incongruencia, f; Mus. disonancia, f

dishearten /dɪs'hartn̩/ vt desalentar, desanimar; desesperar; disuadir (de)

disheveled /dɪ'ʃɛvəld/ a despeinado, desgreñado; (untidy) desaseado

dishonest /dɪs'ɒnɪst/ a falto de honradez, tramposo; fraudulento; falso, desleal

dishonestly /dɪs'ɒnɪstli/ adv de mala fe, sin honradez; fraudulentamente; deslealmente

dishonesty /dɪs'ɒnɪsti/ n falta de honradez, falta de integridad, f; fraude, m; falsedad, deslealtad, f

dishonor /dɪs'ɒnər/ n deshonra, f, vt deshonrar; Com. no pagar, o no aceptar, un giro

dishonorable /dɪs'ɒnərəbəl/ a deshonroso

disillusion /ˌdɪsɪ'luʒən/ vt desengañar, desilusionar

disillusionment /ˌdɪsɪ'luʒənmənt/ n desilusión, f, desengaño, desencanto, m

disinfect /ˌdɪsɪn'fɛkt/ vt desinfectar

disinfectant /ˌdɪsɪn'fɛktənt/ a and n desinfectante m.

disingenuous /ˌdɪsɪn'dʒɛnyuəs/ a tortuoso, doble, falso, insincero

disinherit /ˌdɪsɪn'hɛrɪt/ vt desheredar

disintegrate /dɪs'ɪntəˌgreɪt/ vt despedazar, disgregar. —vi disgregarse; desmoronarse

disintegration /dɪsˌɪntə'greɪʃən/ n disgregración, f; disolución, f, desmoronamiento, m

disinter /ˌdɪsɪn'tɜr/ vt desenterrar

disinterested /dɪs'ɪntəˌrɛstɪd, -trɪstɪd/ a desinteresado

disinterment /ˌdɪsɪn'tɜrmənt/ n desenterramiento, m

disjointed /dɪs'dʒɔɪntɪd/ a dislocado; desarticulado; incoherente, inconexo; (of a speech, etc.) descosido

disk /dɪsk/ n disco, m

dislike /dɪs'laɪk/ n aversión, f; antipatía, f; (hostility) animosidad, f. —vt desagradar, no gustar; repugnar. **I d. the house,** No me gusta la casa. **I d. them,** No me gustan

dislocate /'dɪsloʊˌkeɪt/ vt dislocar, descoyuntar; Fig. interrumpir

dislocation /ˌdɪsloʊ'keɪʃən/ n dislocación, f, descoyuntamiento, m; Fig. interrupción, f

dislodge /dɪs'lɒdʒ/ vt desalojar

disloyal /dɪs'lɔɪəl/ a desleal, infiel, falso

disloyalty /dɪs'lɔɪəlti/ n deslealtad, infidelidad, falsedad, f

dismal /'dɪzməl/ a lóbrego, sombrío; lúgubre; funesto; triste

dismantle /dɪs'mæntl̩/ vt (a ship or fort) desmantelar; (a machine) desmontar; (a house, etc.) desamueblar

dismay /dɪs'meɪ/ n desmayo, desaliento, m; consternación, f; espanto, terror, m. —vt desanimar; consternar; espantar, horrorizar

dismember /dɪs'mɛmbər/ vt desmembrar

dismiss /dɪs'mɪs/ vt (from a job) despedir (de); (from an official position) destituir (de); (bid good-bye to) despedirse de; (after military parade) dar la orden de romper filas; (thoughts) apartar de sí; ahuyentar; (discard) desechar, descartar; (omit) pasar por alto de; (disregard) rechazar; (a parliament, etc.) disolver; (a law case) absolver de la instancia. **to d. in a few words,** tratar someramente; hablar brevemente de

dismissal /dɪs'mɪsəl/ n despedida, f; (from an official post) destitución, f; apartamiento, m; (discard) descarte, m; (of a parliament, etc.) disolución, f

dismount /v dɪs'maunt; n also 'dɪs,maunt/ vi apearse, desmontar, echar pie a tierra; bajar. —vt desmontar; (dismantle) desarmar

disobedience /,dɪsə'bidiəns/ n desobediencia, f

disobedient /,dɪsə'bidiənt/ a desobediente

disobey /,dɪsə'bei/ vt and vi desobedecer

disobliging /,dɪsə'blaidʒɪŋ/ a poco servicial

disorder /dɪs'ɔrdər/ n desorden, m; confusión, f; (unrest) perturbación del orden público, f; motín, m; (disease) enfermedad, f; (mental) enajenación mental, f; trastorno, m. —vt desordenar, desarreglar; (of health) perjudicar; (the mind) trastornar. **in d.,** en desorden, desarreglado; (helter-skelter) atropelladamente

disordered /dɪs'ɔrdərd/ a en desorden; irregular, desordenado; (of the mind and bodily organs) trastornado; (ill) enfermo; (confused) confuso

disorganization /dɪs,ɔrgənə'zeiʃən/ n desorganización, f

disorganize /dɪs'ɔrgə,naiz/ vt desorganizar

disorientate /dɪs'ɔriən,teit/ vt desorientar

disown /dɪs'oun/ vt repudiar; negar; renegar de

disparage /dɪ'spærɪdʒ/ vt menospreciar; desacreditar; denigrar; (spoil) perjudicar; (scorn) despreciar

disparagement /dɪ'spærɪdʒmənt/ n menosprecio, m; denigración, f; desprecio, m

disparagingly /dɪ'spærɪdʒɪŋli/ adv con desprecio

disparity /dɪ'spærɪti/ n disparidad, f

dispassionate /dɪs'pæʃənɪt/ a desapasionado, sereno; imparcial; moderado

dispatch /dɪ'spætʃ/ n despacho, m; Com. envío, m; (message) mensaje, m; (communiqué) parte, f; (cable) telegrama, m; (promptness) prontitud, presteza, f; (execution) ejecución, muerte, f. —vt despachar; enviar, remitir; (Fam. kill) despachar. **d.-case,** cartera, f. **d.-rider,** mensajero motociclista, m

dispel /dɪ'spel/ vt disipar

dispensary /dɪ'spensəri/ n dispensario, m

dispensation /,dɪspən'seiʃən/ n dispensación, f; (of the Pope, etc.) dispensa, f; (decree) ley, f, decreto, m; (of justice) administración, f

dispense /dɪ'spens/ vt dispensar; (of justice) administrar. **to d. with,** pasar sin, prescindir de

dispersal /dɪ'spɜrsəl/ n dispersión, f; disipación, f; esparcimiento, m

disperse /dɪ'spɜrs/ vt dispersar; disipar; esparcir. —vi dispersarse disiparse

dispirited /dɪ'spɪrɪtɪd/ a abatido, desanimado, deprimido; lánguido

displace /dɪs'pleis/ vt desalojar; cambiar de situación; (of liquids) desplazar; (oust) quitar el puesto (a), destituir

displacement /dɪs'pleismənt/ n desalojamiento, m; cambio de situación, m; (of liquid) desplazamiento, m; (from a post) destitución, f

display /dɪ'splei/ n exhibición, f; ostentación, f; presentación, f; (development) desarrollo, m; manifestación, f; (naval or military) maniobras, f pl; espectáculo, m; (pomp) pompa, f; fausto, m. —vt exhibir; mostrar, manifestar, ostentar; (unfold) desplegar, extender; (develop) desarrollar. **d. cabinet,** vitrina, f

displease /dɪs'pliz/ vt desagradar; ofender; enojar

displeasing /dɪs'plizɪŋ/ a desagradable

displeasure /dɪs'plɛʒər/ n desagrado, m; disgusto, m; disfavor, m; indignación, f; enojo, m; (grief) angustia, f

disport /dɪ'spɔrt/ vi (oneself), divertirse, entretenerse, recrearse; retozar, jugar

disposal /dɪ'spouzəl/ n disposición, f; (transfer) cesión, enajenación, f; (sale) venta, f; (gift) donación, f. **I am at your d.,** Estoy a la disposición de Vd. **the d. of the troops,** la disposición de las tropas

dispose /dɪ'spouz/ vt disponer; inclinar. —vi disponer. **to d. of,** disponer de; (finish) terminar, concluir; (get rid of) deshacerse de; (give away) regalar; (sell) vender; (transfer) ceder; (of houses, etc.) traspasar; (kill) matar; (send) enviar; (use) servirse de; (refute) refutar. **"To be disposed of,"** (a business, etc.) «Se traspasa»

disposed /dɪ'spouzd/ a (in compounds) intencionado, dispuesto. **well-d.,** bien intencionado

disposition /,dɪspə'zɪʃən/ n disposición, f; (temperament) naturaleza, índole, f, temperamento, carácter, m; (humor) humor, m

dispossess /,dɪspə'zɛs/ vt desposeer (de); privar (de); desahuciar

dispossession /,dɪspə'zɛʃən/ n desposeimiento, m; desahúcio, m

disproportion /,dɪsprə'pɔrʃən/ n desproporción, f

disproportionate /,dɪsprə'pɔrʃənɪt/ a desproporcionado

disprove /dɪs'pruv/ vt refutar

disputable /dɪˈspyutəbəl/ a disputable; discutible

dispute /dɪˈspyut/ n disputa, controversia, f; altercación, f; discusión, f; debate, m. —vt and vi disputar. **beyond d.,** a incontestable. —adv incontestablemente; fuera de duda

disqualification /dɪs,kwɒləfɪˈkeɪʃən/ n incapacidad, f; inhabilitación, f; impedimento, m; Sports. descalificación, f

disqualify /dɪsˈkwɒləˌfaɪ/ vt incapacitar; inhabilitar; Sports. descalificar

disquiet /dɪsˈkwaɪɪt/ n desasosiego, m; intranquilidad, inquietud, agitación, f. —vt desasosegar, intranquilizar, perturbar, agitar

disquieting /dɪsˈkwaɪɪtɪŋ/ a intranquilizador, perturbador

disquisition /ˌdɪskwəˈzɪʃən/ n disquisición, f

disregard /ˌdɪsrɪˈgɑrd/ n indiferencia, f; omisión, f; descuido, m; (scorn) desdén, m. —vt no hacer caso de, desatender; omitir; desconocer; descuidar; despreciar

disregardful /ˌdɪsrɪˈgɑrdfəl/ a indiferente; negligente; desatento; desdeñoso

disrepair /ˌdɪsrɪˈpɛər/ n deterioro, mal estado, m

disreputable /dɪsˈrɛpyətəbəl/ a de mala fama; (shameful) vergonzoso, vil; (compromising) comprometedor; de mal aspecto, horrible; ruin

disreputably /dɪsˈrɛpyətəbli/ adv ruinmente; vergonzosamente

disrepute /ˌdɪsrɪˈpyut/ n disfavor, m; mala fama, f; deshonra, f; descrédito, m. **to come into d.,** caer en disfavor; perder su reputación

disrespect /ˌdɪsrɪˈspɛkt/ n falta de respeto, f; irreverencia, f

disrespectful /ˌdɪsrɪˈspɛktfəl/ a irrespetuoso, irreverente

disrobe /dɪsˈroʊb/ vt desnudar. —vi desnudarse

disrupt /dɪsˈrʌpt/ vt quebrar; desorganizar; interrumpir; separar

disruption /dɪsˈrʌpʃən/ n quebrantamiento, m; desorganización, f; interrupción, f; separación, f

dissatisfaction /ˌdɪssætɪsˈfækʃən/ n descontento, desagrado, disgusto, m

dissatisfied /dɪsˈsætɪsˌfaɪd/ a descontentado, malcontento, no satisfecho

dissect /dɪˈsɛkt/ vt disecar; Fig. analizar

dissection /dɪˈsɛkʃən/ n disección, f; análisis, m

dissemble /dɪˈsɛmbəl/ vt and vi disimular, fingir

dissembler /dɪˈsɛmblər/ n hipócrita, mf; disimulador (-ra)

disseminate /dɪˈsɛməˌneɪt/ vt diseminar; propagar, sembrar

dissension /dɪˈsɛnʃən/ n disensión, f; disidencia, f

dissent /dɪˈsɛnt/ n disentimiento, m, vi disentir, disidir

dissentient /dɪˈsɛnʃənt/ a disidente,

divergente. **without one d. voice,** unánimemente

dissertation /ˌdɪsərˈteɪʃən/ n disertación, f

disservice /dɪsˈsɜrvɪs/ n deservicio, m

dissimilar /dɪˈsɪmələr/ a disímil, desemejante, diferente

dissimilarity /ˌdɪˌsɪməˈlærɪti/ n desemejanza, diferencia, disparidad, f

dissimulation /dɪˌsɪmyəˈleɪʃən/ n disimulación, f, disimulo, m

dissipate /ˈdɪsəˌpeɪt/ vt disipar; dispersar; (waste) derrochar, desperdiciar. —vi disiparse; dispersarse; (vanish) desvanecerse; (of persons) ser disoluto

dissipated /ˈdɪsəˌpeɪtɪd/ a (of persons) disipado, disoluto, vicioso

dissipation /ˌdɪsəˈpeɪʃən/ n disipación, f; (waste) derroche, m; libertinaje, m

dissociate /dɪˈsoʊʃiˌeɪt/ vt disociar

dissociation /dɪˌsoʊsiˈeɪʃən/ n disociación, f

dissolute /ˈdɪsəˌlut/ a disoluto, vicioso, licencioso

dissolution /ˌdɪsəˈluʃən/ n disolución, f; separación, f; muerte, f

dissolvable /dɪˈzɒlvəbəl/ a soluble

dissolve /dɪˈzɒlv/ vt disolver; derretir; (of parliament) prorrogar; (a marriage, etc.) anular; Fig. disipar. —vi disolverse; derretirse; (vanish) desvanecerse, disiparse, evaporarse. **to d. into tears,** deshacerse en lágrimas

dissolvent /dɪˈzɒlvənt/ a disolutivo. —n disolvente, m

dissonance /ˈdɪsənəns/ n disonancia, f; Fig. discordia, falta de armonía, f

dissonant /ˈdɪsənənt/ n disonancia, f, a disonante

dissuade /dɪˈsweɪd/ vt disuadir (de), apartar (de)

distaff /ˈdɪstæf/ n rueca, f

distance /ˈdɪstəns/ n distancia, f; lontananza, f; lejanía, f; trecho, m; (of time) intervalo, m; (difference) diferencia, f. **at a d.,** a alguna distancia; lejos; (from afar) desde lejos. **from a d.,** desde (or de) lejos. **in the d.,** a lo lejos, en lontananza. **to keep at a d.,** mantener lejos; guardar las distancias (con). **to keep one's d.,** mantenerse a distancia; no intimarse, guardar las distancias. **What is the d. from London to Madrid?** ¿Qué distancia hay desde Londres a Madrid?

distant /ˈdɪstənt/ a distante; lejano; remoto; (of manner) frío, reservado; (slight) ligero; (of references, etc.) indirecto. **He is a d. relation,** Es un pariente lejano. **They are always rather d. with her,** La tratan siempre con bastante frialdad

distantly /ˈdɪstəntli/ adv a distancia; a lo lejos; desde lejos; remotamente; (of manner) con frialdad; (slightly) ligeramente

distaste /dɪsˈteɪst/ n aversión, repugnancia, f; disgusto, hastío, m

distasteful /dɪsˈteɪstfəl/ a desagradable

distemper /dɪs'tempər/ n enfermedad, f; (in animals) moquillo, m; *Fig.* mal, m; (for walls) pintura al temple, f. —vt desordenar, perturbar; (walls) pintar al temple

distend /dɪ'stɛnd/ vt ensanchar; dilatar; inflar, henchir; *Med.* distender. —vi ensancharse, dilatarse

distension /dɪs'tɛnʃən/ n dilatación, f; inflación, f; henchimiento, m; *Med.* distensión, f

distillation /ˌdɪstlˈeɪʃən/ n destilación, f; extracción, f; exudación, f

distiller /dɪ'stɪlər/ n destilador (-ra)

distillery /dɪ'stɪləri/ n destilería, f, destilatorio, m

distinct /dɪ'stɪŋkt/ a distinto; diferente; claro; notable, evidente

distinction /dɪ'stɪŋkʃən/ n distinción, f

distinctive /dɪ'stɪŋktɪv/ a distintivo; característico

distinctly /dɪ'stɪŋktli/ adv claramente; distintamente

distinctness /dɪ'stɪŋktnɪs/ n claridad, f; distinción, f; carácter distintivo, m

distinguish /dɪ'stɪŋgwɪʃ/ vt distinguir; discernir; caracterizar; (honor) honrar. —vi distinguir, diferenciar

distinguishable /dɪ'stɪŋgwɪʃəbəl/ a distinguible; perceptible, discernible

distinguished /dɪ'stɪŋgwɪʃt/ a distinguido; eminente; famoso, ilustre, egregio

distort /dɪ'stɔrt/ vt (twist) torcer; deformar; falsear; pervertir

distortion /dɪ'stɔrʃən/ n deformación, f; torcimiento, m; contorsión, f; perversión, f; *Radio.* deformación, f

distract /dɪ'strækt/ vt distraer; interrumpir; perturbar; (turn aside) desviar, apartar; (madden) enloquecer, volver loco (a)

distracted /dɪ'stræktɪd/ a aturdido; demente, loco

distraction /dɪ'strækʃən/ n distracción, f; (amusement) diversion, f, pasatiempo, m; (bewilderment) confusión, f, aturdimiento, m; (madness) locura, f; **to drive to d.,** trastornar, sacar de quicio.

distrain /dɪ'streɪn/ vi embargar

distraint /dɪ'streɪnt/ n embargo, m

distraught /dɪ'strɔt/ a aturdido; desesperado; enloquecido

distress /dɪ'strɛs/ n dolor, m, aflicción, f; pena, f; miseria, penuria, f; (exhaustion) fatiga, f, cansancio, m; (pain) dolor, m; (misfortune) desdicha, f; apuro, m; (danger) peligro, m; *Law.* embargo, m. —vt afligir, dar pena (a), llenar de angustia; cansar, fatigar; (pain) doler

distressed /dɪ'strɛst/ a afligido; necesitado, pobre

distressing /dɪ'strɛsɪŋ/ a congojoso, doloroso, penoso

distribute /dɪ'strɪbyut/ vt (of justice, etc.) administrar; distribuir; repartir

distribution /ˌdɪstrə'byuʃən/ n (of jus-

tice) administración, f; distribución, f; reparto, m

district /'dɪstrɪkt/ n distrito, m; comarca, f; (of a town) barrio, m; (judicial) partido judicial, m; jurisdicción, f; región, zona, f

distrust /dɪs'trʌst/ n desconfianza, f; recelo, m, sospecha, f. —vt desconfiar de, sospechar

distrustful /dɪs'trʌstfəl/ a desconfiado, receloso, suspicaz

disturb /dɪ'stɜrb/ vt perturbar; interrumpir; incomodar; (make anxious) inquietar; (alter) cambiar; (disarrange) desordenar, desarreglar. **to d. the peace,** perturbar el orden público

disturbance /dɪ'stɜrbəns/ n perturbación, f; disturbio, m, conmoción, f; incomodidad, f; agitación, f; confusión, f; tumulto, m; desorden, m; *Radio.* parásitos, m pl

disturbing /dɪ'stɜrbɪŋ/ a perturbador; inquietador; conmovedor, impresionante, emocionante

disunion /dɪs'yunyən/ n desunión, f; discordia, f

disunite /ˌdɪsyu'naɪt/ vt desunir; separar, dividir. —vi separarse

disuse /n dɪs'yus; v -'yuz/ n desuso, m. —vt desusar; desacostumbrar. **to fall into d.,** caer en desuso

ditch /dɪtʃ/ n zanja, f; (for defense, etc.) foso, m; (irrigation) acequia, f. —vt zanjar; abarrancar. **to die in the last d.,** morir en la brecha

ditto /'dɪtou/ adv ídem; también

diuretic /ˌdaɪə'rɛtɪk/ a diurético

dive /daɪv/ n buceo, m; *Aer.* picada, f, vi bucear; sumergirse (en); *Aer.* volar en picado; penetrar (en); (into a book) enfrascarse en. **to d. out,** salir precipitadamente. **to d.-bomb,** bombardear en picado. **d.-bomber,** avión en picado, m. **d.-bombing,** bombardeo en picado, m

diver /'daɪvər/ n buceador, m; buzo, m; (bird) somorgujo, m

diverge /dɪ'vɜrdʒ/ vi divergir

divergence /dɪ'vɜrdʒəns/ n divergencia, f

divergent /dɪ'vɜrdʒənt/ a divergente

diverse /dɪ'vɜrs/ a diverso, vario

diversify /dɪ'vɜrsə,faɪ/ vt diversificar

diversion /dɪ'vɜrʒən/ n diversión, f; entretenimiento, m, recreación, f; pasatiempo, m; placer, m; *Mil.* diversión, f

diversity /dɪ'vɜrsɪti/ n diversidad, variedad, f

divert /dɪ'vɜrt/ vt desviar; (amuse) divertir, entretener

diverting /dɪ'vɜrtɪŋ/ a divertido, entretenido

divide /dɪ'vaɪd/ vt dividir; partir; separar; (cut) cortar; (share) repartir, distribuir; (hair) hacer la raya (del pelo); (of voting) provocar una votación. —vi dividirse; separarse; (of roads, etc.) bifurcarse; (of voting) votar. **divided skirt,** n falda pantalón, f

dividend /'dɪvɪˌdɛnd/ n dividendo, m. **d. warrant,** cupón de dividendo, m

divine /dɪ'vaɪn/ a divino; sublime; *Inf.* estupendo. —n teólogo, m. —vt (foretell) vaticinar, pronosticar; presentir; (guess) adivinar

diving /'daɪvɪŋ/ n buceo, m; *Aer.* picado, m. **d.-bell,** campana de bucear, f. **d.-board,** (low) trampolín, m; (high) palanca, f. **d.-suit,** escafandra, f

divinity /dɪ'vɪnɪti/ n divinidad, f; teología, f

division /dɪ'vɪʒən/ n división, f; separación, f; (distribution) repartimiento, m; (*Mil. Math.*) división, f; sección, f; grupo, m; (voting) votación, f; (discord) discordia, desunión, f. **without a d.,** por unanimidad, sin votar

divorce /dɪ'vɔrs/ n divorcio, m. —vt divorciarse de; *Fig.* divorciar, separar. **to file a petition of d.,** poner una petición de divorcio

divorcee /dɪvɔr'sei/ n (wife) divorciada, f; (husband) divorciado, m

divulge /dɪ'vʌldʒ/ vt divulgar, revelar

dizziness /'dɪzɪnɪs/ n vértigo, m; mareo, m; (bewilderment) aturdimiento, m, confusión, f

dizzy /'dɪzi/ a vertiginoso; mareado; confuso, perplejo, aturdido

do /du/ vt hacer; ejecutar; (one's duty, etc.) cumplir con; concluir; (cause) causar; (homage) rendir; (commit) cometer; (arrange) arreglar; (cook) cocer, guisar; (roast) asar; (*Fam.* cheat) engañar; (suit) convenir; (suffice) bastar; (act) hacer el papel (de); (*Fam.* treat) tratar (bien o mal); (learn) aprender; (exhaust) agotar; (walk) andar; (travel, journey) recorrer; (translate) traducir; (prepare) preparar. —vi hacer; (behave) conducirse; (of health) estar (bien o mal); (act) obrar; (get on) ir; (be suitable, suit) convenir; (suffice) bastar; (of plants) florecer; (cook) cocerse; (last) durar. **Don't!** ¡No lo hagas! ¡Quieto! ¡Calla! **How do you do?** ¿Cómo está Vd.? ¡Buenos días! **Have done!** ¡Acaba de una vez! **It will do you good,** Te conviene; Te hará bien; Te sentará bien. **It will do you no harm,** No te perjudicará; No te hará daño. **I could do with one,** Me gustaría (tener) uno; (of drinks) Me bebería uno con mucho gusto. **That will do,** Eso basta; Se puede servirse de eso; Está bien así; (leave it alone) ¡Déjate de eso! (be quiet!) ¡No digas más! ¡Cállate! **That won't do,** Eso no es bastante; Eso no sirve; Eso no se hace así; Eso no se hace. **That will never do,** Eso no servirá; Eso no puede ser. **This will do,** (when buying an article) Me quedaré con éste; Me serviré de esto; Esto basta; Esto será suficiente; (is all right) Está bien así. **Thy will be done!** ¡Hágase tu voluntad! **to be doing,** estar haciendo; estar ocupado en (or con) hacer; (of food) estar cocinando. **to be done for,** estar perdido; estar muerto. **to do bet-**

ter, hacer mejor (que); (mend one's ways) enmendarse, corregirse; (improve) mejorar, hacer progresos; (in health) encontrarse mejor. **to do nothing,** no hacer nada. **to do reverence,** rendir homenaje; inclinarse. **to do to death,** matar; asesinar; ejecutar. **to do violence to,** *Fig.* hacer fuerza a. **to do well,** hacer bien; obrar bien; (be successful) tener éxito; hacer buena impresión; (prosperous) tener una buena posición. **to do wonders,** hacer maravillas. **to have done with,** renunciar (a); dejar de hacer, cesar; concluir, terminar; no tener más que ver con; (forsake) abandonar; (a person) romper con. **to have nothing to do,** no tener nada que hacer. **to have nothing to do with,** no tener nada que ver con; (of people) no tratar; (end a friendship) romper su amistad con, dejar de ver. **well done,** bien hecho; (of food) bien guisado; (of meat) bien asado. **What is to be done?** ¿Qué hay que hacer? ¿Qué se puede hacer? **What is to do?** ¿Qué pasa? ¿Qué hay? **When he had done speaking,** Cuando hubo terminado de hablar. **to do again,** hacer de nuevo, volver a hacer, rehacer; repetir. **He will not do it again,** No lo hará más. **to do away with,** quitar; eliminar; suprimir; hacer desaparecer; poner fin a; hacer cesar; destruir; matar. **to do by,** tratar (a), portarse con. **to do for,** arruinar; matar; (suffice) bastar para; ser a propósito para, servir para; (look after) cuidar; (as a housekeeper) dirigir la casa para. **to do out,** (a room) limpiar. **to do out of,** quitar; privar de; (steal) robar. **to do up,** (tie) atar; (fold) enrollar, plegar; (envolver; (parcel) empaquetar; (arrange) arreglar; decorar; poner en orden; poner como nuevo; (iron) planchar; (launder) lavar y planchar; (tire) fatigar. **to do with,** (of people) tratar; (of things) tener que ver con; (put up with) poder con; poder sufrir. **to do without,** prescindir de; pasarse sin

do /du/ as an auxiliary verb is not translated in Spanish, e.g. *I do believe,* creo. *Do not do that,* no hagas eso. *I did not know,* no sabía. When it is used for emphasis, *do* is translated by *sí, ciertamente, claro* and similar words, e.g.: *She did not know, but he did,* Ella no lo sabía pero él sí. *You do paint well,* Pintas muy bien por cierto. *Do come this time,* No dejes de venir esta vez

docile /'dɒsəl/ a dócil

dock /dɒk/ n dique, m, dársena, f; (wharf) muelle, m; (in a law court) banquillo de los acusados, m; *Bot.* romaza, f. —vt (a tail) descolar; cortar, cercenar; reducir; (money) descontar; (a ship) poner en dique. —vi entrar en dársena, entrar en dique, entrar en muelle. **dry-d.,** dique seco, m. **floating-d.,** dique flotante, m. **d.-dues,** muellaje, m. **d. rat,** (thief) raquero, m

docket /'dɒkɪt/ n (bundle) legajo, m; extracto, m; minuta, f; (label) etiqueta, f, marbete, m

dockyard /'dɒk,yɑrd/ n arsenal, astillero, m

doctor /'dɒktər/ n doctor (-ra); (medical practitioner) médico (-ca), asistir; (repair) reparar, componer; adulterar; mezclar drogas con; falsificar. —vi ejercer la medicina. **family d.**, médico de cabecera, m. **to graduate as a d.**, doctorarse. **d. of divinity, laws, medicine,** doctor (-ra) en teología, en derecho, en medicina, m

doctorate /'dɒktərɪt/ n doctorado, m

doctrinaire /'dɒktrə'neər/ a and n doctrinario (-ia)

doctrine /'dɒktrɪn/ n doctrina, f

document /n 'dɒkyəmənt; v -,mɛnt/ n documento, m. —vt documentar; probar con documentos. **d.-case,** carpeta, f

documentary /,dɒkyə'mɛntəri/ a documental; escrito, auténtico. **d. film,** película documental, f

documentation /,dɒkyəmən'teiʃən/ n documentación, f

dodge /dɒdʒ/ n esquince, regate, m; evasiva, f; (trick) estratagema, m, maniobra, f; artefacto, m. —vt esquivar, evadir

doeskin /'dou,skɪn/ n ante, m, piel de gama, f

doff /dɒf/ vt quitar; (of hats, etc.) quitarse; desnudarse de

dog /dɒg/ n perro, m; (male) macho, m; (andiron) morillo, m; Astron. Can Mayor (or Menor), Sirio, m. —vt perseguir; seguir los pasos de; espiar. **You can't deceive an old dog,** A perro viejo no hay tus tus. **to go to the dogs,** ir a las carreras de galgos; Fig. ir cuesta abajo. **mongrel dog,** perro mestizo, m. **thoroughbred dog,** perro de raza pura, m. **dog-collar,** collar de perro, m; Eccl. alzacuello, m. **dog-days,** días caniculares, m pl, canícula, f. **dog-eared** (of books) con las puntas de las hojas dobladas. **dog-fight,** lucha de perros, f; combate aéreo, m. **dog-fish,** lija, f, cazón, m. **dog in the manger,** el perro del hortelano. **dog-kennel,** perrera, f. **dog-latin,** bajo latín, m. **dog license,** matrícula de perros, f. **dog-racing,** carrera de galgos, f. **dog-rose,** escaramujo, m. **dog show,** exposición canina, f. **dog-tooth,** diente de perro, m. **dog-vane,** Naut. cataviento, m

dogged /'dɔgɪd/ a persistente, tenaz, pertinaz, obstinado

doggerel /'dɔgərəl/ n malos versos, m pl; aleluyas, coplas de ciego, f pl, a malo, irregular

dogma /'dɔgmə/ n dogma, m

dogmatic /dɔg'mætɪk/ a dogmático

doily /'dɔili/ n carpeta, f, pañito de adorno, m

doings /'duɪŋz/ n pl acciones, f pl; (deeds) hechos, m pl; (behavior) conducta, f; (happenings) acontecimientos, m pl; (works) obras, f pl; (things) cosas, f pl

doldrums /'douldrəmz/ n pl calmas ecuatoriales, f pl

dole /doul/ n limosna, f; porción, f. **to d. out,** repartir; distribuir en porciones pequeñas; racionar; dar contra la voluntad de uno.

doleful /'doulfəl/ a triste, lúgubre, melancólico; doloroso

doll /dɒl/ n muñeca, f

dollar /'dɒlər/ n dólar, m

dolly /'dɒli/ n muñeca, f; (for clothes) moza, f. **d.-tub,** cubo para la colada, m

dolphin /'dɒlfɪn/ n delfín, m

dolt /doult/ n cabeza de alcornoque, mf, zamacuco, m

domain /dou'mein/ n territorio, m; heredad, posesión, propiedad, f; (empire) dominio, m

dome /doum/ n cúpula, f; bóveda, f; (palace) palacio, m

domestic /də'mɛstɪk/ a doméstico; familiar; (home-loving) casero; (of animals) doméstico; (national) interior, nacional. —n doméstico, sirviente, m; criada, f. **d. economy,** economía doméstica, f

domesticate /də'mɛstɪ,keit/ vt domesticar

domesticated /də'mɛstɪ,keitɪd/ a (of animals) domesticado; (of persons) casero

domicile /'dɒmə,sail/ n domicilio, m, vt domiciliar

dominant /'dɒmənənt/ a dominante; imperante. —n Mus. dominante, f. **to be d.,** prevalecer

dominate /'dɒmə,neit/ vt and vi dominar

domination /,dɒmə'neiʃən/ n dominación, f

domineer /,dɒmə'nɪər/ vi dominar, tiranizar. **to d. over,** mandar en

domineering /,dɒmə'nɪərɪŋ/ a dominante, mandón, tiránico

Dominican Republic, the la República Dominicana, f

dominion /də'mɪnyən/ n dominio, m; autoridad, soberanía, f; imperio, m; pl **dominions,** Eccl. dominaciones, f pl

domino /'dɒmə,nou/ n dominó, m. **to go d.,** hacer domino

don /dɒn/ n (Spanish and Italian title) don, m; señor, m. —vt ponerse, vestirse

donation /dou'neiʃən/ n donación, dádiva, f; contribución, f

done /dʌn/ a and past part hecho; (of food) cocido; (roasted) asado; (tired) rendido; (Fam. deceived) engañado. **Well d.!** ¡Bien hecho! **d. for,** arruinado; muerto; perdido; vencido; (spoilt) estropeado

donkey /'dɒŋki/ n borrico (-ca), burro (-rra). **d.-engine,** máquina auxiliar, f

donor /'dounər/ n donador (-ra); dador (-ra)

doodle /'dudl/ v borrajear, garabatear, hacer garabatos

doom /dum/ n condena, f; (fate) suerte, f; (judgment) destino, m; ruina, f; juicio, m. —vt sentenciar; condenar

doomsday /'dumz,dei/ n día del juicio final, m

door /dɔr/ n puerta, f; entrada, f. **front d.,** puerta de entrada, f. **next d.,** la casa vecina; la puerta de al lado, la puerta vecina. **next d. neighbor,** vecino (-na) de al lado. **out of doors,** al aire libre; en la calle. **to knock at the d.,** llamar a la puerta. **to slam the d. in a person's face,** dar con la puerta en las narices de alguien. **d.-bell,** timbre (non-electric, campanilla, f) de llamada, m. **d.-jamb,** quicial, m. **d. keeper,** portero, m. **d.-knob,** tirador, m. **d.-knocker,** manija, f; picaporte, m, aldaba, f. **d.-plate,** placa, f. **d.-shutter,** cierre metálico, m. **d.-step,** peldaño de la puerta, m; umbral, m. **d.-way,** portal, m

dope /doup/ n drogas, f pl, narcóticos, m pl; (news) información, f. **d. fiend,** morfinómano (-na)

dope-pusher /'doup ,puʃər/ n narcotraficante, mf

dormant /'dɔrmənt/ a durmiente; latente; secreto; inactivo. **to go d.,** dormirse

dormitory /'dɔrmɪ,tɔri/ n dormitorio, m

dorsum /'dɔrsəm/ n dorso, m

dossier /'dɒsi,ei/ n documentación, f

dot /dɒt/ n punto, m; Mus. puntillo, m; pl **dots,** Gram. puntos suspensivos, m pl. —vt poner punto (a una letra); (scatter) salpicar. **on the dot,** (of time) en punto. **to dot one's i's,** poner los puntos sobre las íes

dotage /'doutɪdʒ/ n senectud, chochera, f

dotard /'doutərd/ n viejo chocho, m; vieja chocha, f; Inf. carcamal, m

dote /dout/ vi chochear. **to d. on,** adorar en, idolatrar

doting /'doutɪŋ/ a chocho

double /'dʌbəl/ a and adv doble; dos veces; (in a pair) en par; en dos; doblemente; (deceitful) doble, de dos caras, falso; ambiguo. —n doble, m; duplicado, m; Theat. contrafigura, f; pl **doubles,** (tennis) dobles, m pl, juego doble, m. —vt doblar; duplicar; (fold) doblegar; (the fist) cerrar (el puño); (Theat. and Naut.) doblar. —vi doblarse; (dodge) volverse atrás, hacer un rodeo, dar una vuelta; esquivarse. **to d. up,** vt envolver; arrollar; (a person) doblar. —vi doblegarse; arrollarse; (collapse) desplomarse. **at the d.,** corriendo. **He was doubled up with pain,** El dolor se le hacía retorcer. **mixed doubles,** parejas mixtas, f pl; dobles mixtos, m pl. **double two,** (telephone) dos dos. **with a d. meaning,** con segunda intención. **d.-barrelled,** de dos cañones. **d.-bass,** contrabajo, m. **d. bed,** cama de matrimonio, f. **d.-bedded,** con cama de matrimonio; con dos camas. **d.-breasted,** cruzado. **d.-chin,** papada, f. **d.-dealing,** duplicidad, f. **d.-edged,** de doble filo. **d.-entry,** Com. partida doble, f. **d.-faced,** de dos caras. **d.-jointed,** con articulaciones dobles

double-spaced /'dʌbəl 'speist/ a a doble espacio, a dos espacios

doubling /'dʌblɪŋ/ n doblamiento, m; doblez, plegadura, f; duplicación, f; (dodging) evasiva, f, esguince, m

doubt /daut/ n duda, f; incertidumbre, f; sospecha, f. —vt and vi dudar; sospechar; titubear, hesitar; temer. **beyond all d.,** fuera de duda. **no d.,** sin duda. **There is no d. that,** No hay duda de que, No cabe duda de que. **When in d....,** En caso de duda...

doubtful /'dautfəl/ a dudoso; incierto; perplejo; ambiguo; (of places) sospechoso

doubtfully /'dautfəli/ adv dudosamente; inciertamente; irresolutamente; ambiguamente

doubtless /'dautlɪs/ adv sin duda, por supuesto; probablemente

douche /duʃ/ n ducha, f, vt duchar

dough /dou/ n pasta, masa, f; (money) lana, f

dour /dʊr/ a huraño, adusto, austero

douse /daus/ vt zambullir; (a sail) recoger; Inf. apagar

dove /dʌv/ n paloma, f. **d.-cote,** palomar, m

dovetail /'dʌv,teil/ n cola de milano, f, vt machihembrar, empalmar; Fig. encajar

dowager /'dauədʒər/ n viuda, f; matrona, f. **d. countess,** condesa viuda, f

dowdy /'daudi/ a desaliñado, desaseado; poco elegante. —n mujer poco elegante, f

dowel /'dauəl/ n espiga, clavija, f, zoquete, m, vt enclavijar

down /daun/ n (of a bird) plumón, m; (on a peach, etc.) pelusilla, f; (hair) vello, m; (before the beard) bozo, m; (of a thistle, etc.) vilano, m. **ups and downs,** vicisitudes, f pl

down /daun/ a pendiente; (of trains, etc.) descendente. —adv abajo; hacia abajo; (lowered) bajado; (of the eyes) bajos; (on the ground) en tierra, por tierra; (stretched out) tendido a lo largo; (depressed) triste, abatido; (ill) enfermo; (fallen) caído; (of the wind) cesado; (closed) cerrado; (exhausted) agotado; Com. al contado; (of temperature) más bajo. —prep abajo de; abajo; en la dirección de; (along) a lo largo de; por. **"Down"** (on elevators) «Para bajar». —interj ¡Abajo!; ¡A tierra! **He went d. the hill,** Bajaba la colina. **He is d. now,** Ha bajado ahora; Está abajo ahora; Está derribado ahora. **The sun has gone d.,** Se ha puesto el sol. **His stock has gone d.,** Fig. Inf. Ha caído en disfavor. **Prices have come d.,** Los precios han bajado. **Their numbers have gone d.,** Sus números han disminuido. **to be d. and out,** estar completamente arruinado, ser pobre de solemnidad. **to boil d.,** reducir hirviendo. **to come d. in the world,** venir a menos. **while I was going d. the river,** mientras iba río abajo, mientras bajaba al río. **d. below,** allá abajo; abajo; en el piso de abajo. **D. on your knees!**

¡De rodillas! **d. to,** hasta. **d. spout,** tubo de bajada, *m.* **D. with!** ¡Abajo! ¡Muera! **d.-stream,** agua abajo.

down /daun/ *vt* derribar; vencer. **to d. tools,** declararse en huelga

downcast /'daun,kæst/ *a* bajo; cabizbajo, deprimido, abatido

downfall /'daun,fɔl/ *n* caída, *f;* derrumbamiento, *m;* (failure) fracaso, *m;* (*Fig.* ruin) decadencia, ruina, *f*

downhearted /'daun'hɑrtɪd/ *a* descorazonado, alicaído, desalentado

downhill / *adv* 'daun'hɪl; *a* 'daun,hɪl/ *adv* cuesta abajo, hacia abajo. —*a* en declive, inclinado. **to go d.,** ir cuesta abajo

downpour /'daun,pɔr/ *n* chubasco (Mexico), aguacero, chaparrón, *m*

downright /'daun,rait/ *a* franco, sincero; categórico, terminante; absoluto. —*adv* muy; completamente

downstairs /'daun'steərz/ *adv* escalera abajo; al piso de abajo; en el piso bajo; abajo. —*a* del piso de abajo. —*n* planta baja, *f;* piso de abajo, *m.* **to go d.,** bajar la escalera; ir al piso de abajo

downtrodden /'daun,trɒdn/ *a* oprimido, esclavizado

downward /'daunwərd/ *a* descendente; inclinado. —*adv* hacia abajo

downy /'dauni/ *a* velloso; (*Fam.* of persons) con más conchas que un galápago

dowry /'dauri/ *n* dote, *mf.* **to give as a d.,** dotar

dowse /dauz/ *vt.* See **douse**

doze /douz/ *vi* dormitar. —*n* sueño ligero, *m*

dozen /'dʌzən/ *n* docena, *f*

drab /dræb/ *a* pardo, parduzco, grisáceo; *Fig.* gris, monótono. —*n* (slut) pazpuerca, *f;* (prostitute) ramera, *f*

draft /dræft/ *n* (act of drawing) tiro, *m;* (of liquid) trago, *m;* (of a ship) calado, *m;* (of air) corriente de aire, *f; Com.* giro, *m,* letra de cambio, *f;* (for the army, navy) conscripción, leva, *f;* (outline) bosquejo, *m;* proyecto, *m;* borrador, *m.* —*vt* (recruit) reclutar; (outline) bosquejar, delinear; (draw up) redactar, proyectar. **on d.,** (of beer, etc.) por vaso. **d. horse,** caballo de tiro, *m.*

draft card *n* cartilla (Mexico), libreta de enrolamiento (Argentina), *m*

draft dodger *n* emboscado, prófugo, *m*

drafting /'dræftɪŋ/ *n* (*Mil. Nav.*) reclutamiento, *m;* (of a bill, etc.) redacción, *f;* (wording) términos, *m pl*

draftsman /'dræftsmən/ *n* dibujante, *m;* delineante, *m;* redactor, *m*

drag /dræg/ *n* (for dredging) draga, *f;* (harrow) rastrillo, *m;* (break) freno, *m;* (obstacle) estorbo, *m; Aer.* sonda. *f.* —*vt* arrastrar; (fishing nets) rastrear; (harrow) rastrillar. —*vi* (of the anchor) garrar; arrastrarse por el suelo; (of time) pasar lentamente; ir más despacio (que); (of interest) decaer, disminuir. **d.-hook,** garfio, *m.* **d.-net,** brancada, *f*

draggled /'drægəld/ *a* mojado y sucio

dragon /'drægən/ *n* dragón, *m.* **d.-fly,** libélula, *f,* caballito del diablo, *m*

dragoon /drə'gun/ *n Mil.* dragón, *m, vt* someter a una disciplina rigurosa; obligar a la fuerza (a)

drain /drein/ *n* desaguadero, *m;* (sewer) cloaca, alcantarilla, *f;* sumidero, *m; Agr.* acequia, *f.* —*vt* desaguar; sanear; (lakes, etc.) desangrar; secar; (bail) achicar; (empty and drink) vaciar; (swallow) tragar; (*Fig.* of sorrow, etc.) apurar; (despoil) despojar; (deprive) privar (de); (impoverish) empobrecer; (exhaust) agotar. —*vi* desaguarse; vaciarse; (with off) escurrirse. **to be well drained,** tener buen drenaje. **to d. the sump,** vaciar la culata. **to d. away,** vaciar. **d.-pipe,** tubo de desagüe, *m*

drainage /'dreinɪdʒ/ *n* (of land) drenaje, *m;* desagüe, *m;* (of wounds) drenaje, *m;* (sewage) aguas del alcantarillado, *f pl.* **main d.,** drenaje municipal, *m*

draining /'dreinɪŋ/ *a* de desagüe; de drenaje. **d.-board,** escurridor, *m*

drake /dreik/ *n* ánade macho, *m*

drama /'drɑmə, 'dræmə/ *n* drama, *m*

dramatic /drə'mætɪk/ *a* dramático

dramatis personae /'dræmətɪs pər'souni/ *n pl* personajes, *m, pl*

dramatist /'dræmətɪst, 'drɑmə-/ *n* dramaturgo, *m*

dramatization /,dræmətə'zeiʃən, ,drɑmə-/ *n* versión escénica, *f;* descripción dramática, *f;* (of emotions) dramatización, *f*

drape /dreip/ *vt* colgar, cubrir; vestir

drapery /'dreipəri/ *n* colgaduras, *f pl;* ropaje, *m,* ropas, *f pl;* pañería, *f*

drastic /'dræstɪk/ *a* drástico; enérgico, fuerte; **a drastic measure,** una medida avanzada, *f*

draw /drɔ/ *vt* tirar; arrastrar; traer; (pluck) arrancar; (attract) atraer; (extract) extraer; sacar; hacer salir; (unsheath) desenvainar; (a bow-string) tender; (cards, dominoes) tomar, robar; (threads) deshilar; (disembowel) destripar; (a check, etc.) girar, librar; (of a ship) calar; (of lines) hacer (rayas); (curtains) correr; (to draw curtains back) descorrer; (salary, money) cobrar, percibir; (obtain) obtener; (persuade) persuadir, inducir; (inhale) respirar; (a sigh) dar; (win) ganar; (a conclusion) deducir, inferir; (a distinction) hacer formular; *Sports.* empatar; (a number, etc.) sortear; (suck) chupar; (tighten) estirar; (lengthen) alargar; (comfort, etc.) tomar; (inspiration) inspirarse en; (obtain money) procurarse (recursos); (withdraw funds) retirar; (write) escribir; (draw) dibujar; (trace) trazar; (provoke) provocar. **to be drawn,** (of tickets in a lottery and cards) salir. **to d. lots,** echar suertes. **to d. water,** sacar agua. **to d. along,** arrastrar; conducir. **to d. aside,** tomar a un lado, tomar aparte; quitar de en medio, poner a un lado; (curtains) descorrer. **to d. away,** (remove) quitar; (a person) llevarse (a); apartar. **to d. back,** hacer recular; hacer retirarse; hacer volverse atrás; (curtains) descorrer. **to d. down,** hacer bajar; tirar a lo largo de (or por); bajar; (attract) atraer. **to d. forth,** hacer salir; hacer avanzar; tirar hacia adelante; conducir; (develop) desarrollar; sacar; hacer aparecer; (comment, etc.) suscitar. **to d. in,** tirar hacia adentro; sacar; acercar; atraer. **to d. off,** sacar; retirar; quitar; (water from pipes, etc.) vaciar; *Print.* tirar; (turn aside) desviar. **to d. on,** (of apparel) ponerse; (boots) calzarse; (occasion) ocasionar. **to d. out,** sacar fuera; hacer salir; tirar (de); (extract) extraer; (trace) trazar; (a person) hacer hablar. **to d. over,** poner encima de; arrastrar por; hacer acercarse (a), tirar hacia; atraer; persuadir. **d. prestige (from),** cobrar prestigio (de). **to d. round,** poner alrededor de. **to d. together,** reunir; acercar. **to d. up,** tirar hacia arriba; subir; sacar; extraer; (raise) levantar, alzar; (bring) traer; (bring near) acercar; (order) ordenar; *Mil.* formar; (a document) redactar; formular. **to d. oneself up,** erguirse

draw /drɔ/ *vi* tirar, tirar, (shrink) encogerse; (wrinkle) arrugarse; (of chimneys, etc.) tirar; (a picture) dibujar; *Sports.* empatar; (move) moverse; avanzar, adelantarse; (of a ship) calar; (a sword) desnudar (la espada); (lots) echar suertes; (attract people) atraer gente; *Com.* girar. **to d. aside,** ponerse a un lado; retirarse. **to d. back,** retroceder, recular; retirarse; vacilar. **to d. in,** retirarse; (of days) hacerse corto; (of dusk) caer. **to d. off,** alejarse; apartarse, retirarse. **to d. on,** (approach) acercarse; avanzar; *Com.* girar contra; inspirarse en. **to d. out,** hacerse largo; (of a vehicle) ponerse en marcha, empezar a andar. **to d. round,** ponerse alrededor; reunirse alrededor. **to d. together,** reunirse. **to d. up,** parar.

draw /drɔ/ *n* tirada, *f;* (of lotteries) sorteo, *m; Sports.* empate, *m;* atracción, *f;* (*Fig.* feeler) tanteo, *m.* **to be a big d.,** ser una gran atracción

drawback /'drɔ͵bæk/ *n* desventaja, *f,* inconveniente, *m*

drawee /drɔ'i/ *n Com.* girado, *m*

drawer /'drɔər *for :* drɔr *for /* *n* tirador (-ra); (of water) aguador (-ra); extractor (-ra); (in a public-house) mozo de taberna, *m;* (designer) diseñador, *m;* (sketcher) dibujante, *mf; Com.* girador, *m;* (receptacle) cajón, *m; pl* drawers, (men's) calzoncillos, *m pl;* (women's) pantalones, *m pl*

drawing /'drɔɪŋ/ *n* (pulling) tiro, *m;* atracción, *f;* (extraction) extracción, *f;* saca, *f;* (in raffles, etc. and of lots) sorteo, *m;* (of money) percibo, *m; Com.* giro, *m;* (sketch) dibujo, *m;* (plan) esquema, *f.* **free-hand d.,** dibujo a pulso, *m.* **d. from life,** dibujo del natural, *m.* **d.-board,**

tablero de dibujo, *m.* **d.-paper,** papel para dibujar, *m.* **d.-room,** salón, *m*

drawl /drɔl/ *vi* hablar arrastrando las palabras

drawn /drɔn/ *past part* See **draw.** *a* (tired) ojeroso, con ojeras, con un aspecto de cansancio; (with pain) desencajado. **long d. out,** demasiado largo. **d. sword,** espada desnuda, *f.* **d.-thread work,** deshilados, *m pl*

dread /drɛd/ *n* pavor, temor, terror, espanto, *m;* trepidación, *f,* miedo, *m.* —*a* temible, espantoso, terrible; augusto. —*vt* temer. —*vi* tener miedo, temer. **in d. of,** con miedo de, con terror de

dreadful /'drɛdfəl/ *a* terrible, pavoroso, espantoso, horroroso; formidable; augusto

dream /drim/ *n* sueño, *m;* ilusión, *f;* ensueño, *m;* fantasía, *f.* —*vt and vi* soñar; imaginar. **He dreamed the hours,** Pasaba las horas soñando. **I wouldn't d. of it!** ¡Ni por sueño! **in a d.,** en sueños; (waking) como en sueños; mecánicamente. **Sweet dreams!** ¡Duerme bien! **to d. of,** soñar con

dreamily /'drimɪli/ *adv* como en sueños; soñolientamente; vagamente

dreaming /'drimɪŋ/ *n* sueños, *m pl*

dreamland /'drim͵lænd/ *n* reino de los sueños, *m*

dreamy /'drimi/ *a* soñador; soñoliento; fantástico; (empty) vacío

dreary /'drɪəri/ *a* triste; melancólico; lóbrego

dredge /drɛdʒ/ *vt* dragar; (with sugar, etc.) espolvorear

dregs /drɛgz/ *n pl* heces, *f pl,* posos, *m pl.* **to drain to the d.,** vaciar hasta las heces

drench /drɛntʃ/ *vt* mojar, calar. **He is drenched to the skin,** Está calado hasta los huesos

dress /drɛs/ *vt* (with clothes) vestir; (arrange) arreglar; (the hair) peinar(se); (a wound) curar; (hides) adobar; (cloth) aprestar; (flax) rastrillar; (stone) labrar; (wood) desbastar; (prune) podar; (a garden) cultivar; (manure) abonar; *Cul.* aderezar; preparar; (season) condimentar; (a table) poner; (adorn) ataviar, adornar; revestir; (a dead body) amortajar. —*vi* vestirse; ataviarse; (of troops) alinearse. **all dressed up and nowhere to go,** compuesta y sin novio. **dressed up to the nines,** vestido de veinticinco alfileres. **Left (Right) d.!** ¡A la izquierda (A la derecha) alinearse! **to d. down,** (scold) poner como un trapo (a), dar una calada (a). **to d. up,** *vt* ataviar; (disguise) disfrazar. —*vi* ponerse muy elegante; disfrazarse

dress /drɛs/ *n* (in general) el vestir; (clothes) ropa, *f;* (frock) vestido, traje, *m;* (uniform) uniforme, *m;* (*Fig.* covering) hábitos, *m pl;* (appearance) aspecto, *m;* forma, *f.* **full d.,** (uniform) uniforme de gala, *m;* (civilian, man's) traje de etiqueta, *m;* (woman's) traje de gala, *m.* **morn-**

ing d., (man's) traje de paisano, *m;*
(woman's) vestido de todos los días, *m;*
(man's formal dress) chaqué, *m.* **ready-
made d.,** traje hecho, *m.* **d. allowance,**
alfileres, *m pl.* **d.-circle,** anfiteatro, *m.* **d.-
coat,** frac, *m.* **d. protector,** sobaquera, *f.*
d. rehearsal, ensayo general, *m.* **d. shirt,**
camisa de pechera dura, *f.* **d. suit,** (with
white tie) traje de frac, *m;* (with black
tie) smoking, *m.* **d. sword,** espada de
gala, *f.* **d. tie,** corbata de smoking (or de
frac), *f*

dresser /'drɛsər/ *n* el que adereza; (of
wounds) practicante (de hospital), *m;*
(valet) ayuda de cámara, *m;* (maid) doncella, *f;* (of skins) adobador de pieles, *m;*
(furniture) aparador, *m;* (in the kitchen)
armario de la cocina, *m*

dressing /'drɛsɪŋ/ *n* el vestir(se); aderezamiento, *m;* (for cloth) apresto, *m;* (of
leather) adobo, *m;* (of wood) desbaste,
m; (of stone) labrado, *m;* (manuring) estercoladura, *f;* (sauce) salsa, *f;* (seasoning) condimentación, *f;* (of a wound)
cura, *f;* (bandage) apósito, *m,* vendaje, *m.*
d.-case, neceser, saco de noche, *m.* **d.-
down,** *Inf.* rapapolvo, *m.* **d.-gown,**
(woman's) salto de cama, quimono, *m;*
(man's) batín, *m.* **d.-jacket,** chambra, *f,*
peinador, *m.* **d.-room,** *Theat.* camarín, *m;*
(in a house) trasalcoba, recámara, *f.* **d.-
station,** puesto de socorro, *m.* **d.-table,**
tocador, *m,* mesa de tocador, *f*

dressmaker /'drɛs,meikər/ *n* modista, *mf*

dressmaking /'drɛs,meikɪŋ/ *n* confección
de vestidos, *f;* arte de la modista, *mf*

dribble /'drɪbəl/ *vi* gotear; (slaver) babear. —*vt* (in football) regatear. —*n* (in
football) regate, *m*

dried /draid/ *a* seco; (of fruit) paso. **d.
up,** (withered) marchito; (of people) enjuto. **d. fish,** cecial, *m.* **d. meat,** cecina, *f*

drift /drɪft/ *n* (in a ship or airplane's
course) deriva, *f;* (of a current) velocidad,
f; (tendency) tendencia, *f;* (meaning)
significación, *f;* (heap) montón, *m;* (aim)
objeto, propósito, fin, *m; Mineral.* galería,
f; (of dust, etc.) nube, *f;* (shower) lluvia,
f; (impulsion) impulso, *m;* violencia, *f.*
—*vi* flotar, ir arrastrado por la corriente;
amontonarse; *Naut.* derivar; *Aer.* abatir.
—*vt* llevar; amontonar. **drifts of sand,**
arena movediza, *f.* **to d. into,** (war, etc.)
entrar sin querer en; (habits) dar en la
flor de; (a room, etc.) deslizarse en. **d.-
wood,** madera de deriva, *f*

drill /drɪl/ *n* (instrument) taladro, perforador, *m,* barrena, *f;* ejercicio, *m,* educación
física, *f; Mil.* instrucción militar, *f;* (cloth)
dril, *m; Agr.* sembradora mecánica, *f;* (for
seeds) hilera, *f;* (discipline) disciplina, *f;*
(teaching) instrucción, *f.* —*vt* taladrar,
barrenar; enseñar el ejercicio (a); enseñar
la instrucción; disciplinar; (seed) sembrar
en hileras. —*vi* hacer el ejercicio; hacer la
instrucción militar. **d. ground,** (in a
barracks) patio de un cuartel, *m;* (in a

school) patio de recreo, *m.* **d.-sergeant,**
sargento instructor, *m*

drilling /'drɪlɪŋ/ *n* (boring) perforación, *f,*
barrenamiento, *m;* (of seeds) sembradura
en hileras, *f;* ejercicios, *m pl;*
(maneuvers) maniobras, *f pl*

drink /drɪŋk/ *n* bebida, *f;* (glass of wine,
etc.) copita, *f;* (of water, etc.) vaso, *m.*
—*vt* beber; tomar; (empty) vaciar. —*vi*
beber. **to d. the health of,** beber a la salud de, brindar por. **to give someone a
d.,** dar a beber. **Would you like a d.?**
¿Quieres tomar algo? **to d. in,** absorber.
to d. off, up, beber de un trago

drinkable /'drɪŋkəbəl/ *a* potable, bebedero

drinker /'drɪŋkər/ *n* bebedor (-ra)

drinking /'drɪŋkɪŋ/ *n* acción de beber, *f;*
el beber, *m;* (alcoholism) bebida, *f.* —*a*
que bebe; aficionado a la bebida; (of
things) para beber; (drinkable) potable;
(tavern) de taberna. **d.-fountain,** fuente
pública para beber agua, *f.* **d. place,** bebedero, *m;* bar, *m.* **d.-song,** canción de
taberna, *f.* **d.-trough,** abrevadero, *m;* **d.-
water,** agua potable, *f*

drip /drɪp/ *vi and vt* chorrear, gotear; caer
gota a gota; escurrir; destilar; chorrear.
—*n* goteo, *m;* gota, *f; Archit.* goterón, *m*

dripping /'drɪpɪŋ/ *n* goteo, *m;* chorreo,
m; (fat) grasa, *f, a* que gotea; mojado;
que chorrea agua. **d.-pan,** grasera, *f*

drive /draiv/ *vt* empujar; arrojar; conducir; (grouse, etc.) batir; (a ball) golpear;
(a nail, etc.) clavar; (oblige) compeler,
forzar a; (a horse, plough, etc.) manejar;
(*Mech.* work) mover; (cause to work, of
machines) hacer funcionar; (a tunnel,
etc.) abrir, construir; (a bargain, etc.)
hacer; (cause) impulsar, hacer; (mad,
etc.) volver. —*vi* lanzarse; (of rain) azotar; (a vehicle) conducir; (in a vehicle) ir
en (coche, etc.). **to let d. at,** (aim)
asestar. **to d. a wedge,** hacer mella. **to
d. home an argument,** convencer; hacer
convincente. **What is he driving at?**
¿Qué se propone? ¿Qué quiere?; ¿Qué
quiere decir con sus indirectas? ¿A dónde
quiere llegar con esto? **to d. along,** ir en
coche o carruaje por; pasearse en coche o
carruaje; conducir un auto, etc., por. **to
d. away,** *vt* echar; (chase) cazar; (flies,
etc.) sacudirse, espantar; (care, etc.)
ahuyentar; (of persons) apartar, alejar.
—*vi* (depart) marcharse (en coche, etc.).
to d. back, *vt* rechazar; (a ball) devolver.
—*vi* volver (en auto, etc.); (arrive) llegar.
to d. down, hacer bajar; arrojar hacia
abajo; (in a vehicle) bajar (por). **to d. in,
into,** *vt* hacer entrar; (of teeth, etc.) hincar; (nails) clavar; *Fig.* introducir. —*vt*
entrar (en coche, carruaje); llegar (en coche, etc.). **to d. off,** See **away. to d. off
the stage,** hacer dejar la escena, silbar.
to d. on, *vt* empujar; hacer avanzar; (attack) atacar. —*vi* seguir su marcha;
seguir avanzando; emprender la marcha.
to d. out, *vt* expulsar; hacer salir;

(chase) cazar. —*vi* salir (en coche, etc.).

to d. up, *vi* llegar (en coche, etc.); parar.

to d. up to, avanzar hasta, llegar hasta; conducir (el coche, etc.) hasta

drive /draɪv/ *n* paseo (en coche, etc.), *m;* (avenue) avenida, *f;* (distance) trayecto, *m;* (journey) viaje, *m;* Mech. acción, *f;* conducción, *f; m;* Mil. ataque, *m;* (of a person) energía, *f;* campaña vigorosa, *f;* impulso, *m.* **left (right) hand d.**, conducción a la izquierda (derecha). **to take a d.**, dar un paseo en (auto, etc.). **to take for a d.**, llevar a paseo en (auto, etc.)

drive-in /ˈdraɪv‚ɪn/ *n* autocine, autocinema, *m*

drivel /ˈdrɪvəl/ *n* vaciedades, patrañas, *f pl,* disparates, *m pl, vi* decir disparates, chochear

driver /ˈdraɪvər/ *n* conductor (-ra); chófer, *m;* (of an engine) maquinista, *m;* (of a cart) carretero, *m;* (of a coach, carriage) cochero, *m;* (of cattle, etc.) ganadero, *m;* (golf) conductor, *m*

"Driveway" «Vado Permanente», «Paso de Carruajes»

driving /ˈdraɪvɪŋ/ *n* conducción, *f;* modo de conducir, *m;* paseo (en coche, etc.), *m;* impulsión, *f.* —*a* de conducir; de chófer; para chóferes; motor; propulsor; impulsor; de transmisión; Fig. impulsor; (violent) violento, impetuoso. **to go d.**, ir de paseo (en auto o carruaje). **d. license**, carnet de chófer, *m.* **d. mirror**, espejo retrovisor, *m.* **d. seat**, asiento del conductor, *m;* (of an old-fashioned coach, etc.) pescante, *m.* **d.-shaft**, Mech. árbol motor, *m.* **d. test**, examen para chóferes, *m.* **d.-wheel**, volante, *m;* rueda motriz, *f.* **d.-whip**, látigo, *m*

drizzle /ˈdrɪzəl/ *n* llovizna, *f, vi* lloviznar

droll /droul/ *a* chusco, gracioso. —*n* bufón, *m*

drone /droun/ *n* abejón, *m; Fig.* zángano, *m;* (hum) zumbido, *m;* (of a song, voice) salmodia, *f, vt and vi* (hum) zumbar; (of a song, voice) salmodiar; (idle) zanganear

droop /drup/ *vi* inclinarse; colgar; caer; (wither) marchitarse; (fade) consumirse; (pine) desanimarse. —*vt* bajar; dejar caer. —*n* caída, *f;* inclinación, *f*

drooping /ˈdrupɪŋ/ *a* caído; debilitado; lánguido; (of ears) gacho; (depressed) alicaído, deprimido

drop /drɒp/ *n* gota, *f;* (tear) lágrima, *f;* (for the ear) pendiente, *m;* (sweet) pastilla, *f;* (of a chandelier) almendra, *f;* (fall) caída, *f;* (in price, etc.) baja, *f;* (slope) pendiente, cuesta, *f.* **by drops**, a gotas. **d. bottle**, frasco cuentagotas, *m.* **d.-curtain**, telón de boca, *m.* **d.-hammer**, martinete, *m.* **d.-head coupé**, cupé descapotable, *m.* **d.-scene**, telón de foro, *m*

drop /drɒp/ *vt* verter a gotas; destilar; (sprinkle) salpicar, rociar; dejar caer; soltar; (lower) bajar; (of clothes, etc.) desprenderse de, quitar; (lose) perder; (a letter in a mailbox) echar; (leave) dejar; (give up) renunciar (a); desistir (de);

abandonar; (kill) tumbar; (a hint) soltar; (a curtsey) hacer. —*vi* gotear, caer en gotas, destilar; (descend) bajar, descender; caer muerto; caer desmayado; (sleep) dormirse; (fall) caer; (of the wind) amainar; (of prices, temperature) bajar. **to let the matter d.**, poner fin a una cuestión. **to d. a line**, poner unas líneas. **to d. anchor**, anclar. **to d. behind**, quedarse atrás. **to d. down**, caer (a tierra). **to d. in**, entrar al pasar. **d. in on somebody**, pasarse por casa de fulano, pasarse por el despacho de (etc.). **to d. off**, separarse (de); disminuir; (sleep) quedar dormido; (die) morir de repente. **to d. out**, separarse; (from a race, etc.) retirarse (de); quedarse atrás; desaparecer; ausentarse, apartarse; (decrease) disminuir; decaer. **He has dropped out of my life**, Le he perdido de vista. **to d. through**, caer por; frustrarse; no dar resultado

dropping /ˈdrɒpɪŋ/ *n* gotera, *f;* gotas, *f pl;* (fall) caída, *f; pl* **droppings** (of a candle) moco, *m;* (dung) cagadas, *f pl.* **Constant d. wears away the stone**, La gotera cava la piedra

dropsy /ˈdrɒpsi/ *n* hidropesía, *f*

dross /drɒs/ *n* escoria, *f;* (rubbish) basura, *f*

drought /draut/ *n* aridez, *f;* (thirst) sed, *f;* (dry season) sequía, *f*

drove /drouv/ *n* manada, *f,* hato, *m;* (of sheep) rebaño, *m;* (crowd) muchedumbre, *f*

drown /draun/ *vi* ahogarse. —*vt* ahogar; sumergir; inundar; (Fig. of cries, sorrow, etc.) ahogar

drowse /drauz/ *vi* adormecerse

drowsiness /ˈdrauzɪnɪs/ *n* somnolencia, *f;* sueño, *m;* (laziness) indolencia, pereza, *f*

drowsy /ˈdrauzi/ *a* soñoliento; adormecedor, soporífero; (heavy) amodorrado. **to grow d.**, adormecerse. **to make d.**, adormecer

drudgery /ˈdrʌdʒəri/ *n* trabajo arduo, *m,* faena monótona, *f*

drug /drʌg/ *n* droga, *f;* medicamento, *m;* narcótico, *m.* —*vt* mezclar con drogas; administrar drogas (a); narcotizar. —*vi* tomar drogas. **d. trade**, comercio de drogas, *m.* **d. traffic**, contrabando de drogas, narcotráfico *m*

drug addict *n* toxicómano, *m*

drug addiction *n* toxicomanía, *f*

druggist /ˈdrʌgɪst/ *n* droguero (-ra)

drum /drʌm/ *n* tambor, *m;* (of the ear) tímpano (del oído), *m;* (cylinder) cilindro, *m;* (box) caja, *f; Archit.* cuerpo de columna, *m.* **bass d.**, bombo, *m.* **with drums beating**, con tambor batiente, *f.* **d.-head**, parche (del tambor), *m.* **d.-head service**, misa de campaña, *f.* **d.-major**, tambor mayor, *m*

drum /drʌm/ *vt and vi* tocar el tambor; (with the fingers) tabalear, teclear; (with the heels) zapatear; (into a person's head) machacar. **to d. out,** *Mil.* expulsar a tambor batiente

drummer /'drʌmər/ *n* tambor, *m*

drumstick /'drʌm,stɪk/ *n* palillo (de tambor), *m*

drunk /drʌŋk/ *a* borracho, ebrio. —*n* borracho, *m*. **to be d.,** estar borracho. **to get d.,** emborracharse; *Inf.* pillar un lobo. **to make d.,** emborrachar

drunkard /'drʌŋkərd/ *n* borracho (-cha)

drunken /'drʌŋkən/ *a* borracho, ebrio

dry /draɪ/ *vi* secarse. —*vt* secar; desaguar; (wipe) enjugar. **to dry one's tears,** enjugarse las lágrimas; *Fig.* secarse las lágrimas. **to dry up,** secarse; (of persons) acecinarse; (with old age) apergaminarse; (of ideas, etc.) agotarse; (be quiet) callarse

dry /draɪ/ *a* seco; árido; estéril; (thirsty) sediento; (of wine) seco; (U.S.A.) prohibicionista; (squeezed) exprimido; (of toast) sin mantequilla; (*Fig.* chilly) aburrido; (sarcastic) sarcástico; (of humour) agudo. **on dry land,** en seco. **dry battery,** pila seca, *f.* **to dry-clean,** lavar al seco. **dry-cleaner,** tintorero (-ra). **dry-cleaning,** lavado al seco, *m.* **dry-cleaning shop,** tintorería, *f.* **dry goods,** lencería, *f.* **dry land,** tierra firme, *f.* **dry measure,** medida para áridos, *f.* **dry-nurse,** ama seca, *f.* **dry-point,** punta seca, *f.* **dry-rot,** carcoma, *f.* **dry-shod,** con los pies secos

drying /'draɪɪŋ/ *n* secamiento, *m*; desecación, *f* a secante; seco; para secar. **d. ground,** tendedero, *m.* **d. machine,** secadora, *f*; (for the hair) secadora de cabello, *f.* **d. room,** secadero, *m*

dual /'duəl/ *a* doble; *Gram.* dual. **d. control,** mandos gemelos, *m pl.* **d. personality,** conciencia doble, *f*

dub /dʌb/ *vt* (a knight) armar caballero; (call) apellidar; (nickname) motejar, apodar

dubbing /'dʌbɪŋ/ *n* (of films) doblaje, *m*

dubious /'dubiəs/ *a* dudoso, incierto; indeciso; problemático; ambiguo

dubiousness /'dubiəsnɪs/ *n* carácter dudoso, *m*; incertidumbre, *f*; ambigüedad, *f*

duck /dʌk/ *n* pato (-ta), ánade, *mf*; *Sports.* cero, *m*; (darling) vida mía, querida, *f*; (jerk) agachada, *f*; (under the water) chapuz, *m*; (material) dril, *m*; *Mil.* auto anfibio, *m*; *pl* **ducks,** pantalones de dril, *m pl.* —*vi* agacharse; (under water) chapuzarse. —*vt* zabullir, sumergir; bajar, inclinar

ducking /'dʌkɪŋ/ *n* chapuz, *m.* **d.-stool,** silla de chapuzar, *f*

duckling /'dʌklɪŋ/ *n* anadino (-na)

duct /dʌkt/ *n* conducto, canal, *m*; *Bot.* tubo, *m*

ductless /'dʌktlɪs/ *a* sin tubos

due /du/ *a* debido; (payable) pagadero; (fallen due) vencido; (fitting) propio; (expected) esperado. —*n* impuesto, *m*; derecho, *m.* **in due form,** en regla. **in its due time,** a su tiempo debido. **to fall**

due, vencerse. **due bill,** *Com.* abonaré, *m.* **due west,** poniente derecho, *m*

duel /'duəl/ *n* duelo, lance de honor, *m*; *Fig.* lucha, *f.* **to fight a d.,** batirse en duelo

duelist /'duəlɪst/ *n* duelista, *m*

duet /du'ɛt/ *n* dúo, *m*

duffer /'dʌfər/ *n* estúpido (-da); ganso, *m*; (at games, etc.) maleta, *m*

dug /dʌg/ *n* teta, *f*

dugout /'dʌg,aut/ *n* trinchera, *f*

duke /duk/ *n* duque, *m*

dull /dʌl/ *a* (stupid) lerdo, estúpido, obtuso; (boring, tedious) aburrido; (of pain, sounds) sordo; (of colors and eyes) apagado; (of light, beams, etc.) sombrío; (not polished) mate; (pale) pálido; (insipid) insípido, insulso; (of people) soso, poco interesante; (dreary, sad) triste; (gray) gris; (of mirrors, etc.) empañado; (of weather) anublado; (of hearing) duro; (slow) lento; lánguido; insensible; (blunt) romo; *Com.* encalmado, inactivo. **to find life d.,** encontrar la vida aburrida. **d. pain,** dolor sordo, *m.* **d. season,** temporada de calma, *f.* **d.-eyed,** con ojos apagados. **d.-witted,** lerdo

dull /dʌl/ *vt* (make stupid) entontecer; (lessen) mitigar; (weaken) debilitar; (pain) calmar, aliviar; (sadden) entristecer; (blunt) embotar; (spoil) estropear; (a mirror, etc.) empañar; (a polished surface) hacer mate, deslustrar; (of enthusiasm, etc.) enfriar; (tire) fatigar; (obstruct) impedir

dullness /'dʌlnɪs/ *n* (stupidity) estupidez, *f*; (boredom) aburrimiento, *m*; (heaviness) pesadez, *f*; (drowsiness) somnolencia, *f*; (insipidity) insipidez, insulsez, *f*; (of literary style) prosaísmo, *m*; (of persons) sosería, *f*; (of a surface) deslustre, *m*; (laziness) pereza, languidez, *f*; (slowness) lentitud, *f*; (tiredness) cansancio, *m*; (sadness) tristeza, *f*; (bluntness) embotamiento, *m*; (of hearing) dureza, *f*; *Com.* desanimación, *f*

dully /'dʌli/ *adv* (stupidly) estúpidamente; sin comprender; (insipidly) insípidamente; (not brightly) sin brillo; (slowly) lentamente; (sadly) tristemente; (tiredly) con cansancio; (of sound) sordamente

duly /'duli/ *adv* debidamente; puntualmente

dumb /dʌm/ *a* mudo; callado; silencioso; *Inf.* tonto, estúpido. **to become d.,** enmudecer. **to strike d.,** dejar sin habla. **d.-bell,** barra con pesas, *f.* **d. show,** pantomima, *f.* **d. waiter,** bufete, *m*

dumbfound /dʌm'faund/ *vt* dejar sin habla; confundir; pasmar

dumbness /'dʌmnɪs/ *n* mudez, *f*, mutismo, *m*; silencio, *m*

dummy /'dʌmi/ *n* (tailor's, etc.) maniquí, *m*; (puppet) títere, *m*; cabeza para pelucas, *f*; (figurehead) hombre de paja, testaferro, *m*; (baby's) chupador, *m*; (at cards) el muerto. —*a* fingido. **to be d.,** (at cards) ser el muerto

dump /dʌmp/ n depósito, m; vaciadero, m. —vt depositar; (goods on a market) inundar (con)

dumping /'dʌmpɪŋ/ n depósito, m; vaciamiento, m; (of goods on a market) inundación, f. **"D. prohibited,"** «Se prohibe arrojar la basura»

dumps /dʌmps/ n murria, f

dun /dʌn/ vt apremiar, importunar

dunce /dʌns/ n asno, bobo, zoquete, m. **dunce's cap,** coroza, f

dun-colored /'dʌn,kʌlərd/ a pardo

dune /dun/ n duna, f

dung /dʌŋ/ n estiércol, m; (of rabbits, mice, deer, sheep, goats) cagarruta, f; (of cows) boñiga, f; (of hens) gallinaza, f. **d.-cart,** carro de basura, m

dungarees /,dʌŋgə'riz/ n mono, m, pantalones-vaquero, m pl

dungeon /'dʌndʒən/ n mazmorra, f, calabozo, m

dupe /dup/ n víctima, f; tonto (-ta). —vt embelecar, engañar. **to be a d.,** Inf hacer el primo

duplicate /a, n 'duplɪkɪt, 'dyu-; v -,keɪt/ a duplicado, doble. —n duplicado, m, copia, f. —vt duplicar

durability /,durə'bɪlɪti/ n duración, f. **This is a cloth of great d.,** Este es un paño que dura mucho, Este es un paño muy duradero

durable /'durəbəl/ a duradero

duration /du'reiʃən/ n duración, f

duress /du'rɛs/ n compulsión, f; (prison) prisión, f

during /'durɪŋ/ prep durante

dusk /dʌsk/ n atardecer, anochecer, m; (twilight) crepúsculo, m; (darkness) oscuridad, f. **at d.,** al atardecer, a la caída de la tarde

dusky /'dʌski/ a (swarthy) moreno; (black) negro; (dim, dark) oscuro; (of colors) sucio

dust /dʌst/ n polvo, m; (cloud of dust) polvareda, f; (ashes) cenizas, f pl; (of coal) cisco, m; (sweepings) barreduras, f pl; (of grain) tamo, m. —vt desempolvar, quitar (or sacudir) el polvo de; (cover with dust) polvorear; (scatter) salpicar; (sweep) barrer; (clean) limpiar. **d.-bin,** basurero, m. **d.-cart,** carro de la basura, m. **d. cloud,** polvareda, f. **d. jacket,** (books) sobrecubierta, f. **d.-pan,** recogedor de basura, m. **d.-sheet,** guardapolvo, m. **d. storm,** vendaval de polvo, m

duster /'dʌstər/ n el, m, que quita el polvo; paño (para quitar el polvo), m; (of feathers) plumero, m

dustiness /'dʌstɪnɪs/ n empolvoramiento, m; estado polvoriento, m

dusting /'dʌstɪŋ/ n limpieza, f; (sweeping) barreduras, f; (powder) polvos antisépticos, m pl

dusty /'dʌsti/ a polvoriento, polvoroso, empolvado; del color del polvo; (of colours) sucio. **It is very d.,** Hay mucho polvo. **to get d.,** llenarse (or cubrirse) de polvo

Dutch /dʌtʃ/ a holandés. **the D.,** los holandeses. **double D.,** griego, galimatías, m. **D. cheese,** queso de bola, m. **D. courage,** coraje falso, m. **D. woman,** holandesa, f

Dutchman /'dʌtʃmən/ n holandés, m

dutiable /'dutiəbəl/ a sujeto a derechos de aduana

dutiful /'dutəfəl/ a que cumple con sus deberes; obediente, sumiso; respetuoso; excelente, muy bueno

dutifully /'dutəfəli/ adv obedientemente; respetuosamente

duty /'duti/ n deber, m; obligación, f; (greetings) respetos, m pl; (charge, burden) carga, f; (tax) derecho, impuesto, m; Mil. servicio, m; (guard) guardia, f. **off d.,** libre. **on d.,** de servicio. **to be on sentry d.,** estar de guardia. **to do d. as,** servir como. **to do one's d.,** hacer (or cumplir con) su deber. **to pay d. on,** pagar derechos de aduana sobre. **d.-free,** franco de derechos

dwarf /dwɔrf/ a enano. —n enano (-na). —vt impedir el crecimiento de; empequeñecer

dwell /dwɛl/ vi vivir, habitar; (with on, upon) (think about) meditar sobre, pensar en; (deal with) tratar de; hablar largamente de; (insist on) insistir en; apoyarse en, hacer hincapié en; (pause over) detenerse en

dweller /'dwɛlər/ n habitante, mf; (more poetic) morador (-ra)

dwelling /'dwɛlɪŋ/ n vivienda, f; (abode) morada, habitación, f; residencia, f; casa, f; (domicile) domicilio, m. **d.-house,** casa, f

dwindle /'dwɪndl/ vi disminuirse; consumirse; (decay) decaer; (degenerate) degenerar. **to d. to,** reducirse a

dwindling /'dwɪndlɪŋ/ n disminución, f

dye /dai/ vt teñir, colorar. —vi teñirse. —n tinte, m; (colour) color, m. **fast dye,** tinte estable, m. **dye-house,** tintorería, f. **dye-stuff,** materia colorante, f. **dye-works,** tintorería, f

dyed-in-the-wool /'daid ən ðə 'wul/ a de pies a cabeza

dyeing /'daiɪŋ/ n teñidura, tintura, f; (as a trade) tintorería, f. **d. and dry-cleaning shop,** tintorería, f

dyer /'daiər/ n tintorero (-ra)

dyestuff /'dai,stʌf/ n materia colorante, materia de tinte, materia tintórea, f

dying /'daiɪŋ/ a moribundo, agonizante; de la muerte; (of light) mortecino; (last) último; supremo; (languishing) lánguido; (deathbed) hecho en su lecho mortuorio. **to be d.,** estar agonizando; (of light) fenecer. **to be d. for,** estar muerto por

dynamic /dai'næmɪk/ a dinámico

dynamite /'dainə,mait/ n dinamita, f

dynasty /'dainəsti/ n dinastía, f

dysentery /'dɪsən,tɛri/ n disentería, f

dyspepsia /dɪs'pɛpsə/ n dispepsia, f

E

e /i/ *n* (letter) e, *f*; *Mus.* mi, *m*

each /itʃ/ *a* cada (invariable), todo.
—*pron* cada uno, *m*; cada una, *f*. **e. of them,** cada uno de ellos. **They help e. other,** Se ayudan mutuamente, Se ayudan entre sí. **to love e. other,** amarse

eager /'igər/ *a* impaciente; ansioso, deseoso; ambicioso

eagerly /'igərli/ *adv* con impaciencia; con ansia; ambiciosamente

eagerness /'igərnɪs/ *n* impaciencia, *f*; ansia, *f*, deseo, *m*; (promptness) alacridad, *f*; (zeal) fervor, *m*

eagle /'igəl/ *n* águila, *f*. **royal e.,** águila caudal, águila real, *f*. **e.-eyed,** con ojos de lince, de ojo avizor. **have the eyes of an e.,** tener ojos de lince, tener vista de lince

ear /ɪər/ *n* (outer ear) oreja, *f*; (inner ear and sense of hearing) oído, *m*; *Bot.* espiga, panoja, *f*. **to begin to show the ear,** (grain) espigar. **to be all ears,** ser todo oídos. **to give ear,** dar oído. **to have a good ear,** tener buen oído. **to play by ear,** tocar de oído. **to turn a deaf ear,** hacerse el sordo. **ear-ache,** dolor de oídos, *m*. **ear-drum,** tímpano (del oído), *m*. **ear-flap,** orejera, *f*. **ear-phone,** **ear-piece,** auricular, *m*. **ear-piercing,** penetrante, agudo. **ear-shot,** alcance del oído, *m*. **to be within ear-shot,** estar al alcance del oído. **ear-trumpet,** trompetilla, *f*. **ear wax,** cerilla, *f*

earl /ɜrl/ *n* conde, *m*

earliness /'ɜrlinɪs/ *n* lo temprano; antigüedad, *f*; lo primitivo; (precocity) precocidad, *f*. **The e. of his arrival,** Su llegada de buena hora

early /'ɜrli/ *a* temprano; primitivo; (of fruit, etc.) temprano, adelantado; (movement) primero (e.g. *early Romanticism*, el primer romanticismo); (person) de la primera época (e.g. *the early Cervantes,* Cervantes de la primera época); (work) un primer (e.g. *an early work of Unamuno's,* una primera obra de Unamuno); (advanced) avanzado; (precocious) precoz; (first, of time) primero; (in the morning) matutino; (near) próximo, cercano; (premature) prematuro; (of child's age) tierno; joven. **in the e. hours,** en las primeras horas; en las altas horas (de la noche). **e. age,** edad temprana, tierna edad, *f*. **e.-fruiting,** *Agr.* tempranal. **e. riser,** madrugador (-ra). **e.-rising,** *a* madrugador. **e. years,** primeros años, años de la niñez, *m pl*

early /'ɜrli/ *adv* temprano; al principio (de); en los primeros días (de); desde los primeros días (de); (in the month, year) a principios (de); (in time) a tiempo; (in the day) de buena hora; (soon) pronto; (among the first) entre los primeros (de). **as e. as possible,** lo más temprano posible; lo más pronto posible. **to be e.,** llegar antes de tiempo; llegar de buena hora. **to get up e.,** madrugar. **to go to bed e.,** acostarse temprano. **too e.,** demasiado temprano. **e. in the morning,** de madrugada

earmark /'ɪər,mɑrk/ *vt* marcar; *Fig.* destinar, reservar

earn /ɜrn/ *vt* ganar; obtener, adquirir; (deserve) merecer

earnest /'ɜrnɪst/ *a* serio; fervoroso; diligente; sincero. **to be in e. about something,** tomarlo en serio; ser sincero (en). **e. money,** arras, *f pl*

earnestly /'ɜrnɪstli/ *adv* seriamente; fervorosamente; con diligencia; sinceramente, de buena fe

earnings /'ɜrnɪŋz/ *n pl Com.* ingresos, *m pl*; (salary) salario, *m*; estipendio, *m*; (of a workman) jornal, *m*

earring /'ɪər,rɪŋ/ *n* pendiente, arete, *m*

earth /ɜrθ/ *n* tierra, *f*; (of a badger, etc.) madriguera, *f*; *Radio.* tierra, *f*. —*vt* cubrir con tierra; *Radio.* conectar con tierra. **clod of e.,** terrón, *m*. **half the e.,** *Inf.* medio mundo, *m*. **on e.,** en este mundo, sobre la tierra

earthen /'ɜrθən/ *a* terrizo, terroso; (of mud) de barro

earthenware /'ɜrθən,wɛər/ *n* alfar, *m*, —*a* de loza, de barro

earthiness /'ɜrθinɪs/ *n* terrosidad, *f*

earthly /'ɜrθli/ *a* terrestre, terrenal; de la tierra; (fleshly) carnal; (worldly) mundano; material. **There is not an e. chance,** No hay la más mínima posibilidad

earthquake /'ɜrθ,kweik/ *n* terremoto, temblor de tierra, *m*

earthy /'ɜrθi/ *a* térreo, terroso

ease /iz/ *n* bienestar, *m*; tranquilidad, *f*; descanso, *m*; (leisure) ocio, *m*; (comfortableness) comodidad, *f*; (freedom from embarrassment) naturalidad, *f*, desembarazo, desenfado, *m*; (from pain) alivio, *m*; (simplicity) facilidad, *f*. —*vt* (widen) ensanchar; aflojar; (pain) aliviar; (lighten) aligerar; (moderate) moderar; (soften) suavizar; (free) librar; (one's mind) tranquilizar. **in my moments of e.,** en mis ocios, en mis momentos de ocio. **Stand at e.!** *Mil.* ¡En su lugar descansen! **to be at e.,** estar a sus anchas; encontrarse bien; comportarse con toda naturalidad. **with e.,** fácilmente. **to e. off,** *vt* (*Naut.* cables, sails) arriar. —*vi* sentirse menos, cesar

easel /'izəl/ *n* caballete (de pintor) *m*

east /ist/ *n* este, *m*; oriente, *m*, (of countries) Oriente, *m*; Levante, *m*. —*a* del este; del oriente; (of countries) de Oriente, oriental; levantino. **e. North e.,** estenordeste, *m*. **e. South e.,** estesudeste, *m*. **e. wind,** viento del este, *m*

Easter /'istər/ *n* Pascua de Resurrección, *f*. **E. egg,** huevo de Pascua, *m*. **E. Saturday,** sábado de gloria, *m*. **E. Sunday,** domingo de Pascua, *m*

eastern /'istərn/ *a* del este; de Oriente; oriental. —*n* oriental, *mf*

eastward /'istwərd/ *adv* hacia el este, hacia oriente

easy /'izi/ *a* fácil; sencillo; (comfortable) cómodo; (free from pain) aliviado; *Com.* flojo; (well-off) acomodado, holgado; (calm) tranquilo; tolerante; natural; afable, condescendiente; (of virtue, women) fácil. —*adv* con calma; despacio. **I must make myself e. about,** he de tranquilizarme sobre. **Stand e.!** ¡En su lugar descansen! **to take it e.,** tomarlo con calma. **e.-chair,** (silla) poltrona, *f.* **easy come, easy go,** lo que por agua, agua (Mexico and Colombia), los dineros del sacristán cantando vienen y cantando se van (Spain). **e.-going,** acomodadizo; indolente; (morally) de manga ancha; (casual) descuidado

eat /it/ *vt* comer; (meals, soup, refreshments) tomar; (with a good, bad appetite) hacer; consumir; (corrode) corroer; desgastar. —*vi* comer; (*Fam.* of food) ser de buen (or mal) comer. **to eat one's breakfast (lunch),** tomar el desayuno, desayunar (almorzar). **to eat one's words,** retractarse. **to eat away,** comer; consumir; corroer. **to eat into,** (of chemicals) morder; (a fortune) consumir; gastar. **eat out of s.b.'s hand,** comer de la mano de fulano, comer en la mano de fulano. **to eat up,** devorar (also *Fig.*)

eating /'itɪŋ/ *n* el comer; comida, *f.* **e. and drinking,** el comer y beber. **e.-house,** casa de comidas, *f*

eau de cologne /'ou də kə'loun/ *n* agua de Colonia, *f*

eaves /ivz/ *n* rafe, alero, *m.* **under the e.,** debajo del alero

eavesdrop /'ivz,drɒp/ *vi* escuchar a las puertas; fisgonear, espiar

eavesdropper /'ivz,drɒpər/ *n* fisgón (-ona)

ebb /eb/ *n* (of the tide) reflujo, *m*; menguante, *f*; *Fig.* declinación, *f*; *Fig.* decadencia, *f*; (of life) vejez, *f.* —*vi* (of tide) menguar; declinar; decaer. **to ebb and flow,** fluir y refluir. **to ebb away from,** dejar; dejar aislado. **ebb-tide,** marea menguante, *f*

ebony /'ebəni/ *n* ébano, *m*

ebullient /ɪ'bʌlyənt/ *a* efervescente, exuberante

eccentric /ɪk'sɛntrɪk/ *a Geom.* excéntrico; raro, original; extravagante, excéntrico. —*n* persona excéntrica, *f*, original, *m*

eccentricity /,ɛksən'trɪsɪti/ *n Geom.* excentricidad, *f*; rareza, extravagancia, excentricidad, *f*

echo /'ɛkou/ *n* eco, *m*; reverberación, resonancia, *f.* —*vt* repercutir; *Fig.* repetir. —*vi* resonar, retumbar, reverberar

eclectic /ɪ'klɛktɪk/ *a* and *n* ecléctico (-ca)

eclipse /ɪ'klɪps/ *n Astron.* eclipse, *m*, *vt* eclipsar, hacer eclipse a. **to be in e.,** estar en eclipse

economic /,ɛkə'nɒmɪk, ,ikə-/ *a* económico

economical /,ɛkə'nɒmɪkəl, ,ikə-/ *a* económico

economics /,ɛkə'nɒmɪks, ,ikə-/ *n* economía política, *f*

economist /ɪ'kɒnəmɪst/ *n* economista, *mf*

economize /ɪ'kɒnə,maiz/ *vt* economizar, ahorrar. —*vi* hacer economías

economy /ɪ'kɒnəmi/ *n* economía, *f.* **domestic e.,** economía doméstica, *f.* **political e.,** economía política, *f*

ecstasy /'ɛkstəsi/ *n* éxtasis, arrebato, *m*; transporte, *m.* **to be in e.,** estar en éxtasis

ecstatic /ɛk'stætɪk/ *a* extático

Ecuador /'ɛkwə,dɔr/ el Ecuador

Ecuadorian /,ɛkwə'dɔriən/ *a* and *n* ecuatoriano (-na)

ecumenical /'ɛkyu'mɛnɪkəl/ *a* ecuménico

eczema /'ɛksəmə/ *n* eczema, *f*

eddy /'ɛdi/ *n* remolino, *m*, *vi* remolinar; *Fig.* remolinear

edema /ɪ'dimə/ *n Med.* edema, *m*

edge /ɛdʒ/ *n* (of sharp instruments) filo, *m*; (of a skate) cuchilla, *f*; margen, *mf*; (shore) orilla, *f*; (of two surfaces) arista, *f*; (of books) borde, *m*, (of a coin) canto, *m*; (of a chair, a precipice, a forest, a curb, etc.) borde, *m*; (extreme) extremidad, *f.* **on e.,** de canto; *Fig.* ansioso. **to be on e.,** *Fig.* tener los nervios en punta. **to set on e.,** poner de canto; (of teeth) dar dentera

edge /ɛdʒ/ *vt* (sharpen) afilar; *Sew.* ribetear; orlar; poner un borde (a); (cut) cortar. **to e. away,** escurrirse. **to e. into,** *vt* insinuarse. —*vi* deslizarse en. **to e. out,** salir poco a poco

edged /ɛdʒd/ *a* afilado, cortante; (in compounds) de... filos; (bordered) bordeado; (of books) de bordes...

edgeways /'ɛdʒweiz/ *adv* de lado; de canto. **He couldn't get a word in e.,** No pudo meter baza en la conversación

edging /'ɛdʒɪŋ/ *n* borde, *m*; ribete, *m*

edible /'ɛdəbəl/ *a* comestible

edict /'idɪkt/ *n* edicto, *m*

edifice /'ɛdəfɪs/ *n* edificio, *m*

edify /'ɛdə,fai/ *vt* edificar

edifying /'ɛdə,faiɪŋ/ *a* edificante, edificador, de edificación

edit /'ɛdɪt/ *vt* editar; (a newspaper, journal) ser director de; (prepare for press) redactar; (correct) corregir

edition /ɪ'dɪʃən/ *n* edición, *f*; *Print.* tirada, *f.* **first e.,** edición príncipe, *f.* **miniature e.,** edición diamante, *f*

editor /'ɛdɪtər/ *n* (of a book) editor (-ra); (of a newspaper, journal) director (-ra)

editorial /,ɛdɪ'tɔriəl/ *a* de redacción; editorial. —*n* editorial, artículo de fondo, *m.* **e. staff,** redacción, *f*

educate /'ɛdʒʊ,keit/ *vt* educar; formar; (accustom) acostumbrar

educated /'ɛdʒʊ,keitɪd/ *a* culto

education /ˌedʒʊ'keiʃən/ n educación, f; enseñanza, f; pedagogía, f. **chair of e.**, cátedra de pedagogía, f. **early e.**, primeras letras, f pl. **higher e.**, enseñanza superior, f

educational /ˌedʒʊ'keiʃənl/ a educativo; pedagógico; instructivo

educationalist /ˌedʒə'keiʃənlɪst/ n pedagogo, m

educator /'edʒʊˌkeitər/ n educador (-ra)

educe /ɪ'dus/ vt educir; deducir; Chem. extraer

eduction /ɪ'dʌkʃən/ n educción, f

eel /il/ n anguila, f. **electric eel**, gimnoto, m. **eel-basket**, nasa para anguilas, f

eerie /'ɪəri/ a misterioso, fantástico; sobrenatural; lúgubre

efface /ɪ'feis/ vt borrar, destruir; quitar. **to e. oneself**, retirarse; permanecer en el fondo

effect /ɪ'fɛkt/ n efecto, m; impresión, f; (result) resultado, m, consecuencia, f, (meaning) substancia, f, significado, m; pl **effects**, efectos, bienes, m pl. —vt efectuar; producir. **in e.**, en efecto, efectivamente. **of no e.**, inútil. **striking after e.**, efectismo, m. **to feel the effects of**, sentir los efectos de; padecer las consecuencias de. **to put into e.**, poner en práctica; hacer efectivo. **to take e.**, producir efecto; ponerse en vigor

effective /ɪ'fɛktɪv/ a eficaz; (striking) de mucho efecto, poderoso, vistoso. **to make e.**, llevar a efecto

effectively /ɪ'fɛktɪvli/ adv eficazmente; (strikingly) con gran efecto; efectivamente, en efecto

effectiveness /ɪ'fɛktɪvnɪs/ n eficacia, f; efecto, m

effectuate /ɪ'fɛktʃuˌeit/ vt efectuar

effeminate /ɪ'fɛmənɪt/ a afeminado, adamado. **to make e.**, afeminar

effervesce /ˌɛfər'vɛs/ vi estar efervescente, hervir

effervescence /ˌɛfər'vɛsəns/ n efervescencia, f

effervescent /ˌɛfər'vɛsənt/ a efervescente

effete /ɪ'fit/ a gastado; estéril; decadente

efficacious /ˌɛfɪ'keiʃəs/ a eficaz

efficacy /'ɛfɪkəsi/ n eficacia, f

efficiency /ɪ'fɪʃənsi/ n eficiencia, f; buen estado, m; habilidad, f; Mech. rendimiento, m

efficient /ɪ'fɪʃənt/ a (e.g. medicine) eficaz; eficiente; (person) competente, capaz

effigy /'ɛfɪdʒi/ n efigie, imagen, f

effort /'ɛfərt/ n esfuerzo, m. **to make an e.**, hacer un esfuerzo. **make every effort to**, hacer lo posible por + Inf.; empeñar sus máximos esfuerzos en el sentido de + Inf.

effortless /'ɛfərtlɪs/ a sin esfuerzo

effrontery /ɪ'frʌntəri/ n descaro, m, insolencia, f

effulgent /ɪ'fʌldʒənt/ a fulgente, resplandeciente

effusive /ɪ'fyusɪv/ a efusivo, expansivo

egg /ɛg/ n huevo, m. **to egg on**, incitar (a). **boiled egg**, huevo cocido, m. **fried egg**, huevo frito, m. **hard egg**, huevo duro, m. **poached egg**, huevo escalfado, m. **scrambled egg**, huevos revueltos, m pl. **soft egg**, huevo pasado por agua, m. **to lay eggs**, poner huevos. **to put all one's eggs in one basket**, Fig. poner toda la carne en el asador. **egg-cup**, huevera, f. **egg dealer**, vendedor (-ra) de huevos. **egg flip**, huevo batido con ron, m. **eggplant**, berenjena, f. **egg-shaped**, aovado. **egg-shell**, cascarón, m, cáscara de huevo, f. **egg-shell china**, loza muy fina, f. **egg-spoon**, cucharita para comer huevos, f. **egg-whisk**, batidor de huevos, m

ego /'igou/ n yo

egoism /'igouˌizəm/ n egoísmo, m

egoist /'igouɪst/ n egoísta, mf

egoistic /ˌigou'ɪstɪk/ a egoísta

egregious /ɪ'gridʒəs/ a notorio

egress /'igrɛs/ n salida, f

Egypt /'idʒɪpt/ Egipto, m

Egyptian /ɪ'dʒɪpʃən/ a egipcio. —n egipcio (-ia); cigarrillo egipcio, m

eh? /ei/ interj ¿eh? ¿qué?

eiderdown /'aidərˌdaun/ edredón, m

eight /eit/ a and n ocho m. **He is e. years old**, Tiene ocho años. **It is e. o'clock**, Son las ocho. **e.-day clock**, reloj con cuerda para ocho días, m. **e. hundred**, a and n ochocientos m.. **e.-syllabled**, octosilábico

eighteen /'ei'tin/ a and n diez y ocho, m.

eighteenth /'ei'tinθ/ a décimoctavo; (of the month) (el) diez y ocho, dieciocho; (of monarchs) diez y ocho. —n décimoctava parte, f. **Louis the E.**, Luis diez y ocho

eighth /eitθ/ a and n octavo, m; (of the month) (el) ocho; (of monarchs) octavo. —n octavo, m

eightieth /'eitiθ/ a octogésimo

eighty /'eiti/ a and n ochenta, m.

either /'iðər/ a and pron uno u otro, cualquiera de los dos; ambos (-as). —conjunc o (becomes u before words beginning with o or ho). —adv tampoco. **I do not like e.**, No me gusta ni el uno ni el otro (ni la una ni la otra). **e.... or**, o... o

ejaculate /ɪ'dʒækyəˌleit/ vt exclamar, lanzar; Med. eyacular

ejaculation /ɪˌdʒækyə'leiʃən/ n exclamación, f; Med. eyaculación, f

ejaculatory /ɪ'dʒækyələˌtori/ a jaculatorio

eject /ɪ'dʒɛkt/ vt echar, expulsar; Law. desahuciar; (emit) despedir, emitir

ejection /ɪ'dʒɛkʃən/ n echamiento, m, expulsión, f; Law. desahúcio, m; (emission) emisión, f

eke /ik/ (out) vt aumentar, añadir a

elaborate /a ɪ'læbərɪt; v -əˌreit/ a elaborado; primoroso; elegante; complicado; (detailed) detallado; (of meals) de muchos platos; (of courtesy, etc.) estudiado. —*vt* elaborar; amplificar

elaborately /ɪ'læbərɪtli/ *adv* primorosamente; elegantemente; complicadamente; con muchos detalles

elaboration /ɪ,læbə'reiʃən/ *n* elaboración, *f*

elapse /ɪ'læps/ *vi* transcurrir, andar, pasar

elastic /ɪ'læstɪk/ *a* elástico. —*n* elástico, *m*. **e. band,** anillo de goma, *m*; cinta de goma, *f*. **e. girdle,** faja elástica, *f*

elate /ɪ'leit/ *vt* alegrar; animar

elation /ɪ'leiʃən/ *n* alegría, *f*, júbilo, *m*; triunfo, *m*

elbow /'elbou/ *n* codo, *m*; ángulo, *m*; (of a chair) brazo, *m*. —*vt* codear, dar codazos (a). **at one's e.,** a la mano. **nudge with the e.,** codazo, *m*. **to be out at e.,** enseñar los codos, tener los codos raídos; ser harapiento. **to e. one's way,** abrirse paso a codazos. **e.-chair,** silla de brazos, *f*. **e. grease,** jugo de muñeca, *m*. **e.-piece** or **patch,** codera, *f*. **e. room,** libertad de movimiento, *f*

elder /'eldər/ *a compar* mayor. —*n* persona mayor, *f*; señor mayor, *m*; (among Jews and in early Christian Church) anciano, *m*; *Bot.* saúco, *m*

elderly /'eldərli/ *a* mayor

eldest /'eldɪst/ *a superl* old (el, la, etc.) mayor. **e. daughter,** hija mayor, *f*. **e. son,** hijo mayor, *m*

elect /ɪ'lekt/ *vt* elegir. —*a* elegido; predestinado. —*n* electo, *m*, elegido, *m*

election /ɪ'lekʃən/ *n Theol.* predestinación, *f*; elección, *f*. **by-e.,** elección parcial, *f*

electioneer /ɪ,lekʃə'nɪər/ *vi* solicitar votos; distribuir propaganda electoral

electioneering /ɪ,lekʃə'nɪərɪŋ/ *n* solicitación de votos, *f*; propaganda electoral, *f*

elective /ɪ'lektɪv/ *a* electivo. —*n* (subject at school) materia optativa, *f*

elector /ɪ'lektər/ *n* elector (-ra); (prince) elector, *m*

electoral /ɪ'lektərəl/ *a* electoral. **e. register,** lista electoral, *f*

electoral college colegio de compromisarios, *m*

electorate /ɪ'lektərɪt/ *n* electorado, *m*

electrician /ɪlek'trɪʃən/ *n* electricista, *mf*

electricity /ɪlek'trɪsɪti/ *n* electricidad, *f*

electrify /ɪ'lektrə,fai/ *vt* electrificar; *Fig.* electrizar

electro- *prefix* (in compounds) electro. **e.-chemistry,** electroquímica, *f*. **e.-dynamics,** electrodinámica, *f*. **e.-magnet,** electroimán, *m*. **e.-magnetic,** electromagnético. **e.-plate,** *vt* galvanizar, platear. —*n* artículo galvanizado, *m*. **e.-therapy,** electroterapia, *f*

electrocute /ɪ'lektrə,kyut/ *vt* electrocutar

electrocution /ɪ,lektrə'kyuʃən/ *n* electrocución, *f*

electrolysis /ɪlek'trɒləsɪs/ *n* electrólisis, *f*

electron /ɪ'lektrɒn/ *n* electrón, *m*

elegance /'eləgəns/ *n* elegancia, *f*

elegant /'eləgənt/ *a* elegante; bello

elegy /'elɪdʒi/ *n* elegía, *f*

element /'eləmənt/ *n* elemento, *m*; factor, *m*; ingrediente, *m*; *Elec.* par, elemento, *m*; *Chem. Phys.* cuerpo simple, *m*; *pl* **elements,** rudimentos, *m pl*, nociones, *f pl*; (weather) intemperie, *f*; (Eucharist) el pan y el vino. **to be in one's e.,** estar en su elemento

elemental /,elə'mentl/ *a* elemental; rudimentario, lo elemental

elementary /,elə'mentəri/ *a* elemental; rudimentario; primario. **e. education,** enseñanza primaria, *f*

elephant /'eləfənt/ *n* elefante (-ta). **e. keeper** or **trainer,** naire, *m*

elevate /'elə,veit/ *vt* (the Host) alzar; elevar; (the eyes, the voice) levantar; (honor) enaltecer

elevated /'elə,veitɪd/ *a* noble, elevado, sublime; edificante; (drunk) achispado

elevation /,elə'veiʃən/ *n* elevación, *f*; enaltecimiento, *m*; (of style, thought) nobleza, sublimidad, *f*; (hill) eminencia, altura, *f*

elevator /'elə,veitər/ *n* (lift) ascensor, *m*; (for grain, etc.) transportador, *m*

elevator shaft caja, *f*, hueco pozo, *m*

eleven /ɪ'levən/ *a* once. —*n* once, *m*. **It is e. o'clock,** Son las once

eleventh /ɪ'levənθ/ *a* onceno, undécimo; (of month) (el) once; (of monarchs) once. —*n* onzavo, *m*; undécima parte, *f*. **at the e. hour,** *Fig.* a última hora. **Louis the E.,** Luis once (XI)

elf /elf/ *n* elfo, duende, *m*; (child) trasgo, *m*; (dwarf) enano, *m*

elicit /ɪ'lɪsɪt/ *vt* sacar; hacer contestar; hacer confesar; descubrir

elicitation /ɪ,lɪsɪ'teiʃən/ *n* descubrimiento, *m*

elide /ɪ'laid/ *vt* elidir

eligibility /,elɪdʒə'bɪlɪti/ *n* elegibilidad, *f*

eligible /'elɪdʒəbəl/ *a* elegible; deseable

eliminate /ɪ'lɪmə,neit/ *vt* eliminar; quitar

elimination /ɪ,lɪmə'neiʃən/ *n* eliminación, *f*

eliminatory /ɪ'lɪmənə,tɔri/ *a* eliminador

elite /ɪ'lit/ *n* nata, flor, *f*

elk /elk/ *n* ante, *m*

ellipse /ɪ'lɪps/ *n Geom.* elipse, *f*; óvalo, *m*

elm /elm/ *n* olmo, *m*. **e. grove,** olmeda, *f*

elocution /,elə'kyuʃən/ *n* elocución, *f*; (art of elocution) declamación, *f*

elongate /ɪ'lɒŋgeit/ *vt* alargar; extender. —*vi* alargarse; extenderse. —*a* alargado; (of face) perfilado

elongation /ɪlɒŋ'geiʃən/ *n* alargamiento, *m*; prolongación, *f*; extensión, *f*

elope /ɪ'loup/ *vi* evadirse, huir; fugarse (con un amante)

elopement /ɪ'loupmənt/ *n* fuga, *f*

eloquence /'eləkwəns/ *n* elocuencia, *f*

eloquent /'eləkwənt/ *a* elocuente

else /els/ *adv* (besides) más; (instead)

otra cosa, más; (otherwise) si no, de otro modo. **anyone e.,** (cualquier) otra persona; alguien más. **Anything e.?** ¿Algo más? **everyone e.,** todos los demás. **everything e.,** todo lo demás. **nobody e.,** ningún otro, nadie más. **nothing e.,** nada más. **or e.,** o bien, de otro modo; si no. **someone e.,** otra persona, otro. **somewhere e.,** en otra parte. **There's nothing e. to do,** No hay nada más que hacer; No hay más remedio

elsewhere /'ɛls,wɛər/ *adv* a, o en, otra parte

elucidate /ɪ'lusɪ,deɪt/ *vt* elucidar, aclarar

elucidation /ɪ,lusɪ'deɪʃən/ *n* elucidación, aclaración, *f*

elude /ɪ'lud/ *vt* eludir, evitar

elusive /ɪ'lusɪv/ *a* (of persons) esquivo; fugaz; difícil de comprender

emaciate /ɪ'meɪʃi,eɪt/ *vt* extenuar, demacrar, enflaquecer

emaciated /ɪ'meɪʃi,eɪtɪd/ *a* extenuado, demacrado. **to become e.,** demacrarse

emaciation /ɪ,meɪʃi'eɪʃən/ *n* demacración, emaciación, *f*; *Med.* depauperación, *f*

e-mail /'i,meɪl/ *n* correo electrónico, *m*

emanate /'ɛmə,neɪt/ *vi* emanar (de), proceder (de)

emanation /,ɛmə'neɪʃən/ *n* emanación, *f*; exhalación, *f*

emancipate /ɪ'mænsə,peɪt/ *vt* emancipar

emancipation /ɪ,mænsə'peɪʃən/ *n* emancipación, *f*

emasculate /*a* ɪ'mæskyəlɪt; *v* -,leɪt/ *a* afeminado. —*vt* emascular; *Fig.* afeminar; mutilar

embalm /ɛm'bam/ *vt* embalsamar; *Fig.* conservar el recuerdo de; perfumar

embalmer /ɛm'bamər/ *n* embalsamador, *m*

embalmment /ɛm'bammənt/ *n* embalsamamiento, *m*

embankment /ɛm'bæŋkmənt/ *n* declive, *m*; ribera, *f*; terraplén, *m*; dique, *m*; (quay) muelle, *m*

embargo /ɛm'bargou/ *n* embargo, *m*, *vt* embargar. **to put an e. on,** embargar. **to remove an e.,** sacar de embargo

embark /ɛm'bark/ *vi* embarcarse; lanzarse (a). —*vt* embarcar

embarkation /,ɛmbar'keɪʃən/ *n* (of persons) embarcación, *f*; (of goods) embarque, *m*

embarrass /ɛm'bærəs/ *vt* impedir; (financially) apurar; (perplex) tener perplejo; (worry) preocupar; (confuse) desconcertar, turbar; (annoy) molestar

embarrassed /ɛm'bærəst/ *a* turbado

embarrassing /ɛm'bærəsɪŋ/ *a* embarazoso; desconcertante; molesto

embarrassment /ɛm'bærəsmənt/ *n* impedimento, *m*; (financial) apuro, *m*; (obligation) compromiso, *m*; (perplexity) perplejidad, *f*; (worry) preocupación, *f*; (confusion) turbación, *f*

embassy /'ɛmbəsi/ *n* embajada, *f*

embattled /ɛm'bætld/ *a* en orden de batalla; *Herald.* almenado

embed /ɛm'bɛd/ *vt* empotrar, enclavar; fijar

embellish /ɛm'bɛlɪʃ/ *vt* embellecer; adornar

embellishment /ɛm'bɛlɪʃmənt/ *n* embellecimiento, *m*; adorno, *m*

ember /'ɛmbər/ *n* rescoldo, *m*. **E. days,** témporas, *f pl*

embezzle /ɛm'bɛzəl/ *vt* desfalcar

embezzlement /ɛm'bɛzəlmənt/ *n* desfalco, *m*

embezzler /ɛm'bɛzlər/ *n* desfalcador (-ra)

embitter /ɛm'bɪtər/ *vt* *Fig.* amargar; envenenar

emblem /'ɛmbləm/ *n* emblema, *m*

embodiment /ɛm'bodɪmənt/ *n* incarnación, *f*; expresión, *f*; personificación, *f*; símbolo, *m*; síntesis, *f*

embody /ɛm'bodi/ *vt* encarnar; expresar; personificar; incorporar; contener; formular; sintetizar. **to be embodied in,** quedar plasmado en

embolden /ɛm'bouldən/ *vt* animar, dar valor (a)

embolism /'ɛmbə,lɪzəm/ *n* *Med.* embolia, *f*

emboss /ɛm'bɔs/ *vt* repujar, abollonar; estampar en relieve

embrace /ɛm'breɪs/ *n* abrazo, *m*. —*vt* abrazar, dar un abrazo (a); (*Fig..* seize) aprovechar; (accept) aceptar; adoptar; (engage in) dedicarse a; (comprise) incluir, abarcar; (comprehend) comprender. **They embraced,** Se abrazaron

embroider /ɛm'brɔɪdər/ *vt* bordar; embellecer; (a tale, etc.) exagerar; *vi* hacer bordado

embroiderer /ɛm'brɔɪdərər/ *n* bordador (-ra)

embroidery /ɛm'brɔɪdəri, -dri/ *n* bordado, *m*; labor, *f*. **e.-frame,** bastidor, *m*. **e. silk,** hilo de bordar, *m*

embroil /ɛm'brɔɪl/ *vt* enredar, embrollar; desordenar

embryo /'ɛmbri,ou/ *n* embrión, *m*; *Fig.* germen, *m*. —*a* embrionario

emend /ɪ'mɛnd/ *vt* enmendar; corregir

emendation /,imən'deɪʃən/ *n* enmienda, *f*; corrección, *f*

emerald /'ɛmərəld/ *n* esmeralda, *f*, *a* de color de esmeralda. **e. green,** verde esmeralda, *m*

emerge /ɪ'mɜrdʒ/ *vt* emerger; surgir; *Fig.* salir; aparecer

emergence /ɪ'mɜrdʒəns/ *n* emergencia, *f*; salida, *f*; aparición, *f*

emergency /ɪ'mɜrdʒənsi/ *n* urgencia, *f*; necesidad, *f*; emergencia, *f*; aprieto, *m*. **e. exit,** salida de urgencia, *f*. **e. port,** *Naut.* puerto de arribada, *m*

emergent /ɪ'mɜrdʒənt/ *a* emergente; que sale; saliente

emery /'ɛməri/ *n* esmeril, *m*. **to polish with e.,** esmerilar. **e.-paper,** papel de lija, *m*

emetic /ɪ'mɛtɪk/ *a* and *n* emético, vomitivo, *m.*

emigrant /'ɛmɪgrənt/ *a* emigrante. —*n* emigrante, *mf* emigrado, *m*

emigrate /'ɛmɪ,greɪt/ *vi* emigrar; *Inf.* trasladarse

emigration /,ɛmə'greɪʃən/ *n* emigración, *f.* **e. officer,** oficial de emigración, *m*

eminence /'ɛmənəns/ *n* (hill) elevación, prominencia, *f;* eminencia (also as title), *f;* distinción, *f*

eminent /'ɛmənənt/ *a* distinguido, eminente; famoso, ilustre; notable; conspicuo

emissary /'ɛmə,sɛri/ *n* emisario (-ia); embajador (-ra); agente, *m*

emission /ɪ'mɪʃən/ *n* emisión, *f*

emit /ɪ'mɪt/ *vt* despedir; exhalar; emitir

emollient /ɪ'mɒlyənt/ *a* emoliente, lenitivo. —*n* emoliente, *m*

emolument /ɪ'mɒlyəmənt/ *n* emolumento, *m*

emotion /ɪ'moʊʃən/ *n* emoción, *f.* **to cause e.,** emocionar

emotional /ɪ'moʊʃənl/ *a* emocional, sentimental; emocionante

emotionless /ɪ'moʊʃənlɪs/ *a* sin emoción

emotive /ɪ'moʊtɪv/ *a* emotivo

emperor /'ɛmpərər/ *n* emperador, *m*

emphasis (on) /'ɛmfəsɪs/ *n* énfasis (en), *mf;* insistencia especial (en), especial atención (a), *f;* accentuación, *f*

emphasize /'ɛmfə,saɪz/ *vt* subrayar, dar énfasis a, poner de relieve, hacer resaltar, dar importancia a; acentuar; insistir en, hacer hincapié (en)

emphatic /ɛm'fætɪk/ *a* enfático

emphatically /ɛm'fætɪkəli/ *adv* con énfasis

empire /'ɛmpaɪər/ *n* imperio, *m*

empiric /ɛm'pɪrɪk/ *a* empírico

employ /ɛm'plɔɪ/ *n* empleo, *m;* servicio, *m.* —*vt* emplear; ocupar; tomar; servirse de, usar. **How do you e. yourself?** ¿Cómo te ocupas? ¿Cómo pasas el tiempo?

employable /ɛm'plɔɪəbəl/ *a* empleable; utilizable

employee /ɛm'plɔɪi/ *n* empleado (-da)

employer /ɛm'plɔɪər/ *n* el, *m,* (*f,* la) que emplea; dueño (-ña), amo (-a); patrón (-ona)

employment /ɛm'plɔɪmənt/ *n* empleo, *m;* uso, *m;* ocupación, *f;* aprovechamiento, *m;* (post) puesto, cargo, *m;* (situation) colocación, *f.* **e. exchange,** bolsa de trabajo, *f*

emporium /ɛm'pɔriəm/ *n* emporio, *m;* (store) almacén, *m*

empower /ɛm'paʊər/ *vt* autorizar; permitir; ayudar (a); dar el poder (para)

empress /'ɛmprɪs/ *n* emperatriz, *f*

emptiness /'ɛmptɪnɪs/ *n* vaciedad, *f;* futilidad, *f;* vacuidad, *f;* (verbosity) palabrería, *f*

empty /'ɛmpti/ *a* vacío; (of a house, etc.) deshabitado, desocupado; (deserted) desierto; (vain) vano, inútil; frívolo; (hungry) hambriento. —*n* envase vacío, *m.*

—*vt* vaciar; descargar. —*vi* vaciarse; (river, etc.) desembocar, venir a morir en. **e.-handed,** con las manos vacías. **e.-headed,** casquivano

emptying /'ɛmptiɪŋ/ *n* vaciamiento, *m;* abandono, *m; pl* **emptyings,** heces de la cerveza, *f pl*

emu /'imyu/ *n* emu, *m*

emulate /'ɛmyə,leɪt/ *vt* emular

emulation /,ɛmyə'leɪʃən/ *n* emulación, *f*

emulsify /ɪ'mʌlsɪfaɪ/ *vt* emulsionar

emulsion /ɪ'mʌlʃən/ *n* emulsión, *f*

enable /ɛn'eɪbəl/ *vt* (to) hacer capaz (de); ayudar (a); autorizar (para); permitir (de)

enact /ɛn'ækt/ *vt Law.* promulgar; decretar; (a part) hacer, desempeñar (un papel); (a play) representar; (happen) ocurrir, tener lugar

enaction /ɛn'ækʃən/ *n Law.* promulgación, *f*

enamel /ɪ'næməl/ *n* esmalte, *m, vt* esmaltar

enameling /ɪ'næməlɪŋ/ *n* esmaltadura, *f*

enamor /ɪ'næmər/ *vt* enamorar. **to be enamored of,** estar enamorado de; estar aficionado a

encamp /ɛn'kæmp/ *vt* and *vi* acampar

encase /ɛn'keɪs/ *vt* encajar; encerrar; (line) forrar

encasement /ɛn'keɪsmənt/ *n* encaje, *m;* encierro, *m*

encephalitis /ɛn,sɛfə'laɪtɪs/ *n* encefalitis, *f.* **e. lethargica,** encefalitis letárgica, *f*

enchant /ɛn'tʃænt/ *vt* encantar, hechizar; fascinar, embelesar, deleitar

enchanting /ɛn'tʃæntɪŋ/ *a* encantador, fascinador

enchantment /ɛn'tʃæntmənt/ *n* encantamiento, *m,* fascinación, *f,* encanto, deleite, *m*

encircle /ɛn'sɜrkəl/ *vt* cercar; rodear; dar la vuelta (a)

enclose /ɛn'klouz/ *vt* cercar; meter dentro de; encerrar; (with a letter, etc.) incluir, adjuntar

enclosed /ɛn'klouzd/ *a* (of letters) adjunto

enclosure /ɛn'klouʒər/ *n* cercamiento, *m;* cercado, *m;* recinto, *m;* (wall) tapia, cerca, *f;* (with a letter) contenido adjunto, *m*

encomium /ɛn'koumiəm/ *n* encomio, *m*

encompass /ɛn'kʌmpəs/ *vt* cercar, rodear

encore /'ɑŋkɔr/ *n* repetición, *f, interj* ¡bis!

encounter /ɛn'kaʊntər/ *n* encuentro, *m;* combate, *m;* conflicto, *m;* lucha, *f.* —*vt* encontrar; atacar; tropezar con

encourage /ɛn'kɜrɪdʒ/ *vt* animar; alentar; estimular; incitar; ayudar; (approve) aprobar; (foster) fomentar

encouragement /ɛn'kɜrɪdʒmənt/ *n* ánimos, *m pl;* estímulo, incentivo, *m;* ayuda, *f;* (approval) aprobación, *f;* (promotion) fomento, *m*

encourager /ɛn'kɜrɪdʒər/ *n* instigador (-ra); ayudador (-ra); aprobador (-ra); fomentador (-ra)

encouraging /ɛnˈkɔrɪdʒɪŋ/ a alentador; estimulante; fomentador; (favorable) halagüeño, favorable

encroach /ɛnˈkroutʃ/ vi usurpar; abusar (de); invadir; robar; (of sea, river) hurtar

encroachment /ɛnˈkroutʃmənt/ n usurpación, f; abuso, m; invasión, f

encrust /ɛnˈkrʌst/ vt encostrar; incrustar

encumber /ɛnˈkʌmbər/ vt impedir, estorbar; llenar; (burden) cargar; (mortgage) hipotecar; (overwhelm) agobiar

encumbrance /ɛnˈkʌmbrəns/ n impedimento, estorbo, m; gravamen, m; carga, f; (mortgage) hipoteca, f

encyclical /ɛnˈsɪklɪkəl/ n encíclica, f

encyclopedia /ɛnˌsaɪkləˈpidiə/ n enciclopedia, f

end /ɛnd/ n fin, m; extremidad, f; extremo, m; conclusión, f; (point) punta, f; cabo, m; (district) barrio, m; cabeza, f; (death) muerte, f; (aim) objeto, intento, m; (purpose) propósito, m; (issue) resultado, m; (bit) fragmento, pedazo, m; (of a word) terminación, f. —vi terminar; acabar; concluir; cesar; (in) terminar en; resultar en; (with) terminar con. —vt terminar; acabar, dar fin a. **at an end,** terminado. **at the end,** al cabo (de); al extremo (de). **end of quotation,** fin de cita, final de la cita, m. **from end to end,** de un extremo a otro; de un cabo a otro. **in the end,** por fin, finalmente. **on end,** de pie, de cabeza, derecho; de punta; (of hair) erizado. **no end of,** un sinnúmero de. **to make both ends meet,** pasar con lo que se tiene. **to make an end of,** acabar con. **to put an end to,** poner fin a. **to the end that,** a fin de que, para que; con objeto de. **toward the end of,** (months, years, etc.) a fines de, a últimos de; hacia el fin de. **two hours on end,** dos horas seguidas. **end-paper,** guarda, f

endanger /ɛnˈdeɪndʒər/ vt arriesgar, poner en peligro

endear /ɛnˈdɪər/ vt hacer querer

endearing /ɛnˈdɪərɪŋ/ a que inspira cariño; atrayente; cariñoso

endearment /ɛnˈdɪərmənt/ n cariño, amor, m; caricia, terneza, f; palabra de cariño, f

endeavor /ɛnˈdɛvər/ vi procurar, intentar, hacer un esfuerzo. —n esfuerzo, m, tentativa, f

endemic /ɛnˈdɛmɪk/ a Med. endémico

ending /ˈɛndɪŋ/ n fin, m; conclusión, f; Gram. terminación, f; cesación, f; (climax) desenlace, m

endive /ˈɛndaɪv/ n Bot. escarola, f

endless /ˈɛndlɪs/ a eterno; inacabable; infinito; sin fin; interminable; incesante

endlessly /ˈɛndlɪsli/ adv sin fin; incesantemente; sin parar

endocrine /ˈɛndəkrɪn/ a endocrino. —n secreción interna, f

end-of-season /ˈɛnd əv ˈsizən/ a por final de temporada (e.g., end-of-season reductions, rebajos por final de temporada,

m pl. end-of-season sale, liquidación por final de temporada, f)

endorse /ɛnˈdɔrs/ vt Com. endosar; garantizar; (uphold) apoyar; confirmar

endorsee /ɛndɔrˈsi/ n endosatario (-ia)

endorsement /ɛnˈdɔrsmənt/ n Com. endoso, m; aval, m, garantía, f; corroboración, confirmación, f

endorser /ɛnˈdɔrsər/ n Com. endosante, m

endow /ɛnˈdaʊ/ vt dotar; fundar; crear

endowment /ɛnˈdaʊmənt/ n dotación, f; fundación, f; creación, f; (mental) inteligencia, f; cualidad, f, don, m. **e. policy,** póliza dotal, f

endurance /ɛnˈdʊrəns/ n aguante, m; resistencia, f; sufrimiento, m; tolerancia, f; paciencia, f; (lastingness) duración, continuación, f. **beyond e.,** intolerable, inaguantable. **e. test,** prueba de resistencia, f

endure /ɛnˈdʊr/ vt soportar; tolerar, aguantar; sufrir; resistir. —vi sufrir; (last) durar, continuar

enduring /ɛnˈdʊrɪŋ/ a permanente, perdurable; continuo; constante

enema /ˈɛnəmə/ n lavativa, enema, f

enemy /ˈɛnəmi/ n enemigo (-ga); adversario (-ia); (in war) enemigo, m. —a del enemigo, enemigo. **to be one's own e.,** ser enemigo de sí mismo. **to become an e. of,** enemistarse con; hacerse enemigo de, volverse hostil a

energetic /ˌɛnərˈdʒɛtɪk/ a enérgico

energy /ˈɛnərdʒi/ n energía, fuerza, f, vigor, m

enervate /ˈɛnərˌveɪt/ a ˈɪnɜrvɪt/ vt enervar; debilitar. —a enervado

enfeeble /ɛnˈfibəl/ vt debilitar

enforce /ɛnˈfɔrs/ vt (a law) poner en vigor; (impose) imponer a la fuerza; hacer cumplir; conseguir por fuerza; (demonstrate) demostrar

enforcement /ɛnˈfɔrsmənt/ n (of a law) ejecución (de una ley), f; imposición a la fuerza, f; observación forzosa, f

enfranchise /ɛnˈfræntʃaɪz/ vt emancipar; conceder derechos civiles (a)

engage /ɛnˈgeɪdʒ/ vt empeñar; contratar; tomar en alquiler; tomar a su servicio; (seats, etc.) reservar; (occupy) ocupar; (attention) atraer; (in) aplicarse a, dedicarse a; Mil. combatir con, librar batalla con; atacar; (of wheels) endentar con. —vi obligarse; dedicarse (a); tomar parte (en); (bet) apostar; Mil. librar batalla; (fight) venir a las manos. **to be engaged in,** traer entre manos, ocuparse en. **to become engaged,** prometerse. **Number engaged!** (telephone) ¡Están comunicando!

engaged /ɛnˈgeɪdʒd/ a ocupado; (betrothed) prometido; reservado

engagement /ɛnˈgeɪdʒmənt/ n obligación, f; compromiso, m; (date) cita, f; (betrothal) palabra de casamiento, f; (battle) combate, m, batalla, f. **I have an e. at two o'clock.** Tengo una cita a las dos

engagement gift regalo de esponsales, *m*

engaging /ɛnˈgeidʒɪŋ/ *a* simpático, atractivo

engender /ɛnˈdʒɛndər/ *vt Fig.* engendrar; excitar

engine /ˈɛndʒən/ *n* máquina, *f;* motor, *m;* (locomotive) locomotora, *f;* (pump) bomba, *f.* **to sit with one's back to the e.,** estar sentado de espaldas a la máquina (or locomotora). **e. builder,** constructor de máquinas, *m.* **e. driver,** maquinista, *mf.* **e. room,** cuarto de máquinas, *m.* **e. works,** taller de maquinaria, *m*

engineer /ˌɛndʒəˈniər/ *n* ingeniero, *m;* mecánico, *m.* —*vt Fig.* gestionar, arreglar. **civil e.,** ingeniero de caminos, canales y puertos, *m.* **Royal Engineers,** Cuerpo de Ingenieros, *m*

engineering /ˌɛndʒəˈniərɪŋ/ *n* ingeniería, *f; Fig.* manejo,' *m.* —*a* de ingeniería

England /ˈɪŋglənd/ Inglaterra, *f*

English /ˈɪŋglɪʃ/ *a* inglés. —*n* (language) inglés, *m.* in **E. fashion,** a la inglesa. to **speak E.,** hablar inglés. **to speak plain E.,** hablar sin rodeos; hablar en cristiano. **E. Church,** iglesia anglicana, *f.* **E.-teacher,** maestro (-ra) de inglés. **English-translator,** traductor al inglés, *m*

English Channel, the el Canal de la Mancha

Englishman /ˈɪŋglɪʃmən/ *n* inglés, *m*

Englishwoman /ˈɪŋglɪʃˌwumən/ *n* inglesa, *f*

engrain /ɛnˈgrein/ *vt* inculcar

engrave /ɛnˈgreiv/ *vt* grabar; esculpir; cincelar; *Fig.* grabar

engraver /ɛnˈgreivər/ *n* grabador (-ra); (tool) cincel, *m*

engraving /ɛnˈgreivɪŋ/ *n* grabadura, *f;* (picture) grabado, *m.* **e. needle,** punta seca, *f*

engross /ɛnˈgrous/ *vt* (a document) poner en limpio; redactar; (absorb) absorber

engrossing /ɛnˈgrousɪŋ/ *a* absorbente

engulf /ɛnˈgʌlf/ *vt* hundir, sumir, sumergir

enhance /ɛnˈhæns/ *vt* realzar; intensificar; aumentar; mejorar

enhancement /ɛnˈhænsmənt/ *n* realce, *m;* intensificación, *f;* aumento, *m;* mejoría, *f*

enigma /əˈnɪgmə/ *n* enigma, *m*

enigmatic /ˌɛnɪgˈmætɪk/ *a* enigmático

enjoin /ɛnˈdʒɔin/ *vt* imponer; ordenar; mandar; encargar

enjoy /ɛnˈdʒɔi/ *vt* disfrutar; gustar de; gozar de; poseer, tener. **to e. oneself,** recrearse, regocijarse; (amuse oneself) divertirse; entretenerse; pasarlo bien. **Did you e. yourself?** ¿Lo pasaste bien?

enjoyable /ɛnˈdʒɔiəbəl/ *a* agradable; divertido, entretenido

enjoyment /ɛnˈdʒɔimənt/ *n* posesión, *f;* goce, disfrute, *m;* (pleasure) placer, *m;*

aprovechamiento, *m;* utilización, *f;* (satisfaction) satisfacción, *f*

enlarge /ɛnˈlɑrdʒ/ *vt* agrandar; aumentar; ensanchar; extender; *Photo.* ampliar; dilatar; (the mind, etc.) ensanchar. —*vi* agrandarse; ensancharse; aumentarse; extenderse. **an enlarged heart,** dilatación del corazón, *f.* **to e. upon,** tratar detalladamente, explayarse en

enlargement /ɛnˈlɑrdʒmənt/ *n* engrandecimiento, *m;* ensanchamiento, *m; Photo.* ampliación, *f; Med.* dilatación, *f;* aumento, *m;* amplificación, *f;* (of a town, etc.) ensanche, *m*

enlighten /ɛnˈlaitn̩/ *vt* iluminar; aclarar; informar

enlightened /ɛnˈlaitn̩d/ *a* culto; ilustrado; inteligente

enlightening /ɛnˈlaitn̩ɪŋ/ *a* instructivo

enlightenment /ɛnˈlaitn̩mənt/ *n* ilustración, *f;* cultura, civilización, *f*

enlist /ɛnˈlɪst/ *vt Mil.* reclutar; alistar; obtener, conseguir. —*vi Mil.* sentar plaza, sentar plaza de soldado; engancharse; alistarse

enlistment /ɛnˈlɪstmənt/ *n Mil.* enganche, *m;* reclutamiento, *m;* alistamiento, *m*

enliven /ɛnˈlaivən/ *vt* animar; avivar; alegrar

enmity /ˈɛnmɪti/ *n* enemistad, enemiga, hostilidad, *f*

enormity /ɪˈnɔrmɪti/ *n* enormidad, *f;* gravedad, *f;* atrocidad, *f*

enormous /ɪˈnɔrməs/ *a* enorme, colosal

enough /ɪˈnʌf/ *a* bastante, suficiente. —*n* lo bastante, lo suficiente. —*adv* bastante; suficientemente. —*interj* ¡bastante! ¡basta! **to be e.,** ser suficiente; bastar. **two are enough,** con dos tenemos bastante, con dos tengo bastante

enquire /ɛnˈkwaiər/. See **inquire**

enrage /ɛnˈreidʒ/ *vt* enfurecer, hacer furioso; *Inf.* hacer rabiar

enraged /ɛnˈreidʒd/ *a* furioso

enrapture /ɛnˈræptʃər/ *vt* entusiasmar, extasiar; (intoxicate) embriagar; (charm) encantar, deleitar

enrich /ɛnˈrɪtʃ/ *vt* enriquecer; (adorn) adornar, embellecer; (the land) fertilizar

enrichment /ɛnˈrɪtʃmənt/ *n* enriquecimiento, *m;* embellecimiento, *m;* (of the land) abono, *m*

enroll /ɛnˈroul/ *vt* alistar; matricular; inscribir; (perpetuate) inmortalizar

ensconce /ɛnˈskɒns/ *vt* acomodar, colocar; ocultar

ensemble /ɑnˈsɑmbəl/ *n* conjunto, *m*

enshrine /ɛnˈʃrain/ *vt* poner en sagrario; guardar con cuidado; *Fig.* guardar como una reliquia

enshroud /ɛnˈʃraud/ *vt* amortajar; envolver; esconder

ensign /ˈɛnsən/ *n* (badge) insignia, *f;* (flag) enseña, bandera, *f;* pabellón, *m;* bandera de popa, *f; Mil.* alférez, *m;* (U. S.A. navy) subteniente, *m*

enslave /ɛnˈsleiv/ vt esclavizar; Fig. dominar

ensue /ɛnˈsu/ vt conseguir. —vi resultar; suceder, sobrevenir

ensuing /ɛnˈsuɪŋ/ a (next) próximo; (resulting) resultante

ensure /ɛnˈʃur/ vt asegurar; estar seguro de que; garantizar

entail /ɛnˈteil/ vt traer consigo, acarrear; Law. ▪incular; n Law. vinculación, f; herencia, f

entangle /ɛnˈtæŋgəl/ vt enredar; coger; Fig. embrollar

entanglement /ɛnˈtæŋgəlmənt/ n enredo, m; complicación, f; intriga, f; (Mil. of wire) alambrada, f

enter /ˈɛntər/ vt entrar en; penetrar; (of thoughts) ocurrirse; (join) ingresar en; entrar en; (become a member of) hacerse miembro de; (enroll) alistarse; (a university) matricularse; (inscribe) inscribir, poner en la lista; (note) anotar, apuntar; (a protest) hacer constar; (make) hacer; formular. —vi entrar; Theat. salir (a la escena); penetrar; Com. anotarse. **to e. for,** vt inscribir. —vi inscribirse, tomar parte en. **to e. into,** entrar en; formar parte de; (conversation) entablar (conversación); (negotiations) iniciar; considerar; (another's emotion) acompañar en; (an agreement, etc.) hacer; (sign) firmar; (bind oneself) obligarse a, comprometerse a; tomar parte en; (undertake) emprender; empezar; adoptar. **to e. up,** anotar; poner en la lista; registrar. **to e. upon,** comenzar, emprender; tomar posesión de; encargarse de, asumir; inaugurar, dar principio a

enterprise /ˈɛntərˌpraiz/ n empresa, f; aventura, f; (spirit) iniciativa, f, empuje, m

enterprising /ˈɛntərˌpraizɪŋ/ a emprendedor, acometedor; de mucha iniciativa

entertain /ˌɛntərˈtein/ vt (an idea, etc.) acariciar, abrigar; considerar; (as a guest) agasajar, obsequiar; recibir en casa; (amuse) divertir, entretener. —vi ser hospitalario; tener invitados en casa; dar fiestas

entertaining /ˌɛntərˈteinɪŋ/ a entretenido, divertido

entertainment /ˌɛntərˈteinmənt/ n convite, m; fiesta, f; reunión, f; banquete, m; (hospitality) hospitalidad, f; (amusement) diversión, f, entretenimiento, m; espectáculo, m; función, f; concierto, m

enthrall /ɛnˈθrɔl/ vt seducir, atraer, encantar; absorber, captar la atención

enthralling /ɛnˈθrɔlɪŋ/ a absorbente; atrayente, halagüeño

enthusiasm /ɛnˈθuziˌæzəm/ n entusiasmo, m

enthusiast /ɛnˈθuziˌæst, -ɪst/ n entusiasta, mf

enthusiastic /ɛnˌθuziˈæstɪk/ a entusiasta. **to make e.,** entusiasmar. **to be e.,** entusiasmarse

entice /ɛnˈtais/ vt tentar, inducir; atraer, seducir

enticement /ɛnˈtaismənt/ n tentación, f; atractivo, m

enticing /ɛnˈtaisɪŋ/ a seduciente, atrayente; halagüeño

entire /ɛnˈtaiər/ a entero; completo; intacto; absoluto; perfecto; íntegro; total

entirely /ɛnˈtaiərli/ adv enteramente; completamente; integralmente; totalmente

entirety /ɛnˈtaiərti/ n totalidad, f; integridad, f; todo, m

entitle /ɛnˈtaitl/ vt (designate) intitular; dar derecho (a); autorizar. **to be entitled to,** tener derecho a

entity /ˈɛntɪti/ n entidad, f; ente, ser, m

entourage /ˌɑntuˈrɑʒ/ n séquito, m; (environment) medio ambiente, m

entrails /ˈɛntreilz/ n entrañas, tripas, f pl, intestinos, m pl

entrain /ɛnˈtrein/ vi tomar el tren, subir al tren

entrance /ˈɛntrəns/ n entrada, f; Theat. salida (a la escena), f; (into a profession, etc.) ingreso, m; alistamiento, m; (beginning) principio, m; (door) puerta, f; (porch) portal, m; (of a cave) boca, f. **e. fee,** cuota de entrada, f. **e. hall,** zaguán, m. **e. money,** entrada, f

entrance /ɛnˈtræns/ vt Fig. encantar, fascinar; extasiar

entrancing /ɛnˈtrænsɪŋ/ a encantador

entreat /ɛnˈtrit/ vt suplicar, implorar, rogar

entreating /ɛnˈtritɪŋ/ a suplicante, implorante

entreaty /ɛnˈtriti/ n súplica, instancia, f, ruego, m

entree /ˈɑntrei/ n entrada, f

entrench /ɛnˈtrɛntʃ/ vt atrincherar

entrust /ɛnˈtrʌst/ vt confiar a (or en), encomendar a; encargar

entry /ˈɛntri/ n entrada, f; (passage) callejuela, f; (note) inscripción, apuntación, f; Com. partida, f; (registration) registro, m. **double e.,** Com. partida doble, f. **single e.,** Com. partida simple, f

entwine /ɛnˈtwain/ vt entrelazar, entretejer

enumerate /ɪˈnuməˌreit/ vt enumerar

enumeration /ɪˌnuməˈreiʃən/ n enumeración, f

enunciate /ɪˈnʌnsiˌeit/ vt enunciar; articular

enunciation /ɪˌnʌnsiˈeiʃən/ n enunciación, f; articulación, f

envelop /ɛnˈvɛləp/ vt envolver, cubrir

envelope /ˈɛnvəˌloup/ n sobre, m

envelopment /ɛnˈvɛləpmənt/ n envolvimiento, m; cubierta, f

enviable /ˈɛnviəbəl/ a envidiable

envious /ˈɛnviəs/ a envidioso. **an e. look,** una mirada de envidia

enviously /ˈɛnviəsli/ adv con envidia

environment /ɛnˈvairənmənt/ n medio ambiente, m

environs /ɛn'vairənz/ *n* inmediaciones, *f pl*, alrededores, *m pl*

envisage /ɛn'vɪzɪdʒ/ *vt* hacer frente a; contemplar; imaginar

envoy /'ɛnvɔi/ *n* enviado, *m*; mensajero (-ra)

envy /'ɛnvi/ *n* envidia, *f*. *vt* envidiar

enzyme /'ɛnzaim/ *n* fermento, *m*, enzima, *f*

eon /'iən/ *n* eón, *m*

ephemeral /ɪ'fɛmərəl/ *a* efímero; *Fig.* fugaz, pasajero

epic /'ɛpɪk/ *a* épico. —*n* epopeya, *f*

epicenter /'ɛpə,sɛntər/ *n* epicentro, *m*

epicure /'ɛpɪ,kyur/ *n* epicúreo (-ea)

epicurean /,ɛpɪkyu'riən/ *a* epicúreo

epidemic /,ɛpɪ'dɛmɪk/ *n* epidemia, *f*; plaga, *f* epidémico

epidermis /,ɛpɪ'dɜrmɪs/ *n* epidermis, *f*

epiglottis /,ɛpɪ'glotɪs/ *n* epiglotis, *f*

epigram /'ɛpɪ,græm/ *n* epigrama, *m*

epigrammatic /,ɛpɪgrə'mætɪk/ *a* epigramático

epigraph /'ɛpɪ,græf/ *n* epígrafe, *m*

epilepsy /'ɛpə,lɛpsi/ *n* epilepsia, alferecía, *f*

epileptic /,ɛpə'lɛptɪk/ *a* and *n* epiléptico (-ca). **e. fit**, ataque epiléptico, *m*. **e. aura**, aura epiléptica, *f*

epiphany /ɪ'pɪfəni/ *n* epifanía, *f*

episcopacy /ɪ'pɪskəpəsi/ *n* episcopado, *m*

episcopalianism /ɪ,pɪskə'peilyə,nɪzəm/ *n* episcopalismo, *m*

episode /'ɛpə,soud/ *n* suceso, incidente, *m*; *Lit.* episodio, *m*

epistle /ɪ'pɪsəl/ *n* epístola, *f*

epistolary /ɪ'pɪstl,ɛri/ *a* epistolar

epitaph /'ɛpɪ,tæf/ *n* epitafio, *m*

epithet /'ɛpə,θɛt/ *n* epíteto, *m*

epitome /ɪ'pɪtəmi/ *n* epítome, *m*

epitomize /ɪ'pɪtə,maiz/ *vt* resumir, abreviar

epoch /'ɛpək/ *n* época, edad, *f*

Epsom salts /'ɛpsəm/ *n* sal de la Higuera, *f*

equability /,ɛkwə'bɪlɪti/ *n* igualdad (de ánimo), ecuanimidad, *f*; uniformidad, *f*

equable /'ɛkwəbəl/ *a* igual, ecuánime; uniforme

equably /'ɛkwəbli/ *adv* con ecuanimidad; igualmente; uniformemente

equal /'ikwəl/ *a* igual; uniforme; imparcial; equitativo, justo. —*n* igual, *mf*. —*vt* ser igual a; equivaler a; igualar; *Sports.* empatar. **to be e. to**, (of persons) ser capaz de; servir para; atreverse a; (circumstances) estar al nivel de; sentirse con fuerzas para. **without e.**, sin igual; (of beauty, etc.) sin par. **e. sign**, *Math.* igual, *m*

equality /ɪ'kwɒlɪti/ *n* igualdad, *f*; uniformidad, *f*

equalization /,ikwələ'zeiʃən/ *n* igualación, *f*

equalize /'ikwə,laiz/ *vt* igualar

equalizing /'ikwə,laizɪŋ/ *a* igualador; compensador

equally /'ikwəli/ *adv* igualmente; imparcialmente

equanimity /,ikwə'nɪmɪti/ *n* ecuanimidad, *f*

equation /ɪ'kweiʒən/ *n* ecuación, *f*

equator /ɪ'kweitər/ *n* ecuador, *m*

equatorial /,ikwə'tɔriəl/ *a* ecuatorial

equerry /'ɛkwəri/ *n* caballerizo del rey, *m*

equestrian /ɪ'kwɛstriən/ *a* ecuestre

equiangular /,ikwi'æŋgyələr/ *a* equiángulo

equidistance /,ikwɪ'dɪstəns/ *n* equidistancia, *f*

equidistant /,ikwɪ'dɪstənt/ *a* equidistante

equilateral /,ikwə'lætərəl/ *a* equilátero

equilibrium /,ikwə'lɪbriəm/ *n* equilibrio, *m*

equine /'ikwain/ *a* equino; hípico; de caballo

equinox /'ikwə,noks/ *n* equinoccio, *m*

equip /ɪ'kwɪp/ *vt* proveer; pertrechar; equipar

equipage /'ɛkwəpɪdʒ/ *n* (train) séquito, tren, *m*; (carriage) carruaje, *m*

equipment /ɪ'kwɪpmənt/ *n* habilitación, *f*; equipo, *m*; pertrechos, *m pl*; material, *m*; aparatos, *m pl*; armamento, *m*

equitable /'ɛkwɪtəbəl/ *a* equitativo, justo

equitably /'ɛkwɪtəbli/ *adv* equitativamente, con justicia

equity /'ɛkwɪti/ *n* equidad, *f*; imparcialidad, justicia, *f*

equivalence /ɪ'kwɪvələns/ *n* equivalencia, *f*

equivalent /ɪ'kwɪvələnt/ *a* and *n* equivalente, *m*. **to be e. to**, equivaler a

equivocal /ɪ'kwɪvəkəl/ *a* equívoco, ambiguo

equivocally /ɪ'kwɪvəkəli/ *adv* equivocadamente

equivocate /ɪ'kwɪvə,keit/ *vi* usar frases equívocas, emplear equívocos, tergiversar

equivocation /ɪ,kwɪvə'keiʃən/ *n* equívoco, *m*

era /'ɪərə, 'ɛrə/ *n* época, era, *f*

eradiation /ɪ,reidi'eiʃən/ *n* irradiación, *f*

eradicable /ɪ'rædɪkəbəl/ *a* erradicable

eradicate /ɪ'rædɪ,keit/ *vt* erradicar; destruir, extirpar; suprimir

eradication /ɪ,rædɪ'keiʃən/ *n* erradicación, *f*; destrucción, *f*; supresión, *f*

erasable /ɪ'reisəbəl/ *a* borrable

erase /ɪ'reis/ *vt* borrar; tachar

eraser /ɪ'reisər/ *n* goma de borrar, *f*. **ink e.**, goma para tinta, *f*

erasure /ɪ'reiʃər/ *n* borradura, *f*; tachón, *m*

ere /ɛər/ *conjunc* antes de (que), antes de. —*prep* antes de

erect /ɪ'rɛkt/ *a* (upright) derecho; erguido; vertical; (uplifted) levantado; (standing) de pie; (firm) firme, resuelto; (alert) vigilante. —*vt* (build) edificar, construir; instalar; (raise) alzar; convertir

erection /ɪ'rɛkʃən/ *n* erección, *f*; construcción, edificación, *f*; (building) edificio, *m;* (structure) estructura, *f;* instalación, *f;* (assembling) montaje, *m*

erectly /ɪ'rɛktli/ *adv* derecho

ermine /'ɜrmɪn/ *n* armiño, *m, a* de armiño

erode /ɪ'roud/ *vt* corroer; comer; *Geol.* denudar

erosion /ɪ'rouʒən/ *n* erosión, *f*

erotic /ɪ'rɒtɪk/ *a* erótico

err /ɜr, ɛr/ *vi* desviarse; errar; desacertar; pecar

errand /'ɛrənd/ *n* mensaje, recado, *m;* encargo, *m;* misión, *f.* **e.-boy,** mandadero, mensajero, motril, mozo, recadero, *m*

errant /'ɛrənt/ *a* errante; (of knights) andante

erratic /ɪ'rætɪk/ *a* (of conduct) excéntrico, irresponsable; (of thoughts, etc.) errante; *Med.* errático

erratum /ɪ'rɑtəm/ *n* errata, *f*

erring /'ɛrɪŋ/ *a* extraviado; pecaminoso

erroneous /ə'rouniəs/ *a* erróneo; falso; injusto

error /'ɛrər/ *n* error, *m;* equivocación, *f,* desacierto, *m;* (sin) pecado, *m.* **in e.,** por equivocación

erudite /'ɛryu,dait/ *a* erudito; sabio

erudition /,ɛryu'dɪʃən/ *n* erudición, *f*

erupt /ɪ'rʌpt/ *vi* entrar en erupción, estar en erupción; *Fig.* salir con fuerza

eruption /ɪ'rʌpʃən/ *n* erupción, *f*

erysipelas /,ɛrə'sɪpələs/ *n* erisipela, *f*

escalade /,ɛskə'leid/ *n* escalada, *f, vt* escalar

escalator /'ɛskə,leitər/ *n* escalera automática, escalera eléctrica, escalera mecánica, escalera móvil, escalera rodante, *f*

escapable /ɪ'skeipəbəl/ *a* evitable, eludible

escapade /'ɛskə,peid/ *n* escapada, *f;* aventura, *f*

escape /ɪ'skeip/ *n* huida, fuga, *f;* evasión, evitación, *f;* (leak) escape, *m; Fig.* salida, *f.* —*vt* eludir, evitar; (of cries, groans, etc.) dar, salir de. —*vi* huir, fugarse, escapar; (slip away) escurrirse; librarse; salvarse; (leak) escaparse. **His name escapes me,** Se me escapa (or se me olvida) su nombre. **to e. notice,** pasar inadvertido. **to have a narrow e.,** salvarse en una tabla. **to e. from,** escaparse de; librarse de; huir de

escape clause *n* cláusula de salvaguardia, *f*

escaping /ɪ'skeipɪŋ/ *a* fugitivo

escarpment /ɪ'skɑrpmənt/ *n* escarpa, *f*

eschew /ɛs'tʃu/ *vt* evitar

eschewal /ɛs'tʃuəl/ *n* evitación, *f*

escort /*n* 'ɛskɔrt; *v* ɪ'skɔrt/ *n Mil.* escolta, *f;* (of ships) convoy, *m;* acompañamiento, *m;* acompañante, *m.* —*vt Mil.* escoltar; (of ships) convoyar; acompañar

escritoire /,ɛskri'twɑr/ *n* escritorio, *m*

Eskimo /'ɛskə,mou/ *a* and *n* esquimal *mf*

esoteric /,ɛsə'tɛrɪk/ *a* esotérico

especial /ɪ'spɛʃəl/ *a* especial; particular

especially /ɪ'spɛʃəli/ *adv* especialmente; ante todo; en particular

Esperanto /,ɛspə'rɑntou/ *n* esperanto, *m*

espionage /'ɛspiə,nɑʒ/ *n* espionaje, *m*

esplanade /'ɛsplə,nɑd/ *n Mil.* explanada, *f;* bulevar, paseo, *m*

espousal /ɪ'spauzəl/ *n* desposorio, *m; Fig.* adhesión (a una causa), *f*

espouse /ɪ'spauz/ *vt* desposar; (a cause) abrazar; defender

espy /ɪ'spai/ *vt* divisar, ver, observar

esquire /'ɛskwaiər/ *n* escudero, *m;* (landowner) hacendado, *m;* (as a title) don (before given name)

essay /'ɛsei; *v* ɛ'sei/ *n* tentativa, *f; Lit.* ensayo, *m, vt* probar; procurar; (on an examination) tema, *m.* **essay question,** tema, *m*

essayist /'ɛseiɪst/ *n* ensayista, *mf*

essence /'ɛsəns/ *n* esencia, *f*

essential /ə'sɛntʃəl/ *a* esencial; indispensable, imprescindible; intrínseco. —*n* artículo de primera necesidad, *m;* elemento necesario, *m*

establish /ɪ'stæblɪʃ/ *vt* establecer; fundar; crear; erigir; (constitute) constituir; (order) disponer; (prove) demostrar, probar; (take root, settle) arraigarse

established /ɪ'stæblɪʃt/ *a* establecido; arraigado; (proved) demostrado; bien conocido; (author) consagrado; (of churches) oficial

establishment /ɪ'stæblɪʃmənt/ *n* establecimiento, *m;* fundación, *f;* creación, *f;* institución, *f;* (building) erección, *f;* arraigo, *m;* (house) casa, *f;* (church) iglesia oficial, *f;* demostración, *f;* reconocimiento, *m*

estate /ɪ'steit/ *n* estado, *m;* clase, *f;* condición, *f;* (land) propiedad, finca, *f;* fortuna, *f;* (inheritance) heredad, *f,* patrimonio, *m; Law.* bienes, *m pl.* **personal e.,** bienes muebles, *m pl;* fortuna personal, *f.* **third e.,** estado llano, *m.* **e. agent,** agente de fincas, *m;* agente de casas, *m*

esteem /ɪ'stim/ *n* estima, *f,* aprecio, *m;* consideración, *f, vt* estimar, apreciar; creer, juzgar

esthete /'ɛsθit/ *n* estético, *m*

esthetic /ɛs'θɛtɪk/ *a* estético

esthetics /ɛs'θɛtɪks/ *n* estética, *f*

estimable /'ɛstəməbəl/ *a* apreciable, estimable

estimate /*n* 'ɛstə,mɪt; *v* -,meit/ *n* estimación, tasa, *f;* cálculos, *m pl;* apreciación, *f;* opinión, *f; pl* **estimates,** presupuesto, *m.* —*vt* (value) avalorar, tasar; calcular, computar; considerar. —*vi* hacer un presupuesto

estimation /,ɛstə'meiʃən/ *n* opinión, *f;* cálculo, cómputo, *m;* (esteem) aprecio, *m,* estima, *f*

Estonian /ɛ'stouniən/ *a* and *n* estonio (-ia); (language) estonio, *m*

estrange /ɪ'streindʒ/ *vt* enajenar; ofender

estrangement /ɪˈstreɪndʒmənt/ n enajenación, alienación, f

estuary /ˈestʃu,erɪ/ n estuario, m, ría, f

etcetera /etˈsetərə/ etcétera. (Used as noun, f)

etch /etʃ/ vt grabar al agua fuerte

etcher /ˈetʃər/ n grabador (-ra) al agua fuerte

etching /ˈetʃɪŋ/ n aguafuerte, f; grabado al agua fuerte, m. **e. needle**, punta seca, aguja de grabador, f

eternal /ɪˈtɜrnḷ/ a eterno; incesante. —n (E.) el Eterno

eternity /ɪˈtɜrnɪtɪ/ n eternidad, f

ether /ˈiθər/ n éter, m

ethereal /ɪˈθɪərɪəl/ a etéreo; vaporoso, aéreo

ethical /ˈeθɪkəl/ a ético, moral; n droga de ordenanza, f

ethics /ˈoθɪks/ n ética, f (filosofía) moral, f

Ethiopia /,iθiˈoupiə/ Etiopia, f

ethnic /ˈeθnɪk/ a étnico

ethyl /ˈeθəl/ n Chem. etilo, m

ethylene /ˈeθə,lin/ n Chem. etileno, m

etiquette /ˈetɪkɪt/ n etiqueta, f

Etruscan /ɪˈtrʌskən/ a and n etrusco (-ca) f

eucalyptus /,yukəˈlɪptəs/ n eucalipto, m

Eucharist /ˈyukərɪst/ n Eucaristía, f

eugenic /yuˈdʒenɪk/ a eugenésico

eugenics /yuˈdʒenɪks/ n eugenesia, f

eulogist /ˈyulədʒɪst/ n elogiador (-ra), loador (-ra)

eulogistic /,yuləˈdʒɪstɪk/ a elogiador

eulogize /ˈyulə,dʒaɪz/ vt elogiar, alabar, encomiar

eulogy /ˈyulədʒi/ n elogio, encomio, m; alabanza, f; panegírico, m

eunuch /ˈyunək/ n eunuco, m

euphemism /ˈyufə,mɪzəm/ n eufemismo, m

euphonious /yuˈfouniəs/ a eufónico

euphony /ˈyufəni/ n eufonía, f

eurhythmic /yuˈrɪðmɪk/ a eurítmico

eurhythmics /yuˈrɪðmɪks/ n euritmia, f

European /,yurəˈpiən/ a and n europeo (-ea)

europeanize /,yurəˈpiə,naɪz/ vt europeanizar

euthanasia /,yuθəˈneɪʒə, -ʒiə, -ziə/ n eutanasia, f

evacuate /ɪˈvækyu,eɪt/ vt evacuar

evacuation /ɪ,vækyuˈeɪʃən/ n evacuación, f

evade /ɪˈveɪd/ vt evadir, eludir; evitar, esquivar; rehuir

evaluate /ɪˈvælyu,eɪt/ vt evaluar, estimar; calcular

evaluation /ɪ,vælyuˈeɪʃən/ n evaluación, estimación, f

evanescent /,evəˈnesənt/ a transitorio, fugaz, pasajero

evangelical /,ivænˈdʒelɪkəl/ a evangélico

evangelicalism /,ivænˈdʒelɪkə,lɪzəm/ n evangelismo, m

evangelist /ɪˈvændʒəlɪst/ n evangelista, m

evangelize /ɪˈvændʒə,laɪz/ vt evangelizar

evaporate /ɪˈvæpə,reɪt/ vi evaporarse; desvanecerse. —vt evaporar

evaporation /ɪ,væpəˈreɪʃən/ n evaporación, f; desvanecimiento, m

evaporative /ɪˈvæpə,reɪtɪv/ a evaporatorio

evasion /ɪˈveɪʒən/ n (escape) fuga, f; evasión, f; evasiva, f, efugio, m

evasive /ɪˈveɪsɪv/ a evasivo, ambiguo

evasively /ɪˈveɪsɪvli/ adv evasivamente

evasiveness /ɪˈveɪsɪvnɪs/ n carácter evasivo, m

eve /iv/ n víspera, f; Eccl. vigilia, f. **on the eve of,** la víspera de; Fig. en vísperas de

even /ˈivən/ a (flat) llano; (smooth) liso; igual; (level with) al mismo nivel (de); uniforme; (of numbers) par; (approximate, of sums) redondo; rítmico; invariable, constante; (of temper) apacible; (just) imparcial; (monotonous) monótono, igual; (paid) pagado; (Com. of date) mismo. **to get e. with,** pagar en la misma moneda, vengarse de

even /ˈivən/ adv siquiera; aun; hasta; (also) también. **not e.,** ni siquiera. **e. as,** así como, del mismo modo que. **e. if,** aun cuando, si bien. **e. now,** aun ahora; ahora mismo. **e. so,** aun así; (nevertheless) sin embargo. **e. though,** aunque; suponiendo que

even /ˈivən/ vt igualar; (level) allanar, nivelar; (accounts) desquitar; compensar; hacer uniforme

evening /ˈivnɪŋ/ n tarde, f, atardecer, m; noche, f; Fig. fin, m, a vespertino, de la tarde. **Good e.!** ¡Buenas tardes! ¡Buenas noches! **in the e.,** al atardecer. **tomorrow e.,** mañana por la tarde. **yesterday e.,** ayer por la tarde. **e. class,** clase nocturna, f. **e. dress,** (women) traje de noche, m; (men) traje de etiqueta, m. **e. meal,** cena, f. **e. paper,** periódico (or diario) de la noche, m. **evening primrose,** hierba del asno, onagra, f. **e. star,** estrella vespertina, estrella de la tarde, f; (Venus) lucero de la tarde, m

evenly /ˈivənli/ adv igualmente; (on a level) a nivel; uniformemente; imparcialmente; (of speech) con suavidad

evenness /ˈivənnɪs/ n igualdad, f; (smoothness) lisura, f; uniformidad, f; imparcialidad, f; (of temper) ecuanimidad, serenidad, f

evensong /ˈivən,sɔŋ/ n vísperas, f pl

event /ɪˈvent/ n incidente, suceso, acontecimiento, m; (result) consecuencia, f; resultado, m; caso, m; (athletics) prueba, f; (race) carrera, f. **at all events,** de todas maneras. **in such an e.,** en tal caso. **in the e. of,** en tal caso de

eventful /ɪˈventfəl/ a lleno de acontecimientos; accidentado; memorable

eventual /ɪˈventʃuəl/ a eventual; final, último

eventuality /ɪ,ventʃuˈælɪti/ n eventualidad, f

eventually /ɪ'vɛntʃuəli/ adv a la larga, al fin

ever /'ɛvər/ adv siempre; (at any time) jamás; alguna vez; nunca; (even) siquiera; (very) muy; (in any way) en modo alguno. **As fast as e. he can,** Lo más aprisa que pueda. **Be it e. so big,** Por grande que sea. **Did you e.!** ¡Habráse visto! ¡Qué cosa! **for e.,** para siempre. **for e. and e.,** para siempre jamás; (mostly ecclesiastical) por los siglos de los siglos; eternamente. **He is e. so nice,** Es muy simpático. **Hardly e.,** casi nunca. **I don't think I have e. been there,** No creo que haya estado nunca allí. **if e.,** si alguna vez; (rarely) raramente. **nor... e.,** ni nunca. **not... e.,** nunca. **e. after,** desde entonces; (afterward) después. **e. and anon,** de vez en cuando. **e. so little,** siquiera un poco; muy poco

evergreen /'ɛvər‚grin/ a siempre verde. —n planta vivaz, f. **e. oak,** encina, f

everlasting /‚ɛvər'læstɪŋ/ a eterno, perpetuo; (of colors) estable; incesante. **e. flower,** perpetua, f

evermore /‚ɛvər'mɔr/ adv eternamente

every /'ɛvri/ a todo; cada (invariable); todos los, m pl; todas las, f pl. **e. day,** todos los días, cada día. **e. now and then,** de cuando en cuando. **e. other day,** cada dos días

everybody /'ɛvri‚bɒdi, -‚bʌdi/ n todo el mundo, m; todos, m pl; todas, f pl; cada uno, m; cada una, f

everyday /'ɛvri‚dei/ a diario, cotidiano; corriente, de cada día, usual

everything /'ɛvri‚θɪŋ/ n todo, m; (e. that, which) todo lo (que). **e. possible,** todo lo posible

everywhere /'ɛvri‚wɛər/ adv por todas partes

evict /ɪ'vɪkt/ vt desahuciar; expulsar

eviction /ɪ'vɪkʃən/ n evicción, f, desahúcio, m; expulsión, f

evidence /'ɛvɪdəns/ n Law. testimonio, m, deposición, f; indicios, m pl; evidencia, f; prueba, f; hecho, m, vt patentizar, probar. **to give e.,** dar testimonio, deponer

evident /'ɛvɪdənt/ a evidente, patente, manifiesto; claro. **to be e.,** ser patente, estar a la vista

evidently /'ɛvɪdəntli/ adv evidentemente; claramente

evil /'ivəl/ a malo; malvado, perverso; de maldad; (unfortunate) aciago; de infortunio; (of spirits) diabólico, malo. —n mal, m; maldad, perversidad, f; (misfortune) desgracia, f. **the E. one,** el Malo. **e. -doer,** malhechor (-ra). **e. eye,** mal de ojo, aojo, m. **e.-minded,** mal pensado; malintencionado. **e.-speaking,** maledicencia, calumnia, f. **e. spirit,** demonio, espíritu malo, m

evince /ɪ'vɪns/ vt evidenciar; mostrar

eviscerate /ɪ'vɪsə‚reit/ vt destripar, desentrañar

evocation /‚ɛvə'keiʃən/ n evocación, f

evocative /ɪ'vɒkətɪv/ a evocador

evoke /ɪ'vouk/ vt evocar

evolution /‚ɛvə'luʃən/ n evolución, f; desarrollo, m; (Nav. Mil.) maniobra, f; Math. extracción de una raíz, f; (revolution) revolución, vuelta, f

evolutionism /‚ɛvə'luʃə‚nɪzəm/ n evolucionismo, m

evolutive /‚ɛvə'lutɪv/ a evolutivo

evolve /ɪ'vɒlv/ vi evolucionar; desarrollarse. —vt producir por evolución; desarrollar; pensar

ewe /yu/ n oveja, f. **ewe lamb,** cordera, f

ewer /'yuər/ n aguamanil, m

exacerbate /ɪg'zæsər‚beit/ vt exacerbar; agravar, empeorar

exacerbation /ɪg‚zæsər'beiʃən/ n exacerbación, f; agravación, f

exact /ɪg'zækt/ a exacto; fiel; metódico; estricto. —vt exigir

exacting /ɪg'zæktɪŋ/ a exigente; severo, estricto; (hard) agotador, arduo

exaction /ɪg'zækʃən/ n exigencia, f; extorsión, exacción, f

exactness /ɪg'zæktnɪs/ n exactitud, f

exaggerate /ɪg'zædʒə‚reit/ vt exagerar; acentuar. —vi exagerar

exaggerated /ɪg'zædʒə‚reitɪd/ a exagerado

exaggeration /ɪg‚zædʒə'reiʃən/ n exageración, f

exaggerator /ɪg'zædʒə‚reitər/ n exagerador (-ra)

exalt /ɪg'zɔlt/ vt exaltar; enaltecer, elevar; (praise) glorificar, magnificar; (intensify) realzar; intensificar

exaltation /‚ɛgzɔl'teiʃən/ n exaltación, elevación, f; alegría, f, júbilo, m; (ecstasy) éxtasis, arrobamiento, m; (of the Cross) exaltación, f

exalted /ɪg'zɔltɪd/ a exaltado, eminente

examination /ɪg‚zæmə'neiʃən/ n examen, m; inspección, f; investigación, f; Law. interrogatorio, m; prueba, f. **to sit an e.,** examinarse. **written e.,** prueba escrita, f

examine /ɪg'zæmɪn/ vt examinar; inspeccionar; investigar; Law. interrogar; (search) reconocer; (by touch) tentar; observar; analizar. **to e. into,** examinar; considerar detenidamente; ahondar en

examinee /ɪg‚zæmə'ni/ n examinando (-da)

examiner /ɪg'zæmɪnər/ n examinador (-ra); inspector (-ra)

examining /ɪg'zæmɪnɪŋ/ a que examina; de examen; Law. interrogante

example /ɪg'zæmpəl/ n ejemplo, m; ilustración, f; (parallel) ejemplar, m; (warning) escarmiento, m. **for e.,** por ejemplo. **to set an e.,** dar ejemplo, dar el ejemplo

exasperate /ɪg'zæspə‚reit/ vt exasperar, irritar; (increase) aumentar; (worsen) agravar

exasperating /ɪg'zæspə‚reitɪŋ/ a exasperante, irritante, provocador

exasperation /ɪg,zæspə'reiʃən/ n exasperación, irritación, f; (worsening) agravación, f; enojo, m

excavate /'ɛkskə,veit/ vt excavar; (hollow) vaciar

excavation /,ɛkskə'veiʃən/ n excavación, f; Archit. vaciado, m

excavator /'ɛkskə,veitər/ n excavador (-ra); (machine) excavadora, f

exceed /ɪk'sid/ vt exceder; (excel) superar, aventajar; (one's hopes, etc.) sobrepujar. —vi excederse. **e. all expectations**, exceder a toda ponderación. **to e. one's rights**, abusar de sus derechos, ir demasiado lejos

exceedingly /ɪk'sidɪŋli/ adv sumamente, extremadamente; sobre manera

excel /ɪk'sɛl/ vt aventajar, superar; vencer. —vi sobresalir; distinguirse, señalarse; ser superior

excellence /'ɛksələns/ n excelencia, f; superioridad, f; perfección, f; mérito, m; buena calidad, f

excellency /'ɛksələnsi/ n (title) Excelencia, f. **Your E.**, Su Excelencia

excellent /'ɛksələnt/ a excelente; superior; perfecto; magnífico; (in examinations) sobresaliente

except /ɪk'sɛpt/ vt exceptuar; omitir

except, excepting /ɪk'sɛpt; ɪk'sɛptɪŋ/ prep excepto, con excepción de; exceptuando; menos; salvo; fuera de. —conjunc a menos que. **except for**, si no fuese por; con excepción de; fuera de

exception /ɪk'sɛpʃən/ n excepción, f; objeción, protesta, f. **to make an e.**, hacer una excepción. **to take e. to**, protestar contra; tachar, criticar; desaprobar

excerpt /n 'ɛksɜrpt; v ɪk'sɜrpt/ n excerpta, f, extracto, m. —vt extraer

excess /ɪk'sɛs, 'ɛksɛs/ n exceso, m; superabundancia, f; demasía, f; Com. superávit, m. **in e.**, en exceso, de sobra. **in e. of**, en exceso de; arriba de. **e.** excesivamente, demasiado. **e. fare**, suplemento, m. **e. luggage**, exceso de equipaje, m; (overweight) exceso de peso, m

excessive /ɪk'sɛsɪv/ a excesivo; superabundante; inmoderado, desmesurado; exagerado

exchange /ɪks'tʃeɪndʒ/ n cambio, trueque, m; (of prisoners) canje, m; (financial) cambio, m; (building) bolsa, lonja, f; (telephone) oficina central de teléfonos, f. —vt cambiar (for, por); trocar; (replace) reemplazar; (prisoners) canjear; (of blows) dar; (pass from, into) pasar de... a. —vi hacer un cambio. **in e. for**, en cambio de, a trueque de; por. **to e. greetings**, saludarse; cambiar saludos. **They exchanged looks**, Se miraron. **What is the rate of e.?** ¿Cuál es el tipo de cambio? **e. of prisoners**, canje de prisioneros, m

exchangeable /ɪks'tʃeɪndʒəbəl/ a cambiable; trocable

exchequer /'ɛkstʃɛkər/ n (public finance) Hacienda pública, f; tesorería, f;

(funds) fondos, m pl. **Chancellor of the E.**, Ministro de Hacienda, m

excise /n 'ɛksaiz; v ɪk'saiz/ n contribución indirecta, f; (customs and e.) Aduana, f. —vt (cut) cortar, extirpar; imponer una contribución indirecta. **e. duty**, derecho de aduana, m

excision /ɛk'sɪʒən/ n excisión, f; extirpación, f

excite /ɪk'sait/ vt emocionar; conmover; agitar; excitar; suscitar, provocar; incitar, instigar; (attention, interest) despertar; estimular. **to become excited**, emocionarse; exaltarse; (annoyed) acalorarse; (upset) agitarse

excitedly /ɪk'saitɪdli/ adv con emoción; acaloradamente; agitadamente

excitement /ɪk'saitmənt/ n conmoción, f; agitación, f; (annoyance) acaloramiento, m; emoción, f; estímulo, m; instigación, f, fomento, m; (amusement) placer, m

exciting /ɪk'saitɪŋ/ a emocionante; conmovedor; agitador; muy interesante

exclaim /ɪk'skleim/ vt and vi exclamar. **to e. against**, clamar contra

exclamation /,ɛksklə'meiʃən/ n exclamación, f. **e. mark**, punto de exclamación, m

exclude /ɪk'sklud/ vt excluir; exceptuar; evitar; (refuse) rechazar

exclusion /ɪk'skluʒən/ n exclusión, f; exceptuación, f; eliminación, f

exclusive /ɪk'sklusɪv/ a exclusivo; (snobbish) exclusivista. **e. of**, no incluido; aparte de

exclusively /ɪk'sklusɪvli/ adv exclusivamente; únicamente

excommunicate /v ,ɛkskə'myuni,keit; -kɪt/ vt excomulgar. —a excomulgado

excommunication /,ɛkskə,myuni'keiʃən/ n excomunión, f

excrement /'ɛkskrəmənt/ n excremento, m

excrescence /ɪk'skrɛsəns/ n excrecencia, f

excrescent /ɪk'skrɛsənt/ a que forma excrecencia; superfluo

excrete /ɪk'skrit/ vt excretar

excretion /ɪk'skriʃən/ n excreción, f

excruciating /ɪk'skruʃi,eitɪŋ/ a atormentador, angustioso; (of pain) agudísimo

excursion /ɪk'skɜrʒən/ n excursión, f; expedición, f; (digression) digresión, f. **e. ticket**, billete de excursión, m. **e. train**, tren de excursionistas, m

excursionist /ɪk'skɜrʒənɪst/ n excursionista, mf; turista, mf

excusable /ɪk'skyuzəbəl/ a disculpable, excusable

excuse /ɪk'skyus/ n excusa, f; disculpa, f; pretexto, m; justificación, defensa, f. **to give as an e.**, pretextar

excuse /ɪk'skyuz/ vt disculpar, excusar; dispensar (de); librar (de); (forgive) perdonar; (defend) justificar, defender; (minimize) paiar; (oneself) disculparse. **E. me!** ¡Con permiso!; ¡Perdone Vd.!; ¡Dispense Vd.!

execrate /'ɛksɪ,kreɪt/ vt execrar, abominar. —vi maldecir

execute /'ɛksɪ,kyut/ vt (perform) ejecutar, poner en efecto, realizar; (Art. Mus.) ejecutar; (part in a play) hacer, desempeñar; (fulfil) cumplir; Law. otorgar (un documento); (kill) ajusticiar

execution /,ɛksɪ'kyuʃən/ n efectuación, realización, f; (Art., Mus.) ejecución, f; (of part in a play) desempeño (de un papel), m; (fulfilment) cumplimiento, m; Law. otorgamiento (de un documento), m; (killing) suplicio, m, ejecución de la pena de muerte, f; (Law. seizure) ejecución, f

executioner /,ɛksɪ'kyuʃənər/ n verdugo, m

executive /ɪg'zɛkyətɪv/ a ejecutivo; administrativo. —n poder ejecutivo, m

executor /ɪg'zɛkyətər/ n administrador testamentario, m

executrix /ɪg'zɛkyətrɪks/ n administradora testamentaria, f

exegesis /,ɛksɪ'dʒɪsɪs/ n exégesis, f

exemplary /ɪg'zɛmplərɪ/ a ejemplar

exemplify /ɪg'zɛmplə,faɪ/ vt ejemplificar; ilustrar, demostrar

exempt /ɪg'zɛmpt/ vt exentar, eximir; librar; dispensar, excusar. —a exento; libre; excusado; inmune

exemption /ɪg'zɛmpʃən/ n exención, f; libertad, f; inmunidad, f

exercise /'ɛksər,saɪz/ n ejercicio, m; uso, m; (essay) ensayo, m; pl **exercises**, (on land or sea) maniobras, f pl. —vt ejercer; usar, emplear; (train) ejercitar, entrenar; adiestrar; pasear, dar un paseo; (worry) preocupar. —vi hacer ejercicio; ejercitarse; adiestrarse. **spiritual exercises**, ejercicios espirituales, m pl. **to take e. in the open air**, tomar ejercicio al aire libre. **to write an e.**, escribir un ejercicio. **e. book**, cuaderno de ejercicios, m

exert /ɪg'zɜrt/ vt hacer uso de, emplear, ejercer, poner en juego; (deploy) desplegar. **to e. oneself**, hacer un esfuerzo (para); esforzarse (de); trabajar mucho; tratar (de); apurarse, tomarse mucha molestia; preocuparse

exertion /ɪg'zɜrʃən/ n esfuerzo, m; uso, m; (exercise) ejercicio, m; (good offices) diligencias, gestiones, f pl; buenos oficios, m pl

exhalation /,ɛkshə'leɪʃən/ n exhalación, f; efluvio, m; vapor, m; humo, m

exhale /ɛks'heɪl/ vt exhalar; emitir, despedir. —vi evaporarse; disiparse

exhaust /ɪg'zɔst/ vt agotar; (empty) vaciar; (end) acabar; apurar; consumir; (tire) rendir, cansar mucho; (weaken) debilitar; (a subject) tratar detalladamente. —n Mech. escape, m; emisión de vapor, f; vapor de escape, m. **e. pipe**, tubo de escape, m

exhausting /ɪg'zɔstɪŋ/ a cansado, agotador

exhaustion /ɪg'zɔstʃən/ n agotamiento, m; rendimiento, cansancio, m; lasitud, f; postración, f

exhaustive /ɪg'zɔstɪv/ a completo; minucioso

exhaustively /ɪg'zɔstɪvlɪ/ adv detenidamente; detalladamente; minuciosamente

exhibit /ɪg'zɪbɪt/ vt exhibir; manifestar, ostentar; revelar, descubrir; presentar. —vi exhibir, ser expositor. —n objeto exhibido, m; Law. prueba, f

exhibition /,ɛksə'bɪʃən/ n exposición, f; (performance) función, f; espectáculo, m; exhibición, f; (showing) manifestación, f; (grant) bolsa de estudio, beca, f

exhibitionist /,ɛksə'bɪʃənɪst/ n exhibicionista, mf

exhibitor /ɪg'zɪbɪtər/ n expositor (-ra)

exhilarate /ɪg'zɪlə,reɪt/ vt alegrar, alborozar

exhilarating /ɪg'zɪlə,reɪtɪŋ/ a alegre; estimulador; vigorizador, tonificante

exhilaration /ɪg,zɪlə'reɪʃən/ n alegría, f, alborozo, regocijo, m

exhort /ɪg'zɔrt/ vt and vi exhortar

exhortation /,ɛgzɔr'teɪʃən/ n exhortación, f

exhume /ɪg'zum/ vt exhumar

exigence /'ɛksɪdʒəns/ n exigencia, f; urgencia, f; (need) necesidad, f

exigent /'ɛksɪdʒənt/ a exigente; urgente

exiguous /ɪg'zɪgyuəs/ a exiguo

exile /'ɛgzaɪl/ n destierro, m; (person) desterrado (-da). —vt desterrar

exist /ɪg'zɪst/ vi existir

existence /ɪg'zɪstəns/ n existencia, f; (being) ser, m; (life) vida, f. **to bring into e.**, causar; producir

existing /ɪg'zɪstɪŋ/ a existente

exit /'ɛgzɪt, 'ɛksɪt/ n salida, f; partida, f; (death) muerte, f; Theat. mutis, m. —vi Theat. hacer mutis. **to make one's e.**, salir; marcharse; irse; morir; Theat. hacer mutis

exodus /'ɛksədəs/ n éxodo, m; salida, f; emigración, f; (Old Testament) Éxodo, m

exonerate /ɪg'zɒnə,reɪt/ vt exonerar

exorbitant /ɪg'zɔrbɪtənt/ a exorbitante

exorcize /'ɛksər,saɪz/ vt exorcizar, conjurar

exotic /ɪg'zɒtɪk/ a exótico. —n planta exótica, f; Fig. flor de estufa, f

expand /ɪk'spænd/ vt extender; abrir; (wings, etc.) desplegar; (the chest, etc.) expandir; dilatar; (amplify) ampliar; (an edition) ampliar, aumentar; (develop) desarrollar; Fig. ensanchar; (increase) aumentar. —vi dilatarse; hincharse; abrirse; extenderse; Fig. ensancharse; (increase) aumentarse

expanse /ɪk'spæns/ n extensión, f

expansible /ɪk'spænsəbəl/ a Phys. expansible; dilatable

expansion /ɪk'spænʃən/ n expansión, f; extensión, f; dilatación, f; (amplification) ampliación, f; (development) desarrollo, m; Fig. ensanchamiento, m; (increase) aumento, m

expansionism /ɪkˈspænʃəˌnɪzəm/ n expansionismo, m

expansive /ɪkˈspænsɪv/ a expansivo; (of persons) efusivo, expresivo, comunicativo, afable

expansiveness /ɪkˈspænsɪvnɪs/ n expansibilidad, f; (of persons) afabilidad, f

expatiate /ɪkˈspeɪʃiˌeɪt/ (upon) vi extenderse en

expatiation /ɪkˌspeɪʃiˈeɪʃən/ n discurso, m; digresión, f

expect /ɪkˈspɛkt/ vt esperar; (await) aguardar; (suppose) suponer; (demand) exigir; (count on) contar con. —vi creer

expectant /ɪkˈspɛktənt/ a expectante; (hopeful) esperanzudo; (pregnant) embarazada

expectantly /ɪkˈspɛktəntli/ adv con expectación

expectation /ˌɛkspɛkˈteɪʃən/ n expectación, f; (hope) esperanza, expectativa, f; probabilidad, f

expectorate /ɪkˈspɛktəˌreɪt/ vt expectorar. —vi escupir

expedience /ɪkˈspidiəns/ n conveniencia, f; oportunidad, f; aptitud, f; (self-interest) egoísmo, m

expedient /ɪkˈspidiənt/ a conveniente, oportuno; apto; prudente; político. —n expediente, recurso, medio, m

expedite /ˈɛkspɪˌdaɪt/ vt acelerar; facilitar; (send off) despachar

expedition /ˌɛkspɪˈdɪʃən/ n expedición, f; (haste) celeridad, diligencia, f

expeditionary /ˌɛkspɪˈdɪʃəˌnɛri/ a expedicionario. **e. force,** fuerza expedicionaria, f

expeditious /ˌɛkspɪˈdɪʃəs/ a expedito, pronto

expel /ɪkˈspɛl/ vt expeler, expulsar; echar, arrojar; despedir

expend /ɪkˈspɛnd/ vt gastar, expender; (time) perder

expenditure /ɪkˈspɛndɪtʃər/ n gasto, desembolso, m; (of time) pérdida, f

expense /ɪkˈspɛns/ n gasto, m; pérdida, f; costa, f; pl gastos, expensas, f pl, gastos, m pl. **at the e. of,** a costa de. **to be put to great e.,** tener que gastar mucho. **to pay one's expenses,** pagar sus gastos

expensive /ɪkˈspɛnsɪv/ a costoso; caro

experience /ɪkˈspɪriəns/ n experiencia, f. —vt experimentar; sentir; sufrir. **by e.,** por experiencia

experienced /ɪkˈspɪriənst/ a experimentado; experto; hábil; (lived) vivido

experiment /n ɪkˈspɛrəmənt; v -ˌmɛnt/ n experimento, m; prueba, f; ensayo, m, tentativa, f. —vi experimentar; hacer una prueba

experimental /ɪkˌspɛrəˈmɛntl/ a experimental; tentativo

expert /ˈɛkspɜrt/ a experto; perito; hábil;

(finished) acabado. —n experto, m, especialista, mf

expertness /ˈɛkspɜrtnɪs/ n pericia, f; maestría, f; habilidad, f; (knowledge) conocimiento, m

expiate /ˈɛkspiˌeɪt/ vt expiar; reparar

expiration /ˌɛkspəˈreɪʃən/ n (breathing out) espiración, f; (ending) expiración, f; terminación, f; Com. vencimiento, m; (death) muerte, f

expiration date fecha de caducidad, f

expire /ɪkˈspaɪər/ vi (exhale) espirar; (die) morir, dar el último suspiro; (of fire, light) extinguirse; (end) expirar; terminar; Com. vencer

explain /ɪkˈspleɪn/ vt explicar; aclarar; demostrar; exponer; (justify) justificar, defender. —vi explicarse. **to e. away,** explicar; justificar

explanation /ˌɛkspləˈneɪʃən/ n explicación, f; aclaración, f

explanatory /ɪkˈsplænəˌtɔri/ a explicativo, aclaratorio

expletive /ˈɛksplɪtɪv/ a expletivo. —n interjección, f

explicit /ɪkˈsplɪsɪt/ a explícito

explode /ɪkˈsploʊd/ vi estallar; detonar; reventar. —vt hacer estallar; (a mine) hacer saltar; (a belief, etc.) hacer abandonar; desechar

exploit /ɪkˈsplɔɪt/ n hazaña, proeza, f; aventura, f. —vt explotar

exploitation /ˌɛksplɔɪˈteɪʃən/ n explotación, f

exploiter /ɪkˈsplɔɪtər/ n explotador (-ra)

exploration /ˌɛkspləˈreɪʃən/ n exploración, f

exploratory /ɪkˈsplɔrəˌtɔri/ a exploratorio

explore /ɪkˈsplɔr/ vt explorar; examinar; averiguar; investigar; (Med. Surg.) explorar

explorer /ɪkˈsplɔrər/ n explorador (-ra)

explosion /ɪkˈsploʊʒən/ n explosión, f; estallido, m, detonación, f

explosive /ɪkˈsploʊsɪv/ a and n explosivo, m. **high e.,** explosivo violento, m. **explosives chamber,** recámara, f

export /n ˈɛkspɔrt; v ɪkˈsport/ n exportación, f. —vt exportar. **e. license,** permiso de exportación, m. **e. trade,** comercio de exportación, m

exportation /ˌɛkspɔrˈteɪʃən/ n exportación, f

exporter /ɪkˈspɔrtər/ n exportador (-ra)

expose /ɪkˈspoʊz/ vt exponer; arriesgar; (exhibit) exhibir, (unmask) desenmascarar; descubrir; revelar; Photo. exponer; (ridicule) ridiculizar

exposed /ɪkˈspoʊzd/ a descubierto; no abrigado; expuesto; peligroso

exposition /ˌɛkspəˈzɪʃən/ n explicación, interpretación, f; declaración, f; (exhibition) exposición, f

expostulate /ɪkˈspɒstʃəˌleɪt/ vi protestar, **to e. with,** reprochar; reconvenir

expostulation /ɪk,spɒstʃəˈleɪʃən/ *n* protesta, *f*; reconvención, *f*

exposure /ɪkˈspouʒər/ *n* exposición, *f*; (aspect) orientación, *f*; (scandal) revelación, *f*, escándalo, *m*; peligro, *m*; exposición al frío or al calor, *f*

expound /ɪkˈspaund/ *vt* exponer, explicar; comentar

expounder /ɪkˈspaundər/ *n* intérprete, *mf*; comentador (-ra)

express /ɪkˈspres/ *a* (clear) categórico, explícito, claro; expreso; (exact) exacto; (quick) rápido. —*n* (messenger, post) expreso, *m*; (train) (tren) expreso, (tren) rápido, *m*; (goods) exprés, *m*. —*vt* expresar; (a letter, etc.) mandar por expreso

expression /ɪkˈspreʃən/ *n* expresión, *f*

expressionless /ɪkˈspreʃənlɪs/ *a* sin expresión

expressive /ɪkˈspresɪv/ *a* expresivo; que expresa

expropriate /ɛksˈprouprɪˌeit/ *vt* expropiar

expropriation /ɛks,prouprɪˈeiʃən/ *n* expropiación, *f*

expulsion /ɪkˈspʌlʃən/ *n* expulsión, *f*

expunge /ɪkˈspʌndʒ/ *vt* borrar; testar; omitir

expurgate /ˈɛkspərˌgeit/ *vt* expurgar

exquisite /ɪkˈskwɪzɪt/ *a* exquisito, precioso, primoroso; excelente; (acute) agudo, intenso; (keen) vivo. —*n* elegante, petimetre, *m*

exquisitely /ɪkˈskwɪzɪtli/ *adv* primorosamente, pulcramente; a la perfección

exquisiteness /ɪkˈskwɪzɪtnɪs/ *n* primor. *m*; pulcritud, perfección, *f*; excelencia, *f*; (of pain) intensidad, *f*; (keenness) viveza, *f*

ex-serviceman /ˈɛksˈsɜrvɪsmən/ *n* excombatiente, antiguo soldado, *m*

extant /ˈɛkstənt/ *a* estante; existente; viviente

extempore /ɪkˈstempəri/ *a* improvisado

extemporize /ɪkˈstempəˌraiz/ *vt and vi* improvisar

extend /ɪkˈstend/ *vt* extender; (hold out) tender, alargar; (lengthen) prolongar; (a period of time) prorrogar, diferir; (make larger) ensanchar; (increase) aumentar; dilatar; ampliar; (offer) ofrecer; *vi* extenderse; dilatarse; continuar; (give) dar de sí, estirarse; (last) prolongarse, durar; (become known) propagarse

extension /ɪkˈstenʃən/ *n* extensión, *f*; expansión, *f*; (increase) aumento, *m*; prolongación, *f*; ampliación, *f*; *Com.* prórroga, *f*; (telephone number) extensión, *f*, interno, *m*

extension cord *n* cordón de extensión, *m*; ladrón *m*, (Mexico; slang)

extensive /ɪkˈstensɪv/ *a* extenso, ancho, vasto; grande, considerable; (comprehensive) comprensivo

extent /ɪkˈstent/ *n* extensión, *f*; (degree) punto, *m*; (limit) límite, *m*. **to a great e.**, en gran parte; considerablemente. **to**

some e., hasta cierto punto. **to the full e.**, en toda su extensión; completamente. **to what e.?** ¿hasta qué punto?

extenuate /ɪkˈstenyu,eit/ *vt* atenuar, desminuir, mitigar, paliar

extenuating /ɪkˈstenyu,eitɪŋ/ *a* atenuante

extenuation /ɪk,stenyuˈeiʃən/ *n* atenuación, mitigación, *f*

exterior /ɪkˈstɪriər/ *a* exterior, externo; de fuera; (foreign) extranjero. —*n* exterior, *m*; aspecto, *m*; forma, *f*

exterminate /ɪkˈstɜrmə,neit/ *vt* exterminar

extermination /ɪk,stɜrməˈneiʃən/ *n* exterminio, *m*

exterminator /ɪkˈstɜrmə,neitər/ *n* exterminador (-ra)

external /ɪkˈstɜrnl/ *a* externo, exterior; (foreign) extranjero. —*n pl* **externals**, apariencias, *f pl*; aspecto exterior, *m*; comportamiento, *m*

extinct /ɪkˈstɪŋkt/ *a* extinto; (of light, fire) extinguido; suprimido

extinction /ɪkˈstɪŋkʃən/ *n* extinción, *f*

extinguish /ɪkˈstɪŋgwɪʃ/ *vt* extinguir; apagar; *Fig.* eclipsar

extinguisher /ɪkˈstɪŋgwɪʃər/ *n* apagador (-ra); (for fires) extintor, *m*; (snuffer) matacandelas, *m*

extinguishment /ɪkˈstɪŋgwɪʃmənt/ *n* apagamiento, *m*; extinción, *f*; abolición, *f*; (destruction) aniquilamiento, *m*

extirpate /ˈɛkstər,peit/ *vt* extirpar

extol /ɪkˈstoul/ *vt* elogiar, encomiar, alabar; cantar

extort /ɪkˈstɔrt/ *vt* arrancar, sacar por fuerza; exigir por amenazas

extortion /ɪkˈstɔrʃən/ *n* extorsión, *f*; exacción, *f*

extortionate /ɪkˈstɔrʃənɪt/ *a* injusto; opresivo; (of price) exorbitante, excesivo

extra /ˈɛkstrə/ *a* and *adv* adicional, extraordinario; suplementario; (spare) de repuesto. —*prefix* (in compounds) extra. —*n* extra, *m*; suplemento, *m*; (of a paper) hoja extraordinaria, *f*; (actor) supernumerario (-ia). **e. charge**, gasto suplementario, *m*; (on the railway, etc.) suplemento, *m*. **e.-mural**, *a* de extramuros

extract /*v* ɪkˈstrækt; *n* ˈɛkstrækt/ *vt* sacar; (*Chem. Math.*) extraer; extractar; (obtain) obtener. —*n Chem.* extracto, *m*; (excerpt) cita, *f*

extraction /ɪkˈstrækʃən/ *n* saca, *f*; extracción, *f*; obtención, *f*

extradite /ˈɛkstrə,dait/ *vt* entregar por extradición

extraneous /ɪkˈstreiniəs/ *a* extraño; (irrelevant) ajeno (a)

extraordinarily /ɪk,strɔrdnˈerəli/ *adv* extraordinariamente, singularmente

extraordinariness /ɪkˈstrɔrdn,erinɪs/ *n* lo extraordinario; singularidad, *f*; (queerness) rareza, *f*

extraordinary /ɪkˈstrɔrdn,eri/ *a* extraordinario; singular; (queer) raro, excéntrico; (incredible) increíble

extravagance /ɪk'strævəgəns/ *n* (in spending) prodigalidad, *f,* derroche, *m;* (of dress, speech) extravagancia, *f;* (foolishness) disparate, *m;* (luxury) lujo, *m*

extravagant /ɪk'strævəgənt/ *a* extravagante; (queer) extraño, raro; (wasteful) pródigo; (of persons) gastador, manirroto; (of price) exorbitante; excesivo

extravagantly /ɪk'strævəgəntli/ *adv* extravagantemente; de un modo extraño; pródigamente; profusamente; excesivamente

extreme /ɪk'strim/ *a* extremo. —*n* extremo, *m.* **in e.**, extremamente, en extremo, en sumo grado. **to carry to extremes,** llevar a extremos; **E. Unction,** Extremaunción, *f*

extremely /ɪk'strimli/ *adv* sumamente; *Inf.* muy

extremism /ɪk'stri,mɪzəm/ *n* extremismo, *m*

extremist /ɪk'strimɪst/ *a* and *n* extremista, *mf*

extremity /ɪk'stremɪti/ *n* extremidad, *f;* (point) punta, *f;* necesidad, *f; pl* **extremities,** *Anat.* extremidades, *f pl;* (measures) medidas extremas, *f pl*

extricate /'ɛkstrɪ,keit/ *vt* desenredar; librar; sacar

extrovert /'ɛkstrə,vɜrt/ *n Psychol.* extravertido, *m*

exuberance /ɪg'zubərəns/ *n* exuberancia, *f*

exuberant /ɪg'zubərənt/ *a* exuberante

exude /ɪg'zud/ *vt* exudar; rezumar; sudar. —*vi* exudar; rezumarse

exult /ɪg'zʌlt/ *vi* exultar; alegrarse

exultant /ɪg'zʌltnt/ *a* exultante, triunfante

exultantly /ɪg'zʌltntli/ *adv* con exultación; triunfalmente

exultation /,ɛgzʌl'teiʃən/ *n* exultación, *f;* triunfo, *m*

eye /ai/ *n* ojo, *m;* (sight) vista, *f;* (look)

mirada, *f;* atención, *f;* (opinion) opinión, *f,* juicio, *m;* (of a needle, of cheese) ojo, *m;* (of a hook) corcheta, *f; Bot.* yema, *f;* (of a potato) grillo, *m.* —*vt* ojear; fijar los ojos en; examinar, mirar detenidamente. **bright eyes,** ojos vivos, *m pl.* **prominent eyes,** ojos saltones, *m pl.* **He couldn't keep his eyes off Mary,** Se le fueron los ojos tras María. **as far as the eye can reach,** hasta donde alcanza la vista. **before one's eyes,** a la vista de uno, ante los ojos de uno. **in my (etc.) eyes,** *Fig.* según creo yo, en mi opinión. **in the twinkling of an eye,** en un abrir y cerrar de ojos. **with an eye to,** pensando en. **with my own eyes,** con mis propios ojos. **with the naked eye,** con la simple vista. **to keep an eye on,** vigilar. **to make eyes at,** guiñar el ojo; mirar con ojos de enamorado. **to have one's eyes opened,** *Fig.* caérsele la venda. **eye-bath,** ojera, *f.* **eye-opener,** revelación, sorpresa, *f.* **eye-pencil,** pincel para las cejas, *m.*

eye-piece, objetivo, ocular, *m.* **eye-shade,** visera, *f.* **eye-tooth,** colmillo, *m.* **eye-witness,** testigo ocular, testigo de vista, testigo presencial, *mf*

eyeball /'ai,bɔl/ *n* globo ocular, *m*

eyebrow /'ai,brau/ *n* ceja, *f*

eye care atención de la vista, *f*

eyed /aid/ *a* que tiene ojos; (in compounds) de ojos..., con ojos...; con los ojos; (of a needle) con el ojo... **She is a blue-eyed child,** Es una niña de ojos azules

eyeglass /'ai,glæs/ *n* lente, *m*

eyelash /'ai,læʃ/ *n* pestaña, *f*

eyelet /'ailɪt/ *n* ojete, *m*

eyelid /'ai,lɪd/ *n* párpado, *m*

eyesight /'ai,sait/ *n* vista, *f*

eyewash /'ai,wɔʃ/ *n* colirio, *m; Inf.* camelo, *m.* **That's all e.!** ¡Eso es un camelo!

eyrie /'ɛəri/ *n* nido (of any bird of prey), nido de águila (eagle's) *m*

F

f /ɛf/ n (letter) efe, f; Mus. fa, m. **f sharp,** fa sostenido, m

fa /fɑ/ n Mus. fa, m

fable /'feibəl/ n fábula, leyenda, historia, f, apólogo, cuento, m; (untruth) invención, mentira, f

fabled /'feibəld/ a celebrado, famoso

fabric /'fæbrɪk/ n obra, fábrica, f; estructura, construcción, f; (making) manufactura, f; (cloth) tejido, paño, m; textura, f

fabricate /'fæbrɪ,keit/ vt fabricar, construir; (invent) fingir, inventar

fabrication /,fæbrɪ'keiʃən/ n fabricación, manufactura, f; construcción, f; (lie) invención, ficción, f

fabulous /'fæbyələs/ a fabuloso

façade /fə'sɑd/ n fachada, frente, f

face /feis/ n superficie, f; (of persons) cara, f, rostro, m; (look) semblante, aire, m; (of coins) anverso, m; (grimace) mueca, f, gesto, m; (dial) esfera, f; (of gems) faceta, f; (of a wall) paramento, m; (front) fachada, frente, f; (effrontery) cara dura, f, descaro, m. **in the f. of,** ante; en presencia de. Mil. Left f.! ¡Izquierda! **on the f. of it,** juzgando por las apariencias. **to bring f. to f.,** confrontar (con). **to laugh in a person's f.,** reírse a la cara (de). **to make a f.,** hacer muecas. **to my f.,** en mi cara, en mis barbas. **to put a good f. on,** Fig. poner (o hacer) buena cara a. **to set one's f. against,** oponerse resueltamente a. **to straighten one's f.,** componer el semblante. **to throw in one's f.,** Fig. dar en rostro, dar en cara. **to wash one's f.,** lavarse la cara. **f. card,** figura (de la baraja), f. **f.-cloth,** paño para lavar la cara, m. **f. downward,** boca abajo. **f. lift,** operación estética facial, f. **f. of the waters,** faz de las aguas, f. **f. powder,** polvos de arroz, m pl. **f. to f.,** cara a cara, de persona a persona; frente a frente. **f. value,** significado literal, m; Com. valor nominal, m

face /feis/ vt mirar hacia; confrontar, hacer cara (a); (of buildings, etc.) mirar a, caer a (or hacia); Fig. arrostrar, enfrentarse con; Sew. guarnecer, aforrar. —vi estar orientado. **to f. the facts,** enfrentarse con la realidad. **to f. the music,** Fig. arrostrar las consecuencias. **to f. about,** volver la espalda; Mil. dar una vuelta, cambiar de frente. **to f. up to,** Fig. hacer cara a

faced /feist/ a con cara..., de cara...; Sew. forrado (de). **to be two-f.,** Fig. ser de dos haces

facer /'feisər/ n puñetazo en la cara, m; Fig. dificultad insuperable, f, problema muy grande, m

facet /'fæsɪt/ n faceta, f

facetious /fə'siʃəs/ a chancero, chistoso, jocoso

facial /'feiʃəl/ a facial. **f. expression,** expresión de la cara, f, semblante, m

facile /'fæsɪl/ a (frivolous) ligero (e.g., a deduction or inference)

facilitate /fə'sɪlɪ,teit/ vt facilitar

facility /fə'sɪlɪti/ n facilidad, f; habilidad, destreza, f

facing /'feisɪŋ/ n Sew. vuelta, f; (of a building) paramento, m; (of lumber) chapa f; encaramiento, m

facsimile /fæk'sɪməli/ n facsímile, m

fact /fækt/ n (event) hecho, suceso, m; (datum) dato, m; realidad, verdad, f. **as a matter of f.,** en realidad. **in f.,** en efecto, en realidad. **I know as a f.,** Tengo por cierto. **The f. is...,** La verdad es (que)... **the f. that,** el hecho de que

fact-finding /'fækt ,faindɪŋ/ informador (e.g. send s.b. on a fact-finding mission, enviar a fulano en misión informadora)

faction /'fækʃən/ n facción, f, partido, bando, m; (tumult) alboroto, m

factional /'fækʃən/ a partidario

factious /'fækʃəs/ a faccioso, sedicioso

factor /'fæktər/ n (fact) factor, elemento, m; consideración, f; Math. factor, m; Com. agente, factor, m

factory /'fæktəri/ n fábrica, manufactura, f; taller, m. **F. Act,** ley de trabajadores industriales, f. **f. hand,** operario (-ia)

factual /'fæktʃuəl/ a basado en hechos, objetivo

faculty /'fækəlti/ n facultad, f; (talent) habilidad, f, talento, m; (university division) facultad, f; (teachers as a group) claustro de profesores, claustro, profesorado, m; (authorization) privilegio, m, autoridad, f

fad /fæd/ n capricho, m, chifladura, f, dengue, m

fade /feid/ vi (of plants) marchitarse, secarse; (of color) palidecer, descolorarse; (vanish) disiparse, desaparecer; (of persons) desmejorarse; (of stains) salir. —vt descolorar, Fig. desvanecer; (of persons) consumirse. **to f. away,** desvanecer; **f.-out,** n (cinema) desaparecimiento gradual, m

faded /'feidɪd/ a (of plants) seco, marchito, mustio; (of colors) descolorado, pálido; (of people) desmejorado

fading /'feidɪŋ/ a (of flowers) medio marchito; (of light) mortecino, pálido; decadente. —n desaparecimiento, m, marchitez, f; decadencia, f

fag /fæg/ n Inf. pitillo, m. **f.-end,** fin, m; restos, m pl, sobras, f pl; (of a cigarette) colilla, f; (offensive) maricón. —vi trabajar mucho. —vt fatigar mucho; hacer trabajar.

faience /fai'ɑns/ n fayenza, f

fail /feil/ vi faltar; fracasar, malograrse; no tener éxito, salir mal; (of strength) decaer, acabarse; (be short of) carecer (de); Com. hacer bancarrota, suspender pagos. —vt abandonar; (disappoint) decepcionar, engañar; (in exams) suspender. **Do not f.**

to see her, No dejes de verla. **He failed to do his duty,** Faltó a su deber

fail /feil/ n without f., sin falta

failing /'feiliŋ/ n falta, f; (shortcoming) vicio, flaco, m, debilidad, f; malogro, fracaso, m; decadencia, f

failure /'feiljər/ n fracaso, m; falta de éxito, f; (in exams) suspensión, f; (of power) no funcionamiento, m; omisión, f, descuido, m; *Com.* quiebra, bancarrota, f; (decay) decadencia, f. **on f. of,** al fracasar; bajo pena de

fain /fein/ a deseoso, muy contento. **He was f. to...,** Se sintió obligado a...; Quería

faint /feint/ a débil; (dim) indistinto, vago, borroso; (of colors) pálido, desmayado; (weak) lánguido, desfallecido; (slight) superficial, rudimentario. —vi perder el sentido, desmayarse. —n desmayo, m. **to be f. with hunger,** estar muerto de hambre. **to cause to f.,** hacer desmayar. **f.-hearted,** pusilánime, medroso. **f.-heartedness,** pusilanimidad, f

fair /fɛər/ n feria, f; (sale) mercado, m; (exhibition) exposición, f

fair /fɛər/ a (beautiful) hermoso, lindo, bello; (of hair) rubio; (of skin) blanco; (clear, fresh) limpio, claro; (good) bueno; (favorable) favorable, propicio, próspero; (of weather) despejado, sereno; (just) imparcial; (straightforward) honrado, recto, justo; (passable) regular, mediano; (of writing) legible; (proper) conveniente. —adv honradamente; (politely) cortésmente; exactamente. **by f. means,** por medios honrados. **It's not f.!** ¡No hay derecho! **to become f.,** (of weather) serenarse. **to give a f. trial,** juzgar imparcialmente; dar una buena oportunidad; *Law.* procesar imparcialmente. **to make a f. copy,** poner en limpio. **f.-haired,** de pelo rubio, rubio. **f. one,** una beldad, f. **f. play,** *Sports.* juego limpio, m; proceder leal, m. **f.-skinned,** de tez blanca, rubio. **f.-weather,** buen tiempo, m, bonanza, f. **f.-weather friends,** amigos de los días prósperos, m pl

fairly /'fɛərli/ adv (justly) con imparcialidad; (moderately) bastante; totalmente, enteramente. **f. good,** bastante bueno; regular

fairness /'fɛərnɪs/ n belleza, hermosura, f; (of skin) blancura, f; (justness) imparcialidad, f; (reasonableness) justicia, equidad, f; (of hair) color rubio, oro, m

fairy /'fɛəri/ n hada, f, duende, m. —a de hada, de duendes; *Fig.* delicado. **f.-gold,** tesoro de duendes, m; **f.-light,** lucecillo, m; luminaria, f. **f.-like,** aduendado, como una hada. **f.-ring,** círculo mágico, m. **f.-tale,** cuento de hadas, m; patraña, f, cuento de viejas, m

faith /feiθ/ n fe, f; confianza, f; (doctrine) creencia, religión, filosofía, f; (honor) palabra, f. **in good f.,** de buena fe. **to break f.,** faltar a la palabra dada. **f.-healing,** curanderismo, m

faithful /'feiθfəl/ a fiel, leal; (accurate) exacto; (trustworthy) veraz. **the f.,** los creyentes

faithfully /'feiθfəli/ adv fielmente, lealmente; (accurately) con exactitud. **Yours f.,** Queda de Vd. su att. s.s.

faithfulness /'feiθfəlnɪs/ n fidelidad, lealtad, f; (accuracy) exactitud, f

faithless /'feiθlɪs/ a infiel, desleal, pérfido.

fake /feik/ vt imitar, falsificar. —n imitación, falsificación, f. **to f. up,** inventar

fall /fɔl/ n caída, f; (of temperature, mercury) baja, f; (of water) salto de agua, m, catarata, cascada, f; (in value) depreciación, f; (in price and Stock Exchange) baja, f; (descent) bajada, f; (autumn) otoño, m; (declivity) declinación, f, declive, desnivel, m; (ruin) ruina, f; destrucción, f; (of night, etc.) caída (de la noche), f; (of snow) nevada, f; (of rain) golpe, m; (*Theat.* of curtain) caída, bajada, f; (surrender) capitulación, rendición, f; (of earth) desprendimiento de tierras, m; (of the tide) reflujo, m

fall /fɔl/ vi caer; (of mercury, temperature) bajar; (collapse) desplomarse, hundirse, derrumbarse; (die) caer muerto; (descend) descender; (*Theat.* of the curtain) bajar, caer; (of a river into the sea, etc.) desembocar, desaguar; (of hair, draperies) caer; (decrease) disminuir; (of spirits) ponerse triste, sentirse deprimido; (sin) caer; (come upon) sobrevenir; (of dusk, etc.) caer, llegar; (strike, touch) tocar; (as a share) tocar en suerte; (as a duty, responsibility) tocar, corresponder; (of seasons) caer en; (of words from the lips) caer de (los labios); (say) decir, pronunciar palabras; (of exclamations) escaparse; (become) venir a ser; (happen) suceder; (be) ser. **fallen upon evil days,** venido a menos. **His face fell,** Puso una cara de desengaño. **Christmas falls on a Thursday this year,** Navidad cae en jueves este año. **to let f.,** dejar caer. **to f. a-** (followed by verb) empezar a. **He fell a-crying,** Empezó a llorar. **to f. again,** volver a caer, recaer. **to f. among,** caer entre. **to f. astern,** quedarse atrás. **to f. away,** (leave) abandonar, dejar; (grow thin) enflaquecer; marchitarse; (crumble) desmoronarse. **to f. back,** retroceder, volver hacia atrás. **to f. back upon,** recurrir a; *Mil.* replegarse hacia. **to f. backward,** caer de espaldas, caer hacia atrás. **to f. behind,** quedarse atrás. **to f. down,** venirse a tierra; venirse abajo; dar consigo en el suelo, caer. **to f. due,** vencer. **to f. flat,** caer de bruces; (be unsuccessful) no tener éxito. **to f. in,** caer en; (collapse) desplomarse; *Mil.* alinearse; (expire) vencer. **to f. into,** caer en. **to f. in with,** tropezar con; reunirse con, juntarse con; (agree) convenir en; *Mil.* **to f. off,** caer de; (of leaves, etc.) desprenderse de, separarse de; (abandon) abandonar; (diminish) disminuir. **to f. on**, caer de (e.g. *to f. on one's back*, caer de espaldas); (of seasons) caer en; (attack) echarse encima de, atacar. **to f. out**, (of a window, etc.) caer por; (happen) acontecer, suceder; (quarrel) pelearse, reñir; *Mil.* romper filas. **to f. out with**, reñir con. **to f. over**, volcar, caer; (stumble) tropezar con. **to f. short**, faltar; carecer, ser deficiente; (fail) malograrse, no llegar a sus expectaciones; (of shooting) errar el tiro. **to f. through**, caer por; (fail) malograrse, fracasar. **to f. to**, empezar a, ponerse a; (be incumbent on) tocar a, corresponder a; (attack) atacar. **to f. under**, caer debajo; caer bajo; sucumbir, perecer; (incur) incurrir en, merecer. **to f. upon**, (attack) caer sobre, acometer; acaecer, tener lugar; (be incumbent) tocar a

fallacious /fəˈleiʃəs/ a falaz, engañoso, ilusorio

fallacy /ˈfæləsi/ n error, m, ilusión, f

fallen /ˈfɔlən/ a caído; arruinado; degradado. **f. angel**, ángel caído, m. **f. woman**, perdida, mujer caída, f

fallible /ˈfæləbəl/ a falible

falling /ˈfɔliŋ/ a que cae, cayente. —n caída, f; (of mercury, temperature) baja, f; (crumbling) desmoronamiento, m; (collapse) hundimiento, derrumbamiento, m; (of tide) reflujo, m; (of waterlevel) bajada, f; (in value) depreciación, f; (of prices and Stock Exchange) baja, f; (diminishment) disminución, f; (in level of earth) declinación, f; (Com. expiry) vencimiento, m; (Theat. of curtain) bajada, caída, f. **f. away**, (crumbling) desmoronamiento, m; desprendimiento de tierras, m; (desertion) deserción, f, abandono, m. **f. back**, retirada, f, retroceso, m. **f. down**, caída, f; derrumbamiento, m. **f. due**, vencimiento, m. **f. in**, hundimiento, m; (crumbling) desmoronamiento, m. **f. off**, caída de, f; (disappearance) desaparición, f; (diminution) disminución, f; (deterioration) deterioración, f. **f. out**, caída por, f; disensión, f. **f. short**, falta, f; carácter inferior, m; frustración, f. **f. star**, estrella fugaz, f

fallout /ˈfɔl,aut/ caída radiactiva, llovizna radiactiva, precipitación radiactiva, f

fallow /ˈfæloʊ/ a (of color) leonado; Agr. barbechado; descuidado. —n barbecho, m. —vt barbechar. **to leave f.**, dejar en barbecho. **f. deer**, corzo (-za)

false /fɔls/ a incorrecto, erróneo, equivocado; falso; (unfounded) infundado; (disloyal) infiel, traidor, desleal; (not real) postizo; artificial; de imitación; *Mus.* desafinado; (pretended) fingido; engañoso, mentiroso. **to play a person f.**, traicionar (a). **f. bottom**, fondo doble, m; **f. claim**, pretensión infundada, f. **f. door**, surtida, f. **f.-hearted**, pérfido, desleal. **f. teeth**, dientes postizos, m pl, dentadura postiza, f

falsehood /ˈfɔlshʊd/ n mentira, f

falsetto /fɔlˈsɛtoʊ/ n falsete, m, voz de cabeza, f

falsification /ˌfɔlsəfiˈkeiʃən/ n falsificación, f; (of texts) corrupción, f

falsify /ˈfɔlsəfai/ vt falsear, falsificar; (disappoint) defraudar, frustrar, contrariar

falter /ˈfɔltər/ vi (physically) titubear; (of speech) balbucir, tartamudear; (of action) vacilar. **to f. out**, balbucir; hablar con voz entrecortada; decir con vacilación

faltering /ˈfɔltəriŋ/ a titubeante; (of speech) entrecortado; vacilante. —n temblor, m; vacilación, f

fame /feim/ n fama, f; reputación, f; (renown) celebridad, f, renombre, m. **of ill f.**, de mala fama

famed /feimd/ a reputado; renombrado, célebre, famoso

familiar /fəˈmilyər/ a íntimo, familiar; afable, amistoso; (ill-bred) insolente, demasiado familiar; (usual) corriente, usual, común; conocido. —n amigo (-ga) íntimo (-ma); *Eccl.* familiar, m; demonio familiar, m. **to be f. with**, (a subject) estar versado en, conocer muy bien; (a person) tratar con familiaridad. **to become f. with**, acostumbrarse a; familiarizarse con; (a person) hacerse íntimo de

familiarity /fəˌmiliˈæriti/ n intimidad, familiaridad, confianza, f; (friendliness) afabilidad, f; (over-familiarity) insolencia, demasiada familiaridad, f; (with a subject) conocimiento (de), m, experiencia (de), f

familiarize /fəˈmilyə,raiz/ vt familiarizar, acostumbrar, habituar. —vr familiarizarse

family /ˈfæmli/ n familia, f; (lineage) linaje, abolengo, m; (Bot. Zool.) familia, f; (of languages) grupo, m. —a de familia; familiar; casero. **f. doctor**, médico de cabecera, m. **f. life**, vida de familia, f; hogar, m. **f. man**, padre de familia, m. **f. name**, apellido, m. **f. seat**, casa solar, f. **f. tree**, árbol genealógico, m

famine /ˈfæmin/ n hambre, f; carestía, escasez, f

famish /ˈfæmiʃ/ vt matar de hambre. —vi morirse de hambre

famished /ˈfæmiʃt/ a hambriento

famous /ˈfeiməs/ a famoso, célebre, renombrado; insigne, distinguido; *Inf.* excelente

famously /ˈfeiməsli/ adv *Inf.* muy bien, excelentemente

fan /fæn/ n abanico, m; Agr. aventador, m; Mech. ventilador, m; (on a windmill) volante, m; (amateur) aficionado (-da); (admirer) admirador (-ra); Archit. abanico, m. —vt abanicar; Agr. aventar; ventilar. **fan oneself**, hacerse viento. **tap with a f.**, abanicazo, golpecito con el abanico, m. **f.-belt**, Mech. correa de transmisión del ventilador, f. **f.-light**, tragaluz, m. **f. maker** or **seller**, abaniquero (-ra). **f.-shaped**, en abanico, abanicado, en forma de abanico

fanatic /fəˈnætɪk/ a and n fanático (-ca)

fanaticism /fə'nætə,sɪzəm/ n fanatismo, m

fancied /'fænsɪd/ a imaginario

fancier /'fænsɪər/ n aficionado (-da); (of animals) criador (-ra)

fanciful /'fænsɪfəl/ a romántico, caprichoso; fantástico

fancy /'fænsi/ n fantasía, imaginación, f; (idea) idea, f, ensueño, m; (caprice) capricho, antojo, m; (liking) afecto, cariño, m; gusto, m, afición, f; (wish) deseo, m; (fantasy) quimera, f, a imaginario; elegante, ornado; *Com.* de capricho, de fantasía; fantástico, extravagante. —vt imaginar, figurarse; (like) gustar de; aficionarse a; antojarse. **I have a f. for...,** Se me antoja.... **Just f.!** ¡Toma! ¡Quia! ¡Parece mentira! **to take a f. to,** (things) tomar afición a; (people) tomar cariño (a). **f.-dress,** disfraz, m. **f.-dress ball,** baile de trajes, m

fancy goods n pl artículos suntuarios m pl

fanfare /'fænfɛər/ n tocata de trompetas, f

fang /fæŋ/ n colmillo, m; raíz de un diente, f

fantastic /fæn'tæstɪk/ a fantástico; extravagante

fantasy /'fæntəsi/ n imaginación, f; fantasía, quimera, visión, f; creación imaginativa, f

far /fɑr/ adv lejos; a lo lejos; (much, greatly) mucho, en alto grado; (very) muy; (mostly) en gran parte. —a lejano, distante; (farther) ulterior. **as far as,** tan lejos como; (up to, until) hasta; en cuanto, por lo que, según que. (e.g. *As far as we know,* Por lo que nosotros sepamos. *As far as we are concerned,* En cuanto a nosotros toca). **by far,** con mucho. **from far and near,** de todas partes. **from far off,** desde lejos. **He read far into the night,** Leyó hasta las altas horas de la noche. **how far?** ¿a qué distancia?; (to what extent) ¿hasta qué punto? ¿hasta dónde? **How far is it to...?** ¿Qué distancia hay a...? **in so far as,** en tanto que. **on the far side,** al lado opuesto; al otro extremo. **so far,** tan lejos; (till now) hasta ahora. **to go far,** ir lejos. **far away,** a distante, remoto, lejano; *Fig.* abstraído. —adv muy lejos. **far beyond,** mucho más allá. **far-fetched,** increíble, improbable. **far-off,** a distante. —adv a lo lejos, en lontananza. **far-reaching,** de gran alcance. **far-sighted,** sagaz, presciente, previsor. **far-sightedness,** sagacidad, previsión, f

farce /fɑrs/ n farsa, f. —vt *Cul.* embutir, rellenar

farcical /'fɑrsɪkəl/ a burlesco, cómico, sainetesco; absurdo, grotesco, ridículo

fare /fɛər/ n (price) pasaje, precio del billete, m; (traveler) viajero (-ra), pasajero (-ra); (food) comida, f. —vi pasarlo (e.g. *to f. well,* pasarlo bien). **bill of f.,** menú,

m. **full f.,** billete entero, m. **f. stage,** trayecto, m

farewell /,fɛər'wɛl/ n despedida, f, adiós, m. —a de despedida. —interj ¡adiós! ¡quede Vd. con Dios! **to bid f. to,** despedirse de

farflung /'fɑr'flʌŋ/ de gran alcance, extenso, vasto; (empire) dilatado

farina /fə'rinə/ n harina (de cereales), f; *Chem.* fécula, f, almidón, m; *Bot.* polen, m

farm /fɑrm/ n granja, hacienda, quintería, finca, chacra, f, cortijo, m. —vt cultivar, labrar (la tierra); (taxes) arrendar. —vi ser granjero. **to f. out,** (taxes) dar en arriendo. **f. girl,** labradora, f. **f. house,** alquería, casa de labranza, granja, f. **f. laborer,** labriego, peón, m. **f. yard,** corral de una granja, m

farmer /'fɑrmər/ n granjero, hacendado, quintero, m, agrícola, mf; (small) colono, labrador, m; (of taxes) arrendatario, m

farmhand /'fɑrm,hænd/ gañán, mozo, mozo de granja, peón m

farming /'fɑrmɪŋ/ n labranza, f, cultivo, m; agricultura, labor agrícola, f; (of taxes) arriendo, m. —a de labranza, labradoril; agrícola

farrago /fə'ragou/ n fárrago, m, mezcla, f

farther /'fɑrðər/ adv más lejos; (beyond) más adelante; (besides) además. —a ulterior; más distante. **at the f. end,** al otro extremo; en el fondo. **f. on,** más adelante; más allá

farthest /'fɑrðɪst/ adv más lejos. —a más lejano, más distante; extremo

fascinate /'fæsə,neit/ vt fascinar; encantar, hechizar, seducir

fascinating /'fæsə,neɪtɪŋ/ a fascinador; encantador, seductor

fascination /,fæsə'neɪʃən/ n fascinación, f; encanto, hechizo, m

Fascism /'fæʃ,ɪzəm/ n fascismo, m

Fascist /'fæʃɪst/ a and n fascista mf

fashion /'fæʃən/ n (form) forma, hechura, f; (way) modo, m; (custom) costumbre, f, uso, m; (vogue) moda, f; (high life) alta sociedad, f; (tone) buen tono, m. —vt hacer, labrar; inventar. **in Spanish f.,** a la española, al uso de España. **the latest f.,** la última moda. **to be in f.,** estar de moda. **to go out of f.,** dejar de ser de moda, perder la popularidad. **f. book,** revista de modas, f. **f. plate,** figurín, m

fashionable /'fæʃənəbəl/ a de moda; elegante; de buen tono. **to be f.,** estar en boga, ser de moda. **f. world,** mundo elegante, mundo de sociedad, m

fashion show desfile de modas, m, exhibición de modas, f

fast /fæst/ a (firm) firme; (secure) seguro; (strong) fuerte; (fixed) fijo; (closed) cerrado; (of boats) amarrado; (tight) apretado; (of colors) estable; (of trains) rápido; (of sleep) profundo; (of friends) leal, seguro; (quick) rápido, veloz; (of a watch) adelantado; (dissipated) disoluto. —*adv* firmemente, seguramente; (quickly) rápidamente; (of sleep) profundamente; (tightly) estrechamente, apretadamente; (of rain) (llover) a cántaros; (ceaselessly) continuamente; (often) frecuentemente; (entirely) completamente. **to be f.**, (clocks) adelantar. **to make f.**, *Naut.* amarrar, trincar. **f. asleep**, profundamente dormido. **f. color**, color estable, color sólido, *m*

fast /fæst/ *n* ayuno, *m*, *vi* ayunar. **to break one's f.**, romper el ayuno. **f.-day**, día de ayuno, día de vigilia, *m*

fasten /'fæsən/ *vt* (tie) atar; (fix) fijar; sujetar; (stick) pegar; (a door) cerrar; (bolt) echar el cerrojo; *Naut.* trincar; (together) juntar, unir; (with buttons, hooks, etc.) abrochar; (on, upon) fijar en; *Fig.* imputar (a). —*vi* fijarse; pegarse; (upon) agarrarse a, asir. **to f. one's eyes on**, fijar los ojos en. **to f. up**, cerrar; atar; (nail) clavar

fastener /'fæsənər/ *n* (bolt) pasador, *m*; (for bags, jewelery, etc.) cierre, *m*; (buckle) hebilla, *f*; (of a coat, etc.) tiador, *m*; (of a book, file) sujetador, *m*; (lock) cerrojo, *m*. **paper-f.**, sujetador de papeles, *m*. **patent-f.**, botón automático, *m*

fastening /'fæsəniŋ/ *n* atadura, *f*; sujeción, *f*, afianzamiento, *m*; (together) union, *f*; (of a garment) brochadura, *f*; (of a handbag) cierre, *m*

fastidious /fæ'stidiəs/ *a* dengoso, melindroso, desdeñoso; (sensitive) sensitivo, delicado; (critical) discerniente, crítico

fasting /'fæstiŋ/ *n* ayuno, *m*. —*a* and *part* de ayuno; en ayunas

fastness /'fæstnis/ *n* firmeza, solidez, *f*; (stronghold) fortaleza, *f*; (retreat) refugio, *m*; (speed) velocidad, rapidez, *f*; (dissipation) disipación, *f*, libertinaje, *m*

fat /fæt/ *a* (stout) gordo, grueso; mantecoso, graso, seboso; (greasy) grasiento; (rich) fértil, pingüe; (productive) lucrativo. —*n* (stoutness) gordura, *f*; (for cooking) manteca, *f*; (lard) lardo, *m*; (of animal or meat) grasa, *f*; sebo, saín, *m*; *Fig.* riqueza, *f*; *Fig.* fertilidad, *f*. **to grow fat**, engordarse, ponerse grueso

fatal /'feitl/ *a* fatal, mortal; funesto

fatality /fei'tæliti/ *n* fatalidad, *f*; infortunio, *m*, calamidad, *f*; muerte, *f*

fate /feit/ *n* destino, sino, hado, *m*; providencia, *f*; fortuna, suerte, *f*; destrucción, ruina, *f*; muerte, *f*. **the Three Fates**, las Parcas

fated /'feitid/ *a* fatal, destinado; predestinado

fateful /'feitfəl/ *a* decisivo, fatal; aciago, ominoso

father /'faðər/ *n* padre, *m*. —*vt* prohijar, adoptar; (on or upon) atribuir (a), imputar (a). **Eternal F.**, Padre Eterno, *m*. **Holy F.**, Padre Santo, *m*. **indulgent f.**, padre indulgente, padrazo, *m*. **Like f. like son**, De tal palo tal astilla. **f. confessor**, *Eccl.*

director espiritual, *m*. **f.-in-law**, suegro, *m*

fatherhood /'faðər,hʊd/ *n* paternidad, *f*

fatherland /'faðər,lænd/ *n* patria, madre patria, *f*

fatherless /'faðərlis/ *a* sin padre, huérfano de padre

fatherly /'faðərli/ *a* paternal, de padre

fathom /'fæðəm/ *n* *Naut.* braza, *f*. —*vt* sondear; *Fig.* profundizar, tantear; (a mystery) desentrañar

fathomless /'fæðəmlis/ *a* insondable; *Fig.* incomprensible, impenetrable

fatigue /fə'tig/ *n* fatiga, *f*, cansancio, *m*; *Mil.* faena, *f*; *Mech.* pérdida de resistencia, *f*. —*vt* fatigar, cansar. **to be fatigued**, estar cansado, cansarse, fatigarse. **f. party**, *Mil.* pelotón de castigo, *m*

fatiguing /fə'tigiŋ/ *a* fatigoso

fatness /'fætnis/ *n* (stoutness) gordura, carnosidad, *f*; grasa, *f*, gordo, *m*; (richness) fertilidad, *f*; lo lucrativo

fatten /'fætn/ *vt* engordar; (animals) cebar, sainar; (land) abonar, fertilizar. —*vi* ponerse grueso, echar carnes

fatty /'fæti/ *a* untoso, grasiento; *Chem.* graso. **f. acid**, ácido graso, *m*. **f. degeneration**, degeneración grasienta, *f*

fatuous /'fætʃuəs/ *a* fatuo, necio, lelo

faucet /'fɔsit/ *n* canilla, llave, *f*, grifo, *m*

fault /fɔlt/ *n* defecto, *m*, imperfección, *f*; (blame) culpa, *f*; (mistake) falta, *f*, error, *m*; (in cloth) canilla, barra, *f*; *Geol.* falla, quiebra, *f*; *Elec.* avería, *f*; *Sports.* falta, *f*, *vi Sports.* cometer una falta. **to a f.**, excesivamente. **to be at f.**, (to blame) tener la culpa; (mistaken) estar equivocado; (puzzled) estar perplejo; (of dogs) perder el rastro. **to find f.**, tachar, culpar, criticar. **Whose f. is it?** ¿Quién tiene la culpa?

faultfinder /'fɔlt,faindər/ *n* criticón (-ona)

faultless /'fɔltlis/ *a* sin faltas; perfecto, sin tacha; impecable

faulty /'fɔlti/ *a* defectuoso, imperfecto

fauna /'fɔnə/ *n* fauna, *f*

favor /'feivər/ *n* favor, *m*; (protection) amistad, protección, *f*, amparo, *m*; (permission) permiso, *m*, licencia, *f*; (kindness) merced, gracia, *f*; (gift) obsequio, *m*; (favoritism) favoritismo, *m*, preferencia, *f*; (benefit) beneficio, *m*; (badge) colores, *m pl*; *Com.* grata, atenta, *f*. —*vt* favorecer, apoyar; mirar con favor, mostrar parcialidad (hacia); (suit) favorecer; (be advantageous) ser propicio (a); (contribute to) contribuir a, ayudar; (resemble) parecerse (a). **Circumstances f. the idea**, Las circunstancias son propicias a la idea, Las circunstancias militan en pro de la idea. **I f. the teaching of modern languages**, Soy partidario de la enseñanza de lenguas vivas. **in f. of**, a favor de, en pro de. **in the f. of**, en el favor de. **out of f.**, fuera de favor; (not fashionable) fuera de moda. **to count on the f. of**, tener de su parte (a), contar con el apoyo de. **to do a f.,** hacer un favor. **to enjoy the f. of,** gozar del favor de. **to fall out of f.,** caer en desgracia; (go out of fashion) pasar de moda. **to grow in f.,** aumentar en favor

favorable /'feivərəbəl/ *a* favorable; propicio, próspero

favored /'feivərd/ *a* favorecido; predilecto; (in compounds) parecido, encarado

favorite /'feivərit/ *a* favorito; predilecto, preferido. —*n* favorito (-ta). **court f.,** valido, privado, *m;* (mistress) querida (de un rey), *f;* (lover) amante (de una reina), *m.* **to be a f.,** ser favorito

fawn /fɔn/ *n Zool.* cervato, *m;* (color) color de cervato, color de ante, *m.* —*a* de color de cervato, anteado, pardo; (of animals) rucio, pardo. —*vt* and *vi* parir la cierva. —*vi* acariciar; (on, upon) adular, lisonjear

fawning /'fɔniŋ/ *n* adulación, *f, a* adulador, lisonjero

fear /fiər/ *n* miedo, temor, *m;* (apprehension) ansiedad, aprensión, *f,* recelo, *m;* (respect) veneración, *f.* —*vt* temer; recelar; (respect) reverenciar. —*vi* tener miedo; estar receloso, estar con cuidado. **for f. of,** por miedo de. **for f. that,** por temor de que, por miedo de que. **from f.,** por miedo. **There is no f. of...,** No hay miedo de (que)...

fearful /'fiərfəl/ *a* miedoso, aprensivo, receloso; (cowardly) tímido, pusilánime; (terrible) horrible, espantoso, pavoroso; *Inf.* tremendo, enorme

fearfully /'fiərfəli/ *adv* con miedo; tímidamente; (terribly) horriblemente; *Inf.* enormemente

fearless /'fiərlɪs/ *a* sin miedo, intrépido, audaz

fearsome /'fiərsəm/ *a* temible, horrible, espantoso

feasibility /,fizə'bɪlɪti/ *n* practicabilidad, posibilidad, *f*

feasible /'fizəbəl/ *a* factible, hacedero, practicable, ejecutable

feast /fist/ *n Eccl.* fiesta, *f;* banquete, *m; Fig.* abundancia, *f, vi* regalarse. —*vt* festejar, agasajar; (delight) recrear, deleitar. **immovable f.,** *Eccl.* fiesta fija, *f.* **movable f.,** fiesta movible, *f.* **f. day,** día de fiesta, *m,* festividad *f*

feat /fit/ *n* hazaña, proeza, *f,* hecho, *m*

feather /'fɛðər/ *n* pluma, *f;* (of the tail) pena, *f; pl* **feathers,** plumaje, *m;* plumas, *f pl.* —*vt* emplumar; adornar con plumas; (rowing) poner casi horizontal la pala del remo. **to f. one's nest,** *Inf.* hacer su agosto. **f.-bed,** plumón, colchón de plumas, *m.* **f.-brained,** casquivano, alocado, aturdido. **f.-duster,** plumero, *m.* **f.-stitch,** *Sew.* diente de perro, *m.* **f. weight,** (boxing) peso pluma, *m*

feature /'fitʃər/ *n* rasgo, *m,* característica, *f;* (cinema) número de programa, *m; pl* **features** (of the face) facciones, *f pl.* —*vt* dar importancia (a); (cinema) presentar. **f. film,** documentaria, *f*

February /'fɛbru,ɛri, 'fɛbyu-/ *n* febrero, *m*

feces /'fisiz/ *n* heces, *f pl;* excremento, *m*

fecund /'fikʌnd/ *a* fecundo, fértil

fecundate /'fikən,deit/ *vt* fecundar

fecundity /fɪ'kʌndɪti/ *n* fecundidad,· fertilidad, *f*

federal /'fɛdərəl/ *a* federal, federalista

federate /*v* 'fɛdə,reit/ -ərɪt/ *vt* confederar. —*vi* confederarse. —*a* confederado

federation /,fɛdə'reiʃən/ *n* confederación, federación, *f;* liga, unión, asociación, *f*

fee /fi/ *n* (feudal law) feudo, *m;* (homage) homenaje, *m;* (duty) derecho, *m;* (professional) honorario, estipendio, *m;* (to a servant) gratificación, *f;* (entrance, university, etc.) cuota, *f;* (payment) paga, *f*

feeble /'fibəl/ *a* débil; lánguido; enfermizo; (of light, etc.) tenue; *Fig.* flojo. **to grow f.,** debilitarse; disminuir. **f.-minded,** anormal

feed /fid/ *n* alimento, *m;* (meal) comida, *f;* (of animals) pienso, forraje, *m; Mech.* alimentación, *f.* —*vt* alimentar; dar de comer (a); (animals) cebar; *Mech.* alimentar; mantener; *Fig.* nutrir. —*vi* comer, alimentarse; (graze) pastar. **to be fed up,** *Inf.* estar hasta la coronilla, estar harto. **to f. on,** alimentarse de; *Fig.* nutrirse de. **f. pipe,** tubo de alimentación, *m*

feedback /'fid,bæk/ *n* retrocomunicación, *f*

feeder /'fidər/ *n* el, *m,* (f, la) que da de comer a; (eater) comedor (-ra); (of a river) tributario, afluente, *m;* (bib) babero, *m; Mech.* alimentador, *m;* (cup for invalids) pistero, *m*

feeding /'fidiŋ/ *n* alimentación, *f, a* alimenticio, de alimentación. **f.-bottle,** biberón, *m.* **f.-cup,** pistero, *m.* **f.-trough,** pesebre, *m*

feel /fil/ *n* (touch) tacto, *m;* (feeling) sensación, *f;* (instinct) instinto, *m,* percepción innata, *f*

feel /fil/ *vt* (touch) tocar, tentar, palpar; (experience) sentir, experimentar; (understand) comprender; (believe) creer; (be conscious of) estar consciente de; (the pulse) tomar; examinar. —*vi* sentir, ser sensible; sentirse, encontrarse; (to the touch) ser... al tacto, estar. **How do you f.?** ¿Cómo se siente Vd.? **I f. cold,** Tengo frío. **I f. for you,** Lo siento en el alma; Estoy muy consciente de ello. **I f. strongly that...,** Estoy convencido de que... **I f. that it is a difficult question,** Me parece una cuestión difícil. **It feels like rain,** Creo que va a llover. **to f. at home,** sentirse a sus anchas, sentirse como en su casa. **to f. hungry (thirsty),** tener hambre (sed). **to f. one's way,** andar a tientas; *Fig.* medir el terreno. **to f. soft,** ser blando al tacto. **to make itself felt,** hacerse sentir. **Your hands f. cold,** Tus manos están frías

feeler /'filər/ *n* (of insects) palpo, *m,* antena, f; tentáculo, m; Fig. tentativa, f, balón de ensayo, m

feeling /'filɪŋ/ n (touch) tacto, m; (sensation) sensación, f; (sentiment) sentimiento, m; emoción, f; (premonition) corazonada, intuición, premonición, f; (tenderness) ternura, f; (perception) sensibilidad, percepción, f; (passion) pasión, f; (belief) opinión, f, sentir, m. —a sensible; tierno; (compassionate) compasivo; apasionado; (moving) conmovedor

feelingly /'filɪŋli/ adv con emoción; (strongly) enérgicamente, vivamente; (understandingly) comprensivamente

feign /fein/ vt fingir; (invent) inventar, imaginar; simular; (allege) pretextar; (dissemble) disimular. —vi disimular

feint /feint/ n artificio, engaño, m; (in fencing) treta, finta, f. —vi hacer finta

felicitation /fɪ,lɪsɪ'teiʃən/ n felicitación, f, parabién, m

felicitous /fɪ'lɪsɪtəs/ a feliz, dichoso, afortunado; (of phrases, etc.) feliz, acertado; oportuno

felicity /fɪ'lɪsɪti/ n felicidad, dicha, f

feline /'filain/ a felino, gatuno, de gato. —n felino, m

fell /fel/ n (skin) piel, f; (upland) altura, cuesta de montaña, f. —a cruel, feroz; (unhappy) aciago, funesto. —vt talar, cortar; (knock down) derribar; Sew. sobrecoser

fellow /'felou/ n compañero (-ra); (equal) igual, mf; (in crime) cómplice, mf; (man) hombre, m; (boy, youth) chico, m; (colleague) colega, m; (of a society) miembro, m; (of a pair of objects) pareja, f; Inf. tipo, chico, m. **He's a good f.,** Es un buen chico. **How are you, old f.?** ¡Hombre! ¿Cómo estás? **f.-citizen,** conciudadano (-na). **f.-countryman,** compatriota, m; paisano (-na). **f.-creature,** semejante, mf **f.-feeling,** simpatía, comprensión mutua, f **f.-member,** compañero (-ra); colega, m. **f.-passenger,** compañero (-ra) de viaje. **f.-prisoner,** compañero (-ra) de prisión. **f.-student,** condiscípulo (-la). **f.-worker,** compañero (-ra) de trabajo; (collaborator) colaborador (-ra); (colleague) colega, m

fellowship /'felou,ʃɪp/ n coparticipación, f; (companionship) compañerismo, m; (brotherhood) comunidad, confraternidad, f; (society) asociación, f; (grant) beca, f; (of a university) colegiatura, f

felon /'felən/ n reo, criminal, mf; felón (-ona); malvado (-da); (swelling) panadizo, m

felonious /fə'louniəs/ a criminal; pérfido, traidor

felony /'feləni/ n felonía, f

felt /felt/ n fieltro, m. **a f. hat,** un sombrero de fieltro

female /'fimeil/ n hembra, f, a femenino. (f. is often rendered in Sp. by the feminine ending of the noun, e.g. a f. cat, una gata; a f. friend, una amiga.) **This is a f.**

animal, Este animal es una hembra. **f. screw,** hembra de tornillo, tuerca, f

feminine /'femənɪn/ a femenino; mujeril, afeminado. **in the f. gender,** en el género femenino

feminism /'femə,nɪzəm/ n feminismo, m

feminist /'femənɪst/ n feminista, mf

femur /'fimər/ n Anat. fémur, m

fen /fɛn/ n marjal, pantano, m

fence /fɛns/ n cerca, f; (of stakes) estacada, palizada, f; (hedge) seto, m; (fencing) esgrima, f; Mech. guía, f; Inf. comprador (-ra) de efectos robados. —vi esgrimir; Fig. defenderse; Inf. recibir efectos robados. —vt cercar; estacar; Fig. defender; proteger. **to sit on the f.,** Fig. estar a ver venir

fencer /'fɛnsər/ n esgrimidor, m

fencesitter /'fɛns,sɪtər/ bailarín de la cuerda flaja, m

fencing /'fɛnsɪŋ/ n esgrima, f; palizada, empalizada, f. **f. mask,** careta, f. **f. master,** maestro de esgrima, maestro de armas, m. **f. match,** asalto de esgrima, m

fend /fɛnd/ (**off**) vt parar; defenderse de, guardarse de. —vi (for) mantener, cuidar de. **to f. for oneself,** ganarse la vida; defenderse

fender /'fɛndər/ n (round hearth) guardafuegos, m; Naut. espolón, m, defensas, f pl; Auto. parachoques, m

ferment /n 'fɜrmənt; v fər'mɛnt/ n fermento, m; fermentación, f; Fig. agitación, conmoción, efervescencia f. —vt hacer fermentar; Fig. agitar, excitar. —vi fermentar, estar en fermentación; Fig. hervirse, agitarse, excitarse

fermentation /,fɜrmən'teiʃən/ n fermentación, f

fern /fɜrn/ n helecho, m

ferocious /fə'rouʃəs/ a feroz, bravo, salvaje

ferocity /fə'rɒsɪti/ n ferocidad, braveza, fiereza, f

ferret /'fɛrɪt/ n Zool. hurón (-ona); **to f. out,** cazar con hurones; (discover) husmear, descubrir

Ferris wheel /'fɛrɪs/ n estrella giratoria, gran rueda, novia, rueda de feria, f

ferry /'fɛri/ n barca de transporte, f; barca de pasaje, f, transbordador, m. —vt transportar de una a otra orilla, llevar en barca. —vi cruzar un río en barca. **ferry across** vt transbordar. **F.-Command,** servicio de entrega y transporte de aeroplanos, m

ferryman /'fɛrimən/ n barquero, m

fertile /'fɜrtl/ a fértil, fecundo; (rich) pingüe; Fig. prolífico, abundante

fertility /fər'tɪlɪti/ n fertilidad, fecundidad, f

fertilization /,fɜrtlə'zeiʃən/ n Biol. fecundación, f; Agr. fertilización, f, abono, m

fertilize /'fɜrtl,aiz/ vt Biol. fecundar; Agr. fertilizar, abonar

fertilizer /'fɜrtl,aizər/ n abono, m

fervent /'fɜrvənt/ a ardiente; fervoroso, intenso; (enthusiastic) entusiasta, apasionado

fervor /'fɜrvər/ n ardor, fervor, m, pasión, f; (enthusiasm) entusiasmo, celo, m; vehemencia, f

fester /'fɛstər/ vi ulcerarse, enconarse; Fig. inflamarse, amargarse. —vt ulcerar

festival /'fɛstəvəl/ a de fiesta. —n festividad, f; Eccl. fiesta, f; (musical, etc.) festival, m

festive /'fɛstɪv/ a de fiesta; festivo, alegre

festivity /fɛ'stɪvɪti/ n festividad, fiesta, f; (merriment) alegría, f, júbilo, m

festoon /fɛ'stun/ n festón, m, guirnalda, f. —vt festonear

fetal /'fitl/ a fetal

fetch /fɛtʃ/ vt traer; ir a buscar; ir por; llevar; (conduct) conducir; (of tears) hacer derramar lágrimas, hacer saltársele las lágrimas; (blood) hacer correr la sangre; (produce, draw) sacar; (a blow, a sigh) dar; (acquire) conseguir; (charm) fascinar; (of price) venderse por. **to go and f.,** ir a buscar. **to f. and carry,** vt (news) divulgar, publicar. —vi estar ocupado en oficios humildes, trajinar. **to f. away,** llevarse; ir a buscar; venir a buscar. **to f. back,** devolver; (of persons) traer (a casa, etc.); traer otra vez. **to f. down,** bajar, llevar abajo; hacer bajar. **to f. in,** hacer entrar; (place inside) poner adentro; (persons and things) llevar adentro. **to f. out,** hacer salir; (bring out things) sacar; (put out) poner afuera; (an idea, etc.) sacar a relucir. **to f. up,** (a parcel, etc.) subir; (a person) hacer subir; llevar arriba

fete /feit/ n fiesta, f

fetid /'fɛtɪd/ a fétido, hediondo

fetish /'fɛtɪʃ/ n fetiche, m

fetishism /'fɛtɪˌʃɪzəm/ n fetichismo, m

fetter /'fɛtər/ n grillete, m; pl **fetters,** grillos, m pl, cadenas, f pl; prisión, cárcel, f. —vt encadenar, atar

fetus /'fitəs/ n feto, m

feud /fyud/ n enemistad, riña, f; (feudal law) feudo, m

feudal /'fyudl/ a feudal. **f. lord,** señor feudal, señor de horca y cuchillo, m

feudalism /'fyudlˌɪzəm/ n feudalismo, m

fever /'fivər/ n fiebre, f; calentura, f; (enthusiasm) pasión, afición, f. **to be in a f.,** tener fiebre; (agitated) estar muy agitado. **to be in a f. to,** estar muy impaciente de. **puerperal f.,** fiebre puerperal, f. **tertian f.,** fiebre terciana, f. **yellow f.,** fiebre amarilla, f

feverish /'fivərɪʃ/ a febril; Fig. ardiente, febril, vehemente. **to grow f.,** empezar a tener fiebre, acalenturarse

few /fyu/ a and n pocos, m pl; pocas, f pl; algunos, m pl; algunas, f pl; (few in number) número pequeño (de), m. **a good f.,** bastantes, mf pl. **not a f.,** no pocos, m pl, (pocas, f pl). **the f.,** la minoría, f. **f. and far between,** raramente, en raras ocasiones; pocos y contados

fewer /'fyuər/ a compar menos. **The f. the better,** Cuantos menos mejor

fewest /'fyuɪst/ a superl (el) menos, m; el menor número (de), m; (el) menos posible de, m

fiancé(e) /ˌfiɑn'sei/ n novio (-ia); desposado (-da), prometido (-da)

fiasco /fi'æskou/ n fiasco, mal éxito, fracaso, malogro, m

fiat /'fiat/ n fiat, mandato, m, orden, f

fib /fɪb/ n mentirilla, f, vt decir mentirillas, mentir

fibber /'fɪbər/ n embustero (-ra), mentiroso (-sa)

fiber /'faibər/ n fibra, f; filamento, m, hebra, f; (of grass, etc.) brizna, f; Fig. naturaleza, f

fickle /'fɪkəl/ a inconstante; mudable; (of persons) liviano, ligero, voluble

fiction /'fɪkʃən/ n ficción, f; invención, f; literatura narrativa, f; novelas, f pl. **legal f.,** ficción legal, ficción de derecho, f

fictitious /tɪk'tɪjəs/ a ficticio; imaginario; fingido

fiddle /'fɪdl/ n violín, m. —vt tocar... en el violín. —vi tocar el violín; (fidget) jugar; perder el tiempo. **to play second f.,** tocar el segundo violín; Fig. ser plato de segunda mesa

fiddler /'fɪdlər/ n violinista, mf

fiddling /'fɪdlɪŋ/ a insignificante, trivial, frívolo

fidelity /fɪ'dɛlɪti/ n fidelidad, f

fidget /'fɪdʒɪt/ vi estar nervioso, estar inquieto; impacientarse; trajinar; (with) jugar con. —vt molestar; impacientar

fidgety /'fɪdʒɪti/ a inquieto, nervioso. **to be f.,** tener hormiguillo

field /fild/ n campo, m; (meadow) prado, m, pradera, f; (sown field) sembrado, m; (Phys. Herald.) campo, m; (of ice) banco, m; Mineral. yacimiento, m; (background) fondo, m; (campaign) campaña, f; (battle) batalla, lucha, f; (space) espacio, m; (of knowledge, etc.) especialidad, esfera, f; (hunting) caza, f; Sports. campo, m; (competitors) todos los competidores en una carrera, etc.; (horses in a race) el campo. —a campal, pradeño; de campo; de los campos. —vt Sports. parar y devolver la pelota. **in the f.,** en el campo de batalla, en campaña. **magnetic f.,** campo magnético, m. **to take the f.,** entrar en campaña. **f.-artillery,** artillería ligera, artillería montada, f. **f.-day,** (holiday) día de asueto, m; (day out) día en el campo, m; Mil. día de maniobras, m. **f.-glasses,** anteojos, gemelos, m pl. **f.-hospital,** hospital de sangre, m; ambulancia fija, f. **f.-kitchen,** cocina de campaña, f. **f.-marshal,** capitán general de ejército, m. **f.-mouse,** ratón silvestre, m. **f. of battle,** campo de batalla, m. **f. of vision,** campo visual, m. **f.-telegraph,** telégrafo de campaña, m

fielder /'fildər/ n (baseball) jardinero (-ra)

field work prácticas de campo, f pl

fiend /find/ n diablo, demonio, m; malvado (-da); (addict) adicto (-ta). **morphia f.**, morfinónamo (-ma)

fiendish /'findɪʃ/ a diabólico, infernal; malvado, cruel, malévolo

fierce /fɪərs/ a salvaje, feroz, cruel; (of the elements) violento, furioso; (intense) intenso, vehemente

fiercely /'fɪərsli/ adv ferozmente; violentamente, con furia; intensamente, con vehemencia

fierceness /'fɪərsnɪs/ n ferocidad, fiereza, f; violencia, furia, f; intensidad, vehemencia, f

fieriness /'faɪərinɪs/ n ardor, m; (flames) las llamas, f pl; (redness) rojez, f; (irritability) ferocidad, irritabilidad, f; (vehemence) pasión, vehemencia, f; (of horses) fogosidad, f

fiery /'faɪəri/ a ardiente; (red) rojo; (irritable) feroz, colérico, irritable; (vehement) apasionado, vehemente; (of horses) fogoso

fifteen /'fɪf'tin/ a and n quince m.; (of age) quince años, m pl

fifteenth /'fɪf'tinθ/ a and n décimoquinto m.; (part) quinzavo, m, décimoquinta parte, f; (of the month) (el) quince, m; (of monarchs) quince, Mus. quincena, f

fifth /fɪfθ/ a quinto; (of monarchs) quinto; (of the month) (el) cinco. —n quinto, m; (part) quinto, m, quinta parte, f; Mus. quinta, f. **Charles V,** Carlos quinto. **f. column,** quinta columna, f

fiftieth /'fɪftiɪθ/ a quincuagésimo; (part) quincuagésima parte, f, cincuentavo, m

fifty /'fɪfti/ a and n cincuenta m.; (of age) cincuenta años, m pl

fig /fɪg/ n higo, m; (tree) higuera, f; Fig. bledo, ardite, m. **green fig,** higo, m, breva, f. **I don't care a fig,** No se me da un higo. **to be not worth a fig,** no valer un ardite. **fig-leaf,** hoja de higuera, f; Fig. hoja de parra, f

fight /faɪt/ n lucha, pelea, f, combate, m; batalla, f; (struggle) lucha, f; (quarrel) riña, pelea, f; (conflict) conflicto, m; (valor) coraje, brío, m. **hand-to-hand f.,** cachetina, f. **in fair f.,** en buena lid. **to have a f.,** tener una pelea. **to show f.,** mostrarse agresivo

fight /faɪt/ vt luchar contra, batirse con; (a battle) dar (batalla); (oppose) oponer; (defend) defender, pelear por; hacer batirse. —vi luchar, batirse, pelear; (with words) disputar; (struggle) luchar; (make war) hacer la guerra; (in a tournament) tornear. **to f. one's way,** abrirse paso con las armas. **to f. against,** luchar contra. **to f. off,** librarse de; sacudirse. **to f. with,** luchar con; pelear con; reñir con

fighter /'faɪtər/ n luchador (-ra); combatiente, m; guerrero, m; duelista, m; (boxer) boxeador, m; Aer. (avión de

caza, m. **night f.,** Aer. (avión de) caza nocturno, m. **f.-bomber,** Aer. caza bombardero, m. **F. Command,** Aer. servicio de aviones de caza, m

fighting /'faɪtɪŋ/ n lucha, f, combate, m; el pelear; (boxing) boxeo, m, a combatiente; (bellicose) agresivo, belicoso. **f.-man,** combatiente, guerrero, m

figment /'fɪgmənt/ n ficción, invención, f

figurative /'fɪgyərətɪv/ a figurado, metafórico; figurativo; simbólico

figuratively /'fɪgyərətɪvli/ adv en sentido figurativo; metafóricamente

figure /'fɪgyər/ n figura, f; forma, f; (statue) estatua, figura, f; (of a person) silueta, f; talle, m; (number) cifra, f; número, m; (quantity) cantidad, f; (price) precio, m; Geom. Gram. Dance. (skating) figura, f; (appearance) presencia, f, aire, m; (picture) imagen, m; (on fabric) diseño, m; Mus. cifra, f, pl figures, aritmética, f, matemáticas, f pl. —vt figurar; (imagine) figurarse, imaginar; Mus. cifrar. —vi figurar, hacer un papel; (calculate) calcular, hacer cuentas. **to f. out,** calcular; (a problem, etc.) resolver. **a fine f. of a woman,** Inf. una real hembra. **lay f.,** maniquí, m. **to be good at figures,** estar fuerte en matemáticas. **to cut a f.,** Fig. hacer figura. **to have a good f.,** tener buen talle. **f. of speech,** figura retórica, figura de dicción, f; (manner of speaking) metáfora f. **f. dance,** baile de figuras, m, contradanza, f. **f.-head,** Naut. mascarón, m, (or figura, f) de proa; Fig. figura decorativa, f

figurine /ˌfɪgyə'rin/ n figurilla, f

filament /'fɪləmənt/ n filamento, m; hebra, f

filamentous /ˌfɪlə'mɛntəs/ a filamentoso, fibroso

filbert /'fɪlbərt/ n avellana, f; (tree) avellano, m

filch /fɪltʃ/ vt sisar, ratear

file /faɪl/ n (line) fila, hilera, sarta, línea, f; Mil. fila, f; (tool) lima, f; (rasp) escofina, f; (list) lista, f, catálogo, m; (for documents) carpeta, f, cartapacio, m; (bundle of papers) legajo, m; (for bills, letters, etc.) clasificador, m; archivo, m; (in an archives) expediente m. **in a f.,** en fila; en cola

file /faɪl/ vt hacer marchar en fila; (smooth) limar; (literary work) pulir; (classify) clasificar; (note particulars) fichar; (keep) guardar; (a petition, etc.) presentar, registrar. —vi marchar en fila. **to f. in,** entrar en fila. **to f. off,** desfilar. **to file a brief,** presentar un escrito. **to f. letters,** clasificar correspondencia. **to f. past,** Mil. desfilar

filibuster /'fɪləˌbʌstər/ n filibustero, pirata, m

filigree /'fɪləˌgri/ n filigrana, f, a afiligranado

filing /'faɪlɪŋ/ n (with a tool) limadura, f; clasificación, f; (of a petition, etc.) presentación, f, registro, m; pl **filings,** limaduras, *f pl*, retales, *m pl*. **f.-cabinet**, fichero, *m*. **f.-card**, ficha, *f*

fill /fɪl/ *vt* llenar; (stuff) rellenar; (appoint to a post) proveer; (occupy a post) desempeñar; (imbue) henchir; (saturate) saturar; (occupy) ocupar; (a tooth) empastar; (fulfil) cumplir; (charge, fuel) cargar; (with food) hartar. —*vi* llenarse. **fill an order**, servir un pedido. **fill a prescription**, surtir una receta. **to f. the chair**, ocupar la presidencia; (university) ocupar la cátedra. **to f. the place of**, ocupar el lugar de; substituir; suplir. **It will be difficult to find someone to f. his place**, Será difícil de encontrar uno que haga lo que hizo él. **to f. to the brim**, llenar hasta los bordes. **to f. in, f. out**, (a form) llenar (or completar) (una hoja); (insert) insertar, añadir; (a hollow) terraplenar. **to f. out**, *vt* hinchar. —*vi* hincharse; echar carnes, (of the face) redondearse. **to f. up**, colmar, llenar hasta los bordes; (an office) proveer; (block) macizar; (a form) completar, llenar

fillet /'fɪlɪt/ *n* venda, cinta, *f*; (of meat or fish) filete, *m*; (of meat) solomillo, *m*; *Archit*. filete, *m*. —*vt* atar con una venda o cinta; *Cul*. cortar en filetes

filling /'fɪlɪŋ/ *n* envase, *m*; (swelling) henchimiento, *m*; (of a tooth) empastadura, *f*; (in or up, of forms, etc.) llenar, *m*. **f. station**, depósito de gasolina, *m*

fillip /'fɪləp/ *n* capirotazo, *m*; (stimulus) estímulo, *m*; (trifle) bagatela, *f*. —*vt* and *vi* dar un capirotazo (a); *vt* estimular, incitar

filly /'fɪli/ *n* jaca, potra, *f*

film /fɪlm/ *n* (on liquids) tela, *f*; (membrana, *f*; (coating) capa ligera, *f*; (on eyes) tela, *f*; (cinema) película, cinta, *f*; *Photo*. película, *f*; *Fig*. velo, *m*; nube, *f*, *vi* cubrirse de un velo, etc. —*vt* cubrir de un velo, etc.; filmar, fotografiar para el cine. **roll f.**, película fotográfica, *f*. **silent f.**, película muda, *f*. **talking f.**, película sonora, *f*. **to shoot a f.**, hacer una película. **to take part in a f.**, actuar, o tomar parte, en una película. **f. pack**, película en paquetes *f*. **f. star**, estrella de la pantalla (or del cine), *f*

film industry industria fílmica, *f*

filmy /'fɪlmi/ *a* transparente, diáfano

filter /'fɪltər/ *n* filtro, *m*. —*vt* filtrar. —*vi* infiltrarse; (*Fig*. of news) trascender, divulgarse. **f.-bed**, filtro, *m*. **f.-paper**, papel filtro, *m*

filth /fɪlθ/ *n* inmundicia, suciedad, *f*; *Fig*. corrupción, *f*; *Fig*. obscenidad, *f*

filthy /'fɪlθi/ *a* inmundo, sucio; escuálido; *Fig*. asqueroso; *Fig*. obsceno

fin /fɪn/ *n* (of fish) aleta, ala, *f*; (of whale) barba, *f*; *Aer*. aleta, *f*

final /'faɪnl/ *a* último, final; (conclusive) conclusivo, decisivo, terminante. —*n* *Sports*. finales, *m pl*; *Educ*. último examen, *m*. **f. blow**, *Fig*. golpe decisivo, *m*. **f. cause**, *Philos*. causa final, *f*

finale /fɪ'næli/ *n* final, *m*

finalist /'faɪnlɪst/ *n* *Sports*. finalista, *mf*

finality /faɪ'nælɪti/ *n* finalidad, *f*; (decision) determinación, resolución, decisión, *f*

finally /'faɪnli/ *adv* por fin, finalmente, por último, a la postre; (irrevocably) irrevocablemente

finance /'faɪnæns/ *n* hacienda pública, *f*, asuntos económicos, *m pl*; finanzas, *f pl*. —*vt* financiar

financial /fɪ'nænʃəl/ *a* financiero, monetario. **f. year**, año económico, *m*

financially /fɪ'nænʃəli/ *adv* del punto de vista financiero

financier /,fɪnən'sɪər, ,faɪnən-/ *n* financiero, *m*

find /faɪnd/ *vt* encontrar, hallar; (discover) descubrir, dar con; (invent) inventar, crear; (supply) facilitar, proporcionar; (provide) proveer; (instruct) instruir; *Law*. declarar. —*vi* *Law*. fallar, dar sentencia. —*n* hallazgo, *m*; descubrimiento, *m*. **I found him out a long time ago**, *Fig*. Hace tiempo que me di cuenta de cómo era él. **I found it possible to go out**, Me fue posible salir. **The judge found them guilty**, El juez les declaró culpables. **to f. a verdict**, *Law*. dar sentencia, fallar. **to f. one's way**, encontrar el camino. **to f. oneself**, hallarse, verse, encontrarse. **to f. out**, averiguar, descubrir. **to f. out about**, informarse sobre (or de)

finder /'faɪndər/ *n* hallador (-ra); (inventor) inventor (-ra), descubridor (-ra); (telescope, camera) buscador, *m*

finding /'faɪndɪŋ/ *n* hallazgo, *m*; (discovery) descubrimiento, *m*; *Law*. fallo, *m*, sentencia, *f*

fine /faɪn/ *n* multa, *f*; (end) fin, *m*. **in f.**, en fin, en resumen

fine /faɪn/ *vt* multar, cargar una multa de

fine /faɪn/ *a* (thin) delgado; (sharp) agudo; (delicate) fino, delicado; (minute) menudo; (refined) refinado, puro; (healthy) saludable; (of weather) bueno; magnífico; (beautiful) hermoso, lindo; excelente; (perfect) perfecto; (good) bueno; elegante; (showy) ostentoso, vistoso; (handsome) guapo; (subtle) sutil; (acute) agudo; (noble) noble; (eminent, accomplished) distinguido, eminente; (polished) pulido; (affected) afectado; (clear) claro; (transparent) transparente, diáfano. —*adv* muy bien. **a f. upstanding young man**, un buen mozo. **a f. upstanding young woman**, una real moza. **He's a f. fellow**, (ironically) Es una buena pieza. **That is all very f. but...**, Todo eso está muy bien pero.... **to become f.**, (weather) mejorar

finely /'faɪnli/ *adv* finamente; menudamente; elegantemente; (ironically) lindamente

fineness /'faɪnnɪs/ *n* (thinness) delgadez, *f*; (excellence) excelencia, *f*; delicadeza, *f*; (softness) suavidad, *f*; elegancia, *f*; (subtlety) sutileza, *f*; (acuteness) agudeza, *f*;

(perfection) perfección, *f;* (nobility) nobleza, *f;* (beauty) hermosura, *f*

finery /'fainəri/ *n* galas, *f pl,* atavíos magníficos, *m pl;* adornos, *m pl;* primor, *m,* belleza, *f*

finesse /fɪ'nes/ *n* sutileza, diplomacia, *f;* estratagema, artificio, *m;* (cunning) astucia, *f, vi* valerse de estratagemas y artificios

finger /'fiŋgər/ *n* dedo, *m;* (of a clock, etc.) manecilla, *f;* (measurement) dedada, *f; Fig.* mano, *f.* —*vt* manosear, tocar; (soil) ensuciar con los dedos; (steal) sisar; (*Mus.* a keyed instrument) teclear, (a stringed instrument) tocar. **first f.,** dedo índice, *m.* **fourth f.,** dedo anular, *m.* **little f.,** dedo meñique, *m.* **second f.,** dedo de en medio, dedo del corazón, *m.* **to burn one's fingers,** quemarse los dedos; *Fig.* cogerse los dedos. **to have at one's f.-tips,** *Fig.* saber al dedillo. **f.-board,** (of piano) teclado, *m;* (of stringed instruments) diapasón, *m.* **f.-bowl,** lavadedos, lavafrutas, *m.* **finger's breadth,** dedo, *m.* **f.-mark,** huella digital, *f.* **f.-nail,** uña del dedo, *f.* **f.-print,** impresión digital, *f.* **f.-stall,** dedil, *m.* **f.-tip,** punta del dedo, yema del dedo, *f.* **f.-wave,** peinado al agua, *m*

fingering /'fiŋgəriŋ/ *n* (touching) manoseo, *m; Mus.* digitación, *f;* (*Mus.* the keys) tecleo, *m;* (wool) estambre, *m*

finial /'finiəl/ *n* pináculo, *m*

finicky /'finiki/ *a* (of persons) dengoso, remilgado; (of things) nimio

finish /'finiʃ/ *n* fin, *m,* conclusión, terminación, *f;* (final touch) última mano, *f;* perfección, *f;* (of an article) acabado, *m; Sports.* llegada, (horse race) meta, *f.* —*vt* terminar, acabar, concluir; llevar a cabo, poner fin a; (perfect) perfeccionar; (put finishing touch to) dar la última mano a; (kill) matar; (exhaust) agotar, rendir; (overcome) vencer. —*vi* acabar; concluirse. **to f. off,** acabar, terminar; (kill) matar, acabar con; (destroy) destruir. **to f. up,** acabar; (eat) comer; (drink) beber

finished goods *n pl* bienes terminados, *m pl*

finisher /'finiʃər/ *n* terminador (-ra), acabador (-ra); pulidor (-ra); (final blow) golpe de gracia, *m*

finishing /'finiʃiŋ/ *a* concluyente. —*n* terminación, *f,* fin, *m;* perfección, *f;* (last touch) última mano, *f.* **to put the f. touch,** dar la última pincelada

finite /'fainait/ *a* finito

Finland /'finlənd/ Finlandia, *f*

Finn /fin/ *n* finlandés (-esa)

Finnish /'finiʃ/ *a* finlandés. —*n* (language) finlandés, *m*

fir /fər/ *n* abeto, sapino, pino, *m.* **red fir,** pino silvestre, *m.* **fir-cone,** piña de abeto, *f.* **fir grove,** abetal, *m*

fire /faiᵊr/ *n* fuego, *m;* (conflagration) incendio, *m;* (on the hearth) lumbre, *f,* fuego, *m; Fig.* ardor, *m,* pasión, *f;* (shooting) fuego, tiro, *m.* **by f. and sword,** a

sangre y fuego. **by the f.,** cerca del fuego; (in a house) al lado de la chimenea. **long-range f.,** *Mil.* fuego de largo alcance, *m.* **short-range f.,** *Mil.* fuego de corto alcance, *m.* **on f.,** en fuego, ardiendo, en llamas; *Fig.* impaciente; *Fig.* lleno de pasión. **to be between two fires,** *Fig.* estar entre dos aguas. **to make a f.,** encender un fuego. **to miss f.,** no dar en el blanco, errar el tiro. **to open f.,** *Mil.* hacer una descarga. **to set on f.,** prender fuego a, incendiar. **to take f.,** encenderse. **under f.,** bajo fuego. **f.-alarm,** alarma de incendios, *f.* **f.-arm,** arma de fuego, *f.* **f.-box,** hogar, *m.* **f.-brand,** tizón, *m.* **f.-brigade,** cuerpo de bomberos, *m.* **f.-damp,** aire detonante, grisú, *m,* mofeta, *f.* **f.-dog,** morillo, *m.* **f.-drill,** (firefighters') instrucción de bomberos, *f,* (others') simulacro de incendio, *m.* **f.-engine,** autobomba, bomba, de incendios, *f.* **f.-escape,** escalera de incendios, *f.* **f.-extinguisher,** apagador de incendio, extintor, matafuego, *m.* **f.-guard,** vigilante de incendios *m;* alambrera, *f.* **f.-hose,** manguera de incendios, *f.* **f.-insurance,** seguro contra incendios, *m.* **f.-irons,** badil *m.* y tenazas *f pl.* **f.-lighter,** encendedor, *m.* **f.-screen,** pantalla, *f.* **f.-ship,** brulote, *m.* **f.-shovel,** badil, *m,* paleta, *f.* **f.-spotter,** vigilante de incendios, *m.* **f.-sprite,** salamandra, *f.* **f.-watching,** servicio de vigilancia de incendios, *m*

fire /faiᵊr/ *vt* incendiar, prender (or pegar) fuego a; quemar; (bricks) cocer; (fire-arms) disparar; (cauterize) cauterizar; (*Fig.* stimulate) estimular, excitar; (inspire) inspirar; (*Inf.* of questions) disparar; (*Inf.* sack) despedir. —*vi* encenderse; (shoot) hacer fuego, disparar (un tiro); (*Inf.* away) disparar; (up) enojarse. **to f. a salute,** disparar un saludo. *Mil.* **F.!** ¡Fuego!

fire department *n* parque de bomberos, servicis de bomberos, servicio de incendios, parque de bombas (Puerto Rico), *m*

firefly /'faiᵊr,flai/ *n* cocuyo, *m*

fireman /'faiᵊrmən/ *n* bombero, *m;* (of an engine, etc.) fogonero, *m.* **fireman's lift,** silleta, *f*

fireplace /'faiᵊr,pleis/ *n* chimenea francesa, chimenea, *f;* (hearth) hogar, *m*

fireproof /'faiᵊr,pruf/ *a* a prueba de incendios; incombustible

firewood /'faiᵊr,wʊd/ *n* leña, *f.* **f. dealer,** leñador (-ra), vendedor (-ra) de leña

firework /'faiᵊr,wɜrk/ *n* fuego artificial, *m*

firing /'faiᵊriŋ/ *n* (of fire-arms) disparo, *m;* (burning) incendio, *m,* quema, *f;* (of bricks, etc.) cocimiento, *m;* (of pottery) cocción, *f;* (cauterization) cauterización, *f;* (fuel) combustible, *m;* (*Inf.* sacking) despedida, *f.* **within f. range,** a tiro. **f.-line,** línea de fuego, *f.* **f.-oven,** (pottery) horno alfarero, *m.* **f.-squad,** pelotón de ejecución, *m*

firm /fɜrm/ *a* firme; (strong) fuerte; (secure) seguro; sólido; (resolute) inflexible, resoluto; severo; (steady) constante; (persistent) tenaz. —*n Com.* casa (de comercio), empresa, *f;* razón social, *f*

firmament /'fɜrməmənt/ *n* firmamento, *m*

firmness /'fɜrmnɪs/ *n* firmeza, *f;* solidez, *f;* inflexibilidad, resolución, *f;* severidad, *f;* constancia, *f;* tenacidad, *f*

first /fɜrst/ *a* primero (primer before *m sing* nouns); (of monarchs) primero; (of dates) (el) primero. —*n* primero, *m;* (beginning) principio, *m.* —*adv* primero, en primer lugar; (before, of time) antes; (for the first time) por primera vez; (at the beginning) al principio; (ahead) adelante. **at f.,** al principio. **from the very f.,** desde el primer momento. **to appear for the f. time,** aparecer (or presentarse) por primera vez; *Theat.* debutar. **to go f.,** ir delante de todos, ir a la cabeza; ir adelante. **f. and foremost,** en primer lugar; ante todo. **f.-aid,** primera cura, *f.* **f.-aid post,** casa de socorro, *f.* **f.-aider,** practicante, *m.* **f.-born,** *a* and *n* primogénito (-ta). **f.-class,** *a* de primera clase; *Fig.* excelente. **f.-cousin,** primo (-ma) carnal, primo (-ma) hermano (-na). **f. edition,** edición príncipe, *f.* **f. floor,** primer piso, *m.* **f. fruits,** frutos primerizos, *m pl; Fig.* primicias, *f pl.* **f.-hand,** *a* original, de primera mano. **f. letters,** primeras letras, *f pl.* **f. night,** *Theat.* estreno, *m.* **f. of all,** primero, ante todo. **f.-rate,** *a* de primera clase

fiscal /'fɪskəl/ *a* and *n* fiscal *m..* **f. year,** año económico, *m*

fish /fɪʃ/ *n* pez, *m;* (out of the water) pescado, *m; Inf.* tipo, indivíduo, *m* —*vt* pescar; (out) sacar. —*vi* pescar; *Fig.* buscar. **fried f.,** pescado frito, *m.* **He is a queer f.,** Es un tipo muy raro. **to be neither f. nor fowl,** no ser ni carne ni pescado. **to feel like a f. out of water,** sentirse fuera de su ambiente. **to f. in troubled waters,** A río revuelto ganancia de pescadores. **f.-eating,** *a* ictiófago. **f.-fork,** tenedor de pescado, *m.* **f.-glue,** cola de pescado, *f.* **f.-hook,** anzuelo, *m.* **f.-knife,** cuchillo de pescado, *m.* **f.-like,** de pez; como un pez, parecido a un pez. **f. roe,** hueva, *f.* **f.-server,** pala para pescado, *f*

fishbone /'fɪʃ,boun/ *n* espina de pescado, raspa de pescado, *f*

fisherman /'fɪʃərmən/ *n* pescador, *m*

fishery /'fɪʃəri/ *n* pesquería, *f*

fishing /'fɪʃɪŋ/ *n* pesca, *f,* *a* de pescar. **to go f.,** ir de pesca. **f.-boat,** bote de pesca, *m.* **f.-floats,** levas, *f pl.* **f.-line,** sedal, *m.* **f.-net,** red de pesca, *f.* **f.-reel,** carretel, carrete, *m.* **f.-rod,** caña de pescar, *f.* **f.-tackle,** aparejo de pesca, *m.* **f. village,** pueblo de pesca, *m*

fishmeal /'fɪʃ,mil/ *n* harina de pescado, *f*

fishy /'fɪʃi/ *a* de pescado; (of eyes, etc.) de pez, como un pez; (in smell) que

huele a pescado; *Inf.* sospechoso; (of stories) inverosímil

fissure /'fɪʃər/ *n* grieta, hendidura, rendija, *f;* (*Anat. Geol.*) fisura, *f*

fist /fɪst/ *n* puño, *m; Print.* manecilla, *f;* (handwriting) letra, *f.* **with clenched fists,** a puño cerrado

fisticuff /'fɪsti,kʌf/ *n* puñetazo, *m; pl* **fisticuffs,** agarrada, riña, *f*

fit /fɪt/ *n* espasmo, paroxismo, *m;* ataque, *m;* (impulse) acceso, arranque, *m;* (whim) capricho, *m;* (of a garment) corte, *m;* (adjustment) ajuste, encaje, *m.* **by fits and starts,** a tropezones, espasmódicamente

fit /fɪt/ *a* a propósito (para), bueno (para); (opportune) oportuno; (proper) conveniente; apto; (decent) decente; (worthy) digno; (ready) preparado, listo; (adequate) adecuado; (capable) capaz, en estado (de); (appropriate) apropiado; (just) justo. **It is not in a fit state to be used,** No está en condiciones para usarse. **to be not fit for,** no servir para; (through ill-health) no tener bastante salud para. **to think fit,** creer (or juzgar) conveniente. **fit for use,** usable. **fit to eat,** comestible

fit /fɪt/ *vt* ajustar, acomodar, encajar; adaptar (a); (furnish) proveer (de), surtir (con); (of tailor, dressmaker) entallar, probar; (of shoemaker) calzar; (of garments, shoes) ir (bien o mal); (prepare) preparar; (go with) ser apropiado (a); (adapt itself to) adaptarse a. —*vi* ajustarse, acomodarse, encajarse; adaptarse; (clothes) ir (bien o mal). **to fit in,** *vt* encajar; incluir. —*vi* encajarse; caber; adaptarse. **to fit out,** equipar, proveer (de); preparar. **to fit up,** montar, instalar; proveer (de). **to fit with,** proveer de

fitful /'fɪtfəl/ *a* intermitente; espasmódico; caprichoso

fitfully /'fɪtfəli/ *adv* por intervalos, a ratos; caprichosamente

fitment /'fɪtmənt/ *n* equipo, *m;* instalación, *f;* (of bookcase, etc.) sección, *f;* (furniture) pieza, *f,* mueble, *m*

fitness /'fɪtnɪs/ *n* conveniencia, *f;* aptitud, capacidad, *f;* oportunidad, *f;* salud, *f;* (good health) vigor, *m*

fitted /'fɪtɪd/ *a* (of clothes) ajustado

fitter /'fɪtər/ *n* ajustador, *m;* (mechanic) armador, mecánico, *m;* (tailoring) cortador, *m;* (dressmaking) probador (-ra)

fitting /'fɪtɪŋ/ *n* encaje, ajuste, *m;* adaptación, *f;* (of a garment) prueba, *f;* (size) medida, *f;* (installation) instalación, *f;* **pl. fittings,** guarniciones, *f pl;* instalaciones, *f pl;* accesorios, *m pl.* —*a* conveniente, justo; apropiado; adecuado; (worthy) digno; (of coats, etc.) ajustado. **f. room,** cuarto de pruebas, *m.* **f. in,** encaje, *m.* **f. out,** equipo, *m.* **f. up,** arreglo, *m;* (of machines) montaje, *m;* (of a house) mueblaje, *m*

five /faiv/ *a* and *n* cinco *m.;* (of the clock) las cinco, *f pl;* (of age) cinco años, *m pl.* **to be f.,** tener cinco años. **f. feet deep,** de cinco pies de profundidad. **f. feet high,** cinco pies de altura. **f.-finger exercises,** ejercicios de piano, *m pl.* **F.-Year Plan,** Plan Quinquenal, *m*

fix /fɪks/ *n* aprieto, apuro, *m;* callejón sin salida, *m.* —*vt* fijar; sujetar, afianzar; (bayonets) calar; (with nails) clavar; (*Photo., Chem., Med.*) fijar; (decide) establecer; (a date) señalar; (eyes, attention) clavar; (on the mind) grabar, estampar; (one's hopes) poner; (base) basar, fundar; (*Inf.* put right) arreglar, componer. —*vi* fijarse; establecerse; determinarse. **to get in a fix,** hacerse un lío. **to fix a price,** fijar un precio. **to fix on, upon,** elegir, escoger; decidir, determinar. **to fix up,** arreglar; decidir; organizar; (differences) olvidar (sus disensiones)

fixation /fɪkˈseɪʃən/ *n* obsesión, idea fija, *f;* (scientific) fijación, *f*

fixative /ˈfɪksətɪv/ *n* (*Med., Photo.*) fijador, *m;* (dyeing) mordiente, *m.* —*a* que fija

fixed /fɪkst/ *a* fijo; inmóvil; permanente; (of ideas) inflexible. **f. bayonet,** bayoneta calada, *f.* **f. price,** precio fijo, *m.* **f. star,** estrella fija, *f*

fixing /ˈfɪksɪŋ/ *n* fijación, *f;* afianzamiento, *m;* arreglo, *m;* (of a date) señalamiento, *m.* **f. bath,** *Photo.* baño fijador, *m*

fixture /ˈfɪkstʃər/ *n* instalación, *f;* accesorio fijo, *m; Sports.* partido, *m; Inf.* permanencia, *f.* **f. card,** *Sports.* calendario deportivo, *m*

fizz /fɪz/ *n* espuma, *f;* chisporroteo, *m. Inf.* champaña, *m.* —*vi* (liquids) espumear; (sputter) chisporrotear

fizzle /ˈfɪzəl/ *n* (failure) fiasco, fracaso, *m.* —*vi* chisporrotear; (out) apagarse; (fail) fracasar, no tener éxito

fjord /fyord/ *n* fiordo, *m*

flabbergast /ˈflæbərˌgæst/ *vt* dejar con la boca abierta, dejar de una pieza

flag /flæg/ *n* bandera, *f;* pabellón, estandarte, *m;* (small) banderola, *f;* (iris) (yellow) cala, *f;* (purple) lirio cárdeno, *m;* (stone) losa, *f.* **to dip the f.,** saludar con la bandera. **to hoist the f.,** izar la bandera. **to strike the f.,** bajar la bandera; (in defeat) rendir la bandera. **f. bearer,** portaestandarte, abanderado, *m.* **f.-day,** día de la banderita, *m;* (in U.S.A.) día de la bandera, *m.* **f.-officer,** almirante, *m;* vicealmirante, *m;* jefe de escuadra, *m.* **f. of truce,** bandera blanca, bandera de paz, *f*

flag /flæg/ *vi* flaquear, debilitarse; languidecer; (wither) marchitarse; decaer, disminuir. —*vt* adornar con banderas; (signal) hacer señales con una bandera; (for a race, etc.) marcar con banderas; (with stones) enlosar, embaldosar.

flagrant /ˈfleɪgrənt/ *a* escandaloso, notorio

flagship /ˈflæg,ʃɪp/ *n* capitana, *f*

flagstaff /ˈflæg,stæf/ *n* asta de bandera, *f*

flagstone /ˈflæg,stoun/ *n* losa, lancha, *f*

flair /fleər/ *n* instinto natural, *m,* comprensión innata, *f;* habilidad natural, *f*

flak /flæk/ *n* cortina (or barrera) anti-aérea, *f*

flake /fleɪk/ *n* escama, *f;* laminilla, hojuela, *f;* (of snow) copo, *m;* (of fire) chispa, *f.* —*vt* cubrir con escamas, etc.; exfoliar; (crumble) hacer migas de, desmigajar. —*vi* escamarse; (off) exfoliarse; caer en copos

flaky /ˈfleɪki/ *a* escamoso; en laminillas; (of pastry) hojaldrado. **f. pastry,** hojaldre, *f*

flamboyance /flæmˈbɔɪəns/ *n* extravagancia, *f, Lit.* ampulosidad, *f*

flamboyant /flæmˈbɔɪənt/ *a Archit.* flamígero; extravagante, llamativo, rimbombante; (of style) ampuloso. **f. gothic,** gótico florido, *m*

flame /fleɪm/ *n* llama, *f; Fig.* fuego, *m. Inf.* amorío, *m.* —*vi* flamear, llamear; arder, abrasarse; (shine) brillar; (up, *Fig.*) inflamarse; acalorarse. **f.-colored,** de color de llama, anaranjado. **f.-thrower,** lanzallamas, *m*

flaming /ˈfleɪmɪŋ/ *a* llameante; abrasador; (of colors) llamativo, chillón; (of feelings) ardiente, fervoroso, apasionado

flamingo /fləˈmɪŋgou/ *n Ornith.* flamenco, *m*

flange /flændʒ/ *n Mech.* reborde, *m, vt* rebordear

flank /flæŋk/ *n* (of animal) ijada, *f;* (human) costado, *m;* (of hill, etc.) lado, *m,* falda, *f; Mil.* flanco, *m.* —*a* (*Mil. Nav.*) por el flanco. —*vt* lindar con, estar contiguo a; (*Mil., Nav.*) flanquear. —*vi* estar al lado de; tocar a, lindar con.

flannel /ˈflænl/ *n* franela, *f, a* de franela

flannelette /ˌflænlˈet/ *n* moletón, *m*

flap /flæp/ *n* golpe, *m;* (of a sail) zapatazo, *m,* sacudida, *f;* (of a pocket) cartera, tapa, *f;* (of skin) colgajo, *m;* (of a shoe, etc.) oreja, *f;* (of a shirt, etc.) falda, *f;* (of a hat) ala, *f;* (of trousers) bragueta, *f;* (rever) solapa, *f;* (of a counter) trampa, *f;* (of a table) hoja plegadiza, *f;* (of the wings) aletazo, *m;* (of w.c.) tapa, *f.* —*vt* sacudir, golpear, batir; agitar; (the tail) menear. —*vi* agitarse; (of wings) aletear; (of sails) zapatear, sacudirse; colgar. **f.-eared,** de orejas grandes y gachas

flapjack /ˈflæp,dʒæk/ *n Cul.* torta de sartén, *f;* (for powder) polvorera, *f*

flapping /ˈflæpɪŋ/ *n* batimiento, *m;* (waving) ondulación, *f;* (of sails) zapatazo, *m;* (of wings) aleteo, *m*

flare /fleər/ *n* fulgor, *m,* llama, *f;* hacha, *f; Aer.* cohete de señales, *m; Sew.* vuelo, *m.* —*vi* relampaguear, fulgurar; brillar; (of a lamp) llamear; (up) encolerizarse, salirse de tino; (of epidemic) declararse; (war, etc.) desencadenarse

flash /flæʃ/ *n* relámpago, centelleo, *m,* ráfaga de luz, *f;* brillo, *m;* (from a gun) fuego, fogonazo, *m;* (of wit, genius) rasgo, *m;* (of joy, etc.) acceso, *m.* —*vi* relampaguear, fulgurar, centellear; brillar; cruzar rápidamente, pasar como un relámpago. —*vt* hacer relampaguear; hacer brillar; (a look, etc.) dar; lanzar; (light) encender; (powder) quemar; transmitir señales por heliógrafo; *Inf.* sacar a relucir, enseñar. **shoulder-f.,** *Mil.* emblema, *m.* **to be gone like a f.,** desaparecer como un relámpago. **to f. out,** brillar, centellear. **f. of lightning,** relámpago, rayo, *m.* **f. of wit,** agudeza, *f,* rasgo de ingenio, *m*

flashback /'flæʃˌbæk/ *n* episodio intercalado, *m,* retrospección, *f*

flashlight /'flæʃˌlait/ *n* luz de magnesio, *f;* (torch) lamparilla eléctrica, *f,* rayo, *m* (Mexico); **f. photograph,** magnesio, *m*

flashy /'flæʃi/ *a* llamativo, de mal gusto, charro; frívolo, superficial

flask /flæsk/ *n* frasco, *m,* redoma, botella, *f;* (for powder) frasco, *m;* (vacuum) termos, *m*

flat /flæt/ *a* llano; (smooth) liso; (lying) tendido, tumbado; (flattened) aplastado; (destroyed) arrasado; (stretched out) extendido; (of nose, face) chato, romo, *m,* (of tire) desinflado; (uniform) uniforme; (depressed) desanimado; (uninteresting) monótono; (boring) aburrido; *Com.* paralizado; (downright) categórico; absoluto; (net) neto; *Mus.* bemol; (of boats) de fondo plano. —*adv* See **flatly.** *n* planicie, *f;* (of a sword) hoja, *f;* (of the hand) palma, *f;* (land) llanura, *f;* (apartment) piso, *m; Mus.* bemol, *m.* **to fall f.,** caer de bruces; *Fig.* no tener éxito. **to make f.,** allanar. **to sing f.,** desafinar. **f. boat,** barco de fondo plano, *m.* **f.-footed,** de pies achatados; *Fig.* pedestre. **f.-iron,** plancha, *f.* **f. roof,** azotea, *f*

flatly /'flætli/ *adv* de plano; a nivel; (plainly) llanamente, netamente; (dully) indiferentemente; (categorically) categóricamente

flatness /'flætnis/ *n* planicie, *f;* llanura, *f;* (smoothness) lisura, *f;* (evenness) igualdad, *f;* (uninterestingness) insulsez, insipidez, *f;* aburrimiento, *m;* (depression) desaliento, abatimiento, *m*

flatten /'flætn/ *vt* aplanar, allanar; aplastar; (smooth) alisar; (even) igualar; (destroy) derribar, arrasar, destruir; (dismay) desconcertar; (out) extender. —*vi* aplanarse, allanarse; aplastarse

flatter /'flætər/ *vt* adular, lisonjear, halagar; (of a dress, photograph, etc.) favorecer, (please the senses) regalar, deleitar; (oneself) felicitarse

flatterer /'flætərər/ *n* adulador (-ra), lisonjero (-ra)

flattering /'flætərɪŋ/ *a* adulador, lisonjero; (promising) halagüeño; favoreciente; deleitoso

flattery /'flætəri/ *n* adulación, *f*

flat tire llanta desinflada, *f*

flatulence /'flætʃələns/ *n* flatulencia, *f*

flaunt /flɔnt/ *vi* (flutter) ondear; pavonearse. —*vt* desplegar; ostentar, sacar a relucir; enseñar

flaunting /'flɔntɪŋ/ *n* ostentación, *f;* alarde, *m.* —*a* ostentoso; magnífico; (fluttering) ondeante

flautist /'flɔtɪst/ *n* flautista, *mf*

flavor /'fleivər/ *n* sabor, gusto, *m; Cul.* condimento, *m; Fig.* dejo, *m.* —*vt Cul.* sazonar, condimentar; dar un gusto (de), hacer saborear (a); *Fig.* dar un dejo (de)

flavoring /'fleivərɪŋ/ *n Cul.* condimento, *m; Fig.* sabor, dejo, *m*

flaw /flɔ/ *n* desperfecto, *m,* imperfección, *f;* (crack) grieta, hendedura, *f;* (in wood, metals) quebraja, *f;* (in gems) pelo, *m;* (in fruit) maca, *f;* (in cloth) gabarro, *m; Fig.* defecto, error, *m;* (wind) ráfaga de viento, *f*

flawless /'flɔlɪs/ *a* sin defecto; perfecto; impecable

flax /flæks/ *n* lino, *m.* **to dress f.,** rastrillar lino. **f.-comb,** rastrillo, *m.* **f. field,** linar, *m*

flaxen /'flæksən/ *a* de lino; (hair) rubio, blondo. **f.-haired,** de pelo rubio

flay /flei/ *vt* desollar; (criticize) despellejar

flea /fli/ *n* pulga, *f.* **f. bite,** picada de pulga, *f*

fleck /flɛk/ *n* pinta, mancha, *f,* lunar, *m;* (of sun) mota, *f;* (speck) partícula, *f;* (freckle) peca, *f.* —*vt* abigarrar; manchar; (dapple) salpicar, motear

flee /fli/ *vi* huir, fugarse, escapar; (vanish) desaparecer; (avoid) evitar, huir de. —*vt* abandonar

fleece /flis/ *n* vellón, *m;* lana, *f;* toisón, *m.* —*vt* esquilar; *Fig. Inf.* pelar. **Order of the Golden F.,** Orden del Toisón de Oro, *f*

fleecy /'flisi/ *a* lanudo, lanar; (white) blanquecino; (of clouds) borreguero. **f. clouds,** borregos, *m pl*

fleet /flit/ *n* (navy) armada, *f;* escuadra, flota, *f; Fig.* serie, *f, a* alado, rápido, veloz. **F. Air Arm,** Aviación Naval, *f.* **f.-footed,** ligero de pies

fleeting /'flitɪŋ/ *a* fugaz, momentáneo, efímero, pasajero

flesh /flɛʃ/ *n* carne, *f;* (mankind) género humano, *m,* humanidad, *f;* (of fruit) pulpa, *f. a* **man of f. and blood,** un hombre de carne y hueso. **of one's own f. and blood,** de la misma sangre de uno. **to make one's f. creep,** dar carne de gallina (a). **f.-coloured,** encarnado, de color de carne. **f.-eating,** carnívoro. **f. wound,** herida superficial, *f*

fleshpot /'flɛʃˌpɒt/ *n* marmita, *f; Fig.* olla, *f.* **the fleshpots of Egypt,** las ollas de Egipto

fleshy /'flɛʃi/ *a* carnoso, grueso; (of fruit) pulposo; suculento

flex /flɛks/ *n Elec.* flexible, *m, vt* doblar. —*vi* doblarse

flexibility /ˌflɛksə'bɪliti/ *n* flexibilidad, *f;* (of style) plasticidad, *f;* docilidad, *f*

flexible /'flɛksəbəl/ *a* flexible; dúctil, maleable; (of style) plástico; of) voice) quebradizo; adaptable; dócil

flick /flɪk/ n golpecito, toque, m; (of the finger) capirotazo, m; Inf. cine, m, vt dar un golpecito a; dar ligeramente con un látigo; sacudir. **flick one's wrist** hacer girar la muñeca **to f. over the pages of,** hojear

flicker /'flɪkər/ n estremecimiento, temblor, m; fluctuación, f; (of bird) aleteo, m; (of flame) onda (de una llama), f; (of eyelashes) pestañeo, m; (of a smile) indicio, f, vi agitarse; (of flags) ondear; vacilar

flickering /'flɪkərɪŋ/ a tenue; vacilante

flier /'flaɪər/ n volador (-ra); aviador (-ra); piloto, m; fugitivo (-va)

flight /flaɪt/ n vuelo, m; (of bird of prey) colada, f; (flock of birds) bandada, f; (migration) migración, f; (of time) transcurso, m; (of imagination, etc.) arranque, m; (volley) lluvia, f; (of aeroplanes) escuadrilla (de aviones), f; (of stairs) tramo, tiro, m; (staircase) escalera, f; (of locks on canal, etc.) ramal, m; (escape) huida, fuga, f. **long-distance f.,** Aer. vuelo de distancia, m. **non-stop f.,** Aer. vuelo sin parar, m. **reconnaissance f.,** Aer. vuelo de reconocimiento, vuelo de patrulla, m. **test f.,** Aer. vuelo de pruebas, m. **to put to f.,** ahuyentar, poner en fuga. **to take f.,** alzar el vuelo. **f.-lieutenant,** teniente aviador, m. **f.-sergeant,** sargento aviador, m

flight attendant sobrecarbo mf

flighty /'flaɪti/ a frívolo, inconstante, veleidoso

flimsy /'flɪmzi/ a endeble; frágil; fútil, insubstancial

flinch /flɪntʃ/ vi echarse atrás, retirarse (ante); vacilar, titubear. **without flinching,** sin vacilar; sin quejarse

fling /flɪŋ/ vt arrojar, echar, tirar; lanzar; (scatter) derramar; (oneself) echarse; (oneself upon) echarse encima, f; Fig. confiar en. —vi lanzarse; marcharse precipitadamente; saltar. —n tiro, m; (of dice, etc.) echada, f; (gibe) sarcasmo, m, burla, chufleta, f; (of horse) respingo, brinco, m; baile escocés, m. **in full f.,** en plena operación; en progreso. **to have one's f.,** darse un verde, correrla. **to f. away,** vt desechar; (waste) desperdiciar, malgastar, perder. —vi marcharse enfadado; marcharse rápidamente. **to f. back,** (a ball) devolver; (the head) echar atrás. **to f. down,** tirar al suelo; arrojar; derribar. **to f. off,** vt rechazar; apartar; (a garment, etc.) quitar. —vi marcharse sin más ni más. **to f. oneself down,** tumbarse, echarse; despeñarse (por). **to f. oneself headlong,** despeñarse. **to f. open,** abrir violentamente, abrir de repente. **to f. out,** vt echar a la fuerza; (a hand) alargar, extender. —vi salir apresuradamente. **to f. over,** (upset) volcar; arrojar por; abandonar. **to f. up,** lanzar al aire; levantar, erguir; renunciar (a), abandonar; dejar

flint /flɪnt/ n pedernal, m; (for producing fire) piedra de encendedor, f

flippant /'flɪpənt/ a poco serio, ligero; frívolo; impertinente

flipper /'flɪpər/ n aleta, f

flirt /flɜrt/ n (man) coquetón, castigador, m; (woman) coqueta, castigadora, f. —vt (shake) sacudir; (move) agitar; (wave) menear. —vi flirtear, coquetear; (toy with) jugar con; divertirse con

flirtation /flɜr'teɪʃən/ n flirteo, amorío, m

flirtatious /flɜr'teɪʃəs/ a (of men) galanteador, castigador; (of women) coqueta

flit /flɪt/ vi revolotear, mariposear; (move silently) deslizarse, pasar silenciosamente; (depart) irse, marcharse; mudarse por los aires. **to f. about,** ir y venir silenciosamente. **to f. past,** pasar como una sombra

float /floʊt/ n masa flotante, f; (raft) balsa, f; Mech. flotador, m; (of fishing rod or net) corcho, m; (of fish) vejiga natatoria, f; (for swimming) nadadera, calabaza, f; (for tableaux) carroza, f; pl **floats,** Theat. candilejas, f pl. —vi flotar; (flags, hair, etc.) ondear; (wander) vagar; Naut. boyar. —vt poner a flote; hacer flotar; (a grounded ship) desencallar; (Com. a company) fundar; (a loan, etc.) emitir, poner en circulación; (launch a ship) botar; (flood) inundar

floating /'floʊtɪŋ/ n flotación, f, flote, m; Com. fundación (de una compañía), f; (of a loan) emisión, f; (of a ship) botadura, f. —a flotante; boyante; Com. en circulación, flotante; fluctuante, variable. **f. capital,** capital fluctuante, m. **f. debt,** deuda flotante, f. **f. dock,** dique flotante, m. **f. light,** buque faro, m. **f. population,** población flotante, f. **f. rib,** costilla flotante, f

flock /flɒk/ n rebaño, m, manada, f; (of birds) bandada, f; Fig. grey, f; (crowd) multitud, muchedumbre, f; (parishioners) congregación, f; (of wool or cotton) vedija (de lana or de algodón), f; pl **flocks,** (for stuffing) borra, f. —vi concurrirse, reunirse, congregarse; ir en tropel, acudir; (birds) volar en bandada. **f.-bed,** colchón de borra, m

floe /floʊ/ n banco de hielo, m

flog /flɒg/ vt azotar; castigar

flood /flʌd/ n inundación, f; (Bible) diluvio, m; (of the tide) flujo, m; Fig. torrente, m; (abundance) copia, abundancia, f; (fit) paroxismo, m. —vt inundar; sumergir; (of tears) mojar. —vi desbordar. **f. lighting,** iluminación intensiva, f

floor /flɔr/ n suelo, piso, m; (wooden) entarimado, m; (story) piso, m; (of a cart) cama, f; Agr. era, f. —vt entablar; echar al suelo, derribar; Fig. desconcertar, confundir. **on the f.,** en el suelo. **on the ground f.,** en el piso bajo. **to take the f.,** Fig. tener la palabra. **f.-polisher,** lustrador de piso, m

flop /flɒp/ *n* golpe, *m;* ruido sordo, *m;* (splash) chapoteo, *m; Inf.* fiasco, *m:* —*vi* dejarse caer

flora /'flɔrə/ *n* flora, *f*

florid /'flɒrɪd/ *a* florido; demasiado ornado, cursi, llamativo; (of complexion) rubicundo

florist /'flɒrɪst/ *n* florista, *mf*

floss /flɒs/ *n* seda floja, filoseda, *f;* (of maize) penacho, *m;* (of a cocoon) cadarzo, *m.* **f. silk,** seda floja, *f*

flotsam /'flɒtsəm/ *n* pecio, *m*

flounce /flauns/ *n* volante, *m, vi* saltar de impaciencia. **to f. out,** salir airadamente

flounder /'flaundər/ *n* (nearest equivalent) *Ichth.* platija, *f;* tumbo, *m.* —*vi* tropezar; revolcarse; andar dificultosamente

flour /flauᵊr/ *n* harina, *f, vt* enharinar. **f.-bin,** tina, *f,* harinero, *m.* **f. merchant,** harinero, *m*

flourish /'flɜrɪʃ/ *n* movimiento, *m;* gesto, saludo, *m;* (of a pen) plumada, *f;* (on the guitar, in fencing) floreo, *m;* preludio, *m;* (fanfare) tocata (de trompetas), *f;* (of a signature) rúbrica, *f;* (in rhetoric) floreo, *m.* —*vi* (of plants) vegetar; (prosper) prosperar, medrar; florecer; (of the guitar, in fencing) florear; *Mus.* preludiar; (with a pen) hacer plumadas (or rasgos de pluma); (of a signature) firmar con rúbrica; (sound a fanfare) hacer una tocata (de trompetas). —*vt* agitar en el aire, blandir

flourishing /'flɜrɪʃɪŋ/ *a* (of plants) lozano; floreciente; (prosperous) próspero; (happy) feliz

flout /flaut/ *vt* burlarse de; despreciar, no hacer caso de

flow /flou/ *n* flujo, *m;* corriente, *f;* chorro, *m;* (of water) caudal, *m;* (output) producción total, cantidad, *f;* (of the tide) flujo (de la marea), *m;* (of words) facilidad, *f.* —*vi* fluir, manar; correr; (of the tide) crecer (la marea); (pass) pasar, correr; (result) resultar (de); provenir (de); (of hair, drapery) caer, ondular; (abound) abundar. **to f. away,** escaparse, salir. **to f. back,** refluir. **to f. down,** descender, fluir hacia abajo; (of tears) correr por. **to f. from,** dimanar de; manar de; *Fig.* provenir de. **to f. in,** llegar en abundancia. **to f. into,** (rivers) desaguar en, desembocar en. **to f. over,** derramarse por. **to f. through,** (water) regar, atravesar; (water) regar. **to f. together,** (rivers) confluir

flower /'flauər/ *n* flor, *f;* (best) flor y nata, crema, *f.* —*vi* florecer. **in f.,** en flor. **No flowers by request,** (for a funeral) No flores por deseo del finado. **f.-bud,** capullo, *m.* **f.-garden,** jardín, *m.* **f. girl,** florista, vendedora de flores, *f.* **f. market,** mercado de flores, *m.* **f.-piece,** florero, *m.* **f. pot,** tiesto, *m,* maceta, *f.* **f. show,** exposición de flores, *f.* **f. vase,** florero, *m*

flowerbed /'flauər,bɛd/ *n* cuadro, macizo, *m*

flowering /'flauərɪŋ/ *n* florecimiento, *m.* —*a* floreciente; con flores; (of shrubs) de adorno. **f. season,** época de la floración, *f*

flowery /'flauəri/ *a* florido

flowing /'flouɪŋ/ *n* flujo, *m;* derrame, *m.* —*a* fluente, corriente; (of tide) creciente; (waving) ondeante; suelto; (of style) fluído

flow of capital corriente de capital, *f*

fluctuate /'flʌktʃu,eit/ *vi* fluctuar, vacilar; variar

fluctuation /,flʌktʃu'eiʃən/ *n* fluctuación, *f;* cambio, *m,* variación, *f;* (hesitancy) indecisión, vacilación, *f*

fluency /'fluənsi/ *n* fluidez, *f*

fluent /'fluənt/ *a* flúido; fácil

fluently /'fluəntli/ *adv* corrientemente, con facilidad, de corrido

fluff /flʌf/ *n* borra, pelusa, *f,* tamo, *m*

fluffy /'flʌfi/ *a* velloso; (feathered) plumoso; (woolly) lanudo; (of hair) encrespado

fluid /'fluɪd/ *n* flúido, líquido, *m,* a flúido

fluke /fluk/ *n* (in billiards) chiripa, *f; Naut.* uña, *f; Inf.* carambola, chiripa, chambonada, *f.* **by a f.,** de carambola, por suerte. **f.-worm,** duela del hígado, *f*

flunkey /'flʌŋki/ *n* lacayo, *m; Fig.* adulador, *m*

fluorescence /flu'resəns/ *n* fluorescencia, *f*

flurry /'flɜri/ *n* (of wind) ráfaga, *f;* (squall) chubasco, *m;* agitación, *f;* conmoción, *f.* —*vt* agitar

flush /flʌʃ/ *n* rubor, *m;* (in the sky) arrebol, rojo, color de rosa, *m;* emoción, *f,* acceso, *m;* sensación, *f;* (at cards) flux, *m;* vigor, *m;* (flowering) floración, *f;* abundancia, *f.* (of youth, etc.) frescura, *f.* —*a* (level) igual, parejo; abundante; (generous) pródigo, liberal; (rich) adinerado. —*vi* ruborizarse, enrojecerse, ponerse colorado; (flood) inundarse, llenarse (de agua, etc.); (of sky) arrebolarse. —*vt* inundar, limpiar con un chorro de agua, etc., lavar; (of blood) circular por; (redden) enrojecer; (make blush) hacer ruborizarse; (exhilarate) excitar, animar; (inflame) inflamar, encender; (make level) igualar, nivelar. **f. with,** a ras de

flushing /'flʌʃɪŋ/ *n* rojez, *f;* (cleansing) limpieza, lavadura, *f;* (flooding) inundación, *f*

fluster /'flʌstər/ *n* agitación, confusión, *f,* aturdimiento, *m.* —*vt* agitar, poner nervioso (a), aturdir; (oneself) preocuparse. —*vi* agitarse; estar nervioso, estar perplejo; (with drink) estar entre dos velas

flute /flut/ *n* flauta, *f; Archit.* estría, *f;* (organ-stop) flautado, *m.* —*vi* tocar la flauta, flautear; tener la voz flauteada. —*vt* tocar (una pieza) en la flauta; (groove) encanutar, acanalar, estriar. **f. player,** flautista, *mf*

flutter /'flʌtər/ *n* (of wings) aleteo, *m;* (of leaves, etc.) murmurio, *m;* (of eyelashes) pestañeo, *m;* (of flags, etc.) ondeo, *m,* ondulación, *f;* (excitement) agitación, f; (stir) sensación, f; (gamble) jugada, f. —vi (of birds) aletear; revolotear; (of butterflies) mariposear; (of flags) ondear; palpitar; (of persons) estar agitado. —vt agitar; (the eyelashes) pestañear; (agitate) agitar, alarmar

fluttering /'flʌtərɪŋ/ n mariposeo, m; revoloteo, m; (of birds) aleteo, m; (of leaves, etc.) murmurio, m; (of flags, etc.) ondeo, m, ondulación, f; (of eyelashes) pestañeo, m

flux /flʌks/ n flujo, m

fly /flai/ n (insect) mosca, f; (on a fishhook) mosca artificial, f; (carriage) calesín, m; (of breeches) bragueta, f; Theat. bambalina, f; (of a tent) toldo, m; (flight) vuelo, m; (of a flag) vuelo, m. **fly-blown**, manchado por las moscas. **fly-by-night**, trasnochador (-ra). **fly-catcher**, Ornith. papamoscas, m; matamoscas, m. **fly-fishing**, pesca con moscas artificiales, f. **fly-leaf**, guarda (de un libro), f. **fly-paper**, papel matamoscas, m. **fly-swatter**, matamoscas, m. **fly-wheel**, Mech. volante, m

fly /flai/ vi volar; (flutter) ondear; (jump) saltar; (rush) lanzarse, precipitarse; (pass away) pasar volando, volar; (run off) marcharse a todo correr; (escape) huir, escapar; (seek refuge) refugiarse; (to the head, of intoxicants) subirse; (vanish) desaparecer. —vt hacer volar; hacer ondear, enarbolar; (an airplane) pilotar, dirigir; (flee from) huir de; evitar. **to let fly (at)**, descargar, tirar; Fig. saltar la sinhueso. **to fly about**, volar en torno de; revolotear. **to fly at**, lanzarse sobre; acometer, asaltar. **to fly away**, emprender el vuelo. **to fly back**, volar hacia el punto de partida; (of doors, etc.) abrir, or cerrar, de repente. **to fly down**, volar abajo. **to fly in**, volar dentro de; volar adentro; (of airplanes) llegar (el avión). **to fly to pieces**, hacerse pedazos. **to fly into a rage**, montarse en cólera. **to fly low**, rastrear; Aer. volar a baja altura. **to fly off**, emprender el vuelo; (hasten) marcharse volando; (of buttons, etc.) saltar (de), separarse (de). **to fly open**, abrirse de repente. **to fly over**, volar por, volar por encima de. **to fly upwards**, volar hacia arriba; subir

flying /'flaiɪŋ/ n vuelo, m. —a volante, volador; que vuela; de volar; volátil; (hasty) rápido; (flowing) ondeante, ondulante. **to shoot f.**, tirar al vuelo. **with f. colors**, con banderas desplegadas, triunfante. **f.-boat**, hidroavión, m. **f.-buttress**, botarel, arbotante, m. **f.-column**, Mil. cuerpo volante, m. **f.-fish**, (pez) volador, m. **f.-fortress**, Aer. fortaleza volante, f. **f.-officer**, oficial de aviación, m. **f.-sickness**, mal de altura, m. **f.-squad**, escuadra ligera, f. **f.-test**, Aer. examen de pilotaje, m

foam /foum/ n espuma, f. —vi espumar; (of horses, etc.) echar espumarajos. **to f.**

and froth, (of the sea) hervir. **f. at the mouth**, echar espuma por la boca.

foam rubber n caucho esponjoso, m, espuma de caucho, f, espuma sintética, f

foamy /'foumi/ a espumoso

fob /fob/ n bolsillo del reloj, m; faltriquera pequeña, f. —vt (off) engañar con

focus /'foukəs/ n foco, m; centro, m. —vt enfocar; concentrar. —vi convergir. **in f.**, en foco

fodder /'fodər/ n Agr. pienso, forraje, m. —vt dar forraje (a)

foe /fou/ n enemigo, m

fog /fɒg/ n neblina, niebla, f; Fig. confusión, f; Fig. perplejidad, f, vt obscurecer; Photo. velar; Fig. ofuscar. —vi hacerse nebuloso; Photo. velarse. **fog-signal**, señal de niebla, f

fogey /'fougi/ n obscurantista, m. **He is an old f.**, Es un señor chapado a la antigua

foggy /'fɒgi/ a nebuloso; Photo. velado. **It is f.**, Hay niebla

foghorn /'fɒg,hɔrn/ n sirena, f; bocina, f

foible /'fɔibəl/ n flaco, m, debilidad, f

foil /fɔil/ n (sword) florete, m; (coat) hoja, f; (of a mirror) azogado, m. —vt frustrar. **f. a plot**, desbaratar un complot. **She makes a good f. for her sister's beauty**, Hace resaltar la belleza de su hermana

foist /fɔist/ vt imponer; insertar, incluir; engañar (con)

fold /fould/ n doblez, f, pliegue, m; arruga, f; Sew. cogido, m; (for sheep) redil, aprisco, m; Fig. iglesia, congregación de los fieles, f; (in compounds) vez, f. —vt doblar, plegar, doblegar; (the arms) cruzar (los brazos); (embrace) abrazar; (wrap) envolver; (clasp) entrelazar; (sheep) meter en redil, encerrar. —vi doblarse, plegarse; cerrarse

folding /'fouldɪŋ/ n plegadura, f, doblamiento, m; (of sheep) encerramiento, m, a plegadizo. **f.-door**, puerta plegadiza, f. **f.-machine**, plegador, m. **f.-seat**, Auto. traspuntín, m. **f.-table**, mesa de tijeras, f; mesa plegadiza, f

foliage /'foulɪɪdʒ/ n follaje, m, frondas, f pl. **thick f.**, frondosidad, f

folio /'fouli,ou/ n folio, m; (a volume) infolio, m. —a de infolio. —vt foliar

folk /fouk/ n (nation) pueblo, m, nación, f; gente, f; pl **folks**, Inf. familia, f; parientes, m pl. **f.-dance**, danza popular, f

folklore /'fouk,lor/ n folclore, m, tradiciones folclóricas, f pl

folksong /'fouk,sɔŋ/ n canción popular, f; romance, m; copla, f

folktale /'fouk,teil/ n conseja, f, cuento popular, m

follicle /'fɒlɪkəl/ n (Anat., Bot.) folículo, m

follow /'fɒlou/ vt seguir; (pursue) perseguir; (hunt) cazar; (adopt) adoptar; (understand) comprender; (notice) observar. —vi ir, or venir, detrás; (of time) venir después; (gen. impers.) seguir, resultar; seguirse. **as follows,** como sigue. **I shall f. your advice,** Seguiré tus consejos. **to f. on the heels of,** *Fig.* pisar los talones (a). **to f. suit,** (at cards) asistir, jugar el mismo palo; *Fig.* imitar. **to f. up,** proseguir; continuar; (pursue) perseguir; (enhance) reforzar. **f.-me-lads,** *Inf.* siguemepollo, *m*

follower /ˈfɒloʊər/ *n* seguidor (-ra); adherente, secuaz, *mf;* (imitator) imitador (-ra); (lover) novio, *m; pl* **followers,** acompañamiento, séquito, *m*

following /ˈfɒloʊɪŋ/ *n* séquito, acompañamiento, *m,* comitiva, *f;* partidarios, *m pl,* adherentes, *mf pl. —a* siguiente; próximo. **f. wind,** viento en popa, *m*

folly /ˈfɒli/ *n* locura, extravagancia, absurdidad, tontería, *f,* disparate, *m*

foment /foʊˈmɛnt/ *vt* (poultice) fomentar; provocar, incitar, instigar; (assist) fomentar, proteger, promover

fond /fɒnd/ *a* (credulous) vano, crédulo, vacío; (doting) demasiado indulgente; (loving) cariñoso, tierno, afectuoso; (addicted to) aficionado a, adicto a, amigo de. **to be f. of,** (things) tener afición a, estar aficionado de; (people) tener cariño (a). **to grow f. of,** (things) aficionarse a; (people) tomar cariño (a)

fondle /ˈfɒndl/ *vt* mimar, acariciar; jugar (con.)

fondness /ˈfɒndnɪs/ *n* cariño, afecto, *m;* (for things) afición, inclinación, *f;* gusto, *m*

font /fɒnt/ *n* pila bautismal, *f; Poet.* fuente, *f; Print.* fundición, *f*

food /fud/ *n* alimento, *m;* comida, *f,* el comer, *m;* (of animals) pasto, *m; Fig.* pábulo, *m;* materia, *f.* **She gave him f.** Le dio de comer. **You have given me f. for thought,** Me has dado en qué pensar. **f.-card,** cartilla de racionamiento, *food, clothing, and shelter* comida, abrigo y vivienda, *f.* **F. Ministry,** Ministerio de Alimentación, *m.* **f. value,** valor nutritivo, *m.* **food poisoning,** intoxicación alimenticia, *f*

foodstuffs /ˈfudˌstʌfs/ *n pl* comestibles, víveres, *m pl*

fool /ful/ *n* tonto (-ta), mentecato (-ta), majadero (ra) necio (-ia); (jester) bufón, *m;* (butt of jest) hazmerreír, *m;* víctima, *f; Cul.* compota de frutas con crema, *f, vi* tontear, hacer tonterías. *—vt* poner en ridículo (a); (deceive) engañar, embaucar; (with) jugar con. **to make a f. of oneself,** ponerse en ridículo. **to f. about,** *vi* perder el tiempo, vagabundear. **to f. away,** malgastar, malbaratar. **fool's bauble,** cetro de bufón, *m.* **fool's cap,** gorro de bufón, *m*

foolhardy /ˈfulˌhɑrdi/ *a* temerario, atrevido

foolish /ˈfulɪʃ/ *a* imprudente; estúpido, tonto; ridículo, absurdo; imbécil

foolproof /ˈfulˌpruf/ *a* (of utensils, etc.) con garantía absoluta

foot /fʊt/ *n* pie, *m;* (of animals, furni-

ture) pata, *f;* (of bed, sofa, grave, ladder, page, etc.) pie, *m;* (hoof) pezuña, *f;* (metric unit and measure) pie, *m; Mil.* infantería, *f;* (base) base, *f;* (step) paso, *m. —a Mil.* de a pie *a pie. —vi* ir a pie; venir a pie; bailar. *—vt* hollar; (account) pagar (una cuenta); (stockings) poner pie (a). **on f.,** a pie; (of soldiers) de a pie; (in progress) en marcha. **to go on f.,** ir a pie, andar. **to put one's best f. forward,** apretar el paso; *Fig.* hacer de su mejor. **to put one's f. down,** poner pies en pared, pararle pararle fulano el alto. **to put one's f. in it,** meter la pata. **to rise to one's feet,** ponerse de pie. **to set f. on,** pisar, hollar. **to set on f.,** poner en pie; *Fig.* poner en marcha. **to trample under f.,** pisotear. **f.-and-mouth disease,** glosopeda, *f.* **f.-brake,** freno de pedal, *m.* **f.-pump,** fuelle de pie, *m.* **f.-rule,** (nearest equivalent) doble decímetro, *m.* **f.-soldier,** soldado de a pie, infante, *m*

football /ˈfʊtˌbɔl/ *n* (game) fútbol, *m;* (ball) pelota de fútbol, *f.* **f. field,** campo de fútbol, *m.* **f. match,** partida de fútbol, *f.* **f. pools,** apuestas de fútbol, *f pl;* (in Spain) apuestas benéficas de fútbol, *f pl*

footbridge /ˈfʊtˌbrɪdʒ/ *n* puente para peatones, *m*

foothills /ˈfʊtˌhɪlz/ *n pl* faldas de la montaña, *f pl*

foothold /ˈfʊtˌhoʊld/ *n* hincapié, *m;* posición establecida, *f*

footing /ˈfʊtɪŋ/ *n* hincapié, *m;* posición firme, *f;* condiciones, *f pl;* relaciones, *f pl.* **on a peacetime f.,** en pie de paz. **to be on an equal f.,** estar en pie de igualdad, estar en iguales condiciones. **to miss one's f.,** resbalar

footlights /ˈfʊtˌlaɪts/ *n pl* canilejas, candilejas, *f pl.* **to get across the f.,** hacer contacto con el público

footnote /ˈfʊtˌnoʊt/ *n* llamada a pie de página, nota a pie de página, *f*

footpath /ˈfʊtˌpæθ/ *n* senda, vereda, *f* sendero, *m*

footprint /ˈfʊtˌprɪnt/ *n* huella, pisada, *f,* vestigio, *m*

footstep /ˈfʊtˌstɛp/ *n* paso, *m;* (trace) pisada, huella, *f.* **to follow in the footsteps of,** *Fig.* seguir las pisadas de

footwear /ˈfʊtˌwɛər/ *n* calzado, *m*

fop /fɒp/ *n* petimetre, *m*

foppish /ˈfɒpɪʃ/ *a* presumido, afectado; elegante

for /fɔr; *unstressed* fər/ *prep* (expressing exchange, price or penalty of, instead of, in support or favor of, on account of) por; (expressing destination, purpose, result) para; (during) durante, por; (for the sake of) para; (because of) a causa de; (in spite of) a pesar de; (as) como; (with) de; (in favor of) en favor de; (in election campaign) con (e.g., "Ecuadorians for Martínez!" ¡Ecuatorianos con Martínez!) (toward) hacia; (that) que, para que (with *subjunc*); a, (before) antes de; (searching for) en busca de; (bound for) con rumbo a; (regarding) en cuanto a; (until) hasta. What's for dinner? ¿Qué hay de comida? **center for...** centro de... (e.g., *Center for Applied Linguistics,* Centro de Lingüística Aplicada). **He is in business for himself,** Tiene negocios por su propia cuenta. **It is raining too hard for you to go there,** Llueve demasiado para que vayas allí. **It is not for him to decide,** No le toca a él decidirlo. **Were it not for...,** Si no fuese por... **She has not been to see me for a week,** Hace una semana que no viene a verme. **It is impossible for them to go out,** Les es imposible salir. **but for all that,** pero con todo. **for ever,** por (or para) siempre. **for fear that,** por miedo de que. **for myself,** en cuanto a mí, personalmente. **for the present,** por ahora. **for what reason?** ¿para qué? ¿por cuál motivo? **for brevity's sake, for the sake of brevity,** por causa de la brevedad

for /fɔr; *unstressed* fər/ *conjunc* porque; visto que, pues, puesto que, en efecto, ya que

forage /'fɔrɪdʒ/ *n* forraje, *m.* —*vt* and *vi* forrajear. **to f. for,** buscar. **f. cap,** gorra de cuartel, *f*

foray /'fɔreɪ/ *n* correría, cabalgada, *f*; saqueo, *m*

forbear /'fɔr,bɛər/ *vt* and *vi* dejar (de); guardarse (de); abstenerse de; evitar; reprimirse (de); rehusarse (de); (cease) cesar (de); (be patient) ser paciente; ser tolerante

forbearance /fɔr'bɛərəns/ *n* abstención, *f*; tolerancia, transigencia, *f*; indulgencia, *f*; paciencia, *f*

forbearing /fɔr'bɛərɪŋ/ *a* tolerance, transigente; generoso, magnánimo; paciente

forbid /fər'bɪd/ *vt* prohibir, defender (de); impedir. **I f. you to do it,** Te prohíbo hacerlo. **The game is forbidden,** El juego está prohibido. **They have forbidden me to...,** Me han defendido de... **Heaven f.!** ¡Dios no lo quiera!

forbidden /fər'bɪdn/ *a* prohibido; ilícito. **f. fruit,** fruto prohibido, *m*

forbidding /fər'bɪdɪŋ/ *a* repugnante, horrible; antipático, desagradable; (dismal) lúgubre; (threatening) amenazador. —*n* prohibición, *f*

force /fɔrs/ *n* fuerza, *f*; violencia, *f*; vigor, *m*; (efficacy) eficacia, *f*; (validity) validez, *f*; (power) poder, *m*; (motive) motivo, *m*, razón, *f*; (weight) peso, *m*, importancia, *f*; (police) policía, *f*; *pl* **forces,** *Mil.* fuerzas, tropas, *f pl.* **by main f.,** por fuerza mayor. **in f.,** vigente, en vigor. **to be in f.,** estar vigente

force /fɔrs/ *vt* forzar; (compel) obligar, constreñir, precisar; (ravish) violar; *Cul.* rellenar; (impose) imponer; (plants) forzar; (the pace) apresurar; (cause) hacer; (a lock, etc.) forzar. **to f. oneself into,** entrar a la fuerza en; (a garment) ponerse con dificultad; imponerse a la fuerza. **to**

f. oneself to, esforzarse a. **to f. the pace,** forzar el paso. **to f. away,** ahuyentar. **to f. back,** hacer retroceder; rechazar; (a sigh, etc.) ahogar. **to f. down,** hacer bajar, obligar a bajar; (make swallow) hacer tragar; (of airplanes) hacer tomar tierra. **to f. in,** introducir a la fuerza; obligar a entrar. **to f. into,** meter a la fuerza; obligar a entrar (en). **to f. on, upon,** imponer. **to f. open,** abrir a la fuerza; (a lock) romper, forzar. **to f. out,** hacer salir; empujar hacia fuera; (words) pronunciar con dificultad. **to f. up,** obligar a subir; hacer subir; hacer vomitar

forced /fɔrst/ *a* forzado; forzoso; afectado. **f. landing,** *Aer.* aterrizaje forzoso, *m.* **f. march,** *Mil.* marcha forzada, *f*

forceful /'fɔrsfəl/ *a* See **forcible**

forcemeat /'fɔrs,mit/ *n* picadillo, *m;* relleno, *m.* **f. ball,** albóndiga, *f*

forceps /'fɔrsəps/ *n pl* fórceps, *m pl;* pinzas, *f pl.* **arterial f.,** pinzas hemostáticas, *f pl*

forcible /'fɔrsəbəl/ *a* fuerte; a la fuerza; violento; enérgico, vigoroso; poderoso; *Lit.* vívido, gráfico, vehemente. **f. feeding,** alimentación forzosa, *f*

forcibly /'fɔrsəbli/ *adv* a la fuerza

forcing /'fɔrsɪŋ/ *n* forzamiento, *m;* compulsión, *f.* **f. frame,** semillero, *m,* especie de invernadero, *f*

ford /fɔrd/ *n* esguazo, vado, *m.* —*vt* esguazar, vadear

fore /fɔr/ *a* delantero; *Naut.* de proa. —*adv* delante; *Naut.* de proa. **f.-and-aft,** *Naut.* de popa a proa.

forearm /'fɔrˌɑrm/ *n* antebrazo, *m.* —*vt* armar de antemano; preparar

forebear /'fɔr,bɛər/ *n* antecesor, *m,* ascendiente, *mf*

forebode /fɔr'boud/ *vt* presagiar, augurar, anunciar; presentir

foreboding /fɔr'boudɪŋ/ *n* presagio, augurio, *m;* presentimiento, *m,* corazonada, *f*

forecast /'fɔr,kæst/ *n* pronóstico, *m;* proyecto, plan, *m, vt* pronosticar; proyectar. **weather f.,** pronóstico del tiempo, *m*

foreclose /fɔr'klouz/ *vt* excluir; impedir; vender por orden judicial; anticipar el resultado de; decidir de antemano

foreclosure /fɔr'klouʒər/ *n* venta por orden judicial, *f;* juicio hipotecario, *m*

forefather /'fɔr,fɑðər/ *n* antepasado, antecesor, *m*

forefinger /'fɔr,fɪŋgər/ *n* índice, dedo índice, *m*

forefront /'fɔr,frʌnt/ *n* delantera, primera línea, *f;* frente, *m;* vanguardia, *f.* **in the f.,** en la vanguardia; en el frente

foregoing /fɔr'gouɪŋ/ *a* precedente, anterior

foregone /fɔr'gɔn/ *a* decidido de antemano; previsto

foreground /'fɔr,graʊnd/ *n* primer plano, primer término, frente, *m.* **in the f.,** *Art.* en primer término

forehead /'fɔrɪd/ *n* frente, *f*

foreign /'fɔrɪn/ a extranjero; extraño; exótico; exterior; (alien) ajeno. **f. affairs,** asuntos extranjeros, m pl. **f. body,** cuerpo extraño, m. **f. debt,** deuda exterior, f. **F. Legion,** tercio extranjero, m. **F. Office,** Ministerio de Relaciones Extranjeras, m. **f. parts,** extranjero, m. **f. policy,** política internacional, f. **F. Secretary,** Secretario de Asuntos Extranjeros, Secretario de Asuntos Exteriores, Ministro de Relaciones Extranjeras, m. **f. trade,** comercio con el extranjero, m

foreigner /'fɔrənər/ n extranjero (-ra)

foreknowledge /'fɔr,nɒlɪdʒ/ n presciencia, precognición, f

forelock /'fɔr,lɒk/ n guedeja, vedeja, f; (of a horse) copete, tupé, m. **to take time by the f.,** asir la ocasión por la melena

foreman /'fɔrmən/ n. (of jury) presidente (del jurado), m; (of a farm) mayoral, m; (in a works) capataz, m

foremost /'fɔr,moust/ a delantero; de primera fila; más importante. —adv en primer lugar; en primera fila

forensic /fə'rɛnsɪk/ a forense, legal. **f. medicine,** medicina legal, f

forerunner /'fɔr,rʌnər/ n precursor (-ra), predecessor (-ra); (presage) anuncio, presagio, m

foresee /fɔr'si/ vt prever, anticipar

foreshadow /fɔr'ʃædou/ vt anunciar, prefigurar; simbolizar; hacer sentir.

foreshorten /fɔr'ʃɔrtn/ vt Art. escorzar

foresight /'fɔr,sait/ n presciencia, f; previsión, prudencia, f; (of gun) punto de mira, m; (optical) croquis de nivel, m

forest /'fɔrɪst/ n bosque, m, selva, f. —vt arbolar

forestall /fɔr'stɔl/ vt anticipar, saltear; prevenir; Com. acaparar

forestation /,fɔrə'steɪʃən/ n repoblación forestal, f

forester /'fɔrəstər/ n silvicultor, guardamonte, ingeniero forestal, m; habitante de los bosques, m

forest fire incendio forestal, m

forestry /'fɔrəstri/ n silvicultura, f

foretaste /n 'fɔr,teist; v fɔr'teist/ n muestra, f; presagio, m. —vt gustar con anticipación

foretell /fɔr'tɛl/ vt predecir, profetizar; anunciar, presagiar

forethought /'fɔr,θɔt/ n presciencia, previsión, f; prevención, f

forewarn /fɔr'wɔrn/ vt prevenir

foreword /'fɔr,wɜrd/ n prefacio, m, introducción, f

forfeit /'fɔrfɪt/ n pérdida, f; (fine) multa, f; (in games) prenda, f; (of rights, goods, etc.) confiscación, f. —a confiscado. —vt perder; perder el derecho o el título de

forfeiture /'fɔrfɪtʃər/ n pérdida, f; confiscación, f; secuestro, m

forge /fɔrdʒ/ n fragua, f; (smithy) herrería, f. —vt and vi fraguar, forjar; (fabricate) inventar, fabricar; falsificar; (advance) avanzar lentamente. **to f. ahead,** abrirse camino; avanzar

forged /fɔrdʒd/ a (of iron) forjado; (of checks, etc.) falso, falsificado

forger /'fɔrdʒər/ n falsificador (-ra), falsario (-ia); (creator) artífice, mf

forgery /'fɔrdʒəri/ n falsificación, f

forget /fər'gɛt/ vt olvidar; descuidar. —vi olvidarse. **to f. about,** olvidarse de, desacordarse de. **to f. oneself,** olvidarse de sí mismo; propasarse; (in anger) perder los estribos

forgetful /fər'gɛtfəl/ a olvidadizo; descuidado, negligente

forgive /fər'gɪv/ vt perdonar, disculpar, condonar; (debts) remitir

forgiveness /fər'gɪvnɪs/ n perdón, m; condonación, f; (remission) remisión, f

forgiving /fər'gɪvɪŋ/ a misericordioso, clemente, dispuesto a perdonar

forgo /fɔr'gou/ vt renunciar, sacrificar, privarse de; abandonar, ceder

forgoing /fɔr'gouɪŋ/ n renunciación, f, sacrificio, m; cesión, f

"For Immediate Occupancy" «De Ocupación Inmediata»

fork /fɔrk/ n Agr. horca, horquilla, f; (table fork) tenedor, m; bifurcación, f; (of rivers) confluencia, f; (of branches) horcadura, f; (of legs) horcajadura, f; (for supporting trees, etc.) horca, f; Mus. diapasón normal, m. —vt hacinar con horca. —vi bifurcarse; ramificarse

forlorn /fɔr'lɔrn/ a abandonado, desamparado, desesperado. **f. hope,** aventura desesperada, f

form /fɔrm/ n forma, f; figura, f; (shadowy) bulto, m; (formality) formalidad, f; ceremonia, f; Eccl. rito, m; método, m; regla, f; (in a school) clase, f; (lair) cama, f; (seat) banco, m; (system) sistema, m; (ghost) espectro, m; aparición, f; (to fill up) documento, m; hoja, f; (state) condición, f; Lit. construcción, forma, f. **It is a matter of f.,** Es una pura formalidad. **in due f.,** en debida forma, en regla. **in the usual f.,** Com. al usado. **It is not good f.,** No es de buena educación

form /fɔrm/ vt formar; (a habit) contraer; (an idea) hacerse (una idea). —vi formarse. **to f. fours,** Mil. formar a cuatro

formal /'fɔrməl/ a esencial; formal; ceremonioso, solemne; (of person) etiquetero, formalista. **f. call,** visita de cumplido, f

formality /fɔr'mælɪti/ n formalidad, f; ceremonia, solemnidad, f

format /'fɔrmæt/ n formato, m

formation /fɔr'meɪʃən/ n formación, f; disposición, f; arreglo, m; organización, f; (Mil., Geol.) formación, f

former /'fɔrmər/ a primero; antiguo; anterior; pasado. **in f. times,** antes, antiguamente. **the f.,** ése, aquél, m; ésa, aquélla, f; aquéllos, m pl; aquéllas, f pl

former /'fɔrmər/ n formador (-ra); creador (-ra), autor (-ra)

formerly /'fɔrmərli/ *adv* antiguamente, antes

formidable /'fɔrmɪdəbəl/ *a* formidable; terrible, espantoso

formless /'fɔrmlɪs/ *a* informe

formula /'fɔrmyələ/ *n* fórmula, *f.* **standard f.**, (*Math.,Chem.*) fórmula clásica, *f*

formulate /'fɔrmyə,leɪt/ *vt* formular

fornicate /'fɔrnɪ,keɪt/ *vi* fornicar

forsake /fɔr'seɪk/ *vt* dejar, desertar; abandonar, desamparar; separarse de; (of birds, the nest) aborrecer; (one's faith) renegar de

"For Sale" «Se Vende»

forsooth /fɔr'suθ/ *adv* ciertamente, claro está

forswear /fɔr'swɛər/ *vt* abjurar; renunciar a. **to f. oneself**, perjurarse

fort /fɔrt/ *n* fortaleza, *f*, fuerte, *m*

forte /'fɔrteɪ/ *n* fuerte, *m.* —*a Mus.* fuerte

forth /fɔrθ/ *adv* (on) adelante, hacia adelante; (out) fuera; (in time) en adelante, en lo consecutivo; (show) a la vista. **and so f.**, y así en lo sucesivo; etcétera

forthcoming /'fɔrθ'kʌmɪŋ/ *a* próximo; futuro; en preparación

forthwith /,fɔrθ'wɪθ/ *adv* en seguida, sin tardanza

fortieth /'fɔrtiɪθ/ *a* cuadragésimo; cuarenta. —*n* cuarentavo, *m*

fortify /'fɔrtə,faɪ/ *vt* fortificar; fortalecer; confirmar; *Fig.* proveer (de)

fortitude /'fɔrtɪ,tud/ *n* aguante, *m*, fortaleza, *f*, estoicismo, *m*

fortnight /'fɔrt,naɪt/ *n* quince días, *m pl*, dos semanas, *f pl*; quincena, *f.* **a f. ago**, hace quince días. **a f. tomorrow**, mañana en quince. **in a f.**, dentro de quince días; al cabo de quince días. **once a f.**, cada quince días

fortnightly /'fɔrt,naɪtli/ *a* quincenal. —*adv* cada dos semanas, dos veces al mes. —*n* revista quincenal, *f*

fortress /'fɔrtrɪs/ *n* fortaleza, plaza fuerte, *f*

fortuitous /fɔr'tuɪtəs/ *a* fortuito, accidental

fortuitously /fɔr'tuɪtəsli/ *adv* accidentalmente

fortunate /'fɔrtʃənɪt/ *a* dichoso, feliz; afortunado; próspero. **to be f.**, (of persons) tener suerte

fortunately /'fɔrtʃənɪtli/ *adv* afortunadamente, por dicha, felizmente

fortune /'fɔrtʃən/ *n* suerte, fortuna, *f*, destino, *m*; (money) caudal, *m*, fortuna, *f*; bienes, *m pl*; buena ventura, *f.* **good f.**, buena fortuna, dicha, *f.* **ill f.**, mala suerte, *f.* **to cost a f.**, costar un sentido. **to make one's f.**, enriquecerse; *Inf.* hacer su pacotilla. **to tell fortunes**, echar las cartas. **f. hunter**, buscador de dotes, cazador de dotes, cazador de fortunas, aventurero, *m.* **f.-teller**, adivinadora, *f*; echadora de cartas, *f.* **f.-telling**, buenaventura, *f*

forty /'fɔrti/ *a* and *n* cuarenta, *m.* **He is turned f.**, Ha cumplido los cuarenta. **person of f.**, cuarentón (-ona). **She is f.**, Tiene cuarenta años

forum /'fɔrəm/ *n* foro, tribuna *f*, (e.g., *to serve as a forum for discussion*, servir de tribuna de discusión)

forward /'fɔrwərd/ *a* avanzado; adelantado; (of position) delantero; (ready) preparado; (eager) pronto, listo, impaciente; activo, emprendedor; (of persons, fruit, etc.) precoz; (pert) insolente, desenvuelto, atrevido. —*adv* adelante; hacia adelante; (of time) en adelante; (farther on) más allá; hacia el frente; en primera línea. —*vt* ayudar, promover; adelantar; (letters) hacer seguir; *Com.* expedir, remitir; (a parcel) despachar; (hasten) apresurar; (plants) hacer crecer. —*n Sports.* delantero, *m.* **center-f.**, *Sports.* delantero centro, *m.* **from this time f.**, de hoy en adelante. **Please f.**, ¡Haga seguir! **putting f. of the clock**, el adelanto de la hora. **to carry f.**, *Com.* pasar a cuenta nueva. **to go f.**, adelantarse; estar en marcha, estar en preparación. **f. line**, *Sports.* delantera, *f.* **F.!** ¡Adelante!

forwarding /'fɔrwərdɪŋ/ *n* fomento, *m*, promoción, *f*; *Com.* expedición, *f*, envío, *m*

forwardness /'fɔrwərdnɪs/ *n* progreso, adelantamiento, *m*; (haste) apresuramiento, *m*; (of persons, fruit, etc.) precocidad, *f*; (pertness) desenvoltura, insolencia, frescura, *f*, descaro, *m*; (eagerness) impaciencia, *f*

fosse /fɒs/ *n* foso, *m*

fossil /'fɒsəl/ *a* and *n* fósil, *m*.

fossilize /'fɒsə,laɪz/ *vt* fosilizar; petrificar. —*vi* fosilizarse

foster /'fɒstər/ *vt* provocar, promover, suscitar; (favor) favorecer, ser propicio a. **f.-brother**, hermano de leche, *m.* **f.-child**, hijo (-ja) de leche. **f.-father**, padre adoptivo, *m.* **f.-mother**, ama de leche, *f.* **f.-sister**, hermana de leche, *f*

foul /faul/ *a* sucio, asqueroso, puerco; (evil-smelling) hediondo, fétido; (of air) viciado; impuro; (language) ofensivo; (coarse) indecente, obsceno; (harmful) nocivo, dañino; (wicked) malvado; infame; vil; (unfair) injusto; *Sports.* sucio; (ugly) feo; (entangled) enredado; (with corrections) lleno de erratas; (choked) atascado; (of weather) borrascoso, tempestuoso; malo, desagradable; (repulsive) repugnante. —*n Sports.* juego sucio, *m.* —*vt* ensuciar; *Naut.* chocar, abordar; (block) atascar; (the anchor) enredar; (dishonor) deshonrar. —*vi* atascarse; (anchor) enredarse; *Naut.* chocar. **to fall f. of**, *Naut.* abordar (un buque); *Fig.* habérselas con. **by fair means or f.**, a las buenas o a las malas. **f. breath**, aliento fétido, aliento corrompido, *m.* **f. brood**, peste de las abejas, *f.* **f. language**, palabras ofensivas, *f pl*; lenguaje obsceno, *m*.

f. play, juego sucio, *m.* **f. weather,** mal
tiempo, tiempo borrascoso, *m*
found /faund/ *vt* fundar; (metal, glass)
fundir; (create, etc.) establecer
foundation /faun'deiʃən/ *n* fundación, *f;*
establecimiento, *m;* creación, *f; Archit.* cimiento, embasamiento, *m;* (basis) base, *f;*
(cause) causa, *f,* origen, principio, *m;* (endowment) dotación, *f; Sew.* refuerzo, *m.*
to lay the f., poner las fundaciones. **f.
stone,** piedra angular, *f. Fig.* primera piedra, *f.* **to lay the f. stone,** poner la piedra angular
founder /'faundər/ *n* fundador (-ra); (of
metals) fundidor, *m.* —*vt* (a ship) hacer
zozobrar. —*vi* zozobrar, irse a pique; *Fig.*
fracasar
founding /'faundɪŋ/ *n* fundación, *f;* establecimiento, *m;* (of metals) fundición, *f*
foundling /'faundlɪŋ/ *n* hijo (-ja) de la
cuna, expósito (-ta). **f. hospital or home,**
casa de cuna, casa de expósitos, inclusa, *f*
foundry /'faundri/ *n* fundición, *f*
fountain /'fauntn/ *n* fuente, *f;* (spring)
manantial, *m;* (jet) chorro, *m;* (artificial)
fuente, *f,* surtidero, *m;* (source) origen,
principio, *m.* **f.-head,** fuente, *f.* **Fountain
of Youth,** Fuente de la juventud, Fuente
de Juventio, *f.* **f. pen,** pluma estilográfica, *f*
four /fɔr/ *a* and *n* cuatro, *m.* **It is f.
o'clock,** Son las cuatro. **She is f.,** Tiene
cuatro años. **on all fours,** a gatas. **f.-
course,** (of meals) de cuatro platos. **f.-
engined,** cuadrimotor. **f.-engined plane,**
cuadrimotor, *m.* **f.-footed,** cuadrúpedo.
f.-horse, de cuatro caballos. **f. hundred,**
cuatrocientos. **f.-inhand,** tiro par, *m.* **f.-
part,** (of a song) a cuatro voces. **f.-wheel
brakes,** freno en las cuatro ruedas, *m*
fourfold /'fɔr,fould/ *a* cuádruple
fourscore /'fɔr'skɔr/ *a* and *n* ochenta, *m.*
fourteen /'fɔr'tin/ *a* and *n* catorce, *m.*
He is f., Tiene catorce años
fourteenth /'fɔr'tinθ/ *a* and *n* décimo-
cuarto *m.;* (of the month) (el) catorce, *m;*
(of monarchs) catorce. **April f.,** El 14 (catorce) de abril
fourth /fɔrθ/ *a* cuarto; (of the month) el
cuatro; (of monarchs) cuarto. —*n* (fourth
part) cuarta parte, *f; Mus.* cuarta, *f.* **f. dimension,** cuarta dimensión, *f.* **f. term,**
(U.S.A. *Polit.*) cuarto mandato, *m*
fowl /faul/ *n* gallo, *m;* gallina, *f;*
(chicken) pollo, *m;* (bird) ave, *f;* (barn-
door f.) ave de corral, *f.* —*vi* cazar aves.
f.-house or run, gallinero, *m*
fox /fɒks/ *n* zorro, *m;* (vixen) zorra,
raposa, *f. Fig.* zorro, taimado, *m.* —*vi*
disimular. —*vt* (books) descolorar. **f.-
brush,** cola de raposa, *f.* **f.-earth,** zorrera, *f.* **f.-hunting,** caza de zorras, *f.* **f. ter-
rier,** fox-térrier, *m*
foxy /'fɒksi/ *a* de zorro; zorrero, astuto
foyer /'fɔiər/ *n* foyer, salón de descanso,
m
fraction /'frækʃən/ *n Math.* fracción, *f,*
número quebrado, *m;* pequeña parte, *f;*

fragmento, *m.* **improper f.,** *Math.* fracción impropia, *f.* **proper f.,** *Math.* fracción propia, *f*
fractional /'frækʃənḷ/ *a* fraccionario
fractious /'frækʃəs/ *a* malhumorado,
enojadizo
fracture /'fræktʃər/ *n Surg.* fractura, *f.*
—*vt* fracturar. **compound f.,** fractura conminuta, *f*
fragile /'frædʒəl/ *a* frágil, quebradizo; (of
persons) delicado
fragment /'frægmənt/ *n* fragmento, *m;*
trozo, pedazo, *m.* **to break into fragments,** hacer pedazos, hacer añicos
fragmentary /'frægmən,teri/ *a* fragmentario
fragrance /'freigrəns/ *n* fragancia, *f,*
buen olor, perfume, aroma, *m*
fragrant /'freigrənt/ *a* fragante, oloroso.
to make f., perfumar
frail /freil/ *a* frágil, quebradizo; débil, endeble. —*n* capacho, *m,* espuerta, *f*
frailty /'freilti/ *n* fragilidad, *f;* debilidad, *f*
frame /freim/ *n* constitución, *f;* sistema,
m; organización, *f;* (of the body) figura,
f, talle, *m;* (of window, picture) marco,
m; (of machine, building) armadura, *f;*
(of a bicycle) cuadro (de bicicleta), *m;*
Agr. cajonera, *f;* (embroidery) bastidor
(para bordar), *m;* (skeleton) esqueleto, *m;*
Lit. composición, construcción, *f;* (of
spectacles) armadura, *f;* (of mind) disposición (de ánimo), *f;* humor, *m.* —*vt*
formar; construir; arreglar; ajustar; (a
picture) enmarcar; componer, hacer;
(draw up) redactar; (think up) idear, inventar; (words) articular, pronunciar. **f. a
constitution,** elaborar una constitución
framework /'freim,wɜrk/ *n* armadura,
armazón, *f,* esqueleto, *m;* organización, *f;*
(basis) base, *f*
franc /fræŋk/ *n* (coin) franco, *m*
France /fræns/ *n* Francia, *f*
franchise /'fræntʃaiz/ *n* (exemption)
franquicia, *f;* privilegio, *m;* (vote) derecho de sufragio, *m;* (citizenship) derecho político, *m*
Frank /fræŋk/ *n* franco (-ca), galo (-la)
frank /fræŋk, frɒŋk/ *a* franco, cándido,
sincero; abierto. —*vt* franquear
frankly /'fræŋkli/ *adv* francamente; sinceramente; cara a cara; sin rodeos, claramente; abiertamente. **to speak f.,** hablar
claro, hablar sin rodeos
frankness /'fræŋknɪs/ *n* franqueza, *f;*
sinceridad, *f,* candor, *m*
frantic /'fræntɪk/ *a* frenético, furioso,
loco. **He drives me f.,** Me vuelve loco
fraternal /frə'tɜrnḷ/ *a* fraterno, fraternal
fraternity /frə'tɜrnɪti/ *n* fraternidad, hermandad, *f*
fraternization /,frætərnə'zeiʃən/ *n* fra-
ternización, *f*
fraternize /'frætər,naiz/ *vi* fraternizar
fratricidal /,frætrɪ'saidḷ/ *a* fratricida
fratricide /'frætrɪ,said/ *n* (person) fratricida, *mf;* (action) fratricidio, *m*

fraud /frɔd/ *n* fraude, *m;* engaño, embuste, *m;* (person) farsante, *m,* embustero (-ra)

fraudulence /'frɔdʒələns/ *n* fraudulencia, fraude, *f*

fraudulent /'frɔdʒələnt/ *a* fraudulento

fraught /frɔt/ *a* (with) cargado de; lleno de, preñado de

fray /frei/ *n* refriega, riña, *f;* combate, *m,* batalla, *f;* (rubbing) raedura, *f.* —*vt* raer, tazar. —*vi* tazarse, deshilarse

frayed /freid/ *a* raído

fraying /'freiŋ/ *n* raedura, deshiladura, *f*

freak /frik/ *n* monstruo, *m;* fenómeno, *m;* (whim) capricho, *m*

freakish /'frikiʃ/ *a* monstruoso; caprichoso; extravagante; raro, singular

freakishness /'frikiʃnɪs/ *n* carácter caprichoso, *m;* extravagancia, *f;* rareza, extrañeza, *f*

freckle /'frɛkəl/ *n* peca, *f.* —*vi* tener pecas; salir pecas (a la cara, etc.)

freckled /'frɛkəld/ *a* pecoso, con pecas

free /fri/ *a* (in most senses) libre; independiente; emancipado; desembarazado; abierto; limpio de; franco; (voluntary) voluntario; (self-governing) autónomo, independiente; accesible; (disengaged) desocupado; (vacant) vacío; (exempt) exento (de); (immune) immune (de); ajeno; gratuito; (loose) suelto; (generous) generoso, liberal; (vicious) disoluto, licencioso; (bold) atrevido; (impudent) insolente, demasiado familiar. —*adv* gratis, gratuitamente. **There are two f. seats in the train,** Hay dos asientos libres en el tren. **to get f.,** libertarse. **to make f. with,** tomarse libertades con; usar como si fuera suyo. **to set f.,** poner en libertad. **f. agent,** libre albedrío, *m.* **f. and easy,** familiar, sin ceremonia. **f. gift,** *Com.* objeto de reclamo, *m.* **f.-hand drawing,** dibujo a pulso, *m.* **f. kick,** *Sports.* golpe franco, *m.* **f. love,** amor libre, *m.* **f. play,** rienda suelta, *f; Mech.* holgura, *f.* **f. port,** puerto franco, *m.* **f. speech,** libertad de palabra, *f.* **f. thought,** libre pensamiento, *m.* **f. ticket,** *Theat.* billete de favor, *m.* **f. trade,** *a* librecambista. —*n* librecambio, *m.* **f. trader,** librecambista, *mf.* **f. verse,** verso libre, verso suelto, *m.* **f.-wheeling,** desenfrenado, libre. **f. will,** propia voluntad, *f;* (theology) libre albedrío, *m*

free /fri/ *vt* libertar, poner en libertad (a); librar (de); (slave) salvar; emancipar; exentar; (of obstacles, difficulties) desembarazar; **to f. from,** libertar de; librar de; (clean) limpiar de

freedom /'fridəm/ *n* libertad, *f;* independencia, *f;* exención, *f;* inmunidad, *f;* soltura, facilidad, *f,* franqueza, *f;* (overfamiliarity) insolencia, *f;* (boldness) audacia, intrepidez, *f;* (of customs) licencia, *f.* **to receive the f. of a city,** ser recibido como ciudadano de honor. **f. of speech,** libertad de palabra, *f.* **f. of the press,** libertad de la prensa, *f.* **f. of worship,** libertad de cultos, *f*

freeing /'friŋ/ *n* liberación, *f;* emancipación, *f;* salvación, *f;* (from obstruction) desembarazo, *m;* limpieza, *f*

freelance /'fri,læns/ *n Mil.* soldado libre, *m; Polit.* independiente, *m;* aventurero (-ra). **f. journalist,** periodista libre, *m*

freethinker /'fri'θɪŋkər/ *n* librepensador (-ra)

freeze /friz/ *vt* helar; (meat, etc.) congelar; *Fig.* helar. —*vi* helarse; congelarse; (*impers.* of the weather) helar. **to f. to death,** morir de frío

freezing /'frizɪŋ/ *n* hielo, *m;* congelación, *f.* —*a* glacial; congelante, frigorífico. **f. mixture,** mezcla frigorífica, *f.* **f. of assets,** bloqueo de los depósitos bancarios, *m.* **f.-point,** punto de congelación, *m.* **above f.-point,** sobre cero. **below f.-point,** bajo cero

freight /freit/ *n* flete, *m;* porte, *m.* —*vt* fletar

freighter /'freitər/ *n* fletador, *m;* (ship) buque de carga, *m*

French /frɛntʃ/ *a* francés. —*n* (language) francés, *m;* (people) los franceses, *m pl.* **in F. fashion,** a la francesa. **to take F. leave,** despedirse a la inglesa. **What is the F. for "hat"?** ¿Cómo se dice «sombrero» en francés? **F. spoken,** Se habla francés. **F. bean,** judía, *f.* **F. chalk,** jabón de sastre, *m.* **F. horn,** trompa, *f.* **F. lesson,** lección de francés, *f.* **F. marigold,** flor del estudiante, *f.* **F. polish,** barniz de muebles, *m.* **F. poodle,** perro (-rra) de aguas. **F. roll,** panecillo, *m.* **F. window,** puerta ventana, *f*

Frenchman /'frɛntʃmən/ *n* francés, *m.* **a young F.,** un joven francés

Frenchwoman /'frɛntʃ,wumən/ *n* francesa, mujer francesa, *f.* **a young F.,** una joven francesa, una muchacha francesa, *f*

frenzied /'frɛnzid/ *a* frenético

frenzy /'frɛnzi/ *n* frenesí, delirio, paroxismo, *m*

frequency /'frikwənsi/ *n* frecuencia, *f.* **high f.,** alta frecuencia, *f.* **low f.,** baja frecuencia, *f*

frequent /'frikwənt/ *v* frɪ'kwent/ *a* frecuente; (usual) común, corriente. —*vt* frecuentar

frequently /'frikwəntli/ *adv* frecuentemente, con frecuencia, muchas veces; comúnmente

fresco /'frɛskou/ *n Art.* fresco, *m,* pintura al fresco, *f.* —*vt* pintar al fresco

fresh /frɛʃ/ *a* fresco; nuevo; reciente; (newly arrived) recién llegado; (inexperienced) inexperto, bisoño, *f;* (of water, not salt) dulce; puro; (healthy) sano; (brisk) vigoroso, enérgico; (vivid) vivo, vívido; (bright) brillante; (cheeky) fresco. —*adv* nuevamente, recién (with past participle). **He came to us f. from school,** Vino a nosotros recién salido de su colegio. **We are going to take the f. air,** Vamos a tomar el fresco. **The milk is not f.,** La leche no está fresca. **f.-complexioned,** de buenos colores. **f. news**, noticias nuevas, *f pl.* **f. troops**, tropas nuevas, *f pl,* (reinforcements) tropas de refuerzo, *f pl.* **f. water**, agua fresca, *f;* (not salt) agua dulce, *f.* **f. wind**, viento fresco, *m*

freshen /'frɛʃən/ *vt* refrescar; (remove salt) desalar. —*vi* (wind) refrescar. **to f. up**, renovar; refrescar; (of dress, etc.) arreglar

freshly /'frɛʃli/ *adv* nuevamente; recientemente

freshness /'frɛʃnɪs/ *n* frescura, *f;* (newness) novedad, *f;* (vividness, brightness) intensidad, *f;* pureza, *f;* (beauty) lozanía, hermosura, *f;* (cheek) frescura, *f*, descaro, *m*

freshwater /'frɛʃˌwɔtər/ *n* agua dulce, *f.* **f. sailor**, marinero de agua dulce, *m*

fret /frɛt/ *n* agitación, *f;* ansiedad, preocupación, *f; Archit.* greca, *f;* (of stringed instrument) traste, *m.* —*vt* roer; (of a horse) bocezar; (corrode) desgastar, corroer; (of the wind, etc.) rizar; (worry) tener preocupado (a); irritar, enojar; (lose) perder; (oneself) apurarse, consumirse; *Archit.* calar. —*vi* torturarse, preocuparse, inquietarse; (complain) quejarse; (mourn) lamentarse, estar triste

fretful /'frɛtfəl/ *a* mal humorado, mohíno, quejoso, irritable

Freudian /'frɔɪdiən/ *a* freudiano

friar /'fraɪər/ *n* fraile, *m.* **Black f.,** dominicano, *m.* **Gray f.,** franciscano, *m.* **White f.,** carmelita, *m.* **f.-like,** frailesco

friction /'frɪkʃən/ *n* frote, frotamiento, roce, *m; Phys.* rozamiento, *m;* fricción, *f.* **to give a f.,** friccionar, dar fricciones (a). **f. gearing,** engranaje de fricción, *m.* **f. glove,** guante de fricciones, *m*

Friday /'fraɪdeɪ/ *n* viernes, *m.* **Good F.,** Viernes Santo, *m*

fried /fraɪd/ *a* frito. **f. egg,** huevo frito, *m*

friend /frɛnd/ *n* amigo (-ga); (acquaintance) conocido (-da); (Quaker) cuáquero (-ra); (follower) adherente, *m;* partidario (-ia); (ally) aliado (-da); *pl* **friends,** amistades, *f pl;* amigos, *m pl.* **a f. of yours,** un amigo tuyo, uno de tus amigos. **to make friends,** hacer amigos; (become friends) hacerse amigos; (after a quarrel) hacer las paces. **Friends!** (to sentinel) ¡Gente de paz!

friendless /'frɛndlɪs/ *a* sin amigos; desamparado

friendliness /'frɛndlinɪs/ *n* amabilidad, afabilidad, cordialidad, amigabilidad, *f*

friendly /'frɛndli/ *a* amistoso, amigable, amigo; afable, acogedor, simpático; propicio, favorable. **to be f. with,** ser amigo de. **f. society,** sociedad de socorros, *f*

friendship /'frɛndʃɪp/ *n* amistad, intimidad, *f*

fright /fraɪt/ *n* terror, susto, *m;* (guy) espantajo, *m.* —*vt* asustar. **to have a f.,** tener un susto. **to take f.,** asustarse

frighten /'fraɪtn/ *vt* espantar, dar un susto (a), alarmar, asustar; horrorizar;

(overawe) acobardar. **to be frightened out of one's wits,** estar muerto de miedo. **to f. away,** ahuyentar, espantar

frightened /'fraɪtnd/ *a* miedoso, tímido, medroso, nervioso

frightening /'fraɪtnɪŋ/ *a* que da miedo; alarmante, amedrentador; horrible

frightful /'fraɪtfəl/ *a* horrible, espantoso, horroroso; *Inf.* tremendo, enorme

frightfully /'fraɪtfəli/ *adv* horrorosamente; *Inf.* enormemente

frigid /'frɪdʒɪd/ *a* frío; helado; *Med.* impotente

frigidity /frɪ'dʒɪdɪti/ *n* frialdad, frigidez, *f; Med.* impotencia, *f*

frill /frɪl/ *n Sew.* volante, *m;* (jabot) chorrera, *f;* (round a bird's neck) collarín de plumas, *m;* (of paper) frunce, *m.* —*vt* alechugar; fruncir

fringe /frɪndʒ/ *n* fleco, *m*, franja, *f;* (of hair) flequillo, *m;* (edge) borde, *m*, margen, *mf.* —*vt* guarnecer con fleco, franjar; adornar; (grow by) crecer al margen (de)

frisk /frɪsk/ *vi* retozar, brincar

frisky /'frɪski/ *a* retozón, juguetón

fritter /'frɪtər/ *n Cul.* fruta de sartén, *f.* —*vt* (away) malgastar, desperdiciar; perder

frivolity /frɪ'vɒlɪti/ *n* frivolidad, ligereza, *f;* futilidad, *f*

frivolous /'frɪvələs/ *a* frívolo, ligero, liviano; (futile) trivial, fútil

frizzy /'frɪzi/ *a* (of hair) crespo, rizado

fro /froʊ/ *adv* hacia atrás. **movement to and fro,** vaivén, *m.* **to and fro,** de un lado a otro. **to go to and fro,** ir y venir

frog /frɒg/ *n* rana, *f.* **to have a f. in the throat,** padecer carraspera

frolic /'frɒlɪk/ *n* (play) juego, *m;* (mischief) travesura, *f;* (folly) locura, extravagancia, *f;* (joke) chanza, *f;* (amusement) diversión, *f;* (wild party) holgorio, *m*, parranda, *f.* —*vi* retozar, juguetear; divertirse

frolicsome /'frɒlɪksəm/ *a* retozón, juguetón

from /frʌm, from; *unstressed* frəm/ *prep* de; desde; (according to) según; (in the name of, on behalf of) de parte de; (through, by) por; (beginning on) a contar de; (with) con; **F.** (on envelope) Remite, Remitente. **He is coming here f. the dentist's,** Vendrá aquí desde casa del dentista. **Give him this message f. me,** Dale este recado de mi parte. **Judging f. his appearance,** Juzgando por su apariencia. **prices f. five hundred pesetas upward,** precios desde quinientos pesetas en adelante. **f. what I hear,** según mi información, según lo que oigo. **f. above,** desde arriba. **f. among,** de entre. **f. afar,** de lejos, desde lejos. **f. time to time,** de cuando en cuando, de vez en cuando

front /frʌnt/ *n* frente, *f;* cara, *f; Mil.* frente, *m;* (battle line) línea de combate, *f;* (of a building) fachada, *f;* (of shirt) pechera, *f;* (at the seaside) playa, *f;* (promenade) paseo de la playa, *m;* (forefront) primera línea, f; (forepart) parte delantera, f; *Theat.* auditorio, m; (organization) organización de fachada, f; (impudence) descaro, m, a delantero; anterior; de frente; primero. —*adv* hacia delante. —*vi* mirar a, dar a; hacer frente a. **in f.**, en frente. **in f. of**, en frente de; (in the presence of) delante de, en la presencia de. **to face f.**, hacer frente. **to put on a bold f.**, hacer de tripas corazón. **f. door**, puerta de entrada, puerta principal, f. **f. line**, *Mil.* línea del frente, f; primera línea, f. **f. seat**, (at an entertainment, etc.) delantera, f. **f. organization** organización de fachada f. **f. tooth**, diente incisivo, m. **f. view**, vista de frente, f; vista de cerca, f

frontage /'frʌntɪdʒ/ n (of a building) fachada, f; (site) terreno de... metros de fachada, m

frontal /'frʌntl/ a *Mil.* de frente; *Anat.* frontal

frontier /frʌn'tɪər/ n frontera, f; *Fig.* límite, m. —a fronterizo

frost /frɒst/ n escarcha, f; helada, f. —*vt* helar; *Cul.* escarchar; (glass) deslustrar; *Fig.* escarchar. —*vi* helar. **f.-bitten,** helado

frostbite /'frɒst,baɪt/ n efectos del frío, m pl

frosted /'frɒstɪd/ a escarchado; helado; (of glass) deslustrado, opaco; *Cul.* escarchado

frosting /'frɒstɪŋ/ n escarcha, f; (of glass) deslustre, m; *Cul.* cobertura, escarcha, f

frosty /'frɒsti/ a helado; de hielo; (of hair) canoso; *Fig.* glacial, frío. **It was f. last night,** Anoche heló

froth /frɒθ/ n espuma, f; *Fig.* frivolidad, vanidad, f, *vi* espumar, hacer espuma; echar espuma. —*vt* hacer espumar; hacer echar espuma

frothy /'frɒθi/ a espumoso, espumajoso; *Fig.* frívolo, superficial

frown /fraun/ n ceño, m; cara de juez, expresión severa, f; desaprobación, f; (of fortune) revés, golpe, m. —*vi* fruncir el ceño. **to f. at, on, upon,** mirar con desaprobación, ver con malos ojos; ser enemigo de; desaprobar

frowning /'fraunɪŋ/ a ceñudo; severo; amenazador

frowsy /'frauzi/ a fétido, mal oliente; mal ventilado; (dirty) sucio; (untidy) desaliñado, desaseado

frozen /'frouzən/ a helado; cubierto de hielo; congelado; (*Geog.* and *Fig.*) glacial. **to be f. up,** estar helado. **f. meat,** carne congelada, f

frugal /'frugəl/ a económico; frugal; sobrio

frugality /fru'gælɪti/ n economía, f; frugalidad, sobriedad, f

fruit /frut/ n (in general sense) fruto, m; (off a tree or bush) fruta, f; *Fig.* fruto, m; resultado, m, consecuencia, f. —*vi* frutar, dar fruto. **bottled f.**, fruta en almíbar, f

candied f., fruta azucarada, f. **dried f.,** fruta seca, f. **first fruits,** primicias, f pl. **soft f.**, frutas blandas, f pl. **stone f.,** fruta de hueso, f. **f.-bearing,** frutal. **f.-cake,** pastel de fruta, m. **f.-dish,** frutero, m. **f. farming,** fruticultura, f. **f.-knife,** cuchillo de postres, m. **f. shop,** frutería, f. **f. tree,** frutal, m

fruiterer /'frutərər/ n frutero (-ra)

fruitful /'frutfəl/ a fructuoso, fértil; prolífico, fecundo; provechoso

fruitfulness /'frutfəlnɪs/ n fertilidad, f; fecundidad, f; provecho, m

fruition /fru'ɪʃən/ n fruición, f

fruitless /'frutlɪs/ a infructuoso, estéril; inútil

fruity /'fruti/ a de fruta; (wines) vinoso; (of voice) melodioso

frump /frʌmp/ n estantigua, f

frumpish /'frʌmpɪʃ/ a estrafalario; fuera de moda

frustrate /'frʌstreɪt/ vt frustrar; defraudar; malograr; destruir; anular

frustration /frʌ'streɪʃən/ n frustración, f; defraudación, f; malogro, m; destrucción, f; desengaño, m

fry /fraɪ/ n *Cul.* fritada, f, vt freír. —*vi* freírse. **small fry,** *Inf.* gente menuda, f

frying /'fraɪɪŋ/ n fritura, f, el freír. **to fall out of the f.-pan into the fire,** ir de mal en peor, andar de zocos en colodros, ir de Guatemala en Guatapeor. **f.-pan,** sartén, f

fuddle /'fʌdl/ vt atontar, aturdir; embriagar, emborrachar

fudge /fʌdʒ/ n patraña, tontería, f, disparate, m. —*interj* ¡qué disparate! ¡qué va!

fuel /'fyuəl/ n combustible, m; *Fig.* cebo, pábulo, m. —*vt* cebar, echar combustible en. —*vi* tomar combustible. **to add f. to the flame,** echar leña al fuego. **f. consumption,** consumo de combustible, m. **f.-oil,** aceite combustible, aceite de quemar, m. **f.-tank,** depósito de combustible, m

fugitive /'fyudʒɪtɪv/ a fugitivo; pasajero, perecedero; transitorio, efímero, fugaz. —*n* fugitivo (-va); (from justice) prófugo (-ga); *Mil.* desertor, m; (refugee) refugiado (-da)

fugue /fyug/ n *Mus.* fuga, f

fulcrum /'fʊlkrəm/ n *Mech.* fulcro, m

full /fʊl/ a lleno; colmado; todo; pleno; (crowded) atestado; (replete) harto; abundante; (intent on) preocupado con, pensando en; (loose) amplio; (plentiful) copioso; (occupied) ocupado; completo; (resonant) sonoro; (mature) maduro; puro, perfecto; (satiated) saciado (de); (of the moon, sails) lleno; (weighed down) agobiado, abrumado; (detailed) detallado; (with uniform, etc.) de gala; (with years, etc.) cumplido. —*n* colmo, m; totalidad, f. —*adv* muy; completamente, totalmente. **f. many a flower,** muchas flores. **at f. gallop,** a galope tendido. **at f. speed,** a todo correr; a toda velocidad. **His hands are f.,** Sus manos están llenas. **The moon was at the**

f., La luna estaba llena. **in f.,** por completo; sin abreviaciones; integralmente. **in f. swing,** en plena actividad. **in f. vigor,** en pleno vigor. **to the f.,** completamente; hasta la última gota; a la perfección. **to be f. to the brim,** estar lleno hasta el tope. **f.-blooded,** sanguíneo; de pura raza; *Fig.* viril, vigoroso; *Fig.* apasionado. **f.-blown,** en plena flor, abierto. **f. dress,** *a* de gala. —*n* traje de etiqueta, traje de ceremonia, *m.* **f.-face,** de cara. **f. -flavored,** (wine) abocado. **f.-grown,** adulto; completamente desarrollado. **f.- length,** de cuerpo entero. **f. moon,** luna llena, *f;* plenilunio, *m.* **f. name,** nombre y apellidos, *m.* **f. powers,** plenos poderes, *m pl.* **f. scale,** tamaño natural, *m.* **f. scope,** carta blanca, *f;* toda clase de facilidades. **f. steam ahead,** a todo vapor. **f. stop,** *Gram.* punto final, *m*

full /fʊl/ *vt* (cloth) abatanar

full-color /'fʊl 'kʌlər/ *a* a todo color. **full-color plates,** láminas a todo color

fullness /'fʊlnɪs/ *n* abundancia, *f;* plenitud, *f;* (repletion) hartura, *f;* (of clothes) amplitud, *f;* (stoutness) gordura, *f;* (swelling) hinchazón, *f.* **She wrote with great f.** of all that she had seen, Describía muy detalladamente todo lo que había visto. **in the f. of time,** andando el tiempo

full-page /'fʊl 'peɪdʒ/ *a* a toda plana. **full-page advertisement,** anuncio a toda plana.

full-time /'fʊl 'taɪm/ *a* de tiempo completo

fully /'fʊli/ *adv* plenamente; enteramente. **It is f. six years since...,** Hace seis años bien cumplidos que... **It is f. 9 o'clock,** Son las nueve bien sonadas. **f. dressed,** completamente vestido

fulminous /'fʌlmənəs/ *a* fulmíneo, fulminoso

fulsome /'fʊlsəm/ *a* servil; insincero, hipócrita; asqueroso, repugnante

fumble /'fʌmbəl/ *vi* (grope) ir a tientas; procurar hacer algo; chapucear (con); (for a word) titubear

fumbling /'fʌmblɪŋ/ *n* hesitación, *f;* tacto incierto, *m.* —*a* incierto; vacilante

fumblingly /'fʌmblɪŋli/ *adv* de manera incierta; a tientas

fume /fyum/ *n* vaho, humo, gas, *m;* emanación, *f;* mal olor, *m,* fetidez, *f; Fig.* vapor, *m;* (state of mind) agitación, *f;* frenesí, *m.* —*vi* humear; refunfuñar, echar pestes

fumigate /'fyumɪˌgeɪt/ *vt* fumigar; sahumar, perfumar; desinfectar

fumigation /ˌfyumɪˈgeɪʃən/ *n* fumigación, *f;* sahumerio, *m*

fumigator /'fyumɪˌgeɪtər/ *n* fumigador (-ra); (apparatus) fumigador, *m*

fuming /'fyumɪŋ/ *n* refunfuño, *m.* —*a* refunfuñador

fun /fʌn/ *n* diversión, *f,* entretenimiento, *m;* (joke) chanza, broma, *f.* **for fun,** para divertirse; en chanza. **in fun,** de burlas.

to have fun, divertirse. **to poke fun at,** burlarse de, mofarse de, ridiculizar

function /'fʌŋkʃən/ *n* función, *f.* —*vi* funcionar

functional /'fʌŋkʃənl/ *a* funcional

functionary /'fʌŋkʃəˌneri/ *n* funcionario, *m.* —*a* funcional

functioning /'fʌŋkʃənɪŋ/ *n* funcionamiento, *m*

fund /fʌnd/ *n* fondo, *m; pl* **funds,** fondos, *m pl; Inf.* dinero, *m.* **public funds,** fondos públicos, *m pl.* **sinking f.,** fondo de amortización, *m*

fundamental /ˌfʌndəˈmentl/ *a* fundamental, básico; esencial. —*n* fundamento, *m*

funeral /'fyunərəl/ *a* funeral, fúnebre, funerario. —*n* funerales, *m pl;* entierro, *m.* **to attend the f. (of),** asistir a los funerales (de). **f. feast,** banquetes fúnebres, *m pl.* **f. director, f. furnisher,** director de pompas fúnebres, *m.* **f. procession,** cortejo fúnebre, *m.* **f. pyre,** pira funeraria, *f.* **f. service,** misa de difuntos, *f*

fungicide /'fʌndʒəˌsaɪd/ *n* anticriptógamo, *m*

fungous /'fʌŋgəs/ *a* fungoso

fungus /'fʌŋgəs/ *n* hongo, *m*

funicular /fyuˈnɪkyələr/ *a* funicular. **f. railway,** ferrocarril funicular, *m*

funnel /'fʌnl/ *n Chem.* embudo, *m; Naut.* chimenea, *f;* (of a chimney) cañón (de chimenea), *m.* **f.-shaped,** en forma de embudo

funny /'fʌni/ *a* cómico, gracioso; divertido; (strange) extraño, raro; (mysterious) misterioso. **It struck me as f.,** (amused me) Me hizo gracia; (seemed strange) Me pareció raro. **f.-bone,** hueso de la alegría, *m*

fur /fɜr/ *n* piel, *f;* depósito, sarro, *m;* (on tongue) saburra, *f.* —*a* hecho de pieles. —*vt* forrar, or adornar, or cubrir, con pieles; depositar sarro sobre; (the tongue) ensuciarse la lengua. —*vi* estar forrado, or adornado, or cubierto, con pieles; formarse incrustaciones; (of the tongue) tener la lengua sucia. **fur cap,** gorra de pieles, *f.* **fur cape,** cuello de piel, *m;* capa de pieles, *f.* **fur trade,** peletería, *f*

furbish /'fɜrbɪʃ/ *vt* pulir; renovar; limpiar

furious /'fyʊriəs/ *a* furioso. **to become f.,** ponerse furioso, enfurecerse

furl /fɜrl/ *vt* plegar; enrollar; *Naut.* aferrar

furlough /'fɜrloʊ/ *n Mil.* permiso, *m.* —*vt* conceder un permiso (a). **on f.,** de permiso

furnace /'fɜrnɪs/ *n* horno, *m;* (of steam boiler) fogón, *m;* (for central heating) caldera de calefacción central, *f;* (for smelting) cubilote, *m*

furnish /'fɜrnɪʃ/ *vt* proveer (de), equipar (de), suplir (de); amueblar; (an opportunity) proporcionar; producir

furnished /'fɜrnɪʃt/ *a* amueblado, con muebles. **f. house,** casa amueblada, *f*

furnishing /'fɜrnɪʃɪŋ/ *n* provisión, *f,*

equipo, *m; pl* **furnishings,** accesorios, *m pl;* mobiliario, mueblaje, *m*

furniture /'fɜrnɪtʃər/ *n* mobiliario, mueblaje, *m;* ajuar, *equipo, m;* avíos, *m pl; Naut.* aparejo, *m.* **a piece of f.,** un mueble. **to empty of f.,** desamueblar, quitar los muebles (de). **f. dealer** or **maker,** mueblista, *mf.* **f. factory,** mueblería, *f.* **f. polish,** crema para muebles, *f.* **f. mover,** transportador de muebles, *m;* (packer) embalador, *m.* **f. repository,** guardamuebles, *m.* **f. van,** carro de mudanzas, *m*

furor /'fyʊrɔr/ *n* furor, *m*

furred /fɜrd/ *a* forrado or cubierto or adornado de piel; (of the tongue) sucia

furrier /'fɜriər/ *n* peletero, *m.* **furrier's shop,** peletería, *f*

furrow /'fɜrou/ *n* surco, *m;* muesca, *f; Archit.* estría, *f;* (wrinkle) arruga, *f.* —*vt* surcar

furry /'fɜri/ *a* cubierto de piel; parecido a una piel; hecho de pieles

further /'fɜrðər/ *a* ulterior, más distante; (other) otro; opuesto; adicional, más. —*adv* más lejos; más allá; además; también; por añadidura. —*vt* promover, fomentar; ayudar. **on the f. side,** al otro lado. **till f. orders,** hasta nueva orden. **f. on,** más adelante; más allá

furtherance /'fɜrðərəns/ *n* fomento, *m,* promoción, *f;* progreso, avance, *m*

furthermore /'fɜrðər,mɔr/ *adv* además, por añadidura

furthest /'fɜrðɪst/ *a* (el, la, lo) más lejano or más distante; extremo. —*adv* más lejos

furtive /'fɜrtɪv/ *a* furtivo

furtively /'fɜrtɪvli/ *adv* furtivamente, a hurtadillas. **to look at f.,** mirar de reojo

fury /'fyʊri/ *n* furor, enfurecimiento, *m,* rabia, *f;* violencia, *f;* frenesí, arrebato, *m;* furia, *f.* **like a f.,** hecho una furia. **to breathe forth f.,** echar rayos

fuse /fyuz/ *n* (of explosives) espoleta, mecha, *f; Elec.* fusible, *m.* —*vt* (metals) fundir; fusionar, mezclar. —*vi* (metals) fundirse; mezclarse. **safety-f.,** espoleta de seguridad, *f.* **time-f.,** espoleta de tiempo, *f.* **to blow a f.,** fundir un fusible. **f. box,** caja de fusibles, *f.* **f. wire,** fusible, *m*

fuselage /'fyusə,laʒ/ *n Aer.* fuselaje, *m*

fusion /'fyuʒən/ *n* fusión, *f;* unión, *f;* (melting) fundición, *f*

fuss /fʌs/ *n* agitación, *f;* (bustle) conmoción, bulla, *f;* bullicio, *m.* —*vi* agitarse, preocuparse. —*vt* poner nervioso. **There's no need to make such a f.,** No es para tanto. **to make a f. of,** (a person) hacer la rueda (a), ser muy atento (a); (spoil) mimar mucho (a). **to f. about,** andar de acá para allá

fussy /'fʌsi/ *a* meticuloso, nimio; nervioso; (of style) florido, hinchado; (of dress) demasiado adornado

fustigate /'fʌsti,geit/ *vt* fustigar

fusty /'fʌsti/ *a* (moldy) mohoso; mal ventilado; mal oliente; (of views, etc.) pasado de moda

futile /'fyutl/ *a* fútil, superficial, frívolo; inútil

futility /fyu'tɪlɪti/ *n* futilidad, superficialidad, frivolidad, *f;* (action) tontería, estupidez, *f*

future /'fyutʃər/ *a* futuro, venidero. —*n* futuro, porvenir, *m.* **in the f.,** en adelante, en lo venidero, en lo sucesivo. **for f. reference,** para información futura. **f. perfect tense,** *Gram.* futuro perfecto, *m.* **f. tense,** *Gram.* futuro, *m*

fuzz /fʌz/ *n* tamo, *m,* pelusa, *f.* **f.-ball,** *Bot.* bejín, *m*

fuzzy /'fʌzi/ *a* crespo rizado; velloso

g /dʒi/ n (letter) ge, f; Mus. sol, m. **G clef**, clave de sol, f

gab /gæb/ n Inf. labia, f. **to have the gift of the gab**, tener mucha labia

gabble /'gæbəl/ vi chacharear, garlar; hablar indistintamente; (of goose and some birds) graznar. —vt decir indistintamente; decir rápidamente; (a language) chapurrear; masculiar. —n cháchara, f; vocerío, m; (of goose and some birds) graznido, m

gabbler /'gæblər/ n charlatán (-ana), chacharero (-ra)

gad /gæd/ vi corretear, callejear. **to gad about**, correr por todos lados; divertirse.

gadabout /'gædə,baut/ n azotacalles, mf; gandul (-la), vagabundo (-da)

gadding /'gædɪŋ/ a callejero; vagabundo. —n vagancia, f; vida errante, f; gandulería, f

gadfly /'gæd,flai/ n Ent. tábano, m; Inf. moscardón, m

gadget /'gædʒɪt/ n accesorio, m; aparato, m; chuchería, f

Gadsden Purchase /'gædzdən/ la Venta de la Meseta, f

gaff /gæf/ n (hook) garfio, m; Naut. pico de cangrejo, m; Theat. teatrucho, m

gag /gæg/ n mordaza, f; Theat. morcilla, f. —vt amordazar; Fig. hacer callar. —vi Theat. meter morcillas

gage /geidʒ/ n prenda, fianza, f; (symbol of challenge) guante, m; (challenge) desafío, m. See **gauge**

gaggle /'gægəl/ n (cry) graznido, m; (of geese) manada (de ocas), f. —vi graznar; cacarear

gaiety /'geiiti/ n alegría, f; animación, vivacidad, f; (entertainment) diversión, festividad, f

gain /gein/ n ganancia, f; provecho, beneficio, m; (increase) aumento, m; (riches) riqueza, f. —vt ganar; (acquire) conseguir; adquirir; obtener; conquistar, captar; (friends) hacerse; (reach) llegar a, alcanzar. —vi ganar; (improve) mejorar; (of a watch) adelantarse. **What have they gained by going to Canada?** ¿Qué han logrado con marcharse al Canadá? **to g. ground**, Fig. ganar terreno. **to g. momentum** adquirir velocidad **to g. time**, ganar tiempo. **to g. on, upon**, acercarse a; (overtake) alcanzar; (outstrip) dejar atrás, pasar; (of sea) invadir; (of habits) imponerse

gainful /'geinfəl/ a ganancioso, lucrativo; ventajoso

gainfully /'geinfəli/ adv ventajosamente; lucrativamente

gainsay /'gein,sei/ vt contradecir; oponer; negar

gait /geit/ n porte, andar, m; paso, m, andadura, f

gala /'geilə/ n gala, fiesta, f. **g.-day**, día de fiesta, m. **g.-dress**, traje de gala, m

galaxy /'gæləksi/ n Astron. vía láctea, f; Fig. constelación, f; grupo brillante, m

gale /geil/ n vendaval, ventarrón, m; (storm) temporal, m; tempestad, f

Galician /gə'lɪʃən/ a and n gallego (-ga).

Galilean /,gælə'leiən/ a and n galileo (-ea)

Galilee /'gælə,li/ Galilea, f

gall /gɔl/ n (on horses) matadura, f; (abrasion) rozadura, f; hiel, bilis, f; Fig. hiel, amargura, f; rencor, m; (American slang) descaro, m, impertinencia, f; Bot. agalla, f. —vt rozar; Fig. mortificar, herir. **g.-apple**, agalla, f. **g.-bladder**, vejiga de la hiel, f. **g.-stone**, cálculo hepático, m

gallant /'gælənt, gə'lænt, -'lɑnt/ a hermoso; (imposing) imponente, majestuoso; (brave) valiente, gallardo, valeroso, intrépido; (chivalrous) caballeroso; noble; (attentive to ladies, or amorous) galante. —n galán, m. —vt galantear, cortejar

gallantly /'gæləntli/ adv (bravely) valientemente; caballerosamente; cortésmente; galantemente

gallantry /'gæləntri/ n (bravery) valentía, f, valor, m; heroísmo, m, proeza, f; (chivalry) caballerosidad, f; (toward women, or amorousness) galantería, f

gallery /'gæləri/ n galería, f; pasillo, m; (of a cloister) tránsito, m; (cloister) claustro, m; (for spectators) tribuna, f; Theat. paraíso, gallinero, m; (theater audience) galería, f; (of portraits, etc.) galería, colección, f; (Mineral., Mil.) galería, f; (building) museo, m. **art g.**, museo de pinturas, m

galley /'gæli/ n (Naut., Print.) galera, f; (kitchen) cocina, f; (rowboat) falúa de capitán, f. **to condemn to the galleys**, echar a galeras. **wooden g.**, Print. galerín, m. **g.-proof**, galerada, f. **g.-slave**, galeote, m

galling /'gɔlɪŋ/ a Fig. irritante; mortificante

gallivant /'gælə,vænt/ vi callejear, corretear; divertirse; ir de parranda

gallon /'gælən/ n galón, m

gallop /'gæləp/ n galope, m. —vi galopar; ir aprisa. —vt hacer galopar, **at full g.**, a rienda suelta, a galope tendido. **to g. back**, volver a galope. **to g. down**, bajar a galope. **to g. off**, marcharse galopando; alejarse galopando. **to g. past**, desfilar a galope ante. **to g. through**, cruzar a galope. **to g. up**, vt subir a galope. —vi llegar a galope

gallopade /,gælə'peid/ n (dance) galop, m

galloping /'gæləpɪŋ/ n galope, m; galopada, f. —a que va a galope; Med. galopante. **g. consumption**, tisis galopante, f

gallows /'gælouz/ n patíbulo, m, horca, f; (framework) montante, m. **g.-bird**, criminal digno de la horca, m

galop /'gæləp/ n galop, m

galore /gə'lɔr/ adv a granel, en abundancia (e.g. **sunshine galore**, sol a granel)

galosh /gə'lɒʃ/ n chanclo, m

gambit /'gæmbɪt/ n (chess) gambito, m; *Fig.* táctica, f

gamble /'gæmbəl/ n juego de azar, m; jugada, f; aventura, f; *Com.* especulación, f. —vi jugar por dinero; especular; (with) *Fig.* aventurar, arriesgar. **to g. on the Stock Exchange,** jugar en la bolsa. **to g. away,** perder al juego

gambler /'gæmblər/ n jugador (-ra)

gambling /'gæmblɪŋ/ n juego, m. —a jugador; de juego. **g.-den,** casa de juego, f, garito, m

gambol /'gæmbəl/ n salto, brinco, retozo, m; cabriola, f; juego, m. —vi saltar, brincar, retozar; juguetear

game /geim/ n juego, m; (match) partido, m; (jest) chanza, f; (trick) trampa, f; (birds, hares, etc.) caza menor, f; (tigers, lions, etc.) caza mayor, f; (flesh of game) caza, f; pl **games,** deportes, m pl. —a de caza; (courageous) valiente, animoso, brioso; resuelto. —vi jugar por dinero. **He is g. for anything,** Se atreve a todo. **big g. hunting,** caza mayor, f. **head of g.,** pieza de caza, f. **It is a g. at which two can play,** Donde las dan las toman. **The g. is not worth the candle,** La cosa no vale la pena. **The g. is up,** *Fig.* El proyecto se ha frustrado. **to make g. of,** (things) burlarse de; (persons) tomar el pelo a; mofarse de. **to play the g.,** *Fig.* jugar limpio. **to g. away,** perder al juego. **g. of cards,** juego de naipes, m. **g. of chance,** juego de azar, m. **g.-bag,** morral, m. **g. drive,** batida de caza, f. **g.-laws,** leyes de caza, f pl. **g.-licence,** licencia de caza, f. **g.-pie,** tortada, f. **g. preserve,** coto de caza, m

gamely /'geimli/ adv valientemente

gaming /'geimɪŋ/ n juego, m, a de juego. **g.-house,** garito, m. **g.-table,** mesa de juego, f; *Fig.* juego, m

gamut /'gæmət/ n gama, f

gander /'gændər/ n ganso, m

gang /gæŋ/ n cuadrilla, pandilla, f; (squad) pelotón, m; (of workers) brigada, cuadrilla, f; group, m. **g.-plank,** plancha, f

ganglion /'gæŋgliən/ n ganglio, m; *Fig.* centro, m

gangrene /'gæŋgrin/ n gangrena, f. —vt gangrenar. —vi gangrenarse

gangster /'gæŋstər/ n pistolero, gángster, m

gangway /'gæŋ,wei/ n pasillo, m; *Naut.* plancha, f, pasamano, m; (opening in ship's side) portalón, m. **midship g.,** crujía, f

gap /gæp/ n brecha, f; abertura, f; (hole) boquete, m; (pass) desfiladero, paso, m; (ravine) hondonada, barranca, f; (blank) laguna, f, vacío, m; (crack) intersticio, m, hendedura, f, resquicio, m. **to fill a gap,** llenar un boquete; llenar un vacío

gape /geip/ vi estar con la boca abierta, papar moscas. **to g. at,** mirar con la boca abierta

gaping /'geipɪŋ/ n huelgo, m; abertura, f, a que bosteza; boquiabierto; abierto

garage /gə'raʒ/ n garaje, m. —vt poner (un coche, etc.) en un garaje. **g. owner,** garajista, mf

garb /garb/ n traje, vestido, m; uniforme, m; *Herald.* espiga, f. —vt vestir, ataviar

garbage /'garbɪdʒ/ n basura, inmundicia, f

garbage can basurero, tarro de la basura, m

garble /'garbəl/ vt falsear, mutilar, pervertir

garden /'gardn/ n jardín, m; huerto, m; (fertile region) huerta, f. —a de jardín. —vi trabajar en el jardín, cultivar un huerto. **g. city,** ciudad jardín, f. **g.-frame,** semillero, m. **g. mold,** tierra vegetal, f. **g.-party,** fiesta de jardín, f. **g.-plot,** parterre, m. **g. produce,** hortalizas, legumbres, f pl. **g. roller,** rodillo, m. **g.-seat,** banco de jardín, m. **g. urn,** jarrón, m

gardener /'gardnər/ n jardinero, m

gardening /'gardnɪŋ/ n jardinería, f; horticultura, f. —a de jardinería

gargantuan /gar'gæntʃuən/ a gargantuesco; tremendo, enorme

gargle /'gargəl/ n (liquid) gargarismo, m; gárgaras, f pl. —vi hacer gárgaras, gargarizar

garish /'gɛərɪʃ/ a cursi, llamativo, charro, chillón

garishness /'gɛərɪʃnɪs/ n cursería, ostentación, f, lo llamativo

garland /'garlənd/ n guirnalda, f; corona, f; (anthology) florilegio, m; *Archit.* festón, m. —vt enguirnaldar

garlic /'garlɪk/ n ajo, m

garment /'garmənt/ n prenda de vestir, f; traje, vestido, m; *Fig.* vestidura, f; (*Fig.* cloak) capa, f

garner /'garnər/ n granero, m; tesoro, m; colección, f. —vt atesorar, guardar

garnet /'garnɪt/ n granate, m

garnish /'garnɪʃ/ n *Cul.* aderezo, m; adorno, m. —vt *Cul.* aderezar; embellecer, adornar

garret /'gærɪt/ n guardilla, buhardilla, f, desván, m

garrison /'gærəsən/ n guarnición, f, presidio, m. —vt guarnecer, presidiar. **g. town,** plaza de armas, f

garrulous /'gærələs/ a gárrulo, locuaz, charlatán

garter /'gartər/ n liga, f; (G.) Jarretera, f, vt atar con liga; investir con la Jarretera. **Order of the G.,** Orden de la Jarretera, f

gas /gæs/ n gas, m; *Fig. Inf.* palabrería, f; (petrol) bencina, f, (de gas; con gas; para gases. —vt asfixiar con gas; *Mil.* atacar con gas; saturar de gas, gasear. **gas attack,** ataque con gases asfixiantes, m. **gas-bag,** bolsa de gas, f; *Inf.* charlatán (-ana). **gas-burner,** mechero de gas, m. **gas-chamber,** cámara de gas, f. **gas detector,** detector de gases, m. **gas-fire,** estufa de gas, f. **gas-fitter,** gasista, m. **gas-fittings,**

lámparas de gas, *f pl.* **gas-light,** luz de gas, *f;* mechero de gas, *m.* **gas-main,** cañería maestra de gas, *f.* **gas-man,** gasista, *m.* **gas-mantle,** camiseta incandescente, *f.* **gas-mask,** máscara para gases, *f.* **gas-meter,** contador de gas, *m.* **gas-pipes,** cañerías (or tuberías) de gas, *f pl.* **gas-ring,** fogón de gas, *m.* **gas-shell,** obús de gases asfixiantes, *m.* **gas-stove,** cocina de gas, *f.* **gas warfare,** guerra química, *f.* **gas-works,** fábrica de gas, *f*

gaseous /'gæsiəs/ *a* gaseoso

gash /gæʃ/ *n* cuchillada, *f;* herida extensa, *f.* —*vt* acuchillar; herir extensamente

gasket /'gæskɪt/ *n* aro de empaquetadura, *m*

gasoline /,gæsə'lin/ *n* gasolina, *f*

gasp /gæsp/ *n* boqueada, *f.* —*vi* boquear. **to be at the last g.,** estar agonizando. **to g. for breath,** luchar por respirar. **to g. out,** decir anhelante, decir con voz entrecortada

gastritis /gæ'straitis/ *n* gastritis, *f*

gate /geit/ *n* puerta, *f;* cancela, verja, *f;* entrada, *f;* (of a lock, etc.) compuerta, *f;* (across a road, etc.) barrera, *f;* (money) entrada, *f; Fig.* puerta, *f.* **automatic g.,** (at level crossings, etc.) barrera de golpe, *f.* **to g.-crash,** asistir sin invitación. **g.-keeper,** portero, *m;* guardabarrera, *mf* **g.-money,** entrada, *f.* **g.-post,** soporte de la puerta, *m*

gateway /'geit,wei/ *n* entrada, *f;* puerta, *f;* paso, *m;* vestíbulo, *m; Fig.* puerta, *f*

gather /'gæðər/ *vt* (assemble) reunir; (amass) acumular, amontonar; (acquire) obtener, adquirir; hacer una colección (de); cobrar; (harvest) cosechar, recolectar; (pick up) recoger; (pluck) coger; (infer) sacar en limpio, aprender; *Sew.* fruncir; (the brows) fruncir (el ceño). —*vi* reunirse, congregarse; amontonarse; (threaten) amenazar; (sadden) amargar; (*Fig.* hover over) cernerse (sobre); (increase) aumentar, crecer; (be covered) cubrirse; (fester) supurar. —*n Sew.* frunce, pliegue, *m.* **to g. breath,** tomar aliento. **to g. speed,** ganar velocidad. **to g. strength,** cobrar fuerzas. **I g. from Mary that they are going abroad,** Según lo que me ha dicho María, van al extranjero. **to g. in,** juntar; reunir; (harvest) cosechar; coger. **to g. together,** *vt* reunir. —*vi* reunirse. **to g. up,** recoger; coger; tomar; (one's limbs) encoger. **to g. up the threads,** *Fig.* recoger los hilos.

gatherer /'gæðərər/ *n* cogedor, colector, *m;* (harvester) segador, *m;* (of grapes) vendimiador (-ra); (of taxes) recaudador, *m*

gathering /'gæðərɪŋ/ *n* cogedura, *f;* (fruit, etc.) recolección, *f;* (of taxes) recaudación, *f;* amontonamiento, *m;* colección, *f; Med.* absceso, *m; Sew.* fruncimiento, *m;* (assembly) reunión, asamblea, *f;* (crowd) concurrencia, muchedumbre, *f*

gathers /'gæðərz/ *n Sew.* fruncidos, pliegues, *m pl*

gauche /gouʃ/ *a* torpe, huraño

gaudily /'gɔdəli/ *adv* ostentosamente; brillantemente

gaudy /'gɔdi/ *a* llamativo, vistoso, brillante, ostentoso

gauge /geidʒ/ *n* (of gun) calibre, *m;* (railway) entrevía, *f;* (for measuring) indicator, *m;* regla de medir, *f; Naut.* calado, *m; Fig.* medida, *f;* (test) indicación, *f;* (model) norma, *f.* —*vt* calibrar; medir; estimar; (ship's capacity) arquear; (judge) juzgar; (size up) tomar la medida (de); *Fig.* interpretar; *Sew.* fruncir; (liquor) aforar. **broad (narrow) g. railway,** ferrocarril de vía ancha (estrecha), *m.* **pressure g.,** manómetro, *m.* **water g.,** indicador del nivel de agua, *m*

gauging /'geidʒɪŋ/ *n* medida, *f;* (of ship's capacity) arqueo, *m;* (of liquor) aforamiento, *m; Fig.* apreciación, *f;* interpretación, *f*

gaunt /gɔnt/ *a* anguloso, huesudo, desvaído; (of houses, etc.) lúgubre

gauntlet /'gɔntlɪt/ *n* guante de manopla, *m;* (part of armor) manopla, *f,* guantelete, *m.* **to throw down the g.,** echar el guante, desafiar

gauze /gɔz/ *n* gasa, *f;* (mist) bruma, *f.* **wire-g.,** tela metálica, *f*

gauzy /'gɔzi/ *a* diáfano; de gasa

gawky /'gɔki/ *a* anguloso, desgarbado, torpe

gay /gei/ *a* alegre; festivo, animado; ligero de cascos, disipado; homosexual; (of colors) brillante, llamativo

Gaza Strip /'gazə/ la franja de Gaza, *f*

gaze /geiz/ *n* mirada, *f;* mirada fija, *f.* —*vi* mirar; mirar fijamente, contemplar

gazing /'geizɪŋ/ *n* contemplación, *f, a* contemplador; que presencia, que asiste a

gear /giər/ *n* (apparel) atavíos, *m pl;* (harness) guarniciones, *f pl,* arneses, *m pl;* (tackle) utensilios, *m pl,* herramientas, *f pl; Naut.* aparejo, *m; Mech.* engranaje, *m;* juego, *m,* marcha, *f.* —*vt* aparejar, enjaezar; *Mech.* poner en marcha, hacer funcionar. —*vi Mech.* engranar, endentar. **low g.,** pimera velocidad, *f.* **neutral g.,** punto muerto, *m.* **reverse g.,** marcha atrás, *f.* **second g.,** segunda velocidad, *f.* **three-speed g.,** cambio de marchas de tres velocidades, *m.* **top g.,** tercera (or cuarta--according to gear-box) velocidad, *f.* **to change g.,** cambiar de marcha, cambiar de velocidad. **to throw out of g.,** *Fig.* desquiciar. **g.-box,** caja de velocidades, *f.* **g.-changing,** cambio de velocidad, *m.* **g.-changing lever,** palanca de cambio de velocidad, palanca de cambio de marchas, *f*

gehenna /gɪ'henə/ *n* gehena, *m*

geld /geld/ *vt* capar, castrar

gelding /'gɛldɪŋ/ *n* castración, capadura, *f;* caballo castrado, *m;* animal castrado, *m*

gelid /'dʒɛlɪd/ a gélido, helado; *Fig.* frío, frígido

gem /dʒɛm/ n piedra preciosa, f; joya, alhaja, f; *Fig.* joya, f. —vt adornar con piedras preciosas; enjoyar

gender /'dʒɛndər/ n *Gram.* género, m; sexo, m

gene /dʒin/ n *Biol.* gene, m

genealogical /,dʒiniə'lɒdʒɪkəl/ a genealógico. **g. tree**, árbol genealógico, m

general /'dʒɛnərəl/ a general; universal; común; corriente; (usual) acostumbrado, usual; del público, público. —n lo general; (*Mil.*, *Eccl.*) general, m; *Inf.* criada para todo, f. **in g.**, por lo general, en general, generalmente. **to become g.**, generalizarse. **to make g.**, generalizar, hacer general. **g. average**, (marine insurance) avería gruesa, f. **g. election**, elección general, f. **g. meeting**, pleno, mitin general, m. **g. opinion**, voz común, opinión general, f. **G. Post Office**, Oficina Central de Correos, f. **g. practitioner**, médico (-ca) general. **g. public**, público, m. **the general reader** el lector de tipo general m

generality /,dʒɛnə'rælɪti/ n generalidad, f

generalization /,dʒɛnərələ'zeiʃən/ n generalización, f

generalize /'dʒɛnərə,laiz/ vt and vi generalizar

generally /'dʒɛnərəli/ adv en general, por regla general, por lo general, generalmente; comúnmente, por lo común

generalship /'dʒɛnərəl,ʃɪp/ n *Mil.* generalato, m; (strategy) táctica, estrategia, f; dirección, jefatura, f

generate /'dʒɛnə,reit/ vt (beget) engendrar, procrear; (*Phys.*, *Chem.*) generar; *Fig.* producir, crear

generation /,dʒɛnə'reiʃən/ n procreación, f; generación, f; *Fig.* producción, creación, f. **the younger g.**, los jóvenes

generative /'dʒɛnərətɪv/ a generador

generator /'dʒɛnə,reitər/ n *Mech.* generador, m; dínamo, f

generic /dʒə'nɛrɪk/ a genérico

generosity /,dʒɛnə'rɒsɪti/ n generosidad, f; liberalidad, f

generous /'dʒɛnərəs/ a generoso; liberal, dadivoso; magnánimo; (plentiful) abundante; (of wines) generoso

generously /'dʒɛnərəsli/ adv generosamente; abundantemente

genesis /'dʒɛnəsɪs/ n principio, origen, m; (G.) Génesis, m

genetic /dʒə'nɛtɪk/ a genético

genetics /dʒə'nɛtɪks/ n genética, f

Geneva /dʒə'nivə/ Ginebra f

genial /'dʒinyəl/ a (of climate) agradable, bueno; (of persons) afable, bondadoso; de buen humor, bonachón

geniality /,dʒini'ælɪti/ n afabilidad, bondad, f; buen humor, m

genially /'dʒinyəli/ adv afablemente

genie /'dʒini/ n genio, m

genital /'dʒɛnɪtl/ a genital, sexual. —n pl **genitals**, genitales, m pl

genius /'dʒinyəs/ n genio, m; carácter, m, índole, f; ingenio, m; *Inf.* talento, m

Genoa /'dʒɛnouə/ Genova, f

Genoese /,dʒɛnou'iz/ a and n genovés (-esa)

genre /'ʒɑnrə/ n género, m. **g. painting**, cuadro de género, m

genteel /dʒɛn'til/ a fino; (affected) remilgado, melindroso; de buen tono; de buena educación

gentile /'dʒɛntail/ a and n gentil mf

gentility /dʒɛn'tɪlɪti/ n aristocracia, f; respetabilidad, f

gentle /'dʒɛntl/ a noble, bien nacido, de buena familia; amable; suave; ligero; dulce; (docile) manso, dócil; (affectionate) cariñoso; bondadoso; sufrido, paciente; cortés; pacífico, tolerante. **He was a man of g. birth**, Era un hombre bien nacido. **"G. reader,"** «Querido lector»

gentlefolk /'dʒɛntl,fouk/ n pl gente de bien, gente fina, f; gente de buena familia, f

gentleman /'dʒɛntlmən/ n caballero, señor, m; gentilhombre, m. **Ladies and gentlemen**, Señoras y caballeros, Señores. **young g.**, señorito, m. **to be a perfect g.**, ser un caballero perfecto. **g.-inwaiting**, gentilhombre de la cámara, m

gentlemanliness /'dʒɛntlmənlinɪs/ n caballerosidad, f

gentlemanly /'dʒɛntlmənli/ a caballeroso

gentleness /'dʒɛntlnɪs/ n amabilidad, f; suavidad, f; dulzura, f; mansedumbre, docilidad, f; bondad, f; paciencia, f; cortesía, f; tolerancia, f

gentlewoman /'dʒɛntl,wumən/ n dama, f; dama de servicio, f

gently /'dʒɛntli/ adv suavemente; dulcemente; silenciosamente, sin ruido; (slowly) despacio, poco a poco. **g. born**, bien nacido

gentry /'dʒɛntri/ n pequeña aristocracia, alta clase media, f; (disparaging) gentle, f

genuflect /'dʒɛnyu,flɛkt/ vi doblar la rodilla

genuine /'dʒɛnyuɪn/ a puro; genuino; verdadero; real; sincero; auténtico

genuinely /'dʒɛnyuɪnli/ adv genuinamente; verdaderamente; realmente; sinceramente

genus /'dʒinəs/ n género, m

geographer /dʒi'ɒgrəfər/ n geógrafo, m

geographical /,dʒiə'græfɪkəl/ a geográfico

geography /dʒi'ɒgrəfi/ n geografía, f

geologist /dʒi'ɒlədʒɪst/ n geólogo, m

geology /dʒi'ɒlədʒi/ n geología, f

geometric /,dʒiə'mɛtrɪk/ a geométrico

geometry /dʒi'ɒmɪtri/ n geometría, f

geranium /dʒə'reiniəm/ n geranio, m

germ /dʒɜrm/ n embrión, germen, m; microbio, bacilo, m; *Fig.* germen, m. **g.-cell**, célula germinal, f

German /'dʒɜrmən/ a alemán; germánico. —n alemán (-ana); (language) alemán, m; germano (-na), germánico (-ca). **Sudeten G.,** alemán (-ana) sudete. **G. measles,** rubeola, f. **G. silver** alpaca, f, melchor m, plata alemana f

germane /dʒər'mein/ a pertinente (a), a propósito (a)

Germanic /dʒər'mænɪk/ a germánico. —n (language) germánico, m

Germanize /'dʒɜrmə,naiz/ vt germanizar. —vi germanizarse

Germany /'dʒɜrməni/ Alemania, f

germicidal /,dʒɜrmə'saidl/ a bactericida

germicide /'dʒɜrmə,said/ n desinfectante, m

germinal /'dʒɜrmənl/ a germinal. —n (G.) germinal, m

germinate /'dʒɜrmə,neit/ vi germinar, brotar. —vt hacer germinar

germination /,dʒɜrmə'neiʃən/ n germinación, f

germinative /'dʒɜrmə,neitɪv/ a germinativo

gerund /'dʒɛrənd/ n gerundio, m

gerundive /dʒə'rʌndɪv/ n gerundio adjetivado, m

Gestapo /gə'stɑpou/ n Gestapo, f

gestation /dʒɛ'steiʃən/ n gestación, f

gesticulate /dʒɛ'stɪkyə,leit/ vi gesticular, hacer gestos; accionar. —vt expresar por gestos

gesticulation /dʒɛ,stɪkyə'leiʃən/ n gesticulación, f

gesticulatory /dʒɛ'stɪkyələ,tɔri/ a gesticular

gesture /'dʒɛstʃər/ n movimiento, m; gesticulación, f; (of the face) gesto, m, mueca, f; ademán, m, acción, f. —vt gesticular. —vt decir por gestos; acompañar con gestos

get /gɛt/ vt (obtain) obtener; (acquire) adquirir; (buy) comprar; (take) tomar; (receive) recibir; (gain, win) ganar; (hit) acertar, dar; (place) poner; (achieve) alcanzar, lograr; (make) hacer; (call) llamar; (understand) comprender; (catch) coger; (procreate) procrear, engendrar; (induce) persuadir; (invite) convidar, invitar; (cause) hacer; (with have and past part.) tener; (with have and past part. followed by infin.) tener que; (followed by noun and past part.) hacer; (fetch) buscar, ir a buscar; (order) mandar, disponer; (procure) procurar; (bring) traer; (money) hacer; (a reputation, etc.) hacerse; (a prize, an advantage) llevar; (learn) aprender; (be) ser. —vi (become) hacerse; ponerse; venir a ser; (old) envejecerse; (angry) montar (en cólera), enojarse; (arrive) llegar a; (attain) alcanzar; (accomplish) conseguir, lograr; (drunk) emborracharse; (hurt) hacerse daño; (wet) mojarse; (cool) enfriarse; (money) hacer (dinero); (of health) ponerse; (find oneself) hallarse, encontrarse; (late) hacerse (tarde); (dark) empezar a caer (la noche), empezar a caer (la noche), empe-

zar a oscurecer; (put oneself) meterse; (grow, be) estar; (on to or on top of) montar sobre, subir a. **He has got run over,** Ha sido atropellado. **It gets on my nerves,** Se me pone los nervios en punta. **Let's get it over!** ¡Vamos a concluir de una vez! **How do you get on with her?** ¿Cómo te va con ella? **She must be getting on for twenty,** Tendrá alrededor de veinte años. **to get a suit made,** mandar hacerse un traje. **to get better,** (in health) mejorar de salud; hacer progresos adelantar. **to get dark,** obscurecer. **to get into conversation with,** trabar conversación con. **to get into bad company,** frecuentar malas compañías. **to get in the habit of,** acostumbrarse a. **to get married,** casarse. **to get near,** acercarse. **to get one's own way,** salir con la suya. **to get oneself up as,** disfrazarse de. **to get out in a hurry,** salir apresuradamente, marcharse rápidamente, Inf. salir pitando. **to get out of the way,** quitarse de en medio, apartarse. **to get rid of,** desembarazarse de, librarse de; salir de; perder. **to have got,** poseer, tener; padecer. **Get on!** ¡Adelante!; (to a horse) ¡Arre!; (continue) ¡Sigue! **Get out!** ¡Fuera! ¡Largo de aquí! ¡Sal! **Get up!** ¡Levántate!; (to a horse) ¡Arre! **to get about,** moverse mucho; andar mucho; (attend to business affairs) ir a sus negocios; (travel) viajar; (get up from sick bed) levantarse; (go out) salir; (be known) saberse, divulgarse, hacerse público. **to get above,** subir a un nivel más alto (de). **to get across,** vi cruzar, atravesar. —vt hacer cruzar. **to get along,** vi (depart) marcharse; (continue) seguir, vivir; (manage) ir, ir tirando. —vt llevar; traer; hacer andar por. **How are you getting along?** ¿Cómo le va? **I am getting along all right, thank you,** Voy tirando, gracias. **to get along without,** pasarse sin. **to get at,** (remove) sacar; (find) encontrar; (reach) llegar a; alcanzar; (discover) descubrir; (allude to) aludir a; (understand) comprender. **to get away,** vi dejar (un lugar); marcharse, irse; (escape) escaparse. —vt ayudar a marcharse; ayudar a escaparse. **to get away with,** llevarse, marcharse con; Inf. salir con la suya. **to get back,** vi regresar, volver; (get home) volver a casa; (be back) estar de vuelta. —vt (recover) recobrar; (receive) recibir; (find again) hallar de nuevo. **to get down,** vi bajar, descender. —vt bajar; (take off a hook) descolgar; (swallow) tragar; (note) anotar; escribir. **to get down on all fours,** ponerse en cuatro patas. **to get down to,** ponerse a (estudiar, trabajar, etc.). **to get in,** vi entrar en; lograr entrar en; (slip in) colarse en; (of political party) entrar en el poder; (of a club) hacerse socio de; (return) regresar; (home) volver a casa; (find oneself) hallarse, estar; (a habit) adquirir. —vt hacer entrar en; (a club, etc.) hacer socio de; (a word) decir.

to get into. See **to get in. to get off,** *vt* apearse de; bajar de; (send) enviar; (from punishment) librar; (bid goodbye) despedirse de; (remove) quitar, sacar. —*vi* apearse; bajar; (from punishment) librarse; (leave) ponerse en camino, marcharse. **to get on,** *vi* (wear) tener puesto; (progress) hacer progresos, adelantar; (prosper) medrar, prosperar; (succeed) tener éxito; avanzar; seguir el camino; (agree) avenirse. —*vt* (push) empujar; (place) poner; (cause) hacer; (clothes) ponerse; (mount) subir a. **to get open,** abrir. **to get out,** *vt* hacer salir; sacar; (publish) publicar; divulgar. —*vi* salir; escapar; **to get out of a jam,** salir de un paso; (descend) bajar (de). **to get over,** (cross) atravesar, cruzar; (an illness, grief, etc.) reponerse, reponerse de; (excuse) perdonar; (surmount) superar; (ground) recorrer. **to get round,** (a person) persuadir; (surround) rodear; (avoid) evitar; (difficulties) superar, vencer. **to get through,** pasar por; (time) pasar, entretener; (money) gastar; (finish) terminar, acabar; (pierce or enter) penetrar; (communicate) comunicar (con); (difficulties) vencer; (an exam) aprobar. **to get to,** llegar a; encontrar; (begin) empezar. **to get together,** *vt* reunir, juntar. —*vi* reunirse, juntarse. **to get under,** ponerse debajo de; (control) dominar. **to get up,** *vt* (raise) alzar, levantar; (carry up things) subir; hacer subir; organizar; preparar; (learn) aprender; (linen) blanquear, colar; (ascend) subir; hacer; (dress) ataviar; (steam) generar; (a play) ensayar, poner en escena. —*vi* levantarse; (on a horse) montar a caballo; (of the wind) refrescarse; (of the fire) avivarse; (of the sea) embravecerse. **to get up to,** llegar a; alcanzar

get-at-able /'gɛt ,æt əbəl/ *a* accesible

getting /'gɛtɪŋ/ *n* adquisición, *f*; (of money) ganancia, *f*. **g. up,** preparación, *f*; organización, *f*; (of a play) representación (de una comedia), puesta en escena, *f*

get-up /'gɛt ,ʌp/ *n* atavío, *m*; (of a book, etc.) aspecto, *m*

gewgaw /'gyugɔ/ *n* chuchería, *f*

geyser /'gaɪzər/ *n* géiser, *m*; (for heating water) calentador (de agua), *m*

ghastly /'gæstli/ *a* horrible; (of a pallidez mortal; cadavérico; (boring) aburrido; muy desagradable

gherkin /'gɜrkɪn/ *n* cohombrillo, *m*

ghetto /'gɛtoʊ/ *n* gueto *m*

ghost /goʊst/ *n* fantasma, espectro, aparecido, *m*; (spirit) alma, *f*; espíritu, *m*; (shadow) sombra, *f*; (writer) mercenario, *m*. Holy G., Espíritu Santo, *m*. **to give up the g.,** entregar el alma; perder la esperanza, desesperarse. **to look like a g.,** parecer un fantasma

ghostly /'goʊstli/ *a* espiritual; espectral; misterioso; pálido; vaporoso, tenue; indistinto

ghost town *n* pueblo-fantasma, *m*

ghoul /gul/ *n* vampiro, *m*

ghoulish /'gulɪʃ/ *a* insano; cruel; sádico

giant /'dʒaɪənt/ *n* gigante, *m*; *Fig.* coloso, *m*, *a* gigantesco; de gigantes; de los gigantes. **g.-killer,** matador de gigantes, *m*. **g.-stride,** (gymnastics) paso volante, *m*

gibber /'dʒɪbər/ *vi* hablar incoherentemente, hablar entre dientes; farfullar, hablar atropelladamente; decir disparates

gibberish /'dʒɪbərɪʃ/ *n* galimatías, *m*; jerigonza, *f*, griego, *m*

gibbet /'dʒɪbɪt/ *n* horca, *f*, patíbulo, *m*. **to die on the g.,** morir ahorcado

gibe /dʒaɪb/ *n* improperio, escarnio, *m*, burla, mofa, *f*. —*vi* criticar. **to g. at,** burlarse de, ridiculizar, mofarse de

giblets /'dʒɪblɪts/ *n pl* menudillos, *m pl*

giddily /'gɪdli/ *adv* vertiginosamente; frívolamente, atolondradamente

giddiness /'gɪdinəs/ *n* vértigo, *m*; atolondramiento, *m*; inconstancia, *f*; frivolidad, ligereza de cascos, *f*

giddy /'gɪdi/ *a* vertiginoso; mareado; atolondrado, casquivano, frívolo; inconstante. **She felt very g.,** Se sintió muy mareada. **to make g.,** dar vértigo (a), marear

gift /gɪft/ *n* regalo, *m*, dádiva, *f*; (quality) don, talento, *m*; prenda, *f*; poder, *m*; *Law.* donación, *f*; (offering) ofrenda, oblación, *f*. —*vt* dotar. **deed of g.,** *Law.* escritura de donación, *f*. **in the g. of,** en el poder de, en las manos de. **I wouldn't have it as a g.,** No lo tomaría ni regalado. **Never look a g. horse in the mouth,** A caballo regalado no se le mira el diente. **g. of tongues,** don de las lenguas, genio de las lenguas, *m*

gifted /'gɪftɪd/ *a* talentoso

gig /gɪg/ *n* (carriage) carrocín, *m*; (boat) falúa, lancha, *f*; (for wool) máquina de cardar paño, *f*; (harpoon) arpón, *m*

gigantic /dʒaɪˈgæntɪk/ *a* gigantesco; colosal, enorme

giggle /'gɪgəl/ *vi* reírse sin motivo; reírse disimuladamente. —*n* risa disimulada, *f*

giggling /'gɪglɪŋ/ *n* risa estúpida, *f*; risa nerviosa, *f*

gigolo /'dʒɪgə,loʊ/ *n* gigolo, mantenido, jinetero (Cuba), *m*

gild /gɪld/ *vt* dorar; (metals) sobredorar; embellecer. **to g. the pill,** dorar la píldora

gill /gɪl/ *n* (of fish) agalla, branquia, *f*; (ravine) barranco, *m*;

gill /dʒɪl/ *n* (measure) cierta medida de líquidos, *f*, (¼ litro)

gilt /gɪlt/ *n* dorado, *m*; pan de oro, *m*; relumbrón, *m*; *Fig.* encanto, *m*, a dorado, áureo. **g.-edged,** (of books) con los bordes dorados. **g.-edged security,** papel del Estado, *m*; valores de toda confianza, *m pl*

gimcrack /'dʒɪm,kræk/ *n* chuchería, *f*. —*a* de baratillo, cursi; mal hecho

gimlet /'gɪmlɪt/ *n* barrena, *f*, taladro, *m*

gin /dʒɪn/ *n* (drink) ginebra, *f*; (snare)

trampa, *f.* —*vt* (snare) coger con trampa.
g. block, *Mech.* garrucha, *f*

ginger /'dʒɪndʒər/ *n* jengibre, *m; Inf.* energía, *f,* brío, *m, a* rojo. —*vt* sazonar con jengibre; *Inf.* animar, estimular. **g.-beer,** gaseosa, *f*

gingerly /'dʒɪndʒərli/ *adv* con gran cuidado; delicadamente

gingham /'gɪŋəm/ *n* guinga, *f*

gingivitis /ˌdʒɪndʒə'vaitɪs/ *n* gingivitis, *f*

gipsy /'dʒɪpsi/ *n.* See **gypsy**

giraffe /dʒə'ræf/ *n* jirafa, *f*

gird /gɜrd/ *vt* ceñir; (invest) investir; (surround) cercar, rodear; (put on) revestir. **to g. oneself for the fray,** prepararse para la lucha

girder /'gɜrdər/ *n* viga, jácena, *f.* **main g.,** viga maestra, *f*

girdle /'gɜrdl/ *n* (belt) cinturón, *m;* (corset) faja, *f;* circunferencia, *f;* zona, *f.* —*vt* ceñir; *Fig.* cercar, rodear

girl /gɜrl/ *n* niña, *f;* (maidservant) criada, muchacha, *f;* (young lady) señorita, *f.* **a young g.,** una jovencita; (a little older) una joven. **old g.,** (of a school) antigua alumna, *f; Inf.* vieja, *f;* (*Inf.* affectionate) chica, *f.* **g. friend,** amiguita, *f.* **g. guide, girl scout,** exploradora, *f.* **girls' school,** colegio de niñas, colegio de señoritas, *m*

girlhood /'gɜrlhʊd/ *n* niñez, *f;* juventud, *f*

girlish /'gɜrlɪʃ/ *a* de niña, de muchacha; (of boys) afeminado; joven

girth /gɜrθ/ *n* (of horse, etc.) cincha, *f;* circunferencia, *f;* (of person) talle, *m;* (obesity) corpulencia, obesidad, *f*

gist /dʒɪst/ *n* esencia, substancia, *f,* importe, *m*

give /gɪv/ *vt* dar; (a present) regalar; (infect) contagiar; (impart) comunicar; (grant) otorgar; (allow, concede) conceder; (assign) asignar, señalar; (appoint) nombrar; (a toast) brindar (a la salud de); (a party, ball, etc.) dar; (a bill) presentar; (wish) desear; (punish) castigar; (pay) pagar; (hand over) entregar; (names at baptism) imponer; (produce) producir; dar; (cause) causar; (of judicial sentences) condenar a; (evoke) proporcionar; (provoke) provocar; (devote) dedicar, consagrar; (sacrifice) sacrificar; (evidence, an account, orders, a lesson, a performance, a concert) dar; (a cry, shout) lanzar, proferir; (a laugh) soltar; (describe) describir; (paint) pintar; (write) escribir; (offer) ofrecer; (show) mostrar; (transmit) transmitir; (heed, pay attention) hacer; (a speech) pronunciar, hacer; (award, adjudge) adjudicar; (ear) prestar (oído (a)). —*vi* dar; ser dadivoso, mostrarse generoso; (give in) ceder; (be elastic) dar de sí; ablandarse; (collapse) hundirse. **G. them my best wishes!** ¡Dales mis mejores recuerdos! **G. us a song!** ¡Cántanos algo! **I can g. him a lift in my car,** Puedo ofrecerle un asiento en mi auto. **I g. you my word,** Os doy mi palabra. **to g. a**

good account of oneself, defenderse bien; hacer bien; salir bien. **to g. a person a piece of one's mind,** contarle cuatro verdades. **to g. chase,** dar caza (a). **to g. it to a person,** poner a uno como nuevo; reprender; (beat) pegar, dar de palos. **to g. of itself,** dar de sí. **to g. rise to,** dar lugar a, ocasionar, causar. **to g. way,** no poder resistir; (break) romperse; (yield) ceder; (collapse) hundirse; (retreat) retroceder. **to g. way to,** (retreat before) retirarse ante; (abandon oneself to) entregarse a, abandonarse a. **to g. away,** enajenar; dar; regalar; (sell cheaply) vender a un precio muy bajo; (get rid of) deshacerse de; (sacrifice) sacrificar; (a secret) revelar; (betray) traicionar; (expose) descubrir; (tell) contar; (a bride) conducir al altar. **He gave himself away,** Reveló su pensamiento sin querer. **to g. back,** *vt* devolver; restituir. —*vi* retirarse, cejar. **to g. forth,** divulgar, publicar; (scatter) derramar; (emit) emitir, despedir; (smoke, rays) echar. **to g. in,** *vt* entregar; presentar. —*vi* darse por vencido. **to g. in to,** (agree with) asentir en, consentir en; rendirse ante. **Mary always gives in to George,** María hace siempre lo que Jorge quiere. **to g. off,** (of odors, etc.) emitir, exhalar, despedir. **to g. out,** *vt* (distribute) distribuir, repartir; (allocate) asignar; (publish) publicar; (announce) anunciar; (reveal) divulgar; (allege) afirmar, hacer saber; (emit) emitir. —*vi* (be exhausted) agotarse; (end) acabarse; (be lacking) faltar. **to g. over,** *vt* entregar; (transfer) traspasar; cesar de. —*vi* cesar. **to g. up,** entregar; ceder; (renounce) renunciar (a); (sacrifice) sacrificar; (abandon) abandonar; (cease) dejar de; (as lost) dar por perdido; (of a patient) desahuciar; (a post) dimitir de; (return) devolver, restituir; (a problem) renunciar (a resolver un problema); (lose hope) perder la esperanza; (give in) darse por vencido. **I had given you up,** (didn't expect you), Creí que no ibas a venir. **to g. oneself up to,** entregarse a; dedicarse a; *Mil.* rendirse a. **to g. up one's seat,** ceder su sitio (or asiento). **to g. upon,** (overlook) dar sobre

give /gɪv/ *n* elasticidad, *f;* el dar de sí; (concession) concesión, *f.* **g. and take,** concesiones mutuas, *f pl.* **g. away,** *Inf.* revelación indiscreta, *f*

given /'gɪvən/ *a* dado; especificado; convenido; (with to) dado a, adicto a. **in a g. time,** en un tiempo dado. **g. that,** dado que

gizzard /'gɪzərd/ *n* molleja, *f.* **It sticks in my g.,** *Inf.* No lo puedo tragar

glacial /'gleiʃəl/ *a* glacial

glacier /'gleiʃər/ *n* glaciar, *m*

glad /glæd/ *a* feliz, alegre; contento, satisfecho; *Inf.* elegante. **to be g.,** alegrarse, estar contento; estar satisfecho. **to give the g. eye,** hacer ojos

gladden /'glædn/ *vt* alegrar, regocijar

glade /gleid/ *n* claro, *m;* rasa, *f*

gladiator /ˈglædiˌeitər/ *n* gladiador, *m*

gladly /ˈglædli/ *adv* alegremente; con mucho gusto, gustoso, de buena gana

glamorous /ˈglæmərəs/ *a* exótico; garboso

glamour /ˈglæmər/ *n* encanto, *m,* fascinación, *f;* garbo, *m.* **g. girl,** belleza exótica, *f*

glance /glæns/ *n* (of a projectile) desviación, *f;* (of light) vislumbre, *m;* relumbrón, centelleo, *m;* (look) vistazo, *m,* ojeada, *f;* mirada, *f, vi* desviarse; relumbrar, centellear, brillar; (with at) ojear, echar un vistazo a, lanzar miradas a; (a book) hojear; mirar; mirar de reojo; *Fig.* indicar brevemente. **at a g.,** con un vistazo; en seguida. **at the first g.,** a primera vista. **to g. off,** desviarse (al chocar). **to g. over,** repasar, echar un vistazo a; (a book) hojear

gland /glænd/ *n* (*Anat., Bot.*) glándula, *f;* (in the neck) ganglio, *m.* **to have swollen glands,** tener inflamación de los ganglios

glare /glɛər/ *n* brillo, fulgor, *m;* luminosidad, *f;* reflejo, *m;* (look) mirada feroz, *f.* —*vi* relumbrar, centellear; (stare) mirar con ferocidad, mirar fijamente

glaring /ˈglɛərɪŋ/ *a* deslumbrante, brillante; (of colors) chillón, llamativo; (of looks) de mirada feroz; (flagrant) notorio, evidente

glaringly /ˈglɛərɪŋli/ *adv* brillantemente; con mirada feroz; notoriamente

glass /glæs/ *n* vidrio, *m;* cristal, *m;* (glassware) artículos de vidrio, *m pl;* cristalería, *f;* (for drinking) vaso, *m,* copa, *f;* (pane) cristal, *m;* (mirror) espejo, *m;* (telescope) telescopio, *m;* catalejo, *m;* (barometer) barómetro, *m;* (hour-glass) reloj de arena, *m;* (of a watch) vidrio (de reloj), *m;* *pl* **glasses,** (binoculars) anteojos, *m pl;* (spectacles) gafas, lentes, *m pl;* (opera glasses) gemelos de teatro, *m pl, a* de vidrio; de cristal. —*vt* vidriar. **John wears glasses,** Juan lleva gafas. **The g. is falling (rising),** El barómetro baja (sube). **to clink glasses,** trincar las copas. **to look in the g.,** mirarse en el espejo. **clear g.,** vidrio trasparente, *m.* **cut g.,** cristal tallado, *m.* **frosted g.,** vidrio jaspeado, *m.* **plate-g.,** vidrio plano, *m;* **safety g.,** vidrio inastillable, *m.* **stained g.,** vidrio de color, vidrio pintado, *m.* **under g.,** bajo vidrio; en invernáculo. **g. bead,** abalorio, *m;* cuenta de vidrio, *f.* **g.-blower,** soplador de vidrio, *m.* **g.-blowing,** el soplar de vidrio. **g. case,** escaparate, *m.* **g.-cloth,** paño para vasos, *m.* **g. eye,** ojo de cristal, *m.* **g. paper,** papel de vidrio, *m.* **g. roof,** techo de cristal, *m.* **g. window,** vidriera, *f*

glassful /ˈglæsfʊl/ *n* contenido de un vaso, *m;* vaso, vaso lleno, *m,* copa, *f*

glassware /ˈglæsˌwɛər/ *n* cristalería, *f*

glaucous /ˈglɔkəs/ *a* de color verdemar; *Bot.* glauco

glaze /gleiz/ *n* barniz, *m:* lustre, brillo, *m.* —*vt* poner vidrios (a); vidriar; barnizar; (paper, leather, etc.) satinar. —*vi* (of eyes) vidriarse, ponerse vidrioso

glazier /ˈgleizər/ *n* vidriero, *m*

gleam /glim/ *n* rayo, destello, *m;* (of color) viso, *m,* mancha, *f;* *Fig.* rayo, *m;* (in the eye) chispa, *f.* —*vi* relucir, centellear, resplandecer; brillar; reflejar la luz; *Fig.* brillar. **g. of hope,** rayo de esperanza, *m*

gleaming /ˈglimɪŋ/ *a* reluciente, centelleante; brillante. —*n* see **gleam**

glean /glin/ *vt* espigar, rebuscar; recoger. —*vi* espigar

gleaning /ˈglinɪŋ/ *n* espigueo, *m;* rebusca, recolección, *f;* *pl* **gleanings,** fragmentos, *m pl*

glee /gli/ *n* alegría, *f,* júbilo, alborozo, *m;* *Mus.* canción para voces solas, *f*

gleeful /ˈglifəl/ *a* alegre, jubiloso, gozoso

glen /glɛn/ *n* cañada, *f,* cañón, *m,* hondonada, *f*

glib /glɪb/ *a* locuaz, voluble; (easy) fácil

glide /glaid/ *n* deslizamiento, *m;* *Aer.* planeo, *m.* —*vi* deslizarse; resbalar; *Aer.* planear. **to g. away,** escurrirse; desaparecer silenciosamente

glider /ˈglaidər/ *n* *Aer.* deslizador, planeador, *m*

gliding /ˈglaidɪŋ/ *n* *Aer.* vuelo sin motor, *m*

glimmer /ˈglɪmər/ *n* luz trémula, luz débil, *f,* tenue resplandor, *m;* vislumbre, *m.* —*vi* brillar con luz trémula, rielar *Fig.;* tener vislumbres (de)

glimpse /glɪmps/ *n* vistazo, *m;* vislumbre, *m;* indicio, *m;* impresión, *f;* vista, *f.* —*vt* entrever, divisar; tener una vista (de); ver por un instante; vislumbrar

glint /glɪnt/ *n* tenue resplandor, *m;* lustre, *m;* centelleo, *m;* reflejo, *m;* (in the eye) chispa, *f.* —*vi* relucir, destellar, rutilar; reflejar

glisten /ˈglɪsən/ *vi* brillar, relucir

glistening /ˈglɪsənɪŋ/ *a* coruscante; brillante, reluciente

glitter /ˈglɪtər/ *n* brillo, resplandor, *m,* rutilación, *f.* —*vi* brillar, resplandecer, relucir; rutilar. **All that glitters is not gold,** Todo lo que reluce no es oro

glittering /ˈglɪtərɪŋ/ *a* reluciente, resplandeciente; *Fig.* brillante

gloat (over) /glout/ *vi* recrearse en, gozarse en, deleitarse en

globe /gloub/ *n* globo, *m;* esfera, *f;* (for fish) pecera, *f;* (for gas, electric light) globo, *m.* **geographical g.,** globo terrestre, *m.* **g.-trotter,** trotamundos, *m*

gloom /glum/ *n* obscuridad, *f;* lobreguez, *f,* tinieblas, *f pl;* *Fig.* melancolía, tristeza, *f;* taciturnidad, *f.* —*vi* *Fig.* ponerse melancólico; ser taciturno

gloomy /ˈglumi/ *a* obscuro; sombrío, lóbrego; melancólico, triste; taciturno; (of prospects, etc.) poco halagüeño, nada atrayente

glorify /'glɔrə,fai/ vt glorificar; exaltar; alabar

glorious /'glɔriəs/ a glorioso; espléndido, magnífico, insigne; Inf. estupendo

glory /'glɔri/ n gloria, f; esplendor, m, magnificencia, f; Art. gloria, f. —vi recrearse, gozarse; glorificarse, jactarse. **to be in one's g.,** estar en la gloria. **to g. in,** hacer gala de, glorificarse en

gloss /glɒs/ n (sheen) lustre, brillo, m; Fig. apariencia, f; (note) glose, m; (excuse) disculpa, f. —vt pulir; glosar. **to g. over,** (faults) disculpar, excusar

glossary /'glɒsəri/ n glosario, m

glossy /'glɒsi/ a lustroso, terso; brillante; (of hair) liso

glove /glʌv/ n guante. **evening gloves,** guantes largos, m pl. **to be hand in g. with,** juntar diestra con diestra. **to fit like a g.,** sentar como un guante. **to put on one's gloves,** ponerse los guantes. **g. shop,** guantería, f. **g.-stretcher,** ensanchador (or abridor) de guantes, m

glove compartment gaveta, guantera, f, guantero, portaguantes m

glow /glou/ n incandescencia, f; claridad, f; luz difusa, f; (heat) calor, m; (of color) intensidad, f; color vivo, m; (enthusiasm) ardor, entusiasmo, m; (redness) rojez, f; (in the sky) arrebol, m; (of pleasure, etc.) sentimiento de placer, m; sensación de bienestar, f. —vi estar incandescente; arder; abrasarse; sentir entusiasmo; mostrarse rojo; experimentar un sentimiento de placer o una sensación de bienestar. **to g. with health,** estar rebosando de salud. **g.-worm,** luciérnaga, f

glower /'glauər/ n ceño, m; mirada amenazadora, f. —vi poner cara de pocos amigos, mirar airadamente; tener los ojos puestos (en)

glowing /'glouɪŋ/ a candente, incandescente; ardiente; entusiasta; satisfecho; intenso; (bright) vivo; (red) encendido; (with health) rebosante de salud. —n see glow

glue /glu/ n engrudo, m, cola, f. —vt encolar, engrudar; pegar; Fig. fijar, poner. **He kept his eyes glued on them,** Tenía los ojos fijados (or pegados) en ellos. **g.-pot,** pote de cola, m

gluey /'glui/ a gomoso; pegajoso, viscoso

glum /glʌm/ a deprimido, taciturno, sombrío

glut /glʌt/ n superabundancia, f, exceso, m. —vt (satiate) hartar; Fig. saciar; (the market) inundar

glutton /'glʌtn/ n glotón (-ona); Fig. ávido (-da)

gluttonous /'glʌtnəs/ a glotón, comilón

gnarled /nɑrld/ a nudoso; (of human beings) curtido

gnash /næʃ/ vt rechinar, crujir (los dientes)

gnat /næt/ n mosquito, m

gnaw /nɔ/ vt roer; morder; (of wood by worms) carcomer; Fig. roer

go /gou/ vi ir; (depart) irse, marcharse;

(go toward) dirigirse a, encaminarse a; (lead to, of roads, etc.) conducir a, ir a; (vanish) desaparecer; (leave) dejar, salir de; (lose) perder; (pass) pasar; (of time) transcurrir, pasar; (be removed) quitarse; (be prohibited) prohibirse; (fall) caer; (collapse) hundirse; (be worn off) desprenderse; desgajarse; Mech. funcionar, trabajar, andar; (sound) sonar; (of the heart) palpitar, latir; (follow) seguir; (gesture) hacer un gesto; (be stated) decirse, afirmarse; (live) vivir; (wear) llevar; (turn out) salir, resultar; (improve) mejorar; (prosper) prosperar; (turn, become) ponerse; volverse; (to sleep) dormirse; (into a faint) desmayarse; (decay) echarse a perder, estropearse; (turn sour) agriarse; (become, adopt views, etc.) hacerse; (be sold) venderse; (be decided) decidirse, ser decidido; (have) tener; (by will) pasar; (belong) pertenecer; (receive) recibir; (have its place) estar; (put) ponerse; (going plus infin.) ir a; (die) morir, irse; (do a journey, a given distance) hacer; (a pace, step) dar; (take) tomar; (escape) escaparse; (contribute) contribuir (a); (harmonize) armonizar (con); (be current) ser válido; (be) ser; (of a document, etc., run) rezar, decir; (attend) asistir a; (be broken) estar roto; (be worn) estar raído; (be granted) darse, otorgarse. **It's gone five,** Ya dieron las cinco. **It's time to be going,** Es hora de marcharse. **Let's go!** ¡Vamos! **These two colours go well together,** Estos colores armonizan bien. **Well, how goes it?** Bueno, ¿qué tal? ¿Cómo te va? **Who goes there?** Mil. ¿Quién va? **to go and fetch,** ir a buscar. **to let go,** soltar; dejar ir. **to go one's way,** seguir su camino. **to go wrong,** salir mal, fracasar; (sin) descarriarse. **"Go!"** (traffic sign) «¡Siga!» **Go on!** ¡Adelante!; (continue) ¡Siga!; Inf. ¡Qué va! **to go about,** dar la vuelta a; rodear; recorrer; (undertake) emprender, hacer; intentar; (of news, etc.) circular; Naut. virar de bordo. **Go about your business!** ¡Métete en lo que to importa! **to go abroad,** ir al extranjero; salir a la calle; publicarse, divulgarse. **to go across,** cruzar, atravesar; pasar. **to go after,** andar tras; seguir; (seek) ir a buscar; (persecute) perseguir. **to go again,** ir de nuevo; (be present) asistir otra vez; volver. **to go against,** ir contra; militar contra; oponerse a; ser desfavorable a. **to go ahead,** adelantar, avanzar; progresar; prosperar; (lead) ir a la cabeza (de), conducir; Naut. marchar hacia adelante. **to go along,** andar por; recorrer; (depart) irse, marcharse. **go apartment-hunting,** ir en busca de piso. **to go along with,** acompañar (a). **to go aside,** quitarse de en medio; apartarse, retirarse. **to go astray,** perderse; extraviarse, descarriarse. **to go at,** atacar, acometer; (undertake) emprender; empezar a. **to go at it again,** Inf. volver a la carga. **to go away,** irse, marcharse; ausentarse; alejarse; desaparecer. **to go away with,** marcharse con; (an object) llevarse. **to go back,** volver; (retreat) retroceder, volverse atrás; (in history) remontarse a. **to go back on,** (a promise, etc.) faltar a; (retract) retractarse; (betray) traicionar. **to go backwards and forwards,** ir y venir; oscilar. **to go before,** (lead) ir a la cabeza de, conducir; anteceder; proceder; (a judge, etc.) comparecer ante. **to go behind,** ir detrás de; esconderse detrás de; seguir; (evidence, etc.) mirar más allá de. **to go between,** ponerse entre; interponerse; (as a mediator) mediar; (insert) intercalarse; (travel) ir entre; llevar cartas entre, ser mensajero de. **to go beyond,** ir más allá; exceder. **to go by,** pasar por; pasar cerca de, pasar junto a; ir por; (of time) transcurrir, pasar; (follow) seguir; guiarse por, atenerse a; (judge by) juzgar por; (a name) pasar por; tomar el nombre de. **to go down,** bajar, descender; (of the sun) ponerse; (sink) hundirse; sumergirse; (fall) caer; (be remembered) ser recordado; (believe) tragar; ser creído. **to go down again,** bajar de nuevo; volver a caer. **go Dutch,** ir a escote, ir a la gringa, ir a la par, ir a limón. **to go far,** ir lejos; influir mucho (en); impresionar mucho; (contribute) contribuir (a). **to go for,** (seek) ir en busca de; procurar tener; (attack) echarse encima de, atacar. **to go for a ride (by car, bicycle, on horseback),** dar un paseo (en coche, en bicicleta, a caballo). **to go forth,** salir; publicarse. **to go forward,** adelantar, avanzar; progresar; continuar; (happen) tener lugar. **to go from,** dejar, abandonar; separarse de, apartarse de; marcharse de. **to go in,** entrar en; (a railway carriage, etc.) subir a; (compete) concurrir. **to go in again,** volver a entrar en, entrar de nuevo en. **to go in and out,** entrar y salir; ir y venir. **to go in for,** entrar a buscar; dedicarse a, entregarse a; (buy) comprarse; tomar parte en; (an examination) tomar (un examen); (for a competition) entrar en (un concurso); (try) ensayar; arriesgar. **to go into,** entrar en; examinar; investigar; ocuparse con. **to go near,** acercarse a. **to go off,** marcharse; (explode) estallar; (of firearms) dispararse; (of the voice, etc.) perder (la voz, etc.); (run away) huir, fugarse. **to go off badly,** salir mal, fracasar, no tener éxito. **to go off well,** salir bien, tener éxito. **to go on,** subirse a; continuar; durar; avanzar; proseguir su marcha; progresar; prosperar; *Theat.* entrar en escena; (of clothes) ponerse; (rely on) apoyarse en. **Don't go on like that,** No seas así, No te pongas así. **This glove will not go on me,** No puedo ponerme este guante. **to be gone on a person,** *Inf.* estar loco por. **I went on to say...,** Después dije; Continuando mi discurso dije... **It was going on for six o'clock**

when... Serían alrededor de las seis cuando... **He is going on for fifty,** Raya en los cincuenta años. **to go on foot,** ir a pie. **to go on with,** continuar con; empezar. **to go out,** salir; (descend) bajar; (of fires, lights) extinguirse, apagarse; (of fashion, etc.) pasar (de); (the tide) menguar; (retire) retirarse; (in society) frecuentar la alta sociedad; (die) morir; (arouse) excitar. **to go out of fashion,** pasar de moda. **to go out of one's way (to),** dejar su camino (para); (lose oneself) perder el camino, extraviarse; (take trouble) desvivirse (por), tomarse molestia (para). **to go over,** cruzar; pasar por encima; (to another party or to the other side) pasarse a; (read) repasar; examinar. **to go past,** pasar; pasar en frente de. **to go round,** dar la vuelta a; (revolve) girar; (surround) rodear; (of news, etc.) divulgarse; (be enough) ser suficiente para todos. **to go through,** ir por, pasar por; recorrer; (pierce) penetrar, atravesar; (examine) examinar; (suffer) padecer, sufrir; (experience) experimentar; (live) vivir; (of time) pasar; (of money) malgastar, derrochar. **to go through with,** llevar a cabo, terminar. **to go to,** ir a, encaminarse a; (a person) acercarse a, dirigirse a; (help, be useful) servir para; (be meant for) destinarse a; (rise of price) subir a; (find) encontrar; (of a bid) subir una apuesta hasta. **to go to war,** declarar la guerra. **to go together,** ir juntos (juntas). **to go toward,** encaminarse hacia; ir hacia; (help) ayudar a. **to go under,** pasar por debajo de; (sink) hundirse; (fail) fracasar; (be bankrupt) arruinarse, declararse en quiebra; (the name of) hacerse pasar por. **to go up,** subir, ir arriba; (a tree) trepar; (a ladder, etc.) subir; (a river) ir río arriba; (to town) ir a; (explode) estallar. **to go up and down,** subir y bajar; oscilar; ir de una parte a otra. **to go upon,** subirse a; (rely on) apoyarse en; obrar según; emprender. **to go upstairs,** ir arriba; (to another story, as in a flat) subir al otro piso; subir la escalera. **to go up to,** acercarse a; (of a bid) subir una apuesta hasta. **to go with,** acompañar; (agree with) estar de acuerdo con; (of principles) seguir, ser fiel a; (harmonize) armonizar con; (be suitable to) ir bien con; convenir a; (*Inf.* get along) ir. **to go without,** marcharse sin; (lack) pasarse sin. **It goes without saying that...,** Huelga decir que **Where are you going with this?** (What do you mean?) ¿A dónde quieres llegar con esto?

go /gou/ *n* (fashion) moda, boga, *f;* (happening) suceso, *m;* (fix) apuro, *m;* (energy) energía, *f,* empuje, brío, *m;* (turn) turno, *m;* (attempt) tentativa, *f;* (action) movimiento, *m,* acción, *f;* (bargain) acuerdo, *m.* **It's a go!** (agreed) ¡Trato hecho! ¡Acordado! ¡Entendidos! ¡Entendidas! **It is all the go,** Hace furor, Es la gran moda. **It is no go,** No puede ser, Es imposible. **Now it's my go,** Ahora me toca a mí, Ahora es mi turno. **on the go,** en movimiento; entre manos; ocupado. **to have a go,** probar suerte; procurar, tratar de; tener un turno

goad /goud/ *n* garrocha, aguijada, *f*, aguijón, *m; Fig.* acicate, estímulo, *m.* —*vt* aguijar, picar; *Fig.* incitar, estimular, empujar. **prick with a g.,** aguijonazo, *m*

go-ahead /'gou ə,hɛd/ *a* emprendedor; progresivo

goal /goul/ *n* (posts in football, etc.) meta, portería, *f;* (score) gol, *m;* (in racing) meta, *f;* (destination) destinación, *f; Fig.* ambición, *f;* (purpose, objective) fin, objeto, *m.* **to score a g.,** marcar un gol. **g.-keeper,** guardameta, *m,* portero (-ra). **g.-post,** palo de la portería, *m*

goat /gout/ *n* cabra, *f; Astron.* capricornio, *m.* **he-g.,** cabrón, *m.* **young g.,** cabrito, *m,* chivo (-va). **g.-herd,** cabrero, *m.* **g. skin,** piel de cabra, *f;* (wineskin) odre, *m*

goatee /gou'ti/ *n* pera, perilla, *f*

gobble /'gɒbəl/ *vt* and *vi* engullir, tragar. —*vi* (of turkey) gluglutear. —*n* glugluteo, *m,* voz del pavo, *f*

go-between /'gou bɪ,twin/ *n* trotaconventos, *f;* alcahuete, *m;* (mediator) medianero (-ra)

goblet /'gɒblɪt/ *n* copa, *f*

goblin /'gɒblɪn/ *n* trasgo, duende, *m*

go-cart /'gou ,kart/ *n* andaderas, *f pl;* pollera, *f;* cochecito de niño, *m*

god /gɒd/ *n* dios, *m; pl* **gods,** dioses, *m pl;* (in a theater) público del paraíso, *m;* paraíso, *m.* **By God!** ¡Vive Dios! **For God's sake,** ¡Por el amor de Dios!; ¡Por Dios! **Please God,** ¡Plegue a Dios! **Thank God!** ¡Gracias a Dios! **God Bless You!** (to someone who has sneezed) ¡Jesús! **God forbid!** ¡No lo quiera Dios! **God grant it!** ¡Dios lo quiera! **God keep you!** ¡Dios le guarde! ¡Vaya Vd. con Dios! **God willing,** Dios mediante. **My father, God rest his soul, was...,** Mi padre, que Dios perdone, era...

godchild /'gɒd,tʃaɪld/ *n* ahijado (-da)

goddaughter /'gɒd,dɔtər/ *n* ahijada, *f*

goddess /'gɒdɪs/ *n* diosa, *f; Poet.* dea, *f*

godfather /'gɒd,faðər/ *n* padrino, *m.* **to be a g. to,** ser padrino de, sacar de pila (a)

godfearing /'gɒd,fɪərɪŋ/ *a* timorato, temeroso de Dios; religioso

godforsaken /'gɒdfər,seikən/ *a* dejado de la mano de Dios; (of places) remoto, solitario

Godhead /'gɒd,hɛd/ *n* divinidad, *f*

godless /'gɒdlɪs/ *a* impío, irreligioso; sin Dios

godlessness /'gɒdlɪsnɪs/ *n* impiedad, irreligiosidad, *f*

godlike /'gɒd,laik/ *a* divino

godliness /'gɒdlɪnɪs/ *n* piedad, *f;* santidad, *f*

godly /'gɒdli/ *a* devoto, piadoso, religioso

godmother /'gɒd,mʌðər/ *n* madrina, *f.*

fairy g., hada madrina, *f.* **to be a g. to,** ser madrina de

godparent /'gɒd,pɛərənt/ *n* padrino, *m;* madrina, *f pl.* **godparents,** padrinos, *m pl*

godsend /'gɒd,sɛnd/ *n* bien, *m;* buena suerte, *f;* fortuna, *f*

go-getter /'gou ,gɛtər/ *n* buscavidas, *mf*

goggle /'gɒgəl/ *n* mirada fija, *f; pl* **goggles,** anteojos, *m pl,* gafas, *f pl;* (of a horse) anteojeras, *f pl.* —*vi* mirar fijamente; salirse a uno los ojos de la cabeza. **g.-eyed,** de ojos saltones. **g.-eyes,** ojos saltones, *m pl*

going /'gouɪŋ/ *n* ida, *f;* (departure) partida, marcha, *f;* salida, *f;* (pace) paso, *m;* (speed) velocidad, *f.* **It was heavy g.,** El avance era lento; El progreso era lento; (of parties, etc.) Era aburrido. **The g. was difficult on those mountainous roads,** El conducir (o el ir o el andar) era difícil en aquellos caminos de montaña. **g. back,** vuelta, *f,* regreso, *m.* **g. down,** bajada, *f,* descenso, *m;* (of the sun, etc.) puesta, *f.* **g. forward,** avance, *m;* progreso, *m.* **g. in,** entrada, *f.* **g. in and out,** idas y venidas, *f pl.* **g. out,** salida, *f;* (of a fire, light) apagamiento, *m*

going /'gouɪŋ/ *a* and *pres part* que va, yendo; que funciona. **G., g., gone** (at an auction) A la una, a las dos, a las tres.

goings-on, (tricks) trapujos, *m pl;* (conduct) conducta, *f.* **g. concern,** empresa próspera, *f.* **g. to,** con destino a

going-away present /'gouɪŋ ə,wei/ *n* regalo de despedida, *m*

goiter /'gɔitər/ *n* bocio, *m*

gold /gould/ *n* oro, *m;* color de oro, *m.* —*a* de oro; áureo. **All that glitters is not g.,** No es oro todo lo que reluce. **cloth of g.,** tela de oro, *f.* **dull g.,** oro mate, *m.* **light g.,** oro pálido, *m.* **old g.,** oro viejo, *m.* **g.-beater,** batidor de oro, *m.* **g.-digger,** minero de oro, *m;* (woman) aventurera, *f.* **g. dust,** oro en polvo, *m.* **g.-fever,** fiebre de oro, *f.* **g. lace,** galón de oro, *m.* **g. lacquer,** sisa dorada, *f.* **g. leaf,** pan de oro, oro batido, *m.* **g. mine,** mina de oro, *f.* **g. piece,** moneda de oro, *f.* **g. plate,** vajilla de oro, *f.* **g. standard,** patrón oro, *m.* **g.-thread,** hilo de oro, *m.* **g.-yielding,** *a* aurífero

golden /'gouldən/ *a* de oro; dorado; áureo; amarillo; *Fig.* feliz; excelente. **to become g.,** dorarse. **g. age,** edad de oro, *f.* **g.-crested wren,** abadejo, *m.* **g. hair,** cabellos dorados (or de oro), *m pl.* **G. Legend,** leyenda áurea, *f.* **g. mean,** justo medio, *m.* **g. rose,** rosa de oro, *f.* **g. rule,** regla áurea, *f.* **g. syrup,** jarabe de arce, *m.* **g. voice,** voz de oro, *f.* **g. wedding,** bodas de oro, *f pl*

goldfish /'gould,fɪʃ/ *n* carpa dorada, *f.* **g. bowl,** pecera, *f*

goldsmith /'gould,smɪθ/ *n* orfebre, oribe, orífice, *m*

golf /gɒlf/ *n* golf, *m.* **g.-club,** (stick) palo

de golf, *m;* (organization) club de golf, *m.*
g.-course, campo de golf, *m*

golfer /'gɒlfər/ *n* jugador (-ra) de golf

gone /gɒn/ *a* and *past part* ido; (lost)
perdido; (ruined) arruinado; (dead)
muerto; (past) pasado; (disappeared)
desaparecido; (fainted) desmayado; (sup-
pressed) suprimido; (pregnant) encinta;
(drunk) borracho; (ended) terminado;
(exhausted) agotado; (ill) enfermo. **far
g.,** avanzado; (in years) de edad avanzada; (of illness) cerca de la muerte, muy
enfermo; (in love) loco de amor; (drunk)
muy borracho. **It is all g.,** No hay más. **It
is g. seven o'clock,** Son las siete y pico,
Son las siete ya

gonorrhea /,gɒnə'riə/ *n* gonorrea, *f*

good /gʊd/ *a* bueno (before *m sing
nouns*) buen; agradable; afortunado; (appropriate) apropiado, oportuno; (beneficial) provechoso, ventajoso; (wholesome)
sano, saludable; (suitable) apto; (useful)
útil; (kind) bondadoso; (much) mucho;
(obliging) amable; (virtuous) virtuoso;
(skilled) experto; (fresh) fresco; (genuine)
genuino, legítimo; verdadero. *—adv* bien.
—interj ¡bueno! ¡bien! **a g. deal,** mucho.
a g. many, bastantes. **a g. turn,** un favor. **a g. way,** (distance) un buen trecho;
mucho. **a g. while,** un buen rato. **as g.
as,** tan bueno como. **Be so g. as to...!**
Haga el favor de, Tenga Vd. la bondad de
(followed by infin.). **fairly g.,** *a* bastante
bueno. *—adv* bastante bien. **I'm g. for
another five miles,** Tengo fuerzas para
cinco millas más. **It was g. of you to do
it,** Vd. fue muy amable de hacerlo, Vd.
tuvo mucha bondad de hacerlo. **to be no
g. at this sort of thing,** no servir para
tales cosas. **to have a g. time,** pasarlo
bien. **to make g.,** reparar; indemnizar;
(accomplish) llevar a cabo, poner en práctica; justificar; (a promise) cumplir. **very
g.,** *a* muy bueno. *—adv* muy bien. **g.-
feeling,** buena voluntad, *f.* **g.-
fellowship,** compañerismo, *m;* buena
compañía, *f.* **g.-for-nothing,** *n* papanatas,
badulaque, *m.* **to be g.-for-nothing,** no
servir para nada. **g. luck,** buena suerte, *f.*
g. manners, buenos modales, *m pl;*
buena crianza, educación, *f.* **g. nature,**
buen natural, *m;* buen humor, *m.* **g.-
natured,** de buen natural; de buen humor, bonachón. **g. offices,** buenos oficios, *m pl.* **g.-tempered,** de buen humor

good /gʊd/ *n* bien, *m;* provecho, *m;* utilidad, *f; pl* **goods.** See separate entry. **I
am saying this for your g.,** Lo digo para
tu bien. **Much g. may it do you!** ¡Buen
provecho te haga! **for g. and all,** para
siempre jamás. **It is no g.,** Es inútil; No
vale la pena. **the g.,** el bien; (people) los
buenos. **They have gone for g.,** Se han
marchado para no volver. **to do one g.,**
hacer bien a uno; mejorar; ser provechoso (a uno); (suit) sentar bien (a uno).
What is the g. of...? ¿Para qué sirve...?;
¿Qué vale...? **g. and evil,** el bien y el mal

good-bye /,gʊd 'bai/ *interj* ¡adiós! *—n*
adiós, *m,* despedida, *f.* **to bid g.-b.,** decir
adiós. **G.-b. for the present!** ¡Hasta la
vista! ¡Hasta luego! **G.-b. until tomorrow, then,** Hasta mañana pues, adiós,
Hasta mañana entonces

goodness /'gʊdnɪs/ *n* bondad, *f;* (of
quality) buena calidad, *f;* (of persons)
amabilidad, benevolencia, *f;* (essence) esencia, substancia, *f;* bien, *m:* excelencia,
f; interj ¡Jesús! ¡Dios mío! **For g. sake!**
¡Por Dios! **I wish to g. that,** ¡Ojalá
que...!

goods /gʊdz/ *n pl* bienes, efectos, *m pl;*
artículos, *m pl; Com.* mercancías, *f pl,*
géneros, *m pl.* **by g.-train,** en pequeña
velocidad. **stolen g.,** objetos robados, *m
pl.* **g. lift,** montacargas, *m.* **g. office,** depósito de mercancías, *m.* **g. station,** estación de carga, *f.* **g.-train,** tren de mercancías, *m.* **g. van,** furgón, *m.* **g. wagon,**
vagón de mercancías, *m*

goodwill /'gʊd'wɪl/ *n* benevolencia, *f;*
buena voluntad, *f;* (of a business) clientela, *f*

goose /gus/ *n* oca, *f,* ganso (-sa); plancha
de sastre, *f. —a* de oca. **g.-flesh,** *Fig.*
carne de gallina, *f.* **g. girl,** ansarera, *f.* **g.-
step,** paso de oca, *m*

gooseberry /'gus,beri/ *n* uva espina, *f*

gore /gɔr/ *n* sangre, *f; Sew.* sesga, nesga,
f. —vt acornear; desgarrar; herir (con
arma blanca)

gorge /gɔrdʒ/ *n* (valley) cañón, barranco,
m; (heavy meal) comilona, *f,* atracón, *m.*
—vt engullir, tragar. *—vi* hartarse, atracarse

gorgeous /'gɔrdʒəs/ *a* magnífico; espléndido, suntuoso; *Inf.* maravilloso, estupendo

gorilla /gə'rɪlə/ *n* gorila, *m*

gormandize /'gɔrmən,daiz/ *vi* glotonear

gory /'gɔri/ *a* ensangrentado; sangriento

gosh /gɒʃ/ *interj* ¡caray! ¡caramba!

gospel /'gɒspəl/ *n* evangelio, *m;* doctrina, *f.* **The G. according to St. Mark,**
El Evangelio según San Marcos. **to believe as g. truth,** creer como si fuese el
evangelio. **to preach the G.,** predicar el
evangelio

gossamer /'gɒsəmər/ *n* hilo de araña, *m,*
red de araña, telaraña, *f;* (filmy material)
gasa, *f;* hilo finísimo, *m, a* de gasa; sutil,
delgado, fino

gossip /'gɒsəp/ *n* murmurador (-ra), chismoso (-sa), hablador (-ra); (scandal)
chisme, *m;* habladuría, murmuración, *f;*
(obsolete, of a woman) comadre, *f;* (talk)
charla, *f. —vi* charlar, conversar; (in bad
sense) murmurar, chismear; criticar. **to
g. about,** charlar de; poner lenguas en,
cortar un sayo (a); hablar mal de. **g. column,** gacetilla, *f*

gouge /gaʊdʒ/ *n* gubia, *f. —vt* escoplear.
to g. out, vaciar; sacar

gourd /gɔrd/ *n* calabaza, *f*

gourmand /gʊr'mɒnd/ *n* glotón, *m*

gourmet /gʊr'mei/ *n* gastrónomo, *m*

gout /gaut/ n Med. gota, f

govern /'gʌvərn/ vt gobernar; regir; (guide) guiar; dominar; domar, refrenar; Gram. regir; (regulate) regular

governess /'gʌvərnɪs/ n institutriz, f; (in a school) maestra, f

governing /'gʌvərnɪŋ/ a gobernante; director; (with principle, etc.) directivo. —n See government

government /'gʌvərnmənt, -ərmənt/ n gobierno, m; dirección, f; autoridad, f. **g. bond,** bono del gobierno, m. **g. house,** palacio del gobernador, m. **g. office,** oficina del gobierno, f. **g. stock,** papel del Estado, m

governmental /,gʌvərn'mɛntḷ, ,gʌvər-/ a gubernamental, gubernativo

Government Printing Office Talleres Gráficos de la Nación, m pl

governor /'gʌvərnər/ n gobernador (-ra); vocal de la junta de gobierno, mf, (of a prison) director (-ra) (de una prisión); Mech. regulador, m. **g.-general,** gobernador general, m

gown /gaun/ n toga, f; (cassock) sotana, f; (dressing-g.) bata, f; (for sleeping) camisa de noche, f; (bathing-wrap) albornoz, m; (dress) vestido, traje, m

grab /græb/ n asimiento, m, presa, f; Mech. gancho, m, —vt arrebatar, asir, agarrar; Fig. alzarse con, tomar

grace /greis/ n elegancia, f; simetría, armonía, f; gracia, gentileza, f; donaire, m; encanto, m; (goodness) bondad, f; gracia, f; merced, f; favor, m; (period of time) plazo, m; (privilege) privilegio, m; Theol. gracia divina, f; (at table) bendición de la mesa, f; (as a title) excelentísimo, (to an archbishop) ilustrísimo. —vt adornar; favorecer; honrar. **airs and graces,** humos, m pl. **the Three Graces,** las Gracias. **three days' g.,** plazo de tres días, m. **to get into a person's good graces,** congraciarse con; caer en gracia con. **to say g.,** bendecir la mesa. **with a bad g.,** a regañadientes. **with a good g.,** de buena gana. **g.-note,** Mus. nota de adorno, f

graceful /'greisfəl/ a airoso, gentil, gracioso; elegante; bonito

graceless /'greislɪs/ a réprobo; dejado de la mano de Dios; sin gracia

gracious /'greiʃəs/ a (merciful) piadoso, clemente; (urbane) afable, condescendiente, agradable. **Good g.!** ¡Vamos!, ¡Dios mío!

graciously /'greiʃəsli/ adv afablemente; con benevolencia. **to be g. pleased,** tener a bien

graciousness /'greiʃəsnɪs/ n amabilidad, afabilidad, condescendencia, f

gradation /grei'deiʃən/ n graduación, f; Mus. gradación, f; paso gradual, m; serie, f

grade /greid/ n grado, m; (quality) calidad, clase, f; (in a school) clase, f; (gradient) pendiente, f, declive, m. —vt graduar, clasificar; (cattle breeding) cru-

zar. **down g.,** cuesta abajo. **up g.,** cuesta arriba. **highest g.,** n primera clase, f. —a de primera clase; de calidad excelente

gradient /'greidiənt/ n declive, m. cuesta, pendiente, f

gradual /'grædʒuəl/ a gradual. —n Eccl. gradual, m

gradually /'grædʒuəli/ adv gradualmente; poco a poco

graduate / n, a 'grædʒuɪt; v -,eit/ n licenciado (-da). —a graduado. —vt graduar. —vi graduarse; (as a doctor) doctorarse. **to g. as,** recibirse de

graduation /,grædʒu'eiʃən/ n graduación, f

graft /græft/ n Bot. injerto, m; Surg. injerto de piel, m; (swindle) estafa, f; (bribery) soborno, m. —vt Bot. injertar; Surg. injertar un trozo de piel; Fig. inferir

grain /grein/ n (corn) grano, m; (cereal) cereal, m, or f; (seed, weight) grano, m; (trace) pizca, f; (of wood, etc.) hila, m, fibra, hebra, veta, f; (of leather) flor, f; (texture) textura, f. —vt granear; granular; (wood, marble, etc.) vetear. **against the g.,** a contrapelo. **g. lands,** mieses, f pl

gram /græm/ n gramo, m

grammar /'græmər/ n gramática, f. **g. school,** instituto de segunda enseñanza, m

grammatically /grə'mætɪkəli/ adv gramaticalmente, como la gramática lo quiere. (e.g., She now speaks Catalan g., Ahora habla el catalán como la gramática lo quiere)

granary /'greinəri/ n granero, hórreo, m, troj, f. **g. keeper,** trojero, m

grand /grænd/ a magnífico, soberbio; imponente; (of dress) espléndido, vistoso; (of people) distinguido, importante; aristocrático; (proud) orgulloso; (of style) elevado, sublime; (morally) noble; augusto; (main) principal; (full) completo; Inf. estupendo, magnífico; (with duke, etc.) gran. —n piano de cola, m. **g.-aunt,** tía abuela, f. **g. cross,** gran cruz, f. **g. duchess,** gran duquesa, f. **g. duke,** gran duque, m. **g. lodge,** (of freemasons) Gran Oriente, m. **g. master,** gran maestre, m. **g.-nephew,** resobrino, m. **g.-niece,** resobrina, f. **g. opera,** ópera, f. **g. piano,** piano de cola, m. **g.-stand,** tribuna, f. **g.-uncle,** tío abuelo, m. **g. vizier,** gran visir, m

grandchild /'græn,tʃaild/ n nieto (-ta). **great-g.,** bisnieto (-ta). **great-great-g.,** tataranieto (-ta)

granddaughter /'græn,dɔtər/ n nieta, f. **great-g.,** bisnieta, f. **great-great-g.,** tataranieta, f

grandeur /'grændʒər/ n magnificencia, f; grandiosidad, f; magnitud, grandeza, f; (pomp) pompa, f, fausto, m

grandfather /'græn,faðər/ n abuelo, m. **great-g.,** bisabuelo, m. **great-great-g.,** tatarabuelo, m

grandiloquent /græn'dɪləkwənt/ *a* grandilocuo

grandiose /'grændɪ,ous/ *a* grandioso, sublime; impresionante; imponente; (in a bad sense) extravagante: (of style) bombástico, hinchado

grand jury *n* jurado de acusación, jurado de jucio, *m*

grandmother /'græn,mʌðər/ *n* abuela, *f*. **great-g.,** bisabuela, *f*. **great-great-g.,** tatarabuela, *f*

grandness /'grændnɪs/ *n* magnificencia, *f*; aristocracia, *f*; (pride) orgullo, *m*; grandiosidad, *f*; (of style) sublimidad, *f*; (of character) nobleza, *f*

grandparent /'græn,pɛərənt/ *n* abuelo, *m*; abuela, *f*; *pl* **grandparents,** abuelos, *m pl*. **great-great-grandparents,** bisabuelos, *m pl*. **great-great-grandparents,** tatarabuelos, *m pl*

grandson /'græn,sʌn/ *n* nieto, *m*. **great-g.,** bisnieto, *m*. **great-great-g.,** tataranieto, *m*

granny /'græni/ *n* abuelita, nana, *f*; abuela, *f*. **g. knot,** nudo al revés, *m*

grant /grænt/ *n* concesión, *f*; otorgamiento, *m*; donación, *f*; privilegio, *m*; (for study) beca, bolsa de estudio, *f*; (transfer) traspaso, *m*, cesión, *f*. —*vt* conceder; (bestow) otorgar, dar; donar; (agree to) acceder a, asentir en; permitir; (transfer) traspasar; (assume) suponer. **to g. a degree,** expedir un título. **to g. a motion,** dar por entrada a una moción. **to take for granted,** descontar; dar por hecho, dar por sentado. **God g. it!** ¡Dios lo quiera! **granted that,** dado que

granulated /'grænyə,leitɪd/ *a* granulado

grape /greip/ *n* uva, *f*. **bunch of grapes,** racimo de uvas, *m*. **muscatel g.,** uva moscatel, *f*. **sour grapes,** uvas agrias, *f pl*; (phrase) ¡están verdes! **g.-fruit,** toronja, *f*. **g. gatherer,** vendimiador (-ra). **g. harvest,** vendimia, *f*. **g. juice,** mosto, *m*. **g.-shot,** metralla, *f*. **g. stone,** granuja, *f*. **g.-sugar,** glucosa, *f*. **g.-vine,** vid, parra, *f*

graph /græf/ *n* gráfica, *f*; diagrama, *m*

graphic /'græfɪk/ *a* gráfico

grapple /'græpəl/ *n Naut.* rezón, arpeo, *m*; lucha a brazo partido, *f*. —*vt Naut.* aferrar; asir, agarrar. —*vi Naut.* aferrarse. **to g. with,** luchar a brazo partido (con); *Fig.* luchar con

grasp /græsp/ *n* agarro, *m*; (reach) alcance, *m*; (of a hand) apretón, *m*; (power) garras, *f pl*, poder, *m*; (understanding) comprensión, *f*, inteligencia, capacidad intelectual, *f*. —*vt* agarrar, asir; empuñar; abrazar; *Fig.* comprender, alcanzar; (a hand) estrechar. —*vi* agarrarse. **within one's g.,** al alcance de uno. **to g. at,** asirse de

grasping /'græspɪŋ/ *n* asimiento, *m*; (understanding) comprensión, *f*, *a* codicioso, tacaño, mezquino

grass /græs/ *n* hierba, *f*; (pasture) pasto, herbaje, *m*; (sward) césped, *m*. —*vt* cubrir de hierba; sembrar de hierba; apacentar. **to hear the g. grow,** sentir crecer la hierba. **to let the g. grow,** *Fig.* dejar crecer la hierba. **to turn out to g.,** echar al pasto. **g.-blade,** brizna de hierba, *f*. **g.-green,** *a* and *n* verde como la hierba *m*.. **g.-grown,** cubierto de hierba. **g.-land,** pradera, *f*. **g.-snake,** culebra *f*. **g. widow,** mujer cuyo marido está ausente

grasshopper /'græs,hopər/ *n* saltamontes, *m*. **grasshopper's chirp,** chirrido (del saltamontes), *m*

grassy /'græsi/ *a* parecido a la hierba, como la hierba; cubierto de hierba; de hierba

grate /greit/ *n* parrilla, *f*; (grating) reja, *f*. —*vt* raspar, raer; *Cul.* rallar; (make a noise) hacer rechinar. —*vi* rozar; rechinar, chirriar. **to g. on, upon,** (of sounds) irritar, molestar; chocar con. **to g. on the ear,** herir el oído

grateful /'greitfəl/ *a* agradecido, reconocido; (pleasant) agradable, grato

gratefulness /'greitfəlnɪs/ *n* agradecimiento, *m*, gratitud, *f*; (pleasantness) agrado, *m*

grater /'greitər/ *n Cul.* rallador, *m*

gratification /,grætəfɪ'keiʃən/ *n* satisfacción, *f*; (pleasure) placer, gusto, *m*

gratified /'grætə,faid/ *a* satisfecho, contento

gratify /'grætə,fai/ *vt* satisfacer; (please) gratificar, agradar

gratifying /'grætə,faiŋ/ *a* satisfactorio, agradable

grating /'greitiŋ/ *n* reja, *f*; rejilla, *f*; *Naut.* jareta, *f*; (optics) retículo, *m*; (sound) rechinamiento, chirrido, *m*. —*a* rechinante, chirriador; áspero

gratis /'grætis/ *a* and *adv* gratis

gratitude /'græti,tud/ *n* agradecimiento, *m*, gratitud, *f*

gratuitous /grə'tuitəs/ *a* gratuito

gratuity /grə'tuiti/ *n* gratificación, propina, *f*

grave /greiv/ *n* (hole) sepultura, fosa, *f*; (monument) tumba, *f*, sepulcro, *m*; *Fig.* muerte, *f*. **g.-digger,** enterrador, sepulturero, *m*

grave /*a* greiv; *n* grɒv/ *a* grave; importante; serio; sobrio; (anxious) preocupado; (of accent) grave. —*n* (grave accent) acento grave, *m*

gravel /'grævəl/ *n* grava, *f*; cascajo, casquijo, *m*; *Med.* arenillas, *f pl*, cálculo, *m*

Graves' disease /greivz/ *n* bocio exoftálmico, *m*

gravitate /'grævɪ,teit/ *vi* gravitar; tender

gravity /'græviti/ *n Phys.* gravedad, *f*; seriedad, *f*; solemnidad, *f*; gravedad, *f*; (weight) peso, *m*; importancia, *f*; (enormity) enormidad, *f*; (danger) peligro, *m*. **center of g.,** centro de gravedad, *m*. **law of g.,** ley de la gravedad, *f*. **specific g.,** peso específico, *m*

gravy /'greivi/ n salsa, f; jugo (de la carne), m. **g.-boat**, salsera, f

gray /grei/ a gris; (of animals) rucio. —n color gris, gris, m; caballo gris, m. **His hair is turning g.**, El pelo se le vuelve gris. **g.-haired**, de pelo gris. **g. matter**, materia gris, f; cacumen, m. **g. mullet**, *Ichth*. mújol, m. **g. squirrel**, gris, m. **g. wolf**, lobo gris, m

grayish /'greiʃ/ a grisáceo, agrisado; (of hair) entrecano

graze /greiz/ n abrasión, f; (brush) roce, m, vi pacer, apacentarse. —vt pastorear, apacentar; (brush) rozar

grazing /'greiziŋ/ n *Agr.* apacentamiento, pastoreo, m; (brushing) rozadura, f. —a que pace, herbívoro; (of land) pacedero. **g. land**, pasto, m

grease /gris/ n grasa, f; (dirt) mugre, f; (of a candle) sebo, m, cera, f. —vt engrasar; manchar con grasa; *Fig. Inf.* untar. **to g. the wheels**, *Fig.* untar el carro. **g.-box**, *Mech.* caja de sebo, f. **g.-gun**, engrasador de compresión, m. **g.-paint**, afeites de actor (or de actriz), m pl. **g.-proof paper**, papel impermeable, m. **g. spot**, lámpara, mancha de grasa, f, saín, m

greasy /'grisi/ a grasiento; (oily) aceitoso; (grubby) mugriento, bisunto; *Fig.* lisonjero. **g. pole**, cucaña, f

great /greit/ a gran; grande; enorme; vasto; (much) mucho; (famous) famoso, ilustre; noble, sublime; (intimate) íntimo; importante; principal; poderoso; magnífico, impresionante; *Inf.* famoso, estupendo; (of time) largo; (clever) fuerte. **Alexander the G.**, Alejandro Magno. **the G. Mogul**, el Gran Mogul. **a g. deal**, mucho. **a g. man**, un grande hombre, un hombre famoso. **a g. many**, muchos (muchas). **He lived to a g. age**, Vivió hasta una edad avanzada. **so g.**, tan grande, tamaño. **the g.**, los grandes hombres. **g. on**, aficionado a. **g.-aunt**, tía abuela, f. **g.-grandchild**, etc. See **grandchild**, etc. **g.-hearted**, valeroso; magnánimo, generoso. **g. power**, gran poder, m. **G. War**, Gran Guerra, f. **the Great Schism**, el Gran Cisma, m

greater /'greitər/ a comp. of **great**, mayor; más grande. **to make g.**, agrandar. **G. London**, el Gran Londres, m

greatest /'greitist/ a sup. of **great**, más grande; mayor; máximo; más famoso; sumo

greatly /'greitli/ adv mucho; con mucho; (very) muy; noblemente

greatness /'greitnis/ n grandeza, f; grandiosidad, f; extensión, vastedad, f; importancia, f; poder, m; majestad, f; esplendor, m; (intensity) intensidad, f; (enormity) enormidad, f

Greece /gris/ Grecia, f

greed /grid/ n (cupidity) codicia, rapacidad, avaricia, f; avidez, ansia, f; (of food) gula, glotonería, f

greedy /'gridi/ a (for food) glotón; codicioso; ambicioso; ávido; deseoso

Greek /grik/ a and n griego (-ga); (language) griego, m. **It's all G. to me**, Para mí es como si fuese en latín, Me es chino. **G. tunic**, peplo, m

green /grin/ a verde; (inexpert) inexperto, bisoño; (recent) nuevo, reciente; (fresh) fresco; (of complexion) pálido, descolorido; (flowery) floreciente; (vigorous) lozano; (young) joven; (unripe) verde; (credulous) crédulo; (raw) crudo; (of wood, vegetables) verde. —n verde, color verde, m; (vegetables) verdura, f; (meadow) prado, m; (turf) césped, m; (grass) hierba, f; (bowling) campo de juego, m. —vt teñir (or pintar) de verde. **bright g.**, n verdegay, verde claro, m. **dark g.**, n verdinegro, m. **light g.**, n verde pálido, m. **to grow** or **look g.**, verdear. **g.-eyed**, de ojos verdes. **g. peas**, guisantes, m pl. **g. table**, tapete verde, m

greenery /'grinəri/ n follaje, m; verdura, f

greenhorn /'grin,hɔrn/ n bisoño (-ña); papanatas, m

greenhouse /'grin,haus/ n invernáculo, invernadero, m

greenish /'griniʃ/ a verdoso. **g.-yellow**, cetrino

greet /grit/ vt saludar; recibir; (express pleasure) dar la bienvenida (a)

greeting /'gritiŋ/ n salutación, f, saludo, m; recepción, f; (welcome) bienvenida, f; pl **greetings**, recuerdos, m pl

gregarious /gri'gɛəriəs/ a gregario

grenade /grɪ'neid/ n granada, bomba, f. **hand-g.**, bomba de mano, f

grey /grei/ See **gray**

greyhound /'grei,haund/ n galgo, lebrel, m. **g. bitch**, galga, f; **g. racing**, carreras de galgos, f pl

grid /grɪd/ n (of electric power) red, f; rejilla, f; (for water, etc.) alcantarilla, f

gridiron /'grɪd,aiərn/ n *Cul.* parrilla, f; (of electric power) red, f; *Theat.* telar, m

grief /grif/ n angustia, pena, aflicción, f; dolor, suplicio, m. **to come to g.**, pasarlo mal, tener un desastre

grievance /'grivəns/ n injusticia, f; motivo de queja, m

grieve /griv/ vt entristecer, afligir, angustiar; atormentar. —vi entristecerse, afligirse, acongojarse. **to g. for**, lamentar; echar de menos

grievous /'grivəs/ a (heavy) oneroso, gravoso; opresivo; doloroso, penoso; lamentable; cruel. **g. error**, error lamentable

grill /grɪl/ n *Cul.* parrilla, f; (grating) rejilla, f; (before a window) reja, f; (food) asado a la parrilla, m. —vt *Cul.* asar a la parrilla; (burn) quemar; (question) interrogar; (torture) torturar. —vi *Cul.* asarse a la parrilla; (be burnt) quemarse. **g.-room**, parrilla, f

grille /grɪl/ n reja, f; rejilla, f; (screen) verja, f

griller /'grɪlər/ n Cul. parrilla, f

grim /grɪm/ a (fierce) feroz, salvaje; (severe) severo, ceñudo, adusto; inflexible; (frightful) horrible

grimace /'grɪməs/ n mueca, f, gesto, mohín, visaje, m. vi hacer muecas

grime /graɪm/ n mugre, f; suciedad, f. **to cover with g.**, enmugrecer

grimly /'grɪmli/ adv severamente; sin sonreír; inflexiblemente; (without retreating) sin cejar; (frightfully) horriblemente; de un modo espantoso

grimy /'graɪmi/ a mugriento, sucio

grin /grɪn/ n sonrisa grande, f; sonrisa burlona, f; (grimace) mueca, f. vi sonreír mostrando los dientes; sonreír bonachonamente; sonreír de un modo burlón

grind /graɪnd/ vt (to powder) pulverizar; moler; (break up) quebrantar; (oppress) agobiar, oprimir; (sharpen) afilar, amolar; (a barrel-organ) tocar (un manubrio); (the teeth) crujir, rechinar (los dientes); (into) reducir a; (Inf. teach) empollar. vi moler; Fig. Inf. trabajar laboriosamente. n Fig. Inf. trabajo pesado, m; n Fig. Inf. estudiantón, m

grinder /'graɪndər/ n (of scissors, etc.) afilador, m; (of an organ) organillero; (mill-stone) piedra de moler, f; (molar) muela, f

grinding /'graɪndɪŋ/ a (tedious) cansado, aburrido; opresivo; (of pain) incesante. n pulverización, f; amoladura, f; (of grain) molienda, f; (polishing) pulimento, bruñido, m; (oppression) opresión, f; (of teeth) rechinamiento, m

grindstone /'graɪnd,stoʊn/ n amoladera, afiladera, piedra de amolar, f. **to have one's nose to the g.**, batir el yunque

grinning /'grɪnɪŋ/ a sonriente, riente; (mocking) burlón

grip /grɪp/ n asimiento, agarro, m; (claws, clutches) garras, f pl; (hand) mano, f; (of shaking hands) apretón de manos, m; (of a weapon, etc.) empuñadura, f; (reach) alcance, m; (understanding) comprensión, f; (control) dominio, m; (bag) portamanteo, m; maleta, f. vt asir, agarrar; (of wheels) agarrarse; Mech. morder; (a sword, etc.) empuñar; (pinch) pellizcar; (surround) cercar; (understand) comprender; (press; to grip the hand and Fig. the heart) apretar; (fill) llenar; (the attention) atraer, llamar; (sway, hold) dominar

gripe /graɪp/ n (Inf. pain) retortijón (de tripas), m

grisly /'grɪzli/ a espantoso; repugnante

grist /grɪst/ n molienda, f. **Everything is g. to their mill**, Sacan partido de todo

gristle /'grɪsəl/ n cartílago, m, ternilla, f

grit /grɪt/ n cascajo, m; polvo, m; Fig. firmeza (de carácter), f; (courage) valor, m; (endurance) aguante, m

gritty /'grɪti/ a arenoso, arenisco

groan /groʊn/ n gemido, m. vi gemir; (creak) crujir. **to g. out**, decir (or contar) entre gemidos. **to g. under**, sufrir bajo, gemir bajo; (of weight) crujir bajo

groaning /'groʊnɪŋ/ n gemidos, m pl. a que gime, gemidor; (under a weight) crujiente

grocer /'groʊsər/ n abacero (-ra) vendedor (-ra) de comestibles. **grocer's shop**, tienda de comestibles, bodega, f

grocery /'groʊsəri/ n tienda de comestibles, tienda de ultramarinos, abarrotería, lonja, bodega, f, negocio de comestibles, m; pl **groceries**, provisiones, f pl, comestibles, m pl

groin /grɔɪn/ n Anat. ingle, f

groom /grum/ n (in a royal household) gentilhombre, m; lacayo, m; mozo de caballos, m; (of a bride) novio, m. vt (a horse) cuidar; (oneself) arreglarse. **She is always well groomed**, Está siempre muy bien arreglada

groove /gruv/ n ranura, muesca, f; estría, f; surco, m; Fig. rutina, f. vt entallar; estriar

grope /groʊp/ vi andar a tientas; (with for) buscar a tientas; procurar, encontrar, buscar. **to g. one's way toward**, avanzar a tientas hacia; Fig. avanzar poco a poco hacia

gropingly /'groʊpɪŋli/ adv a tientas; irresolutamente

gross /groʊs/ n Com. gruesa, f; totalidad, f, a grueso; denso, espeso; (unrefined) grosero; (great) grande; (crass) craso; total; Com. bruto; (tremendous) enorme. **in g.**, en grueso. **g. amount**, total, m; Com. importe bruto, m. **g. weight**, peso bruto, m

grotesque /groʊ'tɛsk/ a grotesco; extravagante, estrambótico; ridículo. n grotesco, m

grotto /'grɒtoʊ/ n gruta, f

ground /graʊnd/ n suelo, m; (of water and Naut.) fondo, m; (earth) tierra, f; Fig. terreno, m; (strata) capa, f; Sports. campo, m; (parade) plaza (de armas), f; (background) fondo, m; (basis) base, f, fundamento, m; (reason) causa, f; motivo, m; (excuse) pretexto, m; (bag) **grounds**, jardines, m pl, parque, m; (sediment) sedimento, m, heces, f pl; (reason) causa, f. vi Naut. varar, encallar. vt poner en tierra; Naut. hacer varar; Elec. conectar con tierra; (base) fundar (en), basar (en); (teach) enseñar los rudimentos (de). a molido; en polvo; (of floors, stories) bajo; (of glass) deslustrado; Bot. terrestre. **common g.**, tierra comunal, f; Fig. tierra común, f. **He is on his own g.**, Está en terreno propio. **It fell to the g.**, Cayó al suelo; Fig. Fracasó. **It is on the g.**, Está en el suelo. **It suits me to the g.**, Me viene de perilla. **to break fresh g.**, Fig. tratar problemas nuevos. **to be well grounded in**, conocer bien los elementos (or rudimentos) de. **to cover g.**, cubrir terreno; recorrer; (in discussion) tocar muchos puntos. **to cut the g. from beneath one's feet,** hacer perder la iniciativa (a). **to give g.,** retroceder; perder terreno. **to raze to the g.,** echar por tierra, arrasar. **to stand one's g.,** resistir el ataque; no darse por vencido; *Fig.* mantenerse firme, mantenerse en sus trece. **to win g.,** ganar terreno. **g. coffee,** café molido, *m.* **g.-color,** (of paint) primera capa, *f.* (color de) fondo, *m;* **g.-floor,** piso bajo, *m.* **g. glass,** vidrio deslustrado, *m.* **g.-ivy,** hiedra terrestre, *f.* **g. nut,** cacahuete, *m.* **g.-plan,** *Archit.* planta, *f.* **g.-rent,** censo, *m.* **g.-sheet,** tela impermeable, *f;* **g. staff,** *Aer.* personal del aeropuerto, *m.* **g.-swell,** mar de fondo, *m*

grounded /ˈgraundɪd/ *a* fundado. **The airplanes are g.,** Los aviones están sin volar. **His suspicions are well g.,** Tiene motivos para sus sospechas

groundless /ˈgraundlɪs/ *a* sin fundamento, inmotivado, sin causa, sin motivo

groundwork /ˈgraund,wɜrk/ *n* fundamento, *m;* base, *f;* principio, *m*

group /grup/ *n* grupo, *m.* —*vt* agrupar. —*vi* agruparse. **g. captain,** coronel de aviación, *m*

grove /grouv/ *n* soto, boscaje, *m;* arboleda, *f*

grovel /ˈgrɒvəl/ *vi* arrastrarse; *Fig.* humillarse

groveling /ˈgrɒvəlɪŋ/ *a Fig.* servil; ruin

grow /grou/ *vi* crecer; (increase) aumentar; (become) hacerse; empezar a, llegar a; (turn) volverse, ponerse; (flourish) progresar, adelantar; (develop) desarrollarse; (extend) extenderse. —*vt* cultivar; dejar crecer. **I grew to fear it,** Llegué a temerlo. **to g. cold,** ponerse frío; enfriarse; (of weather) empezar a hacer frío. **to g. fat,** engordar. **to g. hard,** ponerse duro; *Fig.* endurecerse. **to g. hot,** ponerse caliente; calentarse; (of weather) empezar a hacer calor. **to g. like Topsy,** crecer a la buena de Dios. **to g. old,** envejecer. **to g. tall,** crecer mucho; ser alto. **to g. again,** crecer de nuevo. **to g. into,** hacerse, llegar a ser; venir a ser. **to g. out of,** brotar de; originarse en; (a habit) desacostumbrarse poco a poco. **He is growing out of his clothes,** La ropa se le hace pequeña. **to g. up,** (of persons) hacerse hombre (mujer); desarrollarse; (of a custom, etc.) imponerse. **to g. on, upon,** crecer sobre; llegar a dominar; (make think) hacer creer, empezar a pensar; (of a habit) arraigar en

grower /ˈgrouər/ *n* cultivador (-ra)

growing /ˈgrouɪŋ/ *n* crecimiento, *m;* desarrollo, *m;* (increase) aumento, *m;* (of flowers, etc.) cultivación, *f,* *a* creciente

growing pains *n pl* crisis de desarrollo, *f*

growl /graul/ *n* gruñido, *m;* reverberación, *f;* trueno, *m.* —*vi* gruñir; (of guns) tronar; (of thunder) reverberar. **to g. out,** decir gruñendo

grown /groun/ *a* crecido; maduro; adulto. **a g. up,** una persona mayor. **to be full-g.,** estar completamente desarrollado; haber llegado a la madurez. **g. over with,** cubierto de

growth /grouθ/ *n* crecimiento, *m;* (development) desarrollo, *m;* (progress) progreso, adelanto, *m;* (increase) aumento, *m;* (cultivation) cultivo, *m;* (vegetation) vegetación, *f; Med.* tumor, *m.* **He has a week's g. on his chin,** Tiene una barba de una semana

grub /grʌb/ *n* larva, *f,* gusano, *m.* —*vt* (with up, out) desarraigar; cavar; desmalezar; *Fig. Inf.* buscar

grubby /ˈgrʌbi/ *a* lleno de gusanos; sucio; bisunto; desaliñado

grudge /grʌdʒ/ *n* motivo de rencor, *m;* rencor, resentimiento, *m,* ojeriza, *f;* mala voluntad, *f,* aversión, *f.* —*vt* envidiar. **to bear a g.,** tener ojeriza

grudging /ˈgrʌdʒɪŋ/ *a* (niggardly) mezquino; envidioso; poco generoso; de mala gana; nada afable

grudgingly /ˈgrʌdʒɪŋli/ *adv* de mala gana, contra su voluntad; con rencor; a regañadientes

gruel /ˈgruəl/ *n* gachas, *f pl*

gruesome /ˈgrusəm/ *a* pavoroso, horrible; macabro

gruff /grʌf/ *a* (of the voice) bronco, grave, áspero; (of manner) brusco, malhumorado

gruffly /ˈgrʌfli/ *adv* en una voz bronca (or áspera), con brusquedad, con impaciencia, malhumoradamente

grumble /ˈgrʌmbəl/ *n* ruido sordo, trueno, *m;* estruendo, *m;* (complaint) refunfuño, rezongo, *m.* —*vi* tronar; refunfuñar, rezongar; hablar entre dientes; quejarse; protestar (contra). —*vt* decir refunfuñando

grumbling /ˈgrʌmblɪŋ/ *a* gruñón, refunfuñador; regañón; descontento. —*n* See **grumble**

grumpy /ˈgrʌmpi/ *a* malhumorado, irritable

grunt /grʌnt/ *n* gruñido, *m.* —*vi* gruñir

guarantee /ˌgærənˈti/ *n Law.* persona de quien otra sale fiadora, *f;* garantía, *f;* abono, *m.* —*vt* garantizar; responder de; abonar; asegurar, acreditar

guarantor /ˈgærənˌtɔr/ *n* garante, *mf*

guard /gɑrd/ *n* (watchfulness) vigilancia, *f;* (in fencing) guardia, *f;* (of a sword) guarnición, *f;* (sentry) centinela, *m;* (soldier) guardia, *m;* (body of soldiers) guardia, *f;* (escort) escolta, *f;* (keeper) guardián, *m;* (protection) protección, defensa, *f;* (of a train) jefe de tren, *m.* —*vt* guardar; proteger, defender; vigilar; (escort) escoltar. **to g. against,** guardarse de. **the changing of the g.,** el relevo de la guardia. **to be on g.,** *Mil.* estar de guardia; (in fencing) estar en guardia. **to be on one's g.,** estar prevenido, estar alerta. **to be off one's g.,** estar desprevenido. **to mount g.,** *Mil.* montar la guardia; vigilar. **guard's van,** furgón de equipajes, *m.* **g.-house,** cuerpo de guardia, *m;* prisión militar.

guarded /'gɑrdɪd/ *a* (reticent) reservado, circunspecto, prudente, discreto

guardedly /'gɑrdɪdli/ *adv* prudentemente, con circunspección, discretamente

guardian /'gɑrdɪən/ *n* protector (-ra); guardián (-ana); *Law.* tutor, *m.* —*a* que guarda; tutelar. **g. angel,** ángel de la guarda, ángel custodio, *m;* deidad tutelar, *f*

guardianship /'gɑrdɪən,ʃɪp/ *n* protección, *f;* patronato, *m; Law.* curaduría, tutela, *f*

Guatemalan /,gwɑtə'mɑlən/ *a* and *n* guatemalteco (-ca)

guava /'gwɑvə/ *n Bot.* guayaba, *f*

guerrilla /gə'rɪlə/ *n* guerrilla, *f;* (soldier) guerrillero, *m.* —*a* de guerrilla. **g. warfare,** guerra de guerrillas, *f*

guess /gɛs/ *n* adivinación, *f;* estimación, *f;* conjetura, *f;* sospecha, *f.* —*vt* and *vi* adivinar; conjeturar; sospechar; imaginar; (suppose) suponer, creer; calcular. **to g. at,** formar una opinión sobre; imaginar. **a rough g.,** estimación aproximada, *f.* **at a g.,** a poco más o menos, a ojo de buen cubero. **g.-work,** conjeturas, suposiciones, *f pl*

guest /gɛst/ *n* (at a meal) convidado (-da), invitado (-da); (at a hotel, etc.) cliente (-da); *Biol.* parásito, *m.* **g.-room,** alcoba de respeto, alcoba de honor, alcoba de huéspedes, *f,* cuarto de amigos, cuarto para invitados, *m*

guffaw /gʌ'fɔ/ *n* carcajada, *f.* —*vi* reírse a carcajadas, soltar el trapo

guidance /'gaɪdns/ *n* dirección, *f;* gobierno, *m;* (advice) consejos, *m pl;* inspiración, *f*

guide /gaɪd/ *n* (person) guía, *mf;* (girl g.) exploradora, *f;* (book and *Fig.*) guía, *f;* mentor, *m;* modelo, *m; Mech.* guía, *f.* —*vt* guiar; conducir; encaminar; dirigir; (govern) gobernar. **g.-book,** guía de turistas, *f.* **g.-post,** poste indicador, *m*

guided tour /'gaɪdɪd/ *n* visita explicada, visita programada, *f*

guideline /'gaɪd,laɪn/ *Lit.* falsarregla, falsilla, *f; Fig.* pauta, *f*

guile /gaɪl/ *n* astucia, superchería, maña, *f*

guileless /'gaɪllɪs/ *a* cándido, sin malicia, inocente

guilt /gɪlt/ *n* culpabilidad, *f;* crimen, *m;* (sin) pecado, *m*

guilt complex complejo de culpa, *m*

guiltily /'gɪltəli/ *adv* culpablemente; como si fuese culpable

guiltless /'gɪltlɪs/ *a* libre de culpa, inocente; puro; ignorante

guilty /'gɪlti/ *a* culpable; delincuente; criminal. **to find g.,** encontrar culpable. **to plead g.,** confesarse culpable. **g. party,** culpable, *m*

guise /gaɪz/ *n* manera, guisa, *f;* (garb)

traje, *m;* máscara, *f; Fig.* pretexto, *m.* **under the g. of,** bajo el pretexto de; bajo la apariencia de

guitar /gɪ'tɑr/ *n* guitarra, *f*

guitarist /gɪ'tɑrɪst/ *n* guitarrista, *mf*

gulf /gʌlf/ *n* golfo, *m;* abismo, *m*

Gulf Stream, the la Corriente del Golfo

gullet /'gʌlɪt/ *n* esófago, *m;* garganta, *f*

gullible /'gʌləbəl/ *a* crédulo

gully /'gʌli/ *n* hondonada, barranca, *f;* (gutter) arroyo, *m*

gulp /gʌlp/ *n* trago, sorbo, *m.* —*vt* engullir, tragar; (repress) ahogar; (believe) tragar. **to g. up,** vomitar

gum /gʌm/ *n* (of the mouth) encía, *f;* goma, *f.* —*vt* engomar; pegar con goma. **gum arabic,** goma arábiga, *f.* **gum boots,** botas de goma, *f.* **gum-resin,** gomorresina, *f.* **gum starch,** aderezo, *m.* **gum tree,** eucalipto, *m*

gummy /'gʌmi/ *a* gomoso

gumption /'gʌmpʃən/ *n* sentido común, seso, *m*

gun /gʌn/ *n* arma de fuego, *f;* (handgun) fusil, *m;* (sporting g.) escopeta, *f;* (pistol) pistola, *f,* revólver, *m;* (cannon) cañón, *m;* (firing) cañonazo, *m.* **big gun,** *Inf.* pájaro gordo, *m.* **heavy gun,** cañón de grueso calibre, *m.* **gun-barrel,** cañón de escopeta, *m.* **gun-carriage,** cureña, *f.* **gun-cotton,** pólvora de algodón, *f.* **gunfire,** cañonazos, *m pl,* fuego, *m.* **gunmetal,** bronce de cañón, *m;* pavón, *m.* **gun-room,** armería, *f;* (on a ship) polvorín, *m.* **gun-running,** contrabanda de armas, *f.* **gun-turret,** torre, *f.* **gun wound,** balazo, *m*

gunman /'gʌnmən/ *n* escopetero, armero, *m;* bandido armado, *m;* gángster, apache, *m*

gunner /'gʌnər/ *n* artillero, *m;* escopetero, *m*

gun permit *n* licencia de armas, *f,* permiso de armas, *m*

gunpowder /'gʌn,paudər/ *n* pólvora, *f*

gunshot /'gʌn,ʃɒt/ *n* escopetazo, *m;* tiro de fusil, *m*

gurgle /'gɜrgəl/ *n* murmullo, murmurio, gorgoteo, *m;* gluglú, *m;* (of a baby) gorjeo, *m.* —*vi* murmurar; hacer gluglú; (of babies) gorjear

gurgling /'gɜrglɪŋ/ *a* murmurante; (of babies) gorjeador. —*n* See **gurgle**

gush /gʌʃ/ *n* chorro, *m;* (of words) torrente, *m;* (of emotion) efusión, *f.* —*vi* chorrear, borbotar; surtir, surgir. **to g. out,** saltar, brotar a borbotones, salir a borbollones, salira borbotones. **to g. over,** *Fig.* hablar con efusión de

gushing /'gʌʃɪŋ/ *a* hirviente; (of people) efusivo, extremoso, empalagoso

gusset /'gʌsɪt/ *n Sew.* escudete, *m*

gust /gʌst/ *n* (of wind) ráfaga, bocanada (de aire), *f; Fig.* arrebato, acceso, *m*

gusto /'gʌstou/ *n* brío, *m;* entusiasmo, *m*

gut /gʌt/ *n* intestino, *m,* tripa, *f;* (catgut) cuerda de tripa, *f; Naut.* estrecho, *m;* pl

guts, tripas, *f pl;* (content) meollo, *m,* substancia, *f;* (stamina) aguante, espíritu, *m.* —*vt* (of fish, etc.) destripar; (plunder) saquear; destruir por completo; quemar completamente

gutter /'gʌtər/ *n* canal, *m;* (of a street) arroyo (de la calle), *m;* (ditch) zanja, *f; Fig.* hampa, *f.* —*vt* surcar. —*vi* gotear; (of a candle) cerotear, gotear la cera. **g. spout,** canalón, *m*

guy /gai/ *n* (rope) viento, *m; Naut.* guía, *f;* (effigy) mamarracho, *m;* (scarecrow) espantajo, *m, vt* sujetar con vientos o guías; burlarse de

guzzle /'gʌzəl/ *vt* tragar, engullir. —*vi* atracarse, engullir; emborracharse. —*n* comilón, *m;* borrachera, *f*

guzzler /'gʌzlər/ *n* tragador (-ra); borracho (-cha)

gymnasium /dʒɪm'nɑziəm/ *n* gimnasio, *m*

gymnast /'dʒɪmnæst/ *n* gimnasta, *mf*

gymnastic /dʒɪm'næstɪk/ *a* gimnástico. **g. rings,** anillas, *f pl*

gymnastics /dʒɪm'næstɪks/ *n* gimnasia, *f*

gynecological /,gainɪkə'lɒdʒɪkəl/ *a* ginecológico

gynecology /,gainɪ'kɒlədʒi/ *n* ginecología, *f*

gypsum /'dʒɪpsəm/ *n* yeso, *m*

gypsy /'dʒɪpsi/ *n* gitano (-na). —*a* gitano, gitanesco; (music) flamenco

gyrate /'dʒaireit/ *vi* girar, rodar

H

h /eitʃ/ *n* (letter) hache, *f*

ha /hɑ/ *interj* ¡ah!

haberdasher /'hæbər,dæʃər/ *n* mercero, *m*

haberdashery /'hæbər,dæʃəri/ *n* mercería, *f*

habiliment /hə'bɪləmənt/ *n* vestidura, *f*; *pl* **habiliments**, indumentaria, *f*

habit /'hæbɪt/ *n* costumbre, *f*, hábito, *m*; (temperament) temperamento, carácter, *m*; (use) uso, *m*; (of body) complexión, constitución, *f*; *Eccl.* hábito, *m*. **to be in the h. of**, soler, acostumbrar, estar acostumbrado a. **to have bad habits**, estar malacostumbrado. **to have the bad h. of**, tener el vicio (or la mala costumbre) de. **to contract the h. of**, contraer la costumbre de. **h. maker**, sastre de trajes de montar, *m*

habitable /'hæbɪtəbəl/ *a* habitable, vividero

habitat /'hæbɪ,tæt/ *n* (*Bot., Zool.*) medio, *m*, habitación, *f*

habitation /,hæbɪ'teɪʃən/ *n* habitación, *f*

habit-forming /'hæbɪt,fɔrmɪŋ/ *a* enviciador, que crea vicio

habitual /hə'bɪtʃuəl/ *a* habitual, acostumbrado, usual; constante; común

habitually /hə'bɪtʃuəli/ *adv* habitualmente; constantemente; comúnmente

habituate /hə'bɪtʃu,eɪt/ *vt* habituar, acostumbrar

habitué /hə'bɪtʃu,ei/ *n* parroquiano (-na); veterano (-na)

hack /hæk/ *n* caballo de alquiler, *m*; rocín, jaco, *m*; (writer) escritor mercenario, *m*. —*vt* acuchillar; tajar, cortar. —*vi* cortar. **to h. to pieces**, cortar en pedazos; pasar a cuchillo

hacking /'hækɪŋ/ *a* (of coughs) seco

hackle /'hækəl/ *n* (for flax, hemp) rastrillo, *m*

hackneyed /'hæknid/ *a* gastado, trillado, muy usado, repetido, resobado

hacksaw /'hæk,sɔ/ *n* sierra de cerrajero, sierra para metal, *f*

hackwork /'hæk,wɜrk/ *n* trabajo de rutina, *m*

haddock /'hædək/ *n* merlango, *m*, pescadilla, *f*

hag /hæg, hɑg/ *n* bruja, *f*

haggard /'hægərd/ *a* ojeroso, trasnochado, trasojado

haggle /'hægəl/ *vi* regatear; vacilar

haggling /'hæglɪŋ/ *n* regateo, *m*, *a* regatón

Hague, The /heɪg/ La Haya

ha, ha! /'hɑ 'hɑ/ *interj* ¡ja, ja!

hail /heɪl/ *n* (salutation) saludo, *m*; (shout) grito, *m*; (frozen rain) granizo, *m*; (of blows) lluvia, *f*. —*interj* ¡salve! —*vt* saludar; llamar; aclamar; *Fig.* lanzar, echar. —*vi* (hailstones) granizar; (blows, etc.) llover. **to h. from**, proceder de, ser natural de. **within h.**, al habla. **H. Mary**, Salve Regina, Avemaría, *f*

hailstone /'heɪl,stoun/ *n* granizo, pedrisco, *m*

hailstorm /'heɪl,stɔrm/ *n* granizada, *f*

hair /hɛər/ *n* (single h.) cabello, *m*; (*Zool. Bot.*) pelo, *m*; (of horse's mane) crin, *f*; (head of h.) cabellera, mata de pelo, *f*, pelo, *m*; (superfluous) vello, *m*; (fiber) fibra, *f*, filamento, *m*; (on the pen) raspa, *f*, pelo, *m*; *Fig.* pelo, *m*. **lock of h.**, bucle, rizo, *m*; mecha, *f*. **to dress one's h.**, peinarse. **to have one's h. cut**, hacerse cortar el pelo. **to part the h.**, hacer(se) la raya del pelo. **to put up one's h.**, hacerse el moño; (to "come out") ponerse de largo. **to tear one's h.**, mesarse los cabellos. **h. combings**, peinaduras, *f pl*. **h.-curler**, tirabuzón, *m*. **h. dryer**, secadora de cabello, *f*. **h. dye**, tinte para el pelo, *m*. **h.-net**, redecilla, *f*. **h.-oil**, brillantina, *f*. **h.-raising**, horripilante, espeluznante. **h.-ribbon**, cinta para el pelo, *f*. **h.-shirt**, cilicio, *m*. **h. slide**, pasador, *m*. **h.-splitting**, sofistería, argucia, *f*; mez quinas argucias, quis quillas, *f pl*. **h.-spring**, muelle del volante, *m*. **h.-switch**, añadido, *m*. **h.-trigger**, pelo de una pistola, *m*

hairbrush /'hɛər,brʌʃ/ *n* cepillo para el cabello, *m*

hairdresser /'hɛər,drɛsər/ *n* peluquero (-ra), peinadora, *f*

hairdressing /'hɛər,drɛsɪŋ/ *n* peinado, *m*. **h. establishment** or **trade**, peluquería, *f*

hairless /'hɛərlɪs/ *a* sin pelo; calvo

hairpin /'hɛər,pɪn/ *n* horquilla, *f*. **h. bend**, viraje en horquilla, *m*

hairy /'hɛəri/ *a* peludo; velloso; *Bot.* hirsuto

Haiti /'heɪti/ Haití, *m*

Haitian /'heɪʃən/ *a* and *n* haitiano (-na)

hake /heɪk/ *n* merluza, *f*

halcyon /'hælsiən/ *n* alción, martín pescador, *m*. —*a* *Fig.* feliz, sereno, tranquilo

hale /heɪl/ *a* fuerte, sano, robusto. —*vt* hacer comparecer

half /hæf/ *n* mitad, *f*; (school term) trimestre, *m*. —*a* medio; semi-. —*adv* a medias; mitad; (almost) casi; insuficientemente; imperfectamente. **I don't h. like it**, No me gusta nada. **It is h.-past two**, Son las dos y media. **an hour and a h.**, una hora y media. **better h.**, *Inf.* media naranja, cara mitad, *f*. **by halves**, a medias. **in h.**, en dos mitades. **one h.**, la mitad, *f*. **to go halves**, ir a medias a. **to h. close**, entornar. **to h. open**, entreabrir. **h. a bottle**, media botella, *f*. **h. a crown**, media corona, *f*. **h.-alive**, semivivo. **h. an hour**, media hora, *f*. **h.-and-h.**, mitad y mitad; en partes iguales. **h.-asleep**, semidormido, medio dormido. **h.-awake**, medio despierto, entre duerme y vela. **h.-back**, *Sports.* medio, *m*. **h.-baked**, medio cocido, crudo; *Fig.* poco maduro. **h.-binding,** encuadernación en media pasta, *f.* **h.-breed,** *a* mestizo. —*n* cruce, *m.* **h.-brother,** hermanastro, hermano de padre, hermano de madre, *m.* **h.-caste,** mestizo. **h. circle,** semicírculo, *m.* **h.-closed,** entreabierto; medio cerrado. **h.-dead,** medio muerto; más muerto que vivo. **h.-done,** hecho a medias, sin acabar. **h.-dozen,** media docena, *f.* **h.-dressed,** medio desnudo. **h. fare,** medio billete, *m.* **h.-full,** medio lleno. **h.-hearted,** débil, poco eficaz, lánguido; indiferente, sin entusiasmo. **h.-heartedness,** debilidad, *f.* indiferencia, *f.* **h. holiday,** media fiesta, *f.* **h.-hourly,** cada media hora. **h.-length,** (portrait) de medio cuerpo. **h.-length coat,** abrigo de tres cuartos, *m.* **h.-light,** media luz, *f.* **h.-mast,** a media asta. **h.-measure,** medida poco eficaz, *f.* **h.-moon,** *n* media luna, *f; Astron.* semilunio, *m;* (of a nail) blanco (de la uña), *m.* **h.-mourning,** medio luto, *m.* **h.-pay,** media paga, *f.* **h.-price,** a mitad de precio. *Inf.* **h.-seas-over.** entre dos velas. **h.-sister,** hermanastra, hermana de padre, hermana de madre, *f.* **h.-time,** *Sports.* media parte, *f.* medio tiempo, *m.* **h.-tone,** de medio tono. **h.-tone illustration,** fotograbado a media tinta, *m.* **h.-truth,** verdad a medias, *f.* **h.-turn,** media vuelta, *f.* **h.-way,** a medio camino; medio. **h.-witted,** medio loco, tonto, imbécil. **h.-year,** medio año, *m.* **h.-yearly,** semestral

halibut /'hælɪbət/ *n* halibut, *m;* (genus) hipogloso, *m*

halitosis /,hælɪ'tousɪs/ *n* halitosis, *f*

hall /hɔl/ *n* (mansion) mansión, casa de campo, *f,* caserón, *m;* (public building) edificio, *m,* casa (de); (town h.) casa del ayuntamiento, *f;* (room) sala, *f;* (entrance) vestíbulo, *m;* (dining room) comedor, *m;* (of residence for students) residencia, *f.* **h. door,** portón, *m,* puerta del vestíbulo, *f.* **h. porter,** conserje, *m.* **h.-stand,** perchero, *m.*

hallelujah /,hælə'luyə/ *n* aleluya, *f*

hallmark /'hɔl,mɑrk/ *n* marca de ley, *f; Fig.* señal, *f;* indicio, *m.* —*vt* poner la marca de ley sobre; *Fig.* sellar

hallow /'hælou/ *vt* santificar; reverenciar; (consecrate) consagrar

Halloween /,hælə'win/ *n* la víspera de Todos los Santos, *f*

hallucination /hə,lusə'neɪʃən/ *n* alucinación, ilusión, *f;* visión, *f;* fantasma, *m*

hallucinatory /hə'lusənə,tɔri/ *a* alucinador

halo /'heilou/ *n* halo, nimbo, *m*

halogen /'hælədʒən/ *n Chem.* halógeno, *m*

halt /hɔlt/ *n Mil.* alto, *m;* cesación, *f;* interrupción, *f;* (on a railway) apeadero, *m;* (for trams, buses) parada, *f.* —*vt* parar, detener. —*vi* pararse, detenerse; *Mil.* hacer alto; cesar; interrumpirse; (in speech) titubear; (of verse) estar cojo;

(doubt) dudar; (limp) cojear. **H.!** *Mil.* ¡Alto!

halter /'hɔltər/ *n* ronzal, cabestro, *m;* (for hanging) dogal, *m.* —*vt* encabestrar, cabestrar

halting /'hɔltɪŋ/ *n* parada, *f;* interrupción, *f.* —*a* (of gait) cojo; incierto; vacilante; (of speech) titubeante

halve /hæv/ *vt* partir (or dividir) en dos mitades

ham /hæm/ *n* jamón, *m; Anat.* pernil, *m;* (radio-operator) radioaficionado, *m*

hamlet /'hæmlɪt/ *n* aldea, *f,* pueblecito, *m*

hammer /'hæmər/ *n* martillo, *m;* (stone cutter's) maceta, *f;* (mason's) piqueta, *f;* (of fire-arms) percusor, *m;* (of piano) macillo, *m.* —*vt* amartillar, martillar, batir. **to throw the h.,** lanzar el martillo. **under the h.,** en subasta, al remate. **h. blow,** martillazo, *m*

hammock /'hæmək/ *n* hamaca, *f; Naut.* coy, *m*

hamper /'hæmpər/ *n* banasta, canasta, *f,* cesto grande, *m.* —*vt* estorbar, dificultar, impedir; *Fig.* embarazar

hamster /'hæmstər/ *n Zool.* hámster, *m,* marmota de Alemania, rata del trigo, *f*

hand /hænd/ *n* mano, *f;* (of animal) pata, mano, *f;* (worker) operario (-ia); obrero (-ra); (skill) habilidad, *f;* (side) mano, *f,* lado, *m;* (measure) palmo, *m;* (of a clock) manecilla, *f;* (of instruments) aguja, *f;* (applause) aplauso, *m;* (power) poder, *m;* las manos; (at cards) mano, *f;* (card player) jugador, *m;* (signature) firma, *f;* (handwriting) letra, escritura, *f;* (influence) influencia, parte, mano, *f.* **old h.,** veterano; perro viejo. **at h.,** a mano, al lado, cerca. **have at hand,** tener a la mano. **at the hands of,** de manos de. **by h.,** a mano; (on the bottle) con biberón. **from h. to h.,** de mano a mano. **in h.,** entre manos; (of money) de contado. **in the hands of,** *Fig.* en el poder de. **"Hands wanted,"** «Se desean trabajadores.» **h. over h.,** mano sobre mano. **hand's breadth,** palmo, *m.* **Hands off!** ¡Fuera las manos! **Hands up!** ¡Manos arriba! **lost with all hands,** (of a ship) perdido con toda su tripulación. **off one's hands,** despachado; (of a daughter) casada. **on all hands,** por todas partes. **on h.,** entre manos; (of goods) existente; (present) presente. **on one's hands,** a cargo de uno. **on the one h.,** por un lado; a un lado. **on the other h.,** por otra parte; en cambio. **out of h.,** luego, inmediatamente; revoltoso. **to come to h.,** venir a mano; (of letters) llegar a las manos (de). **to get one's h. in,** ejercitarse. **to have a h. in,** tener parte en; intervenir en. **to have no h. in,** no tener arte ni parte en. **to have on h.,** traer entre manos. **to have the upper h.,** tener la sartén por el mango, llevar la ventaja. **to hold one's h.,** abstenerse; detenerse. **to hold hands,** cogerse de las manos. **to**

lay **hands** on, tocar; poner mano en; echar manos a. **to set one's h.** to, emprender; (sign) firmar. **to shake hands,** estrechar la mano. **to stretch out one's hands,** tender las manos. **to take one's hands off,** no tocar. **with folded hands,** mano sobre mano. **with his hands behind his back,** con las manos en la espalda. **h.-in-h.,** cogidos (cogidas) de las manos. **h.-lever,** manija, f. **h.-loom,** telar de mano, m. **h. luggage,** equipaje de mano, m. **h.-made,** hecho a mano. **h.-mill,** molinillo, m. **h.-pump,** n Naut. sacabuche, m. **h. rail,** pasamano, m, baranda, balustrada, f. **h.-sewn,** cosido a mano. **h.-to-h.,** de mano en mano; (of a fight) a brazo partido, cuerpo a cuerpo. **h.-to-h. fight,** cachetina, f. **h.-to-mouth,** precario. **to live from h.-to-mouth,** vivir de día en día

hand /hænd/ vt dar; entregar; alargar. **to h. down,** bajar; (a person) ayudar a bajar; transmitir. **to h. in,** entregar; (a person) ayudar a entrar; (one's resignation) dimitir; (send) mandar, enviar. **to h. on,** transmitir. **to h. out,** vt distribuir; (a person) ayudar a salir; (from a vehicle) ayudar a bajar. —vi Inf. pagar. **to h. over,** vt entregar. —vi Mil. traspasar los poderes (a). **to h. round,** pasar de mano en mano; pasar; ofrecer. **to h. up,** subir; (a person) ayudar a subir

handbag /'hænd,bæg/ n bolso, saco, monedero, m

handbill /'hænd,bɪl/ n anuncio, m

handbook /'hænd,bʊk/ n manual, compendio, tratado, m; anuario, m; (guide) guía, f

handcuff /'hænd,kʌf/ n esposa, f, grillo, m, (gen. —pl.). —vt poner las esposas (a), maniatar

handful /'hændfʊl/ n puño, puñado, manojo, m. **to be a h.,** Inf. tener el diablo en el cuerpo. **in handfuls,** a manojos

handicap /'hændi,kæp/ n desventaja, f; obstáculo, m; Sports. handicap, m; ventaja, f. —vt Fig. perjudicar, impedir, dificultar. **the handicapped,** los lisiados, m pl

handicraft /'hændi,kræft/ n mano de obra, f; (skill) destreza manual, f

handiwork /'hændi,wɜrk/ n mano de obra, f; trabajo manual, m; obra, f; (deed) acción, f, hecho, m

handkerchief /'hæŋkərtʃɪf/ n pañuelo, m

handle /'hændl/ n mango, puño, m; (lever) palanca, f; (of baskets, dishes, jugs) asa, f; (of doors, windows, drawers) pomo, m, (of a car door) picaporte m; (to one's name) designación, f; título, m; (excuse) pretexto, m. —vt (touch) tocar; manejar, manipular; (treat) tratar; **h. with kid gloves,** tratar con guantes de seda; (deal in) comerciar en; tomar; (paw) manosear; (direct) dirigir; (control) gobernar; (pilot) pilotar; (a theme) expli-

car, tratar de. **h.-bar,** manillar, m. **h.-bar grip,** puño de un manillar, m

handling /'hændlɪŋ/ n manejo, m; manipulación, f; (treatment) trato, m, relaciones (con), f pl; (thumbing) manoseo, m; interpretación, f; Art. tratamiento, m, técnica, f

handshake /'hænd,ʃeik/ n apretón de manos, m

handsome /'hænsəm/ a (generous) generoso; magnánimo; considerable; hermoso, bello; elegante; (of people) guapo, distinguido; excelente; (flattering) halagüeño. **He was a very h. man,** Era un hombre muy guapo

handsomely /'hænsəmli/ adv generosamente; con magnanimidad; elegantemente; bien

handspring /'hænd,sprɪŋ/ n voltereta sobre las manos, f

handwork /'hænd,wɜrk/ n obra hecha a mano, f, trabajo a mano, m; (needlework) labor de aguja, f

handworked /'hænd,wɜrkt/ a hecho a mano; (embroidered) bordado

handwriting /'hænd,raitɪŋ/ n caligrafía, letra, escritura, f. **the h. on the wall,** la mano que escribía en la pared, f

handy /'hændi/ a (of persons) diestro, mañoso, hábil; (of things) conveniente, útil; (near) cercano, a mano. —adv cerca. **h.-man,** hombre de muchos oficios, m; factótum, m

hang /hæŋ/ vt colgar; suspender; (execute) ahorcar; (the head) bajar; dejar caer; (upholster) entapizar; (with wallpaper) empapelar; (drape) poner colgaduras en; (place) poner; (cover) cubrir. —vi colgar, pender; estar suspendido; (be executed) ser ahorcado; (of garments) caer. —n (of garments) caída, f; (of a machine) mecanismo, m; (meaning) sentido, m, significación, f. **to h. by a thread,** pender de un hilo. **to h. in the balance,** estar en la balanza. **to h. fire,** estar (una cosa) en suspenso. **to h. loose,** caer suelto; (clothes) venir ancho. **to h. about,** (surround) rodear, pegarse a; (frequent) frecuentar; (haunt) rondar; (be imminent) ser inminente, amenazar; (embrace) abrazar. **to h. back,** retroceder; quedarse atrás; Fig. vacilar, titubear. **to h. down,** colgar, pender; estar caído; caerse. **to h. on,** seguir agarrado (a); apoyarse en; Fig. persistir; (a person's words) estar pendiente de, beber; (remain) quedarse. **to h. out,** vt tender. —vi (lean out) asomarse (por); (Inf. live) habitar. **to h. over,** colgar por encima; (brood) cernerse sobre; (lean over) inclinarse sobre; quedarse cerca de; (overhang) sobresalir; (overarch) abovedar; (threaten) amenazar. **to h. together,** (of persons) permanecer unidos; (of things) tener cohesión; (be consistent) ser lógico, ser consistente. **to h. up,** colgar; suspender; Fig. dejar pendiente, interrumpir.

to h. upon, apoyarse en; (a person's words) beber las palabras de uno

hangar /'hæŋər/ n cobertizo; Aer. hangar, m

hanger /'hæŋər/ n colgadero, m; percha f. **h.-on,** parásito, m; dependiente, m

hanging /'hæŋɪŋ/ n colgamiento, m; (killing) ahorcamiento, m; pl **hangings,** colgaduras, f pl, cortinajes, m pl. —a pendiente colgante; péndulo; (of gardens) pensil. **It's not a h. matter,** No es una cuestión de vida y muerte. **h. bridge,** - puente colgante, m. **h. committee,** junta (de una exposición,) f. **h. lamp,** lámpara de techo, f

hangman /'hæŋmən/ n verdugo, m

hangnail /'hæŋ,neil/ n padrastro, m

hangover /'hæŋ,ouvər/ n (after drinking) resaca, cruda (Mexico), f

hanker /'hæŋkər/ vi (with after) ansiar, ambicionar; (with for) anhelar, suspirar por, desear con vehemencia

hanky-panky /'hæŋki 'pæŋki/ n super-chería; f; engaño, m

haphazard /n 'hæp,hæzərd/ a hæp'hæzərd/ n casualidad, f. —a fortuito, casual

hapless /'hæplɪs/ a desgraciado, desdi-chado

happen /'hæpən/ vi suceder, acontecer, ocurrir, pasar; (to be found, be) hallarse por casualidad; (take place) tener lugar, verificarse; (arise) sobrevenir. **Do you know what has happened to...?** ¿Sabes qué se ha hecho de...? **as if nothing had happened,** como si no hubiese pasado nada. **He turned up as if nothing had happened,** Se presentó como si tal cosa. **How did it h.?** ¿Cómo fue esto? **If they h. to see you,** Si acaso te vean. **I happened to be in London,** Me hallaba por casualidad en Londres. **It won't h. again,** No volverá a suceder. **whatever happens,** venga lo que venga

happening /'hæpənɪŋ/ n suceso, aconte-cimiento, hecho, m, ocurrencia, f

happiness /'hæpinɪs/ n felicidad, dicha, f; alegría, f, regocijo, m

happy /'hæpi/ a (lucky) afortunado; (fe-licitous) feliz, oportuno; feliz, dichoso; alegre, regocijado. **to be h.,** estar con-tento, ser feliz. **to be h. about,** alegrarse de. **to make h.,** hacer feliz, alegrar. **h.-go-lucky,** irresponsable, descuidado

harangue /hə'ræŋ/ n arenga, f. —vt arengar. —vi pronunciar una arenga

harass /hə'ræs/ vt hostigar, acosar; ator-mentar; preocupar; Mil. picar. **to h. the rear-guard,** picar la retaguardia

harbinger /'harbɪndʒər/ n Fig. precursor, heraldo, m; presagio, anuncio, m. —vt anunciar, presagiar

harbor /'harbər/ n puerto, m; (bay) ba-hía, f; (haven) asilo, refugio, m. —vt dar refugio (a), albergar, acoger; (cherish) abrigar, acariciar; (conceal) esconder. **in-ner h.,** puerto, m. **outer h.,** rada del puerto, f. **to put into h.,** entrar en el

puerto. **h. bar,** barra del puerto, f. **h.-dues,** derechos de puerto, m pl. **h.-master,** capitán de puerto, contramaestre de puerto, m

hard /hard/ a duro; (firm) firme; difícil; laborioso, agotador; violento; poderoso; arduo; fuerte, recio; vigoroso, robusto; insensible, inflexible, cruel; (of weather) inclemente, severo; (unjust) injusto, opre-sivo; (stiff) tieso; (of water) cruda; (of wood) brava. —adv duro; duramente; con ahínco; con fuerza; de firme; difícil-mente; (of gazing) fijamente; severa-mente; (firmly) firmemente; vigorosa-mente; (of raining) a cántaros, mucho; (quickly) rápidamente; excesivamente; (much) mucho; (of bearing misfortune) a pechos; (attentively) atentamente; (heav-ily) pesadamente; (badly) mal; (closely) de cerca, inmediatamente. **It was a h. blow,** Fue un golpe recio. **to be h. put to,** encontrar difícil. **to go h.,** endurecer-se. **to go h. with,** irle mal a uno. **to have a h. time,** pasar apuros, pasarlo mal. **to look h. at,** mirar atentamente, examinar detenidamente; mirar fijamente. **to be a h. drinker,** ser un bebedor em-pedernido. **h. and fast rule,** regla inalter-able, f. **h.-bitten,** de carácter duro. **a h.-boiled egg,** un huevo duro. **h. breath-ing,** resuello, m. **h. by,** muy cerca. **h. cash,** efectivo, m. **h.-earned,** difícilmente conseguido; ganado con el sudor de la frente. **h.-featured,** de facciones duras. **h.-fisted,** tacaño. **h.-fought,** arduo, re-ñido. **h.-headed,** práctico, perspicaz. **h.-hearted,** duro de corazón, insensible. **h.-heartedness,** insensibilidad, f. **h. labor,** Law. trabajos forzados, m pl, presidio, m. **h.-mouthed,** (of horses) boquiduro. **h. of hearing,** duro de oído. **h.-up,** apurado. **to be very h.-up,** ser muy pobre; Inf. es-tar a la cuarta pregunta. **h.-wearing,** duradero; sufrido. **h.-won,** See h.-earned. **h.-working,** trabajador, hacen-doso, diligente

harden /'hardn/ vt endurecer; (metal) templar; robustecer; (to war) aguerrir; (make callous) hacer insensible. —vi endurecerse; hacerse duro; templarse; ro-bustecerse; (of shares) entonarse

hardening /'hardnɪŋ/ n endurecimiento, m; (of metal) temple, m. **h. of the arte-ries,** arteriosclerosis, f

hardly /'hardli/ adv duramente; difícil-mente; (badly) mal; severamente; (scarcely) apenas, casi. **h. ever,** casi nunca

hardness /'hardnɪs/ n dureza, f; severi-dad, f; inhumanidad, insensibilidad, f; (stiffness) tiesura, f; (difficulty) dificultad, f; (of water) crudeza, f; (of hearing) dureza de oído, f

hardship /'hardʃɪp/ n penas, f pl, traba-jos, m pl; infortunio, m, desdicha, f; (suf-fering) sufrimiento, m; (affliction) aflic-ción, f; (privation) privación, f. **to undergo h.,** pasar trabajos

hardware /'hard,wɛər/ n ferretería, f

hardy /'hardi/ a audaz, intrépido; (strong) fuerte, robusto; Bot. resistente

hare /hɛər/ n liebre, f. **young h.**, lebrato, m. **h. and hounds**, rally paper, m, caza de papelitos, f. **h.-brained**, casquivano, atronado, con cabeza de chorlito. **hare's foot**, mano de gato, f. **h.-lip**, labio leporino, m. **h.-lipped**, labihendido

haricot /'hærə,kou/ n (green bean) judia, f; (dried bean) alubia, f

hark /hark/ vt escuchar; oír. **to h. back**, volver al punto de partida; volver a la misma canción

harlot /'harlət/ n ramera, prostituta, meretriz, f

harm /harm/ n mal, m; daño, m; perjuicio, m; (danger) peligro, m; (detriment) menoscabo, m; (misfortune) desgracia, f, vt hacer mal (a); dañar, hacer daño (a); perjudicar. **And there's no h. in that,** Y en eso no hay mal. **to keep out of harm's way,** evitar el peligro; guardarse del mal

harmful /'harmfəl/ a malo; dañino, perjudicial, nocivo; (dangerous) peligroso. **to be h.,** (of food, etc.) hacer mal (a); (of pests) ser dañino; (of behavior, etc.) perjudicar

harmless /'harmlɪs/ a innocuo; inofensivo; inocente

harmonic /har'mɒnɪk/ n (Phys. Math.) harmónica, f; Mus. armónico, m, a Mus. armónico

harmonica /har'mɒnɪkə/ n armónica, f

harmonious /har'mouniəs/ a armonioso

harmonize /'harmə,naiz/ vt armonizar. —vi armonizarse, estar en armonía

harmony /'harməni/ n armonía, f; Fig. paz, f, buenas relaciones, f pl; música, f. **to live in h.,** vivir en paz

harness /'harnɪs/ n guarniciones, f pl; jaeces, m pl; (armor) arnés, m. —vt enjaezar; (yoke) enganchar; (water) represar. **to die in h.,** Fig. morir en la brecha. **h. maker,** guarnicionero, m. **h. room,** guadarnés, m

harp /harp/ n arpa, f. **to h. on,** volver a la misma canción, volver a repetir

harpist /'harpɪst/ n arpista, mf

harpoon /har'pun/ n arpón, m. —vt arponear

harpsichord /'harpsɪ,kɔrd/ n arpicordio, m

harrow /'hærou/ n Agr. rastra, f, escarificador, m. —vt Agr. escarificar; Fig. lastimar, atormentar

harrowing /'hærouɪŋ/ a patibulario, conmovedor, atormentador, angustioso

harry /'hæri/ vt devastar, asolar; (persons) robar; perseguir; (worry) atormentar; (annoy) molestar

harsh /harʃ/ a áspero; (of voice) ronco; (of sound) discordante; (of colors) áspero; duro; chillón; severo, duro; (of features) duro; (of taste) ácido, acerbo

harshness /'harʃnɪs/ n (roughness) aspereza, f; (of voice) ronquedad, aspereza,

f; (of sound) disonancia, f; (of colors) aspereza, f; severidad, f; dureza, f; (of taste) acidez, f

harum-scarum /'hɛərəm 'skɛərəm/ n tronera, saltabarrancos, mf molino, m, a irresponsable

harvest /'harvɪst/ n cosecha, siega, f; recolección, f; Fig. producto, fruto, m. —vt cosechar; recoger. **h. festival,** fiesta de la cosecha, f

harvester /'harvəstər/ n segador, m, cosechero (-ra); (machine) segadora, f

hash /hæʃ/ n Cul. picado, m. —vt Cul. picar

hashish /'hæʃɪʃ/ n hachich, hachís, quif, m

hasp /hæsp/ n pasador, m; sujetador, m

hassock /'hæsək/ n cojín, m

haste /heist/ n prisa, rapidez, f; precipitación, f; urgencia, f. —vt dar prisa (a); acelerar; precipitar. —vi darse prisa; acelerarse; precipitarse. **in h.,** de prisa, aprisa. **to be in h.,** estar de prisa, llevar prisa. **in great h.,** muy aprisa, aprisa y corriendo, precipitadamente; con mucha prisa. **More h. less speed,** (Spanish equivalent. Words said by Charles III of Spain to his valet) Vísteme despacio que voy de prisa!

hasten /'heisən/ vt acelerar, apresurar; precipitar. —vi darse prisa, apresurarse; moverse con rapidez; correr. **to h. one's steps,** apretar el paso. **to h. away,** marcharse rápidamente. **to h. back,** regresar apresuradamente. **to h. down,** bajar rápidamente. **to h. on,** seguir el camino sin descansar; seguir rápidamente. **to h. out,** salir rápidamente. **to h. towards,** ir rápidamente hacia; correr hacia. **to h. up,** subir aprisa, correr hacia arriba; darse prisa

hastily /'heistli/ adv de prisa, rápidamente; con precipitación, precipitadamente; (angrily) impacientemente, airadamente; (thoughtlessly) sin reflexión

hastiness /'heistɪnɪs/ n rapidez, f; precipitación, f; (anger) impaciencia, irritación, f

hasty /'heisti/ a rápido, apresurado; precipitado; (superficial) superficial, ligero; (ill-considered) desconsiderado, imprudente; (angry) impaciente, irritable; violento, apasionado

hat /hæt/ n sombrero, m. **to pass round the h.,** pasar el platillo. **Andalusian h.,** sombrero calañés, m. **bowler h.,** sombrero hongo, m. **broad-brimmed h.,** sombrero chambergo, m. **Panama h.,** sombrero de jipijapa, m. **picture h.,** pamela, f. **shovel h.,** sombrero de teja, m. **soft felt h.,** sombrero flexible, m. **straw h.,** sombrero de paja, m. **three-cornered h.,** sombrero de tres picos, m. **top-h.,** sombrero de copa, m. **h. shop** or **trade,** sombrerera, f

hatch /hætʃ/ n (wicket) compuerta, f; (trap-door) puerta caediza, f; Naut. escotilla, f; compuerta de esclusa, f; (of chickens) pollada, _f;_ (of birds) nidada, _f._ —_vt_ (birds) empollar; incubar, encobar; _Fig._ tramar, urdir. —_vi_ empollarse, salir del cascarón; incubarse; _Fig._ madurarse. **to h. a plot,** urdir un complot, conspirar. **to h. chickens,** sacar pollos.

hatchet /'hætʃɪt/ _n_ hacha pequeña, _f,_ machado, _m._ **to bury the h.,** hacer la paz. **h.-faced,** de cara de cuchillo

hate /heit/ _n_ odio, aborrecimiento, _m,_ aversión, _f;_ abominación, _f._ —_vt_ odiar, aborrecer, detestar; repugnar; saber mal, sentir. **I h. to trouble you,** Me sabe mal molestarle, Siento mucho molestarle. **to h. the sight of,** _Inf._ no poder ver (a)

hateful /'heitfəl/ _a_ odioso, aborrecible; repugnante

hater /'heitər/ _n_ aborrecedor (-ra). **to be a good h.,** saber odiar

hatred /'heitrɪd/ _n_ odio, aborrecimiento, _m,_ detestación, _f;_ aversión, enemistad. _f_

hatter /'hætər/ _n_ sombrerero, _m._ **as mad as a h.,** loco como una cabra

haughtiness /'hɔtinɪs/ _n_ altanería, arrogancia, altivez, soberbia, _f,_ orgullo, _m_

haughty /'hɔti/ _a_ altanero, arrogante, altivo, orgulloso

haul /hɔl/ _n_ (pull) tirón, _m;_ (of fish) redada, _f;_ (booty) botín, _m._ —_vt_ arrastrar, tirar de; _Naut._ halar. **to h. at, upon,** (ropes, etc.) aflojar, soltar, arriar. **to h. down,** (flags, sails) arriar

haunch /hɔntʃ/ _n_ anca, culata, _f;_ (of meat) pierna, _f._ **h.-bone,** hueso ilíaco, _m_

haunt /hɔnt/ _n_ punto de reunión, lugar frecuentado (por), _m;_ (lair) cubil, nido, _m,_ guarida, _f._ —_vt_ frecuentar; rondar; (of ideas) perseguir; (of ghosts) aparecer, visitar. **It is a h. of thieves,** Es una cueva de ladrones

haunted /'hɔntɪd/ _a_ (by spirits) encantado

hauteur /hou'tɜr/ _n_ altivez, _f_

Havana /hə'vænə/ la Habana, _f._ —_n_ (cigar) habano, _m._ (native) habanero (-ra), habano (-na)

have /hæv/ _unstressed_ həv, əv/ _vt_ tener; poseer; (suffer) padecer; (spend) pasar; (eat or drink) tomar; (eat) comer; (a cigarette) fumar; (a bath, etc.) tomar; (a walk, a ride) dar; (cause to be done) mandar (hacer), hacer (hacer); (deceive) engañar; (defeat) vencer; (catch) coger; (say) decir; (allow) permitir; (tolerate) tolerar, sufrir; (obtain) lograr, conseguir; (wish) querer; (know) saber; (realize) realizar; (buy) comprar; (acquire) adquirir. As an auxiliary verb, haber (e.g. _I h. done it,_ Lo he hecho, etc.). **As fate would h. it,** Según quiso la suerte. **Do you h. to go?** ¿Tiene Vd. que marcharse? **H. him come here,** Hazle venir aquí. **I h. been had,** Me han engañado. **I h. a good mind to...,** Tengo ganas de... **I had all my books stolen,** Me robaron todos los libros. **You had better go,** Es mejor que te vayas. **I had rather,** Preferiría, Me gustaría más bien. **I h. had a suit made,**

Mandé hacerme un traje, Hice hacerme un traje. **I would not h. had it otherwise,** No lo hubiese querido de otra manera. **I will not h. it,** No lo quiero; No quiero tomarlo; (object) No lo permitiré. **If we had known,** Si lo hubiésemos sabido. **It has to do with the sun,** Está relacionado con el sol, Tiene que ver con el sol. **Have a good trip!** ¡Buen viaje!, ¡Feliz viaje! **What are you going to h.?** ¿Qué quiere Vd. tomar? **Will you h. some jam?** ¿Quiere Vd. mermelada? **to h. breakfast,** desayunar. **to h. dinner, supper,** cenar. **to h. lunch,** almorzar. **to h. for tea,** invitar a tomar el té; (of food) merendar. **to h. tea,** tomar el té. **to h. it out with,** habérselas con. **to h. just,** acabar de. **I h. just done it,** Acabo de hacerlo. **to h. on hand,** traer entre manos. **to h. one's eye on,** no perder de vista (a), vigilar. **to h. one's tail between one's legs,** ir rabo entre piernas. **to h. to,** tener que; deber. **It has to be so,** Tiene que ser así. **to h. too much of,** sobrar, tener demasiado de. **He has too much time,** Le sobra tiempo. **to h. about one,** tener (o llevar) consigo. **to h. back,** aceptar; recibir. **to h. down,** hacer bajar. **She had her hair down,** El pelo le caía por las espaldas. **to h. in,** hacer entrar. **to h. on,** vestir, llevar puesto; (engagements) tener (compromisos). **to h. out,** hacer salir; llevar a paseo; llevar fuera; (have removed) hacerse sacar; quitar. **to h. up,** (persons) hacer subir; (things) subir; _Law._ llevar a (ante) los tribunales. **to h. with one,** tener consigo. **I h. her with me,** La tengo conmigo, Ella me acompaña

haven /'heivən/ _n_ puerto, _m,_ abra, _f; Fig._ oasis, abrigo, refugio, _m_

havoc /'hævək/ _n_ destrucción, ruina, _f; Fig._ estrago, _m._ **to wreak h. among,** destruir; _Fig._ hacer estragos entre (o en)

Hawaii /hə'waii/ Hawai, _m_

hawk /hɔk/ _n_ halcón, _m;_ gavilán, milano, _m._ —_vi_ cazar con halcón. —_vt_ vender mercancías por las calles; _Fig._ difundir. **h.-eyed,** de ojos de lince. **h.-nosed,** de nariz aguileña

hawker /'hɔkər/ _n_ halconero, _m;_ (vendor) buhonero, _m,_ vendedor (-ra) ambulante

hay /hei/ _n_ heno, _m._ **to make hay while the sun shines,** hacer su agosto. **hay fever,** fiebre del heno, _f._ **hay-fork,** horca, _f_

haystack /'hei,stæk/ _n_ almiar, _m,_ niara, _f_

hazard /'hæzərd/ _n_ azar, _m,_ suerte, _f;_ riesgo, peligro, _m;_ (game) juego de azar, _m._ —_vt_ arriesgar, aventurar. **at all hazards,** a todo riesgo

hazardous /'hæzərdəs/ _a_ azaroso, arriesgado, peligroso

haze /heiz/ _n_ bruma, _f;_ confusión, _f_

hazel /'heizəl/ _n_ avellano, _m._ **h.-nut,** avellana, _f_

hazy /'heizi/ _a_ brumoso, calinoso; confuso

he /hi/ *pers pron* él. —*n* (of humans) varón, *m*; (of animals) macho, *m*. **he who,** el que, quien. **he-goat,** macho cabrío, *m*. **he-man,** todo un hombre, hombre cabal, *m*

head /hɛd/ *vt* golpear con la cabeza; encabezar; (lead) capitanear; (direct) dirigir, guiar; (wine) cabecear. —*vi* estar a la cabeza de; dirigirse a. **headed for,** con rumbo a, en dirección a. **to h. off,** interceptar; desviar; *Fig.* distraer

head /hɛd/ *n Anat.* cabeza, *f*; (upper portion) parte superior, *f*; (of a coin) cara, *f*; (hair) cabellera, *f*; (individual) persona, *f*; (of cattle) res, *f*; (of a mountain) cumbre, *f*; (of a ladder) último peldaño, *m*; (of toadstools) sombrero, *m*; (of trees) copa, *f*; (of a stick) puño, *m*; (of a cylinder) culata, *f*; (of a river, etc.) manantial, origen, *m*; (of a bed) cabecera, *f*; (of nails, pins) cabeza, *f*; (froth) espuma, *f*; (flower) flor, *f*; (leaves) hojas, *f pl*; (first place) primer puesto, *m*; (of game, fish) pieza, *f*; (of a page, column) cabeza, *f*; (cape) cabo, *m*; (of an arrow, dart, lance) punta, *f*; (front) frente, *m*; (leader) jefe, cabeza, *m*; (chief) director (-ra), superior (-ra); presidente (-ta); (of a school) director (-ra); (of a cask) fondo, *m*; *Mech.* cabezal, *m*; (of an ax) filo, *m*; (of a bridge) cabeza, *f*; (of a jetty, pier) punta, *f*; (of a ship) proa, *f*; (of a flower) cabezuela, *f*; (of asparagus) punta, *f*; (of a table) cabeza, *f*; (of the family) jefe, cabeza, *m*; (seat of honor) cabecera, *f*; (title) título, *m*; (aspect) punto de vista, *m*; (division) capítulo, *m*; (management, direction) dirección, *f*; (talent) talento, *m*, cabeza, *f*; (intelligence) inteligencia, *f*. —*a* principal; primero; en jefe. **at the h. of,** a la cabeza de. **crowned h.,** testa coronada, *f*. **from h. to foot,** de pies a cabeza; de hito en hito; de arriba abajo. **He took it into his h. to...,** Se le ocurrió de... **This story has neither h. nor tail,** Este cuento no tiene pies ni cabeza. **with h. held high,** con la frente levantada. **to come to a h.,** llegar a la crisis; llegar al punto decisivo. **to get an idea out of a person's h.,** *Fig.* quitar una idea a uno de la cabeza. **to keep one's h.,** *Fig.* conservar la sangre fría, no perder la cabeza. **to lose one's h.,** *Fig.* perder la cabeza. **to put into a person's h.,** *Fig.* meter a (uno) en la cabeza. **to run one's h. against,** golpear la cabeza contra. **h. first,** de cabeza. **h. of cattle,** res, *f*. **h. office,** central, *f*. **h. of hair,** cabellera, *f*; mata de pelo, *f*. **h.-on,** de cabeza. **h.-on collision,** choque de frente, *m*. **h. opening,** (of a garment) cabezón, *m*. **heads or tails,** cara o cruz, águila y sol (Mexico). **h. over heels,** de patas arriba. **h. over heels in love,** calado hasta los huesos. **h.-dress,** tocado, *m*; peinado, *m*; sombrero, *m*. **h. voice,** voz de cabeza, *f*. **h. waiter,** encargado de comedor, jefe de camareros, *m*

headache /'hɛd,eik/ *n* dolor de cabeza, *m*; *Fig.* quebradero de cabeza, *m*

headboard /'hɛd,bɔrd/ *n* cabecera de una cama, *f*

headed /'hɛdɪd/ *a* con cabeza...; que tiene la cabeza...; de cabeza...; (of an article) intitulado. **large h.,** cabezudo

header /'hɛdər/ *n* caída de cabeza, *f*; salto de cabeza, *m*

headgear /'hɛd,gɪər/ *n* tocado, *m*; sombrero, gorro, *m*

heading /'hɛdɪŋ/ *n Naut.* el poner la proa en dirección (a); el guiar en dirección (a); (of a book, etc.) título, encabezamiento, *m*; (soccer) golpe de cabeza, *m*. **to come under the h. of,** estar incluido entre; clasificarse bajo

headlight /'hɛd,lait/ *n Auto.* faro, *m*; (Rail. Naut.) farol, *m*. **to dip the headlights,** bajar los faros. **to switch on the headlights,** encender los faros (or los faroles)

headline /'hɛd,lain/ *n* (of a newspaper) titular, *m*; (to a chapter) título de la columna, *m*

headlong /'hɛd,lɔŋ/ *a* precipitado; despeñado. —*adv* de cabeza; precipitadamente. **to fall h.,** caer de cabeza

headman /'hɛd,mæn/ *n* cacique, cabecilla, *m*; (foreman) capataz, contramaestre, *m*

headmaster /'hɛd'mæstər/ *n* director de colegio, rector, *m*

headmistress /'hɛd'mɪstrɪs/ *n* directora de colegio, rectora, *f*

head nurse enfermero-jefe, *m*

head-on collision /'hɛd ,ɒn/ *n* choque frontal, *m*

headphones /'hɛd,founz/ *n pl* auriculares, *m pl*

headquarters /'hɛd,kwɔrtərz/ *n Mil.* cuartel general, *m*; oficina central, *f*; jefatura, *f*; centro, *m*

headrest /'hɛd,rɛst/ *n* respaldo, *m*; apoyo para la cabeza, *m*

headstrong /'hɛd,strɔŋ/ *a* impetuoso, terco, testarudo

headway /'hɛd,wei/ *n* marcha, *f*; *Fig.* progreso, avance, *m*. **to make h.,** avanzar; *Fig.* hacer progresos; *Fig.* prosperar

heady /'hɛdi/ *a* apasionado, violento; impetuoso, precipitado; (obstinate) terco; (of alcohol) encabezado; *Fig.* embriagador

heal /hil/ *vt* curar, sanar; (flesh) cicatrizar. —*vi* curar, sanar; cicatrizarse; (superficially) sobresanar

healer /'hilər/ *n* sanador (-ra), curador (-ra); curandero, *m*

health /hɛlθ/ *n* salud, *f*; higiene, sanidad, *f*. **Here's to your very good h.!** ¡Salud y pesetas! **to drink a person's h.,** Disfruta de buena salud. **to drink a person's h.,** beber a la salud de. **to enjoy good h.,** gozar de buena salud. **to look full of h.,** vender salud. **h.-giving,** saludable. **h. inspection,** visita de sanidad, *f*. **h. officer,** inspector de sanidad, *m*. **h. resort,** balneario, *m*

healthy /'hɛlθi/ *a* sano; con buena salud;

(healthful) saludable. **to be h.,** tener buena salud

heap /hip/ n montón, m; rima, pila, f, acervo, m; (of people) muchedumbre, f, tropel, m. —vt amontonar; apilar; colmar. **in heaps,** a montones. **We have heaps of time,** Nos sobra tiempo, Tenemos tiempo de sobra. **to h. together,** juntar, mezclar. **to h. up, upon,** colmar; amontonar; Agr. hacinar; Fig. acumular

hear /hɪər/ vt oír; (listen) escuchar; (attend) asistir a; (give audience) dar audiencia (a); (a lawsuit) ver (un pleito); (speak) hablar; (be aware of, feel) sentir. —vi oír; tener noticias; (learn) enterarse de; (allow) permitir. **H.! H.!** ¡Muy bien! ¡Bravo! **I have heard it said that...** He oído decir que... **Let me h. from you!** ¡Mándame noticias tuyas! **They were never heard of again,** No se volvió a saber de ellos, No se supo más de ellos. **to h. about,** oír de; (know) saber de, tener noticias de; recibir información sobre. **to h. from,** ser informado por; tener noticias de: recibir carta de. **to h. of,** enterarse de, saber; recibir información sobre; (allow) permitir

hearing /'hɪərɪŋ/ n (sense of) oído, m; alcance del oído, m; presencia, f; audición, f; Law. vista (de una causa) f. **It was said in my h.,** Fue dicho en mi presencia. **out of h.,** fuera del alcance del oído. **within h.,** al alcance del oído. **have a h. problem,** ser parcialmente sordo

hearing aid acústica, aparato auditivo, aparato acústico, audífono, m

hearsay /'hɪər,seɪ/ n fama, f, rumor, m. **by h.,** de oídas

hearse /hɜrs/ n coche fúnebre, m

heart /hɑrt/ n corazón, m; (feelings) entrañas, f pl; (of the earth, etc.) seno, corazón, m; (of lettuce, etc.) cogollo, repollo, m; (suit in cards) copas, f pl; Bot. médula, f; (soul) alma, f; (courage) valor, m; ánimo, m. **at h.,** en el fondo, esencialmente. **by h.,** de memoria. **from the h.,** con toda sinceridad, de todo corazón. **He is a man after my own h.,** Es un hombre de los que me gustan. **I have no h. to do it,** No tengo valor de hacerlo. **in the h. of the country,** en medio del campo. **to break one's h.,** partirse el corazón. **to have one's h. in one's mouth,** tener el alma en un hilo, estar muerto de miedo. **to have no h.,** Fig. no tener entrañas. **to lose h.,** desanimarse, descorazonarse. **to set one's h. on,** poner el corazón en. **to take h.,** cobrar ánimo; Inf. hacer de tripas corazón. **to take to h.,** tomar a pechos. **to wear one's h. on one's sleeve,** tener el corazón en la mano. **with all my h.,** con toda el alma. **h.-ache,** angustia, pena, f; **h.-beat,** latido del corazón, m. **h.-breaker,** (woman) coqueta, f; (man) ladrón de corazones, m. **h. disease,** enfermedad del corazón, enfermedad cardíaca, f. **h. failure,** colapso

cardíaco, m. **h.-rending,** desgarrador, angustioso. **h.-searching,** examen de conciencia, m. **h.-shaped,** acorazonado, en forma de corazón. **h.-strings,** fibras del corazón, f pl. **h.-to-h. talk,** conversación íntima, f. **h.-whole,** libre de afectos

heartbreaking /'hɑrt,breɪkɪŋ/ a desgarrador, angustioso, lastimoso

heartbroken /'hɑrt,broʊkən/ a acongojado, afligido, transido de dolor

heartburn /'hɑrt,bɜrn/ n acidez del estómago, acedia, pirosis, rescoldera, f

hearten /'hɑrtn/ vt alentar, animar

heartfelt /'hɑrt,fɛlt/ a hondo; de todo corazón, sincero; más expresivo

hearth /hɑrθ/ n hogar, m; chimenea, f; Fig. hogar, m.

heartily /'hɑrtli/ adv cordialmente; sinceramente; enérgicamente; con entusiasmo; (of eating) con buen apetito; (very) muy, completamente. **I am h. sick of it all,** Inf. Estoy harto hasta los dientes

heartless /'hɑrtlɪs/ a sin corazón, sin piedad, despiadado, inhumano, cruel

hearty /'hɑrti/ a cordial; sincero; enérgico; vigoroso; robusto; (frank) campechano; (of appetite) voraz; bueno; (big) grande

heat /hit/ n calor, m; (in animals) celo, m; (of an action) calor, m; Fig. vehemencia, fogosidad, f; Fig. fuego, m; (passion) ardor, m, pasión, f; (of a race) carrera eliminatoria, f. —vt calentar; (excite) conmover, acalorar, excitar; (annoy) irritar. —vi calentarse. **dead h.,** empate, m. **in h.,** en celo. **in the h. of the moment,** en el calor del momento. **to become heated,** Fig. acalorarse, exaltarse. **white h.,** candencia, incandescencia, f. **h. lightning,** fucilazo, m. **h. spot,** pápula, f; terminación sensible, f. **h. stroke,** insolación, f. **h. wave,** onda de calor, f

heater /'hitər/ n calentador, m; calorífero, m; (stove) estufa, f; (for plates) calientaplatos, m. **water-h.,** calentador de agua, m

heath /hiθ/ n brezal, m; yermo, páramo, m; Bot. brezo, m

heathen /'hiðən/ n pagano (-na); idólatra, mf; ateo (-ea), descreído (-da). —a pagano; ateo; bárbaro

heating /'hitɪŋ/ n calefacción, f, a calentador; (of drinks) fortificante. **central h.,** calefacción central, f

heave /hiv/ vt alzar, levantar; Naut. izar; (the anchor, etc.) virar; (throw) arrojar, lanzar; elevar; (extract) extraer; (emit) dar, exhalar. —vi subir y bajar; palpitar; agitarse. —n tirón, m; (of the sea) vaivén, m. **to h. in sight,** aparecer, surgir. **to h. out sail,** Naut. desenvergar. **to h. the lead,** Naut. escandallar. **to h. to,** Naut. estarse a la capa

heaven /'hɛvən/ n cielo, m; firmamento, m; paraíso, m. **Heavens!** ¡Cielos! **For Dios! Thank H.!** ¡Gracias a Dios! **h.-born,** celeste. **h.-sent,** Fig. providencial

heavenly /'hɛvənli/ a celeste, celestial; divino; Fig. delicioso. **h. body**, astro, m

heavily /'hɛvəli/ adv pesadamente; torpemente; penosamente; (slowly) lentamente; severamente; excesivamente; (of sighing) hondamente; (sadly) tristemente; (of rain, etc.) reciamente; fuertemente; (of wind) con violencia. **He fell h.**, Cayó de plomo. **to lie h. upon**, pesar mucho sobre. **to rain h.**, llover mucho, diluviar

heaviness /'hɛvɪnɪs/ n peso, m; (lethargy) torpor, letargo, m; sueño, m, languidez, f; (clumsiness) torpeza, f; (severity) severidad, f; importancia, responsabilidad, f; dificultad, f; (gravity) gravedad, f; tristeza, melancolía, f; (boredom) sosería, insulsez, f; (of style) monotonía, ponderosidad, f

heaving /'hivɪŋ/ n levantamiento, m; (of the anchor, etc.) virada, f; (of the sea) vaivén, m; (of the breast) palpitación, f

heavy /'hɛvi/ a pesado; torpe; sin gracia; (slow) lento; (thick) grueso; (strong) fuerte; (hard) duro; grave; difícil; oneroso; responsable, importante; (oppressive) opresivo; penoso; grande; (sad) triste, melancólico; (of the sky) anublado; (of food) indigesto; (tedious) aburrido, soso; (pompous) pomposo; (of roads) malo; (of scents) fuerte, penetrante; (of sleep, weather) pesado; (weary) rendido; (charged with) cargado de; (of a meal) grande, abundante; (violent) violento; (of a cold, etc.) malo; (drowsy) soñoliento; (torpid) tórpido; (of rain, snow, hail) fuerte, recio; (of firing) intenso; (of sighs) profundo; (of soil) recio, de mucha miga; (Phys. Chem.) pesado. **to be h.**, pesar mucho. **How h. are you?** ¿Cuánto pesa Vd.? **h.-armed**, armado hasta los dientes. **h.-eyed**, con ojeras. **h. guns**, artillería pesada, f. **h.-handed**, de manos torpes; Fig. tiránico, opresivo. **h.-hearted**, triste, apesadumbrado. **h. industry**, la gran industria, la industria pesada, f. **h.-laden**, muy cargado. **h. losses**, Mil. pérdidas cuantiosas, f pl. **h. weight**, Sports. peso pesado, m

Hebrew /'hibru/ n hebreo (-ea), judío (-ía); (language) hebreo, m

heckle /'hɛkəl/ vt Fig. interrumpir, importunar con preguntas

heckler /'hɛklər/ n perturbador (-ra)

hectare /'hɛktɛər/ n hectárea, f

hectic /'hɛktɪk/ a (consumptive) hético; (feverish) febril; Fig. Inf. agitado

hector /'hɛktər/ vt intimidar, amenazar

hectoring /'hɛktərɪŋ/ a imperioso; amenazador

hedge /hɛdʒ/ n seto, m; barrera, f. —vt cercar con un seto; rodear. —vi Fig. titubear, vacilar. **h.-hopping**, Aer. vuelo a ras de tierra, m. **h.-sparrow**, acentor de bosque, m

hedgehog /'hɛdʒˌhɒg/ n erizo, m. **h. position**, Mil. puesto fuerte, m

hedonism /'hidnˌɪzəm/ n hedonismo, m

heed /hid/ n atención, f, cuidado, m. —vt

atender; observar, considerar; escuchar. —vi hacer caso

heedful /'hidfəl/ a atento; cuidadoso

heedless /'hidlɪs/ a desatento; descuidado, negligente; distraído

heel /hil/ n Anat. talón, calcañar, m; (of shoe) tacón, m; (of a violin, etc., bow) talón, m; (remains) restos, m pl. —vt poner tacón a; poner talón a; Naut. hacer zozobrar. —vi Naut. zozobrar. **rubber h.**, tacón de goma, m. **She let him cool his heels for half an hour**, le dio un plantón de media hora. **to follow on a person's heels**, pisarle (a uno) los talones. **to be down at h.**, (of shoes) estar gastados los tacones; estar desaseado. **to take to one's heels**, apretar a correr, poner pies en polvorosa. **to turn on one's h.**, dar media vuelta. **h.-bone**, zancajo, m. **h.-piece**, talón, m

heft /hɛft/ vt sopesar, tomar al peso

hegemony /hɪ'dʒɛməni/ n hegemonía, f

heifer /'hɛfər/ n ternera, vaquilla, f

heigh /hei/ interj (calling attention) ¡oye! ¡oiga! **h.-ho!** ¡ay!

height /hait/ n altura, f; elevación, f; altitud, f; (stature) estatura, f; (high ground) cerro, m, colina, f; (sublimity) sublimidad, excelencia, f; colmo, m; (zenith) auge, m, cumbre, f

heighten /'haitn/ vt hacer más alto; (enhance) realzar; (exaggerate) exagerar; (perfect) perfeccionar; (intensify) intensificar

heightening /'haitnɪŋ/ n elevación, f; (enhancement) realce, m; (exaggeration) exageración, f; (perfection) perfección, f; (intensification) intensificación, f

heinous /'heinəs/ a atroz, nefando, horrible

heir /ɛər/ n heredero, m. **h. apparent**, heredero aparente, m. **h.-at-law**, heredero forzoso, m. **h. presumptive**, presunto heredero, m

heiress /'ɛərɪs/ n heredera, f

heirloom /'ɛərˌlum/ n reliquia de familia, f; Fig. herencia, f

helicopter /'hɛliˌkɒptər/ n helicóptero, m

helium /'hiliəm/ n Chem. helio, m

hell /hɛl/ n infierno, m. **h.-fire**, fuego del infierno, m, llamas del infierno, f pl

hellish /'hɛliʃ/ a infernal; Inf. horrible, detestable

hello /hɛ'lou/ interj ¡hola!; (on telephoning someone) ¡oiga! ¡alo!; (answering telephone) ¡diga! ¡alo!

helm /hɛlm/ n caña del timón, f; timón, gobernalle, m. **to obey the h.**, obedecer el timón. **to take the h.**, gobernar el timón; ponerse a pilotar

helmet /'hɛlmɪt/ n casco, m; (in olden days) yelmo, capacete, m; (sun) casco colonial, m

help /hɛlp/ n ayuda, f; auxilio, socorro, m; (protection) favor, m, protección, f; (remedy) remedio, m; (cooperation) cooperación, f, concurso, m; (domestic) criada, f. **A little h. is worth a lot of**

sympathy, Más vale un toma que dos te daré. **There's no h. for it,** No hay más remedio. **to call for h.,** pedir socorro a gritos. **without h.,** a solas, sin la ayuda de nadie

help /help/ vt ayudar; socorrer, auxiliar; (favor) favorecer; (mitigate) aliviar; (contribute to) contribuir a, facilitar; (avoid) evitar. —vi ayudar. **He cannot h. worrying,** No puede menos de preocuparse. **God h. you!** ¡Dios te ampare! **So h. me God!** ¡Así Dios me salve! **to h. one another,** ayudarse mutuamente, ayudarse los unos a los otros. **to h. oneself,** (to food) servirse. **to h. down, off,** ayudar a bajar; a apearse. **to h. in,** ayudar a entrar. **to h. along, forward, on,** avanzar, fomentar, promover; contribuir a. **Shall I h. you on with the dress?** ¿Quieres que te ayude a ponerte el vestido? **to h. out,** ayudar a salir; (from a vehicle) ayudar a bajar; (of a difficulty, etc.) sacar; suplir la falta de; ayudar. **to h. over,** ayudar a cruzar; (a difficulty) ayudar a salir (de un apuro); ayudar a vencer (un obstáculo, etc.); (a period) ayudar a pasar. **to h. to,** contribuir a, ayudar en; (food) servir. **to h. up,** ayudar a subir; ayudar a levantarse, levantar

helper /helpər/ n auxiliador (-ra); asistente (-ta); (protector) favorecedor (-ra); bienhechor (-ra); (colleague) colega, m; (co-worker) colaborador (-ra). **He thanked all his helpers,** Dio las gracias a todos los que le habían ayudado

helpful /helpfəl/ a útil, provechoso; (obliging) servicial, atento; (favorable) favorable; (healthy) saludable

helping /helpɪŋ/ n ayuda, f; (of food) porción, ración, f; plato, m. **Won't you have a second h.?** ¿No quiere usted servirse más (or otra vez)? ¿No quiere usted repetir? **to lend a h. hand (to),** prestar ayuda (a)

helpless /helplɪs/ a desamparado, abandonado; (through infirmity) imposibilitado; impotente, sin fuerzas (para); (shiftless) incompetente, inútil

helpmeet /help,mit/ n compañero (-ra) perfecto (-ta); esposa, f

helter-skelter /heltər 'skeltər/ adv atropelladamente; en desorden. —n barahunda, f

hem /hem/ n Sew. dobladillo, filete, m, bastilla, f; (edge) orilla, f. —interj ¡ejem! —vt hacer dobladillo en, dobladillar. —vi (cough) fingir toser. **false hem,** Sew. dobladillo falso, m. **running hem,** Sew. jareta, f. **to hem and haw,** tartamudear; vacilar. **to hem in,** cercar, sitiar

hemisphere /hemɪ,sfɪər/ n hemisferio, m

hemlock /hem,lɒk/ n Bot. cicuta, f

hemoglobin /himə,gloubɪn/ n Chem. hemoglobina, f

hemophilia /,himə'fɪliə/ n Med. hemofilia, f

hemorrhage /hemərɪdʒ/ n hemorragia, f, flujo de sangre, m

hemorrhoids /hemə,rɔidz/ n pl Med. hemorroides, f

hemp /hemp/ n cáñamo, m. **h. cloth,** lienzo, m. **h.-seed,** cañamón, m

hemstitch /hem,stɪtʃ/ n vainica, f. —vt hacer vainica en

hen /hen/ n gallina, f; (female bird) hembra, f. **the hen pheasant,** la hembra del faisán. **hen bird,** pájara, f. **hen-coop** or **house,** gallinero, m. **hen party,** Inf. reunión de mujeres, f. **hen-roost,** nidal, ponedero, m

hence /hens/ adv (of place) de aquí; (of time) de ahora, de aquí a, al cabo de, en; (therefore) por eso, por lo tanto, por consiguiente. —interj ¡fuera! ¡fuera de aquí! **I shall come to see you a month h.,** Vendré a verte en un mes (or al cabo de un mes). **ten years h.,** de aquí a diez años. **h. the fact that...,** de aquí que.... **H. it happens that...,** Por eso sucede que...

henceforth /,hens'fɔrθ/ adv desde aquí en adelante, de hoy en adelante

henchman /hentʃmən/ n escudero, m; satélite, secuaz, m

henpecked /hen,pekt/ a gobernado por su mujer, que se deja mandar por su mujer

her /hər; unstressed hər, ər/ pers pron direct object la; (with prepositions) ella. —pers pron indirect object le, a ella. —poss a sus, mf; sus, mf pl, de ella. **I saw her on Wednesday,** La vi el miércoles. **The message is for her,** El recado es para ella. **It is her book,** Es su libro, Es el libro de ella

herald /herəld/ n heraldo, m; presagio, anuncio, m. —vt proclamar; anunciar; presagiar

herb /ɜrb; esp. Brit. hɜrb/ n hierba, f

herby /ɜrbi, 'hɜr-/ a herbáceo

Herculean /,hɜrkyə'liən/ a hercúleo

herd /hɜrd/ n manada, f; (of cattle) hato, m; (race) raza, f; (Fig. contemptuous) populacho, m, masa, f. —vt reunir en manadas; reunir en hatos; (sheep) reunir en rebaños; guiar las manadas, etc. —vi ir en manadas, hatos o rebaños; asociarse, reunirse. **h.-instinct,** instinto gregario, m; instinto de las masas, m

herdsman /hɜrdzmən/ n ganadero, pastor, manadero, m; (head herdsman) rabadán, m

here /hɪər/ adv aquí; (at roll-call) ¡presente!; acá; en este punto; ahora. —n presente, m. **And h. he looked at me,** Y a este punto me miró. **Come h.!** ¡Ven acá! **in h.,** aquí dentro. **h. below,** aquí abajo, en la tierra. **h. and there,** aquí y allá. **h., there and everywhere,** en todas partes. **H. I am,** Heme aquí. **h. is...,** he aquí... **H. they are,** Aquí los tienes, Aquí están. **Here's to you!** (on drinking) ¡Salud y pesetas! ¡A tu salud!

hereabouts /'hɪərə,bauts/ *adv* por aquí cerca

hereafter /hɪər'æftər/ *adv* en lo futuro; desde ahora; en adelante. —*n* futuro, *m*. **the H.,** la otra vida

hereby /hɪər'bai/ *adv* por esto, por las presentes

hereditarily /hə,rɛdɪ'tɛrəli/ *adv* hereditariamente, por herencia

hereditary /hə'rɛdɪ,tɛri/ *a* hereditario

heredity /hə'rɛdɪti/ *n* herencia, *f*

herein /hɪər'ɪn/ *adv* en esto; aquí dentro; incluso

hereinafter /,hɪərɪn'æftər/ *adv* después, más abajo, más adelante, en adelante, en lo sucesivo

heresy /'hɛrəsi/ *n* herejía, *f*

heretic /'hɛrɪtɪk/ *n* hereje, *mf*

heretical /hə'rɛtɪkəl/ *a* herético

hereunder /hɪər'ʌndər/ *adv* abajo

hereupon /,hɪərə'pɒn/ *adv* en esto, en seguida

herewith /hɪər'wɪθ/ *adv* junto con esto, con esto; ahora, en esta ocasión

heritage /'hɛrɪtɪdʒ/ *n* herencia, *f*

hermaphrodite /hər'mæfrə,dait/ *a and n* hermafrodita, *mf*

hermetic /hər'mɛtɪk/ *a* hermético

hermit /'hɜrmɪt/ *n* ermitaño, *m*. **h. crab,** paguro, cangrejo ermitaño, *m*

hernia /'hɜrniə/ *n* hernia, *f*

hero /'hɪərou/ *n* héroe, *m*. **h.-worship,** culto a los héroes, *m*

heroic /hɪ'rouɪk/ *a* heroico, épico

heroin /'herouɪn/ *n* Chem. heroína, *f*

heroine /'herouɪn/ *n* heroína, *f*

heroism /'herou,ɪzəm/ *n* heroísmo, *m*

herpes /'hɜrpiz/ *n pl* herpes, *mf pl*

herring /'herɪŋ/ *n* arenque, *m*

hers /hɜrz/ *poss pron 3rd sing* (el) suyo, *m*; (la) suya, *f*; (los) suyos, *m pl*; (las) suyas, *f pl*; de ella. **This book is h.,** Este libro es suyo, Este libro es de ella. **This book is h.,** not mine, Este libro es el suyo no el mío. **a sister of h.,** una de sus hermanas, una hermana suya

herself /hər'sɛlf/ *pron* sí misma, sí; ella misma; (with reflexive verb) se. **She has done it by h.,** Lo ha hecho por sí misma. **She h. told me so,** Ella misma me lo dijo. **She is by h.,** Está a solas, Está sola

hesitancy /'hɛzɪtənsi/. See **hesitation**

hesitant /'hɛzɪtənt/ *a* indeciso, vacilante, irresoluto. **to be h.,** mostrarse irresoluto

hesitate /'hɛzɪ,teɪt/ *vi* vacilar, dudar; titubear. **I do not h. to say...,** No vacilo en decir... **He hesitated over his reply,** Tardaba en dar su respuesta

hesitatingly /'hɛzɪ,teɪtɪŋli/ *adv* irresolutamente; titubeando

hesitation /,hɛzɪ'teɪʃən/ *n* vacilación, hesitación, *f*; irresolución, indecisión, *f*; (reluctance) aversión, repugnancia, *f*; titubeo, *m*

heterogeneous /,hɛtərə'dʒiniəs/ *a* heterogéneo

hew /hyu/ *vt* cortar, tajar; (trees) talar; (a career, etc.) hacerse

hewer /'hyuər/ *n* partidor, talador, *m*

hey /hei/ *interj* ¡he! ¡oye!

heyday /'hei,dei/ *n* apogeo, colmo, *m*; buenos tiempos, *m pl*; reinado, *m*; pleno vigor, *m*

hi /hai/ *interj* ¡oye! ¡hola!

hiatus /hai'eitəs/ *n* hiato, *m*; laguna, *f*, vacío, *m*

hibernate /'haibər,neit/ *vi* invernar

hibernation /,haibər'neiʃən/ *n* invernada, *f*

hidden /'hɪdn̩/ *a* escondido, secreto, oculto

hide /haid/ *n* piel, *f*; pellejo, cuero, *m*

hide /haid/ *vt* esconder, ocultar; (cover) cubrir, tapar; (dissemble) disimular; (meaning) obscurecer. —*vi* esconderse; ocultarse; refugiarse. **to h. from each other,** esconderse el uno del otro. **h.-and-seek,** escondite, dormirlas, *m*

hidebound /'haid,baund/ *a* Fig. muy conservador, reaccionario, de ideas muy tradicionales

hideous /'hɪdiəs/ *a* horrible, repulsivo, horroroso; repugnante, odioso

hideously /'hɪdiəsli/ *adv* horriblemente. **to be h. ugly,** (of people) ser más feo que Picio

hiding /'haidɪŋ/ *n* ocultación, *f*; encubrimiento, *m*; refugio, *m*; Inf. paliza, tunda, *f*. **h.-place,** escondite, escondrijo, *m*

hie /hai/ *vi* apresurarse, ir a prisa

hierarchical /,haiə'rɑrkikəl/ *a* jerárquico

hierarchy /'haiə,rɑrki/ *n* jerarquía, *f*

hieroglyph /'haiərə,glɪf/ *n* jeroglífico, *m*

higgledy-piggledy /'hɪɡəldi 'pɪɡəldi/ *adv* revueltamente, en confusión; en montón, en desorden

high /hai/ *a* alto; elevado; (with altar, Mass, street, festival) mayor; grande; eminente; aristocrático; (of shooting) fijante; (of quality) superior; excelente; (haughty) orgulloso; (solemn) solemne; (good) bueno; noble; supremo; sumo; (of price) subido; Mus. agudo; (of the sea) tempestuoso, borrascoso; (of wind and explosives) violento, fuerte; (of polish) brillante; (with speed) grande; (with tension, frequency) alto; (with number, etc.) importante, grande; (with colors) subido; (of food) pasado; (angry) enojado, airado; (of cheek bones) saliente, prominente; (well-seasoned) picante; (flattering) lisonjero. —*adv* alto; hacia arriba; arriba; (deeply) profundamente; fuertemente; con violencia; (of price) a un precio elevado; (luxuriously) lujosamente; Mus. agudo. **a room 12 ft. h.,** un cuarto de doce pies de altura. **I knew her when she was so h.,** La conocí tamaña. **It is h. time he came,** Ya es hora de que viniese. **on h.,** en alto, arriba; en los cielos. **h. altar,** altar mayor, *m*. **h. and dry,** en la playa, varado; Fig. en seco. **h. and low,** de arriba abajo; por todas partes. **h.-born,** aristocrático, de alta alcurnia. **h.-**

bred, (of people) de buena familia; (of animals) de buena raza. **h.-class,** de buena clase; de alta calidad. **h. collar,** alzacuello, *m.* **h. colored,** de colores vivos; *Fig.* exagerado. **h. command,** (*Mil. Nav.*) alto mando, *m.* **h. court,** tribunal supremo, *m.* **h. day,** día festivo, *m.* **h. explosive,** explosivo violento, *m.* **h.-flown,** hinchado, retumbante, altisonante. **h. frequency,** alta frecuencia, *f.* **h.-handed,** arbitrario, dominador, despótico. **h.-heeled,** *a* de tacón alto. **h. jump,** salto de altura, *m.* **h. land,** tierras altas, *f pl*; eminencia, *f.* **h. light,** *Art.* realce, *m;* acontecimiento de más interés, *m;* momento culminante, *m.* **h. mass,** misa mayor, *f.* **h.-minded,** de nobles pensamientos; arrogante. **h.-necked,** con cuello alto. **h.-pitched,** de tono alto, agudo. **h.-powered,** de alta potencia. **h.-powered car,** coche de muchos caballos, *m.* **h. precision,** suma precisión, *f.* **h. pressure,** alta presión, *f; Fig.* urgencia, *f; n* de alta presión; *Fig.* urgente. **h.-priced,** caro. **h. priest,** sumo pontífice, sumo sacerdote, alto sacerdote, *m.* **h. relief,** alto relieve, *m.* **h. road,** carretera mayor, *f.* **h. school,** instituto de segunda enseñanza, instituto, colegio, liceo, *m;* colegio, liceo, instituto, *m,* escuela secundaria, secundaria, *f.* **h. sea,** marejada, *f.* **h. seas,** alta mar, *f.* **h.-seasoned,** picante, *h.* **h. society,** alta sociedad, *f.* **h. sounding,** altisonante, bombástico. **h.-speed,** de alta velocidad. **h.-spirited,** brioso; alegre. **h.-strung,** nervioso, excitable, sensitivo. **h. tension,** alta tensión, *f.* **h. tide,** marea alta, *f.* **h.-toned,** *Mus.* agudo; *Inf.* de alto copete; aristocrático. **h. treason,** alta traición, *f.* **h. water,** marea alta, pleamar, *f.* **h.-water mark,** límite de la marea, *m; Fig.* colmo, *m;* apogeo, *m*

highbrow /'hai,brau/ *a* and *n* intelectual, *mf*

higher /'haiər/ *a compar* of **high,** más alto; más elevado; superior. **on a h. plane,** en un nivel más alto. **h. education,** enseñanza superior, *f.* **h. mathematics,** la alta matemática, *f.* **h. criticism,** la alta crítica, *f.* **h. up,** más arriba. **h. up the river,** río arriba

highest /'haiist/ *a superl* of **high,** el más alto; la más alta; los más altos; las más altas; sumo, supremo; excelente. **h. common factor,** *Math.* máximo común divisor, *m.* **h. references,** (of cook, gardener, etc.) informes inmejorables, *m pl;* *Com.* referencias excelentes, *f pl*

highland /'hailənd/ *n* altiplanicie, *f;* montañas, *f pl,* distrito montañoso, *m.* —*a* montañoso

highlight /'hai,lait/ *vt* dar relieve a, destacar

highly /'haili/ *adv* altamente; mucho; muy; extremadamente; grandemente; bien; favorablemente; con lisonja, lisonjeramente. **h. seasoned,** picante. **h. strung,** nervioso, excitable

highness /'hainis/ *n* altura, *f;* elevación, *f;* excelencia, *f;* nobleza, *f;* (title) Alteza, *f.* **His Royal H.,** **Her Royal Highness,** Su Alteza Real

high-ranking /'hai 'ræŋkɪŋ/ *a* de alta jerarquía, de alto rango

highway /'hai,wei/ *n* camino real, *m,* carretera, *f.* **h. code,** código de la vía pública (or de la circulación), *m.* **h. robbery,** salteamiento de caminos, atraco, *m*

highways and byways /'hai,weiz ən 'bai,weiz/ caminos y veredas

hike /haik/ *vi* ir de excursión. —*n* marcha con equipo, *f*

hiker /'haikər/ *n* excursionista, *mf*

hiking /'haikɪŋ/ *n* excursionismo, *m;* marcha con equipo, *f*

hilarious /hɪ'lɛəriəs/ *a* alegre

hill /hɪl/ *n* colina, *f,* cerro, otero, *m;* monte, *m,* montaña, *f;* (pile) montón, *m.* **h.-side,** falda de montaña, ladera de una colina, *f.* **h.-top,** cumbre de una colina, *f*

hilly /'hɪli/ *a* montañoso

hilt /hɪlt/ *n* puño, *m,* empuñadura, *f*

him /hɪm/ *pron 3rd sing direct object* le, lo; (with prep.) él; *indirect object* le, a él; (with a direct obj. in 3rd person) se. **I gave him the magazine,** Le di la revista. **I gave it to him,** Se lo di a él. **This is for him,** Esto es para él

himself /hɪm'sɛlf/ *pron* sí, sí mismo; él mismo; (reflexive) se. **He did it by h.,** Lo hizo por sí mismo. For more examples see **herself**

hind /haind/ *n* corza, cierva, *f.* —*a* trasero, posterior. **h.-quarters,** cuarto trasero, *m;* (of a horse) ancas, *f pl*

hinder /'hindər/ *a* trasero, posterior

hinder /'hindər/ *vt* impedir, estorbar; embarazar, dificultar; interrumpir. —*vi* ser un obstáculo; formar un obstáculo

hindmost /'haind,moust/ *a* posterior, postrero, último

hindrance /'hindrəns/ *n* obstáculo, estorbo, impedimento, *m;* perjuicio, *m;* interrupción, *f*

hinge /hɪndʒ/ *n* gozne, pernio, *m,* bisagra, *f;* articulación, *f; Fig.* eje, *m.* —*vi* moverse (or abrirse) sobre goznes; *Fig.* depender (de). —*vt* engoznar

hint /hint/ *n* indirecta, insinuación, sugestión, *f;* (advice) consejo, *m.* —*vt* dar a entender, decir con medias palabras, insinuar, sugerir. —*vi* insinuar. **to take the h.,** darse por aludido

hinterland /'hintər,lænd/ *n* interior (de un país), *m*

hip /hɪp/ *n Anat.* cadera, *f; Bot.* fruto del rosal silvestre, *m.* **h.-bath,** baño de asiento, *m.* **h.-bone,** hueso ilíaco, *m.* **h.-joint,** articulación de la cadera, *f.* **h.-pocket,** faltriquera, *f*

hippopotamus /,hɪpə'pɒtəməs/ *n* hipopótamo, *m*

hire /haiər/ *n* alquiler, arriendo, *m;* salario, *m.* —*vt* alquilar, arrendar; tomar a su arriendo; (person) contratar; tomar a su servicio. **to h. out,** alquilar. **for** or **on h.,**

de alquiler. **h.-purchase,** compra a plazos, f

hireling /'hai²rlɪŋ/ n mercenario, m

hirer /'hai²rər/ n alquilador (-ra), arrendador (-ra)

hirsute /'hɜrsut/ a hirsuto. **non-h.** Bot. lampiño

his /hɪz; unstressed ɪz/ poss pron 3rd sing (el) suyo, m; (la) suya, f; (los) suyos, m pl; (las) suyas, f pl; de él. —poss a su, mf; sus, mf pl; de él. **his handkerchiefs,** sus pañuelos. **his mother,** su madre, la madre de él. **a sister of his,** una de sus hermanas, una hermana suya. See **hers** for more examples.

Hispano-American /hɪs'pænou ə'mɛrɪkən/ a hispano-americano

hiss /hɪs/ n silbido, m; (sputter) chisporroteo, m. —vi silbar

hissing /'hɪsɪŋ/ n silbido, m; chisporroteo, m. —a silbante

hist /hɪst/ interj ¡chist!

histology /hɪ'stɒlədʒi/ n histología, f

historian /hɪ'stɔriən/ n historiador (-ra)

historic /hɪ'stɒrɪk/ a histórico

historical /hɪ'stɒrɪkəl/ a histórico. **h. truth,** verdad histórica, f

history /'hɪstəri/ n historia, f. **Biblical h.,** historia sagrada, f. **natural h.,** historia natural, f

histrionic /ˌhɪstri'ɒnɪk/ a histriónico

hit /hɪt/ n golpe, m; Aer. impacto, m; (success) éxito, m; (piece of luck) buena suerte, f; (satire) sátira, f. —vt golpear; (buffet) abofetear, pegar; (find) dar con, tropezar con; (attain) acertar; (guess) adivinar; (attract) atraer; (deal) lanzar, dar; (wound) herir, hacer daño a. **The sun hits me right in the eyes,** El sol me da en la cabeza. **direct hit,** Aer. impacto de lleno, m. **lucky hit,** acierto, m. **to hit a straight left,** (boxing) lanzar un directo con la izquierda. **to hit the mark,** dar en el blanco; Fig. dar en el clavo. **hit or miss,** acierto o error. **to hit against,** dar contra, estrellar contra. **to hit back,** defenderse; devolver golpe por golpe. **to hit off,** imitar; (a likeness) coger. **to hit out,** abofetear; Fig. atacar; golpear (la pelota) fuera. **to hit upon,** dar con; tropezar con; encontrar por casualidad; (remember) acordarse de

hitch /hɪtʃ/ n (jerk) sacudida, f; nudo fácil de soltar, m; Fig. obstáculo, m; Fig. dificultad, f. **give s.b. a hitch,** levantar a fulano, m. —vt sacudir; (a chair, etc.) arrastrar, empujar; amarrar, enganchar; atar. —vi (along a seat, etc.) correrse (en); (get entangled) enredarse, cogerse; (rub) rascarse. **without a h.,** sin dificultad alguna, viento en popa; (smoothly) a pedir de boca. **to h. up,** sacudir, dar una sacudida (a)

hitchhike /'hɪtʃˌhaik/ vi ir a dedo (Argentina), pedir aventón (Mexico), pedir botella (Cuba), hacer autostop, ir por autostop (Spain)

hither /'hɪðər/ adv acá, hacia acá; a

citerior, más cercano. **h. and thither,** acá y aculla allá

hitherto /'hɪðər,tu/ adv hasta ahora, hasta el presente

hive /haiv/ n (for bees) colmena, f; (swarm) enjambre, m; Fig. centro, m. —vt (bees) enjambrar. **h. of industry,** centro de industria

hoard /hɔrd/ n acumulación, f; provisión, f; tesoro, m. —vt acumular, amasar, amontonar; guardar

hoarding /'hɔrdɪŋ/ n amontonamiento, m; acaparamiento, m; (fence) empalizada, cerca, f; palizada de tablas, f

hoarfrost /'hɔr,frɔst/ n escarcha, helada blanca, f

hoarse /hɔrs/ a ronco; discordante. **to be h.,** tener la voz ronca. **to grow h.,** enronquecerse

hoarseness /'hɔrsnɪs/ n ronquera, f; Inf. carraspera, f

hoary /'hɔri/ a (of the hair) canoso; blanco; (old) vetusto, antiguo, viejo

hoax /houks/ n estafa, f, engaño, m; broma pesada, f; burla, f. —vt estafar, engañar; burlar

hob /hɒb/ n repisa interior del hogar, f

hobble /'hɒbəl/ n (gait) cojera, f; traba, maniota, f. —vi cojear. —vt manear. **h. skirt,** falda muy estrecha, f

hobby /'hɒbi/ n pasatiempo, m, recreación, f; manía, afición, f. **h.-horse,** caballo de cartón, m; Fig. caballo de batalla, m

hobgoblin /'hɒb,gɒblɪn/ n trasgo, duende, m

hobnail /'hɒb,neil/ n clavo de herradura, clavo de botas, m

hobnailed /'hɒb,neild/ a (of boots) con clavos

hobnob /'hɒb,nɒb/ vi codearse, tratar con familiaridad

hock /hɒk/ n Anat. pernil, m; (wine) vino del Rin, m

hockey /'hɒki/ n chueca, m. **h. ball,** bola, pelota de chueca, f. **h. stick,** bastón de chueca, m

hocus-pocus /'houkəs 'poukəs/ n juego de pasa pasa, m; engaño, m, treta, f

hodgepodge /'hɒdʒ,pɒdʒ/ See **hotchpotch**

hoe /hou/ n azadón, m. —vt azadonar; sachar

hog /hɒg/ n cerdo, puerco, m. **to go the whole hog,** ir al extremo. **hogskin,** piel de cerdo, f

hoggish /'hɒgɪʃ/ a porcuno; (greedy) comilón, tragón; (selfish) egoísta

hoist /hɔist/ n levantamiento, m; (lift) montacargas, m; (winch) cabria, f; (crane) grúa, f. —vt levantar, alzar; (flags) enarbolar; suspender; Naut. izar

hoity-toity /'hɔiti 'tɔiti/ a picajoso, quisquilloso; presuntuoso

hold /hould/ n asimiento, agarro, m; presa, f; asidero, m; Fig. autoridad, f, poder, m; Fig. comprensión, f; (of a ship) cala, bodega, *f.* **to loose one's h.,** aflojar su presa. **to lose one's h.,** perder su presa. **to seize h. of,** asirse de, echar mano de. **h.-all,** funda, *f.* **h.-up,** (robbery) atraco, robo a mano armada, *m;* (in traffic) atasco (or obstáculo) en el tráfico, *m;* (in work) parada, cesación (de trabajo), *f*

hold /hould/ *vt* tener; asir, agarrar; coger; retener; (embrace) abrazar; (a post) ocupar; (a meeting, etc.) celebrar; (bear weight of) aguantar, soportar; (own) poseer; *Mil.* ocupar, defender; (contain) contener; (have in store) reservar; tener capacidad para; (retain) retener; (believe) creer, opinar; (consider) opinar, tener para (mí, etc.); juzgar; (restrain) detener; contener; (of attention, etc.) mantener; (maneuvers) hacer; (observe) guardar. —*vi* resistir, aguantar; (be valid) ser válido; regir; (apply) aplicarse; (last) continuar, seguir. —*interj* ¡tente! ¡para! **The room won't h. more,** En este cuarto no caben más. **They h. him in great respect,** Le tienen mucho respeto. **The theory does not h. water,** La teoría es falsa, La teoría no es lógica. **to h. one's own,** defenderse, mantenerse en sus trece. **to h. one's breath,** contener la respiración. **to h. one's tongue,** callarse. **to h. sway,** mandar; reinar. **to h. tightly,** agarrar fuertemente; (clasp) estrechar. **H. the line!** (telephone) ¡Aguarde un momento! **to h. back,** *vt* detener; contener; retener; esconder; abstenerse de entregar. —*vi* quedarse atrás; vacilar, dudar; tardar en. **to h. by,** seguir; basarse en, apoyarse en. **to h. down,** sujetar; (oppress) oprimir. **to h. fast,** *vt* sujetar fuertemente. —*vi* mantenerse firme; *Fig.* estar agarrado (a). **to h. forth,** *vt* ofrecer; expresar. —*vi* hacer un discurso, perorar. **to h. in,** *vt* contener; retener. —*vi* contenerse. **to h. off,** *vt* apartar, alejar. —*vi* apartarse, alejarse, mantenerse alejado. **to h. on,** seguir, persistir en; aguantar. **to h. out,** *vt* alargar, extender; ofrecer. —*vi* aguantar; durar, resistir. **to h. over,** tener suspendido sobre; (postpone) aplazar; *Fig.* amenazar con. **to h. to,** agarrarse a; atenerse a. **to h. together,** *vt* unir; juntar. —*vi* mantenerse juntos. **to h. up,** *vt* (display) mostrar, enseñar; levantar; sostener, soportar; (rob) atracar, saltear; (delay) atrasar; (stop) interrumpir, parar. —*vi* mantenerse en pie; (of weather) seguir bueno. **The train has been held up by fog,** El tren viene con retraso a causa de la niebla

holder /'houldər/ *n* el *m,* (f, la) que tiene; poseedor (-ra); *Com.* tenedor (-ra); inquilino (-na); propietario (-ia); (support) soporte, *m;* mango, *m;* asa, *f;* (in compounds) porta...

holding /'houldiŋ/ *n* tención, *f;* posesión, *f;* propiedad, *f;* (leasing) arrendamiento, *m;* (celebration) solemnización, *f;* (of a meeting) el celebrar, el tener; *pl* **holdings,** *Com.* valores habidos, *m pl*

holding company *n* compañía de cartera, *f*

hole /houl/ *n* hoyo, *m;* boquete, *m;* agujero, *m;* cavidad, *f;* (hollow) depresión, *f;* hueco, *m;* orificio, *m;* (tear) roto, desgarro, *m;* (eyelet) punto, *m;* (in cheese) ojo, *m;* (in stocking) rotura, *f,* punto, *m;* (lair) madriguera, *f;* (nest) nido, *m;* (golf) hoyo, *m;* (fix) aprieto, *m.* —*vt* agujerear; excavar; (bore) taladrar; *Sports.* meter la pelota (en). **to h. out,** (golf) meter la pelota en el hoyo. **h.-and-corner,** *a Inf.* bajo mano, secreto

hole-puncher /'houl ˌpʌntʃər/ *n* agujereadora, *f*

holiday /'hɒlɪˌdei/ *n* día feriado, *m;* día de fiesta, día festivo, *m;* vacación, *f.* —*a* festivo, alegre; de vacación; de vacaciones; de excursión; (summer) veraniego. **day's h.,** día de asueto, *m.* **to take a h.,** tomar una vacación; hacer fiesta. **h. camp,** colonia veraniega, *f.* **h.-maker,** excursionista, turista, *mf;* (in the summer) veraneante, *mf* **holidays with pay,** vacaciones retribuidas, *f pl*

holiness /'houlinɪs/ *n* santidad, *f*

Holland /'hɒlənd/ Holanda, *f*

holland /'hɒlənd/ *n* lienzo crudo. —*a* holandés. **H. gin,** ginebra holandesa, *f*

hollow /'hɒlou/ *a* hueco; cóncavo; (empty) vacío; (of eyes, etc.) hundido; (of sound) sordo; (of a cough) cavernoso; (echoing) retumbante; (*Fig.* unreal) vacío, falso; insincero. —*adv* vacío; *Inf.* completamente. —*n* hueco, *m;* concavidad, *f;* (hole) hoyo, *m;* cavidad, *f;* (valley) hondanada, *f,* barranco, *m;* (groove) ranura, *f;* (depression) depresión, *f;* (in the back) curvadura, *f.* —*vt* excavar, ahuecar; vaciar. **h.-cheeked,** con las mejillas hundidas. **h.-eyed,** con los ojos hundidos, de ojos hundidos

holocaust /'hɒləˌkɔst/ *n* holocausto, *m*

holster /'houlstər/ *n* pistolera, *f*

holy /'houli/ *a* santo; sagrado; (blessed) bendito. **most h.,** *a* santísimo. **to make h.,** santificar. **H. Father,** Padre Santo, el Papa, *m.* **H. Ghost,** Espíritu Santo, *m.* **H. Office,** Santo Oficio, *m,* Inquisición, *f.* **H. Orders,** órdenes sagradas, *f pl.* **h. places,** santos lugares, *m pl.* **H. Scripture,** Sagrada Escritura, *f.* **H. See,** Cátedra de San Pedro, *f.* **h. water,** agua bendita, *f.* **H. Souls,** las Ánimas Benditas. **h. water stoup,** acetre, *m.* **H. Week,** Semana Santa, *f*

Holy Land, the la Tierra Santa, *f.*

homage /'hɒmɪdʒ/ *n* homenaje, *m;* culto, *m;* reverencia, *f.* **to pay h.,** rendir homenaje

home /houm/ *n* casa, *f;* hogar, *m;* domicilio, *m,* residencia, *f;* (institution) asilo, *m;* (haven) refugio, *m;* (habitation) morada, *f;* (country of origin) país de origen, *m;* (native land) patria, *f;* (environment) ambiente natural, *m; Sports.* meta, *f.* —*a* casero, doméstico; nativo; nacional, del país; indígena. —*adv* a casa, hacia casa; (in one's country) en su patria; (returned) de vuelta; (of the feelings) al corazón, al alma; (to the limit) al límite. **at h.,** en casa; *Fig.* en su elemento; (of games) en campo propio; de recibo. **at-h. day,** día de recibo, *m.* **He shot the bolt h.,** Echó el cerrojo. **one's long h.,** su última morada. **to be at h.,** estar en casa; estar de recibo. **to be away from h.,** estar fuera de casa; estar ausente. **to bring h.,** traer (or llevar) a casa: hacer ver; convencer; llegar al alma; (a crime) probar (contra). **to go h.,** volver a casa; volver a la patria; (be effective) hacer su efecto; (move) herir en lo más vivo. **to make oneself at h.,** ponerse a sus anchas, sentirse como en casa de uno. **Please make yourself at home!** ¡Ha tomado posesión de su casa! **to strike h.,** dar en el blanco; herir; (hit) golpear; herir en lo más vivo; hacerse sentir. **h. affairs,** asuntos domésticos, *m pl,* (Ministry of) Gobernación, *f.* **h.-bred,** criado en el país. **h.-brewed,** fermentado en el país; hecho en casa. **h.-coming,** regreso al hogar, *m.* **h. counties,** condados alrededor de Londres, *m pl.* **H. Defense,** defensa nacional, *f.* **h. farm,** residencia del propietario de una finca, *f.* **h. for the aged,** asilo de ancianos, *m.* **h. front,** frente doméstico, *m.* **H. Guard,** milicia nacional, *f.* **h. life,** vida de familia, *f.* **h.-made** casero, de fabricación casera, hecho en casa. **H. Office,** Ministerio de Gobernación, *m.* **H. Rule,** autonomía, *f.* **H. Secretary,** Ministro de Gobernación, *m.* **h. stretch,** último trecho (de una carrera), *m.* **h. truth,** verdad, *Inf.* fresca, *f.* **to tell someone a few h. truths,** contarle cuatro verdades

homeless /'houmlis/ *a* sin casa; sin hogar. **the h.,** los sin techo

homely /'houmli/ *a* doméstico; familiar; (unpretentious) sencillo; llano; (ugly) feo; desabrido

homeopath /'houmiə,pæθ/ *n* homeópata, *mf*

homeopathic /,houmiə'pæθɪk/ *a* homeópata

homeopathy /,houmi'ɒpəθi/ *n* homeopatía, *f*

homesick /'houm,sɪk/ *a* nostálgico. **to be h.,** tener morriña

homesickness /'houm,sɪknɪs/ *n* nostalgia, añoranza, morriña, *f*

homespun /'houm,spʌn/ *a* tejido en casa; hecho en casa; basto, grueso

homestead /'houmstɛd/ *n* hacienda, *f;* casa solariega, *f;* casa, *f*

homeward /'houmwərd/ *adv* hacia casa, en dirección al hogar; de vuelta; hacia la patria. **h.-bound,** en dirección a casa; (of ships) con rumbo al puerto de origen; (of other traffic) de vuelta

homicidal /,houmə'saɪdl/ *a* homicida

homicide /'homə,saɪd/ *n* (act) homicidio, *m;* (person) homicida, *mf*

homogeneous /,houmə'dʒiniəs/ *a* homogéneo

homosexual /,houmə'sɛkʃuəl/ *a* and *n* homosexual, *mf*

Honduran /hɒn'durən/ *a* and *n* hondureño (-ña)

hone /houn/ *n* piedra de afilar, *f.* —*vt* afilar, vaciar

honest /'ɒnɪst/ *a* honrado; decente, honesto; (chaste) casto; (loyal) sincero, leal; (frank) franco; imparcial. **an h. man,** un hombre de buena fe, un hombre honrado, un hombre decente

honesty /'ɒnəsti/ *n* honradez, *f;* honestidad, *f;* (chastity) castidad, *f;* sinceridad, *f;* rectitud, imparcialidad, *f*

honey /'hʌni/ *n* miel, *f.* **h.-bee,** abeja obrera, *f.* **h.-colored,** melado. **h.-pot,** jarro de miel, *m.* **h.-tongued,** melifluo; de pico de oro

honeydew /'hʌni,du/ *n* mielada, *f; Fig.* ambrosia, *f*

honeyed /'hʌnid/ *a* de miel; *Fig.* meloso, adulador

honeymoon /'hʌni,mun/ *n* luna de miel, *f;* viaje de novios, viaje nupcial, *m.* —*vi* hacer un viaje nupcial

honor /'ɒnər/ *n* honor, *m;* honra, *f;* honradez, rectitud, integridad, *f; pl* **honors,** honores, *m pl;* condecoraciones, *f pl;* (last h.) honras, pompas fúnebres, *f pl.* —*vt* honrar; (God) glorificar; (decorate) condecorar, laurear; (respect) respetar; reverenciar; *Com.* aceptar; (a toast) beber. **On my h.,** A fe mía. **point of h.,** punto de honor, pundonor, *m.* **word of h.,** palabra de honor, *f.* **Your H.,** (to a judge) Excelentísimo Señor Juez

honorable /'ɒnərəbəl/ *a* honorable; glorioso; digno; ilustre; (sensitive of honor) pundonoroso

honorable mention *n* accésit, *m*

honorarium /,ɒnə'rɛəriəm/ *n* honorario, *m*

honorary /'ɒnə,rɛri/ *a* honorario, honorífico. **h. member,** socio (-ia) honorario (-ia). **h. mention,** mención honorífica, *f*

hood /hʊd/ *n* capucha, caperuza, *f;* (folding, of vehicles) capota, cubierta, cubierta del motor *f;* (of a carriage) caparazón, fuelle, *m;* (of a car) capó, *m;* (university) muceta, *f;* (of a fireplace) campana (de hogar), *f;* (cowl of chimney) sombrerete (de chimenea), *m.* —*vt* cubrir con capucha; cubrir; (the eyes) ocultar, cubrir, velar

hoodwink /'hʊd,wɪŋk/ *vt* vendar (los ojos); *Fig.* engañar, embaucar, burlar

hoof /hʊf/ *n* casco, *m;* (cloven) pezuña, *f*

hoof it ir a golpe de calcetín

hook /hʊk/ *n* gancho, garfio, *m;* (boat-) bichero, *m;* (fish-) anzuelo, *m;* (on a dress) corchete, *m;* (hanger) colgadero, *m;* (claw) garra, *f.* —*vt* enganchar; (a dress) abrochar; (fish) pescar, coger; (nab) atrapar, pescar. **by h. or by crook,** a tuertas o a derechas. **left h.,** (boxing) izquierdo, *m.* **right h.,** (boxing) derecho, *m.* **to catch oneself on a h.**, engancharse. **h. and eye**, los corchetes. **h.-nosed**, con nariz de gancho, con nariz aguileña. **h.-up**, *Radio.* circuito, *m;* transmisión en circuito, *f*

hookworm /'hʊk,wɜrm/ *n* anquilostoma, *m*

hooligan /'huligən/ *n* rufián, *m*

hoop /hup/ *n* aro, arco, *m;* (of a skirt) miriñaque, *m;* (croquet) argolla, *f;* (toy) aro, *m;* círculo, *m.* —*vt* poner aros a; *Fig.* rodear

hoot /hut/ *n* (of owls) ululación, *f*, grito, *m;* (whistle) silbido, *m;* ruido, clamor, *m.* —*vi* (of owls) ulular, gritar; silbar; *Auto.* avisar con la bocina. **to h. off the stage**, hacer abandonar la escena. **to h. down**, silbar

hop /hɒp/ *n* salto, brinco, *m; Bot.* lúpulo, *m; Bot.* flores de oblón, *f pl;* (dance) baile, *m.* —*vi* saltar con un pie; andar dando brincos; saltar; (limp) cojear; recoger lúpulo; (of plant) dar lúpulo. —*vt* saltar. **hop-garden**, huerto de lúpulo, *m.* **hop-kiln**, horno para secar lúpulo, *m.* **hop-picker**, recolector (-ra) de lúpulo. **hop-picking**, recolección de lúpulos, *f*

hope /houp/ *n* esperanza, *f;* (faith) confianza, *f;* (expectation) anticipación, expectación, *f;* (probability) probabilidad, *f;* (illusion) ilusión, *f;* sueño, *m.* —*vi* esperar. **to live in h. that**, vivir con la esperanza de que. **to lose h.**, desesperarse. **to h. against h.**, esperar sin motivo, esperar lo imposible. **to h. for**, desear. **to h. in**, confiar en

hopeful /'houpfəl/ *a* lleno de esperanzas, confiado; optimista; (*Fig.*) risueño. —*n Inf* la esperanza de la casa. **to look h.**, *Fig.* prometer bien

hopeless /'houplɪs/ *a* desesperado, sin esperanza; irremediable; (of situations) imposible; (of disease) incurable. **to be h.**, (lose hope) desesperarse; (have no remedy) ser irremediable; (of disease) no tener cura. **to make h.**, hacer perder la esperanza, desesperar; dejar sin remedio; (a situation) hacer imposible; (an illness) hacer imposible de curar

hopelessly /'houplɪsli/ *adv* sin esperanza; sin remedio; imposiblemente; incurablemente

hopscotch /'hɒp,skɒtʃ/ *n* infernáculo, *m*, rayuela, *f*

horizon /hə'raizən/ *n* horizonte, *m*

horizontal /,hɔrə'zɒntl/ *a* horizontal. **h. suspension**, (gymnastics) plancha, *f*

hormone /'hɔrmoun/ *n* hormona, *f*

horn /hɔrn/ *n* (of bull, etc.) cuerno, *m;* (antler) asta, *f;* (of an insect) antena, *f;* (of a snail) tentáculo, *m; Mus.* cuerno, *m;* trompa, *f;* (of motor and phonograph) bocina, *f;* (of moon) cuerno (de la luna), *m.* **article made of h.**, objeto de cuerno, *m.* **on the horns of a dilemma**, entre la espada y la pared. **h. of plenty**, cuerno de abundancia, *m;* cornucopia, *f.* **h.-rimmed**

spectacles, anteojos de concha, *m pl.* **h. thrust**, cornada, *f*

hornet /'hɔrnɪt/ *n* avispón, abejón, *m*

horny /'hɔrni/ *a* córneo; calloso; duro. **h.-handed**, con manos callosas

horoscope /'hɔrə,skoup/ *n* horóscopo, *m*

horrible /'hɔrəbəl/ *a* horrible, repugnante, espantoso; (of price) enorme; *Inf.* horrible

horrid /'hɔrɪd/ *a* horroroso; desagradable

horrific /hɔ'rɪfɪk/ *a* horrífico, horrendo

horrify /'hɔrə,fai/ *vt* horrorizar; escandalizar

horrifying /'hɔrə,faiɪŋ/ *a* horroroso, horripilante

horror /'hɔrər/ *n* horror, *m.* **h.-stricken**, horrorizado

horse /hɔrs/ *n* caballo, *m;* (cavalry) caballería, *f;* (frame) caballete, *m;* (gymnastics and as punishment) potro, *m.* —*vt* caballar, caballuno. —*vt* montar a caballo. **pack of horses**, caballada, *f.* **to ride a h.**, cabalgar, montar a caballo. **H. Artillery**, artillería montada, *f.* **h. blanket**, manta para caballos, *f;* sudadero, *m.* **h.-block**, montador, *m.* **h.-box**, vagón para caballos, *m.* **h.-breaker**, domador de caballos, *m.* **h.-cab**, simón, *m.* **h.-chestnut**, castaña pilonga, *f.* **h.-chestnut flower**, candela, *f.* **h.-collar**, collera, *f.* **h.-dealer**, chalán, *m.* **h.-doctor**, veterinario, *m.* **h.-flesh**, carne de caballo, *f.* **h.-fly**, tábano, *m.* **H. Guards**, guardias montadas, *f pl.* **h.-latitudes**, calmas de Cáncer, *f pl.* **h.-laugh**, carcajada, *f.* **h.-master**, maestro de equitación, *m.* **h. meat**, carne de caballo, *f.* **h. pistol**, pistola de arzón, *f.* **h.-play**, payasada, *f.* **h.-power**, caballo de vapor, *m;* potencia, *f.* **a twelve-h.p. car**, un coche de doce caballos. **h.-race**, carrera de caballos, *f.* **h.-radish**, rábano picante, raíz amarga, *m.* **h.-sense**, sentido común, *m*, gramática parda, *f.* **h. show**, exposición de caballos, feria equina *f;* concurso de caballos, *m.* **h.-trainer**, entrenador de caballos, *m.* **h. tram**, tranvía de sangre, *m.* **h. trappings**, monturas, *f pl*

horseback /'hɔrs,bæk/ *n* lomo de caballo, *m.* **on h.**, a caballo. **to ride on h.**, ir a caballo

horseman /'hɔrsmən/ *n* jinete, cabalgador, *m*

horsemanship /'hɔrsmən,ʃɪp/ *n* equitación, *f*, manejo del caballo, *m*

horseshoe /'hɔrs,ʃu/ *n* herradura, *f.* **h. arch**, arco de herradura, arco morisco, *m*

horsewoman /'hɔrs,wumən/ *n* amazona, *f*

horsey /'hɔrsi/ *a* de caballo; aficionado a caballos; grosero

horticultural /,hɔrtɪ'kʌltʃərəl/ *a* horticultural. **h. show**, exposición de flores, *f*

hose /houz/ *n* (tube) manga, *f;* (breeches) calzón, *m;* (stockings) medias, *f pl;* (socks) calcetines, *m pl.* **h. man**, manguero, *m.* **h.-pipe**, manga de riego, manguera, *f*

hosier /'houʒər/ *n* calcetero (-ra)

hosiery /'houʒəri/ *n* calcetería, *f.* **h. trade**, calcetería, *f*

hospice /'hɒspɪs/ *n* hospicio, *m;* asilo, refugio, *m*

hospitable /'hɒspɪtəbəl/ *a* hospitalario

hospitably /'hɒspɪtəbəli/ *adv* hospitalariamente

hospital /'hɒspɪtl/ *n* hospital, *m;* (school) colegio, *m.* **h. nurse**, enfermera, *f.* **h. ship**, buque hospital, *m*

hospital bed cama hospitalaria, *f*

hospitality /ˌhɒspɪ'tælɪti/ *n* hospitalidad, *f*

host /houst/ *n* huésped, convidador, (of radio or tv program) presentador, *m;* (at an inn) patrón, mesonero, *m;* (army) ejército, *m;* (crowd) multitud, muchedumbre, *f; Eccl.* hostia, *f; pl* **hosts**, huestes, *f pl.* **h.-plant**, planta huésped, *f*

hostage /'hɒstɪdʒ/ *n* rehén, *m; Fig.* prenda, *f*

host country *n* (of an organization) país-sede, *m*

hostel /'hɒstl/ *n* hostería, *f;* club, *m;* residencia de estudiantes, *f*

hostelry /'hɒstlri/ *n* hospedería, *f;* parador, mesón, *m*

hostess /'houstɪs/ *n* ama de la casa, *f;* la que recibe a los invitados; la que convida; (of an inn) patrona, mesonera, *f*

hostile /'hɒstl/ *a* enemigo; hostil, contrario (a); (of circumstances, etc.) desfavorable

hostility /hɒ'stɪlɪti/ *n* enemistad, *f,* antagonismo, *m,* mala voluntad, *f;* hostilidad, guerra, *f.* **suspension of hostilities**, suspensión de hostilidades, *f*

hot /hɒt/ *a* caliente; (of a day, etc.) caluroso; (piquant) picante; ardiente; vehemente, impetuoso; violento; impaciente; colérico; entusiasta; lleno de deseo; *Art.* intenso; (great) grande, mucho; (vigorous) enérgico. **You are getting very hot now,** *Inf.* (in a game, etc.) Te estás quemando. **It is hot,** Está caliente; (of weather) Hace calor. **to grow hot,** calentarse; *Fig.* acalorarse; (of weather) empezar a hacer calor. **to make hot,** calentar; dar calor (a); *Inf.* dar vergüenza. **hotblooded,** de sangre caliente; apasionado; colérico. **hot-foot,** aprisa, apresuradamente. **hot-headed,** impetuoso. **hotplate,** *Elec.* calientaplatos, *m.* **hot springs,** termas, *f pl.* **hot-tempered,** colérico, irascible. **hot water,** agua caliente, *f.* **hot-water bottle,** bolsa de goma, *f.* **hot-water pipes,** las cañerías del agua caliente

hotbed /'hɒt,bed/ *n* semillero, vivero, *m; Fig.* semillero, foco, *m*

hotchpotch /'hɒtʃ,pɒtʃ/ *n* potaje, *m; Fig.* mezcolanza, *f,* fárrago, *m*

hotel /hou'tel/ *n* hotel, *m.* **h.-keeper,** hotelero (-ra)

hothead /'hɒt,hed/ *n* exaltado (-da), fanático (-ca)

hothouse /'hɒt,haus/ *n* invernáculo, *m,* estufa, *f.* **h. plant,** *Fig.* planta de estufa, *f*

hound /haund/ *n* perro de caza, sabueso de artois, *m;* perro, *m; Inf.* canalla, *m.* —*vt* cazar con perros; *Fig.* perseguir; *Fig.* incitar. **master of hounds,** montero, *m.* **pack of hounds,** jauría, *f*

hour /auˀr/ *n* hora, *f;* momento, *m;* ocasión, oportunidad, *f; pl.* **hours,** horas, *f pl.* **after hours,** fuera de horas. **at the eleventh h.,** en el último minuto. **by the h.,** por horas; horas enteras. **small hours,** altas horas de la noche, *Inf.* las tantas, *f pl.* **to keep late hours,** acostarse tarde. **to strike the h.,** dar la hora. **h.-glass,** reloj de arena, *m.* **h.-hand,** horario, *m.* **h. of death,** hora suprema, hora de la muerte, *f*

hourly /'auˀrli/ *a* cada hora; por hora; continuo. —*adv* a cada hora; de un momento a otro

house /*n* haus; *v* hauz/ *n* casa, *f;* (home) hogar, *m;* (lineage) familia, *f,* abolengo, *m;* (*Theat.*) sala, *f,* teatro, *m; Com.* casa comercial, *f;* (takings) entrada, *f;* (audience) público, *m;* (of Lords, Commons) cámara, *f;* (college) colegio, *m;* (parliament) parlamento, *m;* (building) edificio, *m.* —*a* de casa; de la casa; doméstico. —*vt* dar vivienda (a); alojar, recibir (or tener) en casa de uno; (store) poner, guardar. **The cottage will not h. them all,** No habrá bastante lugar para todos ellos en la cabaña, No cabrán todos en la cabaña. **country-h.,** finca, *f;* casa de campo, *f.* **full h.,** casa llena, *f; Theat.* lleno, *m.* **to bring down the h.,** *Theat.* hacer venirse el teatro abajo. **to keep h.,** llevar la casa; ser ama de casa. **to keep open h.,** tener mesa puesta, ser hospitalario. **to set up h.,** poner casa. **h. of cards,** castillo de naipes, *m.* **H. of Commons,** Cámara de los Comunes, *f.* **H. of Lords,** Cámara de los Lores, *f.* **h.-agent,** agente de casas, *m.* **h.-boat,** barco-habitación, *m,* casa flotante, *f.* **h.-dog,** perro de guardia, *m;* perro de casa, *m.* **h.-fly,** mosca doméstica, *f.* **h. furnisher,** mueblista, *mf.* **h. painter,** pintor de brocha gorda, *m.* **h. party,** reunión en una casa de campo, *f.* **h.-physician,** médico (-ca) interno (-na). **h. porter,** portero, *m.* **h. property,** propiedad inmueble, *f.* **h.-room,** capacidad de una casa, *f.* **h. slipper,** zapatilla, *f,* pantuflo, *m.* **h.-surgeon,** cirujano interno, *m.* **h.-to-h.,** de casa en casa. **h.-warming,** reunión para colgar la cremallera, *f*

housebreaker /'haus,breikər/ *n* ladrón de casas, *m*

housebreaking /'haus,breikɪŋ/ *n* robo de una casa, *m*

houseful /'hausfʊl/ *n* casa, *f*

house furnishings *n pl* artefactos para el hogar, accesorios caseros, aparatos electrodomésticos, *m pl*

household /'haus,hould/ *n* casa, *f;* familia, *f;* hogar, *m.* —*a* de la casa;

doméstico; del hogar. **to be a h. word,** andar en lenguas. **h. accounts,** cuentas de la casa, *f pl.* **h. duties,** labores de la casa, *f pl.* **h. gods,** penates, *m pl.* **h. goods,** ajuar, mobiliario, *m.* **h. management,** gobierno de la casa, *m*

householder /'haus,houldər/ *n* padre de familia, *m;* dueño (-ña) (or inquilino (-na)) de una casa

housekeeper /'haus,kipər/ *n* ama de llaves, *f;* mujer de su casa, *f*

housekeeping /'haus,kipiŋ/ *n* gobierno de la casa, *m;* economía doméstica, *f.* —*a* doméstico. **to set up h.,** poner casa

housemaid /'haus,meid/ *n* camarera, sirvienta, *f.* **housemaid's knee,** rodilla de fregona, *f*

house of ill repute *n* burdel, *m,* casa de citas, casa de zorras, casa pública, *f;* lupanar, *m*

housetops /'haus,tɒps/ *n* tejado, *m,* (flat roof) azotea, *f.* **to shout from the h.,** pregonar a los cuatro vientos

housewife /'haus,waif/ *n* madre de familia, mujer de su casa, *f;* (sewing-bag) neceser de costura, *m*

housing /'hauziŋ/ *n* provisión de vivienda, *f;* (storage) almacenaje, *m;* alojamiento, *m; Inf.* casa, vivienda, *f.* **h. scheme,** urbanización, *f.* **h. shortage,** crisis de vivienda, *f,* déficit habitacional, *m*

hovel /'hʌvəl/ *n* casucha, *f*

hover /'hʌvər/ *vi* revolotear; (of hawks, etc.) cernerse; estar suspendido; rondar; seguir de cerca, estar al lado (de); *Fig.* vacilar, dudar

how /hau/ *adv* cómo; (by what means, in what manner) de qué modo; (at what price) a qué precio; qué; cuánto. —*n* el cómo. **to know how,** saber. **For how long?** ¿Por cuánto tiempo? **How are you?** ¿Cómo está Vd.? *Inf.* algo tal. **How do you do!** ¡Mucho gusto (en conocerlo/conocerla/conocerlos/conocerlas)! **How old are you?** ¿Qué edad tiene Vd.? **How beautiful!** ¡Qué hermoso! **How big!** ¡Cuán grande! **How early?** ¿Cuán temprano?; ¿Cuándo a más tardar? **How far?** ¿A qué distancia? ¿Hasta qué punto? ¿Hasta dónde? **How fast?** ¿A qué velocidad? **How few!** ¡Qué pocos! **How little!** ¡Qué pequeño!; ¡Qué poco! **How long?** ¿Cuánto tiempo? **How many?** ¿Cuántos? *m pl;* ¿Cuántas? *f pl.* **How much is it?** ¿Cuánto vale? **How much cloth do you want?** ¿Cuánta tela quieres? **How often?** ¿Cuán a menudo? ¿Cuántas veces? **How would you like to go for a walk?** ¿Te gustaría pasearte? **How are you going to Lisbon?** ¿En qué vas a Lisboa?

however /hau'evər/ *adv* como quiera (que) (followed by subjunctive); por más que (followed by subjunctive); por... que (followed by subjunctive). —*conjunc* (nevertheless) sin embargo, no obstante. **h. good it is,** por bueno que sea. **h. he does it,** como quiera que lo haga. **h. it**

---

may be, sea como sea. **h. much,** por mucho que

howl /haul/ *n* aullido, *m;* (groan) gemido, *m;* (cry) grito, *m;* (roar) rugido, bramido, *m;* lamento, *m.* —*vi* aullar; gemir; gritar; rugir, bramar. —*vt* chillar. **Each time he opened his mouth he was howled down,** Cada vez que abrió la boca se armó una bronca

howler /'haulər/ *n* aullador (-ra); *Zool.* mono (-na) chillón (-ona); (blunder) coladura, plancha, *f*

howling /'hauliŋ/ *a* aullante; gemidor; (crying) que llora; bramante, rugiente. —*n* los aullidos; (groaning) el gemir, los gemidos; (crying) los gritos; (weeping) el lloro; (roaring) los bramidos, el rugir; los lamentos

hub /hʌb/ *n* (of a wheel) cubo (de rueda) *m; Fig.* centro, *m.* **hub cap,** tapa de cubo, *f*

hubbub /'hʌbʌb/ *n* algarada, barahúnda, *f*

huckster /'hʌkstər/ *n* revendedor (-ra). —*vi* revender; (haggle) regatear

huddle /'hʌdl/ *n* (heap) montón, *m;* colección, *f;* (group) corrillo, grupo, *m;* (mixture) mezcla, *f.* —*vt* arrebujar, amontonar; acurrucar, arrebujar; (throw on) echarse. —*vi* amontonarse; apiñarse; acurrucarse, arrebujarse

hue /hyu/ *n* color, *m;* matiz, tono, *m;* (of opinion) matiz, *m;* (clamor) clamor, *m,* gritería, *f.* **hue and cry,** alarma, *f*

huff /hʌf/ *n* acceso de cólera, *m*

hug /hʌg/ *n* abrazo, *m.* —*vt* abrazar, apretujar; *Fig.* acariciar; *Naut.* navegar muy cerca de. **to hug oneself,** *Fig.* congratularse

huge /hyudʒ/ *a* enorme, inmenso; gigante; vasto

hugely /'hyudʒli/ *adv* inmensamente, enormemente

hulk /hʌlk/ *n* barco viejo, *m;* pontón, *m*

hulking /'hʌlkiŋ/ *a* pesado, desgarbado

hull /hʌl/ *n Naut.* casco (de un buque), *m;* (shell) cáscara, *f;* (pod) vaina, *f, vt* mondar

hullabaloo /'hʌləbə,lu/ *n* alboroto, tumulto, *m;* vocerío, *m*

hullo /hə'lou/ *interj* See **hallo**

hum /hʌm/ *n* zumbido, *m;* ruido confuso, *m.* —*vi* (sing) canturrear; zumbar; (confused sound) zurrir; (hesitate) vacilar. —*vt* (a tune) tararear

human /'hyumən/ *a* humano. **the h. touch,** el don de gentes. **h. being,** ser humano, hombre, *m*

humane /hyu'mein/ *a* humanitario, humano

humanitarian /hyu,mæni'teəriən/ *a* humanitario

humanity /hyu'mæniti/ *n* humanidad, *f;* raza humana, *f.* **the humanities,** las humanidades

humanize /'hyumə,naiz/ *vt* humanizar; (milk) maternizar. —*vi* humanizarse

humble /'hʌmbəl/ *a* humilde; modesto;

(cringing) servil; sumiso; pobre. —*vt* humillar; mortificar. **to h. oneself,** humillarse

humbleness /'hʌmbəlnıs/ *n* humildad, *f;* modestia, *f;* (abjectness) servilismo, *m;* sumisión, *f;* pobreza, *f;* (of birth, etc.) obscuridad, *f*

humbling /'hʌmblıŋ/ *n* humillación, *f;* mortificación, *f*

humbly /'hʌmbli/ *adv* humildemente; modestamente; servilmente

humbug /'hʌm,bʌg/ *n* (fraud) embuste, engaño, *m;* (nonsense) disparate, *m,* tontería, *f;* mentira, *f;* (person) farsante, charlatán, *m;* (sweetmeat) caramelo de menta, *m.* —*vt* engañar, embaucar; burlarse de

humdrum /'hʌm,drʌm/ *a* monótono; aburrido

humid /'hyumıd/ *a* húmedo

humidity /hyu'mıdıti/ *n* humedad, *f*

humiliate /hyu'mıli,eit/ *vt* humillar, mortificar. **to h. oneself,** humillarse

humiliating /hyu'mıli,eitıŋ/ *a* humillante; degradante

humiliation /hyu,mıli'eiʃən/ *n* humillación, mortificación, *f;* degradación, *f*

humility /hyu'mılıti/ *n* humildad, *f;* modestia, *f*

humming /'hʌmıŋ/ *n* zumbido, *m;* (of a tune) tarareo, *m.* —*a* zumbador. **h.-bird,** pájaro mosca, colibrí, *m.* **h.-top,** trompa, *f*

humor /'hyumər/ *n* humor, *m;* humorismo, *m;* (temperament) disposición, *f,* carácter, *m;* (whim) capricho, *m.* —*vt* seguir el humor (a), complacer; satisfacer, consentir en; (a lock, etc.) manejar. **in a good (bad) h.,** de buen (mal) humor. **I am not in the h. to...** No estoy de humor para... **sense of h.,** sentido de humor, *m*

humored /'hyumərd/ *a* (in compounds) de humor... **good-h.,** de buen humor. **ill-h.,** malhumorado, de mal humor

humorist /'hyumərıst/ *n* humorista, *mf*

humorless /'hyumərlıs/ *a* sin sentido humorístico, sin sentido de humor

humorous /'hyumərəs/ *a* humorístico; cómico, risible

hump /hʌmp/ *n* joroba, giba, *f;* (hillock) montecillo, *m;* Inf. depresión, *f*

humpback /'hʌmp,bæk/ *n* giba, joroba, *f;* (person) jorobado (-da), giboso (-sa)

humpbacked /'hʌmp,bækt/ *a* jorobado, giboso, corcovado

humph /*an inarticulate expression resembling a snort or grunt; spelling pron.* hʌmf/ *interj* ¡qué va!; ¡patrañas!

humus /'hyuməs/ *n* humus, mantillo, *m*

hunchback /'hʌntʃ,bæk/ *n* joroba, giba, *f;* (person) jorobado (-da), corcovado (-da), giboso (-sa)

hunchbacked /'hʌntʃ,bækt/ *a* jorobado, giboso, corcovado

hundred /'hʌndrıd/ *n* ciento, *m;* centenar, centena, *f.* —*a* ciento; (before nouns and adjectives, excluding numerals,

with the exception of mil and millón) cien. **a h. thousand,** cien mil. **one h. and one,** ciento uno. **by the h.,** a centenares. **hundreds of people,** centenares de personas, *m pl.* **h.-millionth,** *a* and *n* cienmillonésimo *m.* **h.-thousandth,** *a* and *n* cienmilésimo *m.*

hundredth /'hʌndrıdθ/ *a* centésimo, céntimo. —*n* centésimo, *m,* centésima parte, *f*

Hungarian /hʌŋ'gɛəriən/ *a* and *n* húngaro (-ra); (language) húngaro, *m*

Hungary /'hʌŋgəri/ Hungría, *f*

hunger /'hʌŋgər/ *n* hambre, *f;* apetito, *m;* (craving) deseo, *m,* ansia, *f.* —*vi* estar hambriento, tener hambre. **to h. for,** desear, ansiar. **h.-strike,** huelga de hambre, *f*

hungry /'hʌŋgri/ *a* hambriento; (of land) pobre; (anxious) deseoso. **to be h.,** tener hambre. **to make h.,** dar hambre

hunk /hʌŋk/ *n* rebanada, *f,* pedazo, *m*

hunt /hʌnt/ *n* caza, cacería, montería, *f;* grupo de cazadores, *m;* (search) busca, *f;* (pursuit) persecución, *f.* —*vt* cazar; cazar a caballo; (search) buscar; rebuscar, explorar; (pursue) perseguir. **to h. down,** perseguir. **to h. for,** buscar. **to h. out,** buscar; descubrir, desenterrar

hunter /'hʌntər/ *n* cazador, *m;* caballo de caza, *m;* (watch) saboneta, *f*

hunting /'hʌntıŋ/ *n* caza, *f;* caza a caballo, *f;* persecución, *f.* —*a* cazador de caza. **to go h.,** ir a cazar. **h.-box,** pabellón de caza, *m.* **h.-cap,** gorra de montar, *f.* **h.-crop,** látigo para cazar, *m.* **h.-ground,** coto de caza, terreno de caza, *m.* **h.-horn,** cuerno de caza, *m,* corneta de monte, *f.* **h. party,** partido de caza, *m,* cacería, *f*

hurdle /'hʌrdl/ *n* valla, *f;* zarzo, *m.* **h.-race,** carrera de obstáculos, *f;* carrera de vallas, *f*

hurl /hʌrl/ *vt* lanzar, tirar, arrojar, echar. **to h. oneself,** lanzarse. **to h. oneself against,** arrojarse a (or contra). **to h. oneself upon,** abalanzarse sobre

hurly-burly /'hʌrli'bʌrli/ *n* alboroto, tumulto, *m*

hurrah /hə'rɑ/ *interj* ¡hurra! ¡viva! —*n* vítor, *m.* **H. for...!** ¡Viva...!, ¡Vivan...! **to shout h.,** vitorear

hurricane /'hʌrı,kein/ *n* huracán, *m.* **h.-lamp,** lámpara sorda, *f*

hurried /'hʌrid/ *a* apresurado, precipitado; hecho a prisa; superficial

hurriedly /'hʌridli/ *adv* apresuradamente, precipitadamente, con prisa; superficialmente; (of writing) a vuela pluma

hurry /'hʌri/ *n* prisa, *f;* precipitación, *f;* urgencia, *f;* confusión, *f;* alboroto, *m.* **in a h.,** aprisa. **in a great h.,** aprisa y co rriendo. **to be in a h.,** llevar prisa, estar de prisa. **There is no h.,** No corre prisa, No hay prisa

hurry /'hʌri/ *vt* apresurar, dar prisa (a); llevar aprisa; hacer andar aprisa; enviar apresuradamente; precipitar; acelerar.

—*vi* darse prisa; apresurarse. **to h. after,** correr detrás de, seguir apresuradamente. **to h. away,** *vi* marcharse aprisa, marcharse corriendo; huir; salir precipitadamente. —*vt* hacer marcharse aprisa; llevar con prisa. **to h. back,** *vi* volver aprisa, apresurarse a volver. —*vt* hacer volver aprisa. **to h. in,** *vi* entrar aprisa, entrar corriendo. —*vt* hacer entrar aprisa. **to h. off.** See **to h. away. to h. on,** *vi* apresurarse. —*vt* apresurar, precipitar. **to h. out,** salir rápidamente. **to h. over,** hacer rápidamente; concluir aprisa; despachar rápidamente; (travel over) atravesar aprisa; pasar rápidamente por. **to h. toward,** llevar rápidamente hacia; arrastrar hacia; impeler hacia. **to h. up,** *vi* darse prisa. —*vt* apresurar, precipitar; estimular

hurt /hɜrt/ *n* herida, *f*; (harm) daño, mal, *m*; perjuicio, *m.* —*vt* (wound) herir; (cause pain) doler; hacer daño (a); hacer mal (a); (damage) perjudicar, estropear; (offend) ofender; (the feelings) mortificar, lastimar, herir. —*vi* doler; hacer mal; perjudicarse, estropearse. **I haven't h. myself,** No me he hecho daño. **Does it still h. you?** ¿Te duele todavía? **to h. deeply,** *Fig.* herir en el alma. **to h. a person's feelings,** herirle (a uno) el amor propio, lastimar, ofender

hurtful /'hɜrtfəl/ *a* nocivo, dañino; injurioso, pernicioso

hurtle /'hɜrtl/ *vt* lanzar. —*vi* lanzarse; volar; caer

husband /'hʌzbənd/ *n* esposo, marido, *m.* —*vt* economizar, ahorrar. **h. and wife,** los esposos, los cónyuges

husbandry /'hʌzbəndri/ *n* labor de los campos, agricultura, *f*; (thrift) frugalidad, parsimonia, *f*

hush /hʌʃ/ *n* silencio, *m*, tranquilidad, *f.* —*interj* ¡chitón! ¡calla! ¡silencio! —*vt* silenciar, hacer callar, imponer silencio (a); (a baby) adormecer; *Fig.* sosegar, calmar. —*vi* callarse, enmudecer. **to h. up,** mantener secreto, ocultar. **h.-h.,** secreto. **h. money,** so-borno, chantaje, *m*

husk /hʌsk/ *n* (of grain) cascabillo, *m*; zurrón, *m*; cáscara, *f*; (of chestnut) erizo, *m*

husky /'hʌski/ *a* (of voice) ronco; *Bot.* cascarudo; (Eskimo) esquimal; *Inf.* robusto, fuerte. —*n* perro esquimal, *m*

hustle /'hʌsəl/ *vt* empujar, codear; *Fig.* precipitar; *Inf.* acelerar. —*vi* codearse; andarse de prisa

hut /hʌt/ *n* choza, cabaña, barraca, *f*

hutch /hʌtʃ/ *n* (chest) arca, *f*, cofre, *m*; (cage) jaula, *f*; (for rabbits) conejera, *f*; (for rats) ratonera, *f*; *Inf.* choza, *f*

hyacinth /'haɪəsɪnθ/ *n* jacinto, *m*

hybrid /'haɪbrɪd/ *a* híbrido; mestizo, mixto. —*n* híbrido, *m*

hydrant /'haɪdrənt/ *n* boca de riego, *f*

hydraulic /haɪ'drɔlɪk/ *a* hidráulico. **h. engineering,** hidrotecnia, *f*

hydrochloric /,haɪdrə'klɔrɪk/ *a* clorhídrico. **h. acid,** ácido clorhídrico, *m*

hydrogen /'haɪdrədʒən/ *n* hidrógeno, *m.* **h. peroxide,** agua oxigenada, *f*

hydropathic /,haɪdrə'pæθɪk/ *a* hidropático. **h. establishment,** balneario, *m*

hydrophobia /,haɪdrə'foubiə/ *n* hidrofobia, rabia, *f*

hydroplane /'haɪdrə,pleɪn/ *n* hidroplano, *m*

hyena /haɪ'inə/ *n* hiena, *f*

hygiene /'haɪdʒin/ *n* higiene, *f.* **personal h.,** higiene privada, *f*

hygienic /,haɪdʒi'ɛnɪk/ *a* higiénico

hymen /'haɪmən/ *n* *Anat.* himen, *m*; himeneo, *m*

hymn /hɪm/ *n* himno, *m.* **h.-book,** himnario, *m*

hyperbole /haɪ'pɜrbəli/ *n* hipérbole, *f*

hyperbolical /,haɪpər'bɒlɪkəl/ *a* hiperbólico

hypercritic /,haɪpər'krɪtɪk/ *n* hipercrítico, *m*

hypercritical /,haɪpər'krɪtɪkəl/ *a* hipercrítico, criticón

hypersensitive /,haɪpər'sɛnsɪtɪv/ *a* vidrioso, quisquilloso

hypertrophy /haɪ'pɜrtrəfi/ *n* hipertrofia, *f.* —*vi* hipertrofiarse

hyphen /'haɪfən/ *n* guión, *m*

hypnosis /hɪp'nousɪs/ *n* hipnosis, *f*

hypnotic /hɪp'nɒtɪk/ *a* hipnótico. —*n* (person) hipnótico (-ca); (drug) hipnótico, narcótico, *m*

hypnotism /'hɪpnə,tɪzəm/ *n* hipnotismo, *m*

hypnotist /'hɪpnətɪst/ *n* hipnotizador (-ra)

hypnotize /'hɪpnə,taɪz/ *vt* hipnotizar

hypo /'haɪpou/ *n* (sodium hyposulphite) hiposulfito sólido, *m*

hypochondria /,haɪpə'kɒndriə/ *n* hipocondria, *f*

hypochondriac /,haɪpə'kɒndri,æk/ *n* hipocondríaco (-ca)

hypocrisy /hɪ'pɒkrəsi/ *n* hipocresía, *f*; mojigatería, gazmoñería, *f*

hypocrite /'hɪpəkrɪt/ *n* hipócrita, *mf*; mojigato (-ta). **to be a h.,** ser hipócrita

hypocritical /,haɪpə'krɪtɪkəl/ *a* hipócrita; mojigato, gazmoño

hypodermic /,haɪpə'dɜrmɪk/ *a* hipodérmico. **h. syringe,** jeringa de inyecciones, *f*

hypothesis /haɪ'pɒθəsɪs/ *n* hipótesis, *f*

hypothetical /,haɪpə'θɛtɪkəl/ *a* hipotético

hysterectomy /,hɪstə'rɛktəmi/ *n* *Surg.* histerectomía, *f*

hysteria /hɪ'stɛriə/ *n* *Med.* histerismo, *m*; histeria, *f*, ataque de nervios, *m*

hysterical /hɪ'stɛrɪkəl/ *a* histérico. **to become h.,** tener un ataque de nervios

hysterics, *n pl* ataque de nervios, *m*

I

i /ai/ *n* (letter) i. —*1st pers pron* yo. It is I, Soy yo. Normally omitted, the verb alone being used except when yo is needed for emphasis, e.g. Hablo a María, I speak to Mary, *but* Yo toco el violín, pero Juan toca el piano, I play the violin, *but* John plays the piano

Iberian Peninsula, the la Peninsula Ibérica

ice /ais/ *n* hielo, *m*; (ice cream) helado, *m*. —*vt* helar; cubrir de hielo; congelar, cuajar; (a cake, etc.) garapiñar, escarchar, alcorzar. **to ice up,** (*Aer., Auto.*) helarse. **to be as cold as ice,** *Inf.* estar hecho un hielo. **His words cut no ice,** Sus palabras ni pinchan ni cortan. **ice-age,** edad del hielo, *f.* **ice-ax,** piolet, *m.* **ice-box,** nevera, *f.* **ice-cream,** helado, mantecado, *m.* **ice-cream cone,** cucurucho de helado, *m.* **ice-cream freezer,** heladora, *f.* **ice-cream vendor,** mantequero (-ra). **ice-field,** campo de hielo, *m.* **ice-floe,** témpano de hielo flotante, *m.* **ice hockey,** hockey sobre patines, *m.* **ice-pack,** bolsa para hielo, *f.* **ice-skates,** patines de cuchilla, *m pl.* **ice water,** agua helada, *f*

iceberg /'aisbərg/ *n* iceberg, témpano de hielo, banco de hielo, *m*

icebound /'ais,baund/ *a* aprisionado por el hielo; atascado en el hielo; (of roads, etc.) helado

iced /aist/ *a* helado; congelado, cuajado; (cakes) garapiñado, escarchado; (of drinks) con hielo. **i. drink,** sorbete, *m*

Iceland /'aisland/ *n* Islandia, *f*

Icelander /'ais,lændər/ *n* islandés (-esa), *f*

icicle /'aisikəl/ *n* carámbano, canelón, cerrión, *m*

icily /'aisəli/ *adv* fríamente; *Fig.* frígidamente, con indiferencia, con frialdad

icing /'aisıŋ/ *n* helada, *f*, hielo, *m*; (on a cake, etc.) alcorza, capa de azúcar, *f*

icon /'aikɒn/ *n* icono, *m*

iconoclast /ai'kɒnə,klæst/ *n* iconoclasta, *mf*

icy /'aisi/ *a* helado; glacial, frío; *Med.* álgido; *Fig.* indiferente, desabrido; *Poet.* frígido, gélido

idea /ai'diə/ *n* idea, *f*, concepto, *m*; (opinion) juicio, *m*, opinión, *f*; (notion) impresión, noción, *f*; (plan) proyecto, plan, designio, *m.* **to form an i. of,** hacerse una idea de, formar un concepto de. **to have an i. of,** tener una idea de; tener nociones de. **An i. struck me,** Se me ocurrió una idea. **full of ideas,** preñado (or lleno) de ideas. **I had no i. that...** No tenía la menor idea de que... No sabía que... **What an i.!** ¡Qué idea!

ideal /ai'diəl/ *a* ideal; excelente, perfecto; (utopian) utópico; (imaginary) imaginario, irreal, ficticio. —*n* ideal, *m*; modelo, prototipo, *m*

idealism /ai'diə,lızəm/ *n* idealismo, *m*

idealist /ai'diəlıst/ *n* idealista, *mf*

idealistic /ai,diə'lıstık/ *a* idealista

idealize /ai'diə,laiz/ *vt* idealizar

idem /'aidɛm/ ídem

identical /ai'dɛntıkəl/ *a* idéntico, mismo, igual; muy parecido, semejante

identifiable /ai,dɛntı'faiəbəl/ *a* identificable

identification /ai,dɛntəfı'keiʃən/ *n* identificación, *f.* **i. number,** placa de identidad, *f*

identify /ai'dɛntə,fai/ *vt* identificar. **to i. oneself with,** identificarse con

identity /ai'dɛntıti/ *n* identidad, *f.* **i. card,** cédula personal, *f*; carnet de identidad, *m.* **i. disc,** disco de identidad, *m*

ideological /,aidiə'lɒdʒıkəl/ *a* ideológico

ideology /,aidi'ɒlədʒi/ *n* ideología, *f*

idiocy /'ıdiəsi/ *n* idiotez, imbecilidad, *f*; (foolishness) necedad, tontería, sandez, *f*

idiom /'ıdiəm/ *n* idiotismo, *m*; modismo, *m*, locución, *f*; (language) habla, *f*, lenguaje, *m*

idiomatic /,ıdiə'mætık/ *a* idiomático

idiosyncrasy /,ıdiə'sıŋkrəsi/ *n* idiosincrasia, *f*

idiosyncratic /,ıdiousın'krætık/ *a* idiosincrásico

idiot /'ıdiət/ *n* idiota, imbécil, *mf*; (fool) necio (-ia), tonto (-ta), mentecato (-ta)

idiotic /,ıdi'ɒtık/ *a* idiota, imbécil; (foolish) necio, tonto, sandio

idle /'aidl/ *a* desocupado; indolente, ocioso; (unemployed) cesante, sin empleo; (lazy) perezoso, holgazán; (of machines) parado, inactivo; (useless) vano, inútil, sin efecto; (false) falso, mentiroso, infundado; (stupid) fútil, frívolo. —*vi* holgar, estar ocioso; holgazanear, haraganear, gandulear. **to i. away,** malgastar, perder. **to i. away the time,** pasar el rato, matar el tiempo. **i. efforts,** vanos esfuerzos, *m pl.* **i. fancies,** ilusiones, fantasías, *f pl*, sueños, *m pl.* **i. hours,** horas desocupadas, *f pl*, ratos perdidos, *m pl.* **i. question,** pregunta ociosa, *f.* **i. tale,** cuento de viejas, *m.* **i. threat,** reto vacuo, *m*

idleness /'aidlnıs/ *n* ociosidad, indolencia, inacción, *f*; pereza, holgazanería, gandulería, *f*; (uselessness) inutilidad, futilidad, *f*

idler /'aidlər/ *n* ocioso (-sa); haragán (-ana); perezoso (-sa), holgazán (-ana), gandul (-la)

idly /'aidli/ *adv* ociosamente, perezosamente; (uselessly) vanamente

idol /'aidl/ *n* ídolo, *m.* **a popular i.,** el ídolo de las masas, *m*

idolater /ai'dɒlətər/ *n* idólatra, *mf*; (admirer) amante, *mf* esclavo (-va), admirador (-ra)

idolatrous /ai'dɒlətrəs/ *a* idólatra, idolátrico

idolatry /ai'dɒlətri/ *n* idolatría, *f*; (devotion) adoración, pasión, *f*

idolize /'aidl,aiz/ *vt* idolatrar, adorar

idyll /'aidl/ n idilio, m

idyllic /ai'dılık/ a idílico

if /ıf/ conjunc si; (even if) aunque, aun cuando; (whenever) cuando, en caso de que; (whether) si. **as if,** como si (foll. by subjunc.). **If he comes, we shall tell him,** Si viene se lo diremos. **If he had not killed the tiger, she would be dead,** Si él no hubiera matado al tigre, ella estaría muerta. **If ever there was one,** Si alguna vez lo hubiera. **if necessary,** si fuese necesario. **if not,** si no, si no es que (e.g., *Poet and philosopher are twins, if not one and the same,* Poeta y filósofo son hermanos gemelos, si no es que la misma cosa). **If only!** ¡Ojalá que! (foll. by subjunc.)

igloo /'ıglu/ n iglú, m

ignite /ıg'nait/ vt encender, pegar fuego (a), incendiar. —vi prender fuego, incendiarse; arder

ignition /ıg'nıʃən/ n ignición, f; Auto. encendido, m. **i. coil,** Auto. carrete de inducción del encendido, m. **i. key,** Auto. llave del contacto, f

ignoble /ıg'noubəl/ a innoble, vil, indigno

ignominious /ˌıgnə'mıniəs/ a ignominioso

ignominy /'ıgnə.mıni/ n ignominia, deshonra, afrenta, f

ignoramus /ˌıgnə'reıməs/ n ignorante, mf

ignorance /'ıgnərəns/ n ignorancia, f; (unawareness) desconocimiento, m. **to plead i.,** pretender ignorancia

ignorant /'ıgnərənt/ a ignorante; inculto. **He is an i. fellow,** Es un ignorante. **to be i. of,** no saber, ignorar. **to be very i.,** ser muy ignorante, Inf. ser muy burro

ignorantly /'ıgnərəntli/ adv ignorantemente, por ignorancia; neciamente

ignore /ıg'nɔr/ vt no hacer caso de, desatender; (omit) pasar por alto de; Law. rechazar; (pretend not to recognize) hacer semblante de no reconocer; (not recognize) no reconocer

ileac /'ılıæk/ a Anat. ilíaco

ileum /'ılıəm/ n Anat. íleon, m

ilium /'ılıəm/ n Anat. ilion, m

ill /ıl/ n mal, m. —a (sick) enfermo, malo; (bad) malo; (unfortunate) desdichado, funesto. —adv mal. **to be ill,** estar malo. **to be taken ill,** caer enfermo. **ill-advised,** mal aconsejado; desacertado, imprudente. **ill-advisedly,** imprudentemente. **ill at ease,** incómodo. **ill-bred,** mal criado, mal educado, mal nacido. **ill-breeding,** mala crianza, mala educación, f. **ill-disposed,** malintencionado. **ill fame,** mala fama, f. **ill-fated,** malhadado, malaventurado, aciago, fatal. **ill-favored,** mal parecido, feúcho. **ill-feeling,** hostilidad, f, rencor, m. **ill-gotten,** maladquirido. **ill-humor,** mal humor, m. **ill-humored,** de mal humor, malhumorado. **ill-luck,** desdicha, mala suerte, malaventura, f; infortunio, m. **ill-mannered,** mal educado. **ill-**

natured, malévolo, perverso. **ill-naturedly,** malignamente. **ill-omened,** nefasto. **ill-spent,** malgastado, perdido. **ill-spoken,** mal hablado. **ill-suited,** malavenido. **ill-timed,** inoportuno, intempestivo. **ill-treat,** maltratar, malparar, tratar mal. **ill-treated,** que ha sido tratado mal; maltrecho. **ill-treatment,** maltratamiento, m, crueldad, f. **ill-turn,** mala jugada, f. **to do an ill-turn,** hacer un flaco servicio. **ill will,** mala voluntad, f; rencor, m, ojeriza, f. **to bear a person ill will,** guardarle rencor

illegal /ı'ligəl/ a ilegal; indebido, ilícito

illegible /ı'lɛdʒəbəl/ a ilegible, indescrifrable

illegibly /ı'lɛdʒəbli/ adv de un modo ilegible

illegitimacy /ˌılı'dʒıtəməsi/ n ilegitimidad, f; falsedad, f

illegitimate /ˌılı'dʒıtəmıt/ a ilegítimo, bastardo; falso; ilícito, desautorizado

illiberal /ı'lıbərəl/ a iliberal; intolerante, estrecho de miras; (mean) avaro, tacaño, ruin

illicit /ı'lısıt/ a ilícito, indebido, ilegal

illicitly /ı'lısıtli/ adv ilícitamente, ilegalmente

illicitness /ı'lısıtnıs/ n ilicitud, ilegalidad, f

illimitable /ı'lımıtəbəl/ a ilimitado, sin límites, infinito

illiteracy /ı'lıtərəsi/ n analfabetismo, m

illiterate /ı'lıtərıt/ a and n analfabeto (-ta), iliterato (-ta)

illness /'ılnıs/ n enfermedad, dolencia, f, mal, m

illogical /ı'lɒdʒıkəl/ a ilógico; absurdo, irracional

illuminant /ı'lumənənt/ a iluminador, alumbrador

illuminate /ı'lumə.neit/ vt iluminar, alumbrar; Art. iluminar; (explain) aclarar, ilustrar

illuminated /ı'lumə.neitıd/ a iluminado, encendido; Art. iluminado. **i. sign,** letrero luminoso, m

illuminating /ı'lumə.neitıŋ/ a iluminador; (explanatory) aclaratorio. —n Art. iluminación, f

illumination /ı.lumə'neıʃən/ n iluminación, f, alumbrado, m; (for decoration) luminaria, f; Art. iluminación, f; Fig. inspiración, f

illuminator /ı'lumə.neitər/ n Art. iluminador (-ra)

illusion /ı'luʒən/ n ilusión, f, engaño, m; (dream) esperanza, ilusión, f, ensueño, m. **to harbor illusions,** tener ilusiones

illusive /ı'lusıv/ a ilusivo, engañoso, falso

illusory /ı'lusəri/ a ilusorio, deceptivo, falso, irreal

illustrate /'ılə.streit/ vt ilustrar, aclarar, explicar, elucidar; Art. ilustrar; (prove) probar, demostrar

illustration /ˌılə'streıʃən/ n ejemplo, m;

ilustración, f; Art. grabado, m; estampa, f; (explanation) elucidación, aclaración, f

illustrative /ɪ'lʌstrətɪv/ a ilustrativo, ilustrador, explicativo, aclaratorio

illustrator /'ɪlə,streitər/ n ilustrador (-ra), grabador (-ra)

illustrious /ɪ'lʌstriəs/ a ilustre, famoso, renombrado, distinguido

image /'ɪmɪdʒ/ n (optics) imagen, f; efigie, imagen, f; (religious) imagen, estatua, f; Art. figura, f; (metaphor) metáfora, expresión, f; (of a person) retrato, m. **to be the i. of,** ser el retrato de. **sharp i.,** imagen nítida, f. **i. breaker,** iconoclasta, mf. **i. vendor,** vendedor (-ra) de imágenes

imagery /'ɪmɪdʒri/ n Art. imaginería, f; (style) metáforas, f pl

imaginary /ɪ'mædʒə,nɛri/ a imaginario; fantástico, de ensueño

imagination /ɪ,mædʒə'neiʃən/ n imaginación, f; imaginativa, fantasía, inventiva, f, ingenio, m

imaginative /ɪ'mædʒənətɪv/ a imaginativo; fantástico

imagine /ɪ'mædʒɪn/ vt imaginar, concebir; idear, proyectar, inventar; figurarse, suponer. **Just i.!** ¡Imagínese usted!

imam /ɪ'mɑm/ n imán, m

imbecile /'ɪmbəsɪl/ a imbécil; (foolish) necio, estúpido, tonto. —n imbécil, mf; (fool) necio (-ia), tonto (-ta), estúpido (-da)

imbecility /,ɪmbə'sɪlɪti/ n imbecilidad, f; (folly) necedad, sandez, f

imbibe /ɪm'baib/ vt embeber, absorber; (drink) sorber, chupar; empaparse de

imbibing /ɪm'baibɪŋ/ n imbibición, absorción, f

imbroglio /ɪm'brouljou/ n embrollo, lío, m

imbue /ɪm'byu/ vt imbuir, calar, empapar; teñir. **to i. with,** infundir de

imitable /'ɪmɪtəbəl/ a imitable

imitate /'ɪmɪ,teit/ vt imitar; copiar, reproducir; (counterfeit) contrahacer

imitation /,ɪmɪ'teiʃən/ n imitación, f; copia, f; remedo, traslado, m. —a imitado; falso, artificial

imitative /'ɪmɪ,teitɪv/ a imitativo; imitador

imitativeness /'ɪmɪ,teitɪvnɪs/ n facultad imitativa (or de imitacion), f

imitator /'ɪmɪ,teitər/ n imitador (-ra); contrahacedor (-ra), falsificador (-ra)

immaculate /ɪ'mækyələt/ a inmaculado, puro; (of dress) elegante. **I. Conception,** la Purísima Concepción

immaculately /ɪ'mækyəlɪtli/ adv inmaculadamente; elegantemente

immanence /'ɪmənəns/ n inmanencia, inherencia, f

immanent /'ɪmənənt/ a inmanente; inherente

immaterial /,ɪmə'tɪəriəl/ a inmaterial, incorpóreo; sin importancia. **It is i. to me,** Me es indiferente, No me importa, Me da lo mismo, Me da igual

immateriality /,ɪmə,tɪəri'ælɪti/ n inmaterialidad, f

immature /'ɪmə'tʃʊr/ a inmaturo; precoz; (of fruit) verde

immaturity /'ɪmə'tʃʊrɪti/ n falta de madurez, f; precocidad, f

immeasurable /ɪ'mɛʒərəbəl/ a inmensurable, inmenso, imponderable

immeasurably /ɪ'mɛʒərəbli/ adv inmensamente, enormemente

immediate /ɪ'midiɪt/ a (of place) inmediato, cercano, contiguo; (of time) próximo, inmediato, directo; (of action) inmediato, perentorio; (on letters) urgente. **to take i. action,** tomar acción inmediata

immediately /ɪ'midiɪtli/ adv (of place) próximamente, contiguamente; (of time) luego, seguidamente, en el acto, ahora mismo, enseguida; directamente; (as soon as) así que

immemorial /,ɪmə'mɔriəl/ a inmemorial, inmemorable

immemorially /,ɪmə'mɔriəli/ adv desde tiempo inmemorial

immense /ɪ'mɛns/ a inmenso, enorme; vasto, extenso; infinito

immensely /ɪ'mɛnsli/ adv inmensamente, enormemente

immensity /ɪ'mɛnsɪti/ n inmensidad, f; extensión, vastedad, f

immerse /ɪ'mɜrs/ vt sumergir, hundir en, zambullir; bautizar por sumersión. Fig. **to be immersed in,** estar absorto en

immersion /ɪ'mɜrʒən/ n sumersion, f, hundimiento, m; Astron. inmersión, f

immigrant /'ɪmɪgrənt/ a and n inmigrante, mf

immigrate /'ɪmɪ,greit/ vi inmigrar

immigration /,ɪmɪ'greiʃən/ n inmigración, f

imminence /'ɪmənəns/ n inminencia, f

imminent /'ɪmənənt/ a inminente

immobile /ɪ'moubəl/ a inmóvil, inmoble; impasible, imperturbable

immobility /,ɪmou'bɪlɪti/ n inmovilidad, f; impasibilidad, imperturbabilidad, f

immobilization /ɪ,moubələ'zeiʃən/ n inmovilización, f

immobilize /ɪ'moubə,laiz/ vt inmovilizar

immoderate /ɪ'mɒdərɪt/ a inmoderado, excesivo, indebido

immoderately /ɪ'mɒdərɪtli/ adv inmoderadamente, excesivamente

immoderateness /ɪ'mɒdərɪtnɪs/ n inmoderación, f, exceso, m

immodest /ɪ'mɒdɪst/ a inmodesto; indecente, deshonesto; (pert) atrevido, descarado

immodestly /ɪ'mɒdɪstli/ adv impúdicamente, inmodestamente

immodesty /ɪ'mɒdɪsti/ n inmodestia, impudicia, f; deshonestidad, licencia, f; (forwardness) descaro, atrevimiento, m

immolate /'ɪmə,leit/ vt inmolar, sacrificar

immolation /,ɪmə'leiʃən/ n inmolación, f, sacrificio, m

immolator /'ɪmə,leitər/ n inmolador (-ra)

immoral /ɪ'mɔrəl/ a inmoral; licencioso, vicioso; incontinente

immorality /ˌɪmə'ræltɪ/ n inmoralidad, f

immortal /ɪ'mɔrtl/ a inmortal; perenne, eterno, imperecedero. —n inmortal, mf

immortality /ˌɪmɔr'tæltɪ/ n inmortalidad, f; fama inmortal, f

immortalize /ɪ'mɔrtl,aiz/ vt inmortalizar, perpetuar

immovable /ɪ'muvəbəl/ a inmoble, fijo, inmóvil; (of purpose) inconmovible, inalterable, constante. —n pl. **immovables** Law. bienes inmuebles, m pl. Eccl. **i. feast,** fiesta fija, f

immune /ɪ'myun/ a inmune, libre; Med. inmune. **i. from,** exento de; libre de

immunity /ɪ'myunɪtɪ/ n inmunidad, libertad, f; exención, f; Med. inmunidad, f

immunization /ˌɪmyunə'zeiʃən/ n Med. inmunización, f

immunize /'ɪmyə,naiz/ vt inmunizar

immure /ɪ'myʊr/ vt emparedar, recluir, encerrar

immutable /ɪ'myutəbəl/ a inmutable, inalterable, constante

imp /ɪmp/ n trasgo, diablillo, duende, m; (child) picaruelo (-la)

impact /'ɪmpækt/ n impacto, m, impacción, f; choque, m, colisión, f

impair /ɪm'pɛər/ vt perjudicar, echar a perder, deteriorar, empeorar, desmejorar. **to be impaired,** deteriorarse, perjudicarse

impairment /ɪm'pɛərmənt/ n deterioración, perjuicio, empeoramiento, m

impale /ɪm'peil/ vt (punishment) empalar; (with a sword) atravesar, espetar

impalement /ɪm'peilmənt/ n (punishment) empalamiento, m; atravesamiento, m, transfixión, f

impalpable /ɪm'pælpəbəl/ a impalpable, intangible; incorpóreo

impart /ɪm'pɑrt/ vt comunicar, dar parte (de); conferir

impartial /ɪm'pɑrʃəl/ a imparcial, ecuánime

impartiality /ɪm,pɑrʃi'ælɪtɪ/ n imparcialidad, ecuanimidad, entereza, f, desinterés, m

impartially /ɪm'pɑrʃəli/ adv imparcialmente, con desinterés

impassable /ɪm'pæsəbəl/ a intransitable, impracticable; (of water) invadeable

impasse /'ɪmpæs/ n callejón sin salida, m

impassible /ɪm'pæsəbəl/ a impasible, insensible; indiferente, imperturbable

impassion /ɪm'pæʃən/ vt apasionar, conmover

impassioned /ɪm'pæʃənd/ a apasionado, vehemente, ardiente

impassive /ɪm'pæsɪv/ a impasible, insensible; indiferente, imperturbable; apático

impassively /ɪm'pæsɪvli/ adv indiferentemente

impassivity /ˌɪmpæ'sɪvɪti/ n impasibilidad, f; indiferencia, f; apatía, f

impatience /ɪm'peiʃəns/ n impaciencia, f

impatient /ɪm'peiʃənt/ a impaciente; intolerante. **to make i.,** impacientar. **to grow i.,** impacientarse, perder la paciencia. **to grow i. at,** impacientarse ante. **to grow i. to,** impacientarse a or por. **to grow i. under,** impacientarse bajo

impatiently /ɪm'peiʃəntli/ adv con impaciencia, impacientemente

impeach /ɪm'pitʃ/ vt Law. denunciar, delatar, acusar, hacer juicio político (Argentina); censurar, criticar, tachar

impeachable /ɪm'pitʃəbəl/ a Law. delatable, denunciable, acusable; censurable

impeacher /ɪm'pitʃər/ n acusador (-ra), denunciador (-ra), delator (-ra)

impeachment /ɪm'pitʃmənt/ n Law. acusación, denuncia, f; reproche, m, queja, f

impeccable /ɪm'pɛkəbəl/ a impecable, intachable, perfecto; elegante

impeccably /ɪm'pɛkəbli/ adv perfectamente; elegantemente

impecunious /ˌɪmpə'kyuniəs/ a indigente, pobre

impede /ɪm'pid/ vt impedir, obstruir, estorbar; Fig. dificultar, embarazar

impediment /ɪm'pɛdəmənt/ n obstáculo, estorbo, m; Fig. dificultad, f; Law. impedimento, m. **to have an i. in one's speech,** tener una dificultad en el hablar

impel /ɪm'pɛl/ vt impulsar, impeler; Fig. estimular, obligar, mover, constreñir. **I felt impelled (to),** Me sentí obligado (a)

impend /ɪm'pɛnd/ vi ser inminente, amenazar

impending /ɪm'pɛndɪŋ/ a inminente, pendiente

impenetrable /ɪm'pɛnɪtrəbəl/ a impenetrable; intransitable; denso, espeso; Fig. enigmático, insondable, secreto

impenetrably /ɪm,pɛnɪtrə'bɪltɪ/ adv impenetrablemente, densamente

impenitence /ɪm'pɛnɪtəns/ n impenitencia, f

impenitent /ɪm'pɛnɪtənt/ a impenitente, incorregible

impenitently /ɪm'pɛnɪtəntli/ adv sin penitencia

imperative /ɪm'pɛrətɪv/ a imperioso, perentorio; Gram. imperativo; (necessary) esencial, urgente. —n mandato, m, orden, f; Gram. imperativo, m. **in the i.,** en el imperativo

imperativeness /ɪm'pɛrətɪvnɪs/ n perentoriedad, f; urgencia, importancia, f

imperceptible /ˌɪmpər'sɛptəbəl/ a imperceptible, insensible

imperceptive /ˌɪmpər'sɛptɪv/ a insensible

imperfect /ɪm'pɜrfɪkt/ a imperfecto; incompleto, defectuoso. —a and n Gram. imperfecto m

imperfection /ˌɪmpər'fɛkʃən/ n imperfección, f; defecto, desperfecto, m; falta, tacha, f

imperial /ɪm'pɪəriəl/ a imperial, imperatorio. —n (beard) pera, f. **i. preference,** preferencia dentro del Imperio, f

imperial /ɪm'pɪərɪəl/ *vt* arriesgar, poner en peligro, aventurar

imperialism /ɪm'pɪərɪə,lɪzəm/ *n* imperialismo, *m*

imperialist /ɪm'pɪərɪəlɪst/ *n* imperialista, *mf*

imperialistic /ɪm,pɪərɪə'lɪstɪk/ *a* imperialista

imperious /ɪm'pɪərɪəs/ *a* imperioso, altivo, arrogante; (pressing) urgente, apremiante

imperiously /ɪm'pɪərɪəsli/ *adv* imperiosamente, con arrogancia

imperiousness /ɪm'pɪərɪəsnɪs/ *n* autoridad, arrogancia, altivez, *f*; necesidad, urgencia, *f*, apremio, *m*

imperishability /ɪm,perɪʃə'bɪlɪti/ *n* (immortality) inmortalidad, perennidad, *f*

imperishable /ɪm'perɪʃəbəl/ *a* imperecedero, inmarchitable, perenne, eterno

impermanence /ɪm'pɜrmənəns/ *n* inestabilidad, interinidad, *f*; brevedad, fugacidad, *f*

impermanent /ɪm'pɜrmənənt/ *a* interino, no permanente

impermeability /ɪm,pɜrmɪə'bɪlɪti/ *n* impermeabilidad, *f*

impermeable /ɪm'pɜrmɪəbəl/ *a* impermeable

impersonal /ɪm'pɜrsənl/ *a* impersonal, objetivo; *Gram.* impersonal

impersonality /ɪm,pɜrsə'nælɪti/ *n* objetividad, *f*

impersonate /ɪm'pɜrsə,neit/ *vt* personificar, simbolizar; *Theat.* representar

impersonation /ɪm,pɜrsə'neiʃən/ *n* personificación, simbolización, *f*; *Theat.* representación, *f*

impertinence /ɪm'pɜrtnəns/ *n* impertinencia, majadería, insolencia, *f*; inoportunidad, *f*; despropósito, *m*

impertinent /ɪm'pɜrtnənt/ *a* impertinente, insolente; (unseasonable) intempestivo, inoportuno; (irrelevant) fuera de propósito

impertinently /ɪm'pɜrtnəntli/ *adv* con insolencia, impertinentemente

imperturbability /ɪm,ɪmpɜrtɜrbə'bɪlɪti/ *n* imperturbabilidad, serenidad, impasibilidad, *f*; impavidez, *f*

imperturbable /ɪm,ɪmpɜr'tɜrbəbəl/ *a* imperturbable, impasible, sereno; impávido

imperturbably /ɪm,ɪmpɜr'tɜrbəbli/ *adv* con serenidad, imperturbablemente

impervious /ɪm'pɜrvɪəs/ *a* impermeable, impenetrable; *Fig.* insensible. **He is i. to arguments**, No hace caso de argumentos

imperviousness /ɪm'pɜrvɪəsnɪs/ *n* impermeabilidad, impenetrabilidad, *f*; *Fig.* insensibilidad, *f*

impetigo /,ɪmpɪ'taigou/ *n Med.* impétigo, *m*

impetuosity /ɪm,petʃu'ɒsɪti/ *n* impetuosidad, temeridad, irreflexión, *f*

impetuous /ɪm'petʃuəs/ *a* impetuoso, temerario, irreflexivo; violento, vehemente

impetus /'ɪmpɪtəs/ *n Mech.* ímpetu, *m*, impulsión, *f*; *Fig.* incentivo, estímulo, impulso, *m*

impiety /ɪm'paɪti/ *n* impiedad, irreligión, irreligiosidad, *f*

impinge (upon) /ɪm'pɪndʒ/ *vi* chocar con, tropezar con

impious /'ɪmpɪəs/ *a* impío, irreligioso, sacrílego; (wicked) malvado, perverso, malo

impish /'ɪmpɪʃ/ *a* travieso, revoltoso, enredador

implacable /ɪm'plækəbəl/ *a* implacable, inexorable, inflexible, riguroso

implant /ɪm'plænt/ *vt Fig.* implantar, inculcar, instilar

implantation /,ɪmplæn'teiʃən/ *n Fig.* implantación, instilación, inculcación, *f*

implement /*n* 'ɪmpləmənt; *v also* -,ment/ *n* instrumento, utensilio, *m*, herramienta, *f*; (of war) elemento, *m.* —*vt* cumplir, hacer efectivo; llevar a cabo

implicate /'ɪmplɪ,keit/ *vt* enredar, envolver; (imply) implicar, contener, llevar en sí; (in a crime) comprometer. **to be implicated in a crime**, estar implicado en un crimen.

implication /,ɪmplɪ'keiʃən/ *n* implicación, inferencia, repercusión, sugestión, *f*; (in a crime) complicidad, *f*

implicit /ɪm'plɪsɪt/ *a* implícito, virtual, tácito; (absolute) ciego, absoluto, implícito. **with i. faith**, con fe ciega

implied /ɪm'plaid/ *a* tácito, implícito

implore /ɪm'plɔr/ *vt* implorar, suplicar

imploring /ɪm'plɔrɪŋ/ *a* suplicante, implorante

imply /ɪm'plai/ *vt* implicar, indicar, presuponer; (mean) querer decir, significar; (hint) insinuar, sugerir

impolite /,ɪmpə'lait/ *a* descortés, mal educado

impolitely /,ɪmpə'laitli/ *adv* con descortesía

impolitic /ɪm'pɒlɪtɪk/ *a* impolítico

imponderable /ɪm'pɒndərəbəl/ *a* imponderable

import /*v* ɪm'pɔrt; *a, n* 'ɪmpɔrt/ *vt Com.* importar; (mean) significar, querer decir. —*a Com.* importado, de importación. —*n Com.* importación, *f*; (meaning) significado, sentido, *m*; (value) importe, valor, *m*; (contents) contenido, tenor, *m*; importancia, *f.* **i. duty**, derechos de importación derechos de entrada, *m pl*, gravamen a la importación, *m.* **i. licence**, permiso de importación, *m.* **i. trade**, negocios de importación, *m pl*

importance /ɪm'pɔrtəns/ *n* importancia, *f*; valor, alcance, *m*, magnitud, *f*; consideración, eminencia, *f.* **to be fully conscious of one's i.**, tener plena conciencia de su importancia

important /ɪm'pɔrtnt/ *a* importante; distinguido; presuntuoso, vanidoso. **to be i.**, importar, ser importante. **i. person**, personaje, *m*, persona importante, *f*

importation /,ɪmpɔr'teiʃən/ *n* importación, *f; Com.* introducción (or importación) de géneros extranjeros, *f*

importer /ɪm'pɔrtər/ *n* importador (-ra)

importunate /ɪm'pɔrtʃənɪt/ *a* (of a demand) insistente, importuno; (of persons) impertinente, pesado

importune /ɪmpɔr'tun/ *vt* importunar, asediar, perseguir

importuning /ɪmpɔr'tunɪŋ/ *n* persecución, importunación, *f*

importunity /ɪmpɔr'tunɪti/ *n* importunidad, insistencia, impertinencia, *f*

impose /ɪm'pouz/ *vt* (on, upon) imponer, infligir, cargar; *Print.* imponer. —*vi* (on, upon) (deceive) engañar, embaucar

imposing /ɪm'pouzɪŋ/ *a* imponente, impresionante; (of persons) majestuoso, importante

imposition /ˌɪmpə'zɪʃən/ *n* imposición, *f;* (burden) impuesto, tributo, *m,* carga, *f;* (*Print., etc.*) imposición, *f;* (trick) fraude, engaño, *m,* decepción, *f*

impossibility /ɪm,pɒsə'bɪlɪti/ *n* imposibilidad, *f*

impossible /ɪm'pɒsəbəl/ *a* imposible. **Nothing is i.,** No hay nada imposible, *Inf.* De menos nos hizo Dios. **to do the i.,** hacer lo imposible

impost /'ɪmpoust/ *n* impuesto, *m,* contribución, gabela, *f*

impostor /ɪm'pɒstər/ *n* impostor (-ra), bribón (-ona), embustero (-ra)

impotence /'ɪmpətəns/ *n* impotencia, *f*

impotent /'ɪmpətənt/ *a* impotente

impound /ɪm'paund/ *vt* acorralar; (water) embalsar; (goods) confiscar

impoverish /ɪm'pɒvərɪʃ/ *vt* empobrecer, depauperar, arruinar; (health) debilitar; (land) agotar

impoverished /ɪm'pɒvərɪʃt/ *a* indigente, necesitado; (of land) agotado

impoverishment /ɪm'pɒvərɪʃmənt/ *n* empobrecimiento, *m,* ruina, *f;* (of land) agotamiento, *m*

impracticable /ɪm'præktɪkəbəl/ *a* impracticable, no factible, imposible

imprecation /ˌɪmprɪ'keɪʃən/ *n* imprecación, maldición, *f*

impregnable /ɪm'prɛgnəbəl/ *a* inexpugnable, inconquistable

impregnate /ɪm'prɛgneɪt/ *vt* impregnar, empapar; *Biol.* fecundar. **to become impregnated,** impregnarse

impregnation /ˌɪmprɛg'neɪʃən/ *n* impregnación, *f; Biol.* fecundación, fertilización, *f; Fig.* inculcación, *f*

impresario /ˌɪmprə'sɑri,ou/ *n* empresario, *m*

impress /*v* ɪm'prɛs; *n* 'ɪmprɛs/ *vt* imprimir; (on the mind) impresionar; inculcar; imbuir; (with respect) imponer; *Mil.* reclutar; (of goods) confiscar. —*n* impresión, marca, señal, huella, *f*

impression /ɪm'prɛʃən/ *n* impresión, *f;* marca, señal, huella, *f; Print.* impresión, *f;* efecto, *m;* idea, noción, *f.* **He has the i. that they do not like him,** Sospecha

que no les es simpático. **to be under the i.,** tener la impresión

impressionable /ɪm'prɛʃənəbəl/ *a* susceptible, impresionable, sensitivo

impressionism /ɪm'prɛʃə,nɪzəm/ *n* impresionismo, *m*

impressionist /ɪm'prɛʃənɪst/ *n* impresionista, *mf*

impressionistic /ɪm,prɛʃə'nɪstɪk/ *a* impresionista

impressive /ɪm'prɛsɪv/ *a* impresionante; emocionante; imponente, majestuoso; enfático

impressively /ɪm'prɛsɪvli/ *adv* solemnemente, de modo impresionante; enfáticamente

imprint /*n* 'ɪmprɪnt; *v* ɪm'prɪnt/ *n* impresión, señal, marca, huella, *f; Print.* pie de imprenta, *m.* —*vt* imprimir; (on the mind) grabar, fijar

imprison /ɪm'prɪzən/ *vt* encerrar, encarcelar, aprisionar

imprisonment /ɪm'prɪzənmənt/ *n* encarcelación, prisión, *f,* encierro, *m*

improbability /ɪm,prɒbə'bɪlɪti/ *n* improbabilidad, *f;* inverosimilitud, *f*

improbable /ɪm'prɒbəbəl/ *a* improbable; inverosímil

improbity /ɪm'proubɪti/ *n* improbidad, *f*

impromptu /ɪm'prɒmptu/ *a* indeliberado, impremeditado, espontáneo. —*adv* de improviso, in promptu. —*n* improvisación, *f*

improper /ɪm'prɒpər/ *a* impropio, inadecuado; incorrecto; indebido; indecente, indecoroso. **i. fraction,** *Math.* quebrado impropio, *m*

improperly /ɪm'prɒpərli/ *adv* impropiamente, incorrectamente; indecorosamente

impropriety /ˌɪmprə'praɪɪti/ *n* inconveniencia, *f;* incorrección, *f;* (style) impropiedad, *f;* falta de decoro, *f*

improve /ɪm'pruv/ *vt* mejorar; perfeccionar; (beautify) embellecer, hermosear; (land) bonificar; *Lit.* corregir, enmendar; (cultivate) cultivar; (increase) aumentar; (an opportunity) aprovechar; (strengthen) fortificar; (business) sacar provecho de, explotar. —*vi* mejorar; perfeccionarse; (progress) hacer progresos, progresar, adelantarse; *Com.* subir; (become beautiful) hacerse hermoso, embellecerse; (increase) aumentarse. **to i. upon,** mejorar, perfeccionar; pulir

improvement /ɪm'pruvmənt/ *n* mejora, *f;* perfeccionamiento, *m;* aumento, *m;* adelantamiento, progreso, *m;* (in health) mejoría, *f;* embellecimiento, *m;* cultivación, *f;* (of land) abono, *m*

improver /ɪm'pruvər/ *n* aprendiz (-za)

improvidence /ɪm'prɒvɪdəns/ *n* imprevisión, *f;* improvidencia, *f*

improvident /ɪm'prɒvɪdənt/ *a* impróvido, desprevenido

improvisation /ɪm,prɒvə'zeɪʃən/ *n* improvisación, *f*

improvise /'ɪmprə,vaɪz/ *vt* improvisar

imprudence /ɪm'prudns/ *n* imprudencia, *f;* desacierto, *m,* indiscreción, *f*

imprudent /ɪm'prudn̩t/ *a* imprudente; desacertado, indiscreto, mal avisado, irreflexivo

impudence /'ɪmpyədəns/ *n* impudencia, *f*, descaro, *m*, insolencia, desvergüenza, *f*, atrevimiento, *m*

impudent /'ɪmpyədənt/ *a* impudente, descarado, insolente, desvergonzado, atrevido

impugn /ɪm'pyun/ *vt* impugnar, contradecir, atacar

impugnment /ɪm'pyunmənt/ *n* impugnación, *f*

impulse /'ɪmpʌls/ *n* ímpetu, *m*, impulsión, *f*; impulso, estímulo, *m*; incitación, instigación, *f*; motivo, *m*; (fit) arranque, arrebato, acceso, *m*

impulsion /ɪm'pʌlʃən/ *n* ímpetu, *m*, impulsión, *f*; empuje, *m*, arranque, *m*

impulsive /ɪm'pʌlsɪv/ *a* impelente; irreflexivo, impulsivo

impulsively /ɪm'pʌlsɪvli/ *adv* por impulso

impulsiveness /ɪm'pʌlsɪvnɪs/ *n* irreflexión, *f*; carácter impulsivo, *m*

impunity /ɪm'pyunɪti/ *n* impunidad, *f*. **with i.,** impunemente

impure /ɪm'pyʊr/ *a* impuro; adulterado, mezclado; (indecent) deshonesto, indecente; (dirty) turbio, sucio

impurity /ɪm'pyʊrɪti/ *n* impureza, *f*; adulteración, mezcla, *f*; deshonestidad, ljviandad, *f*; suciedad, turbiedad, *f*

imputation /ˌɪmpyu'teɪʃən/ *n* imputación, atribución, *f*; (in a bad sense) acusación, *f*, reproche, *m*

impute /ɪm'pyut/ *vt* imputar, achacar, atribuir; acusar, reprochar

imputer /ɪm'pyutər/ *n* imputador (-ra); recriminador (-ra), acusador (-ra)

in /ɪn/ *prep* en; a; (of duration) durante, mientras; (with) con; (through) por; dentro de; (under) bajo; (following a superlative) de; (of specified time) dentro de, de aquí a; (with afternoon, etc.) por; (out of) sobre. **course in medieval Catalan literature,** curso de literatura catalana medioeval. **dressed in black,** vestido de negro. **in London,** en Londres. **in the morning,** por la mañana; (in the course of) durante la mañana. **in time,** a tiempo; dentro de algún tiempo. **in a week,** dentro de una semana. **in the best way,** del mejor modo. **in writing,** por escrito. **in anger,** con enojo. **in one's hand,** en la mano. **in addition to,** además de, a más de. **in case,** por si acaso, en caso de que. **in order to,** a fin de, para (foll. by infin.). **in order that,** para que (foll. by subjunc.). **in so far as,** en cuanto. **in spite of,** a pesar de. **in the distance,** a lo lejos, en lontananza. **in the meantime,** entre tanto. **in the middle of,** en el medio de; a la mitad de. **in the style of,** al modo de; a la manera de, a la (francesa, etc.)

in /ɪn/ *adv* adentro, dentro; (at home) en casa; (of sun) escondido; (of fire) alumbrado; (in power) en el poder; (of harvest) cosechado; (of boats) entrado (with haber); (of trains) llegado (with haber). **to be in,** estar dentro; haber llegado; estar en casa. **to be in for,** estar expuesto a, correr el riesgo de. **to be in with a person,** ser muy amigo de, estar muy metido con. **Come in!** ¡Adelante!; ¡Pase usted! **ins and outs,** sinuosidades, *f pl*; (of river) meandros, *m pl*; (of an affair) pormenores, detalles, *m pl*. **in less time than you can say Jack Robinson,** en menos de Jesús, en un credo, en menos que canta un gallo, en menos que se persigna un cura loco. **In the middle of nowhere,** donde Cristo dio las tres voces, (Western Hemisphere) donde el diablo perdió el poncho.

in /ɪn/ *a* interno. **in-law** (of relations) político. **in-patient,** enfermo (-ma) de hospital

inability /ˌɪnə'bɪlɪti/ *n* incapacidad, inhabilidad, ineptitud, incompetencia, *f*; impotencia, *f*

inaccessible /ˌɪnək'sɛsəbəl/ *a* inaccesible

inaccuracy /ɪn'ækyərəsi/ *n* inexactitud, incorrección, *f*

inaccurate /ɪn'ækyərɪt/ *a* inexacto, incorrecto

inaccurately /ɪn'ækyərɪtli/ *adv* inexactamente, erróneamente

inaction /ɪn'ækʃən/ *n* inacción, *f*

inactive /ɪn'æktɪv/ *a* inactivo, pasivo; (of things) inerte, (lazy) perezoso, indolente; (machinery) parado; (motionless) inmóvil; (at leisure) desocupado, sin empleo

inactivity /ˌɪnæk'tɪvɪti/ *n* inactividad, pasividad, *f*; (of things) inercia, *f*; pereza, indolencia, *f*; (of machinery) paro, *m*; inmovilidad, *f*; (leisure) desocupación, *f*

inadequacy /ɪn'ædɪkwəsi/ *n* insuficiencia, escasez, *f*; imperfección, *f*, defecto, *m*

inadequate /ɪn'ædɪkwɪt/ *a* inadecuado, insuficiente, escaso; imperfecto, defectuoso

inadvertence /ˌɪnəd'vɜrtn̩s/ *n* inadvertencia, *f*; equivocación, *f*, descuido, *m*

inadvertent /ˌɪnəd'vɜrtn̩t/ *a* inadvertido, accidental, casual; negligente

inalienable /ɪn'eɪlyənəbəl/ *a* inajenable, inalienable

inalterable /ɪn'ɔltərəbəl/ *a* inalterable

inane /ɪ'neɪn/ *a* lelo, fatuo, vacío, necio

inanimate /ɪn'ænɪmɪt/ *a* (of matter) inanimado; sin vida, exánime, muerto

inanition /ˌɪnə'nɪʃən/ *n* inanición, *f*

inanity /ɪ'nænɪti/ *n* vacuidad, fatuidad, necedad, *f*

inappeasable /ˌɪnə'pizəbəl/ *a* implacable, riguroso

inapposite /ɪn'æpəzɪt/ *a* fuera de propósito, no pertinente, inoportuno

inappreciable /ˌɪnə'priʃiəbəl/ *a* inapreciable, imperceptible

inappreciative /ˌɪnə'priʃiətɪv/ *a* desagradecido, ingrato. **i. of,** insensible a, indiferente a

inapproachable /ˌɪnəˈprəʊtʃəbəl/ *a* inaccesible, huraño, adusto

inappropriate /ˌɪnəˈprəʊpriːt/ *a* impropio, inconveniente, inadecuado, incongruente; inoportuno

inappropriately /ˌɪnəˈprəʊpriːtli/ *adv* impropiamente; inoportunamente

inapt /ɪnˈæpt/ *a* inepto, inhábil; impropio

inaptitude /ɪnˈæptɪˌtjuːd/ *n* ineptitud, inhabilidad, *f*; impropiedad, *f*

inarticulate /ˌɪnɑːrˈtɪkjəlɪt/ *a* (of speech) inarticulado; (reticent) inexpresivo, reservado; indistinto; *Anat.* inarticulado

inarticulately /ˌɪnɑːrˈtɪkjəlɪtli/ *adv* indistintamente, de un modo inarticulado

inarticulateness /ˌɪnɑːrˈtɪkjəlɪtnɪs/ *n* tartamudez, *f*; inexpresión, reserva, *f*; silencio, *m*

inartistic /ˌɪnɑːrˈtɪstɪk/ *a* antiartístico, antiestético

inasmuch (as) /ˌɪnəzˈmʌtʃ/ *adv* puesto que, visto que, dado que

inattention /ˌɪnəˈtenʃən/ *n* desatención, inaplicación, abstracción, *f*; falta de solicitud, *f*

inattentive /ˌɪnəˈtentɪv/ *a* desatento, distraído; poco solícito, no atento

inattentively /ˌɪnəˈtentɪvli/ *adv* sin atención, distraídamente

inaudibility /ɪnˌɔːdəˈbɪlɪti/ *n* imposibilidad de oír, *f*

inaudible /ɪnˈɔːdəbəl/ *a* inaudible, no audible, ininteligible

inaudibly /ɪnˈɔːdəbli/ *adv* indistintamente, de modo inaudible

inaugurate /ɪnˈɔːgjəˌreɪt/ *vt* inaugurar; (open) estrenar, abrir, dedicar; (install) investir, instalar; (initiate) originar, iniciar, dar lugar (a)

inauguration /ɪnˌɔːgjəˈreɪʃən/ *n* inauguración, *f*; (opening) estreno, *m*, apertura, *f*; (investiture) instalación, investidura, *f*

inauspicious /ˌɪnəˈspɪʃəs/ *a* poco propicio, desfavorable; ominoso, triste, infeliz

inborn /ˈɪnbɔrn/ *a* innato, instintivo, inherente

inbred /ˈɪnbred/ *a* innato, inherente, instintivo

Inca /ˈɪŋkə/ *a* incaico, de los incas. —*n* inca, *m*

incalculable /ɪnˈkælkyələbəl/ *a* incalculable, innumerable; (of persons) voluble, veleidoso, caprichoso; infinito, immenso

incandescence /ˌɪnkənˈdesəns/ *n* incandescencia, candencia, *f*

incandescent /ˌɪnkənˈdesənt/ *a* incandescente, candente. **i. light,** luz incandescente, *f*. **to make i.,** encandecer

incantation /ˌɪnkænˈteɪʃən/ *n* hechizo, *m*, encantación, *f*, ensalmo, *m*

incapable /ɪnˈkeɪpəbəl/ *a* incapaz; inhábil, incompetente; (physically) imposibilitado

incapacitate /ˌɪnkəˈpæsɪˌteɪt/ *vt* imposibilitar, incapacitar, inutilizar; (disqualify) inhabilitar, incapacitar

incarcerate /ɪnˈkɑːrsəˌreɪt/ *vt* encarcelar

incarceration /ɪnˌkɑːrsəˈreɪʃən/ *n* encarcelación, prisión, *f*

incarnate /a ɪnˈkɑːrnɪt/ *v* -neɪt/ *a* encarnado. —*vt* encarnar

incarnation /ˌɪnkɑːrˈneɪʃən/ *n* encarnación, *f*

incautious /ɪnˈkɔːʃəs/ *a* incauto, imprudente

incautiousness /ɪnˈkɔːʃəsnɪs/ *n* imprudencia, negligencia, falta de cautela, *f*

incendiary /ɪnˈsendiˌeri/ *a* incendiario. **i. bomb,** incendiaria, *f*

incense /ɪnˈsens/ *n* incienso, *m*; *Fig.* adulación, *f*. —*vt Eccl.* incensar; (annoy) irritar, exasperar, enojar. **i. burner,** incensario, *m*

incentive /ɪnˈsentɪv/ *n* incentivo, estímulo, motivo, *m*. —*a* estimulador, incitativo

inception /ɪnˈsepʃən/ *n* comienzo, principio, *m*; inauguración, *f*

incertitude /ɪnˈsɜːrtɪˌtjuːd/ *n* incertidumbre, *f*

incessant /ɪnˈsesənt/ *a* incesante, continuo, constante

incessantly /ɪnˈsesəntli/ *adv* incesantemente, sin cesar

incest /ˈɪnsest/ *n* incesto, *m*

incestuous /ɪnˈsestʃuəs/ *a* incestuoso

inch /ɪntʃ/ *n* pulgada, *f*. **every i. a man,** hombre hecho y derecho. **Not an i.!** ¡Ni pizca! **within an i. of,** a dos dedos de. **i. by i.,** palmo a palmo, paso a paso. **i. tape,** cinta métrica, *f*

inchoate /ɪnˈkoʊɪt/ *a* rudimentario; imperfecto, incompleto

incidence /ˈɪnsɪdəns/ *n* incidencia, *f*

incident /ˈɪnsɪdənt/ *a* propio, característico, incidental. —*n* incidente, acontecimiento, *m*, ocurrencia, *f*

incidental /ˌɪnsɪˈdentl/ *a* incidente, incidental; accidental, accesorio, no esencial. **i. expense,** gasto imprevisto, *m*

incidentally /ˌɪnsɪˈdentli/ *adv* (secondarily) incidentalmente; (by the way) de propósito

incinerate /ɪnˈsɪnəˌreɪt/ *vt* incinerar

incineration /ɪnˌsɪnəˈreɪʃən/ *n* incineración, cremación, *f*

incinerator /ɪnˈsɪnəˌreɪtər/ *n* incinerador, *m*

incipient /ɪnˈsɪpiənt/ *a* incipiente, naciente, rudimentario

incise /ɪnˈsaɪz/ *vt* cortar; *Art.* grabar, tajar

incision /ɪnˈsɪʒən/ *n* incisión, *f*; corte, tajo, *m*; *Med.* abscisión, *f*

incisive /ɪnˈsaɪsɪv/ *a* (of mind) agudo, penetrante; (of words) mordaz, incisivo, punzante

incisively /ɪnˈsaɪsɪvli/ *adv* en pocas palabras; mordazmente, incisivamente

incisiveness /ɪnˈsaɪsɪvnɪs/ *n* (of mind) agudeza, penetración, *f*; (of words) mordacidad, *f*, sarcasmo, *m*

incisor /ɪnˈsaɪzər/ *n* diente incisivo, *m*

incite /ɪnˈsaɪt/ *vt* incitar, estimular, animar; provocar, tentar. **to i. to,** mover a, incitar a

incitement /ɪn'saitmənt/ *n* incitación, instigación, *f;* estímulo, *m;* tentación, *f;* aliciente, *m*

incivility /ˌɪnsə'vɪlɪti/ *n* incivilidad, descortesía, *f*

inclemency /ɪn'klɛmənsi/ *n* inclemencia, *f,* rigor, *m*

inclement /ɪn'klɛmənt/ *a* inclemente, riguroso, borrascoso

inclination /ˌɪnklə'neiʃən/ *n* inclinación, *f;* (slope) declive, *m,* pendiente, cuesta, *f;* (tendency) propensión, tendencia, *f;* (liking) afición, *f;* amor, *m;* (bow) reverencia, *f; Geom.* inclinación, *f*

incline /*v* ɪn'klain; *n* 'ɪnklain/ *vt* inclinar, torcer; doblar; (cause) inclinar (a), hacer. —*vi* inclinarse, torcerse; (tend) tender, propender, inclinarse; (colors) tirar (a). —*n* declive, *m,* pendiente, cuesta, inclinación, *f.* **I am inclined to believe it,** Me inclino a creerlo. **I am inclined to do it,** Estoy por hacerlo, Creo que lo haré

inclined /ɪn'klaind/ *a* torcido, inclinado, doblado; *Fig.* propenso, adicto. **i. plane,** plano inclinado, *m*

include /ɪn'klud/ *vt* incluir, contener, encerrar; comprender, abrazar

including /ɪn'kludɪŋ/ *present part* incluso, inclusive. **not i.,** no comprendido

inclusion /ɪn'kluʒən/ *n* inclusión, *f*

inclusive /ɪn'klusɪv/ *a* inclusivo. **January 2 to January 12 i.,** del 2 al 12 de enero, ambos inclusivos. **not i. of,** sin contar, exclusivo de. **i. of,** que incluye. **i. terms,** todo incluido, todos los gastos incluidos

incognito /ˌɪnkɒg'nitou/ *a and adv* and *n* incógnito, *m.*

incoherence /ˌɪnkou'hɪərəns/ *n* incoherencia, inconsecuencia, *f*

incoherent /ˌɪnkou'hɪərənt/ *a* incoherente, inconexo, inconsecuente. **an i. piece of writing,** un escrito sin pies ni cabeza

incoherently /ˌɪnkou'hɪərəntli/ *adv* con incoherencia

incombustible /ˌɪnkəm'bʌstəbəl/ *a* incombustible

income /'ɪnkʌm/ *n* renta, *f,* ingreso, *m; Com.* rédito, *m.* **i.-tax,** impuesto de utilidades, *m.* **i.-tax commissioners,** inspectores de impuestos de utilidades, *m pl.* **i.-tax return,** declaración de utilidades, *f*

incoming /'ɪn,kʌmɪŋ/ *a* entrante; nuevo. —*n* entrada, llegada, *f.* —*n pl* **incomings,** ingresos, *m pl*

incommensurable /ˌɪnkə'mɛnsərəbəl/ *a* inconmensurable, no conmensurable

incommensurate /ˌɪnkə'mɛnsərɪt/ *a* desproporcionado, desmedido

incommode /ˌɪnkə'moud/ *vt* incomodar, molestar, fastidiar

incommodious /ˌɪnkə'moudiəs/ *a* estrecho; incómodo, inconveniente

incommunicable /ˌɪnkə'myunɪkəbəl/ *a* incomunicable, indecible, inexplicable

incommunicative /ˌɪnkə'myunɪkətɪv/ *a* insociable, intratable, adusto, huraño

incomparable /ɪn'kɒmpərəbəl/ *a* incomparable; sin par, sin igual, excelente

incomparably /ɪn'kɒmpərəbli/ *adv* incomparablemente, con mucho

incompatible /ˌɪnkəm'pætəbəl/ *a* incompatible

incompetence /ɪn'kɒmpɪtəns/ *n* incompetencia, ineptitud, inhabilidad, *f; Law.* incapacidad, *f*

incompetent /ɪn'kɒmpɪtənt/ *a* incompetente, incapaz, inepto, inhábil; *Law.* incapaz

incompetently /ɪn'kɒmpɪtəntli/ *adv* inhábilmente

incomplete /ˌɪnkəm'plit/ *a* incompleto; imperfecto, defectuoso; (unfinished) sin terminar, inacabado, inconcluso. **incomplete sentence,** frase que queda colgando, *f*

incompletely /ˌɪnkəm'plitli/ *adv* incompletamente; imperfectamente

incompleteness /ˌɪnkəm'plitnɪs/ *n* estado incompleto, *m;* imperfección, *f;* inconclusión, *f*

incomprehensible /ˌɪnkɒmprɪ'hɛnsəbəl/ *a* incomprensible

incomprehension /ˌɪnkɒmprɪ'hɛnʃən/ *n* incomprensión, falta de comprensión, *f*

inconceivable /ˌɪnkən'sivəbəl/ *a* inconcebible, inimaginable

inconclusive /ˌɪnkən'klusɪv/ *a* inconcluyente, cuestionable, dudoso, no convincente

incongruity /ˌɪnkən'gruti/ *n* incongruencia, desproporción, disonancia, *f*

incongruous /ɪn'kɒŋgruəs/ *a* incongruente, incongruo; chocante, desproporcionado, disonante

inconsequence /ɪn'kɒnsɪˌkwɛns/ *n* inconsecuencia, *f*

inconsequent, inconsequential /ɪn'kɒnsɪˌkwɛnt; ɪn,kɒnsɪ'kwɛnʃəl/ *a* inconsecuente, ilógico; inconsistente

inconsiderable /ˌɪnkən'sɪdərəbəl/ *a* insignificante

inconsiderate /ˌɪnkən'sɪdərɪt/ *a* desconsiderado, irreflexivo, irrespetuoso

inconsiderately /ˌɪnkən'sɪdərɪtli/ *adv* sin consideración, desconsideradamente

inconsistency /ˌɪnkən'sɪstənsi/ *n* inconsistencia, inconsecuencia, incompatibilidad, contradicción, anomalía, *f*

inconsistent /ˌɪnkən'sɪstənt/ *a* inconsistente, inconsiguiente, incompatible, contradictorio, anómalo

inconsolable /ˌɪnkən'souləbəl/ *a* inconsolable, desconsolado. **to be i.,** estar inconsolable, (*Inf.* of a woman) estar hecha una Magdalena

inconspicuous /ˌɪnkən'spɪkyuəs/ *a* que no llama la atención; insignificante, humilde, modesto

inconspicuously /ˌɪnkən'spɪkyuəsli/ *adv* humildemente, modestamente

inconstancy /ɪn'kɒnstənsi/ *n* inconstancia, movilidad, *f;* mudanza, veleidad, *f*

inconstant /ɪn'kɒnstənt/ *a* inconstante,

mudable, variable; veleidoso, volátil, voluble

incontinence /ɪn'kɒntnəns/ n incontinencia, f

incontinent /ɪn'kɒntnənt/ a incontinente

incontrollable /ˌɪnkən'troʊləbəl/ a ingobernable, indomable

incontrovertible /ˌɪnkɒntrə'vɜrtəbəl/ a incontrovertible, incontrastable

inconvenience /ˌɪnkən'vinyəns/ n incomodidad, inconveniencia, f; (of time) inoportunidad, f. —vt incomodar, causar inconvenientes (a)

inconvenient /ˌɪnkən'vinyənt/ a incómodo, inconveniente, molesto, embarazoso; (of time) inoportuno. **at an i. time,** a deshora

incorporate /v ɪn'kɔrpə,reit; a -pərɪt/ vt incorporar, agregar; comprender, incluir, encerrar. —vi asociarse, incorporarse. —a incorpóreo, inmaterial; incorporado, asociado

incorporation /ɪn,kɔrpə'reiʃən/ n incorporación, agregación, f; asociación, f

incorrect /ˌɪnkə'rekt/ a incorrecto; inexacto, erróneo, falso

incorrigible /ɪn'kɒrɪdʒəbəl/ a incorregible, empecatado

incorrigibly /ɪn'kɒrɪdʒəbli/ adv incorregiblemente, obstinadamente

incorrupt /ˌɪnkə'rʌpt/ a incorrupto; recto, honrado

incorruptibility /ˌɪnkə,rʌptə'bɪlɪti/ n incorruptibilidad, f; honradez, probidad, f

incorruptible /ˌɪnkə'rʌptəbəl/ a incorrupto; honrado, insobornable

increase /v ɪn'kris; n 'ɪnkris/ vt aumentar, acrecentar; (in numbers) multiplicar; (extend) ampliar, extender; (of price) encarecer, aumentar. —vi aumentar, crecer; multiplicarse; extenderse; encarecerse, aumentar. —n aumento, crecimiento, m; multiplicación, f; (in price) encarecimiento, m, alza, f; (of water) crecida, f; (of moon) creciente, f. **It is on the i.,** Va en aumento. **to i. and multiply,** crecer y multiplicar

increasingly /ɪn'krisɪŋli/ adv más y más; en creciente, en aumento

incredible /ɪn'kredəbəl/ a increíble; fabuloso, extraordinario. **It seems i.,** Es increíble, Inf. Parece mentira

incredibly /ɪn'kredəbli/ adv increíblemente

incredulity /ˌɪnkrɪ'dulɪti/ n incredulidad, f, escepticismo, m

incredulous /ɪn'kredʒələs/ a incrédulo, escéptico

incredulously /ɪn'kredʒələsli/ adv con incredulidad, escépticamente

increment /'ɪnkrəmənt/ n aumento, incremento, m; adición, añadidura, f; Math. incremento, m. **unearned i.,** plusvalía, mayor valía, f

incriminate /ɪn'krɪmə,neit/ vt incriminar

incriminating /ɪn'krɪmə,neitɪŋ/ a incriminante, acriminador

incrust /ɪn'krʌst/ vt incrustar, encostrar

incrustation /ˌɪnkrʌ'steiʃən/ n incrustación, f; (scab) costra, f

incubate /'ɪnkyə,beit/ vt empollar; Med. incubar

incubation /ˌɪnkyə'beiʃən/ n empolladura, incubación, f; Med. incubación, f

incubator /'ɪnkyə,beitər/ n incubadora, f

incubus /'ɪnkyəbəs/ n íncubo, m; (burden) carga, f

inculcate /ɪn'kʌlkeit/ vt inculcar, implantar, instilar

inculcation /ˌɪnkʌl'keiʃən/ n inculcación, implantación, instilación, f

incumbency /ɪn'kʌmbənsi/ n posesión, duración de, posesión, duración (de cualquier puesto), f

incumbent /ɪn'kʌmbənt/ a obligatorio. —n Eccl. beneficiado, m. **to be i. on,** incumbir a, ser de su obligación

incur /ɪn'kɜr/ vi incurrir (en), incidir (en). **to i. an obligation,** contraer una obligación

incurable /ɪn'kyurəbəl/ a incurable, insanable; Fig. sin solución, irremediable. —n incurable, mf

incurably /ɪn'kyurəbli/ adv incurablemente, irremediablemente

incurious /ɪn'kyuriəs/ a indiferente, sin interés; incurioso, negligente, descuidado

incursion /ɪn'kɜrʒən/ n incursión, invasión, irrupción, f, acometimiento, m

indebted /ɪn'detɪd/ a empeñado, adeudado; (obliged) reconocido

indebtedness /ɪn'detɪdnɪs/ n deuda, f; (gratitude) obligación, f; agradecimiento, m

indecency /ɪn'disənsi/ n indecencia, f

indecent /ɪn'disənt/ a indecente; obsceno, deshonesto

indecently /ɪn'disəntli/ adv torpemente, indecentemente

indecision /ˌɪndɪ'sɪʒən/ n indecisión, vacilación, irresolución, f

indecisive /ˌɪndɪ'saisɪv/ a indeciso, irresoluto, vacilante

indecorous /ɪn'dekərəs/ a indecoroso, indecente, indigno

indecorum /ˌɪndɪ'kɔrəm/ n indecoro, m, indecencia, f; incorrección, f

indeed /ɪn'did/ adv en efecto, de veras, a la verdad, realmente, por cierto, claro está. —interr ¿de veras? ¿es posible? **I shall be very glad i.,** Estaré contento de veras. **It is i. an excellent book,** Es en efecto un libro excelente. **There are differences i. between this house and the other,** Hay diferencias, claro está, entre esta casa y la otra

indefatigability /ˌɪndɪ,fætɪgə'bɪlɪti/ n resistencia, f, aguante, m, tenacidad, f

indefatigable /ˌɪndɪ'fætɪgəbəl/ a incansable, infatigable, resistente

indefatigably /ˌɪndɪ'fætɪgəbli/ adv infatigablemente

indefensible /ˌɪndɪ'fensəbəl/ a indefendible, insostenible

indefinable /ˌɪndɪ'fainəbəl/ a indefinible

indefinite /ɪn'defənɪt/ a indefinido, incierto; (delicate) sutil, delicado; *Gram.* indefinido; (vague) vago. *Gram.* **i. article**, artículo indefinido, *m*

indefinitely /ɪn'defənɪtli/ adv indefinidamente

indefiniteness /ɪn'defənɪtnɪs/ n lo indefinido, el carácter indefinido, m; vaguedad, f

indelibility /ɪnˌdelə'bɪlɪti/ n resistencia, f, lo indeleble; *Fig.* duración, tenacidad, f

indelible /ɪn'deləbəl/ a indeleble, imborrable; *Fig.* inolvidable

indelibly /ɪn'deləbli/ adv indeleblemente

indelicacy /ɪn'delɪkəsi/ n falta de buen gusto, grosería, f; (tactlessness) indiscreción, falta de tacto, f

indelicate /ɪn'delɪkɪt/ a grosero, descortés; indecoroso, inmodesto; (tactless) inoportuno, indiscreto

indemnification /ɪnˌdemnəfɪ'keiʃən/ n indemnización, compensación, f

indemnify /ɪn'demnə,fai/ vt indemnizar, compensar

indemnity /ɪn'demnɪti/ n indemnización, reparación, f

indent /ɪn'dent/ vt endentar, mellar; *Print.* sangrar

indentation /ˌɪnden'teiʃən/ n impresión, depresión, f; corte, m, mella, f; línea quebrada, f, zigzag, m

indenture /ɪn'dentʃər/ n escritura, f, instrumento, m. —vt escriturar

independence /ˌɪndɪ'pendəns/ n independencia, libertad, f; (autonomy) autonomía, f. **I. Day**, Fiesta de la Independencia, f. **i. movement**, movimiento en favor de la independencia, m

independent /ˌɪndɪ'pendənt/ a independiente; libre; (autonomous) autónomo; **i. of**, libre de; aparte de. **a person of i. means**, una persona acomodada

independently /ˌɪndɪ'pendəntli/ adv independientemente

indescribable /ˌɪndɪ'skraibəbəl/ a indescriptible; indefinible, indecible, inexplicable; incalificable

indestructible /ˌɪndɪ'strʌktəbəl/ a indestructible

indeterminable /ˌɪndɪ'tɜrmənəbəl/ a indeterminable

indeterminate /ˌɪndɪ'tɜrmənɪt/ a indeterminado, indefinido, vago; *Math.* indeterminado

indetermination /ˌɪndɪˌtɜrmə'neiʃən/ f irresolución, indecisión, duda, vacilación, f

index /'ɪndeks/ n (forefinger) dedo índice, m; (of book) tabla de materias, f, índice, m; (on instruments) manecilla, aguja, f; *Math.* índice, m; (sign) señal, indicación, f. —vt poner índice (a); poner en el índice. **i. card**, ficha, f. **I. expurgatorius**, Índice expurgatorio, m

India /'ɪndiə/ n la India, f. **I. paper**, papel de China, m. **i.-rubber**, *Bot.* caucho, m;

(eraser) goma de borrar, f. **i.-rubber tree**, yacio, m

Indian /'ɪndiən/ a and n indio (-ia). **I. chief**, cacique, m. **I. club**, maza, f. **I. corn**, maíz, m. **I. ink**, tinta china, f. **I. summer**, veranillo, veranillo de San Martín, m

Indian Ocean, the el Océano Índico, m

indicate /'ɪndɪ,keit/ vt indicar, señalar; (show) denotar, mostrar, anunciar

indication /ˌɪndɪ'keiʃən/ n indicación, f; señal, f, indicio, síntoma, m; prueba, f

indicative /ɪn'dɪkətɪv/ a indicador, indicativo, demostrativo; *Gram.* indicativo. —n *Gram.* indicativo, m. **to be i. of**, indicar, señalar

indicator /'ɪndɪ,keitər/ n indicador, señalador, m

indict /ɪn'dait/ vt acusar; *Law.* demandar, enjuiciar

indictable /ɪn'daitəbəl/ a procesable, denunciable, enjuiciable

indictment /ɪn'daitmənt/ n acusación, f; *Law.* procesamiento, m

indifference /ɪn'dɪfərəns/ n indiferencia, apatía, f, desinterés, desapego, m; imparcialidad, neutralidad, f; (coldness) frialdad, tibieza, f

indifferent /ɪn'dɪfərənt/ a indiferente, apático; imparcial, neutral; frío; (ordinary) regular, ordinario, ni bien ni mal

indifferently /ɪn'dɪfərəntli/ adv con indiferencia; imparcialmente; friamente

indigence /'ɪndɪdʒəns/ n indigencia, necesidad, penuria, f

indigenous /ɪn'dɪdʒənəs/ a indígena, nativo, natural

indigent /'ɪndɪdʒənt/ a indigente, necesitado, menesteroso

indigestible /ˌɪndɪ'dʒestəbəl/ a indigesto

indigestion /ˌɪndɪ'dʒestʃən/ n indigestión, f; *Fig.* empacho, ahíto, m

indignant /ɪn'dɪgnənt/ a indignado. **to make i.**, indignar

indignantly /ɪn'dɪgnəntli/ adv con indignación

indignation /ˌɪndɪg'neiʃən/ n indignación, cólera, f

indignity /ɪn'dɪgnɪti/ n indignidad, f; ultraje, m

indigo /'ɪndɪ,gou/ n añil, índigo, m

indirect /ˌɪndə'rekt/ a indirecto; oblicuo; tortuoso; *Gram.* **i. case**, caso oblicuo, m

indirectness /ˌɪndə'rektnɪs/ n (of route) rodeo, m, desviación, f; oblicuidad, f; (falsity) tortuosidad, f

indiscernible /ˌɪndɪ'sɜrnəbəl/ a imperceptible

indiscipline /ɪn'dɪsəplɪn/ n indisciplina, falta de disciplina, f

indiscreet /ˌɪndɪ'skrit/ a indiscreto, imprudente, impolítico

indiscretion /ˌɪndɪ'skreʃən/ n indiscreción, imprudencia, f; (slip) desliz, m

indiscriminate /ˌɪndɪ'skrɪmənɪt/ a general, universal; indistinto, promiscuo

indiscriminately /ˌɪndɪˈskrɪmənɪtli/ *adv* promiscuamente

indiscrimination /ˌɪndɪˌskrɪməˈneɪʃən/ *n* universalidad, indistinción, *f*

indispensable /ˌɪndɪˈspɛnsəbəl/ *a* imprescindible, indispensable, insustituible

indispensably /ˌɪndɪˈspɛnsəbli/ *adv* forzosamente, indispensablemente

indispose /ˌɪndɪˈspouz/ *vt* indisponer. **to be indisposed**, estar indispuesto, indisponerse

indisposed /ˌɪndɪˈspouzd/ *a* indispuesto, enfermo, destemplado; (reluctant) maldispuesto

indisposition /ˌɪndɪspəˈzɪʃən/ *n* indisposición, enfermedad, *f*

indisputability /ˌɪndɪˌspyutəˈbɪlɪti/ *n* verdad manifiesta, certeza, evidencia, *f*

indisputable /ˌɪndɪˈspyutəbəl/ *a* innegable, incontestable; irrefutable, evidente

indisputably /ˌɪndɪˈspyutəbli/ *adv* indisputablemente

indissoluble /ˌɪndɪˈsɒlyəbəl/ *a* indisoluble

indistinct /ˌɪndɪˈstɪŋkt/ *a* indistinto; indeterminado, confuso, vago

indistinctly /ˌɪndɪˈstɪŋktli/ *adv* indistintamente; confusamente, vagamente

indistinguishable /ˌɪndɪˈstɪŋgwɪʃəbəl/ *a* indistinguible

individual /ˌɪndəˈvɪdʒuəl/ *a* (single) solo, único; individual, individuo, particular, propio; personal. —*n* individuo, *m*, particular, *mf*

individualism /ˌɪndəˈvɪdʒuəˌlɪzəm/ *n* individualismo, *m*

individualist /ˌɪndəˈvɪdʒuəlɪst/ *n* individualista, *mf*

individualistic /ˌɪndəˌvɪdʒuəˈlɪstɪk/ *a* individualista

individuality /ˌɪndəˌvɪdʒuˈælɪti/ *n* individualidad, personalidad, *f*; carácter, *m*, naturaleza, *f*

individualize /ˌɪndəˈvɪdʒuəˌlaɪz/ *vt* particularizar, individuar

individually /ˌɪndəˈvɪdʒuəli/ *adv* individualmente, particularmente

indivisible /ˌɪndəˈvɪzəbəl/ *a* incompartible, impartible, indivisible

indivisibly /ˌɪndəˈvɪzəbli/ *adv* indivisiblemente

indocile /ɪnˈdɒsɪl/ *a* indócil, desobediente, rebelde

indolence /ˈɪndləns/ *n* indolencia, pereza, desidia, *f*

indolent /ˈɪndlənt/ *a* indolente, perezoso, holgazán; *Med.* indoloro

indomitable /ɪnˈdɒmɪtəbəl/ *a* indomable, indómito

indoor /ˈɪnˌdɔr/ *a* de casa; de puertas adentro, interno. **i. swimming pool**, piscina bajo techo, *f*. **i. tennis**, tenis en pistas cubiertas, tenis bajo techo, *m*

indoors /ɪnˈdɔrz/ *adv* en casa; adentro, bajo techo

indorsee /ɪndɔrˈsi/ *n* endosatario (-ia)

indubitable /ɪnˈdubɪtəbəl/ *a* indudable

induce /ɪnˈdus/ *vt* inducir, mover; instigar, incitar; producir, ocasionar; *Elec.* inducir. **Nothing would i. me to do it**, Nada me induciría a hacerlo

inducement /ɪnˈdusmənt/ *n* incitamento, *m*; estímulo, *m*; aliciente, atractivo, *m*; tentación, *f*

induct /ɪnˈdʌkt/ *vt* instalar; introducir, iniciar

induction /ɪnˈdʌkʃən/ *n* instalación, *f*; iniciación, introducción, *f*; *Phys.* inducción, *f*. **i. coil**, carrete de inducción, *m*

inductive /ɪnˈdʌktɪv/ *a* (of reasoning) inductivo; *Phys.* inductor

indulge /ɪnˈdʌldʒ/ *vt* (children) consentir, mimar; (a desire) satisfacer, dar rienda suelta a; (with a gift) agasajar (con), dar gusto (con). **to i. in**, *vt* consentir en. —*vi* entregarse a, permitirse, gustar de

indulgence /ɪnˈdʌldʒəns/ *n* (of children) mimo, cariño excesivo, *m*; (of a desire) propensión (a), afición (a), *f*; (toward others) tolerancia, transigencia, *f*; *Eccl.* indulgencia, *f*

indulgent /ɪnˈdʌldʒənt/ *a* indulgente; tolerante, transigente

industrial /ɪnˈdʌstriəl/ *a* industrial. **i. alcohol**, alcohol desnaturalizado, *m*. **i. school**, escuela de artes y oficios, *f*, *Com.* **i. shares**, valores industriales, *m pl*

industrialist /ɪnˈdʌstriəlɪst/ *n* industrial, *m*

industrialize /ɪnˈdʌstriəˌlaɪz/ *vt* industrializar

industrious /ɪnˈdʌstriəs/ *a* industrioso, aplicado, diligente

industriousness /ɪnˈdʌstriəsnɪs/ *n* industria, laboriosidad, *f*

industry /ˈɪndəstri/ *n* diligencia, aplicación, *f*; (work) trabajo, *m*, labor, *f*; *Com.* industria, *f*

inebriate /*a, n* ɪˈnibrɪɪt; *v* -briˌeit/ *a* borracho, ebrio. —*n* borracho (-cha). —*vt* embriagar, emborrachar

inedible /ɪnˈɛdəbəl/ *a* incomible, no comestible

ineffable /ɪnˈɛfəbəl/ *a* indecible, inefable

ineffective /ˌɪnɪˈfɛktɪv/ *a* ineficaz; vano, fútil. **to be i.**, (of persons) no pinchar ni cortar. **to prove i.**, quedar sin efecto; no tener influencia

ineffectiveness /ˌɪnɪˈfɛktɪvnɪs/ *n* ineficacia, *f*; futilidad, *f*

inefficiency /ˌɪnɪˈfɪʃənsi/ *n* ineficacia, incompetencia, ineptitud, *f*

inefficient /ˌɪnɪˈfɪʃənt/ *a* ineficaz, incapaz

inelastic /ˌɪnɪˈlæstɪk/ *a* inelástico

inelegance /ɪnˈɛlɪgəns/ *n* inelegancia, fealdad, vulgaridad, *f*

inelegant /ɪnˈɛlɪgənt/ *a* inelegante, ordinario, de mal gusto

inelegantly /ɪnˈɛlɪgəntli/ *adv* sin elegancia

ineligible /ɪnˈɛlɪdʒəbəl/ *a* inelegible

inept /ɪnˈɛpt/ *a* inepto, inoportuno; ab-

surdo, ridículo; (of persons) incompetente, ineficaz

ineptitude /ɪnˈɛptɪˌtud/ n ineptitud, f;
necedad, f; (of persons) incapacidad, incompetencia, f

ineptly /ɪnˈɛptli/ adv ineptamente, neciamente

inequality /ˌɪnɪˈkwɒlɪti/ n desigualdad,
desemejanza, disparidad, f; (of surface)
escabrosidad, aspereza, f; Fig. injusticia,
f; (of opportunity) diferencia, f

inequitable /ɪnˈɛkwɪtəbəl/ a desigual, injusto

inequity /ɪnˈɛkwɪti/ n injusticia, desigualdad, f

ineradicable /ˌɪnɪˈrædɪkəbəl/ a indeleble,
imborrable

inert /ɪnˈɜrt/ a inerte, inactivo, pasivo;
ocioso, flojo, perezoso

inertia /ɪnˈɜrʃə/ n inercia, inacción, f;
abulia, pereza, f; Phys. inercia, f

inertly /ɪnˈɜrtli/ adv indolentemente, sin
mover, pasivamente

inescapable /ˌɪnəˈskeɪpəbəl/ a ineludible,
inevitable

inestimable /ɪnˈɛstəməbəl/ a inestimable

inevitability /ɪnˌɛvɪtəˈbɪlɪti/ n fatalidad,
necesidad, f; lo inevitable

inevitable /ɪnˈɛvɪtəbəl/ a inevitable,
necesario, fatal, forzoso, ineludible

inevitably /ɪnˈɛvɪtəbli/ adv inevitablemente, necesariamente, forzosamente

inexact /ˌɪnɪɡˈzækt/ a inexacto, incorrecto

inexcusable /ˌɪnɪkˈskyuzəbəl/ a imperdonable, inexcusable, irremisible

inexcusableness /ˌɪnɪkˈskyuzəbəlnɪs/ n
enormidad, f; lo inexcusable

inexcusably /ˌɪnɪkˈskyuzəbli/ adv inexcusablemente

inexhaustible /ˌɪnɪɡˈzɔstəbəl/ a inagotable, inexhausto

inexorable /ɪnˈɛksərəbəl/ a inexorable,
inflexible, duro

inexorably /ɪnˈɛksərəbli/ adv inexorablemente, implacablemente

inexpediency /ˌɪnɪkˈspidiənsi/ n inoportunidad, inconveniencia, imprudencia, f

inexpedient /ˌɪnɪkˈspidiənt/ a inoportuno; inconveniente; impolítico, imprudente. **to deem i.,** creer inoportuno

inexpensive /ˌɪnɪkˈspɛnsɪv/ a poco costoso, barato

inexperience /ˌɪnɪkˈspɪəriəns/ n inexperiencia, falta de experiencia, f

inexperienced /ˌɪnɪkˈspɪəriənst/ a inexperto, novato

inexpert /ɪnˈɛkspərt/ a inexperto, imperito

inexpertly /ɪnˈɛkspərtli/ adv sin habilidad

inexpertness /ɪnˈɛkspərtnɪs/ n impericia,
torpeza, f

inexpiable /ɪnˈɛkspɪəbəl/ a inexpiable

inexplicable /ɪnˈɛksplɪkəbəl/ a inexplicable

inexplicit /ˌɪnɪkˈsplɪsɪt/ a no explícito

inexplosive /ˌɪnɪkˈsploʊsɪv/ a inexplosible

inexpressible /ˌɪnɪkˈsprɛsəbəl/ a inexplicable, indecible, inefable

inexpressive /ˌɪnɪkˈsprɛsɪv/ a inexpresivo; (of persons) reservado, callado,
poco expresivo, retraído

inexpugnable /ˌɪnɪkˈspʌɡnəbəl/ a inexpugnable

inextinguishable /ˌɪnɪkˈstɪŋɡwɪʃəbəl/ a
inapagable, inextinguible

inextricable /ɪnˈɛkstrɪkəbəl/ a inextricable, intrincado, enmarañado

infallible /ɪnˈfæləbəl/ a infalible

infamous /ˈɪnfəməs/ a infame, torpe, vil,
ignominioso; odioso, repugnante

infamously /ˈɪnfəməsli/ adv infame-
mente

infamy /ˈɪnfəmi/ n infamia, torpeza,
vileza, ignominia, f; deshonra, f

infancy /ˈɪnfənsi/ n infancia, niñez, f;
Law. minoridad, f

infant /ˈɪnfənt/ n criatura, f; crío (-fa),
niño (-ña); Law. menor, mf **i. school,** escuela de párvulos, f

infanticide /ɪnˈfæntəˌsaɪd/ n (act) infan-
ticidio, m; (person) infanticida, mf

infantile /ˈɪnfənˌtaɪl/ a infantil. **i. paralysis,** parálisis infantil, f

infantry /ˈɪnfəntri/ n Mil. infantería, f

infantryman /ˈɪnfəntrimən/ n Mil. infante, peón, m

infatuate /ɪnˈfætʃuˌeɪt/ vt infatuar, embobar

infatuation /ɪnˌfætʃuˈeɪʃən/ n infatuación, f, encaprichamiento, m

infect /ɪnˈfɛkt/ vt infectar, contagiar; Fig.
pegar, influir; (Fig. in a bad sense) corromper, pervertir, inficionar. **to become
infected,** infectarse

infected /ɪnˈfɛktɪd/ a infecto

infection /ɪnˈfɛkʃən/ n infección, f, contagio, m; Fig. influencia, f; (Fig. in a bad
sense) corrupción, perversión, f

infectious /ɪnˈfɛkʃəs/ a infeccioso, contagioso; (Fig. in a bad sense) corruptor;
Fig. contagioso

infectiousness /ɪnˈfɛkʃəsnɪs/ n contagio-
sidad, f

infelicitous /ˌɪnfəˈlɪsɪtəs/ a poco
apropiado, desacertado

infelicity /ˌɪnfəˈlɪsɪti/ n infelicidad, desdicha, f, infortunio, m; desacierto, m, inoportunidad, f

infer /ɪnˈfɜr/ vt inferir, concluir, educir,
deducir, implicar

inferable /ɪnˈfɜrəbəl/ a deducible, de-
mostrable

inference /ˈɪnfərəns/ n inferencia, deducción, conclusión, f

inferior /ɪnˈfɪəriər/ a inferior; (in rank)
subordinado, subalterno; (of position)
secundario. —n inferior, mf subordinado
(-da). **to be not i.,** no ser inferior, Inf. no
quedarse en zaga

inferiority /ɪnˌfɪəriˈɔrɪti/ n inferioridad,
f. **i. complex,** complejo de inferioridad, m

infernal /ɪnˈfɜrnl/ *a* infernal; *Poet.* inferno, tartáreo

inferno /ɪnˈfɜrnou/ *n* infierno, *m*

infertile /ɪnˈfɜrtl/ *a* infértil, infecundo, estéril

infertility /ˌɪnfərˈtɪlɪti/ *n* infertilidad, infecundidad, esterilidad, *f*

infest /ɪnˈfɛst/ *vt* infestar. **to be infested with,** plagarse de

infestation /ˌɪnfɛsˈteiʃən/ *n* infestación, *f*

infidel /ˈɪnfɪdl/ *n* infiel, gentil, *mf* pagano (-na); (atheist) descreído (-da), ateo (-ea). —*a* pagano; infiel, descreído, ateo

infidelity /ˌɪnfɪˈdɛlɪti/ *n* infidelidad, alevosía, perfidia, *f*

infiltrate /ɪnˈfɪltreit/ *vt* infiltrar. —*vi* infiltrarse

infiltration /ˌɪnfɪlˈtreiʃən/ *n* infiltración, *f*

infinite /ˈɪnfənɪt/ *a* infinito, ilimitado; inmenso, enorme; (of number) innumerable, infinito. —*n* infinito, *m*

infinitesimal /ˌɪnfɪnɪˈtɛsəməl/ *a* infinitesimal. **i. calculus,** cálculo infinitesimal, *m*

infinitive /ɪnˈfɪnɪtɪv/ *a* and *n Gram.* infinitivo, *m*.

infinitude, infinity /ɪnˈfɪnɪtud; ɪnˈfɪnɪti/ *n* infinidad, infinitud, *f*; (extent) inmensidad, *f*; (of number) sinfín, *m*; *Math.* infinito, *m*

infirm /ɪnˈfɜrm/ *a* achacoso, enfermizo, enclenque; (shaky) inestable, inseguro; (of purpose) irresoluto, vacilante

infirmary /ɪnˈfɜrməri/ *n* enfermería, *f*, hospital, *m*

infirmity /ɪnˈfɜrmɪti/ *n* achaque, *m*, enfermedad, dolencia, *f*; (fault) flaqueza, falta, *f*

inflame /ɪnˈfleim/ *vt* encender; (excite) acalorar, irritar, provocar; *Med.* inflamar. —*vi* encenderse, arder; acalorarse, irritarse; *Med.* inflamarse

inflammable /ɪnˈflæməbəl/ *a* inflamable

inflammation /ˌɪnfləˈmeiʃən/ *n* inflamación, *f*

inflammatory /ɪnˈflæməˌtɔri/ *a* inflamador; *Med.* inflamatorio

inflate /ɪnˈfleit/ *vt* inflar, hinchar; (with pride) engreír, ensoberbecer

inflation /ɪnˈfleiʃən/ *n* inflación, hinchazón, *f*; *Com.* inflación, *f*

inflect /ɪnˈflɛkt/ *vt* torcer; (voice) modular; *Gram.* conjugar, declinar

inflection /ɪnˈflɛkʃən/ *n* dobladura, *f*; (of voice) tono, acento, *m*, modulación, *f*; *Gram.* conjugación, declinación, *f*

inflexibility /ɪnˌflɛksəˈbɪlɪti/ *n* inflexibilidad, dureza, rigidez, *f*

inflexible /ɪnˈflɛksəbəl/ *a* inflexible, rígido; *Fig.* inexorable, inalterable

inflict /ɪnˈflɪkt/ *vt* infligir, imponer

infliction /ɪnˈflɪkʃən/ *n* imposición, *f*; castigo, *m*

inflow /ˈɪnˌflou/ *n* afluencia, *f*, flujo, *m*

influence /ˈɪnfluəns/ *n* influencia, *f*, influjo, *m*; ascendiente, *m*; (importance) in-

fluencia, importancia, *f*. —*vt* influir, afectar; persuadir, inducir. **to have i. over,** (a person) tener ascendiente sobre. *Law.* **undue i.,** influencia indebida, *f*

influential /ˌɪnfluˈɛnʃəl/ *a* influyente; (of person) prestigioso, importante

influenza /ˌɪnfluˈɛnzə/ *n Med.* gripe, *f*, trancazo, *m*

influx /ˈɪnˌflʌks/ *n* influjo, *m*; (of rivers) desembocadura, afluencia, *f*

inform /ɪnˈfɔrm/ *vt* (fill) infundir, llenar; (tell) informar, enterar, advertir; instruir; (with about) poner al corriente de, participar. —*vi* (with against) delatar (a), denunciar. **to i. oneself,** informarse, enterarse. **to be informed about,** estar al corriente de

informal /ɪnˈfɔrməl/ *a* irregular; sin ceremonia, de confianza; (meeting) no oficial, extraoficial

informality /ˌɪnfɔrˈmælɪti/ *n* irregularidad, *f*; falta de ceremonia, sencillez, *f*; intimidad, *f*

informally /ɪnˈfɔrməli/ *adv* sin ceremonia

informant /ɪnˈfɔrmənt/ *n* informante, *mf*; informador (-ra)

information /ˌɪnfərˈmeiʃən/ *n* información, instrucción, *f*; noticia, *f*, aviso, *m*; *Law.* denuncia, delación, *f*. **piece of i.,** información, *f*. **i. bureau,** oficina de información, *f*

informative /ɪnˈfɔrmətɪv/ *a* informativo

informer /ɪnˈfɔrmər/ *n* delator (-ra), denunciador (-ra)

infraction /ɪnˈfrækʃən/ *n* contravención, infracción, transgresión, *f*

infrared /ˌɪnfrəˈrɛd/ *a Phys.* infrarrojo, ultrarrojo

infrequency /ɪnˈfrikwənsi/ *n* infrecuencia, rareza, irregularidad, *f*

infrequent /ɪnˈfrikwənt/ *a* infrecuente, raro, irregular

infrequently /ɪnˈfrikwəntli/ *adv* rara vez, infrecuentemente

infringe /ɪnˈfrɪndʒ/ *vt* infringir, violar, contravenir, quebrantar

infringement /ɪnˈfrɪndʒmənt/ *n* contravención, violación, infracción, *f*

infringer /ɪnˈfrɪndʒər/ *n* infractor (-ra), contraventor (-ra), violador (-ra), transgresor (-ra)

infuriate /ɪnˈfyuriˌeit/ *vt* enfurecer, enloquecer, enojar. **to be infuriated,** estar furioso

infuse /ɪnˈfyuz/ *vt* vaciar, infiltrar; *Fig.* infundir, inculcar, instilar

infusion /ɪnˈfyuʒən/ *n* infusión, *f*; *Fig.* instilación, inculcación, *f*

ingathering /ɪnˈɡæðərɪŋ/ *n* cosecha, recolección, *f*

ingenious /ɪnˈdʒinyəs/ *a* ingenioso; mañoso, hábil

ingenuity /ˌɪndʒəˈnuɪti/ *n* ingeniosidad, inventiva, listeza, habilidad, *f*

ingenuous /ɪnˈdʒɛnyuəs/ *a* ingenuo, franco, sincero, cándido, sencillo, inocente

ingest /ɪn'dʒɛst/ vt ingerir

ingestion /ɪn'dʒɛstʃən/ n ingestión, f

inglorious /ɪn'glɔrɪəs/ a vergonzoso, ignominioso, deshonroso; desconocido, obscuro

ingoing /'ɪn,gouɪŋ/ a entrante, que entra. —n ingreso, m, entrada, f; Com. **i. and outgoing**, entradas y salidas, f pl

ingot /'ɪŋgət/ n pepita, f, lingote, m; (of any metal) barra, f

ingrained /ɪn'greind, 'ɪn,greind/ a innato, natural

ingratiate /ɪn'greiʃi,eit/ vt (oneself with) congraciarse con, captarse la buena voluntad de, insinuarse en el favor de

ingratiating /ɪn'greiʃi,eitɪŋ/ a obsequioso

ingratitude /ɪn'grætɪ,tud/ n ingratitud, f, desagradecimiento, m

ingredient /ɪn'gridiənt/ n ingrediente, m

ingress /'ɪŋgrɛs/ n ingreso, m; derecho de entrada, m

ingrowing /'ɪn,grouɪŋ/ a que crece hacia adentro. **i. nail**, uñero, m

inhabit /ɪn'hæbɪt/ vt habitar, ocupar, vivir en, residir en

inhabitable /ɪn'hæbɪtəbəl/ a habitable, vividero

inhabitant /ɪn'hæbɪtənt/ n habitante, residente, m; vecino (-na)

inhabited /ɪn'hæbɪtɪd/ a habitado, poblado

inhalation /,ɪnhə'leiʃən/ n inspiración, f; Med. inhalación, f

inhale /ɪn'heil/ vt aspirar; Med. inhalar

inharmonious /,ɪnhɑr'mouniəs/ a Mus. disonante, inarmónico; desavenido, discorde, desconforme. **to be i.**, disonar; (of people) llevarse mal

inhere /ɪn'hɪər/ vi ser inherente; pertenecer (a), residir (en)

inherence /ɪn'hɪərəns/ n inherencia, f

inherent /ɪn'hɪərənt/ a inherente; innato, intrínseco, natural

inherently /ɪn'hɪərəntli/ adv intrínsecamente

inherit /ɪn'hɛrɪt/ vt heredar

inheritance /ɪn'hɛrɪtəns/ n herencia, f; patrimonio, abolengo, m

inhibit /ɪn'hɪbɪt/ vt inhibir, impedir; Eccl. prohibir. **be inhibited, became inhibited**, cohibirse

inhibition /,ɪnɪ'bɪʃən/ n inhibición, f

inhibitory /ɪn'hɪbɪ,tɔri/ a inhibitorio

inhospitable /ɪn'hɒspɪtəbəl/ a inhospitalario

inhospitably /ɪn'hɒspɪtəbli/ adv desabridamente

inhuman /ɪn'hyumən/ a inhumano; cruel, bárbaro

inhumanity /,ɪnhyu'mænɪti/ n inhumanidad, crueldad, f

inhumanly /ɪn'hyumənli/ adv inhumanamente, cruelmente

inhume /ɪn'hyum/ vt inhumar, sepultar

inimical /ɪ'nɪmɪkəl/ a enemigo, hostil, opuesto, contrario

inimically /ɪ'nɪmɪkəli/ adv hostilmente

inimitable /ɪ'nɪmɪtəbəl/ a inimitable

iniquitous /ɪ'nɪkwɪtəs/ a inicuo, malvado, perverso, nefando; Inf. diabólico

iniquity /ɪ'nɪkwɪti/ n iniquidad, maldad, injusticia, f

initial /ɪ'nɪʃəl/ a inicial. —n inicial, letra inicial, f. —vt firmar con las iniciales

initially /ɪ'nɪʃəli/ adv al principio, en primer lugar

initiate /a ɪ'nɪʃiɪt; v ɪ'nɪʃi,eit/ a iniciado. —vt iniciar, poner en pie, empezar, entablar; (a person) admitir

initiation /ɪ,nɪʃi'eiʃən/ n principio, m; (of a person) iniciación, admisión, f

initiative /ɪ'nɪʃiətɪv/ n iniciativa, f. **to take the i.**, tomar la iniciative

inject /ɪn'dʒɛkt/ vt inyectar

injection /ɪn'dʒɛkʃən/ n inyección, f. **i. syringe**, jeringa de inyecciones, f

injudicious /,ɪndʒu'dɪʃəs/ a imprudente, indiscreto

injunction /ɪn'dʒʌŋkʃən/ n precepto, mandato, m; Law. embargo, m

injure /'ɪndʒər/ vt perjudicar, dañar; menoscabar, deteriorar; (hurt) lastimar, lisiar. **to i. oneself**, hacerse daño

injured /'ɪndʒərd/ a (physically) lisiado; (morally) ofendido

injurer /'ɪndʒərər/ n perjudicador (-ra)

injurious /ɪn'dʒuriəs/ a dañoso, perjudicial, malo; ofensivo, injurioso

injury /'ɪndʒəri/ n perjuicio, daño, m; (physical) lesión, f; (insult) agravio, insulto, m

injustice /ɪn'dʒʌstɪs/ n injusticia, desigualdad, f. **You do him an i.**, Le juzgas mal

ink /ɪŋk/ n tinta, f. —vt entintar. **copying-ink**, tinta de copiar, f. **marking-ink**, tinta indeleble, f. **printer's ink**, tinta de imprenta, f. **ink-stand** or **ink-well**, tintero, m

inkling /'ɪŋklɪŋ/ n sospecha, noción, f

inky /'ɪŋki/ a manchado de tinta. **i. black**, negro como el betún

inland /'ɪnlænd/ n el interior de un país, a interior, mediterráneo; del país, regional. —adv tierra adentro. **to go i.**, internarse en un país. **I. Revenue**, delegación de contribuciones, f. **i. town**, ciudad del interior, f

inlay /'ɪn,lei/ vt taracear, ataracear, embutir; incrustar. —n taracea, f, embutido, m

inlet /'ɪnlɛt/ n entrada, admisión, f; Geog. ensenada, f. **i. valve**, válvula de admisión, f

inmate /'ɪn,meit/ n residente, habitante, m; (of hospital) paciente, mf; enfermo (-ma); (of prison) prisionero

inmost /'ɪnmoust/. See **innermost**

inn /ɪn/ n posada, fonda, venta, f, mesón, m. **Inns of Court**, Colegio de Abogados, m

innate /ɪ'neit/ a innato, inherente, instintivo, nativo

innately /ɪ'neɪtli/ *adv* naturalmente, instintivamente

innavigable /ɪ'nævɪgəbəl/ *a* innavegable

inner /'ɪnər/ *a* interior, interno. **i. tube** *Auto.* cámara de neumatico, cámara de aire, *f*

innermost /'ɪnər,moʊst/ *a* más adentro; *Fig.* más íntimo, más hondo

innings /'ɪnɪŋz/ *n* (sport) turno, *m*

innkeeper /'ɪn,kipər/ *n* fondista, *mf;* taberdhnero (-ra), mesonero (-ra), posadero (-ra)

innocence /'ɪnəsəns/ *n* inocencia, *f;* pureza, *f;* (guilelessness) simplicidad, *f*, candor, *m*

innocent /'ɪnəsənt/ *a* inocente, puro; (guiltless) inocente, inculpable; (foolish) simple, tonto, candoroso, inocentón; (harmless) innocuo. —*n* inocente, *mf* **Holy Innocents**, Santos Inocentes, *m pl*

innocuous /ɪ'nɒkyuəs/ *a* innocuo, inofensivo

innovate /'ɪnə,veɪt/ *vt* innovar

innovation /,ɪnə'veɪʃən/ *n* innovación, *f*

innovator /'ɪnə,veɪtər/ *n* innovador (-ra)

innuendo /,ɪnyu'ɛndoʊ/ *n* indirecta, insinuación, *f*

innumerable /ɪ'numərəbəl/ *a* innumerable, incalculable. **i. things**, un sinfín de cosas

inobservance /,ɪnəb'zɜrvəns/ *n* inobservancia, *f*, incumplimiento, *m*

inoculate /ɪ'nɒkyə,leɪt/ *vt* inocular

inoculation /ɪ,nɒkyə'leɪʃən/ *n* inoculación, *f*

inoffensive /,ɪnə'fɛnsɪv/ *a* inofensivo, innocuo; (of people) pacífico, apacible, manso

inoperable /ɪn'ɒpərəbəl/ *a* inoperable

inoperative /ɪn'ɒpərətɪv/ *a* ineficaz, impracticable, inútil

inopportune /ɪn,ɒpər'tun/ *a* inoportuno, intempestivo, inconveniente

inopportunely /ɪn,ɒpər'tunli/ *adv* inoportunamente, a destiempo

inordinate /ɪn'ɔrdn̩ɪt/ *a* desordenado, excesivo

inordinately /ɪn'ɔrdn̩ɪtli/ *adv* desmedidamente

inorganic /,ɪnɔr'gænɪk/ *a* inorgánico

inoxidizable /ɪn'ɒksɪ,daɪzəbəl/ *a* inoxidadhble

input /'ɪn,pʊt/ *n* capacidad instalada, *f*, insumo, *m*

inquest /'ɪnkwɛst/ *n Law.* indagación, investigación, *f*

inquietude /ɪn'kwaɪɪ,tud/ *n* inquietud, *f*, desasosiego, *m*, agitación, preocupación, *f*

inquire /ɪn'kwaɪər/ *vt and vi* preguntar, averiguar, indagar. **to i. about,** (persons) preguntar por; (things) hacer preguntas sobre. **to i. into,** investigar, examinar, averiguar. **to i. of,** preguntar a. **"I. within,"** «Se dan informaciones»

inquirer /ɪn'kwaɪərər/ *n* indagador (-ra), inquiridor (-ra)

inquiring /ɪn'kwaɪərɪŋ/ *a* indagador, inquiridor

inquiry /ɪn'kwaɪəri/ *n* interrogación, pregunta, *f;* indagación, pesquisa, investigación, *f;* examen, *m.* **i. office,** oficina de informaciones, *f.* **on i.,** al preguntar

inquisition /,ɪnkwə'zɪʃən/ *n* investigación, indagación, *f;* inquisición, *f.* **Holy I.,** Santo Oficio, *m,* Inquisición, *f*

inquisitive /ɪn'kwɪzɪtɪv/ *a* curioso, inquiridor; preguntador, impertinente, mirón

inquisitively /ɪn'kwɪzɪtɪvli/ *adv* con curiosidad, impertinentemente

inquisitiveness /ɪn'kwɪzɪtɪvnɪs/ *n* curiosidad, *f;* impertinencia, *f*

Inquisitor /ɪn'kwɪzɪtər/ *n Eccl.* inquisidor, *m*

inquisitorial /ɪn,kwɪzɪ'tɔriəl/ *a* inquisitorial, inquisidor

inroad /'ɪn,roʊd/ *n* incursión, *f*

insalubrious /,ɪnsə'lubriəs/ *a* malsano, insalubre

insane /ɪn'seɪn/ *a* loco, demente, insano; (senseless) insensato, ridículo. **to become i.,** enloquecer, volverse loco, perder la razón. **to drive i.,** volver a uno el juicio, enloquecer, trastornar. **i. person,** demente, *mf.* loco (-ca)

insanitary /ɪn'sænɪ,tɛri/ *a* antihigiénico, malsano

insanity /ɪn'sænɪti/ *n* demencia, locura, *f;* enloquecimiento, *m;* (folly) insensatez, ridiculez, *f*

insatiable /ɪn'seɪʃəbəl/ *a* insaciable

inscribe /ɪn'skraɪb/ *vt* inscribir

inscription /ɪn'skrɪpʃən/ *n* inscripción, *f;* letrero, *m;* (of a book) dedicatoria, *f; Com.* inscripción, anotación, *f*, asiento, *m*

inscrutable /ɪn'skrutəbəl/ *a* enigmático, insondable, incomprensible, inescrutable

inscrutably /ɪn'skrutəbli/ *adv* incomprensiblemente, enigmáticamente

insect /'ɪnsɛkt/ *n* insecto, *m.* **i. powder,** polvos insecticidas, *m pl*

insecticide /ɪn'sɛktə,saɪd/ *a and n* insecticida *m.*

insecure /,ɪnsɪ'kyʊr/ *a* inseguro, precario

insecurity /,ɪnsɪ'kyʊrɪti/ *n* inseguridad, *f;* incertidumbre, inestabilidad, *f*

inseminate /ɪn'sɛmə,neɪt/ *vt Fig.* implantar; *Med.* fecundar

insemination /ɪn,sɛmə'neɪʃən/ *n Fig.* implantación, *f; Med.* fecundación, *f*

insensate /ɪn'sɛnseɪt/ *a* (unfeeling) insensible, insensitivo; (stupid) insensato, sin sentido, necio

insensibility /ɪn,sɛnsə'bɪlɪti/ *n* insensibilidad, inconsciencia, *f;* (stupor) sopor, letargo, *m;* impasibilidad, indiferencia, *f*

insensible /ɪn'sɛnsəbəl/ *a* insensible, inconsciente; indiferente, impasible, duro de corazón; (scarcely noticeable) imperceptible. **to make i.,** (to sensations) hacer indiferente (a); insensibilizar

insensibly /ɪn'sɛnsəbli/ *adv* insensiblemente, imperceptiblemente

insensitive /ɪn'sɛnsɪtɪv/ a insensible, insensitivo; (person) hecho un tronco, hecho un leño

insentient /ɪn'sɛnʃənt/ a insensible

inseparable /ɪn'sɛpərəbəl/ a inseparable

insert /ɪn'sɜrt/ vt insertar, intercalar; (introduce) meter dentro, introducir, encajar; (in a newspaper) publicar

insertion /ɪn'sɜrʃən/ n inserción, intercalación, f; (introduction) introducción, f; metimiento, encaje, m; Sew. entredós, m; (in a newspaper) publicación, f

inshore /'ɪn'ʃɔr/ a cercano a la orilla.
—adv cerca de la orilla. **i. fishing**, pesca de arrastre, f

inside /ˌɪn'said/ a interior, interno. —adv adentro, dentro. —n interior, m; (contents) contenido, m; (lining) forro, m; (Inf. stomach) entrañas, f pl. **to turn i. out**, volver al revés. **to walk on the i. of the pavement**, andar a la derecha de la acera. **from the i.**, desde el interior; por dentro. **on the i.**, por dentro, en el interior. **i. information**, información confidencial, f. **i. out**, al revés, de dentro afuera

insidious /ɪn'sɪdiəs/ a insidioso, enganoso, traidor

insight /'ɪn,sait/ n percepción, perspicacia, intuición, f. atisbo, m

insignia /ɪn'sɪgniə/ n pl insignias, f pl

insignificance /ˌɪnsɪg'nɪfɪkəns/ n insignificancia, futilidad, pequeñez, f

insignificant /ˌɪnsɪg'nɪfɪkənt/ a insignificante; fútil, trivial

insincere /ˌɪnsɪn'sɪər/ a insincero, hipócrita, falso

insincerity /ˌɪnsɪn'sɛrɪti/ n insinceridad, hipocresía, falsedad, falta de sinceridad, doblez, f

insinuate /ɪn'sɪnyu,eit/ vt insinuar, introducir; (hint) soltar una indirecta, sugerir; (oneself) insinuarse, introducirse con habilidad

insinuation /ɪn,sɪnyu'eiʃən/ n insinuación, introducción, f; (hint) indirecta, f

insipid /ɪn'sɪpɪd/ a insípido, insulso; (dull) soso

insist /ɪn'sɪst/ vi insistir; persistir, obstinarse. **to i. on**, insistir en; obstinarse en, hacer hincapié en, aferrarse en (or a)

insistence /ɪn'sɪstəns/ n insistencia, f; obstinación, pertinacia, f

insistent /ɪn'sɪstənt/ a insistente; porfiado, obstinaz

insistently /ɪn'sɪstəntli/ adv con insistencia; porfiadamente

insobriety /ˌɪnsə'braiɪti/ n falta de sobriedad, f; embriaguez, ebriedad, f

insole /'ɪn,soul/ n (of shoes) plantilla, f

insolence /'ɪnsələns/ n insolencia, altanería, majadería, frescura, f, atrevimiento, descaro, m

insolent /'ɪnsələnt/ a insolente, arrogante, atrevido, descarado, desmesurado, fresco

insoluble /ɪn'sɒlyəbəl/ a insoluble

insolvency /ɪn'sɒlvənsi/ n insolvencia, f

insolvent /ɪn'sɒlvənt/ a insolvente

insomnia /ɪn'sɒmniə/ n insomnio, m

insomuch /ˌɪnsə'mʌtʃ/ adv (gen. with as or that) de modo (que), así (que), de suerte (que)

inspect /ɪn'spɛkt/ vt examinar, investigar, inspeccionar; (officially) registrar, reconocer

inspection /ɪn'spɛkʃən/ n inspección, investigación, f; examen, m; (official) reconocimiento, registro, m

inspector /ɪn'spɛktər/ n inspector, m, veedor, interventor, m

inspiration /ˌɪnspə'reiʃən/ n (of breath) inspiración, aspiración, f; numen, m, inspiración, vena, f. **to find i. in**, inspirarse en.

inspire /ɪn'spaiᵊr/ vt (inhale) aspirar, inspirar; (stimulate) animar, alentar, iluminar; (suggest) sugerir, inspirar; infundir. **to i. enthusiasm**, entusiasmar. **to i. hope**, dar esperanza, esperanzar

inspired /ɪn'spaiᵊrd/ a inspirado, intuitivo, iluminado; (of genius) genial

inspiring /ɪn'spaiᵊrɪŋ/ a alentador, animador; inspirador

inspirit /ɪn'spɪrɪt/ vt alentar, inspirar, estimular, animar

inspiriting /ɪn'spɪrɪtɪŋ/ a alentador, estimulador

instability /ˌɪnstə'bɪlɪti/ n inestabilidad, mutabilidad, inconstancia, f

install /ɪn'stɔl/ vt (all meanings) instalar. **to i. oneself**, instalarse, establecerse

installation /ˌɪnstə'leiʃən/ n (all meanings) instalación, f

installment /ɪn'stɔlmənt/ n (of a story) entrega, f; Com. plazo, m, cuota, f. **by installments**, Com. a plazos. **i. plan**, pago a plazos, pago por cuotas, m

instance /'ɪnstəns/ n ejemplo, caso, m; (request) solicitación, f, ruego, m; Law. instancia, f. —vt citar como ejemplo, mencionar; demostrar, probar. **for i.**, por ejemplo, verbigracia. **in that i....**, en el caso... **in the first i.**, en primer lugar, primero

instant /'ɪnstənt/ a inmediato, urgente; Com. corriente, actual. —n instante, momento, m; Inf. tris, santiamén, m. Com. **the 2nd i.**, el 2° (segundo) del corriente. **this i.**, (immediately) en seguida

instantaneous /ˌɪnstən'teiniəs/ a instantáneo. Photo. **i. exposure**, instantánea, f

instantly /'ɪnstəntli/ adv en seguida, al instante, inmediatamente

instead /ɪn'stɛd/ adv en cambio; (with of) en vez de, en lugar de

instep /'ɪn,stɛp/ n empeine, m

instigate /'ɪnstɪ,geit/ vt instigar, incitar, aguijar, animar, provocar; fomentar

instigating /'ɪnstɪ,geitɪŋ/ a instigador, provocador, fomentador

instigation /ˌɪnstɪ'geiʃən/ n instigación, incitación, f; estímulo, m

instigator /'ɪnstɪ,geitər/ *n* instigador (-ra), provocador (-ra), fomentador (-ra)

instinct /ɪn'stɪŋkt/ *n* instinto, *m.* **i. with,** imbuido de, lleno de. **by i.,** por instinto, movido por instinto

instinctive /ɪn'stɪŋktɪv/ *a* instintivo, espontáneo

instinctively /ɪn'stɪŋktɪvli/ *adv* por instinto

institute /'ɪnstɪ,tut/ *vt* instituir, fundar, establecer; (an inquiry) iniciar, empezar. —*n* instituto, *m*; *pl* **institutes,** *Law.* instituta, *f*

institution /,ɪnstɪ'tuʃən/ *n* (creation) fundación, creación, *f*; institución, *f*, instituto, *m*; (beginning) comienzo, *m*, iniciación, *f*; (charitable) asilo, *m*; (custom) uso, *m*, costumbre, tradición, *f*

institutional /,ɪnstɪ'tuʃənļ/ *a* institucional

instruct /ɪn'strʌkt/ *vt* (teach) instruir, enseñar; (order) mandar, dar orden (a)

instruction /ɪn'strʌkʃən/ *n* (teaching) instrucción, enseñanza, *f*; *pl* **instructions,** (orders) instrucciones, *f pl* orden, *f*, mandato, *m*

instructive /ɪn'strʌktɪv/ *a* instructivo, instructor, informativo

instructor /ɪn'strʌktər/ *n* instructor, preceptor, *m*

instrument /'ɪnstrəmənt/ *n* instrumento, *m*; (tool) herramienta, *f*, utensilio, aparato, *m*; (agent) órgano, agente, medio, *m*; *Law.* instrumento, *m*, escritura, *f*. —*vt Mus.* instrumentar. **percussion i.,** instrumento de percusión, *m.* **scientific i.,** instrumento científico, *m.* **stringed i.,** instrumento de cuerda, *m.* **wind i.,** instrumento de viento, *m*

instrumental /,ɪnstrə'mentļ/ *a* instrumental; influyente. **to be i. in,** contribuir a

instrumentality /,ɪnstrəmen'tælɪti/ *n* mediación, intervención, agencia, *f*, buenos oficios, *m pl*

instrumentation /,ɪnstrəmen'teiʃən/ *n Mus.* instrumentación, *f*; mediación, *f*

insubordinate /,ɪnsə'bɔrdnɪt/ *a* insubordinado, rebelde, desobediente, refractario

insubordination /,ɪnsə,bɔrdn'eiʃən/ *n* insubordinación, rebeldía, desobediencia, *f*

insubstantial /,ɪnsəb'stænʃəl/ *a* irreal; insubstancial

insufferable /ɪn'sʌfərəbəl/. See **intolerable**

insufficiency /,ɪnsə'fɪʃənsi/ *n* insuficiencia, falta, carestía, *f*

insufficient /,ɪnsə'fɪʃənt/ *a* insuficiente, falto. **"I. Postage,"** «Falta de franqueo»

insular /'ɪnsələr/ *a* isleño, insular; (narrow-minded) intolerante, iliberal

insularity /,ɪnsə'lɛərɪti/ *n* carácter isleño, *m*; (narrow-mindedness) iliberalidad, intolerancia, *f*

insulate /'ɪnsə,leit/ *vt* aislar

insulating /'ɪnsə,leitɪŋ/ *a* aislador. **i. tape,** *Elec.* cinta aisladora, *f*

insulation /,ɪnsə'leiʃən/ *n* aislamiento, *m*

insulator /'ɪnsə,leitər/ *n Elec.* aislador, *m*

insulin /'ɪnsəlɪn/ *n Med.* insulina, *f*

insult /*n.* 'ɪnsʌlt; *v.* ɪn'sʌlt/ *n* insulto, agravio, ultraje, *m*, afrenta, ofensa, *f*. —*vt* insultar, ofender, afrentar. **He was insulted,** Fue insultado; Se mostró ofendido

insulting /ɪn'sʌltɪŋ/ *a* insultante, injurioso, ofensivo. **He was very i. to them,** Les insultó, Les trató con menosprecio

insuperable /ɪn'supərəbəl/ *a* insuperable, invencible

insupportable /,ɪnsə'pɔrtəbəl/ *a* insoportable, inaguantable, intolerable, insufrible

insurable /ɪn'ʃurəbəl/ *a* asegurable

insurance /ɪn'ʃurəns/ *n* aseguramiento, *m*; *Com.* seguro, *m*; aseguración, *f.* **accident i.,** seguro contra accidentes, *m.* **fire-i.,** seguro contra incendio, *m.* **life i.,** seguro sobre la vida, *m.* **maritime i.,** seguro marítimo, *m.* **National I. Act,** Ley del Seguro Nacional Obligatorio, *f.* **i. broker,** corredor de seguros, *m.* **i. company,** compañía de seguros, *f.* **i. policy,** póliza de seguros, *f.* **i. premium,** prima de seguros, *f*

insure /ɪn'ʃur, -'ʃɜr/ *vt Com.* asegurar. **to i. oneself,** asegurarse. **the insured,** (person) el asegurado

insurer /ɪn'ʃurər/ *n* asegurador (-ra)

insurgent /ɪn'sɜrdʒənt/ *a* insurgente, rebelde; (of sea) invasor. —*n* rebelde, *mf* insurrecto (-ta)

insurmountable /,ɪnsər'mauntəbəl/ *a* insalvable, insuperable, invencible, intransitable

insurrection /,ɪnsə'rɛkʃən/ *n* insurrección, sublevación, *f*, levantamiento, *m*

intact /ɪn'tækt/ *a* intacto, íntegro, indemne

intake /'ɪn,teik/ *n* (of a stocking) menguado, *m*; *Mech.* aspiración, *f*; válvula de admisión, *f*; *Aer.* admisión, toma, *f*; orificio de entrada, *m*

intangible /ɪn'tændʒəbəl/ *a* intangible; incomprensible

integer /'ɪntɪdʒər/ *n Math.* número entero, *m*

integral /'ɪntɪgrəl/ *a* íntegro, intrínseco, inherente; *Math.* entero. —*n Math.* integral, *f.* **i. calculus,** cálculo integral, *m*

integrate /'ɪntɪ,greit/ *vt* integrar, completar; formar en un todo; *Math.* integrar

integrity /ɪn'tɛgrɪti/ *n* integridad, honradez, rectitud, entereza, *f*

intellect /'ɪntļ,ɛkt/ *n* intelecto, entendimiento, *m*

intellectual /,ɪntļ'ɛktʃuəl/ *a* intelectual, mental. —*n* intelectual

intelligence /ɪn'tɛlɪdʒəns/ *n* inteligencia, comprensión, mente, *f*; (quickness of mind) agudeza, perspicacia, *f*; (news) noticia, *f*, conocimiento, informe, *m.* **the latest i.,** las últimas noticias. **i. quotient,** cociente de inteligencia, *m.* **I. Service,** Inteligencia, *f;* policía secreta, *f.* **i. test,** prueba de inteligencia, *f*

intelligent /ɪnˈtelɪdʒənt/ *a* inteligente

intelligentsia /ɪnˌtelɪˈdʒentsɪə/ *n* clase intelectual, intelectualidad, *f*, *Inf.* masa cefálica, *f*

intelligible /ɪnˈtelɪdʒəbəl/ *a* inteligible, comprensible

intemperance /ɪnˈtempərəns/ *n* intemperancia, inmoderación, *f;* exceso en la bebida, *m*

intemperate /ɪnˈtempərɪt/ *a* intemperante, destemplado, descomedido; inmoderado; bebedor en exceso

intend /ɪnˈtend/ *vt* intentar, proponerse, pensar; destinar, dedicar; (mean) querer decir. **to be intended,** estar destinado; tener por fin; querer decir

intended /ɪnˈtendɪd/ *a* pensado, deseado. —*n Inf.* novio (-ia), futuro (-ra), prometido (-da)

intense /ɪnˈtens/ *a* intenso, vivo, fuerte; (of emotions) profundo, hondo, vehemente; (of colors) subido, intenso; (great) extremado, sumo, muy grande

intensification /ɪnˌtensɪfɪˈkeɪʃən/ *n* intensificación, *f;* aumento, *m*

intensify /ɪnˈtensəˌfaɪ/ *vt* intensar, intensificar; aumentar

intensity /ɪnˈtensɪti/ *n* intensidad, fuerza, *f;* (of emotions) profundidad, vehemencia, violencia, *f;* (of colors) intensidad, *f*

intensive /ɪnˈtensɪv/ *a* intensivo

intensive-care unit /ɪnˈtensɪvˈkeər/ *n* sala de terapia intensiva, unidad de cuidados intensivos, unidad de vigilancia intensiva, *f*

intent /ɪnˈtent/ *n* intento, propósito, deseo, *m.* —*a* atento; (absorbed) absorto, interesado; (on doing) resuelto a, decidido a. **to all intents and purposes,** en efecto, en realidad. **to be i. on,** (reading, etc.) estar absorto en, entregarse a. **with i. to defraud,** con el propósito deliberado de defraudar

intention /ɪnˈtenʃən/ *n* intención, voluntad, *f,* propósito, pensamiento, proyecto, *m*

intentional /ɪnˈtenʃənl/ *a* intencional, deliberado, premeditado

intentionally /ɪnˈtenʃənli/ *adv* a propósito, intencionalmente, de pensado

intentioned /ɪnˈtenʃənd/ *a* intencionado

intently /ɪnˈtentli/ *adv* atentamente

inter /ɪnˈtɜr/ *vt* enterrar, sepultar

inter- *prefix* inter, entre. **i.-allied,** interaliado, de los aliados. **i.-denominational,** intersectario. **i.-university,** interuniversitario. **i.-urban,** interurbano

interaction /ˌɪntərˈækʃən/ *n* interacción, acción recíproca, acción mutua, *f*

intercede /ˌɪntərˈsid/ *vi* interceder, mediar. **to i. for,** hablar por

intercept /ˌɪntərˈsept/ *vt* interceptar, detener; entrecoger, atajar

interception /ˌɪntərˈsepʃən/ *n* interceptación, detención, *f*

intercession /ˌɪntərˈseʃən/ *n* mediación, intercesión, *f*

interchangeable /ˌɪntərˈtʃeɪndʒəbəl/ *a* intercambiable

intercom /ˈɪntərˌkɒm/ *n* teléfono interior, *m*

intercostal /ˌɪntərˈkɒstl/ *a Anat.* intercostal

intercourse /ˈɪntərˌkɔrs/ *n* (social) trato, *m,* relaciones, *f pl; Com.* comercio, tráfico, *m;* (of ideas) intercambio, *m;* (sexual) coito, trato sexual, *m*

interdependence /ˌɪntərdɪˈpendənt/ *n* dependencia mutua, mutualidad, *f*

interdependent /ˌɪntərdɪˈpendənt/ *a* mutuo

interdict /*n* ˈɪntərˌdɪkt/ *v* /ˌɪntərˈdɪkt/ *n* interdicto, veto, *m,* prohibición, *f; Eccl.* entredicho, *m.* —*vt* interdecir, prohibir, privar; *Eccl.* poner entredicho

interdiction /ˌɪntərˈdɪkʃən/ *n* interdicción, prohibición, *f*

interest /ˈɪntərɪst/ *n* interés, *m;* provecho, *m; Com.* premio, rédito, interés, *m;* (in a firm) participación, *f;* (curiosity) interés, *m;* curiosidad, *f;* simpatía, *f;* (influence) influencia, *f.* —*n pl* **interests,** (commercial undertakings) empresas, *f pl,* intereses, negocios, *m pl.* **to be interested in,** interesarse en, (on behalf of) por. **to be in one's own i.,** ser en provecho de uno, ser en su propio interés. **to bear eight per cent. i.,** dar interés del ocho por ciento. **to pay with i.,** pagar con creces. **to put out at i.,** dar a interés. **in the interests of,** en interés de. **compound i.,** interés compuesto, *m.* **simple i.,** interés sencillo, *m.* **vested interests,** intereses creados, *m pl*

interesting /ˈɪntərəstɪŋ/ *a* interesante, curioso, atractivo

interestingly /ˈɪntərəstɪŋli/ *adv* amenamente, de modo interesante

interfere /ˌɪntərˈfɪər/ *vi* intervenir, meterse, entremeterse, mezclarse; *Inf.* mangonear, meter las narices; (with) meterse con; (impede) estorbar, impedir

interference /ˌɪntərˈfɪərəns/ *n* intervención, *f,* entrometimiento, *m;* (obstacle) estorbo, obstáculo, *m; Phys.* interferencia, *f; Radio.* parásitos, *m pl*

interim /ˈɪntərəm/ *n* ínterin, intermedio, *m.* —*a* interino, provisional. **in the i.,** entre tanto, en el ínterin. *Com.* **i. dividend,** dividendo interino, *m*

interior /ɪnˈtɪəriər/ *a* interior, interno; doméstico. —*n* interior, *m*

interject /ˌɪntərˈdʒekt/ *vt* interponer

interjection /ˌɪntərˈdʒekʃən/ *n* exclamación, interjección, *f;* interposición, *f*

interlace /ˌɪntərˈleɪs/ *vt* entrelazar, entretejer

interleave /ˌɪntərˈliv/ *vt* interfoliar, interpaginar

interline /ˈɪntərˌlaɪn/ *vt* entrerrenglonar, interlinear

interlining /ˈɪntərˌlaɪnɪŋ/ *n* entretela, *f*

interlock /ˌɪntərˈlɒk/ *vt* (of wheels, etc.)

endentar; trabar; cerrar. —*vi* endentarse; entrelazarse, unirse; cerrar

interlocutor /,ɪntər'lɒkyətər/ *n* interlocutor (-ra)

interloper /'ɪntər,loupər/ *n* intruso (-sa); *Com.* intérlope, *m*

interloping /,ɪntər'loupɪŋ/ *a* intérlope

interlude /'ɪntər,lud/ *n* intervalo, intermedio, *m*; *Mus.* interludio, *m*; *Theat.* entremés, *m*

intermarriage /,ɪntər'mærɪdʒ/ *n* casamiento entre parientes próximos, entre razas distintas, o entre grupos étnicos distintos, *m*

intermarry /,ɪntər'mæri/ *vi* contraer matrimonio entre parientes próximos, entre personas de razas distintas, o entre grupos étnicos distintos

intermediary /,ɪntər'midi,ɛri/ *a* and *n* intermediario (-ia)

intermediate /,ɪntər'midi,eit/ *a* intermedio, medio, mediañero. —*n* sustancia intermedia, *f*. —*vi* intervenir, mediar

interment /ɪn'tɜrmənt/ *n* entierro, *m*

interminable /ɪn'tɜrmənəbəl/ *a* interminable, inacabable

intermingle /,ɪntər'mɪŋgəl/ *vt* entremezclar, entreverar. —*vi* mezclarse

intermission /,ɪntər'mɪʃən/ *n* intermisión, interrupción, pausa, *f*; *Theat.* entreacto, *m*. **without i.**, sin pausa, sin tregua

intermittence /,ɪntər'mɪtns/ *n* intermitencia, alternación, *f*

intermittent /,ɪntər'mɪtnt/ *a* intermitente, discontinuo; (of fever) intermitente

intermittently /,ɪntər'mɪtntli/ *adv* a intervalos, a ratos, a pausas

intern /ɪn'tɜrn/ *n Med.* practicante de hospital *m*, interno (-na), interno de hospital, alumno interno, *m*. —*vt* confinar, encerrar

internal /ɪn'tɜrnl/ *a* interno, interior; (of affairs) doméstico, civil; intrínseco; íntimo. **i.-combustion engine,** motor de combustión interna, *m*

international /,ɪntər'næʃənl/ *a* internacional. —*n Sports.* un partido internacional. **i. law,** derecho internacional, *m*

internecine /,ɪntər'nisin/ *a* sanguinario, feroz

internee /,ɪntɜr'ni/ *n* internado (-da)

Internet, the /'ɪntər,nɛt/ *n* el Internet, *m*

internment /ɪn'tɜrnmənt/ *n* internamiento, *m*. **i. camp,** campo de internamiento, *m*

interpolate /ɪn'tɜrpə,leit/ *vt* interpolar, intercalar, interponer

interpolation /ɪn,tɜrpə'leiʃən/ *n* interpolación, inserción, añadidura, *f*

interpose /,ɪntər'pouz/ *vt* interponer; (a remark) interpolar. —*vi* interponerse, intervenir; (interfere) entrometerse; interrumpir

interpret /ɪn'tɜrprɪt/ *vt* interpretar;

(translate) traducir; (explain) explicar, descifrar. —*vi* interpretar.

interpretation /ɪn,tɜrprɪ'teiʃən/ *n* interpretación, *f*; (translation) traducción, *f*; (explanation) explicación, *f*

interpretative /ɪn'tɜrprɪ,teitɪv/ *a* interpretativo, interpretador

interpreter /ɪn'tɜrprɪtər/ *n* intérprete, *mf*

interrelation /,ɪntɛrɪ'leiʃən/ *n* relación mutua, *f*

interrogate /ɪn'tɛrə,geit/ *vt* interrogar, examinar, preguntar

interrogating /ɪn'tɛrə,geitɪŋ/ *a* interrogante

interrogation /ɪn,tɛrə'geiʃən/ *n* interrogación, *f*, examen, *m*; pregunta, *f*. **mark of i.,** punto de interrogación, *m*

interrogative /,ɪntə'rɒgətɪv/ *a* interrogativo. —*n* palabra interrogativa, *f*

interrogator /ɪn'tɛrə,geitər/ *n* examinador (-ra), interrogador (-ra)

interrogatory /,ɪntə'rɒgə,tɔri/ *a* interrogativo. —*n* interrogatorio, *m*

interrupt /,ɪntə'rʌpt/ *vt* interrumpir

interrupter /,ɪntə'rʌptər/ *n* interruptor (-ra); *Elec.* interruptor, *m*

interruption /,ɪntə'rʌpʃən/ *n* interrupción, *f*

intersect /,ɪntər'sɛkt/ *vt* cruzar. —*vi* cruzarse, intersecarse

intersection /,ɪntər'sɛkʃən/ *n* intersección, *f*; cruce, *m*, (of streets) bocacalle, *f*

intersperse /,ɪntər'spɜrs/ *vt* diseminar, esparcir; interpolar, entremezclar

interstice /ɪn'tɜrstɪs/ *n* intervalo, intermedio, *m*; (chink) intersticio, *m*, hendedura, *f*

intertwine /,ɪntər'twain/ *vt* entretejer, entrelazar. —*vi* entrelazarse

interval /'ɪntərvəl/ *n* intervalo, intermedio, *m*, pausa, *f*; *Theat.* entreacto, *m*, intermisión, *f*; (in schools) recreo, *m*. **at intervals,** a trechos, de vez en cuando. **lucid i.,** intervalo claro, intervalo lúcido, *m*

intervene /,ɪntər'vin/ *vi* intervenir, tomar parte (en), mediar; (occur) sobrevenir, acaecer; *Law.* interponerse

intervening /,ɪntər'vinɪŋ/ *a* intermedio; interventor

intervention /,ɪntər'vɛnʃən/ *n* intervención, mediación, *f*

interview /'ɪntər,vyu/ *n* entrevista, *f*, interview, *m*. —*vt* entrevistarse con

interviewer /'ɪntər,vyuər/ *n* interrogador (-ra); (reporter) reportero, periodista, *m*

interweave /,ɪntər'wiv/ *vt* entretejer, entrelazar

intestate /ɪn'tɛsteit/ *a* and *n* intestado (-da)

intestinal /ɪn'tɛstənl/ *a* intestinal, intestino. **i. worm,** lombriz intestinal, *f*

intestine /ɪn'tɛstɪn/ *n* intestino, *m*. **large i.,** intestino grueso, *m*. **small i.,** intestino delgado, *m*

intimacy /'ɪntəməsi/ *n* intimidad, *f*,

familiaridad, f; (of nobility and others) privanza, f

intimate /'ɪntəmɪt/ a íntimo; (of relations) entrañable, estrecho; intrínseco, esencial; (of knowledge) profundo, completo, detallado. —n amigo (-ga) de confianza. —vt intimar, dar a entender, indicar. **to become i.,** intimarse. **to be on i. terms with,** tratar de tú (a), ser amigo íntimo de

intimation /ˌɪntə'meɪʃən/ n intimación, indicación, f; (hint) insinuación, indirecta, f

intimidate /ɪn'tɪmɪˌdeɪt/ vt intimidar, aterrar, infundir miedo (a), espantar, acobardar, amedrentar

intimidation /ɪnˌtɪmɪ'deɪʃən/ n intimidación, f

into /'ɪntu; unstressed -tʊ, -tə/ prep en; a, al, a la; dentro, adentro; (of transforming, forming, etc.) en. **Throw it i. the fire,** Échalo al (or en el) fuego. **She went i. the house,** Entró en la casa. **to look i.,** mirar dentro de; mirar hacia el interior (de); investigar

intolerable /ɪn'tɒlərəbəl/ a intolerable, insufrible, inaguantable, insoportable, inllevable

intolerably /ɪn'tɒlərəbli/ adv intolerablemente, insufriblemente

intolerance /ɪn'tɒlərəns/ n intolerancia, intransigencia, f

intolerant /ɪn'tɒlərənt/ a intolerante, intransigente; Med. intolerante

intonation /ˌɪntoʊ'neɪʃən/ n entonación, f

intone /ɪn'toʊn/ vt entonar; Eccl. salmodiar

intoxicant /ɪn'tɒksɪkənt/ a embriagador. —n bebida alcohólica, f

intoxicate /ɪn'tɒksɪˌkeɪt/ vt emborrachar, embriagar; Med. intoxicar, envenenar; (excite) embriagar, embelesar

intoxicated /ɪn'tɒksɪˌkeɪtɪd/ a borracho; (excited) ebrio, embriagado; Med. intoxicado

intoxicating /ɪn'tɒksɪˌkeɪtɪŋ/ a embriagador

intoxication /ɪnˌtɒksɪ'keɪʃən/ n borrachera, embriaguez, f; Med. intoxicación, f, envenenamiento, m; (excitement) entusiasmo, m, ebriedad, f

- **intractability** /ɪnˌtræktə'bɪlɪti/ n insociabilidad, hurañería, f

intractable /ɪn'træktəbəl/ a intratable, insociable, huraño

intransigence /ɪn'trænsɪdʒəns/ n intransigencia, intolerancia, f

intransigent /ɪn'trænsɪdʒənt/ a intransigente, intolerante

intransitive /ɪn'trænsɪtɪv/ a intransitivo, neutro

intrauterine /ˌɪntrə'yutərɪn/ a Med. intrauterino

intravenous /ˌɪntrə'vinəs/ a Med. intravenoso

intrepid /ɪn'trɛpɪd/ a intrépido, osado, audaz

intrepidity /ˌɪntrə'pɪdɪti/ n intrepidez, osadía, audacia, f

intricacy /'ɪntrɪkəsi/ n intrincación, complejidad, f

intricate /'ɪntrɪkɪt/ a intrincado, complejo

intricately /'ɪntrɪkɪtli/ adv intrincadamente

intrigue /ɪn'trig; n. also 'ɪntrig/ n intriga, maquinación, f, enredo, m; (amorous) lío, m. —vi intrigar, enredar; (amorous) tener un lío. —vt (interest) atraer, interesar; (with) intrigar con

intriguer /ɪn'trigər/ n intrigante, mf. urdemalas, m, enredador (-ra)

intriguing /ɪn'trigɪŋ/ a enredador; (attractive) atrayente, interesante, seductor

intrinsic /ɪn'trɪnsɪk/ a intrínseco, innato, inherente, esencial

introduce /ˌɪntrə'dus/ vt introducir; hacer entrar; insertar, injerir; (a person) presentar; poner de moda, introducir; (a bill) presentar; (a person to a thing) llamar la atención sobre. **Permit me to i. my friend,** Permítame que le presente mi amigo

introduction /ˌɪntrə'dʌkʃən/ n introducción, f; (of a book) prefacio, prólogo, m, advertencia, f; (of a person) presentación, f; inserción, f

introductory /ˌɪntrə'dʌktəri/ a introductor, preliminar, preparatorio

introspection /ˌɪntrə'spekʃən/ n introspección, f

introspective /ˌɪntrə'spektɪv/ a introspectivo

introvert /'ɪntrəˌvɜrt/ a and n Psychol. introverso (-sa)

intrude /ɪn'trud/ vt introducir, imponer. —vi entremeterse, inmiscuirse. **Do I i.?** ¿Estorbo?

intruder /ɪn'trudər/ n intruso (-sa)

intrusion /ɪn'truʒən/ n intrusión, f; Geol. intromisión, f

intrusive /ɪn'trusɪv/ a intruso

intuition /ˌɪntu'ɪʃən/ n intuición, f. **to know by i.,** intuir, saber por intuición

intuitive /ɪn'tuɪtɪv/ a intuitivo

inundate /'ɪnənˌdeɪt/ vt inundar, anegar; Fig. abrumar

inundation /ˌɪnən'deɪʃən/ n inundación, anegación, f; Fig. diluvio, m, abundancia, f

inure /ɪn'yʊr/ vt endurecer, habituar

invade /ɪn'veɪd/ vt invadir, irrumpir, asaltar; Med. invadir

invader /ɪn'veɪdər/ n invasor (-ra), acometedor (-ra), agresor (-ra)

invading /ɪn'veɪdɪŋ/ a invasor, irruptor

invalid /ɪn'vælɪd/ a inválido, nulo. **to become i.,** caducar

invalid /'ɪnvəlɪd/ a inválido (-da), enfermo (-ma). **to become an i.,** quedarse inválido. **to i. out of the army,** licenciar por invalidez. **i. carriage,** cochecillo de inválido, m

invalidate /ɪnˈvælɪˌdeɪt/ vt invalidar, anular

invalidity /ˌɪnvəˈlɪdɪti/ n invalidez, nulidad, f

invaluable /ɪnˈvæljuəbəl/ n inestimable

invariability /ɪnˌvɛəriəˈbɪlɪti/ n invariabilidad, invariación, inalterabilidad, inmutabilidad, f

invariable /ɪnˈvɛəriəbəl/ a invariable, inmutable, inalterable

invasion /ɪnˈveiʒən/ n invasión, irrupción, f; Med. invasión, f

invective /ɪnˈvɛktɪv/ n invectiva, diatriba, f

inveigh (against) /ɪnˈvei/ vi desencadenarse (contra), prorrumpir en invectivas (contra)

inveigle /ɪnˈveigəl/ vt seducir, engatusar, persuadir

invent /ɪnˈvɛnt/ vt inventar, descubrir, originar; (a falsehood) fingir; (create) idear, componer

invention /ɪnˈvɛnʃən/ n invención, f, invento, descubrimiento, m; (imagination) ingeniosidad, inventiva, f; (falsehood) ficción, mentira, f; (finding) invención, f, hallazgo, m

inventive /ɪnˈvɛntɪv/ a inventor, inventivo; ingenioso, despejado

inventiveness /ɪnˈvɛntɪvnɪs/ n inventiva, f

inventor /ɪnˈvɛntər/ n inventor (-ra), autor (-ra)

inventory /ˈɪnvənˌtɔri/ n inventario, m; descripción, f. —vt inventariar

inverse /ɪnˈvɜrs/ a inverso. **i. proportion,** razón inversa, f

inversion /ɪnˈvɜrʒən/ n inversión, f, trastrocamiento, m; Gram. hipérbaton, m

invert /ɪnˈvɜrt/ vt invertir, trastornar, trastrocar. **inverted commas,** comilla, f

invest /ɪnˈvɛst/ vt Com. invertir; Mil. sitiar, cercar; (foll. by with) poner, cubrir con; (of qualities) conferir, otorgar, dar. —vi (with in) poner dinero en, echar caudal en; Inf. comprar

investigable /ɪnˈvɛstɪgəbəl/ a averiguable

investigate /ɪnˈvɛstɪˌgeit/ vt investigar, estudiar; examinar, averiguar; explorar

investigation /ɪnˌvɛstɪˈgeiʃən/ n investigación, f, estudio, m; examen, m, averiguación, f; encuesta, pesquisa, f

investigator /ɪnˈvɛstɪˌgeitər/ n investigador (-ra); averiguador (-ra)

investigatory /ɪnˈvɛtɪgəˌtɔri/ a investigador

investment /ɪnˈvɛstmənt/ n (Com. of money) inversión, f, empleo, m; Mil. cerco, m; (investiture) instalación, f; pl **investments,** Com. acciones, f pl, fondos, m pl

investor /ɪnˈvɛstər/ n inversionista, m; accionista, mf

inveterate /ɪnˈvɛtərɪt/ a inveterado, antiguo, arraigado, incurable

invidious /ɪnˈvɪdiəs/ a odioso, repugnante, injusto

invigorate /ɪnˈvɪgəˌreit/ vt vigorizar, dar fuerza (a), avivar

invigorating /ɪnˈvɪgəˌreitɪŋ/ a fortaleciente, fortificador, vigorizador

invincible /ɪnˈvɪnsəbəl/ a invencible, indomable; Fig. insuperable

inviolable /ɪnˈvaiələbəl/ a inviolable

inviolate /ɪnˈvaiəlɪt/ a inviolado

invisible /ɪnˈvɪzəbəl/ a invisible. **i. ink,** tinta simpática, f. **i. mending,** zurcido invisible, m

invitation /ˌɪnvɪˈteiʃən/ n invitación, f; convite, m; (card) tarjeta de invitación, f

invite /ɪnˈvait/ vt invitar, convidar; (request) pedir, rogar; (of things) incitar, tentar

inviting /ɪnˈvaitɪŋ/ a atrayente, incitante; (of food) apetitoso; (of looks) provocativo

invocation /ˌɪnvəˈkeiʃən/ n invocación, f

invoice /ˈɪnvɔis/ n Com. factura, f. —vt facturar. **proforma i.,** factura simulada, f. **shipping i.,** factura de expedición, f. **i. book,** libro de facturas, m

invoke /ɪnˈvouk/ vt invocar; suplicar, implorar; (laws) acogerse (a)

involuntarily /ɪnˌvɒlənˈtɛərəli/ adv sin querer, involuntariamente

involuntary /ɪnˈvɒlənˌtɛri/ a involuntario; instintivo, inconsciente

involve /ɪnˈvɒlv/ vt (entangle) enredar, embrollar, enmarañar; (implicate) comprometer; (imply) implicar, ocasionar, suponer, traer consigo

involved /ɪnˈvɒlvd/ a complejo, intrincado; (of style) confuso, obscuro

invulnerable /ɪnˈvʌlnərəbəl/ a invulnerable

inward /ˈɪnwərd/ a interior, interno; íntimo, espiritual. —adv adentro

inwardly /ˈɪnwərdli/ adv interiormente; para sí, entre sí

inwards /ˈɪnwərdz/ adv hacia dentro; adentro

iodine /ˈaiəˌdain/ n yodo, m. **i. poisoning,** yodismo, m

ion /ˈaiən/ n Chem. ion, m

Ionic /aiˈɒnɪk/ a jónico. **i. foot** Poet. jónico, m

iota /aiˈoutə/ n (letter) iota, f; jota, pizca, f, ápice, m. **not an i.,** ni pizca

I.O.U. n Com. abonaré, m

ipecacuanha /ˌɪpɪˌkækyəˈwanyə/ n ipecacuana, f

Iranian /ɪˈreiniən/ a and n iranio (-ia)

Iraq /ɪˈræk/ Irak, m

irascibility /ɪˌræsəˈbɪlɪti/ n irascibilidad, iracundia, irritabilidad, f

irascible /ɪˈræsəbəl/ a irascible, iracundo, irritable

irate /aiˈreit/ a airado, colérico, enojado

ire /aiər/ n ira, cólera, furia, f

Ireland /ˈaiərlənd/ Irlanda, f

iridescence /ˌɪrɪˈdɛsəns/ n iridiscencia, f

iridescent /ˌɪrɪˈdɛsənt/ a iridiscente. **to look i.,** irisar, tornasolarse

iridium /ɪˈrɪdiəm/ n Chem. iridio, m

iris /ˈaɪrɪs/ n Anat. iris, m; Bot. irídea, f

Irish /ˈaɪrɪʃ/ a and n irlandés (-esa) the L, los irlandeses

irksome /ˈɜːksəm/ a fastidioso, tedioso, aburrido

iron /ˈaɪərn/ n hierro, m; (for clothes) plancha, f; (tool) utensilio, m, herramienta, f; (golf) hierro, m; pl **irons**, grillos, m pl, cadenas, f pl. —a de hierro, férreo; Fig. duro, severo. —vt (linen) planchar; (with out) allanar. **to have too many irons in the fire,** tener demasiados asuntos entre manos. **to put in irons,** echar grillos (a). **to strike while the i. is hot,** A hierro caliente batir de repente. **cast-i.,** hierro colado, m. **scrap i.,** hierro viejo, m. **sheet i.,** hierro en planchas, m. **wrought i.,** hierro dulce, m. **i. age,** edad de hierro, f. **i.-foundry,** fundición de hierro, f. **i. lung,** Med. pulmón de hierro, pulmón de acero, m. **i.-mold,** mancha de orín, f. **i. smelting furnace,** alto horno, m. **i. tonic,** Med. reconstituyente ferruginoso, m. **i. will,** voluntad de hierro, f

ironclad /a ˈaɪərnˈklæd/ n -,klæd/ a blindado, acorazado. —n buque de guerra blindado, acorazado, m

ironer /ˈaɪərnər/ n planchador (-ra)

ironical /aɪˈrɒnɪkəl/ a irónico

ironing /ˈaɪərnɪŋ/ n planchado, m; ropa por planchar, f. —a de planchar. **i. board,** tabla de planchar, f

ironwork /ˈaɪərnˌwɜːk/ n herraje, m; obra de hierro, f

ironworks /ˈaɪərnˌwɜːks/ n herrería, f

irony /ˈaɪrəni/ n ironía, f. —a (like iron) ferruginoso

Iroquois /ˈɪrəˌkwɔɪ/ a and n iroqués (-esa)

irradiate /ɪˈreɪdiˌeɪt/ vt irradiar; Fig. iluminar, aclarar

irradiation /ɪˌreɪdiˈeɪʃən/ n irradiación, f; Fig. iluminación, f

irrational /ɪˈræʃənl/ a ilógico, ridículo, irracional

irreclaimable /ˌɪrɪˈkleɪməbəl/ a irrecuperable, irredimible; (of land) inservible, improductivo; irreformable

irreconcilable /ɪˈrɛkənˌsaɪləbəl/ a irreconciliable

irrecoverable /ˌɪrɪˈkʌvərəbəl/ a irrecuperable, incobrable

irredeemable /ˌɪrɪˈdiməbəl/ a irredimible, perdido. **i. government loan,** deuda perpetua, f

irreducible /ˌɪrɪˈdusəbəl/ a irreducible

irrefutable /ɪˈrɛfyətəbəl/ a irrefutable, indisputable, innegable, irrebatible

irregular /ɪˈrɛgyələr/ a irregular; anormal; (of shape) disforme; desordenado; Gram. irregular; (of surface) desigual, escabroso

irregularity /ɪˌrɛgyəˈlærɪti/ n irregularidad, f; anormalidad, f; (of shape) desproporción, irregularidad, f; (of surface) escabrosidad, desigualdad, f; exceso, m, demasía, f

irrelevance /ɪˈrɛləvəns/ n inconexión, f; inoportunidad, f; futilidad, poca importancia, f; (stupidity) desatino, m, impertinencia, f

irrelevant /ɪˈrɛləvənt/ a inaplicable, fuera de propósito; inoportuno; sin importancia, fútil; (stupid) impertinente

irreligion /ˌɪrɪˈlɪdʒən/ n irreligión, impiedad, f

irreligious /ˌɪrɪˈlɪdʒəs/ a irreligioso, impío

irremediable /ˌɪrɪˈmidiəbəl/ a irremediable, irreparable

irremediably /ˌɪrɪˈmidiəbli/ adv sin remedio, irremediablemente

irreparable /ɪˈrɛpərəbəl/ a irreparable

irreplaceable /ˌɪrɪˈpleɪsəbəl/ a irreemplazable

irrepressible /ˌɪrɪˈprɛsəbəl/ a incontrolable, indomable

irreproachable /ˌɪrɪˈproutʃəbəl/ a irreprochable, intachable

irresistible /ˌɪrɪˈzɪstəbəl/ a irresistible

irresolute /ɪˈrɛzəˌlut/ a irresoluto, indeciso, vacilante

irrespective /ˌɪrɪˈspɛktɪv/ a (with of) independiente de, aparte de, sin distinción de

irresponsible /ˌɪrɪˈspɒnsəbəl/ a irresponsable

irretrievable /ˌɪrɪˈtrivəbəl/ a irrecuperable

irreverence /ɪˈrɛvərəns/ n irreverencia, f

irreverent /ɪˈrɛvərənt/ a irreverente, irrespetuoso

irrevocable /ɪˈrɛvəkəbəl/ a irrevocable; inquebrantable

irrigable /ˈɪrɪgəbəl/ a regadío

irrigate /ˈɪrɪˌgeɪt/ vt Agr. poner en regadío, regar; Med. irrigar

irrigation /ˌɪrɪˈgeɪʃən/ n Agr. riego, m; Med. irrigación, f. **i. channel,** cacera, acequia, f, canal de riego, m

irritability /ˌɪrɪtəˈbɪlɪti/ n irritabilidad, iracundia, f

irritable /ˈɪrɪtəbəl/ a irritable, irascible, iracundo

irritably /ˈɪrɪtəbli/ adv con irritación, airadamente

irritant /ˈɪrɪtənt/ a irritante, irritador. —n irritador, m; Med. medicamento irritante, m

irritate /ˈɪrɪˌteɪt/ vt provocar, estimular; irritar, molestar, exasperar; Med. irritar

irritating /ˈɪrɪˌteɪtɪŋ/ a irritador, irritante

irritatingly /ˈɪrɪˌteɪtɪŋli/ adv de un modo irritante

irritation /ˌɪrɪˈteɪʃən/ n irritación, f, enojo, m; Physiol. picazón, f, picor, m

irruption /ɪˈrʌpʃən/ n irrupción, invasión, f

isinglass /ˈaɪzənˌglæs/ n cola de pescado, f

Islamic /ɪsˈlæmɪk/ a islámico

island /ˈaɪlənd/ n isla, f, a isleño

islander /ˈaɪləndər/ n isleño (-ña)

islet /ˈaɪlɪt/ n isleta, f; isolote, m

isobaric /ˌaisəˈbærɪk/ a isobárico
isolate /v. ˈaisəˌleit/ vt aislar, apartar
isolated /ˈaisəˌleitɪd/ a aislado, apartado, solitario; único, solo
isolation /ˌaisəˈleiʃən/ n aislamiento, apartamiento, m, soledad, f
isolationism /ˌaisəˈleiʃəˌnɪzəm/ n Polit. aislacionismo, aislamientismo, m
isolationist /ˌaisəˈleiʃənɪst/ a and n Polit. aislacionista, aislamientista, mf
isomerism /aiˈsɒməˌrɪzəm/ n Chem. isomería, f
isometric /ˌaisəˈmetrɪk/ a isométrico
isosceles /aiˈsɒsəˌliz/ a isósceles
isotope /ˈaisəˌtoup/ n isotope, isotopo, m
Israelite /ˈɪzriəˌlait/ a and n israelita mf
issue /ˈɪʃu/ n salida, f; (result) resultado, m, consecuencia, f; (of a periodical) número, m; Print. edición, tirada, f; (offspring) proie, sucesión, f; (of notes, bonds) emisión, f; Med. flujo, m; cuestión, f, problema, m. —vi salir, fluir, manar; nacer, originarse; resultar, terminarse. —vt (an order) expedir, emitir, dictar; publicar, dar a luz; (of notes, bonds) poner en circulación, librar. **at i.,** en disputa, en cuestión. **to join i.,** llevar la contraria, oponer
isthmian /ˈɪsmiən/ a ístmico
isthmus /ˈɪsməs/ n istmo, m
it /ɪt/ pron (as subject) él, m; ella, f; (gen. omitted with all verbs in Sp.); (as object) lo, m; la, f; (as indirect object) le (se with an object in 3rd pers.); (meaning that thing, that affair) eso, ello. Sometimes omitted in other cases, e.g. *He has thought it necessary to stay at home,* Ha creído necesario de quedarse en casa. *We heard it said that...,* Oímos decir que... *to make it perfectly clear that...,* dejar bien claro que... —n (slang) garbo, aquél, m;

atractivos, m pl. **Is it not so?** ¿No es así? **That is it,** Eso es. **It's me,** Soy yo
Italian /ɪˈtælyən/ a and n italiano (-na) (language) italiano, m. Art. **I. School,** escuela italiana, f
italic /ɪˈtælɪk/ a (of Italy) itálico; Print. itálico, bastardillo. —n letra bastardilla, bastardilla, letra itálica, f. **italics mine,** el subrayado es mío, los subrayados son míos
italicize /ɪˈtæləˌsaiz/ vt imprimir en bastardilla; dar énfasis (a)
Italy /ˈɪtli/ Italia, f
itch /ɪtʃ/ n sarna, f; Fig. picazón, f; prurito, capricho, m. —vi picar; Fig. sentir picazón; (with to) rabiar por, suspirar por.
itching /ˈɪtʃɪŋ/ n picazón, f, picor, m. —a sarnoso, picante; Med. pruriginoso. **to have an i. palm,** Fig. ser de la virgen del puño
item /n ˈaitəm; adv ˈaitem/ n ítem, artículo, m; Com. partida, f; punto, detalle, m; (of a program) número, m; asunto, m. —adv ítem
iterative /ˈɪtəˌreitɪv/ a iterativo
itinerant /aiˈtɪnərənt/ a nómada, errante
itinerary /aiˈtɪnəˌreri/ n itinerario, m, ruta, f
its /ɪts/ poss a su (with pl. obj.) sus. **a book and its pages,** un libro y sus páginas.
itself /ɪtˈself/ pron él mismo, m; ella misma, f; (with prep.) sí; (with reflex. verb) se; (with noun) el mismo, la misma; (meaning alone) solo. **in i.,** en sí
ivory /ˈaivəri/ n marfil, m. —a ebúrneo, de marfil, marfileño. **vegetable i.,** marfil vegetal, m. **i. carving,** talla de marfil, f
ivory tower n torre de marfil, f
ivory-tower /ˈaivəri ˈtauər/ a de torre de marfil
ivy /ˈaivi/ n hiedra, f

J

j /dʒei/ n (letter) jota, f

jab /dʒæb/ vt (with a hypodermic needle, etc.) pinchar; introducir (en); clavar (con); (scrape) hurgar; (place) poner. —n pinchazo, m; golpe, m. **He jabbed his pistol in my ribs,** Me puso la pistola en las costillas

jabber /'dʒæbər/ vt and vi chapurrear; (of monkeys) chillar

jabbering /'dʒæbərɪŋ/ n chapurreo, m; (of monkeys) chillidos, m pl

Jack /dʒæk/ n Juan, m; (man) hombre, m; (sailor) marinero, m; (in cards) sota, f; (for raising weights) gato, m; (of a spit) torno, m; (of some animals) macho, m; (bowls) boliche, m. —vt (with up) solevantar con gatos. **Union J.,** pabellón británico, m. **j.-boot,** bota de montar, f. **J.-in-office,** mandarín, funcionario impertinente, m. **J.-in-the-box,** faca, f. **j.-knife,** navaja, f. **J. of all trades,** hombre de muchos oficios, m. **jack of all trades, master of none,** aprendiz de todo, oficial de nada. **j.-rabbit,** liebre americana, f. **J.-tar,** marinero, m

jackal /'dʒækəl/ n chacal, adive, m

jackass /'dʒæk,æs/ n asno, m; (fool) tonto, asno, m. **laughing j.,** martín pescador, m

jacket /'dʒækɪt/ n chaqueta, f; americana, f; (for boilers, etc.) camisa, f; (of a book) forro, m, sobrecubierta, f. **strait j.,** camisa de fuerza, f

jacks /dʒæks/ n (game) matatenas, f pl, cantillos, m pl

jade /dʒeid/ n Mineral. jade, m; (horse) rocín, m; (woman) mala pécora, f; (saucy wench) mozuela, picaruela, f

jaded /'dʒeidɪd/ a fatigado, agotado, rendido; (of the palate) saciado

jagged /'dʒægɪd/ a dentado

jaguar /'dʒægwɑr/ n jaguar, m

jail /dʒeil/ cárcel, prisión, f; encierro, m. —vt encarcelar. —a carcelario, carcelero.

jailbird /'dʒeil,bɜrd/ n malhechor, m; presidiario, m

jailer /'dʒeilər/ n carcelero (-ra)

jalopy /dʒə'lɒpi/ carcacho, m, (Mexico), cafetera rusa, f (Spain)

jalousie /'dʒælə,si/ n celosía, f

jam /dʒæm/ vt (ram) apretar; apiñar; estrujar; (a machine) atascar; (radio) causar interferencia (a); (preserve) hacer confitura de. —vi atascarse. —n (of people) agolpamiento, m; (traffic) atasco, m; (preserve) confitura, mermelada, compota, f. **He jammed his hat on,** Se encasquetó el sombrero. **She suddenly jammed down on the brakes,** Frenó de repente. **jam-dish,** compotera, f. **jam-jar,** pote para confitura, m

Jamaican /dʒə'meikən/ a jamaicano, n jamaicano (-na)

jamboree /,dʒæmbə'ri/ campamento, m

jangle /'dʒæŋgəl/ vi cencerrear; chocar; rechinar. —n cencerreo, m; choque, m; rechinamiento, m

janitor /'dʒænɪtər/ n portero, m; (in a university, etc.) bedel, m

January /'dʒænyu,ɛri/ n enero, m

Japan /dʒə'pæn/ el Japón, m

japan /dʒə'pæn/ n charol, m. —vt charolar

Japanese /,dʒæpə'niz/ a japonés. —n japonés (-esa); (language) japonés, m

jar /dʒɑr/ n chirrido, m; choque, m; sacudida, f; vibración, trepidación, f; (quarrel) riña, f; (receptacle) jarra, f; (for tobacco, honey, cosmetics, etc.) pote, m; (Leyden) botella (de Leyden), f. —vi chirriar; vibrar, trepidar; chocar; (of sounds) ser discorde; (of colors) chillar. —vt sacudir; hacer vibrar. **It jarred on my nerves,** Me atacaba los nervios. **It gave me a nasty jar,** Fig. Me hizo una impresión desagradable. **on the jar,** entreabierto

jargon /'dʒɑrgən/ n jerga, jerigonza, f; monserga, f; (technical) lenguaje especial, m

jarring /'dʒɑrɪŋ/ a discorde, disonante; en conflicto, opuesto; (to the nerves) que ataca a los nervios

jasmine /'dʒæzmɪn/ n jazmín, m. **yellow j.,** jazmín amarillo, m

jaundice /'dʒɔndɪs/ n ictericia, f

jaundiced /'dʒɔndɪst/ a envidioso; desengañado, desilusionado

jaunt /dʒɔnt/ n excursión, f, vi ir de excursión

jauntily /'dʒɔntli/ adv airosamente, con garbo

jaunty /'dʒɔnti/ a garboso, airoso

javelin /'dʒævlɪn/ n jabalina, f. **j. throwing,** lanzamiento de la jabalina, m

jaw /dʒɔ/ n quijada, f; maxilar, m; pl **jaws,** boca, f; (of death, etc.) garras, f pl; Mech. quijada, f; (narrow entrance) boca, abertura, f. **jaw-bone,** mandíbula, f; Anat. hueso maxilar, m

jay /dʒei/ n arrendajo, m

jazz /dʒæz/ n jazz, m. —vi bailar el jazz. **j. band,** orquesta de jazz, f

jealous /'dʒɛləs/ a celoso; envidioso. **to be j. of,** tener celos de. **to make j.,** dar celos (a)

jealousy /'dʒɛləsi/ n celos, m pl

jeans /dʒinz/ n vaqueros, m pl

jeep /dʒip/ n Mil. yip, m

jeer /dʒɪər/ n burla, mofa, f; insulto, m, vi burlarse; (with at) mofarse de

jeering /'dʒɪərɪŋ/ a mofador. —n burlas, f pl; insultos, m pl

jellied /'dʒɛlid/ a en gelatina

jelly /'dʒɛli/ n jalea, f; gelatina, f, vi solidificarse. **j.-bag,** manga, f. **j.-fish,** aguamala, aguaviva, malagna, medusa, f

jeopardize /'dʒɛpər,daiz/ vt arriesgar, poner en juego; comprometer

jeopardy /'dʒɛpərdi/ n peligro, m

jerk /dʒɜrk/ n sacudida, f. —vt sacudir;

dar una sacudida (a); lanzar bruscamente; (pull) tirar de; (push) empujar. —*vi* moverse a sacudidas. **I jerked myself free,** Me libré de una sacudida

jerkily /'dʒɜrkəli/ *adv* con sacudidas; espasmódicamente; nerviosamente

jerky /'dʒɜrki/ *a* espasmódico; nervioso (also of style)

jerry-built /'dʒɛri͵bɪlt/ *a* mal construido, de pacotilla

jersey /'dʒɜrzi/ *n* jersey, *m*. —*a* de jersey; de Jersey. **football j.,** camiseta de fútbol, *f*, jersey de fútbol, *m*. **J. cow,** vaca jerseysa, *f*

Jerusalem /dʒɪ'rusələm/ Jerusalén, *m*

jest /dʒɛst/ *n* broma, chanza, *f*; (joke) chiste, *m*; (laughingstock) hazmerreír, *m*. —*vi* bromear; burlarse (de). **in j.,** en broma, de guasa

jester /'dʒɛstər/ *n* burlón (-ona); (practical joker, etc.) bromista, *mf*; (at a royal court) bufón, *m*

jesting /'dʒɛstɪŋ/ *n* bromas, *f pl*; chistes, *m pl*; burlas, *f pl*. —*a* de broma; burlón

jestingly /'dʒɛstɪŋli/ *adv* en broma

Jesuit /'dʒɛʒuɪt/ *n* Jesuita, *m*

jet /dʒɛt/ *n* Mineral. azabache, *m*; (stream) chorro, *m*; (pipe) surtidero, *m*; (burner) mechero, *m*, *vi* chorrear. **jet-black,** negro como el azabache, de azabache. **jet-propelled engine,** motor de retroacción, *m*. **jet-propelled plane,** aeroplano de reacción, *m*

jetsam /'dʒɛtsəm/ *n* echazón, *f*; Fig. víctima, *f*

jettison /'dʒɛtəsən/ *n* echazón, *f*. —*vt* echar (mercancías) al mar; Fig. librarse de, abandonar

jetty /'dʒɛti/ *n* dique, malecón, *m*; (landing pier) embarcadero, muelle, *m*

Jew /dʒu/ *n* judío, *m*. **Jew's harp,** birimbao, *m*

jewel /'dʒuəl/ *n* joya, alhaja, *f*; (of a watch) rubí, *m*; Fig. alhaja, *f*. —*vt* enjoyar, adornar con piedras preciosas. **j.-box, -case,** joyero, *m*

jeweled /'dʒuəld/ *a* adornado con piedras preciosas, enjoyado; (of a watch) con rubíes

jeweler /'dʒuələr/ *n* joyero (-ra). **jeweler's shop,** joyería, *f*

jewelry /'dʒuəlri/ *n* joyas, *f pl*; artículos de joyería, *m pl*

Jewess /'dʒuɪs/ *n* judía, *f*

Jewish /'dʒuɪʃ/ *a* judío

Jewry /'dʒuri/ *n* judería, *f*

jib /dʒɪb/ *n* Naut. foque, *m*. —*vi* (of a horse) plantarse; (refuse) rehusar. **to jib at,** vacilar en; mostrarse desinclinado. **jib-boom,** Naut. botalón de foque, *m*

jiffy /'dʒɪfi/ *n* instante, credo, *m*. **in a j.,** en un decir Jesús, en un credo, en un santiamén

jig /dʒɪg/ *n* (dance) jiga, *f*. —*vi* bailar una jiga; bailar, agitarse, sacudirse. —*vt* agitar, sacudir; (sieve) cribar

jigsaw puzzle /'dʒɪg͵sɔ/ *n* rompecabezas, *m*

jilt /dʒɪlt/ *vt* dar calabazas (a)

jingle /'dʒɪŋgəl/ *n* tintineo, *m*; ruido, *m*; verso, *m*; estribillo, *m*. —*vi* tintinar; sonar; rimar

jitters, to have the /'dʒɪtərz/ no tenerlas todas consigo, no saber dónde meterse

job /dʒɒb/ *n* tarea, *f*; trabajo, *m*; empleo, *m*; (affair) asunto, *m*; (thing) cosa, *f*; (unscrupulous transaction) intriga, *f*. **It is a good (bad) job that...,** Es una buena (mala) cosa que... **He has done a good job,** Ha hecho un buen trabajo. **He has lost his job,** Ha perdido su empleo, Le han declarado cesante. **odd-job man,** factótum, *m*. **job-lot,** colección miscelánea, *f*; Com. saldo de mercancías, *m*

jobber /'dʒɒbər/ *n* (workman) destajista, *m*; (in stocks) agiotista, *m*; Com. corredor, *m*

jobless /'dʒɒblɪs/ *a* sin trabajo

jockey /'dʒɒki/ *n* jockey, *m*. —*vt* engañar; (with into) persuadir, hacer; (with out of) quitar, robar. **j. cap,** gorra de jockey, *f*. **J. Club,** jockey-club, *m*

jocose /dʒou'kous/ *a* jocoso, gracioso, guasón

jocular /'dʒɒkyələr/ *a* gracioso, alegre; chistoso, zumbón

jocularly /'dʒɒkyələrli/ *adv* en broma; alegremente

jocund /'dʒɒkənd/ *a* alegre, jovial; jocundo

jog /dʒɒg/ *vt* empujar; (the memory) refrescar. —*vi* ir despacio; andar a trote corto. —*n* empujón, *m*. **He jogged me with his elbow,** Me dio con el codo. **jogtrot,** trote corto, *m*

joie de vivre /ʒwadə'vivrə/ *n* goce de vivir, arregosto de vivir, *m*

join /dʒɔin/ *vt* juntar; unir; añadir; (railway lines) empalmar; juntarse con; (meet) encontrarse (con); reunirse (con); (a club, etc.) hacerse miembro (de); (share) acompañar; (regiments, ships) volver (a). —*vi* juntarse; unirse; asociarse. —*n* unión, *f*; (railway) empalme, *m*; (roads) bifurcación, *f*. **At what time will you j. me?** ¿A qué hora me vendrás a buscar? **He has joined his ship,** Ha vuelto a su buque. **Will you j. me in a drink?** ¿Me quieres acompañar en una bebida? **to j. battle,** librar batalla. **to j. forces,** combinar; Inf. juntar meriendas. **to j. in,** tomar parte en, participar en. **to j. together,** *vt* unir, juntar. —*vi* juntarse; asociarse. **to j. up,** alistarse

joiner /'dʒɔinər/ *n* carpintero, ensamblador, *m*,

joining /'dʒɔinɪŋ/ *n* juntura, conjunción, *f*; (etc.) ensambladura, *f*; Fig. unión, *f*

joint /dʒɔint/ *n* juntura, junta, *f*; Anat. coyuntura, articulación, *f*; (knuckle) nudillo, *m*; (of meat) cuarto, *m*; (hinge) bisagra, *f*; Bot. nudo, *m*, *a* unido; combinado; colectivo; mixto; mutuo; (in compounds) co. —*vt* juntar; (meat) descuartizar. **out of j.,** dislocado; (of the times) fuera de compás. **j. account,** cuenta corriente mutua, f. **j.-heir,** coheredero, m. **j. stock company,** compañía por acciones, sociedad anónima, f

jointly /'dʒɔintli/ adv juntamente, en común, colectivamente

joist /dʒɔist/ n sopanda, viga, f

joke /dʒouk/ n chiste, m; burla, broma, f. —vi bromear, chancearse. —vt burlarse (de). **Can he take a j.?** ¿Sabe aguantar una broma? **practical j.,** broma pesada, f. **to play a j.,** gastar una broma, hacer una burla

joker /'dʒoukər/ n bromista, mf; (in cards) comodín, m

joking /'dʒoukiŋ/ n chistes, m pl, bromas, f pl. —a chistoso; cómico

jokingly /'dʒoukiŋli/ adv en broma, de guasa

jollity /'dʒɒliti/ n alegría, f, regocijo, m

jolly /'dʒɒli/ a alegre, jovial; (tipsy) achispado; (amusing) divertido; (nice) agradable. —adv muy. **He is a j. good fellow,** Es un hombre estupendo. **I am j. glad,** Estoy contentísimo, Me alegro mucho

jolt /dʒoult/ n sacudida, f. —vt sacudir. —vi (of a vehicle) traquetear

jolting /'dʒoultiŋ/ n sacudidas, f pl, sacudimiento, m; (of a vehicle) traqueteo, m

Jordan /'dʒɔrdn/ Jordania, f

jostle /'dʒɒsəl/ vt empujar, empellar. —vi dar empujones, codear

jot /dʒɒt/ n jota, pizca, f. —vt (down) apuntar. **not a jot,** ni jota, ni pizca. **to be not worth a jot,** no valer un comino

jotter /'dʒɒtər/ n taco para notas, m; (exercise book) cuaderno, m

journal /'dʒɜrnl/ n (diary) diario, m; (ship's) diario de navegación, m; (newspaper) periódico, m; (review) revista, f

journalese /,dʒɜrnl'iz/ n lenguaje periodístico, m

journalism /'dʒɜrnl,izəm/ n periodismo, m

journalist /'dʒɜrnlist/ n periodista, mf

journey /'dʒɜrni/ n viaje, m; expedición, f; trayecto, m; camino, m. —vi viajar. **j. by sea,** viaje por mar. **Pleasant j.!** ¡Buen viaje! ¡Feliz viaje! **outward j.,** viaje de ida, m. **return j.,** viaje de regreso, m

jovial /'dʒouviəl/ a jovial

jowl /dʒaul/ n (cheek) carrillo, m; (of cattle, etc.) papada, f; (jaw) quijada, f

joy /dʒɔi/ n alegría, f; felicidad, f; deleite, placer, m, vi alegrarse. **I wish you joy,** Te deseo la felicidad. **joy-ride,** excursión en coche, f; vuelo en avión, m. **joy-stick,** (of an airplane) palanca de gobierno, f

joyful /'dʒɔifəl/ a alegre

joyless /'dʒɔilis/ a sin alegría, triste

joyous /'dʒɔiəs/. See **joyful**

jubilant /'dʒubələnt/ a jubiloso; triunfante

jubilantly /'dʒubələntli/ adv con júbilo, alegremente; triunfalmente

jubilation /,dʒubə'leiʃən/ n júbilo, m, alegría, f; ruido triunfal, m

jubilee /'dʒubə,li/ n jubileo, m

Judaic /dʒu'deiik/ a judaico

Judaism /'dʒudi,izəm/ n judaísmo, m

Judas /'dʒudəs/ n (traitor and hole) judas, m

Judezmo /dʒu'dezmou/ el judesmo, m

judge /dʒʌdʒ/ n juez, m; (connoisseur) conocedor (-ra) (de); (umpire) arbitrio, m. —vt juzgar; considerar, tener por. —vi servir como juez; juzgar. **judging by,** a juzgar por. **to be a good j. of,** ser buen juez de. **to j. for oneself,** formar su propia opinión

judicature /'dʒudi,keitʃər/ n judicatura, f; (court) juzgado, m

judicial /dʒu'dɪʃəl/ a judicial; legal; (of the mind) juicioso. **j. inquiry,** investigación judicial, f. **j. separation,** separación legal, f

judiciary /dʒu'dɪʃi,eri/ a judicial. —n judicatura, f

judicious /dʒu'dɪʃəs/ a juicioso, prudente

judiciously /dʒu'dɪʃəsli/ adv prudentemente, juiciosamente

judo /'dʒudou/ n yudo, m

judoka /dʒu'dou,ka/ n yudoca, mf

jug /dʒʌg/ n jarro, m; cántaro, m; pote, m. —vt Cul. estofar. —vi (of nightingale) trinar, cantar. **jugged hare,** n liebre en estofado, f

juggle /'dʒʌgəl/ vi hacer juegos malabares. **to j. out of,** (money, etc.) quitar con engaño, estafar. **to j. with,** Fig. (facts, etc.) tergiversar, falsificar; (person) engañar

juggler /'dʒʌglər/ n malabarista, mf; (deceiver) estafador (-ra)

jugular /'dʒʌgyələr/ a Anat. yugular. **j. vein,** yugular, m

juice /dʒus/ n jugo, m; Fig. zumo, m. **digestive j.,** jugo digestivo, m

juiciness /'dʒusinis/ n jugosidad, f; suculencia, f

juicy /'dʒusi/ a jugoso; suculento

jujube /'dʒudʒub/ n pastilla, f

jukebox /'dʒuk,bɒks/ n tocadiscos, vitrola, sinfonola, f

July /dʒu'lai/ n julio, m

jumble /'dʒʌmbəl/ vt mezclar, confundir. —n mezcla confusa, colección miscelánea, confusión, f. **j. sale,** tómbola, f

jump /dʒʌmp/ n salto, m; (in prices, etc.) aumento, m. **at one j.,** de un salto. **high j.,** salto de altura, m. **long j.,** salto de longitud, m. **to be on the j.,** Inf. estar nervioso, tener los nervios en punta

jump /dʒʌmp/ vi saltar; dar un salto; brincar; (of tea-cups, etc.) bailar; (throb) pulsar. —vt saltar; hacer saltar; (a child) brincar; (omit) pasar por alto de, omitir. **The train jumped the rails,** El tren se descarriló. **to j. out of bed,** saltar de la cama. **to j. to the conclusion that...,** darse prisa a concluir que... **to j. about,**

dar saltos, brincar; revolverse, moverse de un lado para otro. **to j. at,** saltar sobre; precipitarse sobre, abalanzarse hacia; (an offer) apresurarse a aceptar; (seize) coger con entusiasmo. **to j. down,** bajar de un salto. **to j. over,** saltar; saltar por encima de. **to j. up,** saltar; (on to a horse, etc.) montar rápidamente; levantarse apresuradamente. **to j. with,** (agree) convenir en, estar conforme con

jumper /'dʒʌmpər/ n saltador (-ra); (sailor's) blusa, f jersey, sweater, m

jumping /'dʒʌmpɪŋ/ n saltos, m pl. —a saltador. **j.-off place,** base avanzada, f; *Fig.* trampolín, m. **j.-pole,** pértiga, f

jumpy /'dʒʌmpi/ a nervioso, agitado

junction /'dʒʌŋkʃən/ n unión, f; (of roads) bifurcación, f; (railway) empalme, m; (connection) conexión, f

juncture /'dʒʌŋktʃər/ n coyuntura, f; momento, m; crisis, f, momento crítico, m; (joint) junta, f

June /dʒun/ n junio, m

jungle /'dʒʌŋɡəl/ n selva, f. **j.-fever,** fiebre de los grandes bosques, f

junior /'dʒunyər/ a joven; hijo; más joven; menos antiguo; subordinado, segundo. —n joven, mf **Carmen is my j. by three years,** Carmen es tres años más joven que yo. **James Thomson, Jr.,** James Thomson, hijo. **the j. school,** los pequeños. **j. partner,** socio menor, m

juniper /'dʒunəpər/ n *Bot.* enebro, m

junk /dʒʌŋk/ n trastos viejos, m pl; (nonsense) patrañas, f pl; *Naut.* junco, m; (salt meat) tasajo, m. **j.-shop,** tienda de trastos viejos, f

junk bond bono-basura, m

juridical /dʒʊ'rɪdɪkəl/ a jurídico

jurisdiction /,dʒʊrɪs'dɪkʃən/ n jurisdicción, f; competencia, f

jurisprudence /,dʒʊrɪs'prudns/ n jurisprudencia, f

jurist /'dʒʊrɪst/ n jurista, legista, mf

juror /'dʒʊrər/ n (miembro del) jurado, m

jury /'dʒʊri/ n jurado, m. **to be on the j.,** formar parte del jurado. **j.-box,** tribuna del jurado, f

juryman /'dʒʊrimən/ n miembro del jurado, m

just /dʒʌst/ a justo; justiciero; exacto; fiel. **Peter the J.,** Pedro el justiciero.

just /dʒʌst/ adv justamente, exactamente;

precisamente; (scarcely) apenas; (almost) casi; (entirely) completamente; (simply) meramente, solamente, tan sólo; (newly) recién (followed by past part.), recientemente. **He only j. missed being run over,** Por poco le atropellan. **It is j. near,** Está muy cerca. **It is j. the same to me,** Me es completamente igual. **J. as he was leaving,** Cuando estaba a punto de marcharse, En el momento de marcharse. **Just as you arrive in Spain, you must...** Nada más llegar a España, tienes que... **That's j. it!** ¡Eso es! ¡Exactamente! **to have j.,** acabar de. **They have j. dined,** Acaban de cenar. **J. as you wish,** Como Vd. quiera. **j. at that moment,** precisamente en aquel momento. **j. by,** muy cerca; al lado. **j. now,** ahora mismo; hace poco; pronto, dentro de poco. **j. yet,** todavía. **They will not come j. yet,** No vendrán todavía. **Just looking** (browser to shopkeeper) Estoy viendo, Estamos viendo

justice /'dʒʌstɪs/ n justicia, f; (judge) juez, m; (magistrate) juez municipal, m. **to bring to j.,** llevar ante el juez (a). **to do j. to,** (a person) hacer justicia (a); (a meal) hacer honor (a). **to do oneself j.,** quedar bien

justifiable /'dʒʌstə,faiəbəl/ a justificable

justifiably /'dʒʌstə,faiəbli/ adv con justicia, justificadamente

justification /,dʒʌstəfɪ'keiʃən/ n justificación, f

justify /'dʒʌstə,fai/ vt justificar, vindicar; (excuse) disculpar; *Print.* justificar. **to be justified (in),** tener derecho (a), tener motivo (para), tener razón (en)

justly /'dʒʌstli/ adv justamente; con justicia; con derecho; con razón; exactamente; debidamente

justness /'dʒʌstnɪs/ n justicia, f; exactitud, f

jute /dʒut/ n yute, m

jut (out) /dʒʌt/ vi salir, proyectar; sobresalir

juvenile /'dʒuvənl/ a juvenil; de la juventud; para la juventud; joven; de niños; para niños. —n joven, mf. **j. court,** tribunal de menores, m. **j. lead,** *Theat.* galancete, galán joven, m. **j. offender,** delincuente infantil, m

juxtapose /'dʒʌkstə,pouz/ vt yuxtaponer

K

k /kei/ n (letter) ka, f

kangaroo /ˌkæŋgəˈruː/ n canguro, m

keel /kiːl/ n quilla, f. —vt carenar. **to k. over,** volcar; caer; Naut. zozobrar

keen /kin/ a (of edges) afilado; agudo; penetrante; vivo; sutil; ardiente; celoso, entusiasta; mordaz; (desirous) ansioso; (of appetite) grande, bueno. **He is a k. tennis player,** Es tenista entusiasta. **Joan has a very k. ear,** Juana tiene un oído muy agudo. **I'm not very k. on apples,** No me gustan mucho las manzanas

keenly /ˈkinli/ adv agudamente; vivamente; (of feeling) hondamente; (of looking) atentamente

keep /kip/ vt guardar; tener; que darse con; retener; conservar; mantener; (a shop, hotel, etc.) dirigir, tener; (a school) ser director de; (a promise, etc.) cumplir; (the law, etc.) observar, guardar; (celebrate) solemnizar; (a secret) guardar; (books, accounts, a house, in step) llevar; (sheep, etc., one's bed) guardar; (a city, etc.) defender; (domestic animals, cars, etc.) tener; (lodge) alojar; (detain) detener; (reserve) reservar; (cause) hacer. **They had kept this room for me,** Me habían reservado este cuarto. **Dorothy has kept the blue dress,** Dorotea se ha quedado con el vestido azul. **The government could not k. order,** El gobierno no sabía mantener el orden. **I did not know how to k. their attention,** No sabía retener su atención. **Carmen kept quiet,** Carmen guardó silencio, Carmen se calló. **Can you k. a secret?** ¿Sabes guardar un secreto? **to k. an appointment,** acudir a una cita. **to k. in repair,** conservar en buen estado. **to k. someone from doing something,** evitar que uno haga algo. **to k. someone waiting,** hacer que espere uno. **to k. something from someone,** ocultar algo de uno. **We were kept at it night and day,** Nos hacían trabajar día y noche. **I always k. it by me,** Lo tengo siempre a mi lado (or conmigo). **to k. away,** alejar; mantener a distancia; no dejar venir. **to k. back,** (a crowd, etc.) detener; cortar el paso (a); no dejar avanzar; (retain) guardar, retener; reservar; (tears, words) reprimir, contener; (evidence, etc.) callar, suprimir. **to k. down,** no dejar subir (a); sujetar; (a nation, etc.) oprimir, subyugar; (emotions) dominar; (prices, expenses) mantener bajo; (check) moderar, reprimir. **to k. in,** (feelings) contener; reprimir; (the house) hacer quedarse en casa, no dejar salir; (imprison) encerrar; (school) hacer quedar en la escuela (a). **to k. off,** alejar; tener a distancia (a); cerrar el paso (a), no dejar avanzar; no andar sobre; no tocar; (a subject) no tratar de, no discutir, no tocar. **K. your hands off!** ¡No toques! **to**

k. on, guardar; retener; (eyes) fijar en, poner en. **to k. out,** no dejar entrar; excluir. **It is difficult to k. him out of trouble,** Es difícil de evitar que se meta en líos. **to k. to,** seguir; limitarse a; adherirse a; **K. to the Left,** «Tome su izquierda», **K. to the right,** «Tome su derecha»; (a path, etc.) seguir por; (one's bed) guardar; (fulfil) cumplir; (oblige) hacer, obligar. **to k. under,** subyugar, oprimir; dominar; controlar. **to k. up,** mantener; (appearances) guardar, conservar; persistir en; (prices) sostener; (in good repair) conservar en buen estado; (go on doing) continuar. **He kept me up late last night,** Anoche me entretuvo hasta muy tarde; Ayer me hizo trasnochar; Anoche me hizo velar. **to k. one's end up,** volver por sí, hacerse fuerte. **to k. up one's spirits,** no desanimarse

keep /kip/ vi quedar; (be) estar; (continue) seguir, continuar; mantenerse; (at home, etc.) quedarse, permanecer; (be accustomed) acostumbrar, soler; (persist) perseverar; (of food) conservarse fresco. **How is he keeping?** ¿Cómo está? **to k. in with someone,** cultivar a alguien. **to k. up with the times,** mantenerse al corriente. **to k. at,** seguir; persistir; perseverar; (pester) importunar. **John keeps at it,** Juan trabaja sin descansar. **to k. away,** mantenerse apartado; mantenerse a distancia; no acudir. **to k. back,** hacerse a un lado, apartarse, alejarse. **to k. down,** quedarse tumbado; seguir acurrucado; no levantarse; esconderse. **to k. from,** (doing something) guardarse de. **to k. off,** mantenerse a distancia. **If the storm keeps off,** Si no estalla una tempestad. **If the rain keeps off,** Si no empieza a llover, Si no hay lluvia. **to k. on,** continuar; seguir. **to k. straight on,** seguir derecho. **I'm tired, but I still k. on,** Estoy cansado, pero sigo trabajando. **to k. out,** quedarse fuera. **to k. out of,** (quarrels, trouble, etc.) no meterse en, evitar. **to k. out of sight,** no dejarse ver, no mostrarse, mantenerse oculto. **to k. together,** quedarse juntos; reunirse

keep /kip/ n (of a castle) mazmorra, f; (maintenance) subsistencia, f; comida, f. **for keeps,** para siempre jamás

keeper /ˈkipər/ n guarda, mf; (in a park, zoo, of a lunatic) guardián, m; (of a museum, etc.) director, m; (of animals) criador (-ra); (gamekeeper) guardabosque, m; (of a boardinghouse, shop, etc.) dueño (-ña); (of accounts, books) tenedor, m. **Am I my brother's k.?** ¿Soy yo responsable por mi hermano?

keeping /ˈkipiŋ/ n guarda, f; conservación, f; protección, f; (of a rule) observación, f; (of an anniversary, etc.) celebración, f; (of a person) mantenimiento, m. **in k. with,** en armonía con; de acuerdo con. **out of k. with,** en desacuerdo con. **to be in safe k.,** estar en buenas manos;

estar en un lugar seguro. **k. back,** retención, *f*

keepsake /'kip,seik/ *n* recuerdo, *m*

keg /kɛg/ *n* barrilete, *m*

ken /kɛn/ *n* alcance de la vista, *m;* vista, *f;* comprensión, *f*

kennel /'kɛnl/ *n* (of a dog) perrera, *f;* (of hounds) jauría, *f;* (dwelling) cuchitril, *m;* (gutter) arroyo, *m.* **k. man,** perrero, *m*

kerchief /'kɔrtʃif/ *n* pañuelo, *m;* pañoleta, *f.* **brightly-colored k.,** pañuelo de hierbas, *m*

kernel /'kɔrnl/ *n* almendra, semilla, *f; Fig.* meollo, *m,* esencia, *f*

kerosene /'kɛrə,sin/ *n* petróleo de lámpara, *m;* kerosén, *m*

ketchup /'kɛtʃəp/ *n* salsa de tomate y setas, *f*

kettle /'kɛtl/ *n* caldero, *m.* **pretty k. of fish,** olla de grillos, *f.* **k.-drum,** timbal, *m.* **k.-drum player,** timbalero, *m*

key /ki/ *n* llave, *f; (Fig. Archit. Mus.)* clave, *f;* (tone) tono, *m;* (of a piano, typewriter, etc.) tecla, *f; Mech.* chaveta, *f;* (of a wind instrument) pistón, *m;* (winged fruit) sámara, *f; Elec.* conmutador, *m.* **major (minor) key,** tono mayor (menor), *m.* **latch-key,** llave de la puerta, *f;* (Yale) llavín, *m.* **master key,** llave maestra, *f.* **skeleton key,** ganzúa, *f.* **He is all keyed up,** Tiene los nervios en punta. **key industry,** industria clave, *f.* **key man,** hombre indispensable, *m.* **key point,** punto estratégico, *m.* **key-ring,** llavero, *m.* **key signature,** *Mus.* clave, *f.* **key word,** palabra clave, *f*

keyboard /'ki,bɔrd/ *n* teclado, *m*

keyhole /'ki,houl/ *n* ojo de la cerradura, *m.* **through the k.,** por el ojo de la cerradura

keynote /'ki,nout/ *n* Mus. tónica, *f; Fig.* piedra clave, idea fundamental, *f*

khaki /'kæki/ *n* caqui, *m*

kick /kɪk/ *vt* dar un puntapié (a); golpear; (a goal) chutar. —*vi* (of horses, etc.) dar coces, cocear; (of guns) recular. to **k. one's heels,** hacer tiempo. **to kick the bucket,** palmarla. to **k. up a row,** hacer un ruido de mil diablos; (quarrel) armar camorra. **to k. about,** dar patadas (a). **to k. away,** quitar con el pie; lanzar con el pie. to **k. off,** quitar con el pie; lanzar; sacudirse. **k.-off,** *n* golpe de salida, puntapié inicial, saque, *m.* **to k. out,** echar a puntapiés

kick /kɪk/ *n* puntapié, *m;* golpe, *m;* coz, *f;* (of guns) culatazo, *m.* **free k.,** golpe franco, *m*

kicking /'kɪkɪŋ/ *n* coces, *f pl;* acoceamiento, *m;* pataleo, *m;* golpeamiento, *m*

kid /kɪd/ *n* cabrito, *m,* chivo (-va); carne de cabrito, *f;* (leather) cabritilla, *f; Inf.* crío, *m.* **kid gloves,** guantes de cabritilla, *m pl*

kidnap /'kɪdnæp/ *vt* secuestrar

kidnapper /'kɪdnæpər/ *n* secuestrador (-ra); ladrón (-ona) de niños

kidnapping /'kɪdnæpɪŋ/ *n* secuestro, *m*

kidney /'kɪdni/ *n* riñón, *m; Fig.* especie, índole, *f.* **k.-bean,** (plant) judía, *f;* (fruit) habichuela, judía, *f,* fréjol, *m*

Kidron /'kɪdrən/ Cedrón, *m*

kill /kɪl/ *vt* matar; destruir; suprimir. to **k. off,** exterminar. **to k. time,** entretener el tiempo, pasarse las horas muertas. to **k. two birds with one stone,** matar dos pájaros de un tiro. **k.-joy,** aguafiestas, *mf*

killer /'kɪlər/ *n* matador (-ra); (murderer) asesino, *m*

killing /'kɪlɪŋ/ *n* matanza, *f;* (murder) asesinato, *m.* —*a* matador; destructivo; (comic) cómico; ridículo, absurdo; (ravishing) irresistible

kiln /kɪl/ *n* horno de cerámica, horno, *m*

kilo /'kilou/ *n* kilo, *m*

kilogram /'kɪlə,græm/ *n* kilogramo, *m*

kilometer /kɪ'lɒmɪtər/ *n* kilómetro, *m*

kilowatt /'kɪlə,wɒt/ *n* Elec. kilovatio, *m*

kilt /kɪlt/ *n* enagüillas, *f pl*

kimono /kə'mounə/ *n* quimono, *m*

kin /kɪn/ *n* parientes, *m pl;* familia, *f;* clase, especie, *f.* **the next of kin,** los parientes próximos, la familia

kind /kaɪnd/ *n* género, *m,* clase, *f;* especie, *f; Inf.* tipo, *m.* **He is a queer k. of person,** Es un tipo muy raro. **What k. of cloth is it?** ¿Qué clase de tela es? **Nothing of the k!** ¡Nada de eso! **payment in k.,** pago en especie, *m*

kind /kaɪnd/ *a* bondadoso, bueno; cariñoso, tierno; amable; favorable, propicio. **Will you be so k. as to...** Tenga Vd. la bondad de... **With k. regards,** Con un saludo afectuoso. **You have been very k. to her,** Vd. ha sido muy bueno para ella. **k.-hearted,** bondadoso. **k.-heartedness,** bondad, benevolencia, *f*

kindergarten /'kɪndər,gɑrtn/ *n* jardín de la infancia, kindergarten, *m*

kindle /'kɪndl/ *vt* encender; hacer arder; *Fig.* avivar. —*vi* prender, empezar a arder; encenderse; *Fig.* inflamarse

kindling /'kɪndlɪŋ/ *n* encendimiento (del fuego), *m;* (wood) leña menuda, *f*

kindly /'kaɪndli/ *a* bondadoso; bueno; benévolo; propicio, favorable; (of climate) benigno. —*adv* con bondad, bondadosamente; fácilmente. **K. sit down,** Haga el favor de sentarse

kindness /'kaɪndnɪs/ *n* bondad, *f;* benevolencia, *f;* amabilidad, *f;* cariño, *m;* favor, *m,* atención, *f*

kindred /'kɪndrɪd/ *n* parentesco, *m;* parientes, *m pl;* familia, *f;* afinidad, *f,* a emparentado; hermano

king /kɪŋ/ *n* (ruler, important person, chess, cards) rey, *m;* (in draughts) dama, *f.* **king's evil,** escrófula, *f.* **k.-bolt,** perno real, *m.* **k.-craft,** arte de reinar, *m,* or *f.* **k.-cup,** *Bot.* botón de oro, *m.* **K.-of-Arms,** rey de armas, *m.* **k.-post,** pendolón, *m*

kingdom /'kɪŋdəm/ *n* reino, *m.* **animal k.,** reino animal, *m*

kink /kɪŋk/ *n* nudo, *m;* pliegue, *m;* (curl) rizo, *m; Fig.* peculiaridad, *f*

kinsfolk /'kɪnz,fouk/ n parientes, m pl, familia, f

kinship /'kɪnʃɪp/ n parentesco, m; afinidad, f

kinsman /'kɪnzmən/ n pariente, deudo, m

kinswoman /'kɪnz,wʊmən/ n parienta, f

kiosk /'kiɒsk/ n quiosco, m

kipper /'kɪpər/ n arenque ahumado, m. —vt ahumar

kiss /kɪs/ n beso, m; (in billiards) pelo, m. —vt besar; dar un beso (a); (of billiard balls) tocar. **to k. each other**, besarse. **k.-curl**, rizo de la sien, m, sortijilla, f

kit /kɪt/ n (tub) cubo, m; (for tools, etc.) cajita, caja, f; (soldier's) equipo, m. **kit-bag**, mochila, f

kitchen /'kɪtʃən/ n cocina, f. **k.-boy**, pinche (de cocina), m. **k.-garden**, huerta, f. **k.-maid**, fregona, f. **k.-range**, cocina económica, f. **k.-sink**, fregadero, m. **k.-stove**, horno de cocina, m. **k. utensils**, batería de cocina, f

kitchenette /,kɪtʃə'nɛt/ n cocinilla, f

kite /kait/ n Ornith. milano, m; cometa, pájara, f. **to fly a k.**, hacer volar una cometa. **box-k.**, cometa celular, f

kith and kin /kɪθ/ n pl parientes y amigos, m pl

kitten /'kɪtn/ n gatito (-ta). —vi (of a cat) parir

kitty /'kɪti/ n michito, m; (in card games) platillo, m

kleptomania /,klɛptə'meiniə/ n cleptomanía, f

kleptomaniac /,klɛptə'meiniæk/ a cleptómano. —n cleptómano (-na)

knack /næk/ n destreza, f; talento, m; (trick) truco, m

knapsack /'næp,sæk/ n mochila, f; Mil. alforja, f

knave /neiv/ n bellaco, truhán, tunante, m; (at cards) sota, f

knavish /'neiviʃ/ a de bribón; taimado, truhanesco

knead /nid/ vt amasar; (massage) sobar; Fig. formar

kneading /'nidɪŋ/ n amasijo, m; (massaging) soba, f. **k.-trough**, amasadera artesa f

knee /ni/ n rodilla, f; Fig. ángulo, codillo, m. **on bended k.**, de hinojos. **on one's knees**, de rodillas, arrodillado. **to go down on one's knees**, arrodillarse, ponerse de rodillas. **k.-breeches**, calzón corto, m; calzón ceñido, m; (Elizabethan) gregüescos, m pl. **k.-cap**, rótula, f. **k.-deep**, hasta las rodillas. **k.-joint**, articulación de la rodilla, f; Mech. junta de codillo, f. **k.-pad**, rodillera, f

kneel (down) /nil/ vi arrodillarse, hincarse de rodillas, ponerse de rodillas

kneeling /'nilɪŋ/ a arrodillado, de rodillas

knell /nɛl/ n toque de difuntos, tañido fúnebre, m; toque de campanas, m; Fig. muerte, f. —vi tocar a muerto. —vt Fig. anunciar, presagiar

knickerbockers /'nɪkər,bɒkərz/ n pl bragas, f pl; calzón corto, m; (women's) pantalones, m pl

knickknack /'nɪk,næk/ n chuchería, f

knife /naif/ n cuchillo, m. **to have one's k. in someone**, tener enemiga (a), querer mal (a). **war to the k.**, guerra a muerte, f. **k.-edge**, filo de cuchillo, m; fiel de soporte, m. **k. grinder**, amolador, m. **k.-handle**, mango de cuchillo, m. **k. thrust**, cuchillada, f

knight /nait/ n caballero, m; (chess) caballo, m. —vt armar caballero, calzar la espuela; (in modern usage) dar el título de caballero. **untried k.**, caballero novel, m. **k. commander**, comendador, m. **k.-errant**, caballero andante, m. **k.-errantry**, caballería andante, f. **Knight of Labor**, Caballero del Trabajo m. **k. of the rueful countenance**, el caballero de la triste figura

knit /nit/ vt and vi hacer calceta, hacer media; juntar; ligar; unir. **Isabel is knitting me a jumper**, Isabel me está haciendo un jersey de punto de media. **to k. one's brows**, fruncir el ceño

knitted /'nitid/ a de punto. **k. goods**, géneros de punto, m pl

knitter /'nitər/ n calcetero (-ra); (machine) máquina de hacer calceta, f

knitting /'nitɪŋ/ n acción de hacer calceta, f; trabajo de punto, m, labor de calceta, f; unión, f. **k.-machine**, máquina de hacer calceta, f. **k.-needle**, aguja de media, aguja de hacer calceta, f

knob /nɒb/ n protuberancia, f; (of a door, etc.) perilla, borlita, f; (ornamental) bellota, f; (of sugar) terrón, m; (of a stick) puño, m

knock /nɒk/ n golpe, m; choque, m; (with a knocker) aldabada, f

knock /nɒk/ vt golpear; chocar (contra). —vi llamar a la puerta; (of an engine) picar. **to k. one's head against**, chocar con la cabeza contra, dar con la cabeza contra. **to k. about**, vt pegar; aporrear. —vi viajar; vagar; rodar; callejear. **to k. against**, golpear contra; chocar contra. **to k. down**, derribar; (of vehicles) atropellar; (houses, etc.) demoler; (an argument, etc.) destruir; (a tender, etc.) rebajar; (of an auctioneer) rematar al mejor postor. **to k. in**, (nails, etc.) clavar. **to k. into one another**, toparse. **to k. off**, hacer caer; sacudir; quitar; (from price) descontar; (from speed, etc.) reducir; (finish) terminar pronto; (runs in cricket) hacer. **to k. out**, (remove) quitar; (boxing) dejar fuera de combate, noquear; (Fig. stun) atontar; (an idea, etc.) bosquejar. **to k. over**, volcar. **to k. up**, hacer saltar; (call) llamar; (runs at cricket) hacer; (tire) agotar, rendir; (building) construir toscamente. **to k. up against**, chocar contra; tropezar con. **k.-kneed**, a patiabierto. **k.-out**, "knock-out," m

knoll /noul/ n altillo, otero, m

knot /nɒt/ n nudo, m; (bow) lazo, m; (of

hair) moño, *m; Naut.* nudo, *m*, milla náutica, *f;* (of people) corrillo, grupo, *m;* (on timber) nudo, *m.* —*vt* anudar. —*vi* hacer nudos; enmarañarse. **to tie a k.,** hacer un nudo

knotty /'nɒti/ *a* nudoso; *Fig.* intrincado, difícil, complicado. **a k. problem,** problema espinoso

know /nou/ *vt* conocer; saber; (understand) comprender; (recognize) reconocer. **I k. her very well by sight,** La conozco muy bien de vista. **John knows Latin,** Juan sabe latín. **How can I k.?** ¿Cómo lo voy a saber yo? **I knew you at once,** Te reconocí en seguida. **They always k. best,** Siempre tienen razón. **Did you k. about Philip?** ¿Has oído lo de Felipe? **to be in the k.,** estar bien informado, saber de buena tinta. **to get to k.,** (a person) llegar a conocer, trabar amistad con. **to make known,** dar a conocer; manifestar. **Who knows?** ¿Quién sabe? **to k. by heart,** saber de coro. **to k. how,** (to do something) saber. **to k. oneself,** conocerse a sí mismo. **k.-it-all,** sabelotodo, *mf,* marisabidilla, *f*

knowing /'nouɪŋ/ *a* inteligente; malicioso; (of animals) sabio. **There is no k.,**

No hay modo de saberlo. **worth k.,** digno de saberse

knowingly /'nouɪŋli/ *adv* a sabiendas, de intento; conscientemente; (cleverly) hábilmente; (with look, etc.) de un aire malicioso

knowledge /'nɒlɪdʒ/ *n* conocimiento, *m.* **To the best of my k. the book does not exist,** El libro no existe que yo sepa. **He has a thorough k. of...,** Conoce a fondo... **lack of k.,** ignorancia, *f.* **He did it without my k.,** Lo hizo sin que lo supiera yo. **It is a matter of common k. that...** Es notorio que...

knowledgeable /'nɒlɪdʒəbəl/ *a* sabedor

knuckle /'nʌkəl/ *n* (of a finger) nudillo, *m,* articulación del dedo, *f;* (of meat) jarrete, *m.* **He knuckled down to his work,** Se puso a trabajar con ahínco. **to k. under,** someterse. **k.-duster,** rompecabezas, *m*

Korea /kə'riə/ Corea, *f*

kosher /'kouʃər/ *a* cosher; (slang) genuino

kowtow /'kau'tau/ *vi* saludar humildemente; *Fig.* bajar la cerviz

kudos /'kudouz/ *n* prestigio, *m,* gloria, *f*

L

l /ɛl/ n (letter) ele, f
la /lɑ/ n Mus. la, m
label /'leibəl/ n etiqueta, (on a garment), rótula, m, (on a can), f; (on a museum specimen, etc.) letrero, m; Fig. calificación, f. —vt poner etiqueta en; marcar, rotular; Fig. calificar, designar, clasificar
labor /'leibər/ n trabajo, m; labor, f; fatiga, pena, f; clase obrera, f; (manual workers) mano de obra, f; (effort) esfuerzo, m; (of childbirth) dolores de parto, m pl. —vi trabajar; (strive) esforzarse, afanarse; (struggle) forcejear, luchar; (try) procurar, tratar de; avanzar con dificultad; (in childbirth) estar de parto. —vt elaborar; pulir, perfeccionar. **to l. under,** sufrir; tener que luchar contra. **hard l.,** trabajo arduo, m; Law. trabajos forzosos, m pl, presidio, m. **Ministry of L.,** Ministerio de Trabajo, m. **to be in l.,** estar de parto. **to l. in vain,** trabajar en balde, arar en el mar. **to l. under a delusion,** estar en el error, estar equivocado. **L. Exchange,** Bolsa de Trabajo, f. **l. leader,** dirigente sindical, m. **L. party,** partido laborista, partido obrero, m. **l. question,** cuestión obrera, f; (domestic) problema del servicio, m. **l.-saving,** a que ahorra trabajo. **l. union,** sindicato, m
laboratory /'læbrə,tɔri/ n laboratorio, m
labored /'leibərd/ a (of style) premioso, artificial; forzado; (of breathing) fatigoso; (slow) torpe, lento
laborer /'leibərər/ n obrero, m; (on the land) labrador, labriego, m; (on the roads, etc.) peón, m; (by the day) jornalero, m
laborious /ləˈbɔriəs/ a laborioso; arduo, difícil, penoso
labyrinth /'læbərɪnθ/ n laberinto, m
lace /leɪs/ n (of shoes, corsets, etc.) cordón, m; (tape) cinta, f; encaje, m; (narrow, for trimming) puntilla, f; (of gold or silver) galón, m. —vt and vi (shoes, etc.) atarse los cordones; (trim) guarnecer con encajes, etc.; Fig. ornar; (a drink) echar (coñac, etc.) en. **blond l.,** blonda, f. **gold l.,** galón de oro, m. **point l.,** encaje de aguja, m. **l. curtain,** cortina de encaje, f; (of net) visillo, m. **l. maker** or **seller,** encajera, f. **l. making,** obra de encaje, f. **l.-pillow,** almohadilla para encajes, f. **l. shoes,** zapatos con cordones, m pl
lacerate /'læsə,reɪt/ vt lacerar
lack /læk/ n falta, f. **l. of evidence,** falta de pruebas, f; carestía, escasez, f; (absence) ausencia, f; (need) necesidad, f. —vt carecer de; no tener; necesitar. —vi hacer falta; necesitarse. **to l. confidence in oneself,** no tener confianza en sí mismo, carecer de confianza en sí mismo. **l.-luster,** (of eyes) apagado, mortecino. **l. of evidence,** falta de pruebas, f
lackadaisical /ˌlækəˈdeɪzɪkəl/ a lánguido;

indiferente; (dreamy) ensimismado, distraído
lackey /'læki/ n lacayo, m
laconic /ləˈkɒnɪk/ a lacónico
lacquer /'lækər/ n laca, f, vt dar laca (a), barnizar con laca. **gold l.,** sisa dorada, f. **l. work,** laca, f
lactate /'lækteɪt/ n lactato, m, vi lactar
lactose /'læktous/ n lactosa, f
lacuna /ləˈkyunə/ n laguna, f
lacy /'leɪsi/ a de encaje; parecido a encaje; Fig. transparente, etéreo
lad /læd/ n muchacho, joven, mozalbete, m; zagal, m; (stable, etc.) mozo, m. **He's some l.!** ¡Qué tío que es! **l. of the village,** chulo, m
ladder /'lædər/ n escalera de mano, f; Naut. escala, f; (in a stocking, etc.) carrera, f. **companion l.,** escala de toldilla, f. **to l. one's stocking,** escurrirse un punto de las medias
Ladies and gentlemen /'leidiz/ n pl Señoras y señores, Señoras y caballeros. **ladies' man,** hombre de salón, Perico entre ellas, mujeriego, m
ladle /'leidl/ n cucharón, cazo, m. —vt servir con cucharón; (a boat) achicar; Inf. distribuir, repartir
lady /'leidi/ n dama, f; señora, f; (English title) milady, f; (woman) mujer, f. **to be a l.,** ser una señora. **leading l.,** Theat. dama primera, f. **Our L.,** Nuestra Señora. **young l.,** señorita, f; Inf. novia, f. **lady's maid,** doncella, f. **l. of the house,** señora de la casa, f. **l. bug,** Ent. catalina mariquita, vaca de San Antonio, f. **L. Chapel,** capilla de la Virgen, f. **L. Day,** día de la Anunciación (de Nuestra Señora), m. **l.-help,** asistenta, f. **l.-in-waiting,** dama de servicio, f. **l.-killer,** ladrón de corazones, castigador, tenorio, m. **l.-love,** querida, amada, f. **l. mayoress,** alcaldesa, f
ladylike /'leidi,laik/ a de dama; elegante; distinguido; bien educado; delicado; (of men) afeminado
lag /læg/ vt recubrir; aislar. —vi retrasarse; quedarse atrás; ir (or andar) despacio; rezagarse; Naut. roncear. —n retraso, m; Mech. retardación de movimiento, f
laggard /'lægərd/ n holgazán (-ana), haragán (-ana)
lagoon /ləˈgun/ n laguna, f
laid /leɪd/ past part of verb **to lay. l. up,** (ill) enfermo; Naut. inactivo; (of cars, etc.) fuera de circulación
lair /lɛər/ n cubil, m; guarida, madriguera, f
laity /'leɪɪti/ n legos, m pl
lake /leɪk/ n lago, m; (pigment) laca, f. **small l.,** laguna, f. **l. dwelling,** vivienda palustre, f
lamb /læm/ n cordero (-ra). —vi parir corderos. **lamb's wool,** lana de cordero. f
lambskin /'læm,skɪn/ n corderina, piel de cordero, f
lame /leɪm/ a estropeado, lisiado; (in the

feet) cojo; (of meter) que cojea, malo; (of arguments) poco convincente; frívolo, flojo. —*vt* lisiar; hacer cojo. **l. excuse,** pretexto frívolo. **to be l.,** (in the feet) (permanently) ser cojo; (temporarily) estar cojo

lament /lə'mɛnt/ *n* lamento, *m;* queja, lamentación, *f.* —*vi* lamentarse; quejarse. —*vt* lamentar, deplorar, llorar

lamentable /lə'mɛntəbəl/ *a* lamentable, deplorable; lastimero

lamentation /,læmən'teiʃən/ *n* lamentación, *f,* lamento, *m.* **Book of Lamentations,** Libro de los lamentos, *m*

lamenting /lə'mɛntɪŋ/ *n* lamentación, *f*

laminate /'læmə,neit/ *a* laminado, laminar. —*vt* laminar

lamp /læmp/ *n* lámpara, *f;* (on vehicles, trains, ships and in the street) farol, *m;* luz, *f;* (oil) candil, *m,* lámpara de aceite, *f.* **safety-l.,** lámpara de seguridad, lámpara de los mineros, *f.* **street l.,** farol (de las calles), *m.* **l.-black,** negro de humo, *m.* **l.-chimney,** tubo de una lámpara, *m.* **l. factory or shop,** lamparería, *f.* **l.-holder,** portalámpara, *f.* **l.-lighter,** farolero, lamparero, *m.* **l.-post,** farola, *f.* **l.-shade,** pantalla (de lámpara,) *f.* **l. stand,** pie de lámpara, *m*

lamplight /'læmp,lait/ *n* luz de la lámpara, *f;* luz artificial, *f.* **in the l.,** a la luz de la lámpara; en luz artificial

lampoon /læm'pun/ *n* pasquinada, *f,* pasquín, *m, vt* pasquinar, satirizar

lance /læns/ *n* lanza, *f;* (soldier) lancero, *m.* —*vt* alancear; *Med.* lancinar. **l. in rest,** lanza en ristre, *f.* **l. thrust,** lanzada, *f.* **l.-corporal,** soldado de primera clase, *m*

land /lænd/ *n* tierra, *f;* terreno, *m;* (country) país, *m;* (region) región, *f;* territorio, *m;* (estate) bienes raíces, *m pl,* tierras, fincas, *f pl.* —*vt* desembarcar; echar en tierra; (*Fig.* place) poner; *Inf.* dejar plantado (con); (obtain) obtener; (a fish) sacar del agua; (a blow) dar (un golpe); (leave) dejar. —*vi* desembarcar; saltar en tierra; (of a plane) aterrizar; (arrive) llegar; (fall) caer. **cultivated l.,** tierras cultivadas, *f pl.* **dry l.,** (not sea) tierra firme, *f.* **native l.,** patria, *f;* suelo natal, *m.* **on l.,** en tierra. **to see how the l. lies,** *Fig.* tantear el terreno. **l. of milk and honey,** jauja, *f,* paraíso, *m.* **l. of promise,** tierra de promisión, *f.* **l. agent,** procurador de fincas, *m.* **l. breeze,** brisa de tierra, *f.* **l. forces,** fuerzas terrestres, *f pl.* **l. law,** leyes agrarias, *f pl.* **l.-locked,** cercado de tierra, mediterráneo **l.-lubber,** marinero de agua dulce, *m.* **l. mine,** mina terrestre, *f.* **l. surveying,** agrimensura, *f.* **l. surveyor,** agrimensor, *m.* **l. tax,** contribución territorial, *f*

landed /'lændid/ *a* hacendado. **l. gentry,** hacendados, terratenientes, *m pl.* **l. property,** bienes raíces, *m pl*

landing /'lændɪŋ/ *n* desembarque, desembarco, *m;* (landing place) desembar-

cadero, *m; Aer.* aterrizaje, *m;* (of steps) descanso, rellano, *m,* mesa, mesilla, *f.* **forced l.,** aterrizaje forzoso, *m.* **l. certificate,** *Com.* tornaguía, *f.* **l. craft,** barcaza de desembarco, *f.* **l. field,** campo de aterrizaje, *m,* pista de vuelo, *f.* **l.-net,** salabardo, *m.* **l. party,** trozo de abordaje, *m.* **l. signal,** *Aer.* señal de aterrizaje, *f.* **l. stage,** desembarcadero, *m;* (jetty) atracadero, *m*

landlady /'lænd,leidi/ *n* patrona, huéspeda, *f*

landlord /'lænd,lord/ *n* (of houses, land) propietario, *m;* hotelero, patrón, *m*

landmark /'lænd,mɑrk/ *n* (of a hill or mountain) punto destacado, *m;* lugar conocido, *m;* característica, *f; Fig.* monumento, *m*

landowner /'lænd,ounər/ *n* hacendado, terrateniente, *m*

landscape /'lænd,skeip/ *n* paisaje, *m;* perspectiva, *f.* **l. gardener,** arquitecto de jardines, *m.* **l. painter,** paisajista, *mf*

landslide /'lænd,slaid/ *n* desprendimiento de tierras, *m; Fig.* cambio brusco de la opinión pública, *m*

lane /lein/ *n* vereda, senda, *f;* (of traffic) carril, *m,* (Argentina, Spain), línea, *f*

language /'læŋgwɪdʒ/ *n* lenguaje, *m;* lengua, *f,* idioma, *m.* **modern l.,** lengua viva, *f.* **strong l.,** palabras mayores, *f pl*

languid /'læŋgwid/ *a* lánguido

languish /'læŋgwɪʃ/ *vi* languidecer

languor /'læŋgər/ *n* languidez, *f*

languorous /'læŋgərəs/ *a* lánguido

lank /læŋk/ *a* flaco, descarnado, alto y delgado; (of hair) lacio

lanky /'læŋki/ *a* larguirucho, descarnado

lantern /'læntərn/ *n* linterna, *f;* (*Naut.* and of a lighthouse) farol, *m; Archit.* linterna, *f;* (small) farolillo, *m.* **dark l.,** linterna sorda, *f.* **magic l.,** linterna mágica, *f.* **l.-jawed,** carilargo. **l. maker,** farolero, *m.* **l. slide,** diapositiva, *f*

lap /læp/ *n* regazo, *m;* falda, *f;* (knees) rodillas, *f pl;* (lick) lamedura, *f;* (of water) murmurio, susurro, *m;* (in a race) vuelta, *f;* (stage) etapa, *f.* —*vt* (wrap) envolver; (cover) cubrir; (fold) plegar; (lick) lamer; (swallow) tragar. —*vi* (overlap) traslaparse; estar replegado; (lick) lamer; (of water) murmurar, susurrar, besar. **l.-dog,** perro de faldas, perro faldero, *m*

lapel /lə'pɛl/ *n* solapa, *f*

lapidary /'læpi,dɛri/ *a* lapidario

lapping /'læpɪŋ/ *n* (licking) lamedura, *f;* (of water) murmurio, susurro, chapaleteo, *m*

lapse /læps/ *n* lapso, *m;* (fault) desliz, *m,* falta, *f;* (of time) transcurso, intervalo, *m;* (fall) caída, *f; Law.* termination) caducidad, *f.* **lapse (into),** *vi* caer (en), recaer (en), reincidir (en); volver a, caer de nuevo (en); (*Law.* cease) caducar; (*Law.* pass to) pasar (a); dejar de existir, desaparecer. **after the l. of three days,** después de tres días, al cabo de tres días.

with the l. of years, en el transcurso de los años

larceny /ˈlɑrsəni/ n latrocinio, m

lard /lɑrd/ n manteca, f; lardo, m. —vt Cul. lardear, mechar; Fig. sembrar (con), adornar (con)

large /lɑrdʒ/ a grande; grueso; amplio; vasto, extenso; (wide) ancho; considerable; (in number) numeroso; (main, chief) principal; liberal; magnánimo. **at l.,** en libertad, suelto. **on the l. side,** algo grande. **l.-headed,** cabezudo. **l.-hearted,** que tiene un gran corazón, magnánimo. **l. mouth,** boca grande, boca rasgada, f. **l.-nosed,** narigudo. **l. scale,** en gran escala. **l.-sized,** de gran tamaño. **l.-toothed,** dentudo, que tiene dientes grandes. **l. type,** letras grandes, f pl

largely /ˈlɑrdʒli/ adv grandemente; en gran manera; en so mayor parte, considerablemente; muy; ampliamente; liberaldhmente; extensamente

largeness /ˈlɑrdʒnɪs/ n gran tamaño, m; (of persons) gran talle, m; amplitud, f; vastedad, extensión, f; (width) anchura, f; liberalidad, f; (generosity) magnanimidad, f; grandeza de ánimo, f

larger /ˈlɑrdʒər/ a compar más grande, etc. See **large.** **to grow l.,** crecer, aumentarse. **to make l.,** hacer más grande; aumentar

largesse /lɑrˈdʒɛs/ n liberalidad, f

lariat /ˈlæriət/ n lazo, m

lark /lɑrk/ n alondra, f; (spree) juerga, f; (joke) risa, f. **to rise with the l.,** levantarse con las gallinas

larva /ˈlɑrvə/ n larva, f

laryngitis /ˌlærənˈdʒaitɪs/ n laringitis, f

larynx /ˈlærɪŋks/ n laringe, f

lascivious /ləˈsɪviəs/ a lascivo, lujurioso

lash /læʃ/ n (thong) tralla, f; (whip) látigo, m; (blow) latigazo, m; azote, m; (of the eye) pestaña, f. —vt dar latigazos (a); azotar; (of waves) romper contra; (of hall, rain) azotar; (excite) provocar; (the tail) agitar (la cola); (scold) fustigar; (fasten) sujetar, atar; Naut. trincar. **to l. out,** (of horses, etc.) dar coces; (in words) prorrumpir (en)

lass /læs/ n muchacha, chica, mozuela, f; zagala, f; niña, f

lassitude /ˈlæsɪˌtud/ n lasitud, f

lasso /ˈlæsoʊ/ n lazo, m, mangana, f, vt lazar, manganear

last /læst/ vi durar; subsistir, conservarse; continuar

last /læst/ a último; (with month, week, etc.) pasado; (supreme) extremo, (el) mayor. —adv al fin; finalmente; por último; después de todos; por última vez; la última vez. —n el, m, (f, la) último (-ma); los últimos, m pl, (f pl, las últimas); (end) fin, m; (for shoes) horma, f. **at l.,** en fin; por fin, a la postre. **at the l. moment,** a última hora. **I have not been there these l. five years,** Hace cinco años que no voy allá. **John spoke l.,** Juan habló el último. **She came at l.,** Por

fin llegó. **to the l.,** hasta el fin. **l. but one,** penúltimo (-ma). **l. hope,** última esperanza, f; último recurso, m. **l. kick,** Inf. último suspiro, m. **l. night,** anoche. **l. week,** la semana pasada

lasting /ˈlæstɪŋ/ a permanente, perdurable; duradero; constante; (of colours) sólido

lastly /ˈlæstli/ adv en conclusión, por fin, finalmente, por último

latch /lætʃ/ n pestillo, m, vt cerrar con pestillo. **l.-key,** llave de la puerta, f; (Yale) llavín, m

late /leit/ a tarde; tardío; (advanced) avanzado; (last) último; reciente; (dead) difunto; (former) antiguo, ex...; (new) nuevo. —adv tarde. **Better l. than never,** Más vale tarde que nunca. **Helen arrived l.,** Elena llegó tarde. **The train arrived five minutes l.,** El tren llegó con cinco minutos de retraso. **He keeps l. hours,** Se acuesta muy tarde, Se acuesta a las altas horas de la noche (Inf. a las tantas). **of l.,** últimamente. **to grow l.,** hacerse tarde. **l.-eighteenth-century poetry,** la poesía de fines del siglo diez y ocho; llorado, malogrado (e.g. the l. Mrs. Smith, la llorada Sra. Smith, la malograda Sra. Smith);

lately /ˈleitli/ adv recientemente; últimamente, hace poco

lateness /ˈleitnɪs/ n lo tarde; lo avanzado; retraso, m. **the l. of the hour,** la hora avanzada

latent /ˈleitn̩t/ a latente

later /ˈleitər/ a más tarde; posterior; más reciente. —adv más tarde; (afterwards) luego, después; posteriormente. **sooner or l.,** tarde o temprano. **l. on,** más tarde

lateral /ˈlætərəl/ a lateral, ladero

late registration n matrícula tardía, f

latest /ˈleitɪst/ a and adv superl último; más reciente, etc. See **late.** **at the l.,** a lo más tarde, a más tardar. **l. fashion,** última moda, f. **l. news,** últimas noticias, f pl; novedad, f

latex /ˈleitɛks/ n (Bot. Chem.) látex, m

lath /læθ/ n listón, m. **to be as thin as a l.,** no tener más que el pellejo, estar en los huesos

lathe /leið/ n torno, m

lather /ˈlæðər/ n espuma de jabón, f, jabonaduras, f pl; (of sweat) espuma, f. —vt enjabonar; Inf. zurrar. —vi hacer espuma

Latin /ˈlætn̩/ n latín, m, a latino. **Low L.,** bajo latín, m. **L.-American,** a latinoamericano. —n latinoamericano (-na)

latitude /ˈlætɪˌtud/ n latitud, f; libertad, f

latrine /ləˈtrin/ n letrina, f

latter /ˈlætər/ a más reciente; último, posterior; moderno. **the l.,** éste, m; ésta, f; esto, neut; éstos, m pl; éstas, f pl. **the l. half,** la segunda mitad. **toward the l. end of the year,** hacia fines del año. **L.-Day Saint,** santo de los últimos días m, santa de los últimos días, f

latterly /ˈlætərli/ adv recientemente, últimamente; en los últimos tiempos; hacia el fin

lattice /'lætɪs/ n rejilla, f; celosía, reja, f. —vt poner celosía (a); entrelazar. **l.-work,** enrejado, m

latticed /'lætɪst/ a (of windows, etc.) con reja

Latvia /'lætvɪə/ Latvia, Letonia, f

Latvian /'lætvɪən/ a latvio. —n latvio (-ia)

laud /lɔd/ n alabanza, f; pl. **lauds,** Eccl. laudes, f pl. —vt alabar, elogiar

laudable /'lɔdəbəl/ a loable, meritorio

laugh /læf/ n risa, f; carcajada, f. —vi reír; (smile) sonreír; reírse. **loud l.,** risa estrepitosa, f. **to l. in a person's face,** reírsele a uno en las barbas. **to l. loudly,** reírse a carcajadas. **to l. to oneself,** reírse interiormente. **to l. to scorn,** poner en ridículo. **to l. at,** reírse de; burlarse de, ridiculizar

laughable /'læfəbəl/ a risible, irrisible, ridículo, absurdo

laughing /'læfɪŋ/ a risueño, alegre; (absurd) risible, n risa, f. **to burst out l.,** reírse a carcajadas. **l.-gas,** gas hilarante, m. **l.-stock,** hazmerreír, m

laughter /'læftər/ n risa, f; (in a report) risas, f pl. **burst of l.,** carcajada, f. **to burst into l.,** soltar el trapo, reírse a carcajadas, desternillarse de risa

launch /lɔntʃ/ n botadura (de un buque), f; lancha, f; bote, m; canoa, f. —vt (throw) lanzar; (a blow) asestar; (a vessel) botar, echar al agua; (begin) iniciar, dar principio a; (make) hacer. **to l. an offensive,** Mil. emprender una ofensiva. **to l. into,** arrojarse en; entregarse a. **motor l.,** canoa automóvil, f. **steam l.,** bote de vapor, m

launching /'lɔntʃɪŋ/ n botadura (de un buque), f; (throwing) lanzamiento, m; (beginning) iniciación, f; inauguración, f; (of a loan, etc.) emisión, f. **l. site,** rampa, f

launder /'lɔndər/ vt lavar y planchar (ropa)

laundress /'lɔndrɪs/ n lavandera, f

laundromat /'lɔndrə,mæt/ n lavandería automática, f

laundry /'lɔndri/ n lavadero, m, lavandería, f; (washing) colada, f; Inf. ropa lavada or ropa para lavar, f. **l.-man,** lavandero, m

laurel /'lɔrəl/ n laurel, cerezo, m, a láureo. **to crown with l.,** laurear. **l. wreath,** lauréola, f

lava /'lɑvə/ n lava, f

lavatory /'lævə,tɔri/ n lavabo, m; retrete, excusado, m

lavender /'lævəndər/ n espliego, m, lavanda, f. **l.-water,** agua de lavanda, f

lavish /'lævɪʃ/ a pródigo; profuso, abundante. —vt prodigar

law /lɔ/ n ley, f; derecho, m; jurisprudencia, f; código de leyes, m. **according to law,** según derecho. **canon law,** derecho civil, m. **constitutional law,** derecho po-

lítico, m. **criminal law,** derecho penal, m. **in law,** por derecho, de acuerdo con la ley; desde el punto de vista legal. **international law,** derecho internacional, m. **maritime law,** código marítimo, m. **sumptuary law,** ley suntuaria, f. **to be the law,** ser la ley. **to go to law,** pleitear (sobre). **to sue at law,** pedir en juicio, poner pleito. **to take the law into one's own hands,** tomar la ley por su propia mano. **law-abiding,** observante de la ley; amigo del orden. **law-breaker,** transgresor (-ra). **law court,** tribunal de justicia, m; palacio de justicia, m. **law of nature,** ley natural, f. **law report,** revista de tribunales, f. **law school,** escuela de derecho, f. **law student,** estudiante de derecho, mf

lawful /'lɔfəl/ a legítimo; legal; lícito; válido

lawfully /'lɔfəli/ adv legalmente, legítimamente, lícitamente

lawfulness /'lɔfəlnɪs/ n legalidad, f; legitimidad, f

lawless /'lɔlɪs/ a ilegal; desordenado; ingobernable, rebelde

lawn /lɔn/ n césped, prado, m; (cloth) estopilla, f. **l.-mower,** cortacésped m, tundidora de césped, f, máquina segadora del césped, f. **l.-tennis,** tenis (en pista de hierba), m

lawsuit /'lɔ,sut/ n pleito, litigio, m, causa, acción, f

lawyer /'lɔyər/ n abogado (-da). **lawyer's office** or **practice,** bufete, m

lax /læks/ a laxo; indisciplinado; vago; descuidado

laxative /'læksətɪv/ n laxante, m, purga, f, a laxativo

lay /lei/ a laico, seglar, lego; profano. —n poema, m, trova, f; romance, m; (song) canción, f. **the lay of the land,** la configuración del terreno. **lay brother,** confeso, monigote, m. **lay figure,** maniquí, m. **lay sister,** (hermana) lega, f

lay /lei/ vt and vi poner; colocar; dejar; (strike) tumbar; (demolish) derribar; (the dust) matar; (pipes, etc.) instalar; (hands on) asentar (la mano en); (deposit) depositar; (beat down corn, etc.) encamar, abatir; (eggs, keel) poner; (the table) cubrir, poner; (stretch) extender(se); (bury) depositar en el sepulcro; (a bet) hacer; (wager) apostar; (an accusation) acusar; (the wind, etc.) sosegar, amainar; (a ghost) exorcizar; (impute) atribuir, imputar; (impose) imponer; (prepare) preparar; (make) hacer; (open) abrir; (blame, etc.) echar; (claim) reclamar; (reveal) revelar. **Don't lay the blame on me!** ¡No me eches la culpa! **We laid our plans,** Hicimos nuestros planes; Hicimos nuestros preparativos. **to lay siege to,** asediar. **to lay the colors on too thick,** Fig. recargar las tintas. **to lay the foundations,** abrir los cimientos; Fig. crear, establecer; fundar. **to lay about one,** dar garrotazos de ciego. **to lay aside,** poner a un lado;

arrinconar; (save) ahorrar; (cast away) desechar; abandonar; (reserve) reservar; (a person) apartar de sí; (incapacitate) incapacitar. **lay something at somebody's feet**, embutir algo en el guante de fulano. **to lay before**, mostrar; presentar; poner a la vista; revelar. **to lay by**, See **to lay aside**. **to lay down**, acostar; depositar; (a burden) posar; (arms) rendir; (one's life) entregar; (give up) renunciar (a); (sketchout) trazar, dibujar; (plan) proyectar; (keep) guardar; (as a principle) establecer, sentar; (the law) dictar. **to lay oneself down**, echarse, tumbarse. **to lay in**, (a stock) proveerse de, hacer provisión de; (hoard) ahorrar; (buy) comprar. **to lay off**, Naut. virar de bordo; Inf. quitarse de encima. **to lay on**, vt colocar sobre; (thrash) pegar; (blows) descargar; (paint, etc.) dar; (water, etc.) instalar; (impose) imponer; (exaggerate) exagerar. —vi atacar. **to lay open**, abrir; descubrir, revelar; manifestar; exponer. **to lay oneself open to attack**, exponerse a ser atacado. **to lay out**, poner; arreglar; (the dead) amortajar; (one's money) invertir, emplear; (at interest) poner a rédito; (plan) planear; (knock down) derribar. **to lay oneself out to**, esforzarse a; tomarse la molestia de. **to lay over**, cubrir; sobreponer; extender sobre. **to lay to**, vi Naut. estar a la capa. **to lay up**, guardar, acumular, atesorar; poner a un lado; (a ship) desarmar; (a car) poner fuera de circulación; (a person) obligar a guardar cama, incapacitar

layer /'leiər/ n capa, f; Geol. estrato, m; Mineral. manto, m; (bird) gallina (pata, etc.) ponedera, f; (one who bets) apostador (-ra); Agr. acodo, m. —vt (of plants) acodar

layette /lei'et/ n canastilla, f

laying /'leiɪŋ/ n colocación, f; puesta, f; (of an egg) postura, f. **l. down**, depósito, m; conservación, f; (explanation) exposición, f. **l. on of hands**, imposición de manos, f. **l. out**, tendedura, f; (of money) empleo, m; inversión, f; (arrangement) arreglo, m

layman /'leimən/ n seglar, mf; profano (-na)

layout /'lei.aut/ n plan, m; diagramación, disposición, f; distribución, f; esquema, m

laze /leiz/ vi holgazanear, gandulear, no hacer nada; encontrarse a sus anchas

laziness /'leizinɪs/ n pereza, holgazanería, f; indolencia, f; lentitud, f

lazy /'leizi/ a perezoso, holgazán; indolente. **l.-bones**, gandul (-la)

lead /lɛd/ n (metal) plomo, m; (in a pencil) mina, f; (plummet) sonda, f; Print. interlínea, f; pl **leads**, (roofs) tejados, m pl. —vt emplomar; guarnecer con plomo; Print. interlinear. **black-l.**, grafito, m. **deep-sea l.**, Naut. escandallo, m. **white l.**, albayalde, m. **to heave the l.**, echar el escandallo, sondar. **l.-colored**, de color de

plomo, plomizo. **l. mine**, mina de plomo, f. **l. poisoning**, saturnismo, m

lead /lid/ n delantera, f; primer lugar, m; dirección, f, mando, m; (suggestion) indicación, f; (influence) influencia, f; (dog's) traílla, f; Theat. protagonista, mf; Theat. papel principal, m; (at cards) mano, f

lead /lid/ vt and vi (conduct) conducir, llevar; guiar; (induce) mover, persuadir, inducir; inclinar; (cause) hacer, causar; (captain) capitanear, encabezar; dirigir; (channel) encauzar; (with life) llevar; (give) dar; (head) ir a la cabeza de; Mil. mandar; (at cards) salir; (at games) jugar en primer lugar; tomar la delantera; Fig. superar a los demás; (of roads) conducir. **to take the l.**, ir delante; ir a la cabeza, tomar la delantera; tomar la iniciativa. **to l. one to think**, hacer pensar. **to l. the way**, mostrar el camino; ir adelante. **to l. along**, llevar (por la mano, etc.), conducir; conducir por; guiar. **to l. astray**, descarriar; desviar (de), seducir (de). **to l. away**, conducir (a otra parte); llevarse (a). **to l. back**, conducir de nuevo; hacer volver. **This path leads back to the village**, Por esta senda se vuelve al pueblo. **to l. in, into**, conducir a (o ante); introducir en, hacer entrar en; invitar a entrar en; (of rooms) comunicarse con (sin, etc.) inducir a. **to l. off**, vi ir adelante; (begin) empezar; (of rooms) comunicarse con. —vt hacer marcharse, llevarse (a). **to l. on**, vt conducir; guiar; hacer pensar en; (make talk) dar cuerda (a). —vi ir a la cabeza; tomar la delantera. **to l. out**, conducir afuera; (to dance) sacar. **to l. to**, conducir a; desembocar en, salir a; (cause) dar lugar a, causar; (make) hacer; (incline) inclinar. **This street leads to the square**, Por esta calle se va a la plaza, Esta calle conduce a la plaza. **to l. up to**, conducir a; (in conversation, etc.) preparar el terreno para; preparar; tener lugar antes de, ocurrir antes de

leaden /'lɛdn/ a hecho de plomo, plúmbeo; (of skies, etc.) plomizo, de color de plomo, aplomado. **l.-footed**, pesado; lento

leader /'lidər/ n conductor (-ra); guía, mf; jefe (-fa); general, m; director (-ra); (in a journal) artículo de fondo, m; (of an orchestra) primer violín, m. **follow-the-l.**, (game) juego de seguir la fila, m

leadership /'lidərˌʃɪp/ n dirección, f; jefatura, f; Mil. mando, m

leading /'lɛdɪŋ/ n (leadwork) emploma dura, f

leading /'lidɪŋ/ n (guidance) dirección, f. —a principal; primero; importante; eminente. **l. article**, artículo de fondo, m; editorial, m. **l. card**, primer naipe, m. **l. counsel**, abogado (-da) principal. **l. lady**, Theat. dama primera, primera actriz, f; (cinema) estrella (de la pantalla), f. **l. man**, Theat. primer galán, m. **l. question**, pregunta que sugiere la respuesta, f;

cuestión importante, *f*. **l. strings**, andadores, *m pl; Fig.* tutelaje, *m*

leaf /lif/ *n* (*Bot*. and of a page, door, window, table, screen, etc.) hoja, *f;* (petal) pétalo, *m, vi* echar hojas. **gold l.**, pan de oro, *m*. **to turn over a new l.**, volver a la hoja, hacer libro nuevo, hacer vida nueva. **to turn over the leaves of a book**, hojear (un libro). **l.-bud**, yema, *f*. **l.-mold**, abono verde, *m*. **l. tobacco**, tabaco en hoja, *m*

leaflet /'liflɪt/ *n* hojuela, *f;* (pamphlet) folleto, *m*

league /lig/ *n* (measure) legua, *f;* liga, federación, sociedad, *f;* (football) liga, *f*. —*vt* aliar; asociar. —*vi* aliarse; asociarse, confederarse. **to be in l.**, *Inf*. estar de manga. **L. of Nations**, Sociedad de las Naciones, *f*

leak /lik/ *n* (hole) agujero, *m*, grieta, *f; Naut*. vía de agua, *f;* (of gas, liquids, etc.) escape, *m;* (in a roof, etc.) gotera, *f; Elec*. resistencia de escape, *f*. —*vi Naut*. hacer agua; (gas, liquids, etc.) escaparse, salirse; (drip) gotear. **to l. out**, (of news, etc.) trascender, saberse. **to spring a l.**, abrirse una vía de agua, hacer agua

leaky /'liki/ *a Naut*. que hace agua; agujereado; poroso; que tiene goteras

lean /lin/ *a* magro, seco, enjuto, delgado; (of meat) magro; *Fig*. pobre, estéril. —*n* carne magra, *f*, magro, *m*. **to grow l.**, enflaquecer

lean /lin/ *vi* inclinarse; apoyarse (en). —*vt* apoyar (en); dejar arrimado (en). **to l. out of the window**, asomarse a la ventana. **to l. against**, apoyarse en, recostarse en (or contra). **to l. back**, echarse hacia atrás; recostarse. **to l. over**, inclinarse. **to l. upon**, apoyarse en; descansar sobre

leaning /'liniŋ/ *n* inclinación, tendencia, *f;* predilección, afición, *f*

leap /lip/ *n* salto, *m;* brinco, *m;* (caper) zapateta, *f; Fig*. salto, *m*. —*vi* saltar, dar un salto; brincar. —*vt* saltar; hacer saltar. **at one l.**, en un salto. **by leaps and bounds**, en saltos. **My heart leaped**, Mi corazón dio un salto. **to l. to the conclusion that...**, saltar a la conclusión de que... **to l. to the eye**, saltar a la vista. **l. frog**, salto, salto de la muerte, *m*, pídola *f*. **l. year**, año bisiesto, *m; salta* cabrillas, *f pl*

learn /lɜrn/ *vt* and *vi* aprender; instruirse; enterarse de. **to l. by heart**, aprender de memoria. **to l. from a reliable source**, saber de buena tinta. **to l. from experience**, aprender por experiencia

learned /'lɜrnɪd/ *a* sabio, docto; erudito; (of professions) liberal; versado (en, entendido (en). **a l. society**, una sociedad erudita

learning /'lɜrnɪŋ/ *n* saber, *m;* conocimientos, *m pl;* erudición, *f;* estudio, *m;* (literature) literatura, *f*

lease /lis/ *n* arrendamiento, arriendo, *m;* contrato de arrendamiento, *m*. —*vt* dar en

arriendo, arrendar. **on l.**, en arriendo. **to take a new l. on life**, recobrar su vigor.

Lend L. Act, ley de préstamo y arriendo, *f*

leash /liʃ/ *n* (of a dog) traílla, *f*

least /list/ *a superl* **little**, mínimo; el (la, etc.) menor; más pequeño. —*adv* menos. —*n* lo menos. **at l.**, siquiera; por lo menos, al menos. **at the very l.**, a lo menos. **not in the l.**, de ninguna manera, nada. **to say the l. of**, sin exagerar, para no decir más

leather /'lɛðər/ *n* cuero, *m;* piel, *f, a* de cuero; de piel. **patent l.**, charol, *m*. **Spanish l.**, cordobán, *m*. **tanned l.**, curtido, *m*. **l. apron**, mandil, *m*. **l. bag**, saco de cuero, *m*. **l. bottle**, bota, *f*. **l. breeches**, pantalón de montar, *m*. **l. jerkin**, coleto, *m*. **l. shield**, adarga, *f*. **l. strap**, correa, *f*. **l. trade**, comercio en cueros, *m*

leatherette /ˌlɛðəˈrɛt/ *n* cartón cuero, *m*

leave /liv/ *n* (permission) permiso, *m;* (*Mil*. etc.) licencia, *f;* (farewell) despedida, *f*. —*vt* and *vi* dejar; abandonar; salir (de), quitar, marcharse (de); (as surety) empeñar; (by will) legar, mandar; (an employment) darse de baja (de); dejar; (give into the keeping of) entregar; (bid farewell) despedirse (de). **By your l.**, Con permiso de Vd. (Vds.). Con la venia de Vd. (Vds.). **on l.**, de permiso. **l.-taking**, despedidas, *f pl*. **to be left**, quedar. **to be left over**, quedar; sobrar. **Two from four leaves two**, De cuatro a dos van dos. **to take French l.**, despedirse a la inglesa. **to take l. of**, despedirse de. **to take one's l.**, marcharse; despedirse. **to l. a deep impression**, *Fig*. impresionar mucho; quedar grabado (en). **to l. undone**, dejar de hacer, no hacer; dejar sin terminar. **to l. about**, *vt* dejar por todas partes. —*vi* (of time) marcharse a eso de... **to l. ajar**, entreabrir, entornar. **to l. alone**, dejar a solas; dejar en paz; no molestar, no meterse con. **to l. aside**, omitir; prescindir de; olvidar. **to l. behind**, dejar atrás; olvidar. **l. much to be desired**, tener mucho que desear. **to l. off**, *vt* dejar de; abandonar; (garments) no ponerse, quitarse. —*vi* terminar. **to l. out**, dejar fuera; dejar a un lado, descontar; omitir; pasar por; (be silent about) callar; suprimir. **to l. to**, dejar para; dejar hacer

leaven /'lɛvən/ *n* levadura, *f*, fermento, *m, vt* fermentar; (*Fig*. permeate) penetrar (en), infiltrar en, imbuir; (a speech) salpimentar (con)

leaving /'liviŋ/ *n* salida, partida, marcha, *f; pl* **leavings**, sobras, *f pl;* desechos, *m pl*

Lebanon /'lɛbənən/ el Líbano, *m*

lecherous /'lɛtʃərəs/ *a* lascivo, lujurioso

lectern /'lɛktərn/ *n* atril, *m;* (in a church) facistol, *m*

lecture /'lɛktʃər/ *n* conferencia, *f;* (in a university) lección, clase, *f;* discurso, *m;* (*Inf*. scolding) sermoneo, *m*. —*vi* dar una

conferencia; (in a university) dar clase.
—*vt* (*Inf.* scold) predicar, sermonear. **l. room,** sala de conferencias, *f;* (in a university) sala de clase, aula, *f*

lecturer /'lɛktʃərər/ *n* conferenciante, *mf;* (in a university) auxiliar, *m;* (professor) catedrático (-ca), profesor (-ra)

ledge /lɛdʒ/ *n* borde, *m;* capa, *f;* (of a window) alféizar, *m;* (shelf) anaquel, *m*

ledger /'lɛdʒər/ *n* libro mayor, *m*

leech /litʃ/ *n* sanguijuela, *f*

leek /lik/ *n* puerro, *m*

leer /lɪər/ *vi* mirar de soslayo; guiñar el ojo; mirar con los ojos llenos de deseo. —*n* mirada de soslayo, *f;* mirada de lascivia, *f*

leeway /'li,wei/ *n* *Naut.* deriva, *f; Fig.* amplitud, margen de holgura, márgenes de maniobra, *f pl*

left /lɛft/ *past part* dejado, etc. See **leave.** *a* izquierdo. —*adv* a la izquierda; hacia la izquierda. —*n* izquierda, *f.* **on the l.,** a la izquierda. **the L.,** *Polit.* las izquierdas. **the Left Bank (of Paris)** la Ribera izquierda, la Orilla izquierda **L. face!** ¡Izquierda! **l.-hand,** mano izquierda, *f;* izquierda, *f.* **l.-hand drive,** conducción a la izquierda, *f.* **l.-handed,** zurdo. **l. luggage office,** consigna, *f.* **l.-overs,** sobras, *f pl,* desperdicios, *m pl*

leg /lɛg/ *n* pierna, *f;* (of animals, birds, furniture) pata, *f;* (of a triangle) cateto, *m;* (of a pair of compasses, trousers, lamb, veal) pierna, *f;* (of boots, stockings) caña, *f;* (of pork) pernil, *m;* (support) pie, *m;* (stage) etapa, *f.* **to be on one's last legs,** estar en las últimas; estar acabándose; estar sin recursos. **to pull a person's leg,** tomar el pelo (a). **leg-pull,** tomadura de pelo, *f.* **leg-of-mutton sleeve,** manga de pernil, *f*

legacy /'lɛgəsi/ *n* legado, *m,* manda, *f;* herencia, *f*

legal /'ligəl/ *a* legal; de derecho; jurídico; (lawful, permissible) legal, lícito; (of a lawyer) de abogado. **l. expenses,** litisexpensas, *f pl.* **l. inquiry,** investigación jurídica, *f*

legalize /'ligə,laiz/ *vt* legalizar; autorizar, legitimar

legally /'ligəli/ *adv* según la ley; según derecho; legalmente

legal tender *n* moneda de curso liberatorio, *f*

legend /'lɛdʒənd/ *n* leyenda, *f*

legendary /'lɛdʒən,dɛri/ *a* legendario

legerdemain /,lɛdʒərdə'mein/ *n* juegos de manos, *m pl*

leggings /'lɛgɪŋz/ *n pl* polainas, *f pl*

legible /'lɛdʒəbəl/ *a* legible

legion /'lidʒən/ *n* legión, *f.* **L. of Honor,** Legión de Honor, *f*

legislate /'lɛdʒɪs,leit/ *vt* legislar

legislation /,lɛdʒɪs'leiʃən/ *n* legislación, *f*

legislator /'lɛdʒɪs,leitər/ *n* legislador (-ra)

legislature /'lɛdʒɪs,leitʃər/ *n* legislatura, *f*

legitimacy /lɪ'dʒɪtəməsi/ *n* legitimidad, *f;* justicia, *f*

legitimate /lɪ'dʒɪtəmɪt/ *a* legítimo; justo

leisure /'liʒər/ *n* ocio, *m,* desocupación, *f;* tiempo libre, *m.* **at one's l.,** con sosiego, despacio. **You can do it at your l.,** Puedes hacerlo cuando tengas tiempo. **to be at l.,** estar desocupado, no tener nada que hacer. **l. moments,** ratos perdidos, momentos de ocio, *m pl*

leisured /'liʒərd/ *a* desocupado, libre; sin ocupación; (wealthy) acomodado

leisurely /'liʒərli/ *a* pausado, lento, deliberado; tardo

lemon /'lɛmən/ *n* limón, *m;* (tree) limonero, *m,* a limonado, de color de limón; hecho o sazonado con limón. **l. drop,** pastilla de limón, *f.* **l.-grove,** limonar, *m.* **l.-squash,** limonada natural, *f.* **l.-squeezer,** exprime limones, *m,* exprimidera, *f*

lemonade /,lɛmə'neid/ *n* limonada, *f.* **l. powder,** limonada seca, *f*

lend /lɛnd/ *vt* prestar. **to l. an ear to l.,** prestar atención a. **It does not l. itself to...,** No se presta a... **to l. a hand,** echar una mano, dar una mano

lender /'lɛndər/ *n* el, *m,* (f, la) que presta; prestador (-ra); (of money) prestamista, *mf; Com.* mutuante, *mf*

lending /'lɛndɪŋ/ *n* prestación, *f,* préstamo, *m.* **l.-library,** biblioteca circulante, *f*

length /lɛŋkθ/ *n* largo, *m;* longitud, *f;* (of fabric) corte, *m;* (of a ship) eslora, *f;* (in racing) largo, *m;* distancia, *f;* (in time) duración, *f;* alcance, *m.* **at l.,** por fin, finalmente; (in full) extensamente, largamente. **by a l.,** por un largo. **full-l.,** de cuerpo entero. **three feet in l.,** tres pies de largo. **to go the l. of...,** llegar al extremo de...

lengthen /'lɛŋkθən/ *vt* alargar; prolongar; extender. —*vi* alargarse; prolongarse; extenderse; (of days) crecer

lengthening /'lɛŋkθənɪŋ/ *n* alargamiento, *m;* prolongación, *f;* crecimiento, *m*

lengthy /'lɛŋkθi/ *a* largo; demasiado largo, larguísimo; (of speech) prolijo; verboso

lenient /'liniənt/ *a* indulgente; poco severo

lens /lɛnz/ *n* lente, *m;* (of the eye) cristalino, *m*

Lent /lɛnt/ *n* Cuaresma, *f*

lentil /'lɛntɪl/ *n* lenteja, *f*

leopard /'lɛpərd/ *n* leopardo, *m*

leper /'lɛpər/ *n* leproso (-sa). **l. colony,** colonia de leprosos, *f*

leprosy /'lɛprəsi/ *n* lepra, *f*

lesbian /'lɛzbiən/ *a and n* lesbiana

lesion /'liʒən/ *n* lesión, *f*

less /lɛs/ *a* menor; más pequeño; menos; inferior. —*adv* menos; sin. **l. than,** menos de (que). **more or l.,** poco más o menos. **no l.,** nada menos. **none the l.,** sin embargo. **to grow l.,** disminuir. **l. and l.,** cada vez menos

lessee /lɛ'siː/ *n* arrendatario (-ia); inquilino (-na)

lessen /'lɛsən/ *vi* disminuir; reducirse. —*vt* disminuir; reducir; (lower) rebajar; (disparage) menospreciar

lessening /'lɛsənɪŋ/ *n* disminución, *f*; reducción, *f*

lesser /'lɛsər/ *a compar* menor; más pequeño. See **little**

lesson /'lɛsən/ *n* lección, *f*. **to give a l.,** dar lección, dar clase; *Fig.* dar una lección (a). **to hear a l.,** tomar la lección

lessor /'lɛsɔr/ *n* arrendador (-ra)

lest /lɛst/ *conjunc* para que no; por miedo de (que), no sea que. **I did not do it l. they should not like it,** No lo hice por miedo de que no les gustase

let /lɛt/ *vt* dejar, permitir; (lease) arrendar. —*vi* alquilarse, ser alquilado. **Let** as an expression of the imperative is rendered in Spanish by the subjunctive or the imperative, e.g. *Let them go!* ¡Que se vayan! ¡Déjalos marchar! *He let them go,* Les dejó marchar. *to let fall,* dejar caer. *to let go,* dejar marchar; soltar; poner en libertad (a). **to let loose,** dar suelta a; *Fig.* desencadenar. **to let one know,** hacer saber, comunicar. **to let the cat out of the bag,** tirar de la manta. **to let th chance slip,** perder la ocasión. **to let alone,** (a thing) no tocar; (a person) dejar en paz, dejar tranquilo; (an affair) no meterse (en or con); (omit) no mencionar, omitir toda mención de. **to let down,** bajar; (by a rope) descolgar; (hair, etc.) dejar caer; (a dress, etc.) alargar; *Naut.* calar; (disappoint) dejar plantado. **to let in,** dejar entrar; hacer entrar; invitar a entrar; recibir; (insert) insertar. **to let into,** (initiate) iniciar en, admitir en; (a secret) revelar. Other meanings, see **to let in.** **to let off,** dejar salir; (free) en libertad; exonerar; perdonar; (a gun) disparar; (fireworks, etc.) hacer estallar. **to let out,** dejar salir; poner en libertad; (from a house) acompañar a la puerta; abrir la puerta; *Sew.* ensanchar; (hire) alquilar; (the fire, etc.) dejar extinguirse. **to let up,** dejar subir; (decrease) disminuir; (end) terminar

let /lɛt/ *n* estorbo, impedimento, obstáculo, *m*. **without let or hindrance,** sin estorbo ni obstáculo

lethal /'liːθəl/ *a* letal. **l. weapon,** instrumento de muerte, *m*

lethargic /lə'θɑrdʒɪk/ *a* aletargado; letárgico

letter /'lɛtər/ *n* (of the alphabet) letra, *f*; (epistle) carta, *f*; *Print.* carácter, *m*; (lessor) arrendador (-ra); *pl* **letters,** letras, *f pl*; (correspondence) correo, *m*; correspondencia, *f.* —*vt* inscribir; imprimir. **capital l.,** letra mayúscula, *f.* **first letters,** *Fig.* primeras letras, *f pl.* **registered l.,** carta certificada, *f*, certificado, *m*. **small l.,** letra minúscula, *f.* **the l. of the law,** la ley escrita, *f.* **to be l.-perfect,** saber de memoria. **to the l.,** *Fig.* a la letra. **letters**

patent, patente, *f*; título de privilegio, *m*. **l.-balance,** pesacartas, *m*. **l.-book,** *Com.* libro copiador, *m*. **l.-box,** buzón de correos, *m*. **l.-card,** tarjeta postal del gobierno, *f*. **l. of credit,** carta de crédito, *f*. **l. of introduction,** carta de presentación, *f*. **l.-writer,** escritor (-ra) de cartas

lettering /'lɛtərɪŋ/ *n* inscripción, *f*; letrero, rótulo, *m*

lettuce /'lɛtɪs/ *n* lechuga, *f*. **l. plant,** lechuguino, *m*. **l. seller,** lechuguero (-ra)

level /'lɛvəl/ *n* nivel, *m*; ras, *m*, flor, *f*; llano, *m*; (plain) llanura, *f*; (instrument) nivel, *m*, *a* llano; igual; al nivel (de); uniforme; imparcial. —*adv* a nivel; igualmente. —*vt* nivelar; igualar; allanar; (a blow) asestar; (a gun) apuntar; (raze) arrasar, derribar; adaptar; hacer uniforme. **on the l.,** a nivel; *Fig.* de buena fe. **spirit l.,** nivel de burbuja, *m*. **to make l. again,** rellanar. **l. country,** campaña, llanura, *f.* **l. with the ground,** a ras de la tierra. **l. with the water,** a flor de agua. **l. crossing,** paso a nivel, *m*. **l.-headed,** sensato, cuerdo. **l. stretch,** rellano, *m*; llanura, *f*

leveling /'lɛvəlɪŋ/ *a* nivelador; de nivelación; igualador. —*n* nivelación, *f*; allanamiento, *m*; (to the ground) arrasamiento, *m*; igualación, *f*

lever /'lɛvər/ *n* palanca, *f*; (handle) manivela, *f*; escape de reloj, *m*; (excuse) pretexto, *m*; (means) modo, *m*. —*vt* sopalancar. **control l.,** *Aer.* palanca de mando, *f*. **hand-l.,** palanca de mano, *f*

leverage /'lɛvərɪdʒ/ *n* sistema de palancas, *m*; acción de palanca, *f*; *Fig.* influencia, fuerza, *f*, poder, *m*

Leviticus /li'vɪtɪkəs/ *n* Levítico, *m*

levity /'lɛvɪti/ *n* levedad, frivolidad, ligereza, *f*

levy /'lɛvi/ *n* exacción (de tributos), *f*; impuesto, *m*; (of a fine) imposición, *f*; *Mil.* leva, *f*. —*vt* (taxes) exigir; (a fine) imponer; (troops) reclutar, enganchar

levying /'lɛviɪŋ/ *n* (of a tax) exacción (de tributos), *f*; (of a fine) imposición, *f*; (of troops) leva, *f*

lewd /lud/ *a* lascivo, lujurioso, impúdico

lewdness /'ludnɪs/ *n* lascivia, lujuria, impudicia, *f*

liability /ˌlaiə'bɪlɪti/ *n* responsabilidad, obligación, *f*; tendencia, *f*; riesgo, *m*; *pl* **liabilities,** obligaciones, *f pl*; *Com.* pasivo, *m*

liable /'laiəbəl/ *a* responsable; propenso (a); expuesto (a); sujeto (a)

liaison /li'eɪzən/ *n* lío, *m*; coordinación, *f*. **l. officer,** oficial de coordinación, *m*

liar /'laiər/ *n* mentiroso (-sa)

libel /'laibəl/ *n* libelo, *m*; difamación, *f*, *vt* difamar, calumniar

libelous /'laibələs/ *a* difamatorio

liberal /'lɪbərəl/ *a* liberal; generoso; abundante. —*n* liberal, *mf.* **l. profession,** carrera liberal, *f.* **l.-minded,** tolerante. **l.-mindedness,** tolerancia, *f*

liberalism /'lɪbərə,lɪzəm/ *n* liberalismo, *m*

liberality /,lɪbə'rælɪti/ *n* liberalidad, *f;* generosidad, *f*

liberalize /'lɪbərə,laɪz/ *vt* liberalizar

liberate /'lɪbə,reɪt/ *vt* (a prisoner) poner en libertad; librar (de); (a gas, etc.) dejar escapar

liberation /,lɪbə'reɪʃən/ *n* liberación, *f;* (of a captive) redención, *f;* (of a slave) manumisión, *f*

liberator /'lɪbə,reɪtər/ *n* libertador (-ra)

libertine /'lɪbər,tin/ *n* libertino, *m*

liberty /'lɪbərti/ *n* libertad, *f;* (familiarity) familiaridad, *f;* (right) privilegio, *m,* pre-rrogativa, *f;* (leave) permiso, *m.* **at l.,** en libertad; desocupado, libre. **I have taken the l. of giving them your name,** Me he tomado la libertad de darles su nombre. **to set at l.,** poner en libertad (a). **to take liberties with,** tratar con familiaridad; (a text) tergiversar. **l. of speech,** libertad de palabra, libertad de expresión, *f.* **l. of thought,** libertad de pensamiento, *f*

libidinous /lɪ'bɪdn̩əs/ *a* libidinoso

librarian /laɪ'brɛriən/ *n* bibliotecario (-ia)

library /'laɪ,brɛri/ *n* biblioteca, *f;* (book shop) librería, *f.* **l. catalog,** catálogo de la biblioteca, *m*

license /'laɪsəns/ *n* licencia, *f,* permiso, *m;* autorización, *f;* (driving) carnet de chófer, permiso de conducción, *m;* (of a car) permiso de circulación, *m;* (for a wireless, etc.) licencia, *f;* (marriage) licencia de casamiento, *f;* (excess) libertinaje, desenfreno, *m.* **import l.,** permiso de importación, *m.* **poetic l.,** licencia poética, *f.* **l. number,** (of a car) número de matriculación, *m.* —*vt* licenciar; autorizar; (a car) sacar la licencia del automóvil

licensee /,laɪsən'si/ *n* concesionario (-ia)

licentious /laɪ'sɛnʃəs/ *a* licencioso, disoluto

licit /'lɪsɪt/ *a* lícito

lick /lɪk/ *vt* lamer; (of waves) besar; (of flames) bailar; (thrash) azotar; (defeat) vencer. **to l. one's lips,** relamerse los labios, chuparse los dedos. **to l. the dust,** morder el polvo

licking /'lɪkɪŋ/ *n* lamedura, *f;* (beating) paliza, tunda, *f;* (defeat) derrota, *f*

lid /lɪd/ *n* cobertera, *f;* tapa, *f;* (of the eye) párpado, *m*

lie /laɪ/ *n* mentira, *f;* invención, falsedad, *f;* mentís, *m, vi* mentir. **to give the lie to,** desmentir, dar el mentís. **to lie barefacedly,** mentir por la mitad de la barba. **white lie,** mentira oficiosa, *f*

lie /laɪ/ *vi* estar tumbado, estar echado; estar recostado; descansar; reposar; (in the grave) yacer; (be) estar; (be situated) hallarse, estar situado; (stretch) extenderse; (sleep) dormir; (depend) depender; (consist) consistir, estribar; (as an obligation) incumbir. **Here lies...,** Aqudh descansa..., Aquí yace... **It does not lie in**

my power, No depende de mí. **to let lie,** dejar; dejar en paz. **to lie at anchor,** estar anclado. **to lie fallow,** estar en barbecho; *Fig.* descansar. **to lie about,** estar esparcido por todas partes; estar en desorden. **to lie along,** estar tendido a lo largo de; *Naut.* dar a la banda. **to lie back,** recostarse; apoyarse (en). **to lie by,** estar acostado al lado de; (of things, places) estar cerca (de); descansar. **to lie down,** tenderse, tumbarse, echarse, acostarse; reposar. **Lie down!** (to a dog) ¡Echate! **to lie down under,** tenderse bajo; (an insult) tragar, sufrir. **to lie in,** consistir en; depender de; (of childbirth) estar de parto. **to lie open,** estar abierto; estar expuesto (a); estar al descubierto, estar a la vista. **to lie over,** (be postponed) quedar aplazado. **to lie to,** *Naut.* estarse a la capa, ponerse en facha. **to lie under,** estar bajo, hallarse bajo; estar bajo el peso de; (be exposed to) estar expuesto a. **to lie with,** dormir con; (concern) tocar (a); corresponder (a)

lie /laɪf/ *n* configuración, *f;* disposición, *f;* posición, *f.* **the lie of the land,** la configuración del terreno

lieu /lu/ *n* lugar, *m.* **in l. of,** en lugar de, en vez de

lieutenant /lu'tɛnənt/ *n* teniente, lugarteniente, *m;* (naval) alférez, *m.* **first l.,** (in the army) primer teniente, teniente, *m;* (in the navy) alférez de navío, *m.* **naval l.,** teniente de navío, *m.* **second l.,** (in the army) segundo teniente, *m;* (in the navy) alférez de fragata, *m.* **l.-colonel,** teniente coronel, *m.* **l.-commander,** capitán de fragata, *m.* **l.-general,** teniente general, *m.* **l.-governor,** subgobernador, *m*

life /laɪf/ *n* vida, *f;* (being) ser, *m;* (society) mundo, *m,* sociedad, *f;* (vitality) vitalidad, *f;* vigor, *m, a* de vida; (of annuities, etc.) vitalicio; (life-saving) de salvamento. **for l.,** de por vida. **from l.,** del natural. **high l.,** gran mundo, *m,* alta sociedad, *f.* **low l.,** vida de los barrios bajos, *f.* **to the l.,** al vivo. **to lay down one's l.,** entregar la vida. **to take one's l. in one's hands,** jugarse la vida. **l. annuity,** fondo vitalicio, *m.* **l.-belt,** (cinturón) salvavidas, *m.* **l.-blood,** sangre vital, *m; Fig.* nervio, *m;* vigor, *m.* **l.-boat,** (on a ship) bote salvavidas, *m;* (on the coast) lancha de salvamento, *f.* **l.-boat station,** estación de salvamento, *f.* **l.-giving,** vivificante, que da vida; tonificante. **l.-guard,** (soldier) guardia militar, *f;* Guardia de Corps, *f,* (at beach or swimming pool) guardavivas, *mf.* **l.-insurance,** seguro sobre la vida, *m.* **l.-interest,** usufructo, *m.* **l.-jacket,** chaleco salvavidas, *m.* **l.-like,** natural. **l.-line,** cable de salvamento, *m.* **l.-saving,** *a* de salvamento; curativo. **l.-saving apparatus,** aparato salvavidas, *m.* **l.-sized,** de tamaño natural

life cycle *n* ciclo vital, *m*

life imprisonment *n* reclusión perpetua, *f*

life jacket n chaleco salvavidas, f

lifeless /'laiflıs/ a sin vida, muerto; ina-nimado; Fig. desanimado

lifelong /'laif,lɒŋ/ a de toda la vida

lifetime /'laif,taim/ n vida, f

lift /lıft/ n esfuerzo para levantar, m; ac-ción de levantar, f; alza, f; (blow) golpe, m; (help) ayuda, f; (elevator) ascensor, m; (for goods) montacargas, m; pl **lifts**, Naut. balancines, m pl. **to give a l. to**, (help) ayudar; (hitchhiker etc.) dar un aventón. **l. attendant**, ascensorista, mf

lift /lıft/ vt levantar; alzar, elevar; (pick up) coger; (raise) subir; (carry off) hurtar; exaltar. —vi (of mist) disiparse; desaparecer. **to l. the elbow**, empinar el codo. **to l. down**, quitar (de); (a person) bajar en brazos. **to l. up**, alzar; erguir; levantar; levantar en brazos

ligament /'lıgəmənt/ n ligamento, m

light /lait/ a (not dark) claro, con mucha luz, bañado de luz; (of colors) claro; (not heavy, and of sleep, food, troops, movements) ligero; (of reading) de entre-tenimiento; (irresponsible) frívolo; (easy) fácil; (slight) leve; (of hair) rubio; (happy) alegre; (fickle) inconstante, livia-no; (of complexion) blanco. —adv ligero. **to be l.**, no pesar mucho; estar de día. **to grow l.**, (dawn) clarear; iluminarse. **to make l. of**, no tomar en serio; no preocu-parse de; (suffering) sufrir sin quejarse. **l.-colored**, (de color) claro. **l.-fingeredness**, sutileza de manos, f. **l.-footed**, ligero de pies. **l.-haired**, de pelo rubio. **l.-headed**, casquivano, ligero de cascos; delirante. **l.-headedness**, ligereza de cascos, frivolidad, f; delirio, m. **l.-hearted**, alegre (de corazón). **l.-heartedness**, alegría, f. **l. horse**, Mil. ca-ballería ligera, f. **l. troops**, tropas ligeras, f pl. **l.-weight**, n (boxing) peso ligero, m, a de peso ligero

light /lait/ n luz, f; (day) día, m; (match) cerilla, f; (of a cigarette, etc.) fuego, m; (of a window) cristal, vidrio, m; (point of view) punto de vista, m; (in a picture) toque de luz, m; pl **lights**, (of-fal) bofes, m pl. **against the l.**, al trasluz. **by the l. of**, a la luz de; según. **half-l.**, media luz, f. **high light** (s), Art. claros, m pl; Fig. momento culminante, m; acon-tecimiento de más interés, m. **to come to l.**, descubrirse. **to put a l. to the fire**, en-cender el fuego. **l.-year**, año de luz, m

light /lait/ vt (a lamp, fire, etc.) encender; iluminar. —vi encenderse; iluminarse; Fig. animarse; brillar. **to l. upon**, encon-trar por casualidad; tropezar con

lighten /'laitṇ/ vt (illuminate) iluminar; (of weight) aligerar; (cheer) alegrar; (mit-igate) aliviar. —vi (grow light) clarear; (of lightning) relampaguear; (become less heavy) disminuir de peso, aligerarse; volverse más alegre

lightening /'laitṇɪŋ/ n aligeramiento, m; (easing) alivio, m; luz, f

lighter /'laitər/ n (boat) lancha, barcaza,

gabarra, f; (device) encendedor, m. **pocket l.**, encendedor de bolsillo, m. **l. man**, gabarrero, m

lighthouse /'lait,haʊs/ n faro, m. **l.-keeper**, guardafaro, m

lighting /'laitıŋ/ n iluminación, f; alum-brado, m. **flood l.**, iluminación intensiva, f. **l.-up time**, hora de encender los faros, f

lightly /'laitli/ adv ligeramente; fácil-mente; (slightly) levemente; ágilmente; sin seriedad. **l. wounded**, levemente herido

lightning /'laitnıŋ/ n relámpago, rayo, m. **as quick as l.**, como un relámpago. **to be struck by l.**, ser herido por un relámpago. **l.-rod**, pararrayos, m

likable /'laikəbəl/ a simpático

like /laik/ a semejante; parecido; igual, mismo; (characteristic) típico, caracterís-tico; (likely) probable; (equivalent) equivalente. —adv como; igual (que); del mismo modo (que). —n semejante, igual, mf; tal cosa, f; cosas semejantes, f pl. **Don't speak to me l. that**, No me hables así. **He was l. a fury**, Estaba hecho una furia. **They are very l. each other**, Se parecen mucho. **to be l.**, parecerse (a), semejar. **to look l.**, parecer ser (que); tener el aspecto de; (of persons) parecerse (a). **to return l. for l.**, pagar en la misma moneda

like /laik/ vt gustar, agradar; estar aficio-nado (a), gustar de; (wish) querer. **As you l.**, Como te parezca bien, Como quieras. **If you l.**, Si quieres. **James likes painting**, Jaime está aficionado a la pin-tura. **Judith does not l. the north of England**, A Judit no le gusta el norte de Inglaterra. **I don't l. to do it**, No me gusta hacerlo. **I should l. him to go to Madrid**, Me gustaría que fuese a Madrid

likelihood /'laikli,hʊd/ n posibilidad, f; probabilidad, f

likely /'laikli/ a probable; verosímil, creíble, plausible; posible; (suitable) satis-factorio, apropiado; (handsome) bien parecido. —adv probablemente. **They are not l. to come**, No es probable que ven-gan

liken /'laikən/ vt comparar

likeness /'laiknıs/ n parecido, m, seme-janza, f; (portrait) retrato, m

likewise /'laik,waiz/ adv igualmente, asi-mismo, tambienwlin. —conjunc además

liking /'laikıŋ/ n (for persons) simpatía, f, cariño, m; (for things) gusto, m, afición, f; (appreciation) aprecio, m. **I have a l. for old cities**, Me gustan (or me atraen) las viejas ciudades. **to take a l. to**, (things) aficionarse a; (persons) prendarse de, tomar cariño (a)

lilac /'lailək/ n lila, f. **l. color**, color de lila, m

lilt /lılt/ n canción, f; ritmo, m; armonía, f

lily /'lıli/ n lirio, m, azucena, f; (of France) flor de lis, f. **l. of the valley**, lirio de los valles, muguete, *m*. **l.-white,** blanco como la azucena

limb /lɪm/ *n Anat.* miembro, *m;* (of a tree) rama, *f*

limbo /'lɪmbou/ *n* limbo, *m*

lime /laim/ *n Chem.* cal, *f;* (for catching birds) liga, hisca, *f;* (linden tree) tilo, *m;* (tree like a lemon) limero, *m;* (fruit) lima, *f.* —*vt* (whiten) encalar; *Agr.* abonar con cal. **slaked l.,** cal muerta, *f.* **l.-flower,** flor del tilo, tila, *f;* flor del limero, *f.* **l.-juice,** jugo de lima, *m.* **l.-kiln,** calera, *f.* **l.-pit,** pozo de cal, *m*

limelight /laim,lait/ *n* luz de calcio, *f; Fig.* centro de atención, *m;* publicidad, *f*. **to be in the l.,** ser el centro de atención, estar a la vista (de público)

limestone /laim,stoun/ *n* piedra caliza, *f.* **l. deposit,** calar, *m*

limit /'lɪmɪt/ *n* límite, *m;* confín, *m;* linde, *m,* or *f;* limitación, *f, vt* limitar; fijar; (restrict) restringir. **This is the l.!** ¡Este es el colmo! ¡No faltaba más!

limitation /,lɪmɪ'teiʃən/ *n* limitación, *f;* restricción, *f*

limousine /'lɪmə,zin/ *n* limousina, *f,* coche cerrado, *m*

limp /lɪmp/ *a* flojo; débil; fláccido; lánguido. —*n* cojera, *f.* —*vi* cojear. **to l. off,** marcharse cojeando. **to l. up,** acercarse cojeando; subir cojeando

limpid /'lɪmpɪd/ *a* límpido, cristalino, puro

linchpin /'lɪntʃ,pɪn/ *n* pezonera, *f*

line /lain/ *vt* (furrow) surcar; (troops, etc.) poner en fila; alinear; (clothes, nests, etc.) forrar; (building) revestir; (one's pocket) llenar. —*vi* estar en línea, alinearse

line /lain/ *n* (most meanings) línea, *f;* (cord) cuerda, *f; Naut.* cordel, *m;* (fishing) sedal, *f;* (railway) vía, *f;* (wrinkle) surco, *m;* arruga, *f;* (row) hilera, ringlera, fila, *f;* (of verse) verso, *m; Print.* renglón, *m;* (of business) ramo, *m;* profesión, *f;* (interest) especialidad, *f.* **bowling or serving l.,** línea de saque, *f.* **hard lines,** mala suerte, *f;* apuro, *m,* situación difícil, *f.* **in a l.,** en fila; en cola. **in direct l.,** (of descent) en línea recta. **It is not in my l.,** No es una especialidad mía; No es uno de mis intereses. **on the lines of,** conforme a; parecido a. **to cross the l.,** (equator) pasar la línea; (railway) cruzar la vía. **to drop a l.,** escribir unas líneas, poner unas líneas. **to read between the lines,** leer entre líneas. **l.-drawing,** dibujo de líneas, *m.* **l. of battle,** línea de batalla, *f*

lineage /'lɪnɪdʒ/ *n* linaje, *m,* familia, raza, *f*

lineament /'lɪnɪəmənt/ *n* lineamento, *m;* (of the face) facciones, *f pl*

linear /'lɪnɪər/ *a* lineal. **l. equation,** ecuación de primer grado, *f*

lined /laind/ *a* rayado, con líneas; (of the face) surcado, arrugado; (of gloves, etc.) forrado. **lined paper,** papel rayado, *m*

linen /'lɪnən/ *n* lino, *m; Inf.* ropa blanca, *f; a* de lino. **clean l.,** ropa limpia, *f.* **dirty l.,** ropa sucia, *f;* ropa para lavar, *f.* **table-l.,** mantelería, *f.* **l. cupboard,** armario para ropa blanca, *m.* **l. draper,** lencero (-ra). **l.-draper's shop,** lencería, *f.* **l. room,** lencería, *f.* **l. tape,** trenzadera, *f.* **l. thread,** hilo de lino, *m*

liner /'lainər/ *n* (ship) transatlántico, *m;* buque de vapor, *m; Aer.* avión de pasaje, *m*

linger /'lɪŋgər/ *vi* (remain) quedarse; tardar en marcharse; ir lentamente; hacer algo despacio

lingerie /,lɑ̃ʒə'rei/ *n* ropa blanca, *f*

lingering /'lɪŋgərɪŋ/ *a* lento; largo; prolongado; melancólico, triste

liniment /'lɪnɪmənt/ *n* linimento, *m*

lining /'lainɪŋ/ *n* (of a garment, etc.) forro, *m;* (building) revestimiento, *m*

link /lɪŋk/ *n* (in a chain) eslabón, *m;* (of beads) sarta, *f; Fig.* enlace, *m,* cadena, *f;* conexión, *f; Mech.* corredera, *f;* (torch) hacha de viento, *f.* —*vt* enlazar, unir; *Fig.* encadenar. **missing l.,** *Fig.* eslabón perdido, *m.* **to l. arms,** cogerse del brazo

links /lɪŋks/ *n pl* campo de golf, *m*

linoleum /lɪ'nouliəm/ *n* linóleo, *m*

linseed /'lɪn,sid/ *n* linaza, *f.* **l. cake,** bagazo, *m.* **l.-oil,** aceite de linaza, *m*

lint /lɪnt/ *n Med.* hilas, *f pl;* (fluff) borra, *f*

lion /'laiən/ *n* león, *m; Fig.* celebridad, *f.* **l. cage or den,** leonera, *f.* **l.-hearted,** valeroso. **l.-hunter,** cazador (-ra) de leones. **l.-keeper,** leonero (-ra). **lion's mane,** melena, *f.* **l.-tamer,** domador (-ra) de leones

lionize /'laiə,naiz/ *vt* dar bombo (a), hacer la rueda (a), tratar como una celebridad (a)

lion's share *n* parte del león, tajada del león, *f*

lip /lɪp/ *n* labio, *m;* (of a vessel) pico, *m;* (of a crater) borde, *m; Fig.* boca, *f.* **to open one's lips,** abrir la boca. **to smack one's lips,** chuparse los dedos. **lip reading,** lectura labial, *f.* **lip-service,** amor fingido, *m;* promesas hipócritas, *f pl.* **lip stick,** lápiz para los labios, *m*

liquefaction /,lɪkwə'fækʃən/ *n* licuefacción, *f*

liquefy /'lɪkwə,fai/ *vt* liquidar. —*vi* liquidarse

liqueur /lɪ'kɜr/ *n* licor, *m.* **l.-glass,** copita de licor, *f.* **l.-set,** licorera, *f*

liquid /'lɪkwɪd/ *n* líquido, *m, a* líquido; límpido. **l. air,** aire líquido, *m.* **l. measure,** medida para líquidos, *f*

liquidate /'lɪkwɪ,deit/ *vt* liquidar; saldar (cuentas); *Mil.* soldar

liquidation /,lɪkwɪ'deiʃən/ *n* liquidación, *f*

liquor /'lɪkər/ *n* licor, *m.* **l. shop,** aguardentería, *f.* **l. traffic,** negocio de vinos y licores, *m;* contrabando, *m*

Lisbon /'lɪzbən/ Lisboa, *f*

lisp /lɪsp/ n ceceo, m; balbuceo, m, vi cecear; balbucir

lissome /'lɪsəm/ a flexible; ágil

list /lɪst/ n lista, f; catálogo, m; matrícula, f; Naut. recalcada, f; inclinación, f; (tournament) liza, f. —vt hacer una lista de; catalogar; matricular, inscribir. —vi Naut. recalcar; inclinarse a un lado. **to enter the lists**, entrar en liza. **l. of wines**, lista de vinos, f

listen /'lɪsən/ vi escuchar; (attend) atender. **Don't you want to l. to the music?** ¿No quieres escuchar la música? **to l. in**, (to the radio) escuchar la radio; (eavesdrop) escuchar a hurtadillas

listener /'lɪsənər/ n oyente, mf; (to radio) radioyente, mf

listless /'lɪstlɪs/ a lánguido, apático, indiferente

litany /'lɪtni/ n letanía, f

liter /'litər/ n litro, m

literal /'lɪtərəl/ a literal. **l.-minded**, sin imaginación

literary /'lɪtə,reri/ a literario

literate /'lɪtərɪt/ a and n literato (-ta)

literature /'lɪtərətʃər/ n literatura, f

lithe /laɪð/ a flexible; sinuoso y delgado; ágil

Lithuania /,lɪθu'einiə/ Lituania, f

Lithuanian /,lɪθu'einiən/ a lituano, m li-tuano (-na); (language) lituano, m

litigant /'lɪtɪgənt/ n litigante, mf

litigate /'lɪtɪ,geit/ vi and vt litigar, pleit-ear

litigation /,lɪtɪ'geiʃən/ n litigación, f

litmus /'lɪtməs/ n tornasol, m. **l. paper**, papel de tornasol, f

litter /'lɪtər/ n litera, f; (stretcher) camilla, f; (bed) lecho, m; cama de paja, f; (brood) camada, cría, f; (rubbish) cosas en desorden, f pl; (papers) papeletas, f pl; (untidiness) desarreglo, desorden, m, confusión, f, vt poner en desorden

little /'lɪtl/ a pequeño; poco; (scanty) escaso; insignificante; bajo, mezquino. —adv poco. **a l.**, un poco (de); un tanto. **in l.**, en pequeño. **not a l.**, no poco; bastante. **l. by l.**, poco a poco. **l. or no**, poco o nada. **however l.**, por pequeño que. **as l. as possible**, lo menos posible. **to make l. of**, no dar importancia a; sacar poco en claro de, no comprender bien; no hacer caso de; (persons) acoger mal. **l. by l.**, poco a poco. **l. finger**, dedo meñique, m. **l. one**, pequeñuela, f, pe-queñito, m

liturgical /lɪ'tɜrdʒɪkəl/ a litúrgico. **l. cal-endar**, calendario litúrgico, m

liturgical vestment n paramento litúr-gico, m

liturgy /'lɪtərdʒi/ n liturgia, f

live /laɪv/ a vivo, viviente; (alight) encendido; (of a wire, etc.) cargado de electricidad. **l. cartridge**, cartucho con bala, m. **l. coal**, ascua, f. **l.-stock**, ganadería, f. **l. wire**, conductor eléctrico, m; Fig. fuerza viva, f

live /laɪv/ vi vivir; residir, habitar; (of ships) mantenerse a flote; salvarse; subsistir. —vt (one's life) llevar, pasar. **Long l.!** ¡Viva! **to have enough to l. on**, tener de que vivir. **to l. together**, convivir. **to l. again**, volver a vivir. **to l. at**, vivir en, habitar. **to l. down**, sobrevivir a; (a fault) lograr borrar. **to l. on**, vivir de. **to l. up to**, vivir con arreglo a, vivir en conformidad con; estar al nivel de, merecer. **to l. up to one's income**, vivir al día, gastarse toda la renta

live broadcast n emisión en directo, f

livelihood /'laɪvli,hʊd/ n vida, subsistencia, f. **to make a l.**, ganarse la vida

livelong /'lɪv,lɔŋ/ a entero, todo; eterno. **all the l. day**, todo el santo día

lively /'laɪvli/ a vivo, vivaracho; brioso, enérgico; alegre; bullicioso; animado; (fresh) fresco; (of colours) brillante; intenso

liver /'lɪvər/ n vividor (-ra), el, m, (f, la) que vive; habitante, m; Anat. hígado, m. **l. cancer**, cáncer del hígado, m. **l. complaint**, mal de hígado, m. **l. extract**, extracto de hígado, m

livery /'lɪvəri/ n librea, f; uniforme, m; Poet. vestiduras, f pl. **l. stables**, pensión de caballos, f; cochería de alquiler, f

livid /'lɪvɪd/ a lívido; cárdeno, amoratado

living /'lɪvɪŋ/ a viviente; vivo, vital. —n vida, f; modo de vivir, m; beneficio eclesiástico, m. **the l.**, los vivos. **to make one's l.**, ganarse la vida. **l. memory**, memoria de personas vivientes, memoria de los que aún viven, f. **l.-room**, sala de estar, f. **l. soul**, ser viviente, m; Inf. bicho viviente, m. **l. wage**, jornal básico, m

lizard /'lɪzərd/ n lagarto (-ta). **giant l.**, dragón, m. **wall l.**, lagartija, f. **l. hole**, la-gartera, f

load /loud/ n carga, f; peso, m; (cart) carretada, f; Elec. carga, f; (quantity) cantidad, f. —vt cargar (con); (with honors) llenar (de); (Fig. weigh down) agobiar (con); (a stick with lead) emplomar; (Elec. and of dice) cargar; (wine) mezclar vino con un narcótico. **to be loaded with fruit**, estar cargado de fruta. **to l. oneself with**, cargarse de. **to l. the dice**, cargar los dados. **to l. again**, recargar

loading /'loudɪŋ/ n carga, f. **l. depot**, cargadero, m

loaf /louf/ n pan, m; (French) barra de pan, f. —vi golfear, vagabundear, gandu-lear. **l. sugar**, azúcar de pilón, m

loafer /'loufər/ n vago (-ga); azotacalles, mf; gandul (-la); golfo (-fa)

loam /loum/ n marga, f

loan /loun/ n empréstito, m; (lending) prestación, f; préstamo, m. —vt prestar. **l. fund**, caja de empréstitos, f. **l. company office**, casa de préstamos, f

loath /louθ/ a desinclinado, poco dispuesto

loathe /louð/ vt abominar, detestar, odiar, aborrecer; repugnar

loathsome /'louðsəm/ a odioso, aborreci-ble; asqueroso; repugnante

lobby /'lɔbi/ n pasillo, m; antecámara, f; (in a hotel, house) vestíbulo, recibidor, m; (waiting-room) sala de espera, f; (in Parliament) sala de los pasos perdidos, f.
—vt and vi cabildear

lobe /loub/ n Bot. lobo, m; (Anat. Archit.) lóbulo, m

lobster /'lɔbstər/ n langosta, f; bogavante, m. **l.-pot**, cambín, m, nasa, f

local /'loukəl/ a local; de la localidad. **l. anesthetic**, anestésico local, m. **l. color**, color local, m

locale /lou'kæl/ n local, m

locality /lou'kæliti/ n localidad, f; situación, f

localize /'louka,laiz/ vt localizar

locate /'loukeit/ vt situar; colocar; localizar. **to be located**, situarse; hallarse

location /lou'keiʃən/ n colocación, f; emplazamiento, m; localidad, f; situación, posición, f

loch /lɔk/ n lago, m

lock /lɔk/ n cerradura (of a door, including a vehicle) f; (of a gun) cerrojo, m; (in wrestling) llave, f; (on rivers, canals) presa, f; (at a dock) esclusa, f; (of hair) mechón, m, guedeja, f; (ringlet) bucle, m; pl **locks**, (hair) cabellos, m pl, pelo, m. **spring l.**, cerradura de golpe, f. **to put a l. on**, poner cerradura a. **under l. and key**, bajo cuatro llaves. **l.-jaw**, trismo, m. **l. keeper**, esclusero, m. **l.-out strike**, huelga patronal, f

lock /lɔk/ vt cerrar con llave; Fig. encerrar; (embrace) abrazar estrechamente; (of wheels, etc.) trabar; (twine) entrelazar. —vi cerrarse con llave. **to l. in**, cerrar con llave; encerrar. **to l. out**, cerrar la puerta (a); dejar en la calle (a). **to l. up**, encerrar; (imprison) encarcelar

locker /'lɔkər/ n (drawer) cajón, m; (cupboard) armario, m; Naut. cajonada, f

locket /'lɔkit/ n guardapelo, m; medallón, m

locksmith /'lɔk,smiθ/ n cerrajero, m. **locksmith's trade**, cerrajería, f

locomotive /,loukə'moutɪv/ a locomotor. —n locomotora, f

locum tenens /'loukəm 'tinɛnz/ n interino (-na)

locust /'loukəst/ n langosta migratoria, f

lode /loud/ n filón, m

lodge /lɔdʒ/ n casita, garita, f; casa de guarda, f; (freemason's) logia, f; (porter's) portería, f, vi hospedarse, alojarse, vivir, parar; penetrar; entrar (en); fijarse (en). —vt hospedar, alojar; albergar; (a blow) asestar; (a complaint) hacer, dar; (money, etc.) depositar. **to l. an accusation against**, querellarse contra, quejarse de. **l.-keeper**, conserje, m

lodger /'lɔdʒər/ n huésped (-eda)

lodging /'lɔdʒɪŋ/ n hospedaje, alojamiento, m; (inn) posada, f; residencia, f; casa, f. **l.-house**, casa de huéspedes, f

loft /lɔft/ n desván, sotabanco, m; pajar, m

lofty /'lɔfti/ a alto; sublime; noble; eminente; (haughty) altanero, soberbio

log /lɔg/ n madero, tronco, m; palo, m; leño, m; Naut., diario de a bordo m, barquilla, f. **to lie like a log**, estar hecho un tronco. **log-book**, Naut. cuaderno de bitácora, m. **log-cabin**, cabañas de troncos, m. **log-wood**, palo campeche, m

logarithm /'lɔgə,rɪðəm/ n logaritmo, m

logic /'lɔdʒɪk/ n lógica, f

logical /'lɔdʒɪkəl/ a lógico

loin /lɔin/ n ijar, m; (of meat) falda, f; pl loins, lomos, riñones m pl. **to gird up one's loins**, Fig. arremangarse los faldones. **l.-cloth**, taparrabo, m

loiter /'lɔitər/ vi vagabundear, vagar, errar; haraganear; rezagarse

loiterer /'lɔitərər/ n haragán (-ana); vago (-ga); rezagado (-da)

loll /lɔl/ vi recostarse (en), apoyarse (en). —vt (the tongue) sacar

London /'lʌndən/ Londres, m

Londoner /'lʌndənər/ n londinense, mf

lone /loun/. See **lonely**

loneliness /'lounlinis/ n soledad, f; aislamiento, m

lonely /'lounli/ a solitario; solo; aislado, remoto; desierto

lonesome /'lounsəm/ a solo, solitario

long /lɔŋ/ a largo; prolongado; de largo; (extensive) extenso; (big) grande; (much) mucho. **a l. time**, mucho tiempo. **It is five feet l.**, Tiene cinco pies de largo. **l.-armed**, que tiene los brazos largos. **l.-boat**, falúa, f. **l. clothes**, (infant's) mantillas, f pl. **l.-distance call**, conferencia telefónica, f. **l.-distance race**, carrera de fondo, f. **l.-eared**, de orejas largas. **l.-faced**, de cara larga, carilargo. **l.-forgotten**, olvidado hace mucho tiempo. **l.-haired**, que tiene el pelo largo. **l.-headed**, dolicocéfalo; Fig. astuto, sagaz. **l.-legged**, zanquilargo, zancudo. **l.-lived**, que vive hasta una edad avanzada; longevo; duradero. **l.-lost**, perdido hace mucho tiempo. **l.-sighted**, présbita; previsor; sagaz. **l.-standing**, viejo, de muchos años. **l.-suffering**, sufrido, paciente. **l.-tailed**, de cola larga. **l.-waisted**, de talle largo. **l.-winded**, prolijo

long /lɔŋ/ adv mucho tiempo; mucho; durante mucho tiempo. **as l. as**, mientras (que). **before l.**, dentro de poco. **the l. and the short of it**, en resumidas cuentas. **How l. has she been here?** ¿Cuánto tiempo hace que está aquí? **not l. before**, poco tiempo antes. **l. ago**, tiempo ha, muchos años ha

long /lɔŋ/ vi anhelar, suspirar (por), desear con vehemencia

longer /'lɔŋgər/ a compar más largo. —adv compar más tiempo. **How much l. must we wait?** ¿Cuánto tiempo más hemos de esperar? **He can no l. walk as he used**, Ya no puede andar como antes

longevity /lɔn'dʒɛviti/ n longevidad, f

longing /'lɔŋiŋ/ a anheloso, ansioso; de envidia. —n anhelo, m, ansia, f; deseo vehemente, m; envidia, f

longitude /'lɒndʒi,tud/ n longitud, f

look /luk/ n mirada, f; (glance) vistazo, m, ojeada, f; (air) semblante, aire, porte, m; (appearance) aspecto, m; apariencia, f. **good looks**, buen parecer, m; guapeza, f. **the new l.**, la nueva línea, la nueva silueta, la nueva moda. **to be on the l.-out**, andar a la mira

look /luk/ vi and vt mirar; considerar, contemplar; (appear, seem) parecer; tener aire (de); tener aspecto (de); hacer el efecto (de); (show oneself) mostrarse; (of buildings, etc.) caer (a); dar (a); mirar (a).; (seem to be) revelar (e.g., You don't l. thirty, No revelas treinta años) **to l. alike**, parecerse. **to l. hopeful**, Fig. prometer bien. **to l. out of the corner of the eye**, mirar de reojo. **to l. (a person) up and down**, mirar de hito en hito. **to l. about one**, mirar a su alrededor; observar. **to l. after**, tener la mirada puesta en, mirar; (care for) cuidar; (watch) vigilar; mirar por. **to l. at**, mirar; considerar; examinar. **He looked at his watch**, Miró su reloj. **He looked at her**, La miró. **to l. away**, desviar los ojos, apartar la mirada. **to l. back**, mirar hacia atrás, volver la cabeza; (in thought) pensar en el pasado. **to l. down**, bajar los ojos; mirar el suelo; mirar hacia abajo. **to l. down upon**, dominar, mirar a; (scorn) despreciar; mirar de arriba para abajo. **to l. for**, buscar; buscar con los ojos; (await) aguardar; (expect) esperar. **to l. forward**, mirar hacia el porvenir; pensar en el futuro; esperar con ilusión. **to l. in**, entrar por un instante, hacer una visita corta. **to l. into**, mirar dentro de; mirar hacia el interior de; estudiar, investigar. **to l. on**, vt mirar; considerar; (of buildings, etc.) dar a. —vi ser espectador. **to l. on to**, dar a. —vi mirar bien; (a house) inspeccionar; (a book) hojear; mirar superficialmente. —vi volver la cabeza, volverse; mirar hacia atrás. **to l. round for**, buscar con los ojos; buscar por todas partes. **to l. through**, mirar por; mirar a través de; examinar; (search) registrar; (understand) registrar. **to l. to**, (be careful of) tener cuidado de; (attend to) atender a; (care for) cuidar de; (count on) contar con; (resort to) acudir a; (await) esperar. **to l. toward**, mirar hacia, mirar en la dirección de; caer a. **to l. up**, vi mirar hacia arriba; (aspire) aspirar; (improve) mejorar. —vt visitar, ir (or venir) a ver; (turn up) buscar; averiguar.

to l. upon, mirar. Other meanings see to l. on. **They l. upon her as their daughter**, La miran como una hija suya. **to l. up to**, Fig. respetar

looked-for /'lukt ,fɔr/ a esperado; deseado

looking /'lukiŋ/ a (in compounds) de... aspecto, de... apariencia. **dirty-l.**, de aspecto sucio. **l.-glass**, espejo, m

lookout /'luk,aut/ n vigilancia, observación, f; (view) vista, f, panorama, m; (viewpoint) miradero, m; Mil. atalaya, m; Naut. gaviero, m; (Fig. prospect) perspectiva, f

loom /lum/ n telar, m, vi asomar, aparecer

loop /lup/ n (turn) vuelta, f; (in rivers, etc.) recodo, m, curva, f; (fold) pliegue, m; bucle, m; (fastening) fiador, m, presilla, f; Aer. rizo, m; (knot) nudo corredizo, m. **to l. the l.**, Aer. hacer el rizo, hacer rizos. **l.-line**, empalme de ferrocarril, m

loophole /'lup,houl/ n saetera, aspillera, f; Fig. escapatoria, f; pretexto, m, excusa, f

loose /lus/ a suelto; (free) libre; (slack) flojo; (of garments) holgado; (untied) desatado; (unfastened) desprendido; (movible) (unchained) desencadenado; en libertad; (pendulous) colgante; (of a nail, tooth, etc.) inseguro; poco firme; que se mueve; (of knots, etc.) flojo; (of the mind, etc.) incoherente, ilógico; poco exacto; (of style, etc.) vago, impreciso; (of conduct) disoluto, vicioso; (careless) negligente, descuidado. —vt (untie) desatar; desprender; soltar; aflojar; (of a priest) absolver; Fig. desencadenar. **to break l.**, desprenderse; soltarse; libertarse; escapar; Fig. desencadenarse. **to let l.**, desatar; aflojar; poner en libertad; soltar; Fig. desencadenar; (interject) lanzar. **to turn l.**, poner en libertad; dar salida (a); echar de casa, poner en la calle. **to work l.**, desprenderse; aflojarse; desvencijarse. **l.-box**, caballeriza, f. **l.-change**, suelto, m. **l.-leaf notebook**, libreta de hojas sueltas, f

loosely /'lusli/ adv flojamente; sueltamente; (vaguely) vagamente; incorrectamente; incoherentemente; (carelessly) negligentemente; (viciously) disolutamente

loosen /'lusən/ vt (untie) desatar; aflojar; soltar; desasir; (the tongue) desatar; Fig. hacer menos riguroso, ablandar

loot /lut/ n botín, m, vt saquear

looter /'lutər/ n saqueador (-ra)

looting /'lutiŋ/ n saqueo, pillaje, m, a saqueador

lop /lɒp/ vt mochar; podar; destroncar; cortar de un golpe. —a (of ears) gacho. **to lop off the ends**, cercenar. **to lop off the top**, desmochar. **lop-sided**, desproporcionado; desequilibrado

loquacious /lou'kweiʃəs/ a locuaz, gárrulo

lord /lɔrd/ n señor, m; (husband) esposo, m; (English title) lord, m, (pl lores); (Christ) Señor, m. **feudal l.**, señor de horca y cuchillo, m. **my l.**, milord. **my lords,** milores. **Our L.**, Nuestro Señor. **the Lord's Prayer,** el Padrenuestro. **to l. it over,** mandar como señor, mandar a la baqueta. **L. Chamberlain,** camarero mayor, m. **L. Chancellor,** gran canciller, m. **L. Chief Justice,** presidente del tribunal supremo, m. **L.-Lieutenant,** virrey, m. **L. Mayor,** alcalde, m. **L. Privy Seal,** guardasellos del rey, m

lordly /'lɔrdli/ a señorial, señoril; altivo, arrogante

lore /lɔr/ n saber, m; erudición, f; tradiciones, f pl

lorry /'lɔri/ n camión, m; carro, m

lose /luz/ vt perder; hacer perder, quitar; (forget) olvidar. —vi perder; (of clocks) atrasar. **to be lost in thought,** estar ensimismado, estar absorto. **to l. oneself (in)** perderse (en); abstraerse (en); entregarse (a). **to l. one's footing,** resbalar. **to l. one's way,** extraviarse, perder el camino. **to l. one's self-control,** perder el tino. **to l. one's head,** perder la cabeza. **to l. ground,** perder terreno. **to l. one's voice,** perder la voz. **to l. patience,** perder la paciencia, perder los estribos

loser /'luzər/ n perdedor (-ra)

losing /'luzɪŋ/ a perdedor. —n pérdida, f

loss /lɔs/ n pérdida, f. **at a l.,** Com. con pérdida; perplejo, dudoso. **heavy losses,** Mil. pérdidas cuantiosas, f pl. **We are at a l. for words...,** No tenemos palabras para...

lot /lɒt/ n suerte, f; fortuna, f; lote, m; parte, porción, cuota, f; (for building) solar, m. **a lot of people,** muchas personas. **Our lot would have been very different,** Nuestra suerte hubiera sido muy distinta, Otro gallo nos cantara. **to draw lots,** echar suertes, sortear. **to take the lot,** Inf. alzarse con el santo y la limosna

lotion /'louʃən/ n loción, f

lottery /'lɒtəri/ n lotería, f. **l. ticket,** billete de la lotería, m

loud /laud/ a fuerte; (noisy) ruidoso, estrepitoso; alto; (gaudy) chillón, llamativo, cursi. —adv ruidosamente. **l.-speaker,** Radio. altavoz, altoparlante, m

loudly /'laudli/ adv en alta voz; fuertemente; ruidosamente, con estrépito

loudness /'laudnɪs/ n (noise) ruido, m; sonoridad, f; (force) fuerza, f; (of colors, etc.) mal gusto, m, vulgaridad, f

lounge /laundʒ/ n sala de estar, f; salón, m, vi reclinarse; ponerse a sus anchas; apoyarse (en); gandulear; vagar. **l. chair,** poltrona, f. **l.-lizard,** Inf. pollo pera, m. **l. -suit,** traje americano, m

lounger /'laundʒər/ n holgazán (-ana); golfo (-fa), azotacalles, mf

louse /laus/ n piojo, m

lousy /'lauzi/ a piojoso

lout /laut/ n patán, zamacuco, m

loutish /'lautɪʃ/ a rústico

lovable /'lʌvəbəl/ a amable; simpático

love /lʌv/ n amor, m; (friendship) amistad, f; (enthusiasm, liking) afición, f; (in tennis) cero, m, vt querer, amar; gustar mucho; tener afición (a). —vi estar enamorado. **I should l. to dine with you,** Me gustaría mucho cenar con Vds. **to be in l. with,** estar enamorado de. **to fall in l. with,** enamorarse de. **They l. each other,** Se quieren. **to make l. to,** hacer el amor (a), galantear. **l. affair,** amorío, lance de amor, m. **l.-bird,** periquito, m. **l.-letter,** carta amatoria, carta de amor, f. **l.-making,** galanteo, m. **l.-philtre,** filtro, m. **l.-song,** canción de amor, f. **l.-story,** historia de amor, f. **l.-token,** prenda de amor, f

lovely /'lʌvli/ a hermoso, bello; delicioso; amable; Inf. estupendo

lover /'lʌvər/ n amante, mf; aficionado (-da)

lovesick /'lʌv,sɪk/ a enfermo de amor, enamorado

loving /'lʌvɪŋ/ a amoroso; cariñoso; (friendly) amistoso; de amor

low /lou/ a bajo; de poca altura; (of dresses, etc.) escotado; (of musical notes) grave; (soft) suave; (feeble) débil; (depressed) deprimido, triste, abatido; (plain) sencillo; (of a fever) lento; (of a bow) profundo; pequeño; inferior; humilde; (ill) enfermo; (vile) vil, ruin; obsceno, escabroso. —adv bajo; cerca de la tierra; en voz baja; (cheaply) barato, a bajo precio. **in a low voice,** en voz baja, paso. **to lay low,** (kill) tumbar; (knock down) derribar; incapacitar. **to lie low,** descansar; estar muerto; esconderse, agacharse; callar. **to run low,** escasear. **low-born,** de humilde cuna. **low-brow,** nada intelectual. **low comedy,** farsa, f. **low flying,** n bajo vuelo, m, a que vuela bajo; terrero, rastrero; que vuela a ras de tierra. **low frequency,** baja frecuencia, f. **low Latin,** bajo latín, m. **Low Mass,** misa rezada, f. **low neck,** escote, m. **low-necked,** escotado. **low-pitched,** grave. **low-spirited,** deprimido. **Low Sunday,** domingo de Cuasimodo, m. **low tension,** baja tensión, f. **low trick,** mala pasada, f. **low water,** marea baja, bajamar, f; (of rivers) estiaje, m

low /lou/ vi berrear, mugir. —n berrido, mugido, m

lower /'louər/ vt bajar; descolgar; disminuir; (price) rebajar; (a boat, sails) arriar. —vi (of persons) fruncir el ceño, mostrarse malhumorado; (of the sky) encapotarse, cargarse; (menace) amenazar. **to l. a boat,** arriar un bote. **to l. oneself,** (by a rope, etc.) descolgarse. **to l. the flag,** abatir la bandera

lower /'louər/ a compar más bajo; menos alto; bajo; inferior. **l. classes,** clase obrera, f, clases bajas, f pl. **l. down,** más abajo. **L. House,** Cámara de los Comunes, f; cámara baja, f. **l. jaw,** mandíbula inferior, f. **l. storey,** piso bajo, m; piso de abajo, m

lowest /'lovist/ a superl el (la, etc.) más bajo; el (la, etc.) más profundo; ínfimo

lowland /'lovlənd/ n tierra baja, f. **the Lowlands,** las tierras bajas de Escocia

lowly /'lovli/ a humilde

lowness /'lovnis/ n poca altura, f; situación poco elevada, f; pequeñez, f; (of musical notes) gravedad, f; (softness) suavidad, f; (feebleness) debilidad, f; (sadness) tristeza, f, abatimiento, m; (of price) baratura, f; inferioridad, f; humildad, f; (vileness) bajeza, f; obscenidad, f

loyal /'lɔiəl/ a leal, fiel

loyalist /'lɔiəlist/ n realista, mf; defensor (-ra) del gobierno legítimo

loyalty /'lɔiəlti/ n lealtad, fidelidad, f

lozenge /'lɒzindʒ/ n pastilla, f

lubricant /'lubrikənt/ a and n lubricante m

lubricate /'lubri,keit/ vt lubricar, engrasar

lubricating oil n aceite lubricante, m

lubrication /,lubri'keiʃən/ n lubricación, f, engrasado, m

lucid /'lusid/ a lúcido; claro

luck /lʌk/ n destino, azar, m; (good) buenaventura, suerte, f. **to bring bad l.,** traer mala suerte. **to try one's l.,** probar fortuna

luckily /'lʌkəli/ adv por fortuna, afortunadamente, felizmente

luckless /'lʌklis/ a desdichado

lucky /'lʌki/ a afortunado; dichoso; venturoso; feliz. **to be l.,** tener buena suerte

lucrative /'lukrətiv/ a lucrativo

lucre /'lukər/ n lucro, m

lucubration /,lukyʊ'breiʃən/ n lucubración, f

ludicrous /'ludikrəs/ a absurdo, risible, ridículo

lug /lʌg/ n tirón, m; (ear and projection) oreja, f, vt tirar (de); arrastrar. **to lug about,** arrastrar (por); llevar con dificultad. **to lug in,** arrastrar adentro; introducir; hacer entrar. **to lug out,** arrastrar afuera; hacer salir

luggage /'lʌgidʒ/ n equipaje, m. **excess l.,** exceso de equipaje, m. **piece of l.,** bulto, m. **to register one's l.,** facturar el equipaje. **l. carrier,** (on buses, etc.) baca, f; (on a car) portaequipajes, m. **l. porter,** mozo de equipajes, m. **l. rack,** (on a car) portaequipajes, m; (in a train) rejilla para el equipaje, f. **l. receipt,** talón de equipaje, m. **l. room,** consigna, f. **l. van,** furgón de equipajes, m

lugubrious /lʊ'gubriəs/ a lúgubre

lukewarm /'luk'wɔrm/ a tibio, templado; Fig. indiferente, frío

lull /lʌl/ n momento de calma, m; tregua, f; silencio, m, vt (a child) arrullar, adormecer; (soothe) sosegar, calmar; disminuir, mitigar

lullaby /'lʌlə,bai/ n canción de cuna, f

lumbago /lʌm'beigou/ n lumbago, m

lumber /'lʌmbər/ n (wood) maderas de sierra, f pl; (rubbish) trastos viejos, m pl. —vt amontonar trastos viejos; obstruir. —vi andar pesadamente; avanzar ruidosamente, avanzar con ruido sordo. **l.-jack,** maderero, ganchero, m. **l.-room,** leonera, f. **l.-yard,** maderería, f, depósito de maderas, m

lumbering /'lʌmbəriŋ/ a pesado

luminary /'lumə,nɛri/ n lumbrera, f

luminous /'lumənəs/ a luminoso

lump /lʌmp/ n masa, f; bulto, m; pedazo, m; (of sugar) terrón m; (swelling) hinchazón, f; protuberancia, f. —vt amontonar. **to l. together,** mezclar; incluir. **in the l.,** en la masa; en grueso. **Let him l. it!** ¡Que se rasque! **l. in one's throat,** nudo en la garganta, m. **l. of sugar,** terrón de azúcar, m. **l. sum,** cantidad gruesa, f

lunacy /'lunəsi/ n locura, f

lunar /'lunər/ a lunar

lunatic /'lunətik/ n loco (-ca); demente, mf a de locos; loco. **l. asylum,** manicomio, m

lunch, luncheon /lʌntʃ; 'lʌntʃən/ n almuerzo, m; (snack) merienda, f. —vi almorzar. **l. basket** or **pail,** fiambrera, f

lung /lʌŋ/ n pulmón, m

lunge /lʌndʒ/ n (fencing) estocada, f; embestida, f, vi dar una estocada; abalanzarse sobre

lurch /lɜrtʃ/ n sacudida, f; Naut. guiñada, f; tambaleo, m; movimiento brusco, m. —vi Naut. guiñar; tambalearse; andar haciendo eses. **to leave in the l.,** dejar plantado

lure /lʊr/ n añagaza, f; reclamo, m; aliciente, atractivo, m; seducción, f. —vt atraer, tentar

lurid /'lʊrid/ a misterioso, fantástico; cárdeno; ominoso; funesto, triste; (orange) anaranjado; (vicissitudinous) accidentado

lurk /lɜrk/ vi acechar, espiar; esconderse

lurking /'lɜrkiŋ/ a (in ambush) en acecho; (of fear, etc.) vago

luscious /'lʌʃəs/ a delicioso; suculento; meloso; atractivo, apetitoso; sensual

lush /lʌʃ/ a jugoso; fresco y lozano; maduro

lust /lʌst/ n lujuria, lascivia, f; codicia, f; deseo, m. **l. for revenge,** deseo de venganza, m

luster /'lʌstər/ n lustre, brillo, m; brillantez, f

lustful /'lʌstfəl/ a lujurioso, lúbrico, lascivo

lustrous /'lʌstrəs/ a lustroso

lusty /'lʌsti/ a vigoroso, fuerte, lozano

lute /lut/ n laúd, m, vihuela, f. **l.-player,** vihuelista, mf

Lutheran /'luθərən/ a luterano. —n luterano (-na)

luxuriance /lʌg'ʒuriəns/ n lozanía, f; exuberancia, superabundancia, f

luxuriant /lʌɡ'ʒʊriənt/ a lozano; fértil; exuberante

luxuriate /lʌɡ'ʒʊri,eit/ vi crecer con exuberancia; complacerse (en); disfrutar (de), gozar (de)

luxurious /lʌɡ'ʒʊriəs/ a lujoso

luxuriously /lʌɡ'ʒʊriəsli/ adv lujosamente, con lujo

luxury /'lʌkʃəri/ n lujo, m. **l. goods**, artículos de lujo, m pl

lyceum /lai'siəm/ n liceo, m

lye /lai/ n lejía, f

lying /'laiiŋ/ a (recumbent) recostado; (untrue) mentiroso, falso. —n mentiras, f pl. **l.-in**, parto, m

lymph /limf/ n linfa, f; vacuna, f

lymphatic /lim'fætik/ a linfático; flemático

lynch /lintʃ/ vt linchar

lynching /'lintʃiŋ/ n linchamiento, m

lynx /liŋks/ n lince, m. **l.-eyed**, de ojos de lince

lyre /lai²r/ n lira, f. **l.-bird**, pájaro lira, m

lyric /'lirik/ n poesía lírica, f; poema lírico, m; letra (de una canción,) f

lyrical /'lirikəl/ a lírico

lyricism /'lirə,sizəm/ n lirismo, m

M

m /em/ n (letter) eme, f
ma'am /mæm/ n señora, f
macabre /mə'kɑbrə/ a macabro
macadam /mə'kædəm/ n macadán, m, a
de macadán
macadamize /mə'kædə,maiz/ vt maca-
danizar
macaroni /,mækə'rouni/ n macarrones, m
pl
macaronic /,mækə'rɒnɪk/ a macarrónico
macaroon /,mækə'run/ n macarrón de almendras, m
Macassar oil /mə'kæsər/ n aceite de Ma-
casar, m
macaw /mə'kɔ/ n macagua, f, guacamayo, m
mace /meis/ n maza, f; Cul. macis, f. m.-
bearer, macero, m
Macedonian /,mæsɪ'douniən/ a mace-
dón, macedonio. —n macedonio (-ia)
macerate /'mæsə,reit/ vt macerar. —vi
macerarse
Machiavellian /,mækiə'veliən/ a maquiavélico
machination /,mækə'neiʃən/ n maquinación, f
machine /mə'ʃin/ n máquina, f; mecanismo, m; aparato, m; instrumento, m; organización, f, vt trabajar a máquina; Sew.
coser a máquina. m.-gun, n ametralladora, f. —vt ametrallar. m.-gun carrier,
portametralladoras, m. m.-gunner, ametrallador, m. m.-made, hecho a máquina.
m.-oil, aceite de motores, m. m.-shop,
taller de maquinaria, m. m.-tool,
máquina herramienta, f
machinery /mə'ʃinəri/ n maquinaria, f;
mecanismo, m; organización, f; sistema,
m
mackerel /'mækərəl/ n caballa, f. m.
sky, cielo aborregado, m
mad /mæd/ a loco; fuera de sí; (of a dog,
etc.) rabioso; furioso. as mad as a hatter, loco como una cabra. to drive mad,
volver loco (a). to go mad, volverse
loco, enloquecer, perder el seso. mad
with joy (pain), loco de alegría (dolor).
mad dog, perro rabioso, m
madam /'mædəm/ n señora, f; (French
form) madama, f. Yes, madam, Sí señora
madcap /'mæd,kæp/ n locuelo (-la), f,
botarate, m; tarambana, mf
madden /'mædn/ vt enloquecer; enfurecer, exasperar
maddening /'mædnɪŋ/ a exasperante,
irritador
made /meid/ past part and a hecho; formado. self-m. man, un hombre hecho y
derecho. m.-to-measure, hecho a la
medida. m.-up, compuesto; (of clothes)
confeccionado, ya hecho; (of the face)
pintado; (fictitious) inventado, ficticio; artificial
madhouse /'mæd,haus/ n casa de locos,
f, manicomio, m
madman /'mæd,mæn/ n loco, m

madness /'mædnɪs/ n locura, f; (of a
dog, etc.) rabia, f; furia, f
Madonna /mə'dɒnə/ n Madona, f
madrigal /'mædrɪgəl/ n madrigal, m
Madrilenian /,mædrə'liniən/ a madrileño, matritense. —n madrileño (-ña)
madwoman /'mæd,wʊmən/ n loca, f
Maecenas /mi'sinəs/ n mecenas, m
maelstrom /'meilstrəm/ n remolino, vórtice, m
magazine /,mægə'zin/ n (store) almacén,
m; (for explosives) polvorín, m, santabárbara, f; (periodical) revista, f. m. rifle, rifle de repetición, m
maggot /'mægət/ n gusano, m, cresa, f;
Fig. manía, f, capricho, m
magic /'mædʒɪk/ n magia, f; mágica, f;
Fig. encanto, m, a mágico. as if by m.,
por ensalmo. m. lantern, linterna mágica,
f
magically /'mædʒɪkli/ adv por encanto
magician /mə'dʒɪʃən/ n mago, mágico,
brujo, m; (conjurer) jugador de manos, m
magisterial /,mædʒə'stɪriəl/ a magistral
magistracy /'mædʒəstrəsi/ n magistra-
tura, f
magistrate /'mædʒə,streit/ n magistrado,
m; juez municipal, m
Magi, the /'meidʒai/ n pl los reyes magos
Magna Carta /'mægnə 'kɑrtə/ n Carta
Magna, f
magnanimity /,mægnə'nɪmɪti/ n magnanimidad, generosidad, f
magnanimous /mæg'nænəməs/ a magnánimo, generoso
magnate /'mægneit/ n magnate, m
magnesia /mæg'niʒə/ n magnesia, f
magnet /'mægnɪt/ n imán, m
magnetic /mæg'netɪk/ a magnético; Fig.
atractivo. m. field, campo magnético, m.
m. needle, brújula, f
magnetize /'mægnɪ,taiz/ vt magnetizar,
imanar; (hypnotize) magnetizar; Fig.
atraer
magnification /,mægnəfɪ'keiʃən/ n (by
a lens, etc.) aumento, m; exageración, f
magnificence /mæg'nɪfəsəns/ n magnificencia, f
magnificent /mæg'nɪfəsənt/ a magnífico
magnify /'mægnə,fai/ vt (by lens) aumentar; exagerar; (praise) magnificar
magnifying /'mægnə,faiɪŋ/ a de aumento, vidrio de aumento. m. glass, lente
de aumento, m
magniloquent /mæg'nɪləkwənt/ a
grandílocuo
magnitude /'mægnɪ,tud/ n magnitud, f
magnolia /mæg'noulyə/ n magnolia, f
magnum /'mægnəm/ n botella de dos
litros, f
magpie /'mæg,pai/ n marica, picaza, f

mahogany /mə'hɒgəni/ n caoba, f, a de caoba

maid /meid/ n doncella, muchacha, f; virgen, f; soltera, f; (servant) criada, f; (daily) asistenta, f. **old m.,** solterona, f. **m.-of-all-work,** criada para todo, f. **m.-of-honor,** dama de honor, f

maiden /'meidn/ n doncella, joven, soltera, f; virgen, f; zagala, f. —a de soltera; soltera f; virginal; (of speeches, voyages, etc.) primero. **m. lady,** dama soltera, f. **m.-name,** apellido de soltera, m. **m. speech,** primer discurso, m

maidenhood /'meidn,hʊd/ n doncellez, f virginidad, f

maidenly /'meidnli/ a virginal; modesto, modoso; tímido

maidservant /'meid,sɜrvənt/ n criada, sirvienta, f

mail /meil/ n mala, f; (bag) valija, f; correo, m; correspondencia, f; (armour) cota de malla, f. —vt mandar por correo; armar con cota de malla. **coat of m.,** cota de malla, f. **royal m.,** malla real, f. **m.-bag,** valija de correo, f; portacartas, m. **m.-boat,** buque correo, m. **m.-cart,** ambulancia de correos, f. **m.-clad,** vestido de cota de malla; armado. **m.-coach,** coche correo, m, diligencia, f. **m.-order,** pedido postal, m. **m.-order business,** negocio de ventas por correo, m. **m.-plane,** avión postal, m. **m. service,** servicio de correos, m. **m. steamer,** vapor correo, m. **m. train,** tren correo, m. **m. van,** (on a train) furgón postal, m

mailed /meild/ a de malla; armado. **m. fist,** Fig. puño de hierro, m

maim /meim/ vt mancar; mutilar, tullir; estropear

maimed /meimd/ a manco; tullido, mutilado

main /mein/ a mayor; principal; más importante, esencial; maestro. —n (mainland) continente, m; (sea) océano, m; (pipe) cañería maestra, f. **by m. force,** por fuerza mayor. **in the m.,** en general, generalmente; en su mayoría. **m. beam,** viga maestra, f. **m. body,** (of a building) ala principal, f; (of a church) cuerpo (de iglesia), m; (of an army) cuerpo (del ejército), m; mayor parte, mayoría, f. **m. line,** línea principal, f. **m. mast,** palo mayor, m. **m. thing,** cosa principal, f, lo más importante. **m. wall,** pared maestra, f

mainland /'mein,lænd/ n continente, m; tierra firme, f

mainly /'meinli/ adv principalmente; en su mayoría; generalmente

mainspring /'mein,sprɪŋ/ n (of a watch) muelle real, m; motivo principal, m; origen, m

mainstay /'mein,stei/ n estay mayor, m; Fig. sostén principal, m

maintain /mein'tein/ vt mantener; sostener; tener; guardar; afirmar

maintenance /'meintənəns/ n manteni-

miento, m; manutención, f, sustento, m; conservación, f, subsistencia, f

maize /meiz/ n maíz, m. **m. field,** maizal, m

majestic /mə'dʒɛstɪk/ a majestuoso

majesty /'mædʒəsti/ n majestad, f; majestuosidad, f. **His** or **Her M.,** Su Majestad

majolica /mə'dʒɒlɪkə/ n mayólica, f

major /'meidʒər/ a mayor; principal. —n mayor de edad, m; Mil. comandante. **anthropology major,** alumno con la especialidad en antropología m. **m.-domo,** mayordomo, m. **m.-general,** general de división, m. **m. road,** carretera, f; ruta de prioridad, f. **m. scale,** escala mayor, f

Majorca /mə'dʒɔrkə/ Mallorca, f

majority /mə'dʒɔrɪti/ n mayoría, f; mayor número, m; generalidad, f. **to have attained one's m.,** ser mayor de edad

make /meik/ vt hacer; crear, formar; (manufacture) fabricar, confeccionar; construir; (produce) producir; causar; (prepare) preparar; (a bed, a fire, a remark, poetry, friends, enemies, war, a curtsey) hacer; (earn, win) ganar; (a speech) pronunciar; (compel) obligar (a), forzar (a); inclinar (a); (arrive at) alcanzar, llegar (a); (calculate) calcular; (arrange) arreglar; deducir; (be) ser; (equal) ser igual a; (think) creer; (appoint as) constituir (en), hacer; (behave) portarse (como). —vi (begin) ir (a), empezar (a); (make as though) hacer (como si); (of the tide) crecer; contribuir (a); tender (a). **He made as if to go,** Hizo como si de marchara. **to m. as though...,** aparentar, fingir. **It made me ill,** Me hizo sentir mal. **They have made it up,** Han hecho las paces. **They m. a great deal of money,** Hacen (or ganan) mucho dinero. **You cannot m. me believe it,** No puedes hacerme creerlo. **He is making himself ridiculous,** Se está poniendo en ridículo. **to m. ready,** preparar. **to m. the tea,** hacer el té; preparar el té. **Two and two m. four,** Dos y dos son cuatro. **to m. oneself known,** darse a conocer. **to m. one of...,** ser uno de... **to m. after,** seguir; correr detrás de. **to m. again,** hacer de nuevo, rehacer. **to m. away with,** quitar; suprimir; destruir; (kill) matar; (squander) derrochar; (steal) llevarse; hurtar. **to m. away with oneself,** quitarse la vida, suicidarse. **to m. for,** encaminarse a, dirigirse a; (attack) abalanzarse sobre, atacar; (tend to) contribuir a, tender a. **to m. off,** marcharse corriendo, largarse; huir, escaparse. **to m. out,** (discern) distinguir; descifrar; (understand) comprender; (prove) probar, justificar; (draw up) redactar; (fill in a form) completar, llenar; (a check, etc.) extender; (an account) hacer; (get on, succeed or otherwise) ir (with bien or mal); (convey) dar la impresión de que; sugerir. **I cannot m. it out,** No lo puedo comprender.

How did you m. out (get on)? ¿Cómo te fue? **to m. over**, hacer de nuevo, rehacer; (transfer) ceder, traspasar. **to m. up**, hacer; acabar; concluir; (clothes) confeccionar; fabricar; (the face) pintarse, maquillarse; (the fire) echar carbón, etc. a; *Print.* compaginar; (invent) inventar; (lies) fabricar; (compose) formar; (package) empaquetar; reparar; indemnizar; compensar; (an account) ajustar; preparar; arreglar; (conciliate) conciliar; enumerar; *Theat.* caracterizarse. **to m. up for**, reemplazar; compensar; (lost time, etc.) recobrar. **to m. up to**, compensar; indemnizar; (flatter) adular, halagar; procurar congraciarse con, procurar obtener el favor de; (court) galantear (con). **m. an impression (on)**, dejar(le a fulano) una impresión

make /meik/ *n* forma, *f*; hechura, *f*; estructura, *f*; confección, *f*; manufactura, *f*; producto, *m*; (trade name) marca, *f*; (character) carácter, temperamento, *m*. **m.-believe**, *n* artificio, pretexto, *m*, *a* fingido, *vi* fingir. **land of m.-believe**, reino de los

os, *m*. **m.-up**, (for the face, etc.) maquillaje, *m*; *Theat.* caracterización, *f*; *Print.* imposición, *f*; (whole) conjunto, *m*; (character) carácter, modo de ser, *m*

maker /'meikər/ *n* creador, *m*; autor (-ra); artífice, *mf*; (manufacturer) fabricante, *m*; constructor, *m*; (of clothes, etc.) confeccionador (-ra); (worker) obrero (-ra)

makeshift /'meik,ʃɪft/ *n* expediente, *m*, *a* provisional

makeweight /'meik,weit/ *n* añadidura (de peso), *f*, contrapeso, *m*; *Fig.* suplente, *m*

making /'meikɪŋ/ *n* creación, *f*; hechura, *f*; (manufacture) fabricación, *f*; construcción, *f*; (of clothes, etc.) confección, *f*; formación, *f*; preparación, *f*; estructura, *f*; composición, *f*; *pl* **makings**, (profits) ganancias, *f pl*; (elements) elementos, *m pl*; germen, *m*; rasgos esenciales, *m pl*, características, *f* —*pl* **m.-up**, (of clothes) confección, *f*; *Print.* ajuste, *m*; (of the face) maquillaje, *m*; (invention) invención, *f*; fabricación, *f*

maladjustment /ˌmælə'dʒʌstmənt/ *n* mal ajuste, *m*; inadaptación, *f*

maladministration /ˌmæləd,mɪnə'streiʃən/ *n* desgobierno, *m*, mala administración, *f*; (of funds) malversación, *f*

maladroit /ˌmælə'drɔit/ *a* torpe

malady /'mælədi/ *n* enfermedad, *f*; mal, *m*

malaria /mə'lɛəriə/ *n* paludismo, *m*

malarial /mə'lɛəriəl/ *a* palúdico. **m. fever**, fiebre palúdica, *f*

malcontent /ˌmælkən'tɛnt/ *n* malcontento (-ta). —*a* descontento

male /meil/ *a* macho; masculino. —*n* macho, *m*; varón, *m*. **m. child**, niño, *m*; niño varón, *m*; (son) hijo varón, *m*. **m.**

flower, flor masculina, *f*. **m. issue**, sucesión masculina, *f*. **m. nurse**, enfermero, *m*. **m. sex**, sexo masculino, *m*

malediction /ˌmælɪ'dɪkʃən/ *n* maldición, *f*

malefic /mə'lɛfɪk/ *a* maléfico

malevolence /mə'lɛvələns/ *n* malevolencia, *f*

malevolent /mə'lɛvələnt/ *a* malévolo, maligno

malformation /ˌmælfɔr'meiʃən/ *n* formación anormal, deformidad, deformación congénita, *f*

malice /'mælɪs/ *n* malicia, *f*; *Law.* alevosía, *f*. **to bear m.**, guardar rencor

malicious /mə'lɪʃəs/ *a* malicioso; maligno, rencoroso

malign /mə'lain/ *vt* calumniar, difamar. —*a* maligno; malévolo

malignant /mə'lɪgnənt/ *a* maligno; malévolo; *Med.* maligno

malinger /mə'lɪŋgər/ *vi* fingirse enfermo

malingerer /mə'lɪŋgərər/ *n* enfermo (ma) fingido (-da)

mallard /'mælərd/ *n* pato (-ta), silvestre

malleable /'mæliəbəl/ *a* maleable

mallet /'mælɪt/ *n* mazo, *m*; (in croquet) pala, *f*, mazo, *m*; (in polo) maza (de polo), *f*

mallow /'mælou/ *n* malva, *f*

malnutrition /ˌmælnu'trɪʃən/ *n* desnutrición, alimentación deficiente, *f*

malodorous /mæl'oudərəs/ *a* de mal olor, hediondo, fétido

malpractice /mæl'præktɪs/ *n* (wrongdoing) maleficencia, *f*; (by a doctor) tratamiento equivocado, perjudicial o ilegal, *m*; (malversation) malversación, *f*; inmoralidad, *f*

malt /mɔlt/ *n* malta, *m*. —*vt* preparar el malta. **m.-house**, fábrica de malta, *f*. **m. vinegar**, vinagre de malta, *m*

malted milk /'mɔltɪd/ *n* leche malteada, *f*

maltreat /mæl'trit/ *vt* maltratar

mamma /'mæmə for 1; 'mamə for 2/ *n* *Anat.* mama, *f*; (mother) mamá, *f*

mammal /'mæməl/ *n* mamífero, *m*

mammalian /mə'meiliən/ *a* mamífero

mammary /'mæməri/ *a* mamario. **m. gland**, mama, teta, *f*

mammoth /'mæməθ/ *n* mamut, *m*, *a* gigantesco, enorme

man /mæn/ *n* hombre, *m*; varón, *m*; persona, *f*; (servant) criado, *m*; (workman) obrero, *m*; (soldier) soldado, *m*; (sailor) marinero, *m*; (humanity) raza humana, *f*; (husband) marido, *m*; (chess) peón, *m*; (checkers) dama, *f*; (a ship) buque, *m*. **no man**, nadie; ningún hombre. **young man**, joven, *m*. **to a man**, como un solo hombre. **to come to man's estate**, llegar a la edad viril. **Man overboard!** ¡Hombre al agua! **man and wife**, marido y mujer, *m*, cónyuges, esposos, *m pl*. **man about town**, hombre de mundo, señorito, *m*. **man-at-arms**, hombre de armas, *m*.

man-eater, caníbal, *mf;* tigre, *m.* **man-eating,** *a* antropófago. **man hater,** misántropo, *m;* mujer que odia a los hombres, *f.* **man-hole,** pozo, *m.* **man-hunter,** caníbal, *mf;* (woman) castigadora, *f.* **man in charge,** encargado, *m.* **man in the moon,** mujer de la luna, *f.* **man in the street,** hombre de la calle, hombre medio, *m.* **man of letters,** hombre de letras, literato, *m;* **man of straw,** bausán, *m;* (figure-head) testaferro, *m.* **man of the world,** hombre del mundo, *m.* **man of war,** buque de guerra, *m.* **man-power,** mano de obra, *f,* brazos, *m pl,* (e.g. *lack of manpower,* falta de brazos, *f).* **man servant,** criado, *m*

man /mæn/ *vt* armar; *Mil.* poner guarnición (a); ocupar; *Naut.* tripular; dirigir; *Fig.* fortificar

manacle /'mænəkəl/ *n* manilla, *f; pl* **manacles,** esposas, *f pl;* grillos, *m pl.* —*vt* poner esposas (a)

manage /'mænɪdʒ/ *vt* manejar; (animals) domar; dirigir; gobernar; administrar; (arrange) agenciar, arreglar; (work) explotar; (do) hacer; (eat) comer. —*vi* arreglárselas (para); (get along) ir tirando; (know how) saber hacer; (succeed in) lograr; (do) hacer

manageable /'mænɪdʒəbəl/ *a* manejable; flexible; (of persons, animals) dócil

management /'mænɪdʒmənt/ *n* manejo, *m;* dirección, *f;* gobierno, *m;* administración, *f;* arreglo, *m;* (working) explotación, *f; Com.* gerencia, *f; Theat.* empresa, *f;* conducta, *f;* (economy) economía, *f;* (skill) habilidad, *f;* prudencia, *f.* **the m.,** la dirección, el cuerpo de directores. **domestic m.,** economía doméstica, *f*

manager /'mænɪdʒər/ *n* director, *m;* administrador, *m;* jefe, *m; Theat.* empresario, *m; Com.* gerente, *m;* regente, *m.* **She is not much of a m.,** No es una mujer de su casa. **manager's office,** dirección, *f*

managerial /,mænɪ'dʒɪəriəl/ *a* directivo; administrativo. **m. board,** junta directiva, *f*

managership /'mænɪdʒərˌʃɪp/ *n* puesto de director, *m;* jefatura, *f*

managing /'mænɪdʒɪŋ/ *a* directivo; (officious) mandón, dominante; (niggardly) tacaño

mandarin /'mændərɪn/ *n* mandarín, *m;* (language) mandarina, *f.* **m. orange,** mandarina, *f*

mandate /'mændeit/ *n* mandato, *m.*

mandated territory, territorios bajo mandato, *m pl*

mandatory /'mændəˌtɔri/ *a* obligatorio

mandible /'mændəbəl/ *n* mandíbula, *f*

mandolin /'mændlɪn/ *n* bandolín, *m,* bandurria, *f*

mane /mein/ *n* melena, *f;* (of a horse) crines, *f pl*

maneuver /mə'nuvər/ *n* maniobra, *f.* —*vi* maniobrar, hacer maniobras. —*vt* hacer maniobrar; manipular

maneuvering /mə'nuvərɪŋ/ *n* maniobras, *f pl;* maquinaciones, intrigas, *f pl*

manfully /'mænfəli/ *adv* valientemente; vigorosamente

mange /meindʒ/ *n* sarna, *f;* (in sheep) roña, *f*

manger /'meindʒər/ *n* pesebre, *m*

mangle /'mæŋgəl/ *n* (for clothes) exprimidor de la ropa, *m.* —*vt* pasar por el exprimidor; (mutilate) mutilar, lacerar, magullar; (a text) mutilar

mango /'mæŋgou/ *n* mango, *m*

mangy /'meindʒi/ *a* sarnoso

manhandle /'mæn,hændl/ *vt* maltratar

manhood /'mænhʊd/ *n* virilidad, *f;* edad viril, *f;* masculinidad, *f;* los hombres; (manliness) hombradía, *f,* valor, *m*

mania /'meiniə/ *n* manía, *f;* obsesión, *f;* capricho, *m,* chifladura, *f*

maniac /'meini,æk/ *n* maníaco (-ca). —*a* maníaco, maniático

manicure /'mænɪ,kyʊr/ *n* manicura, *f.* —*vt* arreglar las uñas. **m.-set,** estuche de manicura, *m*

manicurist /'mænɪ,kyʊrɪst/ *n* manicuro (-ra)

manifest /'mænə,fɛst/ *n Naut.* manifiesto, *m.* —*vt* mostrar; hacer patente, probar; manifestarse. —*vi* publicar un manifiesto; (of spirits) manifestarse. —*a* manifiesto, evidente, claro, patente. **to make m.,** poner de manifiesto

manifestation /,mænəfə'steiʃən/ *n* manifestación, *f*

manifestly /'mænə,fɛstli/ *adv* evidentemente, manifiestamente

manifesto /,mænə'fɛstou/ *n* manifiesto, *m*

manifold /'mænə,fould/ *a* múltiple; numeroso; diverso, vario

manikin /'mænɪkɪn/ *n* enano, *m;* muñeco, *m; Art.* maniquí, *m*

manipulate /mə'nɪpyə,leit/ *vt* manipular

manipulative /mə'nɪpyə,leitɪv/ *a* manipulador

mankind /'mæn'kaind/ *n* humanidad, *f,* raza humana, *f,* género humano, *m*

manlike /'mæn,laik/ *a* de hombre, masculino; varonil; (of a woman) hombruno

manliness /'mænlinɪs/ *n* masculinidad, hombradía, *f;* virilidad, *f;* valor, *m;* (of a woman) aire hombruno, *m*

manly /'mænli/ *a* masculino, de hombre; varonil, viril; valiente; fuerte. **to be very m.,** ser muy hombre, ser todo un hombre

manna /'mænə/ *n* maná, *m*

mannequin /'mænɪkɪn/ *n* maniquí, modelo, *f.* **m. parade,** exposición de modelos, *f*

manner /'mænər/ *n* manera, *f,* modo, *m;* aire, porte, *m;* conducta, *f;* (style) estilo, *m;* (sort) clase, *f; Gram.* modo, *m; pl* **manners,** modales, *m pl,* crianza, educación, *f;* (customs) costumbres, *f pl.* **after the m. of,** en (or según) el estilo de. **in a m. of speaking,** en cierto modo, para decirlo así. **in this m.,** de este modo. **to have bad (good) manners,** tener malos (buenos) modales, ser mal (bien) criado. **the novel of manners,** la novela de costumbres

mannered /'mænərd/ *a* amanerado; (in compounds)... educado, de... modales; de costumbres... **well-m.,** bien educado, de buenos modales

mannerism /'mænə‚rızəm/ *n* amaneramiento, *m;* afectación, *f; Theat.* latiguillo, *m.* **to acquire mannerisms,** amanerarse

mannerly /'mænərli/ *a* cortés, bien educado, atento

mannish /'mænıʃ/ *a* (of a woman) hombruno; de hombre, masculino

manor /'mænər/ *n* feudo, *m;* finca, hacienda, *f;* casa solariega, *f;* señorío, *m*

manorial /məˈnɔriəl/ *a* señorial

mansion /'mænʃən/ *n* mansión, *f;* casa solariega, *f;* hotel, *m.* **m.-house,** casa solariega, *f;* residencia del alcalde de Londres, *f*

manslaughter /'mæn‚slɔtər/ *n* homicidio, *m; Law.* homicidio sin premeditación, *m*

mantelpiece /'mæntl‚pis/ *n* repisa de chimenea, *f*

mantilla /mænˈtılə/ *n* mantilla, *f*

mantle /'mæntl/ *n* capa, *f,* manto, *m; Fig.* cubertura, *f;* (gas) camiseta, *f,* manguito, *mf; Zool.* manto, *m.* —*vt* cubrir; envolver; ocultar. —*vi* extenderse; (of blushes) inundar, subirse (a las mejillas)

manual /'mænyuəl/ *a* manual. —*n* manual, *m; Mus.* teclado de órgano, *m.* **m. work,** trabajo manual, *m*

manufactory /‚mænyə'fæktəri/ *n* fábrica, *f,* taller, *m*

manufacture /‚mænyə'fæktʃər/ *n* fabricación, *f;* manufactura, *f.* —*vt* manufacturar, fabricar

manufacturer /‚mænyə'fæktʃərər/ *n* fabricante, industrial, *m.* **manufacturer's price,** precio de fábrica, *m*

manufacturing /‚mænyə'fæktʃərıŋ/ *a* manufacturero, fabril. —*n* fabricación, *f*

manure /məˈnʊr/ *n* estiércol, abono, *m.* —*vt* estercolar, abonar. **m. heap,** estercolero, *m*

manuring /məˈnʊrıŋ/ *n* estercoladura, *f*

manuscript /'mænyə‚skrıpt/ *n* manuscrito, *m,* a manuscrito

many /'mɛni/ *a* muchos (-as); numeroso; diversos (-as); varios (-as). —*n* muchos (-as); la mayoría; las masas; muchedumbre, multitud, *f.* **a great m.,** muchísimos, *m pl,* muchísimas, *f pl;* un gran número. **as m. as...,** tantos como... **How m. are there?** ¿Cuántos hay? ¿Cuántas hay? **m. a time,** muchas veces. **three too m.,** tres de más. **for m. long years,** por largos años. **m.-colored,** multicolor. **m.-headed,** con muchas cabezas. **m.-sided,** multilátero; polifacético; complicado

map /mæp/ *n* mapa, *m;* plano, *m;* (chart) carta, *f.* —*vt* hacer un mapa (or plano)

de. **to map out,** *Surv.* apear; trazar; (plan) proyectar. **ordnance map,** mapa del estado mayor, *m.* **map of the world,** mapamundi, mapa del mundo, *m.* **map-making,** cartografía, *f*

maple /'meipəl/ *n* (tree) arce, *m;* (wood) madera de arce, *f.* **m.-syrup,** jarabe de arce, *m*

mapping /'mæpıŋ/ *n* cartografía, *f*

mar /mar/ *vt* estropear; desfigurar; (happiness) destruir, aguar; frustrar

marauder /məˈrɔdər/ *n* merodeador, *m*

marauding /məˈrɔdıŋ/ *a* merodeador, *n* merodeo, *m*

marble /'marbəl/ *n* mármol, *m;* (for playing with) canica, *f,* a de marmol, marmóreo; *Fig.* insensible; (of paper, etc.) jaspeado. —*vt* jaspear. **m. cutter,** marmolista, *m.* **m. works,** marmolería, *f*

March /martʃ/ *n* marzo, *m.* **as mad as a M. hare,** loco como una cabra, loco de atar

march /martʃ/ *n* marcha, *f;* (step) paso, *m; Fig.* marcha, *f,* progreso, *m.* **forced m.,** marcha forzada, *f.* **quick m.,** paso doble, *m.* **to steal a m. on,** tomar la delantera (a), ganar por la mano (a). **to strike up a m.,** batir la marcha. **m.-past,** desfile, *m*

march /martʃ/ *vi* marchar; (of properties) lindar (con). —*vt* hacer marchar, poner en marcha (a). **to m. back,** *vi* regresar (or volver) a pie. —*vt* hacer volver a pie. **to m. in,** entrar (a pie) en. **to m. off,** marcharse. **to m. on,** seguir marchando; seguir adelante; avanzar. **to m. past,** desfilar ante

marching /'martʃıŋ/ *n* marcha, *f.* —*a* en marcha; de marcha. **to receive one's m. orders,** recibir la orden de marchar; *Inf.* ser despedido. **m. order,** orden de marcha, *m.* **m. song,** canción de marcha, *f*

mardi gras /'mardi ‚gra/ *n* martes de carnaval, *m*

mare /mɛər/ *n* yegua, *f*

margarine /'mardʒərın/ *n* margarina, *f*

margin /'mardʒın/ *n* borde, lado, *m,* orilla, *f;* (of a page) margen, *mf;* reserva, *f;* sobrante, *f.* **m. in the m.,** al margen

marginal /'mardʒənl/ *a* marginal. **m. note,** acotación, nota marginal, *f*

marine /məˈrin/ *a* marino, de mar; marítimo; naval. —*n* (fleet) marina, *f;* (soldier) soldado de marina, *m.* **Tell that to the marines!** ¡Cuéntaselo a tu tía! **mercantile m.,** marina mercante, *f.* **m. forces,** infantería de marina, *f.* **m. insurance,** seguro marítimo, *m*

mariner /'mærənər/ *n* marinero, marino, *m.* **mariner's compass,** aguja de marear, brújula, *f*

marionette /‚mæriə'nɛt/ *n* marioneta, *f,* títere, *m*

marital /'mærıtl/ *a* marital

maritime /'mærı‚taım/ *a* marítimo

mark /mark/ *n* marca, *f;* señal, *f;* mancha, *f;* impresión, *f;* (target) blanco, *m;* (standard) norma, *f;* (level) nivel, *m;*

(distinction) importancia, distinción, f; (in examinations) nota, f; calificación, f; (signature) cruz, f; (coin) marco, m. —vt marcar; señalar; (price) poner precio (a); (notice) observar, darse cuenta (de); (characterize) caracterizar. **trade-m.**, marca de fábrica, f. **to be beside the m.**, no dar en el blanco; errar el tiro; Fig. no tener nada que ver con; equivocarse. **to hit the m.**, dar en el blanco; Fig. dar en el clavo. **to make one's m.**, firmar con una cruz; distinguirse. **to m. time**, marcar el paso; Fig. hacer tiempo. **to m. down**, (a person) señalar; escoger; (in price) rebajar. **to m. out**, marcar; trazar; definir; (erase) borrar; (a person) escoger; destinar **to m. somebody absent**, ponerle a fulano su ausencia. **m. somebody present**, ponerle a fulano su asistencia.

Mark /mɑrk/ n Marcos. **the Gospel according to St. M.**, el Evangelio de San Marcos

marked /mɑrkt/ a marcado; señalado; notable; acentuado; particular, especial. **He speaks with a m. Galician accent**, Habla con marcado acento gallego

markedly /'mɑrkɪdli/ adv marcadamente; notablemente; especialmente, particularmente

marker /'mɑrkər/ n (billiards) marcador, m; (football, etc.) tanteador, m

market /'mɑrkɪt/ n mercado, m; tráfico, m; venta, f; (price) precio, m; (shop) bazar, emporio, m. —vt and vi comprar en un mercado; vender en un mercado. **black m.**, mercado negro, estraperlo, m. **open m.**, mercado al aire libre, m; Fig. mercado libre, m. **m. day**, día de mercado, m. **m. garden**, huerto, m, huerta, f. **m. gardener**, hortelano, m. **m.-place**, plaza de mercado, f; Fig. mercado, m. **m. price**, precio corriente, m. **m. stall**, tabanco, puesto de mercado, m. **m.-woman**, verdulera, f

marketable /'mɑrkɪtəbəl/ a comerciable, vendible; corriente

marketing /'mɑrkɪtɪŋ/ n venta, f; compra en un mercado, f; mercado, m. **to go m.**, ir al mercado

marking /'mɑrkɪŋ/ n marca, f; (spot on animals, etc.) pinta, f. **m.-ink**, tinta de marcar, f. **m.-iron**, ferrete, hierro de marcar, m

marksman /'mɑrksmən/ n tirador (-ra)

marksmanship /'mɑrksmən,ʃɪp/ n puntería, f

marmalade /'mɑrmə,leɪd/ n mermelada de naranjas amargas, f

marmoset /'mɑrmə,zɛt/ n tití, m

maroon /mə'run/ n (color) marrón, m; (slave) cimarrón (-ona); (firework) petardo, m. —a de marrón. —vt abandonar, dejar

marquee /mɑr'ki/ n marquesina, f

marriage /'mærɪdʒ/ n matrimonio, m; unión, f; (wedding) boda, f, casamiento, m. **by m.**, (of relationship) político. **She**

is an aunt by m., tía política. **m. articles**, capitulaciones (matrimoniales), f pl. **m. contract**, contrato matrimonial, m. **m. license**, licencia de casamiento, f. **m. portion**, dote, mf. **m. rate**, nupcialidad, f. **m. register**, acta matrimonial, f. **m. song**, epitalamio, m

marriageable /'mærɪdʒəbəl/ a casadero

married /'mærɪd/ past part and a casado; matrimonial, conyugal. **newly-m. couple**, los recién casados. **to get m. to**, casarse con. **m. couple**, matrimonio, m, cónyuges, m pl. **m. life**, vida conyugal, f

married name n nombre de casada, f

marrow /'mæroʊ/ n tuétano, m, médula, f; Fig. meollo, m. **to the m. of one's bones**, hasta los tuétanos

marrowbone /'mæroʊ,boʊn/ n hueso medular, m. **on one's marrowbones**, de rodillas

marry /'mæri/ vt casarse con, contraer matrimonio con; casar; (of a priest) unir en matrimonio; Fig. juntar, unir. —vi casarse. **to m. again**, volver a casarse

marsh /mɑrʃ/ n marjal, pantano, m. **m.-mallow**, Bot. malvavisco, m. **m. marigold**, calta, f

marshal /'mɑrʃəl/ n mariscal, m, vt poner en orden, arreglar; dirigir. **field-m.**, capitán general de ejército, m

mart /mɑrt/ n Poet. plaza de mercado, f; mercado, m; emporio, m; (auction rooms) martillo, m

martial /'mɑrʃəl/ a militar; marcial, belicoso. **m. array**, orden de batalla, m. **m. law**, derecho militar, m; estado de guerra, m. **m. spirit**, marcialidad, f, espíritu belicoso, m

martinet /,mɑrtn'ɛt/ n Mil. ordenancista, m; rigorista, mf

Martinique /,mɑrtn'ik/ Martinica, f

martyr /'mɑrtər/ n mártir, mf vt martirizar

martyrdom /'mɑrtərdəm/ n martirio, m

marvel /'mɑrvəl/ n maravilla, f. **to m. at**, maravillarse de, admirarse de

marvelous /'mɑrvələs/ a maravilloso

marvelousness /'mɑrvələsnɪs/ n maravilla, f, carácter maravilloso, m, lo maravilloso

marzipan /'mɑrzə,pæn/ n mazapán, m

mascot /'mæskɒt/ n mascota, f

masculine /'mæskyəlɪn/ a masculino; varonil, macho; de hombre; (of a woman) hombruno. —n masculino, m

masculinity /,mæskyə'lɪnɪti/ n masculinidad, f

mash /mæʃ/ n mezcla, f; amasijo, m; pasta, f, puré, m. —vt mezclar; amasar. **mashed potatoes**, puré de patatas (de papas), m

mask /mæsk/ n máscara, f; antifaz, m; (death) mascarilla, f; (person) máscara, mf. —vt enmascarar; Fig. encubrir, disimular. —vi ponerse una máscara; disfrazarse. **masked ball**, n baile de máscaras, m

masochism /'mæsə,kɪzəm/ n masoquismo, m

mason /'meisən/ n albañil, m; (freemason) francmasón, masón, m

masonic /mə'sɒnɪk/ a masónico. **m.
lodge,** logia de francmasones, f

masonry /'meisənri/ n (trade) albañilería,
f; mampostería, f

masque /mæsk/ n mascarada, f

masquerade /,mæskə'reid/ n mascarada,
f

masquerader /,mæskə'reidər/ n máscara, mf

mass /mæs/ n misa, f. **to hear m.,** oír
misa. **to say m.,** celebrar misa. **high m.,**
misa mayor, f. **low m.,** misa rezada, f.
m. book, libro de misa, m

mass /mæs/ n masa, f; (shape) bulto, m;
(heap) montón, m; (great number) muchedumbre, f; (cloud of steam, etc.)
nube, f. —vt amasar; Mil. concentrar.
—vi congregarse en masa. **in a m.,** en
masa; en conjunto. **the m. (of)...,** la
mayoría (de)... **the masses,** las masas, el
vulgo, el pueblo. **m. formation,** columna
cerrada, f. **m.-meeting,** mitin, mitin popular, m. **m.-production,** fabricación en
serie, f

massacre /'mæsəkər/ n matanza, carnicería, f, vt hacer una carnicería (de)

massage /mə'sɑʒ/ n masaje, m; (friction)
fricción, f. —vt dar un masaje (a)

masseur, masseuse /mə'sɜr; mə'sus/ n
masajista, mf

massive /'mæsɪv/ a macizo; sólido

mast /mæst/ n Naut. palo, árbol, m; (for
wireless) mástil, m; poste, m; (beech)
hayuco, m; (oak) bellota, f. —vt Naut. arbolar. **at half-m.,** a media asta. **m.-head,**
calcés, tope, m

masted /'mæstɪd/ a arbolado; (in compounds) de... palos

master /'mæstər/ n (of the house, etc.)
señor, amo, m; maestro, m; Naut. patrón,
m; (owner) dueño, m; (teacher) profesor,
maestro, m; (young master and as address) señorito, m; director, m; jefe, m;
(expert) perito, m; (of a military order)
maestre, m, a maestro; superior. —vt
dominar; ser maestro en; dominar, conocer a fondo. **This picture is by an old
m.,** Este cuadro es de un gran maestro
antiguo. **to be m. of oneself,** ser dueño
de sí. **to be one's own m.,** ser dueño de
sí mismo; trabajar por su propia cuenta;
ser independiente; estar libre. **m. builder,**
maestro de obras, m. **m. hand,** mano maestra, f. **M. of Arts,** maestro (-tra) en
artes. **M. of Ceremonies,** maestro de
ceremonias, m. **M. of Foxhounds,** cazador mayor, m. **M. of the Horse,** caballerizo mayor del rey, m. **M. of the Rolls,**
archivero mayor, m. **m.-key,** llave maestra, f. **m. mind,** águila, f, ingenio, m.
m. stroke, golpe maestro, m

masterful /'mæstərfəl/ a imperioso,
dominante; autoritario, arbitrario

masterliness /'mæstərlinɪs/ n maestría,
f; excelencia, f; perfección, f

masterly /'mæstərli/ a maestro; excelente; perfecto. **m. performance,** obra
maestra, f; Theat. representación perfecta,
f; ejecución excelente, f

masterpiece /'mæstər,pis/ n obra maestra, f

master plan n plan regulador, m

masterstroke /'mæstər,strouk/ n golpe
magistral, golpe de maestro, m

mastery /'mæstəri/ n dominio, m; autoridad, f; poder, m; ventaja, f; superioridad,
maestría, f; conocimiento profundo, m.
to gain the m. of, hacerse el señor de;
llegar a dominar

mastic /'mæstɪk/ n masilla, almáciga, f

masticate /'mæstɪ,keit/ vt masticar,
mascar

mastiff /'mæstɪf/ n mastín, alano, m

mastoid /'mæstɔid/ a mastoides. —n
apófisis mastoides, f

masturbate /'mæstər,beit/ vi masturbarse

masturbation /,mæstər'beiʃən/ n masturbación, f

mat /mæt/ n esterilla, f; alfombrilla, f;
(on the table) tapete individual, m. —vt
(tangle) enmarañar, desgreñar. —vi
enmarañarse

match /mætʃ/ n Sports. partido, m;
(wrestling, boxing) lucha, f; (fencing)
asalto, m; (race) carrera, f; (contest) concurso, m; (equal) igual, mf; (pair) pareja,
f; compañero (-ra); (marriage) boda, f,
casamiento, m; (for lighting) cerilla, f,
fósforo, m; (for guns) mecha, f. —vt
competir con; (equal) igualar; ser igual
(a); hacer juego con; emparejar, aparear;
armonizar. —vi ser igual; hacer juego; armonizarse. **good m.,** Inf. buen partido,
m. **as thin as a m.,** más delgado que una
cerilla. **to meet one's m.,** dar con la
horma de su zapato. **to play a m.,** jugar
un partido. **m.-box,** cajita de cerillas, fosforera, f. **m.-seller,** fosforero (-ra)

matchless /'mætʃlɪs/ a incomparable, sin
igual, sin par

mate /meit/ n compañero, camarada, m;
(spouse) compañero (-ra); pareja, f; (on
merchant ships) piloto, m; (assistant)
ayudante, m; (at chess) mate, m. —vt
(marry) casar, desposar; (animals, birds)
aparear, acoplar; (chess) dar jaque mate
(a). —vi casarse; aparearse, acoplarse

maté /'mɑtei/ n maté, té del Paraguay, m

material /mə'tɪriəl/ a material; importante, esencial; considerable; sensible, notable; grave. —n material, m; materia, f;
(fabric) tela, f; tejido, m. **raw materials,**
materias primas, f pl. **writing materials,**
utensilios de escritorio, m pl; papel de escribir, m

materiality /mə,tɪri'æliti/ n materiali-
dad, f; importancia, f

materialize /mə'tɪriə,laiz/ vt materializar

maternal /mə'tɜrnl/ a materno, maternal. **m. grandparents,** abuelos maternos, *m pl*

maternity /mə'tɜrniti/ n maternidad, *f.* **m. center,** centro de maternidad, *m.* **m. hospital,** casa de maternidad, *f*

mathematical /,mæθə'mætikəl/ a matemático

mathematician /,mæθəmə'tiʃən/ n matemático, *m*

mathematics /,mæθə'mætiks/ n *pl;* matemáticas, *f pl.* **applied m.,** matemáticas prácticas, *f pl.* **higher m.,** matemáticas superiores, *f pl.* **pure m.,** matemáticas teóricas, *f pl*

matinee /,mætn'ei/ n función de tarde, *f*

mating /'meitiŋ/ n (of animals) apareamiento, acoplamiento, *m;* unión, *f;* casamiento, *m*

matins /'mætnz/ n *pl Eccl.* maitines, *m pl*

matriarch /'meitri,ark/ n matriarca, *f*

matriculate /mə'trikyə,leit/ vt matricular. —vi matricularse

matrimonial /,mætrə'mouniəl/ a matrimonial, de matrimonio; marital. **m. agency,** agencia de matrimonios, *f*

matrimony /'mætrə,mouni/ n matrimonio, *m*

matrix /'meitriks/ n matriz, *f*

matron /'meitrən/ n matrona, mujer casada, madre de familia, *f;* (of a hospital) matrona, *f;* (of a school) ama de llaves, *f;* directora, *f.* **m. of honor,** (at a wedding) madrina, *f*

matted /'mætid/ a enmarañado, enredado

matter /'mætər/ n materia, *f;* substancia, *f;* caso, *m;* cuestión, *f;* asunto, *m;* causa, *f;* (distance) distancia, *f;* (amount) cantidad, *f;* (duration) espacio de tiempo, *m;* (importance) importancia, *f; Med.* pus, *m; pl* matters, asuntos, *m pl,* etc.; situación, *f.* as if nothing were the m., como si no hubiese pasado nada. **for that m.,** en cuanto a eso. **grey m.,** substancia gris, *f.* **in the m. of,** en el caso de. **It is a m. of taste,** Es cuestión de gusto. **printed m.,** impresos, *m pl.* **What is the m.?** ¿Qué pasa? **What is the m. with him?** ¿Qué tiene? ¿Qué le pasa? **m.-of-course,** cosa natural, *f.* **m.-of-fact,** práctico; sin imaginación; positivista. **m. of fact,** n hecho positivo, *m,* realidad, *f.* **As a m. of fact...,** En realidad..., El caso es que... **m. of form,** cuestión de fórmula, *f;* pura formalidad, *f*

matter /'mætər/ vi importar; (discharge) supurar. **What does it m.?** ¿Qué importa? **It doesn't m.,** Es igual, No importa, Da lo mismo

mattress /'mætris/ n colchón, *m.* spring-m., colchón de muelles, *m.* m.-maker, colchonero, *m*

mature /mə'tʃʊr/ a maduro; *Com.* vencido. —vt madurar. —vi madurarse; *Com.* vencer

maturity /mə'tʃʊriti/ n madurez, *f;* edad madura, *f;* (*Com.* of a bill) vencimiento, *m*

maudlin /'mɔdlin/ a sensiblero; lacrimoso; (tipsy) calamocano

maul /mɔl/ vt maltratar; herir

mausoleum /,mɔsə'liəm/ n mausoleo, *m*

mauve /mouv/ n color purpúreo delicado, color de malva, *m,* a de color de malva

maw /mɔ/ n (of a ruminant) cuajar, *m;* (of a bird) buche, *m; Fig.* abismo, *m*

mawkish /'mɔkiʃ/ a insípido, insulso; sensiblero; asqueroso

maxim /'mæksim/ n máxima, *f*

maximum /'mæksəməm/ a máximo. —n máximo, *m*

may /mei/ v aux poder; ser posible; (expressing wish, hope) ojalá que..., Dios quiera que..., or the present subjunctive may be used, e.g. *May you live many years!* ¡(qué) Viva Vd. muchos años! (to denote uncertainty, the future tense of the verb is often used, e.g. *You may perhaps remember the date,* Vd. quizás se acordará de la fecha. *Who may he be?* ¿Quién será?) **May God grant it!** ¡(que) Dios lo quiera! **It may be that...,** Puede ser que..., Es posible que..., Quizás... **He may come on Saturday,** Es posible que venga el sábado; Puede venir el sábado. **May I come in?** ¿Puedo entrar? ¿Se puede entrar? **May I come and see you?** ¿Me das permiso para hacerte una visita? ¿Me dejas venir a verte? **May I go then?** ¿Puedo irme pues? ¿Tengo permiso para marcharme entonces?

May /mei/ n mayo, *m; Fig.* abril, *m; Bot.* espina blanca, *f.* **May Day,** primero de mayo, *m.* **mayflower,** flor del cuclillo, *f.* **mayfly,** cachipolla, *f.* **May queen,** maya, *f*

maybe /'meibi/ adv quizás, tal vez

mayonnaise /,meiə'neiz/ n mayonesa, *f.* **m. sauce,** salsa mayonesa, *f*

mayor /'meiər/ n alcalde, *m*

mayoral /'meiərəl/ a de alcalde

mayoress /'meiəris/ n alcaldesa, *f*

maze /meiz/ n laberinto, *m; Fig.* perplejidad, *f.* —vt dejar perplejo, aturdir

me /mi/ pron me; (after a preposition only) mí. **They sent it for me,** Lo mandaron para mí. **Dear me!** ¡Ay de mí!

meadow /'mɛdou/ n prado, *m,* pradera, *f.* **m.-sweet,** reina de los prados, *f*

meager /'migər/ a magro, enjuto, flaco; (scanty) exiguo, escaso, insuficiente; pobre; *Fig.* árido

meagerly /'migərli/ adv pobremente

meal /mil/ n comida, *f;* (flour) harina, *f.* **to have a good m.,** comer bien. **test m.,** *Med.* comida de prueba, *f.* **m.-time,** hora de comida, *f*

mealy /'mili/ a harinoso; (of the complexion) pastoso

mean /min/ a (middle) medianero; (average) mediano; (humble) humilde; pobre; inferior; bajo, vil, ruin; (avaricious) tacaño, mezquino. **m.-spirited,** vil, de alma ruin

mean /min/ n medio, *m;* medianía, *f; pl* means, medio, *m;* expediente, *m;* me-

dios, *m pl;* (financial) recursos, *m pl;*
modo, *m,* manera, *f.* **by all means,** por
todos los medios; (certainly) ¡ya lo creo!
¡no faltaba más! ¡naturalmente! **by
means of,** mediante, por medio de; con
la ayuda de. **by no means,** de ningún
modo; nada. **by some means,** de algún
modo, de alguna manera

mean /min/ *vt* destinar (para); pretender,
proponerse; intentar, pensar; querer decir, significar; importar; (wish) querer;
(concern, speak about) tratarse (de). —*vi*
tener el propósito, tener la intención. **I
did not m. to do it,** Lo hice sin querer.
What does this word m.? ¿Qué significa
esta palabra? **What do you m. by that?**
¿Qué quieres decir con eso? **This portrait
is meant to be Joan,** Este retrato quiere
ser Juana. **What do they m. to do?**
¿Qué piensan (or se proponen) hacer? **Do
you really m. it?** ¿Lo dices en serio?
Charles always means well, Carlos siempre tiene buenas intenciones

meander /mi'ændər/ *n* meandro, serpenteo, *m;* camino tortuoso, *m, vi* serpentear; errar, vagar; (in talk) divagar

meandering /mi'ændərɪŋ/ *n* meandros,
m pl, serpenteo, *m;* (in talk) divaga-
ciones, *f pl, a* serpentino, tortuoso

meaning /'minɪŋ/ *n* intención, voluntad,
f; significación, *f,* significado, *m;* (of
words) acepción, *f;* (sense) sentido, *m;*
(thought) pensamiento, *m.* —*a*
significante. **double m.,** doble intención,
f. **He gave me a m. look,** Me miró con
intención. **What is the m. of it?** ¿Qué
significa? ¿Qué quiere decir?

meaningful /'minɪŋfəl/ *a* significante

meaningless /'minɪŋlɪs/ *a* sin sentido;
insensato; insignificante

meaningly /'minɪŋli/ *adv* significativa-
mente; con intención

meanness /'minnɪs/ *n* pobreza, *f;* inferioridad, *f;* mediocridad, *f;* bajeza, ruindad, *f;* (stinginess) mezquindad, tacade-
hería, *f*

meantime, meanwhile /'min,taim;
'min,wail/ *n* ínterin, *m, adv* entre tanto,
mientras tanto, a todo esto. **in the m.,**
mientras tanto, en el ínterin

measles /'mizəlz/ *n* sarampión, *m.* **German m.,** rubéola, *f*

measurable /'mɛʒərəbəl/ *a* mensurable

measure /'mɛʒər/ *n* medida, *f;* capacidad, *f;* (for measuring) regla, *f;* número,
m; proporción, *f;* (limit) límite, *m;* (Fig.
step) medida, *f;* (metre) metro, *m; Mus.*
compás, *m;* (degree) grado, *m;* manera, *f;*
(parliamentary) proyecto (de ley), *m.* —*vt*
medir; proporcionar, distribuir; (water)
aforar; (land) apear; (height of persons)
tallar; (for clothes) tomar las medidas (a);
(judge) juzgar; (test) probar, (*Poet.* traverse) recorrer. **a suit made to m.,** un
traje hecho a medida. **in great m.,** en
gran manera, en alto grado. **in some m.,**
hasta cierto punto. **to m. one's length,**
caer tendido. **to take a person's m.,** *Fig.*

tomar las medidas (a). **to m. up to,** *Fig.*
estar al nivel de, ser igual a

measured /'mɛʒərd/ *a* mesurado, moderado; uniforme; limitado. **to walk with
m. tread,** andar a pasos contados

measurement /'mɛʒərmənt/ *n* medición,
f; medida, *f;* dimensión, *f*

meat /mit/ *n* carne, *f;* (food) alimento,
m; (meal) comida, *f; Fig.* substancia, *f.*
to sit at m., estar a la mesa. **cold meats,**
fiambres, *m pl.* **m.-ball,** albóndiga, *f.* **m.-
chopper,** picador, *m.* **m.-dish,** fuente, *f.*
m.-eater, comedor (-ra) de carne. **m. extract,** carne concentrada, *f.* **m.-market,**
carnicería, *f.* **m.-pie,** pastel de carne, *m.*
m.-safe, fresquera, *f*

meaty /'miti/ *a* carnoso; *Fig.* substancial

mechanic /mə'kænɪk/ *n* mecánico, *m*

mechanical /mə'kænɪkəl/ *a* mecánico;
maquinal

mechanical pencil *n* lapicero, *m*

mechanics /mə'kænɪks/ *n* mecánica, *f*

mechanism /'mɛkə,nɪzəm/ *n* mecanismo,
m, (philosophy) mecanicismo, *m*

mechanize /'mɛkə,naɪz/ *vt* convertir en
máquina; (gen. *Mil.*) mecanizar; motori-
zar

medal /'mɛdl/ *n* medalla, *f*

medallion /mə'dælyən/ *n* medallón, *m*

meddle /'mɛdl/ *vi* tocar; meterse (con or
en); entremeterse, inmiscuirse; intrigar

meddler /'mɛdlər/ *n* entremetido (-da);
intrigante, *mf*

meddlesome /'mɛdlsəm/ *a* entremetido;
oficioso; impertinente; enredador, intrigante. **to be very m.,** meterse en todo

median /'midiən/ *a* del medio

mediate /*v* 'midi,eit; *a* -ɪt/ *vi* intervenir, mediar, arbitrar; abogar (por). —*a*
medio; interpuesto

media /'midiə/, **the** los medios informa-
tivos, *m pl*

mediation /,midi'eiʃən/ *n* mediación, intervención, *f;* intercesión, *f;* interposición,
f

mediator /'midi,eitər/ *n* mediador (-ra);
arbitrador, *m;* intercesor (-ra)

medical /'mɛdɪkəl/ *a* médico; de medicina; de médico. —*n Inf.* estudiante de
medicina, *m.* **Army M. Service,** Servicio
de Sanidad Militar, *m.* **m. books,** libros
de medicina, *m pl.* **m. examination,** examen médico, *m,* exploración médica, *f.*
m. jurisprudence, medicina legal, *f.* **m.
knowledge,** conocimientos médicos, *m
pl.* **m. practitioner,** médico (-ca). **m.
school,** escuela de medicina, *f*

medicament /mə'dɪkəmənt/ *n* medicamento, *m*

medicate /'mɛdɪ,keit/ *vt* medicar; medicinar

medication /,mɛdɪ'keiʃən/ *n* medicación,
f

medicinal /mə'dɪsənl/ *a* medicinal

medicine /'mɛdəsɪn/ *n* medicina, *f;*
medicamento, *m;* (charm) ensalmo,
hechizo, *m.* **patent m.,** específico far-

macéutico, *m.* **m. ball,** balón medical, *m.*
m. chest, botiquín, *m.* **m. man,** hechizador, *m*

medieval /ˌmidí'ivəl/ *a* medieval

mediocre /ˌmidi'oukər/ *a* mediocre

meditate /'mɛdɪˌteit/ *vt* idear, proyectar,
meditar. —*vi* meditar, reflexionar; pensar,
intentar

meditation /ˌmɛdɪ'teiʃən/ *n* meditación,
f

meditative /'mɛdɪˌteitɪv/ *a* meditabundo,
contemplativo; de meditación

Mediterranean /ˌmɛdɪtə'reiniən/ *a* mediterráneo. —*n* Mar Mediterráneo, *m*

medium /'midiəm/ *n* medio, *m;* (cooking) término medio, a medio cocer, a medio asar, *m;* (environment) medio ambiente, *m;* (agency) intermediario, *m;*
(spiritualism) médium, *m; Art.* medio, *m,*
a mediano; regular; mediocre. **through
the m. of,** por medio de. **m.-sized,** de tamaño regular

medlar /'mɛdlər/ *n* (fruit) níspola, *f;*
(tree) níspero, *m*

medley /'mɛdli/ *n* mezcla, *f;* miscelánea,
f, a mezclado, mixto

medulla /mə'dʌlə/ *n* medula, *f*

meek /mik/ *a* dulce, manso; humilde;
modesto; pacífico

meekly /'mikli/ *adv* mansamente;
humildemente; modestamente

meet /mit/ *vt* encontrar; encontrarse con;
tropezar con; (by arrangement) reunirse
con; (make the acquaintance of) conocer
(a); (satisfy) satisfacer; cumplir (con); (a
bill) pagar, saldar; (refute) refutar; (fight)
batirse (con); (confront) hacer frente (a).
—*vi* juntarse; encontrarse; reunirse;
verse; (of rivers) confluir. —*n* montería,
f, a conveniente. **I shall m. you at the
station,** Te esperaré en la estación. **Until
we m. again!** ¡Hasta la vista! **to go to
m.,** ir al encuentro de. **to m. half-way,**
encontrar a la mitad del camino; partir la
diferencia (con); hacer concesiones (a). **to
m. the eye,** saltar a la vista. **to m. with,**
encontrar; experimentar; sufrir

meeting /'mitɪŋ/ *n* encuentro, *m;* reunión, *f;* (interview) entrevista, *f;* (of rivers, etc.) confluencia, *f;* (public, etc.) mitin, *m;* (council) concilio, *m;* concurso,
m; (race) concurso de carreras de caballos, *m.* **creditors' m.,** concurso de acreedores, *m.* **m.-house,** templo de los
Cuáqueros, *m.* **m.-place,** lugar de reunión, *m;* lugar de cita, *m;* centro, *m.* **to
adjourn the m.,** levantar la sesión. **to
call a m.,** convocar una sesión. **to open
the m.,** abrir la sesión

megalomania /ˌmɛgəlou'meiniə/ *n* me-
galomanía, monomanía de grandezas, *f*

megalomaniac /ˌmɛgəlou'meiniæk/ *a*
megalómano (-na)

megaphone /'mɛgəˌfoun/ *n* megáfono,
portavoz, *m*

melancholia /ˌmɛlən'koulia/ *n* melancolía, *f*

melancholy /'mɛlənˌkɒli/ *a* melancólico.
—*n* melancolía, *f*

mellifluous /mə'lɪfluəs/ *a* melifluo;
dulce

mellow /'mɛlou/ *a* maduro; dulce; (of
wine) rancio; blando; suave; (of sound)
melodioso; (slang) alegre; (tipsy) entre
dos luces. —*vt* madurar; ablandar; suavizar. —*vi* madurarse

mellowing /'mɛlouɪŋ/ *n* maduración, *f*

melodic /mə'lɒdɪk/ *a* melódico

melodious /mə'loudiəs/ *a* melodioso

melodrama /'mɛləˌdrɑmə/ *n* melodrama,
m

melodramatic /ˌmɛlədrə'mætɪk/ *a* melodramático

melody /'mɛlədi/ *n* melodía, *f*

melon /'mɛlən/ *n* melón, *m;* sandía, *f.*
slice of m., raja de melón, *f.* **m. bed,**
sandiar, *m.* **m.-shaped,** amelonado

melt /mɛlt/ *vi* derretirse; deshacerse; disolverse; evaporarse; desaparecer; (of
money, etc.) hacerse sal y agua; (relent)
enternecerse, ablandarse. —*vt* fundir;
(snow, etc.) derretir; (Fig. soften) ablandar. **He melted away,** *Inf.* Se escurri. **to
m. into tears,** deshacerse en lágrimas. **to
m. down,** fundir

melting /'mɛltɪŋ/ *a* fundente; (forgiving)
indulgente; (tender) de ternura; lánguido;
dulce. —*n* fusión, *f;* derretimiento, *m.* **m.
point,** punto de fusión, *m.* **m. pot,** *Metall.* crisol, *m; Fig.* caldera de razas, *f, m*

member /'mɛmbər/ *n* miembro, *m;* (of a
club, etc.) socio (-ia). **M. of Parliament,**
diputado a Cortes, *m*

membership /'mɛmbərˌʃɪp/ *n* calidad de
miembro, socio(-ia); número de miembros
(or socios), *m,* composición, integración, *f*

membrane /'mɛmbrein/ *n* membrana, *f*

memento /mə'mɛntou/ *n* recuerdo, *m*

memoir /'mɛmwɑr/ *n* memoria, *f*

memorable /'mɛmərəbəl/ *a* memorable

memorandum /ˌmɛmə'rændəm/ *n* memorándum, *m*

memorial /mə'mɔriəl/ *a* conmemorativo.
—*n* monumento conmemorativo, *m;* memorial, *m*

memorize /'mɛməˌraiz/ *vt* aprender de
memoria

memory /'mɛməri/ *n* memoria, *f;* recuerdo, *m.* **from m.,** de memoria. **If my
m. does not deceive me,** Si mal no me
acuerdo. **in m. of,** en conmemoración de;
en recuerdo de

memory span *n* retentiva memorística, *f*

menace /'mɛnɪs/ *n* amenaza, *f, vt* amenazar

menacing /'mɛnəsɪŋ/ *a* amenazador

menacingly /'mɛnəsɪŋli/ *adv* con
amenazas

menagerie /mə'nædʒəri/ *n* colección de
fieras, *f;* casa de fieras, *f*

mend /mɛnd/ *vt* remendar; componer; reparar; (darn) zurcir; (rectify) remediar;
reformar; enmendar; (a fire) echar carbón
(or leña, etc.) a; (one's pace) avivar. —*vi*

(in health and of the weather) mejorar.
—*n* remiendo, *m;* (darn) zurcido, *m.* **to
be on the m.,** ir mejorando. **to m. one's
ways,** reformarse, enmendarse

mendacious /mɛnˈdeɪʃəs/ *a* mendaz

mender /ˈmɛndər/ *n* componedor (-ra);
(darner) zurcidor (-ra); reparador (-ra);
(cobbler and tailor) remendón, *m*

mendicant /ˈmɛndɪkənt/ *a* mendicante.
—*n* mendicante, *mf.* **m. friar,** fraile
mendicante, *m*

mending /ˈmɛndɪŋ/ *n* compostura, *f;* reparación, *f;* (darning) zurcidura, *f;* ropa
por zurcir, *f*

menial /ˈminiəl/ *a* doméstico; servil;
bajo, ruin. —*n* criado (-da); lacayo, *m*

meningitis /ˌmɛnɪnˈdʒaɪtɪs/ *n* meningitis,
f

menopause /ˈmɛnəˌpɔz/ *n* menopausia, *f*

menses /ˈmɛnsiz/ *n* menstruación, *f*

menstrual /ˈmɛnstruəl/ *a* menstrual

menstruate /ˈmɛnstruˌeɪt/ *vi* menstruar

menstruation /ˌmɛnstruˈeɪʃən/ *n*
menstruación, *f.*

mental /ˈmɛntl/ *a* mental; intelectual. **m.
derangement,** enajenación mental, *f.* **m.
hospital,** manicomio, *m*

mentality /mɛnˈtælɪti/ *n* mentalidad, *f*

mention /ˈmɛnʃən/ *n* mención, *f;* alusión, *f.* —*vt* hacer mención (de), mencionar, mentar, hablar (de); aludir (a);
(quote) citar; (in dispatches) nombrar.
Don't m. it! (keep silent) ¡No digas
nada!; (you're welcome) ¡No hay de que!

mentor /ˈmɛntɔr/ *n* mentor, *m*

menu /ˈmɛnyu/ *n* menú, *m;* lista de
platos, *f*

meow /miˈaʊ/ *vi* maullar. —*n* maullido,
m

mephitic /məˈfɪtɪk/ *a* mefítico

mercantile /ˈmɜrkənˌtil/ *a* mercantil;
mercante. **m. law,** derecho mercantil, *m.*
m. marine, marina mercante, *f*

mercenary /ˈmɜrsəˌnɛri/ *a* mercenario.
—*n* (soldier) mercenario, *m*

merchandise /ˈmɜrtʃənˌdaɪz/ *n* mercancía, *f*

merchant /ˈmɜrtʃənt/ *n* traficante (en),
mf, negociante (en), *m;* comerciante, *mf*
mercader, *m.* —*a* mercante. **The M. of
Venice,** El Mercader de Venecia. **m.
navy, service,** marina mercante, *f.* **m.
ship,** buque mercante, *m*

merchantman /ˈmɜrtʃəntmən/ *n* buque
mercante, *m*

merciful /ˈmɜrsɪfəl/ *a* misericordioso, piadoso; compasivo; clemente; indulgente

mercifully /ˈmɜrsɪfəli/ *adv* misericordio-
samente; compasivamente; con indulgencia

merciless /ˈmɜrsɪlɪs/ *a* despiadado, inhumano

mercilessly /ˈmɜrsɪlɪsli/ *adv* sin piedad

mercurial /mərˈkyuriəl/ *a* mercurial;
(changeable) volátil; (lively) vivo

mercury /ˈmɜrkyəri/ *n* mercurio, *m;*

(*Astron.* and *Myth.*) Mercurio, *m.* **Mercury's wand,** caduceo, *m*

mercy /ˈmɜrsi/ *n* misericordia, *f;* compasión, *f;* clemencia, *f;* indulgencia, *f;* merced, *f.* **at the m. of the elements,** a la
intemperie. **to be at the m. of,** estar a la
merced de

mere /mɪər/ *a* mero; simple; no más que,
solo. —*n* lago, *m*

merely /ˈmɪərli/ *adv* meramente, solamente; simplemente, sencillamente

meretricious /ˌmɛrɪˈtrɪʃəs/ *a* (archaic)
meretricio; (flashy) de oropel; llamativo,
charro

merge /mɜrdʒ/ *vt* fundir; *Com.* fusionar;
mezclar. —*vi* fundirse; *Com.* fusionarse;
mezclarse

merger /ˈmɜrdʒər/ *n* combinación, *f;*
Com. fusión, *f*

meridian /məˈrɪdiən/ *n* (*Geog. Astron.*)
meridiano, *m;* (noon) mediodía, *m;*
(peak) apogeo, *m*

meringue /məˈræŋ/ *n* merengue, *m*

merino /məˈrinoʊ/ *a* de merino; merino.
—*n* (fabric and sheep) merino, *m*

merit /ˈmɛrɪt/ *n* mérito, *m,* *vt* merecer,
ser digno de

meritorious /ˌmɛrɪˈtɔriəs/ *a* meritorio

merlon /ˈmɜrlən/ *n* merlón, *m,* almena, *f*

mermaid /ˈmɜrˌmeɪd/ *n* sirena, *f*

merrily /ˈmɛrɪli/ *adv* alegremente

merriment /ˈmɛrɪmənt/ *n* alegría, *f;* júbilo, *m;* regocijo, *m;* diversión, *f;* juego,
m

merriness /ˈmɛrɪnɪs/ *n* alegría, *f;* regocijo, *m;* *Inf.* ebriedad, *f*

merry /ˈmɛri/ *a* alegre; jovial; feliz; regocijado, divertido; (tipsy) calamocano. **to
make m.,** divertirse. **to make m. over,**
reírse de. **M. Christmas!** ¡Felices Navidades! **m.-andrew,** bufón, *m.* **m. m.-go-
round,** caballitos, *m pl,* tiovivo, *m.* **m.-
making,** festividades, fiestas, *f pl*

meseta *n* meseta, *f*

mesh /mɛʃ/ *n* malla, *f;* *Mech.* engranaje,
m; (network) red, *f;* (snare) lazo, *m.* —*vt*
coger con red; *Mech.* endentar

mesmerism /ˈmɛzməˌrɪzəm/ *n*
mesmerismo, *m*

mesmerize /ˈmɛzməˌraɪz/ *vt* hipnotizar

mess /mɛs/ *n* (of food) plato de comida,
m; porción, ración, *f;* rancho, *m;* (mixture) mezcla, *f;* (disorder) desorden, *m;*
suciedad, *f;* (failure) fracaso, *m.* —*vt*
(dirty) ensuciar; desordenar; (mismanage)
echar a perder. **to be in a m.,** *Inf.* estar
aviado. **to get in a m.,** *Inf.* hacerse un
lío. **to make a m. of,** ensuciar; desordenar; (spoil) echarlo todo a rodar

message /ˈmɛsɪdʒ/ *n* mensaje, *m;* recado, *m;* (telegraphic) parte, *m.* **I have
to take a m.,** Tengo que hacer un recado

messenger /ˈmɛsəndʒər/ *n* mensajero
(-ra); (of telegrams) repartidor, *m;* heraldo, *m;* anuncio, *m*

Messiah /mɪˈsaɪə/ *n* Mesías, *m*

Messianic /ˌmɛsiˈænɪk/ *a* mesiánico

messrs. /'mɛsərz/ n pl (abbreviation) sres. (from señores), m pl

metabolism /mə'tæbə,lɪzəm/ n metabolismo, m

metabolize /mə'tæbə,laɪz/ vt metabolizar

metal /'mɛtḷ/ n metal, m; vidrio en fusión, m; (road) grava, f; Herald. metal, m; (mettle) temple, temperamento, m; brío, fuego, m; pl metals, (of a railway) rieles, m pl. **m. engraver,** grabador en metal, m. **m. polish,** limpiametales, m. **m. shavings,** cizallas, f pl. **m. work,** metalistería, f. **m. worker,** metalario, m

metallic /mə'tælɪk/ a metálico

metalliferous /,mɛtḷ'ɪfərəs/ a metalífero

metalloid /'mɛtḷ,ɔɪd/ n metaloide, m

metallurgic /,mɛtḷ'ɜrdʒɪk/ a metalúrgico

metamorphosis /,mɛtə'mɔrfəsɪs/ n metamorfosis, f

metaphor /'mɛtə,fɔr/ n metáfora, f

metaphorical /,mɛtə'fɔrɪkəl/ a metafórico

meteor /'mitiər/ n meteoro, m

meteoric /,miti'ɔrɪk/ a meteórico

meteorite /'mitiə,raɪt/ n meteorito, m

meteorological /,mitiərə'lɒdʒɪkəl/ a meteorológico

meteorologist /,mitiə'rɒlədʒɪst/ n meteorologista, mf

meteorology /,mitiə'rɒlədʒi/ n meteorología, f

meter /'mitər/ n (for gas, etc.) contador, m; (verse and measure) metro, m

methane /'mɛθeɪn/ n metano, m

method /'mɛθəd/ n método, m; técnica, f; táctica, f

methodical /mə'θɒdɪkəl/ a metódico; ordenado, sistemático

methyl /'mɛθəl/ n metilo, m. **m. alcohol,** alcohol metílico, m

methylated spirit /'mɛθə,leɪtɪd/ n alcohol desnaturalizado, m

meticulous /mə'tɪkyələs/ a meticuloso; minucioso

meticulously /mə'tɪkyələsli/ adv con meticulosidad

meticulousness /mə'tɪkyələsnɪs/ n meticulosidad, f; minuciosidad, f

metric /'mɛtrɪk/ a métrico. **m. system,** sistema métrico, m

metrics /'mɛtrɪks/ n métrica, f

metronome /'mɛtrə,noʊm/ n metrónomo, m

metropolis /mɪ'trɒpəlɪs/ n metrópoli, f; capital, f

metropolitan /,mɛtrə'pɒlɪtḷ/ a metropolitano; de la capital. —n Eccl. metropolitano, m

mettle /'mɛtḷ/ n temple, temperamento, m; fuego, brío, m; valor, m. **You have put him on his m.,** Le has picado en el amor propio

mew /myu/ n (gull) gaviota, f; (of a cat) maullido, m; (of sea-birds) alarido, m. —vi (of a cat) maullar; (of sea-birds) dar alaridos. **to mew up,** encerrar

Mexican /'mɛksɪkən/ a mejicano. —n mejicano (-na)

Mexico /'mɛksɪ,koʊ/ Méjico, m

mezzanine /'mɛzə,nin/ n entresuelo, m

mezzo soprano /'mɛtsou sə'prænoʊ/ n mezzo-soprano

mi /mi/ n Mus. mi, m

miasma /mai'æzmə/ n miasma, m

mica /'maikə/ n mica, f

microbe /'maikroʊb/ n microbio, m

microbiologist /,maikroʊbai'ɒlədʒɪst/ n microbiólogo, m

microbiology /,maikroʊbai'ɒlədʒi/ n microbiología, f

microcosm /'maikrə,kɒzəm/ n microcosmo, m

microphone /'maikrə,foʊn/ n micrófono, m

microscope /'maikrə,skoʊp/ n microscopio, m

microscopic /,maikrə'skɒpɪk/ a microscópico

microwave /'maikroʊ,weiv/ n microonda, f

mid /mɪd/ a medio. —prep entre; en medio de; a mediados de. **from mid May to August,** desde mediados de mayo hasta agosto. **a mid-fourteenth century castle,** un castillo de mediados del siglo catorce. **in mid air,** en medio del aire. **in mid channel,** en medio del canal. **in mid winter,** en medio del invierno

midday /'mɪd'dei/ n mediodía, m, a del mediodía, meridional. **at m.,** a mediodía

middle /'mɪdḷ/ a medio; en medio de; del centro; intermedio; (average) mediano. —n medio, m; mitad, f; centro, m; (waist) cintura, f. **in the m. of,** en medio de. **in the m. of nowhere,** donde Cristo dio las tres voces. **toward the m. of the month,** a mediados del mes. **m. age,** edad madura, f. **m.-aged,** de edad madura, de cierta edad. **M. Ages,** edad media, f. **m. class,** clase media, burguesía, f, a de la clase media, burgués. **m. distance,** término medio, m. **m. ear,** oído medio, m. **m. finger,** dedo de en medio (or del corazón), m. **m. way,** Fig. término medio, m. **m. weight,** peso medio, m

Middle East, the el Oriente Medio, el Levante, m

middleman /'mɪdḷ,mæn/ n agente de negocios, m; (retailer) revendedor, m; intermediario, m

middling /'mɪdlɪŋ/ a mediano; mediocre; regular, así, así

midge /mɪdʒ/ n mosquito, m, mosca de agua, f

midget /'mɪdʒɪt/ n enano (-na). **m. submarine,** submarino de bolsillo, m

midnight /'mɪd,naɪt/ n medianoche, f. —a de medianoche; nocturno. **at m.,** a medianoche. **to burn the m. oil,** quemarse las cejas. **m. mass,** misa del gallo, f

midriff /'mɪdrɪf/ n diafragma, m

midship /'mɪd,ʃɪp/ a maestro. —n medio

del buque, *m.* **m. beam,** bao maestro, *m.*
m. gangway, crujía, *f*

midshipman /'mɪd,ʃɪpmən/ *n* guardia-
marina, *m*

midst /mɪdst/ *n* medio, *m;* seno, *m, prep*
entre. **in the m. of,** en medio de. **There
is a traitor in our m.,** Hay un traidor entre nosotros (or en nuestra compañía)

midstream /'mɪd'strim/ *n* **in m.** *m.* en
medio de la corriente

midsummer /'mɪd'sʌmər/ *n* pleno verano, *m;* solsticio estival, *m;* fiesta de San
Juan, *f.* **A M. Night's Dream,** El Sueño
de la Noche de San Juan

midway / *adv* a, 'mɪd'wei; *n* -,wei/ *a*
and *adv* situado a medio camino; a medio camino, a la mitad del camino; entre.
—*n* mitad del camino, *f;* medio, *m.* **m.
between...,** equidistante de..., entre

midwife /'mɪd,waif/ *n* comadrona, partera, *f*

midwifery /mɪd'wɪfəri/ *n* obstetricia, *f*

midwinter /n 'mɪd'wɪntər, -,wɪn-; *a*
-,wɪn-/ *n* medio del invierno, *m*

mien /min/ *n* aire, *m;* porte, semblante,
m

might /mait/ *vi* poder. **It m. or m. not
be true,** Podría o no podría ser verdad.
How happy Mary m. have been! ¡Qué
feliz pudo haber sido María! **I thought
that you m. have seen him in the theater,** Creí que pudieras haberle visto en el
teatro. **That I m....!** ¡Que yo pudiese...!
This m. have been avoided if... Esto
podía haberse evitado si...

might /mait/ *n* fuerza, *f;* poder, *m.* **with
m. and main,** con todas sus fuerzas

mightily /'maitʃli/ *adv* fuertemente;
poderosamente; *Inf.* muchísimo, sumamente

mighty /'maiti/ *a* fuerte, vigoroso;
poderoso; grande; *Inf.* enorme; (proud)
arrogante. —*adv Inf.* enormemente, muy

migraine /'maigrein/ *n* migraña, jaqueca,
f

migrant /'maigrənt/ *a* migratorio, de
paso. —*n* ave migratoria, ave de paso, *f*

migrate /'maigreit/ *vi* emigrar

migration /mai'greiʃən/ *n* migración, *f*

migratory /'maigrə,tɔri/ *a* migratorio, de
paso; (of people) nómada, pasajero

migratory worker *n* trabajador golon-
drino, *m*

milch /mɪltʃ/ *a f,* (of cows) lechera

mild /maild/ *a* apacible, pacífico; manso;
dulce; suave; (of the weather) blando;
Med. benigno; (light) leve; (of drinks)
ligero; (weak) débil

mildew /'mil,du/ *n* mildiu, añublo, *m;*
moho, *m.* —*vt* anublar; enmohecer. —*vi*
anublarse; enmohecerse

mildly /'maildli/ *adv* suavemente; dulcemente; con indulgencia

mile /mail/ *n* milla, *f*

mileage /'mailɪdʒ/ *n* distancia en millas,
f; kilometraje, *m*

milestone /'mail,stoun/ *n* hito, *m,* piedra
miliaria, *f;* mojón kilométrico, *m*

militancy /'mɪlɪtənsi/ *n* carácter militante, *m;* belicosidad, *f*

militant /'mɪlɪtənt/ *a* militante, combatiente; belicoso; agresivo. —*n*
combatiente, *mf*

militarism /'mɪlɪtə,rɪzəm/ *n* militarismo,
m

militarist /'mɪlɪtərɪst/ *n* militarista, *mf*

militarize /'mɪlɪtə,raiz/ *vt* militarizar

military /'mɪlɪ,teri/ *a* militar; de guerra.
the m., los militares. **m. academy,**
colegio militar, *m.* **m. camp,** campo militar, *m.* **m. law,** código militar, *m.* **m.
man,** militar, *m.* **m. police,** policía militar, *f.* **m. service,** servicio militar, *m*

militate /'mɪlɪ,teit/ *vi* militar
contra **(against)**

militia /mɪ'lɪʃə/ *n* milicia, *f*

militiaman /mɪ'lɪʃəmən/ *n* miliciano, *m*

milk /mɪlk/ *n* leche, *f.* —*vt* ordeñar. —*vi* dar leche. **to have
m. and water in one's veins,** tener san-
gre de horchata. **condensed m.,** leche
condensada, leche en lata, *f.* **m.-can,**
lechera, *f.* **m.-cart,** carro de la leche, *m.*
m. chocolate, chocolate con leche, *m.* **m.
of magnesia,** leche de magnesia, *f.* **m.-
pail,** ordeñadero, *m.* **m.-tooth,** diente de
leche, *m.* **m.-white,** blanco como la leche

milking /'mɪlkɪŋ/ *n* ordeño, *m.* **m.-
machine,** máquina ordeñadora, *f.* **m.-
stool,** taburete, banquillo, *m*

milkmaid /'mɪlk,meid/ *n* lechera, *f*

milkman /'mɪlk,mæn/ *n* lechero, *m*

milksop /'mɪlk,sop/ *n* marica, *m*

milky /'mɪlki/ *a* lechero; de leche;
lechoso, como leche; *Astron.* lácteo. **the
Milky Way** la Vía láctea *f*

mill /mɪl/ *n* molino, *m;* (for coffee, etc.)
molinillo, *m;* (factory) fábrica, *f;* taller,
m; (textile) hilandería, *f;* fábrica de teji-
dos, *f;* (fight) riña a puñetazos, *f;*
pugilato, *m.* —*vt* (grind) moler; (coins)
acordonar; (cloth) abatanar; (chocolate)
batir. **cotton m.,** hilandería de algodón, *f.*
hand-m., molinillo, *m.* **paper-m.,** fábrica
de papel, *f.* **saw-m.,** serrería, *f.* **spinning
m.,** hilandería, *f.* **water m.,** molino de
agua, *m.* **m.-course,** saetín, canal de
molino, *m.* **m.-dam,** esclusa de molino, *f.*
m.-hand, obrero (-ra). **m.-pond,** cubo, *m.*
m.-race, caz, *m.* **m.-wheel,** rueda de
molino, *f*

millennial /mɪl'lɛniəl/ *a* milenario, *m*

millennium /mɪ'lɛniəm/ *n* milenario, *m*

miller /'mɪlər/ *n* molinero, *m.* **miller's
wife,** molinera

millet /'mɪlɪt/ *n* mijo, *m*

milligram /'mɪlɪ,græm/ *n* miligramo, *m*

millimeter /'mɪlə,mitər/ *n* milímetro, *m*

milliner /'mɪlənər/ *n* sombrerero (-ra),
modista, *mf* **milliner's shop,** sombrerería,
tienda de modista, *f*

millinery /'mɪlə,neri/ *n* sombreros, *m pl;*
modas, *f pl;* tienda de modista, *f*

milling /'mɪlɪŋ/ *n* molienda, *f;* acuñación, *f;* (edge of coin) cordoncillo, *m.* **m. machine,** fresadora, *f*

million /'mɪlyən/ *n* millón, *m.* **the m.,** las masas

millionaire /,mɪlyə'neər/ *a* millonario. —*n* millonario, *m*

millionth /'mɪlyənθ/ *a* millonésimo

millstone /'mɪl,stoun/ *n* piedra de moler, muela, *f*

mime /maim/ *n* (Greek farce and actor) mimo, *m;* (mimicry) mímica, *f;* pantomima, *f.* —*vi* hacer en pantomima

mimetic /mɪ'metɪk/ *a* mímico, imitativo

mimic /'mɪmɪk/ *a* mímico; (pretended) fingido. —*n* imitador (-ra). —*vt* imitar, contrahacer; *Biol.* imitar, adaptarse a

mimicry /'mɪmɪkri/ *n* mímica, imitación, *f; Biol.* mimetismo, *m*

minaret /,mɪnə'ret/ *n* minarete, *m;* (of a mosque) alminar, *m*

minatory /'mɪnə,tori, -,touri/ *a* amenazador

mince /mɪns/ *vt* desmenuzar; (meat) picar; (words) medir (las palabras). —*vi* andar con pasos menuditos; andar o moverse con afectación; hacer remilgos. **m.-meat,** carne picada, *f;* (sweet) conserva de fruta y especias, *f*

mincing /'mɪnsɪŋ/ *a* afectado. —*n* acción de picar carne, *f.* **m. machine,** máquina de picar carne, *f*

mind /maind/ *n* inteligencia, *f;* espíritu ánimo, *m;* imaginación, *f;* alma, *f;* (memory) memoria, *f;* recuerdo, *m;* (understanding) entendimiento, *m;* (genius) ingenio, *m;* (cast of mind) mentalidad, *f;* (opinion) opinión, *f;* (liking) gusto, *m;* (thoughts) pensamiento, *m;* (intention) propósito, *m,* intención, *f;* (tendency) propensión, inclinación, *f.* **I have a good m. to go away,** Por poco me marcho; Tengo ganas de marcharme. **I have changed my m.,** He cambiado de opinión. **out of m.,** olvidado. **I shall give him a piece of my m.,** Le diré cuatro verdades. **It had quite gone out of my m.,** Lo había olvidado completamente. **I can see it in my mind's eye,** Está presente a mi imaginación. **I shall bear it in m.,** Lo tendré en cuenta. **I thought in my own m. that...,** Pensé por mis adentros que... **We are both of the same m.,** Ambos somos de la misma opinión. **to be out of one's m.,** estar fuera de juicio. **to call to m.,** acordarse de. **to have something on one's m.,** estar preocupado. **to make up one's m. (to),** resolverse (a), decidirse (a), determinar; animarse (a). **m.-reader,** adivinador (-ra) del pensamiento

mind /maind/ *vt* (remember) recordar, no olvidar; (heed) atender a; hacer caso de; tener cuidado de; (fear) tener miedo de; (obey) obedecer; preocuparse de; (object to) molestar; importar; (care for) cuidar. —*vi* tener cuidado; molestar; (feel) sentir; (fear) tener miedo; (be the same thing) ser igual. **Do you m. being quiet a mo-**

ment? ¿Quieres hacer el favor de callarte un momento? **Do you m. if I smoke?** ¿Le molesta si fumo? **They don't m.,** No les importa, Les da igual. **Never m.!** ¡No se moleste!; ¡No se preocupe!; ¡No importa! ¡Vaya! **M. what you are doing!** ¡Cuidado con lo que haces! **M. your own business!** ¡No te metas donde no te llaman!

mindful /'maindfəl/ *a* atento (a), cuidadoso (de); que se acuerda (de)

mine /main/ *a poss* mío, *m,* (mía, *f;* míos, *m pl;* mías, *f pl);* el mío, *m,* (la mía, *f;* lo mío, *neut;* los míos, *m pl;* las mías, *f pl);* mi *(pl* mis). **a friend of m.,** un amigo mío; uno de mis amigos

mine /main/ *n* mina, *f.* —*vt* minar; extraer; sembrar minas en, colocar minas en. —*vi* minar; hacer una mina; dedicarse a la minería. **drifting m.,** mina a la deriva, *f.* **land m.,** mina terrestre, *f.* **magnetic m.,** mina magnética, *f.* **to lay mines,** colocar (or sembrar) minas. **m.-sweeper,** dragaminas, buque barreminas, *m*

minefield /'main,fild/ *n* campo de minas, *m;* barrera de minas, *f*

minelayer /'main,leiər/ *n* barca plantaminas, *f,* barco siembraminas, lanzaminas, *m*

miner /'mainər/ *n* minero, *m; Mil.* zapador minador, *m*

mineral /'mɪnərəl/ *n* mineral, *m, a* mineral. **m. baths,** baños, *m pl.* **m. water,** agua mineral, *f;* gaseosa, *f*

mingle /'mɪŋgəl/ *vt* mezclar; confundir. —*vi* mezclarse; confundirse

mingling /'mɪŋglɪŋ/ *n* mezcla, *f*

miniature /'mɪniətʃər/ *n* miniatura, *f.* —*a* en miniatura. **m. edition,** edición diamante, *f*

miniature golf *n* minigolf, *m*

miniaturist /'mɪniətʃərɪst/ *n* miniaturista, *mf*

minimize /'mɪnə,maiz/ *vt* aminorar, reducir al mínimo; mitigar; (underrate) tener en menos, despreciar

minimum /'mɪnəməm/ *n* mínimo, *m, a* mínimo

mining /'mainɪŋ/ *n* minería, *f, a* minero; de mina; de minas; de minero. **m. engineer,** ingeniero de minas, *m*

minion /'mɪnyən/ *n* favorito (-ta); satélite, *m; Print.* miñona, *f*

minister /'mɪnəstər/ *n* ministro, *m.* —*vi* servir; suministrar, proveer de; (contribute) contribuir (a). **m. of health,** ministro de sanidad, *m.* **m. of war,** ministro de la guerra, *m*

ministry /'mɪnəstri/ *n* ministerio, *m.* **m. of food,** Ministerio de Abastecimientos, *m*

mink /mɪŋk/ *n* visón, *m*

minor /'mainər/ *a* menor. —*n* menor de edad, *m;* (logic) menor, *f; Mus.* tono menor, *m; Eccl.* menor, *m.* **to be a m.,** ser menor de edad. **m. key,** tono menor,

m. **m. orders**, *Eccl.* órdenes menores, *f
pl.* **m. scale**, escala menor, *f*

minority /mɪˈnɔrɪti/ *n* minoría, *f;* (of age) minoridad, *f.* **in the m.**, en la minoría

minster /ˈmɪnstər/ *n* catedral, *f;* monasterio, *m*

minstrel /ˈmɪnstrəl/ *n* trovador, juglar, *m;* músico, *m;* cantante, *m*

mint /mɪnt/ *n Bot.* menta, hierbabuena, *f;* casa de moneda, casa de la moneda, ceca, *f; Fig.* mina, *f;* (source) origen, *m.* —*vt* (money) acuñar; *Fig.* inventar, *a* (postage stamp) en estado nuevo

minus /ˈmaɪnəs/ *a* menos; negativo; desprovisto de; sin. —*n* signo menos, *m;* cantidad negativa, *f*

minute /maɪˈnut/ *a* menudo, diminuto; insignificante; minucioso

minute /ˈmɪnɪt/ *n* minuto, *m;* momento, *m;* instante, *m;* (note) minuta, *f; pl* **minutes**, actas, *f pl.* **in a m.**, en un instante. **m.-book**, libro de actas, minutario, *m.* **m.-hand**, minutero, *m*

minutely /maɪˈnutli/ *adv* minuciosamente; en detalle; exactamente

minx /mɪŋks/ *n* picaruela, *f;* coqueta, *f*

miracle /ˈmɪrəkəl/ *n* milagro, *m.* **m.-monger**, milagrero (-ra). **m. play**, milagro, *m*

miraculous /mɪˈrækyələs/ *a* milagroso

mirage /mɪˈrɑʒ/ *n* espejismo, *m*

mire /maɪr/ *n* fango, lodo, *m;* (miry place) lodazal, *m*

mirror /ˈmɪrər/ *n* espejo, *m.* —*vt* reflejar. **to look in the m.**, mirarse al espejo. **full-length m.**, espejo de cuerpo entero, *m.* **small m.**, espejuelo, *m*

mirth /mɜrθ/ *n* alegría, *f,* júbilo, *m;* risa, *f;* hilaridad, *f*

mirthful /ˈmɜrfəl/ *a* alegre

miry /ˈmaɪri/ *a* lodoso, fangoso, cenagoso

misadventure /ˌmɪsədˈventʃər/ *n* desgracia, *f;* accidente, *m*

misanthrope /ˈmɪsənˌθroup/ *n* misántropo, *m*

misanthropic /ˌmɪsənˈθrɒpɪk/ *a* misantrópico

misapply /ˌmɪsəˈplaɪ/ *vt* aplicar mal; hacer mal uso de; abusar de

misapprehend /ˌmɪsæprɪˈhɛnd/ *vt* comprender mal; equivocarse sobre

misapprehension /ˌmɪsæprəˈhɛnʃən/ *n* concepto erróneo, *m;* equivocación, *f,* error, *m*

misappropriate /ˌmɪsəˈproupriˌeit/ *vt* malversar

misbehave /ˌmɪsbɪˈheɪv/ *vi* portarse mal; (of a child) ser malo

misbehavior /ˌmɪsbɪˈheɪvyər/ *n* mala conducta, *f*

miscalculate /mɪsˈkælkyəleit/ *vt* calcular mal; engañarse (sobre)

miscalculation /ˌmɪskælkyəˈleiʃən/ *n* mal cálculo, error, *m;* desacierto, *m*

miscall /mɪsˈkɔl/ *vt* mal nombrar; llamar equivocadamente; (abuse) insultar

miscarriage /mɪsˈkærɪdʒ/ *n Med.* aborto, *m;* (failure) malogro, fracaso, *m;* (of goods) extravío, *m*

miscarriage of justice *n* yerro en la administración de la justicia, *m*

miscarry /mɪsˈkæri/ *vi Med.* abortar, malparir; (fail) malograrse, frustrarse; (of goods) extraviarse

miscellaneous /ˌmɪsəˈleiniəs/ *a* misceláneo; vario, diverso

mischance /mɪsˈtʃæns/ *n* mala suerte, *f;* infortunio, *m,* desgracia, *f;* accidente, *m*

mischief /ˈmɪstʃɪf/ *n* daño, *m;* mal, *m;* (wilfulness) travesura, *f;* (person) diablillo, *m.* **m.-maker**, enredador (-ra), chismoso (-sa); alborotador, *m;* malicioso (-sa). **m.-making**, *a* enredador; chismoso; malicioso; alborotador

mischievous /ˈmɪstʃəvəs/ *a* dañino, perjudicial, malo; malicioso; chismoso; (wilful) travieso; juguetón; (of glances, etc.) malicioso

misconceive /ˌmɪskənˈsiv/ *vt* formar un concepto erróneo de; concebir mal, juzgar mal

misconception /ˌmɪskənˈsɛpʃən/ *n* concepto erróneo, *m,* idea falsa, *f;* error, *m,* equivocación, *f;* engaño, *m*

misconduct / *n* mɪsˈkɒndʌkt; *v* ˌmɪskənˈdʌkt/ *n* mala conducta, *f.* **to m. oneself**, portarse mal

misconstruction /ˌmɪskənˈstrʌkʃən/ *n* mala interpretación, *f;* falsa interpretación, *f;* tergiversación, *f;* mala traducción, *f*

misconstrue /ˌmɪskənˈstru/ *vt* interpretar mal; entender mal; tergiversar; traducir mal

miscount / *v* mɪsˈkaunt; *n* ˈmɪsˌkaunt/ *vt* contar mal, equivocarse en la cuenta de; calcular mal. —*n* error, *m;* yerro de cuenta, *m*

miscreant /ˈmɪskriənt/ *n* malandrín, *m;* bribón, *m,* a vil, malandrín

misdeed /mɪsˈdid/ *n* delito, malhecho, crimen, *m*

misdemeanor /ˌmɪsdɪˈminər/ *n* mala conducta, *f; Law.* delito, *m;* ofensa, *f,* malhecho, *m*

misdirect /ˌmɪsdɪˈrekt/ *vt* informar mal (acerca del camino); (a letter) dirigir mal, poner unas señas incorrectas en

miser /ˈmaɪzər/ *n* avaro (-ra)

miserable /ˈmɪzərəbəl/ *a* infeliz, desgraciado; miserable; despreciable; sin valor

miserably /ˈmɪzərəbli/ *adv* miserablemente

miserly /ˈmaɪzərli/ *a* avaro, tacaño

misery /ˈmɪzəri/ *n* miseria, *f;* sufrimiento, *m;* dolor, tormento, *m*

misfire /mɪsˈfɪr/ *vi* no dar fuego; (of a motor-car, etc.) hacer falsas explosiones, errar el encendido

misfit /mɪsˈfɪt; ˈmɪsˌfɪt for person/ *n* traje que no cae bien, *m;* zapato que no va bien, *m;* (person) inadaptado, *m*

misfortune /mɪsˈfɔrtʃən/ *n* infortunio,

m, mala suerte, adversidad, *f;* desdicha, desgracia, *f;* mal, *m*

misgive /mɪs'gɪv/ *vt* hacer temer; llenar de duda; hacer recelar; hacer presentir

misgiving /mɪs'gɪvɪŋ/ *n* temor, *m;* duda, *f;* recelo, *m;* presentimiento, *m*

misgovern /mɪs'gʌvərn/ *vt* gobernar mal; administrar mal; dirigir mal

misgovernment /mɪs'gʌvərnmənt/ *n* desgobierno, *m;* mala administración, *f*

misguided /mɪs'gaɪdɪd/ *a* mal dirigido; extraviado; engañado; (blind) ciego

mishap /'mɪshæp/ *n* desgracia, *f;* contratiempo, accidente, *m.* **to have a m.,** sufrir una desgracia; tener un accidente

misinform /,mɪsɪn'fɔrm/ *vt* informar mal; dar informes erróneos (a)

misinformation /,mɪsɪnfər'meɪʃən/ *n* noticia falsa, *f;* información errónea, *f*

misinterpret /,mɪsɪn'tɜrprɪt/ *vt* interpretar mal; entender mal; torcer; tergiversar; traducir mal

misinterpretation /,mɪsɪn,tɜrprɪ'teɪʃən/ *n* mala interpretación, *f;* interpretación falsa, *f;* tergiversación, *f;* mala traducción, *f*

misjudge /mɪs'dʒʌdʒ/ *vt* juzgar mal; equivocarse (en or sobre); tener una idea falsa de

misjudgment /mɪs'dʒʌdʒmənt/ *n* juicio errado, *m;* idea falsa, *f;* juicio injusto, *m*

mislay /mɪs'leɪ/ *vt* extraviar, perder

mislead /mɪs'lid/ *vt* extraviar; llevar a conclusiones erróneas, despistar; engañar

misleading /mɪs'lidɪŋ/ *a* de falsas apariencias; erróneo, falso; engañoso

mismanage /mɪs'mænɪdʒ/ *vt* administrar mal; dirigir mal; echar a perder

misname /mɪs'neɪm/ *vt* mal nombrar; llamar equivocadamente

misnomer /mɪs'noumər/ *n* nombre equivocado, *m;* nombre inapropiado, *m*

misogynist /mɪ'sɒdʒənɪst/ *n* misógino, *m*

misogyny /mɪ'sɒdʒəni/ *n* misoginia, *f*

misplace /mɪs'pleɪs/ *vt* colocar mal; poner fuera de lugar

misplaced /mɪs'pleɪst/ *a* mal puesto; inoportuno; equivocado

misprint /*n.* mɪs,prɪnt/ *v.* mɪs'prɪnt/ *n* error de imprenta, *m,* errata, *f, vt* imprimir con erratas

mispronounce /,mɪsprə'naʊns/ *vt* pronunciar mal

mispronunciation /,mɪsprənʌnsi'eɪʃən/ *n* mala pronunciación, *f*

misquote /mɪs'kwoʊt/ *vt* citar mal, citar erróneamente

misrepresent /,mɪsreprɪ'zɛnt/ *vt* desfigurar; tergiversar; falsificar

misrepresentation /mɪs,reprɪzɛn'teɪʃən/ *n* desfiguración, *f;* tergiversación, *f;* falsificación, *f*

misrule /mɪs'rul/ *vt* gobernar mal. —*n* mal gobierno, desgobierno, *m;* confusión, *f*

miss /mɪs/ *n* señorita, *f*

miss /mɪs/ *vt* (one's aim) errar (el tiro, etc.); no acertar (a); (let fall) dejar caer; (lose a train, the post, etc., one's footing, an opportunity, etc.) perder; (fall short of) dejar de; no ver; no notar; pasar por alto de; omitir; echar de menos; notar la falta de; no encontrar. —*vi* errar; (fail) salir mal, fracasar. **I m. you,** Te echo de menos. **to be missing,** faltar; estar ausente; haberse marchado; haber desaparecido. **to m. one's mark,** errar el blanco. **to m. out,** omitir, pasar por alto de. **She doesn't miss a beat,** (fig.) No se le escapa nada

missal /'mɪsəl/ *n* misal, *m*

misshapen /mɪs'ʃeɪpən/ *a* deforme

missile /'mɪsəl/ *n* arma arrojadiza, *f;* proyectil, *m*

missing /'mɪsɪŋ/ *a* que falta; perdido; ausente; *Mil.* desaparecido

mission /'mɪʃən/ *n* misión, *f*

missionary /'mɪʃə,neri/ *n* misionero, *m*

missive /'mɪsɪv/ *n* misiva, *f*

misspend /mɪs'spend/ *vt* malgastar; desperdiciar; perder

mist /mɪst/ *n* bruma, neblina, *f;* vapor, *m;* (drizzle) llovizna, *f; Fig.* nube, *f.* —*vt* anublar, empañar. —*vi* lloviznar

mistake /mɪ'steɪk/ *vt* comprender mal; equivocarse sobre; errar; (with for) confundir con, equivocarse con. —*n* equivocación, *f;* error, *m;* inadvertencia, *f;* (in an exercise, etc.) falta, *f.* **And no m.!** *Inf.* Sin duda alguna. **by m.,** por equivocación; (involuntarily) sin querer. **If I am not mistaken,** Si no me engaño, Si no estoy equivocado. **to make a m.,** equivocarse

mistaken /mɪ'steɪkən/ *a* (of persons and things) equivocado; (of things) erróneo; incorrecto

mistakenly /mɪ'steɪkənli/ *adv* equivocadamente; injustamente, falsamente

mister /'mɪstər/ *n* señor, *m*

mistimed /mɪs'taɪmd/ *a* intempestivo; inoportuno

mistletoe /'mɪsəl,toʊ/ *n* muérdago, *m*

mistranslate /,mɪstrænz'leɪt/ *vt* traducir mal; interpretar mal

mistranslation /,mɪstrænz'leɪʃən/ *n* mala traducción, *f;* traducción inexacta, *f*

mistress /'mɪstrɪs/ *n* señora, *f;* maestra, *f;* (fiancée) prometida, *f;* (beloved) amada, dulce dueña, *f;* (concubine) amiga, querida, *f.* **M. (Mrs.) Gómez,** Sra Gómez. **m. of the robes,** camarera mayor, *f*

mistrust /mɪs'trʌst/ *vt* desconfiar de, no tener confianza en; dudar de. —*n* desconfianza, *f;* recelo, *m,* suspicacia, *f;* aprensión, *f*

mistrustful /mɪs'trʌstfəl/ *a* desconfiado; receloso, suspicaz. **to be m. of,** recelarse de

misty /'mɪsti/ *a* brumoso, nebuloso; vaporoso; (of the eyes) anublado; (of windows, etc.) empañado

misunderstand /,mɪsʌndər'stænd/ *vt*

comprender mal; tomar en sentido erróneo; interpretar mal

misunderstanding /,misʌndər'stændiŋ/ *n* concepto erróneo, error, *m;* equivocación, *f;* (disagreement) desavenencia, *f*

misuse /*n* mis'yus; *v* -'yuz/ *vt* emplear mal; abusar de; (funds) malversar; (illtreat) tratar mal. —*n* abuso, *m;* (of funds) malversación, *f*

mite /mait/ *n* (coin) ardite, *m;* (trifle) pizca, *f;* óbolo, *m; Ent.* ácaro, *m*

mitigate /'miti,geit/ *vt* (pain) aliviar; mitigar; suavizar

mitigation /,miti'geiʃən/ *n* (of pain) alivio, *m;* mitigación, *f*

mitten /'mitn/ *n* mitón, *m*

mix /miks/ *vt* mezclar; (salad) aderezar; (concrete, etc.) amasar; combinar, unir; (sociably) alternar (con); (confuse) confundir. —*vi* mezclarse; frecuentar la compañía (de); frecuentar; (get on well) llevarse bien

mixed /mikst/ *a* mezclado; vario, surtido; mixto; (confused) confuso. **m. doubles,** parejas mixtas, *f pl.* **m. up,** (in disorder) revuelto; confuso. **m. up with,** implicado en; asociado con

mixer /'miksər/ *n* mezclador, *m;* (person) mezclador (-ra); *Inf.* persona sociable, *f.* **electric m.,** mezclador eléctrico, *m*

mixture /'mikstʃər/ *n* mezcla, *f;* (medicine) poción, medicina, *f*

mnemonics /ni'moniks/ *n* mnemotecnia, *f*

moan /moun/ *vt* lamentar; llorar. —*vi* gemir; quejarse, lamentarse. —*n* gemido, *m;* lamento, *m;* quejido, *m*

moaning /'mouniŋ/ *n* gemidos, *m pl*

moat /mout/ *n* foso, *m*

mob /mob/ *n* (crowd) muchedumbre, multitud, *f;* (rabble) populacho, *m,* gentuza, *f.* —*vt* atropellar; atacar. **mob-cap,** cofia, *f*

mobile /'moubil/ *a* móvil; ambulante; (fickle) voluble. **m. canteen,** cantina ambulante, *f*

mobility /mou'biliti/ *n* movilidad, *f*

mobilization /,moubələ'zeiʃən/ *n* movilización, *f*

mobilize /'moubə,laiz/ *vt* movilizar. —*vi* movilizarse

moccasin /'mokəsin, -zən/ *n* mocasín, *m*

mocha /'moukə/ *n* café de Moca, *m*

mock /mok/ *vt* ridiculizar; burlarse (de), mofarse (de); (cause to fail) frustrar; (mimic) imitar; (delude) engañar. —*vi* mofarse, burlarse, reírse. —*a* cómico, burlesco; falso; fingido; imitado. **to make a m. of,** poner en ridículo; hacer absurdo; burlarse de. **m.-heroic,** heroico-cómico. **m.-orange,** *Bot.* jeringuilla, *f.* **m.-turtle soup,** sopa hecha con cabeza de ternera a imitación de tortuga, *f*

mocker /*n* mofador (-ra); el, *m,* (*f,* la) que se burla de

mockery /'mokəri/ *n* mofa, burla, *f;* ridículo, *m;* ilusión, apariencia, *f.* **to make a m. of,** mofarse de; hacer ridículo

mocking /'mokiŋ/ *a* burlón. **m. bird,** pájaro burlón, *m*

mode /moud/ *n* modo, *m;* manera, *f;* (fashion) moda, *f;* uso, *m,* costumbre, *f*

model /'modl/ *n* modelo, *m;* (artist's) modelo vivo, *m, a* modelo; en miniatura. —*vt* modelar; moldear; formar; hacer; planear. **m. display,** (hats, etc.) exposición de modelos, *f.* **m. railway,** ferrocarril en miniatura, *m*

modeling /'modliŋ/ *n* modelado, *m;* modelo, *m.* **m. wax,** cera para moldear, *f*

modem /'moudəm, -dɛm/ *n* módem, *m*

moderate /*a, n.* 'modərit *v.* -ə,reit/ *a* moderado; (of prices, etc.) módico; (fair, medium) regular, mediano; razonable; mediocre. —*n* moderado, *m.* —*vt* moderar; modificar; calmar. —*vi* moderarse; calmarse

moderately /'modəritli/ *adv* moderadamente; módicamente; medianamente; bastante; razonablemente; mediocremente

moderation /,modə'reiʃən/ *n* moderación, *f.* **in m.,** en moderación

modern /'modərn/ *a* moderno. —*n* modernista, *mf.* **in the m. way,** a la moderna. **m. language,** lengua viva, *f*

modernize /'modər,naiz/ *vt* modernizar

modest /'modist/ *a* modesto; (of a woman) púdico

modesty /'modisti/ *n* modestia, *f;* (of a woman) pudor, *m*

modicum /'modikəm/ *n* porción pequeña, *f;* poco, *m*

modifiable *a* modificable

modification /,modəfi'keiʃən/ *n* modificación, *f*

modify /'modə,fai/ *vt* modificar. **It has been much modified,** Se ha modificado mucho; Se han hecho muchas modificaciones

modifying *a* modificante, modificador

modish /'moudiʃ/ *a* de moda en boga; elegante

modiste /mou'dist/ *n* modista, *mf*

modulate /'modʒə,leit/ *vt and vi* modular

modulation /,modʒə'leiʃən/ *n* modulación, *f*

modus vivendi /'moudəs vi'vɛndi, -dai/ *n* modo de conveniencia, *m*

moiré /mwa'rei, mɔ-/ *n* muaré, *m*

moist /mɔist/ *a* húmedo

moisten /'mɔisən/ *vt* humedecer, mojar

moisture /'mɔistʃər/ *n* humedad, *f*

molar /'moulər/ *n* muela, *f, a* molar

molasses /mə'læsiz/ *n pl* melaza, *f*

mold /mould/ *n* (fungus) moho, *m;* (humus) mantillo, *m;* (iron-mould) mancha de orín, *f;* (matrix) molde, *m,* matriz, *f; Cul.* cubilete, *m; Naut.* gálibo, *m;* (for jelly, etc.) molde, *m; Archit.* moldura, *f;* (temperament) temple, *m,* disposición, *f.* —*vt* moldear; (cast) vaciar; moldurar; *Naut.* galibar; *Fig.* amoldar, formar; *Agr.* cubrir con mantillo. **to m. oneself on,**

modelarse sobre. **m.-board,** (of a plough) orejera, f

molder /'moʊldər/ n moldeador, m; Fig. amolador (-ra); creador (-ra). —vi desmoronarse, convertirse en polvo; Fig. decaer, desmoronarse; vegetar

molding /'moʊldɪŋ/ n amoldamiento, m; vaciado, m; Archit. moldura, f; Fig. formación,

moldy /'moʊldi/ a mohoso, enmohecido; Fig. anticuado

mole /'moʊleɪ/ n (animal) topo, m; (spot) lunar, m; (breakwater) dique, malecón, m; muelle, m

molecular /mə'lɛkyələr/ a molecular

molecule /'moli,kyul/ n molécula, f

molehill /'moʊl,hɪl/ n topera, f

moleskin /'moʊl,skɪn/ n piel de topo, f

molest /mə'lɛst/ vt molestar; perseguir, importunar; faltar al respeto (a)

molestation /,moʊlə'steɪʃən/ n importunidad, persecución, f; molestia, incomodidad, f

mollification /,moləfɪ'keɪʃən/ n apaciguamiento, m; mitigación, f

mollify /'molə,faɪ/ vt apaciguar, calmar; mitigar

mollusk /'moləsk/ n molusco, m

mollycoddle /'moli,kodl/ n alfeñique, mírame y no me toques, m; niño (-ña), mimado (-da)

Moloch /'moʊlok/ n Moloc, m

molt /moʊlt/ vi mudar, n muda, f

molten /'moʊltn/ a fundido; derretido

moment /'moʊmənt/ n momento, m; instante m; (importance) importancia, f. **at this m.,** en este momento. **Do it this m.!** ¡Hazlo al instante (or en seguida)!

momentarily /,moʊmən'tɛrəli, 'moʊmən,ter-/ adv momentáneamente; cada momento

momentary /'moʊmən,tɛri/ a momentáneo

momentous /moʊ'mɛntəs/ a de suma importancia; crítico; grave

momentum /moʊ'mɛntəm/ n momento, m, velocidad adquirida f; Fig. ímpetu, m. **to gather m.,** cobrar velocidad, acelerar

monarch /'monərk/ n monarca, m

monarchy /'monərki/ n monarquía, f

monastery /'monə,stɛri/ n monasterio, m

monastic /mə'næstɪk/ a monástico. **m. life,** vida de clausura, f

monasticism n vida monástica, f

Monday /'mʌndeɪ, -di/ n lunes, m

monetary /'moni,tɛri/ a monetario

money /'mʌni/ n dinero, m; (coin) moneda, f; sistema monetario, m. **paper m.,** papel moneda, m. **ready m.,** dinero contante, m. **to make m.,** ganar (or hacer) dinero; enriquecerse. **M. talks,** Poderoso caballero es Don Dinero. **m.-bag,** talega, f; (person) ricacho (-cha). **m.-bags,** riqueza, f. **m.-box,** alcancía, hucha, f. **m.-changer,** cambista, mf **m.-lender,** prestamista, mf **m.-making,** n el

hacer dinero; prosperidad, ganancia, f. —a lucrativo. **m.-order,** giro postal, m

moneyed /'mʌnid/ a adinerado; acomodado

mongoose /'moŋ,gus/ n mangosta, f

mongrel /'mʌŋgrəl/ a mestizo, atravesado. —n perro mestizo, m; (in contempt) mestizo. m

monitor /'monɪtər/ n monitor, m

monitory /'monɪ,tɔri/ a monitorio. —n Eccl. monitorio, m

monk /mʌŋk/ n monje, m. **to become a m.,** hacerse monje, tomar el hábito. **monk's-hood,** acónito, m

monkey /'mʌŋki/ n mono (-na); (imp) diablillo, m; (of a pile-driver) pilón de martinete, m; (in glass-making) crisol, m. **to m. with,** meterse con; entremeterse. **m. nut,** cacahuete, m. **m.-puzzle,** (tree) araucaria, f. **m. tricks,** monadas, travesuras, diabluras, f pl. **m.-wrench,** llave inglesa, f

monochromatic /,monəkroʊ'mætɪk/ a monocromo

monocle /'monəkəl/ n monóculo, m

monogamous /mə'nogəməs/ a monógamo

monogamy /mə'nogəmi/ n monogamia, f

monogram /'monə,græm/ n monograma, m

monograph /'monə,græf/ n monografía, f, opúsculo, m

monolithic /,monə'lɪθɪk/ a monolítico

monologue /'monə,lɔg/ n monólogo, m

monomania /,monə'meɪniə/ n monomanía, f

monoplane /'monə,pleɪn/ n monoplano, m

monopolization /mə,nopələ'zeɪʃən/ n monopolio, m

monopolize /mə'nopə,laɪz/ vt monopolizar

monopoly /mə'nopəli/ n monopolio, m

monotheism /'monəθi,ɪzəm/ n monoteísmo, m

monotheist /'monəθiɪst/ n monoteísta, mf

monotone /'monə,toʊn/ n monotonía, f

monotonous /mə'notnəs/ a monótono

monotony /mə'notni/ n monotonía, f

Monroe doctrine /mən'roʊ/ n monroísmo, m

monsoon /mon'sun/ n monzón, mf

monster /'monstər/ n monstruo, m

monstrosity /mon'strosɪti/ n monstruosidad, f

monstrous /'monstrəs/ a monstruoso; horrible, atroz; enorme

montage /mon'taʒ/ n montaje, m

month /mʌnθ/ n mes, m. **He arrived a m. ago,** Llegó hace un mes

monthly /'mʌnθli/ a mensual. —adv mensualmente, cada mes. —n revista (or publicación) mensual, f; pl **monthlies,** menstruación, regla, f. **m. salary** or **payment,** mensualidad, f

monument /'mɒnyəmənt/ *n* monumento, *m*

monumental /ˌmɒnyə'mentl/ *a* monumental

moo /mu/ *vi* (of cattle) mugir. —*n* mugido, *m*

mood /mud/ *n* humor, *m*; espíritu, *m*; *Gram.* modo, *m*

moodily /'mudli/ *adv* taciturnamente; tristemente, pensativamente

moodiness /'mudinis/ *n* mal humor, *m*, taciturnidad, *f*; melancolía, tristeza, *f*

moody /'mudi/ *a* taciturno, de mal humor; triste, melancólico, pensativo

moon /mun/ *n* luna, *f*; satélite, *m*; mes lunar, *m*; luz de la luna, *f*. **full m.,** plenilunio, *m*; luna llena, *f*. **new m.,** novilunio, *m*, luna nueva, *f*

moonless /'munlɪs/ *a* sin luna

moonlight /'mun,laɪt/ *n* luz de la luna, *f*. **in the m.,** a la luz de la luna. **to do a m. flit,** *Inf.* mudarse por el aire

moonlighting /'mun,laɪtɪŋ/ *n* el pluriempleo, *m*

moonlit /'mun,lɪt/ *a* iluminado por la luna. **moonlit night,** noche de luna, *f*

moonshine /'mun,ʃaɪn/ *n* claridad de la luna, *f*; *Fig.* música celestial, ilusión, *f*

moonstone /'mun,stoʊn/ *n* adularia, *f*

moonstruck /'mun,strʌk/ *a* lunático

Moor /mʊr/ *n* moro (-ra)

moor /mʊr/ *n* páramo, brezal, *m*; (marsh) pantano, *m*; (for game) coto, *m*. —*vt* amarrar, aferrar; afirmar con anclas o cables. **m.-hen,** polla de agua, *f*

mooring /'mʊrɪŋ/ *n* amarre, *m*. **m.-mast,** *Aer.* poste de amarre, *m*

moorings /'mʊrɪŋz/ *n pl* amarradero, *m*

Moorish /'mʊrɪʃ/ *a* moro; árabe. **M. architecture,** arquitectura árabe, *f*. **M. girl,** mora, *f*

moorland /'mʊrlənd/ *n* páramo, brezal, *m*

moose /mus/ *n* anta, *f*

moot /mut/ *n* junta, *f*; ayuntamiento, *m*. —*a* discutible. —*vt* (bring up) suscitar; (discuss) discutir, debatir

mop /mɒp/ *n* (implement) trapeador, *m* (Ecuador), escoba con fleco, *f*; (of hair) mata (de pelo), *f*. —*vt* trapear (Ecuador); (dry) enjugar, secar. **to mop up,** *Inf.* limpiar; *Mil.* acabar con (el enemigo)

mope /moʊp/ *vi* replace by tristear. **to m. about,** vagar tristemente

moral /'mɒrəl/ *a* moral; (chaste) casto, virtuoso; honrado. —*n* (maxim) moraleja, *f*; *pl* **morals,** moralidad, *f*; ética, *f*; moral, *f*; (conduct) costumbres, *f pl*. **m. philosophy,** filosofía moral, *f*. **m. support,** apoyo moral, *m*. **m. tale,** apólogo, *m*

morale /mə'ræl/ *n* moral, *f*

moralist /'mɒrəlɪst/ *n* moralista, *m*

morality /mə'rælɪti/ *n* moralidad, *f*; virtud, *f*; castidad, *f*. **m. play,** moralidad, *f*, drama alegórico, *m*

moralize /'mɒrə,laɪz/ *vt and vi* moralizar

morals /'mɒrəlz/. See **moral**

morass /mə'ræs/ *n* marisma, ciénaga, *f*

moratorium /ˌmɒrə'tɔriəm/ *n* moratoria, *f*

morbid /'mɔrbɪd/ *a* mórbido, morboso; (of the mind, etc.) insano

morbidity /mɔr'bɪdɪti/ *n* morbidez, *f*

mordant /'mɔrdnt/ *a* mordaz; (of acid) mordiente. —*n* mordiente, *m*

more /mɔr/ *a and adv* más. **The m. he earns, the less he saves,** Cuanto más gana, menos ahorra. **the m. the better,** cuanto más, tanto mejor. **without m. ado,** sin más ni más; sin decir nada. **Would you like some m.?** ¿Quiere Vd. más? (of food) ¿Quiere Vd. repetir? **no m.,** no más; (never) nunca más; (finished) se acabó. **once m.,** otra vez, una vez más. **m. and m.,** cada vez más, más y más. **m. or less,** más o menos; (about) poco más o menos

moreover /mɔr'oʊvər/ *adv* además, también; por otra parte

morgue /mɔrg/ *n* depósito de cadáveres, *m*

moribund /'mɔrə,bʌnd/ *a* moribundo

Mormon /'mɔrmən/ *a* mormónico. —*n* mormón (-ona)

Mormonism /'mɔrmə,nɪzəm/ *n* mormonismo, *m*

morning /'mɔrnɪŋ/ *n* mañana, *f*, *a* matutino, de la mañana. **Good m.!** ¡Buenos días! **the next m.,** la mañana siguiente. **very early in the m.,** muy de mañana. **m. coat,** chaqué, *m*. **m. dew,** rocío de la mañana, *m*. **m. paper,** periódico de la mañana, *m*. **m. star,** lucero del alba, *m*. **m. suit,** chaqué, *m*

Moroccan /mə'rɒkən/ *a* marroquí, marrueco. —*n* marrueco (-ca), marroquí, *mf*

Morocco /mə'rɒkou/ Marruecos, *m*

morocco /mə'rɒkou/ *n* (leather) marroquí, tafilete, *m*

morose /mə'rous/ *a* sombrío, taciturno, malhumorado

morrow /'mɒrou/ *n* mañana, *f*; día siguiente, *m*

morsel /'mɔrsəl/ *n* pedazo, *m*; (mouthful) bocado, *m*

mortal /'mɔrtl/ *a* mortal. —*n* mortal, *mf*. **m. sin,** pecado mortal, pecado capital, *m*

mortality /mɔr'tælɪti/ *n* mortalidad, *f*

mortally wounded /'mɔrtli/ *adv* herido de muerte

mortar /'mɔrtər/ *n* (for building) argamasa, *f*; (for mixing and *Mil.*) mortero, *m*. **m. and pestle,** mortero y majador, *m*. **m.-board,** (in building) cuezo, *m*; (academic cap) birrete, *m*

mortgage /'mɔrgɪdʒ/ *n* hipoteca, *f*. —*vt* hipotecar. —*a* hipotecario. **to pay off a m.,** redimir una hipoteca

mortgageable /'mɔrgɪdʒəbəl/ *a* hipotecable

mortgaged debt /'mɔrgɪdʒd/ *n* deuda garantizada con una hipoteca, *f*

mortgagee /ˌmɔrgə'dʒi/ *n* acreedor (-ra) hipotecario (-ia)

mortgagor /'mɔrgədʒər/ n deudor (-ra) hipotecario (-ia)

mortification /ˌmɔrtəfɪ'keiʃən/ n mortificación, f; humillación, f; Med. gangrena, f

mortify /'mɔrtə,fai/ vt mortificar; humillar. —vi Med. gangrenarse

mortifying /'mɔrtə,faiɪŋ/ a humillante

mortise /'mɔrtɪs/ n muesca, f. —vt hacer muescas (en); ensamblar

mortuary /'mɔrtʃu,eri/ a mortuorio. —n depósito de cadáveres, m

Mosaic /mou'zeiik/ a mosaico

mosaic /mou'zeiik/ n mosaico, m

Moscow /'mɒskou,-kau/ Moscú, m

mosque /mɒsk/ n mezquita, f

mosquito /mə'skitou/ n mosquito, m. **m. net**, mosquitero, m

moss /mɒs/ n musgo, m; moho, m; (swamp) marjal, m

mossiness /'mɒsɪnɪs/ n estado musgoso, m

mossy /'mɒsi/ a musgoso

most /moust/ a el (la, los, etc.) más; la mayor parte de; la mayoría de; (el, etc.) mayor. —adv más; el (la, etc.) más; (extremely) sumamente; (very) muy; (before adjectives sometimes expressed by superlative, e.g. m. reverend, reverendísimo, m. holy, santísimo, etc.). —n (highest price) el mayor precio; la mayor parte; el mayor número; lo más. **m. of all**, sobre todo. **m. people**, la mayoría de la gente. **at the m.**, a lo más, a lo sumo. **for the m. part**, en su mayor parte; casi todos; generalmente, casi siempre. **to make the m. of**, sacar el mayor partido posible de; aprovechar bien; exagerar

mostly /'moustli/ adv principalmente; en su mayoría; en su mayor parte; casi siempre; en general, generalmente

mote /mout/ n átomo, m; mota, f. **to see the m. in our neighbor's eye and not the beam in our own**, ver la paja en el ojo del vecino y no la viga en el nuestro

motet /mou'tet/ n motete, m

moth /mɔθ/ n mariposa nocturna, f; polilla, f. **m.ball**, bola de naftalina, f. **m.-eaten**, apolillado

mother /'mʌðər/ n madre, f; madre de familia, f; (of alcoholic beverages) madre, f. —vt cuidar como una madre (a); servir de madre (a); (animals) ahijar. **M. Church**, madre iglesia, f; iglesia metropolitana, f. **m.-in-law**, suegra, f. **m. land**, (madre) patria, f. **m.-of-pearl**, madreperla, f, nácar, m. —a nacarado, nacáreo. **M. Superior**, (madre) superiora, f. **m. tongue**, lengua materna, f

motherhood /'mʌðər,hud/ n maternidad, f

motherless /'mʌðərlɪs/ a huérfano de madre, sin madre

motherlike a de madre, como una madre

motherliness /'mʌðərlinɪs/ n cariño maternal, m

motherly /'mʌðərli/ a maternal

motif /mou'tif/ n motivo, m; tema, m; Sew. adorno, m

motion /'mouʃən/ n movimiento, m; Mech. marcha, operación, f; mecanismo, m; (sign) seña, señal, f; (gesture) ademán, gesto, m; (carriage) aire, porte, m; (of the bowels) movimiento del vientre, m, deyección, f; (will) voluntad, f, deseo, m; (proposal in an assembly or debate) proposición, moción, f; Law. pedimento, m. —vt hacer una señal (a). —vi hacer señas. **to set in m.**, poner en marcha. **m. picture**, fotografía cinematográfica, película, f. **m.-picture theater**, cine, m

motionless /'mouʃənlɪs/ a inmóvil

motivate /'moutə,veit/ vt motivar

motive /'moutɪv/ n motivo, m. —a motor motivo. **with no m.**, sin motivo. **m. power**, fuerza motriz, f

motley /'mɒtli/ a abigarrado, multicolor; (mixed) diverso, vario. —n traje de colores, m, botarga, f

motor /'moutər/ n motor, m; automóvil, m, a motor; movido por motor; con motor; (traveling) de viaje. —vi ir en automóvil. —vt llevar en automóvil (a). **m. boat**, lancha automóvil, f. **m.bus**, autobús, ómnibus, m. **m.car**, automóvil, m. **m.-coach**, autobús, m. **m.cycle**, motocicleta, f. **m.cyclist**, motociclista, mf. **m.-launch**, canoa automóvil, f. **m.oil**, aceite para motores, m. **m.-road**, autopista, f. **m.-rug**, manta de viaje, f. **m.-scooter**, bicicleta con motor, f. **m.-spirit**, bencina, f

motoring /'moutərɪŋ/ n automovilismo, m

motorist /'moutərɪst/ n automovilista, motorista, mf

mottled /'mɒtld/ a abigarrado; (of marble, etc.) jaspeado, esquizado; manchado (con), con manchas (de); pintado (con)

motto /'mɒtou/ n Herald. divisa, f; mote, m; (in a book, etc.) tema, m

mound /maund/ n montón, m; (knoll) altozano, m; (for defence) baluarte, m; (for burial) túmulo, m

mount /maunt/ n (hill, and in palmistry) monte, m; (for riding) cabellería, f; montadura, f; (for a picture) borde, m. —vt subir; (machines, etc.) montar; (jewels) engastar; (a picture) poner un borde a; (a play) poner en escena; poner a caballo; proveer de caballo. —vi montar; subir; (increase) aumentar. **to m. a horse**, subir a caballo, montar. **to m. guard**, Mil. montar la guardia. **to m. the throne**, subir al trono

mountain /'maunt̩n/ n montaña, f; (mound) montón, m. —a de montaña(s); montañés; alpino, alpestre. **to make a m. out of a molehill**, convertir un grano de arena en una montaña. hacer de una pulga un camello, hacer de una pulga un elefante. **m.-chain**, cadena de montañas, f. **m. dweller**, montañés (-esa). **m. railway**, ferrocárril de cremallera, m. **m.-side**, falda de una montaña, f

mountaineer /ˌmaunt̩n'iər/ n (inhabit-

ant) montañés (-esa); (climber) alpinista,
mf. —*vi* hacer alpinismo

mountaineering /ˌmauntɪˈɪərɪŋ/ *n* alpinismo, *m*

mountainous /ˈmauntɲəs/ *a* montañoso; (huge) enorme

mountebank /ˈmauntəˌbæŋk/ *n* saltabanco, *m*; charlatán, *m*

mounting /ˈmauntɪŋ/ *n* (ascent) subida, *f*; ascensión, *f*; (of machinery, etc.) armadura, *f*; montadura, *f*; (of a precious stone) engaste, *m*. **m.-block,** subidero, *m*

mourn /mɔrn/ *vi* afligirse, lamentarse; (wear mourning) estar de luto. —*vt* llorar; lamentar; llevar luto por

mourner /ˈmɔrnər/ *n* lamentador (-ra); (paid) plañidera, *f*; el, *m*, (*f*, la) que acompaña al féretro

mournful /ˈmɔrnfəl/ *a* triste, acongojado; funesto, lúgubre; fúnebre; lamentable

mourning /ˈmɔrnɪŋ/ *n* aflicción, *f*; lamentación, *f*; luto, *m*. **deep m.,** luto riguroso, *m*. **half m.,** medio luto, *m*. **to be in m.,** estar de luto. **to be in m. for,** llevar luto por. **to come out of m.,** dejar el luto. **m.-band,** (on the hat) tira de gasa, *f*; (on the arm) brazal de luto, *m*. **m.-coach,** coche fúnebre, *m*

mouse /n. maus; v. mauz/ *n* ratón (-na); *Naut.* barrilete, *m*. —*vi* cazar ratones. **m.-coloured,** de color de rata. **m.-hole, m.-trap,** ratonera, *f*

moustache /ˈmʌstæʃ, məˈstæʃ/ *n* bigote, *m*; mostacho, *m*

mousy /ˈmausi/ *a* ratonesco, ratonil

mouth /n. mauθ; v. mauð/ *n* (*Anat.* human being, of a bottle, cave) boca, *f*; entrada, *f*; (of a river) desembocadura, *f*; (of a channel) embocadero, *m*; (of a wind instrument) boquilla, *f*. —*vt* pronunciar con afectación; (chew) mascar. —*vi* clamar a gritos, vociferar. **down in the m.,** *Inf.* con las orejas caídas. **It makes my m. water,** Se me hace la boca agua. **large m.,** boca rasgada, *f*. **m.-gag,** abrebocas, *m*. **m.-organ,** armónica, *f*. **m.-wash,** antiséptico bucal, *m* (Argentina), enjuague, *m*

mouthed /mauðd, mauθt/ *a* que tiene boca...; de boca... **open-m.,** boquiabierto

mouthful /ˈmauθˌful/ *n* bocado, *m*; (of smoke, air) bocanada, *f*

mouthpiece /ˈmauθˌpis/ *n* (of wind instruments, tobacco-pipe, waterpipe) boquilla, *f*; (of a wineskin) brocal, *m*; (spokesman) portavoz, *m*; intérprete, *mf*

movable /ˈmuvəbəl/ *a* movible; (of goods) mobiliario. **m. feast,** fiesta movible, *f*

move /muv/ *n* movimiento, *m*; (of household effects) mudanza, *f*; (motion) marcha, *f*; (in a game) jugada, *f*; (*Fig.* step) paso, *m*; (device) maniobra, *f*. **Whose m. is it?** ¿A quién le toca jugar? **to be on the m.,** estar en movimiento; estar de viaje. **to be always on the m.,** *Inf.* parecer una lanzadera

move /muv/ *vt* mover; poner en marcha;

(furniture) trasladar; cambiar de lugar; (stir) remover; (shake) agitar, hacer temblar; (transport) transportar; (a piece in chess, etc.) jugar; (pull) arrancar; (impel) impulsar; (incline) inclinar, disponer; (affect emotionally) conmover, emocionar, enternecer; impresionar. —*vi* moverse; ponerse en marcha; (walk) andar; ir; avanzar; (a step forward, etc.) dar; (move house) trasladarse; (act) entrar en acción; (in games) hacer una jugada; (progress) progresar; (shake) agitarse, temblar; removerse; (propose in an assembly) hacer una proposición; (in a court of law) hacer un pedimento; (grow) crecer. **to m. about,** pasearse; ir y venir; (of traffic) circular; (remove) trasladarse; (stir, tremble) agitarse. **to m. along,** caminar por; avanzar por. **to m. aside,** *vt* apartar; poner a un lado; (curtains) descorrer —*vi* ponerse a un lado; quitarse de en medio. **to m. away,** *vt* alejar. —*vi* alejarse; marcharse; trasladarse; mudar de casa. **to m. back,** retroceder; volver hacia atrás. **to m. down,** bajar, descender. **to m. forward,** adelantarse; avanzar; progresar. **to m. in,** entrar (en); tomar posesión de una casa. **to m. off,** *vt* quitar. —*vi* marcharse; ponerse en marcha; alejarse; apartarse. **to m. on,** avanzar; ponerse en marcha; circular; (of time) pasar, correr. **to m. out,** *vt* sacar, quitar. —*vi* salir; (from a house) mudarse, abandonar (una casa, etc.). **to m. round,** dar vueltas, girar; (turn round) volverse. **to m. to,** (make) hacer, animar (a); causar. **to m. up,** *vt* montar, subir. —*vi* montar; avanzar

movement /ˈmuvmənt/ *n* movimiento, *m*; *Mech.* mecanismo, *m*; (Stock Exchange) actividad, *f*. **encircling m.,** *Mil.* movimiento envolvente, *m*

mover /ˈmuvər/ *n* motor, *m*; móvil, *m*; promotor (-ra); (of a motion, proposer) autor (-ra) de una moción

movie /ˈmuvi/ *n* *Inf.* cine, *m*. **m. camera,** máquina de impresionar, *f*. **m. star,** estrella de la pantalla, *f*

moving /ˈmuvɪŋ/ *a* móvil; motor; (affecting) emocionante, conmovedor; impresionante; patético. —*n* movimiento, *m*; traslado, *m*; cambio de domicilio, *m*. **m. picture,** fotografía cinematográfica, *f*. **m. staircase,** escalera móvil, *f*

movingly /ˈmuvɪŋli/ *adv* con emoción; patéticamente

mow /mou/ *vt* segar.

mowing /ˈmouɪŋ/ *n* siega, *f*. **m.-machine,** segadora, *f*

Mr. /ˈmɪstər/ See **mister**

Mrs. /ˈmɪsəz/ See **mistress**

much /mʌtʃ/ *a* mucho. —*adv* mucho; (by far) con mucho; (with past part.) muy; (pretty nearly) casi, más o menos. **m. of a size,** más o menos del mismo tamaño. **I was m. angered,** Estuve muy enfadado. **as m. as,** tanto como. **as m. more,** otro tanto. **How m. is it?** ¿Cuánto es? ¿Cuánto

cuesta? **however m....,** por mucho que...
not m., no mucho. **not to think m. of,**
tener en poco (a). **so m. so that,** tanto
que. **too m.,** demasiado. **to make m. of,**
dar grande importancia a; (a person)
apreciar, querer; agasajar; (a child) mimar, acariciar

mucilage /'myusəlɪdʒ/ *n* muciflago, *m*

muck /mʌk/ *n* (dung) estiércol, *m*; (filth)
porquería, inmundicia, *f*; suciedad, *f*;
(rubbish, of a literary work, etc.) porquería, *n*. **to m. up,** ensuciar; (spoil) estropear por completo

mucous /'myukəs/ *a* mucoso. **m. membrane,** mucosa, *f*

mucus /'myukəs/ *n* mucosidad, *f*; (from
the nose) moco, *m*

mud /mʌd/ *n* lodo, barro, fango, *m*. **to
stick in the mud,** (of a ship, etc.) embarrancarse. **mudbath,** baño de barro, *m*.
mud wall, tapia, *f*

muddle /'mʌdl/ *vt* (bewilder) dejar perplejo, aturdir; (intoxicate) emborrachar;
(stupefy) entontecer; (spoil) estropear;
embarullar, dejar en desorden; hacer un
lío de. —*n* desorden, *m*; confusión, *f*; lío,
embrollo, *m*. **in a m.,** en desorden; en
confusión. **to make a m.,** armar un lío.
to m. away, derrochar sin ton ni son

muddled /'mʌdld/ *a* desordenado; confuso; estúpido; torpe; (drunk) borracho

muddy /'mʌdi/ *a* fangoso, lodoso, barro-
so; cubierto de lodo; (of liquids, etc.)
turbio; (of the complexion) cetrino. —*vt*
enlodar, cubrir de lodo; ensuciar; (liquids) enturbiar

mudguard /'mʌd,gɑrd/ *n* guardabarro, *m*

muezzin /myu'ɛzɪn, mu-/ *n* almuecín, almuédano, *m*

muff /mʌf/ *n* manguito, *m*; (for a car radiator) cubierta para radiador, *f*; (Inf. at
games, etc.) maleta, *m*. —*vt* dejar escapar
(una pelota); (an opportunity) perder

muffin /'mʌfɪn/ *n* mollete, *m*

muffle /'mʌfəl/ *vt* embozar, arrebozar;
envolver; encubrir, ocultar, tapar; (stifle
sound of) apagar; (oars, bells) envolver
con tela para no hacer ruido; *Fig.* ahogar.
to m. oneself up, embozarse

muffled /'mʌfəld/ *a* (of sound) sordo;
confuso; apagado. **m. drum,** tambor en-
lutado, *m*

muffler /'mʌflər/ *n* bufanda, tapaboca, *f*;
(furnace) mufla, *f*; (of a car radiator) cubierta para radiador, *f*; (silencer) silencioso, *m*

mug /mʌg/ *n* vaso, *m*; (tankard) pichel,
tarro, *m*; (face) jeta, *f*; (dupe) primo, *m*;
(at games, etc.) maleta, *m*

mulatto /mə'lætou/ *a* mulato. —*n*
mulato (-ta). **m.-like,** amulatado

mulberry /'mʌl,bɛri/ *n* (fruit) mora, *f*;
(bush) morera, *f*. **m. plantation,** moreral,
m

mule /myul/ *n* mulo (-la); (slipper) mula,
chinela, *f*; (spinning-jenny) huso mecánico, *m*

mulish /'mulɪʃ/ *a* mular; terco como
una mula

mullet /'mʌlɪt/ *n* (red) salmonete, *m*,
trilla, *f*; (grey) mújol, *m*

multicolored /'mʌlti,kʌlərd/ *a* multicolor

multifarious /,mʌltə'fɛəriəs/ *a*
numeroso, mucho; diverso, vario

multiform /'mʌlti,fɔrm/ *a* multiforme

multilateral /,mʌltɪ'lætərəl/ *a* multilátero

multimillionaire /,mʌltɪ'mɪlyə,nɛər/ *a*
archimillonario, multimillonario, *n* multimillonario, *m*

multiple /'mʌltəpəl/ *a* múltiple, múltiplo.
—*n* múltiplo, *m*

multiple-choice question *n* pregunta
optativa, *f*

multiplicand /,mʌltəplɪ'kænd/ *n* multi-
plicando, *m*

multiplication /,mʌltəplɪ'keiʃən/ *n* multiplicación, *f*. **m. table,** tabla de multiplicación, *f*

multiplier /'mʌltə,plaiər/ *n Math.* multiplicador, *m*; máquina de multiplicar, *f*

multiply /'mʌltəpli/ *vt* multiplicar. —*vi*
multiplicarse

multitude /'mʌltɪ,tud/ *n* multitud, *f*. **the
m.,** las masas

multitudinous /,mʌltɪ'tudnəs/ *a* muy
numeroso

mumble /'mʌmbəl/ *vi* and *vt* musitar, hablar entre dientes; refunfuñar; (chew)
mascullar

mummify /'mʌmə,fai/ *vt* momificar. —*vi*
momificarse

mummy /'mʌmi/ *n* momia, *f*; carne de
momia, *f*; (Inf. mother) mama, *f*. **m.
case,** sarcófago, *m*

mumps /mʌmps/ *n pl* parotiditis, papera,
f

munch /mʌntʃ/ *vt* másticar, mascullar,
mascar

mundane /mʌn'dein/ *a* mundano

municipal /myu'nɪsəpəl/ *a* municipal. **m.
charter,** fuero municipal, *m*. **m. government,** gobierno municipal, *m*

municipality /myu,nɪsə'pælɪti/ *n* municipio, *m*

munificent /myu'nɪfəsənt/ *a* munífico,
generoso

munition /myu'nɪʃən/ *n* munición, *f*.
—*vt* municionar. **m. dump,** depósito de
municiones, *m*. **m. factory,** fábrica de
municiones, *f*. **m. worker,** obrero (-ra) de
una fábrica de municiones

mural /'myʊrəl/ *a* mural. —*n* pintura mural, *f*

murder /'mɜrdər/ *n* asesinato, *m*. —*vt*
asesinar; dar muerte (a), matar; (a work,
etc.) degollar. **He was murdered,** Fue
asesinado. **wilful m.,** homicidio premeditado, *m*

murderer /'mɜrdərər/ *n* asesino, *m*

murderous /'mɜrdərəs/ *a* homicida;
cruel, sanguinario; fatal; imposible, intolerable

murky /'mɜrki/ *a* lóbrego, negro, obscuro;
(of one's past, etc.) negro, accidentado

murmur /'mɜrmər/ n murmullo, m; rumor, m; susurro, m; (grumble) murmurio, m. —vi murmurar, susurrar; (complain) murmurar, quejarse. —vt murmurar, decir en voz baja

murmuring /'mɜrmərɪŋ/ n murmurio, m, a que murmura, susurrante

muscatel /ˌmʌskə'tɛl/ a moscatel. —n moscatel, m. **m. grape,** uva moscatel, f

muscle /'mʌsəl/ n músculo, m

muscular /'mʌskyələr/ a muscular, musculoso; (brawny) membrudo, fornido. **m. pains,** (in the legs, etc.) agujetas, f pl

musculature /'mʌskyələtʃər/ n musculatura, f

Muse /myuz/ n musa, f

muse /myuz/ n meditación, f. —vi meditar, reflexionar, rumiar; mirar las musarañas, estar distraído. **to m. on,** meditar en (or sobre)

museum /myu'ziəm/ n museo, m

mushroom /'mʌʃrum/ n seta, f. —a de setas; de forma de seta; (upstart) advenedizo; (ephemeral) efímero, de un día. **m.-bed,** setal, m. **m. m.-spawn,** esporas de setas, f pl

music /'myuzɪk/ n música, f; armonía, f; melodía, f. —a de música. **to set to m.,** poner en música. **m.-hall,** teatro de variedades, m; salón de conciertos, m. **m. master,** profesor de música, m. **m. publisher,** editor de obras musicales, m. **m. stand,** atril, m; tablado para una orquesta, m. **m. stool,** taburete de piano, m

musical /'myuzɪkəl/ a musical; de música; armonioso, melodioso. **She is very m.,** Es muy aficionada a la música; Tiene mucho talento para la música. **m.-box,** caja de música, f. **m. comedy,** zarzuela, f. **m. instrument,** instrumento de música, m

musical chairs n escobas, f pl, el juego de sillas, m sing

musician /myu'zɪʃən/ n músico (-ca)

musing /'myuzɪŋ/ n meditación, f; ensueños, m pl, a pensativo, meditabundo

musk /mʌsk/ n (substance) almizcle, m; perfume de almizcle, m. —a de almizcle; almizclero; (of scents) almizcleño. **m.-deer,** almizclero, m. **m.-rat,** rata almizclera, f

Muslim /'mʌzlɪm/ a musulmán, mahometano. —n musulmán (-ana)

muslin /'mʌzlɪn/ n muselina, f, a de muselina

mussel /'mʌsəl/ n mejillón, m. **m.-bed,** criadero de mejillones, m

must /mʌst/ vi haber de; tener que; deber; (expressing probability) deber de, ser. **This question m. be settled without delay,** Esta cuestión debe ser resuelta sin demora. **You m. do it at once,** Tienes que hacerlo en seguida. **I m. have seen him in the street sometime,** Debo haberle visto en la calle alguna vez. **One m. eat to live,** Se ha de comer para vivir. **Well, go if you m.,** Bueno, vete si no hay más remedio. **It m. be a difficult de-**

cision for him, Debe ser una decisión difícil para él. **It m. have been about twelve o'clock when...,** Serían las doce cuando...

must /mʌst/ n mosto, zumo de la uva, m; (mould) moho, m

mustard /'mʌstərd/ n mostaza, f. **m. gas,** iperita, f. **m. plaster,** sinapismo, m. **m. pot,** mostacera, f. **m. spoon,** cucharita para la mostaza, f

muster /'mʌstər/ n lista, f, rol, m; revista, f; reunión, f, vt pasar lista (de); pasar revista (a); reunir. —vi juntarse, reunirse. **to m. out,** (from the army) dar de baja (a). **to m. up sufficient courage,** cobrar ánimos suficientes. **to pass m.,** pasar revista; ser aceptado. **m.-roll,** Mil. muestra, f; Naut. rol de la tripulación, m

mustiness /'mʌstɪnɪs/ n moho, m; ranciedad, f; (of a room, etc.) olor de humedad, m

musty /'mʌsti/ a mohoso; rancio; que huele a humedad. **to go m.,** enmohecerse

mutable /'myutəbəl/ a mudable; inconstante, inestable

mutation /myu'teɪʃən/ n mutación, f

mute /myut/ a mudo; silencioso. —n mudo (-da); Mus. sordina, f; (phonetics) letra muda, f. **deaf m.,** sordomudo (-da)

muted /'myutɪd/ a (of sounds) sordo, apagado

mutilate /'myutˌleit/ vt mutilar; estropear

mutineer /ˌmyutn̩'ɪər/ n amotinador, rebelde, m

mutinous /'myutn̩əs/ a amotinado; rebelde, sedicioso; turbulento

mutiny /'myutn̩i/ n motín, m; sublevación, insurrección, f, vi amotinarse, sublevarse

mutt /mʌt/ n chucho, m

mutter /'mʌtər/ vt and vi murmurar, musitar; mascullar, decir (or hablar) entre dientes; gruñir, refunfuñar; (of thunder, etc.) tronar, retumbar. —n murmurio, m; rumor, m; retumbo, m

mutton /'mʌtn̩/ n carnero, m, a de carnero. **m.-chop,** chuleta, f

mutual /'myutʃuəl/ a mutuo, recíproco; común. **by m. consent,** de común acuerdo. **m. aid society,** sociedad de socorros mutuos, f. **m. insurance company,** sociedad de seguros mutuos, f

mutual fund n fondo de inversiones rentables, m

muzzle /'mʌzəl/ n (snout) hocico, m; (for a dog) bozal, m; (of a gun) boca, f. —vt abozalar, poner un bozal (a); (Fig. gag) amordazar, imponer silencio (a)

muzzling /'mʌzlɪŋ/ n acción de abozalar, f; (Fig. gagging) amordazamiento, m

my /mai/ a poss mi, mf; mis, mf pl **my relatives,** mis parientes. **My goodness!** ¡Dios mío!

myelitis /ˌmaiə'laitɪs/ n mielitis, f

myopia /mai'oupiə/ n miopía, f

myopic /mai'ɒpɪk/ a miope

myriad /'mɪrɪəd/ n miríada, f

myrrh /mɜr/ n mirra, f

myrtle /'mɜrtl/ n mirto, arrayán, m

myself /mai'self/ pron yo mismo; (as a reflexive with a preposition) mí; (with a reflexive verb) me. **I m. sent it,** yo mismo (-ma) lo mandé

mysterious /mɪ'stɪərɪəs/ a misterioso

mystery /'mɪstəri/ n misterio, m. **m. play,** (religious) misterio, drama litúrgico,

m; (thriller) comedia de detectives, f. **m. story,** novela policíaca, f; novela de aventuras, f

mystic /'mɪstɪk/ a místico

mysticism /'mɪstə,sɪzəm/ n misticismo, m

mystify /'mɪstə,fai/ vt mistificar

myth /mɪθ/ n mito, m

mythical /'mɪθɪkəl/ a mítico

mythology /mɪ'θɒlədʒi/ n mitología, f

n /ɛn/ *n* (letter) ene, *f*
nab /næb/ *vt Inf.* atrapar, apresar, agazapar
nacre /'neikər/ *n* nácar, *m*, madreperla, *f*
nadir /'neidər/ *n* nadir, *m*
nag /næg/ *n* jaca, *f*; (wretched hack) rocín, jamelgo, penco, *m.* —*vt* zaherir, echar en cara, regañar; (of one's conscience) remorder. —*vi* criticar, regañar
nagging /'nægɪŋ/ *n* zaherimiento, *m.* —*a* zaheridor, criticón; (pain) continuo, incesante, constante
nail /neil/ *vt* clavar, enclavar; (for ornament) clavetear, tachonar, adornar con clavos. —*n* uña, *f*; *Mech.* clavo, *m*; (animal's) garra, *f.* **to n. down**, sujetar (or cerrar) con clavos. **to n. to (on to)**, clavar en. **to n. together**, fijar con clavos. *Inf.* **on the n.**, en el acto, en seguida. *Inf.* **to hit the n. on the head**, dar en el clavo. **brass-headed n.**, tachón, *m.* **French n.**, punta de París, *f.* **headless n.**, puntilla, *f.* **hob-n.**, clavo de herradura, *m.* **hook n.**, gancho, *m.* **round-headed n.**, bellota, *f.* **n.-brush**, cepillo para las (or de) uñas, *m.* **n.-file**, lima para las uñas, *f.* **n. head**, cabeza de un clavo, *f.* **n.-puller**, sacaclavos, arrancaclavos, botador, *m.* **n.-scissors**, tijeras para las uñas, *f pl.* **n. trade**, ferretería, *f.* **n. varnish**, barniz para las uñas, *m*
naive /nɑ'iv/ *a* ingenuo, candoroso, espontáneo
naively /nɑ'ivli/ *adv* ingenuamente, espontáneamente
naiveté /nɑiv'tei, -,ivə'tei, -'ivtei, -'ivə-/ *n* ingenuidad, naturalidad, franqueza, *f*; candor, *m*
naked /'neikɪd/ *a* desnudo, nudo; desabrigado, indefenso, desamparado; (birds) implume; calvo; (truth) simple, sencillo, puro; evidente, patente. **stark n.**, en cueros vivos, tal como le parió su madre. **with the n. sword**, con la espada desnuda. **n. eye**, simple vista, *f.* **n. light**, llama descubierta, *f*
nakedly /'neikɪdli/ *adv* nudamente; desabrigadamente; abiertamente, claramente
nakedness /'neikɪdnɪs/ *n* desnudez, *f*; *Fig.* desabrigo, *m*, aridez, *f*; *Fig.* claridad, *f.* **the truth in all its n.**, la verdad desnuda
namby-pamby /'næmbi'pæmbi/ *a* soso, insípido, ñoño
name /neim/ *n* nombre, *m*; título, *m*; fama, opinión, *f*; renombre, crédito, *m*; autoridad, *f*; apodo, mal nombre, *m.* —*vt* nombrar, llamar, imponer el nombre de, apellidar; mencionar, señalar; (appoint) designar, elegir; (ships) bautizar. **by n.**, por nombre. **Christian n.**, nombre de pila, *m.* **in his n.**, en nombre de él, en nombre suyo; de parte de él. **in n. only**, nada más que en nombre. **to be named**, llamarse. **to call (a person) names**, poner como un trapo (a). **to go under the n. of**, vivir bajo el nombre de. **to have a good n.**, tener buena fama. **What is her**

N

n.? ¿Cómo se llama? **n. day**, santo, *m.* **n. plate**, (machinery) placa de fábrica, *f*; (streets) rótulo, *m*; (professional) placa profesional, *f*
nameless /'neimlɪs/ *a* anónimo; desconocido; (inexpressible) vago, indecible
namely /'neimli/ *adv* a saber, es decir
namesake /'neim,seik/ *n* tocayo (-ya)
nap /næp/ *n* (cloth) pelusa, *f*, pelo, tamo, *m*; (plants) vello, *m*, pelusilla, *f*; (sleep) siesta, *f*, sueño, *m*; (cards) napolitana, *f.* **to take a nap**, *vi* dormitar, echar un sueño, echar una siesta. **to take an afternoon nap**, dormir la siesta. **to be caught napping**, estar desprevenido
nape /neip/ *n* nuca, *f*, cogote, *m*; (animal's) testuz, *m*
naphtha /'næfθə, 'næp-/ *n Chem.* nafta, *f.* **wood n.**, alcohol metílico, *m*
naphthalene /'næfθə,lin, 'næp-/ *n Chem.* naftalina, *f*
napkin /'næpkɪn/ *n* (table) servilleta, *f*; (babies') pañal, *m.* **n.-ring**, servilletero, *m*
Naples /'neipəlz/ Nápoles, *m*
narcotic /nɑr'kɒtɪk/ *a Med.* narcótico, calmante, soporífero. —*n Med.* narcótico, *m*, opiata, *f*
narrate /'næreit/ *vt* narrar, contar; referir, relatar
narration /næ'reiʃən/ *n* narración, narrativa; relación, descripción, *f*, relato, *m*
narrative /'nærətɪv/ *a* narrador, narrativo, narratorio. —*n* narrativa, *f*; descripción, *f*
narrow /'nærou/ *vt* estrechar, angostar; reducir, limitar. —*vi* reducirse, hacerse más estrecho; (eyes) entornarse; (knitting) menguar. —*a* estrecho, angosto; limitado, restringido, reducido, corto; (avaricious) ruin, avaro, mezquino; (ideas) intolerante, intransigente. **"Narrow Road," «Camino Estrecho».** —*n pl* **narrows,** *Naut.* estrecho, *m*; desfiladero, paso estrecho, *m.* **to have a n. escape,** escapar en una tabla. **n.-brimmed** (hats), de ala estrecha. **n. circumstances,** estrechez, escasez de medios, *f.* **n.-gauge railway,** ferrocarril de vía estrecha (or de vía angosta), *m.* **n. life,** vida de horizontes estrechos, *f.* **n. majority,** escasa mayoría, *f.* **n.-minded,** cerrado al mundo, intolerante, intransigente. **n.-mindedness,** intolerancia, intransigencia, estrechez de miras, *f*
narrowly /'nærouli/ *adv* estrechamente; por poco, con dificultad; atentamente, cuidadosamente. **I escaped being run over,** Por poco me atropellan
nascent /'næsənt, 'neisənt/ *a* naciente
nastiness /'næstinɪs/ *n* suciedad, inmundicia, porquería, *f*; (indecency) obscenidad, indecencia, *f*; (rudeness) insolen-

cia, impertinencia, grosería, f; (difficulty) dificultad, f, lo malo

nasty /'næsti/ a nauseabundo, repugnante; asqueroso, inmundo, sucio; (obscene) indecente, obsceno; desagradable, malo; (malicious) rencoroso, malicioso; violento; malévolo, amenazador; peligroso; difícil. Fig. **to be in a n. mess,** tener el agua al cuello. **to turn n.,** Inf. ponerse desagradable

natal /'neitl/ a natal, natalicio, de nacimiento, nativo

nation /'neiʃən/ n nación, f, estado, país, m; (people) pueblo, m

national /'næʃənl/ a nacional; público; patriótico. —n nacional, mf. **n. anthem,** himno nacional, m. **n. debt,** deuda pública, f. **n. schools,** escuelas públicas, f pl. **n. socialism,** nacionalsocialismo, m. **n. socialist,** a and n nacionalsocialista mf. **n. syndicalism,** Polit. nacionalsindicalismo, m. **n. syndicalist,** a and n Polit. nacionalsindicalista, mf

nationalism /'næʃənl,izəm/ n nacionalismo, patriotismo, m

nationalist /'næʃənlist/ a and n nacionalista, mf

nationality /,næʃ ə'næliti/ n nacionalidad, f; nación, f

nationalization /,næʃənlə'zeiʃən/ n nacionalización, f

nationalize /'næʃənl,aiz, 'næʃnə,laiz/ vt nacionalizar

National Labor Relations Board n Junta Nacional de Relaciones Laborales

nationally /'næʃənli/ adv nacionalmente, como nación; del punto de vista nacional

native /'neitiv/ a (of a place) nativo, natal, oriundo; indígena; nacional, típico, del país; (vocabulary) patrimonial (as opposed to borrowed vocabulary); (of genius) natural, innato, instintivo; Mineral. nativo; (language) vernáculo. —n nacional, mf; natural, mf; ciudadano (-na) indígena, aborigen (gen. pl.), mf; producto nacional, m. **He is a n. of Madrid,** Nació en Madrid, Es natural de Madrid, Es madrileño. **native informant,** sujeto, m. **n. land,** patria, tierra, f. **n. place,** lugar natal, m. **n. region,** patria chica, f. **n. soil,** terruño, m. **n. tongue,** lengua materna, f

nativity /nə'tiviti/ n navidad, natividad, f; (manger) nacimiento, m

natty /'næti/ a Inf. chulo, majo; coquetón

natural /'nætʃərəl/ a natural; (wild) virgen, salvaje; nativo; (of products) crudo; normal; (usual) acostumbrado, corriente, natural; (of likeness) fiel, verdadero; (illegitimate) ilegítimo, bastardo; (of qualities) innato, instintivo; físico; característico, propio; (of people) inafectado, sencillo, genuino; Mus. natural. —n Mus. becuadro, m; Mus. nota natural, f; imbécil, mf **n. features,** geografía física, f. **n. history,** historia natural, f. **n. philosophy,** filosofía natural, f. **n. science,** ciencias naturales, f pl. **n. selection,** selección natural, f. **n. state,** estado virgen, m

natural child n hijo ilegítimo, m

natural daughter n hija ilegítima, f

naturalism /'nætʃərə,lizəm/ n naturalismo, m

naturalist /'nætʃərəlist/ n (Lit. and Science.) naturalista, mf

naturalistic /,nætʃərə'listik/ a naturalista

naturalization /,nætʃərələ'zeiʃən/ n naturalización, f; aclimatación, f. **n. papers,** carta de naturaleza, f

naturalize /'nætʃərə,laiz/ vt naturalizar; aclimatar. **to become naturalized,** naturalizarse

naturally /'nætʃərəli/ adv naturalmente, por naturaleza; normalmente; sin afectación; instintivamente; por instinto; (without art) al natural

nature /'neitʃər/ n naturaleza, f; (of people) carácter, fondo, temperamento, genio, natural, modo de ser, m; (kind) género, m, especie, f; (essence) condición, esencia, cualidad, f, Art. from n., del natural. **good n.,** bondad natural, afabilidad, f. **ill n.,** mala índole, f. **nature cure,** naturismo, m. **n. curist,** naturalista, mf. **n. study,** historia natural, f. **n. worship,** panteísmo, culto de la naturaleza, m

natured /'neitʃərd/ a de carácter, de índole, con un modo de ser, de condición

naught /nɔt/ n nada, f; cero, m. —a inútil, sin valor. **all for n.,** todo en balde. **to come to n.,** malograrse. **to set at n.,** tener en menos; despreciar

naughty /'nɔti/ a travieso, pícaro, revoltoso, malo; salado, escabroso, verde (stories, etc.). **to be n.,** (children) ser malo

nausea /'nɔziə, -ʒə/ n náusea, f, bascas, f pl, mareo, m; Fig. asco, m

nauseate /'nɔzi,eit, -ʒi-/ vt dar náuseas; Fig. repugnar, dar asco

nauseating /'nɔzi,eitiŋ, -ʒi-/ a repugnante, horrible; asqueroso

nauseous /'nɔʃəs/ a nauseabundo, asqueroso; Fig. repugnante

nauseousness /'nɔʃəsnis/ n náusea, asquerosidad, f; Fig. repugnancia, f, asco, m

nautical /'nɔtikəl/ a náutico, marítimo. **n. day, twenty-four hours,** singladura, f

naval /'neivəl/ a naval; de marina, marítimo. **n. base,** base naval, f. **n. engagement,** batalla naval, f. **n. hospital,** hospital de marina, m. **n. law,** código naval, m. **n. officer,** oficial de marina, m. **n. power,** poder marítimo, m. **n. reservist,** marinero de reserva, m. **n. yard,** arsenal, m

nave /neiv/ n Archit. nave, f; (of wheels) cubo, m

navel /'neivəl/ n ombligo, m. **n. string,** cordón umbilical, m

navigable /'nævigəbəl/ a navegable, practicable

navigate /'nævi,geit/ vt navegar, marear, dirigir (unbuque) Fig. conducir, guiar. —vi navegar

navigation /,nævi'geiʃən/ n navegación,

f; (science of) náutica, marina, *f.* **n. company,** empresa naviera, *f.* **n. laws,** derecho marítimo, *m.* **n. lights,** luces de navegación, *f pl*

navigator /ˈnævɪˌgeitər/ *n* navegador, navegante, *m;* piloto, *m*

navvy /ˈnævɪ/ *n* peón, bracero, jornalero, *m; Mech.* máquina, excavadora, *f.* **road n.,** peón caminero, *m.* **to work like a n.,** estar hecho un azacán, sudar la gota gorda

navy /ˈneivɪ/ *n* marina, *f;* armada, *f;* (color) azul marino, *m.* **n. board,** consejo de la armada, *m.* **n. department** ministerio de marina, *m.* **n. estimates,** presupuesto de marina, *m.* **n. list,** escalafón de marina, *m*

nay /nei/ *adv* no; al contrario, más bien, mejor dicho. —*n* negativa, *f,* voto contrario, *m*

Nazi /ˈnɑtsi/ *a* and *n* nacionalsocialista, naci, *mf*

Nazism /ˈnɑtsɪzəm/ *n* nacismo, *m*

n.d. (no date) *s.f,* (sin fecha)

near /nɪər/ *vi* acercarse, aproximarse. —*a* cercano, inmediato, contiguo; (of time) inminente, próximo; (relationship) cercano, consanguíneo; (of friends) íntimo, entrañable; (mean) tacaño, avariento

near /nɪər/ *prep* cerca de, junto a; hacia, en la dirección de; (of time) cerca de, casi. —*adv* cerca; (time) cerca, próximamente. **to be n. to,** estar cerca de. **to bring n.,** acercar, aproximar. **It was a n. thing,** Escapамos por un pelo. **n. at hand,** a la mano; (time) cerca, inminente. **n.-by,** *a* cercaño, inmediato. —*adv* cerca. **n. side,** (of vehicles) lado de la acera, *m.* **n.-sighted,** corto de vista, miope. **n.-sightedness,** miopía, cortedad de vista, *f*

nearest /ˈnɪərɪst/ *a* compar and superl más cercano, más cerca; más corto. **the n. way,** el camino más corto, el camino directo

nearly /ˈnɪərli/ *adv* casi; cerca de, aproximadamente; estrechamente; íntimamente. **It touches me n.,** Me toca de cerca, Es de sumo interés para mí. **They n. killed me,** Por poco me matan. **to be n.,** (of age) frisar en, rayar en

nearness /ˈnɪərnɪs/ *n* (of place) cercanía, proximidad, contigüidad, *f;* (of time) inminencia, proximidad, *f;* (relationship) consanguinidad, *f;* (avarice) avaricia, tacañería, *f;* (dearness) intimidad, amistad estrecha, *f*

neat /nit/ *a Zool.* vacuno; elegante, sencillo, de buen gusto; (of the body) bien hecho, airoso, esbelto; (clean) limpio, aseado; (of handwriting) legible, bien proporcionado; pulido, esmerado, acabado; hábil, astuto, diestro; (of liquor, spirits) puro, solo. **to make a n. job of,** hacer (algo) bien

neatly /ˈnitli/ *adv* sencillamente, con elegancia, con primor; con aseo, limpiamente; bien (proporcionado); diestramente, hábilmente

neatness /ˈnitnɪs/ *n* aseo, *m,* limpieza, *f;* elegancia, sencillez, *f;* buen gusto, *m;* destreza, habilidad, *f;* (aptness) pertinencia, *f*

nebula /ˈnɛbyələ/ *n Astron.* nebulosa, *f*

nebulous /ˈnɛbyələs/ *a* nebuloso; vago, impreciso, confuso

necessarily /ˌnɛsəˈsɛrəli/ *adv* necesariamente; inevitablemente, sin duda

necessary /ˈnɛsəˌsɛri/ *a* necesario, inevitable; imprescindible, preciso, indispensable, esencial; obligatorio, debido, forzoso. —*n* requisito esencial, *m.* **if n.,** en caso de necesidad; si fuera necesario. **to be n.,** hacer falta; necesitarse

necessitate /nəˈsɛsɪˌteit/ *vt* necesitar, exigir, requerir, obligar

necessitous /nəˈsɛsɪtəs/ *a* pobre, indigente, miserable, necesitado

necessity /nəˈsɛsɪti/ *n* necesidad, *f:* menester, *m,* (e.g., *an indispensable n.,* un menester imprescindible); consecuencia, *f,* resultado, efecto, *m;* inevitabilidad, fatalidad, *f,* (poverty) indigencia, pobreza, *f.* **Fire and clothing are necessities,** El fuego y el vestir son cosas necesarias. **from n.,** por necesidad. **in case of n.,** si fuese necesario, en caso de necesidad. **of n.,** de necesidad, sin remedio. **physical necessities,** menesteres físicos, *m pl.* **prime n.,** artículo de primera necesidad, *m.* **to be under the n. of,** tener que, tener la necesidad de

Necessity is the mother of invention La necesidad es una gran inventora, La necesidad aguza el ingenio

neck /nɛk/ *n* cuello, *m,* garganta, *f;* (of bottles) gollete, cuello, *m;* (of animals) pescuezo, *m; Geog.* istmo, *m,* lengua de tierra, *f;* (of musical instruments) clavijero, mástil, *m; Sew.* escote, *m.* **low-necked,** (of dresses) escotado. **She fell on his n.,** Se colgó de su cuello. **He won by a n.,** Ganó por un cuello; *Fig.* Ganó por un tris. **to break anyone's n.,** romperle el pescuezo. **to wring the n. of,** torcer el pescuezo (a). **n. and n.,** parejos. **n. or nothing,** todo o nada, perdiz o no comerla. **n. stock,** alzacuello, *m*

necklace /ˈnɛklɪs/ *n* collar, *m*

necktie /ˈnɛkˌtai/ *n* corbata, *f*

nectar /ˈnɛktər/ *n* néctar, *m*

nectarine /ˌnɛktəˈrin/ *n Bot.* variedad de melocotón, *f*

need /nid/ *vt* necesitar, haber menester, requerir, exigir. —*vi* ser necesario, hacer falta, carecer; haber (de). **N. I obey?** ¿He de obedecer? **You need to write carefully,** Hay que escribir con cuidado. **The work n. not be done for tomorrow,** No es preciso hacer el trabajo para mañana

need /nid/ *n* necesidad, *f;* cosa necesaria, *f;* falta; (poverty) indigencia, pobreza, *f;* urgencia, *f;* (shortage) escasez, carestía, *f.* **in case of n.,** en caso de necesidad, en caso de urgencia. **I have n. of two more books,** Me hacen falta dos libros más

needful /'nidfəl/ *a* necesario, preciso; indispensable, esencial. **the n.,** lo necesario

neediness /'nidinis/ *n* pobreza, penuria, miseria, estrechez, *f*

needle /'nidl/ *n Sew.* aguja, *f;* (of compass) brújula, aguja imanada, *f;* (monument) obelisco, *m;* (of scales) field, *m,* lengüeta, *f;* (of phonograph) púa, *f,* (of measuring instruments) índice, *m; Med.* aguja de inyecciones, *f. Inf.* **to be as sharp as a n.,** no tener pelo de tonto. **pack n.,** aguja espartera, *f.* **n.-case,** alfiletero, agujero, *m.* **n. maker,** fabricante de agujas, *m.* **n.-shaped,** en forma de aguja, acicular

needle and thread hilo y aguja

needless /'nidlis/ *a* innecesario, supérfluo. **n. to say,** claro está que..., huelga decir que...

needlessly /'nidlisli/ *adv* innecesariamente, inútilmente; en vano, de balde

needlework /'nidl,wɜrk/ *n* labor de aguja, labor blanca, costura, *f;* bordado, *m.* **to do n.,** hacer costura

needs /nidz/ *adv* necesariamente, sin remedio *n pl* necesidades, *f pl.* **if n. must,** si hace falta. **N. must when the devil drives,** A la fuerza ahorcan

needy /'nidi/ *a* necesitado, menesteroso, corto de medios, pobre, apurado

ne'er-do-well /'nɛrdu,wɛl/ *n* calavera, perdido, *m.* **to be a n.,** ser de mala madera

nefarious /nɪ'fɛəriəs/ *a* nefario, vil, nefando

negative /'nɛgətɪv/ *vt* negar, denegar; votar en contra (de), oponerse (a); (prevent) impedir, imposibilitar. —*a* negativo. —*n* negativa, negación, *f;* repulsa, denegación, *f; Photo.* negativo, *m,* prueba negativa, *f; Elec.* electricidad negativa, *f.* **to reply in the n.,** dar una respuesta negativa

neglect /nɪ'glɛkt/ *vt* descuidar, desatender; abandonar, dejar; (ignore) despreciar, no hacer caso (de); omitir, olvidar. —*n* descuido, *m,* desatención, *f;* inobservancia, *f;* abandono, olvido, *m;* desdén, *m,* frialdad, *f.* **to fall into n.,** caer en desuso. **to n. one's obligations,** descuidar sus obligaciones

neglectful /nɪ'glɛktfəl/ *a* negligente, descuidado, omiso

negligee /,nɛglɪ'ʒei/ *n* salto de cama, quimono, *m,* bata, *f*

negligence /'nɛglɪdʒəns/ *n* negligencia, *f,* descuido, *m;* flojedad, pereza, *f;* (of dress) desaliño, *m*

negligent /'nɛglɪdʒənt/ *a* negligente, descuidado; remiso, flojo, perezoso

negligible /'nɛglɪdʒəbəl/ *a* insignificante, escaso, insuficiente; sin importancia, desdeñable

negotiable /nɪ'gouʃiəbəl, -ʃəbəl/ *a* negociable; (of a road) practicable, transitable

negotiate /nɪ'gouʃi,eit/ *vt* gestionar, agenciar, tratar; (a bend) tomar; (an obstacle) salvar, franquear; *vi* negociar. **to**

n. a bill of exchange, descontar una letra de cambio. **to n. for a contract,** tratar un contrato

negotiation /nɪ,gouʃi'eiʃən/ *n* negociación, *f; Com.* gestión, transacción, *f;* (of a bend) toma, *f;* (of an obstacle) salto, *m*

neigh /nei/ *vi* relinchar. —*n* relincho, relinchido, *m*

neighbor /'neibər/ *n* vecino (-na); (biblical) prójimo (-ma)

neighborhood /'neibər,hʊd/ *n* vecindad, *f,* vecindario, *m;* cercanía, *f,* afueras, *f pl,* alrededores, *m pl;* a de barrio (e.g. *neighborhood moviehouse,* cine del barrio)

neighboring /'neibərɪŋ/ *a* vecino; cercano, inmediato, adyacente

neighborliness /'neibərlinis/ *n* buena vecindad, *f*

neighborly /'neibərli/ *a* amistoso, sociable, bondadoso. **to be n.,** ser de buena vecindad

neither /'niðər, 'nai-/ *a* ningún; ninguno de los dos, e.g. *N. explanation is right,* Ninguna de las dos explicaciones es correcta. —*conjunc* ni, tampoco, e.g. *N. Mary nor John,* Ni María ni Juan. *N. will he give it to her,* Tampoco se lo dará. —*pron* ni uno ni otro, ninguno, e.g. *N. of them heard it,* Ni uno ni otro lo oyó.

nemesis /'nɛməsɪs/ *n* némesis, *f;* justicia, *f*

neon /'niɒn/ *n Chem.* neón, *m*

neon sign anuncio luminoso, *m*

neophyte /'niə,fait/ *n* neófito (-ta); aspirante, *mf*

nephew /'nɛfyu/ *n* sobrino, *m*

nephritis /nə'fraitɪs/ *n Med.* nefritis, *f*

nepotism /'nɛpə,tɪzəm/ *n* nepotismo, *m*

nerve /nɜrv/ *n* (*Anat. Bot.*) nervio, *m;* valor, ánimo, *m;* vitalidad, *f; Inf.* descaro, *m,* desvergüenza, frescura, *f.* —*vt* animar, alentar, envalentonar; esforzar; dar fuerza (a). —*vi* animarse, esforzarse (a). **My nerves are all on edge,** Se me crispan los nervios. **n.-cell,** neurona, *f.* **to lose one's n.,** perder la cabeza; perder los nervios. **to strain every n.,** hacer un esfuerzo supremo. **n. center,** centro nervioso, *m.* **n.-racking,** espantoso, horripilante. **n. strain,** tensión nerviosa, *f*

nerveless /'nɜrvlɪs/ *a* sin nervio; enervado

nervous /'nɜrvəs/ *a* nervioso, asustadizo, tímido; agitado, excitado; (of style) vigoroso. **n. breakdown,** crisis nerviosa, *f.* **n. system,** sistema nervioso, *m*

nervousness /'nɜrvəsnɪs/ *n* nervosidad, timidez, *f;* agitación, *f;* (of style) vigor, *m;* energía, *f*

nervy /'nɜrvi/ *a* nervioso

nest /nɛst/ *vi* anidar, hacerse un nido. —*n* (bird's) nido, *m;* (animal's) madriguera, *f;* (of drawers) juego, *m,* serie, *f;* (of thieves) cueva, guarida, *f; Inf.* casita, *f,* hogar, *m.* **to feather one's n.,** hacer su agosto. **n.-egg,** *Fig.* nidal, *m.* **n. of eggs,** nidada de huevos, *f*

nestle /'nɛsəl/ *vt* apoyar. —*vi* apiñarse,

hacerse un ovillo. **to n. up to a person,** apretarse contra

nestling /'nɛstlɪŋ/ n pichón, pollo, m; pajarito, m

net /nɛt/ vt coger con redes; obtener, coger; cubrir con redes. —vi hacer redes. —n red, f; (mesh) malla, f; (fabric) tul, m. **net making,** manufactura de redes, f

net /nɛt/ a Com. líquido, neto, limpio; (of fabric) de tul. **net amount,** importe líquido, importe neto, m. **net balance,** saldo líquido, m. **net cost,** precio neto, m. **net profit,** beneficio neto (or líquido), m

nether /'nɛðər/ a inferior, bajero, más bajo. **n. regions,** infierno, m

Netherlander /'nɛðər,lændər/ n neerlandés (-esa), holandés (-esa)

Netherlands, the /'nɛðərləndz/ los Países Bajos m pl

nethermost /'nɛðər,moust/ a lo más bajo, ínfimo, más hondo

netting /'nɛtɪŋ/ n red, (obra de) malla, f; Naut. jareta, f; manufactura de redes, f; pesca con redes, f. **wire-n.,** tela metálica, malla de alambre, f

nettle /'nɛtl/ vt picar; Fig. irritar, picar, fastidiar, disgustar. —n ortiga, f. **n.-rash,** urticaria, f

network /'nɛt,wɜrk/ n red, malla, randa, f; (of communications) sistema, m, red, f

neuralgia /nʊ'rældʒə/ n neuralgia, f

neuralgic /nʊ'rældʒɪk/ a neurálgico

neurasthenia /,nʊrəs'θiniə/ n neurastenia, f

neurasthenic /,nʊrəs'θɛnɪk/ a and n neurasténico (-ca)

neurologist /nʊ'rolədʒɪst/ n neurólogo, m

neurosurgeon /'nʊrou,sɜrdʒən/ n neurocirujano, m

neurotic /nʊ'rotɪk/ a and n neurótico (-ca)

neuter /'nutər/ a neutro; (of verbs) intransitivo; (Zool. Bot.) sin sexo

neutral /'nutrəl/ a neutral; (Chem. Mech.) neutro; (of colors) indeciso, indeterminado; (of persons) imparcial, indiferente. —n neutral, mf Mech. **to go into n.,** pasar a marcha neutra

neutrality /nu'trælti/ n neutralidad, f; indiferencia, f; imparcialidad, f

neutralize /'nutrə,laiz/ vt neutralizar

never /'nɛvər/ adv nunca, jamás; de ningún modo, no; ni aun, ni siquiera. **Better late than n.,** Más vale tarde que nunca. **Never look a gift horse in the mouth,** A caballo regalado no se le mira el diente. **Were the hour n. so late,** Por más tarde que fuese la hora. **n. again,** nunca jamás. **n. a one,** ni siquiera uno. **n. a whit,** ni pizca. **N. mind!** ¡No importa! ¡No te preocupes! ¡No hagas caso! **n.-ceasing,** continuo, incesante. **n.-ending,** inacabable, eterno, sin fin. **n.-failing,** infalible. **n.-to-be-forgotten,** inolvidable

nevermore /,nɛvər'mɔr/ adv nunca jamás

nevertheless /,nɛvərðə'lɛs/ adv sin embargo, no obstante, con todo

new /nu/ a nuevo; novel, fresco; distinto, diferente; moderno; (inexperienced) novato, no habituado; reciente. —adv (in compounds) recién. **as good as new,** como nuevo. **brand-new,** flamante, nuevecito. **new-born,** recién nacido. **new-comer,** recién llegado (-da). **new-fashioned,** de última moda. **new-found,** recién hallado. **new-laid egg,** huevo fresco, m. **new moon,** luna nueva, f, novilunio, m. **new rich,** ricacho (-cha); indio, m. **new student,** alumno de nuevo ingreso. **New Testament,** Nuevo Testamento, m. **New World,** Nuevo Mundo, m. **New York** (er), a and n neoyorquino (-na). **New Zealand** (er), a and n neozelandés (esa)

newest /'nuist/ a superl. novísimo; más reciente

Newfoundland /'nufənlənd/ Terranova, f. **N. dog,** perro de Terranova, m

newish /'nuiʃ/ a bastante nuevo

newly /'nuli/ adv nuevamente; hace poco, recientemente. The abb. form **recién** is used only with past part, e.g. the n. painted door, la puerta recién pintada. the n.-weds, los desposados, los recién casados

newness /'nunɪs/ n novedad, f; inexperiencia, falta de práctica, f; innovación, f

New Orleans /'ɔrlɪənz, ɔr'linz/ Nueva Orleans, f

news /nuz/ n pl noticias, f pl; nueva, f; reporte, aviso, m; novedad, f. **No n. is good n.,** Falta de noticias, buena señal. **piece of n.,** noticia, f. **What's the n.?** ¡Qué hay de nuevo? **n. agency,** agencia de noticias, agencia periodística, f. **n.-agent,** agente de la prensa, m; vendedor (-ra) de periódicos. **n. bulletin,** Radio. boletín de noticias, m. Inf. **n.-hound,** gacetillero (-ra). **n. item,** noticia de actualidad, f. **n.-print,** papel para periódicos, m. **n.-room,** gabinete de lectura, m. **n. reel,** película noticiera, revista cinematográfica, f, noticiario cinematográfico, noticiero m, actualidades, f pl. **n.-stand,** puesto de periódicos, quiosco de periódicos, m. **n. theater,** cine de actualidades, m

newscast /'nuz,kæst/ n noticiario, m

newspaper /'nuz,peipər/ n periódico, diario, noticiero, m. **n. clipping, n. cutting,** recorte de periódico, m. **n. paragraph,** suelto, m. **n. reporter,** reportero (-ra); periodista, mf **n. reporting,** reporterismo, m. **n. serial,** folletín, m, novela por entregas, f. **n. vendor,** vendedor (-ra) de periódicos, n

news report n reportaje, m

New York /yɔrk/ Nueva York, f

New Zealand /'ziland/ Nueva Zelandia, f

next /nɛkst/ a (of place) siguiente, vecino, contiguo; (of time) próximo, siguiente. **on the n. page,** en la página siguiente. **the n. day,** el día siguiente. **the n.-door house,** la casa vecina. **the n. life,** la otra vida. **n. month (yesar),** el mes (año) próximo (or que viene). **n. time,** otra vez, la próxima vez

next /nɛkst/ *adv* (of time) luego, en seguida; (of place) inmediatamente después. **I come n.,** Ahora me toca a mí. **It is n. to a certainty that...,** Es casi seguro que... **the n. best,** el segundo. **the n. of kin,** los pariente más cercarro, *m,* parientes más cercanos, *m pl.* **to wear n. to the skin,** llevar sobre la piel. **n. to,** al lado de, junto a; primero después de; casi. **n. to nothing,** casi nada, muy poco. **What n.?** ¿Qué más?; ¿Y ahora qué?

nibble /'nɪbəl/ *vt* mordiscar, mordisquear, roer; (horses) rozar; (fish) picar; *Fig.* considerar, tantear; *vi* picar. —*n* mordisco, *m;* roedura, *f*

Nicaraguan /,nɪkə'ragwən/ *a* and *n* nicaragüeño (-ña)

Nice /nis/ Niza, *f*

nice /nais/ *a* escrupuloso, minucioso, exacto; (of persons) simpático, afable, amable; fino; (of things) agradable, bonito; bueno; sutil, delicado; (*Inf. Ironic.*) bonito. **a n. point,** un punto delicado. **a n. view,** una vista agradable (or bonita). **n.-looking,** guapo. **n. people,** gente fina, *f;* gente simpática, *f*

nicely /'naisli/ *adv* muy bien; con elegancia; primorosamente; con amabilidad, gentilmente; agradablemente

niceness /'naisnis/ *n* exactitud, minuciosidad, *f;* (of persons) bondad, amabilidad, *f;* amenidad, hermosura, *f;* lo bonito; sutileza, *f;* refinamiento, *m*

nicety /'naisiti/ *n* exactitud, *f;* sutileza, *f,* refinamiento, *m.* **niceties,** *n pl* detalles, *m pl.* **to a n.,** con la mayor precisión; a la perfección

niche /nɪtʃ/ *n* nicho, templete, *m;* (vaulted) hornacina, *f, Fig.* **to find a n. for oneself,** encontrarse una buena posición; situarse

nick /nɪk/ *vt* cortar en muescas, mellar, tarjar. —*n* mella, muesca, *f.* **in the n. of time,** en el momento oportuno, a tiempo

nickel /'nɪkəl/ *n* níquel, *m; Com.* moneda de níquel, *f.* **n.-plated,** niquelado

nickname /'nɪk,neim/ *vt* apodar, motejar, apellidar. —*n* apodo, sobrenombre, mote, mal nombre, *m*

nicotine /'nɪkə,tin/ *n* nicotina, *f*

niece /nis/ *n* sobrina, *f*

niggardly /'nɪgərdli/ *a* tacaño, avaricioso, mezquino, ruin, miserable

niggling /'nɪglɪŋ/ *a* nimio, meticuloso; escrupuloso, minucioso

nigh. /nai/ See **near**

night /nait/ *n* noche, *f; Fig.* oscuridad, *f,* tinieblas, *f pl.* **all n.,** toda la noche, la noche entera. **all n. service,** servicio nocturno permanente, *m.* **at or by n.,** de noche. **every n.,** todas las noches, cada noche. **Good n.!** ¡Buenas noches! **last n.,**

ayer por la noche, anoche, la noche pasada. **restless n.,** noche mala, noche toledana, *f.* **the n. before last,** anteayer por la noche, *m.* **to-n.,** esta noche. **tomorrow n.,** mañana por la noche. **to be n.,** ser de noche. **to spend the n.,** pernoctar, pasar la noche. **n.-bird,** pájaro nocturno, *m; Inf.* trasnochador (-ra). **n.-blindness,** nictalopia, *f.* **n.-cap,** gorro de dormir, *m.* **n. clothes,** traje de dormir, *m.* **n. club,** cabaré *m.* **n. dew,** relente, sereno, *m.* **n. flying,** vuelo nocturno, *m.* **n.-jar,** *Ornith.* chotacabras, *m.* **n.-light,** mariposa, lamparilla, *f.* **n. mail,** último correo, *m;* tren correo de la noche, *m.* **n. school,** escuela nocturna, *f.* **n. shift,** turno de noche, *m.* **n. watch,** ronda de noche, *f; Naut.* sonochada, *f.* **n. watchman,** (in the street) sereno, *m;* (of a building) vigilante nocturno, *m*

nightfall /'nait,fɔl/ *n* anochecer, crepúsculo, atardecer, *m*

nightgown /'nait,gaun/ *n* camisa de noche, *f*

nightingale /'naitŋ,geil, 'naitɪŋ-/ *n* ruiseñor, *m*

nightly /'naitli/ *a* de noche; nocturno, nocturnal. —*adv* todas las noches, cada noche

nightmare /'nait,mɛər/ *n* pesadilla, *f*

Nile /nail/ el Nilo, *m*

nimble /'nɪmbəl/ *a* ágil, activo; vivo, listo. **n.-fingered,** ligero de dedos. **n.-witted,** despierto, vivo

nimbly /'nɪmbli/ *adv* ágilmente, ligeramente

nincompoop /'nɪnkəm,pup, 'nɪŋ-/ *n* papirote, *m,* papanatas, *mf* tonto (-ta)

nine /nain/ *a* and *n* nueve, *m.* **He is n.,** Tiene nueve años. **the N.,** las nueve Musas. **n. o'clock,** las nueve. **to be dressed up to the nines,** estar hecho un brazo de mar

ninefold /a 'nain,fould; *adv.* 'nain'fould/ *a* and *adv* nueve veces

nineteen /'nain'tin/ *a* and *n* diez y nueve, diecinueve *m*

nineteenth /'nain'tinθ/ *a* décimonono. —*n* (of month) el diez y nueve; (of monarchs) diez y nueve. **the n. century,** el siglo diez y nueve

ninetieth /'naintiəθ/ *a* nonagésimo, noventa

ninety /'nainti/ *a* and *n* noventa *m.* **n.-one,** noventa y uno. **n.-two,** noventa y dos. **n.-first chapter,** el capítulo noventa y uno

ninny /'nini/ *n* parapoco, chancleta, *mf;* mentecato (-ta)

ninth /nainθ/ *a* noveno, nono. —*n* nueve, *m;* (of the month) el nueve (of sovereigns) nono. **one n.,** un noveno

nip /nɪp/ *vt* pellizcar, pinchar; mordiscar, morder; (wither) marchitar; (freeze) helar; (run) correr. —*vi* pinchar; picar (el viento). —*n* pellizco, pinchazo, *m;* mordisco, *m;* (of spirits) trago, *m;* copita, *f;* (in the air) viento frío, hielo, *m.* **to nip**

in, colarse dentro, deslizarse en. **to nip off,** pirarse, mudarse. *Fig.* **to nip in the bud,** cortar en flor

nippers /ˈnɪpərz/ *pl* alicates, *m pl;* tenacillas, pinzas, *f pl*

nipple /ˈnɪpəl/ *n* pezón, *m;* pezón artificial, *m*

nit /nɪt/ *n* Ent. liendre, *f*

nitrogen /ˈnaɪtrədʒən/ *n* Chem. nitrógeno, *m*

no /nou/ *a* ningún, ninguno, ninguna, e.g. *by no means,* de ningún modo, *No* is often not translated in Sp., e.g. *I have no time,* No tengo tiempo. —*adv* no. —*n* voto negativo, no, *m.* *to be of no account,* no tener importancia; no significar nada. *to be no good for,* no servir para. *to be of no use,* ser inútil. *to have no connection with,* no tener nada que ver con. *for no reason,* sin motivo alguno. *"No Admittance,"* «Entrada Prohibida.» *no, indeed,* Cierto que no. *no-man's land,* tierra de nadie, *f. no more,* no más. *No more of this!* ¡No hablemos más de eso! *no one,* nadie, ninguno. *no sooner,* no bien, tan pronto (como). **no such thing,** no tal. **"No Thoroughfare,"** «Prohibido el Paso.» **whether or not,** sea o no sea

Noah's Ark /ˈnouəz/ *n* arca de Noé, *f*

nobility /nouˈbɪlɪti/ *n* nobleza, *f;* (of rank) aristocracia, nobleza, *f;* (of conduct) caballerosidad, hidalguía, generosidad, bondad, *f;* (grandeur) grandeza, sublimidad, *f.* **the higher n.,** los nobles de primera clase

noble /ˈnoubəl/ *a* noble; (in rank) aristocrático, noble, linajudo; (of conduct) caballeroso, generoso; (of buildings) sublime, magnífico. —*n* noble, *m,* aristócrata, *mf* **to make n.,** ennoblecer. **n.-mindedness,** generosidad, grandeza de alma, *f.* **n. title,** título de nobleza, título del reino, *m*

noblewoman /ˈnoubəlˌwʊmən/ *n* dama noble, mujer noble, aristócrata, *f*

nobly /ˈnoubli/ *adv* noblemente, generosamente. **n. born,** noble de nacimiento

nobody /ˈnouˌbɒdi/ *n* nadie, ninguno. **There was n. there,** No había nadie allí. *Inf.* **a n.,** un (una) cualquiera, una persona insignificante. **n. else,** nadie más, ningún otro

nocturnal /nɒkˈtɜrnl/ *a* nocturno, nocherniego, nocturnal

nocturne /ˈnɒktɜrn/ *n* Mus. nocturno, *m*

nod /nɒd/ *vt* inclinar la cabeza; hacer una señal (or señas) con la cabeza; *vi* dar cabezadas; cabecear; (of trees) mecerse, inclinarse; inclinar la cabeza. —*n* señal (or seña) con la cabeza, *f;* inclinación de la cabeza, *f;* cabeceo, *m,* cabezada, *f.* **A nod is as good as a wink,** A buen entendedor pocas palabras. **He nodded to me as he passed,** Me saludó con la cabeza al pasar. **He signed to me with a nod,** Me hizo una señal con la cabeza

nodding /ˈnɒdɪŋ/ *a* que cabecea; *Bot.*

colgante, inclinado; temblante. —*n* cabeceo, *m;* saludo con la cabeza, *m*

noddle /ˈnɒdl/ *n* mollera, *f*

node /noud/ *n* (Bot. Med.) nudo, *m*

nodule /ˈnɒdʒul/ *n* nódulo, *m;* nudillo, *m*

noise /nɔɪz/ *n* ruido, son, *m;* tumulto, clamor, estruendo, alboroto, *m.* **to make a n.,** hacer ruido. **to n. abroad,** divulgar, publicar

noiseless /ˈnɔɪzlɪs/ *a* silencioso, callado, sin ruido

noisily /ˈnɔɪzəli/ *adv* ruidosamente

noisiness /ˈnɔɪzɪnɪs/ *n* ruido, estrépito, tumulto, clamor, *m;* (of voices) gritería, *f*

noisome /ˈnɔɪsəm/ *a* ofensivo; fétido, apestoso

noisy /ˈnɔɪzi/ *a* ruidoso; estruendoso; estrepitoso, clamoroso

nomad /ˈnoumæd/ *a* nómada, errante; (of flocks) trashumante. —*n* nómada, *mf*

nomenclature /ˈnoumənˌkleɪtʃər/ *n* nomenclatura, *f*

nominal /ˈnɒmənl/ *a* nominal; titular; insignificante, de poca importancia. **the n. head,** el director en nombre

nominally /ˈnɒmənli/ *adv* nominalmente, en nombre

nominate /ˈnɒməˌneɪt/ *vt* nombrar, designar, elegir; fijar, señalar

nominating /ˈnɒməˌneɪtɪŋ/ *a* nominador

nomination /ˌnɒməˈneɪʃən/ *n* nombramiento, *m,* nominación, *f;* señalamiento, *m*

nominee /ˌnɒməˈni/ *n* nómino propuesto, *m*

non /nɒn/ *adv* non; des-; in-; falta de. **non-acceptance,** rechazo, *m.* **non-acquaintance,** ignorancia, *f.* **non-admission,** no admisión, *f;* denegación, *f,* rechazo, *m.* **non-aggression,** no agresión, *f.* **non-alcoholic,** no alcohólico. **non-appearance,** ausencia, *f; Law.* no comparecencia, contumacia, *f.* **non-arrival,** ausencia, *f;* falta de recibo, *f.* **non-attendance,** falta de asistencia, ausencia, *f.* **non-carbonated,** sin gas. **non-combatant,** no combatiente. **non-commissioned officer,** oficial subalterno, *m.* **non-committal,** evasivo, equívoco, ambiguo. **non-compliance,** falta de obediencia, *f.* **non-concurrence,** falta de acuerdo, *f.* **non-conducting,** no conductivo. **non-conductor,** mal conductor, *m; Elec.* aislador, *m.* **non-contagious,** no contagioso. **non-cooperation,** *Polit.* resistencia pasiva, *f;* no cooperación, *f.* **non-delivery,** falta de entrega, *f.* **non-essential,** no esencial, prescindible. **non-execution,** no cumplimiento, *m.* **non-existence,** no existencia, *f.* **non-existent,** inexistente, no existente. **non-intervention,** no intervención, *f.* **non-manufacturing,** no industrial. **non-member,** visitante, *mf* **non-observance,** incumplimiento, *m;* violación, *f.* **non-payment,** falta de pago, *f.* **non-performance,** falta de ejecución, *f.* **non-poisonous,** no venenoso, innocuo. **non-**

resistance, falta de resistencia, *f*; obediencia pasiva, *f*. **non-skid**, antideslizante, antirresbaladizo. **non-smoking**, que no fuma; (of a railway compartment, etc.) para no fumadores. **non-stop**, continuo, incesante; directo, sin parar; *Aer.* sin escalas

non-aligned /ˌnɒn əˈlaind/ *a* no abanderado

non-alignment /ˌnɒn əˈlainmənt/ *n* no abanderamiento *m*

nonchalance /ˌnɒnʃəˈlɑns/ *n* aplomo, *m*, indiferencia, frialdad, calma, *f*

nonchalant /ˌnɒnʃəˈlɑnt/ *a* indiferente, frío, impasible

nonchalantly /ˌnɒnʃəˈlɑntli/ *adv* con indiferencia

nonconformist /ˌnɒnkənˈfɔrmɪst/ *a* and *n* disidente *mf*; *a* inconforme, *n*, inconformista, *mf*

nondescript /ˌnɒndɪˈskrɪpt/ *a* indeterminado, indefinido, indeciso, mediocre

none /nʌn/ *pron* nadie, ninguno; nada. —*a* and *n* ninguno (-na). —*adv* no; de ningún modo, de ninguna manera. **I have n.**, No lo tengo, No tengo ninguno. **We have n. of your things**, No tenemos ninguna de tus cosas. **I was n. the worse**, No me hallaba peor. **N. can read his account with pleasure**, Nadie puede leer su narración con gusto. **n. the less**, no menos; sin embargo

nonentity /nɒnˈɛntɪti/ *n* persona sin importancia, medianía, *f*, cero, *m*

nonplussed /nɒnˈplʌst/ *a* cortado, perplejo, confuso

non-profit /nɒn ˈprɒfɪt/ *a* sin fines de lucro, sin fines lucrativos

nonsense /ˈnɒnsɛns/ *n* disparate, despropósito, desatino, *m*, absurdidad, *f*; *Inf.* galimatías, *m*; pamplina, patraña, *f*. **to talk n.**, hablar sin ton ni son. **N.!** ¡A otro perro con este hueso! ¡Patrañas!

nonsensical /nɒnˈsɛnsɪkəl/ *a* absurdo, ridículo, disparatado

noodle /ˈnudl/ *n Cul.* tallarín, *m*; *Inf.* mentecato (-ta), bobo (-ba)

nook /nuk/ *n* escondrijo, lugar retirado, rincón, *m*

noon /nun/ *n* mediodía, *m*; *Fig.* punto culminante, apogeo, *m*, *a* de mediodía, meridional. **at n.**, a mediodía

noose /nus/ *vt* coger con lazos. —*n* lazo corredizo, dogal, *m*

nopal /ˈnoupəl/ *n Bot.* nopal, *m*

No Parking «Se Prohíbe Estacionar,» «Se Prohíbe Estacionarse»

nor /nɔr/ *unstressed* nər/ *conjunc* ni, ni, tampoco. **He removed neither his coat nor his hat**, No se quitó ni el gabán ni el sombrero. **Nor was this the first time**, Y no fue ésta la primera vez. **Nor I**, Ni yo tampoco

norm /nɔrm/ *n* modelo, *m*, norma, regla, pauta, *f*; (of size) marca, *f*; (*Bot. Zool.*) tipo, *m*

normal /ˈnɔrməl/ *a* normal; común, natural, corriente, regular; *Math.* perpendicu-

lar, normal. —*n* condición normal, *f*, estado normal, *m*; *Math.* normal, *f*. **to become n.**, normalizarse, hacerse normal. **to make n.**, normalizar. **n. school**, escuela normal, *f*

normalize /ˈnɔrməˌlaiz/ *vt* normalizar

north /nɔrθ/ *n* norte, *m*. —*a* del norte, septentrional. **n. by west**, norte, cuarta noroeste. **n. of the city**, al norte de la ciudad. **N.-American**, *a* and *n* norteamericano (-na). **n.-east**, *a* and *n* nordeste *m*. **n.-easter**, viento del nordeste, *m*. **n.-easterly**, del nordeste (winds). **n.-eastern**, del nordeste (places). **n.-eastward**, hacia el nordeste. **n.-n.-east**, nornordeste, *m*. **n.-n.-west**, nornoroeste, *m*. **n.-polar**, ártico. **N. Star**, estrella del norte, estrella polar, *f*. **n.-west**, noroeste, *m*. **n.-wester**, viento del noroeste, *m*. **n.-westerly**, del noroeste (winds). **n.-westerly gale**, temporal del noroeste, *m*. **n.-western**, del noroeste; situado al noroeste. **n.-westwards**, hacia el noroeste. **n. wind**, el viento del norte, el cierzo

North America, Norteamérica, América del Norte, *f*

northern /ˈnɔrðərn/ *a* del norte, septentrional, norteño; (of races) nórdico. **N. Cross**, crucero, *m*. **n. lights**, aurora boreal, *f*

northerner /ˈnɔrðərnər/ *n* hombre del norte, *m*, habitante del norte, *mf*

northernmost /ˈnɔrðərnˌmoust/ *a superl* al extremo norte, más septentrional

northwards /ˈnɔrθwərdz/ *adv* hacia el norte

Norway /ˈnɔrwei/ Noruega, *f*

Norwegian /nɔrˈwidʒən/ *a* and *n* noruego (-ga); (language) noruego, *m*

nose /nouz/ *n* nariz, *f*; (of animals) hocico, *m*; (sense of smell) olfato, *m*; (of ships) proa, *f*; (of jug) pico, *m*, boca, *f*; (projecting piece) cuerno, *m*, nariz, *f*; (of airplane) cabeza, *f*, *vt* acariciar con la nariz; avanzar lentamente. —*vi* husmear, olfatear. **to n. into**, *Inf.* meter las narices, poner baza. **to n. out**, descubrir, averiguar. **to bleed at the n.**, echar sangre por las narices. **to blow one's n.**, sonar (or limpiarse) las narices. **to keep one's n. to the grindstone**, estar sobre el yunque, batir el cobre. *Fig.* **to lead by the n.**, tener a uno agarrado por las narices. **to pay through the n.**, costar un ojo de la cara. **to speak through the n.**, ganguear. **to turn up one's n.**, *Fig.* hacer gestos (a), volver la cara. **flat n.**, nariz chata, *f*. **snub n.**, nariz respingona, *f*. **well-shaped n.**, nariz perfilada, *f*. **under one's n.**, bajo las narices de uno. **n.-bag**, cebadera, mochila, *f*; morral, *m*. **n.-bleeding**, *Med.* epistaxis, *f*; hemorragia de las narices, *f*. **n.-dive**, *Aer.* descenso de cabeza, picado, *m*. —*vi* picar. **n.-piece**, (of microscope) ocular, *m*. **n.-ring**, (of a bull, etc.) narigón, *m*

-nosed *a* de nariz..., con la nariz...

nosegay /ˈnouzˌgei/ *n* ramillete, *m*

No Smoking «Prohibido Fumar», Se Prohibe Fumar

nostalgia /nɒˈstældʒə/ n nostalgia, añoranza, f

nostalgic /nɒˈstældʒɪk/ a nostálgico

nostril /ˈnɒstrəl/ n ventana de la nariz, f, n pl **nostrils**, narices, f pl

nostrum /ˈnɒstrəm/ n panacea, f, curalotodo, m; medicina patentada, f

not /nɒt/ adv no; sin; ni, ni siquiera. Is it not true? We think not, ¿No es verdad? No lo creemos. You have seen Mary, have you not? Vd. ha visto a María, ¿verdad? not caring whether he came or not, sin preocuparse de que viniese o no. not that he will come, no es decir que venga. not at all, de ningún modo; (courtesy) ¡de nada! not even, ni siquiera. not guilty, no culpable. not one, ni uno. not so much as, no tanto como; ni siquiera. It is not so much that, as It is... No es tanto eso, cuanto que... not to say, por no decir

notable /ˈnoutəbəl/ a notable, señalado, memorable; digno de atención. —n persona eminente, f, notable, mf

notary /ˈnoutəri/ n notario, escribano, m

notation /nouˈteiʃən/ n notación, f

notch /nɒtʃ/ vt cortar muescas (en); mellar, ranurar, entallar. —n muesca, mella, ranura, entalladura, f

note /nout/ vt notar, observar; anotar, apuntar; advertir, hacerse cuenta de. —n Mus. nota, f; son, acento, m; (letter) recado, billete, m; anotación, glosa, f; apuntación, f; apunte, m, nota, f; (importance) importancia, distinción, f; Com. vale, abonaré, m; (sign) marca, señal, f. to n. down, anotar. worthy of note, digno de atención. **n.-book,** libro de apuntes, cuaderno, m, libreta, f. **n.-case,** cartera, f. **n.-paper,** papel de escribir, m. **n.-taker,** apuntador (-ra)

noted /ˈnoutid/ a célebre, famoso, ilustre, eminente, insigne

noteworthy /ˈnoutˌwɜrði/ a digno de nota, notable, digno de atención

nothing /ˈnʌθiŋ/ n nada, f; la nada; cero, m. —adv en nada. to come to n., anonadarse, fracasar. to do n., no hacer nada. to do n. but, no hacer más que. to have n. to do with, no tener nada que ver con; Inf. no tener arte ni parte en. There is n. else to do, No hay nada más que hacer; No hay más remedio. There is n. to fear, No hay de que tener miedo. We could make n. of the book, No llegamos a comprender el libro. for n., de balde, en vano; gratis. next to n., casi nada. n. else or more, nada más. n. like, ni con mucho. n. much, poca cosa. n. new, nada nuevo. n. similar, nada semejante. n. to speak of, poca cosa

notice /ˈnoutis/ vt observar, reparar en, darse cuenta (de), marcar, caer en la cuenta (de), fijarse (en). —n observación, atención, f; aviso, m, notificación, f; anuncio, m; (term) plazo, m; (review) crítica, f. at short n., a corto aviso. until further n., hasta nuevo aviso (or orden). to attract n., atraer la atención. I hadn't noticed, No me había fijado. to be beneath one's n., no merecer su atención. to be under n., estar dimitido. to bring to the n. of, dar noticia de. to escape n., pasar desapercibido. to give n., hacer saber, informar; (of employer) despedir (a); (of employee) dimitir, dar la dimisión. to take n. of, notar, darse cuenta de; hacer caso, atender (a). n. board, letrero, tablero de anuncios, m. n. to quit, desahúcio, m

noticeable /ˈnoutisəbəl/ a perceptible, evidente; digno de observación, notable

noticeably /ˈnoutisəbli/ adv perceptiblemente; notablemente

notification /ˌnoutəfiˈkeiʃən/ n notificación, intimación, advertencia, f, aviso, m

notify /ˈnoutəˌfai/ vt notificar, comunicar, avisar, intimar, hacer saber

notion /ˈnouʃən/ n noción, idea, f, concepto, m; (view) opinión, f, parecer, m; (novelty) novedad, f; artículo de fantasía, m. I have a n. that..., Tengo la idea de que..., Sospecho que... I haven't a n., No tengo idea

No Tipping «No Se Admiten Propinas»

notoriety /ˌnoutəˈraiiti/ n notoriedad, publicidad, f; escándalo, m; persona notoria, f

notorious /nouˈtɔriəs/ a notorio, famoso, conocido; escandaloso, sensacional

notwithstanding /ˌnɒtwiðˈstændiŋ/ prep a pesar de. —adv sin embargo, no obstante. —conjunc aunque, bien que, por más que

nougat /ˈnugət/ n turrón, m

nought /nɒt/ n Math. cero, m; nada, f

noun /naun/ n substantivo, nombre, m

nourish /ˈnɜriʃ/ vt sustentar, alimentar, nutrir; Fig. fomentar, favorecer

nourishing /ˈnɜriʃiŋ/ a nutritivo, alimenticio, nutricio

nourishment /ˈnɜriʃmənt/ n nutrición, f; sustento, m; alimento, m; Fig. fomento, pasto, m

Nova Scotia /ˈnouvə ˈskouʃə/ Nueva Escocia, f

novel /ˈnɒvəl/ a nuevo, original, inacostumbrado. —n novela, f.

novelette /ˌnɒvəˈlet/ n novela corta, f

novelist /ˈnɒvəlist/ n novelista, mf

novelty /ˈnɒvəlti/ n novedad, f; innovación, f; cambio, m

November /nouˈvembər/ n noviembre, m

novice /ˈnɒvis/ n Eccl. novicio (-ia); comenzante, principiante, mf, aspirante, m

novocain /ˈnouvəˌkein/ n Med. novocaína, f

now /nau/ adv ahora, actualmente, al presente, a la fecha; en seguida, ahora, inmediatamente; poco ha, hace poco; pues bien. —interj ¡A ver! ¡Vamos! —conjunc pero, mas. —n presente, m, actualidad, f. before now, antes, en otras ocasiones, ya, previamente. just now, ahora mismo, hace poco. **now... now,** ya... ya; sucesivamente, en turno. **now and then,** de vez en cuando, de tarde en tarde. **now that,** ya que, ahora que, dado que. **until now,** hasta el presente, hasta aquí, hasta ahora

nowadays /'nauə,deiz/ adv hoy en día, actualmente, en nuestros días

nowhere /'nou,wɛər/ adv en ninguna parte. **in the middle of n.,** donde Cristo dio las tres voces. **n. else,** en ninguna otra parte. Inf. **n. near,** ni con mucho; muy lejos (de)

nowise /'nou,waiz/ adv de ningún modo, en modo alguno, de ninguna manera

noxious /'nɒkʃəs/ a dañoso, nocivo; pestífero

nozzle /'nɒzəl/ n (of a hose-pipe) boquilla, f; Mech. gollete, m; tubo de salida, m, tobera, f; inyector, m

n.p. (no place) s.l. (sin lugar)

nuance /'nuɑns/ n matiz, m, gradación, sombra, f

nubile /'nubil, -bail/ a núbil

nuclear /'nukliər/ a nuclear

nucleus /'nukliəs/ n núcleo, m; centro, foco, m

nude /nud/ a desnudo, nudo

nudge /nʌdʒ/ vt dar un codazo (a). —n codazo, m

nudism /'nudizəm/ n nudismo, m

nudist /'nudist/ n nudista, mf

nudity /'nuditi/ n desnudez, f

nugget /'nʌgit/ n Mineral. pepita, f

nuisance /'nusəns/ n molestia, incomodidad, f, fastidio, m; Inf. tostón, m, lata, f. **to make a n. of oneself,** meterse donde no le llaman, ser un pelmazo. **What a n.!** ¡Qué lata! ¡Qué fastidio!

null /nʌl/ a nulo, inválido, sin fuerza legal. **n. and void,** nulo, írrito

nullification /,nʌləfɪ'keiʃən/ n anulación, invalidación, f

nullity /'nʌliti/ n nulidad, f

numb /nʌm/ vt entumecer, entorpecer. —a entumecido; torpe, dormido; paralizado; Fig. insensible, pasmado. **n. with cold,** entumecido de frío

number /'nʌmbər/ vt numerar, contar; poner número (a); (pages of a book) foliar; ascender a. —n número, m; (figure) cifra, f; (crowd) multitud, muchedumbre, f; cantidad, f; (of a periodical) ejemplar, m; Gram. número, m; pl versos, m pl. **Numbers,** (Bible) Números, m pl; **to be numbered among,** figurar entre. **among the n. of,** entre la muchedumbre de. **a n. of,** varios, muchos, una cantidad de. **in great n.,** en gran número; en su mayoría. **6 Peace Street,** Calle de la Paz Nº (número) 6. **one of their n.,** uno entre ellos. **n. board,** (racing) indicador, m. **n. plate,** Auto. chapa de identidad, placa de número, f

numbering /'nʌmbərɪŋ/ n numeración, f

numberless /'nʌmbərlɪs/ a innumerable, sin número, sin fin, infinito

numbness /'nʌmnɪs/ n entumecimiento, entorpecimiento, m; Fig. insensibilidad, f

numeral /'numərəl/ a numeral. —n número, m, cifra, f; Gram. nombre o adjetivo numeral, m

numerical /nu'merikəl/ a numérico

numerous /'numərəs/ a numeroso; nutrido, grande; muchos (-as)

numismatic /,numiz'mætik/ a numismático. —n pl **numismatics,** numismática, f

numskull /'nʌm,skʌl/ n zote, topo, m

nun /nun/ n monja, religiosa, f. **to become a nun,** profesar, tomar el hábito, meterse monja

nuptial /'nʌpʃəl/ a nupcial. —n pl **nuptials,** nupcias, f pl, enlace, m. **n. mass,** Eccl. misa de velaciones, f. **n. song,** epitalamio, m

nurse /nɜrs/ vt criar; dar de mamar (a), amamantar; (the sick) cuidar, asistir; (fondle) acariciar, mimar; Fig. fomentar, promover. —vi trabajar como enfermera. —n (of the sick) enfermera, f; (wet) nodriza, ama de leche, f; (children's) niñera, f; Fig. fomentador, m. **male n.,** enfermero, m

nursery /'nɜrsəri/ n Agr. plantel, vivero semillero, criadero, m; (children's room) cuarto de los niños, m; Fig. sementera, f; semillero, m. **n. governess,** aya, f. **n. rhyme,** canción infantil, f

nurseryman /'nɜrsərimən/ n horticultor, m; jardinero, m

nursing /'nɜrsɪŋ/ n lactancia, crianza, f; (of the sick) asistencia, f, cuido, m. **n. home,** clínica, f. **n. mother,** madre lactante, f

nurture /'nɜrtʃər/ vt alimentar; criar, educar. —n nutrición, alimentación, f; crianza, educación, f

nut /nʌt/ vi coger nueces. —n Bot. nuez, f; Mech. tuerca, hembra de tornillo, f, Inf. **to be a tough nut to crack,** ser un tío de cuidado. **to crack nuts,** cascar nueces. **to go nutting,** coger nueces. **cashew nut,** anacardo, m. **loose nut,** Mech. tuerca aflojada, f. **nut-brown,** castaño. **nut tree,** nogal, m

nutcrackers /'nʌt,krækərz/ n pl cascanueces, quebrantanueces, m

nutmeg /'nʌtmɛg/ n nuez moscada, nuez de especia, f

nutrition /nu'trɪʃən/ n nutrición, alimentación, f

nutritious, nutritive /nu'trɪʃəs; 'nutritɪv/ a nutritivo, alimenticio, alible

nutshell /'nʌt,ʃɛl/ n cáscara de nuez, f. **to put in a n.,** decir en resumidas cuentas, decir en forma apastillada

nutty /'nʌti/ a de nuez

nuzzle /'nʌzəl/ vt acariciar con la nariz

nylon /'nailɒn/ n nilón, nylon, m. **n. stockings,** medias de cristal (or de nilón), f pl

nymph /nimf/ n ninfa, f; Ent. crisálida, f. **n.-like,** como una ninfa; de ninfa

nymphomania /,nimfə'meiniə/ n ninfomanía, f, furor uterino, m

O

o /ou/ *n* (letter) o, *f*, *interj* ¡o! **O that...!** ¡Ojalá que!

oaf /ouf/ *n* zoquete, zamacuco, *m*

oafish /'oufiʃ/ *a* lerdo, torpe

oak /ouk/ *n* (tree and wood) roble, *m*, *a* de roble. **carved oak,** roble tallado, *m*. **holm-oak,** encina, *f*. **oak-apple,** agalla, *f*. **oak grove,** robledo, *m*

oar /ɔr/ *n* remo, *m*. **to lie on the oars,** cesar de remar. **to pull at the oars,** bogar, remar. **to put in one's oar,** *Inf.* meter baza. **to ship the oars,** armar los remos. **to unship the oars,** desarmar los remos. **oar-stroke,** palada, *f*

oarsman /'ɔrzmən/ *n* remero, bogador, *m*

oasis /ou'eɪsɪs/ *n* oasis, *m*

OAS (Organization of American States) OEA (Organización de los Estados Americanos)

oat /out/ *n Bot.* avena, *f*. **wild oat,** avena silvestre, *f*. **to sow one's wild oats,** correrla, andarse a la flor del berro. **oat field,** avenal, *m*

oath /ouθ/ *n* juramento, *m*; (curse) blasfemia, *f*, reniego, *m*. **on o.,** bajo juramento. **to break an o.,** violar el juramento. **to put on o.,** tomar juramento, hacer prestar juramento. **to take an o.,** prestar (or hacer) juramento. **to take the o. of allegiance,** jurar la bandera

oatmeal /'out,mil/ *n* harina de avena, *f*

obdurate /'ɒbdʊrɪt/ *a* obstinado, terco, porfiado. **He is o. to our requests,** Es sordo a nuestros ruegos

obedience /ou'bidiəns/ *n* obediencia, sumisión, docilidad, *f*. **blind o.,** obediencia ciega, *f*. **in o. to,** conforme a, de acuerdo con

obedient /ou'bidiənt/ *a* obediente, sumiso, dócil. **to be o. to,** ser obediente (a), obedecer (a)

obeisance /ou'beisəns, ou'bi-/ *n* reverencia, cortesía, *f*, saludo, *m*; (homage) homenaje, *m*

obese /ou'bis/ *a* obeso, corpulento, grueso, gordo

obesity /ou'bisɪti/ *n* obesidad, gordura, corpulencia, *f*

obey /ou'bei/ *vt* and *vi* obedecer. —*vt* (carry out) cumplir, observar. **to be obeyed,** ser obedecido

obfuscate /'ɒbfə,skeit/ *vt* ofuscar, cegar

obituary /ou'bɪtʃu,eri/ *a* mortuorio, necrológico. —*n* obituario, *m*, necrología, *f*. **o. column,** (in newspaper) sección necrológica, *f*. **o. notice,** esquela de defunción, *f*

object /*n.* 'ɒbdʒɪkt; *v.* əb'dʒɛkt/ *n* objeto, artículo, *m*, cosa, *f*; (purpose) propósito, intento, *m*; (aim) fin, término, *m*; *Gram.* complemento, *m*; *Inf.* individuo, *m*. —*vt* objetar, poner reparos (a). —*vi* oponerse, poner objeciones. **I o. to that remark,** Protesto contra esa observación. **If you don't o.,** Si Vd. no tiene inconveniente. **o. finder,** objetivo, *m*. **o. lesson,** lección de cosas, *f*; lección práctica, *f*

objection /əb'dʒɛkʃən/ *n* objeción, protesta, *f*, reparo, *m*; (obstacle) dificultad, *f*, inconveniente, *m*. **to have no o.,** no tener inconveniente. **to raise an o.,** hacer constar una protesta, poner una objeción

objectionable /əb'dʒɛkʃənəbəl/ *a* censurable, reprensible; desagradable, molesto

objective /əb'dʒɛktɪv/ *a* objetivo; *Gram.* acusativo. —*n* objeto, propósito, *m*; destinación, *f*; *Mil.* objetivo, *m*, *Gram.* **o. case,** caso acusativo, *m*,

objector /əb'dʒɛktər/ *n* objetante, *mf*, impugnador (-ra). **conscientious o.,** (dissident) el, *m*, (*f*, la) que protesta contra; (pacifist) pacifista, *mf*

obligation /,ɒblɪ'geiʃən/ *n* obligación, *f*; deber, *m*, precisión, *f*; compromiso, *m*. **of o.,** de deber; de precepto. **to be under an o.,** estar bajo una obligación; deber un favor. **to place under an o.,** poner bajo una obligación

obligatory /ə'blɪgə,tɔri/ *a* obligatorio, forzoso

oblige /ə'blaidʒ/ *vt* (insist on) obligar, hacer, forzar; (gratify) hacer un favor (a), complacer. **He obliged me with a match,** Me hizo el favor de una cerilla. **They are much obliged to you,** Le están muy reconocidos. **Much obliged!** ¡Se agradece!

obliging /ə'blaidʒɪŋ/ *a* atento, condescendiente, complaciente, servicial

obligingly /ə'blaidʒɪŋli/ *adv* cortésmente

oblique /ə'blik/ *a* oblicuo, sesgado; (indirect) indirecto, evasivo; *Gram.* oblicuo

obliquely /ə'blikli/ *adv* oblicuamente, al sesgo, sesgadamente; indirectamente. **to place o.,** poner al sesgo

obliterate /ə'blɪtə,reit/ *vt* borrar; destruir, aniquilar. **to be obliterated,** borrarse; quedar destruido

obliteration /ə,blɪtə'reiʃən/ *n* testación, *f*; destrucción, *f*. **o. raid,** bombardeo de saturación, *m*

oblivion /ə'blɪviən/ *n* olvido, *m*. **to cast into o.,** echar al olvido

oblivious /ə'blɪviəs/ *a* olvidadizo, descuidado

oblong /'ɒb,lɒŋ/ *a* oblongo, cuadrilongo, rectangular. —*n* rectángulo, cuadrilongo, *m*

obloquy /'ɒblɒkwi/ *n* infamia, maledicencia, deshonra, *f*

obnoxious /əb'nɒkʃəs/ *a* odioso, ofensivo, aborrecible

oboe /'oubou/ *n Mus.* oboe, *m*. **o. player,** oboe, *m*

obscene /əb'sin/ *a* indecente, obsceno, escabroso

obscenity /əb'senɪti/ *n* indecencia, obscenidad, *f*

obscure /əb'skyur/ *a* (indistinct) obscuro, indistinto; (dark) lóbrego, tenebroso; (remote) retirado, apartado; (puzzling) confuso; (unknown) desconocido; humilde; (difficult to understand) abstruso, obscuro; (vague) vago. —*vt* obscurecer; (hide) esconder; (eclipse) eclipsar. **to o. the issue,** hacer perder de vista el problema

obscurity /əb'skyʊrɪti/ *n* (darkness) obscuridad, lobreguez, *f*; (difficulty of meaning) ambigüedad, confusión, vaguedad, *f*; humildad, *f*

obsequious /əb'sikwiəs/ *a* servil, empalagoso, zalamero

observable /əb'zɜrvəbəl/ *a* observable, perceptible, visible; notable

observance /əb'zɜrvəns/ *n* observancia, *f*, cumplimiento, *m*; práctica, costumbre, *f*; (religious) rito, *m*

observant /əb'zɜrvənt/ *a* observador; obediente, atento. **o. of,** observador de; atento a

observation /ˌɒbzər'veɪʃən/ *n* observación, *f*, examen, escrutinio, *m*; (experience) experiencia, *f*; (remark) advertencia, *f*, comento, *m*. **to escape o.,** no ser advertido. **o. car.,** vagón-mirador, *m*, **o. post,** puesto de observación, *m*

observatory /əb'zɜrvəˌtɔri/ *n* observatorio, *m*

observe /əb'zɜrv/ *vt* (laws) cumplir; (holy days, etc.) guardar; (notice) observar, mirar, notar, ver, reparar en; (remark) decir, advertir; (examine) vigilar, atisbar, examinar; *Astron.* observar. —*vi* ser observador. **to o. silence,** guardar silencio

observer /əb'zɜrvər/ *n* observador (-ra)

obsess /əb'sɛs/ *vt* obsesionar, obcecar

obsessed /əb'sɛst/ *a* obseso

obsession /əb'sɛʃən/ *n* obsesión, obcecación, idea fija, manía, *f*

obsolescent /ˌɒbsə'lɛsənt/ *a* que se hace antiguo, que cae en desuso

obsolete /ˌɒbsə'lit/ *a* obsoleto, anticuado; *Biol.* rudimentario, atrofiado

obstacle /'ɒbstəkəl/ *n* obstáculo, impedimento, *m*; dificultad, *f*, inconveniente, *m*. **to put obstacles in the way of,** *Fig.* dificultar, hacer difícil. **o. race,** carrera de obstáculos, *f*

obstetrician /ˌɒbstɪ'trɪʃən/ *n* obstétrico (-ea), médico (-ca) partero (-ra)

obstetrics /əb'stɛtrɪks/ *n* obstetricia, tocología, *f*

obstinacy /'ɒbstənəsi/ *n* obstinación, terquedad, tenacidad, porfía, *f*, tesón, *m*; persistencia, *f*

obstinate /'ɒbstənɪt/ *a* terco, porfiado, obstinado, tenaz; refractario; persistente, pertinaz. **to be o.,** ser terco; porfiar. **to be o. about,** obstinarse en.

obstreperous /əb'strɛpərəs/ *a* turbulento, ruidoso

obstruct /əb'strʌkt/ *vt* obstruir: impedir; cerrar; (thwart) estorbar; (hinder) dificultar, embarazar; (the traffic) obstruir, atascar. —*vi* estorbar. **to become obstructed,** obstruirse, cerrarse

obstruction /əb'strʌkʃən/ *n* obstrucción,

f; estorbo, obstáculo, *m*. **to cause a street o.,** obstruir el tráfico

obtain /əb'tein/ *vt* obtener, conseguir, lograr; recibir; (by threats) arrancar. —*vi* estar en boga, estar en vigor, predominar. **to o. on false pretences,** conseguir por engaño

obtainable /əb'teinəbəl/ *a* asequible, alcanzable. **easily o.,** fácil a obtener

obtrude /əb'trud/ *vt* imponer

obtrusion /əb'truʒən/ *n* imposición, *f*; importunidad, *f*

obtrusive /əb'trusɪv/ *a* importuno; entremetido; pretencioso

obtuse /əb'tus/ *a* (blunt) obtuso, romo; (stupid) estúpido, torpe, lerdo. **o. angle,** obtusángulo, *m*

obtuseness /əb'tusnɪs/ *n* (bluntness) embotamiento, *m*; (stupidity) estupidez, torpeza, *f*

obverse / *a* ɒb'vɜrs; *n.* 'ɒbvɜrs/ *a* del anverso. —*n* anverso, *m*

obviate /'ɒbviˌeit/ *vt* obviar, evitar

obvious /'ɒbviəs/ *a* evidente, manifiesto, patente, obvio, aparente, transparente; poco sutil

obviously /'ɒbviəsli/ *adv* evidentemente, patentemente

occasion /ə'keiʒən/ *n* ocasión, *f*; oportunidad, *f*, momento oportuno, tiempo propicio, *m*; (reason) motivo, origen, *m*, causa, razón, *f*; (need) necesidad, *f*. —*vt* ocasionar, causar, producir. **as o. demands,** cuando las circunstancias lo exigen, en caso necesario. **for the o.,** para la ocasión. **on one o.,** una vez. **on the o. of,** en la ocasión de. **on that o.,** en tal ocasión, en aquella ocasión. **He has given me no o. to say so,** No me ha dado motivos de decirlo. **There is no o. for it,** No hay necesidad para ello. **to have o. to,** haber de, tener que, necesitar. **to lose no o.,** no perder ripio (or oportunidad). **to rise to the o.,** estar al nivel de las circunstancias. **to take this o.,** aprovechar esta oportunidad

occasional /ə'keiʒənl/ *a* (occurring at times) de vez en cuando, intermitente; poco frecuente, infrecuente; (of verse) de ocasión. **o. table,** mesilla, *f*

occasionally /ə'keiʒənli/ *adv* de vez en cuando

occlude /ə'klud/ *vt* obstruir, cerrar; *Med.* ocluir; *Chem.* absorber

occlusion /ə'kluʒən/ *n* cerramiento, *m*; *Med.* oclusión, *f*; *Chem.* absorción de gases, *f*

occult /ə'kʌlt/ *a* oculto, escondido, misterioso; mágico. **o. sciences,** creencias ocultas, *f pl*

occupancy /'ɒkyəpənsi/ *n* ocupación, posesión, *f*; (tenancy) tenencia, *f*

occupant /'ɒkyəpənt/ *n* habitante, *mf*; ocupante, *mf*; (tenant) inquilino (-na)

occupation /ˌɒkyə'peiʃən/ *n* ocupación *f*; (tenure) inquilinato, *m*, tenencia, *f*; (work) trabajo, quehacer, *m*, labor, *f*;

(employment) empleo, oficio, *m;* profesión, *f*

occupational /ˌɒkjəˈpeiʃənl/ *a* de oficio. **o. disease,** enfermedad profesional, *f*

occupier /ˈɒkjəˌpaiər/ *n* ocupante, *mf,* inquilino (-na)

occupy /ˈɒkjəˌpai/ *vt* ocupar; (live in) vivir en, habitar; (time) emplear, pasar; (take over) apoderarse de, ocupar. **to o. oneself in** or **with,** ocuparse en, ocuparse con. **to be occupied in** or **with,** estar ocupado con, ocuparse en

occur /əˈkɜr/ *vi* (happen) suceder, tener lugar, acaecer; (exist) encontrarse, existir; (of ideas) ocurrirse, venirse. **to o. to one's mind,** venírsele a las mientes. **to o. again,** volver a suceder, ocurrir de nuevo. **An idea occurred to her,** Se le ocurrió una idea

occurrence /əˈkɜrəns/ *n* ocurrencia, *f;* incidente, suceso, acontecimiento, *m.* **to be of frequent o.,** ocurrir con frecuencia, acontecer a menudo

ocean /ˈoʊʃən/ *n* océano, *m; Fig.* mar, abundancia, *f.* **o.-going vessel,** buque de alta mar, *m*

Oceania /ˌoʊʃiˈæniə/ el Mundo Novísmo, *m*

octagon /ˈɒktəˌgɒn/ *n* octágono, *m*

octave /ˈɒktiv/ *n* (*Eccl.* metrics, *Mus.*) octava, *f*

octavo /ɒkˈteivou, -ˈtɑ-/ *n Print.* libro, etc. en octavo (8°), *m.* **in o.,** en octavo. **large o.,** octavo mayor, *m.* **small o.,** octavo menor, *m*

octet /ɒkˈtet/ *n Mus.* octeto, *m*

October /ɒkˈtoubər/ *n* octubre, *m,* 2 October 1996, el segundo (2°) de octubre de mil novecientos noventa y seis

octogenarian /ˌɒktədʒəˈnɛəriən/ *a and n* octogenario (-ia)

octopus /ˈɒktəpəs/ *n* pulpo, *m*

ocular /ˈɒkyələr/ *a* ocular, visual. —*n* ocular, *m*

oculist /ˈɒkyəlɪst/ *n* oculista, *mf*

odd /ɒd/ *a* (of numbers) impar; (of volumes, etc.) suelto; (strange) raro, curioso, extraño, extravagante; (casual) casual, accidental; (extra) y pico, y tantos, sobrante; (of gloves, etc.) sin pareja. **at odd moments,** en momentos de ocio. **at odd times,** de vez en cuando. **thirty odd,** treinta y pico. **odd number,** número impare, *m.* **odd or even,** pares o impares. **odd trick,** (at cards) una baza más

oddity /ˈɒditi/ *n* excentricidad, rareza, extravagancia, *f;* (person) ente singular, *m;* (curio) objeto curioso, *m,* antigüedad, *f*

oddly /ˈɒdli/ *adv* singularmente

odds /ɒdz/ *n pl* diferencia, desigualdad, *f;* (superiority) ventaja, superioridad, *f;* (quarrel) disputa, riña, *f.* **The o. are that...,** Lo más probable es que... **to fight against dreadful o.,** luchar contra fuerzas muy superiores. **o. and ends,**

(remains) sobras y picos, *f pl;* (trifles) ñaques, *m pl,* chucherías, *f pl*

odious /ˈoudiəs/ *a* odioso, detestable, aborrecible, repugnante

odium /ˈoudiəm/ *n* odio, *m*

odor /ˈoudər/ *n* olor, *m,* (fragrance) perfume, aroma, *m,* fragancia, *f; Fig.* sospecha, *f.* **in bad o.,** *Fig.* en disfavor. **o. of sanctity,** olor de santidad, *m*

odorless /ˈoudərlɪs/ *a* inodoro

odorous /ˈoudərəs/ *a* fragante, oloroso

odyssey /ˈɒdəsi/ *n* odisea, *f*

of /əv/ *prep.* **of** has many idiomatic translations which are given as far as possible under the heading of the word concerned. It is also not translated. **I robbed him of his reward,** Le robé su recompensa. **I was thinking of you,** Pensaba en tí. **It was very good of you to...,** Vd. ha tenido mucha bondad de... **Your naming of the child Mary,** El que Vd. haya dado el nombre de María al niño. **29th of Sept., 1936,** el 29 de septiembre de 1936. **Of course!** ¡Claro está! ¡Ya lo creo! ¡Naturalmente! **of late,** últimamente. **of the** (before *m, sing*) del; (before *f, sing*) de la; (before *m pl*) de los; (before *f pl*) de las. **to dream of,** soñar con. **to smell of,** oler a tener olor de. **to taste of, etc.,** saber a, tener gusto de.

off /ɔf/ *prep* de; fuera de; cerca de; desde; *Naut.* a la altura de. **from off,** de. **Take your gloves off the table!** ¡Quítate los guantes de la mesa! **The wheel was off the car,** La rueda se había desprendido del coche. **to be off duty,** no estar de servicio; *Mil.* no estar de guardia. **to lunch off cold meat,** almorzar de carne fría. **off one's head,** chiflado

off /ɔf/ *a* (contrasted with near) de la derecha, derecho; (unlikely) improbable, remoto. —*adv* (with intransitive verbs of motion) se (e.g. *He has gone off,* Se ha marchado); (contrasted with on) de (e.g. *He has fallen off the horse,* Ha caído del caballo); (of place at a distance) lejos, a distancia de; (of time) generally a verb is used (e.g. *The wedding is three months off,* Faltan tres meses para la boda); (completely) enteramente. **Off** is often not translated in Sp. (e.g. *to put off,* aplazar, *to cut off,* cortar). **day off,** día libre, día de asueto, *m.* **How far off is the house from here? The house is five miles off.** ¿Cuántas millas está la casa de aquí? La casa está a cinco millas de aquí. **His hat is off,** Está sin sombrero, Se ha quitado el sombrero. **The cover is off,** La cubierta está quitada. **The party is off,** Se ha anulado la reunión. **6% off,** un descuento de seis por ciento. —*interj* Off **with you!** ¡Márchate! ¡Fuera! **off and on,** de, de vez en cuando, espasmódicamente. **off color,** (ill) malucho; (of jokes) verde. **off season,** estación muerta, *f.* **off-shore,** a vista de tierra. **off-stage,** entre bastidores

offal /ˈɔfəl/ *n* (butchers') menudencias, *f*

pl, asadura, *f,* menudos, despojos, *m pl;* desperdicio, *m*

offend /ə'fend/ *vt* ofender; agraviar, insultar; herir; desagradar, disgustar; *vi* ofender, pecar. **to be offended,** resentirse, insultarse. **This offends my sense of justice,** Esto ofende mi sentimiento de justicia. **to o. against,** pecar contra; violar

offender /ə'fendər/ *n* delincuente, *mf;* agraviador (-ra), pecador (-ra), transgresor (-ra). **old o.,** *Law.* criminal inveterado, *m*

offense /ə'fens/ *n* ofensa, transgresión, violación, *f;* pecado, *m; Law.* delito, crimen, *m;* (insult) agravio, *m,* afrenta, *f.* **the first o.,** el primer delito, *m.* **fresh o.,** nuevo delito, *m.* **political o.,** crimen político, *m.* **technical o.,** *Law.* cuasidelito, *m.* **to commit an o. against,** ofender contra. **to take o.,** resentirse, darse por ofendido

offensive /ə'fensɪv/ *a* ofensivo, desagradable, repugnante; (insulting) injurioso, agraviador, agresivo. —*n Mil.* ofensiva, *f.* **to take the o.,** tomar la ofensiva

offer /'ɔfər/ *n* oferta, *f;* ofrecimiento, *m;* (of help) promesa, *f;* proposición, *f; Com.* oferta, *f.* —*vt* ofrecer; prometer; (opportunities, etc.) deparar, brindar; tributar. —*vi* ofrecerse, ocurrir, surgir. **to o. up,** ofrecer; inmolar, sacrificar. **He did not offer to go,** No hizo además de marcharse. **to o. resistance,** oponer resistencia. **o. of marriage,** oferta de matrimonio, *f*

offhand /'ɔf'hænd/ *a* sin preparación, de repente; (casual) casual, despreocupado; (discourteous) brusco, descortés

offhandedly /'ɔf'hændɪdli/ *adv* sin preparación, espontáneamente; negligentemente; bruscamente

office /'ɔfɪs/ *n* oficina, *m;* (post) cargo, puesto, destino, *m;* (state department) ministerio, *m;* (of a Cabinet minister) cartera, *f;* (room) oficina, *f;* despacho, escritorio, *m;* (of a newspaper) redacción, *f;* (lawyer's) bufete, *m;* departamento, *m; Eccl.* oficio, *m pl.* **offices,** negocio, *m;* oficinas, *f pl;* (prayers) rezos, *m pl; Eccl.* oficios, *m pl.* **domestic offices,** dependencias, *f pl.* **good offices,** *Fig.* buenos oficios, *m pl.* **head o.,** casa central, oficina principal, *f.* **private o.,** despacho particular, *m.* **to be in o.,** estar en el poder. **o.-bearer,** miembro de la junta, *m;* funcionario, *m.* **o.-boy,** mozo de oficina, *m.* **o. employee,** oficinista, *mf.* **o. hours,** horas de oficina, *f pl;* (professions) horas de consulta, *f pl.* **o.-seeker,** aspirante, *m;* pretendiente, *m.* **o: work,** trabajo de oficina, *m*

officer /'ɔfəsər/ *n* oficial, funcionario, *m;* (police) agente de policía, *m;* (of the Church) dignatario, *m; (Mil. Nav. Aer.)* oficial, *m.* —*vt* mandar. **commissioned o.,** oficial, *m.* **non-commissioned o.,** oficial subalterno, *m.* **to be well officered,**

tener buena oficialidad. **Officers' Training Corps,** Escuela de Oficiales, *f*

office worker *n* oficinista, *mf*

official /ə'fɪʃəl/ *a* oficial; autorizado; ceremonioso, grave. —*n* funcionario, *m;* oficial público, *m.* **high o.,** funcionario importante. *m.* **o. mourning,** duelo oficial, *m.* **o. receiver,** fiscal de quiebras, *m*

officiate /ə'fɪʃi,eit/ *vi* celebrar; oficiar; funcionar

officious /ə'fɪʃəs/ *a* oficioso, entremetido

offing /'ɔfɪŋ/ *n Naut.* mar afuera, *m.* **in the o.,** cerca

off season fuera de temporada

offset /*n* 'ɔf,set; *v.* ,ɔf'set/ *n* compensación, *f, vt* compensar, neutralizar

offshoot /'ɔf,ʃut/ *n* renuevo, vástago, *m*

offside /'ɔf'said/ *a* (of a car) del lado derecho (or izquierda); *Sports.* fuera de juego

offspring /'ɔf,sprɪŋ/ *n* vástago, *m;* descendiente, *mf;* prole, *f;* hijos, *m pl*

often /'ɔfən/ *adv* a menudo, mucho, con frecuencia, frecuentemente, muchas veces. **as o. as,** tan a menudo como, siempre que. **as o. as not,** no pocas veces. **How o.?** ¿Cuántas veces? **It is not o. that...,** No ocurre con frecuencia que... **so o.,** tantas veces, con frecuencia. **Do you go there o.?** ¿Va Vd. allí con frecuencia (or frecuentemente)? **Not o.,** Voy rara vez allá

ogle /'ougəl/ *vt and vi* comer(se) con los ojos (a), ojear, guiñar el ojo (a). —*n* ojeada, *f,* guiño, *m*

ogling /'ouglɪŋ/ *n* guiño, *m,* ojeada, *f*

ogre /'ougər/ *n* ogro, *m*

oh! /ou/ *interj* ¡o! **O no!** ¡Ca! ¡Claro que no!

oil /ɔil/ *n* aceite, *m;* petróleo, *m;* óleo, *m.* —*vt* aceitar, engrasar; olear, ungir, untar; (bribe) sobornar, untar la mano; *Fig.* suavizar. —*a* aceitero; petrolero. **to pour oil on troubled waters,** echar aceite sobre aguas turbulentas. **to strike oil,** encontrar un pozo de petróleo; *Fig.* encontrar un filón. **crude oil,** petróleo bruto, *m.* **heavy oil,** aceite pesado, *m.* **thin oil,** aceite ligero, *m. Art.* **in oils,** al óleo. **oil-bearing,** petrolífero. **oil-box,** engrasador, *m.* **oil-burner,** quemador de petróleo, *m.* **oil-can,** aceitera, *f.* **oil-colors,** pinturas al óleo, *f pl.* **oil field,** yacimiento petrolífero, campo de petróleo, *m.* **oil-filter,** separador de aceite, *m.* **oil-gauge,** nivel de aceite, *m.* **oil lamp,** velón, candil, quinqué, *m.* **oil of turpentine,** aceite de trementina, aguarrás, *m.* esencia de trementina, *f.* **oil-painting,** pintura al óleo, *f.* **oil pipeline,** oleoducto, *m.* **oil shop,** aceitería, *f.* **oil-silk,** encerado, *m.* **oil stove,** estufa de petróleo, *f.* **oil tanker,** *Naut.* petrolero, *m.* **oil-well,** pozo de petróleo, *m*

oilcloth /'ɔil,klɔθ/ *n* hule, *m;* linóleo, *m*

oilskin /'ɔil,skɪn/ *n* encerado, *m*

oily /'ɔili/ *a* aceitoso, grasiento

ointment /'ɔintmənt/ n ungüento, m, pomada, f

old /ould/ a viejo; antiguo, anciano; (of wines, etc.) añejo; (worn out) usado, gastado; (inveterate) arraigado, inveterado. **How old are you?** ¿Cuántos años tiene usted? **to be sixteen years old,** tener dieciséis años. **He is old enough to know his own mind,** Tiene bastante edad para saber lo que quiere. **to grow old,** envejecer. **to remain an old maid,** quedar soltera; Inf. quedarse para vestir imágenes. **of old,** antiguamente. **prematurely old,** revejido averiado. **old age,** vejez, senectud, f. **old bachelor,** solterón, m. **old clothes,** ropa vieja (or usada), ropa de segunda mano, f. **old-clothes dealer,** ropavejero (-ra). **old-clothes shop,** ropavejería, f. **old-established,** viejo. **old-fashioned,** pasado de moda, viejo, (of people) chapado a la antigua. **old lady,** anciana, dama vieja, f. **old-looking,** de aspecto viejo, avejentado. **old maid,** solterona, f. **old-maidish,** remilgado. **old man,** viejo, m; Theat. barba, m. **old salt,** lobo de mar, m. **Old Testament,** Antiguo Testamento, m. **old wives' tale,** cuento de viejas, m. **old woman,** vieja, f. **Old World,** Viejo Mundo, mundo antiguo, m

old-age home /'ould 'eidʒ/ n asilo de ancianos, m

olden /'ouldən/ a antiguo. **o. days,** días pasados, m pl

older /'ouldər/ a compar más viejo, mayor. **The older the madder,** A la vejez viruelas

old hat n viejo conocido

oldish /'ouldiʃ/ a bastante viejo, de cierta edad

olfactory /ɒl'fæktəri/ a olfatorio, olfativo

olive /'ɒlɪv/ n (tree) olivo, m; (fruit) aceituna, oliva, f, a aceitunado. **wild o. tree,** acebuche, m. **o.-complexioned,** con tez aceitunada. **o. green,** verde oliva, m. **o. grove,** olivar, m. **o. oil,** aceite de oliva, m

olympian /ə'lɪmpiən/ a olímpico

olympic /ə'lɪmpɪk/ a olímpico. **o. games,** juegos olímpicos, m pl

olympus /ə'lɪmpəs/ n olimpo, m

omelet /'ɒmlɪt/ n tortilla, f. **sweet o.,** tortilla dulce, f

omen /'oumən/ n pronóstico, presagio, agüero, m, vt agorar, anunciar

ominous /'ɒmənəs/ a ominoso, azaroso, siniestro, amenazante

omission /ou'mɪʃən/ n omisión, f; olvido, descuido, m; supresión, f

omit /ou'mɪt/ vt omitir; olvidar, descuidar; (suppress) suprimir, excluir, callar, dejar a un lado

omitting /ou'mɪtɪŋ/ pres part salvo, excepto

omnibus /'ɒmnə,bʌs/ n ómnibus, autobús, m. **o. conductor,** cobrador de autobús, m. **o. driver,** conductor de autobús, m. **o. route,** trayecto de autobús, m. **o.**

service, servicio de autobuses, m. **o. volume,** volumen de obras coleccionadas, m

omnipotent /ɒm'nɪpətənt/ a omnipotente, todopoderoso

omniscience /ɒm'nɪʃəns/ n omnisciencia, f

omniscient /ɒm'nɪʃənt/ a omniscio, omnisciente

omnivorous /ɒm'nɪvərəs/ a omnívoro

on /ɒn/ prep (upon) sobre, en, encima de; (concerning) de, acerca de, sobre; (against) contra; (after) después; (according to) según; (with gerund) en; (with infin.) al; (at) a; (connected with, employed in) de; (by means of) por, mediante; (near to) cerca de, sobre; (into) en. Untranslated before days of week, dates of month or time of day (e.g. on Monday, el lunes. on Friday afternoons, los viernes por la tarde). **She has a bracelet on her wrist,** Tiene una pulsera en la muñeca. **He will retire on a good income,** Se jubilará con una buena renta. **on my uncle's death,** después de la muerte (or a muerte) de mi tío, al morir. **On seeing them, he stopped,** Al verles se paró. **on leave,** con licencia, en uso de licencia. **on the next page,** en la página siguiente. **on this occasion,** en esta ocasión. **on the other hand,** en cambio. **on second thoughts,** luego de pensarlo bien. **on the way,** en camino. **on one side,** a un lado. **on the left,** a la izquierda. **on time,** a tiempo. **on my honor,** bajo palabra de honor. **on pain of death,** so pena de muerte, bajo pena de muerte. **on an average,** por término medio. **on his part,** por su parte. **on and after,** desde, a partir de. **on credit,** de fiado. **on fire,** ardiendo, en llamas. **on foot,** a pie. **on purpose,** a propósito; con intención. **on,** adv puesto (e.g. She has her gloves on, Tiene los guantes puestos); (forward) adelante, hacia adelante; (continue, with a verb) seguir, continuar (e.g. He went on talking, Siguió hablando). Often **on** is included in Sp. verb (e.g. The new play is on, Se ha estrenado la nueva comedia. The fight is on, Ya ha empezado la lucha). **On!** interj ¡Adelante! **and so on,** y así sucesivamente. **to have on,** llevar puesto. **on and off,** de vez en cuando. **on and on,** sin cesar

once /wʌns/ adv una vez; (formerly) en otro tiempo, antiguamente; conjunc si (e.g. O. you give him the opportunity, Si le das la oportunidad). **all at o.,** todo junto, a un mismo tiempo; simultáneamente; (suddenly) súbitamente, de repente. **at o.,** en seguida, inmediatamente. **for o.,** por una vez. **more than o.,** más de una vez. **not o.,** ni siquiera una vez. **o. before,** una vez antes. **o. and for all,** una vez para siempre; por última vez. **o. in a while,** de vez en cuando. **o. more,** otra vez. **o. or twice,** una vez o dos, algunas veces. **o. too often,** una vez demasiado. **O. upon a time,** En tiempos pasados, En tiempos de Maricastaña; (as beginning of a story) Érase una vez, Había una vez, Hubo una vez

once in a blue moon a cada muerte de un obispo

one /wʌn/ *a* un, uno, una; (first) primero; (single) único, solo; (indifferent) igual, indiferente; (some, certain) algún, cierto, un (e.g. *one day*, cierto día). —*n* uno; (hour) la una; (of age) un año. Often not translated in Sp. (e.g. *I shall take the blue one*, Tomaré el azul). —*pron* se; uno. **one's**, su, de uno (e.g. *one's work*, el trabajo de uno). **I for one do not think so,** Yo por uno no lo creo. **It is all one,** Es igual, No hace diferencia alguna. **only one,** un solo. **that one,** ése, *m*, ésa, *f*, eso, *neut*. **this one,** éste, *m*, ésta, *f*, esto, *neut*. **these ones,** éstos, etc. **those ones,** ésos, etc. **the one,** el (que), *m*, la (que), *f*. **with one accord,** unánimemente. **one and all,** todos. **one another,** se, uno a otro, mutuamente. **one by one,** uno a uno. **one day,** un día; un día de éstos, algún día. **one-eyed,** tuerto. **one-handed,** manco. **one-sided,** parcial. **one-way street,** calle de dirección única, *f*. **one-way traffic,** tráfico en una sola dirección, *m*

onerous /ˈɒnərəs/ *a* oneroso, pesado, molesto, gravoso

oneself /wʌnˈself/ *pron* se, uno mismo (una misma); (after prep.) sí mismo, sí. **It must be done by o.,** Uno mismo ha de hacerlo

onion /ˈʌnjən/ *n* cebolla, *f*. **string of onions,** ristra de cebollas, *f*. **young o.,** babosa, *f*. **o. bed,** cebollar, *m*. **o. seed,** cebollino, *m*. **o. seller,** cebollero (-ra)

on-line /ˈɒnˌlain, ˈɒn-/ *a* conectado, en línea

onlooker /ˈɒnˌlʊkər/ *n* espectado (-ra), observador (-ra); testigo, *mf*

only /ˈounli/ *a* único, solo. —*adv* únicamente, sólo; no... más (que), tan sólo; con la excepción de, salvo. —*conjunc* pero, salvo (que), si no fuera (que). **I shall o. give you three,** No te daré más de tres. **The o. thing one can do,** Lo único que se puede hacer. **I o. wished to see her,** Quería verla nada más. **if o.,** ¡ojalá (que)! **not o....,** no sólo... **o.-begotten,** *a* unigénito. **o. child,** hijo (-ja) único (-ca)

onrush /ˈɒnˌrʌʃ/ *n* asalto, ataque, acometimiento, *m*, acometida, embestida, *f*; (of water, etc.) acceso, *m*; torrente, *m*, corriente, *f*

onset /ˈɒnˌset/ *n* ataque, *m*, acometida, *f*; (beginning) principio, *m*. **at the first o.,** al primer ímpetu

onslaught /ˈɒnˌslɔt/ *n* asalto, ataque, *m*

onus /ˈounəs/ *n* responsabilidad, *f*. **o. of proof,** obligación de probar, *f*

onward /ˈɒnwərd/ *a* progresivo. —*adv* adelante, hacia adelante; (as a command) ¡Adelante!

onyx /ˈɒniks/ *n Mineral.* ónice, *m*

ooze /uz/ *n* légamo, limo, fango, *m*, lama, *f*. —*vi* exudar, rezumarse; manar; *vt* sudar. **to o. satisfaction,** caérsele (a uno) la baba. **to o. away,** (of money, etc.) desaparecer, volar. **to o. out,** (news) divulgarse

opacity /ouˈpæsɪti/ *n* opacidad, *f*

opal /ˈoupəl/ *n* ópalo, *m*

opaque /ouˈpeik/ *a* opaco

op. cit. /ˈɒpˈsit/ (opere citato) obra cit. (obra citada)

open /ˈoupən/ *vt* abrir; (a package) desempaquetar, desenvolver; (remove lid) destapar; (unfold) desplegar; (inaugurate) inaugurar; iniciar, empezar; establecer; (an abscess) cortar; (with arms, heart, eyes) abrir; (with mind, thought) descubrir, revelar; (make accessible) franquear, hacer accesible; (tear) romper; *vi* abrirse; empezar, comenzar; (of a view, etc.) aparecer, extenderse; inaugurarse; (of a career, etc.) prepararse. **to o. fire against,** abrir el fuego contra. **to o. into,** comunicar con, salir a. **to o. into each other,** (of rooms) comunicarse. **to o. on,** mirar a, dar a, caer a. **to o. out,** *vt* abrir; desplegar; revelar. —*vi* extenderse; revelarse. **to o. the eyes of,** *Fig.* desengañar, desilusionar. **to o. up,** abrir; explorar, hacer accesible; *Fig. Inf.* desabrocharse. **to o. with** or **by,** empezar con

open /ˈoupən/ *a* abierto; descubierto; expuesto; (unfenced) descercado; (not private) público; libre; (unfolded) desplegado, extendido; (persuasible) receptivo; no resuelto, pendiente; (frank) franco, candoroso; (with sea) alto; (liberal) generoso, hospitalario; sin prejuicios; *Com.* abierto, pendiente; sin defensa; (of weather) despejado; (of a letter) sin sellar; (without a lid) destapado; (well-known) manifiesto, bien conocido. —*n* aire libre, *m*. **in the o.,** al descubierto. **in the o. air,** al aire libre, al raso, a cielo abierto. **to break o.,** forzar. **to cut o.,** abrir de un tajo, cortar. **to leave o.,** dejar abierto. **wide o.,** muy abierto; (of doors) de par en par. **o. boat,** barco descubierto, *m*. **o. car,** coche abierto, *m*. **o. carriage,** carruaje descubierto, *m*. **o. cast,** *Mineral.* roza abierta, *f*. **o.-eyed,** con los ojos abiertos. **o.-handed,** generoso, dadivoso. **o. letter,** carta abierta, *f*. **o.-minded,** imparcial. **o.-mouthed,** con la boca abierta, boquiabierto. **o. question,** cuestión por decidir, cuestión discutible, *f*. **o. secret,** secreto a voces, *m*. **o. sea,** alta mar, *f*. **o. town,** ciudad abierta, *f*. **o. tramcar,** jardinera, *f*. **o. truck,** vagoneta, *f*. **o.-work,** *Sew.* calado, enrejado, *m*

opener /ˈoupənər/ *n* abridor, *m*

opening /ˈoupənɪŋ/ *n* abertura, brecha, *f*; orificio, *m*; inauguración, apertura, *f*; principio, *m*; (chance) oportunidad, *f*; (employment) puesto, *m*. **o. price,** *Com.* (on Exchange) precio de apertura, *m*, primer curso *m*

opera /ˈɒpərə/ *n* ópera, *f*. **comic o.,** zarzuela, f. **o.-cloak,** abrigo de noche, m. **o. -glasses,** gemelos de teatro, m pl. **o.-hat,** clac, m. **o.-house,** teatro de la ópera, m. **o. singer,** cantante de ópera, operista, mf

operate /'ɒpə,reit/ vi funcionar, trabajar; obrar; (with on, upon) producir efecto sobre; influir; Surg. operar; (on Exchange) especular, jugar a la bolsa; vt hacer funcionar, manejar; mover, impulsar; dirigir

operatic /,ɒpə'rætɪk/ a de ópera, operístico

operating /'ɒpə,reitɪŋ/ a (of surgeons) operante; de operación. **o. table,** mesa de operaciones, f. **o. theater,** anfiteatro, m; sala de operaciones, f

operation /,ɒpə'reiʃən/ n funcionamiento, m, acción, f; Surg. intervención quirúrgica, operación, f; (difference) maniobra, f; manipulación, f. **to come into o.,** ponerse en práctica; hacerse efectivo. **to continue in o.,** (laws) seguir en vigor. **to perform an o.,** Surg. operar, praticar una intervención quirúrgica; hacer una maniobra. **to put into o.,** poner en práctica

operative /'ɒpərətɪv/ a operativo, activo. —n operario (-ia), obrero (-ra). **to become o.,** tener efecto

operator /'ɒpə,reitər/ n operario (-ia); (telephone) telefonista, mf; (machines, engines) maquinista, mf; Surg. operador, m

operetta /,ɒpə'rɛtə/ n opereta, f

ophthalmologist /,ɒfθəl'mɒlədʒɪst/ n oftalmólogo, m

ophthalmology /,ɒfθəl'mɒlədʒi/ n oftalmología, f

opine /ou'pain/ vi and vt opinar, creer

opinion /ə'pinyən/ n opinión, f, parecer, juicio, m; concepto, m, idea, f. **in my o.,** según mi parecer. **to be of the o. that,** ser de la opinión que, opinar que. **to be of the same o.,** estar de acuerdo, concurrir. **public o.,** opinión (or voz) pública, f.

opinionated /ə'pinyə,neitɪd/ a terco, obstinado

opium /'oupiəm/ n opio, m. **o. addict,** opiónamo (-ma). **o. den,** fumadero de opio, m. **o. eater,** mascador de opio, opiófago, m. **o. smoker,** fumador (-ra) de opio

opponent /ə'pounənt/ n antagonista, mf, enemigo (-ga); contrario (-ia), adversario (-ia), competidor (-ra)

opportune /,ɒpər'tun/ a oportuno, tempestivo, conveniente, a propósito. **to be o.,** venir al caso. **o. moment,** momento oportuno, m; hora propicia, f

opportunist /,ɒpər'tunɪst/ n oportunista, mf

opportunity /,ɒpər'tunɪti/ n oportunidad, ocasión, posibilidad, f. **to give an o. for,** dar margen para. **to open new opportunities,** abrir nuevos horizontes. **to take the o.,** tomar la oportunidad

oppose /ə'pouz/ vt (counterbalance) oponer, contrarrestar; combatir; hacer

frente (a), contrariar, pugnar contra, oponerse (a)

opposed (to) /ə'pouzd/ a opuesto a, enemigo de, contra

opposing /ə'pouzɪŋ/ a opuesto; enemigo, contrario

opposite /'ɒpəzɪt/ a (facing) de cara a, frente a, del otro lado de; opuesto; (antagonistic) contrario, antagónico; otro, diferente. —n contraria, f, lo opuesto; antagonista, mf; adversario (-ia). **the o. sex,** el otro sexo. **o. leaves,** Bot. hojas opuestas, f pl. **o. to,** frente a; distinto de

opposition /,ɒpə'zɪʃən/ n oposición, f; (obstacle) estorbo, impedimento, m, dificultad, f; resistencia, hostilidad, f; (Astron. Polit.) oposición, f; (difference) contraste, m, diferencia, f. **—a** de la oposición. **in o.,** en oposición; Polit. en la oposición. **to be in o.,** estar en oposición; Polit. ser de la oposición, estar en la oposición

oppress /ə'prɛs/ vt oprimir, tiranizar, subyugar, apremiar; (of moral causes) abrumar, agobiar, desanimar; (of heat, etc.) ahogar

oppression /ə'prɛʃən/ n opresión, tiranía, crueldad, f; (moral) agobio, sufrimiento, m, ansia, f; (difficulty in breathing) sofocación, f, ahogo, m

oppressive /ə'prɛsɪv/ a opresivo, tiránico, cruel; (taxes, etc.) gravoso; (of heat) sofocante, asfixiante; agobiador, abrumador

oppressor /ə'prɛsər/ n opresor (-ra), subyugador (-ra), tirano (-na)

opprobrious /ə'proubriəs/ a oprobioso, vituperioso; infame

opt /ɒpt/ vi optar, escoger, elegir

optician /ɒp'tɪʃən/ n óptico, m

optics /'ɒptɪks/ n óptica, f

optimist /'ɒptəmɪst/ n optimista, mf

optimistic /,ɒptə'mɪstɪk/ a optimista

optimum /'ɒptəməm/ n lo óptimo; (used as adjective) óptimo

option /'ɒpʃən/ n opción, f, (all meanings)

optional /'ɒpʃənḷ/ a discrecional, facultativo

opulence /'ɒpyələns/ n opulencia, riqueza, magnificencia, f; (abundance) abundancia, copia, f

opulent /'ɒpyələnt/ a opulento, rico, acaudalado; abundante

opus /'oupəs/ n obra, composición, f

or /ɔr/ conjunc o; (before a word beginning with o or ho) u; (negative) ni. **—n** Herald. oro, m. **an hour or so,** una hora más o menos, alrededor de una hora. **either... or,** o... o. **or else,** o bien. **whether... or,** que... que, siquiera... siquiera, ya... ya. **without... or,** sin... ni

oracle /'ɔrəkəl/ n oráculo, m

oracular /ɔ'rækyələr/ a profético, vatídico; ambiguo, misterioso, sibilino; dogmático, magistral

oral /'ɔrəl/ a verbal, hablado; Anat. oral, bucal

oral cavity *n* cavidad bucal, *f*

orange /'ɔrɪndʒ/ *n* (tree) naranjo, *m*; (fruit) naranja, *f*; **bitter o.,** naranja amarga, *f*; **blood o.,** naranja dulce, *f*; **tangerine o.,** naranja mandarina, *f*. **o. blossom,** azahar, *m*. **o. color,** color de naranja, *m*. **o.-colored,** de color de naranja, anaranjado. **o.-flower water,** agua de azahar, *f*. **o. grove,** naranjal, *m*. **o. grower** (or **seller**), naranjero (-ra). **o. peel,** piel de naranja, *f*. **o.-stick,** (for nails) limpiauñas, *m*

orangeade /,ɔrɪndʒ'eid/ *n* naranjada, *f*; (mineral water) gaseosa, *f*

oration /ɔ'reiʃən/ *n* oración, declamación, *f*, discurso, *m*

orator /'ɔrətər/ *n* orador (-ra), declamador (-ra)

oratorical /,ɔrə'tɔrɪkəl/ *a* oratorio, declamatorio, retórico

oratorio /,ɔrə'tɔri,ou/ *n* *Mus.* oratorio, *m*

oratory /'ɔrə,tɔri/ *n* oratoria, elocuencia, *f*; *Eccl.* oratorio, *m*, capilla, *f*

orb /ɔrb/ *n* orbe, *m*; esfera, *f*, globo, *m*; astro, *m*; *Poet.* ojo, *m*

orbit /'ɔrbɪt/ *n* *Astron.* órbita, *f*; *Anat.* órbita, cuenca del ojo, *f*

orchard /'ɔrtʃərd/ *n* huerto, vergel, *m*; (especially of apples) pomar, *m*

orchestra /'ɔrkəstrə/ *n* orquesta, *f*. **with full o.,** con gran orquesta. *Theat.* **o. seat, o. stall,** butaca de piatea, *f*

orchestral /ɔr'kɛstrəl/ *a* orquestal, instrumental

orchestrate /'ɔrkə,streit/ *vt* orquestar, instrumentar

orchid /'ɔrkɪd/ *n* orquídea, *f*

ordain /ɔr'dein/ *vt* mandar, disponer, decretar; *Eccl.* ordenar. **to be ordained as,** *Eccl.* ordenarse de

ordeal /ɔr'dil/ *n* *Hist.* ordalías, *f pl*; prueba severa, *f*

order /'ɔrdər/ *n* (most meanings) orden, *m*; (command) precepto, mandamiento, decreto, *m*; orden, *f*; (rule) regla, *f*; (for money) libranza postal, *f*; (for goods) pedido, encargo, *m*; (arrangement) método, arreglo, *m*, clasificación, *f*; (condition) estado, *m*; *Archit.* estilo, *m*; (*Zool. Bot.*) orden, *m*; (sort) clase, especie, *f*; (rank) clase social, *f*; *Eccl.* orden, *f*; (badge) condecoración, insignia, *f*; (association) sociedad, asociación, compañía, *f*; (to view a house, etc.) permiso, *m*; (series) serie, *f*. **His liver is out of o.,** No está bién del hígado. **in good o.,** en buen estado; arreglado. **in o.,** (alphabetical, etc.) en orden; arreglado; (parliamentary) en regla. **in o. that,** para que, a fin de que. **in o. to,** a fin de, para. **out of o.,** estropeado, descompuesto; (on a notice) No funciona; (parliamentary) fuera del orden del día. **till further o.,** hasta nueva orden. **to o.,** *Com.* por encargo especial. **to give an o.,** dar una orden; *Com.* poner un pedido. **to go out of o.,** descomponerse. **to keep in o.,** mantener en orden. **to put in o.,** poner en orden, ordenar. **to take holy orders,** tomar órdenes sagradas. **O.!** ¡Orden! **O. in Council,** orden real, *f*. **o. of knighthood,** orden de caballería, *f*. **o. of the day,** orden del día, *f*. **o. paper,** orden del día, *f*; reglamento, *m*

order /'ɔrdər/ *vt* disponer; arreglar; (command) mandar, ordenar; (request) rogar, pedir; (direct) dirigir, gobernar; *Com.* encargar, cometer; (a meal, a taxi) encargar. **I ordered them to do it,** Les mandé hacerlo. **to o. about,** mandar. **to o. back,** hacer volver, mandar que vuelva. **to o. down,** hacer bajar, pedir (a uno) que baje. **to o. in,** mandar entrar. **to o. off,** despedir, decir (a uno) que se vaya. **to o. out,** mandar salir; (the troops) hacer salir la tropa; echar. **to o. up,** mandar subir, hacer subir

orderly /'ɔrdərli/ *a* bien arreglado, metódico; aseado, en orden; (of behaviour) formal, bien disciplinado. —*n Mil.* ordenanza, *m*; ayudante de hospital *m*

ordinal /'ɔrdn̩l/ *a* and *n* ordinal *m*

ordinance /'ɔrdn̩əns/ *n* ordenanza, *f*, reglamento, *m*; *Archit.* ordenación, *f*; *Eccl.* rito, *m*

ordinarily /,ɔrdn̩'ɛərəli/ *adv* de ordinario, ordinariamente, comúnmente

ordinary /'ɔrdn̩,ɛri/ *a* (usual) corriente, común, usual, ordinario, normal; (average) mediano, mediocre; (somewhat vulgar) ordinario, vulgar. —*n Eccl.* ordinario, *m*. **out of the o.,** excepcional; poco común. **o. seaman,** marinero, *m*. **o. share,** *Com.* acción ordinaria, *f*

ore /ɔr/ *n* *Mineral.* mena, *f*, quijo, *m*

organ /'ɔrgən/ *n* (all meanings) órgano, *m*. **barrel-o.,** organillo, órgano de manubrio, *m*. **o.-blower,** entonador (-ra). **o.-grinder,** organillero (-ra). **o.-loft,** tribuna del órgano, *f*. **o.-pipe,** cañón de órgano, *m*. **o.-stop,** registro de órgano, *m*

organic /ɔr'gænɪk/ *a* orgánico. **o. chemistry,** química orgánica, *f*

organism /'ɔrgə,nɪzəm/ *n* organismo, *m*

organist /'ɔrgənɪst/ *n* organista, *mf*

organization /,ɔrgənə'zeiʃən/ *n* organización, *f*; grupo, *m*, asociación, sociedad, *f*; organismo, *m*

organize /'ɔrgə,naiz/ *vt* organizar; arreglar. —*vi* organizarse; asociarse, constituirse

orgasm /'ɔrgæzəm/ *n* *Med.* orgasmo, *m*

orgy /'ɔrdʒi/ *n* orgía, *f*

orient /'ɔriənt/ *a Poet.* naciente, oriental. —*n* Oriente, Este, *m*. **pearl of fine o.,** perla de hermoso oriente, *f*

oriental /,ɔri'ɛntl/ *a* and *n* oriental, *mf*

orientate /'ɔriən,teit/ *vt* orientar; dirigir, guiar. —*vi* mirar (or caer) hacia el este; orientarse

orifice /'ɔrəfɪs/ *n* orificio, *m*; abertura, boca, *f*

origin /'ɔrɪdʒɪn/ *n* origen, génesis, *m*; raíz, causa, *f*; principio, comienzo, *m*; (extraction) descendencia, procedencia, familia, *f*, nacimiento, *m*

original /əˈrɪdʒənl/ a original; primitivo, primero; ingenioso. —n original, m; prototipo, modelo, m. **o. sin,** pecado original, m

originality /əˌrɪdʒəˈnælɪti/ n originalidad, f

originally /əˈrɪdʒənli/ adv originalmente; al principio; antiguamente

originate /əˈrɪdʒəˌneit/ vt (produce) ocasionar, producir, suscitar, iniciar, engendrar; (create) inventar, crear. —vi originarse, surgir, nacer. **to o. in,** tener su origen en, surgir de, emanar de, venir de

originator /əˈrɪdʒəˌneitər/ n iniciador (-ra), fundador (-ra); autor (-ra), creador (-ra)

ornament /n. ˈɔrnəmənt; v. -ˌment/ n adorno, m; decoración, f; Fig. ornamento, m; (trinket) chuchería, f, n pl. **ornaments,** Eccl. ornamentos, m pl. —vt ornar, adornar, decorar, embellecer

ornamental /ˌɔrnəˈmentl/ a ornamental, decorativo

ornamentation /ˌɔrnəmənˈteiʃən/ n ornamentación, decoración, f

ornate /ɔrˈneit/ a vistoso, ornado en demasía, barroco

orphan /ˈɔrfən/ a and n huérfano (-na)

orphanage /ˈɔrfənɪdʒ/ n orfanato, hospicio, m

orthodox /ˈɔrθəˌdɒks/ a ortodoxo

orthodoxy /ˈɔrθəˌdɒksi/ n ortodoxia, f

orthographic /ˌɔrθəˈgræfɪk/ a ortográfico

orthography /ɔrˈθɒgrəfi/ n ortografía, f

orthopedic /ˌɔrθəˈpidik/ a ortopédico

orthopedics /ˌɔrθəˈpidiks/ n ortopedia, f

orthopedist /ˌɔrθəˈpidɪst/ n ortopedista, mf ortopédico (-ca)

oscillate /ˈɒsəˌleit/ vi oscilar, fluctuar; (hesitate) dudar, vacilar. —vt hacer oscilar

oscillation /ˌɒsəˈleiʃən/ n oscilación, fluctuación, vibración, f; Elec. oscilación, f

oscillator /ˈɒsəˌleitər/ n oscilador, m

osculation /ˌɒskyəˈleiʃən/ n ósculo, m

osier /ˈouʒər/ n Bot. mimbre, m, or f. **o. bed,** mimbrera, f

osmic /ˈɒzmɪk/ a Chem. ósmico

osmosis /ɒzˈmousɪs/ n (Phys. Chem.) ósmosis, f

osseous /ˈɒsiəs/ a óseo

ossify /ˈɒsəˌfai/ vt osificar; vi osificarse

osteitis /ˌɒstiˈaitɪs/ n Med. osteítis, f

ostensible /ɒˈstensəbəl/ a ostensible; aparente, engañoso, ilusorio

ostensibly /ɒˈstensəbli/ adv en apariencia, ostensiblemente

ostentation /ˌɒstenˈteiʃən/ n ostentación, f; aparato, fausto, boato, alarde, m, soberbia, f

ostentatious /ˌɒstenˈteiʃəs/ a ostentoso; aparatoso, fastuoso, rumboso

ostentatiously /ˌɒstenˈteiʃəsli/ adv con ostentación

osteomyelitis /ˌɒstiouˌmaiəˈlaitɪs/ n Med. osteomielitis, f

osteopath /ˈɒstiəˌpæθ/ n osteópata, m

osteopathy /ˌɒstiˈɒpəθi/ n osteopatía, f

ostracize /ˈɒstrəˌsaiz/ vt desterrar; excluir del trato, echar de la sociedad

ostrich /ˈɒstrɪtʃ/ n avestruz, m. **o. farm,** criadero de avestruces, m

otalgia /ouˈtældʒiə/ n Med. otalgia, f, dolor de oídos, m

other /ˈʌðər/ a otro. —pron el otro, m; la otra, f; lo otro, neut adv (with than) de otra manera que, de otro modo que; otra cosa que. **this hand, not the o.,** esta mano, no la otra. **every o. day,** un día sí y otro no, cada dos días. **no o.,** ningún otro, m; otra ninguna, f. **someone or o.,** alguien. **the others,** los (las) demás, m, f pl; los otros, m pl; las otras, f pl. **o. people,** otros, m pl, los demás

otherwise /ˈʌðərˌwaiz/ adv de otra manera, de otro modo, otramente; (in other respects) por lo demás, por otra parte; (if not) si no

otitis /ouˈtaitɪs/ n Med. otitis, f

otologist /ouˈtɒlədʒɪst/ n otólogo, m

otter /ˈɒtər/ n Zool. nutria, f. **o. hound,** perro para cazar la nutria

ottoman /ˈɒtəmən/ a otomano, turco. —n otomana, f

ouch! /autʃ/ interj ¡ax!, ¡huy!

ought /ɔt/ v aux deber, tener la obligación (de); ser conveniente, convenir; ser necesario (que), tener que. **I o. to have done it yesterday,** Debía haberlo hecho ayer. **She o. not to come,** No debe (debiera, debería) venir. **He o. to see them tomorrow,** (should) Conviene que les vea mañana; Tiene la obligación de verles mañana; (must) Es necesario que les vea mañana, Tiene que verles mañana.

ounce /auns/ n (animal and weight) onza, f. **He hasn't an o. of common sense,** No tiene pizca de sentido común

our /auər unstressed ɑr/ a nuestro

ours /auərz/ pron nuestro, m; nuestra, f; nuestros, m pl; nuestras, f pl; de nosotros, m pl; de nosotras, f pl; el nuestro, m; la nuestra, f; lo nuestro, neut; los nuestros, m pl; las nuestras, f pl. **This book is ours,** Este libro es nuestro (or el nuestro)

ourselves /ɑrˈsɛlvz/ pron pl nosotros mismos, m pl; nosotras mismas, f pl

oust /aust/ vt despedir, desahuciar, expulsar, echar

out /aut/ adv afuera; hacia fuera; (gone out) fuera, salido, ausente; (invested) puesto; (published) publicado, salido; (discovered) conocido, descubierto; (on strike) en huelga; (mistaken) en error, equivocado; (of journeys) de ida, (on ships) de navegación (e.g. on the second day out, al segundo día de navegación); (of fire, etc.) extinguido; (at sea) en el mar; (of girls in society) puesta de largo, que ha entrado en sociedad; (of fashion) fuera de moda; (of office) fuera del poder; (in holes) roto, agujereado, andrajoso; (exhausted) agotado; (expired) vencido; (of a watch) llevar... minutos (horas) de atraso or de adelanto; (unfriendly) reñido; (way out) salida, *f;* (sport) fuera de juego; (of flowers) abierto; (of chickens) empollado. **a scene out of one of Shakespeare's plays,** una escena de una de las comedias de Shakespeare. **I am out $6,** He perdido seis dólares. **I am out of tea,** Se me ha acabado el té. **to drink out of a glass,** beber de un vaso. **to read out of a book,** leer en un libro. **to speak out,** hablar claro. **Murder will out,** El asesinato se descubrirá. **out-and-out,** completo; (with rogue, etc.) redomado. **out of,** fuera de; (beyond) más allá de; (through, by) por; (with) con; (without) sin; (from among) entre; (in) en; (with a negative sense) no. **out of breath,** jadeante, sin aliento. **out of character,** impropio. **out of commission,** fuera de servicio. **out of danger,** fuera de peligro. **out of date,** anticuado. **out of hand,** en seguida; indisciplinado. **out of money,** sin dinero. **out of necessity,** por necesidad. **out of one's mind,** loco, demente. **out of order.** See **order. out of print,** agotado. **out of reach,** fuera de alcance, inasequible. **out of season,** fuera de temporada. **out of sight,** fuera del alcance de la vista; invisible. **Out of sight, out of mind,** Ojos que no ven, corazón que no siente. **out of sorts,** indispuesto. **out of temper,** de mal genio. **out of the question,** imposible. **out of the way,** *adv* (of work) terminado, hecho; (remote) fuera del camino; (put aside) arrinconado; donde no estorbe. **out-of-the-way,** *a* remoto, aislado; (unusual) extraordinario, singular. **out of this world,** lo máximo, lo último. **out of touch with,** alejado de; sin relaciones con; sin simpatía con. **out of work,** sin empleo, sin trabajo, en paro forzoso. **out-patient,** enfermo (-ma) de un dispensario. **Out!** *interj* ¡Fuera! ¡Fuera de aquí! ¡Márchate! **Out with it!** ¡Hable Vd.! sin rodeos! ¡Hablen claro!

outbalance /ˌaut'bæləns/ *vt* exceder, sobrepujar

outbid /ˌaut'bɪd/ *vt* pujar, mejorar

outbidding /ˌaut'bɪdɪŋ/ *n* puja, mejora, *f*

outbreak /'aut,breik/ *n* (of war) declaración, *f;* comienzo, *m;* (of disease) epidemia, *f;* (of crimes, etc.) serie, *f*

outbuilding /'aut,bɪldɪŋ/ *n* dependencia, *f,* edificio accesorio, anexo, *m*

outburst /'aut,bərst/ *n* acceso, arranque, *m,* explosión, *f*

outcast /'aut,kæst/ *n* paria, *mf;* desterrado (-da), proscripto (-ta)

outclass /ˌaut'klæs/ *vt* aventajar, ser superior (a), exceder

outcome /'aut,kʌm/ *n* consecuencia, *f,* resultado, *m*

outcry /'aut,krai/ *n* clamor, grito, *m;* protesta, *f*

outdistance /ˌaut'dɪstəns/ *vt* dejar atrás

outdo /ˌaut'du/ *vt* eclipsar, aventajar, sobrepujar

outdoor /'aut,dɔr/ *a* externo; (of activities) al aire libre; fuera de casa

outdoors /ˌaut'dɔrz/ *adv* fuera de casa; al aire libre

outer /'autər/ *a* externo, exterior

outermost /'autər,moust/ *a superl* (el, etc.) más externo, más exterior; extremo, de más allá

outer space espacio extraatmosférico, espacio extraterreste, espacio exterior, espacio sideral, espacio sidéreo, espacio ultraterrestre, *m*

outfit /'aut,fɪt/ *n* equipo, *m;* (of clothes) traje, *m;* (of furniture or trousseau) ajuar, *m;* (gear) pertrechos, avíos, *m pl.* —*vt* aviar equipar

outflank /ˌaut'flæŋk/ *vt Mil.* flanquear; ser más listo (que)

outgoing /'aut,gouɪŋ/ *a* saliente, que sale; cesante. **outgoings,** *n pl* gastos, *m pl*

outgrow /ˌaut'grou/ *vt* hacerse demasiado grande para; crecer más que; (ideas) perder; (illness) curarse de, curarse con la edad; pasar de la edad de, ser ya viejo para. **to o. one's clothes,** quedársele a uno chica la ropa. **to o. one's strength,** estar demasiado crecido para su edad

outgrowth /'aut,grouθ/ *n* excrecencia, *f;* resultado, fruto, *m,* consecuencia, *f*

outhouse /'aut,haus/ *n* edificio accesorio, *m*

outing /'autɪŋ/ *n* excursión, vuelta, *f,* paseo, *m*

outlandish /aut'lændɪʃ/ *a* extraño, singular, raro; absurdo, ridículo

outlast /ˌaut'læst/ *vt* durar más que; (outlive) sobrevivir a

outlaw /'aut,lɔ/ *n* bandido, proscrito, *m, vt* proscribir

outlay /'aut,lei/ *n* gasto, desembolso, *m*

outlet /'autlet/ *n* salida, *f;* orificio de salida, *m;* (of drains, etc.) desagüe, *m;* (of streets, rivers) desembocadura, *f; Fig.* escape, *m,* válvula de seguridad, *f*

outline /'aut,lain/ *n* perfil, contorno, *m;* (drawing) esbozo, bosquejo, *m;* idea general, *f;* plan general, *m, vt* esbozar, bosquejar. **in o.,** en esbozo; en perfil. **to be outlined** (against), dibujarse (contra), destacarse (contra)

outlive /ˌaut'lɪv/ *vt* sobrevivir (a); (live down) hacer olvidar

outlook /'aut,lʊk/ *n* (view) perspectiva, vista, *f;* (opinion) actitud, *f,* punto de vista, *m;* aspecto, *m,* apariencia, *f;* (for trade, etc.) perspectiva, *f,* posibilidades, *f pl.* **o. tower,** atalaya, *f*

outlying /'aut,laiŋ/ *a* remoto, lejano, distante

outmaneuver /ˌautmə'nuvər/ *vt* superar en estrategia

outmatch /ˌaut'mætʃ/ *vt* aventajar, superar

outmoded /ˌaut'moudɪd/ a anticuado, pasado de moda

outnumber /ˌaut'nʌmbər/ vt ser más numerosos que, exceder en número

out-of-court settlement /aut əv ˌkɔrt/ n arreglo pacífico, m

out-of-town a de las provincias

outpost /'aut,poust/ n Mil. avanzada, f, puesto avanzado, m

outpouring /'aut,pɔrɪŋ/ n derramamiento, m; efusión, f

output /'aut,put/ n producción, f. **o. capacity,** capacidad de producción, f

outrage /'autreidʒ/ n barbaridad infamia, atrocidad, f; rapto, m, violación, f. —vt ultrajar; violar; violentar

outrageous /aut'reidʒəs/ a atroz, terrible; desaforado, monstruoso; injurioso; ridículo

outré /u'trei/ a cursi, extravagante

outride /ˌaut'raid/ vt cabalgar más a prisa que

outright /adv. 'aut'rait; a. 'aut,rait/ adv (frankly) de plano (e.g. to reject outright, rechazar de plano), francamente, sin reserva; (immediately) en seguida, immediatamente. —a categórico; completo; franco

outrival /'aut,raivəl/ vt vencer, superar

outrun /ˌaut'rʌn/ vt correr más que

outset /'aut,set/ n principio, comienzo, m

outshine /ˌaut'fain/ vt brillar más que, eclipsar en brillantez; superar, eclipsar

outside /adv., prep., a. 'aut'said; n. 'aut'said/ adv afuera, fuera. —prep fuera de, al otro lado de, al exterior de; (besides) aparte de, fuera de. —a externo, exterior; (of labor, etc.) desde fuera; máximo; ajeno. —n exterior, m, superficie, f; aspecto, m, apariencia, f. **at the o.,** a lo sumo, cuando más. **from the o.,** de (or desde) fuera. **on the o.,** (externally) por fuera. **o. the door,** a la puerta

outsider /ˌaut'saidər/ n forastero (-ra); desconocido (-da); caballo desconocido, m; persona poco deseable, f

outsize /'aut,saiz/ n artículo de talla mayor que las corrientes, m

outskirts /'aut'skərts/ n pl alrededores, m pl, afueras, immediaciones, cercanías, f pl

outspoken /'aut'spoukən/ a franco. **to be o.,** decir lo que se piensa, no tener pelos en la lengua

outspread /'aut,spred/ a extendido; (of wings) desplegadas

outstanding /ˌaut'stændɪŋ/ a excelente; sobresaliente, conspicuo; Com. pendiente, sin pagar. **to be o.,** Com. estar pendiente; Fig. sobresalir. **o. account,** Com. cuenta pendiente, f

outstay /ˌaut'stei/ vt quedarse más tiempo que. **to o. one's welcome,** pegársele la silla

outstretched /ˌaut'stretʃt/ a extendido

outstrip /ˌaut'strip/ vt dejar atrás, pasar; aventajar, superar

outvote /ˌaut'vout/ vt emitir más votos que; rechazar por votación

outward /'autwərd/ a exterior, externo; aparente, visible. —adv exteriormente; hacia fuera; superficialmente. **o. bound,** con rumbo a... **o. voyage,** el viaje de ida

outwardly /'autwərdli/ adv exteriormente; hacia fuera; en apariencia

outwear /ˌaut'wɛər/ vt durar más que; gastar

outweigh /ˌaut'wei/ vt exceder, valer más que

outwit /ˌaut'wit/ vt ser más listo que; vencer

outworn /'aut'wɔrn/ a anticuado, ya viejo

oval /'ouvəl/ n óvalo, m, a oval, ovalado, aovado

ovarian /ou'vɛəriən/ a (Bot. Zool.) ovárico

ovary /'ouvəri/ n ovario, m

ovation /ou'veiʃən/ n ovación, recepción entusiasta, f

oven /'ʌvən/ n horno, m **o. peel,** pala de horno, f. **o. rake,** hurgón, m

over /'ouvər/ prep (above, upon, over) sobre, encima de; (on the other side) al otro lado de; (across) allende, a través de; (more than) más de; (beyond) más allá de; (of rank) superior a; (during) durante; (in addition) además de; (through) por. —n (cricket) serie de saques, f, adv encima; en; por encima; al otro lado; de un lado a otro; enfrente; al lado contrario; de un extremo a otro; (finished) terminado; (ruined) arruinado, perdido; (more) más; (excessively) demasiado, excesivamente; (covered) cubierto (de); (extra) en exceso; (completely) enteramente; (from head to foot) de pies a cabeza, de hito en hito; (of time) pasado. **over** is also used as a prefix. Indicating excess, it is generally translated by demasiado or excesivamente. In other meanings, it is either not translated or its meaning forms part of the verb, being translated as re-, super-, trans-, ultra. Very often a less literal translation is more successful than the employment of the above prefixes. **all o.,** (everywhere) en todas partes; (finished) todo acabado; (covered) cubierto (de); (up and down) de pies a cabeza. **all the world o.,** en todo el mundo. **embroidered all o.,** todo bordado. **He is o. in Germany,** Está en Alemania. **He trembled all o.,** Estaba todo tembloroso. **that which is o.,** el exceso, lo que queda. **to read o.,** leer, repasar. **o. again,** de nuevo. **o. and above,** por encima de, fuera de, en exceso de. **o. and o.,** repetidamente, muchas veces. **o. my signature,** bajo mi firma. **o. six months since...,** más de seis meses desde que...

overabundant /ˌouvərə'bʌndənt/ a sobreabundante

overact /ˌouvər'ækt/ vt exagerar (un papel)

overall /'ouvər,ɔl/ n bata, f; guardapolvo,

m; a deconjunto (e.g., *overall assessment,* evaluación de conjunto) *pl* **overalls,** monó, *m*

overanxious /,ouvər'æŋkʃəs/ *a* demasiado ansioso; demasiado inquieto. **to be o.-a.,** preocuparse demasiado

overarch /,ouvər'artʃ/ *vt* abovedar

overawe /,ouvər'ɔ/ *vt* intimidar, acobardar

overbalance /,ouvər'bæləns/ *vt* hacer perder el equilibrio. hacer caer; preponderar. —*vi* perder el equilibrio, caer

overbalancing /'ouvər,bælənsɪŋ/ *n* pérdida del equilibrio, caída, *f;* preponderancia, *f*

overbearing /,ouvər'bɛərɪŋ/ *a* dominante, autoritario, imperioso

overboard /'ouvər,bɔrd/ *adv* al agua, al mar.

overburden /,ouvər'bərdn/ *vt* sobrecargar, agobiar

overcast /*a.* 'ouvər'kæst; *v.* ,ouvər'kæst/ *a* anublado, cerrado, encapotado. —*vt Sew.* sobrehilar. **to become o.,** anublarse

overcharge /*n.* 'ouvər,tʃardʒ; *v.* ,ouvər'tʃardʒ/ *n* recargo, *m;* (price) recargo de precio, precio excesivo, *m.* —*vt* recargar, cobrar un precio excesivo; *Elec.* sobrecargar. —*vi* cobrar demasiado

overcoat /'ouvər,kout/ *n* abrigo, sobretodo, gabán, *m*

overcome /,ouvər'kʌm/ *vt* vencer, rendir, subyugar; (difficulties) triunfar de, allanar, dominar. —*vi* saber vencer. —*a* (by sleep, etc.) rendido; (at a loss) turbado, confundido; (by kindness) agradecidísimo

overconfidence /,ouvər'kɒnfɪdəns/ *n* confianza excesiva, *f*

overcooked /'ouvər,kukt/ *a* recocido, demasiado cocido

overcrowd /,ouvər'kraud/ *vt* atestar, llenar de bote en bote; (over-populate) sobrepoblar

overcrowding /'ouvər,kraudɪŋ/ *n* sobrepoblación, *f*

overdo /,ouvər'du/ *vt* exagerar; ir demasiado lejos, hacer demasiado; *Cul.* recocer; (overtire) fatigarse demasiado

overdose /'ouvər,dous/ *n* dosis excesiva, *f*

overdraft /'ouvər,dræft/ *n Com.* giro en descubierto, *m*

overdraw /,ouvər'drɔ/ *vt and vi Com.* girar en descubierto

over-dressed /'ouvər 'drest/ *a* que viste demasiado; cursi

overdue /,ouvər'du/ *a* atrasado; *Com.* vencido y no pagado

overeat /,ouvər'it/ *vi* comer demasiado, atracarse

overestimate /,ouvər'estə,meit/ *vt* estimar en valor excesivo; exagerar, sobreestimar, *n* presupuesto excesivo, *m;* estimación excesiva, *f*

overexcite /,ouvərɪk'sait/ *vt* sobreexcitar

overexposure /,ouvərɪk'spouʒər/ *n Photo.* exceso deexposición, *m*

overfatigue /,ouvərfə'tig/ *vt* fatigar demasiado. —*n* cansancio excesivo, *m*

overflow /*v.* ,ouvər'flou; *n.* 'ouvər,flou/ *vt* inundar, derramarse por; *Fig.* cubrir, llenar; desbordarse. —*vi* (with) rebosar de. —*n* inundación, *f,* desbordamiento, derrame, *m; Fig.* residuo, resto, exceso, *m;* (plumbing) sumidero, vertedero, *m,* descarga, *f.* **The river overflowed its banks,** El río se desbordó, El río salió de cauce

overflowing /,ouvər'flouɪŋ/ *a* rebosante; superabundante. **filled to o.,** lleno hasta los bordes. **o. with health,** rebosante de salud, vendiendo salud

overgrown /,ouvər'groun/ *a* (gawky) talludo; (plants) exuberante, vicioso; frondoso, cubierto de verdura

overhang /,ouvər'hæŋ/ *vt* caer a, mirar a; colgar; *Fig.* amenazar. —*vi* colgar, sobresalir; *Fig.* amenazar

overhanging /'ouvər,hæŋɪŋ/ *a* saledizo, sobresaliente; colgante, pendiente

overhaul /*v.* ,ouvər'hɔl; *n.* 'ouvər,hɔl/ *vt* examinar, investigar; componer, hacer una inspección general de; (of boats overtaking) alcanzar. —*n* examen, *m,* investigación, *f; Med.* exploración general, *f*

overhead /'ouvər'hed/ *adv* arriba, en lo alto, encima de la cabeza. —*a* aéreo, elevado; general, fijo. **o. cable,** cable eléctrico, *m.* **o. expenses,** gastos generales, *m pl.* **o. railway,** ferrocarril aéreo (or elevado), *m*

overhear /,ouvər'hɪər/ *vt* (accidentally) oír por casualidad, oír sin querer; (on purpose) alcanzar a oír, lograr oír

overheat /,ouvər'hit/ *vt* acalorar, hacer demasiado caliente, recalentar. —*vi* (in argument) acalorarse; hacerse demasiado caliente

overheating /,ouvər'hitɪŋ/ *n* recalentamiento, *m*

overindulge /,ouvərɪn'dʌldʒ/ *vt* mimar demasiado; dedicarse a algo con exceso; tomar algo con exceso. —*vi* darse demasiada buena vida

overjoyed /'ouvər,dʒɔid/ *a* contentísimo, lleno de alegría, encantado

overland /'ouvər,lænd/ *adv* por tierra. —*a* terrestre, trascontinental

overlap /*v.* ,ouvər'læp; *n.* 'ouvər,læp/ *vi* traslaparse; coincidir. —*n* traslapo, *m*

overlay /,ouvər'lei/ *vt* cubrir, dar una capa; (with silver) platear; (with gold) dorar. —*n* capa, *f;* cubierta, *f*

overload /*v.* ,ouvər'loud; *n.* 'ouvər,loud/ *vt* sobrecargar, recargar. —*n* sobrecarga, *f*

overlook /,ouvər'luk/ *vt* (face) dar a, mirar a, dominar; (supervise) vigilar, examinar, inspeccionar; (not notice) no notar, pasar por alto, no hacer, caso de, no fijarse en; (neglect) desdeñar; (ignore) no darse cuenta de, ignorar; (excuse) perdonar, tolerar, hacer la vista gorda

overlord /'ouvər,lɔrd/ *n* señor de horca y cuchillo, señor, jefe, *m*

overnight /*adv.* 'ouvər'nait; *a.*

'ouvər,nait/ *adv* la noche pasada, durante la noche; toda la noche. —*a* de la víspera, nocturno. **to stay o. with,** pasar la noche con

overpass /'ouvər,pæs/ *n* pasaje elevado, viaducto, *m*

overpay /,ouvər'pei/ *vt* pagar demasiado

overpayment /'ouvər,peimənt/ *n* pago excesivo, *m*

overpopulate /,ouvər'pɒpyə,leit/ *vt* sobrepoblar, become overpopulated recargarse de habitantes (with people), recargarse de animales (with animals)

overpower /,ouvər'pauər/ *vt* vencer, subyugar; (of scents, etc.) trastornar; rendir, dominar

overpowering /,ouvər'pauərɪŋ/ *a* irresistible

overproduce /,ouvərprə'dus/ *vt and vi* sobreproducir

overrate /,ouvər'reit/ *vt* exagerar el valor de; (of property) sobrevalorar

overreach /,ouvər'ritʃ/ *vt* sobrealcanzar. **to o. oneself,** sobrepasarse, ir demasiado lejos

override /,ouvər'raid/ *vt* (trample) pasar por encima (de); *Fig.* rechazar, poner a un lado; (bully) dominar; (a horse) fatigar, reventar

overripe /,ouvər'raip/ *a* demasiado maduro

overrule /,ouvər'rul/ *vt Law.* denegar, no admitir; vencer

overrun /,ouvər'rʌn/ *vt* (flood) inundar; (ravage) invadir; (infest) plagar, infestar; desbordarse, derramarse

oversee /,ouvər'si/ *vt* vigilar, inspeccionar

overseer /'ouvər,siər/ *n* capataz, mayoral, sobrestante, contramaestre, *m;* inspector (-ra), veedor (-ra)

oversensitive /,ouvər'sɛnsɪtɪv/ *a* demasiado sensitivo; vidrioso; susceptible

overshadow /,ouvər'ʃædou/ *vt* sombrear; *Fig.* eclipsar, obscurecer; (sadden) entristecer

overshoe /'ouvər,ʃu/ *n* chanclo, *m;* (for snow) galocha, *f*

overshoot /,ouvər'ʃut/ *vt* tirar más allá del blanco; *Fig.* exceder, rebasar el límite conveniente, **overshoot the target** (fig.) ir más allá del blanco, ir más allá de lo razonable. **to o. oneself,** exagerar; propasarse, descomedirse

oversight /'ouvər,sait/ *n* inadvertencia, omisión, equivocación, *f;* descuido, *m*

oversimplify /,ouvər'sɪmplə,fai/ *vt* simplificar en exceso

oversleep /,ouvər'slip/ *vi* dormir demasiado; *Inf.* pegársele a uno las sábanas, levantarse demasiado tarde

overspend /,ouvər'spɛnd/ *vt and vi* gastar demasiado

overspread /,ouvər'sprɛd/ *vt* desparramar, salpicar, esparcir, sembrar; cubrir

overstate /,ouvər'steit/ *vt* exagerar, encarecer, ponderar

overstatement /,ouvər'steitmənt/ *n* exageración, ponderación, *f*

overstep /,ouvər'stɛp/ *vt* exceder, pasar, violar; rebasar, pasar más allá (de)

overstrain /,ouvər'strein/ *vt* fatigar demasiado, agotar. —*n* fatiga, *f.* **to o. oneself,** esforzarse demasiado, cansarse demasiado

overstrung /,ouvər'strʌŋ/ *a* nervioso, excitable; (piano) de cuerdas cruzadas

overt /ou'vɜrt/ *a* abierto, público; manifiesto, evidente

overtake /,ouvər'teik/ *vt* alcanzar, pasar, dejar atrás; adelantarse (a); (surprise) coger, sorprender; (overwhelm) vencer, dominar

overtax /,ouvər'tæks/ *vt* oprimir de tributos; agobiar, cansar demasiado

overthrow /*v.* ,ouvər'θrou; *n.* 'ouvər,θrou/ *vt* volcar, echar por tierra, derribar; *Fig.* vencer, destruir, destronar. —*n* vuelco, derribo, *m; Fig.* destrucción, ruina, *f*

overtime /'ouvər,taim/ *adv* fuera de las horas estipuladas. —*n* horas extraordinarias de trabajo, *f pl.* **to work o.,** trabajar horas extraordinarias

overture /'ouvərtʃər/ *n Mus.* obertura, *f*

overturn /,ouvər'tɜrn/ *vt* volcar, derribar, echar a rodar, echar abajo; (upset) revolver, desordenar. —*vi* volcar, venirse abajo, allanarse; estar revuelto

overweening /'ouvər'winɪŋ/ *a* arrogante, insolente, altivo

overweight /'ouvər,weit/ *n* sobrepeso, exceso en el peso, *m.* **to be o.,** pesar más de lo debido

overwhelm /,ouvər'wɛlm/ *vt* (conquer) vencer, aplastar, derrotar; (of waves, etc.) sumergir, hundir, inundar, engolfar; (in argument) confundir, dejar confuso, avergonzar; (of grief, etc.) vencer, postrar, dominar; (of work) inundar

overwhelming /,ouvər'wɛlmɪŋ/ *a* irresistible, invencible, abrumador, apabullante

overwind /,ouvər'waind/ *vt* (a watch) dar demasiada cuerda a; romper la cuerda de

overwork /*v.* ,ouvər'wɜrk; *n.* 'ouvər,wɜrk/ *vt* hacer trabajar demasiado (or con exceso); esclavizar. —*vi* trabajar demasiado. —*n* exceso de trabajo, demasiado trabajo, *m*

overwrought /'ouvər'rɔt/ *a* (overworked) agotado por el trabajo, rendido, muy cansado; nerviosísimo, sobreexcitado, exaltado, muy agitado

ovulation /,ɒvyə'leiʃən/ *n Med.* ovulación, *f*

owe /ou/ *vt* deber, tener deudas (de); deber, estar agradecido (por), estar obligado (a). —*vi* estar en deuda, estar endeudado, tener deudas. **He owes his tailor $30,** Le debe treinta dólares a su sastre. **I owe him thanks for his help,** Le estoy agradecido por su ayuda (*or* Le debo las gracias por...). **He owes his success to**

good fortune, Su éxito se debe a la suerte

owing /'ouɪŋ/ *a* sin pagar. **o. to,** debido a, a causa de, por. **We had to stay in o. to the rain,** Tuvimos que quedarnos en casa a causa de la lluvia. **What is o. to you now?** ¿Cuánto se le debe ahora?

owl /aul/ *n* búho, mochuelo, *m.* **barn or screech owl,** lechuza, *f.* **brown owl,** autillo, *m*

owlish /'aulɪʃ/ *a* parecido a un búho, de búho

own /oun/ *a* propio. —*n* (dearest) bien, *m.* —*vt* poseer, tener, ser dueño de; (recognize) reconocer; (admit) confesar. —*vi* confesar. **my (thy, his, our, your) own,** mi (tu, su, nuestro, vuestro) propio, *m,* (*f,* propia); mis (tus, sus, nuestros, vuestros) propios, *m pl,* (*f pl,* propias); (when not placed before a noun) el mío (tuyo, suyo, nuestro, vuestro), la mía (tuya, etc.), los míos (tuyos, etc.), las mías (tuyas, etc.);

(relations) los suyos. **in his own house,** en su propia casa. **my (thy, his, etc.) own self,** yo (tú, él) mismo, *m,* (*f,* misma, *m pl,* mismos, *f pl,* mismas). **a room of one's own,** un cuarto para sí (or para uno mismo). **to be on one's own,** ser independiente; estar a solas. **to hold one's own,** mantenerse en sus trece. **to own up,** confesar

owner /'ounər/ *n* dueño (-ña), propietario (-ia), posesor (-ra)

ownership /'ounərˌʃɪp/ *n* posesión, *f,* dominio, *m;* propiedad, *f*

ox /ɒks/ *n* buey (*pl* bueyes), *m.* **oxeye daisy,** margarita, *f.* **oxstall,** boyera, *f*

oxygen /'ɒksɪdʒən/ *n* oxígeno, *m.* **o. mask,** máscara de oxígeno, *f.* **o. tent,** tienda de oxígeno, *f*

oyster /'ɔistər/ *n* ostra, *f.* **o. bed,** pescadero (or criadero) de ostras, *m.* **o. culture,** ostricultura, *f*

ozone /'ouzoun/ *n* ozono, *m*

p /pi/ *n* (letter) pe, *f.* **to mind one's p's and q's,** poner los puntos sobre las íes; ir con pies de plomo

pabulum /'pæbyələm/ *n* pábulo, *m;* sustento, *m*

pace /peis/ *n* paso, *m;* (gait) andar, *m,* marcha, *f;* (of a horse) andadura, *f;* (speed) velocidad, *f.* —*vi* pasear(se), andar; (of a horse) amblar. —*vt* recorrer, andar por; marcar el paso para; (with out) medir a pasos. **at a good p.,** a un buen paso. **to keep p. with,** ajustarse al paso de, ir al mismo paso que; andar al paso de; (events) mantenerse al corriente de. **to p. up and down,** pasearse, dar vueltas. **p.-maker,** el que marca el paso

paced /peist/ *a* de andar...; (of a horse) de andadura...; de paso...

pacific /pə'sɪfɪk/ *a Geog.* pacífico; sosegado, tranquilo, pacífico. **He is of a p. disposition,** Es amigo de la paz

Pacific, the, el (Océano) Pacífico, *m*

pacifier /'pæsə,faiər/ *n* pacificador (-ra)

pacifist /'pæsəfɪst/ *a* pacifista. —*n* pacifista, *mf*

pacify /'pæsə,fai/ *vt* pacificar; calmar, tranquilizar; aplacar, conciliar

pack /pæk/ *n* (bundle) fardo, lío, *m;* paquete, *m;* (load) carga, *f;* (of hounds) jauría, *f;* (herd) hato, *m;* (of seals) manada, *f;* (of cards) baraja (de naipes), *f;* (of rogues) cuadrilla, *f;* (of lies, etc.) colección, *f;* masa, *f;* (of ice) témpanos flotantes, *m pl;* (Rugby football) delanteros, *m pl;* (for the face) compresa, *f.* **p.-horse,** caballo de carga, *m.* **p.-needle,** aguja espartera, *f.* **p.-saddle,** albarda, *f.* **p.-thread,** bramante, *m*

pack /pæk/ *vt* embalar; empaquetar; envasar; encajonar; (a suit-case, etc.) hacer; (cram) apretar; (crowd) atestar, llenar; (a pipe joint, etc.) empaquetar; (an animal) cargar. —*vi* llenar; (one's luggage) hacer el equipaje, hacer el baúl, arreglar el equipaje. **packed like sardines,** como sardinas en banasta. **The train was packed,** El tren estabaa lleno de bote en bote. **to p. off,** (a person) despachar; poner de partitas en la calle. **to p. up,** hacer el equipaje; empaquetar; embalar; *Inf.* liar el hato

package /'pækɪdʒ/ *n* paquete, *m;* bulto, *m;* (bundle) fardo, *m*

packer /'pækər/ *n* embalador, *m;* envasador (-ra)

packet /'pækɪt/ *n* paquete, *m;* (of cigarettes, etc.) cajetilla, *f;* (boat) paquebote, *m.* **to make one's p.,** *Inf.* hacer su pacotilla

packing /'pækɪŋ/ *n* embalaje, *m;* envoltura, *f;* envase, *m;* (on a pipe, etc.) guarnición, *f.* **I must do my p.,** Tengo que hacer las maletas. **p.-case,** caja de embalaje, *f.* **p.-needle,** aguja espartera, *f*

pact /pækt/ *n* pacto, convenio, *m.* **to make a p.,** pactar

pad /pæd/ *n* almohadilla, *f,* cojinete, *m;* (on a bed, chair) colchoneta, *f;* (on a

wound) cabezal, *m;* (for polishing) muñeca, *f;* (hockey) defensa, *f;* (cricket) espinillera, *f;* (writing) bloque, *m;* (of a calendar) taco, *m;* (blotting) secafirmas, *m;* (of a quadruped's foot) pulpejo, *m;* (of fox, hare) pata, *f;* (leaf) hoja grande, *f, vt* almohadillar; acolchar; rellenar, forrar; (out, a book, etc.) meter paja en. **inking-pad,** almohadilla de entintar, *f.* **padded cell,** celda acolchonada, *f.* **shoulder-pad,** (in a garment) hombrera, *f*

padding /'pædɪŋ/ *n* relleno, *m,* almohadilla, *f;* (material) borra, *f,* algodón, *m; Fig.* paja, *f,* ripio, *m,*

paddle /'pædl/ *n* (oar) canalete, zagual, *m;* paleta, *f;* (flipper) aleta, *f, vt* and *vi* remar con canalete, (dabble) chapotear. **double p.,** remo doble, *m.* **p.-steamer,** vapor de ruedas, vapor de paleta, *m.* **p.-wheel,** rueda de paletas, *f*

padlock /'pæd,lɒk/ *n* candado, *m, vt* cerrar con candado, acerrojar

pagan /'peigən/ *a* and *n* pagano (-na)

page /peidʒ/ *n* (boy) paje, *m;* (squire) escudero, *m;* (of a book, etc.) página, *f; Fig.* hoja, *f.* —*vt* compaginar; (a person) vocear. **on p. nine,** en la página nueve. **to turn the p.,** *Fig.* volver la hoja

pageant /'pædʒənt/ *n* espectáculo, *m;* (procession) desfile, *m;* representación teatral, *f;* fiesta, *f; Fig.* pompa, *f,* aparato, *m*

pageantry /'pædʒəntri/ *n* pompa, *f,* aparato, *m,* magnificencia, *f*

pager /'peidʒər/ *n* buscapersonas, *m,* bip, *m* (Mexico)

paid /peid/ *a* pagado; (on a parcel) porte pagado. **p. mourner,** plañidera, *f.* **p.-up share,** acción liberada, *f*

pail /peil/ *n* cubo, pozal, *m,* cubeta, *f*

pain /pein/ *n* dolor, *m;* sufrimiento, *m;* (mental) tormento, *m,* angustia, *f; Law.* pena, *f; pl* **pains,** (effort) trabajo, esfuerzo, *m.* —*vt* doler; atormentar, afligir. **dull p.,** dolor sordo, *m.* **I have a p. in my head,** Me duele la cabeza. **on p. of death,** so pena de muerte. **to be in great p.,** sufrir mucho. **to take pains,** tomarse trabajo, esforzarse, esmerarse

painful /'peinfəl/ *a* doloroso; angustioso; fatigoso; (troublesome) molesto; (embarrassing) embarazoso; difícil; (laborious) arduo

painless /'peinlɪs/ *a* sin dolor, indoloro

painstaking /'peinz,teikɪŋ, 'pein,stei-/ *a* concienzudo; diligente, industrioso; cuidadoso. —*n* trabajo, *m;* diligencia, industria, *f;* cuidado, *m*

paint /peint/ *n* pintura, *f;* (for preserving metal) pavón, *m;* (rouge) colorete, *m.* —*vt* pintar. —*vi* pintar; pintarse. **The door is painted blue,** La puerta está pintada de azul. **p.-box,** caja de pinturas, *f.*

p.-brush, pincel, *m;* (for house painting) brocha, *f*

painter /'peɪntər/ *n* pintor (-ra); (house) pintor de brocha gorda, pintor de casas, *m;* (of a boat) boza, *f.* **sign-p.,** pintor de muestras, *m*

painting /'peɪntɪŋ/ *n* pintura, *f;* (picture) cuadro, *m,* pintura, *f*

pair /pɛər/ *n* par, *m;* (of people) pareja, *f;* (of oxen) yunta, *f.* —*vt* parear, emparejar; (persons) unir, casar; (animals) aparear. —*vi* parearse; casarse; aparearse. **a carriage and p.,** un landó con dos caballos. **a p. of steps,** una escalera de mano. **a p. of pants a p.** of trousers, unos pantalones. **in pairs,** de dos en dos; por parejas. **to p. off,** *vi* formar pareja; *Inf.* casarse

pal /pæl/ *n* camarada, compinche, *mf;* amigote, *f*

palace /'pælɪs/ *n* palacio, *m*

palatable /'pælətəbəl/ *a* sabroso, apetitoso; *Fig.* agradable, aceptable

palate /'pælɪt/ *n* paladar, *m.* **hard p.,** paladar, *m.* **soft p.,** velo del paladar, *m*

palatial /pə'leɪʃəl/ *a* (of a palace) palaciego; (sumptuous) magnífico, suntuoso

pale /peɪl/ *n* (stake) estaca, *f;* límite, *m; Herald.* palo, *m, a* pálido; (wan) descolorido; (of colours) claro, desmayado; (of light) tenue, mortecino; (lustreless) sin brillo, muerto. —*vi* palidecer, perder el color; *Fig.* eclipsarse

palette /'pælɪt/ *n* paleta, *f.* **p.-knife,** espátula, *f*

palisade /,pælə'seɪd/ *n* palenque, *m,* tranquera, palizada, *f; Mil.* estacada, *f*

pall /pɔl/ *n* (on a coffin) paño mortuorio, *m;* (*Fig.* covering) manto, *m,* capa, *f; Eccl.* palio, *m;* (over a chalice) palia, *f.* —*vi* perder el sabor, hacerse insípido; saciarse (de); aburrirse (de), cansarse (de). **The music of Bach never palls on me,** No me canso nunca de la música de Bach

palliate /'pæli,eɪt/ *vt* (pain) paliar, aliviar; mitigar; (excuse) disculpar, excusar

palliative /'pæli,eɪtɪv, -iətɪv/ *a* paliativo; (extenuating) atenuante. —*n* paliativo, *m*

pallid /'pælɪd/ *a* pálido

pallor /'pælər/ *n* palidez, *f*

palm /pɑm/ *n* (of the hand, and *Fig.,* victory) palma, *f;* (measurement) ancho de la mano, *m;* (tree) palmera, *f.* —*vt* empalmar; (with off) defraudar (con); dar gato por liebre (a). **to bear away the p.,** llevar la palma. **p. branch,** palma, *f.* **p. grove,** palmar, *m.* **p.-oil,** aceite de palma, *m;* (bribe) soborno, *m.* **P. Sunday,** Domingo de Ramos, *m.* **p. tree,** palmera, *f*

palmy /'pɑmi/ *a* palmar; (flourishing) floreciente; (happy) dichoso, feliz; (prosperous) próspero; triunfante

palp /pælp/ *n* palpo, *m*

palpable /'pælpəbəl/ *a* palpable

palpate /'pælpeɪt/ *vt* palpar

palpitate /'pælpɪ,teɪt/ *vi* palpitar

palpitation /,pælpɪ'teɪʃən/ *n* palpitación, *f*

palsy /'pɔlzi/ *n* parálisis, *f, vt* paralizar

paltry /'pɔltri/ *a* mezquino, insignificante, pobre

pampas /'pæmpəz; *attributively* 'pæmpəs/ *n* pampa, *f*

pamper /'pæmpər/ *vt* mimar, consentir demasiado; criar con mimos, regalar; alimentar demasiado bien

pampered /'pæmpərd/ *a* mimado, consentido; demasiado bien alimentado

pamphlet /'pæmflɪt/ *n* folleto, *m*

pan /pæn/ *n* (vessel) cazuela, *f,* cacerola, *f;* (brain) cráneo, *m;* (of a balance) platillo, *m;* (of a firelock) cazoleta, *f; Cinema.* toma panorámica *f, prefix* pan-. **to pan off,** separar el oro en una gamella. **to pan out,** dar oro; *Fig.* suceder. **Pan-Americanism,** panamericanismo, *m*

Pan /pæn/ *n* Pan, *m.* **pipes of Pan,** flauta de Pan, *f*

panacea /,pænə'siə/ *n* panacea, *f*

panache /pə'næʃ/ *n* penacho, *m*

panada /pənə'dɑ/ *n Cul.* panetela, *f*

Panama /'pænə,mɑ/ *el* Panamá, *m*

Panama /'pænə,mɑ/ *a* panameño. (-ña). **P. hat,** sombrero de jipijapa, panamá *m*

pancake /'pæn,keɪk/ *n* fruta de sartén, hojuela, *f.* **p. landing,** *Aer.* aterrizaje brusco, *m.* **P. Tuesday,** martes de Carnaval, *m*

pancreas /'pæŋkriəs, 'pæŋ-/ *n* páncreas, *m*

panda /'pændə/ *n Zool.* panda, *mf*

pandemic /pæn'dɛmɪk/ *a* pandémico

pandemonium /,pændə'mouniəm/ *n* pandemonio

pander /'pændər/ *n* alcahuete, *m, vi* alcahuetear. **to p. to,** prestarse a; favorecer, ayudar

pane /peɪn/ *n* hoja de vidrio, hoja de cristal, *f;* cuadro, *m*

panegyric /,pænɪ'dʒɪrɪk/ *a* panegírico. —*n* panegírico, *m*

panel /'pænl/ *n* panel, entrepaño, *m; Art.* tabla, *f;* (in a dress) paño, *m;* (list) lista, *f,* registro, *m;* (jury) jurado, *m;* lista de jurados, *f, vt* labrar a entrepaños; artesonar. **p. doctor,** médico (-ca) de seguros

paneled /'pænld/ *a* entrepañado; (of ceilings) artesonado. **p. ceiling,** artesonado, *m*

paneling /'pænlɪŋ/ *n* entrepaños, *m pl;* artesonado, *m*

panful /'pæn,fʊl/ *n* cazolada, *f*

pang /pæŋ/ *n* punzada (de dolor), *f,* dolor agudo, *m;* dolor, *m;* (anguish of mind) angustia, *f,* tormento, *m;* (of conscience) remordimiento, *m*

panic /'pænɪk/ *n* pánico, *m;* pavor, espanto, *m;* terror súbito, *m, a* pánico. —*vi* espantarse. **p.-monger,** alarmista, *mf* **p.-stricken,** aterrorizado, despavorido

panicky /'pæniki/ *a Inf.* lleno de pánico; nervioso

panicle /'pænɪkəl/ *n Bot.* panoja, *f*

panoply /'pænəpli/ *n* panoplia, *f*

panorama /ˌpænəˈræmə, -ˈrɑmə/ *n* panorama, *m*

panoramic /ˌpænəˈræmɪk/ *a* panorámico

pansy /ˈpænzi/ *n* pensamiento, *m*, trinitaria, *f*

pant /pænt/ *vi* jadear; (of dogs) hipar; resollar; (of the heart) palpitar. —*n* jadeo, *m*; palpitación, *f*. **to p. after,** suspirar por

pantaloon /ˌpæntlˈun/ *n* (trouser) pantalón, *m*; (Pantaloon) Pantalón, *m*

pantechnicon /pænˈtɛknɪˌkɒn/ *n* almacén de muebles, *m*; (van) carro de mudanzas, *m*

pantheon /ˈpænθiˌɒn, -ən *or, esp. Brit.*, pænˈθiən/ *n* panteón, *m*

panther /ˈpænθər/ *n* pantera, *f*

panties /ˈpæntiz/ *n pl* pantalones, *m pl*

panting /ˈpæntɪŋ/ *a* jadeante, sin aliento. —*n* jadeo, *m*; resuello, *m*; respiración difícil, *f*; palpitación, *f*

pantomime /ˈpæntəˌmaɪm/ *n* pantomima, *f*; revista, *f*. **in p.,** en pantomima; por gestos

pantry /ˈpæntri/ *n* despensa, *f*

pants /pænts/ *n pl* calzoncillos, *m pl*; (trousers) pantalones, *m pl*

pap /pæp/ *n* (nipple) pezón, *m*; (soft food) papilla, *f*

papa /ˈpɑpə, pəˈpɑ/ *n* papá, *m*

papacy /ˈpeɪpəsi/ *n* papado, pontificado, *m*

papal /ˈpeɪpəl/ *a* papal, pontificio. **p. bull,** bula pontificia, *f*. **p. nuncio,** nuncio del Papa, nuncio apostólico, *m*. **p. see,** sede apostólica, *f*

paper /ˈpeɪpər/ *n* papel, *m*; hoja de papel, *f*; documento, *m*; (lecture) comunicación, *f*; (newspaper) periódico, *m*; (journal) revista, *f*; (exam.) examen escrito, trabajo, *m*; ejercicio, *m*; *pl* **papers,** (credentials) documentación, *f*, credenciales, *f pl*; *Com.* valores negociables, *m pl*; (packet) paquete, *m*, a de papel; para papeles; parecido al papel. —*vt* (a room) empapelar; (a parcel) envolver. **daily p.,** diario, *m*. **in p. covers,** (of books) en rústica. **slip of p.,** papeleta, *f*. **to send in one's papers,** entregar su dimisión. **p. bag,** saco de papel, *m*. **p.-chase,** rally-paper, *m*. **p. clip,** prendedero de oficina, "sujeta papels," *m*. **p.-cutting machine,** guillotina, *f*. **p. folder,** plegadera, *f*. **p.-hanger,** empapelador, *m*. **p.-hanging,** empapelado, *m*. **p.-knife,** cortapapel, *m*. **p.-maker,** fabricante de papel, *m*. **p.-making,** manufactura de papel, *f*. **p.-mill,** fábrica de papel, *f*. **p.-money,** papel moneda, *m*. **p.-pulp,** pasta, *f*. **p.-streamer,** serpentina, *f*. **p.-weight,** pisapapeles, *m*

papering /ˈpeɪpərɪŋ/ *n* (of a room) empapelado, *m*

papier-mâché /ˌpeɪpərməˈʃeɪ, pɑˌpyeɪ-/ *n* cartón piedra, *m*

papillary /ˈpæpəˌlɛri/ *a* papilar

papoose /pæˈpus/ *n* niño indio, *m*

paprika /pæˈprikə, pə-, pɑ-, ˈpæprɪkə/ *n* pimienta húngara, *f*

papyrus /pəˈpaɪrəs/ *n* papiro, *m*

par /pɑr/ *n* par, *f*. **at par,** *Com.* a la par. **above (below) par,** *Com.* por encima (or debajo) de la par. **He is a little below par,** No está muy bien de salud. **to be on par with,** ser el equivalente de; ser igual a. **par excellence,** por excelencia

parable /ˈpærəbəl/ *n* parábola, *f*

parachute /ˈpærəˌʃut/ *n* paracaídas, *m*; *Bot.* vilano, *m*. **to p. down,** lanzarse en paracaídas. **p. troops,** cuerpo de paracaidistas, *m*

parachutist /ˈpærəˌʃutɪst/ *n* paracaidista, *mf*

parade /pəˈreɪd/ *n* alarde, *m*; *Mil.* parada, revista, *f*; (procession) desfile, *m*, procesión, *f*; (promenade) paseo, *m*. —*vt* (display) hacer alarde de, hacer gala de, ostentar; (troops) formar en parada; pasar revista (a); (patrol) recorrer. —*vi Mil.* tomar parte en una parada; desfilar. **to p. up and down,** pasearse. **p.-ground,** campo de instrucción, *m*; plaza de armas, *f*

paradigm /ˈpærəˌdaɪm/ *n* paradigma, *m*

paradise /ˈpærəˌdaɪs/ *n* paraíso, edén, *m*; *Fig.* jauja, *f*. **bird of p.,** ave del paraíso, *f*

paradox /ˈpærəˌdɒks/ *n* paradoja, *f*

paradoxical /ˌpærəˈdɒksɪkəl/ *a* paradójico

paraffin /ˈpærəfɪn/ *n* parafina, *f*. —*vt* parafinar. **p.-oil,** parafina líquida, *f*

paragon /ˈpærəˌgɒn/ *n* modelo perfecto, dechado, *m*

paragraph /ˈpærəˌgræf/ *n* párrafo, *m*; (in a newspaper) suelto, *m*. —*vt* dividir en párrafos; escribir un suelto sobre. **new p.,** párrafo aparte, *m*

Paraguay /ˈpærəˌgwaɪ, -ˌgweɪ/ el Paraguay, *m*

Paraguayan /ˌpærəˈgwaɪən/ *a* and *n* paraguayo (-ya)

parakeet /ˈpærəˌkit/ *n Ornith.* perico, *m*

parallel /ˈpærəˌlɛl/ *a* paralelo; igual; semejante, análogo. —*n* línea paralela, *f*; paralelo, *m*; *Mil.* paralela, *f*; *Geog.* paralelo, *m*; *Print.* pleca, *f*. —*vt* poner en paralelo; cotejar, comparar; igualar. **to run p. to,** ser paralelo a; ser conforme a. **p. bars,** paralelas, *f pl*

paralysis /pəˈræləsɪs/ *n* parálisis, *f*

paralytic /ˌpærəˈlɪtɪk/ *a* and *n* paralítico (-ca)

paramount /ˈpærəˌmaunt/ *a* supremo, sumo

paramour /ˈpærəˌmʊr/ *n* amante, querido, *m*; querida, amiga, *f*

paranoia /ˌpærəˈnɔɪə/ *n* paranoia, *f*

paranoiac /ˌpærəˈnɔɪæk/ *n* paranoico, *m*

parapet /ˈpærəpɪt, -ˌpɛt/ *n* (*Archit.* and *Mil.*) parapeto, *m*

paraphernalia /ˌpærəfərˈneɪlyə, -fəˈneɪl-/ *n Law.* bienes parafernales, *m pl*; (finery) atavíos, adornos, *m pl*; equipo, *m*; arreos, *m pl*; insignias, *f pl*

paraphrase /'pærə,freiz/ n paráfrasis, f, vt parafrasear

parasite /'pærə,sait/ n parásito, m; Inf. zángano, m, gorrista, mf

parasitic /,pærə'sitik/ a parásito, parasitario; Med. parasítico

parasol /'pærə,sɔl, -,sɒl/ n parasol, quitasol, m

parboil /'pɑr,bɔil/ vt sancochar

parcel /'pɑrsəl/ n paquete, m; fardo, m; (of land) parcela, f. **to p. out**, repartir, distribuir; dividir. **to p. up**, envolver, empaquetar. **p. post**, servicio de paquetes, m

parch /pɑrtʃ/ vt secar; abrasar, quemar; (roast) tostar. —vi secarse; quemarse, abrasarse

parched /pɑrtʃt/ a seco, sediento. **p. with thirst**, muerto de sed

parchment /'pɑrtʃmənt/ n pergamino, m; (of a drum) parche, m. **p.-like**, apergaminado

pardon /'pɑrdn/ n perdón, m; Eccl. indulgencia, f. —vt perdonar; indultar, amnistiar. **a general p.**, una amnistía. **I beg your p.!** ¡Vd. dispense!; ¡Perdone Vd.! **to beg p.**, pedir perdón; disculparse. **P.?** ¿Cómo?

pardonable /'pɑrdnəbəl/ a perdonable, disculpable, excusable

pardonableness /'pɑrdnəbəlnis/ n disculpabilidad, f

pardonably /'pɑrdnəbli/ adv disculpablemente, excusablemente

pardoner /'pɑrdnər/ n vendedor de indulgencias, m; perdonador (-ra)

pardoning /'pɑrdnɪŋ/ n perdón, m; remisión, f

pare /pɛər/ vt (one's nails) cortar; (fruit) mondar; (potatoes, etc.) pelar; (remove) quitar; (reduce) reducir

parent /'pɛərənt, 'pær-/ n padre, m; madre, f; (ancestor) antepasado, m; (origin) origen, m, fuente, f; (cause) causa, f; (author) autor, m; autora, f; pl **parents**, padres, m pl. —a madre, materno; principal

parentage /'pɛərəntɪdʒ, 'pær-/ n parentela, f; linaje, m, familia, alcurnia, f; procedencia, f; nacimiento, origen, m

parental /pə'rɛntl/ a paternal; maternal, de madre

parentally /pə'rɛntli/ adv como un padre; como una madre

parenthesis /pə'rɛnθəsɪs/ n paréntesis, m

parenthetical /,pɛərən'θɛtɪkəl/ a entre paréntesis; de paréntesis

parenthood /'pɛərənt,hʊd, 'pær-/ n paternidad, f; maternidad, f

pariah /pə'raiə/ n paria, mf

parietal /pə'raiɪtl/ a parietal

paring /'pɛərɪŋ/ n (act) raedura, f; peladura, mondadura, f; (shred) brizna, f; (refuse) desecho, desperdicio, m. **p.-knife**, trinchete, m

Paris /'pærɪs/ París, m

parish /'pærɪʃ/ n parroquia, f; feligresía,

f, a parroquial. **p. church**, parroquia, f. **p. clerk**, sacristán de parroquia, m. **p. priest**, párroco, m. **p. register**, registro de la parroquia, m

parishioner /pə'rɪʃənər/ n parroquiano (-na); feligrés (-esa)

Parisian /pə'rɪʒən, -'rɪʒən, -'rɪziən/ a parisiense. —n parisiense, mf

parity /'pærɪti/ n paridad, f

park /pɑrk/ n parque, m; jardín, m. —vt (vehicles) estacionar; (dump) depositar. **car p.**, parque de automóviles, m. **p.-keeper**, guardián del parque, m

parking /'pɑrkɪŋ/ n (of vehicles) estacionamiento, m; (dumping) depósito, m. **p. lights**, Auto. luces de estacionamiento, f pl. **p. place**, parque de estacionamiento, m

parking meter n parquímetro, m (Argentina)

parlance /'pɑrləns/ n lenguaje, m. **in common p.**, en lenguaje vulgar

parley /'pɑrli/ n plática, conversación, f; discusión, f; Mil. parlamento, m. —vi Mil. parlamentar; discutir; conversar. —vt hablar

parliament /'pɑrləmənt/ n parlamento, m; cortes, f pl; cuerpo legislativo, m

parliamentarian /,pɑrləmən'tɛəriən/ a and n parlamentario; (of an academy) censor, m

parliamentary /,pɑrlə'mɛntəri, -tri; sometimes ,pɑrljə-/ a parlamentario. **p. immunity**, inviolabilidad parlamentaria, f

parlor /'pɑrlər/ n salón, gabinete, m; sala de recibo, f; (in a convent) locutorio, m. **p. games**, diversión de salón, f, juego de sociedad, m. **p.-maid**, camarera, f

parlous /'pɑrləs/ a crítico, malo. —adv sumamente, muy

Parmesan /'pɑrmə,zɑn, ,pɑrmə'zɑn/ a parmesano, de Parma. —n parmesano (-na). **P. cheese**, queso de Parma, m

parochial /pə'roukiəl/ a parroquial, parroquiano; Fig. provincial

parochialism /pə'roukiə,lizəm/ n provincialismo, m

parodist /'pærədist/ n parodista, mf

parody /'pærədi/ n parodia, f, vt parodiar

parole /pə'roul/ n (of convict) libertad vigilada, f

paroxysm /'pærək,sizəm/ n paroxismo, m; ataque, acceso, m

parquet /pɑr'kei/ (floor) entarimado m; (of theater) platea, f

parrot /'pærət/ n papagayo, loro, m

parry /'pæri/ vt (a blow, and in fencing) parar; rechazar; evitar. —n parada, f; (in fencing) quite, m, parada, f

parse /pɑrs, pɑrz/ vt analizar

parsimonious /,pɑrsə'mouniəs/ a parsimonioso

parsimoniously /,pɑrsə'mouniəsli/ adv con parsimonia

parsimony /'pɑrsə,mouni/ n parsimonia, f

parsley /'pɑrsli/ n perejil, m

parsnip /'pɑrsnɪp/ n chirivía, f

part /pɑrt/ n parte, f; porción, f; trozo, m; Mech. pieza, f; (Gram. and of a literary work) parte, f; (of a living organism) miembro, m; (duty) deber, m, obligación, f; Theat. papel, m; Mus. voz, f; pl **parts**, (region) partes, f pl, lugar, m; (talents) partes, dotes, f pl. **foreign parts**, países extranjeros, m pl, el extranjero. **For my p....**, Por lo que a mí toca, Por mi parte. **for the most p.**, en su mayoría. **from all parts**, de todas partes. **in p.**, en parte; parcialmente. **spare p.**, pieza de recambio, f. **The funny p. of it is...**, Lo cómico del asunto es... **the latter p. of the month**, los últimos días del mes, la segunda quincena del mes. **to form p. of**, formar parte de. **to play a p.**, hacer un papel. **to take a person's p.**, apoyar a alguien, ser partidario de alguien. **to take in good p.**, tomar bien. **to take p. in**, tomar parte en, participar en. **p. of speech**, parte de la oración, f. **p.-owner**, copropietario (-ia). **p.-time job**, trabajo de unas cuantas horas, m

part /pɑrt/ vt distribuir, repartir; dividir; separar (de); (open) abrir. —vi partir, marcharse; despedirse; (of roads, etc.) bifurcarse; dividirse; (open) abrirse. **to p. one's hair**, hacerse la raya. **to p. from**, (things) separarse de; (people) despedirse de. **to p. with**, separarse de; deshacerse de; perder; (dismiss) despedir (a)

partake /pɑr'teik/ vt participar de, compartir; tomar parte en. —vi tomar algo (de comer, de beber). **to p. of**, comer (beber) de; tener rasgos de

Parthian /'pɑrθiən/ a parto. —n parto (-ta). **P. shot**, la flecha del parto

partial /'pɑrʃəl/ a parcial; (fond of) aficionado (a). **p. eclipse**, eclipse parcial, m

participant /pɑr'tɪsəpənt/ a participante. —n partícipe, mf

participate /pɑr'tɪsə,peit/ vi participar (de), compartir; tomar parte (en)

participation /pɑr,tɪsə'peiʃən/ n participación, f

particle /'pɑrtɪkəl/ n partícula, f; Fig. átomo, grano, m, pizca, f; Gram. partícula, f

parti-colored /'pɑrti,kʌlərd/ a bicolor

particular /pər'tɪkyələr/ a particular; especial; individual; singular; cierto; exacto; escrupuloso; difícil, exigente. —n detalle, pormenor, m; circunstancia, f; caso particular, m; pl **particulars**, informes, detalles, m pl. **further particulars**, más detalles. **in p.**, en particular; sobre todo. **He is very p. about...**, Es muy exigente en cuanto a...; Le es muy importante..., Le importa mucho...

particularize /pər'tɪkyələ,raiz/ vt particularizar, detallar; especificar

particularly /pər'tɪkyələrli/ adv en particular; particularmente; sobre todo

parting /'pɑrtɪŋ/ n despedida, f; partida, f; separación, f; (of the hair) raya, crencha, f; (cross roads) bifurcación, f.

—a de despedida. **at p.**, al despedirse. **to reach the p. of the ways**, Fig. llegar al punto decisivo

partisan /'pɑrtəzən, -sən/ n partidario (-ia); (fighter) guerrillero, m, a partidario; de guerrilleros

partisanship /'pɑrtə,zənʃɪp/ n partidarismo, m

partition /pɑr'tɪʃən, pər-/ n partición, f; división, f; (wall) pared, f, tabique, m. **the p. of Ireland**, la división de Irlanda

partly /'pɑrtli/ adv en parte

partner /'pɑrtnər/ n asociado (-da); Com. socio (-ia); (dancing) pareja, f; (in games, and companion) compañero (-ra); (spouse) consorte, mf; (in crime) codelincuente, mf **sleeping p.**, socio comanditario, m. **working p.**, socio industrial, m

partnership /'pɑrtnər,ʃɪp/ n asociación, f; Com. sociedad, compañía, f. **deed of p.**, artículos de sociedad, m pl. **to take into p.**, tomar como socio (a). **to form a p.**, asociarse

partridge /'pɑrtrɪdʒ/ n Ornith. perdiz, f. **young p.**, perdigón, m

parturition /,pɑrtu'rɪʃən, -tʃu-/ n parto, m

party /'pɑrti/ n partido, m; grupo, m; (of pleasure, etc.) partida, f; reunión, fiesta, f; Mil. pelotón, destacamento, m; Law. parte, f; (person) interesado (-da); (accessory) cómplice, mf. **rescue p.**, pelotón de salvamento, m. **to be a p. to**, prestarse a; ser cómplice en. **to give a p.**, dar una fiesta, dar una reunión. **p.-spirit**, espíritu del partido, m. **p.-wall**, pared medianera, f

parvenu /'pɑrvə,nu/ n advenedizo (-za)

pass /pæs/ n (in an exam.) aprobación, f; (crisis) crisis, situación crítica, f; estado, m; (with the hands) pase, m; (permit) permiso, m; Mil. licencia, f; (safe-conduct) salvoconducto, m; (in football, etc.) pase, m; (membership card) carnet, m; (defile) desfiladero, paso, puerto, m; Naut. rebasadero, m; (fencing) estocada, f. **free p.**, billete de favor, m. **p.-book**, libreta de banco, f. **p. certificate**, (in exams.) aprobado, m. **p.-key**, llave maestra, f

pass /pæs/ vi pasar; (of time) correr, pasar, transcurrir; (happen) ocurrir, tomar lugar; (end) cesar, desaparecer; (die) morir. —vt pasar; hacer pasar; (the butter, etc.) dar, alargar; (in football, hockey) pasar; (excel) aventajar, exceder; (a bill, an examination) aprobar; (sentence) fallar, pronunciar; (a remark) hacer; (transfer) traspasar; (tolerate) sufrir, tolerar; evacuar. **He passed in psychology**, Aprobó sicología. **to allow to p.**, ceder el paso (a). **to bring to p.**, ocasionar. **to come to p.**, suceder. **to let p.**, (put up with) dejar pasar; no hacer caso de; (forgive) perdonar. **to p. a vote of confidence**, votar una proposición de confianza. **to p. the buck**, Inf. echarle a uno el muerto. **pass the hat, pass the plate,** pasar la gorra. **to p. along,** pasar por; pasar. **to p. away,** pasar; desaparecer; (die) morir, fallecer; (of time) transcurrir. **to p. by,** pasar por, pasar delante de, pasar al lado de; (omit) pasar por alto de, omitir; (ignore) pasar sin hacer caso de. **to p. for,** pasar por. **to p. in,** entrar. **to p. in and out,** entrar y salir. **to p. off,** *vi* pasar; cesar, acabarse; desaparecer; evaporarse, disiparse; (of events) tener lugar. —*vt* (oneself) darse por; dar por, hacer pasar por. **to p. a cat off as hare,** dar gato por liebre. **to p. on,** *vi* pasar; seguir su camino, continuar su marcha. —*vt* pasar algo de uno a otro. **to p. out,** salir. **to p. over,** pasar por encima de; pasar; cruzar, atravesar; (transfer) traspasar; (disregard) pasar por alto de, dejar a un lado; omitir. **to p. over in silence,** pasar en silencio (por). **to p. round,** circular. **to p. through,** cruzar, atravesar, pasar por; (pierce) traspasar; *Fig.* experimentar

passable /'pæsəbəl/ *a* transitable, pasadero; (fairly good) regular, mediano; tolerable

passably /'pæsəbli/ *adv* medianamente, pasaderamente, tolerablemente

passage /'pæsɪdʒ/ *n* pasaje, *m;* paso, tránsito, *m;* (voyage) viaje, *m,* travesía, *f;* (corridor) pasillo, *m;* (entrance) entrada, *f;* (way) camino, *m;* (alley) callejón, *m;* (in a mine) galería, *f;* (of time) transcurso, *m;* (of birds) pasa, *f;* (in a book, and *Mus.*) pasaje, *m;* (occurrence) episodio, incidente, *m;* (of a bill) aprobación, *f.* **p. money,** pasaje, *m.* **p. of arms,** lucha, *f,* combate, *m;* disputa, *f*

passenger /'pæsəndʒər/ *n* viajero (-ra); (on foot) peatón, *m.* **by p. train,** en gran velocidad

passerby /'pæsər'bai/ *n* transeúnte, paseante, *mf*

passing /'pæsɪŋ/ *a* pasajero; fugitivo; momentáneo. —*adv* sumamente, extremadamente. —*n* pasada, *f;* paso, *m;* (death) muerte, *m;* (disappearance) desaparición, *f;* (of a law) aprobación, *f.* **in p.,** de paso. **p.-bell,** toque de difuntos, *m*

passing grade *n* mínima calificación aprobatoria, *f*

passion /'pæʃən/ *n* pasión, *f;* (Christ's) Pasión, *f;* (anger) cólera, *f.* **to fly into a p.,** montar en cólera. **p.-flower,** pasionaria, granadilla, *f.* **P. play,** drama de la Pasión, *m.* **P. Sunday,** Domingo de Pasión, *m.* **P. Week,** Semana Santa, *f*

passionate /'pæʃənɪt/ *a* apasionado; (quick-tempered) irascible, colérico; (fervid) vehemente, intenso, ardiente

passive /'pæsɪv/ *a* pasivo. —*n Gram.* pasiva, *f.* **p. resistance,** resistencia pasiva, *f*

Passover /'pæs,ouvər/ *n* Pascua de los judíos, *f*

passport /'pæsport/ *n* pasaporte, *m*

password /'pæs,wɜrd/ *n* contraseña, *f*

past /pæst/ *a* pasado; último; (expert) consumado; (former) antiguo, ex-. —*n* pasado, *m;* historia, *f,* antecedentes, *m pl,* *prep* después de; (in front of) delante de; (next to) al lado de; (beyond) más allá de; (without) sin; fuera de; (of age) más de; (no longer able to) incapaz de. —*adv* más allá. (The translation of **past** as an adverb is often either omitted, or included in the verb, e.g. *The years flew p.,* Los años transcurrieron. *for centuries p.,* durante siglos.) **I am p. caring,** Nada me importa ya. **It is a quarter p. ten,** Son las diez y cuarto. **It is p. four o'clock,** Son las siete pasadas, Son después de las cuatro. **what's p. is p.,** lo pasado, pasado. **p. doubt,** fuera de duda. **p. endurance,** insoportable. **p. help,** sin remedio, irremediable. **p. hope,** sin esperanza. **p.-master,** maestro, consumado, experto, *m.* **p. participle,** participio pasado, *m.* **p. president,** ex-presidente, *m.* **p. tense,** (tiempo) pasado, *m*

paste /peist/ *n* pasta, *f;* (gloy) engrudo, *m.* —*vt* (affix) pegar; (glue) engomar, engrudar

pastel /pæ'stɛl/ *n Art.* pastel, *m.* **p. drawing,** pintura al pastel, *f*

pasteurize /'pæstʃə,raiz/ *vt* pasteurizar

pastime /'pæs,taim/ *n* pasatiempo, entretenimiento, *m,* diversión, recreación, *f*

pastor /'pæstər/ *n* pastor, *m*

pastoral /'pæstərəl/ *a* pastoril; *Eccl.* pastoral. —*n Eccl.* pastoral, *f;* (Poet. Mus.) pastorela, *f*

pastry /'peistri/ *n* (dough) pasta, *f;* pastel, *m,* torta, *f;* pastelería, *f.* **p.-cook,** repostero, *m,* pastelero (-ra)

pasture /'pæstʃər/ *n* (grass, etc.) pasto, herbaje, *m;* pasturaje, *m;* (field) prado, *m,* pradera, dehesa, *f.* —*vi* pacer, pastar. —*vt* apacentar, pastar

pasty /'pæsti/ *a* pastoso; (pale) pálido. —*n* empanada, *f*

pat /pæt/ *n* toque, *m;* caricia, *f;* (for butter) molde (de mantequilla), *m.* —*vt* tocar; acariciar, pasar la mano (sobre). —*adv* a propósito; oportunamente; fácilmente. **pat of butter,** pedacito de mantequilla, *m.* **pat on the back,** golpe en la espalda, *m; Fig.* elogio, *m*

Patagonian /,pætə'gouniən/ *a* and *n* patagón (-ona)

patch /pætʃ/ *n* (mend) remiendo, *m;* (piece) pedazo, *m;* (plaster and *Auto.*, etc.) parche, *m;* (beauty spot) lunar postizo, *m;* (of ground) parcela, *f;* (of flowers, etc.) mancha, *f;* (stain and *Fig.*) mancha, *f.* —*vt* (mend) remendar; poner remiendo (a); pegar; (roughly) chafallar; (the face) ponerse lunares postizos. **p. of blue sky,** pedazo de cielo azul. **patch of green grass,** mancha de hierba verde. **to be not a p. on,** no ser de la misma clase que; (of persons) no llegarle a los zancajos de. **to p. up a quarrel,** hacer las paces

patchwork /'pætʃ,wɜrk/ *n* labor de retazos, obra de retacitos, f; *Fig.* mezcla, mezcolanza, f. **p. quilt,** centón, m

patchy /'pætʃi/ a desigual; manchado

patent /'pætnt/ a evidente, patente; patentado. —n patente, f. —vt patentar. **p. of nobility,** carta de hidalguía, ejecutoria, f. **"P. Applied For,"** «Patente Solicitada.» **Patent Pending** marca en trámite. **p. leather,** n charol, m. —a de charol. **p. medicine,** específico farmacéutico, m

patentee /,pætn'ti/ n el, m, (f, la) que obtiene una patente; inventor (-ra)

patently /'pætntli/ adv evidentemente, claramente

paternal /pə'tɜrnl/ a paterno, paternal

paternity /pə'tɜrnɪti/ n paternidad, f

path /pæθ/ n senda, vereda, f, sendero, m; camino, m; (track) pista, f; (traject) trayectoria, f. **the beaten p.,** el camino trillado

pathetic /pə'θɛtɪk/ a patético

pathology /pə'θɑlədʒi/ n patología, f

pathos /'peɪθɒs/ n lo patético

patience /'peɪʃəns/ n paciencia, f. **He tries my p. very much,** Me cuesta mucho no impacientarme con él. **to lose p.,** perder la paciencia; (grow angry) perder los estribos. **to play p.,** hacer solitarios

patient /'peɪʃənt/ a paciente. —n paciente, mf; (ill person) enfermo (-ma); (of a physician) cliente, mf

patiently /'peɪʃəntli/ adv con paciencia, pacientemente

patina /'pætnə, pə'tinə/ n pátina, f

patriarch /'peɪtri,ɑrk/ n patriarca, m

patrician /pə'trɪʃən/ a and n patricio (-ia)

patrimony /'pætrə,mouni/ n patrimonio, m

patriot /'peɪtriət/ n patriota, mf

patriotic /,peɪtri'ɒtɪk/ a patriótico

patriotism /'peɪtri,tɪzəm/ n patriotismo, m

patrol /pə'troul/ n patrulla, f; ronda, f, vi and vt patrullar; rondar; recorrer. **p. boat,** lancha escampavía, f. **p. flight,** vuelo de patrulla, m

patron /'peɪtrən/ n (of a freed slave) patrono, m; (of the arts, etc.) mecenas, protector, m; (customer) parroquiano (-na), cliente, mf. **p. saint,** santo (-ta) patrón (-ona)

patronage /'peɪtrənɪdʒ/ n (protection) patrocinio, m; protección, f; *Eccl.* patronato, m; (regular custom) clientela, f; (of manner) superioridad, f

patronize /'peɪtrə,naɪz/ vt patrocinar; proteger, favorecer; (a shop) ser parroquiano de; (treat arrogantly) tratar con superioridad

patronizing /'peɪtrə,naɪzɪŋ/ a (with air, behavior, etc.) de superioridad, de altivez

patter /'pætər/ n (jargon) jerga, f; charla, f; (of rain) azotes, m pl; (of feet) son, m; golpecitos, m pl. —vt (repeat) decir mecánicamente. —vi (chatter) charlar; (of rain) azotar, bailar; correr ligeramente

pattern /'pætərn/ n modelo, m; (Sew. and dressmaking) patrón, m; (in founding) molde, m; (template) escantillón, m; (of cloth, etc.) muestra, f; (design) dibujo, diseño, m; (example) ejemplar, m. —vt diseñar; estampar. **p. book,** libro de muestras, m

patty /'pæti/ n empanada, f, pastelillo, m

paucity /'pɔsɪti/ n poquedad, f; corto número, m; insuficiencia, escasez, f

paunch /pɔntʃ/ n panza, barriga, f

pauper /'pɔpər/ n pobre, mf

pauperism /'pɔpə,rɪzəm/ n pauperismo, m

pauperize /'pɔpə,raɪz/ vt empobrecer, reducir a la miseria

pause /pɔz/ n pausa, f; intervalo, m; silencio, m; interrupción, f; *Mus.* pausa, f. —vi pausar, hacer una pausa; detenerse, interrumpirse; vacilar. **to give p. to,** hacer vacilar (a)

pave /peiv/ vt empedrar, enlosar. **to p. the way for,** facilitar el paso de, preparar el terreno para, abrir el camino de

pavement /'peɪvmənt/ n pavimento, m; (sidewalk) acera, f. **p.-artist,** pintor callejero, m

pavilion /pə'vɪlyən/ n pabellón, m; (for a band, etc.) quiosco, m; (tent) tienda de campaña, f

paving /'peɪvɪŋ/ n pavimentación, f; empedrado, m; see **pavement. p.-stone,** losa, f

paw /pɔ/ n pata, f; (with claws) garra, f; *Inf.* manaza, f. —vt tocar con la pata; (scratch) arañar; (handle) manosear. —vi (of a horse) piafar

pawn /pɔn/ n (chess) peón (de ajedrez), m; empeño, m; *Fig.* prenda, f. —vt empeñar, pignorar; dar en prenda. **p.-ticket,** papeleta de empeño, f

pawnbroker /'pɔn,broukər/ n prestamista, mf

pawnshop /'pɔn,ʃɒp/ n casa de préstamos, casa de empeño, f, monte de piedad, m

pay /pei/ n paga, f; (*Mil. Nav.*) soldada, f; salario, m; (of a workman) jornal, m; (reward) recompensa, compensación, f; (profit) beneficio, provecho, m. **pay-day,** día de paga, m. **pay-office,** pagaduría, f. **pay-sheet,** nómina, f

pay /pei/ vt pagar; (a debt) satisfacer; (spend) gastar; (recompense) remunerar, recompensar; (hand over) entregar; (yield) producir; (a visit) hacer; (attention) prestar; (homage) rendir; (one's respects) presentar. —vi pagar; producir ganancia; sacar provecho; ser una ventaja, ser provechoso. **It would not pay him to do it,** No le saldría a cuenta hacerlo. **This job doesn't pay,** Este trabajo no da dinero. **to pay a compliment (to),** cumplimentar, decir alabanzas (a), echar una flor (a). **to pay attention,** prestar atención; hacer caso. **to pay cash,** pagar al contado. **to pay in advance,** pagar adelantado. **to pay in full,**

saldar. **to pay off old scores,** ajustar cuentas viejas. **to pay one's addresses to,** hacer la corte (a), pretender en matrimonio (a). **to pay the penalty,** sufrir el castigo, hacer penitencia. **to pay with interest,** pagar con creces. **to pay again,** volver a pagar, pagar de nuevo. **to pay back,** devolver, restituir; (money only) reembolsar; *Fig.* pagar en la misma moneda, vengarse (de). **to pay down,** pagar al contado. **to pay for,** pagar, costear; satisfacer. **to pay in,** ingresar. **to pay off,** (persons) despedir; (a debt) saldar; (a mortgage) cancelar, redimir. **to pay out,** (persons) vengarse de; (money) pagar; (ropes, etc.) arriar. **to pay up,** pagar; pagar por completo; (shares, etc.) redimir

payable /'peɪəbəl/ a pagadero; a pagar; que puede ser pagado

payee /peɪ'iː/ n tenedor, m

paymaster /'peɪˌmæstər/ n pagador, m; tesorero, m. **P.-General,** ordenador general de pagos, m

payment /'peɪmənt/ n pago, m, paga, f; remuneración, f; *Fig.* recompensa, satisfacción, f; *Fig.* premio, m. **in p. of,** en pago de. **on p. of,** mediante el pago de. **p. in advance,** pago adelantado, anticipo, m

pea /piː/ n guisante, m. **dry or split pea,** guisante seco, m. **sweet pea,** guisante de olor, m. **pea-flour,** harina de guisantes, f. **pea-green,** verde claro, m. **pea-jacket,** chaquetón de piloto, m. **pea-shooter,** cerbatana, f

peace /piːs/ n paz, f; tranquilidad, quietud, f, sosiego, m; *Law.* orden público, m. **P.!** ¡Silencio! **to hold one's p.,** callarse, guardar silencio. **to make p.,** hacer las paces. **P. be upon this house!** ¡Paz sea en esta casa! **p.-footing,** pie de paz, m. **p.-loving,** pacífico. **p.-offering,** sacrificio propiciatorio, m; satisfacción, oferta de paz, f

peaceable /'piːsəbəl/ a pacífico; apacible; tranquilo, sosegado

peaceful /'piːsfəl/ a pacífico; tranquilo; silencioso. **to come with p. intentions,** venir de paz

peacefully /'piːsfəli/ adv en paz; pacíficamente; tranquilamente

peacemaker /'piːsˌmeɪkər/ n pacificador (-ra), conciliador (-ra)

peach /piːtʃ/ n (fruit) melocotón, m; (tree) melocotonero, melocotón, m; (girl) breva, f. **p.-colour,** color de melocotón, m

peacock /'piːˌkɒk/ n pavo real, pavón, m. —vi pavonearse; darse humos. **The p. spread its tail,** El pavo real hizo la rueda

peak /piːk/ n punta, f; (of a cap) visera, f; (of a mountain) peñasco, m, cumbre, cima, f; (mountain itself) pico, m; (Naut. of a hull) pico, m; *Fig.* auge, apogeo, m; punto más alto, m. —vi consumirse, enflaquecer. **p. hours,** horas de mayor tráfico, f pl

peaked /'piːkɪd/ a en punta; puntiagudo; picudo; (of a cap) con visera; (wan) ojeroso; (thin) delgaducho, macilento, consumido

peal /piːl/ n toque (or repique) de campanas, m; campanillazo, m; carillón, m; (noise) estruendo, ruido, m; (of thunder) trueno, m; (of an organ) sonido, m. —vi repicar; sonar. —vt tañer, echar a vuelo (las campanas); (of a bell that one presses) hacer sonar, tocar. **a p. of laughter,** una carcajada

peanut /'piːˌnʌt/ n cacahuete, m. **p. butter,** mantequilla de cacahuete, f

pear /pɛər/ n pera, f. **p.-shaped,** piriforme, de figura de pera. **p. tree,** peral, m

pearl /pɜːrl/ n perla, f; (mother-of-pearl) nácar, m, a de perla; perlero. —vt (dew) rociar, aljofarar. —vi pescar perlas; formar perlas. **seed p.,** aljófar, m. **p.-ash,** carbonato potásico, m. **p.-barley,** cebada perlada, f. **p.-button,** botón de nácar, m. **p.-fisher,** pescador de perlas, m. **p.-fishery,** pescadería de perlas, f. **p.-grey,** gris de perla, m

peasant /'pɛzənt/ n campesino (-na), labrador (-ra). —a campesino

peasantry /'pɛzəntri/ n campesinos, m pl, gente del campo, f

peat /piːt/ n turba, f. **p.-bog,** turbera, f

pebble /'pɛbəl/ n guijarro, m, pedrezuela, guija, f; (gravel) guijo, m; cristal de roca, m; lente de cristal de roca, m

peccadillo /ˌpɛkə'dɪloʊ/ n pecadillo, m

peck /pɛk/ n (of a bird) picotazo, m, picada, f; (kiss) besito, m; (large amount) montón, m; multitud, f. —vt (of a bird) picotear; sacar (or coger) con el pico; (kiss) besar rápidamente. —vi (with at) picotear; picar

peculiar /pɪ'kyulyər/ a particular, peculiar, individual; propio, característico; (marked) especial; (unusual) extraño, raro, extraordinario

peculiarity /pɪˌkyuli'ærɪti/ n peculiaridad, particularidad, f; singularidad, f; (eccentricity) excentricidad, rareza, f

peculiarly /pɪ'kyulyɔrli/ adv particularmente, peculiarmente; especialmente; extrañamente

pecuniary /pɪ'kyuniˌɛri/ a pecuniario

pedagogic /ˌpɛdə'gɒdʒɪk/ a pedagógico

pedagogue /'pɛdəˌgɒg/ n pedagogo, m

pedagogy /'pɛdəˌgoudʒi, -ˌgɒdʒi/ n pedagogía, f

pedal /'pɛdl/ n pedal, m. —vi pedalear

pedant /'pɛdnt/ n pedante, mf

pedantic /pə'dæntɪk/ a pedante

pedantry /'pɛdntri/ n pedantería, f

peddle /'pɛdl/ vi ser buhonero. —vt revender

pedestal /'pɛdəstl/ n pedestal, m; *Fig.* fundamento, m, base, f. **to put on a p.,** *Fig.* poner sobre un pedestal

pedestrian /pə'dɛstriən/ n peatón, peón, m, a pedestre; *Fig.* patoso. **p. traffic,** circulación de los peatones, f

pedestrian crosswalk, cruce peatonal (Argentina), cruce de peatones, *m*

pediatrician /ˌpidiə'trɪʃən/ *n* pediatra, *mf*

pedigree /'pɛdɪˌgri/ *n* genealogía, *f*; raza, *f*; (of words) etimología, *f*. —*a* (of animals) de raza, de casta. **p. dog**, perro de casta, *m*

pedlar /'pɛdlər/ *n* buhonero, *m*

pedometer /pə'dɒmɪtər/ *n* pedómetro, cuentapasos, *m*

peel /pil/ *n* (baker's) pala, *f*; (of fruit, etc.) piel, *f*, hollejo, *m*. —*vt* pelar, mondar; (bark) descortezar. —*vi* descascararse, desconcharse; (of the bark of a tree) descortezarse

peeling /'pilɪŋ/ *n* (of fruit, etc.) peladura, monda, *f*; (of bark) descortezadura, *f*; (of paint, etc.) desconchadura, *f*

peep /pip/ *vi* (of birds) piar; (of mice) chillar; (peer) atisbar, mirar a hurtadillas; (appear) asomar; mostrarse; (of the dawn) despuntar. —*n* (of birds) pío, *m*; (of mice) chillido, *m*; (glimpse) vista, *f*; (glance) ojeada, mirada furtiva, *f*. **at the p. of day**, al despuntar el día. **p.-hole**, mirilla, *f*, atisbadero, *m*; escucha, *f*. **p.-show**, óptica, *f*

peer /pɪər/ *n* par, *m*; igual, *mf*. —*vi* atisbar; escudriñar; *Fig.* asomar, aparecer

peerless /'pɪərlɪs/ *a* sin par, incomparable, sin igual

peevish /'pivɪʃ/ *a* displicente, malhumorado; picajoso, vidrioso, enojadizo

peg /pɛg/ *n* clavija, *f*; (of a tent) estaca, *f*; (of a barrel) estaquilla, *f*; (of a violin, etc.) clavija, *f*; (for coats, etc.) colgadero, *m*; (of whisky, etc.) trago, *m*; *Fig.* pretexto, *m*. —*vt* clavar, enclavijar, empernar. **to take down a peg**, bajar los humos (a). **to peg away**, batirse el cobre. **to peg down**, fijar con clavijas; (a tent) sujetar con estacas; (prices) fijar

peignoir /pein'war/ *n* peinador, salto de cama, *m*, bata, *f*

pekinese /ˌpikə'niz/ *n* perro (-rra) pequinés (-esa)

pelican /'pɛlɪkən/ *n* pelícano, *m*

pellagra /pə'lægrə/ *n* *Med.* pelagra, *f*

pellet /'pɛlɪt/ *n* bolita, *f*; (pill) píldora, *f*; (shot) perdigón, *m*

pellmell /'pɛl'mɛl/ *adv* a trochemoche; atropelladamente

pellucid /pə'lusɪd/ *a* diáfano

pelota /pə'loutə/ *n* pelota vasca, *f*. **p. player**, pelotari, *m*

pelt /pɛlt/ *n* pellejo, *m*; cuero, *m*; (fur) piel, *f*; (blow) golpe, *m*. —*vt* llover (piedras, etc.) sobre, arrojar... sobre; (questions) disparar; (throw) tirar. —*vi* (of rrain) azotar, diluviar

pelvis /'pɛlvɪs/ *n* pelvis, *f*

pen /pɛn/ *n* (for sheep, etc.) aprisco, *m*; corral, *m*; (paddock) parque, *m*; (for hens) pollera, *f*; (for writing and *Fig.*, author, etc.) pluma, *f*. —*vt* (shut up) acorralar; encerrar; (write) escribir (con pluma). **pen-and-ink drawing**, dibujo a

la pluma, *m*. **pen-holder**, portaplumas, *m*. **pen-name**, seudónimo, *m*. **pen-wiper**, limpiaplumas, *m*

penal /'pinḷ/ *a* penal. **p. code**, código penal, *m*. **p. colony**, colonia penal, *f*. **p. servitude**, trabajos forzados (or forzosos), *m pl*. **p. servitude for life**, cadena perpetua, *f*

penalize /'pinḷˌaiz/ *vt* penar, imponer pena (a); castigar

penalty /'pɛnḷti/ *n* *Law.* penalidad, *f*; castigo, *m*; (fine) multa, *f*; (risk) riesgo, *m*; *Sports.* sanción, *m*. **the p. of**, la desventaja de. **under p. of**, so pena de. **p. kick**, (football) penalty, *m*

penance /'pɛnəns/ *n* penitencia, *f*. **to do p.**, hacer penitencia

penchant /'pɛntʃənt/ *n* tendencia, *f*; inclinación, *f*

pencil /'pɛnsəl/ *n* lápiz, *m*; (automatic) lapicero, *m*. —*vt* escribir (or dibujar or marcar) con lápiz. **p.-case**, estuche para lápices, *m*. **p.-holder**, lapicero, *m*. **p.-sharpener**, cortalápices, afilalápices, *m*

pendant /'pɛndənt/ *n* (jewel) pendiente, *m*; *Archit.* culo de lámpara, *m*; (Naut. rope) amantillo, *m*; (flag) gallardete, *m*

pending /'pɛndɪŋ/ *a* pendiente. —*prep* durante. **to be p.**, pender; amenazar

pendulous /'pɛndʒələs/ *a* péndulo; colgante; oscilante

pendulum /'pɛndʒələm/ *n* péndola, *f*, péndulo, *m*

penetrable /'pɛnɪtrəbəl/ *a* penetrable

penetrate /'pɛnɪˌtreit/ *vt and vi* penetrar

penetrating /'pɛnɪˌtreitɪŋ/ *a* penetrante

penetration /ˌpɛnɪ'treiʃən/ *n* penetración, *f*

penguin /'pɛŋgwɪn/ *n* pingüino, pájaro bobo, *m*

penicillin /ˌpɛnə'sɪlɪn/ *n* penicilina, *f*

peninsula /pə'nɪnsələ, -'nɪnsyələ/ *n* península, *f*

peninsular /pə'nɪnsələr, -'nɪnsyələr/ *a* peninsular. **P. War**, Guerra de la Independencia, *f*

penis /'pinɪs/ *n* pene, *m*

penitence /'pɛnɪtəns/ *n* penitencia, *f*

penitent /'pɛnɪtənt/ *a* penitente. —*n* penitente, *mf*

penitentiary /ˌpɛnɪ'tɛnʃəri/ *n* *Eccl.* penitenciaria, *f*; casa de corrección, *f*; penitenciaria, *f*; presidio, *m*; cárcel modelo, *f*, *a* penitenciario

penknife /'pɛnˌnaif/ *n* cortaplumas, *m*

penmanship /'pɛnmənˌʃip/ *n* caligrafía, *f*

pennant /'pɛnənt/ *n* *Naut.* gallardete, *m*; banderola, *f*; (ensign) insignia, bandera, *f*

penniless /'pɛnɪlɪs/ *a* sin un penique, sin blanca; indigente, pobre de solemnidad. **to leave p.**, dejar en la miseria; *Inf.* dejar sin camisa

penning /'pɛnɪŋ/ *n* escritura, *f*; (drawing up) redacción, *f*; (of bulls, etc.) acorralamiento, *m*

penny /'pɛni/ *n* de un centavo, penique, *m*; perra gorda, *f*. —*a* de un penique. **p.-**

a-liner, gacetillero, *m.* **p. dreadful,** folletín, *m,* novela por entregas, *f.* **p.-in-the-slot machine,** tragaperras, *f*

pension /'pɛnʃən/ *n* pensión, *f; Mil.* retiro, *m;* (grant) beca, *f;* (boardinghouse) pensión de familia, *f.* —*vt* pensionar, dar una pensión (a); (with off) jubilar. **old age p.,** pensión para la vejez, *f.* **retirement p.,** pensión vitalicia, *f*

pensioner /'pɛnʃənər/ *n* pensionista, *mf;* (Mil. and Nav.) inválido, *m*

pensive /'pɛnsɪv/ *a* pensativo, meditabundo; cabizbajo, triste

pentagon /'pɛntəˌgɒn/ *n* pentágono, *m*

Pentateuch /'pɛntəˌtuk/ *n* pentateuco, *m*

Pentecost /'pɛntɪˌkɔst/ *n* Pentecostés, *m,* Pascua, *f*

pentecostal /ˌpɛntɪˈkɔstl/ *a* de Pentecostés, pascual

penthouse /'pɛntˌhaʊs/ *n* cobertizo, tinglado, *m,* tejavana, *f*

pent-up /pɛnt ˈʌp/ *a* encerrado; enjaulado; (of emotion) reprimido

penurious /pəˈnʊriəs/ *a* pobre; escaso; (stingy) tacaño, avaro

penury /'pɛnyəri/ *n* penuria, *f*

people /'pipəl/ *n* pueblo, *m;* nación, *f;* gente, *f;* personas, *f pl;* (used disparagingly, mob) populacho, vulgo, *m;* (inhabitants) habitantes, *m pl;* (subjects) súbditos, *m pl;* (relations) parientes, *m pl;* familia, *f.* —*vt* poblar. **little p.,** (children) gente menuda, *f.* **respectable p.,** gente de bien, *f.* **the p. of Burgos,** los habitantes de Burgos. **P. say,** Se dice, La gente dice. **Very few p. think as you do,** Hay muy pocas personas que opinan como Vd. **How are your p.** (family)? ¿Cómo están los de tu casa? ¿Cómo está tu familia? **"People Working"** «Trabajadores»

pep /pɛp/ *n Inf.* energía, *f,* ánimo, *m.* **p. talk,** discurso estimulante, *m.* **p. up,** animar

pepper /'pɛpər/ *n* pimienta, *f;* (plant) pimentero, pimiento, *m, vt* sazonar con pimienta; (pelt) acribillar; (with questions) disparar; (a literary work with quotations, etc.) salpimentar. **black p.,** pimienta negra, *f.* **red p.,** pimiento, *m;* (cayenne) pimentón, *m.* **p.-castor,** pimentero, *m*

peppercorn /'pɛpərˌkɔrn/ *n* grano de pimienta, *m*

peppermint /'pɛpərˌmɪnt/ *n* menta, *f.* **p. drop,** pastilla de menta, *f*

peppery /'pɛpəri/ *a* picante; (irascible) colérico, irascible

peptic /'pɛptɪk/ *a* péptico

per /pər; *unstressed* pər/ *prep* por. **ninety miles per hour,** noventa millas por hora. **ten pesetas per dozen,** diez pesetas la docena. **$60 per annum,** sesenta dólares al año. **per cent.,** por ciento

perambulate /pərˈæmbyəˌleit/ *vt* recorrer

perambulator /pərˈæmbyəˌleitər/ *n* cochecito para niños, *m*

percale /pərˈkeil/ *n* percal, *m*

percaline /ˌpərkəˈlin/ *n* percalina, *f*

perceive /pərˈsiv/ *vt* percibir, comprender, darse cuenta de; percibir, discernir

percentage /pərˈsɛntɪdʒ/ *n* tanto por ciento, *m;* porcentaje, *m*

perceptible /pərˈsɛptəbəl/ *a* perceptible, visible; sensible

perception /pərˈsɛpʃən/ *n* percepción, *f;* sensibilidad, *f*

perceptive /pərˈsɛptɪv/ *a* perceptivo

perch /pərtʃ/ *n Ichth.* perca, *f;* (for birds) percha, *f;* (measure) pértiga, *f.* —*vi* posarse (en or sobre). —*vt* posar (en or sobre)

percolate /'pərkəˌleit/ *vi* filtrar; *Fig.* penetrar. —*vt* filtrar, colar

percolation /ˌpərkəˈleiʃən/ *n* filtración, *f*

percolator /'pərkəˌleitər/ *n* filtro, *m.* **coffee p.,** colador de café, *m*

percussion /pərˈkʌʃən/ *n* percusión, *f;* choque, *m.* **p. cap,** fulminante, *m.* **p. instrument,** instrumento de percusión, *m*

perdition /pərˈdɪʃən/ *n* perdición, *f;* ruina, *f*

peremptory /pəˈrɛmptəri/ *a* perentorio; (of manner, etc.) imperioso, autoritario

perennial /pəˈrɛniəl/ *a Bot.* vivaz; perenne; eterno, perpetuo. —*n* planta vivaz, *f*

perfect /*a.*, *n.* 'pərfɪkt; *v.* pərˈfɛkt/ *a* perfecto; (of a work) acabado; completo. —*n Gram.* (tiempo) perfecto, *m.* —*vt* perfeccionar; (oneself) perfeccionarse. **to have a p. knowledge of...,** conocer a fondo... **They are p. strangers to me,** Me son completamente desconocidos

perfectible /pərˈfɛktəbəl/ *a* perfectible

perfection /pərˈfɛkʃən/ *n* perfección, *f;* excelencia, *f.* **to p.,** a la perfección, a las mil maravillas

perfectionist /pərˈfɛkʃənɪst/ *n* perfeccionista, *mf*

perfidious /pərˈfɪdiəs/ *a* pérfido

perfidy /'pərfɪdi/ *n* perfidia, *f*

perforate /'pərfəˌreit/ *vt* perforar, agujerear

perforating /'pərfəˌreitɪŋ/ *a* perforador

perforation /ˌpərfəˈreiʃən/ *n* perforación, *f;* agujero, *m*

perforce /pərˈfɔrs/ *adv* a la fuerza, forzosamente

perform /pərˈfɔrm/ *vt* hacer; poner por obra, llevar a cabo; desempeñar, cumplir; ejercer; (a piece of music, etc.) ejecutar; realizar; (a play) representar, dar; (a part in a play) desempeñar (el papel de...); (Divine Service) oficiar. —*vi Theat.* trabajar, representar un papel; (a musical instrument) tocar; (sing) cantar; (of animals) hacer trucos

performable /pərˈfɔrməbəl/ *a* hacedero, practicable, ejecutable; *Theat.* que puede representarse; *Mus.* tocable

performance /pərˈfɔrməns/ *n* ejecución, realización, *f;* desempeño, ejercicio, *m;* cumplimiento, *m;* acción, *f;* hazaña, *f;* (work) obra, *f; Theat.* función, repre-

sentación, f; (*Theat.* acting of a part) interpretación, f; *Mus.* ejecución, f; *Mech.* potencia, f. **first p.,** *Theat.* estreno, m
performer /pər'fɔrmər/ n *Mus.* ejecutante, mf, músico, m; *Theat.* actor (-triz), representante, mf; artista, mf
performing /pər'fɔrmɪŋ/ a (of animals) sabio. **p. dog,** perro sabio, m
perfume /n. 'pɜrfyum; v. pər'fyum/ n perfume, m; fragancia, f; aroma, m. —vt perfumar; embalsamar, aromatizar, llenar con fragancia. **p. burner,** perfumador, m
perfumery /pər'fyuməri/ n perfumería, f
perfunctorily /pər'fʌŋktərəli/ adv perfunctoriamente, sin cuidado; superficialmente
perfunctory /pər'fʌŋktəri/ a perfunctorio, negligente; superficial; ligero, de cumplido
pergola /'pɜrgələ/ n emparrado, cenador, m
perhaps /pər'hæps/ adv quizá, quizás(s), tal vez
peril /'perəl/ n peligro, m; riesgo, m. —vt poner en peligro; arriesgar. **at one's p.,** a su riesgo. **in p.,** en peligro
perilous /'perələs/ a peligroso, arriesgado
perimeter /pə'rɪmɪtər/ n perímetro, m
period /'pɪəriəd/ n período, m; época, f; edad, f, tiempo, m; duración, f; término, plazo, m; *Gram.* período, m; (full stop) punto final, m; *Med.* menstruación, regla, f. **p. furniture,** muebles de época, m pl
periodic /ˌpɪəri'ɒdɪk/ a periódico
periodical /ˌpɪəri'ɒdɪkəl/ a periódico. —n publicación periódica, revista, f
peripatetic /ˌperəpə'tetɪk/ a peripatético
peripheral /pə'rɪfərəl/ a periférico
periphery /pə'rɪfəri/ n periferia, f
periscope /'perəˌskoup/ n periscopio, m
perish /'perɪʃ/ vi perecer; marchitarse; desaparecer, acabar. **to be perished with cold,** estar muerto de frío
perishable /'perɪʃəbəl/ a perecedero, frágil
peritonitis /ˌperɪtɪ'naɪtɪs/ n peritonitis, f
periwinkle /'perɪˌwɪŋkəl/ n *Zool.* caracol marino, m; *Bot.* vincapervinca, f
perjure /'pɜrdʒər/ vt perjurar. **to p. oneself,** perjurarse
perjurer /'pɜrdʒərər/ n perjuro (-ra); perjurador (-ra)
perjury /'pɜrdʒəri/ n perjurio, m. **to commit p.,** jurar en falso, perjurar
perk (up) /pɜrk/ vi levantar la cabeza; recobrar sus bríos, alzar la cabeza; sacar la cabeza
perky /'pɜrki/ a desenvuelto, gallardo; coquetón; atrevido; (gay) alegre
permanence /'pɜrmənəns/ n permanencia, f; estabilidad, f
permanent /'pɜrmənənt/ a permanente; estable; (of posts, etc.) fijo. **p. wave,** ondulación permanente, f. **p. way,** *Rail.* vía, f
permeable /'pɜrmiəbəl/ a permeable

permeate /'pɜrmi,eit/ vt penetrar; impregnar; *Fig.* infiltrar (en)
permissible /pər'mɪsəbəl/ a permisible, admisible; lícito
permission /pər'mɪʃən/ n permiso, m, licencia, f
permissive /pər'mɪsɪv/ a permisivo, tolerado; (optional) facultativo
permit /v pər'mɪt; n 'pɜrmɪt/ vt permitir; dar permiso (a), dejar; tolerar, sufrir; admitir. —n permiso, m; licencia, f; pase, m. **Will you p. me to smoke?** ¿Me permites fumar?
permutation /ˌpɜrmyu'teiʃən/ n permutación, f
permute /pər'myut/ vt permutar
pernicious /pər'nɪʃəs/ a pernicioso. **p. anemia,** anemia perniciosa, f
pernickety /pər'nɪkɪti/ a tiquismiquis
peroration /ˌperə'reiʃən/ n peroración, f
peroxide /pə'rɒksaid/ n peróxido, m
perpendicular /ˌpɜrpən'dɪkyələr/ a perpendicular. —n perpendicular, f
perpetrate /'pɜrpɪ,treit/ vt *Law.* perpetrar; cometer
perpetrator /'pɜrpɪ,treitər/ n el, m, (f, la) que comete; *Law.* autor (-ra); perpetrador (-ra)
perpetual /pər'petʃuəl/ a perpetuo, perdurable, eterno; incesante, constante; (life-long) perpetuo
perpetually /pər'petʃuəli/ adv perpetuamente; sin cesar; continuamente; constantemente
perpetuate /pər'petʃu,eit/ vt perpetuar, eternizar; inmortalizar
perpetuity /ˌpɜrpɪ'tuiti/ n perpetuidad, f. **in p.,** para siempre
perplex /pər'pleks/ vt dejar perplejo, aturdir, confundir; embrollar
perplexed /pər'plekst/ a perplejo, irresoluto; confuso; (of questions, etc.) complicado, intrincado
perplexing /pər'pleksɪŋ/ a difícil; complicado; confuso
perplexity /pər'pleksɪti/ n perplejidad, f; confusión, f
perquisites /'pɜrkwəzɪts/ n pl emolumentos, m pl; gajes, percances, m pl; (tips) propinas, f pl
persecute /'pɜrsɪ,kyut/ vt perseguir; importunar, molestar
persecution /ˌpɜrsɪ'kyuʃən/ n persecución, f
persecutor /'pɜrsɪ,kyutər/ n perseguidor (-ra)
perseverance /ˌpɜrsə'vɪərəns/ n perseverancia, f
persevere /ˌpɜrsə'vɪər/ vi perseverar
persevering /ˌpɜrsə'vɪərɪŋ/ a perseverante
perseveringly /ˌpɜrsə'vɪərɪŋli/ adv con perseverancia, perseverantemente
Persia /'pɜrʒə/ (la) Persia, f
Persian /'pɜrʒən/ a persa; de Persia; pérsico. —n persa, mf; (language) persa, m.

P. blinds, persianas, f pl. P. cat, gato
(-ta) de Angora

persist /pər'sɪst/ vi persistir; persistir
(en), empeñarse (en), obstinarse (en)

persistence /pər'sɪstəns/ n persistencia, f

persistent /pər'sɪstənt/ a persistente

persistently /pər'sɪstəntli/ adv con persistencia, persistentemente

person /'pɜrsən/ n persona, f. first p.,
Gram. primera persona, f. in p., en persona. no p., nadie

personable /'pɜrsənəbəl/ a bien parecido

personage /'pɜrsənɪdʒ/ n personaje, m

personal /'pɜrsənəl/ a personal; íntimo;
particular; en persona; (movable) mueble. He is to make a p. appearance, Va
a estar presente en persona. p. column,
(in a newspaper) columna de los suspiros,
f. p. equation, ecuación personal, f. p.
estate, (goods) bienes muebles, m pl

personality /,pɜrsə'nælɪti/ n personalidad, f; (insult) personalismo, m. dual p.,
conciencia doble, f

personate /'pɜrsə,neit/ vt (in a play)
hacer el papel de; (impersonate) hacerse
pasar por

personification /pər,sɒnəfɪ'keiʃən/ n
personificación, f

personify /pər'sɒnə,fai/ vt personificar

personnel /,pɜrsə'nel/ n personal, m

perspective /pər'spektɪv/ n perspectiva,
f, a en perspectiva

perspicacious /,pɜrspɪ'keiʃəs/ a perspicaz, clarividente, sagaz

perspicacity /,pɜrspɪ'kæsɪti/ n perspicacia, clarividencia, sagacidad, f

perspicuity /,pɜrspɪ'kyuɪti/ n perspicui-
dad, claridad, lucidez, f

perspicuous /pər'spɪkyuəs/ a perspicuo,
claro

perspiration /'pɜrspə'reiʃən/ n sudor, m

perspire /pər'spaiˀr/ vi sudar, transpirar

persuadable /pər'sweidəbəl/ a persuasible

persuade /pər'sweid/ vt persuadir; inducir (a), instar (a), mover (a), inclinar (a)

persuasion /pər'sweiʒən/ n persuasión,
f; persuasiva, f; opinión, f; creencia, f;
religión, f; secta, f

persuasive /pər'sweisɪv/ a persuasivo.
—n persuasión, f; aliciente, atractivo, m

persuasively /pər'sweisɪvli/ adv de un
modo persuasivo, persuasivamente

persuasiveness /pər'sweisɪvnɪs/ n persuasiva, f

pert /pɜrt/ a petulante; respondón, des-
parpajado

pertain /pər'tein/ vi pertenecer (a); tocar
(a), incumbir (a), convenir (a); estar relacionado (con)

pertinacious /,pɜrtn̩'eiʃəs/ a pertinaz

pertinaciously /,pɜrtn̩'eiʃəsli/ adv con
pertinacia

pertinacity /,pɜrtn̩'æsɪti/ n pertinacia, f

pertinence /'pɜrtn̩əns/ n pertinencia, f

pertinent /'pɜrtn̩ənt/ a pertinente,
atinado

pertinently /'pɜrtn̩əntli/ adv atinada-
mente

pertly /'pɜrtli/ adv con petulancia; con
descaro

pertness /'pɜrtnɪs/ n petulancia, f; desparpajo, descaro, m

perturb /pər'tɜrb/ vt perturbar, agitar,
turbar, inquietar

perturbation /,pɜrtər'beiʃən/ n perturbación, agitación, inquietud, f; confusión, f;
desorden, m

perturbed /pər'tɜrbd/ a perturbado,
agitado, ansioso, intranquilo

perturbing /pər'tɜrbɪŋ/ a perturbador,
inquietador

Peru /pə'ru/ el Perú

perusal /pə'ruzəl/ n lectura, f; examen,
m

peruse /pə'ruz/ vt leer con cuidado, estudiar, examinar

Peruvian /pə'ruvi ən/ a and n peruano
(-na)

pervade /pər'veid/ vt penetrar; llenar, saturar; difundirse por; reinar en

pervasive /pər'veisɪv/ a penetrante

perverse /pər'vɜrs/ a (wicked) perverso,
depravado; obstinado; travieso; intratable

perversion /pər'vɜrʒən/ n perversión, f

perversity /pər'vɜrsɪti/ n (wickedness)
perversidad, f; obstinacia, f; travesura, f

perversive /pər'vɜrsɪv/ a perversivo

pervert /pər'vɜrt/ vt pervertir; (words,
etc.) torcer, tergiversar

pervious /'pɜrviəs/ a penetrable; permeable

pessimism /'pesə,mɪzəm/ n pesimismo,
m

pessimist /'pesəmɪst/ n pesimista, mf

pessimistic /,pesə'mɪstɪk/ a pesimista

pessimistically /,pesə'mɪstɪkli/ adv con
pesimismo

pest /pest/ n insecto nocivo, m; animal
dañino, m; parásito, m; (pestilence)
peste, f; Fig. plaga, f; (person) mosca, f

pester /'pestər/ vt importunar, molestar,
incomodar. to p. constantly, Inf. no dejar a sol ni a sombra

pestering /'pestərɪŋ/ n importunaciones,
f pl

pestilence /'pestləns/ n pestilencia,
peste, f; plaga, f

pestilential /,pestl̩'enʃəl/ a pestilente,
pestífero; pernicioso

pestle /'pesəl/ n mano de mortero, f, vt
pistar, machacar, majar

pet /pet/ n animal doméstico, m; niño
(-ña) mimado (-da); favorito (-ta); (dear)
querido (-da); (peevishness) despecho,
malhumor, m. —vt acariciar; (spoil) mimar. to be a great pet, ser un gran favorito

petal /'petl/ n pétalo, m, hoja, f

peter (out) vi desaparecer; agotarse

petition /pə'tɪʃən/ n petición, f; súplica,
f; instancia, solicitud, f; memorial, m.
—vt suplicar; pedir, demandar; dirigir un

memorial (a). **to file a p.,** elevar una instancia

petitioner /pə'tɪʃənər/ n peticionario (-ia)

petrifaction /ˌpetrə'fækʃən/ n petrificación, f

petrify /'petrəˌfaɪ/ vt petrificar; Inf. dejar seco. **to become petrified,** petrificarse

petrol /'petrəl/ n bencina, gasolina, f. —a de gasolina, de bencina. **to run out of p.,** tener una pana de bencina. **p. gauge,** indicador del nivel de gasolina, m. **p. pump,** surtidor de gasolina, m. **p. station,** puesto de bencina, m, estación de servicio, f. **p. tank,** depósito de bencina, m

petroleum /pə'trouliəm/ n petróleo, m. —a petrolero; de petróleo. **p. works,** refinería de petróleo, f

petrology /pɪ'trɒlədʒi/ n petrografía, f

petrous /'petrəs/ a pétreo

petticoat /'petiˌkout/ n enagua, f; pl **petticoats,** (slang) faldas, f pl. —a de faldas, de mujeres; de mujer

pettifogger /'petiˌfɒgər/ n (lawyer) picapleitos, m, rábula, mf; (quibbler) sofista, mf

pettifogging /'petiˌfɒgɪŋ/ a charlatán, mezquino, trivial

pettiness /'petinɪs/ n trivialidad, insignificancia, f; pequeñez, f; mezquindad, f; ruindad, bajeza, f

petty /'peti/ a trivial, sin importancia, insignificante; inferior; pequeño; mezquino; ruin; bajo. **p. cash,** gastos menores de caja, m pl. **p. expense,** gasto menudo, m. **p. officer,** suboficial, m. **p. thief,** ratero (-ra)

petulance /'petʃələns/ n mal humor, m, displicencia, irritabilidad, f

petulant /'petʃələnt/ a malhumorado, displicente, enojadizo, irritable

petulantly /'petʃələntli/ adv displicentemente, con mal humor

pew /pyu/ n banco (de iglesia), m. **p.-opener,** sacristán, m

pewter /'pyutər/ n peltre, m, a de peltre

phalanx /'feilæŋks/ n falange, f

phallic /'fælɪk/ a fálico

phallus /'fæləs/ n falo, m

phantasmagoria /fænˌtæzmə'gɔriə/ n fantasmagoría, f

phantasmagoric /fænˌtæzmə'gɔrɪk/ a fantasmagórico

phantom /'fæntəm/ n fantasma, espectro, m; sombra, ficción, f; visión, f

pharmaceutical /ˌfɑrmə'sutɪkəl/ a farmacéutico; n producto farmacéutico, m

pharmacist /'fɑrməsɪst/ n farmacéutico, m

pharmacologist /ˌfɑrmə'kɒlədʒɪst/ n farmacólogo, m

pharmacology /ˌfɑrmə'kɒlədʒi/ n farmacología, f

pharmacy /'fɑrməsi/ n farmacia, f

pharyngitis /ˌfærɪn'dʒaɪtɪs/ n faringitis, f

pharynx /'færɪŋks/ n faringe, f

phase /feiz/ n fase, f; aspecto, m; Astron. fase, f

pheasant /'fezənt/ n faisán, m. **hen p.,** faisana, f. **p. shooting,** caza de faisanes, f

phenomenal /fɪ'nɒmənl/ a fenomenal

phenomenon /fɪ'nɒməˌnɒn/ n fenómeno, m

phial /'faiəl/ n redoma, f

philander /fɪ'lændər/ vi galantear

philanderer /fɪ'lændərər/ n Tenorio, galanteador, m

philanthropic /ˌfɪlən'θrɒpɪk/ a filantrópico

philanthropist /fɪ'lænθrəpɪst/ n filántropo, m

philanthropy /fɪ'lænθrəpi/ n filantropía, f

philatelic /ˌfɪlə'telɪk/ a filatélico

philatelist /fɪ'lætɪst/ n filatelista, mf

philately /fɪ'lætli/ n filatelia, f

philharmonic /ˌfɪlhɑr'mɒnɪk/ a filarmónico

Philippine /'fɪləˌpin/ a and n filipino (-na)

Philippines, the /'fɪləˌpinz/ las (Islas) Filipinas, f pl

Philistine /'fɪləˌstin/ a and n filisteo (-ea)

philological /ˌfɪlə'lɒdʒɪkəl/ a filológico

philologist /fɪ'lɒlədʒɪst/ n filólogo, m

philology /fɪ'lɒlədʒi/ n filología, f

philosopher /fɪ'lɒsəfər/ n filósofo, m. **philosopher's stone,** piedra filosofal, f

philosophical /ˌfɪlə'sɒfɪkəl/ a filosófico

philosophize /fɪ'lɒsəˌfaɪz/ vi filosofar

philosophy /fɪ'lɒsəfi/ n filosofía, f. **moral p.,** filosofía moral, f. **natural p.,** filosofía natural, f

philter /'fɪltər/ n filtro, m

phlebitis /flə'baitɪs/ n flebitis, f

phlebotomist /flə'bɒtəmɪst/ n sangrador, flebotomiano, m

phlebotomy /flə'bɒtəmi/ n flebotomía, f

phlegm /flɛm/ n flema, f

phlegmatic /flɛg'mætɪk/ a flemático

phoenix /'finɪks/ n fénix, f

phonetic /fə'nɛtɪk/ a fonético

phonetics /fə'nɛtɪks, fou-/ n fonética, f

phony /'founi/ a falso; espurio. **p. war,** guerra tonta, guerra falsa, f

phosphate /'fɒsfeit/ n fosfato, m

phosphorescence /ˌfɒsfə'resəns/ n fosforescencia, f

phosphorescent /ˌfɒsfə'resənt/ a fosforescente

phosphorus /'fɒsfərəs/ n fósforo, m

photo /'foutou/ n foto, f

photochemistry /ˌfoutou'kɛməstri/ n fotoquímica, f

photogenic /ˌfoutə'dʒɛnɪk/ a fotogénico

photograph /'foutəˌgræf/ n fotografía, f. —vt fotografiar, retratar. **to have one's p. taken,** hacerse retratar

photographer /fə'tɒgrəfər/ n fotógrafo, m

photographic /ˌfoutə'græfɪk/ a fotográfico

photography /fə'tɒgrəfi/ n fotografía, f

photogravure /,foutəgrə'vyur/ n fotograbado, m

photostat /'foutə,stæt/ n fotostato, m

photosynthesis /,foutə'sɪnθəsɪs/ n fotosíntesis, f

phrase /freiz/ n frase, f; Mus. frase musical, f. —vt expresar, frasear; redactar. **p.-book**, libro de frases, m

phraseology /,freizi'ɒlədʒi/ n fraseología, f

phrasing /'freiziŋ/ n (drawing up) redacción, f; (style) estilo, m; Mus. frases, f pl

phrenetic /frɪ'nɛtɪk/ a frenético

phthisis /'θaɪsɪs/ n tisis, f

phylactery /fɪ'læktəri/ n filactria, f

physical /'fɪzɪkəl/ a físico. **p. fitness,** buen estado físico, m. **p. geography,** geografía física, f. **p. jerks,** ejercicios físicos, m pl. **p. sciences,** ciencias físicas, f pl. **p. training,** educación física, f

physician /fɪ'zɪʃən/ n médico (-ca)

physicist /'fɪzəsɪst/ n físico, m

physics /'fɪzɪks/ n física, f

physiognomy /,fɪzi'ɒgnəmi/ n fisonomía, f

physiological /,fɪziə'lɒdʒɪkəl/ a fisiológico

physiologist /,fɪzi'ɒlədʒɪst/ n fisiólogo, m

physiology /,fɪzi'ɒlədʒi/ n fisiología, f

physiotherapy /,fɪziou'θerəpi/ n fisioterapia, f

physique /fɪ'zik/ n físico, m

pianist /pi'ænɪst, 'pɪənɪst/ n pianista, mf

pianola /,pɪə'noulə/ n piano mecánico, m

piano, pianoforte /pi'ænou; pi'ænə,fɔrt/ n piano, m. **baby grand p.,** piano de media cola, m. **grand p.,** piano de cola, m. **upright p.,** piano vertical, m. **p. maker,** fabricante de pianos, m. **p. stool,** taburete de piano, m. **p. tuner,** afinador de pianos, m

picaresque /,pɪkə'rɛsk/ a picaresco

piccolo /'pɪkə,lou/ n flautín, m

pick /pɪk/ n (tool) pico, zapapico, m; (mattock) piqueta, f; (choice) selección, f; derecho de elección, m; (best) lo mejor, lo más escogido; (Fig. cream) flor, nata, f. **tooth-p.,** mondadientes, m. **p.-a-back,** sobre los hombros, a cuestas. **p.-ax,** zapapico, m, alcotana, f. **p.-me-up,** tónico, m; trago, m

pick /pɪk/ vt (with a pick-ax, make a hole) picar; (pluck, pick up) coger; (remove) sacar; (clean) limpiar; (one's teeth) mondarse (los dientes); (one's nose) hurgarse (las narices); (a bone) roer; (a lock) abrir con ganzúa; (a pocket) bolsear, robar del bolsillo; (peck) picotear; (choose) escoger; (a quarrel) buscar. — vi (steal) hurtar, robar; (nibble) picar. **I have a bone to p. with you,** Tengo que ajustar unas cuentas contigo. **Take your p.!** ¡Escoja! **to p. and choose,** mostrarse difícil. **to p. to pieces,** Fig. criticar severamente. **to p. one's way**

through, abrirse camino entre; andar con precaución por; andar a tientas por. **to p. off,** coger; arrancar; quitar; (shoot) disparar; fusilar. **to p. out,** entresacar; escoger; (recognize) reconocer; (understand) llegar a comprender; (a tune) tocar de oídas; (a song) cantar de oídas; (of colours) contrastar, resaltar. **to p. up,** vt (ground, etc.) romper con pico; coger; tomar; recoger; (raise) levantar, alzar; (information, etc.) cobrar, adquirir; (a living) ganar; (make friends with) trabar amistad con; (recover) recobrar; (find) encontrar, hallar; (buy) comprar; (learn) aprender; (a wireless message) interceptar; (a radio station) oír, tener. — vi recobrar la salud; reponerse; mejorar. —n Mech. recobro, m

picket /'pɪkɪt/ n estaca, f; (Mil. and during strikes) piquete, m. — vt cercar con estacas; poner piquetes ante (or alrededor de); poner de guardia; estacionar

picking /'pɪkɪŋ/ n (gathering) recolección, f; (choosing) selección, f; (pilfering) robo, m; pl **pickings,** desperdicios, m pl; (perquisites) gajes, m pl; ganancias, f pl

pickle /'pɪkəl/ n (solution) escabeche, m; (vegetable, etc.) encurtido, m; (plight) apuro, m; (child) diablillo, m. — vt encurtir, escabechar

picklock /'pɪk,lɒk/ n (thief and instrument) ganzúa, f

pickpocket /'pɪk,pɒkɪt/ n carterista, mf ratero (-ra)

picnic /'pɪknɪk/ n partida de campo, jira, f, picnic, m. — vi llevar la merienda al campo, hacer un picnic

pictorial /pɪk'tɔriəl/ a pictórico; ilustrado. —n revista ilustrada, f

picture /'pɪktʃər/ n cuadro, m; (of a person) retrato, m; imagen, f; (illustration) grabado, m, lámina, f; fotografía, f; (outlook) perspectiva, f; idea, f. —vt pintar; describir; imaginar. **to go to the pictures,** ir al cine. **motion p.,** película, f. **talking p.,** película sonora, f. **p. book,** libro con láminas, m. **p. frame,** marco, m. **p. gallery,** museo de pinturas, m; galería de pinturas, f. **p. hat,** pamela, f. **p. palace,** cine, m. **p. postcard,** tarjeta postal, f. **p. restorer,** restaurador de cuadros, m. **p. writing,** pictografía, f

picturesque /,pɪktʃə'rɛsk/ a pintoresco

pie /pai/ n (savoury) empanada, f; (sweet) pastel, m, torta, f; (of meat) pastelón, m; Print. pastel, m. **apple pie,** torta de manzanas, f. **to eat humble pie,** bajar las orejas. **to have a finger in the pie,** meter baza

piebald /'pai,bɒld/ a pío; tordo

piece /pis/ n pedazo, m; trozo, m; parte, porción, f; (literary, artistic work, coin, of fabric, at chess, etc. and slang) pieza, f; (of luggage) bulto, m; (of paper) hoja, f; (of ground) parcela, f; (of money) moneda, f, vt remendar; unir, juntar. **a p. of advice,** un consejo. **a p. of bread,** un pedazo de pan; una rebanada de pan. **a**

p. of folly, un acto de locura. a p. of furniture, un mueble. a p. of insolence, una insolencia. a p. of news, una noticia. a p. of paper, un papel, una hoja de papel, una cuartilla. a p. of poetry, una poesía. Peter has a five-shilling p., Pedro tiene una moneda de cinco chelines. to break in pieces, vt hacer pedazos, romper. —vi hacerse pedazos, romperse. to come or fall to pieces, deshacerse; (of machines) desarmarse. to cut in pieces, cortar en pedazos; (an army) destrozar. to give a p. of one's mind (to), decir cuatro verdades (a), decir cuántas son cinco (a). to go to pieces, (of persons) hacerse pedazos. to take to pieces, (a machine) desmontar; deshacer. to tear or pull to pieces, hacer pedazos, despedazar; desgarrar. p. goods, géneros en piezas, m pl. p.-work, trabajo a destajo, m. to do p.-work, trabajar a destajo. p.-worker, destajista, mf

piecemeal /'pis,mil/ adv a pedazos; a remiendos; en detalle; poco a poco

piecrust /'pai,krʌst/ n pasta, f

pied /paid/ a bicolor; abigarrado, de varios colores

pier /pɪər/ n (jetty) dique, m; embarcadero, m; malecón, m; (of a bridge) pila, f; (pillar) columna, f; (between windows, etc.) entrepaño, m. **p.-glass**, espejo de cuerpo entero, m. **p. head**, punta del dique, f. **p. table**, consola, f

pierce /pɪərs/ vt penetrar; (of sorrow, etc.) traspasar, herir; (bore) agujerear, taladrar. —vi penetrar

pierced ear /pɪərst/ n oreja perforada, f

piercing /'pɪərsɪŋ/ a penetrante; (of the wind, etc.) cortante; (of the voice, etc.) agudo. —n penetración, f

piety /'paɪɪti/ n piedad, devoción, f

piffle /'pɪfəl/ n patrañas, tonterías, f pl

pig /pɪg/ n puerco, cerdo, m; Inf. cochino, m; (metal) lingote, m. **to buy a p. in a poke**, cerrar un trato a ciegas. **p.-eyed**, de ojos de cerdo. **p.-iron**, arrabio, m; hierro colado en barras, lingote de fundición, m

pigeon /'pɪdʒən/ n paloma, f, palomo, m; Inf. primo, m. —vt embaucar, engañar. **carrier p.**, paloma mensajera, f. **clay p.**, pichón de barro, platillo de arcilla, m. **male p.**, pichón, m. **pouter p.**, paloma buchona, f. **young p.**, palomino, m. **p. fancier**, palomero, m. **p.-hole**, casilla, f. —vt encasillar. **set of p.-holes**, encasillado, m. **p.-shooting**, tiro de pichón, m. **p.-toed**, patituerto

piggy bank /'pɪgi/ n alcancía, f

pigheaded /'pɪg,hedɪd/ a terco, testarudo

pigment /'pɪgmənt/ n pigmento, m

pigskin /'pɪg,skɪn/ n piel de cerdo, f

pigsty /'pɪg,staɪ/ n pocilga, f

pigtail /'pɪg,teɪl/ n coleta, f

pike /paɪk/ n Mil. pica, f, chuzo, m; (peak) pico, m

pilaster /pɪ'læstər/ n pilastra, f

pile /paɪl/ n estaca, f; poste, m; (engi-

neering) pilote, m; (heap) pila, f, montón, m; (pyre) pira, f; (building) edificio grande, m; Elec. pila, f; (hair) pelo, m; (nap) pelusa, f; pl piles, Med. almorranas, f pl. —vt clavar pilotes en; apoyar con pilotes; (heap) amontonar; (load) cargar. **to make one's p.**, Inf. hacer su pacotilla. **to p. arms**, poner los fusiles en pabellón. **to p. on**, (coal, etc.) echar; (increase) aumentar. **to p. it on**, exagerar, intensificar; (a table) cargar. **to p. up**, amontonarse; acumularse; (of a ship) encallar. **p.-driver**, machina, f; martinete, m. **p. dwelling**, vivienda palustre, sostenida por pilares, f

pilfer /'pɪlfər/ vt sisar, sonsacar, hurtar, ratear

pilferer /'pɪlfərər/ n sisador (-ra), ratero (-ra)

pilgrim /'pɪlgrɪm/ n peregrino (-na). **pilgrim's staff**, bordón, m

pilgrimage /'pɪlgrəmɪdʒ/ n peregrinación, f; romería, f. **to make a p.**, hacer una peregrinación, peregrinar; ir en romería

piling /'paɪlɪŋ/ n amontonamiento, m; (of buildings) pilotaje, m

pill /pɪl/ n píldora, f. **to gild the p.**, Fig. dorar la píldora. **p.-box**, caja de píldoras, f; casamata, f, Mil. nido de ametralladoras, m

pillage /'pɪlɪdʒ/ vt pillar, saquear. —n saqueo, m

pillager /'pɪlɪdʒər/ n saqueador (-ra)

pillar /'pɪlər/ n pilar, m, columna, f; (person) sostén, soporte, m. **from p. to post**, de Ceca en Meca. **p. of salt**, estatua de sal, f. **the Pillars of Hercules**, las Columnas de Hércules. **to be a p. of strength**, Inf. ser una roca. **p.-box**, buzón, m

pillared /'pɪlərd/ a con columnas, sostenido por columnas; en columnas

pillory /'pɪlɔri/ n picota, argolla, f. —vt empicotar; Fig. poner en ridículo; censurar duramente

pillow /'pɪlou/ n almohada, f; (for lacemaking) cojín, m; (of a machine) cojinete, m. —vt apoyar; reposar; servir como almohada. **to take counsel of one's p.**, consultar con la almohada. **p.-case**, funda de almohada, f

pilot /'paɪlət/ n piloto, m; Naut. práctico, piloto (de puerto), m. —vt guiar, conducir; (Naut. Aer.) pilotar, pilotear. **p. boat**, vaporcito del práctico, m. **p. jacket**, chaquetón de piloto, m. **p. officer**, oficial de aviación, m

pimento /pɪ'mentou/ n pimiento, m

pimp /pɪmp/ n rufián, alcahuete, m, vi alcahuetear

pimple /'pɪmpəl/ n grano, m

pimply /'pɪmpli/ a con granos

pin /pɪn/ n alfiler, m; prendedor, m; clavija, f; clavo, m, chaveta, f; (bolt) perno, m. —vt prender con alfileres; (with a peg) enclavijar; fijar; sujetar. **to pin up**, sujetar con alfileres; (the hair) sujetar con horquillas. **I don't care a pin,**

No me importa un bledo. **to be on pins, needles,** tener aguijones. **pin-head,** cabeza de alfiler, f. **pin-money,** alfileres, m pl. **pin-oak,** Bot. pincarrasca, m, carrasca, f. **pin point,** punta de alfiler, f. **pin-prick,** alfilerazo, m

pinafore /'pɪnə.fɔr/ n delantal de niño, m

pincers /'pɪnsərz/ n pl pinzas, tenazas, f pl, alicates, m pl; (of crustaceans) pinzas, f pl. **p. movement,** movimiento de pinzas, m

pinch /pɪntʃ/ vt pellizcar; (crush) estrujar; aplastar; apretar; (of the cold) helar; (steal) hurtar, birlar; (arrest) coger, prender. —n pellizco, torniscón, m; pulgarada, f; (of snuff) polvo, m; (distress) miseria, f; (pain) dolor, m, angustia, f. **at a p.,** en caso de apuro. **to know where the shoe pinches,** saber dónde le aprieta el zapato

pincushion /'pɪn.kʊʃən/ n acerico, m

pine /paɪn/ n Bot. pino, m. —vi languidecer, marchitarse, consumirse. **to p. for,** anhelar, suspirar por, perecer por. **pitch-p.,** pino de tea, m. **p.-apple,** piña de las Indias, f, ananás, m. **p. cone,** piña, f. **p. kernel,** piñón, m. **p. needle,** pinocha, f. **p. wood,** pinar, m, pineda, f

pinion /'pɪnyən/ n (wing) ala, f; (small feather) piñón, m; (in carving) alón, m; (wheel) piñón, m. —vt atar las alas de; cortar un piñón de; (a person) atar; (the arms of) trincar, asegurar

pink /pɪŋk/ n Bot. clavel, m; color de rosa, m; (perfection) modelo, m; colmo, m; (hunting) color rojo, m; levitín rojo de caza, m. —a de color de rosa, rosado. —vt Sew. picar; (pierce) penecrar, atravesar. —vi (of an engine) picar

pinking /'pɪŋkɪŋ/ n Sew. picadura, f

pinnacle /'pɪnəkəl/ n Naut. pinaza, f

pinnacle /'pɪnəkəl/ n pináculo, m

pinpoint /'pɪn.pɔɪnt/ vt precisar

pint /paɪnt/ n (measure) pinta, f

pioneer /ˌpaɪə'nɪər/ n pionero, explorador, m; introductor, m. **to be a p. in...,** ser el primero en (or a)... **pioneering role,** papel de iniciador (as: She played a pioneering role, jugó un papel de iniciadora)

pious /'paɪəs/ a pío, devoto, piadoso

pip /pɪp/ n (of fruit) pepita, f; (on cards, dice) punto, m; (disease) moquillo, m; (of an army, etc., officer) insignia, f

pipe /paɪp/ n (for tobacco) pipa de fumar, f; Mus. caramillo, m; (boatswain's) pito, m; (of a bird) trino, m; (voice) voz aguda, f; tubo, m; (for water, etc.) cañería, f; (of a hose) manga, f; (of an organ) cañón, m; (of wine) pipa, f; pl **pipes,** Mus. gaita, f. —vi tocar el caramillo (or la gaita); empezar a cantar; silbar; (of birds) trinar. —vt (a tune) tocar; (sing) cantar; (whistle) llamar con pito; conducir con cañerías; instalar cañerías en. **He smokes a p.,** Fuma una pipa. **I**

smoked a p. (of tobacco) before I went to bed, Fumé una pipa antes de acostarme. **Put that in your p. and smoke it!** ¡Chúpate eso! **p. clay,** blanquizal, m. **p. cleaner,** limpiapipas, m. **p. layer,** cañero, fontanero, m. **p. laying,** instalación de cañerías, f. **p.-line,** cañería, f; (oil) oleoducto, m. **p. tobacco,** tabaco de pipa, m

piper /'paɪpər/ n (bagpiper) gaitero, m; flautista, mf

pipette /paɪ'pɛt/ n Chem. pipeta, f

piping /'paɪpɪŋ/ n sonido del caramillo, m; música de la flauta, etc., f; (of birds) trinos, m pl; voz aguda, f; (for water, etc.) cañería, tubería, f; Sew. cordoncillo, m. **p.-hot,** hirviente

pippin /'pɪpɪn/ n (apple) camuesa, f

piquant /'pikənt/ a picante

pique /pik/ n (resentment, and score in game) pique, m. **to p. oneself upon,** preciarse de, jactarse de. **to be piqued,** estar enojado. Inf. amoscarse

piracy /'paɪrəsi/ n piratería, f

pirate /'paɪrət/ n pirata, mf. —vi piratear. —vt publicar una edición furtiva de. **p. edition,** edición furtiva, f

pirouette /ˌpɪru'ɛt/ n pirueta, f

pistachio /pɪ'stæʃiˌou/ n pistacho, m

pistol /'pɪstl/ n pistola, f. **p. belt,** charpa, f, cinto de pistolas, m. **p. case,** pistolera, f. **p. shot,** pistoletazo, m

piston /'pɪstən/ n Mech. émbolo, pistón, m; Mus. pistón, m, llave, f. **p. ring,** anillo de émbolo, segmento de émbolo, m. **p. rod,** biela, f. **p. stroke,** carrera del émbolo, f

pit /pɪt/ n hoyo, m; foso, m; (in a garage) foso de reparación, m; Theat. platea, f; (trap) trampa, f; (scar) hoyo, m; precipicio, m; (hell) infierno, m. —vt (with smallpox) marcar con viruelas; (against) competir con. **pithead,** boca de mina, f. **pit of the stomach,** boca del estómago, f. **pit stall,** butaca de platea, f

pitch /pɪtʃ/ n Chem. pez, brea, f, alquitrán, m; (place) puesto, m; (throwing) lanzamiento, m; (distance thrown) alcance, m; (for cricket) cancha, f; (bowling) saque, m; (slope) pendiente, inclinación, f; (height) elevación, f; Mus. tono, m; (Fig. degree) grado, extremo, m; (Naut. Aer.) cabeceo, m; (of threads of a screw, etc.) paso, m. —vt (camp) asentar; (a tent, etc.) colocar, poner; (throw) lanzar, arrojar, tirar; (cricket, etc.) lanzar; (fix in) clavar; Mus. graduar el tono de; (tell) narrar. —vi (fall) caer; Naut. cabecear, zozobrar; Aer. cabecear. **to paint with p.,** embrear. **to p. into,** (attack) acometer, atacar; (scold) desatarse contra; (food) engullir. **p.-black,** negro como la pez; oscuro como boca de lobo. **p.-pine,** pino de tea, m. **p.-pipe,** diapasón vocal, m

pitched battle /pɪtʃt/ n batalla campal, f

pitcher /'pɪtʃər/ n jarro, cántaro, m; (in baseball) lanzador de pelota, m

pitchfork /'pɪtʃˌfɔrk/ n horquilla, f, aventador, m. —vt levantar con horquilla; *Fig.* lanzar

pitching /'pɪtʃɪŋ/ n (pavement) adoquinado, m; (of a ship) socollada, f; cabeceo, m

piteous /'pɪtiəs/ a lastimero; triste; plañidero; compasivo, tierno

pitfall /'pɪtˌfɔl/ n trampa, f; *Fig.* añagaza, f, lazo, peligro, m

pith /pɪθ/ n *Bot.* médula, f; médula espinal, f; *Fig.* meollo, m; fuerza, f, vigor, m; substancia, f; quinta esencia, f; importancia, f

pithiness /'pɪθɪnɪs/ n jugosidad, f; fuerza, f, vigor, m

pithy /'pɪθi/ a meduloso; *Fig.* jugoso; enérgico, vigoroso

pitiable /'pɪtiəbəl/ a lastimoso, digno de compasión; (paltry) despreciable

pitiful /'pɪtɪfəl/ a piadoso, compasivo; conmovedor, doloroso, lastimero; (contemptible) miserable

pitifully /'pɪtɪfəli/ adv lastimosamente

pitiless /'pɪtɪlɪs/ a sin piedad, despiadado

pittance /'pɪtns/ n pitanza, f; pequeña porción, f; ración de hambre, f

pitted /'pɪtɪd/ a picoso

pituitary /pɪ'tuɪˌteri/ a pituitario

pity /'pɪti/ n piedad, compasión, f, lástima, f. —vt compadecerse de, tener lástima (a); compadecer. **It is a p. that...,** Es lástima que... **Have p.!** ¡Ten piedad! **to take p. on,** tener lástima (a). **to move to p.,** dar lástima (a), enternecer

pivot /'pɪvət/ n pivote, m; eje, m; *Fig.* punto de partida, m, vi girar sobre un pivote o eje

pivotal /'pɪvətl/ a *Fig.* cardinal, principal, fundamental

pixy /'pɪksi/ n duende, m. **p. hood,** caperuza, f

pizzicato /ˌpɪtsɪ'kɑtou/ a pichigato

placable /'plækəbəl/ a aplacable, placable

placard /'plækard/ n cartel, m. —vt fijar carteles (en); publicar por carteles

placate /'pleikeit/ vt aplacar, ablandar, apaciguar

placatory /'pleikəˌtɔri/ a placativo

place /pleis/ n lugar, m; sitio, m; (position) puesto, m; (seat) asiento, m; (laid at table) cubierto, m; (square) plaza, f; (house) residencia, f; (in the country) casa de campo, finca, f; (in a book) pasaje, m; (in an examination) calificación, f; (rank) posición, f, rango, m; (employment) empleo, m, colocación, f. —vt poner; colocar; (in employment) dar empleo (a); (appoint) nombrar; (an order) dar; (money) invertir; (remember) recordar, traer a la memoria; (size up) fijar; (confidence) poner. **in p.,** en su lugar; apropiado. **in p. of,** en vez de, en lugar de. **in the first p.,** en primer lugar, primero. **in the next p.,** luego, después. **out of p.,** fuera de lugar; inoportuno. **It is not my p. to...,** No me toca a mí de... **to give p. to,** ceder el paso (a); ceder

(a). **to take p.,** verificarse, tener lugar, ocurrir. **p. of business,** establecimiento, local de negocios, m. **p. of worship,** edificio de culto, m

placenta /plə'sentə/ n placenta, f

placid /'plæsɪd/ a plácido, apacible; calmoso; sereno, sosegado; dulce

placing /'pleisɪŋ/ n colocación, f; posición, f; localización, f

placket /'plækɪt/ n abertura (en una falda), f

plagiarism /'pleidʒəˌrɪzəm/ n plagio, m

plagiarist /'pleidʒərɪst/ n plagiario (-ia)

plagiarize /'pleidʒəˌraɪz/ vt plagiar, hurtar

plague /pleig/ n plaga, f; peste, pestilencia, f. —vt importunar, atormentar; plagar

plaid /plæd/ n manta escocesa, f; género de cuadros, m, a a cuadros

plain /plein/ a claro; evidente; (simple) sencillo; llano; sin adorno; (flat) liso, igual; (candid) franco; (with truth, etc.) desnudo; mero; puro, sin mezcla; (of words) redondo; (ugly) feo. —adv claramente, llanamente; sencillamente; francamente. —n llanura, f, llano, m. **the p. truth,** la pura verdad, f. **p. clothes,** traje de paisano, m. **p. clothes man,** detective, m. **p. cooking,** cocina sencilla, cocina casera, f. **p. dealing,** buena fe, sinceridad, f. **p. dweller,** llanero (-ra). **p. living,** vida sencilla, f. **p. people,** gente sencilla, f. **p. sailing,** *Fig.* camino fácil, m. **p. sewing,** costura, f. **p.-song,** canto llano, m. **p. speaking,** franqueza, f. **p. spoken,** franco. **in p. English,** sin rodeos, en cristiano (e.g. *Speak in p. English!* Habla sin rodeos! Habla en cristiano!)

plainly /'pleinli/ adv claramente; sencillamente; llanamente; francamente; rotundamente

plainsman /'pleinzmən/ n hombre de las llanuras, m

plaint /pleint/ n queja, f, lamento, m; *Law.* demanda, querella, f

plaintiff /'pleintɪf/ n demandante, mf, actor, m, parte actora, actora, f

plaintive /'pleintɪv/ a quejumbroso, dolorido; patético

plait /pleit/ n trenza, f. —vt trenzar; tejer. **in plaits,** (of hair) en trenzas

plan /plæn/ n plan, m; (map) plano, m; proyecto, m. —vt planear; proyectar; proponerse. **the Marshall P.,** el Plan Marshall. **to make a p. of,** trazar un plano de. **to make plans,** hacer planes

plane /plein/ n (tree) plátano, m; (tool) cepillo, m; *Geom.* plano, m; (level) nivel, m; *Aer.* avión, m, plano. —vt acepillar, alisar. —vi *Aer.* planear

planet /'plænɪt/ n planeta, m

planetarium /ˌplænɪ'teəriəm/ n planetario, m

planetary /'plænɪˌteri/ a planetario

plank /plæŋk/ n tabla, f; *Fig.* fundamento, principio, m; pl **planks,** tablazón, f. —vt entablar, enmaderar

plankton /'plæŋktən/ n plancton, m

planned /plænd/ a proyectado, planeado; dirigido. **p. economy,** economía dirigida, f

planner /'plænər/ n proyectista, mf; autor (-ra) de un plan

planning /'plænɪŋ/ n proyecto, m; concepción, f

plant /plænt/ n Bot. planta, f; instalación, f, material, m. —vt plantar; (place) colocar; fijar; (a blow) asestar; (people) establecer; (instil) inculcar, imbuir (con); (conceal) esconder. **p. pot,** florero, m. **p. stand,** jardinera, f

plantain /'plæntɪn/ n Bot. llantén, m

plantation /plæn'teɪʃən/ n plantación, f; plantío, m; Fig. colonia, f; introducción, f, establecimiento, m

planter /'plæntər/ n plantador, cultivador, m

planting /'plæntɪŋ/ n plantación, f; Fig. colonia, f; introducción, f. **p. out,** trasplante, m

plaque /plæk/ n placa, f; medalla, f

plash /plæʃ/ n (puddle) charco, m; (sound) chapaleteo, m. —vt and vi chapotear, chapalear

plasma /'plæzmə/ n plasma, m

plaster /'plæstər/ n (for walls, etc.) argamasa, f; yeso, m; Med. parche, emplasto, m. —vt (walls, etc.) enlucir, enyesar; poner emplastos (a or en); (daub) embadurnar manchar; (cover) cubrir. **p. cast,** vaciado, yeso, m. **p. of Paris,** escayola, f

plasterer /'plæstərər/ n yesero, m

plastering /'plæstərɪŋ/ n revoque, enyesado, guarnecido, m. **p. trowel,** fratás, m

plastic /'plæstɪk/ a plástico. —n plástica, f; pl **plastics,** materias plásticas, f pl. **p. surgery,** cirugía plástica, cirugía estética, f

plasticine /'plæstə,sin/ n plasticina, f

plate /pleɪt/ n plancha, chapa, f; (engraving and Photo., of a doctor, etc.) placa, f; (illustration) lámina, f, (cutlery, etc.) vajilla, f; (for eating) plato, m; (for money) platillo, m; electrotipo, m; (dental) dentadura postiza, f. —vt (with armor) blindar; (with metal) planchear; (silver) platear; (electro-plate) niquelar. **silver p.,** vajilla de plata, plata, f. **p.-armor,** armadura, f; (of a ship) blindaje, m. **p.-draining rack,** escurreplatos, m. **p.-glass,** vidrio plano, m. **p.-rack,** escurridero para platos, m. **p. warmer,** calientaplatos, m

plateau /plæ'toʊ/ n meseta, altiplanicie, f

plater /'pleɪtər/ n plateador, m; platero, m

platform /'plætfɔrm/ n plataforma, f; (railway) andén, m. **p. ticket,** billete de andén, m

plating /'pleɪtɪŋ/ n niquelado, m; electrogalvanización, f; (with armor) blindaje, m

platinum /'plætnəm/ n platino, m. **p. blonde,** rubia platino, f

platitude /'plætɪ,tud/ n perogrullada, f, lugar común, m; trivialidad, vulgaridad, f

platitudinous /,plætɪ'tudnəs/ a lleno de perogrulladas; trivial

platonic /plə'tɒnɪk/ a platónico

platoon /plə'tun/ n Mil. pelotón, m

platter /'plætər/ n fuente, f, trinchero, m; plato, m

plaudit /'plɔdɪt/ n aplauso, m, aclamación, f; (praise) elogio, m, alabanza, f

plausible /'plɔzəbəl/ a plausible

play /pleɪ/ vi jugar; (frolic) juguetear, retozar; recrearse, divertirse; Mech. moverse; (on a musical instrument) tocar; (wave) ondear, flotar; Theat. representar; (behave) conducirse. —vt jugar; (of a searchlight, etc.) enfocar; (direct) dirigir; (a fish) agotar; (a joke, etc.) hacer; (a piece in a game) mover; (a musical instrument or music) tocar; (a string instrument) tañer; (a character in a play) hacer el papel de; (a drama, etc.) representar, poner en escena. **to p. a joke,** gastar una broma, hacer una burla. **to p. fair,** jugar limpio. **to p. false,** jugar sucio, engañar. **to p. the fool,** hacerse el tonto, hacerse el payaso. **to p. at,** jugar a; (pretend) fingir; hacer sin entusiasmo. **to p. off,** confrontar, contraponer. **to p. on.** See **to p. upon. to p. on the...,** (of musical instruments) tocar. **to p. to,** (a person) tocar para. **to p. upon,** tocar; (a person's fears, etc.) explotar. **to p. up to,** (a person) adular, hacer la rueda (a). **to p. with,** jugar con; burlarse de; (an idea) acariciar play, n juego, m; diversión, f, recreo, m; (reflection) reflejo, m; movimiento libre, m; (to the imagination, etc.) rienda suelta, f; Mech. holgura, f; Lit. pieza dramática, comedia, f; (performance) función, representación, f; (Theater.) teatro, m. **fair p.,** juego limpio, m. **foul p.,** juego sucio, m; traición, perfidia, f. **to bring into p.,** poner en juego. **to come into p.,** entrar en juego. **to give p. to,** dar rienda a. **p. on words,** juego de palabras, m. **p.-pen,** cuadro enrejado, m

playact /'pleɪˌækt/ vi hacer la comedia

playbill /'pleɪˌbɪl/ n cartel, m; programa, m

played-out /,pleɪd 'aʊt/ a agotado; viejo

player /'pleɪər/ n jugador (-ra); Theat. actor (-triz), representante, mf; Mus. músico (-ca), tocador (-ra)

playfellow /'pleɪˌfɛloʊ/ n camarada, mf; compañero (-ra) de juego, compañero de juegos

playful /'pleɪfəl/ a juguetón; travieso; alegre

playfully /'pleɪfəli/ adv en juego, de broma; alegremente

playgoer /'pleɪˌɡoʊər/ n persona que frecuenta los teatros, f; espectador de comedias, m

playground /'pleɪˌɡraʊnd/ n patio de recreo, m

playing /'pleɪɪŋ/ n juego, m. **p.-cards,** naipes, m pl, cartas, f pl. **p.-field,** campo de deportes, m

playlet /'pleɪlɪt/ n comedia corta, f

playmate /'plei,meit/. See **playfellow**

plaything /'plei,θiŋ/ n juguete, m

playtime /'plei,taim/ n recreación, f; (in schools) hora de recreo, f, recreo, m

playwright /'plei,rait/ n dramaturgo, m, autor (-ra) de comedias

plea /pli/ n Law. informe, m; declaración, f; Law. acción, f, proceso, m; (excuse) pretexto, m, excusa, f; (entreaty) súplica, f. **under p. of**, bajo pretexto de, con excusa de

plead /plid/ vi Law. pleitear; Law. declarar; suplicar; (of counsel, etc.) abogar (por); interceder (por). —vt defender en juicio; aducir, alegar; pretender. **to p. guilty**, confesarse culpable. **to p. not guilty**, negar la acusación. **to p. ignorance**, pretender ignorancia

pleading /'plidiŋ/ n súplicas, f pl; Law. defensa, f; pl **pleadings**, alegatos, m pl, a implorante

pleasant /'plezənt/ a agradable; placentero; ameno; encantador; dulce; alegre; (of persons) simpático, amable; bueno; divertido

pleasantly /'plezəntli/ adv agradablemente; de un modo muy amable; alegremente

pleasantry /'plezəntri/ n jocosidad, f; broma, chanza, f

please /pliz/ vi dar placer, gustar, dar gusto, agradar; parecer bien, querer, servirse; tener a bien, placer. —vt deleitar, agradar, gustar; halagar; contentar, satisfacer. **I will do what I p.**, Haré lo que me parezca bien. **If you p.**, Si te parece bien; Con tu permiso. **She is very easy to p.**, Es muy fácil de darle placer. **When you p.**, Cuando Vd. quiera, Cuando a Vd le venga bien Cuando Vd. guste. **"Please Do Not Disturb,"** «No Molesten.» **P. sit down!** ¡Haga el favor de sentarse! ¡Sírvase de sentarse! **P. God!** ¡Plegue a Dios!

pleased /plizd/ a contento (de or con); encantado (de); alegre (de); satisfecho (de or con). **I am p. with my new house**, Estoy contento con mi nueva casa. **I'm p. to meet you**, Mucho gusto (en conocerle), Mucho gusto (en conocerla). **to be p.**, estar contento; complacerse en

pleasing /'plizin/ a agradable, grato; placentero; halagüeño

pleasurable /'pleʒərəbəl/ a agradable; divertido, entretenido

pleasure /'pleʒər/ n placer, m; gusto, m; satisfacción, f; (will) voluntad, f; recreo, m; diversión, distracción, f. **to give p. (to)**, dar placer (a); deleitar, agradar; complacer. **to take p. in**, gustar de, disfrutar de; complacerse en. **I shall do it with great p.**, Lo haré con mucho gusto, Lo haré con mucho placer. **p.-boat**, barco de recreo, m. **p.-ground**, parque de atracciones, m. **p.-seeking**, amigo de placeres, frívolo. **p. trip**, viaje de recreo, m; excursión, f

pleasure craft n barco de recreo, m,

(one vessel); barcas de recreo (collectively), m pl

pleat /plit/ n pliegue, m, vt plegar, hacer pliegues en

pleating /'plitiŋ/ n plegado, m

plebeian /plɪ'biən/ a plebeyo. —n plebeyo (-ya)

plebiscite /'plebə,sait/ n plebiscito, m. **to take a p.**, hacer un plebiscito

pledge /plɛdʒ/ n prenda, f; empeño, m; garantía, f; (hostage) rehén, m; (toast) brindis, m. —vt empeñar, dar en prenda; garantizar; brindar por; prometer. **to p. oneself**, comprometerse. **to p. support for**, prometer apoyo para

plenitude /'plenɪ,tud/ n plenitud, f

plentifully /'plentəfəli/ adv en abundancia

plenty /'plenti/ n abundancia, f; en abundancia; de sobra; mucho. —adv Inf. bastante. **There is p. of food**, Hay comida en abundancia. **We have p. of time**, Tenemos tiempo de sobra

plethora /'plɛθərə/ n plétora, f

pleurisy /'plʊrəsi/ n pleuresía, f

plexus /'plɛksəs/ n plexo, m

pliable, pliant /'plaiəbəl; 'plaiənt/ a flexible; dócil

pliers /'plaiərz/ n pl pinzas, f pl, alicates, m pl, tenazas, f pl

plight /plait/ vt (one's word) empeñar, dar; prometer en matrimonio. —n (fix) aprieto, apuro, m. **to p. one's troth**, dar palabra de matrimonio

plinth /plɪnθ/ n Archit. plinto, m

plod /plɒd/ vi andar despacio, caminar con trabajo; Fig. trabajar con ahínco

plodder /'plɒdər/ n trabajador lento y concienzudo, m; (student) empollón (-ona)

plot /plɒt/ n (of land) parcela, f; terreno, solar, m; (plan) proyecto, m; estratagema, f; (literary) intriga, trama, f; (story) argumento, m; (conspiracy) conjuración, f, complot, m. —vt trazar (un plano, etc.); urdir, tramar. —vi conspirar, intrigar

plotter /'plɒtər/ n conspirador (-ra conjurado (-da)

plotting /'plɒtiŋ/ n trazado (de un plano, una gráfica), m; (conspiracy) conspiración, f; maquinaciones, f pl; (hatching) trama, f

plow /plau/ n arado, m; Astron. el Carro, la Osa Mayor; (in an examination) escabechina, f. —vt and vi arar; Fig. surcar; (in examinations) escabechar (an calabazas (a), suspender. **plow the sands**, arar en el mar. **p. handle**, esteva, f. **to p. up**, roturar

pluck /plʌk/ vt (pick) coger; (a bird) desplumar; Mus. puntear; (in an examination) calabacear escabechar. —vi tirar (de). —n (tug) tirón, m; (of an animal) asadura, f; (courage) coraje, m. **to p. up courage**, tomar coraje, sacar ánimos. **to p. off**, quitar. **to p. out**, arrancar; quitar

plucky /'plʌki/ a valiente, esforzado, resuelto, animoso

plug /plʌg/ n tapón, tarugo, m; (in building) nudillo, m; (of a switchboard) clave, f; Elec. enchufe, m; (of a w.c.) tirador, m; (of a bath, etc.) tapón, m; (of tobacco) rollo, m. —vt atarugar, taponar, obturar; (in building) rellenar. —vi (with away) batirse el cobre, sudar la gota gorda. **to p. in,** enchufar

plum /plʌm/ n (tree) ciruelo, m; (fruit) ciruela, f; (raisin) pasa, f; (Inf. prize) breva, golosina, f. **p. cake,** pastel de fruta, m

plumage /'plumidʒ/ n plumaje, m

plumb /plʌm/ n plomada, f; (sounding-lead) escandallo, m. —a perpendículo; recto; completo. —adv a plomo, verticalmente; exactamente. —vt aplomar; Naut. sondar; (Fig. pierce) penetrar; (understand) comprender. —vi trabajar como plomero. **p.-line,** plomada, f

plumber /'plʌmər/ n plomero, fontanero, m; instalador de cañerías, m

plumbing /'plʌmɪŋ/ n plomería, fontanería, f; instalación de cañerías, m

plume /plum/ n pluma, f; penacho, m. —vt adornar con plumas; desplumar; **to p. itself,** (of a bird) limpiarse las plumas. **to p. oneself on,** echárselas de, hacer alarde de; jactarse de

plummet /'plʌmɪt/ n plomada, f; (weight) plomo, m; (sounding-lead) sonda, f

plump /plʌmp/ a gordito, llenito; rollizo; hinchado. ◆—adv de golpe; claramente. —vt (swell) hinchar, rellenar; (make fall) hacer (or dejar) caer. —vi (swell) hincharse; engordar; (fall) caer; dejarse caer. **to p. for,** escoger, dar apoyo (a); votar por. **p.-cheeked,** mofletudo

plunder /'plʌndər/ vt saquear; pillar; despojar. —n saqueo, pillaje, m; (booty) botín, despojo, m

plunderer /'plʌndərər/ n saqueador (-ra); ladrón (-ona)

plundering /'plʌndərɪŋ/ n saqueo, m; despojo, m. —a saqueador

plunge /plʌndʒ/ vt chapuzar; sumergir; hundir; meter. —vi sumergirse; (into water) zambullirse; (rush) precipitarse, lanzarse; Naut. zozobrar; (of a horse) encabritarse; (gamble) jugarse el todo. —n sumersión, f; zambullida, f; chapuz, m; (rush) salto, m; (Fig. step) paso, m

plunger /'plʌndʒər/ n Mech. émbolo, m

plunging /'plʌndʒɪŋ/ n (of a ship) zozobra, f; (of a horse) cabriolas, f pl; saltos, m pl, For other meanings, see **plunge**

plural /'plʊrəl/ a plural. —n plural, m. **in the p.,** en el plural. **to make p.,** poner en plural

plurality /plʊ'ræliti/ n pluralidad, f

plus /plʌs/ prep and a más; (Math. Elec.) positivo. —n signo más, m; Math. cantidad positiva, f. **p. fours,** pantalones de golf, m pl

plush /plʌʃ/ n felpa, f; velludo, m

plushy /'plʌʃi/ a felpudo; de felpa

plutocrat /'pluţə,kræt/ n plutócrata, mf

ply /plai/ n cabo, m. —vt emplear, usar; manejar; ejercer; ofrecer, servir (con); importunar (con). —vi hacer el trayecto; hacer el servicio; ir y venir; hacer viajes. **to ply for hire,** tomar viajeros; ofrecerse para ser alquilado

plywood /'plai,wʊd/ n madera contrachapada, f

pneumatic /nʊ'mætɪk/ a neumático. —n (tire) neumático, m. **p. drill,** barreno neumático, m

pneumococcus /,numə'kɒkəs/ n neumococo, m

pneumonia /nʊ'mounyə/ n pulmonía, f. **double p.,** pulmonía doble, f

poach /poutʃ/ vt cazar (or pescar) en vedado. —vt robar caza de un vedado; Fig. invadir; (Fig. steal) hurtar; (eggs) escalfar. **to p. upon another's preserves,** meterse en los asuntos de otro

poacher /'poutʃər/ n cazador furtivo, m

poaching /'poutʃɪŋ/ n caza (or pesca) furtiva, f

pock /pɒk/ n pústula, f. **p.-mark,** hoyo, m. **p.-marked,** picado de viruelas

pocket /'pɒkɪt/ n bolsillo, m; bolsillo del reloj, m; faltriquera, f; Mineral. bolsa, f, depósito, m; Fig. bolsa, f; (in billiards) tronera, f. —vt meter (or poner) en el bolsillo; (an insult) tragarse; (in billiards) entronerar; (a profit) ganar; apropiarse. **air-p.,** bolsa de aire, f. **to be out of p.,** haber perdido, tener una pérdida. **to have a person in one's p.,** calzarse a una persona. **to p. one's pride,** olvidarse de su orgullo. **p. battleship,** acorazado de bolsillo, m. **p.-book,** cartera, f. **p. dictionary,** diccionario de bolsillo, m. **p.-flap,** portezuela, f. **p.-handkerchief,** pañuelo (de bolsillo), m. **p.-knife,** cortaplumas, m. **p.-lighter,** encendedor de bolsillo, m. **p.-money,** alfileres, m pl, dinero del bolsillo, m. **p. picking,** ratería de carterista, f

pocketful /'pɒkɪt,fʊl/ n bolsillo lleno (de), m; lo que cabe en un bolsillo

pocket of resistance n foco de resistencia, m

pod /pɒd/ n Bot. vaina, f; (of a silkworm) capullo, m. —vt desvainar; mondar. —vi hincharse, llenarse

podgy /'pɒdʒi/ a gordo, grueso

poem /'pouəm/ n poema, m; pl poems, poesías, f pl, versos, m pl

poet /'pouɪt/ n poeta, m. **p. laureate,** poeta laureado, m

poetic /pou'etɪk/ a poético. **p. licence,** licencia poética, f

poetics /pou'etɪks/ n poética, f

poetry /'pouɪtri/ n poesía, f; versos, poemas, m pl

pogrom /pə'grʌm/ n pogrom, m

poignancy /'pɔinyənsi/ n (of emotions) profundidad, violencia, f, lo patético (of a retort, etc.) mordacidad, acerbidad, f

poignant /'pɔinyənt/ a (moving) conmovedor, hondo, agudo; patético; (mordant) mordaz, agudo

poignantly /'pɔinyɑntli/ *adv* de un modo conmovedor, patéticamente; mordazmente

poinsettia /pɔin'sɛtiə/ *n* flor de nochebuena, *f*

point /pɔint/ *n* (usual meanings and *Astrol., Math.*, in cards, in a speech, etc.) punto, *m;* característica, *f;* cualidad, *f;* (purpose) motivo, fin, *m;* (question) cuestión, *f;* asunto, *m;* (wit) agudeza, *f;* (significance) significación, *f;* (detail) detalle, *m;* (in rationing) cupón, *m;* (sharp end) punta, *f;* (of a shawl, etc.) pico, *m;* (of land) promontorio, cabo, *m;* (engraving) buril, *m;* (railway) aguja, *f;* (of horses) cabo, *m.* **Mary has many good points,** María tiene muchas cualidades buenas. **There is no p. in being angry,** No hay para que enfadarse. **in p.,** en cuestión; a propósito. **in p. of fact,** en efecto, en verdad. **on the p. of,** a punto de. **to be to the p.,** venir al caso; ser apropiado. **to carry one's p.,** salir con la suya. **to come to the p.,** ir al grano, ir al caso, ir al mollo del asunto. **to make a p. of,** insistir en; tener por principio. **to win on points,** (boxing) ganar por puntos. **p. at issue,** cuestión bajo consideración, *f,* punto en cuestión, *m.* **p.-blank,** a boca de jarro. **p.-duty,** regulación de tráfico, *f.* **p. lace,** encaje de aguja, *m.* **p. of honor,** punto de honor, *m;* cuestión de honor, *f.* **p. or order,** cuestión de orden, *f.* **p. of view,** punto de vista, *m.* **What's your p.?** ¿A dónde quieres llegar con esto?

point /pɔint/ *vt* sacar punta (a), afilar; (a moral, etc.) inculcar; (in building) rejuntar; *Gram.* puntuar; (of dogs) mostrar la caza. **He pointed his gun at them,** Les apuntó con su fusil. **The hands of the clock pointed to seven o'clock,** Las agujas del reloj marcaban las siete. **to p. with the finger,** señalar con el dedo. **to p. at,** señalar, indicar; (with a gun) apuntar; dirigir. **to p. out,** señalar, indicar; enseñar, mostrar; advertir

pointed /'pɔintid/ *a* (sharpened) afilado; (in shape) puntiagudo; picudo; *Archit.* ojival; *Fig.* mordaz; satírico; (of a remark, etc.) directo; personal; aparente, evidente

pointedly /'pɔintidli/ *adv* explícitamente, categóricamente; mordazmente; directamente; satíricamente

pointer /'pɔintər/ *n* (of a clock, weighing-machine, etc.) aguja, *f;* (of a balance) fiel, *m;* (wand) puntero, *m;* *Fig.* índice, *m;* (dog) perro de muestra, *m*

pointing /'pɔintiŋ/ *n* (in building) rejuntado, *m;* (of a gun) puntería, *f*

pointless /'pɔintlis/ *a* sin motivo, innecesario; fútil; sin importancia

poise /pɔiz/ *vt* balancear; pesar. —*vi* balancearse; posar, estar suspendido. —*n* equilibrio, *m;* (of mind) serenidad de ánimo, sangre fría, *m;* aplomo, *m;* (bearing) porte, aire, *m*

poison /'pɔizən/ *n* veneno, *m; Fig.* ponzoña, *f,* veneno, *m.* —*vt* envenenar; intoxicar; *Fig.* emponzoñar. **p. gas,** gas asfixiante, *m*

poisoning /'pɔizəniŋ/ *n* envenenamiento, *m;* intoxicación, *f*

poisonous /'pɔizənəs/ *a* venenoso; tóxico; *Fig.* ponzoñoso, pernicioso. **p. snake,** serpiente venenosa

poke /pouk/ *vt* (thrust) clavar; (make) hacer; (the fire) atizar; hurgar; (push) empujar; (put away) arrinconar. —*vi* andar a tientas; meterse. **Don't p. your nose into other people's business!** ¡No te metas donde no te llaman! **They poked his eyes out,** Le saltaron los ojos. **to p. fun at,** burlarse de, mofarse de. **to p. the fire,** atizar la lumbre (or el fuego). **to p. about for,** buscar a tientas. **p.-bonnet,** capelina, *f*

poker /'poukər/ *n* (game) póker, *m;* (for the fire) hurgón, atizador, *m.* **p. work,** pirograbado, *m*

poky /'pouki/ *a* estrecho, ahogado, pequeño; miserable

Poland /'poulənd/ Polonia, *f*

polar /'poulər/ *a* polar. **p. bear,** oso (-sa) blanco (-ca). **p. lights,** aurora boreal, *f*

polarize /'poulə,raiz/ *vt* polarizar

pole /poul/ *n* palo largo, *m;* poste, *m;* (of a tent) mástil, *m;* (of a cart) pértiga, *f;* *Sports.* pértiga, garrocha, *f;* (measurement) percha, *f;* (*Astron. Geog. Biol. Math. Elec.*) polo, *m.* —*vt* (a punt) impeler con pértiga. **from p. to p.,** de polo a polo. **greasy p.,** cucaña, *f.* **under bare poles,** *Naut.* a palo seco. **p.-ax,** hachuela de mano, *f;* hacha de marinero, *f;* (butcher's) mazo, *m.* **p. jumping,** salto de pértiga, salto a la garrocha, *m.* **p.-star,** estrella polar, *f*

Pole /poul/ *n* polaco (-ca)

polemic /pə'lɛmik/ *n* polémica, *f*

polemical /pə'lɛmikəl/ *a* polémico

police /pə'lis/ *n* policía, *f.* —*vt* mantener servicio de policía en; mantener el orden público en; administrar, regular. **mounted p.,** policía montada, *f.* **p. constable,** (agente de) policía, guardia urbano, *m.* **p. court,** tribunal de la policía, *m.* **p. dog,** perro de policía, *m.* **p. force,** cuerpo de policía, *m,* policía, *f.* **p. magistrate,** juez municipal, *m.* **p. station,** comisaría de policía, *f.* **p. trap,** puesto oculto de la policía del tráfico, *m.* **p. woman,** policía, *f*

policeman /pə'lismən/ *n* policía, guardia, *m*

policy /'pɑləsi/ *n* política, *f;* táctica, *f;* sistema, *m;* norma de conducta, *f;* ideas, *f pl;* principios, *m pl;* prudencia, *f;* (insurance) póliza, *f.* **fixed premium p.,** póliza a prima fija, *f.* **p.-holder,** asegurado (-da), tenedor (de una póliza), *m*

poliomyelitis /,pouliou,maiə'laitis/ *n* poliomielitis, *f*

polish /'pɑliʃ/ *vt* (metals and wood) pulir; (furniture and shoes) dar brillo (a); (*Lit.*

works) pulir, limar; (persons) descortezar, civilizar. **—n** (shine) brillo, *m;* (furniture) cera para los muebles, *f;* (metal, silver) líquido para limpiar metales, *m;* (for shoes) betún para zapatos, *m;* (varnish) barniz, *m;* (of Lit. works) pulidez, elegancia, *f;* (of persons) urbanidad, cultura, *f.* **to p. off,** terminar a prisa; (a person) acabar con; (food) engullir

Polish /'poulɪʃ/ *a* polaco, polonés. **—n** (language) polaco, *m*

polished /'polɪʃt/ *a* (of verses, etc.) pulido, elegante; (of person) culto, distinguido; (of manners) fino, cortés

polisher /'polɪʃər/ *n* (machine) pulidor, *m;* lustrador, *n.* **floor-p.,** lustrador de piso, *m.* **French p.,** barnizador, *m*

polite /pə'laɪt/ *a* cortés, bien educado; atento; elegante

politeness /pə'laɪtnɪs/ *n* cortesía, *f.* **for p. sake,** por cortesía

politic /'polɪtɪk/ *a* político

political /pə'lɪtɪkəl/ *a* político. **p. agent,** agente político, *m.* **p. economist,** hacendista, *mf* **p. economy,** economía política, *f*

politician /,polɪ'tɪʃən/ *n* político (-ca)

politics /'polɪtɪks/ *n* política, *f.* **to dabble in p.,** meterse en política

polity /'polɪti/ *n* forma de gobierno, constitución política, *f*

polka-dot /'poukə,dot/ *a* con puntos

poll /poul/ *n* (head of person) cabeza, *f;* (voters' register) lista electoral, *f;* (voting) votación, *f;* (polling booth) colegio electoral, *m;* (counting of votes) escrutinio, *m.* **—vt** (trees) desmochar; (vote) votar, dar su voto (a); (obtain votes) obtener, recibir; (count votes) escrutar. **p.-tax,** capitación, *f*

pollen /'polən/ *n* polen, *m*

pollinate /'polə,neɪt/ *vt* fecundar con polen

pollination /,polə'neɪʃən/ *n* polinización, *f*

polling /'poulɪŋ/ *n* votación, *f.* **p. booth,** colegio electoral, *m*

pollute /pə'lut/ *vt* contaminar; ensuciar; profanar; (corrupt morally) corromper

pollution /pə'luʃən/ *n* contaminación, *f;* profanación, *f;* corrupción, *f*

polo /'poulou/ *n* polo, *m.* **p. mallet,** maza de polo, *f.* **p. player,** jugador de polo, *m,* polista, *mf*

poltroon /pol'trun/ *n* cobarde, *m*

polychrome /'poli,kroum/ *a* policromo

polygamist /pə'lɪgəmɪst/ *n* polígamo (-ma)

polygamous /pə'lɪgəməs/ *a* polígamo

polygenesis /,poli'dʒɛnəsɪs/ *n* poligenismo, *m*

polyglot /'poli,glot/ *n* polígloto (-ta). **p.** Bible, poliglota, *f*

polygon /'poli,gon/ *n* polígono, *m*

polyp /'polɪp/ *n* pólipo, *m*

polyphonic /,poli'fonɪk/ *a* polifónico

polyphony /pə'lɪfəni/ *n* polifonía, *f*

polytechnic /,poli'tɛknɪk/ *a* politécnico

pomade /po'meɪd/ *n* pomada, *f*

pomegranate /'pom,grænɪt/ *n* granada, *f*

pommel /'pʌməl/ *n* pomo, *m, vt* aporrear

pomp /pomp/ *n* pompa, magnificencia, *f,* fausto, aparato, *m;* ostentación, *f*

Pompeii /pom'peɪ/ Pompeya, *f*

pompom /'pom,pom/ *n* pompón, *m*

pomposity /pom'posɪti/ *n* pomposidad, presunción, *f;* (of language) ampulosidad, *f*

pompous /'pompəs/ *a* pomposo, ostentoso; (of style) ampuloso, hinchado; importante. **to be p.,** (of persons) darse tono

pond /pond/ *n* charca, *f,* estanque, *m*

ponder /'pondər/ *vt* ponderar, estudiar, considerar. **—vi** meditar (sobre), reflexionar (sobre)

ponderous /'pondərəs/ *a* pesado; macizo, abultado; grave; (dull) pesado, aburrido

poniard /'ponyərd/ *n* puñal, *m, vt* apuñalar

pontiff /'pontɪf/ *n* pontífice, *m*

pontifical /pon'tɪfɪkəl/ *a* pontificio

pontificate /pon'tɪfɪ,kɪt/ *n* pontificado, *m*

pontoon /pon'tun/ *n* pontón, *m.* **p. bridge,** puente de pontones, *m*

pony /'pouni/ *n* jaca, *f*

poodle /'pudl/ *n* perro (-rra) de aguas, perro de lanas, perro lanudo

pooh-pooh /'pu'pu/ *vt* despreciar, desdeñar. **Pooh!** ¡Bah!

pool /pul/ *n* (in a river) rebalsa, *f;* charca, *f,* estanque, *m;* (of blood, etc.) charco, *m;* (in cards) baceta, *f; Com.* asociación, *f; Fig.* fuente, *f; pl* **pools,** (football) apuestas benéficas de fútbol, *f pl.* **—vt** (resources, etc.) combinar; juntar

poop /pup/ *n* popa, *f.* **p. lantern,** fanal, *m*

poor /pur/ *a* pobre; malo; (insignificant or unfortunate) infeliz, desgraciado. **the p.,** los pobres. **to be in p. health,** estar mal de salud. **to be p. stuff,** ser de pacotilla. **to be poorer than a church mouse,** ser más pobre que las ratas. **to have a p. opinion of,** tener en poco (a). **P. me!** ¡Ay de mí! ¡Pecador de mí! **p.-box,** cepillo, *m.* **p.-law,** ley de asistencia pública, *f.* **p.-spirited,** apocado

poorhouse /'pur,haus/ *n* asilo, *m*

pop /pop/ *n* (of a cork) taponazo, *m;* (of a gun) detonación, *f;* (drink) gaseosa, *f, adv* ¡pum! **—vi** (of a cork) saltar; (of guns) detonar. **—vt** (corks) hacer saltar; (a gun, a question, etc.) disparar. **pop-gun,** escopeta de aire comprimido, *f.* **to pop down,** bajar a presuradamente. **to pop in,** (visit) dejarse caer; entrar rápidamente. **to pop off,** marcharse a prisa; (die) estirar la pata. **to pop up,** subir corriendo; aparecer de pronto

pope /poup/ *n* Papa, *m*

popinjay /'pɒpɪn,dʒei/ n (fop) pisaverde, m

poplar /'pɒplər/ n (black) chopo, álamo, m; (white) álamo blanco, m. **p. grove,** alameda, f

poplin /'pɒplɪn/ n popelina, f

poppy /'pɒpi/ n amapola, adormidera, f

populace /'pɒpyələs/ n pueblo, m; (scornful) populacho, m

popular /'pɒpyələr/ a popular; en boga, de moda; común. **He is a p. hero,** Es un héroe popular

popularity /,pɒpyə'lærɪti/ n popularidad, f

popularization /,pɒpyələrə'zeiʃən/ n vulgarización, f

popularize /'pɒpyələ,raiz/ vt popularizar, vulgarizar

populate /'pɒpyə,leit/ vt poblar

population /,pɒpyə'leiʃən/ n población, f

populous /'pɒpyələs/ a populoso; muy póblado

porcelain /'pɔrsəlɪn/ n porcelana, f

porch /pɔrtʃ/ n pórtico, m; (of a house) portal, m

porcupine /'pɔrkyə,pain/ n puerco espín, m

pore /pɔr/ n poro, m. **to p. over,** estar absorto en; examinar cuidadosamente

pork /pɔrk/ n carne de cerdo, f. **salt p.,** tocino, m. **p. butcher,** tocinero, m. **p. pie,** pastel de carne de cerdo, m

pornographic /,pɔrnə'græfɪk/ a pornográfico

pornography /pɔr'nɒgrəfi/ n pornografía, f

porosity /pə'rɒsɪti/ n porosidad, f

porous /'pɔrəs/ a poroso

porphyry /'pɔrfəri/ n pórfido, m

porpoise /'pɔrpəs/ n marsopa, f, puerco marino, m

porridge /'pɒrɪdʒ/ n gachas, f pl, m

port /pɔrt/ n puerto, m; (in a ship) porta, f; (larboard) babor, m; (wine) vino de Oporto, m; (mien) porte, m, presencia, f. —vt (the helm) poner a babor; Mil. llevar un fusil terciado. **to put into p.,** tomar puerto. **to stop at a p.,** hacer escala en un puerto. **p. dues,** derechos de puerto, m pl

portable /'pɔrtəbəl/ a portátil; móvil. **p. typewriter,** máquina de escribir portátil (or de viaje), f. **p. wireless,** radio portátil, f

portal /'pɔrtl/ n portal, m

portcullis /pɔrt'kʌlɪs/ n rastrillo, m

portend /pɔr'tend/ vt presagiar, anunciar

portent /'pɔrtent/ n augurio, presagio, m; portento, m

portentous /pɔr'tentəs/ a ominoso; portentoso; importante

porter /'pɔrtər/ n (messenger) mozo de cordel, m; (of a university, hotel) portero, m; (of a block of flats) conserje, m; (railway) mozo de estación, m; (drink) cerveza negra, f. **porter's lodge,** portería, f; conserjería, f

portfolio /pɔrt'fouli,ou/ n carpeta, f; (Polit. of a minister) cartera, f; (Polit. ministry) ministerio, m

porthole /'pɔrt,houl/ n tronera, f

portico /'pɔrtɪ,kou/ n pórtico, m

portiere /pɔr'tyeər/ n antepuerta, f

portion /'pɔrʃən/ n porción, f; parte, f; (marriage) dote, mf; (piece) pedazo, m; (in a restaurant) ración, f; (in life) fortuna, f. —vt dividir; repartir; (dower) dotar

portly /'pɔrtli/ a corpulento, grueso

portmanteau /pɔrt'mæntou/ n maleta, f

portrait /'pɔrtrɪt/ n retrato, m. **p. painter,** pintor (-ra) de retratos

portraiture /'pɔrtrɪtʃər/ n retratos, m pl; descripción, pintura, f

portray /pɔr'trei/ vt retratar; pintar, representar; (in words) describir, pintar

portrayal /pɔr'treiəl/ n pintura, f; retrato, m; (in words) descripción, f

portrayer /pɔr'treiər/ n retratista, mf, pintor (-ra)

Portuguese /,pɔrtʃə'giz/ a portugués. —n portugués (-esa); (language) portugués, m

pose /pouz/ vt colocar; (a problem, etc.) plantear; (a question) hacer; vi colocarse; (with as) echárselas de, dárselas de, fingir ser; hacerse pasar por. —n actitud, postura, f; (affected) pose, f; (deception) engaño, m

poser /'pouzər/ n problema difícil, m; (in an examination) pega, f; pregunta embarazosa, f

position /pə'zɪʃən/ n posición, f; situación, f; actitud, postura, f; condición, f; estado, m; (post) puesto, empleo, m. **He is not in a p. to...,** No está en condiciones de..., No está para... **to place in p.,** poner en posición, colocar

positive /'pɒzɪtɪv/ a positivo; absoluto; (convinced) convencido, seguro; (downright) categórico; Inf. completo. —n realidad, f; Photo. (prueba) positiva, f

positively /'pɒzɪtɪvli/ adv positivamente; categóricamente

posse /'pɒsi/ n pelotón, m; multitud, muchedumbre, f

possess /pə'zes/ vt poseer; gozar (de); (of ideas, etc.) dominar. **to p. oneself of,** apoderarse de, apropiarse. **What possessed you to do it?** ¿Qué te hizo hacerlo?

possession /pə'zeʃən/ n posesión, f. **to take p. of,** tomar posesión de; hacerse dueño de, apoderarse de; (a house, etc.) entrar en, ocupar

possessor /pə'zesər/ n poseedor (-ra); dueño (-ña); propietario (-ia)

possibility /,pɒsə'bɪlɪti/ n posibilidad, f

possible /'pɒsəbəl/ a posible. **as soon as p.,** cuanto antes, lo más pronto posible. **to make p.,** hacer posible, posibilitar

possibly /'pɒsəbli/ adv posiblemente; (perhaps) quizás. **I shall come as soon as I p. can,** Vendré lo más pronto posible

post /poust/ *n* (pole) poste, *m*; (of a sentry, etc.) puesto, *m*; (employment) empleo, *m*; (mail) correo, *m*; *Mil.* toque, *m*. —*vt* (a notice) fijar; anunciar; (to an appointment) destinar; (letters, etc.) echar al correo; *Com.* pasar al libro mayor; (inform) tener al corriente. —*vi* viajar en posta. **"P. no bills!"** «Se prohibe fijar carteles.» **registered p.,** correo certificado, *m.* **p. card,** postal, *f.* **p.-chaise,** silla de posta, *f.* **p.-date,** posfecha, *f.* **p.-free,** franco de porte. **p.-haste,** con gran celeridad. **p.-horse,** caballo de posta, *m.* **p.-impressionism,** post-impresionismo, *m.* **p.-mortem,** *n* autopsia, *f.* **p.-natal,** postnatal. **p.-nuptial,** postnupcial. **p. office,** correo, *m,* correos, *m pl;* (on a train) ambulancia de correos, *f.* **p. office box,** apartado de correos, *m.* **p. office savings bank,** caja postal de ahorros, *f.* **p.-paid,** porte pagado; franco. **p.-war,** *n* postguerra, *f.* —*a* de la postguerra

postage /'poustɪdʒ/ *n* porte de correos, franqueo, *m.* **p. stamp,** sello postal, *m*

postage meter *n* franqueadora, *f*

postal /'poustl/ *a* postal. **p. order,** orden postal de pago, *f.* **p. packet,** paquete postal, *m*

poster /'poustər/ *n* cartel, *m.* —*vt* fijar carteles (a or en); anunciar por carteles. **bill-p.,** fijador de carteles, *m*

poste restante /,poust rɛ'stɑnt/ *n* lista de correos, *f*

posterior /pɒ'stɪəriər/ *a* posterior. —*n* trasero, *m,* asentaderas, *f pl*

posterity /pɒ'stɛrɪti/ *n* posteridad, *f*

postgraduate /poust'grædʒuɪt/ *n* estudiante graduado que hace estudios avanzados, *m* —*a* avanzado; para estudiantes graduados

posthumous /'pɒstʃəməs/ *a* póstumo

posthumously /'pɒstʃəməsli/ *adv* después de la muerte

postman /'poustmən/ *n* cartero, *m*

postmark /'poustmɑrk/ *n* matasellos, *m, vt* poner matasellos (a)

postmaster /'poust,mæstər/ *n* administrador de correos, *m*

postpone /poust'poun/ *vt* aplazar, diferir; retrasar; (subordinate) postergar

postponement /poust'pounmənt/ *n* aplazamiento, *m;* tardanza, *f*

postscript /'poust,skrɪpt/ *n* posdata, *f*

postulate /*n.* 'pɒstʃəlɪt; *v.* -,leɪt/ *n* postulado, *m, vt* postular

posture /'pɒstʃər/ *n* postura, actitud, *f;* (of affairs) estado, *m,* situación, *f.* —*vi* tomar una postura

pot /pɒt/ *n* pote, *m;* tarro, *m;* (flower-) tiesto, *m;* (for cooking) olla, marmita, *f;* jarro, *m.* —*vt* plantar en tiestos; conservar en potes. **pot-bellied,** panzudo. **pot-boiler,** obra literaria escrita con el sólo propósito de ganar dinero, *f.* **pot-herb,** hierba que se emplea para sazonar, hortaliza, *f.* **pot-hole,** bache, **pot-luck,** comida ordinaria, *f.* **pot-shot,** tiro fácil, *m;* tiro al azar, *m*

potable /'poutəbəl/ *a* potable

potage /pou'tɑʒ/ *n* potaje, *m*

potash /'pɒt,æʃ/ *n* potasa, *f.* **caustic p.,** potasa cáustica, *f*

potassium /pə'tæsiəm/ *n* potasio, *m*

potato /pə'teitou/ *n* patata, *f.* **sweet p.,** batata, *f.* **p. beetle,** coleóptero de la patata, *m.* **p. omelet,** tortilla a la española, *f.* **p. patch,** patatal, *m.* **p. peeler,** pelapatatas, *m*

potency /'poutnsi/ *n* potencia, *f;* fuerza, eficacia, *f*

potent /'poutnt/ *a* potente, fuerte; eficaz

potentate /'poutn,teit/ *n* potentado, *m*

potential /pə'tɛnʃəl/ *a* potencial; virtual; (*Phys. Gram.*) potencial, *n* poder, *m; Gram.* modo potencial, *m; Phys.* energía potencial, *f; Elec.* tensión potencial, *f*

potion /'pouʃən/ *n* poción, *f,*

potpourri /,poupu'ri/ *n* popurrí, *m*

potter /'pɒtər/ *n* alfarero, *m.* —*vi* gandulear. —*vt* perder. **potter's clay,** barro de alfarero, *m.* **potter's wheel,** tabanque, *m.* **potter's workshop,** alfar, *m*

pottery /'pɒtəri/ *n* alfarería, *f;* (china) loza, porcelana, *f*

pouch /pautʃ/ *n* bolsa, *f; Zool.* bolsa marsupial, *f;* (for tobacco) tabaquera, *f;* (for cartridges) cartuchera, *f.* —*vt* embolsar. —*vi* bolsear

poultice /'poultɪs/ *n* apósito, emplasto, *m, vt* poner emplastos (a or en)

poultry /'poultri/ *n* volatería, *f.* **p. dealer,** gallinero (-ra) vendedor (-ra) de volatería. **p. yard,** gallinero, *m*

poultry farming *n* avicultura, *f*

pounce /pauns/ *n* (swoop) calada, *f.* —*vi* (swoop) calarse; saltar (sobre); agarrar, hacer presa (en); *Fig.* atacar; descubrir, hacer patente

pound /paund/ *n* (weight and currency) libra, *f;* (for cattle) corral de concejo, *m;* (thump) golpe, *m.* —*vt* (break up) machacar, pistar; (beat) batir; (thump) golpear, aporrear. —*vi* dar golpes. **p. sterling,** libra esterlina, *f.* **p. troy,** libra medicinal, *f*

pour /por/ *vt* vaciar, verter; derramar. —*vi* correr; (of rain) diluviar, llover a cántaros; (fill) llenar; (of crowds, words, etc.) derramarse. **to p. out the tea,** servir el té. **The crowd poured in,** La multitud entró en tropel

pouring /'pɔriŋ/ *a* (of rain) torrencial

pout /paut/ *vi* torcer el gesto; hacer pucheritos

poverty /'pɒvərti/ *n* pobreza, *f.* **p.-stricken,** menesteroso, indigente, necesitado

powder /'paudər/ *n* polvo, *m;* (face) polvos de arroz, *m pl;* (gun) pólvora, *f.* —*vt* polvorear; (crush) reducir a polvo, pulverizar. —*vi* ponerse polvos. **p.-flash,** fogonazo, *m.* **p.-flask,** polvorín, *m.* **p.-magazine,** santabárbara, *f* fábrica de pólvora, *f.* **p.-mill,** fábrica de pólvora, *f.* **p.-puff,** polvera, borla de empolvarse, *f*

powdered /'paudərd/ *a* en polvo

powdery /'paudəri/ *a* polvoriento; friable

power /'pauər/ *n* poder, *m*; facultad, capacidad, *f*; vigor, *m*, fuerza, *f*; (*Polit.* and *Math.*) potencia, *f*; *Mech.* fuerza, *m*. influencia, **f. as far as lies within my p.,** en cuanto me sea posible. **It does not lie within my p.,** No está dentro de mis posibilidades, No está en mi poder. **the Great Powers,** las grandes potencias. **powers that be,** los que mandan. **to be in p.,** estar en el poder. **p.-house, p.-station,** central eléctrica, *f*. **p. of attorney,** poderes, *m pl*, procuración, *f*. **to grant p. of attorney (to),** dar poderes (a)

powerful /'pauərfəl/ *a* poderoso; fuerte; eficaz; potente; (of arguments, etc.) convincente

powerless /'pauərlıs/ *a* impotente

power steering *n* dirección asistida *f* (Spain); servo dirección *f*

powwow /'pau,wau/ *n* conferencia, *f*, conversación, *f*

pox /pɒks/ *n* sífilis, *f*; (smallpox) viruelas, *f pl*; (chicken-pox) viruelas falsas, *f pl*

practicable /'præktɪkəbəl/ *a* practicable, factible, posible; viable, transitable

practical /'præktɪkəl/ *a* (doable) factible; práctico; virtual. **p. joke,** burla de consecuencias

practically /'præktɪkli/ *adv* prácticamente; en práctica; virtualmente; (in fact) en efecto. **p. nothing,** casi nada

practice /'præktɪs/ *n* (custom) costumbre, *f*; práctica, *f*; ejercicio, *m*; (of a doctor, etc.) clientela, *f*; profesión, *f*; (religious) rito, *m*, ceremonias, *f pl*; (experience) experiencia, *f*. **It is not his p. to...,** No es su costumbre de... **to be out of p.,** estar desentrenado. **to put into p.,** poner en práctica. **P. makes perfect,** El ejercicio hace maestro. —*vt* tener la costumbre de; practicar; (a profession) ejercer; (a game) entrenarse en; (work at) estudiar; (a musical instrument) tocar; (accustom) acostumbrar. **to p. what one preaches,** predicar con el ejemplo

practiced /'præktɪst/ *a* experimentado; experto

practitioner /præk'tɪʃənər/ *n* médico (-ca). **general p.,** médico (-ca) general

pragmatic /præg'mætɪk/ *a* pragmatista; (historical) pragmático; práctico

prairie /'prɛəri/ *n* pradera, sabana, pampa, *f*, *a* de la pradera, etc.

praise /preiz/ *vt* alabar; ensalzar, glorificar; elogiar. —*n* alabanza, *f*; elogio, *m*; glorificación, *f*, ensalzamiento, *m*. **to p. to the skies,** poner en los cuernos de la luna poner por las nubes, poner sobre las estrellas hacerse lenguas de

praiseworthy /'preiz,wɜrði/ *a* digno de alabanza, laudable

prance /præns/ *vi* (of a horse) caracolear, encabritarse, cabriolar; saltar; andar airosamente. —*n* corveta, cabriola, *f*; salto, *m*

prank /præŋk/ *n* travesura, diablura, *f*. **to play pranks,** hacer diabluras

prate, prattle /preit; 'prætl/ *vi* charlar, chacharear; (lisp) balbucir; (of brooks, etc.) murmurar, susurrar. —*vt* divulgar. —*n* charla, cháchara, *f*; balbuceo, *m*

prattler /'prætlər/ *n* parlanchín (-ina); (gossip) chismoso (-sa); (child) niño (-ña) parlero

prattling /'prætlıŋ/ *n* charla, *f*; (lisping) balbuceo, *m*; (of brooks, etc.) murmullo, susurro, ruido armonioso, *m*. —*a* charlatán, gárrulo; balbuciente; (of brooks, etc.) parlero

prawn /prɔn/ *n* camarón, *m*

pray /prei/ *vt* and *vi* suplicar; implorar; rezar, orar. **P. be seated,** Haga el favor de sentarse

prayer /preiər/ *n* rezo, *m*, plegaria, oración, *f*; súplica, *f*; *Law.* petición, *f*. **p. book,** libro de devociones, devocionario, *m*. **p.-meeting,** reunión para rezar, *f*. **p.-rug,** alfombra de rezo, *f*

praying /'preiŋ/ *n* rezo, *m*; suplicación, *f*

pre- *prefix* de antes de (e.g. *pre-World-War-1 publications,* publicaciones de antes de la Primera Guerra Mundial)

preach /pritʃ/ *vt* and *vi* predicar

preacher /'pritʃər/ *n* predicador (-ra). **to turn p.,** meterse a predicar

preaching /'pritʃɪŋ/ *n* predicación, *f*, *a* predicador

preamble /'pri,æmbəl/ *n* preámbulo, *m*

prearrange /,priə'reindʒ/ *vt* preparar de antemano, predisponer

precarious /prɪ'kɛəriəs/ *a* precario; inseguro; incierto, arriesgado

precaution /prɪ'kɔʃən/ *n* precaución, *f*. **to take precautions,** tomar precauciones

precautionary /prɪ'kɔʃə,nɛri/ *a* de precaución; preventivo

precede /prɪ'sid/ *vt* preceder (a), anteceder (a); tomar precedencia (a), exceder en importancia (a). —*vi* ir delante; tener la precedencia

precedence /'prɛsɪdəns/ *n* precedencia, *f*; prioridad, *f*; superioridad, *f*. **to take p. over,** tomar precedencia (a), preceder (a)

precedent /*n*. 'prɛsɪdənt/ *a*. prɪ'sidnt/ *n* precedente, *m*, *a* precedente. **without p.,** sin precedente

preceding /prɪ'sidɪŋ/ *a* anterior, precedente

precept /'prisɛpt/ *n* precepto, *m*

precinct /'prisɪŋkt/ *n* (police station) comisaría de sección (Argentina), delegación (Mexico), *f*

precincts /'prisɪŋkts/ *n pl* recinto, *f*; ámbito, *m*; distrito, barrio, *m*

preciosity /,prɛʃi'ɒsɪti/ *n* afectación, *f*

precious /'prɛʃəs/ *a* precioso; de gran valor; hermoso; amado; muy querido; (with rogue, etc.) redomado; completo. **p. little,** muy poco. **p. nearly,** casi, por poco... **p. stone,** piedra preciosa, *f*

precipice /'prɛsəpɪs/ *n* precipicio, *m*

precipitant /prɪ'sɪpɪtənt/ *a* precipitado

precipitate /*v*. prɪ'sɪpɪ,teit/ *n*., *a*. -tɪt/ *vt* precipitar, despeñar, arrojar; acelerar;

Chem. precipitar. —*vi* precipitarse. —*n* precipitado, *m.* —*a* precipitado, súbito. **to p. oneself,** tirarse, lanzarse

precipitation /prɪˌsɪpɪˈteɪʃən/ *n Chem.* precipitación, *f; Chem.* precipitado, *m;* (rain, etc.) precipitación pluvial, *f*

precipitous /prɪˈsɪpɪtəs/ *a* precipitoso, escarpado, acantilado

precipitously /prɪˈsɪpɪtəsli/ *adv* en precipicio

precise /prɪˈsaɪs/ *a* preciso; exacto; justo; puntual; escrupuloso; formal; claro; pedante, afectado; ceremonioso

precisely /prɪˈsaɪsli/ *adv* precisamente; exactamente; puntualmente; escrupulosamente; claramente; con afectación; ceremoniosamente. **at six o'clock p.,** a las seis en punto

precision /prɪˈsɪʒən/ *n* precisión, *f;* exactitud, *f;* puntualidad, *f;* escrupulosidad, *f;* claridad, *f;* afectación, *f;* ceremonia, *f*

preclude /prɪˈklud/ *vt* excluir; impedir; hacer imposible

preclusion /prɪˈkluʒən/ *n* exclusión, *f;* imposibilidad, *f*

precocious /prɪˈkouʃəs/ *a* precoz

preconceived /ˌprikənˈsivd/ *a* preconcebido

preconception /ˌprikənˈsɛpʃən/ *n* idea preconcebida, *f;* (prejudice) prejuicio, *m*

preconcerted /ˌprikənˈsɛrtɪd/ *a* concertado de antemano

precursor /prɪˈkɜrsər/ *n* precursor (-ra)

precursory /prɪˈkɜrsəri/ *a* precursorio

predatory /ˈprɛdəˌtɔri/ *a* rapaz; de rapiña; voraz

predecease /ˌpridɪˈsis/ *vt* morir antes (de or que); *Law.* premorir. —*n Law.* premuerto, *m*

predecessor /ˈprɛdəˌsɛsər/ *n* predecesor (-ra); (ancestor) antepasado, *m*

predicament /prɪˈdɪkəmənt/ *n* /ˈprɛdɪkəmənt/ (logic) predicamento, *m;* situación, *f;* (fix) apuro, *m; pl* **predicaments,** categorías, *f pl*

predicate /v. ˈprɛdɪˌkeit; n. -kɪt/ *vt* afirmar. —*n* (logic, *Gram.*) predicado, *m*

predict /prɪˈdɪkt/ *vt* predecir, pronosticar, profetizar

prediction /prɪˈdɪkʃən/ *n* predicción, *f;* pronóstico, vaticinio, *m,* profecía, *f*

predilection /ˌprɛdlˈɛkʃən/ *n* predilección, *f*

predispose /ˌpridɪˈspouz/ *vt* predisponer

predominance /prɪˈdɑmənəns/ *n* predominio, *m*

predominant /prɪˈdɑmənənt/ *a* predominante

predominate /prɪˈdɑməˌneit/ *vi* predominar

preeminence /priˈɛmənəns/ *n* preeminencia, *f;* primacía, superioridad, *f*

preeminent /priˈɛmənənt/ *a* preeminente; superior; extraordinario

preeminently /priˈɛmənəntli/ *adv* preeminentemente; extraordinariamente; por excelencia; entre todos

preen /prin/ *vt* (of birds) limpiarse; (of people) darse humos, jactarse

prefabricated /priˈfæbrɪˌkeitɪd/ *a* prefabricado

preface /ˈprɛfɪs/ *n* prólogo, *m; Eccl.* prefacio, *m;* introducción, *f.* —*vt* dar principio (a), empezar. **He prefaced his remarks by...,** Dijo a modo de introducción

prefatory /ˈprɛfəˌtɔri/ *a* preliminar, introductorio; a manera de prólogo

prefer /prɪˈfɜr/ *vt* preferir, gustar más (a); (promote) ascender, elevar; (a charge, etc.) presentar. **to p. a charge against,** pedir en júicio (a). **I p. oranges to apples,** Me gustan más las naranjas que las manzanas, Prefiero las naranjas a las manzanas

preferable /ˈprɛfərəbəl/ *a* preferible

preferably /ˈprɛfərəbli/ *adv* preferiblemente, con preferencia

preference /ˈprɛfərəns/ *n* preferencia, *f;* privilegio, *m.* **p. share,** acción privilegiada, acción preferente, *f*

preferential /ˌprɛfəˈrɛnʃəl/ *a* preferente

preferment /prɪˈfɜrmənt/ *n* promoción, *f,* ascenso, *m;* puesto eminente, *m*

preferred /prɪˈfɜrd/ *a* preferente; favorito, predilecto. **p. share,** acción preferente, *f*

prefix /ˈprifɪks/ *vt* anteponer, prefijar; (to a word) poner prefijo (a). —*n* prefijo, *m*

pregnancy /ˈprɛgnənsi/ *n* embarazo, *m,* preñez, *f*

pregnant /ˈprɛgnənt/ *a* embarazada, encinta, preñada, *f; Fig.* fértil; *Fig.* preñado

prehensile /prɪˈhɛnsɪl/ *a* prensil

prehistoric /ˌprihɪˈstɔrɪk/ *a* prehistórico

prehistory /priˈhɪstəri/ *n* prehistoria, *f*

prejudge /priˈdʒʌdʒ/ *vt* prejuzgar

prejudice /ˈprɛdʒədɪs/ *n* prejuicio, *m; Law.* perjuicio, *m.* —*vt* influir, predisponer; (damage) perjudicar. **without p.,** sin perjuicio

prejudiced /ˈprɛdʒədɪst/ *a* parcial; con prejuicios

prejudicial /ˌprɛdʒəˈdɪʃəl/ *a* perjudicial

preliminary /prɪˈlɪməˌnɛri/ *a* preliminar. —*n* preliminar, *m*

prelude (to) /ˈprɛlyud/ *n* preludio (de) *m;* presagio (de) *m, vt* and *vi* preludiar

premature /ˌpriməˈtʃʊr/ *a* prematuro

premeditate /prɪˈmɛdɪˌteit/ *vt* premeditar

premeditatedly /prɪˈmɛdɪˌteitɪdli/ *adv* premeditadamente, con premeditación

premeditation /prɪˌmɛdɪˈteiʃən/ *n* premeditación, *f*

premier /prɪˈmɪər/ *a* primero, principal. —*n* primer ministro, *m;* (in Spain) presidente del Consejo de Ministros, *m*

premiere /prɪˈmɪər/ *n* estreno, *m*

premiership /prɪˈmɪərʃɪp/ *n* puesto de primer ministro, *m;* (in Spain) presidencia del Consejo de Ministros, *f*

premise /ˈprɛmɪs/ *n* (logic) premisa, *f; pl* **premises,** local, *m;* recinto, *m;* establecimiento, *m;* propiedad, *f;* tierras, *f pl.* **on**

the premises, en el local; en el establecimiento

premium /'primiəm/ n (prize) premio, m, recompensa, f; Com. prima, f; precio, m. **at a p.,** a premio; a una prima; (of shares) sobre la par; Fig. en boga, muy solicitado, en gran demanda

premonition /,primə'niʃən/ n presentimiento, presagio, m

prenatal /pri'neitl/ a prenatal, antenatal

preoccupation /pri,ɒkyə'peiʃən/ n preocupación, f

preoccupied /pri'ɒkyə,paid/ a preocupado; abstraído, absorto

preoccupy /pri'ɒkyə,pai/ vt preocupar

prepaid /pri'peid/ a porte pagado, franco de porte

preparation /,prepə'reiʃən/ n preparación, f; preparativo, m, disposición, f; (patent food) preparado, m. **I have made all my preparations,** He hecho todos mis preparativos. **The book is in p.,** El libro está en preparación

preparative /pri'pærətiv/ a preparativo. —n preparativo, m

preparatory /pri'pærə,tɔri/ a preparatorio, preparativo; preliminar. **p. school,** escuela preparatoria, f, m. **p. to,** como preparación para; antes de

prepare /pri'pɛər/ vt preparar; aparejar, aviar; equipar; (cloth) aprestar. —vi prepararse; hacer preparativos

preparedness /pri'pɛəridnis/ n estado de preparación, m; preparación, f, apercibimiento, m

prepay /pri'pei/ vt pagar adelantado; (a letter, etc.) franquear

prepayment /pri'peimənt/ n pago adelantado, m; (of a letter, etc.) franqueo, m

preponderance /pri'pɒndərəns/ n preponderancia, f

preponderant /pri'pɒndərənt/ a preponderante, predominante

preponderate /pri'pɒndə,reit/ vi preponderar; prevalecer (sobre), predominar (sobre)

preposition /,pripə'ziʃən/ n preposición, f

prepossess /,pripə'zɛs/ vt predisponer; causar buena impresión (a)

prepossessing /,pripə'zɛsiŋ/ a atractivo

preposterous /pri'pɒstərəs/ a ridículo, absurdo

Prep School /prep/ n preparatoria, f

prepuce /'pripyus/ n prepucio, m

prerequisite /pri'rɛkwəzit/ n requisito necesario, esencial, m, a previamente necesario, esencial

prerogative /pri'rɒgətiv/ n prerrogativa, f

presage /'presidʒ/ n presagio, m; anuncio, m. —vt presagiar; anunciar

Presbyterian /,prezbi'tiəriən/ a and n presbiteriano (-na)

prescient /'preʃənt/ a presciente

prescind /pri'sind/ vt prescindir (de); separar (de). —vi separarse

prescribe /pri'skraib/ vt and vi prescribir; Med. recetar; dar leyes; Law. prescribir

prescription /pri'skripʃən/ n prescripción, f; Med. receta, f

presence /'prezəns/ n presencia, f; (ghost) aparición, f. **in the p. of,** en presencia de, delante; a vista de. **p. of mind,** presencia de ánimo, serenidad de ánimo, f

present /'prezənt/ a presente; actual; (with month) corriente; Gram. presente. **at p.,** al presente, actualmente. **at the p. day,** a la fecha, en la actualidad, hoy día. **P. company excepted!** ¡Mejorando lo presente! **the present writer,** el que suscribe, el que esto escribe, el que estas líneas traza. **to be p. at,** presenciar, ser testigo de; asistir a, acudir a; hallarse en. **p.-day,** de hoy, actual. **p. tense,** Gram. tiempo presente, m

present /'prezənt/ n (time) presente, m; actualidad, f; Gram. tiempo presente, m; (gift) regalo, m, dádiva, f. **By these presents...,** Law. Por estas presentes... **to make a p. of,** regalar. **Jane made me a p. of a watch,** Juana me regaló un reloj

present /pri'zɛnt/ vt presentar; ofrecer; manifestar; (a gift) regalar, dar; (Eccl. Mil.) presentar. **New problems presented themselves,** Nuevos problemas surgieron. **to p. arms,** presentar las armas. **He presented himself in the office,** Se presentó en la oficina. **He presented his friend Mr. Moreno to me,** Me presentó a su amigo el Sr. Moreno

presentation /,prezən'teiʃən/ n presentación, f; homenaje, m; (exhibition) exposición, f. **on p.,** Com. a presentación

presentiment /pri'zɛntəmənt/ n presentimiento, m, corazonada, f. **I had a p. that...,** Tuve el presentimiento de que..., Tuve una corazonada que... **to have a p. about,** presentir

presently /'prezəntli/ adv pronto; en seguida; dentro de poco

preservation /,prezər'veiʃən/ n conservación, f; (from harm) preservación, f

preservative /pri'zɜrvətiv/ a preservativo. —n preservativo, m

preserve /pri'zɜrv/ vt preservar (de); guardar; proteger; conservar; Cul. hacer conservas de; (in syrup) almibarar. —n Cul. conserva, f; (of fruit) compota, confitura, f; (covert) coto, m. **preserved fruit,** dulce de almíbar, m. **p. dish,** compotera, f

preserver /pri'zɜrvər/ n conservador (-ra); (saviour) salvador (-ra); (benefactor) bienhechor (-ra)

preserving /pri'zɜrviŋ/ n (from harm) preservación, f; conservación, f. **p. pan,** cazuela para conservas, f

preside /pri'zaid/ vi (over) presidir; dirigir, gobernar. **He presided at the meeting,** Presidió la reunión

presidency /'prezidənsi/ n presidencia, f

president /'prezidənt/ n presidente, m;

(of a college) rector, *m.* **lady p.**, presidenta, *f*

presidential /ˌprezɪˈdenʃəl/ *a* presidencial

press /pres/ *vt* prensar; (juice out of) exprimir; (clothes) planchar; (a bell, a hand, and of a shoe, etc.) apretar; (embrace) dar un abrazo (a); (a stamp, a kiss, etc.) imprimir; (an enemy) hostigar, acosar; (in a game) apretar; (crowd upon) oprimir; (emphasize) insistir en; (urge) instar, instigar; (compel) obligar; apremiar; (oppress) abrumar, agobiar; (paper) satinar; (an advantage) aprovecharse de. **Lola pressed his hand,** Lola le apretó la mano. **Time presses,** El tiempo es breve. **I did not p. the point,** No insistí. **to p. against,** pegar(se) contra. **to p. down,** comprimir; *Fig.* agobiar. **to p. for,** exigir, reclamar. **to p. forward, on,** avanzar; seguir el camino, continuar la marcha; (hurry) apretar el paso

press /pres/ *n* (pressure) apretón, *m*; (push) golpe, *m*; (throng) muchedumbre, *f*; (of business, etc.) urgencia, *f*; (apparatus) prensa, *f*; (printing press and publishing firm) imprenta, *f*; (cupboard) armario, *m*. **Associated P.**, Prensa Asociada, *f*. **freedom of the p.**, libertad de la prensa, *f*. **in p.**, **in the p.**, en prensa. **in the p. of battle**, en lo más reñido de la batalla. **to go to p.**, entrar en prensa. **p.-agent**, agente de publicidad, *m*. **p.-box**, tribuna de la prensa, *f*. **p. clipping, p.-cutting**, recorte de prensa, *m*. **p.-gallery**, tribuna de la prensa, *f*. **p.-gang**, ronda de enganche, *f*. **p.-mark**, número de catálogo, *m*. **p. proof**, prueba de imprenta, *f*. **p.-room**, taller de imprenta, *m*. **p.-stud**, botón automático, *m*. **p. conference**, rueda de prensa, entrevista de prensa, conferencia de pensa, *f*

pressing /ˈpresɪŋ/ *a* urgente, apremiante; importuno. —*n* prensado, *m*, prensadura, *f*; expresión, *f*; (of a garment) planchado, *m*

pressure /ˈpreʃər/ *n* presión, *f*; (of the hand) apretón, *m*; apremio, *m*; opresión, *f*; (weight) peso, *m*; (force) fuerza, *f*; urgencia, *f*. **p.-cooker**, cazuela de presión, olla de presión, *f*, presto, *m*. **p.-gauge**, manómetro, *m*

prestidigitation /ˌprestɪˌdɪdʒɪˈteɪʃən/ *n* prestidigitación, *f*, juegos de manos, *m pl*

prestige /preˈstiʒ/ *n* prestigio, *m*

prestigious /preˈstɪdʒəs/ *a* prestigiado

presume /prɪˈzum/ *vt* presumir; suponer; sospechar; (attempt) pretender. —*vi* presumir; tomarse libertades; abusar (de)

presumption /prɪˈzʌmpʃən/ *n* presunción, *f*; suposición, *f*; (effrontery) atrevimiento, *m*; insolencia, *f*

presumptive /prɪˈzʌmptɪv/ *a* presuntivo; (with heir, etc.) presunto

presumptuous /prɪˈzʌmptʃuəs/ *a* presumido, insolente, presuntuoso; atrevido

presuppose /ˌprisəˈpouz/ *vt* presuponer

presupposition /ˌprisʌpəˈzɪʃən/ *n* presuposición, *f*

pretence /prɪˈtens/ *n* (claim) pretensión, *f*; afectación, *f*; (simulation) fingimiento, *m*; pretexto, *m*. **false pretences,** apariencias fingidas, *f pl*; engaño, *m*, estafa, *f*. **to make a p. of,** fingir. **under p. of,** bajo pretexto de

pretend /prɪˈtend/ *vt* dar como pretexto de; aparentar, fingir, simular, hacer el papel (de). —*vi* pretender (a); tener pretensiones (de); ser pretendiente (a); fingir

pretended /prɪˈtendɪd/ *a* supuesto, fingido; falso

pretender /prɪˈtendər/ *n* pretendiente, *m*; hipócrita, *mf*

pretension /prɪˈtenʃən/ *n* pretensión, *f*; afectación, simulación, *f*

pretentious /prɪˈtenʃəs/ *a* pretencioso; (of persons) presumido

pretentiousness /prɪˈtenʃəsnɪs/ *n* pretensiones, *f pl*, lo pretencioso

preterite /ˈpretərɪt/ *n* (tiempo) pretérito, *m*, *a* pretérito, pasado

pretext /ˈpritekst/ *n* pretexto, *m*. —*vt* pretextar. **under p. of,** bajo pretexto de, so color de

pretty /ˈprɪti/ *a* bonito; (of women, children) guapo, mono; (of men) lindo; elegante; excelente; *Ironic.* bueno. —*adv* bastante; medianamente; (very) muy; (almost) casi. **p. good,** bastante bueno. **p.-p.,** de muñeca; mono. —*n* chuchería, *f*, guapos, *m pl*. **p. ways,** monerías, *f pl*

prevail /prɪˈveɪl/ *vi* prevalecer, predominar; ser la costumbre. **to p. against or over,** triunfar de, vencer (a). **to p. on, upon,** inducir, convencer, persuadir. **to be prevailed upon to,** dejarse persuadir a

prevailing /prɪˈveɪlɪŋ/ *a* prevaleciente; dominante; predominante, reinante; general; común; (fashionable) en boga

prevalence /ˈprevələns/ *n* predominio, *m*; existencia, *f*; (habit) costumbre, *f*; (fashion) boga, *f*

prevalent /ˈprevələnt/ *a* prevaleciente, predominante; general; común; corriente; (fashionable) en boga

prevaricate /prɪˈværɪˌkeɪt/ *vi* tergiversar; *Law.* prevaricar

prevaricator /prɪˈværɪˌkeɪtər/ *n* tergiversador (-ra)

prevent /prɪˈvent/ *vt* evitar; (hinder) impedir (a)

prevention /prɪˈvenʃən/ *n* prevención, *f*; (preventive) estorbo, obstáculo, *m*

preventive /prɪˈventɪv/ *a* preventivo. —*n* preservativo, *m*

preview /ˈpriˌvyu/ *n* vista de antemano, *f*; (of a film) avances, *m pl* (Cuba, Mexico), colas, *f pl* (Argentina), cortos *m pl* (Venezuela), sinopsis, *f* (Uruguay), tráiler, *m* (Spain)

previous /ˈpriviəs/ *a* previo, anterior. **p. to,** antes de

previously /ˈpriviəsli/ *adv* anteriormente, antes, previamente

prewar /'pri'wɔr/ *a* de antes de la guerra

prey /prei/ *n* presa, *f;* *Fig.* víctima, *f;* (booty) botín, *m.* —*vi* (of animals) devorar; (plunder) robar, pillar; (of sorrow, etc.) hacer presa (de); agobiar, consumir; (sponge on) vivir a costa de. **to fall a p. to,** ser víctima de

price /prais/ *n* precio, *m;* valor, *m;* costa, *f.* —*vt* evaluar, tasar; poner precio a; preguntar el precio de; fijar el precio de. **at any p.,** a cualquier precio; (whatever the cost) cueste lo que cueste. **at a reduced p.,** a precio reducido. **fixed p.,** precio fijo, *m.* **p. ceiling,** precio máximo, precio tope, *m.* **p. control,** control de precios, *m.* **price list,** lista de precios, *f;* tarifa, *f;* (of shares, etc.) boletín de cotización, *m.* **Prices are subject to change without notice,** Los precios están sujetos a variación sin previo aviso.

priceless /'praislɪs/ *a* sin precio; (amusing) divertidísimo. **These jewels are p.,** Estas joyas no tienen precio

prick /prɪk/ *n* pinchazo, *m;* picadura, *f;* punzada, *f;* (prickle) espina, *f;* (with a goad) aguijonazo, *m;* (with a pin) alfilerazo, *m;* (with a spur) espolada, *f;* (of conscience) remordimiento, escrúpulo, *m.* —*vt* pinchar, punzar; picar; (with remorse) atormentar, causar remordimiento (a); (urge on) incitar. **to p. the ears,** aguzar las orejas

prickle /'prɪkəl/ *n* espina, *f;* (irritation) escozor, *m*

prickly /'prɪkli/ *a* espinoso; erizado. **p. heat,** salpullido causado por exceso de calor, *m.* **p. pear,** higo chumbo, *m,* chumbera, *f*

pride /praid/ *n* orgullo, *m;* arrogancia, *f;* (splendour) pompa, *f,* fausto, aparato, *m;* belleza, *f;* vigor, *m;* (of lions) manada, *f.* **to take p. in,** estar orgulloso de. **to p. oneself,** sentirse orgulloso, ufanarse. **to p. oneself upon,** jactarse de, preciarse de

priest /prist/ *n* sacerdote, *m;* cura, *m.* **high-p.,** sumo sacerdote, *m.* **p.-ridden,** dominado por el clero

prig /prɪg/ *n* fatuo (-ua), mojigato (-ta)

priggish /'prɪgɪʃ/ *a* fatuo, gazmoño

prim /prɪm/ *a* almidonado, etiquetero; peripuesto; afectado

primacy /'praiməsi/ *n* primacía, *f*

prima donna /,primə 'donə/ *n* cantatriz, *f*

primarily /prai'mɛərəli/ *adv* en primer lugar principalmente

primary /'praimeri/ *a* primario; primitivo; principal. **p. education,** enseñanza primaria, *f.* **p. color,** color primario, *m.* **p. school,** escuela primaria, *f.* **p. election,** elección interna (dentro de un partido), *f*

prime /praim/ *a* primero; principal; excelente; de primera calidad; de primera clase. —*n* (spring) primavera, *f;* (of life, etc.) flor, *f,* vigor, *m;* (best) nata, crema, *f; Eccl.* prima, *f;* (number) número primo, *m.* —*vt* preparar, aprestar; (fire-arms) cebar. **p. the pump,** cebar la bomba; (with

paint, etc.) imprimar; (instruct) dar instrucciones (a), informar. **in his p.,** en la flor de su edad. **of p. quality,** de primera calidad. **P. Minister,** Primer Ministro, *m.* **p. necessity,** artículo de primera necesidad, *m*

primer /'praimər/ *n* cartilla, *f,* abecedario, *m;* libro de lectura, *m;* (prayer book) devocionario, *m*

primeval /prai'mivəl/ *a* primevo, primitivo

priming /'praimiŋ/ *n* preparación, *f;* (of fire-arms) cebo, *m;* (of paint, etc.) imprimación, *f;* instrucción, *f*

primitive /'primitiv/ *a* primitivo; anticuado. —*n* primitivo, *m*

primrose /'prim,rouz/ *n* primavera, *f;* color amarillo pálido, *m*

prince /prins/ *n* príncipe, *m.* **P. Consort,** príncipe consorte, *m.* **P. of Wales,** (Britain) príncipe heredero, *m;* (Spanish equivalent) Príncipe de Asturias, *m.* **p. regent,** príncipe regente, *m.* **P. Charming,** el Príncipe Azul, *m*

princely /'prinsli/ *a* principesco; magnífico; noble

princess /'prinsis/ *n* princesa, *f*

principal /'prinsəpəl/ *a* principal; fundamental; mayor. —*n* principal, jefe, *m;* (of a university) rector, *m;* (of a school) director (-ra); *Law.* causante, *m; Com.* capital, *m*

principle /'prinsəpəl/ *n* principio, *m.* **in p.,** en principio

print /print/ *n* (mark) impresión, marca, *f;* (type) letra de molde, *f,* tipo, *m;* (of books) imprenta, *f;* (fabric) estampado, *m;* (picture) grabado, *m;* (photograph) positiva impresa, *f;* (mold) molde, *m.* —*vt* marcar; imprimir; (on the mind) grabar; *Print.* tirar, hacer una tirada (de); (in photography) tirar una prueba (de); (publish) sacar a luz, publicar; (fabrics) estampar. **in p.,** impreso; publicado; **He likes to see his name in print,** Le gusta ver su nombre en letras de molde; (available) existente. **to be out of p.,** estar agotado. **p. dress,** vestido estampado, *m*

printed /'printid/ *a* impreso. **p. fabric,** estampado, *m.* **p. matter,** impresos, *m pl*

printer /'printər/ *n* impresor, *m;* tipógrafo, *m.* **printer's devil,** aprendiz de impresor, *m.* **printer's ink,** tinta de imprenta, tinta tipográfica, *f.* **printer's mark,** pie de imprenta, *m*

printing /'printiŋ/ *n* imprenta, *f;* impresión, *f;* (of fabrics) estampación, *f;* (art of) tipografía, *f.* **p. house,** imprenta, *f.* **p. machine,** máquina de imprimir, *f.* **p. press,** prensa tipográfica, *f.* **p. types,** caracteres de imprenta, *m pl*

prior /'praiər/ *n* prior, *m,* a anterior, previo. **p. to,** anterior a, antes de

priority /prai'ɔriti/ *n* prioridad, *f*

prism /'prizəm/ *n* prisma, *m;* espectro solar, *m*

prison /'prizən/ *n* prisión, cárcel, *f.* **p.-breaking,** huida de la prisión, *f.* **p. camp,**

campo de prisioneros, *m.* **p. van**, coche celular, *m.* **p. yard**, patio de la prisión, *m*

prisoner /'prɪzənər/ *n* prisionero (-ra), preso (-sa). **to take p.**, prender, hacer prisionero (a)

pristine /'prɪstin/ *a* pristino, original

privacy /'praɪvəsi/ *n* soledad, *f,* aislamiento, retiro, *m;* intimidad, *f;* secreto, *m*

private /'praɪvɪt/ *a* particular; privado; secreto; confidencial; reservado; íntimo; personal; doméstico; (of hearings, etc.) a puertas cerradas; (own) propio. —*n* (soldier) soldado raso, *m.* **in p.**, en secreto; confidencialmente, de persona a persona. **They wish to be p.**, Quieren estar a solas. **p. company**, sociedad en comandita, *f.* **p. hotel**, pensión, *f.* **p. house**, casa particular, *f.* **p. individual**, particular, *mf.* **p. interview**, entrevista privada, *f.* **p. life**, vida privada, *f.* **p. office**, despacho particular, *m.* **p. secretary**, secretario (-ia) particular. **p. viewing**, (of a film) función privada, *f.* **(of an exhibition)** día de inauguración, *m*

privately /'praɪvɪtli/ *adv* privadamente; en secreto; personalmente; confidencialmente; (of hearings) a puertas cerradas

privation /praɪ'veɪʃən/ *n* privación, *f;* carencia, escasez, *f*

privilege /'prɪvəlɪdʒ/ *n* privilegio, *m;* derecho, *m;* inmunidad, *f.* —*vt* privilegiar

privy /'prɪvi/ *a* privado; cómplice; enterado; personal, particular. —*n* (latrine) retrete, *m.* **p. council**, consejo privado, *m*

prize /praɪz/ *n* premio, *m;* recompensa, *f,* galardón, *m;* (capture) presa, *f.* —*a* que ha ganado un premio; premiado; (huge) enorme; (complete) de primer orden. —*vt* estimar, apreciar. **to p. open**, abrir con una palanca. **to carry off the p.**, ganar el premio. **cash p.**, premio en metálico, *m.* **first p.**, primer premio, *m;* (in a lottery) premio gordo, *m.* **p. court**, tribunal de presas, *m.* **p. fight**, partido de boxeo, *m.* **p. fighter**, boxeador, *m.* **p. giving**, distribución de premios, *f.* **p. money**, premio en metálico, *m;* (boxing) bolsa, *f*

probability /ˌprɒbə'bɪlɪti/ *n* probabilidad, *f*

probable /'prɒbəbəl/ *a* probable

probate /'proubeit/ *n* verificación de un testamento, *f*

probation /prou'beiʃən/ *n* probación, *f; Law.* libertad vigilada, *f*

probe /proub/ *n Surg.* sonda, cala, tienta, *f.* —*vt Surg.* tentar; escudriñar

probity /'proubiti/ *n* probidad, integridad, *f*

problem /'prɒbləm/ *n* problema, *m;* cuestión, *f.* **p. play**, drama de tesis, *m*

problematic /ˌprɒblə'mætɪk/ *a* problemático

problem child *n* niño problemático, *m* (male), niña problemática, *f* (female)

proboscis /prou'bɒsɪs/ *n* (of an elephant) trompa, *f;* (of an insect) trompetilla, *f*

procedure /prə'sidʒər/ *n* procedimiento, *m*

proceed /prə'sid/ *vi* seguir el camino, continuar la marcha; avanzar; seguir adelante; ir; proceder; ponerse (a); empezar (a); (say) proseguir; (come to) llegar a, ir a; (of a play, etc.) desarrollarse. **Before we p. any further...** Antes de ir más lejos... **to p. to blows**, llegar a las manos. **to p. against**, proceder contra, procesar. **to p. from**, venir de. **to p. with,** proseguir; poner por obra; usar

proceeding /prə'sidɪŋ/ *n* modo de obrar, *m;* conducta, *f;* procedimiento, *m;* transacción, *f; pl* **proceedings**, (measures) medidas, *f pl,* actos, *m pl;* (of a learned society or a conference) actas, *f pl.* **to take proceedings against,** *Law.* procesar

proceeds /'prousidz/ *n pl* producto, *m;* ganancias, *f pl;* beneficios, *m pl.* **net p.**, producto neto, *m*

process /'prɒsɛs/ *n* proceso, *m;* (method) procedimiento, *m;* (course) curso, *m;* marcha, *f;* (*Law. Zool.*) proceso, *m.* —*vt* beneficiar (ore); trasformar, elaborar. **in p. of**, en curso de. **in the p. of time**, con el tiempo marchando el tiempo

processing industry /'prɒsɛsɪŋ/ *n* industria de trasformación, industria de elaboración, *f*

procession /prə'sɛʃən/ *n* desfile, *m;* cortejo, *m;* (religious) procesión, *f.* **funeral p.**, cortejo fúnebre, *m.* **to walk in p.**, desfilar

proclaim /prou'kleɪm/ *vt* proclamar; publicar, pregonar; anunciar; (reveal) revelar; (outlaw) denunciar

proclamation /ˌprɒklə'meɪʃən/ *n* proclamación, *f;* proclama, *f,* anuncio, *m;* declaración, *f*

proclivity /prou'klɪvɪti/ *n* proclividad, propensión, *f*

procrastinate /prou'kræstə,neɪt/ *vi* tardar (en decidirse), aplazar su decisión; vacilar; perder el tiempo

procrastination /prou,kræstə'neɪʃən/ *n* dilación, tardanza, *f;* vacilación, *f;* pereza, *f*

procreate /'proukri,eit/ *vt* procrear

procreation /ˌproukri'eiʃən/ *n* procreación, *f*

proctor /'prɒktər/ *n* procurador, *m; Educ.* censor, *m*

procurable /prou'kyʊrəbəl/ *a* procurable; asequible

procure /prou'kyʊr/ *vt* obtener, conseguir, lograr

procurement /prou'kyʊrmənt/ *n* obtención, *f,* logro, *m*

procurer /prou'kyʊrər/ *n* alcahuete, *m*

prod /prɒd/ *n* (with a bayonet, etc.) punzada, *f;* Fig. pinchazo, *m.* —*vt* punzar; (in the ribs, etc.) clavar; *Fig.* pinchar

prodigal /'prɒdɪgəl/ *a and n* pródigo (-ga)

prodigious /prə'dɪdʒəs/ *a* prodigioso

prodigy /'prɒdɪdʒi/ *n* prodigio, *m;* portento, *m.* **child p.**, niño prodigio

produce /*v.* prə'dus; *n.* 'prɒdus, 'proudus/ *vt* producir; dar frutos; (show) mostrar, presentar; (take out) sacar; (occasion) causar, traer consigo, ocasionar; (goods) fabricar, manufacturar; (of shares, etc.) rendir; *Geom.* prolongar; (a play) poner en escena. —*n* producto, *m*; víveres, comestibles, *m pl*

producer /prə'dusər/ *n* productor (-ra); *Theat.* director de escena, *m*

product /'prɒdʌkt/ *n* producto, *m*; (result) fruto, resultado, *m*, consecuencia, *f*; *Math.* producto, *m*

production /prə'dʌkʃən/ *n* producción, *f*; producto, *m*; *Geom.* prolongación, *f*; (of a play) dirección escénica, *f*; (performance) producción, *f*. **p. cost,** coste de producción, *m*

productive /prə'dʌktɪv/ *a* productivo

profane /prə'fein/ *a* profano; sacrílego, blasfemo. —*vt* profanar

profanity /prə'fænɪti/ *n* profanidad, *f*; blasfemia, *f*

profess /prə'fɛs/ *vt* (assert) afirmar, manifestar; declarar; (a faith, a profession, teach) profesar; (feign) fingir; (pretend) tener pretensiones de. —*vi* (as a monk or nun) tomar estado, entrar en religión. **He professed himself surprised,** Se declaró sorprendido

professed /prə'fɛst/ *a* declarado; *Eccl.* profeso; ostensible, fingido

profession /prə'fɛʃən/ *n* profesión, *f*; carrera, *f*; declaración, *f*. **p. of faith,** profesión de fe, *f*. **the learned professions,** las carreras liberales

professional /prə'fɛʃənl/ *a* profesional; de la profesión; de profesión; de carrera. **p. diplomat,** diplomático (-ca) de carrera. **p. etiquette,** etiqueta profesional, *f*. **p. man,** hombre profesional, *m*; hombre de carrera liberal, *m*

professor /prə'fɛsər/ *n* catedrático (-ca), profesor (-ra)

professorship /prə'fɛsər,ʃɪp/ *n* cátedra, *f*

proffer /'prɒfər/ *vt* proponer; ofrecer. —*n* oferta, *f*

proficiency /prə'fɪʃənsi/ *n* pericia, habilidad, *f*

proficient /prə'fɪʃənt/ *a* proficiente, experto, adepto, perito

profile /'proufail/ *n* perfil, *m*. —*vt* perfilar. **in p.,** de perfil

profit /'prɒfɪt/ *n* provecho, *m*; utilidad, *f*; ventaja, *f*; *Com.* ganancia, *f*, *vt* aprovechar. —*vi* ganar; *Com.* sacar ganancia. **to p. by,** aprovechar. **gross p.,** ganancia total, *f*. **p. and loss,** ganancias y pérdidas, *f pl*. **p. sharing,** participación en las ganancias, participación de utilidades, *f*

profitable /'prɒfɪtəbəl/ *a* provechoso, útil, ventajoso; lucrativo. **p. use,** aprovechamiento, *m*

profitably /'prɒfɪtəbli/ *adv* con provecho, provechosamente; lucrativamente

profiteer /,prɒfɪ'tɪər/ *n* estraperlista, *mf*

profit incentive *n* acicate del lucro, *m*

profligate /'prɒflɪgɪt/ *a* licencioso, disoluto. —*n* libertino, *m*

profound /prə'faund/ *a* profundo

profundity /prə'fʌndɪti/ *n* profundidad, *f*

profuse /prə'fyus/ *a* profuso; pródigo; lujoso

profusion /prə'fyuʒən/ *n* profusión, abundancia, *f*; prodigalidad, *f*; exceso, *m*

progenitor /prou'dʒɛnɪtər/ *n* progenitor, *m*; (ancestor) antepasado, *m*

progeny /'prɒdʒəni/ *n* prole, *f*

prognosis /prɒg'nousɪs/ *n* prognosis, *f*; presagio, *m*; *Med.* pronóstico, *m*

prognosticate /prɒg'nɒstɪ,keit/ *vt* pronosticar, presagiar

program /'prougræm/ *n* programa, *m*

progress /n. 'prɒgrɛs; v. prə'grɛs/ *n* progreso, *m*; avance, *m*; (betterment) mejora, *f*; (of events) marcha, *f*. —*vi* avanzar, marchar; (improve) progresar, adelantar; mejorar. **to make p.,** adelantarse; hacer progresos

progression /prə'grɛʃən/ *n* progresión, *f*

progressive /prə'grɛsɪv/ *a* progresivo; avanzado; *Polit.* progresista. —*n Polit.* progresista, *mf*

prohibit /prou'hɪbɪt/ *vt* prohibir; defender; (prevent) impedir, privar. **His health prohibited him from doing it,** Su salud le impidió hacerlo

prohibition /,prouə'bɪʃən/ *n* prohibición, *f*; interdicción, *f*; (of alcohol) prohibicionismo, *m*

prohibitive /prou'hɪbɪtɪv/ *a* prohibitivo, prohibitorio

project /v. prə'dʒɛkt; n. 'prɒdʒɛkt/ *vt* (all meanings) proyectar, —*vi* sobresalir; destacarse. —*n* proyectil, plan, *m*

projectile /prə'dʒɛktɪl/ *n* proyectil, *m*, *a* arrojadizo

projecting /prə'dʒɛktɪŋ/ *a* saliente; (of teeth) saltón

projection /prə'dʒɛkʃən/ *n* (hurling) lanzamiento, *m*; prominencia, protuberancia, *f*; (other meanings) proyección, *f*

projector /prə'dʒɛktər/ *n* proyectista, *mf*; proyector, *m*

proletarian /,proulɪ'tɛəriən/ *a* proletario

proletariate /,proulɪ'tɛəriɪt/ *n* proletariado, *m*

prolific /prə'lɪfɪk/ *a* prolífico; fecundo; fértil

prolix /prou'lɪks/ *a* prolijo

prolog /'prou,lɒg/ *n* prólogo, *m*, *vt* prologar

prolong /prə'lɒŋ/ *vt* prolongar

promenade /,prɒmə'neid, -'nɑd/ *n* paseo, *m*; bulevar, *m*; avenida, *f*. —*vi* pasearse. —*vt* recorrer, andar por, pasearse por. **p. deck,** cubierta de paseo, *f*

prominence /'prɒmənəns/ *n* prominencia, *f*; protuberancia, *f*; eminencia, *f*; importancia, *f*

prominent /'prɒmənənt/ *a* prominente, saliente; (of eyes, teeth) saltón; (distinguished) eminente, distinguido. **They placed the vase in a p. position,** Pusieron el florero muy a la vista. **to play a p. part,** desempeñar un papel importante. **p. eyes,** ojos saltones, *m pl*

promiscuous /prə'mɪskyuəs/ *a* promiscuo

promise /'promɪs/ *n* promesa, *f;* (hope) esperanza, *f;* (word) palabra, *f;* (future) porvenir, *m.* —*vt* and *vi* prometer. **a young man of p.,** un joven de porvenir. **to break one's p.,** faltar a su palabra; no cumplir una promesa. **to keep one's p.,** guardar su palabra; cumplir su promesa. **to p. and do nothing,** apuntar y no dar. **under p. of,** bajo palabra de. **p. of marriage,** palabra de matrimonio, *f*

promised /'promɪst/ *a* prometido. **P. Land,** Tierra de promisión, *f*

promising /'proməsɪŋ/ *a* que promete bien, que promete mucho; prometedor; (of the future, etc.) halagüeño; (of persons) que llegará

promissory /'promə,sɔri/ *a* promisorio. **p. note,** pagaré, abonaré, *m*

promontory /'promən,tɔri/ *n* promontorio, *m*

promote /prə'mout/ *vt* fomentar, promover; provocar; (aid) favorecer, proteger; avanzar; estimular; (to a post) ascender; (an act bill) promover; *Com.* negociar

promoter /prə'moutər/ *n* promotor (-ra); instigador (-ra); (*Theat.* etc.) empresario, *m*

promotion /prə'mouʃən/ *n* (encouragement) fomento, *m;* (furtherance) adelanto, *m;* protección, *f,* favorecimiento, *m;* (in employment, etc.) promoción, *f,* ascenso, *m;* (of a company, etc.) creación, *f*

prompt /prompt/ *a* pronto; diligente; presuroso; puntual; rápido; *Com.* inmediato. —*vt* impulsar, incitar, mover; dictar; insinuar; *Theat.* apuntar; (remind) recordar. **He came at five o'clock p.,** Vino a las cinco en punto. **p. book,** libro del traspunte, *m.* **p. box,** concha (del apuntador), *f*

prompter /'promptər/ *n Theat.* apuntador, (in the wings) traspunte, *m*

prompting /'promptɪŋ/ *n* sugestión, *f;* instigación, *f; pl* **promptings,** impulso, *m;* (of the heart, etc.) dictados, *m pl*

promptly /'promptli/ *adv* inmediatamente, en seguida; con prontitud, con celeridad; puntualmente

promulgate /'promǝl,geit/ *vt* promulgar; divulgar, diseminar

promulgation /'promǝl'geiʃǝn/ *n* promulgación, *f;* divulgación, diseminación, *f*

prone /proun/ *a* postrado; inclinado, propenso

prong /prɔŋ/ *n* (pitchfork) horquilla, *f;* (of a fork) diente, *m,* púa, *f*

pronged /prɔŋd/ *a* dentado, con púas

pronoun /'prou,naun/ *n* pronombre, *m*

pronounce /prə'nauns/ *vt* pronunciar; declarar; articular

pronounced /prə'naunst/ *a* marcado; perceptible; bien definido

pronunciation /prə,nʌnsi'eiʃǝn/ *n* pronunciación, *f;* articulación, *f*

proof /pruf/ *n* prueba, *f;* demostración, *f;* ensayo, *m; Law.* testimonio, *m;* (*Photo. Print.*) prueba, *f; Math.* comprobación, *f,* a hecho a prueba (de); impenetrable (a); *Fig.* insensible (a). —*vt* (raincoats, etc.) impermeabilizar. **in p. whereof,** en fe de lo cual. **p. against bombs,** a prueba de bombas. **p. reading,** corrección de pruebas, *f*

prop /prop/ *n* apoyo, puntal, estribadero, *m;* (for a tree) horca, *f,* rodrigón, *m; Naut.* escora, *f; Fig.* báculo, *m,* columna, *f,* apoyo, *m.* —*vt* apoyar; apuntalar; (a tree) ahorquillar; (a building) acodalar; *Naut.* escorar; *Fig.* sostener. **He propped himself against the wall,** Se apoyó en el muro, Se arrimó al muro

propaganda /,propǝ'gændǝ/ *n* propaganda, *f*

propagandist /,propǝ'gændɪst/ *n* propagandista, *mf*

propagate /'propǝ,geit/ *vt* propagar. —*vi* propagarse

propagation /,propǝ'geiʃǝn/ *n* propagación, *f*

propel /prǝ'pɛl/ *vt* propulsar, empujar, mover

propeller /prǝ'pɛlǝr/ *n* propulsor, *m; Mech.* hélice, *f*

propensity /prǝ'pɛnsɪti/ *n* propensión, tendencia, inclinación, *f*

proper /'propǝr/ *a* propio; apropiado; correcto; decente; (prim) afectado; serio, formal; (exact) justo, exacto; (suitable (for)) bueno (para), apto (para); (true) verdadero; (characteristic) peculiar; *Herald.* natural; (with rascal, etc.) redomado; (handsome) guapo. **If you think it p.,** Si te parece bien. **p. noun,** nombre propio, *m*

properly /'propǝrli/ *adv* decentemente; correctamente; propiamente; bien. **to do (a thing) p.,** hacer algo bien. **p. speaking,** propiamente dicho, hablando con propiedad

propertied /'propǝrtid/ *a* propietario, hacendado; (rich) pudiente, adinerado

property /'propǝrti/ *n* propiedad, *f;* (belongings) bienes, *m pl;* posesiones, *f pl;* (estate) hacienda, *f;* (quality) cualidad, *f pl* **properties,** *Theat.* accesorios, *m pl.* **personal p.,** bienes muebles, *m pl;* cosas personales, *f pl.* **real p.,** bienes raíces, *m pl.* **p. man,** *Theat.* encargado de los accesorios, *m.* **p. owner,** propietario (-ia). **p. tax,** contribución sobre la propiedad, *f*

prophecy /'profǝsi/ *n* profecía, *f;* predicción, *f*

prophesy /'profǝ,sai/ *vt* profetizar; presagiar, predecir. —*vi* hacer profecías

prophet /'profɪt/ *n* profeta, *m*

prophetic /prǝ'fɛtɪk/ *a* profético

prophylactic /,proufǝ'læktɪk/ *a* and *n* profiláctico, *m*

propinquity /prou'pɪŋkwɪti/ *n* propincuidad, proximidad, *f;* (relationship) parentesco, *m*

propitiate /prə'pɪʃi,eit/ vt propiciar; apaciguar, conciliar

propitious /prə'pɪʃəs/ a propicio, favorable

proportion /prə'pɔrʃən/ n proporción, f; parte, f; porción, f; pl **proportions**, proporciones, f pl; dimensiones, f pl. —vt proporcionar; repartir, distribuir. **in p.**, en proporción; conforme (a), según; Com. a prorrata. **in p. as**, a medida que. **out of p.**, desproporcionado. **He has lost all sense of p.**, Ha perdido su equilibrio (mental)

proportional /prə'pɔrʃənl/ a proporcional; en proporción (a); proporcionado (a). **p. representation**, representación proporcional, f

proportionate /a. prə'pɔrʃənit; v. -,neit/ a proporcionado; proporcional. —vt proporcionar

proposal /prə'pouzəl/ n proposición, f; oferta, f; (plan) propósito, proyecto, m. **p. of marriage**, oferta de matrimonio, f

propose /prə'pouz/ vt proponer; ofrecer; (a toast) dar, brindar. —vi pretender, intentar, tener la intención de; pensar; (marriage) declararse

proposer /prə'pouzər/ n proponente, m; (of a motion) autor (-ra) de una proposición

proposition /,prɒpə'zɪʃən/ n proposición, f; (plan) proyecto, propósito, m

propound /prə'paund/ vt proponer; plantear, presentar

proprietary /prə'praii,teri/ a propietario; de propiedad

proprietor /prə'praiitər/ n propietario, m; dueño, m

propriety /prə'praiiti/ n decoro, m; conveniencia, f; corrección, f

propulsion /prə'pʌlʃən/ n propulsión, f

prorogation /,prourou'geiʃən/ n prorrogación, f

prorogue /prou'roug/ vt prorrogar, suspender (la sesión de una asamblea legislativa)

prosaic /prou'zeiik/ a prosaico

pros and cons /'prouz ən 'kɒnz/ el pro y el contra

proscenium /prou'siniəm/ n proscenio, m

proscribe /prou'skraib/ vt proscribir

proscription /prou'skrɪpʃən/ n proscripción, f

prose /prouz/ n prosa, f. **p. writer**, prosista, mf

prosecute /'prɒsɪ,kyut/ vt proseguir, llevar adelante; (Law. a person) procesar; (Law. a claim) pedir en juicio

prosecution /,prɒsɪ'kyuʃən/ n prosecución, f; cumplimiento, m; Law. acusación, f; (Law. party) parte actora, f. **in the p. of his duty**, en el cumplimiento de su deber

prosecutor /'prɒsɪ,kyutər/ n demandante, actor, m. **public p.**, fiscal, m

proselyte /'prɒsə,lait/ n prosélito, m

prose writer n prosador, m

prospect /'prɒspɛkt/ n perspectiva, f; esperanza, f; probabilidad, f; (in mining) indicio de filón, m; criadero (de oro, etc.), m. —vi explorar; (of a mine) prometer (bien), dar buenas esperanzas. —vt explorar, inspeccionar; examinar. **He is a man with good prospects**, Es un hombre de porvenir

prospecting /'prɒspɛktɪŋ/ n la prospección, f

prospective /prə'spɛktɪv/ a en expectativa, futuro; previsor

prospector /'prɒspɛktər/ n explorador, operador, m

prospectus /prə'spɛktəs/ n prospecto, programa, m

prosper /'prɒspər/ vi prosperar. —vt favorecer, prosperar

prosperity /prɒ'spɛriti/ n prosperidad, f

prosperous /'prɒspərəs/ a próspero; favorable

prostate /'prɒsteit/ n próstata, f

prostitute /'prɒstɪ,tut/ n prostituta, f, vt prostituir

prostitution /,prɒstɪ'tuʃən/ n prostitución, f

prostrate /'prɒstreit/ a tendido; postrado; abatido. —vt derribar; arruinar; (by grief, etc.) postrar; (oneself) postrarse

prostration /prɒ'streiʃən/ n postración, f; abatimiento, m. **nervous p.**, neurastenia, f

prosy /'prouzi/ a aburrido, árido; pedestre, prosaico; verboso, prolijo

protagonist /prou'tægənist/ n protagonista, mf

protean /'proutiən/ a proteico

protect /prə'tɛkt/ vt proteger

protection /prə'tɛkʃən/ n protección, f; defensa, f; garantía, f; abrigo, m; refugio, m; (passport) salvoconducto, m; Polit. proteccionismo, m

protective /prə'tɛktɪv/ a protector; Polit. proteccionista

protector /prə'tɛktər/ n protector, m

protein /'proutin, -tiin/ n proteína, f

protest /v. prə'tɛst, 'proutɛst; n. 'proutɛst/ vt protestar; Law. hacer el protesto de una letra de cambio. —vi declarar; insistir (en); hacer una protesta. —n protesta, f; Law. protesto, m. **under p.**, bajo protesta. **to p. against**, protestar contra

Protestant /'prɒtəstənt/ a and n protestante, mf

Protestantism /'prɒtəstən,tizəm/ n protestantismo, m

protestation /,proutə'steiʃən/ n protestación, f

protester /'proutɛstər/ n el, m, (f, la) que protesta

protest literature n literatura de denuncia, f

protocol /'proutə,kɔl/ n protocolo, m, vt protocolizar

protoplasm /'proutə,plæzəm/ *n* proto-
plasma, *m*

prototype /'proutə,taip/ *n* prototipo, *m*

protract /prou'trækt/ *vt* prolongar; dilatar

protracted /prou'træktɪd/ *a* prolongado;
largo

protraction /prou'trækʃən/ *n* prolongación, *f*

protractor /prou'træktər/ *n* (*Geom.* and
Surv.) transportador, *m.* **p. muscle,**
músculo extensor, *m*

protrude /prou'trud/ *vt* sacar fuera. —*vi*
salir fuera; sobresalir

protuberance /prou'tubərəns/ *n* protuberancia, *f*

protuberant /prou'tubərənt/ *a* protube-
rante, prominente

proud /praud/ *a* orgulloso; arrogante; noble; glorioso; magnífico; soberbio. **to be
p.,** enorgullecerse. **to make p.,** enorgullecer; hacer orgulloso. **to be p. of,** ser orgulloso de, pagarse de, gloriarse en. **p.
flesh,** carnosidad, *f,* bezo, *m*

proudly /'praudli/ *adv* con orgullo, orgu-
llosamente

prove /pruv/ *vt* probar; demostrar; (experience) experimentar, sufrir; poner a
prueba; (a will) verificar; (show) mostrar;
confirmar. —*vi* resultar, salir (bien o
mal)

provenance /'prɒvənəns/ *n* origen, *m*

proverb /'prɒvərb/ *n* refrán, *m;* proverbio, *m.* **collection of proverbs,** refranero,
m. **Book of Proverbs,** Proverbios, *m pl*

proverbial /prə'vərbiəl/ *a* proverbial

provide /prə'vaid/ *vt* proporcionar, dar;
proveer, surtir, suplir; (stipulate) estipular; preparar (por); tomar precauciones
(contra); sufragar los gastos (de); proporcionar medios de vida (a); señalar una
pensión (a). **to p. oneself with,**
proveerse de

provided (that) /prə'vaidid/ *conjunc* si;
a condición de que, siempre que, con tal
que

providence /'prɒvidəns/ *n* providencia, *f*

provident /'prɒvidənt/ *a* próvido, previsor, prudente; económico

providential /,prɒvi'dɛnʃəl/ *a* providencial

providently /'prɒvidəntli/ *adv* próvida-
mente, prudentemente

provider /prə'vaidər/ *n* proveedor (-ra)

province /'prɒvins/ *n* provincia, *f;* esfera,
f; función, incumbencia, *f*

provincial /prə'vinʃəl/ *a* provincial, de
provincia; provinciano. —*n* provinciano
(-na); *Eccl.* provincial, *m*

provincialism /prə'vinʃə,lizəm/ *n*
provincialismo, *m*

provision /prə'viʒən/ *n* provisión, *f;*
(stipulation) estipulación, *f;* **pl.
provisions,** provisiones, *f pl;* víveres,
comestibles, *m pl.* —*vt* abastecer, aprovisionar. **to make p. for,** hacer provisión
para, proveer de. **to make p. for one's**

family, asegurar el porvenir de su familia.
p. merchant, vendedor (-ra) de
comestibles

provisional /prə'viʒənl/ *a* provisional,
interino

proviso /prə'vaizou/ *n* condición, estipulación, disposición, *f*

provocation /,prɒvə'keiʃən/ *n* provocación, *f*

provocative /prə'vɒkətiv/ *a* provocativo,
provocador

provoke /prə'vouk/ *vt* provocar; suscitar;
incitar, excitar; (irritate) sacar de madre
(a), indignar

provoker /prə'voukər/ *n* provocador
(-ra); instigador (-ra)

provoking /prə'voukiŋ/ *a* provocativo;
(irritating) enojoso, irritante

provost /'prouvoust/ *or, esp. in military
usage,* 'prouvou/ *n* preboste, *m;* (of a college) director, *m;* (in Scotland) alcalde,
m. **p.-marshal,** capitán preboste, *m*

prow /prau/ *n* proa, *f*

prowess /'prauis/ *n* valor, *m,* destreza, *f;*
proeza, *f*

prowl /praul/ *vi* and *vt* rondar; cazar al
acecho

prowler /'praulər/ *n* rondador (-ra); ladrón (-ona)

proximity /prɒk'simiti/ *n* proximidad, *f*

proximo /'prɒksə,mou/ *adv* en (o del)
mes próximo

proxy /'prɒksi/ *n* poder, *m;* delegación, *f;*
apoderado, *m;* delegado (-da); substituto
(-ta). **to be married by p.,** casarse por
poderes

prude /prud/ *n* mojigata, beata, *f*

prudence /'prudns/ *n* prudencia, *f*

prudent /'prudnt/ *a* prudente

prudently /'prudntli/ *adv* con prudencia

prudery /'prudəri/ *n* mojigatería, beatería,
damería, gazmoñería, *f*

prudish /'prudiʃ/ *a* mojigato, gazmoño,
remilgado

prune /prun/ *n* ciruela pasa, *f;* color de
ciruela, *m, vt* podar; (cut) cortar; reducir

pruning /'pruniŋ/ *n* poda, *f;* reducción, *f.*
p. knife, podadera, *f*

prurient /'pruriənt/ *a* lascivo, lujurioso,
salaz

pry /prai/ *vi* escudriñar; acechar, espiar,
fisgonear; (meddle) entremeterse, meterse
donde no le llaman. —*vt* See **prize**

prying /'praiŋ/ *n* fisgoneo, *m;* curiosidad, *f,* a fisgón, curioso

psalm /sɑm/ *n* salmo, *m.* **to sing
psalms,** salmodiar

psalmist /'sɑmist/ *n* salmista, *m*

pseudo- *a* seudo. **p.-learned,** erudito a
la violeta

pseudonym /'sudnim/ *n* seudónimo, *m*

psychiatrist /si'kaiətrist, sai-/ *n*
siquiatra, *m*

psychiatry /si'kaiətri, sai-/ *n* siquiatría, *f*

psychic /'saikik/ *a* síquico

psychoanalysis /,saikou'næləsis/ *n* sicoanálisis, *mf*

psychoanalyst /ˌsaikou'ænlɪst/ n sicoanalista, mf

psychoanalyze /ˌsaikou'ænlˌaiz/ vt sicoanalizar

psychological /ˌsaikə'lɒdʒɪkəl/ a sicológico

psychologist /sai'kɒlədʒɪst/ n sicólogo (-ga)

psychology /sai'kɒlədʒi/ n sicología, f

psychopathic /ˌsaikə'pæθɪk/ a sicopático

psychosis /sai'kousɪs/ n sicosis, f

psychotherapy /ˌsaikou'θerəpi/ n sicoterapia, f

ptomaine poisoning /'toumein/ n intoxicación por tomaínas, f

puberty /'pyubərti/ n pubertad, f

pubescent /pyu'besənt/ a púber

pubic /'pyubɪk/ a púbico

public /'pʌblɪk/ a and n público m. **in p.,** en público. **p. assistance,** asistencia pública, f. **p. funds,** hacienda pública, f. **p. health,** higiene pública, f. **p.-house,** taberna, f. **p. opinion,** opinión pública, f. Inf. el qué dirán. **p.-spirited,** patriótico. **p. thoroughfare,** vía pública, f. **p. works,** obras públicas, f pl

publication /ˌpʌblɪ'keiʃən/ n publicación, f

publicist /'pʌbləsɪst/ n publicista, mf

publicity /pʌ'blɪsɪti/ n publicidad, f

publicity agent n publicista, mf

publish /'pʌblɪʃ/ vt publicar, divulgar, difundir; (a book, etc.) dar a luz, dar a la prensa, publicar; (of a publisher) editar. **to p. abroad,** pregonar a los cuatro vientos. **to p. banns of marriage,** correr las amonestaciones

publisher /'pʌblɪʃər/ n publicador (-ra); (of books) editor (-ra)

publishing /'pʌblɪʃɪŋ/ n publicación, f. **p. house,** casa editorial, f. **the p. world,** el mundo de la edición, m

puck /pʌk/ n trasgo, m; diablillo, picaruelo, m

pucker /'pʌkər/ vt (one's brow, etc.) fruncir; (crease) arrugar. —vi arrugarse. —n frunce, m; arruga, f; (fold) bolsa, f

puckish /'pʌkɪʃ/ a travieso

pudding /'pudɪŋ/ n pudín, budín, m. **black p.,** morcilla, f

puddle /'pʌdl/ n charco, m

puerile /'pyuərɪl/ a pueril

puerperal /pyu'ɜrpərəl/ a puerperal. **p. fever,** fiebre puerperal, f

Puerto Rican /'pwertə 'rikən, 'pɔr-/ a and n puertorriqueño (-ña)

puff /pʌf/ vt and vi (blow) soplar; (at a pipe, etc.) chupar; (smoke) lanzar bocanadas de humo; (make pant) hacer jadear; (advertise) dar bombo (a); (distend) hinchar; (make conceited) envanecerse; (of a train, etc.) bufar; resoplar. —n soplo, m; (of smoke, etc.) bocanada, f; (of an engine, etc.) resoplido, bufido, m; (for powder) borla (para polvos), f; (pastry) bollo, m; (advertisement) bombo, m. **to be puffed up,** Fig. hincharse, inflarse.

p. of wind, ráfaga de aire, f. **p.-ball,** bejín, m. **p.-pastry,** hojaldre, m, or f. **p.-sleeve,** manga de bullón, f

puffy /'pʌfi/ a (of the wind) a ráfagas; (panting) jadeante; (swollen) hinchado

pug /pʌg/ n (dog) doguino, m. **p.-nosed,** de nariz respingona

pugilist /'pyudʒəlɪst/ n pugilista, mf; boxeador, m

pugnacious /pʌg'neiʃəs/ a pugnaz, belicoso

pugnacity /pʌg'næsɪti/ n pugnacidad, belicosidad, f

pull /pul/ n tirón, m; sacudida, f; golpe, m; (row) paseo en barco, m; (with the oars) golpe (de remos), m; (at a bell) tirón, m; (bell-rope) tirador, m; (at a bottle) trago, m; (strain) fuerza, f; atracción, f; (struggle) lucha, f; (advantage) ventaja, f; (influence) influencia, f. **to give a p.,** tirar (de), dar un tirón (a). **to have plenty of p.,** Inf. tener buenas aldabas

pull /pul/ vt tirar (de); (drag) arrastrar; (extract) sacar; (a boat) remar; (gather) coger; Print. imprimir. He pulled the trigger (of his gun), Apretó el gatillo. He was sitting by the fire pulling at his pipe, Estaba sentado cerca del fuego fumando su pipa. **to p. a hat well down on the head,** calarse el sombrero. **to p. a person's leg,** tomar el pelo (a). **to p. oneself together,** componer el semblante, serenarse; recobrar el aplomo; (tidy oneself) arreglarse. **to p. apart,** vt separar; romper en dos. —vi separarse; romperse en dos. **to p. away,** vt arrancar; quitar. —vi tirar con esfuerzo. **to p. back,** tirar hacia atrás; hacer retroceder (a); retener. **to p. down,** hacer bajar, obligar a bajar; (objects) bajar; (buildings) derribar, demoler; (humble) humillar; degradar; (weaken) debilitar. **to p. in,** tirar hacia dentro; hacer entrar; (a horse) enfrenar; (expenditure) reducir. **to p. off,** arrancar; (clothes) quitarse; (a deal) cerrar (un trato), concluir con éxito; (win) ganar. **to p. on,** vt (gloves, etc.) meterse, ponerse. —vi seguir remando. **to p. open,** abrir; abrir rápidamente. **to p. out,** hacer salir; obligar a salir; (teeth, daggers, etc.) sacar; (hair) arrancar. **to p. round, through,** vt ayudar a reponerse (a); sacar de un aprieto. —vi restablecerse; reponerse, cobrar la salud, sanar. **to p. together,** obrar de acuerdo, (get on) llevarse (bien or mal). He pulled himself together very quickly, Se repuso muy pronto. **to p. up,** vt montar, subir; (a horse) sofrenar; (stop) parar; (by the root) desarraigar, extirpar; (interrupt) interrumpir; (scold) reñir. —vi pararse; (restrain oneself) reprimirse, contenerse

pullet /'pulɪt/ n polla, f

pulley /'puli/ n polea, f; Naut. garrucha, f. **p. wheel,** roldana, f

pulling /'pulɪŋ/ n tracción, f; tirada, f; arranque, m

pullover /'pulˌouvər/ n jersey, m

pulmonary /'pʌlmə,neri/ a pulmonar

pulp /pʌlp/ n pulpa, f; (of fruit) carne, f; (paper) pasta, f; (of teeth) bulbo dentario, m. —vt reducir a pulpa; deshacer (el papel). **to beat to a p.,** Inf. poner como un pulpo

pulpit /'pulpɪt, 'pʌl-/ n púlpito, m

pulsate /'pʌlseɪt/ vi pulsar, latir

pulsation /pʌl'seɪʃən/ n pulsación, f, latido, m

pulse /pʌls/ n pulso, m; pulsación, f, latido, m; vibración, f; (vegetable) legumbre, f, vi pulsar, latir; vibrar. **to take a person's p.,** tomar el pulso a

pulverize /'pʌlvə,raɪz/ vt pulverizar

pumice /'pʌmɪs/ n piedra pómez, f

pummel /'pʌməl/ vt aporrear

pump /pʌmp/ n Mech. bomba, f; (for water, etc.) aguatocha, f; Naut. pompa, f; (slipper) escarpín, m, vt bombear, extraer por medio de una bomba; (inflate) inflar; (for information) sondear, sonsacar. **hand-p.,** bomba de mano, f. **to work a p.,** darle a la bomba

pumpkin /'pʌmpkɪn/ n calabaza, f, (Chile) zapallo m; (plant) calabacera, f

pun /pʌn/ n retruécano, m

punch /pʌntʃ/ n (drink) ponche, m; (blow) puñetazo, golpe, m; Mech. punzón, m; (for tickets, etc.) taladro, m; Inf. fuerza, f. —vt (perforate) taladrar, punzar; estampar; (hit) dar un puñetazo (a). **p.-ball,** pelota de boxeo, f. **p.-bowl,** ponchera, f

punctilious /pʌŋk'tɪliəs/ a formal, puntual, puntilloso

punctual /'pʌŋktʃuəl/ a puntual

punctuate /'pʌŋktʃu,eɪt/ vt puntuar

punctuation /,pʌŋktʃu'eɪʃən/ n puntuación, f

puncture /'pʌŋktʃər/ n pinchazo, m; perforación, f; Surg. punción, f. —vt pinchar; perforar; punzar. **We have a p. in the right tire,** Tenemos un pinchazo en el neumático derecho

pungency /'pʌndʒənsi/ n picante, m; acerbidad, mordacidad, f

pungent /'pʌndʒənt/ a picante; acerbo, mordaz

punish /'pʌnɪʃ/ vt castigar; maltratar

punishable /'pʌnɪʃəbəl/ a punible

punishment /'pʌnɪʃmənt/ n castigo, m; pena, f; maltrato, m

punitive /'pyunɪtɪv/ a punitivo

puny /'pyuni/ a débil, encanijado; insignificante; pequeño

pup /pʌp/ n cachorro (-rra). —vi parir la perra

pupil /'pyupəl/ n alumno (-na), discípulo (-la); (of the eye) pupila, niña (del ojo), f; Law. pupilo (-la). —a escolar. **day p.,** alumno (-na) externo (-na). **p. teacher,** maestro (-tra) alumno (-na)

puppet /'pʌpɪt/ n títere, m, marioneta, f; muñeca, f; (person) maniquí, m, pl. **show,** función de títeres, f. **p. showman,** titiritero, titerero, m

puppy /'pʌpi/ n perrito (-ta), cachorro (-rra)

purblind /'pər,blaind/ a ciego; (short-sighted and Fig.) miope

purchasable /'pərtʃəsəbəl/ a comprable, que puede comprarse; Fig. sobornable

purchase /'pərtʃəs/ vt comprar; adquirir; Fig. lograr, conseguir. —n compra, f; adquisición, f; Mech. apalancamiento, m; fuerza, f; (lever) palanca, f, aparejo, m; Fig. influencia, f. **p. tax,** impuesto de lujo, m

purchaser /'pərtʃəsər/ n comprador (-ra)

purchasing /'pərtʃəsɪŋ/ n See **purchase. p. power,** poder de adquisición, m

pure /pyur/ a puro. **p.-bred,** de raza

purgative /'pərgətɪv/ a purgativo. —n purga, f

purgatory /'pərgə,tɔri/ n purgatorio, m

purge /pərdʒ/ n purgación, f; (laxative) purga, f; Polit. depuración, f; purificación, f. —vt purgar; Polit. depurar; purificar; expurgar

purging /'pərdʒɪŋ/ n purgación, f; Polit. depuración, f; Fig. purificación, f

purifier /'pyorə,faɪər/ n purificador (-ra)

purify /'pyorə,faɪ/ vt purificar; (metals) acrisolar; refinar; depurar; (purge) purgar

purist /'pyorɪst/ n purista, mf

puritan /'pyorɪtn/ a and n puritano (-na)

purity /'pyorɪti/ n pureza, f

purl /pərl/ vi (of a stream, etc.) murmurar, susurrar. —n (of a stream, etc.) susurro, murmullo, m

purlieu /'pərlu/ n límite, m; pl **purlieus,** alrededores, m pl, inmediaciones, f pl; (slums) barrios bajos, m pl

purling /'pərlɪŋ/ a murmurante, que susurra, parlero. —n murmullo, susurro, m

purloin /pər'lɔɪn/ vt hurtar, robar

purple /'pərpəl/ n púrpura, f, a purpúreo. —vt purpurar, teñir de púrpura. —vi purpurear

purport /v. pər'pɔrt; n. 'pərpɔrt/ vt dar a entender, querer decir; significar; indicar; parecer; tener el objeto de; pretender. —n importe, m; sentido, significado, m; objeto, m

purpose /'pərpəs/ n objeto, m; propósito, fin, m; intención, f; proyecto, m; designio, m; determinación, voluntad, f; efecto, m; ventaja, utilidad, f, vi and vt proponerse; pensar, tener el propósito (de), intentar. **It will serve my p.,** Servirá para lo que yo quiero. **for the p. of...,** con el propósito de..., con el fin de... for purposes of... para efectos de... **on p.,** de propósito, expresamente. **to no p.,** inútilmente; en vano

purposeful /'pərpəsfəl/ a resuelto; de substancia

purposeless /'pərpəslɪs/ a irresoluto, vacilante, vago; sin objeto; inútil

purposely /'pərpəsli/ adv expresamente, de intento

purr /pər/ vi ronronear. —n ronroneo, m

purse /pərs/ n bolsa, f; monedero, portamonedas, *m*. **to p. one's lips,** apretar los labios

purser /'pɜrsər/ *n Naut.* contador, sobrecargo, *m*. **purser's office,** contaduría, *f*

pursuance /pər'suəns/ *n* cumplimiento, desempeño, *m*, prosecución, *f*. **in p. of,** en cumplimiento de; en consecuencia de

pursuant /pər'suənt/ *a* and *adv* según; conforme (a), de acuerdo (con); en consecuencia (de)

pursue /pər'su/ *vt* perseguir; seguir; (search) buscar; (hunt) cazar; (a submarine, etc.) dar caza (a); (continue) proseguir, continuar; (an occupation) dedicarse (a), ejercer

pursuer /pər'suər/ *n* perseguidor (-ra)

pursuit /pər'sut/ *n* perseguimiento, *m*; (search) busca, *f*; (hunt) caza, *f*; (performance) prosecución, *f*, desempeño, *m*; (employment) ocupación, *f*. **in p. of,** en busca de, **p. plane,** avión de caza, *m*

purulent /'pyurələnt/ *a* purulento

purvey /pər'vei/ *vt* proveer, surtir, suministrar; abastecer; procurar

purveyance /pər'veiəns/ *n* suministro, abastecimiento, *m*; provisión, *f*

purveyor /pər'veiər/ *n* suministrador (-ra), proveedor (-ra), bastecedor (-ra)

pus /pʌs/ *n* pus, *m*

push /puʃ/ *n* empujón, *m*; empellón, *m*; impulso, *m*; (of a person) empuje, *m*, energía, *f*; (attack) ataque, *m*, ofensiva, *f*; (effort) esfuerzo, *m*; crisis, *f*, momento crítico, *m*. **at a push,** *Inf.* en caso de necesidad; en un aprieto, si llegara el caso. **to give the p. to,** *Inf.* despedir (a). **p.-bicycle,** bicicleta, *f*. **p.-button,** botón, *m*; botón de llamada, *m*. **p.-cart,** carretilla de mano, *f*; (child's) cochecito de niño, *m*

push /puʃ/ *vt* empujar; (jostle) empellar, dar empellones (a); (a finger in one's eye, etc.) clavar; (a button) apretar; (*Fig.* a person) proteger, ayudar; dar publicidad (a); (a claim, etc.) insistir en; (compel) obligar. —*vi* empujar; dar empujones, empellar. **I am pushed for time,** Me falta tiempo. **He is pushed for money,** Está apurado por dinero. **I have pushed my finger in my eye,** Me he clavado el dedo en el ojo. **to p. against,** empujar contra; lanzarse contra; empellar, dar empellones (a). **to p. aside, away,** apartar con la mano; rechazar, alejar. **to p. back,** (hair, etc.) echar hacia atrás; (people) hacer retroceder; rechazar. **to p. by,** pasar. **to p. down,** hacer bajar; hacer caer; (demolish) derribar. **to p. forward,** *vt* empujar hacia delante, hacer avanzar; (a plan, etc.) llevar adelante. —*vi* adelantarse a empujones; avanzar; seguir el camino. **to p. oneself forward,** *Fig.* abrirse camino; entremeterse; darse importancia. **to p. in,** *vt* empujar; hacer entrar; clavar, hincar. —*vi* entrar a la fuerza; entremeterse. **to p. off,** *vt* quitar con la mano (a); *Inf.* quitar de encima (a). —*vi Naut.* desatracar; *Inf.* ponerse en camino. **to p. open,**

empujar, abrir. **to p. out,** *vt* empujar hacia fuera; hacer salir; echar. —*vi Naut.* zarpar. **to p. through,** *vt* (business, etc.) despachar rápidamente; (a crowd) abrirse camino por. —*vi* aparecer, mostrarse. **to p. to,** cerrar. **to p. up,** empujar; hacer subir; (windows, etc.) levantar. **be pushing up the daises,** mirar los árboles de raíz

pushing /'puʃiŋ/ *a* enérgico, emprendedor; ambicioso; agresivo. **by p. and shoving,** a empellones, a empujones

pusillanimous /,pyusə'læniməs/ *a* pusilánime

pustule /'pʌstʃul/ *n* pústula, *f*

put /put/ *vt* poner; colocar; (pour out) echar; aplicar; emplear; (estimate) calcular; presentar; (ask) preguntar; (say) decir; (express) expresar; (a question) hacer; (a problem) plantear; (the weight) lanzar; (rank) estimar. **As the Spanish put it,** Cómo dicen los españoles. **If I may put it so,** Si puedo expresarlo así, Por así decirlo. **hard put to it,** en dificultades, apurado. **How will you put it to her?** ¿Cómo se lo vas a explicar a ella? **to put ashore,** echar en tierra (a). **to put a child to bed,** acostar a un niño. **to put in order,** arreglar; ordenar. **to put out of joint,** dislocar. **to put out of order,** estropear. **to put to death,** matar; (judicially) ajusticiar. **to put about,** *vt* (a rumor) diseminar, divulgar; (worry) preocupar. —*vi Naut.* virar, cambiar de rumbo. **to put aside,** poner a un lado; descartar; (omit) omitir, pasar por alto de; (fears, etc.) desechar. **to put away,** quitar; guardar; poner en salvo; arrinconar; (thoughts) desechar, ahuyentar; (save) ahorrar; (banish) despedir, alejar; (a wife) repudiar, divorciar; (food) tragar. **to put back,** *vt* echar hacia atrás; hacer retroceder; (replace) devolver, restituir; (the clock) retrasar; (retard) retardar, atrasar. —*vi Naut.* volver a puerto. **to put down,** depositar; poner en el suelo; (the blinds) bajar; (an umbrella) cerrar; (a rebellion) sofocar; (gambling, etc.) suprimir; (humble) abatir, humillar; degradar; (silence) hacer callar; (reduce) reducir, disminuir; (write) apuntar, anotar; (a name) inscribir; (to an account) poner a la cuenta de; (estimate) juzgar, creer; (impute) atribuir. **The book is so interesting that it's hard to put down,** El libro es tan interesante que es difícil dejarlo. **to put forth,** (leaves, flowers, sun's rays) echar; (a book) publicar, dar a luz; (a hand) alargar; (an arm) extender; (show) manifestar, mostrar; (strength, etc.) desplegar; (use) emplear. **to put forward,** avanzar; (a clock) adelantar; (a suggestion, etc.) hacer; (propose) proponer; (a case) presentar. **to put oneself forward,** ponerse en evidencia. **to put in,** poner dentro; (a hand, etc.) introducir; (liquids) echar en; (a government) poner en el poder; (an employment) nombrar, colocar; (insert) insertar; (a claim) presentar; (say) decir. **I shall put in two hours' work before bedtime,** Trabajaré por dos horas antes de acostarme. **He put in a good word for you,** Habló en tu favor. **to put in writing,** poner por escrito. **to put in for,** (an employment) solicitar (un empleo); (as a candidate) presentarse como candidato para. **to put into,** meter dentro (de); (words) expresar; (port) arribar, hacer escala en (un puerto). **to put off,** desechar; (garments) quitarse, despojarse (de); (postpone) diferir, aplazar; (evade) evadir, entretener; quitarse de encima (a), desembarazarse (de); (confuse) desconcertar; (discourage) desanimar; quitar el apetito (a). **to put on,** poner sobre; (clothes) ponerse; (pretend) fingir, afectar; poner; (a play) poner en escena; (the hands of a clock) adelantar; (weight) engordar, poner carnes; (add) añadir; (*Sports.* score) hacer; (bet) apostar; (the light) encender; (assume) tomar; (the brake) frenar; (abuse) abusar (de). engañar. **He put the kettle on the fire,** Puso la tetera en el fuego. **to put on airs and graces,** darse humos. **to put on probation,** dar el azul a, poner a prueba a. **to put on more trains,** poner más trenes. **put one's foot down,** ponerle a fulano el alto. **to put out,** *vt* (eject) echar, expulsar; hacer salir; poner en la calle; (a tenant) desahuciar; (one's hand) alargar; (one's arm) extender; (one's tongue) sacar; (eyes) saltar; (fire, light) apagar, extinguir; (leaves, etc.) echar; (horns) sacar; (head) asomar, sacar; (use) emplear; (give) entregar, dar; (at interest) dar a interés; (finish) terminar; (dislocate) dislocar; (worry) desconcertar, turbar; poner los nervios en punta (a); (anger) enojar; (inconvenience) incomodar; (a book) publicar; (a boat) echar al mar. —*vi* (of a ship) hacerse a la vela, zarpar. **to put out to grass,** mandar a pacer. **We put out to sea,** Nos hicimos a la mar. **to put the cart before the horse,** poner la carreta por delante de los bueyes. **to put through,** (perform) desempeñar; concluir, terminar; (thrust) meter; (subject to) someter a; (exercise) ejercitar; (on the tele-

phone) poner en comunicación (con). **to put together,** juntar; (a machine, etc.) montar, armar. **to put two and two together,** atar cabos. **to put up,** *vt* (sails, a flag) izar; (raise a window) levantar, cerrar; (open a window, or an umbrella) abrir; (one's hands, etc.) poner en alto; (one's fists) alzar; (a prayer) ofrecer; hacer; (as a candidate) nombrar; (for sale) poner (a la venta); (the price) aumentar; (a prescription) preparar; (food) conservar; (pack) empaquetar; (a sword) envainar; (lodge) alojar; (a petition) presentar; (build) construir; *Mech.* montar; (*Inf.* plan) arreglar. —*vi* alojarse. **to put upon,** abusar (de); oprimir; (accuse) imputar, acusar (de). **to put up to,** incitar (a), instigar (a); dar informaciones sobre; poner al corriente (de). **to put up with,** tolerar, soportar, aguantar; resignarse a; contentarse con, conformarse con

putative /'pyutətɪv/ *a* supuesto; (of relationship) putativo

putrefy /'pyutrə,fai/ *vt* pudrir. —*vt* pudrirse, descomponerse

putrid /'pyutrɪd/ *a* pútrido; *Inf.* apestoso

putting /'putɪŋ/ *n* acción de poner, *f*; colocación, *f*. **p. forward of the clock,** adelanto de la hora, *m*. **p. off,** tardanza, dilación, *f*. **p. the weight,** lanzamiento del peso, *m*. **p. up,** (for office) candidatura, *f*. /'pʌtɪŋ/ **p. green,** pista de golf en miniatura, *f*

putty /'pʌti/ *n* masilla, *f*, *vt* enmasillar, rellenar con masilla

puzzle /'pʌzəl/ *vt* dejar perplejo; desconcertar; confundir; embrollar. —*n* problema, *m*; dificultad, *f*; enigma, *m*; (perplexity) perplejidad, *f*; (game) rompecabezas, *m*. **to p. out,** procurar resolver; encontrar la solución de. **to p. over,** pensar en, meditar sobre. **I am puzzled by...,** Me trae (or tiene) perplejo...

pygmy /'pɪgmi/ *a* and *n* pigmeo (-ea)

pyjamas /pə'dʒɑməz, -'dʒæməz/ *n* pijama, *m*

pyramid /'pɪrəmɪd/ *n* pirámide, *f*

pyre /paiʳr/ *n* pira, *f*

Pyrenees, the /'pɪərə,niz/ los Pirineos, *m pl*

python /'paiθɒn/ *n* pitón, *m*

q /kyu/ *n* (letter) cu, *f*

Q

quackery /'kwækəri/ *n* charlatanería, *f*, charlatanismo, *m*

quadrangle /'kwɒd,ræŋgəl/ *n* cuadrángulo, *m*; (courtyard) patio, *m*

quadrant /'kwɒdrənt/ *n* (*Geom. Astron.* etc.) cuadrante, *m*

quadratic /kwɒ'drætɪk/ *a* cuadrático. **q. equation,** cuadrática, ecuación de segundo grado, *f*

quadrilateral /,kwɒdrə'lætərəl/ *a* and *n* cuadrilátero *m*

quadruped /'kwɒdru,pɛd/ *a* and *n* cuadrúpedo *m*

quadruple /kwɒ'drupəl/ *a* cuádruple. —*vt* cuadruplicar. —*n* cuádruplo, *m*

quadruplet /kwɒ'drʌplɪt/ *n* serie de cuatro cosas, *f*; bicicleta de cuatro asientos, *f*; uno (una) de cuatro niños (-as) gemelos (-as)

quaff /kwɒf/ *vt* beber a grandes tragos, vaciar de un trago

quagmire /'kwæg,maɪər/ *n* tremedal, pantano, *m*; *Fig.* cenagal, *m*

quail /kweil/ *n* codorniz, *f*, (U.S.A.) parpayuela, *f*. —*vi* cejar, retroceder; temblar, acobardarse

quaint /kweint/ *a* pintoresco; curioso, raro; (eccentric) excéntrico, extravagante

quaintly /'kweintli/ *adv* de un modo pintoresco; curiosamente; con extravagancia

quake /kweik/ *vi* estremecerse, vibrar; temblar. —*n* estremecimiento, *m*; (of the earth) terremoto, *m*. **to q. with fear,** temblar de miedo

Quaker /'kweikər/ *n* cuáquero (-ra)

quaking /'kweikɪŋ/ *a* temblón; tembloroso. —*n* temblor, *m*; estremecimiento, *m*. **q. ash,** álamo temblón, *m*

qualification /,kwɒləfɪ'keiʃən/ *n* calificación, *f*; requisito, *m*; capacidad, aptitud, *f*; (reservation) reservación, salvedad, *f*

qualified /'kwɒlə,faid/ *a* apto, competente; (of professions) con título universitario; habilitado; limitado

qualify /'kwɒlə,fai/ *vt* habilitar; calificar; modificar; suavizar; *vi* habilitarse; prepararse; llenar los requisitos

qualitative /'kwɒlɪ,teitiv/ *a* cualitativo

quality /'kwɒlɪti/ *n* cualidad, *f*; calidad, *f*; propiedad, *f*. **This cloth is of good q.,** Esta tela es de buena calidad. **the q.,** la alta sociedad, la aristocracia

qualm /kwɑm/ *n* náusea, *f*; mareo, desmayo, *m*; (of conscience) escrúpulo, remordimiento, *m*

quandary /'kwɒndəri/ *n* incertidumbre, perplejidad, *f*; dilema, apuro, *m*. **to be in a q.,** estar perplejo

quantitative /'kwɒntɪ,teitiv/ *a* cuantitativo

quantity /'kwɒntɪti/ *n* cantidad, *f*; gran cantidad, *f*. **unknown q.,** incógnita, *f*

quarantine /'kwɒrən,tin/ *n* cuarentena, *f*, *vt* someter a cuarentena

quarrel /'kwɒrəl/ *vi* pelear, disputar; (scold) reñir; (find fault) criticar. —*n*

pelea, disputa, *f*; (glazier's) diamante de vidriero, *m*. **to pick a q. with,** armar pleito con, reñir con. **to q. with,** reñir con, romper con; quejarse de

quarrelling /'kwɒrəlɪŋ/ *n* disputas, altercaciones, *f pl*

quarrelsome /'kwɒrəlsəm/ *a* pendenciero, peleador, belicoso

quarry /'kwɒri/ *n* cantera, *f*; *Fig.* mina, *f*; (prey) presa, *f*; víctima, *f*. —*vt* explotar una cantera; examinar

quart /kwɔrt/ *n* cuarto de galón, *m*

quarter /'kwɔrtər/ *n* (fourth part) cuarta parte, *f*, cuarto, *m*; (of a year) trimestre, *m*; (of an hour, the moon, a ton, an animal, etc.) cuarta, *f*; *Naut.* cuartelada, *f*; (of a town) barrio, *m*, (mercy) cuartel, *m*; *Herald.* cuartel, *m*; dirección, *f*; origen, fuente, *f*; *pl* **quarters,** vivienda, *f*; alojamiento, *m*; (barracks) cuartel, *m*. —*vt* cuartear; (a body) descuartizar, hacer cuartos (a); (troops) alojar; (in barracks) acuartelar; *Herald.* cuartelar. **a q. of an hour,** un cuarto de hora. **at close quarters,** de cerca. **hind quarters,** cuartos traseros, *m pl*. **It is a q. to four,** Son las cuatro menos cuarto. **It is a q. past four,** Son las cuatro y cuarto. **q.-day,** primer día de un trimestre, *m*. **q.-deck,** alcázar, *m*; cuerpo de oficiales de un buque, *m*. **q.-mile,** cuarto de milla, *m*. **q.-plate,** cuarto de placa, *m*. **q.-sessions,** sesión trimestral de los juzgados municipales, *f*. **q.-staff,** barra, *f*. **q.-tone,** cuarto de tono, *m*

quartering /'kwɔrtərɪŋ/ *n* (punishment) descuartizamiento, *m*; *Herald.* cantón, *m*

quarterly /'kwɔrtərli/ *a* trimestral, trimestre. —*n* publicación trimestral, *f*, *adv* trimestralmente

quartet /kwɔr'tɛt/ *n* cuarteto, *m*

quarto /'kwɔrtou/ *n* papel en cuarto, *m*; libro en cuarto, *m*. **in q.,** en cuarto

quartz /kwɔrts/ *n* cuarzo, *m*

quash /kwɒʃ/ *vt Law.* anular, derogar; *Inf.* sofocar, reprimir

quasi /'kweizai, 'kwɑsi/ *a* and *adv* cuasi

quaver /'kweivər/ *vi* vibrar; temblar; (trill) trinar, hacer quiebros. —*vt* decir con voz temblorosa. —*n* vibración, *f*; trémolo, *m*; (trill) trino, *m*; (musical note) corchea, *f*

quaveringly /'kweivərɪŋli/ *adv* con voz temblorosa

quavery /'kweivəri/ *a* trémulo, tembloroso

quay /ki, kei/ *n* muelle, *m*

queasiness /'kwizinɪs/ *n* náusea, *f*; escrupulosidad, *f*

queasy /'kwizi/ *a* propenso a la náusea; nauseabundo; delicado, escrupuloso

queen /kwin/ *n* reina, *f*; (in a Spanish pack of cards) caballo, *m*; (in a French or English pack and in chess) reina, *f*. **to q.**

it, conducirse como una reina; mandar.
q. bee, maestra, abeja reina, *f.* **q. cell,**
maestril, *m.* **q. mother,** reina madre, *f.*
q. regent, reina regente, *f.*

queenly /'kwinli/ *a* de reina; regio

queer /kwɪər/ *a* raro; extraño, singular;
ridículo; (shady) sospechoso; (ill)
malucho, algo enfermo; (mad) chiflado

queerly /'kwɪərli/ *adv* extrañamente;
ridículamente

queerness /'kwɪərnɪs/ *n* rareza, extrañeza, singularidad, *f;* ridiculez, *f*

quell /kwɛl/ *vt* subyugar; reprimir; apaciguar, calmar

quench /kwɛntʃ/ *vt* apagar; calmar; satisfacer. **to q. one's thirst,** apagar la sed

quenching /'kwɛntʃɪŋ/ *n* apagamiento,
m; satisfacción, *f*

querulous /'kwɛrələs/ *a* quejumbroso

query /'kwɪəri/ *n* pregunta, *f;* duda, *f;*
punto de interrogación, *m.* —*vt* preguntar;
dudar (de); poner en duda. —*vi* hacer
una pregunta; expresar una duda

quest /kwɛst/ *n* busca, *f;* (adventure) demanda, *f.* **in q. of,** en busca de

question /'kwɛstʃən/ *n* pregunta, *f;* problema, *m;* asunto, *m;* cuestión, *f;* (discussion) debate, *m,* discusión, *f.* —*vt* and *vi*
interrogar; examinar; poner en duda, dudar de; preguntarse; hacer preguntas. **be-**
yond q., fuera de duda. **to ask a q.,**
hacer una pregunta. **without q.,** sin
duda. **It is out of the q.,** Es completamente imposible. **It is a q. of whether...,**
Se trata de si... **q.-mark,** punto interrogante, *m*

questionable /'kwɛstʃənəbəl/ *a* cuestionable, discutible, dudoso; equívoco,
sospechoso

questioner /'kwɛstʃənər/ *n* preguntador
(-ra); interrogador (-ra)

questioning /kwɛstʃənɪŋ/ *n* preguntas, *f*
pl; interrogatorio, *m*

questioningly /kwɛstʃənɪŋli/ *adv* inter-
rogativamente

questionnaire /ˌkwɛstʃəˈnɛər/ *n* cuestionario, *m*

quetzal /ˈkɛtsɑl/ *n* (money and *Ornith.*)
quetzal, *m*

queue /kyu/ *n* coleta, *f;* cola, *f, vi* formar
cola; hacer cola

quibble /'kwɪbəl/ *n* equívoco, subterfugio, *m;* sutileza, *f;* (pun) retruécano, *m.*
—*vi* hacer uso de subterfugios; sutilizar

quibbler /'kwɪblər/ *n* sofista, *mf*

quibbling /'kwɪblɪŋ/ *n* sofistería, *f,* sofis-
mas, *m pl,* sutilezas, *f pl*

quick /kwɪk/ *a* vivo; agudo; penetrante;
sagaz; rápido, veloz; (ready) pronto; ágil,
activo; (light) ligero. —*adv* rápidamente;
(soon) pronto. —*n* carne viva, *f; Fig.* lo
vivo; **Be q.!** ¡Date prisa! **He was very q.,**
Lo hizo muy aprisa; Volvió (or Fue, according to sense) rápidamente. **the q.**
and the dead, los vivos y los muertos.
to cut to the q., herir en lo más vivo. **q.**
march, paso doble, *m.* **q.-sighted,** de
vista aguda, perspicaz. **q. step,** paso rá-

pido, *m.* **q.-tempered,** de genio vivo,
colérico. **q. time,** compás rápido, *m; Mil.*
paso doble, *m.* **q.-witted,** de ingenio
agudo

quicken /'kwɪkən/ *vt* vivificar; animar;
acelerar; excitar, avivar. —*vi* vivificarse;
despertarse; renovarse; acelerarse; (stir)
moverse. **to q. one's step,** acelerar el
paso

quicklime /'kwɪkˌlaim/ *n* cal viva, *f*

quickly /'kwɪkli/ *adv* rápidamente; (soon)
pronto; (immediately) en seguida;
(promptly) con presteza; vivamente

quickness /'kwɪknɪs/ *n* viveza, *f;* (of wit,
etc.) agudeza, *f;* rapidez, velocidad, *f;*
(promptness) prontitud, *f;* agilidad, *f;*
(lightness) ligereza, *f;* (understanding) penetración, sagacidad, *f*

quicksand /'kwɪkˌsænd/ *n* arena movediza, *f; Fig.* cenagal, *m*

quicksilver /'kwɪkˌsɪlvər/ *n* azogue, mercurio, *m, vt* azogar

quiescence /kwiˈɛsəns/ *n* reposo, *m;*
quietud, tranquilidad, *f;* inactividad, *f;*
pasividad, *f*

quiescent /kwiˈɛsənt/ *a* quieto; inactivo;
pasivo

quiet /'kwaiɪt/ *a* tranquilo; quieto; silencioso; quedo; monótono; inactivo; (informal) sin ceremonia; (simple) sencillo; (of
the mind) sereno; (of colours, etc.) suave.
—*n* tranquilidad, quietud, *f;* silencio, *m;*
paz, *f;* (of mind) serenidad, *f.* —*vt*
tranquilizar, sosegar; calmar. **to be q.,**
callarse; no hacer ruido. **Be q.!** ¡Estate
quieto! ¡A callar!

quietly /'kwaiɪtli/ *adv* tranquilamente; en
silencio; sin ruido; en calma; (simply)
sencillamente; dulcemente

quill /kwɪl/ *n* pluma de ave, *f;* (of a
feather) cañón, *m;* (pen) pluma, *f;* (of a
porcupine) púa, *f.* **q.-driver,** cagatintas,
mf

quilt /kwɪlt/ *n* colcha, *f,* edredón, *m.* —*vt*
acolchar. **q. maker,** colchero, *m*

quilting /'kwɪltɪŋ/ *n* acolchamiento, *m;*
colchadura, *f*

quince /kwɪns/ *n* (tree and fruit) membrillo, *m.* **q. cheese,** carne de membrillo,
f. **q. jelly,** jalea de membrillo, *f*

quinine /'kwainain/ *n* quinina, *f*

quinsy /'kwɪnzi/ *n* angina, *f*

quintessence /kwɪnˈtɛsəns/ *n* quinta
esencia, *f*

quintessential /ˌkwɪntəˈsɛnʃəl/ *a* quin-
taesenciado

quintet /kwɪnˈtɛt/ *n* quinteto, *m*

quintuple /kwɪnˈtupəl/ *a* quíntuplo

quip /kwɪp/ *n* agudeza, salida, *f;* (hint)
indirecta, *f;* donaire, *m,* chanza, burla, *f*

quirk /kwɜrk/ *n* (quip) agudeza, salida, *f;*
(quibble) sutileza, evasiva, *f,* (gesture)
gesto, *m*

quit /kwɪt/ *vt* abandonar; dejar; renunciar (a). —*vi* marcharse, *Inf.* tomar las de
Villadiego, poner pies en polvorosa;
(slang) dejar de, cesar de. **notice to q.,**
aviso de desahúcio, *m*

quite /kwait/ *adv* completamente, enteramente; totalmente; del todo; (very) muy; (fairly) bastante. **It is not q. the thing to do,** Esto es algo que no se hace. **Q. so!** ¡Claro!; ¡Eso es! Se comprende. **It is not q. so good as we hoped,** No es tan bueno como esperábamos. **Peter is q. grown-up,** Pedro está hecho un hombre (*or* es todo un hombre)

quits /kwɪts/ *adv* quito, descargado. **be q.,** estar en paz

quitter /'kwɪtər/ *n* desertor (-ra); cobarde, *mf*

quiver /'kwɪvər/ *vi* temblar; vibrar; estremecerse; palpitar; (of light) titilar. —*n* (for arrows) aljaba, *f*, carcaj, *m*. See also **quivering**

quivering /'kwɪvərɪŋ/ *a* tremulante; vibrante; palpitante. —*n* temblor, *m*; estremecimiento, *m*

quixotic /kwɪk'sɒtɪk/ *a* quijotesco

quiz /kwɪz/ *n* examen parcial, *m*. —*vt* tomar el pelo (a), burlarse (de); (stare) mirar de hito en hito (a)

quizzical /'kwɪzɪkəl/ *a* burlón; cómico; estrafalario

quoin /kɔin, kwɔin/ *n* piedra angular, *f*; ángulo, *m*; (wedge) cuña, *f*. —*vt* meter cuñas (a)

quoit /kwɔit/ *n* tejo, *m*; *pl* **quoits,** juego de tejos, *m*

quondam /'kwɒndəm/ *a* antiguo

quorum /'kwɔrəm/ *n* quórum, *m*. **to form a q.,** hacer un quórum

quota /'kwoutə/ *n* cuota, *f*

quotable /'kwoutəbəl/ *a* citable; (Stock Exchange) cotizable

quota system *n* tablas diferenciales, *f pl*

quotation /kwou'teiʃən/ *n* citación, *f*; cita, *f*; *Com.* cotización, *f*. **q. mark,** comilla, *f*

quote /kwout/ *vt* citar; *Com.* cotizar. —*n Inf.* comilla, *f*

quoth /kwouθ/ *vt* **q. I,** dije yo. **q. he,** dijo él

quotient /'kwouʃənt/ *n* cociente, *m*. **intelligence q.,** cociente intelectual, *m*

R

r /ar/ *n* (letter) erre, *f*
rabbi /'ræbai/ *n* rabí, rabino, *m*. **grand r.**, gran rabino, *m*
rabbinical /rə'bınıkəl/ *a* rabínico
rabbit /'ræbıt/ *n* conejo (-ja). —*a* conejuno, de conejo. —*vi* cazar conejos. **young r.**, gazapo, *m*. **r.-hutch**, jaula para conejos, *f*. **r.-warren**, conejera, *f*
rabble /'ræbəl/ *n* populacho, vulgo, *m*, plebe, *f*
rabid /'ræbıd/ *a* rabioso; fanático; furioso, violento
rabies /'reibiz/ *n* rabia, hidrofobia, *f*
raccoon /ræ'kun/ *n* mapache, *m*
race /reis/ *n* carrera, *f*, (current) corriente, *f*; (prize) premio, *m*; (breed) raza, *f*; casta, estirpe, *f*; (family) linaje, *m*, familia, *f*; (scornful) ralea, *f*; (struggle) lucha, *f*. —*vi* tomar parte en una carrera; correr de prisa; asistir a concursos de carreras de caballos; (of a machine) dispararse. —*vt* (hacer) correr; competir en una carrera (con); desafiar a una carrera. **flat r.**, carrera llana, *f*. **mill-r.**, caz, *m*. **to run a r.**, tomar parte en una carrera; *Fig.* hacer una carrera. **r.-card**, programa de carreras de caballos, *m*. **r. hatred**, odio de razas, *m*. **r.-meeting**, concurso de carreras de caballos, *m*. **r. suicide**, suicidio de la raza, *m*. **r.-track**, pista, *f*
racecourse /'reis,kɔrs/ *n* hipódromo, *m*; estadio, *m*
racehorse /'reis,hɔrs/ *n* caballo de carrera, *m*
racer /'reisər/ *n* (horse) caballo de carreras, *m*; (person) carrerista, *mf*; (car) coche de carreras, *m*; (boat) yate de carreras, *m*; (bicycle) bicicleta de carreras, *f*
rachitic /rə'kıtık/ *a* raquítico
racial /'reiʃəl/ *a* racial, de raza
racialism /'reiʃə,lızəm/ *n* rivalidad de razas, *f*
raciness /'reisınıs/ *n* sabor, *m*; savia, *f*, picante, *m*
racing /'reisıŋ/ *n* carreras, *f pl*; *Mech.* disparo, *m*, *a* de carreras; hípico. **r. calendar**, calendario de concursos de carreras de caballos, *m*. **r. car**, coche de carreras, *m*. **r. cycle**, bicicleta de carreras, *f*
rack /ræk/ *n* (for hay) percha (del pesebre), *f*; (in a railway compartment) rejilla, *f*; (for billiard cues) taquera, *f*; (for clothes) percha, *f*; (for torture) potro, *m*; *Mech.* cremallera, *f*. —*vt* poner en el potro, torturar; atormentar. **to be on the r.**, estar en el potro **to r. one's brains**, devanarse los sesos, quebrarse la cabeza. **r. and ruin**, ruina total, *f*. **r. railway**, ferrocarril de cremallera, *m*,
racket /'rækıt/ *n* *Sports.* raqueta, *f*; (din) barahúnda, *f*; ruido, estrépito, *m*; confusión, *f*; (bustle) bullicio, *m*, agitación, *f*; (swindle) estafa, *f*; (binge) parranda, *f*. **to play rackets**, jugar a la raqueta

racoon /ræ'kun/ *n* mapache, *m*
racy /'reisi/ *a* picante; sabroso
radar /'reidɑr/ *n* radar, *m*
raddled /'rædld/ *a* pintado de almagre; mal pintado
radial /'reidiəl/ *a* radial
radiance /'reidiəns/ *n* resplandor, brillo, *m*, luminosidad, *f*
radiant /'reidiənt/ *a* radiante; brillante, luminoso. —*n* *Geom.* línea radial, *f*. **r. heat**, calor radiante, *m*
radiantly /'reidiəntli/ *adv* con resplandor; brillantemente; con alegría
radiate /'reidi,eit/ *vi* radiar. —*vt* irradiar
radiation /,reidi'eiʃən/ *n* irradiación, *f*; *Geom.* radiación, *f*
radiator /'reidi,eitər/ *n* (for central heating and of a car) radiador, *m*; (stove) calorífero, *m*
radical /'rædıkəl/ *a* radical. —*n* (*Math. Chem.*) radical, *m*; *Polit.* radical, *mf*
radio /'reidi,ou/ *n* radio, *f*; radiocomunicación, *f*. **r. amateur, r. enthusiast**, radioaficionado (-da). **r. announcer**, locutor (-ra). **r. broadcast**, radioemisión, radiodifusión, *f*. **r. listener**, radiooyente, *mf f*. **r. receiver**, (technical) radiorreceptor, *m*; (usual word) aparato de radio, *m*. **r. transmitter**, radiotransmisor, *m*
radioactive /,reidiou'æktıv/ *a* radiactivo
radioactive fallout *n* caída radiactiva, llovizna radiactiva, precipitación radiactiva, *f*
radiofrequency /,reidiou'frikwənsi/ *n* radiofrecuencia, *f*
radiologist /,reidi'ɒləgıst/ *n* radiólogo, *m*
radiology /reidi'ɒlədʒi/ *n* radiología, *f*
radish /'rædıʃ/ *n* rábano, *m*. **horse-r.**, rábano picante, *m*
radium /'reidiəm/ *n* radio, *m*
radius /'reidiəs/ *n* (*Geom. Anat.*) radio, *m*; (of a wheel) rayo, *m*; (scope) alcance, *f*
raffish /'ræfıʃ/ *a* disoluto, libertino
raffle /'ræfəl/ *n* rifa, *f*, sorteo, *m*; lotería, *f*. —*vt* rifar, sortear
raft /ræft/ *n* balsa, *f*; (timber) armadía, *f*. —*vt* transportar en balsa; cruzar en balsa
rafter /'ræftər/ *n* (of a roof) viga, traviesa, *f*; (raftsman) balsero, *m*
rag /ræg/ *n* jirón, guiñapo, *m*; (for cleaning) paño, trapo, *m*; (for papermaking) estraza, *f*; (of smoke, etc.) penacho, *m*; (newspaper) papelucho, *m*; *pl* **rags**, harapos, *m pl*, *Inf.* viejos hábitos, *m pl*. —*vt* (tease) tomar el pelo (a); burlarse de; hacer una broma pesada (a). **r.-and-bone-man, ragpicker**, andrajero, trapero (Mexico), pepinador, *m*. **r. doll**, muñeca de trapo, *f*
ragamuffin /'rægə,mʌfın/ *n* galopín, *m*
rage /reidʒ/ *n* (anger) cólera, rabia, ira, *f*; (of the elements) furia, violencia, *f*; (ardor) entusiasmo, ardor, *m*; (fashion) boga, moda, *f*; (craze) manía, *f*; (of the poet) furor, *m*. —*vi* (be angry) rabiar, estar furioso; (of the sea) encresparse, al-

borotarse, enfurecerse; (of wind, fire, animals) bramar, rugir; (of pain) rabiar; (be prevalent) prevalecer, desencadenarse. **to r. against,** protestar furiosamente contra; culpar amargamente (de). **to be all the r.,** *Inf.* ser la ultima moda. **to fly into a r.,** montar en cólera. **to put into a r.,** hacer rabiar

ragged /'rægɪd/ *a* harapiento, andrajoso; roto; (uneven) desigual; (rugged) peñascoso, áspero, escabroso; (serrated) serrado; dentellado; (of a coastline) accidentado; (unfinished) inacabado, sin terminar; (of style) descuidado, sin pulir

raging /'reidʒɪŋ/ *a* furioso, rabioso; violento; (roaring) bramante; (of the sea) bravío; intenso. —*n* furia, *f*; violencia, *f*; intensidad, *f*

raglan /'ræglən/ *n* raglán, *m*. **r. sleeve,** manga raglán, *f*

ragout /'ræ'gu/ *n* estofado, *m*

ragpicker /'ræg,pɪkər/ *n* trapero (-ra)

raid /reid/ *n* incursión, correría, *f*; asalto, ataque, *m*; (by the police) razzia, *f*; (by aircraft) bombardeo, *m*, *vt* invadir; atacar, asaltar; apoderarse de; hacer una razzia en; (by aircraft) bombear, bombardear; (pillage) pillar, saquear. **obliteration r.,** hombardeo de saturación, *m*

raider /'reidər/ *n* corsario, *m*; atacador, asaltador, *m*; (aircraft) avión enemigo, *m*

rail /reil/ *n* barra, *f*; antepecho, *m*; (of a staircase) barandilla, *f*, pasamano, *m*; (track) riel, *m*; (railway) ferrocarril, *m*; (of a ship) barandilla, *f*; (of a chair) travesaño, *m pl.* **rails,** (fence) cerca, barrera, palizada, *f.* —*vt* cercar con una palizada, poner cerca a; mandar por ferrocarril. **by r.,** por ferrocarril. **to run off the rails,** descarrilar. **to r. at,** protestar contra; prorrumpir en invectivas contra, injuriar (de palabra (a)

railing /'reilɪŋ/ *n* barandilla, *f*; antepecho, *m*, enrejado, *m*; (grille) reja, *f*; (jeers) burlas, *f pl*; insultos, *m pl*, injurias, *f pl*; quejas, *f pl*

raillery /'reiləri/ *n* jocosidad, tomadura de pelo, *f*; sátiras, *f pl*

railway /'reil,wei/ *n* ferrocarril, *m*; vía férrea, *f*, camino de hierro, *m*, *a* de ferrocarril, ferroviario. **elevated r.,** ferrocarril aéreo, *m*. **narrow gauge r.,** ferrocarril de vía estrecha, *m*. **r. buffet,** fonda, *f*, (or restaurante, *m*) de estación. **r. carriage,** departamento de tren, *m*. **r. company,** compañía de ferrocarriles, *f*. **r. crossing,** paso a nivel, *m*. **r. engine,** locomotora, *f*. **r. guard,** jefe del tren, *m*. **r. guide,** guía de ferrocarriles, *f*. **r. line,** vía férrea, *f*. **r. marshalling yard,** apartadero ferroviario, *m*. **r. passenger,** viajero (-ra) en un tren. **r. platform,** andén, *m*. **r. porter,** mozo de estación, *m*. **r. siding,** vía muerta, *f*. **r. signal,** disco de señales, *m*. **r. station,** estación (de ferrocarril), *f*. **r. system,** sistema ferroviario, *m*. **r. ticket,** billete de tren, *m*

railwayman /'reil,weimən/ *n* ferroviario, empleado de los ferrocarriles, *m*

raiment /'reimənt/ *n* ropa, *f*; *Poet.* hábitos, *m pl*

rain /rein/ *n* lluvia, *f.* —*vi and vt* llover. **a r. of arrows,** una lluvia de flechas. **fine r.,** llovizna, *f.* **to r. cats and dogs,** llover a cántaros. **to r. hard,** diluviar. **r. cloud,** nubarrón, *m.* **r.-gauge,** pluviómetro, *m*

rainbow /'rein,bou/ *n* arco iris, arco de San Martín, *m*

raincoat /'rein,kout/ *n* abrigo impermeable, *m*

raindrop /'rein,drɒp/ *n* gota de lluvia, *f*

rainfall /'rein,fɔl/ *n* cantidad llovida, *f*; (shower) aguacero, *m*

rainy /'reini/ *a* lluvioso. **r. day,** día de lluvia, *m*; *Fig.* tiempo de escasez, *m*

raise /reiz/ *vt* levantar; alzar; (the hat) quitar; solevantar; (dough) fermentar; (erect) erigir, edificar; (dust) levantar; (promote) ascender; (increase) aumentar; hacer subir; (spirits, memories) evocar; (the dead) resucitar; (cause) causar; dar lugar (a); hacer concebir; (a question, a point) hacer; plantear; (breed or educate) criar; (a crop) cultivar; (an army) alistar; (gather together) juntar; (a subscription) hacer; (money, etc.) obtener, hallar; (a siege, etc.) levantar, alzar; (a laugh, a protest, etc.) suscitar, provocar; (utter) poner, dar; (a fund) abrir. **to r. oneself,** incorporarse. **He succeeded in raising himself,** Logró alzarse; Logró mejorar su posición. **He raised their hopes unduly,** Les hizo concebir esperanzas desmesuradas. **to r. an objection (to),** poner objeción (a). **to r. an outcry,** armar un alboroto. **to r. a point,** hacer una observación; plantear una cuestión. **to r. a siege,** levantar un sitio. **to r. Cain,** armar lo de Dios es Cristo. **to r. one's voice,** alzar la voz

raisin /'reizin/ *n* pasa, *f*

raising /'reizɪŋ/ *n* levantamiento, *m*; alzamiento, *m*; (of a building, monument) erección, *f*; elevación, *f*; (increase) aumento, *m*; provocación, *f*; fundación, *f*; (breeding or education) crianza, *f*; (of spirits) evocación, *f*; (of the dead) resucitación, *f*; producción, *f*; (of crops) cultivo, *m*

rake /reik/ *n Agr.* rastrillo, *m*, rastra, *f*; (for the fire) hurgón, *m*; (croupier's) raqueta, *f*; (of a mast, funnel) inclinación, *f*; (person) tenorio, calavera, *m.* —*vt Agr.* rastrillar; (a fire, etc.) hurgar; (sweep) barrer; recoger; (ransack) buscar (en); (with fire) enfilar, tirar a lo largo de; (scan) escudriñar. —*vi* trabajar con el rastrillo; (slope) inclinarse. **r. off,** tajada, *f.* **to r. together,** juntar con el rastrillo; amontonar; ahorrar. **to r. up,** (revive) resucitar, desenterrar

rakish /'reikɪʃ/ *a* (of a ship) de palos muy inclinados, (dissolute) disoluto, libertino; (dashing) elegante

rally /'ræli/ *vt* reunir; *Mil.* rehacer; (faculties) concentrar; (tease) tomar el pelo (a). —*vi* reunirse; *Mil.* rehacerse; (revive) mejorar, recobrar las fuerzas; (of markets, etc.) mejorar *n* reunión, *f*

rallying /'ræliŋ/ *n* reunión, *f*; (of faculties, etc.) concentración, *f*; (recovery) mejora, *f*. **r. point,** punto de reunión, *m*

ram /ræm/ *n* Zool. carnero, morueco, *m*; *Astron.* Aries, Carnero, *m*; (Mil. etc.) ariete, *m*; (tool) pisón, *m*; *Nav.* espolón, *m*, *vt* golpear con ariete o espolón; (of a gun) atacar; apisonar; meter a la fuerza; hacer tragar a la fuerza; (squeeze) apretar; (crowd) atestar

ramble /'ræmbəl/ *vi* vagar, vagabundear; hacer una excursión. —*vt* errar por

rambler /'ræmblər/ *n* excursionista, *mf*; paseante, *mf*; *Bot.* rosa trepante, *f*

rambling /'ræmbliŋ/ *a* (of houses) encantado; laberíntico; (straggly) disperso; (of thought, etc.) incoherente, inconexo. —*n* vagabundeo, *m*; excursiones, *f pl*; paseo, *m*; (digression) digresiones, *f pl*; (delirium) desvaríos, *m pl*

ramification /,ræməfɪ'keiʃən/ *n* ramificación, *f*

ramify /'ræmə,fai/ *vi* ramificarse, tener ramificaciones. —*vt* ramificar; dividir en ramales

ramp /ræmp/ *n* rampa, *f*; (swindle) estafa, *f*; (storm, commotion) tormenta, *f*

rampage /'ræmpeidʒ/ *vi* alborotarse; bramar

rampant /'ræmpənt/ *a* salvaje; *Herald.* rampante; (of persons) impaciente, furioso; (of plants, growth) lozano, exuberante; desenfrenado; (rife) prevaleciente, predominante

rampart /'ræmpɑrt/ *n* muralla, *f*; terraplén, *m*; *Fig.* baluarte, *m.* —*vt* abaluartar, abastionar

ramshackle /'ræm,ʃækəl/ *a* destartalado, ruinoso; desvencijado; (badly made) mal hecho

ranch /ræntʃ/ *n* rancho, *m*, hacienda (de ganado), *f*

rancher /'ræntʃər/ *n* ranchero, *m*

rancid /'rænsɪd/ *a* rancio

rancor /'ræŋkər/ *n* rencor, encono, *m*

random /'rændəm/ *n* azar, *m*, *a* fortuito, al azar; sin orden ni concierto. **at r.,** a la ventura, al azar; sin pensar; (of shooting) sin apuntar. **to talk at r.,** hablar a trochemoche

range /reindʒ/ *n* línea, hilera, *f*; (of mountains) cadena, *f*; serie, *f*; clase, *f*; variedad, *f*; (of goods) surtido, *m*; (of a gun, voice, vision, etc.) alcance, *m*; (area) extensión, área, *f*; esfera de actividad, *f*; (scope) alcance, *m*; (of voice, musical instrument) compás, *m*; (of colors) gama, *f*; (for shooting) campo de tiro, *m*; (for cooking) cocina económica, *f*. **at close r.,** de cerca. **out of r.,** fuera de alcance. **within r.,** al alcance. **r.-finder,** (of guns, cameras) telémetro, *m*. **r. of mountains,** cadena de montañas, *f*; sierra, *f*

range /reindʒ/ *vt Poet.* arreglar; alinear; ordenar, clasificar; (a gun, etc.) apuntar; (place oneself) ponerse; sumarse (a); (roam) recorrer; (scan) escudriñar. —*vi* extenderse; (roam) vagar; (of plants) crecer (en); variar, fluctuar; oscilar, vacilar; (of guns, etc.) alcanzar; (of the mind) pasar (por); (include) incluir

ranger /'reindʒər/ *n* (wanderer) vagabundo, *m*; (keeper) guardabosque, *m*; *Mil.* batidor, *m*

rank /ræŋk/ *n* línea, *f*; fila, *f*; grado, *m*; clase, *f*; rango, *m*; categoría, *f*; posición, *f*; calidad, *f*; distinción, *f.* —*vt* ordenar; clasificar; (estimate) estimar; poner (entre). —*vi* ocupar un puesto; tener un grado, rango, etc.; estar al nivel (de); ser igual (a); contarse (entre). —*a* (luxuriant) lozano, exuberante; fértil; (thick) espeso; (rancid) rancio; (complete) consumado; completo; (foul-smelling) fétido; *Fig.* repugnante, aborrecible; (very) muy. **of the first r.,** de primera calidad; de primera clase; de distinción. **the r. and file,** los soldados, la tropa; las masas, hombres de filas, *m pl*, mujeres de fila, *f pl*, la mayoría; los socios ordinarios (de un club, etc.). **to break ranks,** *Mil.* romper filas. **to rise from the ranks,** ascender de las filas. **to r. high,** ocupar alta posición; ser de los mejores (de). **to r. with,** estar al nivel de; (be numbered among) contarse entre, figurar entre

rankle /'ræŋkəl/ *vi Fig.* irritar, molestar; envenenarse la vida, hacerse odioso

ransack /'rænsæk/ *vt* (search) registrar; (pillage) saquear; *Fig.* buscar en

ransacking /'rænsækiŋ/ *n* (searching) registro, *m*; (sacking) saqueo, *m*

ransom /'rænsəm/ *n* rescate, *m*, redención, *f*; liberación, *f.* —*vt* rescatar, redimir

ransomer /'rænsəmər/ *n* rescatador (-ra)

ransoming /'rænsəmiŋ/ *n* redención, *f*; liberación, *f*

rant /rænt/ *vi* declamar a gritos, vociferar; despotricar (contra); desvariar; hablar por hablar, hablar sin ton ni son. —*n* declamación, vociferación, *f*; desvarío, *m*

ranter /'ræntər/ *n* declamador (-ra); agitador populachero, *m*; predicador chillón, *m*

rap /ræp/ *n* golpecito, *m*; toque, *m*; (with the knocker) aldabada, *f*; (worthless trifle) ardite, maravedí, *m.* —*vt* and *vi* golpear; tocar. **He doesn't care a rap,** No le importa un ardite. **to rap at the door,** tocar a la puerta. **to rap with the knuckles,** golpear con los nudillos. **to rap out an oath,** proferir una blasfemia

rapacious /rə'peiʃəs/ *a* rapaz

rapaciously /rə'peiʃəsli/ *adv* con rapacidad

rapacity /rə'pæsɪti/ *n* rapacidad, *f*

rape /reip/ *n* (carrying off) rapto, *m.* **the Rape of the Sabine Women,** el Rapto de las Sabinas, *m*; *Law.* estupro, *m*; violación, *f*; *Bot.* nabo silvestre, *m.* —*vt* (carry off) raptar, robar; violar, forzar

rapid /'ræpɪd/ a rápido. —n rápido, m. **r.-combustion,** combustión activa, f

rapidity /rə'pɪdɪtɪ/ n rapidez, f

rapidly /'ræpɪdlɪ/ adv rápidamente, con rapidez

rapier /'reipiər/ n estoque, m; espadín, m

rapine /'ræpɪn/ n rapiña, f

rapping /'ræpɪŋ/ n golpecitos, m pl; golpeo, m; toques, m pl; (of the knocker) aldabeo, m

rapscallion /ræp'skælyən/ n bribón, m

rapt /ræpt/ past part and a arrebatado; absorto; extático, extasiado

rapture /'ræptʃər/ n arrebato, m; éxtasis, m; transporte, m; embriaguez, f; entusiasmo, m

rapturous /'ræptʃərəs/ a embelesado; extático; entusiasta

rare /rɛər/ a raro; extraordinario; exótico; infrecuente

rarefy /'rɛərəˌfai/ vt rarefacer. —vi rarefacerse

rareness /'rɛərnɪs/ n rareza, f; singularidad, f; infrecuencia, f

rarity /'rɛərɪtɪ/ n rareza, f; (uncommonness and rare object) rareza, f

rascal /'ræskəl/ n sinvergüenza, m; truhán, bribón, pícaro, m; (affectionately) picaruelo, m

rascality /ræ'skælɪtɪ/ n bellaquería, truhanería, f

rash /ræʃ/ a temerario, precipitado; imprudente. —n erupción, f, salpullido, m

rasher /'ræʃər/ n magra, f; (of bacon) torrezno, m

rashly /'ræʃlɪ/ adv temerariamente, precipitadamente; imprudentemente, con imprudencia

rasp /ræsp/ n escofina, f, rallo, m; sonido áspero, m. —vt raspar, escofinar; (get on one's nerves) poner los nervios en punta (a)

raspberry /'ræz,bɛrɪ/ n frambuesa, f. **r.-cane,** frambueso, m. **r. jam,** mermelada de frambuesa, f

rasping /'ræspɪŋ/ a (of the voice) áspero, estridente

rat /ræt/ n rata, f; desertor, m; (black leg) esquirol, m. —vi cazar ratas; ser desertor; ser esquirol. **rat-catcher,** cazador de ratas, m. **rat poison,** matarratas, m, raticida, f. **rat-trap,** ratonera, f

ratchet /'rætʃɪt/ n Mech. trinquete, m; (of a watch) disparador, m. **r.-drill,** carraca, f. **r.-wheel,** rueda dentada con trinquete, f

rate /reit/ n velocidad, f; razón, proporción, f; (of exchange) tipo, m; tanto, m; precio, m; clase, f; modo, m, manera, f; Naut. clasificación, f; (tax) contribución, f, impuesto, m; pl **rates,** (of a house) inquilinato, m. —vt tasar; estimar; fijar el precio (a); Naut. clasificar; imponer una contribución (de); (scold) reñir. **at a great r.,** rápidamente, velozmente. **at a r. of,** a razón de; a una velocidad de. **at any r.,** de todos modos; por lo menos; sea como fuere. **at this r.,** de este modo;

a este paso; a esa cuenta; en esta proporción; (with seguir) así. **first-r.,** de primera clase. **rates and taxes,** contribuciones e impuestos, f pl. **r. of climb,** Aer. velocidad ascensional, f. **r. of exchange,** tipo de cambio, m. **r.-payer,** contribuyente, mf

rather /'ræðər/ adv más bien; antes; (more willingly) de mejor gana; (somewhat) algo, un poco; (perhaps) quizás; mejor dicho; (fairly) bastante; (very) muy; mucho; al contrario. **R.!** ¡Ya lo creo! **or r.,** o más bien. **anything r. than...,** cualquier cosa menos... **He had r.,** Preferiría. **r. than,** antes que, en vez de

ratification /ˌrætəfɪ'keiʃən/ n ratificación, f; (of a bill) aprobación, f

ratify /'rætəˌfai/ vt ratificar

rating /'reitɪŋ/ n tasación, f; valuación, f; clasificación, f; impuesto, m, contribución, f; repartición de impuestos, f; (of a ship's company) graduación, f; (scolding) represión, f

ratio /'reiʃou/ n razón, f; proporción, f. **In direct r.,** En razón directa

ratiocination /ˌræʃɪˌɒsə'nɛiʃən/ n raciocinación, f

ration /'ræʃən, 'reiʃən/ n ración, f. —vt racionar. **r.-book,** cartilla de racionamiento, f

rational /'ræʃənl/ a racional; razonable, juicioso. —n ser racional, m

rationalist /'ræʃənlɪst/ n racionalista, mf

rationalistic /ˌræʃənl'ɪstɪk/ a racionalista

rationality /ˌræʃə'nælɪtɪ/ n racionalidad, f; justicia, f

rationalization /ˌræʃənlə'zeiʃən/ n racionalización, f; justificación, f

rationalize /'ræʃənlˌaiz/ vt hacer racional; concebir racionalmente; Math. quitar los radicales (a); justificar

rationing /'ræʃənɪŋ, 'rei-/ n racionamiento, m

rattan /ræ'tæn/ n rota, f, bejuco, m; junquillo, m

ratteen /ræ'tin/ n ratina, f

rattle /'rætl/ vi hacer ruido; rechinar, crujir; (of loose windows, etc.) zangolotearse; (knock) golpear; tocar; (patter) bailar; sonar; (of the dying) dar un estertor. —vt (shake) sacudir; hacer vibrar; (jolt) traquetear; (do rapidly) acabar rápidamente; (confuse) aturdir, hacer perder la cabeza (a); desconcertar. **to r. along,** deslizarse (or correr) rápidamente. **to r. off,** (repeat) decir rápidamente; terminar apresuradamente. **to r. on about,** charlar mucho de, hablar sin cesar sobre

rattle /'rætl/ n rechinamiento, crujido, m; zangoloteo, m; ruido, m; son (de la lluvia, etc.), m; (in the throat) estertor, m; (of a rattlesnake) cascabel, m; (child's) sonajero, m; matraca, f; carraca, f; (chatter) charla, f. **r.-headed,** de cabeza de chorlito, casquivano

rattlesnake /'rætlˌsneik/ n serpiente de cascabel, f, crótalo, m

raucous /'rɔkəs/ a ronco, estridente

ravage /'rævɪdʒ/ *vt* devastar; (pillage)
saquear; destruir; (spoil) estropear. —*n*
devastación, *f;* destrucción, *f;* estrago, *m*

ravager /'rævɪdʒər/ *n* devastador (-ra);
saqueador (-ra)

rave /reiv/ *vi* desvariar, delirar; (of the
elements) bramar, rugir. **to r. about,** hablar con entusiasmo de; delirar por. **to r.
against,** vociferar contra, despotricarse
contra

ravel /'rævəl/ *vt* deshilar, destejer; *Fig.*
enredar. **to r. out,** deshilarse; *Fig.* desenredarse, desenmarañarse

raven /'reivən/ *n* cuervo, *m, a* negro
como el azabache

ravening /'rævənɪŋ/ *a* rapaz, salvaje

ravenous /'rævənəs/ *a* voraz

ravine /rə'vin/ *n* cañada, *f,* barranco, cañón, *m*

raving /'reivɪŋ/ *n* delirio, *m,* desvaríos, *m
pl.* —*a* delirante; violento; bravío

ravioli /,rævi'ouli/ *n pl* ravioles, *m pl*

ravish /'rævɪʃ/ *vt* (carry off) arrebatar,
raptar; extasiar, encantar; (rape) violar,
forzar

ravisher /'rævɪʃər/ *n* raptador, *m;* violador, *m*

ravishing /'rævɪʃɪŋ/ *n* violación, *f, a* encantador

ravishment /'rævɪʃmənt/ *n* violación, *f;*
arrobamiento, *m;* transporte, éxstasis, *m*

raw /rɔ/ *a* (of meat, etc., silk, leather,
weather) crudo; bruto; (inexpert) bisoño;
(of flesh) vivo; *Com.* en bruto. **raw-
boned,** huesudo, flaco. **raw hand,** novato (-ta).
raw material, primera materia, *f.* **raw
materials,** materias primas, *f pl.* **raw
score,** puntuación bruta, *f.* **raw silk,** seda
cruda, seda en rama, *f.* **raw sugar,** azúcar bruto, *m*

rawhide /'rɔ,haid/ *a* de cuero crudo

rawness /'rɔnɪs/ *n* crudeza, *f;* inexperiencia, *f;* (of weather) humedad, *f*

ray /rei/ *n* rayo, *m;* (line) raya, *f;* (radius)
radio, *m;* (fish) raya, *f.* **cathode rays,**
rayos catódicos, *m pl*

rayon /'reiɒn/ *n* rayón, *m*

raze /reiz/ *vt* arrasar, asolar; demoler;
(erase) borrar, tachar

razor /'reizər/ *n* navaja, *f.* **electric r.,**
máquina de afeitar eléctrica, *f.* **safety r.,**
máquina de afeitar, *f.* **slash with a r.,**
navajada, *f.* **r. blade,** hoja de afeitar, *f.* **r.
case,** navajero, *m.* **r. strop,** suavizador, *m*

re /ri, rei/ *n Mus.* re, *m; prep Law.* causa,
f; Com. concerniente a

re /ri/ *prefix* (attached to verb) re-; (after
the verb) de nuevo; (followed by infin.)
volver a... **to re-count,** volver a contar,
contar de nuevo, recontar

reabsorb /,riəb'sɔrb, -'zɔrb/ *vt* resorber

reabsorption /,riəb'sɔrpʃən, -'zɔrp-/ *n*
reabsorción, resorción, *f*

reach /ritʃ/ *vt* (stretch out) alargar; extender; alcanzar; llegar hasta; (arrive at)
llegar a; (achieve) lograr, obtener. —*vi*
extenderse; alcanzar; penetrar. —*n*
alcance, *f;* extensión, *f;* poder, *m;* capacidad, *f;* (of a river) tabla, *f.* **as far as
the eye could r.,** hasta donde alcanzaba
la vista. **He reached home very soon,**
Llegó muy pronto a casa. **out of r.,** fuera
de alcance. **to r. a deadlock,** llegar a un
punto muerto. **within r.,** al alcance.
within easy r., de fácil acceso; a corta
distancia. **to r. after,** procurar alcanzar;
hacer esfuerzos para obtener. **to r. back,**
(of time) remontarse. **to r. down,** bajar.
r.-me-downs, ropa hecha, *f*

react /ri'ækt/ *vi* reaccionar. —*vt* hacer de
nuevo; *Theat.* volver a representar

reaction /ri'ækʃən/ *n* reacción, *f*

reactionary /ri'ækʃə,neri/ *a* and *n* reaccionario (-ia)

read /rid/ *vt* leer; (a riddle, etc.) adivinar;
descifrar; interpretar; (study) estudiar;
(the Burial Service, etc.) decir; (correct)
corregir; (of thermometers, etc.) marcar.
—*vi* leer; estudiar; (be written) estar escrito, decir. **The play acts better than it
reads,** La comedia es mejor representada
que leída. **to r. aloud,** leer en voz alta.
to r. between the lines, leer entre
líneas. **to r. proofs,** corregir pruebas. **to
r. to oneself,** leer para sí. **to r. about,**
leer; (learn) enterarse de. **to r. again,**
volver a leer, leer otra vez. **to r. on,** continuar leyendo. **to r. out,** leer en alta
voz. **to r. over,** leer; leerlo todo. **to r.
over and over again,** leer muchas veces,
leer y releer.

read /rɛd/ *past part* leído, etc. **well-r.,** re-
leído; instruido, culto

readable /'ridəbəl/ *a* legible; interesante

reader /'ridər/ *n* lector (-ra); *Eccl.* lector,
m; (proof) corrector de pruebas, *m;* (citation collector for a dictionary) cedulista,
mf; (university) profesor (-ra) auxiliar a
cátedra; (book) libro de lectura, *m.* **to be
a great r.,** leer mucho. **the Spanish r.**
(reader of Spanish books) el lector de español

readily /'rɛdli/ *adv* fácilmente; en
seguida, inmediatamente; de buena gana,
con placer

readiness /'rɛdinɪs/ *n* prontitud, expedición, *f;* buena voluntad, *f;* (of speech,
etc.) facilidad, *f.* **in r.,** preparado. **r. of
wit,** viveza de ingenio, *f*

reading /'ridɪŋ/ *n* lectura, *f;* (erudition)
conocimientos, *m pl;* (recital) declamación, *f;* (lecture) conferencia, *f;* (study)
estudio, *m;* interpretación, *f;* (of a thermometer, etc.) registro, *m;* (of a will)
apertura, *f.* **r.-book,** libro de lectura, *m.*
r.-desk, atril, *m.* **r.-glass,** lente para leer,
m, carlita, *f.* **r.-lamp,** lámpara de sobremesa, *f.* **r.-matter,** material de lectura,
m. **r.-room,** gabinete de lectura, *m,* sala
de lectura, *f*

readjourn /,riə'dʒɜrn/ *vt* (a meeting) suspender (la sesión) de nuevo

readjust /,riə'dʒʌst/ *vt* reajustar, reacomo-
dar; *vi* reacomodarse

readjustment /ˌriə'dʒʌ½stmənt/ n reajuste, m, reacomodación, f

readmission /ˌriəd'miʃən/ n readmisión, f

readmit /ˌriəd'mit/ vt readmitir

ready /'redi/ a listo, preparado; dispuesto; pronto; (on the point of) a punto de; (easy) fácil; (near at hand) a la mano; (with money) contante; (with wit, etc.) vivo; (available) disponible; (nimble) ágil, ligero. **I am r. to do it,** Estoy dispuesto a hacerlo. **in r. cash,** en dinero contante. **to get r.,** prepararse; (dress) vestirse. **to make r.,** vt preparar; aprestar; Print. imponer. —vi prepararse, disponerse. **r.-made,** hecho; confeccionado. **r.-made clothing,** ropa hecha, f. **r. money,** dinero contante, m. **r.-witted,** de ingenio vivo

reaffirm /ˌriə'fɜrm/ vt afirmar de nuevo; reiterar, volver a repetir

reaffirmation /ˌriæfər'meiʃən/ n reiteración, f

real /'reiəl/ a real; verdadero; efectivo; (with silk, etc.) puro; sincero. **r. estate, r. property,** bienes raíces, m pl

realism /'riəˌlizəm/ n realismo, m

realist /'riəlist/ n realista, mf

realistic /ˌriə'listik/ a realista

reality /ri'æliti/ n realidad, f; verdad, f

realize /'riəˌlaiz/ vt (understand) darse cuenta de, hacerse cargo de; realizar; (make real) dar vida (a); (accomplish) llevar a cabo; Com. realizar; (gain) adquirir

really /'riəli/ adv realmente; en verdad; en realidad; en efecto; (frankly) francamente. **R.?** ¿De veras?

realm /relm/ n reino, m, dominios, m pl; Fig. esfera, f

realty /'riəlti/ n bienes raíces, m pl

reanimate /ri'ænəˌmeit/ vt reanimar

reap /rip/ vt segar; Fig. cosechar, recoger

reaper /'ripər/ n segador (-ra); (machine) segadora mecánica, f

reaping /'ripiŋ/ n siega, f; Fig. cosecha, f. **r.-machine,** segadora mecánica, f

reappear /ˌriə'piər/ vi reaparecer

reappearance /ˌriə'piərəns/ n reaparición, f

reapplication /ˌriæplɪ'keiʃən/ n nueva aplicación, f; (of paint, etc.) otra capa, f; (for a post, etc.) nueva solicitud, f

reapply /ˌriə'plai/ vt aplicar de nuevo; (paint, etc.) dar otra capa (de); (for a post, etc.) mandar una nueva solicitud

reappoint /ˌriə'point/ vt designar de nuevo

rear /riər/ vt (lift) alzar, levantar; (breed, educate) criar; (build) erigir, construir. —vi (of horses) encabritarse, corcovear

rear /riər/ n cola, f; parte de atrás, f; parte posterior, f; última fila, f; (background) fondo, m; Inf. trasera, f; Mil. retaguardia, f. —a de atrás; trasero; último; posterior; de última fila; Mil. de retaguardia. **in the r.,** por detrás; a la cola; en retaguardia. **to bring up the r.,** cerrar la marcha. **r.-admiral,** contra almirante, m. **r.-axle,** eje trasero, m. **r.-guard,** retaguardia, f. **r. lamp,** faro trasero, m. **r. rank,** última fila, f. **r. view,** vista por detrás, f; vista posterior, f

rearm /ri'arm/ vt rearmar. —vi rearmarse

rearmament /ri'arməmənt/ n rearmamento, m

rearrange /ˌriə'reindʒ/ vt volver a arreglar; arreglar de otra manera; (a literary work) refundir, adaptar

rearrangement /ˌriə'reindʒmənt/ n nuevo arroglo, m; (of a literary work) refundición, adaptación, f

reason /'rizən/ n razón, f. **I have plenty of r. to...** No me faltarían motivos para... —vi and vt razonar. **to r. out of,** disuadir de. **by r. of,** a causa de, con motivo de; en virtud de. **for this r.,** por esto, por esta razón. **out of all r.,** fuera de razón. **to stand to r.,** ser lógico, estar puesto en razón. **with r.,** con razón. **r. of state,** razón de estado, f

reasonable /'rizənəbəl/ a razonable; racional

reasoning /'rizəniŋ/ n razonamiento, m

reassemble /ˌriə'sɛmbəl/ vt reunir otra vez. —vi juntarse de nuevo

reassess /ˌriə'sɛs/ vt tasar de nuevo; repartir de nuevo; (a work of art) hacer una nueva apreciación (de)

reassessment /ˌriə'sɛsmənt/ n nueva tasación, f; nuevo repartimiento, m; (of a work of art) nueva estimación, f

reassume /ˌriə'sum/ vt reasumir

reassure /ˌriə'ʃʊr/ vt asegurar de nuevo; tranquilizar, confortar

reassuring /ˌriə'ʃʊriŋ/ a tranquilizador, consolador

rebate /'ribeit/ n rebaja, f, descuento, m; reducción, f. —vt rebajar, descontar; reducir. **to r. pro rata,** ratear

rebel /n. 'rɛbəl; v. ri'bɛl/ n rebelde, mf, insurrecto (-ta). —vi rebelarse, sublevarse. **r. leader,** cabecilla, m

rebellion /ri'bɛljən/ n rebelión, f

rebellious /ri'bɛljəs/ a rebelde; revoltoso; refractario

rebirth /ri'bɜrθ/ n renacimiento, m

rebound /v. ri'baund; n. 'ri,baund/ a (of books) reencuadernado. —vi rebotar; repercutir; (revive) reavivarse. —n rebote, resalto, m; reacción, f, rechazo, m

rebuff /ri'bʌf/ n repulsa, f, desaire, m; contrariedad, f. —vt rechazar; contrariar

rebuild /ri'bild/ vt reedificar

rebuke /ri'byuk/ n reconvención, reprensión, censura, f, reproche, m, vt reprender, censurar, reprochar

rebukingly /ri'byukiŋli/ adv en tono de censura; con reprensión, con reprobación

rebut /ri'bʌt/ vt refutar

rebuttal /ri'bʌtl/ n refutación, f

recalcitrance /ri'kælsitrəns/ n terquedad, obstinacia, f; rebeldía, f

recalcitrant /ri'kælsitrənt/ a reacio, recalcitrante

recall / v. rɪ'kɔl; n. also 'rikɔl/ vt llamar; hacer volver; (dismiss) destituir; (ambassador, etc.) retirar; (remind or remember) recordar; (revoke) revocar. —n llamada, f; Mil. toque de llamada, m; (of ambassadors, etc.) retirada, f; (dismissal) destitución, f. **beyond r.,** irrevocable; (forgotten) olvidado

recant /rɪ'kænt/ vt retractar, retirar. —vi desdecirse (de), retractarse

recantation /,rikæn'teiʃən/ n recantación, f

recapitulate /,rikə'pɪtʃə,leit/ vt recapitular, resumir

recapture /ri'kæptʃər/ vt volver a prender, hacer prisionero nuevamente; (a place) volver a tomar; (a ship) represar

recast /ri'kæst/ vt (metals, a literary work) refundir; (alter) cambiar; (reckon) volver a calcular

recede /ri'sid/ vi retroceder; alejarse (de), separarse (de); desviarse (de); retirarse; desaparecer; (diminish) disminuir; (of prices) bajar

receding /ri'sidɪŋ/ a que retrocede, etc.

receipt /ri'sit/ n recibo, m; (for money) recibí, m; (recipe) receta, f; pl **receipts,** ingresos, m pl. —vt firmar (or extender) recibo. **on r. of,** al recibir. **to acknowledge the r. of,** acusar recibo de. **r. book,** libro talonario, m

receive /ri'siv/ vt and vi recibir; admitir, aceptar, acoger; (money) percibir, cobrar; (lodge) hospedar, alojar; (contain) contener. **to be well received,** tener buena acogida

receiver /ri'sivər/ n recibidor (-ra); (of stolen goods) receptador (-ra); (in bankruptcies) síndico, m; (for other legal business) receptor, m; (of a telephone) auricular, m; Elec. receptor, m; Radio. radiorreceptor, m. **to hang up (the r.),** colgar (el auricular)

receivership /ri'sivər,ʃip/ n sindicatura, f; receptoría, f

receiving /ri'sivɪŋ/ n recibimiento, m; (of money, etc.) cobranza, f, percibo, m; (of stolen goods) encubrimiento, m. —a que recibe; recipiente; de recepción. **r. set,** aparato de radio, m

recent /'risənt/ a reciente; nuevo. **in r. years,** en estos últimos años

recently /'risəntli/ adv recientemente; (before past participles) recién. **until r.,** hasta hace poco. **r. painted,** recién pintado

receptacle /ri'sɛptəkəl/ n receptáculo, recipiente, m; Bot. receptáculo, m

reception /ri'sɛpʃən/ n recepción, f; recibo, m; (welcome) acogida, f; (of evidence) recepción, f. **r. room,** pieza de recibo, f, gabinete, m

receptive /ri'sɛptɪv/ a receptivo; susceptible

recess /ri'sɛs, 'risɛs/ n (holiday) vacaciones, f pl; (during school hours) hora de recreo, f; (Fig. heart) seno, m, entrañas, f pl; (of the soul, heart) hondón, m; (in a

coastline, etc.) depresión, f; (in a wall) nicho, m; (alcove) alcoba, f. **parliamentary r.,** interregno parlamentario, m

recharge /ri'tʃɑrdʒ/ vt (a gun, etc.) recargar; acusar de nuevo

recipe /'rɛsəpi/ n receta, f

recipient /ri'sɪpiənt/ n recibidor (-ra); el, m, (f, la) que recibe. —a recipiente; receptivo

reciprocal /ri'sɪprəkəl/ a recíproco

reciprocate /ri'sɪprə,keit/ vt reciprocar; Mech. producir movimiento de vaivén. —vi Mech. oscilar, tener movimiento alternativo; corresponder; ser recíproco

reciprocity /,rɛsə'prɒsiti/ n reciprocidad, f

recital /ri'saitl/ n narración, relación, f; enumeración, f; recitación, f; Mus. recital, m

recitation /,rɛsi'teiʃən/ n recitación, f

recitative /,rɛsitə'tiv/ n recitado, m

recite /ri'sait/ vt recitar, repetir; narrar; declamar. —vi decir una recitación

reckless /'rɛklɪs/ a temerario, audaz; precipitado; descuidado (de); indiferente (a); excesivo; imprudente

recklessly /'rɛklɪsli/ adv temerariamente; descuidadamente; imprudentemente

reckon /'rɛkən/ vt calcular, computar; contar; enumerar; (believe) considerar, juzgar; (attribute) atribuir; (think) creer (que). **to r. up,** echar cuentas, calcular. **to r. with,** contar con; tomar en serio

reckoner /'rɛkənər/ n calculador (-ra). **ready r.,** tablas matemáticas, f pl

reckoning /'rɛkənɪŋ/ n cálculo, m, calculación, f; cuenta, f; Fig. retribución, f, castigo, m; Naut. estima, f. **the day of r.,** el día de ajuste de cuentas; el día del juicio final. **to be out in one's r.,** equivocarse en el cálculo; engañarse en el juicio

reclaim /ri'kleim/ vt (land) entarquinar; (reform) reformar; (tame) domesticar; (claim) reclamar; (restore) restaurar

reclamation /,rɛklə'meiʃən/ n (of land) entarquinamiento, m; cultivo, m; (reform) reformación, f; (restoration) restauración, f; (claiming) reclamación, f

recline /ri'klain/ vt apoyar; recostar; reclinar; descansar, reposar. —vi recostarse, reclinarse; estar tumbado; apoyarse; descansar

reclining /ri'klainɪŋ/ n reclinación, f. —a inclinado; acostado; (of statues) yacente

recluse /'rɛklus, ri'klus/ a solitario, n recluso (-sa); solitario (-ia); ermitaño, m, anacoreta, mf

recognition /,rɛkəg'nɪʃən/ n reconocimiento, m

recognizance /ri'kɒgnəzəns, -'kɒnə-/ n reconocimiento, m; Law. obligación, f

recognize /'rɛkəg,naiz/ vt reconocer; confesar

recoil /n. 'ri,kɔil; v. ri'kɔil/ n. reculada, f; (of a gun) culatazo, m; (refusal) rechazo, m; (result) repercusión, f; (repugnance) aversión, repugnancia, f. —vi recular; retroceder; repercutir; sentir repugnancia

recollect /ˌrɛkəˈlɛkt/ vt acordarse de, recordar. **to r. oneself,** reponerse, recobrarse

recollection /ˌrɛkəˈlɛkʃən/ n recuerdo, m, memoria, f

recommence /ˌrikəˈmɛns/ vt and vi empezar de nuevo

recommend /ˌrɛkəˈmɛnd/ vt recomendar; aconsejar; encargar

recommendation /ˌrɛkəmənˈdeiʃən/ n recomendación, f

recommendatory /ˌrɛkəˈmɛndə,tɔri/ a recomendatario

recompense /ˈrɛkəm,pɛns/ n recompensa, f, vt recompensar

reconcilable /ˌrɛkənˈsailəbəl/ a reconciliable; compatible; conciliable

reconcile /ˈrɛkən,sail/ vt reconciliar; (quarrels) componer, ajustar; (opposing theories, etc.) conciliar. **to r. oneself ( ),** aceptar; acostumbrarse (a); resignarse (a)

reconciliation /ˌrɛkən,sɪliˈeiʃən/ n reconciliación, f; (of theories, etc.) conciliación, f

reconciliatory /ˌrɒkənˈsɪliə,tɔrɪ/ a reconciliador

recondite /ˈrɛkən,dait/ a recóndito

reconnaissance /rɪˈkɒnəsəns, -zəns/ n reconocimiento, m; exploración, f. **r. flight,** vuelo de reconocimiento, m. **r. plane,** avión de reconocimiento, m

reconnoiter /ˌrikəˈnɔitər/ vt Mil. reconocer; explorar. —vi Mil. practicar un reconocimiento; correr la campaña

reconnoitering /ˌrikəˈnɔitərɪŋ/ n reconocimiento, m, a de reconocimiento

reconquest /riˈkɒŋkwɛst/ n reconquista, f

reconsider /ˌrikənˈsɪdər/ vt considerar de nuevo, volver a considerar; volver a discutir

reconstitute /riˈkɒnstɪ,tut/ vt reconstituir

reconstruct /ˌrikənˈstrʌkt/ vt reconstruir

reconstruction /ˌrikənˈstrʌkʃən/ n reconstrucción, f

recopy /riˈkɒpi/ vt copiar de nuevo

record /v. rɪˈkɔrd; n. ˈrɛkərd/ vt apuntar; inscribir; (recount) contar, escribir; recordar; registrar; (of thermometers, etc.) marcar, registrar; hacer un disco de gramófono de; (radio, cinema) impresionar. —n relación, f; crónica, f; historia, f; (soldier's) hoja de servicios, f; (past) antecedentes, m pl; documento, m; inscripción, f; (entry) partida, f; testimonio, m; (memory) recuerdo, m; registro, m; (gramophone) disco de gramófono, m; Sports. record, m, plusmarca, f; pl **records,** m pl; (notes) notas, f pl; (facts) datos, m pl; anales, m pl. **keeper of the records,** archivero, m. **off the r.,** confidencialmente. **on r.,** escrito; registrado; inscrito en los anales de la historia. **to break a r.,** supremar precedentes. **r.-holder,** plusmarquista, mf

recorder /rɪˈkɔrdər/ n registrador, m; ar-

chivero, m; Law. juez, m; (historian) historiador, m; Mus. caramillo, m; Mech. contador, indicador, m; (scientific) aparato registrador, m

recording /rɪˈkɔrdɪŋ/ a registrador. **r. apparatus,** (cinema, radio, gramophone) máquina de impresionar, f; (scientific) aparato registrador, m. **r. van,** carro de sonido, m

recount /rɪˈkaunt/ vt contar de nuevo; (tell) referir, narrar, contar

recoup /rɪˈkup/ vt compensar, indemnizar; recobrar, desquitarse de

recourse /ˈrikɔrs/ n recurso, m. **to have r. to,** recurrir, a

recover /rɪˈkʌvər/ vt (regain) recobrar; Fig. reconquistar; (retrieve) rescatar; Law. reivindicar. —vi reponerse; (in health) recobrar la salud, sanar, curarse; Law. ganar un pleito. **to r. consciousness,** volver en sí

recoverable /rɪˈkʌvərəbəl/ a recuperable

recovery /rɪˈkʌvəri/ n (regaining) recobro, m, recuperación, f; (of money) cobranza, f, (retrieval) rescate, m; Fig. reconquista, f; (from illness) mejoría, convalecencia, f; restablecimiento, m; Law. reivindicación, f

recreant /ˈrɛkriənt/ a traidor, falso, desleal. —n apóstata, mf traidor (-ra)

recreate /ˈrɛkri,eit/ vt recrear

recreation /ˌrɛkriˈeiʃən/ n recreación, f; (break in schools) recreo, m. **r. hall,** sala de recreo, f

recreative /ˈrɛkri,eitɪv/ a recreativo

recriminate /rɪˈkrɪmə,neit/ vi recriminar

recrimination /rɪ,krɪməˈneiʃən/ n recriminación, reconvención, f

recriminatory /rɪˈkrɪmənə,tɔri/ a recriminador

recross /riˈkrɔs/ vt volver a cruzar, cruzar de nuevo

recrudesce /ˌrikruˈdɛs/ vi recrudecer

recrudescent /ˌrikruˈdɛsənt/ a recrudescente

recruit /rɪˈkrut/ n recluta, m. —vt reclutar; (restore) reponer

recruiting /rɪˈkrutɪŋ/ n reclutamiento, m. **r. office,** caja de reclutamiento, f

rectal /ˈrɛktl/ a rectal

rectangle /ˈrɛk,tæŋgəl/ n rectángulo, m

rectangular /rɛkˈtæŋgələr/ a rectangular

rectifiable /ˈrɛktə,faiəbəl/ a rectificable

rectification /ˌrɛktəfɪˈkeiʃən/ n rectificación, f

rectify /ˈrɛktə,fai/ vt rectificar

rectilinear /ˌrɛktlˈɪniər/ a rectilíneo

rectitude /ˈrɛktɪ,tud/ n rectitud, f

rector /ˈrɛktər/ n (of a university or school) rector, m; (priest) párroco, m

rectum /ˈrɛktəm/ n recto, m

recumbent /rɪˈkʌmbənt/ a recostado, reclinado; (of a statue) yacente

recuperable /rɪˈkupərəbəl/ a recuperable

recuperate /rɪˈkupə,reit/ vt recuperar, recobrar. —vi restablecerse, reponerse; recuperarse

recuperation /rɪkupəˈreɪʃən/ n recuperación, f

recuperative /rɪˈkupərətɪv/ a recuperativo

recur /rɪˈkɜr/ vi presentarse a la imaginación; volver (sobre); presentarse de nuevo, aparecer otra vez; repetirse; reproducirse

recurrence /rɪˈkɜrəns/ n reaparición, f; repetición, f

recurrent /rɪˈkɜrənt/ a periódico; Med. recurrente

red /rɛd/ a rojo; (of wine) tinto. —n color rojo, m; (in billiards) mingo, m, bola roja, f; Polit. rojo, m. **to catch red-handed,** coger con el hurto en las manos; coger con las manos en la masa, coger en el acto. **to grow red,** enrojecerse, ponerse rojo; volverse rojo. **red-berried,** con bayas rojas. **red cabbage,** lombarda, f. **red cedar,** cedro dulce, m. **red corpuscle,** glóbulo rojo, m. **Red Cross,** Cruz Roja, f. **red currant,** grosella, f. **red currant bush,** grosellero, m. **red-eyed,** con los ojos inyectados. **red fir,** pino silvestre, m. **red flush,** (in the sky) arrebol, m. **red-gold,** bermejo; (of hair, etc.) rojo. **red-haired,** pelirrojo, de pelo rojo. **red-handed,** con las manos ensangrentadas; Fig. en el acto. **red-head** (person) pelirrojo (-ja). **red-heat,** incandescencia, f. **red-hot,** candente, m. **red-lead,** minio, m. **red-letter,** de fiesta; extraordinario. **red-letter day,** día de fiesta, m; día extraordinario, m. **red mullet,** salmonete, m, trilla, f. **red ocher,** almagre, m. **red pepper,** pimiento, m; (cayenne) pimentón, m, Red Sea, mar Rojo, mar Bermejo, m. **red tape,** balduque, m; formulismo, m; burocracia, f. **red wine,** vino tinto, m

redden /ˈrɛdn/ vt rojear, enrojecer; pintar de rojo. —vi enrojecerse, ponerse rojo; volverse rojo

reddish /ˈrɛdɪʃ/ a rojizo

redeem /rɪˈdim/ vt (a mortgage, bonds, etc.) amortizar; (from pawn) desempeñar; (a promise, etc.) cumplir; libertar; redimir; compensar; (a fault) expiar; (reform) reformar; (rescue) rescatar

redeemable /rɪˈdiməbəl/ a redimible; amortizable

redeemer /rɪˈdimər/ n rescatador (-ra); salvador (-ra); Theol. Redentor, m

redeeming /rɪˈdimɪŋ/ a redentor; compensatorio. **r. feature,** compensación, f; rasgo bueno, m. **There is no r. feature in his work,** No hay nada bueno en su obra

redemption /rɪˈdɛmpʃən/ n (of a mortgage, etc.) amortización, f; (from pawn) desempeño, m; (of a promise, etc.) cumplimiento, m; (ransom, and rescue) rescate, m; Theol. redención, f; compensación, f; (of a fault) expiación, f; reformación, f

redemptive /rɪˈdɛmptɪv/ a redentor

redescend /ˌridɪˈsɛnd/ vi bajar de nuevo

rediscovery /ˌridəˈskʌvəri/ n nuevo descubrimiento, m

redistribute /ˌridɪˈstrɪbyut/ vt distribuir de nuevo, volver a distribuir

redistribution /ˌridɪstrəˈbyuʃən/ n nueva distribución, f

redolent /ˈrɛdlənt/ a fragante, oloroso; Fig. evocador (de)

redouble /riˈdʌbəl/ vt redoblar. —vi redoblarse

redoubling /riˈdʌblɪŋ/ n redoblamiento, m

redoubt /rɪˈdaut/ n reducto, m

redoubtable /rɪˈdautəbəl/ a formidable, terrible; valiente

redound /rɪˈdaund/ vi redundar (en)

redress /rɪˈdrɛs/ vt rectificar; reparar; remediar; hacer justicia (a); corregir

reduce /rɪˈdus/ vt reducir; disminuir; (in price) rebajar; abreviar; (exhaust, weaken) agotar; (impoverish) empobrecer; (degrade) degradar. **to r. to the ranks,** Mil. volver a las filas; degradar. **to be in reduced circumstances,** estar en la indigencia

reduction /rɪˈdʌkʃən/ n reducción, f; (in price) rebaja, f

redundance /rɪˈdʌndəns/ n redundancia, f

redundant /rɪˈdʌndənt/ a redundante; superfluo, excesivo

reduplicate /rɪˈduplɪˌkeit/ vt reduplicar

reecho /riˈɛkou/ vt repetir; devolver el son de, hacer reverberar. —vi repercutirse, reverberar

reed /rid/ n Bot. caña, f; (arrow) saeta, f; (pipe) caramillo, m; (in wind-instruments) lengüeta, f; Archit. junquillo, m; (in a loom) peine, m; (pastoral poetry) poesía bucólica, f. —vt (thatch) bardar con cañas

reef /rif/ n arrecife, escollo, encalladero, m; Mineral. filón, m; Naut. rizo, m. —vt Naut. arrizar. **to take in reefs,** Naut. hacer el rizo. **r.-knot,** nudo de marino, m

reek /rik/ n humo, m; olor, m. —vi humear; oler (de); Fig. recordar, hacer pensar (en)

reel /ril/ n carrete, m; devanadera, f; (of a fishing rod) carrete, carretel, m; (cinema) cinta, f; (dance) baile escocés, m. —vt devanar. —vi tambalear, titubear; (of ships, etc.) cabecear; temblar; oscilar. **to r. about drunkenly,** (of persons) andar haciendo eses, arrimarse a las paredes. **to r. off,** recitar; enumerar; decir rápidamente

reelect /ˌriɪˈlɛkt/ vt reelegir

reeling /ˈrilɪŋ/ n tambaleo, m; andar vacilante, m; (of a ship, etc.) cabeceo, m; oscilación, f

reembarcation /ˌriɛmbarˈkeiʃən/ n reembarque, m

reembark /ˌriɛmˈbark/ vt reembarcar. —vi reembarcarse

reemerge /ˌriɪˈmɜrdʒ/ vi reaparecer

reenact /ˌriːˈnækt/ vt revalidar (una ley); decretar de nuevo

reenactment /ˌriːˈnæktmənt/ n revalidación (de una ley), f; nuevo decreto, m

reengage /ˌriːnˈgeidʒ/ vt contratar de nuevo

reenlist /ˌriːnˈlɪst/ vt and vi alistar(se) de nuevo

reenlistment /ˌriːnˈlɪstmənt/ n reenganche, m

reenter /riˈentər/ vt volver a entrar (en); reingresar (en)

reentry /riˈentri/ n segunda entrada, f, reingreso, m

reequip /ˌriːˈkwɪp/ vt equipar de nuevo

reestablish /ˌriːˈstæblɪʃ/ vt restablecer; restaurar

reestablishment /ˌriːˈstæblɪʃmənt/ n restablecimiento, m; restauración, f

reexamination /ˌriːgˌzæmɪˈneiʃən/ n reexaminación, f; nuevo examen, m; Law. nuevo interrogatorio, m

reexamine /ˌriːgˈzæmɪn/ vt reexaminar; Law. interrogar de nuevo

reexport /ˌriːkˈspɔrt/ vt reexportar

reexportation /ˌriːkspɔrˈteiʃən/ n reexportación, f

refashion /riˈfæʃən/ vt volver a hacer; formar de nuevo

refectory /riˈfektəri/ n refectorio, m

refer /riˈfɜr/ vt atribuir (a); (send) enviar, remitir; (assign) referir (a), relacionar (con). —vi referirse (a); aludir (a); hablar (de)

referee /ˌrefəˈri/ n árbitro, m; Law. juez arbitrador, m; (reference) garante, mf fiador (-ra). —vi servir de árbitro

reference /ˈrefərəns/ n referencia, f; consulta, f; mención, f; alusión, f; (relation) relación, f; pl **references**, Com. referencias, f pl. **for r.**, para consulta. **in r. to**, con referencia a, respecto a, en cuanto a. **terms of r.**, puntos de consulta, m pl. **work of r.**, libro de consulta, m

reference book n libro de consulta, m

referendum /ˌrefəˈrendəm/ n referéndum, m

refill /v. riˈfɪl; n. ˈriˌfɪl/ vt rellenar; rehenchir; (pen) llenar de nuevo con tinta. —n (for a pencil) mina de recambio, f

refine /riˈfain/ vt refinar; (metals) acrisolar; (fats) clarificar; Fig. perfeccionar, pulir, refinar

refined /riˈfaind/ a refinado; fino; culto; cortés; elegante; delicado; (subtle) sutil; (affected) afectado

refinement /riˈfainmənt/ n refinamiento, m; finura, f; cultura, f; cortesía, f; elegancia, f; delicadeza, f; (subtlety) sutileza, f; (affectation) afectación, f

refinery /riˈfainəri/ n refinería, f

refit /riˈfɪt/ vt reparar; Naut. embonar

refitting /riˈfɪtɪŋ/ n reparación, f; Naut. embonada, f

reflect /riˈflekt/ vt reflejar; reflexionar. —vi reflejar; reflexionar (sobre), pensar (en), meditar (sobre). **This offer reflects**

credit on him, Esta oferta le hace honor. **to r. on, upon**, reflexionar sobre; (disparage) desacreditar; (affect unfavorably) perjudicar

reflection /riˈflekʃən/ n Phys. reflexión, f; reflejo, m; consideración, f, pensamiento, m; (aspersion) censura, f, reproche, m. **upon mature r.**, después de pensarlo bien

reflective /riˈflektɪv/ a Phys. reflector; reflexivo, pensativo, meditabundo

reflex /ˈriːfleks/ a reflejo. —n reflejo, m; acción refleja, f. **r. action**, acción refleja, f

refloat /riˈflout/ vt (a ship) poner otra vex a flote, desvarar

reflux /ˈriːˌflʌks/ n reflujo, m

reform /riˈfɔrm/ n reforma, f. —a de reforma; reformista. —vt reformar; formar de nuevo. —vi reformarse

reformation /ˌrefərˈmeiʃən/ n reformación, f; **Reformation**, Reforma, f

reformatory /riˈfɔrməˌtɔri/ a reformatorio, reformador. —n reformatorio, m, casa de corrección, f

reformer /riˈfɔrmər/ n reformador (-ra), reformista, mf

refract /riˈfrækt/ vt refractar

refractive /riˈfræktɪv/ a refringente

refractoriness /riˈfræktərinəs/ n terquedad, obstinacia, f; rebeldía, indocilidad, f

refractory /riˈfræktəri/ a (of substances) refractario; recalcitrante, intratable, rebelde

refrain /riˈfrein/ n estribillo, estrambote, m

refrain /riˈfrein/ vi abstenerse (de), evitar

refresh /riˈfreʃ/ vt refrescar

refreshing /riˈfreʃɪŋ/ a refrescante; atractivo; estimulante; interesante

refreshment /riˈfreʃmənt/ n (solace) solaz, reposo, m; recreación, f, deleite, m; (food and (or) drink) refresco, m. **r.-room**, (at a station) fonda, f

refrigerate /riˈfrɪdʒəˌreit/ vt refrigerar; enfriar; refrescar

refrigeration /riˌfrɪdʒəˈreiʃən/ n refrigeración, f; enfriamiento, m. **r. chamber**, cámara frigorífica, f

refrigerator /riˈfrɪdʒəˌreitər/ n refrigerador, m, nevera, f

refuel /riˈfyuəl/ vt (a furnace) cargar con carbón, etc.; (of a ship) tomar carbón; (of an airplane, motor vehicle) tomar bencina

refuge /ˈrefyudʒ/ n refugio, m; asilo, m; (resort) recurso, m; subterfugio, m; (traffic island) refugio para peatones, m. **to take r.**, refugiarse; resguardarse (de)

refugee /ˌrefyuˈdʒi/ a refugiado. —n refugiado (-da)

refulgent /riˈfʌldʒənt/ a refulgente

refund /riˈfʌnd/ vt reembolsar; devolver

refunding /riˈfʌndɪŋ/ n reembolso, m; devolución, f

refurbish /riˈfɜrbɪʃ/ vt restaurar; renovar; (a literary work) refundir

refurnish /ri'fɛrnɪʃ/ *vt* amueblar de nuevo

refusal /rɪ'fyuzəl/ *n* negativa, *f*; (rejection) rechazo, *m*; (option) opción, *f*; preferencia, *f*

refuse /rɪ'fyuz/ *vt* negar; (reject) rechazar. —*vi* negarse (a), rehusar; (of a horse) resistirse a saltar

refuse /'refyus/ *n* desecho, *m*; desperdicios, *m pl*; residuo, *m*; basura, *f*. —*a* de desecho. **r. dump,** muladar, *m*

refute /rɪ'fyut/ *vt* refutar

regain /ri'gein/ *vt* recobrar, recuperar; cobrar; ganar de nuevo, *Fig.* reconquistar. **to r. one's breath,** cobrar aliento. **to r. consciousness,** volver en sí

regal /'rigəl/ *a* regio, real

regale /rɪ'geil/ *vt* regalar, agasajar; recrear, deleitar

regard /rɪ'gɑrd/ *vt* mirar; observar; considerar; (respect) respetar; (concern) importar, concernir; relacionarse con. —*n* mirada, *f*; atención, *f*; (esteem) aprecio, *m*, estimación, *f*; respeto, *m*; veneración, *f*; (relation) referencia, *f*; *pl* **regards,** recuerdos, saludos, *m pl*. **He has little r. for their feelings,** Le importan poco sus susceptibilidades. **With kindest regards,** Con mis saludos más afectuosos. **as regards, with r. to,** con referencia a, respecto a, en cuanto a

regardful /rɪ'gɑrdfəl/ *a* atento (a), cuidadoso (de); que se preocupa (de)

regarding /rɪ'gɑrdɪŋ/ *prep* tocante a, en cuanto a, respecto de

regardless /rɪ'gɑrdlɪs/ *a* negligente (de); indiferente (a), insensible (a); que no se interesa (en); que no se inquieta (por); sin preocuparse (de)

regatta /rɪ'gætə, -'gɑtə/ *n* regata, *f*

regenerate /rɪ'dʒɛnə,reit/ *vt* regenerar. —*a* regenerado

regenerative /rɪ'dʒɛnərətɪv/ *a* regenerador

regent /'ridʒənt/ *n* regente, *mf*

régime /rei'ʒim/ *n* régimen, *m*

regimen /'rɛdʒəmən/ *n* (*Gram. Med.*) régimen, *m*,

regiment /*n.* 'rɛdʒəmənt; *v.* -,mɛnt/ *n* regimiento, *m*. —*vt* regimentar. **r. of the line,** tropa de línea, *f*

regimentation /,rɛdʒəmən'teiʃən/ *n* regimentación, *f*

region /'ridʒən/ *n* región, *f*

regional /'ridʒənl/ *a* regional

regionalist /'ridʒənlɪst/ *n* regionalista, *mf*

register /'rɛdʒəstər/ *n* (record and *Mech. Mus. Print.*) registro, *m*; (of ships, etc.) matrícula, *f*; lista, *f*. —*vt* registrar; matricular; (a ship) abanderar; inscribir; (one's child in a school) anotar (Argentina), inscribir; (of thermometers, etc.) marcar; (letters) certificar; (luggage) facturar; (in one's mind) grabar; (emotion) mostrar, manifestar. —*vi* (at a hotel, etc.) registrarse; *Print.* estar en registro. **cash r., caja registradora,** *f*. **r. of births, marriages and deaths,** registro civil, *m*

registered letter /'rɛdʒəstərd/ *n* carta certificada, *f*

registrar /'rɛdʒə,strɑr/ *n* registrador, *m*; archivero, *m*; secretario, *m*; (of a school) jefe de inscripciones, secretario general (the latter has many more duties). **r. of births, marriages and deaths,** secretario del registro civil, *m*. **registrar's office,** oficina del registro civil, *f*

registration /,rɛdʒə'streiʃən/ *n* registro, *m*; inscripción, *f*; (of a vehicle, etc.) matrícula, *f*; *Naut.* abanderamiento, *m*; (of a letter, etc.) certificación, *f*. **r. number,** número de matrícula, *m*

registry /'rɛdʒəstri/ *n* registro, *m*; inscripción, *f*; matrícula, *f*. **r. office,** oficina del registro civil, *f*; (for servants) agencia doméstica, *f*

regression /rɪ'grɛʃən/ *n* regresión, *f*, retroceso, *m*

regret /rɪ'grɛt/ *vt* sentir; lamentar, pesar; arrepentirse (de); (miss) echar de menos (a). —*n* sentimiento, pesar, *m*; (remorse) remordimiento, *m*. **I r. very much that...,** Me pesa mucho que..., Siento mucho que... **to send one's regrets,** mandar sus excusas

regretful /rɪ'grɛtfəl/ *a* lleno de pesar; arrepentido; lamentable, deplorable. **He was most r. that...,** Lamentaba mucho que...

regretfully /rɪ'grɛtfəli/ *adv* con pesar

regrettable /rɪ'grɛtəbəl/ *a* lamentable, deplorable; doloroso; (with loss, etc.) sensible

regrettably /rɪ'grɛtəbli/ *adv* lamentablemente; sensiblemente

regroup /ri'grup/ *vt* arreglar de nuevo; formar de nuevo; reorganizar

regular /'rɛgyələr/ *a* regular; normal; (ordinary) corriente, común; (in order) en regla; (*Gram. Bot. Eccl. Mil. Geom.*) regular. —*n Eccl.* regular, *m*; (soldier) soldado de línea, *m*; (officer) militar de carrera, *m*; (client) parroquiano habitual, *m*

regularize /'rɛgyələ,raiz/ *vt* regularizar

regulate /'rɛgyə,leit/ *vt* regular; ajustar, arreglar; (direct) dirigir; reglamentar

regulation /,rɛgyə'leiʃən/ *n* regulación, *f*; arreglo, *m*; (rule) reglamento, *m*, *a* de reglamento; normal

regulative /'rɛgyə,leitɪv/ *a* regulador

regurgitate /rɪ'gɜrdʒɪ,teit/ *vt and vi* regurgitar

rehabilitate /,rihə'bɪlɪ,teit/ *vt* rehabilitar

rehash /ri'hæʃ/ *vt* (a literary work, etc.) refundir

rehearing /ri'hɪərɪŋ/ *n* nueva audición, *f*, (of a case) revisión, *f*

rehearsal /rɪ'hɜrsəl/ *n Theat.* ensayo, *m*; recitación, *f*; relación, narración, *f*. **dress r.,** ensayo general, *m*

rehearse /rɪ'hɜrs/ *vt Theat.* ensayar; recitar; (narrate) narrar; enumerar

reheat /ri'hit/ *vt* recalentar

reign /rein/ n reinado, m. —vi reinar; predominar

reigning /'reiniŋ/ a reinante; predominante

reimburse /,riim'bɜrs/ vt reembolsar

reimbursement /,riim'bɜrsmənt/ n reembolso, m

reimport /ri'impɔrt/ vt importar de nuevo, reimportar, n reimporte, m

reimpose /,riim'pouz/ vt reimponer

reimprison /,riim'prizən/ vt encarcelar de nuevo, reencarcelar

rein /rein/ n rienda, f. —vt llevar las riendas (de); (hold back) refrenar. **to give r. to,** Fig. dar rienda suelta (a)

reincarnation /,riinkɑr'neiʃən/ n reencarnación, f

reincorporate /,riin'kɔrpə,reit/ vt reincorporar

reindeer /'rein,diər/ n reno, m

reinforce /,riin'fɔrs/ vt reforzar; (concrete) armar; fortalecer. **reinforced concrete,** n hormigón armado, m

reinforcement /,riin'fɔrsmənt/ n reforzamiento, m; (Mil. Nav. Fig.) refuerzo, m

reinsert /,riin'sɜrt/ vt volver a insertar

reinstall /,riin'stɔl/ vt reinstalar; rehabilitar

reinstate /,riin'steit/ vt reponer, restablecer, reinstalar; rehabilitar

reinstatement /,riin'steitmənt/ n restablecimiento, m; rehabilitación, f

reinsurance /,riinʃurəns/ n reaseguro, m

reinsure /,riin'ʃur, -'ʃɜr/ vt reasegurar

reintegrate /ri'intə,greit/ vt reintegrar

reintegration /,riintə'greiʃən/ n reintegración, f

reinter /,riin'tɜr/ vt enterrar de nuevo

reinvest /,riin'vest/ vt reinvertir

reinvestment /,riin'vestmənt/ n reinversión, f

reinvigorate /,riin'vigə,reit/ vt reanimar, dar nuevo vigor (a)

reinvite /,riin'vait/ vt invitar de nuevo (a)

reissue /ri'iʃu/ n nueva emisión, f; (of a book, etc.) nueva edición, reimpresión, f. —vt hacer una nueva emisión (de); reeditar, publicar de nuevo

reiterate /ri'itə,reit/ vt reiterar, repetir

reject /v. ri'dʒekt/ vt rechazar, rehusar; repudiar; repulsar; desechar

rejection /ri'dʒekʃən/ n rechazamiento, m; repudiación, refutación, f; repulsa, f

rejoice /ri'dʒɔis/ vt alegrar, regocijar. —vi alegrarse (de), regocijarse (de), gloriarse (en)

rejoicing /ri'dʒɔisiŋ/ n regocijo, júbilo, m, alegría, f; algazara, f, fiestas, f pl

rejoin /ri'dʒɔin/ vt and vi juntar de nuevo; volver a; reunirse con; (reply) contestar, replicar

rejoinder /ri'dʒɔindər/ n contestación, respuesta, f

rejuvenate /ri'dʒuvə,neit/ vt rejuvenecer

rekindle /ri'kindl/ vt encender de nuevo;

despertar, reavivar. —vi encenderse de nuevo; reavivarse

relapse /ri'læps; n. also 'rilæps/ n reincidencia, recaída, f; Med. recidiva, f. —vi reincidir (en); Med. recaer

relapsed /ri'læpst/ a relapso

relate /ri'leit/ vt (recount) relatar, narrar; relacionar; unir; (of kinship) emparentar. —vi ajustarse (a); referirse (a). **The first fact is not related to the second,** El primer hecho no tiene nada que ver con el segundo

related /ri'leitid/ a relacionado; (by kinship) emparentado. **John is well-r.,** Juan es de buena familia; Juan es de familia influyente; Juan tiene buenas relaciones

relation /ri'leiʃən/ n (narrative) relación, narración, f; conexión, f; relación, f; (kinship) parentesco, m; (person) pariente (-ta). **in r. to,** con relación a, en cuanto a

relationship /ri'leiʃən,ʃip/ n parentesco, m; conexión, relación, f

relative /'relətiv/ a relativo. —n pariente (-ta), pl **relatives,** parientes, m pl, parentela, f

relax /ri'læks/ vt relajar; aflojar; soltar; (make less severe) ablandar; (decrease) mitigar. —vi relajarse; aflojar; (rest) descansar

relaxation /,rilæk'seiʃən/ n relajación, f; aflojamiento, m; ablandamiento, m; mitigación, f; (rest) descanso, reposo, m; (pastime) pasatiempo, m; (amusement) diversión, f

relaxing /ri'læksiŋ/ a relajante; (of climate) enervante

relay /'rilei; v. ri'lei/ n (of horses) parada, f; (shift) tanda, f; relevo, m; Elec. relais, m; Radio. redifusión, f. —vt enviar por posta; Elec. reemitir; Radio. retransmitir; (lay again) colocar de nuevo. **r. race,** carrera de equipo, carrera de relevos, f

release /ri'lis/ vt soltar; (hurl) lanzar; (set free) poner en libertad (a); librar (de); absolver; (surrender) renunciar (a); dar al público, poner en circulación; (lease again) realquilar. —n soltura, f; lanzamiento, m; liberación, f; (from pain) alivio, m; remisión, f; exoneración, f; publicación, f; (of films) representación, f; Law. soltura, f

relegate /'reli,geit/ vt relegar

relent /ri'lent/ vi ablandarse, enternecerse; ceder

relenting /ri'lentiŋ/ n enternecimiento, desenojo, m

relentless /ri'lentlis/ a implacable, inexorable; despiadado

relentlessly /ri'lentlisli/ adv inexorablemente; sin piedad

relet /ri'let/ vt realquilar

relevance /'reləvəns/ n conexión, f; pertinencia, f; aplicabilidad, f

relevant /'reləvənt/ a relativo; pertinente, a propósito, oportuno; aplicable

reliability /ri,laiə'biliti/ n seguridad, f;

formalidad, f; confianza, f; exactitud, f;
veracidad, f

reliable /rɪˈlaɪəbəl/ a seguro; formal;
digno de crédito, de confianza, solvente
digno de confianza; exacto; veraz

reliably /rɪˈlaɪəbli/ adv seguramente; de
una manera digna de confianza; exactamente

reliance /rɪˈlaɪəns/ n confianza, f. **to
place r. on,** tener confianza en

reliant /rɪˈlaɪənt/ a confiado

relic /ˈrelɪk/ n vestigio, rastro, m; Eccl. reliquia, f

relief /rɪˈlif/ n (alleviation) alivio, m;
desahogo, m; (help) socorro, m, ayuda, f;
beneficencia, f; Mil. relevo, m; (pleasure)
placer, m, satisfacción, f; (consolation)
consuelo, m; Law. remisión, f; Art. relieve, m. **high r.,** alto relieve, m. **low r.,**
bajo relieve, m. **r. map,** mapa en relieve,
m. **r. train,** tren de socorro, m

relieve /rɪˈliv/ vt aliviar; aligerar, suavizar; mitigar; (one's feelings, etc.) desahogar; (Mil. and to take the place of) relevar; (free) librar; (dismiss) destituir;
(remove) quitar; (rob) robar; (help) socorrer, remediar; (redeem) redimir; (ornament) adornar; (from a wrong) hacer justicia (a)

relieving /rɪˈlivɪŋ/ n alivio, m; aligeramiento, m; mitigación, f; (of the feelings)
desahogo, m; Mil. relevo, m; (help) socorro, m. **r. arch,** sobrearco, m

relight /riˈlaɪt/ vt volver a encender. —vi
encenderse de nuevo

religion /rɪˈlɪdʒən/ n religión, f

religiosity /rɪˌlɪdʒɪˈɒsɪti/ n religiosidad, f

religious /rɪˈlɪdʒəs/ a religioso; en religión; piadoso, creyente; devoto. —n
religioso (-sa). **r. orders,** órdenes religio-
sas, f pl. **r. toleration,** libertad de cultos,
f

relinquish /rɪˈlɪŋkwɪʃ/ vt abandonar;
(one's grip) soltar; renunciar; desistir
(de), dejar (de); (a post) dimitir (de)

relinquishment /rɪˈlɪŋkwɪʃmənt/ n
abandono, m; renuncia, f; dejamiento, m;
(of a post) dimisión, f

relish /ˈrelɪʃ/ n gusto, m; sabor, m;
(touch, smack) dejo, m; condimento, m;
apetito, m, gana, f. —vt gustar de; comer
con apetito; saborear, paladear; Fig. seducir, atraer, gustar. —vi tener gusto (de). **I
do not much r. the idea,** No me seduce
la idea

relishing /ˈrelɪʃɪŋ/ n saboreo, m; (enjoyment) goce, m, fruición, f; consideración,
f

relive /riˈlɪv/ vt vivir de nuevo, volver a
vivir

reload / riˈloud/ vt recargar

reluctance /rɪˈlʌktəns/ n repugnancia,
desgana, f. **with r.,** a regañadientes, de
mala gana

reluctant /rɪˈlʌktənt/ a poco dispuesto
(a), que tiene repugnancia a (hacer algo),
sin gana; (forced) forzado; artificial; (hesitating) vacilante

reluctantly /rɪˈlʌktəntli/ adv de mala
gana, con repugnancia, a disgusto

rely on /rɪˈlaɪ/ vi contar con, confiar en,
depender de

remain /rɪˈmein/ vi quedar; permanecer;
(be left over) sobrar; continuar. **I r. yours
faithfully...,** (in a letter) Queda de Vd. su
att. s.s.... **It remains to be written,**
Queda por escribir

remainder /rɪˈmeindər/ n resto, m; restos, m pl, sobras, f pl; residuo, m. **The r.
of the people went away,** Los demás se
marcharon

remaining /rɪˈmeinɪŋ/ pres part and a
que queda; sobrante

remains /rɪˈmeinz/ n pl restos, m pl; sobras, f pl, desperdicios, m pl; ruinas, f pl

remake /vi riˈmeik/ vt rehacer; reformar

remand /rɪˈmænd/ vt Law. reencarcelar.
—n Law. reencarcelamiento, m

remark /rɪˈmɑrk/ n observación, f; nota,
f; comentario, m. —vt and vi observar;
notar. **to r. on,** comentar, hacer una observación sobre

remarkable /rɪˈmɑrkəbəl/ a notable, singular, extraordinario

remarriage /ˈriˌmærɪdʒ/ n segundas nupcias, f pl, segundo casamiento, m

remarry /ˈriˈmæri/ vt volver a casar (a).
—vi casarse en segundas nupcias; volver
a casarse

remedial /rɪˈmidiəl/ a remediador; curativo, terapéutico

remedy /ˈremɪdi/ n remedio, m; recurso,
m, vt remediar; curar

remember /rɪˈmembər/ vt recordar; tener
presente; acordarse de. —vi acordarse; no
olvidarse. **R. me to your mother,** Dale
recuerdos míos a tu madre. **If I r.
rightly...,** Si bien me acuerdo... **And r.
that I shall do no more!** ¡Y no olvides
que no haré más!

remembrance /rɪˈmembrəns/ n recuerdo, m; memoria, f; pl
remembrances, recuerdos, m pl

remind /rɪˈmaind/ vt recordar

reminder /rɪˈmaindər/ n recuerdo, m;
(warning) advertencia, f. **a gentle r.,** una
indirecta, una insinuación

reminisce /ˌremɪˈnɪs/ vi Inf. recordar viejas historias

reminiscence /ˌreməˈnɪsəns/ n reminiscencia, f, recuerdo, m

reminiscent /ˌreməˈnɪsənt/ a evocador,
que recuerda; de reminiscencia; que
piensa en el pasado. **to be r. of,** recordar; Inf. oler a

remiss /rɪˈmɪs/ a negligente, descuidado

remission /rɪˈmɪʃən/ n remisión, f

remit /rɪˈmɪt/ vt remitir; Com. remesar,
enviar. —vi (pay) pagar

remittance /rɪˈmɪtns/ n remesa, f; envío,
m

remitter /rɪˈmɪtər/ n remitente, mf

remnant /ˈremnənt/ n resto, m; (of fabric) retal, retazo, m; (relic) vestigio, m,
reliquia, f. **r. sale,** saldo, m

remodel /rɪ'mɒdl/ vt rehacer; reformar; modelar de nuevo; (a play, etc.) refundir

remodeling /rɪ'mɒdlɪŋ/ n reformación, f; (of a play, etc.) refundición, f

remonstrance /rɪ'mɒnstrəns/ n protesta, f; reconvención, f

remonstrate /rɪ'mɒnstreit/ vi protestar, objetar. **to r. with,** reprochar, reconvenir

remorse /rɪ'mɔrs/ n remordimiento, m

remorseful /rɪ'mɔrsfəl/ a lleno de remordimientos; penitente, arrepentido

remorsefully /rɪ'mɔrsfəli/ adv con remordimiento

remorseless /rɪ'mɔrslɪs/ a sin conciencia, sin remordimientos; despiadado, inflexible

remote /rɪ'mout/ a distante, lejano; remoto; aislado; ajeno; (slight) leve, vago. **r. control,** mando a distancia, m

remoteness /rɪ'moutnɪs/ n distancia, f; aislamiento, m; alejamiento, m; (vagueness) vaguedad, f

remount /v. ri'maunt/ n. 'ri,maunt/ vt subir de nuevo, montar de nuevo; Mil. remontar. —vi (go back to) remontar (a), derivarse (de). —n Mil. remonta, f

removable /rɪ'muvəbəl/ a que puede quitarse; (of collars, etc.) de quita y pon; transportable; (of officials, etc.) amovible

removal /rɪ'muvəl/ n acción de quitar o levantar, f; sacamiento, m; separación, f; eliminación, f; alejamiento, m; traslado, m; (from office, etc.) deposición, f; supresión, f; asesinato, m. **r. van,** carro de mudanzas, m

remove /rɪ'muv/ vt quitar; retirar; levantar; sacar; apartar; separar; eliminar; trasladar; (from office) destituir; suprimir; asesinar. —vi trasladarse. —n grado, m; distancia, f; (departure) partida, f. **to r. oneself,** quitarse de en medio. **to r. one's hat,** descubrirse. **first cousin once removed,** hijo de primo carnal, primo hermano del padre, primo hermano de la madre, m

remunerate /rɪ'myunə,reit/ vt remunerar

remuneration /rɪ,myunə'reiʃən/ n remuneración, f

remunerative /rɪ'myunərətɪv/ a remunerador

renaissance /'rɛnə,sans/ n renacimiento, m, a renacentista

renal /'rinl/ a renal

rename /ri'neim/ vt poner otro nombre (a)

renascent /rɪ'næsənt, -'neisənt/ a renaciente, que renace

rend /rɛnd/ vt desgarrar, rasgar; Fig. lacerar; (split) hender; Fig. dividir. **to r. from,** arrancar (a). **to r. the air,** (with cries, etc.) llenar el aire

render /'rɛndər/ vt (return) devolver; dar; rendir; (make) hacer; (help, service) prestar; interpretar; (translate) traducir; (fat) derretir y clarificar

rendering /'rɛndərɪŋ/ n versión, f; interpretación, f

rendezvous /'rɒndə,vu, -dei-/ n cita, f; lugar de cita, m; reunión, f. —vi reunirse

renegade /'rɛnɪ,geid/ a renegado. —n renegado (-da)

renew /rɪ'nu/ vt renovar; (resume) reanudar; (a lease, etc.) prorrogar

renewal /rɪ'nuəl/ n renovación, f; (resumption) reanudación, f; (of a lease, etc.) prorrogación, f

renewed /rɪ'nud/ a renovado; nuevo

rennet /'rɛnɪt/ n cuajo, m

renounce /rɪ'nauns/ vt renunciar; (a throne) abdicar; renegar (de), repudiar; abandonar. —vi Law. desistir; (cards) renunciar

renouncement /rɪ'naunsmənt/ n renuncia, f; (of a throne) abdicación, f; repudiación, f

renovate /'rɛnə,veit/ vt renovar; limpiar; restaurar

renovation /,rɛnə'veiʃən/ n renovación, f; limpiadura, f; restauración, f

renovator /'rɛnə,veitər/ n renovador (-ra)

renown /rɪ'naun/ n renombre, m, fama, f

renowned /rɪ'naund/ a renombrado, famoso

rent /rɛnt/ n (tear) rasgadura, f; desgarro, m; abertura, f; raja hendedura, f; (discord) división, f; (hire) alquiler, m; arrendamiento, m. —vt arrendar, alquilar. **r.- free,** sin pagar alquiler

rentable /'rɛntəbəl/ a alquilable, arrendable

renter /'rɛntər/ n arrendador (-ra)

renunciation /rɪ,nʌnsi'eiʃən/ n renunciación, renuncia, f

reoccupy /ri'ɒkyu,pai/ vt volver a ocupar, ocupar otra vez

reopen /ri'oupən/ vt abrir de nuevo, volver a abrir. —vi abrirse nuevamente, abrirse otra vez

reopening /ri'oupənɪŋ/ n reapertura, f

reorder /ri'ɔrdər/ vt ordenar de nuevo, Com. volver a pedir. —n Com. nuevo pedido, m

reorganize /ri'ɔrgə,naiz/ vt reorganizar

reorganizing /ri'ɔrgə,naizɪŋ/ a reorganizador

repack /ri'pæk/ vt reembalar; reenvasar; volver a hacer (una maleta)

repaint /ri'peint/ vt pintar de nuevo

repair /rɪ'pɛər/ vt arreglar (e.g. a machine) componer, remendar; reparar; restaurar; rehacer. —vi (with to) dirigirse a, ir a; acudir a. —n arreglo m, reparación, f; compostura, f; restauración, f. **to keep in r.,** conservar en buen estado

repairer /rɪ'pɛərər/ n componedor (-ra); restaurador (-ra)

repairing /rɪ'pɛərɪŋ/ a reparador

repartee /,rɛpər'ti, -'tei, -ɑr-/ n respuestas, agudezas, f pl; Inf. dimes y diretes, m pl

repast /rɪ'pæst/ n comida, f; (light) colación, f

repatriate /v. ri'peitri,eit/ vt repatriar

repay /rɪ'peɪ/ vt reembolsar; recompensar, pagar; pagar en la misma moneda. —vi pagar. It well repays a visit, Vale la pena de visitarse

repayable /rɪ'peɪəbəl/ a reembolsable

repayment /rɪ'peɪmənt/ n reembolso, m; pago, retorno, m

repeal /rɪ'pil/ n abrogación, revocación, f, vt abrogar, rescindir, revocar

repeat /rɪ'pit/ vt repetir; reiterar; (renew) renovar; duplicar. —n repetición, f

repeated /rɪ'pitɪd/ a reiterado; redoblado

repeater /rɪ'pitər/ n repetidor (-ra); reloj de repetición, m; arma de repetición, f

repel /rɪ'pɛl/ vt repeler; ahuyentar; (spurn) rechazar; Phys. resistir; repugnar

repellent /rɪ'pɛlənt/ a repulsivo

repent /rɪ'pɛnt/ vt arrepentirse de. —vi arrepentirse

repentance /rɪ'pɛntṇs/ n arrepentimiento, m, penitencia, f

repentant /rɪ'pɛntṇt/ a arrepentido, penitente, contrito

repeople /ri'pipəl/ vt repoblar

repercussion /,ripər'kʌʃən/ n repercusión, f

repertory /'rɛpər,tɔri/ n repertorio, m

repetition /,rɛpɪ'tɪʃən/ n repetición, f; recitación, f

repetitive /rɪ'pɛtɪtɪv/ a iterativo

repine /rɪ'paɪn/ vi afligirse (de); quejarse (de); padecer nostalgia

repining /rɪ'paɪnɪŋ/ n pesares, m pl; quejas, f pl, descontento, m; nostalgia, f

replace /rɪ'pleɪs/ vt (put back) reponer, colocar de nuevo; restituir, devolver; (renew) renovar; (in a post, etc.) reemplazar, substituir

replaceable /rɪ'pleɪsəbəl/ a restituible; renovable; reemplazable

replacement /rɪ'pleɪsmənt/ n reposición, f; restitución, devolución, f; renovación, f; reemplazo, m

replant /ri'plænt/ vt replantar

replenish /rɪ'plɛnɪʃ/ vt rellenar

replete /rɪ'plit/ a repleto

replica /'rɛplɪkə/ n réplica, f

reply /rɪ'plaɪ/ n respuesta, contestación, f, vi responder, contestar. Awaiting your r., En espera de sus noticias. in his r., en su respuesta

repopulate /ri'pɒpyə,leɪt/ vt repoblar

repopulation /ri,pɒpyə'leɪʃən/ n repoblación, f

report /rɪ'pɔrt/ n (rumor) voz, f, rumor, m; (reputation) fama, f; (news) noticia, f; (journalistic) reportaje, m; (Mil. Nav. and from school) parte, f; (weather) boletín, m; (proceedings) actas, f pl; (statement) informe, m; relación, f; (of a gun, etc.) detonación, f; explosión, f. —vt dar cuenta de, relatar; informar; (measure) registrar; (Mil. Nav.) dar parte de; comunicar; (journalistic) hacer un reportaje de; (transcribe) transcribir; (accuse) denunciar; quejarse de. —vi presentar informe; ser reportero; (present oneself)

presentarse, comparecer. It is reported that..., Se informa que...

report card n boletín de calificaciones, m

reporter /rɪ'pɔrtər/ n reportero (-ra); Law. relator, m

reporting /rɪ'pɔrtɪŋ/ n reporterismo, m

repose /rɪ'pouz/ n reposo, m; quietud, f; tranquilidad, serenidad, f. —vt reposar, descansar; reclinar; (place) poner. —vi reposar; tener confianza (en); basarse (en)

repository /rɪ'pɒzɪ,tɔri/ n repositorio, depósito, m; almacén, m; (furniture) guardamuebles, m; (person) depositario (-ia)

reprehend /,rɛprɪ'hɛnd/ vt reprender, reprobar

reprehensible /,rɛprɪ'hɛnsəbəl/ a reprensible

represent /,rɛprɪ'zɛnt/ vt representar; significar

representation /,rɛprɪzɛn'teɪʃən/ n representación, f

representative /,rɛprɪ'zɛntətɪv/ a que representa; representativo. —n representante, mf

repress /rɪ'prɛs/ vt reprimir

repression /rɪ'prɛʃən/ n represión, f

repressive /rɪ'prɛsɪv/ a represivo

reprieve /rɪ'priv/ vt Law. aplazar la ejecución (de); Fig. dar una tregua (a)

reprimand /'rɛprə,mænd/ n reprimenda, f, vt reprender

reprint /n. 'ri,prɪnt; v. ri'prɪnt/ n reimpresión, tirada aparte, separata, f, vt reimprimir

reprinting /'ri,prɪntɪŋ/ n reimpresión, f

reprisal /rɪ'praɪzəl/ n represalia, f. to take reprisals, tomar represalias

reproach /rɪ'proutʃ/ n reproche, m; censura, f; (shame) vergüenza, f. —vt reprochar; censurar; echar en cara; afear

reproachful /rɪ'proutʃfəl/ a severo; lleno de reproches; de censura; (shameful) vergonzoso

reproachfully /rɪ'proutʃfəli/ adv con reprobación, con reprensión, severamente

reprobate /'rɛprə,beɪt/ n réprobo (-ba)

reproduce /,riprə'dus/ vt reproducir. —vi reproducirse

reproducible /,riprə'dusəbəl/ a reproductible

reproductive /,riprə'dʌktɪv/ a reproductor; de reproducción

reproof /rɪ'pruf/ n reconvención, f

reprove /rɪ'pruv/ vt censurar, culpar; reprender

reptile /'rɛptɪl, -taɪl/ a and n reptil, m

republic /rɪ'pʌblɪk/ n república, f. the r. of letters, la república de las letras

republican /rɪ'pʌblɪkən/ a and n republicano (-na)

republish /ri'pʌblɪʃ/ vt publicar de nuevo; volver a editar

repudiate /rɪ'pyudi,eɪt/ vt repudiar; negar, rechazar

repudiation /rɪ,pyudi'eiʃən/ n repudiación, f

repugnance /rɪ'pʌgnəns/ n repugnacia, f

repugnant /rɪ'pʌgnənt/ a repugnante; contrario; opuesto. **to be r. to,** repugnar (a)

repulse /rɪ'pʌls/ vt repulsar, repeler; rebatir, refutar; (refuse) rechazar, n repulsa, f; refutación, f; rechazo, m

repulsion /rɪ'pʌlʃən/ n Phys. repulsión, f; repugnancia, aversión, f

repulsive /rɪ'pʌlsɪv/ a repulsivo, repugnante, repelente

reputable /'rɛpyətəbəl/ a honrado, respetable, formal

reputation /,rɛpyə'teiʃən/ n reputación, f; fama, f, renombre, m. **to have the r. of,** ser reputado como, pasar por

reputed /rɪ'pyutɪd/ a supuesto; putativo

reputedly /rɪ'pyutɪdli/ adv según la opinión común, según dice la gente

request /rɪ'kwɛst/ n ruego, m, petición, f; instancia, f; solicitud, f; Com. demanda, f. —vt pedir, rogar; suplicar; solicitar. **in r.,** en boga; solicitado; en demanda, **on r.,** a solicitud. **r. stop,** (for buses) parada discrecional, f

requiem /'rɛkwiəm/ n réquiem, m. **r. mass,** misa de difuntos, f

require /rɪ'kwaiᵊr/ vt exigir, requerir; necesitar; (wish) desear; invitar. —vi ser necesario

required /rɪ'kwaiərd/ a necesario; obligatorio

requirement /rɪ'kwaiᵊrmənt/ n deseo, m; requisito, m; formalidad, f; estipulación, f; necesidad, f

requisite /'rɛkwəzɪt/ n requisito, m. —a necesario, requisito, preciso. **to be r.,** ser necesario, ser menester hacer falta

requisition /,rɛkwə'zɪʃən/ vt Mil. requisar

requital /rɪ'kwaitl/ n recompensa, f; compensación, satisfacción, f

requite /rɪ'kwait/ vt pagar, recompensar; (affection) corresponder a

resale /'ri,seil/ n reventa, f

rescind /rɪ'sɪnd/ vt rescindir

rescission /rɪ'sɪʒən/ n rescisión, f

rescue /'rɛskyu/ vt salvar; librar; Mil. rescatar. —n socorro, m; salvamento, m; Mil. rescate, m. **to go to the r. of,** ir al socorro de. **r. party,** expedición de salvamento, f; Mil. expedición de rescate, f

rescuer /'rɛskyuər/ n salvador (-ra)

research /rɪ'sɜrtʃ, 'risɜrtʃ/ n investigación, f, vt investigar

researcher /rɪsɜrtʃər, 'risɜrtʃər/ n investigador (-ra)

resell /ri'sɛl/ vt revender

resemblance /rɪ'zɛmbləns/ n parecido, m, semejanza, f. **The two sisters bear a strong r. to each other,** Las dos hermanas se parecen mucho

resemble /rɪ'zɛmbəl/ vt parecerse a (a). **Mary doesn't r. her mother,** María no se parece a su madre

resent /rɪ'zɛnt/ vt resentirse de; ofenderse por, indignarse por; tomar a mal

resentful /rɪ'zɛntfəl/ a resentido; ofendido, indignado, agraviado; vengativo

resentfully /rɪ'zɛntfəli/ adv con resentimiento; con indignación

resentment /rɪ'zɛntmənt/ n resentimiento, m

reservation /,rɛzər'veiʃən/ n reservación, f; reserva, f; territorio reservado, m; santuario, m. **mental r.,** reserva mental, f

reserve /rɪ'zɜrv/ n reserva, f. —vt reservar. —a de reserva. **without r.,** sin reserva

reserved /rɪ'zɜrvd/ a reservado; callado, taciturno. **r. compartment,** reservado, m. **r. list,** (Mil. Nav.) sección de reserva, f

reservedly /rɪ'zɜrvɪdli/ adv con reserva

reservist /rɪ'zɜrvɪst/ n reservista, mf

reservoir /'rɛzər,vwar/ n depósito, m; cisterna, f, aljibe, tanque, m

reset /v. ri'sɛt/ vt montar de nuevo

resettle /ri'sɛtl/ vt repoblar; rehabilitar; (a dispute) llegar a un nuevo acuerdo sobre

resettlement /ri'sɛtl̩mənt/ n repoblación, f; rehabilitación, f; (of a dispute) nuevo acuerdo, m

reshape /ri'ʃeip/ vt reformar

reship /ri'ʃɪp/ vt reembarcar

reshipment /ri'ʃɪpmənt/ n reembarque, m

reshuffle /ri'ʃʌfəl/ vt volver a barajar; Fig. cambiar

reside /rɪ'zaid/ vi residir, habitar; vivir

residence /'rɛzɪdəns/ n residencia, f, permanencia, estada, f; domicilio, m

resident /'rɛzɪdənt/ a residente; (of a servant) que duerme en casa; interno. —n residente, mf; (diplomacy) residente, m

residential /,rɛzɪ'dɛnʃəl/ a residencial

residue /'rɛzɪ,du/ n resto, m; (Law., Chem.) residuo, m

residuum /rɪ'zɪdʒuəm/ n residuo, m

resign /rɪ'zain/ vt renunciar a; ceder; resignar. —vi dimitir. **to r. oneself,** resignarse

resignation /,rɛzɪg'neiʃən/ n resignación, f; (from a post) dimisión, f. **to send in one's r.,** dimitir

resigned /rɪ'zaind/ a resignado

resilient /rɪ'zɪlyənt/ a elástico

resin /'rɛzɪn/ n resina, f; (solid, for violin bows, etc.) colofonia, f

resist /rɪ'zɪst/ vt and vi (bear) aguantar; (impede) impedir; (repel, ward off) resistir; rechazar; hacer frente a; oponerse (a); negarse (a)

resistance /rɪ'zɪstəns/ n resistencia, f; aguante, m, tenacidad, f; oposición, f; repugnancia, f. **passive r.,** resistencia pasiva, f. **r. coil,** Elec. resistencia, f. **r. movement,** movimiento de resistencia, m

resistant /rɪ'zɪstənt/ a resistente

resister /rɪ'zɪstər/ n el, m, (f, la) que re-
siste

resole /ri'soul/ vt remontar

resolute /'rezə,lut/ a resuelto, decidido

resolution /,rezə'luʃən/ n resolución, f;
(proposal placed before a legislative body,
etc.) proposición, f; propósito, m

resolve /rɪ'zɒlv/ vt resolver; desarrollar,
deshacer (an abbreviation, acronym, or
initialism). —vi resolverse. —n propósito,
m; (of character) resolución, firmeza, f

resonance /'rezənəns/ n resonancia, f;
sonoridad, f

resonant /'rezənənt/ a resonante; rever-
berante, sonoro

resort /rɪ'zɔrt/ n recurso, m; punto de
reunión. m; (frequentation) frecuentación,
f; (gathering) concurrencia, f; reunión, f.
—vi acudir (a), acogerse (a); hacer uso
(de); pasar (a); (frequent) frecuentar,
concurrir. **health r.**, balneario, m. **holiday r.**, playa de verano, f; pueblo de veraneo, m. **in the last r.**, en último recurso

resound /rɪ'zaund/ vi resonar, retumbar,
retronar; Fig. tener fama, ser celebrado.
—vt hacer reverberar; Fig. celebrar

resounding /rɪ'zaundɪŋ/ a retumbante,
resonante

resource /'risɔrs/ n recurso, m; (of character) inventiva, f; pl resources; recursos, fondos, m pl

resourceful /rɪ'sɔrsfəl/ a ingenioso

respect /rɪ'spɛkt/ n respeto, m; consideración, f; (reference, regard) respecto, m;
pl respects, (greetings) saludos, m pl; homenaje, m. —vt respetar; honrar; (concern, regard) concernir, tocar (a). **in
other respects**, por lo demás. **in r. of**,
tocante a, respecto a. **in some respects**,
desde algunos puntos de vista. **out of r.
for**, por consideración a

respectable /rɪ'spɛktəbəl/ a respetable;
pasable; considerable

respected /rɪ'spɛktɪd/ a and part res-
petado; apreciado, estimado; digno de
respeto, honrado

respectful /rɪ'spɛktfəl/ a respetuoso

respectfully /rɪ'spɛktfəli/ adv respetuosamente

respecting /rɪ'spɛktɪŋ/ prep con respecto
a, en cuanto a, tocante a; a propósito de

respective /rɪ'spɛktɪv/ a respectivo; relativo

respectively /rɪ'spɛktɪvli/ adv respectiva-
mente

respiration /,rɛspə'reɪʃən/ n respiración,
f

respirator /'rɛspə,reɪtər/ n respirador, m

respiratory /'rɛspərə,tɔri/ a respiratorio

respire /rɪ'spaɪər/ vt and vi respirar; exhalar; descansar

respite /'rɛspɪt/ n tregua, pausa, f; respiro, m; Law. espera, f. —vt dar tregua
(a); (postpone) aplazar; (relieve) aliviar

resplendence /rɪ'splɛndəns/ n resplan-

dor, m, refulgencia, f, esplendor, fulgor,
m

resplendent /rɪ'splɛndənt/ a resplandeciente, refulgente, relumbrante. **He was r.
in a new uniform**, Lucía (or Ostentaba)
un nuevo uniforme. **to be r.**, ser resplandeciente; relumbrar, refulgir

respond /rɪ'spɒnd/ vi responder; contestar; (obey) obedecer; reaccionar

respondent /rɪ'spɒndənt/ n (in a suit)
demandado (-da)

response /rɪ'spɒns/ n respuesta, f; Eccl.
responso, m

responsibility /rɪ,spɒnsə'bɪlɪti/ n responsabilidad, f

responsible /rɪ'spɒnsəbəl/ a responsable

responsive /rɪ'spɒnsɪv/ a simpático; sensible, sensitivo

rest /rɛst/ n descanso, m; reposo, m; (the
grave) última morada, f; tranquilidad,
paz, f; inacción, f; (prop) soporte, apoyo,
m; base, f; (for a lance) ristre, m; (for a
rifle) apoyo, m; Mus. silencio, m, pausa,
f; (in verse) cesura, f. **in r.**, en ristre. **the
r.**, el resto; los demás, los otros. **to set
at r.**, calmar, tranquilizar; (remove) quitar. **r.-cure**, cura de reposo, f. **r.-house**,
hospedería, f; refugio, m. **r.-room,
lounge**, sala de descanso, f; (toilet) excusado, retrete, m; (in theaters) saloncillo,
m

rest /rɛst/ vi reposar, descansar; (lie
down) acostarse, echarse; (stop) cesar,
parar; estar en paz; apoyarse (en); descansar (sobre); posar; depender (de);
(remain) quedar. —vt descansar; dar un
descanso (a); (lean) apoyar; basar (en).
It rests with them, Depende de ellos.
**These valuable documents now rest in
the Library of Congress**, Estos valiosos
documentos han parado en la Biblioteca
del Congreso. **May he r. in peace!** ¡Que
en paz descanse! **to r. assured**, estar
seguro. **to r. on one's oars**, cesar de remar; descansar

restate /ri'steit/ vt repetir, afirmar de
nuevo

restaurant /'rɛstərənt/ n restaurante, restorán, m. **r.-car**, coche-comedor, m

restful /'rɛstfəl/ a descansado; tranquilo,
sosegado

resting /'rɛstɪŋ/ n reposo, m. **last r.-
place**, última morada, f. **r.-place**, descan-
sadero, m; refugio, m

restitution /,rɛstɪ'tuʃən/ n restitución, f

restive /'rɛstɪv/ a (of a horse) repropio,
ingobernable; inquieto, agitado; impaciente

restless /'rɛstlɪs/ a agitado; inquieto, intranquilo; turbulento; sin reposo; (wakeful) desvelado; (ceaseless) incesante. **r.
night**, noche desvelada, noche intran-
quila, Inf. noche toledana, f

restlessly /'rɛstlɪsli/ adv agitadamente;
con inquietud; turbulentamente; incesantemente

restock /ri'stɒk/ vt (with goods) surtir de

nuevo; proveer de nuevo; restablecer; repoblar

restoration /ˌrɛstəˈreɪʃən/ n restauración, f; renovación, f; restablecimiento, m; (returning) restitución, f

restore /rɪˈstɔr/ vt restaurar; restituir; devolver; restablecer; reponer; (repair) reformar, reparar; reconstruir; (to former rank, etc.) rehabilitar. **He restored the book to its place,** Devolvió el libro a su sitio

restrain /rɪˈstreɪn/ vt refrenar; reprimir; (restrict) limitar, restringir; (prevent) impedir; desviar; (detain) recluir. **to r. oneself,** contenerse

restrained /rɪˈstreɪnd/ a moderado, mesurado; sobrio; (of emotion) contenido

restraining /rɪˈstreɪnɪŋ/ a restrictivo; moderador, calmante

restraint /rɪˈstreɪnt/ n freno, m; restricción, f; limitación, f; prohibición, f; compulsión, f; (reserve) reserva, f; moderación, f

restrict /rɪˈstrɪkt/ vt restringir; limitar

restriction /rɪˈstrɪkʃən/ n restricción, f; limitación, f

restrictive /rɪˈstrɪktɪv/ a restrictivo

result /rɪˈzʌlt/ n resultado, m; consecuencia, resulta, f; solución, f. —vi resultar. **as the r. of,** de resultas de

resultant /rɪˈzʌltnt/ a resultante; con secuente. —n resultado, m; Mech. resultante, f

resume /rɪˈzum/ vt reasumir; (continue) reanudar, continuar; (summarize) resumir

résumé n resumen, m

resumption /rɪˈzʌmpʃən/ n (renewal) reanudación, f; reasunción, f

resurgence /rɪˈsɜrdʒəns/ n resurgimiento, m

resurrect /ˌrɛzəˈrɛkt/ vt Inf. desenterrar; resucitar

resurrection /ˌrɛzəˈrɛkʃən/ n resurrección, f

resuscitate /rɪˈsʌsɪˌteɪt/ vt and vi resucitar

resuscitation /rɪˌsʌsɪˈteɪʃən/ n resurrección, f; renovación, f; renacimiento, m

retail /ˈriteɪl/ n venta al por menor, reventa, f. —adv al por menor. —vt (goods) vender al por menor, revender; (tell) contar; repetir. **r. trade,** comercio al por menor, m

retailer /ˈriteɪlər/ n vendedor (-ra) al por menor; (of a story) narrador (-ra); el, m, (f, la) que cuenta algo

retain /rɪˈteɪn/ vt retener; guardar; conservar; (a barrister) ajustar; (hire) contratar

retainer /rɪˈteɪnər/ n (dependent) criado, dependiente, m; partidario, adherente, m; (fee) honorario, m; pl retainers, séquito, m, adherentes, m pl, gente, f

retaining wall /rɪˈteɪnɪŋ/ n muro de contención, m

retake /riˈteɪk/ vt volver a tomar; reconquistar

retaliate /rɪˈtæliˌeɪt/ vt vengarse de, desquitarse de. —vi vengarse, tomar represalias

retaliation /rɪˌtæliˈeɪʃən/ n represalias, f pl; desquite, m, satisfacción, f. **law of r.,** talión, m,

retard /rɪˈtɑrd/ vt retardar

retch /rɛtʃ/ vi tener náuseas, procurar vomitar

retention /rɪˈtɛnʃən/ n retención, f; conservación, f

retentive /rɪˈtɛntɪv/ a retentivo

reticence /ˈrɛtəsəns/ n reticencia, reserva, f

reticent /ˈrɛtəsənt/ a reservado, inexpresivo, taciturno

retina /ˈrɛtnə, ˈrɛtnə/ n retina, f

retinue /ˈrɛtn̩ˌu, -ˌyu/ n séquito, acompañamiento, m, comitiva, f

retire /rɪˈtaɪ³r/ vi retirarse; (to bed) recogerse, acostarse; (from a post) jubilarse —vt retirar; jubilar. **to r. from a post,** Mil. rendir el puesto

retired /rɪˈtaɪ³rd/ a retirado; (remote) apartado, aislado; (hidden) escondido; (former) antiguo; (from employment, etc.) jubilado; (of an officer) retirado. **to place on the r. list,** jubilar; (Mil. Nav.) dar el retiro (a)

retirement /rɪˈtaɪ³rmənt/ n retirada, f; (solitude) apartamiento, aislamiento, m; retiro, m; (superannuation) jubilación, f

retiring /rɪˈtaɪ³rɪŋ/ a que se retira; (from a post) dimitente; (with pension, etc.) de jubilación; (reserved) reservado; modesto

retort /rɪˈtɔrt/ vi replicar. —vt retorcer; devolver (una acusación, etc.). —n réplica, f; contestación, f; Chem. retorta, f

retouch /v. riˈtʌtʃ/ vt retocar

retrace /rɪˈtreɪs/ vt volver a trazar; volver a andar (un camino); (one's steps) volver sobre sus pasos, volver atrás; (in memory) rememorar, recordar; buscar el origen (de); (recount) narrar, contar

retract /rɪˈtrækt/ vt retractar, retirar; (draw back) retraer. —vi retractarse

retread /v. riˈtrɛd/ vt pisar de nuevo; (tires) recauchetear

retreat /rɪˈtrit/ n retirada, f; (Mil. signal) retreta, f; (refuge and Eccl.) retiro, m. —vi retirarse; retroceder; refugiarse

retreating /rɪˈtritɪŋ/ a que se retira; que retrocede; Mil. que se bate en retirada

retrench /rɪˈtrɛntʃ/ vt reducir; disminuir; vi economizar, hacer economías

retrial /ˈrɪtraɪl/ n (of a person) nuevo proceso, m; (of a case) revisión, f

retribution /ˌrɛtrəˈbyuʃən/ n retribución, f; justo castigo, m, pena merecida, f

retrieval /rɪˈtrivəl/ n recuperación, f; reparación, f; (of game) cobra, f; (of one's character) rehabilitación, f

retrieve /rɪˈtriv/ vt (game, of dogs) cobrar; (regain) recobrar, recuperar; restaurar; reparar; restablecer; (one's character) rehabilitar. —vi cobrar la caza

retroactive /ˌrɛtrouˈæktɪv/ a retroactivo

retrocede /ˌretrə'sid/ *vi* retroceder

retrograde /'retrə,greid/ *a* retrógrado

retrogression /ˌretrə'grɛʃən/ *n* retrogradación, regresión, *f; Med.* retroceso, *m*

retrogressive /ˌretrə'grɛsɪv/ *a* retrógrado

retrospect /'retrə,spɛkt/ *n* mirada retrospectiva, *f*, examen del pasado, *m.* **in r.,** retrospectivamente

retrospection /ˌretrə'spɛkʃən/ *n* retrospección, *f*

retry /ri'trai/ *vt* (a case) rever; (a person) procesar de nuevo

return /rɪ'tɜrn/ *vi* regresar; volver; reaparecer; presentarse de nuevo; *Law.* revertir; (answer) contestar, responder. —*vt* (give back or put back) devolver; (a ball) restar; (a kindness, visit) pagar; restituir; (reciprocate) corresponder (a); recompensar; contestar (a); dar; rendir; (yield) producir; (a verdict) fallar, pronunciar; (report) dar parte de; anunciar; (exchange) cambiar; (elect) elegir. —*n* regreso, *m;* vuelta, *f;* (giving or putting back) devolución, *f;* pago, *m;* restitución, *f;* correspondencia, *f;* recompensa, *f;* (reply) respuesta, *f;* (reappearance) reaparición, *f;* reinstalación, *f;* repetición, *f;* (gain) ganancia, *f,* provecho, *m;* rendimiento, *m;* (exchange) cambio, *m;* (report) parte oficial, *f;* informe, *m;* lista, *f;* (election) elección, *f; pl* **returns,** tablas estadísticas, *f pl;* (of an election) resultados, *m pl.* **Many happy returns!** ¡Feliz cumpleaños! **by return mail,** a vuelta de correo. **on my (his, etc.) r.,** a la vuelta, cuando vuelva. **to r. like for like,** pagar en la misma moneda. **r. journey, r. trip,** viaje de vuelta, *m.* **r. match,** partido de vuelta, *m.* **r. ticket,** billete de ida y vuelta, *m;* billete de vuelta, *m*

returnable /rɪ'tɜrnəbəl/ *a* restituible; susceptible a ser devuelto; (on approval) a prueba; *Law.* devolutivo

"Return to Sender" «Al remitente»

reunion /ri'yunyən/ *n* reunión, *f*

reunite /ˌriyu'nait/ *vt* reunir. —*vi* reunirse

revaccinate /ri'væksə,neit/ *vt* revacunar

revaccination /ri,væksə'neiʃən/ *n* revacunación, *f*

reveal /rɪ'vil/ *vt* revelar; descubrir

revealing /rɪ'vilɪŋ/ *a* revelador. —*n* revelación, *f;* descubrimiento, *m*

reveille /'rɛvəli; *Brit.* rɪ'væli/ *n Mil.* diana, *f*

revel /'rɛvəl/ *vi* divertirse; regocijarse (en), gozarse (en); entregarse (a); (carouse) ir de parranda; emborracharse. —*n* algazara, jarana, *f; pl* **revels,** fiestas, festividades, *f pl*

revelation /ˌrɛvə'leiʃən/ *n* revelación, *f;* descubrimiento, *m;* (in the Bible) Apocalipsis, *m*

reveler /'rɛvələr/ *n* convidado alegre, *m;* (at night) trasnochador (-ra), *m;* (drunk) borracho (-cha); (masked) máscara, *mf*

revelry /'rɛvəlri/ *n* festividades, *f pl,* regocijo, *m;* orgías, *f pl*

revenge /rɪ'vɛndʒ/ *n* venganza, *f.* —*vt* vengarse de; desquitarse de

revengeful /rɪ'vɛndʒfəl/ *a* vengativo

revenue /'rɛvən,yu, -ə,nu/ *n* rentas públicas, *f pl;* (treasury) fisco, *m; Com.* rédito, *m,* ingresos, *m pl;* beneficio, *m.* **Inland R.,** delegación de contribuciones, *f.* **r. officer,** agente fiscal, *m*

reverberate /rɪ'vɜrb@,reit/ *vt* and *vi* (of sound) retumbar, resonar; (of light, etc.) reverberar

reverberation /rɪ,vɜrbə'reiʃən/ *n* (reflection) reverberación, *f;* (of sound) retumbo, eco, *m*

revere /rɪ'vɪər/ *vt* reverenciar, venerar, honrar

reverence /'rɛvərəns/ *n* reverencia, *f,* *vt* reverenciar

reverend /'rɛvərənd/ *a* reverendo

reverent /'rɛvərənt/ *a* reverente

reverie /'rɛvəri/ *n* ensueño, *m*

reversal /rɪ'vɜrsəl/ *n* inversión, *f;* (of a verdict) revocación, *f*

reverse /rɪ'vɜrs/ *vt* invertir; (a steam engine) dar contra vapor (a); (a vehicle) poner en marcha atrás; (arms) llevar a la funerala; (a judgment, etc.) revocar, derogar. —*vi* (dancing) dar vueltas al revés. —*n* lo contrario, lo opuesto; (back) dorso, revés, *m;* (change) cambio, *m;* (check) revés, *m,* vicisitud, *f;* (loss) pérdida, *f;* (defeat) derrota, *f; Mech.* marcha atrás, *f, a* inverso; contrario, opuesto. **quite the r.,** todo el contrario. **r. turn,** (of an engine) cambio de dirección, *m;* (in dancing) vuelta al revés, *f*

reversion /rɪ'vɜrʒən, -ʃən/ *n* reversión, *f; Biol.* atavismo, *m;* (of offices) futura, *f;* (of property) reversión, *f*

revert /rɪ'vɜrt/ *vi Law.* revertir; volver (a)

review /rɪ'vyu/ *n* examen, análisis, *m;* juicio crítico, *m;* (journal and *Mil.*) revista, *f;* (criticism) revista, reseña, *f; Law.* revisión, *f.* —*vt* examinar, analizar; (*Mil.* etc.) pasar revista (a); revisar; repasar; (a book, etc.) reseñar; *Law.* revisar. —*vi* escribir revistas

revile /rɪ'vail/ *vt* injuriar, maldecir, difamar

reviling /rɪ'vailɪŋ/ *n* insultos, *m pl,* injurias, *f pl*

revisal /rɪ'vaizəl/ *n* revisión, *f*

revise /rɪ'vaiz/ *vt* revisar; repasar; corregir; (change) cambiar

reviser /rɪ'vaizər/ *n* revisor, *m;* corrector de pruebas, *m*

revision /rɪ'vɪʒən/ *n* revisión, *f;* repaso, *m;* corrección de pruebas, *f*

revival /rɪ'vaivəl/ *n* resurgimiento, *m;* renovación, *f;* (awakening) despertamiento, *m;* restablecimiento, *m;* resurrección, *f;* (of learning) renacimiento, *m; Theat.* reposición, *f;* (religious) despertar religioso, *m*

revive /rɪ'vaiv/ *vi* reponerse; restablecerse; resucitar; renovarse; renacer; cobrar fuerzas; (recover consciousness) volver en sí. —*vt* hacer revivir; resucitar; restablecer; renovar; restaurar; despertar; (fire, colours) avivar

revivify /rɪ'vɪvəˌfaɪ/ *vt* revivificar

revocation /ˌrevə'keɪʃən/ *n* revocación, *f*

revoke /rɪ'vouk/ *vt* revocar, anular, derogar; (wills) quebrantar. —*vi* revocar, anular; (at cards) renunciar. —*n* (cards) renuncio, *m*

revolt /rɪ'voult/ *n* rebelión, *f*, *vi* rebelarse, sublevarse. —*vt* repugnar, indignar, dar asco (a)

revolting /rɪ'voultɪŋ/ *a* repugnante, asqueroso; (rebellious) rebelde

revolution /ˌrevə'luʃən/ *n* revolución, *f*; (turn) vuelta, *f*, giro, *m*

revolutionary /ˌrevə'luʃəˌneri/ *a* and *n* revolucionario (-ia)

revolutionize /ˌrevə'luʃəˌnaɪz/ *vt* revolucionar

revolve /rɪ'vɒlv/ *vi* dar vueltas, girar; suceder periódicamente. —*vt* hacer girar; (ponder) revolver, discurrir

revolver /rɪ'vɒlvər/ *n* revólver, *m*

revolving /rɪ'vɒlvɪŋ/ *a* giratorio, que vuelve; periódico. **r. chair,** silla giratoria, *f*. **r. door,** puerta giratoria, *f*. **r. stage,** escenario giratorio, *m*

revue /rɪ'vyu/ *n Theat.* revista, *f*

revulsion /rɪ'vʌlʃən/ *n* revulsión, *f*

rev up /rev/ *vt* (an engine) calentar

reward /rɪ'wɔrd/ *n* recompensa, *f*; retribución, *f*. —*vt* recompensar; satisfacer, premiar

rewarding /rɪ'wɔrdɪŋ/ *a* premiador; que recompensa. —*n* recompensación, *f*. **a rewarding experience,** una experiencia compensadora, *f*

rewrite /v. ri'raɪt/ *vt* escribir de nuevo; volver a escribir; (adapt) redactar otra vez

rhapsody /'ræpsədi/ *n* rapsodia, *f*

rhetoric /'retərɪk/ *n* retórica, *f*

rhetorical /rɪ'tɔrɪkəl/ *a* retórico; declamatorio

rheumatic /rʊ'mætɪk/ *a* reumático. **r. fever,** reumatismo poliarticular agudo, *m*

rheumatism /'rumaˌtɪzəm/ *n* reumatismo, reuma, *m*

rheumy /'rumi/ *a* catarroso; (of the eyes) legañoso

rhinestone /'raɪnˌstoun/ circón, *m*

Rhine, the /raɪn/ el Rin, *m*

rhinoceros /raɪ'nɒsərəs/ *n* rinoceronte, *m*

rhubarb /'rubɑrb/ *n* ruibarbo, *m*

rhyme /raɪm/ *n* rima, *f*; verso, *m*. —*vi* and *vt* rimar. **without r. or reason,** sin ton ni son; a tontas y a locas

rhyming /'raɪmɪŋ/ *a* rimador

rhythm /'rɪðəm/ *n* ritmo, *m*

rhythmic /'rɪðmɪk/ *a* rítmico

rib /rɪb/ *n* (*Anat. Bot. Aer. Naut. Archit.*) costilla, *f*; (of an umbrella or fan) varilla, *f*; (in cloth) cordoncillo, *m*, lista, *f*

ribald /'rɪbəld/ *a* escabroso, ribaldo, indecente

ribaldry /'rɪbəldri/ *n* ribaldería, escabrosidad, indecencia, *f*

ribbed /rɪbd/ *a* con costillas; (of cloth) listado, con listas

ribbon /'rɪbən/ *n* cinta, *f*; tira, *f*; (tatter) jirón, *m*. **to tear to ribbons,** hacer jirones

rice /raɪs/ *n* arroz, *m*. —*a* de arroz; con arroz. **r. field,** arrozal, *m*. **r.-paper,** papel de paja de arroz, *m*. **r.-pudding,** arroz con leche, *m*

rich /rɪtʃ/ *a* rico; opulento; (happy) dichoso; (of land, etc.) fértil; abundante; (of objects) magnífico, suntuoso, hermoso; precioso; (of food) exquisito; suculento; (highly seasoned) muy sazonado; (creamy) con mucha nata; (of colours) brillante, vivo. **new r.,** ricacho (-cha). **newly-r.,** advenedizo. **to grow r.,** enriquecerse

riches /'rɪtʃɪz/ *n* riqueza, *f*

richness /'rɪtʃnɪs/ *n* riqueza, *f*; opulencia, *f*; (of land, etc.) fertilidad, *f*; abundancia, *f*; (of objects) magnificencia, suntuosidad, hermosura, *f*; preciosidad, *f*; (of food) gusto exquisito, *m*; suculencia, *f*; (piquancy) gusto picante, *m*; (of colours) viveza, *f*

rickets /'rɪkɪts/ *n* raquitismo, *m*

rickety /'rɪkɪti/ *a Med.* raquítico; destartalado, desvencijado; (unsteady) tambaleante; cojo

ricochet /ˌrɪkə'ʃeɪ/ *n* rebote, *m*, *vi* rebotar

rid /rɪd/ *vt* librar (de). **to get rid of,** librarse de; quitarse de encima (a); perder, quitarse; (dismiss) despedir. **to rid oneself of,** librarse de, deshacerse de

riddance /'rɪdns/ *n* libramiento, *m*

riddle /'rɪdl/ *n* acertijo, *m*; enigma, problema, *m*; misterio, *m*; (sieve) tamiz de alambre, *m*; *vt* (guess) adivinar; (sift) cribar; (with holes) acribillar

ride /raɪd/ *vi* (a horse) montar a caballo, cabalgar; pasear a caballo; (a mule, a bicycle) montar en, pasear en; (a vehicle, train) ir en; (a carriage, car) andar en, pasear en; (float) flotar; (on the wind) dejarse llevar por el viento; ser llevado por el viento; (go) ir; (come) venir; (a distance) hacer... a caballo, en coche, etc.; *Naut.* estar al ancla; *Mech.* tener juego. —*vt* (a horse, mule, bicycle) montar; ir montado sobre; manejar; (a race) hacer; (float) flotar en; (cleave, the sea, etc.) surcar. —*n* paseo (a caballo, en bicicleta, en coche, etc.), *m*; viaje (en un autobús, de tren, etc.), *m*; (bridle path) camino de herradura, *m*; cabalgata, *f*, desfile a caballo, *m*. **a r. on horseback,** un paseo a caballo. **They gave me a r. in their car,** (e.g. to see the sights) Me llevaron a paseo en su auto, (a lift to a certain place) Me dieron un aventón. **ride at anchor,** estar fondeado. **to r. a bicycle,** montar en bicicleta. **to r. roughshod over,** mandar a la baqueta (a), mandar a puntapiés (a). **to r. sidesaddle,** cabalgar a mujeriegas. **to r. at,** embestir con. **to r. away,** marcharse, alejarse; marcharse a caballo, etc. **to r. back,**

rider   748

volver; volver a caballo, en bicicleta, etc. **to r. behind,** seguir a caballo; ir inmediatamente detrás (de); (on the back seat) ocupar el asiento de atrás; (on the same animal) cabalgar en la grupa. **to r. down,** atropellar; (trample) pisotear, pasar por encima de. **to r. on,** seguir su camino. **to r. out,** salir a paseo en caballo, etc.; irse a paseo en coche, etc.; (a storm) hacer frente a, luchar con. **to r. over,** pasar por encima de; recorrer. **to r. up,** *vi* llegar, acercarse; (of a tie, etc.) subir. —*vt* montar

rider /'raidər/ *n* cabalgador (-ra); jinete, *m;* persona que va en coche, etc., *f;* (on a bicycle) ciclista, *mf;* (on a motorcycle) motociclista, *mf;* (horsebreaker) domador de caballos, *m;* (clause) añadidura, *f;* corolario, *m*

ridge /ridʒ/ *n* cumbre, cima, *f;* (of mountains) cordillera, sierra, *f;* (of a roof, of a nose) caballete, *m; Agr.* lomo, caballón, *m;* (wrinkle) arruga, *f;* (on coins) cordoncillo, *m.* —*vt* surcar; formar lomos (en); (wrinkle) arrugar

ridicule /'ridɪˌkyul/ *n* ridículo, *m, vt* poner en ridículo, ridiculizar; burlarse (de), mofarse (de)

ridiculous /ri'dɪkyələs/ *a* ridículo, absurdo

riding /'raidɪŋ/ *a* cabalgante; que va a caballo; montado (a, en, sobre); *Naut.* al ancla; (in compounds) de equitación; de montar. —*n* equitación, *f;* paseo a caballo; en bicicleta, etc., *m;* acción de ir a caballo, etc., *f;* (district) comarca, *f.* **r.-boots,** botas de montar, *f pl.* **r.-habit,** traje de montar, *m;* (woman's) amazona, *f.* **r.-master,** profesor de equitación, *m.* **r.-saddle,** silla de montar, *f.* **r.-school,** escuela de equitación, *f*

rife /raif/ *a* común; corriente; frecuente; prevalente; abundante; general. **r. with,** abundante en; lleno de

riffraff /'rɪfˌræf/ *n* desperdicios, *m pl;* (rabble) gentuza, canalla, *f*

rifle /'raifəl/ *n* rifle, fusil rayado, *m.* —*vt* robar; (a suitcase, etc.) desvalijar; (a gun) rayar. **r.-range,** campo de tiro, *m.* **r.-sling,** portafusil, *m.* **r.-shot,** fusilazo, *m*

rifleman /'raifəlmən/ *n* fusilero, *m*

rift /rɪft/ *n* hendedura, abertura, *f;* grieta, *f*

rig /rɪg/ *n Naut.* aparejo, *m; Inf.* atavío, *m.* —*vt* (a ship) aparejar; equipar; (elections) falsificar. **to rig out,** proveer de; equipar con; ataviar. **to rig up,** arreglar; armar, construir

rigging /'rɪgɪŋ/ *n* (of a ship) aparejo, *m*

right /rait/ *a* recto; correcto; conveniente, debido; apropiado; exacto; (opposite of left hand) derecho; (straight) directo; en línea recta; razonable; (true) verdadero, genuino, legítimo; (just) justo; (prudent) prudente; (in health) sano. **All r.!** ¡Está bien! **I feel all r.,** Me siento perfectamente bien, Estoy bien. **He is the r. man for the job,** Él es el hombre que hace

falta para el puesto. **It is the r. word,** Es la palabra apropiada. **on the r.,** a la derecha. **to be r.,** (of persons) tener razón. **to make r.,** poner en orden; arreglar. **r.-angle,** ángulo recto, *m.* **r.-angled,** rectangular. **r.-angled triangle,** triángulo rectángulo, *m.* **the R. Bank (of Paris),** la Orilla derecha, la Ribera derecha, *f.* **r. hand,** *m* (mano) derecha, diestra, *f;* derecha, *f;* (person) brazo derecho, *m.* —*a* de la mano derecha; de la derecha; a la derecha. **r.-handed,** derecho; diestro, hábil. **r. mind,** entero juicio, *m.* **r.-minded,** juicioso, prudente; honrado. **r.-of-way,** derecho a la vía, *m*

right /rait/ *adv* directamente; inmediatamente; derechamente; correctamente; debidamente; exactamente; bien; (quite, thoroughly) completamente; honradamente; (very) muy. **r. on,** adelante; en frente. **R. about face!** ¡Media vuelta a la derecha! **r. at the bottom,** al fondo; al final; el último (de la clase, etc.). **r. at the end of his speech,** al fin de su discurso. **r. away,** en seguida, inmediatamente

right /rait/ *n* razón, *f;* verdad, *f;* justicia, *f;* (good) bien, *m;* derecho, *m;* (not left side) derecha, *f;* (of political parties) derechas, *f pl.* **r. and wrong,** el bien y el mal. **"All rights reserved,"** «Derechos reservados.» **by rights,** por derecho. **It is on the r.,** Está a la derecha. **to exercise one's r.,** usar de su derecho. **r. of association,** derecho de asociación, *m.* **r. of way,** derecho de paso, *m.* **to be in the r.,** tener razón; estar en su derecho

right /rait/ *vt* enderezar; rectificar; corregir; poner en orden; *Naut.* enderezar; hacer justicia (a). **to r. wrongs,** deshacer agravios

righteous /'raitʃəs/ *a* recto, virtuoso, justo; justificado

righteousness /'raitʃəsnɪs/ *n* rectitud, integridad, virtud, *f;* justicia, *f*

rightful /'raitfəl/ *a* justo; legítimo; verdadero

rightfully /'raitfəli/ *adv* justamente; legítimamente; verdaderamente

rightly /'raitli/ *adv* justamente; legítimamente; correctamente; bien. **r. or wrongly,** mal que bien

rightness /'raitnɪs/ *n* rectitud, *f;* derechura, *f;* justicia, *f;* exactitud, *f*

rigid /'rɪdʒɪd/ *a* rígido; inflexible; severo, riguroso

rigidity /ri'dʒɪdɪti/ *n* rigidez, *f;* inflexibilidad, *f;* severidad, *f*

rigmarole /'rɪgməˌroul/ *n* monserga, *f,* galimatías, *m,* jerigonza, *f*

rigor /'rɪgər/ *n* rigor, *m*

rigorous /'rɪgərəs/ *a* riguroso

rile /rail/ *vt Inf.* irritar, sacar de tino (a)

rim /rɪm/ *n* borde, *m;* orilla, *f;* (of a wheel) llanta, *f,* aro, *m*

rime /raim/ *n* escarcha, *f, vt* cubrir con escarcha. See also **rhyme**

rind /raind/ *n* (of fruit) cáscara, corteza, *f;* (of cheese) costra, *f;* (of bacon) piel, *f*

ring /rɪŋ/ n círculo, m; (round the eyes) ojera, f; (for curtains, etc.) anilla, f; (for the finger) anillo, m, sortija, f; (for children's games, etc.) corro, m; (for the ears) arete, m; (of smoke and for the nose) anillo, m; (for hitching, etc.) argolla, f; (for boxing) cuadrilátero, m; (on a racecourse) picadero, m; (at a circus, bull-fight) ruedo, redondel, m; Fig. arena, f; (group) camarilla, f, grupo, m; (metallic sound) sonido metálico, m; resonancia, f; (tinkle) tintín, m; (of a bell) repique, tañido, son (de la campana), m; (of bells) juego de campanas, m; (of laughter, etc.) ruido, m; (of truth, etc.) apariencia, f. **r.-bolt,** Naut. cáncamo, m. **r. finger,** dedo anular, m. **r.-master,** director de circo, m

ring /rɪŋ/ vt (surround) cercar, rodear; (a bull, etc.) poner un anillo (a); (sound) hacer sonar; sonar; (a door bell, etc.) tocar, apretar; (bells) echar a vuelo; (announce by pealing the bells) anunciar, proclamar; sonar, tañer. —vi (of bells) sonar; (re-echo) resonar; (of the ears) zumbar; (tinkle) tintinar. **to r. the bell,** tocar la campana; tocar el timbre. **to r. off,** colgar el teléfono. **to r. up,** llamar por teléfono, telefonear

ringing /'rɪŋɪŋ/ n acción de tocar las campanas o el timbre, f; toque, m; repique, m; campanilleo, m; (in the ears) zumbido, m. —a resonante, sonoro. **r. signal,** señal de llamada, f. **the r. of the bells,** el son de las campanas

ringleader /'rɪŋ,lidər/ n cabecilla, m

ringlet /'rɪŋlɪt/ n rizo, bucle, m

ringworm /'rɪŋ,wɜrm/ n tiña, f

rink /rɪŋk/ n pista, f. **skating-r.,** sala de patinar, f; pista de patinar, f

rinse /rɪns/ n enjuague, m; enjuagadura, f; (of clothes) aclarado, m. —vt enjuagar; (clothes) aclarar; lavar

riot /'raɪət/ n motín, m; tumulto, m; desorden, m; exceso, m; orgía, f; disipación, f. —vi amotinarse; alborotarse; entregarse a la disipación (or al placer); (enjoy) gozar, disfrutar. **to run r.,** hacer excesos; perder el freno; desmandarse; Fig. extenderse por todas partes; crecer en abundancia, cubrir todo

rioter /'raɪətər/ n amotinador (-ra); alborotador (-ra)

riotous /'raɪətəs/ a sedicioso; bullicioso; disoluto; desordenado; desenfrenado

rip /rɪp/ vt rasgar; (unsew) descoser; (wood, etc.) partir; (make) hacer. —vi rasgarse. —n rasgón, m; rasgadura, f; desgarro, m; (libertine) calavera, m. **to rip off,** arrancar; quitar. **to rip open,** abrir; (an animal) abrir en canal

ripe /raɪp/ a maduro; preparado; perfecto, acabado

ripen /'raɪpən/ vt and vi madurar

ripeness /'raɪpnɪs/ n madurez, f

ripple /'rɪpəl/ n rizo, m; onda, f; (of sound) murmullo, m. —vt rizar. —vi rizarse; murmurar

rise /raɪz/ vi ascender; subir; levantarse; ponerse de pie; (of a meeting) suspenderse; (from the dead) resucitar; (grow) crecer; (swell) hincharse; (of sun, moon) salir; (of sound, gradient, price, stock exchange quotations) subir; (of river source) nacer; (in revolt) sublevarse, rebelarse; (to the mind) presentarse, surgir; (appear) aparecer; (of buildings, etc.) elevarse, alzarse; (in the world) mejorar de posición; (originate) originarse (en), proceder (de); (of mercury) alzarse; (of fish) picar. **He has risen in my estimation,** Ha ganado en mi estimación. **She rose early,** Se levantó temprano. **The color rose in her cheeks,** Se le subieron los colores a la cara. **to r. to the occasion,** estar al nivel de las circunstancias. **to r. to one's feet,** ponerse de pie. **to r. to the bait,** morder el anzuelo. **to r. again,** levantarse de nuevo; resucitar; renovarse, suscitarse otra vez. **to r. above,** alzarse por encima de; mostrarse superior a

rise /raɪz/ n ascensión, f; subida, f; levantamiento, m; (in price, temperature) alza, f; (increase) aumento, m; (of the sun, moon) salida, f; (of a river) nacimiento, m; (origin) origen, m; (growth, development) desarrollo, crecimiento, m; (promotion) ascenso, m; (slope) cuesta, f; pendiente, f; (high ground) eminencia, altura, f. **to give r. to,** dar lugar a, causar. **r. and fall,** subida y baja, f; (of the voice) ritmo, m; (of music) cadencia, f; (of institutions) grandeza y decadencia, f. **r. to power,** subida al poder, f

riser /'raɪzər/ n el, m, (f, la) que se levanta; (of a step) contrahuella, f. **early r.,** madrugador (-ra). **late r.,** el, m, (f, la) que se levanta tarde

risibility /,rɪzə'bɪlɪti/ n risibilidad, f

rising /'raɪzɪŋ/ n subida, f; (of the source of rivers) nacimiento, m; (overflowing of rivers) crecimiento, m; (of sun, moon) salida, f; (from the dead) resurrección, f; (rebellion) sublevación, insurrección, f; (of the tide) crecida, f; (of bread) levadura, f; (of an assembly) suspensión, f; (of a theater curtain) subida, f; (literary) renacimiento, m, a creciente; naciente; saliente; (promising) de porvenir; (young) joven. **the r. generation,** los jóvenes, la generación joven. **He is r. forty,** Raya en los cuarenta. **He likes early r.,** Le gusta madrugar. **On the r. of the curtain...,** Al levantarse el telón... **the r. of the moon,** la salida de la luna, f. **the r. tide,** la marea creciente

risk /rɪsk/ n riesgo, m; peligro, m. —vt arriesgar; atreverse (a), osar. **at the r. of,** al riesgo de. **to take a r.,** tomar un riesgo; correr peligro. **to r. everything on the outcome,** jugar el todo por el todo

risk capital n capital-riesgo, m

riskiness /'rɪskɪnɪs/ n peligro, m

risky /'rɪski/ a arriesgado, peligroso

rissole /'rɪ'soul/ n risol, m, (pl risoles)

rite /rait/ n rito, m

ritual /'rɪtʃuəl/ a ritual. —n rito, m, ceremonia, f

rival /'raivəl/ n rival, mf a competidor; rival. —vt rivalizar con, competir con

rivalry /'raivəlri/ n rivalidad, f

river /'rɪvər/ n río, m. —a del río; fluvial. **r.-basin,** cuenca de un río, f. **r.-bed,** lecho, cauce (de un río), m. **r. civilization,** civilización fluvial, f. **r.-god,** dios de los ríos, m. **r.-mouth,** ría, f. **r. port,** puerto fluvial, m

riverside /'rɪvər,said/ n ribera, orilla de un río, f. —a de la(s) orilla(s) de un río; situado a la orilla de un río; ribereño

rivet /'rɪvɪt/ n remache, roblón, m. —vt remachar; clavar; Fig. fijar, concentrar; Fig. cautivar, absorber

road /roud/ n camino, m; carretera, f; ruta, f; pl roads, Naut. rada, f. **high r.,** camino real, m. **main r.,** carretera, f. **secondary r.,** carretera de segunda clase, f. **on the r. to...,** en el camino de... **to get out of the r.,** Inf. quitarse de en medio. **to go by r.,** ir por carretera. **"R. up!"** «Carretera en reparaciones.» **r.-book,** guía de carreteras, f. **r. house,** albergue de carretera, m. **r. maker,** constructor de caminos, m; (navvy) peón caminero, m. **r. making,** construcción de caminos, f. **r. map,** mapa de carreteras, m. **r. sign,** señal de carretera, señal de tránsito, señal vial, f, poste indicador, m. **The r. to hell is paved with good intentions,** El camino del infierno está empedrado de buenas intenciones. **"R. Repairs,"** «Camino en Reparación»

roadside /'roud,said/ n borde del camino, m, a al lado del camino

roadway /'roud,wei/ n calzada, carretera, f

roam /roum/ vi vagar, vagabundear, andar errante. —vt errar por

roar /rɔr/ vi rugir; (of a bull, of the wind, of a person in anger) bramar; dar voces; (of the fire) crepitar; (of cannon) retumbar; (of thunder) estallar. —vt gritar. —n rugido, bramido, m; (shout) grito, m; (of the fire) crepitación, f; (of cannon, thunder) estallido, m; (noise) ruido, m. **to r. with laughter,** reírse a carcajadas

roaring /'rɔrɪŋ/ n (of horses) asma de los caballos, f, For other meanings, see under **roar.** a rugiente, bramante; Inf. magnífico. **to do a r. trade,** hacer un buen negocio

roast /roust/ n asado, m, carne asada, f. —a asado; tostado. —vt asar; (coffee and to warm one's feet, etc.) tostar; (metals) calcinar; (scold) desollar vivo (a). —vi asarse; tostarse. **r. beef,** rosbif, m

roaster /'roustər/ n asador, m; (for coffee or peanuts) tostador, m; (for chestnuts, etc.) tambor, m

rob /rɒb/ vt robar; quitar, privar (de). **They have robbed her of her pocketbook,** Le han robado la cartera

robber /'rɒbər/ n ladrón (-ona); (footpad) salteador de caminos, m; (brigand) bandido, m

robbery /'rɒbəri/ n robo, m. **It's daylight r.!** ¡Es un desuello! **to commit a r.,** cometer un robo. **r. with violence,** robo armado, m

robe /roub/ n traje talar, m, toga, f; (of a monk, nun) hábito, m; (of a priest, etc.) sotana, f; Poet. manto, m; (infant's) mantillas, f pl; pl **robes,** traje de ceremonia, m. —vt vestir; cubrir, revestir (de). —vi vestirse. **bath r.,** albornoz, m

robot /'roubɒt, -bɒt/ n hombre mecánico, m; Aer. piloto mecánico, m. **traffic r.,** torre del tráfico, f, aparato automático, m. **r. plane,** avión sin piloto, m

robust /rou'bʌst/ a robusto; fuerte, vigoroso. **to make r.,** robustecer

rock /rɒk/ n roca, f; (in the sea) abrojo, escollo, m; peña, f, peñasco, m. **as firm as a r.,** como una roca. **to be on the rocks,** Inf. estar a la cuarta pregunta. **r. bottom,** n fondo, m. —a mínimo, más bajo. **r. crystal,** cuarzo, m. **r.-garden,** jardincito rocoso, jardín alpestre, m. **r.-plant,** planta alpestre, f. **r.-rose,** heliantemo, m. **r.-salt,** sal gema, f

rock /rɒk/ vt mecer; (shake) hacer temblar, sacudir; (to sleep) arrullar. —vi mecerse, balancearse; tambalearse; agitarse; temblar

rocker /'rɒkər/ n (of a chair, cradle) balancín, m; (chair) mecedora, f

rocket /'rɒkɪt/ n cohete, volador, m. —vi lanzarse. **r.-launching aircraft,** caza lanzacohetes, f

rocking /'rɒkɪŋ/ n balanceo, m; (staggering) tambaleo, m; oscilación, f; (of an infant) arrullo, m. **r.-chair,** mecedora, f. **r.-horse,** caballo balancín, caballo mecedor, m

rocky /'rɒki/ a rocoso; de roca; roqueño; (rough) fragoso, escabroso; (rugged) peñascoso, escarpado. **the R. Mountains,** las Montañas Rocosas, f pl

rod /rɒd/ n vara, f; bastón de mando, m; (for fishing) caña, f; (measure) pértiga, f; (surveying) jalón, m; palo, m; (for punishment) vergajo, m; Mech. vástago, m. **connecting rod,** biela, f. **to fish with rod and line,** pescar con caña

rodent /'roudṇt/ a and n roedor, m

roe /rou/ n (deer) corzo (-za); (of fish) hueva, f; **soft roes,** lechas, f pl

rogue /roug/ n bribón, pícaro, pillo, m; Law. vago, m; (affectionate) picaruelo (-la)

roguish /'rougɪʃ/ a picaresco, bellaco; (mischievous) travieso, juguetón; malicioso

role /roul/ n papel, m

roll /roul/ n rollo, m; (list) rol, m, lista, f; (of bread) panecillo, m; (of a drum) redoble, m; (of thunder) tronido, m; (of cloth) pieza, f; (of tobacco) rollo, m; (of meat, etc.) pastel, m; (of a ship) balanceo, m; pl **rolls,** (records) archivos, m pl. **He has**

a nautical r., Tiene un andar de marinero. **to call the r.,** pasar lista. **r. film,** película fotográfica, f. **r. of honour,** lista de honor, f. **r.-on corset,** faja elástica, f, corsé de goma, m. **r.-top desk,** buró de cierre enrollable, m

roll /roul/ vi rodar; dar vueltas; (wallow) revolcarse; (of a ship) balancearse, bambolearse; (in money, etc.) nadar; (flow) correr, fluir; (Fig. of time) pasar tranquilamente; (of vehicle) rodar; pasar rodando; (of country) ondular; (of the sea) ondear; (of drums) redoblar; (of thunder) retumbar. —vt hacer rodar; arrollar; (a cigarette) liar; (metals) laminar; (move) mover; (the eyes) guiñar (los ojos); (the ground) apisonar; (pastry) aplanar; (of an organ) sonar; (a drum) redoblar. **Mary rolled her eyes heavenwards,** María puso los ojos en blanco. **to r. away,** alejarse; desaparecer; (of time) pasar. **to r. back,** volver, retirarse; desaparecer. **to r. by,** pasar rodando; desaparecer. **to r. down,** bajar rodando, rodar por. **to r. in,** llegar en gran cantidad (or en gran número). **to r. off,** caer de. **to r. on,** seguir su marcha; fluir sin cesar; seguir su curso; (of time) avanzar. **to r. out,** (metal) laminar; (pastry) aplanar; (bring out) sacar; desenrollar. **to r. over,** vt volcar; tumbar; dar la vuelta (a). —vi dar la vuelta; volverse al otro lado. **to r. up,** arrollar; envolver; (of hedgehogs, etc.) enroscarse, hacerse un ovillo

roller /'roulər/ n rodillo, m; cilindro, m; (wheel, castor) rueda, f; (for flattening the ground) apisonadora, f; Print. rodillo, m; (wave) ola grande, f. **r.-bandage,** venda, f. **r. canary,** canario de raza flauta, m. **r.-skate,** patín de ruedas, m. **r.-skating,** patinaje de ruedas, m. **r.-towel,** toalla continua, f

rollicking /'rɪlɪkɪŋ/ a alegre, jovial; juguetón

rolling /'roulɪŋ/ a rodante; (of landscape) ondulante, quebrado. —n rodadura, f; (wallowing) revuelco, m; (of metals) laminación, f; (of a ship) balanceo, m; (rolling up) enrollamiento, m. **r.-pin,** rollo, rodillo de pastelero, m. **r.-stock,** material móvil ferroviario, m

Roman /'roumən/ a romano, de los romanos; (of noses and Print.) romano. —n romano (-na). **in R. fashion,** a la romana. **R. Catholic,** a católico; católico apostólico romano. —n el católico (-ca). **R. Catholicism,** catolicismo, m. **R. figures,** números romanos, m pl. **R. nose,** nariz romana, f. **R. road,** vía romana, f. **R. type,** Print. tipo romano, m

Romance /'roumæns/ a (of languages) romance. —n (language) romance, m

romance /rou'mæns/ n novela de caballería, f; romance, m; aventura, f; cuento, m, novela, f; romanticismo, m; Mus. romanza, f. —vi inventar ficciones; exagerar

romantic /rou'mæntɪk/ a and n romántico (-ca)

Rome /roum/ Roma, f

romp /romp/ vi juguetear, brincar, retozar, loquear; correr rápidamente. —n locuelo (-la), saltaparedes, mf; (game) retozo, m. **The horse romped home easily,** El caballo ganó la carrera fácilmente

rompers /'rompərz/ n mono, m

romping /'rompɪŋ/ n juegos, m pl, travesuras, f pl

roof /ruf/ n tejado, techado, m; (of a motor-car, bus) tejadillo, m; (of coaches, etc.) imperial, f; cubierta, f; (of the mouth) paladar, m; (bower) enramada, f; (of heaven) bóveda (del cielo), f. —vt techar, tejar; (shelter) abrigar. **r.-garden,** azotea, f. **r.-gutter,** canalera, f

roofer /'rufər/ n techador, m; constructor de tejados, m

rook /ruk/ n chova, f, grajo, m; (chess) torre, f. —vt engañar, estafar; (overcharge) desollar vivo (a)

room /rum/ n (in a house) habitación, f, cuarto, m; sala, f; cámara, f; (behind a shop) trastienda, f; (space) sitio, espacio, m; lugar, m; (opportunity) oportunidad, f; (cause) motivo, m, causa, f. —vi alojarse. **bath-r.,** cuarto de baño, m. **dining-r.,** comedor, m. **drawing-r.,** salón, m. **There is no r. for us in this car,** No cabemos en este coche. **There is still r. for improvement,** Se puede mejorar todavía. **There isn't r. for anything else,** No cabe más. **to be r.,** caber, haber sitio. **to make r.,** hacer sitio

rooming house /'rutɪd/ n casa de huéspedes, f

roommate /'rum,meit, 'rʌm-/ n compañero de cuarto, compañero de pieza, m

roomy /'rumi, 'rʌmi/ a espacioso, amplio; (of garments) holgado

roost /rust/ n percha de gallinero, f. —vi dormir en una percha; recogerse. **to rule the r.,** ser el amo del cotarro

rooster /'rustər/ n gallo, m,

root /rut or, sometimes, rʊt/ n raíz, f; Gram. radical, m; Mus. base, f; origen, m; explicación, f. —vt arraigar; Fig. fijar, clavar. —vi echar raíces; Fig. arraigarse; (of pigs, etc.) hozar, escarbar; revolver. **to r. out,** arrancar de raíz; Fig. desarraigar; (destroy) extirpar. **cubed r.,** raíz cúbica, f. **from the r.,** (entirely) de raíz. **square r.,** raíz cuadrada, f. **to cut close to the r.,** cortar a raíz

rope /roup/ n soga, cuerda, f; (hawser) maroma, f; Naut. cabo, m; (tight-rope) cable, m, cuerda de volatinero, f; (string) ristra, sarta, f; hilo, m; pl ropes, (boxing) cuerdas del cuadrilátero, f pl. —vt encordelar, atar con cuerdas. **to r. in,** encerrar; (a person) enganchar, coger. **a r. of pearls,** una sarta de perlas. **to give a person plenty of r.,** dar mucha latitud (a). **to know the ropes,** conocer todos los trucos. **r.-ladder,** escala de cuerda, f. **r.-maker,** cordelero (-ra), soguero, m. **r.-**

making, cordelería, soguería, *f.* **r.-trick,** truco de la cuerda, *m.* **r.-walk,** cordelería, *f.* **r.-yarn,** *Naut.* filástica, *f*

rosary /'rouzəri/ *n* rosario, *m.* **to say the r.,** rezar el rosario

rose /rouz/ *n* rosa, *f;* color de rosa, *m;* (rosette) roseta, *f; Archit.* rosetón, *m;* (of watering-can) pomo, *m,* roseta, *f.* —*a* de rosa, rosado. **to see the world through r.-colored spectacles,** ver las cosas en color de rosa. **to turn to r.,** volverse color de rosa, rosear. **r.-bay,** *Bot.* rododafne, adelfa, *f.* **r.-bush,** rosal, *m.* **r.-color,** color de rosa, rosa, *m.* **r.-colored,** de color de rosa, rosado. **r.-garden,** rosalera, rosaleda, *f.* **r. grower,** cultivador (-ra) de rosas. **r. hip,** escaramujo, *m.* **r.-leaf,** hoja de rosa, *f;* pétalo de rosa, *m.* **r.-like,** como una rosa, de rosa. **r.-red,** de color de rosa; como una rosa. **climbing r.-tree,** rosal trepador, *m.* **dwarf r.-tree,** rosal bajo, *m.* **standard r.-tree,** rosal de tallo, *m.* **r.-water,** agua de rosas, *f.* **r.-window,** rosetón, *m,* rosa, *f.* **r.-wood,** palo de rosa, *m*

rosé *a* (of wines) rosado

rosebud /'rouz,bʌd/ *n* capullo de rosa, *m*

rosemary /'rouz,mɛəri/ *n* romero, *m*

rosin /'rɒzin/ *n* (solid, for violin-bows, etc.) colofonia, *f;* resina, *f.* —*vt* dar con colofonia; dar con resina

roster /'rɒstər/ *n* lista, *f;* registro, *m,* matrícula, *f*

rostrum /'rɒstrəm/ *n* tribuna, *f; Zool.* pico, *m;* (of a ship) espolón, *m*

rosy /'rouzi/ *a* róseo, rosado; sonrosado; *Fig.* de color de rosa, halagüeño; optimista. **r.-cheeked,** con (de) mejillas sonrosadas

rot /rɒt/ *n* putrefacción, podredumbre, *f;* (in trees) caries, *f;* (in sheep) comalía, *f;* (slang) patrañas, *f pl,* disparates, *m pl, vi* pudrirse; descomponerse; *Fig.* echarse a perder; (slang) decir disparates. —*vt* pudrir; *Fig.* corromper; (slang) tomar el pelo (a)

rotary /'routəri/ *a* rotativo. **r. printing press,** rotativa, *f*

rotary telephone *n* teléfono de discado, *m*

rotate /'routeit/ *vi* girar, dar vueltas; alternarse. —*vt* hacer girar

rotation /rou'teiʃən/ *n* rotación, *f;* turno, *m.* **in r.,** por turnos. **r. of crops,** rotación de cultivos, *f*

rote, to learn by /rout/ *vt* aprender de memoria, aprender por repetición, aprender de cotorra

rotogravure /,routəgrə'vyur/ *n* rotograbado, *m*

rotten /'rɒtn/ *a* putrefacto; podrido; (of bones, teeth) cariado; dañado, echado a perder; *Fig.* corrompido; (slang) pésimo. **to smell r.,** oler a podredumbre; apestar

rotting /'rɒtiŋ/ *n* pudrición, *f, a* que se pudre

rotund /rou'tʌnd/ *a* rotundo

rotunda /rou'tʌndə/ *n* rotonda, *f*

roué /ru'ei, 'ruei/ *n* calavera, libertino, *m*

rouge /ruʒ/ *n* colorete, *m, vt* and *vi* pintar de rojo, poner(se) colorete

rough /rʌf/ *a* áspero; duro; (of country) fragoso, escabroso; (uneven) desigual; (stormy) borrascoso, tempestuoso; (of the sea) encrespado, bravo; (of movement) violento; (bristling) erizado; (of the hair) despeinado; (unpolished) tosco; basto; (unskilled, clumsy) torpe; (of sounds, tastes) áspero; (of persons) rudo, inculto; (severe) severo; (of behavior) brutal; (of manners) brusco; (rude) grosero; (approximate) aproximado. —*adv* duramente, mal. —*n* estado tosco, *m;* (person) matón, *m.* **in the r.,** en bruto; (roughed out) bosquejado. **to grow r.,** (of the sea) encresparse, embravecerse. **to take the r. with the smooth,** *Fig.* aceptar la realidad; tomar lo bueno con lo malo. **to r. it,** luchar contra las dificultades, pasar apuros; llevar una vida sencilla; vivir mal. **to r. out,** bosquejar. **r. and ready,** improvisado; provisional. **r. and tumble,** *n* camorra, pendencia, *f.* **r.-cast,** *vt* dar una primera capa de mezcla gruesa (a); bosquejar. **r. diamond,** diamante bruto (or en bruto), *m.* **r.-draft,** borrador, *m;* bosquejo, *m.* **r.-haired,** (of a dog) de pelo crespo. **r.-hewn,** modelado toscamente; desbastado; *Fig.* cerril, tosco. **r.-house,** jarana, *f.* **r.-rider,** domador (de caballos), *m.* **r. sketch,** bosquejo, esbozo, *m.* **r.-spoken,** malhablado

roughen /'rʌfən/ *vt* poner áspero. —*vi* ponerse áspero

roughly /'rʌfli/ *adv* rudamente, toscamente; duramente; brutalmente; bruscamente; (of tastes, sounds) ásperamente; (approximately) aproximadamente, más o menos

roughness /'rʌfnis/ *n* aspereza, *f;* dureza, *f;* tosquedad, *f;* rudeza. *f;* (of the sea, wind) braveza, *f;* violencia, *f;* (of manner) brusquedad, *f;* brutalidad, *f;* (vulgarity) grosería, *f.* **the r. of the way,** la aspereza del camino

roulette /ru'lɛt/ *n* ruleta, *f*

round /raund/ *a* redondo; (plump) rollizo; rotundo, categórico; sonoro. **a r. sum,** una cantidad redonda; un número redondo. **to walk at a r. pace,** andar a un buen paso. **r. dance,** baile en ruedo, *m.* **r.-faced,** carilleno, de cara redonda. **r.-house,** cuerpo de guardia, *m; Naut.* tumbadillo, *m.* **r.-shouldered,** cargado de espaldas. **r. table,** mesa redonda, *f;* (of King Arthur) Tabla Redonda, *f.* **r. trip,** viaje redondo, viaje de ida y vuelta, *m.* **r.-up,** rodeo de ganado, *m;* arresto, *m*

round /raund/ *n* círculo, *m;* esfera, *f;* redondez, *f;* (slice) rodaja, *f;* (of a ladder) peldaño, *m;* (patrol and *Mil.*) ronda, *f;* circuito, *m;* vuelta, *f,* giro, *m;* serie, *f;* rutina, *f;* (of ammunition) andanada, descarga, *f;* (of cartridge) cartucho lleno, *m;* (of applause, etc.) salva, *f;* (of golf) partido, *m;* (in a fight) asalto, *m; Sports.*

vuelta, *f*; (of drinks) ronda, *f*; (doctor's) visitas, *f pl*

round /raund/ *vt* redondear; (*Fig.* complete) acabar, perfeccionar; (go round, e.g. a corner) dar vuelta (a), doblar, trasponer; rodear, cercar; (of a ship) doblar. —*vi* redondearse. **to r. off**, redondear; terminar; coronar. **to r. up**, (cattle) rodear. **to r. upon**, volverse contra

round /raund/ *adv* en derredor; por todos lados; a la redonda, en torno; en circunferencia; en conjunto (**r. is not** translated in Spanish, e.g. *I shall come r. to your house,* Vendré a tu casa). —*prep* alrededor de. **all the year r.,** todo el año, el año entero. **r. about,** a la redonda de. al derredor de; (nearly) cerca de; (of time by the clock) a eso de. **The road is closed and we shall have to go r.,** El camino está cerrado y tendremos que dar una vuelta. **to come r.,** volver; dejarse persuadir; recobrar su buen humor. **to go r.,** (spin) dar vueltas; (of the wind) cambiar. **There is enough to go r.,** Hay bastante para todos

roundabout /a. ,raundə'baut, *n.* 'raundə,baut/ *a* indirecto; desviado; vago. —*n* tiovivo, *m*; (traffic) redondel, *m*. **He spoke in a r. way,** Hablaba con circunloquios. **We went there by a r. way,** Fuimos dando un rodeo

roundly /'raundli/ *adv* en redondo; rotundamente, claramente

rouse /rauz/ *vt* despertar; animar; excitar; suscitar, provocar. **to r. oneself,** despertarse; animarse (a hacer algo)

rousing /'rauziŋ/ *a* que despierta; (moving) emocionante; (enthusiastic) entusiasta; grande, bueno

rout /raut/ *n* (rabble) chusma, *f*; (party) sarao, *m*; (defeat) derrota, *f*; (meeting) reunión, *f*. —*vt* derrotar, poner en fuga; vencer

route /rut, raut/ *n* ruta, *f*; camino, *m*; itinerario, *m*. **r. march,** marcha de maniobras, *f*

routine /ru'tin/ *n* rutina, *f*, *a* rutinario, de rutina

rove /rouv/ *vi* vagar, errar

roving /'rouviŋ/ *a* vagabundo, errante; ambulante

row /rou/ *n* (line) hilera, fila, hila, *f*; (in a theater, etc.) fila, *f*; (string) ristra, *f*; (in a boat) paseo en bote, *m*; (commotion) alboroto, *m*; (noise) ruido, *m*; (shindy) gresca, camorra, *f*; (scolding) regaño, *m*, *vi* (a boat) remar, bogar. —*vt* conducir remando; (scold) regañar. **to be a row,** (shindy) haber la de San Quintín. **to start a row,** (shindy) armar camorra.

rowboat /'rou,bout/ *n* bote de remos, *m*

rowdy /'raudi/ *a* alborotador. —*n* trafalmejas, *mf* rufián, *m*

rower /'rouər/ *n* remero (-ra), bogador (-ra)

rowing /'rouiŋ/ *a* que rema; de remos. —*n* deporte del remo, *m*; paseo en bote, *m*. **r.-boat,** bote de remos, *m*. **r.-club,**

club náutico, *m*. **r.-seat,** bancada, *f*. **r.-stroke,** bogada, *f*

royal /'rɔiəl/ *a* real; regio. —*n Naut.* sobrejuanete, *m*. **r. academy,** real academia, *f*. **r. eagle,** águila real, *f*. **R. Highness,** Alteza Real, *f*. **r. letters patent,** cédula real, *f*. **R. Mail,** mala real, *f*. **R. Standard,** estandarte real, *m*

royalty /'rɔiəlti/ *n* realeza, *f*; miembro de la familia real, *m*; tanto por ciento de los ingresos, *m*; derechos de autor, *m pl*

R.R. (abbrev. of *Railroad*) F.R. (abbrev. of *ferrocarril*)

rub /rʌb/ *vt* frotar, estregar; fregar; rozar; friccionar; (make sore) raspar. **to rub one's hands together,** frotarse las manos. **to rub the wrong way,** frotar a contrapelo. **to rub against,** rozar. **to rub along,** *Inf.* ir tirando. **to rub down,** (a horse) bruzar; limpiar; (dry) secar; (wear down) desgastar. **to rub in,** dar fricciones con; frotar con; (an idea, etc.) machacar. **to rub off,** *vt* quitar (frotando); borrar. —*vi* borrarse; separarse (de). **to rub out,** *vt* borrar. —*vi* borrarse. **to rub up,** (polish) limpiar; *Fig.* refrescar

rub /rʌb/ *n* frotación, *f*; roce, *m*; fricción, *f*; *Fig.* obstáculo, *m*; dificultad, *f*. **to give a rub,** frotar, etc. **rub-a-dub,** rataplán, *m*

rubber /'rʌbər/ *a* de caucho, de goma. —*n* caucho, *m*, goma, *f*; (for erasing) goma de borrar, *f*; (masseur) masajista, *mf*; (at whist, etc.) partida, *f*; *pl* **rubbers,** zapatos de goma, chanclos, *m pl*. **synthetic r.,** caucho artificial, *m*. **r. band,** goma, banda de goma, *f*. **r. belt,** *Mech.* correa de transmisión de caucho, *f*. **r.-plant, tree,** cauchera, *f*. **r. plantation,** cauchal, *m*. **r. planter,** cauchero, *m*. **r. stamp,** estampilla, *f*

rubbing /'rʌbiŋ/ *n* frotación, *f*; fricción, *f*; roce, *m*; (of floors, dishes, etc.) fregado, *m*

rubbish /'rʌbiʃ/ *n* basura, *f*; desperdicios, *m pl*, desecho, *m*; (of goods) pacotilla, *f*; (nonsense) pamplinas, patrañas, *f pl*, disparates, *m pl*. **r. cart,** carro del basurero, *m*

rubble /'rʌbəl or, for , 'rʌbəl/ *n* escombros, *m pl*; cascote, *m*; piedra bruta, *f*

rubicund /'rubi,kʌnd/ *a* rubicundo

rubric /'rubrik/ *n* rúbrica, *f*

ruby /'rubi/ *n* rubí, *m*. —*a* de rubíes; de rubí. **r. lips,** labios de rubí, *m pl*

rucksack /'rʌk,sæk, 'ruk-/ *n* mochila, *f*

rudder /'rʌdər/ *n* timón, gobernalle, *m*

ruddy /'rʌdi/ *a* rubicundo; rojo; fresco(te); (of animals) barcino

rude /rud/ *a* rudo; tosco; vigoroso; grosero, descortés

rudeness /'rudnis/ *n* rudeza, *f*; tosquedad, *f*; grosería, incivilidad, descortesía, *f*

rudiment /'rudəmənt/ *n* rudimento, *m*

rudimentary /,rudə'mɛntəri/ *a* rudimentario

rue /ru/ *vt* lamentar, llorar. —*n Bot.* ruda, *f*

rueful /'rufəl/ *a* triste, melancólico; ladhmentable

ruff /rʌf/ *n* golilla, lechuguilla, *f*; (of a bird) collarín de plumas, *m*; (of an animal) collarín de pelo, *m*

ruffian /'rʌfiən/ *n* rufián, *m*

ruffle /'rʌfəl/ *n Sew.* volante fruncido, *m*; (of a bird) collarín de plumas, *m*; (of an animal) collarín de pelo, *m*; (ripple) rizo, *m*; (annoyance) irritación, *f*. —*vt* (ripple) rizar; (pleat) fruncir; (feathers) erizar; (hair) despeinar; agitar; (annoy) irritar, incomodar

ruffling /'rʌflɪŋ/ *n* (rippling) rizado, *m*; (pleating) fruncido, *m*; (of the temper) irritación, *f*

rug /rʌg/ *n* (floor) alfombra, *f*; manta de viaje, *f*. **rug strap**, portamantas, *m*

rugged /'rʌgɪd/ *a* áspero, escabroso; escarpado, abrupto; (wrinkled) arrugado; tosco; (harsh) duro, severo; inculto; rudo; mal acabado; vigoroso

ruggedness /'rʌgɪdnɪs/ *n* aspereza, escabrosidad, *f*; lo escarpado; dureza, severidad, *f*; rudeza, *f*; vigor, *m*

ruin /'ruɪn/ *n* ruina, *f*. —*vt* arruinar; echar a perder, estropear por completo; (a woman) perder

ruination /,ruə'neɪʃən/ *n* ruina, perdición, *f*

ruined /'ruɪnd/ *a* arruinado; en ruinas

ruinous /'ruənəs/ *a* ruinoso; en ruinas

rule /rul/ *n* regla, *f*; gobierno, *m*; autoridad, *f*; mando, *m*; administración, *f*; (reign) reinado, *m*; (of a court, etc.) orden, *f*; (for measuring) regla, *f*; *Print.* regleta, *f*; *pl* **rules**, reglas, *f pl*; reglamento, *m*. —*vt* gobernar; regentar, regir; (control) dominar; (of a chairman, etc.) disponer, decidir; (guide) guiar; (lines) reglar. —*vi* gobernar; (of a monarch) reinar; (of prices) mantenerse; estar en boga, prevalecer. **as a r.**, por regla general, en general. **slide-r.**, regla de cálculo, *f*. **to make it a r.**, tener por regla; tener por costumbre; tener por máxima. **to r. out**, excluir; *Law.* no admitir. **to r. over**, (of a king, etc.) reinar sobre. **r. of the road**, reglamento del tráfico, *m*. **r. of thumb**, regla empírica, *f*; rutina, *f*

ruler /'rulər/ *n* gobernador (-ra); soberano (-na); (master) amo (ama); (for ruling lines) regla, *f*

ruling /'rulɪŋ/ *a* regente; dominante; (current) vigente. —*n* gobierno, *m*; *Law.* decisión, *f*; fallo, *m*; (with lines) rayado, *m*. **r. pen**, tiralíneas, *m*

rum /rʌm/ *n* ron, *m*

rumble /'rʌmbəl/ *vi* retumbar, tronar; (of vehicles) rugir; crujir. —*n* retumbo, trueno, *m*; rugido, *m*; ruido sordo, *m*; rumor, *m*; crujido, *m*

rumbling /'rʌmblɪŋ/ *a* que retumba, etc. —*n* ruido sordo, *m*; retumbo, *m*; crujido, *m*; (in the bowels) rugido, *m*

ruminant /'rumənənt/ *a* and *n* rumiante, *mf*

ruminate /'rumə,neɪt/ *vi* and *vt* rumiar

rumination /,rumə'neɪʃən/ *n* rumia, *f*; meditación, reflexión, *f*

rummage /'rʌmɪdʒ/ *vt* revolver, desordenar, trastornar; explorar. **to r. out**, desenterrar

rumor /'rumər/ *n* rumor, *m*, fama, *f*. **It is rumored that...**, Hay rumores de que..., La voz corre que..., Se dice que...

rump /rʌmp/ *n* (of an animal) nalgas, ancas, *f pl*; cuarto trasero, *m*; (of a bird) rabadilla, *f*; (scornful) culo, *m*, posaderas, *f pl*. **r.-steak**, solomillo, *m*

rumple /'rʌmpəl/ *vt* arrugar; desordenar

run /rʌn/ *vi* correr; acudir; (flee) huir; (rush) precipitarse, lanzarse; (in a race) tomar parte en una carrera; competir; (pass over) deslizarse (por); (of machines) andar, marchar; (of traffic) circular; (leave, of trains, ships, etc.) salir; (ply between) hacer el trayecto entre... y...; (flow) fluir, correr; (into the sea, of rivers) desembocar (en); (spurt) chorrear, manar; (drip) gotear; (leak) dejar fugar (el agua, etc.); (of colors) correrse; caer; (of tears) correr; derramarse; (of eyes) llorar; (melt) derretirse; (of a sore) supurar; (travel or go) ir; moverse; (work) trabajar; funcionar; (of editions of a book) agotarse; (of a play) representarse; (cross) cruzar; (elapse) correr; transcurrir, pasar; (become) hacerse; (of wording) decir; (be current) correr; (for parliament, etc.) hacerse candidato; (navigate) navegar; (spread) extenderse; (be) estar; (of thoughts) pasar; (last) durar; (tend) tender (a). —*vt* (a race, a horse) correr; (drive) conducir; (a business, etc.) administrar; dirigir; (govern) gobernar; regir; (hunt) cazar; perseguir; (water, etc.) hacer correr; (pierce) clavar; introducir; (push) empujar; (one's hand, eye, etc.) pasar; (risks, etc.) correr; (possess) tener; establecer un servicio de (autobuses, etc.); (smuggle) hacer contrabando de. **The ship ran aground**, El barco encalló. **to run dry**, secarse; agotarse. **to run in the family**, estar en la familia. **to run into debt**, endeudarse; contraer deudas. **to run to seed**, granar; agotarse. **Steamers run daily between Barcelona and Mallorca**, Hay servicio diario de vapores entre Barcelona y Mallorca. **A stab of pain ran up his leg**, Sintió un dolor agudo en la pierna. **Feeling was running high**, Los ánimos estaban excitados. **My arrangements ran smoothly**, Mis planes marchaban bien. **Funds are running low**, El dinero escasea. **The tune runs in my head**, Tengo la canción metida en la cabeza. **The message runs like this**, El mensaje reza así, El mensaje dice así. **He ran his fingers through his hair**, Se mesaba los cabellos. **to run about**, andar de un lado a otro, correr por todas partes; (gad) corretear. **to run across**, cruzar corriendo; (meet) topar con, tropezar con. **to run after**, correr detrás (de); perseguir; buscar. **to**

run against, (collide with) dar contra; (meet) tropezar con. **to run at,** abalanzarse hacia, precipitarse sobre; atacar. **to run away,** huir, escaparse; (slip away) escurrirse; (of a horse) dispararse, desbocarse. **to run away with,** huir con, fugarse con; (carry off) arrebatar; (steal) llevarse; (imagine) imaginarse, figurarse; (of temper, etc.) dominar, poseer. **to run back,** volver corriendo; llegar corriendo; retroceder rápidamente, correr hacia atrás. **to run backwards,** correr hacia atrás; **to run backwards and forwards,** ir y venir. **to run behind,** correr detrás (de); quedarse atrás; (be late) estar atrasado. **to run down,** *vi* bajar corriendo; descender, bajar; (of a clock) parar; (of a battery) gastarse; (of liquids) correr; fluir; (drop by drop) destilar. —*vt* (capture) coger; alcanzar; (a person by a vehicle) atropellar; (a ship) echar a pique; (disparage) hablar mal de. **run-down,** (in health) agotado; (of a clock) parado. **to run for,** buscar corriendo; correr para coger (el autobús, etc.); (president, etc.) ser candidato para. **to run in,** *vi* entrar corriendo. —*vt* arrestar; hacer prisionero; *Print.* encerrar. **to run into,** tropezar con; chocar con; (plunge into) meterse de cabeza en; (of sums of money, etc.) ascender a; (of streets, rivers, etc.) desembocar en. **to run off,** *vi* escaparse corriendo; marcharse corriendo. —*vt* deslizarse por; (drain) vaciar; *Print.* imprimir; (compose) componer. **to run off with,** huir con. **to run on,** correr delante; continuar; (of the mind) pensar en, entregarse a; hablar sin cesar; *Print.* recorrer. **to run out,** *vi* salir corriendo; (of liquids) derramarse; salir; (end) acabarse; agotarse; (project) sobresalir. —*vt* (cricket) coger al lanzador fuera de la línea de saque. **to run out of,** no tener más de, haber terminado. **to run over,** *vi* rebosar; derramarse. —*vt* (of a vehicle) atropellar, pasar por encima de; (peruse) repasar; revisar. **run pell-mell,** salir pitando, salir volando, salvarse por pies. **to run through,** correr por; pasar por; recorrer; (go directly) ir directamente (a); (pierce) traspasar, pasar de parte a parte; (squander) derrochar, malbaratar; (read) hojear, leer por encima a. **to run up,** *vt* (hoist) izar; hacer de prisa; construir rápidamente; (incur) incurrir. —*vi* subir corriendo; (of plants) trepar (por); (shrink) encogerse; (of expenses) aumentar. **to run up to time,** llegar a su hora. **to run up against,** tropezar con; (opposition, etc.) encontrar.

run /rʌn/ *n* carrera, corrida, *f;* (excursion) visita, excursión, *f;* (cricket) carrera, *f;* (walk) paseo, *m;* (by train or sea) viaje, *m;* (by bus, tram) trayecto, *m;* (sea crossing) travesía, *f;* (distance run) recorrido, *m;* (of events, etc.) curso, *m;* marcha, *f;* (of markets, etc.) tendencia, *f;* (rhythm) ritmo, *m;* dirección, *f;* distancia, *f; Mus.* serie de notas, *f;* serie, *f;* duración, *f;*

Theat. serie de representaciones, *f;* (freedom to use) libre uso, *m;* (majority) mayoría, *f;* (on a bank) asedio, *m;* (on a book, etc.) d > f; (for sheep, etc.) terreno de pasto, *m;* (for fowls) gallinero, *m.* **a run of bad luck,** una temporada de mala suerte. **at a run,** corriendo. **in the long run,** a la larga, al fin y al cabo. **on the run,** en fuga; ocupado. **Prices came down with a run,** Los precios bajaron de golpe. **take-off run,** *Aer.* recorrido de despegue, *m*

runaway /'rʌnə,wei/ *a* fugitivo; (of a horse) desbocado

rung /rʌŋ/ *n* (of a ladder) peldaño, *m;* (of a chair) travesaño, *m;* (lath) listón, *m*

runner /'rʌnər/ *n* corredor (-ra); (carrier of sedan chair, etc.) silletero, *mf;* (smuggler) contrabandista, *m;* (courier) estafeta, *f;* (messenger) mensajero, *m;* (ring) anillo movible, pasador corredizo, *m;* rueda móvil, *f;* (of a sledge) patín, *m; Bot.* tallo rastrero, *m.* **r.-up,** el segundo

running /'rʌnɪŋ/ *a* corredor; (of water, bank accounts) corriente; (of a knot) corredizo; (of a sore) supurante; (continuous) continuo; (consecutive) consecutivo. —*n* carrera, *f;* marcha, *f;* funcionamiento, *m;* administración, *f;* gobierno, *m;* dirección, *f;* (flowing) derrame, *m;* (of trains, buses, etc.) servicio, *m;* (smuggling) contrabando, *m;* (of a sore) supuración, *f.* **six times r.,** seis veces consecutivas. **The car is in r. order,** El auto está en buen estado. **r. away,** fuga, *f.* **r.-board,** (of a car, etc.) estribo, *m;* (of a locomotive) plataforma, *f.* **r. costs,** gastos de mantenimiento, *m pl;* (railway) gastos de tracción, *m pl.* **r. fight,** acción de retirada, *f.* **r.-knot,** lazo corredizo, *m.* **r. title,** *Print.* título de la columna, *m*

run-off match /'rʌnɒf/ *n* desempate, *m*

runway /'rʌn,wei/ *n* (for launching a ship) grada, *f;* (of an airfield) pista de aterrizaje, *f*

rupture /'rʌptʃər/ *n* rompimiento, *m,* rotura, *f;* ruptura, *f; med* hernia, *f*

ruptured /'rʌptʃərd/ *a med* herniado, quebrado

rural /'rʊrəl/ *a* rural, campestre, del campo; agrario

ruse /ruz/ *n* artimaña, treta, ardid, *f*

rush /rʌʃ/ *n Bot.* junco, *m;* acometida, *f;* ataque, *m;* (of water) torrente, *m;* (bustle) bullicio, *m;* (speed) prisa, *f;* precipitación, *f;* acceso, *m;* (crowd) tropel, *m,* masa, *f;* (struggle) lucha, *f;* furia, *f.* —*vi* precipitarse, lanzarse; agolparse. —*vt* llevar rápidamente (a); despachar rápidamente; precipitar; (attack) asaltar, atacar; (capture) tomar, capturar; hacer de prisa; (a bill) hacer aprobar de prisa. **to r. upon,** abalanzarse hacia; embestir. **in a r.,** en tropel, en masa; de prisa. **to r. to a conclusion,** precipitarse a una conclusión. **r.-bottomed,** con asiento de enea. **r. hour,** hora de mayor circulación, *f,* hora de aglomeración, hora-pico (Argentina), hora brava (Argentina, informal). **r. order,** pedido urgente, *m*

russet /'rʌsɪt/ *a* rojizo; rojo. **r. apple,** manzana asperiega, *f*

Russia /'rʌʃə/ Rusia, *f*

Russian /'rʌʃən/ *a* ruso. —*n* ruso (-sa); (language) ruso, *m*. **R. leather,** piel de Rusia, *f*

rust /rʌst/ *n* herrumbre, *f*, orín, *m;* moho, *m;* (disease) añublo, tizón, *m*. —*vt* aherrumbrar; enmohecer. —*vi* aherrumbrarse; enmohecerse

rustic /'rʌstɪk/ *a* rústico; campesino, aldeano; (scornful) palurdo, grosero. —*n* aldeano, *m;* (scornful) patán, *m*

rusticate /'rʌstɪˌkeit/ *vi* rusticar, vivir en el campo. —*vt* enviar al campo

rustiness /'rʌstinɪs/ *n* herrumbre, *f;* en-

mohecimiento, *m;* color rojizo, *m; Fig.* falta de práctica, *f*

rustle /'rʌsəl/ *n* susurro, *m;* murmurio, *m;* (of silk, a dress, etc.) frufrú, *m;* (of paper, etc.) crujido, *m*. —*vi* susurrar; murmurar; crujir. —*vt* (a paper) hacer crujir

rusty /'rʌsti/ *a* herrumbroso; enmohecido, mohoso; (red) rojizo, (worn out) usado, viejo; (out of practice) desacostumbrado; (forgotten) empolvorado, oxidado (e.g. *My Portuguese is rusty,* Mi portugués está empolvorado)

rut /rʌt/ *n* rodera, *f,* bache, surco, *m; fig* sendero trillado, *m; fig* rutina, *f;* (sexual appetite) celo, *m, vi* estar en celo

ruthless /'ruθlɪs/ *a* inhumano, insensible, despiadado; inexorable, inflexible

rye /rai/ *n* centeno, *m*. **rye field,** centenar, *m*

s /ɛs/ n (letter) ese, f

Sabbath /'sæbəθ/ n (Jewish) sábado, m; (Christian) domingo, m

sabbatical /sə'bætɪkəl/ a sabático

sable /'seibəl/ n (animal and fur) marta, f; herald sable, m. —a herald sable; poet negro

sabotage /'sæbə,tɑʒ/ n sabotaje, m, vt cometer un acto de sabotaje en

saboteur /,sæbə'tɜr/ n saboteador, m

sac /sæk/ n biol saco, m

saccharin /'sækərɪn/ n sacarina, f

sachet /sæ'ʃei/ n sachet, m; bolsa, f. **handkerchief s.,** bolsa para pañuelos, f

sack /sæk/ n (bag) saco, m; mil saqueo, saqueamiento, saco, m. —vt meter en sacos; (dismiss) dar pasaporte (a), despedir; mil saquear. **to get the s.,** recibir el pasaporte. **to give the s.,** dar el pasaporte (a), poner de patitas en la calle (a). **s. coat,** saco, m

sackcloth /'sæk,klɔθ/ n harpillera, f. **to repent in s. and ashes,** ponerse cenizas en la cabeza

sacrament /'sækrəmənt/ n sacramento, m; Eucaristía, f. **the Blessed S.,** el Santisimo Sacramento. **to receive the Holy S.,** comulgar. **to receive the last sacraments,** recibir los sacramentos, recibir la Extremaunción

sacred /'seikrɪd/ a sagrado; sacro, santo; consagrado. **Nothing is s. to them,** No hay nada sagrado para ellos, No respetan nada. **the S. Heart of Jesus,** el Sagrado Corazón (de Jesús). **S. to the memory of...** Consagrado a la memoria de... **s. music,** música sagrada, f

sacrifice /'sækrə,fais/ n sacrificio, m. —vt and vi sacrificar. **s. of the mass,** sacrificio del altar, m

sacrilege /'sækrəlɪdʒ/ n sacrilegio, m

sacrilegious /,sækrɪ'lɪdʒəs/ a sacrílego

sacrosanct /'sækrou,sæŋkt/ a sacrosanto

sad /sæd/ a triste; melancólico; (of a mistake) deplorable, funesto; Inf. redomado; (pensive) pensativo. **How s!** ¡Qué lástima! ¡Qué triste! **It made me s.,** Me entristeció

sadden /'sædn/ vt entristecer, acongojar, afligir

saddle /'sædl/ n (riding) silla de montar, f; (of a bicycle, etc.) sillín, m; mech silla, f; Anat. espalda, f. —vt ensillar. **s. with the responsibility of,** echar la responsabilidad de (a). **s. of mutton,** lomo de carnero, m. **s.-bag,** alforja, f. **s.-cloth,** mantilla de silla, f. **s.-tree,** arzón, m

sadism /'seidɪzəm/ n sadismo, m

sadist /'seidɪst/ n sadista, mf

sadistic /sə'dɪstɪk/ a sadístico

sadness /'sædnɪs/ n tristeza, melancolía, f

safe /seif/ a al abrigo (de); seguro; salvo; (certain) cierto; prudente; digno de confianza. —n caja de caudales, f; (for food) alacena, f. **I stood beneath a tree s. from the rain,** Estaba de pie bajo un árbol, al abrigo de la lluvia. **to put something in a s. place,** poner algo en salvo; poner algo en un lugar seguro. **s. and sound,** sano y salvo. **s.-conduct,** salvoconducto, m. **s.-keeping,** lugar seguro, m; (of a person) buenas manos, f pl

safeguard /'seif,gɑrd/ n protección, garantía, f; precaución, f. —vt proteger, guardar; tomar precauciones (contra)

safely /'seifli/ adv seguramente; sin accidente, sin novedad, sano y salvo; sin peligro. **You may s. tell him,** Puedes decírselo con toda seguridad. **to put (something) away s.,** poner (algo) en un lugar seguro

safety /'seifti/ n seguridad, f. —a de seguridad; (of locks) de golpe. **a place of s.,** un lugar seguro. **in s.,** en salvo, en seguro; con seguridad. **to believe in s. first,** poner la seguridad en primer lugar. **to play for s.,** jugar seguro. **with complete s.,** con toda seguridad. **s.-belt,** (cinto) salvavidas, m. **s.-catch,** fiador, m. **s.-curtain,** telón de seguridad, telón contra incendios, m. **s.-fuse,** espoleta de seguridad, f. **s.-glass,** vidrio inastillable, m. **s.-island,** refugio para peatones, m. **s.-lamp,** lámpara de seguridad, f. **s.-latch,** pestillo de golpe, m. **s.-lock,** (of firearms) seguro, m; (of doors, etc.) cerradura de seguridad, f. **s.-pin,** imperdible, m. **s.-razor,** máquina de afeitar, f. **s.-valve,** válvula de seguridad, f

saffron /'sæfrən/ n azafrán, m, a azafranado, de color de azafrán.

sag /sæg/ vi doblegarse, ceder; inclinarse; naut caer a sotavento; (of prices) bajar; (of spirits, etc.) flaquear

saga /'sɑgə/ n saga, f; epopeya, f

sagacious /sə'geiʃəs/ a sagaz, perspicaz; (of animals) sabio

sagacity /sə'gæsɪti/ n sagacidad, perspicacia, f; (of animals) sabiduría, f

sage /seidʒ/ n sabio, m; bot salvia, f. —a sabio; sagaz; cuerdo

said /sɛd/ a antedicho; tal dicho. **No sooner s. than done,** Dicho y hecho. **the s. Mr. Martínez,** el tal Sr. Martínez

sail /seil/ n (of a ship) vela, f; (sailing-ship) velero, m; (of a windmill) aspa, f; mech ala, f; (trip) paseo en barco, m. —vi navegar; ir en barco; dar un paseo en barco; (leave) salir en barco; zarpar; (of swans, etc.) deslizarse; (of clouds, etc.) flotar. —vt (a ship) gobernar; (the sea) navegar por. **She sailed into the room,** Entró majestuosamente en la sala. **The ship sailed at eight knots,** El buque navegaba a ocho nudos. **to go for a s.,** dar un paseo en barco. **to s. round the world,** dar la vuelta al mundo. **to s. the seas,** navegar por los mares. **to set s.,** darse a la vela, zarpar. **to take in the sails,** amainar. **s.-maker,** velero, m. **to s.**

into, entrar en. **to s. round,** (the Cape, etc.) doblar. **to s. up,** subir en barco; (of a boat) ir río arriba

sailing /'seiliŋ/ *n* navegación, *f*; (departure) salida, *f.* **It's all plain s.,** Todo va viento en popa. **s.-boat,** bote de vela, *m.* **s.-ship,** buque de vela, velero, *m*

sailor /'seilər/ *n* marinero, *m.* **John is a bad s.,** Juan se marea fácilmente. **to be a good s.,** no marearse. **s.-blouse,** marinera, *f.* **s.-suit,** traje de marinero, *m*

saint /seint/ *n* santo (-ta); (before masculine names of Sts., excluding Sts. Dominic and Thomas) San; *Inf.* ángel, *m.* **All Saints' Day,** el día de Todos los Santos. **saint's day,** fiesta de un santo (or de una santa), *f*; (of a person) santo, *m.* **St. Bernard dog,** perro de San Bernardo, *m.* **St. John the Baptist,** San Juan Bautista. **St. Martin's summer,** el veranillo de San Martín. **St. Vitus's dance,** el baile de San Vito

sainthood /'seinthud/ *n* santidad, *f*

saintly /'seintli/ *a* de santo; de santa; santo; inf angelical

sake /seik/ *n* amor, *m*; causa, *f.* **for God's s.,** por el amor de Dios. **for the s. of,** para; por amor de. **to talk for talking's s.,** hablar por hablar

salable /'seiləbəl/ *a* vendible

salad /'sæləd/ *n* ensalada, *f*; (lettuce) lechuga, *f.* **fruit s.,** macedonia de frutas, *f.* **s.-bowl,** ensaladera, *f.* **s.-dressing,** aderezo, aliño, *m*, salsa para ensalada, *f.* **s.-oil,** aceite para ensaladas, *m*

salamander /'sælə,mændər/ *n* salamandra, *f*

salary /'sæləri/ *n* sueldo, salario, *m*

sale /seil/ *n* venta, *f*; (auction) almoneda, subasta pública, *f.* **clearance s.,** liquidación, *f*, saldo, *m.* **to be on s.,** estar de venta. «Piano for s.,» «Se vende un piano.» **s. price,** precio de venta, *m*; precio de saldo, *m*

salesman /'seilzmən/ *n* dependiente de tienda, *m*; (traveller) viajante, *m*

salesroom /'seilz,rum/ *n* salón de ventas, *m*

salient /'seiliənt/ *a* saliente; *Fig.* prominente, conspicuo, notable, *n* saliente, *m.* **s. angle,** ángulo saliente, *m*

saliva /sə'laivə/ *n* saliva, *f*

sallow /'sælou/ *a* cetrino, oliváceo, lívido

sally /'sæli/ *n* (mil. etc) salida, *f*; (quip) ocurrencia, salida, *f.* **—vi** hacer una salida, salir. **to s. forth,** ponerse en camino

salmon /'sæmən/ *n* salmón, *m*; color de salmón, *m.* **s.-net,** salmonera, *f.* **s. trout,** trucha asalmonada, *f*

salon /sə'lɒn/ *n* salón, *m*

saloon /sə'lun/ *n* sala, *f*; (of a steamer) cámara, *f*, salón, *m*; (on train, for sleeping) departamento de coche cama, *m*; (on train, for dining) coche comedor, *m*; *auto* coche cerrado, *m.* **billiard s.,** salón de billares, *m.* **dancing s.,** salón de baile, *m.*

hair-dresser's s., salón de peluquero, *m.* **s. bar,** bar, *m*

salt /sɔlt/ *n* sal, *f*; (spice) sabor, *m*; (wit) sal, agudeza, *f.* **—a** salobre, salino; salado; (of land) salitroso. **—vt** (season) poner sal en; (cure) salar. **kitchen s.,** sal de cocina, *f.* **old s.,** inf lobo de mar, *m.* **rock s.,** sal gema, *f.* **sea s.,** sal marina, *f.* **to be not worth one's s.,** no merecer el pan que se come. **to take with a pinch of s.,** tomar con su grano de sal. **s.-cellar,** salero, *m.* **s. lagoon,** albufera, *f.* **s. lake,** lago salado, *m.* **s. marsh,** saladar, *m.* **s. meat,** carne salada, cecina, *f.* **s. merchant,** salinero, *m.* **s.-mine,** mina de sal, *f.* **s.-spoon,** cucharita de sal, *f.* **s. water,** agua salada, *f*; agua de mar, *f.* **s.-water fish,** pez de mar, *m.* **s.-works,** salinas *f pl*

salty /'sɔlti/ *a* salado; salobre

salubrious /sə'lubriəs/ *a* salubre, saludable, sano

salutary /'sælyə,tɛri/ *a* saludable, beneficioso

salutation /,sælyə'teiʃən/ *n* salutación, *f*, saludo, *m*

salute /sə'lut/ *vt* and *vi* saludar. **—n** saludo, *m*; (of guns) salva, *f.* **to fire a s.,** hacer salvas, saludar con... salvas. **The soldier saluted them,** El soldado les saludó. **to take the s.,** tomar el saludo. **saluting base,** puesto de mando, *m*

Salvadoran, Salvadorian /,sælvə'dɔrən; -'dɔriən/ *a* and *n* salvadoreño (-ña)

salvage /'sælvidʒ/ *n* salvamento, *m*, *vt* salvar

salvation /sæl'veiʃən/ *n* salvación, *f.* **to work out one's own s.,** salvar el alma. **the S. Army,** el Ejército de la Salvación, *m*

salve /sælv/ *n* pomada, *f*; fig bálsamo, *m.* **—vt** curar; (overcome) vencer; (soothe) tranquilizar; *naut* salvar. **to s. one's conscience,** tranquilizar la conciencia

salvo /'sælvou/ *n* (of guns or applause) salva, *f*; (reservation) salvedad, reservación, *f.* **s. of applause,** salva de aplausos, *f*

same /seim/ *a* mismo; igual; parecido; idéntico. **—adv** lo mismo; del mismo modo. **all the s.,** sin embargo; con todo, a pesar de eso. **at the s. time,** al mismo tiempo; a la vez. **just the s.,** igual; (nevertheless) sin embargo. **He bowed deeply and I did the s.,** Él hizo una profunda reverencia y yo hice lo mismo. **They do not look at things the s. as we do,** No ven las cosas del mismo modo que nosotros. **If it is the s. to her,** Si le da igual. **It's all the s.,** Es igual, Lo mismo da, Es todo uno. Ávila, **capital of the province of the s. name,** Ávila, capital de la provincia de su nombre

"Same-Day Service" /'seimdei/ «En el día» (Argentina)

sample /'sæmpəl/ *n* muestra, *f*; prueba, *f*;

ejemplo, *m.* —*vt* sacar una muestra de; (try) probar. **s. book,** muestrario, *m*

sampler /'sæmplər/ *n* probador, *m;* (of wines) catador, *m;* (sew) dechado, *m*

sanatorium /ˌsænə'tɔriəm/ *n* sanatorio, *m*

sanctify /'sæŋktəˌfai/ *vt* santificar; consagrar

sanctimonious /ˌsæŋktə'mouniəs/ *a* santurrón, mojigato, beato

sanction /'sæŋkʃən/ *n* sanción, *f.* —*vt* sancionar; autorizar. **to apply sanctions,** *polit* aplicar sanciones

sanctity /'sæŋktɪti/ *n* santidad, *f;* lo sagrado; inviolabilidad, *f.* **odor of s.,** olor de santidad, *f*

sanctuary /'sæŋktʃuˌɛri/ *n* santuario, *m;* (historical) sagrado, sagrado asilo, *m;* refugio, asilo, *m.* **to take s.,** acogerse a sagrado; refugiarse

sand /sænd/ *n* arena, *f;* (for drying writing) arenilla, *f;* granos de arena, *m pl; pl* **sands,** playa, *f;* (of life) horas de la vida, *f pl.* —*vt* arenar. **to plough the s.,** arar en el mar. **s.-bag,** *n* saco de arena, *m.* —*vt* (a building) proteger con sacos de arena; (a person) golpear con un saco de arena. **s.-bank,** banco de arena, *m,* barra, *f.* **to run on a s.-bank,** encallar. **s.-colored,** de color de arena. **s.-dune,** médano, *m.* **s.-paper,** *n* papel de lija, *m.* —*vt* pulir con papel de lija, lijar. **s.-pit,** arenal, *m.* **s. shoes,** alpargatas, *f pl*

sandal /'sændl/ *n* sandalia, *f;* (rope-soled) alpargata, *f.* **s.-wood,** sándalo, *m*

sandstorm /'sænd,stɔrm/ *n* tempestad de arena, *f;* simún, *m*

sandwich /'sændwɪtʃ, 'sæn-/ *n* emparedado, bocadillo, *m.* —*vt* insertar. **I found myself sandwiched between two fat men,** Me encontré aplastado entre dos hombres gordos. **s.-man,** hombre sándwich, *m*

sandy /'sændi/ *a* arenoso; sabuloso; (of hair) rojo, rufo, bermejo. **a s. beach,** una playa arenosa

sane /sein/ *a* de juicio sano; razonable, prudente; sesudo. **He is a very s. person,** Es un hombre con mucho sentido común. **to be s.,** estar en su juicio; (of a policy, etc.) ser prudente, ser razonable

sangfroid /san'frwa/ *n* sangre fría, *f;* aplomo, *m*

sanguine /'sæŋgwɪn/ *a* (of complexion) rubicundo; sanguíneo; optimista, confiado. —*n* (drawing) sanguina, *f.* **to be s. about the future,** ser optimista acerca del porvenir, tener confianza en el porvenir

sanitary /'sænɪˌtɛri/ *a* sanitario; higiénico, **s. inspector,** inspector de sanidad, *m.* **s. napkin, s. towel,** servilleta higiénica, toalla sanitaria, *mf,* paño higiénico, *m*

sanitation /ˌsænɪ'teiʃən/ *n* higiene, *f;* sanidad pública, *f;* (apparatus) instalación sanitaria, *f*

sanity /'sænɪti/ *n* juicio sano, *m;* pruden-

cia, *f;* (common sense) sentido común, *m,* sensatez, *f*

Santa Claus /'sæntə klɔz/ *n* (Spanish equivalent) los Reyes Magos, *m pl*

São Paulo /'sau 'paulou, -lu/ San Pablo, *m*

sap /sæp/ *n* (bot and fig) savia, *f; mil* zapa, *f.* —*vt* (undermine) debilitar, agotar; *mil* zapar

sapphire /'sæfaiªr/ *n* zafiro, *m.* —*a* de zafiros; cerúleo, de zafiro

Saragossa /ˌsærə'gosə/ Zaragoza, *f*

sarcasm /'sɑrkæzəm/ *n* sarcasmo, *m*

sarcastic /sɑr'kæstɪk/ *a* sarcástico

sarcophagus /sɑr'kɒfəgəs/ *n* sarcófago, *m*

sardine /sɑr'din/ *n* sardina, *f.* **packed like sardines,** como sardinas en banasta. **s.-net,** sardinal, *m*

Sardinia /sɑr'dɪniə/ Cerdeña, *f*

Sardinian /sɑr'dɪniən/ *a* and *n* sardo (-da)

sardonic /sɑr'dɒnɪk/ *a* sardónico

sash /sæʃ/ *n* (with uniform) faja, *f;* (belt) cinto, cinturón, *m;* (of a window) cerco, *m.* **s. window,** ventana de guillotina, *f*

Satan /'seitn/ *n* Satanás, *m*

satanic /sə'tænɪk, sei-/ *a* satánico

satchel /'sætʃəl/ *n* saquito de mano, *m,* bolsa, *f;* (school) vademécum, *m;* cartapacio, *m,* cartera, *f*

sate /seit/ *vt* saciar, hartar; satisfacer

satellite /'sætlˌait/ *n* satélite, *m*

satiate /*v.* 'seiʃiˌeit; -ɪt, -ˌeit/ *vt* saciar, hartar; satisfacer. —*a* harto; repleto

satin /'sætn/ *n* raso, *m.* —*a* de raso; (glossy) lustroso, terso. —*vt* (paper) satinar

satire /'sætaiªr/ *n* sátira, *f*

satiric /sə'tɪərɪk/ *a* satírico

satirist /'sætərɪst/ *n* escritor (-ra) satírico (-ca)

satirize /'sætəˌraiz/ *vt* satirizar

satisfaction /ˌsætɪs'fækʃən/ *n* satisfacción, *f;* (contentment) contento, *m,* satisfacción, *f;* (for sin) expiación,. *f;* (of a debt) pago, *m;* desquite, *m;* recompensa, *f.* **to demand s.,** pedir satisfacción. **to give (someone) s.,** dar contento (a), alegrar

satisfactory /ˌsætɪs'fæktəri/ *a* satisfactorio; (for sin) expiatorio

satisfy /'sætɪsˌfai/ *vt* satisfacer; (convince) convencer; (allay) tranquilizar, apaciguar. **I am satisfied with him,** Estoy satisfecho (Estoy contento) con él. **The explanation did not s. me,** La explicación no me convenció. **to s. oneself that...,** asegurarse de que... **to s. one's thirst,** apagar la sed

satisfying /'sætɪsˌfaiɪŋ/ *a* que satisface; satisfactorio; (of food) nutritivo

saturate /'sætʃəˌreit/ *vt* saturar (de), empapar (de); *chem* saturar; *fig* imbuir; *fig* empapar. **to s. oneself in,** (a subject) empaparse en

saturation /ˌsætʃə'reiʃən/ *n* saturación,

f. **s. point,** (*chem* etc.) punto de saturación, *m*

Saturday /'sætər,dei/ *n* sábado, *m*

Saturn /'sætərn/ *n* Saturno, *m*

sauce /sɔs/ *n* salsa, *f*; (thick fruit) compota, *f*; *inf* insolencia, *f*. **s.-boat,** salsera, *f*

saucepan /'sɔs,pæn/ *n* cazuela, cacerola, *f*. **double s.,** baño de María, *m*

saucer /'sɔsər/ *n* platillo, *m*. **flying s.,** platillo volante, *m*. **s.-eyed,** con ojos redondos

saucy /'sɔsi/ *a* respondón, descarado; (cheerful) alegre; (of hats, etc.) coquetón, majo

sauerkraut /'sauᵊr,kraut/ *n* chucruta, *f*

saunter /'sɔntər/ *vi* pasearse, vagar, *n* paseo, *m*, vuelta, *f*

sausage /'sɔsɪdʒ/ *n* chorizo, *m*; salchicha, *f*. **s.-balloon,** globo cautivo, *m*. **s.-curl,** bucle, *m*. **s.-machine,** choricera, *f*. **s.-maker,** choricero (-ra)

savage /'sævɪdʒ/ *a* salvaje; feroz; (cruel) inhumano, cruel; (furious) furioso. —*n* salvaje, *mf*

savagery /'sævɪdʒri/ *n* salvajismo, *m*; ferocidad, *f*; brutalidad, crueldad, *f*

savannah /sə'vænə/ *n* sabana, *f*. **s. dweller,** sabanero (-ra)

save /seiv/ *vt* salvar; (keep) guardar; conservar; reservar; (money, one's clothes, etc.) ahorrar; (time) ganar; (avoid) evitar. —*vi* salvar; hacer economías; ahorrar. **He saved my life,** Me salvó la vida. **They have saved a room for me,** Me han reservado una habitación. **to s. appearances,** guardar las apariencias. **to s. oneself trouble,** ahorrarse molestias. **to s. the situation,** estar al nivel de las circunstancias

save /seiv/ *prep* salvo, excepto, menos. —*conjunc* sino, a menos que; con la excepción de. **all s. one,** todos menos uno. **all the conspirators s. he,** todos los conspiradores con la excepción de él

saving /'seivɪŋ/ *a* frugal, económico; (stingy) tacaño, avaricioso; (clause) condicional. —*n* salvación, *f*; (of money, time, etc.) ahorro, *m*, economía, *f*; *pl* **savings,** ahorros, *m pl*. —*prep* salvo, excepto, fuera de. —*conjunc* con excepción de que, fuera de que. **s. grace,** único mérito, *m*. **savings bank,** caja de ahorros, *f*. **savings fund,** montepío, *m*

savior /'seivyər/ *n* salvador (-ra). **the S.,** el Salvador, el Redentor

savor /'seivər/ *n* sabor, gusto, *m*; (aftertaste) dejo, *m*; (zest) salsa, *f*. —*vi* saber (a), tener sabor (de); *fig* oler (a). —*vt* saborear, paladear; (flavor) sazonar

savory /'seivəri/ *a* sabroso, apetitoso; (not sweet) no dulce; (of places) respetable; (of reputation, etc.) bueno. —*n* entremés salado, *m*. **s. omelette,** tortilla, *f*

saw /sɔ/ *n* (maxim) sentencia, *f*; (proverb) refrán, decir, *m*; (tool) sierra, *f*. —*vt* aserrar; (the air) cortar. —*vi* usar

una sierra. **two-handled saw,** tronzador, *m*. **saw-fish,** pez sierra, *m*. **saw-mill,** molino de aserrar, *m*. **saw-pit,** aserradero, *m*

sawdust /'sɔ,dʌst/ *n* aserrín, *m*

saxophone /'sæksə,foun/ *n* saxófono, *m*, saxofón *m*

say /sei/ *vt* decir; recitar. —*vi* decir. **Let us say that the house is worth $100,000,** Pongamos por ejemplo que la casa vale cien mil dólares. **He has no say in the matter,** No entra ni sale en el asunto. **I have said my say,** He dicho lo que quería. **They say,** Se dice, Dicen, La gente dice. **You don't say!** ¡Calle! ¿De veras? ¡Imposible! **that is to say...,** es decir...; esto es..., a saber... **to say one's prayers,** rezar, decir sus oraciones. **to say again,** volver a decir; decir otra vez, repetir. **to say over and over again,** repetir muchas veces, decir repetidamente. **What do you say to that?** ¿Qué dices a esto?

saying /'seiɪŋ/ *n* decir, *m*; (proverb) refrán, *m*; (maxim) sentencia, *f*. **As the s. is,** Como suele decirse; Según el refrán. **It goes without s.,** Huelga decir. **It's only a s.,** Es nada más

scab /skæb/ *n* (of a wound) costra, *f*; (disease) escabro, *m*; (blackleg) esquirol, *m*

scabby /'skæbi/ *a* costroso; (diseased) roñoso, sarnoso

scabies /'skeibiz/ *n* sarna, *f*. **s. mite,** arador de la sarna, *m*

scaffold /'skæfəld/ *n* (in building) andamio, *m*; (for execution) cadalso, patíbulo, *m*. **to go to the s.,** ir al patíbulo; acabar en el patíbulo

scald /skɔld/ *vt* escaldar; quemar; (instruments) esterilizar. —*n* quemadura, escaldadura, *f*. **to s. oneself,** escaldarse. **scalding hot,** hirviendo

scale /skeil/ *n* (of a balance) platillo, *m*; *zool* escama, *f*; *bot* bráctea, *f*; *bot* hojuela, *f*; (flake) laminita, *f*; (*mus, math*) escala, *f*; (of charges, etc.) tarifa, *f*; (of salaries) escalafón, *m*; (of a thermometer) escala, *f*. —*vt* escalar; (fish) escamar. **major s.,** escala mayor, *f*. **minor s.,** escala menor, *f*. **on a grand s.,** en gran escala. **on a small s.,** en pequeña escala. **pair of scales,** balanza, *f*; (for heavy weights) báscula, *f*. **social s.,** escala social, *f*. **The Scales,** *Astron.* Libra, *f*. **to draw to s.,** dibujar a escala. **to turn the scales,** pesar; *Fig.* inclinar la balanza. **to s. down,** (*Art.* and of charges) reducir

scaling /'skeilɪŋ/ *n* (of fish) escamadura, *f*; (of buildings) desconchadura, *f*; (ascent) escalamiento, *m*

scallop /'skoləp, 'skæl-/ *n* (*ichth* and badge) venera, *f*; concha, *f*; sew onda, *f*, festón, *m*. —*vt Cul.* guisar en conchas; *sew* ondear, festonear

scalp /skælp/ *n* anat pericráneo, *m*; cuero cabelludo, *m*; *fig* trofeo, *m*. —*vt* escalpar. **s.-hunter,** cazador de cabelleras, *m*

scalpel /'skælpəl/ n escalpelo, m

scaly /'skeili/ a escamoso, conchado; (of boilers) incrustado

scamp /skæmp/ n bribón, granuja, m, vt (work) frangollar

scamper /'skæmpər/ vi retozar, brincar; correr. —n carrerita, f. **to s. off,** salvarse por los pies, huir; marcharse corriendo

scan /skæn/ vt (verse) medir, escandir; (examine) escudriñar, examinar; (glance at) dar un vistazo (a)

scandal /'skændl/ n escándalo, m; maledicencia, f; (slander) calumnia, f. **to talk s.,** murmurar

scandalize /'skændl,aiz/ vt escandalizar

scandalous /'skændləs/ a escandaloso; infame; calumnioso

Scandinavia /,skændə'neiviə/ Escandinavia, f

Scandinavian /,skændə'neiviən/ a escandinavo. —n escandinavo (-va)

scant /skænt/ a escaso; insuficiente

scantiness /'skæntinis/ n escasez, f; insuficiencia, f

scanty /'skænti/ a insuficiente; escaso; (of hair) ralo; (of crops, etc.) pobre

scapegoat /'skeip,gout/ n víctima propiciatoria, f; cabeza de turco, f. **to be a s. for,** pagar el pato por

scapegrace /'skeip,greis/ n bribón, m

scapula /'skæpyələ/ n anat escápula, f

scar /skar/ n cicatriz, f; fig señal, f. —vt marcar con una cicatriz. **to s. over,** cicatrizarse

scarce /skɛərs/ a escaso; insuficiente; raro. —adv poet apenas. **to make oneself s.,** largarse, pirarse, escabullirse; ausentarse, esconderse

scarcely /'skɛərsli/ adv apenas; no bien; casi; (with difficulty) a duras penas, con dificultad. **It is s. likely he said that,** No es muy probable que lo hubiese dicho. **There were s. twenty people in the building,** Había apenas veinte personas en el edificio. **S. anyone likes his pictures,** Sus cuadros no le gustan a casi nadie

scarcity /'skɛərsiti/ n escasez, insuficiencia, f; (famine) carestía, f; (rarity) rareza, f

scare /skɛər/ vt asustar, espantar, llenar de miedo (a); intimidar. —n susto, pánico, m; alarma, f. **What a s. I got!** ¡Qué susto me he llevado! **to s. away,** ahuyentar

scarecrow /'skɛər,krou/ n espantapájaros, m; Inf. estantigua, f, mamarracho, espantajo, m

scarf /skarf/ n bufanda, f; (tie) corbata, f; mil faja, f

scarlatina /,skɑrlə'tinə/ n med escarlatina, f

scarlet /'skɑrlit/ n escarlata, f. —a de color escarlata. **to turn s.,** (of persons) enrojecerse. **s. fever,** escarlatina, f. **s. hat,** eccl capelo (cardenalicio), m. **s. runner,** bot judía verde, f

scathing /'skeiðiŋ/ a mordaz, cáustico

scatter /'skætər/ vt esparcir, sembrar con; (benefits, etc.) derramar; (put to flight) derrotar; dispersar; disipar; fig frustrar; (squander) derrochar, desparramar. —vi dispersarse. **The crowd scattered,** La muchedumbre se dispersó. **s.-brained,** de cabeza de chorlito, atolondrado

scattered /'skætərd/ a disperso; esparcido

scattered showers n lluvias aisladas, f pl

scavenge /'skævindʒ/ vt (streets) recoger la basura de, barrer

scavenger /'skævindʒər/ n (of the streets) barrendero, m; (dustman) basurero, m; zool animal que se alimenta de carne muerta, m; insecto que se alimenta de estiércol, m. —vt See **scavenge**

scenario /sɪ'nɛəri,ou, -'nɑr-/ n escenario, m

scene /sin/ n escena, f; teatro, lugar, m; espectáculo, m; (theat décor) decoración, f; (of a play) escena, f; (view) vista, perspectiva, f. **behind the scenes,** entre bastidores. **The s. is laid...,** La acción pasa..., **to come on the s.,** entrar en escena. **to make a s.,** hacer una escena. **s.-painter,** n escenógrafo (-fa). **s.-shifter,** tramoyista, mf

scenery /'sinəri/ n theat decorado, m; (landscape) paisaje, m

scenic /'sinik/ a dramático; escénico; pintoresco. **s. railway,** montaña rusa, f

scent /sɛnt/ vt perfumar; (smell) oler; (out) husmear, olfatear; (suspect) sospechar. —n perfume, m; fragancia, f, aroma, m; (smell) olor, m; (of hounds) viento, m; (of game, etc.) rastro, viento, m; (fig of person) nariz, f; (trail) pista, f. **to lose the s.,** perder la pista. **to s. danger,** oler el peligro. **to throw off the s.,** despistar. **s.-bottle,** frasco de perfume, m. **s.-spray,** pulverizador, m

sceptic /'skɛptik/ n escéptico (-ca)

sceptical /'skɛptikəl/ a escéptico

schedule /'skɛdʒul/ n lista, m; programa, m; (of taxes) clase, f; (of trains, etc.) horario, m. —vt poner en una lista; inventariar

scheme /skim/ n plan, m; proyecto, m; diagrama, esquema, m; (summary) resumen, m; (of colors, etc.) combinación, f; (plot) intriga, maquinación, f. —vt proyectar. —vi planear, formar planes; (intrigue) intrigar, conspirar. **color s.,** combinación de colores, f

schemer /'skimər/ n (plotter) intrigante, mf

scheming /'skimiŋ/ a intrigante; astuto. —n planes, proyectos, m pl; intrigas, maquinaciones, f pl

schism /'sizəm, 'skiz-/ n cisma, mf

scholar /'skɒlər/ n (at school) colegial (-la); (disciple) alumno (-na); (student) estudiante, mf; (learned person) erudito (-ta), hombre de letras, m; (scholarship holder) becario, m.

scholarly /'skɒlərli/ a de sabio, de hombre de letras; erudito

scholarship /'skɒlər,ʃip/ n erudición, f; saber, m; (exhibition) beca, f. **s. holder,** becario, m

scholastic /skə'læstik/ a escolar, escolástico; pedante; (medieval) escolástico. —n escolástico, m. **the s. profession,** el magisterio

school /skul/ n escuela, f; colegio, m; academia, f; educ departamento, m; (faculty) facultad, f; (of fish) banco, m. —vt enseñar, instruir; formar; disciplinar. **in s.,** en clase. **day s.,** escuela, f, colegio, m. **the Florentine s.,** (of painting) la escuela florentina. **the lower s.,** los alumnos del preparatorio. **private s.,** colegio particular, m. **s.-bag,** vademécum, m. **s.-book,** libro escolar, m. **s.-days,** los días de escuela; los años de colegio. **in his s.-days,** cuando él iba a la escuela. **s.-fees,** gastos de la enseñanza, m pl, cuota escolar, f,

schoolboy /'skul,bɔi/ n muchacho de escuela, colegial, m

school district n sector escolar, m

schoolfellow /'skul,fɛlou/ n compañero de colegio, condiscípulo, m

schoolgirl /'skul,gɜrl/ n colegiala, f

schooling /'skuliŋ/ n educación, enseñanza, f

schoolmaster /'skul,mæstər/ n maestro de escuela, professor, m

schoolmistress /'skul,mistris/ n maestra de escuela, profesora, f

school of hard knocks n universidad sin tejados, f

schoolroom /'skul,rum/ n aula, sala de clase, salón de clase, m

sciatic /sai'ætik/ a ciático

sciatica /sai'ætikə/ n ciática, f

science /'saiəns/ n ciencia, f

scientific /,saiən'tifik/ a científico; exacto, sistemático

scientist /'saiəntist/ n hombre de ciencia, m, científico (-ca)

scintilla /sin'tilə/ n fig átomo, vestigio, m

scintillate /'sintḷ,eit/ vi centellear, lucir, chispear; (of persons) brillar

scion /'saiən/ n (sucker) acodo, m; (shoot) vástago, renuevo, m; (human) descendiente, mf. **s. of a noble race,** vástago de una raza noble, m

scissors /'sizərz/ n pl tijeras, f pl. **s.-sharpener,** amolador, m

sclerosis /sklɪ'rousis/ n med esclerosis, f

sclerotic /sklɪ'rɒtik/ a anat esclerótica, f

scoff /skɔf, skɒf/ n burla, mofa, f. —vi burlarse. **to s. at,** burlarse de, mofarse de

scoffer /'skɔfər, 'skɒf-/ n mofador (-ra); (at religion, etc.) incrédulo (-la)

scold /skould/ n virago, f, vt reñir, reprender

scolding /'skouldiŋ/ n reprensión, increpación, f

scone /skoun, skɒn/ n bollo, m

scoop /skup/ n pala de mano, f; cuchara de draga, f; (boat) achicador, m; (financial) golpe, m; (journalistic) éxito periodístico, m. —vt sacar con pala (de); sacar con cuchara (de); (shares, etc.) comprar, obtener. **to s. out,** vaciar; excavar; (bail) achicar

scooter /'skutər/ n (child's) patinete, patín del diablo, m; monopatín, m

scope /skoup/ n alcance, m; esfera de acción, f; lugar, m. **to give full s. to,** dar rienda suelta a. **to have full s.,** tener plena oportunidad; tener todas las facilidades. **within the s. of,** dentro del alcance de

scorch /skɔrtʃ/ vt chamuscar; (the skin) tostar; (of the sun) abrasar, quemar; (wither) agostar. **to s. along,** ir como un relámpago. **scorching,** a abrasador, ardiente; fig mordaz

score /skɔr/ n (scratch) rasguño, m; señal, f; (crossing out) raya, f; (reckoning) cuenta, f, escote, m; (notch) muesca, f; sports tanteo, m, puntuación, f; (point) punto, tanto, m; (twenty) veintena, f; (reason) motivo, m, causa, f; respecto, m; mus partitura, f. —vt marcar; rayar; (erase) tachar, borrar; (cricket runs, etc.) hacer; (goals) marcar; (points) ganar; (reckon) apuntar. **s. a triumph,** apuntarse un triunfo; mus instrumentar; (for orchestra) orquestar. —vi (be fortunate) llevar la ventaja. **to pay off old scores,** ajustar cuentas viejas. **to s. off someone,** ganar un punto (a), triunfar de. **upon that s.,** a ese respecto; por esa causa. **Upon what s.?** ¿Con qué motivo? **s.-board,** marcador, m

scorer /'skɔrər/ n (of a goal, etc.) tanteador, m; (keeper of score) marcador, m

scorn /skɔrn/ n desprecio, desdén, m. —vt despreciar, desdeñar; reírse de. **to s. to do,** no dignarse hacer

scornful /'skɔrnfəl/ a desdeñoso, despreciativo

Scorpion /'skɔrpiən/ n Escorpión, m

scorpion /'skɔrpiən/ n escorpión, alacrán, m; astron Escorpión, m

Scot /skɒt/ n escocés, m

scotch /skɒtʃ/ vt (kill) matar; (thwart) frustrar; (a wheel) calzar

Scotland /'skɒtlənd/ n Escocia, f

Scotswoman /'skɒts,wumən/ n escocesa, f

Scottish /'skɒtiʃ/ a escocés

scoundrel /'skaundrəl/ n canalla, sinvergüenza, mf

scour /'skauər/ vt (traverse) recorrer, batir; (pans, etc.) fregar, estregar; (free from) limpiar (de); (of water) arrastrar

scourge /skɜrdʒ/ vt azotar, flagelar; castigar, mortificar. —n disciplinas, f pl; fig verdugo, m, plaga, f

scout /skaut/ n mil batidor, explorador, m. —vi mil explorar, reconocer. —vt (flout) rechazar a mano airada, rechazar con desdén. **boy s.,** muchacho explorador, m

scowl /skaul/ vi fruncir el ceño. —n ceño, m. **to s. at,** mirar con ceño

scraggy /'skrægi/ *a* flaco, magro, descarnado

scramble /'skræmbəl/ *vi* trepar. —*vt* (throw) arrojar; (eggs) revolver. **scrambled eggs,** huevos revueltos, *m pl.* **to s. for,** andar a la rebatiña por; (for coins, etc.) luchar para. **to s. up,** escalar; subir a gatas

scrap /skræp/ *n* pedazo, *m;* fragmento, *m;* pizca, brizna, *f;* (shindy) suiza, camorra, *f;* (boxing) combate de boxeo, *m; pl* **scraps,** desperdicios, *m pl;* (food) restos de la comida, *m pl.* —*vt* desechar; (expunge) borrar; *vi* (fight) armar camorra. **a few scraps of news,** algunas noticias. **Do you mind not coming? Not a s.,** ¿Te importa no venir? Ni pizca. **s.-book,** álbum de recortes, *m;* **s.-heap,** depósito de basura, *m; fig* olvido, *m.* **s.-iron,** chatarra, *f,* hierro viejo, *m*

scrape /skreip/ *vt* raspar, rascar, raer; (one's shoes) restregar; (a musical instrument) rascar. —*n* raoguño, *m,* ruido de raspar, *m;* (predicament) lío, apuro, *m;* dificultad, *f.* **to s. acquaintance with,** trabar amistad con. **to s. along,** *inf* ir tirando. **to s. away,** rascar; quitar. **to s. through,** (an examination) aprobar justo. **to s. together,** amontonar poco a poco

scrappy /'skræpi/ *a* escaso; fragmentario; (incoherent) descosido. **a s. meal,** una comida escasa

scratch /skrætʃ/ *vt* arañar; (the earth) escarbar; (rub) rascar; (a hole) hacer; (sketch) dibujar, trazar; (a horse) retirar de una carrera. —*vi* arañar; rascar; escarbar; (of a pen) rasguear; (back out) retirarse. —*n* arañazo, *m;* (of a pen) rasguco, *m;* (in a race) línea de salida, *f;* (in games) cero, *m.* —*a* improvisado. **The dog scratched at the door,** El perro arañó la puerta. **to come up to s.,** estar al nivel de las circunstancias. **to s. one's head,** rascarse la cabeza. **to s. a person's eyes out,** sacar los ojos con las uñas (a). **to s. the surface of,** (a subject) tratar superficialmente. **to s. out,** tachar

scrawl /skrɔl/ *vi* hacer garabatos. —*vt* garabatear, garrapatear. —*n* garabato, *m*

scream /skrim/ *vt* and *vi* chillar. —*n* chillido, *m.* **It was a perfect s.** Era para morirse de risa. **to s. with laughter,** reírse a carcajadas, morirse de risa

screaming /'skrimɪŋ/ *n* chillidos, *m pl.* —*a* chillador; (piercing) penetrante, agudo; (funny) divertidísimo

screech /skritʃ/ *vi* chillar; (of owls, etc.) ulular; graznar. —*n* chillido, *m,* ululación, *f;* graznido, *m.* **s.-owl,** úlula, *f*

screed /skrid/ *n* arenga, *f;* cita larga, *f*

screen /skrin/ *n* biombo, *m;* (wire) tela metálica, *f;* (nonfolding) mampara, *f;* (ecol) cancel, *m;* (cinema, television) pantalla, *f;* (of trees, etc., and *mil*) cortina, *f;* (fig protection) abrigo, *m.* —*vt* proteger; (shelter) abrigar; (hide) esconder, ocultar; (a light) proteger con pantalla; (a film) proyectar; (sieve) cribar, cerner; (exam-

ine) investigar. **to s. from view,** ocultar la vista (de), esconder. **s. star,** estrella de la pantalla, *f*

screw /skru/ *n* tornillo, *m;* (propeller) hélice, *f;* vuelta de tornillo, *f;* presión, *f;* (miser) tacaño, *m;* (salary) salario, *m.* —*vt* atornillar; torcer; apretar, oprimir. **He has a s. loose,** Le falta un tornillo. **to s. down,** sujetar con tornillos. **to s. up,** cerrar con tornillos. **to s. up one's courage,** tomar coraje. **to s. up one's eyes,** desojarse, entornar los ojos. **s.-driver,** destornillador, *m*

scribble /'skrɪbəl/ *vt* escribir de prisa, *vi* garabatear, garrapatear; escribir, ser autor. —*n* garabato, garrapato, *m;* mala letra, letra ilegible, *f;* (note) billete, *m*

scribe /skraib/ *n* escribiente, copista, *mf;* (Jewish history) escriba, *m*

scrimmage /'skrimidʒ/ *n* reyerta, pelea, camorra, *f;* (Rugby) mêlée, *f*

script /skript/ *n* letra cursiva, *f,* pluma plumilla, *f;* manuscrito, *m; law* escritura, *f;* examen escrito, *m;* (film) escenario, *m*

Scripture /'skriptʃər/ *n* Sagrada Escritura, *f.* **Scriptures,** Escrituras, *f pl;* (of non-Christian religions) los libros sagrados

scrofula /'skrɒfyələ/ *n* escrófula, *f*

scroll /skroul/ *n* (of paper, etc.) rollo, *m;* pergamino, *m;* (flourish) rúbrica, *f;* (of an Ionic capital) voluta, *f.* **s. of fame,** lista de la fama, *f*

scrotum /'skroutəm/ *n* anat escroto, *m*

scrounge /skraundʒ/ *vi* sablear. —*vt* dar un sablazo (a); hurtar

scrub /skrʌb/ *vt* fregar; limpiar; restregar. —*n* fregado, *m;* limpieza, *f;* fricción, *f;* (brushwood) matorral, breñal, *m,* maleza, *f*

scrubbing /'skrʌbɪŋ/ *n* fregado, *m.* **s.-brush,** cepillo para el suelo, *m*

scrubby /'skrʌbi/ *a* (of plants) anémico; (of persons) insignificante, pobre; (of land) cubierto de maleza

scruff /skrʌf/ *n* nuca, *f,* pescuezo, *m*

scruple /'skrupəl/ *n* escrúpulo, *m.* —*vi* tener escrúpulos. **to have no scruples,** no tener escrúpulos

scrupulous /'skrupyələs/ *a* escrupuloso; exacto, meticuloso

scrutinize /'skrutn̩aiz/ *vt* escudriñar, examinar; (votes) escrutar

scrutiny /'skrutni/ *n* escrutinio, *m*

scud /skʌd/ *vi* correr; deslizarse; flotar. **to s. before the wind,** ir viento en popa

scuffle /'skʌfəl/ *vi* pelear, forcejear, andar a la rebatiña. —*n* refriega, pelea, sa rracina, arrebatiña, *f*

scull /skʌl/ *n* remo, *m,* *vi* remar

scullery /'skʌləri/ *n* fregadero, *m.* **s. maid,** fregona, *f*

sculptor /'skʌlptər/ *n* escultor, *m,* escultora, *f*

sculpture /'skʌlptʃər/ *n* escultura, *f, vt* esculpir

scum /skʌm/ *n* espuma, *f;* (dregs) heces,

f pl. —vt espumar. **s. of the earth,** las heces de la sociedad

scurrilous /'skɜrələs/ a grosero, indecente

scurry /'skɜri/ vi echar a correr. —n fuga precipitada, f; (of rain) chaparrón, m; (of snow) remolino, m. **to s. off,** escabullirse. **to s. through,** hacer de prisa, terminar rápidamente

scurvy /'skɜrvi/ a tiñoso, vil, ruin. —n escorbuto, m. **a s. trick,** una mala pasada

scuttle /'skʌtl/ n (trap-door) escotillón, m; naut escotilla, f; (for coal) carbonera, f; (flight) huida precipitada, f. —vt (a boat) echar a pique, vi (run away) escabullirse, apretar a correr

scythe /saið/ n dalle, m, guadaña, f, vt dallar, segar

sea /si/ n mar, m, or f; ola, f; multitud, f. **Black Sea,** Mar Negro. **Mediteranean Sea,** (Mar) Mediterráneo, m. **at sea,** en el mar; perplejo. **beyond the seas,** allende los mares. **by sea,** por mar, m. **by the sea,** a la orilla del mar. **high seas,** alta mar, f. **the seven seas,** todos los mares del mundo. **to go to sea,** hacerse marinero. **to put to sea,** hacerse a la mar, hacerse a la vela. **sea-anemone,** anémone de mar. f. **sea-bathing,** baños de mar, m pl. **sea-breeze,** brisa de mar, f. **sea captain,** capitán de mar, m. **sea chart,** carta de marear, f. **sea-coast,** litoral, m, costa marítima, f. **sea-cow,** manatí, m. **sea dog,** lobo de mar, m. **sea-fight,** combate naval, m. **sea-foam,** espuma de mar, f. **sea-girt,** rodeado por el mar. **sea-going,** de altura, navegante. **sea-going craft,** embarcación de alta mar, f. **sea-green,** verdemar, m. **sea-gull,** gaviota, f. **sea-horse,** caballo marino, m. **sea-legs,** piernas de marino, f pl. **sea-level,** nivel del mar, m. **sea-lion,** león marino, m. **sea-mist,** bruma, f. **sea-nymph,** nereida, f. **sea-power,** potencia naval, f. **sea-serpent,** serpiente de mar, f. **sea-sick,** mareado. **to be sea-sick,** marearse. **sea-sickness,** mal de mar, m. **sea-trip,** viaje por mar, m. **sea-urchin,** erizo de mar, m. **sea-wall,** dique de mar, m.

seafarer /'si,fɛərər/ n (traveller) viajero (-ra) por mar; (sailor) marinero, m

seal /sil/ n zool foca, f, lobo marino, m; piel de foca, f, sello, m; (stamp) estampillo, timbre, m; vt sellar; (stamp) estampar; (letters, etc.) cerrar; vi cazar focas. **His fate is sealed,** Su suerte está determinada. **His lips were sealed,** Sus labios estaban cerrados. **under my hand and s.,** firmado y sellado por mí. **s.-ring,** sortija de sello, f

sealskin /'sil,skɪn/ n piel de foca, f

seam /sim/ n sew costura, f; naut costura de los tablones, f; anat sutura, f; surg cicatriz, f; (wrinkle) arruga, f, surco, m; geol capa, f; yacimiento, m; mineral vena, f, filón, m. —vt coser; juntar; (a face) surcar, arrugar

seaman /'simən/ n marinero, m; hombre

de mar, m; navegante, m. **able-bodied s.,** marinero práctico, m

seamstress /'simstrɪs/ n costurera, f

seamy /'simi/ a con costuras. **the s. side of life,** el lado peor de la vida

seaplane /'si,plein/ n hidroavión, hidroplano, m

seaport /'si,pɔrt/ n puerto de mar, m

sear /sɪər/ a marchito. —vt agostar, secar; (a wound) cauterizar; marchitar, ajar; (a conscience) endurecer

search /sɜrtʃ/ vt registrar; (a wound) explorar; examinar; escudriñar; investigar. —vi buscar. —n busca, f; (of luggage, etc.) reconocimiento, m. **in s. of,** en busca de. **to s. after, for,** buscar; ir al encuentro de. **to s. out,** ir en busca de; preguntar por. **right of s.,** (international law) derecho de visita, m. **s.-party,** pelotón de salvamento, m. **s.-warrant,** auto de reconocimiento, auto de registro domiciliario, orden de allanamiento, orden de cateo, m

searching /'sɜrtʃɪŋ/ a escrutador; penetrante; minucioso. **a s. look,** una mirada penetrante. **a s. wind,** un viento penetrante. **a s. question,** una pregunta perspicaz

searchlight /'sɜrtʃ,lait/ n reflector, proyector, m

seashore /'si,ʃɔr/ n playa, f; orilla del mar, f

seaside /'si,said/ n orilla del mar, f; playa, f. **to go to the s.,** ir al mar, ir a la playa

season /'sizən/ n estación, f; sazón, f; temporada, f; tiempo, m. —vt (food) sazonar; (wood, wine) madurar; (accustom) acostumbrar, aclimatar; (with wit, etc.) salpimentar; (temper) templar, moderar. —vi madurarse. **at that s.,** a la sazón. **close s.,** veda, f. **in s.,** en sazón; a su tiempo. **out of s.,** fuera de sazón; fuera de tiempo, inoportuno. **the dead s.,** la estación muerta. **the autumn s.,** el otoño; (for social functions, etc.) la temporada de otoño. **s.-ticket,** billete de abono, m

seasonable /'sizənəbəl/ a de estación; tempestivo, oportuno

seasonably /'sizənəbli/ adv en sazón; oportunamente

seasonal /'sizənl/ a estacional; de temporada

seasonal worker n trabajador por temporada, m

seasoned /'sizənd/ a (of food) sazonado; (of wood, etc.) maduro. **highly-s.,** (of a dish) picante, con muchas especies

seasoning /'sizənɪŋ/ n cul condimento, m; madurez, f; aclimatación, f; fig salsa, sal, f

seat /sit/ n asiento, m; (bench) banco, m; (chair) silla, f; (in a cinema, etc.) localidad, f; (theat etc., ticket) entrada, f; (of a person) trasero, m, asentaderas, f pl; (of trousers) fondillos, m pl; (of government, etc.) sede, capital, f; (of war, etc.) teatro, *m;* (place) sitio, lugar, *m;* (house) casa solar, *f.* —*vt* sentar; poner en una silla (a); encontrar sitio; (of buildings) tener asientos; (a chair) poner asiento (a). **The hall seats a thousand,** La sala tiene mil asientos, Hay mil asientos en la sala. **Please be seated!** ¡Haga el favor de sentarse! **to be seated,** estar sentado; sentarse. **to have a good s.,** (on a horse) caer bien a caballo. **to hold a s. in parliament,** ser diputado a Cortes. **to keep one's s.,** permanecer sentado. **to take a s.,** tomar asiento, sentarse. **s.-back,** respaldo, *m.* **s. belt,** cinturón de seguridad, *m*

seaweed /'si,wid/ *n* alga marina, *f*
secede /sɪ'sid/ *vi* retirarse (de); separarse (de)
secession /sɪ'sɛʃən/ *n* secesión, *f*
seclusion /sɪ'kluʒən/ *n* reclusión, *f;* apartamiento, retiro, *m;* soledad, *f*
second /'sɛkənd/ *a* segundo; otro; igual. —*adv* en segundo lugar; después. —*n* segundo, *m;* (in a duel) padrino, *m;* (helper) ayudante, *m;* (boxing) segundo, *m;* (railway compartment) departamento de segunda (clase), *m; mus* segunda, *f;* (of time) segundo, *m;* (moment) instante, momento, *m.* —*vt* secundar; (a motion) apoyar; *mil* ayudar. **the s. of May,** el dos de mayo. **James the S.,** Jaime el segundo. **on s. thoughts,** después de pensarlo bien. **every s. day,** cada dos días. **They live on the s. floor,** Viven en el primer piso (since the ground floor is not counted separately in Spanish speaking areas, the American second floor = the Spanish **primer piso**). **the s. largest,** el más grande menos uno. **to be s. to none,** no ser inferior a ninguno; (of persons) no ser inferior a nadie; no ceder a nadie. **to come off s.,** llegar el segundo; ser vencido. **seconds hand,** (of watch) segundero, *m.* **s.-in-command,** segundo, *m;* subjefe, *m.* **s.-best,** segundo. **My s.-best hat,** Mi sombrero número dos. **to come off s.-best,** salir mal parado, ser vencido. **s. class,** segunda clase, *f.* **s.-class,** de segunda clase; de calidad inferior; mediocre. **s. cousin,** primo (-ma) segundo (-a). **s. gear,** segunda velocidad, *f.* **s.-hand,** *a* usado; de ocasión; no nuevo. —*adv* de segunda mano. **s.-hand car,** un coche de segunda mano. **s.-hand clothing,** ropa usada, *f.* **s. lieutenant,** *mil* subteniente, segundo teniente, *m; nav* alférez de fragata, *m.* **s.-rate,** *a* inferior, mediocre. **s. sight,** doble vista, *f*
secondary /'sɛkənˌdɛri/ *a* secundario; subordinado; accesorio; poco importante. **s. education,** enseñanza secundaria, *f*
secrecy /'sikrəsi/ *n* secreto, *m;* reserva, *f,* silencio, *m.* **in the s. of one's own heart,** en lo más íntimo de su corazón
secret /'sikrɪt/ *a* secreto; clandestino; (of persons) reservado, taciturno; (secluded) remoto, apartado; oculto; misterioso. —*n* secreto, *m;* (key) clave, *f.* **a s. code,** un

código secreto. **in s.,** en secreto, secretamente. **open s.,** secreto a voces. **to keep a s.,** guardar un secreto. **to keep s.,** tener secreto, ocultar. **s. drawer,** secreto, *m*.
secretary /'sɛkrɪˌtɛri/ *n* secretario (-ia). **private s.,** secretario (-ia) particular. **S. of State,** ministro, *m;* Ministro de Estado, *m*
secrete /sɪ'krit/ *vt* esconder, ocultar; *med* secretar
secretion /sɪ'kriʃən/ *n* escondimiento, *m; med* secreción, *f*
secretive /'sikrɪtɪv/ *a* reservado, callado
sect /sɛkt/ *n* secta, *f*
section /'sɛkʃən/ *n* sección, *f;* porción, *f;* subdivisión, *f;* (of a law) artículo, *m.* —*vt* seccionar. **conic s.,** sección cónica, *f*
sectional /'sɛkʃənl/ *a* en secciones. **s. bookcase,** biblioteca desmontable, *f*
sector /'sɛktər/ *n* sector, *m*
secular /'sɛkyələr/ *a* (very old) secular; (lay) seglar; laico; profano. **s. music,** música profana, *f.* **s. school,** escuela laica, *f*
secularize /'sɛkyələˌraɪz/ *vt* secularizar
secure /sɪ'kyʊr/ *a* seguro; (certain) asegurado; (safe) en seguridad; sano y salvo; (firm) firme; fijo; (confident (in)) confiado (en). —*vt* asegurar; (insure) garantizar; (lock) cerrar; (confine) prender; (acquire) adquirir, obtener; lograr, conseguir
securely /sɪ'kyʊrli/ *adv* seguramente; en seguridad, sin peligro, con confianza; (firmly) firmemente
security /sɪ'kyʊrɪti/ *n* seguridad, *f;* protección, defensa, *f;* garantía, *f;* (faith) confianza, *f; com* fianza, *f;* (person) fiador, *m; pl* **securities,** valores, títulos, *m pl.* **government securities,** papel del Estado, *m.* **to give s.,** *com* dar fianza. **to stand s. for,** *com* salir fiador de
sedate /sɪ'deɪt/ *a* tranquilo, sosegado; formal, serio, grave
sedative /'sɛdətɪv/ *a and n* sedativo, calmante *m*
sedentary /'sɛdnˌtɛri/ *a* sedentario
sediment /'sɛdəmənt/ *n* sedimento, *m*
sedition /sɪ'dɪʃən/ *n* sedición, *f*
seditious /sɪ'dɪʃəs/ *a* sedicioso
seduce /sɪ'dus/ *vt* seducir
seduction /sɪ'dʌkʃən/ *n* seducción, *f*
seductive /sɪ'dʌktɪv/ *a* seductivo, atractivo; persuasivo
sedulous /'sɛdʒələs/ *a* asiduo, diligente
see /si/ *n* sede, *f.* **The Holy S.,** la Santa Sede, *f*
see /si/ *vt and vi* ver; mirar; (understand) comprender; (visit) visitar; (attend to) atender a; ocuparse de. **He sees the matter quite differently,** Él mira el asunto de un modo completamente distinto, Su punto de vista sobre el asunto es completamente distinto. **You are not fit to be seen,** No eres nada presentable. **See you next Tuesday!** ¡Hasta el miércoles que viene! **I see!** ¡Ya! ¡Ahora comprendo! **Let's see!** ¡Vamos a ver! **Shall I see you home?** ¿Quieres que te acom-

pañe a casa? **to go and see,** ir a ver. **to see red,** echar chispas. **to see the sights,** visitar los monumentos. **to see life,** ver mundo. **to see service,** servir (en el ejército, etc.). **to see about,** atender a; pensar en; ocuparse de. **to see after,** cuidar de; atender (a); ocuparse de. **to see again,** volver a ver. **to see into,** investigar, examinar. **to see off,** (at the station, etc.) ir a despedir; acompañar. **to see out,** (a person) acompañar a la puerta; (a play, etc.) quedarse hasta el fin (de); no dejar el puesto. **to see over,** inspeccionar. **to see through,** (a house, etc.) inspeccionar; (a person) calarle las intenciones; (a mystery) penetrar; (a person through trouble) ayudar. **to see it through,** llevarlo al cabo; quedarse hasta el fin. **to see to,** atender a; ocuparse de; encargarse de. **to see to everything,** encargarse de todo

seed /sid/ *n* semilla, *f;* simiente, *f;* (of fruit) pepita, *f,* grano, *m; fig* germen, *m;* (offspring) prole, descendencia, *f. —vt* granar. —*vt* sembrar. **s.-bed,** almáciga, *f,* semillero, *m.* **s.-pearl,** aljófar, *m.* **s.-plot,** sementera, *f; fig* semillero, *m.* **s.-time,** tiempo de sembrar, *m*

seedling /'sidlɪŋ/ *n* planta de semilla, *f*

seedy /'sidi/ *a* granado; (of clothes) raído, roto; (of persons) andrajoso, desharrapado; (ill) infeliz, desgraciado; (ill) indispuesto, malucho

seeing /'siɪŋ/ *n* vista, *f;* visión, *f.* **It is worth s.,** Vale la pena de verse. **s. that...,** visto que, dado que, como que. **S. is believing,** Ver es creer

seek /sik/ *vt* buscar; solicitar, pretender; (demand) pedir; (investigate) investigar; (to do something) procurar, tratar de. **They are much sought after,** Son muy populares, Están en demanda. **to s. after,** buscar; perseguir. **to s. for,** buscar

seeker /'sikər/ *n* el, *m,* (*f,* la) que busca; investigador (-ra)

seem /sim/ *vi* parecer. **He seemed honest,** Parecía honrado. **It seemed to me,** Me pareció a mí. **It seems that they were both at home last night,** Parece ser que ambos estaban en casa anoche

seeming /'simɪŋ/ *a* aparente; supuesto

seemingly /'simɪŋli/ *adv* aparentemente; en apariencia

seemly /'simli/ *a* decoroso, decente

seep /sip/ *vi* filtrar; rezumarse

seer /sɪər/ *n* profeta, *m*

seesaw /'si,sɔ/ *n* columpio, *m;* vaivén, *m. —vi* columpiarse; balancearse, oscilar. —*a* de vaivén, oscilante

seethe /sið/ *vi* hervir; *fig* bullir

segment /'sɛgmənt/ *n* segmento, *m*

segregate /*v.* 'sɛgrɪ,geit; *a.* -gɪt/ *vt* segregar. —*vi* segregarse. —*a* segregado

segregation /,sɛgrɪ'geiʃən/ *n* segregación, *f*

Seine, the /sɛn/ *n* el Sena, *m*

seize /siz/ *vt law* embargar; apoderarse de; asir; (a person) prender; coger; (a

meaning) comprender; (an occasion, etc.) aprovecharse de; (of emotions) dominar; (of illnesses) atacar. —*vi mech* atascarse. **He was seized by fear,** Le dominó el miedo. **to s. the opportunity,** aprovecharse de la oportunidad. **to s. upon a pretext,** valerse de un pretexto

seizure /'siʒər/ *n* asimiento, *m;* (of property) embargo, secuestro, *m;* (of a person) captura, *f;* arresto, *m; med* ataque, *m*

seldom /'sɛldəm/ *adv* rara vez, raramente; pocas veces

select /sɪ'lɛkt/ *a* escogido, selecto; exclusivista. —*vt* escoger

selection /sɪ'lɛkʃən/ *n* selección, *f.* **selections from Cervantes,** trozos escogidos de Cervantes, *m pl.* **to make a s. from,** escoger entre. **s. committee,** comité de selección, *m*

selective /sɪ'lɛktɪv/ *a* selectivo

self /sɛlf/ *n* mismo (-a), propio (-a); sí mismo (-a), se; personalidad, *f;* ser, *m.* **all by one's s.,** sin ayuda de nadie; solo; *inf* solito. **my other s.,** mi otro yo. **my better s.,** mi mejor parte. **the s.,** el yo. **s.-abasement,** humillación de sí mismo, *f.* **s.-acting,** automático. **s.-apparent,** evidente, patente. **s.-appointed,** nombrado por uno mismo. **s.-assertion,** presunción, *f.* **s.-assertive,** presumido. **s.-assurance,** confianza en sí mismo, *f;* aplomo, *m;* (impertinence) cara dura, frescura, *f.* **s.-centered,** egocéntrico. **s.-colored,** del mismo color; de su color natural. **s.-command,** dominio de sí mismo, *m;* sangre fría, ecuanimidad, *f.* **s.-complacent,** satisfecho de sí mismo. **s.-conceit,** vanidad, arrogancia, petulancia, *f.* **s.-confidence,** confianza en sí mismo, *f;* aplomo, *m.* **s.-confident,** seguro de sí mismo, lleno de confianza en sí mismo. **s.-conscious,** turbado, confuso, apocado. **s.-consciousness,** turbación, confusión, *f,* apocamiento, azoramiento, *m.* **s.-contained,** (of a person) reservado, poco comunicativo; dueño de sí mismo; (of things) completo; (of flats, etc.) independiente; con entrada independiente. **s.-contradictory,** contradictorio. **s.-control,** dominio de sí mismo, *m;* ecuanimidad, serenidad, sangre fría, *f.* **s.-controlled,** dueño de sí mismo; ecuánime, sereno. **s.-deception,** engaño de sí mismo, *m;* ilusiones, *f pl.* **s.-defense,** defensa propia, *f.* **s.-denial,** abnegación, *f;* renunciación, *f;* frugalidad, *f.* **s.-destruction,** suicidio, *m.* **s.-determination,** libre albedrío, *m;* (of peoples) autonomía, *f;* independencia, *f.* **s.-educating,** autodidacto. **s.-esteem,** respeto para uno mismo, *m;* amor propio, *m.* **s.-evident,** aparente, que salta a la vista. **s.-explanatory,** que se explica a sí mismo; evidente. **s.-generating,** autógeno. **s.-government,** (of a person) dominio de sí mismo, *m;* (of a state) autonomía, *f.* **s.-importance,** presunción, petulancia, *f.* **s.-important,** pagado de sí mismo. **to be s.-important,** darse importancia, darse tono. **s.-indulgence,** indulgencia con sí mismo, f; (of food, drink, etc.) excesos, m pl, falta de moderación, f. **s.-indulgent,** indulgente con sí mismo; dado a los placeres, sibarita. **s.-interest,** propio interés, m. **s.-knowledge,** conocimiento de sí mismo, m. **s.-love,** egolatría, f. **s.-made man,** hombre que ha llegado a su posición actual por sus propios esfuerzos, m. **self-medication,** automedicación, f. **s.-opinionated,** terco, obstinaz. **s.-portrait,** autorretrato, m. **s.-possessed,** dueño de sí mismo; reservado; de sangre fría. **s.-possession,** aplomo, m, sangre fría, serenidad, f. **s.-preservation,** protección de sí mismo, f. **s.-reliance,** independencia, f; confianza en sí mismo, f. **s.-reliant,** independiente; confiado en sí mismo. **s.-reproach,** remordimiento, m. **s.-respect,** respeto de sí mismo; amor propio, m, dignidad, f. **s.-respecting,** que se respeta; que tiene amor propio. **s.-restraint,** dominio de sí mismo, m; moderación, f. **s.-righteous,** farisaico. **s.-sacrifice,** abnegación, f. **s.-sacrificing,** abnegado. **s.-same,** mismo, idéntico. **s.-satisfaction,** satisfacción de sí mismo, f; vanidad, f; (of desires, etc.) satisfacción, indulgencia, f. **s.-satisfied,** satisfecho de sí mismo, pagado de sí mismo. **s.-seeking,** a egoísta, interesado. —n egoísmo, m. **s.-starter,** Mech. arranque automático, m. **s.-styled,** autodenominado, autotitulado, llamado por sí mismo. **s.-sufficiency,** suficiencia, f; presunción, f. **s.-sufficient,** que basta a sí mismo; contento de sí mismo. **s.-supporting,** que vive de su propio trabajo; (of an institution, business) independiente. **s.-taught,** autodidacto. **s.-willed,** voluntarioso

selfish /'sɛlfɪʃ/ a egoísta, interesado

selfishness /'sɛlfɪʃnɪs/ n egoísmo, m

sell /sɛl/ vt vender. —vi vender; venderse. **They sold him to his enemies,** Le vendieron a sus enemigos. **House to s.,** «Se vende una casa.» **to s. at a loss,** malvender, vender con pérdida. **to s. for cash,** vender al contado. **to s. retail,** vender al por menor. **to s. wholesale,** vender al por mayor. **to s. one's life dearly,** vender cara la vida. **They sold the chair for $10,** Vendieron la silla por diez dólares. **to s. off,** (goods) liquidar, saldar. **to s. out,** vender; agotar. **The best edition is sold out,** La mejor edición está agotada. **All the nylons have been sold out,** Se han vendido todas las medias de nilón (de cristal). **to s. up,** vender

seller /'sɛlər/ n vendedor (-ra); comerciante (en), m

selling /'sɛlɪŋ/ n venta, f. **s. off,** liquidación, f. **s. price,** precio de venta, m

selvage /'sɛlvɪdʒ/ n (in cloth) orillo, m

semblance /'sɛmbləns/ n apariencia, f.

to put on a s. of woe, aparentar ser triste

semen /'simən/ n semen, m, esperma, f

semester /sɪ'mɛstər/ n semestre, m

semi- prefix semi; medio. **s.-conscious,** medio consciente. **s.-detached house,** casa doble, f

semicircle /'sɛmɪ,sɜrkəl/ n semicírculo, m

semicolon /'sɛmɪ,koulən/ n punto y coma, m

semidetached /,sɛmɪdɪ'tætʃt, ,sɛmai-/ a (house) apartado

seminarist /'sɛmɪnərɪst/ n seminarista, mf

seminary /'sɛmə,nɛri/ n seminario, m; (for girls) colegio interno, m

semolina /,sɛmə'linə/ n sémola, f

senate /'sɛnɪt/ n senado, m

senator /'sɛnətər/ n senador, m

send /sɛnd/ vt enviar, mandar; com remitir; (a ball) lanzar; (grant) conceder, permitir; (inflict) afligir (con). **I sent Jane for it,** Envié a Juana a buscarlo. **He sent us word that he could not come,** Nos mandó un recado diciéndonos que no podía venir. **to s. mad,** hacer enloquecer. **to s. packing,** mandar a paseo. **to s. again,** volver a mandar. **to s. away,** vt enviar; (dismiss) destituir; despedir; (scare off) ahuyentar, vi enviar a otra parte. **to s. back,** (goods) devolver; (persons) volver. **to s. down,** hacer bajar; (rain, etc.) mandar, derramar; (a student) suspender, expulsar. **to s. in,** mandar; (persons) hacer entrar, introducir; (food) servir; (a bill) presentar; (note, etc.) dar. **Please s. him in!** ¡Sírvase de invitarle a entrar! **to s. in one's resignation,** mandar su dimisión. **to s. off,** enviar, mandar; (goods) despachar; (persons) destituir; (scare) ahuyentar. **s.-off,** n despedida, f. **a good s.-off,** una despedida afectuosa. **to s. on,** (a letter) hacer seguir; (instructions) trasmitir. **to s. out,** hacer salir; mandar; (emit) despedir, dar; (new shoots, etc.) echar. **to s. round,** (the hat, etc.) hacer circular. **to s. up,** enviar arriba; mandar subir, hacer subir; mandar, enviar; (a ball) lanzar

sender /'sɛndər/ n remitente, mf; elec transmisor, m

senile /'sinail/ a senil

senior /'sinyər/ a mayor, de mayor edad; más antiguo. **Martínez s.,** Martínez padre. **Charles is Mary's s. by five years,** Carlos es cinco años mayor que María. **s. member,** decano, m

seniority /sin'yɔrɪti/ n ancianidad, f; antigüedad, f

sensation /sɛn'seɪʃən/ n sensación, f; sentimiento, m; impresión, f. **to create a s.,** causar una sensación

sensational /sɛn'seɪʃənl/ a sensacional

sense /sɛns/ n sentido, m. —vt sentir. **in a s.,** hasta cierto punto; desde un punto de vista. **in the full s. of the word,** en toda la extensión de la palabra. **common**

s., sentido común, *m*. **He has no s. of smell,** No tiene olfato. **the five senses,** los cinco sentidos. **to be out of one's senses,** estar fuera de sí, estar trastornado. **You must be out of your senses!** ¡Debes de haber perdido el juicio! ¡Estás loco! **to come to one's senses,** (after unconsciousness) volver en sí; (after folly) recobrar el sentido común. **to talk s.,** hablar con sentido común, hablar razonablemente. **s. organ,** órgano de los sentidos, *m*. **have a good s. of direction,** saber orientarse, tener buena orientación. **have no s. of smell,** ser incapaz de percibir olores. **have no s. of taste,** ser incapaz de distinguir gustos

senseless /'sɛnslɪs/ *a* (unconscious) sin sentido, insensible; desmayado; (silly) necio, estúpido. **to knock s.,** derribar, tumbar

sensible /'sɛnsəbəl/ *a* sensible; (conscious) consciente (de); sesudo. **to be s. of,** estar consciente de; estar persuadido de

sensitive /'sɛnsɪtɪv/ *a* sensitivo; susceptible (a); impresionable. **s. plant,** sensitiva, *f*

sensitivity /ˌsɛnsɪ'tɪvɪti/ *n* sensibilidad, *f*; susceptibilidad, *f*; delicadeza, *f*

sensitize /'sɛnsɪˌtaɪz/ *vt photo* sensibilizar

sensual /'sɛnʃʊəl/ *a* sensual; voluptuoso

sensuous /'sɛnʃʊəs/ *a* sensorio

sentence /'sɛntns/ *n law* sentencia, *f*; (penalty) pena, *f*; *gram* frase, *f*; (maxim) máxima, sentencia, *f*. —*vt* sentenciar, condenar. **to pass s.,** pronunciar sentencia, fallar. **under s. of,** bajo pena de

sententious /sɛn'tɛnʃəs/ *a* sentencioso

sentient /'sɛnʃənt/ *a* sensible

sentiment /'sɛntəmənt/ *n* sentimiento, *m*; (sentimentality) sentimentalismo, *m*; opinión, *f*

sentimental /ˌsɛntə'mɛntl/ *a* sentimental; (mawkish) sensiblero

sentimentalist /ˌsɛntə'mɛntlɪst/ *n* romántico (-ca), persona sentimental, *f*

sentimentality /ˌsɛntəmɛn'tælɪti/ *n* sentimentalismo, *m*, sensiblería, *f*

sentimentalize /ˌsɛntə'mɛntlˌaɪz/ *vt* idealizar

sentinel /'sɛntnl/ *n* centinela, *mf*

sentry /'sɛntri/ *n* centinela, *m*. **to be on s. duty,** estar de guardia. **s.-box,** garita de centinela, *f*

separate /*a.* 'sɛpərɪt; *v.* ˌreɪt/ *a* separado; distinto; independiente. —*vt* separar; dividir. —*vi* separarse; (of husband and wife) separarse de bienes y de cuerpos

separately /'sɛpərɪtli/ *adv* separadamente; aparte

separatism /'sɛpərəˌtɪzəm/ *n* separatismo, *m*

separatist /'sɛpərətɪst/ *a and n* separatista *mf*

Sephardic /sə'fardɪk/ *a* Sefaradí

sepia /'sipiə/ *n* (color and fish) sepia, *f*

September /sɛp'tɛmbər/ *n* setiembre, septiembre, *m*

septic /'sɛptɪk/ *a* séptico

septicemia /ˌsɛptə'simiə/ *n* septicemia, *f*

septuagenarian /ˌsɛptʃuədʒə'nɛəriən/ *n* setentón (-ona); septuagenario (-ia)

septum /'sɛptəm/ *n* septo, tabique, *m*

sepulcher /'sɛpəlkər/ *n* sepulcro, *m*

sequel /'sikwəl/ *n* (of a story, etc.) continuación, *f*; consecuencia, *f*; resultado, *m*

sequence /'sikwəns/ *n* sucesión, *f*; serie, *f*; orden, *mf*; (at cards) serie, *f*; *gram* correspondencia, *f*; (*eccl* and cinema) secuencia, *f*. **s. of tenses,** correspondencia de los tiempos, *f*

sequestered /sɪ'kwɛstərd/ *a* aislado, remoto

sequestrate /sɪ'kwɛstreɪt/ *vt* secuestrar

sequestration /ˌsikwɛs'treɪʃən/ *n* secuestro, *m*,

sequin /'sikwɪn/ *n* lentejuela, *f*

Serbia /'sɜrbiə/ Servia, *f*

Serbian /'sɜrbiən/ *a* servio. —*n* servio (-ia); (language) servio, *m*

serenade /ˌsɛrə'neɪd/ *n* serenata, *f*, *vt* dar una serenata (a)

serene /sə'rin/ *a* sereno. **His S. Highness,** Su Alteza Serenísima

serenity /sə'rɛnɪti/ *n* serenidad, *f*; tranquilidad, *f*

serf /sɜrf/ *n* siervo (-va)

serfdom /'sɜrfdəm/ *n* servidumbre, *f*

serge /sɜrdʒ/ *n* estameña, *f*; (silk) sarga, *f*

sergeant /'sardʒənt/ *n mil* sargento, *m*; (police) sargento de policía, *m*. **s.-at-arms,** macero, *m*. **s.-major,** sargento instructor, *m*

serial /'sɪəriəl/ *a* en serie; (of a story) por entregas. —*n* novela por entregas, *f*. **s. number,** número de serie, *m*

series /'sɪəriz/ *n* serie, *f*; cadena, *f*; *math* serie, progresión, *f*. **in s.,** en serie

serious /'sɪəriəs/ *a* serio; sincero; verdadero; (of illness, etc.) grave; importante. **He was s.** (not laughing) **when he said it,** Lo dijo en serio. **He is very s. about it,** Lo toma muy en serio. **to grow s.,** (of persons) ponerse serio; (of events) hacerse grave

seriously /'sɪəriəsli/ *adv* seriamente; en serio; gravemente. **to take** (something) **s.,** tomar (algo) en serio. **to take oneself s.,** tomarse muy en serio

seriousness /'sɪəriəsnɪs/ *n* seriedad, *f*; gravedad, *f*. **in all s.,** en serio, seriamente

sermon /'sɜrmən/ *n* sermón, *m*

serpent /'sɜrpənt/ *n* serpiente, *f*; *mus* serpentón, *m*

serpentine /'sɜrpənˌtin, -ˌtaɪn/ *a* serpentino; (of character) tortuoso. —*n mineral* serpentina, *f*

serrated /'sɛreɪtɪd/ *a* serrado; dentellado

serum /'sɪərəm/ *n* suero, *m*

servant /'sɜrvənt/ *n* servidor (-ra); (domestic) criado (-da); (employee) empleado (-da); (slave and *fig*) siervo (-va);

pl **servants,** (domestic) servidumbre, *f,* servicio, *m.* **I remain your obedient s.,** Quedo de Vd. atento y seguro servidor (att. y s.s.s.). **civil s.,** empleado del estado, *m.* **general s.,** criada para todo, *f.* **man s.,** criado, *m.* **the s. problem,** el problema del servicio. **Your s., sir,** Servidor de Vd., señor. **s.-girl,** criada, *f*

serve /sɜrv/ *vt* servir (a); ser útil (a); satisfacer; (in a shop) despachar; (an apprenticeship, etc.) hacer; (a prison sentence) cumplir; (treat) tratar; (of stallion) cubrir; (a warrant, etc.) ejecutar; (a notice) entregar; (a ball) servir; (on a jury, etc.) formar parte de; *naut* aforrar. —*vi* servir; (*mil, nav*) hacer el servicio. —*n sports* saque, *m.* **It serves you right!** ¡Lo tienes merecido! **to s. at table,** servir a la mesa. **to s. as,** servir de. **to s. out,** distribuir; servir. **Serves 8,** (recipe) Da 8 porciones

server /'sɜrvər/ *n eccl* acólito, *m., sports* saque, *m;* (tray) bandeja, *f;* (for fish, etc.) pala, *f*

service /'sɜrvɪs/ *n* servicio, *m;* *eccl* oficio, *m;* servicio de mesa, *m;* (of a writ) entrega, *f; sports* saque, *m.* **coffee s.,** juego de café, *m.* **diplomatic s.,** cuerpo diplomático, *m.* **At your s.,** Para servir a Vd., A su disposición. **on active s.,** en acto de servicio; en el campo de batalla. **to go into s.,** (of servants) ir a servir. **to render s.,** prestar servicios. **s. tree,** serbal, *m*

serviceable /'sɜrvəsəbəl/ *a* (of persons) servicial; (of things) servible, utilizable; útil; práctico; (lasting) duradero

service road *n* vía de servicio, *f*

servile /'sɜrvil/ *a* servil

serving /'sɜrvɪŋ/ *a* sirviente; al servicio (de). **s. maid,** criada, *f.* **s. table,** trinchero, *m*

servitude /'sɜrvɪˌtud/ *n* servidumbre, esclavitud, *f.* **penal s.,** cadena perpetua, *f*

session /'sɛʃən/ *n* sesión, *f;* junta, *f.* **petty sessions,** tribunal de primera instancia, *m*

set /sɛt/ *vt* poner; colocar; fijar; (seeds, etc.) plantar; (bones) reducir, componer; (gems) engastar, montar; (a clock) regular; (sails) desplegar; (the teeth of a saw) trabar, triscar; (congeal) hacer coagular; (a trap) armar; (a snare) tender; (a razor) afilar; (make ready) preparar; (type) componer; (cause) hacer; *mus* poner en música; *mus* adaptar; (order) mandar; (prescribe) dar, asignar; (estimate) estimar, evaluar; (an example, etc.) dar; (establish) establecer, crear. —*vi* (of the sun, etc.) ponerse; (solidify) coagularse, solidificarse; (of tides) fluir; (of the wind) soplar; (of dogs) hacer punta. **The joke set him laughing,** El chiste le hizo reír. **set an example,** dar ejemplo, dar el ejemplo. **set a precedent,** sentar precedente. **to set a person's mind at rest,** tranquilizar, sosegar. **to set a trap,** armar lazo. **to set at ease,** poner a sus anchas (a), hacer cómodo (a). **to set at naught,** despre-

ciar. **to set eyes on,** poner los ojos en. **to set fire to,** pegar fuego a, incendiar. **to set free,** poner en libertad, librar (de). **to set in motion,** poner en marcha. **to set one's teeth,** apretar los dientes. **to set people talking,** dar que hablar a la gente. **to set the fashion,** fijar la moda; poner de moda. **to set the alarm at seven o'clock,** poner el despertador a las siete. **to set the table,** poner la mesa. **to set to work,** ponerse a trabajar. **to set about,** *vi* (begin) ponerse (a); empezar; (undertake) emprender. —*vt* (a rumour, etc.) divulgar. **They set about each other,** Empezaron a golpearse, Vinieron a las manos. **to set against,** indisponer (con), enemistar (con); hacer el enemigo (de), ser hostil (a); (balance) oponer, balancear. **to set oneself against,** oponerse a; atacar, luchar contra. **to set aside,** poner a un lado; apartar; (discard) desechar; (omit) omitir, pasar por alto de; dejar aparte, excluir; (keep) reservar; (money, etc.) ahorrar; (reject) rechazar; (quash) anular. **to set back,** hacer retroceder. **set-back,** *n* revés, *m;* contrariedad, *f.* **to set before,** poner ante; (facts) exponer; (introduce) presentar. **to set down,** poner en tierra; depositar; (of a bus, etc.) dejar; (in writing) poner por escrito; anotar, apuntar; narrar, contar; (attribute) atribuir; (fix) fijar, formular; (believe to be) creer. **Passengers are set down at...,** Los viajeros pueden apearse en... **to set forth,** *vt* (one's opinions, etc.) exponer; publicar; (display) exhibir, mostrar; (make) hacer. —*vi* ponerse en camino. **to set going,** poner en marcha; echar a andar. **to set in,** empezar; (of the tide) fluir. **A reaction has set in,** Se ha hecho sentir una reacción. **to set off,** *vt* (explode) hacer estallar; (cause) hacer; (heighten) realzar; hacer resaltar; (counterbalance) contraponer. —*vi* partir; ponerse en camino. **set-off,** *n* contraste, *m,* contraposición, *f.* **to set off against,** contraponer. **to set on,** *vt* (a dog) azuzar; (incite) instigar, incitar. —*vi* atacar. **to set out,** *vt* (state) exponer, manifestar; (embellish) realzar; (display) arreglar, disponer. —*vi* ponerse en camino, partir. **to set over,** (rule) tener autoridad sobre, gobernar. **to set to,** (begin to) ponerse a, empezar a; (work) ponerse a trabajar. **set-to,** *n* lucha, *f;* (boxing) asalto, *m;* (quarrel) pelea, riña, *f.* **to set up,** *vt* (a monument, etc.) erigir, levantar; (fix) fijar; (apparatus, machinery) montar; (exalt) exaltar; (found) establecer; crear; (propound) exponer; (a howl, etc.) dar; (equip with) proveer de; instalar; (make strong) robustecer; fortificar; (type) componer; (raise) alzar. —*vi* establecerse; dárselas de. **He sets himself up as a painter,** Se las da de pintor. **to set** (a person) **up as a model,** poner como modelo (a). **to set up house,** poner casa. **to set up a business,** establecer un comercio. **set-up**, *n* establecimiento, *m*; arreglo, *m*. **to set upon**, atacar

set /sɛt/ *n* (of sun, etc.) puesta, *f*, ocaso, *m*; (of the head, etc.) porte, *m*; (of a garment) corte, *m*; (of the tide, etc.) dirección, *f*; (slant) inclinación, *f*; (*fig* drift) tendencia, *f*, movimiento, *m*; (of the teeth of a saw) triscamiento, *m*; (of men, houses, etc.) grupo, *m*; (of tools, golf clubs, china, etc.) juego, *m*; (gang) pandilla, camarilla, *f*; clase, *f*; (*dance*) tanda, *f*; (tennis) partido, *f*; *theat* decoración, *f*; *radio* aparato de radio, *m*, radio, *f*. **coffee set**, juego de café, *m*. **all-mains set**, radio de corriente eléctrica, *f*. **battery set**, radio de batería, *f*. **portable set**, radio portátil, *f*. **the smart set**, el mundo elegante. **to have a shampoo and set**, hacerse lavar y marcar (el pelo). **to make a set**, hacer juego. **to make a dead set at**, hacer un ataque vigoroso (a), atacar resueltamente; procurar insinuarse en el favor de. **set of teeth**, dentadura, *f*

set /sɛt/ *a* fijo; inmóvil; (of a smile) forzado; (of a task) asignado; (of times) señalado, fijo; (prescribed) prescrito, establecido; (firm) firme; (resolved) resuelto; (well-known) consabido; (obstinate) terco, nada adaptable. **well set-up**, apuesto, bien plantado. **He is set on doing it**, Se empeña en **to be dead set against**, estar completamente opuesto a. **set phrase**, frase hecha, *f*. **set-square**, cartabón, *m*

setting /ˈsɛtɪŋ/ *n* (of the sun, etc.) puesta, *f*; (of mortar, etc.) fraguado, *m*; (of a jelly) solidificación, *f*; (of jewels) engaste, *m*, montadura, *f*; (of bones) aliño, *m*; (of teeth of saw) traba, *f*; (of razor) afiladura, *f*; (of a trap) armadura, *f*; (of a machine, etc.) ajuste, *m*; (frame) marco, *m*; *mus* arreglo, *m*; *theat* decorado, *m*; (emplacement) lecho, *m*. **the s. sun**, el sol poniente. **s. free**, liberación, *f*. **s. off**, partida, salida, *f*. **s. out**, ida, marcha, *f*; principio, *m*. **s.-up**, creación, institución, *f*, establecimiento, *m*; (of a machine) montaje, *m*; *print* composición, *f*

settle /ˈsɛtl/ *vt* colocar; asegurar, afirmar; (a country) colonizar; (live in) establecer (en); (populate) poblar; (in a profession, etc.) dar; (install) instalar; (the imagination, etc.) sosegar, calmar; (resolve) resolver; (arrange) disponer, arreglar; (differences) componer, concertar; (an opponent, etc.) confundir; (a bill) saldar, pagar; (a claim) satisfacer; (clarify) depositar, clarificar; (end) poner fin (a). —*vi* establecerse; (of weather) serenarse; (to work, etc.) empezar a, ponerse a; (applicarse a; (decide) decidirse; (alight) posarse; (of foundations, etc.) asentarse; (of a ship) zozobrar; (of sediment) depositarse; (of liquid) clarificarse. **to s. accounts with**, *fig* ajustar cuentas con. **to s. down**, establecerse, arraigarse; adap-

tarse (a); (become calm) sosegarse, calmarse; sentar el juicio; (of foundations) asentarse; (of ship) depositarse; (of sediment) depositarse. **to s. in**, *vt* instalar. —*vi* instalarse. **to s. on**, (choose) escoger; (decide on) decidirse (a). **to s. a pension on**, señalar pensión (a). **to s. up**, *vt* (one's affairs) poner en orden; (bill) pagar, saldar. —*vi* llegar a un acuerdo; pagar cuentas

settled /ˈsɛtld/ *a* fijo; permanente; invariable; (of countries) colonizado; (of weather) sereno

settlement /ˈsɛtlmənt/ *n* (of a country) colonización, *f*; (of a dispute) arreglo, ajuste, *m*; (of a question) solución, *f*; decisión, *f*; (of a bill) saldo, pago, *m*, liquidación, *f*; (of an obligation) satisfacción, *f*; (colony) colonia, *f*; (creation) creación, institución, *f*; establecimiento, arraigo, *m*. **deed of s.**, escritura de donación, *f*. **marriage s.**, contrato matrimonial, *m*; **s. out of court**, arreglo pacífico, *m*

settler /ˈsɛtlər/ *n* colono, *m*; colonizador (-ra)

seven /ˈsɛvən/ *a* and *n* siete *m*. **It is s. o'clock**, Son las siete. **the s. deadly sins**, los siete pecados capitales

seventeen /ˈsɛvənˈtin/ *a* diecisiete, diez y siete. —*n* diecisiete, *m*. **She is just s.**, Acaba de cumplir los diez y siete años

seventeenth /ˈsɛvənˈtinθ/ *a* décimoséptimo; (of monarchs and of the month) diez y siete. —*n* décimoséptimo, *m*. **Louis the S.**, Luis diez y siete. **the s. of June**, el diez y siete de junio

seventh /ˈsɛvənθ/ *a* séptimo; (of the month) siete. —*n* séptimo, *m*; séptima parte, *f*; *mus* séptima, *f*. **Edward the S.**, Eduardo séptimo. **the s. of August**, el siete de agosto

seventieth /ˈsɛvəntiɪθ/ *a* septuagésimo, setentavo. —*n* setentavo, *m*

seventy /ˈsɛvənti/ *a* and *n* setenta, *m*

sever /ˈsɛvər/ *vt* separar; romper; dividir

several /ˈsɛvərəl/ *a* distinto, diferente; respectivo; varios, *m pl*, (*f pl*, varias); algunos, *m pl*, (*f pl*, algunas)

severally /ˈsɛvərəli/ *adv* separadamente; individualmente; independientemente

severance /ˈsɛvərəns/ *n* separación, *f*; (of friendship, etc.) ruptura, *f*

severe /səˈvɪər/ *a* severo; riguroso; fuerte; duro; (of style) austero; (of pain) agudo; (of illness) grave

severity /səˈvɛrɪti/ *n* severidad, *f*; intensidad, *f*; (of weather) inclemencia, *f*; (of illness) gravedad, *f*

sew /sou/ *vt* and *vi* coser. **to sew on**, coser, pegar

sewage /ˈsuɪdʒ/ *n* aguas residuales, *f pl*. **s. system**, alcantarillado, *m*

sewer /ˈsuər/ *n* alcantarilla, cloaca, *f*, albañal, *m*

sewing /ˈsouɪŋ/ *n* costura, *f*. **s. bag**, costurero, *m*. **s. cotton**, hilo de coser, *m*. **s. machine**, máquina de coser, *f*. **s. silk**, torzal, *m*

sex /sɛks/ n sexo, m. **the fair sex,** el bello sexo. **the weaker sex,** el sexo débil. **sex appeal,** atractivo, m

sh! /ʃ/ interj ¡Chitón! ¡Chis!

shabbily /'ʃæbəli/ adv (of dressing) pobremente; (of treatment) mezquinamente

shabby /'ʃæbi/ a (of persons) desharrapado, andrajoso; (of garments) raído, roto; (of a neighborhood, etc.) pobre; (mean) ruin, mezquino

shack /ʃæk/ n choza, f

shackle /'ʃækəl/ n traba, f; pl **shackles,** grillos, m pl, esposas, f pl; fig cadenas, f pl. —vt poner esposas (a), encadenar; (a horse) apear; fig atar; (impede) estorbar

shad /ʃæd/ n sábalo, m

shade /ʃeid/ n sombra, f; (in a picture) toque de obscuro, m; (for the eyes) visera, f; (of a lamp) pantalla, f; (ghost) espectro, fantasma, m; (of color) matiz, m; (tinge) dejo, m. —vt sombrear, dar sombra (a); (the face, etc.) proteger, resguardar; (a drawing) esfumar. **in the s.,** a la sombra. **80° in the s.,** ochenta grados a la sombra. **to put** (a person) **in the s.,** eclipsar

shadow /'ʃædou/ n sombra, f; obscuridad, f; (in a picture) toque de obscuro, m. —vt sombrear; obscurecer; (a person) seguir. **to cast a s.,** proyectar una sombra. **to s. forth,** indicar; simbolizar. **s. show,** sombras chinescas, f pl

shadowy /'ʃædoui/ a umbroso; vago, indistinto, indefinido

shady /'ʃeidi/ a sombreado, umbrío; sombrío; (of persons, etc.) sospechoso. **It was s. in the wood,** Hacía sombra en el bosque

shaft /ʃæft/ n fuste, m; (arrow) flecha, saeta, f, dardo, m; (of a golf club, etc.) mango, m; (of a cart) vara, f; mech árbol, eje, m; (of a column and a feather) cañón, m; (of light) rayo, m; (of a mine) pozo, tiro, m; (air-shaft) conducto de aire, ventilador, m. **cam-s.,** árbol de levas, m. **driving s.,** árbol motor, m

shaggy /'ʃægi/ a peludo; lanudo

shake /ʃeik/ vt sacudir; agitar; hacer temblar; (weaken) debilitar, hacer flaquear. —vi estremecerse; temblar; (trill) trinar. **He managed to s. himself free,** Consiguió librarse por una sacudida. **to s. hands,** darse la mano, estrecharse la mano. **to s. one's finger at,** señalar con el dedo (a). **to s. one's fist at,** amenazar con el puño (a). **to s. one's head,** mover la cabeza; negar con la cabeza. **to s. one's sides,** (with laughter) reírse a carcajadas. **to s. with fear,** temblar de miedo. **to s. down,** sacudir, hacer caer. **s.-down,** n cama improvisada, f. **to s. off,** sacudirse; librarse (de), perder; quitar de encima (a). **to s. out,** (unfurl) desplegar; sacudir. **to s. up,** agitar; sacudir, remover

shake /ʃeik/ n sacudida, f; (of the head) movimiento (de la cabeza), m; (of the hand) apretón (de manos), m; temblor,

---

m; mus trino, gorjeo, m. **in two shakes,** Inf. en un periquete. **to give a person a good s.,** sacudir violentamente (a)

shaking /'ʃeikiŋ/ n sacudimiento, m; temblor, m; (of windows, etc.) zangoloteo, m

shaky /'ʃeiki/ a inestable; poco firme; (of hands, etc.) tembloroso; (of the voice) trémulo; (of gait) vacilante; dudoso

shall /ʃæl; unstressed ʃəl/ v aux (expressing simple future) **I s. arrive tomorrow,** Llegaré mañana. **S. we go to the sea next week?** ¿Iremos al mar la semana próxima?; (expressing obligation, compulsion) **You s. not go out,** No has de salir, No quiero que salgas. **He s. see her immediately,** Tiene que verla en seguida; (as a polite formula) **S. I go?** ¿Quiere Vd. que vaya? **S. we buy the soap?** ¿Quiere Vd. que compremos el jabón? ¿Compraremos el jabón?

shallot /'ʃɒlət, ʃə'lɒt/ n bot chalote, m, ascalonia, f

shallow /'ʃælou/ a poco profundo; (of a receptacle) llano; (of persons) superficial, frívolo; (of knowledge, etc.) superficial, ligero, somero. —n bajío, m

sham /ʃæm/ vt fingir, simular. —n farsa, f; imitación, f; engaño, m; (person) farsante, m. —a fingido; falso; espurio. **to s. illness,** fingirse enfermo. **to s. dead,** hacer la mortecina. **You're just a s.,** Eres un farsante

shamble /'ʃæmbəl/ vi andar arrastrándose. —n andar pesado, m; pl **shambles,** matadero, m; fig carnicería, f

shame /ʃeim/ n vergüenza, f; ignominia, f; deshonra, f. —vt avergonzar; deshonrar. **For s.!** ¡Qué vergüenza! **What a s.!** ¡Qué lástima! **to put to s.,** avergonzar

shamefaced /'ʃeim,feist/ a (bashful) vergonzoso, tímido; (ashamed) avergonzado

shameful /'ʃeimfəl/ a vergonzoso, escandaloso; indecente

shameless /'ʃeimlis/ a desvergonzado; impúdico, indecente

shamelessly /'ʃeimlisli/ adv desvergonzadamente

shampoo /ʃæm'pu/ n champú, m. —vt dar un champú (a); dar un masaje (a). **dry s.,** champú seco, m

shank /ʃæŋk/ n zanca, f; mech pierna, f; (handle) mango, m; (of a button) rabo, m, cola, f. **go on Shank's mare, ride on Shank's mare,** caminar en coche de San Francisco, ir en la boridad de Villadiego

shanty /'ʃænti/ n choza, f

shanty town n barriada (Peru), callampa, población, población callampa (Chile), f. Rancho (Venezuela), m, villa-miseria (Argentina), f

shape /ʃeip/ n forma, f; bulto, m; fantasma, m; (of a garment) corte, m; (of a person) talle, m; cul molde, m; (of a hat) forma, f. —vt formar; (a garment) cortar; (ideas) dar forma (a); adaptar; (stone, etc.) labrar; (one's life) dominar. —vi (of events) desarrollarse. **to go out of s.,** perder la forma. **to take s.,** tomar forma. **to s. one's course,** dirigirse (hacia, a); *naut* dar el rumbo. **to s. well,** prometer bien

shapeless /'ʃeiplɪs/ *a* informe; disforme

shapely /'ʃeipli/ *a* bien formado; simétrico

share /ʃeər/ *n* porción, *f;* parte, *f;* cuota, *f;* contribución, *f;* (part ownership) interés, *m;* (in a company) acción, *f.* —*vt* distribuir; compartir; dividir; tomar parte en. —*vi* participar (de); tomar parte (en). **to fall to one's s.,** tocar, corresponder. **to go shares with,** dividir con, compartir con. **to take a s. in the conversation,** tomar parte en la conversación. **paid-up s.,** *com* acción liberada, *f.* **to s. out,** repartir, distribuir

shareholder /'ʃeər,houldər/ *n* accionista, *mf*

shark /ʃɑrk/ *n ichth* tiburón, *m; inf* caimán, *m*

sharp /ʃɑrp/ *a* (of edges) afilado, cortante; (of points) punzante, puntiagudo; (of features, etc.) anguloso; (of bends, etc.) brusco; (of outlines, etc.) definido, distinto; (of pain, sound) agudo; (marked) marcado; (intense) intenso; (of winds, glance, etc.) penetrante; (of hearing) fino; (of appetite) bueno; (of showers) fuerte; (quick) rápido; (clever, etc.) vivo, listo; perspicaz; (of children) despierto, precoz; (unscrupulous) astuto, sin escrúpulos; (of criticism, remarks) mordaz; (of rebukes, sentences, etc.) severo; (of winters, etc.) riguroso; (of fighting) encarnizado; (of taste) picante; (sour) ácido; *mus* sostenido. —*adv* en punto; *mus* sostenido. —*n mus* sostenido, *m.* **at five o'clock s.,** a las cinco en punto. **Look s.!** ¡Date prisa! **s.-edged,** afilado. **s.-eyed,** con ojos de lince; de mirada penetrante. **s.-featured,** de facciones angulosas. **s.-nosed,** de nariz puntiaguda. **s.-pointed,** puntiagudo. **s. practice,** procedimientos poco honrados, *m pl.* **s.-tongued,** de lengua áspera. **s. turn,** curva brusca, curva cerrada, *f.* **s.-witted,** de inteligencia viva, listo

sharpen /'ʃɑrpən/ *vt* (knives) afilar, amolar; (pencils, etc.) sacar punta (a); (wits, etc.) despabilar; (appetite) abrir. **This walk has sharpened my appetite,** Este paseo me ha abierto el apetito. **to s. one's claws,** afilarse las uñas

sharper /'ʃɑrpər/ *n inf* caballero de industria, timador, *m;* (at cards) fullero, *m*

sharpshooter /'ʃɑrp,ʃutər/ *n* franco tirador, *m*

sharpsighted /'ʃɑrp,saitɪd/ *a* de vista penetrante, listo, perspicaz

shatter /'ʃætər/ *vt* romper, quebrantar; hacer añicos; *fig* destrozar. **You have shattered my illusions,** Has destrozado todas mis ilusiones

shave /ʃeiv/ *vt* afeitar, rasurar; (wood, etc.) acepillar. —*vi* afeitarse; (of razors)

afeitar. —*n* afeitada, *f.* **to have a s.,** hacerse afeitar. **to have a close s.,** *inf* escapar por un pelo

shaving /'ʃeivɪŋ/ *n* afeitada, *f;* (of wood, etc.) viruta, acepilladura, *f.* **s.-bowl,** bacía, *f.* **s.-brush,** brocha de afeitar, *f.* **s.-glass,** espejo de afeitar, *m.* **s.-soap,** jabón de afeitar, *m.* **s.-stick,** barra de jabón de afeitar, *f*

shawl /ʃɔl/ *n* chal, mantón, rebozo, *m*

she /ʃi/ *pers pron* ella; la; (female) hembra, *f;* (translated by fem. ending in the case of animals, etc., e.g. *she bear,* osa, *she cat,* gata). **It is her,** Es ella. **she who is dancing,** la que baila

sheaf /ʃif/ *n* (of corn, etc.) gavilla, garba, *f;* (of arrows) haz, *m;* (of papers, etc.) paquete, atado, *m.* **to bind in sheaves,** agavillar

shear /ʃɪər/ *vt.* (sheep) esquilar, trasquilar; tonsurar; cortar; (cloth) tundir

shears /ʃɪərz/ *n pl* tijeras grandes, *f pl,* cizalla, *f*

sheath /ʃiθ/ *n* vaina, *f.* **s.-knife,** cuchillo de monte, *m*

shed /ʃed/ *vt* derramar; (skin, etc.) mudar; perder; (remove) quitarse, desprenderse de; (get rid of) deshacerse de. —*n* cobertizo, sotechado, *m;* cabaña, *f.* **to s. light on,** echar luz sobre, iluminar

sheen /ʃin/ *n* lustre, *m;* brillo, *m*

sheep /ʃip/ *n* oveja, *f;* carnero, *m;* ganado lanar, *m.* **He is the black s. of the family,** Es el garbanzo negro de la familia. **to cast sheep's eyes at,** lanzar miradas de carnero degollado. **s. breeder,** ganadero, *m.* **s.-dip,** desinfectante para ganado, *m.* **s.-dog,** perro de pastor, *m.* **s.-like,** ovejuno, de oveja. **s.-shearing,** esquileo, *m*

sheepish /'ʃipɪʃ/ *a* tímido, vergonzoso; estúpido

sheepskin /'ʃip,skɪn/ *n* piel de carnero, *f.* **s. jacket,** zamarra, *f*

sheer /ʃɪər/ *a* puro; completo, absoluto; (steep) escarpado, acantilado; a pico; (of fabrics) transparente; ligero, fino. —*adv* completamente; de un golpe; (perpendicularly) a pico. **to s. off,** desviarse; largarse, marcharse

sheet /ʃit/ *n* (bed) sábana, *f;* (shroud) mortaja, *f;* (of paper) hoja, *f;* cuartilla, *f;* (pamphlet) folleto, *m;* (news) periódico, *m,* hoja, *f;* (of metal, etc.) lámina, plancha, *f;* (of water, etc.) extensión, *f;* *naut* escota, *f.* —*vt* poner sábanas en; envolver en sábanas; (a corpse) amortajar. **to be as white as a s.,** estar pálido como un muerto. **s. bend,** (knot) nudo de tejedor, *m.* **s. glass,** vidrio en lámina, *m.* **s. iron,** hierro en planchas, *m*

shekel /'ʃekəl/ *n* (coin) siclo, *m; pl* **shekels,** dinero, *m*

shelf /ʃelf/ *n* estante, anaquel, *m;* (reef) banco de arena, bajío, *m;* (of rock) escalón, *m.* **to be on the s.,** *inf* quedarse para tía, quedarse para vestir imágenes

shell /ʃel/ *n* (of small shellfish) concha, *f;*

(of tortoise) coraza, *f;* (of insects, lobsters, etc.) caparazón, *m;* (of a nut) cáscara, *f;* (of an egg) cascarón, *m;* (of peas, beans) vaina, *f;* (*com* and *mus*) concha, *f;* (of a building) casco, *m;* (outside) exterior, *m;* (empty form) apariencia, *f; mil* granada, *f.* —*vt* pelar; (nuts) descascarar; (beans, etc.) desvainar; *mil* bombardear. **to be under s.-fire,** sufrir un bombardeo. **s..shock,** neurosis de guerra, *f*

shellfish /'ʃel,fiʃ/ *n* crustáceo, *m;* (as food) marisco, *m*

shelling /'ʃeliŋ/ *n mil* bombardeo, *m*

shelter /'ʃeltər/ *n* abrigo, amparo, *m;* refugio, *m;* asilo, *m.* —*vt* dar asilo (a); abrigar; (defend) amparar, proteger; (hide) esconder. —*vi* refugiarse; resguardarse; esconderse

shelve /ʃelv/ *vt* (books) poner en un estante; (persons) destituir; (questions, etc.) aplazar, arrinconar; proveer de estantes, *vi* (slope) inclinarse, formar declive; (of sea bed) formar escalones

shepherd /'ʃepərd/ *n* pastor, *m.* —*vt* guardar; guiar, conducir. **s. boy,** zagal, *m.* **shepherd's pouch,** zurrón, *m*

sherbet /'ʃərbɪt/ *n* sorbete, *m*

sheriff /'ʃerɪf/ *n* (in U.K.) sheriff, *m;* (U.S.A.) jefe de la policía, *m*

sherry /'ʃeri/ *n* (vino de) jerez, *m.* **dry s.,** jerez seco, *m*

shield /ʃild/ *n* escudo, *m;* (round) rodela, *f; herald* escudo de armas, *m; fig* defensa, *f,* amparo, *m.* —*vt* proteger, amparar. **to s. a person,** proteger a una persona. **to s. one's eyes from the sun,** proteger los ojos del sol. **s.-bearer,** escudero, *m*

shift /ʃɪft/ *vt* mover; trasladar; quitar, librarse de; cambiar. —*vi* moverse; (of the wind) girar; cambiar. —*n* cambio, *m;* (expedient) recurso, expediente, *m;* (dodge) artificio, *m,* trampa, *f;* (of workmen) tanda, *f,* turno, *m.* **to make s.,** arreglárselas (para hacer algo); procurar (hacer algo); (manage) ir tirando. **to s. for oneself,** compenérselas, arreglárselas. **to s. the scenes,** *theat* cambiar de decoración. **to s. the helm,** *naut* cambiar el timón. **to work in shifts,** trabajar por turnos

shifting /'ʃɪftɪŋ/ *a* (of light, etc.) cambiante; (of sand, etc.) movedizo; (of wind) mudable; (of moods) voluble. **s. sand,** arena movediza, *f*

shiftless /'ʃɪftlɪs/ *a* perezoso; sin energía, ineficaz

shifty /'ʃɪfti/ *a* (tricky) tramposo, astuto; (dishonest) informal, falso; (of gaze) furtivo. **s.-eyed,** *a* de mirada furtiva

shilling /'ʃɪlɪŋ/ *n* chelín, *m.* **nine shillings in the £,** nueve chelines por libra. **to cut off with a s.,** desheredar

shilly shally /'ʃɪli ˌʃæli/ *n* irresolución, vacilación, *f, vi* estar irresoluto, titubear, no saber qué hacer

shimmer /'ʃɪmər/ *vi* rielar; relucir. —*n* luz trémula, *f;* resplandor, *m;* viso, *m*

shin /ʃɪn/ *n* espinilla, *f;* (of beef) corvejón, *m.* **to s. up,** trepar

shindy /'ʃɪndi/ *n* suiza, reyerta, tasquera, *f.* **to kick up a s.,** armar camorra

shine /ʃain/ *vi* brillar; resplandecer, relucir, relumbrar. —*vt* (shoes) dar lustre a. —*n* brillo, *m;* lustre, *m.* **in rain or s.,** en buen o mal tiempo. **to s. with happiness,** radiar felicidad. **to take the s. out of,** eclipsar

shingle /'ʃɪŋgəl/ *n* (pebbles) guijarros, *m pl;* cascajo, *m;* barda, *f;* (hair) pelo a la garçonne, *m; pl* **shingles,** *med* zona, *f,* herpe zóster, *m.* —*vt* (the hair) cortar a la garçonne

shining /'ʃainɪŋ/ *a* resplandeciente, brillante, reluciente; radiante. **s. with happiness,** radiante de felicidad. **s. example,** ejemplo notable, *m*

shiny /'ʃaini/ *a* brillante; lustroso; terso; (of trousers, etc.) reluciente; (of paper) glaseado

ship /ʃɪp/ *n* buque, barco, *m;* (sailing) velero, *m.* —*vt* embarcar; (oars) armar. —*vi* embarcar; (as a member of crew) embarcarse. **on board s.,** a bordo. **to s. a sea,** embarcar agua. **to take s.,** embarcar. **to s. off,** mandar. **ship's boat,** lancha, *f.* **ship's boy,** grumete, *m.* **ship's carpenter,** carpintero de ribera, *f.* **ship's company,** tripulación, *f.* **s.-breaker,** desguazador, *m.* **s.-canal,** canal de navegación, *m.* **s.-load,** cargamento, *m*

shipment /'ʃɪpmənt/ *n* embarque, *m;* despacho por mar, *m;* (consignment) remesa, *f*

shipowner /'ʃɪpˌounər/ *n* naviero, *m*

shipper /'ʃɪpər/ *n* naviero, *m;* importador, *m;* exportador, *m*

shipping /'ʃɪpɪŋ/ *n* embarque, *m;* buques, barcos, *m pl;* (of a country) marina, *f.* **s. agent,** consignatario de buques, *m.* **s. company,** compañía de navegación, *f.* **s. offices,** oficinas de una compañía de navegación, *f pl*

shipshape /'ʃɪpˌʃeip/ *a* en buen orden; bien arreglado

shipwreck /'ʃɪpˌrek/ *n* naufragio, *m, vt* hacer naufragar, echar a pique

shipwrecked person /'ʃɪpˌrekt/ *n* náufrago (-ga). **to be shipwrecked,** naufragar

shipyard /'ʃɪpˌyard/ *n* astillero, varadero, *m*

shire /ʃaiᵊr/ *n* condado, *m*

shirk /ʃərk/ *vt* eludir, esquivar; desentenderse de. —*vi* faltar al deber

shirr /ʃər/ *vt* fruncir

shirt /ʃərt/ *n* camisa, *f.* **dress s.,** camisa de pechera dura, *f.* **hair-s.,** cilicio, *m.* **in one's s.-sleeves,** en mangas de camisa. **s.-blouse,** blusa sencilla, *f.* **s.-collar,** cuello de camisa, *m.* **s. factory** or **shop,** camisería, *f.* **shirt-front,** pechera, *f.* **s.-maker,** camisero (-ra)

shirting /'ʃərtɪŋ/ *n* tela para camisas, *f*

shiver /'ʃɪvər/ *vi* temblar, tiritar; dar diente con diente; (of a boat) zozobrar.

—*vt* (break) hacer añicos, romper; (sails) sacudir. —*n* temblor, estremecimiento, *m*; escalofrío, *m*; (of glass, etc.) fragmento, *m*, astilla, *f*. **You give me the shivers,** Me das escalofríos

shoal /ʃoul/ *n* (of fish) banco, *m*; gran cantidad, *f*; (of people) multitud, muchedumbre, *f*; (water) bajo fondo, *m*; (sand-bank) banco, bajío, *m*, *a* poco profundo. **I know shoals of people in Valencia,** Conozco a muchísima gente de Valencia

shock /ʃɒk/ *n* choque, *m*; *elec* conmoción, *f*; *med* shock, *m*; (*med* stroke) conmoción cerebral, *f*; (fright) sobresalto, susto, *m*. —*vt* sacudir, dar una sacudida (a); chocar; escandalizar, horrorizar. —*vi* chocar. **electric s.,** conmoción eléctrica, *f*. **She is easily shocked,** Ella se escandaliza fácilmente. **s. of hair,** mata de pelo, *f*. **s. absorber,** *ech* amortiguador, *m*; *auto* amortiguador (de los muelles), *m*. **s. troops,** tropas de asalto, *f pl*, elementos de choque, *m pl*

shocking /ˈʃɒkɪŋ/ *a* escandaloso; repugnante, horrible; espantoso. **How s.!** ¡Qué horror! **s. bad,** malísimo

shod /ʃɒd/ *a* calzado; (of horses) herrado

shoddy /ˈʃɒdi/ *n* pacotilla, *f*. —*a* de pacotilla; espurio, falso

shoe /ʃu/ *n* zapato, *m*; (horse) herradura, *f*; (*naut mech*) zapata, *f*. —*vt* (horses) herrar. **I should not like to be in his shoes,** No me gustaría estar en su pellejo. **That is quite another pair of shoes,** Eso es harina de otro costal. **to cast a s.,** (of horses) desherrarse, perder una herradura. **to put on one's shoes,** ponerse los zapatos, calzarse. **to remove one's shoes,** quitarse los zapatos, descalzarse. **wooden shoes,** zuecos, *m pl*. **s.-buckle,** hebilla de zapato, *f*. **s.-lace,** cordón de zapato, *m*. **s.-leather,** cuero para zapatos, *m*; calzado, *m*. **s.-scraper,** limpiabarros, *m*, estregadera, *f*. **s.-shop,** zapatería, *f*

shoeblack /ˈʃublæk/ *n* betún, *m*; (person) limpiabotas, *m*

shoehorn /ˈʃuhɔrn/ *n* calzador, *m*

shoemaker /ˈʃumeɪkər/ *n* zapatero (-ra)

shoo! /ʃu/ *interj* ¡fuera!; ¡zape! —*vt* ahuyentar

shoot /ʃut/ *vt* (throw) lanzar; precipitar; (empty) vaciar; (a rapid) salvar; (rays, etc.) echar; (an arrow, a gun, etc.) disparar; (a person, etc.) pegar un tiro (a); *sports* tirar; *mil* fusilar, pasar por las armas; (a film) hacer, impresionar. —*vi* lanzarse, precipitarse; (of pain) latir; (sprout) brotar; disparar; tirar; (at football) tirar a gol, chutar. **to s. a glance at,** lanzar una mirada (a). **I was shot in the foot,** Una bala me hirió en el pie. **to s. the sun,** *naut* tomar el sol. **to s. ahead,** tomar la delantera. **to s. at,** tirar a. **to s by,** pasar como una bala. **to s. down,** *aer* derribar; matar de un tiro. **to s. up,** (of children) espigarse; (of prices) subir mucho; (of cliffs, etc.) elevarse

shoot /ʃut/ *n* partida de caza, *f*; tiro, *m*; *bot* renuevo, retoño, *m*

shooting /ˈʃutɪŋ/ *n* tiro, *m*; caza con escopeta, *f*; (of guns) tiroteo, *m*; (of an arrow) disparo, *m*; (of a film) rodaje, *m*. **to go s.,** ir a cazar con escopeta. **s.-box,** pabellón de caza, *m*. **s. butts,** tiradero, *m*. **s. dog,** perro de caza, *m*. **s.-gallery,** tiro al blanco, *m*. **s. match,** concurso de tiro, *m*. **s. pain,** punzada de dolor, *f*. **s. party,** partida de caza, *f*. **s. practice,** ejercicios de tiro, *m pl*. **s.-range,** campo de tiro, *m*. **s. star,** estrella fugaz, *f*

shop /ʃɒp/ *n* tienda, *f*; (workshop) taller, *m*. —*vi* ir de compras, ir de tiendas; comprar. **to talk s.,** hablar de negocios. **s.-assistant,** dependiente (-ta). **s.-soiled,** deslucido. **s.-steward,** representante de los obreros de una fábrica o taller, *m*. **s. window,** escaparate, *m*

shopkeeper /ˈʃɒpˌkipər/ *n* tendero (-ra)

shoplifter /ˈʃɒpˌlɪftər/ *n* ladrón (-ona) de tiendas, ratero (-ra) de las tiendas

shopper /ˈʃɒpər/ *n* comprador (-ra)

shopping /ˈʃɒpɪŋ/ *n* compra, *f*; compras, *f pl*. **to go s.,** ir de compras. **s. basket,** cesta para compras, *f*. **s. center,** centro comercial, *m*

shopwalker /ˈʃɒpˌwɔkər/ *n* jefe de recepción, *m*

shore /ʃɔr/ *n* orilla, ribera, *f*; costa, *f*; (sands) playa, *f*. **off s.,** en alta mar. **on s.,** en tierra. **to come on s.,** desembarcar. **to s. up,** apuntalar, acodalar; *fig* apoyar

short /ʃɔrt/ *a* corto; (of persons) bajo; breve; (of temper) vivo; insuficiente; distante (de); (brusque) seco; (of money) alcanzado. —*adv* súbitamente; brevemente. —*n* (vowel) vocal breve, *m*; *pl* **shorts,** calzones cortos, *m pl*. **for s.,** para mayor brevedad. **for a s. time,** por poco tiempo. **in a s. time,** dentro de poco. **in s.,** en breve, en resumen, en pocas palabras. **on s. notice,** con poco tiempo de aviso. **s. of,** con la excepción de, menos. **to be s.,** faltar, ser escaso. **to be s. with someone,** tratar con sequedad (a). **to fall s. of expectations,** no cumplir las esperanzas. **to go s. of,** pasarse sin. **to grow s.,** escasear. **s.-circuit,** corto circuito, *m*. **s. cut,** atajo, *m*. **s.-haired,** pelicorto. **s.-handed,** falto de mano de obra. **s.-lived,** de vida corta; efímero, fugaz. **to be short-lived,** tener vida corta. **s.-sighted,** corto de vista. **s.-sightedness,** miopía, cortedad de vista, *f*. **s. story,** cuento, *m*. **s.-tempered,** irascible, irritable, de genio vivo. **s.-waisted,** corto de talle. **s.-winded,** corto de resuello; asmático

shortage /ˈʃɔrtɪdʒ/ *n* falta, escasez, *f*; carestía, *f*. **water s.,** carestía de agua, *f*

shortcoming /ˈʃɔrtˌkʌmɪŋ/ *n* defecto, *m*; imperfección, *f*

shorten /ˈʃɔrtn̩/ *vt* acortar; reducir, disminuir; abreviar. —*vi* acortarse

shorthand /ˈʃɔrtˌhænd/ *n* taquigrafía, estenografía, *f*. —*a* taquigráfico, estenográfico. **to take down in s.,** taquigrafiar. **s. writer,** estenógrafo (-fa); taquígrafo (-fa)

shortly /'ʃɔrtli/ *adv* dentro de poco, pronto; brevemente, en resumen, en pocas palabras; (curtly) bruscamente, secamente

shortness /'ʃɔrtnɪs/ *n* cortedad, *f*; brevedad, *f*; (of a person) pequeñez, (lack) falta, *f*; (of memory, sight) cortedad, *f*; brusquedad, *f*. **s. of breath,** falta de aliento, respiración difícil, *f*

shot /ʃɒt/ *n* perdigón, *m*; *inf* perdigones, *m pl*; bala, *f*; (firing) tiro, *m*; (person) tirador (-ra); (stroke, etc.) golpe, *m*, tirada, *f*; (cinema) fotograma, *m*. —*a* (of silk) tornasolado. **at one s.,** de un tiro. **like a s.,** *fig* como una bala. **to exchange shots,** tirotearse. **to fire a s.,** disparar un tiro. **to have a s. at,** probar suerte. **s.-gun,** escopeta, *f*. **s. silk,** seda tornasolada, *f*

should /ʃʊd/ *v aux* (expressing future) I **s. like to go to the sea,** Me gustaría ir al mar; (expressing conditional) **I s. like to see them if I could,** Me gustaría verlos si pudiera; (expressing obligation) **You s. go at once,** Debes ir en seguida; (expressing probability) **They s. arrive tomorrow,** Seguramente llegarán mañana; (expressing doubt) **If the moment s. be opportune,** Si el momento fuera oportuno. **I s. just think so!** ¡Ya lo creo! ¡No lo dudo!

shoulder /'ʃoʊldər/ *n* hombro, *m*; (of mutton) espalda, *f*; (of a hill) falda, *f*. —*vt* echar al hombro, echar sobre sí; (a responsibility) cargar con, hacerse responsable para; (jostle) dar codazos (a). **s. to s.,** hombro a hombro. **s. arms!** ¡Armas al hombro! **s.-blade,** omoplato, *m*. **s.-knot,** charretera, *f*. **s.-pad,** hombrera, *f*. **s.-strap,** *mil* dragona, *f*; (of a dress, etc.) tirante, *m*; (of a water carrier, etc.) correón, *m*

shout /ʃaʊt/ *vi* gritar, hablar a gritos. —*vt* gritar. —*n* grito, *m*. **shouts of applause,** aclamaciones, *f pl*, aplausos, *m pl*. **to s. from the housetops,** pregonar a los cuatro vientos. **to s. with laughter,** reírse a carcajadas. **to s. down,** silbar. **to s. out,** gritar

shove /ʃʌv/ *vt* empujar; poner. —*n* empujón, *m*. **to s. along,** empujar. **to s. aside,** empujar a un lado; apartar a codazos. **to s. away,** rechazar. **to s. back,** hacer retroceder. **to s. forward,** hacer avanzar, empujar hacia adelante. **to s. off,** (a boat) echar afuera. **to s. out,** empujar hacia fuera

shovel /'ʃʌvəl/ *n* pala, *f*. —*vt* traspalar. **s. hat,** sombrero de teja, *m*

show /ʃoʊ/ *vt* mostrar; hacer ver; (disclose) descubrir; revelar; (exhibit) exhibir; (indicate) indicar; (prove) demostrar, probar; (conduct) conducir, llevar, guiar; (explain) explicar; (oneself) presentarse. —*vi* mostrarse; verse; parecer. **to s.**

cause, mostrar causa. **to s. fight,** ofrecer resistencia. **s. signs of,** dar señales de. **to s. itself,** declararse, asomarse, surgir. **to s. to the door,** acompañar a la puerta. **to s. in,** (a person) hacer entrar, introducir (en). **to s. off,** *vt* exhibir; realzar; (new clothes, etc.) lucir. —*vi* darse importancia; pavonearse. **to s. out,** (a person) acompañar a la puerta; (in anger) poner de patitas en la calle. **to s. through,** *vi* trasparentarse. —*vt* conducir por. **to s. up,** *vt* invitar a subir; (a fraud, etc.) descubrir; (a swindler) desenmascarar; (defects) revelar. —*vi* (stand out) destacarse; (be present) asomarse, asistir

show /ʃoʊ/ *n* (exhibition) exposición, *f*; espectáculo, *m*; (sign) indicio, *m*, señal, *f*; (ostentation) pompa, *f*, aparato, *m*, ostentación, *f*; (appearance) apariencia, *f*; (affair) negocio, *m*. **to give the s. away,** echar los títeres a rodar. **to make a s. of,** hacer gala de. **s.-case,** escaparate, *m*, vitrina, *f*. **s. of hands,** votación por manos levantadas, *f*. **s.-room,** salón de muestras, *m*

showdown /'ʃoʊˌdaʊn/ *n* cartas boca arriba, *m*

shower /'ʃaʊər/ *n* chaparrón, chubasco, *m*; (of spray, etc.) chorro, *m*; (of stones, arrows, etc.) lluvia, *f*; (of honors) cosecha, *f*; (bridal) despedida de soltera, despedida de soltería, *f*. —*vt* derramar, rociar; mojar; llover. —*vi* chaparrear, llover. **s.-bath,** ducha, *f*

showy /'ʃoʊi/ *a* vistoso; ostentoso

shrapnel /'ʃræpnl/ *n* granada, *m*, granada de metralla, *f*

shred /ʃrɛd/ *n* fragmento, *m*; (of cloth) jirón, *m*; brizna, *f*; *fig* pizca, *f*. —*vt* desmenuzar. **to tear in shreds,** hacer pedazos

shrew /ʃru/ *n zool* musaraña, *f*; (woman) fiera, *f*

shrewd /ʃrud/ *a* sagaz, perspicaz; prudente; (of the wind) penetrante; (pain) punzante. **to have a s. idea of,** tener una buena idea de. **a s. diplomat,** un fino diplomático

shrewish /'ʃruɪʃ/ *a* regañón

shriek /ʃrik/ *vi* chillar, gritar. —*vt* decir a voces, gritar. —*n* chillido, *m*; grito agudo, *m*. **shrieks of laughter,** carcajadas, *f pl*

shrift /ʃrɪft/ *n*. **to give short,** enviar normal (a), enviar a paseo (a)

shrill /ʃrɪl/ *a* estridente, agudo

shrimp /ʃrɪmp/ *n* camarón, *m*, gamba, *f*, *vi* pescar camarones

shrine /ʃraɪn/ *n* relicario, *m*; sepulcro de santo, *m*; templete, *m*, capilla, *f*; santuario, *m*

shrink /ʃrɪŋk/ *vi*. encogerse; contraerse; disminuir, reducirse. —*vt* encoger; reducir, disminuir; desaparecer; disiparse. **I shrank from doing it,** Me repugnaba hacerlo. **to s. away from,** retroceder ante; recular ante; huir de. **to s. back,** recular (ante)

shrinkage /'ʃrɪŋkɪdʒ/ n encogimiento, m; contracción, f; reducción, disminución, f

shrivel /'ʃrɪvəl/ vi avellanarse; (of persons, through old age) acartonarse, apergaminarse; (wither) marchitarse; arrugarse. —vt arrugar; secar, marchitar

shroud /ʃraud/ n sudario, m, mortaja, f; Naut. obenque, m. **to wrap in a s.,** amortajar

shrub /ʃrʌb/ n arbusto, m; matajo, m

shrubbery /'ʃrʌbəri/ n arbustos, m pl, maleza, f; bosquecillo, m

shrug /ʃrʌg/ vi encogerse de hombros. —n encogimiento de hombros, m

shrunken /'ʃrʌŋkən/ a contraído; acartonado, apergaminado; seco, marchito. **shrunken head,** cabeza reducida, f

shudder /'ʃʌdər/ vi estremecerse; vibrar. —n estremecimiento, m; escalofrío, m; (of an engine, etc.) vibración, f

shuffle /'ʃʌfəl/ vt (the feet) arrastrar; (scrape) restregar; (cards) barajar; (papers) mezclar. —vi arrastrar los pies, arrastrarse; (cards) barajar; fig tergiversar. —n (of the cards) barajadura, f; fig evasiva, f; embuste, m. **to s. along,** andar arrastrando los pies

shun /ʃʌn/ vt evitar, rehuir, esquivar

shunt /ʃʌnt/ vt rail apartar; elec shuntar. —vi rail hacer maniobras

shut /ʃʌt/ vt and vi cerrar. **to s. again,** volver a cerrar. **to s. down,** vt cerrar; (a machine) parar. —vi (of factories, etc.) cerrar. **to s. in,** encerrar; (surround) cercar, rodear. **to s. off,** (water, etc.) cortar; (isolate) aislar (de). **to s. out,** excluir; obstruir, impedir; negar la entrada (a). **to s. up,** vt cerrar; encerrar; inf hacer callar (a); vi inf callarse, cerrar la boca. **to s. oneself up,** encerrarse

shutter /'ʃʌtər/ n (window) contraventana, f, postigo, m; (of a camera) obturador, m; (of a fireplace) campana (de hogar), f. —vt poner contraventanas (a); cerrar los postigos de

shuttle /'ʃʌtl/ n (weaver's, and sewing-machine) lanzadera, f. (airplane service) puente aéreo, m. **s.-cock,** volante, gallito, m

shy /ʃai/ a (of animals) tímido, salvaje; (of persons) huraño, tímido; vergonzoso. —vi (of a horse) respingar; (of persons) asustarse (de). —vt (a ball, etc.) lanzar. —n (of a horse) respingo, m; (of a ball) lanzamiento, m; (try) prueba, tentativa, f. **to fight shy of,** procurar evitar. **to have a shy at,** probar

shyness /'ʃainɪs/ n timidez, f; huraña, f; vergüenza, f

Siamese /,saiə'miz/ a siamés. —n siamés (-esa); (language) siamés, m. **S. cat,** gato siamés, m

sic /sɪk/ vt atacar; abijar, azuzar (a dog); adv así (in academic prose)

sick /sɪk/ a enfermo; mareado. **the s.,** los enfermos. **to be s.,** vomitar; estar enfermo. **to be s. of,** estar harto de. **to feel s.,** sentirse mareado. **to be on the s.-list,**

estar enfermo. **s.-bed,** lecho de dolor, m. **s.-headache,** jaqueca, con náusea, f. **s.-leave,** mil permiso por enfermedad, m. **s. -nurse,** enfermera, f

sicken /'sɪkən/ vi caer enfermo, enfermar; (feel sick) marearse; (recoil from) repugnar; (weary of) cansarse (de); aburrirse (de). —vt marear; dar asco (a), repugnar; cansar, aburrir. **It sickens me,** Me da asco. **He is sickening for measles,** Muestra síntomas de sarampión

sickly /'sɪkli/ a enfermizo, achacoso, malucho; (of places, etc.) malsano; (pale) pálido; débil; (of a smell) nauseabundo; (mawkish) empalagoso

sickness /'sɪknɪs/ n enfermedad, f; mal, m; náusea, f, mareo, m

side /said/ n lado, m; (hand) mano, f; (of a river, etc.) orilla, f, margen, m; (of a person) costado, m; (of an animal) ijada, f; (of a hill) falda, pendiente, ladera, f; (of a ship) banda, f, costado, m; (aspect) aspecto, m; punto de vista, m; (party) partido, grupo, m; (team) equipo, m; (of descent) lado, m. —a lateral, de lado; oblicuo. **on all sides,** por todas partes. **on both sides,** por ambos lados. **s. by s.,** lado a lado. **the other s. of the picture,** el revés de la medalla. **to change sides,** cambiar de partido. **to pick sides,** escoger el equipo. **to put on s.,** darse tono, alzar el gallo. **to split one's sides,** desternillarse de risa, reírse a carcajadas. **to s. with,** declararse por, ponerse al lado de, tomar el partido de. **wrong s. out,** al revés. **s.-car,** sidecar, asiento lateral, m. **s.-chain,** chem cadena lateral, f. **s.-dish,** entremés, m. **s. door,** puerta lateral, f. **s.-face,** a de perfil. —n perfil, m. **s.-glance,** mirada de soslayo, f. **s.-issue,** cuestión secundaria, f. **s.-line,** negocio accesorio, m; ocupación secundaria, f; rail vía secundaria, f. **s.-saddle,** silla de señora, silla de montar de lado, f. **s.-show,** (at a fair) barraca, f, puesto de feria, f; exhibición secundaria, f; función secundaria, f. **s.-table,** trinchero, m. **s.-track,** n rail apartadero, m. —vt desviar (de), apartar (de). **s.-view,** perfil, m. **s.-walk,** acera, f. **s.-whiskers,** patillas, f pl

sidelight /'said,lait/ n luz lateral, f; (on a ship) ojo de buey, m; fig información incidental, f

side road n camino lateral, m

sideways /'said,weiz/ adv oblicuamente, de lado; (edgewise) de soslayo. —a de soslayo

sidle /'saidl/ vi andar (or ir) de lado. **to s. up to,** acercarse servilmente a; arrimarse (a)

siege /sidʒ/ n asedio, sitio, cerco, m. **to lay s. to,** poner cerco (a), sitiar, asediar cercar. **to raise a s.,** levantar un sitio

sieve /sɪv/ n cedazo, tamiz, m, criba, f, vt tamizar, cerner, cribar

sift /sɪft/ vt (sieve) cerner, cribar; (sugar, etc.) salpicar (con); (a question) escudriñar, examinar minuciosamente

sigh /sai/ *vi* suspirar; (of the wind) susurrar. —*n* suspiro, *m*; (of the wind) susurro, *m*. **to s. for**, suspirar por; lamentar

sight /sait/ *n* vista, *f*; visión, *f*; espectáculo, *m*; (fright) estantigua, *f*. —*vt* ver, divisar; (aim) apuntar. **front s.**, (of guns) alza, *f*. **short s.**, (of eyes) vista corta, *f*. **at first s.**, a primera vista. **in s.**, a la vista. **in s. of**, a vista de. **out of s.**, que no está a la vista; perdido de vista. **Out of s., out of mind**, Ojos que no ven, corazón que no siente. **to be lost to s.**, perderse de vista. **to catch a s. of**, vislumbrar. **to come in s.**, aparecer, asomarse. **to know by s.**, conocer de vista (a). **s.-reading**, lectura a primera vista, *f*

sightly /'saitli/ *a* hermoso; deleitable

sightseeing /'sait,siŋ/ *n* turismo, *m*. **to go s.**, visitar los monumentos, ver los puntos de interés

sightseer /'sait,siər/ *n* curioso (-sa); turista, *mf*

sign /sain/ *n* señal, *f*; seña, *f*; indicio, *m*; (of the zodiac and *mus*) signo, *m*; marca, *f*; *eccl* símbolo, *m*; (of a shop, etc.) muestra, *f*; rótulo, *m*; (symptom) síntoma, *m*. —*vt* firmar; indicar; *eccl* persignar. **as a s. of**, en señal de. **to converse by signs**, hablar por señas. **to make the s. of the cross**, santiguar. **to show signs (of)**, dar señas (de); indicar. **s.-painter**, pintor de muestras, *m*

signal /'signl/ *n* señal, *f*. —*vt* señalar; hacer señales (a). —*vi* hacer señales. —*a* insigne, notable. **fog-s.**, señal de niebla, *f*. **landing s.**, *aer* señal de aterrizaje, *f*. **to give the s. for**, dar la señal para. **s.-box**, garita de señales, *f*. **s. code**, *naut* código de señales, *m*

signature /'signətʃər/ *n* firma, *f*; (*mus* and *print*) signatura, *f*

signboard /'sain,bɔrd/ *n* letrero, *m*, muestra, *f*

significance /sig'nifikəns/ *n* significación, *f*; significado, *m*; importancia, *f*

significant /sig'nifikənt/ *a* significativo, significante; expresivo; importante

signify /'signə,fai/ *vt* significar; querer decir; importar. —*vi* significar, tener importancia; importar

signpost /'sain,poust/ *n* indicador de dirección, *m*

silence /'sailəns/ *n* silencio, *m*, *interj* ¡silencio! —*vt* hacer callar, imponer silencio (a); silenciar. **to keep s.**, guardar silencio, callarse. **to pass over in s.**, pasar en silencio (por), pasar por alto de. **S. gives consent**, Quien calla otorga

silencer /'sailənsər/ *n* (of fire-arms) silencioso, *m*; *auto* silenciador, silencioso, *m*

silent /'sailənt/ *a* silencioso. **to become s.**, enmudecer; callar. **to remain s.**, callarse, guardar silencio; permanecer silencioso. **s. partner**, *n* socio (-ia) comanditario (-ia)

silhouette /,silu'et/ *n* silueta, *f*. —*vt* representar en silueta; destacar. **in s.**, en

silueta. **to be silhouetted against the sky**, destacarse contra el sielo

silica /'silikə/ *n* sílice, *f*

silk /silk/ *n* seda, *f*, *a* de seda. **artificial s.**, seda artificial, *f*. **floss s.**, seda ocal, *f*. **sewing s.**, seda de coser, *f*. **twist s.**, seda cordelada, *f*. **as smooth as s.**, como una seda. **s. growing**, sericultura, *f*. **s. hat**, sombrero de copa, *m*. **s. merchandise**, sedería, *f*. **s. stocking**, media de seda, *f*

silken /'silkən/ *a* de seda; sedoso

silk-screen process /'silk,skrin/ *n* imprenta por tamiz, imprenta serigráfica, imprenta tamigráfica, impresión con estarcido de seda, *f*, proceso tamigráfico, *m*, serigrafía, tamigrafía, *f*

silkworm /'silk,wɜrm/ *n* gusano de seda, *m*

silky /'silki/ *a* sedoso; (of wine) suave

sill /sil/ *n* (of a window) alféizar, antepecho, *m*; (of a door) umbral, *m*

silly /'sili/ *a* tonto, estúpido; imbécil. —*n* tonto (-ta). **You are a s. ass**, Eres un imbécil

silt /silt/ *n* aluvión, *m*, sedimentación, *f*. **to s. up**, *vt* cegar (or obstruir) con aluvión. —*vi* cegarse con aluvión

silver /'silvər/ *n* plata, *f*. —*a* de plata; argénteo; (of the voice, etc.) argentino. —*vt* platear; (mirrors) azogar; (hair) blanquear. **s. birch**, abedul, *m*. **s. fox**, zorro plateado, *m*. **s.-gry**, gris perla, *m*. **s.-haired**, de pelo entrecano. **s.-paper**, papel de estaño, *m*. **s.-plate**, *n* vajilla de plata, *f*. —*vt* platear. **s.-tongued**, de pico de oro; de voz argentina. **s. wedding**, bodas de plata, *f pl*

silversmith /'silvər,smiθ/ *n* platero, *m*. **silversmith's shop**, platería, *f*

similar /'simələr/ *a* parecido (a), semejante (a); similar; *geom* semejante. **to be s. to**, asemejarse (a), parecerse (a)

similarity /,simə'læriti/ *n* parecido, *m*, semejanza, similitud, *f*

similarly /'simələrli/ *adv* de un modo parecido, asimismo

simile /'siməli/ *n* símil, *m*

simmer /'simər/ *vi* hervir a fuego lento; *fig* estar a punto de estallar. **to s. down**, *fig* moderarse poco a poco. **to s. over**, *fig* estallar

simper /'simpər/ *vi* sonreírse bobamente

simple /'simpəl/ *a* sencillo; simple; ingenuo, inocente; crédulo; (humble) humilde; (mere) mero. **s.-hearted**, inocente, cándido, sin malicia. **s.-minded**, ingenuo; crédulo. **s.-mindedness**, ingenuidad, *f*; credulidad, *f*

simpleton /'simpəltən/ *n* primo (-ma); papanatas, *m*, tonto (-ta)

simplicity /sim'plisiti/ *n* sencillez, *f*; simplicidad, candidez, *f*

simplifiable /,simplə'faiəbəl/ *a* simplificable

simplify /'simplə,fai/ *vt* simplificar

simply /'simpli/ *adv* sencillamente; simplemente, meramente; absolutamente

simulate /'sɪmyə,leɪt/ vt fingir, aparentar, simular

simultaneous /,saɪməl'teɪnɪəs/ a simultáneo

sin /sɪn/ n pecado, m, vi pecar; faltar (a)

since /sɪns/ adv desde entonces, desde (que). —prep desde. —conjunc desde que; ya que, puesto que. **a long time s.**, hace mucho. **not long s.**, hace poco. **How long is it s...?** ¿Cuánto tiempo hace que...? **s. then**, desde entonces

sincere /sɪn'sɪər/ a sincero

sincerely /sɪn'sɪərli/ adv sinceramente. **Yours s.**, Su afectísimo...

sincerity /sɪn'sɛrɪti/ n sinceridad, f

sine /saɪn/ n math seno, m

sinecure /'saɪnɪ,kyʊr/ n canonjía, sinecura, f, empleo de aviador (Mexican slang), m

sinew /'sɪnyu/ n tendón, m; pl sinews, nervio, m, fuerza, f

sinful /'sɪnfəl/ a (of persons) pecador; (of thoughts, acts) pecaminoso

sing /sɪŋ/ vi cantar; (of the ears) zumbar; (of wind, water) murmurar, susurrar; (of a cat) ronronear. —vt cantar. **to s. a child to sleep**, dormir a un niño cantando. **to s. another song**, inf bajar el tono. **to s. small**, hacerse el chiquito. **to s. the praises of**, hacer las alabanzas de. **to s. out**, vocear, gritar. **s.-song**, n canturía, f; concierto improvisado, m. —a monótono

singe /sɪndʒ/ vt chamuscar; (a fowl) aperdigar; (hair) quemar las puntas de los cabellos

singer /'sɪŋər/ n cantor (-ra); (professional) cantante, mf; (bird) ave cantora, f

singing /'sɪŋɪŋ/ n canto, m; (of the ears) zumbido, m. —a cantante. **s.-bird**, ave cantora, f. **s.-master**, maestro de cantar, m

single /'sɪŋgəl/ a único, sencillo; solo; simple; (individual) particular; individual; (unmarried) soltero. —n (tennis) juego sencillo, individual, m. **in s. file**, de reata. **to s. out**, escoger; singularizar. **s. bed**, cama de monja, f. **s. bedroom**, habitación individual, habitación con una sola cama, f. **s.-breasted**, (of coats) recto. **s. combat**, combate singular, m. **s. entry**, Com. partida simple, f. **s.-handed**, de una mano; para una sola persona; sin ayuda, solo, en solitario. **s.-minded**, sin doblez, sincero de una sola idea. **s. ticket**, billete sencillo, m

singleness /'sɪŋgəlnɪs/ n celibato, m, soltería, f. **with s. of purpose**, con un solo objeto

singly /'sɪŋgli/ adv separadamente, uno a uno; a solas, solo; sin ayuda

singular /'sɪŋgyələr/ a and n singular, m

sinister /'sɪnəstər/ a siniestro

sink /sɪŋk/ vi ir al fondo; bajar; hundirse; (of ships) irse a pique, naufragar; sumergirse; disminuir; caer (en); penetrar; (of persons, fires) morir; (of the sun, etc.) ponerse. —vt (a ship) echar a pique;

sumergir; hundir; dejar caer; bajar; (wells) cavar; reducir, disminuir; (invest) invertir; (one's identity, etc.) tener secreto; (differences) olvidar; (engrave) grabar. **My heart sank**, Se me cayeron las alas del corazón. **He sank to his knees**, Cayó de rodillas. **He is sinking fast**, Está en las últimas. **Their words began to s. in**, Sus palabras empezaban a tener efecto (or hacer mella). **I found her sunk in thought**, La encontré ensimismada. **to s. one's voice**, bajar la voz. **to s. down on a chair**, dejarse caer en una silla. **to s. into misery**, caer en la miseria. **to s. under**, (a responsibility, etc.) estar agobiado bajo

sink /sɪŋk/ n (kitchen) fregadero, m; sumidero, m, sentina, f. **s. of iniquity**, sentina, f

sinker /'sɪŋkər/ n (engraver) grabador (-ra); (of a fishing line) plomada, f

sinking /'sɪŋkɪŋ/ n hundimiento, m; (of the sun) puesta, f; (of wells) cavadura, f; sumergimiento, m. **the s. of a boat**, el hundimiento de un buque. **with s. heart**, con la muerte en el alma. **s. fund**, fondo de amortización, m

sinner /'sɪnər/ n pecador (-ra)

sinuous /'sɪnyuəs/ a sinuoso, tortuoso; flexible, ágil

sinus /'saɪnəs/ n (anat etc.) seno, m

sip /sɪp/ vt sorber; (wine) saborear, paladear. —n sorbo, m

siphon /'saɪfən/ n sifón, m, vt sacar con sifón

sir /sɜr/ n señor, m; (British title) sir. **Dear s.**, Muy Señor mío

sire /saɪər/ n (to a monarch) Señor, m; (father) padre, m; (stallion) semental, m. —vt procrear, engendrar

siren /'saɪrən/ n sirena, f. **s. suit**, mono, m

sirloin /'sɜrlɔɪn/ n solomillo, m

sister /'sɪstər/ n hermana, f; (before nun's christian name) Sor; (hospital) hermana del hospital, f; enfermera, f. **s. language**, lengua hermana, f. **s. ship**, buque gemelo, m. **s.-in-law**, cuñada, hermana política, f. **S. of Mercy**, Hermana de la Caridad, f

sisterhood /'sɪstər,hʊd/ n hermandad, f; comunidad de monjas, f

sisterly /'sɪstərli/ a de hermana

sit /sɪt/ vi sentarse; estar sentado; (of birds) posarse; (of hens) empollar; (in Parliament, etc.) ser diputado; (of a committee, etc.) celebrar sesión; (on a committee, etc.) formar parte de; (function) funcionar; (of garments, food, and fig) sentar. **to sit a horse**, mantenerse a caballo; montar a caballo. **to sit oneself**, sentarse, tomar asiento. **to sit by**, (a person) sentarse (or estar sentado) al lado de. **to sit for** (a portrait) servir de modelo para; hacerse retratar. **to sit tight**, no moverse. **to sit down**, sentarse; (besiege) sitiar. **to sit on**, sentarse (en or sobre); (eggs) empollar; (a committee, etc.) formar parte de; (investigate) investigar; (snub) dejar aplastado (a). **to sit out,** quedarse hasta el fin (de). **to sit out a dance,** conversar un baile. **to sit up,** incorporarse en la cama; tenerse derecho; (at night) velar; (of dogs, etc.) pedir. **to sit up and take notice,** abrir los ojos. **to sit up in bed,** incorporarse en la cama. **to sit up late,** estar de pie hasta muy tarde

sit-down strike /'sɪt,daun/ n huelga de brazos caídos, huelga de sentados, f

site /sait/ n sitio, local, m; (for building) solar, m

sitting /'sɪtɪŋ/ n asentada, f; (of Parliament, etc.) sesión, f; (for a portrait) estadia, f; (of eggs) nidada, f. **at a s.,** de una sentada. **s.-room,** sala de estar, f

situated /'sɪtʃu,eitid/ a situado. **How is he s.?** ¿Cómo está situado? ¿Cuál es su situación?

situation /,sɪtʃu'eiʃən/ n situación, f; (job) empleo, m

six /sɪks/ a and n seis, m. **It is six o'clock,** Son las seis. **Everything is at sixes and sevens,** Todo está en desorden. **six-foot,** de seis pies. **six hundred,** seiscientos (-as)

sixteen /'sɪks'tin/ a and n diez y seis, dieciséis, m. **John is s.,** Juan tiene dieciséis años

sixteenth /'sɪks'tinθ/ a décimosexto; (of the month) (el) diez y seis; (of monarch) diez y seis. —n diecíseisavo, m

sixth /sɪksθ/ a sexto; (of the month) (el) seis; (of monarchs) sexto. —n seisavo, m; sexta parte, f; mus sexta, f. **Henry the S.,** Enrique sexto. **May the s.,** el seis de mayo

sixtieth /'sɪkstiɪθ/ a sexagésimo. —n sesentavo, m; sexagésima parte, f

sixty /'sɪksti/ a and n sesenta m. **John has turned s.,** Juan ha pasado los sesenta

sizable /'saizəbəl/ a bastante grande

size /saiz/ n tamaño, m; dimensión, f; (height) altura, f; (measurement) medida, f; talle, m; (in gloves, etc.) número, m; (glue) cola, f. —vt clasificar por tamaños; (glaze, etc.) encolar. **to s. up,** tomar las medidas (a).

sizzle /'sɪzəl/ vi chisporrotear, chirriar. —n chisporroteo, chirrido, m

skate /skeit/ n patín, m; ichth raya, f, vi patinar

skater /'skeitər/ n patinador (-ra)

skating /'skeitɪŋ/ n patinaje, m. **s. rink,** sala de patinar, f; pista de hielo, pista de patinar, f, patinadero, m

skein /skein/ n madeja, f

skeleton /'skelɪtn/ n esqueleto, m; (of a building) armadura, f; (of a literary work) esquema, m. **s. key,** ganzúa, f

sketch /skɛtʃ/ n croquis, apunte, m; (for a literary work) esbozo, esquema, m; (article) cuadro, artículo, m; descripción, f; theat entremés, sainete, m. —vt dibujar; esbozar, bosquejar; trazar; describir. **s.-book,** álbum de croquis, m

sketching /'skɛtʃɪŋ/ n arte de dibujar, mf. **He likes s.,** Le gusta dibujar

sketchy /'skɛtʃi/ a bosquejado; incompleto; escaso

skewer /'skyuər/ n broqueta, f, vt espetar

ski /ski/ n esquí, m, vi esquiar

skid /skɪd/ n (of a vehicle) patinazo, m, vi patinar

skier /'skiər/ n esquiador, m

skiing /'skiɪŋ/ n patinaje sobre la nieve, m, el esquiar. **to go s.,** ir a esquiar

skill /skɪl/ n habilidad, f

skilled /skɪld/ a hábil; experto

skilled worker n obrero calificado, m

skillful /'skɪlfəl/ a hábil

skim /skɪm/ vt espumar; (milk) desnatar; (touch lightly) deslizarse sobre, rozar; (a book) hojear

skimp /skɪmp/ vt escatimar; escasear; (work) frangollar. —vi ser parsimonioso

skimpy /'skɪmpi/ a escaso

skin /skɪn/ n tez, f, cutis, m, piel, f; (of fruit) pellejo, m, piel, f; (for wine) odre, pellejo, m; (on milk) espuma, f —vt despellejar; pelar, mondar; (graze) hacerse daño (a); inf desollar. **next to one's s.,** sobre la piel. **to s. over,** cicatrizarse. **to have a thin s.,** fig ser muy susceptible. **to save one's s.,** salvar el pellejo. **s.-deep,** superficial. **s.-tight,** escurrido, muy ajustado

skinflint /'skɪn,flɪnt/ n avaro (-ra)

skinny /'skɪni/ a flaco, descarnado, magro

skip /skɪp/ vi retozar, brincar, saltar; saltar a la comba; (bolt) largarse, escaparse. —vt saltar; (a book) hojear; (omit) omitir; pasar por alto de. —n brinco, pequeño salto, m

skipper /'skɪpər/ n naut patrón, m; (inf and sports) capitán, m

skirmish /'skɜrmɪʃ/ vi escaramuzar. —n escaramuza, f

skirt /skɜrt/ n falda, f; (edge) margen, borde, m, orilla, f; (of a jacket, etc.) faldón, m —vt ladear; (hug) rodear, ceñir

skit /skɪt/ n sátira, f; parodia, f

skittish /'skɪtɪʃ/ a (of a horse) retozón; (of persons) frívolo; caprichoso

skulk /skʌlk/ vi estar en acecho; esconderse; rondar

skull /skʌl/ n cráneo, m; calavera, f. **s.-cap,** gorro, casquete, m; (for ecclesiastics) solideo, m

skunk /skʌŋk/ n zool mofeta, f, chingue, mapurite, yaguré, zorrillo, zorrino, zorro hediondo, m

sky /skai/ n cielo, m. **to praise to the skies,** poner en los cuernos de la luna. **s.-blue,** n azul celeste, m. —a de color azul celeste, cerúleo, s. **s.-high,** hasta las nubes, hasta el cielo. **s.-line,** horizonte, m. **s.-sign,** anuncio luminoso, m

skylight /'skai,lait/ n claraboya, f, tragaluz, m

slab /slæb/ n bloque, m; losa, f; plancha, f

slack /slæk/ *a* lento; flojo; (lazy) perezoso; negligente, descuidado; *com* encalmado; débil. —*vi* ser perezoso. **the s. season,** la estación muerta. **to be s. in one's work,** ser negligente en el trabajo. **to s. off,** disminuir sus esfuerzos; dejar de trabajar

slacken /'slækən/ *vt and vi* aflojar; disminuir, reducir. **The wind slackened,** El viento amainaba, El viento aflojaba. **to s. one's efforts,** disminuir sus esfuerzos. **to s. speed,** disminuir la velocidad

slacker /'slækər/ *n* gandul (-la)

slacks /slæks/ *n pl* pantalones, *m pl*

slake /sleik/ *vt* (one's thirst and lime) apagar; satisfacer

slam /slæm/ *vt* cerrar de golpe; golpear. —*n* (of a door) portazo, *m;* golpe, *m;* (cards) capote, *m.* **He went out and slammed the door,** Salió dando un portazo

slander /'slændər/ *n* calumnia, *f, vt* calumniar

slanderous /'slændərəs/ *a* calumnioso

slang /slæŋ/ *n* argot, *m,* jerga, *f, vt* poner como un trapo (a), llenar de insultos

slant /slænt/ *vi* estar al sesgo; inclinarse; ser oblicuo. —*vt* inclinar. —*n* inclinación, *f;* oblicuidad, *f.* **on the s.,** inclinado; oblicuo

slap /slæp/ *vt* pegar con la mano. —*n* bofetada, *f;* palmada, *f.* **to s. on the back,** golpear en la espalda. **s.-dash,** (of persons) irresponsable, descuidado; (of work) chapucero, sin cuidado

slash /slæʃ/ *vt* (gash, also sleeves, etc.) acuchillar; cortar; (with a whip) dar latigazos (a). —*n* cuchillada, *f;* corte, *m;* latigazo, *m*

slat /slæt/ *n* tablilla, *f, vi* (of sails) dar zapatazos, zapatear

slate /sleit/ *n* pizarra, *f,* esquisto, *m;* (for roofs and for writing) pizarra, *f, vt* (a roof) empizarrar; (censure) criticar severamente, censurar. **s.-colored,** apizarrado. **s. pencil,** pizarrín, *m.* **s. quarry,** pizarrería, *f,* pizarral, *m*

slating /'sleitiŋ/ *n* empizarrado, *m;* (criticism) crítica severa, censura, *f;* (scolding) peluca, *f*

slattern /'slætərn/ *n* pazpuerca, *f*

slaughter /'slɔtər/ *n* matanza, *f;* carnicería, *f.* —*vt* (animals) sacrificar, matar; matar, hacer una carnicería de. **s.-house,** matadero, *m*

slaughterer /'slɔtərər/ *n* jifero, carnicero, *m*

Slav /slɑv, slæv/ *a and n* eslavo (-va)

slave /sleiv/ *n* esclavo (-va). —*vi* trabajar mucho. **white s. traffic,** trata de blancas, *f.* **s.-bangle,** esclava, *f.* **s.-driver,** capataz de esclavos, negrero, *m; fig* negrero, sayón de esclavos, *m.* **s.-trade,** trata de esclavos, *f*

slaver /'sleivər/ *n* negrero, *m*

slaver /'slævər/ *vi* babear. —*n* baba, *f*

slavering /'slævəriŋ/ *a* baboso

slavery /'sleivəri/ *n* esclavitud, *f;* trabajo muy arduo, *m*

slavish /'sleiviʃ/ *a* de esclavo; servil

Slavonic /slə'vɒnɪk/ *a* eslavo. —*n* (language) eslavo, *m,* lengua eslava, *f*

slay /slei/ *vt* matar; asesinar

slaying /'sleiiŋ/ *n* matanza, *f;* asesinato, *m*

sledge /sledʒ/ *n* trineo, *m.* —*vi* ir en trineo. —*vt* transportar por trineo. **s.-hammer,** acotillo, *m*

sleek /slik/ *a* liso, lustroso; (of general appearance) pulcro, bien aseado, elegante; (of manner) obsequioso

sleep /slip/ *n* sueño, *m.* —*vi* dormir; reposar, descansar. —*vt* dormir. **a deep s.,** un sueño pesado. **He walks in his s.,** Es un sonámbulo. **to court s.,** conciliar el sueño. **to go to s.,** dormirse; entumecerse. **My foot has gone to s.,** Se me ha dormido (*or* Se me ha entumecido) el pie. **to send a person to s.,** adormecer. **to s. like a top,** dormir como un lirón. **to s. oneself sober,** dormir la mona. **to s. in,** dormir tarde; dormir en casa. **to s. off,** (a cold, etc.) curarse... durmiendo; (drunkenness) dormirla. **to s. on,** *vt* (consider) dormir sobre, consultar con la almohada. —*vi* seguir durmiendo. **to s. out,** dormir fuera de casa; dormir al aire libre

sleeper /'slipər/ *n* durmiente, *mf; rail* traviesa, *f;* (on a train) coche cama, *m.* **to be a bad s.,** dormir mal. **to be a good s.,** dormir bien

sleeping /'slipiŋ/ *a* durmiente. —*n* el dormir. **between s. and waking,** entre duerme y vela. **s.-bag,** saco-cama, *m.* **s.-car,** coche cama, *m.* **s.-draught,** narcótico, *m.* **s. partner,** *n* socio (-ia) comanditario (-ia). **s. sickness,** enfermedad del sueño, *f*

sleepless /'sliplɪs/ *a* (of persons) insomne, desvelado; (unremitting) incansable; (of the sea, etc.) en perpetuo movimiento. **to spend a s. night,** pasar una noche en vela, pasar una noche toledana, pasar una noche sin dormir

sleepwalker /'slip,wɔkər/ *n* sonámbulo (-la)

sleepwalking /'slip,wɔkiŋ/ *n* sonambulismo, *m*

sleepy /'slipi/ *a* soñoliento; letárgico. **to be s.,** tener sueño. **s.-head,** lirón, *m,* marmota, *f*

sleet /slit/ *n* aguanieve, cellisca, nevisca, *f, vi* caer aguanieve, cellisquear, neviscar

sleeve /sliv/ *n* manga, *f;* (of a hose pipe, etc.) manguera, *f; mech* manguito, *m.* **to have something up one's s.,** traer algo en la manga

sleeveless /'slivlɪs/ *a* sin manga

sleigh /slei/ *n* trineo, *m, vi* ir en trineo

sleight of hand /sleit/ *n* prestidigitación, *f;* juego de manos, *m*

slender /'slendər/ *a* delgado; esbelto; tenue; escaso; pequeño; ligero. **Their means are very s.,** Sus recursos son muy escasos. **It is a very s. hope,** Es una esperanza muy remota

sleuth /sluθ/ n (dog) sabueso, m; inf detective, m

slice /slais/ n lonja, tajada, f; (of fruit) raja, f; (of bread, etc.) rebanada, f; (share) parte, porción, f; (for fish, etc.) pala, f. —vt cortar en tajadas, etc.; rajar; cortar

slick /slɪk/ a hábil, diestro

slide /slaid/ vi deslizarse, resbalar; (over a question) pasar por alto de; (into a habit, etc.) caer (en). —n resbalón, m; pista de hielo, f; (chute) tobogán, m; (of a microscope) portaobjetos, m; (lantern) diapositiva, f; (for the hair) pasador, m; (of rock, etc.) desprendimiento, m; mech guía, f. **to let things s.,** dejar rodar la bola. **s.-rule,** regla de cálculo, f

sliding /'slaidɪŋ/ a resbaladizo; corredizo; movible. **s.-door,** puerta corrediza, puerta de corradera, f. **s.-roof,** techo corredizo, m. **s.-scale,** escala graduada, f. **s.-seat,** asiento movible, m; (in a rowing-boat) bancada corrediza, f

slight /slait/ a delgado; débil, frágil; ligero; (small) pequeño; escaso; (trivial) insignificante, poco importante. —vt desairar, despreciar. —n desaire, desprecio, m; falta de respeto, f

slighting /'slaitɪŋ/ a despreciativo, de desprecio

slightly /'slaitli/ adv ligeramente; poco. **I only know her s.,** La conozco muy poco. **s. built,** de talle delgado

slim /slɪm/ a delgado; escaso. —vi adelgazarse. **He has very s. chances of success,** Tiene muy pocas posibilidades de conseguir el éxito

slime /slaim/ n légamo, limo, lodo, cieno, m; (of a snail) limazo, m; fig cieno, m

slimy /'slaimi/ a limoso, legamoso; pecinoso, viscoso; (of persons) rastrero, servil

sling /slɪŋ/ vt arrojar, lanzar; tirar con honda; (a sword, etc.) suspender; (lift) embragar; (a limb) poner en cabestrillo. —n (for missiles) honda, f; Naut balso, m; (for a limb) cabestrillo, m, charpa, f

slink /slɪŋk/ vi (away, off) escurrirse, escabullirse

slip /slɪp/ vi resbalar, deslizar; (stumble) resbalar, tropezar; (fall) caer; (out of place) salirse; (become untied) desatarse; (steal away) escabullirse; (glide) deslizarse; (of years) correr, pasar; (skid) patinar. —vt deslizar; (garments, shoes) ponerse; (dogs, cables) soltar; (an arm round, etc.) pasar; Rail desacoplar; (escape) escaparse de; (free oneself of) librarse de. —n resbalón, m; (skid) patinazo, m; (stumble) tropezón, traspié, m; (oversight) inadvertencia, f; (mistake) falta, equivocación, f; (moral lapse) desliz, m; (petticoat) combinación, f; (cover) funda, f; Bot vástago, m; Print galerada, f; (of paper) papeleta, f; pl slips, Naut anguilas, f pl. **It slipped my memory,** Se

me fue de la memoria. **There's many a s. 'twixt the cup and the lip,** Del dicho al hecho hay muy gran trecho, De la mano a la boca desaparece la sopa. **to give** (someone) **the slip,** escaparse de. **You ought not to let the opportunity s.,** No debes perder la oportunidad. **to let s. a secret,** revelar un secreto. **to let s. an exclamation,** soltar (dar) una exclamación. **to s. into,** colarse en, deslizarse en. **to s. into,** colarse en, deslizarse en. **to s. into one's clothes,** vestirse rápidamente. **to s. on,** (a garment) ponerse. **to s. out,** salir a hurtadillas; escaparse; (of information) divulgarse. **s. of a boy,** mozalbete, joven imberbe, m. **s. of the tongue,** error de lengua, m. **s.-knot,** nudo corredizo, m

slipcover /'slɪp,kʌvər/ n cubierta, cubierta para muebles, funda, funda para muebles, f

slipper /'slɪpər/ n babucha, chinela, f, pantuflo, m; (heelless) chancleta, f; (dancing) zapatilla de baile, f **s.-shaped,** achinelado

slippery /'slɪpəri/ a resbaladizo; poco firme, inestable; (of persons) informal, sin escrúpulos

slipshod /'slɪp,ʃod/ a descuidado, negligente; poco correcto

slit /slɪt/ vt cortar; hender, rajar; (the throat) degollar. —n cortadura, f; resquicio, m. **to s. open,** abrir de un tajo

slither /'slɪðər/ vi resbalar; deslizarse

sliver /'slɪvər/ n raja, f; (of wood) astilla, f; (of cloth) tira, f

slobber /'slɒbər/ vi babear; (blubber) gimotear, n baba, f

slog /slog/ vt golpear duramente. **to s. away,** batirse el cobre, trabajar como un negro

slogan /'slougən/ n grito de batalla, m; reclamo, f; frase hecha, f; mote, m

slop /slop/ n charco, m; pl slops, agua sucia, f; alimentos líquidos, m pl. —vi derramarse, verterse. —vt verter, derramar

slope /sloup/ n inclinación, f; pendiente, f; (of a mountain, etc.) falda, ladera, cuesta, f; vertiente, mf. —vi inclinarse; estar en declive; bajar (hacia). **to s. down,** declinar

sloping /'sloupɪŋ/ a inclinado; en declive; (of shoulders) caídos, m pl

sloppy /'slopi/ a casi líquido; (muddy) lodoso, lleno de barro; (of work) chapucero; (of persons) baboso, sobón. **s. sentiment,** sensiblería, f

slot /slot/ n ranura, muesca, f. **s.-machine,** máquina expendedora, f, expendedor, m; (in amusement arcades, etc.) tragaperras, m

sloth /sloθ or, esp. for 2, slouθ/ n pereza, indolencia, f; zool perezoso, m

slothful /'sloθfəl, 'slouθ-/ a perezoso, indolente

slouch /slautʃ/ n inclinación del cuerpo, f. —vi andar cabizbajo, andar arrastrando los pies. **to s. about,** vagar, golfear. **s.-hat,** sombrero gacho, *m*

slough /slʌf/ *n* (bog) cenagal, pantano, *m,* marisma, *f;* (of a snake) camisa, *f.* —*vt* (a skin) mudar; (prejudices, etc.) desechar

sloven /'slʌvən/ *n* puerco, *m;* (at work) chapucero, *m*

slovenly /'slʌvənli/ *a* desgarbado, desaseado; (careless) descuidado, negligente; (of work) chapucero

slow /slou/ *a* despacio; lento; (stupid) torpe; tardo; (of clocks) atrasado; (boring) aburrido; (inactive) flojo. —*adv* despacio, lentamente. **I was not s. to...,** No tardé en... **The clock is ten minutes s.,** El reloj lleva diez minutos de atraso. **to s. down,** aflojar el paso; ir más despacio. **s.-motion,** velocidad reducida, *f.* **s. train,** tren ómnibus, *m.* **s.-witted,** lerdo tardo

"Slow Down" «Moderar Su Velocidad»

slow learner *n* alumno de lento aprendizaje, *m*

slowly /'slouli/ *adv* despacio, lentamente; poco a poco

slug /slʌg/ *n* babosa, *f*

sluggard /'slʌgərd/ *n* gandul (-la), perezoso (-a)

sluggish /'slʌgɪʃ/ *a* perezoso; (of the market) flojo; (of temperament, etc.) calmoso, flemático; (slow) lento

sluice /slus/ *n* esclusa, *f;* canal, *m,* acequia, *f* **to s. down,** lavar; echar agua sobre; (a person) dar una ducha (a), dar un baño (a). **s.-gate,** compuerta de esclusa, *f;* tajaderas, *f pl,* tablacho, *m*

slum /slʌm/ *n* barrio pobre, *m,* banda de miseria (Argentina), barriada (Peru), población (Chile), villa-miseria (Argentina), *f,* tugurio (Colombia), *m; pl* **slums,** barrios bajos, *m pl*

slumber /'slʌmbər/ *vi* dormir; (go to sleep) dormirse, caer dormido; (be latent) estar latente. —*n* sueño, *m*

slump /slʌmp/ *n com* baja repentina, *f; fig* baja, racha mala, *f.* —*vi com* bajar repentinamente. **the s.,** la crisis económica. **to s. into an armchair,** dejarse caer en un sillón

slur /slɜr/ *vt* (words) comerse sílabas o letras (de); (in writing) unir (las palabras); (mus of notes) ligar. **to cast a s. on,** difamar, manchar. **to s. over,** pasar por alto de, omitir, suprimir

slush /slʌʃ/ *n* lodo, *m;* agua nieve, *f;* (sentimentality) ñoñería, *f*

slut /slʌt/ *n* pazpuerca, marrana, *f*

sly /slai/ *a* astuto, taimado, socarrón; disimulado; (arch) malicioso. **on the sly,** a hurtadillas

slyly /'slaili/ *adv* astutamente; disimuladamente; (archly) maliciosamente

smack /smæk/ *n* (taste) sabor, gusto, *m;* (tinge) dejo, *m;* (blow) golpe, *m;* (with the hand) bofetada, palmada, *f;* (with a whip) latigazo, *m;* (crack of whip) restallido, chasquido, *m;* (kiss) beso sonado,

m; (boat) lancha de pescar, *f.* —*vi* (taste of) tener gusto de, saber a; (be tinged with) oler a. —*vt* (a whip) hacer restallar; (slap) pegar con la mano. **to s. one's lips over,** chuparse los dedos

small /smɔl/ *a* pequeño; menudo; menor; poco; (petty) mezquino, vulgar. —*n* parte estrecha, *f.* **a s. number,** un pequeño número. **to make a person look s.,** humillar. **to make oneself s.,** hacerse chiquito. **s.-arms,** armas portátiles, *f pl.* **s. change,** suelto, *m.* **s. craft,** embarcaciones menores, *f pl.* **s. fry,** pececillos, *m pl;* (children) gente menuda, *f;* gente sin importancia, *f.* **s. hours,** altas horas de la noche, *f pl.* **s.-minded,** adocenado, de cortos alcances. **s.-talk,** trivialidades, *f pl,* charla frívola, *f*

smallish /'smɔlɪʃ/ *a* bastante pequeño; más bien pequeño que grande

smallpox /'smɔl,pɒks/ *n* viruelas, *f pl*

smart /smart/ *vi* picar; dolerse (de). —*n* escozor, *m;* dolor, *m.* —*a* severo; vivo; rápido; pronto; (competent) hábil; (clever) listo; (unscrupulous) cuco, astuto; (of personal appearance) majo; elegante, distinguido; (neat) aseado; (fashionable, etc.) de moda; de buen tono. **to s. for,** ser castigado por. **to s. under,** sufrir

smarten /'smartņ/ *vt* embellecer. —*vi* (up) ponerse elegante; mejorar. **I must go and s. myself up a little,** Tengo que arreglarme un poco

smartly /'smartli/ *adv* severamente; vivamente; rápidamente; hábilmente; elegantemente

smash /smæʃ/ *vt* romper, quebrar; (a ball, etc.) golpear; (annihilate) destruir; (an opponent) aplastar. —*vi* romperse, quebrarse; hacerse pedazos; (collide) chocar (con, contra); estallarse (contra); (financially) hacer bancarrota. —*n* rotura, *f;* quebrantamiento, *m;* estruendo, *m;* (financial) quiebra, ruina, *f;* (car, etc.) accidente, *m;* desastre, *m,* catástrofe, *f.* **to s. to atoms,** hacer trizas. **to s. up,** hacer pedazos. **s. and grab raid,** atraco a mano armada, *m*

smash hit *n* éxito arrollador, éxito rotundo, *m*

smattering /'smætərɪŋ/ *n* conocimiento superficial, *m,* tintura, *f,* barniz, *m*

smear /smɪər/ *n* mancha, *f; biol* frotis, *m.* —*vt* embadurnar (de); manchar (con), ensuciar (con); (oneself) untarse; (blur) borrar

smell /smɛl/ *n* (sense of) olfato, *m;* (odor) olor, *m.* —*vt* oler. —*vi* oler; tener olor; (disagreeably) oler mal, tener mal olor; (stink) apestar. **How good it smells!** ¡Qué bien huele! **to s. of,** oler a. **to s. out,** husmear

smelling /'smɛlɪŋ/ *n* olfateo, *m.* **s.-bottle,** frasco de sales, *m.* **s.-salts,** sales (inglesas), *f pl*

smelt /smɛlt/ *vt* fundir. —*n ichth* eperlano, *m*

smile /smail/ vi sonreír; reírse. —vt expresar con una sonrisa. —n sonrisa, f. **Mary smiled her thanks,** María dio las gracias con una sonrisa. **smile at adversity,** ponerse buena cara a mal tiempo. **to s. at threats,** reírse de las amenazas

smirch /smɜrtʃ/ vt manchar. —n mancha, f

smirk /smɜrk/ vi sonreír con afectación; hacer visajes. —n sonrisa afectada, f

smite /smait/ vt golpear; (kill) matar; (punish) castigar; (pain) doler; (of bright light, sounds, etc.) herir; (cause remorse) remorder. **My conscience smites me,** Tengo remordimientos de conciencia. **to be smitten by,** inf estar prendado de. **I was smitten by a desire to smoke,** Me entraron deseos de fumar

smith /smiθ/ n herrero, m. **smith's hammer,** destajador, m

smithereens /ˌsmiðə'rinz/ n pl añicos, m pl

smithy /'smiθi, 'smiði/ n herrería, f

smock /smɒk/ n blusa, f; (child's) delantal, m

smoke /smouk/ n humo, m. —vi humear, echar humo; (tobacco) fumar. —vt ahumar; ennegrecer; (tobacco) fumar. **smoked glasses,** gafas ahumadas, f pl. **s. helmet,** casco respiratorio, m. **s.-screen,** cortina de humo, f. **s. signal,** ahumada, f. **s.-stack,** chimenea, f

smoker /smoukər/ n fumador (-ra)

smoking /'smoukiŋ/ a humeante. —n el fumar. **"S. Prohibited,"** «Se prohibe fumar.» **non-s. compartment,** rail departamento de no fumadores, m. **s.-carriage,** rail departamento para fumadores, m. **s.-room,** fumadero, m

smooth /smuð/ a liso; igual; (of the skin, etc.) suave; (of water) calmo, tranquilo; (flattering, etc.) lisonjero; obsequioso; afable. —vt allanar; (hair, etc.) alisar; (paths, etc.) igualar. **to s. down,** (a person) tranquilizar, calmar. **to s. over,** (faults) exculpar. **to s. the way for,** allanar el camino para. **s.-faced,** barbilampiño, lampiño, bien afeitado, todo afeitado; fig obsequioso, untuoso. **s.-haired,** de pelo liso. **s.-spoken,** de palabras lisonjeras; obsequioso

smoothly /'smuðli/ adv lisamente; (of speech) afablemente; con lisonjeras. **Everything was going s.,** Todo iba viento en popa

smother /'smʌðər/ vt ahogar, sofocar; (a fire) apagar; (cover) envolver, cubrir

smoulder /'smouldər/ vi arder sin llama, arder lentamente; (of passions, etc.) arder; estar latente

smudge /smʌdʒ/ vt manchar, ensuciar; (blur) borrar. —n mancha, f

smug /smʌɡ/ a satisfecho de sí mismo, pagado de sí mismo; farisaico

smuggle /'smʌɡəl/ vt pasar de contrabando. —vi hacer contrabando

smuggler /'smʌɡlər/ n contrabandista, mf

smut /smʌt/ n copo de hollín, m; mancha, f; (disease) tizón, m

smutty /'smʌti/ a tiznado; ahumado; inf verde

snack /snæk/ n tentempié, piscolabis, bocado, m. **to take a s.,** tomar un piscolabis

snack bar n merendero, m

snag /snæɡ/ n (of a tree) tocón, m; (of a tooth) raigón, m; (problem) busilis, m; obstáculo inesperado, m

snail /sneil/ n caracol, m. **at a snail's pace,** a paso de tortuga

snake /sneik/ n serpiente, f. **s.-charmer,** encantador de serpientes, m

snap /snæp/ vt morder; (break) romper; (one's fingers) castañetear; (a whip) chasquear; (down a lid, etc.) cerrar de golpe; (beaks, etc.) cerrar ruidosamente; photo sacar una instantánea de. —vi partirse; quebrarse; hablar bruscamente. —n (bite) mordedura, f; golpe seco, m; chasquido, m; rotura, f; (clasp) cierre, m; (of weather) temporada, f; (spirit) vigor, brío, m; photo instantánea, f. **to s. at,** procurar morder; (an invitation, etc.) aceptar gustoso. **to s. one's fingers at,** fig burlarse de. **to s. up,** coger, agarrar; (a person) cortar la palabra (a), interrumpir. **s.-fastener,** botón de presión, m

snapdragon /'snæp.dræɡən/ n dragón, m, becerra, boca de dragón, f

snappily /'snæpəli/ adv irritablemente

snappy /'snæpi/ a irritable; vigoroso

snapshot /'snæp.ʃɒt/ n instantánea, foto, f

snare /snɛər/ n cepo, lazo, m, trampa, f; fig red, f. —vt coger en el lazo; fig enredar

snarl /snɒrl/ vi (of dogs) regañar; (cats, etc.) gruñir. —n regañamiento, m; gruñido, m

snarling /'snɒrliŋ/ n regañamiento, m; gruñidos, m pl, a gruñidor

snatch /snætʃ/ vt asir; agarrar; (enjoy) disfrutar; (an opportunity) tomar, aprovecharse de. —n asimiento, agarro, m; (of time) rato, m; instante, m; (of song) fragmento, m. **to make a s. at,** procurar agarrar; alargar la mano hacia. **to s. a hurried meal,** comer aprisa. **to s. away,** arrebatar, quitar; (carry off) robar. **to s. up,** coger rápidamente; coger en brazos

sneak /snik/ vi deslizarse (en), colarse (en); (lurk) rondar; (inform) acusar. —n mandilón, m; (accuser) acusón (-ona). **to s. off,** escabullirse, irse a hurtadillas. **s.-thief,** n garduño (-ña)

sneaker /'snikər/ n (shoe) zapatilla de tenis, f

sneaking /'snikiŋ/ a furtivo, ruin, mezquino; secreto

sneer /snɪər/ vi sonreír irónicamente; burlarse, mofarse. —n sonrisa sardónica, sonrisa de desprecio, f; burla, mofa, f. **to s. at,** mofarse de, burlarse de; hablar con desprecio de

sneering /'snɪərɪŋ/ a mofador, burlón

sneeringly /'snɪərɪŋli/ *adv* con una sonrisa sardónica; burlonamente

sneeze /sniz/ *vi* estornudar. —*n* estornudo, *m*. **It's not to be sneezed at,** No es moco de pavo

sniff /snɪf/ *vi* respirar fuertemente; resollar. —*vt* oler, olfatear; aspirar. **to s. at,** oler. **to s. out,** *Inf.* husmear

snigger /'snɪɡər/ *vi* reírse por lo bajo, reírse disimuladamente. —*n* risa disimulada, *f*

snip /snɪp/ *vt* cortar con tijeras; cortar, quitar. —*n* tijeretada, *f*; (of cloth, etc.) recorte, pedacito, *m*

snipe /snaɪp/ *n ornith* agachadiza, *f*. **to s. at,** *Mil.* pacar

sniper /'snaɪpər/ *n Mil.* paco, *m*

snippet /'snɪpɪt/ *n* pedacito, fragmento, *m*; (of prose, etc.) trocito, *m*; (of news) noticia, *f*

snivel /'snɪvəl/ *vi* lloriquear, gimotear

sniveling /'snɪvəlɪŋ/ *n* lloriqueo, gimoteo, *m*. —*a* llorón; mocoso

snob /snɒb/ *n* esnob, *mf*

snobbery /'snɒbəri/ *n* snobismo, *m*

snobbish /'snɒbɪʃ/ *a* esnob

snood /snud/ *n* (for the hair) redecilla, *f*; (turkey's) moco (de pavo), *m*; (fishing) cendal, *m*

snoop /snup/ *vi* espiar; entremeterse

snooze /snuz/ *vi* dormitar, echar un sueño. —*n* sueñecito, *m*; (afternoon) siesta, *f*

snore /snɔr/ *vi* roncar. —*n* ronquido, *m*

snoring /'snɔrɪŋ/ *n* ronquidos, *m pl*

snort /snɔrt/ *vi* bufar; resoplar. —*n* bufido, *m*; resoplido, *m*

snout /snaʊt/ *n* hocico, *m*; (of a pig) jeta, *f*

snow /snoʊ/ *n* nieve, *f*. —*vi* nevar. —*vt* nevar; *fig* inundar. **to s. under** (with), inundar con. **to be snowed up,** estar aprisionado por la nieve. **s.-blindness,** deslumbramiento causado por la nieve, *m*. **s.-boot,** bota para la nieve, *f*. **s.-bound,** aprisionado por la nieve; bloqueado por la nieve. **s.-capped,** coronado de nieve. **s.-clad,** cubierto de nieve. **s.-drift,** acumulación de nieve, *f*. **s.-field,** ventisquero, *m*. **s.-goggles,** gafas ahumadas, *f pl*. **s.-line,** límite de las nieves perpetuas, *m*. **s.-man,** figura de nieve, *f*. **s.-plough,** quitanieves, *m*. **s.-shoe,** raqueta de nieve, *f*. **s.-white,** blanco como la nieve

snowball /'snoʊˌbɔl/ *n* bola de nieves, *f*; *bot* bola de nieve, *f*

snowfall /'snoʊˌfɔl/ *n* nevada, *f*

snowflake /'snoʊˌfleɪk/ *n* copo de nieve, *m*

snowstorm /'snoʊˌstɔrm/ *n* ventisca, *f*

snowy /'snoʊi/ *a* nevoso; de nieve

snub /snʌb/ *vt* repulsar; desairar, tratar con desdén. —*n* repulsa, *f*, desaire, *m*; (nose) nariz respingona, *f*. **s.-nosed,** de nariz respingona

snuff /snʌf/ *vt* (breathe) oler, olfatear; inhalar; (a candle) atizar, despabilar. —*n* (of a candle) moco, *m*, despabiladura, *f*; (tobacco) rapé, *m*. **to take s.,** tomar rapé. **to s. out,** extinguir. **s.-box,** caja de rapé, tabaquera, *f*

snuffle /'snʌfəl/ *vi* hacer ruido con la nariz; respirar fuerte; (in speaking) ganguear

snuffling /'snʌflɪŋ/ *a* mocoso; (of the voice) gangoso

snug /snʌɡ/ *a* caliente; cómodo; (hidden) escondido, **to have a s. income,** tener el riñón bien cubierto, ser acomodado

snuggle /'snʌɡəl/ *vi* hacerse un ovillo; acomodarse; ponerse cómodo. **to s. up to,** arrimarse, apretarse contra

so /soʊ/ *adv* así; de este modo, de esta manera; por lo tanto; tanto; (before adjs. and advs. but not before **más, mejor, menos, peor,** where **tanto** is used) tan; (in the same way) del mismo modo, de igual modo; (therefore) de modo que, de manera que; (also) también; (approximately) más o menos, aproximadamente. **Is that so?** ¡De veras? **If so...,** si así es... **He has not yet done so,** no lo ha hecho todavía. **I told you so!** ¡Ya te lo dije yo! **So be it!** ¡Así sea! **So far,** hasta aquí; hasta ahora. **so forth,** etcétera. **So long!** ¡Nos vemos! **so much,** tanto. **So much the worse for them,** Tanto peor para ellos. **so to speak,** por decirlo así. **so as to,** a fin de, para. **so long as,** con tal que, a condición de que. **so on,** etcétera. **so soon as,** tan pronto como. **so that,** de suerte que, de modo que, para que; con que. **so-and-so,** *n* fulano (-na); mengano (-na). **so-called,** así llamado, supuesto. **so-so,** así-así, regular

soak /soʊk/ *vt* remojar; empapar; (skins) abrevar. —*vi* estar en remojo. —*n* remojo, *m*; (rain) diluvio, *m*; (booze) borrachera, *f*. **to s. into,** filtrar en; penetrar. **to s. through,** penetrar; filtrar **so-called,** así llamado, supuesto. **so-so,** así, regular

soaked /soʊkt/ *a* remojado. **He is s. to the skin,** Está calado hasta los huesos

soap /soʊp/ *n* jabón, *m*. —*vt* jabonar; (flatter) enjabonar. **a tablet of s.,** una pastilla de jabón. **soft s.,** jabón blando, *m*. **toilet s.,** jabón de tocador, jaboncillo, *m*. **s.-bubble,** burbuja de jabón, *f*. **s. dish,** jabonera, *f*. **s. factory,** jabonería, *f*. **s.-flakes,** copos de jabón, *m pl*

soap box *n lit* caja de jabón, *f*; *fig* tribuna callejera, *f*

soap opera /'ɒpərə/ *n* radionovela (on radio), *f*; telenovela (on television), *f*, serial lacrimógeno (derogatory), *m*

soapsuds /'soʊpˌsʌdz/ *n pl* jabonaduras, *f pl*

soar /sɔr/ *vi* remontarse; *fig* elevarse; (of prices, etc.) subir de golpe

soaring /'sɔrɪŋ/ *n* remonte, vuelo, *m*; *fig* aspiración, *f*; (of prices, etc.) subida repentina, *f*

sob /sɒb/ *vi* sollozar. —*n* sollozo, *m*. **to**

sob one's heart out, llorar a lágrima viva. **to sob out,** decir sollozando, decir entre sollozos

sober /'soubər/ a sobrio; moderado; (of colors) obscuro. **s.-minded,** serio; reflexivo

sobriety /sə'braiiti/ n sobriedad, f; moderación, f; seriedad, f; calma, tranquilidad, f

sobriquet /'soubrı,kei, -,ket/ n apodo, m

soccer /'sɒkər/ n fútbol (Asociación), m

sociable /'souʃəbəl/ a sociable; amistoso

social /'souʃəl/ a social; sociable. —n reunión, velada, f. **s.-democrat,** a and n socialdemócrata, mf. **s. event,** acontecimiento social, m. **s. insurance,** previsión social, f. **s. services,** servicios sociales, m pl. **s. work,** asistencia social, f

socialism /'souʃə,lızəm/ n socialismo, m

socialist /'souʃəlɪst/ a socialista, laborista. —n socialista, mf

socialize /'souʃə,laiz/ vt socializar

society /sə'saiiti/ n sociedad, f; (fashionable) mundo elegante, m, alta sociedad, f; compañía, f. **to go into s.,** (of girls) ponerse de largo; entrar en el mundo elegante. **s. hostess,** dama de sociedad, f. **Society for the Prevention of Cruelty to Animals,** sociedad protectora de animales, f. **s. news,** noticias de sociedad, f pl

sociologist /,sousi,ɒlədʒɪst/ n sociólogo (-ga)

sociology /,sousi'ɒlədʒi/ n sociología, f

sock /sɒk/ n calcetín, m; (for a shoe) plantilla, f

socket /'sɒkɪt/ n mech encaje, cubo, ojo, m; (of a lamp, and elec) enchufe, m; (of the eye) órbita, cuenca, f; (of a tooth) alvéolo, m; (of a joint) fosa, f. **His eyes started out of their sockets,** Sus ojos estaban fuera de su órbita

sod /sɒd/ n césped, m; (cut) tepe, m

soda /'soudə/ n sosa, f. **caustic s.,** sosa cáustica, f. **s.-ash,** carbonato sódico, m. **s.-fountain,** aparato de aguas gaseosas, m. **s.-water,** sifón, m

sodden /'sɒdn/ a saturado, empapado

sodium /'soudiəm/ n sodio, m

sofa /'soufə/ n sofá, m

soft /sɒft/ a blando; suave; muelle; (flabby) flojo; (of disposition, etc.) dulce; (effeminate) muelle, afeminado; (lenient) indulgente; (easy) fácil; (silly) tonto. **to have a s. spot for,** (a person) tener una debilidad para. **s. coal,** carbón bituminoso, m. **s. drink,** bebida no alcohólica, f. **s. felt hat,** sombrero flexible, m. **s. fruit,** fruta blanda, f. **s.-boiled,** (of eggs) pasado por agua; (of persons) inocente, ingenuo. **s.-hearted,** de buen corazón; compasivo, bondadoso. **s.-heartedness,** buen corazón, m, bondad, f. **s.-spoken,** de voz suave; que habla con dulzura, meloso. **s. water,** agua blanda, f

soften /'sɒfən/ vt ablandar, reblandecer (weaken) debilitar; (mitigate) mitigar, suavizar; (the heart, etc.) enternecer. —vi reblandecerse; enternecerse

softening /'sɒfənɪŋ/ n reblandecimiento, m; (relenting) enternecimiento, m

softly /'sɒftli/ adv suavemente; dulcemente, tiernamente; sin ruido, silenciosamente

soggy /'sɒgi/ a empapado de agua; saturado

soil /sɔil/ n tierra, f; (country) país, m, tierra, f. —vt ensuciar; Fig. manchar. **my native s.,** mi tierra, mi patria

soiled /sɔild/ a sucio. **s. linen,** ropa sucia, f

sojourn /'soudʒɜrn/ vi morar, residir, permanecer. —n residencia, permanencia, f

solace /'sɒlɪs/ n consuelo, solaz, m. —vt consolar; solazar

solar /'soulər/ a solar. **s. plexus,** anat plexo solar, m. **s. system,** sistema solar, m

solder /'sɒdər/ n soldadura, f, vt soldar

soldering /'sɒdərɪŋ/ n soldadura, f

soldier /'souldʒər/ n soldado, m; militar, m. **He wants to be a s.,** Quiere ser militar

soldierly /'souldʒərli/ a militar; marcial

soldiery /'souldʒəri/ n soldadesca, f

sole /soul/ n (of a foot) planta, f; (of a shoe) suela, f; (of a plough) cepa, f; ichth lenguado, m, suela, f. —vt (shoes) solar, poner suela (a). —a solo, único; exclusivo. **s. right,** exclusiva, f, derecho exclusivo, m

solely /'soulli/ adv sólo; únicamente, puramente; meramente

solemn /'sɒləm/ a solemne; grave; serio; (sacred) sagrado. **Why do you look so s.?** ¿Por qué estás tan serio?

solemnity /sə'lemnɪti/ n solemnidad, f

solemnize /'sɒləm,naiz/ vt solemnizar

solicit /sə'lɪsɪt/ vt solicitar; implorar; rogar encarecidamente

solicitor /sə'lɪsɪtər/ n abogado (-da)

solicitous /sə'lɪsɪtəs/ a ansioso (de), deseoso (de); solícito, atento; (worried) preocupado

solicitude /sə'lɪsɪ,tud/ n solicitud, f, cuidado, m; (anxiety) preocupación, f

solid /'sɒlɪd/ a sólido; macizo; (of persons) serio, formal; (unanimous) unánime. —n sólido, m. **a s. meal,** una comida fuerte. **He slept for ten s. hours,** Durmió por diez horas seguidas. **solid-colored material,** tela lisa, f. **s. food,** alimentos sólidos, m pl. **s. geometry,** geometría del espacio, f. **s. gold,** oro de ley, m. **s. tire,** llanta de goma maciza, f

solidarity /,sɒlɪ'dærɪti/ n solidaridad, f

solidify /sə'lɪdə,fai/ vt solidificar. —vi solidificarse; congelarse

solidity /sə'lɪdɪti/ n solidez, f; unanimidad, f

soliloquize /sə'lɪlə,kwaiz/ vi soliloquiar, hablar a solas

soliloquy /sə'lɪləkwi/ n soliloquio, m

solitaire /'sɒlɪ,tɛər/ n (diamond and game) solitario, m

solitary /'sɒlɪ,teri/ a solitario; solo, aislado, único. **He was in s. confinement for three months,** Estuvo incomunicado durante tres meses. **There is not a s. one,** No hay ni uno

solitude /'sɒlɪˌtud/ n soledad, f

solo /'soulou/ n (performance and cards) solo, m. **to sing a s.,** cantar un solo. **It was his first s. flight,** Era su primer vuelo a solas

soloist /'soulouɪst/ n solista, mf

solstice /'sɒlstɪs, 'soul-/ n solsticio, m. **summer s.,** solsticio vernal, m. **winter s.,** solsticio hiemal, m

soluble /'sɒlyəbəl/ a soluble

solution /sə'luʃən/ n solución, f

solvable /'sɒlvəbəl/ a que se puede resolver, soluble

solve /sɒlv/ vt resolver, hallar la solución de

solvency /'sɒlvənsi/ n solvencia, f

solvent /'sɒlvənt/ a com solvente; (chem and fig) disolvente. —n disolvente, m

somber /'sɒmbər/ a sombrío

some /sʌm; unstressed səm/ a alguno (-a), algunos (-as); (before a masculine sing. noun) algún; unos (-as); un poco de, algo de; (as a partitive, often not translated, e.g. Give me s. wine, Dame vino); (approximately) aproximadamente, unos (-as). —pron algunos (-as), unos (-as); algo, un poco. **I should like s. strawberries,** Me gustaría comer unas fresas. **s. day,** algún día. **S. say yes, others no,** Algunos dicen que sí, otros que no. **There are s. sixty people in the garden,** Hay unas sesenta personas en el jardín

somebody, someone /'sʌmbɒdi; 'sʌm,wʌn/ n alguien, mf. **s. else,** otro (-a), otra persona, f. **S. or other said that the book is worth reading,** No sé quién dijo que el libro vale la pena de leerse. **to be s.,** inf ser un personaje

somehow /'sʌm,hau/ adv de un modo u otro, de alguna manera. **S. I don't like them,** No sé por qué, pero no me gustan

somersault /'sʌmər,sɔlt/ n salto mortal, m, vi dar un salto mortal

something /'sʌm,θɪŋ/ n algo, m, alguna cosa, f. —adv algún tanto. **Would you like s. else?** ¿Quiere Vd. otra cosa? **He left s. like fifty thousand pounds,** Dejó algo así como cincuenta mil libras. **He has s. to live for,** Tiene para que vivir

sometime /'sʌm,taim/ adv algún día, alguna vez; en algún tiempo. —a ex-. **Come and see me s. soon,** Ven a verme algún día de estos. **He will have to go abroad s. or another,** Tarde o temprano, tiene que ir al extranjero. **s. last month,** durante el mes pasado

sometimes /'sʌm,taimz/ adv algunas veces, a veces. **s. happy, s. sad,** algunas veces feliz y otras triste, ora feliz ora triste

somewhat /'sʌm,wʌt/ adv algo; algún tanto, un tanto; un poco. **I am s. busy,** Estoy algo ocupado. **He is s. of a lady-**killer, Tiene sus puntos de castigador, Tiene algo de castigador

somewhere /'sʌm,wɛər/ adv en alguna parte. **s. about,** por ahí. **s. else,** en otra parte

somnambulism /sɒm'næmbyə,lɪzəm/ n somnambulismo, m

somnambulist /sɒm'næmbyəlɪst/ n somnámbulo (-la)

somnolence /'sɒmnələns/ n somnolencia, f

somnolent /'sɒmnələnt/ a soñoliento; soporífero

son /sʌn/ n hijo, m. **son-in-law,** yerno, hijo político, m

song /sɒŋ/ n canto, m; canción, f; (poem) poema, verso, m. **It's nothing to make a s. about,** No es para tanto. **to break into s.,** ponerse a cantar. **to be not worth an old s.,** no valer un pito. **the S. of Songs,** Cantar de los Cantares, m. **s.-bird,** ave canora, f. **s.-book,** libro de canciones, m. **s.-writer,** compositor (-ra) de canciones

sonic /'sɒnɪk/ a sónico. **sonic boom,** estampido sónico, m

sonnet /'sɒnɪt/ n soneto, m

sonorous /sə'nɔrəs/ a sonoro

soon /sun/ adv pronto; dentro de poco, luego. **as s. as,** así que, en cuanto, luego que, no bien... **as s. as possible,** lo antes posible, lo más pronto posible, con la mayor antelación posible, cuanto antes. **s. after,** poco después (de). **See you s.!** ¡Hasta pronto! **sooner or later,** tarde o temprano. **the sooner the better,** cuanto antes mejor. **No sooner had he left the house, when...** Apenas hubo dejado la casa, cuando... **Emily would sooner go to London,** Emilia preferiría ir a Londres (A Emilia le gustaría más ir a Londres)

soot /sut/ n hollín, m, vt cubrir de hollín

soothe /suð/ vt tranquilizar, calmar, (pain) aliviar, mitigar

soothing /'suðɪŋ/ a calmante, tranquilizador, sosegador; (of powders, etc.) calmante

soothsaying /'suθ,seiɪŋ/ n adivinanza, f

sooty /'suti/ a cubierto de hollín; negro como el hollín

sop /sɒp/ n sopa, f; (bribe) soborno, m

sophist /'sɒfɪst/ n hist sofista, m; (quibbler) sofista, mf

sophistic /sə'fɪstɪk/ a philos sofista; (of persons, arguments) sofístico

sophisticated /sə'fɪstɪ,keitɪd/ a nada ingenuo; mundano; (cultured) culto

sophistication /sə,fɪstɪ'keiʃən/ n falta de simplicidad, f; mundanería, f; cultura, f

sophistry /'sɒfəstri/ n sofistería, f

soporific /,sɒpə'rɪfɪk/ a soporífico

sopping /'sɒpɪŋ/ a muy mojado. **s. wet,** hecho una sopa

soprano /sə'prænou/ n (voice and part) soprano, m; (singer) soprano, tiple, mf

sorcerer /'sɔrsərər/ n encantador, mago, brujo, m

sorcery /'sɔrsəri/ *n* sortilegio, *m*, hechicería, brujería, *f*; encanto, *m*

sordid /'sɔrdɪd/ *a* sórdido, *f*; (of motives, etc.) ruin, vil

sore /sɔr/ *a* doloroso, malo; (sad) triste; (annoyed) enojado; (with need, etc.) extremo. —*n* llaga, *f*; (on horses, etc., caused by girths) matadura, *f*; *Fig.* herida, *f*; recuerdo doloroso, *m*. **to open an old s.,** *Fig.* renovar la herida. **running s.,** úlcera, *f*. **s. throat,** dolor de garganta, *m*

sorely /'sɔrli/ *adv* grandemente; muy; urgentemente. **He was s. tempted,** Tuvo grandes tentaciones

soreness /'sɔrnɪs/ *n* dolor, *m*; (resentment) amargura, *f*, resentimiento, *m*; (ill-feeling) rencor, *m*

sorrow /'sɔrou/ *n* pesar, *m*, aflicción, pesadumbre, *f*; tristeza, *f*. —*vi* afligirse; entristecerse. **To my great s.,** Con gran pesar mío. **s.-stricken,** afligido, agobiado de pena

sorrowful /'sɔrəfəl/ *a* afligido, angustiado; triste

sort /sɔrt/ *n* especie, *f*; clase, *f*; tipo, *m*. —*vt* separar (de); clasificar. **a s. of hat,** una especie de sombrero. **all sorts of,** toda clase de. **He is a good s.,** Es buen chico. **He is a queer s.,** Es un tipo raro. **in some s.,** hasta cierto punto. **I am out of sorts,** Estoy destemplado. **Nothing of the s.!** ¡Nada de eso!

sorter /'sɔrtər/ *n* oficial de correos, *m*; clasificador (-ra)

sorting /'sɔrtɪŋ/ *n* clasificación, *f*

sot /sɒt/ *n* zaque, pellejo, *m*

sotto voce /'sɒt'ou vout'ʃi/ *adv* a sovoz, en voz baja

soul /soul/ *n* alma, *f*; espíritu, *m*; (departed) ánima, *f*; (being) ser, *m*; (life) vida, *f*; (heart) corazón, *m*. **All Souls' Day,** Día de los Difuntos, *m*. **He is a good s.!** ¡Es un bendito! **She is a simple s.,** Ella es una alma de Dios. **without seeing a living s.,** sin ver un bicho viviente. **Upon my s.!** ¡Por mi vida! **s. in purgatory,** alma en pena, *f*. **s.-stirring,** emocionante

soulful /'soulfəl/ *a* sentimental, emocional; espiritual; romántico

sound /saund/ *n* sonido, *m*; son, *m*; ruido, *m*; (strait) estrecho, *m*. —*vi* sonar; hacer ruido; resonar; (seem) parecer. —*vt* sonar; (the horn, the alarm, musical instrument) tocar; (express) expresar; proclamar; (praise) celebrar; *Naut.* hondear; *Med.* tentar; (the chest) auscultar; (try to discover) tentar, sondar; (experience) experimentar. **to the s. of,** al son de. **s.-box,** (of a gramophone) diafragma, *m*. **s.-detector,** fonolocalización de aviones, *f*. **s.-film,** película sonora, *f*. **s.-proof,** (of radio studios, etc.) aislado de todo sonido. **s.-track,** guía sonora, banda sonora, *f*. **s.-wave,** onda sonora, *f*

sound /saund/ *a* sano; (of a person) perspicaz; (reasonable) lógico, razonable; (of a policy, etc.) prudente; (of an argu-ment, etc.) válido; (of an investment) seguro; (solvent) solvente; (good) bueno; (deep) profundo. —*adv* profundamente, bien

sounding /'saundɪŋ/ *n Naut.* sondeo, *m*; *pl* **soundings,** sondas, *f pl*. —*a* sonoro. **to take soundings,** sondar, echar la plomada. **s.-board,** tabla de armonía, *f*

soundly /'saundli/ *adv* sanamente; juiciosamente, prudentemente; bien; (deeply) profundamente

soup /sup/ *n* sopa, *f*. **clear s.,** consommé, *m*. **thick s.,** puré, *m*. **to be in the s.,** *Inf.* estar aviado. **s.-ladle,** cucharón, *m*. **s.-plate,** plato sopero, *m*. **s.-tureen,** sopera, *f*

sour /sauər/ *a* ácido, agrio; (of milk) agrio; (of persons, etc.) agrio, desabrido. —*vt* agriar. —*vi* volverse agrio. **S. grapes!** ¡Están verdes!

source /sɔrs/ *n* (of a river, etc.) nacimiento, *m*; fuente, *f*; (of infection) foco, *m*. **to know from a good s.,** saber de buena tinta

south /sauθ/ *n* sur, *m*; mediodía, *m*. —*a* del sur. —*adv* hacia el sur. **S. African,** *a* and *n* sudafricano (-na). **S. American,** *a* and *n* sudamericano (-na). **s.-east,** *n* sudeste, *m*. —*a* del sudeste. —*adv* hacia el sudeste. **s.-easter,** viento del sudeste, *m*. **s.-easterly,** *a* del sudeste; al sudeste. —*adv* hacia el sudeste. **s.-eastern,** del sudeste. **s.-s.-east,** *n* sudsudeste, *m*. **s.-s.-west,** sudsudoeste, *m*. **s.-west,** *n* sudoeste, *m*. —*a* del sudoeste. —*adv* hacia el sudoeste. **s.-west wind,** viento sudoeste, ábrego, *m*. **s.-westerly,** *a* del sudoeste. —*adv* hacia el sudoeste. **s.-western,** *a* del sudoeste

South Africa República Sudafricana, *f*

South America América del Sur, Sudamérica, *f*

southerly /'sʌðərli/ *a* del sur; hacia el sur. **The house has a s. aspect,** La casa está orientada al sur

southern /'sʌðərn/ *a* del sur; del mediodía; meridional. **S. Cross,** Cruz, *f*, Crucero, *m*. **s. express,** sudexpreso, *m*

southerner /'sʌðərnər/ *n* habitante del sur, *m*

southward /'sauθwərd/ *Naut.* 'sʌðərd/ *a* del sur; al sur. —*adv* hacia el sur

souvenir /,suvə'nɪər/ *n* recuerdo, *m*

sovereign /'sɒvrɪn/ *a* soberano. —*n* soberano (-na); (coin) soberano, *m*

sovereignty /'sɒvrɪnti/ *n* soberanía, *f*

Soviet Union, the la Unión Soviética, *f*

sow /sau/ *n* cerda, puerca, marrana, *f*; (of a wild boar) jabalina, *f*; (of iron) galápago, *m*

sow /sou/ *vt* sembrar; esparcir; diseminar

sowing /'souɪŋ/ *n* sembradura, siembra, *f*. **s. machine,** sembradera, *f*. **s. time,** tiempo de la siembra, *m*

soya bean /'sɔiə/ *n* soja, *f*

spa /spa/ *n* balneario, *m*; (spring) manantial mineral, *m*, caldas, *f pl*

space /speis/ *n* espacio, *m*; (of time) temporada, f; intervalo, m; (Print., Mus.) espacio, m. —vt espaciar. **blank s.,** blanco, m. **s.-bar,** tecla de espacios, f, espaciador, m

spacious /'speiʃəs/ a espacioso; amplio

spade /speid/ n pala, azada, f; (cards) espada, f. **to call a s. a s.,** llamar al pan pan y al vino vino, llamar a las cosas por su nombre. **s.-work,** trabajo preparatorio, m, labor de pala, f

spaghetti /spə'gɛti/ n fideos, macarrones, m pl

Spain /spein/ España, f

span /spæn/ vt medir a palmos; rodear; medir; (cross) atravesar, cruzar. —n palmo, m; espacio, m; duración, f; (of a bridge) vano, m; (of wing, Aer., Zool.) envergadura, f; (distance) distancia, f. **single-s. bridge,** puente de vano único. **the brief s. of human life,** la corta duración de la vida humana

spangle /'spæŋgəl/ n lentejuela, f; (tinsel) oropel, m. —vt adornar con lentejuelas; sembrar (de), esparcir (de). **spangled with stars,** sembrado de estrellas

Spaniard /'spænyərd/ n español (-la). **a young s.,** un joven español

Spanish /'spænɪʃ/ a español. —n (language) español, castellano, m. **a S. girl,** una muchacha española. **in S. fashion,** a la española. **S. American,** a and n hispanoamericano (-na). **S. broom,** retama de olor, f. **S. fly,** cantárida, f

Spanish America Hispanoamérica, f

spank /spæŋk/ vt pegar con la mano, azotar. —n azotazo, m. **to s. along,** correr rápidamente; (of a horse) galopar

spanking /'spæŋkɪŋ/ n azotamiento, vapuleo, m

spanner /'spænər/ n llave inglesa, llave de tuercas, f

spar /spar/ n Naut. mastel, m; Mineral. espato, m; (boxing) boxeo, m; (quarrel) disputa, f. —vi boxear; (argue) disputar

spare /spɛər/ a (meager) frugal, escaso; (of persons) enjuto, flaco; (available) disponible; (extra) de repuesto. —n recambio, m. **s. part,** pieza de recambio, pieza de repuesto, f. **s. room,** cuarto de amigos, m. **s. time,** ratos de ocio, m pl, tiempo disponible, m. **s. wheel,** rueda de repuesto, f

spare /spɛər/ vt (expense, etc.) escatimar; ahorrar; (do without) pasarse sin; (give) dar; (a life, etc.) perdonar; (avoid) evitar; dispensar de; (grant) hacer gracia de; (time) dedicar. **I cannot s. her,** No puedo estar sin ella. **They have no money to s.,** No tienen dinero de sobra. **to be sparing of,** ser avaro de

sparingly /'spɛərɪŋli/ adv frugalmente; escasamente. **to eat s.,** comer con frugalidad

spark /spark/ n chispa, f; (gallant) pisaverde, m. —vi chispear, echar chispas

sparking /'sparkɪŋ/ a chispeante. —n emisión de chispas, f. **s.-plug,** bujía de encendido, f

sparkle /'sparkəl/ vi centellear, rutilar, destellar; Fig. brillar; (of wines) ser espumoso. —n centelleo, destello, m; Fig. brillo, m

sparkling /'sparklɪŋ/ a rutilante, centelleante, reluciente; Fig. brillante, chispeante; (of wines) espumante

sparse /spars/ a claro, ralo; esparcido

Spartan /'spartn/ a and n espartano (-na)

spasm /'spæzəm/ n espasmo, m; ataque, m; acceso, m

spasmodic /spæz'mɒdɪk/ a espasmódico; intermitente

spat /spæt/ n (gaiter) polaina de tela, f

spate /speit/ n crecida, f; Fig. torrente, m. **in s.,** crecido

spatter /'spætər/ vt salpicar; (Fig. smirch) manchar. —vi rociar. —n salpicadura, f; rociada, f

spatula /'spætʃələ/ n espátula, f

spawn /spɔn/ vt and vi desovar; engendrar. —n huevas, f pl, freza, f; (offspring) producto, m

speak /spik/ vi hablar; pronunciar un discurso; (sound) sonar. —vt decir, (French, etc.) hablar. **She never spoke to him again,** Nunca volvió a dirigirle la palabra. **roughly speaking,** aproximadamente, más o menos. **Speaking for myself,** En cuanto a mí, Por mi parte. **without speaking,** sin decir nada, sin hablar. **to s. for,** (a person) hablar por. **to s. for itself,** hablar por sí mismo, ser evidente. **to s. one's mind,** decir lo que se piensa. **to s. of,** hablar de. **to s. out,** hablar claro; hablar alto. **to s. up for,** (a person) hablar en favor de (alguien)

speaker /'spikər/ n el, m, (f, la) que habla; (public) orador (-ra). **the S.,** el Presidente de la Cámara de los Comunes

speaking /'spikɪŋ/ a hablante; para hablar; elocuente, expresivo. —n habla, f, discurso, m. **They are not on s. terms,** No se hablan. **within s. distance,** al habla. **s.-trumpet,** portavoz, m. **s.-tube,** tubo acústico, m

spear /spɪər/ n lanza, f; (javelin) venablo, m; (harpoon) arpón, m. —vt herir con lanza, alancear; (fish) arponear. **s.-head,** punta de la lanza, f. **s.-thrust,** lanzada, f

special /'spɛʃəl/ a especial; particular; extraordinario; n (train) tren extraordinario, m. **s. correspondent,** corresponsal extraordinario, m. **s. friend,** amigo (-ga) del alma, amigo íntimo

specialist /'spɛʃəlɪst/ n especialista, mf

specialization /,spɛʃələ'zeiʃən/ n especialización, f

specialize /'spɛʃə,laiz/ vt especializar. —vi especializarse

specially /'spɛʃəli/ adv especialmente; particularmente; sobre todo

species /'spiʃiz, -siz/ n especie, f; raza, f

specific /spɪ'sɪfɪk/ a específico; explícito. —n específico, m. **s. gravity,** peso específico, m, densidad, f

specify /'spɛsə,fai/ vt especificar

specimen /'spɛsəmən/ *n* espécimen, *m*; ejemplo, *m*; *Inf.* tipo, *m*

specious /'spiʃəs/ *a* especioso

speck /spɛk/ *n* pequeña mancha, *f*; punto, *m*; átomo, *m*; (on fruit) maca, *f*

speckle /'spɛkəl/ *vt* motear, manchar

spectacle /'spɛktəkəl/ *n* espectáculo, *m*; escena, *f*; *pl* **spectacles**, gafas, *f pl*, anteojos, *m pl*. **s.-case**, cajita para las gafas, *f*

spectacular /spɛk'tækyələr/ *a* espectacular

spectator /'spɛkteitər/ *n* espectador (-ra)

specter /'spɛktər/ *n* espectro, fantasma, *m*

spectrum /'spɛktrəm/ *n Phys.* espectro, *m*

speculate /'spɛkyə,leit/ *vi* especular (sobre, acerca de); *Com.* especular (en)

speculative /'spɛkyə,lətɪv/ *a* especulativo

speculator /'spɛkyə,leitər/ *n* especulador (-ra)

speech /spitʃ/ *n* habla, *f*; palabra, *f*; (idiom) lenguaje, *m*; (language) idioma, *m*; *Gram.* oración, *f*; (address) discurso, *m*; disertación, *f*. **part of s.**, parte de la oración, *f*. **to make a s.**, pronunciar un discurso. **s.maker**, orador (-ra)

speechless /'spitʃlis/ *a* mudo; sin habla; desconcertado, turbado

speed /spid/ *n* prisa, rapidez, *f*; velocidad, *f* —*vt* dar la bienvenida (a); conceder éxito (a); (accelerate) acelerar. —*vi* darse prisa; correr a toda prisa; (of arrows) volar. **at full s.**, a toda prisa; a toda velocidad; a todo correr. **maximum s.**, velocidad máxima, *f*. **with all s.**, a toda prisa. **s. of impact**, velocidad del choque, *f*. **s.-boat**, lancha de carrera, *f*. **s.-limit**, velocidad máxima, *f*, límite de velocidad, *f*

speedily /'spidli/ *adv* aprisa, rápidamente; prontamente

speeding /'spidɪŋ/ *n* exceso de velocidad, *m*. **s. up**, aceleración, *f*

speedometer /spi'dɒmɪtər/ *n* cuentakilómetros, *m*

speedway /'spid,wei/ *n* autódromo, *m*, pista de ceniza, *f*

speedy /'spidi/ *a* rápido; pronto

spell /spɛl/ *n* ensalmo, hechizo, *m*; encanto, *m*; (bout) turno, *m*; (interval) rato, *m*; temporada, *f*. —*vt* (a word) deletrear; (a word in writing) escribir; (mean) significar; (be) ser. **a s. of good weather**, una temporada de buen tiempo. **by spells**, a ratos. **to learn to s.**, aprender la ortografía. **s.-bound**, encantado, fascinado; asombrado

spelling /'spɛlɪŋ/ *n* deletreo, *m*; ortografía, *f*. **s.-book**, silabario, *m*; **s. mistake**, falta de ortografía, *f*

spelling bee *n* certamen de deletreo, *m*

spend /spɛnd/ *vt* gastar; (time, etc.) pasar; (spend; consumir, agotar. —*vi* gastar, hacer gastos. **to s. oneself**, agotarse

spendthrift /'spɛnd,θrɪft/ *n* derrochador

(-ra), manirroto (-ta). —*a* despilfarrado, pródigo

spent /spɛnt/ *a* agotado, rendido. **The night is far s.**, La noche está avanzada. **s. bullet**, bala fría, *f*

sperm /spɜrm/ *n Biol.* esperma, *f*; (whale) cachalote, *m*

spermaceti /,spɜrmə'sɛti/ *n* esperma de ballena, *f*

sphere /sfɪər/ *n* esfera, *f*. **s. of influence**, zona de influencia, *f*

spice /spais/ *n* especia, *f*; *Fig.* sabor, *m*; (trace) dejo, *m*. —*vt* especiar. **s. cupboard**, especiero, *m*

spick and span /'spɪk ən 'spæn/ *a* limpio como una patena; (brand-new) flamante; (of persons) muy compuesto

spicy /'spaisi/ *a* especiado; aromático; *Fig.* picante

spider /'spaidər/ *n* araña, *f*. **spider's web**, telaraña, *f*

spigot /'spɪgət/ *n* espiche, *m*

spike /spaik/ *n* punta (de hierro, etc.), *f*; escarpia, *f*; (for boots) clavo, *m*; *Bot.* espiga, *f*. —*vt* clavetear; (a cannon) clavar

spill /spɪl/ *vt* derramar. —*n* (fall) caída, *f*

spilling /'spɪlɪŋ/ *n* derramamiento, derrame, *m*

spin /spɪn/ *vt* hilar; (a cocoon) tejer; (a top) bailar; (a ball) tornear; (a coin) lanzar. —*vi* hilar; girar, bailar. —*n* vuelta, *f*; paseo, *m*. **to send spinning downstairs**, hacer rodar por la escalera (a). **to s. a yarn**, contar un cuento. **to s. out**, prolongar

spinach /'spɪnɪtʃ/ *n* espinaca, *f*

spinal /'spainl/ *a* espinal. **s. anaesthesia**, raquianestesia, *f*. **s. column**, columna vertebral, *f*

spine /spain/ *n Anat.* espinazo, *m*, columna vertebral, *f*; *Bot.* espina, *f*; (of a porcupine, etc.) púa, *f*

spinner /'spinər/ *n* hilandero (-ra); máquina de hilar, *f*

spinning /'spinɪŋ/ *n* hilado, *m*; hilandería, *f*. **s.-machine**, máquina de hilar, *f*. **s.-top**, trompo, *m*, peonza, *f*. **s.-wheel**, rueca, *f*

spinster /'spinstər/ *n* soltera, *f*. **confirmed s.**, solterona, *f*

spiral /'spairəl/ *a* espiral; en espiral. —*n* espiral, *f*

spire /spaiᵊr/ *n* (of a church) aguja, *f*; espira, *f*

spirit /'spirit/ *n* espíritu, *m*; alma, *f*; (ghost) aparecido, fantasma, *m*; (outstanding person) ingenio, *m*, inteligencia, *f*; (disposition) ánimo, *m*; (courage) valor, espíritu, *m*; (for a lamp, etc.) alcohol, *m*. **the Holy S.**, El Espíritu Santo. **to be in high spirits**, no caber de contento, saltar de alegría. **to be in low spirits**, estar desalentado, estar deprimido. **to be full of spirits**, ser bullicioso, tener mucha energía. **to keep up one's spirits**, sostener el valor. **to s. away**, quitar secretamente, hacer desaparecer; (kidnap) secuestrar. **s.-level,** nivel de burbuja, *m.* **s.-stove,** cocinilla, *f*

spirited /'spɪrɪtɪd/ *a* animado, vigoroso; fogoso, animoso, brioso

spiritless /'spɪrɪtlɪs/ *a* sin espíritu, apático; flojo, débil; (depressed) abatido, desalentado; (cowardly) sin valor, cobarde

spiritual /'spɪrɪtʃuəl/ *a* espiritual

spirituality /ˌspɪrɪtʃuˈælɪti/ *n* espiritualidad, *f*

spirituous /'spɪrɪtʃuəs/ *a* espiritoso

spirt /spɜrt/ *vi, vt, n.* See **spurt**

spit /spɪt/ *n* (for roasting) espetón, asador, *m;* (sand-bank) banco de arena, *m;* (of land) lengua de tierra, *f;* (spittle) saliva, *f.* **the spit of, the spit and image of, the spitting image of,** la imagen viva de, la segunda edición de, *f* —*vt* (skewer) espetar; (saliva, etc.) escupir; (curses, etc.) vomitar. —*vi* escupir, expectorar; (of a cat) fufear, decir fu; (sputter) chisporrotear; (rain) lloviznar

spite /spaɪt/ *n* malevolencia, mála voluntad, hostilidad, *f;* rencor, *m,* ojeriza, *f.* —*vt* contrariar, hacer daño (a). **He has a s. against them,** Les tiene rencor. **in s. of,** a pesar de; a despecho de

spiteful /'spaɪtfəl/ *a* rencoroso, malévolo

spitefully /'spaɪtfəli/ *adv* malévolamente; con rencor; por maldad; por despecho

spitfire /'spɪtˌfaɪər/ *n* cascarrabias, *mf,* furia, *f*

spittle /'spɪtl/ *n* saliva, *f*

splash /splæʃ/ *vt* salpicar (de); manchar (con). —*vi* derramarse, esparcirse; chapotear, chapalear. —*n* chapoteo, *m;* (of rain, etc.) chapaleteo, *m;* (stain or patch) mancha, *f.* **John was splashing about in the sea,** Juan chapoteaba en el mar. **to make a s.,** *Fig.* causar una sensación. **s.-board,** alero, *m*

spleen /splin/ *n Anat.* bazo, *m;* esplín, *m*

splendid /'splɛndɪd/ *a* espléndido; magnífico; glorioso; excelente

splendor /'splɛndər/ *n* resplandor, *m;* magnificencia, *f;* (of exploits, etc.) esplendor, brillo, *m*

splice /splaɪs/ *vt* (ropes, timbers) empalmar; (marry) unir, casar. —*n* empalme, *m*

splint /splɪnt/ *n Surg.* férula, *f.* **to put in a s.,** entablar

splinter /'splɪntər/ *vt* astillar, hacer astillas. —*vi* hacerse astillas

split /splɪt/ *vi* henderse; resquebrajarse; (of seams) nacerse; abrirse; dividirse. —*vt* hender; partir; dividir; abrir; (the atom) escindir. —*n* hendedura, *f;* grieta, *f;* división, *f;* (in fabric) rasgón, *m;* (quarrel) ruptura, *f.* **to s. hairs,** andar en quisquillas, pararse en pelillos, sutilizar. **I have a splitting headache,** Tengo un dolor de cabeza que me trae loco. **to s. one's sides,** reírse a carcajadas, desternillarse de risa. **to s. on a rock,** estrellarse contra una roca. **to s. the difference,** partir la diferencia. **The blow s. his head**

open, El golpe le abrió la cabeza. **to s. on,** *Inf.* delatar, denunciar

splotch /splɒtʃ/ *n* mancha, *f,* borrón, *m*

splutter /'splʌtər/ *vi* chisporrotear; (of a person) balbucir. —*n* chisporroteo, *m.* **to s. out,** decir tartamudeando

spoil /spɔɪl/ *n* botín, despojo, *m;* (of war) trofeo, *m.* —*vt* estropear; echar a perder; (diminish) mitigar; (a child) mimar; (injure) dañar; (destroy) arruinar, destruir. —*vi* estropearse; echarse a perder. **to be spoiling for a fight,** tener ganas de pelearse. **You have spoilt my fun,** Me has aguado la fiesta. **s.-sport,** aguafiestas, *mf*

spoke /spouk/ *n* (of a wheel) rayo, *m;* (of a ladder) travesaño, peldaño, *m; Naut.* cabilla (de la rueda del timón), *f*

spoken /'spoukən/ *a* hablado. **well-s.,** bien hablado; cortés

spokesman /'spouksmən/ *n* portavoz, *m.* **to be s.,** llevar la palabra

sponge /spʌndʒ/ *n* esponja, *f;* (cadger) gorrón (-ona); (cake) bizcocho, *m.* —*vt* limpiar con esponja. **to s.,** *Inf.* vivir de gorra. **s.-holder,** esponjera, *f*

sponger /'spʌndʒər/ *n* gorrón (-ona), vividor, *m,* sablista, *mf*

sponging *n* esponjadura, *f; Inf.* sablazo, *m*

spongy /'spʌndʒi/ *a* esponjoso

sponsor /'spɒnsər/ *n* garante, *mf;* valedor (-ra), patron (-na); (godfather) padrino, *m;* (godmother) madrina, *f,* (radio and TV) auspiciador, patrocinador, *m*

spontaneous /spɒnˈteɪniəs/ *a* espontáneo. **s. combustion,** combustión espontánea, *f*

spook /spuk/ *n* fantasma, espectro, *m*

spool /spul/ *n* (for thread) bobina, *f,* carrete, *m;* (in a sewing machine) canilla, *f;* (of a fishing rod) carrete, *m*

spoon /spun/ *n* cuchara, *f.* —*vt* sacar con cuchara. —*vi* (slang) besuquearse. **to s.-feed,** dar de comer con cuchara (a); tratar como un niño (a)

spoonful /'spunfʊl/ *n* cucharada, *f*

spoor /spʊr, spɔr/ *n* pista, huella de animal, *f;* rastro, *m*

sporadic /spəˈrædɪk/ *a* esporádico

sport /spɔrt/ *n* deporte, sport, *m;* deportismo, *m;* (jest) broma, *f;* (game) juego, *m;* (plaything) juguete, *m;* (pastime) pasatiempo, *m.* —*vi* jugar; recrearse, divertirse. —*vt* llevar; ostentar, lucir. **He is a s.,** Es un buen chico. **to make s. of,** burlarse de. **sports car,** coche de deporte, *m.* **sports ground,** campo de recreo, *m.* **sports jacket,** chaqueta de deporte, americana, *f.* **sports shirt,** camisa corta, *f*

sporting /'spɔrtɪŋ/ *a* deportista; caballeroso. **I think there is a s. chance,** Me parece que hay una posibilidad de éxito

sporting goods *n* artículos de deporte, efectos de deportes, *m pl*

sportive /'spɔrtɪv/ *a* juguetón; bromista

sportsman /'spɔrtsmən/ *n* deportista, *m;* aficionado al sport, *m; Fig.* caballero, señor, *m;* buen chico, *m*

sportsmanlike /'spɔrtsmən,laik/ a de deportista; caballeroso

sportsmanship /'spɔrtsmən,ʃɪp/ n deportividad, f

spot /spɒt/ n mancha, f; pinta, f; (on the face, etc.) peca, f; grano, m; (place) sitio, m; lugar, m; (of liquor) trago, m; (of food) bocado, m; (of rain) gota, f. —vt manchar; motear; (recognize) reconocer; (understand) darse cuenta de, comprender. **a tender s.**, Fig. debilidad, f. **on the s.**, en el acto. **s. ball**, (billiards) pinta, f. **s. cash**, dinero contante, m

spotless /'spɒtlɪs/ a saltando de limpio; sin mancha; inmaculado; puro; virgen

spotlight /'spɒt,lait/ n luz del proyector, f; proyector, m

spotted /'spɒtɪd/ a (stained) manchado; (of animals, etc.) con manchas; (of garments, etc.) con pintas

spotty /'spɒti/ a lleno de manchas; moteado; (pimply) con granos

spouse /spaus/ n esposo, m; esposa, f

spout /spaut/ vi chorrear; Inf. hablar incesantemente. —vt arrojar; vomitar; Inf. declamar, recitar. —n (of a jug, etc.) pico, m; (for water, etc.) tubo, m, cañería, f; canalón, m; (gust) ráfaga, nube, f. **down s.**, tubo de bajada, m

spouting /'spautɪŋ/ n chorreo, m; Inf. declamación, f

Sprachgefühl /'ʃpraxgə,fil/ n sentido del idioma, m

sprain /sprein/ vt dislocar, torcer. —n dislocación, f, esguince, m. **Victoria has sprained her foot**, Victoria se ha torcido el pie

sprat /spræt/ n sardineta, f

sprawl /sprɔl/ vi recostarse (en); extenderse; (of plants) trepar. **He went sprawling**, Cayó cuan largo era

spray /sprei/ n (branch) ramo, m; (of water, etc.) rocío, m; (of the sea) espuma, f; (mechanical device) pulverizador, m. —vt pulverizar; rociar; regar; (the throat) jeringar

spread /spred/ vt tender; cubrir (de); poner; (stretch out) extender; (open out) desplegar; (of disease, etc.) propagar; diseminar; divulgar, difundir. —vi extenderse; propagarse; difundirse; divulgarse; (become general) generalizarse. —n extensión, f; expansión, f; propagación, f; divulgación, f; (Aer. and of birds) envergadura, f. **Carmen s. her hands to the fire**, Carmen extendió las manos al fuego. **The peacock s. its tail**, El pavo real hizo la rueda. **The dove s. its wings**, La paloma desplegó sus alas. **to s. out**, vt extender; desplegar; (scatter) esparcir, vi extenderse. **spread like wildfire**, correr como pólvora en reguero, propagarse como un reguero de pólvora, ser un reguero de pólvora

spreading /'spredɪŋ/ n (of a disease) propagación, f; (of knowledge, etc.) divulgación, f; expansión, f; extensión, f

spreadsheet /'spred,ʃit/ n hoja de cálculo, f

spree /spri/ n juerga, parranda, f; excursión, f. **to go on the s.**, ir de juerga, ir de picos pardos

sprig /sprɪg/ n ramita, f; (of heather, etc.) espiga, f; (scion) vástago, m

sprightly /'spraitli/ a vivaracho, despierto; enérgico

spring /sprɪŋ/ vi saltar, brincar; (become) hacerse; (seek) buscar; (of plants, water) brotar; (of tears) arrasar, llenar; (from) originarse (en), ser causado (por); inspirarse (en). —vt (a mine) volar; (a trap) soltar. **to s. a surprise**, dar una sorpresa. **to s. a surprise on a person**, coger a la imprevista (a). **to s. at a person**, precipitarse sobre. **to s. to one's feet**, ponerse de pie de un salto. **to s. back**, saltar hacia atrás; recular; volver a su sitio. **to s. open**, abrirse súbitamente. **to s. up**, (of plants) brotar, crecer; (of difficulties, etc.) surgir, asomarse

spring /sprɪŋ/ n (jump) salto, brinco, m; (of water) fuente, f, manantial, m; (season) primavera, f; (of a watch, etc.) re sorte, m; (of a mattress, etc.) muelle, m. —a primaveral. —vi saltar, brincar. **at one s.**, en un salto. **to give a s.**, dar un salto. **s.-board**, trampolín, m. **s.-mattress**, colchón de muelles, m. **s.-tide**, marea viva, f

sprinkle /'sprɪŋkəl/ vt esparcir; salpicar; rociar

sprinkling /'sprɪŋklɪŋ/ n salpicadura, f; rociadura, f; pequeño número, m. **a s. of snow**, una nevada ligera

sprint /sprɪnt/ vi sprintar. —n sprint, m

sprout /spraut/ vi brotar, despuntar, retoñar, tallecer; germinar. —vt salir. —n brote, retoño, pimpollo, m; germen, m. **Brussels sprouts**, coles de Bruselas, f pl

spruce /sprus/ a peripuesto, muy aseado, pulido; elegante, n Bot. pícea, f. **to s. oneself up**, arreglarse, ponerse elegante

spry /sprai/ a activo, ágil

spur /spɜr/ n espuela, f; aguijada, f; (of a bird) espolón, m; Bot. espuela, f; (of a mountain range) espolón, estribo, m; Fig. estímulo, m. —vt espolear, picar con la espuela; calzarse las espuelas; Fig. estimular, incitar. **on the s. of the moment**, bajo el impulso del momento

spurious /'spyuriəs/ a espurio; falso

spurn /spɜrn/ vt rechazar; tratar con desprecio; menospreciar

spurt /spɜrt/ vi (gush) chorrear, borbotar; brotar, surgir; (in racing, etc.) hacer un esfuerzo supremo. —vt hacer chorrear; lanzar. —n (jet) chorro, m; esfuerzo supremo, m

sputter /'spʌtər/ vi chisporrotear; crepitar; (of a pen) escupir; (of a person) balbucir

sputum /'spyutəm/ n esputo, m

spy /spai/ vt observar, discernir. —vi espiar, ser espía. —n espía, mf. **to spy out the land**, explorar el terreno. **to spy**

upon, espiar; seguir los pasos (a). **spyglass**, catalejo, *m*

squabble /'skwɒbəl/ *n* disputa, *f*; riña, *f*. —*vi* pelearse; disputar

squabbling /'skwɒblɪŋ/ *n* riñas, querellas, *f pl*; disputas, *f pl*

squad /skwɒd/ *n* escuadra, *f*; pelotón, *m*

squadron /'skwɒdrən/ *n* Mil. escuadrón, *m*; Nav. escuadra, *f*; Aer. escuadrilla, *f*; (of persons) pelotón, *m*. **s.-leader**, comandante, *m*

squalid /'skwɒlɪd/ *a* escuálido; (of quarrels, etc.) sórdido, mezquino

squall /skwɔl/ *vi* berrear; chillar. —*n* berrido, *m*; chillido, *m*; (storm) chubasco, turbión, *m*; (storm) chubasco, turbión, *m*; Fig. tormenta, tempestad, *f*

squalor /'skwɒlər/ *n* escualidez, *f*; sordidez, mezquindad, *f*

squander /'skwɒndər/ *vt* derrochar, tirar, desperdiciar; (time, etc.) malgastar

square /skwɛər/ *n* Math. cuadrado, *m*; rectángulo, *m*; (of a chessboard) escaque, *m*; (of a draughtboard and of graph paper) casilla, *f*; (in a town) plaza, *f*; (of troops) cuadro, *m*, *a* cuadrado; justo; igual; (honest) honrado, formal; (unambiguous) redondo, categórico; Math. cuadrado. **She wore a silk s. on her head**, Llevaba un pañuelo de seda en la cabeza. **five s. feet**, cinco pies cuadrados. **nine feet s.**, nueve pies en cuadro. **on the s.**, honradamente. **a s. dance**, contradanza, *f*. **a s. meal**, una buena comida. **s. dealing**, trato limpio, *m*. **The account is s.**, La cuenta está justa. **to get s. with**, desquitarse (de), vengarse de. **s. measure**, medida de superficie, *f*. **s. root**, raíz cuadrada, *f*. **s.-shouldered**, de hombros cuadrados

square /skwɛər/ *vt* cuadrar; escuadrar; (arrange) arreglar; (bribe) sobornar; (reconcile) acomodar; Math. cuadrar. —*vi* conformarse (con), cuadrar (con). **to s. the circle**, cuadrar el círculo. **to s. one's shoulders**, enderezarse. **to s. accounts with**, saldar cuentas con. **to s. up to**, (a person) avanzar belicosamente hacia

squarely /'skwɛərli/ *adv* en cuadro; directamente; sin ambigüedades, rotundamente; (honestly) de buena fe, honradamente

squash /skwɒʃ/ *vt* aplastar. —*vi* aplastarse; apretarse. —*n* aplastamiento, *m*; (of fruit, etc.) pulpa, *f*; (of people) agolpamiento, *m*; muchedumbre, *f*; (drink) refresco (de limón, etc.), *m*, (sport) frontón con raqueta, *m*

squat /skwɒt/ *vi* acuclillarse, agacharse, agazaparse ponerse en cuclillas; estar en cuclillas; (on land, etc.) apropiarse sin derecho. —*a* rechoncho

squatter /'skwɒtər/ *n* intruso (-sa); colono usurpador, *m*

squawk /skwɔk/ *vi* graznar; lanzar gritos agudos. —*n* graznido, *m*; grito agudo, *m*

squeak /skwik/ *vi* (of carts, etc.) chirriar, rechinar; (of shoes) crujir; (of persons,

mice, etc.) chillar; (slang) cantar. —*n* chirrido, crujido, *m*; chillido, *m*. **to have a narrow s.**, escapar por un pelo

squeal /skwil/ *vi* lanzar gritos agudos, chillar; (complain) quejarse; (slang) cantar. —*n* grito agudo, chillido, *m*

squeamish /'skwimɪʃ/ *a* que se marea fácilmente; mareado; (nauseated) asqueado; delicado; remilgado

squeeze /skwiz/ *vt* apretar; estrujar; (fruit) exprimir; (extort) arrancar; (money from) sangrar. —*n* (of the hand, etc.) apretón, *m*; estrujón, *m*; (of fruit juice) algunas gotas (de). **It was a tight s. in the car**, Íbamos muy apretados en el coche. **He was in a tight s.**, Se encontraba en un aprieto. **to s. one's way through the crowd**, abrirse camino a codazos por la muchedumbre. **to s. in**, *vt* hacer sitio para. —*vi* introducirse con dificultad (en)

squelch /skwɛltʃ/ *vi* gorgotear, chapotear. —*vt* aplastar

squib /skwɪb/ *n* (firework) rapapiés, buscapiés, *m*; (lampoon) pasquinada, *f*

squid /skwɪd/ *n* calamar, *m*

squint /skwɪnt/ *n* estrabismo, *m*; mirada furtiva, *f*; Inf. vistazo, *m*, mirada, *f*. —*vi* ser bizco; bizcar. **to s. at**, mirar de soslayo. **s.-eyed**, bizco. **to be s.-eyed**, mirar contra el gobierno

squire /skwaɪər/ *n* escudero, *m*; hacendado, *m*. —*vt* escoltar, acompañar

squirm /skwɜrm/ *vi* retorcerse; (with embarrassment) no saber dónde meterse. —*n* retorcimiento, *m*. **to s. along the ground**, arrastrarse por el suelo

squirrel /'skwɜrəl/ *n* ardilla, *f*

squirt /skwɜrt/ *vt* (liquids) lanzar. —*vi* chorrear, salir a chorros. —*n* chorro, *m*; (syringe) jeringa, *f*

stab /stæb/ *vt* apuñalar, dar de puñaladas (a); herir. —*n* puñalada, *f*; herida, *f*; (of pain, and Fig.) pinchazo, *m*. **a s. in the back**, una puñalada por la espalda

stability /stə'bɪlɪti/ *n* estabilidad, *f*; solidez, firmeza, *f*

stabilize /'steɪbə‚laɪz/ *vt* estabilizar

stable /'steɪbəl/ *a* estable; fijo, firme. —*n* cuadra, caballeriza, *f*; (for cows, etc.) establo, *m*. —*vt* poner en la cuadra; alojar. **s.-boy**, mozo de cuadra, *m*

stack /stæk/ *n* (of hay) niara, *f*, almiar, *m*; (heap) montón, *m*; (of rifles) pabellón, *m*; (of a chimney) cañón, *m*. —*vt* Agr. hacinar; amontonar; Mil. poner (las armas) en pabellón

stacked /stækt/ *a* (woman) abultada de pechera

stadium /'steɪdiəm/ *n* estadio, *m*

staff /stæf/ *n* vara, *f*; (bishop's, and Fig.) báculo, *m*; (pilgrim's) bordón, *m*; (pole) palo, *m*; (flagstaff) asta, *f*; (of an office, etc.) personal, *m*; (editorial) redacción, *f*; (corps) cuerpo, *m*; Mil. plana mayor, *f*, estado mayor, *m*; Mus. pentagrama, *m*. —*vt* proveer de personal. **general s.**, estado mayor general, *m*. **s. officer**, Mil. oficial de estado mayor, *m*

stag /stæg/ *n* ciervo, *m*. **s.-beetle,** ciervo volante, *m*. **s.-hunting,** caza del ciervo, *f*

stage /steidʒ/ *n* (for workmen) andamio, *m*; (of a microscope) portaobjetos, *m*; *Theat.* escena, *f*, tablas, *f pl*; teatro, *m*; (of development, etc.) etapa, *f*; fase, *f*. —*vt Theat.* escenificar, poner en escena; *Theat.* representar; (a demonstration, etc.) arreglar. **by easy stages,** poco a poco; (of a journey) a pequeñas etapas. **to come on the s.,** salir a la escena. **to go on the s.,** hacerse actor (actriz), dedicarse al teatro. **s. carpenter,** tramoyista, *m*. **s.-coach,** diligencia, *f*. **s.-craft,** arte de escribir para el teatro, *f*; arte escénica, *f*. **s.-direction,** acotación, *f*. **s.-door,** entrada de los artistas, *f*. **s.-effect,** efecto escénico, *m*. **s.-fright,** miedo al público, *m*. **s.-hand,** tramoyista, sacasillas, metesillas y sacamuertos, *m*. **s. manager,** director de escena, *m*. **s.-whisper,** aparte, *m*

stagger /stægər/ *vi* tambalear; andar haciendo eses; (hesitate) titubear, vacilar. —*vt* desconcertar. —*n* titubeo, tambaleo, *m*; *Aer.* decalaje, *m*. **staggered working hours,** horas de trabajo escalonadas, *f pl*

staggering /stægərɪŋ/ *a* tambaleante; (surprising) asombroso, sorprendente; (dreadful) espantoso. **a s. blow,** un golpe que derriba

stagnant /stægnənt/ *a* estancado; paralizado. **to be s.,** estar estancado. **s. water,** agua estancada, *f*

stagnate /stægneit/ *vi* estancarse; estar estancado; (of persons) vegetar

stagnation /stægˈneiʃən/ *n* (of water) estancación, *f*; estagnación, *f*; parálisis, *f*

staid /steid/ *a* serio, formal, juicioso

stain /stein/ *vt* manchar; (dye) teñir. —*n* mancha, *f*; colorante, *m*. **without a s.,** *Fig.* sin mancha. **stained glass,** vidrio de color, *m*. **s.-remover,** quitamanchas, *m*

stainless /steinlɪs/ *a* sin mancha; inmaculado, puro

stair /steɪr/ *n* escalón, peldaño, *m*; escalera, *f*; *pl* **stairs,** escalera, *f*. **a flight of stairs,** una escalera; un tramo de escaleras. **below stairs,** escalera abajo. **s.-carpet,** alfombra de escalera, *f*. **s.-rod,** varilla para alfombra de escalera, *f*

staircase /steərˌkeis/ *n* escalera, *f*. **spiral s.,** escalera de caracol, *f*

stake /steik/ *n* estaca, *f*; (for plants) rodrigón, *m*; (gaming) envite, *m*, apuesta, *f*; (in an undertaking) interés, *m*; *pl* **stakes,** (prize) premio, *m*; (race) carrera, *f*. —*vt* estacar; (plants) rodrigar; (bet) jugar. **at s.,** en juego; en peligro. **to be burnt at the s.,** morir en la hoguera. **to s. one's all,** jugarse el todo por el todo. **to s. a claim,** hacer una reclamación. **to s. out,** jalonar

stale /steil/ *a* no fresco; (of bread, etc.) duro, seco; (of air) viciado; viejo; pasado de moda; (tired) cansado

stalemate /steilˌmeit/ *n* (chess, checkers) tablas, *f pl*; *Fig.* punto muerto,

m. **to reach a s.,** llegar a un punto muerto

stalk /stɔk/ *n Bot.* tallo, *m*; *Bot.* pedúnculo, *m*; (of a glass) pie, *m*. —*vi* andar majestuosamente; *Fig.* rondar. —*vt* (game) cazar al acecho; (a person) seguir los pasos (a)

stall /stɔl/ *n* (in a stable) puesto (individual), *m*; (stable) establo, *m*; (choir) silla de coro, *f*; (in a fair, etc.) barraca, *f*, puesto, *m*; *Theat.* butaca, *f*; (finger-stall) dedal, *m*. —*vi* (an engine) cortar accidentalmente. —*vi Auto.* pararse de pronto; *Aer.* perder velocidad; (of a cart, etc.) atascarse. **pit s.,** *Theat.* butaca de platea, *f*

stallion /stælyən/ *n* semental, *m*

stalwart /stɔlwərt/ *a* robusto, fornido; leal; valiente

stamina /stæmənə/ *n* resistencia, *f*

stammer /stæmər/ *vi* tartamudear; (hesitate in speaking) titubear, balbucir. —*n* tartamudez, *f*; titubeo, balbuceo, *m*

stamp /stæmp/ *vt* estampar; imprimir; (documents) timbrar; pegar el sello de correo (a); (characterize) sellar; (*Fig.* engrave) grabar; (coins) acuñar; (press) apisonar; (with the foot) golpear con los pies, patear; (in dancing) zapatear. —*n* (with the foot) patada, *f*, golpe con los pies, *m*; (mark, etc.) marca, *f*; (rubber, etc.) estampilla, *f*; matasellos, *m*; cuño, *m*; (for documents) póliza, *f*; timbre, *m*; (for letters) sello, *m*; (machine) punzón, *m*; mano de mortero, *f*; (*Fig.* sign) sello, *m*; (kind) temple, *m*, clase, *f*. **The events of that day are stamped on my memory,** Los acontecimientos de aquel día están grabados en mi memoria. **to s. out,** (a fire, etc.) extinguir, apagar; (resistance, etc.) vencer; destruir. **postage-s.,** sello de correos, *m*. **s.-album,** álbum de sellos, *m*. **s.-duty,** impuesto del timbre, *m*. **s.-machine,** expendedor automático de sellos de correo, *m*

stampede /stæmˈpid/ *n* fuga precipitada, *f*; pánico, *m*. —*vi* huir precipitadamente; (of animals) salir en estampía; huir en desorden. —*vt* hacer perder la cabeza (a), sembrar el pánico entre

stance /stæns/ *n* posición de los pies, *f*; postura, *f*

stanch /stɔntʃ/ *vt* restañar

stand /stænd/ *vi* estar de pie; ponerse de pie, incorporarse; estar; hallarse; sostenerse; ser; ponerse; (halt) parar; (remain) permanecer, quedar. —*vt* poner; (endure) resistir; tolerar; sufrir; (entertain) convidar. **S.!** ¡Alto! **as things s.,** tal como están las cosas. **I cannot s. any more,** No puedo más. **I cannot s. him,** No le puedo ver. **Nothing stands between them and ruin,** No hay nada entre ellos y la ruina. **I stood him a drink,** Le convidé a un trago. **How do we s.?** ¿Cómo estamos? **It stands to reason that...,** Es lógico que... **Edward stands six feet,** Eduardo tiene seis pies de altura.

to s. accused of, ser acusado de. to s. godfather (or godmother) to, sacar de pila (a). to s. in need (of), necesitar, tener necesidad (de). to s. on end, (of hair) ponerse de punta, despeluzarse, to s. one in good stead, ser útil, ser ventajoso. to s. one's ground, no ceder, tenerse fuerte. to s. to attention, cuadrarse, permanecer en posición de firmes. to s. well with, tener buenas relaciones con, ser estimado de. to s. aside, tenerse a un lado; apartarse; (in favor of someone) retirarse. to s. back, quedarse atrás; recular, retroceder. to s. by, estar de pie cerca de; estar al lado de; estar presente (sin intervenir); ser espectador; estar preparado; (one's friends) ayudar, proteger; (a promise), etc.) atenerse (a); ser fiel (a); (of a ship) mantenerse listo. s.-by, n recurso, m. to s. for, representar; simbolizar; (mean) significar; (Parliament, etc.) presentarse como candidato; (put up with) tolerar, sufrir. to s. in, colaborar. to s. in with, estar de acuerdo con, ser partidario de; compartir. to s. off, mantenerse a distancia. to s. out, (in relief, and Fig. of persons) destacarse; (be firm) resistir, mantenerse firme; Naut. gobernar más afuera. S. out of the way! ¡Quítate del medio! to s. over, (be postponed) quedar aplazado. to s. up, estar de pie; ponerse de pie, incorporarse; tenerse derecho. to s. up against, resistir; oponerse a. to s. up for, defender; volverpor. to s. up to, hacer cara a

stand /stænd/ n puesto, m; posición, actitud, f; (for taxis, etc.) punto, m; (in a market, etc.) puesto, m; Sports. tribuna, f; (for a band) quiosco, m; (of a dish, etc.) pie, m; Mech. sostén, m; (opposition) resistencia, oposición, f. to make a s. against, oponerse resueltamente (a); ofrecer resistencia (a). to take one's s., fundarse (en), apoyarse (en). to take up one's s. by the fire, ponerse cerca del fuego

standard /'stændərd/ n (flag) estandárte, m, bandera, f; (for gold, weights, etc.) marco, m; norma, f; convención, regla, f; (of a lamp) pie, m; (pole) poste, m; columna, f; (level) nivel, m. —a corriente; normal; típico; clásico. It is a s. type, Es un tipo corriente. gold s., patrón de oro, m. s. author, autor clásico, m. s. formula, fórmula clásica, f. s. of living, nivel de vida, m. s.-bearer, abanderado, m. s.-lamp, lámpara vertical, f

standardization /,stændərdə'zeifən/ n (of armaments, etc.) unificación de tipos, f; (of dyestuffs, medicinals, etc.) control, m, estandardización, f

standardize /'stændər,daiz/ vt hacer uniforme; controlar

standing /'stændiŋ/ a de pie, derecho; permanente, fijo; constante. —n posición, f; reputación, f; importancia, f; antigüedad, f. It is a quarrel of long s., Es una

riña antigua. s. committee, comisión permanente, f. s. room, sitio para estar de pie, m. s. water, agua estancada, f.

standoffish, frío, etiquetero; altanero.

stand-offishness, frialdad, f; altanería, f.

standpoint, punto de vista, m

standstill /'stænd,stɪl/ n parada, f; pausa, f. at a s., parado; (of industry) paralizado

stanza /'stænzə/ n estrofa, estancia, f

staple /'steipəl/ n (fastener) grapa, f; (of wool, etc.) hebra, fibra, f; producto principal (de un pais), m; (raw material) materia prima, f; a principal; más importante; corriente

stapler /'steiplər/, (device) cosepapeles, engrapador, m, atrochadora (Argentina), f

star /star/ n (all meanings) estrella, f; (asterisk) asterisco, m. —vt estrellar, sembrar de estrellas; marcar con asterisco. —vi (Theat. cinema) presentarse como estrella, ser estrella. stars and stripes, las barras y las estrellas. to be born under a lucky s., tener estrella. to see stars, ver estrellas. s.-gazing, observación de las estrellas, f; ensimismamiento, m. s.-spangled, estrellado, tachonado de estrellas, sembrado de estrellas. s.-turn, gran atracción, f

starboard /'starbərd/ n Naut. estribor, m

starch /startʃ/ n almidón, m, las harinas, f pl, vt almidonar

stare /stɛər/ vi mirar fijamente; abrir mucho los ojos. —n mirada fija, f. stony s., mirada dura, f. to s. at, (a person) clavar la mirada en; mirar de hito en hito (a). The explanation stares one in the face, La explicación salta a la vista (or está evidente). to s. into space, mirar las telarañas. to s. out of countenance, avergonzar con la mirada

stark /stark/ a rígido; Poet. poderoso; absoluto. s. staring mad, loco de atar. s.-naked, en cueros vivos, en pelota

start /start/ vi estremecerse, asustarse; saltar; (set out) salir; ponerse en camino; (of a train, a race) arrancar; ponerse en marcha; Aer. despegar; (begin) empezar; (of timbers) combarse. —vt empezar; (a car, etc.) poner en marcha; (a race) dar la señal de partida; (a hare, etc.) levantar; (cause) provocar, causar; (a discussion, etc.) abrir; iniciar. —n (fright) susto, m; (setting out) partida, salida, f; (beginning) principio, comienzo, m; (starting-point of a race) arrancadero, m; Aer. despegue, m; (advantage) ventaja, f. at the s., al principio. for a s., para empezar. from s. to finish, desde el principio hasta el fin. She started to cry, Se puso a llorar. He has started his journey to Canada, Ha empezado su viaje al Canadá. I started up the engine, Puse el motor en marcha. to get a s., asustarse; tomar la delantera. to give (a person) a s., asustar, dar un susto (a); dar la ventaja (a). to give (a person) a s. in life, ayudar a alguien a situarse en la vida. to make a fresh s. (in life), hacer vida nueva, empezar la vida de nuevo. **to s. after,** lanzarse en busca de; salir tras. **to s. back,** retroceder; emprender el viaje de regreso; marcharse. **to s. off,** salir, partir; ponerse en camino. **to s. up,** *vi* incorporarse bruscamente, ponerse de pie de un salto; (appear) surgir, aparecer. —*vt* (an engine) poner en marcha

starter /'stɑrtər/ *n* iniciador (-ra); (for a race) starter, juez de salida, *m*; (competitor in a race) corredor, *m*; (of a car, etc.) arranque, *m*

starting /'stɑrtɪŋ/ *n* (setting out) salida, partida, *f*; (beginning) principio, *m*; (fear) estremecimiento, *m*; susto, *m*. **s.-gear,** palanca de arranque, *f*. **s.-handle,** manivela de arranque, *f*. **s.-point,** punto de partida, *m*. *Fig*. arrancadero, punto de arranque, *m*. **s.-post,** puesto de salida, *m*

startle /'stɑrtl/ *vt* asustar, sobresaltar, alarmar. **The news startled him out of his indifference,** Las noticias le hicieron salir de su indiferencia

startling /'stɑrtlɪŋ/ *a* alarmante; (of dress, etc.) exagerado; (of colors) chillón

starvation /stɑr'veɪʃən/ *n* hambre, *f*; *Med*. inanición, *f*. **s. diet,** régimen de hambre, *m*. **s. wage,** ración de hambre, *f*

starve /stɑrv/ *vi* morir de hambre; pasar hambre, no tener bastante que comer; no comer. —*vt* matar de hambre; privar de alimentos (a). **I am simply starving,** Tengo una hambre canina, Me muero de hambre. **to s. with cold,** *vi* morir de frío. —*vt* matar de frío

starved /stɑrvd/ *a* muerto de hambre, hambriento. **s. of affection,** hambriento de cariño

state /steɪt/ *n* estado, *m*; condición, *f*; (anxiety) agitación, ansiedad, *f*; (social) rango, *m*; (pomp) magnificencia, pompa, *f*; (government, etc.) Estado, *m*; nación, *f*. —*a* de Estado; de gala, de ceremonia. **the married s.,** el estado matrimonial. **s. of war,** estado de guerra. **in s.,** con gran pompa. **to lie in s.,** (of a body) estar expuesto. **s. apartments,** habitaciones de gala, *f pl*. **s. banquet,** comida de gala, *f*. **s. coach,** coche de gala, *m*. **s. control,** control por el Estado, *m*. **S. Department,** Ministerio de Estado, *m*. **s. education,** instrucción pública, *f*. **State of the Union message,** Mensaje al Congreso, *m*. **s. papers,** documentos de Estado, *m pl*

state /steɪt/ *vt* decir (que); afirmar (que); (one's case, etc.) exponer; explicar; *Math*. proponer

statecraft /'steɪt,kræft/ *n* arte de gobernar, *m*

stated /'steɪtɪd/ *a* arreglado, indicado; fijo. **the s. date,** la fecha indicada. **at s. intervals,** a intervalos fijos

statehood /'steɪthʊd/ *n* estadidad, *f*

stately /'steɪtli/ *a* majestuoso; imponente; noble; digno

statement /'steɪtmənt/ *n* afirmación, declaración, *f*; resumen, *m*; exposición, *f*;

Law. deposición, *f*; *Com*. estado de cuenta, *m*. **to make a s.,** hacer una declaración

stateroom /'steɪt,rum/ *n* sala de recepción, *f*; (on a ship) camarote, *m*

statesman /'steɪtsmən/ *n* hombre de estado, *m*

static /'stætɪk/ *a* estático

station /'steɪʃən/ *n* (place) puesto, sitio, *m*; (*Rail.* and *Eccl.*) estación, *f*; (social) posición social, *f*; *Naut*. apostadero, *m*; *Surv*. punto de marca, *m*. —*vt* estacionar, colocar, poner. **to s. oneself,** colocarse. **Stations of the Cross,** Estaciones, *f pl*. **s.-master,** jefe de la estación, *m*

stationary /'steɪʃə,nɛri/ *a* estacionario; inmóvil; *Astron*. estacional

stationer /'steɪʃənər/ *n* papelero (-ra). **stationer's shop,** papelería, *f*

stationery /'steɪʃə,nɛri/ *n* papelería, *f*, efectos de escritorio, *m pl*; papel de escribir, *m*

station wagon *n* pisicorre, coche camioneta, coche rural, *m*

statistical /stə'tɪstɪkəl/ *a* estadístico

statistician /,stætɪs'tɪʃən/ *n* estadista, *m*

statistics /stə'tɪstɪks/ *n* estadística, *f*

statue /'stætʃu/ *n* estatua, *f*; imagen, *f*

statuesque /,stætʃu'ɛsk/ *a* escultural

statuette /,stætʃu'ɛt/ *n* figurilla, *f*

stature /'stætʃər/ *n* estatura, *f*; (moral, etc.) valor, *m*

status /'steɪtəs, 'stætəs/ *n* (*Law*. etc.) estado, *m*; posición, *f*; rango, *m*. **What is his s. as a physicist?** ¿Cómo se le considera entre los físicos? **social s.,** posición social, *f*; rango social, *m*

statute /'stætʃut/ *n* ley, *f*; acto legislativo, *m*; estatuto, *m*; regla, *f*. **s. book,** código legal, *m*

statutory /'stætʃu,tɔri/ *a* establecido; reglamentario; estatutario

staunch /stɔntʃ/ *a* leal, fiel; firme, constante. —*vt* restañar

stave /steɪv/ *n* (of a barrel, etc.) duela, *f*; (of a ladder) peldaño, *m*; (stanza) estrofa, *f*; *Mus*. pentagrama, *m*. **to s. in,** abrir boquete en; romper a golpes; quebrar. **to s. off,** apartar, alejar; (delay) aplazar, diferir; (avoid) evitar; (thirst, etc.) dominar

stay /steɪ/ *vt* detener; (a judgment, etc.) suspender. —*vi* permanecer; quedarse; detenerse; (of weather, etc.) durar; (lodge) hospedarse, vivir. **to come to s.,** venir a ser permanente. **to s. a person's hand,** detenerle a fulano el brazo. **to s. at home,** quedarse en casa. **s.-at-home,** *a* casero. —*n* persona casera, *f*. **to s. the course,** terminar la carrera. **S.! Say no more!** ¡Calle! ¡No diga más! **to s. away,** ausentarse. **to s. up,** no acostarse; velar. **to s. with,** quedarse con; alojarse con; quedarse en casa de, vivir con

stay /steɪ/ *n* estancia, permanencia, *f*; residencia, *f*; (restraint) freno, *m*; *Law*. suspensión, *f*; (endurance) aguante, *m*, resistencia, *f*; *Naut*. estay, *m*; (prop) puntal, *m; Fig.* apoyo, soporte, *m; pl* **stays,** corsé, *m*

stead /stɛd/ *n* lugar, *m.* **in the s. of,** en el lugar de, como substituto de. **It has stood me in good s.,** Me ha sido muy útil

steadfast /'stɛd,fæst/ *a* fijo; constante; firme; tenaz. **s. gaze,** mirada fija, *f*

steadily /'stɛdli/ *adv* firmemente; (without stopping) sin parar; continuamente; (assiduously) diligentemente; (uniformly) uniformemente. **Prices have gone up s.,** Los precios no han dejado de subir. **He looked at it s.,** Lo miraba sin pestañear (or fijamente)

steady /'stɛdi/ *a* firme; seguro; fijo; constante; uniforme; continuo; estacionario; (of persons) serio, formal, juicioso; (of workers) diligente, asiduo. —*vt* afirmar; (persons) hacer más serio (a); (nerves, etc.) calmar, fortificar. **a s. job,** un empleo seguro. **S.!** ¡Calma!; *Naut.* ¡Seguro! **He steadied himself against the table,** Se apoyó en la mesa

steak /steik/ *n* tajada, *f;* biftec, *m*

steal /stil/ *vt* robar, hurtar; tomar. —*vi* robar, ser ladrón; (glide) deslizarse; (overwhelm) dominar, ganar insensiblemente (a). **to s. a kiss,** robar un beso. **to s. a look,** mirar de soslayo (or de lado). **to s. away,** escurrirse, escabullirse; marcharse a hurtadillas. **to s. in,** deslizarse en, colarse en

stealthy /'stɛlθi/ *a* furtivo; cauteloso

steam /stim/ *n* vapor, *m.* —*a* de vapor. —*vi* echar vapor. —*vt Cul.* cocer al vapor; (clothes) mojar; (windows, etc.) empañar. **to have the s. up,** estar bajo presión. **The windows are steamed,** Los cristales están empañados. **s.-boiler,** caldera de vapor, *f.* **s.-engine,** máquina de vapor, *f.* **s.-hammer,** maza de fragua, *f.* **s.-heat,** calefacción por vapor, *f.* **s.-roller,** *Lit.* apisonadora, *Fig.* fuerza arrolladora, *f*

steamship /'stim,ʃɪp/ *n* buque de vapor, piróscafo, *m*

steel /stil/ *n* (metal, and *Poet.* sword) acero, *m;* (for sharpening) afilón, *m.* —*a* de acero; acerado. —*vt* acerar; *Fig.* endurecer. **to be made of s.,** *Fig.* ser de bronce. **He cannot s. himself to do it,** No puede persuadirse a hacerlo. **to s. one's heart,** hacerse duro de corazón. **cold s.,** arma blanca, *f.* **stainless s.,** acero inoxidable, *m.* **s.-engraving,** grabado en acero, *m*

steel mill *n* fábrica de acero, *f*

steep /stip/ *a* acantilado, escarpado; precipitoso; (of stairs, etc.) empinado; (of price) exorbitante. —*vt* (soak) remojar, empapar; *Fig.* absorber; (in a subject) empaparse (en). —*n* remojo, *m.* **It's a bit s.!** *Inf.* ¡Es un poco demasiado!

steeple /'stipəl/ *n* campanario, *m,* torre, *f;* aguja, *f*

steer /stɪər/ *vt Naut.* gobernar; (a car, etc.) conducir; *Fig.* guiar, conducir. —*vi Naut.* timonear; *Naut.* navegar; *Auto.*

conducir. —*n Zool.* novillo, *m.* **to s. clear of,** evitar. **to s. one's way through the crowd,** abrirse paso entre la muchedumbre

steerage /'stɪərɪdʒ/ *n* gobierno, *m;* (stern) popa, *f;* (quarters) entrepuente, *m.* **to go s.,** viajar en tercera clase

steering /'stɪrɪŋ/ *n Naut.* gobierno, *m;* (tiller, etc.) gobernalle, timón, *m;* (of a vehicle) conducción, *f.* **s.-column,** barra de dirección, *f.* **s.-wheel,** *Auto.* volante de dirección, *m; Naut.* rueda del timón, *f*

stem /stɛm/ *n* (of a tree) tronco, *m;* (of a plant) tallo, *m;* (of a glass, etc.) pie, *m;* (*Mus.* of a note) rabo, *m;* (of a pipe) tubo, *m;* (of a word) radical, *m.* —*vt* (check) contener; (the tide) ir contra; (the current) vencer; (dam) estancar. **from s. to stern,** de proa a popa

stench /stɛntʃ/ *n* tufo, hedor, *m,* hediondez, *f*

stencil /'stɛnsəl/ *n* patrón para estarcir, *m;* estarcido, *m.* —*vt* estarcir

stenography /stə'nɒgrəfi/ *n* estenografía, taquigrafía, *f*

step /stɛp/ *n* paso, *m;* (footprint) huella, *f;* (measure) medida, *f;* (of a stair, etc.) escalón, peldaño, *m,* grada, *f;* (of a ladder) peldaño, *m;* (of vehicles) estribo, *m;* (grade) escalón, *m; Mus.* intervalo, *m.* **at every s.,** a cada paso. **flight of steps,** escalera, *f;* (before a building, etc.) escalinata, *f.* **in steps,** en escalones. **to bend one's steps towards,** dirigirse hacia. **to keep in s.,** llevar el paso. **to take a s.,** dar un paso. **to take steps,** tomar medidas. **s. by s.,** paso a paso; poco a poco. **s.-dance,** baile típico, *m.* **s.-ladder,** escalera de tijera, *f*

step /stɛp/ *vi* dar un paso; pisar; andar. **Please s. in!** Sírvase de entrar. **Will you s. this way, please?** ¡Haga el favor de venir por aquí! **to s. aside,** ponerse a un lado; desviarse; *Fig.* retirarse (en favor de). **to s. in,** entrar; intervenir (en); (meddle) entrometerse. **He stepped into the train,** Subió al tren. **to s. on,** pisar. **to s. on board,** *Naut.* ir a bordo. **to s. out,** salir; (from a vehicle) bajar; (a dance) bailar. **He stepped out a moment ago,** Salió hace un instante

stepbrother /'stɛp,brʌðər/ *n* hermanastro, medio hermano, *m*

stepchild /'stɛp,tʃaɪld/ *n* hijastro (-ra)

stepdaughter /'stɛp,dɔtər/ *n* hijastra, *f*

stepfather /'stɛp,faðər/ *n* padrastro, *m*

stepmother /'stɛp,mʌðər/ *n* madrastra, *f*

steppingstone /'stɛpɪŋ,stoun/ *n* pasadera, *f; Fig.* escabel, escalón, *m*

stepsister /'stɛp,sɪstər/ *n* hermanastra, media hermana, *f*

stepson /'stɛp,sʌn/ *n* hijastro, *m*

stereotype /'stɛriə,taip/ *n* estereotipia, *f,* clisé, *m, vt* (*Print.* and *Fig.*) estereotipar

sterile /'stɛrɪl/ *a* estéril; árido

sterility /stə'rɪlɪti/ *n* esterilidad, *f;* aridez, *f*

sterilize /'stɛrə,laiz/ *vt* esterilizar

sterling /'stɜrlɪŋ/ a esterlina f; Fig. genuino. **pound s.,** libra esterlina, f

stern /stɜrn/ a severo, austero; duro. —n Naut. popa, f

stevedore /'stivɪˌdɔr/ n estibador, m

stew /stu/ vt guisar a la cazuela, estofar; (mutton, etc.) hervir; (fruit) cocer. —n estofado, m; Inf. agitación, f. **to be in a s.,** Inf. sudar la gota gorda. **stewed fruit,** compota de frutas, f. **s.-pot,** cazuela, olla, f, puchero, m

steward /'stuərd/ n administrador, m; mayordomo, m; (provision) despensero, m; Naut. camarero, m

stewardess /'stuərdɪs/ n Naut. camarera, f

stick /stɪk/ vt clavar (en), hundir (en); (put) poner; sacar; (stamps, etc.) pegar; fijar; (endure) resistir; tolerar. —vi clavarse, hundirse; estar clavado; pegarse; (remain) quedar; (in the mud, etc.) atascarse, embarrancarse, (on a reef) encallarse; (in the throat, etc.) atravesarse; (stop) detenerse. **It sticks in my throat,** Inf. No lo puedo tragar. **Friends always s. together,** Los amigos no se abandonan. **The nickname stuck to him,** El apodo se le quedó. **to s. at,** persistir en; desistir (ante); pararse (ante); tener escrúpulos sobre. **to s. at nothing,** no tener escrúpulos. **He stuck at his work,** Siguió trabajando. **to s. down,** pegar. **to s. out,** vi proyectar; sobresalir. —vt (one's chest) inflar; (one's tongue) sacar. **His ears s. out,** Tiene las orejas salientes. **to s. to,** (one's job) no dejar; (one's plans) adherirse (a); (one's principles) ser fiel (a); (one's friends) no abandonar; (one's word, etc.) cumplir; atenerse a. **to s. up,** vi (of hair) erizarse, ponerse de punta: salirse. —vt clavar; (a notice) fijar. **to s. up for,** (a person) defender

stick /stɪk/ n estaca, f; (for the fire) leña, f; (walking-s.) bastón, m; (of office) vara, f; (of sealing-wax, etc.) barra, f; palo, m; (baton) batuta, f; (of celery) tallo, m. **in a cleft s.,** entre la espada y la pared. **to give** (a person) **the s.,** dar palo (a)

stickler /'stɪklər/ n rigorista, mf. **to be a s. for etiquette,** ser etiquetero

sticky /'stɪki/ a pegajoso, viscoso; Fig. difícil

stiff /stɪf/ a rígido; inflexible; tieso; (of paste, etc.) espeso; (of manner) distante; (of a bow, etc.) frío; (of a person) almidonado, etiquetero; severo; (of examinations, etc.) difícil; (strong) fuerte; (of price, etc.) alto, exorbitante; (of a shirt front, etc.) duro. **s. with cold,** aterido de frío. **s. neck,** torticolis, m. **s.-necked,** terco, obstinado

stiffen /'stɪfən/ vt reforzar; atiesar; (paste, etc.) hacer más espeso; (Fig. strengthen) robustecer; (make more obstinate) hacer más tenaz. —vi atiesarse; endurecerse; (straighten oneself) enderezarse; (of manner) volverse menos cordial; (become firmer) robustecerse;

(become more obstinate) hacerse más tenaz. **The breeze stiffened,** Refrescó el viento

stifle /'staifəl/ vt ahogar, sofocar; apagar; suprimir

stigma /'stɪgmə/ n estigma, m

stile /stail/ n (nearest equivalent) portilla con escalones, f

still /stɪl/ a tranquilo; inmóvil; quedo; silencioso; (of wine) no espumoso. —n silencio, m. **in the s. of the night,** en el silencio de la noche. **Keep s.!** ¡Estate quieto! **to keep s.,** quedarse inmóvil, no moverse. **s.-birth,** nacimiento de un niño muerto, m. **s.-born,** nacido muerto. **s. life,** Art. bodegón, m, naturaleza muerta, f

still /stɪl/ vt hacer callar, acallar; calmar, tranquilizar; apaciguar; (pain) aliviar

still /stɪl/ adv todavía, aún; (nevertheless) sin embargo, no obstante; (always) siempre. **I think she s. visits them every week,** Me parece que sigue visitándoles cada semana. **s. and all,** con todo y eso. **s. more,** aún más

still /stɪl/ n alambique, m. **salt water s.,** adrazo, m

stillness /'stɪlnɪs/ n quietud, tranquilidad, f; silencio, m. **in the s. of the night,** en el silencio de la noche

stilted /'stɪltɪd/ a ampuloso, campanudo, hinchado

stimulant /'stɪmyələnt/ a and n estimulante, m

stimulate /'stɪmyəˌleit/ vt estimular; incitar (a), excitar (a)

stimulating /'stɪmyəˌleitɪŋ/ a estimulante; (encouraging) alentador; (inspiring) sugestivo, inspirador

stimulation /ˌstɪmyəˈleiʃən/ n excitación, f; (stimulus) estímulo, m

stimulus /'stɪmyələs/ n estímulo, m; Med. estimulante, m; (incentive) impulso, incentivo, m; acicate, aguijón, m

sting /stɪŋ/ vt picar, pinchar; (of snakes, etc.) morder; (of hot dishes) resquemar; (of hail, etc.) azotar; (pain) atormentar; (provoke) provocar (a), incitar (a). —n (Zool. organ) aguijón, m; Bot. púa, f; (of a scorpion) uña, f; (of a serpent) colmillo, m; (pain and wound) pinchazo, m; (serpent's) mordedura, f; (stimulus) acicate, estímulo, m; (torment) tormento, dolor, m

stingy /'stɪndʒi/ a tacaño, avaro, mezquino

stink /stɪŋk/ vi apestar, heder, oler mal. —n tufo, m, hediondez, f

stinking /'stɪŋkɪŋ/ a apestoso, hediondo, fétido, mal oliente

stint /stɪnt/ vt escatimar; limitar. —n límite, m, restricción, f. **without s.,** sin límite; sin restricción

stipend /'staipɛnd/ n estipendio, salario, m

stipulate /'stɪpyəˌleit/ vi estipular, poner como condición. —vt estipular, especificar. **They stipulated for a five-day**

week, Pusieron como condición (*or* Estipularon) que trabajasen cinco días por semana

stir /stɜr/ *vt* agitar; revolver; (the fire) atizar; (move) mover; (emotionally) conmover, impresionar; (the imagination) estimular. —*vi* moverse. —*n* movimiento, *m;* conmoción, *f;* (bustle) bullicio, *m;* sensación, *f.* **to make a s.,** causar una sensación. **to s. one's coffee,** revolver el café. **to s. up discontent,** fomentar el descontento

stirring /ˈstɜrɪŋ/ *a* conmovedor, emocionante, impresionante; (of times, etc.) turbulento, agitado

stirrup /ˈstɜrəp, ˈstɪr-/ *n* estribo, *m.* **s.-cup,** última copa, *f.* **s.-pump,** bomba de mano (para líquidos), *f*

stitch /stɪtʃ/ *n* (action) puntada, *f;* (result) punto, *m; Surg.* punto de sutura, *m;* (pain) punzada, *f,* pinchazo, *m.* —*vt* coser; *Surg.* suturar

stock /stɒk/ *n* (of a tree) tronco, *m;* (of a rifle) culata, *f;* (handle) mango, *m;* (of a horse's tail) nabo, *m;* (stem for grafting etc.) injerto, *m;* (race) raza, *f;* (lineage) linaje, *m,* estirpe, *f;* (supply) provisión, *f;* reserva, *f;* (of merchandise) surtido, *m; Cul.* caldo, *m;* (collar) alzacuello, *m; Bot.* alhelí, *m;* (government) papel del estado, *m,* valores públicos, *m pl;* (financial) valores, *m pl,* (of a company) capital, *m; pl* **stocks,** *Hist.* cepo, *m;* (of goods) existencias, *f pl,* stock, *m,* a corriente; del repertorio. **in s.** en existencia. **lives.,** ganado *m.* **rolling-s.,** *Rail.* materia móvil ferroviario, *m.* **s. phrase** frase hecha, *f.* **s. size,** talla corriente, *f.* **to lay in a s. of,** hacer provisión de, almacenar, **to stand s.-still,** quedarse completamente inmóvil. **to take s.,** *Com.* hacer inventario. **to take s. of,** inventariar; examinar, considerar. **s.-breeder,** ganadero, *m.* **s.-broker,** corredor de bolsa, bolsista, *m.* **s. exchange,** bolsa, *f.* **s.-in-hand,** *Com.* existencias, *f pl.* **s.-in-trade** (*Com.* etc.) capital, *m.* **s.-raising,** cría de ganados, ganadería, *f.* **s.-taking,** *Com.* inventario, *m*

stock /stɒk/ *vt* proveer (de), abastecer (de); (of shops) tener existencia de

stockade /stɒˈkeɪd/ *n* estacada, empalizada, *f, vt* empalizar

stocking /ˈstɒkɪŋ/ *n* media, *f.* **nylon stockings,** medias de cristal (or de nilón), *f pl*

stocky /ˈstɒki/ *a* rechoncho, doblado, achaparrado

stodgy /ˈstɒdʒi/ *a* (of food) indigesto; (of style, etc.) pesado, amazacotado

stoic /ˈstoʊɪk/ *a and n* estoico (-ca)

stoke /stoʊk/ *vt* (a furnace, etc.) cargar, alimentar; (a fire) echar carbón, etc., en. **s.-hole,** cuarto de fogoneros, *m; Naut.* cámara de calderas, *f*

stole /stoʊl/ *n* (*Eccl.* and of fur, etc.) estola, *f*

stolid /ˈstɒlɪd/ *a* impasible, imperturbable

stomach /ˈstʌmək/ *n* estómago, vientre, *m;* apetito, estómago, *m;* (courage) corazón, valor, *m.* —*vt* digerir; (tolerate) tragar, sufrir. **s.ache,** dolor de estómago, *m*

stone /stoʊn/ *n* piedra, *f;* (gem) piedra preciosa, *f;* (of cherries, etc.) hueso, *m;* (of grapes, etc.) pepita, *f; Med.* cálculo, *m.* —*a* de piedra. —*vt* apedrear; (a wall, etc.) revestir de piedra; (fruit) deshuesar. **to pave with stones,** empedrar. **to leave no s. unturned,** no dejar piedra sin remover. **within a stone's throw,** a corta distancia, a un paso. **S. Age,** edad de piedra, *f.* **s.-breaker,** cantero, picapedrero, *m.* **s.-cold,** muy frío, completamente frío. **s.-deaf,** *a* completamente sordo. **s.-fruit,** fruta de hueso, *f.* **s.-mason,** mazonero, albañil, *m;* picapedrero, *m.* **s.-quarry,** pedrera, cantera, *f*

stony /ˈstoʊni/ *a* pedregoso; (of hearts, etc.) duro, insensible, empedernido; (of a stare, etc.) fijo, duro

stool /stul/ *n* banquillo, taburete, *m;* (feces) excremento, *m*

stoop /stup/ *vi* inclinarse, doblarse; encorvarse; ser cargado de espaldas; andar encorvado; (demean oneself) rebajarse (a). —*vt* inclinar, doblar. —*n* inclinación, *f;* cargazón de espaldas, *f*

stop /stɒp/ *vt* (a hole) obstruir, atascar; (a leak) cegar, tapar; (a tooth) empastar; (stanch) restañar; (the traffic, etc.) parar; detener; (prevent) evitar; (discontinue) cesar (de), dejarse de; (cut off) cortar; (end) poner fin (a), acabar con; (payment) suspender. —*vi* parar; detenerse; cesar; terminar; (stay) quedarse, permanecer. **I stopped myself from saying what I thought,** Me abstuve de decir lo que pensaba, Me mordí la lengua. **They stopped the food-supply,** Cortaron las provisiones. **to s. beating about the bush,** dejarse de historias. **to s. one's ears,** *Fig.* taparse los oídos. **to s. payments,** suspender pagos

stop /stɒp/ *n* parada, *f;* pausa, *f;* interrupción, *f;* cesación, *f;* (of an organ) registro, *m.* **"Stop,"** (road sign) «Alto.» **full s.,** *Gram.* punto, *m.* **tram s.,** parada de tranvía, *f.* **to come to a full s.,** pararse de golpe; cesar súbitamente. **to put a s. to,** poner fin a, poner coto a, acabar con. *f pl.* **s.-watch,** cronógrafo, *m*

stopgap /ˈstɒpˌɡæp/ *n* (person) tapagujeros, *m;* substituto, *m*

stoppage /ˈstɒpɪdʒ/ *n* parada, *f;* cesación, *f;* suspensión, *f;* interrupción, *f;* pausa, *f;* (obstruction) impedimento, *m;* obstrucción, *f.* **s. of work,** suspensión de trabajo, *f*

stopper /ˈstɒpər/ *n* tapón, *m;* obturador, *m, vt* cerrar con tapón, taponar

stopping /ˈstɒpɪŋ/ *n* parada, *f;* cesación, *f;* suspensión, *f;* (of a tooth) empaste, *m.* **without s.,** sin parar. **without s. to draw breath,** de un aliento. **s.-place,** paradero, *m;* (of buses, etc.) parada, *f.* **s.**

train, tren ómnibus, *m.* **s. up,** obturación, *f*

storage /'stɔrɪdʒ/ *n* almacenamiento, *m;* (charge) almacenaje, *m;* (place) depósito, *m.* **cold s.,** cámara frigorífica, *f.* **s. battery,** acumulador, *m*

store /stɔr/ *n* provisión, *f;* abundancia, *f;* reserva, *f;* (of knowledge, etc.) tesoro, *m;* (for furniture, etc.) depósito, almacén, *m; pl* **stores,** (shop) almacenes, *m pl;* (food) provisiones, *f pl; (Mil.* etc.) pertrechos, *m pl.* —*vt* proveer; guardar, acumular; tener en reserva; (furniture, etc.) almacenar; (hold) caber en, tomar. **in s.,** en reserva; en depósito, en almacén. **to set s. by,** estimar en mucho; dar importancia a. **to set little s. by,** estimar en poco; conceder poca importancia a. **s.-room,** despensa, *f*

storehouse /'stɔr,haus/ *n* almacén, *m; Fig.* mina, *f,* tesoro, *m*

stork /stɔrk/ *n* cigüeña, *f*

storm /stɔrm/ *n* tempestad, tormenta, *f,* temporal, *m; Fig.* tempestad, *f; Mil.* asalto, *m* —*vt Mil.* tomar por asalto, asaltar. —*vi* (of persons) bramar de cólera. **to take by s.,** tomar por asalto; *Fig.* cautivar, conquistar. **s. cloud,** nubarrón, *m.* **s.-signal,** señal de temporal, *f.* **s.-tossed,** *a* sacudido por la tempestad. **s. troops,** tropas de asalto, *f pl.* **s. window,** contravidriera, *f*

stormy /'stɔrmi/ *a* tempestuoso; de tormenta; (of life, etc.) borrascoso; (of meetings, etc.) tempestuoso

story /'stɔri/ *n* historia, *f;* cuento, *m;* anécdota, *f;* (funny) chiste, *m;* (plot) argumento, enredo, *m;* (fib) mentira, *f;* (floor) piso *m.* **It's always the same old s.,** Es siempre la misma canción (or historia). **That is quite another s.,** Eso es harina de otro costal. **short s.,** cuento, *m.* **s. book,** libro de cuentos, *m.* **s. teller,** cuentista, *mf;* (fibber) mentiroso (-sa)

stout /staut/ *a* fuerte; (brave) intrépido, indómito; (fat) gordo, grueso; (firm) sólido, firme; (decided) resuelto, vigoroso. —*n* (drink) cerveza negra, *f.* **s.-hearted,** valiente, intrépido

stove /stouv/ *n* estufa, *f;* (open, for cooking) cocina económica, *f;* (gas, etc., for cooking) cocina, *f,* fogón, *m.* **s. pipe,** tubo de la chimenea, *m*

stow /stou/ *vt* meter, poner; colocar; (hide) esconder; (cargo) estibar, arrimar

stowaway /'stoua,wei/ *n* polizón, llovido, *m, vi* embarcarse secretamente

straddle /'strædl/ *vi (Nav.* etc.) graduar el tiro. —*vt* montar a horcajadas en. **s.-legged,** patiabierto

strafe /streif/ *vt* bombardear concentradamente; castigar; reñir

straggle /'strægəl/ *vi* rezagarse; vagar en desorden; dispersarse; estar esparcido; extenderse

straight /streit/ *a* derecho; recto; (of hair) lacio; directo; (tidy) en orden; (frank) franco; (honest) honrado. —*adv* derecho; en línea recta; directamente.

Keep s. on! ¡Siga Vd. derecho! **to go s. to the point,** dejarse de rodeos; ir al grano. **to look s. in the eyes,** mirar derecho en los ojos. **s. away,** inmediatamente, en seguida. **s. out,** sin rodeos

straighten /'streitn/ *vt* enderezar; poner derecho; poner en orden; arreglar. —*vi* ponerse derecho; enderezarse. **to s. one's face,** componer el semblante. **to s. the line,** *Mil.* rectificar el frente. **to s. out,** poner en orden; *Fig.* desenredar. **to s. oneself up,** erguirse

straightforward /,streit'fɔrwərd/ *a* honrado, sincero; franco; (simple) sencillo. **s. answer,** respuesta directa, *f*

straightway /'streit'wei, -,wei/ *adv* al instante, inmediatamente

strain /strein/ *vt* estirar, forzar; esforzar; (one's eyes) quebrarse; (one's ears) aguzar (el oído); (a muscle, etc.) torcer; (a friendship) pedir demasiado (a), exigir demasiado (de); (a person's patience, etc.) abusar (de); (words) tergiversar; (embrace) abrazar estrechamente (a); (filter) filtrar; *Cul.* colar. —*vi* hacer un gran esfuerzo, esforzarse (para). —*n* tirantez, *f;* tensión, *f;* (effort) esfuerzo, *m;* (sprain) torcedura, *f;* (nervous) tensión nerviosa, *f; Mech.* esfuerzo, *m;* (breed) raza, *f; Biol.* cepa, *f;* (tendency) tendencia, *f;* (heredity) herencia, *f;* rasgo, *m,* vena, *f;* (style) estilo, *m; Mus.* melodía, *f;* (of mirth, etc.) son, ruido, *m;* (poetry) poesía, *f.* **to s. a point,** hacer una excepción. **to s. after effect,** buscar demasiado el efecto

strained /streind/ *a* tenso; (of muscles, etc.) torcido; (of smiles, etc.) forzado. **s. relations,** *Polit.* estado de tirantez, *m*

strainer /'streinər/ *n* filtro, *m;* coladero, *m*

strait /streit/ *n Geog.* estrecho, *m.* **to be in great straits,** estar en un apuro. **s. laced,** *Fig.* de manga estrecha

straiten /'streitn/ *vt* estrechar; limitar, **in straitened circumstances,** en la necesidad

Strait of Magellan /mə'dʒɛlən/ Estrecho de Magallanes, *m*

strand /strænd/ *n* (shore) playa, *f;* (of a river) ribera, orilla, *f;* (of rope) cabo, ramal, *m;* (of thread, etc.) hebra, *f;* (of hair) trenza, *f.* —*vt* and *vi* (a ship) encallar, varar. **to be stranded,** hallarse abandonado; (by missing a train, etc.) quedarse colgado. **to leave stranded,** abandonar, dejar plantado (a)

strange /streindʒ/ *a* (unknown) desconocido; nuevo; (exotic, etc.) extraño, singular; extraordinario; raro; exótico. **I felt very s. in a s. country,** Me sentía muy solo en un país desconocido. **He is a very s. person,** Es una persona muy rara

stranger /'streindʒər/ *n* desconocido (-da); (from a foreign country) extranjero (-ra); (from another region, etc.) forastero (-ra).

strangle /'stræŋgəl/ vt estrangular; (a sob, etc.) ahogar

stranglehold /'stræŋgəl,hould/ n collar de fuerza, m. **to have a s. (on),** tener asido por la garganta; paralizar

strap /stræp/ n correa, f; tirante de botas, m, vt atar con correas

strapping /'stræpɪŋ/ a rozagante, robusto

stratagem /'strætədʒəm/ n estratagema, f, ardid, m

strategic /strə'tidʒɪk/ a estratégico

strategy /'strætɪdʒi/ n estrategia, f

stratum /'streitəm, 'strætəm/ n Geol. estrato, m, capa, f; (social, etc.) estrato, m

straw /strɔ/ n paja, f. **I don't care a s.,** No se me da un bledo. **to be not worth a s.,** no valer un ardite. **to be the last s.,** ser el colmo. **to drink through a s.,** sorber con una paja. **s. hat,** sombrero de paja, m. **s.-coloured,** pajizo

strawberry /'strɔ,bɛri/ n (plant and fruit, especially small or wild) fresa, f; (large cultivated) fresón, m. **s. bed,** fresal, m. **s. ice,** helado de fresa, m

stray /strei/ vi errar, vagar; perderse; (from a path, etc., also Fig.) descarriarse. —n animal perdido, m; niño (-ña) sin hogar. —a descarriado, perdido; errante; (sporadic) esporádico

stray bullet n bala perdida, f

streak /strik/ n raya, f; (in wood and stone) vena, f; (of light) rayo, m; (of humor, etc.) rasgo, m. —vt rayar. **like a s. of lightning,** como un relámpago

streaky /'striki/ a rayado; (of bacon) entreverado

stream /strim/ n arroyo, riachuelo, m; río, m; (current) corriente, f; (of words, etc.) torrente, m. —vi correr, fluir; manar, brotar; (float) flotar, ondear. —vt (blood, etc.) manar, echar. **The tears streamed down Jean's cheeks,** Las lágrimas corrían por las mejillas de Juana. **s.-lined,** fuselado

streamer /'strimər/ n gallardete, m, serpentina, f; (on a hat, etc.) cinta colgante, f, siguemepollo, m

stream-of-consciousness n escritura automática, f, fluir de la conciencia, m; flujo de la subconciencia, m; monólogo interior, m

street /strit/ n calle, f. **the man in the s.,** el hombre medio. **at s. level,** a ras de suelo. **s. arab,** golfo, m. **s. cries,** gritos de vendedores ambulantes, m pl. **s. entertainer,** saltabanco, m. **s. brawl, s. fight,** algarada callejera, f. **s. fighting,** luchas en las calles, f pl. **s. musician,** músico ambulante, m. **s.-sweeper,** barrendero, m. **s.-walker,** buscona, prostituta, f

strength /strɛŋkθ, strɛnθ/ n fuerza, f; (of colors, etc.) intensidad, f; (of character) firmeza (de carácter), f; (of will) resolución, decisión, f; Mil. complemento, m. **The enemy is in s.,** El enemigo está presente en gran número. **by sheer s.,** a viva fuerza. **on the s. of,** confiando en, en razón de

strengthen /'strɛŋkθən, 'strɛn-/ vt fortificar; consolidar; reforzar. —vi fortificarse; consolidarse; reforzarse

strenuous /'strɛnyuəs/ a activo, enérgico; vigoroso; (arduous) arduo

stress /strɛs/ n tensión, f; impulso, m; importancia, f, énfasis, m; Gram. acento (tónico), m; acentuación, f; Mech. esfuerzo, m. —vt acentuar; poner énfasis en, insistir en. **under s. of circumstance,** impulsado por las circunstancias. **times of s.,** tiempos turbulentos, m pl. **to lay great s. on,** insistir mucho en; dar gran importancia a

stretch /strɛtʃ/ vt (make bigger) ensanchar; (pull) estirar; (one's hand, etc.) alargar, extender; (knock down) tumbar. —vi ensancharse; dar de sí; ceder; extenderse. **to s. oneself,** estirarse, desperezarse. **to s. as far as,** llegar hasta, extenderse hasta. **to s. a point,** hacer una concesión. **to s. one's legs,** estirar las piernas

stretch /strɛtʃ/ n estirón, m; tensión, f; (of country, etc.) extensión, f; (scope) alcance, m. **by a s. of the imagination,** con un esfuerzo de imaginación. **He can sleep for hours at a s.,** Puede dormir durante horas enteras

stretcher /'strɛtʃər/ n (for gloves) ensanchador, m; dilatador, m; (for canvas) bastidor, m; (for wounded, etc.) camilla, f. **s.-bearer,** camillero, m

strew /stru/ vt esparcir; derramar

stricken /'strɪkən/ a (wounded) herido; (ill) enfermo; (with grief) afligido, agobiado de dolor. **s. in years,** entrado en años

strict /strɪkt/ a exacto; estricto; escrupuloso; severo

strictly /'strɪktli/ adv exactamente; estrictamente; severamente, con severidad. **s. speaking,** en rigor, en realidad

stricture /'strɪktʃər/ n Fig. crítica severa, censura, f. **to pass strictures on,** criticar severamente

stride /straid/ vi andar a pasos largos, dar zancadas; cruzar a grandes trancos. —vt cruzar de un tranco; poner una pierna en cada lado de. —n zancada, f, paso largo, tranco, m. **to s. up and down,** dar zancadas

strident /'straidnt/ a estridente; (of colors) chillón

strife /straif/ n lucha, f, conflicto, m

strike /straik/ vt golpear; pegar, dar una bofetada (a); (wound) herir; (a coin) acuñar; (a light) encender; (of a snake) morder; (a blow) asestar, dar; (of ships, a rock, etc.) chocar contra; estrellarse contra; (flags) bajar, arriar; (a tent) desmontar; (camp) levantar; (come upon) llegar a; (discover) encontrar por casualidad; tropezar con; hallar, descubrir; (seem) parecer; (impress) impresionar; (of ideas) ocurrirse; (an attitude) tomar, adoptar;

(of a clock) dar; (a balance) hacer; (a bargain) cerrar, llegar a; (level) nivelar; (cuttings) enraciar. —*vi* golpear; (of a clock) dar la hora; (of a ship) encallar; (go) ir; (penetrate) penetrar; (of a cutting) arraigar; (sound) sonar. **He struck the table with his fist,** Golpeó la mesa con el puño. **I was very much struck by the city's beauty,** La belleza de la ciudad me impresionó mucho. **The news struck fear into their hearts,** La noticia les llenó el corazón de miedo. **The clock struck three,** El reloj dio las tres. **The hour has struck,** *Fig.* Ha llegado la hora. **How did the house s. you?** ¿Qué te pareció la casa? **to s. a bargain,** cerrar un trato. **to s. a blow,** asestar un golpe. **to s. across country,** ir a campo traviesa. **to s. an attitude,** tomar una actitud. **to s. home,** dar en el blanco; herir; herir en lo más vivo; hacerse sentir. **to s. at,** asestar un golpe a); acometer, embestir; atacar. **to s. down,** derribar; (of illness) acometer. **to s. off,** (a head, etc.) cortar; (a name) borrar, tachar; (print) imprimir. **to s. out,** *vi* asestar un golpe a); (of a swimmer) nadar; echarse, lanzarse. —*vt* (a word, etc.) borrar, rayar; (begin) iniciar. **to s. through,** (cross out) rayar, tachar; (of the sun's rays, etc.) penetrar. **to s. up,** *vt* tocar; empezar a cantar; (a friendship) trabar. —*vi* empezar a tocar. **to s. up a march,** *Mil.* batir la marcha

strike /straik/ *n* huelga, *f.* —*vi* declararse en huelga. **go-slow s.,** tortuguismo, *m.* **lock-out s.,** huelga patronal, *f.* **sit-down s.,** huelga de brazos caídos, *f.* **to go on s.,** declararse en huelga. **s.-breaker,** esquirol, *m.* **s.-pay,** subsidio de huelga, *m*

striker /'straikər/ *n* huelguista, *mf*

striking /'straikiŋ/ *a* notable, sorprendente; (impressive) impresionante; que llama la atención; llamativo

string /striŋ/ *n* bramante, *m*; cuerda, *f*; (ribbon) cinta, *f*; (of beads, etc.) sarta, *f*; (of onions) ristra, *f*; (of horses, etc.) reata, *f*; hilera, *f*; (of a bridge) cable, *m*; (of oaths, lies) sarta, serie, *f*; (of beans) fibra, *f*. —*vt* encordar; (beads, etc.) ensartar; (beans) quitar las fibras (de). **He is all strung up,** Se le crispan los nervios. **the strings,** los instrumentos de cuerda. **a s. of pearls,** un collar de perlas. **for strings,** *Mus.* para arco. **to pull strings,** *Fig.* manejar los hilos. **to s. up,** (an instrument) templar; (a person) pender, ahorcar. **s. bean,** judía verde, *f*

stringed /striŋd/ *a* (of musical instruments) de cuerda. **s. instrument,** instrumento de cuerda, *m*

stringent /'strindʒənt/ *a* estricto, severo

stringy /'striŋi/ *a* fibroso; filamentoso; correoso; arrugado

strip /strip/ *vt* desnudar; despojar (de), quitar; robar; (a cow) ordeñar hasta agotar la leche. —*vi* desnudarse. —*n* (tatter) jirón, *m*; tira, lista, *f*; (of wood) listón, *m*; (of earth) pedazo, *m*; (*Geog.* of land)

zona, *f.* **to s. off,** *vt* quitar; (bark from a tree) descortezar; (one's clothes) despojarse de. —*vi* desprenderse, separarse

stripe /straip/ *n* raya, lista, *f*; (*Mil.* etc.) galón, *m*; (lash) azote, *m.* —*vt* rayar. **the stripes of the tiger,** las rayas del tigre

striped /straipt, 'straipɪd/ *a* listado, a rayas; con rayas. **s. trousers,** pantalón de corte, *m*

stripling /'striplɪŋ/ *n* joven imberbe, pollo, mancebo, *m*

strive /straiv/ *vi* esforzarse (a); pugnar (por, para); trabajar (por); (fight against) luchar contra; pelear con. **He was striving to understand,** Pugnaba por (or Se esforzaba a) comprender

stroke /strouk/ *n* (blow) golpe, *m*; (of the oars) golpe del remo, *m*, remada, *f*; (at billiards) tacada, *f*; (in golf) tirada, *f*; (in swimming) braza, *f*; (of a clock) campanada, *f*; (of a pen) rasgo de la pluma, *m*; (of a brush) pincelada, *f*; *Mech.* golpe de émbolo, *m*; (caress) caricia con la mano, *f.* —*vt* acariciar con la mano. **on the s. of six,** al acabar de dar las seis. **to have a s.,** tener un ataque de apoplejía. **s. of genius,** rasgo de ingenio, *m.* **s. of good luck,** racha de buena suerte, *f*

stroll /stroul/ *vi* pasearse, vagar. —*n* vuelta, *f*, paseo, *m.* **to go for a s.,** dar una vuelta

stroller /'stroulər/ *n* paseante, *mf*

strolling /'stroulɪŋ/ *a* errante; ambulante. **s. player,** *n* cómico (-ca) ambulante

strong /strɔŋ/ *a* fuerte; vigoroso; robusto; enérgico; firme; poderoso; (of colors) intenso, vivo; (of tea, coffee) cargado; *Gram.* fuerte. **The government took s. measures,** El gobierno tomó medidas enérgicas. **They gave very s. reasons,** Alegaron unas razones muy poderosas. **Grammar is not his s. point,** La gramática no es su punto fuerte. **The enemy is s. in numbers,** El enemigo es numéricamente fuerte. **The society is four thousand s.,** La sociedad tiene cuatro mil miembros. **s. box,** caja de caudales, *f.* **s. man,** hombre fuerte, *m*; (in a circus) hércules, *m.* **s.-minded,** de espíritu fuerte; independiente. **s. room,** cámara acorazada, *f*

stronghold /'strɔŋˌhould/ *n* fortaleza, *f*; refugio, *m*

structural /'strʌktʃərəl/ *a* estructural

structure /'strʌktʃər/ *n* estructura, *f*; edificio, *m*; construcción, *f*

struggle /'strʌgəl/ *vi* luchar; pelear; disputarse. —*n* lucha, *f*; combate, *m*; conflicto, *m.* **to s. to one's feet,** luchar por levantarse. **without a s.,** sin luchar

strum /strʌm/ *vt* (a stringed instrument) rascar; tocar mal

strut /strʌt/ *vi* pavonearse. —*vt* (prop) apuntalar. —*n* pavonada, *f*; (prop) puntal, *m.* **to s. out,** salir de un paso majestuoso

stub /stʌb/ *n* (of a tree) tocón, *m*; (of a pencil, candle, etc.) cabo, *m*; pedazo, fragmento, m; (of a cigarette or cigar) colilla, f. **s.-book,** talonario, m

stubble /'stʌbəl/ n rastrojo, m; (beard) barba de tres días, f

stubborn /'stʌbərn/ a inquebrantable, tenaz; persistente; (pig-headed) terco, testarudo

stucco /'stʌkou/ n estuco, m, vt estucar

stud /stʌd/ n (of horses) caballeriza, f; (nail) tachón, m; (for collars) pasador para camisas, m. —vt tachonar; sembrar **dress s.,** botón de la pechera, m. **s.-farm,** potrero, m

student /'studnt/ n estudiante, mf. —a estudiantil

studied /'stʌdid/ a estudiado; calculado; (of style) cerebral, reflexivo; (intentional) deliberado

studio /'studi,ou/ n estudio, m. **broadcasting s.,** estudio de emisión, m

studious /'studiəs/ a estudioso, aplicado; (deliberate) intencional, deliberate; (eager) solícito, ansioso

study /'stʌdi/ n estudio, m; solicitud, f, cuidado, m; investigación, f; (room) gabinete, cuarto de trabajo, m. —vt ocuparse de, cuidar de, atender a; considerar; estudiar; examinar; (the stars) observar; (try) procurar. —vi estudiar. **in a brown s.,** en Babia. **to make a s. of,** hacer un estudio de, estudiar. **to s. for an examination,** prepararse para un examen

stuff /stʌf/ n substancia, materia, f; (fabric) tela, f, paño, m; (rubbish) cachivaches, m pl, cosas, f pl. —a de estofa. —vt henchir; llenar; Cul. rellenar; (with food) ahitar (de); (cram) atestar, apretar; (furniture) rehenchir; (an animal, bird) disecar; (put) meter, poner. **S. and nonsense!** ¡Patrañas! **to be poor s.,** ser de pacotilla; no valer para nada

stuffing /'stʌfɪŋ/ n (of furniture) rehenchimiento, m; Cul. relleno, m

stuffy /'stʌfi/ a mal ventilado, poco aireado, ahogado

stultify /'stʌltə,fai/ vt hacer inútil; invalidar; hacer ridículo

stumble /'stʌmbəl/ vi tropezar; dar un traspié; (in speaking) tartamudear. —n tropezón, m; traspié, m. **to s. through a speech,** pronunciar un discurso a tropezones. **to s. against,** tropezar contra. **to s. upon, across,** tropezar con; encontrar por casualidad

stumbling block n tropiezo, impedimento, m

stump /stʌmp/ n (of a tree) tocón, m; (of an arm, leg) muñón, m; (of a pencil, candle) cabo, m; (of a tooth) raigón, m; (of a cigar) colilla, f; (cricket) poste, montante, m; Art. esfumino, m; (leg) pata, f. —vt (disconcert) desconcertar; Art. esfumar; recorrer. **to s. up,** Inf. pagar

stun /stʌn/ vt dejar sin sentido (a); aturdir de un golpe (a); (astound) pasmar

stunning /'stʌnɪŋ/ a aturdidor; que pasma; Inf. estupendo

stunt /stʌnt/ vt impedir el crecimiento de;

encanijar. —n (advertising) anuncio de reclamo, m; recurso (para conseguir algo), m; proeza, f

stunted /'stʌntɪd/ a (of trees, etc.) enano; (of children) encanijado; (of intelligence) inmaduro

stupefy /'stupə,fai/ vt atontar, embrutecer; causar estupor (a), asombrar

stupendous /stu'pɛndəs/ a asombroso; enorme

stupid /'stupɪd/ a (with sleep, etc.) atontado; (silly) estúpido, tonto. —n tonto (-ta)

stupidity /stu'pɪdɪti/ n estupidez, f; tontería, f

stupor /'stupər/ n estupor, m

sturdy /'stɜrdi/ a robusto, vigoroso, fuerte; firme, tenaz

sturgeon /'stɜrdʒən/ n Ichth. esturión, m

stutter /'stʌtər/ vi tartamudear. —vt balbucir. —n tartamudeo, m

sty /stai/ n (pig) pocilga, f; Med. orzuelo, m

style /stail/ n (for etching) buril, m; (Lit., Art., Archit., etc.) estilo, m; (fashion) moda, f; (model) modelo, m; (behavior, etc.) tono, m; elegancia, f; (kind) especie, clase, f; (designation) tratamiento, m; vt llamar, nombrar. **the latest styles from Madrid,** los últimos modelos de Madrid. **He has a very individual s.,** Su estilo es muy personal. **They live in great s.,** Viven en gran lujo

stylish /'stailɪʃ/ a elegante

suasive /'sweisɪv/ a suasorio, persuasivo

suave /swɑv/ a afable, cortés, urbano; (of wine) suave

subaltern /sʌb'ɔltərn/ n Mil. subalterno, m, a subalterno, subordinado

subconscious /sʌb'kɒnʃəs/ a subconsciente. **the s.,** la subconsciencia

subcutaneous /,sʌbkyu'teiniəs/ a subcutáneo

subdivide /,sʌbdɪ'vaid/ vt subdividir. —vi subdividirse

subdue /səb'du/ vt subyugar, sojuzgar, vencer; (one's passions) dominar; (colors, voices) suavizar; (lessen) mitigar, apagar

subdued /səb'dud/ a (of colors) apagado; (of persons) sumiso; (depressed) deprimido, melancólico. **in a s. voice,** en voz baja

subheading /'sʌb,hedɪŋ/ n subtítulo, m

subhuman /sʌb'hyumən/ a subhumano

subject /n. 'sʌbdʒɪkt; v. səb'dʒɛkt/ a sujeto; sometido (a); expuesto (a). —n (of a country) súbdito (-ta); sujeto, m; (of study) asignatura, materia, f; (theme) tema, m; (Gram., Philos.) sujeto, m. —vt subyugar; someter. **It can only be done s. to his consent,** Podrá hacerse únicamente si él lo consiente. **He is a British s.,** Es súbdito británico. **to change the s.,** cambiar de conversación. **to s. to criticism,** criticar (a). **s.-matter,** materia, f; (of a letter) contenido, m

subjection /səb'dʒɛkʃən/ n sujeción, f; sometimiento, m. **He was in a state of**

complete s., Estaba completamente sumiso. **to bring into s.,** subyugar

subjective /səb'dʒɛktɪv/ a subjetivo

subjoin /səb'dʒɔɪn/ vt añadir, adjuntar

subjugate /'sʌbdʒə,geit/ vt subyugar, someter

subjunctive /səb'dʒʌŋktɪv/ a and n subjuntivo m

sublet /v. sʌb'lɛt; n. 'sʌb,lɛt/ vt subarrendar. —n subarriendo, m

sublimate /v. 'sʌblə,meit; n. -mɪt/ vt sublimar. —n sublimado, m

sublime /sə'blaim/ a sublime; absoluto, completo; extremo. **the s.,** lo sublime

submarine /,sʌbmə'rin/ a submarino. —n submarino, m. **midget s.,** submarino enano, submarino de bolsillo, m. **s. chaser,** cazasubmarino, m

submerge /səb'mɜrdʒ/ vt sumergir; inundar. —vi sumergirse. **The submarine submerged,** El submarino se sumergió

submergence /səb'mɜrdʒəns/ n sumergimiento, m, sumersión, f; hundimiento, m

submersible /səb'mɜrsəbəl/ a sumergible

submersion /səb'mɜrʒən/ n sumersión, f; hundimiento, m

submission /səb'mɪʃən/ n sometimiento, m; sumisión, resignación, f; docilidad, f

submissive /səb'mɪsɪv/ a sumiso, dócil, manso

submit /səb'mɪt/ vt someterse (a); doblarse ante; (a scheme, etc.) someter; presentar; (urge) proponer. —vi someterse; resignarse; (surrender) rendirse, entregarse. **to s. to arbitration,** someter a arbitraje

subnormal /sʌb'nɔrməl/ a anormal

subordinate /adj., n. sə'bɔrdnɪt; v. -dn,eit/ a subordinado; subalterno, inferior; secundario. —n subordinado (-da). —vt subordinar

subordination /sə,bɔrdn̩'eiʃən/ n subordinación, f

subplot /'sʌb,plɒt/ n intriga secundaria, trama secundaria, f

subscribe /səb'skraib/ vt and vi subscribir; (to a periodical, etc.) abonarse (a)

subscriber /səb'skraibər/ n subscriptor (-ra); abonado (-da)

subscription /səb'skrɪpʃən/ n subscripción, f; (to a periodical, series of concerts, etc.) abono, m; (to a club) cuota, f

subsequent /'sʌbsɪkwənt/ a subsiguiente, subsecuente; posterior. **s. to,** después de, posterior a. **s. upon,** de resultas de

subsequently /'sʌbsɪkwəntli/ adv más tarde; subsiguientemente; posteriormente

subservient /səb'sɜrviənt/ a servil; subordinado; útil

subside /səb'said/ vi (of water) bajar; (of ground) hundirse; (of foundations) asentarse; disminuir; calmarse; (be quiet) callarse. **to s. into a chair,** dejarse caer en un sillón

subsidence /səb'saidn̩s/ n hundimiento, m; desplome, derrumbamiento, m; (of

floods) bajada, f; (of anger, etc.) apaciguamiento, m

subsidiary /səb'sɪdi,ɛri/ a subsidiario

subsidize /'sʌbsɪ,daiz/ vt subvencionar

subsidy /'sʌbsɪdi/ n subvención, f, subsidio, m; prima, f

subsist /səb'sɪst/ vi subsistir

subsoil /'sʌb,sɔil/ n subsuelo, m

substance /'sʌbstəns/ n substancia, f

substantial /səb'stænʃəl/ a substancial; sólido; importante

substantiate /səb'stænʃi,eit/ vt establecer, verificar; justificar

substantive /'sʌbstəntɪv/ a real, independiente; Gram. substantivo. —n Gram. substantivo, m

substitute /'sʌbstɪ,tut/ n substituto (-ta); (material) substituto, m. —vt substituir, reemplazar. **to be a s. for,** hacer las veces de

substitution /,sʌbstɪ'tuʃən/ n substitución, f, reemplazo, m

subterfuge /'sʌbtər,fyudʒ/ n subterfugio, m; evasiva, f

subterranean /,sʌbtə'reiniən/ a subterráneo

subtitle /'sʌb,taitl/ n subtítulo, m; (on films) guión, m

subtle /'sʌtl/ a sutil; delicado; penetrante; (crafty) astuto

subtlety /'sʌtlti/ n sutileza, f; delicadeza, f; (craftiness) astucia, f

subtract /səb'trækt/ vt restar, substraer

subtraction /səb'trækʃən/ n resta, f, substracción, f

suburb /'sʌbɜrb/ n suburbio, m; pl suburbs, las afueras, f pl los arrabales, m pl

suburban /sə'bɜrbən/ a suburbano

subversion /səb'vɜrʒən/ n subversión, f

subversive /səb'vɜrsiv/ a subversivo

subvert /səb'vɜrt/ vt subvertir

subway /'sʌb,wei/ n (passageway) pasaje subterráneo, m; (underground railway) metro (Spain, Puerto Rico), subte (Argentina), m

succeed /sək'sid/ vt seguir (a); suceder (a); heredar. —vi seguir (a); suceder (a); (be successful) tener éxito. **I did not s. in doing it,** No logré hacerlo. **to s. to the throne,** subir al trono

succeeding /sək'sidɪŋ/ a subsiguiente; futuro; consecutivo; sucesivo

success /sək'sɛs/ n éxito, m; triunfo, m. **to be a s.,** tener éxito. **The film was a great s.,** La película tuvo mucho éxito

successful /sək'sɛsfəl/ a que tiene éxito; afortunado, venturoso; próspero

successfully /sək'sɛsfəli/ adv con éxito; prósperamente

succession /sək'sɛʃən/ n sucesión, f; (series) serie, f; (inheritance) herencia, f; (descendants) descendencia, f. **in s.,** sucesivamente

successive /sək'sɛsɪv/ a sucesivo

successor /sək'sɛsər/ n sucesor (-ra)

succinct /sək'sɪŋkt/ a sucinto, conciso

succor /'sʌkər/ vt socorrer, auxiliar. —n socorro, m, ayuda, f

succulent /'sʌkyələnt/ a suculento

succumb /sə'kʌm/ vi sucumbir; someterse, ceder

such /sʌtʃ/ a tal; parecido, semejante; así; tanto; (before an adjective, adverb) tan. —n el, m, (f, la) que, los, m pl, (f pl, las) que; tal. **s. men,** tales hombres. **I have never seen s. magnificence,** Nunca he visto tanta magnificencia. **s. an important man,** un hombre tan importante. **s. pictures as these,** cuadros como estos. **S. is life!** ¡Así es la vida! **science as s.,** la ciencia como tal. **s.-and-s.,** tal y tal

suchlike /'sʌtʃ,laik/ a parecido, semejante; de esta clase

suck /sʌk/ vt chupar; (the breast) mamar; sorber; (of a vacuum cleaner, etc.) aspirar. —n chupada, f, succión, f. **to s. down,** tragar. **to s. up,** aspirar; absorber

sucker /'sʌkər/ n Zool. ventosa, f; Bot. acodo, mugrón, m; (greenhorn) primo, m; (pig) lechón, m

suckle /'sʌkəl/ vt amamantar, dar el pecho (a)

suction /'sʌkʃən/ n succión, f; aspiración, f. **s.-pump,** bomba aspirante, f

sudden /'sʌdn/ a súbito; (unexpected) inesperado, impensado; (of bends) brusco. **all of a s.,** de repente; súbitamente

suddenly /'sʌdnli/ adv súbitamente; de pronto, de repente

suds /sʌdz/ n pl jabonaduras, f pl; espuma, f

sue /su/ vt Law. proceder contra, pedir en juicio; Law. demandar; (beg) suplicar. **to sue for peace,** pedir la paz

suede /sweid/ n ante, m. **s. glove,** guante de ante, m

suet /'suit/ n sebo, m

suffer /'sʌfər/ vt sufrir, padecer; pasar; experimentar; (tolerate) tolerar, sufrir; (allow) permitir. —vi sufrir. **She suffers from her environment,** es la víctima de su medio ambiente

sufferance /'sʌfərəns/ n tolerancia, f. **on s.,** por tolerancia

sufferer /'sʌfərər/ n enfermo (-ma); víctima, f

suffering /'sʌfərɪŋ/ n sufrimiento, padecimiento, m; dolor, m. —a sufriente

suffice /sə'fais/ vi ser suficiente, bastar. —vt satisfacer

sufficiency /sə'fɪʃənsi/ n suficiencia, f; (of money) subsistencia, f

sufficient /sə'fɪʃənt/ a suficiente, bastante. **to be s.,** bastar, ser suficiente

sufficiently /sə'fɪʃəntli/ adv suficientemente, bastante

suffix /'sʌfɪks/ n Gram. sufijo, m

suffocate /'sʌfə,keit/ vt ahogar, sofocar, asfixiar. —vi sofocarse, asfixiarse

suffocating /'sʌfə,keitɪŋ/ a sofocante, asfixiante

suffocation /,sʌfə'keiʃən/ n sofocación, asfixia, f; ahogo, m

suffrage /'sʌfrɪdʒ/ n sufragio, m; voto, m. **universal s.,** sufragio universal, m

suffragette /,sʌfrə'dʒɛt/ n sufragista, f

suffuse /sə'fyuz/ vt bañar, inundar, cubrir

sugar /'ʃugər/ n azúcar, m. —vt azucarar. **brown s.,** azúcar moreno, m. **loaf s.,** azúcar de pilón, m. **white s.,** azúcar blanco, m. **to s. the pill,** dorar la píldora. **s.-almond,** peladilla, f. **s.-basin,** azucarera, f. **s.-beet,** remolacha, f. **s.-candy,** azúcar candi, m. **s.-cane,** caña de azúcar, f. **s.-cane syrup,** miel de caña, f. **s.-paste,** alfeñique, m, alcorza, f. **s.-refinery,** fábrica de azúcar, f. **s.-tongs,** tenacillas para azúcar, f pl

sugary /'ʃugəri/ a azucarado; Fig. meloso, almibarado

suggest /səg'dʒɛst/ vt implicar; indicar, dar a entender; sugerir; (advise) aconsejar; (hint) insinuar; (evoke) evocar. **I suggested they should go to London,** Les aconsejé que fueran a Londres. **An idea suggested itself to him,** Se le ocurrió una idea

suggestion /səg'dʒɛstʃən/ n sugestión, f; insinuación, f

suggestive /səg'dʒɛstɪv/ a sugestivo; estimulante

suicidal /,suə'saidl/ a suicida. **s. tendency,** tendencia suicida, tendencia al suicidio, f

suicide /'suə,said/ n (act) suicidio, m; (person) suicida, mf. **to commit s.,** darse la muerte, quitarse la vida suicidarse

suit /sut/ n (request) petición, súplica, f; oferta de matrimonio, f; Law. pleito, m; (of clothes) traje, m; (cards) palo, m; (of cards held) serie, f, vt convenir; sentar; ir bien (a); venir bien (a); (adapt) adaptar. **S. yourself!** ¡Haz lo que quieras! **The arrangement suits me very well,** El arreglo me viene muy bien. **The climate doesn't s. me,** El clima no me sienta bien. **The color does not s. you,** El color no te va bien. **to follow s.,** seguir en el ejemplo (de); (cards) jugar el mismo palo. **s.-case,** maleta, f

suitable /'sutəbəl/ a conveniente; apropiado; apto; a propósito. **Not s. for children,** No apto para menores. **to make s. for,** adaptar a las necesidades de

suite /swit/ n (of retainers, etc.) séquito, acompañamiento, m; (of furniture, etc.) juego, m; Mus. suite, f. **private s.,** habitaciones particulares, f pl. **s. of rooms,** apartamiento, m

suitor /'sutər/ n Law. demandante, m; pretendiente, m

sulk /sʌlk/ vi ponerse malhumorado, mohíno

sulky /'sʌlki/ a mohíno, malhumorado

sullen /'sʌlən/ a taciturno, hosco; malhumorado, sombrío; (of a landscape, etc.) triste, sombrío

sully /'sʌli/ vt desdorar, empañar; manchar

sulphur /'sʌlfər/ n azufre, m

sultan /'sʌltn̩/ n sultán, m

sultry /'sʌltri/ a bochornoso, sofocante

sum /sʌm/ n suma, f; total, m; cantidad, f; (in arithmetic) problema (de aritmética), m. —vt sumar, calcular. **in sum**, en suma; en resumen. **to sum up**, recapitular; resumir; (a person) tomar las medidas (a)

summarize /'sʌmə,raiz/ vt resumir brevemente; compendiar

summary /'sʌməri/ a somero; Law. sumario. —n resumen, sumario, compendio, m. **summary records**, actas resumidas, f pl

summer /'sʌmər/ n verano, estío, m. **to spend the s.**, veranear. **s.-house**, cenador, m. **s.-time**, verano, m; hora de verano, f. **s. wheat**, trigo tremesino, m

summit /'sʌmɪt/ n cima, cumbre, f; Fig. apogeo, m

summitry /'sʌmɪtri/ n diplomacia en la cumbre, f

summon /'sʌmən/ vt llamar, hacer venir; mandar, requerir; Law. citar. **to s. up one's courage**, cobrar ánimos

summons /'sʌmənz/ n llamamiento, m; Mil. intimación, f; Law. citación, f. —vt Law. citar

sumptuous /'sʌmptʃuəs/ a suntuoso, lujoso, magnífico

sun /sʌn/ n sol, m. **The sun was shining**, Hacía sol, El sol brillaba. **to bask in the sun**, tomar el sol. **sun-bathing**, baños de sol, m pl. **sun-blind**, toldo para el sol, m. **sun-bonnet**, capelina, f. **sunglasses**, gafas ahumadas, f pl. **sunhelmet**, casco colonial, m. **sun-spot**, Astron. mancha del sol, f; (freckle) peca, f. **sun-worship**, adoración del sol, f

sunburn /'sʌn,bɜrn/ n quemadura del sol, f; bronceado, m

sunburnt /'sʌn,bɜrnt/ a quemado por el sol; bronceado, tostado por el sol

sundae /'sʌndei/ n helado de frutas, m

Sunday /'sʌndei/ n domingo, m. **in his S. best**, en su traje dominguero, endomingado. **S. school**, escuela dominical, f

Sunday's child n niño nacido de pies, niño nacido un domingo, niño mimado de la fortuna

sunder /'sʌndər/ vt dividir en dos, hender; separar

sundial /'sʌn,daiəl/ n reloj de sol, reloj solar, m

sundown /'sʌn,daun/ n puesta del sol, f

sundry /'sʌndri/ a varios (-as). —n pl **sundries**, artículos diversos, m pl; Com. varios, m pl. **all and s.**, todo el mundo, todos y cada uno

sunflower /'sʌn,flauər/ n girasol, tornasol, m, trompeta de amor, f

sunken /'sʌŋkən/ a (of eyes, etc.) hundido

sunlight /'sʌn,lait/ n luz del sol, f, rayos

del sol, m pl. **artificial s.**, sol artificial, m. **in the s.**, al sol

sunny /'sʌni/ a de sol; bañado de sol; asoleado; expuesto al sol; (face) risueño; (of disposition, etc.) alegre. **to be s.**, hacer sol

sunrise /'sʌn,raiz/ n salida del sol, f. **from s. to sunset**, de sol a sol

sunset /'sʌn,sɛt/ n puesta del sol, f. **at s.**, a la caída (or puesta) del sol

sunshade /'sʌn,ʃeid/ n parasol, quitasol, m, sombrilla, f

sunshine /'sʌn,ʃain/ n luz del sol, f. **in the s.**, al sol

sunstroke /'sʌn,strouk/ n insolación, f

sup /sʌp/ vt sorber. —vi cenar. —n sorbo, m

super /'supər/ n (actor) comparsa, mf; (film) superproducción, f; (of a beehive) alza, f

superabundance /,supərə'bʌndəns/ n superabundancia, sobreabundancia, f

superabundant /,supərə'bʌndənt/ a superabundante, sobreabundante. **to be s.**, sobreabundar

superannuated /,supər'ænyu,eitɪd/ a (retired) jubilado; (out-of-date) anticuado

superannuation /,supər,ænyu'eiʃən/ n (retirement and pension) jubilación, f

superb /su'pɜrb/ a magnífico, espléndido

supercargo /'supər'kɑrgou/ n Naut. sobrecargo, m

supercilious /,supər'siliəs/ a altanero, altivo, orgulloso; desdeñoso

superciliousness /,supər'siliəsnɪs/ n altanería, altivez, f; orgullo, m; desdén, m

superficial /,supər'fiʃəl/ a superficial

superficiality /,supər,fiʃi'ælɪti/ n superficialidad, f

superfine /,supər'fain/ a superfino

superfluity /,supər'fluti/ n superfluidad, f

superfluous /su'pɜrfluəs/ a superfluo. **to be s.**, sobrar

superfortress /'supər,fɔrtrɪs/ n Aer. superfortaleza volante, f

superhuman /,supər'hyumən/ a sobrehumano

superimpose /,supərɪm'pouz/ vt sobreponer

superintend /,supərɪn'tɛnd/ vt superentender, dirigir

superintendent /,supərɪn'tɛndənt/ n superintendente, mf; director (-ra); (school) inspector; (police) subjefe de la policía, m

superior /sə'pɪəriər/ a superior; (in number) mayor; (smug) desdeñoso. —n superior (-ra). **Mother S.**, (madre) superiora, f. **s. to**, superior a; encima de

superiority /sə,pɪəri'ɔriti/ n superioridad, f

superlative /sə'pɜrlətɪv/ a extremo, supremo; Gram. superlativo. —n Gram. superlativo, m

superlatively /sə'pɜrlətɪvli/ adv en sumo grado, superlativamente

superman /'supər,mæn/ n superhombre, m

supernatural /,supər'nætʃərəl/ a sobrenatural

superscribe /'supər,skraib/ vt sobrescribir; poner el sobrescrito (a)

superscription /,supər'skrɪpʃən/ n (on letters, documents) sobrescrito, m; leyenda, f

supersede /,supər'sid/ vt reemplazar; suplantar

superstition /,supər'stɪʃən/ n superstición, f

superstitious /,supər'stɪʃəs/ a supersticioso

supervene /,supər'vin/ vi sobrevenir

supervise /'supər,vaiz/ vt superentender, vigilar; dirigir

supervision /,supər'vɪʒən/ n superintendencia, f; dirección, f

supervisor /'supər,vaizər/ n superintendente, mf; inspector (-ra); director (-ra)

supine /a. su'pain; n. 'supain/ a supino; indolente, negligente. —n Gram. supino, m

supper /'sʌpər/ n cena, f. **the Last S.**, la Última Cena. **to have s.**, cenar. **s.-time**, hora de cenar, f

supplant /sə'plænt/ vt suplantar; usurpar; reemplazar

supple /'sʌpəl/ a flexible; dócil, manso; (fawning) adulador, servil, lisonjero

supplement /'sʌpləmənt/ n suplemento, m; (of a book) apéndice, m

supplementary /,sʌplə'mɛntəri/ a suplementario; adicional

supplicate /'sʌplɪ,keit/ vt and vi suplicar

supply /sə'plai/ vt proveer (de); suministrar; proporcionar, dar; (a deficiency) suplir; (a post) llenar; (a post temporarily) reemplazar. —n suministro, surtimiento, m; provisión, f; (of electricity, etc.) suministro, m; Com. oferta, f; (person) substituto (-ta), pl supplies, Com. existencias, f pl; Mil. pertrechos, m pl; víveres, m pl, provisiones, f pl. **s. and demand**, oferta y demanda, f

support /sə'pɔrt/ vt apoyar, sostener; mantener; (endure) soportar; (a cause) apoyar, defender; (corroborate) confirmar, vindicar. —n apoyo, m; sostén, m; soporte, m. **to speak in s. of**, defender, abogar por. **to s. oneself**, ganarse la vida, mantenerse

supporter /sə'pɔrtər/ n apoyo, m; defensor (-ra); partidario (-ia)

suppose /sə'pouz/ vt suponer; imaginar(se); creer. **always supposing**, dado que, en el caso de que. **Supposing he had gone out?** ¿Y si hubiera salido? **I don't s. they will go to Spain**, No creo que vayan a España. **He is supposed to be clever**, Tiene fama de listo

supposed /sə'pouzd, -'pouzɪd/ a supuesto; que se llama a sí mismo

supposition /,sʌpə'zɪʃən/ n suposición, hipótesis, f

suppress /sə'prɛs/ vt reprimir; (yawns,

etc.) ahogar; contener; (heresies, rebellions, books, etc.) suprimir; (dissemble) disimular, esconder; (a heckler, etc.) hacer callar

suppression /sə'prɛʃən/ n represión, f; supresión, f; disimulación, f

suppurate /'sʌpyə,reit/ vi supurar

supremacy /sə'prɛməsi/ n supremacía, f

supreme /sə'prim/ a supremo; sumo. **with s. indifference**, con suma indiferencia. **s. court**, tribunal supremo, m

surcharge /'sɜr,tʃɑrdʒ/ n sobrecarga, f

sure /ʃur/ a seguro; cierto. —adv seguramente. **Be s. to...!** ¡Ten cuidado de...! ¡No dejes de...! **to be s.**, seguramente, sin duda; ¡claro!; (fancy!) ¡no me digas!; ¡qué sorpresa! **I am not so s. of that**, No diría yo tanto. **Come on Thursday for s.**, Venga el jueves sin falta. **It is s. to rain tomorrow**, Seguramente va a llover mañana. **to make s. of**, asegurarse de. **to be (or feel) s.**, estar seguro. **s.-footed**, de pie firme, seguro

surely /'ʃurli/ adv seguramente; sin duda, ciertamente; por supuesto

sureness /'ʃurnes/ n seguridad, f; certeza, f

surety /'ʃuriti/ n garantía, fianza, f; (person) garante, mf. **to go s. for**, ser fiador (de), salir garante (por)

surf /sɜrf/ n resaca, f; rompiente, m; oleaje, m. **s.-board**, aquaplano, m. **s.-riding**, patinaje sobre las olas, m

surface /'sɜrfɪs/ n superficie, f; exterior, m. —a superficial. —vi (of a submarine) salir a la superficie. **on the s.**, en apariencia

surface mail n correo por vía ordinaria, servicio ordinario, servicio per vía de superficie, m

surfeit /'sɜrfɪt/ n exceso, m, superabundancia, f; saciedad, f. —vt hartar; saciar

surge /sɜrdʒ/ vi (of waves) embravecerse, hincharse; (of crowds) agitarse, bullir; (of emotions) despertarse. —n (of sea, crowd, blood) oleada, f; (of anger) ola, f. **The blood surged into his face**, La sangre se le subió a las mejillas

surgeon /'sɜrdʒən/ n cirujano, m; (Nav., Mil.) médico, m

surgery /'sɜrdʒəri/ n cirugía, f; (doctor's) consultorio, m; (dispensary) dispensario, m

surgical /'sɜrdʒɪkəl/ a quirúrgico

surly /'sɜrli/ a taciturno, huraño, malhumorado; brusco

surmise /sər'maiz/ n conjetura, suposición, f. —vt conjeturar, adivinar; imaginar, suponer. —vi hacer conjeturas

surmount /sər'maunt/ vt superar, vencer; coronar

surname /'sɜr,neim/ n apellido, m, vt denominar, nombrar

surpass /sər'pæs/ vt superar, exceder; aventajarse (a); eclipsar

surpassing /sər'pæsɪŋ/ a sin par, incomparable

surplus /'sɜrplʌs/ n exceso, sobrante, m;

(*Com.* of accounts) superávit, *m.* **sale of s. stock,** liquidación de saldos, *f*

surprise /sər'praiz, sə-/ *n* sorpresa, *f;* asombro, *m.* —*vt* sorprender; asombrar. **to s.** (someone) **in the act,** coger en el acto. **to take** (a person) **by s.,** sorprender (a). **He was surprised into admitting it,** Cogido a la imprevista, lo confesó

surprising /sər'praiziŋ, sə-/ *a* sorprendente

surrealism /sə'riə,lizəm/ *n* surrealismo, *m*

surrender /sə'rɛndər/ *vt* rendir, entregar; (goods) ceder, renunciar (a). —*vi* rendirse, entregarse; abandonarse. —*n* rendición, capitulación, *f;* entrega, *f;* (of goods) cesión, *f;* (of an insurance policy) rescate, *m.* **to s. oneself to remorse,** abandonarse (or entregarse) al remordimiento. **to s. unconditionally,** entregarse a discreción

surreptitious /,sʌrəp'tɪʃəs/ *a* subrepticio

surround /sə'raund/ *vt* rodear, cercar, *Mil.* asediar, sitiar. —*n* borde, *m.* **Peter was surrounded by his friends,** Pedro estaba rodeado por sus amigos

surrounding /sə'raundɪŋ/ *a* (que está) alrededor de; vecino. **the s. country,** los alrededores

surroundings /sə'raundɪŋz/ *n pl* cercanías, *f pl*, alrededores, *m pl;* (environment) medio, *m;* (medio) ambiente, *m*

surtax /'sɜr,tæks/ *n* impuesto suplementario, *m*

surveillance /sər'veiləns/ *n* vigilancia, *f*

survey /*v.* sər'vei; *n.* 'sɜrvei/ *vt* contemplar, mirar; (events, etc.) pasar en revista; estudiar; (land, etc.) apear; (a house, etc.) inspeccionar. —*n* vista general, *f;* inspección, *f;* (of facts, etc.) examen, *m;* estudio, *m;* (of land, etc.) apeo, *m;* (of literature, etc.) bosquejo, breve panorama, *m*

surveying /sər'veiɪŋ/ *n* agrimensura, *f*

surveyor /sər'veiər/ *n* agrimensor, *m;* (superintendent) inspector, *m;* superintendente, *m*

survival /sər'vaivəl/ *n* supervivencia, *f.* **s. of the fittest,** supervivencia de los más aptos, *f*

survive /sər'vaiv/ *vt* sobrevivir a. —*vi* sobrevivir; (of customs) subsistir, durar

survivor /sər'vaivər/ *n* sobreviviente, *mf*

susceptible /sə'sɛptəbəl/ *a* susceptible; impresionable; sensible; (to love) enamoradizo. **He is s. to bronchitis,** Es susceptible a la bronquitis

suspect /*a., n.* 'sʌspɛkt; *v.* sə'spɛkt/ *a* and *n* sospechoso (-sa). —*vt* sospechar; dudar; imaginar, suponer. —*vi* tener sospechas

suspend /sə'spɛnd/ *vt* suspender. **suspended animation,** muerte aparente, *f*

suspender /sə'spɛndər/ *n* liga, *f; pl* **suspenders,** (braces) tirantes del pantalón, *m pl.* **s.-belt,** faja, *f*

suspense /sə'spɛns/ *n* incertidumbre, *f.*

to keep (a person) **in s.,** dejar en la incertidumbre (a)

suspension /sə'spɛnʃən/ *n* suspensión, *f.* **s.-bridge,** puente colgante, *m.* **s. of payments,** suspensión de pagos, *f,*

suspicion /sə'spɪʃən/ *n* sospecha, *f;* (touch) dejo, *m;* cantidad muy pequeña, *f.* **to be above s.,** estar por encima de toda sospecha. **to be under s.,** estar bajo sospecha. **I had no suspicions...,** No sospechaba...

suspicious /sə'spɪʃəs/ *a* (by nature) suspicaz; sospechoso. **to make s.,** hacer sospechar

sustain /sə'stein/ *vt* sostener; mantener; sustentar; apoyar; corroborar, confirmar; (a note) prolongar. **to s. injuries,** recibir heridas

sustenance /'sʌstənəns/ *n* mantenimiento, *m;* sustento, *m,* alimentos, *m pl*

svelte /svɛlt/ *a* esbelto, gentil

swab /swɒb/ *vt Naut.* lampacear; limpiar con lampazo; *Surg.* tamponar. —*n* lampazo, *m; Surg.* torunda, *f,* tampón, *m*

swaddle /'swɒdl/ *vt* envolver; (infants) fajar

swaddling clothes /'swɒdlɪŋ/ *n pl* pañales, *m pl.* **to be still in s. clothes,** *Fig.* estar en mantillas, estar en pañales

swag /swæg/ *n* botín, *m*

swagger /'swægər/ *vi* fanfarronear, pavonearse; darse importancia. —*n* pavoneo, *m;* aire importante, *m;* (coat) tonto, *m.* —*a* majo; de última moda

swain /swein/ *n* zagal, *m;* enamorado, *m;* pretendiente, amante, *m*

swallow /'swɒlou/ *vt* tragar, engullir. —*n* trago, *m;* sorbo, *m; Ornith.* golondrina, *f.* **to s. an insult** (a story), tragar un insulto (una historia). **to s. one's words,** retractarse. **to s. one's pride,** bajar la cerviz, humillarse. **to s. up,** tragar; absorber. **s.-tailed coat,** frac, *m*

swamp /swɒmp/ *n* pantano, *m,* marisma, *f.* —*vt* sumergir; (a boat) echar a pique, hundir; (inundate) inundar

swan /swɒn/ *n* cisne, *m.* **swan's down,** plumón de cisne, *m.* **s.-song,** canto del cisne, *m*

swank /swæŋk/ *n* pretensiones, *f pl,* *vi* darse humos

sward /swɔrd/ *n* césped, *m,* hierba, *f*

swarm /swɔrm/ *n* enjambre, *m;* (of people) muchedumbre, multitud, *f;* tropel, *m.* —*vi* (of bees) enjambrar; (of other insects) pulular; (of people) hormiguear, bullir, pulular. —*vt* (climb) trepar. **to s. with,** estar infestado de

swarthy /'swɔrði/ *a* moreno

swashbuckler /'swɒʃ,bʌklər, 'swɔʃ-/ *n* perdonavidas, matasiete, *m*

swastika /'swɒstɪkə/ *n* esvástica, cruz gamada, *f*

swathe /swɒð/ *vt* envolver; fajar; (with bandages) vendar

sway /swei/ *vi* balancearse; oscilar; (stagger, of persons) bambolearse; (totter, of things) tambalearse; (of carriages) cabecear; (gracefully, in walking) cimbrarse. —*vt* balancear, mecer; oscilar; hacer tambalear; (influence) influir, inclinar; (govern) regir, gobernar. —*n* balanceo, *m*; oscilación, *f*; vaivén, *m*; tambaleo, *m*; (influence) ascendiente, dominio, *m*, influencia, *f*; (rule) imperio, poder, *m*. **to hold s. over,** gobernar, regir

swear /swɛər/ *vt* jurar; (*Law.* etc.) declarar bajo juramento. —*vi* jurar; (curse) echar pestes, blasfemar. **to s. at,** maldecir. **to s. by,** jurar por; poner fe implícita en. **to be sworn in,** prestar juramento. **to s. in,** tomar juramento (a). **to s. to,** atestiguar

sweat /swɛt/ *n* sudor, *m*; *Inf.* trabajo arduo, *m*. —*vi* sudar. —*vt* sudar; hacer sudar; (workers) explotar. **by the s. of one's brow,** con el sudor de la frente, con el sudor del rostro. **s.-gland,** glándula sudorípara, *f*

sweater /ˈswɛtər/ *n* suéter, jersey, *m*

sweating /ˈswɛtɪŋ/ *n* transpiración, *f*; (of workers) explotación, *f*

sweaty /ˈswɛti/ *a* sudoroso

Swede /swid/ *n* sueco (-ca); (vegetable) naba, *f*

Sweden /ˈswidn/ Suecia, *f*

Swedish /ˈswidɪʃ/ *a* sueco. —*n* (language) sueco, *m*

sweep /swip/ *vi* extenderse (por); (cleave) surcar; pasar rápidamente (por); invadir; dominar; andar majestuosamente; (with a brush) barrer. —*vt* barrer; pasar (por); (the strings of a musical instrument) rasguear; (the sea) navegar por; (mines) barrer; (the horizon, etc.) examinar; (a chimney) deshollinar; (with a brush) barrer; (remove) arrebatar; quitar; llevarse; (abolish) suprimir. **to s. along,** *vt* (of the current, crowds, etc.) arrastrar. —*vi* pasar majestuosamente; correr rápidamente (por). **to s. aside,** apartar con la mano; abandonar; (a protest) desoír, no hacer caso de. **to s. away,** barrer; (remove) llevarse; destruir; suprimir. **to s. down,** *vt* barrer; (carry) arrastrar. —*vi* (of cliffs, etc.) bajar; (of an enemy) abalanzarse (sobre); lanzarse (por). **to s. off,** barrer; (a person) llevarse sin perder tiempo; arrebatar con violencia (a). **to be swept off one's feet,** ser arrastrado (por); perder el balance; (of emotion) ser dominado por. **to s. on,** seguir su avance inexorable; seguir su marcha. **to s. up,** recoger, barrer

sweep /swip/ *n* barredura, *f*; (of a chimney) deshollinador, *m*; (of the tide) curso, *m*; (of a scythe, etc.) golpe, *m*; (range) alcance, *m*; (fold) pliegue, *m*; (curve) curva, *f*; (of water, etc.) extensión, *f*; (of wings) envergadura, *f*. **with a s. of the arm,** con un gesto del brazo. **to make a clean s. of,** hacer tabla rasa de

sweeping /ˈswipɪŋ/ *a* completo; comprensivo; demasiado general; radical. **a s. judgment,** un juicio demasiado general.

s. change, cambio radicale, *m pl.* **s. brush,** escoba, *f*

sweepings /ˈswipɪŋz/ *n pl* barreduras, *f pl*; residuos, *m pl*; (of society) heces, *f pl*

sweepstake /ˈswip,steik/ *n* lotería, *f*

sweet /swit/ *a* dulce; (of scents) oloroso, fragante; (of sounds) melodioso, dulce; (charming) encantador; amable; (pretty) bonito. —*n* bombón, *m*; golosina, *f*; (at a meal) (plato) dulce, *m*; dulzura, *f*; (beloved) amor, *m*, querido (-da). **How s. it smells!** ¡Qué buen olor tiene! **the sweets of life,** las dulzuras de la vida. **s.-pea,** guisante de olor, *m*, haba de las Indias, *f*. **s.-potato,** batata, *f*. **s.-scented, s.-scented,** perfumado, fragante. **s.-tempered,** amable, de carácter dulce. **s.-toothed,** goloso. **s.-william,** *Bot.* clavel de la China, clavel de ramillete, clavel de San Isidro, ramillete de Constantinopla, *m*, minutisa, *f*

sweetbread /ˈswit,brɛd/ *n* lechecillas, *f pl*

sweeten /ˈswitn/ *vt* azucarar; endulzar. **Cervantes sweetens one's bitter moments,** Cervantes endulza los momentos ásperos

sweetheart /ˈswit,hɑrt/ *n* amante, *mf*, amado (-da); (as address) querido (-da)

sweet potato *n* batata, *f*, boniato, buniato, camote, *m*

sweet sixteen *n* (age) los dieciséis abriles, *m pl*; (party) quinceañera (at age fifteen) *f*

swell /swɛl/ *vi* hincharse; (of the sea) entumecerse; crecer; aumentarse. —*vt* hinchar; aumentar. —*n* (of the sea) oleada, *f*, oleaje, *m*; (of the ground) ondulación, *f*; (of sound) crescendo, *m*; (increase) aumento, *m*; (dandy) pisaverde, elegante, *m*; (important person) pájaro gordo, *m*; (at games, etc.) espada, *m*. —*a* estupendo; elegantísimo; de primera, excelente. **to suffer from swelled head,** tener humos, darse importancia. **This foot is swollen,** Este pie está hinchado (or tumefacto). **The refugees have swelled the population,** Los refugiados han aumentado la población. **eyes swollen with tears,** ojos arrasados de lágrimas. **to s. with pride,** hincharse de orgullo

swelling /ˈswɛlɪŋ/ *n* hinchazón, *f*; *Med.* tumefacción, *f*; (bruise, etc.) chichón, *m*

swelter /ˈswɛltər/ *vi* abrasarse; arder. —*n* bochorno, calor sofocante, *m*

swerve /swɜrv/ *vi* desviarse; apartarse (de); torcerse. —*n* desvío, *m*

swift /swɪft/ *a* rápido, veloz; pronto. —*adv* velozmente, rápidamente. —*n* *Ornith.* vencejo, *m*. **s.-flowing,** (of rivers, etc.) de corriente rápida. **s.-footed,** de pies ligeros

swim /swɪm/ *vi* nadar; flotar; (glide) deslizarse; (fill) inundarse. —*vt* (a horse) hacer nadar; pasar a nado; nadar. —*n* natación, *f*. **eyes swimming with tears,** ojos inundados de lágrimas. **He enjoys a s.,** Le gusta nadar. **My head swims,** Se me va la cabeza. **Everything swam before my eyes,** Todo parecía bailar ante mis ojos. **to be in the s.,** formar parte (de), ser (de); (be up to date) estar al corriente. **to s. the Channel,** atravesar el canal de la Mancha a nado. **to s. with the tide,** ir con la corriente

swimmer /'swɪmər/ n nadador (-ra). **He is a bad s.,** Él nada mal

swimming /'swɪmɪŋ/ n natación, f; (of the head) vértigo, m. **s.-bath,** piscina, f. **s.-costume,** traje de baño, m. **s.-pool,** piscina al aire libre, f

swindle /'swɪndl/ vt engañar, estafar; defraudar (de). —n estafa, f, timo, m; engaño, m; impostura, f

swindler /'swɪndlər/ n estafador (-ra), trampeador (-ra); engañador (-ra)

swine /swaɪn/ n cerdo, puerco, m; (person) cochino (-na). **a herd of s.,** una manada de cerdos

swing /swɪŋ/ vi balancearse; oscilar; (hang) colgar, pender; columpiarse; girar; dar la vuelta; (of a boat) bornear. —vt balancear; (hang) colgar; (rock) mecer; (in a swing, etc.) columpiar; hacer oscilar; (raise) subir. —n oscilación, f; vaivén, m; balanceo, m; (rhythm) ritmo, m; (seat, etc.) columpio, m; (reach) alcance, m. **The door swung open,** La puerta se abrió silenciosamente. **He swung the car round,** Dio la vuelta al auto. **He swung himself into the saddle,** Montó de un salto. **to be in full s.,** estar a toda marcha. **to go with a s.,** tener mucho éxito. **s.-boat,** columpio, m. **s.-bridge,** puente giratorio, m. **s.-door,** puerta giratoria, f

swinging /'swɪŋɪŋ/ a oscilante; pendiente; rítmico. —n balanceo, m; oscilación, f; vaivén, m; ritmo, m. **s. stride,** andar rítmico, m

swipe /swaɪp/ vt golpear duro; aplastar. —n golpe fuerte, m

swirl /swɜrl/ vi arremolinarse. —n remolino, m

swish /swɪʃ/ vt (of an animal's tail) agitar, mover, menear; (of a cane) blandir; (thrash) azotar. —vi silbar; (of water) susurrar; (of a dress, etc.) crujir. —n silbo, m; (of water) susurro, murmullo, m; (of a dress, etc.) crujido, m

Swiss /swɪs/ a and n suizo (-za)

switch /swɪtʃ/ n vara, f; (riding) látigo, m; (of hair) trenza, f; Elec. interruptor, m; Rail. aguja, f; (Rail. siding) desviadero, m. —vt azotar; (a train) desviar; Elec. interrumpir; (transfer) trasladar; (of an animal, its tail) remover, mover rápidamente. **to s. off,** (Elec. and telephone) cortar; (Radio. and Auto.) desconectar. **to s. on,** conectar; (a light) poner (la luz); (a radio) encender

switchboard /'swɪtʃˌbɔrd/ n cuadro de distribución, m

Switzerland /'swɪtsərlənd/ Suiza, f

swivel /'swɪvəl/ n torniquete, m; anillo móvil, m; pivote, m. —vi girar sobre un

eje; dar una vuelta. **s.-chair,** silla giratoria, f. **s.-door,** puerta giratoria, f

swoon /swun/ vi desvanecerse, desmayarse. —n desmayo, desvanecimiento, m

swoop /swup/ vi calarse, abatirse; (of robbers, etc.) abalanzarse (sobre). —n calada, f. **at one fell s.,** de un solo golpe

sword /sɔrd/ n espada, f; sable, m. **to measure swords with,** cruzar espadas con. **to put to the s.,** pasar a cuchillo (a). **s.-arm,** brazo derecho, m. **s.-belt,** talabarte, m. **s.-cut,** sablazo, m. **s.-dance,** danza de espadas, f. **s.-fish,** pez espada, pez sierra, espadarte, m, jifia, f. **s.-play,** esgrima, f; manejo de la espada, m. **s.-stick,** bastón de estoque, m. **s.-thrust,** golpe de espada, m, estocada, f

sybarite /'sɪbəˌraɪt/ a and n sibarita, mf

sycophant /'sɪkəfənt/ n sicofanta, f

syllable /'sɪləbəl/ n sílaba, f

syllabus /'sɪləbəs/ n programa, m; compendio, m

sylvan /'sɪlvən/ a selvático, silvestre; rústico

symbiosis /ˌsɪmbiˈousɪs/ n simbiosis, f

symbol /'sɪmbəl/ n símbolo, emblema, m; Math. símbolo, m; (of rank, etc.) insignia, f

symbolize /'sɪmbəˌlaɪz/ vt simbolizar

symmetrical /sɪˈmɛtrɪkəl/ a simétrico

symmetry /'sɪmɪtri/ n simetría, f

sympathetic /ˌsɪmpəˈθɛtɪk/ a simpático; compasivo; (of the public, etc.) bien dispuesto. —n Anat. gran simpático, m. **s. words,** palabras de simpatía, f pl. **s. ink,** tinta simpática, f

sympathize /'sɪmpəˌθaɪz/ vi simpatizar (con); (understand) comprender; (condole) compadecerse (de), condolerse (de); dar el pésame

sympathizer /'sɪmpəˌθaɪzər/ n partidario (-ia)

sympathy /'sɪmpəθi/ n simpatía, f; compasión, f. **Paul is in s. with their aims,** Pablo está de acuerdo con sus objetos. **Please accept my s.,** (on a bereavement) Le acompaño a Vd. en su sentimiento

symphonic /sɪmˈfɒnɪk/ a sinfónico

symphony /'sɪmfəni/ n sinfonía, f

symposium /sɪmˈpouziəm/ n colección de artículos, m

symptom /'sɪmptəm/ n síntoma, m; señal, f, indicio, m. **to show symptoms of,** dar indicios de

symptomatic /ˌsɪmptəˈmætɪk/ a sintomático

synagogue /'sɪnəˌgɒg/ n sinagoga, f

synchronize /'sɪŋkrəˌnaɪz/ vi coincidir, tener lugar simultáneamente; sincronizarse. —vt sincronizar

synchronous /'sɪŋkrənəs/ a sincrónico

syncopate /'sɪŋkəˌpeɪt/ vt (Gram. Mus.) sincopar

syncopation /ˌsɪŋkəˈpeɪʃən/ n Mus. síncopa, f

syncope /'sɪŋkəˌpi/ n (Med. Gram.) síncope, m

syndical /'sɪndɪkəl/ a sindical
syndicalist /'sɪndɪkəlɪst/ n sindicalista, mf
syndicate /n. 'sɪndɪkɪt; v. -ˌkeit/ n sindicato, m, vt sindicar
synod /'sɪnəd/ n Eccl. sínodo, m
synonym /'sɪnənɪm/ n sinónimo, m
synonymous /sɪ'nɒnəməs/ a sinónimo
synopsis /sɪ'nɒpsɪs/ n sinopsis, f
syntax /'sɪntæks/ n sintaxis, f
synthesis /'sɪnθəsɪs/ n síntesis, f
synthetic /sɪn'θetɪk/ a sintético
synthetize /'sɪnθəˌtaiz/ vt sintetizar
syphilis /'sɪfəlɪs/ n sífilis, f

Syria /'sɪərɪə/ Siria, f
Syrian /'sɪərɪə/ a and n siríaco (-ca), sirio (-ia)
syringe /sə'rɪndʒ/ n jeringa, f, vt jeringar
syrup /'sɪrəp, 'sɜr-/ n jarabe, m; (for bottling fruit, etc.) almíbar, m
system /'sɪstəm/ n sistema, m; régimen, m; método, m; (body) organismo, m. **He has no s. in his work,** No tiene método en su trabajo. **the nervous s.,** el sistema nervioso. **the feudal s.,** el feudalismo, el sistema feudal
systematic /ˌsɪstə'mætɪk/ a sistemático, metódico
systole /'sɪstəˌli/ n Med. sístole, f

t /ti/ n (letter) te, f. —a en T, en forma de T. **T bandage,** vendaje en T, m. **T square,** regla T, f

tab /tæb/ n oreja, f

tabernacle /'tæbər,nækəl/ n tabernáculo, m; templo, m; Archit. templete, m; Eccl. custodia, f

tabes /'teibiz/ n Med. tabes, f

table /'teibəl/ n mesa, f; (food) comida, mesa, f; (of the law, weights, measures, contents, etc.) tabla, f; (of land) meseta, f; (of prices) lista, tarifa, f. —vt (parliament) poner sobre la mesa; enumerar, apuntar, hacer una lista de. **to clear the t.,** alzar (or levantar) la mesa. **to lay the t.,** cubrir (or poner) la mesa. **to have a table d'hôte meal,** tomar el menú. **to rise from the t.,** levantarse de la mesa. **to sit down at the t.,** ponerse a la mesa. **The tables are turned,** Se volvió la tortilla. **side t.,** aparador, trinchero, m. **small t.,** mesilla, f. **t. of contents,** tabla de materias, f, índice, índice de materias, índice general, m. **t.-centrepiece,** centro de mesa, m. **t.-cloth,** mantel, m. **t.-companion,** comensal, mf **t.-knife,** cuchillo de mesa, m **t.-lamp,** quinqué, m; lampara de mesa, f. **t.-land,** meseta, f. **t.-leg,** pata de una mesa, f. **t.-linen,** mantelería, f. **t.-napkin,** servilleta, f. **t.-runner,** camino de mesa, m. **t.-spoon,** cuchara para los legumbres, f. **t.-talk,** conversación de sobremesa, f. **t.-turning,** mesas que dan vueltas, f pl. **t.-ware,** artículos para la mesa, m pl

tableau /tæ'blou/ n cuadro, m. **tableaux vivants,** cuadros vivos, m pl

tablespoonful /'teibəlspun,ful/ n cucharada, f

tablet /'tæblɪt/ n tabla, f; (with inscription) tarjeta, losa, lápida, f; Med. comprimido, m, tableta, f; (of soap, chocolate) pastilla, f; (of song, poem) refrán, m. **writing t.,** taco de papel, m

tabloid /'tæblɔɪd/ n comprimido, m, pastilla, f

taboo /tə'bu, tæ-/ n tabú, m. —vt prohibido, tabú. —vt declarar tabú, prohibir

tabor /'teibər/ n Mus. tamboril, tamborín, m. **t. player,** tamborilero, m

tabulate /'tæbyə,leit/ vt resumir en tablas; hacer una lista de, catalogar

tacit /'tæsɪt/ a tácito

taciturn /'tæsɪ,tɜrn/ a taciturno, sombrío, reservado, de pocas palabras

tack /tæk/ n (nail) tachuela, puntilla, f; Sew. hilván, embaste, m; Naut. amura, f; Naut. puño de amura, m; Naut. bordada, f; Fig. cambio de política, m. —vt clavar con tachuelas; Sew. hilvanar, embastar; Fig. añadir. —vi Naut. virar; Fig. cambiar de política, adoptar un nuevo plan de acción. **t. puller,** sacabrocas, m

tackle /'tækəl/ n aparejo, m; maniobra, f; Naut. cuadernal, m, jarcia, f; (gear) aparejos, avíos, m pl; (football) carga, f. —vt agarrar, asir; Fig. atacar, abordar; (foot-ball) cargar; (undertake) emprender; (a problem) luchar con. **t.-block,** polea, f

tacky /'tæki/ a pegajoso, viscoso

tact /tækt/ n tacto, m, discreción, diplomacia, delicadeza, f

tactful /'tæktfəl/ a lleno de tacto, diplomático, discreto

tactical /'tæktɪkəl/ a táctico

tactics /'tæktɪks/ n pl táctica, f.

tactile /'tæktɪl/ a táctil; tangible

tactless /'tæktlɪs/ a que no tiene tacto, sin tacto alguno, indiscreto

tadpole /'tædpoul/ n renacuajo, m

taffeta /'tæfɪtə/ n tafetán, m

tag /tæg/ n herrete, m; (label) marbete, m, etiqueta, f; (of tail) punta del rabo, f; (of boot) tirador de bota, m; (game) marro, m; (rag) arrapiezo, m; (quotation) cita bien conocida, f; (of song, poem) refrán, m. **to play t.,** jugar al marro

Tagus /'teigəs/ el Tajo, m

tail /teil/ n cola, f, rabo, m; (plait) trenza, f; (wisp of hair) mechón, m; (of a comet) cola, cabellera, f; (of a note in music) rabito, m; (of a coat) faldón, m; (of a kite) cola, f; (of the eye), rabo, m; (retinue) séquito, m, banda, f; (of an aeroplane) cola, f; (end) tin, m; (of coin) cruz, f; (line) fila, cola, f. —vt seguir de cerca, pisarle (a uno) los talones. **to t. after,** seguir de cerca. **to t. away,** disminuir; desaparecer, perderse de vista. **to t. on,** unir, juntar. **to turn t.,** volver la espalda, poner los pies en polvorosa. **with the t. between the legs,** con el rabo entre piernas. **t.-board,** (of a cart) escalera, f. **t.-coat,** frac, m. **t.-end,** extremo, m; fin, m; lo último. **t.-feather,** pena, f. **t.-fin,** aleta caudal, f; Aer. timón de dirección, m. **t.-light,** farol trasero, m. **t.-piece,** (of a violin, etc.) cola, f; Print. marmosete, culo de lámpara, m. **t. spin** Aer. barrena de cola, f. **t. wind,** viento de cola, m

tailed /teild/ a de cola. **big-t.,** rabudo, de cola grande. **long-t.,** rabilargo. **short-t.,** rabicorto

tailless /'teillɪs/ a rabón, sin rabo

tailor /'teilər/ n sastre (-ra). **t.-made,** n traje sastre, m, a de hechura de sastre. **tailor's shop,** sastrería, f

tailoring /'teilərɪŋ/ n sastrería, f; (work) corte, m

taint /teint/ n corrupción, f; infección, f; (blemish) mancha, f; (tinge) dejo, m. —vt corromper, pervertir; inficionar; (meat) corromper. —vi corromperse, inficionarse; (meat) corromperse

take /teik/ vt tomar; (receive) aceptar; (remove) quitar; (pick up) coger; (grab) asir, agarrar; Math. restar; (carry) llevar; (a person) traer, llevar; (guide) conducir, guiar; (win) ganar; (earn) cobrar, percibir; obtener; (make prisoner) hacer prisionero, prender; (a town, etc.) tomar, rendir, conquistar; (appropriate) apoderarse de, apropiarse; (steal) robar, hurtar; (ensnare) coger, cazar con trampas; (fish) pescar, coger; (a trick, in cards) hacer (una baza); (an illness) contraer, coger; (by surprise) sorprender, coger desprevenido (a); (attract) atraer; (drink) beber; (a meal) tomar; (select) escoger; (hire) alquilar; (suppose) suponer; (use) emplear, usar; (impers., require) necesitarse, hacer falta; (purchase) comprar; (assume) adoptar, asumir; (a leap) dar (un salto); (a walk) dar (un paseo); (a look) echar (un vistazo); (measures) tomar (medidas); (the chair) presidir; (understand) comprender; (a photograph) sacar (una fotografía); (believe) creer; (consider) considerar; (a note) apuntar; (jump over) saltar; (time) tomar, emplear. **I t.** **size three in shoes,** Calzo el número tres. **to t. to be,** (believe) suponer; (mistake) creer quivocadamente. **to t. (a thing) badly,** tomarlo (or llevarlo) a mal. **The book took me two hours to read,** Necesité dos horas para leer el libro, Leí el libro en dos horas. **And this, I t. it, is Mary?** ¿Y supongo que ésta será María? **to be taken with,** ser entusiasta de; (of persons) estar prendado de. **to t. aback,** desconcertar, coger desprevenido (a). **to t. again,** volver a tomar; llevar otra vez; (a photograph) retratar otra vez. **to t. along,** llevar; traer. **to t. away,** quitar; llevarse. **to t. back,** devolver; (retract) retractar; (receive) recibir (algo) devuelto. **to t. down,** bajar; (a building) derribar; (machinery) desmontar; (hair) deshacerse (el cabello); (swallow) tragar; (in writing) apuntar; (humble) quitar los humos (a), humillar. **to t. for,** creer, imaginar; (a walk, etc.) llevar a; (mistake) creer erróneamente; tomar por. **Whom do you t. me for?** ¿Por quién me tomas? **to. t. for granted (assume),** dar por descontado, dar por lecho, dar por sentado, dar por supuesto; (underestimate) no hacer caso de, tratar con indiferencia. **t. the lion's share (of),** llevarse la parte del león (de), llevarse la tajada del león (de). **t shape,** cobrar perfiles más nítidos, estructurarse con más nitidez, ir adquiriendo consistencia, tomar forma. **t. the law into one's own hands,** tomar la justicia por la mano. **to t. from,** privar, quitar de; (subtract) restar; substraer de. **to t. in,** (believe) tragar, creer; (sail) acortar las velas; (deceive) engañar; (lead in) hacer entrar; (accept) recibir, aceptar. **to t. off,** quitar; (surgically) amputar; (one's hat, etc.) quitarse (el sombrero); (eyes) sacar; (take away) llevarse; (mimic) imitar; (ridicule) ridiculizar; (unstick) despegar; (discount) descontar. **to t. on,** emprender; aceptar; (at sports) jugar. **to t. on oneself,** encargarse de, tomar por su cuenta, asumir. **to t. out,** sacar; extraer; (remove) quitar; (outside) llevar fuera; (for a walk) llevar a paseo; (obtain) obtener, sacar; (tire) agotar, rendir. **to t. over,** tomar posesión de; asumir; (show) mostrar, conducir por. **t. the bull by the horns,** ir al toro por los cuernos. **take seriously,** tomar en serio. **to t. up,** subir; (pick up) recoger; (a challenge, etc.) aceptar; (a dress, etc.) acortar; (absorb) absorber; (of space) ocupar; (of time) ocupar, hacer perder; (buy) comprar; (adopt) dedicarse a; (arrest) arrestar, prender; (criticize) censurar, criticar; (begin) empezar; (resume) continuar

take /teik/ *vi* tomar; (be successful) tener éxito; (of vaccination, etc.) prender; (a good (bad) photograph) salir bien (mal). **to t. after,** salir a, parecerse a; (of conduct) seguir el ejemplo de; **to t. off,** salir; *Aer.* despegar. **to t. on,** *Inf.* lamentarse. **to t. to,** dedicarse a; darse a; (of persons) tomar cariño a; (grow accustomed) acostumbrarse a. **to t. up with,** hacerse amigo de

take /teik/ *n* toma, *f*; cogida, *f*; *Print.* tomada, *f*; *Theat.* taquilla, *f*. **t.-in,** engaño, *m*. **t.-off,** *Aer.* (recorrido del) despegue, *m*; caricatura, *f*; sátira, *f*

taking /ˈteikiŋ/ *n* toma, *f*; secuestro, *m*, *n pl* **takings,** ingresos, *m pl; Theat.* taquilla, entrada, *f*. —*a* atractivo, encantador; simpático; (of disease) contagioso

talcum powder /ˈtælkəm/ *n* talco, polvo de talco, *m*

tale /teil/ *n* (recital) narración, historia, *f*; relato, *m*; cuento, *m*; leyenda, historia, fábula, *f*; (number) cuenta, *f*, número, *m*; (gossip) chisme, *m*. **old wives' t,** cuento de viejas, *m*. **to tell a t.,** contar una historia. **to tell tales,** contar cuentos; revelar secretos, chismear

talebearer /ˈteilˌbɛərər/ *n* correveidile, *mf*; chismoso (-sa), soplón (-ona)

talent /ˈtælənt/ *n* (coin) talento, *m*; (ability) ingenio, *m*; habilidad, *f*. **the best t. in Spain,** la flor de la cultura española

talented /ˈtæləntid/ *a* talentoso, ingenioso

talisman /ˈtælismən/ *n* talismán, *m*

talit /ˈtalis, talit/ taled, *m*

talk /tɔk/ *vi* and *vt* hablar, decir. **to t. business,** hablar de negocios. **to t. for talking's sake,** hablar por hablar. **to t. French,** hablar francés. **to t. nonsense,** decir disparates. **to t. too much,** hablar demasiado; *Inf.* hablar por los codos, irse (a uno) la lengua. **to t. about,** hablar de; conversar sobre. **to t. at,** decir algo a alguien para que lo entienda otro. **Are you talking at me?** ¿Lo dices por mí? **to t. away,** seguir hablando; disipar. **to t. into,** persuadir, inducir (a) a. **to t. of,** hablar de; charlar sobre. **to t. on,** hablar acerca de (or sobre); (continue) seguir hablando. **to t. out of,** disuadir de. **to t. out of turn,** meterse donde no le llaman, meter la pata. **to t. over,** hablar de; discutir, considerar. **to t. round,** persuadir. **to t. to,** (address) hablar a; (consult) hablar con; (scold) reprender. **to t. to each other,** hablarse. **to t. up,** hablar claro

talk /tɔk/ *n* conversación, *f;* (informal lecture) charla, *f;* (empty words) palabras, *f pl;* (notoriety) escándalo, *m;* rumor, *m*. **There is t. of...,** Se dice que...; Se habla de que. **to give a t.,** dar una charla. **to indulge in small t.,** hablar de cosas sin importancia, hablar de naderías

talkative /'tɔkətɪv/ *a* locuaz, gárrulo, hablador, decidor. **to be very t.,** ser muy locuaz; *Inf.* tener mucha lengua

talker /'tɔkər/ *n* hablador (-ra), conversador (-ra); (lecturer) orador (-ra); (in a derogatory sense) fanfarrón (-ona), charlatán (-ana). **to be a good t.,** hablar bien, ser buen conversacionista

talking /'tɔkɪŋ/ *a* que habla, hablante; (of birds, dolls, etc.) parlero. **to give a good t. to,** dar una peluca (a). **t.-film,** película sonora, *f.* **t.-machine,** fonógrafo, *m*

tall /tɔl/ *a* alto; (of stories) exagerado. **five feet tall,** de cinco pies de altura

tallboy /'tɔl,bɔi/ *n* cómoda alta, *f*

tallow /'tæloʊ/ *n* sebo, *m.* **t. candle,** vela de sebo, *f.* **t. chandler,** velero (-ra). **t.-faced,** con cara de color de cera

tally /'tæli/ *n* tarja, tara, *f;* cuenta, *f.* —*vt* llevar la cuenta (de). —*vi* estar conforme, cuadrar

Talmud /'talmʊd/ *n* Talmud, *m*

Talmudic /tal'mʊdɪk/ *a* talmúdico

tambour /'tæmbʊr, tæm'bʊr/ *n Mus.* tambor, *m;* (for embroidery) tambor (or bastidor) para bordar, *m*

tambourine /,tæmbə'rin/ *n* pandereta, *f*

tame /teim/ *a* domesticado, manso; (spiritless) sumiso; (dull) aburrido, soso. —*vt* domar, domesticar; (curb) reprimir, gobernar, domar, suavizar. **to grow t.,** domesticarse

taming /'teimɪŋ/ *n* domadura, *f.* **The T. of the Shrew,** La Fierecilla Domada

tamp /tæmp/ *vt* apisonar; (in blasting) atacar (un barreno)

tamper /'tæmpər/ *vi* (with) descomponer, estropear; (meddle with) meterse con; (witnesses) sobornar; (documents) falsificar

tampon /'tæmpɒn/ *n Surg.* tampón, tapón, *m, vt* taponar

tan /tæn/ *vt* curtir, adobar; (of sun) tostar, quemar; (slang) zurrar. —*vi* tostarse por el sol. —*n* color café claro, *m;* bronceado, cutis tostado, *m.* —*a* de color café claro

tandem /'tændəm/ *n* tándem, *m*

tang /tæŋ/ *n* (of sword, etc.) espiga, *f;* (flavor) fuerte sabor, *m;* (sound) retintín, *m*

tangent /'tændʒənt/ *a* and *n* tangente *f.* **to go off on a t.,** *Fig.* salir por la tangente

tangerine /'tændʒə'rin/ *a* and *n* tangerino (-na). **t. orange,** naranja mandarina, *f*

tangible /'tændʒəbəl/ *a* tangible; *Fig.* real

tangle /'tæŋgəl/ *n* embrollo, enredo,

nudo, *m;* (of streets) laberinto, *m; Fig.* confusión, *f.* —*vt* embrollar, enmarañar; (entangle) enredar; *Fig.* poner en confusión, complicar. —*vi* enmarañarse

tank /tæŋk/ *n* tanque, depósito (de agua, etc.), *m;* cisterna, *f;* (as a reservoir) aljibe, estanque, *m; Mil.* tanque, carro de asalto, *m*

tanker /'tæŋkər/ *n* petrolero, *m*

tanned /tænd/ *a* bronceado, quemado por el sol, dorado por el sol

tannery /'tænəri/ *n* curtiduría, *f*

tantalize /'tæntḷ,aiz/ *vt* tentar, atormentar, provocar

tantalizing /'tæntḷ,aizɪŋ/ *a* tentador, atormentador; provocativo

tantamount /'tæntə,maunt/ *a* equivalente, igual. **to be t. to,** ser equivalente a

tantrum /'tæntrəm/ *n* pataleta, rabieta, *f,* berrinche, *m*

tap /tæp/ *n* (blow) pequeño golpe, toque ligero, *m;* palmadita, *f;* (for drawing water, etc.) grifo, *m,* llave, *f;* (of a barrel) canilla, *f;* (brew of liquor) clase de vino, *f;* (tap room) bar con mostrador, *m;* (tool) macho de terraja, *m;* (piece of leather on shoe) tapa, *f; pl* taps, *Mil.* toque de apagar las luces, *m.* —*vt* (strike) golpear ligeramente, dar una palmadita a; (pierce) horadar; (a barrel) decentar; *Surg.* hacer una puntura en; (trees) sangrar; *Elec.* derivar (una corriente); (of water, current) tomar; (information) descubrir; (telephone) escuchar las conversaciones telefónicas. —*vi* golpear ligeramente. **to tap at the door,** llamar suavemente a la puerta. **on tap,** en tonel. **screw-tap,** terraja, *f.* **tap-dance,** claqué, *m.* **tap-root,** raíz pivotante, *f*

tape /teip/ *n* (linen) cinta de hilo, *f;* (cotton) cinta de algodón, *f;* (telegraph machine) cinta de papel, *f;* (surveying) cinta para medir, *f.* **t. adhesive t.,** cinta adhesiva, *f.* **red t.,** balduque, *m; Fig.* burocracia, *f;* formulismo, *m.* **t.-machine,** telégrafo de cotizaciones bancarias, *m.* **t.-measure,** cinta métrica, *f*

taper /'teipər/ *n* bujía, cerilla, *f; Eccl.* cirio, *m.* —*vi* ahusarse, rematar en punta. —*vt* afilar

tapering /'teipərɪŋ/ *a* cónico, piramidal; (of fingers) afilado

tapestry /'tæpəstri/ *n* tapiz, *m.* **t. weaver,** tapicero, *m*

tapeworm /'teip,wɜrm/ *n* tenia, lombriz solitaria, *f*

tar /tɑr/ *n* alquitrán, *m,* brea, *f.* —*vt* embrear, alquitranar. **to tar and feather,** emplumar. **coal t.,** alquitrán mineral, *m*

tarantula /tə'ræntʃələ/ *n* tarántula, *f*

tardy /'tɑrdi/ *a* (late) tardío, (slow) lento; (reluctant) desinclinado

tare /tɛər/ *n Bot.* yero, *m;* (in the Bible) cizaña, *f; Com.* tara, *f;* (of a vehicle) peso en vacío, *m*

target /'tɑrgɪt/ *n* blanco (de tiro), *m;* (shield) rodela, tarja, *f.* **t. practice,** tiro al blanco, *m*

tariff /'tærɪf/ n tarifa, f. **to put a t. on,** tarifar

tarmac /'tɑrmæk/ n alquitranado, m

tarn /tɑrn/ n lago de montaña, m

tarnish /'tɑrnɪʃ/ n deslustre, m. —vt deslustrar, empañar; Fig. obscurecer, manchar. —vi deslustrarse

tarpaulin /tɑr'pɔlɪn, 'tɑrpəlɪn/ n alquitranado, encerado, m

tarry /'tɑri/ vi tardar, detenerse

tart /tɑrt/ a ácido, acerbo, agridulce; Fig. áspero. —n tarta, f; pastelillo de fruta, m

tartar /'tɑrtər/ n Chem. tártaro, m; (in teeth) sarro, tártaro, m; **cream of t.,** (cremor) tártaro, m. **t. emetic,** tártaro emético, m. **Tartar,** a and n tártaro (-ra)

task /tæsk/ n tarea, labor, f; empresa, f; misión, f. **to take to t.,** regañar, censurar. **t.-force,** (naval or military) contingente, m

taskmaster /'tæsk,mæstər/ n el que señala una tarea; amo, m

tassel /'tæsəl/ n borla, f; (of corn) panoja, espiga, f

taste /teist/ n gusto, m; (flavor) sabor, m; (specimen) ejemplo, m, idea, f; (small quantity) un poco, muy poco; (liking) afición, inclinación, f; (of drink) sorbo, trago, m; (tinge) dejo, m. —vt (appraise) probar; gustar, percibir el gusto de; (experience) experimentar, conocer. —vi tener gusto, tener sabor. **a matter of t.,** cuestión de gusto. **Each to his own t.,** Entre gustos no hay disputa. **He had not tasted a bite,** No había probado bocado. **in bad (good) t.,** de mal (buen) gusto; de mal (buen) tono. **to have a t. for,** ser aficionado a, gustar de. **to t.,** Cul. a gusto, a sabor. **to t. of,** tener gusto de, saber a

tasted /'teistɪd/ a (in compounds) de sabor...

tasteful /'teistfəl/ a de buen gusto

tastefully /'teistfəli/ adv con buen gusto

tasteless /'teistlɪs/ a insípido, soso, insulso; de mal gusto

taster /'teistər/ n catador, m; (vessel) catavino, m

tasting /'teistɪŋ/ n saboreo, m, gustación, f, a (in compounds) de sabor...

tasty /'teisti/ a apetitoso, sabroso

tatter /'tætər/ n andrajo, harapo, m; jirón, m. **to tear in tatters,** hacer jirones

tattered /'tætərd/ a andrajoso, haraposo

tattoo /tæ'tu/ n tatuaje, m; Mil. retreta, f; (display) parada militar, f. —vt tatuar

taunt /tɔnt/ n mofa, f, insulto, escarnio, m. —vt insultar, atormentar. **to t. with,** echar en cara

taunting /'tɔntɪŋ/ a insultante, burlón, insolente

tauntingly /'tɔntɪŋli/ adv burlonamente, insolentemente

taut /tɔt/ a tieso, tirante, tenso; en regla; Naut. **to make t.,** tesar

tauten /'tɔtn/ vt tesar; poner tieso

tautological /,tɔt'ɒdʒɪkəl/ a tautológico

tavern /'tævərn/ n taberna, f; (inn) mesón, m, posada, f. **t.-keeper,** tabernero, m

tawdrily /'tɔdrɪli/ adv llamativamente, de un modo cursi

tawdry /'tɔdri/ a chillón, charro, cursi

tawny /'tɔni/ a leonado

tax /tæks/ n contribución, gabela, imposición, f; Fig. carga, f; vt imponer contribuciones (a); Law. tasar; Fig. cargar, abrumar. **to tax with,** tachar (de), acusar (de). **direct (indirect) tax,** contribución directa (indirecta), f. **tax-collector,** recaudador de contribuciones, m. **tax-free,** libre de impuestos. **tax-rate,** tarifa de impuestos, f, cupo, m. **tax-register,** lista de contribuyentes, f

taxable /'tæksəbəl/ a imponible, sujeto a impuestos

taxation /tæk'seiʃən/ n imposición de contribuciones (or impuestos), f

tax evasion n evasión tributaria, f

taxi /'tæksi/ n taxi, m. —vi ir en un taxi; Aer. correr por tierra. **t. driver,** chófer de un taxi, taxista, m. **t. rank, taxi stand,** parada de taxis, f

taxidermist /'tæksɪ,dɜrmɪst/ n taxidermista, mf

taxpayer /'tæks,peiər/ n contribuyente, mf

taxpaying /'tæks,peiɪŋ/ a tributario, que paga contribuciones

tax reform n reforma impositiva, reforma tributaria, f

tea /ti/ n (liquid) té, m; (meal) merienda, f. **to have tea,** tomar el té, merendar. **tea-caddy,** bote para té, m. **tea-chest,** caja para té, f. **tea-cosy,** cubretetera, m. **tea-cup,** taza para té, f. **tea-dance,** té baile, m. **tea-kettle** or **tea-pot,** tetera, f. **tea-leaf,** hoja de té, f. **tea-party,** reunión para tomar el té, f. **tea-room,** salón de té, m. **tea-rose,** rosa de té, f. **tea-set,** juego de té, m. **tea-strainer,** colador de té, m. **tea-time,** hora de té, f. **tea-urn,** samowar, m, tetera para hacer té, f. **tea-waggon,** carrito para el té, m.

teach /titʃ/ vt (a person) enseñar, instruir; (a subject) enseñar; (to lecture on) ser profesor de; (a lesson) dar una lección (de). —vi (be a teacher) dedicarse a la enseñanza. **to teach at...,** desempeñor una cátedra en... **to t. a person Spanish,** enseñar el castellano a alguien. **to t. how to,** enseñar a (followed by infin.)

teachable /'titʃəbəl/ a educable; dócil

teacher /'titʃər/ n preceptor, m; profesor, maestro, m. **woman t.,** profesora, maestra, f

teaching /'titʃɪŋ/ n enseñanza, f; (belief) doctrina, f, a docente. **t. profession,** magisterio, m

teak /tik/ n Bot. teca, f; (wood) madera de teca, f

team /tim/ n (of horses) tiro, m; (of oxen, mules) par, m, pareja, yunta, f; Sports. partido, equipo, m; compañía, f, grupo, m. —vt enganchar, uncir. **t.-work,** cooperación, f

teamster /'timstər/ n gañán, m

tear /tɪər/ vt rasgar; romper; lacerar; (in pieces) hacer pedazos, despedazar; (scratch) arañar; Fig. atormentar. **to t. asunder,** romper; desmembrar. **to t. away,** arrancar, quitar violentamente. **to t. down,** derribar, echar abajo. **to t. off,** arrancar; desgajar. **to t. oneself away,** arrancarse, desgarrarse. **to t. one's hair,** arrancarse los pelos, mesarse. **to t. open,** abrir apresuradamente. **to t. up,** hacer pedazos; (uproot) arrancar, desarraigar.

tear /tɛər/ vi rasgarse; romper; correr precipitadamente. **to t. along,** correr rápidamente (por). **to t. away,** marcharse corriendo. **to t. down,** bajar corriendo. **to t. into,** entrar corriendo en. **to t. off,** irse precipitadamente, marcharse corriendo. **to t. up,** subir corriendo; llegar corriendo; atravesar rápidamente

tear /tɛər/ n lágrima, f; (drop) gota, f. **with tears in one's eyes,** con lágrimas en los ojos. **to shed tears,** llorar, lagrimear. **to wipe away one's tears,** secarse las lágrimas. **t.-drop,** lágrima, f. **t.-duct,** conducto lacrimal, m. **t.-gas,** gas lacrimante, m. **t.-stained,** mojado de lágrimas

tear /tɛər/ n (rent) rasgón, m

tearful /'tɪərfəl/ a lloroso, lacrimoso

tearjerker /'tɪər,dʒɜrkər/ n drama lacrimón, m

tease /tiz/ vt (card) cardar; (annoy) fastidiar, irritar, molestar; (chaff) tomar el pelo (a), embromar; (pester) importunar. —n bromista, mf

teaser /'tizər/ n (problem) rompecabezas, m; (person) bromista, mf

teaspoon /'ti,spun/ n cucharita, f

teaspoonful /'tispun,fʊl/ n cucharadita, f

teat /tit, tɪt/ n pezón, m; (of animals) teta, f

technical /'tɛknɪkəl/ a técnico. **t. offence,** Law. cuasidelito, m. **t. school,** escuela industrial, f

technicality /,tɛknɪ'kælɪti/ n carácter técnico, m; tecnicismo, m; detalle técnico, m

technician /tɛk'nɪʃən/ n técnico, m

technicolor /'tɛknɪ,kʌlər/ n tecnicolor, m

technique /tɛk'nik/ n técnica, f; ejecución, f; mecanismo, m

technological /,tɛknə'lɒdʒɪkəl/ a tecnológico

technology /tɛk'nɒlədʒi/ n tecnología, f

teddy bear /'tɛdi/ n osito de trapo, m

tedious /'tidiəs/ a aburrido, tedioso, pesado

tedium /'tidiəm/ n tedio, m, monotonía, f

tee /ti/ n Sports. meta, f; (golf) tee, m; (letter) te, f; cosa en forma de te, f. —vt (golf) colocar la pelota en el tee

teem /tim/ vi rebosar (de), abundar (en); pulular, hormiguear, estar lleno (de); (with rain) diluviar

teeming /'timɪŋ/ a prolífico, fecundo. **t. with,** abundante en, lleno de

teens /tinz/ n pl números y años desde trece hasta diez y nueve; edad de trece a diez y nueve años de edad. **to be still in one's t.,** no haber cumplido aún los veinte

teeter /'titər/ vi balancearse, columpiarse

teethe /tið/ vi endentecer, echar los dientes

teething /'tiðɪŋ/ n dentición, f. **t.-ring,** chupador, m

teetotaller /'ti,toutlər/ n abstemio (-ia)

teetotum /'ti'toutəm/ n perinola, f

telecast /'tɛlɪ,kæst/ vt telefundir

telecommunication /,tɛlɪkə,myunɪ'keɪʃən/ n telecomunicación, f

telegram /'tɛlɪ,græm/ n telegrama, m

telegraph /'tɛlɪ,græf/ n telégrafo, m. —vi telegrafiar; Fig. hacer señas. —vt telegrafiar, enviar por telégrafo **t line,** línea telegráfica, f. **t. office,** central de telégrafos, f. **t. pole,** poste telegráfico, m. **t. wire,** hilo telegráfico, m

telegraphic /,tɛlɪ'græfɪk/ a telegráfico

telepathic /,tɛlə'pæθɪk/ a telepático

telepathy /tə'lɛpəθi/ n telepatía, f

telephone /'tɛlə,foun/ n teléfono, m. —vi telefonear. —vt telefonear, llamar por teléfono. **to be on the t.,** (speaking) estar comunicando; (of subscribers) tener teléfono. **dial t.,** teléfono automático, m. **t. call,** comunicación telefónica, f; conversación telefónica, f. **t. call box,** teléfono público, m. **t. directory,** guía de teléfonos, f. **t. exchange,** central telefónica, f. **t. number,** número de teléfono, m. **t. operator,** telefonista, mf **t. receiver,** receptor telefónico, m. **t. wire,** hilo telefónico, m

telephony /tə'lɛfəni/ n telefonía, f. **wireless t.,** telefonía sin hilos, f

teleprinter /'tɛlə,prɪntər/ n teletipo, m

telescope /'tɛlə,skoup/ n telescopio, catalejo, m. —vt enchufar. —vi enchufarse, meterse una cosa dentro de otra

telescopic /,tɛlə'skɒpɪk/ a telescópico; de enchufe

televise /'tɛlə,vaiz/ vt trasmitir por televisión

television /'tɛlə,vɪʒən/ n televisión, f. **on television,** por televisión. **I saw her on television,** La vi por televisión

television series n serie televisiva, f

tell /tɛl/ vt contar, narrar; decir; revelar; expresar; (the time, of clocks) marcar; (inform) comunicar, informar; (show) indicar, manifestar; (explain) explicar; distinguir; (order) mandar; (compute) contar. —vi decir; (have effect) producir efecto. **We cannot t.,** No sabemos. **Who can t.?** ¿Quién sabe? **T. that to the marines!,** ¡Cuéntaselo a tu tía! **to t. its own tale,** hacer ver por sí mismo lo que hay. **to t. again,** volver a decir; contar otra vez. **to t. off,** regañar, reñir; (on a

mission) despachar, mandar. **to t. on,** delatar. **to t. upon,** afectar

teller /'tɛlər/ n narrador (-ra); (of votes)
escrutador (-ra) de votos; (payer) pagador; (bank) cajero (-ra), m

telling /'tɛlɪŋ/ a notable, significante.
—n narración, f

telltale /'tɛl,teil/ n chismoso (-sa), soplón
(-ona); (informer) acusón (-ona); *Fig.* indicio, m, señal, f, a revelador

temerity /tə'mɛriti/ n temeridad, f

temper /'tɛmpər/ n (of metals) temple,
m; (nature) naturaleza, f, carácter, m; espíritu, m; (mood) humor, m; (anger) mal
genio, m. —vt (of metals) templar; moderar, mitigar; mezclar. —vi templarse. **bad
(good) t.,** mal (buen) humor. **to keep
one's t.,** no enojarse, no impacientarse.
to lose one's t., enojarse, perder la paciencia

temperament /'tɛmpərəmənt, -prəmənt/
n temperamento, m; modo de ser, natural, m, naturaleza, índole, f; *Mus.* temple,
m

temperamental /,tɛmpərə'mɛntl,
-prə'mɛn-/ a natural, innato; caprichoso

temperance /'tɛmpərəns/ n moderación,
templanza, f; sobriedad, abstinencia, f

temperate /'tɛmpərɪt/ a moderado; sobrio; (of regions) templado. **t. zone,** zona
templada, f

temperature /'tɛmpərətʃər/ n temperatura, f. **to have a t.,** tener fiebre

tempered /'tɛmpərd/ a de humor..., de
genio... **to be good (bad) t.,** ser de buen
(mal) humor

tempering /'tɛmpərɪŋ/ n temperación, f

tempest /'tɛmpɪst/ n tempestad, borrasca, f, temporal, m; *Fig.* tormenta, f

tempest in a teapot borrasca en un
vaso de agua, m

tempestuous /tɛm'pɛstʃuəs/ a tempestuoso, borrascoso; *Fig.* impetuoso,
violento

temple /'tɛmpəl/ n templo, m; *Anat.*
sien, f

tempo /'tɛmpou/ n *Mus.* tiempo, m

temporal /'tɛmpərəl/ a temporal; (transient) transitorio, fugaz; *Anat.* temporal.
—n *Anat.* hueso temporal, m

temporarily /,tɛmpə'rɛərəli/ adv provisionalmente

temporary /'tɛmpə,rɛri/ a provisional,
interino

temporize /'tɛmpə,raiz/ vi ganar tiempo;
contemporizar

tempt /tɛmpt/ vt tentar; atraer, seducir

temptation /tɛmp'teiʃən/ n tentación, f;
aliciente, atractivo, m

tempting /'tɛmptɪŋ/ a tentador, atrayente; seductor

ten /tɛn/ a diez; (of the clock) las diez, f
pl; (of age) diez años, m pl, n diez, m; (a
round number) decena, f; ten-millionth,
a and n diezmillonésimo m. **ten months
old,** diezmesino. **ten syllable,** decasílabo.
ten thousand, a and n diez mil m.

There are ten thousand soldiers, Hay
diez mil soldados. **ten-thousandth,** a
and n diezmilésimo m

tenable /'tɛnəbəl/ a sostenible, defendible

tenacious /tə'neiʃəs/ a tenaz; (stubborn)
porfiado, obstinaz, terco; (sticky) adhesivo. **to be t. of life,** estar muy apegado
a la vida

tenacity /tə'næsɪti/ n tenacidad, f; porfía, f; tesón, m

tenant /'tɛnənt/ n arrendatario (-ia), inquilino (-na); habitante, m; morador (-ra)

tend /tɛnd/ vt cuidar, atender; guardar;
vigilar. —vi tender; inclinarse (a), propender (a)

tendency /'tɛndənsi/ n tendencia, inclinación, propensión, f; proclividad, f

tendentious /tɛn'dɛnʃəs/ a tendencioso

tender /'tɛndər/ n guardián, m; *Com.*
oferta, propuesta, f; *Naut.* falúa, f; (of a
railway engine) ténder, m. **legal t.,**
moneda corriente, f

tender /'tɛndər/ a tierno; delicado; (of
conscience) escrupuloso; (of a subject)
espinoso; compasivo, afectuoso, sensible;
muelle, blando. **t.-hearted,** compasivo,
tierno de corazón

tender /'tɛndər/ vt ofrecer; dar; presentar. —vi hacer una oferta. **to t.
condolences,** dar el pésame. **to t. one's
resignation,** presentar la dimisión. **to t.
thanks,** dar las gracias

tenderness /'tɛndərnɪs/ n ternura, f;
sensibilidad, f; delicadeza, f; dulzura, f;
indulgencia, f; compasividad, benevolencia, f; escrupulosidad, f; mimo, cariño, m

tendon /'tɛndən/ n *Anat.* tendón, m. **t.
of Achilles,** tendón de Aquiles, m

tenement /'tɛnəmənt/ n casa de vecindad, f; vivienda, f; *Poet.* morada, f

tenet /'tɛnɪt/ n principio, dogma, m, doctrina, f

tenfold /a.'tɛn,fould; adv. -'fould/ a dé-
cuplo. —adv diez veces

tennis /'tɛnɪs/ n tenis, m. **to play t.,** jugar al tenis. **t. ball,** pelota de tenis, f. **t.
court,** campo de tenis, m, cancha de
tenis, pista de tenis, f. **tennis club,** club
de tenis, m. **t. racket,** raqueta de tenis, f;
tennis shoe, zapatilla de tenis, f

tenon /'tɛnən/ n espiga, f, vt espigar

tenor /'tɛnər/ n curso, m; tenor, contenido, m; *Mus.* tenor, m; *Mus.* alto, m;
(mus. instrument) viola, f. —a *Mus.* de
tenor

tense /tɛns/ n *Gram.* tiempo, m. —a
tirante, estirado, tieso; tenso

tension /'tɛnʃən/ n tensión, f; *Elec.*
voltaje, m, tensión, f; (of sewing-
machine) tensahílo, m. **state of t.,** (diplomatic) estado de tirantez, f

tent /tɛnt/ n tienda (de campaña), f;
(bell) pabellón, m; *Surg.* tienda, f. **oxygen t.,** tienda oxígena, f. **to pitch tents,**
armar las tiendas de campaña; acam-
parse. **to strike tents,** plegar tiendas. **t.
fly,** toldo de tienda, m. **t. maker,**

tendero, *m.* **t. peg,** clave que sujeta las cuerdas de una tienda, *f.* **t. pole,** mástil (or montante) de tienda, *m*

tentacle /'tɛntəkəl/ *n* tentáculo, *m*

tentative /'tɛntətɪv/ *a* tentativo, interino, provisional, de prueba, *n* tentativa, *f,* ensayo, *m*

tentatively /'tɛntətɪvli/ *adv* por vía de ensayo, experimentalmente

tenth /tɛnθ/ *a* décimo; (of monarchs) diez; (of the month) (el) diez. —*n* décimo, *m;* (part) décima parte, *f; Mus.* decena, *f*

tenthly /'tɛnθli/ *adv* en décimo lugar

tenuous /'tɛnyuəs/ *a* tenue; sutil; delgado; fino

tenure /'tɛnyər/ *n* tenencia, posesión, *f;* (duration) duración, *f;* (of office) administración, *f*

tepid /'tɛpɪd/ *a* tibio

tercentenary /ˌtɜrsɛn'tɛnəri/ *n* tercer centenario, *m*

tercet /'tɜrsɪt/ *n* terceto, *m*

term /tɜrm/ *n* (limit) límite, fin, *m;* (period) plazo, tiempo, período, *m;* (schools, universities) trimestre, *m;* (*Math. Law. Logic.*) término, *m;* (word) expresión, palabra, *f pl.* terms, (conditions) condiciones, *f pl;* (charges) precios, *m pl,* tarifa, *f;* (words) términos, *m pl,* palabras, *f pl.* —*vt* llamar, calificar. **for a t. of years,** por un plazo de años. **in plain terms,** en palabras claras. **on equal terms,** en condiciones iguales. **to be on bad (good) terms with,** estar en (or tener) malas (buenas) relaciones con. **to come to terms,** llegar a un acuerdo; hacer las paces. **What are your terms?** ¿Cuáles son sus condiciones? (price) ¿Cuáles son sus precios? **terms of sale,** condiciones de venta, *f pl*

termagant /'tɜrməgənt/ *n* arpía, fiera, *f*

terminable /'tɜrmənəbəl/ *a* terminable

terminal /'tɜrmənl/ *a* terminal, final; (of schools, universities) trimestre. —*n* término, *m; Elec.* borne, *m;* (schools, universities) examen de fin de trimestre, *m;* (railway) estación terminal, *f;* (*Archit.* and figure) término, *m; Archit.* remate, *m*

terminate /'tɜrmə,neit/ *vt* limitar; terminar, concluir, poner fin (a). —*vi* terminarse, concluirse (por); cesar

termination /ˌtɜrmə'neiʃən/ *n* terminación, conclusión, *f;* fin, *m; Gram.* terminación, *f;* cabo, remate, *m*

terminology /ˌtɜrmə'nɒlədʒi/ *n* nomenclatura, terminología, *f*

terminus /'tɜrmənəs/ *n* (railway) estación terminal, *f;* (*Archit.* and figure) término, *m; Archit.* remate, *m; Myth.* Término, *m*

termite /'tɜrmait/ *n Ent.* termita, *m*

term paper *n* trabajo de examen, *m*

terrace /'tɛrəs/ *n* terraza, *f, vt* terraplenar

terracotta /ˌtɛrə'kɒtə/ *n* terracota, *f*

terrain /tə'rein/ *n* terreno, campo, *m,* región, *f*

terrapin /'tɛrəpɪn/ *n* tortuga de agua dulce, *f*

terrestrial /tə'rɛstriəl/ *a* terrestre, terrenal

terrible /'tɛrəbəl/ *a* terrible, pavoroso, espantoso; *Inf.* tremendo

terrific /tə'rɪfɪk/ *a* espantoso, terrible; *Inf.* atroz, tremendo

terrify /'tɛrə,fai/ *vt* aterrorizar, espantar, horrorizar

terrifying /'tɛrə,faiɪŋ/ *a* aterrador, espantoso

territorial /ˌtɛrɪ'tɔriəl/ *a* territorial. —*n* soldado del ejército territorial, *m*

territory /'tɛrɪ,tɔri/ *n* región, comarca, *f;* (state) territorio, *m;* jurisdicción, *f.* **mandated territory,** territorio bajo mandato, *m pl*

terror /'tɛrər/ *n* terror, pavor, espanto, *m.* **the Reign of T.,** el Reinado del Terror, *m.* **t.-stricken,** espantado, muerto de miedo

terrorism /'tɛrə,rɪzəm/ *n* terrorismo, *m*

terrorist /'tɛrərɪst/ *n* terrorista, *m*

terrorize /'tɛrə,raiz/ *vt* aterrorizar

terse /tɜrs/ *a* conciso, sucinto; seco, brusco

tertiary /'tɜrʃi,eri, -ʃəri/ *a* tercero; *Geol.* terciario. —*n Eccl.* terciario, *m*

test /tɛst/ *n* (proof) prueba, *f;* examen, *m;* investigación, *f;* (standard) criterio, *m,* piedra de toque, *f; Chem.* análisis, *m;* (trial) ensayo, *m; Zool.* concha, *f.* —*vt Chem.* ensayar; probar, poner a prueba; examinar; (eyes) graduar (la vista). **to put to the t.,** poner a prueba. **to stand the t.,** soportar la prueba. **t. match,** partido internacional de cricket, *m.* **t. meal,** *Med.* comida de prueba, *f.* **t. pilot,** *Aer.* piloto de pruebas, *m.* **t. tube,** tubo de ensayo, *m*

testament /'tɛstəmənt/ *n* testamento, *m.* **the New T.,** el Nuevo Testamento, *m.* **the Old T.,** el Antiguo Testamento, *m*

testate /'tɛsteit/ *a* testado

testator /'tɛsteitər/ *n* testador, *m,* (**testatrix,** testadora, *f*)

testicle /'tɛstɪkəl/ *n* testículo, *m*

testify /'tɛstə,fai/ *vt and vi* declarar, atestar; *Law.* atestiguar, testificar, dar fe

testimonial /ˌtɛstə'mouniəl/ *n* recomendación, *f;* certificado, *m;* (tribute) homenaje, *m*

testimony /'tɛstə,mouni/ *n* testimonio, *m,* declaración, *f;* (proof) prueba, *f.* **in t. whereof,** en fe de lo cual. **to bear t.,** atestar

testing grounds /'tɛstɪŋ/ *n* campo de experimentación, campo de pruebas, *m*

testy /'tɛsti/ *a* enojadizo, irritable, irascible, quisquilloso

tetanus /'tɛtnəs/ *n* tétano, *m*

tether /'tɛðər/ *n* traba, atadura, maniota, *f.* —*vt* atar con una correa. **to be at the end of one's t.,** acabarse la resistencia; acabarse la paciencia

text /tɛkst/ *n* texto, *m;* (subject) tema,

m; (motto) lema, *m;* (of a musical composition) letra, *f.* **t.-book,** libro de texto, *m*

textile /'tɛkstail/ *a* textil, de tejer. —*n* textil, *m,* materia textil, *f;* tejido, *m*

texture /'tɛkstʃər/ *n* (material and *Biol.*) tejido, *m;* textura, *f*

thalamus /'θæləməs/ *n* (*Anat., Bot.*) tálamo, *m*

Thames, the /tɛmz/ *n* el Támesis, *m.* **to set the T. on fire,** descubrir la pólvora

than /ðæn, ðɛn; *unstressed* ðən, ən/ *conjunc* que; (between **more, less,** or **fewer** and a number) que; (in comparisons of inequality) que, but que becomes(*a*) del (de la, de los, de las) que if the point of comparison is a noun in the principal clause, which has to be supplied mentally to fill up the ellipsis; (*b*) de lo que if there is no noun to act as a point of comparison, e.g. **He was older than I thought,** Era más viejo de lo que yo pensaba. **They have less than they deserve,** Tienen menos de lo que merecen. **They lose more money than (the money) they earn,** Pierden más dinero del que ganan. **He will meet with more opposition than he thought,** Va a encontrar más oposición de la que pensaba. **I have more books than you,** Tengo más libros que tú. **She has fewer than nine and more than five,** Ella tiene menos de nueve y más de cinco

thank /θæŋk/ *vt* agradecer, dar las gracias (a). **to t. for,** agradecer. **I will t. you to be more polite,** Le agradecería que fuese más cortés. **He has himself to t. for it,** Él mismo tiene la culpa de ello. **No, t. you,** No, muchas gracias. **T. goodness!** ¡Gracias a Dios!

thank /θæŋks/ *n* (now in pl. only, **thanks**) gracias, *f pl.* **a vote of thanks,** un voto de gracias. **Many thanks!** ¡Muchas gracias! **to return thanks,** dar las gracias. **thanks to,** merced a, debido a. **thanks to you,** gracias a tí. **t.-offering,** ofrecimiento en acción de gracias, *m*

thankful /'θæŋkfəl/ *a* agradecido. **I am t. to see,** Me alegro de ver, Me es grato ver

thankfully /'θæŋkfəli/ *adv* con gratitud, agradecido

thankless /'θæŋklɪs/ *a* ingrato; desagradecido; desagradable

thanksgiving /,θæŋks'gɪvɪŋ/ *n* acción de gracias, *f.* **T. service,** servicio de acción de gracias, *m.* **Thanksgiving (Day),** *n* día de acción de dar gracias, día de gracias, *m*

that /ðæt; *unstressed* ðət/ *dem a* ese, *m;* esa, *f;* aquel, *m;* aquella, *f.* **dem. pron** ése, *m;* ésa, *f;* eso, *neut;* aquél, *m;* aquélla, *f;* aquello, *neut;* (standing for a noun) el, *m;* la, *f;* lo, *neut* **All t. there is,** Todo lo que hay. **His temperament is t. of his mother,** Su temperamento es el de su madre. **We have not come to t. yet,** Todavía no hemos llegado a ese punto. **T.**

is what I want to know, Eso es lo que quiero saber. **with t.,** con eso; (thereupon) en eso. **Go t. way,** Vaya Vd. por allí; Tome Vd. aquel camino. **T. is to say...,** Es decir.... **What do you mean by t.?** ¿Qué quieres decir con eso? **The novel is not as bad as all t.,** La novela no es tan mala como tú piensas (*or* como dicen, etc.)

that /ðæt; *unstressed* ðət/ *pron rel* que; el cual, *m;* la cual, *f;* lo cual, *neut;* (of persons) a quien, *mf;* a quienes, *mf pl;* (with from) de quien, *mf;* de quienes, *mf pl;* (of place) donde. **The letter t. I sent you,** la carta que te mandé. **The box t. John put them in,** la caja en la cual los puso Juan. **The last time t. I saw her,** La última vez que la vi

that /ðæt; *unstressed* ðət/ *conjunc* que; (of purpose) para que; afin de que; (before infin.) para; (because) porque. **So t. he would come!** ¡Ojalá que viniese! **so t.,** para que; (before infin.) para; (as a result) de manera que; de modo que. **It is better t. he should not come,** Es mejor que no venga. **now t.,** ahora que

thatch /θætʃ/ *n* barda, *f;* v bardar

thaw /θɔ/ *n* deshielo, *m.* —*vt* deshelar; derretir. —*vi* deshelarse; derretirse

the /*stressed* ði; *unstressed before a consonant* ðə, *unstressed before a vowel* ði/ *def art* el, *m;* la, *f;* lo, *neut;* los, *m pl;* las, *f pl;* (before feminine sing. noun beginning with stressed a or ha) el; (untranslated between the name and number of a monarch, pope, ruler, e.g. *Charles the Tenth,* Carlos diez). —*adv* (before a comparative) cuanto, tanto más. **at the** or **to the,** al, *m,* (also before feminine sing. noun beginning with a or ha); a la, *f;* a lo, *neut;* a los, *m pl;* a las, *f pl.* **from the** or **of the,** del, *m,* (also before feminine sing. noun beginning with stressed a or ha); de la, *f;* de lo, *neut;* de los, *m pl;* de las, *f pl.* **the one,** see one. **The sooner the better,** Cuanto antes mejor. **The room will be all the warmer,** El cuarto estará tanto más caliente

theater /'θiətər/ *n* teatro, *m;* (lecture) anfiteatro, *m;* (drama) teatro, *m,* obra dramática, *f;* (scene) teatro, *m,* escena, *f.* **t. attendant,** acomodador (-ra)

theater-in-the-round /'θiətɔrɪnðə'raund/ *n* teatro circular, teatro en círculo, *m*

theatrical /θi'ætrɪkəl/ *a* teatral. —*n pl* **theatricals,** funciones teatrales, *f pl.* **amateur theatricals,** función de aficionados, *f.* **t. company,** compañía de teatro, *f.* **t. costumier,** mascarero (-ra), alquilador (-ra) de disfraces. **t. manager,** empresario de teatro, *m*

theatricality /θi,ætrɪ'kælɪti/ *n* teatralidad, *f*

thee /ði/ *pers pron* te; (after prep.) tí. **with t.,** contigo

theft /θɛft/ *n* robo, hurto, *m*

their /ðɛər; *unstressed* ðər/ *poss a* su, *mf*

sing; sus, *pl;* de ellos, *m pl;* de ellas, *f pl.* **They have t. books,** Tienen sus libros. **I have t. books,** Tengo los libros de ellos

theirs /ðɛərz/ *poss pron* (el) suyo, *m;* (la) suya, *f;* (los) suyos, *m pl;* (las) suyas, *f pl;* de ellos, *m pl;* de ellas, *f pl.* **These hats are t.,** Estos sombreros son los suyos

them /ðɛm; *unstressed* ðəm, əm/ *pers pron* ellos, *m pl;* ellas, *f pl;* (as object of a verb) las, *f pl;* (to them) les

thematic /θiˈmætɪk/ *a* temático

theme /θim/ *n* tema, asunto, *m;* tesis, *f; Mus.* tema, motivo, *m*

themselves /ðəmˈsɛlvz, ˌðɛm-/ *pers pron pl* ellos mismos, *m pl;* ellas mismas, *f pl, reflexive pron* sí; sí mismos; (with a reflexive verb) se. **They t. told me about it,** Ellos mismos me lo dijeron. **They left it for t.,** Lo dejaron para sí (mismos)

then /ðɛn/ *adv* (of future time) entonces; (of past time) a la sazón, en aquella época, entonces; (next, afterwards) luego, después, en seguida; (in that case) en este caso, entonces; (therefore) por consiguiente. —*a* de entonces. —*n* entonces, *m.* —*conjunc* (moreover) además; pues. **And what t.?** ¿Y qué pasó después?; ¿Y qué pasará ahora?; ¿Y qué más? **by t.,** por entonces. **now and t.,** de vez en cuando. **now... t.,** ya... ya, ora... ora. **since t.,** desde aquel tiempo; desde entonces; desde aquella ocasión. **until t.,** hasta entonces; hasta aquella época. **well t.,** bien, pues. **t. and there,** en el acto, en seguida; allí mismo

thence /ðɛns/ *adv* desde allí, de allí; (therefore) por eso, por esa razón, por consiguiente

thenceforth /ˌðɛnsˈfɔrθ/ *adv* de allí en adelante, desde entonces

theocracy /θiˈɒkrəsi/ *n* teocracia, *f*

theologian /ˌθiəˈloudʒən/ *n* teólogo, *m*

theological /ˌθiəˈlɒdʒɪkəl/ *a* teológico, teologal

theology /θiˈɒlədʒi/ *n* teología, *f*

theorem /ˈθiərəm/ *n* teorema, *m*

theoretical /ˌθiəˈrɛtɪkəl/ *a* teórico

theorist /ˈθiərɪst/ *n* teórico, *m*

theorize /ˈθiəˌraɪz/ *vi* teorizar

theory /ˈθiəri/ *n* teoría, *f*

therapeutic /ˌθɛrəˈpyutɪk/ *a* terapéutico. —*n* therapeutics, terapéutica, *f*

therapeutist /ˌθɛrəˈpyutɪst/ *n* terapeuta, *mf*

therapy /ˈθɛrəpi/ *suffix* terapia, *f*

there /ðɛər; *unstressed* ðər/ *adv* allí; ahí, allá; (at that point) en eso; (used pronominally as subject of verb) haber, e.g. *T. was once a king,* Hubo una vez un rey; *What is t. to do here?* ¿Qué hay que hacer aquí? —*interj* ¡vaya!; (I told you so!) ¡ya ves! ¡ya te lo dije yo!; (in surprise) ¡toma! **about t.,** cerca de allí. **down t.,** allí abajo. **in t.,** allí dentro. **out t.,** allí fuera. **over t.,** ahí; allá a lo lejos. **up t.,** allí arriba. **T. came a time when...,** Llegó la hora cuando... **T. it is!** ¡Allí está! **t. is**

or **t. are,** hay. **t. was** or **t. were,** había, hubo. **t. may be,** puede haber, quizás habrá. **t. must be,** tiene que haber. **t. will be,** habrá. **T., t.!** (to a child, etc.) ¡Vamos!

thereabouts /ˈðɛrəˌbauts/ *adv* (near to a place) cerca de allí, por ahí, allí cerca; (approximately) approximadamente, cerca de

thereafter /ˌðɛərˈæftər/ *adv* después, después de eso

thereby /ˌðɛərˈbai/ *adv* (near to that place) por allí cerca; (by that means) con lo cual, de este modo

therefore /ˈðɛərˌfɔr/ *adv* por lo tanto, por eso, así, por consiguiente; por esta razón

therein /ˌðɛərˈɪn/ *adv* (inside) allí dentro; (in this, that particular) en estre, en eso, en ese particular

thereinafter /ˌðɛərɪnˈæftər/ *adv* posteriormente, más adelante

thereupon /ˈðɛərəˌpɒn/ *adv* (in consequence) por consiguiente, por lo tanto; (at that point) luego, en eso; (immediately afterwards) inmediatamente después, en seguida

thermal /ˈθərməl/ *a* termal. **t. springs,** aguas termales, termas, *f pl*

thermodynamics /ˌθərmoudaiˈnæmɪks/ *n* termodinámica, *f*

thermoelectric /ˌθərmoʊˈlɛktrɪk/ *a* termoeléctrico

thermometer /θərˈmɒmɪtər/ *n* termómetro, *m*

thermos flask /ˈθərməs/ *n* termos, *m*

thermostat /ˈθərməˌstæt/ *n* termostato, *m*

thesaurus /θɪˈsɔrəs/ *n* tesoro, tesauro, *m*

these /ðiz/ *dem pron pl* of **this,** éstos, *m pl;* éstas, *f pl, dem a* estos, *m pl;* estas, *f pl.* **Aren't t. your flowers?** ¿No son éstas tus flores? **T. pictures have been sold,** Estos cuadros se han vendito

thesis /ˈθisɪs/ *n* tesis, *f*

they /ðei/ *pers pron* ellos, *m pl;* ellas, *f pl;* (people) se (followed by sing. verb). **T. say,** Dicen, Se dice

thick /θɪk/ *a* espeso; (big) grueso, (wall) grueso, (string, cord) gordo; (vapors) denso; (muddy) turbio; (dense, close) tupido apretado; (numerous) numeroso, repetido, continuo; (full of) lleno (de); (of voice) velado, indistinto; (obtuse) estúpido, lerdo; (friendly) íntimo. —*adv* densamente; continuamente, sin cesar. **three feet t.,** de tres pies de espesor. **That's a bit t.!** ¡Eso es un poco demasiado! **to be as t. as thieves,** estar unidos como los dedos de la mano. **t.-lipped,** con labios gruesos, bezudo. **t.-headed,** estúpido, lerdo. **t.-skinned,** de piel gruesa; *Zool.* paquidermo; *Fig.* sin vergüenza, insensible. **t. stroke,** (of letters) grueso, *m*

thick /θɪk/ *n* espesor, *m;* parte gruesa, *f;* lo más denso; (of a fight) lo más reñido;

centro, *m.* **in the t. of,** en el centro (de), en medio de

thicken /'θɪkən/ *vt* espesar; (increase) aumentar, multiplicar; *Cul.* espesar. —*vi* espesarse; condensar; aumentar; multiplicarse; (of a mystery, etc.) complicarse; hacerse más denso; *Cul.* espesarse

thicket /'θɪkɪt/ *n* matorral, soto, *m,* maleza, *f;* (grove) boscaje, *m*

thickness /'θɪknɪs/ *n* espesor, *m;* grueso, *m;* densidad, *f;* (of liquids) consistencia, *f;* (layer) capa, *f;* (of speech) dificultad (en el hablar), *f*

thickset /'θɪk'sɛt/ *a* doblado

thief /θif/ *n* ladrón (-ona); (in a candle) moco de vela, *m.* **Stop t.!** ¡Ladrones! **thieves' den,** *Fig.* cueva de ladrones, *f*

thieve /θiv/ *vi* hurtar, robar. —*vt* robar

thievish /'θiviʃ/ *a* ladrón

thigh /θai/ *n* muslo, *m.* **t.-bone,** fémur, *m*

thimble /'θɪmbəl/ *n* dedal, *m*

thin /θɪn/ *a* delgado; (lean) flaco; (small) pequeño; delicado; fino; (of air, light) tenue, sutil; (clothes) ligero; (sparse) escaso; transparente; (watery) aguado; (of wine) bautizado; (not close) claro; (of arguments) flojo. —*vt* adelgazar; aclarar; *Agr.* limpiar; reducir. —*vi* adelgazarse; afilarse; reducirse. **somewhat t.,** (of persons) delgaducho, algo flaco. **to grow t.,** enflaquecer; afilarse. **to make t.,** hacer adelgazar volver flaco. **t.-clad,** ligero de ropa; mal vestido. **t.-faced,** de cara delgada. **t.-lipped,** de labios apretados. **t.-skinned,** de piel fina; *Fig.* sensitivo, sensible

thine /ðain/ See **theirs.** *poss pron* (el) tuyo, *m;* (la) tuya, *f;* (los) tuyos, *m pl;* (las) tuyas, *f pl;* tus, *mf* tus, *mf pl;* de ti. **The fault is t.,** La culpa es tuya, La culpa es de ti

thing /θɪŋ/ *n* cosa, *f;* objeto, artículo, *m;* (affair) asunto, *m;* (contemptuous) sujeto, tipo, *m;* (creature) ser, *m,* criatura, *f;* pl **things,** (belongings) efectos, trastos, *m pl;* (luggage) equipaje, *m;* (clothes) trapitos, *m pl;* (circumstances) circunstancias, condiciones, *f pl.* **above all things,** ante todo, sobre todo. **a very pretty little t.,** (child) una pequeña muy mona. **as things are,** tal como están las cosas. **for one t.,** en primer lugar. **Her behavior is not quite the t.,** La conducta de ella no está bien vista. **The bad t. is that...,** Lo malo es que...; **The good t. is that...,** Menos mal que...; Lo bueno es que... **No such t.!** ¡No hay tal!; ¡Nada de eso! **Poor t.!** ¡Pobrecito!; (woman) ¡Pobre mujer!; (man) ¡Pobre hombre! **to be just the t.,** venir al pelo. **with one t. and another,** entre unas cosas y otras. **I like things Spanish,** Me gusta lo español

think /θɪŋk/ *vt* and *vi* pensar; (believe) creer; (deem) considerar, juzgar; imaginar; (suspect) sospechar, (opine) ser de opinión (que). **And to t. that...!** ¡Y pensar que...! **As you t. fit,** Como usted

quiera, Como a usted le parezca bien. **He thought as much,** Se lo figuraba. **He little thought that...!** ¡Cuán lejos estaba de pensar que...! **He thinks nothing of...,** No le importa...; Desprecia..., Tiene una opinión bastante mala de.... **I don't t. so,** No lo creo. **I should t. not!** ¡Claro que no! **¡Eso sí que no! I should t. so!** ¡Claro! ¡Ya lo creo! **It makes me t. of...,** Me hace pensar en... **One might t.,** Podría creerse... **to t. better of something,** cambiar de opinión, considerar mejor. **to t. highly (badly) of,** tener buen (mal) concepto sobre. **to t. over carefully,** pensarlo bien, considerar detenidamente; *Inf.* consultar con la almohada. **to t. proper,** creer conveniente. **to t. to oneself,** pensar para sí (o entre sí). **to t. too much of oneself,** pensar demasiado en sí; tener demasiada buena opinión de sí mismo; tener humos. **What do you t. about it?** ¿Qué te parece? **to t. about,** (of persons) pensar en; (of things) pensar en (o sobre); meditar, considerar, reflexionar sobre. **to t. for,** pensar por. **to t. of,** pensar en; pensar de (o sobre). **What do you t. of this?** ¿Qué te parece esto? **to t. out,** idear, proyectar, hacer planes para; (a problem) resolver. **to t. over,** pensar; reflexionar sobre, meditar sobre. **I shall t. it over,** Lo pensaré.

thinker /'θɪŋkər/ *n* pensador, *m*

thinking /'θɪŋkɪŋ/ *n* pensamiento, *m,* reflexión, meditación, *f;* juicio, *m;* opinión, *f,* parecer, *m.* —*a* pensador; inteligente; racional; serio. **To my way of t.,** Según pienso yo, A mi parecer. **way of t.,** modo de pensar, *m*

third /θɜrd/ *a* tercero (tercer before *m,* *sing* noun); (of monarchs) tercero; (of the month) (el) tres. —*n* tercio, *m,* tercera parte, *f; Mus.* tercera, *f.* **T. time lucky!** ¡A la tercera va la vencida! **t. class,** *n* tercera clase, *f.* —*a* de tercera clase. **t. party,** tercera persona, *f.* **t-party insurance,** seguro contra tercera persona, *m.* **t. person,** tercero (-ra); *Gram.* tercera persona, *f.* **t.-rate,** de tercera clase

thirst /θɜrst/ *n* sed, *f; Fig.* deseo, *m,* ansia, *f;* entusiasmo, *m.* **to satisfy one's t.,** apagar (or matar) la sed

thirsty /'θɜrsti/ *a* sediento. **to be t.,** tener sed. **to make t.,** dar sed.

thirteen /'θɜr'tin/ *a* and *n* trece *m.* **t. hundred,** *a* and *n* mil trescientos *m*

thirteenth /θɜr'tinθ/ *a* décimotercio; (of monarchs) trece; (of month) (el) trece, *m,* *n* décimotercio, trezavo, *m*

thirtieth /'θɜrtiəθ/ *a* trigésimo; (of month) (el) treinta, *m.* —*n* treintavo, *m*

thirty /'θɜrti/ *a* and *n* treinta, *m.* **t.-first,** treinta y uno

this /ðɪs/ *dem a* este, *m;* esta, *f,* dem *pron* éste, *m;* ésta, *f;* esto, *neut* **by t. time,** a esta hora, ya. **like t.,** de este modo, así. **T. is Wednesday,** Hoy es miércoles. **What is all t.?** ¿Qué es todo esto?

thistle /'θɪsəl/ n cardo, m. **t.-down**, papo de cardo, vilano de cardo, m

thither /'θɪðər, 'ðɪð-/ adv allá, hacia allá; a ese fin. —a más remoto

thong /θɒŋ/ n correa, tira, f

thorax /'θɔræks/ n tórax, m

thorn /θɔrn/ n espina, f; (tree) espino, m; Fig. abrojo, m, espina, f. **to be a t. in the flesh of**, ser una espina en el costado de. **t. brake**, espinar, m

thorny /'θɔrni/ a espinoso; Fig. difícil, arduo

thorough /'θɜrou/ a completo; perfecto; (conscientious) concienzudo; (careful) cuidadoso. **t.-bred**, (of animals) de pura raza, de casta; (of persons) bien nacido. **t.-paced**, cabal, consumado

thoroughfare /'θɜrə‚fɛər/ n vía pública, f. **"No t."**, «Prohibido el paso», «Calle cerrada»

thoroughly /'θɜrəli/ adv completamente; (of knowing a subject) a fondo; concienzudamente

those /ðouz/ dem a pl of **that**, esos, m pl; esas, f pl; aquellos, m pl; aquellas, f pl, dem pron ésos, m pl; ésas, f pl; aquéllos, m pl; aquéllas, f pl; (standing for a noun) los, m pl; las, f pl. **t. who**, quienes, mf pl; los que, m pl; las que, f pl. **t. that** or **which**, los que, m pl; las que, f pl. **Your eyes are t. of your mother**, Tus ojos son los de tu madre

thou /ðau/ pers pron tú

though /ðou/ conjunc (followed by subjunc. when doubt is implied or uncertain future time) aunque, bien que; (nevertheless) sin embargo, no obstante; (in spite of) a pesar de que; (but) pero. **as t.**, como si (followed by subjunc.). **even t.**, aunque (followed by subjunc.)

thought /θɔt/ n pensamiento, m; meditación, reflexión, f. **some thoughts on...** algunas reflexiones sobre...; opinión, f; consideración, f; idea, f, propósito, m; (care) cuidado, m, solicitud, f; Inf. pizca, f. **on second thought**, después de pensarlo bien. **The t. struck him**, Se le ocurrió la idea. **to collect one's thoughts**, orientarse; informarse (de). **t.-reading**, adivinación del pensamiento, f. **t.-transference**, telepatía, transmisión del pensamiento, f

thoughtful /'θɔtfəl/ a pensativo, meditabundo; serio; especulativo; (provident) previsor, f; (kind) atento, solícito; cuidadoso; (anxious) inquieto, intranquilo

thoughtfully /'θɔtfəli/ adv pensativamente; seriamente; (providently) con previsión; (kindly) atentamente, solícitamente

thoughtless /'θɔtlɪs/ a irreflexivo; (careless) descuidado, negligente; (unkind) inconsiderado; (silly) necio, estúpido

thoughtlessly /'θɔtlɪsli/ adv sin pensar, irreflexivamente; negligentemente

thousand /'θauzənd/ a mil, m. —n mil, m; millar, m. **one t.**, mil, m. **one t. three hundred**, a mil trescientos, m pl; mil

trescientas, f pl. —n mil trescientos, m pl. **two (three) t.**, dos (tres) mil. **by thousands**, por millares; por miles. **t.-fold**, mil veces más

thrash /θræʃ/ vt azotar, apalear; Agr. trillar, desgranar; Inf. triunfar sobre, derrotar. —vi Agr. trillar el grano; arrojarse, agitarse. Fig. **to t. out**, ventilar

thread /θrɛd/ n hilo, m; (fibre) hebra, fibra, f, filamento, m; (of a screw) filete, m; Fig. hilo, m, a de hilo. —vt (a needle) enhebrar; (beads) ensartar; (make one's way) colarse a través de, atravesar; pasar por. **to hang by a t.**, pender de un hilo. **to lose the t. of**, Fig. perder el hilo de

threadbare /'θrɛd‚bɛər/ a raído; muy usado; Fig. trivial, viejo

threadworm /'θrɛd‚wɜrm/ n m, lombriz intestinal, f

threat /θrɛt/ n amenaza, f

threaten /'θrɛtn/ vt and vi amenazar. **to t. with**, amenazar con

threatening /'θrɛtnɪŋ/ a amenazador. —n amenazas, f pl

three /θri/ a and n tres m; (of the clock) las tres, f pl; (of one's age) tres años, m pl. **t.-color process**, tricromía, f. **t.-colored**, tricolor. **t.-cornered**, triangular; (of hats) de tres picos, tricornio. **t.-cornered hat**, sombrero de tres picos, tricornio, m. **t. decker**, Naut. navío de tres puentes, m; novela larga, f. **t. deep**, en tres hileras. **t. hundred**, a and n trescientos m. **t.-hundredth**, a and n tricentésimo m. **t.-legged**, de tres patas. **t.-legged stool**, banqueta, f. **t.-per-cents**, acción al tres por ciento (3%), f. **t.-phase**, Elec. trifásico, m. **t.-ply**, (of yarn) triple; (of wood) de tres capas. **t.-quarter**, de tres cuartos. **t. quarters of an hour**, tres cuartos de hora, m pl. **t.-sided**, trilátero. **t. speed gear box**, cambio de marcha de tres velocidades, m. **t.-stringed**, Mus. de tres cuerdos. **t. thousand**, a tres mil, mf pl; n tres mil, m

threefold /'θri‚fould/ a triple

Three Musketeers, the los Tres Mosqueteros

threescore /'θri'skɔr/ a and n sesenta, f pl

threesome /'θrisəm/ n partido de tres, m

thresh /θrɛʃ/ vt trillar, desgranar. —vi trillar el grano. **to t. out**, ventilar

threshold /'θrɛʃould/ n umbral, m; Psychol. limen, m; Fig. comienzo, principio, m; (entrance) entrada, f. **to cross the t.**, atravesar (o pisar) los umbrales

thrice /θrais/ adv tres veces

thrift /θrift/ n frugalidad, parsimonia, f

thrifty /'θrifti/ a frugal, económico

thrill /θril/ n estremecimiento, m; emoción, f. —vt conmover, emocionar; penetrar. —vi estremecerse, emocionarse

thriller /'θrilər/ n libro, m, (or comedia, f) sensacional; (detective novel) novela policíaca, f

thrilling /'θrilɪŋ/ a sensacional, espeluznante; (moving) emocionante, conmovedor

thrive /θraiv/ vi prosperar, medrar; enriquecerse, tener éxito; (grow) desarrollarse, robustecerse; florecer; (of plants) acertar

thriving /'θraiviŋ/ a próspero; floreciente; robusto, vigoroso

throat /θrout/ n garganta, f; orificio, m; (narrow entry) paso, m. **sore t.**, dolor de garganta, m. **to cut one's t.**, cortarse la garganta. **to take by the t.**, asir (or agarrar) por la garganta

throat cancer n cáncer de la garganta, m

throb /θrɒb/ n latido, m; pulsación, f; vibración, f; Fig. estremecimiento, m. —vi palpitar, latir; vibrar

throbbing /'θrɒbiŋ/ n pulsación, f; vibración, f. —a palpitante; vibrante. **t. pain**, dolor pungente, m

throe /θrou/ n dolor, m, agonía, angustia, f. **in the throes of**, en medio de; luchando con; en las garras de. **throes of childbirth**, dolores de parto, m pl. **throes of death**, agonía de la muerte, f

thrombosis /θrɒm'bousis/ n Med. trombosis, f

throne /θroun/ n trono, m; (royal power) corona, f, poder real, m. —vt elevar al trono. **speech from the t.**, el discurso de la corona, m

throng /θrɒŋ/ n muchedumbre, multitud, f. —vi apiñarse remolinarse, acudir. —vt atestar, llenar de bote en bote

throttle /'θrɒtl/ n Mech. regulador, m; Auto. estrangulador, m; Inf. garganta, f. —vt estrangular; Fig. ahogar, suprimir. **to open (close) the t.**, abrir (cerrar) el estrangulador

through /θru/ prep por; al través de; de un lado a otro de; por medio de; (between) entre; por causa de; gracias a. —adv al través; de un lado a otro; (whole) entero, todo; (from beginning to end) desde el principio hasta el fin; (to the end) hasta el fin. —a (of passages, etc.) que va desde... hasta...; (of trains) directo. **to look t. the window**, mirar por la ventana, asomarse a la ventana. **to be wet t.**, estar calado hasta los huesos; estar muy mojado. **to carry t.**, llevar a cabo. **to fall t.**, caer por; (fail) fracasar. **to sleep the whole night t.**, dormir durante toda la noche, dormir la noche entera. **t. and t.**, completamente. **through the length and breadth of**, a lo largo y a lo ancho de, hasta los últimos rincones de. **t. traffic**, tráfico directo, m. **t. train**, tren directo, m

throughout /θru'aut/ prep por todo; durante todo. —adv completamente; (from beginning to end) desde el principio hasta el fin; (everywhere) en todas partes

throw /θrou/ vt arrojar, lanzar, echar; (fire) disparar; (pottery) plasmar; (knock down) derribar; (slough) mudar (la piel); (cast off) despojarse de; (a rider) desmontar; (a glance) echar, dirigir (una mirada,

etc.); (silk) torcer; (dice) echar; (light) dirigir, enfocar. **to t. oneself at the head of**, echarse a la cabeza de. **to t. open**, abrir de par en par; abrir. **to t. overboard**, Naut. echar al mar; desechar; (desert) abandonar. **to t. about**, esparcir, desparramar; derrochar. **to t. aside**, echar a un lado, desechar; abandonar, dejar. **to t. away**, tirar; desechar; (spend) malgastar, derrochar; (waste) sacrificar; (of opportunities) malograr, perder. **to t. back**, devolver; echar hacia atrás. **to t. down**, derribar, dar en el suelo con; echar abajo; (arms) rendir. **to t. down the glove**, arrojar el guante. **to t. oneself down**, tumbarse, echarse; (descend) echarse abajo. **to t. oneself down from**, arrojarse de. **to t. in**, echar dentro; (give extra) añadir; (the clutch) embragar; insertar; (a remark) hacer (una observación). **to t. off**, despojarse de; quitarse; (refuse) rechazar; sacudirse; (get rid of) despedir; (renounce) renunciar; (exhale) emitir, despedir; (verses) improvisar. **to t. on**, echar sobre; (garments) ponerse. **to t. oneself upon**, lanzarse sobre. **to t. out**, expeler; hacer salir; plantar en la calle; (utter) proferir, soltar; (one's chest) inflar. **to t. over**, (desert) abandonar, dejar. **to t. up**, (build) levantar; lanzar en el aire; (a post, etc.) renunciar (a), abandonar; vomitar

thrum /θrʌm/ vt and vi tocar mal; (keyed instruments) teclear; (of stringed instruments) rascar las cuerdas (de)

thrust /θrʌst/ n empujón, m; (with a sword) estocada, f; (fencing) golpe, m; (with a lance) bote, m; ataque, m; asalto, m. —vt empujar; (put) meter; (insert) introducir; (pierce) atravesar; (out, through, of the head, etc.) asomar. —vi acometer, atacar, embestir; meterse, introducirse; (intrude) entrometerse; (fencing) dar un golpe. **to t. aside**, empujar a un lado; (proposals) rechazar. **to t. back**, hacer retroceder, empujar hacia atrás; (words) tragarse; (thoughts) apartar, rechazar. **to t. down**, empujar hacia abajo; hacer bajar; Fig. reprimir. **to t. forward**, empujar hacia delante; hacer seguir. **to t. oneself forward**, adelantarse; Fig. ponerse delante de los otros, darse importancia. **to t. in**, introducir; (stick) hincar; (insert) intercalar. **to t. on**, hacer seguir; empujar sobre; (garments) ponerse rápidamente. **to t. oneself in**, introducirse; entrometerse. **to t. out**, echar fuera; hacer salir, echar; expulsar; (the tongue) sacar (la lengua); (the head, etc.) asomar. **to t. through**, atravesar; (pierce) traspasar. **to t. one's way through**, abrirse paso por. **to t. upon**, imponer, hacer aceptar

thud /θʌd/ n sonido sordo, m; golpe sordo, m

thug /θʌg/ n asesino, criminal, m

thumb /θʌm/ n pulgar, m. —vt hojear; ensuciar con los dedos. **under the t. of,** Fig. en el poder de. **t. index,** índice pulgar, m. **t.-mark,** huella del dedo, f. **t.-screw,** tornillo de orejas, m, **t.-stall,** dedil, m. **t.-tack,** chinche, m

thump /θʌmp/ n golpe, porrazo, m. —vt and vi golpear, aporrear; (the ground, of rabbits) zapatear

thunder /'θʌndər/ n trueno, m; (of hooves, etc.) estampido, m; estruendo, m. —vi tronar; retumbar; Fig. fulminar. —vt gritar en una voz de trueno, rugir. to **t. along,** avanzar como el trueno; galopar ruidosamente. **t.-clap,** trueno, m. **t.-cloud,** nube de tormenta, f, nubarrón, m. **t.-storm,** tronada, f. **t. struck,** muerto, estupefacto. **to be thunderstruck,** quedarse frío

thunderbolt /'θʌndər,boult/ n rayo, m

thunderer /'θʌndərər/ n fulminador, m. **the Thunderer,** Júpiter tonante, Júpiter tronante, m; el «Times» londinense, m

Thursday /'θɜrzdei/ n jueves, m. **Holy T.,** Jueves Santo, m

thus /ðʌs/ adv así; de este modo; en estos términos; hasta este punto. **t. far,** hasta ahora; hasta este punto; hasta aquí. **Thus it is that...,** Así es que...

thwart /θwɔrt/ vt frustrar, impedir

thyme /taim/ n Bot. tomillo, m

thymus /'θaiməs/ n Anat. timo, m

thyroid /'θairɔid/ a tiroideo. **t. gland,** tiroides, f

thyself /ðai'self/ poss pron tu mismo, m; tu misma, f; (with prep.) tí mismo, m; tí misma, f; (in a reflexive verb) te

Tiberias /tai'biəriəs/ Tiberíades, f

Tibetan /tɪ'betn/ a and n tibetano (-na); (language) tibetano, m

tic /tɪk/ n (twitch) tic nervioso, m

tick /tɪk/ n Ent. ácaro, m; (sound) tictac, m; (cover) funda de colchón, f; Inf. fiado, crédito, m; (mark) marca, f vt hacer tic-tac. —vt poner una marca contra. **on t.,** Inf. al fiado. **to t. off,** poner una marca contra; Inf. reñir. **to t. over,** Auto. andar, marchar

ticket /'tɪkɪt/ n billete, m; (for an entertainment) entrada, localidad, f; (label) etiqueta, f; (pawn) papeleta de empeño, f; (for luggage) talón, m (Polit. U.S.A.) candidatura, f, vt marcar. **to take one's t.,** sacar el billete (for an entertainment) la entrada, f). **excursion t.,** billete de excursión, m. **return t.,** billete de ida y vuelta, m. **season t.,** billete de abono, m. **single t.,** billete sencillo, m. **t. agency,** (for travel) agencia de viajes, f; (for entertainments) agencia de teatros, f. **t. collector or inspector,** revisor, m. **t. holder,** tenedor de billete, m; abonado (-da). **t. office,** (railway) despacho de billetes, m; taquilla, f. **t.-of-leave,** libertad condi-

cional, f. **t. punch,** sacabocados, m; (on tramcars) clasificador de billetes, m

tickle /'tɪkəl/ vt hacer cosquillas (a), cosquillear; irritar; (gratify) halagar; (amuse) divertir. —vi tener cosquillas; hacer cosquillas; ser irritante

ticklish /'tɪklɪʃ/ a cosquilloso; (of persons) difícil, vidrioso; (of affairs) espinoso, delicado

tidal /'taidl/ a de marea. **t. wave,** marejada, f; Fig. ola popular, f

tidbit /'tɪd,bɪt/ n See titbit

tide /taid/ n marea, f; (season) tiempo, m, estación, f; (trend) corriente, f; (progress) curso, m; marcha, f. —vi (with over) vencer, superar; aguardar la ocasión. **to go against the t.,** ir contra la corriente. **to go with the t.,** seguir la corriente. **high t.,** marea alta, f. **low t.,** marea baja, f, bajamar, m. **neap t.,** marea muerta, f. **t. mark,** lengua del agua, f

tidings /'taidɪŋz/ n pl noticias, nuevas, f pl

tidy /'taidi/ a aseado; metódico, en orden; pulcro; Inf. considerable. —vt poner en orden, asear; limpiar; (oneself) arreglarse

tie /tai/ n lazo, m, atadura, f; (knot) nudo, m; (for the neck) corbata, f; Sports. empate, m; Mus. ligado, m; Archit. tirante, m; (spiritual bond) lazo, m; (burden) carga, responsabilidad, f. **tie clasp,** pisa corbata, mf. **tie-pin,** alfiler de corbata, m. **tie seller,** corbatero (-ra)

tie /tai/ vt atar; (bind) ligar; (lace) lacear; (a knot) hacer; (with a knot) anudar; (unite) unir; (Fig. bind) constreñir, obligar; (limit) restringir; (occupy) ocupar, entretener; (hamper) estorbar, impedir. —vi atarse; Sports. empatar. **to tie one's tie,** hacer la corbata. **to tie down,** atar a; limitar; obligar. **They tied him down to a chair,** Le ataron a una silla. **to tie together,** enlazar, ligar; unir. **to tie up,** liar, atar; (wrap) envolver; recoger; Naut. amarrar, atracar; (restrict) limitar, restringir; (invest) invertir

tie-breaker /'tai,breikər/ n desempate, m

tier /'tiər/ n fila, hilera, f. **in tiers,** en gradas; (of a dress) en volantes

tiff /tɪf/ n disgusto, m

tiger /'taigər/ n tigre, m. **t.-cat,** gato (-ta) atigrado (-da). **t.-lily,** tigridia, f

tight /tait/ a apretado; (not leaky) hermético, impermeable; (taut) tieso, tirante; (narrow) estrecho; (trim) compacto; (of clothes) muy ajustado; (shut) bien cerrado; Naut. estanco; (risky) peligroso, difícil; (miserly) tacaño; (of money, goods) escaso; **to be t.-fisted,** ser como un puño. **to hold t.,** agarrar fuerte. **t. corner,** Fig. aprieto, lance apretado, m. **t.-rope,** cuerda de volatinero, f. **t.-rope walker,** alambrista, equilibrista, mf; volatinero (-ra), bailarín de la cuerda floja, m. **t.-rope walker's pole,** balancín, m

tighten /'taitn/ vt estrechar, apretar;

(stretch) estirar; (of saddle girths) cinchar. —*vi* estrecharse; estirarse

tights /taits/ *n pl* mallas, *f pl*

tile /tail/ *n* teja, *f;* (for flooring) baldosa, losa, *f;* (ornamental) azulejo, *m;* (hat) chistera, *f.* —*vt* tejar; embaldosar. **t. floor,** enlosado, embaldosado, *m.* **t. manufacturer,** tejero, *m.* **t. works** or **yard,** tejar, *m,* (Colombia) galpón *m*

till /til/ *n* (for money) cajón, *m.* —*vt Agr.* cultivar, labrar. —*prep* hasta. —*conjunc* hasta que

tilt /tilt/ *n* inclinación, *f;* ladeo, *m;* (fight) torneo, *m,* justa, *f.* —*vt* inclinar; ladear; (a drinking vessel) empinar. —*vi* inclinarse; ladearse; (fight) justar. **to t. against,** *Fig.* arremeter contra, atacar. **at full t.,** a todo correr. **t. hammer,** martinete de báscula, *m.* **t.-yard,** palestra, *f*

timber /'tɪmbər/ *n* madera de construcción, *f;* (trees) árboles de monte, *m pl;* bosque, *m;* (beam) viga, *f; Naut.* cuaderna, *f.* —*vt* enmaderar. **t. line,** límite del bosque maderable, *m.* **t. merchant,** maderero, *m.* **t. wolf,** lobo gris, *m.* **t. work,** maderaje, *m.* **t. yard,** maderería, *f,* corral de madera, *m*

time /taim/ *n* (in general) tiempo, *m;* (epoch) época, edad, *f;* tiempos, *m pl;* (of the year) estación, *f;* (by the clock) hora, *f;* (lifetime) vida, *f;* (particular moment of time) momento, *m;* (occasion) sazón, ocasión, *f;* (day) día, *m;* (time allowed) plazo, *m;* (in repetition) vez, *f; Mus.* compás, *m; Mil.* paso, *m.* —*vt* ajustar al tiempo; hacer con oportunidad; (regulate) regular; calcular el tiempo que se emplea en hacer una cosa; (a blow) calcular. **all the t.,** todo el tiempo; continuamente, sin cesar. **a long t.,** mucho tiempo. **a long t. ago,** mucho tiempo ha, hace mucho. **at a t.,** a la vez, al mismo tiempo; (of period) en una época. **at any t.,** a cualquier hora; en cualquier momento; (when you like) cuando gustes. **at no t.,** jamás, nunca. **at some t.,** alguna vez; en alguna época. **at some t. or another,** un día u otro; en una u otra ocasión; en alguna época. **at that t.,** en aquella época; en la sazón; en aquel instante. **at the one t.,** de una vez. **at the present t.,** en la actualidad, al presente. **at the proper t.,** a su debido tiempo; a la hora señalada; a la hora conveniente. **at the same t.,** al mismo tiempo. **at the same t. as,** mientras, a medida que; al mismo instante que, **at times,** a veces, en ocasiones. **behind the times,** *Fig.* atrasado de noticias; pasado de moda. **behind t.,** atrasado. **by that t.,** para entonces. **every t.,** cada vez; siempre. **for some t.,** durante algún tiempo. **for some t. past,** de algún tiempo a esta parte. **for the t. being,** de momento, por ahora, por lo pronto. **from this t.,** desde hoy; desde esta fecha. **from this t. forward,** de hoy en adelante. **from t. to t.,** de vez en cuando, de cuando en cuando, de tarde

en tarde. **in a month's t.,** en un mes. **in a short t.,** en breve, dentro de poco. **in good t.,** puntualmente; temprano. **in my t.,** en mis días, en mis tiempos. **in olden times,** antiguamente, en otros tiempos. **in the course of t.,** andando el tiempo, en el transcurso de los años. **in the t. of,** en la época de. **in t.,** (promptly) a tiempo; con el tiempo. **in t. to come,** en el porvenir. **It is t. to...,** Es hora de.... **many times,** frecuentemente, muchas veces. **Once upon a t.,** Érase una vez, Una vez había, Érase que érase, Érase que se era. **Since t. out of mind,** Desde tiempo inmemorial. **the last (next) t.,** la última (próxima) vez. **this t. of year,** esta estación del año. **T. hangs heavy on his hands,** El tiempo se le hace interminable. **T. flies,** El tiempo vuela. **T. will tell!** ¡El tiempo lo dirá! ¡Veremos lo que veremos! **What t. is it?** ¿Qué hora es? **The t. is...,** La hora es... **within a given t.,** dentro de un plazo dado. **to be out of t.,** estar fuera de compás. **to gain t.,** ganar tiempo. **to have a good t.,** pasarlo bien, divertirse. **to have a bad t.,** pasarlo mal; *Inf.* tener un mal cuarto de hora. **to have no t. to,** no tener tiempo para + noun or pronoun, no tener tiempo de + infinitive. **to keep t.,** guardar el compás. **to kill t.,** engañar (or entretener) el tiempo. **to mark t.,** marcar el paso; *Fig.* hacer tiempo. **to pass the t.,** pasar el rato; pasar el tiempo. **to pass the t. of day,** saludar. **to serve one's t.,** (to a trade) servir el aprendizaje; (in prison) cumplir su condena; *Mil.* hacer el servicio militar. **to take t. to,** tomar tiempo para. **to take t. by the forelock,** asir la ocasión por la melena. **to waste t.,** perder el tiempo. **t. exposure,** pose, *f.* **t. fuse,** espoleta de tiempo, espoleta graduada, *f.* **t.-honored,** tradicional, consagrado por el tiempo. **t.-keeper,** capataz, *m;* reloj, *m.* **t.-saving,** que ahorra el tiempo. **t.-server,** lamelos, *mf.* **t.-signal,** señales horarias, *f pl.* **t.-table,** horario, *m;* itinerario, programa, *m* (railway) guía de ferrocarriles, *f.* **t. to come,** porvenir, *m,* lo venidero

timed /taimd/ *a* calculado; (ill-) intempestivo; (well-) oportuno

timeless /'taimlɪs/ *a* eterno

timely /'taimli/ *a* oportuno

timepiece /'taim,pis/ *n* reloj, *m*

time zone *n* huso esférico, huso horario, *m*

timid /'tɪmɪd/ *a* tímido, asustadizo, medroso; (shy) vergonzoso

timing /'taimɪŋ/ *n* medida del tiempo, *f; Mech.* regulación, *f;* (timetable) horario, *m*

timorous /'tɪmərəs/ *a* timorato, apocado, asustadizo

tin /tɪn/ *n* (metal) estaño, *m;* (container) lata, *f;* (sheet) hojalata, *f;* (money) plata, *f.* —*vt* estañar; (place in tins) envasar en lata; cubrir con hojalata, hoja de aluminio, *f.* **tin-foil,** papel de estaño, *m.* **tin**

hat, casco de acero, *m.* **tin opener,** abrelatas, abridor de latas, *m.* **tin-plate,** hojalata, *f.* **tin soldier,** soldado de plomo, *m.* **tin ware,** hojalatería, *f*

tincture /'tɪŋktʃər/ *n* tintura, *f*, tinte, *m; Med.* tintura, *f;* (trace) dejo, *m;* (veneer) capa, *f.* —*vt* teñir, tinturar

tinder /'tɪndər/ *n* yesca, *f.* **t. box,** yescas, lumbres, *f pl*

tinge /tɪndʒ/ *n* tinte, matiz, *m; Fig.* dejo, toque, *m.* —*vt* matizar, tinturar; *Fig.* tocar

tingle /'tɪŋgəl/ *n* picazón, comezón, *f;* (thrill) estremecimiento, *m.* —*vi* picar; (of ears) zumbar; (thrill) estremecerse (de); vibrar

tinker /'tɪŋkər/ *n* calderero remendón, *m.* —*vt* remendar. —*vi* chafallar. **to t. with,** jugar con

tinkle /'tɪŋkəl/ *n* tilín, retintín, *m;* campanilleo, *m;* cencerreo, *m.* —*vi* tintinar. —*vt* hacer tintinar

tinsel /'tɪnsəl/ *n* oropel, *m;* (cloth) lama de oro o plata, *f*, brocadillo, *m; Fig.* oropel, *m.* —*a* de oropel; de brocadillo; *Fig.* charro. —*vt* adornar con oropel

tint /tɪnt/ *n* tinta, *f*, color, *m;* matiz, *m;* tinte, *m.* —*vt* colorar, teñir; matizar

tiny /'taini/ *a* diminuto, minúsculo, menudo, chiquito

tip /tɪp/ *n* punta, *f;* cabo, *m,* extremidad, *f;* (of an umbrella, etc.) regatón, *m;* (of a lance) borne, *m;* (of a cigarette) boquilla, *f;* (of a shoe) puntera, *f;* (of a finger) yema, *f;* (for rubbish) depósito de basura, *m;* (gratuity) propina, *f;* (information) informe oportuno, *m;* (tap) golpecito, *m.* **to have on the tip of one's tongue,** tener en la punta de la lengua. **tip-cart,** volquete, *m.* **tip-up seat,** asiento plegable, *m*

tip /tɪp/ *vt* inclinar; volcar, voltear; (drinking vessel) empinar; poner regatón, etc. (a); *Poet.* tocar, golpear ligeramente; (reward) dar propina (a). —*vi* inclinarse; (topple) tambalearse; (reward) dar propina. **to tip the wink,** guiñar el ojo (a). **to tip off,** (liquids) echar; hacer caer; (inform) decir en secreto; informar oportunamente. **to tip over,** *vt* volcar; hacer caer. —*vi* volcarse; caer; (of a boat) zozobrar. **to tip up,** *vt* (a seat) levantar; (money) proporcionar (al dinero); (upset) volcar; hacer perder el equilibrio. —*vi* volcarse; (of a seat) levantarse; (lose the balance) perder el equilibrio

tipple /'tɪpəl/ *n* bebida, *f.* —*vt* beber, sorber. —*vi* empinar el codo

tipsy /'tɪpsi/ *a* achispado, algo borracho. **to be t.,** estar entre dos luces, estar entre dos velas

tiptoe /'tɪp,tou/ (on) *adv* de puntillas; *Fig.* excitado, ansioso. **to stand on t.,** ponerse de puntillas, empinarse

tirade /'taireid/ *n* diatriba, *f*

tire /taiər/ *n* (of a cart, etc.) llanta, *f; Auto.* neumático, *m;* (of a perambulator, etc.) rueda de goma, *f.* **balloon t.,** neu-

mático balón, *m.* **pneumatic t.,** neumático, *m.* **slack t.,** neumático desinflado, *m.* **solid t.,** neumático macizo, *m.* **spare t.,** neumático de recambio (or de repuesto), *m.* **t. burst,** estallido de un neumático, *m.* **t. valve,** válvula de cámara (del neumático), *f*

tire /taiər/ *vt* cansar, fatigar; (bore) aburrir. —*vi* cansarse, fatigarse; aburrirse. **to be tired of,** estar cansado de. **to grow tired,** empezar a cansarse. **to t. out,** rendir de cansancio

tired /taiərd/ *a* cansado, fatigado. **to be sick and t. of,** estar hasta la coronilla (de), (of persons) con. **t. of,** cansado de; disgustado de

tireless /'taiərlɪs/ *a* infatigable, incansable

tiresome /'taiərsəm/ *a* fastidioso, molesto, pesado; (dull) aburrido

tiring /'taiərɪŋ/ *a* fatigoso

tissue /'tɪʃu/ *n* (cloth) tisú, *m,* lama, *f;* (paper) pañuelito *m; Biol.* tejido, *m;* (series) serie, sarta, *f.* **t. paper,** papel de seda, *m*

tit /tɪt/ *n Ornith.* paro, *m.* **tit for tat,** tal para cual

titbit /'tɪt,bɪt/ *n* golosina, *f*

titillate /'tɪtl̩,eit/ *vt* titilar, estimular

titivate /'tɪtə,veit/ *vi* arreglarse

title /'taitl̩/ *n* título, *m;* (right) derecho, *m;* documento, *m.* **to give a t. to,** intitular; ennoblecer. **t. deed,** títulos de propiedad, *m.* **t. page,** portada, *f.* **t. role,** papel principal, *m*

titter /'tɪtər/ *vi* reírse disimuladamente. —*n* risa disimulada, *f*

tittle /'tɪtl̩/ *n* adarme, tilde, ápice, *m*

to /tu; *unstressed* tʊ, tə/ *prep* a; (as far as) hasta; (in the direction of) en dirección a, hacia; (with indirect object) a; (until) hasta; (compared with) en comparación con, comparado con; (against) contra; (according to) según; (as) como; (in) en; (so that, in order to, for the purpose of) para; (indicating possession) a, de; (of time by the clock) menos; (by) por; (before verbs of motion or which imply motion) a (sometimes para); (before some other verbs) de; en; (before verbs of beginning, inviting, exhorting, obliging) a; (indicating indirect object) a; (before a subjunctive or infinitive indicating future action or obligation) que. **To** is often not translated. With most Spanish infinitives no separate translation is necessary, e.g. *leer, decir, to read, to speak.* Some verbs are always followed by a preposition (e.g. *to begin to speak,* empezar a hablar, etc.). —*adv* (shut) cerrado. **to come to,** volver en sí. **to lie to,** *Naut.* ponerse a la capa. **to and from,** de un lado a otro. **face to face,** cara a cara. **He has been a good friend to them,** Ha sido un buen amigo para ellos. **That is new to me,** Eso es nuevo para mí. **He went to London,** Se fue a Londres. **to go to France (Canada),** ir a Francia (al Canadá). **the road to Madrid,** la carretera de Madrid. **She**

kept the secret to herself, Guardó el secreto para sí. **to go to the dentist**, ir al dentista. **We give it to them**, Se lo damos a ellos. **It belongs to me**, Pertenece a mí. **What does it matter to you?** ¿Qué te importa a tí? **I wish to see him**, Quiero verle. **They did it to help us**, Lo hicieron para ayudarnos. **I have to go to see her**, Tengo que ir a verla. **to this day**, hasta hoy, hasta el presente. **It is a quarter to six**, Son las seis menos cuarto. **to the last shilling**, hasta el último chelín. **the next to me**, el que me sigue. **closed to the public**, cerrado para el público

toad /toud/ n sapo, m

toady /'toudi/ n lameculos, mf adulador (-ra). —vt lamer el culo (a), adular

toast /toust/ n Cul. tostada, f; (drink) brindis, m. —vt tostar; brindar, beber a la salud de. —vi brindar. **buttered t.**, mantecada, f. **t.-rack**, portatostadas, m

toaster /'toustər/ n (device) tostador, m; (person) brindador, m

tobacco /tə'bækou/ n tabaco, m. —a tabacalero. **black** or **cut t.**, picadura, f. **leaf t.**, tabaco de hoja, m. **mild t.**, tobaco flojo, m. **pipe t.**, tabaco de pipa, m. **plug t.**, tabaco para mascar, m. **strong t.**, tabaco fuerte, m. **Turkish t.**, tabaco turco, m. **Virginian t.**, tabaco rubio, m. **t.-pipe**, pipa (de tabaco), f. **t.-pipe cleaner**, escobillón para limpiar pipas, m. **t. plantation**, tabacal, m. **t. planter**, tabacalero (-ra). **t. poisoning**, tabaquismo, m. **t.-pouch** or **jar**, tabaquera, f

toboggan /tə'bogən/ n tobogán, m. —vi ir en tobogán. **t. run**, pista de tobogán, f

today /tə'dei/ adv hoy; ahora, actualmente, al presente, hoy día. —n el día de hoy. **from t.**, desde hoy. **from t. forward**, de hoy en adelante

toddle /'todl/ vi hacer pinos, empezar a andar; (stroll) dar una vuelta; (leave) marcharse

toddy /'todi/ n ponche, m

toe /tou/ n dedo del pie, m; (cloven) pezuña, f; uña, f; (of furniture) base, f, pie, m; (of stockings, shoes) punta, f. **He stepped on my toe**, Me pisó el dedo del pie. **big toe**, dedo pulgar del pie, dedo gordo del pie, m. **little toe**, dedo pequeño del pie, m. **to toe the line**, ponerse en la raya, m; Fig. cumplir con su deber. **toe-cap**, puntera, f. **toe-dancing**, baile de puntillas, m. **toe-nail**, uña del dedo del pie, f

toffee /'tofi/ n caramelo, m

together /tə'gɛðər/ adv junto; (uninterruptedly) sin interrupción; (in concert) simultáneamente, a la vez, al mismo tiempo; (consecutively) seguido. **t. with**, con; junto con; en compañía de; (simultaneously) a la vez que

toil /toil/ n labor, f, trabajo, m —pl. **toils**, lazos, m pl; Fig. redes, f pl. —vi trabajar, afanarse. **to t. along**, caminar penosamente (por); adelantar con dificultad. **to t. up**, subir penosamente

toilet /'toilit/ n tocado, m; atavío, m; vestido, m; (w.c.) retrete, excusado, m; (for ladies) tocador, m. **to make one's t.**, arreglarse. **t. case**, neceser, m. **t.-paper**, papel higiénico, m. **t.-powder**, polvos de arroz, m pl. **t. roll**, rollo de papel higiénico, m. **t.-set**, juego de tocador, m. **t. soap**, jabón de olor, jabón de tocador, m

token /'toukən/ n señal, muestra, f; prueba, f; (presage) síntoma, indicio, m; (remembrance) recuerdo, m. **as a t. of**, en señal de; como recuerdo de

tolerable /'tolərəbəl/ a tolerable, soportable, llevadero; (fairly good) mediano, mediocre, regular

tolerably /'tolərəbli/ adv bastante

tolerance /'tolərəns/ n tolerancia, f; paciencia, indulgencia, f

tolerant /'tolərənt/ a tolerante; indulgente

tolerate /'tolə,reit/ vt tolerar, sufrir, soportar; permitir

toleration /,tolə'reiʃən/ n tolerancia, f; indulgencia, paciencia, f. **religious t.**, libertad de cultos, f

toll /toul/ n (of a bell) tañido, doble, m; (for passage) peaje, portazgo, m; (for grinding) derecho de molienda, m —vt and vi doblar, tañer. **to t. the hour**, dar la hora. **t. call**, conferencia telefónica interurbana, llamada a larga distancia, f. **t. gate**, barrera de peaje, f. **t. house**, oficina de portazgos, f

toll booth n caseta de pago, f

tomahawk /'toma,hok/ n hacha de guerra de los indios, f

tomato /tə'meitou/ n tomate, jitomate, (Mexico) m. **t. plant**, tomatera, f. **t. sauce**, salsa de tomate, f

tomb /tum/ n tumba, f, sepulcro, m

tomboy /'tom,boi/ n muchachote, torbellino, m

tombstone /'tum,stoun/ n piedra mortuoria, f, monumento funerario, m

tome /toum/ n tomo, volumen, m

tomfoolery /,tom'fuləri/ n necedad, tontería, f; payasada, f

tomorrow /tə'morou/ adv and n mañana, f. **a fortnight t.**, mañana en quince. **the day after t.**, pasado mañana. **t. afternoon (morning)**, mañana por la tarde (mañana). **T. is Friday**, Mañana es viernes

ton /tʌn/ n tonelada, f

tone /toun/ n tono, m; (Mus. Med. Art.) tono, m; (of the voice) acento, m, entonación, f; (of musical instruments) sonido, m; (shade) matiz, m. —vt entonar; Photo. virar. **to t. down**, vt (Art. Mus.) amortiguar; Fig. suavizar, modificar. —vi (Art. Mus.) amortiguarse; Fig. suavizarse, modificarse. **to t. in with**, (of colors) vt armonizar con. —vi armonizarse, corresponder en tono o matiz. **to t. up**, vt subir de color, intensificar el color de; Med. entonar, robustecer. **t. poem**, poema sinfónico, m

tongs /tonz/ n pl tenazas, f pl; tenacillas,

f pl. **curling t.**, tenacillas para el pelo, *f*
pl. **sugar t.**, tenacillas para azúcar, *f pl*
tongue /tʌŋ/ *n Anat.* lengua, *f;* (language) idioma, *m,* lengua, *f;* (speech) modo de hablar, *m,* habla, *f; Mus.* lengüeta, *f;* (of buckle) diente, *m;* (of shoe) oreja, *f;* (of land) lengua, *f;* (of a bell) badajo, *m;* (flame) lengua, *f.* **My t. ran away with me,** *Inf.* Se me fue la mula. **to give t.**, ladrar. **to hold one's t.**, cerrar el pico, tener la boca. **t.** of fire, lengua de fuego, *f.* **t. tied,** con impedimento en el habla; turbado, confuso; mudo. **t.-twister,** trabalenguas, *m*
-tongued *a* de voz...
tonic /'tɒnɪk/ *a* tónico. —*n Med.* tónico, reconstituyente, *m; Mus.* tónica, *f*
tonight /tə'naɪt/ *adv* and *n* esta noche
tonnage /'tʌnɪdʒ/ *n* tonelaje, porte, *m;* (duty) derecho de tonelaje, *m*
tonsil /'tɒnsəl/ *n* amígdala, *f*
tonsillitis /ˌtɒnsə'laɪtɪs/ *n* amigdalitis, *f*
too /tu/ *adv* demasiado; (very) muy; también; además. **too hard,** demasiado difícil, demasiado rígido; (of persons) demasiado duro. **too much,** demasiado. **too often,** con demasiada frecuencia
tool /tul/ *n* herramienta, *f;* utensilio, *m;* instrumento, *m;* (person) criatura, *f.* —*vt* labrar con herramienta; (a book) estampar en seco. **t.-bag,** capacho, *m.* **t. box,** caja de herramientas, *f*
toot /tut/ *n* sonido de bocina, *m, vi* sonar una bocina
tooth /tuθ/ *n* diente, *m;* muela, *f;* (of comb) púa, *f;* (taste) gusto, paladar, *m;* (cog) diente de rueda, *m;* (of saw) diente, *m.* —*vt* dentar; mellar. —*vi Mech.* engranar. **armed to the teeth,** armado hasta los dientes. **double t.**, muela, *f.* **false teeth,** dentadura postiza, *f.* **set of teeth,** dentadura, *f.* **to cut one's teeth,** echar los dientes. **to have a sweet t.**, ser muy goloso. **to show one's teeth,** enseñar los dientes. **t.-brush,** cepillo para los dientes, *m.* **t. drawing,** extracción de un diente, *f.* **t.-paste,** pasta dentífrica, *f*
toothache /'tuθˌeɪk/ *n* dolor de muelas, *m*
toothless /'tuθlɪs/ *a* desdentado, sin dientes; (of combs) sin púas
toothpick /'tuθˌpɪk/ *n* mondadientes, *m*
top /tɒp/ *n* (summit) cima, cumbre, *f;* (of a tree) copa, *f;* (of the head) coronilla, *f;* (of a page) cabeza, *f;* (crest) copete, *m,* cresta, *f;* (surface) superficie, *f;* (of a wall) coronamiento, *m;* (tip) punta, *f;* (point) ápice, *m;* (of a tram, bus) imperial, baca, *f;* (of a wave) cresta, *f;* (acme) auge, *m;* (of a class) primero (de la clase), *m;* (highest rank) último grado, *m;* (of a plant) hojas, *f pl;* (of a piano) cima, *f; Naut.* cofa, *f;* (head of a bed, etc.) cabeza, *f;* (lid) tapadera, *f;* (toy) trompo, peón, *m;* (humming) trompa, *f. a* más alto; máximo; (chief) principal, primero. —*vt* (cover) cubrir de; (cut off) desmochar; (come level with) llegar a la cima

de; (rise above) elevarse por encima (de), coronar, dominar; (be superior to) exceder, aventajar; (golf) topear. **at the top,** a la cabeza; a la cumbre. **from top to bottom,** de arriba abajo. **on top of,** encima de; (besides) en adición a, además de. **to be top-dog,** ser un gallito. **to sleep like a top,** dormir como un lirón. **top boots,** botas de campaña, *f pl.* **top-dog,** vencedor, *m;* poderoso, *m.* **top-hat,** sombrero de copa, *m.* **top-heavy,** más pesado por arriba que por abajo
topaz /'toupæz/ *n* topacio, jacinto occidental, *m*
topcoat /'tɒpˌkout/ *n* sobretodo, gabán, *m*
top floor *n* piso alto, *m*
topic /'tɒpɪk/ *n* asunto, tema, *m*
topical /'tɒpɪkəl/ *a* tópico; actual
topmost /'tɒpˌmoust/ *a* más alto; más importante
topple /'tɒpəl/ *vi* tambalearse, estar al punto de caer. **to t. down,** volcarse; derribarse; caer. **to t. over,** *vi* venirse abajo; perder el equilibrio. —*vt* derribar, hacer caer
topsy-turvy /'tɒpsi'tɜrvi/ *a* desordenado. —*adv* en desorden, patas arriba, de arriba abajo
torch /tɔrtʃ/ *n* antorcha, hacha, tea, *f.* **electric t.,** lamparilla eléctrica, *f.* **t.-bearer,** hachero, *m*
torchlight /'tɔrtʃˌlaɪt/ *n* luz de antorcha, *f.* **by t.,** a la luz de las antorchas
torment /*v.* tɔr'mɛnt, *n.* 'tɔrmɛnt/ *n* tormento, *m,* angustia, *f;* (torture) tortura, *f;* suplicio, *m;* mortificación, *f;* disgusto, *m.* —*vt* atormentar, martirizar; (torture) torturar; molestar
tornado /tɔr'neɪdou/ *n* tornado, *m*
torpedo /tɔr'pidou/ *n* torpedo, *m; Ichth.* pez torpedo, *m.* —*vt* torpedear. **self-propelling t.,** torpedo automóvil, *m.* **t.-boat,** torpedero, *m.* **t.-boat destroyer,** cazatorpedero, contratorpedero, *m.* **t. netting,** red contra torpedos, *f.* **t. station,** base de torpederos, *f.* **t. tube,** tubo lanzatorpedos, *m*
torpid /'tɔrpɪd/ *a* aletargado, entorpecido; (of the mind) torpe, tardo, apático
torrent /'tɔrənt/ *n* torrente, *m*
torrential /tə'rɛnʃəl/ *a* torrencial
torrid /'tɔrɪd/ *a* tórrido. **t. zone,** zona tórrida, *f*
torso /'tɔrsou/ *n* torso, *m*
tort /tɔrt/ *n Law.* tuerto, *m*
tortoise /'tɔrtəs/ *n* tortuga, *f.* **t.-shell,** carey, *m.* —*a* de carey
tortuous /'tɔrtʃuəs/ *a* tortuoso
torture /'tɔrtʃər/ *n* tortura, *f,* tormento, *m;* angustia, *f.* —*vt* torturar, dar tormento (a); martirizar
torturing /'tɔrtʃərɪŋ/ *a* torturador, atormentador; angustioso
toss /tɒs/ *n* sacudimiento, *m,* sacudida, *f;* (of the head) movimiento (de cabeza), *m;* (bull fighting) cogida, *f;* (from a horse) caída de caballo, *f.* —*vt* echar, lan-

zar; agitar, sacudir; (of bulls) acornear.
—*vi* agitarse; (of plumes, etc.) ondear; (in a boat) balancearse a la merced de las olas; jugar a cara o cruz. **to t. in a blanket,** mantear, dar una manta (a). **to t. aside,** echar a un lado; abandonar. **to t. off,** beber de un trago. **to t. up,** jugar a cara o cruz

tot /tɒt/ *n* (child) nene (-na), crío (-ía); (of drink) vaso pequeño, *m*. **to tot up,** sumar

total /'toutl/ *a* total; absoluto, completo, entero. —*n* total, *m*, suma, *f*. —*vt* sumar. —*vi* ascender (a). **t. employment,** ocupación total, *f*. **t. war,** guerra total, *f*

totalitarian /tou,tælɪ'teərɪən/ *a* totalitario

totality /tou'tælɪti/ *n* totalidad, *f*

totem /'toutəm/ *n* tótem, *m*

totter /'tɒtər/ *vi* (of persons) bambolearse; tambalear, estar al punto de caer; *Fig.* aproximarse a su fin

touch /tʌtʃ/ *vt* tocar; (brush against) rozar; (reach) alcanzar; (musical instruments) tocar; (move) emocionar, enternecer; (spur on) aguijar; (food) tomar; (affect) influir, afectar; (arouse) despertar, estimular; (equal) compararse con, igualar; (consider) tratar ligeramente (de); (money) dar un sablazo (a). —*vi* tocarse; imponer las manos para curar. **I have not touched a bite,** No he probado un bocado. **This touches me dearly,** Esto me toca de cerca. **to t. at,** hacer escala en, tocar en (un puerto). **to t. off,** descargar. **to t. up,** retocar; corregir. **to t. upon,** (a subject) tratar superficialmente de, tratar ligeramente de; hablar de; considerar

touch /tʌtʃ/ *n* (sense of) tacto, *m*; (contact) toque, contacto, *m*; (brushing) roce, *m*; (tap) golpe ligero, *m*; palmadita, *f*; (of an illness) ataque ligero, *m*; *Mus.* dedeo, *m*; (little) dejo, *m*; (test) prueba, *f*, toque, *m*; *Art.* toque, *m*, pincelada, *f*. **by the t.,** a tiento. **in t. with,** en relaciones con; en comunicación con; al corriente de. **to give the finishing t.,** dar la última pincelada; dar el último toque. **t.-line,** (football) línea de toque, línea lateral, *f*. **t.-me-not,** *Inf.* erizo, *m*. **t.-stone,** piedra de toque, *f*

touched /tʌtʃt/ *a* emocionado, conmovido

touching /'tʌtʃɪŋ/ *a* patético, conmovedor. —*prep* tocante a, acerca de. —*n* tocamiento, *m*

touchy /'tʌtʃi/ *a* susceptible, quisquilloso, vidrioso

tough /tʌf/ *a* (hard) duro; vigoroso, fuerte, robusto; resistente; (of character) tenaz, firme; (of a job) difícil; espinoso. —*n* chulo, *m*

toughen /'tʌfən/ *vt* endurecer. —*vi* endurecerse

toughness /'tʌfnɪs/ *n* dureza, *f*; vigor, *m*, fuerza, *f*; resistencia, *f*; tenacidad, firmeza, *f*; dificultad, *f*

toupee /tu'pei/ *n* tupé, *m*

tour /tʊr/ *n* viaje, *m*, excursión, *f*. —*vi* viajar. —*vt* viajar por. **circular t.,** viaje redondo, *m*. **on t.,** *Theat.* en tour, de gira

touring /'tʊrɪŋ/ *a* de turismo. —

tourist /'tʊrɪst/ *n* turista, *mf*; viajero (-ra). **t. agency,** agencia de turismo, *f*, patronato de turismo, *m*. **t. ticket,** billete kilométrico, *m*

tournament /'tʊrnəmənt/ *n* torneo, *m*, justa, *f*; (of games) concurso, *m*

tourniquet /'tʊrnɪkɪt, 'tʊr-/ *n* torniquete, *m*

tousle /'tauzəl, -səl/ *vt* despeinar; desordenar el pelo

tout /taut/ *n* buhonero, *m*. **to t. for,** pescar, solicitar

tow /tou/ *n* remolque, *m*; (rope) estopa, *f*. —*vt* (*Naut. Auto.*) remolcar. **on tow,** a remolque. **tow-path,** camino de sirga, *m*. **tow rope,** cable de remolque, *m*

towards /tɔrdz/ *prep* hacia, en dirección a; (of time) sobre, cerca de; (concerning) tocante a; (with persons) para, con

towel /'tauəl/ *n* toalla, *f*. **roller t.,** toalla continua, *f*. **t. rail,** toallero, *m*

tower /'tauər/ *n* torre, *f*; (fortress) fortaleza, *f*; (belfry) campanario, *m*; (large) torreón, *m*. —*vi* elevarse. **to t. above,** destacarse sobre, sobresalir; *Fig.* sobrepujar, superar

towering /'tauərɪŋ/ *a* elevado; dominante; orgulloso; *Fig.* violento, terrible

town /taun/ *n* población, *f*, pueblo, *m*; ciudad, *f*. **t. clerk,** secretario de ayuntamiento, *m*. **t. council,** concejo municipal, *m*. **t. councilor,** concejero municipal, *m*. **t. crier,** pregonero, *m*. **t. hall,** (casa de) ayuntamiento, casa consistorial, *f*. **t. house,** casa de ciudad, *f*. **t. planning,** urbanismo, *m*; reforma urbana, *f*. **t. wall,** muralla, *f*

"Town Ahead" «Poblado Próximo»

town worthy *n* persona principal de la ciudad, *f*

toxic /'tɒksɪk/ *a* tóxico

toy /tɔi/ *n* juguete, *m*. —*vi* (with) jugar con; acariciar. **toy maker,** fabricante de juguetes, *m*

toyshop /'tɔi,ʃɒp/ *n* juguetería, tienda de juguetes, *f*

trace /treis/ *n* huella, pista, *f*, rastro, *m*; vestigio, *m*; indicio, *m*, evidencia, *f*; (of a harness) tirante, *m*; (touch) dejo, *m*; (of fear, etc.) sombra, *f*. —*vt* trazar; (through transparent paper) calcar; seguir la pista (de); (write) escribir; (discern) distinguir; investigar; descubrir; determinar; (walk) atravesar, recorrer. **to t. back,** (of ancestry, etc.) hacer remontar (a)

tracer /'treisər/ *n* trazador (-ra). **t. bullet,** bala luminosa, *f*

trachea /'treikiə/ *n* *Anat.* tráquea, *f*

trachoma /trə'koumə/ *n* *Med.* tracoma, *f*

tracing /'treisɪŋ/ *n* calco, *m*; trazo, *m*;

seguimiento, *m.* **t.-paper,** papel de calcar, *m*

track /træk/ *n* huella, *f,* rastro, *m;* (for racing, etc.) pista, *f;* (of wheels) rodada, *f;* (railway) vía, *f;* (of a boat) estela, *f;* (path) senda, vereda, *f;* (sign) señal, evidencia, *f;* (course) ruta, *f.* —*vt* rastrear, seguir la pista (de); *Naut.* sirgar. **to t. down,** seguir y capturar. **double t.,** vía doble, *f.* **off the t.,** extraviado; (of a train) descarrilado; *Fig.* por los cerros de Úbeda. **side t.,** desviadero, *m.* **to keep t. of,** *Inf.* no perder de vista (a); seguir las fortunas de

tract /trækt/ *n* tracto, *m;* región, *f; Anat.* vía, *f;* (written) tratado, *m*

tractable /'træktəbəl/ *a* dócil

traction /'trækʃən/ *n* tracción, *f.* **t.-engine,** máquina de arrastre (or de tracción), *f*

tractor /'træktər/ *n* máquina de arrastre, *f;* tractor, *m*

trade /treid/ *n* comercio, *m;* tráfico, *m;* negocio, *m;* industria, *f;* (calling) oficio, *m,* profesión, *f;* (dealers) comerciantes, *mf pl.* —*vi* comerciar, traficar —*vt* cambiar. **to t. on,** explotar, aprovecharse de. **by t.,** de oficio, por profesión. **t.-mark,** marca de fábrica, *f.* **t.-name,** razón social, *f.* **t. price,** precio para el comerciante, *m.* **t. union,** sindicato, *m.* **T. Union Congress,** Congreso de Sindicatos, *m.* **t. unionism,** sistema de sindicatos obreros, *m.* **t.-winds,** vientos alisios, *m pl.*

trader /'treidər/ *n* comerciante, traficante, *mf;* mercader, *m;* (boat) buque mercante, *m*

tradesman /'treidzmən/ *n* tendero, *m.* **tradesmen's entrance,** puerta de servicio, *f*

trading /'treidɪŋ/ *n* comercio, tráfico, *m.* —*a* mercantil, comerciante, mercante. **t. ship,** buque mercante, *m.* **t. station,** factoría, *f*

tradition /trə'dɪʃən/ *n* tradición, *f*

traditional /trə'dɪʃənl/ *a* tradicional; del lugar

traduce /trə'dus/ *vt* calumniar, denigrar, vituperar

traffic /'træfɪk/ *n* comercio, negocio, tráfico, *m;* (in transit) transporte, *m;* (in movement) circulación, *f.* —*vi* comerciar, traficar, negociar. **to cause a block in the t.,** interrumpir la circulación. **t. block,** obstrucción del tráfico, *f,* atasco en la circulación, *m.* **t. indicator,** (on a car) indicador de dirección, *m.* **t. island,** refugio para peatones, salvavidas, *m.* **t. light,** disco, *m,* luz (de tráfico), *f,* semáforo, *m.* **t. roundabout,** redondel, *m*

tragedy /'trædʒɪdi/ *n* tragedia, *f*

tragic /'trædʒɪk/ *a* trágico

tragicomedy /ˌtrædʒɪ'kɒmɪdi/ *n* tragicomedia, *f*

trail /treil/ *n* rastro, *m,* pista, huella, *f;* (path) sendero, *m;* (of a comet) cola, cabellera, *f.* —*vt* rastrear, seguir el rastro de; (drag) arrastrar; (the anchor) garrar.

—*vi* arrastrar; (of plants) trepar. **on the t. of,** en busca de; siguiendo el rastro de; **put somebody on the t. of...** darle a fulano la pista de...

trailer /'treilər/ *n* cazador (-ra); perseguidor (-ra); *Auto.* remolque, *m;* (cinema) anuncio de próximas atracciones, *m; Bot.* talle rastrero, *m*

train /trein/ *n* (railway) tren, *m;* (of a dress) cola, *f;* (retinue) séquito, *m;* (procession) desfile, *m,* comitiva, *f;* (series) serie, sucesión, *f;* (of gunpowder) reguero de pólvora, *m.* **down t.,** tren descendente, *m.* **excursion t.,** tren de excursionistas, *m.* **express t.,** exprés, tren expreso, *m.* **fast t.,** rápido, *m.* **goods t.,** tren de mercancías, *m.* **mail t.,** tren correo, *m.* **next t.,** próximo tren, *m.* **passenger t.,** tren de pasajeros, *m.* **stopping t.,** tren ómnibus, *m.* **through t.,** tren directo, *m.* **up t.,** tren ascendente, *m.* **t.-bearer,** paje que lleva la cola, *m;* dama de honor, *f;* (of a cardinal, etc.) caudatario, *m.* **t.-ferry,** buque transbordador, *m.* **t.-oil,** aceite de ballena, *m.* **t. service,** servicio de trenes, *m*

train /trein/ *vt* educar; adiestrar; enseñar; *Sports.* entrenar; (firearms) apuntar; (plants) guiar; (accustom) habituar, acostumbrar; (a horse for racing) entrenar; (circus) amaestrar. —*vi* educarse; adiestrarse; *Sports.* entrenarse

trainer /'treinər/ *n* (of men and racehorses) entrenador, *m;* (of performing animals) domador, *m*

training /'treiniŋ/ *n* educación, *f,* enseñanza, instrucción, *f; Sports.* entrenamiento, *m.* **t.-college,** escuela normal, *f.* **t.-ship,** buque escuela, *m*

trait /treit/ *n* rasgo, *m,* característica, *f*

traitor /'treitər/ *n* traidor, *m*

trajectory /trə'dʒɛktəri/ *n* trayectoria, *f*

tram /træm/ *n* tranvía, *m.* —*a* tranviario. **t. conductor,** cobrador de tranvía, *m.* **t. depot,** cochera de tranvías, *f.* **t. stop,** parada de tranvía, *f*

trammel /'træməl/ *n* (of a horse) traba, *f; Fig.* obstáculo, estorbo, *m.* —*vt* travar; *Fig.* estorbar, impedir

tramp /træmp/ *n* (person) vagabundo (-da); vago (-ga); (walk) caminata, *f,* paseo largo, *m;* ruido de pasos, *m; Naut.* vapor volandero, *m.* —*vi* ir a pie; patear; vagabundear. —*vt* vagar por

trample /'træmpəl/ *n* pisoteo, *m;* (of feet) ruido de pasos, *m.* —*vt* pisotear, pisar, hollar. —*vi* pisar fuerte. **to t. on,** *Fig.* atropellar humillar

trance /træns/ *n* rapto, arrobamiento, *m; Med.* catalepsia, *f*

tranquil /'træŋkwɪl/ *a* tranquilo, apacible; sereno, sosegado

tranquility /træŋ'kwɪlɪti/ *n* tranquilidad, paz, quietud, *f;* serenidad, *f,* sosiego, *m;* calma, *f*

tranquilize /'træŋkwə,laiz/ *vt* tranquilizar, sosegar, calmar

tranquilizer /'træŋkwə,laizər/ n calmante, m

trans- prefix trans-. **t.-Pyrenean,** a traspirenaico. **to t.-ship,** trasbordar. **t.-shipment,** trasbordo, m. **t.-Siberian,** trasiberiano

transact /træn'sækt/ vt despachar, hacer. —vi despachar un negocio

transaction /træn'sækʃən/ n desempeño, m; negocio, m; transacción, operación, f; pl **transactions** (of a society) actas, f pl

transatlantic /,trænsət'læntik/ a transatlántico. **t. liner,** transatlántico, m

transcend /træn'sɛnd/ vt exceder, superar, rebasar. —vi trascender

transcribe /træn'skraib/ vt trascribir, copiar; Mus. trascribir, adaptar

transcript /'trænskript/ n traslado, trasunto, m; (student's) certificado de estudios, certificado de materias aprobadas, m, constancia de estudios, copia del expediente académico, hoja de estudios, f

transfer /v. træns'fɜr, n. 'trænsfər/ n traslado, m; trasferencia, f, traspaso, m; Law. cesión, enajenación, f; (picture) calcomanía, f. —vt trasladar; trasferir; pasar; Law. enajenar, ceder; estampar; calcografiar. —vi trasbordarse. **deed of t.,** escritura de cesión, f. **t.-paper,** papel de calcar, m

transferable /træns'fɜrəbəl/ a trasferible

transference /'trænsfərəns/ n traslado, m; transferencia, f; Law. cesión, enajenación, f

transfigure /træns'fɪgyər/ vt trasfigurar, trasformar

transfix /træns'fiks/ vt traspasar, Fig. paralizar

transform /træns'fɔrm/ vt trasformar; convertir, cambiar. **It is completely transformed,** Está completamente trasformado

transformation /,trænsfər'meiʃən/ n trasformación, f; conversión, f, cambio, m

transformer /træns'fɔrmər/ n Elec. trasformador, m

transfuse /træns'fyuz/ vt trasfundir

transfusion /træns'fyuʒən/ n trasfusión, f. **blood t.,** trasfusión de sangre, f•

transgress /træns'grɛs/ vt exceder, sobrepasar; (violate) contravenir, violar, pecar contra. —vi pecar

transgression /træns'grɛʃən/ n contravención, trasgresión, f; pecado, m

transgressor /træns'grɛsər/ n trasgresor (-ra), pecador (-ra)

transient /'trænʃənt, -ʒənt/ a transitorio, fugaz, pasajero; perecedero

transit /'trænsit/ n tránsito, paso, m; trasporte, m; Astron. tránsito, m. **in t.,** de tránsito

transition /træn'zɪʃən/ n transición, f; cambio, m; tránsito, paso, m

transitional /træn'zɪʃənl/ a de transición, transitorio

transitively /'trænsɪtɪvli/ adv transitivamente

transitorily /,trænsɪ'tɔrəli/ adv transitoriamente; provisionalmente

transitory /'trænsɪ,tɔri/ a transitorio, fugaz, pasajero, breve

translatable /træns'leitəbəl/ a traducible

translate /træns'leit/ vt traducir; interpretar; (transfer) trasladar

translation /træns'leiʃən/ n traducción, f; versión, f; traslado, m

translator /træns'leitər/ n traductor (-ra)

translucent /træns'lusənt/ a traslúcido, transparente

transmigrate /træns'maigreit/ vi trasmigrar

transmissible /træns'mɪsəbəl/ a trasmisible

transmission /træns'mɪʃən/ n trasmisión, f

transmit /træns'mɪt/ vt. trasmitir; remitir, dar

transmitter /træns'mɪtər/ n trasmisor (-ra); Radio. radiotrasmisor, m; Elec. trasmisor, m

transmute /træns'myut/ vt trasmutar

transoceanic /,trænsouʃi'ænɪk/ a transoceánico

transom /'trænsəm/ n travesaño, m; Naut. yugo de popa, m

transparency /træns'pɛərənsi/ n trasparencia, f; diafanidad, f; (picture) trasparente, m

transparent /træns'pɛərənt/ a trasparente; diáfano; (of style) claro, limpio

transpire /træn'spaiər/ vi traspirar; rezumarse; hacerse público; Inf. acontecer. —vt exhalar

transplant /træns'plænt/ vt trasplantar

transport /v. træns'pɔrt, n. 'trænspɔrt/ n trasporte, m; Naut. navío de trasporte, m; Aer. avión de trasporte, m; (fit) acceso, paroxismo, m. —vt trasportar; (convicts) deportar; Fig. (joy) colmar; (rage) llenar

transportation /,trænspɔr'teiʃən/ n trasporte, m; (convicts) deportación, f

transpose /træns'pouz/ vt trasponer; Mus. trasportar

transverse /træns'vɜrs/ a trasverso, trasversal

trap /træp/ n trampa, f; cepo, m; (net) lazo, m, red, f; (for mice, rats) ratonera, f; Mech. sifón de depósito, m; pequeño carruaje de dos ruedas, m; (door) puerta caediza, f; Theat. escotillón, m; pl **traps,** trastos, m pl; equipaje, m. —vt coger con trampa; hacer caer en el lazo; Fig. tender el lazo. —vi armar una trampa; armar lazo. **to fall into a t.,** Fig. caer en la trampa. **to pack one's traps,** liar el hato

trapeze /træ'piz/ n trapecio (de gimnasia), m

trapper /'træpər/ n cazador de animales de piel, m

trappings /'træpɪŋz/ n pl arneses, jaeces, m pl; arreos, aderezos, m pl, galas, f pl

trash /træʃ/ n paja, hojarasca, f; (of sugar, etc.) bagazo, m; trastos viejos, m pl; cachivaches, m pl; (literary) paja, f

trashy /'træʃi/ *a* de ningún valor, inútil, despreciable

traumatic /trə'mætɪk/ *a Med.* traumático

travail /trə'veil/ *n* dolores de parto, *m pl.* —*vi* estar de parto; trabajar

travel /'trævəl/ *n* el viajar, viajes, *m pl.* —*vi* viajar; ver mundo; (of traffic) circular, pasar, ir. —*vt* viajar por; recorrer; (with number of miles) hacer. **to t. over,** viajar por; recorrer. **t. worn,** fatigado por el viaje

travel agent *n* agente de viajes, *mf*

traveled /'trævəld/ *a* que ha viajado, que ha visto muchas partes

traveler /'trævələr/ *n* viajero (-ra); pasajero (-ra). **commercial t.,** viajante, *mf* **traveler's check,** cheque de viajeros, *m.* **traveler's joy,** *Bot.* clemátide, *f*

traveling /'trævəlɪŋ/ *n* viajes, *m pl.* —*a* viajero; para (or de) viajar; (itinerant) ambulante. **t. crane,** grúa móvil, *f.* **t. expenses,** gastos de viaje, *m pl.* **t. requisites,** objetos de viaje, *m pl.* **t. rug,** manta, *f.* **t. show,** circo ambulante, *m*

traverse /*n., a.* 'trævərs; *v.* trə'vərs/ *n* travesaño, *m; Law.* negación, *f; (Mil. Archit.)* través, *m;* (crossing) travesía, *f, a* transversal. —*vt* atravesar, cruzar; *Law.* negar

travesty /'trævəsti/ *n* parodia, *f, vt* parodiar

trawl /trɔl/ *vt* rastrear. —*vi* pescar a la rastra. **t.-net,** red de arrastre, *f*

trawler /'trɔlər/ *n* barco barredero, *m;* pescador a la rastra, *m*

tray /trei/ *n* bandeja, *f;* (of a balance) platillo, *m;* (in a wardrobe, etc.) cajón, *m;* (trough) artesa, *f*

treacherous /'trɛtʃərəs/ *a* traidor, falso, pérfido, fementido; (of memory) infiel; engañoso; (of ice, etc.) peligroso

treachery /'trɛtʃəri/ *n* perfidia, traición, falsedad, *f*

treacle /'trikəl/ *n* melado, *m*

tread /trɛd/ *n* pisada, *f;* paso, *m;* (of a stair) peldaño, *m;* (of tire) pastilla, *f;* (walk) andar, porte, *m, vi* pisar; (trample) pisotear; hollar; (oppress) oprimir. —*vt* hollar; (a path) abrir; recorrer; caminar por; bailar. **to t. the grapes,** pisar las uvas. **to t. the stage,** pisar las tablas. **to t. under foot,** hollar; pisotear. **to t. on,** pisar. **to t. on one's heels,** pisarle los talones a uno; seguir de cerca. **to t. out,** (a measure) bailar

treadle /'trɛdl/ *n* pedal, *m;* (of a loom) cárcola, *f*

treadmill /'trɛd,mɪl/ *n* molino de rueda de escalones, *m; Fig.* rueda, *f*

treason /'trizən/ *n* traición, *f.* **high t.,** alta traición, lesa majestad, *f*

treasure /'trɛʒər/ *n* tesoro, *m;* riqueza, *f,* caudal, *m; Fig.* perla, *f.* —*vt* atesorar; acumular (or guardar) riquezas; (a memory) guardar. **t. trove,** tesoro hallado, *m*

treasurer /'trɛʒərər/ *n* tesorero (-ra)

treasury /'trɛʒəri/ *n* tesorería, *f;* (government department) Ministerio de Hacienda,

m; (anthology) tesoro, *m.* **t. bench,** banco del Gobierno, *m*

treat /trit/ *n* (pleasure) gusto, placer, *m;* (present) obsequio, *m;* (entertainment) fiesta, *f.* —*vt* tratar; *Med.* tratar, curar; (regale) obsequiar. —*vi* (stand host) convidar; (of) tratar de, versar sobre; (with) negociar con

treatise /'tritɪs/ *n* tesis, monografía, disertación, *f,* tratado, *m*

treatment /'tritmənt/ *n* tratamiento, *m;* (of persons) conducta hacia, *f,* modo de obrar con, *m; Med.* tratamiento, *m;* (Lit., Art.) procedimiento, *m,* técnica, *f*

treaty /'triti/ *n* tratado, pacto, *m;* (bargain) contrato, *m*

treble /'trɛbəl/ *n Mus.* tiple, *m;* voz de tiple, *f.* —*a* triple; *Mus.* sobreagudo. —*vt* triplicar; *vi* triplicarse. **t. clef,** clave de sol, *f*

tree /tri/ *n* árbol, *m;* (for shoes) horma, *f;* (of a saddle) arzón, *m.* **breadfruit t.,** árbol del pan, *m.* **Judas t.,** árbol de amor, *m.* **t. of knowledge,** árbol de la ciencia, *m.* **t.-covered,** arbolado. **t-frog,** rana de San Antonio, *f*

trek /trɛk/ *vi* caminar, andar

trellis /'trɛlɪs/ *n* enrejado, *m;* (for plants) espaldera, *f.* —*vt* cercar con un enrejado; construir espalderas

tremble /'trɛmbəl/ *vi* temblar; estremecerse; trepidar; vibrar; (sway) oscilar; (of flags) ondear; agitarse; ser tembloroso. **His fate trembled in the balance,** Su suerte estaba en la balanza. **to t. all over,** temblar de pies a cabeza

trembling /'trɛmblɪŋ/ *n* temblor, *m;* estremecimiento, *m;* trepidación, *f;* vibración, *f;* (fear) agitación, ansiedad, *f;* temor, *m.* —*a* tembloroso; trémulo

tremendous /trɪ'mɛndəs/ *a* terrible, espantoso; formidable; grande; importante; *Inf.* tremendo; enorme

tremendously /trɪ'mɛndəsli/ *adv* terriblemente; *Inf.* enormemente

tremor /'trɛmər/ *n* temblor, movimiento sísmico, *m;* (thrill) estremecimiento, *m;* vibración, *f*

tremulous /'trɛmyələs/ *a* trémulo, tembloroso; vacilante; tímido

trench /trɛntʃ/ *n* zanja, *f,* foso, *m;* (for irrigation) acequia, *f; Mil.* trinchera, *f.* —*vt* hacer zanjas (en); acequiar; *Mil.* atrincherar. **t.-fever,** tifus exantemático, *m.* **t.-foot,** pie de trinchera, *m.* **t.-mortar,** mortero de trinchera, *m*

trenchant /'trɛntʃənt/ *a* mordaz

trencher /'trɛntʃər/ *n* trinchero, *m*

trend /trɛnd/ *n* curso, rumbo, *m; Fig.* tendencia, *f;* dirección, *f.* —*vi Fig.* tender

trepan /trɪ'pæn/ *vt Surg.* trepanar

trepanning /trɪ'pænɪŋ/ *n Surg.* trepanación, *f*

trepidation /,trɛpɪ'deiʃən/ *n* trepidación, *f*

trespass /'trɛspəs, -pæs/ *n* violación de propiedad, *f;* ofensa, *f;* pecado, *m;* (in the Lord's Prayer) deuda, *f.* —*vi* (on land) entrar sin derecho, violar la propiedad; (upon) entrar sin permiso en; (with patience, etc.) abusar de; (against) pecar contra, infringir

trespasser /'trɛspəsər, -pæs-/ n violador (-ra) de la ley de propiedad. **"Trespassers will be prosecuted,"** «Entrada prohibida,» «Prohibido el paso»

tress /trɛs/ n (plait) trenza, f; rizo, bucle, m; pl **tresses,** cabellera, f

trestle /'trɛsəl/ n caballete, m; armazón, m. **trestle-table,** mesa de caballete, f

triad /'traɪæd/ n terna, f; Mus. acorde, m

trial /'traɪəl/ n prueba, f, ensayo, m; examen, m; (experiment) tentativa, f, experimento, m; (misfortune) desgracia, pena, f; (nuisance) molestia, f; Law. vista de una causa, f. **on t.,** a prueba; Law. en proceso. **to bring to t.,** procesar. **to stand one's t.,** ser procesado. **t. run,** marcha de ensayo, f. **t. trip,** Naut. viaje de ensayo, m

trial and error n tanteos, m. **by trial and error,** por tanteos

triangle /'traɪˌæŋgəl/ n triángulo, m. **acute-angled t.,** triángulo acutángulo, m. **obtuse-angled t.,** triángulo obtusángulo, m. **right-angled t.,** triángulo rectángulo, m. **the eternal t.,** el eterno triángulo

triangular /traɪ'æŋgyələr/ a triangular, triángulo

triangulation /traɪˌæŋgyə'leɪʃən/ n (in surveying) triangulación, f

tribal /'traɪbəl/ a tribal

tribe /traɪb/ n tribu, f

tribesman /'traɪbzmən/ n miembro de una tribu, m

tribulation /ˌtrɪbyə'leɪʃən/ n tribulación, f; pena, aflicción, desgracia, f

tribunal /traɪ'byunl/ n (seat) tribunal, m; (court) juzgado, m; (confessional) confesionario, m

tribune /'trɪbyun/ n (person) tribuno, m; tribuna, f

tributary /'trɪbyəˌtɛri/ a and n tributario, m

tribute /'trɪbyut/ n tributo, m; contribución, imposición, f

trice /traɪs/ n tris, soplo, m. **in a t.,** en un periquete, en un avemaría, en dos trancos

tricentennial /ˌtraɪsɛn'tɛniəl/ a de trescientos años; n tercer centenario, tricentenario, m

trick /trɪk/ n (swindle) estafa, f, engaño, m; (ruse) truco, m, estratagema, ardid, f; (mischief) travesura, f; burla, f; (illusion) ilusión, f; (habit) costumbre, f; (affectation) afectación, f; (jugglery) juego de manos, m; (knack) talento, m; (at cards) baza, f. —vt engañar, estafar; (with out) adornar, ataviar; (with into) inducir fraudulentamente. —vi trampear. **dirty t.,** Inf. mala pasada, perrada, f. **His memory plays him tricks,** La memoria le engaña. **to play a t. on,** gastar una broma (a). **to play tricks,** hacer travesuras. **t. riding,** acrobacia ecuestre, f

trickery /'trɪkəri/ n maullería, superchería, f; fraude, engaño, m

trickle /'trɪkəl/ n chorrito, hilo (de agua, etc.) m. —vi gotear. **to t. down,** deslizar por, correr por, escurrir por

trickling /'trɪklɪŋ/ n goteo, m; (sound) murmullo, m

trickster /'trɪkstər/ n embustero (-ra), trampeador (-ra). **to be a t.,** ser buena maula

tricky /'trɪki/ a informal, maullero; (of things) difícil; complicado; (clever) ingenioso

tricycle /'traɪsɪkəl/ n triciclo, m

tried /traɪd/ a probado

trifle /'traɪfəl/ n (object) baratija, fruslería, f; pequeñez, tontería, bagatela, f; Culin. f; (small amount) pequeña cantidad, f, muy poco (de); (adverbially) algo. —vi entretenerse, jugar. —vt (away) malgastar. **to t. with,** jugar con

trifler /'traɪflər/ n persona frívola, f; (with affections) seductor (-ra)

trifling /'traɪflɪŋ/ a insignificante, sin importancia, trivial

trigger /'trɪgər/ n (of a fire-arm) gatillo, m; Mech. tirador, m

trigonometry /ˌtrɪgə'nɒmɪtri/ n trigonometría, f

trilingual /traɪ'lɪŋgwəl/ a trilingüe

trill /trɪl/ n trino, m, vi trinar

trillion /'trɪlyən/ n trillón, m

trilogy /'trɪlədʒi/ n trilogía, f

trim /trɪm/ a aseado; bien arreglado; bien ajustado; elegante; bonito; (of sail) orientado. **She has a t. waist,** Inf. Tiene un talle juncal. —n orden, m; buen estado, m; buena condición, f; (toilet) atavío, m. —vt arreglar; (tidy) asear; pulir; (ornament) ornar, adornar; (adapt) ajustar, adaptar; Sew. guarnecer; (lamps) despabilar; (a fire) atizar; (hair, moustache) atusar, recortar; (trees) mondar, atusar; alisar; (sails) templar, orientar; (distribute weight in a boat) equilibrar; (of quill pens) tajar. —vi (waver) nadar entre dos aguas. **to t. oneself up,** arreglarse

trimly /'trɪmli/ adv aseadamente; lindamente

trimmer /'trɪmər/ n guarnecedor (-ra); contemporizador (-ra)

trimming /'trɪmɪŋ/ n arreglo, m; guarnición, f; (on a dress) pasamanería, f; adorno, m; Agr. poda, f; adaptación, f; ajuste, m; pl **trimmings,** accesorios, m pl

trimness /'trɪmnɪs/ n aseo, buen orden, m; buen estado, m; elegancia, lindeza, f; (slimness) esbeltez, f

Trinity /'trɪnɪti/ n Trinidad, f

trinket /'trɪŋkɪt/ n joya, alhaja, f; dije, m, chuchería, baratija, f

trinomial /traɪ'noumiəl/ a Math. de tres términos. —n Math. trinomio, m

trio /'triou/ n trío, m

trip /trɪp/ n excursión, f; viaje, m; (slip) traspié, tropiezo, m; (in wrestling) zancadilla, f; (mistake) desliz, m. —vi (stumble) tropezar, caer; (move nimbly) andar airosamente, ir (or correr) ligeramente; (frolic) bailar, saltar; (wrestling, games) echar la zancadilla; (err) equivocarse; cometer un desliz. —vt (up) hacer caer; echar la zancadilla (a); coger en una falta; hacer desdecirse; coger en un desliz; Naut. levantar (el ancla)

tripartite /traɪˈpɑːrtaɪt/ a tripartito

tripe /traɪp/ n callos, m pl

triple /ˈtrɪpəl/ a triple. —vt triplicar. —vi triplicarse

triplet /ˈtrɪplɪt/ n Poet. terceto, m; Mus. tresillo, m; cada uno (una) de tres hermanos (hermanas) gemelos (-as)

triplicate /a. ˈtrɪplɪkɪt, v. -ˌkeɪt/ a triplicado. —vt triplicar

triplication /ˌtrɪplɪˈkeɪʃən/ n triplicación, f

tripod /ˈtraɪpɒd/ n trípode, m

tripper /ˈtrɪpər/ n turista, excursionista, mf

tripping /ˈtrɪpɪŋ/ a ligero, ágil

trite /traɪt/ a vulgar, trivial

triteness /ˈtraɪtnɪs/ n trivialidad, vulgaridad, f

triumph /ˈtraɪəmf/ n triunfo, m. —vi triunfar; (over) triunfar de, vencer

triumphal /traɪˈʌmfəl/ a triunfal. **t. arch,** arco de triunfo, m

triumphant /traɪˈʌmfənt/ a triunfante, victorioso

trivet /ˈtrɪvɪt/ n trébedes, f pl, trípode, m

trivial /ˈtrɪviəl/ a trivial, frívolo; insignificante, sin importancia

triviality /ˌtrɪviˈælɪti/ n trivialidad, frivolidad, f; insignificancia, f

trodden /ˈtrɒdn̩/ a trillado, batido

Trojan /ˈtroʊdʒən/ a and n troyano (-na). **the T. War,** la guerra de Troya, f

trolley /ˈtroʊli/ n Elec. trole, m; (for children) carretón, m. **t.-bus,** trolebús, m. —n trolley car tranvía, m. **t.-pole,** trole, m

trollop /ˈtrɒləp/ n tarasca, ramera, f

trombone /trɒmˈboʊn/ n trombón, m. **t. player,** trombón, m

troop /truːp/ n banda, muchedumbre, f; Theat. compañía, f; (of cavalry) escuadrón, m; pl Mil. tropas, f pl; ejército, m. —vi ir en tropel, congregarse; (with away) marcharse en tropel, retirarse; (with out) salir en masa. **fresh troops,** tropas frescas, f pl. **storm troops,** tropas de asalto, f pl. **t.-ship,** transporte de guerra, m

trooper /ˈtruːpər/ n soldado de caballería, m

trope /troʊp/ n tropo, m

trophy /ˈtroʊfi/ n trofeo, m

tropic /ˈtrɒpɪk/ a and n trópico, m

tropical /ˈtrɒpɪkəl/ a tropical

trot /trɒt/ n trote, m. —vi trotar. —vt hacer trotar. **to t. out,** Inf. sacar a relucir

troth /trɒθ/ n fe, f; palabra, f. **to plight**

one's t., dar palabra de matrimonio, desposarse

trotting /ˈtrɒtɪŋ/ a trotón. —n trote, m

troubadour /ˈtruːbəˌdɔːr/ n trovador, m, a trovadoresco

trouble /ˈtrʌbəl/ n (grief) aflicción, angustia, f; (difficulty) dificultad, f; (effort) esfuerzo, m; pena, desgracia, f; (annoyance) disgusto, sinsabor, m; (unrest) confusión, f, disturbio, m; (illness) enfermedad, f; mal, m; (disagreement) desavenencia, f. **The t. is....,** Lo malo es; La dificultad está en que... **to be in t.,** estar afligido; estar en un apuro, estar entre la espada y la pared. **to be not worth the t.,** no valer la pena. **to stir up t.,** revolver el ajo; armar un lío. **to take the t. to,** tomarse la molestia de

trouble /ˈtrʌbəl/ vt turbar; agitar; afligir, inquietar; (badger) importunar; (annoy) molestar; (cost an effort) costar trabajo (e g. *Learning Spanish did not t. him much,* No le costó mucho trabajo aprender el castellano). —vi preocuparse; darse la molestia; inquietarse

troubled /ˈtrʌbəld/ a agitado; inquieto; preocupado; (of life) accidentado, borrascoso. **to fish in t. waters,** pescar en agua turbia, pescar en río revuelto

troublesome /ˈtrʌbəlsəm/ a dificultoso; molesto; inconveniente; importuno; fastidioso

trough /trɒf/ n gamella, f; (for kneading bread) artesa, f; (of the waves) seno, m; (meteorological) mínimo, m. **drinking t.,** abrevadero, m. **stone t.,** pila, f

trounce /traʊns/ vt zurrar, apalear; Fig. fustigar

troupe /truːp/ n compañía, f

trousers /ˈtraʊzərz/ n pl pantalones, m pl. **plus four t.,** pantalones de golf, m pl. **striped t.,** pantalón de corte, m. **t. pocket,** bolsillo del pantalón, m. **t. press,** prensa para pantalones, f

trousseau /ˈtruːsoʊ/ n ajuar de novia, m

trout /traʊt/ n trucha, f

trowel /ˈtraʊəl/ n Agr. almocafre, m; (mason's) paleta, f, palustre, m

troy weight n peso de joyería, m

truant /ˈtruːənt/ n novillero, m; haragán (-ana). —a haragán, perezoso. **to play t.,** (from school) hacer novillos; ausentarse

truce /truːs/ n tregua, f; suspensión, cesación, f

truck /trʌk/ n (lorry) camión, m; carretilla de mano, f; (railway) vagón de carga, m; (intercourse) relaciones, f pl; (trash) cachivaches, m pl, cosas sin valor, f pl

truckle /ˈtrʌkəl/ vi humillarse, no levantar los ojos. **t. bed,** carriola, f

truculent /ˈtrʌkələnt/ a truculento, agresivo

trudge /trʌdʒ/ vi caminar a pie; andar con dificultad, caminar lentamente, andar trabajosamente, n caminata, f

true /truː/ a verdadero; real; leal, sincero; fiel; exacto; honesto; genuino; auténtico;

alineado, a plomo. **That is t. of...** Es propio de.... **—**adv realmente; exactamente. **t.-bred**, de casta legítima. **t.-hearted**, leal, fiel, sincero

truffle /'trʌfəl/ n trufa, f. **to stuff with truffles**, trufar

truism /'truɪzəm/ n perogrullada, f

truly /'truli/ adv lealmente; realmente, verdaderamente; en efecto, por cierto; sinceramente, de buena fe. **Yours t.**, su seguro servidor (su s.s.)

trump /trʌmp/ n (cards) triunfo, m; son de la trompeta, m; *Inf.* gran persona, joya, f. **—**vt ganar con el triunfo. **to t. up**, inventar. **t.-card**, naipe de triunfo, m

trumpet /'trʌmpɪt/ n trompeta, f. **—**vt trompetear; *Fig.* pregonar. **—**vi (of elephant) barritar. **ear.-t.**, trompetilla (acústica), f. **speaking t.**, portavoz, m. **t. blast**, trompetazo, m. **t. shaped**, en trompeta

trumpeter /'trʌmpɪtər/ n trompetero, trompeta, m

truncheon /'trʌntʃən/ n porra (de goma), f; bastón de mando, m. **blow with a t.**, porrazo, m

trundle /'trʌndl/ vt and vi rodar

trunk /trʌŋk/ n (*Anat. Bot.*) tronco, m; (elephant's) trompa, f; (railway) línea principal, f; baúl, m; coíre, m; pl **trunks**, (Elizabethan, etc.) trusas, f pl; calzoncillos cortos, m pl. **wardrobe t.**, baúl mundo, m. **t.-call**, conferencia telefónica, f. **t.-line**, tronco, m. **t.-road**, carretera de primera clase, carretera mayor, f

truss /trʌs/ n *Med.* braguero, m; (of straw, etc.) haz, m; (of blossom) racimo, m; (framework) armazón, f. **—**vt atar; *Cul.* espetar; (a building) apuntalar

trust /trʌst/ n fe, confianza, f; deber, m; *Law.* fideicomiso, m; (credit) crédito, m; esperanza, expectación, f; *Com.* trust, m. **—**vt tener confianza en; confiar en; esperar; creer; *Com.* dar crédito (a). **—**vi confiar; *Com.* dar crédito. **in t.**, en confianza; en administración, en depósito. **on t.**, al fiado

trustee /trʌ'sti/ n guardián, m; *Law.* fideicomisario, depositario, consignatario, m

trustful /'trʌstfəl/ a confiado

trustworthy /'trʌst,wɜrði/ a digno de confianza, honrado; fidedigno, seguro; exacto

trusty /'trʌsti/ a leal, fiel; firme, seguro

truth /truθ/ n verdad, f; realidad, f; exactitud, f. **the plain t.**, la pura verdad. **to tell the t.**, decir la verdad

truthful /'truθfəl/ a veraz; exacto, verdadero

try /trai/ vt and vi procurar, tratar de; (test) probar, ensayar; (a case, *Law.*) ver (el pleito); (strain) poner a prueba, (tire) cansar, fatigar; (annoy) molestar, exasperar; (afflict) hacer sufrir, afligir; (attempt) intentar; (judge) juzgar; (the weight of) tomar a pulso; (assay) refinar. **—**n tentativa, f; (football) tiro, m. **Try as he**

would...., Por más que hizo... **to try hard to**, hacer un gran esfuerzo para. **to try one's luck**, probar fortuna. **to try on clothes**, probarse (un vestido, etc.). **to try out**, poner a prueba, probar. **to try to**, tratar de, procurar

trying /'traiŋ/ a molesto; fatigoso; irritante; (painful) angustioso, penoso

tryst /trɪst/ n cita, f; lugar de cita, m. **—**vt citar. **—**vi citarse

tsar /zar, tsar/ n zar, m

tub /tʌb/ n cuba, f, artesón, m; cubeta, f. **—**vi bañarse. **tub thumper**, *Inf.* gerundio, m

tuba /'tubə/ n *Mus.* tuba, f

tube /tub/ n tubo, m; (railway) metro, ferrocarril subterráneo, m; tubo, m; *Anat.* trompa, f. **Eustachian t.**, *Anat.* trompa de Eustaquio, f. **Fallopian t.**, trompa de Falopio, f. **inner t.**, *Auto.* cámara de aire, f. **speaking t.**, tubo acústico, m. **test t.**, tubo de ensayo, m

tuber /'tubər/ n tubérculo, m

tuberculosis /tʊ,bɜrkyə'lousɪs/ n tuberculosis, f

tuberose /'tub,rouz/ n nardo, m, tuberosa, f

tuck /tʌk/ n *Sew.* alforzar, f; pliegue, m. **—**vt recoger; *Sew.* alforzar. **—**vi hacer alforzas. **to t. in**, (in bed) arropar; *Inf.* tragar. **to t. under**, poner debajo; doblar. **to t. up**, (in bed) arropar; (skirt) sofaldar; (sleeves) arremangar

Tuesday /'tuzdei/ n martes, m. **Shrove T.**, martes de carnaval, m

tuft /tʌft/ n (bunch) manojo, m; (on the head) copete, moño, m, cresta, f; (tassel) borla, f; mechón, m

tug /tʌg/ n tirón, m; sacudida, f; (boat) remolcador, m. **—**vt tirar de; halar; sacudir. **—**vi tirar con fuerza. **to give a tug**, dar una sacudida. **tug of war**, *Lit.* lucha de la cuerda, f; *Fig.* estira y afloja, m sing

tuition /tu'ɪʃən/ n (teaching) instrucción, enseñanza, f; lecciones, f pl; (fee) cuota, f

tulip /'tulɪp/ n tulipán, m. **t. wood**, palo de rosa, m

tulle /tul/ n tul, m

tumble /'tʌmbəl/ n caída, f; (somersault) tumbo, m; voltereta, f. **—**vi caer; (acrobats) voltear, dar saltos. **—**vt hacer caer; desarreglar. **to t. down**, venirse abajo; caer por. **t. down**, ruinoso, destartalado. **to t. off**, caer de. **to t. out**, vt hacer salir; arrojar. **—**vi salir apresuradamente. **to t. over**, vt tropezar con. **—**vi volcarse. **to t. to**, *Inf.* caer en la cuenta

tumbler /'tʌmblər/ n (acrobat) volteador (-ra); vaso para beber, m

tumid /'tumɪd/ a túmido, hinchado

tumor /'tumər/ n tumor, m

tumult /'tumʌlt/ n alboroto, tumulto, m; conmoción, agitación, f; confusión, f

tumultuous /tu'mʌltʃuəs/ a tumultuoso, alborotado; ruidoso; confuso; turbulento, violento

tun /tʌn/ n tonel, m; cuba, f; vt entonelar, embarrilar

tune /tun/ n melodía, f; son, m; armonía, f; Fig. tono, m; Inf. suma, f. —vt Mus. afinar, templar; Radio. sintonizar; (up, an engine) ajustar (un motor). —vi (in) sintonizar el receptor; (up, Mus.) templar (afinar) los instrumentos. **in t.,** Mus. afinado, templado; Fig. armonioso; (agreement) de acuerdo, conforme. **out of t.,** Mus. desafinado, destemplado. **to be out of t.,** desentonar, discordar; Fig. no armonizar, no estar en armonía. **to go out of t.,** desafinar. **to put out of t.,** destemplar. **to change one's t.,** Inf. bajar el tono

tuneful /'tunfəl/ a melodioso

tuner /'tunər/ n afinador, templador, m; Radio. sintonizador, m

tunic /'tunɪk/ n túnica, f

tuning /'tunɪŋ/ n afinación, f; Radio. sintonización, f. **t. fork,** diapasón normal, m. **t. key,** templador, m

tunnel /'tʌnl/ n túnel, m. —vt hacer (or construir) un túnel por. —vi hacer un túnel

turbid /'tɜrbɪd/ a turbio; Fig. confuso, **to make t.,** enturbiar

turbine /'tɜrbɪn, -baɪn/ n turbina, f

turbulence /'tɜrbyələns/ n turbulencia, f; desorden, m; agitación, f

turbulent /'tɜrbyələnt/ a turbulento; alborotado; (stormy) borrascoso; agitado

tureen /tʊ'rin/ n sopera, f

turf /tɜrf/ n césped, m; (fuel) turba, f; (racing) carreras de caballos, f pl

turgid /'tɜrdʒɪd/ a turgente, hinchado; (of style) pomposo

Turk /tɜrk/ n turco (-ca). **Turk's head,** (duster) deshollinador, m; Naut. cabeza de turco, f

Turkey /'tɜrki/ Turquía, f

turkey /'tɜrki/ n (cock) pavo, m; (hen) pava, f. **t. red,** rojo turco, m

Turkish /'tɜrkɪʃ/ a turco. —n (language) turco, idioma turco, m. **T. bath,** baño turco, m. **T. slipper,** babucha, f. **T. towel,** toalla rusa, f

turmoil /'tɜrmɔɪl/ n alboroto, tumulto, desorden, m

turn /tɜrn/ n turno, m; (twist) torcimiento, m; (bend) recodo, m, vuelta, f; (in a river) meandro, m; (in a road) viraje, m; (revolution) vuelta, revolución, f; (direction) dirección, f; (in spiral stair) espira, f; Theat. número, m; (change) cambio, m; vicisitud, f; (appearance) aspecto, m; (service) servicio, m; (nature) índole, naturaleza, f; (of phrase) giro, m, expresión, f; (walk) vuelta, f, paseo, m; (talent) talento, m. **a sharp t.,** (in a road) un viraje rápido. **at every t.,** a cada instante; en todas partes. **bad t.,** flaco servicio, m. **by turns,** por turnos. **good t.,** servicio, favor, m. **in its t.,** a su vez. **Now it's my t.,** Ahora me toca a mí. **The affair has taken a new t.,** El asunto ha cambiado de aspecto. **turn of the century,** vuelta del siglo, f. **turn of the millenium,** vuelta del milenio, f. **to a t.,** Cul. a la perfección. **to have a t. for,** tener talento para. **to take turns at,** alternar en. **t.-table,** (railway) plataforma, f; (of a gramophone) disco giratorio, m. **t. up,** barahúnda, conmoción, f; (of trousers) dobladillo (del pantalón), m

turn /tɜrn/ vt (on a lathe) tornear; (revolve) dar vueltas a, girar; (a key, door handle, etc.) torcer; (the leaves of a book) hojear; (the brain) trastornar; (a screw) enroscar; (the stomach) revolver (el estómago), marear; (go round) doblar, dar la vuelta a; (change) cambiar, mudar; (translate) traducir, verter; (dissuade) disuadir; (deflect) desviar; (apply) adaptar; (direct, move) volver; (concentrate) dirigir; concentrar; (turn over) volver del revés al derecho; (upside-down) volver lo de arriba abajo; (make) hacer, volver; (make sour) volver agrio; (transform) transformar convertir; Mil. envolver. **He has turned thirty,** Ha cumplido los treinta. **He said it without turning a hair,** Lo dijo sin pestañear. **He turned his head,** Volvió la cabeza. **They have turned the corner,** Han doblado la esquina; Fig. Han pasado la crisis. **"Please t. over,"** «A la vuelta (de la página).» **to t. a deaf ear to,** no dar oídos a, no hacer caso de. **to t. one's hand to,** aplicarse a. **to t. to account,** sacar ventaja (de). **to t. adrift,** dejar a la merced de las olas; echar de casa, poner en la calle; abandonar. **to t. against,** causar aversión, hacer hostil. **to t. aside,** desviar. **to t. away,** despedir; rechazar; (the head, etc.) volver; desviar. **to t. back,** hacer volver; enviar de nuevo; (raise) alzar; (fold) doblar; (the clock) retrasar. **to t. down,** doblar; (gas) bajar; (a glass, etc.) poner boca abajo; (reject) rechazar; (a suitor) dar calabazas a. **to t. from,** alejar de, desviar de. **to t. in,** doblar hacia dentro; entregar. **to t. in one's toes,** ser patizambo. **to t. inside out,** volver al revés. **to t. into,** (enter) entrar en; (change) cambiar en, transformar en; convertir en; (translate) traducir a. **to t. off,** (dismiss) despedir; (from) desviarse de, dejar; (light) apagar; (water) cortar; Mech. cerrar; (disconnect) desconectar; (avoid) evitar; (refuse) rechazar. **to t. off the tap,** (water, gas) cerrar la llave (del agua, del gas). **to t. on,** (light) encender; (water, gas, etc.) abrir la llave (del agua, del gas); (steam) dar (vapor); (electric current) establecer (la corriente eléctrica); (eyes) fijar. **to t. out,** (expel) expeler, echar; (dismiss) despedir; (animals) echar al campo; (produce) producir; (dress) vestir; (equip) equipar, guarnecer; (a light) apagar. **to t. over,** (the page) volver (la hoja); (transfer) ceder, traspasar; revolver; (upset) volcar; considerar, pensar. **to t. round,** dar vuelta a; girar; (empty) descargar. **to t. up,** levantar; apuntar; hacia arriba;

(the earth) labrar, cavar; (a glass) poner boca arriba; (one's sleeves, skirt) arremangar; (fold) doblar. **to t. up one's nose at,** mirar con desprecio. **to t. upon,** atacar, volverse contra, acometer; depender de, estribar en. **to t. upside down,** volver lo de arriba abajo; revolver; revolcar

turn /tɜrn/ *vi* (in a lathe) tornear; (revolve) girar, dar vueltas; (depend) depender (de); torcer; volverse; dar la vuelta; girar sobre los talones; dirigirse (a, hacia); (move) mudar de posición; (deviate) desviarse (de); (be changed) convertirse (en); (become) hacerse, venir a ser; (begin) meterse a; (take to) dedicarse a; (seek help) acudir; (change behavior) enmendarse, corregirse; (the stomach) revolver (el estómago); (go sour) agriarse, avinagrarse; (rebel) sublevarse. **He turned to the left,** Dio la vuelta a la izquierda; Torció hacia la izquierda. **My head turns,** (with giddiness) Se me va la cabeza. **to t. about,** voltearse, dar la vuelta. **to t. against,** coger aversión (a), disgustarse con; volverse hostil (a). **to t. aside,** desviarse; dejar el camino. **to t. away,** volver la cabeza; apartarse; alejarse. **to t. back,** volver atrás; volver de nuevo; retroceder; volver sobre sus pasos. **to t. down,** doblarse; reducirse. **to t. from,** alejarse de; apartarse de, huir de. **to t. in,** doblarse hacia dentro; (retire) acostarse. **to t. into,** transformarse en; convertirse en. **to t. off,** (depart from) desviarse (de); (fork) torcer, bifurcarse. **to t. out,** estar vuelto hacia fuera; (leave ome) salir de casa; (rise) levantarse (de la cama); (arrive) llegar, presentarse; (attend) asistir, acudir; (result) resultar. **to t. over,** mudar (or cambiar) de posición, revolverse; (upset) voltearse, volcarse. **to t. round,** girar; volverse; cambiar de frente; cambiar de dirección, dar la vuelta; (*Auto., Aer.*) virar; (change views) cambiar de opinión; (change sides) cambiar de partido. **to t. round and round,** dar vueltas, girar. **to t. to,** (apply to) acudir a; (begin) ponerse a; (become) convertirse en; (face) dirigirse hacia; (address) dirigirse a. **to t. up,** (crop up) surgir, aparecer; (arrive) llegar; (happen) acontecer; (be found again) volver a hallarse, reaparecer; (cards) venir; (of hats) levantar el ala; (of hair, etc.) doblarse. **His nose turns up,** Tiene la nariz respingona

turncoat /'tɜrn,kout/ *n* desertor (-ra), renegado (-da). **to become a t.,** volver la casaca

turning /'tɜrnɪŋ/ *n* (bend) vuelta, *f;* (turnery) tornería, *f;* (of milk, etc.) agrura, *f; pl* **turnings,** *Sew.* ensanche, *m.* **t.-point,** punto decisivo, *m,* crisis, *f*

turnip /'tɜrnɪp/ *n* nabo, *m.* **t. field,** nabar, *m*

turnover /'tɜrn,ouvər/ *n Com.* ventas, *f pl; Cul.* pastelillo, *m*

turnpike /'tɜrn,paik/ *n* barrera de portazgo, *f*

turnstile /'tɜrn,stail/ *n* torniquete, *m*

turpentine /'tɜrpən,tain/ *n* aguarrás, *m,* trementina, *f*

turpitude /'tɜrpɪ,tud/ *n* infamia, maldad, *f*

turquoise /'tɜrkɔiz, -kwɔiz/ *n* turquesa, *f*

turret /'tɜrɪt/ *n* torrecilla, almenilla, *f; Naut.* torre blindada, *f*

turreted /'tɜrɪtɪd/ *a* con torres, guarnecido de torres; en forma de torre

turtle /'tɜrtl/ *n* tortuga (dove) tórtolo (-la); (sea) tortuga de mar, *f.* **to turn t.,** voltearse patas arriba; *Naut.* zozobrar. **t. soup,** sopa de tortuga, *f*

tusk /tʌsk/ *n* colmillo, *m*

tussle /'tʌsəl/ *n* lucha, *f;* agarrada, *f.* —*vi* luchar, pelear; tener una agarrada

tutelage /'tutlɪdʒ/ *n* tutela, *f*

tutor /'tutər/ *n* (private) ayo, *m;* profesor (-ra); (Roman law) tutor, *m;* (supervisor of studies) preceptor. —*vt* enseñar, instruir. —*vi* ser profesor, dar clases

tutorial /tu'tɔriəl/ *n* (university) seminario, *m;* (private) clase particular, *f*

tutoring /'tutərɪŋ/ *n* enseñanza, instrucción, *f*

twaddle /'twɒdl/ *n* disparates, *m pl,* tonterías, patrañas, *f pl*

twain /twein/ *a* and *n* dos, *m*

twang /twæŋ/ *n* punteado de una cuerda, *m;* (of a guitar) zumbido, *m;* (in speech) gangueo, *m.* —*vt* puntear; (las cuerdas de un instrumento) rasguear. —*vi* zumbar. **to speak with a t.,** hablar con una voz gangosa

tweak /twik/ *n* pellizco, *m;* sacudida, *f;* tirón, *m.* —*vt* pellizcar; sacudir, tirar

tweed /twid/ *n* mezcla, *f,* cheviot, *m*

tweezers /'twizərz/ *n pl* pinzas, tenacillas, *f pl*

twelfth /twelfθ/ *a* duodécimo; (of the month) (el) doce; (of monarchs) doce. —*n* duodécimo, *m;* (part) dozavo, *m,* duodécima parte, *f.* **T.-night,** Día de Reyes, *m,* Epifanía, *f*

twelve /twelv/ *a* and *n* doce *m;* (of age) doce años, *m pl.* **o'clock,** las doce; (mid-day) mediodía, *m;* (midnight) media noche, *f,* las doce de la noche. **t.-syllabled,** dodecasílabo

twentieth /'twɛntiɪθ/ *a* vigésimo; (of the month) (el) veinte; (of monarchs) veinte, *n* vigésimo, *m;* (part) vigésima parte, *f*

twenty /'twɛnti/ *a* veinte; (of age) veinte años, *m pl,* n veinte, *m;* (score) veintena, *f.* **t.-first,** vigésimo primero; (of date) (el) veintiuno, *m,* (In modern Spanish the ordinals above *décimo* "tenth" are generally replaced by the cardinals, e.g. *the twenty-ninth chapter,* el capítulo veintinueve.)

twice /twais/ *adv* dos veces. **t. as many** or **as much,** el doble

twiddle /'twɪdl/ *vt* jugar con; hacer girar. —*vi* girar; vibrar. —*n* vuelta, *f.* **to t.**

one's thumbs, dar vuelta a los pulgares, estar mano sobre mano

twig /twɪg/ n ramita, pequeña rama, f

twilight /'twai,lait/ n crepúsculo, m; media luz, f. —a crepuscular. **in the t.,** en el crepúsculo; en la media luz. **t. sleep,** parto sin dolor, m

twin /twɪn/ a gemelo, mellizo; doble. —n gemelo (-la), mellizo (-za); (of objects) pareja, f, par, m. **t.-engined,** bimotor. **t. screw,** (Naut. Aer.) de dos hélices

twine /twain/ n bramante, cordel, m; guita, f. —vt enroscar; (weave) tejer; (encircle) ceñir; (round, about) abrazar. —vi (of plants) trepar; entrelazarse; (wind) serpentear

twinge /twɪndʒ/ n punzada, f, dolor agudo, m; Fig. remordimiento, tormento, m. —vi causar un dolor agudo

twinkle /'twɪŋkəl/ vi centellear, chispear, titilar; (of eyes) brillar; (of feet) moverse rápidamente, bailar. —n (in the eye) chispa, f

twinkling /'twɪŋklɪŋ/ n centelleo, m; titilación, f; (of the eye) brillo, m; (glimpse) vislumbre, m, Fig. instante, momento, m. —a titilante, centelleador. **in a t.,** en un dos por tres. **in the t. of an eye,** en un abrir y cerrar de ojos

twirl /twɜrl/ n rotación, vuelta, f; pirueta, f. —vi hacer girar; voltear; torcer; (a stick, etc.) dar vueltas (a). —vi girar, dar vueltas; dar piruetas

twirp /twɜrp/ n Inf. renacuajo, m

twist /twɪst/ n (skein) mecha, f; trenza, f; (yarn) torzal, m; (of tobacco) rollo, m; (of bread) rosca de pan, f; (act of twisting) torcimiento, m, torsión, f; (in a road, etc.) recodo, m, curva, vuelta, f; (pull) sacudida, f; (contortion) regate, esguince, m; (in a winding stair) espira, f; (in ball games) efecto, m; (in a person's nature) peculiaridad, f; falta de franqueza, f; (to words) interpretación, f. —vt torcer; enroscar; (plait) trenzar; (wring) estrujar; (weave) tejer; (encircle) ceñir; (a stick, etc.) dar vueltas a; (of hands) crispar; (distort) interpretar mal, torcer. —vi torcerse; enroscarse; (wind) serpentear; dar vueltas; (coil) ensortijarse; (writhe) undular, retorcerse; (of a stair) dar vueltas

twitch /twɪtʃ/ n sacudida, f, tirón, m; (nervous) contracción nerviosa, f. —vt tirar bruscamente, quitar rápidamente; agarrar; (ears, etc.) mover; (hands) crispar, retorcer. —vi crisparse; (of ears, nose) moverse

twitter /'twɪtər/ n piada, f, gorjeo, m. —vi piar, gorjear

two /tu/ a and n dos, m; (of the clock) (las) dos, f pl; (of age) dos años, m pl. —a de dos. **in two,** en dos partes. **in two's,** de dos en dos. **one or two,** uno o dos; algunos, m pl; algunas, f pl. **two against two,** dos a dos. **two by two,** de dos en dos, a pares. **Two can live as cheaply as one,** Donde come uno comen dos. **to put two and two together,** atar cabos. **two-edged,** de dos filos. **two-faced,** de dos caras; Fig. de dos haces. **to be two-faced,** hacer a dos caras. **two-headed,** de dos cabezas; bicéfalo. **two hundred,** a and n doscientos, m. **two hundredth,** a ducentésimo. —n ducentésima parte, f; doscientos, m. **two-legged,** bípedo. **two-ply,** de dos hilos. **two-seater,** a de dos asientos. **two-speed gear box,** cambio de marcha de dos velocidades, m. **two step,** paso doble, m. **two of a kind,** (well-matched) tal para cual. **two-way switch,** Elec. interruptor de dos direcciones, m

twofold /a. 'tu,fould/ adv. -'fould/ a doble. —adv doblemente, dos veces

twosome /'tusəm/ n partido de dos, m

type /taip/ n. tipo, m; Print. carácter, m, letra de imprenta, f, tipo, m. —vt and vi escribir a máquina. **t. case,** caja de imprenta, f. **t. founder,** fundidor de letras de imprenta, m. **t. foundry,** fundición de tipos, f. **t.-setter,** cajista, mf **t.-setting,** composición tipográfica, f

typewrite /'taip,rait/ vt and vi escribir a máquina

typewriter /'taip,raitər/ n máquina de escribir, f

typhoid /'taifɔid/ n tifoidea, fiebre tifoidea, f

typhoon /tai'fun/ n tifón, m

typhus /'taifəs/ n tifus, tabardillo pintado, m

typical /'tɪpɪkəl/ a típico, característico; simbólico

typify /'tɪpə,fai/ vt simbolizar, representar; ser ejemplo de

typist /'taipɪst/ n mecanografista, mf; mecanógrafo (-fa)

tyrannical /tɪ'rænɪkəl/ a tiránico, despótico

tyrannize /'tɪrə,naiz/ vi tiranizar

tyranny /'tɪrəni/ n tiranía, f, despotismo, m

tyrant /'tairənt/ n déspota, m, tirano (-na)

U

u /yu/ *n* (letter) u, *f*. **U-boat,** submarino, *m*. **u-shaped,** en forma de U

ubiquitous /yu'bɪkwɪtəs/ *a* ubicuo, omnipresente

udder /'ʌdər/ *n* ubre, teta, mama, *f*

ugh /ʊx, ʌg/ *interj* ¡uf!

ugliness /'ʌglinɪs/ *n* fealdad, *f*; (moral) perversidad, *f*; (of a situation) peligro, *m*, lo difícil

ugly /'ʌgli/ *a* feo; (morally) repugnante, asqueroso, perverso; (of a situation) peligroso, difícil; (of a wound) grave, profundo; (of a look) amenazador; *Inf.* desagradable; (of weather) borrascoso. **to make u.,** afear, hacer feo

Ukraine /yu'kreɪn/ Ucrania, *f*

Ukrainian /yu'kreɪniən/ *a* and *n* ucranio (-ia)

ulcer /'ʌlsər/ *n* úlcera, *f*

ulcerate /'ʌlsə,reɪt/ *vt* ulcerar. —*vi* ulcerarse

ulterior /ʌl'tɪəriər/ *a* (of place) ulterior; (of time) posterior, ulterior; (of motives) interesado, oculto; **ulterior motive,** segunda intención, *f*

ultimate /'ʌltəmɪt/ *a* último; fundamental, esencial

ultimately /'ʌltəmɪtli/ *adv* por fin, al final; esencialmente

ultimatum /,ʌltə'meɪtəm/ *n* ultimátum, *m*

ultra /'ʌltrə/ *a* exagerado, extremo. —*prefix* ultra-. **u.-red,** ultrarrojo. **u.-violet,** ultravioleta

ultramarine /,ʌltrəmə'rin/ *a* ultramarino. —*n* azul de ultramar, *m*

umbilicus /ʌm'bɪlɪkəs/ *n* ombligo, *m*

umbrage /'ʌmbrɪdʒ/ *n Poet.* sombra, *f*; resentimiento, enfado, *m*. **to take u.,** ofenderse, resentirse

umbrella /ʌm'brɛlə/ *n* paraguas, *m*. **u. maker,** paragüero (-ra). **u. shop,** paragüería, *f*. **u. stand,** paragüero, *m*

umpire /'ʌmpaɪər/ *n Sports.* árbitro, *m*; *Law.* juez arbitrador, tercero en discordia, *m*. —*vt* arbitrar

un- *prefix* Used before adjectives, adverbs, abstract nouns, verbs and translated in Spanish by **in-, des-, nada, no, poco, sin,** as well as in other ways

unabashed /,ʌnə'bæʃt/ *a* desvergonzado, descarado, insolente; (calm) sereno, sosegado

unabashedly /,ʌnə'bæʃɪdli/ *adv* sin rubor

unabated /,ʌnə'beɪtɪd/ *a* no disminuido; cabal, entero

unabbreviated /,ʌnə'brivi,eɪtɪd/ *a* íntegro, sin abreviar

unable /ʌn'eɪbəl/ *a* incapaz, impotente; (physical denso) imposibilitado. **to be u. to,** no poder, serle a uno imposible. **to be u. to control,** no poder controlar

unabridged /,ʌnə'brɪdʒd/ *a*. See **unabbreviated**

unaccented /ʌn'æksɛntɪd/ *a* sin acento

unacceptable /,ʌnæk,sɛptəbəl/ *a* inaceptable

unaccepted /,ʌnæk,sɛptɪd/ *a* rechazado, no aceptado

unaccommodating *a* poco complaciente, nada servicial

unaccompanied /,ʌnə'kʌmpənid/ *a* solo, sin compañía; *Mus.* sin acompañamiento

unaccomplished /,ʌnə'komplɪʃt/ *a* incompleto, sin terminar, inacabado; (not clever) sin talento

unaccountable /,ʌnə'kauntəbəl/ *a* inexplicable; irresponsable

unaccountably /,ʌnə'kauntəbli/ *adv* inexplicablemente, extrañamente

unaccredited /,ʌnæ'krɛdɪtɪd/ *a* no acreditado; extraoficial

unaccustomed /,ʌnə'kʌstəmd/ *a* no habituado; (unusual) desacostumbrado, insólito, inusitado

unacknowledged /,ʌnæk'nɒlɪdʒd/ *a* no reconocido; (of letter) sin contestación, por contestar; no correspondido, sin devolver; (of crimes, etc.) inconfeso, no declarado

unacquainted /,ʌnə'kweɪntɪd/ *a* que no conoce; que desconoce, que ignora; no habituado. **to be u. with,** no conocer; ignorar; no estar acostumbrado a

unadaptable /,ʌnə'dæptəbəl/ *a* inadaptable (also of persons)

unadorned /,ʌnə'dɔrnd/ *a* sin adorno sencillo, que no tiene adornos

unadulterated /,ʌnə'dʌltə,reɪtɪd/ *a* sin mezcla, no adulterado, natural; genuino, verdadero; puro

unadventurous /ʌn'æd'vɛntʃərəs/ *a* nada aventurero, que no busca aventuras, tímido; tranquilo, sin incidente

unadvisability /,ʌnæd,vaɪzə'bɪlɪti/ *n* imprudencia, *f*; inoportunidad, *f*

unadvisable /,ʌnæd,vaɪzə'bəl/ *a* imprudente; inoportuno, no conveniente

unadvisedly /,ʌnæd,vaɪzɪdli/ *adv* imprudentemente

unaffected /,ʌnə'fɛktɪd/ *a* natural, llano, sin melindres; impasible; genuino, sincero. **u. by,** no afectado por

unaffectedly /,ʌnə'fɛktɪdli/ *adv* sin afectación

unaffectedness /,ʌnə'fɛktɪdnɪs/ *n* naturalidad, sencillez, *f*; sinceridad, franqueza, *f*

unaffiliated /,ʌnə'fɪli,eɪtɪd/ *a* no afiliado

unafraid /,ʌnə'freɪd/ *a* sin temor

unaided *a* sin ayuda, solo a solas

unaired /ʌn'ɛərd/ *a* sin ventilar, no ventilado; húmedo, sin airear

unalloyed /,ʌnə'lɔɪd/ *a* sin mezcla, puro

unalterability /ʌn,ɔltərə'bɪlɪti/ *n* lo inalterable; constancia, *f*

unalterable /ʌn'ɔltərəbəl/ *a* inalterable; invariable, constante

unambiguous /ˌʌnæmˈbɪgyuəs/ *a* no ambiguo, nada dudoso, claro

unambitious /ˌʌnæmˈbɪʃəs/ *a* sin ambición; modesto

unamusing /ˌʌnəˈmyuzɪŋ/ *a* nada divertido

unanimity /ˌyunəˈnɪmɪti/ *n* unanimidad, *f*

unanimous /yuˈnænəməs/ *a* unánime

unanimously /yuˈnænəməsli/ *adv* unánimemente, por unanimidad. **carried u.**, adoptado por unanimidad

unanswerable /ʌnˈænsərəbəl/ *a* incontestable, incontrovertible, incontrastable, irrefutable

unanswered /ʌnˈænsərd/ *a* no contestado, sin contestar; (unrequited) no correspondido

unapparent /ˌʌnəˈpærənt/ *a* no aparente

unappealable /ˌʌnəˈpiləbəl/ *a* inapelable

unappeasable /ˌʌnəˈpizəbəl/ *a* implacable

unappeased /ˌʌnəˈpizd/ *a* no satisfecho; implacable

unappetizing /ʌnˈæpɪˌtaizɪŋ/ *a* no apetitoso; (unattractive) repugnante, feo

unappreciated /ˌʌnəˈpriʃiˌeitɪd/ *a* desestimado, no apreciado, tenido en poco; (misunderstood) mal comprendido

unapproachable /ˌʌnəˈproutʃəbəl/ *a* inaccesible

unapproved /ˌʌnəˈpruvd/ *a* sin aprobar, no aprobado

unarm /ʌnˈɑrm/ *vt* desarmar. —*vi* desarmarse, quitarse las armas

unarmed /ʌnˈɑrmd/ *a* desarmado; indefenso; (*Zool., Bot.*) inerme

unartistic /ˌʌnɑrˈtɪstɪk/ *a* no artístico

unascertainable /ˌʌnæsərˈteinəbəl/ *a* no verificable

unashamed /ˌʌnəˈʃeimd/ *a* sin vergüenza; tranquilo, sereno; insolente, descarado

unasked /ʌnˈæskt/ *a* sin pedir; no solicitado; espontáneo; (uninvited) no convidado

unassailable /ˌʌnəˈseiləbəl/ *a* inexpugnable; irrefutable; incontestable

unassisted /ˌʌnəˈsɪstɪd/ *a*. See **unaided**

unassuming /ˌʌnəˈsumɪŋ/ *a* modesto, sin pretensiones

unattached /ˌʌnəˈtætʃt/ *a* suelto; *Law.* no embargado; *Mil.* de reemplazo; independiente

unattainable /ˌʌnəˈteinəbəl/ *a* inasequible, irrealizable

unattended /ˌʌnəˈtendɪd/ *a* solo, sin acompañamiento; (of ill person) sin tratamiento; (of entertainment, etc.) no concurrido

unattested /ˌʌnəˈtestɪd/ *a* sin atestación

unattractive /ˌʌnəˈtræktɪv/ *a* poco atrayente, desagradable, antipático, feo

unauthentic /ˌʌnɔˈθɛntɪk/ *a* no auténtico, sin autenticidad; apócrifo

unauthorized /ʌnˈɔθəˌraizd/ *a* no autorizado

unavailable /ˌʌnəˈveiləbəl/ *a* inaprovechable

unavailing /ˌʌnəˈveilɪŋ/ *a* inútil, vano

unavenged /ˌʌnəˈvɛndʒd/ *a* no vengado, sin castigo

unavoidable /ˌʌnəˈvɔidəbəl/ *a* inevitable, preciso, necesario. **to be u.**, no poder evitarse, no tener remedio

unavoidably /ˌʌnəˈvɔidəbli/ *adv* irremediablemente

unaware /ˌʌnəˈwɛər/ *a* ignorante; inconsciente. **to be u. of**, ignorar, desconocer; no darse cuenta de

unawareness /ˌʌnəˈwɛərnɪs/ *n* ignorancia, *f*, desconocimiento, *m*; inconsciencia, *f*

unawares /ˌʌnəˈwɛərz/ *adv* (by mistake) sin querer, inadvertidamente; (unprepared) de sobresalto, de improviso, inopinadamente. **He caught me u.**, Me cogió desprevenido

unbalance /ʌnˈbæləns/ *vt* desequilibrar, hacer perder el equilibrio; *Fig.* trastornar

unbalanced /ʌnˈbælənst/ *a* desequilibrado; *Fig.* trastornado; *Com.* no balanceado

unbar /ʌnˈbɑr/ *vt* desatrancar; *Fig.* abrir

unbearable /ʌnˈbɛərəbəl/ *a* intolerable, insufrible, inaguantable, inllevable, insoportable

unbeatable /ʌnˈbitəbəl/ *a* inmejorable

unbeaten /ʌnˈbitn/ *a* (of paths) no frecuentado, no pisado; (of armies) no derrotado, no batido; invicto

unbecoming /ˌʌnbɪˈkʌmɪŋ/ *a* impropio, inapropiado, inconveniente; indecoroso, indigno; indecente; (of clothes) que no va bien, que sienta mal

unbelievable /ˌʌnbɪˈlivəbəl/ *a* increíble

unbeloved /ˌʌnbɪˈlʌvd/ *a* no amado

unbend /ʌnˈbɛnd/ *vt* desencorvar, enderezar; entretenerse, descansar; *Naut.* of sails) desenvergar; (*Naut.* of cables) desamarrar. —*vi* enderezarse; mostrarse afable

unbending /ʌnˈbɛndɪŋ/ *a* inflexible, rígido, tieso; *Fig.* inexorable, inflexible, duro, terco; (amiable) afable, jovial

unbiased /ʌnˈbaiəst/ *a* imparcial, ecuánime

unbidden /ʌnˈbɪdn/ *a* espontáneo; (uninvited) no convidado, no invitado

unbind /ʌnˈbaind/ *vt* desligar, desatar; (bandages) desvendar; (books) desencuadernar

unbleached /ʌnˈblitʃt/ *a* crudo, sin blanquear

unblemished /ʌnˈblɛmɪʃt/ *a* no manchado; (pure) sin mancha, inmaculado, puro

unblessed /ʌnˈblɛst/ *a* no bendecido, no consagrado; (accursed) maldito; (unhappy) desdichado

unblushing /ʌnˈblʌʃɪŋ/ *a* desvergonzado, insolente

unbolt /ʌnˈboult/ *vt* descerrojar, desempernar

unborn /ʌn'bɔrn/ *a* sin nacer, no nacido todavía; venidero

unbosom /ʌn'buzəm/ *vt* confesar, declarar. **to u. oneself,** abrir su pecho (a) or (con)

unbought /ʌn'bɔt/ *a* no comprado; gratuito, libre; (not bribed) no sobornado

unbound /ʌn'baund/ *a* suelto, libre; (of books) en rama, no encuadernado

unbounded /ʌn'baundɪd/ *a* ilimitado, infinito; inmenso

unbowed /ʌn'baud/ *a* erguido; no encorvado; (undefeated) invicto

unbreakable /ʌn'breikəbəl/ *a* irrompible, inquebrantable

unbridled /ʌn'braidld/ *a* desenfrenado, violento; licencioso

unbroken /ʌn'broukən/ *a* no quebrantado, intacto, entero; continuo, incesante; no interrumpido; (of soil) virgen; (of a horse) indomado; inviolado; (of the spirit) indómito; (of a record) no batido

unbuckle /ʌn'bʌkəl/ *vt* deshebillar

unburden /ʌn'bɜrdn̩/ *vt* descargar; aliviar. **to u. oneself,** (express one's feelings) desahogarse

unburnt /ʌn'bɜrnt/ *a* no quemado; incombusto

unbusinesslike /ʌn'bɪznɪs,laik/ *a* informal; poco comercial, descuidado

unbutton /ʌn'bʌtn̩/ *vt* desabrochar, desabotonar

uncalled /ʌn'kɔld/ *a* no llamado, no invitado. **u.-for,** impertinente; innecesario

uncanny /ʌn'kæni/ *a* misterioso, horroroso, pavoroso

uncared-for /ʌn'keərd,fɔr/ *a* abandonado, desatendido, desamparado

unceasing /ʌn'sisɪŋ/ *a* continuo, incesante, sin cesar, constante

unceasingly /ʌn'sisɪŋli/ *adv* incesantemente, sin cesar

uncensored /ʌn'sɛnsərd/ *a* no censurado

unceremonious /,ʌnsɛrə'mouniəs/ *a* sin ceremonia, familiar; descortés, brusco

uncertain /ʌn'sɜrtn̩/ *a* incierto, dudoso; inseguro; precario; (hesitant) indeciso, vacilante, irresoluto

uncertainty /ʌn'sɜrtn̩ti/ *n* incertidumbre, duda, *f*; inseguridad, *f*; irresolución, *f*

uncertificated /,ʌnsər'tɪfɪ,keitɪd/ *a* sin certificado (of teachers, etc.) sin título

uncertified /ʌn'sɜrtə,faid/ *a* sin garantía; no garantizado; (of lunatics) sin certificar

unchain /ʌn'tʃein/ *vt* desencadenar

unchallenged /ʌn'tʃæləndʒd/ *a* incontestable

unchangeable /ʌn'tʃeindʒəbəl/ *a* invariable, inalterable, inmutable

unchanging /ʌn'tʃeindʒɪŋ/ *a* inmutable, invariable

uncharitable /ʌn'tʃærɪtəbəl/ *a* nada caritativo, duro; intolerante, intransigente

uncharitableness /ʌn'tʃærɪtəbəlnɪs/ *n* falta de caridad, *f*; intolerancia, intransigencia

uncharitably /ʌn'tʃærɪtəbli/ *adv* sin caridad; con intolerancia

unchaste /ʌn'tʃeist/ *a* incasto, incontinente; deshonesto, impuro, lascivo

unchecked /ʌn'tʃɛkt/ *a* desenfrenado; (unproved) no comprobado; *Com.* no confrontado

unchivalrous /ʌn'ʃɪvəlrəs/ *a* nada galante, nada caballeroso

uncircumcised /ʌn'sɜrkəm,saizd/ *a* incircunciso

uncivil /ʌn'sɪvəl/ *a* descortés, incivil

uncivilized /ʌn'sɪvə,laizd/ *a* no civilizado, bárbaro, salvaje, inculto

unclad /ʌn'klæd/ *a* sin vestir; desnudo

unclasp /ʌn'klæsp/ *vt* (jewelery) desengarzar; desabrochar; (of hands) soltar, separar

unclassifiable /ʌn'klæsə,faiəbəl/ *a* inclasificable

unclassified /ʌn'klæsə,faid/ *a* sin clasificar

uncle /'ʌŋkəl/ *n* tío, *m*; (pawnbroker) prestamista, *m*

unclean /ʌn'klin/ *a* sucio, puerco, inmundo; desaseado; impuro, obsceno; (ritually) poluto

uncleanliness /ʌn'klɛnlinɪs/ *n* suciedad, porquería, *f*; desaseo, *m*; falta de limpieza, *f*

uncleanly /ʌn'klɛnli/ *a* sucio, puerco; desaseado

unclench /ʌn'klɛntʃ/ *vt* (of hands) abrir

Uncle Tom's Cabin La Cabaña del Tío Tom

uncoil /ʌn'kɔil/ *vt* desarrollar. —*vi* desovillarse; (of snakes) desanillarse

uncollected /,ʌnkə'lɛktɪd/ *a* disperso; no cobrado; (in confusion) confuso, desordenado

uncolored /ʌn'kʌlərd/ *a* incoloro; *Fig.* imparcial, objetivo, sencillo

uncombed /ʌn'koumd/ *a* despeinado, sin peinar

uncomfortable /ʌn'kʌmftəbəl/ *a* incómodo; (anxious) intranquilo, inquieto, desasosegado, preocupado; (awkward) molesto, difícil, desagradable. **to be u.,** (people) estar incómodo; (anxious) estar preocupado; (of things) ser incómodo

uncomfortably /ʌn'kʌmfərtəbli/ *adv* incómodamente; intranquilamente; desagradablemente

uncomforted /ʌn'kʌmfərtɪd/ *a* desconsolado, sin consuelo

uncommon /ʌn'kɒmən/ *a* poco común, extraordinario, singular, raro, extraño; infrecuente; insólito

uncommonly /ʌn'kɒmənli/ *adv* extraordinariamente, muy; infrecuentemente, raramente

uncommunicative /,ʌnkə'myunɪkətɪv/ *a* reservado, poco expresivo

uncommunicativeness /,ʌnkə'myunɪkətɪvnɪs/ *n* reserva, *f*

uncomplaining /,ʌnkəm'pleinɪŋ/ *a* resignado, que no se queja

uncomplainingly /ˌʌnkəm'pleinɪŋli/ *adv* con resignación

uncompliant /ˌʌnkəm'plaiant/ *a* sordo, inflexible

uncomplicated /ʌn'kɒmplɪˌkeitɪd/ *a* sencillo, sin complicaciones

uncomplimentary /ˌʌnkɒmplə'mentəri/ *a* descortés, poco halagüeño, ofensivo

uncompromising /ʌn'kɒmprəˌmaizɪŋ/ *a* inflexible, estricto, intolerante; irreconciliable

unconcealed /ˌʌnkən'sild/ *a* no oculto; abierto

unconcern /ˌʌnkən'sɜrn/ *n* indiferencia, frialdad, *f,* desapego, *m;* (lack of interest) apatía, despreocupación, *f;* (nonchalance) desenfado, *m,* frescura, *f*

unconcerned /ˌʌnkən'sɜrnd/ *a* indiferente, frío, despegado; apático, despreocupado; desenfadado, fresco

unconcernedly /ˌʌnkən'sɜrnɪdli/ *adv* con indiferencia; sin preocuparse; con desenfado

unconditional /ˌʌnkən'dɪʃən/ *a* incondicional, absoluto. **u. surrender,** rendición incondicional, *f*

unconfined /ˌʌnkən'faind/ *a* suelto, libre; ilimitado; sin estorbo

unconfirmed /ˌʌnkən'fɜrmd/ *a* no confirmado; (report) sin confirmar

uncongenial /ˌʌnkən'dʒinyəl/ *a* incompatible, antipático; desagradable, repugnante

uncongeniality /ˌʌnkənˌdʒini'ælɪti/ *n* incompatibilidad, antipatía, *f;* repugnancia, *f;* lo desagradable

unconnected /ˌʌnkə'nektɪd/ *a* inconexo; *Mech.* desconectado; (relationship) sin parentesco; (confused) incoherente

unconquerable /ʌn'kɒŋkərəbəl/ *a* invencible, indomable, inconquistable

unconquered /ʌn'kɒŋkərd/ *a* no vencido

unconscientious /ˌʌnkɒnʃi'enʃəs/ *a* poco concienzudo

unconscionable /ʌn'kɒnʃənəbəl/ *a* excesivo, desmedido; sin conciencia

unconscious /ʌn'kɒnʃəs/ *a* inconsciente; (senseless) insensible, sin sentido; (spontáneo) espontáneo; (unaware) ignorante. **to be u. of,** ignorar; perder la consciencia de. **to become u.,** perder el sentido

unconsciously /ʌn'kɒnʃəsli/ *adv* inconscientemente, involuntariamente

unconsciousness /ʌn'kɒnʃəsnɪs/ *n* inconsciencia, *f;* (hypnosis, swoon) insensibilidad, *f;* (unawareness) ignorancia, falta de conocimiento, *f*

unconsecrated /ʌn'kɒnsɪˌkreitɪd/ *a* no consagrado

unconsidered /ˌʌnkən'sɪdərd/ *a* indeliberado; sin importancia, trivial

unconstitutional /ˌʌnkɒnstɪ'tuʃən/ *a* anticonstitucional, inconstitucional

unconstrained /ˌʌnkən'streind/ *a* libre; voluntario; sin freno

uncontaminated /ˌʌnkən'tæmɪˌneitɪd/ *a* incontaminado; puro, sin mancha, impoluto

uncontested /ˌʌnkən'testɪd/ *a* sin oposición

uncontradicted /ˌʌnkɒntrə'dɪktɪd/ *a* sin contradicción; incontestable

uncontrollable /ˌʌnkən'trouləbəl/ *a* irrefrenable, incontrolable, inmanejable; (temper) ingobernable; indomable

uncontrolled /ˌʌnkən'trould/ *a* libre, no controlado; desenfrenado, desgobernado

unconventional /ˌʌnkən'venʃən/ *n* poco convencional; bohemio, excéntrico, extravagante; original

unconventionality /ˌʌnkənˌvenʃə'nælɪti/ *a* excentricidad, extravagancia, independencia de ideas, *f;* (of a design) originalidad, *f*

unconversant /ˌʌnkən'vɜrsənt/ *a* poco familiar, poco versado (en)

unconverted /ˌʌnkən'vɜrtɪd/ *a* no convertido; sin transformar

unconvinced /ˌʌnkən'vɪnst/ *a* no convencido

unconvincing /ˌʌnkən'vɪnsɪŋ/ *a* no convincente, poco convincente, que no me (nos, etc.) convence; frívolo

uncooked /ʌn'kʊkt/ *a* crudo, no cocido, sin cocer

uncork /ʌn'kɔrk/ *vt* destapar, descorchar, quitar el corcho

uncorrected /ˌʌnkə'rektɪd/ *a* sin corregir, no corregido

uncorroborated /ˌʌnkə'rɒbəˌreitɪd/ *a* no confirmado, sin confirmar

uncorrupted /ˌʌnkə'rʌptɪd/ *a* incorrupto; puro, no pervertido; (unbribed) no sobornado, honrado

uncorruptible /ˌʌnkə'rʌptəbəl/ *a* incorruptible

uncounted /ʌn'kauntɪd/ *a* no contado, sin cuenta

uncouple /ʌn'kʌpəl/ *vt* soltar; desenganchar, desconectar

uncouth /ʌn'kuθ/ *a* grosero, chabacano, tosco, patán

uncouthness /ʌn'kuθnɪs/ *n* grosería, tosquedad, patanería, *f*

uncover /ʌn'kʌvər/ *vt* descubrir; (remove lid of) destapar; (remove coverings of) desabrigar, desarropar; (leave unprotected) desamparar; (disclose) revelar, dejar al descubierto. —*vi* descubrirse, quitar el sombrero

uncovered /ʌn'kʌvərd/ *a* descubierto; desnudo; sin cubierta

uncreated /ˌʌnkri'eitɪd/ *a* increado

uncritical /ʌn'krɪtɪkəl/ *a* sin sentido crítico, poco juicioso

uncross /ʌn'krɔs/ *vt* (of legs) descruzar

uncrossed /ʌn'krɔst/ *a* (of check) sin cruzar

uncrowned /ʌn'kraund/ *a* antes de ser coronado; sin corona

unction /'ʌŋkʃən/ *n* unción, *f;* untadura, *f,* untamiento, *m;* (unguent) ungüento, *m;* (zeal) fervor, *m;* (flattery) insinceridad, hipocresía, *f;* (relish) gusto, entusiasmo, *m.* **extreme u.,** extremaunción, *f*

unctuous /'ʌŋktʃuəs/ *a* untuoso, craso; insincero, zalamero

uncultivable /ʌn'kʌltəvəbəl/ *a* incultivable

uncultivated /ʌn'kʌltə,veitid/ *a* inculto, yermo; (barbarous) salvaje, bárbaro; (uncultured) inculto, tosco; no cultivado

uncultured /ʌn'kʌltʃərd/ *a* inculto, iletrado

uncurbed /ʌn'kɜrbd/ *a* sin freno; *Fig.* desenfrenado

uncurl /ʌn'kɜrl/ *vt* desrizar *vi* desrizarse; desovillarse

uncut /ʌn'kʌt/ *a* sin cortar, no cortado; (of gems) sin labrar

undamaged /ʌn'dæmidʒd/ *a* indemne, sin daño

undated /ʌn'deitid/ *a* sin fecha

undaunted /ʌn'dɔntid/ *a* intrépido, atrevido

undeceive /,ʌndɪ'siv/ *vt* desengañar, desilusionar

undecided /,ʌndɪ'saidid/ *a* (of question) pendiente, indeciso; dudoso; vacilante, irresoluto

undefended /,ʌndɪ'fɛndɪd/ *a* indefenso

undeferable /,ʌndɪ'fɜrəbəl/ *a* inaplazable

undefiled /,ʌndɪ'faild/ *a* impoluto, incontaminado; puro

undefinable /,ʌndɪ'fainəbəl/ *a* indefinible; inefable, vago

undefined /,ʌndɪ'faind/ *a* indefinido; indeterminado

undelivered /,ʌndɪ'livərd/ *a* no recibido; (speech) no pronunciado; (not sent) no enviado

undemonstrative /,ʌndə'mɒnstrətɪv/ *a* poco expresivo, reservado

undeniable /,ʌndɪ'naiəbəl/ *a* incontestable, innegable, indudable; excelente; inequívoco, evidente

undeniably /,ʌndɪ'naiəbli/ *adv* indudablemente

undependable /,ʌndɪ'pɛndəbəl/ *a* indigno de confianza

under /'ʌndər/ *prep* debajo de; bajo; (in) en; (less than) menos de, menos que; (at the orders of) a las órdenes de, al mando de; (in less time than) en menos de; (under the weight of) bajo el peso de; (at the foot of) al abrigo de; (for less than) por menos de; (at the time of) en la época de, en tiempos de; (according to) según, conforme a, en virtud de (e.g. *under the law*, en virtud de la ley); (of monarchs) bajo (or durante) el reinado de; (of rank) inferior a; (in virtue of) en virtud de; (of age) menor de; (with penalty, pretext, etc.) so; en; a (see below for examples); (*Agr.* of fields) plantado de, sembrado de. **u. arms,** bajo las armas. **u. contract,** bajo contrato. **u. cover,** al abrigo, bajo cubierto. **u. cover of,** bajo pretexto de, so color de. **u. fire,** bajo fuego. **u. oath,** bajo juramento. **u. pain of,** so pena de.

u. sail, a la vela. **u. separate cover,** bajo cubierta separada, en sobre apartado, por separado. **u. steam,** al vapor. **u. way,** en camino; en marcha; en preparación. **to be u. an obligation,** deber favores; (to) tener obligacion de; estar obligado a

under /'ʌndər/ *a* inferior; (of rank) subalterno, subordinado; bajo, bajero. —*adv* debajo; abajo; más abajo; menos; (for less) para menos; (ill) mal; (insufficient) insuficiente. **to bring u.,** someter. **to keep u.,** dominar, subyugar

underact /,ʌndər'ækt/ *vt* hacer un papel sin fogosidad

underarm /'ʌndər,ɑrm/ *n* sobaco, *m.* —*a* sobacal; (of bowling) de debajo del brazo. **to serve u.,** sacar por debajo

underbid /,ʌndər'bid/ *vt* ofrecer menos que

undercharge /,ʌndər'tʃɑrdʒ/ *vt* cobrar menos de lo debido

underclothes /'ʌndər,klouz, -,klouðz/ *n* ropa interior, *f,* paños menores, *m pl*

undercurrent /'ʌndər,kɜrənt/ *n* corriente submarina, *f; Fig.* tendencia oculta

underdeveloped /,ʌndərdɪ'vɛləpt/ *a* de desarrollo atrasado; *Photo.* no revelado lo suficiente

underdog /'ʌndər,dɔg/ *n* víctima, *f;* débil, paciente, *m.* **underdogs,** los de abajo, *m pl*

underdone /'ʌndər'dʌn/ *a* (of meat) crudo, medio asado

underestimate /,ʌndər'ɛstə,meit/ *vt* tasar en menos; desestimar, menospreciar

underfeed /,ʌndər'fid/ *vt* alimentar insuficientemente

underfoot /,ʌndər'fut/ *adv* debajo de los pies, en el suelo

undergo /,ʌndər'gou/ *vt* sufrir, padecer, pasar por. **undergo surgery,** someterse a la cirugía

undergraduate /,ʌndər'grædʒuit/ *n* estudiante no graduado, *m*

underground /*a., n.* 'ʌndər,graund; *adv.* -'graund/ *a* subterráneo; *Fig.* oculto, secreto. —*adv* bajo tierra, debajo de la tierra; *Fig.* en secreto, ocultamente. —*n* sótano, *m;* metro, ferrocarril subterráneo, *m*

undergrowth /'ʌndər,grouθ/ *n* maleza, *f*

underhand /'ʌndər,hænd/ *adv Fig.* bajo mano, ocultamente, a escondidas. —*a Fig.* secreto, oculto

underlie /,ʌndər'lai/ *vt* estar debajo de; servir de base a, caracterizar

underline /,ʌndər'lain/ *vt* subrayar

underling /'ʌndərlɪŋ/ *n* subordinado (-da)

underlying /'ʌndər,laiɪŋ/ *a* fundamental, básico, esencial

undermine /,ʌndər'main/ *vt* socavar, excavar; minar, destruir poco a poco

undermining /'ʌndər,mainɪŋ/ *n* socava, excavación, *f;* destrucción, *f;* a minador

underneath /,ʌndər'niθ/ *adv* debajo. —*prep* bajo, debajo de

undernourished /ˌʌndər'nɜrɪʃt/ a mal alimentado

undernourishment /ˌʌndər'nɜrɪʃmənt/ n desnutrición, f

underpaid /ˌʌndər'peid/ a insuficientemente retribuido, mal pagado

underpass /ˈʌndərˌpæs, -ˌpɑs/ n pasaje por debajo, m

underpay /ˌʌndər'pei/ vt pagar mal, remunerar (or retribuir) deficientemente

underpayment /ˈʌndərˌpeimənt/ n retribución mezquina, f, pago insuficiente, m

underpin /ˌʌndər'pɪn/ vt apuntalar, socalzar

underpopulated /ˌʌndər'pɒpyəˌleitid/ a con baja densidad de población

underprivileged /ˌʌndər'prɪvəlɪdʒd/ a menesteroso, pobre, necesitado

underrate /ˌʌndər'reit/ vt tasar en menos; tener en poco, desestimar, menospreciar

undersecretary /ˈʌndərˌsɛkrəˌtɛri/ n subsecretario (-ia)

undersell /ˌʌndər'sɛl/ vt vender a un precio más bajo que

underside /ˈʌndərˌsaid/ n revés, envés, m

undersigned /ˈʌndərˌsaind/ a infrascrito, suscrito. **the u.**, el abajo firmado, el infrascrito

undersized /ˌʌndər'saizd/ a muy pequeno, enclenque, enano

understand /ˌʌndər'stænd/ vt comprender, entender; (know) saber; (be acquainted with) conocer; (hear) oír, tener entendido; (mean) sobrentender. —vi comprender, entender; oír, tener entendido. **to u. each other,** comprenderse. **It being understood that...,** Bien entendido que...

understandable /ˌʌndər'stændəbəl/ a comprensible; inteligible. **It is very u. why he does not wish to come,** Se comprende muy bien por qué no quiere venir

understanding /ˌʌndər'stændɪŋ/ n (intelligence) entendimiento, m, inteligencia, f; (agreement) acuerdo, m; (knowledge) conocimiento, m; (wisdom) comprensión, sabiduría, f. —a inteligente; sabio; (sympathetic) comprensivo, simpático. **to come to an u.,** ponerse de acuerdo

understate /ˌʌndər'steit/ vt decir menos que, rebajar, describir sin énfasis

understudy /ˈʌndərˌstʌdi/ n sobresaliente, mf. —vt sustituir

undertake /ˌʌndər'teik/ vt comprometerse a, encargarse de; emprender, abarcar, acometer

undertaker /ˈʌndərˌteikər/ n empresario, director de pompas fúnebres, m

undertaking /ˌʌndər'teikɪŋ/ n empresa, tarea, f; garantía, promesa, f; (funerals) funeraria, f

undertone /ˈʌndərˌtoun/ n voz baja, f; Art. color tenue (or apagado), m. **in an u.,** en voz baja

undervalue /ˌʌndər'vælyu/ vt tasar en menos; tener en poco, despreciar

underwater /ˈʌndər'wɔtər/ a subacuático, submarino. **underwater flipper,** aleta de bucear

underweight /ˈʌndər'weit/ a de bajo peso, que pesa menos de lo debido, flaco

underworld /ˈʌndərˌwɜrld/ n (hell) infierno, averno, m; (slums) hampa, f, fondos bajos de la sociedad, m pl; heces de la sociedad, f pl

underwrite /ˌʌndər'rait/ vt Com. asegurar contra riesgos; reasegurar; obligarse a comprar todas las acciones de una compañía no subscritas por el público, mediante un pago convenido

underwriter /ˈʌndərˌraitər/ n asegurador, m; reasegurador, m

undeserved /ˌʌndɪ'zɜrvd/ a inmerecido, no merecido

undeserving /ˌʌndɪ'zɜrvɪŋ/ a indigno, desmerecedor; que no merece

undesirable /ˌʌndɪ'zaiərəbəl/ a no deseable; nocivo, pernicioso; (unsuitable) inconveniente

undesirous /ˌʌndɪ'zaiərəs/ a no deseoso

undestroyed /ˌʌndɪ'strɔid/ a sin destruir, no destruido, intacto

undetected /ˌʌndɪ'tɛktɪd/ a no descubierto

undeveloped /ˌʌndɪ'vɛləpt/ a no desarrollado; rudimentario; inmaturo; (of a country) no explotado, virgen; Photo. no revelado; (of land) sin cultivar

undigested /ˌʌndɪ'dʒɛstɪd/ a no digerido, indigesto

undignified /ʌn'dɪgnəˌfaid/ a sin dignidad; poco serio; indecoroso

undiluted /ˌʌndɪ'lutɪd/ a sin diluir, puro

undiminished /ˌʌndɪ'mɪnɪst/ a no disminuido, sin disminuir, cabal, íntegro

undiplomatic /ˌʌndɪplə'mætɪk/ a impolítico, indiscreto

undirected /ˌʌndɪ'rɛktɪd/ a sin dirección; (of letters) sin señas

undiscernible /ˌʌndɪ'sɜrnəbəl/ a imperceptible, invisible

undiscerning /ˌʌndɪ'sɜrnɪŋ/ a sin percepción, obtuso, sin discernimiento

undisciplined /ʌn'dɪsəplɪnd/ a indisciplinado

undisclosed /ˌʌndɪ'sklouzd/ a no revelado, secreto

undiscovered /ˌʌndɪ'skʌvərd/ a no descubierto, ignoto

undiscriminating /ˌʌndɪ'skrɪməˌneitɪŋ/ a sin distinción; sin sentido crítico

undisguised /ˌʌndɪ'skaizd/ a sin disfraz; abierto, claro

undismayed /ˌʌndɪs'meid/ a intrépido, impávido; sin desaliento

undisposed /ˌʌndɪ'spouzd/ a desinclinado; (of property) no enajenado, no invertido

undisputed /ˌʌndɪ'spyutɪd/ a incontestable, indisputable

undistinguished /ˌʌndɪ'stɪŋgwɪʃt/ a (of writers) poco conocido; indistinto; sin distinción

undisturbed /ˌʌndɪ'stɜrbd/ a sin tocar; tranquilo, sereno, impasible

undivided /ˌʌndɪ'vaɪdɪd/ a indiviso, íntegro; junto; completo, entero

undo /ʌn'du/ vt anular; reparar; desatar, deshacer; desasir; abrir

undoing /ʌn'duɪŋ/ n anulación, f; (reparation) reparación, f; (opening) abrir, m; ruina, f

undomesticated /ˌʌndə'mɛstɪˌkeɪtɪd/ a salvaje, no domesticado; poco casero

undone /ʌn'dʌn/ a and part sin hacer; deshecho; arruinado, perdido. **I am undone!** ¡Estoy perdido! **to come u.**, desatarse. **to leave u.**, dejar sin hacer

undoubted /ʌn'daʊtɪd/ a indudable, evidente, incontestable

undoubtedly /ʌn'daʊtɪdli/ adv sin duda

undreamed /ʌn'drimd/ a no soñado. **u. of**, inopinado, no imaginado

undress /ʌn'drɛs/ vt desnudar, desvestir. —vi desnudarse. —n traje de casa, m; paños menores, m pl; Mil. traje de cuartel, m

undressed /ʌn'drɛst/ a desnudo; en paños menores; (of wounds) sin curar; Com. en rama, en bruto

undrinkable /ʌn'drɪŋkəbəl/ a impotable

undue /ʌn'du/ a excesivo, indebido; injusto; impropio; (of a bill of exchange) por vencer

undulant /ˈʌndʒələnt/ a ondulante. **u. fever**, fiebre mediterránea, fiebre de Malta, f

undulate /ˈʌndʒəˌleɪt/ vi ondular, ondear

undulating /ˈʌndʒəˌleɪtɪŋ/ a ondulante

undulatory /ˈʌndʒələˌtɔri/ a ondulatorio, undoso

unduly /ʌn'duli/ adv excesivamente, demasiado, indebidamente; injustamente

undutiful /ʌn'dutəfəl/ a desobediente, irrespetuoso

undying /ʌn'daɪɪŋ/ a inmortal, imperecedero; eterno

unearned /ʌn'ɜrnd/ a no ganado; inmerecido

unearth /ʌn'ɜrθ/ vt desenterrar; Fig. descubrir, sacar a luz

unearthly /ʌn'ɜrθli/ a sobrenatural; misterioso, aterrador, espantoso

uneasily /ʌn'izəli/ adv con dificultad; incómodamente; inquietamente

uneasiness /ʌn'izɪnɪs/ n malestar, m; (discomfort) incomodidad, f; (anxiety) inquietud, intranquilidad, f, desasosiego, m

uneasy /ʌn'izi/ a incómodo, inseguro; inquieto, intranquilo, desasosegado; aturdido, turbado. **to become u.**, inquietarse

uneatable /ʌn'itəbəl/ a incomible

uneconomical /ˌʌnɛkə'nɒmɪkəl/ a poco económico, costoso, caro

unedifying /ʌn'ɛdəˌfaɪɪŋ/ a poco edificante

uneducated /ʌn'ɛdʒəˌkeɪtɪd/ a ignorante; ineducado, inculto, indocto

unembarrassed /ˌʌnɛm'bærəst/ a sereno, tranquilo, imperturbable; (financially) sin deudas, acomodado

unemotional /ˌʌni'moʊʃənļ/ a frío, impasible

unemployable /ˌʌnɛm'plɔɪəbəl/ a sin uso, inservible; (of persons) inútil para el trabajo

unemployed /ˌʌnɛm'plɔɪd/ a sin empleo; (out of work) sin trabajo, parado; desocupado, ocioso; inactivo. —n paro obrero, m. **the u.**, los sin trabajo, los cesantes, los desocupados

unemployment /ˌʌnɛm'plɔɪmənt/ n paro forzoso, m. **u. benefit**, subvención contra el paro obrero, f. **u. insurance**, seguro contra el paro obrero, m.

unencumbered /ˌʌnɛn'kʌmbərd/ a libre, independiente; (of estates) libre de gravamen; (untaxable) saneado

unending /ʌn'ɛndɪŋ/ a perpetuo, eterno, sin fin; inacabable, constante, continuo, incesante

unendurable /ˌʌnɛn'dʊrəbəl/ a insoportable, insufrible, intolerable

unenlightened /ˌʌnɛn'laɪtņd/ a ignorante

unenterprising /ʌn'ɛntərˌpraɪzɪŋ/ a poco emprendedor, tímido

unenthusiastic /ˌʌnɛnˌθuzi'æstɪk/ a sin entusiasmo, tibio

unequal /ʌn'ikwəl/ a desigual; inferior; (out of proportion) desproporcionado; injusto; insuficiente; incapaz; (of ground) escabroso. **to be u. to the task**, ser incapaz de la tarea; no tener fuerzas para la tarea

unequalled /ʌn'ikwəld/ a sin igual, incomparable, sin par, único

unequally /ʌn'ikwəli/ adv desigualmente

unequivocal /ˌʌni'kwɪvəkəl/ a inequívoco; redondo, claro, franco

unerring /ʌn'ɜrɪŋ, -'ɛr-/ a infalible; seguro

unerringly /ʌn'ɜrɪŋli, -'ɛr- adv infaliblemente; sin equivocarse

unesthetic /ˌʌnɛs'θɛtɪk/ a antiestético

uneven /ʌn'ivən/ a desigual; (of roads) escabroso, quebrado; (of numbers) impar; irregular

unevenly /ʌn'ivənli/ adv desigualmente

unevenness /ʌn'ivənnɪs/ n desigualdad, f; desnivel, m, irregularidad, f. **the unevenness of the terrain**, lo desigual del terreno, lo accidentado del terreno, m

uneventful /ˌʌni'vɛntfəl/ a sin incidentes, sin aconfecimientos notables; tranquilo

unexampled /ˌʌnɪg'zæmpəld/ a sin igual, sin par

unexceptionable /ˌʌnɪk'sɛpʃənəbəl/ a intachable, irreprensible; correcto; impecable, perfecto

unexpected /ˌʌnɪk'spɛktɪd/ a inesperado, imprevisto, inopinado, impensado; repentino, súbito

unexpectedly /ˌʌnɪk'spɛktɪdli/ *adv* inesperadamente; de repente

unexpectedness /ˌʌnɪk'spɛktɪdnɪs/ *n* lo inesperado

unexpired /ˌʌnɪk'spaiᵊrd/ *a* (of bill of exchange) no vencido; (of lease) no caducado

unexplored /ˌʌnɪk'splɔrd/ *a* inexplorado

unexpressed /ˌʌnɪk'sprɛst/ *a* no expresado; tácito, sobrentendido

unexpurgated /ʌn'ɛkspər,geitɪd/ *a* sin expurgar, completo

unfading /ʌn'feidɪŋ/ *a* inmarcesible, inmarchitable; eterno, inmortal

unfailing /ʌn'feilɪŋ/ *a* inagotable; inexhausto; seguro; indefectible

unfailingly /ʌn'feilɪŋli/ *adv* siempre, constantemente; sin faltar

unfair /ʌn'fɛər/ *a* injusto; vil, bajo, soez; de mala fe, engañoso; (of play) sucio

unfairly /ʌn'fɛrli/ *adv* injustamente; de mala fe

unfairness /ʌn'fɛrnɪs/ *n* injusticia, *f*; mala fe, *f*

unfaithful /ʌn'feiθfəl/ *a* infiel; desleal; inexacto, incorrecto. **to be u. to,** ser infiel a; faltar a

unfaltering /ʌn'fɔltərɪŋ/ *a* sin vacilar; resuelto, firme

unfamiliar /ˌʌnfə'mɪlyər/ *a* poco familiar; desconocido. **to be u. with,** ser ignorante de

unfashionable /ʌn'fæʃənəbəl/ *a* pasado de moda, fuera de moda; poco elegante

unfashionably /ʌn'fæʃənəbli/ *adv* contra la tendencia de la moda; sin elegancia

unfasten /ʌn'fæsən/ *vt* desatar; desabrochar, desenganchar; abrir; aflojar; soltar

unfathomable /ʌn'fæðəməbəl/ *a* insondable; impenetrable, inescrutable

unfavorable /ʌn'feivərəbəl/ *a* desfavorable, adverso, contrario

unfeeling /ʌn'filɪŋ/ *a* insensible, impasible, frío; duro, cruel

unfeigned /ʌn'feind/ *a* sincero, natural, verdadero

unfenced /ʌn'fɛnst/ *a* descercado, sin tapia; abierto

unfetter /ʌn'fɛtər/ *vt* desencadenar, destrabar; poner en libertad, librar

unfinished /ʌn'fɪnɪʃt/ *a* incompleto, inacabado; sin acabar; imperfecto

unfit /ʌn'fɪt/ *a* incapaz; incompetente, inepto; (unsuitable) impropio; (useless) inservible, inadecuado; (unworthy) indigno; (ill) enfermo, malo. —*vt* inhabilitar, incapacitar. **u. for human consumption,** impropio para el consumo humano

unfitness /ʌn'fɪtnɪs/ *n* incapacidad, *f*; incompetencia, ineptitud, *f*; impropiedad, *f*; falta de mérito, *f*; falta de salud, *f*

unfix /ʌn'fɪks/ *vt* desprender, despegar, descomponer; soltar. **to come unfixed,** desprenderse

unflagging /ʌn'flægɪŋ/ *a* incansable, infatigable; persistente, constante

unflattering /ʌn'flætərɪŋ/ *a* poco halagüeño

unflinching /ʌn'flɪntʃɪŋ/ *a* inconmovible, resuelto, firme

unfold /ʌn'fould/ *vt* desplegar, desdoblar; tender; abrir; (plans) revelar, descubrir; contar, manifestar. —*vi* abrirse

unfolding /ʌn'fouldɪŋ/ *a* que se abre. —*n* despliegue, *m*; revelación, *f*; narración, *f*

unforced /ʌn'fɔrst/ *a* libre; espontáneo; fácil; natural

unforeseen /ˌʌnfɔr'sin/ *a* imprevisto, inesperado

unforgettable /ˌʌnfər'gɛtəbəl/ *a* involvidable

unforgivable /ˌʌnfər'gɪvəbəl/ *a* inexcusable, imperdonable

unforgiving /ˌʌnfər'gɪvɪŋ/ *a* implacable, que no perdona, inexorable

unformed /ʌn'fɔrmd/ *a* informe; rudimentario; inmaduro, (inexperienced) inexperto, sin experiencia

unfortunate /ʌn'fɔrtʃənɪt/ *a* desdichado, infortunado, desgraciado, desventurado. —*n* desdichado (-da); pobre, *mf*; (prostitute) perdida, *f*

unfortunately /ʌn'fɔrtʃənɪtli/ *adv* por desdicha, desgraciadamente

unfounded /ʌn'faundɪd/ *a* infundado, inmotivado, sin fundamento, injustificado

unfrequented /ʌn'frikwɛntɪd/ *a* poco frecuentado, solitario, retirado, aislado

unfriendliness /ʌn'frɛndlinɪs/ *n* hostilidad, falta de amistad, frialdad, *f*; huraña, insociabilidad, *f*

unfriendly /ʌn'frɛndli/ *a* hostil, enemigo; (of things, events) perjudicial; huraño, insociable

unfruitful /ʌn'frutfəl/ *a* estéril, infecundo; infructuoso, improductivo, vano

unfulfilled /ˌʌnfəl'fɪld/ *a* incumplido, sin cumplir; malogrado

unfurl /ʌn'fɜrl/ *vt* desplegar; *Naut.* izar (las velas)

unfurnished /ʌn'fɜrnɪʃt/ *a* desamueblado, sin muebles; desprovisto (de), sin

ungainliness /ʌn'geinlinɪs/ *n* falta de gracia, torpeza, *f*, desgarbo, *m*

ungainly /ʌn'geinli/ *a* desgarbado

ungenerous /ʌn'dʒɛnərəs/ *a* poco generoso; avaro, tacaño, mezquino; injusto

ungentlemanly /ʌn'dʒɛntļmənli/ *a* poco caballeroso, indigno de un caballero

ungodliness /ʌn'gɒdlinɪs/ *n* impiedad, *f*

ungodly /ʌn'gɒdli/ *a* impío, irreligioso

ungovernable /ʌn'gʌvərnəbəl/ *a* ingobernable, indomable; irrefrenable

ungraceful /ʌn'greisfəl/ *a* desagraciado, desgarbado, sin gracia

ungracious /ʌn'greiʃəs/ *a* desagradable, poco cortés, desdeñoso

ungraciousness /ʌn'greiʃəsnɪs/ *n* descortesía, aspereza, inurbanidad, *f*

ungrammatical /ˌʌŋɡrə'mætɪkəl/ a antigramatical, incorrecto

ungrateful /ʌn'ɡreitfəl/ a ingrato, desagradecido; desagradable, odioso

ungratefulness /ʌn'ɡreitfəlnɪs/ n ingratitud, f; lo desagradable

ungrounded /ʌn'ɡraundɪd/ a infundado; sin motivo

ungrudging /ʌn'ɡrʌdʒɪŋ/ a no avaro, liberal; generoso, magnánimo

ungrudgingly /ʌn'ɡrʌdʒɪŋli/ adv de buena gana

unguarded /ʌn'ɡɑrdɪd/ a indefenso, sin protección; descuidado; indiscreto, imprudente; sin reflexión

unguided /ʌn'ɡaidɪd/ a sin guía

unhallowed /ʌn'hæloud/ a impío, profano

unhampered /ʌn'hæmpərd/ a desembarazado, libre

unhappily /ʌn'hæpəli/ adv desafortunadamente, por desgracia

unhappiness /ʌn'hæpɪnɪs/ n infelicidad, desgracia, desdicha, tristeza, f

unhappy /ʌn'hæpi/ a infeliz, desgraciado, desdichado, triste; (ill-fated) aciago, funesto, malhadado; (remark) inoportuno, inapropiado

unharmed /ʌn'hɑrmd/ a ileso, sano y salvo; (of things) indemne, sin daño

unharness /ʌn'hɑrnɪs/ vt desaparejar; desenganchar; desarmar

unhealthiness /ʌn'hɛlθinɪs/ n falta de salud, f; (of place) insalubridad, f

unhealthy /ʌn'hɛlθi/ a enfermizo; malsano, insalubre

unheard /ʌn'hɜrd/ a no oído; sin ser escuchado; desconocido. **u.-of**, inaudito, no imaginado

unheeding /ʌn'hidɪŋ/ a distraído; desatento, sin prestar atención (a); descuidado

unhelpful /ʌn'hɛlpfəl/ a poco servicial; inútil

unhesitating /ʌn'hɛzɪˌteitɪŋ/ a resuelto, decidido; pronto, inmediato

unhesitatingly /ʌn'hɛzɪˌteitɪŋli/ adv sin vacilar

unhitch /ʌn'hitʃ/ vt desenganchar; descolgar

unholy /ʌn'houli/ a impío, sacrílego

unhook /ʌn'hʊk/ vt desenganchar; desabrochar; descolgar

unhoped-for /ʌn'houptfɔr/ a inesperado

unhurt /ʌn'hɜrt/ a ileso, incólume, sano y salvo; (of things) sin daño

unicorn /'junɪˌkɔrn/ n unicornio, m

unidentified /ˌʌnai'dɛntəˌfaid/ a no reconocido, no identificado

unification /ˌjunəfɪ'keiʃən/ n unificación, f

uniform /'junəˌfɔrm/ a uniforme; igual, constante, invariable; homogéneo. —n uniforme, m. **in full u.**, de gran uniforme. **to make u.**, uniformar, igualar, hacer uniforme

uniformity /ˌjunə'fɔrmɪti/ n uniformidad, igualdad, f

uniformly /'junəˌfɔrmli/ adv uniformemente

unify /'junəˌfai/ vt unificar; unir

unilateral /ˌjunə'lætərəl/ a unilateral

unimaginable /ˌʌnɪ'mædʒənəbəl/ a inimaginable, no imaginable

unimaginative /ˌʌnɪ'mædʒənətɪv/ a sin imaginación

unimpaired /ˌʌnɪm'peərd/ a no disminuido; sin alteración; intacto, entero; sin menoscabo

unimpeachable /ˌʌnɪm'pitʃəbəl/ a irreprochable, intachable

unimportance /ˌʌnɪm'pɔrtns/ n no importancia, insignificancia, trivialidad, f

unimportant /ˌʌnɪm'pɔrtnt/ a sin importancia, nada importante, insignificante, trivial

unimpressive /ˌʌnɪm'prɛsɪv/ a poco impresionante; nada conmovedor; (of persons) insignificante

uninflammable /ˌʌnɪn'flæməbəl/ a no inflamable, incombustible

uninfluenced /ˌʌnɪn'fluənsd/ a no afectado (por), libre (de)

uninformed /ˌʌnɪn'fɔrmd/ a ignorante

uninhabitable /ˌʌnɪn'hæbɪtəbəl/ a inhabitable

uninhabited /ˌʌnɪn'hæbɪtɪd/ a deshabitado, inhabitado, vacío, desierto

uninjured /ʌn'ɪndʒərd/ a ileso; sin daño

uninspired /ˌʌnɪn'spaiərd/ a sin inspiración; pedestre, mediocre

uninstructive /ˌʌnɪn'strʌktɪv/ a nada instructivo

uninsured /ˌʌnɪn'ʃʊrd/ a no asegurado

unintelligent /ˌʌnɪn'tɛlɪdʒənt/ a nada inteligente, corto de alcances, tonto

unintelligible /ˌʌnɪn'tɛlɪdʒəbəl/ a ininteligible, incomprensible

unintentional /ˌʌnɪn'tɛnʃənl/ a involuntario, inadvertido

unintentionally /ˌʌnɪn'tɛnʃənli/ adv sin querer, involuntariamente

uninterested /ʌn'ɪntərəstɪd/ a no interesado, despreocupado

uninteresting /ʌn'ɪntərəstɪŋ/ a sin interés, poco interesante, soso

uninterrupted /ˌʌnɪntə'rʌptɪd/ a ininterrumpido, sin interrupción; continuo, incesante

uninvited /ˌʌnɪn'vaitɪd/ a no invitado, no convidado, sin invitación; (unlooked-for) no buscado

uninviting /ˌʌnɪn'vaitɪŋ/ a poco atrayente; inhospitalario

union /'junyən/ n unión, f; Mech. manguito de unión, m; conexión, f; (poverty) asociación, f; (of trade) gremio de oficios, m; sindicato (obrero), m; (workhouse) asilo, m; (U.S.A.) Estados Unidos de América, m pl

unique /yu'nik/ a único, sin igual, sin par

uniqueness /yu'niknɪs/ n unicidad, f; lo singular

unison /'junəsən, / n unisonancia, f. **in u.**, al unísono

unit /'yunɪt/ n unidad, f. **u. bookcase**, librería en secciones, f

unite /yu'nait/ vt unir, juntar; combinar, incorporar; (of countries) unificar; (of energies, etc.) reunir. —vi unirse, juntarse; reunirse, concertarse; convenirse

united /yu'naitɪd/ a unido; junto. **the U. Nations**, las Naciones Unidas, f pl

United States of America los Estados Unidos, m pl

unity /'yunɪti/ n unidad, f; Math. la unidad; unión, f; conformidad, armonía, f. **the three unities**, las tres unidades

universal /ˌyunə'vɜrsəl/ a universal; general; común. **to make u.**, universalizar, generalizar. **u. joint**, junta universal, f; Auto. cardán, m

universe /'yunə,vɜrs/ n universo, m; creación, f, mundo, m

university /ˌyunə'vɜrsɪti/ n universidad, f. —a universitario. **u. degree**, grado universitario, m

unjust /ʌn'dʒʌst/ a injusto

unjustifiable /ʌn,dʒʌstə'faiəbəl/ a injustificable, indisculpable, inexcusable

unjustifiably /ʌn,dʒʌstə'faiəbli/ adv injustificadamente, inexcusablemente

unjustly /ʌn'dʒʌstli/ adv injustamente, sin razón

unkempt /ʌn'kɛmpt/ a despeinado; desaseado, sucio

unkind /ʌn'kaind/ a nada bondadoso, nada amable; poco complaciente; duro, cruel; desfavorable, nada propicio

unkindly /ʌn'kaindli/ adv sin bondad; con dureza, cruelmente

unkindness /ʌn'kaindnɪs/ n falta de bondad, f; severidad, crueldad, dureza, f, rigor, m; acto de crueldad, m

unknowable /ʌn'nouəbəl/ a impenetrable, incomprehensible, insondable

unknowingly /ʌn'nouɪŋli/ adv sin querer, involuntariamente; sin saberlo; insensiblemente

unknown /ʌn'noun/ a ignoto, desconocido; Math. incógnito. —n lo desconocido, misterio, m; Math. incógnita, f; (person) desconocido (-da), forastero (-ra). Math. **u. quantity**, incógnita, f

unlabeled /ʌn'leibəld/ a sin etiqueta

unlace /ʌn'leis/ vt desenlazar; desatar

unladylike /ʌn'leidi,laik/ a indigno (or impropio) de una dama; vulgar, ordinario, cursi

unlamented /ˌʌnlə'mɛntɪd/ a no llorado, no lamentado

unlatch /ʌn'lætʃ/ vt alzar el pestillo de, abrir

unlawful /ʌn'lɔfəl/ a ilegal, ilícito

unlawfulness /ʌn'lɔfəlnɪs/ n ilegalidad, f

unlearn /ʌn'lɜrn/ vt olvidar, desaprender

unleash /ʌn'liʃ/ vt soltar

unleavened /ʌn'lɛvənd/ a ázimo, sin levadura

unless /ʌn'lɛs/ conjunc a no ser que, a menos que, como no, si no (all followed by subjunc.); salvo, excepto, con excepción de

unlicensed /ʌn'laisənst/ a no autorizado, sin licencia

unlike /ʌn'laik/ a disímil, desemejante; distinto, diferente. —prep a distinción de, a diferencia de, al contrario de. **They are quite u.**, No se parecen nada

unlikely /ʌn'laikli/ a improbable, inverosímil; arriesgado

unlimited /ʌn'lɪmɪtɪd/ a ilimitado, infinito, inmenso; sin restricción; exagerado. **unlimited telephone**, teléfono no medido (Argentina)

unlined /ʌn'laind/ a no forrado, sin forro; sin rayas; (of face) sin arrugas

unlit /ʌn'lɪt/ a no iluminado, oscuro, sin luz

unload /ʌn'loud/ vt descargar; aligerar; Naut. hondear; (of shares) deshacerse de. —vi descargar

unloading /ʌn'loudɪŋ/ n descarga, f, descargue, m

unlock /ʌn'lɒk/ vt desencerrar, abrir; Fig. revelar, descubrir

unloose /ʌn'lus/ vt desatar; soltar; poner en libertad

unlovable /ʌn'lʌvəbəl/ a indigno del querer; antipático, poco amable; repugnante

unluckily /ʌn'lʌkəli/ adv desafortunadamente, por desgracia

unluckiness /ʌn'lʌkɪnɪs/ n mala suerte, f; (unsuitability) inoportunidad, f; lo nefasto, lo malo

unlucky /ʌn'lʌki/ a de mala suerte; desdichado, desgraciado, infeliz; (ill-omened) funesto, nefasto, fatal; inoportuno, inconveniente

unmanageable /ʌn'mænɪdʒəbəl/ a indomable, indócil; ingobernable, inmanejable; (unwieldy) difícil de manejar, pesado

unmannerly /ʌn'mænərli/ a mal educado, descortés

unmarketable /ʌn'markɪtəbəl/ a invendible

unmarriageable /ʌn'mærɪdʒəbəl/ a incasable

unmarried /ʌn'mærid/ a soltero, célibe

unmask /ʌn'mæsk/ vt desenmascarar; Fig. quitar la careta (a). —vi quitarse la máscara; Fig. quitarse la careta, descubrirse

unmeaning /ʌn'minɪŋ/ a sin sentido, vacío, sin significación

unmentionable /ʌn'mɛnʃənəbəl/ a que no se puede mencionar; indigno de mencionarse

unmerciful /ʌn'mɜrsɪfəl/ a sin piedad, sin compasión; cruel, despiadado, duro

unmerited /ʌn'mɛrɪtɪd/ a inmerecido, desmerecido

unmindful /ʌn'maindfəl/ a olvidadizo; desatento; negligente. **u. of**, sin pensar en, olvidando unmistakable /ˌʌnmɪˈsteɪkəbəl/ a inequívoco; manifiesto, evidente, indudable

unmistakably /ˌʌnmɪˈsteɪkəbli/ adv indudablemente

unmitigated /ʌnˈmɪtɪˌgeɪtɪd/ a no mitigado; completo, absoluto; (of rogue) redomado

unmixed /ʌnˈmɪkst/ a sin mezcla; puro, sencillo; (free) limpio

unmoor /ʌnˈmʊr/ vt desamarrar

unmoral /ʌnˈmɔrəl, -ˈmɒr-/ a amoral, no moral; sin fin didáctico

unmounted /ʌnˈmaʊntɪd/ a desmontado

unmoved /ʌnˈmuvd/ a fijo; (unemotional) impasible, frío; (determined) firme, inflexible, inexorable

unmusical /ʌnˈmyuzɪkəl/ a sin afición a la música; sin oído (para la música); inarmónico

unnatural /ʌnˈnætʃərəl/ a desnaturalizado; (of vices, etc.) contra natural; innatural; (of style) rebuscado; artificial; inhumano, cruel

unnavigable /ʌnˈnævɪgəbəl/ a innavegable, no navegable

unnecessarily /ˌʌnnesəˈserəli/ adv inútilmente, innecesariamente, sin necesidad

unnecessary /ʌnˈnesəˌseri/ a innecesario, superfluo, inútil

unneighborly /ʌnˈneibərli/ a de mala vecindad, impropio de vecinos, poco servicial

unnerve /ʌnˈnɜrv/ vt acobardar quitar el valor, desanimar

unnoticed /ʌnˈnoutɪst/ a inadvertido, no observado

unobliging /ʌnəˈblaidʒɪŋ/ a nada servicial

unobservable /ˌʌnbəˈzɜrvəbəl/ a inobservable

unobservant /ˌʌnəbˈzɜrvənt/ a inobservante

unobserved /ˌʌnəbˈzɜrvd/ a sin ser notado, desapercibido

unobstructed /ˌʌnəbˈstrʌktɪd/ a no obstruido; sin obstáculos; libre

unobtainable /ˌʌnəbˈteinəbəl/ a inalcanzable, inasequible

unobtrusive /ˌʌnəbˈtrusɪv/ a discreto, modesto

unoccupied /ʌnˈɒkyəˌpaid/ a (at leisure) desocupado, ocioso, sin ocupación; vacío, vacante, libre; (untenanted) deshabitado

unofficial /ˌʌnəˈfɪʃəl/ a no oficial

unopened /ʌnˈoupənd/ a sin abrir, ce rrado; (of exhibitions, etc.) no inaugurado

unopposed /ˌʌnəˈpouzd/ a sin oposición

unoriginal /ˌʌnəˈridʒənl/ a poco original

unostentatious /ˌʌnɒstənˈteiʃəs/ a sencillo, modesto, sin ostentación

unostentatiousness /ˌʌnɒstənˈteiʃəsnɪs/ n sencillez, modestia, falta de ostentación, f

unpack /ʌnˈpæk/ vt desempaquetar; (trunks) vaciar; (bales) desembalar. —vi desempaquetar; deshacer las maletas

unpacking /ʌnˈpækɪŋ/ n desembalaje, m

unpaid /ʌnˈpeid/ a sin pagar, no pagado

unpalatable /ʌnˈpælətəbəl/ a de mal sabor; desagradable

unparalleled /ʌnˈpærəˌleld/ a sin paralelo, sin par, sin igual

unpardonable /ʌnˈpardnəbəl/ a imperdonable, inexcusable, irremisible

unpatriotic /ˌʌnpeitriˈɒtɪk/ a antipatriótico

unpaved /ʌnˈpeivd/ a sin empedrar

unperceived /ˌʌnpərˈsivd/ a inadvertido, sin ser notado

unperturbed /ˌʌnpərˈtɜrbd/ a impasible, sin alterarse, sereno

unpleasant /ʌnˈplezənt/ a desagradable, desapacible; ofensivo; (troublesome) enfadoso, molesto

unpleasantly /ʌnˈplezəntli/ adv desagradablemente

unpleasantness /ʌnˈplezəntnɪs/ n lo desagradable; disgusto, sinsabor, m; (disagreement) disputa, riña, f

unpleasing /ʌnˈplizɪŋ/ a nada placentero; desagradable, sin atractivos

unplug /ʌnˈplʌg/ vt desenchufar

unpolished /ʌnˈpɒlɪʃt/ a sin pulir, tosco, mate; Fig. inculto, cerril. u. diamond, diamante en bruto, m

unpolluted /ˌʌnpəˈlutɪd/ a impoluto, incontaminado; puro, sin pervertir

unpopular /ʌnˈpɒpyələr/ a impopular

unpopularity /ˌʌnpɒpyəˈlærɪti/ n impopularidad, f

unpractical /ʌnˈpræktəkəl/ a impracticable, imposible; (of persons) sin sentido práctico

unpracticed /ʌnˈpræktɪst/ a no practicado; inexperto, inhábil

unpraiseworthy /ʌnˈpreizˌwɜrði/ a inmeritorio

unprecedented /ʌnˈpresɪˌdentɪd/ a sin precedente, inaudito

unprejudiced /ʌnˈpredʒədɪst/ a sin prejuicios, imparcial

unpremeditated /ˌʌnpriˈmedɪˌteitɪd/ a sin premeditación, indeliberado, impremeditado

unprepared /ˌʌnprɪˈpeərd/ a sin preparación, no preparado; desprevenido; desapercibido (unready)

unpreparedness /ˌʌnprɪˈpeərɪdnɪs/ n falta de preparación, imprevisión, f, desapercibimiento, m

unprepossessing /ˌʌnpripəˈzesɪŋ/ a poco atrayente, antipático

unpresentable /ˌʌnprɪˈzentəbəl/ a impresentable

unpretentious /ˌʌnprɪˈtenʃəs/ a sin pretensiones, modesto

unprincipled /ʌnˈprɪnsəpld/ a sin consciencia, sin escrúpulos

unprocurable /ˌʌnprouˈkyurəbəl/ a inalcanzable, inasequible

unproductive /ˌʌnprəˈdʌktɪv/ a improductivo; infructuoso, estéril

unproductiveness /ˌʌnprəˈdʌktɪvnɪs/ n infructuosidad, f; esterilidad, f

unprofessional /ˌʌnprə'feʃən/ a sin profesión; contrario a la ética profesional

unprofitable /ʌn'prɒfɪtəbəl/ a improductivo, infructuoso; sin provecho; inútil; nada lucrativo

unpromising /ʌn'prɒməsɪŋ/ a poco halagüeño

unpronounceable /ˌʌnprə'naunsəbəl/ a impronunciable

unpropitious /ˌʌnprə'pɪʃəs/ a desfavorable, nada propicio, nada halagüeño

unprotected /ˌʌnprə'tɛktɪd/ a sin protección; (of persons) indefenso, desválido

unproved /ʌn'pruvd/ a no probado, sin demostrar

unprovided /ˌʌnprə'vaɪdɪd/ a desapercibido, desprovisto. u. for, sin provisión (para); sin medios de vida, desamparado

unprovoked /ˌʌnprə'voukt/ a no provocado, sin provocación; sin motivo

unpublished /ʌn'pʌblɪʃt/ a inédito, no publicado, sin publicar

unpunctual /ʌn'pʌŋktʃuəl/ a no puntual, retrasado

unpunished /ʌn'pʌnɪʃt/ a impune, sin castigo

unqualified /ʌn'kwɒlə,faɪd/ a incapaz, incompetente; (with professions) sin título; (downright) incondicional, absoluto

unquenchable /ʌn'kwɛntʃəbəl/ a inextinguible, inapagable; insaciable

unquestionable /ʌn'kwɛstʃənəbəl/ a indiscutible, indudable, indubitable

unquestionably /ʌn'kwɛstʃənəbli/ adv indudablemente

unquiet /ʌn'kwaɪɪt/ a inquieto, intranquilo; agitado

unravel /ʌn'rævəl/ vt deshilar; destejer; (a mystery, etc.) desentrañar, desembrollar, descifrar

unraveling /ʌn'rævəlɪŋ/ n deshiladura, f; aclaración, f

unreadable /ʌn'ridəbəl/ a ilegible

unreadiness /ʌn'redɪnɪs/ n falta de preparación, f, desapercibimiento, m; lentitud, f

unready /ʌn'redi/ a desapercibido, desprevenido; lento

unreal /ʌn'rɪəl/ a irreal; falso, imaginario, ilusorio; ficticio; artificial; insincero, hipócrita; ideal; incorpóreo

unreality /ˌʌnrɪ'ælɪti/ n irrealidad, f; falsedad, f; artificialidad, f; lo quimérico

unreasonable /ʌn'rizənəbəl/ a irrazonable, irracional; disparatado, extravagante; (with price, etc.) exorbitante, excesivo

unreasonableness /ʌn'rizənəbəlnɪs/ n irracionalidad, f; exorbitancia, f

unreasonably /ʌn'rizənəbli/ adv irracionalmente

unreasoning /ʌn'rizənɪŋ/ a irracional; sin motivo, sin causa

unrecognizable /ʌn'rekəg,naizəbəl/ a que no puede reconocerse; imposible de reconocer

unrecognized /ʌn'rekəg,naizd/ a no reconocido

unreconciled /ˌʌn'rekən,saɪld/ a no resignado, no reconciliado

unrectified /ʌn'rektə,faɪd/ a no corregido, sin rectificar

unredeemed /ˌʌnrɪ'dimd/ a no redimido; no mitigado; (of pledges) sin desempeñar

unrefined /ˌʌnrɪ'faɪnd/ a no refinado, impuro; inculto, grosero

unreformed /ˌʌnrɪ'fɔrmd/ a no reformado

unrefuted /ˌʌnrɪ'fyutɪd/ a no refutado

unregenerate /ˌʌnrɪ'dʒenərɪt/ a no regenerado

unregretted /ˌʌnrɪ'gretɪd/ a no llorado, sin lamentar

unrehearsed /ˌʌnrɪ'hɜrst/ a sin preparación; Theat. sin ensayar; (extempore) improvisado

unrelated /ˌʌnrɪ'leɪtɪd/ a inconexo; (of persons) sin parentesco

unrelenting /ˌʌnrɪ'lentɪŋ/ a implacable, inflexible, inexorable

unreliability /ˌʌnrɪˌlaɪə'bɪlɪti/ n incertidumbre, f; el no poder confiar en, informalidad, inestabilidad, f

unreliable /ˌʌnrɪ'laɪəbəl/ a incierto, dudoso, indigno de confianza; (of persons) informal

unrelieved /ˌʌnrɪ'livd/ a no aliviado; absoluto, complete, total

unremitting /ˌʌnrɪ'mɪtɪŋ/ a incansable

unrepealed /ˌʌnrɪ'pild/ a vigente

unrepentant /ˌʌnrɪ'pentn̩t/ a impenitente

unrepresentative /ˌʌnreprɪ'zentətɪv/ a poco representativo

unrepresented /ˌʌnreprɪ'zentɪd/ a sin representación

unrequited /ˌʌnrɪ'kwaɪtɪd/ a no correspondido

unreserved /ˌʌnrɪ'zɜrvd/ a no reservado; expresivo, comunicativo, expansivo, franco

unreservedly /ˌʌnrɪ'zɜrvɪdli/ adv sin reserva; con toda franqueza

unresisting /ˌʌnrɪ'zɪstɪŋ/ a sin oponer resistencia

unresolved /ˌʌnrɪ'zɒlvd/ a sin resolverse, vacilante; incierto, dudoso, inseguro; sin solución

unresponsive /ˌʌnrɪ'spɒnsɪv/ a flemático; insensible, sordo

unresponsiveness /ˌʌnrɪ'spɒnsɪvnɪs/ n flema, f; insensibilidad, f

unrest /ʌn'rest/ n desasosiego, m, agitación, inquietud, f

unrestful /ʌn'restfəl/ a agitado, inquieto, intranquilo

unrestrained /ˌʌnrɪ'streɪnd/ a desenfrenado; ilimitado, sin límites; sin reserva

unrestricted /ˌʌnrɪ'strɪktɪd/ a sin restricción; ilimitado

unrewarded /ˌʌnrɪ'wɔrdɪd/ a sin premio, no recompensado

unrighteous /ʌn'raɪtʃəs/ a injusto, malo, perverso

unripe /ʌn'raɪp/ a verde, inmaturo

unrivaled /ʌn'raivəld/ a sin igual, sin par

unroll /ʌn'roul/ vt desarrollar. —vi desarrollarse; (unfold) desplegarse (a la vista)

unromantic /ˌʌnrou'mæntɪk/ a poco (or nada) romántico

unruffled /ʌn'rʌfəld/ a sereno, plácido, ecuánime; no arrugado; (of hair) liso

unruliness /ʌn'rulinɪs/ n turbulencia, indisciplina, f; insubordinación, rebeldía, f

unruly /ʌn'ruli/ a ingobernable, revoltoso; refractario, rebelde; (of hair) indomable

unsaddle /ʌn'sædl/ vt desensillar; derribar (del caballo, etc.)

unsafe /ʌn'seif/ a inseguro; peligroso; arriesgado; (to eat) nocivo

unsaid /ʌn'sɛd/ a sin decir, no dicho

unsalable / ½n'seiləbəl/ a invendible

unsalaried /ʌn'sælərid/ a no asalariado

unsalted /ʌn'sɔltid/ a soso, sin sal

unsanctioned /ʌn'sæŋkʃənd/ a no permitido, sin sancionar

unsanitary /ʌn'sænɪˌteri/ a antihigiénico

unsatisfactory /ˌʌnsætɪs'fæktɔri/ a poco (or nada) satisfactorio; no aceptable

unsatisfied /ʌn'sætɪsˌfaid/ a no satisfecho; descontento; no convencido; (hungry) no harto; Com. no saldado

unsatisfying /ʌn'sætɪsˌfaiɪŋ/ a que no satisface

unsavoriness /ʌn'seivərɪnɪs/ n insipidez, f, mal sabor, m; lo desagradable; sordidez, suciedad, f

unsavory /ʌn'seivəri/ a insípido, de mal sabor; desagradable; sórdido, sucio

unscathed /ʌn'skeiðd/ a sin daño, ileso

unscented /ʌn'sɛntid/ a sin perfume, sin olor, no fragante

unscholarly /ʌn'skɒlərli/ a nada erudito; indigno de un erudito

unscientific /ˌʌnsaiən'tɪfɪk/ a no científico

unscrew /ʌn'skru/ vt destornillar. —vi destornillarse

unscrupulous /ʌn'skrupyələs/ a sin escrúpulos, poco escrupuloso, desaprensivo

unseal /ʌn'sil/ vt desellar, romper (or quitar) el sello (de)

unseasonable /ʌn'sizənəbəl/ a intempestivo, fuera de sazón; inoportuno, inconveniente. **at an u. hour,** a una hora inconveniente, a deshora

unseasonably /ʌn'sizənəbli/ /adv intempestivamente; a deshora; inoportunamente

unseasoned /ʌn'sizənd/ a Cul. sin sazonar, soso; (wood) verde; no maduro, sin madurar

unseat /ʌn'sit/ vt (from horse) tirar, echar al suelo; Polit. desituir

unseaworthy /'ʌn'si,wɜrði/ a innavegable

unseemly /ʌn'simli/ a indecoroso, indigno; indecente; impropio

unseen /ʌn'sin/ a no visto, invisible; inadvertido; secreto, oculto. f. versión al libro abierto, f. **the u.,** lo invisible

unselfish /ʌn'sɛlfɪʃ/ a desinteresado, abnegado, nada egoísta; generoso

unselfishness /ʌn'sɛlfɪʃnɪs/ n abnegación, f; desinterés, m; generosidad, f

unsentimental /ˌʌnsɛntə'mɛntl/ a no sentimental

unserviceable /ʌn'sɜrvisəbəl/ a inservible, inútil, que no sirve para nada, sin utilidad

unsettle /ʌn'sɛtl/ vt desarreglar; desorganizar; hacer inseguro; agitar, perturbar

unsettled /ʌn'sɛtld/ a inconstante, variable; Com. pendiente, sin pagar; incierto; sin resolver; (of estates) sin solucionar

unshackle /ʌn'ʃækəl/ vt desencadenar

unshakable /ʌn'ʃeikəbəl/ a inconmovible, firme

unshapely /ʌn'ʃeipli/ a desproporcionado

unshaven /ʌn'ʃeivən/ a sin afeitar

unsheathe /ʌn'ʃið/ vt desenvainar, sacar

unsheltered /ʌn'ʃɛltərd/ a desabrigado, desamparado; no protegido, sin protección; (of places) sin abrigo, expuesto; (from) sin defensa contra

unship /ʌn'ʃɪp/ vt desembarcar; (the oars) desarmar

unshod /ʌn'ʃɒd/ a descalzo; (of a horse) sin herraduras

unshrinkable /ʌn'ʃrɪŋkəbəl/ a que no se encoge

unshrinking /ʌn'ʃrɪŋkɪŋ/ a intrépido; resoluto, sin vacilar

unsightly /ʌn'saitli/ a feo, horrible, repugnante, antiestético

unsinkable /ʌn'sɪŋkəbəl/ a insumergible

unskilled /ʌn'skɪld/ a inexperto, inhábil, imperito, torpe

unsociability /ˌʌnsouʃə'bɪlɪti/ n insociabilidad, huraña, esquivez, f

unsociable /ʌn'souʃəbəl/ a insociable, huraño, esquivo, arisco

unsocial /ʌn'souʃəl/ a insocial, antisocial

unsold /ʌn'sould/ a no vendido, sin vender

unsolder /ʌn'sɒdər/ vt desoldar, desestañar

unsoldierly /ʌn'souldʒɜrli/ a indigno de un soldado; poco marcial

unsophisticated /ˌʌnsə'fɪstɪˌkeitɪd/ a ingenuo, inocente, cándido

unsought /ʌn'sɔt/ a no solicitado; no buscado

unsound /ʌn'saund/ a enfermo; defectuoso; (rotten) podrido; (fallacious) erróneo, poco convincente; (of persons) informal, indigno de confianza; (of religious views) heterodoxo. **of u. mind,** insáno

unsparing /ʌn'spɛərɪŋ/ a severo, implacable; generoso, pródigo

unspeakable /ʌn'spikəbəl/ a indecible, inefable; que no puede mencionarse, horrible

unspecified /ʌn'spɛsəˌfaid/ a no especificado

unspoken /ʌn'spoukən/ a no pronunciado

unsportsmanlike /ʌn'spɔrtsmən,laik/ *a*
indigno de un cazador; indigno de un deportista; nada caballeroso. **to play in an
u. way,** jugar sucio

unstable /ʌn'steibəl/ *a* inestable; variable; inconstante; vacilante, irresoluto

unstained /ʌn'steind/ *a* no manchado;
no teñido; inmaculado, sin mancha

unstatesmanlike /ʌn'steitsmən,laik/ *a*
impropio (*or* indigno) de un hombre de
estado

unsteadiness /ʌn'stɛdinɪs/ *n* inestabilidad, falta de firmeza, *f;* inconstancia, *f*

unsteady /ʌn'stɛdi/ *a* inestable, inseguro;
inconstante

unstitch /ʌn'stɪtʃ/ *vt* desapuntar

unstudied /ʌn'stʌdid/ *a* no estudiado;
natural, espontáneo

unsubstantial /,ʌnsəb'stænʃəl/ *a* insubstancial; ligero; irreal, imaginario; incorpóreo; aparente

unsuccessful /,ʌnsək'sɛsfəl/ *a* sin éxito;
infructuoso. **to be u.,** no tener éxito

unsuccessfully /,ʌnsək'sɛsfəli/ *adv* en
vano, sin éxito

unsuitable /ʌn'sutəbəl/ *a* inapropiado;
inconveniente; impropio; inservible; incapaz; inoportuno

unsung /ʌn'sʌŋ/ *a* no cantado; no celebrado en verso

unsupported /,ʌnsə'pɔrtɪd/ *a* sin apoyo;
sin defensa; no favorecido

unsurmountable /,ʌnsər'mauntəbəl/ *a*
insuperable, infranqueable

unsurpassable /,ʌnsər'pæsəbəl/ *a* inmejorable, insuperable

unsurpassed /,ʌnsər'pæst/ *a* sin par

unsuspecting /,ʌnsə'spɛktɪŋ/ *a* no suspicaz, confiado, no receloso

unswerving /ʌn'swɜrvɪŋ/ *a* directo; sin
vacilar, constante

unsymmetrical /,ʌnsɪ'mɛtrɪkəl/ *a* asimétrico

unsympathetic /,ʌnsɪmpə'θɛtɪk/ *a* indiferente, incompasivo; antipático

unsystematic /,ʌnsɪstə'mætɪk/ *a* sin
sistema, asistemático, no metódico

untalented /ʌn'tæləntɪd/ *a* sin talento

untamed /ʌn'teimd/ *a* indomado, cerril,
bravío, no domesticado; desenfrenado,
violento

untenable /ʌn'tɛnəbəl/ *a* insostenible

untenanted /ʌn'tɛnəntɪd/ *a* desalquilado, deshabitado; vacío, desierto

unthankful /ʌn'θæŋkfəl/ *a* ingrato, desagradecido

unthinkable /ʌn'θɪŋkəbəl/ *a* inconcebible; imposible

unthinking /ʌn'θɪŋkɪŋ/ *a* sin reflexión;
desatento; indiscreto

unthinkingly /ʌn'θɪŋkɪŋli/ *adv* sin pensar

untidily /ʌn'taidɪli/ *adv* en desorden, sin
aseo

untidy /ʌn'taidi/ *a* desarreglado; desaseado; abandonado; en desorden, sin
concierto

untie /ʌn'tai/ *vt* desatar, desanudar;
(knots) deshacer

until /ʌn'tɪl/ *prep* hasta. —*conjunc* hasta
que. (The subjunc. is required in clauses
referring to future time, e.g. *No venga
usted hasta que le avise yo,* Don't come
until I tell you. In clauses referring to past
or present time the indicative is generally
used, e.g. *No la reconocí hasta que se
volvió,* I didn't recognize her until she
turned round)

untimely /ʌn'taimli/ *a* inoportuno, intempestivo; prematuro

untiring /ʌn'tai°rɪŋ/ *a* incansable, infatigable

unto /'ʌntu; *unstressed* -tə/ *prep* hacia

untold /ʌn'tould/ *a* no revelado; no na-
rrado; sin decir, no dicho; incalculable

untouchable /ʌn'tʌtʃəbəl/ *a* que no
puede tocarse, intangible; (of castes) into-
cable

untouched /ʌn'tʌtʃt/ *a* sin tocar; intacto, incólume

untrained /ʌn'treind/ *a* indisciplinado;
inexperto; no adiestrado

untranslatable /,ʌntræns'leitəbəl/ *a* intraducible

untraveled /ʌn'trævəld/ *a* no frecuentado; (of persons) provinciano

untried /ʌn'traid/ *a* no experimentado. **u.
knight,** caballero novel, *m*

untrodden /ʌn'trɒdn/ *a* no hollado, no
frecuentado; inexplorado, virgen

untroubled /ʌn'trʌbəld/ *a* tranquilo,
sosegado

untrue /ʌn'tru/ *a* mentiroso, falso, engañoso; ficticio, imaginario; traidor, desleal; infiel

untrustworthiness /ʌn'trʌst,wɜrðinɪs/ *n*
incertidumbre, inseguridad, *f;* (of persons)
informalidad, *f*

untrustworthy /ʌn'trʌst,wɜrði/ *a* indigno de confianza; incierto, dudoso; desleal

untruth /ʌn'truθ/ *n* mentira, falsedad, *f;*
ficción, *f*

untruthful /ʌn'truθfəl/ *a* mentiroso;
falso

unused /ʌn'yuzd/ *a* no empleado;
/ʌn'yust/ desacostumbrado; inusitado;
(postage stamp) sin sellar

unusual /ʌn'yuʒuəl/ *a* fuera de lo común,
desacostumbrado; extraño, raro, peregrino, extraordinario

unusually /ʌn'yuʒuəli/ *adv* excepcional-
mente; infrecuentemente

unvarnished /ʌn'vɑrnɪʃt/ *a* sin barnizar;
Fig. sencillo

unvarying /ʌn'vɛəriɪŋ/ *a* invariable,
constante, uniforme

unveil /ʌn'veil/ *vt* quitar el velo; (memorial) descubrir; *Fig.* revelar. —*vi* quitarse
el velo; revelarse, quitarse la careta

unventilated /ʌn'vɛntʃeitɪd/ *a* sin ventilación; sin aire, ahogado; (of topics) no
discutido

unverifiable /ʌn,verə'faiəbəl/ a que no puede verificarse

unverified /ʌn,verə'faid/ a sin verificar

unvisited /ʌn 'vɪsɪtɪd/ no visitado; no frecuentado

unvoiced /ʌn'vɔist/ a no expresado

unwanted /ʌn'wɒntɪd/ a no deseado; superfluo, de más

unwarranted /ʌn'wɒrəntɪd/ a sin garantía; inexcusable, injustificable

unwary /ʌn'weəri/ a incauto, imprudente

unwashed /ʌn'wɒʃt/ a sin lavar; sucio

unwavering /ʌn'weivərɪŋ/ a resuelto, firme; inexorable; (gaze) fijo

unwaveringly /ʌn'weivərɪŋli/ adv sin vacilar; inexorablemente

unwelcome /ʌn'welkəm/ a mal acogido; inoportuno; desagradable

unwell /ʌn'wel/ a indispuesto

unwholesome /ʌn'houlsəm/ a malsano, nocivo, insalubre

unwieldy /ʌn'wildi/ a pesado, abultado, difícil de manejar

unwilling /ʌn'wɪlɪŋ/ a desinclinado, reluctante

unwillingly /ʌn'wɪlɪŋli/ adv de mala gana

unwillingness /ʌn'wɪlɪŋnɪs/ n falta de inclinación, repugnancia, f

unwind /ʌn'waind/ vt desenvolver; (thread) desdevanar, desovillar. —vi desarrollarse; desdevanarse

unwise /ʌn'waiz/ a imprudente, indiscreto, incauto; (lacking wisdom) tonto

unwisely /ʌn'waizli/ adv imprudentemente, indiscretamente

unwitting /ʌn'wɪtɪŋ/ a inconsciente

unwittingly /ʌn'wɪtɪŋli/ adv sin darse cuenta

unwomanly /ʌn'wumənli/ a poco femenino

unworkable /ʌn'wɜrkəbəl/ a impráctico

unworkmanlike /ʌn'wɜrkmən,laik/ a chapucero, charanguero

unworldly /ʌn'wɜrldli/ a poco, mundano, espiritual

unworn /ʌn'wɔrn/ a sin llevar, nuevo

unworthy /ʌn'wɜrði/ a indigno

unwounded /ʌn'wundɪd/ a no herido, sin herida, ileso

unwrap /ʌn'ræp/ vt desenvolver, desempapelar

unwritten /ʌn'rɪtn/ a no escrito. **u. law,** ley consuetudinaria, f

unyielding /ʌn'yildɪŋ/ a duro, firme; (of persons) inflexible, terco, resuelto, obstinado

up /ʌp/ adv (high) arriba, en alto; (higher) hacia arriba; (out of bed) levantado; (standing) de pie; (finished) concluido, terminado; (of time) llegado; (excited) agitado; (rebellious) sublevado; (of sun, etc.) salido; (come or gone up) subido; (of universities) en residencia; (for discussion) bajo consideración; (abreast of) al lado, al nivel; (incapable) incapaz, incompetente; (ill) enfermo, indispuesto. **"Up,"** (on elevators) «Para subir.» (For various idiomatic uses of **up** after verbs, see verbs themselves.) a (in a few expressions only) ascendente. —prep en lo alto de; hacia arriba de; a lo largo de; (with country) en el interior de; (with current) contra. **to be up in arms,** sublevarse, rebelarse. **to be very hard up,** ser muy pobre, estar a la cuarta pregunta. **to drink up,** beberlo todo. **to go or come up,** subir. **to lay up,** acumular. **to speak up,** hablar en voz alta. **He has something up his sleeve,** Tiene algo en la manga. **It is all up,** Todo se acabó, Mi gozo en el pozo. **It is not up to much,** Vale muy poco; No es muy fuerte. **It is up to you,** Tú dirás, Tú harás lo que te parezca. **What is he up to?** ¿Qué está tramando? **What's up?** ¿Qué pasa? ¿Qué hay? **up and down,** adv bajando y subiendo, de arriba abajo; de un lado a otro; por todas partes. **up-and-down,** a fluctuante; (of roads) ondulante; (of life) accidentado, borrascoso. **ups and downs,** vicisitudes, f pl, altibajos, m pl. **upgrade,** subida, f, up in, versado en, perito en. **well up in,** fuerte en. **up North,** al norte; en el norte; hacia el norte. **up there,** allí arriba, allí en lo alto. **up to,** hasta; (aware) al corriente de, informado de. **up to date,** adv hasta la fecha. **up-to-date,** a de última moda; al día. **up to now,** hasta ahora. **up train,** tren ascendente. **Up with...!** ¡Arriba! **Up you go!** (to children) ¡Upa!

upbraid /ʌp'breid/ vt reprender, echar en cara

upbringing /'ʌp,brɪŋɪŋ/ n crianza, educación, f

upcountry /n., a 'ʌp,kʌntri; adv. ʌp'kʌntri/ n tierra adentro, f; lo interior (de un país). —a de tierra adentro, del interior. —adv tierra adentro, hacia el interior

update /'ʌp,deit/ vt actualizar, poner al día

upheaval /ʌp'hivəl/ n solevantamiento, m; trastorno, m

uphill /a, adv. 'ʌp'hɪl; n. 'ʌp,hɪl/ a ascendente; penoso, fatigoso, difícil. —adv cuesta arriba, pecho arriba

uphold /ʌp'hould/ vt sostener, apoyar; (help) ayudar, consolar; (protect) defender; (countenance) aprobar; Law. confirmar

upholster /ʌp'houlstər, ə'poul-/ vt entapizar, tapizar

upholsterer /ʌp'houlstərər; ə'poulʌ/ n tapicero, m

upholstery /ʌp'houlstəri, ə'poulʌ/ n tapicería, f; (of car) almohadillado, m

upkeep /'ʌp,kip/ n mantenimiento, m, conservación, f

upland /'ʌplənd/ n tierra alta, f, a alto, elevado

uplift /v. ʌp'lɪft; n. 'ʌp,lɪft/ vt elevar. —n elevación, f; Inf. fervor, m

upon /ə'pɒn/ prep. See **on**

usual

upper /'ʌpər/ a compar superior; alto; de arriba. —n (of shoe) pala, f, Sports. **u.-cut,** golpe de abajo arriba, upper-cut, m. **U. Egypt,** Alto Egipto, m. **u. hand,** dominio, m; superioridad, ventaja, f. **u. house,** cámara alta, f; senado, m. **u. ten,** los diez primeros

upper classes a clases altas, capas altas, f pl

uppermost /'ʌpər,moust/ a más alto, más elevado; predominante, principal; más fuerte. —adv en primer lugar; en lo más alto. **to be u.,** predominar

upright /'ʌp,rait/ a recto, derecho; vertical; (honorable) honrado, digno, recto. —n (stanchion) mástil, soporte, palo derecho, montante, m. —adv en pie; derecho

uprightly /'ʌp,raitli/ adv rectamente, honradamente

uprising /'ʌp,raiziŋ/ n insurrección, sublevación, f

uproar /'ʌp,rɔr/ n alboroto, tumulto, estrépito, m, conmoción, f

uproarious /ʌp'rɔriəs/ a tumultuoso, es trepitoso

uproot /ʌp'rut/ vt desarraigar; Fig. arrancar; (destroy) extirpar

upset /v. ʌp'sɛt; n. 'ʌp,sɛt/ vt volcar; (overthrow) derribar, echar abajo; (frustrate) contrariar; desarreglar; (distress) trastornar, turbar; (of food) hacer mal. —vi volcarse. —n vuelco, m; trastorno, m. **u. price,** tipo de subasta, m

upshot /'ʌp,ʃɒt/ n resultado, m; consecuencia, f

upside /'ʌp,said/ n lado superior, m; parte superior, f; (of trains) andén ascendente, m. **u. down,** al revés, de arriba abajo; en desorden

upstairs /'ʌp'stɛərz/ adv arriba, en el piso de arriba; (with go or come) al piso de arriba

upstanding /ʌp'stændiŋ/ a gallardo, guapo. **an u. young man (woman),** un buen mozo (una buena moza)

upstart /'ʌp,stɑrt/ n arribista, mf; advenedizo (-za), insolente, mf; presuntuoso (-sa)

upstream /'ʌp'strim/ a and adv contra la corriente, agua arriba, río arriba

upward /'ʌpwərd/ a ascendente, hacia arriba

upwards /'ʌpwərdz/ adv hacia arriba; en adelante. **u. of,** más de

uranium /yʊ'reiniəm/ n Mineral. uranio, m

urban /'ɜrbən/ a urbano, ciudadano

urbane /ɜr'bein/ a cortés, urbano, fino

urbanity /ɜr'bænɪti/ n urbanidad, cortesía, finura, f

urban renewal n renovación urbana, renovación urbanística, f

urchin /'ɜrtʃɪn/ n galopín, granuja, pilluelo, m

urethra /yʊ'riθrə/ n Anat. uretra, f

urge /ɜrdʒ/ vt empujar, impeler; incitar; estimular, azuzar, animar; pedir con urgencia, recomendar con ahínco, instar, insistir (en). —n instinto, impulso, m; deseo, m; ambición, f

urgency /'ɜrdʒənsi/ n urgencia, f; importancia, perentoriedad, f

urgent /'ɜrdʒənt/ a urgente; importante, apremiante, perentorio. **to be u.,** urgir

urinal /'yʊrənl/ n orinal, urinario, m

urinalysis /,yʊrə'næləsɪs/ n análisis de orina, urinálisis, m

urinary tract n conducto urinario, m, vías urinarias, f pl

urinate /'yʊrə,neit/ vi orinar

urine /'yʊrɪn/ n orín, m

urn /ɜrn/ n urna, f; (for coffee) cafetera, f; (for tea) tetera, f

urticaria /,ɜrtɪ'kɛəriə/ n Med. urticaria, f

Uruguayan /,yʊrə'gweiən/ a and n uruguayo (-ya)

us /ʌs/ pron nos; (with prep.) nosotros. **He came toward us,** Vino hacia nosotros

usable /'yuzəbəl/ a aprovechable, servible

usage /'yusɪdʒ/ n (handling) tratamiento, m; uso, m, costumbre, f

use /yus/ n uso, m; manejo, empleo, m; (custom) costumbre práctica, f; (need) necesidad, f; (usefulness) aprovechamiento, m; Law. usufructo, m. **directions for use,** direcciones para el uso, f pl, **for the use of...,** para uso de... **in use,** en uso. **out of use,** anticuado; fuera de moda. **to be of no use,** no servir; ser inútil. **to have no use for,** no tener necesidad de; Inf. tener en poco. **to make use of,** servirse de, aprovechar; Law. ejercer. **to put to use,** poner en uso, poner en servicio

use /yuz/ vt usar; (employ) emplear; (utilize) servirse de, utilizar; (handle) manejar; hacer uso de; (consume) gastar, consumir; (treat) tratar; practicar. **to use up,** agotar, acabar con; consumir. —vi impers acostumbrar, soler (e.g. It used to happen that..., Solía ocurrir que...). (Used to and the verb which follows are often translated simply by the imperfect tense of the following verb, e.g. I used to see her every day, La veía todos los días. Use of the verbs acostumbrar or soler to translate used to adds emphasis to the statement)

used /yuzd/ a and past part /yust/ acostumbrado, habituado; empleado; (clothes) usado; (postage stamp) sellado. **to become u. to,** acostumbrarse a

useful /'yusfəl/ a útil; provechoso; servicial

usefulness /'yusfəlnɪs/ n utilidad, f; valor, m

useless /'yuslɪs/ a inútil; vano, infructuoso. **to render u.,** inutilizar

user /'yuzər/ n el, m, (f, la) que usa, comprador (-ra)

usher /'ʌʃər/ n ujier, m; (in a theater) acomodador (-ra). —vt introducir, anunciar; acomodar

usual /'yuʒuəl/ a usual, acostumbrado,

habitual; normal, común. **as u.,** como siempre. **in the u. form,** *Com.* al usado; como de costumbre. **with their usual courtesy,** con la cortesía que les es característica

usually /'yuʒuəli/ *adv* por lo general, ordinariamente. **We u. go out on Sundays,** Acostumbramos salir los domingos

usurer /'yuʒərər/ *n* usurero (-ra)

usurp /yu'sɔrp/ *vt* usurpar; asumir, arrogarse

usury /'yuʒəri/ *n* usura, *f.* **to practice u.,** usurear, dar (or tomar) a usura

utensil /yu'tɛnsəl/ *n* utensilio, instrumento, *m*; herramienta, *f.* **kitchen utensils,** batería de cocina, *f*

uterine /'yutərɪn/ *a Med.* uterino

uterus /'yutərəs/ *n* útero, *m*

utilitarian /yu,tɪlɪ'tɛəriən/ *a* utilitario

utility /yu'tɪlɪti/ *n* utilidad, *f*; ventaja, *f*, beneficio, provecho, *m*. **u. goods,** artículos fabricados bajo la autorizacion del gobierno, *m pl*

utilizable /,yutɪl'aizəbəl/ *a* utilizable, aprovechable

utilization ,yutWə'zeiSən/ *n* empleo, aprovechamiento, *m*

utilize /'yutl,aiz/ *vt* utilizar, servirse de; aprovechar

utmost /'ʌt,moust/ *a* (outermost) extremo; (farthest) más remoto, más distante; (greatest) mayor, más grande. —*n* lo más; todo lo posible. **to do one's u.,** hacer todo lo posible, hacer todo lo que uno pueda

utopian /yu'toupiən/ *a* utópico

utter /'ʌtər/ *a* completo, total; terminate, absoluto; sumo, extremo. **He is an u. fool,** Es un tonto de capirote

utter /'ʌtər/ *vt* pronunciar, proferir, decir, hablar; (a sigh, cry, etc.) dar; (express) manifestar, expresar, explicar; (coin) poner en circulación; (a libel) publicar; (disclose) revelar, descubrir

utterance /'ʌtərəns/ *n* expresión, manifestación, *f*; pronunciación, *f*; (style) lenguaje, *m*

utterly /'ʌtərli/ *adv* enteramente, completamente

uttermost /'ʌtər,moust/ *a*. See **utmost**

v /vi/ *n* (letter) ve, *f*; pieza en forma de V, *f*

vacancy /'veikənsi/ *n* vacío, *m*; vacancia, *f*; (mental) vacuidad, *f*; (of offices, posts) vacante, *f*; (leisure) desocupación, ociosidad, *f*; (gap, blank) vacío, *m*, laguna, *f*

vacant /'veikənt/ *a* vacío; despoblado, deshabitado; (free) libre; (of offices, etc.) vacante; (leisured) ocioso; (absent-minded) distraído; (vague) vago; (foolish) estúpido, estólido

vacate /'veikeit/ *vt* dejar vacío; (a post) dejar; (a throne) renunciar a; dejar vacante; *Mil.* evacuar; *Law.* anular, rescindir

vacation /vei'keiʃən/ *n* (of offices) vacante, *f*; (holiday) vacaciones, *f pl*, *f*. **the long v.**, las vacaciones de verano. **to be on a v.**, estar de vacaciones

vaccinate /'væksə,neit/ *vt* vacunar

vaccination /,væksə'neiʃən/ *n* vacunación, *f*

vaccine /væk'sin/ *n* vacuna, *f*

vacillate /'væsə,leit/ *vi* (sway) oscilar; (hesitate) vacilar, titubear, dudar

vacillating /'væsə,leitɪŋ/ *a* vacilante

vacuous /'vækyuəs/ *a* desocupado, ocioso; estúpido, vacío

vacuum /'vækyum/ *n* vacío, *m*. **v. brake**, freno al vacío, *m*. **v. cleaner**, aspirador de polvo, *m* **v. flask**, termos, *m*. **v. pump**, bomba neumática, *f*. **vacuum-shelf dryer**, secador al vacío, *m*

vagabond /'vægə,bɒnd/ *n* vagabundo (-da); vago, *m*; (beggar) mendigo (-ga). —*a* vagabundo, errante

vagary /və'geəri, 'veigəri/ *n* (whim) capricho, antojo, *m*, extravagancia, *f*; (of the mind) divagación, *f*

vagina /və'dʒainə/ *n* vagina, *f*

vaginal /'vædʒənl/ *a* vaginal

vagrancy /'veigrənsi/ *n* vagancia, *f*

vagrant /'veigrənt/ *n* vago, *m*, *a* vagabundo, errante

vague /veig/ *a* vago; indistinto; equívoco, ambiguo; (uncertain) incierto

vagueness /'veignɪs/ *n* vaguedad, *f*

vain /vein/ *a* vano; (fruitless) infructuoso; (useless) inútil; (unsubstantial) fútil, insubstancial; fantástico; (empty) vacío; (worthless) despreciable; (conceited) vanidoso, presumido. **in v.**, en vano, en balde, inútilmente. **v. about**, orgulloso de

vainglorious /vein'glɔriəs, -'glour-/ *a* vanaglorioso

vainly /'veinli/ *adv* vanamente; inútilmente; (conceitedly) vanidosamente, con vanidad

valance /'væləns/ *n* cenefa, *f*

vale /veil/ *n* (valley) valle, *m*. —*interj* ¡adiós! —*n* (good-bye) vale, *m*

valediction /,væli'dikʃən/ *n* despedida, *f*; vale, *m*

valedictory /,væli'diktəri/ *a* de despedida

Valencian /və'lenʃiən/ *a* and *n* valenciano (-na)

valency /'veilənsi/ *n Chem.* valencia, *f*

valet /væ'lei, 'vælɪt/ *n* criado, *m*. **v. de chambre**, ayuda de cámara, *m*

valetudinarian /,væli,tudn'eəriən/ *a* valetudinario

valiant /'vælyənt/ *a* valiente, esforzado, animoso, bravo

valid /'vælɪd/ *a* válido, valedero; (of laws in force) vigente

validate /'væli,deit/ *vt* validar

validity /və'lɪdɪti/ *n* validez, *f*

valise /və'lis/ *n* valija, *f*, saco de viaje, *m*

valley /'væli/ *n* valle, *m*

valor /'vælər/ *n* valor, *m*, valentía, *f*

valorous /'vælərəs/ *a* valoroso, esforzudo, intrépido

valuable /'vælyuəbəl/ *a* valuoso; costoso; precioso; estimable; excelente. —*n pl* **valuables**, objetos de valor, *m pl*

valuation /,vælyu'eiʃən/ *n* valuación, tasación, *f*; estimación, *f*

value /'vælyu/ *n* valor, *m*; precio, *m*; estimación, *f*; importancia, *f*; (*Gram. Mus.*) valor, *m*; *pl* **values**, valores morales, principios, *m pl.* —*vt* tasar, valorar; estimar; apreciar; tener en mucho; hacer caso de; considerar. **to be of v.**, ser de valor

valued /'vælyud/ *a* apreciado, estimado; precioso

valueless /'vælyulɪs/ *a* sin valor; insignificante

valuer /'vælyuər/ *n* tasador, *m*

valve /vælv/ *n* (Elec., Mech., Anat.) válvula, *f*; (*Bot., Zool.*) valva, *f*

vamp /væmp/ *n* (of a shoe) pala (de zapato), *f*; (patch) remiendo, *m*; *Mus.* acompañamiento improvisado, *m*; *Inf.* aventurera, *f*. —*vt* (of shoes) poner palas (a); (patch) remendar; *Mus.* improvisar un acompañamiento; (of a woman) fascinar, engatusar

vampire /'væmpaiᵊr/ *n* vampiro, *m*

van /væn/ *n* (*Mil., Nav., Fig.*) vanguardia, *f*; camión, *m*; (for delivery) camión de reparto, *m*; (for furniture) conductora de muebles, *f*; (removal) carro de mudanzas, *m*; (mail) camión postal, *m*; (for bathing) caseta de baño, *f*; (for guard on trains) furgón de equipajes, *m*; (railroad car) vagón, *m*

vandal /'vændl/ *a* and *n* vándalo (-la); bárbaro (-ra)

vandalism /'vændl,izəm/ *n* vandalismo, *m*

Vandyke /væn'daik/ *n* cuadro de Vandyke, *m*. **V. beard**, perilla, *f*. **V. collar**, cuello de encaje, *m*

vane /vein/ *n* (weathercock) veleta, *f*; (of a windmill) aspa, *f*; (of a propeller) paleta, *f*; (of a feather) barba, *f*; (of a surveying instrument) pínula, *f*

vanguard /'væn,gɑrd/ *n* vanguardia, *f*.

in the v., a vanguardia; *Fig.* en la vanguardia

vanilla /vəˈnɪlə/ *n* vainilla, *f*

vanish /ˈvænɪʃ/ *vi* desaparecer; desvanecerse; disiparse

vanishing /ˈvænɪʃɪŋ/ *n* desaparición, *f*; disipación, *f*. **v. cream**, crema desvanecedora, *f*. **v. point**, punto de la vista, *m*

vanity /ˈvænɪti/ *n* vanidad, *f*. **v. case**, polvera de bolsillo, *f*

vanquish /ˈvæŋkwɪʃ/ *vt* vencer, derrotar

vantage /ˈvæntɪdʒ, ˈvɑn-/ *n* ventaja (also in tennis), *f*. **v.-ground**, posición ventajosa, *f*, sitial de privilegio, *m*

vapid /ˈvæpɪd/ *a* insípido, insulso; (of speeches, etc.) soso, aburrido, insípido

vapidity /væˈpɪdɪti/ *n* insipidez, sosería, *f*

vapor /ˈveɪpər/ *n* vapor, *m*; *pl* **vapors**, (hysteria) vapores, *m pl*. —*vi* (boast) jactarse, baladronear; decir disparates. **v. bath**, baño de vapor, *m*

vaporize /ˈveɪpəˌraɪz/ *vt* vaporizar. —*vi* vaporizarse

vaporizer /ˈveɪpəˌraɪzər/ *n* vaporizador, *m*

vaporous /ˈveɪpərəs/ *a* vaporoso

variable /ˈvɛəriəbəl/ *a* variable. —*n Math.* variable, *f*

variance /ˈvɛəriəns/ *n* variación, *f*, cambio, *m*; desacuerdo, *m*, disensión, *f*; diferencia, contradicción, *f*. **at v.,** en desacuerdo, reñidos; hostil (a), opuesto (a); (of things) distinto (de), en contradicción (con)

variant /ˈvɛəriənt/ *n* variante, *f*

variation /ˌvɛəriˈeɪʃən/ *n* variación, *f*; cambio, *m*; variedad, *f*; diferencia, *f*; (*Mus.* magnetism) variación, *f*

varicose /ˈværɪˌkous/ *a* varicoso

varied success /ˈvɛərid/ éxito vario, *m*

variegate /ˈvɛəriˌgeɪt/ *vt* abigarrar, matizar, salpicar

variegated /ˈvɛəriˌgeɪtɪd/ *a* abigarrado; variado; mezclado

variety /vəˈraɪɪti/ *n* variedad, *f*; diversidad, *f*; (choice) surtido, *m*. **v. show**, función de variedades, *f*

various /ˈvɛəriəs/ *a* vario, diverso; diferente

variously /ˈvɛəriəsli/ *adv* diversamente

varnish /ˈvɑrnɪʃ/ *n* barniz, *m*. —*vt* barnizar; (pottery) vidriar; (conceal) disimular. **copal v.,** barniz copal, *m*. **japan v.,** charol japonés, *m*. **lacquer v.,** laca, *f*. **v. remover,** (for nails) quitaesmalte, *m*

varnishing /ˈvɑrnɪʃɪŋ/ *n* barnizado, *m*; (of pottery) vidriado, *m*

vary /ˈvɛəri/ *vt* variar; cambiar; diversificar; modificar. —*vi* variar; cambiar; (be different) ser distinto (de); (deviate) desviarse (de); (disagree) estar en desacuerdo, distar, estar en contradicción. **to v. directly (indirectly),** *Math.* variar en razón directa (inversa)

varying /ˈvɛəriŋ/ *a* variante, cambiante, diverso

vase /veis, veiz, vɑz/ *n* vaso, jarrón, *m*; urna, *f*

vaseline /ˈvæsəˌlin/ *n* vaselina, *f*

vast /væst/ *a* vasto, extenso; enorme; grande. —*n* vastedad, inmensidad, *f*

vat /væt/ *n* cuba, tina, *f*; alberca, *f*, estanque, *m*. **dyeing vat**, cuba de tintorero, *f*. **tanning vat**, noque, *m*. **wine vat**, lagar, *m*

Vatican /ˈvætɪkən/ *a* and *n* Vaticano, *m*

vaudeville /ˈvɔdvɪl/ *n* vodevil, *m*, zarzuela cómica, *f*

vault /vɔlt/ *n Archit.* bóveda, *f*; caverna, *f*; (for wine) bodega, cueva, *f*; (in a bank) cámara acorazada, *f*; (in a church) cripta, *f*; sepultura, *f*; (of the sky) bóveda celeste, *f*; (leap) salto, *m*; voltereta, *f*. —*vi* (jump) saltar; (with a pole) saltar con pértiga; saltar por encima de; voltear. —*vt Archit.* abovedar; saltar

vaulter /ˈvɔltər/ *n* saltador (-ra)

vaulting /ˈvɔltɪŋ/ *n* construcción de bóvedas, *f*; bóvedas, *f pl*; edificio abovedado, *m*; (jumping) salto, *m*. **v.-horse**, potro de madera, *m*

vaunt /vɔnt/ *vi* jactarse (de); hacer gala (de); triunfar (sobre). —*vt* ostentar, sacar a relucir; (praise) alabar. —*n* jactancia, *f*

veal /vil/ *n* ternera, *f*. **v.-cutlet**, chuleta de ternera, *f*

veer /vɪər/ *vi* (of the wind) girar; (of a ship) virar; *Fig.* cambiar (de opinión, etc.). —*vt* virar

vegetable /ˈvɛdʒtəbəl/ *n* vegetal, *m*; legumbre, *f*; *pl* **vegetables**, (green and generally cooked) verduras, *f pl*; (raw green) hortalizas, *f pl*. **v. dish**, fuente de legumbres, *f*. **v. garden**, huerto de legumbres, *m*; **v. ivory**, marfil vegetal, *m*. **v. kingdom**, reino vegetal, *m*. **v. soup**, sopa de hortelano, *f*

vegetal /ˈvɛdʒɪtl/ *a* vegetal

vegetarian /ˌvɛdʒɪˈtɛəriən/ *a* and *n* vegetariano (-na)

vegetate /ˈvɛdʒɪˌteɪt/ *vi* vegetar

vehemence /ˈviəməns/ *n* vehemencia, *f*; violencia, *f*; impetuosidad, *f*; pasión, *f*; ardor, *m*

vehement /ˈviəmənt/ *a* vehemente; violento; impetuoso; apasionado

vehemently /ˈviəməntli/ *adv* con vehemencia; violentamente; con impetuosidad; apasionadamente

vehicle /ˈviɪkəl/ *n* vehículo, *m*; (means) medio, *m*; instrumento, *m*

vehicular /viˈhɪkyələr/ *a* vehicular, de los vehículos o los coches. **v. traffic**, circulación de los coches, *f*, los vehículos

veil /veil/ *n* velo, *m*; (curtain) cortina, *f*; (disguise) disfraz, *m*; (excuse) pretexto, *m*; (appearance) apariencia, *f*. —*vt* velar; cubrir con un velo; (hide) tapar, encubrir; (dissemble) disimular; (disguise) disfrazar. **to take the v.,** tomar el velo, profesar

vein /vein/ *n* (*Anat.*, *Bot.*) vena, *f*; (*Geol.*, *Mineral.*) veta, *f*, filón, *m*; (in wood) fibra, hebra, f; (*Fig.* streak) rasgo, m; (inspiration) vena, f; (mood) humor, m

velocity /vəˈlɒsɪtɪ/ n velocidad, f; rapidez, f

velours /vəˈlʊr/ n terciopelo, m

velvet /ˈvɛlvɪt/ n terciopelo, m, a hecho de terciopelo; aterciopelado

vendor /ˈvɛndɔr/ n vendedor (-ra)

veneer /vəˈnɪər/ vt chapear, taracear; (conceal) disimular, disfrazar. —n taraceado, chapeado, m; (plate) chapa, hoja para chapear, f; (*Fig.* gloss) barniz, m, apariencia, f

venerate /ˈvɛnəˌreɪt/ vt venerar, reverenciar

venereal /vəˈnɪərɪəl/ a venéreo. **v. disease,** enfermedad venérea.

Venetian /vəˈniʃən/ a and n veneciano (-na). **v. blinds,** persianas, celosías, f pl

Venezuelan /ˌvɛnəˈzweɪlən/ a and n venezolano (-na)

vengeance /ˈvɛndʒəns/ n venganza, f

vengeful /ˈvɛndʒfəl/ a vengativo

venial /ˈvinɪəl/ a venial

Venice /ˈvɛnɪs/ Venecia, f

venom /ˈvɛnəm/ n veneno, m

venomous /ˈvɛnəməs/ a venenoso; maligno, malicioso

vent /vɛnt/ n abertura, f; salida, f; (airhole) respiradero, m; (in pipes) ventosa, f; (in fire-arms) oído, m; *Anat.* ano, m; (*Fig.* outlet) desahogo, m; expresión, f. —vt dejar escapar; (pierce) agujerear; (discharge) emitir, vomitar; (relieve) desahogar; expresar, dar expresión (a), dar rienda suelta (a)

ventilate /ˈvɛntlˌeɪt/ vt ventilar; discutir

ventilator /ˈvɛntlˌeɪtər/ n ventilador, m

ventricle /ˈvɛntrɪkəl/ n ventrículo, m

ventriloquist /vɛnˈtrɪləkwɪst/ n ventrílocuo (-ua)

venture /ˈvɛntʃər/ n ventura, f; riesgo, m; aventura, f; especulación, f. —vt arriesgar, aventurar; (stake) jugar; (state) expresar. —vi aventurarse; (dare) atreverse, osar; permitirse. **at a v.,** a la ventura. **to v. on,** arriesgarse a; probar ventura con; lanzarse a; (a remark) permitirse. **to v. out,** atreverse a salir

venturesome /ˈvɛntʃərsəm/ a atrevido, audaz; (dangerous) arriesgado, peligroso

Venus /ˈvinəs/ n (planet) Venus, m; (woman) venus, f

veracious /vəˈreɪʃəs/ a veraz, verídico; verdadero

veracity /vəˈræsɪtɪ/ n veracidad, f; verdad, f

veranda /vəˈrændə/ n veranda, f

verb /vɜrb/ n verbo, m. **auxiliary v.,** verbo auxiliar, m. **intransitive v.,** verbo intransitivo (neutro), m. **reflexive v.,** verbo reflexivo, m. **transitive v.,** verbo transitivo, m

verbal /ˈvɜrbəl/ a verbal

verbally /ˈvɜrbəlɪ/ adv de palabra, verbalmente

verbatim /vərˈbeɪtɪm/ a textual. —adv textualmente, palabra por palabra

verbiage /ˈvɜrbɪɪdʒ/ n verbosidad, palabrería, f

verbose /vərˈbous/ a verboso, prolijo

verdant /ˈvɜrdnt/ a verde

verdict /ˈvɜrdɪkt/ n *Law.* veredicto, fallo, m, sentencia, f; opinión, f, juicio, m. **to bring in a v.,** fallar sentencia.

verdure /ˈvɜrdʒər/ n verdura, f, verdor, m; *Fig.* lozanía, f

verge /vɜrdʒ/ n (wand) vara, f; (edge) margen, borde, m; (of a lake, etc.) orilla, f; (horizon) horizonte, m; *Fig.* víspera, f, punto, m. **on the v. of,** al margen de, a la orilla de. **to be on the v. of,** *Fig.* estar a punto de; estar en vísperas de

verifiable /ˌvɛrəˈfaiəbəl/ a verificable

verify /ˈvɛrəˌfai/ vt verificar, confirmar; probar

verily /ˈvɛrəlɪ/ adv de veras, en verdad

verisimilitude /ˌvɛrəsɪˈmɪlɪˌtud/ n verosimilitud, f

veritable /ˈvɛrɪtəbəl/ a verdadero

verity /ˈvɛrɪtɪ/ n verdad, f

vermicelli /ˌvɜrmɪˈtʃɛlɪ/ n fideos, m pl

vermilion /vərˈmɪljən/ n bermellón, m

vermin /ˈvɜrmɪn/ n bichos dañinos, m pl; (insects) parásitos, m pl

vermouth /vərˈmuθ/ n vermut, m

vernacular /vərˈnækjələr/ a vernáculo; nativo; vulgar. —n lengua popular, f; lenguaje vulgar, m

versatile /ˈvɜrsətl/ a *Zool.* versátil; inconstante, voluble; (clever) de muchos talentos; de muchos intereses; adaptable; completo, cabal

verse /vɜrs/ n verso, m; (stanza) estrofa, f; (in the Bible) versículo, m; (poetry) poesía, f, versos, m pl **to make verses,** escribir versos

versed /vɜrst/ a versado, experimentado

version /ˈvɜrʒən/ n versión, f; traducción, f; interpretación, f

versus /ˈvɜrsəs/ prep contra

vertebra /ˈvɜrtəbrə/ n vértebra, f

vertebrate /ˈvɜrtəbrɪt/ n vertebrado, m

vertical /ˈvɜrtɪkəl/ a vertical

vertiginous /vərˈtɪdʒənəs/ a vertiginoso

vertigo /ˈvɜrtɪˌgou/ n vértigo, m

verve /vɜrv/ n brío, m, fogosidad, f

very /ˈvɛrɪ/ a mismo; (mere) mero; (true) verdadero; (with adjective and comparative) más grande; *Inf.* mismísimo; (complete) perfecto, completo. **The v. thought of it made him laugh,** Sólo con pensarlo se rió (or La mera idea le hizo reír). **this v. minute,** este mismísimo instante. **the v. day,** el mismo día

very /ˈvɛrɪ/ adv muy; mucho; demasiado; (exactly) exactamente; completamente; absolutamente. **He is v. worried,** Está muy preocupado. **He is not v. well,** (i.e. rather ill) Está bastante bien. **This cloth is the v. best,** Esta tela es la mejor que hay. **I like it v. much,** Me gusta muchísimo. **He is v. much pleased,** Está muy contento. **so v. little,** tan poco; tan pequeño. **v. well,** muy bien

vesper /'vɛspər/ n estrella vespertina, f, héspero, m; pl **vespers,** Eccl. vísperas, f pl

vessel /'vɛsəl/ n vasija, f, recipiente, m; (boat) barco, buque, m; (Anat., Bot.) vaso, m

vest /vɛst/ n camiseta, f; (waistcoat) chaleco, m. —vt vestir; (with authority, etc.) revestir de; (property, etc.) hacer entrega de, ceder. —vi tener validez; (dress) vestirse. **vested interests,** intereses creados, m pl. **v.-pocket,** bolsillo del chaleco, m. **v.-pocket camera,** cámara de bolsillo, f

vestibule /'vɛstə,byul/ n vestíbulo, m; (anteroom) antecámara, f; (of a theatre box) antepalco, m; Anat. vestíbulo, m

vestige /'vɛstɪdʒ/ n vestigio, rastro, m; sombra, f; Biol. rudimento, m

vestry /'vɛstri/ n vestuario, m, sacristía, f

veteran /'vɛtərən/ a veterano; de los veteranos; aguerrido; anciano; experimentado. —n veterano (-na)

veterinary /'vɛtərə,nɛri/ a veterinario. **v. science,** veterinaria, f. **v. surgeon,** veterinario, m

veto /'vitou/ n veto, m; prohibición, f. —vt poner el veto; prohibir

vex /vɛks/ vt contrariar, irritar; enojar; (make impatient) impacientar; fastidiar; (afflict) afligir, acongojar; (worry) inquietar

vexation /vɛk'seiʃən/ n contrariedad, irritación, f; enojo, enfado, m; (impatience) impaciencia, f; fastidio, m; aflicción, f; inquietud, f; disgusto, m

vexatious /vɛk'seiʃəs/ a irritante; enojoso, enfadoso; fastidioso, molesto

vexed /vɛkst/ a discutido; contencioso; (thorny) espinoso, difícil

vexing /'vɛksɪŋ/ a irritante; molesto; enfadoso

via /'vaiə, 'viə/ n vía, f, prep por, por la vía de

viable /'vaiəbəl/ a viable

viaduct /'vaiə,dʌkt/ n viaducto, m

vial /'vaiəl/ n frasco, m, ampolleta, f

vibrant /'vaibrənt/ a vibrante

vibrate /'vaibreit/ vi vibrar; (of machines) trepidar; oscilar. —vt hacer vibrar, vibrar

vibration /vai'breiʃən/ n vibración, f; trepidación, f; oscilación, f

vibrator /'vaibreitər/ n Elec. vibrador, m; Radio. oscilador, m

vicarious /vai'kɛəriəs/ a vicario; sufrido por otro; experimentado por otro

vicariously /vai'kɛəriəsli/ adv por delegación; por substitución. **I know it only vicariously,** Lo conozco sólo por referencia

vice /vais/ n vicio, m; defecto, m; (in a horse) vicio, resabio, m; (tool) tornillo de banco, m, prefix vice. **v.-admiral,** vicealmirante, m. **v.-chairman,** vice-presidente (-ta). **v.-chancellor,** vicecanciller, m. **v.-**

consul, vice-cónsul, m. **v.-consulate,** vice-consulado, m. **v.-president,** vicepresidente (-ta)

viceroy /'vaisrɔi/ n virrey, m

vice versa /'vaisə,vɜrsə, 'vais-/ adv viceversa

vicinity /vɪ'sɪnɪti/ n vecindad, f; (nearness) cercanía, proximidad, f. **to be in the v. of,** estar en la vecindad de

vicious /'vɪʃəs/ a vicioso. **v. circle,** círculo vicioso, m

vicissitude /vɪ'sɪsɪ,tud/ n vicisitud, f

victim /'vɪktəm/ n víctima, f

victimize /'vɪktə,maiz/ vt hacer víctima (de); sacrificar; ser víctima (de), sufrir; (cheat) estafar, engañar

victor /'vɪktər/ n víctor, vencedor, m

victorious /vɪk'tɔriəs/ a victorioso, triunfante. **to be v.,** triunfar, salir victorioso

victory /'vɪktəri/ n victoria, f

victual /'vɪtl/ n vitualla, vianda, f; pl **victuals,** víveres, m pl, provisiones, f pl. —vt avituallar; abastecer. —vi tomar provisiones

victualler /'vɪtlər/ n abastecedor (-ra), proveedor (-ra)

vide /waidə, 'vaidi, 'videi/ Latin imperative véase, véanse

video /'vidi,ou/, n vídeo, m

videotape /'vidiou,teip/ n videograbación, videocinta, f

vie /vai/ vi (with) competir con; rivalizar con; (with a person for) disputar; luchar con

Vienna /vi'ɛnə/ Viena, f

view /vyu/ n vista, f; perspectiva, f, panorama, m; (landscape) paisaje, m; escena, f; inspección, f; (judgment) opinión, f, parecer, m; consideración, f; (appearance) apariencia, f; aspecto, m; (purpose) propósito, m, intención, f; (sight) alcance de la vista, m; (show) exposición, f. —vt examinar; inspeccionar; (look at) mirar; (see) ver, contemplar; considerar. **in v. of,** en vista de. **in my v.,** en mi opinión, segun creo yo. **on v.,** a la vista. **to keep in v.,** no perder de vista; Fig. no olvidar, tener presente. **to take a different v.,** pensar de un modo distinto. **to v. a house,** inspeccionar una casa. **with a v. to,** con el propósito de. **v.-finder,** enfocador, m. **v.-point,** punto de vista, m

viewer /'vyuər/ n espectador (-ra); examinador (-rà)

vigil /'vɪdʒəl/ n vela, vigilia, f; Eccl. vigilia, f

vigilance /'vɪdʒələns/ n vigilancia, f, desvelo, m

vigilant /'vɪdʒələnt/ a vigilante, desvelado

vignette /vɪn'yɛt/ n viñeta, f

vigor /'vɪgər/ n vigor, m, fuerza, f

vigorous /'vɪgərəs/ a vigoroso, enérgico, fuerte

vigorously /'vɪgərəsli/ adv con vigor

Viking /'vaikɪŋ/ n vikingo, m

vile /vail/ a vil; bajo; despreciable; infame; *Inf.* horrible

vilification /ˌvɪləfɪ'keɪʃən/ n vilipendio, m, difamación, f

vilifier /'vɪləˌfaɪər/ n difamador (-ra)

vilify /'vɪləˌfaɪ/ vt vilipendiar, difamar

villa /'vɪlə/ n villa, torre, casa de campo, f; hotel, m

village /'vɪlɪdʒ/ n aldea, f, pueblo, m

villager /'vɪlɪdʒər/ n aldeano (-na)

villain /'vɪlən/ n *Hist.* villano, m; malvado, m

villainous /'vɪlənəs/ a malvado; infame; vil

villainy /'vɪləni/ n vileza, infamia, maldad, f

vindicate /'vɪndɪˌkeɪt/ vt vindicar, justificar; defender

vindictive /vɪn'dɪktɪv/ a vengativo; rencoroso

vindictiveness /vɪn'dɪktɪvnɪs/ n deseo de venganza, m; rencor, m

vine /vaɪn/ n vid, parra, f; (twining plant) enredadera, f. **v.-arbor,** emparrado, m. **v.-branch,** sarmiento, m. **v.-clad,** cubierto de parras. **v.-grower,** vinicultor, m. **v.-growing,** vinicultura, f. **v.-leaf,** hoja de parra, f. **v.-pest,** filoxera, f. **v.-stock,** cepa, f

vinegar /'vɪnɪgər/ n vinagre, m. **v.-cruet,** vinagrera, f. **v.-sauce,** vinagreta, f

vineyard /'vɪnyərd/ n viña, f, viñedo, m. **v.-keeper,** viñador, m

vinous /'vaɪnəs/ a vinoso

vintage /'vɪntɪdʒ/ n vendimia, f; (of wine) cosecha (de vino), f

vintner /'vɪntnər/ n vinatero, m

violate /'vaɪəˌleɪt/ vt (desecrate) profanar; (infringe) contravenir, infringir; (break) romper; (ravish) violar

violation /ˌvaɪə'leɪʃən/ n profanación, f; (infringement) contravención, f; (rape) violación, f

violence /'vaɪələns/ n violencia, f

violent /'vaɪələnt/ a violento

violently /'vaɪələntli/ adv con violencia

violet /'vaɪəlɪt/ n violeta, f. —a violado, v. color, violeta, color violado, m

violin /ˌvaɪə'lɪn/ n violín, m

violinist /ˌvaɪə'lɪnɪst/ n violinista, mf

violoncello /ˌvaɪələn'tʃɛlou/ n violoncelo, m

viper /'vaɪpər/ n víbora, f

virgin /'vɜrdʒɪn/ n virgen, f; (sign of the zodiac) Virgo, m. —a virginal; (untouched) virgen. **the V.,** la Virgen. **v. soil,** tierra virgen, f

virginity /vər'dʒɪnɪti/ n virginidad, f

virile /'vɪrəl/ a viril

virility /və'rɪlɪti/ n virilidad, f

virtual /'vɜrtʃuəl/ a virtual

virtue /'vɜrtʃu/ n virtud, f

virtuosity /ˌvɜrtʃu'ɒsɪti/ n virtuosidad, f

virtuoso /ˌvɜrtʃu'ousou/ n virtuoso (-sa)

virtuous /'vɜrtʃuəs/ a virtuoso

virulent /'vɪryələnt/ a virulento

virus /'vaɪrəs/ n virus, m

visa /'vizə/ n visado, m

visage /'vɪzɪdʒ/ n cara, f, rostro, m; semblante, aspecto, m

viscera /'vɪsərə/ n víscera, f

viscous /'vɪskəs/ a viscoso

visé /'vizei/ n visado, m, vt visar

visibility /ˌvɪzə'bɪlɪti/ n visibilidad, f. **poor v.,** mala visibilidad, f

visible /'vɪzəbəl/ a visible; aparente, evidente

vision /'vɪʒən/ n visión, f; (eyesight) vista, f. **field of v.,** campo visual, m

visionary /'vɪʒəˌnɛri/ a and n visionario (-ia)

visit /'vɪzɪt/ n visita, f; (inspection) inspección, f; (doctor's) visita de médico, f. —vt visitar; hacer una visita (a); ir a ver; inspeccionar; (frequent) frecuentar; (Biblical) visitar. **to be visited by an epidemic,** sufrir una epidemia. **to go visiting,** ir de visita. **to pay a v.,** hacer una visita

visitation /ˌvɪzɪ'teɪʃən/ n visita, f; *Eccl.* visitación, f; (inspection) inspección, f; (punishment) castigo, m

visiting /'vɪzɪtɪŋ/ a de visita. **v. card,** tarjeta de visita, f. **v. card case,** tarjetero, m. **visiting hours,** horas de visita, f pl

visitor /'vɪzɪtər/ n visita, f; (official) visitador, m

visor /'vaɪzər/ n víscera, f

vista /'vɪstə/ n vista, perspectiva, f

visual /'vɪʒuəl/ a visual. **the v. arts,** las artes visuales

visualize /'vɪʒuəˌlaɪz/ vt and vi imaginarse, ver mentalmente

vital /'vaɪtl/ a vital; esencial; trascendental

vitality /vaɪ'tælɪti/ n vitalidad, f

vitamin /'vaɪtəmɪn/ n vitamina, f

vitiate /'vɪʃiˌeɪt/ vt viciar; corromper, contaminar

vitriolic /ˌvɪtri'ɒlɪk/ a vitriólico

vituperate /vaɪ'tupəˌreɪt/ vt vituperar

vituperation /vaɪˌtupə'reɪʃən/ n vituperio, m

vivacious /vɪ'veɪʃəs, vaɪ-/ a animado, vivaracho

vivacity /vɪ'væsɪti, vaɪ-/ n vivacidad, animación, f

viva voce /'vaɪvə vousi, 'vivə/ a oral. —n examen oral, m

vivid /'vɪvɪd/ a vivo; brillante; intenso; (of descriptions, etc.) gráfico

vividness /'vɪvɪdnɪs/ n vivacidad, f; intensidad, f; (strength) fuerza, f

vivify /'vɪvəˌfaɪ/ vt vivificar, avivar

vivisection /ˌvɪvə'sɛkʃən/ n vivisección, f

vixen /'vɪksən/ n raposa, zorra, f; (woman) arpía, f

viz. a saber

vocabulary /vou'kæbyəˌlɛri/ n vocabulario, m

vocal /'voukəl/ a vocal. **v. cords,** cuerdas vocales, f pl

vocalist /'voukəlıst/ n cantante, mf. voz, f

vocation /vou'keiʃən/ n vocación, f; oficio, m; empleo, m; profesión, f

vocational /vou'keiʃənl/ a profesional; práctico. **vocational guidance**, guía vocacional, orientación profesional, f. **v. training**, instrucción práctica, f; enseñanza de oficio, f

vociferate /vou'sıfə,reit/ vt gritar. —vi vociferar, vocear

vociferous /vou'sıfərəs/ a (noisy) ruidoso; vocinglero, clamoroso

vodka /'vɒdkə/ n vodca, m

vogue /voug/ n moda, f. **in v.**, en boga, de moda

voice /vɔis/ n voz, f. —vt expresar, interpretar, hacerse eco de; hablar. **in a loud v.**, en voz alta. **in a low v.**, en voz baja

void /vɔid/ a (empty) vacío; (vacant) vacante; deshabitado; (lacking in) privado (de), desprovisto (de); (without) sin; Law. inválido, nulo; sin valor. —n vacío, m. —vt evacuar; Law. anular; invalidar

voile /vɔil/ n espumilla, f

volatile /'vɒlətl/ a volátil; (light) ligero; (changeable) mudable, inconstante

volatility /,vɒlə'tılıti/ n volatilidad, f; ligereza, f; volubilidad, f

volcanic /vɒl'kænık/ a volcánico

volcano /vɒl'keinou/ n volcán, m. **extinct v.**, volcán extinto, m

volition /vou'lıʃən/ n volición, f; voluntad, f

volley /'vɒli/ n (of stones, etc.) lluvia, f; (of fire-arms) descarga, f; (of cannon, naval guns) andanada, f; Sports. voleo, m; (of words, etc.) torrente, m; (of applause and as a salute) salva, f. —vt Sports. volear; (abuse, etc.) dirigir. —vi lanzar una descarga, hacer una descarga

volt /voult/ n Elec. voltio, m; (of a horse and in fencing) vuelta, f. **v.-ampere**, voltamperio, m

voltage /'voultıdʒ/ n voltaje, m. **v. control**, mando del voltaje, m

voluble /'vɒlyəbəl/ a gárrulo, locuaz

volume /'vɒlyum/ n (book) tomo, m; (amount, size, space) volumen, m; (of water) caudal (de río), m; (mass) masa, f; (of smoke) humareda, f, nubes de humo, f pl

voluminous /və'lumənəs/ a voluminoso

voluntary /'vɒlən,teri/ a voluntario; espontáneo; libre; (charitable) benéfico; (intentional) intencional, deliberado. —n solo de órgano, m

volunteer /,vɒlən'tıər/ n Mil. voluntario (-ia). —a de voluntarios. —vt ofrecer; contribuir; expresar. —vi ofrecerse para hacer algo; Mil. alistarse, ofrecerse a servir como voluntario

voluptuous /və'lʌptʃuəs/ a voluptuoso

vomit /'vɒmit/ vt and vi vomitar; arrojar, devolver. —n vómito, m

voodoo /'vudu/ n vudú, m

voracious /vɔ'reiʃəs/ a voraz

vortex /'vɔrteks/ n torbellino, m, vorágine, f; Fig. vórtice, m

vote /vout/ n voto, m; (voting) votación, f; (suffrage) sufragio, m; (election) elección, f. —vt votar; asignar; nombrar; elegir; (consider) tener por. —vi votar, dar el voto. **casting v.**, voto de calidad, m. **to put to the v.**, poner a votación. **to v. down**, desechar, rechazar. **v. of confidence**, voto de confianza, m. **v. of thanks**, voto de gracias, m

voter /'voutər/ n votante, mf, votador (-ra); elector (-ra)

voting /'voutıŋ/ n votación, f; elección, f. —a de votar; electoral. **v. paper**, papeleta de votación, f

votive /'voutıv/ a votivo. **v. offering**, exvoto, m

vouch /vautʃ/ vi atestiguar, afirmar; garantizar; responder (de)

voucher /'vautʃər/ n (guarantor) fiador (-ra); (guarantee) garantía, f; (receipt) recibo, m; (proof) prueba, f; documento justificativo, m; vale, bono, m

vouchsafe /vautʃ'seif/ vt conceder, otorgar

vow /vau/ n voto, m; promesa solemne, f. —vt hacer voto (de), hacer promesa solemne (de); jurar. **to take a vow**, hacer un voto

vowel /'vauəl/ n vocal, f

voyage /'vɔiıdʒ/ n viaje (por mar), m; travesía, f. —vi viajar por mar. **Good v.!** ¡Buen viaje!, Feliz viaje!

voyager /'vɔiıdʒər/ n viajero (-ra)

vulgar /'vʌlgər/ a vulgar; (ill-bred) ordinario, cursi; (in bad taste) de mal gusto; trivial; adocenado; (coarse) grosero. —n vulgo, populacho, m. **v. fraction**, fracción común, f

vulgarism /'vʌlgə,rızəm/ n vulgarismo, m; vulgaridad, f

vulgarity /vʌl'gærıti/ n vulgaridad, f; grosería, f; mal tono, m, cursilería, f

Vulgate /'vʌlgeit/ n Vulgata, f

vulture /'vʌltʃər/ n buitre, m

w /'dʌbəl,yu/ n ve doble, f
wabble /'wɒbəl/ vi. See **wobble**
wad /wɒd/ n (of straw, etc.) atado, m; (of notes, etc.) rollo, m; (in a gun) taco, m. —vt Sew. acolchar; (furniture) emborrar; (guns) atacar; (stuff) rellenar
wadding /'wɒdɪŋ/ n borra, f; (lining) entretela, f; (for guns) taco, m; (stuffing) relleno, m
waddle /'wɒdl/ n anadeo, m, vi anadear
wade /weid/ vi and vt andar (en el agua, etc.); vadear; (paddle) chapotear. **to w. in**, entrar en (el agua, etc.); Fig. meterse en. **to w. through**, (a book) leer con dificultad; estudiar detenidamente; ir por
wafer /'weifər/ n (host) hostia, f; (for sealing) oblea, f; (for ices) barquillo, m
waffle /'wɒfəl/ n Cul. fruta de sartén, f
waft /wɒft/ vt llevar por el aire o encima del agua; hacer flotar; (stir) mecer; (of the wind) traer. —n (fragrance) ráfaga de olor, f
wag /wæg/ n (of the tail) coleada, f; movimiento, m; meneo, m; (jester) bromista, m/f. —vt mover ligeramente; agitar; (of the tail) menear (la cola), colear. —vi menearse; moverse; oscilar; (of the world) ir. **And thus the world wags**, Y así va el mundo
wage /weidʒ/ vt emprender; sostener; hacer. **to w. war**, hacer guerra. —n pl. **wages**, salario, m
wager /'weidʒər/ n (bet) apuesta, f; (test) prueba, f, vt (bet) apostar; (pledge) empeñar. **to lay a w.**, hacer una apuesta
waggish /'wægɪʃ/ a zumbón, jocoso; cómico
waggle /'wægəl/ vt menear; mover; agitar; oscilar. —vi menearse; moverse; agitarse; oscilar. —n meneo, movimiento, m; oscilación, f
wagon /'wægən/ n carro, m; carreta, f; (railway) vagón, m. **w.-lit**, coche cama, m. **w.-load**, carretada, f; vagón, m
waif /weif/ n niño (-ña) sin hogar; animal perdido o abandonado, m; objeto extraviado, m; objeto sin dueño, m. **waifs and strays**, niños abandonados, m pl
wail /weil/ n lamento, gemido, m; (complaint) queja, f. —vi lamentarse, gemir; quejarse (de). —vt lamentar, deplorar
wainscot /'weinskət, -skɒt/ n entablado de madera, m. —vt enmaderar; poner friso de madera (á)
waist /weist/ n cintura, f; (blouse) blusa, f; (belt) cinturón, m; (bodice) corpiño, m; (narrowest portion) cuello, m, garganta, f; Naut. combés, m. **w.-band**, pretina, f. **w.-deep**, hasta la cintura. **w.-line**, cintura, f. **w. measurement**, medida de la cintura, f. **w.-coat**, chaleco, m. **w. strap**, trincha, f
wait /weit/ vi and vt esperar, aguardar; (serve) servir. **to keep waiting**, hacer esperar. **to w. at table**, servir a la mesa. **to w. on oneself**, servirse a sí mismo; cuidarse a sí mismo; hacer las cosas por sí solo. **to w. one's time**, aguardar la

ocasión. **to w. for**, (until) esperar hasta que; (of persons) esperar (a), aguardar (a); (in ambush) acechar. **to w. upon**, (serve) servir (a); (visit) visitar; (present sus respetos (a); (Fig. accompany) acompañar; (follow) seguir a
wait /weit/ n espera, f; (pause) pausa, f, intervalo, m; (ambush) asechanza, f; pl **waits**, coro de nochebuena, m. **to lie in w. for**, estar en acecho para
waiter /'weitər/ n camarero, mozo, m; (tray) bandeja, f
waiting /'weitɪŋ/ n espera, f. —a que espera; de espera; de servicio. **lady-in-w.**, dama de servicio, f. **w.-maid**, camarera, doncella, f. **w.-room**, (of a bus station, etc.) sala de espera, f; (of an office) antesala, f
waitress /'weitrɪs/ n camarera, f
waive /weiv/ vt renunciar (a); desistir (de)
wake /weik/ vi estar despierto; despertarse; (watch) velar. —vt despertar; (a corpse) velar. —n vela, f; vigilia, f; (of a corpse) velatorio, m; (holiday) fiesta, f; (of a ship) estela, f. **in the w. of**, Naut. en la estela de; después de; seguido por
wakeful /'weikfəl/ a vigilante; (awake) despierto. **to be w.**, pasar la noche en vela
waken /'weikən/ vi despertarse. —vt despertar; (call) llamar
waking /'weikɪŋ/ a despierto; de vela. —n despertar, m; (watching) vela, f
wale /weil/ n (weal) verdugo, m, huella de azote, f, vt azotar
Wales /weilz/ (País de) Gales, m
walk /wɔk/ n (pace) paso, m; (modo de andar, m; (journey on foot) paseo, m, vuelta, f; (long) caminata, f; (promenade) paseo, m, avenida, f; (path) senda, f; (rank) clase social, f; esfera, f; profesión, f; ocupación, f. **quick w.**, paseo rápido, m; (pace) andar rápido, m. **to go for a w.**, ir de paseo. **to take a w.**, dar un paseo (or una vuelta), pasear. **to take for a w.**, llevar a paseo, sacar a paseo. **w.-out**, (strike) huelga, f. **w.-over**, triunfo, m, (or victoria, f) fácil. **w. past**, desfile, m
walk /wɔk/ vi andar; caminar; ir a pie; (take a walk) pasear, dar un paseo; (of ghosts) aparecer; (behave) conducirse. —vt hacer andar; (take for a walk) sacar a paseo; andar de una parte a otra (de), recorrer; (a specified distance) hacer a pie, andar; (a horse) llevar al paso. **to w. abroad**, dar un paseo; salir. **to w. arm in arm**, ir de bracero. **to w. past**, pasar; (in procession) desfilar. **to w. quickly**, andar de prisa. **to w. slowly**, andar despacio, andar lentamente. **to w. the hospitals**, estudiar en los hospitales. **to w. the streets**, recorrer las calles; vagar por

las calles. **to w. about,** pasearse; ir y venir. **to w. after,** seguir (a), ir detrás de. **to w. along,** andar por; recorrer. **to w. away,** marcharse, irse. **to w. away with,** (win) ganar, llevarse; (steal) quitar, tomar, alzarse con. **to w. back,** volver; volver a pie, regresar a pie. **to w. down,** bajar; bajar a pie; andar por. **to w. in,** entrar en; entrar a pie en; (walk about) pasearse en. **to w. on,** seguir andando; (step on) pisar. **to w. out,** salir. **to w. over,** andar por; llevar la victoria (a); triunfar fácilmente sobre. **to w. round,** dar la vuelta a. **to w. round and round,** dar vueltas. **to w. up,** subir andando; subir. **to w. up and down,** dar vueltas, ir y venir

walker /'wɔkər/ n (pedestrian) peatón, m; andador (-ra); (promenader) paseante, mf

walking /'wɔkɪŋ/ n el andar; (excursion on foot) paseo, m. —a andante; de andar; a pie; ambulante. **at a w. pace,** a un paso de andadura. **w. encyclopedia,** enciclopedia ambulante, f. **w. match,** marcha atlética, f. **w.-stick,** bastón, m. **w. tour,** excursión a pie, f

wall /wɔl/ n muro, m; (rampart) muralla, f; (Fig. and of an organ, cavity, etc.) pared, f. **partition w.,** tabique, m. **Walls have ears,** Las paredes oyen. **w. lizard,** lagartija, f. **w. map,** mapa mural, m. **w.-painting,** pintura mural, f. **w.-paper,** papel pintado, m. **w. socket,** Elec. enchufe, m

wall /wɔl/ vt cercar con un muro; amurallar. **to w. in,** murar. **to w. up,** tapiar, tabicar

wallet /'wɒlɪt/ n cartera, f; bolsa de cuero, f

wallop /'wɒləp/ n golpe, m, vt tundir, zurrar

wallow /'wɒlou/ vi revolcarse; encenagarse; (in riches, etc.) nadar (en). —n revuelco, m

walnut /'wɔl,nʌt/ n (tree and wood) nogal, m; (nut) nuez de nogal, f

walrus /'wɔlrəs/ n morsa, f

waltz /wɔlts/ n vals, m, vi valsar

wan /wɑn/ a ojeroso, descolorido; (of the sky, etc.) pálido, sin color

wand /wɒnd/ n vara, f; (conductor's) batuta, f. **magic w.,** varita mágica, f

wander /'wɒndər/ vi errar, vagar; (deviate) extraviarse; (from the subject) desviarse del asunto; divagar; (be delirious) delirar. —vt vagar por, errar por, recorrer

wanderer /'wɒndərər/ n vagabundo (-da); hombre, m. (f, mujer) errante; (traveler) viajero (-ra)

wandering /'wɒndərɪŋ/ a errante; vagabundo; nómada; (traveling) viajero; (delirious) delirante; (of thoughts, the mind) distraído; (of cells, kidneys, etc.) flotante. —n vagancia, f; viaje, m; (delirium) delirio, m; (digression) divagación, f; (of a river, etc.) meandro, m. **the w. Jew,** el judío errante

wane /wein/ vi (of the moon, etc.) menguar; (decrease) disminuir; (Fig. decay) decaer. —n (of the moon) menguante de la luna, f; mengua, f; disminución, f; decadencia, f

waning /'weinɪŋ/ a menguante

wanly /'wɒnli/ adv pálidamente; Fig. tristemente

want /wɒnt/ vt (lack) carecer de, faltar; (need) necesitar, haber menester de; (require or wish) querer, desear; (demand) exigir; (ought) deber; (do without) pasarse sin. —vi hacer falta; carecer (de); (be poor) estar necesitado. **I don't w. to,** No quiero, No me da la gana. **to be wanted,** hacer falta; (called) ser llamado. **You are wanted on the telephone,** Te llaman por teléfono

want /wɒnt/ n (lack) falta, f; escasez, carestía, f; (need) necesidad, f; (poverty) pobreza, indigencia, f; (absence) ausencia, f; (wish) deseo, m; exigencia, f. **in w. of,** por falta de; en la ausencia de. **to be in w.,** estar en la necesidad, ser indigente

wanted /'wɒntɪd/ se necesita; (advertisement) demanda, f. **Estelle wants me to write a letter,** Estrella quiere que escriba una carta. **What do you w. me to do?** ¿Qué quiere Vd. que haga?; ¿En qué puedo servirle? **What does Paul w.?** ¿Qué quiere Pablo?; (require) ¿Qué necesita Pablo? **He wants (needs) a holiday,** Le hacen falta unas vacaciones, Necesita unas vacaciones

wanting /'wɒntɪŋ/ a deficiente (en); falto (de); (scarce) escaso; ausente; (in intelligence) menguado. —prep (less) menos; (without) sin. **to be w.,** faltar. **to be w. in,** carecer de

wanton /'wɒntn/ a (playful) juguetón; (wilful) travieso; (loose) suelto, libre; (unrestrained) desenfrenado; extravagante; excesivo; caprichoso; (dishevelled) en desorden; (reckless) indiscreto; (of vegetation) lozano; (purposeless) inútil; imperdonable; frívolo; (unchaste) disoluto; lascivo. —n mujer disoluta, f; ramera, f; (child) niño (-ña) juguetón (-ona)

wantonly /'wɒntnli/ adv innecesariamente; sin motivo; excesivamente; lascivamente

war /wɔr/ n guerra, f. —a de guerra; guerrero. —vi guerrear. **at war with,** en guerra con. **cold war,** guerra tonta, f. **on a war footing,** en pie de guerra. **We are at war,** Estamos en guerra. **to be on the war-path,** Fig. Inf. buscar pendencia, tratar de armarla. **to declare war on,** declarar la guerra (a). **to make war on,** hacer la guerra (a). **war to the death,** guerra a muerte, **war correspondent,** corresponsal en el teatro de guerra, m. **war-cry,** alarido de guerra, grito de combate, grito de guerra m. **war-dance,** danza guerrera, f. **war horse,** caballo de batalla, m. **war loan,** empréstito de guerra, m. **war-lord,** adalid, caudillo, jefe militar, m. **war ma-**

terial, pertrechos de guerra, *m pl*; municiones, *f pl.* **war memorial,** monumento a los caídos, *m.* **war minister,** Ministro de la Guerra, *m.* **war neurosis,** neurosis de guerra, *f.* **War Office,** Ministerio de la Guerra, *m.* **war plane,** avión de guerra, *m.* **war-ship,** barco (or buque) de guerra, *m.* **war-wearied,** agotado por la guerra

warble /'worbəl/ *vt* and *vi* trinar; gorjear; murmurar. —*n* trino, *m*; gorjeo, *m*; murmurio, *m*

ward /word/ *n* protección, *f*; (of a minor) pupilo (-la); (of locks, keys) guarda, *f*; (of a city) barrio, distrito, *m*; (of a hospital, etc.) sala, *f*; (of a prison) celda, *f*; (fencing) guardia, *f.* **w.-room,** cuarto de los oficiales, *m.* **w. sister,** hermana de una sala de hospital, *f*

ward /word/ *vt* proteger, defender. **to w. off,** desviar; evitar

warden /'wordn/ *n* guardián, *m*; director (-ra); (of a prison) alcaide, *m*; (of a church) mayordomo de la iglesia, *m*; (of a port) capitán, *m*

wardrobe /'wordroub/ *n* guardarropa, ropero, *m*; (clothes) ropa, *f*; *Theat.* vestuario, *m.* **w. trunk,** baúl mundo, *m*

ware /wɛər/ *n* mercadería, *f*; (pottery) loza, *f*; *pl* **wares,** mercancías, *f pl*

war effort *n* esfuerzo bélico, esfuerzo de guerra, esfuerzo guerrero, *m*

warehouse /n. 'wɛərˌhaus; v. -ˌhauz/ *n* almacén, *m*, *vt* almacenar

warfare /'worˌfɛər/ *n* guerra, *f*; lucha, *f*; arte militar, *m*, or *f.* **chemical w.,** guerra química, *f*

war head *n* (of torpedo) cabeza de combate, punto de combate, *f*; (of missile) detonante, *m*

war heroine *n* heroína de guerra, *f*

warily /'wɛərəli/ *adv* con cautela, cautelosamente; prudentemente

wariness /'wɛərinis/ *n* cautela *f*; prudencia, *f*

warlike /'worˌlaik/ *a* belicoso, guerrero; militar, de guerra; marcial. **war-spirit,** espíritu belicoso, *m*, marcialidad, *f*

warm /worm/ *a* caliente; (lukewarm) tibio; (hot) caluroso; (affectionate) cordial, cariñoso, afectuoso; (angry) acalorado; (enthusiastic) entusiasta, ardiente; (art) cálido; (of coats, etc.) de abrigo; (fresh) fresco, reciente; *Inf.* adinerado. —*vt* calentar; *Fig.* encender; entusiasmar. —*vi* calentarse; *Fig.* entusiasmarse (con). **to have a w. at the fire,** calentarse al lado del fuego. **to be w.,** (of things) estar caliente; (of coats, etc.) ser de abrigo; (of the weather) hacer calor; (of people) tener calor. **to grow w.,** calentarse; (grow angry) excitarse, agitarse; (of a discussion) hacerse acalorado. **to keep w.,** conservar caliente; calentar. **to keep oneself w.,** estar caliente, no enfriarse. **to w. up,** calentar. **w.-blooded,** de sangre caliente; ardiente. **w.-hearted,** de buen corazón; generoso; afectuoso, cor-

dial. **w.-heartedness,** buen corazón, *m*; generosidad, *f*; cordialidad, *f*

warming /'wormɪŋ/ *n* calentamiento, *m*; calefacción, *f.* —*a* calentador; para calentar. **w.-pan,** calentador, *m*

warmly /'wormli/ *adv* (affectionately) cordialmente, afectuosamente; con entusiasmo; (angrily) acaloradamente. **to be w. wrapped up,** estar bien abrigado

warmonger /'worˌmʌŋgər/ *n* atizador de guerra, belicista, fautor de guerra, fomentador de guerra, propagador (-ra) de guerra

warmth /wormθ/ *n* calor, *m*

warn /worn/ *vt* advertir; prevenir; amonestar; (inform) avisar

warning /'wornɪŋ/ *n* advertencia, *f*; aviso, *m*; amonestación, *f*; (lesson) lección, *f*, escarmiento, *m*; alarma, *f.* —*a* amonestador; de alarma. **to give w.,** prevenir, advertir; (dismiss) despedir. **to take w.,** escarmentar

warp /worp/ *vt* torcer; combar; *Naut.* espiar; (the mind) pervertir. —*vi* torcerse; combarse, bornearse; *Naut.* espiarse. —*n* (in a fabric) urdimbre, *f*; (in wood) comba, *f*, torcimiento, *m*; *Naut.* espía, *f.* **w. and woof,** trama y urdimbre, *f*

warping /'worpɪŋ/ *n* (of wood) combadura, *f*; (weaving) urdidura, *f*; *Naut.* espía, *f*; (of the mind) perversión, *f.* **w. frame,** urdidera, *f*

warrant /'worant, 'wor-/ *n* autoridad, *f*; justificación, *f*; autorización, *f*; garantía, *f*; decreto de prisión, *m*; orden, *f*; *Com.* orden de pago, *f*; *Mil.* nombramiento, *m*; motivo, *m*, razón, *f.* —*vt* justificar; autorizar; garantizar, responder por; asegurar. **pay w.,** boletín de pago, *m*

warranty /'worǝnti/ *n* autorización, *f*; justificación, *f*; *Law.* garantía, *f*

warren /'worǝn/ *n* (for hunting) vedado, *m*; (rabbit) conejera, *f*; vivar, *m*, madriguera, *f*

warrior /'worɪər/ *n* guerrero, *m*; soldado, *m*

Warsaw /'worsɔ/ Varsovia, *f*

wart /wort/ *n* verruga, *f*

wary /'wɛəri/ *a* cauto, cauteloso; prudente

wash /wɒʃ/ *vt* lavar; (dishes) fregar; (lave) bañar; (clean) limpiar; (furrow) surcar; (wet) regar, humedecer; (with paint) dar una capa de color o de metal. —*vi* lavarse; lavar ropa. **Two of the crew were washed overboard,** El mar arrastró a dos de los tripulantes. **Will this material w.?** ¿Se puede lavar esta tela? ¿Es lavable esta tela? **to w. ashore,** echar a la playa. **w. away,** (remove by washing) quitar lavando; derrubiar; (water or waves) arrastrar, llevarse. **to w. one's hands,** lavarse las manos. **to look washed out,** estar ojeroso. **to w. down,** lavar; limpiar; (remove) llevarse; (accompany with drink) regar. **to w. off,** *vt* quitar lavando; hacer desaparecer; borrar; (of waves, etc.) llevarse; (of color) desteñir. —*vi* borrarse; desteñirse. **to w. up,** lavar los platos, fregar la vajilla; (cast up) desechar. **w. one's dirty laundry in public,** sacar los más sucios trapillos a la colada

wash /wɒʃ/ *n* lavadura, *f*, lavado, *m;* baño, *m;* (clothes) ropa para lavar, ropa sucia, *f;* colada, *f;* (of the waves) chapoteo, *m;* (lotion) loción, *f;* (coating) capa, *f;* (silt) aluvión, *m.* **w.-basin,** palangana, *f.* **w.-board,** tabla de lavar, *f.* **w.-house,** lavadero, *m.* **w.-leather,** gamuza, badana, *f.* **w.-out,** fracaso, *m.* **w.-stand,** aguamanil, lavabo, *m.* **w.-tub,** cuba de lavar, *f*

washable /'wɒʃəbəl/ *a* lavable

washer /'wɒʃər/ *n* lavador (-ra); (washerwoman) lavandera, *f;* (machine) lavadora, *f; Mech.* arandela, *f*

washerwoman /'wɒʃər,wʊmən/ *n* lavandera, *f*

washing /'wɒʃɪŋ/ *n* lavamiento, *m;* ropa sucia, ropa para lavar, *f;* ropa limpia, *f;* ropa, *f;* (bleaching) blanqueadura, *f;* (toilet) abluciones, *f pl; Eccl.* lavatorio, *m; pl* **washings,** lavazas, *f pl.* **There is a lot of w.** to be done, Hay mucha ropa que lavar. **w.-board,** tabla de lavar, *f.* **w.-day,** día de colada, *m.* **w.-machine,** lavadora, máquina de lavar, *f.* **w.-soda,** carbonato sódico, *m.* **w.-up,** lavado de los platos, *m.* **w.-up machine,** fregador mecánico de platos, *m*

wasp /wɒsp/ *n* avispa, *f.* **wasp's nest,** avispero, *m.* **w.-waisted,** (of clothes) ceñido, muy ajustado

waspish /'wɒspɪʃ/ *a* enojadizo, irascible; malicioso; mordaz

waste /weist/ *vt* desperdiciar, derrochar, malgastar; (time) perder; consumir; corroer; (devastate) asolar, devastar; echar a perder; malograr; disipar; agotar. —*vi* gastarse; consumirse; perderse. **to w. time,** perder el tiempo. **to w. away,** (of persons) demacrarse, consumirse

waste /weist/ *n* (wilderness) yermo, desierto, *m;* (vastness) inmensidad, vastedad, *f;* (loss) pérdida, *f;* (squandering) despilfarro, derroche, *m;* disminución, *f;* (refuse) desechos, *m pl;* (of cotton, etc.) borra, *f;* disipación, *f.* —*a* (of land) sin cultivar; yermo, inútil; desechado, de desecho; superfluo. **to lay w.,** devastar. **w. land,** yermo, *m;* tierras sin cultivar, *f pl.* **w. paper,** papel usado, papel de desecho, *m.* **w.-paper basket,** cesto para papeles, *m.* **w.-pipe,** desaguadero, tubo de desagüe, *m*

wasteful /'weistfəl/ *a* pródigo, derrochador, manirroto; antieconómico; ruinoso; inútil

waster /'weistər/ *n* gastador (-ra); disipador (-ra); (loafer) golfo, *m*

watch /wɒtʃ/ *vi* velar; mirar. —*vt* mirar; observar; guardar; (await) esperar; (spy upon) espiar, acechar. **to w. for,** buscar aguardar. **to w. over,** vigilar, guardar; (care for) cuidar; proteger

watch /wɒtʃ/ *n* (at night) vela, *f;* (wakefulness) desvelo, *m;* observación, vigilancia, *f;* (*Mil. Naut.*) guardia, *f;* (sentinel) centinela, *m;* (watchman) sereno, vigilante, *m;* (guard) ronda, *f;* (timepiece) reloj de bolsillo, *m.* **to be on the w.,** estar al acecho, estar al alerta, estar a la mira. **to keep w.,** vigilar. **dog w.,** media guardia, *f.* **pocket w.,** reloj de bolsillo, *m.* **wrist w.,** reloj de pulsera, *m.* **w.-case,** caja de reloj, relojera, *f.* **w.-chain,** cadena de reloj, leontina, *f.* **w.-dog,** perro guardián, *m.* **w.-glass,** cristal de reloj, *m.* **w.-making,** relojería, *f.* **w.-night,** noche vieja, *f.* **w.-spring,** muelle de reloj, *m,* espiral, *f.* **w.-tower,** vigía, atalaya, *f*

watcher /'wɒtʃər/ *n* observador (-ra); espectador (-ra); (at a sick bed) el, *m,* (*f,* la) que vela a un enfermo

watchful /'wɒtʃfəl/ *a* vigilante, alerto; observador; atento, cuidadoso

watchfully /'wɒtʃfəli/ *adv* vigilantemente; atentamente

watching /'wɒtʃɪŋ/ *n* observación, *f;* (vigil) vela, *f*

watchmaker /'wɒtʃ,meikər/ *n* relojero (-ra). **watchmaker's shop,** relojería, *f*

watchman /'wɒtʃmən/ *n* vigilante, sereno, *m;* guardián, *m*

watchword /'wɒtʃ,wɜrd/ *n* (password) consigna, contraseña, *f;* (motto) lema, *m*

water /'wɒtər/ *n* agua, *f;* (tide) marea, *f;* (of precious stones) aguas, *f pl;* (urine) orina, *f;* (quality) calidad, clase, *f.* —*a* de agua; por agua; acuático; hidráulico. **fresh w.,** (not salt) agua dulce, *f;* agua fresca, *f.* **hard w.,** agua cruda, *f.* **high w.,** marea alta, *f.* **low w.,** marea baja, *f.* **of the first w.,** de primera clase. **running w.,** agua corriente, *f.* **soft w.,** agua blanda, *f.* **to make w.,** *Naut.* hacer agua; orinar. **to take the waters,** tomar las aguas. **under w.,** debajo del agua. —*a* acuático. **w.-bird,** ave acuática, *f.* **w.-blister,** ampolla, *f.* **w.-boatman,** chinche de agua, *f.* **w.-borne,** flotante. **w.-bottle,** cantimplora, *f.* **w.-brash,** acedia, *f.* **w.-butt,** barril, *m,* pipa, *f.* **w.-carrier,** aguador (-ra). **w.-cart,** carro de regar, *m.* **w.-closet,** retrete, excusado, *m.* **w.-color,** acuarela, *f.* **w.-color painting,** pintura a la acuarela, *f.* **w.-colorist,** acuarelista, *mf* **w.-cooled,** enfriado por agua. **w.-cooler,** cantimplora, *f.* **w.-finder,** zahorí, *m.* **w.-front,** (wharf) muelle, *m;* puerto, *m;* litoral, *m.* **w.-gauge,** indicador de nivel de agua, *m,* vara de aforar, *f.* **w.-glass,** vidrio soluble, silicato de sosa, *m.* **w.-heater,** calentador de agua, *m.* **w.-ice,** helado, *m.* **w.-level,** nivel de las aguas, *m.* **w.-lily,** nenúfar, *m,* azucena de agua, *f.* **w.-line,** lengua de agua, *f;* (of a ship) línea de flotación, *f.* **w.-logged,** anegado en agua. **w.-main,** cañería maestra de agua, *f.* **w. man,** barquero, *m.* **w.-melon,** sandía, *f.* **w. mill,** aceña, *f.* **w.-nymph,** náyade, *f.* **w.-pipe,** cañería del agua, *f.* **w. pitcher,** jarro, *m.* **w. plant,** planta acuática, f. **w.-polo**, polo acuático, *m*. **w. -power**, fuerza hidráulica, f. **w.-rate**, cupo del consumo de agua, *m*. **w. snake**, culebra de agua, f. **w. softener**, generador de agua dulce, *m*; purificador de agua, *m*. **w. spaniel**, perro (-rra) de aguas. **w. sprite**, ondina, f. **w.-supply**, abastecimiento de agua, *m*; traída de aguas, f. **w. tank**, depósito para agua, *m*. **w. tower**, arca de agua, f. **w. wave**, ondulado al agua, *m*. **w.-way**, canal, río *m*, o vía f, navegable. **w.-wheel**, rueda hidráulica, f. azud, *m*; (for irrigation) aceña, f. **w. wings**, nadaderas, f pl

water /'wɔtər/ vt (irrigate, sprinkle) regar; (moisten) mojar; (cattle, etc.) abrevar; (wine, etc.) aguar; diluir con agua; (bathe) bañar. —*vi* (of animals) beber agua; (of engines, etc.) tomar agua; (of the eyes, mouth) hacerse agua. **My mouth waters**, Se me hace agua la boca

watercourse /'wɔtər,kɔrs/ *n* corriente de agua, f. cauce, *m*; lecho de un río, *m*

watered-down /'wɔtərd'daʊn/ *Fig.* pasado por agua

waterfall /'wɔtər,fɔl/ *n* salto de agua, *m*, cascada, catarata, f

watering /'wɔtərɪŋ/ *n* riego, *m*; irrigación, f; (of eyes) lagrimeo, *m*; (of cattle, etc.) el abrevar (a); *Naut.* aguada, f. **w.-can**, regadera, f. **w.-cart**, carro de regar, *m*. **w.-place**, (for animals) aguadero, *m*; (for cattle) abrevadero, *m*; (spa) balneario, *m*; (by the sea) playa de veraneo, f

watermark /'wɔtər,mɑrk/ *n* (in paper) filigrana, f; nivel del agua, *m*. —*vt* filigranar

waterproof /'wɔtər,pruf/ *a* impermeable; a prueba de agua. —*n* impermeable, *m*. —*vt* hacer impermeable, impermeabilizar

water-repellent /'wɔtərɪ,pɛlənt/ *a* repelente al agua

watershed /'wɔtər,ʃɛd/ *n* vertiente, f; línea divisoria de las aguas, f; (riverbasin) cuenca, f

watertight /'wɔtər,taɪt/ *a* impermeable, estanco; a prueba de agua; (of arguments, etc.) irrefutable

waterworks /'wɔtər,wɜrks/ *n* establecimiento para la distribución de las aguas, *m*; obras hidráulicas, f pl

watery /'wɔtəri/ *a* (wet) húmedo; acuoso; (of the sky) de lluvia; (of eyes) lagrimoso, lloroso; (sodden) mojado; (of soup, etc.) claro; insípido

watt /wɒt/ *n* vatio, *m*. **w. hour**, vatio hora, *m*. **w.-meter**, vatímetro, *m*

wave /weɪv/ vi ondear; ondular; flotar; hacer señales. —vt (brandish) blandir; agitar; (the hair) ondular; ondear; hacer señales (de). **They waved goodby to him**, Le hicieron adiós con la mano; Le hicieron señas de despedida; Se despidieron de él agitando el pañuelo

wave /weɪv/ *n* (of the sea) ola, f; *Phys.* onda, f; (in hair or a surface) ondulación, f; (movement) movimiento, *m*; (of anger, etc.) ráfaga, f. **long w.**, onda larga, f.

medium w., onda media, f. **short w.**, onda corta, f. **sound w.**, onda sonora, f. **to have one's hair waved**, hacerse ondular el pelo. **w. band**, franja undosa, escala de longitudes de onda, f. **w. crest**, cresta de la ola, cabrilla, f. **w.-length**, longitud de onda, f

waver /'weɪvər/ vi ondear; oscilar; (hesitate) vacilar, titubear; (totter) tambalearse; (weaken) flaquear

waverer /'weɪvərər/ *n* irresoluto (-ta), vacilante, *m*

wavering /'weɪvərɪŋ/ *n* vacilación, irresolución, f. —*a* oscilante; vacilante, irresoluto; flotante

waving /'weɪvɪŋ/ *n* ondulación, f; oscilación, f; agitación, f; movimiento, *m*. —*a* ondulante; oscilante; que se balancea

wavy /'weɪvi/ *a* ondulado; flotante

wax /wæks/ *n* cera, f; (cobblers') cerote, *m*; (in the ear) cerilla, f. —*a* de cera, vt encerar. —*vi* crecer; hacerse; ponerse. **to wax enthusiastic**, entusiasmarse. **waxed paper**, papel encerado, *m*. **wax chandler**, cerero, *m*. **wax doll**, muñeca de cera, f. **wax modeling**, modelado en cera, *m*, ceroplástica, f. **wax taper**, blandón, *m*

waxen /'wæksən/ *a* de cera; como la cera; de color de cera

waxing /'wæksɪŋ/ *n* enceramiento, *m*; (of the moon) crecimiento, *m*; aumento, *m*

wax museum *n* museo de cera, *m*

waxwork /'wæks,wɜrk/ *n* figura de cera, f

waxy /'wæksi/ *a*. See **waxen**

way /weɪ/ *n* camino, *m*; senda, f; paso, *m*; ruta, f; (railway, etc.) vía, f; dirección, f; rumbo, *m*; distancia, f; (journey) viaje, *m*; (sea crossing) travesía, f; avance, progreso, *m*; (Naut. etc.) marcha, f; método, *m*; modo, *m*; (means) medio, *m*; manera, f; (habit) costumbre, f; (behavior) conducta, f, modo de obrar, *m*; (line of business, etc.) ramo, *m*; (state) estado, *m*, condición, f; (course) curso, *m*; (respect) punto de vista, *m*; (particular kind) género, *m*; (scale) escala, f. **a long way off**, a gran distancia, a lo lejos. **a short way off**, a poca distancia, no muy lejos. **by way of**, pasando por; por vía de; como; por medio de; a modo de. **by the way**, de paso; durante el viaje; durante la travesía; a propósito, entre paréntesis. **in a small way**, en pequeña escala. **in a way**, hasta cierto punto; desde cierto punto de vista. **in many ways**, de muchos modos; por muchas cosas. **in no way**, de ningún modo; nada. **in the way**, en el medio. **in the way of**, en cuanto a, tocante a; en materia de. **I went out of my way to**, Dejé el camino para; Me di la molestia de. **Is this the way to...?** ¿Es este el camino a...? **Make way!** ¡Calle! **Milky Way**, vía láctea, f. **on the way**, en camino; al paso; durante el viaje. **out of the way**, puesto a un lado; arrinconado; apartado, alejado; (imprisoned) en prisión; fuera del camino; re- moto; (unusual) original. **over the way,** en frente; al otro lado (de la calle, etc.). **right of w.,** derecho de paso, *m.* **The ship left on its way to...,** El barco zarpó con rumbo a... **the Way of the Cross,** vía crucis, *f.* **This way!** ¡Por aquí!; De este modo, Así. **this way and that,** en todas direcciones, por todos lados. **"This way to...,"** «Dirección a...» A... **under way,** en camino; en marcha; en prepara- ción. **to bar the way,** cerrar el paso. **to be in the way,** estorbar. **to be out of the way of doing,** haber perdido la cos- tumbre de hacer (algo). **to clear the way,** abrir paso, abrir calle; *Fig.* preparar el terreno. **to force one's way through,** abrirse paso por. **to find a way,** encon- trar un camino; *Fig.* encontrar medios. **to find one's way,** hallar el camino; orien- tarse. **to get into the way of,** contraer la costumbre de. **to get under way,** *Naut.* zarpar, hacerse a la vela; ponerse en marcha. **to give way,** ceder; (break) romper. **to go a long way,** ir lejos; con- tribuir mucho (a). **to have one's own way,** salir con la suya. **to keep out of the way,** *vt* and *vi* esconder(se); man- tener(se) alejado; mantener(se) apartado. **to lose one's way,** perder el camino; desorientarse; *Fig.* extraviarse. **to make one's way,** abrirse paso. **to make one's way down,** bajar. **to make one's way round,** dar la vuelta a. **to make one's way up,** subir. **to make way,** hacer lu- gar; hacer sitio; dar paso (a). **to pay one's way,** ganarse la vida; pagar lo que se debe. **to prepare the way for,** prepa- rar el terreno para. **to put out of the way,** poner a un lado; apartar; (kill) ma- tar; (imprison) poner en la cárcel; hacer cautivo (a). **to see one's way,** poder ver el camino; poder orientarse; ver el modo de hacer algo; ver cómo se puede hacer algo. **ways and means,** medios y ar- bitrios, *m pl.* **way back,** camino de re- greso, *m;* vuelta, *f.* **way down,** bajada, *f.* **way in,** entrada, *f.* **way out,** salida, *f.* **way round,** camino alrededor, *m;* solu- ción, *f;* modo de evitar..., *m.* **way through,** paso, *m.* **way up,** subida, *f*

wayfarer /ˈweiˌfɛərər/ *n* transeúnte, *mf;* viajero (-ra)

waylay /ˈweiˌlei/ *vt* asechar, salir al paso (de)

wayside /ˈweiˌsaid/ *n* borde del camino, *m.* —*a* (of flowers) silvestre; (by the side of the road) en la carretera

wayward /ˈweiwərd/ *a* caprichoso; deso- bediente; voluntarioso; travieso; rebelde

waywardness /ˈweiwərdnɪs/ *n* desobe- diencia, indocilidad, *f;* voluntariedad, *f;* travesura, *f;* rebeldía, *f*

we /wi/ *pron* nosotros, *m pl;* nosotras, *f pl.* (Usually omitted except for emphasis or for clarity.) **We are in the garden,** Es- tamos en el jardín. **We have come, but**
they are not here, Nosotros hemos venido pero ellos no están aquí

weak /wik/ *a* débil; flojo; frágil; delicado; (insecure) inseguro; (of arguments) poco convincente; (of prices, markets, etc.) flojo, en baja. **w.-eyed,** de vista floja. **w.- kneed,** débil de rodillas; *Fig.* sin volun- tad. **w.-minded,** sin carácter; pusilánime. **w. spot,** debilidad, *f;* flaco, *m;* lado dé- bil, *m;* desventaja, *f*

weaken /ˈwikən/ *vt* debilitar; (diminish) disminuir. —*vi* debilitarse; flaquear, des- fallecer; (give way) ceder

weakening /ˈwikənɪŋ/ *n* debilitación, *f.* —*a* debilitante; enervante

weaker /ˈwikər/ *a compar* más débil. **the w. sex,** el sexo débil

weakling /ˈwiklɪŋ/ *n* ser delicado, *m,* persona débil, *f;* cobarde, *m; Inf.* al- feñique, *m*

weakly /ˈwikli/ *a* enfermizo, delicado, en- clenque. —*adv* débilmente

weakness /ˈwiknɪs/ *n* debilidad, *f;* imper- fección, *f*

weal /wil/ *n* bienestar, *m;* prosperidad, *f;* (blow) verdugo, *m*

wealth /wɛlθ/ *n* riqueza, *f;* abundancia, *f;* bienes, *m pl*

wealthy /ˈwɛlθi/ *a* rico, adinerado, acau- dalado; abundante (en)

wean /win/ *vt* destetar, ablactar; separar (de); privar (de); enajenar el afecto de; (of ideas) desaferrar (de)

weaning /ˈwinɪŋ/ *n* ablactación, *f,* des- tete, *m*

weapon /ˈwɛpən/ *n* arma, *f; pl* weap- ons, (*Zool., Bot.*) medios de defensa, *m pl.* **steel w.,** arma blanca, *f*

wear /wɛər/ *n* uso, *m;* gasto, *m;* deterio- ro, *m;* (fashion) moda, boga, *f.* **for hard w.,** para todo uso. **for one's own w.,** para su propio uso. **for evening w.,** para llevar de noche. **for summer w.,** para lle- var en verano. **w. and tear,** uso y des- gáste, *m;* deterioro natural, *m*

wear /wɛər/ *vt* llevar; llevar puesto; traer; usar; (have) tener; (exhibit) mos- trar; (be clad in) vestir; (waste) gastar; deteriorar; (make) hacer; (exhaust) ago- tar, cansar, consumir. —*vi* (last) durar; (of persons) conservar(se); (of time) co- rrer; avanzar. **She wears well,** Está bien conservada. **to w. one's heart on one's sleeve,** tener el corazón en la mano. **to w. the trousers,** *Fig. Inf.* llevar los panta- lones. **to w. well,** durar mucho. **to w. away,** *vt* gastar, roer; (rub out) borrar; consumir. —*vi* (of time) pasar lenta- mente, transcurrir despacio. **to w. down,** gastar; consumir; reducir; agotar las fuerzas de; destruir; (tire) fatigar. **to w. off,** *vt* destruir; borrar. —*vi* quitarse; bo- rrarse; *Fig.* desaparecer, pasar. **to w. on,** (of time) transcurrir, correr, pasar. **to w. out,** *vt* usar; romper con el uso; con- sumir, acabar con; (exhaust) agotar; (tire) rendir. —*vi* usarse; romperse con el uso; consumirse

weariness /'wɪərɪnɪs/ n cansancio, m, fatiga, lasitud; f; aburrimiento, m; aversión, repugnancia, f

wearing /'wɛərɪŋ/ n uso, m; desgaste, m. —a (tiring) agotador; cansado. **w. apparel,** ropa, f

wearisome /'wɪərɪsəm/ a cansado; laborioso; aburrido, tedioso, pesado

weary /'wɪəri/ a cansado, fatigado; aburrido; hastiado; impaciente; tedioso, enfadoso. —vt cansar, fatigar; aburrir; hastiar; molestar. —vi cansarse, fatigarse; aburrirse. **to w. for,** anhelar, suspirar por; (miss) echar de menos (a). **to w. of,** aburrirse de; (things) impacientarse de; (people) impacientarse con

weasel /'wizəl/ n comadreja, f

weather /'wɛðər/ n tiempo, m; intemperie, f; (storm) tempestad, f. —a Naut. del lado del viento; de barlovento. —vt (of rain, etc.) desgastar; curtir; secar al aire; Naut. pasar a barlovento; (bear) aguantar, capear; (survive) sobrevivir a; luchar con. —vi curtirse a la intemperie. **Andrew is a little under the w.,** Andrés está algo destemplado; (with drink) Andrés tiene una mona; (depressed) Andrés está melancólico. **to be bad (good) w.,** hacer mal (buen) tiempo. **What is the w. like?** ¿Qué tiempo hace? ¿Cómo está el tiempo? **w.-beaten,** curtido por la intemperie. **w. chart,** carta meteorológica, f. **w. conditions,** condiciones meteorológicas, f pl. **w. forecast,** pronóstico del tiempo, m. **w.-hardened,** endurecido a la intemperie. **w. prophet,** meteorologista, mf **w. report,** boletín meteorológico, m. **w.-worn,** gastado por la intemperie; curtido por la intemperie

weathercock /'wɛðər,kɒk/ n veleta, f

weather-resistant /'wɛðərɪ,zɪstənt/ a resistente a la intemperie

weave /wiv/ vt tejer; trenzar; entrelazar; Fig. tejer. —vi tejer. —n tejido, m; textura, f

weaver /'wivər/ n tejedor (-ra)

weaving /'wivɪŋ/ n tejido, m; tejeduría, f. **w. machine,** telar, m

web /wɛb/ n tejido, m; tela, f; (network) red, f; (spider's) telaraña, f; (of a feather) barba, f; (of birds, etc.) membrana interdigital, f; (of intrigue) red, f; (snarl) lazo, m, trampa, f. **web-foot,** pie palmado, m. **web-footed,** palmípedo.

wed /wɛd/ vt casarse con; (join in marriage, cause to marry) casar; Fig. unir. —vi estar casado; casarse

wedded /'wɛdɪd/ a casado; matrimonial, conyugal; Fig. unido (a); aficionado (a), entusiasta (de), devoto (de); aferrado (a). **to be w. to one's own opinion,** estar aferrado a su propia opinión

wedding /'wɛdɪŋ/ n boda, f, casamiento, m; (with golden, etc.) bodas, f pl; (union) enlace, m, a de boda, nupcial, matrimonial, conyugal; de novios, de la novia. **golden w.,** bodas de oro, f pl. **silver w.,** bodas de plata, f pl. **w. bouquet,** ramo

de la novia, m. **w.-breakfast,** banquete de bodas, m. **w.-cake,** torta de la boda, f, pan de la boda, m. **w.-day,** día de la boda, m. **w.-march,** marcha nupcial, f. **w.-present,** regalo de boda, regalo de la boda, m. **w.-ring,** anillo de boda, m. **w. trip,** viaje de novios, m

wedge /wɛdʒ/ n cuña, f; (under a wheel) calza, alzaprima, f; Mil. cuña, mella, f; (of cheese) pedazo, m. —vt acuñar, meter cuñas; (a wheel) calzar; (fix) sujetar. **to be the thin end of the w.,** ser el principio, ser el primer paso. **to drive a w.,** Mil. hacer mella, hacer practicar una cuña. **to w. oneself in,** introducirse con dificultad (en). **w.-shaped,** cuneiforme

wedlock /'wɛd,lɒk/ n matrimonio, m

Wednesday /'wɛnzdei/ n miércoles, m

wee /wi/ a pequeñito, chiquito. **a wee bit,** un poquito

weed /wid/ n mala hierba, f; tabaco, m; (cigar) cigarro, m; (person) madeja, f; (Fig. evil) cizaña, f. —vt carpir, desherbar, sachar, sallar, escardar; Fig. extirpar, arrancar. **w.-grown,** cubierto de malas hierbas. **to w. out,** extirpar; quitar

weedy /'widi/ a lleno de malas hierbas; Fig. raquítico

week /wik/ n semana, f. **in a w.,** de hoy en ocho (días); en una semana; después de una semana. **once a w.,** una vez por semana. **a w. ago,** hace una semana. **Michael will come a w. from today,** Miguel llegará hoy en ocho. **w. in, w. out,** semana tras semana. **w.-day,** día de trabajo, día laborable, día de la semana que no sea el domingo. **on weekdays,** entre semana, m. **w.-end,** fin de semana, m. **w.-end case,** saco de noche, m

weekly /'wikli/ a semanal, semanario; de cada semana. —adv semanalmente, cada semana. —n semanario, m, revista semanal, f

weep /wip/ vt and vi llorar. **to w. for,** (a person) llorar (a); (on account of) llorar por; (with happiness, etc.) llorar de. **They wept for joy,** Lloraron de alegría

weevil /'wivəl/ n gorgojo, m

weigh /wei/ vt pesar; (consider) considerar, ponderar, tomar en cuenta; comparar; (the anchor) levar. —vi pesar; ser de importancia. **to w. anchor,** zarpar, levar el ancla, hacerse a la vela. **to w. down,** pesar sobre; sobrecargar; hacer inclinarse bajo; Fig. agobiar. **to be weighed down,** hundirse por su propio peso; Fig. estar agobiado. **to w. out,** pesar. **to w. with,** influir (en). **w.-bridge,** báscula, f

weight /weit/ n peso, m; (heaviness) pesantez, f; cargo, m; (of a clock and as part of a system) pesa, f; Fig. peso, m, importancia, f. —vt cargar; (a stick) emplomar; aumentar el peso (de); poner un peso (a). **gross w.,** peso bruto, m. **heavy w.,** peso pesado, m. **light w.,** peso ligero, m. **middle w.,** peso medio, m. **net w.,** peso neto, m. **to lose w.,** adelgazar. **loss of w.,** (of a person) adelgazamiento, m.

to put on w., cobrar carnes, hacerse más gordo. **to put the w.,** *Sports.* lanzar el peso. **to throw one's w. about,** *Inf.* darse importancia. **to try the w. of,** sopesar. **weights and measures,** pesas y medidas, *f pl.* **weightlifting,** halterofilia, *f*

weighty /'weiti/ *a* pesado; (influential) influyente; importante, de peso; grave

weird /wiərd/ *a* misterioso, sobrenatural; fantástico; mágico; (queer) raro, extraño. **the W. Sisters,** las Parcas

welcome /'welkəm/ *a* bienvenido; (pleasant) grato, agradable. —*n* bienvenida, *f*; buena acogida, *f*; (reception) acogida, *f*. —*vt* dar la bienvenida (a); acoger con alegría, acoger con entusiasmo; agasajar, festejar; (receive) acoger, recibir; recibir con gusto. **W.!** ¡Bienvenido! **to bid w.,** dar la bienvenida (a). **You are w.,** Estás bienvenido. **You are w. to it,** Está a su disposición

welcoming /'welkəmɪŋ/ *a* acogedor, cordial, amistoso

weld /weld/ *vt* soldar; combinar; unificar

welder /'weldər/ *n* soldador, *m*

welding /'weldɪŋ/ *n* soldadura, *f*; unión, fusión, *f*

welfare /'wel,feər/ *n* bienestar, bien, *m*; (health) salud, *f*; prosperidad, *f*; intereses, *m pl.* **w. state,** estado benefactor, estado de beneficencia, estado socializante, *m.* **w. work,** trabajo social, *m*

well /wel/ *a* bien; bien de salud; bueno; conveniente; (advantageous) provechoso; favorable; (happy) feliz; (healed) curado; (recovered) repuesto. **I am very w.,** Estoy muy bien. **to get w.,** ponerse bien. **to make w.,** curar. **w. enough,** bastante bien

well /wel/ *adv* bien; (very) muy; favorablemente; convenientemente; (easily) sin dificultad. **as w.,** también. **as w. as,** tan bien como; además de. **That is all very w. but...,** Todo eso está muy bien pero... **to be w. up in,** estar versado en. **to get on w. with,** llevarse bien con. **Very w.!** ¡Está bien! Muy bien. **w. and good,** bien está. **w. now,** ahora bien. **w. then,** conque; pues bien. **w.-advised,** bien aconsejado; prudente. **w.-aimed,** certero. **w.-appointed,** bien provisto; (furnished) bien amueblado. **w.-attended,** concurrido. **w.-balanced,** bien equilibrado. **w.-behaved,** bien educado; (of animals) manso. **w.-being,** bienestar, *m*; felicidad, *f*. **w.-born,** bien nacido, de buena familia. **w.-bred,** bien criado, bien educado; (of animals) de pura raza. **w.-chosen,** bien escogido. **w.-defined,** bien definido. **w.-deserved,** bien merecido. **w.-disposed,** bien dispuesto; favorable; bien intencionado. **w.-doing,** *n* el obrar bien; obras de caridad, *f pl*, *a* bondadoso, caritativo. **w.-done,** *a* bien hecho. —*interj* ¡bravo! **w.-educated,** instruido, culto. **w.-favored,** guapo, de buen parecer. **w.-founded,** bien fundado. **w.-groomed,**

elegante. **w.-grounded,** bien fundado; bien instruido. **w.-informed,** instruido; culto, ilustrado. **w.-intentioned,** bien intencionado. **w.-known,** bien conocido, notorio. **w.-meaning,** bien intencionado. **w.-modulated,** armonioso. **w.-off,** acomodado, adinerado; feliz. **w.-read,** culto, instruido. **w.-shaped,** bien hecho; bien formado. **w.-shaped nose,** nariz perfilada, *f*. **w.-spent,** bien empleado. **w.-spoken,** bien hablado; bien dicho. **w.-stocked,** bien provisto. **w.-suited,** apropiado. **w.-timed,** oportuno. **w.-to-do,** acomodado, rico. **w.-wisher,** amigo (-ga). **w.-worn,** raído; (of paths) trillado

well /wel/ *n* pozo, *m*; (of a stair) caja, *f*; cañón de escalera, *m*; (fountain) fuente, *f*, manantial, *m*; (of a fishing boat) vivar, *m*; (of a ship) sentina, *f*. **w.-sinker,** pocero, *m*

well /wel/ *vi* chorrear, manar, brotar, fluir

Welsh /welʃ/ *a* galés, de Gales. —*n* (language) galés, *m*. **the W.,** los galeses

Welshman /'welʃmən/ *n* galés, *m*

Welshwoman /'welʃ,wumən/ *n* galesa, *f*

welt /welt/ *n* (of shoe) vira, *f*, cerquillo, *m*; (in knitting) ribete, *m*; (weal) verdugo, *m*

Weltanschauung /'veltan,ʃauən/ *n* cosmovisión, postura de vida, *f*

welter /'weltər/ *vi* revolcarse; bañarse (en), nadar (en). —*n* confusión, *f*, tumulto, *m*; mezcla, *f*. **w.-weight,** peso welter, *m*

wench /wentʃ/ *n* mozuela, muchacha, *f*

wend /wend/ *vt* dirigir, encaminar. —*vi* ir. **to w. one's way,** dirigir sus pasos, seguir su camino

west /west/ *n* oeste, *m*; poniente, *m*; occidente, *m*. —*a* del oeste; occidental. —*adv* hacia el oeste, a poniente; al occidente. **W. Indian,** de las Antillas, de las Indias Occidentales. **w.-north-w.,** oesnorueste, *m*. **w.-south-w.,** oessudueste, *m*. **w. wind,** viento del oeste, poniente, *m*

westerly /'westərli/ *a* del oeste; hacia el oeste; occidental

western /'westərn/ *a* occidental; del oeste. —*n* (novel) novela caballista, *f*; (film) película del oeste, *f*

westernized /'westər,naizd/ *a* influido por el occidente

westernmost /'westərn,moust/ *a* más al oeste

West Indies Indias Occidentales, *f pl*

westward /'westwərd/ *a* que está al oeste. —*adv* hacia el oeste; hacia el occidente

wet /wet/ *a* mojado; húmedo; (rainy) lluvioso. —*vt* mojar; humedecer. —*n* (rain) lluvia, *f*. **"Mind the wet paint!"** «¡Cuidado, recién pintado!» **to be wet,** estar mojado; (of the weather) llover. **to get wet,** mojarse. **wet blanket,** *Fig.* aguafiestas, *mf* **wet through,** (of persons) calado, hecho una sopa. **wet-nurse,** nodriza, *f*

whack /wæk/ n golpe, m; (try) tentativa, f; (portion) porción, parte, f. —vt golpear, aporrear, pegar

whale /weil/ n ballena, f. **sperm w.**, cachalote, m. **w.-oil**, aceite de ballena, m

wharf /wɔrf/ n muelle, embarcadero, descargadero, m, vt amarrar al muelle

what /wʌt; unstressed wət/ a pron (interrogative and exclamatory) qué; cómo; (relative) que; el que, m; la que, f; lo que, neut; los que, m pl; las que, f pl; (which, interrogative) cuál, mf; cuáles, mf pl; (how many) cuantos, m pl; cuantas, f pl; (interrogatory and exclamatory) cuántos, m pl; cuántas, f pl; (how much, interrogative and exclamatory) cuánto, m; cuánta, f. **And w. not,** Y qué sé yo qué más. **Make w. changes you will,** Haz los cambios que quieras. **W. confidence he had...,** La confianza que tenía... **W. is this called?** ¿Cómo se llama esto? **W. did they go there for?** ¿Por qué fueron? **W. do you take me for?** ¿Por quién me tomas? **That was not w. he said,** No fue eso lo que dijo. **to know what's w.,** saber cuántas son cinco. **You have heard the latest news, w.?** Has oído las últimas noticias, ¿verdad? **W. a plty!** ¡Qué lástima! **W., do you really believe it?** ¿Lo crees de veras? **W. else?** ¿Qué más? **W. for?** ¿Para qué? **what's-his-name,** fulano (-na) de tal, m. **W. ho!** ¡Hola! **W. if...?** ¿Qué será si...? **W. is the matter?** ¿Qué pasa? **W. though...,** aun cuando...; ¿Qué importa qué? **w. with one thing, w. with another,** entre una cosa y otra. **What's more,...** Es más,...

whatever /wʌt'evər/ a pron cuanto; todo lo que; cualquier cosa que; cualquier. **W. sacrifice is necessary,** Cualquier sacrificio que sea necesario. **W. I have is yours,** Todo lo que tenga es vuestro. **W. happens,** Venga lo que venga. **It is of no use w.,** No sirve absolutamente para nada

wheal /wil/ n. See **weal**

wheat /wit/ n trigo, m. —a de trigo. **summer w.,** trigo tremesino, m. **whole w.,** a de trigo entero. **w.-ear,** espiga de trigo, f. **w.-field,** trigal, m. **w.-sheaf,** gavilla de trigo, f

wheedle /'widl/ vt lagotear, engatusar; (flatter) halagar; (with out) sacar con mimos

wheedling /'widlɪŋ/ a zalamero, mimoso; marrullero. —n lagotería, f, mimos, m pl; (flattery) halagos, m pl; marrullería, f

wheel /wil/ n rueda, f; (bicycle) bicicleta, f; (for steering a ship) timón, m; rueda del timón, f; (for steering a car) volante, m; (for spinning) rueca, f; (potter's) rueda de alfarero, f; (of birds) vuelo, m; (turn) vuelta, f; Mil. conversión, f. **Catherine w.,** (firework) rueda de Santa Catalina, f. **back w.,** rueda trasera, f. **front w.,** rueda delantera, f. **to break on the w.,** enrodar. **to go on wheels,** ir en

ruedas; Fig. ir viento en popa. **to take the w.,** (in a ship) tomar el timón; tomar el volante. **w. of fortune,** rueda de la fortuna, f. **w.-chair,** silla de ruedas, f. **w.-house,** timonera, f. **w.-mark,** rodada, f

wheel /wil/ vt hacer rodar; (push) empujar; (drive) conducir; transportar; llevar; pasear; (turn) hacer girar. —vi girar; dar vueltas; ir en bicicleta. **to w. about,** cambiar de frente; volverse; cambiar de rumbo

wheelbarrow /'wil,bærou/ n carretilla, f

wheeled /wild/ a de... ruedas; con ruedas. **w. chair,** silla de ruedas, f

wheeze /wiz/ vi ser asmático, jadear, respirar fatigosamente, resollar

wheezing /'wizɪŋ/ n resuello, jadeo, m; respiración fatigada, f

whelp /wɛlp/ n cachorro (-rra). —vi and vt parir

when /wɛn; unstressed wən/ adv cuando (interrogative, cuándo); (as soon as) tan pronto como, en cuanto; (meaning "and then") y luego, y entonces, (although) aunque. **I will see you w. I return,** Te veré cuando vuelva. **W. he came to see me he was already ill,** Cuando vino a verme estaba enfermo ya. **We returned a week ago, since w. I have not been out,** Volvimos hace ocho días y desde entonces no he salido. **Since w.?** ¿Desde cuándo?

whence /wɛns/ adv de donde (interrogative, de dónde); a donde (interrogative a dónde); por donde, de que; por lo que. **W. does he come?** ¿De dónde viene? **W. comes it that?** ¿Cómo es que...?

whenever /wɛn'evər/ adv cuando quiera que, siempre que; cada vez que, todas las veces que; cuando

where /wɛər/ adv pron donde (interrogative, dónde); en donde; en que (interrogative, en qué); (to where with verbs of motion) a donde (interrogative, a dónde); (from where with verbs of motion) de donde (interrogative, de dónde). **W. are you going to?** ¿A dónde va Vd.? **This is w. we get out,** (of a bus, etc.) Nos apeamos aquí

whereabouts /'wɛərə,bauts/ adv (interrogative) dónde; (relative) donde. —n paradero, m

whereas /wɛər'æz/ conjunc (inasmuch as) visto que, ya que; (although) mientras (que)

whereat /wɛər'æt/ adv por lo cual; a lo cual

whereby /wɛər'bai/ adv cómo; por qué; por el cual, con el cual

wherefore /'wɛər,fɔr/ adv (why) por qué; por lo cual. —n porqué, m

wherein /wɛər'ɪn/ adv en donde (interrogative, en dónde); en que (interrogative, en qué)

whereinto /wɛər'ɪntu/ adv en donde; dentro del cual; en lo cual

whereof /wɛər'ʌv/ adv de que; (whose) cuyo

whereon /wɛər'ɒn/ *adv* sobre que; en qué

whereto /wɛər'tu/ *adv* adonde; a lo que

whereupon /ˌwɛərə'pɒn/ *adv* dónde; sobre lo cual, con lo cual; en consecuencia de lo cual

wherever /wɛər'ɛvər/ *adv* dondequiera (que), en cualquier sitio; adondequiera (que). **Sit w. you like,** Siéntate donde te parezca bien

wherewith /wɛər'wɪθ, -'wɪð/ *adv* con que (*interrogative,* con qué)

wherewithal /ˌwɛərwɪð,ɔl, -wɪθ-/ *n* lo necesario; dinero necesario, *m*

whet /wɛt/ *vt* (knives, etc.) afilar, amolar, aguzar; (curiosity, etc.) excitar, estimular

whether /'wɛðər/ *conjunc* si; que; sea que, ya que. **W. he will or no,** Que quiera, que no quiera. **w. or not,** si o no

whetstone /'wɛt,stoun/ *n* afiladera, amoladera, piedra de amolar, *f*

whey /wei/ *n* suero (de la leche), *m*

which /wɪtʃ/ *a* and *pron* cuál, *mf;* cuáles, *mf pl;* que (interrogative, qué); el cual, *m;* la cual, *f;* lo cual, *neut;* los cuales, *m pl;* las cuales, *f pl;* el que, *m;* la que, *f;* lo que, *neut;* los que, *m pl;* las que, *f pl;* (who) quien. **all of w.,** todo lo cual, etc. **in w.,** en donde, en el que; donde. **the w.,** el cual, la cual, etc. **W. would you like?** ¿Cuál quieres? **The documents w. I have seen,** Los documentos que he visto. **W. way have we to go?** ¿Por dónde hemos de ir?

whichever /wɪtʃ'ɛvər/ *a* and *pron* cualquiera (que), *mf;* cualesquiera, *mf pl;* el que, *m;* la que, *f;* (of persons only) quienquiera (que), *mf;* quienesquiera (que), *mf pl* **Give me w. you like,** Dame el que quieras. **I shall take w. of you would like to come,** Me llevaré a cualquiera de Vds. que guste de venir

whiff /wɪf/ *n* (of air) soplo, *m;* vaho, *m;* fragancia, *f*

while /wail/ *n* rato, *m;* momento, *m;* tiempo, *m.* **after a w.,** al cabo de algún tiempo, después de algún tiempo. **a little w. ago,** hace poco. **all this w.,** en todo este tiempo. **at whiles,** a ratos, de vez en cuando. **between whiles,** de cuando en cuando; entre tanto. **It is worth your w. to do it,** Vale la pena de hacerse. **Mary smiled the w.,** María mientras tanto se sonreía. **once in a w.,** de vez en cuando; en ocasiones

while /wail/ *conjunc* mientras (que); al (followed by an infinitive); al mismo tiempo que; a medida que; (although) aunque; si bien. **w. I was walking down the street,** mientras andaba por la calle, al andar yo por la calle. —*vt* to w. (away), pasar, entretener. **to w. away the time,** pasar el rato

whim /wɪm/ *n* capricho, antojo, *m;* manía, *f;* extravagancia, *f;* fantasía, *f*

whimper /'wɪmpər/ *n* quejido, sollozo, gemido, *m, vi* lloriquear, quejarse, sollozar, gemir

whimsical /'wɪmzɪkəl/ *a* antojadizo, caprichoso; fantástico

whine /wain/ *vi* gimotear, lloriquear; quejarse

whining /'wainɪŋ/ *n* gimoteo, lloriqueo, *m;* quejumbres, *f pl.* —*a* que lloriquea; quejumbroso

whinny /'wɪni/ *n* relincho, hin, *m, vi* relinchar

whip /wɪp/ *vt* azotar; pegar; *Cul.* batir; *Sew.* sobrecoser; (ropes, etc.) ligar; (defeat) vencer. —*vi* moverse rápidamente. **to w. down,** *vi* bajar volando, bajar corriendo. —*vt* arrebatar (de). **to w. in,** entrar precipitadamente (en), penetrar apresuradamente (en). **to w. off,** cazar a latigazos, despachar a golpes; (remove) quitar rápidamente; (persons) llevar corriendo, llevar aprisa. **to w. open,** abrir rápidamente. **to w. out,** *vt* (draw) sacar rápidamente; (utter) saltar diciendo (que); proferir. —*vi* escabullirse, escaparse, salir apresuradamente. **to w. round,** volverse de repente. **to w. up,** *vt* (horses, etc.) avivar con el látigo; (snatch) coger de repente agarrar; (gather) reunir. —*vi* (mount) subir corriendo

whip /wɪp/ *n* azote, zurriago, *m;* (riding) látigo, *m.* **blow with a w.,** latigazo, *m.* **to have the w.-hand,** mandar, tener la sartén por el mango; tener la ventaja. **w.-cord,** tralla del látigo, *f*

whipping /'wɪpɪŋ/ *n* paliza, *f,* vapuleo, azotamiento, *m.* **w. post,** picota, *f.* **w. top,** trompo, *m,* peonza, *f*

whirl /wɜrl/ *n* vuelta, *f,* giro, *m;* rotación, *f; Fig.* torbellino, *m.* —*vi* girar; dar vueltas; (dance) bailar, danzar. —*vt* hacer girar; dar vueltas (a); (carry) llevar rápidamente. **to w. along,** volar (por), pasar aprisa (por); dejar atrás los vientos, correr velozmente. **to w. past,** pasar volando (por); pasar como una exhalación. **to w. through,** atravesar rápidamente, cruzar volando

whirligig /'wɜrlɪ,gɪg/ *n* perinola, *f;* (merry-go-round) tiovivo, *m*

whirlpool /'wɜrl,pul/ *n* vórtice, remolino, *m; Fig.* vorágine, *f*

whirlwind /'wɜrl,wɪnd/ *n* torbellino, *m,* manga de viento, *f*

whirr /wɜr/ *n* zumbido, *m;* (of wings) ruido (de las alas), *m.* —*vi* girar; zumbar

whisk /wɪsk/ *n* cepillo, *m; Cul.* batidor, *m;* (movement) movimiento rápido, *m.* —*vt Cul.* batir; (wag) menear, mover rápidamente; (with off, away) quitar rápidamente; sacudirse; arrebatar; (take away a person) llevarse (a). —*vi* moverse rápidamente; andar rápidamente

whiskers /'wɪskərz/ *n pl* mostacho, *m,* patillas, barbas, *f pl;* (of a feline) bigotes, *m pl*

whisky /'wɪs-/ *n* güisqui, *m*

whisper /'wɪspər/ *n* cuchicheo, (rumor) voz, *f;* (of leaves, etc.) susurro, murmullo, *m.* —*vi* and *vt* cuchichear, hablar al oído; (of leaves, etc.) susurrar; (of rumors) murmurar. **in a w.**, al oído, en un susurro

whisperer /'wɪspərərsol; *n* cuchicheador (-ra); (gossip) murmurador (-ra)

whispering /'wɪspərɪŋ/ *n* cuchicheo, *m;* susurro, *m;* (gossip) murmurio, *m.* **w. gallery,** galería de los murmullos, *f. Inf.* sala de los secretos, *f.*

whistle /'wɪsəl/ *n* (sound) silbido, silbo, *m;* (instrument) pito, silbato, *m; Inf.* gaznate, *m.* —*vi* and *vt* silbar. **blast on the w.**, pitido, *m.* **to w. for,** llamar silbando; *Inf.* esperar sentado, buscar en vano

whit /wɪt/ *n* pizca, *f;* bledo, *m.* **not a w.,** ni pizca

white /wait/ *a* blanco; pálido; puro. —*n* color blanco, blanco, *m;* (pigment) pintura blanca, *f;* (whiteness) blancura, *f;* (of egg) clara (del huevo), *f;* (person) blanco, *m.* **Elizabeth went w.,** Isabel se puso pálida. **the w.,** (billiards) la blanca. **the w. of the eye,** lo blanco del ojo. **w. ant,** hormiga blanca, termita, *f.* **w. cabbage,** repollo, *m.* **w. caps,** (of waves) cabrillas, *f pl;* (of mountains) picos blancos, *m pl.* **w. clover,** trébol blanco, *m.* **w. corpuscle,** glóbulo blanco, m. **w. currant,** grosella blanca, *f.* **w. elephant,** elefante (-ta) blanco (-ca). **w. ensign,** pabellón blanco, *m.* **w.-faced,** de cara pálida. **w. fish,** pescado blanco, *m.* **w. flag,** bandera blanca, *f.* **w.-haired,** de pelo blanco. **w. heat,** calor blanco, *m,* candencia, *f;* ardor, *m.* **w. horses,** cabrillas, palomas, *f pl.* **w.-hot,** incandescente. **W. House, the,** la Casa Blanca, *f.* **w. lead,** albayalde, *m.* **w. lie,** mentira inocente, mentira oficiosa, mentira piadosa, la mentirilla, *f.* **w. man,** blanco, hombre de raza blanca, *m.* **the white man's burden,** la misión sagrada de la civilización blanca, *f.* **w. meat,** carne blanca, pechuga, *f.* **w. paper,** libro blanco, *m.* **w. sauce,** salsa blanca, *f.* **w. slave,** víctima de la trata de blancas, *f.* **w. slavery,** trata de blancas, *f.* **w. sugar,** azúcar blanco, azúcar de flor, *m.* **w. woman,** mujer de raza blanca, *f.*

whiten /'waitn/ *vt* blanquear. —*vi* blanquearse

whitewash /'wait,wɒʃ/ *vt* blanquear, jalbegar, encalar; (*Fig.* of faults) disculpar, justificar

whither /'wɪðər/ *adv* (interrogative) adónde; (with a clause) adonde

whithersoever /,wɪðərsou'ɛvər/ *adv* adondequiera

whiting /'waitɪŋ/ *n* blanco de España, *m;* blanco para los zapatos, *m;* (fish) pescadilla, *f,* merlango, *m*

whittle /'wɪtl/ *n* navaja, *f.* —*vt* cercenar, cortar; (sharpen) afilar, sacar punta (a); tallar; *Fig.* reducir. **to w. away, down,** *Fig.* reducir a nada

whizz /wɪz/ *n* silbido, zumbido, *m, vi* silbar, zumbar

who /hu/ *pron* (interrogative) quién, *mf;* quiénes, *mf pl;* (relative) quien, *mf;*

quienes, *mf pl;* que; (in elliptical constructions the person that, etc.) el que, *m;* la que, *f;* los que, *m pl;* las que, *f pl*

whoa /wou/ *interj* ¡so!

whoever /hu'ɛvər/ *pron* quienquiera (que); cualquiera (que); quien.

whole /houl/ *a* (healthy) sano; (uninjured) ileso, entero; todo. —*n* todo, *m;* total, *m;* totalidad, *f;* conjunto, *m.* **on the w.,** por regla general, en general; en conjunto. **the w. week,** la semana entera, toda la semana. **w.-hearted,** sincero, genuino; entusiasta. **w.-heartedly,** de todo corazón. **w.-heartedness,** sinceridad, *f;* entusiasmo, *m.* **w. length,** *a* de cuerpo entero. **w. number,** número entero, *m*

wholemeal /'houl'mil/ *n* harina de trigo entero, *f,* a de trigo entero

wholeness /'houlnɪs/ *n* totalidad, *f;* integridad, *f;* todo, *m*

wholesale /'houl,seil/ *a Com.* al por mayor; en grueso; *Fig.* general; en masa. —*n* venta al por mayor, *f.* **w. price,** precio al por mayor, *m.* **w. trade,** comercio al por mayor, *m*

wholesaler /'houl,seilər/ *n* comerciante al por mayor, *mf* mercader de grueso, *m*

wholesome /'houlsəm/ *a* sano; saludable; (edifying) edificante

wholly /'houli/ *adv* completamente, enteramente, totalmente; integralmente; del todo

whom /hum/ *pron* quien; a quien, *mf;* a quienes, *mf pl;* (interrogative) a quién, *mf;* a quiénes *mf pl;* al que, *m;* a la que, *f;* a los que, *m pl;* a las que, *f pl.* **from w.,** de quien; (interrogative) de quién. **the man w. you saw,** el hombre a quien viste

whoop /wup, wʊp/ *n* alarido, grito, *m;* estertor de la tos ferina, *m.* —*vi* dar gritos, chillar; /hup/ (whooping-cough) toser

whooping cough /'hupɪŋ/ *n* tos ferina, coqueluche, *f*

whore /hɔr/ *n* puta, ramera, *f*

whorl /wɔrl, worl/ *n* (of a shell) espira, *f; Bot.* verticilo, *m;* (of a spindle) tortera, *f*

whose /huz/ *pron* cuyo, *m;* cuya, *f;* cuyos, *m pl;* cuyas, *f pl;* de quien, *mf;* de quienes, *mf pl;* (interrogative) de quién, de quiénes; **W. daughter is she?** ¿De quién es ella la hija? **This is the writer w. name I always forget,** Este es el autor cuyo nombre siempre olvido

whosoever /,husou'ɛvər/ *pron.* See whoever

why /wai/ *adv* (interrogative) por qué; (on account of which) por el cual, *m;* por la cual, *f;* por la cual, neut; por los cuales, *m pl;* por las cuales, *f pl;* (how) cómo. —*n* ni porqué, *m, interj* ¡qué!; ¡cómo!; ¡toma!; si. **not to know the why or wherefore,** no saber ni el porqué ni el cómo, no saber ni el qué ni el por qué. **Why! I have just come,** ¡Si no hago más de llegar! **Why not?** ¿Por qué no? ¡Cómo no!

wick /wɪk/ n mecha, torcida, f

wicked /'wɪkɪd/ a malo; malvado, perverso; pecaminoso; malicioso; (mischievous) travieso

wickedness /'wɪkɪdnɪs/ n maldad, f; perversidad, f; pecado, m; (mischievousness) travesura, f

wicker /'wɪkər/ n mimbre, m, a de mimbre

wicket /'wɪkɪt/ n postigo, portillo, m; (half-door) media puerta, f; (at cricket) meta, f. **w.-keeper,** guardameta, m

wide /waid/ a ancho; (in measurements) de ancho; vasto; extenso; grande; amplio; (loose) holgado; (distant) lejos; liberal; general, comprensivo. —adv lejos; completamente. **far and w.,** por todas partes. **to be too w.,** ser muy ancho; estar muy ancho; (of garments) venir muy ancho. **two feet w.,** dos pies de ancho. **w.-awake,** muy despierto; despabilado; vigilante. **w.-eyed,** con los ojos muy abiertos; asombrado. **w.-open,** abierto de par en par

widely /'waidli/ adv extensamente; generalmente; (very) muy

widen /'waidn/ vt ensanchar; extender. —vi ensancharse; extenderse

widespread /'waid'sprɛd/ a universal, generalizado; extenso; esparcido. **to become w.,** generalizarse

widow /'wɪdou/ n viuda, f. —vt dejar viuda; dejar viudo; Fig. privar. **to be a grass w.,** estar viuda. **to become a w.,** enviudar, perder al esposo. **widow's pension,** viudedad, f. **widow's weeds,** luto de viuda, m

widowed /'wɪdoud/ a viudo

widower /'wɪdouər/ n viudo, m. **to become a w.,** perder a la esposa, enviudar

width /wɪdθ/ n anchura, f; (of cloth) ancho, m; (of mind) liberalismo, m. **double w.,** (cloth) doble ancho, m

wield /wild/ vt (a scepter) empuñar; (power, etc.) ejercer; (a pen, sword) manejar

wife /waif/ n esposa, mujer, f; mujer, f; comadre, f. **husband and w.,** los cónyuges, los esposos. **old wives' tale,** cuento de viejas, m. **The Merry Wives of Windsor,** Las alegres comadres de Windsor. **to take to w.,** contraer matrimonio con, tomar como esposa (a)

wig /wɪg/ n peluca, f; (hair) cabellera, f. **top wig,** peluquín, m. **wigmaker,** peluquero, m

wigwam /'wɪgwɒm/ n tienda de indios, f

wild /waild/ a (of animals, men, land) salvaje; (barren) desierto, yermo; (mountainous) riscoso, montañoso; (of plants, birds) silvestre, montés; (disarranged) en desorden, desarreglado; (complete) absoluto, completo; (dissipated) disipado, vicioso; (foolish) alocado; (of the sea) bravío; (of weather, etc.) borrascoso; (mad with delight, etc.) loco; (frantic, mad) frenético, loco; (with "talk," etc.) extravagante; insensato, desatinado; (shy)

arisco; (incoherent) inconexo, incoherente; (frightened) alarmado, espantado; (wilful) travieso, indomable. —n tierra virgen, f; desierto, m; soledad, f. **It made me w.,** (angry) Me hizo rabiar. **to run w.,** volver al estado silvestre; (of persons) llevar una vida de salvajes; volverse loco. **to shoot w.,** errar el tiro. **to spread like w. fire,** propagarse como el fuego. **w. beast,** fiera, f. **w. boar,** jabalí, m. **w. cat,** gato montés, m. **w. duck,** pato silvestre, m. **w. goat,** cabra montesa, f. **w.-goose chase,** caza infructuosa, f; empresa quimérica, f. **w. oats,** avenas locas, f pl; Fig. indiscreciones de la juventud, f pl. **to sow one's w. oats,** andarse a la flor del berro

wilderness /'wɪldərnɪs/ n desierto, m; yermo, páramo, despoblado, m; soledad, f; (jungle) selva, f; (maze) laberinto, m; infinidad, f

wildly /'waildli/ adv en un estado salvaje; sin cultivo; (rashly) desatinadamente; sin reflexión, sin pensar; (incoherently) incoherentemente; (stupidly, of looking, etc.) tontamente; (in panic) con ojos espantados, con terror en los ojos, alarmado

wildness /'waildnɪs/ n salvajez, f; estado silvestre, m; naturaleza silvestre, f; (ferocity) ferocidad, f; (of the wind, sea) braveza, f; (of the wind) violencia, f; (impetuosity) impetuosidad, f; (of statements, etc.) extravagancia, f; (incoherence) incoherencia, f; (disorder) desorden, m; (wilfulness, of children) travesuras, f pl; (of the expression) gesto espantado, m

wile /wail/ n estratagema, f, engaño, m, ardid, f

will /wɪl/ n voluntad, f; albedrío, m; (wish) deseo, m; (pleasure) discreción, f, placer, m; (legal document) testamento, m. **against my w.,** contra mi voluntad. **at w.,** a voluntad; a gusto, a discreción. **free w.,** libre albedrío, m. **of one's own free w.,** por su propia voluntad. **iron w.,** voluntad de hierro, f. **last w. and testament,** última disposición, última voluntad, f. **to do with a w.,** hacer con toda el alma, hacer con entusiasmo. **to make one's w.,** otorgar (hacer) su testamento. **w.-power,** fuerza de voluntad, f

will /wɪl/ vt querer; disponer, ordenar; (bequeath) legar, dejar en testamento; mandar; (oblige) sugestionar (a una persona) para que haga algo; hipnotizar. —vi aux querer; (As a sign of the future it is not translated separately in Spanish) **I w. come tomorrow,** Vendré mañana. **John does not approve, but I w. go,** Juan no lo aprueba pero yo quiero ir. **Do what you w.,** Haga lo que a Vd. le parezca bien, Haga lo que Vd. quiera; Haga lo que haga. **Boys w. be boys,** Los niños son siempre niños. **He w. not (won't) do it,** No lo hará; No quiere hacerlo

willful /'wɪlfəl/ a rebelde, voluntarioso;

(of children) travieso; (of crimes, etc.) premeditado

willfully /'wɪlfəli/ adv voluntariosamente; intencionadamente; (of committing crimes) con premeditación

willing /'wɪlɪŋ/ a dispuesto, inclinado; (serviceable) servicial; deseoso; espontáneo; complaciente; gustoso; (willingly) de buena gana. **to be w.,** estar dispuesto (a), querer; consentir (en)

willingly /'wɪlɪŋli/ adv de buena gana, con gusto

willingness /'wɪlɪŋnɪs/ n buena voluntad, f; deseo de servir, m; complacencia, f; (consent) consentimiento, m

will-o'-the-wisp /'wɪləðə'wɪsp/ n fuego fatuo, m

willow /'wɪlou/ n sauce, m. **weeping w.,** sauce llorón, m. **w.-pattern china,** porcelana de estilo chino, f. **w. tree,** sauce, m

willy nilly /'wɪli 'nɪli/ adv de buen o mal grado, mal que bien

wilt /wɪlt/ vi (of plants) marchitarse, secarse; Fig languidecer; ajarse. —vt marchitar; Fig ajar; hacer languidecer

wily /'waɪli/ a astuto, chuzón

win /wɪn/ vt ganar; (reach) alcanzar, lograr; (a victory, etc.) llevarse; conquistar. —vi ganar; triunfar. —n triunfo, m. **to win back,** volver a ganar; recobrar

wince /wɪns/ vi retroceder, recular; (flinch) quejarse; (of a horse) respingar. —n respingo, m. **without wincing,** sin quejarse; estoicamente

winch /wɪntʃ/ n cabria, f; (handle) manubrio, m

wind /wɪnd/ n viento, m; aire, m; (flatulence) flatulencia, f; (breath) respiración, f, aliento, m; (idle talk) paja, f. **breath of w.,** soplo de viento, m. **following w.,** viento en popa, m. **high w.,** viento alto, viento fuerte, m. **land w.,** viento terrenal, m. **It's an ill w. that blows nobody good,** No hay mal que por bien no venga. **There is something in the w.,** Hay algo en el aire, Se trama algo. **to get w. of,** husmear. **to sail before the w.,** navegar de viento en popa. **The w. stiffened,** Refrescó el viento. **You took the w. out of his sails,** Le deshinchaste las velas. **w.-instrument,** instrumento de viento, m. **w.-proof,** a prueba del viento. **w.-swept,** expuesto a todos los vientos. **w. storm,** ventarrón, m

wind /waɪnd/ vi serpentear; desfilar lentamente; torcerse. —vt (turn) dar vueltas (a); (a handle) manejar, mover; (a watch) dar cuerda (a); (wool, etc.) devanar, ovillar; (wrap) envolver; (of arms, embrace) rodear (con); (a horn) tocar. **to w. off,** devanar; desenrollar. **to w. round,** (wrap) envolver; (skirt) rodear; (embrace) ceñir con (los brazos); (pass by) pasar por; deslizarse por; (of snakes) enroscarse. **to w. up,** (a watch) dar cuerda (a); (thread) devanar; (conclude)

concluir; Com. liquidar; (excite) agitar, emocionar

windbag /'wɪnd,bæg/ n pandero, m, sacamuelas, mf

windfall /'wɪnd,fɔl/ n fruta caída del árbol, f; (good luck) breva, f; ganancia inesperada, lotería, f

winding /'waɪndɪŋ/ a tortuoso; (e.g., road) sinuoso; serpentino; en espiral. —n tortuosidad, f; meandro, recoveco, m, vuelta, curva, f. **w. sheet,** mortaja, f, sudario, m. **w. stair,** escalera de caracol, f. **w.-up,** conclusión, f; Com. liquidación, f

windmill /'wɪnd,mɪl/ n molino de viento, m

window /'wɪndou/ n ventana, f; (of a shop) escaparate, m; (in a train, car, bank, etc.) ventanilla, f; (booking office) taquilla, f; (of a church) vidriera, f. **casement w.,** ventana, f. **sash w.,** ventana de guillotina, f. **small w.,** ventanilla, f. **stained glass w.,** vidriera, f. **to lean out of the w.,** asomarse a la ventana. **to look out of the w.,** mirar por la ventana. **w. blind,** (Venetian) persiana, f; transparente, m; (against the sun) toldo, m. **w.-dresser,** decorador (-ra) de escaparates. **w. frame,** marco de ventana, m. **w.-pane,** cristal (de ventana), m. **w.-shutter,** contraventana, f. **w.-sill,** repisa de la ventana, f, alféizar, m

windpipe /'wɪnd,paɪp/ n tráquea, f

windscreen /'wɪnd,skrin/ n parabrisas, guardabrisa, m. **w.-wiper,** limpiaparabrisas, limpiavidrios, m

windward /'wɪndwərd/ n barlovento, m. —a de barlovento. —adv a barlovento

windy /'wɪndi/ a ventoso; expuesto al viento; (of style) hinchado, pomposo. **It is w.,** Hace viento

wine /waɪn/ n vino, m; zumo fermentado (de algunas frutas), m. —a de vino; de vinos; para vino. **in w.,** Cul. en vino; (drunk) ebrio, borracho. **heavy w.,** vino fuerte, m. **light w.,** vino ligero, m. **local w.,** vino del país, m. **matured w.,** vino generoso, m. **red w.,** vino tinto, m. **thin w.,** vinillo, m. **white w.,** vino blanco, m. **w.-cellar,** bodega, cueva, f. **w.-colored,** de color de vino. **w.-cooler,** cubo para enfriar vinos, m. **w. country,** tierra de vino, f. **w. decanter,** garrafa para vino, f. **w.-grower,** vinicultor (-ra). **w.-growing,** n vinicultura, f. —a vinícola. **w. lees,** zupia, f. **w. merchant,** comerciante en vinos, mf. vinatero, m. **w.-press,** lagar, m. **w.-taster,** catavinos, m. **w. waiter,** bodeguero, m

wineskin /'waɪn,skɪn/ n bota, f, odre, m, pellejo, m

wing /wɪŋ/ n (of a bird and Zool. Archit. Aer. Mil. Bot.) ala, f; (flight) vuelo, m; Theat. bastidor, m; Fig. protección, f. —vt dar alas (a); llevar sobre las alas; (wound) herir en el ala; herir en el brazo; volar por. —vi volar. **beating of wings,** batir de alas, aleteo, m. **in the wings,** Theat. entre bastidores. **on the w.,** al vuelo. **to clip a (person's) wings,** cortar (or quebrar) las alas (a). **under his w.,** bajo su protección. **w.-case,** élitro (de un insecto), *m.* **w. chair,** sillón con orejas, *m.* **w.-commander,** teniente coronel de aviación, *m.* **w.-span,** (*Zool.* and *Aer.*) envergadura, *f.* **w.-spread,** extensión del ala, *f.* **w.-tip,** punta del ala, *f*

wink /wɪŋk/ *vi* (blink) pestañear; (as a signal, etc.) guiñar; (of stars, etc.) titilar, parpadear, centellear. —*vt* guiñar (el ojo). —*n* pestañeo, *m;* guiño, *m.* **not to sleep a w.,** no pegar los ojos. **to take forty winks,** echar una siesta. **to w. at,** guiñar el ojo (a); (ignore) hacer la vista gorda

winner /'wɪnər/ *n* ganador (-ra); vencedor (-ra)

winning /'wɪnɪŋ/ *a* ganador; vencedor; (attractive) encantador. —*n* ganancia, *f.* **w. number,** número galardonado, número premiado, número vencedor, *m.* **w.-post,** meta, *f.* **w. side,** *Sports.* equipo vencedor, *m;* (politics, etc.) partido vencedor, *m*

winnings /'wɪnɪŋz/ *n* ganancias, *f pl*

winnow /'wɪnoʊ/ *vt* aventar, abalear; *Fig.* separar

winsome /'wɪnsəm/ *a* sandunguero; dulce, encantador

winter /'wɪntər/ *n* invierno, *m.* —*a* de invierno; hiemal. —*vi* pasar el invierno, invernar. —*vt* (of cattle, etc.) guardar en invierno. **in w.,** en invierno, durante el invierno. **w. clothes,** ropa de invierno, *f.* **w. palace,** palacio de invierno, *m.* **w. quarters,** invernadero, *m.* **w. season,** invierno, *m;* temporada de invierno, *f.* **w. sleep,** invernada, *f.* **w. solstice,** solsticio hiemal, *m.* **w. sports,** deportes de nieve, *m pl.* **w. wheat,** trigo de invierno, *m*

wintry /'wɪntri/ *a* de invierno; invernal; (of a smile, etc.) glacial

wipe /waɪp/ *vt* limpiar; (rub) frotar; (dry) secar; (remove) quitar. —*n* limpión, *m;* (blow) golpe de lado, *m.* **to w. one's eyes,** enjugarse las lagrimas. **to w. off, out,** limpiar; (remove) quitar; (erase) borrar; (kill) destruir completamente, exterminar; (a military force) destrozar; (a debt) cancelar

wire /waɪr/ *n* alambre, *m;* hilo metálico, *m;* telégrafo (eléctrico), *m; Inf.* telegrama, *m.* —*vt* atar con alambre; (fence) alambrar; (snare) coger con lazo de alambre; (of electrical equipment, etc.) instalar; (telegraph) telegrafiar. —*vi* (telegraph) telegrafiar. **barbed w.,** alambre espinoso, *m.* **live w.,** alambre cargado (de electricidad), *m;* (person) fuerza viva, *f.* **w.-cutters,** cortaalambres, *m pl.* **w.-entanglement,** *Mil.* alambrada, *f.* **w. fence,** alambrera, *f;* cercado de alambre, *m.* **w. gauze,** tela metálica, *f.* **w. nail,** punta de París, *f.* **w.-netting,** malla de alambre, *f;* alambrado, *m.* **w.-pulling,** influencias secretas, *f pl;* intrigas políticas, *f pl*

wireless /'waɪrlɪs/ *a* sin hilos; (of a mes-

sage) radiotelegráfico; por radio. —*n* telegrafía sin hilos, *f;* radiotelefonía, *f;* (telegram) radiocomunicación, *f;* (broadcasting) radio, *f.* —*vt* radiotelegrafiar. **Let's listen to the w.,** Vamos a escuchar la radio. **portable w.,** radio portátil, *f.* **w. engineer,** ingeniero radio-telegráfica, *m.* **w. enthusiast,** radioaficionado (-da). **w. licence,** permiso de radiorreceptor, *m.* **w. operator,** radiotelegrafista, *mf.* **w. room,** cuarto de telegrafía sin hilos, *m.* **w. set,** aparato de radio, *m.* **w. station,** estación de radiotelegrafía, *f;* (broadcasting) radioemisora, *f.* **w. telegraph,** telégrafo sin hilos, *m.* **w. telegraphy,** telegrafía sin hilos, radiotelegrafía, *f.* **w. telephony,** telefonía sin hilos, *f.* **w. transmission,** radioemisión, *f*

wiretap /'waɪərˌtæp/ *vi* poner escucha. —*vt* poner escucha a

wiring /'waɪrɪŋ/ *n* instalación de alambres eléctricos, *f*

wiry /'waɪəri/ *a* semejante a un alambre; (of persons) nervudo

wisdom /'wɪzdəm/ *n* sabiduría, *f;* (learning) saber, *m;* (judgment) juicio, *m.* **Book of W.,** Libro de la Sabiduría, *m.* **w.-tooth,** muela del juicio, *f*

wise /waɪz/ *a* sabio; juicioso, prudente; (informed) enterado, informado. **a w. man,** un sabio. **in no w.,** de ningún modo. **the W. Men of the East,** los magos. **w. guy,** *Inf.* toro corrido, *m*

wish /wɪʃ/ *n* deseo, *m.* **Best wishes for the New Year,** Los mejores deseos para el Año Nuevo. **w.-bone,** espoleta, *f*

wish /wɪʃ/ *vt* querer; desear; ansiar; (with "good morning", etc.) dar. **I w. he were here!** ¡Ojalá que estuviera aquí! **Theresa wishes us to go,** Teresa quiere que vayamos. **I w. it had happened otherwise,** Quisiera que las cosas hubiesen pasado de otra manera. **I w. you would make less noise,** Me gustaría que hicieses menos ruido. **I only w. one thing,** Solamente deseo una cosa. **I w. you good luck,** Te deseo mucha suerte. **I wished him a merry Christmas,** Le deseé unas Pascuas muy felices, Le felicité las Pascuas. **to w. a prosperous New Year,** desear un próspero Año Nuevo. **to w. good-by,** despedirse (de). **to w. good day,** dar los buenos días. **to w. for,** desear

wishful /'wɪʃfəl/ *a* deseoso; ansioso; ávido. **w. thinking,** ilusiones, *f pl;* optimismo injustificado, optimismo exagerado, *m*

wisp /wɪsp/ *n* mechón, *m;* jirón, *m;* trozo, pedazo, *m*

wistful /'wɪstfəl/ *a* ansioso; triste; patético; (envious) envidioso; (regretful) de pesar; (remorseful) de remordimiento; (thoughtful) pensativo

wit /wɪt/ *n* (reason) juicio, *m;* agudeza, gracia, *f,* rasgo de ingenio, *m;* ingenio, *m;* inteligencia, *f,* talento, *m;* (person) hombre de ingenio, *m;* mujer de ingenio, *f.*

my five wits, mis cinco sentidos. **to be at one's wits' end**, no saber qué hacer. **to live by one's wits**, ser caballero de industria. **to lose one's wits**, perder el juicio

witch /wɪtʃ/ n bruja, f. **witches' sabbath**, aquelarre, m. **w.-doctor**, hechizador, mago, m. **witch-hazel**, carpe, m; loción de carpe, f

witchcraft /'wɪtʃ,kræft/ n brujería, f; sortilegio, encantamiento, m

with /wɪθ, wɪð/ prep con; en compañía de; en casa de; (against) contra; (among) entre; en; (by) por; (towards) hacia; para con; (according to) según; (notwithstanding) a pesar de; a; (concerning) con respecto a; en el caso de. **Rose is w. Antony**, Rosa está con Antonio. **He was w. his dog**, Estaba acompañado por su perro. **He pulled at it w. both hands**, Lo tiró con las dos manos. **filled w. fear**, lleno de miedo. **to shiver w. cold**, temblarse de frío. **the girl w. golden hair**, la muchacha del pelo dorado. **They killed it w. one blow**, Lo mataron de un sólo golpe. **It rests w. you to decide**, Tú tienes que decidirlo; Te toca a tí decidirlo. **to begin w.**, adv para empezar; v empezar por. **w. all speed**, a toda prisa. **to part w.**, desprenderse de; (of people) despedirse de; separarse de. **w. that...**, (at once) en esto... (disease and poverty, etc.) **are still with us**, están todavía en el mundo

withal /wɪð'ɔl, wɪθ-/ adv además; al mismo tiempo. —prep con

withdraw /wɪð'drɔ, wɪθ-/ vt retirar; (words) retractar; (remove) quitar, privar (de); (a legal action) apartar. —vi retirarse; retroceder; apartarse; irse

withdrawal /wɪð'drɔəl, wɪθ-/ n retirada, f; (retirement) retiro, m; apartamiento, m

withdrawn /wɪð'drɔn, wɪθ-/ a (abstracted) ensimismado, meditabundo

wither /'wɪðər/ vi marchitarse, secarse, ajarse. —vt marchitar, secar, ajar; Fig. hacer languidecer, matar; (snub) avergonzar

withered /'wɪðərd/ a marchito, mustio; muerto; (of persons) acartonado, seco

withering /'wɪðərɪŋ/ a que marchita; (scorching) abrasador, ardiente; (scornful) despreciativo, desdeñoso; (biting) mordaz, cáustico

withhold /wɪθ'hould, wɪð-/ vt retener; detener; (restrain) refrenar; apartar; (refuse) negar; abstenerse de; (refuse to reveal) ocultar

within /wɪð'ɪn, wɪθ-/ adv dentro, adentro; en el interior; en casa; Fig. en lo interior. **He stayed w.**, Se quedó dentro. **Is Mrs. González w.?** ¿Está en casa la Sra. González?

within /wɪð'ɪn, wɪθ-/ prep dentro de; el interior de; en; entre; (within range of) al alcance de; a la distancia de; (near) cerca de; a poco de; (of time) en el espacio de, en; dentro de; (almost) por poco, casi.

He was w. an inch of being killed, Por poco le matan. **to be w. hearing**, estar al alcance de la voz. **seen from w.**, visto desde dentro. **twice w. a fortnight**, dos veces en quince días. **w. himself**, por sus adentros, entre sí. **w. an inch of**, Fig. a dos dedos de. **a few miles of Edinburgh**, a unas millas de Edimburgo. **w. a short distance**, en una corta distancia; a poca distancia

without /wɪð'aut, wɪθ-/ prep sin; falto de; (outside) fuera de; (beyond) más allá de. —adv exteriormente; por fuera; hacia afuera; fuera. **It goes w. saying**, No hay que decir. **w. more ado**, sin más ni más. **w. my knowledge**, sin que yo lo supiese. **w. regard for**, sin miramientos por. **w. saying more**, sin decir más. **without batting an eyelash**, sin sobresaltos

withstand /wɪð'stænd, wɪθ-/ vt resistir, oponerse (a); soportar

witless /'wɪtlɪs/ a sin seso, tonto, necio

witness /'wɪtnɪs/ n (evidence) testimonio, m; (person) testigo, mf; espectador (-ra). **in w. whereof**, en fe de lo cual. **to bear w.**, atestiguar, dar testimonio. **to bring forward witnesses**, hacer testigos. **w. my hand**, en fe de lo cual, firmo. **w.-box**, puesto de los testigos, m. **w. for the defence**, testigo de descargo, mf. **w. for the prosecution**, testigo de cargo, mf

witness /'wɪtnɪs/ vt (show) mostrar, señalar; (see) ser testigo de, ver, presenciar; Law. atestiguar. —vi dar testimonio; servir de testigo

witticism /'wɪtə,sɪzəm/ n rasgo de ingenio, donaire, m, agudeza, f

wittily /'wɪtɪli/ adv ingeniosamente, donairosamente, agudamente

witty /'wɪti/ a salado, gracioso. **w. sally**, agudeza, f

wizard /'wɪzərd/ n mago, hechicero, m

wizened /'wɪzənd/ a seco, arrugado; (of persons) acartonado

wobble /'wɒbəl/ vi tambalearse, balancearse; (quiver) temblar; oscilar; Mech. galopar; (stagger) titubear; Fig. vacilar

woe /wou/ n dolor, m; congoja, aflicción, f; mal, desastre, infortunio, m. **Woe is me!** ¡Ay de mí! ¡Desdichado de mí!

woebegone /'woubɪ,gɔn/ a angustiado

woeful /'woufəl/ a triste; doloroso; funesto

wolf /wʊlf/ n lobo (-ba). **a w. in sheep's clothing**, un lobo en piel de cordero. **to cry w.**, gritar «el lobo!» **to keep the w. from the door**, ponerse a cubierto del hambre. **w.-cub**, lobezno, m. **w.-hound**, perro lobo, m. **w. pack**, manada de lobos, f

woman /'wʊmən/ n mujer, f; hembra, f; (lady-in-waiting) dama de servicio, f. **a fine figure of a w.**, una real hembra. **w. doctor**, médica, f. **w.-hater**, misógino, m. **w. of the town**, mujer de la vida airada, f. **w. of the world**, mujer de mundo, f

womanish /'wʊmənɪʃ/ a afeminado

womankind /'womən,kaind/ n el sexo femenino, las mujeres

womanly /'womənli/ a femenino, de mujer

womb /wum/ n útero, m, matriz, f; Fig. seno, m

wonder /'wʌndər/ n maravilla, f; prodigio, m; portento, milagro, m; (surprise) sorpresa, f; admiración, f; asombro, m; (problem) enigma, m; misterio, m. —vi admirarse, asombrarse, maravillarse; sorprenderse. —vt (ask oneself) preguntarse; desear saber. **I wondered what the answer would be,** Me preguntaba qué sería la respuesta. **It is no w. that...,** No es mucho que..., No es sorprendente que... **It is one of the wonders of the world,** Es una de las maravillas del mundo. **to work wonders,** hacer milagros. **to w. at,** asombrarse de, maravillarse de; sorprenderse de. **w.-working,** milagroso

wonderful /'wʌndərfəl/ a maravilloso; magnífico; asombroso; Inf. estupendo

wonderland /'wʌndər,lænd/ n mundo fantástico, m; reino de las hadas, m; país de las maravillas, m. **"Alice in W.,"** Alicia en el país de las maravillas

wondrous /'wʌndrəs/ a maravilloso. —adv extraordinariamente

wont /wɔnt, wount/ n costumbre, f. —vi soler. **as he was w.,** Como solía

won't /wount/. See **will not**

woo /wu/ vt galantear; hacer la corte (a), solicitar amores a; cortejar; Fig. solicitar; perseguir

wood /wʊd/ n bosque, m; madera, f; (for the fire, etc.) leña, f; (cask) barril, m. —a de madera; (of the woods) selvático. **dead w.,** ramas muertas, f pl; Fig. paja, f. **w. alcohol,** alcohol metílico, m. **w.-anemone,** anémona de los bosques, f. **w.-block floor,** entarimado, m. **w.-borer,** xiló-fago, m. **w.-carver,** tallista, mf **w.-carving,** talla en madera, f. **w.-craft,** conocimiento del campo, m. **w.-cut,** grabado en madera, m. **w.-cutter,** leñador, m. **w.-engraver,** grabador (-ra) en madera. **w.-engraving,** grabado al boj, m. **w.-fibre,** fibra de madera, f. **w.-louse,** cochinilla, f. **w.-nymph,** ninfa de los bosques, f. **w.-pigeon,** paloma torcaz, f. **w.-pile,** pila de leña, leñera, f. **w.-pulp,** pulpa de madera, f. **w.-shaving,** acepilladura, f. **w.-splinter,** tasquil, m, astilla, f. **w.-wind,** Mus. madera, f. **w.-worm,** carcoma, f

wooded /'wʊdɪd/ a provisto de árboles, plantado de árboles, arbolado

wooden /'wʊdn/ a de madera; de palo; (of smiles) mecánico; (stiff) indiferente, sin emoción; (clumsy) torpe; (of character) inflexible. **He has a w. leg,** Tiene una pata de palo. **w. beam,** madero, m; viga de madera, f. **w. bridge,** pontón, m. **w. galley,** Print. galerín, m

woodland /n. 'wʊd,lænd/ a -lənd/ n bosques, m pl. —a de bosque; silvestre

woodpecker /'wʊd,pɛkər/ n pájaro carpintero, picamaderos, m

woodshed /'wʊd,ʃɛd/ n leñera, f

woodwork /'wʊd,wɜrk/ n maderaje, m; molduras, f pl; carpintería, f

woof /wʊf/ n trama, f

wool /wʊl/ n lana, f. —a de lana; lanar. **to go w.-gathering,** estar distraído. **to pull the w. over a person's eyes,** engañar como a un chino. **w.-bearing,** lanar. **w.-carding,** cardadura de lana, f. **w.-growing,** cría de ganado lanar, f. **w. merchant,** comerciante en lanas, mf, lanero. **w.-pack,** fardo de lana, m. **w. trade,** comercio de lana, m

woollen /'wʊlən/ a de lana; lanar. —n paño de lana, m; género de punta de lana, m

woolly /'wʊli/ a lanudo, lanoso; de lana; Bot. velloso; (of hair) lanoso, crespo. —n género de punta de lana, m; (sweater) jersey, m

word /wɜrd/ n palabra, f; Gram. vocablo, m; Theol. verbo, m; (maxim) sentencia, f, dicho, m; (message) recado, m; (news) aviso, m, noticias, f pl; (Mil. command) voz de mando, f; (order) orden, f; (password) contraseña, f; (term) término, m. —vt expresar; formular; (draw up) redactar; escribir. **He was as good as his w.,** Fue hombre de palabra. **I do not know how to w. this letter,** No sé cómo redactar esta carta. **in a w.,** en una palabra; en resumidas cuentas. **by w. of mouth,** de palabra. **I give you my w. for it,** Le doy mi palabra de honor. **in other words,** en otros términos; en efecto. **the W. (of God),** el Verbo (de Dios). **to have a w. with,** hablar con; conversar con; entablar conversación con. **to leave w.,** dejar recado. **to have words with,** tener palabras con. **to keep one's w.,** cumplir su palabra

wording /'wɜrdɪŋ/ n fraseología, f; expresión, f; estilo, m; (terms) términos, m pl; (drawing up) redacción, f

word processing /'wɜrd ,prɔsɛsɪŋ/ n tratamiento de textos, procesamiento de textos, m

wordy /'wɜrdi/ a verboso, prolijo

work /wɜrk/ n trabajo, m; (sewing) labor, f; (literary, artistic production and theological) obra, f; (behavior) acción, f, acto, m; (employment) empleo, m; (business affairs) negocios, m pl; pl **works,** obras, fortificaciones, f pl; obras públicas, f pl; construcciones, f pl; (of a machine) mecanismo, m; motor, m; (factory) fábrica, f, taller, m. **w. of art,** obra de arte. **w. accident,** accidente del trabajo, m. **w.-bag,** bolsa de costura, f, saco de labor, m. **w.-box,** (on legs) costurero, m; (small) neceser de costura, m. **w.-people,** obreros (-as). **w.-room,** taller, m; (study) estudio, m; (for sewing) cuarto de costura, m. **w.-table,** banco de taller, m; (for writing) mesa de escribir, f

work /wɜrk/ vi trabajar; Sew. hacer labor

de aguja, coser; (embroider) bordar; *Mech.* funcionar, marchar; (succeed) tener éxito; ser eficaz; (be busy) estar ocupado; (be employed) tener empleo; (of the face) demudarse, torcerse; (ferment) fermentar; (operate) obrar *vt* trabajar; operar, hacer funcionar; mover; (control) manejar; (a mine) explotar; (embroider) bordar; (wood) tallar; (a problem) resolver; calcular; (iron, etc.) labrar; (the soil) cultivar; (a ship) maniobrar; (do) hacer; (bring about) efectuar; traer consigo; producir; (agitate oneself) agitarse, emocionarse, excitarse. **to w. in repoussé,** repujar. **to w. loose,** desprenderse. **to w. one's passage,** trabajar por el pasaje. **to w. overtime,** trabajar horas extraordinarias. **to w. two ways,** ser espada de dos filos. **to w. at,** trabajar en; ocuparse en; dedicarse a; elaborar. **to w. in,** *vt* introducir; insinuar. —*vi* combinarse. **to w. into,** penetrar en. **to w. off,** usar, emplear; (get rid of) deshacerse de, librarse de. **to w. on, upon,** influir en; obrar sobre; estar ocupado en. **to w. out,** *vt* calcular; resolver; (a mine, a topic, etc,) agotar; (develop) elaborar, desarrollar; trazar, planear; (find) encontrar. —*vi* llegar (a); resultar; venir a ser. **to w. up,** crear; (promote) fomentar; producir; (excite) agitar, excitar; (fashion) dar forma (a), labrar; (finish) terminar

workable /'wɜrkəbəl/ *a* laborable; factible, practicable; (of a mine) explotable

workaday /'wɜrkə,dei/ *a* de todos los días; prosaico

workbench /'wɜrk,bentʃ/ *n* banco de mecánico, *f*, banco de taller, banco de trabajo, *m*, mesa de trabajo, *f*

workday /'wɜrk,dei/ *n* día de trabajo, día laborable, *m*

worker /'wɜrkər/ *n* trabajador (-ra); (manual) obrero (-ra); (of a machine) operario (-ia). **w.-ant,** hormiga obrera, *f.* **w.-bee,** abeja obrera, *f*

working /'wɜrkɪŋ/ *a* de trabajo; (of capital) de explotación; trabajador, que trabaja; obrero. —*n* trabajo, *m*; (of a machine, organism, institution) funcionamiento, *m*; explotación, *f*; (of a mine) laboreo, *m*; (of a ship) maniobra, *f*; (of metal, stone, wood) labra, *f*; operación, *f*; (result) efecto, resultado, *m*; (calculation) cálculo, *m*. "Not w.," «No funciona.» **to be in w. order,** funcionar bien. **w.-class,** clase obrera, *f*; pueblo, *m*. **w.-clothes,** ropa de trabajo, *f.* **w.-day,** día de trabajo, *m.* **w.-hours,** horas de trabajo, horas hábiles, *f pl.* **w. hypothesis,** postulado, *m.* **w.-man,** obrero, *m*; trabajador, *m.* **w.-out,** elaboración, *f*; ensayo, *m.* **w.-plan,** plan de trabajo, *m.* **w.-woman,** obrera, *f.* **Your W.,** vuestra merced

workman /'wɜrkmən/ *n* obrero, *m*; (agricultural) labrador, *m*

workmanlike /'wɜrkmən,laik/ *a* bien hecho, bien acabado; (clever) hábil

workmanship /'wɜrkmən,ʃip/ *n* trabajo,

m; manufactura, *f*; hechura, *f*; (cleverness) habilidad, *f*

workshop /'wɜrk,ʃop/ *n* taller, *m*

world /wɜrld/ *n* mundo, *m.* **For all the w. as if...,** Exactamente como si... **to see the w.,** ver mundo. **to treat the w. as one's oyster,** ponerse el mundo por montera. **w. without end,** por los siglos de los siglos. **w.-power,** potencia mundial, gran potencia, *f.* **w.-wide,** mundial, universal

worldliness /'wɜrldlinis/ *n* mundanería, *f*, conocimiento del mundo, *m*; frivolidad, vanidad mundana, *f*; egoísmo, *m*; prudencia, *f*

worldly /'wɜrldli/ *a* de este mundo; mundano; humano; profano; frívolo. **to be w.-wise,** tener mucho mundo

worm /wɜrm/ *n* gusano, *m*; lombriz, *f*; *Chem.* serpentín, *m*; (of a screw) tornillo sinfín, *m*; (person) gusano, *m*; *Fig.* gusano roedor, remordimiento, *m.* **intestinal w.,** lombriz intestinal, *f*, gusano de la conciencia. **w. eaten,** carcomido. **w.-hole,** picadura de gusano, lombriguera, *f.* **w.-powder,** polvos antihelmínticos, *m pl.* **w.-shaped,** vermiforme

worm /wɜrm/ *vt* (a dog) dar un vermífugo (a). —*vi* arrastrarse como un gusano. **to w. one's way into,** deslizarse en; *Fig.* insinuarse en, introducirse en. **to w. out,** (secrets, information) sonsacar

wormy /'wɜrmi/ *a* gusanoso, lleno de gusanos

worn /wɔrn/ *a* (of garments) raído; estropeado, gastado; (of paths) trillado; (of the face) arrugado, cansado. **w. out,** acabado; muy usado; (tired) rendido; (exhausted) agotado

worry /'wɜri/ *n* preocupación, inquietud, ansiedad, *f*; problema, cuidado, *m.* —*vt* (prey) zamarrear; preocupar, inquietar; molestar; importunar. —*vi* estar preocupado, estar intranquilo, inquietarse. **Don't worry,** Pierda cuidado, No pase cuidado

worse /wɜrs/ *a compar* peor; inferior. —*adv* peor; menos. —*n* lo peor. **so much the w.,** tanto peor. **to be w. off,** estar peor; estar en peores circunstancias; ser menos feliz. **to be the w. for wear,** ser muy usado; estar ajado; ser ya viejo. **to grow w.,** empeorarse; (of an ill person) ponerse peor. **w. and w.,** de mal en peor, peor que peor. **w. than ever,** peor que nunca

worsen /'wɜrsən/ *vt* agravar, hacer peor; exasperar. —*vi* agravarse, empeorarse; exasperarse

worship /'wɜrʃip/ *n* culto, *m*; adoración, *f*; veneración, *f.* —*vt* adorar; reverenciar. —*vi* adorar; rezar; dar culto (a). **place of w.,** edificio de culto, *m.* **Your W.,** vuestra merced

worshipful /'wɜrʃipfəl/ *a* venerable, respetable

worshipper /'wɜrʃipər/ *n* adorador (-ra); *pl* **worshippers,** (in a church, etc.) fieles, *m pl*, congregación, *f*

worst /wɜrst/ a el (la, etc.) peor; más malo. —adv el (la, etc.) peor. —n el (la, etc.) peor; lo peor. —vt vencer, derrotar; triunfar sobre **If the w. comes to the w.,** En el peor de los casos. **The w. of it is that...,** Lo peor es que... **to have the w. of it,** salir perdiendo, llevar la peor parte

worsted /'wʊstid, 'wɜrstid/ n estambre, m, a de estambre

worth /wɜrθ/ n valor, m; precio, m; mérito, m, a (que) vale; de precio de; cuyo valor es de; equivalente a; (que) merece; digno de. **He bought six hundred pesetas w. of sweets,** Compró seiscientas pesetas de dulces. **He sang for all he was w.,** Cantó con toda su alma. **It is w. seeing,** Es digno de verse, Vale la pena de verse. **to be w.,** valer. **to be w. while,** valer la pena, merecer la pena

worthless /'wɜrθlɪs/ a sin valor; sin mérito; inútil; malo; (of persons) vil, despreciable, indigno

worthy /'wɜrði/ a digno de respeto, benemérito, respetable; digno, merecedor; meritorio. —n varón ilustre, hombre célebre, m; héroe, m; (Inf. Ironic.) tío, m. **to be w. of,** ser digno de, merecer

would /wʊd/ unstressed wəd/ preterite and subjunctive of **will.** (indicating a conditional tense) **They w. come if...,** Vendrían si...; (indicating an imperfect tense) **Often he w. sing,** Muchas veces cantaba, **Now and then a blackbird w. whistle,** De vez en cuando silbó un mirlo; (expressing wish, desire) **What w. they?** ¿Qué quieren? **The place where I w. be,** El lugar donde quisiera estar. **W. I were at home!** ¡Ojalá que estuviese en casa! **I thought that I w. tell you,** Se me ocurrió la idea de decírselo. **It w. seem that...,** Parece ser que..., Según parece...; Se diría que... **He said that he w. never have done it,** Dijo que no lo hubiera hecho nunca. **They w. have been killed if he had not rescued them,** Habrían sido matados si él no los hubiese salvado. **He w. go,** Se empeñó en ir. **He w. not do it,** Rehusó hacerlo, Se resistió a hacerlo; No quiso hacerlo. **This w. probably be the house,** Sin duda esta sería la casa. **W. you be good enough to...,** Tenga Vd. la bondad de..., Haga el favor de...

would-be /'wʊdbi/ a supuesto; llamado; aspirante (a); en esperanza de (followed by infin.); (frustrated) frustrado, malogrado

wound /wund/ n herida, f. —vt herir; (the feelings) lastimar, lacerar. **deep w.,** herida penetrante, f. **the wounded,** los heridos.

wraith /reiθ/ n fantasma, espectro, m, sombra, f

wrangle /'ræŋgəl/ vi discutir; altercar, disputar acaloradamente; reñir; (bargain) regatear. —n argumento, m; disputa, f, altercado, m; riña, f

wrap /ræp/ vt envolver; arrollar; cubrir; abrigar; (conceal) ocultar. —n envoltorio, m; abrigo, m; pl **wraps,** abrigos y mantas de viaje, m pl. **W. yourself up well!** ¡Abrígate bien! **to be wrapped up in,** estar envuelto en; Fig. estar entregado a, estar absorto en; (a person) estar embelesado con

wrapper /'ræpər/ n envoltura, f; embalaje, m; (of a newspaper) faja, f; (of a book) sobrecubierta, f; (dressing-gown) bata, f, salto de cama, m

wrapping /'ræpɪŋ/ n envoltura, cubierta, f. **w.-paper,** papel de envolver, m

wrath /ræθ/ n ira, f

wrathful /'ræθfəl/ a airado

wreak /rik/ vt ejecutar; (anger, etc.) descargar. **to w. one's vengeance,** vengarse

wreath /riθ/ n guirnalda, f; corona, f; trenza, f. **funeral w.,** corona funeraria, f

wreathe /rið/ vt trenzar; (entwine) entrelazar (de); (garland) coronar (de), enguirnaldar (con); (encircle) ceñir, rodear; (a face in smiles) iluminar

wreck /rek/ n naufragio, m; buque naufragado, m; destrucción, f; Fig. ruina, f; (remains) restos, m pl; (person) sombra, f. —vt hacer naufragar; destruir; Fig. arruinar; hacer fracasar. **I am a complete w.,** Inf. Estoy hecho una ruina. **to be wrecked,** irse a pique, naufragar; Fig. arruinarse; frustrarse

wreckage /'rekɪdʒ/ n naufragio, m; restos de naufragio, m pl; ruinas, f pl; (of a car, plane, etc.) restos, m pl; accidente, m

wrench /rentʃ/ n (jerk) arranque, m; (pull) tirón, m; (sprain) torcedura, f; (tool) llave, f; (pain) dolor, m. —vt arrancar; forzar; torcer, dislocar. **He has wrenched his arm,** Se ha torcido el brazo

wrest /rest/ vt arrebatar, arrancar

wrestle /'resəl/ vi luchar. —n lucha grecorromana, f; Fig. lucha, f. **to w. with,** Fig. luchar con; luchar contra

wrestler /'reslər/ n luchador, m

wrestling /'reslɪŋ/ n lucha grecorromana, f. **all-in-w.,** lucha libre, f. **w.-match,** lucha, f

wretch /retʃ/ n infeliz, mf; (ruffian) infame, mf; (playful) picaruelo (-la). **a poor w.,** un pobre diablo

wretched /'retʃɪd/ a (unhappy) infeliz, desdichado; miserable; pobre; (ill) enfermo; horrible; malo; mezquino; despreciable; lamentable

wriggle /'rɪgəl/ vi agitarse, moverse; menearse; serpear, culebrear; retorcerse. —n See under **wriggling. to w. into,** insinuarse en, deslizarse dentro (de). **to w. out,** escaparse. **to w. out of a difficulty,** extricarse de una dificultad

wring /rɪŋ/ vt torcer; estrujar; exprimir; arrancar; (force) forzar. **to w. one's hands,** restregarse las manos. **to w. the neck of,** torcer el pescuezo (a). **to w. out,** exprimir; estrujar

wrinkle /'rɪŋkəl/ n arruga, f; pliegue, m; Inf. noción, f. —vt arrugar. —vi arrugarse. **to w. one's brow,** (frown) fruncir el ceño; (in perplexity) arrugar la frente

wrist /rɪst/ n muñeca, f. **w.-band,** tira del puño de la camisa, f. **w. bandage,** pulsera, f

writ /rɪt/ n escritura, f; Law. decreto judicial, mandamiento, m; orden, f; título ejecutorio, m; hábeas corpus, m. **Holy W.,** la Sagrada Escritura. **to issue a w.,** dar orden. **to serve a w.,** notificar una orden. **w. of privilege,** auto de excarcelación, m

write /rait/ vt and vi escribir; Fig. mostrar. **He writes a good hand,** Tiene buena letra. **I shall w. to them for a list,** Les escribiré pidiendo una lista. **to w. back,** contestar por escrito; contestar a una carta. **to w. down,** poner por escrito; anotar, apuntar; describir. **to w. for,** escribir para; escribir para pedir algo; escribir algo en vez de otra persona. **to w. off,** escribir; escribir rápidamente; cancelar. **to w. on,** seguir escribiendo; escribir sobre. **to w. out,** copiar; redactar. **to w. over again,** escribir de nuevo, escribir otra vez, volver a escribir. **to w. up,** redactar; Com. poner al día; (praise) escribir alabando

writer /'raitər/ n escritor (-ra); autor (-ra). **the present w.,** el que, m, (f, la que) esto escribe. **writer's cramp,** calambre del escribiente, m

writhe /raið/ vi retorcerse

writing /'raitɪŋ/ n escritura, f; (work) escrito, m; inscripción, f; documento, m; (style) estilo, m; (hand) letra, f; el arte de escribir; trabajo literario, m. **in one's own w.,** de su propia letra. **in w.,** por escrito. **w.-case,** escribanía, f. **w.-desk,** escritorio, m. **w.-pad,** taco de papel, m. **w.-paper,** papel de escribir, m. **w.-table,** mesa de escribir, f

wrong /rɒŋ/ a injusto; mal; equivocado, erróneo; inexacto; falso; incorrecto; desacertado; inoportuno. **It is the w. one,** No es el que hacía falta; No es el que quería. **to be in the w. place,** estar mal situado; estar mal colocado. **to be w.,** estar mal;

no tener razón; (mistaken) estar equivocado; (of deeds or things) estar mal hecho; (be unjust) ser injusto; (of clocks) andar mal. **to do w.,** hacer mal; obrar mal. **to get out of bed on the w. side,** levantarse del izquierdo. **to go w.,** (of persons) descarriarse; (of affairs) ir mal; salir mal; frustrarse; (of apparatus) estropearse, no funcionar. **We have taken the w. road,** Nos hemos equivocado de camino. **You were very w. to...,** Has hecho muy mal en... **w.-headed,** terco, obstinado; disparatado. **w.-headedness,** terquedad, obstinación, f. **w. number,** (telephone) número errado, m. **w. side,** revés, m; lado malo, m. **w. side out,** al envés; al revés

wrong /rɒŋ/ adv mal; injustamente; sin razón; incorrectamente; equivocadamente; (inside out) al revés. **to get it w.,** (a sum) calcular mal; (misunderstand) comprender mal

wrong /rɒŋ/ n mal, m; injusticia, f; perjuicio, m; ofensa, f, agravio, m; culpa, f; error, m. **to be in the w.,** no tener razón; haber hecho mal. **to put one in the w.,** echar la culpa (a), hacer responsable (de)

wrong /rɒŋ/ vt hacer mal (a); perjudicar; ser injusto con; ofender

wrongdoer /'rɒŋˌduər/ n malhechor (-ra); pecador (-ra); perverso (-sa)

wrongdoing /'rɒŋˌduɪŋ/ n maldad, maleficencia, f; pecado, m; injusticia, f

wrongful /'rɒŋfəl/ a injusto; perjudicial; falso

wrongly /'rɒŋli/ adv injustamente; erróneamente, equivocadamente; perversamente; mal

wrought /rɔt/ a forjado; labrado; (hammered) batido; trabajado. **w. iron,** hierro dulce, hierro forjado, m. **w. up,** muy excitado, muy agitado, muy nervioso

wry /rai/ a torcido; tuerto; triste; pesimista; desilusionado; irónico. **wry face,** mueca f, de desengaño, de ironía, de disgusto, etc. **make a wry face,** torcer el gesto. **wry neck,** Ornith. torcecuello, m

XYZ

x /ɛks/ n equis, f

x-ray /'ɛks,rei/ vt tomar una radiografía (de). **x-ray,** rayo x, m pl. **x-ray examination,** examen con rayos x, m. **x-ray photograph,** radiografía, f

xylophone /'zailə,foun/ n xilófono, m

y /wai/ n (letter) i griega, ye, f

yacht /yɒt/ n yate, m. **y. club,** club marítimo, m. **y. race,** regata de yates, f

yank /yæŋk/ n tirón, m, sacudida, f. —vt dar un tirón (a); sacar de un tirón

Yankee /'yæŋki/ a and n yanqui, mf

yap /yæp/ vi ladrar. —n ladrido, m

yard /yɑrd/ n (measure) yarda, f; Naut. verga, f; corral, m; (courtyard) patio, m. —vt acorralar. **goods y.,** estación de mercancías, f. **y.-arm,** penol (de la verga), m. **y.-stick,** vara de medir de una yarda, f

yarn /yɑrn/ n hilaza, f; hilo, m; (story) historia, f, cuento, m. **to spin a y.,** contar una historia

yaw /yɔ/ vi Naut. guiñar; Aer. serpentear. —n Naut. guiñada, f; Aer. serpenteo, m

yawn /yɔn/ vi bostezar; quedarse con la boca abierta; (of chasms, etc.) abrirse. —n bostezo, m. **to stifle a y.,** ahogar un bostezo

yea /yei/ adv en verdad, ciertamente; y aun... no sólo... sino. —n sí, m

year /yɪər/ n año, m; pl years, años, m pl, edad, f. **We are getting on in years,** Nos vamos haciendo viejos. **He is five years old,** Tiene cinco años. **all the y. round,** todo el año, el año entero. **by the y.,** al año. **every other y.,** cada dos años, un año sí y otro no. **in after years,** en años posteriores. **last y.,** el año pasado. **next y.,** el año próximo, el año que viene. **y. after y.,** año tras año. **New Y.,** Año Nuevo, m. **to see the New Y. in,** ver empezar el Año Nuevo. **New Year's Day,** día de Año Nuevo, m. **(A) Happy New Y.!** ¡Feliz Año Nuevo! **y.-book,** anuario, m

yearly /'yɪərli/ a anual. —adv anualmente, cada año; una vez al año

yearn /yɜrn/ vi anhelar, suspirar (por); desear vivamente

yearning /'yɜrnɪŋ/ n sed, ansia, f; anhelo, deseo vehemente, m. —a ansioso; anhelante; (tender) tierno

yeast /yist/ n levadura, f

yell /yɛl/ vi and vt chillar; gritar. —n chillido, m; grito, m

yellow /'yɛlou/ a amarillo; (of hair) rubio; (cowardly) cobarde; (newspaper) amarillista, sensacionalista. **to turn y.,** vi ponerse amarillo; amarillear. —vt volver amarillo. **y. fever,** fiebre amarilla, f. **y.-hammer,** Ornith. emberizo, m

yellow pages n páginas amarillas, páginas doradas, f pl

yelp /yɛlp/ vi gañir. —n gañido, m

yen /yɛn/ n (currency) yen, m; (desire) deseovivo, m

yes /yɛs/ adv sí. **Yes?** ¿De verdad? ¿Y qué pasó después? ¿Y entonces? **to say yes,** decir que sí; dar el sí. **yes-man,** amenista, sacristán de amén, m

yesterday /'yɛstər,dei/ adv ayer. —n ayer, m. **the day before y.,** anteayer

yet /yɛt/ adv aún, todavía. **as yet,** hasta ahora; todavía. **He has not come yet,** No ha venido todavía. **yet again,** otra vez

yet /yɛt/ conjunc sin embargo, no obstante, con todo; pero. **The book is well written and yet I do not like it,** El libro está bien escrito, y sin embargo no me gusta

Yiddish /'yɪdɪʃ/ n yídis, yídish, yídico, m; a yídico

yield /yild/ vt producir; dar; (grant) otorgar; (afford) ofrecer; (surrender) ceder. —vi producir; (submit) rendirse, someterse; (of disease) responder; (give way) flaquear, doblegarse; dar de sí; (consent) consentir (en); (to circumstances, etc.) ceder (a), sucumbir (a). —n producción, f, producto, m; Com. rédito, m; (crop) cosecha, f. **to y. to temptation,** ceder a la tentación. **to y. up,** entregar; devolver

yielding /'yildɪŋ/ a flexible; (soft) blando; dócil, sumiso; fácil; condescendiente

yogurt /'yougərt/ n yogur, m

yoke /youk/ n yugo, m; (of oxen) yunta, f; (for pails) balancín, m; (of a garment) canesú, m; Fig. férula, f, yugo, m. —vt uncir, acoplar. **to throw off the y.,** sacudir el yugo

yokel /'youkəl/ n patán, rústico, m

yolk /youk/ n (of an egg) yema, f

yonder /'yɒndər/ a aquel; aquella, f; aquellos, m pl; aquellas, f pl. —adv allí; allá a lo lejos

yore /yɔr/ n **in days of y.,** antaño; en otro tiempo

you /yu/ pers pron; unstressed yʊ, yə/ pers pron nominative (polite form) usted (Vd.), mf; ustedes (Vds.), mf pl; (familiar form) sing tu, mf; (pl) vosotros, m pl; vosotras, f pl; (one) uno, m; una, f; se (followed by 3rd pers. sing. of verb). —pers pron acc (polite form) le, m; la, f; les, m pl; las, f pl; a usted, a ustedes; (informal form) te, mf; os, mf pl; (after most prepositions) ti, mf; vosotros, m pl; vosotras, f pl. **Are you there?** (telephone) ¡Oiga! **I gave the parcel to you,** Te (os) di el paquete; Di el paquete a usted (a ustedes). **I shall wait for you in the garden,** Te (os) esperaré en el jardín; Esperaré a Vds. (a Vd.) en el jardín. **This present is for you,** Este regalo es para ti (para vosotros, para Vd. (Vds.)). **Away with you!** ¡Vete! ¡Marchaos! **Between you and me,** Entre tú y yo. **you can't eat your cake and have it too,** no hay rosa sin espinas. **You never**

can tell, No se sabe nunca, Uno no sabe nunca

young /yʌŋ/ a joven; nuevo, reciente; inexperto; poco avanzado. —*n* cría, *f,* hijuelos, *m pl.* **y. blood,** *Inf.* pollo pera, *m.* **y. girl,** jovencita, *f.* **y. man** joven, *m.* **y. people,** jóvenes, *m pl.* **in his y. days,** en su juventud. **The night is y.,** La noche está poca avanzada. **to grow y. again,** rejuvenecer. **with y.,** (of animals) preñada *f*

younger /ˈyʌŋgər/ a más joven; menor. **Peter is his y. brother,** Pedro es su hermano menor. **to look y.,** parecer más joven

youngster /ˈyʌŋstər/ n jovencito, chico, muchacho, *m;* niño, *m*

your /yʊr, yɔr; *unstressed* yər/ a *poss* (polite form) su (*pl* sus); de usted (Vd.), (*pl* de ustedes (Vds.)); (familiar form) tu (*pl* vuestro). **I have y. papers,** Tengo tus (vuestros) papeles; Tengo los papeles de Vd. (*or de* Vds.). **How is y. mother?** ¿Cómo está su (tu) madre? **It is y. turn,** Te toca a ti, Le toca a Vd.

yours /yʊrz, yɔrz/ pron poss (polite form) (el) suyo, *m;* (la) suya, *f;* (los) suyos, *m pl;* (las) suyas, *f pl;* el, *m;* la, *f;* lo, *neut;* los, *m pl;* las, *f pl;* de usted (Vd.), *mf sing* or de ustedes (Vds.), *mf pl;* (familiar form) (el) tuyo, *m,* (la) tuya, *f;* (los) tuyos, *m pl;* (las) tuyas, *f pl;* (el) vuestro, *m;* (la) vuestra, *f;* (los) vuestros, *m pl;* (las) vuestras, *f pl.* **This is a picture of y.,** (addressing one person), Este es uno de los cuadros de usted (Vd.), Este es uno de los cuadros. **This hat is mine, it is not y.,** Este sombrero es el mío, no es el tuyo. **The horse is y.,** El caballo es tuyo (de Vd.). **Y. affectionately,** Un abrazo de tu amigo... **Y. faithfully,** Queda de Vd. su att. (atentísimo) s.s. (seguro servidor). **Y. sincerely,** Queda de Vd. su aff. (afectuoso)

yourself /yʊrˈsɛlf, yər- yər-/ pers pron (familiar form sing) tú mismo, *m;* tú misma, *f;* (after a preposition) tí, *mf;* (polite form) usted (Vd.) mismo, *m;* usetd misma, *f; pl* **yourselves,** (familiar form) vosotros mismos, *m pl;* vosotras mismas, *f pl;* (polite form) ustedes (Vds.) mismos,

m pl; ustedes mismas, *f pl.* **This is for y.,** Esto es para ti; Esto es para Vd.

youth /yuθ/ n juventud, *f;* (man) joven, chico, mozalbete, *m;* (collectively) jóvenes, *m pl,* juventud, *f*

youthful /ˈyuθfəl/ a joven, juvenil; de la juventud

Yucatan /ˌyukəˈtæn/ a yucateco

Yule /yul/ n Navidad, *f.* **y.-log,** leño de Navidad, *m.* **y-tide,** Navidades, *f pl*

z /zi/ n (letter) zeda, zeta, *f*

zeal /zil/ n celo, entusiasmo, *m;* ardor, fervor, *m*

zealot /ˈzɛlət/ n fanático (-ca)

zealous /ˈzɛləs/ a celoso, entusiasta

zebra /ˈzibrə/ n cebra, *f*

zenith /ˈziniθ/ n cenit, *m; Fig.* apogeo, punto culminante, *m*

zephyr /ˈzɛfər/ n céfiro, *m,* brisa, *f*

zero /ˈzɪərou/ n cero, *m.* **below z.,** bajo cero. **z. hour,** hora cero, *f*

zest /zɛst/ n sabor, gusto, *m;* entusiasmo, *m.* **to eat with z.,** comer con buen apetito. **to enter on with z.,** emprender con entusiasmo

zigzag /ˈzɪgˌzæg/ n zigzag, *m.* —*a* and *adv* en zigzag. —*vi* zigzaguear, hacer zigzags, serpentear; (of persons) andar haciendo eses

zinc /zɪŋk/ n cinc, *m.* **z. oxide,** óxido de cinc, *m*

Zion /ˈzaiən/ n Sión, *m*

Zionism /ˈzaiəˌnɪzəm/ n sionismo, *m*

Zionist /ˈzaiənɪst/ n and a sionista

zip /zɪp/ n (of a bullet) silbido, *m; Inf.* energía, *f.* **zip fastener,** cierre de cremallera, *m*

zip code n código postal, *m*

zipper /ˈzɪpər/ n cremallera, *f,* cierre relámpago, cierre, cerrador, *m*

zither /ˈzɪθər/ n cítara, *f*

zodiac /ˈzoudiˌæk/ n zodiaco, *m*

zone /zoun/ n zona, *f;* faja, *f*

zoo /zu/ n jardín zoológico, *m*

zoological /ˌzouəˈlɒdʒɪkəl/ a zoológico. **Z. garden,** jardín zoológico, *m*

zoom /zum/ n zumbido, *m.* —*vi* zumbar; *Aer.* empinarse

Spanish Irregular Verbs

Infinitive	Present	Future	Preterit	Past Part.
andar	ando	andaré	anduve	andado
caber	quepo	cabré	cupe	cabido
caer	caigo	caeré	caí	caído
conducir	conduzco	conduciré	conduje	conducido
dar	doy	daré	di	dado
decir	digo	diré	dije	dicho
estar	estoy	estaré	estuve	estado
haber	he	habré	hube	habido
hacer	hago	haré	hice	hecho
ir	voy	iré	fui	ido
jugar	juego	jugaré	jugué	jugado
morir	muero	moriré	morí	muerto
oir	oigo	oiré	oí	oído
poder	puedo	podré	pude	podido
poner	pongo	pondré	puse	puesto
querer	quiero	querré	quise	querido
saber	sé	sabré	supe	sabido
salir	salgo	saldré	salí	salido
ser	soy	seré	fui	sido
tener	tengo	tendré	tuve	tenído
traer	traigo	traeré	traje	traído
valer	valgo	valdré	valí	valido
venir	vengo	vendré	vine	venido
ver	veo	veré	vi	visto

Las formas del verbo inglés

1. Se forma la 3ª persona singular del tiempo presente exactamente al igual que el plural de los sustantivos, añadiendo **-es** o **-s** a la forma sencilla según las mismas reglas, así:

(1)	teach	pass	wish	fix	buzz		
	teaches	passes	wishes	fixes	buzzes		

(2)	place	change	judge	please	freeze		
	places	changes	judges	pleases	freezes		

(3a)	find	sell	clean	hear	love	buy	know
	finds	sells	cleans	hears	loves	buys	knows

(3b)	think	like	laugh	stop	hope	meet	want
	thinks	likes	laughs	stops	hopes	meets	wants

(4)	cry	try	dry	carry	deny		
	cries	tries	dries	carries	denies		

Cinco verbos muy comunes tienen 3ª persona singular irregular:

(5)	go	do	say	have	be
	goes	does	says	has	is

2. Se forman el tiempo pasado y el participio de modo igual, añadiendo a la forma sencilla la terminación **-ed** o **-d** según las reglas que siguen:

(1) Si la forma sencilla termina en **-d** o **-t**, se le pone **-ed** como sílaba aparte:

end	fold	need	load	want	feast	wait	light
ended	folded	needed	loaded	wanted	feasted	waited	lighted

(2) Si la forma sencilla termina en cualquier otra consonante, se añade también **-ed** pero sin hacer sílaba aparte:

(2a)
bang	sail	seem	harm	earn	weigh
banged	sailed	seemed	harmed	earned	weighed

(2b)
lunch	work	look	laugh	help	pass
lunched	worked	looked	laughed	helped	passed

(3) Si la forma sencilla termina en **-e**, se le pone sólo **-d:**

(3a)
hate	taste	waste	guide	fade	trade
hated	tasted	wasted	guided	faded	traded

(3b)
free	judge	rule	name	dine	scare
freed	judged	ruled	named	dined	scared

(3c)
place	force	knife	like	hope	base
placed	forced	knifed	liked	hoped	based

(4) Una **-y** final que sigue a cualquier consonante se cambia en **-ie** al añadir la **-d** del pasado/participio:

cry	try	dry	carry	deny
cried	tried	dried	carried	denied

3. Varios verbos muy comunes forman el tiempo pasado y el participio de manera irregular. Pertenecen a tres grupos.

(1) Los que tienen una sola forma irregular para tiempo pasado y participio, como los siguientes:

bend	bleed	bring	build	buy	catch	creep	deal
bent	bled	brought	built	bought	caught	crept	dealt
dig	feed	feel	fight	find	flee	get	hang
dug	fed	felt	fought	found	fled	got	hung
have	hear	hold	keep	lead	leave	lend	lose
had	heard	held	kept	led	left	lent	lost
make	mean	meet	say	seek	sell	send	shine
made	meant	met	said	sought	sold	sent	shone
shoot	sit	sleep	spend	stand	strike	sweep	teach
shot	sat	slept	spent	stood	struck	swept	taught

(2) Los que tienen una forma irregular para el tiempo pasado y otra forma irregular para el participio, como los siguientes:

be	beat	become	begin	bite
was	beat	became	began	bit
been	beaten	become	begun	bitten
blow	break	choose	come	do
blew	broke	chose	came	did
blown	broken	chosen	come	done
draw	drink	drive	eat	fall
drew	drank	drove	ate	fell
drawn	drunk	driven	eaten	fallen
fly	forget	freeze	give	go
flew	forgot	froze	gave	went
flown	forgotten	frozen	given	gone
grow	hide	know	ride	ring
grew	hid	knew	rode	rang
grown	hidden	known	ridden	rung
rise	run	see	shake	shrink
rose	ran	saw	shook	shrank
risen	run	seen	shaken	shrunk
sing	sink	speak	steal	swear
sang	sank	spoke	stole	swore
sung	sunk	spoken	stolen	sworn
swim	tear	throw	wear	write
swam	tore	threw	wore	wrote
swum	torn	thrown	worn	written

(3) Los que no varían del todo, la forma sencilla funcionando también como pasado/participio; entre éstos son de mayor frecuencia:

bet	burst	cast	cost	cut
hit	hurt	let	put	quit
read	set	shed	shut	slit
spit	split	spread	thrust	wet

Numbers/Números

Cardinal/Cardinales

one	1	uno, una
two	2	dos
three	3	tres
four	4	cuatro
five	5	cinco
six	6	seis
seven	7	siete
eight	8	ocho
nine	9	nueve
ten	10	diez
eleven	11	once
twelve	12	doce
thirteen	13	trece
fourteen	14	catorce
fifteen	15	quince
sixteen	16	dieciséis
seventeen	17	diecisiete
eighteen	18	dieciocho
nineteen	19	diecinueve
twenty	20	veinte
twenty-one	21	veinte y uno (*or* veintiuno)
twenty-two	22	veinte y dos (*or* veintidós)
thirty	30	treinta
thirty-one	31	treinta y uno
thirty-two	32	treinta y dos
forty	40	cuarenta
fifty	50	cincuenta
sixty	60	sesenta
seventy	70	setenta
eighty	80	ochenta
ninety	90	noventa

one hundred	100	cien
one hundred one	101	ciento uno
one hundred two	102	ciento dos
two hundred	200	doscientos, -as
three hundred	300	trescientos, -as
four hundred	400	cuatrocientos, -as
five hundred	500	quinientos, -as
six hundred	600	seiscientos, -as
seven hundred	700	setecientos, -as
eight hundred	800	ochocientos, -as
nine hundred	900	novecientos, -as
one thousand	1,000	mil
two thousand	2,000	dos mil
one hundred thousand	100,000	cien mil
one million	1,000,000	un millón
two million	2,000,000	dos millones

Ordinal/Ordinales

first	1st / 1°	primero
second	2nd / 2°	segundo
third	3rd / 3°	tercero
fourth	4th / 4°	cuarto
fifth	5th / 5°	quinto
sixth	6th / 6°	sexto
seventh	7th / 7°	séptimo
eighth	8th / 8°	octavo
ninth	9th / 9°	noveno
tenth	10th / 10°	décimo

Days of the Week/Días de la Semana

Sunday	domingo	Thursday	jueves
Monday	lunes	Friday	viernes
Tuesday	martes	Saturday	sábado
Wednesday	miércoles		

Months/Meses

January	enero	July	julio
February	febrero	August	agosto
March	marzo	September	septiembre
April	abril	October	octubre
May	mayo	November	noviembre
June	junio	December	diciembre

Weights and Measures/Pesos y Medidas

1 centímetro	=	.3937 inches		1 kilolitro	=	264.18 gallons
1 metro	=	39.37 inches		1 inch	=	2.54 centímetros
1 kilómetro	=	.621 mile		1 foot	=	.305 metros
1 centigramo	=	.1543 grain		1 mile	=	1.61 kilómetros
1 gramo	=	15.432 grains		1 grain	=	.065 gramos
1 kilogramo	=	2.2046 pounds		1 pound	=	.455 kilogramos
1 tonelada	=	2.204 pounds		1 ton	=	.907 toneladas
1 centilitro	=	.338 ounces		1 ounce	=	2.96 centilitros
1 litro	=	1.0567 quart (liquid);		1 quart	=	1.13 litros
		.908 quart (dry)		1 gallon	=	4.52 litros

Signs/Señales

Caution	Precaución	No smoking	Prohibido fumar
Danger	Peligro	No admittance	Entrada prohibida
Exit	Salida	One way	Dirección única
Entrance	Entrada	No entry	Dirección prohibida
Stop	Alto	Women	Señoras, Mujeres, Damas
Closed	Cerrado	Men	Señores, Hombres, Caballeros
Open	Abierto	Ladies' Room	El cuarto de damas
Slow	Despacio	Men's Room	El servicio

Useful Phrases/Locuciones Útiles

Good day, Good morning. Buenos días.

Good afternoon. Buenas tardes.

Good night, Good evening. Buenas noches.

Hello. ¡Hola!

Welcome! ¡Bienvenido!

See you later. Hasta luego.

Goodbye. ¡Adiós!

How are you? ¿Cómo está usted?

I'm fine, thank you. Estoy bien, gracias.

I'm pleased to meet you. Mucho gusto en conocerle.

May I introduce . . . Quisiera presentar . . .

Thank you very much. Muchas gracias.

You're welcome. De nada or No hay de qué.

Please. Por favor.

Excuse me. Con permiso.

Good luck. ¡Buena suerte!

To your health. ¡Salud!

Please help me. Ayúdeme, por favor.

I don't know. No sé.

I don't understand. No entiendo.

Do you understand? ¿Entiende usted?

I don't speak Spanish. No hablo español.

Do you speak English? ¿Habla usted inglés?

How do you say . . . in Spanish? ¿Cómo se dice . . . en español?

What do you call this? ¿Cómo se llama esto?

Speak slowly, please. Hable despacio, por favor.

Please repeat. Repita, por favor.

I don't like it. No me gusta.

I am lost. Ando perdido; Me he extraviado.

What is your name? ¿Cómo se llama usted?

My name is . . . Me llamo . . .

I am an American. Soy norteamericano.

Where are you from? ¿De dónde es usted?

I'm from . . . Soy de . . .

How is the weather? ¿Qué tiempo hace?
It's cold (hot) today. Hace frío (calor) hoy.
What time is it? ¿Qué hora es?

How much is it? ¿Cuánto es?
It is too much. Es demasiado.
What do you wish? ¿Qué desea usted?
I want to buy . . . Quiero comprar . . .
May I see something better? ¿Podría ver algo mejor?
May I see something cheaper? ¿Podría ver algo menos caro?
It is not exactly what I want. No es exactamente lo que quiero.

I'm hungry. Tengo hambre.
I'm thirsty. Tengo sed.
Where is there a restaurant? ¿Dónde hay un restaurante?
I have a reservation. Tengo una reservación.
I would like . . . Quisiera . . .; Me gustaría . . .
Please give me . . . Por favor, déme usted . . .
Please bring me . . . Por favor, tráigame usted . . .
May I see the menu? ¿Podría ver el menú?
The bill, please. La cuenta, por favor.
Is service included in the bill? ¿El servicio está incluido en la cuenta?
Where is there a hotel? ¿Dónde hay un hotel?
Where is the post office? ¿Dónde está el correo?
Is there any mail for me? ¿Hay correo para mí?
Where can I mail this letter? ¿Dónde puedo echar esta carta al correo?

Take me to . . . Lléveme a . . .
I believe I am ill. Creo que estoy enfermo.

Please call a doctor. Por favor, llame al médico.
Please call the police. Por favor, llame a la policía.
I want to send a telegram. Quiero poner un telegrama.
As soon as possible. Cuanto antes.

Round trip. Ida y vuelta.
Please help me with my luggage. Por favor, ayúdeme con mi equipaje.
Where can I get a taxi? ¿Dónde puedo coger un taxi?
What is the fare to . . . ¿Cuánto es el pasaje hasta . . . ?
Please take me to this address. Por favor, lléveme a esta dirección.
Where can I change my money? ¿Dónde puedo cambiar mi dinero?
Where is the nearest bank? ¿Dónde está el banco más cercano?
Can you accept my check? ¿Puede aceptar usted mi cheque?
Do you accept traveler's checks? ¿Aceptan cheques de viaje?
What is the postage? ¿Cuánto es el franqueo?
Where is the nearest drugstore? ¿Dónde está la farmacia más cercana?
Where is the men's (women's) room? ¿Dónde está el servicio de caballeros (de señoras)?
Please let me off at . . . Por favor, déjeme bajar en . . .
Right away. ¡Pronto!
Help. ¡Socorro!
Who is it? ¿Quién es?
Just a minute! ¡Un momento no más!
Come in. ¡Pase usted!
Pardon me. Dispense usted.
Stop. ¡Pare!
Look out. ¡Cuidado!
Hurry. ¡De prisa! *or* ¡Dése prisa!
Go on. ¡Siga!
To (on, at) the right. A la derecha.
To (on, at) the left. A la izquierda.
Straight ahead. Adelante.

As the world gets smaller, we need to communicate with more people than ever. Don't miss this valuable tool:

RANDOM HOUSE JAPANESE-ENGLISH ENGLISH-JAPANESE DICTIONARY

Reliable, detailed, and up-to-date.

Featuring more than 50,000 entries, including the most common meanings, romanization and Japanese characters, and hundreds of new words.

Also with explanatory glosses to specify meaning and assure appropriate translation!

RANDOM HOUSE JAPANESE-ENGLISH ENGLISH-JAPANESE DICTIONARY
by Seigo Nakao
Published by Ballantine Books.
Available in bookstores everywhere.

Express yourself with precision . . .

RANDOM HOUSE WEBSTER'S POWER VOCABULARY BUILDER

teaches how words work—and how to make them work for you!

- Strengthen your word power and expertise!
- Learn proper pronunciation!
- Try your skill at numerous vocabulary tests and entertaining word puzzles to gauge your mastery of English!

RANDOM HOUSE WEBSTER'S POWER VOCABULARY BUILDER

Published by Ballantine Books.
Available in bookstores everywhere.

The authoritative, comprehensive, and handy reference for writers, students, and businesspeople alike:

RANDOM HOUSE WEBSTER'S SPELL CHECKER & ABBREVIATIONS DICTIONARY

- 50,000 entries spelled and divided
- Preferred hyphenation breaks
- Vocabulary featuring business and computer terms
- More than 10,000 abbreviations for common words and phrases
- Covers all areas of school, business, and science
- Includes acronyms, initialisms, and symbols

RANDOM HOUSE WEBSTER'S SPELL CHECKER & ABBREVIATIONS DICTIONARY

Published by Ballantine Books.
Available in bookstores everywhere.

Articles, memos, letters, scripts, essays, fiction—you can improve them all when you use the

RANDOM HOUSE GUIDE TO GOOD WRITING

Featuring exercises and examples from great writers to help you master style, usage, grammar, and punctuation.

Clear, concise, effective—it's a must for anyone who wishes to communicate well in writing.

RANDOM HOUSE GUIDE TO GOOD WRITING
by Mitchell Ivers

Published by Ballantine Books.
Available in bookstores everywhere.

When you are looking for just the
right word, turn to:

RANDOM HOUSE
ROGET'S THESAURUS

With more than 11,000 main entries and
200,000 synonyms and antonyms, this is
the authoritative, comprehensive, and
easy-to-use thesaurus favored by writers
and students alike!

RANDOM HOUSE
ROGET'S THESAURUS
Third Edition

Published by Ballantine Books.
Available in bookstores everywhere.